Oxford Dictionary of National Biography

Volume 26

Oxford Dictionary of National Biography

IN ASSOCIATION WITH
The British Academy

From the earliest times to the year 2000

Edited by
H. C. G. Matthew
and
Brian Harrison

Volume 26
Haycock–Hichens

Ashland
Community & Technical College
Library

College Drive Campus

OXFORD
UNIVERSITY PRESS

OXFORD
UNIVERSITY PRESS

Great Clarendon Street, Oxford OX2 6DP

Oxford University Press is a department of the University of Oxford.
It furthers the University's objective of excellence in research, scholarship,
and education by publishing worldwide in

Oxford New York

Auckland Bangkok Buenos Aires Cape Town
Chennai Dar es Salaam Delhi Hong Kong Istanbul Karachi
Kolkata Kuala Lumpur Madrid Melbourne Mexico City Mumbai Nairobi
São Paulo Shanghai Taipei Tokyo Toronto

Oxford is a registered trade mark of Oxford University Press
in the UK and in certain other countries

Published in the United States
by Oxford University Press Inc., New York

© Oxford University Press 2004

Illustrations © individual copyright holders as listed in
'Picture credits', and reproduced with permission

Database right Oxford University Press (maker)

First published 2004

All rights reserved. No part of this material may be reproduced,
stored in a retrieval system, or transmitted, in any form or by any means,
without the prior permission in writing of Oxford University Press,
or as expressly permitted by law, or under terms agreed with the appropriate
reprographics rights organization. Enquiries concerning reproduction
outside the scope of the above should be sent to the Rights Department,
Oxford University Press, at the address above

You must not circulate this book in any other binding or cover
and you must impose this same condition on any acquirer

British Library Cataloguing in Publication Data
Data available

Library of Congress Cataloging in Publication Data
Data available: for details see volume 1, p. iv

ISBN 0-19-861376-8 (this volume)
ISBN 0-19-861411-X (set of sixty volumes)

Text captured by Alliance Phototypesetters, Pondicherry
Illustrations reproduced and archived by
Alliance Graphics Ltd, UK
Typeset in OUP Swift by Interactive Sciences Limited, Gloucester
Printed in Great Britain on acid-free paper by
Butler and Tanner Ltd,
Frome, Somerset

LIST OF ABBREVIATIONS

1 General abbreviations

AB	bachelor of arts
ABC	Australian Broadcasting Corporation
ABC TV	ABC Television
act.	active
A$	Australian dollar
AD	*anno domini*
AFC	Air Force Cross
AIDS	acquired immune deficiency syndrome
AK	Alaska
AL	Alabama
A level	advanced level [examination]
ALS	associate of the Linnean Society
AM	master of arts
AMICE	associate member of the Institution of Civil Engineers
ANZAC	Australian and New Zealand Army Corps
appx *pl.* appxs	appendix(es)
AR	Arkansas
ARA	associate of the Royal Academy
ARCA	associate of the Royal College of Art
ARCM	associate of the Royal College of Music
ARCO	associate of the Royal College of Organists
ARIBA	associate of the Royal Institute of British Architects
ARP	air-raid precautions
ARRC	associate of the Royal Red Cross
ARSA	associate of the Royal Scottish Academy
art.	article / item
ASC	Army Service Corps
Asch	Austrian Schilling
ASDIC	Antisubmarine Detection Investigation Committee
ATS	Auxiliary Territorial Service
ATV	Associated Television
Aug	August
AZ	Arizona
b.	born
BA	bachelor of arts
BA (Admin.)	bachelor of arts (administration)
BAFTA	British Academy of Film and Television Arts
BAO	bachelor of arts in obstetrics
bap.	baptized
BBC	British Broadcasting Corporation / Company
BC	before Christ
BCE	before the common (*or* Christian) era
BCE	bachelor of civil engineering
BCG	bacillus of Calmette and Guérin [inoculation against tuberculosis]
BCh	bachelor of surgery
BChir	bachelor of surgery
BCL	bachelor of civil law

BCnL	bachelor of canon law
BCom	bachelor of commerce
BD	bachelor of divinity
BEd	bachelor of education
BEng	bachelor of engineering
bk *pl.* bks	book(s)
BL	bachelor of law / letters / literature
BLitt	bachelor of letters
BM	bachelor of medicine
BMus	bachelor of music
BP	before present
BP	British Petroleum
Bros.	Brothers
BS	(1) bachelor of science; (2) bachelor of surgery; (3) British standard
BSc	bachelor of science
BSc (Econ.)	bachelor of science (economics)
BSc (Eng.)	bachelor of science (engineering)
bt	baronet
BTh	bachelor of theology
bur.	buried
C.	command [identifier for published parliamentary papers]
c.	*circa*
c.	*capitulum pl. capitula*: chapter(s)
CA	California
Cantab.	Cantabrigiensis
cap.	*capitulum pl. capitula*: chapter(s)
CB	companion of the Bath
CBE	commander of the Order of the British Empire
CBS	Columbia Broadcasting System
cc	cubic centimetres
C$	Canadian dollar
CD	compact disc
Cd	command [identifier for published parliamentary papers]
CE	Common (*or* Christian) Era
cent.	century
cf.	compare
CH	Companion of Honour
chap.	chapter
ChB	bachelor of surgery
CI	Imperial Order of the Crown of India
CIA	Central Intelligence Agency
CID	Criminal Investigation Department
CIE	companion of the Order of the Indian Empire
Cie	Compagnie
CLit	companion of literature
CM	master of surgery
cm	centimetre(s)

Cmd	command [identifier for published parliamentary papers]
CMG	companion of the Order of St Michael and St George
Cmnd	command [identifier for published parliamentary papers]
CO	Colorado
Co.	company
co.	county
col. *pl.* cols.	column(s)
Corp.	corporation
CSE	certificate of secondary education
CSI	companion of the Order of the Star of India
CT	Connecticut
CVO	commander of the Royal Victorian Order
cwt	hundredweight
$	(American) dollar
d.	(1) penny (pence); (2) died
DBE	dame commander of the Order of the British Empire
DCH	diploma in child health
DCh	doctor of surgery
DCL	doctor of civil law
DCnL	doctor of canon law
DCVO	dame commander of the Royal Victorian Order
DD	doctor of divinity
DE	Delaware
Dec	December
dem.	demolished
DEng	doctor of engineering
des.	destroyed
DFC	Distinguished Flying Cross
DipEd	diploma in education
DipPsych	diploma in psychiatry
diss.	dissertation
DL	deputy lieutenant
DLitt	doctor of letters
DLittCelt	doctor of Celtic letters
DM	(1) Deutschmark; (2) doctor of medicine; (3) doctor of musical arts
DMus	doctor of music
DNA	dioxyribonucleic acid
doc.	document
DOL	doctor of oriental learning
DPH	diploma in public health
DPhil	doctor of philosophy
DPM	diploma in psychological medicine
DSC	Distinguished Service Cross
DSc	doctor of science
DSc (Econ.)	doctor of science (economics)
DSc (Eng.)	doctor of science (engineering)
DSM	Distinguished Service Medal
DSO	companion of the Distinguished Service Order
DSocSc	doctor of social science
DTech	doctor of technology
DTh	doctor of theology
DTM	diploma in tropical medicine
DTMH	diploma in tropical medicine and hygiene
DU	doctor of the university
DUniv	doctor of the university
dwt	pennyweight
EC	European Community
ed. *pl.* eds.	edited / edited by / editor(s)
Edin.	Edinburgh
edn	edition
EEC	European Economic Community
EFTA	European Free Trade Association
EICS	East India Company Service
EMI	Electrical and Musical Industries (Ltd)
Eng.	English
enl.	enlarged
ENSA	Entertainments National Service Association
ep. *pl.* epp.	*epistola(e)*
ESP	extra-sensory perception
esp.	especially
esq.	esquire
est.	estimate / estimated
EU	European Union
ex	sold by (*lit.* out of)
excl.	excludes / excluding
exh.	exhibited
exh. cat.	exhibition catalogue
f. *pl.* ff.	following [pages]
FA	Football Association
FACP	fellow of the American College of Physicians
facs.	facsimile
FANY	First Aid Nursing Yeomanry
FBA	fellow of the British Academy
FBI	Federation of British Industries
FCS	fellow of the Chemical Society
Feb	February
FEng	fellow of the Fellowship of Engineering
FFCM	fellow of the Faculty of Community Medicine
FGS	fellow of the Geological Society
fig.	figure
FIMechE	fellow of the Institution of Mechanical Engineers
FL	Florida
fl.	*floruit*
FLS	fellow of the Linnean Society
FM	frequency modulation
fol. *pl.* fols.	folio(s)
Fr	French francs
Fr.	French
FRAeS	fellow of the Royal Aeronautical Society
FRAI	fellow of the Royal Anthropological Institute
FRAM	fellow of the Royal Academy of Music
FRAS	(1) fellow of the Royal Asiatic Society; (2) fellow of the Royal Astronomical Society
FRCM	fellow of the Royal College of Music
FRCO	fellow of the Royal College of Organists
FRCOG	fellow of the Royal College of Obstetricians and Gynaecologists
FRCP(C)	fellow of the Royal College of Physicians of Canada
FRCP (Edin.)	fellow of the Royal College of Physicians of Edinburgh
FRCP (Lond.)	fellow of the Royal College of Physicians of London
FRCPath	fellow of the Royal College of Pathologists
FRCPsych	fellow of the Royal College of Psychiatrists
FRCS	fellow of the Royal College of Surgeons
FRGS	fellow of the Royal Geographical Society
FRIBA	fellow of the Royal Institute of British Architects
FRICS	fellow of the Royal Institute of Chartered Surveyors
FRS	fellow of the Royal Society
FRSA	fellow of the Royal Society of Arts

FRSCM	fellow of the Royal School of Church Music		ISO	companion of the Imperial Service Order
FRSE	fellow of the Royal Society of Edinburgh		It.	Italian
FRSL	fellow of the Royal Society of Literature		ITA	Independent Television Authority
FSA	fellow of the Society of Antiquaries		ITV	Independent Television
ft	foot *pl.* feet		Jan	January
FTCL	fellow of Trinity College of Music, London		JP	justice of the peace
ft-lb per min.	foot-pounds per minute [unit of horsepower]		jun.	junior
FZS	fellow of the Zoological Society		KB	knight of the Order of the Bath
GA	Georgia		KBE	knight commander of the Order of the British Empire
GBE	knight or dame grand cross of the Order of the British Empire		KC	king's counsel
GCB	knight grand cross of the Order of the Bath		kcal	kilocalorie
GCE	general certificate of education		KCB	knight commander of the Order of the Bath
GCH	knight grand cross of the Royal Guelphic Order		KCH	knight commander of the Royal Guelphic Order
GCHQ	government communications headquarters		KCIE	knight commander of the Order of the Indian Empire
GCIE	knight grand commander of the Order of the Indian Empire		KCMG	knight commander of the Order of St Michael and St George
GCMG	knight or dame grand cross of the Order of St Michael and St George		KCSI	knight commander of the Order of the Star of India
GCSE	general certificate of secondary education		KCVO	knight commander of the Royal Victorian Order
GCSI	knight grand commander of the Order of the Star of India		keV	kilo-electron-volt
GCStJ	bailiff or dame grand cross of the order of St John of Jerusalem		KG	knight of the Order of the Garter
GCVO	knight or dame grand cross of the Royal Victorian Order		KGB	[Soviet committee of state security]
			KH	knight of the Royal Guelphic Order
GEC	General Electric Company		KLM	Koninklijke Luchtvaart Maatschappij (Royal Dutch Air Lines)
Ger.	German			
GI	government (*or* general) issue		km	kilometre(s)
GMT	Greenwich mean time		KP	knight of the Order of St Patrick
GP	general practitioner		KS	Kansas
GPU	[Soviet special police unit]		KT	knight of the Order of the Thistle
GSO	general staff officer		kt	knight
Heb.	Hebrew		KY	Kentucky
HEICS	Honourable East India Company Service		£	pound(s) sterling
HI	Hawaii		£E	Egyptian pound
HIV	human immunodeficiency virus		L	lira *pl.* lire
HK$	Hong Kong dollar		l. *pl.* ll.	line(s)
HM	his / her majesty('s)		LA	Lousiana
HMAS	his / her majesty's Australian ship		LAA	light anti-aircraft
HMNZS	his / her majesty's New Zealand ship		LAH	licentiate of the Apothecaries' Hall, Dublin
HMS	his / her majesty's ship		Lat.	Latin
HMSO	His / Her Majesty's Stationery Office		lb	pound(s), unit of weight
HMV	His Master's Voice		LDS	licence in dental surgery
Hon.	Honourable		*lit.*	literally
hp	horsepower		LittB	bachelor of letters
hr	hour(s)		LittD	doctor of letters
HRH	his / her royal highness		LKQCPI	licentiate of the King and Queen's College of Physicians, Ireland
HTV	Harlech Television			
IA	Iowa		LLA	lady literate in arts
ibid.	*ibidem*: in the same place		LLB	bachelor of laws
ICI	Imperial Chemical Industries (Ltd)		LLD	doctor of laws
ID	Idaho		LLM	master of laws
IL	Illinois		LM	licentiate in midwifery
illus.	illustration		LP	long-playing record
illustr.	illustrated		LRAM	licentiate of the Royal Academy of Music
IN	Indiana		LRCP	licentiate of the Royal College of Physicians
in.	inch(es)		LRCPS (Glasgow)	licentiate of the Royal College of Physicians and Surgeons of Glasgow
Inc.	Incorporated			
incl.	includes / including		LRCS	licentiate of the Royal College of Surgeons
IOU	I owe you		LSA	licentiate of the Society of Apothecaries
IQ	intelligence quotient		LSD	lysergic acid diethylamide
Ir£	Irish pound		LVO	lieutenant of the Royal Victorian Order
IRA	Irish Republican Army		M. *pl.* MM.	Monsieur *pl.* Messieurs
			m	metre(s)

m. *pl.* mm.	membrane(s)	ND	North Dakota
MA	(1) Massachusetts; (2) master of arts	n.d.	no date
MAI	master of engineering	NE	Nebraska
MB	bachelor of medicine	*nem. con.*	*nemine contradicente*: unanimously
MBA	master of business administration	new ser.	new series
MBE	member of the Order of the British Empire	NH	New Hampshire
MC	Military Cross	NHS	National Health Service
MCC	Marylebone Cricket Club	NJ	New Jersey
MCh	master of surgery	NKVD	[Soviet people's commissariat for internal affairs]
MChir	master of surgery		
MCom	master of commerce	NM	New Mexico
MD	(1) doctor of medicine; (2) Maryland	nm	nanometre(s)
MDMA	methylenedioxymethamphetamine	no. *pl.* nos.	number(s)
ME	Maine	Nov	November
MEd	master of education	n.p.	no place [of publication]
MEng	master of engineering	NS	new style
MEP	member of the European parliament	NV	Nevada
MG	Morris Garages	NY	New York
MGM	Metro-Goldwyn-Mayer	NZBS	New Zealand Broadcasting Service
Mgr	Monsignor	OBE	officer of the Order of the British Empire
MI	(1) Michigan; (2) military intelligence	obit.	obituary
MI1c	[secret intelligence department]	Oct	October
MI5	[military intelligence department]	OCTU	officer cadets training unit
MI6	[secret intelligence department]	OECD	Organization for Economic Co-operation and Development
MI9	[secret escape service]		
MICE	member of the Institution of Civil Engineers	OEEC	Organization for European Economic Co-operation
MIEE	member of the Institution of Electrical Engineers		
		OFM	order of Friars Minor [Franciscans]
min.	minute(s)	OFMCap	Ordine Frati Minori Cappucini: member of the Capuchin order
Mk	mark		
ML	(1) licentiate of medicine; (2) master of laws	OH	Ohio
MLitt	master of letters	OK	Oklahoma
Mlle	Mademoiselle	O level	ordinary level [examination]
mm	millimetre(s)	OM	Order of Merit
Mme	Madame	OP	order of Preachers [Dominicans]
MN	Minnesota	op. *pl.* opp.	opus *pl.* opera
MO	Missouri	OPEC	Organization of Petroleum Exporting Countries
MOH	medical officer of health		
MP	member of parliament	OR	Oregon
m.p.h.	miles per hour	orig.	original
MPhil	master of philosophy	OS	old style
MRCP	member of the Royal College of Physicians	OSB	Order of St Benedict
MRCS	member of the Royal College of Surgeons	OTC	Officers' Training Corps
MRCVS	member of the Royal College of Veterinary Surgeons	OWS	Old Watercolour Society
		Oxon.	Oxoniensis
MRIA	member of the Royal Irish Academy	p. *pl.* pp.	page(s)
MS	(1) master of science; (2) Mississippi	PA	Pennsylvania
MS *pl.* MSS	manuscript(s)	p.a.	per annum
MSc	master of science	para.	paragraph
MSc (Econ.)	master of science (economics)	PAYE	pay as you earn
MT	Montana	pbk *pl.* pbks	paperback(s)
MusB	bachelor of music	*per.*	[during the] period
MusBac	bachelor of music	PhD	doctor of philosophy
MusD	doctor of music	pl.	(1) plate(s); (2) plural
MV	motor vessel	priv. coll.	private collection
MVO	member of the Royal Victorian Order	pt *pl.* pts	part(s)
n. *pl.* nn.	note(s)	pubd	published
NAAFI	Navy, Army, and Air Force Institutes	PVC	polyvinyl chloride
NASA	National Aeronautics and Space Administration	q. *pl.* qq.	(1) question(s); (2) quire(s)
NATO	North Atlantic Treaty Organization	QC	queen's counsel
NBC	National Broadcasting Corporation	R	rand
NC	North Carolina	R.	Rex / Regina
NCO	non-commissioned officer	*r*	recto
		r.	reigned / ruled
		RA	Royal Academy / Royal Academician

RAC	Royal Automobile Club
RAF	Royal Air Force
RAFVR	Royal Air Force Volunteer Reserve
RAM	[member of the] Royal Academy of Music
RAMC	Royal Army Medical Corps
RCA	Royal College of Art
RCNC	Royal Corps of Naval Constructors
RCOG	Royal College of Obstetricians and Gynaecologists
RDI	royal designer for industry
RE	Royal Engineers
repr. *pl.* reprs.	reprint(s) / reprinted
repro.	reproduced
rev.	revised / revised by / reviser / revision
Revd	Reverend
RHA	Royal Hibernian Academy
RI	(1) Rhode Island; (2) Royal Institute of Painters in Water-Colours
RIBA	Royal Institute of British Architects
RIN	Royal Indian Navy
RM	Reichsmark
RMS	Royal Mail steamer
RN	Royal Navy
RNA	ribonucleic acid
RNAS	Royal Naval Air Service
RNR	Royal Naval Reserve
RNVR	Royal Naval Volunteer Reserve
RO	Record Office
r.p.m.	revolutions per minute
RRS	royal research ship
Rs	rupees
RSA	(1) Royal Scottish Academician; (2) Royal Society of Arts
RSPCA	Royal Society for the Prevention of Cruelty to Animals
Rt Hon.	Right Honourable
Rt Revd	Right Reverend
RUC	Royal Ulster Constabulary
Russ.	Russian
RWS	Royal Watercolour Society
S4C	Sianel Pedwar Cymru
s.	shilling(s)
s.a.	*sub anno*: under the year
SABC	South African Broadcasting Corporation
SAS	Special Air Service
SC	South Carolina
ScD	doctor of science
S$	Singapore dollar
SD	South Dakota
sec.	second(s)
sel.	selected
sen.	senior
Sept	September
ser.	series
SHAPE	supreme headquarters allied powers, Europe
SIDRO	Société Internationale d'Énergie Hydro-Électrique
sig. *pl.* sigs.	signature(s)
sing.	singular
SIS	Secret Intelligence Service
SJ	Society of Jesus
Skr	Swedish krona
Span.	Spanish
SPCK	Society for Promoting Christian Knowledge
SS	(1) Santissimi; (2) Schutzstaffel; (3) steam ship
STB	bachelor of theology
STD	doctor of theology
STM	master of theology
STP	doctor of theology
supp.	supposedly
suppl. *pl.* suppls.	supplement(s)
s.v.	*sub verbo / sub voce*: under the word / heading
SY	steam yacht
TA	Territorial Army
TASS	[Soviet news agency]
TB	tuberculosis (*lit.* tubercle bacillus)
TD	(1) *teachtaí dála* (member of the Dáil); (2) territorial decoration
TN	Tennessee
TNT	trinitrotoluene
trans.	translated / translated by / translation / translator
TT	tourist trophy
TUC	Trades Union Congress
TX	Texas
U-boat	*Unterseeboot*: submarine
Ufa	Universum-Film AG
UMIST	University of Manchester Institute of Science and Technology
UN	United Nations
UNESCO	United Nations Educational, Scientific, and Cultural Organization
UNICEF	United Nations International Children's Emergency Fund
unpubd	unpublished
USS	United States ship
UT	Utah
v	verso
v.	versus
VA	Virginia
VAD	Voluntary Aid Detachment
VC	Victoria Cross
VE-day	victory in Europe day
Ven.	Venerable
VJ-day	victory over Japan day
vol. *pl.* vols.	volume(s)
VT	Vermont
WA	Washington [state]
WAAC	Women's Auxiliary Army Corps
WAAF	Women's Auxiliary Air Force
WEA	Workers' Educational Association
WHO	World Health Organization
WI	Wisconsin
WRAF	Women's Royal Air Force
WRNS	Women's Royal Naval Service
WV	West Virginia
WVS	Women's Voluntary Service
WY	Wyoming
¥	yen
YMCA	Young Men's Christian Association
YWCA	Young Women's Christian Association

2 *Institution abbreviations*

All Souls Oxf.	All Souls College, Oxford
AM Oxf.	Ashmolean Museum, Oxford
Balliol Oxf.	Balliol College, Oxford
BBC WAC	BBC Written Archives Centre, Reading
Beds. & Luton ARS	Bedfordshire and Luton Archives and Record Service, Bedford
Berks. RO	Berkshire Record Office, Reading
BFI	British Film Institute, London
BFI NFTVA	British Film Institute, London, National Film and Television Archive
BGS	British Geological Survey, Keyworth, Nottingham
Birm. CA	Birmingham Central Library, Birmingham City Archives
Birm. CL	Birmingham Central Library
BL	British Library, London
BL NSA	British Library, London, National Sound Archive
BL OIOC	British Library, London, Oriental and India Office Collections
BLPES	London School of Economics and Political Science, British Library of Political and Economic Science
BM	British Museum, London
Bodl. Oxf.	Bodleian Library, Oxford
Bodl. RH	Bodleian Library of Commonwealth and African Studies at Rhodes House, Oxford
Borth. Inst.	Borthwick Institute of Historical Research, University of York
Boston PL	Boston Public Library, Massachusetts
Bristol RO	Bristol Record Office
Bucks. RLSS	Buckinghamshire Records and Local Studies Service, Aylesbury
CAC Cam.	Churchill College, Cambridge, Churchill Archives Centre
Cambs. AS	Cambridgeshire Archive Service
CCC Cam.	Corpus Christi College, Cambridge
CCC Oxf.	Corpus Christi College, Oxford
Ches. & Chester ALSS	Cheshire and Chester Archives and Local Studies Service
Christ Church Oxf.	Christ Church, Oxford
Christies	Christies, London
City Westm. AC	City of Westminster Archives Centre, London
CKS	Centre for Kentish Studies, Maidstone
CLRO	Corporation of London Records Office
Coll. Arms	College of Arms, London
Col. U.	Columbia University, New York
Cornwall RO	Cornwall Record Office, Truro
Courtauld Inst.	Courtauld Institute of Art, London
CUL	Cambridge University Library
Cumbria AS	Cumbria Archive Service
Derbys. RO	Derbyshire Record Office, Matlock
Devon RO	Devon Record Office, Exeter
Dorset RO	Dorset Record Office, Dorchester
Duke U.	Duke University, Durham, North Carolina
Duke U., Perkins L.	Duke University, Durham, North Carolina, William R. Perkins Library
Durham Cath. CL	Durham Cathedral, chapter library
Durham RO	Durham Record Office
DWL	Dr Williams's Library, London
Essex RO	Essex Record Office
E. Sussex RO	East Sussex Record Office, Lewes
Eton	Eton College, Berkshire
FM Cam.	Fitzwilliam Museum, Cambridge
Folger	Folger Shakespeare Library, Washington, DC
Garr. Club	Garrick Club, London
Girton Cam.	Girton College, Cambridge
GL	Guildhall Library, London
Glos. RO	Gloucestershire Record Office, Gloucester
Gon. & Caius Cam.	Gonville and Caius College, Cambridge
Gov. Art Coll.	Government Art Collection
GS Lond.	Geological Society of London
Hants. RO	Hampshire Record Office, Winchester
Harris Man. Oxf.	Harris Manchester College, Oxford
Harvard TC	Harvard Theatre Collection, Harvard University, Cambridge, Massachusetts, Nathan Marsh Pusey Library
Harvard U.	Harvard University, Cambridge, Massachusetts
Harvard U., Houghton L.	Harvard University, Cambridge, Massachusetts, Houghton Library
Herefs. RO	Herefordshire Record Office, Hereford
Herts. ALS	Hertfordshire Archives and Local Studies, Hertford
Hist. Soc. Penn.	Historical Society of Pennsylvania, Philadelphia
HLRO	House of Lords Record Office, London
Hult. Arch.	Hulton Archive, London and New York
Hunt. L.	Huntington Library, San Marino, California
ICL	Imperial College, London
Inst. CE	Institution of Civil Engineers, London
Inst. EE	Institution of Electrical Engineers, London
IWM	Imperial War Museum, London
IWM FVA	Imperial War Museum, London, Film and Video Archive
IWM SA	Imperial War Museum, London, Sound Archive
JRL	John Rylands University Library of Manchester
King's AC Cam.	King's College Archives Centre, Cambridge
King's Cam.	King's College, Cambridge
King's Lond.	King's College, London
King's Lond., Liddell Hart C.	King's College, London, Liddell Hart Centre for Military Archives
Lancs. RO	Lancashire Record Office, Preston
L. Cong.	Library of Congress, Washington, DC
Leics. RO	Leicestershire, Leicester, and Rutland Record Office, Leicester
Lincs. Arch.	Lincolnshire Archives, Lincoln
Linn. Soc.	Linnean Society of London
LMA	London Metropolitan Archives
LPL	Lambeth Palace, London
Lpool RO	Liverpool Record Office and Local Studies Service
LUL	London University Library
Magd. Cam.	Magdalene College, Cambridge
Magd. Oxf.	Magdalen College, Oxford
Man. City Gall.	Manchester City Galleries
Man. CL	Manchester Central Library
Mass. Hist. Soc.	Massachusetts Historical Society, Boston
Merton Oxf.	Merton College, Oxford
MHS Oxf.	Museum of the History of Science, Oxford
Mitchell L., Glas.	Mitchell Library, Glasgow
Mitchell L., NSW	State Library of New South Wales, Sydney, Mitchell Library
Morgan L.	Pierpont Morgan Library, New York
NA Canada	National Archives of Canada, Ottawa
NA Ire.	National Archives of Ireland, Dublin
NAM	National Army Museum, London
NA Scot.	National Archives of Scotland, Edinburgh
News Int. RO	News International Record Office, London
NG Ire.	National Gallery of Ireland, Dublin

NG Scot.	National Gallery of Scotland, Edinburgh
NHM	Natural History Museum, London
NL Aus.	National Library of Australia, Canberra
NL Ire.	National Library of Ireland, Dublin
NL NZ	National Library of New Zealand, Wellington
NL NZ, Turnbull L.	National Library of New Zealand, Wellington, Alexander Turnbull Library
NL Scot.	National Library of Scotland, Edinburgh
NL Wales	National Library of Wales, Aberystwyth
NMG Wales	National Museum and Gallery of Wales, Cardiff
NMM	National Maritime Museum, London
Norfolk RO	Norfolk Record Office, Norwich
Northants. RO	Northamptonshire Record Office, Northampton
Northumbd RO	Northumberland Record Office
Notts. Arch.	Nottinghamshire Archives, Nottingham
NPG	National Portrait Gallery, London
NRA	National Archives, London, Historical Manuscripts Commission, National Register of Archives
Nuffield Oxf.	Nuffield College, Oxford
N. Yorks. CRO	North Yorkshire County Record Office, Northallerton
NYPL	New York Public Library
Oxf. UA	Oxford University Archives
Oxf. U. Mus. NH	Oxford University Museum of Natural History
Oxon. RO	Oxfordshire Record Office, Oxford
Pembroke Cam.	Pembroke College, Cambridge
PRO	National Archives, London, Public Record Office
PRO NIre.	Public Record Office for Northern Ireland, Belfast
Pusey Oxf.	Pusey House, Oxford
RA	Royal Academy of Arts, London
Ransom HRC	Harry Ransom Humanities Research Center, University of Texas, Austin
RAS	Royal Astronomical Society, London
RBG Kew	Royal Botanic Gardens, Kew, London
RCP Lond.	Royal College of Physicians of London
RCS Eng.	Royal College of Surgeons of England, London
RGS	Royal Geographical Society, London
RIBA	Royal Institute of British Architects, London
RIBA BAL	Royal Institute of British Architects, London, British Architectural Library
Royal Arch.	Royal Archives, Windsor Castle, Berkshire [by gracious permission of her majesty the queen]
Royal Irish Acad.	Royal Irish Academy, Dublin
Royal Scot. Acad.	Royal Scottish Academy, Edinburgh
RS	Royal Society, London
RSA	Royal Society of Arts, London
RS Friends, Lond.	Religious Society of Friends, London
St Ant. Oxf.	St Antony's College, Oxford
St John Cam.	St John's College, Cambridge
S. Antiquaries, Lond.	Society of Antiquaries of London
Sci. Mus.	Science Museum, London
Scot. NPG	Scottish National Portrait Gallery, Edinburgh
Scott Polar RI	University of Cambridge, Scott Polar Research Institute
Sheff. Arch.	Sheffield Archives
Shrops. RRC	Shropshire Records and Research Centre, Shrewsbury
SOAS	School of Oriental and African Studies, London
Som. ARS	Somerset Archive and Record Service, Taunton
Staffs. RO	Staffordshire Record Office, Stafford
Suffolk RO	Suffolk Record Office
Surrey HC	Surrey History Centre, Woking
TCD	Trinity College, Dublin
Trinity Cam.	Trinity College, Cambridge
U. Aberdeen	University of Aberdeen
U. Birm.	University of Birmingham
U. Birm. L.	University of Birmingham Library
U. Cal.	University of California
U. Cam.	University of Cambridge
UCL	University College, London
U. Durham	University of Durham
U. Durham L.	University of Durham Library
U. Edin.	University of Edinburgh
U. Edin., New Coll.	University of Edinburgh, New College
U. Edin., New Coll. L.	University of Edinburgh, New College Library
U. Edin. L.	University of Edinburgh Library
U. Glas.	University of Glasgow
U. Glas. L.	University of Glasgow Library
U. Hull	University of Hull
U. Hull, Brynmor Jones L.	University of Hull, Brynmor Jones Library
U. Leeds	University of Leeds
U. Leeds, Brotherton L.	University of Leeds, Brotherton Library
U. Lond.	University of London
U. Lpool	University of Liverpool
U. Lpool L.	University of Liverpool Library
U. Mich.	University of Michigan, Ann Arbor
U. Mich., Clements L.	University of Michigan, Ann Arbor, William L. Clements Library
U. Newcastle	University of Newcastle upon Tyne
U. Newcastle, Robinson L.	University of Newcastle upon Tyne, Robinson Library
U. Nott.	University of Nottingham
U. Nott. L.	University of Nottingham Library
U. Oxf.	University of Oxford
U. Reading	University of Reading
U. Reading L.	University of Reading Library
U. St Andr.	University of St Andrews
U. St Andr. L.	University of St Andrews Library
U. Southampton	University of Southampton
U. Southampton L.	University of Southampton Library
U. Sussex	University of Sussex, Brighton
U. Texas	University of Texas, Austin
U. Wales	University of Wales
U. Warwick Mod. RC	University of Warwick, Coventry, Modern Records Centre
V&A	Victoria and Albert Museum, London
V&A NAL	Victoria and Albert Museum, London, National Art Library
Warks. CRO	Warwickshire County Record Office, Warwick
Wellcome L.	Wellcome Library for the History and Understanding of Medicine, London
Westm. DA	Westminster Diocesan Archives, London
Wilts. & Swindon RO	Wiltshire and Swindon Record Office, Trowbridge
Worcs. RO	Worcestershire Record Office, Worcester
W. Sussex RO	West Sussex Record Office, Chichester
W. Yorks. AS	West Yorkshire Archive Service
Yale U.	Yale University, New Haven, Connecticut
Yale U., Beinecke L.	Yale University, New Haven, Connecticut, Beinecke Rare Book and Manuscript Library
Yale U. CBA	Yale University, New Haven, Connecticut, Yale Center for British Art

3 Bibliographic abbreviations

Adams, *Drama* — W. D. Adams, *A dictionary of the drama*, 1: *A–G* (1904); 2: *H–Z* (1956) [vol. 2 microfilm only]

AFM — J O'Donovan, ed. and trans., *Annala rioghachta Eireann / Annals of the kingdom of Ireland by the four masters*, 7 vols. (1848–51); 2nd edn (1856); 3rd edn (1990)

Allibone, *Dict.* — S. A. Allibone, *A critical dictionary of English literature and British and American authors*, 3 vols. (1859–71); suppl. by J. F. Kirk, 2 vols. (1891)

ANB — J. A. Garraty and M. C. Carnes, eds., *American national biography*, 24 vols. (1999)

Anderson, *Scot. nat.* — W. Anderson, *The Scottish nation, or, The surnames, families, literature, honours, and biographical history of the people of Scotland*, 3 vols. (1859–63)

Ann. mon. — H. R. Luard, ed., *Annales monastici*, 5 vols., Rolls Series, 36 (1864–9)

Ann. Ulster — S. Mac Airt and G. Mac Niocaill, eds., *Annals of Ulster (to AD 1131)* (1983)

APC — *Acts of the privy council of England*, new ser., 46 vols. (1890–1964)

APS — *The acts of the parliaments of Scotland*, 12 vols. in 13 (1814–75)

Arber, *Regs. Stationers* — F. Arber, ed., *A transcript of the registers of the Company of Stationers of London, 1554–1640 AD*, 5 vols. (1875–94)

ArchR — *Architectural Review*

ASC — D. Whitelock, D. C. Douglas, and S. I. Tucker, ed. and trans., *The Anglo-Saxon Chronicle: a revised translation* (1961)

AS chart. — P. H. Sawyer, *Anglo-Saxon charters: an annotated list and bibliography*, Royal Historical Society Guides and Handbooks (1968)

AusDB — D. Pike and others, eds., *Australian dictionary of biography*, 16 vols. (1966–2002)

Baker, *Serjeants* — J. H. Baker, *The order of serjeants at law*, SeldS, suppl. ser., 5 (1984)

Bale, *Cat.* — J. Bale, *Scriptorum illustrium Maioris Brytannie, quam nunc Angliam et Scotiam vocant: catalogus*, 2 vols. in 1 (Basel, 1557–9); facs. edn (1971)

Bale, *Index* — J. Bale, *Index Britanniae scriptorum*, ed. R. L. Poole and M. Bateson (1902); facs. edn (1990)

BBCS — *Bulletin of the Board of Celtic Studies*

BDMBR — J. O. Baylen and N. J. Gossman, eds., *Biographical dictionary of modern British radicals*, 3 vols. in 4 (1979–88)

Bede, *Hist. eccl.* — *Bede's Ecclesiastical history of the English people*, ed. and trans. B. Colgrave and R. A. B. Mynors, OMT (1969); repr. (1991)

Bénézit, *Dict.* — E. Bénézit, *Dictionnaire critique et documentaire des peintres, sculpteurs, dessinateurs et graveurs*, 3 vols. (Paris, 1911–23); new edn, 8 vols. (1948–66); 3rd edn (1966); 3rd edn, rev. and enl., 10 vols. (1976); 4th edn, 14 vols. (1999)

BIHR — *Bulletin of the Institute of Historical Research*

Birch, *Seals* — W. de Birch, *Catalogue of seals in the department of manuscripts in the British Museum*, 6 vols. (1887–1900)

Bishop Burnet's History — *Bishop Burnet's History of his own time*, ed. M. J. Routh, 2nd edn, 6 vols. (1833)

Blackwood — *Blackwood's [Edinburgh] Magazine*, 328 vols. (1817–1980)

Blain, Clements & Grundy, *Feminist comp.* — V. Blain, P. Clements, and I. Grundy, eds., *The feminist companion to literature in English* (1990)

BL cat. — *The British Library general catalogue of printed books* [in 360 vols. with suppls., also CD-ROM and online]

BMJ — *British Medical Journal*

Boase & Courtney, *Bibl. Corn.* — G. C. Boase and W. P. Courtney, *Bibliotheca Cornubiensis: a catalogue of the writings … of Cornishmen*, 3 vols. (1874–82)

Boase, *Mod. Eng. biog.* — F. Boase, *Modern English biography: containing many thousand concise memoirs of persons who have died since the year 1850*, 6 vols. (privately printed, Truro, 1892–1921); repr. (1965)

Boswell, *Life* — *Boswell's Life of Johnson: together with Journal of a tour to the Hebrides and Johnson's Diary of a journey into north Wales*, ed. G. B. Hill, enl. edn, rev. L. F. Powell, 6 vols. (1934–50); 2nd edn (1964); repr. (1971)

Brown & Stratton, *Brit. mus.* — J. D. Brown and S. S. Stratton, *British musical biography* (1897)

Bryan, *Painters* — M. Bryan, *A biographical and critical dictionary of painters and engravers*, 2 vols. (1816); new edn, ed. G. Stanley (1849); new edn, ed. R. E. Graves and W. Armstrong, 2 vols. (1886–9); [4th edn], ed. G. C. Williamson, 5 vols. (1903–5) [various reprs.]

Burke, *Gen. GB* — J. Burke, *A genealogical and heraldic history of the commoners of Great Britain and Ireland*, 4 vols. (1833–8); new edn as *A genealogical and heraldic dictionary of the landed gentry of Great Britain and Ireland*, 3 vols. [1843–9] [many later edns]

Burke, *Gen. Ire.* — J. B. Burke, *A genealogical and heraldic history of the landed gentry of Ireland* (1899); 2nd edn (1904); 3rd edn (1912); 4th edn (1958); 5th edn as *Burke's Irish family records* (1976)

Burke, *Peerage* — J. Burke, *A general [later edns A genealogical] and heraldic dictionary of the peerage and baronetage of the United Kingdom [later edns the British empire]* (1829–)

Burney, *Hist. mus.* — C. Burney, *A general history of music, from the earliest ages to the present period*, 4 vols. (1776–89)

Burtchaell & Sadleir, *Alum. Dubl.* — G. D. Burtchaell and T. U. Sadleir, *Alumni Dublinenses: a register of the students, graduates, and provosts of Trinity College* (1924); [2nd edn], with suppl., in 2 pts (1935)

Calamy rev. — A. G. Matthews, *Calamy revised* (1934); repr. (1988)

CCI — *Calendar of confirmations and inventories granted and given up in the several commissariots of Scotland* (1876–)

CCIR — *Calendar of the close rolls preserved in the Public Record Office*, 47 vols. (1892–1963)

CDS — J. Bain, ed., *Calendar of documents relating to Scotland*, 4 vols., PRO (1881–8); suppl. vol. 5, ed. G. G. Simpson and J. D. Galbraith [1986]

CEPR letters — W. H. Bliss, C. Johnson, and J. Twemlow, eds., *Calendar of entries in the papal registers relating to Great Britain and Ireland: papal letters* (1893–)

CGPLA — *Calendars of the grants of probate and letters of administration* [in 4 ser.: *England & Wales, Northern Ireland, Ireland*, and *Éire*]

Chambers, *Scots.* — R. Chambers, ed., *A biographical dictionary of eminent Scotsmen*, 4 vols. (1832–5)

Chancery records — chancery records pubd by the PRO

Chancery records (RC) — chancery records pubd by the Record Commissions

CIPM	*Calendar of inquisitions post mortem*, [20 vols.], PRO (1904–); also *Henry VII*, 3 vols. (1898–1955)
Clarendon, *Hist. rebellion*	E. Hyde, earl of Clarendon, *The history of the rebellion and civil wars in England*, 6 vols. (1888); repr. (1958) and (1992)
Cobbett, *Parl. hist.*	W. Cobbett and J. Wright, eds., *Cobbett's Parliamentary history of England*, 36 vols. (1806–1820)
Colvin, *Archs.*	H. Colvin, *A biographical dictionary of British architects, 1600–1840*, 3rd edn (1995)
Cooper, *Ath. Cantab.*	C. H. Cooper and T. Cooper, *Athenae Cantabrigienses*, 3 vols. (1858–1913); repr. (1967)
CPR	*Calendar of the patent rolls preserved in the Public Record Office* (1891–)
Crockford	*Crockford's Clerical Directory*
CS	Camden Society
CSP	*Calendar of state papers* [in 11 ser.: domestic, Scotland, Scottish series, Ireland, colonial, Commonwealth, foreign, Spain [at Simancas], Rome, Milan, and Venice]
CYS	Canterbury and York Society
DAB	*Dictionary of American biography*, 21 vols. (1928–36), repr. in 11 vols. (1964); 10 suppls. (1944–96)
DBB	D. J. Jeremy, ed., *Dictionary of business biography*, 5 vols. (1984–6)
DCB	G. W. Brown and others, *Dictionary of Canadian biography*, [14 vols.] (1966–)
Debrett's Peerage	*Debrett's Peerage* (1803–) [sometimes *Debrett's Illustrated peerage*]
Desmond, *Botanists*	R. Desmond, *Dictionary of British and Irish botanists and horticulturists* (1977); rev. edn (1994)
Dir. Brit. archs.	A. Felstead, J. Franklin, and L. Pinfield, eds., *Directory of British architects, 1834–1900* (1993); 2nd edn, ed. A. Brodie and others, 2 vols. (2001)
DLB	J. M. Bellamy and J. Saville, eds., *Dictionary of labour biography*, [10 vols.] (1972–)
DLitB	Dictionary of Literary Biography
DNB	*Dictionary of national biography*, 63 vols. (1885–1900), suppl., 3 vols. (1901); repr. in 22 vols. (1908–9); 10 further suppls. (1912–96); *Missing persons* (1993)
DNZB	W. H. Oliver and C. Orange, eds., *The dictionary of New Zealand biography*, 5 vols. (1990–2000)
DSAB	W. J. de Kock and others, eds., *Dictionary of South African biography*, 5 vols. (1968–87)
DSB	C. C. Gillispie and F. L. Holmes, eds., *Dictionary of scientific biography*, 16 vols. (1970–80); repr. in 8 vols. (1981); 2 vol. suppl. (1990)
DSBB	A. Slaven and S. Checkland, eds., *Dictionary of Scottish business biography, 1860–1960*, 2 vols. (1986–90)
DSCHT	N. M. de S. Cameron and others, eds., *Dictionary of Scottish church history and theology* (1993)
Dugdale, *Monasticon*	W. Dugdale, *Monasticon Anglicanum*, 3 vols. (1655–72); 2nd edn, 3 vols. (1661–82); new edn, ed. J. Caley, J. Ellis, and B. Bandinel, 6 vols. in 8 pts (1817–30); repr. (1846) and (1970)
DWB	J. E. Lloyd and others, eds., *Dictionary of Welsh biography down to 1940* (1959) [Eng. trans. of *Y bywgraffiadur Cymreig hyd 1940*, 2nd edn (1954)]
EdinR	*Edinburgh Review, or, Critical Journal*
EETS	Early English Text Society
Emden, *Cam.*	A. B. Emden, *A biographical register of the University of Cambridge to 1500* (1963)
Emden, *Oxf.*	A. B. Emden, *A biographical register of the University of Oxford to AD 1500*, 3 vols. (1957–9); also *A biographical register of the University of Oxford, AD 1501 to 1540* (1974)
EngHR	*English Historical Review*
Engraved Brit. ports.	F. M. O'Donoghue and H. M. Hake, *Catalogue of engraved British portraits preserved in the department of prints and drawings in the British Museum*, 6 vols. (1908–25)
ER	The English Reports, 178 vols. (1900–32)
ESTC	*English short title catalogue, 1475–1800* [CD-ROM and online]
Evelyn, *Diary*	*The diary of John Evelyn*, ed. E. S. De Beer, 6 vols. (1955); repr. (2000)
Farington, *Diary*	*The diary of Joseph Farington*, ed. K. Garlick and others, 17 vols. (1978–98)
Fasti Angl. (Hardy)	J. Le Neve, *Fasti ecclesiae Anglicanae*, ed. T. D. Hardy, 3 vols. (1854)
Fasti Angl., 1066–1300	[J. Le Neve], *Fasti ecclesiae Anglicanae, 1066–1300*, ed. D. E. Greenway and J. S. Barrow, [8 vols.] (1968–)
Fasti Angl., 1300–1541	[J. Le Neve], *Fasti ecclesiae Anglicanae, 1300–1541*, 12 vols. (1962–7)
Fasti Angl., 1541–1857	[J. Le Neve], *Fasti ecclesiae Anglicanae, 1541–1857*, ed. J. M. Horn, D. M. Smith, and D. S. Bailey, [9 vols.] (1969–)
Fasti Scot.	H. Scott, *Fasti ecclesiae Scoticanae*, 3 vols. in 6 (1871); new edn, [11 vols.] (1915–)
FO List	*Foreign Office List*
Fortescue, *Brit. army*	J. W. Fortescue, *A history of the British army*, 13 vols. (1899–1930)
Foss, *Judges*	E. Foss, *The judges of England*, 9 vols. (1848–64); repr. (1966)
Foster, *Alum. Oxon.*	J. Foster, ed., *Alumni Oxonienses: the members of the University of Oxford, 1715–1886*, 4 vols. (1887–8); later edn (1891); also *Alumni Oxonienses … 1500–1714*, 4 vols. (1891–2); 8 vol. repr. (1968) and (2000)
Fuller, *Worthies*	T. Fuller, *The history of the worthies of England*, 4 pts (1662); new edn, 2 vols., ed. J. Nichols (1811); new edn, 3 vols., ed. P. A. Nuttall (1840); repr. (1965)
GEC, *Baronetage*	G. E. Cokayne, *Complete baronetage*, 6 vols. (1900–09); repr. (1983) [microprint]
GEC, *Peerage*	G. E. C. [G. E. Cokayne], *The complete peerage of England, Scotland, Ireland, Great Britain, and the United Kingdom*, 8 vols. (1887–98); new edn, ed. V. Gibbs and others, 14 vols. in 15 (1910–98); microprint repr. (1982) and (1987)
Genest, *Eng. stage*	J. Genest, *Some account of the English stage from the Restoration in 1660 to 1830*, 10 vols. (1832); repr. [New York, 1965]
Gillow, *Lit. biog. hist.*	J. Gillow, *A literary and biographical history or bibliographical dictionary of the English Catholics, from the breach with Rome, in 1534, to the present time*, 5 vols. [1885–1902]; repr. (1961); repr. with preface by C. Gillow (1999)
Gir. Camb. opera	*Giraldi Cambrensis opera*, ed. J. S. Brewer, J. F. Dimock, and G. F. Warner, 8 vols., Rolls Series, 21 (1861–91)
GJ	*Geographical Journal*

Gladstone, *Diaries* — *The Gladstone diaries: with cabinet minutes and prime-ministerial correspondence*, ed. M. R. D. Foot and H. C. G. Matthew, 14 vols. (1968–94)

GM — *Gentleman's Magazine*

Graves, *Artists* — A. Graves, ed., *A dictionary of artists who have exhibited works in the principal London exhibitions of oil paintings from 1760 to 1880* (1884); new edn (1895); 3rd edn (1901); facs. edn (1969); repr. [1970], (1973), and (1984)

Graves, *Brit. Inst.* — A. Graves, *The British Institution, 1806–1867: a complete dictionary of contributors and their work from the foundation of the institution* (1875); facs. edn (1908); repr. (1969)

Graves, *RA exhibitors* — A. Graves, *The Royal Academy of Arts: a complete dictionary of contributors and their work from its foundation in 1769 to 1904*, 8 vols. (1905–6); repr. in 4 vols. (1970) and (1972)

Graves, *Soc. Artists* — A. Graves, *The Society of Artists of Great Britain, 1760–1791, the Free Society of Artists, 1761–1783: a complete dictionary* (1907); facs. edn (1969)

Greaves & Zaller, *BDBR* — R. L. Greaves and R. Zaller, eds., *Biographical dictionary of British radicals in the seventeenth century*, 3 vols. (1982–4)

Grove, *Dict. mus.* — G. Grove, ed., *A dictionary of music and musicians*, 5 vols. (1878–90); 2nd edn, ed. J. A. Fuller Maitland (1904–10); 3rd edn, ed. H. C. Colles (1927); 4th edn with suppl. (1940); 5th edn, ed. E. Blom, 9 vols. (1954); suppl. (1961) [see also *New Grove*]

Hall, *Dramatic ports.* — L. A. Hall, *Catalogue of dramatic portraits in the theatre collection of the Harvard College library*, 4 vols. (1930–34)

Hansard — *Hansard's parliamentary debates*, ser. 1–5 (1803–)

Highfill, Burnim & Langhans, *BDA* — P. H. Highfill, K. A. Burnim, and E. A. Langhans, *A biographical dictionary of actors, actresses, musicians, dancers, managers, and other stage personnel in London, 1660–1800*, 16 vols. (1973–93)

Hist. U. Oxf. — T. H. Aston, ed., *The history of the University of Oxford*, 8 vols. (1984–2000) [1: *The early Oxford schools*, ed. J. I. Catto (1984); 2: *Late medieval Oxford*, ed. J. I. Catto and R. Evans (1992); 3: *The collegiate university*, ed. J. McConica (1986); 4: *Seventeenth-century Oxford*, ed. N. Tyacke (1997); 5: *The eighteenth century*, ed. L. S. Sutherland and L. G. Mitchell (1986); 6–7: *Nineteenth-century Oxford*, ed. M. G. Brock and M. C. Curthoys (1997–2000); 8: *The twentieth century*, ed. B. Harrison (2000)]

HJ — *Historical Journal*

HMC — Historical Manuscripts Commission

Holdsworth, *Eng. law* — W. S. Holdsworth, *A history of English law*, ed. A. L. Goodhart and H. L. Hanbury, 17 vols. (1903–72)

HoP, *Commons* — *The history of parliament: the House of Commons* [1386–1421, ed. J. S. Roskell, L. Clark, and C. Rawcliffe, 4 vols. (1992); 1509–1558, ed. S. T. Bindoff, 3 vols. (1982); 1558–1603, ed. P. W. Hasler, 3 vols. (1981); 1660–1690, ed. B. D. Henning, 3 vols. (1983); 1690–1715, ed. D. W. Hayton, E. Cruickshanks, and S. Handley, 5 vols. (2002); 1715–1754, ed. R. Sedgwick, 2 vols. (1970); 1754–1790, ed. L. Namier and J. Brooke, 3 vols. (1964), repr. (1985); 1790–1820, ed. R. G. Thorne, 5 vols. (1986); in draft (used with permission): 1422–1504, 1604–1629, 1640–1660, and 1820–1832]

IGI — *International Genealogical Index*, Church of Jesus Christ of the Latterday Saints

ILN — *Illustrated London News*

IMC — Irish Manuscripts Commission

Irving, *Scots.* — J. Irving, ed., *The book of Scotsmen eminent for achievements in arms and arts, church and state, law, legislation and literature, commerce, science, travel and philanthropy* (1881)

JCS — *Journal of the Chemical Society*

JHC — *Journals of the House of Commons*

JHL — *Journals of the House of Lords*

John of Worcester, *Chron.* — *The chronicle of John of Worcester*, ed. R. R. Darlington and P. McGurk, trans. J. Bray and P. McGurk, 3 vols., OMT (1995–) [vol. 1 forthcoming]

Keeler, *Long Parliament* — M. F. Keeler, *The Long Parliament, 1640–1641: a biographical study of its members* (1954)

Kelly, *Handbk* — *The upper ten thousand: an alphabetical list of all members of noble families*, 3 vols. (1875–7); continued as *Kelly's handbook of the upper ten thousand for 1878* [1879], 2 vols. (1878–9); continued as *Kelly's handbook to the titled, landed and official classes*, 94 vols. (1880–1973)

LondG — *London Gazette*

LP Henry VIII — J. S. Brewer, J. Gairdner, and R. H. Brodie, eds., *Letters and papers, foreign and domestic, of the reign of Henry VIII*, 23 vols. in 38 (1862–1932); repr. (1965)

Mallalieu, *Watercolour artists* — H. L. Mallalieu, *The dictionary of British watercolour artists up to 1820*, 3 vols. (1976–90); vol. 1, 2nd edn (1986)

Memoirs FRS — *Biographical Memoirs of Fellows of the Royal Society*

MGH — Monumenta Germaniae Historica

MT — *Musical Times*

Munk, *Roll* — W. Munk, *The roll of the Royal College of Physicians of London*, 2 vols. (1861); 2nd edn, 3 vols. (1878)

N&Q — *Notes and Queries*

New Grove — S. Sadie, ed., *The new Grove dictionary of music and musicians*, 20 vols. (1980); 2nd edn, 29 vols. (2001) [also online edn; see also Grove, *Dict. mus.*]

Nichols, *Illustrations* — J. Nichols and J. B. Nichols, *Illustrations of the literary history of the eighteenth century*, 8 vols. (1817–58)

Nichols, *Lit. anecdotes* — J. Nichols, *Literary anecdotes of the eighteenth century*, 9 vols. (1812–16); facs. edn (1966)

Obits. FRS — *Obituary Notices of Fellows of the Royal Society*

O'Byrne, *Naval biog. dict.* — W. R. O'Byrne, *A naval biographical dictionary* (1849); repr. (1990); [2nd edn], 2 vols. (1861)

OHS — Oxford Historical Society

Old Westminsters — *The record of Old Westminsters*, 1–2, ed. G. F. R. Barker and A. H. Stenning (1928); suppl. 1, ed. J. B. Whitmore and G. R. Y. Radcliffe [1938]; 3, ed. J. B. Whitmore, G. R. Y. Radcliffe, and D. C. Simpson (1963); suppl. 2, ed. F. E. Pagan (1978); 4, ed. F. E. Pagan and H. E. Pagan (1992)

OMT — Oxford Medieval Texts

Ordericus Vitalis, *Eccl. hist.* — *The ecclesiastical history of Orderic Vitalis*, ed. and trans. M. Chibnall, 6 vols., OMT (1969–80); repr. (1990)

Paris, *Chron.* — *Matthaei Parisiensis, monachi sancti Albani, chronica majora*, ed. H. R. Luard, Rolls Series, 7 vols. (1872–83)

Parl. papers — *Parliamentary papers* (1801–)

PBA — *Proceedings of the British Academy*

Pepys, *Diary*	*The diary of Samuel Pepys*, ed. R. Latham and W. Matthews, 11 vols. (1970–83); repr. (1995) and (2000)
Pevsner	N. Pevsner and others, Buildings of England series
PICE	*Proceedings of the Institution of Civil Engineers*
Pipe rolls	*The great roll of the pipe for . . .*, PRSoc. (1884–)
PRO	Public Record Office
PRS	*Proceedings of the Royal Society of London*
PRSoc.	Pipe Roll Society
PTRS	*Philosophical Transactions of the Royal Society*
QR	*Quarterly Review*
RC	Record Commissions
Redgrave, *Artists*	S. Redgrave, *A dictionary of artists of the English school* (1874); rev. edn (1878); repr. (1970)
Reg. Oxf.	C. W. Boase and A. Clark, eds., *Register of the University of Oxford*, 5 vols., OHS, 1, 10–12, 14 (1885–9)
Reg. PCS	J. H. Burton and others, eds., *The register of the privy council of Scotland*, 1st ser., 14 vols. (1877–98); 2nd ser., 8 vols. (1899–1908); 3rd ser., [16 vols.] (1908–70)
Reg. RAN	H. W. C. Davis and others, eds., *Regesta regum Anglo-Normannorum, 1066–1154*, 4 vols. (1913–69)
RIBA Journal	*Journal of the Royal Institute of British Architects* [later *RIBA Journal*]
RotP	J. Strachey, ed., *Rotuli parliamentorum ut et petitiones, et placita in parliamento*, 6 vols. (1767–77)
RotS	D. Macpherson, J. Caley, and W. Illingworth, eds., *Rotuli Scotiae in Turri Londinensi et in domo capitulari Westmonasteriensi asservati*, 2 vols., RC, 14 (1814–19)
RS	Record(s) Society
Rymer, *Foedera*	T. Rymer and R. Sanderson, eds., *Foedera, conventiones, literae et cuiuscunque generis acta publica inter reges Angliae et alios quosvis imperatores, reges, pontifices, principes, vel communitates*, 20 vols. (1704–35); 2nd edn, 20 vols. (1726–35); 3rd edn, 10 vols. (1739–45); facs. edn (1967); new edn, ed. A. Clarke, J. Caley, and F. Holbrooke, 4 vols., RC, 50 (1816–30)
Sainty, *Judges*	J. Sainty, ed., *The judges of England, 1272–1990*, SeldS, suppl. ser., 10 (1993)
Sainty, *King's counsel*	J. Sainty, ed., *A list of English law officers and king's counsel*, SeldS, suppl. ser., 7 (1987)
SCH	Studies in Church History
Scots peerage	J. B. Paul, ed. *The Scots peerage, founded on Wood's edition of Sir Robert Douglas's Peerage of Scotland, containing an historical and genealogical account of the nobility of that kingdom*, 9 vols. (1904–14)
SeldS	Selden Society
SHR	*Scottish Historical Review*
State trials	T. B. Howell and T. J. Howell, eds., *Cobbett's Complete collection of state trials*, 34 vols. (1809–28)
STC, 1475–1640	A. W. Pollard, G. R. Redgrave, and others, eds., *A short-title catalogue of . . . English books . . . 1475–1640* (1926); 2nd edn, ed. W. A. Jackson, F. S. Ferguson, and K. F. Pantzer, 3 vols. (1976–91) [see also Wing, *STC*]
STS	Scottish Text Society
SurtS	Surtees Society
Symeon of Durham, *Opera*	*Symeonis monachi opera omnia*, ed. T. Arnold, 2 vols., Rolls Series, 75 (1882–5); repr. (1965)
Tanner, *Bibl. Brit.-Hib.*	T. Tanner, *Bibliotheca Britannico-Hibernica*, ed. D. Wilkins (1748); repr. (1963)
Thieme & Becker, *Allgemeines Lexikon*	U. Thieme, F. Becker, and H. Vollmer, eds., *Allgemeines Lexikon der bildenden Künstler von der Antike bis zur Gegenwart*, 37 vols. (Leipzig, 1907–50); repr. (1961–5), (1983), and (1992)
Thurloe, *State papers*	*A collection of the state papers of John Thurloe*, ed. T. Birch, 7 vols. (1742)
TLS	*Times Literary Supplement*
Tout, *Admin. hist.*	T. F. Tout, *Chapters in the administrative history of mediaeval England: the wardrobe, the chamber, and the small seals*, 6 vols. (1920–33); repr. (1967)
TRHS	*Transactions of the Royal Historical Society*
VCH	H. A. Doubleday and others, eds., *The Victoria history of the counties of England*, [88 vols.] (1900–)
Venn, *Alum. Cant.*	J. Venn and J. A. Venn, *Alumni Cantabrigienses: a biographical list of all known students, graduates, and holders of office at the University of Cambridge, from the earliest times to 1900*, 10 vols. (1922–54); repr. in 2 vols. (1974–8)
Vertue, *Note books*	[G. Vertue], *Note books*, ed. K. Esdaile, earl of Ilchester, and H. M. Hake, 6 vols., Walpole Society, 18, 20, 22, 24, 26, 30 (1930–55)
VF	*Vanity Fair*
Walford, *County families*	E. Walford, *The county families of the United Kingdom, or, Royal manual of the titled and untitled aristocracy of Great Britain and Ireland* (1860)
Walker rev.	A. G. Matthews, *Walker revised: being a revision of John Walker's Sufferings of the clergy during the grand rebellion, 1642–60* (1948); repr. (1988)
Walpole, *Corr.*	*The Yale edition of Horace Walpole's correspondence*, ed. W. S. Lewis, 48 vols. (1937–83)
Ward, *Men of the reign*	T. H. Ward, ed., *Men of the reign: a biographical dictionary of eminent persons of British and colonial birth who have died during the reign of Queen Victoria* (1885); repr. (Graz, 1968)
Waterhouse, *18c painters*	E. Waterhouse, *The dictionary of 18th century painters in oils and crayons* (1981); repr. as *British 18th century painters in oils and crayons* (1991), vol. 2 of *Dictionary of British art*
Watt, *Bibl. Brit.*	R. Watt, *Bibliotheca Britannica, or, A general index to British and foreign literature*, 4 vols. (1824) [many reprs.]
Wellesley index	W. E. Houghton, ed., *The Wellesley index to Victorian periodicals, 1824–1900*, 5 vols. (1966–89); new edn (1999) [CD-ROM]
Wing, *STC*	D. Wing, ed., *Short-title catalogue of . . . English books . . . 1641–1700*, 3 vols. (1945–51); 2nd edn (1972–88); rev. and enl. edn, ed. J. J. Morrison, C. W. Nelson, and M. Seccombe, 4 vols. (1994–8) [see also *STC, 1475–1640*]
Wisden	*John Wisden's Cricketer's Almanack*
Wood, *Ath. Oxon.*	A. Wood, *Athenae Oxonienses . . . to which are added the Fasti*, 2 vols. (1691–2); 2nd edn (1721); new edn, 4 vols., ed. P. Bliss (1813–20); repr. (1967) and (1969)
Wood, *Vic. painters*	C. Wood, *Dictionary of Victorian painters* (1971); 2nd edn (1978); 3rd edn as *Victorian painters*, 2 vols. (1995), vol. 4 of *Dictionary of British art*
WW	*Who's who* (1849–)
WWBMP	M. Stenton and S. Lees, eds., *Who's who of British members of parliament*, 4 vols. (1976–81)
WWW	*Who was who* (1929–)

Haycock, Edward (*bap.* 1790, *d.* 1870), architect, was baptized on 20 September 1790 at St Chad's Church, Shrewsbury, the second of the three sons of John Hiram Haycock (1759–1830), architect and builder, of Shrewsbury, and his wife, Elizabeth (1758/9–1848), daughter of William Trevitt of Newport. He became a pupil of Jeffry Wyatville, entered the Royal Academy Schools in 1809, and exhibited student's work at the Royal Academy from 1808 to 1810. After returning to Shrewsbury to join his father in the family business, he exhibited at the Liverpool Academy from 1812 to 1814 and in the latter year became involved in an ambitious public project in the town, the erection of a monumental column in honour of Rowland Hill, first Viscount Hill. A competition was held, in which Haycock won the second premium; and it was then decided to adopt his design but to put it 'into the hands' of Thomas Harrison of Chester, who made certain minor modifications to it (Colvin, *Archs.*, 479).

On 13 February 1827 Haycock married in St Sepulchre, Holborn, Mary Hatton (*b.* 1801), daughter of Robert Hinckesman of London, with whom he had three sons and four daughters. Thereafter it appears that Haycock himself rather than his father was the main architect member of the family firm, although, in partnership with his brother Robert, he continued to engage in building as well as architecture until *c.*1845, after which he practised as an architect only. From 1834 to 1866 he was also county surveyor for Shropshire, a post previously held by John Hiram Haycock from 1824 until his death. He was a moderately prolific architect with an extensive practice in Shropshire, the Welsh marches, and south Wales, and his output encompassed further public buildings, including the Royal Infirmary, Shrewsbury (1827–30), numerous churches, and country houses. The churches are in a conventional lancet Gothic style, one example of which is St George's, Frankwell, Shrewsbury (1831–2); but in his major country house commissions, notably Clytha Court, Monmouthshire (1824–8) and Millichope Park, Shropshire (1835–40), Haycock confirmed his promise as a neoclassical designer of considerable merit.

Haycock also played an active part in the political life of Shrewsbury: he sat on the council for thirty-four years, rose to become an alderman, and served as mayor in 1842. He was a friend of the Shropshire architect John Carline and also of Dr Robert Waring Darwin, the father of the naturalist Charles Darwin. The eldest son, Edward junior, continued Haycock's practice after his death, which occurred in Shrewsbury on 20 December 1870. Haycock was buried in St Chad's churchyard, Shrewsbury.

PETER LEACH, *rev.*

Sources Colvin, *Archs.* · J. L. Hobbs, 'The Haycocks', *Shropshire Magazine*, 11 (Feb 1960), 17–18 · J. Morris, 'The mayors of Shrewsbury', *Transactions of the Shropshire Archaeological Society*, 4th ser., 9 (1923–4), 1–42, esp. 28–30 · *CGPLA Eng. & Wales* (1871)

Wealth at death under £4000: probate, 4 March 1871, *CGPLA Eng. & Wales*

Haycraft, Colin Berry (1929–1994), publisher, was born in Quetta, India, on 12 January 1929, the younger son of William Church Stacpoole Haycraft (1891–1929), army officer, and his wife, Olive Lillian Esmée, *née* King (*b.* 1901). His father, a major in the 5/8 Punjab regiment, was murdered on the parade ground in Quetta by one of his men, when Haycraft was still an infant; his mother subsequently returned to England. He had one elder brother, John Stacpoole *Haycraft (1926–1996), who became an expert in language teaching.

Following school at Wellington College and two years' national service, Haycraft pursued a distinguished undergraduate career at Oxford. Queen's College (which he entered as a scholar in 1949) remained a love of his life, rewarded almost too late by an honorary fellowship. He graduated with a first in *literae humaniores* and won blues in lawn tennis, rackets, and squash, playing squash for England. With his spare frame and face, his quickness of eye and brain remained all his life. He continued to write Greek verse (and sometimes not altogether polite epigrams), his love of classics being crowned by presidency of the Classical Association.

After graduating Haycraft worked on the *Daily Mirror*, first in Lagos and then as personal assistant to his cousin Cecil Harmsworth King, finding it a more interesting paper than later popular journalism, though the restraints of his position proved tiresome. Following a brief period on *The Observer* he found his true vocation—publishing—at Bodley Head from 1959 onwards, then at Weidenfeld and Nicolson a year or so later. As a director of the latter company he ran Lord Weidenfeld's exceptionally well-illustrated World University Library series with great success. In 1956 he had married Anna Margaret (*b.* 1932), daughter of John and Alexandra Lindholm; she was subsequently to become well known as a novelist, writing as Alice Thomas Ellis. Of their six children one daughter died in infancy, and a son, Joshua, died as a result of an accident when adolescent. This tragedy affected Haycraft and his family very deeply. It may have strengthened Anna's Catholic persuasion (she was a novice nun before their marriage), though Haycraft himself remained a robust non-believer. The religious conflict, half joking, half serious, seemed to strengthen their relationship.

In 1968, with his friend Timothy Simon (who died three years later), Haycraft bought the small but highly regarded publishing house Gerald Duckworth & Co. Ltd from Lord Horder. Mervyn Horder retained his interest in the firm, both professionally and with memorable contributions to the sometimes risqué Duckworth parties, such as playing the piano while wearing a Victorian bathing dress to accompany a Spanish belly dancer. Like its director, Duckworths combined sometimes over-the-top jollity with serious contributions to scholarship.

Haycraft (who succeeded Horder as chairman of Duckworths in 1971) published books that interested him—from knitting patterns to philosophy, as he would say—by eminent authors from the universities, preferably Oxford, and household-name novelists, notably his wife, Anna, and Beryl Bainbridge. He could sometimes find it difficult to deal with women novelists, with few exceptions leaving them for Anna; he was at his happiest in conversation with his fellow men over fine claret, especially at the Beefsteak Club. He was renowned for his wit, sometimes deliberately outrageous, as when, woozy during an illness, he said that now he knew what it was like to be a woman: 'Horrible!—one can't think, or see anything clearly.'

Haycraft seldom left Gloucester Crescent (near Regent's Park in London) where the family lived in a large, ever friendly house in the same road as the scene of his work—the Old Piano Factory. This 22-sided tower of Dickensian charm under Haycraft's management became truly a hive of activity where authors of all kinds and distinction were welcomed. His support of creative thinking and writing—as perhaps the last and certainly the most respected small independent publisher in London—was effective and widely appreciated. Unfortunately, his business sense did not match his editorial skills or his scholarship. Running into severe financial storms, he sold a 50 per cent share in Duckworths to Roger Shashua in 1988. Unfortunately neither this nor a subsequent arrangement with the Rowntree Trust and two other private investors was successful, and in 1991 Haycraft was forced to buy back his shares in order to regain control of the company. The trauma undoubtedly affected his health and very likely killed him. He died in London of a stroke on 24 September 1994. He was buried in the churchyard, close to his son Joshua, near their holiday house at Pennant Melangell, near Llanfyllin, north Wales.

While on holiday in Wales, Haycraft would sit all day reading and writing Greek in a smoke-filled room, drinking whisky—apparently ignoring the superb view of the surrounding landscape with its waterfall and grazing sheep. It was London, literary parties, and good company with gossip and jokes combined with serious ideas that meant most to him. Haycraft was indeed the most sociable and yet the most secret of men; optimistic in business, sometimes too trusting, while sharing others' less intelligent enthusiasms and impractical ideas. With his friends he would convey thoughts beyond words with a glance, and smile at himself with a whimsical, puckish look.

RICHARD L. GREGORY

Sources S. Martin, ed., *Colin Haycraft: maverick publisher, 1929–1994* (1995) · J. Jolliffe, *Wolf at the door. Duckworth: 100 years of Bloomsbury behaviour* (1998) · *The Times* (27 Sept 1994) · *The Independent* (30 Sept 1994) · *WWW* · personal knowledge (2004) · private information (2004) · *Army List*
Archives Bodl. Oxf., corresp. with Kurt Mendelssohn
Likenesses photograph, repro. in *The Times* · photograph, repro. in *The Independent*
Wealth at death £1,105,641: probate, 1 June 1995, *CGPLA Eng. & Wales*

Haycraft, John Stacpoole (1926–1996), English language teacher and author, was born on 11 December 1926 in Quetta, India, the elder of the two sons of William Church Stacpoole Haycraft (1891–1929), Indian army officer, and his wife, Olive Lillian Esmée (1901–1978), daughter of Lucas King, of Dublin, and his wife, Philomene, from Bavaria. His younger brother, Colin Berry *Haycraft (1929–1994), became a successful publisher. When Haycraft was

two years old, his father (a major in the 5/8 Punjab regiment) was murdered by a disaffected soldier. His family then led a roving life, mainly in France, until he was sent with a scholarship to Wellington College. Called up to the Coldstream Guards just before the end of the Second World War, he subsequently transferred to the Queen's Royal regiment, serving in India, Egypt, and Britain. He entered Jesus College, Oxford, in 1948, graduating with a second-class degree in modern history in 1951. He travelled much in vacations, and was awarded an English Speaking Union fellowship to the United States after graduation, following courses at Yale Drama School from 1951 to 1952. He returned to Europe to a lifetime's professional relationship with his Swedish wife, Brita Elisabeth, *née* Langenfelt, whom he married on 17 October 1953 in Bromma, Sweden. The couple immediately set off for Spain. They had a daughter and two sons.

For six years John and Brita Haycraft laid the bases for their careers as language entrepreneurs and teachers, founding their first school in Córdoba in 1953 and negotiating the complexities of life under Franco with humour, skill, and a great sympathy for their students. The school was launched at the beginning of worldwide English teaching's post-war expansion, and was the first school in what became the International House network. Through these schools Haycraft contrived to build a reputation as a creative although somewhat maverick figure, offering (certainly in his own view) a more flexible and dynamic alternative to the ideas on language teaching which emerged from conventional sources in the universities and the British Council. At the same time, he was able to work with these institutions whenever it was beneficial to do so, while similarly using his wide range of social and political contacts to ensure that his schools were as successful as possible across a wide range of different political and social systems.

Haycraft contributed to many language teaching developments of the 1960s and 1970s. He attracted a body of talented teachers, offering relative security in the insecure world of teaching English as a foreign language, and developed such innovations as the English Teaching Theatre, contributions to the BBC's *English by Radio*, magazines for language teachers such as *Modern English Teacher*, and most notably an intensive short programme for teacher induction which eventually became a model for the Royal Society of Arts certificates and diplomas. He also supported the International Association of Teachers of English as a Foreign Language. He thus played a significant role in the professionalization of English teaching, though (as he remarked in his posthumously published autobiography, with reference to the Association of Recognised English Language Schools), 'An uneasy trade association was not my scene' (Haycraft, 258). The only significant area to which he made no contribution was research, with which he had little patience.

Haycraft remained at heart a gifted amateur, perhaps primarily interested in writing. His Spanish experience led to *Babel in Spain* (1958), the success of which led in turn to well-received books that departed from the language teaching theme: *Italian Labyrinth* (1985) and *In Search of the French Revolution* (1989), as well as textbooks for English and teacher training.

International House in London opened in 1959, and affiliated schools developed in many other countries, sometimes encountering political difficulties, as in Lebanon or Libya, but with massive markets, particularly in Spain and Italy. Haycraft's optimism and impatience with protocol were usually assets, as was his manifest idealism; only an optimist would have moved London's International House in 1977 from slightly run-down premises in Shaftesbury Avenue to the old St James's Club in Piccadilly. He inspired many young teachers, while simultaneously benefiting from his establishment connections and skilled public relations, bringing in Harold Macmillan to open the new premises. But he was never just a businessman using the schools as a means of making profit; indeed, his enthusiasm was driven by a creative naïvety which led him to make impulsive decisions and show consistent impatience with more cautious colleagues. His energy and ebullience were his most noted features.

Haycraft combined a military appearance and speech with a modest personal lifestyle and bohemian friends. His London home was in Blackheath. He was appointed CBE in 1982, and in 1990 retired as director-general of International House, but he continued to promote English language teaching, particularly in eastern Europe, where he acted as adviser to the philanthropist George Soros. He died of heart failure on 23 May 1996 and was buried at Walberswick, Suffolk. He was survived by his wife, Brita, and their three children.

CHRISTOPHER BRUMFIT

Sources J. Haycraft, *Adventures of a language traveller* (1998) · *The Guardian* (29 May 1996) · *WWW* · personal knowledge (2004) · private information (2004) · *CGPLA Eng. & Wales* (1996)
Archives priv. coll. | International House, London, archives
Likenesses photograph, repro. in *The Guardian* · photographs, repro. in Haycraft, *Adventures*
Wealth at death £68,786: probate, 1996, *CGPLA Eng. & Wales*

Hayday, Arthur (1869–1956), trade unionist and politician, was born at 36 Roscoe Street, Plaistow, West Ham, London, in 1869, the son of Thomas Bloomfield Hayday, a labourer at a manure works, and his wife, Sarah Susannah Glander. His date of birth was registered as 27 October, although in his *Who's Who* entry he gave it as 24 October. He attended St Luke's national school in Tidal Basin, and left school at the age of nine to work in market gardening. His subsequent employments included work as a kitchen boy, chemical worker, and trimmer and stoker in the merchant navy. West Ham was the birthplace of Will Thorne's National Union of Gasworkers and General Labourers, and Hayday became an early member. His workplace activism led to victimization by his employers in 1893; the following year he joined the Marxist Social Democratic Federation (SDF), the dominant independent labour organization in West Ham.

The weakness of local Liberalism and the enthusiasm of Thorne and his lieutenants with their combination of trade union activism and socialism transformed the character of West Ham's municipal politics. Hayday was elected to the borough council on the SDF ticket in 1896. Two years later West Ham produced Britain's first Labour municipal majority, a coalition of SDF and Independent Labour Party, trades council, and Progressive members. Hayday was the only socialist alderman. The majority embarked on a programme of municipal improvements and increased expenditure. Labour lost its majority in 1900, but Hayday remained on the council until he left West Ham at the beginning of 1909.

Hayday's status in West Ham politics was enhanced by his union base. In 1898 he became a full-time official of the National Union of Gasworkers and General Labourers responsible for organization of what was rather misleadingly entitled the London district. This extended as far north as Nottingham and Derby, and as far west as Plymouth. The optimism of the union's early days had long vanished, and Hayday and his colleagues battled to maintain the union's viability. They depended very much on the organization of municipal employees, and therefore had a keen interest in political representation. Hayday was present at the foundation conference of the Labour Representation Committee (LRC) in February 1900 and his union was one of the first affiliates to the new organization. This connection allowed him, like Thorne, to combine membership of the SDF with involvement in the politics of the LRC (subsequently the Labour Party).

During 1908 members of the Gasworkers' and General Labourers' union in the midlands requested their own district organizer. Hayday was appointed to the new post and moved to Nottingham. The city's politics contrasted with those of West Ham. The Nottingham Trades Council still contained Liberal sympathizers, and working-class Liberalism was strong, not least among the local miners. Tariff reform, promoted by some Conservatives, appealed to many workers within the lace industry. No Labour candidate stood for a Nottingham parliamentary seat before 1914, and Labour's municipal representation was meagre. Hayday's robust style could grate on the respectable both within and beyond the local trade union movement. In May 1910 he created a stir when he characterized the recently deceased King Edward VII as a 'parasite'. Along with other social democrats he joined the British Socialist Party (BSP) in 1912, but was thoroughly pragmatic in his trade union, and in most of his political, activities.

Hayday took a strongly patriotic line in August 1914. He spoke on recruiting platforms and later served on the tribunals set up under the Military Service Act. As a local Conservative newspaper acknowledged, his involvement was robust: 'no one was more prompt in unmasking any shirker who masqueraded as a "conshie"' (*Nottingham Guardian*, 14 Dec 1918). When the BSP split into pro- and anti-war factions in April 1916, he went with the former, which seceded to form the National Socialist Party. His patriotism played well with many members of the Nottingham Trades Council and wartime conditions facilitated his work as a trade union organizer within what had become the National Union of General Workers.

In the general election of December 1918 Hayday fought Nottingham West as the official Labour candidate. His only opponent was a Liberal who had been regarded favourably by the pre-war trades council. Hayday's victory, based on a blend of patriotic and class sentiments, marked a decisive change in the political credibility of the local labour movement. He retained the seat at every inter-war election with the exception of 1931.

Hayday combined his parliamentary duties with a growing status within the trade union movement. He was a member of the general council of the Trades Union Congress from 1922 to 1936; his union was the largest constituent of the 1924 amalgamation that produced the National Union of General and Municipal Workers. His own politics were reflected in those of the new union. It stood unreservedly on the right of the labour movement and took a tough line against communist influence in the recriminations that followed the 1926 general strike.

Within the House of Commons Hayday emerged as one of the most influential Labour backbenchers. In part this reflected his expertise in the fine print of the complex unemployment insurance regulations. An observer noted that he was 'not an expert of the study, trained on scientific lines, and possessed of an abundance of theories, but an expert of experience' (*Yorkshire Post*, 30 June 1930). He also saw himself as representing the trade union interest within the Parliamentary Labour Party (PLP). Early contacts between the TUC and the 1929 Labour government indicated tensions. Hayday was clear about his primary loyalty:

> He was an industrialist before he was a politician. Were they going to leave it to the political intriguers who knew nothing about their movement? It was the industrial side that would have to bear the brunt of the storm.   (TUC general council, 26 June 1929, University of Warwick, TUC Archive, MS 292 75 1/14)

In the second half of 1929 the two themes coalesced. Hayday was appointed by the government to the Morris committee, set up to consider conditions of eligibility for unemployment benefit. The existing 'not genuinely seeking work' disqualification was regarded within the labour movement as both insulting, and, in areas of high unemployment, inoperable. The TUC position presented to the Morris committee was that disqualification should depend on a claimant's definite refusal of a suitable job offer. This became known as the Hayday formula. The Morris committee's recommendations did not unambiguously endorse the Hayday formula, and this ambiguity was reflected in government legislation introduced in November 1929. After much private pressure and some open criticism including a Commons speech from Hayday, the government accepted the formula.

This was the first round in a series of engagements between the TUC general council, influential Labour backbenchers, and Labour ministers that culminated in the crisis of August 1931. Hayday was regularly involved in exchanges between general council members and ministers, particularly once he became TUC chairman for the twelve months from September 1930. Although these critics always distinguished themselves sharply from the small band of left-wing rebels in the parliamentary party, their unhappiness with ministerial style and policies was made evident in private meetings. The bargaining was complex because the principal figures had a range of identities. As a trade unionist Hayday was critical of key government policies; as a party loyalist and member of the PLP consultative committee he took a tough line against open dissent. His adversary on unemployment insurance—the minister of labour, Margaret Bondfield—was also an official in his union, but in these critical encounters collegiality was limited.

Hayday pronounced the authorized requiem on the second Labour government from the chair at the Trades Union Congress held at Bristol in early September 1931: 'courageous and determined action by the national bodies invested with authority in the Labour and Trade Union Movement has saved the working class from destruction' (*TUC Report 1931*, 67). As fraternal delegate at the subsequent Labour Party conference he pronounced an anathema on the Labour ministers who had joined the National Government. They were 'political blacklegs' (*Labour Party Conference Report 1931*, 201). He insisted that future unity must involve a recognition that the Labour government had treated the unions badly.

These sentiments shaped Labour politics for several years; Hayday however was subsequently a marginal figure. He lost his Nottingham seat at the general election held in October 1931, and although he regained it in November 1935 his final period in the Commons, until his retirement in June 1945, was much less active. He died at his home, 28 Stamford Road, West Bridgford, Nottinghamshire, on 28 February 1956. He married twice, the second time in 1910, and according to several accounts fathered eighteen children (his *Who's Who* entry claimed twelve). One son, Frederick, became an official in his father's union and chaired the TUC in 1962–3.

Hayday's robust politics were typically directed to immediate objectives. In this combination he reflected the culture of West Ham Labour, and especially of its dominant figure, Will Thorne. His actions in the critical years of 1929–31 showed an acute sense of the complex relationship between the Labour government, the Labour Party, and the TUC. He articulated a political identity that was loyalist, and yet licensed distance from the actions and styles of Labour ministers. This was a crucial ingredient in the trade union and Labour Party response to the crisis of 1931.   DAVID HOWELL

Sources R. Skidelsky, *Politicians and the slump* (1967) • D. Howell, *MacDonald's party: Labour identities and crisis, 1922–1931* (2002) • H. Clegg, *General union* (1954) • P. Wyncoll, 'A history of the labour movement in Nottingham, 1880–1918', PhD diss., Open University, 1982 • P. Thompson, *Socialists, liberals and labour: the struggle for London, 1885–1914* (1967) • J. Johnston, *A hundred commoners* (1931) • S. V. Bracher, *The Herald book of labour members* (1924) [profile] • *Nottingham Guardian* [election reports] • *NUGMW Journal* • WWW • b. cert. • d. cert.

Archives People's History Museum, Manchester, parliamentary labour party minutes · University of Warwick, Trades Union Congress archives, MS 292 · Working Class Movement Library, Salford, records of National Union of General and Municipal Workers and its predecessors
Likenesses photograph, University of York, *Dictionary of labour biography* files
Wealth at death £8106 2s. 8d.: probate, 27 June 1956, *CGPLA Eng. & Wales*

Hayday, James (1796–1872), bookbinder, was born in London. Of his parents, nothing is known. He was apprenticed to Charles Marchant, vellum binder, 12 Old Gloucester Street, Queen Square, London, and then for some time worked as a journeyman commencing business in a very humble way. In 1825 he became one of the auditors of the Journeymen Bookbinders' Trade Society. In 1833 he rented premises at 31 Little Queen Street, Lincoln's Inn Fields, where he continued until his retirement in 1861. Hayday had long seen the need to make printed books open freely and lie flat as in the example of Samuel Bagster's polyglot Bibles, which were bound by Joseph Welsh of 10 Queen Street, Golden Square, in what was known as 'Bagster's Renowned Binding'. These books were made flexible, and covered with purple pin-headed sealskin with a blind tool ornament. Constant opening of traditionally bound books disfigured the grain of the leather, and to obviate this Hayday introduced the cross or pin-headed grain known as Turkey morocco. In his own binding he sewed the books fully along every sheet, a technique that caused extra thickness that Hayday remedied by sewing with silk, rather than thread. Also, in order to equalize the thickness he rounded the fore edges more than was customary. To make the back tight he dispensed with the ordinary backing of paper, and fastened the leather cover down to the back.

Works bound by Hayday became famous and increased in monetary value. Edward Gardner of the Oxford Warehouse, 7 Paternoster Row, London, secured Hayday's services for the Oxford University Press. William Pickering, bookseller, of 57 Chancery Lane, also introduced him to many wealthy patrons. After entering into a brief partnership with Mr Boyce, 'a finisher', he again started on his own account at 31 Little Queen Street. Unable to compete with other and cheaper binders, he was adjudicated a bankrupt on 10 June 1861. Hayday sold the use of his name to William Mansell, who succeeded to the bookbinding establishment. Retiring to St Leonards Hayday died there on 19 March 1872, aged seventy-six. A number of his bindings are in the National Art Library, Victoria and Albert Museum, London.

G. C. BOASE, *rev.* HELEN CAROLINE JONES

Sources J. Owen, *The sermon on the mount* (1844) [bound by Hayday] · F. Summerly [H. Cole], *Traditional nursery songs of England*, 2nd edn (1846) [bound by Hayday] · G. Daniel, *Democritus in London: with the mad pranks and comical conceits of Motley and Robin Goodfellow* (1852) [bound by Hayday]

Hayden, George (*d.* 1722?), composer, was organist of the church of St Mary Magdalen, Bermondsey, from December 1713 until his death, which probably took place in the summer of 1722. He composed three italianate cantatas, *Martillo*, *Thyrsis*, and *Neptune and Amymone* (1717), which achieved some success and were approved by both Charles Burney and Sir John Hawkins. Two of his songs enjoyed particular success—'New Mad Tom' (performed by Bartholomew Platt at Sadler's Wells) and 'As I saw fair Clora walk alone', which was republished as late as 1930.

L. M. MIDDLETON, *rev.* K. D. REYNOLDS

Sources M. Boyd, 'Hayden, George', *New Grove* · W. H. Husk, 'Hayden, George', Grove, *Dict. mus.* (1927) · Burney, *Hist. mus.*, 4.650 · J. Hawkins, *A general history of the science and practice of music*, 3 (1776), 825

Hayden, Mary Teresa (1862–1942), historian and campaigner for women's causes, was born in Dublin on 19 May 1862, the daughter of Thomas Hayden (1823–1881), physician, and his wife, Mary Anne Ryan (*d.* 1873). Thomas Hayden was born in Parsonsville, co. Tipperary, the son of a Protestant father and a Catholic mother. The children of that marriage were brought up in the Roman Catholic faith, and after completing his medical training Thomas Hayden served as professor of anatomy at the school of medicine in the Catholic University of Ireland (1855–81). He in turn raised his own children, Mary, and her brother, John Joseph (1859–1936), as Catholics, assuming an increasingly active role in their upbringing after the death of his wife in 1873.

Mary Hayden was sent as a boarder to the Ursuline convent at Thurles, co. Tipperary, in 1873, where she excelled academically, distinguishing herself in history, geography, and Christian doctrine. However, she disliked boarding and having been sent in 1875 to Mount Anville, a prestigious convent school, in co. Dublin she left after only two months. She subsequently attended Mount Anville's newly opened day school in Harcourt Street, Dublin. An eager and successful student, Hayden initially benefited from her father's progressive views on education. But when her rebellious streak became apparent and she failed to conform to the 'ladylike' manner he deemed appropriate, her father objected to her academic aspirations and denounced her behaviour as 'fast'. Hayden was frequently expected to serve as hostess at numerous social events at the family home in fashionable Merrion Square, Dublin, but she found such occasions dull, despairing in particular of the well-bred women she was required to entertain and to emulate. Labelled a 'bluestocking' by her closest friends, she took up smoking and, to the despair of her father, continued to protest against her exclusion from such masculine activities as cricket, politics, and intellectual life.

After the death of her father in 1881, Hayden embarked in earnest on her academic career. She attended classes in Dublin at the Dominican convent in Eccles Street and the protestant Alexandra College, the most progressive and genuinely academic women's college in Ireland. She studied languages and literature, winning a scholarship in modern languages and taking a BA with honours at the Royal University of Ireland in 1885. Among the first Irish female graduates, she won further distinction in 1887 when she graduated from the Royal University with an MA with first class honours. In 1895 she was awarded a

Royal University junior fellowship in English and history, but, to her dismay, she was not awarded a university fellowship. Convinced that she was excluded from a senior university post because of her sex, she taught instead at a number of women's colleges, and became increasingly involved in the movement to improve provision for female students and academics.

Hayden made her first public pronouncement on the position of women in the Royal University in 1888, when she participated in the publication of a pamphlet, *The Case of the Catholic Lady Students of the Royal University Stated*. She subsequently led the campaign to have women accepted as full students at University College, Dublin, and in 1902 she co-founded and became vice-president of the Women Graduates and Candidate Graduates Association. An advocate of women's suffrage, she joined the Irish Women's Franchise League, became a member of the Irishwomen's Suffrage and Local Government Association and co-founded the Irish Catholic Women's Suffrage Society in 1915. Hayden was also a founder member and president of the Irish Women Patrols, a volunteer women's police force established in 1914. An energetic philanthropist, she also founded the St Joan of Arc Girls' Club for poor children and supported the Alexandra College Guild for social work.

A member of the National Executive of the Gaelic League, Hayden became increasingly interested in Irish history and language. This was reflected in her appointment in 1909 as lecturer in modern Irish history at University College, Dublin. She was promoted to professor in 1911 and became the only female founder member of the senate of the new National University of Ireland in 1909, a position she held until 1924. In recognition of her contribution to the National University, she was created an honorary DLitt in 1935. A popular professor, she maintained her dedication to women's education, holding the presidency of the National University Women Graduates' Association from 1913 until her death. A prolific writer, Hayden published short stories and scholarly articles and reviews on numerous aspects of Irish history and culture in journals including *Spectre*, *New Ireland Review*, and *Studies*. Published in 1921 and co-authored with George A. Moonan, *A Short History of the Irish People from the Earliest Times to 1920* (1921) was her most important contribution to Irish history. Known popularly as Hayden and Moonan, the book served as the standard Irish history text in schools and universities for over fifty years.

Through her association with the Gaelic League, Hayden befriended many of the men who led the 1916 Easter rising. However, as a constitutional nationalist and a pacifist, she disapproved of the Easter rising and of Irish separatism. She consequently refused to support the 1918 election campaign of Constance Markievicz (a participant in the rising), earning the disapproval of many of fellow feminists and nationalists. Despite rapidly changing political circumstances which saw republican candidates swept into power in the 1918 general election, Hayden joined the Irish Dominion League which campaigned for Irish home rule within the empire and supported the Anglo-Irish treaty of 1921.

Aggrieved by the marginal role women continued to play in Irish political and intellectual life, Hayden became one of the most outspoken critics of public policy in independent Ireland. As an active member of the National Council of Women in Ireland and the Women's Social and Progressive League, she protested against the underrepresentation of women in the Irish senate and new legislation which threatened to weaken women's employment rights. She reserved her harshest criticism for the 1937 Irish constitution, arguing that the clauses concerning the place of women in Irish society represented a return to the middle ages.

Bespectacled and earnest, Hayden's serious demeanour and public commitment to worthy causes belied a lively sense of humour and an enjoyment of domestic activities including baking and sewing. A keen cyclist and swimmer, she also travelled widely throughout Ireland and the continent and journeyed as far as India. Hayden remained a popular and controversial speaker on issues ranging from women's rights to Gaelic Ireland well into her seventies. She died, unmarried, at her home, 26 Cambridge Road, Dublin, on 12 July 1942, and was buried in Dublin on 15 July, leaving an estate of £2726 which was divided among her family and friends. She characteristically bequeathed small sums to charities for animals and children and instructed masses to be said in her local Catholic parish for the repose of her soul and for the souls of her deceased parents. S. PAŠETA

Sources NL Ire., Mary Hayden MSS [incl. diary, 1878–1903] · A. O'Farrelly, 'Mary Hayden', *Alexandra College Magazine* (Dec 1942), 32–5 · M. Macken, 'Professor Mary Hayden; president, 1913–1942', *National University Women Graduates' Association, 1902–1952* (1952), 34–5 · M. T. Downes, *The case of the Catholic lady students of the Royal University stated* (1888) · *Irish Times* (16 July 1942) · K. O'Ceirin and C. O'Ceirin, *Women of Ireland: a biographical dictionary* (1996)
Archives NL Ire., diaries
Wealth at death £2726 11s. 7d.: probate, 1942, *CGPLA Éire*; will, NA Ire.

Haydn, Timothy Joseph (1788/1793–1856), newspaper editor and compiler of reference works, was born in Lisbon on 24 November 1788 or 1793, the son of Thomas Haydn, an expatriate protestant Irishman. In 1809 he fled Napoleon's invading army in a 'once-Danish frigate' sailing to Plymouth. He settled in Dublin and made his début as a writer by ghosting a *History of the Azores* for Thomas Ashe, self-styled 'captain of the light dragoons' in which he drew on his early experience of Portugal and her colonies. His first, short-lived, journalistic venture was *The Stage*, a review journal of Dublin's theatres written jointly with Frederick Conway. But it was as a political journalist that Haydn made his name, winning a reputation for well-written, pro-government newspapers, which sought 'to soften all political asperities, not to provoke the acerbities of party' (*Dublin Evening Mail*, prospectus, 1823). In Dublin he founded *The Statesman*, *The Patriot*, the *Morning Star*, and the *Dublin Evening Mail*. His direction of the last made it, according to Stanley Lees Giffard, the chief protestant newspaper in Ireland, 'much better written and better conducted than it has been since' (letter to Royal Literary Fund, 1851). Journalism was a litigious, even hazardous business, and in 1823 Haydn was physically assaulted, while in 1824–5 he was prosecuted for concealing his ownership of the *Mail* and the *Morning Star* and banned from writing for the Dublin press. He turned to the provinces, writing for the Cork *Bolster's Quarterly* or the *Magazine of Ireland* and editing the *Limerick Star and Evening Post* and the *Limerick Times*. Whether arising from this dispute or some other cause, he moved to London in 1839 and for thirteen years was correspondent of the London *Courier and Evening Gazette*.

Nothing is known of Haydn's first marriage (*c*.1816), of which there were four children—a son, who became a printer (*b. c*.1832), and three daughters. In 1836 he married Mary Johnson (or Johnston); she was sixteen, he in his late forties. A much-loved daughter, Emma, was born in 1841, and sons in 1843 and 1848. Haydn began to write for the booksellers and, although he was known and highly esteemed in government circles, the trade proved sadly exploitative. He worked for Henry George Bohn on a 'classical and historical work' (maybe a revision of John Blair's *Chronology and History of the World*), but 'Mr Bohn flatly refused to pay even the most moderate sum for four months' labour on a book of dates and chronology prepared for him' (letter to Edward Moxon, n.d.). He turned down Thomas Tegg's offer to compile a chronology, reluctant to be associated with 'an ill-digested, servile, clumsy *compilation* merely' (letter to Moxon, n.d.). He revised Samuel Lewis's *Topographical Dictionaries* (10 vols., 1842–9), and Robert Beatson's *Political Index*, published as *The Book of Dignities* (1851) and reissued in an expanded edition, dedicated to W. E. Gladstone, by Horace Ockerby in 1894 (reprinted 1969), a compilation still the most useful for identifying the holders of many British governmental and ecclesiastical posts. Relations with Longman, the publisher, were soured by the task's proving so onerous that Haydn had to turn down more remunerative work and part with his copyright in his profit-sharing contract to make ends meet. By contrast, Edward Moxon was a kind and supportive friend and a fair employer—but then the *Dictionary of Dates* (1841) proved such a money-spinner that it continued to give good profits long after the death of both author and publisher.

The prosperity of the Dublin years fell steadily away and in 1850, Haydn applied for relief to the Royal Literary Fund. His troubles multiplied. In 1852 he fell on his back down a flight of stairs; his landlord died, the widow distrained on the furniture for arrears of rent, and the Haydns moved to a single room. The spectre of a debtor's prison was held off by further grants from the Royal Literary Fund, a loan from Dickens, and from Moxon money gifts as well as advances on the seventh edition of the *Dictionary of Dates*. In June 1854 Sir John Barrow got him work as an extra clerk at the Admiralty at 3 guineas a week; his job was to 'prepare a digest and index of several volumes of dispatches from the Principal Secretaries of State during the last century' (letter to the Royal Literary Fund, 1855), work which he enjoyed and did well. But his luck did not hold, for, on Easter Tuesday 1855, he suffered a stroke; a public subscription, the last humiliating refuge of the destitute public figure, was organized by Moxon and the impresario Alfred Bunn, a friend from Haydn's Dublin days. Meanwhile Mrs Haydn struggled to make ends meet by selling stationery and running a meagre circulating library with books donated by publishers; their twelve-year-old son did a paper round. In his last months Haydn received a civil-list pension of £25 p.a. Benjamin Vincent assisted him on the seventh edition of the *Dictionary of Dates*, which was published after his death. He died at 13 Crowley Street, Oakley Square, London, on 17 January 1856.

Haydn's reputation rests on the *Dictionary of Dates*. Posterity has upheld his own assessment of it as far more accurate, informative and well-organized than any of its rivals, and it is still consulted by historians. Such was the prestige of the work that Haydn's name was later attached to a series of dictionaries with which he had nothing to do, including the *Universal Index of Biography* (1870), edited by J. P. Payne; the *Dictionary of Science* (1870), edited by G. F. Rodwell; Haydn's *Bible Dictionary* (1871), edited by C. Boutell; and the *Dictionary of Popular Medicine and Hygiene* (1877). ROBIN MYERS

Sources R. Myers, 'Writing for the booksellers in the early nineteenth century: a case study', *Author/publisher relations during the eighteenth and nineteenth centuries*, ed. R. Myers and M. Harris (1983), 119–56 • Royal Literary Fund, 1850–78, BL, registered case no. 1239 • autograph letters, 1843–56, priv. coll. [Robin Myers] • *GM*, 2nd ser., 45 (1856), 542 • *The Times* (19 Jan 1856), 10b • *Annual Register* (1856), 232 [of chronicle section: pt 2]
Archives priv. coll., autograph letters | BL, Royal Literary Fund, registered case no. 1239

Haydock, George Leo (1774–1849), editor of the Douai Bible, was born on 11 April 1774 at Cottam, near Woodplumpton, Lancashire. He was the youngest son of George Haydock of The Tagg, Cottam, and his second wife, Ann or Anne, daughter of William Cottam, gentleman, of Bilsborrow. He attended a school run by the Revd Robert Banister at Mowbreck Hall, near Kirkham, and in April 1785 entered the English College at Douai. He escaped from Douai during the French Revolution (in August 1793), accompanied by his brother, the Catholic publisher Thomas *Haydock (1772–1859), and the Revd William Davis, one of the minor professors. After a brief stay at Old Hall Green, near Ware, Hertfordshire, he went home to The Tagg on 3 November 1794, where he remained until January 1796, when he rejoined many of his former Douai companions belonging to the northern vicariate in the newly established college at Crook Hall, Durham. He was ordained priest on 22 September 1798, and appointed general prefect and master of all the schools under poetry. In January 1803 he was appointed to the poor mission of Ugthorpe, Yorkshire.

In 1808 Haydock began work on a new edition of the

Douai Bible and Rheims Testament, which was to be published by his brother Thomas and was fully completed in 1814. Through his work on the Bible he also published *The Tree of Life, or, The one Church of God from Adam until the 19th or 58th Century* (1809). The Douai Bible, a translation of the Old Testament Vulgate for the use of English-speaking Catholics, had first been published by the English College at Douai in 1609 and the New Testament had been brought out by the English College at Rheims in 1582. The Douai text had been updated and reissued (1750) by the recusant bishop Richard Challoner and the Rheims New Testament by Troy in 1794. Haydock's task was to update this standard English Catholic version of the Bible for the use of a new generation. Drawing heavily on earlier critical notes by Bristow, Calmet, Du Hamel, Estius, Menochius, Pastorini (Bishop Charles Walmesley), Tirinus, Worthington, and Witham, Haydock also enlisted the help of the Benedictine monks at Ampleforth, particularly Benedict Rayment and Thomas Gregory Robinson, for his notes to the New Testament. Haydock ensured that notes by the original translators were marked 'H', those by Challoner marked 'C', and those by Rayment 'A'. The new version was first published in a series of shilling pamphlets and then printed in two volumes by a Manchester press in 1812–14. A second edition was published in Dublin in 1812–13 and republished in Dublin and Edinburgh in 1845–8. Until Husenbeth's new edition of the Douai Bible and Rheims text appeared in 1850–53, Haydock's was the standard edition of the Bible for the use of English-speaking Catholics, though it was criticized for the quality of its scholarship by a number of English Catholic clergy and biblical scholars: Archdeacon Cotton thought Haydock 'pious and warm-hearted' but not possessed of 'high scholarship' (Cotton, 85) and, while praising his diligence, thought that the haste with which the critical notes had been prepared had led to some errors of judgement.

In July 1816 Haydock was appointed to the mission of Whitby, but still with the obligation of attending Ugthorpe. It was during this period that he published *Prayers before and after Mass* (1822), *A Key to the Roman Catholic Office* (1823), *A Collection of Catholic Hymns* (1823), and *The Method of Sanctifying the Sabbath Days* (1824). Presently he claimed publicly that bishops Smith and Penswick were defrauding him of income and rejected their denials. He was therefore rusticated to the private chaplaincy of Westby Hall, Lancashire, but that did not silence him. Smith disdained the continuing slanderous attacks, but within three weeks of his death on 30 July 1831 the exasperated Penswick, his successor, interdicted Haydock from saying mass in the northern vicariate. Haydock retired to his estate, The Tagg, where for more than eight years he devoted himself to study. He appealed to *propaganda fide* against the interdict twice in 1832 but the letters were intercepted and passed to Penswick. The reason for his suspension lapsed with Penswick's death in January 1836, his faculties were restored in November 1839, and he was appointed to the mission at Penrith, Cumberland. Haydock died there on 29 November 1849 and was buried in the new chapel he had begun but did not live to see

completed. His library was sold by auction at Preston in 1851 and two portraits of him, one in silhouette and another in oils, turned up in the possession of Joseph Gillow, author of the famous *Biographical Dictionary of English Catholics*, about 1900.

THOMPSON COOPER, rev. LEO GOOCH

Sources Gillow, *Lit. biog. hist.* • A. J. Maas, 'Haydock, George Leo', *The Catholic encyclopedia*, ed. C. G. Herbermann and others, 7 (1910) • G. Anstruther, *The seminary priests*, 4 (1977) • P. R. Harris, ed., *Douai College documents, 1639–1794*, Catholic RS, 63 (1972) • J. Gillow, *The Haydock papers* (1888) • H. Cotton, *Rhemes and Doway: an attempt to show what has been done by Roman Catholics for the diffusion of the Holy Scriptures in English* (1855) • P. Whittle, *The history of the borough of Preston*, 2 (1837) • C. Hardwick, *History of the borough of Preston and its environs* (1857) • C. W. Sutton, *A list of Lancashire authors* (1876) • S. K. Ohlhausen, 'The last Haydock Bible', *Recusant History*, 22 (1994–5), 529–35
Archives Ushaw College, Durham, corresp. and papers

Haydock [Haddock], **Richard** (c.1552–1605), Roman Catholic priest, was the second son of Ewan or Vivian Haydock (d. 1581) and Helen Wesby (d. 1558), of Cottam Hall, near Preston, Lancashire. He was a nephew of William Allen, his mother's sister having married George Allen, a brother of the cardinal. Fifteen years after the death of his mother Haydock accompanied his father to the English College in Douai in 1573. His father was ordained priest in 1575, and Richard was ordained priest two years later, on 23 March 1577, at Cateau Cambrésis. Father and son were followed to Douai by another son, George, who was also ordained, and later executed at Tyburn in 1584.

After ordination and gaining his doctorate in theology in 1578 Richard was sent to Rome by Allen to assist in the founding of the English College in that city. He supported the Jesuits and became involved in the disputes concerning the administration of the college in its early days. He wrote a long letter to his uncle William Allen giving a detailed account of these events. His name is second in the college register immediately following that of Ralph Sherwin. An English spy in Rome described Haydock as 'about 36 years of age, short of stature and lean of body and face; the hair of his beard thin, the hair of his upper lip somewhat long and of a flaxen colour' (Talbot and Aveling, 205).

Haydock was sent to England in January 1580 and worked for some years as a missioner in Lancashire; it was during this time that his younger brother George was captured and executed. When his uncle became a cardinal Haydock returned to Rome and in 1594 he was listed as a member of Allen's household. He remained in Rome after the cardinal's death and although not himself a Jesuit he assisted Robert Persons. When further disturbances occurred in the English College and Cardinal Sega made his visitation in 1596, Haydock was a cause for complaint from the students, who declared 'Mr Haydock who has made himself very busy about these late disturbances should be forbidden the college' (Foley, 6.28). His name is also recorded in the state papers of 1601 where he is referred to as Robert Persons's coachman and president of the council of the English College. On 26 October 1602 Haydock passed through Rheims on a mission to Ireland and in that same year he is referred to as dean of Dublin. In 1603 he returned to Rome and he rented a house, next to the English College, where he died on 13 July 1605. He was buried in the church of the English College. In his last years he translated Bellarmine's *Dichiarazione più copiosa della dottrina cristiana* into English as *An Ample Declaration of the Christian Doctrine* and had it published at Douai. In his will he left money to St Ursula's Augustinian convent in Louvain and various bequests to relatives and friends.

MICHAEL E. WILLIAMS

Sources G. Anstruther, *The seminary priests 1: Elizabethan, 1558–1603* [1966], 159–60 · Gillow, *Lit. biog. hist.*, 3.221–6 · *Dodd's Church history of England*, ed. M. A. Tierney, 5 vols. (1839–43), vol. 2, pp. 350–61 · J. Gillow, *The Haydock papers* (1888) · H. Foley, ed., *Records of the English province of the Society of Jesus*, 2 (1875), 225; 6 (1880), 28, 519, 739 · T. F. Knox and others, eds., *The first and second diaries of the English College, Douay* (1878) · A. F. Allison and D. M. Rogers, eds., *The contemporary printed literature of the English Counter-Reformation between 1558 and 1640*, 2 (1994), 361 · *DNB* · C. Talbot, ed., *Miscellanea: recusant records*, Catholic RS, 53 (1961)
Archives NL Wales, letters to Allen
Likenesses attrib. C. Sledd, 1580–89, BM
Wealth at death 40 gold crowns to St Ursula's Monastery, Louvain; 50 gold crowns to friends and relations; plus 8 Spanish gold crowns, and various gifts: will, extracted Foley, ed., *Records*, vol. 6, p. 519

Haydock, Richard (1569/70–c.1642), physician, was born at Greywell in Hampshire, the son of James Haydock and Margaret, daughter of Thomas Bill of Ashwell, Hertfordshire, physician to Henry VIII and Edward VI; William Bill, dean of Westminster, was her uncle. He was educated at Wykeham's school in Winchester, and on 12 July 1588 matriculated at New College, Oxford, of which he was elected a fellow in 1590. He graduated BA on 16 January 1592, proceeded MA on 31 October 1595, and BM on 14 June 1601. While still a student, he published *A Tracte Containing the Artes of Curious Paintinge, Carvinge and Buildinge* (1598), a translation from the Italian of Giovanni Paolo Lomazzo, and the first treatise on painting to be published in English. The illustrations are Haydock's, including the title-page with a self-portrait.

Haydock travelled for some time on the continent, before returning to Oxford to study medicine. In 1605 he left the university and settled in Salisbury, where he practised as a physician for many years. There he acquired a reputation for preaching sermons in his sleep, often of a puritan, anti-Catholic nature. He was summoned to court to exhibit his powers before James I, who visited him at night to hear him preach. Eventually Haydock admitted that he was not in fact asleep. He said that he had begun the habit of speaking at night to overcome a stutter, and having gained fame for it, now found it difficult to admit the truth. The king pardoned him, and offered him a position in the church if he would take holy orders. Haydock chose instead to continue as a physician in Salisbury.

In January 1607 Haydock married Susan Ramsdell in Ringwood. They had at least one son. With a second wife,

Gertrude Thayne, he had a daughter, Elizabeth, who married the anatomist Nathaniel Highmore on 30 December 1640.

Shortly after Elizabeth's wedding, Haydock retired to London, where he died about 1642 and was buried.

SARAH BAKEWELL

Sources K. J. Höltgen, 'Richard Haydocke: translator, engraver, physician', *The Library*, 5th ser., 33 (1978), 15–32 · J. E. Gordon, 'Richard Haydocke: physician, engraver and nocturnal preacher (1570–1642(c))', *The Practitioner*, 198 (1967), 849–54 · Wood, *Ath. Oxon.* · Foster, *Alum. Oxon.* · J. Stow and E. Howes, *Annales, or, A generall chronicle of England … unto the end of this present yeere, 1631* (1631), 863–4 · A. Wilson, *The history of Great Britain: being the life and reign of King James the First* (1653), 111
Likenesses J. Thayne, engraving, 1772, Wellcome L. · J. Thayne, engraving, 1772, RCP Lond. · R. Haydock, self-portrait, line engraving, BM, NPG; repro. in Lomazzo, *Artes of curious paintinge*, trans. R. Haydock (1598), title-page

Haydock, Roger (1643–1696), Quaker preacher, was born at Coppull, in the parish of Standish, Lancashire, on 1 May 1643, the second son of Roger Haydock (d. 1670), and his wife, Alice Nightingale. He was baptized in the parish the following day. He was educated but where is not known. In 1667 Roger's brother, John, became a Friend. This conversion upset their mother, who is recorded as being inclined to presbyterianism, and she apparently enlisted Roger's help in dissuading his brother. The result, however, was that Roger likewise converted in November 1667. The brothers began to travel to Quaker meetings throughout Lancashire. In April 1668 they were both arrested at a meeting in Bury and were imprisoned at Lancaster Castle for some months. Roger was again apprehended in January 1669 for attending three meetings at Bury and was fined £15 by the Manchester quarter sessions. On the death of his father in 1670, John inherited the estate at Bogburn Hall, Coppull, where Roger acted as steward in his brother's absences.

In 1674, on the information of Ralph Brideoake, bishop of Chichester and rector of Standish, Roger Haydock was prosecuted in the ecclesiastical court at Chester for non-payment of tithes and in May was committed to Lancaster gaol for non-appearance; he was released on 12 January 1675. In July and August 1675 he travelled throughout the midland and northern counties, and on return to Lancashire in August he was fined £20 for attending a meeting at Bury. During the next few years he spent a considerable amount of time in prison for refusal to pay tithes and for preaching. He does, however, appear to have been allowed some measure of liberty, at which times he continued to preach and attend meetings. On 4 June 1676 he engaged in a dispute at Crowton in Weaverham parish, Cheshire, with John Barber, vicar of Weaverham, John Davis, vicar of Frodsham, and John Cheyney, said to be curate at Burtonwood in Warrington parish. In January 1677 Haydock engaged in further dispute with John Cheyney at Arley Hall, Cheshire. These disputes prompted the publication of two works, *The Skirmisher Confounded* (1676) and *A Hypocrite Unveiled* (1677), in which Haydock challenged Cheyney and his anti-Quaker publications.

Between 1677 and 1681 Haydock made several preaching

tours throughout England. In 1681 he made his first overseas tour to the Netherlands and Germany, where at Alzey in Hesse-Darmstadt he was arrested and imprisoned for eleven days. On his return he married Eleanor Low (d. 1723) of Crewood Hall, Crowton, near Northwich, Cheshire, on 6 March 1682 at Newton, near Middlewich. They had four sons, three of whom died in childhood: their surviving son, Robert, was born at Penketh, Lancashire, in 1687. Haydock was imprisoned yet again at Lancaster between August 1683 and May 1684. By July 1684 he was once more indicted, with his wife, for holding conventicles. A further spell of imprisonment followed from December 1684 until March 1686, when he was finally released following a king's pardon. He gained the protection of the earl of Derby, who sympathized with Friends in the Isle of Man. Later in 1686 Haydock embarked on another tour of the Netherlands and Germany, and on his return he visited Friends throughout Scotland and the north of England.

About 1687 Haydock moved to Brick Hall, Penketh, Lancashire, where his ever frail health broke down. However, by 1693 he was sufficiently recovered to enter a public dispute with another Cheshire clergyman, John Hyde, and to resume his travels in England and the Netherlands. Through the years Haydock maintained a regular correspondence with Friends in Europe and America, in which he described his travels and meetings with other Quakers. In May 1696 he succumbed to a fever and, after a short illness, died at Penketh on 11 May 1696. He was buried that same month in the Quaker burial-ground at Greystone, near Penketh.

In 1700 John Haydock published *A Collection of the Christian Writings*, an anthology of his brother's works, which includes an account of Haydock's life and death together with testimonials from Eleanor Haydock and other Friends. It also included the claim that he had travelled nearly 33,000 miles during his career, and ministered to more than 2600 meetings. Haydock's will, proved at Chester in 1701 some five years after his death, bequeathed half his estate to his wife with bequests to his son, nephews, and nieces. Eleanor Haydock outlived her husband by many years. She was also a zealous Quaker, travelling throughout the country to meetings. She died in 1723. In 1743 their son Robert emigrated with his family to America, where they eventually settled in Flushing, Long Island. In 1922 a memorial was raised in Standish parish church to the Haydock family, which commemorates not only Roger Haydock but also his father, his son, and Roger's brother William, rector of Standish from 1678 until 1713.   CATHERINE NUNN

Sources A collection of the Christian writings, labours, travels, and sufferings of ... Roger Haydock, ed. J. Haydock (1700) • T. C. Porteus, 'Roger Haydock of Coppull, a brief biography', *Transactions of the Lancashire and Cheshire Antiquarian Society*, 52 (1937), 1–66 • R. Muschamp, *The story of the Quakers: early happenings in Warrington and district* (1931) • J. Besse, *A collection of the sufferings of the people called Quakers*, 2 vols. (1753) • J. Gough, *History of the people called Quakers* (1789) • N. Morgan, *Lancashire Quakers and the establishment* (1993) • W. C. Braithwaite, *The second period of Quakerism*, ed. H. J. Cadbury, 2nd edn (1961) • *DNB* • Friends' marriage registers, Ches. & Chester ALSS, EFC 1/14/2 [transcript]
Archives Hist. Soc. Penn., Pemberton papers, corresp., collection no. 484
Wealth at death see will, Lancs. RO

Haydock, Thomas (1772–1859), printer, was born on 21 February 1772 at The Tagg, Cottam, near Preston, the second son of George Haydock (1724–1783) and his second wife, Ann, *née* Cottam (1761–1783). His father was a member of the Society of Friends but his mother was a Roman Catholic and Thomas received a Catholic education at Mowbreck Hall School. He then studied for the priesthood at the English colleges at Douai and Lisbon, returning to Crook Hall in co. Durham, where he made his third unsuccessful attempt to become a priest.

In 1796 Haydock moved to Manchester, where he opened a language school, and issued a number of Catholic works (some of which he had translated) at 42 Alport Street. By 1800 he had moved to 16 Tib Lane, Manchester, from which address he also established a printing business. In 1806 he announced the publication of a folio Bible in the Douai version with extensive notes by his brother George Leo *Haydock (1774–1849), but in the same year Haydock left for Ireland and set up business in Dublin. It being thought that he had abandoned the Bible project, the Catholics of Manchester secured the approval of the vicar apostolic of the area for an edition to be printed by Oswald Syers, who announced the commencement in March 1811. Haydock returned to Manchester in July 1811 and began printing his brother's Bible, printing 1500 copies, which were issued in fortnightly, later weekly, parts at 1s. each. It was completed by 1814. A number of subsequent editions appeared throughout the nineteenth century from other printers.

Haydock returned to Dublin and continued printing Catholic works but his business at Lower Ormond Street did not prosper and he was imprisoned for debt. In 1818 he married an Irishwoman, Mary Lynde, who died in 1823. The couple had three children, all of whom died young. His business struggled on for some years but about 1840 Haydock returned first to Liverpool and later to Preston, where he died on 25 August 1859.   BRENDA J. SCRAGG

Sources Gillow, *Lit. biog. hist.* • Ushaw College, Durham, Haydock correspondence • M. Sharratt, ed., *Lisbon College register, 1628–1813*, Catholic RS, 72 (1991) • C. Hardwick, *History of the borough of Preston and its environs* (1857) • H. Fishwick, *The history of the parish of Preston* (1900)
Archives Ushaw College, Durham, corresp.
Wealth at death under £100: probate, 9 Dec 1859, *CGPLA Eng. & Wales*

Haydock, William (c.1483–1537), Cistercian monk, was a younger son of William Haydock, esquire, of Cottam Hall, near Preston, Lancashire, and Joan, daughter of William Heton of Heaton, whom he married in 1480/1481. Having joined the Cistercian abbey of Whalley early in the sixteenth century, Haydock was a monk of some seniority when the Pilgrimage of Grace took place in 1536. Whalley very early became involved in the rising, partly, at least, because of family ties. The abbot and convent of the neighbouring Cistercian house of Sawley, just over the county boundary in Yorkshire, had been forced to surrender their abbey in May 1536, when most of the monks received dispensations to take secular livings or to transfer to another house of the order. Together with two or three other Sawley monks, Richard Eastgate chose to join his brother, John Eastgate, who was a monk of Whalley. Richard Eastgate may well have helped incite unrest at Whalley, where an unnamed monk was later alleged to have asserted at this juncture that no secular knave should be head of the church. The abbot, John Paslew, concealed this traitorous saying from the central government, and furthermore encouraged the Commons to restore the former Sawley monks to their house.

Once the rebellion had been suppressed in the spring of 1537 the king displayed a particular animus against the monks of Whalley and Sawley. Abbot Paslew of Whalley, William Haydock, and both the Eastgate brothers were tried on a charge of high treason at the Lancaster assizes in March 1537, and Paslew, Haydock, and Richard Eastgate were found guilty. The abbot and Richard Eastgate were hanged at Lancaster on 10 March, while Haydock was returned to Whalley and executed there two days later. Haydock's corpse was not dismembered and distributed around the county as a warning against any future unrest, as were the bodies of the abbot and Eastgate, but, after hanging some time, was clandestinely removed by his nephew, another William Haydock, and hidden at Cottam Hall, the seat of the family, where it was discovered when the house was pulled down in the early part of the nineteenth century.

CLAIRE CROSS

Sources LP Henry VIII, vol. 12/1 · J. E. W. Wallis, 'The narrative of the indictment of the traitors of Whalley and Cartmell, 1536–7', Miscellanies, V, Chetham Society, 90 (1931) · D. S. Chambers, Faculty offices registers, 1534–1549 (1966) · Gillow, Lit. biog. hist., vol. 3 · C. Haigh, The last days of the Lancashire monasteries and the Pilgrimage of Grace, Chetham Society, 3rd ser., 17 (1969) · T. D. Whitaker, An history of the original parish of Whalley, 3rd edn (1818) · J. Caley and J. Hunter, eds., Valor ecclesiasticus temp. Henrici VIII, 6 vols., RC (1810–34) · F. R. Raines, The vicars of Rochdale, ed. H. H. Howarth, Chetham Society, new ser., 1 (1883) · D. Knowles [M. C. Knowles], The religious orders in England, [another edn], 3 (1961) · G. W. O. Woodward, The dissolution of the monasteries (1966) · C. Cross and N. Vickers, eds., Monks, friars and nuns in sixteenth century Yorkshire, Yorkshire Archaeological Society, 150 (1995) · W. S. Weeks, 'Abbot Paslew and the Pilgrimage of Grace', Transactions of the Lancashire and Cheshire Antiquarian Society, 47 (1930–31), 199–223

Haydon, Benjamin Robert (1786–1846), history painter and diarist, born in Wimpole Street, Plymouth, Devon, on 26 January 1786, was the son of a printer, publisher, and bookseller, Benjamin Robert Haydon (1758–1813), who came from an old Devon family. His mother, Sarah Cobley (d. 1808), was the daughter of the Revd B. Cobley, curate of Shillingford, Devon, and afterwards rector of Dodbrooke in the same county. Both his father and his grandfather were fond of painting.

Early years At six Haydon was sent to the grammar school at Plymouth under the Revd Dr Bidlake, who encouraged him to sketch from nature; and a Neapolitan called Fenzi, employed by his father as his head bookbinder, excited Haydon's imagination by describing the works of Raphael

Benjamin Robert Haydon (1786–1846), by Georgiana Margaretta Zornlin, 1825

and Michelangelo, and urged him: 'don't draw de landscape; draw de *feegoore*, master Benjamin' (*Life*, 1st edn, 1.8). By his own account Haydon was 'an excessively self-willed, passionate child'. He had an early desire for public recognition, and loved to take centre stage by giving dramatic entertainments to his schoolfellows; but equally he could shut himself up in the attic to paint and give lectures to himself. He read widely in his father's shop, always showing a preference for the lives of ambitious men. His father, thinking a severer discipline might help, sent him in 1798 to the grammar school at Plympton, where he remained under the Revd W. Haynes until 1801. Here the relaxed but superficial tuition of Dr Bidlake was replaced by order and good teaching, and Haydon acquired a fair knowledge of Latin, Greek, and French; but more, this was the school of Sir Joshua Reynolds himself, and Haydon variously indulged his love of art by copying 'caricatures'—satirical prints which he had purchased—or by adorning the hall with a spirited hunting scene drawn with burnt sticks. He rose to be head boy. He taught his schoolfellows drawing, and tried his hand at etching. Before being formally apprenticed to his father in 1801, he was sent to Exeter to study accounting. Haydon, however, was now strongly inclined towards art, and became 'more celebrated for electrifying the cat, killing flies by sparks and doing everything and anything but my duty' (ibid., 1.12). He regarded the seven-year apprenticeship to be a part of his father's 'ceaseless opposition' against his desire to become an artist. He was rude to customers and silent at home. In 1803 a serious illness left him blind for six weeks, and with severe eye problems for the rest of his life: 'see or not see,' he told his father, 'a painter I'll be, and if I am a great one without seeing, I shall be the first' (ibid., 1.13). In that same year Haydon acquired the great anatomical work by Albinus, *Tables of the Skeleton and Muscles of the Human Body*, in the English edition (1749). Starting what was to become a lifelong habit, he bought the book without being able to afford it; when he took it home, his mother 'cried much' and his father 'paid with black looks', but Haydon was triumphant (ibid., 1.15). It was the beginning of his passionate pursuit of anatomical knowledge: 'Oh, the delight of hurrying it away to my bedroom', he noted in his *Autobiography*, 'turning over the plates, copying them out, learning the origin and insertion of the muscles, and then getting my sister to hear me!' (ibid.). A second book of equal importance came as a gift from his father: Sir Joshua Reynolds's *Works* (3 vols., 1798). Half a century later, in his *Lectures on Painting and Design* (1844), an exhausted and more experienced Haydon saw that Reynolds's reliance on an individual's industry was 'certainly a most seducing doctrine; but as likely to lead virtuous men to misery and a mad-house as to happiness and reputation' (vol. 1, p. 3). But for the young Haydon in 1803, Reynolds's *Discourse* convinced him that he must become an artist: Reynolds 'expressed so strong a conviction that all men were equal and that application made the difference' (*Life*, 1st edn, 1.14). On 13 May 1804, with £20 in his pocket, he started for 'London, Sir Joshua—Drawing—Dissection—and High Art' (ibid., 18).

Haydon immediately determined to devote himself to study for two years before beginning to paint: he first took lodgings at 3 Broad Street, Carnaby Market, and then visited the exhibition of the Royal Academy at Somerset House and felt confident with his plan. His commitment to solitary study was finally, and fortunately, interrupted by the artist and author Prince Hoare, who visited him, and it was through Hoare that Haydon met John Opie and James Northcote, both teachers at the Royal Academy. Although Haydon did not wish to have a master, he asked for advice. Northcote, aware of the Boydell family's recent financial disaster from the failure of their project to present the plays of Shakespeare through paintings and related engravings, seriously warned his fellow Devonian, who claimed he wanted to follow Reynolds's recommendation to paint historical pictures: 'Heestoricaul peinter! Why yee'll starve with a bundle of straw under yeer head!' (*Life*, 1st edn, 1.22). Northcote advised Haydon to paint portraits, a pursuit that Haydon despised. Ironically, Haydon is today often admired for his portraits—though too often he painted these for love and affection for the sitter rather than for the money he needed. Haydon later considered that this time of study was 'perhaps too solitary and peculiar' (ibid., 26); and fortunately, in 1805, he met Henry Fuseli, the recently appointed keeper of the Royal Academy, and he became his student. Haydon's world opened out, and his first close friend was the Yorkshire painter John Jackson, who already had a patron in Lord Mulgrave, a close friend of Sir George Beaumont. Haydon had to make a visit to Plymouth because his father was very ill, but returned to meet David Wilkie, and the three artists became friends. It was Wilkie who encouraged Haydon to attend Charles Bell's lectures on anatomy in 1806. But all was not well with Haydon for, whereas Wilkie was finding considerable success with his patrons, Haydon lost direction and retired to Plymouth, where he fell in love. It was Wilkie who brought back Haydon from his despondent life at Plymouth by reporting that Lord Mulgrave was prepared to commission a painting from Haydon. Thus Haydon returned to London to begin his first major painting, *Joseph and Mary Resting on the Road to Egypt* (for a chronological checklist of Haydon's 204 paintings, see (*Diary*, 5.587)), a painting he considered as practice for Mulgrave's commission: *The celebrated old Roman tribune, Dentatus, making his last desperate effort against his own soldiers, who attacked and murdered him in a narrow pass*. Dentatus was the first of Haydon's tragic heroes: Mulgrave had found the story recorded in Nathaniel Hooke's *Roman History*. Dentatus was a soldier who had not been rewarded for his efforts; the Roman decemvirs, finding the people indignant at this injustice, became fearful that Dentatus would be a magnet for popular dissent and arranged for him to be assassinated. Thus he was trapped alone in a mountain defile where, having killed and wounded many of his assassins, he was overwhelmed and crushed by a large boulder. The picture can seem an ambitious but academic exercise but it exemplifies many of Haydon's subsequent concerns. With Wilkie, Haydon had read Charles Bell's *Anatomy and Philosophy of Expression* and this influenced the athletic, muscular figure of Dentatus. Haydon also read Thomas Hope's *Costumes of the Ancients* (1809) (and his own copy is now at the Wordsworth Trust, Grasmere). Hope admired Haydon sufficiently to buy his first painting, *Joseph and Mary Resting on the Road to Egypt*; he also presented a copy of his book to Haydon and introduced him to the idea that paintings should have historically appropriate costumes. But, more, Hope introduced a theme that Haydon was to make his own—the claim that there was a need for a national fund to support historical painting. But there was one new element, and that came from Haydon's sudden and impassioned commitment to studying the great marble figures brought by Lord Elgin from the Parthenon in Athens. It was Wilkie who took Haydon to see these Grecian wonders in the covered yard of Lord Elgin's house in Park Lane, London. Haydon was desperate to learn the skills needed for Mulgrave's commission: at the end of 1807 he had gone to Plymouth and painted the portraits of local figures (at 15 guineas each) as practice for *Dentatus*. Then, in November, his mother became ill and died while travelling with Haydon to London in search of medical advice. It was then, on seeing the sculptures, that Haydon felt he had found the secret of antiquity which would teach him how to make *Dentatus* a worthy painting. He spent up to twelve to fourteen hours a day sketching. It was shortly after this intense period of drawing, and when he had begun his more extensive work on *Dentatus*, that Haydon, on 23 July 1808, began his diary, which in 1842 he recognized as significant: 'It is the history, in fact, of my mind' (ibid., 1.98). It is a document which eventually ran to over a million words, and because of its variety, its personal eccentricity, his own sense of achievement and exultation, it draws in the reader; that Haydon is so often outrageous in his opinions delights because he allows his own ludicrous behaviour to be revealed. The 'incessant labour' on *Dentatus* continued until the painting was finally exhibited on 31 March 1809 at the Royal Academy.

Early commissions Haydon's lifelong feud with the Royal Academy now began. *Dentatus* was hung and then moved to what Haydon considered an unfavourable site. He had a gift for being pugnacious and imprudently so. He was favoured in August 1809 by Sir George Beaumont's commissioning him to paint Macbeth before the murder. Beaumont wanted the painting to be a certain size, and Haydon made it much bigger, so that it was inconvenient for Beaumont's house. Despite this uneasiness, Beaumont did not stand in the way of Haydon being awarded the British Institution prize for *Dentatus* as the best historical picture. Haydon continued to work hard at *Macbeth*, which was finished by the end of 1811, but the painting brought him into debt because his father, halfway through the work on the painting, withdrew his financial support. Haydon began to borrow money, and from this point onwards he was rarely free from debt. When, ultimately, Sir George Beaumont took *Macbeth* and urged Haydon to stick to painting rather than to controversy, Haydon seriously dedicated himself to his art and commenced on 7 March 1812 *The Judgement of Solomon*. The painting occupied him for two years, and what society he had was increasingly literary, including William Hazlitt, Charles Lamb, John Scott, and Leigh Hunt. By the end of 1813 Haydon realized that his life had been dominated by *Solomon* and that he had been four years without a commission. His father had given him no financial aid for three years before his death on 25 June 1813; his only support had come from some funding from the imprisoned brothers Leigh and John Hunt, and from the kindness of restaurateurs who admired his talk and his genius. In April 1814 *Solomon* was exhibited with great success at the Oil and Watercolour Society, but Haydon related that it had involved 'the most dreadful application, influenced by an enthusiasm stimulated by despair almost a delirium' (*Life*, 1.216), and he later claimed (in 1843) that he never entirely recovered. The British Institution wished to buy the painting so that it could join Benjamin West's *Christ Healing the Sick* (1811), as a foundation for the proposed National Gallery. The picture, destined to have many owners, went to private purchasers. Leigh Hunt, despite the fact that he was in the Surrey gaol at Horsemonger Lane for libelling the prince regent, saw the picture because Haydon enterprisingly brought it to the gaol: it was therefore equally possible that Leigh influenced his art-critic brother Robert, who wrote on the painting at length in *The Examiner*, on 1 May 1814; *Solomon* was praised for its Venetian colour, its lustrous texture, its Raphaelesque composition, and its expressive power:

> In all these respects the invention of our young Painter—young in years, but old in genius and study—he is justly classed on a level with the great Masters of the Art … not even Raphael surpassed him in the grand object of Art—the portraiture of the heart.

The striking portrait of Leigh Hunt (NPG) was painted in gratitude, and then Haydon turned to a new subject, even more massive in its physical scale: *Christ's Entry into Jerusalem*. Having made the first sketches between 22 May and 17 July 1814, Haydon went with David Wilkie to France and they visited the Louvre, Versailles, Fontainebleau, and Rambouillet. His diary contains a brilliant account of a Paris still excited by Napoleon, despite his exile to Elba; it also provided an excellent opportunity for Haydon to experience the stolen treasures accumulated by Napoleon in the Louvre, a chance that Haydon did not entirely take amid some of the excitements. On his return he seized the opportunity of publishing in *The Examiner* for late August and September articles under the signature E. S. But more, Haydon returned to England to find his genius as a painter recognized: he was unexpectedly elected on 26 September 1814 to the freedom of his native city of Plymouth (where his *Solomon* now appropriately adorns the town hall). The British Institution awarded him 100 guineas for *Solomon*, but its purchase by Sir William Elford and J. W. Tingcombe, bankers of Plymouth, for 700 guineas, did not pay his debt of over £1000; nor did it bring him new commissions; its exhibition in Exeter, Bath, and London was not a financial success, and the bankers sold it on.

Christ's Entry into Jerusalem Haydon did not learn from mistakes, and for six years he was largely devoted to completing the immense oil painting *Christ's Entry into Jerusalem* (12 ft 6 in. x 15 ft 1 in., with a frame weighing 600 lb; now at St Mary's Seminary, Norwood, Ohio). His diary records his passion for the project: on 29 April 815 he wrote: 'Never have I had such irresistible and perpetual urgings of future greatness. I have been like a man with air-balloons under his armpits and ether in his soul' (*Diary*, 1.430). But the truth is that Haydon had new distractions. Perhaps the weakness of his eyes made painting difficult; but equally he entered into public debate and courageously (some would say obstinately) continued the controversy about the Elgin marbles. Canova arrived from Italy in 1815, and at their meeting on 19 November confirmed Haydon's views as to their supreme merit. A committee was appointed by the House of Commons to consider the question of the purchase of the marbles for the nation, but out of consideration to the connoisseur Richard Payne Knight, who misguidedly had doubted the authenticity and therefore the importance of the brilliant fragments, Haydon's evidence (hostile to Knight) was not used. Haydon, however, continued the dispute, notably in his essay in *The Examiner* of 17 March 1816: 'On the judgement of connoisseurs being preferred to that of professional men,—Elgin marbles, &c'; this was later issued as a pamphlet. Parliament voted to purchase the Elgin marbles on 7 June 1816: Sir Thomas Lawrence wryly noted that Haydon had perhaps saved the marbles but that the controversy itself would ruin Haydon. And certainly, Haydon increasingly made enemies by insisting on the need for funding national art and by gratuitously attacking the Royal Academy: he had a new vehicle, the *Annals of the Fine Arts*, a periodical edited by a friend, the architect James

Elmes (1782–1862), published from 1816 to 1819. 'Elmes', Haydon remembered:

> was a man of considerable talent, of great good-nature, and a thorough admirer of mine. He had been the very first to notice and criticise my early works; I hated the Academy, and was very glad of the use of a publication where I had unlimited control. (*Life*, 1st edn, 1.327)

Haydon's influence ensured that the magazine in 1819 published two of Keats's greatest poems. 'Ode to the nightingale [*sic*]' and 'Ode to a Grecian Urn'.

While Haydon committed himself to painting *Christ's Entry into Jerusalem*, using the heads of his friends, pupils, servants, and hired models, he became a significant witness to the lives of many of the key writers of his time, and the first of these was Wordsworth. Curiously, Sir George Beaumont had warned Haydon and Wilkie in August 1809 against Wordsworth's 'Democratical principles', but when they met in 1815 Haydon was inspired (*Diary*, 5.436). The poet and artist met on 23 May and on 13 June, this last date being when Haydon took Wordsworth's life-mask (Wordsworth Trust). Their correspondence began, and on 21 December 1815 came Wordsworth's fine sonnet addressed to Haydon, 'High is our calling, friend', which Haydon, with due delight, and having sought Wordsworth's permission, had printed in John Scott's weekly newspaper, *The Champion* (4 February 1816), and in Leigh Hunt's *Examiner* (31 March 1816), the two editors still being friendly, but within a year to be enemies. The sonnet put Haydon under an obligation: he would have to provide Wordsworth personally with a portrait—'be assured I will exert myself to make one of my best heads, or sketches for your acceptance—if it be possible it will be worthy of the sonnets—god grant it may.' This portrait (Wordsworth Trust) was additional to Haydon's real need to include Wordsworth's head in *Christ's Entry into Jerusalem*, but Haydon's wish to do it indicated his ambition to model himself upon Wordsworth's capacity for inner direction and self-belief:

> Faith in the whispers of the lonely Muse
> When the whole world seems adverse to desert.
> (Brown, Woof, and Hebron, 31)

In their letters *Christ's Entry* became the centre of a creative discussion: Wordsworth disagreed with Haydon's assertion that his characterization of figures in the crowd watching Christ enter the city was essentially Shakespearian. In particular, Wordsworth detected in Haydon's attempt to criticize, even satirize (such as the proposed character of a supercilious prude) a Hogarthian quality which would spoil the dignity of the picture:

> A character like that of the haughty prude belongs rather to the higher kinds of Comedy, such as the works of Hogarth, than to a subject of this nature, which to use Milton's expression, is 'more than heroic'.—I coincide with you in opinion as to Raphael's characters, but depend upon it he has erred upon the safer side. (ibid., 32)

Haydon's writings Wordsworth certainly urges caution, while not absolutely wanting to discourage Haydon's 'efforts to introduce more of the diversities of actual humanity into the management of sublime and pathetic subjects' (Brown, Woof, and Hebron, 32). The irony is that Haydon had a natural gift for humorous observation which was at odds with his insistent cry for 'high art'. It is undoubtedly true that he was, after his bankruptcy in 1823, at his most effective in domestic pictures, not least in those full of social observation: this is analogous to the fact that in his best writing he is a master of the comedy of things. Aldous Huxley, who was totally unappreciative of Haydon's skill as a draughtsman and real achievement in his painting, too strongly claims that:

> it is … as novelist that Haydon would have best exhibited his powers. I can imagine great rambling books in which absurd sublimities … and much radical philosophising would have alternated in the approved Shakespearean or Faustian style with admirable passages of well-observed, naturalistic comic relief. (*Autobiography*, ed. Taylor, 1926, 1.xvi–xvii)

In truth, Haydon's capacity to write fiction is exhibited in the little-known pamphlets that accompanied paintings such as his excellent *The Mock Election* (1827; Royal Collection) or *Chairing the Member* (1828; Tate collection). Wordsworth, in advising Haydon to avoid the Hogarthian element, did not have Huxley's or our own advantage in seeing how comically Haydon could write in his diary and in his later reworking of that text as autobiography. Those comic capacities are exhibited famously in the diary entry dated 28 December 1817 when Haydon describes the dinner party he gave for Wordsworth, Keats, Lamb, and Thomas Monkhouse (Wordsworth's relative); the later evening party also included John Kingston, deputy controller of stamps, and Wordsworth's superior in the excise, and the scene was set for a confrontation between a drunken Charles Lamb and an unimaginative Kingston, with several guests, including Keats and Haydon, trying to suppress their laughter. Perhaps this double gift of writing and painting, though possessed in different degrees, made Haydon such a sympathetic character to Hazlitt: 'I don't know what it is that attaches me to H[aydon] so much, except that he and I, whenever we meet, sit in judgement on another set of old friends, and "carve them as a dish fit for the Gods"' (Hazlitt, 12.132). Such a sympathy did not prevent Haydon from writing a masterly account of the human chaos in Hazlitt's household in April 1813 when he was invited to the baptism of Hazlitt's child—a baptism indeed in which the child was not even baptized. All things exhibited 'beastliness & indifference to the common comforts of life': Hazlitt's wife was

> in an influenza, thin, pale & spitty; and his chubby child, squalling, obstinate, & half-cleaned. After waiting a little, all looking forlornly at the potatoes for fear they might be the chief dish, in issued a piece of overdone beef, burnt, toppling about on seven or eight corners, with a great bone sticking out like a battering ram; the great difficulty was to make it stand upright! But the greater to discover a *cuttable* place, for all was jagged, jutting, & irregular. Like a true Genius, he forgot to go for a Parson to christen his child. (*Diary*, 1.303)

Part of the friendship between Haydon and Hazlitt was that the painter hoped Hazlitt might praise him in the various papers and periodicals for which he wrote. However, Hazlitt's remarks on *Christ's Entry into Jerusalem* in

1820 were mixed: though Hazlitt could praise Haydon's talents, he found this particular painting had not been sufficiently finished; and further, tellingly, he suggested that Haydon's constant pamphleteering about his own paintings, with their concern with his good intentions, 'deceives the artist himself, and may mislead the public'. But a year later he exuberantly gave a verbal portrait of Haydon's character:

> One great merit of Mr. Haydon's pictures is their size. Reduce him within narrow limits, and you cut off half his resources. His genius is gigantic. He is of the race of Brobdignag [sic], and not of Lilliput. … Vastness does not confound him, difficulty rouses him, impossibility is the element in which he glories.   (Hazlitt, 18.142–3)

Hazlitt's capacity to appreciate the gusto of life allowed him, unlike most of his contemporaries, to see Haydon in the round.

'Great spirits' of the age And it is this which brings Haydon into the context of other 'great spirits' of the age; some of these are reflected in *Christ's Entry*. Hazlitt stands watching Christ on the donkey; Keats is shown talking, possibly irreverently, to his friend William Bewick, a painter who was a pupil of Haydon's; Wordsworth is bowing his head in reverence, standing beside the wrinkled visage of Voltaire and the handsome heroic figure of Newton. Figures not in the picture are those of Leigh Hunt and Shelley, whom Haydon knew but by 1817 had come to dislike, not least because of their atheism. Symbolically, their atheism is present in the image of Voltaire—Haydon's orthodox Christian theology was simply baffled by the scepticism of Shelley, Hunt, Horace Smith, even Keats:

> I dined with Shelley at Horace Smith's—I could not conceive what this slender feeble creature [was that] sat opposite me—eating vegetables at last in a feeble tremulous voice he said 'As to that detestable religion, the Christian religion' &c Hunt chuckled up with a sort of delight as he had now a bolster to support him & finding Keats, Smith all of his own way of thinking set at me immediately.   (Gray and Walker, 23)

Keats was able to remain a friend, even to tease Haydon by placing his hand on his heart and bowing his head to the figure of Voltaire in Haydon's picture, saying 'there is the being I will bow to' (in contrast to Wordsworth who bowed his head to Christ) (*Letters of John Keats*, 2.317). The Keats that Haydon knew from 1816 to 1817 was depicted as most lively, and pleased Haydon by declaring that the three great things to rejoice at in this age were 'The Excursion, Your [Haydon's] Pictures and Hazlitt's depth of taste' (ibid., 1.203). *Christ's Entry into Jerusalem* did not produce the critical éclat of his *Solomon*. When it was exhibited in the Egyptian Hall, despite Mrs Siddons's declaration that the figure of Christ was perfect, Haydon admitted: 'I overdid it; and like all overdoings it was weak … when it ought to have looked best it looked worst, and looked well only when the whole picture could not be seen' (*Life*, 1st edn, 1.376).

The Raising of Lazarus But it was Haydon's ambition to paint a third large picture so that he would have at least three major paintings in his control (*Dentatus* belonged to Lord Mulgrave) which the public would pay to see: *The Raising of Lazarus* (Tate collection) is only adequately described by Haydon's most thoughtful critic, David Blayney Brown:

> Alas the picture is rolled today, but it was evidently a deeply flawed masterpiece. Lazarus—for whom William Bewick sat—was recognised from the first as a triumph of expressive characterisation, worthy of a great master, but the Christ from whom he draws life has always been condemned as limp and sentimental; if Dentatus's heroism had been expressed in a form of almost grotesque superhumanity, now Christ's spirituality glimmered feebly from too ordinary a frame.   (Brown, Woof, and Hebron, 14)

When *The Raising of Lazarus* was exhibited, again at the Egyptian Hall (condemned by some at the Royal Academy as a 'raree show'), disaster struck: on 13 April 1823 the picture was seized; on 21 April Haydon was arrested for debt and taken to the king's bench prison. Haydon was to be imprisoned again in 1827, 1830, and 1836, but this first occasion involved the disastrous loss of all the large pictures that he had hoped to exhibit together as a group of wonders for profit. Thereafter, Haydon considered his situation indeed bitter: he considered that 'B. R. Haydon died' and that some lesser figure emerged who 'painted in imitation of the former a few small works … asked a patron or two to employ him and, in short, did all those things that men must do who prefer their own degradation to the starvation of their children' (ibid., 15). For, importantly, Haydon had married, on 10 October 1821, Mary Cawse Hyman, a widow with two sons. His own son, Frank Scott *Haydon (1822–1887), archivist, was born on 12 December 1822; his daughter, Mary Mordwinoff (after Haydon's mother's sister, who married the Russian admiral Count Nikolay S. Mordvinov), on 17 March 1824; Alfred on 5 December 1825; and Frederick Wordsworth Haydon, memorialist, on 14 September 1827 (there were eight children in all but Alfred and the last four children died between 1831 and 1836, almost certainly from tuberculosis). Haydon took commissions where he could: a chalk drawing of Charles Heathcote Tatham, architect and friend, belongs to September 1823; on 2 April 1824 Haydon declared: 'Shall begin a little insignificant one of Mercury & Argus' (*Diary*, 2.470); but one cannot be really sure he began the work then or later, for on 9 April 1826 the entry reads: 'Began Mercury & Argus. Worked hard. Painted Argus's head' (ibid., 3.90). The painting was not exhibited until 1831 at the British Institution. February 1826 sees him beginning *Venus Appearing to Anchises* (Yale U. CBA) for Sir John Leicester, which he completed in a few weeks; on 12 April 1826 he began *Alexander Taming Bucephalus* (Petworth House, Sussex which the third earl of Egremont (1751–1837) saw in May and commissioned for Petworth. Lord Egremont seemed pleased with the work but it took until 10 March 1827 for Haydon to complete it; and through maladroitness Haydon did not build, as Turner emphatically did, a relationship with his generous patron.

Subject paintings Haydon's imprisonment in June 1827, again for debt, was brought to an end by a subscription arranged by Walter Scott's son-in-law, J. G. Lockhart, but that month led Haydon to one of the best of his subjects:

The Mock Election (Royal Collection), which shows those in gaol imitating the election taking place outside the prison. Haydon completed the painting in five months, and exhibited it in January at the Egyptian Hall, when he had already begun a second painting on a related subject, *Chairing the Member* (Tate collection)—this, too, was based on an incident he witnessed at the king's bench prison when the constable of the gaol called out the Coldstream Guards to quell the supposed riotous behaviour of the prisoners. It was a moment of triumph for Haydon, recently rejected by the Royal Academy as a possible member, when George IV purchased *The Mock Election* for 500 guineas. Haydon was very disappointed that *Chairing the Member* did not so much please the king, and it was finally sold for £300 to 'a young Tanner (Mr. Frances of Exeter)' (*Diary*, 3.352). He then began another painting whose subject was again taken from the streets of London: *Punch, or, May Day* (Tate collection), a good-humoured depiction, which took him over a year to complete. Among these entertaining pictures, his concern for events of his own lifetime led him to one of his most fruitful themes: on 8 December 1830 'Sir Robert Peel called, and gave me a commission to paint Napoleon musing, the size of life' (ibid., 3.498). This was the first of his twenty-three pictures of Napoleon on St Helena. Here humour might have helped, for his work was easily mocked by Turner in *War: the Exile and the Rock Limpet* (1842; Tate collection), in which he revises Haydon's subject by turning the figure of Napoleon so that he looks down, towards the viewer, and contemplates a shrimp in the water. But the one painting that does indeed show effective humour, and is often praised, is *Waiting for 'The Times'*, completed between October and November 1831 (in two versions—one at *The Times*, News International plc): it represents a gentleman in a coffee house, waiting impatiently for *The Times* to be handed over by another reader; it catches the excitement of readers during the progress of the Reform Bill through parliament in 1831.

Among other commissions recording public events, Haydon undertook by subscription a celebratory work, *The Meeting of the Unions on Newhall Hill, Birmingham*, to memorialize the successful agitation in favour of the Reform Bill. He managed only to do a series of sixteen individual portraits and a sketch for the painting (all now at Birmingham Museum and Art Gallery) which, through lack of subscriptions, was not completed. A more ambitious work was begun on 11 July 1832, the very day that Haydon attended the reform banquet by invitation of Lord Grey, who wanted him to paint, for 500 guineas, the memorable scene of the whigs gathered in the Guildhall to mark the triumph of parliamentary reform. As ever, Haydon's method was scarcely economic, for the commission took him over two years and involved at least forty individual portraits; some were issued as prints, but by the time it was completed on 22 March 1834 politics had changed—the whigs were falling from fashion—and the exhibition closed on 29 August with losses of £230. The painting, still in possession of the Grey family, is a wonder of accumulated faces; it was also issued as a print with a

key naming all the persons. The painting itself may not have brought Haydon a financial triumph, but his diary at this time is in heightened mode: almost every day Haydon was meeting major whig ministers in order to draw their portraits; he even made it his business to attend the House of Lords to carry on sketching, and in his journal he recorded a masterful series of prose portraits. He recorded conversations and social habits (such as touching ankles under the table). Amid it all, touchingly and yet ludicrously, he fell in love with the writer Mrs Norton, who had sat as his model for *Cassandra* (1834). A fear that he might be cited (Lord Melbourne was) in the divorce case initiated by Mrs Norton's husband haunted him, even after he had finished the agreeable flirtation (known to his wife, to his great remorse, through her reading of his diary). Out of this socializing with the whigs there emerged something of public significance, for he was able to lobby Melbourne (who succeeded Grey as prime minister in 1834) on the need for public art commissions for the new houses of parliament (the earlier having been destroyed by fire on 16 October 1834); again, he persuaded the whigs that the Royal Academy should not be allowed to take charge of the new National Gallery; finally, his demand that there should be support for teaching the art of drawing led to his examination by the parliamentary select committee on arts and principles of design on 28 June 1836. By August 1837 a parliamentary report recommended the setting up of art education schools throughout the country, and these institutes became a fact in the 1840s. As he continued his work as a controversialist and public figure, Haydon remained committed to high art. One heroic theme was *The Maid of Saragossa* (Plymouth City Museum and Art Gallery), begun in 1836 and finished in 1842: Haydon drew upon a contemporary legend already celebrated by Byron and, significantly, by his friend David Wilkie in a painting of 1822 (Royal Collection). At the same time Haydon began a Roman theme derived from Livy: *Marcus Curtius Leaping into the Gulf* (Royal Albert Memorial Museum, Exeter; version National Gallery of Victoria, Melbourne, Australia): this shows a young soldier leaping fearlessly into a chasm that had mysteriously opened in the forum; he wished to appease the gods and to demonstrate Roman valour. Here the idea of sacrificing one's life parallels Haydon's sense of personal piety (he was very often 'at prayer' in his diary) and his own continuing sense of suffering for high art—the parallel all the more potent because the head of the Roman hero is a self-portrait. Interestingly, the power of the picture is as much in the treatment of the horse as in the man, for in the leap the artist conveys the whole anatomy of the terrified horse. To the end Haydon always made anatomy the basis for drawing the figure, whether it was man or beast (a point that his 'ungrateful' pupil, Edwin Landseer, at least derived from Haydon).

Public life Beyond lobbying, another influential career had begun for Haydon, for on 9 September 1835 he began a series of lectures at the Mechanics' Institution (chaired by Dr George Birkbeck, the institution's founder in 1834). Haydon recorded, 'I laid down principles which must reform English Art, & I had an audience who gloriously comprehended them' (*Diary*, 4.307). For ten years Haydon enjoyed being a public figure, especially away from London: for instance, on 27 April 1837 a dinner for 110 was held in his honour in Edinburgh: 'I was met with such a storm of applause' (ibid., 413, n. 5). He toured Glasgow, Liverpool, Manchester, and Leicester, giving single lectures, but in Manchester he gave a series. His lectures were not published (although there were lengthy newspaper reports) until the end of his life, in 1844 and 1846, but a substantial essay, 'Painting and the fine arts', appeared in 1838, along with an essay by Hazlitt, both essays reprinted from the seventh edition of the *Encyclopaedia Britannica*, issued between 1830 and 1842; to his chagrin, Wilkie told Haydon that 'he had begun it, but it was very learned!' (ibid., 4.506). *The Athenaeum* gave it more respect in three articles, published on 14, 21, and 28 July 1838 (pp. 482–4; 510–12; 526–8).

With some of his paintings Haydon published prose pamphlets: *Description of the Drawings from the Cartoons and Elgin Marbles by Mr. Haydon's Pupils* (1819); *Description of 'Christ's Triumphant Entry into Jerusalem'* (1820); *Explanation of the picture of 'The mock election' which took place at the king's bench prison, July 1827* (1828); *Explanation of the Picture 'Chairing the Member'* (1828), and *A Description of Haydon's Picture of the Reform Banquet* (1834). It was on 7 July 1839 that Haydon began to write his autobiography—a rough draft entitled 'Vita' covers his life to 1825; and his more finished autobiography runs to 1820. It was published by Tom Taylor in three volumes in 1853, and is a brilliant and well-shaped account. He had hoped that Elizabeth Barrett would prepare it for publication, but on the advice of Robert Browning, her future husband, she declined. In his will he makes it clear that he expects his memoir, journal, and letters to be published: 'My Memoirs are to 1820, my journals will supply the rest. The style, the individuality of [Samuel] Richardson, which I wish not curtailed by an Editor. Correspondence & Journals for the rest' (*Diary*, 1.xii). Longman commissioned Tom Taylor to prepare the papers for the press, the first volume being the autobiography and the second two extracts from the journals from 1820 to 1846. Frederick Wordsworth Haydon compiled *Benjamin Robert Haydon: Correspondence and Table-Talk* (2 vols., 1876) and provided letters to and from Haydon, sometimes revised and excerpted. The major contribution to Haydon scholarship is *The Diary of Benjamin Robert Haydon* (ed. W. B. Pope, 5 vols., 1960–63), which reveals a more demanding text for readers but a powerful one with its shifts in mood, its candour, and its indiscretion, a text indeed as detailed as a Richardson novel. Much of his correspondence has not been published.

Later years In some ways Haydon's last years are marked by a need to justify himself, in his journal, in his autobiography, and in his lectures; but throughout his passion for painting remains. Some paintings were very large indeed: *The Black Prince Thanking Lord James Audley for his Gallantry in the Battle of Poitiers* (279 x 305 cm, now at Plymouth City Museum and Art Gallery) was commissioned by George John, Lord Audley (1783–1837), a young man who was possibly mad and certainly proved to have no money; Haydon was rescued by its purchase by his generous patron William Newton. On 21 June 1836 he began an even larger painting, *The Maid of Saragossa* (Plymouth City Museum and Art Gallery), which he raffled for £525. On 31 August he began a painting that took six years to complete, *Marcus Curtius Leaping into the Gulf* (Exeter City Art Gallery)—another of his studies of heroic suicides. One of his largest pictures was *The Anti-Slavery Convention*, begun on 21 June 1840 and completed in less than a year; it was first exhibited at the Egyptian Hall in 1841, and is now at the National Portrait Gallery, London. *The General Anti-Slavery Convention at the Freemasons' Tavern* celebrated the presence of Thomas Clarkson (1760–1846), the pioneer abolitionist who had begun his work in 1785. Haydon, always a historical painter, wished to paint heroes. *Wellington Musing on the Field of Waterloo … Twenty Years after* (St George's Hall, Liverpool) was begun in 1838 and completed in 1839. It was not exhibited until 1842 but Haydon had taken the initiative of having the picture engraved by T. G. Lupton, and that engraving was sent to Wordsworth by the end of August 1840. Wordsworth, while walking up Helvellyn with his daughter, memorably composed his third sonnet to Haydon, 'On a portrait of the duke of Wellington upon the field of Waterloo, by Haydon', with its first line 'By art's bold privilege Warrior and War-Horse stand'. On receiving the sonnet, Haydon was prompted to paint what may be considered his greatest portrait: *Wordsworth on Helvellyn* (NPG). With his egotistical flair, Haydon thinks of Wordsworth not just meditating, but meditating especially upon Haydon's own ambitious picture. Wordsworth is depicted as a standing figure with head bowed, even as he was twenty years previously in *Christ's Entry into Jerusalem*: now Wordsworth's hair is white but the same sketch of 1819 (Wordsworth Museum, Grasmere) provides the basis of the downturned head which Hazlitt praised in his essay 'On my first acquaintance with poets' (1825): this drawing of Wordsworth was 'the most like his drooping weight of thought and expression' (Hazlitt, 17.118).

More paintings of both Napoleon and Wellington were dashed out in these late years. But time was not on Haydon's side—not least because, with the coming of the prince consort and his influence upon the taste of the English court, Haydon found he was sidelined, not only by the Royal Academy, with its acquired taste for German pictures, but also by those on the committee appointing artists to adorn the newly built houses of parliament. On 22 March 1843 he wrote: 'My opposition to the German School, which is strong at court, has effectually excluded all hope from the palace' (*Diary*, 5.255). He was not chosen, and even heard from his old pupil, Charles Eastlake, now director of the National Gallery, that Sir Robert Peel, one of the appointing committee, had said that he was 'annoyed at my restless activity about art—that I interfered in everything' (ibid., 294). Haydon felt bitter at being rejected since he had been the advocate of the need to employ artists to provide new works for the houses of parliament.

His paranoid tendency led Haydon to remember vividly his old quarrels: when the portrait painter Thomas Phillips died on 20 April 1845, he recalled that Phillips (and Martin Archer Shee, president of the Royal Academy, 1830–50) had rehung his painting of *Dentatus* in 1809, and the new positioning, Haydon thought, was much to his disadvantage: 'God forgive him, I can't!—the bitterest enemy from the beginning I ever had, except Shee' (*Diary*, 5.429). He recognized that those appointed to commission works for the houses of parliament 'resolved to employ none but those of German tendency' (ibid., 470). Almost recklessly he painted on: *Uriel Revealing himself to Satan*, completed in March 1845; *The Banishment of Aristides*, completed on 26 September 1845; *Nero Playing on the Lyre*, completed in January 1846 (the last two pictures both priv. coll., on loan to the National Gallery of Victoria, Melbourne, Australia). Only his *Alfred and the First British Jury* remained unfinished at his death. Some of these pictures, intended for parliament, he defiantly exhibited at the Egyptian Hall, Piccadilly, but by 18 May 1846 the exhibition closed and Haydon had lost more than £111. He bitterly noted that a nearby exhibition on the dwarf Tom Thumb was attended by crowds. The more he was neglected, the more he made it his business to write, and, on completing his critical preface for the second volume of *Lectures on Painting and Design* (March 1846), Haydon declared, 'I am not decayed, but the people have been corrupted' (*Diary*, 5.544). Though he had a wonderful capacity for confession, Haydon perhaps lacked self-knowledge. He is an unreliable narrator, not least in his assessment of others: for instance, he loved Keats in 1816, but was harsh on Keats before he left for Italy; he heroized Wordsworth in 1815 and until 1820, when he quarrelled because Wordsworth straightforwardly explained that he could not lend him money. His vituperative account of Wordsworth in a letter to Mary Mitford of 1824, calling him 'an old satyr … lecherous, animal & devouring … an old beast, cloaked in piety and verse', suggests a mental imbalance (Jones). Still, on 12 April 1831 Wordsworth called after an absence of several years.

> I was glad to see him. He spoke of my Napoleon in high poetry of language, with his usual straightforward intensity of diction. We shook hands heartily. He spoke of Napoleon so highly that I wrote & told him to give me a Sonnet. If he would or could, he'd make the fortune of the Picture. (Haydon, *Diary*, 3.515)

Once more Wordsworth complied, and on 12 June Haydon records receiving the sonnet 'To B. R. Haydon, on Seeing his Picture of Napoleon Bonaparte on the Island of St. Helena'. Haydon felt buoyed up, '& fancied myself the greatest of men when I was returning from my walk after indulging on my certain posthumous fame' (ibid., 522–3). But immediately reality intruded, and he found himself in a dispute with a man whose request he refused and who therefore called Haydon 'a shabby fellow, a d—n shabby fellow'. Haydon reflected: 'This is Life—a sonnet in the morning, & damned as a shabby fellow in the evening! One does not like to be called shabby, and it made me uneasy all evening' (ibid.). Wordsworth's sonnet put

Haydon into a genial mood and their friendship was renewed until Wordsworth became poet laureate in 1843. It was the image of Wordsworth attending the court and falling to his knees in front of the young queen which aroused Haydon's contempt, inspiring him to write verses (14 May 1845) which, though scarcely competent, seem to parallel, and probably prompted Robert Browning's 'The Lost Leader', an attack on Wordsworth's becoming poet laureate: 'Just for a handful of silver he left us' (Brown, Woof, and Hebron, 56–61). Wordsworth himself was probably ignorant of Haydon's hostility, and summed up the painter for Frederick Wordsworth Haydon, Haydon's youngest surviving son and Wordsworth's godson:

> Your father was a fine, frank, generous nature, a capital talker, and well-informed. And as to his art, he said, 'He is the first painter in his grand style of art that England or any other country has produced since the days of Titian. He may be disregarded and scorned now by the ignorant and malevolent, but posterity would do him justice. There are things in his works that have never been surpassed, they will be the text books of art hereafter.' (*Correspondence and Table-Talk*, 1.110)

Life, gusto, ambition and a sense of failure mingle in this ambitious artist who, through his writings, allowed himself, with some danger to his reputation, to be wholly known. On Monday, 22 June 1846 Haydon rose early, went to Oxford Street and bought a small pistol: he locked himself in his painting room, and wrote out a considerate and business-like will. His death certificate states that he committed 'suicide—with a razor by cutting his throat after shooting a pistol ball at the upper and back part of his head. Found dead 22nd June 1846 at no. 14 Burwood Place Edgware Road.'. Two days later the jury recorded that Haydon 'was in an unsound state of mind when he committed the act' (*Diary*, 5.559). His gravestone in the old Paddington churchyard, behind Mrs Siddons's grave, beside his five dead children, more fairly records: 'He devoted forty-two years to the improvement of the taste of the English people in high art and died broken-hearted from pecuniary distress' (ibid.).

Haydon's second son, **Frederick Wordsworth Haydon** (1827–1886), was born on 14 September 1827 and was baptized on 18 September, when Wordsworth and David Wilkie were his godfathers. He entered the Royal Navy in August 1841, and served in many ships. On 1 December 1868 at St Saviour, Leeds, he married Robina Fairbairn. He was latterly an inspector of factories but was dismissed in 1867 for publishing a letter addressed to Gladstone, entitled 'Our officials at the home office'. He became his father's memorialist, publishing *Correspondence and Table-Talk* in two volumes in 1876. He died in London at Bethlem Hospital on 12 November 1886.   ROBERT WOOF

Sources *The life of Benjamin Robert Haydon, historical painter, from his autobiography and journals*, ed. T. Taylor, 3 vols. (1853) • *The life of Benjamin Robert Haydon, historical painter, from his autobiography and journals*, ed. T. Taylor, 2nd edn, 3 vols. (1853) • A. Huxley, introduction, in *The autobiography and memoirs of Benjamin Robert Haydon*, ed. T. Taylor, 2 vols. (1926) • E. Blunden, introduction and epilogue, in *Autobiography of Benjamin Robert Haydon*, ed. T. Taylor (1927) • *The autobiography and memoirs of Benjamin Robert Haydon, 1786–1846*, ed. A. P. D. Penrose (1927) • *The diary of Benjamin Robert Haydon*, ed. W. B.

Pope, 5 vols. (1960–63) • *Benjamin Robert Haydon: correspondence and table-talk*, ed. F. W. Haydon, 2 vols. (1876) • B. R. Haydon, *Lectures on painting and design*, 2 vols. (1844) • B. R. Haydon and W. Hazlitt, *Painting and the fine arts, being … articles … contributed to the 'Encyclopedia Britannica'* (1838) • *The correspondence of Elizabeth Barrett Browning and Benjamin Robert Haydon, 1842–1845*, ed. W. B. Pope (Cambridge, Mass., 1972) • *Neglected genius: the diaries of Benjamin Robert Haydon, 1808–1846*, ed. J. Jolliffe (1990) • *Annals of the Fine Arts* (1816–20) • *Elizabeth Barrett to Miss Mitford*, ed. B. Miller (1954) • *The letters of Robert Browning and Elizabeth Barrett Browning, 1845–1846*, ed. R. W. B. Browning (1899) • *The letters of Robert Browning and Elizabeth Barrett Barrett, 1845–1846*, ed. E. Kintner, 2 vols. (Cambridge, Mass., 1969) • *Life and letters of William Bewick (artist)*, ed. T. Landseer, 2 vols. (1871) • F. Blanshard, *Portraits of Wordsworth* (1959) • D. B. Brown, R. Woof, and S. Hebron, *Benjamin Robert Haydon, 1786–1846: painter and writer; friend of Wordsworth and Keats* (1996) [exhibition catalogue Wordsworth Trust, Dove Cottage, Grasmere] • Farington, *Diary*, vols. 15–16 • B. F. Cook, *The Elgin marbles* (1997) • F. Cummings, 'Poussin, Haydon and *The judgement of Solomon*', *Burlington Magazine*, 106 (1962), 146 ff. • F. Cummings, 'Nature and the antique in B. R. Haydon's *Assassination of Dentatus*', *Journal of the Warburg and Courtauld Institutes*, 25 (1962), 147 ff. • F. Cummings, 'Phidias in Bloomsbury: B. R. Haydon's drawings of the Elgin marbles', *Burlington Magazine*, 106 (1962), 325 ff. • E. Fletcher, *Conversations of James Northcote R.A. with James Ward on art and artists* (1901) • C. M. Franzero, *A life in exile: Ugo Foscolo in London, 1816–1827* (1977) • E. George, *The life and death of Benjamin Robert Haydon* (1948) • D. Gray and V. W. Walker, 'Benjamin Robert Haydon on Byron and others', *Keats–Shelley Memorial Bulletin*, 7 (1956) • A. Hayter, *A sultry month: scenes of London literary life in 1846* (1965) • *The complete works of William Hazlitt*, ed. P. P. Howe, 21 vols. (1930–34) • P. Hughes-Hallett, *The immortal dinner* (2000) • I. Jack, *Keats and the mirror of art* (1967) • S. Jones, 'B. R. Haydon on some contemporaries: a new letter', *Review of English Studies*, new ser., 26 (1975), 183–9 • J. Keats, *The complete poems*, ed. J. Barnard, 3rd edn (1988) • *The letters of John Keats*, ed. H. E. Rollins, 2 vols. (Cambridge, Mass., 1958) • W. Knight, 'On the portraits of Wordsworth', *Transactions of the Wordsworth Society*, 3 (1882), 56–76 • L. Campbell, *Landseer: the Victorian paragon* (1976) • J. McCoubrey, 'War and peace in 1842: Turner, Haydon and Wilkie', *Turner Studies*, 4/2 (1984), 2–7 • *Life of Mary Russell Mitford, related in a selection from her letters to her friends*, ed. A. G. L'Estrange, 3 vols. (1870) • C. Olney, *Benjamin Robert Haydon, historical painter* (Atlanta, Georgia, 1952) • F. Owen and D. B. Brown, *Collector of genius: a life of Sir George Beaumont* (1988) • R. Park, ed., *Sale catalogues of libraries of eminent persons*, 9: *Poets and men of letters* (1974) • E. M. Symonds [G. Paston], *B. R. Haydon and his friends* (1905) • M. Pidgley, *Benjamin Robert Haydon: bi-centenary exhibition, drawings from the Exeter collection* (1986) [exhibition catalogue, Exeter] • M. Pidgeley, *The tragicomical history of B. R. Haydon's Marcus Curtius leaping into the gulf* (1986) • D. Robertson, *Sir Charles Eastlake and the Victorian art world* (Princeton, New Jersey, 1978) • H. E. Rollins, ed., *The Keats circle: letters and papers, 1816–1878*, 2 vols. (Cambridge, Mass., 1948) • A. C. Sewter, 'A revaluation of Haydon', *Art Quarterly*, 5 (autumn 1942), 323–37 • R. Walker, *National Portrait Gallery: Regency portraits*, 2 vols. (1985) • D. Watkin, *Thomas Hope, 1769–1831, and the neo-classical idea* (1968) • R. Woof and S. Hebron, *John Keats* (1995) [exhibition catalogue, Wordsworth Trust, Grasmere] • *The poetical works of William Wordsworth*, ed. E. De Selincourt and H. Darbishire, 5 vols. (1940–49) • *The letters of William and Dorothy Wordsworth*, ed. E. De Selincourt, 2nd edn, rev. C. L. Shaver, M. Moorman, and A. G. Hill, 8 vols. (1967–93) • d. cert. • D. H. Solkin, ed., *Art on the line* (2001)

Archives Hunt. L., letters; literary MSS • V&A NAL, MSS of history of art and lectures on art | BL, letters to Leigh Hunt, Add. MSS 38108–38110, 38523, *passim* • BL, corresp. with John Keats, MS Facs 337 • BL, corresp. with Sir Robert Peel, Add. MSS 40392–40593, *passim* • Bodl. Oxf., letters to Sir Thomas Talfourd • Ches. & Chester ALSS, letters to Sir John Leicester • FM Cam., letters to Prince Hoare, John Murray, Sir Robert Peel, and others • FM Cam., letters to Sir Robert Peel • Lambton Park, Chester-le-Street, co. Durham, letters to first earl of Durham • NL Scot., letters to Sir Walter Scott • Staffs. RO, letters to duke of Sutherland • W. Sussex RO, letters to duke of Richmond

Likenesses D. Wilkie, chalk drawing, 1815, NPG • J. P. Davis, drawing, 1816, V&A • G. H. Harlow, oils, 1816, Birmingham Museums and Art gallery • J. Keats, caricature, 1816, NPG • two plastercast life masks, *c.*1820, NPG • G. M. Zornlin, oils, 1825, NPG [*see illus.*] • B. Haydon, self-portrait, *c.*1845, NPG • G. H. Harlow, chalk drawing, Courtauld Inst. • W. Nicholson, oils, Plymouth City Museum and Art Gallery

Haydon, Frank Scott (1822–1887), record scholar, was born on 12 October 1822, the eldest son of Benjamin Robert *Haydon (1786–1846), the painter, and his wife, Mary Cawse Hyman. He was baptized at Paddington, Middlesex, on 13 July 1829, Sir Walter Scott being a godfather (whence came his second name) and Mary Russell Mitford a godmother. He was educated, on his impecunious father's borrowings, at a school at Wappenham, Northamptonshire, and then at Cambridge University, where he entered Gonville and Caius College in 1840 but migrated to Jesus College in January 1842. He came high both in mathematics and classics, but his university career was embarrassed by his father's irregular payments and he took the pass degree of BA in 1845. In that year Haydon secured a nomination from Sir Robert Peel to one of the Public Record Office clerkships, at £80 per annum, with prospects of improvement. He briefly took up a customs appointment in 1846 but soon returned to the junior clerkship of his original department. He was promoted senior clerk in 1860 and assistant keeper in 1885.

Much of Haydon's work was concerned with the calendaring of the patent rolls and he had a high reputation in the office for his palaeographical skill. His other main work was an edition for the Rolls Series of the *Eulogium historiarum* (3 vols., 1858–63): he worked on this out of office hours and was paid an editorial fee.

Haydon married on 14 October 1858 at Merton, Surrey, Ellen Mary (1829–1861), second daughter of Edward Rayne of West Barnes. They had a daughter, Ellen Mary Middleton (b. 1859), who survived him, and two children who died in infancy. From 1854 he was custodian of his father's very extensive manuscript diary, which he annotated discreetly and accurately; it descended to his daughter and was eventually published in full in 1960–63.

Haydon had the reputation among his Public Record Office contemporaries of being 'superior and temperamental', and his sight had been troubling him before his death. He shot himself through the brain on 29 October 1887, at his home, Southey Lodge, Kingston Road, Wimbledon, in circumstances which recalled his father's suicide. ALAN BELL

Sources *The diary of Benjamin Robert Haydon*, ed. W. B. Pope, 5 vols. (1960–63) • *The Times* (1 Nov 1887), 11 • F. S. Haydon, 'A letter of Sir Walter Scott', *The Athenaeum* (21 July 1877), 79–80 • F. S. Haydon, 'Haydon's "correspondence and table-talk", a letter of Sir Walter Scott', 2602 (8 Sept 1877), 307 • Boase, *Mod. Eng. biog.* • Venn, *Alum. Cant.* • J. D. Cantwell, *The Public Record Office, 1838–1958* (1991) • *CGPLA Eng. & Wales* (1887)

Wealth at death £376 15s.: administration, 22 Dec 1887, CGPLA Eng. & Wales

Haydon, Frederick Wordsworth (1827–1886). *See under* Haydon, Benjamin Robert (1786–1846).

Hayek, Friedrich August (1899–1992), economist and political philosopher, was born in Vienna on 8 May 1899, the eldest of three sons of August Josef Gustav von Hayek (1871–1928), physician and botanist, and his wife, Felicitas Johanna Valerie, *née* von Juraschek (1875–1967), daughter of Franz von Juraschek, statistician, professor, and senior civil servant. His great-great-grandfather, Josef von Hayek (1750–1830), gained a minor title of nobility as an enterprising steward for an aristocratic landowner in Moravia. Hayek's English-language opponents insisted on calling him in later life von Hayek. In fact such titles were abolished in the inter-war Austrian republic. The 'von' got back into his name only by an accident, when he submitted his birth certificate for his British naturalization in 1938, and was in too much of a hurry for a passport to correct it. Hayek's mother called him Fritz, an appellation also used by friends and contemporaries, but which he never liked. He was educated at two different *Volkschüler* and two different *Gymnasia*; he later explained his frequent changes of school by saying that he 'ran into difficulties with my teachers, who were irritated by the combination of obvious ability and laziness and lack of interest I showed' (*Hayek on Hayek*, 42). In March 1917 he joined a field artillery regiment in Vienna, and at the end of 1917 he was sent to the Italian front. There he contracted malaria and encountered his cousin Ludwig Wittgenstein. Returning to Vienna, he enrolled at the university in November 1918.

Hayek's father never achieved his ambition to hold a university chair, which helps to explain his son's belief that that was the most desirable of all positions. He afterwards remarked that the decisive aspect of his own student years was that 'you were not expected to confine yourself to your own subject' (*Hayek on Hayek*, 51); and indeed he wavered between psychology and economics, which at the time had to be combined with law. During winter 1919–20 (when the University of Vienna was closed for lack of fuel for heating) he went to Zürich, where he worked briefly in the laboratory of the brain anatomist von Monakow. He once said that he might well have become a biologist had not his father given him two 'heavy volumes' by August Weismann (the biologist who rediscovered Mendel's genetics) at a time when he was too immature to appreciate them. He also remarked that the qualities he had admired in the University of Vienna had disappeared by the Second World War, and he avoided returning to the city.

Hayek graduated with a Dr Jur in 1921, completing his degree in three years rather than the usual four. In October that year a letter of recommendation from his university teacher Friedrich von Wieser to Ludwig von Mises led to a post with the *Abrechnungsamt*, an agency concerned with clearing debts arising from the First World War. While working there he also studied at the University of Vienna for the DScPol., completing his second degree in

Friedrich August Hayek (1899–1992), by Ramsey & Muspratt, 1940s

1923. His real opportunity came when he gained a research assistantship in New York in 1923–4. While there he investigated statistical time series and, more characteristically, wrote a critique of proto-Keynesian underconsumption theories. He also unearthed from American accounts facts about the First World War which had largely been kept from the Austrian population. This may well have been one of the origins of his scepticism about government and all its works.

Back in Austria Hayek became a participant in the economics seminar organized by von Mises, who in 1927 secured for him the post of director of the Austrian Institute for Economic Research, a newly established institute for business cycle research. He also held a lectureship in economics at the University of Vienna, from 1929. Some of his papers caught the attention of Lionel Robbins, professor of economics at the London School of Economics (LSE), and one of the very few British economists who could read German. In 1931 Robbins invited him to give a series of lectures in London, published later that year as *Prices and Production*. Recalling his arrival, Robbins wrote: 'I can still see the door of my room opening to admit the tall, powerful, reserved figure which announced itself quietly and firmly as "Hayek"' (Robbins, 127). In the same year Hayek was appointed visiting professor at the LSE, and in 1932 he was appointed Tooke professor of economic science and statistics, a post he held until 1950. As he subsequently remarked: 'If you are offered a chair in the University of London at the age of 32 you take it.' He was naturalized in 1938.

The London School of Economics Robbins himself had been appointed in 1929, at thirty, the youngest economics professor in the UK. He wanted to establish the LSE as a centre for economic theory; to counteract the insular emphasis of Cambridge; and to combat the influence of John Maynard Keynes, with whom he had already clashed on an official committee in 1930. He believed Hayek could help on all three fronts. Hayek did indeed bring many cosmopolitan contacts to the LSE. He was, for instance, instrumental in the appointment of Karl Popper, the philosopher and author of *The Open Society* (1945). He subsequently looked back on his own work at the LSE in the 1930s as 'intellectually [the] most active and satisfying of my life' (*Hayek on Hayek*, 81).

Hayek's technical work at the LSE had three main but related aspects: capital, monetary, and business cycle theory. He promoted the 'Austrian' capital theory, which emphasized that lower interest rates promoted a more 'roundabout' structure of production—what later would be described as a capital-deepening one. But he eventually abandoned the earlier Austrian concept of an average period of production in favour of the more complex idea of the structure of production. He was himself dissatisfied with his final effort in this direction, *The Pure Theory of Capital*, which appeared in 1941 and which he subsequently said he had rushed out too quickly under the erroneous belief that the war would soon make such publications impossible. An intended sequel covering money and business cycles was never written.

American writers who attempted to relaunch 'Austrian economics' towards the end of the twentieth century tended to treat *The Pure Theory of Capital* as an unfortunate divergence and preferred to base themselves on *Prices and Production* and related works. The issue of 'Austrian economics' did not loom large in the 1930s because during that time the differences between the Austrian and other branches of neo-classical economics were less than at any time before or since. The main intellectual battle line was between neo-classical economics of all kinds and the increasingly heretical work of Keynes at Cambridge which culminated in the latter's *General Theory* (1936). By the time that the large divergencies between post-war mainstream economics and the Austrian tradition had emerged into daylight Hayek had largely switched his interest to political philosophy and broad questions of economic policy. Nevertheless his policy recommendations still had their roots in his earlier work on capital and monetary theory; and he did write the occasional short clarificatory paper well into the 1960s, sometimes in response to queries from John Hicks.

It was ironical that media critics later described Hayek as the 'father of monetarism'. From his early studies of business cycles onwards, he emphasized how difficult it was to define the money supply and that, in any case, variations in velocity were at least as important as changes in quantity. But the special characteristic of his cycle theory was his stress on the divergent movement of different prices during the business cycle, so that general price indices could not convey useful information for policy. In view of his insistence on the importance of changing relative prices in so many contexts, and throughout his career, it is surprising that he never sought to measure or estimate such relative price changes. This cannot be completely explained away by his distrust of index numbers.

Hayek's insistence that, while inflation is a monetary phenomenon, there is no such thing as 'the quantity of money', and no sharp boundary between money and other financial assets, has stood the test of time. The experience of the British governments in the 1980s, which changed their monetary targets so much and to so little avail, was much less puzzling to a Hayekian than to a true monetarist believer. So, too, was the high unemployment cost of reducing inflation, which Hayek insisted was inevitable while labour markets were dominated by the collective bargaining mentality.

Hayek's own business cycle theory started out from the 'natural rate of interest', a concept invented by the Swedish economist Knut Wicksell. This was the rate at which savings and investment were equal and the economy was in equilibrium. In an upturn or downturn the market rate of interest diverges from the natural one and the economy becomes unco-ordinated. In the boom phase banks expand credit, and consumption goods are pushed up in price; thus 'forced savings' are extracted from consumers. A neutral monetary policy would attempt to smooth out the cycle by keeping the market rates equal to the natural rate. But as the latter was unknowable this would, in Hayek's view, be an impossible undertaking. Any attempt to use monetary policy to keep the general price level stable would make matters worse—for instance, central banks would raise interest rates near the top of a boom, thus aggravating the ensuing recession. During the 1970s, when the main questions were no longer those of smoothing the business cycle, but double-digit inflation that threatened world prosperity, Hayek changed his views, at least by implication. He then roundly castigated governments, central banks, and, above all, economists for having allowed inflation to soar out of control, from a misguided 'Keynesian' desire to give priority to output and employment.

Hayek and Keynes During his visit in 1931, Hayek was invited to Cambridge. Richard Kahn, Keynes's closest collaborator, asked why if in the middle of a slump he went out and bought an overcoat he would not help to increase output and employment. Hayek replied that it would take a long mathematical demonstration to explain why not; and according to local reports this incident destroyed Hayek's chances of a Cambridge chair.

Looking back seventy years later, the analyst is struck by the similarity rather than the differences of the business cycle theories of Hayek and Keynes at the time of the latter's *Treatise on Money* of 1931. The controversy between the two is admirably set out in volume 9 of the Routledge edition of the collected works of Hayek. This contains papers by Keynes and others as well as Hayek; and the editor, Bruce Caldwell, contributes a lucid and non-partisan introduction concluding that both men promoted theories with specific application to particular times and place, but that neither produced a *general* theory of the trade cycle. (The Cambridge economist Dennis Robertson quipped that what Hayek called a boom Keynes called a slump.) Ironically, Hayek's over-investment theory of the cycle was least applicable to the depressed 1930s when it was launched, but could have found its application in Japan in the 1980s and 1990s, when excessive investment helped trigger a long-lasting recession. Any attempt, however, to revive the theory in a globalized economy would require an analysis of the effects of supporting investment by overseas capital inflows, as well as by forced domestic savings.

The underlying divergence between Hayek and Keynes was rooted in the latter's growing conviction that a frequent and perhaps normal condition of capitalism was one of unused resources, a doctrine which was not fully set out until the *General Theory*, published in 1936. Hayek on the other hand tended to assume as a first approximation full employment of resources. Keynes's rapid victory was above all due to the fact that his theory was primarily directed to explain severe and persistent unemployment during one of the worst depressions of all time. In addition Keynes's theory was more easily translated into mathematical models which bore the hallmark of what was regarded as serious economics. Last but by no means least, Keynes was able to promote the *General Theory* by various means (including offering the book at an especially low price). By the end of the 1930s even the LSE was largely Keynesian.

Hayek wrote a long review for *Economica* of Keynes's earlier 1931 *Treatise on Money*, only to be told by the author (who was by then working on the *General Theory*), 'Oh, never mind; I no longer believe all that' (*Hayek on Hayek*, 90). Hayek often declared that his greatest regret was his failure to write a critique of the *General Theory*, which after his earlier experience he was initially inclined to dismiss as a mere 'tract for the times'. Nevertheless in the last few pages of *The Pure Theory of Capital* there is in fact a sketch of Hayek's unwritten critique. In a section entitled 'Mr Keynes's economics of abundance', Hayek insisted that abundant reserves of all resources are unlikely except in the depths of a severe depression. This still left open the question of where between the two extremes an economy would tend to be. The answer did not appear until Milton Friedman launched the concept of the 'natural rate of unemployment' (later rechristened the 'non-accelerating inflation rate of unemployment', or NAIRU) in 1967. The implicit answer was that the sustainable limit to economic activity was the point at which inflation began to accelerate.

Prices as signalling devices Hayek himself came to regard a different and less technical essay, 'Economics and knowledge', first published in *Economica* in 1937 and later, with related papers, in *Individualism and the Economic Order* (1948), as 'the most original contribution I have made to the theory of economics' (*Hayek on Hayek*, 79); and it does indeed form the link between his economic ideas and his wider social philosophy. It set itself to answer the question: 'How can a combination of fragments of knowledge existing in different minds bring about results, which if they were to be brought about deliberately would require a knowledge on the part of the directing mind which no single person can possess?' According to Hayek, a market system is a discovery technique. No computer can predict the emergence of new knowledge, original ideas, or innovations—and people's reactions to them. His scepticism about the use of econometric relationships was based on a wider epistemological view. For he insisted that the most important kind of knowledge was not of propositions or theories, but of practical skills and dispositions governed by rules which we may imperfectly discover afterwards, but not formulate in advance.

Contrary to popular repute, Hayek always believed that mathematics had an important role to play in economic theory as 'a beautiful way of describing certain patterns' (*Hayek on Hayek*, 148). But he remarked that mathematical economists usually understood so little real mathematics that they believed their subject had to be quantitative and numerical. Unlike many mainstream neo-classical economists Hayek saw the market as an example of human institutions, like language or law, which have evolved without any conscious plan on anyone's part. Whereas mainstream economists were preoccupied with the optimal allocation of resources in given conditions, Hayek was concerned with the effect of the market system on the evolution and stability of society. He insisted that wants, techniques, and resources are not given, but are constantly changing—in part because of the activities of entrepreneurs who open up possibilities which people did not know existed before. (The dynamic and entrepreneurial aspect was also emphasized by another economist of Austrian origin, Joseph Schumpeter, thus providing a so-called Austrian critique of mainstream neo-classical economics, which overlaps with the objections of 'radical' political economists.)

It was this turn in his economic thinking, quite as much as any political differences, which was responsible for Hayek's growing estrangement from the mainstream economics profession. It was not that they disagreed with his depiction of the market as a signalling and incentive device. It was much more that it was difficult to formulate it in terms of the models fashionable among the new generation of economists. A more legitimate criticism was that just as there could be market failures in traditional economics, due to the divergence of private from social costs, so could there be failures in signalling systems, which policy might try to improve. But Hayek had little to say on these, apart from his specialized work on business cycles which he did not revisit. Another problem was that his depiction of markets did not seem to lead to a research programme for further work. (A reasonably sympathetic critic described it as 'poetry'.) This deficiency was beginning to be remedied at the end of the twentieth century by researchers developing the mathematical theory of complexity, originally derived from physics and applied to phenomena such as earthquakes or biological cataclysms, but which they felt could be developed for the study of social events.

During the war years the LSE was evacuated to Cambridge; and Keynes took care that Hayek had comfortable rooms in King's College. Keynes himself spent weekends in Cambridge and the two became friends, despite differences of outlook. Unlike Keynes, Hayek was in no sense a charismatic personality. But they had many shared interests, for instance in antiquarian books and biography. It was then that Hayek came across the correspondence between John Stuart Mill and his future wife Harriet Taylor, which he subsequently published in 1951.

The Road to Serfdom   Contrary to widespread belief, Hayek did not suddenly 'leave economics' to write a political polemic. His inaugural lecture at the London School of Economics in 1933 was partly devoted to what he saw as the error of socialists who, from the best of motives, were liable to bring about results the very opposite of what they intended. But he was no more happy with conservatives 'who never felt the urge to reconstruct the world and who frequently supported the forces of stability only for reasons of selfishness' (F. A. Hayek, 'The trend of economic thinking', *Collected Works*, 3.34).

The basic idea that a planned economy could not work because it would provide no basis for deciding what to produce and by what methods (the so-called calculation problem) was due not to Hayek but to his mentor von Mises. Hayek became involved through his role as an editor of a book on this debate, *Collectivist Economic Planning* (1935), which also contained essays by socialists who wanted to use the market mechanism. Hayek's main contribution was to explain why it would not be possible for socialist enterprises simply to copy private enterprise principles, while remitting their profits to the state. The unexpected collapse of the Soviet Union and its satellites in 1989–91 supplied a belated vindication of his thesis.

The genesis of *The Road to Serfdom* was a memorandum Hayek wrote in the late 1930s for William Beveridge, then director of the London School of Economics, protesting against the frequent depiction of Nazism and fascism as forms of capitalism. He viewed them as collectivist systems, much closer to Soviet communism than to anything in the USA or Britain. This memorandum was enlarged in 1939 for the Public Policy Pamphlets series of the University of Chicago Press. Hayek was induced to expand it further as a tract for a wider market by his alarm at the number of well-intentioned English writers who naïvely wished to continue wartime planning systems to direct the economy for conscious purposes in times of peace. He saw such centralized control as a threat not only to prosperity but to freedom. He did not pretend that most people enjoyed choice. The question was rather whether people should be left themselves to make inescapable choices or whether the decisions should be made for them by someone else.

A reader several decades later would have had to make some allowance for the historical circumstances. But that would have been all to the good. For Hayek had indeed seen all the supposedly progressive ideas he castigated

advanced a generation earlier among German militaristic as well as socialist circles. Although central planning fell into disrepute among political élites in the last twenty or thirty years of the twentieth century, there is always a danger that, faced with seemingly intractable problems, there will be a cry for a strong government 'to take a lead'. Hayek afterwards regretted that, because of the wartime alliance with the Soviet Union, he had to choose all his examples from German thinking and policy. But it was fortunate that he did so. He thereby removed the work from cold-war polemics and also provided a perennially needed reminder of the roots of collectivism in German metaphysics, which exalted society over the individual and poured scorn on the selfish and commercial motivation of the Anglo-Saxons.

The Road to Serfdom was far and away the most eloquent and straightforward statement of his political and economic outlook that Hayek ever achieved. It also seemed something of a miracle, given the sometimes tortuous nature of his other writing. Perhaps the greatest miracle was his choice of title, which is so important to the success of any popular work of political economy. *The Road to Serfdom* was a very clear statement of certain economic verities, which mainstream economists would find it difficult to deny, but which rarely come out in their work. For instance, it analysed what would happen if a planning authority tried to regulate the numbers in different employments by adjusting pay and other terms of work. Is not this an enlightened application of market principles? No, it is not. When a government authority fixes remuneration for a category of worker and supposedly selects them by merit,

> the strength of their desire for the job will count for very little. The person whose qualifications are not of the standard type, or whose temperament is not of the ordinary kind, will no longer be able to come to special arrangements with an employer.

Someone who prefers irregular hours or even a 'happy-go-lucky existence with a small and perhaps uncertain income to a regular routine will no longer have the choice'. People will 'no longer be free to be rational or efficient only when and where we think it worthwhile' (*Road to Serfdom*, 1976 edn, 71–2). The individual would be used by authority to service such abstractions as the social welfare or the good of the community. These few sentences are worth more than all the 'research-based' studies of minimum-wage laws of later decades.

In his preface to the edition of 1976 Hayek explained that he subsequently 'tried hard to get back to economics proper' but he could not free himself of the feeling 'that the problems on which I had so undesignedly embarked were more challenging and important than those of economic theory; and that much that I had said in my first sketch needed clarification and elaboration' (*Road to Serfdom*, 1976 edn, vii). Not all who criticized Hayek for leaving 'economics proper' were political opponents. Some just did not believe that such questions on the borders of politics, philosophy, and economics lent themselves to academic study, and that they were best discussed over coffee when economists were challenged by sociologists, politicians, or journalists.

With *The Road to Serfdom*, Hayek achieved what the editor of his collected works subsequently called his 'fifteen minutes of fame', and he was invited in 1946 to give a lecture tour of the United States, where he was not always received as politely as in Britain. Although the book became an international best-seller, Hayek dated his ostracism by many fellow economists to that work, which they shunned as a popular polemic. Nevertheless his critique of 'planning' was more sympathetically received in Britain than it was in America. For instance, one leading British Fabian, Barbara Wootton, took pains to try to show that democratic planning need not be a threat to freedom. Some of Hayek's disciples have, however, made too much of Keynes's letter in which he said that 'morally and philosophically' he was 'in deeply moved agreement' with *The Road to Serfdom*. More indicative of their underlying differences was Keynes's remark: 'Dangerous acts can be done safely in a community which thinks and feels rightly, which would be the way to hell if they were executed by those who think wrongly' (Keynes, *The Collected Writings*, 27, 1980, 385–8).

Although no politician, Hayek did indeed try to rally intellectual support. With aid from Swiss and American sympathizers he founded in 1947 the Mont Pélerin group of scholars dedicated to the revival of classical liberalism, of which he was president for the next thirteen years and which continued to meet for the rest of the century and beyond. His most lasting practical legacy was probably the network of free-market think-tanks he helped to inspire all over the world. He later remarked that if he had followed his natural inclination he would eventually have become active in public life; but his migration from one country to another made that impossible.

Chicago and after To add to his problems, Hayek remarried in controversial circumstances. Owing to some misunderstanding, his youthful first love, Hélène Bitterlich, had married someone else, and Hayek himself went on to marry, in 1926, Hélène Berta Marie (Hella) von Fritsch (*d.* 1960), with whom he had a daughter, Christina Maria Felicitas (*b.* 1929), and a son, Lorenz Josef Heinrich Erich (*b.* 1934). But when he returned on a private visit to Vienna after the Second World War he found that he was then free to marry Hélène Bitterlich, which he did, in 1950, after divorcing his first wife. This led to estrangement from many of his closest associates in London, and especially from Lionel Robbins, whose actions have been condemned by some as an example of 'illiberal liberalism' and explained by others as sympathy for Hayek's first wife. It was this combined personal and professional distancing which helped to explain his move to Chicago, where he went in 1950 to take up a chair of social and moral science established by the interdisciplinary committee on social thought, a post he held until 1962. (He had earlier been turned down by the economics faculty.)

Hayek's initial years in Chicago saw the publication in book form of two earlier works. *The Sensory Order* (1952) was the final form of a thesis he had developed in Vienna in the 1920s on philosophical psychology. In oversimplified form, the thesis was that there are inherent limits to the human mind's capacity to understand itself, and that human beings know much more than they can ever explicitly explain. The second book, *The Counter-Revolution of Science* (1952), was based on wartime papers attacking 'scientism', by which he meant the pitfalls which arise when the social sciences believe they can ape too closely the methods of the natural ones. His scepticism was initially based on the 'Austrian' belief that the data of the social sciences were inherently subjective. In later papers, reproduced in *Studies in Philosophy, Politics and Economics* (1967), he shifted his ground—partly under the influence of Popper—somewhat away from subjectivity towards the more persuasive one of the *complexity* of social phenomena. He maintained that the social sciences—in common with biology—dealt with complex phenomena which are susceptible only to predictions of pattern and not to specific forecasts.

For Hayek the cardinal sin of his time was something known under the ungainly label of 'constructivism'. This was akin to what Michael Oakeshott called 'rationalism', and is the error of believing that any order we find in society has been put there by a designing mind—and can be, accordingly, redesigned from scratch. His continuing concern was 'with the results of human action but not of human intention', a phrase which he took from the Scottish philosopher Adam Ferguson (1723–1816). This led him away from the Benthamite utilitarianism which he had originally imbibed from von Mises, towards a version of rule utilitarianism.

The main achievement of Hayek's Chicago years was *The Constitution of Liberty*, published in 1960. His concern in that book was for 'that condition of men in which coercion of some by others is reduced as much as is possible' (p. 11). However, he did not in fact provide any easily recognizable criteria for identifying state interventions of the harmful type. The free-market arguments in *The Road to Serfdom* were based on the incompatibility of central planning with personal liberty. But Hayek now approached the issue indirectly. He argued that the main condition for a free society is what he called 'the rule of law'. By that he meant a presumption in favour of general rules and against discretionary power. He attempted to derive from this conception not only the fundamental political and legal basis, but also the economic policies, of a free society. Many writers of the most diverse political persuasions accepted that general rules were an important protection—perhaps the most important single protection—for freedom. But Hayek was criticized for suggesting that general laws were a *sufficient* condition for a free society. Many policies involving a high degree of coercion can be imposed by general rules—for example, a ban on the teaching of evolution, or on any literature or music which flouts the principles of Marxism–Leninism.

There is no one philosopher's stone for minimizing coercion in society. Hayek's concern to restore a government of laws rather than of men can be seen from his later writings, which warned of the degeneration of democracy into a struggle for spoils among competing groups.

He saw the source of interest-group domination in what he called majoritarian or unlimited democracy. This is the belief that a government elected by a majority of voters (usually a plurality) should be able to enact what it likes without any check—a system which Lord Hailsham was to call an 'elective dictatorship'. Some of Hayek's own later constitutional proposals struck even his admirers as far-fetched. But their underlying aim was important. It was to recover an older idea of a state, which has no purposes of its own, but provides a framework of rules and arrangements under which people can pursue their own individual aims without getting in each other's way. This ideal—which is a long way removed from the practice of any modern government, even of the radical right—has been labelled by Oakeshott as a 'civil association', as opposed to the more usual idea of the state as an 'enterprise association', with its own aims and purposes. The close similarity of the later work of Hayek and Oakeshott, pursued in relative isolation, is a theme which deserves a study of its own.

Politics apart, Hayek ascribed his isolation from postwar economics partly to the fact that he never sympathized with either macroeconomics or econometrics. At a time when most go-ahead economists were raring to equip themselves with forecasting models and computer printouts, Hayek, in contrast to Milton Friedman, seemed an armchair thinker, preoccupied with problems such as the limitations of human knowledge. But in the longer haul the contrast did not necessarily tell against Hayek. A disadvantage of late twentieth-century methodological orthodoxy, carefully explained in *Studies in Philosophy, Politics and Economics*, is that many economists acquired a vested interest in the existence of stable, discoverable, numerical relationships between phenomena such as income and consumption, or short-run changes in the money supply and the price level. Hayek warned that one could not guarantee the successful discovery of such relationships, but that scientific method could still be applied to predict certain general features of interacting systems—as it is, for instance, in biology and linguistics. Despite his friendship and ideological sympathy with Milton Friedman, he regarded the stress on prediction in Friedman's *Essays in Positive Economics* as 'quite as dangerous' as anything that Keynes had written (*Hayek on Hayek*, 145).

Although Hayek spent over a decade in Chicago, he never really felt at home in the United States. He was also growing increasingly deaf and had ceased to go to the theatre—thus leaving mountaineering as his main extracurricular interest. In 1962 he accepted a professorship of economic policy at the University of Freiburg im Breisgau in Germany, where he enjoyed a pretty free rein. This was followed by a less happy period as a professor at the University of Salzburg from 1969 to 1977; he then returned to Freiburg, where he spent the rest of his days.

The Nobel prize Hayek suffered more than one fit of depression in later life. The first was in 1960, which he ascribed to his cessation of smoking because of a medical false alarm. A subsequent depression occurred in the early 1970s, which he attributed to a doctor erroneously treating him for diabetes. But his disappointment with the initial reception of *The Constitution of Liberty* and his own recognition that after his seventieth birthday in 1969 his mental powers 'began noticeably to decline' (*Hayek on Hayek*, 131) could also have been relevant.

The award of a Nobel prize for economics in 1974, jointly with the left-inclined Swedish economist Gunnar Myrdal, was followed by a rejuvenation. Even that award had its bitter-sweet side. His Nobel address, 'The pretence of knowledge', was rejected by *Economica*, the journal of the LSE of which he had previously been editor; and it was eventually published by the free-market Institute of Economic Affairs. But among political theorists and sociologists, even those critical of the new right, he was studied more seriously than the more fashionable economic technicians. (A good example of such studies is Andrew Gamble, *The Iron Cage of Liberty*, 1996.)

Hayek's last major work of social philosophy was entitled *Law, Legislation and Liberty* (3 vols., 1973–9). He originally described it as a tailpiece to *The Constitution of Liberty*. But what attracted most attention was a postscript in which he ascribed the success of human institutions to their evolutionary success in the struggle for survival. This came dangerously near to justifying whatever system happened to exist—including by inference the communist order which still prevailed in Russia. Some of his strongest earlier supporters, such as Norman Barry, complained that his previous critical rationalism had been 'almost completely jettisoned in favour of a curious, neo-Darwinistic form of social evolutionism' (Barry, *Classical Liberalism*, 3).

There were thus great ultimate differences between Hayek and some others who shared a similar outlook. Unlike most classical liberals, Hayek's espousal of liberty turned out to be based neither on ultimate judgements, nor on considerations of welfare, utility, or happiness. He did not even accept the methodological individualism of most mainstream economists. For him, the key to institutions was natural selection among competing traditions. This evolutionary approach remained in the background in the classic politico-economic works of his middle period. But its roots went back to his student reflections on biology.

Meanwhile, in the world of public affairs, Hayek's return to public attention also owed something to the proclaimed adherence of Margaret Thatcher, Britain's 'radical right' prime minister from 1979 to 1990. It was sometimes said that if she was, as she proclaimed, 'a conviction politician', the convictions were those of Hayek. Yet the conclusion was not quite fair to either. Although the former UK Conservative leader was an admirer, Hayek mainly provided articulation and confirmation of convictions she had already reached. The admiration was reciprocated, yet some saw much in his writings that was at variance with Thatcherite practice.

Competitive money Hayek never ceased commenting on topical economic issues. He had always distrusted the idea of purely national currencies floating against each other.

Ashland
Community & Technical College
Library

86142

In a pre-war work, *Monetary Nationalism and International Stability* (1937), he came out in favour of a fixed international standard. This would probably be gold, but he had no particular preference for that over any other reference point. During the Second World War he published, in the *Economic Journal* for 1943, a proposal for an international currency which would be convertible into a basket of commodities on a pre-determined basis. He was here supporting and amplifying similar proposals put forward earlier by Benjamin Graham and Frank D. Graham. Such ideas faded from public view, as the Bretton Woods system developed at the end of the war came to be based on national currencies linked by 'fixed but adjustable' exchange rates. It may or may not be a coincidence (most likely it was common causality) that the breakdown of Bretton Woods coincided with the 'great inflation' of the 1970s, probably the largest peacetime inflation of the twentieth century, apart from the hyperinflations following the two world wars.

In the 1970s Hayek went on to propose free competition, not only between national currencies, but between privately issued ones as well. This started 'as a bitter joke' directed against what he regarded as the chronic inability of governments to provide sound money. But it led him into the 'fascinating problem of what would happen if money were provided competitively' (*Hayek on Hayek*, 150). His analysis of this topic, in *The Denationalisation of Money* (1978), proved to be his most detailed pronouncement on monetary matters for several decades. A number of economists devoted serious attention to these proposals. Indeed, competition between different official (but not private) currencies was the main alternative put forward by the British government, in various guises, to the plan for a European currency—the euro—which was finally launched in 1999. Notions of competitive currencies enjoyed a certain vogue, especially but not only among opponents of European monetary union. But what their exponents could never explain was what prevented this competition from developing in countries such as the UK, where legal tender laws were not restrictive, and people could contract in whatever currencies they chose.

Much more was likely to be heard of competitive private enterprise currencies during the twenty-first century. The progress of electronic money and instant communication via the internet was a long-term threat to the central bank monopoly of base money—cash and bank reserves. Electronic transactions could reach a point where the private sector might make settlements 'without the need for clearing through the central bank'. This threatened the whole concept of an official national money, a possibility outlined by the deputy governor of the Bank of England, Mervyn King, writing in the *Bank of England Bulletin* (November 1999).

An iconoclast to the end In 1988 Hayek produced a final book, *The Fatal Conceit*, which some readers found a refreshingly straightforward guide to his teachings. It needs, however, to be stressed that this book emerged near the end of his life, after an illness, and that it was heavily edited by W. Bartley with the aid of a host of scholars apart from Hayek himself.

Whatever the status of this last volume, Hayek remained to the end much more iconoclastic than his more conventional supporters would have liked. He never subscribed, for instance, to any religious belief; and late in life he reiterated in an interview that he found monotheistic religions more objectionable than some others because they tended to be more intolerant of competition and dissent. As far as the economy was concerned, he never imagined that there was anything just in market rewards. These depended on an unpredictable mixture of effort, ability, and luck. Quite apart from the adverse economic consequences, it was not desirable even to try to reward merit through public policy, which would involve some authority deciding how much pain and effort a task had cost, and how much of a person's achievement was due to outside circumstances.

Hayek was mainly known in the 1930s for technical studies of monetary, business cycle, and capital theory. These were subsequently overshadowed by the 'Keynesian Revolution', but were being re-examined towards the end of the twentieth century. He had a brief period of fame in some circles and notoriety in others for *The Road to Serfdom*, his tract of 1944 against centralized economic planning in time of peace. He was held to have inspired a controversial election broadcast by Winston Churchill a year later, in which the latter warned of a socialist 'gestapo'. He re-emerged in the public eye in the 1970s and 1980s at a time of widespread disillusion both with Keynesian methods for securing full employment and with the apparently relentless expansion in the role of government. The breakdown of the post-war boom, triggered by the oil price explosion of 1973, was no surprise to Hayek—except that he had never expected it to last nearly as long as it did. In the last twenty years of the twentieth century many dozens of books and articles on Hayek appeared, although mostly by political theorists and historians of ideas rather than economists. His most important contribution to political and economic philosophy was almost certainly *The Constitution of Liberty*.

Hayek's own inability to resolve the ultimate conundrums of human conduct should not obscure the range of his achievements. His writings asserted the case for general rules over discretionary authority. They exposed the misleading identification of liberal democracy with the divine right of temporary majorities. They demonstrated the connection between economic and personal freedoms. They showed that the domination of both the political and economic market place by interest group struggles is a source of evil; and they explained why pecuniary rewards neither can nor should reflect merit. In presenting him as a revered thinker with a complete system, his followers may have made his work neater, simpler, and less interesting than it really was. In all these matters Hayek, like Keynes or Friedman or the American philosopher John Rawls, or other such seminal figures, is best treated as an intellectual iconoclast rather than a pundit with all the answers.

Hayek died in Freiburg im Breisgau, Germany, on 23 March 1992. He was survived by his second wife, and the two children of his first marriage. A memorial meeting was held at the London School of Economics on 23 September 1992. SAMUEL BRITTAN

Sources *The collected works of F. A. Hayek*, ed. W. W. Bartley and others (1988–) [incl. introductions and editorial footnotes] · *Hayek on Hayek: an autobiographical dialogue*, ed. S. Kresge and L. Wenar (1994) · L. Robbins, *Autobiography of an economist* (1971) · R. M. Hartwell, *A history of the Mont Pelerin Society* (1995) · S. Brittan, *Essays, moral, political and economic* (1996) · J. R. Hicks, *Critical essays in monetary theory* (1967) · N. Barry, *Hayek's social and economic philosophy* (1979) · S. Frowen, ed., *Hayek: economist and social philosopher* (1997) · E. Streissler, ed., *Essays in honour of F. A. Hayek* (1969) · A. H. Shand, *The capitalist alternative: an introduction to neo-Austrian economics* (1984) · A. Gamble, *The iron cage of liberty* (1996) · J. Hicks, *Capital and time: a neo-Austrian theory* (1973) · S. Brittan, *The role and limits of government* (1983) · O. Issing, *Hayek, currency competition and European monetary union* (1999) · S. Brittan, *A restatement of economic liberalism* (1986) · A. Seldon, ed., *Agenda for a free society: essays on the constitution of liberty* (1961) · M. Blaug, *Economic theory in retrospect* (1964) · N. Barry, *Classical liberalism in the age of post-communism* (1996) · J. Raybould, ed., *Hayek: a commemorative album* (1998) · *WWW* · naturalization cert.
Archives Stanford University, California, Hoover Institution | BLPES, *Economica* papers · BLPES, Theodor Gregory papers · Bodl. Oxf., Society for Protection of Science and Learning papers · CAC Cam., R. G. Hawtrey papers | SOUND BL NSA, 'Hayek, his life and thought', BBC, 20 Nov 1986, V5025/2 · BL NSA, 'Friedrich Hayek', NP3917W BD1 · BL NSA, performance recording · BL NSA, recorded lectures
Likenesses Ramsey & Muspratt, photograph, 1940–49, NPG [*see illus.*] · R. Moynihan, oils, 1982, NPG · photographs, Hoover Institute, Stanford, California, Hayek archive · photographs, repro. in Kresge and Wenar, eds., *Hayek on Hayek*
Wealth at death £13,532—effects in England: administration with will, 28 March 1994, *CGPLA Eng. & Wales*

Hayes [*other married name* Smith], **Alice** (1657–1720), Quaker preacher and autobiographer, was born at Rickmansworth in Hertfordshire, the daughter of 'honest parents', whose names are unknown but who brought her up as a member of the Church of England (Hayes, 3). Her mother, 'a tender, affectionate parent', died during her childhood. Alice was herself ill at the time 'and supposed nigh unto death'; in her account of her life she related how her mother 'fell down upon her knees, and prayed the Lord to take her and spare me; which he did' (ibid., 4). At the age of about sixteen conflict with her stepmother drove Alice to leave home and to go into service. As a young woman she indulged in 'sins' such as dancing, singing, and telling idle stories (ibid., 5) but was also 'close and constant, as opportunity permitted, in going to the publick worship, and very often got alone into private places to pray' (ibid., 7). Learning that a Quaker woman preacher was in the neighbourhood she went to hear her but, though the woman's words made a strong impression, 'the enemy soon prevailed again' (ibid., 10). Nevertheless her employer's wife, noting her piety, often remarked that 'this Alice will be a Quaker' (ibid., 10).

While in service Alice met Daniel Smith, a tenant farmer, whom she married about 1675 and with whom she had five children. A serious illness about a year and a half after her marriage led her to think more seriously of religion:

> morning and evening I failed not to pray, and to read the scriptures, and other books … constantly going to the publick worship … resolving to have a care both of my words and actions, and to act justly by all men. (Hayes, 17)

She joined the Society of Friends about 1680. Her conversion exposed her to considerable antagonism from her Anglican parish priest and from relatives and acquaintances, as well as from her husband, who 'grew very unkind' (ibid., 31) and threatened to leave her if she did not break off her connection with the Friends. However, he later relented and, according to Alice, 'died in the faith' (ibid., 43).

Following her conversion Alice was inspired 'to speak a word in season, both in publick and private, to others that were in exercise' (Hayes, 43). On 31 August 1696 she went with another Friend to the local church and, during morning service, stood up and put a number of questions to the priest, 'but he would not, and hastened out' (ibid., 47). She then addressed the congregation, denying that Quakers rejected the scriptures or the reality of Christ. The death of Daniel Smith left Alice, as his widow, liable for the payment of tithe on the family farm. As a Quaker she felt: 'I could not pay to support that worship which in conscience I believe … not to be acceptable with God' (ibid., 52); but she hesitated to risk prosecution and 'thereby bring sorrow and sufferings upon myself and family' (ibid., 58). However, following prayer and consultation with other Friends she was convinced that she must follow her conscience on the issue and she served a term of thirteen or fourteen weeks' imprisonment in St Albans gaol for non-payment of tithe.

In 1708 Alice wrote an autobiography, which covered her life from childhood to her imprisonment but made no reference to her second marriage, in 1697, to Thomas Hayes, who died in 1699, nor to the preaching tours which Alice undertook throughout Britain and to the Netherlands and Germany, where 'many were reached and tendered by her ministry' (Hayes, 86). In offering this account of her career and spiritual progress she disclaimed any motives of 'self', asserting that she wrote 'for the encouragement of my offspring … and for all the babes and lambs of God' (ibid., 60), and 'that God only may have the praise, who is the Author of all good' (ibid., 61). About 1712 she left Hertfordshire and settled in Tottenham, where she continued to be active in the society. In 1720 she was taken ill while at the Friends' yearly meeting in London. She returned to her home, where she died on 8 July 1720, and she was buried on 13 July 1720 in the Quaker burial-ground at Winchmore Hill. Her autobiography, together with a testimony by the Tottenham Friends and an account of some of her dying sayings, was published in 1723 as *A Legacy, or, Widow's Mite* and was reprinted five times. ROSEMARY RAUGHTER

Sources A. Hayes, *A legacy, or, Widow's mite, left by Alice Hayes, to her children and others: being a brief relation of her life. To which is added, an account of some of her dying sayings*, 4th edn (1786) · S. Mendelson and

P. Crawford, *Women in early modern England, 1550–1720* (1998) • M. R. Brailsford, *Quaker women, 1650–1690* (1915) • Blain, Clements & Grundy, *Feminist comp.* • M. Bell, G. Parfitt, and S. Shepherd, *A biographical dictionary of English women writers, 1580–1720* (1990)

Hayes [*née* Hall], **Catherine** (1690–1726), murderer, was born near Birmingham. Described in her youth as a 'fiery, turbulent … and intractable spirit' (*Tyburn Chronicle*, 2.253), she moved to Great Ombersley, Worcestershire, about 1705. Here she was taken in by members of the Hayes family and their son John Hayes (*c.*1685–1726), carpenter, whom she married in either 1706 or 1707, aged sixteen. The couple later moved to London, taking lodgings first at Tottenham Court Road and then on Tyburn Road, where they earned a living selling sea coal. In 1725 Catherine Hayes was visited by two former associates, Thomas Wood (*c.*1698–1726) and Thomas Billings (*c.*1703–1726), who lodged with the couple. Later trial reports state that Hayes spoke of murdering her husband on account of his alleged atheism and infanticide. Initially reluctant, the two men assisted with the murder on 1 March 1726 after a heavy drinking session, when a drunken John Hayes was beaten to death. His body was then dismembered and hidden (2 March) in different parts of the city: the head in the Thames near Westminster, the limbs and torso in Marylebone Fields. After its discovery on the following day, the head was displayed at St Margaret's, Westminster, and soon after identified; the rest of the body was located on 24 March. By this date Hayes and Billings had been arrested on a warrant by Justice Lambert, Hayes being sent to Tothill Fields bridewell and then to Newgate. She maintained her innocence during a trial which provoked considerable interest in the London press, but was found guilty and sentenced to be burnt at the stake. Billings and Wood—the latter having been arrested soon after his two accomplices—confessed and were sentenced to be hanged. Wood died in prison but Hayes failed in an attempt to poison herself. On 9 May, Billings was hanged at Marylebone Fields and on the same day at Tyburn, Hayes became the last woman in England to be burnt alive for petty treason (though the burning of women's bodies after execution continued until 1790); reports noted the executioner's failure to strangle her before the flames grew too high and the crowd's attempts to kill her by throwing pieces of wood. Interest in the horrific nature of Hayes's crime and execution continued after her death with the publication of *The Life of C.H.*, *A Narrative of the Barbarous and Unheard of Murder of John Hayes* (both 1726), and a ballad reprinted in *The Tyburn Chronicle* (vol. 2). Hayes's life later served as the basis for William Thackeray's story *Catherine*, which was serialized in *Fraser's Magazine* (1st ser., 19–21, 1839–40) and published as a single volume in 1869.

PHILIP CARTER

Sources *The Tyburn chronicle; or, Villany display'd in all its branches*, 4 vols. (1768) • A. Knapp and W. Baldwin, *Criminal chronology, or, The new Newgate calendar*, 4 vols. (1810–11) • *DNB* • R. Norton, *Mother Clap's molly house: the gay subculture in England, 1700–1830* (1992) • V. A. C. Gatrell, *The hanging tree: execution and the English people, 1770–1868* (1994)

Likenesses engraving (of execution), repro. in *The Tyburn chronicle*

Hayes [*married name* Bushnell], **Catherine** (1825–1861), singer, was born at 4 Patrick Street, Limerick, on 25 October 1825, the daughter of Arthur Williamson Hayes, a musician. Through the patronage of Bishop Knox of Limerick, funds were procured to enable her to study in Dublin under Antonio Sapio from 1839 until 1842. Her first public appearance was made on 3 May 1839 at Sapio's annual concert in the Rotunda, Dublin. Early the following year she sang in her native city, and then frequently performed in Dublin. After hearing Grisi and Mario in *Norma* on 13 September 1841, she decided to pursue a career on the operatic stage. She went to Paris on 12 October 1842 and studied under Manuel García, who after a year and a half advised her to proceed to Italy. At Milan she became the pupil of Felice Ronconi, and through the intervention of Madame Grassini was engaged for the Italian Opera House, Marseilles, where on 10 May 1845 she made her first appearance on the stage, as Elvira in *I puritani*, and was enthusiastically applauded. After her return to Milan she continued her studies under Ronconi, until Morelli, the director of La Scala at Milan, offered her an engagement. Here her first character was Linda in Donizetti's *Linda di Chamounix*, which established her reputation as a singer of Italian opera. Her voice had now become a soprano of the sweetest quality and of good compass, ascending with ease to D in alt. The upper notes were limpid, and like a well-tuned silver bell up to A. Her lower tones were considered the most beautiful ever heard in a real soprano, and her trill was remarkably good. Hayes was a touching actress in all her standard parts. She was tall, with a fine figure, and graceful in her movements. She remained at Milan during the autumn of 1845 and the carnival of 1846, and took the characters of Lucia, Zora in *Mosè in Egitto*, Desdemona, and Amina. Later on in 1846 she sang in Vienna, and on the first night of the carnival of 1847 appeared in Venice in a poor opera composed for her by Malespino, a nobleman, entitled *Albergo di Romano*. After returning to Vienna she took part in *Estrella*, expressly written for her by Ricci.

Following a tour of the Italian cities Hayes returned in 1849 to England, where she was engaged for the season at Covent Garden at a salary of £1300. On Tuesday 10 April she made her début, once more in *Linda di Chamounix*, and was received with much warmth. At the close of the season she sang before the queen at Buckingham Palace. On 5 November 1849 she appeared at a concert given by the Dublin Philharmonic Society, and afterwards at the Theatre Royal, Dublin, in *Lucia di Lammermoor*, when the Edgardo was so badly played by Paglieri that an uproar ensued, and Sims Reeves, one of the audience, took his place on the stage. Hayes sang Lucia again at Her Majesty's Theatre, London, on 2 April 1850, again with Sims Reeves. She refused to be suspended from a wire to sing Ariel in *La tempesta*, and the role was taken by Giulia Grisi. At the carnival in Rome in 1851 she was engaged at the Teatro

Catherine Hayes (1825–1861), by Herbert Watkins, late 1850s

d'Apollone, performed in *Maria de Rohan* for twelve nights, and received the diploma of the Academia di Santa Cecilia. From Rome she returned to London, where during the season of 1851 she was the star of the concert room and of the Sacred Harmonic Society's performances of oratorios by Handel, Haydn, and Mendelssohn.

Hayes left England in September 1851, and first sang in New York on the 23rd of that month. By the advice of William Avery Bushnell of Connecticut, an electioneering agent, she forfeited £3000, and gave him the management of her tour. During 1853 she was in California, where fabulous sums were paid for admission to her performances, one ticket selling for $1150. A horse named after her won the Oaks in 1853. She went on to tour South America, and, after giving concerts in Hawaii, arrived at Sydney, Australia, in January 1854. From Sydney, Melbourne, and Adelaide she went to India and Batavia, revisited Australia, and returned to England in August 1856, after an absence of five years. In that year she lost $27,000 by the failure of Saunders and Brennon of San Francisco.

On 8 October 1857, at St George's, Hanover Square, Catherine Hayes married her adviser, William Avery Bushnell. However, he soon fell ill, and died at Biarritz, France, on 2 July 1858, aged thirty-five. She appeared at Jullien's Promenade Concerts at Her Majesty's Theatre in 1857, when her ballad singing was much applauded. After her husband's death she took part in concerts in London and the provinces. She died in the house of a friend, Henry Lee, at Roccles, Upper Sydenham, Kent, on 11 August 1861, and was buried in Kensal Green cemetery on 17 August. In 1852 was published, anonymously, a *Memoir of Miss Catherine Hayes, the 'Swan of Erin'*, recording the sobriquet by which she was popularly known.   G. C. BOASE, *rev.* J. GILLILAND

Sources *The Times* (13 Aug 1861) · C. J. Hamilton, *Notable Irishwomen* (1904) · *Memoir of Miss Catherine Hayes, the 'Swan of Erin'* [1852] · *New Grove* · *ILN* (6 Sept 1851), 285–6 · D. Hyde, *New-found voices: women in nineteenth-century English music* (1984) · 'Our portrait gallery, no. LXI: Catherine Hayes', *Dublin University Magazine*, 36 (1850), 584–95 · *GM*, 3rd ser., 11 (1861), 331 · J. S. Reeves, *My jubilee* (1889) · H. S. Wyndham, *The annals of the Covent Garden Theatre: from 1732 to 1897*, 2 vols. (1906) · E. C. Clayton, *Queens of song*, 2 (1863), 274 · Brown & Stratton, *Brit. mus.* · J. Tallis, *Tallis's drawing room table book of theatrical portraits, memoirs and anecdotes* (1851), 33–5 · H. F. Chorley, *Thirty years' musical recollections*, 2 vols. (1862) · m. cert. · d. cert.
Likenesses portrait, in or before 1850, repro. in *Dublin University Magazine*, 584 · portrait, in or before 1851, repro. in *Tallis's drawing room table book*, 33 · portrait, in or before 1851, repro. in *ILN*, 285 · H. Watkins, albumen print, *c.*1856–1859, NPG [*see illus.*] · E. Grimston, lithograph?, BM, NPG · C. W. Wright, engraving, repro. in *Gleason's Pictorial*, 1 (1851), 296 · daguerreotype (aged twenty-six), repro. in *Century*, 45 (1904), 673 · portraits, Harvard TC · prints, BM, Harvard TC, NPG
Wealth at death £16,000: probate, 26 Aug 1861, *CGPLA Eng. & Wales*

Hayes, Charles (1678–1760), mathematician, was a member of Gray's Inn and the author of *Treatise of Fluxions, or, An Introduction to Mathematical Philosophy*, which appeared in 1704. This was the first English work explaining Newton's method of fluxions—the Newtonian version of the infinitesimal calculus; it covered in more than three hundred pages all the known areas of the early eighteenth-century calculus (finding tangents, areas, maxima and minima, caustics, centres of gravity, percussion, and oscillation, plus a treatment of central forces). It was published just before Newton's masterpiece, *De quadratura curvarum* (1704), which certainly nullified the usefulness of Hayes's laudable effort. In the preface Hayes writes that he asked the advice of John Harris, and his knowledge of contemporary literature on the subject, both continental and British, is remarkable. Hayes's treatise is clearly an attempt to divulge to the general reader the result on the calculus obtained by the most distinguished mathematicians. He claims no originality and in several cases his treatise is quite eclectic: in the section devoted to astronomy, for example, he mixes propositions taken from Newton's *Principia* (1687) with propositions taken from Leibniz's works on dynamics, which were based on completely different conceptions.

In 1710 Hayes printed a pamphlet, *New and Easy Method to Find the Longitude at Land or Sea*, and in 1723 *Of the Moon, a Philosophical Dialogue*, in which he attempted to prove that the moon is not opaque, but has some light of its own. Having made a voyage to Africa and spent some time there, he had considerable repute as a geographer, and was chosen annually to be sub-governor or deputy governor of the Royal African Company. After applying himself for some years to the study of Hebrew, Hayes in 1736 published his *Vindication of the History of the Septuagint*, and in 1738 *Critical Examination of the Holy Gospels According to St Matthew and St Luke*, with regard to the history of Christ's birth and infancy. His studies were afterwards mainly directed to chronology, excepting occasional tracts written to defend the policy of the Royal African Company. In 1741 he published a *Dissertation on the Chronology of the Septuagint*, a defence of the Chaldean and Egyptian chronology and history, and in 1747 there appeared a supplement, *Series of Kings of Argos and of Emperors of China from Fohi to Jesus Christ*, to prove that their dates and order of succession agreed with the Septuagint.

When the Royal African Company was dissolved in 1752 Hayes settled at Downe, Kent, and became absorbed in his great work, *Chronographia Asiatica et Aegyptiaca*, which he did not live to complete. Two parts of it only were published, during the last two years of his life, when he had chambers in Gray's Inn. Part of his argument is that the Septuagint and Josephus made use of writings preserved in the library of the temple of Jerusalem which had been omitted in making up the Old Testament canon. John Nichols remarked that Hayes spent much time in philosophical experiments. Hayes found favour with his contemporaries for his 'sedate temper' and clear method of exposition, and Charles Hutton, who was twenty-three years old at Hayes's death, remarked that he had 'great erudition concealed by modesty' (Hutton, 587). Hayes died at his chambers in Gray's Inn on 18 December 1760.

R. E. ANDERSON, *rev.* NICCOLÒ GUICCIARDINI

Sources *GM*, 1st ser., 31 (1761), 543–7 · Nichols, *Lit. anecdotes*, 2.322–6 · C. Hutton, *A philosophical and mathematical dictionary*, new edn, 1 (1815), 587 · R. V. Wallis and P. J. Wallis, eds., *Biobibliography of British mathematics and its applications*, 2 (1986) · J. Aikin and others, *General biography, or, Lives, critical and historical of the most eminent persons*, 10 vols. (1799–1815) · N. Guicciardini, *The development of Newtonian calculus in Britain, 1700–1800* (1989) · N. A. Hans, *New trends in education in the eighteenth century* (1951)

Hayes, Edmund (1804–1867), judge, was born at Millmount, co. Down, the eldest son of William Hayes of Millmount, merchant and linen manufacturer, and his wife (of whom little is known). He was educated at the Belfast Academical Institution, and in 1820 he entered Trinity College, Dublin, where he graduated BA in 1825, and LLB and LLD in 1832. He entered Gray's Inn in 1825, and in 1827 he was called to the Irish bar and joined the north-eastern circuit, but he subsequently transferred himself to the home circuit. He lectured in constitutional and criminal law at the King's Inns. In 1837 he published reports of cases in the Irish exchequer (1830 to 1832). In 1843, with Thomas Jones, he published a continuation of these from 1832 to 1834. He also wrote in 1843 a treatise on Irish criminal law.

In 1835 Hayes married Grace Mary Anne Shaw of Dublin; they had nine children. After her death (some time between 1852 and 1858) he married Mary Harriet Tranchell, widow of Lieutenant James Shaw. They had one son.

Hayes was appointed a QC in 1852 and was law adviser to the crown under Lord Derby's first administration. He held this post again in 1858 and was subsequently promoted to be Irish solicitor-general. In 1859 he succeeded Mr Justice Crampton in the court of queen's bench, but he

was compelled in 1866 to leave because of poor health. He finally resigned in Michaelmas term of the same year and died at his home, Crinken House, near Bray, co. Wicklow, on 28 or 29 April 1867. He was buried in Mount Jerome cemetery, Dublin.

J. A. HAMILTON, *rev.* SINÉAD AGNEW

Sources F. E. Ball, *The judges in Ireland, 1221–1921*, 2 (1926), 296–7, 328, 361 · Burtchaell & Sadleir, *Alum. Dubl.* · *Law Times* (1 June 1867), 47 · Boase, *Mod. Eng. biog.* · J. S. Crone, *A concise dictionary of Irish biography*, rev. edn (1937), 91 · Allibone, *Dict.* · *The Times* (1 May 1867) · *GM*, 4th ser., 3 (1867), 826
Wealth at death under £9000: probate, 1 June 1867, *CGPLA Ire.*

Hayes, Edward (*b.* *c.*1550, *d.* in or after 1613), seaman and promoter of colonization, was probably born in West Derby, Lancashire, the son of Edward Hayes and his wife, Alice, small landowners in Lancashire. His father moved into Liverpool before 1567 and established himself as a merchant, and the younger Edward probably attended a grammar school there before his admission to King's College, Cambridge, in 1565. His presence was not continuous as he was entered again as a scholar-commoner in 1571; he did not take a degree. Shortly afterwards he apparently became tutor to a son or sons of Sir Thomas Hoby of Bisham Abbey, Berkshire, whose wife, Elizabeth, commended him to her brother-in-law William Cecil (later Baron Burghley), whom Hayes apparently served in unknown capacities for at least twenty years. He may have accompanied Edward Hoby on a continental tour in 1576 or 1577.

Hayes evidently had a taste for the sea and for exploration. In 1578 he subscribed to the first unsuccessful colonizing voyage of Sir Humphrey Gilbert. He acquired a small ship of 40 tons, which he named the *Golden Hind* in honour of Sir Francis Drake. After interminable waiting he accompanied Gilbert to Newfoundland in 1583, witnessed Gilbert's actions there, and survived various disasters, culminating in the loss of Gilbert at sea, to bring his ship home in September 1583 as the sole vessel to survive the expedition. He contributed information on the voyage to *A True Report* by Sir George Peckham before the end of the year, and sat down to record a detailed narrative of the voyage and some description of Newfoundland. This he passed eventually to Richard Hakluyt for publication in his *Principall Navigations* in 1589. It is one of the finest voyage narratives in the collection, vivid and informative, and conveying well the atmosphere of an exploring voyage. This is especially true of the circumstances of Gilbert's death at sea. Sailing, as he insisted on doing, in his tiny 8 ton frigate *Squirrel*, Gilbert kept close company with Hayes's *Golden Hind*, and came on board from time to time. Hayes last saw him:

> sitting abafte with a booke in his hande, cryed out unto us in the Hinde (so often as wee did approche within hearing): Wee are as neere to heaven by Sea, as by lande. Reiterating the same speeche, well beseeming a souldier, resolute in Jesus Christe, as I can testifie he was. The same Mundaye night about twelve of the clocke, or not long after, the Frigat beeing a heade of us in the Golden Hinde, suddenly her lights were out, whereof as it were in a moment we lost the sight, and withall our watch cryed, the Generall was cast

away, which was too true. For in that moment, the Frigat was devoured and swallowed uppe of the Sea.   (Hakluyt, *Principall Navigations*, 1589, 695)

During the Spanish war Hayes is found engaged in privateering between 1589 and 1591, but the rest of his life was spent largely in projecting. He bombarded Burghley with schemes for exploiting Newfoundland in 1585 and 1586, interestingly proposing the financing of one of them on the tontine principle, but they involved impractical proposals, as the international fishery could not be controlled by any one country except at vast expense. In the early 1590s Hayes turned his attention to the maritimes and New England, and his long proposal for colonizing and developing the commerce of this region is one of the fullest and most sensible colonial projects of the period. It was printed in shortened form in the *Briefe and True Relation* (1602) by John Brereton. Hayes kept in close contact with the twists and turns of English interest in North America for nearly thirty years, even if his plans for financing the Virginia Company in 1606 form a mere footnote to the history of that enterprise.

Hayes moved his residence frequently. In 1585 he lived at Charing Cross, in 1589–90 in Writtington, Essex, by 1596 he writes from 'my house in Hamsell Park, Sussex', while early in the 1600s he may have lived for a time in Isleworth, Middlesex. In association with his technically minded relative Thomas Hayes (the exact relationship is not known) he may have had an iron furnace and hammer pond at Hamsell Farm, and possibly a smelter and perhaps a coining press in Isleworth at the end of the century. He wrote numerous promotion schemes, mostly involving the grant of monopolies to himself and his associate. His favourite was the making of a copper coinage for England, with which he approached successive lord treasurers between 1579 and 1613. He acquired his sole opportunity in 1599 when he induced Sir Robert Cecil to approve a copper coinage scheme for Ireland, which was put into operation in 1601, though he was not able to secure a monopoly for its production. He also directed the issue of a debased silver coinage, which caused much hardship in Ireland and was finally withdrawn in 1603. He was for a time in Ireland overseeing the introduction of these changes, and he and Thomas were both given substantial pensions (£100 each) in 1603.

Hayes's other projects from time to time involved the militia, the London water supply, various technical innovations in rolling-mill design, a stamping machine for coinage (these may well have originated with Thomas Hayes), and others. In 1606 he returned to the financing of colonies. With Thomas, he proposed a scheme by which government and private capital could be combined for the financing of the proposed Virginia colony: this is of some interest, but was not taken up. He disappears from view in 1613, and may have died shortly afterwards. He was a typical projector of the period, and he also had gifts as a writer, though some of his projects appear wrapped in airy rhetoric: only his colonizing plans are of enduring interest.   DAVID B. QUINN

Sources R. Hakluyt, *The principall navigations, voiages and discoveries of the English nation*, 3 vols. in 2 (1589); facs. edn, Hakluyt Society, extra ser., 39 (1965), 679–97 · R. Hakluyt, *The principal navigations, voyages, traffiques and discoveries of the English nation*, 2nd edn, 3 (1600), 153–61 · D. B. Quinn, A. M. Quinn, and S. Hillier, eds., *New American world: a documentary history of North America to 1612*, 3, 5 (1979) · D. B. Quinn, ed., *The voyages and colonising enterprises of Sir Humphrey Gilbert*, 2 vols., Hakluyt Society, 2nd ser., 83–4 (1940) · *Calendar of the manuscripts of the most hon. the marquis of Salisbury*, 6, HMC, 9 (1895); 9–13 (1902–15); 17 (1938) · J. Brereton, *A briefe and true relation of the discoverie of the north part of Virginia … whereunto is annexed a treatise, of M. Edward Hayes* (1602) · D. B. Quinn, 'Edward Hayes and the Americas', *England and the discovery of America, 1481–1620* (1974), 227–45 · *The new found land of Stephen Parmenius: the life and writings of a Hungarian poet, drowned on a voyage from Newfoundland, 1583*, ed. and trans. D. B. Quinn and N. M. Cheshire [1972]
Archives CUL, MS DA3, 85 no. 4 · Hatfield House, Hertfordshire, Cecil MSS · Lancs. RO, Molyneaux muniments · Lpool RO, court roll · PRO, SP 125, SP63, HCA1
Wealth at death £100 p.a. pension from 1603 to death

Hayes, Edward Brian [Tubby] (1935–1973), jazz musician and composer, was born on 30 January 1935 at the Royal Free Hospital, St Pancras, London, the son of Edward Kenneth Hayes, a violinist with the BBC Revue Orchestra, and his wife, Dorothy Kathleen Roche. Tubby, as he was known, commenced study of the violin at the age of eight, of the piano two years later, and finally of the tenor saxophone in December 1946. He attended Rutlish grammar school, Merton (John Major, the future prime minister, became a student at the school shortly after Hayes left), and played with semi-professional bands in the late 1940s. He became a full-time musician at the age of sixteen, making his first recordings in the summer of 1951 with trumpeter Kenny Baker's sextet.

Hayes's mastery of the saxophone and his unique talent for jazz improvisation at such an early age marked him as a musician of promise. He played in the big dance bands of Ambrose, Vic Lewis, and Jack Parnell before forming his own octet in April 1955. The following year he took up the vibraphone, and from April 1957 until August 1959 he co-led the Jazz Couriers with fellow tenor saxophonist Ronnie Scott. He subsequently led his own quartet, various other small groups, and a much praised big band which was assembled for television and recording purposes. Hayes himself composed and arranged a great deal of the material for his various bands, and his big band albums titled *100% Proof* and *Tubbs* are among the finest non-American orchestral recordings of their type. Tubby also worked on a number of film soundtracks, including the one for Charlie Chaplin's *A King in New York* (1957).

Hayes's fame as a jazz soloist was international and he visited the United States on a number of occasions in the 1960s, making records there with noted American musicians in 1961 and 1962. He played and recorded with pianist Friedrich Gulda and his Eurojazz Orchestra in Vienna, appeared with international bands in Recklingshausen and Berlin, and worked in Scandinavia as a featured soloist. He bought a flute in 1958 and mastered it within a short time; in the same year he produced a multi-recording (*The Eighth Wonder*), playing alto, tenor, and baritone saxophones, double bass, and drums himself.

Edward Brian [Tubby] **Hayes** (1935–1973), by unknown photographer

Hayes was married twice, first, on 27 October 1953, to Margaret Helen Yates (b. 1929/30), the daughter of Herbert Alexander Yates, a tool examiner. The marriage was dissolved on 1 July 1960. His second marriage, on 9 November 1960, was to Alexandra Souriya Rose Khan (b. 1929/30), daughter of Samunder Khan, a clothing salesman. This ended in divorce in 1966, but not before two sons, Richard Terence and Lewis Alexander, had been born.

During the late 1960s Hayes suffered serious illnesses which prevented him from playing for varying periods. He underwent heart surgery in January 1970 and again in June 1971 but he was able to resume playing at the end of that year. In May 1973 he was taken ill while working in Brighton and admitted to Hammersmith Hospital. He died there on 8 June during an operation to correct a faulty heart valve; his funeral and cremation took place at Golders Green crematorium.

During his comparatively short lifetime Tubby Hayes achieved the rare distinction of being recognized as an outstanding jazz musician not only in his own country but also abroad, including in the United States. An indication of his reputation and stature may be gauged from the fact that he was called upon at short notice to take the place of an absent and important saxophone soloist at a London concert by Duke Ellington and his orchestra in 1964.

ALUN MORGAN

Sources J. Chilton, *Who's who of British jazz* (1997) · B. Schwartz, *Tubby Hayes: a discography* (1990) · *CGPLA Eng. & Wales* (1975) · b. cert. · m. cert. [Margaret Yates] · m. cert. [Alexandra Khan]
Likenesses photograph, 1968, Hult. Arch. · photograph, Redferns Music Picture Library [*see illus.*]
Wealth at death £4276: administration, 30 Jan 1975, *CGPLA Eng. & Wales*

Hayes, Edwin (1819–1904), marine painter, was born on 7 June 1819 at Bristol, the son of Charles Hayes, who left Bristol for Dublin in the early 1830s to run the Bristol and Glasgow Hotel and Tavern in Marlborough Street. Hayes himself wrote that his parents were English, but that he was 'generally considered to be Irish' (Hayes to H. Cundall, c.1878, V&A). His early training was at the Kildare School of Art, Dublin, but he also spent much of his youth at sea, 'to learn more correctly the manner of handling ships and nautical matters generally' (ibid.). His first exhibited works, *A Marine View* and *A Brisk Gale*, were shown in 1842 at the Royal Hibernian Academy, where he exhibited almost every year until his death, being elected an associate in 1853 and a member in 1871. In 1847 he married Ellen, daughter of James Briscoe of Carrick-on-Suir, co. Tipperary; they had eleven children, including the landscape painter Claude Hayes.

In 1852 Hayes moved to London, where he lived for the rest of his life, after 1870 in Hampstead and Brondesbury. His first London exhibit was in 1854 at the British Institution; and in 1855 he first contributed to the Royal Academy exhibition. He also exhibited extensively at the New Watercolour Society, of which he became an associate in 1860 and a member in 1863. Although his work is generally regarded as of the 'older school of marine painters' (Strickland, 1.460) and is conventional in style, showing little influence of contemporary developments in painting in Europe, his watercolours particularly have a freedom of mark-making and expression which helps to explain the exhibition of his work at less academically conventional venues, such as the Grosvenor Gallery and the New Gallery. His painting *Sunset at Sea* (exh. RA, 1894), applauded by the critics, was bought for £175 in 1896 by the Chantrey trustees for the Tate Gallery. He enjoyed a high international reputation during his lifetime, exhibiting at Chicago, St Louis, Paris, and Brussels. The collection of his letters at the Victoria and Albert Museum indicates the eminence of his acquaintances, including the art critic Sir Isidore Spielmann, the painter Sir Edward Poynter, Henry Cundall, and Sir James Linton. He held a retrospective exhibition of 150 works at Dowdeswell and Dowdeswell, Bond Street, London, in March 1888. He died on 7 November 1904 at his home, 20 Aldridge Road Villas, Westbourne Park, London, and was buried at Kensal Green cemetery.

GEOFF QUILLEY

Sources W. G. Strickland, *A dictionary of Irish artists*, 2 vols. (1913) · A. M. Stewart and C. de Courcy, *Royal Hibernian Academy of Arts: index of exhibitors and their works, 1826–1979*, 3 vols. (1985–7) · A. M. Stewart, *Irish societies and sketching clubs: index of exhibitors, 1870–1980*, 2 vols. (Dublin, 1997) · *The Times* (9 Nov 1904) · E. Hayes, letters to E. Poynter (1) and I. Spielmann (6), V&A, 86.GG.Box 3: MSL/1917/229/114; 86.PP.15 Box 14: MSL/1999/2/1188–1193 · E. Hayes, letter to H. Cundall, June c.1878, V&A, RC.U.2: MSL/1934/4195/20 · E. Hayes, letter to J. D. Linton, 17 Oct 1897, V&A, 86.WW.2: MSL/1980/1/96 · Graves, *RA exhibitors* · Graves, *Brit. Inst.* · E. H. H. Archibald, *Dictionary of sea painters* (1980) · A. Wilson, *A dictionary of British marine painters* (1967)
Archives V&A, letters to H. Cundall · V&A, letters to Sir J. D. Linton · V&A, letters to Sir E. Poynter; letters to I. Spielmann
Wealth at death £6150 3s. 7d.: resworn probate, 13 Dec 1904, *CGPLA Eng. & Wales*

Hayes, Sir George (1805–1869), judge, was born on 19 June 1805 at Judd Place, Somers Town, London, the second son of Sheedy Hayes, a landowner in the West Indies, and his wife, Catherine, daughter of John Westgate. He was educated at Highgate School in London and at St Edmund's Roman Catholic College near Ware.

Hayes converted to Anglicanism after leaving school, and then launched himself on a legal career. He was articled to William Francis Patterson, a solicitor in Leamington, and after completing his articles, in November 1824 entered the Middle Temple as a student. He first practised as a special pleader and on 29 January 1830 was called to the bar. He joined the midland circuit, and attended the Warwickshire sessions. He soon acquired an extensive practice especially in sessions' appeal cases. On 3 September 1839 he married Sophia Anne, the eldest daughter of John Hill, a physician from Leicester; they had four sons and four daughters. In 1854 Hayes wrote a humorous elegy lamenting the extinction of the fictitious defendants John Doe and Richard Roe from pleadings in ejectment actions.

In 1856 Hayes was made serjeant-at-law, and on 22 February 1861 obtained a patent of precedence to rank next after Archibald John Stephens QC. In December 1861 he was appointed recorder of Leicester, and on the promotion to the bench of Mr Justice Mellor, he shared the lead of the midland circuit with Kenneth Macaulay QC. Hayes was less successful in common jury cases than in cases before special juries to which his subtle reasoning and refined wit were more suited. In the famous Matlock will case, for instance, where he was the leader, his victory was due to his extensive knowledge of the law and his masterly dissection of the evidence. He had a considerable command of the English classics and was an accomplished pianist, singer, and artist, as well as being well read in Latin, Greek, French, and Italian. He also wrote a humorous song on the 'Dog and the Cock' case which he sometimes sang in public.

On 9 August 1868, under the act appointing additional judges, Hayes was named a justice of the court of queen's bench, sworn in on 24 August, and knighted by the queen at Windsor Castle on 9 December 1868. On 19 November 1869, after sitting all day in the foul air of the bail court at Westminster, he suddenly had a stroke. He was taken to the Westminster Palace Hotel, where he died on 24 November. He was survived by his wife.

G. C. BOASE, rev. HUGH MOONEY

Sources E. Foss, *Biographia juridica: a biographical dictionary of the judges of England … 1066–1870* (1870) · *Law Magazine*, new ser., 29 (1870), 114–25 · *The Times* (25 Nov 1869), 9 · *The Times* (26 Nov 1869), 8 · *Annual Register* (1869), 168 · *Law Times* (27 Nov 1869), 61 · *ILN* (4 Dec 1869), 578 · *GM*, 2nd ser., 12 (1839), 536
Wealth at death under £3000: administration, 23 Dec 1869, *CGPLA Eng. & Wales*

Hayes, John (1775–1838), naval officer, great-nephew of Adam Hayes, master shipwright of Deptford Dockyard, nominally entered the navy aged seven, but really not until 1787, when he was embarked on the *Orion* (74 guns, Sir Hyde Parker). In 1790 he was serving in the frigate *Pearl* under Captain G. W. A. Courtenay, whom in the spring of 1793 he followed to the *Boston* (32 guns), and on 31 July took part in the action with the French frigate *Ambuscade*. Courtenay was killed, and the *Boston* overpowered and compelled to haul off, though the *Ambuscade* was not able to pursue her. On returning to England he was made lieutenant, on 7 October 1793, and appointed to the *Dido* (28 guns) with Sir Charles Hamilton, whom he followed to the frigate *San Fiorenzo* in the Mediterranean.

After serving in the channel and the West Indies, Hayes was promoted on 1 March 1799 by Sir Hyde Parker, then commander-in-chief at Jamaica, to commander, and, continuing on the Jamaica station, was advanced to post rank on 29 April 1802. In January 1809 he commanded the *Alfred* (74 guns) on the coast of Spain, and was in charge of the embarkation of troops after the battle of Corunna. Later he was moved into the *Achille* for the Walcheren expedition, and at the end of the year was appointed to the frigate *Freya*, in which he served under the command of Sir Alexander Cochrane at the capture of Guadeloupe in January 1810. He returned to England in the following autumn, and in September 1812 was appointed to temporary command of the *Magnificent* (74 guns), employed in the Bay of Biscay. On the evening of 16 December she anchored in the entrance to Basque Roads and, during the night, was driven from her anchors by a violent gale towards a dangerous reef. She was saved from what appeared certain destruction by the excellent discipline of the crew and the seamanship of her captain, which won for him the title 'Magnificent Hayes'.

In January 1813 Hayes was appointed to the *Majestic*, a 74 gun ship, which had been cut down, on a plan suggested by him, into the semblance of a frigate, to meet the new demands of war with the United States. She carried an armament of twenty-eight 32-pounders and twenty-eight 42-pounder carronades, and was sent over to look out for the heavy American frigates. She did not fall in with one, but on 15 January 1815 was, with the frigates *Tenedos* and *Pomona*, in company with the *Endymion* when the United States frigate *President* was captured.

On the remodelling of the Order of the Bath in 1815 Hayes was made a CB, and in 1819 he was appointed superintendent of the ordinary at Devonport. In 1829–30 he commanded the *Ganges* at Portsmouth; and from 1830 to 1832 was commodore on the west coast of Africa, with a broad pennant on board the *Dryad* (42 guns). By the very large promotion which took place on 10 January 1837 he became rear-admiral of the white. Hayes died the following year, on 7 April, at Southsea, and was buried at Farlington, Hampshire. Through his whole service he had paid unusual attention to the details of naval construction, a subject for which he appears to have inherited a strong interest, and on which he published pamphlets which were favourably received at the time. He was married and had children, among whom were Admiral Courtenay Osborn Hayes, and Vice-Admiral John Montagu Hayes (d. 1882).

J. K. LAUGHTON, rev. ROGER MORRISS

Sources J. Marshall, *Royal naval biography*, 2/2 (1825), 673, 677 · O'Byrne, *Naval biog. dict.* · *GM*, 2nd ser., 10 (1838), 324–5 · W. James,

The naval history of Great Britain, from the declaration of war by France in 1793, to the accession of George IV, [5th edn], 6 vols. (1859–60), vol. 1, p. 110 • *Naval Chronicle*, 29 (1813), 21 • A. B. Rodger, *The war of the second coalition: 1798–1801, a strategic commentary* (1964) • R. Muir, *Britain and the defeat of Napoleon, 1807–1815* (1996)

Hayes, John (1787/8–1866), portrait painter, was born in Middlesex; of his parents, nothing is known. He entered the Royal Academy Schools in October 1801, when he was thirteen and a half. Of the seventy-seven works he exhibited at the Royal Academy between 1814 and 1851 most were portraits, especially of military and naval officers, including in 1834 *Admiral Sir John Harvey*. He occasionally sent historical pictures, such as, in 1837, *Mary Queen of Scots, when a Prisoner*, and sometimes literary subjects, for example, in 1844, *Jeanie Deans' Interview with her Sister Effie, in the Tolbooth, after her Condemnation*, from Sir Walter Scott's novel *The Heart of Midlothian*. His portraits also included those of actors and actresses in character; *Portrait of a Young Highlander* (exh. RA, 1822); *Portrait of a Polish Jew* (exh. RA, 1827); *Mitai, Chieftain of Otaheite* (exh. RA, 1835), and *Gypsies Reposing* (exh. RA, 1843), suggesting that Hayes had a particular interest in colour and costume. His portrait of the historian *Miss Agnes Strickland* (1846; NPG) was engraved by F. C. Lewis as the frontispiece to her *Lives of the Queens of England* (1851). Hayes exhibited from a number of London addresses: 16 Henrietta Street, Covent Garden (1814–16); 147 Strand (1817–19); 1 Frith Street, Soho (1821–47), and 28 Great Russell Street (1849–51). He also exhibited at the British Institution and at the Society of British Artists, having a considerable and successful practice as a portrait painter. Hayes died at his home, 51A Berners Street, London, on 14 June 1866.

L. H. CUST, *rev.* LIZ MELLINGS

Sources Graves, *RA exhibitors* • Graves, *Artists* • A. Davies and E. Kilmurray, *Dictionary of British portraiture*, 4 vols. (1979–81) • Redgrave, *Artists* • F. Lewis, *A dictionary of British historical painters* (1979) • B. Stewart and M. Cutten, *The dictionary of portrait painters in Britain up to 1920* (1997) • K. K. Yung, *National Portrait Gallery: complete illustrated catalogue, 1856–1979*, ed. M. Pettman (1981) • R. Parkinson, ed., *Catalogue of British oil paintings, 1820–1860* (1990) [catalogue of V&A] • artist's file, archive material, Courtauld Inst., Witt Library • Boase, *Mod. Eng. biog.* • www.npg.org.uk/live/search/a-z/sitA.asp • S. C. Hutchison, 'The Royal Academy Schools, 1768–1830', *Walpole Society*, 38 (1960–62), 123–91, esp. 160
Archives Courtauld Inst., Witt Library, file

Hayes, John Henry [Jack] (1887–1941), police officer, trade unionist, and politician, was born on 14 October 1887 at 11 Mitre Fold, Wolverhampton, Staffordshire, one of seven children of John William Hayes, policeman, and his wife, Sarah (*née* Inchley). His father rose to the rank of chief inspector, and Jack Hayes was brought up in moderately comfortable surroundings. He was educated at St Mark's elementary school and at the Wolverhampton Science and Technical Schools, leaving at the age of thirteen to take up a clerical post with the Wolverhampton Corrugated Iron Company, first in Wolverhampton and later at Ellesmere Port. By attendance at evening classes he became proficient in shorthand, bookkeeping, and accountancy, and also fluent in French. In 1909 he joined the administrative staff of the Metropolitan Police Force,

and rose to the rank of sergeant within four years. On 19 July 1913 he married Ethel Stroudley, the daughter of a schoolmaster from Albrighton, Shropshire. They had one daughter.

In the police Hayes became known as an articulate spokesman for his fellow officers, and an ardent advocate of the right to union organization. There was growing rank and file support for a police union in the metropolitan force, due to discontent over promotion, disciplinary and appeal procedures, and over wages and conditions. In 1913 metropolitan officers were forbidden from union membership, under penalty of dismissal, but the price rises of the war years and the radicalization of politics towards the end of the war only increased dissatisfaction. In 1918 the National Union of Police and Prison Officers (NUPPO), of which Hayes was an early and prominent member, declared a strike of the Metropolitan Police. The union won a pay increase and other improvements, and a verbal promise of recognition from Lloyd George himself. Soon after, Hayes resigned from the police to take up the full-time position of general secretary of NUPPO.

After the deliberations of the Desborough committee on police pay and conditions, to which Hayes gave evidence, the resultant Police Act of 1919 awarded higher wages on a national scale for the first time, but union membership was made unlawful, the internal Police Federation was established, and other NUPPO demands were largely ignored. A national police strike against the Police Act was called in August 1919, but it received majority support only from constables in Liverpool, Birkenhead, and Bootle, and collapsed after three weeks. Strikers were dismissed from the force, with loss of all pension and superannuation rights. Hayes was devastated by this defeat. He demanded a drastic reduction in his own salary, and maintained a long and ultimately fruitless campaign for the reinstatement of the sacked men.

As a result of the 1919 débâcle Hayes was drawn into the politics of Liverpool, where the strike became something of a *cause célèbre* in labour circles. In the municipal elections of November 1919 he stood unsuccessfully as a NUPPO-sponsored Labour candidate in Prince's Park ward. Three years later, Edge Hill Labour Party adopted him as its parliamentary candidate for the constituency, which contained a large proportion of unionized skilled workers, and was largely free of the religious sectarianism which dominated the politics of other Liverpool districts. He was defeated in the 1922 general election, but at a by-election on 6 March 1923 he became the first Labour MP in Liverpool.

Hayes retained the seat until 1931, and became a diligent MP who specialized in representing the interests of lower-ranking police and prison officers. On wider political issues he made few pronouncements, but he was generally counted in the moderate mainstream of his party. When the 1924 Labour government refused reinstatement of the 1919 police strikers he embarrassed the prime minister and home secretary by quoting to the house their earlier written commitment to reinstating the men. He was parliamentary private secretary to the minister of pensions in the 1924 government, and a whip from 1925 to 1931. He was also a member of the national executive of the party in 1926 and 1927. In the 1929 government Hayes accepted the post of vice-chamberlain of his majesty's household.

When Labour split in 1931 Hayes refused to go with MacDonald into the National Government, displaying his best qualities of loyalty and decency, and he lost Edge Hill in the landslide defeat of that year. In 1935 he narrowly missed regaining the seat, and his political career faded rapidly. He remained active on the editorial board of the *Police Review*, and after 1931 he also became registrar of the Joint Council of Qualified Opticians and secretary of the British Optical Association. He died in King's College Hospital, London, on 25 April 1941 as a result of kidney disease and associated complications, being survived by his widow and daughter.

A tall man, notable for his imposing waxed moustache, Hayes aptly described himself thus: 'I was born in the police service. I was brought up in it, and I am of the police service, and I want to see the police service carry out its proper function and be an ennobling profession' (*Hansard* 5C, 166, 1703). These sentiments, rather than any grander political philosophy, were the driving force of his life and the foundation of his political career. The moderate and reformist essence of the Labour Party between the wars can be gauged in part by considering individuals like him.   SAM DAVIES

Sources *Liverpool Daily Post and Mercury* (1919–41) · *Liverpool Daily Post* (28 April 1941) · *Liverpool Echo* (1919–41) · *Liverpool Echo* (26 April 1941) · *The Times* (1919–41) · *Hansard 5C* (1923–31) · P. J. Waller, *Democracy and sectarianism: a political and social history of Liverpool, 1868–1939* (1981) · S. Davies, *Liverpool labour: social and political influences on the development of the labour party in Liverpool, 1900–1939* (1996) · Liverpool Central Library, Local History Department, Liverpool Trades Council and Labour Party MSS · R. Bean, 'Police unrest, unionization and the 1919 strike in Liverpool', *Journal of Contemporary History*, 15 (1980), 633–53 · V. L. Allen, 'The National Union of Police and Prison Officers', *Economic History Review*, 2nd ser., 11 (1958–9), 133–43 · *Liverpool Official Red Book* (1924–31) · *WWBMP*, vol. 3 · *The Labour who's who* (1927) · b. cert. · d. cert.
Archives Liverpool Central Library, Liverpool trades council and labour party MSS
Likenesses photographs, Liverpool Central Library, Local History Department
Wealth at death £809 13s. 2d.: administration, 22 Aug 1941, *CGPLA Eng. & Wales*

Hayes, Sir John Macnamara, first baronet (1750?–1809), military physician, was born in Limerick, the son of John Hayes and Margaret, daughter and coheir of Sheedy Macnamara of Ballyally, co. Clare. Nothing further is known about his early life. Hayes served as a surgeon during the American War of Independence, between 1775 and 1783. In October 1777 he was in charge of a hospital abandoned to the enemy during the retreat to Saratoga, after the battle of Bemis Heights. He was appointed physician to the forces on 26 November 1779, and later he served with the British force which captured Georgia in 1779.

In 1783 Hayes went on half pay. On 20 March 1784, he graduated MD at Rheims, and on 26 June 1786 became a licentiate of the Royal College of Physicians. On 1 May 1787 he married Anne (*d.* 18 Jan 1848), eldest daughter of Henry White (1732–1786), merchant and a member of the council of New York, and his wife, Eva van Cortlandt. They had two sons and two daughters. Hayes was appointed physician-extraordinary to the prince of Wales in 1791, and physician to the Westminster Hospital, London, in 1792, an office which he resigned in 1794.

Hayes also served during the French wars between 1793 and 1798; he was appointed director of hospitals under the earl of Moira on 20 November 1793. In 1795 he supervised the embarkation of the force commanded by Lieutenant-General Sir Ralph Abercromby, which was bound for the West Indies. For his services he was created a baronet in 1797.

On 7 May 1806 Hayes became inspector-general of the ordnance medical department at Woolwich, a post he held until his death from acute laryngitis on 19 July 1809. He was buried later that month at St James's, Piccadilly, London, and was survived by his wife.

                            GORDON GOODWIN, rev. CLAIRE E. J. HERRICK

Sources N. Cantlie, *A history of the army medical department*, 1 (1974), 146–58, 196, 205, 241–3 · A. Peterkin and W. Johnston, *Commissioned officers in the medical services of the British army, 1660–1960*, 1 (1968), 48 · Munk, *Roll* · Burke, *Peerage* · *Who was who in America: historical volume, 1607–1896*, rev. edn (1967)
Archives Wilts. & Swindon RO, letters | U. Nott. L., letters to Charles Mellish
Likenesses N. Branwhite, stipple, pubd 1801 (after S. Medley), BM · S. Medley, portrait

Hayes, Sir John Osler Chattock (1913–1998), naval officer, was born in Bermuda on 9 May 1913, the elder son of Major Lionel Chattock Hayes of the Royal Army Medical Corps, and his wife, Dorothy Christine Osler. He entered the Royal Naval College, Dartmouth, as a naval cadet in 1927 and went to sea in HMS *Royal Oak* in 1930. He specialized in navigation in 1936 and spent two years thereafter in HMS *Fowey* in the Persian Gulf. On 15 April 1939 he married the Hon. Rosalind Mary Finlay, only daughter of William *Finlay, second Viscount Finlay of Nairn, lord justice of appeal; they had two sons and one daughter.

At the outbreak of the Second World War, Hayes joined the light cruiser *Cairo*, escorting convoys up and down the east coast. This entailed constant work on the bridge when at sea and meticulous updating of charted minefields when in harbour. The consequent eyestrain led to his relief, and he spent the next year ashore, training upper yardmen at HMS *St Vincent*. He joined the battlecruiser *Repulse* at the end of 1940 and for the next year, under the leadership of Captain William Tennant, was in a ship that he subsequently regarded as the centre of gravity of his naval life, so high was the efficiency and spirit on board. However, on 10 December 1941, with the battleship *Prince of Wales*, *Repulse* was overwhelmed and sunk by Japanese torpedo aircraft off Malaya. Hayes, thrown off the flag deck as the ship rolled over, was rescued by the destroyer *Electra* and was taken to Singapore, where he was detailed as liaison officer to no. 3 corps for their final withdrawal across the Strait of Johore to Singapore Island itself. He gathered all available craft, and the withdrawal was safely accomplished. He was created an honorary Argyll and Sutherland highlander in recognition of his achievement. He was evacuated to Batavia in the destroyer *Jupiter* just before the fall of Singapore. His report on the indiscipline in particular of some Australian troops in the final days before the Japanese occupation provoked an outcry when it was released fifty years later, but Hayes stuck to the main points of his story.

Ordered to make his own way back to Britain, Hayes adventurously managed a passage home via Ceylon. He was at once appointed staff officer (operations) to Rear-Admiral Louis Hamilton, commanding the 1st cruiser squadron in the Home Fleet. Early in July 1942 Hamilton's force was operating in support of convoy PQ17 bound for north Russia when, on the personal decision of the first sea lord, the convoy was ordered to scatter in the face of what he believed to be the sortie of the German battleship *Tirpitz*. This disastrous decision resulted in the destruction of most of the convoy by submarines and shore-based aircraft. Hayes's narrative, drafted at the time, was many years later instrumental in a successful libel action by Commander J. E. Broome, who had been in charge of the convoy's close escort, against David Irving, the author of *The Destruction of Convoy PQ17* (1968), which implied insubordination and cowardice on Broome's part.

Hayes spent the last eighteen months of the war in Malta on Hamilton's staff, with involvement in the liberation of Greece, a service for which Hayes was appointed OBE. After a year in the carrier *Indomitable*, converted to bring home service personnel from overseas, Hayes went to the training cruiser as cadet training officer. His success in this job was rewarded by promotion to commander in June 1948. Two years on the staff of the Imperial Defence College were followed by appointment as executive officer of the aircraft-carrier *Ocean*, a successful tenure cut short by an unexpected Admiralty appointment. Promoted captain in 1954, he took command of the frigate *Sparrow*, which had a serious disciplinary problem; Hayes quickly restored morale. His command of the boys' training establishment *St Vincent* was followed by a stint in the joint planning staff in the Ministry of Defence and then the offer of the much coveted command of an aircraft-carrier. But a medical examination suggested that Hayes's eyesight was below the standard for sea command, and he went instead to be commodore of HMS *Drake* at Plymouth.

Promoted to rear-admiral in 1962, Hayes became naval secretary, a post of great influence serving two widely different masters: Lord Carrington, the first lord of the Admiralty, and Sir Caspar John, the first sea lord. From there he moved to the post of second in command of the western fleet—ironically, one of only two flag officers' commands afloat. His last visit in his flagship *Tiger* was, appropriately, to Bermuda. As vice-admiral he took up his final appointment as flag officer in Scotland and Northern Ireland, a widespread and highly operational national and NATO command. He was appointed KCB in 1967.

Hayes was always known in the navy as Joc, because of his initials rather than any Scottish descent. But he and his family had for some years had a home at Nigg on the Cromarty Firth, and they remained there after he left the active list in 1968. After some time on the Ross-shire council and chairmanship of the Cromarty port authority he became lord lieutenant of Ross and Cromarty, a post that he held until his seventy-fifth birthday. In 1991 he published an episodic autobiography, *Face the Music*, its title reflecting his lifelong love of that art. He died at the Raigmore Hospital, Inverness, on 7 September 1998, and was survived by his wife and their three children.

RICHARD HILL

Sources J. Hayes, *Face the music* (1991) · *The Times* (16 Sept 1998) · *Daily Telegraph* (23 Sept 1998) · *The Independent* (29 Sept 1998) · *The Scotsman* (3 Oct 1998) · *The Guardian* (5 Nov 1998) · certificate of service · WWW · personal knowledge (2004) · private information (2004) [Lady Hayes, widow; son; colleagues] · m. cert. · d. cert.
Archives IWM, memoirs and papers
Likenesses photograph, 1962, repro. in *The Guardian* · photograph, repro. in *The Times* · photograph, repro. in *Daily Telegraph* · photograph, repro. in *The Independent* · photograph, repro. in *The Scotsman* · photographs, priv. coll.

Hayes, Michael Angelo (1820–1877), watercolour painter, was born at Waterford, Ireland, on 25 July 1820, the son and pupil of the painter Edward Hayes (1797–1864). He made his début as a sporting artist with six illustrations for *Car Driving in the South of Ireland* (1836), engraved by John Harris; he also painted watercolours (now in the National Army Museum, London) of the uniforms of the 46th South Devonshire regiment in 1837. In 1837 Hayes also began exhibiting, showing eventually some fifty paintings at the Royal Hibernian Academy in Dublin. At its exhibition in 1841, the critic of the *Art Union* (3, July 1841, 119) noted: 'This young artist is fast making a name for himself. His contributions show originality as well as a quick perception and close-keeping to natural effects'. In 1844 he showed military drawings at the Society of Artists of Ireland, leading the *Art Union* to opine that he was 'getting beyond the small ambition of barrack repute for correctness of the tags and buttons, and showing the feeling of a real artist by his toning of colour, and disposing and grouping of his materials' (6, Sept 1844, 280). He was appointed military painter-in-ordinary to the lord lieutenant of Ireland in 1842. In that year Hayes went to London, where he exhibited *Videttes—16th Lancers in India* and *The Soldier and the Citizen* (exh. Society of British Artists, 1845), and *Her majesty's 3rd dragoon guards taking the principal Sikh battery at Moodkee, 26 December 1845* (exh. Royal Academy, 1847), his only exhibits at these galleries. He returned to Dublin, where he settled, by 1848.

In 1845 Hayes won a prize from the Irish Art Union for five drawings illustrating *The Ballad of Savourneen Deelish* (published in 1846 as *Prize Outlines*); he also provided illustrations for A. G. Stark's *The South of Ireland* (1850). In 1876 he gave a lecture, 'On the pictorial delineation of animals in rapid motion', with lantern-slides, to the Royal Dublin Society, showing (before Eadweard Muybridge's photographs appeared in 1878) that horses do not gallop with all legs stretched out in a 'flying gallop', as previously depicted. His last exhibit at the Royal Hibernian Academy (in 1876) was *The installation of the prince of Wales as a knight of*

St Patrick in St Patrick's Cathedral, Dublin, on 18 April 1868. He also exhibited thirty-five watercolours at the New Water-colour Society.

Hayes was elected an associate of the Royal Hibernian Academy in 1853 and a full member in 1854, and was appointed its secretary in 1856; a year later he was expelled from the academy after he had antagonized older members by his reorganization of the academy's finances. Under a new charter he returned as a member in 1860 and was reinstated as secretary in 1861; he retired in 1870. Esteemed in Dublin for his 'genial disposition and respected for his varied attainments' (*Art Journal*, 108), he served as Dublin city marshal from 1867, but was involved in a libel action for caricaturing a former lord mayor, Sir W. Carroll. On 31 December 1877, while examining a cistern at the top of his house at 4 Salem Place, Adelaide Place, Dublin, he overbalanced, fell in, and was drowned. He was survived by his wife, Ellen.   DELIA MILLAR

Sources *Art Journal*, 40 (1878), 76, 108 · Mallalieu, *Watercolour artists*, vols. 1–2 · Bénézit, *Dict.*, 3rd edn · S. Mitchell, *The dictionary of British equestrian artists* (1985) · M. A. Wingfield, *A dictionary of sporting artists, 1650–1990* (1992) · H. Boylan, *A dictionary of Irish biography*, 3rd edn (1998) · Wood, *Vic. painters*, 3rd edn · C. Barrett, 'Michael Angelo Hayes, RHA, and the galloping horse', *The Arts in Ireland*, 1/3 (1973), 42–7 · *CGPLA Ire.* (1878)
Wealth at death under £3000: administration, 2 July 1878, *CGPLA Ire.*

Patricia Lawlor Hayes (1909–1998), by unknown photographer

Hayes, Patricia Lawlor (1909–1998), actress, was born on 22 December 1909 at 128 Sternhold Avenue, Streatham, London, the daughter of George Frederick Hayes, an Irish protestant (who converted to Catholicism) working as a civil service clerk in the Admiralty, a job he hated, and his wife, Florence Alice Lawlor, a mother who was keen to achieve her own stage ambitions through her daughter. In a nursing home for the first year of her life, and always physically so small that she was able to portray children much younger than she was (as an adult she was only 4 feet 9 inches tall), Patricia was enrolled by her father into a dancing and elocution class at the age of five and had appeared in many seaside shows by the time she was six. She was educated at the Sacred Heart Convent, Wandsworth, and when she was twelve made her first legitimate stage appearance, at the Court Theatre, London, in the Christmas fantasy *The Great Big World* (1921).

As a schoolgirl Hayes had few friends because her mother regarded most of the local children as 'common and unable to speak properly' (*Daily Telegraph*, 21 Sept 1998). The fact that her parents were too short of money to sustain their social ambitions meant that Hayes, though comradely and genial, was throughout her life so careful with money that she disliked such simple pleasures as eating in restaurants.

At the Royal Academy of Dramatic Art Hayes won the Bancroft gold medal in 1928, her judges being Dame Edith Evans, Sir Gerald Du Maurier, and Frank Cellier. She then went into repertory at Oxford and was for two years with the Jevan Brandon-Thomas touring company. In 1938 J. B. Priestley cast her as Ruby Birtle, the maid, in his *When we are Married* (St Martin's Theatre); the part and the reviews

established her, and she appeared again in the play in 1986 at the Whitehall Theatre, this time playing the charwoman Mrs Northropp. On 8 June 1939 she married Valentine Ernest Brooke, an actor and radio announcer; they had three children before they were divorced in 1946.

Hayes had made broadcasts for the BBC as a child, and in 1943 she played one of two schoolboy detectives in *Norman and Henry Bones, Boy Detectives*. Charles Hawtrey, who later made his reputation in the *Carry on* series of broad comedy British films, played Norman, and Patricia, her name shortened to the more masculine Pat, played Henry. She began to feature regularly on the BBC children's hour. For many years most of her work was for radio, some of it for experimental drama on the Third Programme. The light entertainment producer Pat Dixon suggested to her that she try radio comedy, and she played a switchback showwoman shouting out 'Hup and Dahn! Hup and Dahn!' at the opening of *Hoop-La* (1944) for the lugubrious comedian Rob Wilton, whose catchphrase was 'The day war broke out …'.

Hayes continued this line of work in *Our Shed* (1946), which was billed as 'Max Wall and his trained troupe of performing zombies'. For six years from 1949 she played a number of supporting roles in the comedian Ted Ray's series *Ray's a Laugh*, including the comedian's secretary Gertrude Dobbs and his cleaning lady Mrs Chatsworth. In the 1950s she went on to play a variety of roles, often boys, and in 1958 she began her association with the comedian Tony Hancock. She began in *Hancock's Half Hour* with a small part in a sketch called 'The Prize Money', in which Hancock won a television quiz and one of his co-habitees, Sid

James, tried to think of ways to relieve him of the prize money. A regular part was soon devised for her as an insidious and sententious home help, who duly transferred with Hancock to television.

Hayes had already appeared on television in 1956 in *The Arthur Haynes Show* and in 1961 supported the comedian Arthur Askey in *The Arthur Askey Show*; she also appeared in *The World of Beachcomber* (1968), a screen version of J. B. Morton's humorous column in the *Daily Express*. She made a more serious reputation playing the eponymous lead in Jeremy Sandford's play *Edna the Inebriate Woman*, broadcast in the BBC's Play for Today series in October 1971; she won the British Academy of Film and Television Arts award for best actress for her portrayal of the solitary outcast.

After appearing with many of the comedians of the day, Hayes began to establish herself as a comic character in her own right in the popular *Till Death Us Do Part* series, written by Johnny Speight, in which Warren Mitchell played the xenophobic and profane Alf Garnett, and Hayes, who joined the series towards the end, in 1975, played one of his picturesque neighbours, Min. Her obsessive and reproving voice as she drove Alf into a frenzy with her seeping advice and undermining comments was one of the comic delights of the ground-breaking series, in which bad language was passed off as a joke. She stayed with the show when it transferred from the BBC to ATV in 1981 as *Till Death*, and when Alf retired to Eastbourne she continued in the BBC's *In Sickness and in Health* from 1985.

Films made by Hayes include *Nicholas Nickleby* (1947), *Goodbye Mr Chips* (1969), *Willow* (1988), and *A Fish called Wanda* (1988). She also, in the 1960s, appeared in commercials made by the Egg Marketing Board, pushing the 'little lion' trademark and the slogan 'Go to work on an egg!'

Hayes remained active in her old age, often on stage. She was Mrs Swabb in Alan Bennett's *Habeas corpus* at the Lyric (1973) and Maria in *Twelfth Night* for the Royal Shakespeare Company (1974), and took part in the comedy *Filumena* at the Lyric in 1977 and the National Theatre in 1982. In 1990 she played the Old Nanny in Chekhov's *Three Sisters* at the Dublin Gate Theatre, and in 1991 she was a witch in Peter Hall's production of Tennessee Williams's *The Rose Tattoo*. Three years later she was in John Antrobus's *That Woman* at Riverside Studios, Hammersmith, characteristically as a tenacious old woman on a housing estate who will not be denied a cup of tea and some human interaction—however much mayhem she has to create to get them.

Hayes was appointed OBE in 1987, the same year in which she received the Clarence Derwent award for best supporting performance (as an eerily deranged and wandering grandmother) in Lorca's *The House of Bernarda Alba* (Globe, 1986–7), an illustration of what she could achieve outside the comic confines of most of her idiosyncratic career.

Patricia Hayes died at Springfield Manor Nursing Home, Hogs Back, Puttenham, Surrey, on 19 September 1998, survived by her son, the actor Richard O'Callaghan, and two daughters. Restricted by her size from most of the classical repertory, she found her métier in characters who were battered by life, indomitable, obsessive, slightly demented, and at odds with society, and brought her concentrated skill to bear on them, whether in comedy or tragedy.

DENNIS BARKER

Sources *Daily Telegraph* (21 Sept 1998) · *The Times* (21 Sept 1998) · N. Fountain and P. Cotes, *The Guardian* (21 Sept 1998) · L. Cochrane, *The Scotsman* (21 Sept 1998) · D. Gifford, *The Independent* (21 Sept 1998) · personal knowledge (2004) · b. cert. · m. cert. · d. cert.
Likenesses photograph, 1973, Hult. Arch. · photograph, repro. in *Daily Telegraph* · photograph, repro. in *The Times* · photograph, repro. in *The Guardian* · photograph, repro. in *The Independent* · photograph, repro. in *The Scotsman* · photograph, BFI [*see illus.*]
Wealth at death £730,676: probate, 17 Dec 1998, *CGPLA Eng. & Wales*

Hayes, Philip (*bap.* 1738, *d.* 1797), composer, was baptized at St Peter-in-the-East, Oxford, on 17 April 1738, the second son of William *Hayes (*bap.* 1708, *d.* 1777) and his wife, Anne (*d.* 1786). He became a chorister at the Chapel Royal under Bernard Gates, and matriculated on 3 May 1763 at Magdalen College, Oxford, where he took the degree of BMus on 18 May of the same year. After acting for a short time (until 1765) as organist of Christ Church Cathedral, he became on 30 November 1767 a gentleman of the Chapel Royal, and on 1 January 1769 a member of the Royal Society of Musicians. Seven years later he succeeded Richard Church as organist of New College, Oxford; in 1777, on his father's death, he succeeded him as organist of Magdalen College and professor of music in the university. He was also appointed organist of the university church and received the degree of DMus on 6 November 1777. In 1790 he succeeded Thomas Norris, in whose favour he had been displaced at Christ Church in 1765, as organist to St John's College, and in 1791 he welcomed Haydn to Oxford to receive an honorary doctorate. Hayes died suddenly, apparently of a heart attack, on 19 March 1797 in London, where he had gone to preside at a festival performance in aid of the newly instituted Musical Fund. He was buried on 21 March in St Paul's Cathedral, with the gentlemen of the king's chapel and the choirs of St Paul's and Westminster Abbey attending the funeral.

Hayes was renowned for his corpulence (which gained him the nickname Fill-Chaise, in punning allusion to his normal signature 'Phil Hayes'), and for the most unsociable temper in England. Although an expert in the field of seventeenth- and eighteenth-century music, editing volumes of sacred music by William Boyce and by his own father, much of his own music displays the influence of the classical style, and of Haydn and his contemporaries. His works included *Six concertos, with accompaniments for organ, harpsichord or pianoforte, to which is added a harpsichord sonata* (1769), an oratorio, *Prophecy* (1781), *Catches and Glees, the Muse's Tribute to Beauty* (1789), *Eight Anthems* (c.1790), a masque, *Telemachus*, and a number of separate anthems, songs, catches, and glees. In addition to the works of Boyce and his father already mentioned, he was the editor of *Harmonia Wiccamica* (1780), which was a collection of music sung at meetings of Wykehamists (members of Winchester College or New College, Oxford) in London, and of *Memoirs of Prince William Henry, Duke of Gloucester*

Philip Hayes (*bap.* 1738, *d.* 1797), by John Cooper, 1758

(1789). Hayes presented a number of portraits and busts to the Oxford music school, where his own portrait by John Cooper now hangs.

R. F. SHARP, *rev.* NICHOLAS SALWEY

Sources S. J. Heighes, 'The life and works of William and Philip Hayes', 3 vols., DPhil diss., U. Oxf., 1990 • P. W. Jones, 'Hayes, Philip', *New Grove* • A. Chalmers, ed., *The general biographical dictionary*, new edn, 17 (1814), 266–7 • J. R. Bloxam, *A register of the presidents, fellows … of Saint Mary Magdalen College*, 8 vols. (1853–85) • J. H. Mee, *The oldest music room in Europe* (1911) • *GM*, 1st ser., 67 (1797), 354 • parish register (baptism), St Peter-in-the-East, Oxford, 17 April 1738

Likenesses J. Cooper, oils, 1758, U. Oxf., faculty of music [*see illus.*] • J. Reynolds, oils, 1780–84 • J. Roberts, pastel drawing, St John's College, Oxford

Wealth at death £1000: administration

Hayes, Walter (*b.* c.1618, *d.* before 1696?), maker of mathematical instruments, was the son of Peter Hayes, a merchant from Chichester. He was apprenticed to John Allen in the Grocers' Company on 22 February 1632, taking his freedom on 14 June 1642. His first workshop was in Birchin Lane, off Cornhill, in the City of London. By 1652 he had established a reputation for a high standard of work, and advertisements for his instruments began to appear in books on mathematics, astronomy, navigation, and surveying. These show that by 1653 at the latest he was resident 'at the Cross-daggers in Moor-fields near Bethelem-gate', also sometimes referred to as 'next dore to the Popes head Taverne' (Taylor). He remained at this address until the end of his working life.

Hayes had strong links with several mathematical writers of the time, including George Atwell, William Leybourn, John Eyre, Seth Partridge, Vincent Wing, and Matthew Norwood. He had particularly close relations with

Leybourn, for whose books he not only supplied the instruments discussed in the text but also engraved the plates for the illustrations. According to the advertisements placed in these books he offered a 'full range of mathematical instruments' in brass, silver, and wood, as well as globes.

Hayes was responsible for the training of a large number of apprentices. Between 1648 and 1684 he took fourteen, as well as one probably turned over to him from a former apprentice. His final apprentice was Edmund Culpeper, who was to be highly regarded both for his mathematical instruments and for his microscopes.

Hayes was a member of the Grocers' Company and became prominent in that guild, but he was most active in the Clockmakers' Company. He joined it as a brother on 24 February 1668, along with eighteen other instrument makers. Two years later he was appointed as an assistant of the company. He refused the post of renter warden on 14 January 1678 but he was elected upper warden on 29 September 1679 and was chosen as master of the company in 1680, being sworn in on 15 October of that year. Having entered the livery of the Grocers' Company in 1668 Hayes was appointed steward two years later and rose to the ranks of assistant and warden in 1681 and 1686 respectively. His last appearance in either company's records came on 21 September 1687, when he was present at the court of assistants of the Grocers' Company. He was probably dead by 1696 since a widow named Jane Hayes (almost certainly his wife) was supplying mathematical instruments to Christ's Hospital in 1696 and 1697.

Hayes was arguably the most important instrument maker of his day. He was highly respected for the quality of his work, and recommended by many of the contemporary mathematical writers. Like his forerunner Elias Allen he left an important legacy in the shape of his apprentices, several of whom were known for the excellence of their own work and who carried the tradition of precision instrument making into the eighteenth century.   H. K. HIGTON

Sources E. G. R. Taylor, *The mathematical practitioners of Tudor and Stuart England* (1954) • J. Brown, *Mathematical instrument makers in the Grocers' Company, 1688–1800* (1979) • G. Clifton, *Directory of British scientific instrument makers, 1550–1851*, ed. G. L'E. Turner (1995) • H. K. Higton, 'Elias Allen and the role of instruments in shaping the mathematical culture of seventeenth-century England', PhD diss., U. Cam., 1996 • D. J. Bryden, 'Evidence from advertising for mathematical instrument making in London, 1556–1714', *Annals of Science*, 49 (1992), 301–36

Hayes, William (*bap.* 1708, *d.* 1777), composer and university professor, son of William Hayes (1685–1758), shoemaker, was baptized at St John's, Gloucester, on 26 January 1708. His name first appears among the list of choristers at Gloucester Cathedral in 1717, where it remains for the next ten years, during which time he was articled to the organist, William Hine. On the expiration of his articles he was appointed organist to St Mary's, Shrewsbury, in 1729. In 1731 he became organist of Worcester Cathedral and in 1734 he succeeded Thomas Hecht as organist and master of the choristers at Magdalen College, Oxford.

William Hayes (*bap.* 1708, *d.* 1777), by Thomas Park, pubd 1787 (after John Cornish)

In that year he acted as steward at the meeting of the three choirs at Worcester.

At Oxford Hayes received the BMus degree on 8 July 1735, and not long afterwards was admitted a member of the Royal Society of Musicians. On 14 January 1742 he was unanimously elected professor of music of the university in succession to Richard Goodson the younger. As professor, he presided over the opening of the Holywell Music Room in 1748, and on the occasion of a performance, which he directed, at the opening of the Radcliffe Library, on 14 April 1749, he was awarded the degree of DMus. In 1754 he acted as deputy steward, and in 1763 as conductor, at the meeting of the three choirs at Gloucester. That same year he won three of the six prizes then offered for the first time by the Noblemen's and Gentlemen's Catch Club, with his canons *Alleluja* and *Miserere nobis*, and a glee, 'Melting airs soft joys inspire'. In 1765 he was elected a 'priviledged member of the club'.

Hayes died at Oxford on 27 July 1777, having been incapacitated for the previous three years following a stroke, and he was buried on 30 July in the churchyard of St Peter-in-the-East. His widow, Anne Hayes (*d.* 1786), whom he married in or about 1730, died on 14 January 1786. His second son, Philip *Hayes, succeeded him as professor of music.

Hayes's sacred compositions included two oratorios, *Sixteen Psalms Selected from the Rev. Mr Merrick's New Version* (1773), and a number of anthems, and his secular compositions included *Twelve Arietts or Ballads, and Two Cantatas* (1735), various odes, masques, cantatas, glees, and songs, and a number of concertos and trio sonatas. Hayes was

especially successful in vocal part-writing. His glee 'Melting airs' and a round, 'Wind, gentle evergreen', were great favourites in their day, and Burney stated that he considered his canon 'Let's drink and let's sing together' to be the 'most pleasant' composition he knew in that form, and also commented that the four books of catches, glees, and canons were the compositions that 'gained him the most celebrity' (Rees, *Cyclopaedia*). Much of his work reveals the strong influence of Handel, whom Hayes clearly emulates in his use of French overtures, accompanied recitatives, and large-scale choral writing. Hayes was the author of *Remarks on Mr. Avison's Essay on Musical Expression*, published anonymously in London in 1753, in which Hayes 'felt so indignant at Avison's treatment of Handel, that he not only points out the false reasoning in his essay, but false composition in his own works' (Chalmers, 17.266).

Hayes's third son, **William Hayes** (*bap.* 1741, *d.* 1790), was a chorister at Magdalen College, Oxford, for two years from 27 June 1749. He matriculated at Magdalen Hall on 16 July 1757, graduated BA on 7 April 1761 and MA (from New College) on 15 January 1764, and was successively appointed minor canon and vicar choral of Worcester Cathedral in 1765, and minor canon of St Paul's Cathedral on 14 January 1766, rising to senior cardinal in 1783. On 24 January 1776 he was sworn in as priest at the Chapel Royal, and became vicar of Tillingham, Essex, in 1783. The latter appointment he held until his death on 22 October 1790. He composed some chants, published several sermons, and contributed a paper to the *Gentleman's Magazine* in May 1765: 'Rules necessary to be observed by all cathedral singers in this kingdom'.

R. F. SHARP, rev. NICHOLAS SALWEY

Sources S. J. Heighes, 'The life and works of William and Philip Hayes', 3 vols., DPhil diss., U. Oxf., 1990 · P. W. Jones, 'Hayes, William', *New Grove* · A. Rees and others, *The cyclopaedia, or, Universal dictionary of arts, sciences, and literature*, 45 vols. (1819–20), vol. 17 · A. Chalmers, ed., *The general biographical dictionary*, new edn, 32 vols. (1812–17) · 'Biographical sketch', *The Harmonicon*, 11 (1833), 141 · P. Hayes, *Cathedral music in score* (1795) [incl. biography] · D. Lysons, *History of the origin and progress of the meeting of the three choirs of Gloucester, Worcester and Hereford* (1812) · O. E. Deutsch, 'Inkpot and squirt-gun', *MT*, 93 (1952), 401–3 · J. R. Bloxam, *A register of the presidents, fellows … of Saint Mary Magdalen College*, 8 vols. (1853–85) · *Jackson's Oxford Journal* (21 Jan 1786)
Likenesses J. Cornish, oils, after 1749, U. Oxf., Examination Schools · T. Park, mezzotint, pubd 1787 (after J. Cornish), BM, NPG [*see illus.*]
Wealth at death pictures and music to Philip: will discussed, Heighes, 'Life and works of William and Philip Hayes'

Hayes, William (1729–1799), bird illustrator, is thought to have lived most of his life in Southall, Middlesex. Nothing is known of his parentage and little is known of his life. He married, and fathered twenty-one children, ten of whom survived him, although only the eldest daughter was able to support herself; his eldest son was disabled from infancy.

Hayes engraved and coloured by hand portraits of birds. He was industrious but lacked originality. The portraits are typical of the period and many of the birds appear lifeless. This impression of artificiality is probably compounded by the fact that he preferred to work on exotic species with bright plumage. Many are no more than scantily etched and Hayes's reliance on colouring to make them look authentic sometimes fails because of the variable quality of colouring from one plate to the next. Part of the reason for this is that seven of his children are known to have helped him with the colouring at various times.

A natural history of British birds with their portraits accurately drawn and beautifully coloured from Nature exists in folio (1775). Despite the title, the few birds to be treated include three oriental pheasants and some ornamental ducks. Short Latin and longer English descriptions are given. In 1778 *Portraits of British and Exotic Birds* was published under the patronage of the fourth earl of Sandwich.

Another of Hayes's patrons was the banker Sir Francis Child of Osterley Park. *Portraits of rare and curious birds, with their descriptions, from the menagery of Osterly Park* (1794) consists of forty-two plates in two volumes, the first dedicated to Thomas Pennant, the naturalist and writer, and the second to the Revd G. H. Glasse. The text accompanying each plate is anecdotal as well as descriptive of the bird. Much of what we know about Hayes comes from the introduction to this work, in which he gives as his reasons for publication his precarious income—it rarely exceeded £90 per annum—and his failing health.

In fact Hayes's distress was extreme and, in 1799, Glasse published 'An appeal to the public' on behalf of 'this ingenious artist'. The Literary Fund and the dean and chapter of Canterbury sent liberal subscriptions but it was during this year that Hayes died. His work remains a representative but little-known component of bird illustration, an art which flourished with the awakening awareness of nature in the eighteenth century.

DAVID E. EVANS

Sources DNB · J. E. Gooders, ed., *Gallery of birds* (1971), vol. 10 of *Birds of the world* · F. Lewis, *A dictionary of British bird painters* (1974) · A. M. Lysaght, *The book of birds: five centuries of bird illustration* (1975) **Wealth at death** extremely poor: *DNB*; Gooders, ed., *Gallery of birds*

Hayes, William (*bap.* 1741, *d.* 1790). *See under* Hayes, William (*bap.* 1708, *d.* 1777).

Hayford, Adelaide Casely- [*née* Adelaide Smith] (1868–1960), educationist and author, was born in Gloucester Street, Freetown, Sierra Leone, on 2 June 1868. Her grandfather William Smith, a Yorkshireman, was employed in the Gold Coast, where he married a Fante noblewoman, and in 1825 moved to Freetown and became judge of the court of mixed commission which adjudicated international slave trading cases. His son William Smith (1815–1896) became registrar of the court, and by a second marriage, to Anne Spilsbury (1840–1876), of part European, part Mandinka descent, had seven children, Adelaide being the sixth. In 1871 the court closed. Smith retired with a substantial pension, took his large family to England, and settled in Jersey. Adelaide was educated at Jersey

Ladies' College, and then spent nearly three years in Germany, studying music in Stuttgart.

When her father died in 1896, Adelaide Smith returned unwillingly to Freetown at his wish. Though her years in Europe had given her a strong sense of African identity and racial pride, she always remained distanced from her own Krio people and was openly censorious of them. The dislike tended to be reciprocated. After a tentative attempt to open a school she returned to England with a recently widowed sister and settled in London. There, on 10 September 1903, she married Joseph Ephraim Casely-*Hayford (1866–1930), a Fante barrister, who later had a distinguished career in the Gold Coast. The marriage was unhappy. She disliked the Gold Coast; in 1912 they separated and she went back to Freetown. They had one daughter, Gladys, a talented poet and one of the few to use the Krio language in her poetry, who died young.

Casely-Hayford now began to plan her lifework, a school to provide girls with industrial and vocational training, lacking in the Freetown schools, but seen in America, she was told, as a prerequisite for 'negro' education. The school would instil 'a pride of race, an enthusiasm for a black man's capabilities, and a genuine admiration for Africa's wonderful art work' (Cromwell, 102). Unable to finance it locally, she and her niece Kathleen Easmon set off in 1920 for the United States to study the African-American school systems and raise money by giving lectures emphasizing the positive aspects of African culture and by selling African artefacts. They had introductions to leading educationists and wore African dress (which Casely-Hayford had never worn before), thus finding themselves welcomed as 'African princesses' and able to jump the customary colour bars. For the next two and a half years they travelled round, addressing schools and churches.

After her return to Africa in 1923, Casely-Hayford opened her school in the old family mansion, with a governing body of local notables. She was joined by an English lady, married to a locally employed Nigerian clergyman, who left soon afterwards and started her own school, taking away most of the girls. To raise more money Casely-Hayford returned briefly to the United States, unwisely sending her governing body what she subsequently admitted was a most insulting letter alleging their lack of support. They resigned, and she returned to a hostile Freetown. 'Had I been starting a brothel', she later wrote, 'the antagonism could not have been worse' (Cromwell, 147). Nevertheless she carried on. Lacking the resources for vocational training, she reconstituted the school to take girls between the ages of four and twelve and provide a more socially based education than the Freetown schools offered. Where possible she introduced something African. There were African songs and dances, African-style pottery and basket making were taught, and her sister, who had learned traditional weaving methods up country, taught weaving. After a few years Casely-Hayford managed to get a small government grant but the finances were always shaky, since most of the girls paid only half fees and some none at all. In 1940, aged seventy-two, she closed the school.

Over the years Casely-Hayford wrote articles on education for Africans, including a memorandum for an international conference on the African child in 1931. She also published short stories, one of which, 'Mista Courifer', about an over-Anglicized African who is converted to African ways, has appeared in anthologies. But though she championed African culture, she remained on friendly social terms with successive colonial governors and in 1949 was appointed MBE. She died at her home in Charlotte Street, Freetown, Sierra Leone, on 24 January 1960 and was buried in Freetown.

Adelaide Casely-Hayford was her own worst enemy. She judged by extremes: others were either right or wrong. A friend recalled that she never resented criticism, merely ignored it, knowing it was wrong. Once, when asked for reminiscences of the famous Freetown lawyer Sir Samuel Lewis, she burst out, 'He was a thief' (personal knowledge), and then admitted that she did not in fact know whether he had ever stolen anything. In her old age she was cared for by a few loving relatives and friends, a self-isolated figure in a community for which she never concealed her dislike, and which reciprocated this by showing little appreciation of her achievements.

CHRISTOPHER FYFE

Sources A. M. Cromwell, *An African Victorian feminist: the life and times of Adelaide Smith Casely Hayford, 1868–1960* (1986) · A. Casely-Hayford, 'The life and times of Adelaide Casely-Hayford', *West African Review* (Oct 1953–Aug 1954) · R. Okonkwo, *Heroes of West African nationalism* (1985) · A. Casely-Hayford, 'Mista Courifer', *An African treasury: articles, essays, stories, poems*, ed. L. Hughes (1961) · personal knowledge (2004)
Archives National Library of Sierra Leone, Freetown, papers
Likenesses photographs, repro. in Cromwell, *African Victorian feminist*

Hayford, Denis (*c*.1635–1733), iron- and steelmaster, whose exact parentage is not clear, was probably born at Ferrybridge in Yorkshire. However, he is known to have been the nephew and residuary legatee of William Hayford of Round Green, Silkstone (*d.* 1674). Both came from Ferrybridge, near the Aire River. Several members of the family, including William's father, Denis Hayford (who died about 1646), grandfather of the ironmaster, had been postmasters there. William Hayford became steward of Francis Rockley of Rockley and Worsborough, who had been left greatly impoverished by the steadfast support of his father, Robert Rockley (*d.* 1644), for Charles I. William Hayford conspired, together with his sister Margaret (wife of Thomas West), John Spencer, William Wilkinson, and others, to have his master outlawed and cast into gaol in 1659; there he ended his days twenty years later. Included in the estate was Rockley furnace, built in 1652 by the ironmaster Lionel Copley (*d.* 1675).

Although the terms of the lease allowed the lessor to cast 40 tons of iron at Rockley annually, there is no evidence of William Hayford's involvement in the iron trade. However, Denis Hayford was soon in partnership with William Simpson, who had taken the lease of Wortley forges in 1676. In 1678, soon after the death of the elder Lionel Copley, in partnership with Francis Barlow they took over the Copley interests in the iron industry, which, in addition to Rockley furnace, included the duke of Norfolk's works (Chapel furnace, Attercliffe and Wadsley forges, and Rotherham slitting mill). Hayford and Simpson also partnered William Cotton of Haigh Hall in running Bank furnace in conjunction with Knottingley forge.

In 1684, again in partnership with Cotton, Hayford acquired Lord Paget's works (Abbots Bromley and Cannock forges and Rugeley slitting mill) and, around the same time, the Cheshire ironworks (Lawton furnace, Warmingham forge, and Cranage forge and slitting mill). They could now supply rod and bar iron to Lancashire, north Wales, and the Birmingham markets in addition to the Sheffield area. Although the Paget works were disposed of in 1692, Hayford's marriage in 1689 to the heiress Gwyn Millington (*d.* 1730) of Millington consolidated his position in Cheshire. A new furnace at Vale Royal, which drew supplies of haematite ore from Furness, was built in 1696.

In 1698 Hayford withdrew some of his Cheshire capital, perhaps to finance his involvement in Derbyshire and Nottinghamshire. Together with Barlow, Simpson, and John Fell (clerk of the duke of Norfolk's works), he acquired the former Sitwell works (Staveley and Foxbrook furnaces, Staveley and Carburton forges, and Renishaw slitting mill) together with Roche Abbey forge. About this time Hayford transferred his residence from Millington to Staveley and later to Romeley, in Clowne parish, Derbyshire.

It is as a pioneer of the steel industry on Tyneside through the 'Company in the North', in which Cotton, Simpson, and Fell were all involved, that Hayford deserves wider fame. About 1687 Hayford acquired Blackhall mill on the River Derwent, where he made steel by the cementation process. This move must have been prompted by the establishment in 1686 of the Hollow Sword Blade Company at Shotley Bridge, upstream from Blackhall. Ambrose Crowley (1658–1713) had used the cementation method of steel manufacture at Stourbridge by 1682, with Swedish bar iron among his raw materials. By 1686 there was a cementation furnace at Abbots Bromley, which Hayford could have known, and the north-eastern location would have favoured his use of Swedish iron. However, local non-phosphoric ores were suitable for steel production and in 1692 Hayford acquired the lease of Allensford furnace and forge, further upstream from Shotley Bridge. This lease was not renewed in 1713, following around £1000 worth of rebuilding work at Blackhall, and when the Swede Kalmeter visited Blackhall in 1719, a German, William Bertram, was operating the steel mill for Hayford. Bertram is reputed to have been shipwrecked on the coast about 1693, but this date so neatly coincides with the beginning of steel making in the area as to cast doubt on the tradition.

Blister steel, made by cementation, was converted into shear steel by welding and forging; 'Hayford steel', double shear steel, also known as Newcastle or German steel, was made by repeating this process. Double shear came in five qualities, though not all raw materials were capable of such refinement, and the Hollow Sword Blade Company continued to prefer Hayford steel even after the Crowley works was established at Winlaton in 1701.

In 1727 the aged Hayford's ironworking interests in the Sheffield area were taken over by his son Millington Hayford; another son, Denis, became a Newcastle merchant, but predeceased his father in 1732; a third son, Francis, became a London ironmonger. His daughter Ann was alive in 1732. Hayford himself died in 1733 and was buried at Rostherne, Cheshire, on 26 February of that year.

BRIAN G. AWTY

Sources H. R. Schubert, *History of the British iron and steel industry from c. 450 BC to AD 1775* (1957) · K. C. Barraclough and B. G. Awty, 'Denis Hayford: an early steel master', *Historical Metallurgy*, 21 (1987), 16–17 · G. G. Hopkinson, 'The charcoal iron industry in the Sheffield region, 1500–1775', *Transactions of the Hunter Archaeological Society*, 8 (1960–63), 122–51 · B. G. Awty, 'Charcoal ironmasters of Cheshire and Lancashire, 1600–1785', *Transactions of the Historic Society of Lancashire and Cheshire*, 109 (1957), 71–124 · C. R. Andrews, *The story of Wortley ironworks*, 3rd edn (1975) · P. W. King, 'The Vale Royal Company and its rivals', *Transactions of the Historic Society of Lancashire and Cheshire*, 142 (1992), 1–18 · J. Hunter, *South Yorkshire: the history and topography of the deanery of Doncaster*, 2 vols. (1828–31) · 'The journal of Mr John Hobson', ed. C. Charles, *Yorkshire diaries and autobiographies*, ed. C. Jackson, [1], SurtS, 65 (1877), 320 · W. F. Irvine, ed., *Marriage licences granted within the archdeaconry of Chester in the diocese of Chester*, 7, Lancashire and Cheshire RS, 73 (1918), 167 · Rostherne parish register (burial)

Hayford, Joseph Ephraim Casely- (1866–1930), lawyer and politician, was born in Cape Coast on 28 September 1866. The scion of a prominent Fante coastal family, he was called Ekra Agyiman in Fante although he later used the Europeanized forms of his names bestowed by missionaries on his family. This owed something to the fact that, like others who shared this complex if privileged background, he was not brought up with a good command of his African mother tongue, Twi, while he spoke and wrote elegant Victorian English. His father was the prominent Wesleyan minister the Revd Joseph de Graft Hayford (Kwamina Affua). His mother, Mary, was a daughter of Samuel Collins Brew, from one of the most distinguished Cape Coast trading families. Through these family connections Casely-Hayford was variously descended from and related to many of the families that constituted the burgeoning modern élite of the Gold Coast. His ancestors included Philip Quaque (Kweku) (1741–1816), the first African Anglican clergyman; the royal families of both Cape Coast and Asante; and the Manx trader Richard Brew (d. 1776), who had married a Fante. His relatives were teachers, newspaper editors, lawyers, ministers of religion, and businessmen, as well as 'traditional leaders', the incumbents of Fante 'stools', or thrones. He was educated at the Wesleyan Boys' High School in Cape Coast before spending two years at Fourah Bay College, in Freetown, Sierra Leone, at that time the only tertiary education institution in English-speaking west Africa.

Casely-Hayford returned to the Gold Coast to teach at the Wesleyan High School in Accra before moving into journalism. Initially he worked for his uncle Prince Brew of Dunkwa, who owned and edited the *Western Echo*. In 1893 he moved on to his uncle's *Gold Coast Chronicle*, of which for a brief time he was sub-editor, and then the *Gold Coast Echo*, which for a few weeks he edited. Like much of the west African press at this time these papers began and ended with some rapidity. Although he never stopped writing for newspapers Casely-Hayford then moved towards the law, and in 1893 was articled to a Cape Coast lawyer. Shortly afterwards he left for Britain, where he read for the bar as a member of the Inner Temple, London, and was a non-collegiate student at Cambridge, where he matriculated at Easter 1893. He was called to the bar on 17 November 1896. From then onwards he lived and practised in several of the major Gold Coast towns.

Casely-Hayford extended his links with yet another prominent Gold Coast family when he married Beatrice Madeline Pinnock, who died in 1902 and to whose memory his famous book *Gold Coast Native Institutions* is dedicated. On 10 September 1903 he married the educationist and writer Adelaide Smith [see Hayford, Adelaide Casely- (1868–1960)], of Freetown; they had one daughter, Gladys, who died young, before they separated in 1912. His return to the Gold Coast after his time in London coincided with the urgent stirrings of political dissent occasioned by the passing of the colonial government's unpopular Lands Bill of 1897. Politicized by this issue and strongly influenced by the influential Fante lawyer John Mensah Sarbah (Kofi Mensah), whom he greatly admired, Casely-Hayford immediately joined the protest begun by the Aborigines' Rights Protection Society (ARPS) and began a career as a political activist. Like many from his background he was enraged by the racialism of much that he read and by much of the colonial attitude that he endured. He expressed this in his strange, didactic novel *Ethiopia Unbound* (London, 1911). While his politics were radical at that time his position was essentially modernizing and reformist, while insistent upon the values of African institutions and ideas. His reformism is immediately clear from the full title of his book: *Gold Coast native institutions with thoughts upon a healthy imperial policy for the Gold Coast and Ashanti* (London, 1903).

Casely-Hayford supported Britain in the First World War, raising funds for the British war effort. His dominant position in the development of west African nationalism emerged as he developed the National Congress of British West Africa immediately after the First World War. The Congress, which linked nationalists in Gambia, Nigeria, and Sierra Leone as well as the Gold Coast, was launched at a conference in Accra in 1920, the first such west African meeting. Casely-Hayford became vice-president of the Congress. It was dedicated to extending the franchise and influence of educated Africans and, in effect, to Africanizing the colonial establishment rather than to independence; like Casely-Hayford himself the Congress expressed moderation that was far from the revolutionary appeals of much west African nationalism after 1945. A pioneer of nationalism none the less, he was a dominant figure in the

National Congress that played a significant role in achieving important electoral reform in the constituent territories in the late 1920s, although by 1930 it had become inactive. Casely-Hayford died on 11 August 1930 in Accra. He had been appointed MBE.   RICHARD RATHBONE

Sources M. Priestley, *West African trade and coast society: a family study* (1969) · L. F. Ofusu-Appiah, *Joseph Ephraim Casely Hayford: a man of vision and faith* (Accra, 1975) · D. Kimble, *A political history of Ghana, 1850–1928* (1963) · J. E. Casely Hayford, *Gold Coast native institutions with thoughts upon a healthy imperial policy for the Gold Coast and Ashanti* (1970) · J. E. Casely Hayford, *Ethiopia unbound* (1969) · M. Sampson, *Gold Coast men of affairs* (1937) · J. E. Casely Hayford, *The truth about the West African land question* (1971) · Venn, *Alum. Cant.* · D. Owusu-Ansah and D. M. McFarland, *Historical dictionary of Ghana* (1995)
Likenesses photograph, repro. in Kimble, *Political history*

Haygarth, John (1740–1827), physician, was born at Swarth Gill in the parish of Garsdale in the West Riding of Yorkshire, the son of William Haygarth and Magdalen Metcalfe. He was educated at Sedbergh School, after which he was tutored in mathematics by John Dawson (1734–1820), a surgeon and self-taught mathematician who later provided much of the statistical data for Haygarth's works. Haygarth next matriculated from St John's College, Cambridge, as the Hepplethwaite scholar in 1759; he graduated MB in 1766. After completing his studies at Edinburgh (1762–5), Leiden, where he matriculated in 1765, London, and Paris, Haygarth was appointed physician to Chester Infirmary in 1766. The infirmary, which had been founded in 1755, was already established as a humane and progressive institution. On 23 January 1776 he married Sarah Vere Widdens (d. 1816) at Christleton, Cheshire. They had four daughters and two sons, William (b. 1781/2), who entered the medical profession, and John (1787–1854), rector of Upham-with-Durley from 1814 to 1854.

During his three decades in Chester, Haygarth built a reputation as one of the outstanding medical practitioners of his time. A man of progressive outlook and enquiring mind, his concern for the welfare of the populace extended beyond the sphere of medical treatment. Although an Anglican, he shared the philanthropic ideals of leading dissenters in the medical profession, such as William Cullen, James Currie, and Thomas Percival. His special interests were the treatment of fever patients and the prevention of smallpox, and his pioneering work in these spheres attracted widespread interest. Haygarth's links with a network of dissenting intellectuals was important in promoting his ideas and reputation. In 1774 he conducted a population census in Chester which included questions about typhus fever and smallpox. In his subsequent paper, *Observations on the Population and Diseases of Chester in 1774*, he advocated removing poor fever patients to separate fever wards. He also ascertained that out of a population of 14,713 in 1774, only 1060 had never contracted smallpox. The high mortality rate arising from smallpox in Chester led him to concentrate on investigating how to prevent the disease.

The Smallpox Society founded in Chester in 1778 (largely as a result of Haygarth's initiative) was formed to promote inoculation and to prevent casual contraction of the disease. Haygarth used the term 'casual smallpox', reflecting his belief that it was a preventable casualty rather than a 'natural' disease. By 1782 the number of local deaths from casual smallpox had reduced by nearly half, and Leeds and Liverpool were to follow Chester's example. In recognition of his work Haygarth was elected to the Royal Society on 8 February 1781. In 1784 Haygarth's *Inquiry how to Prevent the Small Pox* was published. This attracted wide interest and approval and its translation into French and German helped to establish Haygarth's international reputation. His theories were further elaborated in his *Sketch of a plan to exterminate the casual small pox from Great Britain and to introduce general inoculation* (1793), which was dedicated to the king. Haygarth's plan involved compulsory inspection of homes and general inoculation, with rewards for information about smallpox outbreaks. He was now at the peak of his fame, but his plan failed to win acceptance in the reactionary political climate of the 1790s, which was hostile to grand reform schemes.

During the early 1780s, in parallel with his work towards smallpox prevention, Haygarth also investigated the laws governing febrile contagion. His researches led him to conclude that it was both safe and wise to admit fever patients into separate wards of the infirmary, rather than to use an adjoining building. In 1783 an attic storey at Chester Infirmary was converted into two wards for the reception and isolation of fever patients. These were the first fever wards in the country and the success of the experiment was immediate. During the first year of the wards, thirty fever patients were admitted to Chester Infirmary, and all except one recovered. The provision for isolation also helped to stop the spread of a typhus epidemic in the city in 1784. On a subsequent visit to Chester, the philanthropist John Howard was deeply impressed with the rules for the fever wards, which he later published.

Haygarth moved to Bath in 1798, where he practised at 17 The Circus and renewed his friendship with William Falconer, a former colleague at Chester Infirmary. No longer having a hospital appointment Haygarth had time to analyse his large collection of clinical records. This led to the publication of treatises on rheumatic fever and on the nodosity of the joints, a term which he proposed to substitute for 'rheumatic gout'. He also published several papers in *Philosophical Transactions* and other scientific journals and was a fellow of the Royal Society both of London and of Edinburgh.

Haygarth's other interests included the state of the free schools in the north of England, which were the subject of his *Letter to Bishop Porteous* (1812). Haygarth strongly believed in a basic education for the poor and the *Letter* includes a plan to provide a good education for all the poor children of England 'at a Moderate Expense'. He also played a leading part in the formation of savings banks, submitting a proposal which was adopted in Bath in 1813. His plan entailed investing all the deposits in the public funds and making the depositors liable to their rise and fall.

During his later years Haygarth often visited his native Garsdale, where he owned several farms. He died at Lambridge House near Bath on 10 June 1827, and was buried at Swainswick church. A memorial pulpit, presented by his granddaughter, stands in Garsdale parish church. A ward at the Chester Infirmary was named in his memory, and for many years the Haygarth medal was awarded to the best nurse at the hospital. SIMON HARRISON

Sources J. Elliott, 'A medical pioneer: John Haygarth of Chester', *BMJ* (1 Feb 1913), 235–42 · F. M. Lobo, 'John Haygarth, smallpox and religious dissent in eighteenth-century England', *The medical enlightenment of the eighteenth century*, ed. A. Cunningham and R. French (1990), 217–53 · 'Memoir of the late Dr Haygarth', *GM*, 1st ser., 97/2 (1827), 305–6 · A. M. Kennett, ed., *Georgian Chester* (1987), 26–7, 30 · Venn, *Alum. Cant.* · private information (2004) [Christopher Booth] · IGI
Likenesses W. Cooke, line engraving, 1801 (after J. H. Bell), BM, NPG, Wellcome L. · J. H. Bell, portrait, repro. in *GM*, facing p. 305 · J. Sharples, pastel, Bristol City Museum and Art Gallery · offset impression, Wellcome L.

Hayler, Guy (1850–1943), temperance advocate, was born, of Huguenot descent, on 5 November 1850 at 3 Market Green, Battle, Sussex, the youngest son of George Hayler, a Chartist tailor of Battle, and his wife, Mary Wood Brignall, eldest daughter of John Brignall of Wittersham, Kent. The family soon moved to nearby Hastings. At six Guy Hayler took the teetotal pledge on a blacksmith's anvil and joined the Band of Hope, a children's temperance organization. In 1864, having been orphaned, he moved to Kent, and a year later he moved to London.

In London Hayler became a working-class temperance enthusiast and political radical while working in the building and decorating trades. He frequently visited the offices of the United Kingdom Alliance, the prohibitionist organization, and William Tweedie's temperance bookshop. In 1870 he joined a Good Templar lodge that met above Tweedie's shop. The Good Templars, a working-class and lower middle-class fraternal temperance society that originated in the United States, had arrived in England two years earlier, and Hayler met his future wife at a lodge meeting. The young Hayler was a political radical; for instance, in 1870 he helped to organize the International Democratic Association's demonstration at Hyde Park in support of the French commune.

On 29 July 1874, at St Mark's, Kennington, Hayler married Ann Elizabeth (1848–1941), only daughter of Henry Hartley Harriss of Maidstone; they had four sons and four daughters. In the same year Hayler left London to spend more than three decades as a temperance organizer in northern England. He lived for sixteen years at Hull, as agent and, later, secretary for the local alliance auxiliary, and then for eighteen years at Newcastle upon Tyne, as general secretary of the North of England Temperance League. He held concurrent temperance offices, was active in the co-operative movement and building societies, and edited several newspapers, the most important of which was the league's *Temperance Witness*; he also founded the National Association of Official Temperance Advocates. While working for the league he became an ally of the aristocratic prohibitionist Rosalind Howard, countess of Carlisle.

When the crushing defeat of the Liberal Party in the general election of 1895 made many of its supporters doubt whether prohibition by local option was practicable, Hayler responded by organizing a national prohibition convention. Always optimistic and cheerful, he never lost faith in a future in which people would embrace prohibition as the only answer to the drink problem. Following the collapse of his health at the end of 1906 he gave up his work as a regional temperance organizer and, in his late fifties, began a new phase of his life, as a propagandist for worldwide prohibition; as early as 1905 he had held international office with the Good Templars. Having returned to London in 1909, after the recovery of his health, he served as honorary president of a propaganda organization, known first as the International Prohibition Confederation and then as the World Prohibition Federation, from its formation in 1909 to 1939. From 1917 until his death he edited a quarterly that reported news about prohibition: the *International Record*. In 1919, when the Anti-Saloon League of America, in the triumphant early days of national prohibition, founded the World League against Alcoholism, the World Prohibition Federation lost prestige.

After his return to London Hayler lived in a villa named Courtfield, at South Norwood Park, that became famous for its temperance library of innumerable books and periodicals, annual reports, pamphlets, and posters. Shortly after his death German bombs demolished the house, but much of the library survived. The University of Wisconsin purchased part of it, and thirty-five volumes of pamphlets at Wisconsin have been preserved on microfilm. In his books and pamphlets Hayler often incorporated excerpts from other temperance and government publications, especially statistics; he was more an editor than an original writer. His best-known publications included *The Master Method: an Enquiry into the Liquor Problem in America* (1901), *Famous Fanatics* (1910), *Prohibition Advance in All Lands: a Study of the World-Wide Character of the Drink Question* (1913), and *The New Europe and Prohibition: a Post War Survey* (1923). He also published a novel, *George Proctor, the Teetotaler* (1895). In 1918 he contested eastern Surrey as an independent Liberal but was defeated by the coalition Conservative, Sir S. A. Coats, of the thread manufacturing company.

All Hayler's children were teetotallers. Mark H. C. Hayler (1887–1986) served as executive secretary of the World Prohibition Federation and after his father's death succeeded him as editor of the *International Record*, which ceased publication in 1968. A member of the United Kingdom Alliance executive council from 1938 to 1984, he is best known as the author of a history of the temperance alliance, *The Vision of a Century, 1853–1953* (1953). He and his brother Glen were imprisoned as conscientious objectors when they refused non-combatant service during the First World War. The eldest son, (Guy) Wilfrid, emigrated to the United States, where he was a successful architect and urban planner.

Hayler's wife, Ann, died on 30 May 1941. He himself died at Mayday Hospital, Croydon, on 23 September 1943, and was cremated at Streatham Park, Wandsworth, on 28 September; a Congregational minister officiated at the funeral. DAVID M. FAHEY

Sources M. H. C. Hayler, *The man from Battle: being a centenary reinterpretation of the life and work of Guy Hayler, social reformer, 1850–1943* (1950) • *WWW, 1941–50* • newspaper clippings, U. Cal., Berkeley, Bancroft Library, (Guy) Wilfrid Hayler papers • *International Record* (July 1941), 8 • *International Record* (Jan 1944), 4–6 • *International Record* (Oct 1944), 7–8 • *International Record* (Oct 1950), 7 • G. Hayler, 'Temperance books and literature that helped me', *International Record* (April 1944), 7 [reprint] • temperance tracts: collection of pamphlets assembled by Guy Hayler, University of Wisconsin, madison [35 vols. on 8 reels (1982)], esp. vol. 14 (reel 4) • E. K. Welsch, introduction, in N. Schrom, *Index to Guy Hayler collection on British temperance* • D. Cherry, 'The Guy Hayler collection on British temperance', *University of Wisconsin Library News* (April 1966), 5–6 • *A record of twenty years' work on behalf of international prohibition: an urgent appeal for increased financial support, twentieth anniversary souvenir*, World Prohibition Federation (1929) • *Norwood News* (24 Sept 1943) • *Norwood News* (4 Oct 1943) • *CGPLA Eng. & Wales* (1944)
Archives University of Wisconsin, collection on British temperance, manuscript minutes and printed documents relating to 1882–1883 campaign for a Sunday closing bill for Yorkshire • University of Wisconsin, collection on British temperance, minutes of early meetings of Newcastle upon Tyne temperance federation | U. Cal., Berkeley, Bancroft Library, (Guy) Wilfrid Hayler papers
Likenesses Elliott & Fry, photograph, 1929, repro. in Hayler, *Man from Battle*, facing p. 3
Wealth at death £952 2s. 11d.: probate, 28 Jan 1944, *CGPLA Eng. & Wales*

Hayley, Robert. *See* Healy, Robert (*c*.1743–1771).

Hayley, Thomas Alphonso (1780–1800), sculptor, was born on 5 October 1870, the natural son of the poet William *Hayley (1745–1820). Hayley inherited from his father an interest in sculpture and, from the age of fourteen, was encouraged to learn drawing, for which he showed a precocious talent, by Joseph Wright of Derby. Hayley quickly attracted the attention and gained the respect of the painter George Romney and the sculptor John Flaxman, by whom he was engaged as a resident pupil in London at the age of fifteen for three years. He was given an almost unprecedented access, for that time, to the art of the ancient world: he copied Flaxman's own casts from the Elgin marbles, and received as a gift Flaxman's tracings from J. Stuart and N. Revett's *Antiquities of Athens* (4 vols., 1762–1816). In return, Flaxman demanded complete dedication, informing Hayley that sculpture was 'a jealous lady' who would 'never be courted by halves' (Whinney, 359). Hayley later repaid his master by modelling a bust of him, in addition to those of Lord Thurlow and James Stainer Clarke, and a medallion of Romney, an engraving of which by Caroline Watson appeared in William Hayley's *Life of Romney* (1809).

In 1798 Hayley became ill from complications arising from a curvature of the spine, and he was compelled to return to his father's cottage at Felpham in Sussex. After two years of suffering, he died there on 2 May 1800 aged just nineteen. He was buried near by at Eartham, where there is a monument to his memory carved and erected by Flaxman inscribed with an epitaph composed by his father. Hayley senior devoted many sonnets to his 'poetic child', a 'youthful Phidias', and included, in his *Essays on Sculpture* (1800), an engraving of his son by William Blake based on a medallion by Flaxman. In 1823 the *Literary Gazette* noted that 'the Genius of Humbug' had 'never produced a more gross piece of absurdity' than John Johnson's edition of *Memoirs of the life and writings of William Hayley, written by himself … and memoirs of his son* (1823) (*Literary Gazette*, 28 June 1823, 405). More recently, Gunnis described him as a 'young man of much ability' (Gunnis, 193), and Whinney as a 'sculptor of much promise' (Whinney, 359). L. H. CUST, *rev.* JASON EDWARDS

Sources W. Hayley, *The life of Romney* (1809) • A. Gilchrist, *Life of William Blake, 'Pictor ignotus'*, 2 vols. (1863) • 'Memoirs of the life and writings of William Hayley', *Literary Gazette* (28 June 1823), 403–5 • R. Gunnis, *Dictionary of British sculptors, 1660–1851* (1953); new edn (1968) • M. Whinney, *Sculpture in Britain, 1530 to 1830*, rev. J. Physick, 2nd edn (1988) • Redgrave, *Artists* • Allibone, *Dict.*
Likenesses G. Romney, oils, 1789–92, Tate collection • G. Romney, group portrait, oils, 1796 (*The four friends*), Abbot Hall Art Gallery, Kendal • W. Blake, stipple, 1880 (after medallion by J. Flaxman), BM, NPG; repro. in W. Hayley, *Essay on sculpture* (1800)

Hayley, William (1745–1820), poet and biographer, was born on 9 November 1745 in Chichester, Sussex, the second son of Thomas Hayley (1715–1748) and his second wife, Mary (1718–1774), daughter of Colonel Thomas Yates, MP for Chichester, and his wife, Margaret. Both parents had an Anglican background: Thomas Hayley's father was dean of Chichester and Mary was brought up by her aunt, the wife of the bishop of Ely. Thomas and Mary married in 1740, Thomas having inherited considerably from his first wife, Pauline Baker, who died earlier in that year. In 1743 he acquired Eartham House, between Chichester and Petworth, which became the family seat.

William Hayley, whose elder brother, Thomas, died in 1750 aged seven years, was initially sent to a dame-school in Chichester kept by the Russell sisters; then, moving to London in 1750, he went to a boarding-school in Kingston. There he contracted a serious illness which left him with a lifelong limp. After being privately tutored he attended Eton College between 1757 and 1763. In 1763 he went up to Trinity Hall, Cambridge. Although he left without a degree, he had proved himself eager for knowledge and self-improvement, having private tuition in Spanish, Italian, art, and, during his vacation, French. In June 1766 he entered himself for the Middle Temple but was neither to reside nor practise there. On 23 October 1769, in Chichester Cathedral, Hayley married Eliza Ball (1750–1797), daughter of the Very Revd Ball, dean of Chichester.

Although affluent, Hayley determined on a literary career having had an early achievement with his 'Ode on the Birth of the Prince of Wales'. This, his first published work, appeared in *Cambridge Verses* and then was reprinted in the *Gentleman's Magazine* (January 1763). His efforts to become a playwright, however, were not so successful. One play, *The Afflicted Father*, was never performed; *The Syrian Queen*, adapted in 1770 from the French, was rejected. A later production, begun in conjunction with Jeremiah Meyer, was an opera, *The Trial of the Rock*, Hayley completing it after Meyer's death. This was a failure. His other plays included the tragedies *Lord Russell* and *Marcella*. In 1793 Anna Seward, praising the sentiments of *Lord Russell*, describing them as 'pleasing, natural and pathetic', also deemed the play as 'lacking spirit and variety' (*Letters of Anna Seward*, 3.212) in style. Earlier, Joseph Wright of Derby had stated that 'never was anything finer wrote than Ld. Russel' (1784?, from photocopies of part of the Gilbert S. Inglefield collection in the possession of the keeper of art at Derby City Museum and Art Gallery). The opinion of each may well have been coloured by the state of their existing relationship with Hayley: Wright and he held a mutual admiration while Seward, suffering a distinct cooling of friendship in contrast to what she had enjoyed some years earlier, became one of Hayley's severest critics. Of *Marcella* she wrote that it had a 'disgusting' plot, and so was 'never likely to please' (*Letters of Anna Seward*, 3.212). Nevertheless, this was staged simultaneously by two rival theatres in 1789. Hayley sought—but failed—to improve morality through his plays and his *Lord Russell* and *Marcella*, both in blank verse, have more recently been referred to as 'pseudo-Shakespearean' (Bishop, 127). Whatever the opinion of his works, Hayley, nevertheless, was deemed to possess 'some skill in moving compassion' (ibid., 128, quoting Cary in the *London Magazine*). *Eudora*, another tragedy, performed in 1790, was believed by Hayley to be so badly produced that he requested it to be withdrawn after just one performance.

Failing to be celebrated as a dramatist Hayley concentrated on poetry, with epitaphs, odes, and sonnets comprising the bulk of his output. Each deftly centred on an individual whether or not he had met the subject. He composed more than 140 epitaphs and his odes, intended to cheer, sympathize, or celebrate, drew the attention of strangers to him from which a firm friendship would often ensue. Friends found that Hayley would unhesitatingly go to extraordinary lengths to assist those experiencing times of distress.

Hayley revelled in being close to talented people; he enjoyed bolstering their confidences, forwarding suggestions for their career advancement, and providing seclusion at Eartham, near Chichester, Sussex (where he had moved in 1774), so that their work might continue uninterrupted. He attempted to exert a near absolute control over his friends, guiding their personal and professional lives. Some, such as George Romney and William Cowper, appreciated his suggestions and willingly acquiesced to his advice but others, William Blake included, rebelled against the suffocating friendship and preferred to distance themselves from this well-meaning man and conduct a cordial relationship from afar.

By 1780 Hayley's marriage was in difficulties; he had had an affair with Miss Betts, the daughter of his former nurse, and their son, Thomas (Tom) Alphonso *Hayley, was born on 5 October 1780. Meanwhile, Eliza was in erratic health; Hayley, ostensibly fearing for her mental state (her mother had been mentally ill), sent her to spend some time in Derby. Although she returned to Eartham briefly, they separated again in 1789 and their marriage finished acrimoniously in February 1795. She died on 8 November

1797, and was buried on 17 November at Eartham parish church.

Romney, introduced to Hayley in 1776, became a lifelong friend and frequent visitor to Eartham. In 1778 Hayley's first major printed work, *Epistle on Painting, Addressed to George Romney*, was published, followed in 1780 by *Ode to Philanthropy*, verses concerning John Howard, prison reformer, and *Essay on History*, addressed to Edward Gibbon, who was to become a friend. The artist Joseph Wright often asked Hayley for suggestions for his canvases, looking to the poet's literary knowledge for advice on detail such as position and light. *Ode to Mr. Wright of Derby* (1783) was included in Hayley's *Poems and Plays* (1788).

Hayley was a prolific poet in spite of the fact that after sailing in an open boat in 1772 his eyes had become inflamed and this resulted in a permanent ophthalmic weakness. This affliction occasioned him to carry, at all times, an umbrella which was used both as a walking aid and, even when riding, as a parasol.

While his plays were generally unsuccessful, Hayley's other publications, revealing his scholarly bent, fared better. *Essay on Epic Poetry* (1781) had appended the first translation into English, in *terza rima*, of the first three cantos of Dante's *Inferno*. Possibly his greatest achievement, however, was his didactic poem *Triumphs of Temper* (1781), which 'was to reform the entire feminine mind of England by the advice' (Bishop, 53). This allegorical work aspired, in rhyming couplets, to teach young women the virtues of a pleasant nature. Its advice was heeded by some: Emma Hamilton thanked Hayley 'for the lessons she had learnt from the poem' (P. Jaffe, *Drawings by George Romney*, 1978, 44) and asked Romney to inform Hayley that his poem 'made me Lady H. ... for Sir W. minds more temper than beauty' (ibid.). *Triumphs of Temper* ran into fourteen editions and proved to be the most durable of all his publications.

Although Hayley was disparaged by some—his work being described as 'void of lyric spirit' (*GM*, 1st ser., 52, 1782, 22) and having 'flimsy tinsel lines' (*Letters of Lady Hesketh*, 22), he was offered the poet laureateship in 1790, an honour which, for reasons unknown, he declined. Anonymously published works included his *Essay on Old Maids* (3 vols., 1785)—which, although deemed 'indelicate' (Bishop, 90) and affronting many, sold well—and his only novel, *The Young Widow, or, The History of Cornelia Sedley* (1789). The publisher who paid him £200 for *Cornelia Sedley* did not profit so Hayley provided him with his (again anonymous) prose *Eulogies of Howard: a Vision* for reprinting, thereby assisting the publisher to recoup some expenses.

In 1792 Hayley agreed to write a life of John Milton for John Boydell to accompany a publication of the works. Although a firm friendship ensued, he was initially devastated to find that William Cowper, whom he had always admired, had embarked on an ostensibly similar commission for a rival publisher. Hayley's submission of his *Life of Milton* resulted in a request to rewrite it, for it was deemed too politically sensitive, and he reluctantly complied. The two publications with which he was connected—*The Poetical Works of John Milton with a Life of the Author by William Hayley* (published by Boydell, 3 vols., 1794, 1795, and 1797) and his own unaltered *Life of Milton* (1796)—were acclaimed, although Anna Seward regarded his involvement as characteristic of a man 'at once the flatterer and foe of royalty' (*Letters of Anna Seward*, 4.48).

Circumstances, combined with the Milton success, persuaded Hayley to turn his attention to biography. He and Lord Sheffield arranged Gibbon's papers in preparation for a posthumous *Autobiography*. Then in 1800, after Hayley had moved to Felpham, the death of his illegitimate son Tom, from curvature of the spine, prompted him to write his biography, which was later incorporated in Hayley's own *Memoirs*.

Within a week of Tom's death—whose funeral his father could not attend, being so distraught—Cowper, for whom Hayley, with dogged persistence, had gained a pension from the Pitt government, also died. Hayley had had a marine turret built at his house at Felpham and here, at The Turret, he became more reclusive than before, signing himself 'the Hermit'. Several sonnets ensued and *Essay on Sculpture* (1800); then he commenced his biography of Cowper. *Life of Cowper* (1803) was a major and successful work which, including further editions, earned Hayley nearly £11,000, although perhaps this was due more to the enduring popularity of Cowper than to Hayley's own literary merit. The death of George Romney in 1802 inspired Hayley to write the artist's biography. Begun in 1803, *Life of Romney* (1809) was not so well received, the Revd John Romney castigating it as late as 1830 in his *Memoirs of the Life and Works of George Romney*. He regarded Hayley, rather than being an asset to his father, as having been an undesirable influence.

By 1800 Hayley was patron to William Blake who had moved nearby in Felpham in order to finish a portrait of Tom, commissioned and begun before the boy's death but not completed to Hayley's satisfaction. One commission was to illustrate a new edition of *Triumphs of Temper*; he was paid 10 guineas for each of the six plates (Bishop, 286). He also designed a series of heads of poets for the library. Hayley, however, proved too domineering for the strong-willed Blake who eventually reacted against his patron: 'I have been forced to insist on his leaving me ... to my Own Self Will; for I am determin'd to be no longer Pester'd with his Genteel Ignorance & Polite Disapprobation' (ibid., 288). While the relationship did become strained, Blake was openly grateful to Hayley after 1803 when he was arrested and his patron stood surety for him. After Blake left Felpham (1803), correspondence indicated that a friendship had developed, probably assisted by Hayley's generosity. He had written some ballads, expressly for Blake to illustrate and to profit by. Collected in one volume, periodical publication having been found to be too costly, *Designs to a Series of Ballads* was eventually published in 1805, Blake sharing the profits only with the publisher.

In 1804 Hayley composed a song entitled *The Loyal Prayer*.

Its theme was the king's health and its success, when performed for the queen, inspired him to write *Triumphs of Music* (1804) which, by common consent, was execrable.

On 28 March 1809 Hayley married his second wife, Mary Welford (1781–1848), daughter of a retired merchant of Blackheath. He was nearly sixty-four, she was twenty-eight years old. By 1812 they had separated. Just before their separation, between 1810 and 1811, Hayley had many works reissued. These were to be his last publications.

As he aged, Hayley became even more reclusive. In the past he had enjoyed swimming and been known as an accomplished horseman, but now his outdoor activities were reduced to walking in his garden. An advocate of fresh air and a teetotaller, he was intrigued by medicine and eager to use new inventions such as the 'electrical machine' and the 'shower-bath'. Generous with his knowledge, unhesitatingly he would doctor villagers and friends alike.

Southey described him as 'confessedly the most popular and the most fashionable of living poets ... by grace of the public King of the bards of Britain', with his *Triumphs of Temper* being, at the time, one of the most successful poems ever, and his *Epistles* succeeding 'because the verse was ... on a level with the taste of the age' (*New Letters*, 2.269–70). As critical of Hayley as of the popular culture, Southey also reflected that 'Everything about that man is good except his poetry'.

Described as a 'large and powerful-looking man with an alert and military bearing' (Bishop, 34) with eyes large and bright 'though with something of an ingratiating expression in them which sometimes inspired mistrust' (ibid., 335), and being benevolent and humorous—an aspect which showed in his work—Hayley suffered from kidney trouble from 1812. He died at Felpham on 12 November 1820 of a bladder-stone, and was buried nine days later in the vault of Robert Steele, an old friend, in Felpham church. His will, dated 1817 but with four codicils, showed the chief beneficiary to be a cousin, Captain Godfrey. His extensive library was auctioned over thirteen days from 13 February 1821. He left his memoirs—which he had elected to write in the third person—to be edited by John Johnson, and these were published in 1823 in two volumes.

VIVIENNE W. PAINTING

Sources M. Bishop, *Blake's Hayley* (1951) · G. E. Bentley, *Blake records* (1969) · *New letters of Robert Southey*, ed. K. Curry, 2 (1965) · A. Nicoll, *A history of English drama, 1660–1900*, 6 vols. (1952–9), vol. 3 · *Letters of Anna Seward: written between the years 1784 and 1807*, ed. A. Constable, 6 vols. (1811) · *DNB* · *GM*, 1st ser., 52 (1782), 22 · *GM*, 1st ser., 90/2 (1820), 469–70 · *GM*, 1st ser., 93/1 (1823), 538–9 · *The letters of William Blake*, 3rd edn, ed. G. Keynes (1980) · W. Hayley, FM Cam. · W. Hayley, *Memoirs of the life and writings of William Hayley esq.* (1823) · *Letters of Lady Hesketh to the Reverend John Johnson*, ed. C. B. Johnson (1901), 22 · Foster, *Alum. Oxon.*

Archives BL, corresp., Add. MSS 30803–30805 · Bodl. Oxf., corresp. · Cornell University, Ithaca, New York · Cowper Memorial Library, Olney, corresp. and MSS · FM Cam., literary MSS and corresp. · Harvard U., Houghton L., corresp. and MSS · Herts. ALS, corresp. and papers · W. Sussex RO, corresp., notebooks, and MSS · Yale U., Beinecke L., corresp. and MSS | BL, corresp. with John Flaxman, Add. MSS 39780–39790 · BL, letters to third Lord

Holland, Add. MSS 51823–51832 · BL, corresp. with William Huskisson, Add. MSS 38734–38737 · BL, letters to Lord Sheffield and Lady Sheffield, Add. MS 61980 · Bodl. Oxf., corresp. with Lady Hesketh · Cornwall RO, letters to John Hawkins with literary MSS · CUL, letters to William Long · Herts. ALS, corresp., incl. with William Cowper · Lancs. RO, letters to Thomas Greene · NL Scot., letters to Sir Walter Scott · W. Sussex RO, letters to William Mason and his wife · Yale U., Beinecke L., letters to Lady Emma Hamilton **Likenesses** G. Romney, group portrait, pen, ink and wash, c.1784, BM · G. Romney, group portrait, oils, 1796 ('The four friends'), Abbot Hall Art Gallery, Kendal · H. R. Cook, stipple, 1807 (after W. Harries), BM, NPG; repro. in *The cabinet* (1807) · R. Cooper, stipple, 1823 (after E. Engleheart), BM, NPG; repro. in Hayley, *Memoirs* · H. Howard, oils, NPG · J. Jacobé, portrait (after G. Romney, c.1778) · attrib. J. Nixon, miniature, V&A · G. Romney, oils, Dulwich College Picture Gallery, London · C. Watson, portrait (after G. Romney, 1796)
Wealth at death affluent; took thirteen days to dispose of library; left valuable paintings: Bishop, *Blake's Hayley*; Munby, *Sale catalogues of eminent persons*, 2.83–173

Hayllar family (*per. c.*1850–*c.*1900), painters, came to prominence with **James Hayllar** (1829–1920), who was born on 3 January 1829, probably at The Hornet, Whyke, Chichester. He was baptized on 13 February at St Pancras, Eastgate Square, Chichester, the son of Thomas Hayllar (1794–1859), coal merchant, farmer, and miller, and his wife, Mary Ann Child (1794–1885). Richard Cobden was his cousin on his father's side. He was educated at Midhurst grammar school and subsequently studied under the marine artists William and John Cantiloe Joy. In 1848 he became a resident pupil of Francis Stephen Cary, who had taken over Henry Sass's academy in Bloomsbury in 1842; he remained with the Carys at 21 Bloomsbury Street until 1851—even after his entry to the Royal Academy Schools in 1849—while working as a portraitist, principally in crayons. In October 1851 he travelled to Italy with his friend John Cavell—to whose sister Ellen he had recently become engaged—and spent two years in Rome (where he met Lord Leighton) and Florence studying from the antique and old masters. On his return in October 1853 he resumed portrait painting, mainly in oils, taking studios in London in Berners Street in 1854 and Great Ormond Street in 1855; *Lady Mynzomdie* (exh. RA, 1854)—a portrait of Ellen Cavell—and *John Cavell* (exh. RA, 1855) were among his first exhibited works. He continued to paint portraits throughout his life, his most famous commissions being for Sir Watkin Williams-Wynn, the duke and duchess of St Albans, and General Hardy.

On 8 March 1855 James Hayllar married Ellen Phoebe Cavell (1827–1899), the daughter of a law stationer, and aunt of Edith Cavell. Although he exhibited from a studio, 1 Langham Chambers, Langham Place, between 1860 and 1864, from 1855 until 1875 they lived at 15 Mecklenburgh Square, where his father-in-law, John Cavell, was head of the household until his death in 1863 and where, between 1856 and 1868, they had nine children, four boys and five girls. Jessica, Edith, Kate, and Mary [*see below*] all became professional painters.

James Hayllar had exhibited at the Royal Academy and the Society of British Artists (SBA) from 1851. From 1855

his work was also shown at the British Institution, the Liverpool Academy (LA), and the Royal Manchester Institution, and in subsequent years at the Royal Hibernian Academy, the New Society of Painters in Water Colours, the Institute of Painters in Oil Colours, and the Atkinson Art Gallery, Southport, among other galleries. In the 1850s he exhibited landscapes and genre subjects such as *The Teetotaller and Tippler* (exh. SBA and LA, 1855) and *Bookworm and Grub* (exh. LA, 1857). During the 1860s he also experimented with historical genre, appending lengthy quotations to titles such as *The incident out of which arose Lord Mansfield's decision that as soon as a slave set his foot upon English territory, he became free* (exh. RA, 1864; V&A), the latter subject having been suggested to him by Richard Cobden. It was not until 1866 that he won acclaim, with a painting entitled *Miss Lily's Carriage Stops the Way* (exh. RA, 1866; exh. Sothebys, 2 November 1994), the first of a series that included *Miss Lily's First Flirtation* (1867; exh. Sothebys, 18 March 1987) and *Miss Lily's Return from the Ball* (exh. RA, 1867; exh. Sothebys, 2 November 1994), depicting one of his small daughters; all three were engraved by Robert Graves. The charm and importance of children in an adult world became James Hayllar's principal and most popular theme. He missed election as an associate of the Royal Academy by one vote, but in 1876 was successfully elected a member of the Society of British Artists.

Between 1865 and 1872 the Hayllars rented a country house called Carlton Rookery, near Saxmundham, in Suffolk, where from April they spent five or six months of every year. The children engaged in numerous outdoor activities and acted in plays written by their father. There are also artistic records (chiefly rural genre scenes and landscapes) of visits to Boulogne between 1862 and 1886. The period 1872–5 was spent in London, at which time all five girls attended a day school in Gower Street that was associated with Bedford College. In 1875 the family settled in the country, at Castle Priory, a large house fronting the Thames at Wallingford, Berkshire, where they remained until 1899. George Dunlop Leslie RA, also with a large family, lived next door. Sport and physical exercise were an important part of life at Castle Priory. Hayllar taught his daughters to swim and also to row, as a result of which the four eldest were all accomplished oarswomen; coxed by their father, they used to row their boat 27 miles in a morning to the Henley regatta. On leaving school Hayllar's daughters and his youngest son, Algernon, received art instruction at home. In an old laundry building converted into a studio their father taught them drawing, painting, and perspective, with evenings devoted to modelling, etching, and engraving. His method, according to his daughter Jessica, was 'never to let anything pass that was not quite correct in form or relation to its surroundings' (Hayllar, 13). Algernon Victor (*b.* 1868), having been apprenticed to Cotton Webb for six months, started a career as an engraver and exhibited two engravings at the Royal Academy in 1889. The four daughters who became painters (primarily in oils) specialized initially in meticulously rendered still life and, throughout their careers, in subjects drawn from their comfortable life at Castle Priory.

Children remained focal in James Hayllar's work, chiefly in the context of local village life, examples being *The Only Daughter* (exh. RA, 1875; Forbes Magazine Collection, New York), *As the Twig is Bent so is the Tree Inclined* (exh. SBA, 1879; exh. Christopher Wood Gallery, March 1983), and *The Centre of Attraction* (exh. RA, 1891; Lady Lever Art Gallery, Port Sunlight), for which he was awarded a silver medal. Jessica described his pictures at this time as 'subjects to bring the poor and well-to-do together, kindly acts and interest shown in various ways' (Hayllar, 11).

James Hayllar last exhibited in 1898, although he continued to sketch landscapes until the end of his life. In 1899 his wife, Ellen, died and he moved with two of his daughters, Jessica and Kate, to Redholme, 14 Cambridge Road, Bournemouth, where he died on 9 March 1920.

The eldest daughter, **Jessica Ellen Hayllar** (1858–1940), was born on 16 September 1858 at 15 Mecklenburgh Square, London. She was the most prolific painter of the five sisters and exhibited at the Society of British Artists and the Dudley Gallery from 1879, the Royal Academy from 1880 (until 1915), the Royal Manchester Institution from 1882, the Institute of Painters in Oil Colours from 1883, and widely in the provinces. After still-life subjects such as *Going to 'my Uncle's'* (exh. RA, 1880; exh. Christies, 6 May 1983) Jessica Hayllar painted domestic scenes, often including children, that depicted everyday occurrences at Castle Priory—for example, *House Cleaning* (exh. SBA, 1882–3)—as well as more important family occasions, such as *Christmas Comes but Once a Year* (exh. RA, 1881), *Fresh from the Font* (exh. RA, 1887), *The Return from Confirmation*, exh. RA, 1888; exh. Christies, 3 February 1978), and *The Day of the Wedding* (exh. Royal Manchester Institution, 1882). Her paintings—which often feature doorways and windows—are notable for their effective perspective and suggestion of depth; the same recessive view through interconnecting rooms characterizes *A Coming Event* (exh. RA, 1886), *Autumn Sunlight* (exh. RA, 1891), and *Teaching* (1895), and windows provide not only interesting effects of light but detailed views of the garden beyond. Figures (usually family members), furnishings, and flowers are painted with equal emphasis by Jessica Hayllar, whose approach has been compared with that of the snapshot photographer (Wood, May 1974, 5). From about 1900 she was confined to a wheelchair as a result of an accident (according to family tradition she was knocked down by a carriage) and during the rest of her life in Bournemouth she chiefly painted flowers, azaleas in particular. She died, unmarried, on 7 November 1940 at Hill House, Perry Hill, Worplesdon, Surrey.

Edith Parvin Hayllar (1860–1948) was born on 15 May 1860, also at 15 Mecklenburgh Square, London. She too depicted daily life at Castle Priory, in paintings such as *Amy's Birthday* (exh. SBA, 1885) and *More Hindrance than Help* (1893; exh. Sothebys, Belgravia, London, 24 October 1978). Her work reveals a particular interest in subjects connected with the family's numerous sporting activities: these included hunting, as depicted in *This Way, Sir!* (exh.

SBA, 1882; exh. Sotheby Beresford Adams, Chester, 31 July 1981); shooting, as in *The 1st of September* (exh. RA, 1887; exh. Sothebys, London, 25 November 1983) and *The 1st of October* (exh. RA, 1888; exh. Christies, London, 18 October 1974); and tennis—*A Summer Shower* (exh. RA, 1883; Forbes Magazine Collection) engagingly portrays an interlude in a mixed doubles. Of the four sisters Edith alone painted the Thames, in works such as *Feeding the Swans* (exh. Sothebys, 6 November 1996) and *A Punting Party*. The settings in Edith Hayllar's figure compositions are always painted in great detail, with careful attention to the particularities of flowers, feathers (in dead game), and household objects, as well as to the social interaction between individuals that forms the subject of a work.

She exhibited at the Society of British Artists (1881/2–1889), the Royal Academy (1882–97), and the Institute of Painters in Oil Colours (1883/4–1895/6). On 9 June 1896 she married the Revd Edward Bruce Mackay (1861–1921), rector of Wallingford and afterwards of Sutton Courtenay, with whom she had four children. She did not paint after her marriage, and died in Guildford, Surrey, on 3 January 1948.

(Alexandra) Mary Hayllar (b. 1862) was born in Mecklenburgh Square on 18 November 1862. She exhibited still lifes, such as *Lawn Tennis Season* (c.1881; Southampton Art Gallery), and figure subjects usually including children—for example, *Helping Gardener* (exh. RA, 1885; exh. Sothebys, 27 March 1996)—with her subject matter, like that of her sisters, drawn entirely from life at Castle Priory. She was mainly represented at the Royal Academy and the Society of British Artists (1880–85), the Dudley Gallery (1881–4), and the Royal Manchester Institution (1882–4). On 1 July 1885 she married Henry Watkins Wells (b. 1855/6), a brewer, and largely abandoned painting, except for miniatures of children. She had died by 1948. **(Beatrice) Kate Hayllar** (b. 1864) was born on 1 September 1864 at 15 Mecklenburgh Square, London. She exhibited still lifes, often featuring flowers, at the Society of British Artists (1883–1888/9)—where her first exhibited painting was bought by the princess of Wales—and the Royal Academy (1885–98). About 1898 she became a nurse and in 1899 she moved to Bournemouth with her father and sister Jessica. A letter that she wrote shows that she was still alive in March 1948. CHARLOTTE YELDHAM

Sources C. Wood, 'The artistic family Hayllar', *Connoisseur*, 186 (April 1974), 266–73; (May 1974), 2–10 • B. Stewart and M. Cutten, *Chichester artists* (1987) • J. E. Hayllar, 'James Hayllar', priv. coll. [manuscript biographical notes] • H. Ottley, *A biographical and critical dictionary of recent and living painters and engravers* (1866) • R. Ormond, *Early Victorian portraits*, 2 vols. (1973) • Graves, *RA exhibitors* • Graves, *Brit. Inst.* • J. Johnson, ed., *Works exhibited at the Royal Society of British Artists, 1824–1893, and the New English Art Club, 1888–1917*, 2 vols. (1975); repr. (1993) • E. Morris and E. Roberts, *The Liverpool Academy and other exhibitions of contemporary art in Liverpool, 1774–1867* (1998) • exhibition catalogues (1855–91) [Royal Manchester Institution] • exhibition catalogues (1879–85) [Dudley Gallery, London] • exhibition catalogues (1883–96) [Institute of Painters in Oil Colours] • exhibition catalogue (1885) [New Society of Painters in Water Colours] • exhibition catalogue (1891) [Atkinson Art Gallery, Southport] • artist's file, archive material, Courtauld Inst., Witt Library [incl. photographs of many Hayllar pictures, with copies of works from *c*.1878, in 6 albums now in a private collection] • *Ladies Pictorial* (28 Dec 1889), 944–5 • d. cert. [James Hayllar] • b. cert. [Jessica Ellen Hayllar] • d. cert. [Jessica Ellen Hayllar] • b. cert. [Edith Parvin Hayllar] • m. cert. [Edward Bruce Mackay] • d. cert. [Edith Parvin Mackay] • b. cert. [Alexandra Mary Hayllar] • m. cert. [Henry Watkins Wells] • b. cert. [Beatrice Kate Hayllar] • census returns, 1861 • *IGI* • L. Lambourne, *Victorian painting* (1999) • *CGPLA Eng. & Wales* (1920) • *CGPLA Eng. & Wales* (1941)

Likenesses J. Hayllar, self-portraits, 1852–64 (James Hayllar); photographs, Courtauld Inst., Witt Library • E. Hayllar, oils, 1896 (James Hayllar), Forbes Magazine Collection, New York • Jessica Hayllar, portrait, 1906 (Beatrice Kate Hayllar), Courtauld Inst., Witt Library • photograph (Edith Parvin Hayllar), Courtauld Inst., Witt Library • photograph (Jessica Ellen Hayllar), Courtauld Inst., Witt Library

Wealth at death £22,857 4*s*. 7*d*.—James Hayllar: probate, 16 April 1920, *CGPLA Eng. & Wales* • £9825 18*s*. 11*d*.—Jessica Hayllar: probate, 22 Feb 1941, *CGPLA Eng. & Wales*

Hayllar, Edith Parvin (1860–1948). *See under* Hayllar family (*per. c*.1850–*c*.1900).

Hayllar, James (1829–1920). *See under* Hayllar family (*per. c*.1850–*c*.1900).

Hayllar, Jessica Ellen (1858–1940). *See under* Hayllar family (*per. c*.1850–*c*.1900).

Hayllar, (Beatrice) Kate (*b*. 1864). *See under* Hayllar family (*per. c*.1850–*c*.1900).

Hayllar, (Alexandra) Mary (*b*. 1862). *See under* Hayllar family (*per. c*.1850–*c*.1900).

Hayls, John (*d*. 1679), portrait painter, is of obscure origins; his surname is presumed to be British. With his daughters Elizabeth and Katherine, Hayls—there described as 'my cozen'—was a beneficiary in the 1672 will of the portrait miniaturist Samuel Cooper. At one time there was professional competition between the two men. In the 1720s the engraver and writer George Vertue described an oval self-portrait miniature by Hayls (now lost) as 'not well drawn but strongly colour'd … this I suppose was one of his essays in Water Colours. with intent to oppose. S. Cooper.limner [i.e. miniaturist]' (Vertue, *Note books*, 2.22). Elsewhere Vertue recorded that 'Samuel Cooper limner, tryd at Oyl Painting. Mr Hayles seeing that turnd to limning & told Cooper that if Quitting limning he would imploy himself that way. For which reason Cooper kept to limning' (ibid., 1.124). Vertue's drawn copy of another now-lost miniature of Hayls, done by John Hoskins (probably the younger) in 1656, is now in the British Museum; Hoskins was Cooper's cousin and thus probably also related to Hayls.

John Hayls may have had contact with the internationally renowned Delft-based portraitist Jan Michiel Mierevelt (1567–1641), whose recipe for vermilion paint—which involved grinding the pigment in urine—he passed on to Richard Symonds. Symonds also described how Hayls cleaned his brushes in 'common oil' and linseed oil, and rinsed them in oil of turpentine, but never in soap. These references in Symonds's notebook for 1651, written in Rome, have led to the supposition that Hayls was living

there too, but it is more likely that Hayls gave this information to Symonds in London. Hayls was active in England as a portraitist from the 1640s until at least the late 1660s, and in 1658 was named by Sanderson among the leading artists there. In London, Hayls lived at Southampton Street in a house taxed at ten hearths, before moving by June 1668 to the south side of Long Acre, in Covent Garden, an area inhabited by a number of artists, including the leading court portraitist of the time, Sir Peter Lely. Hayls also leased three messuages in Hart Street nearby (Edmond, 197 n. 204). According to Buckeridge, Hayls 'was so excellent a copist, that many of the portraits which he did after Vandyck, pass at this day for originals' (Buckeridge, 382). Certainly Van Dyck's influence is evident in the poses and compositions of Hayls's few surviving works.

As Hayls did not sign his paintings, his style has had to be deduced through careful examination of a handful of documented portraits. The most celebrated of these is his comparatively late image of Samuel Pepys (1666; NPG). From 1666 to 1668 Pepys's diary contains many references to Hayls, whom he also commissioned to portray his wife and his father. These start in February 1666 when Hayls began Mrs Pepys's portrait 'in the posture we saw one of my Lady Peters [now unidentified], like a St Katherine' (Pepys, 7.44). On 24 February Pepys visited Hayls's, where his wife was sitting to him among her friends, 'and there sung and was mighty merry' (ibid., 7.53); on 14 March he noted 'how suddenly [Hayls] draws the Heavens, laying a dark ground and then lightening it when and where he will' (ibid., 7.72). On 17 March Pepys paid Hayls £14 for her completed painting (apparently destroyed in the nineteenth century; engraved *c*.1828 by J. Thomson) and 25*s*. for the frame, and began to sit for his own portrait on the same financial terms. 'I sit to have it full of shadows, and do almost break my neck looking over my shoulder to make the posture for him to work by', he complained; all sittings took place at Hayls's premises (ibid., 7.74–5). A fortnight later Hayls and his kinsman Samuel Cooper met Pepys in the Covent Garden coffee house and took him to Cooper's nearby studio. Pepys spent an hour with Hayls in the galleries at Whitehall Palace on 13 April, where the artist pointed out the characteristics of different painters, and Pepys subsequently insisted that Hayls paint out the landscape background in his own portrait: 'I perceived he doth not like it so well—however, is so civil as to say it shall be altered' (ibid., 7.103). On 14 June Pepys accompanied his wife and father to Hayls's, where they viewed the picture of Pepys senior. Two years later, on 19 July 1668, Hayls, Cooper, and others dined at Pepys's, who proudly described them as 'all eminent men in their way' (ibid., 9.265), and on 5 September the diarist visited Hayls's new house in Long Acre (ibid., 9.299).

A 'Mr Hales' appeared before the court of the Painter-Stainers' Company on 29 June 1669 in connection with the 'Lacquery Pattent' (Whinney and Millar, 187 n. 3). A 'Mr Haies' was one of four painters under consideration in 1670 for the major commission to paint a series of twenty-two portraits of judges for the aldermen of the City of London, but lost out to John Michael Wright (Howgego, 21). A 'St Sebastian by … Hayes' was presented to the Painters' Guildhall by the artist (later destroyed; see Vertue, *Note books*, 2.30 and [J. D. Crace], *A Catalogue of the Pictures … at Painters' Hall*, 1908, 11, no. 45). Both these references are thought to be to Hayls.

Vertue recorded Hayls's death, recounted by a Mr Green, thus: 'Mr. Hayls painter. Dyd at his house in long Acre. Comeing from the necessary house [the lavatory] he dropt down dead in the Garden. Being drest in a Velvet suit ready to go to a Ld Mayors feast' (Vertue, *Note books*, 1.31). Hayls was buried at St Martin-in-the-Fields, London, on 27 November 1679, and letters of administration were granted to his widow, Katherine.

Hayls must have had an extensive *œuvre*, but few surviving works have been certainly identified. Robert White's engraving of his image of the miniaturist and poet Thomas Flatman was prefixed to the third edition of Flatman's *Poem and Songs* (1682), and a portrait of the musician Richard Low was mezzotinted by Isaac Beckett as after 'Hays' (both originals are lost). In 1729 three portraits at Woburn Abbey, Bedfordshire, were inventoried as being by 'Hales', two of which, *Colonel John Russell* (c.1645) and *Ladies Diana and Anne Russell* (c.1658), remain there (Vertue, *Note books*, 2.40–41). A few other portraits elsewhere bear inscriptions stating that they are by 'Hales', and from this small group and the Pepys portrait characteristics of his style have been discerned, enabling further works to be attributed to him.   KAREN HEARN

Sources Pepys, *Diary* · C. H. C. Baker, *Lely and the Stuart portrait painters: a study of English portraiture before and after van Dyck*, 2 vols. (1912), vol. 1, pp. 130–37; vol. 2, pp. 121, 182 · M. Edmond, 'Limners and picturemakers', *Walpole Society*, 47 (1978–80), 60–242, esp. 106–7, 111 · M. Beal, *A study of Richard Symonds* (1984), 18, 113, 229, 233 · M. K. Talley, *Portrait painting in England: studies in the technical literature before 1700* (1981), 200, 204–5, 235, 319, 378 · Vertue, *Note books*, 1.22, 31, 43, 83–4, 111, 124, 142; 2.2, 22, 30, 40; 4.3, 31, 101, 108, 173 · W. Sanderson, *Graphice: the use of the pen and pensil, or, The most excellent art of painting* (1658), 20 · D. Piper, *Catalogue of seventeenth-century portraits in the National Portrait Gallery, 1625–1714* (1963), 269–70 · M. Whinney and O. Millar, *English art, 1625–1714* (1957), 187 · [B. Buckeridge], 'An essay towards an English school of painters', in R. de Piles, *The art of painting, and the lives of the painters* (1706), 398–480, esp. 382–3 · E. Croft-Murray and P. H. Hulton, eds., *Catalogue of British drawings*, 1 (1960), 343–5 · D. Foskett, *Samuel Cooper* (1974), 48–50, 56–7 · E. Waterhouse, *Painting in Britain, 1530–1790*, 5th edn (1994), 100–01, 108, 342–3 n.11 · J. L. Howgego, 'The Guildhall fire judges', *Guildhall Miscellany*, 1/2 (1953), 20–30 · M. S. [M. Smith], *The art of painting according to the theory and practice of the best Italian, French and German painters* (1692), 22 · letters of administration, PRO, PROB 6/55, fol. 12v

Likenesses T. Chambars, line engraving, BM · J. Hayls, self-portrait, miniature · G. Vertue, pencil and sepia drawing (after miniature by J. Hoskins, 1656), BM, NPG; repro. in H. Walpole, *Anecdotes of painting in England* (1762)

Haym, Nicola Francesco (1678–1729), composer and librettist, born on 26 June 1678 at Rome, was conjecturally the eldest of three children of a German, Sebastiano Haym (*d.* before 1700), and his wife, Elena. Nicola was a professional violoncellist in 1694, a member of the Accademia di Santa Cecilia in 1695, a violoncello instructor at the Seminario Romano in 1697, and a composer of oratorios in 1699–1700. In March 1701 he and the violinist Nicola Cosimi arrived at London. Their English patron was Wriothesley Russell, marquess of Tavistock (later duke of Bedford); they lived for four years at his London residence, Southampton House in Bloomsbury, and Haym served him for a decade.

In 1703–5 Haym published twenty-four trio sonatas, composed seven cantatas, and prepared a new edition of Corelli's forty-eight trio sonatas, all presumably for use at private concerts, particularly those of Russell, which were organized by Haym, the 'Master of his Chamber Musick'. When Italian operas began to be produced at London in 1705–10, Haym served as cellist, negotiator for the orchestra, and manager for his 'scholar', the singer Joanna Maria *Lindelheim, 'the Baroness', who conjecturally lived with him in Bow Street, not far from the Drury Lane Theatre. He musically adapted the most successful works: Giovanni Bononcini's *Camilla* (sixty-three performances in 1706–9) and Alessandro Scarlatti's *Pyrrhus and Demetrius* (fifty-nine performances in 1708–17). In 1710–20 he adapted text and music for Italian *pasticci*, adapted texts for one to three operas by Handel, and conjecturally wrote a new libretto, *Tito Manlio*, for Attilio Ariosti. Like his adaptations, this libretto shrewdly minimizes the amount of story-telling in simple recitatives; it instead stresses melodramatic incidents that call for accompanied recitatives and culminate with abjectly languorous or thrillingly heroic arias. In spring 1712 Thomas Clayton, Charles Dieupart, and Haym managed eight public concerts at York Buildings. In spring 1713 Haym managed five that featured singing by the Baroness. He also organized annual concerts for her benefit in 1714–17, when they lived on Bridges Street, Covent Garden.

After Russell's death in 1711 Haym's antiquarian work was encouraged by an annual stipend from Charles Montague, Baron Halifax. After Montague died in 1715 Haym's patron became James Brydges, earl of Carnarvon (later duke of Chandos). In 1716 Haym composed six anthems for use at St Lawrence's, Whitchurch, in Cannons, by Brydges' three singers and six instrumentalists. Then in 1719–20 he published *Il tesoro Britannico*, which contains his engravings and historical comments for 780 ancient medals owned by eighteen private British collectors and Oxford University.

In 1720 Haym was named one of the two principal cellists for the new Royal Academy of Music. In 1722–8 he served as its secretary, which required him to stage-manage twenty-four productions and to adapt texts for at least half of them, including seven by Handel, three to eight by Ariosti, and two by Bononcini. He based most adaptations upon the 313 librettos listed in his sale catalogue (Gibson, 439–65). In 1721–4 he edited recent tragedies by Scipione Maffei and Giovanni Battista Recanati, then edited *La Gierusalemme liberata* by Torquato Tasso. He dedicated his Tasso volumes to George I, and dedicated each of their twenty plates to a British nobleman. He was elected to the Society of Antiquaries on 9 December 1724. By then he lived on Wardour Street, and the 'Baronessa d'Haym' was buried at St Anne's, Soho, on 20 December 1724. 'Jack d' Haym' (*b. c.*1710) was presumably their son; Mr Davis (*fl.* 1733–5), a singing actor raised by Haym, was probably a different person.

Haym's most influential scholarly achievement was an annotated bibliography, *Notizia de' libri rari nella lingua italiana* (1726), which reappeared in Italy (as *Biblioteca italiana*) in five editions of 1728–1803. In 1726–9 Haym was a founder member and secretary of the Academy of Vocal (later Ancient) Music. When Haym died on 31 July 1729 John Lockman was translating his history of music into English. The only known remnants of it are a few of the sixty engraved 'heads' that Haym drew for volume 2 (1550–1729). Those of Thomas Tallis and William Byrd must have been drawn from his imagination, but that of Francesca Cuzzoni must provide a good likeness of a singer he knew well. After his death two sale catalogues listed much that 'the Learned and Ingenious Antiquarian' had collected. The first sale (2–6 March 1730) included 413 items: ancient medals, statues and stones, Renaissance and baroque prints, musical instruments, and furniture. The second (9–18 March 1730) included 1380 books, twenty-six musical scores, and two musical instruments. His obituary enumerated 'great Abilities', then emphasized 'uncommon Modesty, Candour, Affability and all the amiable Virtues of Life. He was, by his own Desire, privately interr'd in St Ann's, Westminster; the Aversion he had always shewn to Pomp and Ostentation accompanying him to the Grave' (*Weekly Medley*).

LOWELL LINDGREN

Sources *A catalogue of the entire collection of the learned and ingenious antiquarian, Mr. Nicola Haym*, 2 vols. (1730) [sale catalogue, London, 2–18 Mar 1830] · L. Lindgren, 'The accomplishments of the learned and ingenious Nicola Francesco Haym (1678–1729)', *Studi Musicali*, 16 (1987), 247–380 · L. Lindgren, 'Haym, Nicola Francesco', *New Grove*, 2nd edn · L. Lindgren, 'Nicola Cosimi in London, 1701–5', *Studi Musicali*, 11 (1982), 229–48 · L. Lindgren, 'Camilla and *The beggar's opera*', *Philological Quarterly*, 59 (1980), 44–61 · J. Milhous and R. D. Hume, eds., *Vice Chamberlain Coke's theatrical papers, 1706–1715* (1982) · W. Dean and J. M. Knapp, *Handel's operas, 1704–1726* (1987) · E. Gibson, *The Royal Academy of Music, 1719–1728: the institution and its directors* (1989) · G. Beeks, 'Handel and music for the earl of Carnarvon', *Bach, Handel, Scarlatti: tercentenary essays*, ed. P. Williams (1985), 1–20 · *The diary of Humfrey Wanley, 1715–1726*, ed. C. E. Wright and R. C. Wright, 1 (1966) · *Weekly Medley* (9 Aug 1729)
Wealth at death considerable: *Catalogue*

Hayman, Francis (1707/8–1776), painter, engraver, and book illustrator, was born perhaps in Exeter, the elder of the two recorded children of John Hayman (*d.* 1713) and his wife, Jane Browne. He was apprenticed for the sum of £84 in 1718 to Robert *Browne, a history painter in London who may have been his maternal uncle. He began his career as a scene painter at Goodman's Fields and Drury Lane theatres. He probably made many stage sets, though evidence of only a few survives. Hayman painted a ceiling decoration showing Apollo and the muses for Goodman's Fields Theatre which was in place by 11 February 1734, two years after the theatre opened (a small watercolour copy by William Capon is in the British Museum). Two years later he was painting scenery at Henry Giffard's rival theatre at Drury Lane for William Pritchard's masque *The Fall*

Francis Hayman (1707/8–1776), self-portrait, 1750

of Phaeton which was 'much admired' (*London Daily Post*, 28 Feb 1736). A couple of months later he was providing scenery to imitate Vauxhall Gardens, which, together with other documentary evidence, suggests that he specialized in landscape effects.

The 1740s were Hayman's most productive period. Following the example of William Hogarth, who became a close friend early in the decade, he began to paint conversation pieces, small-scale full-length portraits, and, occasionally, three-quarter-length portraits. Among the best of them are the portraits of members of the family of Jonathan Tyers, the entrepreneurial proprietor of the pleasure gardens at Vauxhall. Examples of these are in the National Portrait Gallery, London, and Yale Center for British Art, New Haven, Connecticut. Most of his sitters were self-made men with literary or artistic backgrounds. Horace Walpole accurately, though unkindly, described his figures as being 'easily distinguishable by the large noses and shambling legs' (Walpole, 2.325).

Tyers invited Hayman to decorate the supper boxes at Vauxhall with a series of large paintings, the earliest of which were unveiled in 1742. Over fifty of Hayman's supper-box subjects, depicting such subjects as children's games, games of chance, and scenes from plays and contemporary novels, are recorded in contemporary guidebooks to Vauxhall Gardens. Fourteen of the paintings survive (some as fragments); these include *May Day, or, The Milkmaids' Garland* and *Sliding upon the Ice* (V&A) and *The Play of See-Saw* (Tate collection). Seven of Hayman's pen-and-brown-ink designs for his supper-box paintings survive (examples are held in Birmingham City Art Gallery, the Courtauld Institute, and Yale Center for British Art, New Haven, Connecticut). Eighteen of the finished paintings were engraved (by various engravers) and published by Thomas and John Bowles in 1743. Tyers also commissioned him to paint pendants of *The Bad Man* and *The Good Man* at the hour of their deaths for one of the buildings in Tyers's macabre garden at Denbies, near Dorking, Surrey. These have not survived but are known through engravings published in 1783, after Hayman's death. About the same time he was also painting the domed ceiling of a staircase at Little Haugh Hall at Nowton, Bury St Edmunds, Suffolk, with *Apollo and the Muses Crowning Archimedes with a Laurel Wreath*, which remains his only extant architectural painting.

Hayman's versatility as an artist is remarkable: for the rest of his life his output embraced history painting, canvases with theatrical subjects, and portraiture. By the end of the 1740s his conversation pieces reflected a reciprocal influence with those of the young Thomas Gainsborough. Gainsborough appears to have worked closely with Hayman and provided the background landscape for at least one of his portraits (that of Elizabeth and Charles Bedford, *c*.1746; priv. coll.). Hayman is also known to have collaborated with George Lambert the landscapist, and his close friend. In the same decade, under the influence of Hubert-François Gravelot and sometimes with his collaboration, he became one of the most prolific designers of book illustrations. He notably illustrated the 1742 edition of Samuel Richardson's novel *Pamela*, Sir Thomas Hanmer's edition of Shakespeare of 1743-4, and Dr Thomas Newton's editions of Milton's *Paradise Lost* and *Paradise Regain'd* in 1749 and 1752 respectively. Pen-and-ink drawings for some book illustrations exist in the British Museum, the Folger Shakespeare Library, Washington, DC, and Waddesdon Manor, Buckinghamshire. These designs frequently provided subject matter for his larger history paintings. Hayman married twice. Nothing is known of his first wife, but his second wife, whom he married on 25 April 1752 at Petersham in Surrey, was Susanna Fleetwood (*née* Williams), the widow of his friend Charles Fleetwood; he outlived her.

In 1742 Hayman became a member of the Sublime Society of Beefsteaks (the Beefsteak Club); by mid-decade he had become, with Gravelot and James Wills, an active promoter and instructor at the St Martin's Lane Academy; and in 1746, through the influence of Hogarth, he donated *The Finding of the Infant Moses in the Bulrushes* to the Foundling Hospital, where it still hangs as one of the four large canvases for the court room. In 1748 he accompanied Hogarth to France, his only recorded trip abroad. By 1753, against Hogarth's will, the St Martin's Lane Academy sought official recognition and Hayman chaired the committee of artists who wished to establish a 'public academy' (*Daily Advertiser*, 23 Oct 1753). The first stage in this long-drawn-out process was the founding of the Society of Artists, which held its first public exhibition in 1760. So as not to

be deflected from an important commission for four history pictures for the rotunda in Vauxhall Gardens (one was engraved by S. F. Ravenet) Hayman resigned the chairmanship. His successor was George Lambert, who died suddenly in 1765 just as the organization received its royal charter of incorporation. Hayman accepted the presidency, and his easy-going character was considered a valuable asset in handling the disagreements that had developed between the committee and the membership. As Thomas Jones remarked, 'Fran. Hayman persuade[d] the disputants to lay aside their mutual Bickerings, and drown their Heartburnings in bumpers of wine' (Oppé, 13-14). These difficulties must have sapped his artistic strength and he produced little work in the late 1760s; indeed, by this time his work had become tired, characterized by clumsy draughtsmanship and garish colouring.

In 1768 Hayman was voted out of the office of president and retired from the furtive negotiations that culminated in the formation of the Royal Academy on 10 December 1768. In 1770 he was given the post of librarian of the Royal Academy as a sinecure. Plagued by gout, he died in London on 2 February 1776 at the age of sixty-eight and was buried in St Anne's Church, Soho, close to where he lived in Dean Street. His only daughter, Susannah, was granted the administration of Hayman's considerable estate. HUGH BELSEY

Sources B. Allen, *Francis Hayman* (1987) · *London Daily Post and General Advertiser* (28 Feb 1736) · H. Walpole, *Anecdotes of painting in England*, ed. R. Wornum, new edn, 3 vols. (1849); repr. (1876), vols. 2, 3 · *Daily Advertiser* [London] (23 Oct 1753) · A. P. Oppé, ed., 'Memoirs of Thomas Jones, Penkerrig, Radnorshire', *Walpole Society*, 32 (1946-8) [whole issue] · B. Allen, 'Jonathan Tyers's other garden', *Journal of Garden History*, 1/3 (1981), 215-38 · B. Allen, 'Joseph Wilton, Francis Hayman and the chimney-pieces from Northumberland House', *Burlington Magazine*, 125 (April 1983), 195-202 · L. Gowing, 'Hogarth, Hayman and the Vauxhall decorations', *Burlington Magazine*, 95 (1953), 4-19 · Langford sale, London, 15 June 1776 · administration, PRO, PROB 6/152, fol. 171 · index of apprentices, 1710-62, GL, XIV 7/13 · exhibition catalogues (1767-76) [Society of Artists] · *Public Advertiser* (3 Feb 1776)
Likenesses F. Hayman, self-portrait, oils, *c*.1735, Royal Albert Memorial Museum, Exeter · F. Hayman, self-portrait, *c*.1745-1748 (with friends), Yale U. CBA · F. Hayman, self-portrait, oils, *c*.1748-1750 (with Grosvenor Bedford?), NPG · F. Hayman, self-portrait, oils, 1750, Royal Albert Memorial Museum, Exeter [*see illus.*] · J. Reynolds, oils, 1756, RA · D. P. Pariset, stipple, 1769 (after P. E. Falconet), BM, NPG · J. Zoffany, group portrait, oils, exh. 1772 (*The Royal Academicians*), Royal Collection · P. E. Falconet, portrait, BM, NPG
Wealth at death estate to daughter, who received £300 p.a.: W. H. Pyne *Wine and Walnuts*, 2 vols. (1823), 2.37 · limited circumstances: Farington, *Diary*, 4.1558

Hayman, Sir (Cecil George) Graham (1893-1966), industrialist, was born on 1 April 1893 at 91 Blair Street, Bromley, Kent, the son of Charles Henry Hayman, engine fitter, and his wife, Clara Annie, *née* Cuthbert. He left school at fifteen to join the office of a manufacturing chemist. This was followed by two years in a solicitor's office and two in a City finance house. In 1914 he enlisted in the 7th London regiment of the 47th London division, transferring in 1916 to the Royal Engineers where he obtained the rank of sergeant. On 19 October 1918 he married Elsie Lilian Leggett (*d.* 1950), the daughter of a house decorator; they had one son and one daughter. After demobilization he was employed by Industrial Appliances, which was bought out by F. A. Hughes & Co. of London, chemical manufacturers. One of Hughes's directors recruited Hayman in 1922 to be secretary of his firm, Herbert Green & Co., industrial alcohol distillers, which was constructing a distillery at Salt End, Hull. Industrial alcohol production was encouraged by a favourable fiscal regime introduced in response to fears of a petrol shortage and because alcohol was a key raw material for science-based industries. New entrants were extremely unwelcome to the Distillers Company Ltd (DCL) which dominated the trade and in 1925 it acquired the Hull distillery. DCL paid Herbert Green £10,000 to stay out of the business and, confident that competition was quelled, raised industrial spirit prices. However, it overlooked Hayman and D. H. Owen Edmunds, Green's former chairman, who together formed Solvent Products Ltd, building another distillery at Dagenham Dock, Essex, and establishing a strong position in the trade which caused DCL to acquire a 50 per cent holding in 1930. Five years later DCL acquired complete control and in November 1936 Hayman was elected to its board.

DCL was diversifying from the drink trade into chemicals and allied products, a difficult process which required senior personnel with first-hand experience of these activities. Hayman fitted the bill and was involved in the team which negotiated the company's agreement with ICI in 1938. This divided much of the British chemical trade between the two firms, lessening the risk of diversification for DCL. Hayman also served on the committee which implemented the agreement; his other pre-war responsibilities included plastics and plasterboard.

During the Second World War Hayman was seconded to the molasses and industrial alcohol control and in 1942 was appointed chairman of DCL's industrial (chemical) activities. His close links with government departments put the company in a favourable position to obtain modern plants in the post-war disposal of government factories. By 1945 Hayman was the senior director on the industrial side, faced with important strategic decisions about the future of petrochemicals.

In the late 1930s DCL had been involved in tortuous negotiations with British and American oil and chemical companies for a joint venture in the production of heavy organic chemicals from oil. Its great anxiety was that the new developments would disrupt its control over the industrial alcohol market and that synthetic processes would displace industrial alcohol made from molasses. When government support for molasses-alcohol was removed in 1945 it became vital for DCL to find a partner in either the chemical or the oil industry. ICI was the obvious choice, but it decided it could make faster progress without DCL (and without the Anglo-Iranian Oil Company with which it had also been negotiating). Hayman had the demanding task of unravelling the 1938 DCL–ICI agreement while seeking a new partner for hydrocarbons. Success came in September 1947 when DCL and Anglo-Iranian (British Petroleum after 1955) announced a £5 million plan for the manufacture of chemicals in the UK through a jointly-owned subsidiary, British Petroleum Chemicals (after 1956 the British Hydrocarbon Company). The physical expression of this was a massive plant at Grangemouth, Scotland. Other plastics and chemical developments in this period included the partnership with the American firms B. F. Goodrich, which formed British Geon (1945) to manufacture polyvinyl chloride, and the Dow Chemical Corporation, which created the Distrene Company (1953) to make polystyrene. These partnerships did not signify a one-way reliance on American technology, for DCL was exploiting fundamental advances made in its laboratories at Great Burgh, Epsom, under the leadership of Dr Herbert Stanley. DCL's plastics interests were also reorganized with the formation of British Resin Products (1947) and a new factory at Barry, south Wales.

Hayman was appointed chairman of DCL's management committee in 1953. He received a knighthood in 1954 and succeeded Sir Henry Ross as board chairman in April 1958, the first non-whisky appointment. By then he had also become chairman of the Association of British Chemical Manufacturers (1950–53), of British Thermoplastics and Rubber Industries Ltd (1952–60), and of British Plaster Board (Holdings) Ltd, and president of the Federation of British Industries (1957–9). Hayman had always been interested in the wider aspects of industrial policy but his presidency covered a difficult period in relationships between government and industry, particularly over public expenditure. Following his presidency he chaired the federation's restrictive practices committee.

Hayman was an outstandingly successful chairman of DCL and largely responsible for its post-war growth. He made the leading whisky company into a dynamic force in the chemical industry. During ten years of progress and expansion the business doubled in size. Hayman attached great importance to maintaining a sense of identity and common purpose within the DCL Group, paying frequent visits to distilleries, industrial plants, and offices which were scattered across Britain, Australia, Canada, South Africa, and the United States. He retired as chairman on 31 March 1963.

Hayman resided at Larchside, Larchwood Avenue, Sunninghill, Berkshire. Except for golf, he had few interests outside business. He died from cancer on 10 March 1966 at Middlesex Hospital, St Marylebone, London, at the age of seventy-two. The attendance at his memorial service included representatives of corporate Britain and provided an interesting reflection on the social mobility provided by an industrial career in twentieth-century Britain. As Sir Norman Kipping said, 'his education was humble: there were no silver spoons'.   RONALD B. WEIR

Sources *DCL Gazette* (spring 1937), 62; (spring 1958), 37; (spring 1963), 4 · R. W. Ferrier, 'Hayman, Sir Cecil George Graham', *DBB* · R. B. Weir, *The history of the Distillers Company, 1877–1939* (1995) · *The Times* (12 March 1966), 10e · *The Times* (8 June 1966), 14e · *Chemistry in Britain*, 2 (1966), 221 · G. B. Ashford, *Chemistry and Industry* (16 April 1966), 646 · b. cert. · m. cert. · d. cert.
Archives U. Warwick Mod. RC, papers as president of Federation of British Industries
Likenesses photographs, repro. in *DCL Gazette*

Wealth at death £80,714: probate, 27 May 1966, *CGPLA Eng. & Wales*

Hayman, Henry (1823–1904), Church of England clergyman and headmaster, was born on 3 March 1823 in Surrey Street, Strand, London, the eldest son of Philip Bell Hayman, clerk in Somerset House (himself son of Henry Hayman, rector of Lewcombe and vicar of Halstock, Dorset), and his wife, Jane, daughter of John Marshall. One of his brothers, John Marshall Hayman, a barrister and member of the staff of the *Saturday Review*, was lost on the Alps near Zermatt in 1876. Another, Edward Hayman (1828–1849), of Clare College, Cambridge, committed suicide 'as a result of religious mania' (Venn, *Alum. Cant.*). Hayman entered Merchant Taylors' School in October 1832, becoming head monitor before passing with a Sir Thomas White scholarship on 28 June 1841 to St John's College, Oxford. There he graduated BA with second classes in classics and mathematics in 1845, and proceeded MA in 1849, BD in 1854, and DD in 1870. He was treasurer of the Oxford Union in Lord Dufferin's presidency, and in 1845 was offered a seat (number five) in the university eight, but family circumstances prevented him from accepting it. He was a fellow of his college from 1844 to 1855, and received the degree of MA, *ad eundem*, at Cambridge in the latter year. He was ordained deacon in 1847 and priest in 1848. He was curate of St Luke's, Old Street, London, from 1848 to 1849, and of St James's, Westminster, from 1849 to 1851, and was assistant preacher at the Temple Church from 1854 to 1857.

In 1852 Hayman became a schoolmaster, and served until 1855 as an assistant master at Charterhouse under Augustus Page Saunders and Edward Elder and became master of the gown boys, a post only once before held by one who was not a Carthusian. On 19 July 1855 he married Matilda Julia, second daughter of George Westby of Mowbreck Hall, Lancashire. In the same year he was elected headmaster of St Olave's Grammar School, Southwark, and was headmaster of Cheltenham grammar school (to be distinguished from Cheltenham College) from 1859 to 1868, and of Bradfield from 1868 to 1869. He introduced science teaching at Bradfield and tried somewhat unsuccessfully to compel the boys to talk exclusively in Latin.

On 20 November 1869 Hayman was elected headmaster of Rugby School in succession to Frederick Temple. The electors, who passed over the superior claims of John Percival and Theodore Walrond, were the trustees of the Rugby charity, who at that date formed the governing body. All the assistant masters but one protested against the appointment. Hayman's conservative predilections, which probably recommended him to the trustees, were held to be in conflict with the liberal traditions of the school. The feeling of hostility grew when it became known that many of Hayman's testimonials referred to his earlier applications for headships and had been used without the consent of the writers. A leader in *The Times* (6 March 1871) spoke of 'the civil war at Rugby', but the trustees initially supported Hayman's disputed authority as headmaster. In December 1871 a new governing body, including Temple, W. H. Bateson, and G. G. Bradley, all of whom were outspoken opponents of Hayman, was constituted under the Public Schools Act of 1868. They passed a censure on the headmaster in November 1872. Meanwhile the school discipline deteriorated, the numbers dwindled, and when a reduction of the assistant masters became necessary, the headmaster resolved on the dismissal of two of his most prominent opponents on the staff, Arthur Sidgwick and the Revd C. J. E. Smith. Hayman's position was further undermined by revelations of the inadequacy of his classical scholarship and another instance of duplicity in his dealings. On 19 December 1873 the new governors passed a resolution removing Hayman from the headmastership. Hayman did not retire without a struggle. On 18 February 1874 he instituted chancery proceedings to restrain the bishop of Exeter (Temple) and the governing body from enforcing his dismissal. The defendants replied by filing a demurrer. After a seven-day hearing (13–19 March 1874), Vice-Chancellor Sir Richard Malins decided against Hayman, but left each side to pay its own costs. Criticizing the conduct of the governing body, Malins admitted that Hayman had suffered a 'grievous hardship'. Although feelings ran high in the academic world, Hayman had many supporters, and they raised a subscription to pay his costs.

In 1874 Hayman was nominated by Disraeli to the lucrative crown living of Aldingham, Lancashire. He became honorary canon of Carlisle in 1884. A well-known lecturer on church defence and against irreligion, Hayman was honorary secretary of the Tithe Owners' Union in 1891, secretary of King Alfred's League of Justice to Voluntary Schools in 1900, and served as proctor in convocation (1887–90).

Latterly, Hayman's reputation was again compromised when a relative of his wife's drew him into the dubious affairs of the Canadian Pacific Colonisation Society. On 21 March 1892 and 23 January 1893 successful actions were brought against Hayman and other directors of the company by two shareholders, claiming the repayment of their investments on grounds that the company's prospectus was fraudulent. Hayman died at Aldingham rectory on 11 July 1904, and was buried in Aldingham churchyard. He was survived by his wife and their numerous family.

Hayman was a cultured scholar and a fluent speaker and preacher. He contributed several articles to the *Edinburgh Review*, mainly on classical subjects, and wrote generally for the leading reviews of the period. He was a voluminous writer for Smith's *Dictionary of the Bible* between 1863 and 1893. His independent works included Greek and Latin verse translations (1864), an edition of Homer's *Odyssey* (3 vols., 1881–6), and miscellaneous works including *Dialogues of the Early Church* (1) Rome, (2) Smyrna, (3) Carthage (1851), *Retail Mammon, or, The Pawnbroker's Daughter* (1853), *Can we Adapt the Public School System to the Middle Class?* (1858), and *The Epistles of the New Testament* (1900), an attempt to present them in current and popular idiom.

[ANON.], rev. M. C. CURTHOYS

Sources *The Times* (13 July 1904) · private information (1912) · *Rugby School: remarks and judgment of vice-chancellor Sir Richard Malins* *on the demurrer to the bill filed by Revd Dr Hayman against the governing body of Rugby School and the bishop of Exeter* (1875) • J. B. H. Simpson, *Rugby since Arnold* (1967) • Venn, *Alum. Cant.* • *Men and women of the time* (1899) • *Wellesley index* • J. R. de S. Honey, *Tom Brown's universe: the development of the Victorian public school* (1977) • *CGPLA Eng. & Wales* (1904)

Archives Rugby School, albums relating to his resignation | BL, corresp. with W. E. Gladstone, Add. MSS 44370–44514, *passim* • Bodl. Oxf., corresp. with Sir Thomas Phillipps • LPL, corresp. with A. C. Tait and related papers • NL Scot., letters to J. S. Blackie
Likenesses oils, 1912, priv. coll. • photograph, 1912, St Olave's Grammar School, Southwark
Wealth at death £1572 19s. 6d.: probate, 4 Nov 1904, *CGPLA Eng. & Wales*

Hayman, Robert (*bap.* 1575, *d.* 1629), colonist and poet, was baptized at Wolborough, Devon (near Newton Abbot), on 14 August 1575, the eldest of nine children of Nicholas Hayman (*d.* 1606), a prosperous citizen who later served as mayor for both Totnes and Dartmouth and MP for both places (Totnes, 1586, and Dartmouth, 1593), and Alice Gaverocke (*d.* 1578). The family moved to Totnes by 1579 and it was there, as a 'little-little' boy, that Robert was given a 'faire red *Orange*' and a kiss by Sir Francis Drake (Hayman, 58). On 15 October 1590 he matriculated at Exeter College, Oxford, aged fifteen (the college register mistakenly has him as eleven years old). He commenced BA on 8 July 1596. In his supplication for the degree he states that he was planning to study abroad and in a letter of 1 July 1600, carried by Robert to Sir Robert Cecil, his father seeks employment for his son and notes that he has studied at Oxford and Poitiers (*Salisbury MSS*, 10.219). On 16 October 1596 he was admitted as a law student at Lincoln's Inn, but there is no indication that he continued with the law. On 21 May 1604, at St Petrock's, Exeter, he married Grace, daughter of Thomas Spicer; she seems to have died young and there is no record of any children.

Hayman's employment or activities are unknown for some twenty years. Edward Sharpham dedicated to him a play called *Cupid's Whirligig* in 1607, but gives no specific information about his friend. In 1617, however, Hayman was made governor of a plantation called Bristol's Hope near Harbour Grace in Newfoundland. The colony had been financed by the Society of Merchant Adventurers of the city of Bristol. Hayman may have become involved in colonial adventure through John Barker, a mayor of the city and the husband of his sister Grace Hayman. During his fifteen months in Bristol's Hope, Hayman used his leisure hours to write and translate, the result published in London in 1628 (entered in the Stationers' register on 4 June 1628) as *Quodlibets, Lately Come over from New Britaniola, Old Newfound-Land*. The work, dedicated to Charles I, contains in the first part a wide variety of epigrams, some comic and satirical, some memorializing his younger days at Lincoln's Inn and the court, some attacking Roman Catholicism, some directed to a circle of his contemporaries, some to his fellow planters, some celebrating his adventure, and one even praising the Newfoundland weather ('Winter is there, short, wholesome, constant, cleare', p. 31). Hayman owes much to the celebrated Latin epigrams (1606–13) of John Owen, and his translation of

Owen's work makes up a second part of *Quodlibets* (because there is a separate paging and signature series, the two parts are sometimes bound separately).

Hayman remained strongly committed to Newfoundland as a potentially wealthy colony, and he wrote to the duke of Buckingham about 1628 (shortly before the duke's assassination) petitioning him to put forward to the king an enclosed 'Proposition of profitt and honor' regarding the need to continue with the work of plantation, specifically to encourage the city he calls 'Carolinople' (near Harbour Grace). In the 'Proposition', Hayman says 'In this Iland at one tyme I lived fifteene Monethes together, and since I have spent allmost every sommer in it' (BL, Egerton MS 2451, fols. 162–9). Despite his special interest in Newfoundland, Hayman was also looking for other ventures, and so about 1628 he engaged himself with another company of adventurers, under the direction of Robert Harcourt, this time proposing to travel to Guiana and the Amazon River. In his will of 17 November 1628 (28 November 1628, PRO, PROB 11/163, sig. 1, transcribed in Moore Smith) he named his nephew Thomas Murchell as his heir, who was to receive the insurance if this project failed. In that same month he set forth in the *Little Hopewell* from London; by February Hayman was looking into establishing trade on the Wiapoco (now called Oiapoque) River. According to a report made by two of his fellow travellers, about 7 October 1629 Hayman set out in a canoe to travel up river and soon contracted a 'burning fever' which swiftly led to his death. His companions lacked shovels, so they used 'paddles and Cassada irons' to bury him 'close by the waters side' (Anderson, 65–9). His will was proved on 23 January 1633, at the request of one of his creditors. WILLIAM BARKER

Sources D. Galloway, 'Robert Hayman (1575–1629): some materials for the life of a colonial governor and first "Canadian" author', *William and Mary Quarterly*, 24 (1967), 75–87 • G. C. Moore Smith, 'Robert Hayman and the plantation of Newfoundland', *EngHR*, 33 (1918), 21–36 • Wood, *Ath. Oxon.*, new edn, 2.545–6 • HoP, *Commons, 1558–1603*, 2.283 • *Reg. Oxf.*, 2/2.178; 2/3.198 • J. Foster, *Men-at-the-bar: a biographical hand-list of the members of the various inns of court*, 2nd edn (1885) • *Calendar of the manuscripts of the most hon. the marquis of Salisbury*, 10, HMC, 9 (1904), 219 • BL, Egerton MS 2451, fols. 162–169 • R. Hayman, *Quodlibets* (1628) • G. T. Cell, 'Hayman, Robert', *DCB*, vol. 1 • R. C. Anderson, ed., *The book of examinations and depositions, 1622–44*, 2, Southampton RS, 31 (1931), 65–9
Wealth at death allowed for insurance payments: will, Moore Smith, 'Robert Hayman'

Hayman, Samuel (1818–1886), Church of Ireland clergyman and writer, eldest son of Matthew Hayman (1789–1867) of South Abbey, Youghal, co. Cork, and Helen (*d.* 1850), third daughter of Arundel Hill of Doneraile, co. Cork, was born at Youghal on 27 July 1818. He was educated at Youghal by the Revd Thomas Nolan, and subsequently at Clonmel, co. Tipperary, by the Revd Robert Bell DD. He entered Trinity College, Dublin, on 18 October 1835, and graduated BA in 1839.

Hayman was curate from 1841 to 1847 of Glanworth, from 1847 to 1849 of Glanmire, and from 1849 to 1863 of Youghal. He was collated in 1863 to the rectory of Ardnageehy, and in 1867 to that of Doneraile, where he remained until 1872, when, after the disestablishment of the Church of Ireland, he was elected to the rectory of Carrigaline, which had the chapelry of Douglas annexed to it. In 1875 Douglas was constituted a separate benefice, and he took charge of it. During his incumbency he made great improvements in the parish. His restoration of the dilapidated church was completed in 1875. Hayman was also a canon of Cork. On 26 September 1854 he married, at St Anne's, Belfast, Emily, daughter of the Revd Marcus Cassidy, chancellor of Kilfenora, co. Clare, and perpetual curate of Newtownards, co. Down. They had one child, Emily Henrietta Anne. Hayman died at Douglas rectory on 15 December 1886, and was buried in the adjacent churchyard.

Hayman wrote articles and poems for the *Dublin University Magazine* when it was edited by Charles Lever, and contributed articles on topographical and genealogical subjects to a number of journals. He wrote a series of historical accounts of Youghal and the surrounding area, and guidebooks to Youghal and towns on the Blackwater estuary. He also edited 'Unpublished Geraldine documents' for the *Journal of the Royal Historical and Archaeological Association of Ireland*, which were published between 1870 and 1881. He may have been A Country Parson, the author of *Concerning Earthly Love* (1869), a volume of poems.

MARIE-LOUISE LEGG

Sources T. A. Lunham, 'Memoir of the late Canon Hayman', *Journal of the Royal Historical and Archaeological Association of Ireland*, 4th ser., 8 (1887–8), 165–70 · D. J. O'Donoghue, *The poets of Ireland: a biographical and bibliographical dictionary* (1912) · Burke, *Gen. GB* · *Irish Ecclesiastical Gazette* (1 Jan 1887), 13
Archives NL Ire., Youghal deeds

Haymo. *See* Haimo (*supp. fl.* 1054).

Haymo of Faversham. *See* Faversham, Haymo of (*c.*1180–1244).

Hayne, Charles Hayne Seale- (1833–1903), politician, born at Brighton on 22 October 1833, was the only son of Charles Hayne Seale-Hayne (1808–1842) of Fuge House, Dartmouth, and his wife, Louisa, daughter of Richard Jennings of Portland Place, London. His father was the second son of Sir John Henry Seale, first baronet (1785–1844) and MP for Dartmouth, whose family had been connected since the seventeenth century with Devon, where they were large landowners, and held many public offices. Seale-Hayne was educated at Eton College, and was called to the bar at Lincoln's Inn on 30 April 1857. In that year, and in 1860, he unsuccessfully contested Dartmouth as a Liberal. In 1885 Seale-Hayne was elected MP for the Mid (or Ashburton) division of Devon, and retained the seat for the Liberals until his death. He was assiduous in his attendance at Westminster, and in 1892 became paymaster-general in Gladstone's fourth administration; he was also made a privy councillor. He held office until the defeat of the Liberal government in 1895. He was treasurer of the Cobden Club, and took an active part in the local affairs of Devon.

For many years Seale-Hayne held the rank of lieutenant-colonel in the South Devon militia (he published its *Annals* in 1873), and afterwards the same rank in the 2nd Devon volunteer artillery. He died, unmarried, at his London residence, 6 Upper Belgrave Street, on 22 November 1903, and was buried at Kensal Green cemetery. His will established a trust to found Seale-Hayne Agricultural College, near Newton Abbot (later a department of the University of Plymouth).

HARRY TAPLEY-SOPER, *rev.* H. C. G. MATTHEW

Sources *The Times* (23 Nov 1903) · *Western Times* (23 Nov 1903) · *Western Magazine and Portfolio* (Jan 1904) · *CGPLA Eng. & Wales* (1903)
Likenesses B. Stone, photograph, Birmingham Reference Library · photographs, University of Plymouth, Seale-Hayne Faculty of Agriculture, Food, and Land Use · portrait, University of Plymouth, Seale-Hayne Faculty of Agriculture, Food, and Land Use
Wealth at death £119,505 3s. 5d.: probate, 1903, *CGPLA Eng. & Wales*

Hayne, Thomas (1581/2–1645), schoolmaster and author, was born in Thrussington, Leicestershire, one of at least four sons and five children of Robert Hayne. He matriculated on 19 October 1599, aged seventeen, from Lincoln College, Oxford, graduated BA in 1605, and proceeded MA in 1612. He was second undermaster at Merchant Taylors' School, London, from 1605 to 1608, and for some years thereafter an usher at Christ Church Hospital school, London.

Lame from birth, Hayne devoted himself to teaching and scholarship. The most notable of his published works is his *Grammatices Latinae compendium* (1640), a school grammar which, probably influenced by the ideas of Comenius, endeavours 'to follow a right and plain method because that maketh all learning more portable' (Hayne, *Grammatices*, Preface). The preface to this book is valuable for the account it gives of the composite authorship of William Lily's standard grammar. Hayne's religious works include a tract in favour of predestination, *The Equall Wayes of God* (1632), and a pedantic 'proof' that Christ's soul did not 'descend into Hell', *Of the Article of our Creed: Christ Descended to Hades* (1642). His *The Life and Death of Dr Martin Luther* (1641), a translation of Melchior Adam's work, was presented in the belief that Luther 'set up God's truth' (Dedication).

Among the generous bequests in Hayne's will, drawn up on 28 September 1640, when he was still living in Christ Church parish, was the gift of most of his books to the Leicester corporation. He also provided for the maintenance of a schoolmaster in Thrussington and two scholars in Lincoln College, Oxford, and for 20s. to be paid each year to a preacher in Leicester to preach a sermon as a thanksgiving for the defeat of the Spanish Armada. He died on 27 July 1645 and was buried at Christ Church Greyfriars, London. A monument over his grave was destroyed by the great fire.

W. R. MEYER

Sources Wood, *Ath. Oxon.*, new edn, 3.173–5 · T. Hayne, *Grammatices Latinae compendium, anno 1637* (1640) · will, PRO, PROB 11/193, fols. 381v–383 · *Reg. Oxf.*, 2/2, 236, 2/3, 252 · Foster, *Alum. Oxon.* · H. B. Wilson, *The history of Merchant-Taylors' School*, 2 (1814), 1182 · *VCH Leicestershire*, 4.365, 413

Likenesses oils, Leicester Museum and Art Gallery • portrait; formerly in town library, Leicester

Wealth at death considerable: will, PRO, PROB 11/193, fols. 381v–383

Hayne [Haynes], **William** (d. 1631?), headmaster, was admitted to Merchant Taylors' School on 28 April 1564 as 'son of … Haynes late of Bristol, yeoman' (Robinson, 6). In 1571 he was elected scholar of Christ's College, Cambridge, where he proceeded MA, and about 1585 became a teacher of grammar.

Partly through the influence of Anthony Watson, bishop of Chichester, and of Gabriel Goodman, dean of Westminster, Hayne was chosen on 19 May 1599 headmaster of Merchant Taylors' School. For twenty-five years he continued in this post, his more distinguished pupils including bishops Matthew Wren, Francis Dee, and George Wilde; James Shirley, the dramatist; Bulstrode Whitelocke; and Edmund Calamy the elder. Hayne, however, had no taste for drama. When James I came to school to dine, on 16 June 1607, John Heming of the King's Men was hurriedly called upon for help.

Hayne stood in high repute as a grammarian. He published *Certaine Epistles of Tully Verbally Translated* (1611), which contains a spirited and controversial defence of studying literature in English translation, as well as a series of textbooks on Latin grammar. He also edited William Lily's *Lilies Rules Construed* (1603) and John Bradford's *Holy Meditations* (1614).

Merchant Taylors' School flourished under Hayne's care, the numbers exceeding the regulations, but his relations with the teaching staff and the governors (the Merchant Taylors' Company) were not always satisfactory. In 1624 he was dismissed from office upon various charges, including 'much weakness of memory', which could not be legally sustained. These may have been concocted by supporters of his eventual successor, Nicolas Grey. Hayne appealed to the lord keeper, preferred a bill of complaint in the court of chancery, and obtained compensation of £130 from the company on the grounds that the infirmities of age rather than 'insufficiency' had caused the alleged misconduct.

Hayne is said to have died in 1631 at an advanced age. He had a son, John Hayne, of St John's College, Oxford, who from 1616 to 1618 was first under-master at Merchant Taylors'; but Thomas Hayne, also a master of the school and a grammarian, does not seem to have been related to him.

C. J. ROBINSON, rev. S. E. MEALOR

Sources H. B. Wilson, *The history of Merchant-Taylors' School*, 2 vols. (1812–14) • C. J. Robinson, ed., *A register of the scholars admitted into Merchant Taylors' School, from AD 1562 to 1874*, 2 vols. (1882–3) • W. C. Farr, *Merchant Taylors' School* (1929), 40–44 • STC, 1475–1640

Archives Berks. RO, letter to Lady Carew

Haynes. *See also* Haines.

Haynes, Denys Eyre Lankester (1913–1994), museum curator, was born on 15 February 1913 in Harrogate, the younger son and the second of the three children of the Revd Hugh Lankester Haynes (1878–1956) and his wife,

Emmeline Marianne Chaldecott (1885–1968). He was educated at Marlborough College (1926–32) and at Trinity College, Cambridge (1932–5), where he specialized in classical archaeology and gained a first in the classical tripos. After a year in Bonn studying Roman provincial archaeology, he was at the British School at Rome in 1936–7 researching for his first publication, *Porta Argentariorum* (1939, with P. E. D. Hirst).

In 1937 Haynes was appointed assistant keeper in the department of metalwork at the Victoria and Albert Museum, London; he transferred on 11 April 1939 to the British Museum's department of Greek and Roman antiquities, a vacancy having arisen following the scandal about the over-cleaning of some of the Elgin marbles in preparation for a new exhibition in the Duveen gallery. On the outbreak of the Second World War he assisted in the enormous task of packing the collection for storage before being transferred to the War Office. He enlisted in the Royal Artillery on 11 September 1941, but later transferred to intelligence, serving in General Alexander's map room during the Italian campaign. He was later reticent about his war service, since he was long under orders not to reveal that his job during the Italian campaign involved the use of intercepted information decoded with the Enigma machine. In 1945 he was posted to Tripoli as antiquities officer. There he wrote the *Historical and Archaeological Guide to Ancient Tripolitania* (1946), revised in 1956 as *Antiquities of Tripolitania*.

After returning to the British Museum in September 1946, Haynes helped to retrieve the collection from storage and to reinstall the exhibitions in those rooms that had survived the war. On 18 January 1951 he married Dr Sybille Edith Overhoff (b. 1926), a distinguished classical archaeologist whose contribution to Etruscology was later recognized by her appointment as MBE (1976). They lived for some years near the museum at 89 Great Russell Street, but moved in 1959 to 24 Hereford Square, South Kensington. They had no children.

In 1953 Haynes was elected a corresponding member of the German Archaeological Institute, full membership following in 1957. In 1954 he was promoted to deputy keeper of Greek and Roman antiquities at the British Museum, and he became keeper in 1956. Most of the collection had by then been reinstalled, but Haynes had to oversee the renewal of the Duveen gallery, which had been bombed in 1940. To mark its opening in 1962 he revised the old guidebook, adding a section on the history of the Elgin marbles to make *An Historical Guide to the Sculptures of the Parthenon*. Meanwhile he had also written *The Parthenon Frieze* (1958). A new exhibition on Greek and Roman daily life was also inaugurated in 1962. *The Portland Vase* (1964) had rather more in the way of scholarly footnotes and analytical bibliography than its companion volumes in the British Museum's series of 'popular' booklets.

Haynes's greatest contribution to the British Museum's permanent exhibition was to transform ten rooms on the ground floor that had been built at intervals in the nineteenth century to display new acquisitions of sculpture.

New walls and floors made it possible for them to become a suite of fourteen rooms adjacent to the Duveen gallery to exhibit selected works in many media, chronologically arranged to illustrate the development of classical art from the Greek Bronze Age to the Roman empire. The new exhibition was opened on 3 July 1969 by the duke of Edinburgh. An album of photographs with commentaries by Haynes, prepared for the occasion, was published in facsimile as *Fifty Masterpieces of Classical Art in the British Museum* (1970).

Outside the museum Haynes was active in the societies for the promotion of Hellenic and Roman studies and served on the council and the executive committee of the British School at Rome. He was elected chairman of the Society for Libyan Studies in 1974.

Witty, cheerful, and ever courteous, Haynes ran his department on a light rein, earning the affection as well as the respect of his staff. Exhibition work and administration limited the time that he had available for scholarship. In 1975 a small book entitled *The Arundel Marbles* was published by the Ashmolean Museum, but it was not until after his retirement in 1976 that he was able to publish as *Greek Art and the Idea of Freedom* (1981) the lectures that he had delivered as Geddes-Harrower professor of Greek art and archaeology at the University of Aberdeen in 1972–3. Throughout his career his major research interest was in ancient bronzes, and his monograph *The Technique of Greek Bronze Statuary* appeared in 1992.

In retirement Haynes lived at Merle Cottage in Dean, Oxfordshire, moving in 1985 to 80 Banbury Road, Oxford. He served as visitor to the Ashmolean Museum from 1979 to 1987. He died of ischaemic heart disease in the Acland Hospital, Oxford, on 27 September 1994, and was cremated at Oxford crematorium on 5 October 1994. He was survived by his wife, Sybille. A memorial meeting was held in the Duveen gallery on 23 November 1994. A series of annual lectures at the British Museum in his memory was inaugurated in 1996.   B. F. COOK

Sources *The Independent* (6 Oct 1994) · *The Times* (11 Oct 1994) · establishments lists and official papers, BM · appreciations by Sir Ernst Gombrich, Professor C. M. Robertson, Professor B. Shefton, and B. F. Cook, read at the memorial meeting, Duveen gallery, BM, 23 Nov 1994, BM, department of Greek and Roman antiquities · registrar-general's indexes to births, 1878, 3rd quarter, Evesham, 6 c 339 [father] · registrar-general's indexes to births, 1885, 1st quarter, Dorking, 2 a 164 [mother] · Marlborough College archives · *WWW*, 1991–5 · private information (2004) [Sybille Haynes, widow] · personal knowledge (2004)
Archives BM, official papers, reports to trustees
Likenesses A. Freeth, pen and wash, 1937, priv. coll. · group portrait, photograph, *c*.1956, BM · photograph, pubd 1956, repro. in *The Times* · group portrait, photograph, 1993, BM
Wealth at death under £125,000: probate, 16 Dec 1994, *CGPLA Eng. & Wales*

Haynes, Edmund Sidney Pollock (1877–1949), lawyer and writer, was born on 26 September 1877 at 9 Upper Bryanston Street, London, the eldest child of Edmund Child Haynes (1846–1907), fellow of Queens' College, Cambridge, and solicitor, and his wife, Grace Mary Nicolas Pollock (1857–1910), daughter of Sir Richard Pollock.

Haynes was a precocious child who was lastingly grateful to have been allowed sufficient freedom and leisure as a king's scholar at Eton College to read voraciously and to think for himself. This he continued to do after his election to a Brakenbury scholarship at Balliol College, Oxford, in 1895.

Placed in the second class by the examiners in the final honour school of history in 1899, Haynes had only a selective respect for dons, and, heeding the advice of his kinsman (and hero) Sir Frederick Pollock, he rejected the possibility of an academic career. He was articled to his father on 1 January 1900 and found congenial the practical atmosphere of the Lincoln's Inn family solicitors' practice which occupied him for forty-eight years.

His practice allowed Haynes to see the harshness of divorce laws at first hand, and he threw himself into the activities of the Divorce Law Reform Union. The reforming bills which he drafted in 1908 and 1915 made no progress, but he tirelessly campaigned for reform in such works as *Divorce Problems of Today* (1917) and *Divorce and its Problems* (1935). Eventually the skilled parliamentary manoeuvring of A. P. Herbert—who dedicated his autobiographical account, *The Ayes Have It* (1937), to 'ESP Haynes and all the veterans'—secured the enactment in 1937 of reforming legislation. But although the Matrimonial Causes Act of 1937 extended the grounds on which divorce could be obtained, its provisions did nothing to interfere with the king's proctor's elaborate machinery of espionage designed to prevent the divorce by consent for which Haynes consistently argued.

Haynes's belief in rationalizing divorce was not founded on any lack of respect for the family. On the contrary, though a strong supporter of women's suffrage, equal pay, and the end of sex discrimination in the professions, he believed that a woman's highest function was to produce and raise children, thereby preserving society from the disintegration resulting from the destruction of the family as an institution.

Although his contribution to the movement for divorce reform may in retrospect constitute Haynes's most significant achievement, his interests were broad and some thirty volumes (many of them collections of essays and notes on literary, political, and philosophical subjects) were published in his lifetime. The starting point of many was his strong commitment to individual liberty and hence to private property, as exemplified in *The Enemy of Liberty* (1923). He believed democracy to be in danger of destruction, if not by trade unions given power to interfere with freedom of labour and contract then by small groups of faddists able to deploy the powers of the modern state to reduce everyone to the same level of servitude, whether by insisting on compulsory social welfare or by prohibiting street gambling, courtship in public, consumption of alcohol, or even nude bathing in the Thames at Eton and elsewhere. Haynes was fiercely critical of organized religion's record of oppression and was for many years a militant supporter of the Rationalist Press Association, but he came to respect the church to the extent that it protected the individual and the family from the state.

Haynes's immutable routine allowed him to savour the pleasures of the table and of conversation in full measure. His conversation and idiosyncratic hospitality (dispensed from a table described by his daughter as embowered in bottles of wine, Worcester sauce, garlic, vinegar, and a variety of patent medicines) inspired—notwithstanding moments of terrifying anger—affectionate friendship with men and women of all ages (including G. K. Chesterton, Hilaire Belloc, John Buchan, Charles Scott-Moncrieff, H. G. Wells, and E. J. Dent).

Haynes married on 1 September 1905 Oriana Huxley Waller, granddaughter of T. H. Huxley and descendant of the poet Edmund Waller; the couple had three daughters, one of whom (Renee) contributed a perceptive biographical memoir to *The Lawyer, a Conversation Piece* (a selection of Haynes's writings published posthumously in 1951). Sadly, Haynes's intolerance of bureaucracy led him, in the stress of wartime conditions, to disregard the accounting formalities imposed on solicitors by the Law Society and in consequence his name was struck off the rolls in 1948 on the thirtieth anniversary of the armistice which had brought to an end the conflict he regarded as marking the world's descent from civilization to barbarism. Haynes was shocked by this disgrace, and did not recover from pneumonia consequent on a domestic accident. He died at home, 5 Marlborough Hill, London, on 5 January 1949; he was survived by his wife.   S. M. CRETNEY

Sources E. S. P. Haynes, *The lawyer, a conversation piece* (1951) [autobiographical introduction] • A. Waugh, 'Introduction', in E. S. P. Haynes, *A lawyer's notebook* (1936) • I. A. Hunter, 'An iconoclastic lawyer: E. S. P. Haynes remembered', *Chesterton Review*, 8 (1987), 193–206 • private information (2004) • WWW • b. cert. • m. cert. • d. cert. • CGPLA Eng. & Wales (1949)

Archives BL, corresp. with G. K. Chesterton and F. A. Chesterton, Add. MSS 73230, fols. 1–6; 73237, fols. 154–159v; 73455 B, fol. 233

Likenesses photographs, priv. coll.

Wealth at death £10,650 18s. 7d.: probate, 24 March 1949, CGPLA Eng. & Wales

Haynes, Sir George Ernest (1902–1983), social work administrator, was born on 24 January 1902 at 27 St Anne's Road, Middlewich, Cheshire, the eldest son of Albert Ernest Haynes, railway porter, and his wife, Sarah Anne Jackson. He was educated at Sandbach School, Cheshire. After graduating BSc from Liverpool University in 1922 Haynes worked as a schoolmaster in a slum area of Liverpool from 1923 to 1928 before taking up the post of warden of the Liverpool University Settlement. He married Kathleen Norris Greenhalgh (b. 1900/01), schoolteacher, on 31 July 1930; they had two daughters.

In 1933 Haynes joined the staff of the National Council of Social Service (NCSS) as a regional organizer in the depressed industrial areas of the north-west. The NCSS (which became the National Council for Voluntary Organisations in 1980), founded in 1919, had grown out of a number of local councils of social service and guilds of help set up before and during the First World War. From the start it saw its role as a co-ordinator of voluntary organizations

and official bodies involved in social work. Haynes moved to the London headquarters of the NCSS in 1936, becoming deputy secretary soon afterwards, and in 1940 he was appointed director.

The NCSS had already set up a Standing Conference of National Organizations in 1938 to enable the statutory authorities to enlist help from voluntary organizations in wartime; this was important in co-ordinating action during the blitz and evacuation. During the war Haynes set in motion a number of new initiatives, including the creation of the rural industries equipment fund: this lent money to village craftsmen, enabling them to buy new equipment. Haynes was appointed CBE in 1945 in recognition of his contribution to the war effort.

One of the aims of the NCSS was to collect and disseminate information. Following discussions during the winter of 1938–9 between various national and local voluntary organizations on how best to help civilians in the event of war, the first 200 Citizens' Advice Bureaux, local centres for advice and information staffed by volunteers, opened the day war broke out in 1939. These were set up mainly by established organizations such as the Charity Organization Society, and the NCSS helped to establish them in areas where no existing organization could set up a bureau. The NCSS, in its *Citizen Advice Notes*, provided information based on official documents but laid out simply and clearly. During the war Haynes set up a department of studies and research, directed by Henry Mess (1884–1944). This prompted several publications, starting with *Our Towns: a Close-up* (1943), based on research done by the women's group on public welfare; then came *Dispersal* (1944), a study, based partly on the experiences of wartime evacuation, of the social consequences of moving office staff permanently out of London and the big cities. There followed *Holidays* (1944), a study of the likely consequences of statutory paid holidays, *British Restaurants* (1946), which considered the lessons to be drawn from wartime developments in communal feeding, and *The Neglected Child and his Family* (1948). Haynes was also responsible for the fortnightly BBC radio programme *Can I Help you?*, broadcast from 1940, dealing with servicemen's problems.

After the war Haynes recognized the need for the NCSS to develop international co-operation in the social services, and helped to set up the Council of British Societies for Relief Abroad to co-ordinate the work of voluntary agencies in Britain dealing with the problems of relief in liberated Europe. In 1947 he chaired a conference of international voluntary organizations at UNESCO headquarters in Paris; this discussed plans for relief and reconstruction following the closing down of the United Nations Relief and Rehabilitation Administration. He also helped to set up the British Council for Aid to Refugees to help displaced people already in Britain or who might go there from refugee camps in Europe. As president of the International Conference of Social Work from 1950 to 1956, and as British delegate to the United Nations Social Commission from 1962 to 1966, Haynes helped to develop exchanges between British social workers and administrators and those in other countries. He was also a member of the Colonial Office advisory committee on social development from 1947 to 1963.

Haynes played an important part in setting up new voluntary organizations, including the National Children's Bureau, the Council of Small Industries in Rural Areas, and the International Council of Social Welfare. Among the many organizations on whose councils and committees he sat were the British National Conference on Social Welfare (1950–67), the British Association of Residential Settlements (1963–8), and the Invalid Aid Association (1964–9). He was vice-chairman of the Family Welfare Association from 1961 to 1966.

Haynes was knighted in 1962. He retired as director of the NCSS in 1967 after twenty-seven years in the post, but he continued to take part in public life, as chairman of the Standing Conference on Legal Aid from 1973 to 1975, and as president of the National Association of Citizens' Advice Bureaux from 1978 to 1981. Sir George Haynes died in Queen Mary's Hospital, Roehampton, on 5 March 1983 from pneumonia. His wife survived him.

ANNE PIMLOTT BAKER

Sources H. Mess, *Voluntary social services since 1918* (1947) · M. Brasnett, *Voluntary social action: a history of the National Council of Social Service, 1919–1969* (1969) · M. E. Brasnett, *The story of the Citizens' Advice Bureaux* (1964) · *The Times* (9 March 1983) · BBC WAC · WWW · b. cert. · m. cert. · d. cert.
Likenesses photograph, repro. in Brasnett, *Voluntary social action*
Wealth at death £43,066: probate, 23 May 1983, *CGPLA Eng. & Wales*

Haynes, Hezekiah (*d.* 1693), parliamentarian army officer and deputy major-general, was the second son of John *Haynes (*d.* 1654) of Copford Hall in Essex and Mary Thornton, daughter of Robert Thornton of Nottingham. A staunch puritan, John Haynes emigrated to New England in 1633 and was later governor of both Massachusetts and Connecticut. Hezekiah returned from New England in 1637 to supervise the sale of some family property. On the outbreak of the first civil war he joined the parliamentarian forces, serving as a captain in Colonel Holborne's regiment of foot. By early 1645 he had risen to the rank of major in Charles Fleetwood's cavalry regiment. He fought at the battle of Preston in 1648, and commanded Fleetwood's regiment at Dunbar in 1650. He probably fought at Worcester in 1651. During the early 1650s he was stationed with Fleetwood's regiment in Essex. In this period he was appointed a JP for Essex, and married Anne, daughter of Thomas Smithsby, former saddler to Charles I. He also purchased some crown lands in Norfolk and Suffolk, but sold these again before the Restoration, though he may have retained some crown property in Essex. Throughout the 1640s and 1650s he was a close friend of the minister of Earls Colne in Essex, Ralph Josselin, who frequently mentions him and his family in his diary.

From the early 1650s Haynes began to carry out administrative as well as military duties for the Commonwealth. In 1653 he served on the committee which investigated how the official posts could be better regulated and the

same year he was appointed to the committee charged with reducing the various government treasuries into a single fund. In 1654 he was named a treasury commissioner and a commissioner for the ejection of scandalous ministers and schoolmasters in Essex and Norfolk. Following the royalist risings of March 1655 Haynes supervised the government's response in Essex and secured a number of prominent royalists who were considered to be major security risks. He remained active in East Anglia throughout the summer, disarming royalist suspects and supervising the raising of the new county troops of horse militia, and on the appointment of the major-generals in the autumn of 1655 he was chosen to act as Charles Fleetwood's deputy in Norfolk, Suffolk, Essex, Cambridgeshire, and the Isle of Ely.

Haynes began work as deputy major-general in early November in Norfolk and over the next few months supervised the taking of security from the royalists of East Anglia and the assessment and imposition of the decimation tax upon them. Among those decimated in Essex was his elder brother, Robert. He also arrested a number of individuals who he believed represented a particular security risk, including the royalist poet John Cleveland, whom he described as 'a most desperate enemy to God and good men' (Bodl. Oxf., MS Rawl. A 32, fols. 647–50). At the end of 1655 he intervened in the election of the chief municipal officers in Colchester, purging the electorate to ensure the return of individuals who supported the government. In July and August 1656 he did all he could to secure the election to the second protectorate parliament of those supportive of Cromwell's regime, but the voters largely rejected his favoured candidates and returned those whom he considered to be the enemies of the godly cause. His letters to John Thurloe, Cromwell's secretary of state, during this period reveal his deep disappointment at the outcome of the election.

Haynes was alarmed by the threat posed by the Quakers in East Anglia, who he reported had held 'considerable meetings' and 'greatly molested' his counties. In the summer of 1656 he arrested a large number and imprisoned them at Bury St Edmunds in Suffolk. He informed Thurloe that some of the local clergy believed the Quakers were 'ripe to cutt throates', and added: 'I thinke their principles would let them if they dared' (Bodl. Oxf., MS Rawl. A 40, fols. 121–4). Haynes sat for Essex in the 1656 parliament. In December, after the house had narrowly rejected a proposal that the Quaker James Nayler should be executed for his blasphemy at Bristol, he suggested that 'his tongue might be slit or bored through, and that he might be stigmatized with the letter B' (*Diary of Thomas Burton*, 1.153). He is not recorded as having taken part in the debates on the Decimation Bill in December 1656 and January 1657. Later in 1657 his elder brother died and left him the family seat of Copford Hall.

Following Oliver Cromwell's death Haynes joined with his commanding officer, Charles Fleetwood, in opposing Richard Cromwell and his parliament and in calling for the return of the Rump Parliament. Later in 1659 he backed Fleetwood and Lambert in their struggle with the

Rump and supported its forcible closure by the army in October. After the Rump's re-assembly in December he lost his commission and was ordered to return home to Essex. He remained there during the summer months of 1660 but was arrested in November on suspicion of involvement in subversive activities and held in the Tower of London for the next eighteen months. He was released in April 1662 after signing a bond of £5000 for his future good behaviour. Following his release he lived quietly at Copford Hall until 1684, when he made the property over to his son and moved to Coggeshall. He died there on 26 August 1693.   CHRISTOPHER DURSTON

Sources W. L. F. Nuttall, 'Hezekiah Haynes: Oliver Cromwell's major-general in the eastern counties', *Transactions of the Essex Archaeological Society*, 3rd ser., 1 (1961–5), 196–209 · Thurloe state papers, Bodl. Oxf., MS Rawl. A · C. H. Firth and G. Davies, *The regimental history of Cromwell's army*, 2 vols. (1940) · PRO, interregnum state papers, SP 18–28 · *The diary of Ralph Josselin, 1616–1683*, ed. A. MacFarlane, British Academy, Records of Social and Economic History, new ser., 3 (1976) · *Diary of Thomas Burton*, ed. J. T. Rutt, 4 vols. (1828) · J. H. Round, 'Colchester during the Commonwealth', *EngHR*, 15 (1900), 641–64 · P. Morant, *The history and antiquities of the county of Essex*, 2 (1768), 195 · I. Gentles, 'The debentures market and military purchases of crown land, 1649–1660', PhD diss., U. Lond., 1969 · PRO, E307, box 10/HI/12 · PRO, C54/3836/28 · PRO, C/54/3872/23 · PRO, C 3972/32 · PRO, C 3876/21
Archives Bodl. Oxf., Thurloe state papers, Rawl. MS A

Haynes, Hopton (*bap.* 1667, *d.* 1749), public official and theological writer, was baptized at Ditcheat, Somerset, on 8 July 1667, the younger son of John Haynes. He may have attended Exeter College, Oxford, matriculating on 22 March 1684. He appears to have entered the Royal Mint as a clerk in 1687. On 23 December 1693 Haynes—then twenty-six and of St Dunstan's, Stepney—was licensed to marry Hannah Sikes (*b.* 1658), the ceremony taking place on the 26th at St Peter Cornhill. In 1695 he was living in Bethnal Green, but a son, Hopton, was baptized on 20 November 1698 at St Mary Colechurch, and another, Samuel, was baptized on 30 November 1701 at St Leonard's, Shoreditch. There were at least two other sons, Newton and Charles, who were admitted to Lincoln's Inn in 1723 as the sons of Hopton Haynes of the Tower of London.

Haynes's administrative ability was much admired by Sir Isaac Newton, master of the mint. He appears to have left his employment in the mint at least twice, only to have been brought back to play a role in the recoinage of 1696–9, specifically instructing the officers and clerks of the five provincial mints. However, despite Newton's support, he was then overlooked for the post of deputy comptroller of the mint and forced to take employment in the excise, under Thomas Hall, who was also an official of the mint. Another mint official, Thomas Neale, employed him as his clerk at £100 until his death in December 1699. Haynes wrote a manuscript entitled 'Brief memoirs relating to the silver and gold coins of England' (1700), which is a major source for studying the recoinage.

Haynes was one of five petitioners for the place of weigher and teller in the mint in August 1701. Newton wrote him a glowing testimonial, in which he referred to Haynes's previous fourteen years' service in the mint 'except two short intermissions' and to his 'general reputation amongst us for integrity, sobriety, good humour and readiness in business. He has a steady hand, writes very fairly, is a very good accountant and skilled in all the business of the Mint' (*Correspondence of Isaac Newton*, 4.375). The Treasury duly appointed him on 30 September 1701.

From about 1710 Haynes was also employed in the tally office of the exchequer, writing to Newton thence in September 1714. In 1718 and 1748 he was described as 'tally-writer', and in 1732 as 'clerk' for the auditor of the receipt, George Montagu, earl of Halifax (in effect his deputy). On 7 February 1723 Haynes overcame the pretensions of Daniel Brattell to succeed to the office of assay-master at the mint. In 1728 he published a defence of the privileges of the mint, *A brief enquiry relating to the right of his majesty's Royal Chapel, and the privileges of his servants within the Tower*. Perhaps in recognition of his long service and advancing years in 1737 he was given a deputy at the mint. In June 1748 there was a complaint made against him that he was no longer capable of fulfilling his duties, and on 7 February 1749 he was retired on full pay.

Much attention has focused on Haynes's religious views. Haynes translated Newton's two letters on the textual criticism of 1 John 5: 7, 8, and 1 Timothy 3: 16. It was through Haynes in 1712 that Whiston corresponded with Newton on the subject of baptism. Richard Baron described Haynes as the 'most zealous unitarian' (*DNB*) he ever knew. Haynes attended Church of England services, but sat down at certain parts to show his dislike; however, the Presbyterian minister at Princes Street, Westminster, Samuel Say, pointed out the inconsistency of this approach, whereupon Haynes never again attended any place of worship. In 1747 he published anonymously *Causa dei contra novatores, or, The religion of the Bible and the religion of the pulpit compared*. The *Scripture Account of the Attributes and Worship of God* was published posthumously in 1750. In it he avowed, 'I will be no Cranmerian, Lutheran, or Calvinist … Fathers and councils, synods and convocations, ancients and moderns, both learned and holy-men, are my fellow servants I embrace them as helps, but I will not follow them as infallible guides' (Haynes, ii).

Haynes died at his house in Queen Square, Westminster, on 18 November 1749, and his will was proved on the 20th. He left his real and personal estate to be divided between his sons, Hopton and Samuel *Haynes, both clergymen. His second wife, Mary Jocelyn (1684/5–1750), survived him, dying on 22 September 1750.   STUART HANDLEY

Sources H. Wagner, 'The descendants of Hopton Haynes', *The Genealogist*, new ser., 20 (1903–4), 280–81 · H. Haynes, *The scripture account of the attributes and worship of God*, 4th edn (1815) · IGI · *The correspondence of Isaac Newton*, ed. H. W. Turnbull and others, 7 vols. (1959–77), vol. 4, pp. 375–6 · J. Redington, ed., *Calendar of Treasury papers*, 6, PRO (1889), 241 · W. A. Shaw, ed., *Calendar of treasury books and papers*, 2, PRO (1898), 236; 3 (1900), 307; 16 (1938), 102, 348, 368, 381 · Foster, *Alum. Oxon.* · C. E. Challis, ed., *A new history of the royal mint* (1992), 380–420 · *London Magazine*, 18 (1749), 529 · will, PRO, PROB 11/774, fols. 282v–283v · J. Craig, *The mint* (1953), 205–31 · G. J. Armytage, ed., *Allegations for marriage licences issued by the vicar-general of the archbishop of Canterbury, July 1687 to June 1694*, Harleian Society, 31 (1890), 277
Archives LUL, memorials relating to the coinage

Likenesses Highmore, oils, DWL · T. Nugent, stipple (after Highmore), BM, NPG; repro. in Harding, *Biographical mirror* (1792)

Haynes, John (1594–1654), colonial governor, was born on 1 May 1594, one of the two sons and nine daughters of John Haynes (d. 1605) of Old Holt, Essex, and his wife, Mary (d. 1619), the daughter of Thomas Mitchell of Hertfordshire. Both of his parents belonged to the locally prominent gentry and Haynes inherited considerable property. At the age of twenty-one, on 11 April 1616, he married Mary Thornton, the daughter of Robert and Anne (*née* Smith) Thornton, of a landed Norfolk family. The couple had six children: John (*b.* 1617), Robert (*b.* 1618), Mary (*b.* 1619), Hezekiah *Haynes (*d.* 1693), a future major-general, Anne (*b.* 1623), and Elizabeth (*b.* 1624). Mary Haynes probably died at or soon after the birth of her last child. About 1625 Haynes purchased the manor of Copford (Coptford) Hall in Essex, a few miles from Epping, which became the home associated with him and his children for generations. The purchase suggests that Haynes expected to remain in England, but within a decade he joined the great puritan migration to New England. Though his attachment to puritanism remains unexplained, he probably became a follower of the great preacher Thomas Hooker in the 1620s. His decision to emigrate in 1633 was surely made in conjunction with Hooker, with whom he sailed. Haynes left his children behind, despite their young ages, opening a wound in the family that was never healed.

Haynes was welcomed to Boston in September 1633 as a godly man of great estate by the governor, John Winthrop, and could have joined the established leadership of the colony, but he preferred to reside in Newtown (Cambridge), where Hooker was pastor and where opposition to Winthrop was centred. Some resented Winthrop because he used his discretionary authority as a magistrate to overlook petty offences while others, like Haynes, wanted to prevent discretionary authority from becoming arbitrary government by adopting a written code of laws, including a magna carta. Haynes, however, had no toleration for dissenting religious opinions and as governor in 1635–6 presided over the expulsion of Roger Williams. In late 1635 or early 1636 he married Mabel Harlakenden (1614–1655), the daughter of Robert Harlakenden, a wealthy and prominent puritan leader, and his wife, Margaret (*née* Hubbart or Hubbard). Haynes had five children with his second wife: Ruth (*b.* c.1636), John (*b.* c.1638), Roger (*b.* 1640), Joseph (*b.* 1642), and Mabel (*b.* 1646). After Haynes's death his widow married Samuel Eaton in November 1654, shortly before her own death in July 1655.

In 1637, after Hooker moved to Hartford, one of the Connecticut River towns, Haynes followed and built a 'mansion house' imposing enough to be used by the colony after his death as an official residence for its governors. For the rest of his life he played a crucial role in the establishment of Connecticut. He helped write the fundamental orders of 1639 and was the first governor elected under that instrument of government. For nearly every year thereafter he was elected governor or deputy governor. In 1643 he helped form the Confederation of New England, an intercolonial union, but because he distrusted Massachusetts Bay, he refused to allow the confederation the authority to interfere in the internal affairs of the member colonies. In late 1646 he was sent on a brief trip to England to try to secure a charter for Connecticut, but returned empty-handed. He was especially important in Connecticut's Indian affairs and though he did much to enforce the protectorate that the English colonists exerted over the Indians of southern New England, he achieved a reputation for being fair and humane. During the 1637 Pequot War, when massacres by both sides were common, he was noted for being 'almost averse from killing women and children' (R. Williams to J. Winthrop Jr, 30 June 1637, *Winthrop Papers*, 2.436–7). After the war, when he was given the duty of parcelling out the captives, he enslaved none for his personal use.

Although Haynes was granted hundreds of acres by Connecticut in reward for his services, he spent much more than he earned. According to his son Hezekiah, Haynes took £10,000 from his English estates to maintain himself and his new family in America, 'to the almost ruine of his family in England' (H. Haynes to J. Winthrop Jr, 27 June 1675, *New England Historical and Genealogical Register*, 24, 1870, 124–5). Even so, he was usually short of cash. He sent two of his sons to Harvard but paid every penny of their fees and tuition in commodities. When he dowered his daughter Ruth, he was unable to provide further for her in his will. His estate was valued at £1540 in 1646 but at £140 less when he died eight years later. Some time in early January 1654, after a convivial evening with friends, he returned home, led his family in prayers, and went to bed in apparent good health. During the night he had trouble breathing and died without saying a word. His death was reported on 9 January. He was buried in the cemetery of the First (Center) Church in Hartford, where a replica of his tombstone, with the death date incorrectly given, still stands.

Haynes seems to have been a friendly, cheerful sort of person whose writings sometimes display a poetic gift for striking imagery. What is most interesting about him is his distrust of Massachusetts Bay and concomitant dedication to Connecticut. He originally envisioned New England as a place where a purified, orthodox form of Christianity was to be practised, and therefore approved the expulsion of dissenters like Roger Williams and Anne Hutchinson. In time, however, he came to believe that 'the most wise God hath provided and cut out this part of his world for a refuge and receptacle for all sorts of consciences' (R. Williams to Major [J.] Mason, 22 June 1670, *Collections of the Massachusetts Historical Society*). For Haynes, it was Connecticut, not Massachusetts Bay, that was more likely to fulfil that providential mission, and so, at great cost, he founded a great state. JAMES P. WALSH

Sources C. E. Cuningham, 'John Haynes of Connecticut', *New England Quarterly*, 12 (1939), 654–80 · H. M. Ward, 'Haynes, John', *ANB* · R. C. Anderson, ed., *The great migration begins: immigrants to New England, 1620–1633*, 3 vols. (Boston, MA, 1995) [incl. genealogical data,

terms of office served, and land transactions.] · *New England Historical and Genealogical Register*, 148 (1994), 240–54 · *The Winthrop papers*, ed. W. C. Ford and others, 6 vols. (1929–92) · J. H. Trumbull, ed., *The public records of the colony of Connecticut*, 1 (1850) · *The journal of John Winthrop, 1630–1649*, ed. R. S. Dunn, J. Savage, and L. Yeandle (1996) · P. Morant, *The history and antiquities of the county of Essex*, 2 vols. (1768) · *Collections of the Massachusetts Historical Society*, 1 (1792), 257–83 · C. W. Manwaring, 'Haynes, John', *A digest of the early Connecticut probate records*, 1 (1904) · I. M. Calder, 'Haynes, John', *DAB* · *DNB*
Archives Connecticut State Library, Hartford, Connecticut archives · Mass. Hist. Soc., Winthrop MSS
Wealth at death £1400 16*s*. 3*d*.: Manwaring, 'Haynes, John', 124–5.

Haynes, John (*fl.* 1735–1753), printmaker and draughtsman, was active between about 1735 and 1753. As no details survive of his birth or life, any information regarding his whereabouts and interests must be derived from his work. From this it seems probable that he was based in York or its environs and this is further supported by George Vertue's reference to a large engraved plan of that city 'by Hains of York' (Vertue, *Note books*, 6.145) published in 1748. John Haynes's earliest known prints were illustrations to Thomas Gent's *Annales regioduni Hullini, or, The history of the royal and beautiful town of Kingston-upon-Hull* (1735). These modest plates of antiquarian monuments and topographical views, such as *The East View of Kingston upon Hull*, were executed in a mixture of etching and engraving. This mixed technique can be seen in a number of his antiquarian-orientated prints of local ruins, as well as in the other bird's-eye prospects and composite plates that he executed at Gent's 'Expence' (T. Gent, *Annales regioduni Hullini*, 1735, title-page). According to Richard Gough, in his *Anecdotes of British Topography* (1768), Haynes was better as a draughtsman providing many 'good drawing[s]' for people such as Henry Toms to engrave.

The publication line on the plates for Gent's book gives further information on John Haynes's career, giving his address as Fossgate, York, and his trade as 'Engraver & Copper plate Printer in York'. His contributions to the architectural designs for Francis Drake's antiquarian account, entitled *Eboracum, or, The History and Antiquities of the City of York* (1736), indicate further connections with this area, as does his own drawing *The Dropping Well at Knaresborough as it Appeared in the Great Frost, January 1739*, which he published as an etching in 1740. Although Haynes did engrave and etch a number of his own designs he was also a draughtsman, occasionally on behalf of the Society of Antiquaries in London and, more frequently, for publishers of local antiquarian and topographical surveys. By 1753 Haynes appears to have moved to London, where his last known work, an engraving of 'the Mandarine yacht belonging to the duke of Cumberland at Windsor' (Dodd, fol. 234), was published.   LUCY PELTZ

Sources Bryan, *Painters* (1903–5) · T. Dodd, 'Memoirs of English engravers, 1550–1800', BL, Add. MS 33401, fols. 234–5 · [R. Gough], *Anecdotes of British topography*, 2 vols. (1768) · Redgrave, *Artists* · Vertue, *Note books*

Haynes, Joseph (1760–1829), etcher, was baptized at the church of St Mary, Shrewsbury, on 20 February 1761, one of several children born to Thomas Haynes and his wife, Margaret, *née* Mills, of that town. He moved to London in his youth to study under John Hamilton Mortimer ARA. After Mortimer's death in 1779, Haynes made etchings from about a dozen of his paintings, including *St Paul Preaching to the Britons* and *Robbers and Banditti*; these were published by Mortimer's widow between 1780 and 1784 and reissued in 1816 by Thomas Palser. In 1782 he etched four of William Hogarth's paintings: *The Staymaker, Debates on Palmistry*, and portraits of James Caulfeild, earl of Charlemount, and Henry Fox, Lord Holland. In the case of the portraits the original paintings were owned by the printmaker Samuel Ireland, a friend of Mortimer. Haynes was also an acquaintance of Sir Joshua Reynolds and made etchings from his paintings. He worked in the free, graphic style of Mortimer, sometimes on an unusually large scale for pure etching. Some of his work was printed in red as well as black. Both the British Museum and the Victoria and Albert Museum hold prints by Haynes; he is said to have worked in mezzotint also and to have produced some paintings.

The later part of Haynes's life was spent in Shrewsbury and Chester, working as a drawing-master, although it is reputed that he lived for a while in Jamaica. He died in Chester on 14 December 1829. No wife or children are mentioned in his will, which divided his possessions between a sister, a brother, and his housekeeper.
                                                                                  MARY GUYATT

Sources Redgrave, *Artists*, 2nd edn, 205 · Bryan, *Painters* (1903–5), 3.635 · G. K. Nagler, ed., *Neues allgemeines Künstler-Lexikon*, 22 vols. (Munich, 1835–52), vols. 21–2 · J. Nichols, *Anecdotes of Hogarth* (1839), 274 · G. Benthall, 'John Hamilton Mortimer', 1959, V&A NAL, 65, 74, 91, 103–4 · E. G. Salisbury, *Border counties worthies* (1880), 84 · will, Ches. & Chester ALSS, WS1829 [Joseph Haynes of Boughton] · *DNB* · parish register, Shrewsbury, St Mary, 20 Feb 1761 [baptism] · IGI
Archives BM · V&A

Haynes, Samuel (*bap.* 1701, *d.* 1752), historian, was baptized on 30 November 1701 at St Leonard's, Shoreditch, London, the second of at least four sons of Hopton *Haynes (*bap.* 1667, *d.* 1749), public official and theological writer, and his first wife, Hannah Sikes (*b.* 1658). He was educated at King's College, Cambridge, where he matriculated in 1719 and graduated BA (1723), proceeding MA in 1727 and DD in 1748. For some time he travelled as tutor to James Cecil, sixth earl of Salisbury, who in 1737 presented him to the valuable rectory of Hatfield. In 1743 he became canon of Windsor, and in 1747 rector of Clothall, Hertfordshire; he held both livings for the rest of his life. Haynes was for some years engaged in preparing an edition of the valuable state papers at Hatfield which dealt with the career of William Cecil, Lord Burghley. The antiquary William Oldys (1696–1761) wrote on 5 February 1738 that Haynes was then engaged on the work, 'that he had two or three transcribers at work', and 'intended to publish a volume at a time'. On 26 March 1738 Oldys discussed the work at Joseph Ames's house and was invited to assist in the undertaking, but declined on the ground that many papers were to be 'stifled' because they dealt too freely with Elizabeth's 'girlish frolics' (*Literary Antiquary*, 19, 26). The original design seems to have been to continue the work to 1612. However, Haynes completed only one volume, which was published, by subscription, as *Collection of state papers relating to affairs in the reigns of Henry VIII, Edward VI, Mary, and Elizabeth, from 1542 to 1570* (1740). Haynes died on 9 June 1752. William Murdin's two-volume edition, which brought the date of the published papers to 1596, appeared in 1759.

W. A. J. ARCHBOLD, *rev.* PHILIP CARTER

Sources Foster, *Alum. Oxon.* • *GM*, 1st ser., 22 (1752), 289 • Nichols, *Lit. anecdotes* • R. Clutterbuck, ed., *The history and antiquities of the county of Hertford*, 2 (1821), 364; 3 (1827), 505 • A. Chalmers, ed., *The general biographical dictionary*, new edn, 17 (1814), 269 • *A literary antiquary: memoir of William Oldys ... together with his diary*, ed. J. Yeowell (1862) • H. Wagner, 'The descendants of Hopton Haynes', *The Genealogist*, new ser., 20 (1903–4), 280–81

Haynes [Heynes], **Simon** (*d.* 1552), clergyman and religious reformer, was educated at Queens' College, Cambridge, graduating BA in 1515/16, MA in 1519, BTh in 1528, and DTh in 1531. He became a fellow of Queens' in 1516, and was president from 27 July 1528 to 1537. He had been ordained in February 1521, and on 28 November 1528 was admitted to the rectory of Barrow, Suffolk. In March 1530 he helped to secure his university's endorsement of Henry VIII's case for a divorce. In 1532–4 he was vice-chancellor.

On 29 January 1535 Haynes was instituted to the vicarage of Stepney, Middlesex (held until 1537). In the same year he was an official anti-papal preacher in Cambridge and from August to December accompanied Christopher Mont on a special embassy to Paris. Haynes was immediately rewarded with the grant of a canonry of Windsor (21 December 1535). On 6 April 1537 the king further nominated him to the deanery of Exeter, vacant and in the crown's gift by the deprivation of Reginald Pole. The conservative chapter objected to Haynes's appointment, and controversy at once arose over its technicalities. He became, as was necessary, first a canon on 21 June, and was elected dean on 16 July. On 27 July he also obtained the rectory of Fulham, Middlesex (held until his death). Quarrels with the Exeter chapter over his rights and emoluments, and about liturgical customs he wished to abolish, were temporarily composed in January 1538. From April to August that year Haynes went (in the unlikely company of the staunchly conservative Edmund Bonner) on a mission to Charles V in Spain, with the hope of dissuading the emperor from attending a general council which might unite Catholic Europe against England. Also in 1538 he acquired the rectory of Newton Ferrers, Devon (which he held until his death). He was also master of St Anthony's Hospital, London.

Haynes had already diagnosed the south-west as 'perilous' country and its clergy as unlearned, few of them 'well persuaded' (*LP Henry VIII*, 12/2, no. 557). Now, as the king's commissioner, he set about preaching reform and destroying images throughout the diocese of Exeter. He made a few converts among the citizens of Exeter itself, but was for the most part, in the words of John Hooker, 'marvellous hated and maligned at' (Whiting, 75). In his

cathedral he caused particular outrage by despoiling the tomb of the revered Bishop Edmund Lacy. In April 1539 he became a member of the short-lived council of the west. Throughout the 1530s he drafted reformist schemes: in 1537 at the time of the compiling of the Bishops' Book, and in 1539 when he noted what he might have said in parliament against the Six Articles Bill. He also planned to replace the Exeter chapter with a body of preachers, and to make the cathedral more of an academic college with university links. In some ways this anticipated the new cathedral foundations of the 1540s. To one of these, Westminster, Haynes was appointed canon in the foundation charter of 17 December 1540. He was given one of the best houses, and was regularly resident. He was also active at Windsor, and investigation into suspected heresies there in 1543 brought him before the privy council on 15 March. He was committed to the Fleet the following day, and renewed complaints against him from the Exeter chapter were simultaneously investigated. He was released on 5 July without charge, but was reprimanded for 'sowing ... many erronious opinions' (*APC, 1542–7*, 150).

In Edward VI's reign Haynes was increasingly employed: in 1547 as justice of the peace for Devon and visitor of the cathedral and diocese of Exeter, and in Lord Northampton's divorce case, in 1549 as visitor of Oxford University and the colleges of Windsor and Winchester, and in 1549 and 1551 on the heresy commissions. He may have had some hand in the 1549 prayer book; he was certainly sent back to the west in the aftermath of the disorders this provoked. But he was now more often at Westminster, where as treasurer he found economic as well as religious motives for disposing of church ornaments. As soon as clerical marriage was permitted (1549) he took Joan (*d.* 1587), daughter of Nicholas Wallron, as his wife. Their elder son, Joseph, was born in the following year; for him and his younger brother, Simon, their father mapped out a detailed educational curriculum (for the most part achieved, since they both went to Cambridge). Haynes made his will on 12 July 1552 and was dead by 24 October. He bequeathed lands at and near Mildenhall, Suffolk, which was probably his birthplace. His widow married first William May, dean of St Paul's, who died in 1560, and then Thomas Yale, dean of arches; she died on 12 September 1587.

C. S. KNIGHTON

Sources *LP Henry VIII*, 9.54, 180, 1063(15); 12/2.557; 13/1.695; 14/1.743, 1035; 18/1.280, 283, 299, 310, 447, 500, 819 • *APC, 1542–7*, 97–8, 117–18, 126–7, 150–51 • *The acts and monuments of John Foxe*, new edn, ed. G. Townsend, 8 vols. (1843–9), vol. 4, pp. 464, 473, 474, 476; vol. 5, pp. 151, 359; vol. 6, p. 298 • *CPR, 1547–53* • N. Orme, *Exeter Cathedral as it was, 1050–1550* (1986), 95–101 • N. Orme, *Education in the west of England, 1066–1548* (1976), 53–5 • BL, Harley MS 604, fols. 164–167v [printed in G. Oliver, *Lives of the bishops of Exeter* (1861), 477–83] • D. MacCulloch, *Thomas Cranmer: a life* (1996), 193, 301, 305, 307, 369–70 • S. L. Ollard, *Fasti Wyndesorienses: the deans and canons of Windsor* (privately printed, Windsor, 1950), 120 • N. Pocock, ed., *Troubles connected with the prayer book of 1549: documents ... in the record office*, CS, new ser., 37 (1884), 75 • F. Rose-Troup, *The western rebellion of 1549* (1913), 173–7 • R. Whiting, *The blind devotion of the people: popular religion and the English Reformation* (1989), 66, 73, 75, 161, 228, 257 • W. T. MacCaffrey, *Exeter, 1540–1640: the growth of an*

English county town, 2nd edn (Cambridge, MA, 1975), 187–8 • H. Reynolds, *A short history of the ancient diocese of Exeter* (1895), 368–9 • G. M. Bell, *A handlist of British diplomatic representatives, 1509–1688*, Royal Historical Society Guides and Handbooks, 16 (1990), 48, 77–8 • C. S. Knighton, ed., *Acts of the dean and chapter of Westminster*, 1 (1997), 22, 27–8, 36, 44–6, 63 • W. H. Rylands, ed., *The visitation of the county of Buckingham made in 1634*, Harleian Society, 58 (1909), 73 • will, PRO, PROB 11/35, fols. 228–30

Archives BL, proposal for reform of Exeter Cathedral, Harley MS 604, fols. 164–167v • BL, proposals for reform, Cotton MS Cleop. E 5, fols. 51–2

Wealth at death £2 8s. 0d. rent p.a. from property at Mildenhall, Suffolk ('ontreat' from 'head mesuage'): will, PRO, PROB 11/35, fols. 228–30

Haynesworth, William (*fl.* 1659), engraver, is known for a half-length engraved portrait of Richard Cromwell as lord protector. Copies of this rare print are in the print room at the British Museum and in the Sutherland collection in the Bodleian Library at Oxford. Haynesworth also engraved a print of Geffroy de Lusignan, a copy from a similar engraving by Jérôme David. He was one of the earliest English engravers.

L. H. CUST, rev. ANNE PUETZ

Sources Redgrave, *Artists* • J. Strutt, *A biographical dictionary, containing an historical account of all the engravers, from the earliest period of the art of engraving to the present time*, 2 vols. (1785–6) • Bryan, *Painters* (1886–9) • T. Dodd, 'Memorials of engravers in Great Britain, 1550–1800', BL, Add. MS 33401 • *Engraved Brit. ports.*, 6.627 • Thieme & Becker, *Allgemeines Lexikon* • Bénézit, *Dict.*, 3rd edn, vol. 5

Hays, Mary (1759–1843), writer, was born on 4 May 1759 in Southwark, London, the daughter of John and Elizabeth Hays, rational dissenters living at 5 Gainsford Street, Southwark, and worshipping at Blacksfields Particular Baptist Chapel on the corner of the street. Her father was a mariner in the merchant fleet and died in or before 1774 when his daughter Sarah married. Mary's siblings included Sarah, Joanna, Elizabeth, John, and 'little Tommy'. The death of her father was the first in a series of 'blows' which encouraged a deep belief in determinism which was to influence Mary's mature life. As a very young woman she cherished 'exquisite sensibility' (Hays to Godwin, 7 Dec 1794) and exhibited a habitual melancholy. In 1778, while living with her widowed mother and two unmarried sisters at Gainsford Street, Southwark, she began a correspondence with John Eccles, and after much opposition from both families, it was agreed that the two could marry. Eccles died weeks before the ceremony, however, and she never fully recovered from the shock.

Despite an 'irascible' temper and a persistent belief that 'much of misery has been my portion' (Hays to Godwin, undated), Hays gained some solace in her religion under the tutelage of Robert Robinson and may have attended the newly established dissenting academy at Hackney. The attack by Gilbert Wakefield there on public worship roused her to produce a pamphlet in its defence, *Cursory Remarks on an Enquiry into the Expediency and Propriety of Public Worship* (1792), under the pseudonym Eusebia. The pamphlet was widely acclaimed and a second edition produced. Its success precipitated her acceptance into the radical circle surrounding the publisher Joseph Johnson,

which included William Blake, Thomas Paine, and William Godwin. The following year she published *Letters and Essays, Moral and Miscellaneous*.

Hays wrote articles for the *Monthly Magazine* during 1796 and 1797, joining in debates about the female intellect and, under the influence of Claude-Adrien Helvétius, insisting on the recognition of environmental and educational influences. She felt that this sensationalism legitimated the passions within rational philosophy which she claimed was 'impotent … against reiterated feeling' (Hays to Godwin, 13 Oct 1795). In 1794–1800 she engaged in a correspondence with the radical William Godwin, who had taken over the educative role vacated by Eccles. Her initial encouragement led to his marriage to her friend Mary Wollstonecraft. The lengthy correspondence between Hays and Godwin displays initial acquiescence and reverence on Hays's part developing into antagonism and later attack on his uncompromisingly rational philosophy. Hays argued instead for an alternative, intuitive logic based on experience which she felt was more appropriate to daily life. As she said, 'how much further … does a little nature go than mere philosophy' (Hays to Godwin, 29 April 1796). The correspondence ended abruptly with the death of Wollstonecraft after Godwin refused Hays admittance to the deathbed and she refused to attend the Anglican funeral service.

Hays had also met and won approval from leading dissenters such as George Dyer, Joseph Priestley, John Disney, and William Frend. She was a worshipper at Salter's Hall and Essex Street Chapel, and was invited to Priestley's farewell gathering before his exile to America in 1794. Through dissent Hays found a 'voice' to articulate her concerns and so contribute to its platform of discussion and controversy. At William Frend's instigation, she formed a close but unresolved relationship with him. According to Henry Crabb Robinson her feelings were reciprocated but Frend claimed to lack the means to support a wife. Their relationship formed the substance of her scandalous first novel *Memoirs of Emma Courtney* (1796). It is unapologetically autobiographical and her frankness about her fictionalized feelings for Frend won her notoriety, despite the preface's insistence that it was 'calculated to operate as a *warning*, rather than as an example'. Her second novel, *The Victim of Prejudice*, was published in 1799 and, according to the 'Advertisement', delineates 'the mischiefs that have ensued from the too great stress laid on the reputation for chastity in women'. She continued to write, producing among other works books for children and an acclaimed *Female Biography, or, Memoirs of Illustrious and Celebrated Women of All Ages and Countries* (6 vols., 1802). Her most radical work was the *Appeal to the Men of Great Britain in behalf of Women* (1798), in which she argued that there were no scriptural or rational arguments to justify the continued subjection of women. It was written at the same time as Wollstonecraft's much more celebrated *Vindication of the Rights of Woman*, though not published until six years later, and echoes many of Wollstonecraft's views on the position of women in society. In particular, Hays joins Wollstonecraft in advising women to throw off their shackles by educating themselves rationally so that they realize their potential as the intellectual equals of men. Hays argued consistently against the disadvantages built into female education and especially against the damaging effects of 'sexual distinctions' (Hays to Godwin, 21 Nov 1795). Her forthright depictions of female passion made her a target for satire, most notably as Bridgetina Botherim in *Memoirs of Modern Philosophers* (1800–01) by Elizabeth Hamilton, and as Lady Gertrude Sinclair in *Edmund Oliver* (1798) by Charles Lloyd.

Hays never married, but had a varied circle of male and female friends. She had a long friendship with the novelist Eliza Fenwick and was considered 'Mamma' to Fenwick's son Orlando. Fenwick invited her to help run a school in Barbados in 1813 and in America in 1821. Despite her wish to become accepted within rational circles she insisted on the acceptance of 'the affections' and may have been instrumental in Godwin's revisions of his writings. Towards the end of her life she confessed to Henry Crabb Robinson that 'I have done with systems. I am a complete and an indifferent skeptic' (Hays to Henry Crabb Robinson, 27 Feb 1802, New York Public Library, Pforzheimer Collection). Her 'exquisite misery' and longevity were ironic comments on her search for happiness and frequent wishes to be dead (Hays to Godwin, 6 Feb 1796). She died in Lower Clapton on 20 February 1843 and was buried in Abney Park cemetery, Stoke Newington, on 25 February. Although she would not have approved of the Anglican service she would have been pleased at Henry Crabb Robinson's observation that the rest of the afternoon was spent in controversial conversation.

MARILYN L. BROOKS

Sources H. C. Robinson, letters, DWL • A. F. Wedd, *The love letters of Mary Hays (1779–1780)* (1925) • A. F. Wedd, *The fate of the Fenwicks* (1927) • M. Hays, letters to William Godwin, NYPL, Humanities and Social Sciences Library, Pforzheimer collection • L. M. Brooks, 'Mary Hays: finding a voice in dissent', *Enlightenment and Dissent*, 14 (1995), 3–24 • J. M. Todd, 'Hays, Mary', *BDMBR*, vol. 1 • G. Luria, 'Mary Hays: a critical biography', PhD diss., New York University, 1972 • Blain, Clements & Grundy, *Feminist comp.* • J. Todd, ed., *A dictionary of British and American women writers, 1660–1800* (1984) • *Selected letters of Mary Hays*, ed. M. L. Brooks [forthcoming]
Archives DWL, letters | NYPL, Pforzheimer Collection

Hays, Matilda Mary (1820?–1897), writer and journal editor, was the daughter of John Hays (*d.* 1862), corn merchant. Details of her early life, such as her place of birth and the identity of her mother, are unknown, although she was referred to as 'half Creole' (letter from Joseph Parkes, Parkes MSS, vol. 2). At eighteen she determined to use her writing to improve women's educational and occupational opportunities. She became a contributor to numerous periodicals, most notably *Ainsworth's Magazine* and *The Mirror*. In 1846 she published a novel, *Helen Stanley*, which indicted the social mores that left women few options for economic security outside marriage. She wrote in *Helen Stanley* that women's conditions would not improve until 'women teach their daughters to respect themselves, … [and] to work for their daily bread, rather than prostitute their persons and hearts' in a loveless marriage (M. Hays, *Helen Stanley*, 1846, 41).

Encouraged by George Henry Lewes and William Charles Macready, in 1847 Hays and Eliza A. Ashurst undertook the publication of the first series of English translations of George Sand's novels, with Hays as editor. The series was partially funded by Edmund Larken, chaplain to Hays's friend and later companion, Theodosia *Monson, dowager Lady Monson (1803–1891). *The Works of George Sand* (1847) was not successful and ceased after the publication of six volumes. Hays's translation of *Fadette* (1851) was published separately.

With support from the author and journalist Mary Howitt, in 1847 Hays explored establishing a periodical that would 'afford free discussion' of women's issues which she felt was not possible 'through ordinary channels of the Press' (Hays, 'Memorial'). Unable to start the journal, and needing to support herself because of her father's 'embarrassed circumstances', she attempted a more lucrative career on the stage. She enlisted the help of American actress Charlotte Cushman (1816–1876), then living and performing with great success in England. Cushman was particularly acclaimed for her breeches roles, and Hays played the female romantic leads opposite her, making her début on 6 October 1848 in Bath. Although critics commented on Hays's promise, her theatrical career lasted less than a year.

Offstage Hays, who, Elizabeth Barrett Browning noted, 'dressed like a man down to the waist' in a fitted jacket, waistcoat, and tie (Browning to H. Barrett, 30 Dec 1853; Browning, 196), lived with Cushman as romantic partners in what Browning called a 'female marriage' (Browning to A. Moulton-Barrett, 22 Oct 1852, Berg Collection). They travelled throughout the United States (1849–52) and lived together in London and Rome (1853–7). Their relationship ended in the spring of 1857, after Cushman became involved with the sculptor Emma Stebbins. Hays threatened to sue Cushman for damages, alleging she had sacrificed her literary career and health to live with Cushman. Cushman agreed to pay her more than $1000 (Anne Brewster diary, 5 June 1876).

Hays returned to London, and with Bessie Rayner Parkes and Barbara Leigh Smith formed the 'women's journal' she had intended a decade earlier. The *English Woman's Journal* was decidedly feminist, although the more radical Hays, whom friends called Max or Mathew, often disagreed with co-editor Parkes about strategies for achieving their goals. The journal's offices at Langham Place served as a nucleus for the Society for Promoting the Employment of Women and the Victoria Press, both of which Hays helped to found. By 1864 Hays's reportedly difficult temperament led to her removal from the journal. In 1865 she petitioned for a pension from the Royal Literary Fund, not on the grounds of her literary merits, but on account of her 'labours on behalf of [her] own sex' and her diminished health from playing 'so arduous a part as Juliet to Miss Cushman's Romeo' (Hays, 'Memorial'). A pension of £100 per year was granted in 1866.

During these years Matilda Hays formed an intense attachment to the poet Adelaide Procter (1825–1864), who was also a member of the Langham Place circle. Procter dedicated her *Legends and Lyrics* (1858) to Hays, and Hays opened her novel *Adrienne Hope* (2 vols., 1866) with one of Procter's poems. After Procter's death, Hays was entrusted with care of her grave. *Adrienne Hope* depicted the pain of a woman in a 'secret marriage'. The novel is partially set in the Anglo-American community in Rome, in which Hays had lived with Cushman and the sculptor Harriet Hosmer, and draws upon details of their relationship. The characters include a Miss Reay, who—like Hays—was 'engaged in editing a philanthropic journal' and felt that her 'best years' had been 'utterly and uselessly sacrificed' in a relationship with an unworthy woman (M. Hays, *Adrienne Hope*, 1, 1866, 217).

Little is known of the last thirty years of Matilda Hays's life (earlier researchers believed, erroneously, that she had died in 1866), other than that she spent many years as companion to Lady Monson. She continued to mourn Adelaide Procter. More than thirty years after Procter's death, when Hays herself died, on 3 July 1897, at 15 Sefton Drive in Toxteth Park, Liverpool, her obituary in the *Liverpool Echo* did not mention her own literary achievements, noting only that she had been 'the dear friend of Adelaide Procter, gone before'.   LISA MERRILL

Sources Girton Cam., vols. 2–10 · J. Rendall, '"A moral engine"? Feminism, liberalism and the *English Woman's Journal*', *Equal or different: women's politics, 1800–1914*, ed. J. Rendall (1987), 112–38 · *Liverpool Echo* (6 July 1897) · J. Leach, *Bright particular star: the life and times of Charlotte Cushman* (1970) · D. Sherwood, *Harriet Hosmer, American sculptor, 1830–1908* (1991) · *Elizabeth Barrett Browning: letters to her sister, 1846–1859*, ed. L. Huxley, cheaper edn (1932) · NYPL, Humanities and Social Sciences Library, Berg collection · A. Brewster, diary, Hist. Soc. Penn., Anne Hampton Brewster papers · M. Howitt to S. J. Hale, 10 Oct 1847, Hunt. L., Huntington miscellaneous papers · *Theatrical Times* (21 Oct 1848), 411 · *Theatrical Times* (27 Jan 1849), 23 · J. Rendall, 'Friendship and politics: Barbara Leigh Smith Bodichon (1827–91) and Bessie Rayner Parkes (1829–1925)', *Sexuality and subordination: interdisciplinary studies of gender in the nineteenth century*, ed. S. Mendus and J. Rendall (1989), 136–70 · L. Cong., manuscript division, Charlotte Cushman MSS · *Dearest Isa: Robert Browning's letters to Isabella Blagden*, ed. E. C. McAleer (1951) · M. M. Hays, 'The memorial of Matilda M. Hays as candidate for a pension from the Governmental Literary Fund', *Parl. papers* (Jan 1866) [Treasury Papers, TI 6650B] · d. cert.
Likenesses cabinet photograph, *c.*1852 (with Charlotte Cushman), Harvard TC · B. R. Parkes, pencil drawing, Girton Cam., Bessie Rayner Parkes MSS

Hayter, Arthur Divett, Baron Haversham (1835–1917). *See under* Hayter, Sir William Goodenough, first baronet (1792–1878).

Hayter, Charles (1761–1835), miniature painter, was born on 24 February 1761, the son of Charles Hayter, an architect and builder, and his wife, Elizabeth Holmes. He was trained in his father's profession but, having developed a talent for drawing small pencil portraits, he entered the Royal Academy Schools in London on 30 January 1786. Thereafter he practised as a miniature painter in London, Essex, and, in 1832, in Winchester, earning a considerable reputation from his portraits in watercolour on ivory and in crayon on vellum, and exhibiting at the Royal Academy between 1786 and 1832. He was professor of perspective

and drawing to Charlotte, princess of Wales, and dedicated to her his *An introduction to perspective, adapted to the capacities of youth, in a series of pleasing and familiar dialogues* (1813). He was also the author of *A New Practical Treatise on the Three Primitive Colours* (1828).

Hayter married, on 15 July 1788, Martha Stevenson (1762–1805), daughter of Thomas and Mary Stevenson of Charing Cross, London. They had two sons and a daughter, all of whom practised as artists: Sir George *Hayter (1792–1871); John Hayter (1800–1895), a portrait and subject painter who exhibited between 1815 and 1879 at the Royal Academy, British Institution, and Old Watercolour Society; and Anne Hayter (*fl.* 1814–1830), who also worked as a miniature painter, exhibiting from her younger brother's address. Charles Hayter died in London on 1 December 1835. An album of 440 sketches by him, together with a manuscript list of his miniatures and several important examples of his miniatures, are in the Victoria and Albert Museum, London.

F. M. O'DONOGHUE, rev. V. REMINGTON

Sources D. Foskett, *Miniatures: dictionary and guide* (1987), 25, 349, 351, 424–5, 561 · B. S. Long, *British miniaturists* (1929), 198 · L. R. Schidlof, *The miniature in Europe in the 16th, 17th, 18th, and 19th centuries*, 4 vols. (1964) · S. Edwards, *Miniatures at Kenwood: the Draper gift* (1997), 204 · K. Coombs, *The portrait miniature in England* (1998), 113 · Graves, *RA exhibitors* · S. C. Hutchison, 'The Royal Academy Schools, 1768–1830', *Walpole Society*, 38 (1960–62), 123–91, esp. 149 · private information (1891)
Likenesses G. Hayter, pencil and wash drawing, 1811, NPG · G. Hayter, etching, 1819, BM, NPG · J. Hayter, group portrait, oils, exh. RA 1823 (*A controversy on colour*), Shipley Art Gallery, Gateshead · G. Hayter, group portrait, oils (*The trial of Queen Caroline, 1820*), NPG

Hayter, Sir George (1792–1871), painter and engraver, was born on 17 December 1792 at 27 St James's Street, Westminster, London, the third of ten children of Charles *Hayter (1761–1835), the son of an architect and a painter in miniature and crayon, and his wife, Martha (1762–1805), daughter of Thomas Stevenson of Charing Cross, London, and his wife, Mary. His parents married in 1788 at St George's, Hanover Square, London.

Early years Hayter's father was a respected miniaturist who exhibited regularly at the Royal Academy from 1786 onwards. After the deaths of his two first-born sons (when aged twelve and four), Charles Hayter came to rely on his son George, who remained at home without benefit of formal education. According to Hayter's memoir, as a young lad he had a thirst for knowledge and benefited from his father's skills as a teacher of geometry and perspective for artists; he also had access to standard books on art. He taught himself to play musical instruments such as the violin, flute, and later the guitar. At about thirteen George frequented a shop making wax dolls at the corner of Bolsover Street and Margaret Street, where the family now lived; here he learned wax modelling. Hayter also copied from plaster casts he hired himself. A portrait drawing by his father of George at this age (1806; priv. coll.; Bryant, 'Drawings at Duncombe Park', fig. 2) shows a confident individual older than his years (he later remarked that the

Sir George Hayter (1792–1871), self-portrait, 1820

death of his mother in 1805 affected him deeply). In copying his father's pencil portraits Hayter developed his skill as a draughtsman, and assisted in the busy miniature practice, but he longed to carry on with his own studies in anatomy in order to progress as an oil painter.

In January 1808 Hayter entered the Royal Academy Schools at the age of fifteen. Both Benjamin West, the president of the Royal Academy, and Martin Archer Shee, the successful portraitist, encouraged him. In 1807 'Dear old Fuseli' (Hayter, 'Account'), then keeper in the academy's schools, saw Hayter's work in miniature, and predicted that 'In all you'll shine, and in this, you'll soar' (Bryant, 'Drawings at Duncombe Park', 241), but he also insisted on the study of anatomy. This early phase of Hayter's life concluded when he and his father fell out over his art studies, and Hayter ran away from home to join the navy as a midshipman at Portsmouth at some time in 1808. With the wars in France in full force, he was not turned away, but after a very brief and apparently happy period at sea, his father arranged his release, agreeing that Hayter would assist him but also be allowed to pursue his own studies in the Royal Academy Schools. There Hayter (and his brother John, who was also training as an artist) befriended Edwin Landseer in particular.

Marriage and miniature painting Hayter fell in love with a lodger in his father's house, Sarah Milton (1779/80–1844), when he was fifteen or sixteen and she was twenty-eight. When his father discovered the attachment Sarah left, but Hayter sought her out, proposed marriage, and she accepted. With the help of friends they married in secret at St Martin-in-the-Fields, London, on 27 May 1809, and continued to live with their respective families. In the same month Hayter showed his first portraits in miniature at the Royal Academy exhibition and gained instant success. He made working visits to Winchester (where his paternal uncle lived) and Southampton. The marriage had become public knowledge by 1811; in that year Sarah Hayter had a baby daughter who, Hayter later wrote, 'died in my arms when I was 18' (Bryant, 'Drawings at Duncombe Park', 243). Sarah seems to have taken up miniature painting at about this time when the couple resided in Woodstock Street off Bond Street, London. They had two more children in quick succession: a daughter, Georgiana (sometimes spelt Giorgina), born in 1813, and a son, William Henry, born in 1814, who was afflicted with blindness.

In 1812 Hayter won the Royal Academy's silver medal for drawing, and in 1814 he won another for a drawing after the antique. Also in that year he exhibited a miniature of Anne Isabella (Annabella) Milbanke, later Lady Byron (priv. coll.; M. Elwin, *Lord Byron's Wife*, 1962, frontispiece), which, together with that of Lady Jane Montague (1813; exh. RA, 1814; on the art market, 1972), set the course of his astonishingly successful career as an artist who produced what William Hazlitt called 'resplendent miniatures, perfect mirrors of the highest heaven of beauty' (Bryant, 'Drawings at Duncombe Park', 241). He commanded the top prices in London for miniatures and found himself admitted at a young age to the most exclusive circles in society by virtue of his talent and increasingly refined social graces. But he 'disliked most exceedingly the minute labour' required, vowing to carry on only to fund his studies as an oil painter (Hayter, 'Account'). He painted his first major work in oil, *St Bernard*, while on a visit to Althorp in 1813.

Hayter's skills as a miniature painter brought him to the attention of Princess Charlotte, daughter of the prince regent and next in line to the throne. In 1815 Hayter was appointed her painter of miniatures and portraits. He interceded for his father, who had published *An Introduction to Perspective* in 1813, proposing that the princess appoint the elder Hayter her professor of perspective; when the second edition was published in 1815 Charles Hayter was granted this honour. The princess of Wales developed her own circle of artists, which included Hayter and his father, John Martin, and George Dawe. When she married Prince Leopold of Saxe-Coburg-Saalfeld in 1816, Hayter's royal appointment was extended to include the position of portrait painter to Leopold, whose friendship and patronage proved of great value in his future career.

Early full-scale works The formation of the British Institution in 1805 with its emphasis on history painting provided a further avenue for Hayter's ambitions as an artist. By now producing commissioned oil portraits, he exhibited a large-scale group of the daughters of the earl of Aberdeen at the British Institution in 1814 as a subject painting, *The Garland* (priv. coll.). In the following year his study of an old man entitled *The Prophet Ezra* (priv. coll.) earned the institution's first premium of 200 guineas and was purchased by the connoisseur Richard Payne Knight. Sir Thomas Lawrence, then the leading portrait painter of the day, wrote: 'a new Prodigy has started up at the British

Institution' (RA, Lawrence Papers, II/98). Joseph Farington recorded in his diary on 7 July 1815 that Hayter:

> married when He was only 16, & has children. His wife also paints miniatures, and they have maintained themselves and their family creditably, and are now in a flourishing way. He being patronised by the Dukes of Devonshire & Newcastle & other distinguished persons, & with those noble Dukes He is upon such terms as to be invited to their public parties, and they write to him in the most familiar and friendly manner.   (Farington, *Diary*, 13.4465)

Hayter's most important patron was no doubt the sixth duke of Bedford (for whom his father had already worked), who introduced him to Antonio Canova in 1815 with a commission for his portrait (Gov. Art Coll., British embassy, Paris), a work completed in Rome when Hayter obtained sittings from the celebrated neo-classical sculptor.

Visit to Italy His brief trip to Paris in 1815 whetted Hayter's appetite for foreign travel. Although his early reputation was secure, his personal life was beginning to disintegrate, despite the birth of another son, Leopold, in 1816 (who died in 1819). By this time he had met Louisa Cauty (1794–1827), who shared his life for the next decade. The strain on his marriage to Sarah from the death of their first baby and the blindness of their son took its toll. When the couple separated the surviving children went to live with their grandfather Charles Hayter, later returning to the care of their father and Louisa Cauty.

In autumn 1816 Hayter left for Italy, probably accompanied by Louisa (she was certainly with him by January 1817) and settled in Rome. They lived openly as man and wife but she could not appear in society; she later called herself Mrs Hayter, despite the fact that Hayter had not obtained a divorce. Having decided to abandon miniature painting, Hayter studied extensively, producing landscapes and academic drawings as well as *The Tribute Money* (art market, 1999) for the duke of Bedford, which gained him election to the Accademia di San Luca in Rome. Even though only an honorary member, Hayter thereafter ostentatiously signed himself with the initials M.A.S.L. This early academic honour was never matched by membership in the Royal Academy at home.

Circle of patrons The death of Princess Charlotte in childbirth in November 1817 meant that Hayter lost his most distinguished patron, and by early 1818 he was back in England cultivating a wide circle of potential new patrons. At Fonthill William Beckford dubbed him 'the Phoenix', and considered that 'an abler artist than he doesn't exist', but by 1819 Beckford found him 'quite foolish, conceited and flattering … it would be impossible to be more pleased with oneself than him' (B. Alexander, ed., *Life at Fonthill, 1807–1822*, 1957, 289). Hayter set up in practice as a portrait painter in London at Wimpole Street; the duke of Bedford commissioned portraits of his children, Samuel Rogers, the artist himself, and a huge portrait of the national hero, the duke of Wellington, resting by his horse Copenhagen (exh. RA, 1820), which remains at Woburn Abbey, Bedfordshire. Hayter's visits to Woburn in these years are evident from his many sketches of Georgiana, duchess of Bedford (for example, Yale U. CBA, and priv. coll.). He sent his more ambitious portraits and large subject paintings of Italian scenes to the British Institution and Royal Academy exhibitions. Louisa gave birth to a son, Angelo Collen (named after the artist Henry Collen, his friend and pupil), in 1819. But living openly with his mistress while his wife was still alive put Hayter beyond the pale of much of the establishment.

In 1820 the 'delicate investigation' of Queen Caroline, wife of George IV, caused a sensation. The introduction of the bill of pains and penalties aimed to 'deprive Her Majesty Caroline Amelia Elizabeth of the Title, Prerogatives, Rights, Privileges and Pretensions of Queen Consort of this Realm, and to dissolve the Marriage between his Majesty and the said Queen' (J. B. Priestley, *The Prince of Pleasure and his Regency*, 1971 edn, 277). Two hundred and sixty peers assembled in the House of Lords on 17 August and Hayter, with a commission from the young politician George Agar Ellis, planned a painting of the remarkable events, sketching tirelessly on the spot in the House of Lords. The painting (NPG) captured the high drama of the scene, and in order to capitalize on the excitement surrounding the event Hayter staged his own exhibition in Pall Mall in June 1823, with a catalogue that anticipated his later aim to be 'the painter of the history of his own time' (Hayter, *Descriptive Catalogue … of the House of Commons*, vii). But further efforts to win commissions to paint grand ceremonials, such as the coronation of George IV or the crowning of the king of France, Charles X, in 1825 (which he tried to persuade Robert Peel to commission) came to nothing.

Nevertheless, Hayter grew ever more confident. Still aged only about thirty, he documented himself in a series of self-portraits that reveal him as a dandy. His many self-portraits, in numerous drawings and paintings, indicate a man concerned with his appearance, as luscious curls spill over his head and bejewelled fingers edge into view. He inserted his own self-portrait into *The Trial of Queen Caroline* (1820–23; NPG), a practice he continued in most of his large contemporary compositions. He constantly sketched; many drawings survive (large collections are held at the British Museum, National Portrait Gallery, and Victoria and Albert Museum), testifying to his prodigious ability to capture a moment. Sheer painterly virtuosity is also evident in his work in the 1820s, as he expressed himself with Romantic vigour on both paper and canvas.

Hayter's personal charm with his many friends, such as the sixth duke of Bedford, meant that he was a favoured guest at country houses, where he depicted members of the family freely. In 1819 Bedford's son Lord John Russell published his *Life of William Lord Russell* and this stimulated Hayter's painting *The Trial of William, Lord Russell, at the Old Bailey in 1638* (priv. coll.). Although poorly hung at the Royal Academy exhibition in 1825, the painting was much praised and engraved with great acclaim. That year Hayter's candidacy for election as an associate member of the Royal Academy failed, owing, it seemed, to his irregular personal life, but no doubt his personality and behaviour also grated on more serious-minded men. He was an astute collector of old-master paintings, many of which he sold on, often acting as an intermediary for his aristocratic friends.

Return to Italy Hayter's large family provided him with distractions; his many drawings of the mid-1820s show music-making with children and include domestic pets. As he had failed to gain academic recognition in his own country, in September 1826 Hayter settled in Florence, where he had friends, including the artist Seymour Kirkup. Other artists, however, found him overbearing. On hearing of his arrival Thomas Uwins quipped: 'How will England go on without the light of this brilliant constellation' (Uwins, 1.181). Hayter's delight in Florentine life was truncated by a scandal that had reverberations throughout Italy. His mistress, Louisa, who had been living in Paris, went to Florence in June 1827, but in a bid for attention she poisoned herself with arsenic and died at once, on 16 October 1827. It was widely assumed that Hayter drove her to suicide, but in a privately printed letter he explained convincingly that the tragic death of the woman 'I had loved best on earth' was an unfortunate accident (Bryant, 'Drawings at Duncombe Park', 248). Memoirs of Henry Fox and Lady Holland (ibid., 243, 245) speak of Hayter's ostracism by society; he had to leave Florence as a result.

Despite these personal setbacks, professionally Hayter gained distinction by his request to submit a work to the gallery of artists' self-portraits in the Uffizi. This work, completed in 1828 (Uffizi gallery, Florence) radiates self-confidence. Election to the academies of Florence, Parma, and Bologna gave Hayter the impetus to move forward. He found a haven in Paris, where he was welcomed with a range of important portrait commissions by eminent expatriates, such as Lord Stuart de Rothesay and his family, which were exhibited at the Salon in 1830. He adopted a smooth, glossy style based on the work of the French painter Baron Gérard and his works displayed a distinctive cosmopolitan chic for the next two years.

Royal patronage Hayter's old friend and patron Prince Leopold, now king of the Belgians, bestowed on him a new title, painter of history and portraits to the king. Plans for a major commission, a full-length portrait of the king's niece Princess Victoria, precipitated Hayter's return to London. On the death of Sir Thomas Lawrence in 1830, Hayter saw the way open for his own advancement. In July 1830, aged thirty-seven, he settled in a fashionable location suitable for his planned position in society. Stratford Place, off Oxford Street, was a street associated with Richard Cosway, a celebrated miniature painter who had many affinities with Hayter, not least their devotion to their own image. Yet his fellow artists continued to find him unsympathetic: in July 1832 John Constable wrote that he went to meet Hayter, 'a very prosperous, disagreeable personage—but a great man in his own opinion, he being a person of consequence' (Bryant, 'Drawings at Duncombe Park', 245).

Hayter's portrait of Princess Victoria remains in the Belgian royal collection. He also painted Princess Victoria's mother, the duchess of Kent. These were prestigious commissions and his stock rose accordingly, but he then planned an unusual work in the year of the Reform Bill, a painting entitled *Moving the address to the crown on the opening of the first reformed parliament in the House of Commons, Feb. 1833* (NPG). The project occupied ten years of his life, much of the time taken up by *ad vivum* portrait studies made for each of the 360 sitters, an enterprise only the most energetic artist would dare to attempt. He offered the oil studies to the sitters for 10 guineas each. When it was completed Hayter staged an exhibition of this work and others at the Egyptian Hall, London, writing in the catalogue that the session of 1833 'presented an event exceeding in interest any previous one in the history of this country' as they met in the old House of Commons, within the walls of St Stephen's Chapel (Hayter, *Descriptive Catalogue ... of the House of Commons*, v).

When, aged seventeen, Princess Victoria came to the throne on the death of William IV in 1837, she had her own ideas about art. She immediately affirmed her patronage by retaining David Wilkie as painter in ordinary and appointing Hayter as her painter of portraits and history painter (the warrant was signed on 5 August 1837). She wrote in her diary that he was 'out and out the *best* Portrait painter in my opinion' (Millar, *Victorian Pictures*, 1.96). Wilkie received the commission to paint her state portrait, but its failure meant that Hayter was called upon. He had already painted a successful portrait of the young queen, given by her to the City of London (exh. RA, 1838; Guildhall Art Gallery); he then produced a new state portrait showing the queen in the imperial Dalmatic robes worn at the coronation (Royal Collection).

Hayter responded enthusiastically to all aspects of court life and enjoyed his visits to Windsor Castle and Buckingham Palace. He taught the queen and Prince Albert how to etch. Haydon lamented what he termed Hayter's 'suppleness', also recording that he behaved in an excessively courtly fashion: 'when the Queen comes in, Hayter bows to the ground 3 or 4 times, and retires with the greatest humility' (*Diary*, ed. Pope, 4.625, 451). He noted further that 'Wilkie had been cut out by Hayter with the Queen' (ibid.). Haydon reported that 'Hayter was allowed such privileges, he bullied the Queen' (ibid., 4.625). His confidence rarely waned; his surviving diary records an individual of prodigious energy, who loved riding around London and seeing his friends and family, as much as promoting his own career.

Hayter was well placed to portray the ceremonial scenes he had long wished to paint. Rather than the queen, the printsellers Hodgson and Graves commissioned him to paint the coronation with a view to issuing an engraving of this national occasion. Initially Hayter demurred because the project might hinder work on his painting of the Reform Parliament but, offered a fee of 2000 guineas, he agreed and his position at court gained him access to Westminster Abbey to make preparatory studies. On the day he had a privileged position from which to record the ceremony. His son Angelo assisted, as did an architectural draughtsman called Ashton. This work secured Hayter's position as the queen's painter and in 1840 she commissioned from him a painting of her marriage to Prince Albert of Saxe-Coburg and Gotha (nephew of Leopold), in the Chapel Royal at St James's Palace (1840–42; Royal Collection). Hayter inserted his own self-portrait in the background.

On the death of David Wilkie in June 1841, Hayter spoke almost too hastily to the queen's adviser and prime minister, Lord Melbourne, about taking up the appointment of principal painter in ordinary. The position was given to him even though the art establishment expected Sir Martin Archer Shee, then president of the Royal Academy, to receive the honour. The *Art Union* stated that the queen had relied more heavily on 'those who have been known to her in youth' such as Hayter, and concluded that the *Coronation* had been 'so perfectly executed to the satisfaction of her Majesty' (*Art Union*, 1841, 120). Since 1838 Hayter had been lobbying for a knighthood, and in 1842 this was bestowed on him. His new title encouraged him to believe that further commissions from the queen, beyond mere repetitions of the state portrait, would follow, but such work did not materialize. He painted *The Christening of the Prince of Wales* (Royal Collection) on speculation without a commission. After her marriage Prince Albert began to direct the queen's tastes in art. He did not warm to Hayter, and preferred the German painter F. X. Winterhalter, who had also gone to the British court with a recommendation from King Leopold.

In 1843 Hayter completed and exhibited his *First Reformed Parliament in the House of Commons* at the Egyptian Hall, using the opportunity to show a range of his work, but the large painting did not sell and he spent many years trying to find a purchaser for this 'national document' including the National Gallery (Hayter to R. Peel, 1 Dec 1845, BM, Add. MS 40580, fol. 129). It was eventually bought by the government in 1858 and was presented to the new National Portrait Gallery. Having exhibited for the final time at the Royal Academy in 1839, Hayter took on commissions from printsellers and painted much of his later output specifically for engraving. In 1843 he travelled to Berlin to deliver to the German court a copy of the state portrait of Queen Victoria.

Later years In his early fifties Hayter was edged out of royal circles, and the prevailing taste shifted away from his style, preferring greater realism. He produced some religious paintings in later years, as well as historical subject paintings such as *Wellington Visiting Napoleon's Effigy at Madame Tussaud's* (1853; burned in 1925) which hung in the Napoleon Room at the famous waxworks almost in the manner of a stage set. He also designed metalwork and produced some sculpture.

In 1844 Hayter's wife, Sarah, died. His spirits were low as he struggled with debts and ill health. He sold his large collection of old-master paintings and other works of art at Christies in May 1845 with the intention of moving to the continent. In July a serious train accident in which Hayter sustained severe leg injuries scotched this plan, but his spirits lifted when on 12 May 1846 he married a widow, (Helena) Cecilia Hyde, *née* Burke (1791/2–1860).

After her death in 1860 he made a late marriage on 23 April 1863 to Martha Carey, *née* Miller (1818–1867), who died four years later. Hayter ended his years alone, satisfied that three of his children were married and self-sufficient; his two daughters lived in France and his blind son Henry was housed in a convent there. To his regret his son Angelo gave up painting as a profession and joined the civil service, rising to become chief reviewer of wills at Somerset House.

Hayter died on 18 January 1871 at his home, 238 Marylebone Road (later named Hayter House), and was buried in St Marylebone cemetery, East Finchley. Soon after his death Queen Victoria purchased *The Christening of the Prince of Wales*. Hayter had designed his own headstone at the time of his third wife's death in 1867. It is inscribed 'Painter, Sculptor, Poet, Musician'. The text enumerates his honours:

> Knight Bachelor of the United Kingdom; Knight of the Lion and Sun of Persia; Painter of History and Portraits and Principal Painter in Ordinary to HM Queen Victoria; Member of the Academies of Fine Arts of Florence, Bologna, Parma, Venice and St. Luke at Rome &c.

Hayter was a distinctly cosmopolitan artist of fluency and glamour. Royal and aristocratic patronage fuelled his ambition to paint large-scale modern history paintings based on portraiture and royal ceremonies. These historical works, especially those in the National Portrait Gallery, remain important visual documents of eminent individuals present at public events in the 1820s, 1830s, and 1840s.

BARBARA COFFEY BRYANT

Sources B. Bryant, 'Sir George Hayter's drawings at Duncombe Park: family ties and a "melancholy event"', *Apollo*, 135 (1992), 240–50 • B. Coffey, *An exhibition of drawings by Sir George Hayter, 1792–1871, and John Hayter, 1800–1895* (1982) [exhibition catalogue, Morton Morris & Co. Gallery, London] • B. Bryant, 'George Hayter', *The dictionary of art*, 14 (1996), 270 • O. Millar, *The Victorian pictures in the collection of her majesty the queen*, 2 vols. (1992) • G. Hayter, 'Account of his own early life by Sir George Hayter from 1792 to 1809 written in 1852', NPG, Heinz Archive and Library [copy of a later transcript from original in priv. coll.] • G. Hayter, diary, 1838–49, NPG, Heinz Archive and Library [after copy of transcript from orig. in priv. coll.] • G. Hayter, *Descriptive catalogue of the historical picture of the interior of the British House of Commons … in 1833* (1843) • G. Hayter, *Descriptive catalogue of the great historical picture representing the trial of her late majesty Queen Caroline of England* (1823) • *The Times* (23 Jan 1871), 9 • *Art Journal*, new ser., 533 (1871), 79 • *ILN* (23 Jan 1871), 91 • *DNB* • Farington, *Diary* • R. Ormond, *Early Victorian portraits*, 2 vols. (1973) • R. Walker, *National Portrait Gallery: Regency portraits*, 2 vols. (1985) • B. S. Long, *British miniaturists* (1929) • *The diary of Benjamin Robert Haydon*, ed. W. B. Pope, 5 vols. (1960–63) • T. Smith, *Recollections of the British Institution* (1860) • D. Alexander, 'George Hayter (1792–1871): a printmaker of the 1820s', *Print Quarterly*, 2 (1985), 218–29 • D. Millar, *The Victorian watercolours and drawings in the collection of her majesty the queen*, 2 vols. (1995) • S. C. Hutchison, 'The Royal Academy Schools, 1768–1830', *Walpole Society*, 38 (1960–62), 123–91, esp. 164 • m. cert. [Helena Cecilia Hyde] • d. cert. • *CGPLA Eng. & Wales* (1871) • S. Uwins, *A memoir of Thomas Uwins*, 2 vols. (1858); repr. in 1 vol. (1978)

Archives Castle Museum, Norwich, letters • FM Cam., letters • Hunt. L., letters • Hunt. L., letters • NPG, family papers; diary [priv. coll., transcript] • priv. coll., family papers, incl. his 'Account of his own early life by Sir George Hayter from 1792 to 1809 written in 1852' [transcript] and family tree • priv. coll., family tree from another branch of family · Royal Arch. · Staffs. RO, letters · V&A NAL, letters | BM, Gladstone papers, letters, Add. MSS

Likenesses C. Hayter, 1806 (aged thirteen), repro. in Bryant, 'Sir George Hayter's drawings', 241, priv. coll. · C. Hayter, drawing, 1807 (aged fourteen), priv. coll. · G. Hayter, self-portrait, miniature, 1810, repro. in Christies, sale catalogue, priv. coll., 1 Dec 1988 · G. Hayter, self-portrait, watercolour and pencil drawing, c.1816, BM · G. Hayter, self-portrait, drawing, 1819, priv. coll. · G. Hayter, self-portrait, oils, 1820, NPG [see illus.] · G. Hayter, self-portraits, seven comic sketches, 1821, NPG · G. Hayter, group portrait, 1823 · J. Hayter, group portrait, oils, exh. RA 1823 (A controversy in colour), Shipley Art Gallery, Gateshead · G. Hayter, self-portrait, drawing, 1824, priv. coll. · G. Hayter, self-portrait, pen-and-ink drawing, c.1826, Bolton Museum and Art Gallery · G. Hayter, self-portrait, oils, 1828, Uffizi Gallery, Florence · G. Hayter, self-portrait, oils, c.1840–1845, priv. coll. · G. Hayter, self-portrait, drawing, 1843, Staatliche Kunstsammlungen, Dresden, Küpferstichkabinett · G. Hayter, self-portrait, miniature, 1845, priv. coll. · G. Hayter, self-portrait, oils, 1863–4, repro. in Sothebys, Belgravia, sale catalogue, 22 Feb 1972, no. 116 · G. Hayter, group portrait, oils (The trial of Queen Caroline), NPG · G. Hayter, group portrait, oils (The House of Commons, 1833), NPG · G. Hayter, self-portrait, etching (after his earlier work), BM, NPG

Wealth at death under £8000: probate, 1 Feb 1871, CGPLA Eng. & Wales

Hayter, Henry Heylyn (1821–1895), statistician, was born at Eden Vale, Wiltshire, on 28 October 1821, the son of Henry Hayter of Eden Vale and Eliza Jane, daughter and heir of John Heylyn of Islington. He was the nephew of Sir William Goodenough Hayter, and was educated privately at Paris and afterwards at Charterhouse School. On leaving school he became a midshipman in the merchant service and made several voyages, first on Wigram's ships, later on West India mail packets. In 1852 he emigrated to Melbourne, Victoria. In June 1855 he married Susan (d. 1911), daughter of William and Sarah Dodd of Porchester Terrace, London; they had one son. In May 1857 he took on temporary assignments as census commissioner for the registrar-general, William Archer.

In his role as census commissioner Hayter was responsible for overseeing the completion of Victoria's second census in 1857. Borrowing ideas which had been developed by William Farr in the 1851 census of Great Britain, Hayter introduced a category for occupation and the use of five-year cohorts for the tabulation of age (rather than using only three categories for age). He also initiated administrative changes when he employed 1005 enumerators for the second census (eight people had been used in Victoria's first census of 1854). These changes eventually became incorporated in the censuses in other colonies of Australia leading to greater uniformity and standardization. Subsequently, Hayter was responsible for the censuses in Victoria from 1861 to 1891.

Hayter was one of the five collectors of statistical data for Victoria in 1859, and he reported on the economy and social conditions of western Victoria. From 1870 to 1872 he served as secretary to the royal commission to inquire into the working of the public service of Victoria. This work led to his construction of a series of annual statistical reports on the colony beginning with the Statistical Register in 1859 (which replaced the Statistics in Victoria), followed by Progress in Victoria in 1873, and ending with the Victorian Year Book in 1874. In 1872 he suffered ill health and went to New Zealand to recuperate. During his visit he helped to bring about extensive improvements in the reporting of statistical data, and before returning to Australia wrote Notes of a Tour to New Zealand.

In May 1874 Hayter was appointed assistant to the registrar-general and the statistical section of the registrar-general's office became a separate office with Hayter in charge as the first government statist. In this capacity he provided the statistical machinery for the colony of Victoria, which formed a model for the whole of Australia. At a conference held in Tasmania in 1875, this model was adopted as the basis of a uniform system of national statistics.

In 1879, when Hayter visited England as secretary to Sir Graham Berry's embassy to the imperial government for the reform of the constitution of Victoria, he was invited twice to give evidence before the House of Commons' committee on statistics. His census of 1881 for Victoria was considered a substantial improvement on previous returns. He became the director of the Metropolitan Bank and the Metropolitan Building Society in 1887. Four years later both institutions went into liquidation; Hayter was by then £36,000 in debt and asked the government to release him from his official post, but the cabinet persuaded him to remain and to represent Victoria at the inter-colonial conference on methods of census which was held at Hobart, Tasmania in 1890 (of which he was elected president), and also to conduct the census of 1891. He held this appointment until his death.

Hayter was a member of various learned societies and was awarded medals at exhibitions at Melbourne, Amsterdam, Calcutta, at the Colonial and Indian Exhibition in 1886, and at Paris in 1889. He was created CMG and an officer of the French Ministre d'Instruction Publique in 1882: two years later he was made a chevalier of the order of the Corona d'Italia. He was also an honorary member of the Royal Statistical Society and of the Statistical and Social Enquiry Society of Ireland.

In addition to his annual statistical reports, Hayter wrote texts for schools such as School History of Victoria and School Geography of Victoria, as well as poems in My Christmas Adventure, and other Poems (1857). He died in Armadale, near Melbourne, on 23 March 1895.

C. A. HARRIS, rev. M. EILEEN MAGNELLO

Sources AusDB · P. Mennell, The dictionary of Australasian biography (1892), 221–2 · P. Serle, Dictionary of Australian biography, 2 vols. (1949) · F. Johns, An Australian biographical dictionary (1934), 163 · J. Camm, The early nineteenth century colonial censuses of Australia (Melbourne, 1988) · private information (1901)

Hayter, John (1755–1818), Church of England clergyman and palaeographer, was born in Chagford, Devon, and baptized there on 19 March 1755, one of two sons of Joshua Hayter, rector of Chagford, and his wife, Frances. Having been educated at Eton College from 1766 to 1772 he matriculated from King's College, Cambridge, in Lent 1774 and graduated BA in 1778. As a student at King's he was awarded, in 1776, the gold medal, presented by Sir William Browne, for the best Greek ode in imitation of

Sappho. From 1776 to 1779 he was a fellow of King's, and in 1780 he was awarded the degree of MA. He was ordained deacon on 15 March 1778 and priest on 28 February 1779, the same day as he succeeded his father as rector of Chagford; he remained in that living until 1810. While at Chagford he married first, on 6 January 1784, Lydia Southmead; and second, on 21 July 1785, Elizabeth Baskerville, with whom he had eight children, including two daughters, Elizabeth and Sophia. In 1797 Elizabeth (who may have been his wife or his daughter) and Sophia Hayter were awarded a contingent pension of £131 in the extraordinary red book 'to commence on the death of the Revd John Hayter' (*GM*, 89/1). In 1810 Hayter was presented by King's College to the rectory of Hepworth, Suffolk, a position that he held until his death. He was also chaplain-in-ordinary to the prince of Wales, later George IV.

In 1800 the prince of Wales undertook to continue at his own expense the unrolling and deciphering of the papyri found at Herculaneum, and selected Hayter to superintend the process. Hayter arrived in Naples in early 1802 and remained there until 1806. During these four years more than 200 scrolls were opened wholly or in part and nearly 100 were copied in lead-pencil facsimiles under his supervision. It is clear that he was a skilful organizer of a group of workers, and his own contribution as a palaeographer was very respectable; without him progress in deciphering the papyri would have been greatly delayed.

With the French invasion of Naples in 1806 Hayter moved to Palermo, and the papyri fell into the hands of the French. At Palermo he contented himself in superintending the engraving of the 'Carmen Latinum' before the prince of Wales recalled him in 1809 to England. In 1811 the prince presented Hayter's copies of the manuscripts to Oxford University, which announced that it would publish the more interesting of them. Accordingly Hayter moved to Oxford to supervise the publication, and during his residence there he was admitted, on 19 February 1812, *ad eundem* to the degree of MA. Little progress was made on the projected publication of the manuscripts and he quit Oxford after a residence there of a few months. Hayter's own publications were confined almost exclusively to the Herculanean manuscripts. In 1800 he published a background to the discovery of the manuscripts, *The Herculanean and Pompeian Manuscripts*, a second edition of which appeared in 1810. In February of that year he contributed a paper to the *Quarterly Review* entitled *Observations upon a Review of the 'Herculanensia'*, while in 1811 there appeared what was probably his most authoritative work, *A Report upon the Herculaneum Manuscripts*. In or about 1815 he was sent to Paris to examine the six Herculanean manuscripts that Napoleon had sent there. While in residence there he died, of an apoplectic stroke, on 2 December 1818.
M. J. MERCER

Sources Venn, *Alum. Cant.*, 2/3.303 · R. A. Austen-Leigh, ed., *The Eton College register, 1753–1790* (1921), 261 · *GM*, 1st ser., 88/2 (1818), 631 · *GM*, 1st ser., 89/1 (1819), 179 · *IGI* · M. Capasso, *Manuale di papirologia ercolanese* (Lecce, 1991), 101–3, 106 · G. Indelli and F. Longo Auricchio, *Contributi alla storia della officina dei papiri ercolanese* (Naples, 1980), 217–25, 159–215
Archives Bodl. Oxf., MSS

Hayter, Richard (1611/12–1684), theological writer, was the son of William Hayter, fishmonger, of Salisbury, Wiltshire. In 1628 he was admitted to Magdalen Hall, Oxford, as a commoner; he matriculated on 4 November 1631 aged nineteen, graduated BA on 26 April 1632, and proceeded MA on 29 January 1635. He returned to Salisbury, but was not ordained. Though millenarianism became less fashionable after the Restoration Hayter was one of those who continued to be interested in it, and in 1675 he published *The meaning of Revelation, or, A paraphrase with questions on the Revelation of St. John, in which the synchronisms of Mr. Joseph Mede, and the expositions of other interpreters, are called into question*, a work reissued the following year under the title *The Apocalypse Unveiled, or, A Paraphrase on the Revelation*. In April 1683, according to Anthony Wood, he had ready for the press 'Errata Mori: the errors of Henry More contained in his epilogue annex'd to his Exposition of the Revelation of St. John' but this appears not to have been published. Hayter died on 30 June 1684 at Salisbury and was buried in the church of St Thomas there.
STEPHEN WRIGHT

Sources R. Benson and H. Hatcher, *The history of modern Wiltshire*, ed. R. C. Hoare, 6 (1843) · Foster, *Alum. Oxon.* · Wood, *Ath. Oxon.*, new edn, vol. 4 · Wing, *STC*

Hayter, Stanley William (1901–1988), painter and printmaker, was born in Hackney on 27 December 1901, the third of four children (two sons and two daughters) of William Harry Hayter, painter, and his wife, Ellen Mercy Palmer. Among his many artist ancestors was Sir George Hayter, portrait and history painter to Queen Victoria. He was educated at Whitgift Middle School, Croydon, and King's College, London (1918–21), where he obtained an honours degree in chemistry. His scientific training, mathematical ability, and lifelong interest in science inform his art. Topological transformations, superimposition of one space upon another, non-Euclidean spaces, wave motion, and moiré interferences of fields in continuous deformation characterize his imagery. The hallmarks of his work—energy, movement, scintillating non-natural colour—reflect both his personality and his investigations into the psychology of vision. His technical innovations in colour printing were the work of a man equally at home in laboratory and in atelier, in whom artistic sensibility and scientific curiosity were fused. Hayter was an intellectual, as well read in poetry and literature as in science. The vibrant tensions in his paintings and prints mirror the taut balance between his reflective analytic abilities and his faith in the irrational, unconscious sources of creativity.

After university Hayter worked as a chemist for the Anglo Persian Oil Company in Abadan, Persia (1922–5). While in Abadan he drew and painted extensively. On his return he exhibited successfully in London. In 1926 he went to Paris, briefly attended the Académie Julian, and gravitated towards avant-garde artistic circles, making friends with Balthus, Alexander Calder, Anthony Gross, André Masson, Joan Miró, and Alberto Giacometti. Joseph Hecht introduced him to engraving. Convinced that the potentialities of gravure had never been realized, he established in 1927 a unique printmaking workshop,

Stanley William Hayter (1901–1988), by Jorge Lewinski, 1968

which became the world famous Atelier 17 (so denominated in 1933)—a powerhouse of innovatory intaglio printmaking for the following sixty years. It was not based on master–pupil relations but on artists sharing ideas, exploring together the expressive possibilities of gravure. The list of those who worked in Atelier 17 between 1928 and 1939 reads like a roll of honour of artists of the interwar years.

Hayter always divided his time equally between painting and printmaking (his output of paintings exceeds that of his prints). Until 1938 he associated with the surrealists, exhibiting with them in Paris, London, and New York and assisting in organizing the 1936 Surrealist Exhibition in London. His imagery focused on mythological themes, war, and violence. His engraved line, the distinctive 'Hayter whiplash', bristled with aggressive energy. He supplemented his vibrant burin work with embossed white line (*gaufrage*), functioning to highlight and to impart depth to the images, and with innovative use of soft ground etching to produce an intaglio equivalent of collage. Though he broke with André Breton over the Éluard affair (1938), remaining loyal to his friend Paul Éluard, he retained his surrealist commitment to automatist creative methods.

In 1939 Hayter returned to England and worked on camouflage techniques. Debarred by injury from military service he went to New York (1940), establishing Atelier 17 at the New School for Social Research. The atelier's exhibition at the Museum of Modern Art (1944) brought renown. Its impact on American printmaking was compared with that of the Armory Show on American painting. In 1945 he moved Atelier 17 to Greenwich Village. During his decade in New York it provided a fertile meeting place for European expatriates, including Marc Chagall, Le Corbusier, Max Ernst, André Masson, Joan Miró, and Yves Tanguy, and American and emigré artists such as Garo Antreasian, William Baziotes, William de Kooning, Matta, Robert Motherwell, Jackson Pollock, and Mark Rothko. As a painter Hayter was recognized as one of the

founders of abstract expressionism. In 1946 he perfected a technique of simultaneous multicolour printing off a single plate in one passage through the press (sometimes misnamed viscosity printing), which, evolving under constant experiment over the years, revolutionized colour printmaking. It made possible subtle gradations of colour, modulations of one band of colour into another, and superimposition of one colour upon another both in relief and in open bitten intaglio. It also integrates colour into the creative process, since it relieves the artist of the need to decompose an image onto different plates for purposes of printing, which minimizes creative interaction with the medium as well as spontaneity in working the plate. The scintillating effects which simultaneous multicolour printing can produce are everywhere evident in his prints over the last three decades of his life.

Hayter returned to Paris (1950), reopening Atelier 17, attracting artists from all over the world, and through them exercising worldwide influence. Prominent themes in his paintings and prints over the next four decades were generalized depiction of light on water, wave motion, water currents, the movement of objects in space or in a fluid medium, and reflections. From 1957 his surrealist imagery gave way to a quasi *tachiste* style, to be followed (mid-1960s) by a decade of preoccupation with undulating line and rhythm. With age his palette became increasingly brilliant, employing fluorescent colours in vibrant, energetic paintings and prints. During his last decade figurative elements reappear in his semi-abstract imagery.

Hayter was awarded the Légion d'honneur (1951), made a chevalier de l'ordre des Arts et Lettres (1968) and commandeur des Arts et Lettres (1986). British recognition came in the form of an OBE (1959), CBE (1968), and honorary RA (1982). In 1988 the British Museum purchased 400 prints from him, the largest purchase from a living artist it had ever made.

His books *New Ways of Gravure* (1949) and *About Prints* (1962) reveal his gifts as a writer. Though he hated to be thought of as a teacher, it was his dynamic personality, charisma, and enthusiasm which made Atelier 17. His Socratic methods of awakening ideas inspired many hundreds of young artists who came to work with him. A true bohemian to the last, Hayter cared little for material comforts or rewards, but cared passionately for honesty in both art and life, and for friendship. His generosity to younger artists was renowned. Hayter was a short, slim, and wiry man of volcanic energy. A shock of hair fell over his forehead. He had bushy eyebrows, piercing blue eyes, and an aquiline nose. In old age, his face was heavily lined—a striking face of great forcefulness, mobile and expressive. His voice was deep and gravelly.

In 1928 Hayter married Edith Fletcher. They had one son, who died of tuberculosis in New York in 1946. The marriage was dissolved in 1929. In 1940 he married the sculptor Helen Phillips, daughter of Lewis Henry Phillips, director of a business college. There were two sons of the marriage, which was dissolved in 1973. In 1974 he married

Désirée, daughter of Aloysius Moorhead, dentist. Hayter died suddenly at his Paris home on 4 May 1988. He was survived by his third wife and two sons.　　P. M. S. HACKER

Sources S. W. Hayter, *New ways of gravure*, rev. edn (1981) • S. W. Hayter, *About prints* (1962) • P. M. S. Hacker, ed., *The renaissance of gravure: the art of S. W. Hayter* (1988) • C. Esposito, *Hayter e l'Atelier 17* (Milan, 1990) [exhibition catalogue, Accademia di San Luca, Rome, 10 May – 1 July 1990] • personal knowledge (2004)
Likenesses J. Lewinski, photograph, 1968, NPG [*see illus.*] • A. Springs, bromide print, 1976, NPG • photograph, repro. in Hacker, ed., *Renaissance of gravure*, frontispiece • photograph, repro. in D. Moorhead, *The prints of Stanley William Hayter* (1952), frontispiece

Hayter, Thomas (*bap.* 1702, *d.* 1762), bishop of London, was baptized at Chagford, Devon, on 17 November 1702, and was the son of George Hayter, rector of the parish, and of his wife, Grace. He was educated at Blundell's School, Tiverton, matriculated at Balliol College, Oxford, in May 1720, and was awarded his BA degree in January 1724. He subsequently became a member of Emmanuel College, Cambridge, and took his MA and DD in 1727 and 1744 respectively. After ordination he was made chaplain to Archbishop Lancelot Blackburne of York (by whose will he benefited handsomely) and obtained many preferments, becoming prebendary of North Muskham at Southwell (1728), rector of Kirkby Overblow (1729), archdeacon of York and subdean of the cathedral (1730), prebendary of Strensall (1735), and rector of Kirkby, Cleveland (1737). He was given a prebend at Westminster in 1739. Hayter was nominated bishop of Norwich in October 1749 and consecrated in December; in 1761 he was translated to London but he died, shortly afterwards, in January 1762.

Respecting politics, Hayter was a whig. In a 30 January sermon, preached before the Lords in 1750, he praised the 'Blessings, of which the Revolution gave us full Possession, *civil* and *religious* Liberty' (T. Hayter, *A Sermon Preached before the Right Honourable the Lords Spiritual and Temporal*, 1750, 6). He attributed the defeat of the Jacobite rising of 1745 to 'the secret, super-intending influence, of the supreme Controller of all events' (T. Hayter, *Sermon Preached before the Honourable House of Commons*, 1746, 23). He was taken up by the whigs, and the duke of Newcastle later claimed that he had 'made him everything that he ever was' (Sykes, 73). As a bishop his attendance in the Lords was irregular. When he did not attend at the time of the Jewish naturalization bill's discussion he was sharply criticized by some of his clergy in Suffolk, who told him that he should have been present and opposed the measure. He preached for a number of charitable bodies, including the charity schools of the Society for Promoting Christian Knowledge in and about London and Westminster, and for the Society for the Propagation of the Gospel. In his sermons he described the role of providence regarding society in general as well as the political order. The social hierarchy was ordained by God; slaves had been placed in their station by him; sickness was rightly viewed as 'a gracious instrument in the hands of Providence, for the moral improvement of such creatures, as we are' (*Sermon Preached before his Grace William Duke of Devonshire*, 1759,

Thomas Hayter (*bap.* 1702, *d.* 1762), attrib. Thomas Hudson, *c.*1755–60 [copy]

12). In Ireland children taking charity should be 'trained up, [so] they will chearfully fill the low laborious Stations for which Providence designed … them' (*Sermon Preach'd before the Society Corresponding with the Incorporated Society in Dublin, for Promoting English Protestant Working-Schools in Ireland*, 1754, 23). To Hayter the dangers to the society of his day were considerable. Popery was the 'determined Enemy of Truth and Liberty' (*A Sermon Preached before the Right Honourable the Lords Spiritual and Temporal*, 1750, 24). Infidelity sapped true religion. In 1755 he claimed that a 'torrent of licentiousness … threatens at present to overwhelm our Laws, our Liberty and our Constitution itself' (*Sermon Preached in the Parish-Church of Christ-Church, London*, 1756, 40). He published seven of his sermons, a charge, as archdeacon of York (1732), and, anonymously, *An examination of a book … entitled, A brief account of many of the prosecutions of the people called Quakers* (1741) and *An Essay on the Liberty of the Press* (1755).

In his private life Hayter was likeable, generous, and hospitable. He was also cultivated and scholarly. '[H]is hours of retirement', the *London Magazine* for 1764 noted, 'were employed in study, and the conversation of those who were most eminent for their parts and learning' (p. 424). Well read with 'an excellent taste of the *belles lettres*' (ibid.), he gathered around himself a circle of literary friends. Charles Godwyn, one of the Bodleian Library's benefactors, thought that he was an outstanding judge of Latin poetry. On account of these accomplishments he seemed admirably suited to direct the education of George, prince of Wales, and of his brother, Prince Edward, following the death of their father, Frederick, prince of Wales, in 1751. He was made preceptor, Earl Harcourt acted as governor, and Andrew Stone and George

Lewis Scott were appointed sub-governor and sub-preceptor respectively.

Hayter's period as preceptor was not a happy one, however, and he felt obliged to resign the position at the end of 1752. The reasons for this were both personal and political. Horace Walpole observed that Hayter was 'sincerely honest and zealous' in discharging his duties (Walpole, 1.194), and certainly this is borne out by the scheme which Hayter produced for the princes' education:

> It is proposed, that their Royal Highnesses do rise at seven o'clock, and translate such parts of Caesar's Commentaries as they had before read … the utmost attention has been, and will be had to explain and inculcate to their Royal Highnesses, the great duties of Religion and Morality, and particularly those that more immediately concern their Royal Highnesses from their high rank and station.
> (*Memoirs and Speeches of … Waldegrave*, 14)

Hayter's earnestness is again illustrated by a sermon preached before the king in 1752 and drawn up for the use of the two princes; it is relentless and austere, expatiating on virtue and duty, reason and passion, pleasure and pain. The prince of Wales may well have been alienated by Hayter's pedantry—much later, as king, he told George Rose MP of his dislike of Hayter—and Walpole felt that the prince's mother, Princess Augusta, found Hayter too strict (though George Bubb Dodington's account of events does not support this contention). Political issues led to a clash with Stone, regarded by Hayter as a crypto-Jacobite intent on instilling into the prince of Wales tory principles. Clearly this was intolerable to Hayter. Consequent on the quarrels about these matters Harcourt resigned on 5 December 1752 and Hayter the next day. The *Gentleman's Magazine* published a poem on the affair:

> envy, faction, and ambitious rage,
> Drove from a guilty court the pious sage.
> (*GM*, 1st ser., 22, 1752, 577)

Lord Waldegrave, by contrast, laid the blame squarely on the bishop's imperious personality. Hayter, he maintained, 'persuaded Harcourt … that they as Governor and Preceptor must be the sole Directors of the young Prince, and that not even the Princess herself ought to have the least Influence over him' (*Memoirs and Speeches of … Waldegrave*, 144). However, according to Edmund Pyle, after the struggle 'all … [Hayter's] view is to be snug & happy in his diocese' (Hartshorne, 192).

The affair's reverberations continued after Hayter's resignation. It had been alleged by the recorder of Newcastle, one Fawcett, that Stone, Bishop Johnson of Gloucester, and William Murray had once been Jacobites, and the matter was discussed in the cabinet council in February 1753. It was also debated in the Lords in March, and Walpole thought that Hayter was desirous of 'inflaming the prejudice against Stone and Murray' but was not given a proper opportunity to do so (Walpole, 1.219). Hayter supported the duke of Bedford's proposal to lay before the house the cabinet council's papers on the matter, but the issue was allowed to drop. None the less Newcastle was furious at Hayter's conduct—Stone, Johnson, and Murray were

some of his closest associates—while Hayter was alienated from the ministry (he voted against the Militia Bill in 1756). His preferment was problematical. Archbishop Herring had urged his elevation to Durham in June 1752, but this came to nothing; George II by that time 'was not at all satisfied with the B. of Norwich' (Taylor, 'Fac totum', 425). After Bishop Sherlock of London died in July 1761, however, it was decided to appoint Hayter his successor. Newcastle had been horrified by the possibility: 'The report that the bishop of Norwich is to be bishop of London, a man … who has acted so ungratefully to me … shews such a disregard to me … that I own it is with difficulty I swallow it' (Sykes, 73). The duke hoped that Hayter might be given Salisbury and even considered resignation, regarding the proposed promotion as 'a personal Declaration against me' (Taylor, 'Fac totum', 431), but the earl of Bute was adamant and Hayter's translation was confirmed on 24 October 1761.

Hayter died, unmarried, on 9 January 1762, of dropsy. He was buried in the churchyard at Fulham; his epitaph speaks of his 'amiable character and conspicuous abilities' (Nichols, 9.506). He left about £25,000, which was to be split among two of his brothers and four sisters. He was a 'Subscriber to almost every public Charity, and innumerable were the Distress'd, who felt his Contribution to many private ones' (Stainsby, 16–17). The chief significance of his career lies in his conduct while the prince of Wales's preceptor; it appeared to provide evidence for the whigs' later claim that George III had been indoctrinated with authoritarian ideas before his accession to the throne.

COLIN HAYDON

Sources parish register, Chagford, Devon, 1702, Devon RO, 1429 A adds 3, 4/PR 2 · L. Blackburne, will, 1743, PRO, PROB 11/725, sig. 144 · T. Hayter, *A short view of some of the general arts of controversy made use of by the advocates for infidelity* (1732) · *The memoirs and speeches of James, 2nd Earl Waldegrave, 1742–1763*, ed. J. C. D. Clark (1988) · H. Walpole, *Memoirs of King George II*, ed. J. Brooke, 1 (1985) · 'Characters of the last two bishops of London', *The London Magazine, or, Gentleman's Monthly Intelligencer*, 424–5 · Nichols, *Lit. anecdotes* · A. Hartshorne, ed., *Memoirs of a royal chaplain, 1729–1763* (1905) · *GM*, 1st ser., 22 (1752) · *The political journal of George Bubb Dodington*, ed. J. Carswell and L. A. Dralle (1965) · S. L. Ollard and P. C. Walker, eds., *Archbishop Herring's visitation returns, 1743*, 5, Yorkshire Archaeological Society, 79 (1931) · T. W. Perry, *Public opinion, propaganda, and politics in eighteenth-century England* (1962) · N. Sykes, 'The duke of Newcastle as ecclesiastical minister', *EngHR*, 57 (1942), 59–84 · S. Taylor, 'The bishops at Westminster in the mid-eighteenth century', *A pillar of the constitution: the House of Lords in British politics, 1640–1784*, ed. C. Jones (1989), 137–63 · S. Taylor, '"The fac totum in ecclesiastic affairs"? The duke of Newcastle and the crown's ecclesiastical patronage', *Albion*, 24 (1992), 409–33 · R. Stainsby, *A sermon preached at St Clement Danes, on Sunday the 17th of January, 1762* (1762) · Foster, *Alum. Oxon.* · E. B. Fryde and others, eds., *Handbook of British chronology*, 3rd edn, Royal Historical Society Guides and Handbooks, 2 (1986) · G. Hennessy, *Novum repertorium ecclesiasticum parochiale Londinense, or, London diocesan clergy succession from the earliest time to the year 1898* (1898) · Venn, *Alum. Cant.*

Archives LPL, corresp. and papers incl. dilapidations accounts for Fulham Palace | Norfolk RO, Norwich diocesan MSS

Likenesses attrib. T. Hudson, oils, *c*.1755–1760 (copy); formerly Fulham Palace, London [*see illus.*]

Wealth at death approx. £25,000: Nichols, *Lit. anecdotes*

Hayter, Sir William Goodenough, first baronet (1792–1878), politician and barrister, youngest son of John Hayter, and his wife, Grace, daughter of Stephen Goodenough of Codford, Wiltshire, was born at Winterbourne Stoke, Wiltshire, on 28 January 1792. He entered Winchester College in 1804 and matriculated on 24 October 1810 from Trinity College, Oxford, where he took his BA in 1814. On being called to the bar at Lincoln's Inn on 23 November 1819, he became an equity draftsman and conveyancer, and attended the Wiltshire sessions, but retired from practice on being made a QC on 21 February 1839; he was, however, bencher of his inn on 15 April 1839, and treasurer in 1853. On 18 August 1832 he married Anne (1806/7–1889), eldest daughter of William Pulsford of Linslade.

On 24 July 1837 Hayter was returned as a Liberal to the House of Commons as one of the members for Wells, and sat for that constituency until 6 July 1865. From 30 December 1847 to 30 May 1849 he was judge-advocate-general. At the latter date he became financial secretary to the Treasury, and in July 1850 was appointed parliamentary and patronage secretary, a post which he held until March 1852, and again from December 1852 to March 1858. Hayter was an effective whip, especially during the minority tory government of 1852 and the early years of the subsequent Aberdeen coalition. He failed to prevent the collapse of the coalition in 1855, and probably preferred working for Palmerston, Aberdeen's successor as prime minister. On 11 February 1848 he was sworn of the privy council. After his retirement, on 19 April 1858, he was created a baronet, and on 27 February 1861, to commemorate his record as whip, he was presented by Lord Palmerston and 365 members of the House of Commons with a service of plate at a banquet in Willis's Rooms (*Illustrated London News*, 9 March 1861, with view of the testimonial).

Hayter was a successful farmer, his farm, Lindsay, near Leighton, Buckinghamshire, being a byword for economy and profitable management. He was one of the council of the Agricultural Society from its commencement in 1838. He voted with C. P. Villiers in 1839 for the repeal of the corn laws, and was present at all the divisions in favour of free trade. He was not a frequent speaker, but took part in debates on matters within his knowledge. In Lord Denman's inquiry into the management of the woods and forests he was a member of the committee, and was chairman of the committee on Feargus O'Connor's land scheme. During 1878 he fell into a depressed state of mind, and on 26 December was found drowned in a small lake in the grounds of his residence, South Hill Park, Easthampstead, Berkshire. He was buried at Easthampstead on 2 January 1879. He was survived by his wife who died in London on 2 June 1889.

Hayter was succeeded by his only son, **Arthur Divett Hayter**, Baron Haversham (1835–1917), politician, who was born on 9 August 1835. After Eton College and Brasenose College, Oxford, Arthur Hayter joined the Grenadier Guards. He was Liberal MP for Wells (1865–8), for Bath (1873–85), and for Walsall (1893–95). Hayter was a reliable Liberal. After succeeding his father as second baronet in 1878, he was a junior whip from 1880 to 1882 and was

Sir William Goodenough Hayter, first baronet (1792–1878), by unknown engraver, pubd 1861 (after John Watkins)

financial secretary to the War Office from 1882 to 1885. He chaired the public accounts committee from 1901 to 1905 and was created Baron Haversham in January 1906. In 1866 he married Henrietta *née* Hope. They had no children and his titles became extinct when he died on 10 May 1917.　　　　　　　　G. C. BOASE, rev. H. C. G. MATTHEW

Sources *The Times* (28 Dec 1878) · *The Times* (30 Dec 1878) · *The Times* (3 Jan 1879) · *Dod's Parliamentary Companion* (1865) · Boase, *Mod. Eng. biog.* · GEC, *Peerage* · GEC, *Baronetage* · Gladstone, *Diaries*
Archives BL, corresp. with Charles Babbage, C. G. A. Dawkins, and W. E. Gladstone · BLPES, corresp. with Joshua Jebb
Likenesses wood-engraving, NPG; repro. in *ILN* (20 July 1850), 64 · wood-engraving (after J. Watkins), NPG; repro. in *ILN* (13 April 1861), 339 [see illus.]
Wealth at death under £100,000: probate, 20 Feb 1879, *CGPLA Eng. & Wales*

Hayter, Sir William Goodenough (1906–1995), diplomatist and college head, was born on 1 August 1906 in Oxford, the only son and eldest of the three children of Sir William Goodenough Hayter (1869–1924), a judge in the Anglo-Egyptian service, and his wife, Alethea, daughter of the Revd John Henry Slessor, rector of Headbourne Worthy, Hampshire. Like his father, he was educated at Winchester College where—also like his father—he was a scholar and became prefect of hall (head boy). His notable school contemporaries included John Sparrow, William Empson, and Richard Crossman. From Winchester he again followed his father as the senior classical scholar to New College, Oxford. After such a promising early academic career his failure to get the expected firsts in both

Sir William Goodenough Hayter (1906–1995), by Walter Stoneman, 1953

moderations and Greats caused much surprise and disappointment. However he won a travelling fellowship at Queen's College, Oxford, and spent the following nine months improving his French and more particularly his German as a prelude to taking the diplomatic service entrance examination in October 1930.

Having passed in third place into the diplomatic service, Hayter was posted for his first year to the League of Nations and the Western department of the Foreign Office. He was then posted to Vienna in October 1931 where he enjoyed cultivating the aristocratic *erste Gesellschaft*. By way of contrast he was posted from April 1934 to January 1937 to Moscow, where Stalin's purges were beginning and where the diplomatic corps was thrown back on its own social resources. He managed none the less to travel widely in the Soviet Union, visiting Ukraine, the Crimea, and the Caucasus—the last in the company of the German ambassador, Count Schulenburg, who was later executed for his part in the plot against Hitler. After another brief spell in the League of Nations department, during which he played a minor part in the preparations for the coronation of King George VI and made a duty visit to Spain during the civil war, he was posted in October 1938 to the embassy in China, then accredited to the Kuomintang government of Chiang Kai-shek at Chungking (Chongqing), which was at war with Japan. Hayter was left in charge for some months in Chungking while his ambassador was based at Shanghai, but he also eventually returned to Shanghai. The prospect for the British mission

in China looked precarious in the extreme (they were later interned by the Japanese) and Hayter was relieved to be posted to Washington as first secretary in December 1940. Arriving shortly before the attack on Pearl Harbor (the news of which he personally passed to London), he subsequently worked closely with both the state department and the American military authorities. On his return to the Foreign Office in May 1944 he worked first in a number of political departments before being promoted in February 1948 to be an assistant under-secretary of state; during this period in London he attended the Potsdam conference as secretary to the British delegation, which was headed successively by Churchill and Attlee, and for three years he held the key post of chairman of the joint intelligence committee of the chiefs of staff. His appointment as minister at the embassy in Paris in December 1949 reintroduced him to the glittering social world he had first known in pre-war Vienna. In his work he tended to be sceptical about the prospect of Britain's requiring or wishing to apply for entry to the European Coal and Steel Community, but he put forward the view that continental European collaboration was in British interests. From Paris in October 1953, at the early age of forty-six, he was appointed ambassador in Moscow. He was appointed KCMG in July 1953, having been made CMG in January 1948.

Hayter's mission to Moscow, which lasted until February 1957, was the high point of his diplomatic career. He arrived shortly after the death of Stalin, when the leadership of the Soviet Union was first in the hands of Malenkov and later of Khrushchov and (to a diminishing extent) Bulganin. The Soviet leadership was accessible for the first time for several decades, and Hayter took full advantage of this to consolidate personal links. He proposed to Eden that Bulganin and Khrushchov should be invited to Britain (the first such post-war visit) and he accompanied them on their tour. Although he had much dialogue with Khrushchov, he never claimed to have influenced fundamentally the latter's policies. One shadow over his mission was subsequently cast by the exposure of the spy Vassal in the naval attaché's office, but Hayter was exonerated from any negligence over this by the subsequent inquiry. His final months in Moscow were dominated by the Soviet intervention in Hungary and by the Anglo-French intervention in Suez. Hayter felt frustrated by being kept in the dark about British intentions over Suez and was privately very critical of the enterprise, which he felt had lessened the chances of any Soviet withdrawal from Hungary; however, when the Soviet government sent a threatening note about Suez to the UK, hinting at the use of rockets, Hayter drafted a robust reply that was accepted by the prime minister. When, shortly after his return to London as deputy under-secretary (political) in the Foreign Office, Hayter was offered the wardenship of New College, Oxford, his acceptance was influenced by his disillusionment over Suez and his failure to see the way clear to any of those top jobs in the diplomatic service to which he aspired. He resigned from the diplomatic service in October 1958.

At New College, where he remained until his retirement in 1976, Hayter was an affable warden who took a keen interest in the undergraduates of the college and assumed the duties of admissions tutor. But he was conscious that being involved in neither teaching nor research limited his role at Oxford, and he did not play much part in university affairs outside his own college. He advocated the admission of women to the college more than a decade before it happened. His other activities included being a fellow of Winchester College (1958–76) and a trustee of the British Museum (1960–70). During his years at Oxford he wrote a number of books mostly about diplomacy and Russia, of which the best known were *The Kremlin and the Embassy* (1966) and an autobiography, *A Double Life* (1974). When eventually he retired to Bassetts House, in the village of Stanton St John, outside Oxford, he continued to write and to entertain his many friends.

Hayter had married on 19 October 1938 Iris Marie (*b.* 1911), the only child of Lieutenant-Colonel Charles Hervey Hoare (who assumed the surname Grey in 1927) and his first wife, Marie Elizabeth, daughter of Ludwig Leupold of Geneva, and widow of Sir Lepel Griffin. Hayter's wife played an exceptionally active and supportive role as a hostees throughout his diplomatic career and at New College, and it was she who provided the warmth for which their official residences were remembered. Their daughter, Teresa, was born in Shanghai in 1940. Hayter was considered by many of his contemporaries to be a quintessential Wykehamist: able, polished, and with an academic turn of mind. It was not coincidence but merit that accounted for his being in so many crucial places at crucial times. To his more astringent colleagues, however, both in the diplomatic service and at Oxford, he sometimes seemed to lack the industry and energy to follow up on detailed and mundane tasks. Only his closest friends broke through the canopy of charm to discover real warmth in his personality. He admitted to having lost his belief in Christianity while at school, but to retaining 'a kind of affectionate loyalty to the Church of England'. He died at Stanton St John, Oxfordshire, on 28 March 1995; he was survived by his wife and daughter.   JOHN URE

Sources W. G. Hayter, *A double life* (1974) · private information (2004) · personal knowledge (2004) · *The Times* (30 March 1995) · *The Independent* (30 March 1995) · *WWW* [forthcoming] · Burke, *Peerage* · FO List
Archives New College, Oxford, papers | FILM BFI NFTVA, news footage | SOUND BFI NFTVA, documentary recording
Likenesses W. Stoneman, photograph, 1953, NPG [*see illus.*] · photograph, repro. in *The Times*
Wealth at death under £125,000: probate, 19 June 1995, CGPLA Eng. & Wales

Haythorne, Sir Edmund (1818–1888), army officer, was the son of John Haythorne of Hill House, Gloucester. He was educated at the Royal Military College, Sandhurst, commissioned ensign in the 98th foot on 12 May 1837, and promoted lieutenant on 4 October 1839.

Under the command of Colin Campbell, later Lord Clyde, Haythorne went with the 98th to China in 1841, and was present with it in the expedition northward in 1842, including the operations on the Yangtze (Yangzi) River,

the attack and capture of Chinkiang (Zhenjiang), and the operations before Nanking (Nanjing). He was Campbell's brigade major at Chushan from July 1843 until the island was given up to the Chinese authorities, and was promoted captain on 11 September 1844.

Haythorne served as Campbell's aide-de-camp in the Second Anglo-Sikh War of 1848–9, when he commanded the 3rd division of Gough's army at the passage of the Chenab, the battles of Sadri, Chilianwala, and Gujrat, and the pursuit of the Afghan contingent to the Khyber Pass. He was awarded the brevet of major on 7 June 1849. He commanded the flank of the 98th at the forcing of the Kohat Pass, under Sir Charles Napier, in 1850, and in 1851 he was again aide-de-camp to Campbell in the operations against the Mohmands on the north-west frontier. He was promoted major on 1 April 1853, lieutenant-colonel on 12 May 1854, and colonel on 28 November 1854.

In June 1855 Haythorne exchanged to the 1st Royals, went to the Crimea, and assumed command of the 1st battalion, with which he was present at the siege and fall of Sevastopol. Afterwards he was brigade major of the Highland brigade under Campbell at Balaklava.

In 1859 Haythorne was nominated chief of staff of the army forming in Hong Kong for service in the north of China, and had sole responsibility for the organization of the force until the arrival of Sir James Hope Grant in March 1860. He was mentioned in dispatches, and especially mentioned by Lord Herbert, secretary of state for war, when proposing a vote of thanks to the China troops.

Haythorne was adjutant-general in Bengal from 1860 to 1865, when he went on half pay. His old chief Lord Clyde spoke with affection of him on his deathbed: 'Good Haythorne, brave Haythorne, as modest as he is brave' (Shadwell, 2.470).

Haythorne married, in 1862, Eliza, daughter of J. Thomas of Bletsoe Castle, Bedfordshire. He became a major-general on 6 March 1868, lieutenant-general on 23 December 1876, and full general on 15 March 1879. He was made KCB in 1873, and colonel of the 37th foot in 1879. He died at his home, Silchester House, Reading, on 18 October 1888, and was buried in Reading on the 23rd.

H. M. CHICHESTER, rev. ALEX MAY

Sources *Army List* · *Hart's Army List* · Burke, *Peerage* (1880) · L. Shadwell, *The life of Colin Campbell*, 2 vols. (1881) · J. Ouchterlony, *The Chinese War* (1844) · C. Hibbert, *The dragon wakes: China and the West, 1793–1911* (1970) · D. Hurd, *The arrow war: an Anglo-Chinese confusion* (1967) · B. Farwell, *Queen Victoria's little wars* (1973) · J. Selby, *The paper dragon* (1968) · G. Bruce, *Six battles for India: the Anglo-Sikh wars, 1845–6, 1848–9* (1969) · B. Bond, ed., *Victorian military campaigns* (1967) · *The Times* (20 Oct 1888) · CGPLA Eng. & Wales (1888)
Archives NAM, letter, 6804/3–31 | BL, Rose MSS, letter
Likenesses wood-engraving, NPG; repro. in *ILN* (10 Nov 1888)
Wealth at death £9140 17s. 3d.: resworn double probate, Aug 1889, CGPLA Eng. & Wales (1888)

Haytley, Edward (*fl.* 1740–1764), portrait and landscape painter, is of unknown origins. Given his professional contacts with Arthur Devis and the connections of many of his sitters he may have come from Lancashire. The earliest reference to him is in a letter, dated 21 August 1740, from Elizabeth Robinson to Anne Donnellan, requesting her to send drawings of flowers by both Haytley and her father. She wanted the studies to help her design the embroidery of an apron that she was making for her friend the duchess of Portland (E. Montagu, 1.57). Haytley's skill as a painter of detail is evident in his accomplished conversation piece showing Elizabeth Robinson with her parents, Edward and Elizabeth Montagu. They sit on a terrace at Sandleford Priory, near Hythe, in Kent, in front of an extensive georgic landscape with haymaking and the village of Newtown in the background (1744; priv. coll., USA). The Montagu papers also contain a description of drawings that Haytley was making of their neighbours the Brockman family, of Beachborough Manor. A description of one drawing corresponds with one of a pair of canvasses, both of which show the newly built Temple Pond at Beachborough (1744; National Gallery of Victoria, Melbourne). The Montagu account books refer to Haytley undertaking a number of other tasks, including repairing pictures.

In 1746 Haytley signed and dated six small-scale full-length portraits of members of the Stanley family (priv. coll.), a triple portrait, possibly representing Matthew and Elizabeth Robinson with their daughter Sarah (priv. coll., USA), and a portrait, known in two versions, of Sir Robert and Lady Bradshaigh posing in front of Haigh Hall (Metropolitan Borough of Wigan and priv. coll.). The settings of the Bradshaigh portraits have the same topographical clarity as the landscapes of Sandleford and Beachborough. Two three-quarters-length portraits, one of Sir Robert Bradshaigh (the other unidentified) are recorded as dated 1750. Two years later Haytley is recorded again painting members of the Montagu family in Kent. In the late 1740s, at the behest of William Hogarth, he donated roundels of Bethlem and Chelsea hospitals to the Foundling Hospital, London; hung in the court room they have become his best-known works.

Haytley contributed two unidentified portraits to the first exhibition at the Incorporated Society of Artists in 1760 and another three to the exhibition of 1761. His last recorded painting, a portrait of Sir William Milner, second baronet, is dated 1764 (Sothebys, 12 March 1980, lot 133). It shares the format of the Stanley portraits, although compositionally it has greater confidence and presence and serves as a pendant to a portrait of Lady Milner by Devis that is dated 1760 (ibid., 132). In the absence of paintings bearing a later date it is presumed that Haytley died soon afterwards. HUGH BELSEY

Sources Hunt. L., Montagu papers, MO 4682 · BL, Montagu account books, Add. MS 42708, CXXIII, 118–202, 214 · E. Devapriam, 'Two conversation pieces by Edward Haytley', *Apollo*, 114 (1981), 85–7 · [D. Posnett], *The Montagu family at Sandleford Priory by Edward Haytley, 1744 … an exhibition of English eighteenth century paintings* [1978] [exhibition catalogue, Leger Galleries, London, June–July 1978] · [D. Posnett], *Realism through informality* (1983), no. 11 [exhibition catalogue, Leger Galleries, London] · S. Sartin, *Polite society by Arthur Devis, 1712–1787: portraits of the English country gentleman and his family* (1983), 66–7 [exhibition catalogue, Preston and London, 1 Oct 1983 – 29 Jan 1984] · E. G. D'Oench, *The conversation piece: Arthur Devis and his contemporaries* (1980), 72–3 [exhibition catalogue, Yale U. CBA, 1 Oct – 30 Nov 1980] · J. Harris, *The artist and the country house: a history of country house and garden view painting in Britain, 1540–1870* (1979), 219–21, 267, 311 · E. Einberg, *Manners and morals: Hogarth and British painting, 1700–1760* (1987), 148–50, 181 [exhibition catalogue, Tate Gallery, London, 15 Oct 1987 – 3 Jan 1988] · *Elizabeth Montagu, the queen of the blue-stockings: her correspondence from 1720 to 1761*, ed. E. J. Cleminson, 1 (1906), 56–7, 61–2 · U. Hoff, *European paintings before 1800 in the National Gallery of Victoria, Melbourne*, 4th edn (1995), 143–4

Archives BL, Brockman account books, Add. MS 42708 · Hunt. L., Montagu papers, MO 4682

Hayward, Abraham (1801–1884), essayist and translator, was born on 22 November 1801 in Wilton, near Salisbury, the eldest son of Joseph Hayward (d. 1844), landed gentleman and writer on agriculture and horticulture, and Mary, daughter of Richard Abraham of White Lackington, Somerset. The product of an old but rather humble Wiltshire family, he was a self-made man of letters. From about 1807 to February 1811 he studied at Bath under Francis Twiss. For the next six years he was a student at Blundell's School in Tiverton. Between January 1817 and September 1818 he was tutored at home, and it was there that he obtained the mastery of German and French which he would later put to profitable literary use. For the next five years he was articled to George Tuson, solicitor, of Northover and later of Ilchester, Somerset, in whose library he discovered his passion for literature.

With his father's blessing Hayward abruptly changed his career plans and enrolled as a student of the Inner Temple in October 1824; after moving to London, he never moved away. Membership in the London Debating Society gave him his first taste of metropolitan intellectual life, and he quickly made a name for himself as one of the few tories who could hold his own against John Stuart Mill and the other young philosophic radicals who ruled the society in the late 1820s. Between rhetorical contests there he practised as a special pleader, and was called to the bar in June 1832. His interest in the law first introduced him to journalism; in June 1828 he became joint editor (with W. F. Cornish) of the *Law Magazine, or, Quarterly Review of Jurisprudence*. He assumed sole editorship after the fourth number and held this position until June 1844.

The young Hayward had never permitted the finer points of the law to distract him from his interest in literature. Thus it is not surprising that his visit to Göttingen in 1831, partly devoted to the study of German jurisprudence, ended with a resolution to translate Goethe's *Faust*. It was this decision which launched him into a literary career. His translation was admired and brought him to public notice in Germany and at home, gaining him admittance into the salons of the German, British, and French capitals. Congratulations were sent to him from poets such as Wordsworth, Southey, and Samuel Rogers, and they were soon followed by invitations to contribute to John Gibson Lockhart's *Quarterly Review* and Edward Bulwer-Lytton's *Monthly Magazine*. As engaging in conversation as he was in prose, Hayward quickly became a regular diner at fashionable tables and hosted his own dinner parties in his bachelor's chambers in the Temple, at 11 King's Bench Walk. Thus, while never winning great

Abraham Hayward (1801–1884), by Lemercier

celebrity for himself, he counted many celebrities among his friends, including Thomas Babington Macaulay, William Makepeace Thackeray (upon whose career his reviews were influential), W. E. Gladstone, J. A. Froude, Joseph Delane, Prince Louis Bonaparte, Nassau Senior, Adolphe Thiers, Laurence Oliphant, François Guizot, Sir George Cornewall Lewis, and Alphonse de Lamartine.

By the 1840s Hayward was devoting much of his time to journalism. While he remained (and apparently chose to remain) virtually briefless, his ties to the political world helped him to secure appointments as a counsel to the Admiralty and a revising barrister. The decision by his friend Lord Chancellor Lyndhurst to give him a silk gown early in 1845 raised eyebrows at the inns of court, and foes in his own inn made this allegedly nepotistic appointment a pretext for refusing to elect him as a bencher. His appointment by Lord John Russell's government to report on the Dublin Improvement Bill in February 1847 helped to take the sting out of this professional rebuff, but, more often than not, his hopes for patronage were dashed. He sought but was denied a commissionership under the Charitable Trusts Bill in 1853 and was once again left empty-handed the following year when, after accepting the lucrative post of secretary to the poor-law board offered to him by the Aberdeen coalition, he was forced to give it up because the incumbent, Lord Courtenay, reneged on his agreement to exchange the secretary's office for that of commissioner of woods and forests.

Hayward, who began his political life as a moderate tory, would never have even been considered for such positions had he not performed useful services for his Peelite friends. His most notable contribution to the Peelite cause came in 1848, when, serving as chief leader writer for the *Morning Chronicle*, he fired regular salvoes at the protectionist rump of the Conservative Party. Like most Peelites, he ended up a moderate Liberal and was a consistent advocate of the timely political concession. The 'paramount excellence of a minister under our system of Government', he concluded in a characteristic tribute to the memory of Lord Melbourne, was skill in:

determining the precise period when the people are ripe for any given change. The evils of procrastination in such a

contingency are obvious enough, but it may be equally dangerous to anticipate; for, if a reaction should be the result, the progress of improvement might be indefinitely delayed. (A. Hayward, *Biographical and Critical Essays*, 1, 1874, 267)

Since they had followed the same political path through most of their lives, it is not surprising that Hayward and Gladstone occasionally corresponded and dined together in the late 1870s and early 1880s. The premier was the most distinguished of the dignitaries at Hayward's funeral, and he 'place[d] on the coffin for Mrs Gladstone a basketful of snowdrops fresh from Hawarden' (*The Times*, 7 Feb 1884, 7).

Political journalism accounts for only a small percentage of Hayward's output, however. He contributed some forty articles to the *Edinburgh Review* between 1841 and 1867, and another eighty to the *Quarterly* between 1834 and his death in 1884, covering such diverse topics as history-writing, foreign travel, French and German novels, fox-hunting, and etiquette. He collected some of his early essays in *The Art of Dining* (1852), which combines all of his characteristic traits as a writer: a sparkling wit, a mock cynicism, a wealth of historical anecdote, a penchant for fashionable gossip and for throwing in a personal tale to illustrate a broader point. Among his few other books are *Biographical and Critical Essays* (2 vols., 1874), which includes revised versions of his favourite pieces; a biography, with letters, of Dr Johnson's friend Mrs Thrale (2 vols., 1861); and a slim biography of Goethe (1878).

Blessed as he was with a keen intellect, a prodigious memory, and remarkable fluency, one could argue that Hayward never quite lived up to his enormous potential. A more charitable conclusion is that he was too fond of his dilettantish way of life to care very much about what posterity might think of it. In his later years it was apparently enough for him to pass much of his comfortable bachelor's existence at the Athenaeum (to which he had been elected in 1835), where he could exchange stories and witticisms over dinner or a rubber of whist, and read books in the members' library and then write about them. He died of heart failure in his rooms at 8 St James's Street, Westminster, London, on 2 February 1884 and was buried four days later in Highgate cemetery.   PHILIP HARLING

Sources DNB · *A selection from the correspondence of Abraham Hayward*, ed. H. E. Carlisle, 2 vols. (1886) · *The Times* (4 Feb 1884), 8 · *The Times* (7 Feb 1884), 7 · *The Athenaeum* (9 Feb 1884), 183–4 · *Saturday Review*, 57 (1884), 176–7 · E. H. Yates, *Fifty years of London life: memoirs of a man of the world* (1885) · G. W. Smalley, *London letters*, 2 vols. (1890) · Wellesley index

Archives BL, corresp. with Charles Babbage, Add. MSS 37189–37200, *passim* · BL, corresp. with W. E. Gladstone, Add. MS 44207 · BL, letters to Lady Holland, Add. MS 52126 · BL, letters to Macvey Napier, Add. MSS 34621–34626, *passim* · Herts. ALS, letters to Lord Lytton · Mitchell L., Glas., Glasgow City Archives, letters to Sir William Stirling-Maxwell · NL Scot., letters to Alexander Campbell Fraser · NL Wales, letters to Sir George Cornewall Lewis · Som. ARS, letters to Lady Waldegrave and Lord Carlingford · St Deiniol's Library, Hawarden, letters to duke of Newcastle · Trinity Cam., letters to Lord Houghton · U. Nott. L., letters to the countess of Charleville and Brinsley and Mrs Marley · UCL, letters to Lord Brougham

Likenesses Ape [C. Pellegrini], watercolour study for a caricature, NPG; repro. in *VF* (27 Nov 1875) · Lemercier, photograph, NPG [*see illus.*]

Wealth at death £1144 4s. 5d.: probate, 5 March 1884, *CGPLA Eng. & Wales*

Hayward, Frank Herbert (1872–1954), inspector of schools and author, was born on 16 December 1872 at Wotton under Edge, Gloucestershire, the son of John Hayward, a bootmaker, later of 56 Seymour Road, Bristol, and his wife, Anne Lydiard. Details of his early education are unknown, but he began teaching in a board school as a pupil teacher in 1887. He was assistant master at St George's School of Science, Bristol (1897–9), and lecturer at Cambridge Day College (1899–1900). He graduated BA at London University in 1894, and BSc and MA in 1898. He was admitted as an advanced student to Gonville and Caius College, Cambridge, in October 1900, having previously kept three terms in Cambridge as a non-collegiate student. He graduated with a BA degree in moral sciences in 1901 and received the moral science prize. He also gained the degree of DLitt from London University in 1901. From 1902 to 1904 he was organizing tutor in mid-Devon, and from 1904 to 1905 principal of the Torquay Pupil-Teacher Centre. Following the reorganization of the London county council inspectorate, which led to an increase in numbers, he was appointed as an assistant inspector in December 1905. He became a district inspector in March 1920 and was responsible for inspecting evening and day schools in Finsbury and Islington, and, from June 1929, in Hackney, Shoreditch, and Stoke Newington.

Hayward was deeply impressed by the writings of the German educator and philosopher Johann Friedrich Herbart (1776–1841), who stated that the most important aim and end of education was morality. Favouring a strictly pedagogic approach, Herbart advocated that teachers develop the many-sided interests of pupils by presenting them with new material which could be associated, appreciated, and then applied. After spending some time researching in Germany, Hayward published in the early years of the twentieth century a number of popular books based on Herbart's ideas, particularly *The Critics of Herbartianism* (1903), based on his London doctoral thesis, *The Secret of Herbart* (1904), and *The Meaning of Education* (1907). He was an early advocate of applying psychology to educational problems, as seen in his *Primary Curriculum* (1909) and *Mental Training and Efficiency* (1921).

Hayward was a great admirer of Frederick James Gould, a leading member of the English positivists, who was concerned with the reform and humanization of education and the promotion of moral instruction in schools. In April 1902, as a member of the Moral Education League, Hayward signed a petition to the school board for London, calling for systematic non-theological moral instruction in all schools 'and to make the formation of character the chief aim of life'. He believed that the failure of the then current educational methods and the incapacity of churches to meet the human and spiritual needs of children needed to be challenged. After the First World War he collaborated with a colleague, Arnold Freeman, in writing a book, *The Spiritual Foundations of Reconstruction*, published in 1919, which suggested that there should be a system of school celebrations, building on the existing empire day, Shakespeare day, and St David's day celebrations, but extending the principle to include a national school liturgy of the Bible, literature, and music. Teachers were to give moral and civic lessons illustrated from the liturgy. In the following year Hayward set out a detailed programme in *A First Book of School Celebrations*. The policy and practice of celebrations, Hayward stated, covered a wide field of topics, ranging from the prophetic utterances of holy men, bards, and seers, to the rise and fall of world conquerors and anniversary celebrations of great men. Thematic celebrations, such as eugenics, temperance, self-control, and avoidance of gambling and the use of narcotics, were also recommended, as well as seasonal and service celebrations. A third volume, *A New Book of Celebrations*, published at Hayward's own expense in 1927, dropped the word 'school' from its title as it was aimed at a wider adult audience. The fourth and final volume of celebrations appeared in 1932. In the preface he wrote that it would be the last 'unless educational leadership comes to my assistance'.

Hayward fully described his long and fruitless battle to persuade his London county council inspectors to adopt the system of celebrations in schools in a book written shortly after his retirement entitled *An Educational Failure: a School Inspector's Story* (1938). Five years earlier he wrote bitterly after a conference of inspectors on civic education:

> Since 1920 I have arranged for probably 150 public Celebrations. Some few of these have been nearly perfect: some few have been disappointing. Most have been good in parts and nearly all have been 'suggestive'. Not 10 times out of the 150 have I seen the face of an L.C.C. inspector. (memorandum, 3 Feb 1933, LMA, EO/PS/2/3)

Apart from a brief reference to celebrations in the 1937 edition of the *Handbook of Suggestions for Teachers*, the plan received no official recognition. He retired from the inspectorate on 16 December 1937.

Hayward served as a councillor for Chingford, Essex (1936–8), but devoted his later years to pamphleteering. His final book was a biography of his hero, F. J. Gould, *The Last Days of a Great Educationist* (1942), written with E. M. White. He died on 16 February 1954 at his home, 19 Heathcote Grove, Chingford, Essex, leaving two sons and two daughters. His wife, Maria Magdalena Hayward, predeceased him. PETER GORDON

Sources R. Aldrich and P. Gordon, *Dictionary of British educationists* (1989) · F. H. Hayward, *An educational failure: a school inspector's story* (1938) · J. Venn and others, eds., *Biographical history of Gonville and Caius College*, 4 (1912) · *London Teacher* (March 1954), 62 · b. cert. · d. cert.

Archives LMA, education officer's MSS · U. Lond., Institute of Education, collection

Wealth at death £5460 2s. 5d.: probate, 4 June 1954, *CGPLA Eng. & Wales*

Hayward, Harry Maxwell [Max] (1924–1979), Russian scholar and translator, was born on 28 July 1924 at 15

Birley Road, Whetstone, north London, the elder of two sons of Harry Hayward and his wife, Emily Schofield. During his early childhood his family moved several times, before settling in Liverpool, where his father worked as an aircraft mechanic. Max won a scholarship to the Liverpool Institute in 1938, where he began to shine at languages. His earliest interests were in Welsh and Romani, and curiosity about Gypsies drew him to Pushkin's work of that name and kindled a desire to learn Russian. In 1942 he went up to Magdalen College, Oxford, to study German, soon switching to Russian. He was becoming a truly remarkable linguist, and friends recall that all his life he retained a command of several languages, such that in different settings he could pass for a Russian, a German, a Czech, or a Greek.

Unfit for military service, Hayward graduated with a first in 1945, and after a year spent at Charles University, Prague, on a British Council scholarship, he was appointed to the British embassy in Moscow in 1947, as one of a group of young British scholars selected by the Foreign Office with a view to improving the quality and flow of information about the USSR. This was the real beginning of a lifelong intense, if troubled, relationship with Russia. Hayward's posting coincided with the onset of the cold war, yet despite official restrictions, he seems to have managed to travel extensively and make some remarkable contacts among 'real' Russians. On returning to Britain in 1949, with both his knowledge of Russia and his command of the language greatly enhanced, Hayward was appointed lecturer in Russian, first at Oxford and then at Leeds University. Having been hitherto purely an exceptional linguist, in his first published articles from the 1950s he began to display a sensitive interest in modern Russian literature and the problems of Soviet society. Still unsure as to his future as an academic, in 1955 he returned to the British embassy in Moscow on a temporary posting. In trying to take up where he had left off previously, however, he kept unorthodox company and got into some alcohol-fuelled scrapes with the secret police, as a result of which he was sent home early. This deeply distressed him, but he was permitted one further trip to Moscow the following year for the *Daily Telegraph*, and reported on the aftermath of the twentieth party congress at which Nikita Khrushchov made his first assault on the cult of Stalin. He never visited Russia again.

Now at a point at which his career seemed at a low ebb, salvation came in the form of a research fellowship at the newly established East European Centre at St Antony's College, Oxford. Hayward remained a fellow from 1956 until his death, and there is no doubt that at St Antony's he found his niche and entered the happiest and most productive period of his life. In the autumn of 1957 the distinguished scholar George Katkov showed him the Russian text of Boris Pasternak's *Doctor Zhivago*, which the author was very anxious to see published in English, as he feared, correctly, that the Soviet authorities would ban publication in the USSR. Hayward was instantly attracted to the work and, though he had never done any professional translation, he convinced Katkov and began a fruitful collaboration with Manya Harari which led to publication a year later. Though he went on to a distinguished career as a translator, *Doctor Zhivago* remains Hayward's best-known and most enduring contribution (significantly, at the end of the twentieth century, this was the only English version of the novel) and it was this work which brought him public recognition.

In November 1958 Hayward began a nine-month research fellowship at Harvard. He clearly took to America, returning regularly during the 1960s, combining academic visits with an active social life. During this time, also, he became increasingly busy organizing visits to Britain by Soviet writers and round-table conferences on the arts in Russia, as well as campaigning publicly on behalf of victims of persecution by the Soviet authorities (for example, his defence of Pasternak's lover, Olga Ivinskaya, arrested in 1960). His diaries and correspondence for this period show the extraordinary range of people with whom he was on first-name terms—W. H. Auden, A. J. Ayer, John Wain, Alexander Kerensky, Arthur Koestler, Teddy Kollek, and Svetlana Stalin, to name but a few. And though in his early Oxford days he had seemed something of a misfit and a loner, in his St Antony's period he appeared equally at home at college high tables, at literary parties, or conversing with regulars in his local pub. At this time he produced some of his best work—often in collaboration with others, for instance his introductions to *Dissonant Voices in Soviet Literature* (1962) and *Literature and Revolution in Soviet Russia* (1963), and his co-editing of the transcript of the Sinyavsky–Daniel trial (1966). Following *Doctor Zhivago*, there were the translations of key works by Tertz and Sinyavsky (whom he seems to have known about before most people) and Isaak Babel, and later on the two volumes of memoirs by Nadezhda Mandelshtam, as well as his many collaborative translations of Aleksandr Solzhenitsyn, Yevgeniya Ginzburg, Anna Akhmatova and others. Nor did he neglect his teaching; the present writer vividly recalls his incisive yet kindly observations and his capacity for transmitting enthusiasm for the subject. Though highly critical of the oppressive nature of the USSR, he was never the stereotypical cold warrior. He remained optimistic about the Russian people and was one of the first to insist that good work could come out of the very travails with which Soviet writers had to contend.

In the 1970s Hayward began to slow down. He had given up the alcohol and nicotine on which he had become heavily dependent, started to build himself a house on the Aegean island of Spetsai, and was spending less and less time in Oxford. He was still full of plans, however, when he was suddenly taken ill in New York in December 1978. Inoperable cancer was diagnosed and he spent the last few months of his life, surrounded by friends and colleagues, back in Oxford, where he died on 18 March 1979 at Michael Sobell House, at the Churchill Hospital. He never married.   MICHAEL FALCHIKOV

Sources P. Blake, 'Introduction', in M. Hayward, *Writers in Russia, 1917–1978*, ed. P. Blake (1983), xv–lxxvi · D. Floyd, *Daily Telegraph* (19

March 1979) · *The Times* (16 Nov 1979) · D. Fanger, 'A diffident custodian', *TLS* (11 Nov 1983), 1251 · E. Acton, 'M. Hayward, *Writers in Russia* (1983)', *Sunday Times* (6 Nov 1983) · personal knowledge (2004) · private information (2004) [R. Hingley, H. Shukman] · b. cert.
Archives St Ant. Oxf., MSS
Wealth at death £13,665: probate, 24 Sept 1979, *CGPLA Eng. & Wales*

Hayward, Sir Isaac James (1884–1976), trade unionist and local politician, was born on 17 November 1884 at Blaenafon, Monmouthshire, the second of five sons in the family of seven children of Thomas Hayward, engine fitter, and his wife, Mary Elizabeth French. He went to the local elementary school, and left aged twelve. His subsequent education was at night school. Hayward remembered Blaenafon 'as a town of 13,000 people, sixty public houses and twenty-two chapels' (Jones, 239), and the necessity of regular Baptist worship and of total abstinence from alcohol was instilled in him by his father from an early age. As with Herbert Morrison, with whom Hayward was later closely associated, his introduction to social problems came through the temperance movement. From the age of twelve to fifteen he worked in the nearby pits, after which he went into engineering. He was soon active in union work in a voluntary capacity, and later he became a full-time official of the National Union of Enginemen, Firemen, Mechanics, and Electrical Workers.

In 1926 the union was affiliated to Ernest Bevin's Transport and General Workers' Union and became known as the Powerworkers' Group of that union: Hayward was first London district secretary, then assistant general secretary, and from 1938 to 1946 general secretary. In his later years he proudly referred to the union card he had held continuously from the age of sixteen. He still held it at his death. Hayward was exempted from military service during the First World War when, in the interest of industrial harmony, there began a new partnership between government and unions. Hayward played his part in this new union role, the work taking him frequently to London, where he and his family moved in 1924. He had married on 13 November 1911 Alice (d. 1944), daughter of Joshua Mayers, a master builder, of Blaenafon; they had four sons, of whom the eldest was killed in action in 1944. In London, Hayward's service on various committees brought him into contact with Clement Attlee and Herbert Morrison. Hayward found Attlee 'cold and aloof' (Jones, 240), but established an instant rapport with Morrison, who was anxious at that time to strengthen his small team, then in opposition at County Hall. Rating Hayward's union experience and balanced judgement very highly, Morrison encouraged him to seek election to the London county council (LCC). Hayward sat for the safe seat of Rotherhithe (1928–37), and later Deptford (1937–55). With Labour's resounding victory at the council elections in 1934 he became, with Lewis Silkin and Charles Latham, a member of Morrison's ruling presidium. This 'quadrumvirate' of close associates effectively governed the council until 1940.

As chief whip Hayward had a special responsibility to

Sir Isaac James Hayward (1884–1976), by Elliott & Fry, 1950

read the mood of the party as well as to maintain discipline within it. He was Morrison's 'eyes and ears and strong arm' (Donoughue and Jones, 193). He was also his trouble shooter and as chairman of the council's public assistance committee (1934–7) steered through the many reforms calculated to ease the existing harshness of the poor law. Hayward aimed to make this 'a genuine welfare service available to all in need, rather than a deterrent system for a narrow category of destitute persons' (*The Times*, 5 Jan 1976). He initiated a more generous and flexible set of scales to be applied to outdoor relief, which became a nationwide model, and set in motion the replacement of the large barrack-like institutions (or workhouses) by the small type of home that became the norm.

For Hayward there were to follow years of service as chairman of important council committees, as the council's representative on outside bodies, and as expert adviser. He became a part-time member of the board of British European Airways on its formation in 1946 and was also chairman of the consultative council of the London Electricity Board (1948–60). In 1947, while he was chairman of the London county council's education committee (1945–7), the development plan required under the Education Act of 1944 came down decisively in favour of a comprehensive school system, which in due course spread across the country. For Hayward, a self-educated man of impressive learning and culture, this was the fulfilment of a dream: 'Why should not the crossing sweeper have a university degree?' The comprehensive principle aroused deep passions, however, and Hayward needed all his polit-ical acumen to restrain the excesses of the enthusiasts on his own side while carrying the case against a determined opposition. In 1952 he was awarded the honorary degree of LLD by the University of London, on whose court he served from 1947, drawing closer the ties between univer-sity and council.

When in 1947 Hayward began his record period of lead-ership of the council (1947–65), he was sixty-three and steeped in the traditions of a council honoured for its integrity. He tolerated no semblance of corruption or impropriety in council affairs and rigidly observed the separation of public duty from private interest. He also kept the council from excessive spending, aware of how damaging this could be to the Labour cause. Hayward was intensely happy on the LCC and had no political ambi-tions beyond it. Mild-mannered and almost diffident, he avoided publicity and stood back to allow others to take the credit for the council's work. At the same time he ruled with a much tighter rein than Morrison had done. Attlee is reported to have remarked privately that under Hayward the LCC was 'the nearest approach to a totalitar-ian state in Western Europe' (Rhodes, 32). An 'old-style Labour political boss', Hayward dealt effectively with the few who dared to challenge him, and, having inherited 'a highly centralised machine', maintained it (Jones, 243). He also used it to good effect, embarking on the much-acclaimed south bank venture—the Royal Festival Con-cert Hall, the Elizabeth and Purcell halls, and the Hayward Gallery (named after him)—partly on land reclaimed from the Thames. He played a major part, too, in the birth of the National Theatre, for when doubt ruled the day he offered a grant from the council of £1 million, from which stemmed the ultimate decision to proceed. As with the south bank, his vision, determination, and clear view of the way forward led to the realization of the Crystal Palace Sports Centre, for which he had carefully assessed the nation's need. He was to be disappointed in his plan for an exhibition centre there, which was abandoned for reasons of finance. In the field of the arts he broke new ground, initiating the role of the public authority as bene-factor, to some extent in place of the private patronage of earlier times. Grants to opera, orchestral music, ballet, sculpture, and painting came to the rescue of the then lan-guishing artistic world. In addition Hayward threw him-self with vigour into the affairs of the International Union of Local Authorities, of whose British section he became chairman.

In his last six years as leader, however, Hayward fought a different battle—to save the LCC from abolition. His great pride in the achievements of the council led him to pre-clude even the possibility of reform at a time when increasing numbers thought this necessary; and he obstinately refused to co-operate with the royal commis-sion on the government of London, withholding advice and even refusing to participate in working parties set up by the government. The cause was eventually lost and he felt some bitterness that the Labour government did not repeal the 1963 act that abolished the council, setting up the greater London council (GLC) in its place. By then Hay-ward was approaching eighty and it was felt by many in the party that he had stayed on too long. His authoritarian style, or 'bossism', was resented by a younger generation of Labour councillor, and when in 1964 he stood as an aldermanic candidate for the GLC he received only a hand-ful of votes. It was a painful lesson: 'He and his style had been rejected' (Jones, 243).

Hayward was knighted under a Conservative govern-ment in 1959 but was overlooked by successive Labour governments for a life peerage, an honour that he had done much to deserve and which was bestowed on col-leagues who had been less than steadfast in their defence of the LCC. He was given the freedoms of the boroughs of Bermondsey and Deptford in 1955 and 1961, and was made an honorary FRIBA in 1970. On 8 December 1951, seven years after the death of his first wife, Hayward had mar-ried Violet Charlotte, daughter of Thomas Henry Cleve-land of Greenwich. He died on 3 January 1976.

FREDA CORBET, *rev.* MARK POTTLE

Sources private information (1986) · personal knowledge (1986) · *The Times* (5 Jan 1976) · *The Times* (6 Jan 1976) · documents (FC, 1986), Greater London council · G. W. Jones, 'Sir Isaac Hayward, 1884–1970', *London Journal*, 2 (1976), 239–44 · K. Young and P. L. Garside, *Metropolitan London: politics and urban change, 1837–1981* (1982) · B. Donoughue and G. W. Jones, *Herbert Morrison: portrait of a politic-ian* (1973) · G. Rhodes, ed., *The new government of London: the first five years* (1972) · Burke, *Peerage* (1967) · *CGPLA Eng. & Wales* (1976)
Likenesses Elliott & Fry, photograph, 1950, NPG [*see illus.*]
Wealth at death £2513: probate, 25 March 1976, *CGPLA Eng. & Wales*

Hayward, Sir John (1564?–1627), historian and civil law-yer, was born in Felixstowe, Suffolk, or in nearby Walton, where a John Haywarde, possibly his father, held modest property. Felixstowe parish subsidized Hayward's educa-tion at Pembroke College, Cambridge, where he gradu-ated BA in 1581 and MA in 1584. In 1591 he became a doctor of laws, the statutory qualification for the practice of civil law in which he was actively engaged throughout his life, certainly from as early as 1595, when the archbishop of Canterbury's warrant admitted him advocate to the court of arches.

In February 1599 Hayward's earliest and most remarked historical work, *The First Part of the Life and Raigne of King Henrie IIII*, was published by John Wolfe. As its title sug-gests, its narrative extends only through the first regnal year of Henry IV, and its greater part consists of a detailed account of the events leading to the downfall of Richard II. Its dedicatory preface, in Latin, seemed to encourage the political ambitions of the earl of Essex, soon to embark upon his misadventured Irish campaign, and in whose behaviour some professed to find evidence of the aspirations of another Bolingbroke.

This connection ensured the book's immediate success, and exposed Hayward to severe criticism. Although for a time the book continued to circulate, its offending pref-ace was suppressed. Queen Elizabeth more than once ascribed dark political motives to its author, instructing

FLY FROM EVEL   DOE   GOOD

Sir John Hayward (1564?–1627), by Willem de Passe, pubd 1630

Francis Bacon to examine the text for evidence of seditious intent. Bacon declined to find treason in it, but reported that it showed evidence of felony, in that Hayward had stolen bits of it from Tacitus (*Sir Francis Bacon his Apologie*, 34–5).

Indeed, the book marked a new departure in British historiography. *Henrie IIII* is the first historical narrative in English to adapt to British material a Tacitean emphasis upon the personal character and behaviour of the participants as the important causal element that lay behind affairs of state. Such demystification took historiography well beyond the sequential narrative of earlier chronicles, and lent itself to the identification of dramatic themes in the historical material. This early British 'politic history' reveals not only substantial borrowings from Tacitus (first published in English only a few years earlier), but the developing influence of more recent continental historiographers, notably Machiavelli, Guicciardini, and Bodin. Hayward's book remained very popular; it was reprinted eight times in the next several decades, the last in 1642 with Sir Robert Cotton's *Life of Henry III*. These subsequent editions are of collateral interest to bibliographical history, as some were counterfeit evasions of the early suppression order, crafted carefully to appear as original editions and bearing a false 1599 imprint.

Later, in June 1599, a second 'corrected' edition of the popular book, bearing a new 'epistle apologetical', was seized and burned while in press, and after Essex's downfall Hayward was interrogated repeatedly by crown officials about his motives in writing it. Hayward's book was cited prominently as evidence against Essex at the earl's hearing in Star Chamber in June 1600, and again in 1601 at the trial following his abortive rebellion.

Hayward had intended a sequel: his manuscript 'Second part of the life and raigne of King Henry IIII' extended the account through Henry's fourth regnal year, to a point just after the battle of Shrewsbury. But events had precluded its publication, and it finally appeared in print only in 1991.

Hayward was remanded to the Tower in July 1600, where he remained until after the queen's death. *The Sanctuarie of a Troubled Soule* (1601) evidently dates from the early months of his imprisonment. Its durable popularity is attested by a dozen editions and issues by 1636, and it brought him more contemporary acclaim than his histories. Similarly successful devotional titles followed in later years: *David's Teares* (1622) and *Christ's Prayer upon the Cross for his Enemies* (1623), both of which were republished often. Much of this religious material reflected intensive private devotion that evidently absorbed much of his study and practice. It was later claimed that he was 'accounted a learned and godly man, being better read in theological authors than in those belonging to his own profession' (Wood, *Ath. Oxon.: Fasti*, 1.368).

None of the unpleasant consequences of *The First Part*'s publication, including nearly three years' imprisonment, appears to have outlived the queen. Released from the Tower upon James's accession, Hayward wrote on 6 June 1603 to the new king urging the importance of contemporary historiography and dedicating to him his scholarly skills (Bodl. Oxf., MS Smith, fols. 23–5); if his pen had incriminated him under Elizabeth, it would soon exculpate him under James.

Only fourteen days after Elizabeth's death, Hayward's *An Answer to the First Part of a Certain Conference Concerning Succession* (1603) was entered for printing, and published soon thereafter. Here Hayward argued the Stuart case against the Spanish preferences of the Jesuits. *A Treatise of the Union of the Two Realms of England and Scotland* appeared in 1604, followed by *A Report of a Discourse Concerning Supreme Power in Affairs of Religion* in 1606, in which he asserted the political government of ecclesiastical affairs to be a right of regality. These treatises were in effect briefs arguing a basis in civil law for the absolute authority of the king, pressing ancient authorities to the service of legal disputation in the best tradition of the civil lawyers (Levack, 86–117). Pleasing to James, they announced Hayward as a vigorous advocate of protestant royalism and its theoretical underpinnings.

By 1610 Hayward's protestant orthodoxy and political

reliability earned his appointment, with William Camden, as official historiographer of the king's new college in Chelsea. Several appointments to judicial posts followed, confirming his good opinion at James's court. There is evidence of prerogative court appointments as early as 1609 when, besides occasional pleadings in admiralty and in the court of common piracy, he appeared as commissioner of admiralty for Middlesex. By 1613 he was serving in the court of delegates (the post-Reformation court of ecclesiastical appeals which had replaced the appellate tribunal of the papacy) and as commissioner for policies and assurances. By c.1617 he was commissioner for Shoreham and Croydon peculiars. He was now prominent among the small coterie of civilians who dominated London civil practice during the period.

Hayward was an acknowledged member of London's intellectual élite from the early days of James I's reign. He was nominated in 1617 as 'a fair and learned historian', one of twenty-seven who might reconstitute the Elizabethan Society of Antiquaries as an academy royal (*Archaeologia*, 1, 1770, xviii). His participation at one antiquarian meeting is recorded:

> Of the precedencye of Doctors and Masters of the Chauncerye before Serieaunts att Lawe, with the arguments for both sides, collected by Sir John Hayward, one of the Masters of said Courte, and answered by Mr. Francis Tate of the Midle Temple. 22 January 1604.   (BL, Add. MS 22587, fols. 33–6)

Degory Wheare, Camden professor of history at Oxford, thought him in 1623 a 'very candid, true and learned writer' (Wheare, 171). Roger Ley, assessing bishops, divines, and scholars notable in his own lifetime, grouped 'the most distinguished John Hayward' with Thomas Bodley, John Cowell, and William Camden; 'He was famous in his time,' he said, 'and wrote very learned books'; Ley enumerated several of Hayward's contributions to history, Stuart orthodoxy, and devotional literature, and confirmed that these had earned Hayward a lucrative appointment as commissary to the dean and chapter of St Paul's (BL, Stowe MS 76, fols. 257–7b).

According to Hayward in its dedication, it was young Henry, prince of Wales, who urged him to make public his next published history, *The Lives of the III Normans, Kings of England* (1613). Apparently, *The Beginning of the Reigne of Queene Elizabeth*, eventually published posthumously in 1636 with a second edition of *The Life and Raigne of King Edward the Sixth* (also a 'politic' history, first published 1630), owed something to the prince's encouragement as well. Hayward's early association with Essex, and his scholarly and literate protestantism, were appropriate to Henry's circle; he may have been the prince's tutor. His emphatic preference for traditional values over upstarts, and his preference for government by a talented and hereditary aristocracy (thematic to his work on Henry IV), appealed to James and Arundel, as it had to the Essex faction.

Hayward collaborated with William Camden and Sir Robert Cotton under Arundel's patronage. In his own somewhat Tacitean assessment of the Essex trial Camden mentioned *Henrie IIII* and its dedication, but appeared to hold Hayward free from the blame attached to the immoderate elements of the Essex faction; he described Hayward as a learned man who suffered an unfortunate reprisal for choosing the wrong season in which to publish that book. Hayward relied upon certain material in Camden's possession for his *Lives of the III Normans*, written before 1612, with which Camden implied a certain professional familiarity in an undated letter to Sir Robert Cotton (BL, Cotton MS Julius C.iii, fol. 60).

Hayward's association with Cotton is better known. It included their collaboration, documented from 1613 into the 1620s, on a private commission from the earl marshal to research the Howard family history. Although late in life he appears to have abandoned writing British history for general publication, he edited Sir Roger Williams's *The Actions of the Lowe Countries*, published with Hayward's introduction in 1618.

Hayward became master in chancery on 13 November 1616. At about this time he was listed among investors in the Bermuda and Virginia ventures. On 5 August 1616 he was admitted to Doctors' Commons, and honorifically, on 1 August 1619, to Gray's Inn. He was granted arms, and was knighted by James at Whitehall on 9 November 1619.

Hayward served on the high commission during the 1620s, and perhaps earlier. This tribunal, like chancery, admiralty, and the ecclesiastical courts, was increasingly resented by supporters of anti-clerical and anti-royalist views. Despite such turmoil Hayward, having gained his mastership under Egerton (c.1596–1617), outlasted both Bacon (c.1617–21) and Williams (c.1621–5), and served until his death under Coventry (c.1625–40).

Hayward and his wife, Jane (d. 1642), a daughter of Andrew Pascall of Springfield, Essex, had only one child, Mary. She married Nicholas Rowe of Muswell Hill, Middlesex, knighted in 1625, but she was already dead when Hayward wrote his will in 1626.

Hayward died a wealthy man on 27 June 1627 in the parish of St Bartholomew-the-Great, Smithfield, where he had lived for many years in the grandest of the glebe houses in Bartholomew Close. His will pointedly spurned his wife and his daughter's relatives by marriage in favour of his only surviving grandchild, also named Mary, to whom he left the greatest part of his fortune. She, however, died as a child in 1634, and the bulk of Hayward's estate thus passed to his wife's nephews, Edward and Thomas Hanchet. Although Hayward's will insistently prescribed precautions to be taken against body-snatchers, and related instructions for an elaborate monument at St Bartholomew's, no indication of his place of burial there survives.   JOHN J. MANNING

Sources *The first and second parts of John Hayward's 'The life and raigne of King Henrie IIII'*, ed. J. J. Manning, Camden 4th ser., 42 (1991), 'Introduction' · J. Hayward, *The life and raigne of King Edward the Sixth*, ed. B. L. Beer (1993), 'Introduction' · J. Hayward, *Annals of the first four years of the reign of Queen Elizabeth*, ed. J. Bruce, CS, 7 (1840) [incl. Hayward's will and burial cert.] · D. R. Woolf, *The idea of history in early Stuart England* (1990) · burial cert. · *DNB* · *Sir Francis Bacon his apologie, in certain imputations concerning the late earle of Essex* (1604), 34–5 · Wood, *Ath. Oxon.: Fasti* (1815) · D. Wheare, *The method* and order of reading both civil and ecclesiastical histories, trans. E. Bohum (1685), 171 · B. P. Levack, *The civil lawyers in England, 1603–1641* (1973) · N. Scarfe, 'Sir John Hayward, his life and disappointments', *Proceedings of the Suffolk Institute of Archaeology and Natural History*, 25 (1949–51), 79–97 · S. L. Goldberg, 'Sir John Hayward, "politic" historian', *Review of English Studies*, new ser., 6 (1955), 233–44 · A. T. Bradford, 'Stuart absolutism and the "utility" of Tacitus', *Huntington Library Quarterly*, 46 (1983), 127–55 · S. M. Kingsbury, ed., *The records of the Virginia Company of London*, 3 (1933), 84, 327; 4 (1935), 306, 365

Likenesses W. Hole, engraving, 1616, BM · T. Cecil, engraving, 1631, repro. in J. Hayward, *The sanctuarie of a troubled soule* (1631), title-page · W. de Passe, line engraving, BM, NPG; repro. in J. Hayward, *The life and raigne of King Edward the sixth* (1630) [*see illus.*] · J. Payne, line engraving (after engraving by W. Hole, 1616), BM; repro. in J. Hayward, *The sanctuarie of a troubled soule* (1623)

Wealth at death holdings near Wood Green and at Felixstowe, Suffolk; £1300 houses and lands in Kentish Town; substantial cash bequests, incl. £20 to the poor of Felixstowe: will, PRO

Hayward, John Davy (1905–1965), literary scholar, was born in London on 2 February 1905, the younger son and second child of John Arthur Hayward, physician and surgeon of Wimbledon, Surrey, and his wife, Rosamond Grace, the daughter of Professor George *Rolleston (1829–1881), physician. His middle name reflected descent from Sir Humphry Davy (1778–1829). Before going up from Gresham's School, Holt, Norfolk, as an exhibitioner to King's College, Cambridge, in 1923, Hayward spent a few months studying in France. At Cambridge he took the English tripos in 1925 and modern and medieval languages in 1927. Fellow undergraduates were impressed that he was at work on an edition of the works of John Wilmot, second earl of Rochester (published before he had completed part two). He further made his mark with his Rabelaisian wit, and the courage with which he defied the muscular dystrophy already beginning to afflict him.

After Cambridge, Hayward lost little time in establishing an independent existence in London and, his wheelchair notwithstanding, pursuing with energy and success the life of a freelance literary man. The magnificent though flawed *Collected Works* of Rochester (1926) was followed by the *Complete Poetry and Selected Prose* of John Donne in 1929. His book built on Herbert Grierson's authoritative 1912 edition of the poems to bring Donne through numerous reprints to a wide audience. Hayward brought out editions and anthologies of works by Saint-Evremond, Jonathan Swift, Robert Herrick, and Samuel Johnson. He edited an anthology of seventeenth-century English poetry and published in 1933 a short biography of Charles II. Post-war achievements included *Donne* (1950) for Penguin Poets, *T. S. Eliot: Selected Prose* (1953), *The Penguin Book of English Verse* (1958), and *The Oxford Book of Nineteenth Century English Verse* (1964). 'I have read', he once quipped to Kathleen Raine, 'the whole of English poetry, *twice*' (Carter, 25).

Hayward acquired an impressive reputation as a book collector. A milestone was his *Catalogue* for the 1947 exhibition of the National Book League. He was an organizer of another exhibition in 1951, 'Le livre anglais', at the Bibliothèque Nationale in Paris, where the opening address was given by T. S. Eliot. For the last dozen years of his life he

John Davy Hayward (1905–1965), by Anthony Devas, c.1950

edited the *Book Collector*, read by collectors, dealers, and librarians throughout the English-speaking world. Among those with whom he worked was Ian Fleming, author of the James Bond novels, who was the *Book Collector*'s founder and chief proprietor. He was made a chevalier of the Légion d'honneur in 1952 and a CBE in 1953.

For later generations it is likely that Hayward's associations and friendships will count for more than his work as a collector. For five years until November 1938 he had a flat at 22 Bina Gardens, near Gloucester Road, London, which soon came to acquire the character of a literary salon. 'Je n'oublierai jamais Bina Gardens', was Paul Valéry's tribute (Gardner, 7). The locale would later gain further renown from *Noctes binanianae*, privately printed in 1939, with poems by Hayward, and by Geoffrey Faber, chairman of Faber and Faber, and T. S. Eliot and F. V. Morley, both partners at Faber. Only twenty-five copies were printed, and the verses were without ascription but humorously characterized by various forms of wildlife. Hayward's persona was a tarantula, reflecting his occasional shafts of venom and the circumstances which brought others to his parlour.

During the Second World War Hayward was evacuated to Merton Hall, Cambridge, as the guest of Lord Rothschild, but he afterwards resumed his earlier social and literary existence in London at a flat, 19 Carlyle Mansions, Cheyne Walk, Chelsea, his home from March 1946 until his death. It was shared for ten years with T. S. Eliot, who was already installed when Hayward took up residence. His 'large and beautiful room, with its massive desk in the window overlooking the river' (Gardner, 12) became a place of pilgrimage. Helen Gardner met Hayward here in August 1947, to discuss a Donne manuscript, and her book *The Composition of 'Four Quartets'* (1978) not only documents his role as consultant in the composition of the poem but also contains an account of the relationship between Eliot and Hayward from its beginnings in 1925. While Hayward's suggestions regarding *Four Quartets* were not perhaps as magisterial as those of Ezra Pound for *The Waste Land* in 1921, they proved to be influential. A prefatory note to the English edition of *Four Quartets* (1944) acknowledges the poet's obligation to the criticism of several friends, 'and particularly to Mr John Hayward for improvements of phrase and construction'. But Hayward's friendship with Eliot was overshadowed by a cloud when, in January 1957, Eliot married his secretary, Valerie Fletcher. Eliot, aware of Hayward's love of gossip, chose not to take him into his confidence, and, with minimal explanation, moved out of Hayward's flat two days before his wedding. Hayward felt his friendship had been betrayed, and he let it be known that Eliot's action rankled. After Eliot's death, however, which occurred only nine months before his own, Hayward spoke of him to a mutual friend, Christopher Sykes, 'with love. I think he had at last acknowledged his terrible misjudgement' (Carter, 36).

Hayward's dandyism was affectionately mocked in Eliot's dedication to him as 'the Man in White Spats' in *Old Possum's Book of Practical Cats* (1939). He died, unmarried, at his home in Chelsea on 17 September 1965 at the age of sixty and was buried in the graveyard of the parish church at Beechingstoke, where his family were small landowners, between Devizes and Pewsey in Wiltshire. A memorial service was held at St Luke's Church, Chelsea, on 1 October. Hayward gave an important collection of papers relating to T. S. Eliot, the Hayward bequest, and another of his own papers, the Hayward collection, to the library of King's College, Cambridge.

ROGER KOJECKÝ

Sources H. Gardner, *The composition of 'Four quartets'* (1978) · J. Carter, ed., *John Hayward, 1904–1965: some memories* (1965) [repr. in *Book Collector* 14, (1965)] · *Annual Report of the Council* [King's College, Cambridge] (1965), 30–33 · A. S. G. Edwards, 'John Davy Hayward: a list of his published writings, 1924–1964', *Analytical and Enumerative Bibliography*, new ser., 1/8 (1994), 1–54 · King's Cam., Hayward MSS · *DNB* · *The Times* (18 Sept 1965) · private information (2004) [D. Oakeley and R. Oakeley] · order of service, St Luke's, Chelsea, London, 1 Oct 1965, BL, X100/26775

Archives King's AC Cam., corresp. and MSS · King's Cam., Hayward bequest | BL, corresp. with Sir Sydney Cockerell, Add. MS 52721 · Bodl. Oxf., corresp. with Graham Pollard · Georgetown University, Washington, DC, Lauinger Library, letters to Graham Greene · King's AC Cam., corresp. with T. S. Eliot [incl. copies] · King's AC Cam., corresp. with A. N. L. Munby

Likenesses A. Devas, ink and wash, c.1950, NPG [*see illus.*] · R. Lutyens, oils, 1957, priv. coll.

Wealth at death £92,303: probate, 25 Jan 1966, *CGPLA Eng. & Wales*

Hayward, (Harold) Richard (1892–1964), writer and actor, was born on 24 October 1892 at 21 Forest Road, Southport, Lancashire, the fourth son and fifth of the seven children of Walter Scott *Hayward (1855–1910), yachtsman and boat designer, and his wife, Louise Eleanor (1859–1932), daughter of John Robson Ivy. His parents came originally from Clerkenwell and Shoreditch, London. The family moved to Ireland about 1894 and lived briefly in Larne, co. Antrim, before settling into Silverstream House, Greenisland, where Hayward grew up. He and his brothers were educated at Larne grammar school. His father, an outstanding amateur yachtsman, was returning from a marine engine export trip to China when he died on 15 August 1910.

Hayward's first work was in connection with ship repair and maintenance in Liverpool, a reserved occupation during the First World War, but after the war he became a representative in the wholesale confectionery trade—for Fox's (makers of Glacier Mints) and Needler's. This involved his travelling throughout Ireland, yielding an income and enough spare time to pursue his myriad other interests. He married, on 9 July 1915, Wilhelmina (known as Elma) Nelson (1896–1961). They lived in the Antrim Road district of Belfast and had two sons: Dion Nelson Hayward, who became a production manager, and Richard Scott Hayward, a molecular biologist.

An interest in the theatre was demonstrated by Hayward in his twenties when he and Elma were acting with the amateur group known as the Ulster Literary Theatre. In 1929 he and J. R. Mageean founded the Empire Players, at the Empire Theatre, Belfast. Hayward hoped that a permanent home would be found for the company, creating a vital force comparable to the Abbey Theatre in Dublin. However, Belfast was not yet ready for this and the Empire Players was wound up in December 1937.

Alongside this involvement with the stage Richard Hayward was quick to appreciate the impact of radio: when the Northern Ireland station of the BBC opened in Belfast in 1924 he was one of the first artists to broadcast. He and Elma were soon taking part in scenes from Shakespeare plays and, with Tyrone Guthrie, founded the Belfast Radio Players. He wrote a variety of sketches, including in 1925 the first long play ever broadcast from Belfast, *A Trip to the Isle of Man: a Saga in Two Parts*. His radio revue *Hip Hip Hooradio* was staged at the Empire Theatre and simultaneously broadcast on 13 December 1927 through the stations of Belfast, Dublin, and Cork (the first broadcast to be made from an Irish theatre). Hayward was the first person to use the Ulster dialect on radio, the moving picture, and the gramophone record. He continued to broadcast intermittently over the rest of his life, but from the 1940s writing took the place of drama.

In 1924 Hayward started making gramophone records, a direct offshoot of his broadcasting, which included some humorous sketches, and led to his being recognized as a traditional ballad singer, with and without the harp. By 1950 he had produced more than 140 records. These were mainly recorded by Decca and included such popular local classics as 'The Ould Orange Flute', 'My Lagan Love', and 'The Inniskilling Dragoon'. His voice was entirely untrained and in no way comparable to that of such singers as John MacCormac, but for that very reason it appeared to have the authentic quality of a ballad singer. His first involvement with films was as a singer and actor, including *The Voice of Ireland* (1932), described as 'the first indigenous Irish sound film', and other films in the 1930s. Hayward even had a small part in *The Quiet Man* (1952), and was also co-producer of *The Luck of the Irish* (1935).

Hayward's first publication was a book of poems, in 1927, followed by a novel, *Sugarhouse Entry* (1936). Two years later he produced *In Praise of Ulster*, which established his reputation as a descriptive writer. Its success lay in its blend of local history, archaeology, and folklore, giving a broad and enthusiastic picture of the village or area. After this came *Where the River Shannon Flows* (1940), *The Corrib Country* (1943), and *In the Kingdom of Kerry* (1950). In all these works Hayward demonstrated a great affection for Ireland as a whole and, while he referred to himself as a northerner, he wrote as an Irishman first and foremost. Hayward's almost total exclusion of religion, politics, and the bitterness which colours much of Irish popular history contributed to the widespread appeal of his writings. Publication of the series of five books, covering the four provinces of Ireland, was spread over the remainder of his life, culminating in *Munster and the City of Cork* only a few months before his death. The series was illustrated with pencil drawings by Raymond Piper, probably the most satisfactory of his collaborations.

Hayward's last major activity was with the Belfast Naturalists' Field Club, which he joined in 1944. Characteristically he threw himself into the club's activities with great enthusiasm: he was soon giving lectures and conducting excursions, and was elected president for 1951–2. In 1951, with his nephew Brendan Adams, he co-founded the folklore and dialect section of the club, and both of them remained its moving spirits until their deaths.

Public recognition of Hayward's work included the award of an honorary DLitt of Lafayette University, Pennsylvania, in 1959, and an OBE in 1964. Following the death of Elma, Hayward married, on 23 February 1962, Dorothy Elizabeth Gamble (*b.* 1916), a hospital secretary. He died at Ballee, Ballymena, co. Antrim, on 13 October 1964, having had a heart attack while driving. He was cremated at Roselawn, near Belfast, on 16 October, and a memorial service was held in Belfast Cathedral on 4 November. He was survived by his wife. RICHARD CLARKE

Sources private information (2004) [Richard Scott Hayward] · J. Bardon, *Beyond the studio: a history of BBC, Northern Ireland* (2000) · O. Byrne, *The stage in Ulster from the 18th century* (1997) · R. Hayward, 'Looking backwards', *The Gramophone Record* (June 1951) · F. McKillop, *History of Larne and East Antrim* (2000) · K. Rockett, *An Irish filmography* (Dun Laoghaire, 1996) · b. cert. · m. cert. · CGPLA NIre. (1965)
Archives Ulster Folk and Transport Museum, Cultra, co. Down, papers, BT 18 OEU | FILM BFI NFTVA
Likenesses H. Craig, portrait, priv. coll. · G. Henry, portrait, priv. coll. · F. McKelvey, portrait, Ulster Folk Museum · R. Piper, portrait, Ulster Folk Museum
Wealth at death £8538 12s.: probate, 1 Sept 1965, CGPLA NIre.

Hayward, Sir Richard Arthur (1910–1994), trade unionist, was born on 14 March 1910 at 117 Brookdale Road, Lewisham, London, one of the three sons of Richard Bolton Hayward, a postman, and his wife, Jessie Emeline Elizabeth Reece. He left Catford central school at the age of fourteen and followed his father and grandfather into the Post Office, first as a messenger boy, then as a counter clerk in south-east London. He joined the Union of Post Office Workers (UPW). In Beckenham on 6 June 1936 he married 25-year-old Ethel Agnes Wheatcroft (*d.* 1993); they had a son and a daughter.

During the Second World War Hayward worked in code-breaking and developed outstanding fluency as a reader of Morse. He went back to his Post Office job in 1945 and rose swiftly in the hierarchy of the UPW, serving as assistant secretary (1947–51) and deputy general secretary (1951–5). The UPW, a medium-sized trade union with more than 100,000 members and fewer than a dozen full-time officials, had a reputation for political moderation. Postal workers, many of them ex-servicemen, generally tolerated poor pay on account of the job security and solid pension rights that they enjoyed as civil servants. Since 1919 management–staff relations in the civil service had been the prime example of Whitleyism, a system of formal and continuous consultation.

From 1955 to 1966 Hayward held the post of secretary-general of the civil service National Whitley Council (staff side), proving exceptionally adept at knitting diverse staff movements into one collective-bargaining entity. The report of the royal commission on the civil service (1953–5) had just established the doctrine of comparison—that the pay of civil servants should correspond to that of similar workers in the private sector—so it fell to Hayward to negotiate the detailed terms. His success in securing improvements won the confidence of union colleagues (such as Ron Smith of the postal workers, Charles Delacourt-Smith of the Post Office Engineering Union, and Leslie Williams of the Society of Civil Servants), while his fundamental fairness and good humour recommended him to the official side. Of medium height, balding, and jovial, Dick Hayward earned the reputation of a fixer, who liked to get pay deals practically sewn up before he lodged the formal claims. Even when bargaining did not go so smoothly, his deft tactics helped the UPW, after a brief work-to-rule, to get a 4 per cent increase in 1962 (when the government was striving to impose a 2 per cent norm). In 1964 a one-day strike in July preceded a victory at arbitration over working hours. Equal pay for women was another of his achievements. At various times he gave advice on industrial relations to the International Labour Organization and public-sector unions in Mauritius, Canada, and Israel.

After retiring from the Whitley Council with a CBE, Hayward was selected in autumn 1966 to chair the new Supplementary Benefits Commission, which replaced the National Assistance Board as the body overseeing means-tested financial help for the needy. Keen to entrench the idea of entitlement and end the stigma of state charity, he worked effectively with social-policy experts such as Richard Titmuss and was knighted in June 1969.

The Post Office ceased to be part of the civil service in

1969, when the final postmaster-general, John Stonehouse, handed over control to a semi-autonomous Post Office Corporation chaired by Viscount Hall. Hayward agreed to join its board as the director responsible for industrial relations. He imagined that he would be able to bring about a better understanding between employers and workers, given his long experience of the industry. However, the advent of a Conservative government in 1970 made the postal unions deeply distrustful of the corporation and its commercial aims. When the UPW demanded a 15 per cent wage increase and the government refused to fund more than 8 per cent, the result was an unprecedented all-out mail strike from 20 January to 8 March 1971. Hayward came under fire from both sides: the UPW expected his support and failed to get it; the government questioned the strength of his commitment to pay restraint. The UPW, driven to the brink of bankruptcy, eventually settled for 9 per cent, and union militants denounced Hayward as a turncoat, seduced by the establishment. An emotional man, he was grieved when the UPW stripped him of his honorary membership in May 1971. In August ill health compelled him to resign from the Post Office Board. A union leader who had thrived in the more consensual labour relations of the public sector in the 1950s and 1960s found himself out of place in the confrontational 1970s.

Though little known to the general public, Sir Richard Hayward continued to serve on numerous quangos. He was chairman of the National Health Service Staff Commission (1972–5) and the new towns staff commission (1976–7), a governor of Guy's Hospital (1949–72), and a member of the civil service security appeals panel (1967–82), the Home Office advisory panel on security (1972–81), and the Parole Board for England and Wales (1975–9). His co-authorship of *A History of Civil Service Cricket* (1993) testified to a lifelong passion. He was also interested in the topography of old London and Southwark and amassed an extensive collection of seventeenth-century trade tokens. Widowed in his eighties, Hayward moved from Southborough, near Tunbridge Wells, to Parracombe, near Barnstaple. He died of heart disease at the cottage hospital in Lynton, Devon, on 26 February 1994.

JASON TOMES

Sources *The Independent* (8 March 1994) · *The Guardian* (26 March 1994) · *The Times* (4 March 1994) · *WWW* · b. cert. · m. cert. · d. cert.
Likenesses photograph, repro. in *The Times* (4 March 1994) · photograph, repro. in *The Independent* (8 March 1994)
Wealth at death £166,042: probate, 1 June 1994, *CGPLA Eng. & Wales*

Hayward, Robert Baldwin (1829–1903), mathematician and schoolteacher, was born on 7 March 1829, probably at Bocking, Essex, the son of Robert Hayward and his wife, Ann Baldwin. His father was from an old Quaker family but withdrew from the Quaker community on his marriage. Hayward was educated at University College School and University College, London, before entering St John's College, Cambridge, in 1846. He graduated as fourth wrangler in 1850, was a fellow from 1852 to 1860, and

assistant tutor in 1852–5. In 1855 he became mathematical tutor and reader in natural philosophy at Durham University, which he left in 1859 to become a mathematics master at Harrow School. He remained there for thirty-four years. In 1860 he married Marianne, daughter of Henry Rowe and sister-in-law of Henry William Watson, an old college friend. They had two sons and four daughters. She died in 1880. From 1856 Hayward produced a number of research papers in applied mathematics and mathematical methods. His early work on moving axes contributed to his election as a fellow of the Royal Society in 1876, a rare distinction for a schoolteacher. In 1871 he was a founder member of the Association for the Improvement of Geometrical Teaching (AIGT), and he was its second president from 1878 to 1889. He played a major part in the AIGT's syllabus and textbook production, and also wrote his own textbooks in geometry and trigonometry. He was instrumental in the organization's gradual transformation into the Mathematical Association in 1897. He was a proponent of the metric system, decimalization, and new methods in arithmetic teaching.

Hayward was a capable mountain climber and an original member of the Alpine Club from its foundation in 1858, withdrawing in 1865. Both at Harrow and during his retirement from 1893 to Shanklin, Isle of Wight, he was active in local politics and championed environmental concerns. He also advocated proportional representation. Hayward largely enjoyed good health, but died at his home, Ashcombe, Shanklin, on 2 February 1903 following a sudden illness.

T. E. JAMES, *rev.* MICHAEL H. PRICE

Sources W. H. B., *PRS*, 75 (1905), 270–72 · *Proceedings of the London Mathematical Society*, 1st ser., 35 (1902–3), 466–70 · *Mathematical Gazette*, 34 (1950), 81 · M. H. Price, *Mathematics for the multitude? A history of the Mathematical Association* (1994) · Venn, *Alum. Cant.* · *The Times* (5 Feb 1903), 1 · *CGPLA Eng. & Wales* (1903)
Likenesses Hills & Saunders, photograph, repro. in *Mathematical Gazette*, facing p. 81 · Maull & Fox, photographs, RS
Wealth at death £6807 6s.: probate, 23 March 1903, *CGPLA Eng. & Wales*

Hayward, Ronald George Still [Ron] (1917–1996), political organizer, was born on 27 June 1917 in Bloxham, Oxfordshire, the son of Ethel Ruth Hayward, milliner. He was brought up by his grandparents. After attending a local Bloxham Church of England school, he was apprenticed at the age of fourteen to a cabinet-maker, a training that was to lead to predictable jokes during the period of the Wilson and Callaghan governments, when he was general secretary of the Labour Party. He served during the war in the RAF. He attended the RAF technical schools at Halton, Cosford, and Locking, and after being appointed a technical training instructor reached senior non-commissioned rank. On 9 October 1943 he married Phyllis Olive Allen (b. 1920/21), a corporal in the Women's Auxiliary Air Force and daughter of Charles Allen, publican. They had three daughters.

At the cessation of hostilities in 1945, Hayward joined the Labour Party agency service and became secretary/

agent to the constituency Labour Party in Banbury, an area held for the Conservatives by Andrew Douglas Dodds-Parker, and then, in 1947, agent for Rochester and Chatham, held by Arthur Bottomley, under-secretary of state for the colonies. Bottomley was away negotiating independence for Burma, which meant that unusual responsibility fell on Hayward. Hayward's success in holding a difficult seat in the general election of 1950 led to promotion as assistant regional organizer for the Labour Party in the southern region. He was appointed to the top post in the same region in 1959.

On the retirement of Dame Sara Barker from the post of national agent of the Labour Party in 1969, Hayward was preferred by a left-wing national executive to the favourite for the job, the assistant national agent, Reg Underhill. Three years later he succeeded Sir Harry Nicholas as general secretary of the party, owing his election to the left in general, and to Tony Benn's casting vote as party chairman in particular. It had been assumed that the deputy general-secretary, Gwynn Morgan, would succeed to the post. Hayward had been a notable opponent of the right-wing bureaucrats who controlled the party machinery in the 1950s and 1960s. Because his regime as general secretary was more open, he was partly blamed for the continual confrontation between right and left, and for the internal warfare that led to the impotence of the party. After defeat in 1979 people tended to forget that it was Hayward, as general secretary, who had delivered two general election victories, against expectation, in 1974. Critics were especially angry that in the wake of Labour's defeat at the general election of 1979, Hayward roundly declared that the election had been lost because the Labour government had failed not merely to carry out conference resolutions and TUC decisions, but even to include them in the party's manifesto; 'I wish sometimes that our prime ministers would act in *our* interests, as a Tory prime minister acts in theirs', he added (*The Times*, 26 March 1996). Asked why there was a 'winter of discontent' in 1978–9, he retorted: 'Because the Cabinet, supported by MPs, ignored Congress and Conference decisions. In my 46 years of membership of this party, I've never yet seen it try Socialism in any sense!' (*Daily Telegraph*, 26 March 1996). If in the end the Trotskyite Militant Tendency went too far for Hayward—one of his last actions before retirement in 1982 was to urge the national executive committee to take action against it—he remained an idealist of the left. He was wonderfully supported by his equally idealist and committed wife, Phyllis. He was appointed CBE in 1970. He died at his home, 37 Sutherland Drive, Birchington, Kent, on 22 March 1996, of heart failure. He was survived by his wife and their three daughters.

TAM DALYELL

Sources *The Times* (26 March 1996) · *The Guardian* (26 March 1996) · *Daily Telegraph* (26 March 1996) · *The Independent* (27 March 1996) · *WWW* · personal knowledge (2004) · private information (2004) · b. cert. · m. cert. · d. cert. · *CGPLA Eng. & Wales* (1996)
Likenesses photograph, 1972, Hult. Arch. · double portrait, photograph, 1974 (with Harold Wilson), repro. in *The Independent* · photograph, 1981, repro. in *Daily Telegraph* · D. McPhee, photograph, repro. in *The Guardian* · photograph, repro. in *The Times*

Hayward [Heyward], **Sir Rowland** (c.1520–1593), merchant and local politician, was the eldest son of George Hayward of Bridgnorth, Shropshire, and his wife, Margaret, daughter of John Whitbrooke. He was educated at Bridgnorth School, and then apprenticed to a London clothworker, becoming a freeman in the Clothworkers' Company of London in 1541 or 1542 (and its master in 1559). By 1560, when he was elected alderman, he was already a substantial figure in London, and he became one of the city's commercial magnates. He was a merchant adventurer (he had traded at Antwerp before 1553), exporting cloth, importing fustians, camlets, and buckram, and dealing in silk. He was a founder member of the Russia Company and remained active in its affairs, serving as governor eight times between 1567 and 1587. He was a promoter of the third slaving voyage of John Hawkins in 1567 and a governor of the Mineral and Battery Works from 1568 onwards. These varied interests brought him considerable wealth and influence. In 1553 he bought property in four counties, some of it formerly monastic, and by his death he had seventeen manors in five counties, besides London property. He had a large house, Elsinge Spital, in the city, and, from 1583, a country residence, King's Place, Hackney, where he entertained the queen, to whom he also lent money.

Hayward married twice, first Joan Tillesworth (d. 1580), daughter of a London goldsmith, and then Catherine, daughter of 'customer' Thomas Smith and granddaughter of alderman Sir Andrew Judde. Nine children survived infancy. The two sons—George, who died childless at the age of twenty-eight, and John, who settled in Kent—were both knighted. Of the seven daughters, Elizabeth married Thomas, Baron Knyvet of Escrick, and Joan [see Thynne, Joan] married John Thynne, son of the builder of Longleat.

A major figure in the politics as well as the business of the city of London, Hayward emerges from the records of the corporation as the most active and energetic of Elizabethan aldermen, a man with a finger in every pie and an obsessive devotion to committee work. He was president of St Bartholomew's Hospital from 1572 to his death, comptroller-general of all the hospitals from 1581, and MP for the city from 1572 to 1583, naturally serving on House of Commons committees concerning London, trade, and industry. He was lord mayor in 1570–71, when he was knighted, and again in 1591, when he stepped in on the death of a mayor in mid-term. As father of the city (senior alderman) from 1586, he was involved in matters as various as military preparations in case of Spanish attack, the management of the city's property, and the furtherance of its interests in parliament. He was a mainstay of city government in the crisis caused by plague in 1593, when he was in his seventies, just as he had been thirty years before, in the devastating epidemic of 1563.

Hayward's fortune was dispersed at his death, his personal estate being divided according to the custom of London between his widow, his children, and various legacies. He left money for the poor and the sick, and an endowment of £20 a year for Bridgnorth School. He died on 5 December 1593, and was buried at St Alfege, London Wall.   PAUL SLACK, rev.

Sources W. Jay, 'Sir Rowland Hayward', *Transactions of the London and Middlesex Archaeological Society*, new ser., 6 (1933), 509–27 · HoP, *Commons, 1558–1603* · T. S. Willan, *The Muscovy merchants of 1555* (1953) · F. F. Foster, *The politics of stability: a portrait of the rulers in Elizabethan London*, Royal Historical Society Studies in History, 1 (1977) · will, PRO, PROB 11/83, sig. 24

Hayward, Thomas (*bap.* 1706, *d.* 1781). *See under* Hayward, Thomas (*d.* 1779?).

Hayward, Thomas (*d.* 1779?), literary editor and lawyer, of whose early life nothing is known, practised law at Hungerford, Berkshire, and in 1738 published, in three volumes, *The British muse, or, A collection of thoughts, moral, natural, and sublime, of our English poets who flourished in the sixteenth and seventeenth centuries*. His friend William Oldys took great interest in the work, and wrote the preface and the dedication to Lady Mary Wortley Montagu. Oldys complained, however, that the publisher employed Dr John Campbell to cut out one-third of his preface before sending it to press. Hayward's anthology, described by Thomas Warton as the best he knew, consists of extracts of varying lengths, arranged alphabetically according to their subject. To each extract the author's name is appended, and a list of 'the author's poems and plays cited' is prefixed to volume 2. A few of the works quoted by Hayward are now lost, and only survive in his quotations. A new edition, entitled *The Quintessence of English Poetry*, appeared in 1740, in 3 volumes. Hayward also compiled, in thirty-four manuscript quarto volumes, with seven volumes of index, a collection of epitaphs from printed books and his own notes. Thirty-two of these volumes (volumes 28 and 29 are missing) and six volumes of the index (volume 1 is missing) were presented to the British Museum in 1842, and are numbered Add. MSS 13916–13953. Hayward was elected a fellow of the Society of Antiquaries on 24 June 1756, but disappears from the list of fellows, probably through death, in 1779.

Two contemporaries belonging to the Gloucestershire family of Hayward bore the same forename. **Thomas Hayward** (*bap.* 1706, *d.* 1781), barrister, the son of William Hayward and his wife, Margaret Selwyn, baptized on 2 August 1706, was MP for Ludgershall, Wiltshire (1741–7 and 1754–6). Educated at Lincoln's Inn, he was called to the bar in 1729 and by 1733 had married Mercy, daughter of Charles Parsons of Bredon, Worcestershire, with whom he had three sons and one daughter. Hayward died at Quedgeley, Gloucestershire, on 14 March 1781. **Sir Thomas Hayward** (1743–1799), government official, was clerk of the cheque to the corps of gentlemen pensioners. He was knighted on retiring from that office in May 1799;

he succeeded to the estate of Carswell, Berkshire, on the death of his maternal uncle, Henry Southby, in 1797, and died there on 7 October 1799.

SIDNEY LEE, rev. MICHAEL BEVAN

Sources *A literary antiquary: memoir of William Oldys … together with his diary*, ed. J. Yeowell (1862) · E. Phillips, *Theatrum poetarum Anglicanorum*, ed. [S. E. Brydges] (1800) · T. Warton, *The history of English poetry*, 4 vols. (1774–81) · R. S. Lea, 'Hayward, Thomas', HoP, *Commons, 1715–54* [Thomas Hayward (bap. 1706, d. 1781)] · *GM*, 1st ser., 51 (1781), 148 [Thomas Hayward (bap. 1706, d. 1781)] · *GM*, 1st ser., 69 (1799), 908 [Thomas Hayward (1743–1799)]

Hayward, Sir Thomas (1743–1799). *See under* Hayward, Thomas (*d.* 1779?).

Hayward, Thomas Walter (1871–1939), cricketer, was born on 29 March 1871 at 55 Regent Street, Cambridge, the fifth of six children (four sons and two daughters) of Daniel Hayward (1832–1910), cricketer and landlord, and his wife, Emma Martin, a nurse by profession. His was a family of noted cricketers, with his grandfather, also Daniel (1808–1852), his father, and his uncle Thomas (1835–1876) all first-class players variously with Surrey and Cambridgeshire (then of first ranking as a county). Locally schooled, Tom Hayward quickly turned his attention to cricket, initially with the Cambridge YMCA and Cambridgeshire, though the latter side was now no longer first-class in grade.

In 1891 Hayward signed professional forms for Surrey County Cricket Club, and in 1893 he made his first-class début. After a stuttering beginning, he settled down by 1895, and was picked to tour South Africa in the winter of 1895–6, when he made both his test début and his maiden test century. Thereafter there were no slip-ups. He continued to score an authoritative 1000 runs a season until his retirement in 1914; he made three trips to Australia and played in thirty-five test matches; he was the first to emulate W. G. Grace when, in 1900, he scored 1000 runs in May; and in 1906 he accumulated 3518 runs, a season's aggregate record which stood until Denis Compton's blistering summer of 1947. In his younger days a useful medium-paced bowler—he did the double (1000 runs and 100 wickets) in 1897—in his last ten seasons he concentrated almost entirely on batting. Although a little disappointing for England—1999 runs in 35 matches at an average of 34.46, and just 3 centuries—he was a most consistent performer in a strong Surrey eleven. During the seasons 1905–14 his opening partnership with Jack Hobbs, to whom he acted as mentor, was one of the most formidable in the history of the game. In all first-class cricket he made an astonishing 43,551 runs, at an average of 41.79, with 104 centuries and a highest score of 315 not out, against Lancashire in 1898, and just one first-class 'pair'.

Hayward was the epitome of Edwardian solidity. In his prime, his rubicund face and military moustache set off his commandingly burly figure, as, seemingly untouched by mortal anxiety, he executed shots, most memorably the off-drive, with masterly skill and painstaking control. 'Unlimited patience, admirable judgement, watchfulness … [and] remarkable powers of endurance' (Green, 403) was how his *Wisden* obituarist characterized him. In his careful living habits he offered a stern, unbending model to his fellow professionals. There was something aldermanic about his demeanour, in that his unvarying dominance was based not on any cavalier or imperious attitude, but on a solemn efficiency, the municipal dignitary making decisive assessments with stately effectiveness.

Hayward married, as his career neared its finale, on 20 January 1914, at Wandsworth register office, Matilda Emma Mitchell, of south London, whose jobs had ranged from railway detective to work with the Royal College of Veterinary Surgeons and at Selfridges. They had no children. During his retirement he was employed for a time as coach for Oxford University Cricket Club. It was, however, at 'the other place' that he lived and there he died, of lung cancer, on 19 July 1939, at his home, 6 Glisson Street, Cambridge, close to Fenner's, a cricket ground he always thought of with fondness. He was buried at Cambridge on 22 July. His wife survived him.   ERIC MIDWINTER

Sources S. Sheen and K. Bartlett, *Tom Hayward*, Association of Cricket Statisticians, Famous Cricketers Series (1997) • E. Midwinter, 'Darling old Oval', *Cricket Lore* (1995) • P. Bailey, P. Thorn, and P. Wynne-Thomas, *Who's who of cricketers* (1984) • B. Green, ed., *The Wisden book of obituaries* (1986) • b. cert.
Archives FILM BFI NFTVA, documentary footage
Likenesses photograph, repro. in D. Lemmon, *The official history of Surrey county cricket club* (1989), 119 • photographs, Marylebone Cricket Club, Lord's, London • photographs, Surrey County Cricket Club, Oval, Kennington, London

Hayward, Walter Scott (1855–1910), yachtsman and boat designer, was born on 17 April 1855 at 20 St James Walk, Clerkenwell, London, the son of James Robertson Hayward (*d.* in or before 1880), ironmonger, and his wife, Eliza Isabella Greely. Nothing is known about his education or early life, but he joined Royal Temple Yacht Club, London, in 1871, sailing at various south coast venues before moving to Manchester in 1877 and joining Cheshire and New Brighton sailing clubs. In 1879 Hayward became one of the very few amateur yachtsmen who passed the Board of Trade's professional examination for yacht masters before the First World War. In Southport on 2 August 1880 he married Louise Eleanor, daughter of John Robson Ivy, a Southport silk merchant; they had one daughter and at least five sons, including the writer and actor (Harold) Richard *Hayward. On the marriage certificate Hayward's occupation is given as manufacturer. Three years later, in 1883 he was elected to membership of the prestigious Royal Mersey Yacht Club as a 'merchant'.

It is probable that by the 1880s Hayward's business interests were in the marine area, and by then he had emerged as the leading small yacht racer in the north west. Although British yacht clubs remained solidly middle-class, Hayward believed that they should widen their membership by reducing the cost of sailing and recruiting far more actively among younger employees in the growing urban professions who, with improved rail networks, could now afford weekend travel to coastal venues. With this in mind, he successfully founded the West Lancashire Yacht Club (WLYC) in 1894 and also established his reputation as a yacht designer. Hayward's contribution became particularly significant in the 1890s because British sailing was then dominated by the conservatively minded Yacht Racing Association (YRA) which supported an elaborate system of rating formulae for all racing boat designs. Its approach inadvertently encouraged wealthy owners to spend heavily, often with scant regard for safety, on new yachts which exploited loopholes in the ratings. The YRA's committee of like-minded yachtsmen could only respond ineffectively with further rules aimed at stopping what was barely distinguishable from cheating.

By contrast, Hayward advocated using small 'one-design' yachts regulated by independent local class associations, with very strict rules giving the wealthy no room for manoeuvre. Indeed, Hayward took a lead of national significance in 1898, when he co-operated with Manchester electrical engineer Herbert Baggs to design the 'Seabird' yacht for the WLYC. The yachting press immediately praised its excellent seaworthiness and extremely low on-the-water price limit of £35, which certainly encouraged wider middle-class participation, with the Seabird being rapidly adopted by other clubs in the north west, Ireland, Scotland, and Wales. Hayward never patented the design, and so did not receive any royalties for what became a very popular boat. He later founded the Seabird Association in 1906, which ultimately enabled the Seabird to become one of the oldest surviving one-design classes in the world.

In the late 1890s Hayward settled near Belfast, where his daughter Gladys, having been taught to sail by her father, became one of the few British women to gain national recognition as competitive helms before 1914. Hayward was a unionist and member of the Church of Ireland, attending Jordanstown church. His restless energy reveals a sociable man who never single-mindedly pursued yachting. He rode with the New Ross harriers and foxhounds, perhaps recalling earlier robust sporting triumphs like his victory in the British amateur single stick championship. Another of his ventures attracted publicity in 1896 when he designed the largest motor yacht to have been launched on the Mersey. From 1906 he followed this up by turning to motor boat racing and establishing Messrs W. Hayward & Co., marine motor engineers, in Belfast, while the congested districts board of Ireland commissioned him to develop the use of motorized fishing boats along the west coast.

In 1910 Hayward travelled to Vladivostok on the Trans-Siberian Railway to advise Russian fishermen about the use of motor boats. He planned to continue to Hong Kong, where two of his sons were opening a car dealership, and then to visit San Francisco on his way home. But he fell ill before arriving at Hong Kong and was admitted to the Peak Hospital. Only partially recovered, he left for England via Suez with one of his sons on the SS *Pembrokeshire*. He died from tubercular disease of the left lung on 15 August 1910 as the ship passed through the Red Sea and he was buried at sea the next day.   ROGER RYAN

Sources R. Ryan, *The West Lancashire Yacht Club, 1894–1994: a centenary history* (1993) • H. C. Folkard, *The sailing boat: a treatise on sailing boats and small yachts*, 6th edn (1906), 261–8 • 'Yachting celebrities

CCXLIX—Mr Walter Scott Hayward', *Yachting World*, 10 (20 Jan 1899), 174 · *Belfast News-Letter* (24 Aug 1910) · *Yachting World*, 33 (25 Aug 1910) · *Southport Guardian* (24 Aug 1910) · *Southport Visiter* (20 Aug 1910) · *British yachts and yachtsmen: a complete history of British yachting from the middle of the sixteenth century to the present day* (1907), 402, 438 · Minute Book of the Secretary, 1862–1913, Royal Mersey Yacht Club, Birkenhead, Liverpool · Register of Admiralty Warrants, *c*.1880–1927, Royal Mersey Yacht Club, Birkenhead, Liverpool · Register of Members, to 1945, Royal Mersey Yacht Club, Birkenhead, Liverpool · J. Coote, *Classic one-designs* (1994) · 'Memorial, the late Walter Scott Hayward', *Yachting World*, 34 (9 March 1911) · private information (2004) · b. cert. · d. cert. · m. cert.
Likenesses photograph, repro. in 'Yachting celebrities CCXLIX' · photographs, priv. coll.

Haywood [*née* Fowler], **Eliza** (1693?–1756), author and actress, was probably born in Shropshire, part of the Fowler family of Harnage Grange. Her use of west country slang and archaic terms in her writing reinforces the circumstantial evidence that Christine Blouch has assembled, although it has been suggested that she was the daughter of Francis and Elizabeth Fowler who was christened at St Sepulchre's in London on 14 October 1693.

By 1714 she was Eliza Haywood and acting in Dublin. To whom she was married has not been discovered, but the long-standing belief that it was the Revd Valentine Haywood has been completely discredited. Haywood identified herself as a widow 'at an age when I was little prepar'd to Stem the Tide of Ill fortune' at least once (Ingrassia, 190–1 n. 20). Whatever the circumstances, by 1719 she was a single woman and describing her marriage as 'unfortunate' (ibid., 193–4 n. 5). Haywood had two children, the elder probably the child of the writer and friend to Samuel Johnson, Richard Savage, who lived with her for a few years, and the younger the son of William Hatchett, the playwright with whom she lived and collaborated for at least twenty years beginning about 1724. At various times in her life Haywood was a political propagandist and, like many writers of her time including Daniel Defoe and Delarivière Manley, wrote effective 'scandalous memoirs' that stigmatized some of the most powerful people of her time. Although Haywood wrote poetry, translated novels, and had some success as a playwright and with her periodical the *Female Spectator*, her prolific and ground-breaking prose fictions are her major claim to fame. She published her first novel in 1719, went on to publish at least fifty-five other fictions, and is now well established as one of the most important founders of the English novel.

Stage career Haywood's first known employment was at the most prestigious theatre outside London, Smock Alley, Dublin. Her earliest known part is in 1715 as Chloe in Thomas Shadwell's adaptation of *Timon of Athens*. While there, she worked under Joseph Ashbury, then reputed to be the greatest living teacher of acting. By 1717 she was acting at Lincoln's Inn Fields. Like so many writers of her time, her first love was the theatre, and she acted periodically into middle age. Her most successful stint was in the 1730s with Henry Fielding's Little Theatre in the Haymarket, where she played parts such as Mrs Screen in his *Historical Register for the Year 1736* (published 1737) and the Muse in his *Eurydice Hiss'd* (published with the *Historical*

Eliza Haywood (1693?–1756), by George Vertue, 1725 (after Jacques Parmentier)

Register). On 23 May 1737, the night before Prime Minister Robert Walpole brought the Licensing Act before the House of Commons, both were performed as her benefit with her in the casts; Sarah, duchess of Marlborough, and other dignitaries attended. By that time Haywood had had four plays performed and had acted many minor parts. *The Fair Captive* (1721), a play written by Captain Robert Hurst that the theatre manager John Rich had given her to make stageworthy, ran three nights, a respectable run at that time, and played a fourth as a special benefit for Haywood, who by that time was admitting she was economically distressed. Her first original play, *A Wife to be Lett* (1724), was performed in August 1724 (a difficult month) and revived a few times. *Frederick, Duke of Brunswick-Lunenburgh* (1729) was written to honour Frederick Louis, who had just arrived in England. This prince of Wales would become a centre of opposition to the Walpole ministry, and her play should be read in that context and as one of the 'patriot' plays produced by James Thomson, David Mallet, Henry Brooke, and others.

Haywood's final and highly successful play, *The Opera of Operas* (1733), was a collaborative adaptation of Fielding's *Tragedy of Tragedies* (1731) with Hatchett, with music by the composers John Frederick Lampe and Thomas Arne; it also had notable political elements. Haywood added a reconciliation scene to the end of Fielding's familiar play, and the king chortles,

My Subjects now no longer by the ears,
But all shake hands, like friends, with one another.

As this play was being written and performed, Queen Caroline was building her Merlin's cave in Richmond Gardens. This bizarre domed building, described by one critic as looking like 'a group of African native huts', had heavily symbolic figures either seated around a table or in tableaux within arches. Haywood's play exploits the queen's emblems and makes a different political statement from that in Fielding's play.

The first woman to write sustained drama criticism, Haywood published *The Dramatic Historiographer* in 1735. It was reprinted as *A Companion to the Theatre* in 1740 and expanded to a two-volume edition with coverage of additional plays in 1747. By 1756 there had been at least seven editions in one or two volumes. In addition to surveying the plays with detailed plot summaries and critical and contextual observations on them, she included firm statements about the 'usefulness' of the theatre and what it ought to be and do. Her point of view is that of a working dramatist, and she consistently evaluates plotting, stage business, liveliness of characters, and, as in William Wycherley's *The Country Wife*, audience tastes, shrewdly.

Miscellaneous writings Haywood's best-known political writings are her scandalous memoirs *Memoirs of a Certain Island, Adjacent to Utopia* (1724–5), *The Secret History of the Present Intrigues of the Court of Caramania* (1727), and *The Adventures of Eovaai* (1736, 1741), which become increasingly sophisticated. *The Adventures of Eovaai*, for example, combines the story of the sexually threatened, kidnapped Princess Eovaai with the plot of the education of Eovaai as a ruler. Thus, we have an imaginative variant on the 'advice to princes' genre. Beginning with her father's lecture, substantial sections of the book are dissertations and dramatizations of forms of government and the relationships they foster between a nation and its people. Near the centre of the book is Eovaai's debate with the old man in Oozoff, who persuades her of the wisdom of an extreme version of the whig revolution principles asserted by her father. Haywood wrote other political pieces and was interrogated about her *A Letter from H— G——g, Esq.* (1750). It, like her second *Parrot* (1746), included dangerous statements about the recent Jacobite rebellion and the Pretender. Many of her prose fictions include pointed, even partisan, political remarks, and some of her last works include specifically political tales as does *The Invisible Spy* (1755) and *The Wife* (1756).

Writers who lived by their pens in the eighteenth century usually depended upon translating for some part of their income, and Haywood was no exception. In 1721 William Chetwood, whom she had met in Dublin, published *Letters from a Lady of Quality to a Chevalier*, a translation of Edmé Boursault's *Treize Lettres amoureuses d'une Dame à un Cavalier* (1709); in 1724 she translated Madeleine

d'Angélique Poisson de Gomez's *La belle assemblée*, and in 1734 its sequel, *L'entretien des beaux esprits*. Her translation *Love in its Variety* (1727) from the Spanish of Matteo Bandello added another fashionable form of European fiction and, as translation did for many other writers, helped familiarize Haywood with popular narrative strategies and expand her stylistic range. These texts were of a piece with contemporary original tales of love and violence. Working in translation, in fact, allowed her to extend her liberating statements and explorations of female sexuality and the permeable boundaries of gender. No decade passed without a few translations, and some, such as *Memoirs of a Man of Honour*, a translation of Abbé Antoine François Prévost d'Exiles's *Memoires et avantures d'un homme de qualité* (1747), were important books in their time and sold well. Just as Haywood maintained some involvement with translation, the theatre, and with politics throughout her life, she never stopped writing poetry. Early in her career she used the popular verse forms, especially heroic couplets and the ode, to write tributes to her friends, about the literary life, and about love. The sixteen-page *Poems on Several Occasions* (1724) is typical.

Also, like most of the writers of her century, she tried writing essay periodicals. *The Tea-Table* in 1724 was her first, and *The Parrot* followed (1728, revived with Hatchett in 1746). The *Female Spectator*, begun in 1744, was a solid success and survived far longer than most London periodicals. At the time of her death Haywood had just given up on the weekly the *Young Lady* because of failing health and inability to 'discharge her Duty as she ought' (*Young Lady*, 42). All of her periodicals cover a wide range of topics, including politics, science, print culture, fashion, literary criticism, and social analysis (especially of courtship and marriage). They conjure up a group of intelligent, engaged women as contributors, readers, and discussants, and set the direction for later periodicals such as Frances Brooke's *Old Maid* and Charlotte Lennox's *Lady's Museum*.

Haywood's early novels It was in the novel, however, that Haywood made a lasting mark. She wrote in every kind of prose fiction then extant, combined and adapted these forms, and created bold new themes and types. William B. Warner has argued that Richardson and Fielding set out rather consciously to disavow, absorb yet erase, and obliterate their female predecessors, including Haywood, whose work is essential to the history of the novel. Feminist critics including Margaret Doody, Jane Spencer, and Ros Ballaster give her credit for initiating major forms of the novel, key character types, and, in Ballaster's words, even 'an autonomous tradition in romantic fiction' (R. Ballaster, *Seductive Forms*, 1992, 158). Doody in *A Natural Passion* argues that Haywood 'established the seduction novel' (Doody, esp. 144–50), and it seems clear that she introduced the themes, issues, and plot lines of many of the mid-century fashion and marriage novels. Today her work appears in anthologies, in collections of her work, and in individual editions that are slowly making her enormous canon available.

Haywood's first prose fiction, *Love in Excess* (1719), along with Defoe's *Robinson Crusoe*, made clear the enormous audience for prose fiction, and in the next decade the percentage of published texts that were novels tripled. Although known as a writer of racy formula fiction who became the author of moral fiction after Samuel Richardson reformed the novel, Haywood was in fact an important experimental novelist who often broke new ground and set trends. As Christopher Flint remarked, 'Haywood, more than any other eighteenth-century writer … bridges the fictional narratives of Behn or Defoe and the works of Burney and Austen' (*Family Fictions*, 219).

Love in Excess is written in the style of the highly popular French romance. Characters both live out and narrate life stories rife with catastrophe, love, lust, intrigue, and emotional excess. Yet *Love in Excess* differs from most of the French romances in ways that 'advance' or point to major types of the English novel. The obstacles lovers encounter in this text tend to come from their actions, personalities, and relationships rather than from accidents, coincidences, or national events, and also, unlike the romances, the hero, D'Elmont, is educated about women and love and genuinely changes. As early as this text Haywood is using mistaken identities, masquerade, and intricate schemes, all more characteristic of the southern European novella than the romance, and all devices that became signature strategies for her. As *Love in Excess* swells to multiple volumes, Haywood uses conventional types of women characters as the means to explore women's sexuality, intelligence, and alleged 'nature', but she also creates Melliora, a complex woman character who introduces complicated subjects for serious discussion. The poles that are Amena and Alovisa, and Melantha and Melliora, give way in part 3 to the rich variety of Ciamara, Camilla, Violetta, and more—characters like those Haywood and other novelists would continue to use and develop for decades.

From the beginning of her career as a novelist Haywood's experimental bent is obvious. *The British Recluse* (1722), her second published fiction, juxtaposes the language and mode of romance and that of the novel. Cleomira tells her story in the ornamented language of the romance, and she has been ruined by the seducer; Belinda relates her isomorphic story in the straightforward prose of the infant novel, and she escapes seduction and becomes an active agent starting a new life. The conclusion of *The British Recluse* has been read both as a lonely, defeated retreat by ruined women and as a daring, triumphant ending in which the women discover they do not need men for happiness. However read, this novel initiates a stream of utopian fictions by women, including the well-respected *Millenium Hall* (1762) by Sarah Scott.

In a series of fictions that have often been regarded as formulaic, repetitious, and filled with eroticism, Haywood's experimental development is rapid. Problems, personalities, desires, and destinies are repeated, reconfigured, developed, and explored in the fictions that follow, among them *The Injur'd Husband* (1723), *Idalia, or, The Unfortunate Mistress* (1723), *The Rash Resolve* (1724), *The Masqueraders* (1724), *Fantomina* (1725), *The Mercenary Lover* (1726), *The City Jilt* (1726), and *Philidore and Placentia* (1727).

She draws freely upon older forms of fiction even as she adapts the work of her contemporaries while creating new plots, characters, and narrative techniques. For example, including elements of travel and voyage literature in fictions such as *Philidore and Placentia* allowed her to contribute to the subgenre of women's travel fictions that provided new ways for women writers to confront the culture's conception of women's nature, and many fictions that distinguished between socialization and essential nature followed by Haywood and others. Haywood occasionally drew on the older tales that incorporated elements of magic and superstition. *The Fruitless Inquiry* (1727) sends a bereaved mother on a quest for a woman 'so compleatly contented in Mind, that there was no Wish but that she enjoy'd'. Should this woman be found, she is to make a shirt for the mother's son, and he will be restored to her. *The Mercenary Lover* is a rather typical southern European tale of seduction, greed, and poison, but it ends with a vicious modern twist—the villain is punished by being completely in the power of his wife. These novels of the 1720s often depicted fashionable pastimes and vacation spots, as *Fantomina*, *The Masqueraders*, and *Bath-Intrigues* (1724) do. If there are elements of soft-core pornography, the fictions are also rich in social commentary and critique. *Fantomina*, for example, exposes the time's stereotypes of the sexuality and availability of servant girls and widows, and *The City Jilt* is set firmly in the predatory economic practices of modern London. *The Rash Resolve* and *The Force of Nature* (1724) are ground-breaking stories of single mothers supporting children. To match her cast of vicious, depraved men, she creates a series of monstrous women as well as her better-known seduced-and-betrayed heroines, and all serve to problematize the platitudes of her society. When the baroness de Tortellée in *The Injur'd Husband*, Gigantilla in *The Perplex'd Dutchess* (1727), and Glicera in *The City Jilt* act like men, they reveal the avarice, lust, and emptiness at the core of modern desire. From beginning to end her fictions show how male privilege is assumed and society implicated. She invents a courtship novel that reveals the rituals of courtship to be destructive to good communication and the happiness of men and women. Many of her fictions depict the shared oppressive situations of women, and she often contests a number of major conceptions about the nature and destiny of women.

Later novels In the wake of the Licensing Act of 1737 and the closing of Fielding's theatre Haywood again became deeply engaged with the contemporary fictional milieu. Her *Anti-Pamela, or, Feign'd Innocence Detected* (1741) joined the ridicule of Samuel Richardson's *Pamela*, and she also wrote *A Present for a Servant-Maid, or, The Sure Means of Gaining Love and Esteem* (1743) and translated *The Virtuous Villager, or, Virgin's Victory* (1742) as part of the contemporary dialogue about *Pamela*. Syrena Tricksy in *Anti-Pamela* is a thoroughly original creation as well as an urban and urbane spoof of Pamela. In this decade she also wrote *The Fortunate Foundlings* (1744), which sends a boy and a girl through Europe, its courts and wars, in a tale that is both an old-fashioned travel romance and a modern depiction of how gender determines life experiences and possibilities. Combining a romance plot with shrewd modern political and social commentary as *The Adventures of Eovaai* had, Haywood depicts major foreign wars and the private interests and deals that influenced them. Part of Haywood's experimental thrust is to treat the same material from opposite perspectives as she does in *The Fortunate Foundlings* and *The History of Jemmy and Jenny Jessamy* (1753). *Anti-Pamela* (1741) and *A Present for a Servant-Maid* (1743) privilege one sex and then the other with cautionary advice, and *The Wife* and *The Husband* (1756) are more obvious examples. The protagonists of her long mid-century novels illustrate Haywood's awareness of the perimeters of gendered spheres and the available and contrasting plots for the lives and opportunities of men and women, real and fictional.

Haywood's best-known novel has become *The History of Miss Betsy Thoughtless* (1751), and its importance to the history of the novel is only now beginning to be understood. It was in a second edition two months after publication, and translations into French and German followed. Jane Spencer, without acknowledging such earlier examples as Mary Davys's *Reform'd coquet* (1724), says that *The History of Betsy Thoughtless* 'outlined the paradigm of the central female tradition in the eighteenth-century novel' with the key character type, 'the mistaken heroine who reforms' (Spencer, 141). It has often been called 'the first important novelistic comedy of manners' (Beasley). An expansion of an inset story in *The British Recluse*, it is perhaps the best example until *Jane Eyre* of the story of an intelligent, independent, wilful woman discovering the full force of the disciplining, transforming forces that create the subdued woman for whom society's gendered commands become willed behaviour. One of the dominant influences on the novel for the next half century, it helped create the domestic novel with its focus on marriage rather than on courtship, which had been the organizing subject and trope through the time of Richardson's *Clarissa*.

Fittingly, Haywood's last major fiction, *The Invisible Spy*, is about the power of print—ethical, economic, and political. Her long and varied career as a writer and political thinker as well as her proprietorship of her publishing shop at the Sign of Fame in the early 1740s provide a nearly unrivalled picture of eighteenth-century print culture. In one of the most interesting segments Haywood examines in detail how the press created, exploited, and fed the Elizabeth Canning case, which came before Henry Fielding in 1753 and haunted him for the rest of his life. Throughout her career she was an astute early literary critic of the novel and her culture's attitudes towards it. Her periodicals include excerpts from novels and many shrewd evaluative statements about the fiction of her time. Her novels refer to fashionable texts and the varying opinions of the effects of reading them. For example, *Love in Excess* dramatizes important debates about reading fiction, and Clitander in *The Mercenary Lover* seduces the virtuous Althea by giving her Ovid, Rochester, and modern novels. In novels such as *Anti-Pamela* and *Betsy Thoughtless* she is clearly in dialogue with the major novelists of her time.

Death and reputation Haywood has been rightly called an emblematic early English woman writer and 'a case study in the politics of literary history' (Blouch, introduction, 7, 8). The time in which she wrote was the moment when the novel was becoming the culture's chief vehicle for moral and social instruction, and her technical innovations were part of this foundation, and she contributed substantially to making the form a serious site for political, moral, and social enquiry and a new hegemonic apparatus.

In the last year of her life Haywood completed her most ambitious, sustained social commentary, *The Invisible Spy*, and published two collections of essays and tales and seven numbers of her periodical the *Young Lady*. At the time of her death she had completed a novel, *The History of Leonora Meadowson*, which Noble would print in 1788. Haywood dates her final illness to around the middle of October 1755, and by February was describing herself as 'incapacitated' by it. She died at her home in New Peter Street, Westminster, on 25 February 1756, and was buried on 3 March in St Margaret's churchyard, Westminster.

PAULA R. BACKSCHEIDER

Sources C. Blouch, 'Eliza Haywood and the romance of obscurity', *Studies in English Literature*, 31 (1991), 535–52 • P. Backscheider, *Selected fiction and drama of Eliza Haywood* (1999) • J. Beasley, 'Haywood', *DLB* • C. Flint, *Family fictions* (Stanford, 1998) • M. A. Doody, *A natural passion* (1974) • C. Ingrassia, *Authorship, commerce, and gender* (1998) • P. Backscheider, 'The shadow of an author', *Eighteenth Century Fiction* (1998), 79–102 • J. Spencer, *The rise of the woman novelist* (1986) • C. Blouch, introduction, *Miss Betsy Thoughtless* (1998)
Likenesses G. Vertue, line engraving, 1725 (after J. Parmentier), BM, NPG [*see illus.*] • E. Kirkall, engraving, repro. in E. Haywood, *The works of Mrs. Eliza Haywood*, 4 vols. (1724) • engraving (with Samuel Johnson), BM; repro. in S. Johnson, *The blazing comet* (1732); *see illus. in* Johnson, Samuel (1690/91–1773) • engraving, repro. in *Female Spectator*, 1 (1744)

Haywood, Francis (1793/4–1858), translator, was born in Manchester. He was baptized in St Mary's Church, Manchester, on 30 April 1794, the son of Francis Haywood, cotton broker, and Hannah, *née* Needham (*bap.* 1769). The family later moved to Liverpool and the younger Francis Haywood became a member of the intellectual circle headed by William Roscoe (biographer of Pope Leo X and Lorenzo de' Medici). Through Roscoe he came to know Antonio Panizzi, one of Roscoe's protégés, who arrived in Liverpool as a political refugee from Italy in 1823. Haywood and Panizzi remained close friends until the former's death, and Haywood was one of Panizzi's sureties when Panizzi was appointed extra assistant librarian in the department of printed books of the British Museum in 1831 (and when he was promoted principal librarian of the museum in 1856).

In May 1826 Haywood married Lucy (*bap.* 1800, *d.* 1871), the widow of Robert Boulton Waldron of Sillins, Callow Hill, Feckenham, Worcestershire, and daughter of Thomas Shrawley Vernon of Hanbury Hall, Worcestershire. Their elder son was Edward Waldron Haywood (1830–1908), high sheriff of Worcestershire in 1875–6, and their daughter, Lucy (1829–1922), married Major-General Charles Trigance Franklin, Royal Artillery, in 1854.

Haywood developed an interest in German culture, and especially in German religion and philosophy, which was unusual in Britain at that time. His work as a cotton broker gave him a comfortable income and time to devote himself to his studies. In 1828 he published an anonymous translation of K. G. Bretschneider's *Reply to the Rev. Hugh J. Rose's Work on the State of Protestantism in Germany*. His main claim to fame, however, is that in 1838 he published the first complete English translation of Immanuel Kant's *Critique of Pure Reason*. In 1829 he had published an article in the *Foreign Review* which referred to the need for an English version of Kant's *Critique*. The philosopher Arthur Schopenhauer wrote to him on the subject but when Haywood suggested that they should collaborate in producing a translation, Schopenhauer took offence. So Haywood proceeded alone, relying considerably on an unpublished partial translation made by Thomas Wirgmann (1777–1840). Haywood's edition was praised by Sir William Hamilton, the chief authority on Kant in Britain, and it remained the standard English translation for some time. It was reprinted with improvements in 1848. Wellek, however, later described Haywood's work as being of little intrinsic value and as clumsy and inaccurate, but of some use in making Kant's work more accessible in England (Wellek, v, 255). Wellek also criticized subsequent translations of the *Critique* by J. M. D. Meiklejohn (1850) and Friedrich Max Müller (1881), and said that the first satisfactory English translation was that of Norman Kemp Smith in 1929 (ibid., 257). In 1844 Haywood published his *Analysis of Kant's 'Critique'*, but this was mainly a compilation of other people's work. His translation of a work by his Liverpool friend Wilhelm Ihne, entitled *Researches into the History of the Roman Constitution* (published in Germany in 1847) appeared in 1853.

In 1855 Haywood's younger son Russell died at Liverpool while waiting to embark with his regiment for the Crimea. In the same year Haywood attempted to help Panizzi who planned to free Luigi Settembrini and other political opponents of Ferdinand II, king of the Two Sicilies. The prisoners were incarcerated on the island of Santo Stefano (45 miles west of Naples) and Haywood tried to hire a steamer to effect their rescue. These negotiations came to nothing, and the ship which Panizzi did manage to hire was wrecked off Yarmouth, and the enterprise had to be abandoned.

Haywood lived for much of his life at Edge Lane Hall, West Derby, on the outskirts of Liverpool. He died, aged sixty-four, on 29 May 1858 at Sillins, Feckenham, and was buried in the churchyard of St John the Baptist, Feckenham. **P. R. HARRIS**

Sources R. Wellek, *Immanuel Kant in England* (1931) · IGI · Boase, *Mod. Eng. biog.*, 2.619 · census returns, 1851, PRO, HO 107/2192, fol. 661 · bond for £500 to the trustees regarding Panizzi's appointment as extra assistant librarian, BM, Add. MS 36714, fol. 229 · Haywood to Panizzi, 7 and 17 Aug 1855, BL, Add. MS 36717, fols. 146, 149 · will, proved, 13 April 1859, Principal Registry of the Family Division, London [Francis Haywood] · will, proved, 24 Feb 1871, Principal Registry of the Family Division, London [Lucy Haywood] · *Liverpool Daily Post* (1 June 1858) · GM, 3rd ser., 5 (1858), 201 · Burke, *Gen. GB* (1886); (1921) · Venn, *Alum. Cant.*, 2/3.305 · *Gore's Liverpool Directory* (1800–34) · *The Post Office directory of Lancashire* (1858) · DNB · memorial tablet, churchyard of St John the Baptist, Feckenham, Worcestershire · L. Fagan, *The life of Sir Anthony Panizzi*, 2 vols. (1880) · d. cert.

Archives BL, corresp. of A. Panizzi, Add. MSS 36714–36727

Likenesses L. Fagan, drawing, repro. in Fagan, *Life of Sir Anthony Panizzi*, vol. 1, p. 54

Wealth at death under £8000: resworn probate, June 1874, *CGPLA Eng. & Wales* (1859)

Haywood, William (1599/1600–1663), Church of England clergyman, was the son of a cooper in Ballance Street, Bristol. He matriculated from St John's College, Oxford, on 15 November 1616, aged sixteen, graduating BA on 11 May 1620 and proceeding MA on 16 April 1624 and BD on 12 May 1630. In 1631 William Laud, former president of St John's and now bishop of London, appointed Haywood as one of his household chaplains. Further preferment quickly followed: he was collated to a prebendal stall in St Paul's, London, on 21 November and presented to the rectory of Laindon, Essex, on 8 December.

One of Haywood's duties as chaplain was to license books for the press. It was later alleged that he had abused his responsibilities by refusing to license some 'good, pious and profitable books' and licensing others that were 'repugnant unto the established doctrine of the Church of England' (Larking, 94). When the sermons of the Canterbury preacher Richard Clerke were submitted to him in 1636, he was said to have demanded 'no lesse than forty shillings as his fee for perusing and licensing them' and to have censored the text very heavily, removing many of the anti-Catholic passages and omitting one sermon entirely 'because the whole scope of it was against Arminius and his errors' (W. Prynne, *Canterburies Doome*, 1646, 2L1v). A list of the alterations survives among the evidence presented at Laud's trial (PRO, SP 16/339/56), from which it appears that the word 'Papist' was altered to the less offensive 'Romanist', and that all references to the pope as Antichrist were removed.

On 8 January 1636 Haywood was presented to the rectory of St Giles-in-the-Fields, London, and on 31 August he proceeded DD. By 1637 he had left Laud's service to become a royal chaplain. Questioned at his trial in 1644 about his relationship with Haywood, Laud declared that he had 'preferred him not to his Majesty till he had preached divers times in court with great approbation; nor then, but with my Lord Chamberlain's love and liking' (*Works*, 4.295–6). However, Haywood's actions as licenser returned to trouble him.

In 1637 *An Introduction to a Devout Life*, an English translation of the work by St Francis de Sales which had been licensed by Haywood, was found to contain Roman Catholic doctrine and was called in by royal proclamation. In his defence Haywood claimed that he had deleted all the Catholic passages from the manuscript before granting it a licence, only to find that they had been surreptitiously inserted into the printed edition. While his account of the case appears to be accurate, a close examination of the text suggests that his alterations were limited and often careless; references to the invocation of saints, for example, were removed by altering 'invocate' to 'call to mind', leaving one sentence that read: 'Call to mind the saints (to whom thou hast a special devotion) to help thee on the way to Heaven'. Haywood later admitted that 'this whole sentence taken together may beare an unsavoury sense' but maintained that 'it may also as properly beare an Orthodox sense'. Other equivocal passages he dismissed as 'slight things, which in a translation might well enough be borne with, though not so well perhaps in a new book' (R. M., C1v).

Despite his eirenical attitude towards Catholicism, there is no evidence that Haywood was himself a crypto-Catholic: during the plague epidemic of 1636–7 he presented a petition to the privy council complaining that many of the parishioners of St Giles had 'become Papists and refuse to come to church', and calling for the arrest of the Jesuit Henry Morse, who had been active in the parish (*Earl of Strafforde's Letters and Dispatches*, 2.57). Furthermore, the de Sales affair does not appear to have damaged Haywood's career. On 28 September 1638 he was appointed a prebendary of Westminster. By about this time he had married Alice Manning (*d.* 1675): their eldest and only surviving son was John (1639–1664), later a fellow of Oriel College, Oxford.

Anthony Wood described Haywood as 'a most excellent preacher of his time', observing that copies of his sermons 'go from hand to hand in manuscript' (Wood, *Ath. Oxon.*). Notes on one of his sermons survive (BL, MS Eng. th. e.14), but the most important record of Haywood's preaching is his own sermon notebook (CUL, Add. MS 3009). One notable feature of his sermons is his emphasis, unusual for a protestant preacher of the period, on the sinlessness of the Virgin Mary: 'I cannot beleeve the streame untainted that was drawne from Adam, but he that purified all the world could easily purifie that' (CUL, Add. MS 3009, fol. 42v). This seems to have been a particular concern of his: the contention that 'Christ was not Mary's Saviour if Mary had no sin' was among the passages that he deleted from Clerke's sermons; and he returned to the topic in a sermon preached at St Giles on 20 January 1638, in which he declared that Mary was 'spotlesse and blameless from any foul sinfull touch' (R. M., B3r).

In June 1641 some of Haywood's parishioners presented a petition to parliament, published as *The Petition and Articles Exhibited … Against Dr Heywood* (1641), complaining that his sermons contained 'most damnable and erronious Doctrines, full of grosse Popish tenets', and that his manner of administering the communion was 'superstitious and idolatrous; manifested by strange anticke jestures of cringings and bowings'. He and his subdeacons were said to wear 'Scarlet, silke, and fine linnen', and to chant the service 'with divers Tones in their voyces, high and low'; he was also alleged to have told a Catholic convert in the parish 'that Salvation might be had in the Church of Rome'. In *An Answer to a Lawless Pamphlet* (1641), the author, R. M., possibly Haywood himself, declared that the petition had been

set on foot by two or three illiterate Trades-men … [who] could draw none of any quality, not a Nobleman, not a Gentleman, not a Vestryman, not a Citizen of any better breeding, but a few such as themselves illiterate and ignorant, many of them not able to write their names.

In a further attempt to vindicate his orthodoxy Haywood published *Two Sermons Preached in the Parish Church of St Giles* (1642), in which he declared that he had already 'gone through the severall Epistles and Gospells, well nigh for every Sunday in the yeare' and now planned to deliver a course of sermons on the creed, the Lord's prayer, and the decalogue. However, on 14 June 1642 he was summoned to appear before the House of Commons and, on confessing that he had commanded his curate to read the king's declaration, was committed to the Fleet prison. On 23 July the Commons released him from prison, but on 2 February 1643 it was agreed that he should remain in safe custody until further order be given. On 23 March 1643 the Lords sequestered him from the parsonage of St Giles, noting that he had continued 'his bowing unto the Altar, and other Superstitions formerly done by him', that he had commanded his curate to read a printed paper 'forbidding the Levies of Soldiers for the Parliament Service', and that he had preached seditiously 'thereby to bring the Parliament into contempt'.

In 1645 Haywood was one of three clergymen chosen by Laud to attend him on the scaffold; this request was refused by parliament, but Laud bequeathed to Haywood 'my ring with an emerald, being my seal ring, with the arms of my see joined to my own' (*Works*, 4.423, 444). The following year Haywood fled to Oxford to join the royalist forces, and on 13 August 1646 he was licensed to preach throughout England. In November 1647 he moved to the Isle of Wight to attend the king in prison at Carisbrooke Castle. One of the sermons he preached before the king was later published as *A Sermon Tending to Peace* (1648), a defence of the treaty with the Scots, in which Haywood declared that the royalists were

still ready to forgive and agree, if our adversaries never so late will come in; though we are smitten on one cheek, turning the other … that so the fault may not lie on our side, but that it may appear to the world, we have done to the utmost of what lieth in us.

During the 1650s Haywood settled at Calne, Wiltshire, where he kept a school in his son's name. Henry Hammond, writing to Gilbert Sheldon in 1652, commended him as a 'very fitt' person to be entrusted with the education of young gentlemen, and noted that he had six pupils under his charge (BL, Harley MS 6942, fols. 81, 98). In 1660 Haywood published a sermon which he had preached at Calne at the funeral of the royalist gentleman Walter Norbane, 'my special friend, one to whom for many real favours and neighborly curtesies, I was much obliged'; the biographical section of the sermon was later reprinted by Clement Barksdale in *A Remembrancer of Excellent Men* (1670). At the Restoration Haywood recovered his preferments, and was appointed a chaplain to Charles II. His final publication was *A Sermon Dissuading from Obloquie Against Governours* (1663), a staunchly royalist sermon on the duty of obedience, ending with an attack on 'virulent tongues … overwhelming both Prince and people in a dark storm of Sedition, and infatuating the Common sort with rage and Madness'. He signed his will on 12 July 1663 and died within a few days; he was buried on 17 July at the foot of the pulpit in Westminster Abbey, although there is no inscription to mark his grave.   ARNOLD HUNT

Sources *The petition and articles exhibited in parliament against Dr Heywood* (1641) • R. M. [W. Haywood?], *An answer to a lawless pamphlet* (1641) • W. Haywood, *Two sermons preached in the parish church of St Giles* (1642) • W. Haywood, *A sermon prepared to be preached at the funerall of Walter Norbane* (1660) • *The works of the most reverend father in God, William Laud*, ed. J. Bliss and W. Scott, 7 vols. (1847–60) • G. Radcliffe, *The earl of Strafforde's letters and dispatches, with an essay towards his life*, ed. W. Knowler, 2 vols. (1739) • N. W. Bawcutt, 'A crisis of Laudian censorship: Nicholas and John Okes and the publication of Sales's *An introduction to a devout life* in 1637', *The Library*, 7th ser., 1/4 (2000) • J. L. Chester, ed., *The marriage, baptismal, and burial registers of the collegiate church or abbey of St Peter, Westminster*, Harleian Society, 10 (1876) • will, PRO, PROB 11/312, sig. 107 • *Walker rev.* • Wood, *Ath. Oxon.* • *JHC* • *JHL* • L. B. Larking, ed., *Proceedings principally in the county of Kent in connection with the parliaments called in 1640, and especially with the committee of religion appointed in that year*, CS, old ser., 80 (1862)
Archives CUL, Add. MS 3009
Wealth at death bequests amounting to £1000: will, PRO, PROB 11/312, sig. 107

Haywood, William (1821–1894), civil engineer and architect, was born on 8 December 1821 at Camberwell in Surrey, one of the three children of William and Mary Haywood. He was educated at Camberwell grammar school before being apprenticed to George Aitchison, architect and surveyor to the St Katharine's Dock Company.

Haywood intended to be an architect, and designed a number of houses early in his career. However in 1845 he entered public service as the assistant surveyor to the commissioners of sewers of the City of London, and was promoted to surveyor a year later. From 1853 until shortly before his death he held the post of engineer and surveyor. He often regretted having forsaken architecture, yet his career placed him in a position of immense influence, such that he can be ranked as one of those who did most to shape Victorian London.

Haywood's duties involved far more than the construction and maintenance of sewers, but in the 1840s and 1850s, when public concern about London's insanitary condition was at its height, his efforts were concentrated on the renewal of the City's sewers, an operation which was largely completed by 1854. In conjunction with Frank Forster, engineer to the metropolitan commissioners of sewers, he devised a scheme in 1851 for diverting sewage from the Thames. After Forster's death Haywood further developed these proposals with Joseph Bazalgette, and they became the basis for the northern outfall sewer scheme carried out in 1858–68.

Haywood's other responsibilities included highways, housing, and burials. He carried out numerous street improvements, and pioneered the use of asphalt for road surfacing in 1869. He laid out the City of London cemetery at Ilford, where eventually his ashes were buried in a mausoleum of his design, and he built a substantial set of artisans' dwellings in Petticoat Square, Whitechapel.

The major achievement of Haywood's career was the construction of Holborn Viaduct in 1863–70. His design to enable traffic to cross the Fleet valley on the level was selected in competition, not without protests about the probity of his entry. Building the new, quarter mile long, street, together with its access streets, involved the demolition of over four thousand buildings, and the result was considered a model of its kind. The viaduct incorporated generously proportioned conduits for sewers, gas, and other services, designed for ease of access.

Haywood had a brilliant command of everything affecting the environment of the City and was a man of strong, though sometimes cynical, feelings. He often gave advice on engineering matters abroad, for which he received a number of foreign honours. He was elected a member of the Institution of Civil Engineers in 1853, and a fellow of the Royal Institute of British Architects four years later. He was probably the author of the letter which led to the foundation of the Geologists' Association in 1858, though he played no subsequent part in the association's development. His main enthusiasm in later life was his membership of the London rifle brigade, of which he was lieutenant-colonel from 1876 to 1882.

Haywood married Jane Rosa Wake on 16 October 1845. They had no children, and appear to have separated by the late 1850s. From about 1870 he lived with Jemima Emma Elbrow in Maida Vale, where their circle of friends included many literary notables of the time. He died at their home, 56 Hamilton Terrace, Maida Vale, London, on 13 April 1894, shortly after resigning the City post which he had held for almost fifty years.   ROBERT THORNE

Sources *PICE*, 117 (1893–4), 376–8 • *City Press* (14 April 1894), 5 • E. F. Freeman, 'The origins of the Geologists' Association', *Archives of Natural History*, 19 (1992), 1–27 • J. Winter, *London's teeming streets, 1830–1914* (1993) • R. Lambert, *Sir John Simon, 1816–1904, and English social administration* (1963) • *CGPLA Eng. & Wales* (1894) • death duty register • D. C. Clow, 'William Haywood and municipal engineering in the Victorian City of London', *Transactions of the Newcomen Society*, 72 (2000–01), 39–76
Archives CLRO, letter-books
Likenesses portrait, repro. in *Builder* (26 Feb 1870), 166
Wealth at death £42,606 13s. 6d.: probate, 13 June 1894, *CGPLA Eng. & Wales*

Hazeldine, William (1763–1840), iron-founder, was born at Waters Upton, Shropshire. His parents moved while he was very young to Sowbatch, near a forge at Moreton Corbet, about 7 miles from Shrewsbury.

In his early years Hazeldine was trained as a millwright by his uncle, himself an able millwright and engineer, who recommended Hazeldine about 1780 to superintend the erection of machinery at Upton forge, of which he subsequently became the tenant. By 1789 he was a millwright in Wyle Cop, Shrewsbury, and shortly afterwards became an iron-founder in Knucking Street in partnership with a Mr Webster, clockmaker and mechanic. The business did well but Webster was not as enterprising as Hazeldine and their partnership was dissolved. Hazeldine subsequently built a new foundry in the suburb of Coleham. He married a Miss Brayne of Ternhill and she, with at least one of his daughters, survived him.

In 1796–7 Hazeldine established an international reputation for innovative cast ironwork when he cast the frame of Ditherington flax mill at Shrewsbury. This was the world's first iron-framed building, and was constructed to the designs of Charles Bage, who had a great understanding of the structural properties of cast iron. Hazeldine became acquainted with Thomas Telford in 1788, through their membership of the Salopian lodge and Hazeldine supplied a pump to Haycock and Telford's new county gaol. Telford had trained as a stonemason, and Hazeldine's experience with the casting and properties of ironwork was to be of particular value on all of Telford's great engineering works. In 1799 Hazeldine leased the Plas Kynaston estate at the north of the rising Pontcysyllte aqueduct and he built there a large new foundry; and in November of that year he won the contract to supply the revolutionary cast-iron bed plates of Chirk aqueduct. In 1800–02 he probably produced the detailed design drawings for the iron deck of the great aqueduct at Pontcysyllte in collaboration with his foreman, William Stuttle, and Thomas Telford; the deck was cast in 1802–3 at his neighbouring foundry and then erected in place.

The real breakthrough in engineering principles applied to cast-iron bridges occurred in 1811–12 with the three-span Bonar Bridge (central span 150 ft) in Scotland. The overall design was by Thomas Telford, and the ironwork was cast by Hazeldine at Plas Kynaston and erected under his supervision. At least a further six bridges of this revolutionary new design were built by this duo at sites in Britain, culminating in the 170 ft Mythe Bridge over the Severn at Tewkesbury (1823–6). The design incorporated perforated plate ribs developed from William Jessop's Bristol bridges, improved lateral bracing, and lozenge-frame spandrels. Hazeldine erected two other bridges of this design without Telford: Eaton Hall, Cheshire (1824), and Cleveland, Bath (1827).

In 1821 Hazeldine contracted to supply the ironwork for Telford's Menai Bridge. At 579 ft span, this was the first major suspension bridge to be built (1819–26). Hazeldine explained the principles of its construction to Princess Victoria in 1832, having also supplied the surviving ironwork for the smaller Conwy suspension bridge in 1824–6. These suspension bridges depended on the tensile strength of wrought iron and this was mostly supplied from Hazeldine's Upton Magna forge. However, the manufacture and testing of the ironwork were at the forefront of the technology of the time and necessitated large new workshops at Coleham. This work resulted in considerable design innovation in respect of a whole range of equipment. By the 1830s there is no evidence for Hazeldine's foundries supplying any large structural castings and these manufactories did not long survive his death. Hazeldine died at his home, Dogpole House, near Shrewsbury, on 26 October 1840, and was buried in St Chad's churchyard, Shrewsbury.

Hazeldine was a founder of the then most important iron-bridge building firm in Britain and an owner of ironworks, mines, and quarries throughout the Welsh marches. His most significant ironwork was produced in collaboration with Thomas Telford, who regarded him as an ingenious inventor and innovator, 'the Arch conjuror himself, Merlin Hazledine' (Thomas Telford to Matthew Davidson, 1796; Ironbridge Gorge Museum Trust).

STEPHEN HUGHES

Sources A. W. Skempton, 'Telford and the design for a new London bridge', Thomas Telford, engineer [Ironbridge 1979], ed. A. Penfold (1980), 62–83 · R. A. Paxton, 'Menai Bridge, 1818–26: evolution of design', Thomas Telford, engineer [Ironbridge 1979], ed. A. Penfold (1980), 84–116 · N. Cossons and B. Trinder, The iron bridge: symbol of the industrial revolution (1979) · C. Hadfield, Thomas Telford's temptation (1993) · B. Trinder, 'Ditherington flax mill, Shrewsbury—a re-evaluation', Textile History, 23 (1992), 189–223 · GM, 2nd ser., 15 (1841), 100–02 · The life of Thomas Telford: civil engineer, written by himself, ed. J. Rickman (1838) · Thomas Telford to Matthew Davidson, 1796, Ironbridge Gorge Museum Trust, Telford MSS
Archives Shrops. RRC, corresp. and papers | Inst. CE, Telford MSS · Ironbridge Gorge Museum Trust, Telford MSS
Likenesses F. Chantrey, pencil drawing, 1831, NPG · F. L. Chantrey, bust, St Chad's Church, Shrewsbury, Shropshire

Hazeltine, Harold Dexter (1871–1960), jurist, was born on 18 November 1871 at Warren, Pennsylvania, USA, the son of an American banker, Abram Jones Hazeltine, and his wife, Harriet Davis. He was descended from a Yorkshire family which had migrated to Massachusetts in 1637. He attended high school at Warren before proceeding to Worcester Academy and then to Brown University. He was fortunate in 1895 to be able to enter the Harvard law school, then in its golden age as the centre of common-law scholarship, where his interest in history was encouraged by J. B. Ames, J. H. Beale, J. B. Thayer, and E. Wambaugh, all of whom regarded legal history as central to the study of law. Fired with enthusiasm for legal history, he moved to Berlin, where he studied with Otto Gierke, and also met Heinrich Brunner. While in Europe he visited England, and made the acquaintance of F. W. Maitland at Cambridge and Sir Frederick Pollock at Oxford. His German doctoral dissertation, published in 1905, was an essay on the early history of mortgages in English law, and this was expanded into *Die Geschichte des englischen Pfandrechts* (Breslau, 1907).

With these impressive qualifications, and with the support of Maitland, Hazeltine was appointed to a lectureship at Emmanuel College, Cambridge, in 1906. However, after only one term of close contact with Maitland, the latter died, leaving Hazeltine to keep the study of legal history alive in Cambridge. The appointment of C. S. Kenny to succeed Maitland freed the university readership in law, and Hazeltine was appointed to it, with a fellowship of Emmanuel, in 1908. Obliged to teach every subject in the law tripos, his wide interests at this period included international law, and he published in 1911 *Law of the Air*, the first major work on this subject. When Kenny retired in 1919, Hazeltine was elected to succeed him in the Downing professorship of the laws of England. As the last holder under the original foundation (altered prospectively in 1926), he was able to move to Downing College as senior fellow and occupy the West Lodge. In 1921 Hazeltine persuaded Cambridge University Press to inaugurate the Cambridge Studies in English Legal History, and he was to write a series of learned prefaces to each of the twelve volumes which appeared under his editorship. His own principal publication as Downing professor was a contribution to the *Cambridge Medieval History* (1926) on Roman and canon law. He was at his best synthesizing, with clarity and elegance, the learning to be found hidden in libraries, but he did not work with manuscripts or produce many original ideas. A man of great charm and easy conversation, his lectures were nevertheless dictated and were said to be appreciated more by those who wished to acquire solid information than by those who sought entertainment or mental stimulation. Although his scholarly achievements justified his election as a fellow of the British Academy in 1924, thereafter he wrote less and less, except for a prodigious quantity of perceptive book reviews.

In 1911, at the age of forty, Hazeltine married Hope Graves, a 27-year-old woman from Vermont, and in 1920 they had a daughter, Georgina, but the marriage ended in divorce and Hazeltine did not remarry. His friend H. A. Holland attributed the decline of his scholarly productivity both to the failure of his marriage and to the collapse of his father's business, which made him financially dependent on his own earnings. In the dark days of 1940, although he was entitled under a special regulation to retain his chair until 1942, he accepted the advice of friends and returned to his country of citizenship. His last twenty years were spent in the other Cambridge, where he had a room in the Harvard law school and enjoyed the companionship of Dean Griswold and the young S. E. Thorne, but his productive career was over. He died on 23 January 1960 at Cambridge, Massachusetts, USA.

J. H. BAKER

Sources H. A. Holland, 'Harold Dexter Hazeltine, 1871–1960', *PBA*, 47 (1961), 311–43 [incl. bibliography] · H. D. Hazeltine, *Englisches Mobiliarpfandrecht im Mittelalter* (Berlin, 1905) · *The Times* (26 Jan 1960)
Archives Emmanuel College, Cambridge, corresp. and notes mainly relating to a projected life of H. M. Gwatkin · Harvard U., law school, corresp. · U. Reading L., legal notes relating to Anglo-Saxon documents
Likenesses Kidd & Baker, photograph, 1939, repro. in Holland, 'Harold Dexter Hazeltine', facing p. 311

Hazlehurst, Thomas (*c.*1740–*c.*1821), miniature painter, was born in Liverpool, the son of Grace, whose surname may have been Leigh, adopted daughter of John (or James) Hardman of Allerton Hall estate, Liverpool; she was disinherited on her marriage to Thomas Hazlehurst's father. His family came from Cheshire. He was a pupil of Sir Joshua Reynolds and was described as such when he exhibited at the Society for Promoting Painting and Design in Liverpool in 1787, while living at 32 Hurst Street. He exhibited with the society between 1760 and 1818. He married Martha Bentley (*d.* 1840), with whom he had thirteen children. Between 1810 and 1812 he exhibited at the Liverpool Academy, having moved to 9 Rodney Street, Liverpool, in 1793. Although he made over £20,000 from his

painting he lost heavily in bad investments and died in poverty, presumably at his last address, Sidney Place, Edge Hill, Liverpool, about 1821. His son Joseph B. Hazlehurst followed in his father's profession as a miniaturist; he died young. Hazlehurst's work is highly finished and of great excellence. He signed his work 'T. H.' in 'neat Roman caps' (D. Foskett, *Miniatures: Dictionary and Guide*, 1987, 561). The sale catalogue of the collection of Joseph Meyer (15 December 1887) included as lot 153 'Scribbleriana by Thomas Hazlehurst, Miniature Painter, with a number of clever sketches interspersed'. A collection of 387 paintings of Lancashire flora by Hazlehurst is in the City of Liverpool Library; examples of his work are also in the British Museum.

EMMA RUTHERFORD

Sources D. Foskett, *A dictionary of British miniature painters*, 2 vols. (1972) · B. S. Long, *British miniaturists* (1929) · D. Foskett, *Collecting miniatures* (1979), 269 · S. Hand, *Signed miniatures* (1925) · Graves, *Artists* · H. Blättel, *International dictionary miniature painters / Internationales Lexikon Miniatur-Maler* (1992) · C. H. Collins Baker, notes on artists, NPG, archive · R. Bayne-Powell, ed., *Catalogue of portrait miniatures in the Fitzwilliam Museum, Cambridge* (1985) · *DNB*
Archives Liverpool Museum, family papers · Lpool RO, notebook
Likenesses T. Hazlehurst, portrait, repro. in Foskett, *Collecting miniatures*, 277; priv. coll.

Hazlewood, Colin Henry (1823–1875), playwright, became a low comedian on the Lincoln, York, and western circuits, but little is known of his origins or early life. In 1850 he wrote and produced at the City of London Theatre a farce entitled *Who's the Victim?* which was a popular success, and he began to write stories for the penny weekly publications. In 1851 he was engaged at the Surrey Theatre, appearing as Bob Blackberry in George Almar's *The Rover's Bride*, and was next engaged by the City of London Theatre as low comedian. Here he remained ten years, producing numerous dramas, farces, and burlesques, among his successes being *The Bonnet Builders' Tea Party* at the Strand Theatre; *Jenny Foster, the Sailor's Child* and *Jessie Vere, or, The Return of the Wanderer*, two dramas each in two acts, produced in 1855 and 1856 respectively at the Britannia Saloon, where they had long runs; and *Waiting for the Verdict*, first performed at the City of London Theatre.

Hazlewood wrote mainly for the Britannia and Pavilion theatres and is said to have been paid at the rate of about 50*s.* an act, with something extra for a very successful piece. He was:

> the most prolific contributor of plays to the Britannia during [the] period and his sources ranged from recently published novels and serialisations in such journals as *The Family*, *The Herald*, and *Bow Bells* to juvenile literature, popular paintings, and newspaper reports. (*Britannia Diaries*, 21)

Among his most popular adaptations were versions of Mary Elizabeth Braddon's sensation novels *Lady Audley's Secret* (1862; dramatization 1863) and *Aurora Floyd* (1863; dramatization 1863). Thirty of his works were printed in T. H. Lacy's *Acting Edition of Plays*.

In his diaries Frederick C. Wilton of the Britannia Theatre recalls a curious incident involving Hazlewood: on 8 September 1865 Wilton notes 'an accident occurring to [Hazlewood's] wife, a drunken woman, from whom he has been a long time separated' (*Britannia Diaries*, 96). *The Times* report refers to 'Henry Fleetwood ... assaulting his wife Ellen' (ibid., 224, 8n.). No other evidence exists to suggest that Hazlewood used this alias.

Hazlewood died at his home, 44 Huntingdon Street, Haggerston, London, on 31 May 1875 at the age of fifty-two, leaving two children, a daughter, and a son, Henry Colin Hazlewood (lessee and manager of the Star Theatre, Wolverhampton, and the author of various burlesques).

G. C. BOASE, *rev.* MEGAN A. STEPHAN

Sources *Era Almanack and Annual* (1869), 18–19, 45 · *The Britannia diaries, 1863–1875: selections from the diaries of Frederick C. Wilton*, ed. J. Davis (1992)

Hazlitt, William (1778–1830), writer and painter, was born on 10 April 1778 at Mitre Close, Maidstone, Kent, the fourth of the seven children of the Revd William Hazlitt (1737–1820), Unitarian minister, and his wife, Grace (1746–1837), *née* Loftus, daughter of an ironmonger of Wisbech, Cambridgeshire.

The family The Hazlitts were an Ulster dissenting family. The writer's grandfather John Hazlitt moved south to Shronell, co. Tipperary, where he was a merchant. He and his wife, Margaret, had three sons, the eldest of whom, William, left home to train for the Presbyterian church, studying under Adam Smith at Glasgow University. On graduating MA in 1760 he joined the Unitarians. In 1764 he was appointed to the ministry at Wisbech, where he met his wife, who herself came from a dissenting family. They moved to Marshfield, near Bath, and then to Maidstone in 1770. The chapel where the Reverend William preached, known as the Earl Street meeting-house, still stands in Bullock Lane, just off the High Street.

The Hazlitt family remained in Maidstone until 1780. During this time the Reverend William was a not inconsiderable figure in dissenting circles. He corresponded with Richard Price and Joseph Priestley, contributing articles to the latter's *Theological Repository*, and he made the acquaintance of Benjamin Franklin. His eldest son, John Hazlitt (1767–1837), became a respected portrait painter, specializing in miniatures. Another son, Loftus, died in infancy, but a daughter, Margaret (1770–1841), was born the same year. Known as Peggy, she remained with her long-lived parents and never married; her journal survives as a valuable family record.

In 1780, when young William was two years old, the family was forced to leave Maidstone as a result of a split in the congregation, partly provoked by the Reverend William's open support for American independence. They returned to Ireland, where William senior served the Unitarian church at Bandon, co. Cork. Another son, Thomas, was born there, but survived only a few weeks; the father, meanwhile, published a number of polemical letters about the maltreatment of American prisoners of war in nearby Kinsale.

The Reverend William Hazlitt, who in 1790 published a collection of discourses under the imprint of the radical bookseller Joseph Johnson, was known as an ultra-dissenter and a republican in politics. Later the family

William Hazlitt (1778–1830), self-portrait, *c*.1802

would befriend Catherine Emmet, niece of the Irish revolutionary Robert Emmet. In 1783 the Reverend William's American sympathies led him to take his family to the United States, where one of his brothers had already emigrated. Hazlitt's fifth birthday coincided with the crossing. The family now included a baby daughter, Harriet, who died from an attack of croup soon after their arrival in New York. A last child, Esther, with whom Grace Hazlitt was pregnant on the crossing, lived only six weeks.

The Reverend William preached to a variety of congregations in New Jersey, Pennsylvania, and New England. In Philadelphia he brought out an edition of Priestley's *Appeal to the Serious and Candid Professors of Christianity*, together with three of his own sermons, and in Boston he played a major role in the conversion of the old King's Chapel into the first Unitarian church in America. But, after failing to find a permanent post, he returned to England.

Hazlitt's earliest surviving letter, written when he was eight, was addressed to his father, as the family waited to hear that they could follow him back across the Atlantic. The liberal politics of the man—he was one of the few English Romantics to remain loyal to the ideals of the French Revolution throughout his life—are anticipated by the words of the boy: 'I think for my part that it would have been a great deal better if the white people had not found [America] out. Let the others [Indians] have it to themselves, for it was made for them' (W. Hazlitt, *Letters*, 43).

The Reverend William was appointed to the ministry at Wem in Shropshire. The family moved there in 1787, though John, now twenty-one, went to London to study painting under Sir Joshua Reynolds, and there he made the acquaintance of the radical philosopher William Godwin.

Hazlitt had happy memories of the countryside around Wem, though he also visited Liverpool, where he saw his first play and engaged in debate about the Test Act. According to his sister, his cheerful childhood disposition turned to sullenness—for which he was afterwards renowned—as a result of excessive study. On turning fifteen he followed his brother to London, where he attended the Unitarian New College in Hackney. Under the guidance of leading intellectuals such as Priestley and Thomas Belsham, the Unitarian academy offered dissenting youths a broader curriculum and a more liberal education than that available at Oxford and Cambridge.

Deciding not to follow his father into the ministry, Hazlitt withdrew from college after two years. He read in recent philosophy and began preparing a metaphysical discourse of his own. He met and deeply admired another great radical, Joseph Fawcett, but also fell under the spell of the prose style of a figure from the opposite end of the political spectrum in the turbulent aftermath of the French Revolution: Edmund Burke. To speak of Burke 'with contempt', said Hazlitt to Coleridge, 'might be made the test of a vulgar democratical mind' (W. Hazlitt, *Complete Works*, ed. P. P. Howe, 21 vols., 1930–34, 17.111).

The painter It was in 1798, which Hazlitt later regarded as a sacred year, that Samuel Taylor Coleridge went to Shrewsbury as minister to the Unitarian congregation. Hazlitt walked the 10 miles from Wem on a raw January morning to hear the great man preach. Twenty-five years later, in his essay 'My first acquaintance with poets', he recollected how he felt inspired by the combination of 'Poetry and philosophy' with 'Truth and genius' in Coleridge's words, first from the pulpit, then in conversation when visiting the Reverend William Hazlitt. But he also noticed that Coleridge couldn't walk in a straight line, a failing he later regarded as symptomatic of the man's political tergiversation. Coleridge invited young Hazlitt to stay with him in Somerset, where he duly met William and Dorothy Wordsworth. Here he read in manuscript, and heard the authors themselves read, the poems that were published as *Lyrical Ballads*.

Later in 1798 Hazlitt viewed the collection of old master paintings from the gallery of the regent, Orléans, which were up for sale in London. Now he was inspired by Titian and Carracci. He determined to become a painter himself, and began studying with his brother John. In 1801, home in Wem, he painted his father 'with a broad light crossing the face, looking down, with spectacles on, reading' (W. Hazlitt, *Complete Works*, ed. P. P. Howe, 21 vols., 1930–34, 8.12). The portrait was accepted for exhibition at the Royal Academy the following year.

Hazlitt undertook a few commissions for portraits of well-to-do manufacturers in Manchester and Liverpool, one of whom asked for five copies of old masters. The 1802 peace of Amiens made it possible for Hazlitt to use this as an opportunity to go to Paris and copy in the Louvre. He

stayed for four months, and Titian's *Young Man in Black with a Glove* became his favourite painting. His commitment to the values of the French Revolution was fortified by this greatest of all art collections being public, not private.

Back in England, Hazlitt based himself in London. He dined at William Godwin's house with Coleridge, the writer Thomas Holcroft, and Charles and Mary Lamb, who soon became fast friends. He painted Lamb in the dress of a Venetian senator and the style of Titian; Hazlitt's finest surviving painting, it now hangs in the National Portrait Gallery. Sir George Beaumont commissioned him to undertake portraits (which do not survive) of Coleridge, young Hartley Coleridge, and Wordsworth.

While in the Lake District for this purpose, Hazlitt—who was inept in his dealings with women—was called 'a black-faced rascal' by a local girl. He pushed her down '"& because, Sir," said Wordsworth, "she refused to gratify his abominable & devilish propensities", he lifted up her petticoats & *smote* her on the *bottom*'. That is how the incident was recollected in the diary (2.470) of Benjamin Robert Haydon (a disinterested party, who incorporated the figures of both Hazlitt and Wordsworth in his historical painting *Christ's Entry into Jerusalem*). When Wordsworth and his circle later fell out with Hazlitt, the story was made public and blown up into a rape attempt which supposedly ended with Hazlitt being run out of town by a posse of angry locals. The truth of the business will probably never be known. There is no evidence for Thomas De Quincey's mischievous claim that Hazlitt also alienated Wordsworth by proposing marriage to his sister Dorothy (seven years Hazlitt's senior).

Hazlitt continued to work on his philosophical discourse, publishing it in 1803 under the title *An Essay on the Principles of Human Action*. It advanced an argument in favour of the natural disinterestedness of the human mind. We know our present through sensation and our past through memory, but we must *imagine* our future. Imagination is a sympathetic projection out from the self, which runs against the grain of the Hobbesian principle that man is ruled by self-interest. The argument was less original than Hazlitt himself claimed—it had antecedents in several Scottish Enlightenment thinkers (Hume, Hutcheson, Smith) and an ultimate source in Shaftesbury's theory of disinterested affection—but it became the underlying principle of his later writings on politics and the arts. He regarded Shakespeare as the greatest of all geniuses because as a dramatist he projected himself into so many different characters and was 'the least of an egotist that it was possible to be' (W. Hazlitt, *Complete Works*, ed. P. P. Howe, 21 vols., 1930–34, 5.47). This claim was a key influence on Keats's ideas of the 'chameleon poet' and 'negative capability'.

Hazlitt gradually became disillusioned with his painting and began to diversify his literary work. *Free Thoughts on Public Affairs*, printed at his own expense in 1806, argued that Charles James Fox, then foreign secretary, should end the war with France; this pamphlet included a scathing 'character' of Pitt the younger, which Hazlitt recycled in several later works. In 1807 Joseph Johnson published his abridgement of Abraham Tucker's *The Light of Nature Pursued*, a philosophical treatise which emphasized the variety and flexibility of human motives and thus offered support for Hazlitt's anti-Hobbesian stance. In the same year another work was published anonymously: *The eloquence of the British senate, or, Select specimens from the speeches of the most distinguished parliamentary speakers, from the beginning of the reign of Charles I to the present time.* Hazlitt selected the extracts and wrote a brief biographical introduction for each speaker, most notably a generous 'character' of his own mighty opposite, Edmund Burke, which he later reprinted in his *Political Essays*. At the same time, he published an attack on Malthus's *Essay on the Principle of Population* (printed first as a series of three letters in Cobbett's *Weekly Political Register*, then in book form). Malthus's theory was based on self-interest, so in attacking it Hazlitt was applying the principles of his own essay on disinterestedness to the political sphere.

The journalist The Lambs introduced Hazlitt to Sarah Stoddart (1774–1840), the independent-minded daughter of a retired naval lieutenant. He proposed to her while she was putting on the kettle (Hazlitt was addicted to tea), and they married by special licence in St Andrew's Church, Holborn, on Sunday 1 May 1808. She brought to the marriage an income of £80 per annum and property in Winterslow, Wiltshire, whither they moved in the autumn. The Lambs enjoyed visiting them there. A son, William, was born on 15 January 1809, but died after six months. On 26 November 1811 a second son, again named William, was born.

In 1809, through the offices of Godwin, Hazlitt published a school textbook, *A New and Improved Grammar of the English Tongue*. Various subsequent literary projects, including a proposed translation of Chateaubriand's *Les martyrs*, petered out. In 1811 he was back in London, taking rooms in Southampton Buildings, resuming with limited success his work as a portrait painter. Early the following year, he delivered a series of ten lectures on English philosophy at the Russell Institution, a subscription library and reading-room in what is now Bloomsbury. The first lecture, poorly delivered, was on Hobbes. Hazlitt's lecturing style improved when in later lectures he turned to his favourite subject of disinterestedness, but attendance remained thin, and the diary of Henry Crabb Robinson records mixed audience reactions.

Later in 1812, Hazlitt obtained his first regular paid employment, as a parliamentary reporter for the *Morning Chronicle* at the rate of 4 guineas per week. One of his fellow reporters was the uninhibited Irish radical Peter Finnerty. Hazlitt's gift for recalling conversations made it easy for him to reproduce—and sometimes embellish—the speeches in the Commons. The secure income from the post enabled him to recall his wife and son from Wiltshire and to take a house in York Street, Westminster. It was owned by Jeremy Bentham and, to Hazlitt's delight, had once been the home of John Milton. At this time Hazlitt formed friendships with a well-established painter, James Northcote, and an enthusiastic tyro in the art, Benjamin Robert Haydon.

Hazlitt's literary style was becoming sharper, his political interventions more incisive. He began to publish, on the one hand, attacks on reactionary politicians and journalists (notably Vetus, Edward Sterling of *The Times*), and on the other, essays on such general topics as patriotism, love of nature, posthumous fame, the disadvantages of a classical education, and 'Why the arts are not progressive'. He was finding his true vocation, that of essayist. One thing that had attracted him to Tucker's *Light of Nature Pursued* had been its preference for instinct over formal reason. He now saw that the occasional essay—light in tone, personal in voice, written to the moment, digressive, enlivened with opinion and quirky detail—was truer to that preference than the abstract, intricately argued, full-scale treatise. He also saw that the painter's arts of *sketching* and of representing the *character* of a subject could be translated into a style of writing.

When the theatre critic of the *Chronicle* departed, Hazlitt took up the post. On 26 January 1814 he witnessed the Drury Lane début of Edmund Kean, in the role of Shylock. His rave reviews of this and subsequent performances virtually single-handedly launched Kean to stardom. The energy of Kean's acting answered to his own ideal of imaginative *gusto*:

> His style of acting is, if we may use the expression, more significant, more pregnant with meaning, more varied and alive in every part, than any we have almost ever witnessed. The character never stands still; there is no vacant pause in the action; the eye is never silent.   (W. Hazlitt, *Complete Works*, ed. P. P. Howe, 21 vols., 1930–34, 5.180)

In 1818 Hazlitt collected his reviews of the Shakespearian and other performances of Kean, John Philip Kemble (whom he admired in a more detached way), Sarah Siddons (whom he worshipped), and Eliza O'Neill (for whom he had high hopes) in a book called *A View of the English Stage*, which has claims to be the first great volume of theatrical notices in the language.

Hazlitt was sometimes unreliable over submitting copy. In May 1814, shortly after the abdication of Napoleon, which he took almost as a personal blow, he was dismissed by James Perry, editor of the *Chronicle*. For the next few years he lived the hand-to-mouth existence of the freelance journalist, writing for a range of publications, including Leigh Hunt's liberal *Examiner*, Francis Jeffrey's whiggish *Edinburgh Review*, and John Hunt's radical *Yellow Dwarf*. In *The Examiner* he mingled praise with damnation of Wordsworth's magnum opus, *The Excursion*, and the rift from Wordsworth and his circle caused by this review was never mended. Relations with Coleridge were not improved by Hazlitt's audacity in writing an account of *The Statesman's Manual* solely on the basis of a publisher's announcement and his own knowledge of Coleridge's apostasy from the radical cause—the review actually appeared before Coleridge had finished writing the book.

Hazlitt always believed that Napoleon was the sword-arm, not the extinguisher, of the principles of the French Revolution; the battle of Waterloo brought him near to distraction. Over the next few years he repeatedly vented his spleen over the pan-European swing to the monarchical politics of what he scathingly termed 'legitimacy'. The Lake poets, whom he regarded as rank turncoats, were the object of special scorn. He became known as a good hater.

Personal stresses were added to political ones. After three miscarriages, Sarah Hazlitt gave birth to another son, John, on 28 November 1815, but, like her eldest born, he died at the age of six months. Hazlitt kept a lock of the infant's hair until his own dying day. His relations with his wife had been cooling for some time.

Relief was found on the fives court. Hazlitt excelled at the game of rackets, which he would play for hours at a time, without braces and stripped to his shirt, contrary to the gentlemanly custom of retaining a waistcoat. His obituary of the racket player John Cavanagh, reprinted at the end of his sinuous essay entitled 'The Indian jugglers', is generous and heartfelt.

The critic In 1816 the *Memoirs of the Late Thomas Holcroft* appeared in three volumes. This had been languishing at the publishers since shortly after Holcroft's death in 1809, when at the behest of Godwin Hazlitt had transcribed Holcroft's diaries, splicing in a variety of other material. A more important publication followed in 1817: *The Round Table* was the first collection of the occasional essays that had first appeared in newspapers and magazines. It came in two volumes, offering forty essays by Hazlitt and twelve by Leigh Hunt (though only Hazlitt's name was on the title-page). Keats admired it greatly and took to imitating Hazlitt's energetic tone. 'It is the finest thing by God—as Hazlitt would say', he wrote in a letter of 9 March 1817 to his friend J. H. Reynolds.

Later in the year Hazlitt published *Characters of Shakespear's Plays*, the first ever economically priced critical survey of all Shakespeare's works. Although like most Shakespearian critics of the age Hazlitt devoted considerable space to analysing the psychological motivation of the central figures in each drama, the word 'characters' in the title did not refer to this. It was the 'character'—the defining characteristics—of the play itself that Hazlitt set out to capture. He did so by means of stylistic sympathy: as if in imitation of the plays in question, the essay on *Hamlet* was speculative, that on *Macbeth* precipitate, on *Coriolanus* politically confrontational ('The language of poetry naturally falls in with the language of power'), and so on. *Characters*, dedicated to Charles Lamb, earned Hazlitt £100. The first edition sold out in six weeks; the second edition did badly, in Hazlitt's view because of the negative review in Gifford's *Quarterly*.

Between 1818 and 1820 Hazlitt gave several series of literary lectures (all published soon after delivery) at the Surrey Institution in Blackfriars Road, to a subscription audience predominantly from the liberal and dissenting communities. *Lectures on the English Poets* (1818) began with a general manifesto on the nature of poetry as an expressive medium ('Poetry is the language of the imagination and the passions', 'Poetry is the universal language which

the heart holds with nature and itself'; W. Hazlitt, *Complete Works*, ed. P. P. Howe, 21 vols., 1930–34, 5.1), then proceeded to Chaucer and Spenser, Shakespeare and Milton, the eighteenth-century tradition, and finally 'the living poets'. At the centre of this last lecture was an analysis of Wordsworth, whom Hazlitt praised highly for his originality but criticized deeply for the 'egotism' of his verse. These lectures were much admired by young Romantic artists, such as Keats and the painter William Bewick, who described Hazlitt as 'the Shakespeare prose writer of our glorious country'—'he outdoes all in truth, style, and originality' (Bewick, 1.42). Bewick's 1824 drawing of Hazlitt is the most fluent image of him that we possess (the version in the National Portrait Gallery is a copy by the artist himself, done the following year).

Hazlitt's *Lectures on the English Comic Writers* (delivered late 1818, published April 1819) began with a distinction between wit and humour, then took on Shakespeare and Ben Jonson, Restoration comedy, the periodical essay from Addison and Steele to Dr Johnson and Oliver Goldsmith, the English novelists (among whom Hazlitt held Fielding in highest regard), and the paintings of Hogarth. This was the first critical history of English comedy.

The final lecture series was on the *Dramatic Literature of the Age of Elizabeth* (delivered late 1819, published January 1820). Hazlitt knew little of Shakespeare's contemporaries, but Charles Lamb lent him a pile of books, which he took down to The Hut, the inn at Winterslow in Wiltshire where he frequently went in order to write. According to his friend Bryan Waller Procter (Barry Cornwall), he successfully mugged up the subject in six weeks. In his opening lecture he argued that the Elizabethan period was the golden age of English literature, thanks to the influence of the questioning spirit of the Reformation, the translation into the vernacular of the Bible and the classics, the birth of the professional playhouse, and the discovery of the New World. Subsequent lectures included brief accounts of most of the dramatists of the day, together with an interesting comparison of the prose styles of Sir Francis Bacon, Sir Thomas Browne, and Jeremy Taylor. Substantial extracts were quoted in each lecture.

The close of the Regency was also a period in which Hazlitt became embroiled in several controversies as a result of his political journalism. John Gibson Lockhart, writing under the pen-name Z in the reactionary *Blackwood's Magazine*, began describing the politically liberal Leigh Hunt and his friends, including Keats, as the 'cockney school'. *Blackwood's* mocked 'Bill Hazlitt' as a failed artist and a mere 'manufacturer' of reviews, essays, and lectures—'pimpled Hazlitt' with his 'coxcomb lectures'. Worse, the incident with the girl in the Lake District was dredged up and dressed up. Hazlitt responded with a libel action, settled out of court.

Another right-wing opponent was Gifford of the *Quarterly Review*. In 1819 Hazlitt published a *Letter to William Gifford Esq.*, a blistering response to the latter's politically motivated negative reception of his books: 'You are the *Government Critic*, a character nicely differing from that of a government spy—the invisible link, that connects literature with the police' (W. Hazlitt, *Complete Works*, ed. P. P. Howe, 21 vols., 1930–34, 9.13). Keats so admired the *Letter* that he copied great chunks of it into his own correspondence. The same year, Hazlitt's *Political Essays, with Sketches of Public Characters* was issued from the press of the radical publisher William Hone. Though a miscellany of previously published occasional journalism, it nevertheless offers a fine introduction to the sharpness of Hazlitt's prose and the spice of his convictions—his faith in Napoleon, his hatred for Pitt, his uneasy admiration of Burke, his dismay at the apostasy of Coleridge and Southey.

In 1820 John Scott founded the monthly *London Magazine*; it became the forum for some of the great works of Romantic prose, such as Lamb's 'Elia' essays and Thomas De Quincey's 'Confessions of an English opium-eater'. Hazlitt became a regular contributor of dramatic notices and general essays. His father died that July, at the age of eighty-four. But it was in the following month that Hazlitt's life was rocked to its foundation.

The lover Hazlitt was living apart from his wife by this time. For 14*s*. a week he rented rooms at 9 Southampton Buildings, off Chancery Lane. His landlady was married to a tailor, Micaiah Walker. Their eldest daughter, Martha, had recently made a very advantageous match to one of their lodgers, Robert Roscoe, son of William Roscoe, the celebrated Liverpool banker and philanthropist whose portrait Hazlitt had painted. A second daughter, Sarah (*b.* 1800), assisted her mother in the lodging-house, and on 16 August 1820 she brought Hazlitt his breakfast. He fell instantly in love and spent the next three years in emotional turmoil.

Hazlitt's friend Procter did not think well of her appearance:

> Her face was round and small, and her eyes were motionless, glassy, and without any speculation (apparently) in them. Her movements in walking were very remarkable, for I never observed her to make a step. She went onwards in a sort of wavy, sinuous manner, like the movement of a snake. She was silent, or uttered monosyllables, and was very demure.
> (*B. W. Procter*, 181)

But Hazlitt himself projected on to her his faith in the transformative magic of art: she was a figure in a painting, an enchantress, Pygmalion's statue.

According to Hazlitt, Sarah flirted with him daily for upwards of a year and a half. She allowed certain sexual liberties, but refused to go the final length. Hazlitt decided to divorce his capable and unromantic wife in order to be free to marry this more tantalizing Sarah. Under Scottish law, but not English, it was possible to remarry after divorce, so it was to Scotland he went early in 1822, in order to fulfil the forty-day residence requirement which would allow him to apply for a divorce there. He broke his journey north at Stamford, to view the pictures at Burghley House. In Edinburgh he visited a brothel, so that there would be evidence for his wife to divorce him. He remained in Scotland for several months, waiting for his wife, making excursions to rural Renton and to Glasgow, where he repeated two of the lectures on the English

poets (one on Shakespeare and Milton, the other on the Scottish poets Thomson and Burns). He returned briefly to London by sea in May, but Sarah Walker avoided him; he was suspicious of her relations with other lodgers, a vulgar Welshman called Griffiths, and Tomkins, a good-looking young gentleman training for the law. Back in Scotland, he waited while the divorce proceedings dragged through the summer, finally being completed in July. Hazlitt returned to London once more. He was on the point of proposing to Sarah when he met her walking with Tomkins. Bitterly disillusioned as he was, he remained obsessed—one moment trying to win her back, the next testing her virtue by engaging an acquaintance to lodge in the building and attempt to seduce her.

In the end Hazlitt could only purge himself of the abortive affair by writing a book about it, *Liber amoris* ('Book of love'), published in May 1823. It consisted of dialogues between 'W' and 'S' written in a style of extreme sensibility, together with edited versions of Hazlitt's own letters to his friends about his feelings for Sarah. Emotionally raw, at times vulgar and embarrassing, *Liber amoris* played into the hands of his enemies in the right-wing press. Though published anonymously, it was quickly identified as Hazlitt's and he was made a laughing-stock for his infatuation with 'the tailor's daughter'. Sarah herself remained loyal to John Tomkins, bearing him a son in 1824 and living with him until his death at the age of sixty in 1858. She lived on for another twenty years. 'To this girl', wrote Procter, Hazlitt 'gave all his valuable time, all his wealthy thoughts, and all the loving frenzy of his heart. For a time, I think that on this point he was substantially insane' (*B. W. Procter*, 182).

The essayist All the while Hazlitt was continuing to support himself financially through his journalism. In April 1821 a volume of *Table-Talk, or, Original Essays* was published by John Warren of Old Bond Street. 'Table-Talk' had been the title of Hazlitt's monthly essay column in the *London*, but this collection consisted mostly of previously unpublished work. Subject matter ranged from low culture ('The Indian jugglers') to memory and time ('On the past and future', 'On living to one's self'). The power of imagination remained a notable concern, most explicitly in the essay 'On genius and common sense'. The death of John Scott, following a duel with a rival literary editor, threw the *London* into disarray and some time later Hazlitt transferred his 'Table-Talk' essays to the *New Monthly Magazine*. It was there that in February 1822 he published his great essay, 'The fight', a memorable account of a prize-fight at Hungerford between Bill Neate and Tom Hickman, known in the ring as the Gas-man. A second volume of *Table-Talk*, again consisting mostly of previously unpublished essays, appeared in May and earned him £80—a poor return for several hundred pages' work, especially when compared to the £56 he was paid for recycling the two old lectures in Glasgow.

In 1824 Hazlitt began publishing a new style of essay in the *New Monthly Magazine*: the pen portrait of a major public figure of the day. A collection of eighteen such pieces was published towards the end of the year (though with

1825 on the title-page) as *The Spirit of the Age, or, Contemporary Portraits*, a work regarded by many as his finest single book. His earlier experience as portrait painter and parliamentary sketch writer prepared him well for the task. The collection gets off to a dazzling start with essays on Jeremy Bentham, William Godwin, Coleridge, and the charismatic preacher Edward Irving. The subsequent portraits of both politicians such as Eldon and Canning, and writers such as Cobbett and Scott, are equally adept, and Wordsworth is treated more generously than in some of Hazlitt's earlier writings. The essay on Byron offers sharp criticisms, but ends with a magnanimous tribute written in the immediate wake of news of the poet's death.

Hazlitt's other publications in this period included the introductions to an anthology of *Select British Poets*, a series of *Sketches of the Principal Picture-Galleries in England* (both 1824), and a collection of aphorisms, entitled *Characteristics: in the Manner of Rochefoucault's Maxims*, published anonymously in 1825 soon after *Liber amoris*, as well as a continuing stream of essays in the periodical press. Hazlitt, who tried to avoid alcohol, was a reluctant socializer, but about this time he attended the regular contributors' dinners hosted by the new publishers of the *London Magazine*, Taylor and Hessey. John Clare, the 'Northamptonshire peasant poet', met him at one of these parties and described him as:

> a middle-sized dark-looking man and his face is deeply lined with a satirical character—his eyes are bright but they are rather buried under his brows—he is a walking satire and you would wonder where his poetry came from that is scattered so thickly over his writings.   (J. Clare, *Prose*, ed. J. W. Tibble and A. Tibble, 1951, 88)

In summer 1823, on the rebound from Sarah Walker, Hazlitt met his second wife, Isabella (1791–1869). She was the ninth child of James Shaw, a freemason from Inverness who enjoyed the company of the military, and his wife, Jean, daughter of an Inverness banker. After various familial disasters, Isabella had found herself with relatives in the Caribbean, where she had married Henry Bridgwater, a lawyer of Grenada, in 1813; he died in 1820, leaving her £300 per annum. She returned to Scotland and, according to a friend of Hazlitt's, met the essayist in a stagecoach and fell in love with him on account of his writings. They married in April 1824 and in the autumn set off on a tour of France and Italy.

In Paris Hazlitt met Stendhal—they admired each other's works and both knew the pangs of disprized love—and arranged with Messrs Galignani for publication of Paris editions of some of his works. Early in 1825 he and his wife arrived in Florence, where acquaintance was renewed with Leigh Hunt and made for the first time with Walter Savage Landor, who found Hazlitt odd. In Rome they stayed in a house in which Salvator Rosa, another artist in Hazlitt's personal pantheon, had once lived. They then returned north to Venice, where the high point was a visit to Titian's studio, then went on to Milan, lakes Como and Maggiore, and over the Simplon Pass to Vevey, with its associations of one of Hazlitt's favourite books, Rousseau's *La nouvelle Héloïse*. Hazlitt and his wife returned

to London in the autumn of 1825 and lodged in Piccadilly. He had described his continental tour in a series of letters in the *Morning Chronicle*; Leigh Hunt and Charles Cowden Clarke republished them in book form in May 1826 with the title *Notes on a Journey through France and Italy*. The same month saw the publication by Colburn of Hazlitt's last collection of miscellaneous essays, *The Plain Speaker: Opinions on Men, Books and Things*, one of his most assured volumes. In 1826 he also published, in the *New Monthly Magazine* under the general title 'Boswell redivivus', a series of 'Conversations' with the painter James Northcote RA. Some of the gossip therein led to a falling-out with Godwin and Leigh Hunt.

Hazlitt and his wife soon returned to Paris. They took a house in the Chaussée d'Antin and he began work on a massive biography of his revered Napoleon. In the autumn of 1827, the marriage came to an end, apparently for mainly financial reasons. Hazlitt's earnings had been dropping; the *London Magazine* paid 15 guineas a sheet and the *New Monthly Magazine* 16. At this rate, he would have earned nearly £200 from his periodical writing in 1824, but only £80 the following year and £40 in 1826, as he began devoting himself to the Napoleon book, for which he received no advance. Hazlitt's son, now a teenager, had joined the Paris household at the end of his summer term, and the second Mrs Hazlitt seems to have resented supporting both a husband and a stepson out of her £300 per annum. Hazlitt took the boy back to London, then wrote to his wife. She refused to join him and went off to Switzerland with her sister.

Little is known about Hazlitt's last years. He suffered from increasing financial difficulties and poor health. The first two volumes of the *Life of Napoleon* were published in February 1828 by Hunt and Clarke, but the firm promptly went bankrupt, and so he earned nothing from them. The remaining two volumes were not published until 1830, about the time of the author's death. The *Life* is his least original work, for it consists mostly of translation or paraphrase of various French histories and biographies, and even Sir Walter Scott's *Life of Napoleon*, though some sections—notably a general introduction to the French Revolution and the 'characters' of Robespierre, Fox, and Pitt—are in Hazlitt's distinctive voice.

Hazlitt continued to write periodical essays until his death, finding new outlets in the weekly *Atlas* and Colburn's *Court Journal*. Further conversations with Northcote appeared in both journals, and were subsequently revised as a book, which was ready for publication in July 1830, but delayed at Northcote's request, finally being issued in the week of Hazlitt's death.

'The sick chamber', a brief essay published in *The Atlas* in August 1830, is a moving account of Hazlitt's own declining health: 'from the crowded theatre to the sick chamber, from the noise, the glare, the keen delight, to the loneliness, the darkness, the dulness, and the pain, there is but one step' (W. Hazlitt, *Complete Works*, ed. P. P. Howe, 21 vols., 1930–34, 17.371). He was at this time living in a room at 6 Frith Street, Soho, in considerable poverty, and in February 1830 he was briefly under arrest for debt.

Seven months later he wrote to Francis Jeffrey of the *Edinburgh*, 'Dear Sir, I am dying; can you send me 10£, and so consummate your many kindnesses to me?' (W. Hazlitt, *Letters*, 378).

George Darling, who had also been doctor to Keats and Clare, was called in, but to no avail. William Hazlitt died about 4.30 p.m. on Saturday 18 September 1830, aged fifty-two, at 6 Frith Street. His son and his dear friend Charles Lamb were present, together with Lamb's friend Edward White of the India House and the publisher J. A. Hessey. Family tradition had it that on his deathbed Hazlitt asked to see his mother and expressed pleasure at his son's engagement to Kitty Reynell. His last words were supposed to have been 'Well, I've had a happy life'. As his best modern biographer remarks, 'there was a world of meaning in that *well*' (Wardle, 485).

Hazlitt's landlady supposedly hid his body under a piece of furniture for some days, so that she could show the room to a prospective new lodger. Charles Lamb made the burial arrangements. Hazlitt was laid to rest in the churchyard of St Anne's, Soho, just off Shaftesbury Avenue, on 23 September, with only his son and a few friends present. A tombstone was erected, on which he was described as:

> The first (unanswered) Metaphysician of the age. A despiser of the merely Rich and Great: A Lover of the People, Poor or Oppressed: A hater of the Pride and Power of the Few … The unconquered Champion of Truth, Liberty, and Humanity.

This was replaced in 1870 by a more sober headstone, which is now attached to the south buttress of the church tower; restored by the writer's grandson in 1901, it has since become badly eroded.

The cause of death has been identified variously as 'weak digestion', 'a species of cholera', and, most likely, cancer of the stomach.

The legacy Hazlitt died penniless; his legacy was his work. His son oversaw the publication of various posthumous essays, including 'The letter-bell', a memorable meditation on the pleasures of the arrival of the mail (*New Monthly Magazine*, March 1831). In 1836 the *Literary Remains of the Late William Hazlitt* were published in two volumes, edited by his son, who contributed an opening biographical essay.

William Hazlitt junior (1811–1893) married Catherine Reynell, daughter of one of the printers of his father's work, in 1833. He eventually became registrar of the London court of bankruptcy, but found time to edit and re-publish about a dozen volumes of his father's essays, reviews, and miscellaneous writings. His own son, William Carew *Hazlitt (1834–1913), a bibliographer, book collector, and editor of Elizabethan literary texts, reissued many of these collections and wrote four memoirs of his grandfather and other members of his family. W. C. Hazlitt's *Memoirs* and *The Hazlitts* include lists of his grandfather's paintings, as does appendix two of P. P. Howe's 1922 biography, but none of these is complete or wholly reliable.

Hazlitt's mother, Grace, who had been shocked by his divorce, lived on in Crediton, Devon, for another seven years. His first wife, Sarah, who always remained close to the family despite the divorce, visited her and Peggy there in 1831. She herself died in 1840.

An annotated collected edition of Hazlitt's works in thirteen volumes, edited by A. R. Waller and Arnold Glover, was published between 1902 and 1906. It was greatly expanded by P. P. Howe into a *Complete Works* of remarkable textual accuracy and with exemplary annotation (21 vols., 1930–34).

Although his life was frowned upon, Hazlitt's writings were held in high regard by the Victorians. 'Though we are mighty fine fellows nowadays', said Robert Louis Stevenson, 'we cannot write like Hazlitt' (Stevenson, 157). But his reputation declined in the twentieth century. With the possible exception of Coleridge, he was the greatest English critic of his age. He was the first great theatre reviewer in the English language. He formed the prototype of the nineteenth- and twentieth-century literary journalist and was a pioneering art critic. He was the father of that tradition of literary passion mingled with political activism which in the later twentieth century was best represented by one of his most ardent advocates, Michael Foot. Yet in 1984 his work was selected as the risibly arcane specialism of the archetypal second-rate academic Philip Swallow in David Lodge's comic novel *Small World*. His fall into literary disrepute may be attributed to the influence of T. S. Eliot and F. R. Leavis. In the 1930s, a century after his death, Hazlitt became a victim of his associations. He had been a close friend of Charles Lamb, who wrote essays in a whimsical style that was regarded by Eliot and his acolytes as the quintessence of that 'belle-lettrism' which they were making it their business to exterminate. Worse still, Hazlitt was a journalist—a word which only ever passed the lips of Leavisites when accompanied by a venomous sneer. And he was committed to popular culture. He brought to his essays on prize-fighters and racket-ball players the same vitality that animated his praise of Edmund Burke's prose, Edmund Kean's Shakespearian acting, and Wordsworth's best poetry. For the puritanical Leavisites, this would never do: they were busy building a high wall between 'mass civilization' and 'minority culture'. Hazlitt was boxed up with Lamb and left on the shelf to gather dust.

Major recuperative work was, however, undertaken by the American scholar David Bromwich (*Hazlitt: the Mind of a Critic*, 1983) and the Northern Irish poet and cultural commentator Tom Paulin (*The Day-Star of Liberty: William Hazlitt's Radical Style*, 1998). They argued for the importance of Hazlitt as the model for a flexible, jargon-free literary critical prose committed to cultural life in the public sphere.

The Sarah Walker affair and the *Liber amoris*, meanwhile, though dismaying to feminists, have inspired a television drama (*Hazlitt in Love*, January 1977) and three novels, Melvyn Bragg's *A Time to Dance* (1990) and, with the debt acknowledged explicitly, Jonathan Bate's *The Cure for Love* (1998), and Anne Haverty's *The Far Side of a Kiss* (2000, told from Sarah Walker's point of view). Hazlitt's childhood home in Wem is privately owned, but bears a plaque. Maidstone, his birthplace, has honoured him by naming its theatre The Hazlitt; the Maidstone Museum owns several of his paintings, including the portrait of his father, though not all are displayed. The house in Frith Street where he died in a small back room is now a hotel, frequented by writers, called Hazlitt's.   JONATHAN BATE

Sources W. Hazlitt, *Letters*, ed. H. M. Sikes, W. H. Bonner, and G. Lahey (1979) • M. Hazlitt, *Journal*, ed. E. J. Moyne (1967) • S. Hazlitt and W. Hazlitt, *Journals, 1822–1831*, ed. W. H. Bonner (1959) • R. M. Wardle, *Hazlitt* (1971) • S. Jones, *Hazlitt: a life: from Winterslow to Frith Street* (1989) • P. P. Howe, *The life of William Hazlitt* (1922); rev. edn with introduction by F. Swinnerton (1949) • W. C. Hazlitt, *Memoirs of William Hazlitt*, 2 vols. (1867) • W. C. Hazlitt, *Four generations of a literary family*, 2 vols. (1897) • W. C. Hazlitt, *Lamb and Hazlitt* (1900) • W. C. Hazlitt, *The Hazlitts: an account of their origin and descent*, 2 vols. (1911) • *Henry Crabb Robinson on books and their writers*, ed. E. J. Morley, 3 vols. (1938) • *The letters of John Keats, 1814–1821*, ed. H. E. Rollins, 2 vols. (1958) • B. W. Procter (Barry Cornwall): *an autobiographical fragment*, ed. C. P. [C. Patmore] (1877) • *The diary of Benjamin Robert Haydon*, ed. W. B. Pope, 5 vols. (1960–63) • T. Paulin, *The day-star of liberty: William Hazlitt's radical style* (1998) • D. Bromwich, *Hazlitt: the mind of a critic* (1983) • H. Baker, *William Hazlitt* (1962) • W. Bewick, *Life and letters*, ed. T. Landseer, 2 vols. (1871) • R. L. Stevenson, *Travels and essays* (1909) • J. W. Kinnaird, *William Hazlitt: critic of power* (1978) • A. C. Grayling, *The quarrel of the age: the life and times of William Hazlitt* (2000)
Archives BL, essays, Egerton MS 3244, Add. MS 61732 | BL, letters to Macvey Napier, Add. MSS 34611–34614 • NL Scot., corresp. with Archibald Constable • State University of New York, Buffalo, Lockwood Memorial Library, A. Conger Goodyear MSS
Likenesses J. Hazlitt, oils, c.1786, Maidstone Museum and Art Gallery • W. Hazlitt, self-portrait, oils, c.1802, Maidstone Museum and Art Gallery [*see illus.*] • J. Hazlitt, oils, c.1813, Maidstone Museum and Art Gallery • B. R. Haydon, oils, 1819 (*Christ's entry into Jerusalem*), Athenaeum of Ohio, St Gregory Seminary, Cincinnati • W. Bewick, chalk drawing, 1824, Maidstone Museum and Art Gallery; 1825 copy, NPG • Horne, death mask, 1830, Maidstone Museum and Art Gallery • J. Durham, bust (after death mask), Maidstone Museum and Art Gallery • line engraving, NPG • plaster mask, Bodl. Oxf.

Hazlitt, William Carew (1834–1913), bibliographer and writer, was born at 76 Charlotte Street, Fitzroy Square, London, on 22 August 1834, the eldest son of William Hazlitt, registrar of the court of bankruptcy, and his wife, Catherine Reynell (*d.* 1860); he was a grandson of William *Hazlitt (1778–1830), the essayist. He was educated at Merchant Taylors' School from 1842 to 1850, and after experimenting with journalism and civil engineering, and serving during the Crimean War as a supernumerary clerk at the War Office, he turned to historical research. In 1858 he published *The History of the Origin and Rise of the Republic of Venice*, which appeared in revised and extended forms in 1860, 1900, and 1915. It played a significant part in the later Victorian rehabilitation of medieval and Renaissance Venice, earlier portrayed by historians as the home of a tyrannous and arbitrary oligarchy.

Hazlitt married, on 10 October 1860, Henrietta Foulkes, the daughter of John Foulkes of Ashfield House, Wrexham, in Denbighshire. They had one son and one daughter. Hazlitt was called to the bar at the Inner Temple in 1861, but instead of practising he became interested in bibliography. In 1867 he published a *Handbook to the popular, poetical and dramatic literature of Great Britain from the invention of printing to the Restoration* (1867). To listing and

editing these early works he devoted much of the rest of his life, examining thousands of old books as they passed through the salerooms. Three series of *Bibliographical Collections and Notes*, with two supplements to the third, were published by him during the years 1876–89, followed by a *General Index*, compiled by G. J. Gray in 1893, and a fourth series in 1903. Written on odd bits of paper in a difficult hand, his notes, when they appeared in print, were sometimes inexact, but the *Collections and Notes* nevertheless became a much used book of reference.

In his old age Hazlitt gave much time to bringing all his notes together, with many new ones, as a *Consolidated Bibliography*, and made the cost of printing this a first charge on a reversionary bequest to the British Museum, the balance of which was to form a fund for purchasing early English books. The preparation of his *Handbook* enabled Hazlitt to give much valuable help to Henry Huth (1815–1876) in the formation of the latter's well-known library, and he frequently offered bargains from the salerooms to the British Museum and elsewhere. His methods of work and experiences are revealed in his *Confessions of a Collector* (1897) and in his two biographical volumes, *The Hazlitts* (1911) and *The Later Hazlitts* (1912).

Hazlitt's chief editorial undertakings were new editions of Robert Dodsley's *Select Collection of Old Plays* in fifteen volumes (1874–6) and of Thomas Warton's *History of English Poetry* (1871), *Shakespeare's Library* in six volumes (1875), *Old English Jest Books* in three volumes (1863–4), and the *Poems and Plays of Thomas Randolph* (1875). He also wrote *Shakespeare: the Man and his Work* (1902), *Coinage of the European Continent* (1893–7), two volumes of poems (1877, 1897), and *Man Considered in Relation to God and a Church* (1905). The record of Hazlitt's publications extends to over sixty items and provides evidence of a busy life. He died at home at 87 Church Road, Richmond, Surrey, on 8 September 1913.   A. W. REED, *rev.* NILANJANA BANERJI

Sources W. C. Hazlitt, *Four generations of a literary family*, 2 vols. (1897) • J. Foster, *Men-at-the-bar: a biographical hand-list of the members of the various inns of court*, 2nd edn (1885) • W. C. Hazlitt, *The Hazlitts* (1911) • W. C. Hazlitt, *The later Hazlitts* (1912) • W. C. Hazlitt, *The confessions of a collector* (1897) • J. Pemble, *Venice rediscovered* (1996) • *CGPLA Eng. & Wales* (1913)
Archives BL, corresp., Add. MSS 38898–38913 • Man. CL, MSS | U. Edin. L., corresp. with James Halliwell-Phillipps
Wealth at death £10,831 1s. 9d.: probate, 4 Oct 1913, *CGPLA Eng. & Wales*

Hazzard [*other married name Kelly*], **Dorothy** (*d.* 1674), Baptist leader, first appears about 1620, when she and her then husband, Anthony Kelly, grocer, who had a shop in High Street, Bristol, between the Guilders Inn and the High Cross, gathered around them a separatist group. Edward Terrill described Dorothy as a 'he-goat before the flock' because she was 'the first woman in this City of Bristol that practized that truth of the Lord ... namely, separation' (Hayden, 85). The group exchanged sermon notes, held days of prayer and fasting, and were ridiculed because 'they had women preachers among them [and] because there were many good women, (that frequented their assembling)' (ibid., 86). Once when they met in the

High Street house they were attacked by the 'rude multitude and seamen, soe that they broake all the windows, because they heard there was Conventicle of Puritans' (ibid.).

When Kelly died Dorothy retained his shop and kept it open 'on the time they called Christmas day, and sit sewing in her shop, as a witness for God in the midst of the Citty, in the face of the Sun, and in the sight of all men' (Hayden, 86). About 1640 she married Matthew Hazzard (1601/2–1671), son of George Hazzard of Lyme Regis, Dorset, and from 19 December 1639 vicar of St Ewin's, Bristol. The couple lived in the parsonage on Sundays and in the High Street for the rest of the week. In the vacant parsonage they sometimes entertained separatist families in Bristol who were waiting for a passage to New England. Dorothy demonstrated her 'unbridled spirit' by using the parsonage as a safe house for women wishing to avoid churching 'at their time for lyeing-in' (Davies, 28, 118). The women were able, by being in Hazzard's parish, 'to avoid the ceremonies of their Churching, the Crosse, and other impositions that most of the Parsons of other parishes did burden them withall, that were delivered within their precincts' (ibid., 88).

The Hazzards supported the parliamentary cause. When Colonel Nathaniel Fiennes was charged by William Prynne with cowardice and dereliction of duty by surrendering Bristol to Prince Rupert in August 1643 Dorothy gave evidence at his trial. Led by Joan Batten, Dorothy, and others, a group of 200 Bristol women and children had defended the Frome Gate against the prince; the women in their evidence said that they had been prepared to 'dead the bullets' of the enemy with the bodies of themselves and their children. Dorothy had put all her goods in the castle on the understanding that Fiennes would defend it and she was angered by his surrender.

When Bristol fell to the king the Hazzards fled. Matthew was for a time rector of East Barnet, Hertfordshire, but by 1645 they had returned to Bristol, where he served as an assistant to the Somerset commission in 1654. In 1662 he was ejected from St Ewin's but he continued to live in Bristol until his death in 1671. Dorothy remained loyal to the Baptist cause at Broadmead and died on or shortly before 14 March 1674, the day on which Edward Terrill noted: 'aged Sister Hazzard departed … she was the First woman member in the Congregation. She lived to a greate age, and came to her grave a shock of Corne fully ripe' (Hayden, 154). ROGER HAYDEN

Sources R. Hayden, ed., *The records of a church in Christ in Bristol, 1640–1687*, Bristol RS, 27 (1974), 12–19, 85, 87–91, 131, 154, 293 · P. McGrath, *Bristol and the civil war* (1981) · J. Latimer, *The annals of Bristol in the seventeenth century* (1900), 148–9, 151, 179, 186 · W. Prynne and C. Walker, *A true and full relation of the prosecution … of Nathaniel Fiennes late colonel and governor of the city and castle of Bristol* (1644), pt 2, catalogue of witnesses, 10 · S. Davies, *Unbridled spirits: women of the English revolution, 1640–1660* (1998) · *Calamy rev.*
Likenesses G. Moira, portrait, Old Council House, Broad Street, Bristol; repro. in McGrath, *Bristol and the Civil War*, facing p. 28

Head, Alice Maud (1886–1981), journalist and businesswoman, was born on 3 May 1886 at 138 High Street, Notting Hill, London, the younger daughter of Frank Dearden Head, a builder, and his wife, Ada Cove, a schoolteacher. After attending school in Acton she was sent to the North London Collegiate School for Girls in Camden Town. She felt that she suffered from a repressive childhood. Her father, a Baptist and strict sabbatarian, believed that 'most forms of pleasure were wrong', and though she acquired a strong sense of duty and discipline she saw herself as unloved (Head, 2). As a result, despite her success in adult life she remained a rather shy and reserved person. Although attractive enough to receive a number of proposals of marriage, she always rejected them.

Despite her education and application Alice Head was never encouraged to pursue a career. Later in life a female relation commented: 'I can't *think* how it is you have got on so well—you have no special gifts, it is *most* extraordinary' (Head, 193). When she expressed a wish to become a journalist she met with discouragement and instead trained to be a secretary. At nineteen, accompanied by her disapproving mother, she was interviewed for a post as a shorthand typist at *Country Life*, and was appointed temporarily at £1 a week: 'the great adventure had begun'. Soon she began to contribute short pieces including minor book reviews and horticultural and agricultural reports. She then worked as a sub-editor to Lord Alfred Douglas at *The Academy*, a literary weekly, but in 1909 she decided to leave and approached Sir George (later Lord) Riddell, the director of George Newnes, for assistance. Riddell appointed her editor of the monthly magazine *Woman At Home* at the age of twenty-two.

Alice Head's life was, however, transformed in 1917 when the American publishing magnate William Randolph Hearst, who was anxious to establish his magazines in Britain, offered her the assistant editorship of *Nash's Magazine* at a weekly salary of £10. In 1923, after the launching of the English edition of *Good Housekeeping*, he employed her as its assistant editor, and in the following year she became editor and managing director, positions which she held until 1939. In this period Alice Head was reputed to be the highest paid woman in Britain. Hearst trusted her so completely that for fifteen years she acted as his personal representative in Europe. On his behalf she made innumerable purchases in order to indulge his whims for items including silver, paintings, antiques, sculpture, St Donats Castle in south Wales, and, most bizarrely, three giraffes ordered at an emporium in the Tottenham Court Road for Hearst's private zoo in California.

Good Housekeeping proved to be a commercial success from the outset. At a time when middle-class women struggled to find domestic help, it offered both practical advice about running a home, and an uplifting view of household management as the equivalent of a profession for married women. During the 1920s Alice Head commissioned articles by prominent feminists including Millicent Fawcett, Rebecca West, and Lady Rhondda, as well as politicians such as Ellen Wilkinson, Margaret Wintringham, and Violet Bonham-Carter. However, the emphasis was heavily on domesticity and on conventional fiction. Her only controversial decision was to publish an attack on female employers and female journalists by Lord Birkenhead in 1927 entitled 'This intrusion of women'. The episode was revealing of her own attitudes. She felt too secure personally to be threatened or irritated by Birkenhead's patronizing remarks, and observed that he had not only accepted employment from a woman but had *asked* for it. Though a suffragist and a successful career woman Alice, like many similar women of her generation, avoided describing herself as a feminist and showed no inclination to campaign for further rights for women.

In 1941, when the fortunes of Randolph Hearst were failing, Head accepted an invitation from George Newnes to rejoin the company to edit *Homes and Gardens*, and, in 1942, to become a director of *Country Life*. She retained these positions until her retirement in 1949. She died at 7 Knaresborough Place, Kensington, London, on 25 July 1981, and was buried at the City Temple on 4 August.

MARTIN PUGH

Sources A. M. Head, *It could never have happened* (1939) · *The Times* (29 July 1981) · *WWW* · M. Pugh, *Women and the women's movement in Britain, 1914–1959* (1992) · b. cert. · d. cert.
Wealth at death £408,062: probate, 25 Nov 1981, *CGPLA Eng. & Wales*

Head, Antony Henry, first Viscount Head (1906–1983), army officer and politician, was born in London on 19 December 1906, the only son and younger child of Geoffrey Head (1872–1955), of 51 South Street, London, and his wife, Ethel Daisy (d. 1965), daughter of Arthur Flower, of Prince's Gate, London. His father, Lloyd's broker, was one of eleven children. One uncle went down with the *Titanic* and another, Sir Henry Head, was an eminent neurologist and FRS.

Educated at Eton College and the Royal Military College, Sandhurst, Head worked for a summer as a stable lad in the well-known racing establishment of Atty Persse. He retained an interest in racing all his life. Tall, slim, and athletic, he was commissioned in the 15th/19th hussars, but an illness which rendered him temporarily unsuited for service abroad led him in 1924 to transfer to the Life Guards; he became an adjutant ten years later. In the intervening years he rode in the Grand National and in many other races as an amateur jockey. In 1932 he obtained leave to sail in the great Finnish four-masted barque *Herzogin Cecilie* in the annual grain-race to Australia. The voyage round the Cape lasted three months and he worked his passage before the mast, receiving at the end of the voyage the able bodied seaman's certificate. In July 1935 Head married Lady Dorothea Louise (d. 1987), daughter of Anthony Ashley-Cooper, ninth earl of Shaftesbury. They had two sons and two daughters, one of whom died in infancy.

In his regiment and elsewhere Head was highly regarded for his energy, enterprise, and love of adventure. A few days before the outbreak of war in 1939 he was engaged in manoeuvres with a Polish cavalry regiment. He contrived to return home before war was finally declared and wrote a report on the Polish cavalry's tactics and equipment. He was sent to the Staff College, Camberley, and by spring 1940 he was brigade-major of the 20th

Antony Henry Head, first Viscount Head (1906–1983), by Elliott & Fry

guards brigade. He took part in the fighting at Boulogne and was awarded the MC. He was then appointed an assistant secretary to the committee of imperial defence; but by 1942 he was GSO2 in the guards armoured division. His clear brain and notable endowment of common sense were recognized in high military quarters. This led to his being appointed chief military planner at combined operations headquarters. From 1943 to 1945 he worked with the directors of plans on amphibious operations, made frequent visits to north Africa, and was much concerned with the planning of the landings in Sicily and Italy. He worked closely with the chiefs of staff and the joint planning staff, with the rank of brigadier. He attended the Casablanca, Tehran, Quebec, and Yalta conferences; and after Yalta he went to Moscow with his close friend Major-General Robert Laycock, chief of combined operations, to discover how best to elicit information about Soviet operational intentions from the Russian general staff who until then had been unco-operatively reticent.

Head was a member of the British delegation at the Potsdam conference in July 1945, but he was already Conservative candidate for Carshalton in the general election of that year. He won the seat with a majority of little more than 1000. His success and popularity in his constituency can be measured by the uninterrupted rise in his majority at subsequent elections until in 1959 it reached 13,244.

While his party was in opposition (1945–51) he made a name for himself in the House of Commons as a fluent and persuasive speaker on defence. So it was not surprising that on 31 October 1951 Winston Churchill, who liked him personally and admired his drive and sharpness of intellect, made him a privy councillor and secretary of state for war—a position he filled to Churchill's satisfaction and continued to hold when Sir Anthony Eden became prime minister in April 1955.

One of his major achievements at the War Office was to establish Welbeck College, which provided a broad education for young men, mostly the sons of artisans, showing an aptitude for technology and mechanization, as a preliminary to entering Sandhurst and obtaining a commission in the technical corps of the army.

On 18 October 1956 Head was appointed minister of defence in succession to Sir Walter Monckton who resigned because he opposed the projected Suez operation. Head was thus placed in a position of vital and immediate significance only a fortnight before the Suez landings, a venture of which the three service ministers had not even been informed and with which the chiefs of staff were not wholly in accord. He was distressed that the operation once begun was not completed. However, he endorsed the policy, and was unshaken in his loyalty to the prime minister, Eden. In January 1957 Harold Macmillan succeeded Eden. Against the advice of Head and the chiefs of staff, Macmillan offered what they considered inadequate financial backing for the armed forces. Head therefore declined an offer to remain minister of defence and retired to the back benches.

In 1960 Head was made a viscount. On Nigerian independence in the same year he became the first British high commissioner in Lagos. Relations with the Nigerian government were at that time excellent and it presented the high commission with the best site in Lagos. The Heads established a close friendship with the prime minister, Sir Abu Bakar Tafawa. They travelled assiduously throughout the country, associated with Nigerian politicians, businessmen, and artists, and their three years' tenure of the post was an undiluted success.

Head, who had been appointed CBE in 1946, and KCMG in 1961, was made GCMG on leaving Lagos in 1963. He was then, until 1966, the first British high commissioner in Malaysia, a duty he performed with his usual enthusiasm, though the political and racial animosity of Malays and Chinese made his task exceedingly difficult and resulted in Singapore's leaving the Malaysian Federation in 1965. The British army was engaged in military operations to oppose the invasion of North Borneo by the Indonesians. Head played an important part in smoothing relations between the British expeditionary force and the Malaysian government which was technically sovereign in the former British North Borneo.

Head was all his life a keen and expert ornithologist and entomologist, and he loved butterflies. When high commissioner in Lagos he would rise early and set forth with a butterfly net in pursuit of rare varieties. His charm never failed, and he had a way of expressing himself which delighted his friends and amused the staff of the offices he held, all of whom were consistently devoted to him.

Sometimes outrageous, especially in his youth, he had an original and decisive mind, and was never anything but honest in speech and action, patriotic, generous, and considerate. He adamantly refused to have his portrait painted, though he himself had skill as an artist.

Lady Head was a portrait painter of outstanding ability and, like her husband, witty and entertaining. She was a constant help to her husband throughout his varied career, and in both Nigeria and Malaysia was a tower of strength to the Red Cross and the order of St John of Jerusalem. On retirement Head and his wife settled at Throope Manor, Bishopstone, near Salisbury and he devoted his energy, still abundant, to helping others. A trustee of the Thomson Foundation from 1967, he was appointed colonel-commandant of the SAS regiment in 1968 (a position he held until 1976) and he became chairman and subsequently president of the Royal National Institute for the Blind and also chairman of the Wessex region of the National Trust. He died at Throope Manor on 29 March 1983 and was succeeded in the viscountcy by his elder son, Richard Antony (b. 1937). JOHN COLVILLE, rev.

Sources *The Times* (30 March 1983) · *WWW* · personal knowledge (1990) · private information (1990) · K. Kyle, *Suez* (1991) · E. Shuckburgh, *Descent to Suez: diaries, 1951–56*, ed. J. Charmley (1986) · Burke, *Peerage* (1980) · *CGPLA Eng. & Wales* (1983)
Archives Bodl. Oxf., corresp. with Lord Monckton · U. Birm. L., corresp. with Lord Avon and Lady Avon
Likenesses Elliott & Fry, photograph, NPG [*see illus.*]
Wealth at death £1,688,854: probate, 8 Aug 1983, *CGPLA Eng. & Wales*

Head, Barclay Vincent (1844–1914), numismatist, the second son of John Head, of Ipswich, and his wife, Elizabeth Bailey, was born at Ipswich on 2 January 1844; his father came of a Quaker family descended from the Quaker apologist Robert Barclay. Educated at the local grammar school under Hubert Holden, he left at the age of seventeen, and entered the department of coins and medals at the British Museum on 12 February 1864, and was promoted to assistant keeper (deputy to the keeper) on 15 February 1871. In 1869 he married Mary Harley (d. 1911), daughter of John Frazer Corkran, of Dublin, author and journalist. They had one daughter.

On 1 February 1893 Head succeeded Reginald Stuart Poole as keeper of his department, a post which he held until 30 June 1906. Through Poole he had some involvement with the Egypt Exploration Fund. His first contributions to numismatic literature were on Anglo-Saxon coins, but by 1868 he had settled down to his life's task. The department of coins and medals began about 1870 to work on the great series of Greek catalogues. With Poole and Percy Gardner, Head produced the first volume, *Italy*, in 1873; he was to write two more volumes in collaboration—*Sicily (Syracuse)* (1876), *Thrace and the Islands* (1877)—and eight alone—*Macedonia* (1879), *Central Greece* (1884), *Attica–Megaris–Aegina* (1888), *Colonies of Corinth* (1889), *Caria, Cos, Rhodes* (1897), *Ionia* (1892), *Lydia* (1901), and *Phrygia* (1906). To these official publications must be added his useful illustrated *Guide to the Coins of the Ancients* (1881) and a number of valuable monographs. He was part editor of the *Numismatic Chronicle* (1869–1910) and president of the Royal Numismatic Society (1908). As early as 1874 his *History of the Coinage of Syracuse* laid the foundations of the modern historical method in Greek numismatics. But the work by which he is best remembered is the *Historia numorum* (1887; 2nd edn, 1911), a system of Greek numismatics. This has been described as the 'bible of numismatics' and remains the most useful general handbook for Greek numismatics.

Head received degrees from Durham in 1887 and Oxford in 1905. His work was much admired abroad: Heidelberg University, the French and Prussian academies, and numerous specialist societies all honoured him. A fine tribute was the dedication to him, on his retirement, of *Corolla numismatica*, which was written by thirty scholars of six nations. He died at his home, 26 Leinster Square, Kensington, London, on 12 June 1914 after a long illness. The Barclay Head prize for numismatics at Oxford commemorates him.

It was said of Head that 'he was the best Greek numismatist this country has produced' (Hill, 39). Although he strictly limited his scope, he was no narrow specialist, his judgement, though deliberate, being instinctively so sound that even his few mistakes are illuminating. He was described as 'sweet-tempered, of infinite patience, perfectly free alike from self-assertion and from jealousy of his colleagues' (*Numismatic Chronicle*, 251).

G. F. HILL, rev. M. L. CAYGILL

Sources *Numismatic Chronicle*, 4th ser., 14 (1914), 168, 249–55 [incl. bibliography] · *WWW* · BM · private information (2004) [A. Burnett, BM] · G. F. Hill, 'Autobiographical fragment', *The Medal*, 12 (1988), 37–48, esp. 39 · *The Athenaeum* (20 June 1914), 861 · private information (1927) · personal knowledge (1927) · *CGPLA Eng. & Wales* (1914)
Archives BM
Likenesses Walery, photograph, 1887, BM, Department of Coins and Medals · photograph, BM, Department of Coins and Medals
Wealth at death £10,219 7s. 10d.: probate, 10 July 1914, *CGPLA Eng. & Wales*

Head, Sir **Edmund Walker**, eighth baronet (1805–1868), governor-in-chief of British North America and scholar, was born on 16 February 1805 at Wiarton Place, near Maidstone, Kent, the son of Revd Sir John Head (*d.* 1838), a clergyman, and his wife, Jane, the daughter of Thomas Walker, a London merchant. He was educated at Winchester College, and in 1823 was matriculated as a fellow-commoner at Oriel College, Oxford, where he took a first in classics and graduated BA in 1827. He was elected a fellow of Merton College, Oxford, in 1830, and held various offices including that of university examiner. Head travelled extensively in Italy, Germany, and Spain between 1828 and 1835, and became well versed in western European languages and culture. His tour of Germany in 1835 was made with his friend George Cornewall Lewis, whose *Essays on the Administrations of Great Britain from 1783 to 1830* he edited for posthumous publication in 1864.

Head entered Lincoln's Inn in 1835, but was never called to the bar. In 1836 he was appointed as an assistant poor-law commissioner, and after 1841 he served as one of the three chief commissioners. He succeeded to the baronetcy on the death of his father in January 1838. On 27 November of that year he married Anna Maria (1808–1890), the daughter of Revd Philip Yorke, prebendary of Ely; they had three children: John (who was drowned in 1859), Caroline, and Amabel Jane. Head was compelled to resign his college fellowship upon his marriage, and he lost his lucrative position on the poor-law commission at its demise in 1847. As compensation, he was offered the lieutenant-governorship of New Brunswick by the secretary of state for the colonies, the third Earl Grey. On arriving to take up the appointment in 1848, he was described as being 5 feet 9 or 10 inches in height, slightly stooped, with a fair complexion, sandy hair, and blue eyes.

As lieutenant-governor, Head inaugurated the system under which the members of the executive council were placed in charge of the various government departments, and on 20 May 1848 he formed what is usually described as the first responsible government in New Brunswick. Since the members of his administration did not form a coherent party he continued to exercise considerable influence over policy. When, in 1850, the executive council members were divided over the appointment of a new chief justice, he unilaterally recommended his own candidate. This provoked considerable anger, and led to the resignation from the council of Charles Fisher, a prominent Reformer, although Head survived the crisis. Among his achievements were the appointment of the agricultural chemist J. F. W. Johnston to undertake an important survey of New Brunswick agriculture and the appointment of a commission of inquiry into King's College, Fredericton, before which he gave evidence based on his Oxford experience. Grey ranked him among his most successful governors, and in 1854 appointed him governor-in-chief of British North America in succession to the earl of Elgin. His crucial function was that of a link between Britain and British North America during a time of change in their political and economic relations. In the United Province of Canada he was unable to exercise as much influence over day-to-day administrative affairs as he had in New Brunswick. He had long favoured some form of colonial union and continued to advocate a federal union of British North America, but recognized that the initiative must come from the colonists themselves. In 1857, when the assembly of the United Province of Canada was unable to agree upon the location of the capital, the question was referred to Queen Victoria, but it was almost certainly Head, who was in England at the time, who persuaded her to select Ottawa. While in England he was sworn of the privy council.

On his return to Canada Head faced a major political crisis. The Conservative administration had been forced to resign over the capital question and a Reform coalition headed by George Brown took office in July 1858, but lasted only four days. Head refused Brown's request to dissolve parliament, and allowed the former ministers to resume office without by-elections in a manoeuvre known as the 'double shuffle', which was strictly legal, but widely condemned. His conduct, although vindicated by the Colonial Office, remained a subject of contention and clouded his final years in office, which were devoted chiefly to maintaining good relations with the United States. His health deteriorated, and after playing host to the prince of Wales and the duke of Newcastle on the first official royal tour to Canada in 1860, he marked time until his replacement by Charles Stanley, fourth Viscount Monck, in October 1861.

Following his return to England, Head became one of the three unpaid civil service commissioners in April 1862, and was elected governor of the reconstituted Hudson's Bay Company in July 1863. He held both positions until his death. Throughout his career he retained a keen interest in many branches of study, including language, philology, law, poetry, ballads, and art. He edited works on western European art (1846, 1848, 1854) and political history (1868), translated the Icelandic saga *The Story of Viga Glum* (1866), and wrote a grammatical essay entitled *Shall and will* (1856, 2nd edn 1858). *Ballads and other Poems*, a volume of his verse, was published posthumously in 1868. He served as secretary and treasurer of the Athenaeum; received honorary degrees from Oxford and Cambridge; and was a fellow of the Royal Society and a KCB. Head died of a heart attack at his home, 29 Eaton Square, London, on 28 January 1868 and was buried in Kensal Green cemetery.

A. St Leger

Sources D. G. G. Kerr, *Sir Edmund Head: a scholarly governor* (1954) · D. G. G. Kerr, 'Head and responsible government in New Brunswick', *Canadian Historical Association Report* (1938), 62–70 · W. S. MacNutt, *New Brunswick: a history, 1784–1867* (1963) · J. M. S. Careless, *Brown of The Globe*, 2 vols. (1959–63) · D. G. Creighton, *John A. Macdonald*, 2 vols. (Toronto, 1952–5) · D. B. Knight, *Choosing Canada's capital* (1977) · G. Martin, *Britain and the origins of Canadian confederation, 1837–67* (1995) · J. A. Gibson, 'Head, Sir Edmund Walker', *DCB*, vol. 9 · *CGPLA Eng. & Wales* (1868) · Foster, *Alum. Oxon.*

Archives Hudson's Bay Company Archives, Winnipeg, Manitoba · NA Canada, New Brunswick, Canada, Governor-General series · NA Canada, MSS · PRO, papers, CO 537/139 | BL, letters to Charles Babbage, Add. MSS 37184–37199 · Bodl. Oxf., corresp. with Sir John Crampton · Herts. ALS, corresp. with Lord Lytton · NA Canada, Baring MSS · NA Canada, Ellice MSS · NA Canada, Howe MSS · NA Canada, Macdonald MSS · New Brunswick Museum, corresp. with Sir William Williams · NL Wales, letters to Sir George Cornewall Lewis · PRO, letters to Sir William Eyre, PRO 30/46 · U. Durham L., corresp. with third Earl Grey · U. Nott. L., letters to duke of Newcastle

Likenesses H. Weigall, oils, exh. RA 1866, Merton Oxf. · W. Holl, stipple (after G. Richmond; *Grillion's Club* series), BM

Wealth at death under £35,000: probate, 9 March 1868, *CGPLA Eng. & Wales*

Head, Sir Francis Bond, first baronet (1793–1875), colonial governor and author, nicknamed Galloping Head for his exploits in South America, was born on 1 January 1793, the son of James Roper Head (formerly Mendes; 1757–1814) of The Hermitage, Higham, Kent, and his wife, Frances Anne Burges, sister of James Bland *Burges. Head's grandfather, Moses Mendes or Mendez, had adopted the surname on marrying Anna Gabriella Head: the family were Jews who had settled in England during the reign of Charles II. Through his mother's connection with the Scottish aristocracy, Head took a ceremonial part in George IV's visit to Edinburgh in 1822, and in the Eglinton

Sir Francis Bond Head, first baronet (1793–1875), by Charles Turner, pubd 1837 (after Nelson Cook)

Tournament in 1839. James Roper Head was a radical, who fled from his creditors to Portugal in 1808. His son was implacably distrustful of radicals and an exaggerated love of all things English suggests sensitivity about his ancestry.

Family financial problems curtailed Head's schooling, and in 1809 he entered the Royal Military Academy, Woolwich. He was commissioned second lieutenant on 1 May 1811, and first lieutenant ten days later. He served in Malta until 1814, visiting Greece in 1813. He fought at Waterloo, and was stationed in France until 1818, and then at Edinburgh where he distinguished himself in 1824 by using explosives to demolish the ruins of the Parliament Square fire. On 20 May 1816, he married his cousin Julia Valenza Somerville (d. 1879), sister of the seventeenth Baron Somerville. Their marriage was very happy, although the birth of four children between 1817 and 1822 probably caused financial strain. Between 1825 and 1828 he three times exchanged regiments, to become a half-pay major in the unglamorous royal wagon train.

In 1825 Head was appointed manager of the Rio Plata Mining Association, and led a party of Cornish miners to Argentina. He found the country in turmoil, with promised franchises sold to rivals. He displayed immense energy, riding to Mendoza and on to Santiago in Chile in search of profitable mines, before abandoning the enterprise. The subsequent dispute with the directors began his career as both a controversialist and a travel writer with the publication of *Rough Notes Taken during some Rapid Journeys across the Pampas and among the Andes* (1826) and *Reports*

Relating to the Failure of the Rio Plata Mining Association (1827).

Head took an interest in social reform, lobbying Peel unsuccessfully for a post in the Metropolitan Police in 1828. He campaigned for the use of the South American lasso to saddle cavalry horses for use as draught animals. In 1831 a demonstration before William IV earned him a knighthood in the Hanoverian order. In 1832 he visited the German spa of Langen-Schwalbach, probably for his wife's health. His account, *Bubbles from the Brunnens of Nassau* (1834), was a popular success. That year he was appointed assistant commissioner for poor law in east Kent. Instead of negotiating the disbandment of existing parochial unions created under Gilbert's Act of 1782, he appealed directly to mass meetings of ratepayers and swept the old system aside. He publicized his achievement in a thinly anonymous article in the *Quarterly Review*.

In December 1835 Head was appointed lieutenant-governor of Upper Canada. Despite a legend that he was confused with his cousin Edmund Walker *Head, the appointment made sense. The whig cabinet sought a practical reformer and Head was acceptable to the king, who was critical of ministerial policy to Canada. On reaching Toronto in January 1836, Head tried to conciliate reformers who wanted a greater say in colonial government. In February he added three reformers to the executive council to make it more representative, but provoked general resignations on 12 March by refusing to be bound by their advice. The elected assembly supported the resigning councillors and refused to vote taxes. Head vetoed all expenditure, and in robust replies to addresses adroitly blamed the ensuing distress on the reformers. Emulating his Kentish tactics, he dissolved the assembly on 28 May and routed the reformers at the polls.

Head threatened several times to resign his post for financial reasons but in 1837 had notice that he was to receive the baronetcy which he had demanded. However his success was short-lived: during an economic recession in 1837 he forced colonial banks to follow the 'honest course' of meeting their obligations in gold; the banks reacted by restricting credit, further depressing the economy. On 10 September 1837 he refused Colonial Office instructions to appoint to office two men whom he regarded as disloyal. With the death of William IV, he lost his protector and his resignation was accepted on 24 November. In November 1837, faced with rising discontent among French Canadians, Sir John Colborne (Head's predecessor, who remained in Canada as commander of the troops) moved most of the garrison from the upper province to Lower Canada. Head grandiosely insisted on sending all the regular troops, throwing himself on the loyalty of the colony's 'yeomanry and peasantry'. This played into the hands of the reckless radical, William Lyon Mackenzie, whose origins in the Dundee weaving industry were as uncongenial to Head as his politics. Head was both to blame the subsequent Upper Canadian uprising on a secret conspiracy and to boast that he had

manipulated Mackenzie into revealing his wicked intentions. The brief uprising was quashed by loyal militia on 7 December. On 27 January 1838 a stunned cabinet listened to 'a most ludicrous' letter from Head which described how at the outbreak of firing, 'down dropped a great rebel, stone dead' (Dorchester, 5.117–18).

Head risked a breach with the United States by authorizing the destruction, on 29 December 1837, of an American steamboat, the *Caroline*, which was supplying rebels on Navy Island above Niagara Falls. He defiantly returned to Britain via New York, arriving on 22 April 1838. He hoped for an appointment to the new Irish poor law but Melbourne dismissed him as 'a damned odd fellow' (Sanders, 423). In February 1839 Head defended his handling of Canadian problems in his *Narrative*, a reply to the report on Canada by Lord Durham, violating protocol by unauthorized publication of dispatches. He urged the Conservative opposition to block the union of Upper and Lower Canada, but was rebuffed by Peel, who thought him 'crack-brained' (Aspinall, 210). In 1840 Head became chairman of the Grand Junction Canal Company. He cut costs and sought toll agreements with other companies, but failed to resist railway competition and was ousted in June 1847. He retired to Great Oxendon in Northamptonshire, moving to Croydon, Surrey, about 1858.

The repeal of the corn laws prompted Head to allege, in *The Emigrant* (1846), a long-standing conspiracy by Peel to subvert British institutions. Undeterred by the derision of reviewers, he espoused other controversial causes. In 1849, in debate with Charles Dickens, he offered a lurid defence of public hanging. In 1850 his warning of imminent French invasion in *The Defenceless State of Great Britain* was savaged by James Gibson Lockhart in the *Quarterly Review*. Its message seemed inconsistent with the moral of his *A Faggot of French Sticks* (1851), an account of a visit to Paris which praised the prince-president, Louis Napoleon, whom Head had known slightly during his exile in England. Head was almost alone in his defence of Louis Napoleon's *coup d'état*. In 1852, in *A Fortnight in Ireland*, written at the invitation of the lord lieutenant, Eglinton, he indicted the Roman Catholic church for that country's miseries. In 1853 the government of Lord Aberdeen awarded Head a literary pension. In July 1864 the fact that he received no pension for his Canadian service was discussed in both houses of parliament, and in 1867 Lord Derby made him a privy councillor. He held the Waterloo medal and the Prussian order of military merit.

Anna Jameson described Head as a small active man, with acute features, and 'an expression of mingled humour and benevolence' (Jameson, 1.153). He rode 16 miles each day until he was seventy-eight. In 1871 Charles (Chinese) Gordon hailed him as 'a very happy man, whose eye is fixed on that land where old friends will meet again' (correspondence in private hands). Head was an Anglican of conventional piety, attracted to presbyterian simplicity but firmly opposed to sabbatarianism. He died at Duppas Hall, Croydon, on 20 July 1875 and was buried at Sanderstead. Despite pleas of poverty, he left a substantial estate. His capital was probably based on his wife's dowry and compensation negotiated after his South American venture. He seems to have regarded his wealth as a trust to be passed on to his children. GED MARTIN

Sources S. W. Jackman, *Galloping Head* (1958) · S. F. Wise, ed., *Sir Francis Bond Head: a narrative* (1969) · S. F. Wise, 'Head, Sir Francis Bond', *DCB*, vol. 10 · G. Martin, 'Sir Francis Bond Head: the private side of a lieutenant-governor', *Ontario History*, 73 (1981), 145–70 · J. A. Gibson, 'The "persistent fallacy" of the governors Head', *Canadian Historical Review*, 19 (1938), 295–300, esp. 295–7 · H. T. Manning and J. S. Galbraith, 'The appointment of Sir Francis Bond Head: a new insight', *Canadian Historical Review*, 42 (1961), 50–52 · G. Martin, 'The appointment of Sir Francis Bond Head as lieutenant-governor of Upper Canada in 1835', *Journal of Imperial and Commonwealth History*, 3 (1974–5), 280–91 · G. Martin, 'Self-defence: Sir Francis Bond Head and Canada, 1841–1875', *Ontario History*, 73 (1981), 3–18 · Baron Broughton [J. C. Hobhouse], *Recollections of a long life*, ed. Lady Dorchester [C. Carleton], 6 vols. (1909–11) · *Lord Melbourne's papers*, ed. L. C. Sanders (1889) · *The correspondence of Charles Arbuthnot*, ed. A. Aspinall, CS, 3rd ser., 65 (1941) · S. Smiles, *A publisher and his friends: memoir and correspondence of the late John Murray*, 2 vols. (1891) · A. Jameson, *Winter studies and summer rambles in Canada*, 3 vols. (1838) · G. M. Craig, *Upper Canada: the formative years, 1784–1841* (1963) · C. Read and R. J. Stagg, eds., *The rebellion of 1837 in Upper Canada* (1985) · *CGPLA Eng. & Wales* (1875)

Archives Bodl. Oxf., corresp. and papers · priv. coll. · PRO, dispatches and papers, CO 537/139 · Public Archives of Ontario, Toronto, corresp. and papers | BL, corresp. with Sir Robert Peel, Add. MSS 40397–40554, *passim* · Lpool RO, letters to fourteenth earl of Derby · NL Ire., letters mainly to Lord Naas · PRO, Upper Canada Series, John Murray & Co. MSS, CO 42 · PRO NIre., letters to Lord Gosford · U. Southampton L., letters to first duke of Wellington · UCL, corresp. with Sir Edwin Chadwick

Likenesses C. Turner, mezzotint, pubd 1837 (after N. Cook), BM, NPG [*see illus.*] · W. B. Gardner, engraving, repro. in *ILN* (31 July 1875), 109 · bust, Langen-Schwalbach, Germany · engraving, repro. in *Graphic* (7 Aug 1875), 128 · engraving, repro. in Jackman, *Galloping Head* · sketches, priv. coll. · wood-engraving, NPG; repro. in *ILN* (31 July 1875)

Wealth at death under £45,000: probate, 3 Sept 1875, *CGPLA Eng. & Wales*

Head, Sir George (1782–1855), commissariat officer, was born at The Hermitage in the parish of Higham, near Rochester, Kent, the son of James Roper Head (formerly Mendes; 1757–1814) and his wife, Frances Anne, daughter of George Burges. Sir Francis Bond *Head was his younger brother. George was educated at Charterhouse School from about 1805 to 1808, in which year he became a captain in the West Kent militia, then at Woodbridge, Suffolk. In the following year he joined the British army at Lisbon as a clerk in the commissariat. He served during the remainder of the Peninsular War, accompanying the army to many actions, including Vitoria, Nivelle, Toulouse, and the Pyrenees. He was promoted deputy assistant commissary-general in 1811 and assistant commissary-general on 25 December 1814. From May 1813 he was in charge of the commissariat of the 3rd division of the Spanish army under Sir Thomas Picton, and later published interesting anecdotes in his *Memoirs of an Assistant Commissary-General*.

Head returned to England in August 1814, and was, on the following 28 October, ordered to Halifax, Nova Scotia; from there he went to Quebec, and was afterwards employed in operations on Lake Huron. After ten months he came back to England, taking a year's leave, and then returned to Halifax, where he remained five years on the peace establishment. Subsequently he served in Ireland, and in 1823 was placed on half pay. In 1829 he published his Canadian reminiscences under the title *Forest Scenery and Incidents in the Wilds of North America*. At the coronation of William IV he acted as deputy knight-marshal, for which he was knighted on 12 October 1831; he subsequently became deputy knight-marshal to Queen Victoria. He published several books, gaining considerable repute for his *A home tour through the manufacturing districts of England in the summer of 1835* and *A home tour through various parts of the United Kingdom in 1837 … being memoirs of an assistant commissary-general*, both works being reprinted in one volume in 1840. He also contributed to the *Quarterly Review*. Head died, unmarried, at Cockspur Street, Charing Cross, London, on 2 May 1855.

G. C. BOASE, rev. JAMES FALKNER

Sources *Army List* · *GM*, 2nd ser., 44 (1855), 97–8 · *Annual Register* (1855), 271–2 · *Colburn's United Service Magazine*, 3 (1849), 141 · Burke, *Peerage* · Boase, *Mod. Eng. biog.*

Head, Guy (*bap.* 1760, *d.* 1800), painter, was baptized in Carlisle on 4 June 1760, the second son of Thomas Head, a butcher, and his wife, Isabella. He studied drawing in Carlisle under J. B. Gilpin (father of the painter Sawrey Gilpin) before enrolling at the Royal Academy Schools in April 1778, when his age was given as '16 4 June next' (Hutchison, 143). He exhibited a variety of works in London: in 1779 two portraits and a small landscape at the Free Society, and a portrait at the Royal Academy; in 1780 a portrait and *The Fire at London Bridge Water Works* at the Society of Artists, and a portrait at the Royal Academy; and in 1781 a *Landscape with Europa*, and *Mr Henderson as Richard III* at the Royal Academy. On 8 June 1783 he married Jane Lewthwaite, the daughter of a wealthy Carlisle businessman, and an amateur landscape painter. Their first child was baptized in London in January 1784, their second in Carlisle in March 1785.

Shortly afterwards Head set out for Holland, with letters of introduction from Sir Joshua Reynolds to the Hope family of merchants in Amsterdam, who 'employed him to paint portraits of some of their families [and] to copy some of their valuable pictures' (*GM*). In 1802 Henry Hope presented to the Royal Academy copies by Head of three paintings by Rubens in Antwerp. The Hopes also gave him £1500 (Farington, *Diary*, 5.1756) and introductions to their associates in Italy, whither Head and his family proceeded in 1786, accompanied by the Dutch painter Daniel Dupré (1752–1817). The painters' progress was marked by their election to the academies of Kassel (March 1786), Bologna (February 1787), and Parma (July 1787). Head's reception pieces remain *in situ*, *Erminia Writing the Name of Tancred* at Bologna, and *The Blind Oedipus* at Parma. In September 1787 Head was elected to the academy at Florence on the strength of a copy he had made 'with such perfect beauty' of Titian's *Venus of Urbino* (J. Robson, journal, 21 Sept 1787, BL, Add. MS 38837; cited in Ingamells, 479). Head had already copied paintings by Guercino and Guido Reni in Bologna and by Correggio in Parma, and he was completing another of the so-called 'Raphael of St John' in the

Uffizi. By means of such careful copies he had already conceived the idea of 'a valuable Gallery ... for the Advantage of his own Countrymen' (Christies sale catalogue, 13 March 1802) and he was to continue making copies throughout his stay in Italy.

By March 1788 Head was in Rome, where he stayed eleven years. He lived with his family in the strada Felice, where children were born in 1790 and 1793, above rooms occupied by the Italian sculptor Vincenzo Pacetti. They were also friendly with John Flaxman and his family (who were in Rome between 1787 and 1794) and Head painted Flaxman's portrait in 1792 (National Portrait Gallery, London). But he was not generally popular within the fractious colony of British artists who thought he was 'determined to stand alone like a great colossus' (James Irvine, letter, 8 April 1791, cited in Ingamells, 480) and called him Guy of Warwick. Head, in turn, was alleged to have called them 'most infamously debauched with respect to women and as he was the only exception he was therefore persecuted by them' (Flaxman, journal, 13 Nov 1790, cited in Ingamells, 480). At least some of the hostility was simple jealousy of Head's successful practice.

Head had arrived in Rome as a member of three Italian academies and he was at once sought after. His first commissions are not identified, but in April 1790 two historical compositions were noticed in his studio, Echo and Antigone, 'a chaste and classical Composition' (Christies sale catalogue, 13 March 1802), and in May 1791 he was painting several (now untraced) portraits. In October 1792 he was elected to the Accademia di San Luca in Rome, and his presentation piece, Iris (of which he painted several versions), attracted the attention of the French academy in Rome in 1795. They also approved other history pieces, including Venus Encircling Juno with the Magic Cestus (Nottingham Art Gallery), and admired his portraits which in 1795 included Thomas and Henry Hope (untraced), the heirs of his former patrons in Holland, and the British traveller and diplomat John Coxe Hippisley (priv. coll.). Head had established a cool, neo-classical style, much favoured by the French but less acceptable to the British; the sculptor Christopher Hewetson, for example, once described Head's Roman portraits as 'painted in his usual style, and with most enormous Cravats and marvelous tight Britches' (C. Hewetson, letter, 14 May 1791, cited in Ingamells, 479).

Apart from his painting Head also collected works of art and antiquities. He commissioned a copy of an antique statue from Pacetti, an engraving after Titian from Raffaele Morghen, and drawings from Vincenzo Camuccini, but his collections principally comprised, apart from the growing number of his own copies, Greek vases and Dutch and Italian old masters.

In February 1798, as the French army invaded Rome, the Heads fled to Naples and thence to Palermo. They met Nelson, of whom Head painted an idealized heroic portrait (National Portrait Gallery, London), and a son born in 1798 was named Horatio Nelson Head. He also met Sir William Hamilton and painted his ebullient second wife, Emma (untraced), who threw a palette at him as he

explained, with a stutter, that her foot was too big for a sandal and would have to have a slipper (P. L. Gordon, *Personal Memoirs*, 1830, 2.384, cited in Ingamells, 480). In the spring of 1799 Head sailed round Sicily with the British consul, Charles Lock, before Nelson finally arranged his passage home.

The Head family were in London by the summer of 1799 and a daughter was baptized in Carlisle in October. They rented a large house at 4 Duke Street, St James's, where Head intended to exhibit his Italian paintings, originals and copies. In 1800 he showed at the Royal Academy three of his Italian pictures: a portrait of Prince Augustus and versions of his *Echo* (Detroit Institute of Arts) and *Iris*. This was to be Head's last exhibition, for on 16 December 1800 he suddenly collapsed and died at his home in Duke Street, barely forty years old. He was buried in St James's, Piccadilly. His collections were dispersed in a number of sales, the most important being three held at Christies in March, April, and May 1802. That of 13 March contained over one hundred of Head's copies, principally of seventeenth-century Flemish and Italian masters, but including some of contemporary English works by Richard Wilson, J. H. Mortimer, Sir Joshua Reynolds, and Nathaniel Dance.   JOHN INGAMELLS

Sources J. Ingamells, ed., *A dictionary of British and Irish travellers in Italy, 1701–1800* (1997), 479–80 · N. Pressly, 'Guy Head: a British artist in Rome in the 1790s', *Detroit Bulletin of Arts*, 60 (1982), 69–79 · F. Salmon, 'Guy Head's *Oedipus* in the Academy at Parma', *Burlington Magazine*, 133 (1991), 514–17 · A. Gunn, 'Guy Head's *Venus and Juno*', *Burlington Magazine*, 133 (1991), 510–13 · S. C. Hutchison, 'The Royal Academy Schools, 1768–1830', *Walpole Society*, 38 (1960–62), 123–91, esp. 143 · Graves, *RA exhibitors* · Graves, *Soc. Artists* · *GM*, 1st ser., 70 (1800), 1298 · Farington, *Diary*, 5.1756 · MS notes by Malcolm Stewart, Paul Mellon Centre, Brinsley Ford archive · *Catalogue*, Christie, Manson, and Wood (1802)

Head, Sir Henry (1861–1940), neurologist, was born at Stamford Hill, Stoke Newington, London, on 4 August 1861, the eldest son of Henry Head, an insurance broker at Lloyd's, and his wife, Hester, daughter of Richard Beck, wine merchant. He was educated for two years at Grove House School, Tottenham, a Quaker establishment, and afterwards at Charterhouse School. He then spent some time in Germany at the University of Halle, before going to Trinity College, Cambridge, in 1880. From 1884 to 1886 he studied under Ewald Hering at the German University of Prague; it is claimed that Head introduced soccer into the city during his stay there. On his return to Cambridge he studied physiology and anatomy and went to University College Hospital, London, for clinical work, before qualifying MB (Cantab.) in 1890, later taking his MD (Cantab.) in 1892. His principal teachers at Cambridge were Michael Foster, W. H. Gaskell, and J. N. Langley.

After qualification Head became successively house physician at University College Hospital, and Victoria Park Hospital for Diseases of the Chest, London, and clinical assistant (1894) at the County Mental Hospital, Rainhill, Liverpool. He then became registrar at the London Hospital and in 1896 assistant physician, becoming in due course physician and consulting physician. His MD thesis, 'On disturbances of sensation, with special reference to the pain of visceral disease', was extended and published in *Brain* (1893, 1894, and 1896). This piece of work established 'Head's areas', the regions of increased cutaneous sensitiveness associated with diseases of the viscera. In 1894 he became MRCP and six years later FRCP, and in 1897 he received the Moxon medal. In 1899 he was elected FRS, and later served on the council (1915–17) and as vice-president (1916–17). From 1910 to 1925 he was editor of *Brain*.

In 1904 Head married Ruth (*d.* 1939), eldest daughter of Anthony Lawson Mayhew, fellow of Wadham College, Oxford; they had no children.

A major event in Head's life was the operation performed on him in April 1903 by James Sherren, an eminent surgeon attached to the London Hospital. Head and Sherren were investigating the physiological basis of sensation through observation of the dissociations produced by injury of the sensory nerve fibres. They found that patients were unable to describe accurately their sensations, or to devote enough time to the experiment. As a result Head decided to make himself the subject of experiment. The operation, the details of which are described by W. H. R. Rivers under the title of 'A human experiment in nerve division' (*Brain*, 31, pt 3, 1908, 323–450), consisted in exposure and excision of small portions of Head's left radial and external cutaneous nerves. To facilitate regeneration of the sensory fibres, the ends of the excised nerves were united with silk sutures. The following results were observed:

> All forms of superficial sensibility were lost over the radial half of the forearm and the back of the hand. There was no interference with deep sensibility, as this is subserved by afferent fibres in the motor nerves. Head recognized two forms of superficial or cutaneous sensibility and called these 'protopathic' and 'epicritic'. Protopathic sensibility, which returned about seven weeks after the nerve had been cut, included sensory response to pain, heat, and cold of a crude nature. Epicritic sensibility, which returned later, was finer and more discriminating; degrees of temperature could be distinguished, light touch was appreciated, and the subject was able to locate accurately the point touched.

Throughout the investigation the tests were applied by Rivers, while Head, whose eyes were closed, was unaware of the nature of the stimuli and of the correctness or error of his replies. The work entitled *Studies in Neurology* (2 vols., 1920) was written by Head in collaboration with Gordon Holmes, George Riddoch, J. Sherren, W. H. R. Rivers, and Theodore Thompson. It consists mainly of seven articles which had appeared in *Brain* between 1905 and 1918. The work also contains an account of the methods employed in testing sensation, an introduction, and an epilogue dealing with the common aims of the writers, and finally a consideration of the most serious criticisms.

Head's last important work, entitled *Aphasia and Kindred Disorders of Speech* (2 vols., 1926), was based on the examination of a large number of men suffering from gunshot wounds of the brain. According to Holmes, these volumes were 'devoted not merely to the clinical and symptomatic aspects of disturbances of speech, but were also an attempt to investigate the psychical processes concerned

therein, and the physiological integrations necessary for the comprehension and expression of ideas in language' (*Obits. FRS*, 676). After completing his work on aphasia, Head began to suffer from a chronic nervous disease which gradually restricted his ability to move.

Head was knighted in 1927, and had been elected an honorary fellow of Trinity College, Cambridge, in 1920. He also received the honorary degree of LLD from Edinburgh University, and that of MD from Strasbourg University.

Head's interests outside medicine were music and literature. It was knowledge of Head's intellectual interests that led Virginia Woolf's husband, Leonard, to consult him about his wife's condition in 1913. Head had two volumes printed for private circulation containing some of his own verse and a translation of some of Heine's poems; these were published in 1919 under the title *Destroyers and other Verses*.

Gordon Holmes believed that:

> Head was an outstanding personality, but in certain respects a complex one. Though he gave the impression of being a severe materialist, he was interested in certain forms of mysticism, probably due to the influence of the Quaker atmosphere in which he was brought up. A rigidly scientific and objective outlook on all matters which he studied was in him combined with a vivid imagination which at times seemed to carry his ideas beyond the bounds of probability. To casual acquaintances his statements in conversation or discussions often appeared extravagant, but they invariably contained a germ of truth. His published writings, on the other hand, were always subjected to a rigid criticism which assured an accurate and reasoned presentation of the conclusions to which he had come.   (*Obits. FRS*, 683)

Head died of pneumonia at his home, Hartley Court, near Reading, on 8 October 1940. He left the greater part of his fortune to the Royal Society for the purpose of the advancement of medical science in England.

J. D. ROLLESTON, *rev.* MICHAEL BEVAN

Sources *The Times* (10 Oct 1940) · G. Holmes, *Obits. FRS*, 3 (1939–41), 665–689 · *BMJ* (19 Oct 1940), 539; (26 Oct 1940), 577 · *The Lancet* (26 Oct 1940), 534 · *Brain*, 63 (1940) · W. Haymaker, ed., *Founders of neurology* (1953) · *CGPLA Eng. & Wales* (1940)
Archives RCP Lond., case records mainly compiled at the London Hospital and the Hospital for Diseases of the Chest, Victoria Park · Wellcome L., corresp. and papers | BL, corresp. with Macmillans, Add. MS 55250 · CUL, letters to Siegfried Sassoon
Likenesses W. Stoneman, photograph, 1917, NPG · F. Dodd, pencil drawing, 1927, Trinity Cam. · photograph, Wellcome L.
Wealth at death £144,588: probate, 8 Jan 1941, *CGPLA Eng. & Wales*

Head, Richard (*c.*1637–1686?), writer, was born in Ireland, the son of a Church of England clergyman who became chaplain to a nobleman and travelled with his patron to Ireland, taking up residence in Carrickfergus. Head's father was murdered in the Irish rising of 1641. Thus far the facts parallel the incidents described in the opening chapters of *The English Rogue* (1665), the fictional autobiography of Meriton Latroon, a professional thief. If Head's most celebrated work is to be trusted in this regard (contemporary accounts corroborate his father's career and death), it can further be stated that the family fled to Belfast, whence they sailed to Barnstaple, where some of his mother's relations lived, before moving to Plymouth, and settling eventually in Bridport, Dorset. It is known that Head attended the town's grammar school in 1650. He is then said to have matriculated at the same Oxford college as his father (he may have been admitted to New Inn Hall, from which a John Head graduated in 1628), but could not afford to stay.

Having left the university, Head was apprenticed to a Latin bookseller in London. About this time he is believed to have published a poem entitled 'Venus' Cabinet Unlock'd', a duodecimo of which no copies are extant. Head married and set himself up as a bookseller, a trade for which he appeared to have considerable aptitude. His passion for gaming ruined his business, however, and in straitened circumstances he retired to Ireland. There he wrote *Hic et ubique, or, The Humors of Dublin*, a comedy which was privately performed to applause. On his return to London in 1663 Head published a text of the play less licentious than that which had been produced, and expressed in the conservative idiom of the English spoken in Ireland. This he dedicated to the duke of Monmouth. No patronage was forthcoming, however, and he set himself up again as a bookseller. Head traded from a variety of addresses throughout his career: his first shop was to be found in Little Britain, according to Sidney Lee, whereas Gerard Langbaine places him, without dates, in Petty Canons Alley, off Paternoster Row and opposite Queen's Head Alley, where his friend William Winstanley found him on his return from Ireland. The earliest imprint to which Head put his name (having now moved to the Heart and Bible in Little Britain) was Samuel Hieron's *Fair Play on both Sides* (1666); early the following year Head and fellow bookseller Francis Kirkman jointly issued *Poor Robin's Jests*. Head was alone responsible for the broadside *The Citizens Joy for the Re-Building of London* (1667).

The business Head thus built up he again gambled away: 'it went out by handfuls', Winstanley observes, 'as it came in piece by piece' (Winstanley, 208). From 1664 he supplemented his income by writing. Head had a shrewd but reckless sense of what would sell: the racy adventures to which *The English Rogue* quickly turns were considered indecent by the licensing authorities, the printers were threatened with imprisonment, and it is likely that the writer went into hiding to escape arrest. Those copies which had already been printed circulated privately before the author submitted a revision. 'If, as seems probable, the extant editions, with their coarse language and episode, present the expurgated version, Head's original draft must have been singularly disreputable', Lee infers (*DNB*). It has long been recognized that Head's picaresque romance draws on beggar-books, cony-catching pamphlets, canting dictionaries, and prison tracts, but what remained in the expurgated edition was also the work of an unblushing plagiary: his writing borrows from Sir John Mandeville's supposed fourteenth-century travels, and includes Theophrastan characters after the manner of John Earle, Richard Brathwait, and Geffray Mynshul. The publishing history of the title is as complicated. The first edition, which sold out within the year, was published by Henry Marsh, who died in 1665 considerably in debt to his

sometime partner Francis Kirkman; to recoup his money, Kirkman secured Marsh's property, reissuing Head's work the following year. It remained popular: second, third, and fourth editions were published in 1666, and by 1667 a fifth had been issued. Kirkman prevailed on Head to write a second part, and when he declined (disingenuously claiming that Latroon's adventures were being taken for episodes in his own life), Kirkman himself wrote an elaboration. This new instalment was licensed on 22 February 1668, but no edition earlier than 1671 is extant. In the same year a third and fourth, and the promise of a fifth, part appeared. Their authorship has been disputed. In the dedication to *Proteus redivivus* (1675) Head explicitly denies a hand in any part but the first: given that 'the *Continuator* hath allready added three *Parts* to the former, and never (as far as I can see) will make an end of pestering the World with more *Volumes*, and large *Editions*', he remarks, 'I diverted my intention into this Subject, *The Art of Wheedling*' (sig. A4r–v), that is, the art of dissembling. Kirkman asserted that he and Head were responsible for the third and fourth parts, however, and the preface to the latter is signed by both men; in view of the shifting monetary and literary alliances of the time, Head's belated disclaimer appears doubtful. It is likely that they worked together. The four parts were published in a uniform edition in 1680. A duodecimo abridgement of the first part, prepared by Head, appeared in 1679 and was reissued in 1688. A fifth part, consisting of a few pages appended to an abridgement of the whole title and which was the work of neither Kirkman nor Head, was published at Gosport in 1688.

Aubrey, who was also acquainted with the author, states that Head's writing sold for 20s. per sheet. His other works, a number of which were published anonymously, include *The Red Sea, or, The description of a most horrid, bloody, and never yet paralel'd sea-fight between the English & Dutch* (1666), dedicated to his friend Richard Uvedale and to which is appended a strained acrostic in memory of Sir Christopher Minns; *The Floating Island* (1673), an account of a debtor's walk from Lambeth to Ram Alley, to the east of the Temple, in the manner of a voyage of discovery; *The Canting Academy* (1673), a compendium of itinerant characters and lore to which is appended a canting dictionary in part extracted from *The English Rogue*; *The Western Wonder, or, O Brazeel, an Inchanted Island Discovered* (1674), a combination of philosophical voyage, moral allegory, and social satire confused with the legend of the Irish Brazil; *Jackson's Recantation* (1674), a highwayman's supposed repentance before the prospect of the gallows; *The Complaisant Companion* (1674), an amusing collection of coarse stories reissued as *Nugae venales* (1686), but in that form known only as a third, corrected edition; *The Miss Display'd, with All her Wheedling Arts and Circumventions* (1675), a compilation similar to that of *Proteus redivivus* which extensively plagiarizes Nicholas Goodman's tale *Holland's Leaguer* (1632); *O Brazile, or, The inchanted island: being a perfect relation of the late discovery … of an island on the north of Ireland* (1675), a sober description of imaginary scenes similar to, but not to be confused with, *The Western Wonder* and its arcadian vein; and *The Life and Death of Mother Shipton* (1677), a popular biography which was often reprinted. Head was regarded by contemporaries as a talented but unsettled man addicted to pleasures beyond his means, temptations which led him eventually to a life of lettered distress as a hack writer. Head is thought to have drowned crossing to the Isle of Wight in 1686. He was about forty-nine.

JONATHAN PRITCHARD

Sources R. Head, *The English rogue* (1665) · W. Winstanley, *The lives of the most famous English poets* (1687), 207–10 · G. Langbaine, *An account of the English dramatick poets* (1691), 246–7 · H. R. Plomer and others, *A dictionary of the booksellers and printers who were at work in England, Scotland, and Ireland from 1641 to 1667* (1907), 94–5 · C. W. R. D. Moseley, 'Richard Head's *The English rogue*: a modern Mandeville?', *Yearbook of English Studies*, 1 (1971), 102–07 · DNB · C. Winton, 'Richard Head and origins of the picaresque in England', *The picaresque: a symposium on the rogue's tale*, ed. C. Benito-Vessels and M. Zappala (1994), 79–93 · J. Caulfield, *Portraits, memoirs, and characters, of remarkable persons, from the reign of Edward the Third, to the revolution*, 3 vols. in 1 (1813), 212–13 · *Letters written by eminent persons … and 'Lives of eminent men' by John Aubrey*, ed. J. Walker, 2 (1813), 439 · M. C. Katanka, 'Goodman's *Holland's leaguer* (1632)—further examples of the plagiarism of Richard Head', *N&Q*, 219 (1974), 415–17 · A. H. Lanner, 'Richard Head's Theophrastan characters', *N&Q*, 215 (1970), 259 · Foster, *Alum. Oxon.*, 1500–1714, 2.684 · R. C. Bald, 'Francis Kirkman, bookseller and author', *Modern Philology*, 41 (1943–4), 17–32 · 'Biographical sketches: some account of the noble family of Chichester', S. McSkimin, *The history and antiquities of the county of the town of Carrickfergus*, new edn, ed. E. J. M'Crum (1909), 469–70
Likenesses engraving, repro. in R. Head, *The English rogue described*, 2nd edn (1666), frontispiece · line engraving, BM, NPG

Headlam, Arthur Cayley (1862–1947), theologian and bishop of Gloucester, was born at Whorlton Hall, co. Durham, on 2 August 1862, the eldest of the five children and four sons of the Revd Arthur Headlam (*d.* 1909) and his first wife, Agnes Sarah Favell (*d.* 1871). His father held successive incumbencies in co. Durham, at Whorlton, St Oswald's, Durham, and Gainford. The Headlam family were Durham gentry with a tradition of public service. One of his younger brothers was Sir James Wycliffe Headlam-*Morley (1863–1929), the historian and public servant, while a cousin was Cuthbert Headlam (1876–1964), the Conservative MP and diarist. Headlam liked to claim descent on his mother's side from both Peter the Great and Oliver Cromwell. His friend Hensley Henson thought that this antecedence may have helped account for his overbearing manner, which earned him the sobriquet the General at Winchester, where he became a scholar in 1876. In 1881 Headlam went with a scholarship to New College, Oxford, where he obtained a second-class degree in classical moderations in 1883, and a first in *literae humaniores* in 1885. That same year he became a fellow of All Souls, where he was a contemporary of Henson and A. V. Dicey; he retained this fellowship until 1897. He was ordained priest in 1889, and spent the following year exploring archaeological sites in Greece and Asia Minor with William Ramsay. In 1898 he became rector of Welwyn, where he met Evelyn Persis Wingfield (1857–1924), whom he married in 1900. The couple had no children.

In 1895 Headlam had collaborated with William Sanday on a commentary on the epistle to the Romans. This was the first of a series of works on the New Testament; later books included *The Life and Teaching of Jesus the Christ* (1923) and *The Fourth Gospel as History*, which was published posthumously in 1948. Headlam's writings combined an openness to new forms of criticism with a staunch opposition to the extremes of the modernists. Indeed, Headlam was an old-fashioned central churchman who rejected extremists of all parties, criticizing them in the pages of the *Church Quarterly Review*, which he edited from 1901 to 1921. In the prayer book controversy of 1927–8 he upheld the church's right to revise its own formularies against the wishes of parliament, believing that this was its inalienable right as a divine institution. But the conflict did not undermine his fervent attachment to the principle of establishment.

In 1903 Headlam became principal of King's College, London. He inherited a ragbag of disparate faculties and institutions which he skilfully consolidated into two parts. The first part, the secular faculties of the college, was successfully incorporated into London University. The second part, the theology department, retained its independence under its own council. This arrangement reflected Headlam's strongly held belief that universities, rather than theological colleges, should be the main centres of ministerial training. Headlam remained at King's until a series of clashes with the Board of Education and the London University senate led to his resignation in 1913. He spent the First World War years writing and studying at Whorlton, before his appointment in 1918 as regius professor of theology at Oxford. In 1923 he was consecrated as bishop of Gloucester.

Headlam was a leading proponent of ecumenism. He promoted relations with the Eastern Orthodox and Swedish Lutheran churches, and was instrumental in securing full intercommunion with the German and Dutch old Catholics in 1931. He also advocated reunion with the nonconformist churches at home, arguing in his 1920 Bampton lectures, *On the Doctrine of the Church and Reunion*, that the Church of England should recognize their orders as valid, in return for nonconformist acceptance of episcopacy. From 1933 to 1945 he chaired the Church of England council on foreign relations. But at the end of his life Headlam became increasingly out of step with the worldwide ecumenical movement, opposing the development of the World Council of Churches on the grounds that it was merely a loose federation of disparate churches which did nothing to work towards removing theological differences.

Headlam's reputation as a pioneering ecumenist was severely compromised by his readiness to defend Nazi policy during the 1930s. He praised the Nazis for their 'self-discipline and self-sacrifice' (*The Times*, 24 Oct 1933, 10). When the German protestant churches split in 1933, Headlam sided with the pro-Nazi German Christians rather than with the rebel Confessing church. He even argued that the prominent Confessing church pastor Martin Niemöller had brought imprisonment upon himself by preaching politics and provoking the Nazi regime (*The*

Times, 14 July 1938, 10). Such comments incurred the wrath of his fellow bishops, including Henson, who dubbed him 'the pertinacious apologist of the Nazi government' (Henson, *Retrospect*, 2.413). Concerned that Headlam could be misconstrued as speaking for the Church of England as a whole, George Bell sought his resignation as chairman of the church's council on foreign relations. But this was not forthcoming, and in July 1938 Bell and Archbishop Cosmo Gordon Lang instead resorted to a public exchange of letters disavowing Headlam's views.

Headlam's failure to condemn Nazism stemmed partly from his vehement anti-socialism. He was an extreme individualist who described himself as the last of the true tories. A vociferous opponent of Christian socialists like William Temple and the Industrial Christian Fellowship, he had condemned their intervention in the miners' strike in 1926. He vigorously opposed state welfare expenditure, arguing that it turned the poor into feckless dependants and impoverished the nation. In the debates which led to the 1944 Education Act he warned that a centralized system of state-controlled education would result in totalitarianism, insisting that the Church of England must fight the state to retain control over its schools.

Headlam received his DD in 1903, was appointed CH in 1921, and became an honorary fellow of New College in 1936. He was again a fellow of All Souls from 1924 until his death. The loneliness of his later years was exacerbated by the death of his wife in 1924, and by severe deafness. In 1945 he resigned his see and went to live at his ancestral home, Whorlton Hall, where he had long been devoted to his rock garden.

A tall and imposing figure with piercing blue-grey eyes, Headlam was one of the last Anglican bishops to wear a top hat, and even insisted on doing so in his car. During his frequent bouts of rage he was given to violently gnawing his knuckles. Even his closest friends conceded that he was often extremely rude, and that he utterly lacked small talk. Hensley Henson likened him to 'a brazil nut, repulsively hard in the shell, and admirable in the kernel' (*Letters*, 250). He died at Whorlton Hall on 17 January 1947, and was buried in the village churchyard alongside his wife three days later.   MATTHEW GRIMLEY

Sources R. C. D. Jasper, *Arthur Cayley Headlam: life and letters of a bishop* (1960) • *The Times* (18 Jan 1947) • E. Pritchard, *Arthur Cayley Headlam: a life* (1989) • E. R. Norman, *Church and society in England, 1770–1970* (1976) • A. Headlam-Morley, 'Biographical essay', in A. C. Headlam, *The fourth gospel as history* (1948) • *Letters of Herbert Hensley Henson*, ed. E. F. Braley (1950) • H. H. Henson, *Retrospect of an unimportant life*, 2: *1920–1939* (1943) • K. Robbins, 'Martin Niemöller, the German church struggle and English opinion', *Journal of Ecclesiastical History*, 21 (1970), 149–70 • K. Robbins, 'Church politics: Dorothy Buxton and the German church struggle', *Church, society and politics*, ed. J. Bulloch, SCH, 12 (1975), 419–33 • *CGPLA Eng. & Wales* (1947) • *DNB*

Archives LPL, MSS 2615–2650 • LPL, papers as editor of *Church Quarterly Review*, MSS 1616–1629 | All Souls Oxf., letters to Sir William Anson • Lancs. RO, letters to T. H. Floyd • LPL, corresp. with John Douglas; corresp. with Edwin James Palmer; letters to Athelstan Riley; corresp. with Persis Louisa Wingfield

Likenesses W. Stoneman, two photographs, 1921–38, NPG • G. Hall Neale, oils, c.1935, bishop's palace, Gloucester • F. Dodd, drawing, priv. coll. • G. Hall Neale, portrait, Gloucester Cathedral • photograph, NPG

Wealth at death £19,010 4s. 6d.: probate, 26 June 1947, *CGPLA Eng. & Wales*

Headlam, Sir Cuthbert Morley, baronet (1876–1964), politician and diarist, was born at Eccles, Lancashire, on 27 April 1876, the third of the five sons of Francis John Headlam (1829–1908), stipendiary magistrate of Manchester, and his wife, Matilda Ann (d. 1921), the daughter of S. Pincofts of Ardwick. The Headlams were a minor gentry family with roots in north Yorkshire and the south of co. Durham who followed careers in the traditional areas of public service. Cuthbert Headlam was educated at King's School, Canterbury, and at Magdalen College, Oxford, where he read modern history and graduated with a second in 1899. In July 1897 he accepted a junior clerkship in the House of Lords, and was called to the bar at the Inner Temple in 1906.

On 22 March 1904 Headlam married Georgina Beatrice Crawley (1880–1968), posthumous daughter of George Baden Crawley, a wealthy City merchant. The marriage was an enduring success founded upon two very different characters: Cuthbert was reserved and sardonic, happiest reading in his study, while Beatrice was energetic and vivacious, a popular figure whose life was spent in a whirl of charitable and social activity. They had no children of their own, but adopted a son, John, a few months after his birth in 1920. Between 1915 and 1918 Headlam served in staff capacities in the army in France, rising to lieutenant-colonel on the general staff; his work was recognized by the award of the DSO in 1918 and appointment as an OBE in 1919.

Headlam chafed at the boredom of his House of Lords clerkship, and aspired to a political career. Lack of money had prevented this, for as the younger son of a younger son he had to make his own living. However, in the early 1920s his salary as editor of the *Army Quarterly* (1920–42) meant that he could afford to resign his clerkship (1924) and look for a Conservative candidacy, although he could not afford the subscriptions demanded by safe seats. Financial insecurity was to remain a constant worry throughout his life, and Headlam always felt that his political hopes were thwarted by his late start and lack of a safe seat, although his acerbic and pessimistic personality was also a factor. A tall, thin figure of striking appearance, he was a successful platform speaker, with 'sincerity, great charm and a beautiful voice' (A. Headlam-Morley, *The Times*, 5 March 1964). His clear and open style was effective in handling hostile audiences in the Labour-dominated north-east, but in the House of Commons he lacked confidence and failed to shine.

Headlam won the difficult marginal of Barnard Castle from Labour in the general election of 1924, and on 16 December 1926 was the first of the new intake to be given office, as parliamentary and financial secretary to the Admiralty. In the Conservative defeat of 1929 Headlam lost his seat, largely because a Liberal candidate intervened. He almost wrested Gateshead from Labour in a by-election in June 1931, and in the general election a few

Ashland
Community & Technical College
Library

86142

months later recovered Barnard Castle. He was given junior office at the Ministry of Pensions on 10 November 1931, and was transferred to the equivalent position at the Ministry of Transport on 29 September 1932. He progressed no further and, disgruntled at being passed over, he resigned on 5 July 1934. He was created a baronet in the coronation honours list of June 1935.

The first half of Headlam's parliamentary career ended with defeat in the general election of November 1935, but by this time he had become the leading active Conservative in the north-east. The chairmanship of the Durham county organization in 1930–37 led to his appointment as chairman of the northern counties area from 1936 to 1946; he was also chairman of the national union in 1941 and sat on its executive committee from 1932 to 1946.

The second phase of Headlam's parliamentary career was as a back-bencher. He won the safe seat of Newcastle North in controversial circumstances in the wartime by-election of June 1940; on the death of the sitting member, Sir N. Grattan-Doyle, the constituency association chose his son to fight the seat, but Headlam defeated him, standing as an independent Conservative, and retained the constituency until his retirement in October 1951. He became a privy councillor on 24 August 1945. From 1925 until 1960 the Headlams lived at Holywell Hall, a few miles from Durham, but he passed his last few years in Bath, where he died at his home, 19 Camden Crescent, on 27 February 1964, and was buried on 2 March in the Lansdown cemetery. The baronetcy became extinct.

Headlam's historical significance lies in his extensive private diary. He kept this regularly from 1910 until 1951, and for the period of his political career it contains more than two and a half million words. Although he observed 'I am not another Pepys' (Headlam's diary, 21 Nov 1944, Headlam MSS), Headlam wrote in a lucid prose style and shrewdly analysed both issues and personalities. When he was at the House of Commons he often recorded the gossip of the lobbies, the mood of his party, and the standing of its leaders. Headlam knew most of the rising Conservative figures of the 1930s and 1940s, and paid particular attention to three of his peers in the 1924 intake—Harold Macmillan, Oliver Stanley, and Anthony Eden.

STUART BALL

Sources Parliament and politics in the age of Baldwin and MacDonald: the Headlam diaries, 1923–1935, ed. S. Ball (1992) · Parliament and politics in the age of Churchill and Attlee: the Headlam diaries, 1935–1951, ed. S. Ball, CS, 5th ser., 14 (1999) · Durham RO, Headlam MSS · The Times (3 March 1964) · The Times (5 March 1964) · Burke, Peerage (1959) · J. Ramsden, The age of Churchill and Eden, 1940–1957 (1995) · private information (2004) [John Headlam, son]
Archives Durham RO, corresp., diaries, and papers · Royal Arch. | St George's Chapel, Windsor, letters, mainly to Stafford Crawley
Likenesses photograph, 1939, Durham RO
Wealth at death £1447: probate, 3 June 1964, CGPLA Eng. & Wales

Headlam, Stewart Duckworth (1847–1924), Church of England clergyman and Christian socialist, was born on 12 January 1847 in Wavertree, near Liverpool, the elder son

Stewart Duckworth Headlam (1847–1924), by F. A. Swaine

and third of four children of Thomas Duckworth Headlam, an insurance underwriter. He was educated at Eton College and at Trinity College, Cambridge, taking a third-class degree in classics in 1869. His theological formation was strongly influenced by Frederick Denison Maurice, whose lectures he attended at Cambridge. In later life he called Maurice his 'great teacher'. Following Maurice, he rejected the doctrine of eternal punishment, marking a decisive break with his father's evangelicalism. He possessed considerable private means, which enabled him to ride out years without church employment and to subsidize his varied religious and political activities.

Headlam was deaconed in 1870 and priested in 1872, serving his title as curate at St John's, Drury Lane, London, from 1870 to 1873, but he was forced to leave when his incumbent took exception to his views on eternal life. This was the first of his many clashes with ecclesiastical authority. From 1873 to 1878 he was curate at St Matthew's, Bethnal Green, where he acquired an intimate knowledge of urban social conditions, and developed his political and social views in a radical direction. It was, however, his open and, at that time, unorthodox support for the theatre and for ballet which led to the bishop of London's ban on his preaching in 1877, and to the withdrawal of his licence by the bishop (John Jackson) early the following year. There followed short curacies at St Thomas's, Charterhouse, and St Michael's, Shoreditch. His chances of a permanent position were ended when, in 1883, he publicly supported abolition of the House of Lords, and his request for a licence was refused. Although his licence was eventually reinstated in 1898 he was never again to hold permanent office in the Church of England.

Headlam's wholehearted endorsement of Maurice's incarnational theology served to unify a wide and seemingly erratic range of social and political interests. He believed the incarnation at once rooted human beings in a filial relationship with God and underscored the social character of humanity. He strenuously opposed puritanism, cultivating friendships with artists, actors, and literary figures, and founding in 1879 the Church and Stage Guild. He defied his bishop by sending a message of sympathy to Charles Bradlaugh in prison, despite having debated with him frequently in public. Characteristically, despite open hostility from friends as well as strangers, he stood bail for Oscar Wilde in 1895. He was an avowed ritualist, with a sacramental personal devotion, and a reverence for Our Lady. His fusion of sacramentalism and Christian socialism was expressed most forcefully in his books *The Laws of Eternal Life* (1884) and *The Meaning of the Mass* (1905), in his Fabian Society pamphlet *The Socialist's Church* (1907), and in the Guild of St Matthew, an association for high-church laity and clergy sympathetic to socialist ideals, which he led from its founding in 1877 until its dissolution in 1909. Even at its peak in the early 1890s the guild never had more than about 360 members; its close identification with socialism meant that it received little support from the church at large, but it was valuable in providing a link between the church and the nascent labour movement.

Christian socialism, in Headlam's hands, became a more strident and yet more practical position than it had ever been to Maurice. He supported trade unionists and socialist politicians, and though he served on the executive committee of the Fabian Society for three periods between 1890 and 1911 he was impatient of its gradualism. He bought and then financed a journal, the *Church Reformer*, for eleven years from 1884, and through its pages supported land reform as advocated by the American Henry George. In later life he became increasingly preoccupied with educational reform. He sat on the London school board from 1882 until its demise in 1903, taking an active role in the promotion of evening classes for adults, especially as chairman of the Evening Continuation Schools Committee from 1897. In 1907 he was elected to the London county council for the Progressive Party, sitting until his death. Despite Headlam's energy, his rebellious character and his unusual combination of socialism with Christian sacramentalism deprived him of much permanent influence either in the church or in the political world. His practical achievements were limited. He was a prophetic figure, whose passion for social justice was to inspire the small group of Anglican clergy exploring the political application of Christian social concern in the late nineteenth and early twentieth centuries.

Headlam was a warm-hearted, buoyant, sociable, and passionate man, with intense convictions and an utter disregard for the personal cost of expressing them. In 1878 he married Beatrice Rosamond, daughter of Charles Plumer Pennington, but they were separated a few years later and Headlam refused to speak of the marriage in later life;

there were no children. A series of heart attacks led to his death at his home, Wavertree, Peter's Road, St Margaret's-on-Thames, Middlesex, on 18 November 1924.

JEREMY MORRIS

Sources F. G. Bettany, *Stewart Headlam* (1926) • K. Leech, 'Stewart Headlam, 1847–1924', *For Christ and the people*, ed. M. Reckitt (1968) • D. Rubinstein, 'Headlam, Stewart Duckworth', *DLB*, vol. 2 • P. D'A. Jones, *The Christian socialist revival, 1877–1914* (1968) • E. R. Norman, *The Victorian Christian socialists* (1987)
Archives BLPES, corresp. with the Fabian Society • Labour History Archive and Study Centre, Manchester, corresp. with War Emergency Workers National Committee
Likenesses F. A. Swaine, photograph, repro. in Bettany, *Stewart Headlam* [*see illus.*]
Wealth at death £5753 4s. 0d.: probate, 1 Jan 1925, *CGPLA Eng. & Wales*

Headlam, Thomas Emerson (1813–1875), barrister and politician, eldest son of John Headlam (1769/70–1854), archdeacon of Richmond and rector of Wycliffe, Yorkshire, and his wife, Maria, daughter of the Revd Thomas W. Morley of Clapham, was born at Wycliffe rectory on 25 June 1813. He was educated at Shrewsbury School and at Trinity College, Cambridge, where he matriculated in 1832, becoming sixteenth wrangler and BA in 1836, and MA in 1839. He was called to the bar at the Inner Temple on 3 May 1839, and practised as an equity draughtsman and conveyancer, going the northern circuit and attending the North Riding sessions.

A Liberal, Headlam was MP for Newcastle upon Tyne from 1847 until 1874. Though he made no great impact in the Commons, he carried through the Trustee Act on 5 August 1850. In 1851 he was appointed a QC and made a bencher of his inn, of which he was reader in 1866, and treasurer in 1867. He was a magistrate and deputy lieutenant for the North Riding of Yorkshire and for Northumberland, and in 1854 became chancellor of the dioceses of Ripon and of Durham. Gilmonby Hall, Bowes, was his Yorkshire residence. At Richmond, Yorkshire, on 1 August 1854 he married Ellen Percival, eldest daughter of Thomas Van Straubenzee, major in the Royal Artillery.

Headlam was judge advocate-general from June 1859 until July 1866, being sworn of the privy council in June 1859. At the 1874 election he lost the support of Newcastle radicals and consequently also his seat (his Liberal colleague, J. Cowen, being elected). He published several pamphlets on the law and *A Speech on Limited Liability* (1849), and he edited and updated several of E. R. Daniell's books on chancery practice. After his retirement from parliamentary life Headlam's health gradually failed, and on his way to winter in a southerly climate, he died at Calais on 3 December 1875. His wife survived him.

G. C. BOASE, *rev.* H. C. G. MATTHEW

Sources *The Times* (9 Dec 1875) • *Law Times* (11 Dec 1875) • *ILN* (11 Dec 1875) • *ILN* (25 Dec 1875) • *Dod's Parliamentary Companion* • J. P. Parry, *Democracy and religion* (1986) • Venn, *Alum. Cant.* • *CGPLA Eng. & Wales* (1876)
Likenesses Spy [L. Ward], chromolithograph caricature, NPG; repro. in *VF* (19 April 1873) • wood-engraving (after photograph by Fradelle & Marshall), NPG; repro. in *ILN* (25 Dec 1875), 269

Wealth at death £14,000: probate, 31 Jan 1876, *CGPLA Eng. & Wales*

Headlam, Walter George (1866–1908), classical scholar and poet, was born at 24 Norfolk Square, Hyde Park, London, on 15 February 1866. He was the second son of Edward Headlam, fellow of St John's College, Cambridge, director of examinations in the civil service commission (nephew of Thomas Emerson Headlam), and his wife, Mary Anne Johnson Sowerby. Through his mother he was a direct descendant of the great classical scholar Richard Bentley, master of Trinity College, Cambridge. After attending Elstree School in Hertfordshire, he went to Harrow School, where the headmaster was Dr H. M. Butler, later master of Trinity College, Cambridge. After a very successful career at school he was a scholar of King's College, Cambridge, from 1884 to 1887; he gained a first class in the classical tripos and a large number of university prizes. His college appointed him to a fellowship in 1890, and he soon afterwards assumed teaching duties. Though his formidable erudition and slightly eccentric personality might have turned out to be drawbacks, he was much appreciated by pupils, including the less able, and many formed lasting friendships with him, which were no doubt facilitated by his lively interest in cricket, music, and hunting. In 1903 he proceeded to the degree of DLitt, and in 1906 became a somewhat hesitant candidate for the vacant regius chair of Greek (he had a great respect for the successful candidate). He chose as the theme of the public lecture he was required to give on this occasion the second chorus of Aeschylus' *Agamemnon*; it was a great success and increased his reputation.

Since about 1890 Headlam had devoted much of his energy to Aeschylus, publishing translations and learned papers; a full edition was planned, and although the enterprise was cut short by his early death, his annotations made on interleaved copies of the text have proved valuable to subsequent scholars. The best modern judge of his work has remarked 'Many of his conjectures were injudicious, but at their best they have a profundity and elegance that Wilamowitz seldom if ever achieved' (M. L. West, *Studies in Aeschylus*, 1990, 369). Headlam was much concerned with textual criticism; in order to elucidate difficult passages he read exceptionally widely in Greek texts of the classical and post-classical periods. He took a deep interest in the causes of textual corruption, giving particular attention to scribal errors of word order and the substitution of explanatory glosses for original words of the text. Discoveries of new Greek texts preserved in papyri also interested him and led to the work which is his greatest monument, an edition of the *Mimes* of Herodas, completed and seen through the press by A. D. Knox (1922); this is a work of massive learning and remains an important source of information for specialists.

During Headlam's lifetime he was well known for his unusual skill in translation from Greek into English, and he wrote English verse which was widely admired. He died suddenly in St George's Hospital, London, on 20 June 1908 from 'an accidental twist of an intestine', and was buried at Wycliffe, Yorkshire.   N. G. WILSON

Walter George Headlam (1866–1908), by Hills & Saunders, c.1884

Sources *Walter Headlam: his letters and poems*, ed. C. Headlam (1910) [incl. a memoir by C. Headlam and a bibliography by L. Haward] · *DNB* · *CGPLA Eng. & Wales* (1908)
Archives King's Cam., annotated copies of editions of Aeschylus
Likenesses Hills & Saunders, photograph, c.1884, King's Cam. [*see illus.*] · group portraits, photographs, repro. in *Walter Headlam*
Wealth at death £409 16s. 10d.: administration, 10 Nov 1908, *CGPLA Eng. & Wales*

Headley. For this title name *see* Winn, Rowland George Allanson Allanson-, fifth Baron Headley (1855–1935).

Headley, Henry (1765–1788), poet and writer on literature, was baptized at Irstead, Norfolk, on 27 April 1765, the only son of Henry Headley (1727/8–1785), rector of that parish, and his wife, Mary Anne, *née* Barchard (1731/2–1818). After his father's death, Headley's mother married Anthony Taylor of Gorleston, Great Yarmouth. Headley was one of Samuel Parr's pupils at Colchester School, and went with him to Norwich. At the former school he was idle, and at Norwich Parr was at first inclined to dismiss him on that ground, but through his father's persuasion was induced to give him another trial, and the experiment was successful. On 14 January 1782 Headley was admitted a commoner of Trinity College, Oxford, under the tuition of the Revd Charles Jesse, and on the following 27 May (Trinity Monday) was elected scholar. William Bowles, the poet, and William Benwell, classicist, were also scholars, and became his friends. Thomas Warton was then a fellow of this college, and Headley fell under his influence.

During his vacation visits from Oxford to his friends in Norfolk, Headley fell in love with a beautiful woman, referred to in his poetry as Myra, but their mutual friends thought the attachment indiscreet, and she was prevailed on to marry a rival. The death of his father freed him from all restraint. He quitted Oxford in 1785, it is said in an agony of disappointment, and without any communication with his friends. At this time, he published anonymously a volume of *Fugitive Pieces* (1785), all of which were written when he was nineteen, and most of which had previously appeared in print. They were reissued with additions in 1786 as *Poems and Other Pieces by Henry Headley*, and the book was inscribed to Dr P—r (Parr). These poems were subsequently included in R. A. Davenport's *British Poets* (vol. 73) and in Park's *Poets* (vol. 41).

On 29 November 1785 Headley was privately married to Elizabeth Carmody at St Marylebone, Middlesex, and it appears that his friends also disapproved of this match. The couple withdrew to Matlock in Derbyshire, and Headley returned to the university to take his degree of BA on 16 May 1786. His next residence was at Norwich, where he occupied himself with the study of the old English poets, and, under the signature C. T. O., contributed several articles to the *Gentleman's Magazine*, most dealing with the works of Milton. Most importantly, however, Headley produced at this time his best-known work, *Select Beauties of English Poetry, with Remarks* (1787). He is also said to have been an early contributor to the *Lounger's Miscellany, or, The Lucubrations of Abel Slug, Esq.*, which ran to twenty numbers in 1788 and 1789.

Headley had been delicate from his youth, and fell a victim to consumption. He went alone to Lisbon in May 1788 in the hope of improving his health. Through a letter of recommendation from Windham he was admitted into the house of M. de Visme at Cintra, but his strength declined. In August he decided to return to Norwich, and after two months of much suffering, he died on 15 November 1788, and was buried at North Walsham on 20 November near his parents and two sisters. An elegant inscription, composed, at his widow's request, by Benwell, for a monument to his memory, was first made public by Kett in 1790. His widow remarried, but died shortly after.

A second edition of Headley's *Select Beauties*, with a biographical sketch by his friend the Revd Henry Kett, appeared in 1810. It had been Headley's intention to have published two more volumes of selections, and to have edited the more valuable poems of Robert Southwell, but death prevented the fulfilment of these designs. *The Critical Remarks of the Late Henry Headley*, which were added to an edition of Phineas Fletcher's *Purple Island* in 1816, were mere extracts from the *Select Beauties*. Headley's selections and notes show a refined taste and much knowledge of English poetry, but the information in Kett's biographical sketch is rather meagre. A writer in *Blackwood's Magazine* (38, 1835, 677) draws attention to the wholesale plagiarisms from his notes and criticisms in Anderson's *Collection of the Poets*. William Beloe identified (Beloe, 1.179, 2.335–45) a song not included in Headley's works and an essay on the character of Timon of Athens. The authenticity of

some lines said to have been written by him in his illness (*GM*, 1st ser., 59, 1789, 649), however, was denied by his friend Benwell (ibid., 679). A few letters from him to John Nichols are printed in the *Illustrations* (4.745–6).

W. P. COURTNEY, *rev.* REBECCA MILLS

Sources H. Kett, 'Biographical sketch of Henry Headley', *Select beauties of ancient English poetry*, ed. H. Headley, 2 vols. in 1 (1810), vol. 1, pp. iii–xix • W. Field, *Memoirs of the life, writings and opinions of the Rev. Samuel Parr*, 2 vols. (1828), vol. 2, pp. 413–15 • E. Phillips, *Theatrum poetarum Anglicanorum*, ed. [S. E. Brydges] (1800), lxx–lxxi • C. J. Palmer, *The perlustration of Great Yarmouth*, 3 vols. (1872–5), vol. 2, p. 80; vol. 3, p. 58 • W. Beloe, *The sexagenarian, or, The recollections of a literary life*, ed. [T. Rennell], 1 (1817), 172–9; 2 (1817), 331–41 • J. Watkins, *The universal biographical dictionary*, new edn (1821), 614 • R. A. Davenport, *A dictionary of biography: comprising the most eminent characters of all ages, nations, and professions* (1831), 331 • J. Gorton, *A general biographical dictionary*, 2 (1828), 40 • Foster, *Alum. Oxon.* • *GM*, 1st ser., 56 (1786), 311 • *GM*, 1st ser., 57 (1787), 1081 • *GM*, 1st ser., 58 (1788), 1033, 1104 • *GM*, 1st ser., 64 (1794), 645 • Nichols, *Illustrations*, 5.210 • Nichols, *Lit. anecdotes*, 8.157–8; 9.28 • IGI • will, PRO, PROB 11/1173, sig. 593

Wealth at death all lands to widow: will, PRO, PROB 11/1173, sig. 593

Headrick, James (*bap.* 1759, *d.* 1841), Church of Scotland minister, agronomist, and geologist, was baptized in the Stirlingshire parish of Logie on 25 March 1759, second of eight children of John Headrick (*b. c.*1730), farmer, and Isabel, *née* Neilson (*b. c.*1735). The family was believed to descend from two German brothers, Cromwellian soldiers settled in Scotland. Educated at the parish school and in Dunblane, Headrick matriculated at Glasgow University in 1774. He did not graduate, though he 'took many prizes' (Lowson and Young, 82), and proceeded to study for the ministry. Licensed by Hamilton presbytery on 25 April 1786, Headrick preached occasionally and evidently did some schoolteaching. He also pursued a lifelong interest in the natural sciences, joining a Glasgow chemical society in the late 1780s. In the 1790s he found employment in the atelier of Sir John Sinclair, probably working on *The Statistical Account of Scotland* and certainly on tasks for the board of agriculture and internal improvement under Sinclair's presidency. Headrick's *Essay on Manures* was published by the board in 1796.

By then Headrick was embroiled, as became almost habitual with him, in controversy. Following the death, in January 1796, of John Anderson (whose student he had doubtless been), Headrick was a candidate for the Glasgow University chair of natural philosophy, with the support (he believed) of William McDowall MP, then rector of the university, and of Henry Dundas, secretary of state for war. Defeated by canvassing on behalf of a rival, Headrick (who later nursed the delusion that he had been appointed to the chair and arbitrarily ejected from it) published, pseudonymously, a scurrilous verse lampoon on the university establishment: *A Peep into the Convent of Clutha* (1797). Having failed likewise to secure appointment as professor in the new institute set up under John Anderson's will, Headrick looked elsewhere for advancement. With the backing of Sir John Dalrymple of Cranston, he wrote to the first lord of the Admiralty (Earl Spencer) and to Dundas with elaborate accounts of weapons designed to facilitate operations (especially at sea) against France.

Neither these (often importunate) approaches nor an attempt in 1798 to secure presentation as minister of Slamannan having borne fruit, Headrick returned to work for Sinclair and others, surveying agrarian and other resources in the Scottish highlands and islands. His travels between 1797 and 1801 took him as far north as Loch Broom on the mainland and to the island of Lewis. On this basis Headrick published an article on the advantages of what became the Caledonian Canal (*Prize Essays and Transactions of the Highland Society*, 1799), and an essay on the improvement of waste lands (1801). In 1802–3 he was in Caithness, surveying mineral resources for the Scottish exchequer chamber and engaging in a somewhat Pickwickian quarrel, with assault threatened and a duel in the offing. He also pre-contracted marriage with Katharine Macbeth (1787–1856), the daughter, not yet sixteen, of a local farmer. The marriage was allegedly solemnized in Edinburgh on 3 September 1804 (though there is some dubiety as to the record of this). Still pursuing preferment, Headrick spent some time in London 'dancing attendance on my Lords of the Admiralty' (Lowson and Young, 89), but with no greater success than his letters had yielded. In the latter part of 1806 he was travelling again—to Skye, to Fort Augustus, and especially to Arran. In 1807 his substantial *View of the Mineralogy, Manufactures, and Fisheries of the Island of Arran*, dedicated to Sir Joseph Banks, was published by Constable.

By then Headrick was at last receiving his long-sought preferment. Through the patronage of George Dempster of Dunnichen, he obtained crown presentation to that Forfarshire parish. He was ordained on 12 August 1807 as assistant and successor to the septuagenarian minister Thomas Masson, who died two years later. Headrick's troubles, however, were far from over. Not only did he find the manse dilapidated, even his stipend was threatened by claims from his predecessor's family. Neither problem had been resolved when Headrick completed his second major work, *A General View of the Agriculture of the County of Angus* (1813). As he neared his sixties, he still cherished hopes of further advancement: in 1817 he tried, but failed, to secure presentation to the parish of Dunblane, where he had been at school.

Dunnichen, however, and the county town of Forfar were, for the rest of his long life, to be Headrick's sphere, or rather, perhaps, his arena. Age did not wither his taste for hot water. In 1827, his *Lecture on geology … to shew, that the Mosaic account of creation is perfectly consistent with the best ascertained facts concerning the mineral structure of our globe* (1828), together with an earlier lecture on the physical sciences, both delivered in Forfar, evoked a vigorous complaint by the minister of the town. Two years later Headrick incurred the Forfar presbytery's censure for having made the Dunnichen pulpit available to James Hawkins, a local landowner who was 'neither a licentiate nor a member of the Church of Scotland' (Forfar presbytery minutes, 21 Oct 1829), and who became an adherent of the 'Row heresy'. Relations between the two, however, were soured

when Hawkins, principal heritor of the parish, supported efforts to have an assistant to the ageing Headrick appointed. Both published pamphlets in the course of the controversy. Eventually, in 1837, Headrick was induced to accept an assistant with right of succession. His later years had brought private as well as public troubles. Two of his five sons figure in the kirk session records of the parish as a result of having fathered illegitimate children. Both predeceased their father, who died at the manse of Dunnichen on 31 March 1841, and was buried in an unmarked grave in Dunnichen churchyard.

Headrick was a man of varied talents, though these were doubtless often misapplied. The 'vice or mole of nature' in his case seems to have been a paranoid tendency to see conspiracy rather than his own inflated expectations as the bar to his fulfilment. Yet he deserves to be remembered, not only as a notable eccentric but as a late representative of the moderate churchmanship which had been a far from negligible factor in the making of the Scottish Enlightenment.   J. H. BURNS

Sources A. Lowson and J. Young, *Portrait gallery of Forfar notables* (1893), 81–100, 125–36, 270 · BL, Althorp MSS, G23, G26 · NA Scot., Melville MSS, GD 51/4, 51/6, 51/9 · J. Headrick, 'On the practicability, and advantages, of opening a navigation', *Prize Essays and Transactions of the Highland Society of Scotland*, 1 (1799), 354–94 · J. Headrick, 'Suggestions respecting various improvements in the highlands of Scotland', *Prize Essays and Transactions of the Highland Society of Scotland*, 2 (1803), 433–69 · NL Scot., Constable MSS · NA Scot., minutes of Dunnichen kirk session · NL Scot., Lee MS 3450 · minutes of Forfar presbytery, 21 Oct 1829, NA Scot. · minutes of Forfar presbytery, 17 Jan 1810, NA Scot. · J. W. Hawkins, *Narrative of the proceedings in the parish of Dunnichen relating to the appointment of an assistant to the minister of that parish* (1835) · W. I. Addison, ed., *The matriculation albums of the University of Glasgow from 1728 to 1858* (1913) · *Fasti Scot.*, new edn, 5.283 · parish records (baptism), Stirlingshire, Logie, 25 March 1759 · *Montrose Review* (9 April 1841)
Archives BL, Althorp MSS · NA Scot., Melville MSS · NL Scot., Constable MSS
Likenesses J. Young, drawing (after a portrait?), repro. in Lowson and Young, *Portrait gallery*

Heaf, Frederick Rowland George [*formerly* Fritz Rudolf Georg Hief] (1894–1973), physician, was born on 21 June 1894 at Desborough, Northamptonshire, the son of Julius Rudolf Hief (1860–1941), watchmaker and maker of scientific instruments, who had emigrated to England from Germany in 1881, and married Alice (d. 1896), a schoolteacher, daughter of Thomas Beavon, ironmaster. Heaf was baptized Fritz Rudolf Georg Hief, but changed his name by deed poll in 1916.

Hief was educated from 1907 at Laxton grammar school and from 1911 at Oundle School, and won a foundation scholarship in 1913 to Sidney Sussex College, Cambridge, where he gained second-class honours in chemistry, physics, and geology. As a conscientious objector he was exempted from military service in 1915, and joined the Friends' Ambulance Unit; however, he was allowed to return to Cambridge to continue a medical education, with clinical studies at St Thomas's Hospital, and qualified in 1918. A short period of service in the Royal Army Medical Corps took him to north Russia and China. Demobilized in April 1919 he obtained resident appointments at the Brompton Hospital and its sanatorium at Frimley. On 25 October 1920 he married Madeleine (d. 1966), daughter of John Denison of Ilkley, Yorkshire. They had two sons and a daughter.

In October 1920 Heaf was appointed senior assistant medical officer to the London county council's Colindale Hospital for tuberculosis, and in September 1922 he moved as medical superintendent to the 200 bed King Edward VII Memorial Sanatorium at Warwick. He returned to the service of the London county council in 1930 as medical superintendent at Colindale. His appointment was part of the comprehensive anti-tuberculosis service, which local authorities were required to provide; and in 1937, he moved to central London as medical officer in charge of the service for London.

At this time the control of tuberculosis depended upon early diagnosis, isolation of infective patients, and public education on the avoidance of infection. Treatment involved long periods of rest in specialized institutions followed by rehabilitation and social support for those who responded well. Increasingly, however, active procedures calling for surgical facilities were being used in selected cases. The task of planning and co-ordinating the activities of tuberculosis dispensaries, hospitals, and sanatoria for the entire metropolitan area in this changing situation, with contributions from the voluntary sector, was challenging; in meeting this challenge, Heaf was greatly helped by his clinical knowledge and experience combined with his friendly, unassuming, and quietly authoritative manner; his administrative ability also became evident. This led to his becoming recognized as an expert in every aspect of tuberculosis. He was elected fellow of the Royal College of Physicians in 1946.

Heaf's concern with the problems of ex-servicemen with tuberculosis led to his becoming honorary medical director of the Preston Hall Village Settlement in 1944. He was active in the affairs of the Tuberculosis Association, of which he was president (1945–9). He was appointed adviser in tuberculosis to the Ministry of Health in 1948 and to the Colonial Office in 1949. In respect of this he was involved in visits to colonies over the next twenty years, and was created CMG in 1956.

In 1949 Heaf was appointed David Davis professor of tuberculosis in the University of Wales at Cardiff. Here a postgraduate course attracted many graduates from overseas. Heaf devised and validated a skin test for tuberculin sensitivity which gave a quantitative result from a single procedure; this procedure was widely used and bore his name. He was active in the scientific and technical committees of the International Union against Tuberculosis. He retired in 1961, but continued until 1966 to work as chest physician in the Caerphilly area. Heaf was co-author with J. B. McDougal of *Rehabilitation of the Tuberculous* (1945) and with J. L. Rusby of *Recent Advances in Tuberculosis* (1949), and he edited *Symposium of Tuberculosis* (1958).

After the death of his wife in 1966, Heaf moved to Freeland, Oxfordshire, where he indulged his lifelong interest in geology and archaeology. He died in Oxford from a heart attack on 4 February 1973.   J. G. SCADDING

Sources personal knowledge (2004) · private information (2004) · N. L. R., *BMJ* (17 Feb 1973), 424–5 · *BMJ* (3 March 1973) · *The Lancet* (17 Feb 1973) · Munk, *Roll* · b. cert. · *CGPLA Eng. & Wales* (1973)
Wealth at death £64,532: probate, 9 March 1973, *CGPLA Eng. & Wales*

Heahberht (*fl.* 764). *See under* Æthelberht II (*d.* 762).

Heal, Sir Ambrose (1872–1959), shopkeeper and furniture designer, was born on 3 September 1872 at Crouch End, London, the eldest child of Ambrose Heal (1847–1913), bedding manufacturer and furnisher, and Emily Maria (1849–1938), daughter of Thomas Stephenson of Finchley. Thus he was born into the family firm of Heal & Son. His great-grandfather, John Harris Heal, started the business in London in 1810. His grandfather, also called John Harris Heal, made the Heals shop in Tottenham Court Road, London, famous for its beds and mattresses in the 1850s and 1860s; they began to sell general and bedroom furniture at this time. His father, a devout Anglican and a pillar of the local community, was a partner in the firm, and chairman from 1906 until his death in 1913. Ambrose Heal himself was educated at Marlborough College and, at some stage, at the Slade School of Fine Art, London. In 1890 he was apprenticed for two years to a cabinet-maker in Warwick with a view to entering the family firm, and he then worked for six months for Graham and Biddle, furnishers, of Oxford Street, London. He joined Heal & Son in 1893 and was put to work in the bedding factory. But he had ideas beyond the technical excellence of mattresses. In the mid-1890s he began designing simple, sturdy pieces of furniture, often in plain oak. They looked out of place among the more conventional designs in Heals shop, and it is said the staff called them 'prison furniture' (Carrington, 36). They were more at home in the exhibitions of the arts and crafts movement, the progressive design movement of the day. But among arts and crafts people Tottenham Court Road was a byword for bad taste. Ambrose Heal, for his part, did not see why there should be a conflict between shopkeeping and good taste.

On 26 February 1895 Heal married Alice Rose Rippingille (1859–1901), daughter of a Birmingham manufacturer. They settled in Pinner, Middlesex, where his father lived, and their only son, Cecil, was born in 1896. In 1900 Ambrose Heal senior built a house for his son and daughter-in-law next-door to his own. It was a modest, white-plastered family house designed by the arts and crafts architect Cecil Brewer, a cousin of the Heals. Named the Fives Court because Ambrose Heal junior enjoyed such active sports, it had a court incorporated in the plan. They moved into the house in March 1901, but Alice Heal was already ill with cancer and died two months later. Three years later, on 20 August 1904, Ambrose Heal married Edith Florence Digby Todhunter (1880–1946), daughter of John Todhunter, the Irish playwright.

Heal was a founding member of the Design and Industries Association (DIA), set up in 1914–15 by a group of architects, designers, shopkeepers, and manufacturers who wanted to bring some of the values of the arts and crafts movement to bear on industrial production, as the

Sir Ambrose Heal (1872–1959), by Edward Irvine Halliday, 1933

Germans had done in the pre-war years. The arts and crafts had been more or less anti-industrial. The DIA wanted a practical campaign for quality in the world of machine production: sound workmanship, the value of everyday things, fitness for purpose. Here was a philosophy for the progressive shopkeeper. The catch-all phrase was 'good design'.

Heal was by this date in control of Heal & Son. On the death of his father in 1913 he became chairman of the firm, a position which he held until 1953. He was a skilful furniture designer, and a collector, but his reputation rests mainly on forty years of discriminating shopkeeping, on his particular mixture of DIA convictions, personal tastes, and opportunism. Beds and mattresses remained the staple of the shop, as in his father's and grandfather's time. (It was Ambrose Heal who designed the shop's well-known four-poster trade mark.) But now Heals began to sell ceramics, glass, and textiles; he shopped in Germany for pots, peasant rugs, and wooden toys. A new shop was built in 1913–16 to Cecil Brewer's designs: an island of architectural quality in Tottenham Court Road. There was an art gallery at the top of this building, showing works by Picasso, Wyndham Lewis, and Modigliani: modern art in a furniture store. Most Heals furniture was simplified, late arts and crafts, but when the shifts of fashion required, the firm could turn to tubular steel or versions of art deco. Such artists as Edward McKnight Kauffer and Claud Lovat Fraser designed Heals posters, and Noel Carrington and John Gloag (both critics and DIA members) wrote persuasive, understated essays in Heals catalogues. The effect was cumulative: looking back on the 1930s, Sir Hugh Casson wrote that 'Heal's was a symbol rather than a shop' (Goodden, 1). In 1933, aged sixty-one, Ambrose Heal was knighted for raising standards of design. Six years later he was appointed a royal designer for industry.

It is not clear how much at Heals was Ambrose Heal's own work and how much that of his senior staff—of Prudence Maufe who ran the Mansard Gallery; of his right-hand man Hamilton Smith, another DIA stalwart; or of the two designers J. F. Johnson and Arthur Greenwood. It was probably largely his, for he kept a tight control over all departments. With his fluffy red-gold hair and high,

slightly condescending voice, he could be seen and heard everywhere on the premises, inspiring respect and fear. Heal had, in effect, made a marketable commodity out of his own tastes and convictions, as did Terence Conran later at Habitat.

In 1917 the Heal family moved to Beaconsfield in Buckinghamshire. The eldest boy, Cecil, had been killed in the war, and Ambrose's and Edith's first child had died in infancy. But there were now three children, Anthony (1907–1995) [see below], Pamela (b. 1908), and Christopher (b. 1911). In 1919 they moved into Baylin's Farm just outside Beaconsfield, a rambling, part-medieval brick farmhouse enlarged for them by Forbes and Tate. Like the Fives Court, this was a domestic haven and a rural retreat—Edith Heal was a keen gardener—but Ambrose Heal was there only at weekends. During the week he stayed in a flat in Fitzroy Square, an arrangement that made his love affairs simpler. Prudence Maufe was his mistress in the early 1920s, and in the late 1920s, oddly seductive with her bobbed hair, Dodie Smith, who bought prints for Heals and later wrote *101 Dalmatians*. His affairs did not, he told her, threaten his family life.

There was a scholarly, acquisitive side to Heal. He made an important collection of eighteenth-century London tradesmen's cards which he bequeathed to the British Museum, and in his later years he compiled long lists of the names, addresses, and visual records of tradesmen, mainly from seventeenth- and eighteenth-century London. These were published as *London Tradesmen's Cards of the Eighteenth Century* (1925), *The English Writing Masters and their Copy Books, 1570–1800* (1931), *The London Goldsmiths, 1200–1800* (1935), *The Signboards of Old London Shops* (1947), and *The London Furniture Makers from the Restoration to the Victorian Era, 1660–1840* (1953). These books are invaluable for researchers. For Heal they perhaps expressed an ambivalence about the past. On the one hand, they created a tradition in which his own work could be seen and valued. On the other, they registered a loss—for, during his lifetime or before, many of these trades had ceased to be important in London's economy.

In the late 1930s Heal began to relax his hold on the firm. His elder surviving son became managing director in 1936. In 1937 he thought of retiring to Bath. But the war came before this move could be made, and he stayed on as chairman. Edith Heal died in 1946, and Ambrose Heal resigned as chairman in 1953. He had worked at Heal & Son for sixty years, and in his last few years at Baylin's Farm he seemed lost. He died at Beaconsfield on 15 November 1959, and was buried on 19 November in Holy Trinity churchyard at Penn near by, next to his wife. His obituary in *The Times* (17 Nov 1959) described him as 'one of the great artists and craftsmen of his time'. This was very wide of the mark, but it showed what a powerful image he had created for his shop, and thus for himself. Most writing about him since his death has had the reverent tone of company hagiography, and he remains, like his friend and fellow furniture designer Gordon Russell, wrapped in the mythology of 'good design'. He deserves an independent study.

Heal's elder surviving son by his second marriage, **Anthony Standerwick Heal** (1907–1995), shopkeeper and businessman, was born on 23 February 1907 and educated at the Quaker School, Leighton Park, Reading (1919–25), Grenoble University (1925–6), and the Münchener Lehrwerkstätten, Munich (1926–7). He then served an apprenticeship at the Gordon Russell furniture workshops in Broadway, Worcestershire (1927–9). In 1929 he joined the family firm and in 1936 became managing director. In 1941 he married Theodora Caldwell, *née* Griffin (*d.* 1992); they had two sons. During the war he served in the Home Guard. As chairman of Heals from 1953, he counted among his particular responsibilities advertising and promotions. His interests in china, glass, and fabrics helped to diversify the stock, and he introduced 'his-and-hers' four-poster beds. He was much concerned with technical education in the furniture industry, and he served as master of the Furniture Makers' Guild (1959–60), president of the Design and Industries Association (1965), and chairman of the Independent Stores Association (1970–72), and was on the council of the City and Guilds of London Institute (1969–81). However, the firm suffered from fashion and market changes, and in 1983 it was bought by Terence Conran's Habitat–Mothercare group. Heal continued his association for another year, working on the company archives, which were given to the Victoria and Albert Museum. He was an enthusiastic owner and racer of veteran and vintage sports cars, especially Sunbeams—on which he published a definitive book in 1989—and was a founder in 1934 and became captain in 1947 of the Vintage Sports Car Club. Also keen on traction engines, he bought a huge 1916 artillery tractor which he drove to rallies. A quiet, reserved man, Heal died on 25 March 1995. He was survived by his two sons.   ALAN CRAWFORD

Sources S. Goodden, *At the sign of the fourposter: a history of Heal's* (1984) · A. Heal, 'Sir Ambrose Heal, 1872–1959: a short biography', *A booklet to commemorate the life and work of Sir Ambrose Heal, 1872–1959*, 2nd edn (1984), 25–8 · N. Carrington, *Industrial design in Britain* (1976) · T. Benton, 'Up and down at Heal's: 1929–35', *ArchR*, 163 (1978), 109–16 · F. MacCarthy, *British design since 1880* (1982) · *Heal's catalogue, 1853–1934: middle class furnishing* (1972) · H. T. Smith, 'The Design and Industries Association, 1: the early years', *Design for To-day*, 3 (1935), 178–80 · N. Pevsner, 'Patient progress three: the DIA', *Studies in art, architecture and design: Victorian and after* (1968), 227–76 · personal papers, V&A, Heals archive · A. Heal and E. Heal, *The records of the Heal family* (privately printed, 1932) · *The Times* (17 Nov 1959) · *The Times* (20 Nov 1959) · J. Golland, *The Fives Court: the centenary history of a house in Pinner* (2000) · V. Grove, *Dear Dodie: the life of Dodie Smith* (1996) · *The Times* (29 March 1995) · *The Guardian* (18 April 1995) · *The Independent* (7 May 1995) · *WWW* · *CGPLA Eng. & Wales* (1960) · *CGPLA Eng. & Wales* (1995)
Archives priv. coll., diaries · V&A NAL, Heals archive | Bodl. Oxf., corresp. with Graham Pollard · Boston University, Dodie Smith MSS · Holborn Library, Camden, London, Camden Local Studies and Archives Centre, collections relating to St Pancras
Likenesses group portrait, photograph, 1889, V&A, Heals archive, AAD/1994/16/1662 · photographs, *c.*1893–1952, V&A, Heals archive, AAD/1994/16/1679 · photograph, *c.*1902, repro. in Golland, *The Fives Court*, 5 · E. I. Halliday, oils, 1933, V&A, Heals archive [*see illus.*] · D. Glass, photographs, 1953, V&A, Heals archive, AAD/1994/16/1491 · photograph, RSA, Royal Designers for Industry Archive

Wealth at death £74,923 4s. 9d.: probate, 21 April 1960, *CGPLA Eng. & Wales* · £318,322—Anthony Standerwick Heal: probate, 1995, *CGPLA Eng. & Wales*

Heal, Anthony Standerwick (1907–1995). *See under* Heal, Sir Ambrose (1872–1959).

Heald, James (1796–1873), philanthropist and politician, second son of James Heald of Brinnington and Disley, Cheshire, merchant, was born on 1 March 1796 at Portwood, near Stockport. He was educated at Rochdale, and entered his father's business. His parents belonged to the Wesleyan connexion, but he contemplated taking orders in the Church of England, and relinquished his work in order to study for that purpose. Through an uncle's influence, however, he rejoined the Wesleyans, and continued for a time as a partner with his father. He became very wealthy, and in 1825 he removed to Parr's Wood, Didsbury, near Manchester, where he lived for the rest of his life. In the latter part of his life he was not actively engaged in business, but greatly assisted in the reconstruction of the Manchester and Liverpool District Bank, and was a shareholder in many Manchester companies. At the general election of 1847 Heald was returned as Conservative MP for Stockport, Richard Cobden being the other member. He joined in founding a prayer meeting for parliamentarians. After declaring himself in favour of free trade he was unseated in 1852.

Heald was extremely charitable. He contributed generously towards various Wesleyan institutions, especially overseas missions, and was treasurer of the Wesleyan Methodist Missionary Society from 1861 to 1874. He became one of the most prominent laymen in the connexion. He was the main supporter of a school for the training of African teachers and candidates for the ministry in southern Africa founded in Healdtown, a settlement named after him in 1867. He also supported the work of missions in Italy. Didsbury Theological Institution, less than a mile from his home, was a special interest, and the young men training for the ministry there found him an intimidating figure. Heald died unmarried at Parr's Wood on 26 October 1873, and was buried in the churchyard at Chapel-en-le-Frith in Derbyshire. The church of St Paul's, Didsbury, built in 1878 next to the theological college he served, was erected in his memory.

W. A. J. ARCHBOLD, *rev.* TIM MACQUIBAN

Sources *Methodist Recorder* (14 Nov 1873) · *Manchester Examiner* (29 Oct 1873) · G. G. Findlay and W. W. Holdsworth, *The history of the Wesleyan Methodist Missionary Society*, 5 vols. (1921–4) · Walford, *County families* · Burke, *Gen. GB* · W. B. Brash and C. J. Wright, *Didsbury College centenary, 1842–1942* (1942), 86–7
Wealth at death under £350,000: probate, 15 Dec 1873, *CGPLA Eng. & Wales*

Heald, Sir Lionel Frederick (1897–1981), lawyer and politician, was born on 7 August 1897 at Parr's Wood, Didsbury, Lancashire, the younger of the two sons of James Heald (1859–1921), and his American wife, Henrietta Stewart, *née* Brown (1867–1961). His father, a solicitor and landowner, was prominent in local government as a Conservative and was an alderman of Liverpool from 1913. Lionel Heald was educated at Charterhouse School, from where, in 1915, he joined the Royal Engineers and served in France and Italy. He was awarded the Italian bronze medal. On demobilization in 1919 he entered Christ Church, Oxford, as a Holford exhibitioner; he graduated BA in 1920 after taking the shortened course in *literae humaniores*. He then read for the bar and was called by the Middle Temple in 1923. He served a pupillage under two pupil masters who differed greatly over politics but were both distinguished lawyers—Donald Somervell, who became a Conservative attorney-general and a lord of appeal in ordinary, and Stafford Cripps, later a Labour chancellor of the exchequer with whom he developed a close friendship and in whose chambers he remained for ten years.

Slightly built, with a pleasing appearance, an attractive voice, and above all an excellent memory, Heald soon built up a substantial practice mainly at the patent bar but also in ecclesiastical law and compensation cases. In 1931 he was junior counsel to the Board of Trade until he took silk in 1937. He also engaged in Conservative politics at the local level and was a St Pancras borough councillor from 1934 until 1937. He was married twice: his first marriage, in 1923, to Flavia, daughter of Lieutenant-Colonel J. S. Forbes, with whom he had a son and a daughter, was dissolved in 1927; he was married second, in 1929, to Daphne Constance Price CBE, daughter of Montague Price, with whom he had two sons and one daughter.

With the outbreak of the Second World War, Heald joined the Royal Air Force Volunteer Reserve and by 1944 he was an air commodore attached to the staff of General Eisenhower. On the coming of peace he returned to practice and stood unsuccessfully as the Conservative candidate at St Pancras in 1945. However in the general election of 1950 he was returned as the member of parliament for Chertsey, a seat he held until he retired from parliament in 1970. When Sir Winston Churchill formed his post-war administration in 1951 it was widely expected that Sir David Maxwell-Scott and Sir Walter Monckton would be appointed the law officers in the new government. However, Sir Winston appointed both to senior cabinet posts and Lionel Heald and Reginald Manningham-Buller were appointed attorney-general and solicitor-general respectively.

The office of attorney-general is the guardian of the public interest and Heald, who was knighted in 1951, was an ideal person to execute these quasi-judicial functions. Apart from the heavy burden of advising the cabinet on matters of law and scrutinizing proposed legislation, the attorney-general in those days was expected regularly to represent the crown in court in both civil and criminal matters, a practice that to the regret of many has declined. Heald duly appeared in appeals over income tax or death duties, and in the admiralty court and the International Court of Justice at The Hague over the claim of the British government to the ownership of Les Minquiers, a group of small islands in the channel. In these courts he acquitted himself with distinction, but he was not so much at ease when prosecuting in the criminal courts, as in the trial of John Christie. After three years' service in the post, the

pressures of which are notorious, he announced his intention to resign and he was succeeded by Sir Reginald Manningham-Buller, whose constitution and resilience permitted him to remain in the office for the next eight years.

In 1954, by then a privy councillor, Heald retired to the back benches and there began a further sixteen fruitful years of parliamentary service during which he exerted much influence. In particular he made an impressive intervention on 13 September 1956 when he expressed his anxiety at the divisions on party lines aroused by the military expedition against Egypt to reverse its seizure of the Suez Canal, and warned the Conservative government that he would not support any action that would involve the United Kingdom in a breach of international obligations. In domestic matters he chaired a committee of Conservative lawyers which foreshadowed the restriction of capital punishment in the legislation of 1957, and in 1960 he served on the Monckton commission on the future of the Central African Federation. His speeches in the house were quietly, sometimes almost diffidently, delivered but he was always listened to with attention because of the respect for his judgement and for his integrity. It caused some surprise that he was never raised to the peerage after his service to government and to the House of Commons, but the absence in him of any personal ambition was widely recognized. He died on 7 November 1981 at Chilworth Manor, Guildford, Surrey, where he had lived for over a quarter of a century, and was buried on 12 November in the graveyard of St Martha's Church, Guildford.   PETER RAWLINSON

Sources *WWW* · personal knowledge (2004) · *Hansard 5C* (1955–6), 558.182–5, 186–7, 252 · *Lancashire: biographies, rolls of honour* (1917) · Walford, *County families* (1919)
Archives FILM BFI NFTVA, documentary footage
Wealth at death £438,572: probate, 1 Feb 1982, *CGPLA Eng. & Wales*

Heald, William Margetson (1767–1837), Church of England clergyman, born at Dewsbury Moor, Yorkshire, the son of John Heald, a farmer and maltster, was educated at Batley grammar school. Intended for the medical profession, he was articled to a Mr Floyd at Leeds before attending medical lectures in Edinburgh and in London. He joined the class of John Hunter during the last course of lectures given by him and commenced practice as a surgeon and apothecary at Wakefield. On deciding to enter the church he abandoned medical practice. In 1790 he was admitted a sizar of St Catharine's College, Cambridge, where he graduated BA in 1794 and MA in 1798.

After taking holy orders in 1794 Heald was curate at Balsham, Cambridgeshire, where he took pupils, among whom were Charles Musgrave, later archdeacon of Craven, and his brother Thomas Musgrave, later archbishop of York. About 1798 he became curate at Birstal, near Leeds, and from 1801 to 1836 he was vicar of the parish, which had a population of 25,000. A liberal in politics, he maintained friendly relations with dissenters. On his resignation (June 1836) the archbishop of York presented the benefice to his son, William Margetson Heald (1801/2–

1875), 'the prototype of Cyril Hall in Charlotte Brontë's *Shirley*' (Venn, *Alum. Cant.*). Heald died in January 1837.

While he was studying medicine at Edinburgh, Heald published a mock heroic poem, in six cantos, called *The Brunoniad* (cf. *Critical Review*, February 1790, 69, 161–3). It gives a humorous account of the medical contests which the eccentricities of Dr John Brown (1735–1788) occasioned. At the time Heald was evidently an adherent of the Brunonian system.

GORDON GOODWIN, rev. M. C. CURTHOYS

Sources R. V. Taylor, ed., *The biographia Leodiensis, or, Biographical sketches of the worthies of Leeds* (1865) · *GM*, 2nd ser., 7 (1837), 435 · Venn, *Alum. Cant.*

Healde, Thomas (*bap.* 1721, *d.* 1789), physician, was baptized at Ashbourne, Derbyshire, on 27 December 1721, the son of Robert Healde of Norwich, who may have been a surgeon. After attending Repton School he was admitted a sub-sizar of Trinity College, Cambridge, on 14 June 1742. He proceeded MB in 1749 and MD in 1754. He began practice at Witham, Essex, and was admitted a candidate of the College of Physicians on 22 December 1759 and a fellow on 22 December 1760. In 1763 he delivered the Goulstonian lectures, and in 1765 he gave the Harveian oration, which was printed during the same year. He moved to London in 1767 and at the college he was censor in 1769 and 1771, Croonian lecturer in 1770, 1784, 1785, and 1786, and Lumleian lecturer from 22 December 1786 until his death. He was elected physician to the London Hospital on 20 June 1770 and became FRS in the same year; in 1771 he was appointed Gresham professor of physic. Healde died on 26 March 1789, leaving his widow and family destitute. The college voted £100 for their relief at the *comitia majora* of 25 June 1789. Mrs Healde practised for many years as a midwife. Healde was the author of *The Use of Oleum asphalti* (1769) and *The New Pharmacopoeia of the Royal College of Physicians, Translated with Notes* (1788).

GORDON GOODWIN, rev. MICHAEL BEVAN

Sources Munk, *Roll* · S. C. Lawrence, *Charitable knowledge: hospital pupils and practitioners in eighteenth-century London* (1996) · Venn, *Alum. Cant.* · P. J. Wallis and R. V. Wallis, *Eighteenth century medics*, 2nd edn (1988) · IGI

Wealth at death 'died destitute'

Heale, William (1581/2–1628), Church of England clergyman and writer on women, was a native of South Heal, Devon. Admitted as a commoner aged eighteen to Exeter College, Oxford, on 14 March 1600, he graduated BA from Broadgates Hall on 13 December 1603, proceeding MA on 3 July 1606. He was admitted to Exeter College as a fellow chaplain on 22 August 1608 in the place of John Raynolds (*d.* 1607) of Corpus Christi, but was expelled on 7 May 1610 for absence. It was during his time at Exeter College that Heale wrote the book for which he is chiefly remembered, against William Gager, who had argued at the University Act of 1608 that it was lawful for husbands to beat their wives.

In *An Apologie for Women* (1609) Heale counter-attacked on many fronts. Such behaviour was against the divinely created order: among human and other species, females and males co-operated harmoniously in accordance with

God's laws. While the tyrants of antiquity treated brutally both wives and subjects, the rulers of great classical civilizations behaved to their wives with respect and love. Heale castigated those of his countrymen who wrote poisonous diatribes against women and 'the multiplicitie of their supposed infirmities', condemning as 'flat impiety' the notion that they embodied evil, 'that old theorem hissed long agoe from off the stage of virtue' (p. 21). He did not advocate equality: 'the stronger in love should demean himself more royally; the weaker for fear should behave herself more curteously. The one valiant and laborious in the fields; the other mild and diligent within the dores' (p. 23). But he found some inequalities repellent. There was in canon and civil law 'a kind of strictness and obdurity against … the estate of wives'; female adulterers could be treated harshly for lapses existing only in the jealous imaginations of their husbands, whereas male offending, though 'as open as the sun, and as odious as hate itself', went unpunished (p. 26).

Heale did not doubt that husbands should wield authority, but opposed its imposition by violence; rebukes should be gentle:

> correction by way of beating … is merely servile … But servility is only to be imposed on such as are servile; and therefore not on wives who are in the law free burgesses of the same city whereof their husbands are free. (p. 49)

This might suggest he was thinking chiefly of a privileged social minority. But other passages suggest a broadly applicable conception of marriage:

> in agreeing matches, where man and wife make up the sweet harmony of mutual love in a reciprocal consent and union, ye may observe a heaven of government, the husband intent on his business, the wife imployed in her house. (p. 12)

A wife was much more than a friend, not only sitting at table, but lying:

> in thy bosome; she shares of thy grievances and lessens the burden; she participates in thy pleasures and augments the joy; in matters of doubt she is thy counsellor; in case of distress thy comforter: she is a co-partner with thee in all the accidents of life. (p. 19)

Such views differed sharply from the rigorous conceptions of many. For Anthony Wood, Heale 'was always esteemed an ingenious man, but weak, as being too much devoted to the female sex' (Wood, *Ath. Oxon.*, 2.89). Little else is known of Heale's life, not even the identity of the wife (possibly Chrispiana or Christiana) who survived him. On 1 December 1610 he was instituted as vicar of Bishopsteignton, Devon; in 1620 he was vicar of Rattery, also in Devon, and this was his residence at the time of his death between 1 January and 16 February 1628; the administration of his property was granted to his widow on 29 April.

STEPHEN WRIGHT

Sources C. W. Boase, *Register of the … members on the foundation of Exeter College, Oxford* (1879) · C. W. Boase, ed., *Registrum Collegii Exoniensis*, new edn, OHS, 27 (1894) · Wood, *Ath. Oxon.*, new edn, 2.89 · G. Oliver, *Ecclesiastical antiquities in Devon* (1840) · will, PRO, PROB 6/13, fol. 21v · M. Ezell, *The patriarch's wife* (1987)

Wealth at death see admin, PRO, PROB 6/13, fol. 21v

Healey, Donald Mitchell (1898–1988), car designer and rally driver, was born on 3 July 1898 in Woodbine Cottage, Perranporth, on the north coast of Cornwall, the elder of the two sons of John Frederick Healey, who ran the village shop, and his wife, Emmie, daughter of Sampson Mitchell, shopkeeper, of Perranporth. His parents were Wesleyan Methodists. After studying engineering at Newquay College, he took up an apprenticeship in 1914 with the Sopwith Aviation Company in Kingston upon Thames, Surrey, while continuing his engineering studies at Kingston Technical College. In 1916 he enlisted in the Royal Flying Corps as an air mechanic, and after qualifying as a pilot he went on night bombing raids, but after a series of crashes he was invalided out of the Royal Flying Corps in November 1917 and was transferred to the aeronautical inspection department of the Air Ministry, and spent the rest of the war checking aircraft components. He returned to Perranporth in 1919, and on 21 October 1921 married Ivy Maud (d. 1980), daughter of Faithful James, a hard rock miner, of Perranporth: they had three sons.

With financial help from his father, Healey opened a garage and car hire business in Perranporth in 1920, but he became more interested in rally driving and motor racing, using the garage to prepare cars for his races. He first entered the Monte Carlo rally in 1929, in a Triumph 7, and after he won at Monte Carlo in 1931 in an Invicta he was in demand as a competition driver. In 1933 he sold the garage business, and moved to the midlands to work for Riley, but later that year joined the Triumph Motor Company as experimental manager. Promoted to the post of technical director in 1934, he was responsible for the design of all Triumph cars, and created the Triumph Dolomite 8 sports car in 1935. At the same time he had many competition successes driving Triumphs, winning the light class at the 1934 Monte Carlo rally in a Triumph Gloria, which he had designed. When the company went into liquidation in 1939, Healey stayed on at the factory as works manager, producing carburettors for aircraft engines for the Ministry of Supply. He later moved to the Humber Car Company, to work on armoured cars.

In 1945 Healey founded the Donald Healey Motor Company Ltd, based in a factory near Warwick, and in 1946 his first car, the Healey Elliot, a saloon car with a Riley engine, went into production. This car scored wins in the 1947 and 1948 alpine rallies, and won the touring class in the Mille Miglia in 1948, the first win by a British car in the history of the race. The Healey Silverstone, a high-performance sports car, appeared in 1949, and its success in the United States led to a contract with Nash Motors, an American company, for Healey to build a car with Nash components. Healey opened a new factory, the Cape Works, to assemble the Nash-Healey, and in 1950 he entered the Le Mans 24 hour race for the first time, driving a Nash-Healey, and he drove Nash-Healeys in the Mille Miglia from 1950 to 1952. But his ambition was to design an inexpensive sports car, capable of speeds over 100 m.p.h., and he launched the Healey 100, with an Austin engine and gearbox, at the 1952 motor show at Earls Court. As the Warwick factory could

not cope with the expected large export orders, he entered into a royalty agreement with the British Motor Corporation—formed by the merger of the Austin Motor Company and Morris Motors in 1952—by which the British Motor Corporation would build the car while Healey would retain control over the design, and the Austin-Healey 100 went into production at the British Motor Corporation's Longbridge factory in 1953. An immediate success, with its aerodynamic shape and excellent performance, the Austin-Healey 100 won many prizes, including the grand prize at the international motor sports show in New York in 1953. By the middle of 1953 they were producing 120 cars a week, all for export, and by the time production ceased in 1967, 74,000 Austin-Healey 100s had been built, 80 per cent of them for export, proving very popular with American servicemen stationed in Britain. In the 100-S, which he developed purely for racing, Healey achieved his greatest ambition when he recorded 203 m.p.h. at Bonneville Salt Flats, Utah, in August 1956.

In 1955 Healey formed Healey Automotive Consultants, and worked on new designs for the British Motor Corporation, including the Austin-Healey Sprite, a small sports car based on the Austin A35 saloon, which was an instant success when it went into production in 1958. In the 1958 alpine trial, Sprites took the first three places in their class. Another venture was Healey Marine Ltd, set up in 1958 to build the Healey sports boat, advertised as being 'as thrilling on the water as the famous Healey sports car is on land'. When he bought a house at Trebah, in Cornwall, in 1963, he converted the outbuildings into workshops where he worked on his designs. He sold the Cape Works in 1963, and opened a car showroom in a disused cinema in Leamington Spa selling all makes of sports car, but this was not a success. When the Leyland Motor Corporation took over the British Motor Corporation in 1967, the new chairman, Sir Donald (later Lord) Stokes, cancelled the agreement with Healey, and stopped the production of Austin-Healey cars at the end of 1967. Healey launched a new sports car, the Jensen-Healey, in 1972, using Vauxhall components, and was chairman of Jensen for a brief period in 1973, but this car fell short of American emission standards. In 1974 he sold his company to the Hamblin Group, keeping Healey Automotive Consultants and the right to the Healey name, but he resisted all offers from companies such as Saab and Ford to produce a new Healey sports car.

Healey loved the competitive side of the motor industry, and was at his happiest driving in a race or a rally: his favourite race was the Mille Miglia, in which he competed eight times between 1948 and 1957. Although he was not interested in serving on committees, and took no part in the activities of the Society of Motor Manufacturers and Traders, he loved to travel, and visited the United States several times a year, promoting the sales of Austin-Healey cars. He was made CBE in 1973 for his services to the British motor industry.

Healey died on 15 January 1988 in the Duchy Hospital,

Truro, Cornwall, and his funeral was held in the Perran-porth Methodist Chapel. The Austin-Healey Club of America raised the money for a memorial window in St Michael's Church, Perranporth.

ANNE PIMLOTT BAKER

Sources P. Garnier and B. Healey, *Donald Healey: my world of cars* (1989) • G. Healey, *The Healey story* (1996) • D. Healey and T. Wisdom, *The Austin-Healey* (1959) • *The Times* (16 Jan 1988) • *WW* • d. cert.
Likenesses Empire Photographers Inc., photograph, repro. in Healey, *Healey story*, 39 • photographs, repro. in Healey, *Healey story*, 27, 91

Healey, John (*b.* in or after **1585**?, *d.* in or before **1616**), translator, can almost certainly be identified with John Healey, traveller and gentleman's steward, who was the son of Richard Healey, servant to the third Baron Sheffield; his mother is recorded as having been alive in 1604. (The John Healey educated at Emmanuel College, Cambridge, and ordained in 1603, who became rector of two Suffolk parishes and died in 1633 was certainly a different person.) Healey the traveller was born in Appleby, Lincolnshire. He attended St John's College, Cambridge, but left to travel, reaching Calais in May 1603 and begging his way through the Low Countries, France, and Germany to Italy, where he was received into or reconciled with the Roman Catholic church. After attempting unsuccessfully to extend his journey to Jerusalem or north Africa, he returned to England in November 1604, and entered the service of the recusant Lancelot Carnaby of Halton, Northumberland, as steward, bailiff, and tutor to his children. When still under twenty-one years of age, he was imprisoned and interrogated in York Castle in 1606 in the aftermath of the Gunpowder Plot, telling his questioners all he knew about recusancy in London, Lincolnshire, and the north, and claiming that a priest had urged him to assassinate the earl of Salisbury. A John Healey sent verses in English and Latin to Lord Salisbury in 1607, presumably in an attempt to obtain his favour or patronage.

Healey the translator has been proposed as the author of a preface to John Smith's *True Relation of … Virginia* (1608). However, the evidence for his career only begins for certain in 1609, with two publications. One, *Philip Mornay, Lord of Plessis, his Teares for the Death of his Sonne*, was a translation of an essay published in Latin and French. Healey's dedication, to an otherwise unknown John Coventry, says that they had both 'long sayled in a deepe, darke sea of misfortunes' (sig. A3r). The other, *The Discoverie of a New World*, was a free translation from the Latin of Joseph Hall's satire *Mundus alter et idem*. Its style is exuberantly colloquial, in the manner of the comic prose of Thomas Nashe and Thomas Dekker, abandoning the decorum of Hall's Latin. Healey dedicated it to the earl of Pembroke, whose patronage John Florio had obtained for it. The preface to a second issue states that Hall had, unfairly, been blamed for the raciness of the translation, and that its faults were due to Healey's youth. In 1610 Healey translated as *Epictetus his Manuall and Cebes his Table* two short philosophical texts which were widely read in early modern Europe, handling the Greek with the assistance of the Latin translation of Hieronymus Wolf.

In the same year Healey's magnum opus, a translation of St Augustine's *The City of God* and the lengthy commentary of Juan Luis Vives, was published; it had been entered in the Stationers' register on 3 May 1608, without a translator's name. Running to more than half a million words, it is one of the largest early modern English translations. Healey's rendering of the Latin is loose but competent, and his rhyming verse translations of the Latin poetry quoted in text and commentary are quite attractive. He worked from at least two editions of the Latin, one of which printed Vives's commentary complete, while the other expurgated passages objectionable to post-Tridentine Roman Catholicism, and he noted which passages these were in a series of marginal comments. He undertook the project at the instigation of William Crashaw. Healey's translation was commercially successful enough to go into a second edition in 1620, and a modernized version was reprinted several times in the popular Everyman series in the twentieth century.

Its publisher, Thomas Thorpe, stated in his dedication of the book to the earl of Pembroke that Healey had recently gone to Virginia (not, as has sometimes been claimed, that he was dead). However, the epistle prefaced to the reissue of *The Discoverie*, probably written in 1613 or 1614, offers to please those who liked the first issue 'with the best inventions that the labours of a yong scholler can produce' (sig. ¶3v), implying that the author intended to continue a literary career in London. It may be that he only stayed in Virginia for a short while; there certainly appear to be no records of his presence there. In 1616 Thorpe reprinted Healey's *Epictetus … and Cebes* with a translation of the *Characters* of Theophrastus which he attributed to Healey. It relies heavily on the Latin translation of Isaac Casaubon. By the time it appeared, according to the dedication Healey had died; the place and cause of his death are unknown.

JOHN CONSIDINE

Sources 'Examinations of John Healey', 1 March–17 April 1606, PRO, SP 14/19, item 6; SP 14/20, items 13, 34–5, 45–7 • R. A. McCabe, 'The relationship of *The discovery of a new world* to *Mundus alter et idem*', *Joseph Hall: a study in satire and meditation* (1982), 321–30 • *Calendar of the manuscripts of the most hon. the marquess of Salisbury*, 19, HMC, 9 (1965) • P. L. Barbour, ed., *The Jamestown voyages under the first charter, 1606–1609*, 2 vols., Hakluyt Society, 2nd ser., 136–7 (1969) • H. B. Lathrop, *Translations from the classics into English from Caxton to Chapman, 1477–1620* (1933)
Archives PRO, SP 14/19–14/20

Healy, Cahir (**1877–1970**), politician, was born on 2 December 1877 at Doorin, near Mountcharles, co. Donegal, the son of Patrick Healy, a Roman Catholic small farmer. He attended the local national school, which was 'mixed' in the religious sense, a factor which inculcated in him a broad-minded tolerance which was to pervade a long political career. Embarking on a career in journalism, he worked with the *Fermanagh News* and *Roscommon Herald* before settling in Enniskillen as an insurance supervisor about 1900. He had already married a local Church of Ireland girl, Catherine Cresswell, in Enniskillen in 1897.

Healy played a prominent role during the Gaelic revival of 1893–1916, contributing articles and verse to the *Shan Van Vocht*, an advanced nationalist journal, and he was a

Cahir Healy (1877–1970), by Lafayette, 1932

founder of both the Gaelic League and the Gaelic Athletic Association in co. Fermanagh in the early 1900s. A separatist, he was present at the historic meeting in Dublin in 1905 when Arthur Griffith launched Sinn Féin with its novel policy of dual monarchy, and subsequently campaigned with Griffith during Sinn Féin's by-election attempt in North Leitrim in 1908.

The by-election defeat marked the beginning of Healy's association with the revolutionary Irish Republican Brotherhood (IRB), though he took no part in the Easter rising. However, following the 'blood sacrifice', his admiration for the executed leaders grew increasingly more intense until he could eulogize them as:

Ye Holy dead,
Who died that we
Might taste the sweet of liberty.
(Phoenix, 'Nationalist father figure')

By 1918 Healy had become prominent in the Sinn Féin movement in Ulster. Prosecuted for opposing conscription, he played a key role in Sinn Féin's general election campaign of December 1918 which witnessed the party's triumph in nationalist Ireland. During the Anglo-Irish war of 1919–21 Healy was able to turn his peripatetic mode of livelihood to the advantage of the revolutionary movement over a large area of counties Fermanagh, Leitrim, and Sligo, where he set up republican arbitration courts.

As a northerner, Healy was preoccupied with preventing partition. However, when the Anglo-Irish treaty was signed in December 1921—with its formal recognition of partition—he professed himself satisfied with the assurances of Griffith and Michael Collins that article 12, with its provision of a boundary commission, would ensure the transfer of Fermanagh and Tyrone to the new Irish Free State.

His membership of Collins's northern advisory committee indicted him in the eyes of the Northern Ireland government and he was interned, along with 500 republican suspects, on the *Argenta*, a converted cargo vessel, in Belfast Lough in May 1922. It was not until he had been twice elected as a Sinn Féin MP for Fermanagh and Tyrone at Westminster that the Unionist government reluctantly bowed to British pressure for his unconditional release in February 1924. The Irish Free State government determined that Healy, as 'one of the sanest and most far-seeing leaders of northern nationalism' (Phoenix, *Northern Nationalism*, 294), should take his seat as a means of focusing attention on the boundary question. While the anti-treaty press attacked his 'fruitless apostasy', Healy saw the real betrayers as Eamon de Valera's irregulars, whose violent activities had forestalled a decision on the boundary.

During 1924–5 Healy worked closely with the Free State's north-eastern boundary bureau in preparing the case of the border nationalists for inclusion in the south. His demand that the Irish government should insist on a plebiscite in border districts went unheeded, and his worst apprehension was realized when the commission collapsed in November 1925 amid well-founded speculation that only minor 'rectification' had been contemplated. The subsequent tripartite agreement of December 1925, with its recognition of the 1920 boundary by the Cosgrave government in return for financial concessions, was to alienate Healy irrevocably from the pro-treaty administration: the northern nationalists, he declaimed, 'had been sold into political servitude for all time' (E. Healy).

Healy was elected to the Northern Ireland parliament in 1925 and took the realistic view that only a *rapprochement* between his border supporters and the home-rule remnant under the Belfast politician Joseph Devlin would serve the demand of the demoralized nationalist minority for political leadership. In 1928 he joined Devlin to form the National League, a constitutional nationalist party pledged to securing Irish unity by consent. However, his hopes of a less sectarian political system were dashed by the Unionists' abolition of proportional representation in 1929, and in 1932 Healy and Devlin led their small party out of the northern parliament in a final gesture of frustration. For a decade after Devlin's death in 1934, Healy assumed his mantle. Until 1945 he and his colleagues boycotted Stormont, preferring instead to rely on de Valera to reopen the partition issue. In 1936, however, Healy instigated an inquiry by the British National Council for Civil Liberties into the operation of the Northern Ireland Special Powers Acts. He always regarded Westminster as a sounding-board for the minority's sense of injustice and played an active role during his two further spells as an MP in 1931–5 and 1950–55.

During the Second World War Healy shared the hope of many nationalists that Britain's defence requirements might hasten Irish unity. In July 1941, following the interception of a letter written by him and apparently containing controversial views on the likelihood of a German victory, he was interned in Brixton prison for eighteen months under the Defence of the Realm Act. Among his prison acquaintances was the blackshirt leader, Sir Oswald Mosley, with whom he formed a lasting friendship. After the war Healy went on to found in 1945 the broad-based Anti-Partition League with the aim of mobilizing world opinion against partition, and assisted Hugh Delargey MP in launching the Friends of Ireland, a parliamentary pressure group within the British Labour Party. The decline of the Anti-Partition League and the IRA revival of the 1950s coincided with the veteran's last years as a nationalist MP. Healy was unequivocal in opposing the use of force to further Irish unity. Moreover, in his later years he became convinced that the policy of abstentionism, which he had formerly advocated, was futile. When Healy finally bowed out of the Irish political scene in 1965 he had attained an almost patriarchal status within the legislature whose very creation he had opposed. His final years were devoted to writing numerous newspaper articles on Irish history and folklore and assisting the work of the Ulster Folk Museum, of which he was proud to be a founder member. He died on 8 February 1970, aged ninety-two, at Erne Hospital, Enniskillen, co. Fermanagh, and was buried three days later.

Healy's career provides a focus for the study of nationalism in Northern Ireland from partition until the late 1960s. He represented a distinctive strand within that movement whose political origins lay with Sinn Féin. From 1921 onwards he combined an aversion to force with an unswerving attachment to the ideal of a united and independent Ireland. In his last years he felt that partition might have been averted had Irish nationalists adopted 'a less aggressive attitude' towards Ulster Unionism before 1916. His political and literary friendships were remarkably eclectic, while his advocacy of a tolerant, non-sectarian Irish nationalism earned him the respect of political opponents. He was the author of *The Mutilation of a Nation* (1945)—a trenchant critique of partition—a volume of poetry (1907), and an unpublished account of his internment experiences. For almost half a century Healy was one of the best-known leaders of the nationalist movement in Northern Ireland. EAMON PHOENIX

Sources PRO NIre., Cahir Healy MSS, D 2991 · E. Phoenix, *Northern nationalism: nationalist politics, partition and the Catholic minority in Northern Ireland, 1890–1940* (1994) · E. Phoenix, 'Introduction and calendar of the Cahir Healy papers', MA diss., Queen's University, Belfast, 1978 · F. J. Whitford, 'Joseph Devlin, Ulsterman and Irishman', MA diss., U. Lond., 1959 · E. Phoenix, 'Nationalist father figure', *Irish Times* (9 June 1982) · E. Healy, letter to editor, *Irish Independent* (30 Nov 1925) [in C. Healy MSS, PRO NIre., D 299/B/1/102] · CGPLA NIre. (1970) · *Irish Weekly* (12 Feb 1970)
Archives PRO NIre., corresp. and papers, D299
Likenesses Lafayette, photograph, 1932, NPG [see illus.]
Wealth at death £10,353 2s.: probate, 17 Dec 1970, CGPLA NIre.

Healy, James (1824–1894), Roman Catholic priest and wit, one of twenty-three children of John Healy, a provision dealer, and his first wife, Mary Meyler, was born in Francis Street, Dublin, on 15 December 1824. From 1834 he was educated at the Vincentian School at Usher's Quay; in 1839 he went to St Vincent's College, Castleknock, co. Dublin, to enter the Vincentian noviciate. He left the college in 1843, however, matriculating on 11 September 1843 at St Patrick's College, Maynooth, where he was a Dunboyne student (1847–8). At the college he studied under the theologians John O'Hanlon and Patrick Aloysius Murray.

After leaving Maynooth in 1850 Healy's first appointment was as reader at St Andrew's, Westland Row, Dublin, and chaplain to the Sisters of Mercy in Bagot Street; his next appointment, in 1852, was to a curacy at St Michael and St John's, Dublin. Here he made a lifelong friend, the eccentric and sharp-tongued scholar Father Charles Meehan. Lodging in the midst of the urban parish in an attic in Smock Alley, Healy proved himself 'the life and soul of his fellow-labourers in parochial work' (*Memories*, 44), bravely risking his life during a cholera epidemic. Both Healy's appointments were owed to Daniel Murray, archbishop of Dublin, with whose moderate Gallican views he sympathized. Like Murray, too, he supported the viceregal establishment in Dublin. In 1852, however, Murray was succeeded by the ultramontane Paul Cullen. In 1858 Healy was transferred to a curacy at Bray, co. Wicklow, and in 1867 Cullen appointed him administrator of the parish of Little Bray, co. Dublin, where he became parish priest in the same year. But his prospects of further promotion seem to have been damaged by his close friendship with William Nicholas Keogh, the judge whose decision in the Galway election trial of 1872 accused the Roman Catholic clergy of exercising undue political influence. Healy remained at Little Bray until 1893, when he was appointed parish priest of Ballybrack and Killiney, co. Dublin, by Cullen's successor.

Healy was a popular and active priest, renowned for his sociability and wit. Despite a modest purse and a single servant, he was the host of a popular Saturday dinner, which was attended by social and political figures including Lord Randolph Churchill, son of the lord lieutenant. In his later years Healy paid almost yearly visits to London, where he met with invitations from Gladstone and Lord Salisbury. In 1879 he visited Rome and Egypt, as the guest of a parishioner; in 1886 he visited America. His health began to fail in 1889, and he paid a recuperative visit to Karlsbad. In 1892 he went on a prolonged tour of Spain and Italy with his friend Henry Arthur Blyth. Another visit to Karlsbad in 1894 failed to restore his health, and he died on 28 October 1894 at Ballybrack, where he was buried.

Although generally conservative in his opinions, Healy was remarkable for his peaceful relations with men of all political and religious persuasions. His wit, which seems often rather ponderous to the modern reader, probably owed much to his spontaneous and appealing delivery. He relied mainly on word play and puns, holding mimicry to be undignified. Contemporaries thought him a brilliant conversationalist, and he may still be admired for the tact with which he adapted his repartee to his audience.

ROSEMARY MITCHELL

Sources *Memories of Father Healy of Little Bray* (1896) · *CGPLA Ire.* (1895)
Likenesses L. Chavalliaud, bronze bust, 1895, NG Ire. · C. A. Tadman, photograph (in old age), repro. in *Memories of Father Healy*, frontispiece
Wealth at death £5039 16s. 10d.: administration, 24 Jan 1895, *CGPLA Ire.*

Healy, John Edward (1872–1934), journalist, was born at Drogheda, co. Louth, Ireland, on 17 March 1872, the eldest child and only son of James Stanislaus Healy, solicitor, and his wife, Kate Mary, daughter of John Edward Appleyard, Church of Ireland clergyman, of Drogheda. He was educated at the local grammar school and in 1892 entered Trinity College, Dublin, as a sizar.

Healy won a classical scholarship in 1895 and in 1896 was first senior moderator in modern literature. He was also junior moderator in classics, was awarded the Brooke prize, and he was in three successive years vice-chancellor's prizeman—twice for English verse and once for English prose. He was well suited for the post when, two years after graduation, he was invited to join the staff of the Dublin *Daily Express*. A few years later he became its editor. In 1899 he married Adeline, daughter of James Poë Alton, of Limerick and later of Dublin, and sister of Dr E. H. Alton, provost of Trinity College. They had two sons.

In 1906 Healy was called to the Irish bar, although he remained Dublin correspondent of *The Times*, to which he had been appointed in 1899. He did not remain at the law long and in 1907 he returned to full-time newspaper work as editor of the *Irish Times*. His editorship, which lasted twenty-seven years, 'was one of the most difficult that have ever fallen to a journalist. For the whole of the period he was the protagonist of a losing cause' (*The Times*, 31 May 1934, 19). Healy was 'an unswerving Unionist' (Oram, 114), believing that Irish nationalism was a backwater away from the main currents of European culture. He promoted the Unionist cause consistently and forcefully through his paper, against the views of the majority of the southern Irish population.

In this time of extreme political turmoil in Ireland, Healy's life was often thought to be in danger, but he refused the protection recommended by his friends. During the Easter rising in 1916, *The Times*, for which Healy was still Dublin correspondent, could obtain no full account of events, as since the evening of Easter Monday Healy 'had been virtually a prisoner in his own office, which at one time was in the line of fire' (*History of The Times*, 4.545). Like Sir Horace Plunkett, with whose projects for economic reform he was closely associated, Healy fought doggedly against the post-war partition of Ireland, and strove to maintain links between the new Irish state and the British empire, opposing any broadening of the gap between Dublin and London. He steadfastly maintained his stance even when it was clear that his cause had been lost.

Healy's unbending response to public opinion and his rejection of political self-determination were characteristics in many ways mirrored in his personal relationships. Hugh Oram describes his manner as chief of the newspaper office. Healy 'remained aloof … he conversed only with other senior members of staff. His austere and impeccably dressed figure, complete with bowler hat and walking stick, struck fear into the more junior members of the firm' (Oram, 114). In 1923 Trinity College, with which Healy had maintained close links (especially with his former tutor J. P. Mahaffy), conferred upon him the honorary degree of MA.

Healy maintained his crusade to the end. Only when he was gone did the 'inflexible Unionism of the paper' disappear. His successor could but then slowly bring the paper 'more into line with the political realities of the day' (Oram, 185). Healy died at Elpis Nursing Home, Lower Mount Street, Dublin, on 30 May 1934, and was buried at Dean's Grange cemetery on 2 June. His wife survived him.   R. J. H. SHAW, *rev.* MARC BRODIE

Sources *The Times* (31 May–1 June 1934) · *Irish Times* (31 May 1934) · personal knowledge (1949) · private information (1949) · H. Oram, *The newspaper book: a history of newspapers in Ireland, 1649–1983* (1983) · [S. Morison and others], *The history of The Times*, 4 (1952) · *WWW* · D. Griffiths, ed., *The encyclopedia of the British press, 1422–1992* (1992) · *CGPLA Eng. & Wales* (1934)
Likenesses photograph, repro. in *The Times*
Wealth at death £3198 11s. 9d.—in England: probate, 16 July 1934, *CGPLA Eng. & Wales*

Healy, Maurice (1859–1923). *See under* Healy, Timothy Michael (1855–1931).

Healy [Hayley], **Robert** (c.1743–1771), artist in chalks, was the son of a Dublin 'mechanical genius' who erected ornamental monuments for aristocratic entertainment and was an 'instrument maker' (*Public Monitor*, 27 March 1773). He had a younger brother, William Healy (or Haly) who was also an artist. Robert Healy is noted principally for an imitation of mezzotint in chalk, and is believed to have been influenced by the mezzotints of Thomas Frye. Healy entered the Royal Dublin Society Schools c.1765, where he probably studied chalk drawing (oil painting was not taught) under Jacob Ennis in the figure school (his self-portrait in chalks of 1766 certainly suggests that this was the case); the renowned teacher Robert West was mentally ill at the time.

Healy exhibited annually at the Society of Artists in Dublin between 1766 and 1770. In 1770 he was awarded the silver palette for the best exhibited drawing of a group of figures. He enjoyed a considerable practice, drawing large portraits of aristocratic ladies, but his contemporary reputation was based on his excellence at drawing animals. Healy received his largest commission in 1768 from Tom Conolly MP, of Castletown, to draw eight outdoor scenes, which all include horses. Conolly paid Healy nearly £200, in five instalments. A colleague of Healy noted that he 'delineated [horses] so admirably that he got plenty of employment from those who had favourite hunters, mares or ladies palfreys' and it is likely that many of the fragile chalk drawings have since been destroyed (Crookshank and the knight of Glin, *Irish Portraits*, 56).

Healy was based in Dublin, and appears to have moved out of his father's house in Essex Quay and bought his own on Dame Street in 1768–9. He died in July 1771 from a cold caught while sketching cattle in Lord Mornington's park at Dangan, co. Meath. Obituary notices lamented the death of 'a gentleman of excellent taste and original genius in his profession' (*Hibernian Magazine*, August 1771, 392) and he received mention in the educated press for a while afterwards, for example in the *Public Monitor* (27 March 1773). His younger brother William imitated his style, and held an exhibition of copies after Robert on graduating from the Royal Dublin Society Schools in 1774. NICHOLAS GRINDLE

Sources D. Guinness, 'Robert Healy: an eighteenth-century sporting artist', *Apollo*, 115 (1982), 80–85 · A. Crookshank and the Knight of Glin [D. Fitzgerald], *The painters of Ireland, c.1660–1920*, 2nd edn (1979), 56 · W. G. Strickland, *A dictionary of Irish artists*, 2 vols. (1913); repr. with introduction by T. J. Snoddy (1989) · *Hibernian Magazine* (Aug 1771) · *Public Monitor* (27 March 1773) · A. Crookshank and the Knight of Glin [D. Fitzgerald], eds., *Irish portraits, 1660–1860* (1969) [exhibition catalogue, Dublin, London, and Belfast, 14 Aug 1969 – 9 March 1970]
Likenesses R. Healy, self-portrait, chalk, 1765, NG Ire. · R. Healy, self-portrait, black and white chalk on paper, 1766, NG Ire.

Healy, Thomas Gerard [Gerry] (1913–1989), Trotskyist leader, was born on 3 December 1913 in Ballybane, co. Galway, Ireland, the son of Michael Healy, a farmer, and his wife, Margaret Mary Rabbitte; he was always known as Gerry Healy. His early life is shrouded in carefully cultivated mythology; all that can be stated with certainty is that in August 1937 he joined the Trotskyist militant group in London, having previously been a member of the Communist Party in Westminster. Within months he resigned to help form a competitor, the Workers' International League, in which he acquired a reputation as an indefatigable organizer and inveterate oppositionalist, resigning and being expelled on several occasions, although always eventually rejoining. Unemployed for much of the 1930s, he spent the war in munitions factories, briefly training as a draughtsman. On 13 December 1941 he married a fellow member of the Workers' International League, Betty Mary Russell (*b*. 1915/16), the 25-year-old daughter of a Streatham estate agent; they had a daughter and a son.

After the Workers' International League fused with the Revolutionary Socialist League to form the Revolutionary Communist Party in 1944, Healy insisted, as he continued to do for four decades, that capitalist crisis was imminent: this required the party to enter the Labour Party, towards which the workers were turning for socialist solutions. When the Revolutionary Communist Party resisted this prescription, the Fourth International split the organization and authorized Healy's followers to enter the Labour Party. He made headway, establishing in 1948, in partnership with Labour MP Tom Braddock and the trade union leader Jack Stanley, an entrist paper, *Socialist Outlook*, and quickly gaining ascendancy in the broad left Socialist Fellowship. The collapse of the Revolutionary Communist Party in 1949 left Healy the unchallenged suzerain of British Trotskyism. But he soon encountered serious reverses. The Labour Party proscribed the Socialist Fellowship in 1951 and *Socialist Outlook* in 1954, and in the latter

year a split in the Fourth International produced significant defections from its British affiliate. Even success in the trade unions, when he influenced the decision of dockers in northern ports to break away from the Transport and General Workers and to join the Amalgamated Stevedores and Dockers, proved ultimately insubstantial.

But Healy demonstrated resilience and flair in turning the crisis of 1956 in the Communist Party of Great Britain over Stalinism and Hungary to political advantage. Tirelessly seeking out disillusioned communists, he recruited some 200 to the Trotskyist entrist group, including talented journalists, thinkers, and trade unionists. In February 1959, emboldened by success and concerned at increased pressure from the Labour Party leadership, he established an open organization: the Socialist Labour League. This, in its turn, was proscribed and its leading members expelled from the Labour Party. Encountering opposition in his own ranks, he emulated those he criticized. By 1961 the majority of recruits from the Communist Party of Great Britain had been expelled or had resigned from the Socialist Labour League.

Continued entry work and temporary control of the Labour Party Young Socialists provided Healy with a sustained flow of young recruits, but by 1965 he had pulled out of the Labour Party and for the remainder of the 1960s built the Socialist Labour League as an exclusive sect on a programme of looming capitalist cataclysm, military dictatorship, and demonization of his competitors on the far left, justified by dogmatic and selective resort to Trotsky's writings. Relative successes, such as the recruitment of a group of car-industry shop stewards in Oxford and the adherence of a range of entertainment-industry luminaries, notably Ken Loach, and Corin and later Vanessa Redgrave, paved the way for the launch of a daily paper, *Workers' Press*, in 1971 and transformation of the Socialist Labour League into the Workers' Revolutionary Party in 1973. By then, world economic problems and political pressures in Britain augured, at least for some, the long-prophesied capitalist crisis. In the changing political climate of the late 1970s, however, the long decline of the Workers' Revolutionary Party began, ushered in by the expulsion in 1974 of its leading trade unionists in a dispute over Healy's catastrophic economic and political perspectives.

Healy was ageing and ailing. With the defection of his French co-thinkers in 1972, he was isolated from the world Trotskyist movement, apart from a handful of satellites. In Britain the Socialist Workers' Party and the militant tendency were overhauling the Workers' Revolutionary Party, increasingly a cult with Healy its guru. He became increasingly paranoid, mounting an expensive investigation which concluded that prominent American Trotskyists were long-standing agents of the CIA and KGB. Long untutored in Marxist theory, he now presented himself as the ultimate authority on dialectical materialism. Bullying and intimidation gave way to violence and his sexual predatoriness, concealed since the 1950s, burgeoned. As the Workers' Revolutionary Party's financial position deteriorated in the early 1980s, Healy obtained funds from

Libya, Iraq, the Gulf states, and the Palestine Liberation Organization, responding with political support. Opposition developed as the defeat of the 1984–5 miners' strike demoralized his organization. On 19 October 1985 Healy was expelled from the Workers' Revolutionary Party after revelations that he had sexually abused at least twenty-six women members.

Until Healy died of a heart attack at St Thomas Hospital, Lambeth, London, on 14 December 1989, he presided over a group of followers, the Marxist Party, scarcely bigger than the band of disciples he had led out of the Revolutionary Communist Party forty years earlier. He was survived by his wife and their children, Alan and Mary. He was memorialized, incompletely and rather flatteringly, by Laurence Olivier in Trevor Griffiths's play *The Party*, as an obdurate, canonical propagandist. In real life he was a talented organizer and orator, and an authoritarian, increasingly brutal dogmatist. He disillusioned thousands with Trotskyism, transforming it in the process into a variant of millenarian cultism.   JOHN MCILROY

Sources S. Bornstein and A. Richardson, *War and the International: a history of the Trotskyist movement in Britain, 1937–1949* (1986) • J. Callaghan, *British Trotskyism: theory and practice* (1984) • J. McIlroy, 'Healy, Thomas Gerard (Gerry)', *DLB* • H. Ratner, *Reluctant revolutionary: memoirs of a Trotskyist, 1936–1960* (1994) • B. Hunter, *Lifelong apprenticeship: the life and times of a revolutionary* (1997) • T. Wohlforth, *The prophet's children: travels on the American left* (New Jersey, 1994) • E. Mandel, *Marxism vs ultra-leftism* (1967) • T. Polan, *The SLL: an autopsy* (1970) • T. Whelan, *The credibility gap: the politics of the SLL* (1970) • 'The disunity of theory and practice: the Trotskyist movement in Britain since 1945', *Revolutionary History*, 6/2 (summer 1996) • C. Lotz and A. Feldman, *Gerry Healy: a revolutionary life* (1994) • B. Pitt, 'The rise and fall of Gerry Healy', *Workers News* (1990–91) [series] • *The Times* (23 Dec 1989) • *The Guardian* (18 Dec 1989) • *The Guardian* (22 Dec 1989) • *The Guardian* (28 Dec 1989) • *The Guardian* (30 Dec 1989) • *Daily Telegraph* (19 Dec 1989) • *The Independent* (21 Dec 1989) • b. cert. • m. cert. • d. cert.
Archives U. Warwick Mod. RC, corresp., MS 325 | U. Hull, Haston papers • U. Warwick Mod. RC, Deane papers, Purdie papers, Tarbuck papers
Likenesses photograph, repro. in *The Times* • photograph, repro. in *The Guardian* • photograph, repro. in *Daily Telegraph* • photograph, repro. in *The Independent*
Wealth at death £48,596: probate, 28 Aug 1990, *CGPLA Eng. & Wales*

Healy, Timothy Michael (1855–1931), politician and first governor-general of the Irish Free State, was born on 17 May 1855. He was the second son of Maurice Healy (*d.* 1906) and his wife, Eliza, *née* Sullivan (*d.* 1859). His elder brother was Thomas J. Healy (1854–1925), a solicitor and MP for North Wexford from 1892 to 1900.

Family and early career The Healy family was closely allied, both by friendship and by intermarriage, with the Sullivans of west Cork. Tim Healy's father was clerk of the Bantry Poor Law Union, and had a local reputation as a Greek scholar. In 1862 he was transferred to a similar post at Lismore in co. Waterford, which he continued to hold for forty-four years until his death in 1906.

Over the next two generations, like many Irish people, Tim Healy attributed the ordinariness of his circumstances to past historic wrongs and his family's religious constancy. His daughter wrote:

Timothy Michael Healy (1855–1931), by Sir William Orpen, 1908

One branch of the O'Healys, who had turned protestant, [claimed] the land of a Catholic cousin … From them the Hely-Hutchinson family are descended. From the Catholic cousin who kept his faith and lost his lands was descended the family of whom Timothy Michael Healy was the second son. (M. Sullivan, 3)

The emphasis on his father's learning was a kind of compensation and proof of a continued, if attenuated, status as a gentleman.

When Tim Healy was four years old his mother died in giving birth to twins. One of these twins, **Maurice Healy** (1859–1923), was Healy's dearest brother. It is said a nurse placed Maurice in the young Tim's arms and said 'This little boy has no mother now and you will have to be a mother to him'. Certainly the two brothers remained very close until Maurice's death and even married two sisters within five years of each other. Maurice was more retiring than his brother but probably also more intelligent. He became one of the leading solicitors in Ireland and a very effective MP (Cork City, 1885–1900, 1909–10, 1910–18). His solid common sense sometimes acted as a corrective to Tim's exuberant impetuosity both in parliament and the courts. Their maternal grandmother, Jane Sullivan, played a significant role in raising both brothers.

Healy was educated at the Christian Brothers' school in Fermoy; but in effect he was largely self-educated, for in 1869 he had to leave for Dublin where he stayed at the house of his uncle Timothy Daniel Sullivan MP. He then went to look for work in England, finally gaining employment in 1871 as a shorthand clerk in the office of the North Eastern Railway Company, Newcastle upon Tyne. In his spare time he became heavily involved in the home-rule politics of the local Irish community.

In 1878, after leaving for London and working as a confidential clerk in a large floor-cloth factory owned by his relative James Barry, Healy became the parliamentary correspondent of *The Nation*, which was owned by his uncle. He wrote numerous articles in support of the newly emergent and more militant home-rule leader C. S. Parnell and his policy of parliamentary 'obstruction'. Healy gradually established himself as part of the broad Parnellite political circle. Parnell admired his undoubted intelligence and energy and in 1880 asked him to organize the Canadian end of his American tour. He became Parnell's secretary but was denied even the rather limited intimacy which Parnell allowed some of his political colleagues. As one of Healy's close relatives, Alexander Sullivan, put it: 'Parnell was more than a bit of a snob. He was always conscious of the vulgarity of the party standard as compared with the culture of his class' (A. M. Sullivan, 49).

Politics and the Commons Parnell did, at least, bring Healy into the parliamentary party by supporting him as nationalist candidate for Wexford against the excellent local claims of John Redmond, the recently deceased MP's own son, in late 1880. After surviving a court case which alleged that he had been guilty of intimidation in an agrarian case, Healy was elected to parliament. Small, bespectacled, speaking in a quick brogue, dressed in rather badly fitting clothing, Healy did not cut an impressive figure—by conventional standards—in the house. He responded by the application of sheer intelligence and diligence: in the debates over the 1881 Land Act he established a personal ascendancy over ministers and brought about the 'Healy clause' which provided that no further rent should in future be charged on tenants' improvements. In a celebrated aside, Healy whispered to a colleague, 'I have added millions to the pockets of the tenants' (T. P. O'Connor, *Memoirs*, 1929, 1.179). However, a later ruling in the Court of Appeal reduced the impact significantly.

Healy was also a keen and voluble supporter of the *United Ireland* newspaper's campaign against the chief secretary, Earl Spencer, nicknamed the duke of Sodom and Gomorrah on account of the homosexuality of some junior Dublin Castle officials. By the mid-1880s Healy had already acquired a reputation for a certain scurrilousness of tone. In 1882 he married his cousin Erina Sullivan: they were to have three daughters and three sons. In 1887 his brother Maurice married Erina's sister Annie Sullivan.

In 1883 Healy was imprisoned for six months following an agrarian case. The sentence was commuted to four months but he later confessed that it had a lasting and negative effect on his peace of mind. Parnell sought to exploit Healy's growing reputation as a friend of the farmers in a Monaghan by-election in June 1883. This was probably the high point of their relationship. Parnell, perhaps for the last time, threw himself into the by-election campaign with vigour and paid unusual attention to detail; it was he who discovered that Healy's victorious poll had been underestimated by 100 votes.

Perhaps unwisely, Healy now became the Parnellite most likely to be chosen for electoral conflicts in Ulster; he won the seat in Londonderry South in 1885 but held it only

for a year. In 1886 he was elected for North Longford, a seat he held until 1892. In 1884 he was called to the Irish bar and eventually took silk in Dublin in 1889 and in London in 1910. His reputation allowed him to do good business in land cases. Nevertheless, Parnell snubbed him by not offering him a brief at the time of the special commission inquiry following *The Times* allegations of 1887; perhaps Parnell acted in retribution for an earlier slight, for in February 1886 the first open clash with Parnell had occurred. Travelling to Galway with another Irish MP, Joseph Biggar, a rather celebrated philanderer, Healy opposed Captain William O'Shea—Parnell's nomination—as member for Galway City. The whiggish O'Shea was not even a nominal or lukewarm home-ruler and the reason for Parnell's support was felt to be obvious: 'the candidate's wife is Parnell's mistress', as Biggar put it rather bluntly. But on this occasion Healy gave way when Parnell appeared unexpectedly in Galway to rally support for O'Shea.

The Home Rule Party divided and reunited After some limited hesitation Healy felt unable to give way again to Parnell following the divorce case revelations of November 1890: his hostility to Parnell at this point had a rational basis; certainly Parnell was recklessly endangering the Irish party's all-important alliance with Gladstonian Liberalism. Nevertheless it is clear that Healy's invective during the divorce crisis contained themes of social resentment ('Mr Landlord Parnell') as well as a more sexually charged language which opened the door ('Who is to be the mistress of the party?' he quipped after John Redmond had referred to Parnell as the 'master of the party') to an onslaught of vulgar public abuse of Katharine O'Shea. It is fair to see Healy in this period as a still young politician who had not thrown off the weight of social and perhaps sexual resentments; in later years, as he became more and more of an established figure, although his tone remained sharp, it was never again quite so hysterical.

In 1892, following Parnell's death, Healy captured North Louth for the anti-Parnellites. But he could never work with the other anti-Parnellite leaders—John Dillon in particular—and he was to be expelled from the national league in 1895. Increasingly, he felt that Dillon was subservient to British Liberalism; Dillon, in turn, felt that Healy was subservient to Irish clericalism. Certainly Healy was able to retain his seat in North Louth only because of his close alliance with Cardinal Logue, who regarded him as the most able parliamentary defender of specifically Catholic interests. He also had the important financial support of William Martin Murphy, another self-made Bantry man and kinsman, an increasingly successful Irish businessman.

Healy played a major role behind the scenes in the reunification of the Irish party in 1900. John Redmond, desperate to sell his ailing *Independent* newspaper, found himself involved with Healy's Bantry ally William Martin Murphy. Healy, by now completely estranged from Dillon, seized the opportunity for intrigue: he played a key role in propelling Redmond into the chair—though not, for another decade, the effective leadership—of the reunited party. Dillon unsurprisingly was alienated by such an action and Redmond soon felt it was wiser to conciliate Dillon, who retained a much wider personal following, than to maintain the alliance with Healy. As a result, Healy never received the rewards—in terms of influence over strategy—that he had expected to flow from his support for Redmond. Instead, the 1900 general election saw both his brothers purged from the party's list of candidates. He became increasingly bitter on this score; in October 1903 he advanced John Howard Parnell against the official Parliamentary Party candidate for a County Meath vacancy. If he was embarrassed by his use of the Parnell name against the official machine, he displayed no sign of it. At the same time Healy again attempted to use Murphy's money to strike a deal with Redmond. This time Murphy offered to buy out the *Freeman's Journal*, the most important journalistic expression of Dillon's views. Horrified at the prospect of another bloody split, Redmond refused; but he suffered a painful consequence: *The Independent*, by now the most successful newspaper in Ireland, never gave wholehearted support to his leadership. Alexander Sullivan, one of Healy's kinsmen and a close political ally up to this point, conceded: 'It was impossible for Redmond to make terms with a man who on the subject of his personal feud was incapable of reason' (A. M. Sullivan, 137).

However, at least after 1903 Healy was to be joined in his estrangement from the party leadership by William O'Brien. O'Brien had been for several years one of Healy's bitterest critics but now he felt more annoyed by Redmond's subservience to Dillon. He and Healy entered into a loose coalition which lasted throughout the effective life of the Irish Parliamentary Party. After the passage of the far-reaching Wyndham Land Act of 1903 both Healy and O'Brien felt (as against Dillon) that the politics of agrarian radicalism was now subject to a sharp law of diminishing returns. They preferred instead to pursue schemes of 'conciliation' designed to move southern landed interests towards some form of acceptance of home rule. Redmond was sympathetic to this policy but inhibited by Dillon's supporters—and also by the volatility of Healy and O'Brien—he felt unable to pursue the policy with any depth of commitment. In 1908 Redmond managed to bring Healy and O'Brien back into the party but by 1909, provoked by differing views of the Birrell Land Act, both men decided to split off again. Headstrong as they were, O'Brien and Healy were responding to real changes in the social basis of Irish politics and Healy was also showing that his intense Catholicism no longer stopped him seeking a better relationship with protestant landlords. In the first general election of 1910, O'Brien and Healy—who retained strong personal support in Cork—managed to inflict a number of significant setbacks on the Redmondite party machine. But as the veto controversy increased Redmond's power at Westminster—and the home-rule cause seemed to prosper—so also did the electoral strength of his critics inevitably weaken.

In the second election of 1910, despite strong support from his clerical ally Cardinal Michael Logue, Healy was defeated in North Louth by 418 votes. He refused to accept the verdict, which ended almost a quarter of a century of

parliamentary representation. On petition his opponent was, however, unseated on the ground of 'corrupt practices, undue influence, bribery, treating, [and] illegal practices' (A. M. Sullivan, *The Last Serjeant*, 1952, 239). Healy's counsel drily commented:

> the evidence was so overwhelming that only one real excuse could have been offered—the city of Dundalk was an essential factor in the electorate … and Dundalk had always refused to vote at all except upon the condition of being primed with drink. (ibid., 29)

Healy found a seat in North-East Cork in July 1911; he was to represent that constituency until 1918.

Sinn Féin and the events of 1916–18 After the Easter rising of 1916, Healy was rapidly convinced that Redmond was doomed. In late 1916 he and O'Brien supported an unsuccessful challenge against the party machine in west Cork; this was proof that Redmondism still had some vitality and that in the event of its eventual collapse, as occurred in the general election of 1918, the new generation of radicals—rather than the dissidents of the old political class—would be the beneficiaries. Taking the point, Healy eased himself out of the forefront of the political conflict; but he did make it clear in 1917 that he was in general sympathy with Sinn Féin, though not with physical force methods. In one notable intervention, he acted as counsel for the family of the dead Sinn Féin hunger striker Thomas Ashe in September of that year; here Healy in cross-examination poured much scorn on the conduct of Max Green, chairman of the prison board and, as it happened, John Redmond's son-in-law. During the 1918 general election he spoke in support of P. J. Little, the Sinn Féin candidate for Rathmines.

Healy in perspective Healy's career is a study in contrasts. There are the outstanding features: the sense of historic destiny and the great ability, evidenced not only by the sharp wit seen both at the bar and in the house—though his most uproarious speech, the 'Uganda' effort of 1902, relies on a racial imagery and vocabulary which has not survived the passage of time—but also by the depth of his political insight. He was particularly astute in his assessments of British political leaders. Set against this is the extraordinary pettiness and fractiousness of the period after 1891: he may have played a key role in destroying Parnell, but in doing so he also permanently diminished his own standing in Irish public life. It was not just that a substantial minority of Irish people found it hard to forgive his role in the divorce crisis, but also, and perhaps more profoundly, that he found it impossible to work under any other leadership in the post-Parnell era. The hero-worship he was prepared to grant the protestant squire, Parnell, he was never prepared to give to others who hailed from rather more familiar religious and social backgrounds. He became a perpetual gadfly: always interesting but always marginal. The fact that he had never been a key figure of the Redmondite party allowed him to make an uneasy peace with Sinn Féin as early as 1917.

Governor-general and last years In 1922 the question of the selection of a suitable governor-general for the recently created Irish Free State came up for settlement. Healy was the obvious choice: finally and ironically a man who had spent much of his political life in controversy and on the margins was acceptable to the British and the new Irish establishment for a key symbolic and reconciling position at the centre of public life. He had also recommended himself to the Catholic hierarchy by a celebrated address in 1921 to the Catholic Truth Society which denounced Darwinism—'the monkey theory'—as a simple excuse for adultery. It is said that towards the end of his life he mellowed and softened; certainly he became more diplomatic: when in 1928 he published his extensive two-volume memoir *Letters and Leaders of my Day*, he omitted many of his scathing epistolary references to the Sinn Féin movement, whose leaders were now the new masters of independent Ireland. He died at Chapelizod, co. Dublin, where he lived, on 26 March 1931, three years after his retirement from the governor-generalship.

Healy enjoyed a very happy and intense family life: the life of his children, and his own, was to be closely interlinked with the Sullivans. His third daughter consoled him after the death of his wife in 1927; and helped him in the social side of his life as governor-general. His second daughter became the wife of Mr Justice Timothy Sullivan, a distinguished lawyer, who later filled the position of president of the high court of the Irish Free State. His third daughter became a nun. His eldest son, Joe, fought with distinction at Gallipoli, and joined the Irish bar. His second, Paul, became a noted Jesuit priest. His third son adopted the medical profession and became the master of an important hospital. His nephew Maurice Healy KC (1888–1943), son of his favourite brother, Maurice, had a successful career both as recorder of Coventry and, alongside J. B. Priestley, as a 'morale-boosting' BBC broadcaster during the early years of the Second World War.

PAUL BEW

Sources T. M. Healy, *Letters and leaders of my day*, 2 vols. (1928) • T. D. Sullivan, *Recollections of troubled times in Irish politics* (1905) • M. Sullivan, *No man's man* (1943) • A. M. Sullivan, *Old Ireland: reminiscences of an Irish KC* (1927) • D. Plunket, *Timothy Healy: memories and anecdotes* [1933] • L. O'Flaherty, *The life of Tim Healy* (1927) • F. Callanan, *Tim Healy* (1996) • P. Bew, *Land and the national question in Ireland, 1858–82* (1978) • *CGPLA Eng. & Wales* (1924) [Maurice Healy] • *Cork Examiner* (10 Nov 1923) • *Cork Examiner* (12 Nov 1923)
Archives University College, Dublin, corresp. and papers | BL, corresp. with Lord Gladstone, Add. MSS 46049–46085, *passim* • Bodl. Oxf., letters to Herbert Asquith • HLRO, letters to Lord Beaverbrook • HLRO, letters to Ralph Blumenfeld • NL Ire., letters to John Redmond • TCD, corresp. with John Dillon
Likenesses B. Stone, photograph, 1898, NPG • W. Orpen, portrait, 1908, priv. coll. [*see illus.*] • J. Davidson, bronze bust, 1914, King's Inns, Dublin • J. Lavery, oils, exh. 1923, Municipal Gallery of Modern Art, Dublin • P. A. de Laszlo, oils, 1929?, Gray's Inn, London • C. Duprechez, portrait, NG Ire. • H. Furniss, group portrait, pen-and-ink sketch for caricature, NPG • S. P. Hall, pencil sketch, NPG • P. A. de Laszlo, portrait, priv. coll. • F. Pegram, pencil sketch, V&A; repro. in *Pictorial World* (1888–9) • Spy [L. Ward], chromolithograph caricature, NPG; repro. in *VF* (3 April 1886)
Wealth at death £18,887 5s. 10d.: probate, 10 June 1931, *CGPLA Eng. & Wales* • £9469 14s. 7d.—Maurice Healy: probate, 1924, *CGPLA Éire*

Heaney, Sheila Anne Elizabeth (1917–1991), army officer, was born on 11 June 1917 at 5 Canning Street, Liverpool, the second of the four children of Francis James Strong Heaney (1874–1950), a consultant general surgeon who specialized in the use of radium, and his wife, Anne Summers, *née* McBurney (1886–1974), an American citizen. Sheila's childhood holidays were often spent in Cornwall, the Lake District, and the counties of Wexford and Kerry. Riding was a favourite pastime, and before the war she enjoyed following hounds. She was educated at Huyton College, Liverpool, and then, in 1935, went to Liverpool University, from where she graduated in 1938. She did a short course at Loughborough College of Technology before joining the personnel department of Marks and Spencer in Liverpool. Her interest in sociology was generated by visiting the less salubrious areas of Liverpool in the company of her father.

Heaney joined the Auxiliary Territorial Service (ATS) in January 1939 and persuaded many of her staff to enlist also. She was posted to 1st west Lancashire platoon as D-company assistant. She was called up for service on 2 September 1939 and promoted junior commander in November 1940. In May 1941 she was given an emergency commission in the ATS as second lieutenant. Thereafter she spent a year at the ATS training centre before becoming second-in-command, Salisbury Plain district group. The first four months of 1944 saw her at the United States Army Staff College in Fort Leavenworth, Kansas, USA. On her return she was posted to ATS clerical group in east Africa and in 1946 to Palestine group. Following this service she was awarded the territorial efficiency medal, the war medal (1939–45) and the general service medal with Palestine clasp. In February 1947 she was promoted captain. She returned to the UK in July 1948 where, following three months at Donnington headquarters, she was posted to the War Office as a deputy assistant adjutant-general.

Heaney decided to make her career with the army and in 1949 was granted a regular army commission with the rank of substantive captain in the Women's Royal Army Corps (WRAC), formed on 1 February that year. In 1951 she was awarded the territorial decoration. She continued at the War Office until 1952 when she went to headquarters 79 anti-aircraft brigade, Royal Artillery, with the rank of major. In 1955, after two years at western command, where her potential as a trainer was recognized, she was appointed MBE. She then went on to 1 independent company, WRAC, followed by another two years at 140 provost company. September 1959 saw her back at the War Office, following which in July 1961 she was posted to the depot and training centre of the WRAC school of instruction. In April 1962 she joined the medical services and WRAC records office, and in February 1963 she was promoted lieutenant-colonel. In October 1965 Heaney was sent to headquarters northern command as assistant director, WRAC, and in June 1967 she was promoted colonel. A month later she became assistant adjutant-general at the Ministry of Defence.

Heaney's promotion to brigadier came in June 1970, and later in the year she was appointed director, WRAC. This was also the year in which she was appointed an honorary aide-de-camp to the queen. In 1972 she visited the USA, where she studied the move towards the integration of servicewomen in the regular army and the campaign for equality in the armed forces. She believed strongly that women should be given more opportunities to achieve their ambitions in the army and prepared the groundwork for women's promotion outside the WRAC. However, she urged caution, and called for evolution rather than revolution. It was largely as a result of her efforts that women were given the chance to fulfil their potential in their chosen arm or service of the army and so achieve greater career opportunities. In February 1973 she was made CB. Her retirement from the WRAC in June 1973 did not lessen her interest in young officers. She served on the military education committee of Edinburgh and Heriot-Watt universities' Officers' Training Corps for some years.

After being widowed Heaney's mother had moved to Edinburgh, and during her years at the War Office, Heaney travelled by train nearly every weekend to care for her. On her retirement she made her home with her mother. But idleness never appealed, so she joined the Women's Royal Voluntary Service (WRVS) and became district organizer for Edinburgh, steering the group through a difficult period of local government re-organization. In 1977 she agreed to become chairman of the WRVS in Scotland. Her genuine interest in people, coupled with her wise judgement and compassion, made her a loved and respected leader. While serving in Kenya she had nearly died as a result of eating tropical mushrooms. Her substantial lameness in later life may have been attributable to this illness; 1981 was the year of the disabled and, with personal knowledge, she was able to set up new projects to help this group.

During her busy life Sheila Heaney managed to find time to give individual help to those who needed it, delivering meals-on-wheels, shopping, and driving the elderly. When she retired from the WRVS in 1981 she became involved in the work of St Columba's Hospice, Edinburgh, serving on its executive committee and providing much of the essential impetus for its development. Having been a heavy smoker during all her adult life, she eventually developed lung cancer, and she spent her last few days in the care of the hospice. She died there on 1 February 1991. She never married. Her funeral and memorial service took place at St James's Episcopal Church in Goldenacre, Edinburgh, on 6 February 1991, and there her ashes were later interred.   MARY CORSAR

Sources ministry of defence archives · Women's Royal Voluntary Service archives · *The Leopard* [journal of WRAC] · archives, St Columba's Hospice, Edinburgh · private information (2004) · personal knowledge (2004) · WWW · *The Times* (8 Feb 1991) · *The Independent* (9 Feb 1991)
Likenesses photograph, repro. in *The Times* · photograph, repro. in *The Independent*
Wealth at death £179,764.33: confirmation, 18 March 1991, NA Scot., SC/CO 225/210

Heaphy, Charles (1820?–1881), artist and colonial official in New Zealand, was born in London, probably in 1820, the younger son (there were also three daughters) of the watercolourist and portrait painter Thomas *Heaphy (1775–1835), and his first wife, Mary Stevenson (*d.* after 1820). The artist Thomas Frank *Heaphy (1813–1873) was his brother. Two of his sisters also painted. After working as a draughtsman for a railway company (1835–6) he attended the Royal Academy intermittently, then in May 1839 he was appointed draughtsman by the New Zealand Company in London, and sent to New Zealand in the *Tory*. He was employed on arrival in preliminary explorations for the company's settlements. In 1840–41 he assisted in the purchase of the Chatham Islands, where he was wounded during a skirmish, and in 1842 he explored the Nelson country for the company's settlement. Throughout this time he painted what he saw, producing notable landscapes and other works. In 1842 he was sent to England to report, using his pictures, on the progress of the Nelson settlement. While there he published some of his works as lithographs and also a book, *Residence in Various Parts of New Zealand* (1842).

After returning to New Zealand, Heaphy made an unsuccessful effort to farm. In 1843 he began a series of journeys as a paid company explorer into the interior. Optimism about settlement possibilities gave way to greater realism, particularly after a journey down the west coast in 1846, when Heaphy and his party survived only through the kindness of the Maori. In 1847 he was employed in watching the New Zealand Company's interests in the marking out of Maori reserves at Massacre Bay (later Golden Bay), and in August 1848 he was appointed draughtsman to the colonial government in Auckland, where he continued to paint, extending his interest to geological and particularly vulcanological subjects. On 30 October 1851 he married Catherine Laetitia, the daughter of Revd Churton. They had no children of their own but adopted two of her relatives.

From 1852 to 1853 Heaphy was commissioner of the Coromandel goldfield, with instructions to secure from the Maori the right of extending the goldfield. From 1854 to 1857 he was district surveyor at Matakama and in 1858 provincial land surveyor for the province of Auckland. In January 1864 he was appointed chief surveyor to the New Zealand government. Heaphy was appointed successively lieutenant and captain in the Auckland rifle volunteers in 1863, and in the Waikato during the war of 1863–6 he distinguished himself when the Maori attacked a bathing party of troops at the Mangapiko River (11 February 1864). Although severely wounded, he continued on active service throughout the day. For this service he was mentioned in dispatches, promoted major in the New Zealand militia (11 February 1864), and in 1867 awarded the Victoria Cross, making him the first soldier of a colonial army to be so honoured.

In 1866 Heaphy was appointed provincial surveyor and deputy waste lands commissioner. From 1867 to 1869 he was a member of the New Zealand house of representatives. In 1869 he was appointed commissioner of native reserves, and in 1878 commissioner of government insurance, judge of the native land court, and commissioner of land claims, appointments which reflected the power of his patron, Donald MacLean. Failing health, caused by early hardships and war wounds, led to his retirement on a pension in June 1881, and his death at Brisbane on 3 August 1881. He was buried at the Toowong cemetery in Brisbane. His wife survived him.

H. M. CHICHESTER, rev. ELIZABETH BAIGENT

Sources M. Fitzgerald, 'Heaphy, Charles', *DNZB*, vol. 1 • D. MacMillan, *Major Charles Heaphy VC and the warrant of 1867* (1990) • B. Gordon and P. Stupples, *Charles Heaphy* (1987) • A. A. St C. Murray Oliver, *A folio of water colours* (1981) • R. Nichol, 'The eruption history of Rangitoto: reappraisal of a small New Zealand myth', *Journal of the Royal Society of New Zealand*, 22 (1992), 159–80 • *LondG* (14 May 1864) [suppl.] • *LondG* (8 Feb 1867)

Heaphy, Thomas (1775–1835), watercolour painter, was born in the parish of St Giles Cripplegate, London, on 29 December 1775, the son of John Gerrard Heaphy, and Katharine Gerard, always referred to as a Frenchwoman, and presumably a member of a family of Huguenot silk weavers in the Spitalfields colony. The romantic tale of the father's noble origins, as given in the *Dictionary of National Biography*, has all the hallmarks of a family legend, but is unmentioned by Thomas Frank *Heaphy in his manuscript in the Royal Watercolour Society archive. Thomas Heaphy showed a love of drawing at an early age, but was first apprenticed to a dyer, before his articles were transferred to the engraver R. M. Meadows. In his spare time he attended a drawing school in Bloomsbury, run either, according to his son, by an otherwise unknown painter named Simpson, or more probably by the caricaturist John Boyne. His first wife, Mary Stevenson, whom he married in 1800, was the sister of a fellow pupil. They had three daughters and two sons, Thomas and Charles *Heaphy. Of the daughters, Mary Anne, Mrs Musgrave, became a miniaturist and watercolour portrait painter who exhibited from the early 1820s; and Elizabeth, Mrs Murray (1815–1882), specialized in Mediterranean and other street and figure subjects. She was elected to the New Society of Painters in Water Colours, now the Royal Institute of Painters in Water Colours, in 1861. Heaphy first exhibited at the Royal Academy in 1797, showing portraits in oil, but he soon realized that his talent was for watercolour, and also that the market for portraits was a crowded one.

From 1807 Heaphy was a regular contributor to the exhibitions of the newly formed Society of Painters in Water Colours (later the Royal Society of Painters in Water Colours), where he made his name with impressive and highly detailed pictures of fish and vegetable markets, inspired by Dutch still lifes with figures, and other scenes of working-class life. These enjoyed a great vogue for several years. His *Hastings Fish Market*, exhibited in 1809, sold for 450 guineas to the daughter of the great collector William Wells of Redleaf, Kent. At this point he returned to portrait painting, with very considerable success and, despite his having objected to the royal family being allowed into the exhibitions before they opened, he painted Princess Charlotte and Prince Leopold and was appointed portrait painter to the princess of Wales. In 1812 he resigned

from the Society of Painters in Water Colours and in the following year he put on an exhibition of his own work. This does not appear to have been a great success, and, on the duke of Wellington's invitation, he accompanied the British army through the Peninsular campaign to its end at the battle of Toulouse. There he painted portraits of both officers and men, and on his return he produced his most important work, a large watercolour of the duke of Wellington giving orders to his staff prior to a battle. It included portraits of about fifty officers. The engraving after the watercolour by Anker Smith, finished and published by Heaphy himself, appeared in 1822 (impression in the NPG, together with three other portraits of Wellington by Heaphy). The National Portrait Gallery also has a watercolour by Heaphy of a youthful Lord Palmerston. In the previous year he had begun to publish a series of prints, in issues of six, *Studies from Nature of British Character*. They were after his chalk studies of the heads of soldiers, sailors, and peasants. In the early 1820s he gave up painting and became a speculator in the development in north-west London of St John's Wood. This sabbatical told on his work when he returned to painting in 1824, and he admitted that 'my power is gone from me' (MS notes by his son, Thomas Heaphy, Royal Watercolour Society archive, J.46). Nevertheless he was a promoter and first president of the Society of British Artists, sending fourteen works to its first exhibition. He resigned a year later, and in 1831 he went to Italy in search of new inspiration. Despite an early dislike of 'academic art' he made fine copies of old masters while there, but after his return to England in mid-1832 he produced little more. He died at his home, 8 St John's Wood Road, London, on 23 October 1835 and was buried in Bunhill Fields. His first wife had died some time after 1820; his second wife, Harriet Jane Mason, survived him.

Heaphy's subject pictures were realistic representations of nature. His miniatures and other portraits, which were also usually on a small scale, were characterized by truthfulness, delicacy of colour, and beauty of finish. He was a versatile and ingenious man, and an enthusiast for mechanical inventions. Though it has been stated that he was always opposed to the Royal Academy—despite Benjamin West's praise for his work—he exhibited there from 1803 to the end of his life. There are examples of his work in the British Museum, the Victoria and Albert Museum, and the National Portrait Gallery, London; the National Gallery of Scotland, Edinburgh; and the Ashmolean Museum, Oxford.

F. M. O'DONOGHUE, rev. HUON MALLALIEU

Sources J. L. Roget, *A history of the 'Old Water-Colour' Society*, 2 vols. (1891); repr. (1972) • Royal Watercolour Society archive, MS J.46 • Faringon, *Diary*

Heaphy, Thomas Frank (1813–1873), painter and writer on art, was born at St John's Wood, London, on 2 April 1813, the eldest son of the six children of the watercolourist Thomas *Heaphy (1775–1835) and his wife, Mary Stevenson (*d.* after 1820). Charles *Heaphy (1820?–1881), a draughtsman and government officer in New Zealand, was his brother, and the miniature painters Elizabeth

Heaphy (afterwards Mrs Henry John Murray; *c.*1815–1882) and Mary Ann Heaphy (afterwards Mrs W. Musgrave; *fl.* 1821–1847) were his sisters. Until about 1850 he used his middle name, Frank, in conjunction with his first, to distinguish himself from his father. In 1831 he accompanied his father on a trip to Italy and also that year exhibited his first painting at the Royal Academy. When the elder Thomas died in 1835, he left his considerable property to his second wife, Harriet Jane Mason; the children of his first marriage—of whom Thomas Frank was one—received nothing. On 10 September 1842 Thomas Frank Heaphy married Eliza, daughter of Joseph Bradstreet of Little Wenham, Suffolk; they had eleven children.

Heaphy's exhibited works until 1859 were chiefly watercolour portraits: his sitters included Signor Fontana, high priest of the order of Saint-Simonians (exh. RA, 1834), John Laurie, sheriff of London (exh. RA, 1848), and Viscount Loftus and Lady Marian Loftus (exh. RA, 1857). He exhibited *La contadina* at the Royal Academy in 1833, but similar foreign peasant subjects did not reappear until much later, in 1859 and 1861. In the 1850s he began to paint light literary narratives, and after 1861 specialized in a mixture of genre and history painting, showing subjects such as Johannes Kepler interrupted by people seeking astrological predictions (exh. RA, 1863) and the potter Bernard Palissy mistaken for a counterfeiter (exh. RA, 1864). The indignity of poverty is a recurrent theme in his work. He exhibited regularly at the Royal Academy and the British Institution, and from 1867, when he became a member, at the Society of British Artists.

In 1844 Heaphy painted an altarpiece for the protestant church at Malta, and he executed a similar commission for Toronto. He travelled to Rome, Genoa, and Arles to investigate the history of the image of Christ, and published his findings in the *Art Journal* in 1861; these articles were republished in 1880 by Wyke Bayliss as *The likeness of Christ: an enquiry into the verisimilitude of the received likeness of our blessed Lord.* His lighter writings include 'A Night in the Catacombs' (*St James's Magazine*, 1861) and 'The beggar saint' (*Once a Week*, 1862). Heaphy, who had become deaf in his later years, died at his home, 46 Sussex Street, Pimlico, London, on 7 August 1873; he was survived by his wife.

Kenneth Bendiner

Sources *Art Journal*, 35 (1873), 308 · *DNB* · H. Hubbard, 'Thomas Heaphy', *Old Water-Colour Society's Club*, 26 (1948), 18–31 · Graves, *RA exhibitors* · M. Bradshaw, ed., *Royal Society of British Artists: members exhibiting, 1824–1892* (1973), 46 · M. Hardie, *Water-colour painting in Britain*, ed. D. Snelgrove, J. Mayne, and B. Taylor, 3: *The Victorian period* (1968), 99–100 · P. G. Nunn, 'The other Heaphys', *Bulletin of New Zealand Art History*, 14 (1993), 3–8 · m. cert. · *CGPLA Eng. & Wales* (1873)
Likenesses T. F. Heaphy, self-portrait, oils, *c.*1831, NPG · T. F. Heaphy, self-portrait, watercolour, *c.*1831, NPG · Bassano, carte-de-visite, NPG
Wealth at death under £100: probate, 30 Aug 1873, *CGPLA Eng. & Wales*

Heard, Henry Fitzgerald [Gerald] (1889–1971), writer and broadcaster, was born on 6 October 1889 at 69 Victoria Park Road, South Hackney, London, the second of three sons of the Revd Henry James Heard (*d.* 1931) and his wife,

Maud Jervis Bannatyne (*d.* 1892). His paternal grandfather, the Revd John Bickford Heard (1828–1908), gave the Hulsean lectures in 1892. At the time of his birth Heard's father was the incumbent of Christ Church, South Hackney. After the death of his mother Heard was looked after by a grandmother who belonged to the Plymouth Brethren.

Heard, who was known as Gerald, was educated first at Hamilton House and Lansdowne Proprietary in Bath, and then at Sherborne School, Dorset, between May 1904 and July 1907. At that time the school was headed by the son of the bishop of Durham, Frederick Brooke Westcott, who excelled in the teaching of divinity and exercised a charismatic influence over his students. Like his father and grandfather, Heard went on to Gonville and Caius College, Cambridge, where he matriculated in 1908 and received his BA in the history tripos (second class) in 1911. Intending to take holy orders as his father and grandfather had done, he became a theological exhibitioner at Caius in 1911. However, he did not take holy orders in the end, although his subsequent career as a peripatetic mystical preacher may be viewed as the fulfilment of his spiritual vocation. He rejected doctrinal Christianity due to the influences of his Cambridge years, when he was exposed to psychical research, anthropology, and the humanist philosophies of Goldsworthy Lowes Dickinson and J. McT. E. McTaggart.

Heard was employed as a private secretary to Lord Robson (1852–1918) between 1913 and 1914. He did not serve in the First World War, having been rejected by the military on physical grounds, and about 1916 he probably suffered a nervous breakdown over his crisis of faith. From 1919 to 1923 he was employed as a live-in secretary to the agricultural expert and retired Irish statesman Sir Horace Plunkett in Foxrock, Ireland. The precise nature of the relationship is unclear. While working for Plunkett, Heard became interested in utopian living and began his career as a writer, although his publications were mostly sporadic until the late 1920s. He wrote for the revived *Irish Statesman* under the editorship of George Russell (A. E.), and worked on his first two books, *Narcissus: an Anatomy of Clothes* (1924) and *The Ascent of Humanity* (1929). In 1923 republican forces tried to burn down Plunkett's house with Heard in it. Their relationship was already floundering at this point, so, although both men moved to London and Heard continued with Plunkett in a secretarial capacity until the statesman's death in 1932, Heard moved in with Christopher (Chris) Wood (*d.* 1976), heir to a jam fortune. Heard was a trustee of the Plunkett Foundation for Agricultural Cooperation from 1924 until 1948, and was both the executor and main beneficiary of Plunkett's will.

From the late 1920s until his emigration to America in 1937 Gerald Heard was an influential figure in intellectual circles in London. Described as 'one of the most penetrating minds in England' by E. M. Forster (Nicolson, 87), 'the cleverest man in the world' by Evelyn Waugh (*Diaries*, 321), and 'our prophet' by Naomi Mitchison (Mitchison, 107), he made, as Aldous Huxley put it, 'his mental home on the vacant spaces between the pigeonholes'. A self-proclaimed 'scientific humanist', Heard sought to reconcile science and religion within a 'third morality'—the title of his 1937 work. Heard's 'third morality' reflected many of the intellectual currents of his day, including idealist philosophy, pacifism, modernist theology, eastern religious philosophy, and psychical research. Heard's writings and influence are significant for their suggestion that philosophical idealism 'relocated' to popular intellectual arenas; that there was a continuing interest in spiritual matters; and that eastern religious ideas offered new ways to approach the spiritual dilemmas previously addressed by psychical research.

Heard expounded his 'third morality' in several books on the 'historical anthropology of consciousness' (Dunaway, 23). These included a trilogy—*The Ascent of Humanity* (1929), *The Social Substance of Religion* (1931), and *The Source of Civilization* (1935)—and *The Emergence of Man* (1931), a reworking of Winwood Reade's *The Martyrdom of Man* (1872). He also proselytized his theories in popular science broadcasts for the BBC, and in articles and reviews which appeared in a range of mostly left-leaning periodicals, particularly the feminist *Time and Tide*. He founded his own magazine, *The Realist—A Journal of Scientific Humanism*, in 1929; it was well received but short-lived. Heard's popular idealism appealed especially to women, both in 1930s Britain and in post-war America, although his work was read by most prominent London intellectuals between the wars.

Like another charismatic religious leader of the 1930s, the Oxford Group movement leader Frank Buchman, Heard sought to promote his views within spiritual groups. These groups were active at Maude Royden's inter-denominational Guildhouse Church, the South Place Ethical Society, and at Dartington Hall, the co-operative educational community founded by Dorothy and Leonard Elmhirst in Devon. These groups are significant both as early examples of group therapy and for reflecting the larger intersection between Pauline theology and psychology in this period. Less successfully, Heard sought to form spiritual groups within H. R. L. Sheppard's Peace Pledge Union, of which he was a leading member and to which he recruited Aldous Huxley. Heard was also involved with the Howard League for Penal Reform, the Society for Psychical Research, the Federation of Progressive Societies and Individuals, and the Cranium Club.

Disillusioned with the future of pacifism and convinced of Europe's imminent destruction, in 1937 Heard emigrated to California with his partner, Chris Wood, along with his friend Aldous Huxley and his family. In the summer of 1937 Heard and Huxley visited Georgia O'Keefe at Ghost Ranch, New Mexico, and O'Keefe painted a symbolic portrait of Heard as a tree (*Gerald's Tree I*, 1937, Georgia O'Keefe Museum, Santa Fe, New Mexico; Mitchell, 3–7). Heard expounded his pacifist 'third morality' throughout the war, founding an eastern-influenced mystical community for the training of pacifists—Trabuco College—near Laguna Beach, California, in 1941. The community was visited by Christopher Isherwood, Aldous Huxley, Ezra Pound, and others, and was taken over by the Vedanta Society in 1949.

Heard continued to promote his spiritual ideas after the war through further books and lectures. The latter were given at the Coronet Theatre in Hollywood (1955–7 and 1959–61), the Harvard Divinity School (1961), and the New School for Social Research (1953), as well as on television and radio. He wrote numerous books on spirituality as well as several acclaimed works of science and detective fiction: these included *Doppelgangers* (1948) and *A Taste for Honey* (1941). The latter became a film, *The Deadly Bees* (1967). He also supplied several celebrities—Dave Brubeck, Clare Boothe Luce, and others—with spiritual counselling, and introduced some to LSD before Timothy Leary. For a time he was seriously preoccupied with flying saucers.

Heard's relationship with Chris Wood ended about 1953, and he lived out the latter years of his life with Jay Michael Barrie (1912–2001), a former singer who lived at Trabuco as a monk until about 1955. Barrie worked for Heard in a secretarial and managerial capacity from the 1950s onwards, and nursed him through a five-year illness and two strokes until his death in 1971.

Slight in stature with striking pale blue eyes, Heard had great presence. This stemmed partly from his reputation as a brilliant 'Wellsian supermind' who read 2000 books a year (Furbank, 136), and partly from his personal charisma and melodious voice. Somerset Maugham described him as a 'scintillating talker', and Leo Charlton noted that his friends spoke of him 'as if he were Jesus Christ' (ibid.). Along with Aldous Huxley and Christopher Isherwood, Heard has been credited with contributing to the spread both of mystical religious ideas and a 'counter-cultural tradition' in America (Robb, 46). By the time of his death in Santa Monica on 14 August 1971, Heard had become a public intellectual in California.   ALISON FALBY

Sources A. Falby, 'Gerald Heard and British intellectual culture between the wars', DPhil diss., U. Oxf., 2000 • D. Robb, 'Brahmins from abroad: English expatriates and spiritual consciousness in modern America', *American Studies*, 26/2 (1985), 45–60 • E. V. Toy, 'The conservative connection: the chairman of the board took LSD before Timothy Leary', *American Studies*, 21/2 (1980), 65–70 • S. Bedford, *Aldous Huxley: a biography*, 2 (1974) • Venn, *Alum. Cant.* • J. M. Barrie, 'Some reminiscences of Gerald Heard', *Parapsychology Review* (May–June 1972), 13–18 • J. Venn and others, eds., *Biographical history of Gonville and Caius College*, 4 (1912) • L. Veysey, *The communal experience: anarchist and mystical counter-cultures in America* (New York, 1973) • D. K. Dunaway, *Aldous Huxley recollected: an oral history* (1995) • P. N. Furbank, *Polycrates' ring (1914–1970)* (1978), vol. 2 of *E. M. Forster: a life* • C. Isherwood, *Diaries*, ed. K. Bucknell, 1: *1939–1960* (1996) • N. Mitchison, *You may well ask: a memoir, 1920–1940* (1979) • H. Nicolson, *Diaries and letters*, ed. N. Nicolson, 1 (1966) • *The diaries of Evelyn Waugh*, ed. M. Davie (1976) • T. West, *Horace Plunkett: co-operation and politics* (1986) • Crockford (1920) • M. Caedel, *Pacifism in Britain, 1914–1945: the defining of a faith* (1980) • C. Isherwood, *My guru and his disciple* (1980) • B. Mitchell, 'O'Keefe's arboreal portraits of D. H. Lawrence and Gerald Heard', *Women's Art Journal* (autumn 1998–winter 9), 3–7

Archives U. Cal., Los Angeles | High Cross House, Dartington, William Curry papers · High Cross House, Dartington, Dorothy Elmhirst papers · High Cross House, Dartington, letters to Margaret Isherwood and Leonard Elmhirst · King's AC Cam., letters to W. G. H. Sprott · L. Cong., letters to Clare Boothe Luce · LPL, corresp. with H. R. L. Sheppard · Plunkett Foundation, Long Hanborough, Oxfordshire, corresp. with Sir Horace Plunkett · Rice University, Houston, Texas, Woodson Research Center, corresp. with Sir Julian Huxley | SOUND BBC WAC

Likenesses A. Huxley, oil on paper, 1933, U. Cal., Los Angeles, special collections · G. L. Bush, bust, 1950, U. Cal., Los Angeles · A. Salemme, bronze bust, 1950, priv. coll. · D. Bachardy, ink drawing, 1962, U. Cal., Los Angeles, special collections · D. Bachardy, colour acrylic wash, U. Cal., Los Angeles, special collections · C. Boothe Luce, oils, L. Cong. · L. M. Jenkins, portrait, U. Cal., Los Angeles

Heard, Sir Isaac (1730–1822), herald, was born on 10 December 1730 at Ottery St Mary, Devon, the elder son of John Heard (1698–1759), of Bridgwater and later of London, and Elizabeth (1705–1778), daughter of Benjamin Michell, of Branscombe and Salcombe Regis, Devon. Educated at Honiton grammar school, he entered the navy as a volunteer aged fifteen. He served in the Mediterranean and on the African coast, and narrowly escaped drowning when, as a midshipman in HMS *Blandford*, he was washed overboard off the coast of Guinea in August 1750. Deeming his prospects in a peacetime navy to be poor he left the service and set up as a merchant at Bilbao in Spain in 1751. The outbreak of hostilities between that country and Britain in 1757 caused his move to London, where he entered the employment of a merchant in the City. Following an introduction to the deputy earl marshal, Thomas Howard, earl of Effingham, who noticed his antiquarian interests, Heard was appointed Bluemantle pursuivant on 5 December 1759. He was advanced to Lancaster herald on 3 July 1761, Norroy king of arms on 18 October 1774, and Clarenceux king of arms on 16 May 1780. He also held the posts of gentleman usher of the scarlet rod of the Order of the Bath, and Brunswick herald (1774–1814), and was secretary to the deputy earl marshal (1774–84). Following the death of Ralph Bigland, he was created Garter king of arms on 1 May 1784. He was knighted at a chapter of the Order of the Garter on 2 June 1786.

Heard had a large heraldic and genealogical practice, which after his death was carried on by James Pulman and George Beltz, both heralds who had begun their working lives at the College of Arms as his clerks. Numerous heroes of the French Revolutionary and Napoleonic wars had grants of arms or augmentations of honour designed by him. Although in many cases, including that of Nelson, he acted to restrain the extravagancies and pomposities suggested by grantees, Heard was largely responsible for the 'landscape' heraldry of the Georgian period which a later age was to regard as debased.

As Garter, Heard firmly defended the rights of the heralds of the college to record the pedigrees of knights of the Order of the Bath of which George Nayler, both genealogist of the order and York herald, claimed a monopoly. He also oversaw the investigation of the forgery of evidence in support of a pedigree by William Radclyffe,

Rouge Croix pursuivant, which led to the latter's conviction for forgery in 1820 and subsequent resignation of his office. Heard travelled abroad on Garter missions to William, landgrave of Hesse-Cassel, in 1786; to Ernest Lewis, duke of Saxe-Gotha-Altenburg in 1791; and to William, king of the Netherlands, and Francis, emperor of Austria, in 1814. He was responsible, at the instigation of William Pitt the younger, for drawing up the statutes of the proposed naval and military order of merit during the winter of 1805–6. During his long tenure as a herald he officiated at the ceremonial funerals of members of six generations of the house of Hanover. At the funeral of Nelson in 1805 he broke with precedent when proclaiming the style of the deceased by adding the words 'and the Hero who in the moment of victory fell, covered with immortal glory' (Wagner, 428).

While trading as a merchant at Bilbao, Heard had made several voyages to Boston, Massachusetts. His first wife, whom he married on 7 March 1770, was Katherine (d. 1783), widow of David Ochterlony of Boston, and daughter of Andrew Tyler, of the same place. By this marriage he became step-father to her three young sons, the eldest of whom was to become General Sir David Ochterlony, first baronet. Heard carried out genealogical work for several American families and corresponded in 1791–2 about his English ancestry with George Washington, for whom he professed a great admiration, and of whom he possessed a portrait. He married second, on 18 August 1787, Alicia (d. 1808), widow of John George Felton, inspector-general of customs for the Leeward Islands, and daughter of Charles Hayes, of Chelsea. He had no children with either wife.

Heard, who was renowned for his 'urbanity of manners' and 'habitual cheerfulness' (*GM*), remained in vigorous health until the last years of his life. He proclaimed the accession of George IV in January 1820, but deputed the work of organizing the coronation to Clarenceux king of arms. He died in the College of Arms on 29 April 1822 and, at his particular request, was buried in St George's Chapel, Windsor, behind the altar. D. V. WHITE

Sources A. Wagner, *Heralds of England: a history of the office and College of Arms* (1967), 425–38, 452–6 · *GM*, 1st ser., 92/1 (1822), 466–7 · *DNB* · registered pedigree, Coll. Arms

Archives Chapter Library, Windsor, notes relating to Garter charters · Coll. Arms, collections · priv. coll., notes on heraldry · Yale U., Beinecke L., notebooks, incl. brief autobiographical notes | Bodl. Oxf., corresp. with William Beckford; corresp. with J. C. Brooke

Likenesses A. W. Devis, oils, 1819, Coll. Arms · C. Turner, mezzotint (after portrait by A. W. Devis, 1819), BM, NPG; repro. in Wagner, *Heralds*

Heard, William (*fl.* 1771–1777), playwright and poet, was the son of a London bookseller. He received a medical education but took to writing for the stage, perhaps influenced by his marriage on 25 May 1771 to the actress and dancer Ann Madden (1750–1797). His first publication was *The Tryal of Dramatic Genius: a Poem*, which discusses the merits and demerits of contemporary playwrights. It appeared anonymously in 1772 together with 'miscellaneous pieces' of verse; one of these is a 'Just Character' of his book-loving father and another a purportedly autobiographical celebration of 'Conjugal Happiness'. Heard wrote a comedy in two acts, *The Snuff Box, or, A Trip to Bath*, performed as an afterpiece at the Haymarket in 1775 and published in the same year. At about this time his daughter, Elizabeth, was born; she would later become a successful actress. Heard's musical drama *Valentine's Day* was performed only once, at Drury Lane, on 23 March 1776. According to the *Westminster Magazine* it 'met with rather an unfavourable reception' (Stone, 3.1963), and was published anonymously.

Heard died at the age of thirty-four, probably by early 1778. He was alive in December 1777, for he wrote a poem praising Hannah More's play *Percy*, first performed in that month. His final publication, *A Sentimental Journey to Bath, Bristol, and their Environs: a Descriptive Poem* (1778), is fulsomely dedicated to More, whom the title poem describes visiting near Bristol and of whose friendship it boasts. She is addressed admiringly in several poems in the collection, which may well have appeared posthumously. It was published by subscription, perhaps to benefit Heard's widow and child.   JOHN MULLAN

Sources Highfill, Burnim & Langhans, *BDA* · *ESTC* · W. Heard, *A sentimental journey to Bath, Bristol, and their environs: a descriptive poem* (1778) · W. Heard, *The tryal of dramatic genius* (1772) · *Critical Review*, 34 (1772) · G. W. Stone, ed., *The London stage, 1660–1800*, pt 4: 1747–1776 (1962)

Heard, William Theodore (1884–1973), cardinal, was born on 24 February 1884 at The Lodge, Fettes College, Edinburgh, the son of William Augustus Heard and his wife, Elizabeth Tamar Burt. His father, from a family originating in Forres, Moray, was headmaster of Fettes, where Heard spent all his early life. His mother was not a Scot but a Lancastrian. She died when her son was only four years old, leaving the father to bring up his son in the manner in which he had been brought up a generation earlier. This included stern discipline and being dressed in old-fashioned clothes.

Heard went on to Balliol College, Oxford, where he went dancing several times a week, became a rowing blue in the boat race of 1907, and joined reading parties at 'Slipper' Urquhart's chalet in the Alps. After obtaining a third in law, he was articled to a legal firm in London and admitted as a solicitor in 1910. The work included tying public houses to breweries, in the course of which he discovered the poverty of youngsters in the East End and joined with the Benedictines in running a club project. He lived with them and after deciding to become a Roman Catholic was received by Father Stanislas St John at Farm Street in the same year. He felt the vocation to go further and offered himself for priestly training to Bishop Amigo of Southwark. He went to Rome and chose the English College rather than the Beda, which took mature students, because he wanted a thorough exposure to the formation. He was still reserved, and it was said 'Heard's breakfast always consisted of black coffee and a frown' (private information). He was ordained, after a course of theology at the Pontifical Gregorian University, in 1918 at the Lateran basilica. He obtained doctorates in theology and

canon law. His father paid the fees. Heard then served as a priest at the Most Holy Trinity parish, Dockhead, Bermondsey, where he remained until 1927.

In 1926 a vacancy appeared on the Sacred Roman Rota, which acts as a court of appeal in marriage cases, and Heard was asked to fill it. He was made a domestic prelate and took up residence in Rome where he was to remain for the rest of his life, for the most part at the English College. As well as being a judge on the Rota, of which he became dean in 1958, he worked at the Sacred Congregation of Rites and was concerned with the canonization of John Fisher and Thomas More and later with the beatification of the English and Welsh martyrs which took place in 1970. He liked to work on marriage annulments in the morning and canonizations in the afternoon, because they were less depressing and even the failed candidates had tried hard. He was also on the pontifical commission for interpreting the code of canon law. It was well known that Heard was consulted by Pope Pius XII as someone who would speak his mind without concern for appearances of any kind, and a number of cardinals were thought to be more than a little frightened of him.

Heard was a stickler for correctness: his motto was *Recte et sapienter*. At the same time he was endlessly accessible to generations of students at the college, and always available for confession before meditation in the morning. It was consoling to know that in his book it was impossible to commit a grave sin if the sirocco was blowing. Heard used especially to enjoy going out to stay at the college villa at Palazzola in the Alban hills in the summer holiday and being at the centre of a group on the terrace. He could talk entertainingly, with common sense disguised as eccentricity, on a variety of subjects from dental surgery to the history of cheese. However, a rock-like integrity was at the base of his remarks.

Late in 1959 Heard had a serious operation, and was too ill to conduct business. During this time a Vatican monsignor called at the college and insisted on speaking with him despite every discouragement. It turned out to be Pope John's special messenger, to tell him of the intention to make him a cardinal. Heard broke down and wept. His health improved in time for him to take charge in June of his titular church of St Theodore.

Heard was made cardinal-protector of the English College in 1961, but this only worsened his relationship with Cardinal Godfrey of Westminster, who had previously been rector of the college. At the Second Vatican Council Heard was very much a member of the curial conservative party. He was a member of the central preparatory commission, but it was not in his nature to take much of a public role in the discussions. He went home to Scotland each summer. He was made an honorary fellow of Balliol College, Oxford. He died on 16 September 1973 at San Stefano Rotondo and was buried three days later in the campo Verano in Rome.   TOM CURTIS-HAYWARD

Sources C. Burns, 'His Eminence Cardinal William Theodore Heard', *Venerabile*, 26/1 (1973), 7–14 · *The Times* (17 Sept 1973) · *WWW* · C. Longley, *The Warlock archive* (2000) · A. Kenny, *A path from Rome* (1985) · *CGPLA Eng. & Wales* (1974)

Likenesses D. Hill, oils, Balliol Oxf. • oils, English College, Rome, Italy • photograph, English College, Rome
Wealth at death £2656: probate, 1 March 1974, *CGPLA Eng. & Wales*

Hearder, Jonathan Nash (1809–1876), electrical engineer, was born on 24 December 1809 at Plymouth, Devon, the eldest son of Jonathan Hearder (1775–1838) and Mary Hannah Parry. He married on 27 October 1837 Susan Plimsaul; she died in 1839. On 21 January 1840 he married his cousin Joanna Sleep Hearder (1809–1887); they had five children. He became interested in science at an early age. He began a career as a schoolmaster, devoting his spare time to science, and he was the first in Plymouth to include science as a school subject. At sixteen he gave his first course of lectures at the Plymouth Mechanics' Institute, where he showed an electric telegraph he had invented. He became well known as a lecturer in the west of England.

At the age of twenty-three Hearder was blinded while experimenting with explosive compounds. His school closed and he turned briefly to music as a profession. In 1838 his father died and he succeeded to the business of making umbrellas and fishing tackle, to which he added the manufacture of gas stoves and electrical engineering. He had a long association with Sir William Snow Harris in his research into lightning conductors. He did important work in the development of the induction coil, attributed to Ruhmkorff, and his son later vouched that he had personally conducted his father to London to demonstrate his coil to Michael Faraday two years before Ruhmkorff produced his coil. About 1850 he was asked to advise on the Atlantic cable and proposed several improvements including the use of gutta percha as an insulator.

He was an active member of the Devonshire Association and the Royal Polytechnic Society and he gave no fewer than fifty-one lectures to the Plymouth Institution. About 1871 the degrees of PhD and DSc were said to have been conferred upon him, though it is not known by which institution. He died of a paralytic attack at 13 Princess Square, Plymouth, on 16 July 1876, and was buried at Ford Park, Plymouth.   IAN G. HEARDER

Sources W. Harpley, *Report and Transactions of the Devonshire Association*, 9 (1877), 55–60 • S. E. Monk, *Annual Report and Transactions of the Plymouth Institution and Devon and Cornwall Natural History Society*, 17 (1937) • *Western Morning News* (17 July 1876) • *South Devon Monthly Museum* [7 vols.] (1833–6) • private information (2004) • m. certs. • d. cert.
Archives Athenaeum, Plymouth • priv. coll., family MSS • Sci. Mus.
Likenesses Heath & Bullingham, cabinet photograph, priv. coll. • oils; formerly in Plymouth Athenaeum; destroyed in the Blitz, 1941 • photograph (after T. H. Williams), priv. coll. • photographs, priv. coll.
Wealth at death under £1500: probate, 2 May 1878, *CGPLA Eng. & Wales*

Hearle, Francis Trounson (1886–1965), aircraft manufacturer, was born at West End Terrace, Penryn, Cornwall, on 12 September 1886, the second child of James Hearle, a dealer in agricultural machinery, and his wife, Helen Trounson. After his education at Trevethan grammar school in Falmouth, he was apprenticed to a local marine engineer, Cox's. In 1907 he left Cornwall to work in north-east London for two bus companies, the Vanguard and the London General. Here he became a friend of another bus company engineer, Geoffrey de Havilland.

De Havilland was enthused by the pioneering flights of the Wright brothers, and although reputed never to have seen an aircraft, he persuaded his grandfather to lend him money to build one. He paid Hearle to join him and the two men attempted to construct the framework in a small workshop in Fulham while de Havilland's new wife sewed the fabric cover. Taken apart for transporting, the aeroplane was reassembled on the Newbury downs near de Havilland's home and made its first flight, crashing after 30 yards. The two men salvaged the wreckage and built a second machine with the same engine which flew in September 1910; de Havilland was at the controls and Hearle became his first passenger. The aircraft was bought by the Royal Aircraft Factory at Farnborough, which hired de Havilland as a designer and Hearle as a mechanic.

In 1912 they parted company when Hearle joined the Deperdussin Company building planes to a French design in Highgate, and after the company failed, the Vickers Company at Erith constructing the Gunbus. In 1915 Vickers asked him to set up an aircraft factory on the site of an old motor works at Weybridge which was to become the centre of the company's aircraft operations. However, Hearle had stayed close to de Havilland, marrying his radical sister, Ione (*d*. 1953) in 1914, and in 1917 resumed his professional partnership with him at the Aircraft Manufacturing Company, where the DH4, a general purpose biplane which had impressed the American military, was being constructed. Hearle took over the experimental department and built prototypes.

The company closed in 1920 but de Havilland, Hearle, and three others formed the De Havilland Aircraft Company that September in Edgware. Starting as works manager, Hearle became general manager in 1927 and took over as managing director in 1938. The company prospered with the success of the 1925 Tiger Moth, a simple, sturdy aircraft which could claim to be the first practical light aeroplane. At £650 it cost less than some motor cars. Over 7000 were sold in seven years and Hearle encouraged the spread of subsidiary companies throughout the former British empire. He was an evangelist for commercial aviation, urging the government to emulate other countries in subsidizing aircraft purchase.

Hearle's management style emphasized team building, with consultative systems and active provision of sports and social clubs. Known to everyone as Daddy Hearle, his friendly good humour coupled with a disciplined firmness encouraged good performance. His enthusiasm for training the young inspired the De Havilland Aeronautical Technical Training School, through which 2900 apprentices had passed by the time Hearle retired. He introduced the American Hamilton propeller in 1934 and De Havillands constructed a 'shadow' factory for production near Bolton, which turned out most of the RAF's propellers in the Second World War. Hearle was largely responsible for the company's production during the war, which amounted to about 12,000 aircraft, nearly half Mosquitos, the highly successful fast light bomber which had been developed using the specialized wooden carapace construction de Havilland had pioneered for a pre-war airliner.

Hearle retired as full-time managing director in 1944 but returned as chairman from 1950 to 1954, remaining on the board until 1956. He was made CBE in the 1950 birthday honours. He and his wife had one son, Patrick Prideaux. Hearle died at his home, Shepherds, Hartsbourne Road, Bushey Heath, Hertfordshire, on 1 September 1965, just a few weeks after de Havilland.   MARTIN ADENEY

Sources C. M. Sharp, *D. H.: an outline of de Havilland history* (1960) · G. de Havilland, *Sky fever: the autobiography of Sir Geoffrey de Havilland* (1961) · d. cert. · C. Martin Sharp, 'Hearle, Francis Trounson', *DBB*
Likenesses Y. Karsh, photographs, 1950–59, British Aerospace Aircraft Group, Hatfield, Hertfordshire · photographs, British Aerospace Aircraft Group, Hatfield, Hertfordshire
Wealth at death £43,526: probate, 15 Nov 1965, *CGPLA Eng. & Wales*

Hearn, (Patricio) Lafcadio Carlos [Yakumo Koizumi]

(1850–1904), author and translator, was born on the Ionian island of Santa Maura, Greece, on 27 June 1850, the eldest surviving child of Surgeon-Major Charles Bush Hearn (*d.* 1866), later of the East India Company, and his first wife, Rosa Antonia Cassimati. The marriage, ever turbulent, failed when Hearn was four, and the boy, abandoned by his parents, spent a troubled childhood in Dublin in the company of Sarah Brenane, his father's aunt. Because of Brenane, who longed for her nephew to become a Roman Catholic priest, Hearn was educated in Jesuit seminaries in Paris and Yvetot, France, as well as at St Cuthbert's College, Ushaw, near Durham, where he lost one of his eyes to schoolboy bullying.

In 1869, when Hearn was nineteen, Brenane was swindled out of her fortune and she cut Hearn adrift. For the next several years he washed dishes and lived in cardboard boxes on the streets of London, New York, and Cincinnati, comparing his life (as Edmund Gosse was to do after him) to Thomas De Quincey's *Confessions of an English Opium-Eater*. Then, in 1873, Hearn got his big break as a newspaper man, first as a typesetter and then as Old Semi-Colon on the *Cincinnati Enquirer*. He quickly achieved notoriety for grisly depictions of death—he once plunged his fingers into the boiling brains of a corpse, he ice-skated on frozen gore, and he drank blood at the abattoirs when that craze had fallen on the people of Cincinnati. But Hearn's popularity as a slaughter-house journalist had little effect on his finances, and his existence was beset by starvation and disease as he migrated from Cincinnati to New Orleans and the West Indies (possibly even taking the voodoo queen, Marie Laveau, as his lover, after a failed marriage to Althea Foley, a cook and former slave). His first stabs at literature, written during this period, were lurid and over-coloured, such as his translation of Gautier, entitled *Cleopatra's Nights and other Fantastic Romances* (1882), and his original volumes of short stories, *Stray Leaves from Strange Literature* (1884) and *Some Chinese Ghosts*

(1887). But the tone of these writings reveals Hearn's growing obsession with the East, which, he said, 'perfumed my mind as with the incense of a strangely new and beautiful worship' (Hearn to W. D. O'Connor, 1883, Wetmore, 1.291).

As a result, in 1890, when Hearn got the chance to go to Japan as a journalist working for *Harper's Weekly*, the experience was profound. Within a week of landing in Yokohama, on 4 April 1890, Hearn quit *Harper's* and found work as an English teacher in the tiny coastal town of Matsue, where, in 1891, he married Setsu Koizumi, daughter of a samurai, converted to Buddhism, and, in 1896, gave up his British passport to become Yakumo Koizumi, a Japanese citizen. For the next fifteen years Hearn specialized as a Western interpreter of Japan, publishing thirteen volumes composed in the Japanese *zuihitsu* style (miscellaneous essays which follow the idiosyncratic flow of the pen). Merging folk superstitions, Buddhist and Shinto philosophy, and ancient stories within his own fleeting impressions, Hearn's project was to present not himself to his readers but the beauties of an 'authentic' Japanese literature. Among his works, published both in London and Boston, were *Glimpses of an Unfamiliar Japan* (1894), *Gleanings in Buddha-Fields* (1897), *Exotics and Retrospectives* (1898), *Kotto: being Japanese Curios with Sundry Cobwebs* (1902), and *Kwaidan: Stories and Studies of Strange Things* (1904). Only *Japan: an Attempt at Interpretation* (1904) had anything analytical about it, while in each book his passionate and sometimes mystical prose so glorified Japan that Hearn has remained a favoured author among the Japanese. Hearn also held a prestigious lectureship in English at the Imperial University of Tokyo from 1896 to 1903. He seems to have been universally beloved by his students, who remembered him as gentle and affectionate, devoid of the anger and paranoia that so upset his human relationships in the West, though partial blindness and chronic illness continued to plague him.

On 26 September 1904, at his *yashiki* in Okubo, Toyko, Hearn died from a heart attack, surrounded by his wife and children—Kazuo, Iwao, Kiyoshi, and Suzuko. He was buried in Tokyo's Zoshigaya Buddhist cemetery in a ceremony attended by more than 200 Japanese. A century after his death, Hearn's popularity is still evident in Japan's wealth of Hearn museums and other 'Hearniana'. His stories are still used to teach children English, and *Kwaidan* was made into a film by the Japanese director Masaki Kobayashi, winner at the Cannes Film Festival in 1965. Wrote Yone Noguchi, the celebrated Japanese poet, 'To denounce Hearn is the same thing as a denunciation of Japan. Lafcadio Hearn was as Japanese as haiku' (Noguchi, 20).   KATHARINE CHUBBUCK

Sources J. Cott, *Wandering ghost: the odyssey of Lafcadio Hearn* (1991) · E. B. Wetmore, ed., *The life and letters of Lafcadio Hearn*, 2 vols. (1906) · E. Gosse, 'Lafcadio Hearn', *Silhouettes* (1925), 219–28 · Y. Noguchi, *Lafcadio Hearn in Japan* (1910) · N. Kennard, *Lafcadio Hearn: his life and works* (1911) · C. Dawson, *Lafcadio Hearn and the vision of Japan* (1992) · Y. Hasegawa, *A walk in Kunamoto: the life and times of Setsu Koizumi, Lafcadio Hearn's Japanese wife* (1997) · K. Koizumi, *Father and I* (1935) · P. Murray, *A fantastic journey: the life and*

literature of Lafcadio Hearn (1993) • S. Koizumi, *Lafcadio Hearn's Japanese wife* (1988) • K. Chubbuck, 'Empire of the spirit: the East, religion and romanticism in the works of some nineteenth-century travel writers', DPhil diss., U. Oxf., 1998
Archives Cincinnati Public Library, Ohio • Col. U. • Harvard U. • L. Cong. • Tulane University, New Orleans • University of Kobe • University of Matsue • University of Tokyo • University of Virginia, Charlottesville
Likenesses photographs, repro. in Wetmore, ed., *Life and letters* • photographs, Tulane University, New Orleans

Hearn, Mary Anne [*pseud.* Marianne Farningham] (1834–1909), religious writer, was born on 17 December 1834 at Farningham, Kent, the eldest child of Joseph Hearn, a small tradesman and village postmaster, and his wife, Rebecca Bowers, the daughter of a paper maker and preacher. Her devout parents, who attended a local (Particular) Baptist church at Eynsford, taught her to read the Bible by the age of six. Her education was mainly informal, although she attended the British and Foreign Society School at Eynsford until her mother's death in 1846, after which she spent most of her time housekeeping. At the age of fourteen she officially joined the (Strict) Baptist church at Eynsford, and at the same time began submitting verses to religious publications. From 1852 to 1853 she taught at Durdham Down School in Bristol, but was called back to Farningham by the death of her sister Rebecca. In 1857 the Baptist minister at Eynsford, Jonathan Whittemore, established a new periodical called the *Christian World*; he invited her to contribute, suggesting the pseudonym of Marianne Farningham, and a verse by her appeared in the first number of the magazine on 9 April. She became a regular contributor of both poetry and prose sketches to this paper, and its companion, also established by Whittemore (in 1860), the *Sunday School Times and Home Educator*. In the same year she published a collection of her poems in *Lays and Lyrics of the Blessed Life*.

In 1857 Mary Anne Hearn took a post as a teacher in Gravesend; here she made a friend who invited her to join her in establishing a school at Northampton. Hearn was the headmistress of the infant department of the British School from 1859 to 1867, before retiring to devote herself entirely to writing. In spring 1867 she was persuaded to teach a Sunday school class of young women, to whom she became much attached. The class expanded, and in 1887 a classroom was donated. In 1885 she was elected to the Northampton school board, on which she served for six years. In 1887 she gave a talk at the Sunday School Union, which was subsequently published as *Will you Take it?* (1887); this was the first of many lectures which she gave over the course of the next six or seven years. She also wrote several biographies, including *Grace Darling* (1876).

In January 1885 Mary Anne Hearn became the editor of the *Sunday School Times*. She contributed two serial stories to the paper, as well as many lesser pieces. She was a keen supporter of the Salvation Army and the temperance movement and, after hearing Benjamin Waugh relating incidents of parental cruelty, she gave her reluctant approval to the Royal Society for the Prevention of Cruelty to Children. The proceeds of her lecturing allowed her to

Mary Anne Hearn [Marianne Farningham] (1834–1909), by T. W. Hunt

buy a house in Northampton, but from the 1890s she also rented a cottage at Barmouth, where she spent an increasingly large amount of her time. In 1901 she gave up teaching her class, but continued to write, publishing her autobiography, *A Working Woman's Life* (1907), among other works. She died at Barmouth on 16 March 1909, and was buried at Northampton on 19 March. She never married, although she was briefly engaged in the 1860s. Her appearance was decidedly plain: photographs show a woman with a round face, a large nose, and slightly protruding teeth. She feared that a portrait which appeared in the *School Sunday Times* to celebrate her new editorship would 'frighten away half the subscribers at one fell blow' (Farningham, 192).

Mary Anne Hearn wrote with great speed and facility, often working against time to meet a deadline: 'Watching and Waiting for Me', one of her most popular hymns, was composed in an hour to catch the post (it was later included in I. D. Sankey's *Sacred Songs and Solos*). Her verse was too plentiful to be uniformly good, but several of her poems, like 'The Night Light' from *Lays and Lyrics*, are engagingly direct; many, such as 'When the grass was green' from *Songs of Sunshine* (1878), show a keen appreciation of nature. Some of her longer poems were popular at recitations. Her large literary output, coupled with her editorial work, made her one of the most influential women members of the nineteenth-century Baptist church.

ROSEMARY MITCHELL

Sources M. Farningham [M. A. Hearn], *A working woman's life* (1907) • 'Death of Marianne Farningham', *Christian World* (18 March

1909), suppl., 23 • W. Glandwr-Morgan, *Marianne Farningham in her Welsh home* (1910) • J. Julian, ed., *A dictionary of hymnology*, rev. edn (1907); repr. in 2 vols. (1957) • *DNB*

Likenesses photograph, *c*.1874, repr. in Farningham, *A working woman's life*, facing p. 138 • photogravure, *c*.1907, repr. in Farningham, *A working woman's life* • T. W. Hunt, stipple and line print, NPG [*see illus.*]

Wealth at death £602 18*s*. 11*d*.: probate, 22 May 1909, *CGPLA Eng. & Wales*

Hearn, William Edward (1826–1888), legal and economic writer, was born on 21 April 1826 at Belturbet, co. Cavan, the second son of the Revd William Edward Hearn (*d*. 1855), vicar of Killargue, co. Leitrim, and his wife, Henrietta Alicia, *née* Reynolds. He was educated at Portora Royal School, Enniskillen, and entered Trinity College, Dublin, in 1842, receiving his BA in 1847, and MA and LLD degrees in 1863. He was married twice: first in Dublin in 1847 to Rose (*d*. 1877), daughter of the Revd W. J. H. Le Fanu; and second in Melbourne in 1878 to Isabel, daughter of Major W. G. St Clair. With his first wife he had six children; his second marriage was childless.

Hearn was professor of Greek in Queen's College, Galway, from 1849 to 1854 when he was nominated as the first professor of modern history, modern literature, logic, and political economy in the new university of Melbourne. He was called to the Irish bar in 1853, and to the bar of Victoria in 1860. On the reorganization of the school of law in 1873 he resigned his professorship and became dean of the faculty of law. From May to October 1886 he was chancellor of the university.

In 1878, after standing unsuccessfully on three previous occasions, Hearn was elected to represent the central province of Victoria in the legislative council. While in parliament he devoted his energies mainly to codification of the law. In 1879 he introduced the Duties of the People Bill, a code of criminal law; in 1881 the Law of Obligations Bill, a code of duties and rights as between subject and subject; in 1884 the Substantive General Law Consolidation Bill. All these bills were in 1887 referred to a joint select committee of both houses for report, and their adoption was recommended, but owing to Hearn's ill health they were dropped for the time being.

Hearn was a prominent member of the Church of England, being chancellor of the diocese of Melbourne from 1877 to 1888, and active in the affairs of Trinity College, the Anglican residential college of the university. In 1886 he was appointed QC. He died on 23 April 1888; four of his children survived him.

As well as writing on *The Condition of Ireland* (1851) and *Plutology* (1864), Hearn published *The Government of England, its Structure and its Development* (1867). This survey of the British constitution was referred to by Herbert Spencer as a work which helped to graft the theory of evolution on to history. In 1879 Hearn's *Aryan Household, its Structure and its Development* continued in a similar vein, tracing a claimed common institutional heritage shared by nations 'of the Aryan stock'. Hearn also made some contributions to the local press.

James Williams, *rev.* Catherine Pease-Watkin

Sources J. A. La Nauze, 'Hearn, William Edward', *AusDB*, vol. 4 • *The Australasian* (28 April 1888) • *The Athenaeum* (28 April 1888), 535–6 • Holdsworth, *Eng. law*, vol. 15 • *BL cat.* • *CGPLA Eng. & Wales* (1888)

Wealth at death £432 15*s*. 1*d*.: resworn administration with will, April 1890, *CGPLA Eng. & Wales* (1888)

Hearne, Mary [*known as* Mrs Hearne] (*fl.* 1718–1720), novelist, is an obscure figure. She may have lived in London, given the references in her novels to such popular London figures as Delariviere Manley and Aphra Behn, established novelists; Lady Katherine Hyde, duchess of Queensberry, a fashionable socialite; and Sir Samuel Garth, whose unflattering portrait as a panderer in Hearne's work is in contrast to his eminent historical reputation. Hearne's *Lover's Week* (1718) and *The Female Deserters* (1719) were among the first novels by a female author to be published by the maverick publisher Edmund Curll; they were conflated into *Honour, the Victory: and Love, the Prize* in 1720 and were serialized in *Heathcote's Original London Post* in 1724.

Hearne's novels depict the young, middle-class woman's London, from bagnio to banqueting house. In *The Lover's Week* the insouciant Amaryllis finds, in exactly six days, a charming nobleman who will satisfy her merry materialism. In this comic novel Hearne produced one of the very few eighteenth-century works to represent a woman gaining romantic happiness while openly rejecting marriage. The two women in *The Female Deserters* represent the other, more realistic, consequences of defying social norms; Calista is drugged, raped, and impounded in a house by her lover, while Isabella's lover is drugged and deported by his disapproving father. Disgraced, Isabella is reduced to taking a position as Calista's maid. This novel represents an early depiction of the drugged rape of a female victim by a predatory aristocrat, a scenario used in other novels throughout the eighteenth century, most notably in Samuel Richardson's *Clarissa*. Hearne's contribution to the genre of the novel resides in her development of autonomous female characters and her realistic portrayal of their various romantic paths.

Joan Cucinotta Reteshka

Sources J. Reteshka, 'A scholarly edition of Mrs Hearne's *The lover's week* and *The female deserters*', PhD diss., Duquesne University, 1998

Hearne, Samuel (1745–1792), explorer and fur trader, was born 'close to London bridge' (Speck, 'Samuel Hearne'), the only son of Samuel Hearne (1707/8–1748) and Diana Hearne, and younger brother to Sarah. His father was managing engineer of the London Bridge waterworks. After receiving some education at Tucker's School—in Beaminster, Dorset, where his mother's family lived— Hearne joined the Royal Navy in 1756 as servant to Captain Samuel (afterwards Viscount) Hood, with whom he saw action during the Seven Years' War. After leaving the navy in 1763 Hearne joined the Hudson's Bay Company (HBC) in 1766 and was posted to Prince of Wales Fort (at what is now Churchill, Manitoba). Native American reports of copper mines near a northern river prompted the HBC to send an expedition led by a European, for which role Hearne was chosen. His initial two expeditions in 1769 and 1770 proved abortive, the second after some privation.

The third expedition benefited considerably from Hearne's choice of Matonabbee, an Ojibwe chief, to guide the party. Hearne travelled 1300 miles on foot to the Coppermine River. He was the first European to cross the Barren Lands to the Arctic Ocean, and in so doing he disproved the existence of the Strait of Anian, a rumoured north-west passage to China. He was also the first to see and cross Great Slave Lake. At 'Bloody Falls' he unwillingly witnessed the massacre of Inuit by Native Americans of his party. Hearne's achievement was recognized by his appointment in 1774 to establish the first HBC interior post at Fort Cumberland, Saskatchewan, and in 1775 as governor of Prince of Wales's Fort. In 1782 he was forced to surrender this fort to the French under Lapérouse. Hearne re-established trading at Prince of Wales Fort until, his health failing, he retired in 1787 to London, where he died, unmarried, in November 1792. His account of his travels was published in 1795, meeting popular success and translation into five languages. W. J. MILLS

Sources G. Speck, *Samuel Hearne and the northwest passage* (1963) · C. S. Mackinnon, 'Hearne, Samuel', *DCB*, vol. 4 · S. Hearne, *A journey from Prince of Wales's Fort in Hudson's Bay to the northern ocean* (1795) · G. Speck, 'Samuel Hearne (1745–1792)', *Arctic*, 36/1 (1983), 100–01 · *DNB* · R. I. Ruggles, *A country so interesting: the Hudson's Bay Company and two centuries of mapping, 1670–1870* (1991)
Archives BL, journal, Add. MS 59237 [copy] · Hudson's Bay Company, Winnipeg, Canada, archives
Likenesses portrait, Champlain Society, Toronto, Canada; repro. in Speck, *Samuel Hearne*, frontispiece · stipple, BM, NPG; repro. in *European Magazine* (1796)

Thomas Hearne (*bap.* 1678, *d.* 1735), by George Vertue, 1723 (after Peter Tillemans)

Hearne, Thomas (*bap.* 1678, *d.* 1735), antiquary and diarist, was born in Little Field Green in the parish of White Waltham, Berkshire, where he was baptized on 11 July 1678. He was the second son of George Hearne (1648–1723), parish clerk of White Waltham, and his first wife, Edith Wise (*d.* 1699), daughter of Thomas Wise of Shottesbrooke and Edith Hearne. A studious boy with serious interests, Hearne was befriended by the Jacobite squire Francis Cherry, who financed his education. In 1692 he was sent to the free school of Bray near Windsor while also receiving private tutoring in classical philology from Cherry and (from 1694) from Cherry's close friend the nonjuring theologian Henry Dodwell. Cherry took the young Hearne into his house in 1695 and sent him to Oxford, where Hearne matriculated from St Edmund Hall on 5 December that year. Hearne took up residence in the hall in 1696 and lived there all his life. He studied classical history, philology, and geography and graduated BA in 1699 and MA in 1703. He gained a reputation as an eager and reliable student and did transcription work for Dodwell and such Oxford scholars as John Mill (working on his edition of the New Testament) and John Ernest Grabe.

Early career at Oxford Hearne started an impressive career at the Bodleian Library when in 1701 he was appointed library assistant (or janitor) through John Hudson, the newly appointed librarian. He was set to work on the planned new edition of Thomas Hyde's 1674 Bodleian catalogue of printed books. Hearne revised the catalogue and compiled an appendix which was to be published separately with the new catalogue. Meanwhile he reviewed the library's catalogues of the manuscripts and the coin collections. He was disappointed when Hudson delayed and finally gave up plans to publish a new catalogue of books. Unfortunately, when the librarian Robert Fysher's Bodleian catalogue was finally published in 1738, he failed to give credit to Hearne's work. Hearne would become second librarian in 1712 and during his Bodleian years developed into one of the 'pioneers of bibliographical methodology' (Birrell, 37) and a scholar of an extensive and minute erudition.

Initially the partnership with Hudson was a success. Both Hudson and Hearne worked to add to the Bodleian's collections at a time when the Licensing Act was not in effect. Under Hudson, Hearne published his first book, *Reliquiae Bodleianae* (1703), an edition of the correspondence of the library's founder, Sir Thomas Bodley, with his first librarian, Thomas James. Hearne edited an expanded edition of De Vallemont's *Ductor historicus* (1704–5) for the publisher Timothy Childe, volume 2 of which was written by Hearne and based on his historical–antiquarian studies in the library. Hudson also financially supported Hearne's generally well-received classical editions of Pliny the younger (1703), Eutropius (1703), Justin (1705), and Livy (1708).

In those years Hearne also supported the work of others. Together with the antiquary and library agent John Bagford, he worked on Bagford's project of a history of printing. Though Bagford never finished the work, much of the bibliographical research was used by others later. Work on the early Chaucer editions by Hearne and Bagford for John Urry of Christ Church eventually led to the edition by William and Timothy Thomas of Chaucer's works (1721). Hearne undertook bibliographical research for many visiting scholars, among them Jeremy Collier and Bishop Francis Atterbury. He contributed to Thomas Smith's edition of the letters of St Ignatius (1709), Joshua Barnes's edition of Homer (1711), and Cuthbert Constable's work on Abraham Woodhead (published in 1736).

High-principled antiquary Hearne arrived in Oxford with nonjuring principles imbibed from his mentors and, though he took the oaths on entering the university—he even wrote a youthful 'Vindication of those who take the oaths' for Cherry—he spent much of his time defending Dodwell's controversial writings on theology and the nonjuring position. However, his ties to the Shottesbrooke nonjurors were mostly emotional. The strongest formative influence was the nonjuror scholar Thomas Smith of Magdalen College. From 1703 until Smith's death in 1710 the two corresponded intensively on a variety of subjects, from politics and religion to English history, book history, antiquarianism, and Oxford academia. Because Smith left Hearne his manuscripts, his scholarship remained an important inspiration to Hearne in his publishing career.

Not surprisingly, the career of a nonjuror and Jacobite did not run smoothly: several nonjurors before Hearne had been deprived of their offices (among them his mentors Dodwell and Smith). Even though the general climate at Oxford was conservative, with a Jacobite chancellor at the time of the Jacobite rising of 1715, the university in Hanoverian times needed to assure the government of its loyalty. Hearne was interested in a university career only if this did not require taking the oaths. In 1707 he had been offered the chaplaincy of Corpus Christi College, and soon after of All Souls College, but Hudson objected to Hearne's taking on more responsibilities. He was a candidate for the position of beadle of divinity in 1709 but stepped down in favour of his older tory friend Edward Lhuyd. Other positions he was offered later—among them the librarianship of the Bodleian Library—he turned down because of the oaths.

Hearne was involved in high-church and nonjuring projects in defence of the Church of England and episcopacy and against presbyterianism and deism. He helped research Hilkiah Bedford's answer to *Priestcraft in Perfection* (1709) by the deist Anthony Collins and proofread Smith's edition of Ignatius, published the same year. Also in 1709 Hearne himself published Sir John Spelman's *Life of Aelfred the Great*, together with an antiquarian essay on a Roman inscription found at Bath. Though he had originally intended to include some of Spelman's royalist pamphlets, he finally decided against it for political reasons. In 1710 Dodwell proclaimed the end of the nonjuring schism and returned to the Anglican church. After some deliberations Hearne decided not to follow Dodwell and Cherry but to join the remaining sectarian group of nonjurors led by George Hickes.

The affairs of post-revolution England as well as of Hearne's turbulent personal life and career are recorded in great detail in his wide correspondence with friends and in his series of 145 octavo diary volumes which he entitled his 'Remarks and collections' (1705–35). His reputation today rests especially on these diaries, which are filled with detailed information about books and manuscripts, contemporary scholarship, and intellectual history. They also contain lively if politically prejudiced portraits of the lives of late seventeenth- and early eighteenth-century scholars and antiquaries and autobiographical pieces. Though less accessible today (as workbooks, the diaries are also filled with scholarly and bibliographical detail) than the more urbane diaries of Evelyn and Pepys, Hearne's volumes are still rewarding when read entire.

After the success of Hearne's edition of Livy (1708), Hudson put him on an edition of Cicero's works, but Hearne was loath to undertake it. From the beginning Hearne's real interests were English history and the antiquities of Roman and pre-Reformation Britain. He finally gave up Cicero in favour of his historical and antiquarian studies. His 'Account of some antiquities between Oxford and Windsor' in the *Monthly Miscellany* (1708–9) was followed by his publication in 1710–12 of the *Itinerary* of the Tudor antiquary John Leland (9 vols.). Hearne's circle of antiquary friends was growing steadily and some contributed work to the *Itinerary* and to Hearne's subsequent edition of Leland's other published and unpublished works in *Collectanea* (5 vols.) in 1715. Among these contributions were John Bagford's essay on London antiquities, Roger Gale's study of the Roman highways, Browne Willis on the parliamentary abbeys, John Woodward on Roman urns, and Ralph Thoresby and Richard Richardson on antiquities found in Yorkshire. Hearne himself contributed an essay on a Roman pavement found at Stonesfield, Oxfordshire. Though less ambitious than the great projects of Edmund Gibson's edition of Camden's *Britannia* and George Hickes's *Thesaurus*, Hearne's volumes give a representative impression of antiquarian studies in the Augustan age.

Problems, 1709–1717 Hearne met increasing opposition from the university authorities, both the curators of the Bodleian Library and the delegates of the university press. In 1709 Arthur Charlett, master of University College and one of the delegates of the university press, had attempted to suppress Hearne's edition of Spelman's *Aelfred*, but without success. The reasons for Charlett's objecting to the book may have had to do with Hearne's nonjuror associations—Charlett's relations with the nonjurors Dodwell, Hickes, and Smith all proved ambivalent. There was opposition from University College as well. William Smith rightly opposed Hearne on his stubbornly held ideas about the myth of the origins and foundation of the college and the university by King Alfred. Smith published the college's *Annals* in 1728, with an attack on Hearne. In 1713 Hearne as keeper of the antiquarian collections of the anatomy school showed a visiting coin collector an engraved portrait of the Pretender (James Francis Edward Stuart). The collector proved to be an Irish whig and the incident was reported in the press. Most problematic for the university, however, in the existing politicized atmosphere, were Hearne's embarrassing and outspoken reflections in his publications about nonjurism, nonjurors, and personalities deemed by Hearne to be enemies of the post-Restoration state and church. Such reflections in a catalogue of Dodwell's works added to Dodwell's *De parma equestri Woodwardiana dissertatio* (1713) led to the suppression of the edition.

In 1715 Hearne published at the Sheldonian Theatre press a facsimile edition of the *Acta apostolorum* from a famous manuscript left to the Bodleian Library by Archbishop Laud. In the same year the university's convocation appointed him architypographer of the press and superior beadle of civil law. However, unprecedented measures were taken by the heads of houses (especially Bernard Gardiner and John Baron) to separate the traditionally linked functions, evidently for political and personal reasons. A press assistant was appointed, it seemed as Hearne's replacement, by the delegates of the press. Hearne regarded these measures as against the university's Laudian statutes. He wished to accept only the traditional position of a learned architypographer as described in these statutes, not that of a more practical assistant desired by the delegates. Subsequently, when Hudson argued to the curators that the beadleship was inconsistent with Hearne's position as second librarian, Hearne relinquished the former.

Hearne's relationship with Hudson sadly deteriorated into mutual acrimony as Hudson wished to dissociate himself from Hearne's nonjuring and Jacobite views. Hearne was now also ousted from the position of second librarian, a position he had clung to even though it paid much less than the beadleship. He was literally locked out of the library when Hudson had the locks changed. Hearne considered himself deprived of his position because he had refused to take the Hanoverian oath of allegiance on 23 January 1716, the last day fixed by the new act. He did not resign and held on to his now obsolete keys. The official reason for his dismissal given by the curators was 'neglect of duty'. Further tensions followed the publications of *Collectanea*, John Rouse's *Historia regum Angliae*, and William Roper's *Life of Thomas More*: Hearne was forbidden the use of the university imprint and new measures also forbade him to print from Bodleian manuscripts. From 1716 he managed to make a living for himself as a private publisher, publishing books by subscription in a regular series. From now on he would obtain access to historical manuscripts mainly from the Ashmolean Museum, the Cottonian and Harleian libraries, Trinity College, Cambridge, and the College of Arms through his growing circle of friends.

With the publication of William Camden's *Annales rerum Anglicarum et Hibernicarum regnante Elizabetha* in 1717, a troubled period began which was to last for about a year and a half and caused Hearne to despair of continuing his publishing career at Oxford. The most complete edition of Camden's *Annals*, for which Hearne used Camden's notes (MS Smith 2), was suppressed and the printing that had

started for his next publication, William of Newburgh's chronicle, was stopped (a move to London in order to continue printing there almost followed, but as always Hearne was reluctant to leave his alma mater). Hearne was summoned to appear before the vice-chancellor's court because of comments in the preface to Camden's *Annals* which appeared to damage the university, and seemed to imply Catholic inclinations. Hearne's patrons—the physician and collector Richard Mead (a whig), John Bridges, John Anstis, and others—did their best to stop the proceedings by influencing the university authorities through prominent tories. Support also came from the Jacobite William King, secretary of the earl of Arran, chancellor of the university. Arran finally ordered the prosecution to be stopped.

An independent publishing career After the prosecution Hearne resumed printing *Guilielmi Neubrigensis historia sive chronica rerum anglicarum* (1719). This was followed by *Thomae Sprotti chronica* in the same year. The next year a series of three publications followed in quick succession: *A Collection of Curious Discourses*, an edition of the papers of the Elizabethan Society of Antiquaries, *Textus Roffensis*, and Robert of Avesbury's chronicle. For some years Hearne also worked on an edition of historical sources for the reign of Charles I. He wrote a preface for the book but was advised not to pursue his pro-Stuart theme by his patrons and advisers, who were wary about what Hearne might say about England's current relations with Spain and the movements of eminent Jacobites. Hearne acquiesced and, with the help of a number of Scottish Jacobite scholars such as the editor Thomas Ruddiman, published instead the Scottish chronicle by John Fordun (1722) without the continuation by Walter Bower. This was followed by the Saxon Hemming's *Chartulary* (1723). Hearne and a considerable number of antiquary friends were much involved with materials related to Glastonbury Abbey. In 1722 Hearne edited the essay on Glastonbury by the Roman Catholic antiquary Charles Eyston in *The History and Antiquities of Glastonbury*, to be followed by editions of John of Glastonbury's chronicle (1726) and Adam of Domerham's history, together with William of Malmesbury's *De antiquitate Glastoniensis ecclesiae* (1727); all books were filled with additional historical documents relating to the abbey and contained in addition the Saxon poem now known as *The Battle of Maldon* and the extant catalogues of Glastonbury Library.

The study of history, book history, historical romances, early printing, ballads, and other works of pre-Reformation traditional literature were scholarly pursuits that Hearne shared with many of his readers. The help of antiquarian book collectors and scholars such as John Anstis, John Bagford, Thomas Baker, Richard Graves, Edward Harley, Thomas and Richard Rawlinson, and Thomas Ward was considerable. These friends played a significant part in publications such as *Robert of Gloucester's Chronicle* (1724) and *Peter Langtoft's Chronicle* (1725) through their many gifts of books and manuscripts and contributions of bibliographical and antiquarian letter-essays, fragments of which were published by Hearne in the glossaries and appendices of these and other volumes. Hearne's bibliographical research also led to new discoveries, for instance of the existence of different textual traditions of Langland's *Pierce the Ploughman* and Chaucer's *Canterbury Tales*. The character of Hearne's private collections has been shown to reflect these friendships and personal interests and convictions.

Historical scholarship today owes its greatest debt to Hearne's accurate editions of the sources of English history: annals, historical biographies, chronicles, and historical documents such as charters, chartularies, catalogues, and lists were published by Hearne in a series of thirty-seven multi-volume publications. Among them was the first English (and the most complete) edition of William of Newburgh's chronicle, followed by editions of the historical writings of Domerham, pseudo-Elmham, the *Liber niger scaccarii* (1728), John Trokelow and Henry of Blaneford (1729), Walter Hemingford (of Guisborough) (1731), Thomas Otterbourne and John Whethamstede (1732), Richard de Morins (1733), and Roger of Howden (1735). Hearne worked in the tradition of historical antiquarianism initiated by Leland and Camden and continued by such editors as Archbishop Matthew Parker, John Joscelyn, Sir Henry Spelman, Bishop John Fell, Thomas Gale, Sir Roger Twysden, and Henry Wharton. His practical concerns about preserving and making available those sources of history not yet in print often merged with ideological concerns: increasingly his choices of additional materials showed a motivation to counter the ongoing formation of a post-Reformation and post-revolution canon of whiggish and anti-Catholic orientation in English history and historiography.

For his series of publications Hearne collaborated with antiquaries who worked as his patrons and agents: Thomas Baker, Hilkiah Bedford, Richard Graves, Richard and Thomas Rawlinson, John Anstis, John Bridges, Richard Mead, and Thomas Tanner (among others) influenced the contents of the books, procured manuscripts as well as subscribers, and supported his work financially. Thus Hearne's publications could be seen as a kind of historical and antiquarian periodical with its own specialized readership. Long and involved prefaces and appendices offered and commented on a great variety of materials (major as well as minor) presented in each volume. Hearne surveyed the work done in the different fields of county history, archaeology, philology, medieval history, bibliography, book history, and historiography. As a textual antiquary he was a provider of materials, who despite his personal shortcomings also knew his scholarly role to be modest: following the advice of Fell and Hickes, he published his manuscripts without editorial emendation. The editors of the Rolls Series were generally appreciative of their predecessor's accuracy and reliability.

Reputation Hearne's difficult personality and outspoken writings about contemporaries and contemporary issues gave him the reputation of an incorrigible, over-confident, naïve, and even cold-hearted person, someone who invited condescension, satire, and ridicule. In 1731 his essay on taking the oaths, written when a student, was published with a hostile preface by John Bilstone and associates mainly from University College. Edmund Curll republished and expanded Bilstone's preface for his *Impartial Memorials* in 1736, after Hearne's death. Non-jurors and antiquaries alike became the butt of satirical jokes by Augustan writers such as Addison and Pope. Alexander Pope's *Dunciad* commemorated Hearne in satirical verses that influenced Curll and others after him who wished to repudiate what they saw as Hearne's useless bookishness and pedantry.

Modern commentators have both praised and denigrated Hearne's personality and his achievements. Generally bibliographers such as Philip Bliss and William Dunn Macray were appreciative of Hearne's detailed knowledge of books and collections. Since the discovery in 1935 of David Casley's transcript of the manuscript of *The Battle of Maldon* from which Hearne printed the poem (the original Cottonian manuscript was lost in the 1731 fire) readers of Saxon and medieval history have found further materials of value in Hearne's books. David Douglas's influential essay gave a fair portrait of Hearne's personality and valued his work in his *English Scholars*, but has often been followed more indiscriminately by later critics. Hearne's *Remarks and Collections* was published, first in a selection by Philip Bliss, then in eleven volumes by the Oxford Historical Society, edited by C. E. Doble, D. W. Rannie, H. E. Salter, and others. The great value of the diaries as a source for such works as Bliss's edition of Wood's *Athenae Oxonienses*, the Victoria county history of Oxfordshire, and the *Dictionary of National Biography* cannot be denied.

Hearne fell ill in 1735 and died, unmarried, in his lodgings at St Edmund Hall on 10 June, possibly of abdominal cancer. He was buried on 14 June, in the graveyard of the parish church of St Peter-in-the-East. His books were sold by Thomas Osborne in 1736 and (ironically, for he had not wished it so) his diaries, correspondence, and manuscript collection went to the Bodleian Library as part of Richard Rawlinson's bequest in 1756. THEODOR HARMSEN

Sources T. Hearne, correspondence, Bodl. Oxf., MSS Rawlinson K (Hearne–Smith) · Bodl. Oxf., MSS Ballard; MSS Cherry; MSS Smith; MSS Rawlinson; MSS Willis; MSS Tanner · *Remarks and collections of Thomas Hearne*, ed. C. E. Doble and others, 11 vols., OHS, 2, 7, 13, 34, 42–3, 48, 50, 65, 67, 72 (1885–1921) · T. H. B. M. Harmsen, *Antiquarianism in the Augustan age: Thomas Hearne, 1678–1735* (2000) · D. C. Douglas, *English scholars, 1660–1730*, 2nd edn (1951) · F. J. M. Korsten, 'Thomas Hearne: the man and his library', *Order and connection*, ed. R. C. Alston (1997) · T. A. Birrell, 'Anthony Wood, John Bagford and Thomas Hearne as bibliographers', *Pioneers in bibliography*, ed. R. Myers and M. Harris (1988), 25–39 · T. Harmsen, 'High-principled antiquarian publishing: the correspondence of Thomas Hearne (1678–1735) and Thomas Smith (1638–1710)', *Lias*, 23 (1996), 69–98 · T. Harmsen, 'Bodleian imbroglios, politics and personalities, 1701–1716: Thomas Hearne, Arthur Charlett and John Hudson', *Neophilologus*, 82/1 (1998), 149–68 · K. Sutherland, 'Byrhtnoth's eighteenth-century context', *The battle of Maldon, AD 991*, ed. D. Scragg (1991) · I. G. Philip, 'Thomas Hearne as a publisher', *Bodleian Library Record*, 3 (1950–51), 146–55 · J. M. Levine, *Dr Woodward's shield: history, science, and satire in Augustan England* (1977), chap. 10 · J. C. Findon, 'The nonjurors and the Church of England, 1689–1716', DPhil diss., U. Oxf., 1978 · W. D. Macray, *Annals of the Bodleian Library, Oxford*, 2nd edn (1890); facs. edn (1984) ·

J. M. Levine, *Humanism and history: origins of modern English historiography* (1987), chap. 4 • J. M. Levine, *The battle of the books: history and literature in the Augustan age* (1991) • S. G. Gillam, 'Thomas Hearne's library', *Bodleian Library Record*, 12 (1985–8), 52–64 • I. G. Philip, 'The genesis of Thomas Hearne's *Ductor Historicus*', *Bodleian Library Record*, 7 (1962–7), 251–64 • S. Briggs, 'Thomas Hearne, Richard Richardson, and the Osmondthick hoard', *Antiquaries Journal*, 58 (1978), 247–59 • H. Carter, *A history of the Oxford University Press*, 1: *To the year 1780* (1975) • [W. Huddesford], ed., *The lives of those eminent antiquaries, John Leland, Thomas Hearne, and Anthony à Wood*, 2 vols. (1772) • *Reliquiae Hearnianae: the remains of Thomas Hearne*, ed. P. Bliss, 2nd edn, 3 vols. (1869) • J. H. Overton, *The nonjurors: their lives, principles, and writings* (1902) • J. M. Bulloch, 'Hearne's first master, the Rev. Patrick Gordon', *N&Q*, 169 (1935), 344–6 • F. Ouvry, *Letters addressed to Thomas Hearne, MA* (1874) • [J. Walker and P. Bliss], eds., *Letters written by eminent persons in the seventeenth and eighteenth centuries*, 2 vols. (1813) • T. Harmsen, 'Letters of learning: a selection from the correspondence of Thomas Hearne and Thomas Smith, 1703–1710', *Lias*, 24 (1997), 37–66 • Wood, *Ath. Oxon.* • R. Easting, 'The middle English "Hearne fragment" of *St Patrick's Purgatory*', *N&Q*, 233 (1988), 436–7 • *DNB*

Archives Bodl. Oxf., collections, diaries, notebooks, and papers; corresp. • Leics. RO, collections relating to Thurnby • Yale U., Beinecke L., papers | BL, letters to Hans Sloane, Sloane MSS 4042–4049 • BL, letters to James West, Lansdowne MS 778 • Bodl. Oxf., letters to George Ballard • Bodl. Oxf., letters to Joshua Barnes • Bodl. Oxf., letters to Hilkiah Bedford • Bodl. Oxf., corresp. with Thomas Carte • Bodl. Oxf., letters to Francis Cherry • Bodl. Oxf., letters to John Murray • Bodl. Oxf., letters to Thomas Rawlinson • Bodl. Oxf., corresp. with Thomas Smith • Bodl. Oxf., letters to Thomas Ward • Bodl. Oxf., letters to Browne Willis • CUL, Baker MSS, MSS Mm. 1. 47 and 48 • NRA, priv. coll., letters to Charles Eyston • priv. coll., letters to John Loveday • W. Yorks. AS, Leeds, Yorkshire Archaeological Society, letters to Cuthbert Constable, MS 47

Likenesses G. Vertue, print, 1723 (after P. Tillemans), BM, NPG [*see illus.*] • G. Vertue, print, BM, NPG; repro. in T. Hearne, *Vindication of the oath of allegiance* (1731)

Wealth at death see *Remarks*, ed. Doble and others; will

Hearne, Thomas (1744–1817), watercolour painter and topographical draughtsman, was born at Marshfield in Gloucestershire on 22 September 1744, the only son of William Hearne (*d.* 1749) and his wife, Prudence (*d.* after 1797). After William Hearne's death his widow and young son moved to Brinkworth in Wiltshire, 5 miles from Malmesbury, where the abbey must have helped to inspire Hearne's interest in Gothic architecture. When he was in his teens Hearne was sent to London to be an apprentice to his uncle, a pastry cook in Maiden Lane; next door was a print shop kept by an engraver called Miller, who probably encouraged Hearne to pursue his artistic inclinations. In 1763 the Society of Arts awarded him a 1 guinea premium for a still life drawing, and 8 guineas the following year for an equestrian subject. From 1765 to 1771 Hearne was indentured to William Woollett, who was considered the finest landscape engraver of his day, but he continued to exhibit landscapes and architectural drawings, and at the end of his apprenticeship he decided to become a draughtsman rather than an engraver. In the spring of 1771 Hearne was introduced to Sir George Beaumont, who was then aged eighteen and who became an important patron. That year Beaumont, Woollett, and Hearne spent six weeks together at the

home of Beaumont's tutor, the Revd Charles Davy, at Henstead in Suffolk.

Later in 1771 Hearne travelled to the Leeward Islands, where he spent three and a half years as draughtsman for Sir Ralph Payne, the newly appointed captain-general and governor-in-chief; his surviving drawings are an almost unique record of colonial life of the period. He never went abroad again. In 1777 Hearne and the engraver William Byrne began a project of recording the historic monuments of Great Britain, entitled *The Antiquities of Great Britain*, which was published in a series of engravings between 1778 and 1806, and subsequently in two volumes. The work was highly influential in promoting the idea that the history and architecture of Britain were as worthy of study as those of Greece and Rome. Hearne was elected to the Society of Antiquaries in 1793. His other engraved work includes illustrations for Fielding's *Joseph Andrews* and Goldsmith's *The Vicar of Wakefield*, and for a series entitled *Rural Sports*.

Hearne travelled extensively within England, Scotland, and Wales. His companions included Beaumont and Joseph Farington, whose diaries are an important source of information about Hearne's life. Among his commissioned works were views of Heveningham Hall in Suffolk, for Sir George Vanneck (1780), and of Downton Castle in Herefordshire, for Richard Payne Knight (1784–6). Hearne sought to create an art comparable to history painting, and his harmonious and atmospheric landscapes mark a considerable advance on earlier topographical drawing. Fine examples include *The Windings of the Forth from Stirling Castle* (*c.*1778; Birmingham Museum and Art Gallery) and *Goodrich Castle on the Wye* (*c.*1794; Paul Mellon collection). His colouring was invariably subdued. According to David Morris, Hearne 'appears to have aimed in his watercolour drawings to have avoided too gross a sensory appeal, in order to elevate his imagery as far as its Academic status allowed'; earlier W. H. Pyne had praised the 'elegance of his chaste pencil' (Morris, 118, 134). The Victoria and Albert Museum, London, has twenty-nine drawings, mostly unsigned.

In all Hearne exhibited forty-two drawings at the Society of Artists, twelve at the Free Society of Artists, and twenty-four at the Royal Academy. Disliking the way in which watercolours were hung by the Royal Academy, however, Hearne did not show there for thirteen years, until the exhibition of 1806; his drawing of that year, *Caister Castle* (V&A), an antiquarian subject surrounded by pastoral scenery, is freer in technique and typical of his later style. One of Hearne's most notable collectors was Dr Thomas Monro, who calculated, in 1810, that £800 of the £3000 that he spent on modern pictures had been for work by Hearne; these drawings were copied at Monro's 'academy' by young artists such as Thomas Girtin and J. M. W. Turner.

A drawing, by Henry Edridge, of Hearne sketching in Ashtead churchyard, in Surrey, depicts him as full-faced and with his receding hair tied back, his hat and cane at one side (1800; V&A). He was a genial but highly fastidious man; in 1816 Beaumont wrote of their forty years of friendship that since they first met 'Hearne has risen daily in my esteem, a man of purer integrity does not exist' (Hardie, 1.175). In his politics Hearne strongly supported the king and the Church of England. By the end of his life his work had been superseded by that of younger and more fashionable painters, whose pictures Hearne frequently disliked: 'the general taste' of the 1808 exhibition of the Society of Painters in Water Colours he pronounced 'deplorable', and the sky in one of Turner's paintings had been done, he said, by 'a mad man' (Morris, 137). Previously he had earned about £150 a year but in old age he was saved from poverty by the generosity of friends, such as Beaumont, and by the family of one of his pupils, Lady Ashburnham. On a visit to Hearne, who was then aged sixty-four, Farington recorded that he was in the habit of rising at half past ten in the morning and working for two and a half to three hours a day before dinner at five; his evenings were spent at Mills' Coffee House. 'He complained of slow circulation & cold feet which Lamb's wool stockings worn in the night & Cloaths heaped upon him will not warm' (Hardie, 1.175).

Hearne died, unmarried, on 13 April 1817 at 5 Macclesfield Street, Soho, London, where he had lived for more than thirty years. Monro was present and paid for the funeral; Hearne's grave at Bushey lies beside that of Edridge and of Monro himself. His pictures and books were sold by Christie and Manson on 11 and 12 June 1817.

SIMON FENWICK

Sources D. Morris, *Thomas Hearne and his landscape* (1989), 118, 137 · M. Hardie, *Water-colour painting in Britain*, ed. D. Snelgrove, J. Mayne, and B. Taylor, 1: *The eighteenth century* (1966), 175 · S. W. Fisher, *A dictionary of watercolour painters, 1750–1900* (1972) · *The exhibition of the Royal Academy* [exhibition catalogues] · *DNB*
Likenesses J. Smart, miniature, *c.*1783, National Museum, Stockholm · G. Dance, portrait, 1795, repro. in Morris, *Thomas Hearne* · H. Edridge, watercolour drawing, 1800, V&A; repro. in Morris, *Thomas Hearne* · H. Edridge, pencil and ink drawing, 1801, BM · W. Daniell, soft-ground etching, pubd 1809 (after G. Dance, 1795), BM, NPG · H. Monro, chalk drawing, NPG

Heath family (*per. c.*1775–1898), engravers and etchers, came to prominence with **James Heath** (1757–1834), who was born on 19 April 1757 in Butcher Hall Lane, Newgate, London, and was baptized on 13 May in Christchurch, Newgate Street, the second son of George Heath (1724–1773), bookbinder, and his wife, formerly Mrs Mary Jacob. The family originated in Nottingham where James Heath's grandfather Joseph Heath was a bookseller and writing-master. In 1771 James Heath was apprenticed to the engraver Joseph Collyer the younger, and by hard application he acquired great skill in execution which established him as one of the leading line engravers of his time. His first major success was in engraving plates for the bookseller John Bell's edition of *The Poets of Great Britain Complete from Chaucer to Churchill* (109 vols., 1777–83). He was employed by the *Robinson family of booksellers, based in Paternoster Row, from 1779 to 1804, and it was reputed that Heath's apprenticeship with Collyer had been funded by George Robinson. Between 1780 and 1788 he produced 100 prints for the publisher Harrison's *Novelist's Magazine* to designs by Thomas Stothard RA. The taste

and dexterity with which he rendered these illustrations brought his style into remarkable popularity. His later engravings after Stothard, Richard Westall RA, and Robert Smirke RA, among others, are very numerous, and examples are to be found in *Harrison's British Classicks* (8 vols., 1785–7); *The Lady's Poetical Magazine* (4 vols., 1781–2); J. C. Lavater's *Essays on Physiognomy* (3 vols., 1789); George Shaw's *General Zoology* (14 vols., 1800–26); George Vancouver's *A voyage of discovery to the north Pacific Ocean, and round the world … in the years 1790–1795* (3 vols., 1798); James Bruce's *Travels to Discover the Source of the Nile* (5 vols., 1790); the works of Horace Walpole; and many editions of popular works. He engraved some plates for John Boydell's *Shakspeare Gallery*, and in 1802 published a six-volume set of Shakespeare illustrated with engravings after works by Stothard and Henry Fuseli, on his own account. While still an apprentice, in 1778, James Heath had married Elizabeth (1758–*c.*1835), daughter of David Thomas, a stocking presser; their son George became a serjeant-at-law. When his wife left him in 1781, Heath lived with Mary Phillipson (1757–1819), with whom he had five daughters and a son, Charles [*see below*].

In 1791 James Heath was elected an associate of the Royal Academy, and in 1794 he was appointed historical engraver to George III, a title which continued under different monarchs until his retirement. He engraved several large plates, notably the *Dead Soldier* after Joseph Wright of Derby; *George Washington* after Gilbert Stuart; *The Death of Nelson* after Benjamin West; *The Riot in Broad Street, 1780* after Francis Wheatley, and his masterpiece *The Death of Major Pierson* after John Singleton Copley, completed in 1796. He worked in line and stipple, also employing etching. Before he retired in 1822, he had re-engraved Stothard's *Canterbury Pilgrims*, left unfinished by Luigi Schiavonetti. He also engraved numerous commissioned portraits, including one of Dr Samuel Johnson, after that by Sir Joshua Reynolds, which was included in Boswell's life of the poet in 1790.

Although James Heath lost much in a fire in his house in 1789, he amassed a considerable fortune, including property in Acton, Middlesex. He was an avid theatregoer, and his many friends included Sir Thomas Lawrence, Richard Brinsley Sheridan, Sir Joshua Reynolds, and actors and actresses including Mrs Siddons, Eliza Farren (later countess of Derby), John Bannister, and Richard Kemble. He was an agreeable and kindly companion with a fund of stories drawn from his experiences. James Heath died in Great Coram Street, London, on 15 November 1834, and was buried on 21 November in Acton parish church.

James Heath trained and employed several pupils and assistants among whom was his only son and second child with Mary Phillipson, **Charles Theodosius Heath** (1785–1848), landscape and figure engraver, who was born on 1 March 1785 at 13 Lisle Street, Leicester Square, London, and baptized in 1791 at St Martin-in-the-Fields. Charles Heath's etched head of a housemaid, of which an impression is in the British Museum, was engraved when he was six years old. He was an apt and brilliant pupil, with his own perfected style, especially of book illustration. At first he specialized in topographical prints, notably in the European Scenery series published by Rodwell and Martin, and also produced some remarkable plates for an edition of the Bible. His smaller engravings for the numerous popular editions of the classics which followed are also executed with great delicacy and taste. Figure work was his forte and some of his portraits are excellent. He branched out into security engraving for banknotes in the 1820s, through the family firm of Perkins, Fairman, and Heath, and in 1840, with his son, Frederick, was responsible for engraving on steel the master die for the world's first postage stamps, from a medal of Queen Victoria by William Wyon. In 1808 Charles Heath married Elizabeth Petch (1787–1861); they had eight children, two of whom died in childhood.

Charles Heath was also a pioneer in new printmaking techniques. From 1802 to 1806 he exhibited lithographs at Somerset House, and in 1820, for an edition of Thomas Campbell's poem *Pleasures of Hope*, he engraved the first plates on mild steel rather than copper, giving much longer production runs from each plate. In larger commercial plates he was less successful. By contrast his *View from Richmond Hill* and his *Gentlemen of the Time of Charles I*, together with his *Christ Healing the Sick*, were masterpieces of their kind.

In 1821 and again in 1826, Charles Heath got into financial difficulties, but quickly recovered following an energetic diversion into the new fashion for illustrated annuals and giftbooks. Although not an originator, he became the chief promoter of these well-known works, and from 1825 onwards he was almost entirely occupied first in engraving for *The Amulet*, *Literary Souvenir*, and *Landscape Annual*, and then in promoting his own productions, notably *The Keepsake*, *Picturesque Annual*, the *Book of Beauty*, and similar publications such as J. M. W. Turner's *Picturesque Views in England and Wales*. For many years he acted as Turner's impresario in enabling the artist's watercolours to be engraved. Apart from many prints in *The Keepsake*, Charles Heath engraved relatively little himself from 1828, but employed assistants and journeymen engravers, including the engravers George T. Doo and James Henry Watt and his two sons, Frederick and Alfred [*see below*]. While the engravings he supervised are for the most part executed with marvellous skill and fidelity, they eventually became somewhat mechanical and out of fashion, as other processes such as lithography and photogravure developed. Owing to the failure of his major debtors, Charles Heath was obliged to sell off his large stock of engravings, and in 1842 trustees were appointed to manage his finances. But he continued to produce fine illustrated books with the help of his publishers, Longmans, until his sudden death at his home, 24 Seymour Place North, Euston, London, on 18 November 1848.

Of Charles Heath's two engraver sons, **Frederick Augustus Heath** (1810–1878), born in the family home, 6 Seymour Place, Euston, was the eldest. He was baptized on 29 January 1824 at St Pancras Old Church. He trained in his father's atelier in Russell Place, Fitzroy Square, and his first engraved plate appeared in *The Keepsake* in 1835. From

1840 he gradually took over the production of *Heath's Picturesque Annual* and of *The Keepsake* until the latter's final demise in 1858. Thereafter he was involved in the engraving of postage stamps in the printing firm of Perkins Bacon (as Perkins, Fairman, and Heath had become), while engraving regularly for George Virtue's *Art Journal*. A fine craftsman, he seems to have lacked his father's business flair. As principal engraver, however, of the master die for the world's first postage stamps including the penny black and twopenny blue in 1840, he has a permanent claim to philatelic as well as artistic fame. In 1844 he had married Mrs Matilda Inwood (*d*. 1869); they had no children. Frederick Heath died at his home, 87 Sussex Road, Holloway, London, on 26 March 1878.

Alfred Theodosius Heath (1812–1896) was born at 6 Seymour Place, and baptized on 29 January 1824 at St Pancras Old Church, the second son of Charles and Elizabeth Heath. His first published print appeared in *The Keepsake* in 1836. His output as an engraver was not large, and is often characterized by a sentimental or religious quality. He worked for many years in later life in the family firm of Perkins Bacon of 69 Fleet Street, London, and as a teacher of engraving. He married Caroline Philpott, with whom he lived at 8 Somerset Street, Battersea, London, until his death there on 30 January 1896.

Charles Heath's son **Henry Charles Heath** (1829–1898), baptized on 22 July 1829 at St Pancras Old Church, London, was also an artist. He was educated at King's College, London, where he gained prizes during his training as an engineer, and took up painting after his father's death. He was helped by the book illustrator and artist Henry Corbould, whose brother, Edward Henry *Corbould, a historical and watercolour painter, had married his sister, Fanny Jemima, in 1839. Henry Heath assisted the miniature painter Robert Thorburn, and also attended the Royal Academy Schools. From 1851 to 1898 he exhibited regularly at the Royal Academy and with the Society of British Artists. On 21 July 1855 he married Mary Ann Smith at St Pancras Old Church. Before 1863 Henry Heath married, second, Georgina Woodcock, who was the mother of his eldest son, Sir (Henry) Frank *Heath (1863–1946), who became an academic and scientific administrator. Having resumed miniature painting after some years as a photographer, Henry Heath was about 1890 appointed miniature painter to Queen Victoria, and in 1894 became a founding member of the Society of Miniature Painters (now the Royal Society of Miniature Painters, Sculptors, and Gravers). He died on 6 January 1898 at his home, 22 Greencroft Gardens, Hampstead, London.

The members of the Heath family of engravers are often confused with two other contemporary engravers of the same name. These were William Heath (1795–1840), printmaker and caricaturist, with whom there appears to be no relationship, and Henry Heath (*d. c.*1835), caricaturist, who was possibly his brother or cousin.

JOHN HEATH

Sources J. Heath, *The Heath family engravers, 1779–1878*, 3 vols. (1993–9) [incl. bibliography and catalogues raisonnés] · G. Heath, *Records of the Heath family, 1744–1913* (privately printed, 1913) · G. W.

Smith, *James Heath: engraver to kings and tutor to many* (privately printed, 1989) · Farington, *Diary* · A. L. Reade, *N&Q*, 9th ser., 12 (11 July 1903) · B. Hunnisett, *An illustrated dictionary of British steel engravers*, new edn (1989) · B. Hunnisett, *Steel engraved book illustration in England* (1980) · D. Foskett, *Miniatures: dictionary and guide* (1987) · IGI · CGPLA Eng. & Wales (1898) [Henry Charles Heath]

Archives Herts. ALS, corresp. with Lord Lytton [Charles Heath]

Likenesses G. Stuart, oils, 1784 (James Heath), Wadsworth Athenaeum, Hartford, Connecticut · T. Kearsley, oils, c.1794–1795 (James Heath) · Mrs Beechey, miniature, exh. RA 1795 (James Heath) · J. Heath, self-portrait, engraving, 1795–6 (James Heath; after Beechey, exh. RA 1795), repro. in *Monthly Mirror* (June 1796) · L. F. Abbott, oils, c.1796 (James Heath) · S. W. Reynolds, mezzotint, pubd 1796 (James Heath; after T. Kearsley, c.1794–1795), BM, NPG · J. R. Smith, mezzotint, 1796 (James Heath; after L. F. Abbott, c.1796), BM, NPG · H. Burch, miniature, exh. RA 1798 (James Heath) · H. Edridge, pencil drawing, c.1810 (James Heath), BM · H. Behnes, bust, c.1819 (James Heath) · A. J. Oliver, miniature?, 1819 (James Heath) · Mrs D. Turner, etching, c.1819 (James Heath; after H. Behnes, c.1819), BM · H. Corbould, portrait, before 1820 (Charles Heath) · E. Turner, drawing, 1820 (James Heath; after H. Behnes, c.1819), V&A · J. Boaden, oils, exh. RA 1827 (James Heath) · S. J. Stump, miniature, exh. RA 1829 (James Heath) · W. Lonsdale, oils, 1830 (James Heath), NPG · T. George, portrait, 1833 (James Heath) · R. J. Lane, lithograph, 1833 (James Heath; after T. George, 1833), BM, NPG · Jackson, oils, exh. NPE 1868 (James Heath) · Mrs D. Turner, etching (Charles Heath; after portrait by H. Corbould, before 1820), BM, NPG; repro. in Hunnisett, *Illustrated dictionary*, p. 46

Wealth at death £670 plus £430 legacy and unvalued landed property in Acton; James Heath: PRO, probate and intestacy · £808 less £2030 owed to creditors; Charles Heath · under £100—Frederick Heath: probate, 11 May 1878, *CGPLA Eng. & Wales* · £105—Alfred Heath: probate, 15 Feb 1896, *CGPLA Eng. & Wales* · £1132 9s. 2d.—Henry Charles Heath: probate, 1 March 1898, *CGPLA Eng. & Wales*

Heath, Adrian Lewis Ross (1920–1992), artist and art teacher, was born on 23 June 1920 at Matmyo, north Burma, the only child of Percy Charles Petgrave Heath, the manager of a rubber plantation for the Bombay Burma Corporation, and his wife, Adria Frederica Ross-Porter. In 1925 Heath was sent from Burma to England to live with his maternal grandmother at Marchwood Park, near Southampton, and in 1929 he became a boarder at Port Regis preparatory school, near Broadstairs in Kent. After this he attended Bryanston School, where he distinguished himself as a sportsman (athletics and cricket) but was disruptive in the classroom. At Bryanston, Heath became more seriously interested in art, but his instruction and exposure to the realities of painting were haphazard, resulting on the one hand in work that was 'very conservative … timid', and on the other in a real enjoyment of the 'deft … brio and brushstroke' handling of paint by Edwardian artists, especially John Singer Sargent (National Life Story Collection).

Heath left Bryanston in 1938 for Newlyn, Cornwall, to study the rudiments of painting with Alexander Stanhope Forbes, and in 1939 entered the Slade School of Fine Art, accompanying the school on its evacuation to Oxford in 1940. An attempt to enlist in the army was rebuffed, but in 1941 Heath was accepted by the RAF. Sidestepping the possibility and responsibilities of a commission, he eventually became a sergeant gunner, flying with 101 squadron. On a cross-channel sortie in January 1942 Heath's aircraft

suffered engine failure: it made a forced landing near the Dutch coast, and Heath was captured. In Stalag 383 near Munich he met Terry Frost, whom he taught to draw and paint by passing on Forbes's basic methods of instruction. Heath became a persistent escaper, and was eventually banished to the isolation of a Silesian Stalag, where he remained until 1945, using his artistic skills as a forger of false papers for other escapers.

After repatriation Heath returned to the Slade. He graduated in 1947, travelled to Paris, and spent a year disengaging from the influence of Cézanne and moving towards the pure abstraction of younger French artists like Serge Poliakoff; his first solo exhibition was held in Carcassonne in 1948. Heath visited Frost in St Ives in 1947, and again in 1951 (when he met Ben Nicholson) but neither event seems to have been crucial to his developing career. Arguably, and unusually, his part-time work as a lecturer in art history (1949–59) at the City Literary Institute, the Hammersmith School of Art, and the Regent Street Polytechnic was just as important. It paid the rent, and Heath freely acknowledged the resulting improvement in his own knowledge and understanding of art. In the same decade his twin careers as artist and teacher of artists gained momentum and began to overlap. Seeking to achieve complete abstraction in his painting, Heath initially inclined towards the 'systems' art (he called it 'dynamic symmetry') then being made by Victor Pasmore, Kenneth Martin, and Anthony Hill. However, in time their focus on mathematical precision became a constraint: Heath veered away from such austere practice, preferring to work intuitively and completely constructively, with what he called 'muck materials' like Polyfilla or cement.

In 1953 Heath began a lifelong association with the Redfern Gallery in London as a regular solo exhibitor and published a rewarding and thought-provoking book, *Abstract Art: its Origin and Meaning*. On 17 July 1952 Heath married Corinne Elizabeth Reid Lloyd (*b.* 1922/3), a designer, daughter of Charles Jesse Lloyd, banker. The newly-weds lived at Heath's house at 22 Fitzroy Street, London, before moving in 1957 to 28 Charlotte Street; they had a son and a daughter. In 1956 Heath was a participant in the important exhibition *This is Tomorrow* at the Whitechapel Art Gallery, and in 1959 he began to exhibit outside London, at venues in Britain and northern Europe, in solo shows or in small, mixed, or group exhibitions of drawing or painting. In later years he travelled widely, drawing single-point motifs in Spain, Morocco, Norway, and Sweden, and 'the barren quality' of the landscape around his own Hebridean croft. These experiences fed an articulate process of painterly self-questioning, and a panoramic intellect developed from hungry and catholic reading.

Heath never denied the many 'happy accidents' that can befall an abstract artist, an openness that helped to establish his charisma as a part-time tutor at the Bath Academy of Art, at Corsham Court (1955–76) alongside Peter Lanyon, Howard Hodgkin, Ayres, and others; and as senior fellow at Cardiff Polytechnic Institute of Higher Education (1977–88). His chairmanship of the Allied Artists'

Association (1954–64) and his service with the Arts Council's art panel (1964–71) were marked by his disarming ability to facilitate, and not to dictate; but perhaps his greatest, unsung service to British art lay in his work during the 1970s and 1980s as standards moderator and troubleshooter for the Council for National Academic Awards. Through his determined promotion of the highest tutorial and academic standards in art education he helped to move British art education forward. Still painting, Heath died in France on 15 September 1992.

JULIAN FREEMAN

Sources interview of Adrian Heath by Norbert Lynton, BL NSA, TAV 1350 AB [transcript] · D. Brown, introduction, *Corsham: a celebration* (1988) [exhibition catalogue, Michael Parkin Gallery, London] · *St. Ives, 1939–64* (1985) [exhibition catalogue, Tate Gallery, London] · *The Independent* (21 Sept 1992) · *The Independent* (28 Sept 1992) · *Daily Telegraph* (3 Oct 1992) · m. cert.
Archives priv. coll., papers and drawings | SOUND BL NSA, national life story collection, Adrian Heath interviewed by Norbert Lynton, 1992; transcript in Tate Archive, TAV 1350 AB
Likenesses I. Kar, photograph, repro. in *St. Ives*, 123 · R. Mayne, photographs, repro. in [J. Poulson], *The ways of Corsham* (1989), 54

Heath, Alfred Theodosius (1812–1896). *See under* Heath family (*per. c.*1775–1898).

Heath, Ambrose (1891–1969), cookery writer and journalist, was born Francis Geoffrey Miller (the second forename was later changed to Gerald) on 7 February 1891 at 16 Broadhurst Gardens, Hampstead, London, the son of Francis Miller (1866–1935), electrical engineer, and his wife, Rose Margaret Bockett. Possibly because his parents thought journalism an unrespectable career, he became known as Ambrose Heath professionally. The decision not to use his real name was taken, he told an interviewer in 1966, because his father was a gentleman. It is hard to believe that he changed his name (and he seems to have used the name Ambrose Heath in most of his dealings; it was not a mere *nom de plume*) because his parents disapproved of the subject of his writing; but he went on to say that 'my parents were supremely uninterested in food' (Bateman, 167).

Heath enjoyed his schooldays at Clifton College (1905–9), 'though I was what you might call—unorthodox … They didn't know what to do with me. I didn't like the formality of ordinary education. I was interested in special things' (Bateman, 167). He spent a lot of time in the company of the masters, but failed the scholarship examination for Christ Church, Oxford. When his father's connections failed to secure him a place in publishing, he escaped to Newlyn, Cornwall, where his father made him an annual allowance of £150 for four years, and he wrote a novel and a children's book, both of which he destroyed. For a time he worked for the Hudson's Bay Company, then in the India Office. He spoke fondly of frequenting Marcel Boulestin's restaurant in the 1920s and 1930s, and in 1933 was a co-founder of the Wine and Food Society, but he had a quarrel with the then secretary and resigned. His journalism began with the 'casual pieces' he submitted to *The Times*, the *News Chronicle*, the *Manchester Guardian*, and the

Ambrose Heath (1891–1969), by Howard Coster, 1939

Yorkshire Post; and he finally became cookery correspondent for the *Morning Post*.

Heath was prodigiously productive; he wrote his first four cookery books in 1933, and had added another eleven by the time the Second World War started, including *Madame Prunier's Fish Cookery Book* (1938), a translation, for which he was best-known. During the war he drew the 'Patsy cookstrip' for the *Daily Mirror*, and should be given the credit for inventing the genre. He also drew the *Daily Mirror's* Saturday gardening strip, 'Digwell', which was still appearing in the late 1960s, though most of the staff of the newspaper did not know the identity of the artist.

Heath wrote more than 100 cookery books. Many of them contained the word 'good' in their titles: 'good food' obviously, but also 'good' potato dishes, savouries, soups, sweets, and ices, to name but a few. They provided directions for cooking almost every conceivable foodstuff, from squirrels—'the recipe does not sound very convincing to me' (Bateman, 201)—to turtle. About the latter he wrote that 'it is not likely that private houses or indeed many establishments will ever want, or be in a position to make turtle soup, but, for the curious, here are details of the way to make it,' starting with a hair-raising passage detailing 'the slaughtering of the turtle' (ibid., 202). He was a very thorough researcher: in a piece he called 'Country dishes', written during the Second World War, he catalogues the eating properties of various birds 'of edible size', common and uncommon, beginning with 'coot: as inedible, I understand, as it appears to be', and ending with a recipe for sparrows (ibid., 200). His other wartime recipes, in such books as *The Good Cook in Wartime* and *From* the Kitchen Front, were more homely, however. His writing was graceful, with an old-fashioned turn of phrase, but with an occasional shaft of self-mockery or irony that makes it enjoyable to read.

Heath was not a very good businessman, and in the 1960s was earning only £1000 a year, surprising for an author with so many titles to his credit. He said that he had sold the copyright in his books for £50 each, with no royalties. Near the end of his life he seemed a little bitter about his poor pay, aware that other cookery writers were getting much larger payments for their books and journalism. He was sacked from *Queen* magazine when he was already elderly, which meant a loss of £900 a year. Aware that copyright in recipes is a difficult matter, he complained that people stole his recipes, but admitted, 'I steal from Escoffier' (Bateman, 173). He had some ambivalence about his subject, and said with reference to a wartime recipe for cod's head soup: 'What I write is dull, very dull. But I don't write dully' (ibid., 170).

Heath's later years were spent at Grange Cottage, Holmbury St Mary, an idyllic house near Dorking—'It's like Walt Disney, isn't it?' (Bateman 170)—with an Aga cooker, and a flower garden but no vegetable garden. He made his own elderberry and other fruit wines. His much younger wife, Violet May, who survived him, called him Loo, and he called her Pooh. They had a daughter, Susan. Heath died at his final home, Pratsham Grange Cottage, Wotton, Surrey, on 31 May 1969.   PAUL LEVY

Sources M. Bateman, *Cookery people* (1966–7) · b. cert. · d. cert. · *Daily Telegraph* (2 June 1969) · *The Times* (2 June 1969)
Likenesses H. Coster, photographs, 1939, NPG [*see illus.*]

Heath, Benjamin (1704–1766), literary scholar and book collector, was born at Exeter on 20 April 1704, the eldest son of Benjamin Heath (1672?–1728), fuller and merchant of Exeter, who married Elizabeth Kelland (buried at St Leonard's, Exeter, in October 1723). His father was a prominent Baptist and he was not baptized in St Leonard's Church until 11 October 1729, by which time both his parents had died. He was educated at the Exeter grammar school, and is said to have been admitted as a student of the Middle Temple in 1721, and again in 1729. On his father's death he inherited the handsome fortune of £30,000 and about 1730 set out on the grand tour. His travels took him to Geneva, where he married Rose Marie (1718–1808), daughter of Jean Michelet, a Genevan merchant, on 12 August 1732, less than two months after she had passed the age of fourteen. She was later naturalized by a special act of parliament about 1760.

In 1725 Heath had been sworn as a freeman of the Weavers' Company at Exeter, but his taste was not for business or a profession, and when he returned to England he abandoned his intention of being called to the bar, and settled in Exeter, where his chief pleasures lay in literature and book collecting. Since the age of thirteen he had been a collector of rare books. In 1740 he published his first work, *An Essay towards a Demonstrative Proof of the Divine Existence, Unity, and Attributes*, dedicated to William Oliver, a physician at Bath. It is said to have followed the lines laid down

in *The Good Man the Living Temple of God* by John Howe, the puritan divine. All his life he studied the classical writers, and the fruit of his labours was shown in the volume of *Notae, sive, Lectiones ad Aeschyli, Sophoclis, Euripidis quae supersunt dramata deperditorumque reliquias*, which was published at Oxford in 1762. On 31 March in the same year the University of Oxford conferred on him the degree of DCL by diploma. Samuel Parr, in a letter to Gilbert Wakefield, defended Heath's scholarship against the criticisms of the German scholar Johann Gottfried Hermann in his *Observationes Criticae* (p. 59), and his note on verse 1002 of the *Hecuba* (*Memoirs of the Life of Gilbert Wakefield*, 2 vols., 1804, 2.439). Heath's object was to restore the metre of the Greek tragedies. In Britain his observations were highly valued, and he was asked to furnish the notes for the Greek tragedies in use at Eton College.

Heath was elected on 23 March 1752 to the post of town clerk of Exeter, which he held until his death. In 1763 there was unrest in cider-producing districts after the imposition of an excise duty on the producer of 4s. a hogshead by the ministry of Lord Bute. Popular meetings were held throughout Devon, Herefordshire, and Worcestershire, and violent attacks were made on the ministry. Heath took a prominent part in the controversy, and was the author of *The case of the county of Devon with respect to the consequences of the new excise duty on cyder and perry* (1763), to which is sometimes ascribed the repeal of the act in 1766. The freeholders of Devon presented him with 'a very large waiter and two pair of candlesticks' in 1764 to mark their appreciation. For some time he retained his interest in politics, and contemplated contesting the city of Exeter, but though he spent £1000 in preliminary expenses, he did not proceed to the poll.

Heath issued anonymously in 1765 *A revisal of Shakespear's text, wherein the alterations introduced into it by the more modern editors and critics are particularly considered*. He praises Lewis Theobald's editions and severely censures William Warburton's conjectural emendations. He owned few critical texts. He did not possess a copy of either of the folio editions of Shakespeare, nor had he seen Sir Thomas Hanmer's edition, but his natural acuteness 'produced a number of very sensible annotations'. His name appeared on the title-pages of two volumes of *Annotations Illustrative of the Plays of Shakespeare, by Johnson, Steevens, Malone, Heath* (1819), but very few of his critical observations are incorporated. Heath was 'always a martyr to bad health, and led the life of a valetudinarian'. He died at Exeter on 13 September 1766, and was buried at St Leonard's, Exeter, on 21 September. Of his large family of seven sons and six daughters, five sons and three daughters lived to middle age. His son Benjamin was headmaster of Harrow School (1771–85), and a younger son, George, became headmaster of Eton College in 1792, and resigned in 1801.

Heath's great-grandson Baron Robert Amadeus Heath preserved four manuscripts by him containing critical notes in Latin on Virgil, Euripides, Catullus, and Tibullus and also a 'Supplement to new edition [by Seward] of

Beaumont and Fletcher's works'. John Forster, in a letter printed in *Heathiana* (Drake, 11), says that Dyce had seen the last manuscript, and had adopted some, but not enough, of its suggested readings. In 1882 it was presented by Baron Heath to the British Museum. In addition to these works Heath left behind him most of the materials for a new edition of Hesiod. He had distributed much of his library between two of his sons during his lifetime but there was still a large collection left at his death, which was sold following the death of his widow in 1808. In 1810 a *Catalogue of books containing all the rare, useful, and valuable publications to the present time to be sold in April and May by Mr. Jeffrey, no. 11 Pall Mall* was printed; it was reissued later in the year with the prices and names of the purchasers.

W. P. COURTNEY, *rev.* IAN MAXTED

Sources W. R. Drake, *Heathiana: notes, genealogical and biographical, of the family of Heath* (privately printed, London, 1881); rev. edn (1882) · Nichols, *Lit. anecdotes*, 2.276–7; 4.285 · S. Halkett and J. Laing, *A dictionary of the anonymous and pseudonymous literature of Great Britain*, 4 vols. (1882–8), vol. 1, p. 319; vol. 3, p. 2204 · T. F. Dibdin, *The bibliographical decameron*, 3 (1817), 368 · G. Oliver, *The history of the city of Exeter* (1861), 216 · J. Davidson, *Bibliotheca Devoniensis* (1852), 109 · J. S. Watson, *The life of William Warburton, D.D.* (1863), 337–8 · *GM*, 1st ser., 34 (1764), 246 · P. Woodland, 'Benjamin Heath and the opposition to the 1763 cider excise', *Parliamentary History*, 4 (1985), 115–36 · T. F. Dibdin, *Bibliomania, or, Book madness: a bibliographical romance*, new edn (1876), 460, 554–62 · IGI

Archives BL, critical notes on Beaumont and Fletcher, Add. MS 31910

Likenesses W. Dickinson, mezzotint, 1773, BM, NPG · J. Dixon, mezzotint (after R. E. Pine), repro. in Drake, *Heathiana*, 8 · R. E. Pine, oils; Exeter Guildhall, 1891

Heath, Charles (1761–1830), topographical printer, was a native of Hurcott, near Kidderminster, Worcestershire, where his father owned extensive paper mills. He was educated in a school at Hartlebury in Worcestershire and served an apprenticeship as a printer in Nottingham. In 1791 he set up his own press at Monmouth, where he wrote and printed topographical works on Monmouthshire, among other 'jobbing' work. The first of these publications was *A Descriptive Account of Raglan Castle* (1792); descriptions of Tintern Abbey (1793), the scenery of the Wye valley (1795), and Monmouth (1804), among others, went into many editions. Heath collected much material on the history and topography of the locality, and though his works show little literary or critical judgement, they were invaluable sources for later historians.

Heath was twice mayor of Monmouth (1819 and 1820). He died on 31 December 1830, and was buried in St Mary's churchyard in Monmouth. His fellow townsmen erected a monument above his grave twenty-five years later: it gave an incorrect date for his death (7 January 1831) but rightly celebrated his picturesque descriptions for encouraging local tourism. [ANON.], *rev.* JOANNE POTIER

Sources DWB · *GM*, 1st ser., 101/1 (1831), 92 · J. P. Anderson, *The book of British topography: a classified catalogue of the topographical works in the library of the British Museum relating to Great Britain and Ireland* (1881)

Likenesses monument, St Mary's churchyard, Monmouth

Heath, Charles Theodosius (1785–1848). *See under* Heath family (*per. c.*1775–1898).

Heath, Christopher (1802–1876), minister of the Catholic Apostolic church, was born in London on 26 March 1802, the son of John and Mary (*née* Potter) Heath. His grandfather, Benjamin Heath, was a velvet manufacturer at Birmingham. His father was a surgeon in the navy, who, after being present in Lord Howe's action of 1 June 1794, left the service and practised at 69 Hatton Garden, London, as a surgeon dentist. Christopher entered St Paul's School, London, on 1 November 1813; in 1817 he became a pupil under his father, and eventually succeeded to his profession. On 20 November 1827 he married Eliza (1805/6–1884), the daughter of James Barclay, at St Bride's Church, Fleet Street.

Although his parents worshipped at St Andrew's, Holborn, Christopher Heath was attracted by the preaching of Edward Irving at the Caledonian Chapel, Cross Street, opposite his surgery in Hatton Garden, and became a member of the congregation there in May 1832. He moved with Irving when he took his congregation to Newman Street Hall on 24 October 1832, and in December 1834 was called to be an elder of the church, but served for a while in the congregation at Islington. Heath was appointed to succeed Irving, who died on 3 June 1835, as angel (or minister) of the congregation, being ordained by John Bate Cardale, the apostle. He gave up his profession and moved from his home in Bedford Row to 14 Newman Street, adjoining the church. In course of time, finding that the Newman Street Hall was small and inconvenient, in conjunction with his deacons he obtained plans from Raphael Brandon for an Early English building in Gordon Square. Of this he laid the first stone in 1851, and it was opened on Christmas eve 1853, being at that time considered perhaps the most beautiful ecclesiastical building erected in England since the Reformation. The west end of the church was, however, never finished, owing to lack of funds. Here he and his congregation continued to be the central point in London of the Catholic Apostolic church (commonly called the Irvingites). Heath paid official visits to the branch churches in continental Europe, but his main work was in London, where, besides the care of his large flock, he was a trustee and administrator of church funds. He was somewhat authoritarian but a man of great energy and industry, trusted for his firmness, tact, and patience. He died of congestion of the lungs at his home, 3 Byng Place, Gordon Square, London, on 1 November 1876 and was buried in Marylebone cemetery, East Finchley. His widow died at 40 Gordon Square on 3 July 1884, aged seventy-eight. Of their eighteen children, the second son, Christopher *Heath, was a well-known surgeon in London. G. C. BOASE, *rev.* TIMOTHY C. F. STUNT

Sources S. Newman-Norton, 'A biographical index of those associated with the Lord's work', Bodl. Oxf., MS facs b.61 · private information (1891) · R. B. Gardiner, ed., *The admission registers of St Paul's School, from 1748 to 1876* (1884) · E. Miller, *The history and doctrines of Irvingism*, 2 vols. (1878) · *A narrative of the proceedings of Mr C. Heath v. Joseph Amesbury* (1849)

Wealth at death £7000: probate, 21 Nov 1876, *CGPLA Eng. & Wales*

Heath, Christopher (1835–1905), surgeon, was born in London on 13 March 1835, the son of Christopher *Heath (1802–1876), minister of the Catholic Apostolic church, and his wife, Eliza Barclay (1805/6–1884).

Heath entered King's College School in May 1845, and after apprenticeship to Nathaniel Davidson of Charles Street, Manchester Square, he began his medical studies at King's College, London, in October 1851. Here he gained the Leathes and Warneford prizes for general proficiency in medical subjects and divinity, and was admitted an associate in 1855. From 11 March to 25 September 1855 he served as hospital dresser on board the steam frigate HMS *Impérieuse* in the Baltic fleet during the Crimean War; he was awarded a medal for his service. He became MRCS in 1856 and FRCS in 1860. He was appointed assistant demonstrator of anatomy at King's College, and served as house surgeon at King's College Hospital to Sir William Fergusson from May to November 1857. In 1856 he was appointed demonstrator of anatomy at the Westminster Hospital, where he was made lecturer on anatomy and assistant surgeon in 1862.

In 1858 Heath was consulting surgeon to the St George and St James Dispensary; in 1860 he was appointed surgeon to the West London Hospital at Hammersmith, and in 1870 he was surgeon to the Hospital for Women in Soho. Meanwhile in 1866 he was appointed assistant surgeon and teacher of operative surgery at University College Hospital, where he became full surgeon on the retirement of Sir John Eric Erichsen in 1871 and Holme professor of clinical surgery in 1875. He resigned his hospital appointments in 1900 when he was elected consulting surgeon and emeritus professor of clinical surgery.

Heath was awarded the Jacksonian prize of the Royal College of Surgeons in 1867 for his essay, 'Injuries and diseases of the jaws, including those of the antrum, with the treatment by operation or otherwise'. This was published in 1868. He was a member of the college board of examiners in anatomy and physiology (1875–80), an examiner in surgery (1883–92) and in dental surgery (1888–92), and he was a member of the council (1881–97). He was Hunterian professor of surgery and pathology (1886–7), Bradshaw lecturer in 1892, and Hunterian orator in 1897, when he chose as his subject 'John Hunter considered as a great surgeon'. He succeeded John Whitaker as president of the college on 4 April 1895, and was re-elected for a second term.

In 1897 Heath visited America to deliver the Lane medical lectures at the Cooper Medical College in San Francisco. During this visit McGill University of Montreal awarded him the honorary degree of LLD. Heath was president of the Clinical Society of London in 1890–91, a fellow of King's College, London, and an associate fellow of the College of Physicians, Philadelphia.

Heath was married twice: first to Sarah, daughter of the Revd Jasper Peck; and second to Gabrielle Nora, daughter of Captain Joseph Maynard RN. Heath lived for many years at 36 Cavendish Square, London, and died there on 8 August 1905, leaving a widow, five sons, and a daughter.

Heath was a brilliant surgeon and a great teacher of both anatomy and surgery. He combined the older methods of the 'coaches' or 'grinders', who prepared pupils for examination, with the practical knowledge of hospital work from which those teachers were debarred. He was a born controversialist, hitting hard and with a confident belief in his own opinion. As an exponent of the rapid style of surgery based on anatomy, he remained sceptical about advances in modern pathology and bacteriology. His published works dealt mainly with general surgical subjects. These included *A Course of Operative Surgery* (1877) and *The Student's Guide to Surgical Diagnosis* (1879).

D'A. POWER, rev. B. A. BRYAN

Sources *The Lancet* (12 Aug 1905), 490–93 · *BMJ* (12 Aug 1905), 359–60 · private information (1912) · personal knowledge (1912)
Archives UCL, letters to Sir Victor Horsley
Likenesses Barraud and Jerrard, photograph, 1873, Wellcome L. · H. J. Brooks, group portrait, oils (*Council of the Royal College of Surgeons of England, 1884–85*), RCS Eng. · H. Pinker, marble bas-relief, University College Hospital, London, Medical School · photograph, Wellcome L.
Wealth at death £7799 4s. 1d.: probate, 22 Aug 1905, *CGPLA Eng. & Wales*

Heath, Cuthbert Eden (1859–1939), underwriter and insurance broker, was born on 23 March 1859 at Forest Lodge, near Southampton, the fourth of the seven children of Captain Leopold George *Heath RN (1817–1907), and his wife, Mary Emma, née Marsh. His father had a brilliant naval career, being knighted in 1868 and promoted to rear-admiral in 1871. Heath was educated privately until the age of eight, then followed his brothers to Temple Grove preparatory school, East Sheen, and to Brighton College. Partial deafness prevented him from entering the navy, and he remained at Brighton College until 1874; he later went to France and Germany for two years to study languages. In 1876 he joined the insurance brokers Henry Head & Co. as a junior clerk. He later said that he was regarded in his youth as 'the fool of his family', 'poor Bertie', who, because of his disability, had to go into a respectable but dull job in the City (Brown, *Cuthbert Heath*, 62).

In 1880, aged twenty-one, Heath joined a Lloyd's syndicate, helped by a loan of £7000 from his father. In 1881 he began marine underwriting for himself and three 'names', and extended this to broking from 1883. In 1885 his father, who was a director of the Hand in Hand Fire Office, invited Heath to reinsure its fire risks. Traditionally Lloyd's had ignored such business, although there was nothing in its rules to prevent it. In the following years Heath instigated a series of radical innovations which amazed his fellow underwriters and changed the face of Lloyd's for ever. He became 'the most original talent ever produced by the insurance industry of this or any other country' (ibid., 75). Heath's innovations included the first American non-marine risk underwritten at Lloyd's, insurance against loss of profits through fire (which the tariff offices complained would ruin fire insurance), 'all risks' policies against accidental loss, 'jeweller's block' policies to cover diamonds in transit, insurance against burglary (1887), earthquakes (1895), smallpox (1901), workmen's compensation (1906), and air-raid damage (1914), and excess of loss reinsurance. From the 1890s he helped to develop trade credit insurance, and became the first chairman of the Trade Indemnity Company in 1918. From 1919 to 1921 he ventured, unsuccessfully, into aviation insurance. In 1926 Heath also helped to introduce to London a cheaper system of establishing premium rates for reinsurances.

In 1890 Heath established C. E. Heath & Co. which became a substantial independent broking firm with considerable overseas business. In 1894, faced with a need for greater capacity for non-marine business, he established the Excess Insurance Company. His practice of writing (doing business) for the Excess from his 'box' (working area) at Lloyd's, however, got him into repeated trouble for breaking the rule banning company underwriting there. Over this and many other matters, Heath had, as one Lloyd's chairman, Neville Dixey, put it 'a fine disregard for conventions' (quoted in obituary, *Post Magazine*). Standing 6 foot 2 inches tall, carrying his familiar black box for his hearing aid, courteous, soft-spoken, and popular with the brokers, Cuthbert Heath was a striking figure at Lloyd's.

In 1902 Heath finally persuaded Lloyd's to accept security deposits for non-marine business. In 1908 Lloyd's also accepted Heath's idea of introducing a compulsory audit of members' accounts. The annual audit, together with the incorporation of non-marine business in the second Lloyd's Act of 1913, became the cornerstone of Lloyd's solidity for most of the twentieth century. Most of Heath's innovations arose, however, from others' suggestions. His flair lay in recognizing opportunities and in rating novel risks quickly and accurately, if sometimes intuitively. He was undoubtedly one of the most dynamic figures at Lloyd's in the early twentieth century. 'No other individual had such a profound effect on the scope of the business, its institutions and its competitive structure' (Westall, 140). He led the market 'in the literal sense that many risks were only undertaken when it was clear that Heath was first involved' (ibid.). In 1911 he was elected to Lloyd's committee, and served for four years. During the 1920s Heath withdrew from daily business at Lloyd's, but his syndicate continued to lead the non-marine market. By the 1930s his annual income was estimated to be £60,000, and his syndicate was writing for 300 members. At the time of his death his estate was valued at just over £1m gross.

In 1891 Heath married Sarah Caroline Gore Gambier (1859–1944), daughter of the Revd Charles Gore Gambier and his wife, Elizabeth. A son, Leopold Cuthbert, and a daughter, Genesta, were born in 1894 and 1897. In 1907 Heath moved into Anstie Grange, Holmwood, near Dorking, which his late father had built in 1863. Heath's wife entertained lavishly—employing fifty servants at Anstie—with guests drawn from London's social élite. Heath himself, diffident, a little austere, and shy by nature, preferred country walks and enjoyed fishing, shooting, and hunting. In 1918 he became joint master of

the Surrey Union hounds. In 1929 he gave 200 acres near Leith Hill to the National Trust for conservation.

During the First World War Heath advised the government on air-raid insurance and was appointed a trustee for Lloyd's Patriotic Fund. Anstie Grange was converted, at his own expense, into an officers' hospital, through which nearly 700 patients passed between 1916 and 1918. Heath was made an OBE in 1920 and was also a knight of grace of the order of St John of Jerusalem. He served as high sheriff of Surrey in 1925–6, and as deputy lieutenant from 1928.

Heath was a member of the Royal Yacht Squadron, and in later years often sailed his yacht in winter in the Mediterranean. In 1930 he purchased a small estate, La Domaine de Savaric, at Èze in the Alpes-Maritimes. He relaxed with reading, and his paint-box of water colours. In 1938 he suffered a stroke, which left him partially paralysed. He died at Anstie Grange on 8 March 1939, and was cremated in a private ceremony. His ashes were interred on 11 March 1939 at Coldharbour church, Holmwood, Surrey.   ROBIN PEARSON

Sources A. Brown, *Cuthbert Heath: maker of the modern Lloyd's of London* (1980) · O. M. Westall, 'Heath, Cuthbert Eden', *DBB* · *The Times* (9 March 1939) · *The Times* (11 March 1939) · *Post Magazine and Insurance Monitor* (18 March 1939) · *The Policyholder* (15 March 1939) · *WWW* · D. E. W. Gibb, *Lloyd's of London: a study in individualism* (1957) · H. Cockerell, *Lloyd's of London: a portrait* (1984) · R. Strauss, *Lloyd's: a historical sketch* (1937) · A. Brown, *Hazard unlimited: from ships to satellites, 300 years of Lloyd's of London*, 3rd edn (1987) · C. Wright and C. E. Fayle, *A history of Lloyd's from the founding of Lloyd's Coffee House to the present day* (1928) · W. A. Dinsdale, *History of accident insurance in Great Britain* (1954)
Likenesses W. Orpen, oils, 1921, C. E. Heath & Co. · J. Hay, oils, 1928, Excess Insurance Co. Ltd · J. Hay, oils, 1936, Lloyd's of London
Wealth at death £1,031,060 17s. 5d.: probate, 20 May 1940, *CGPLA Eng. & Wales*

Heath, Douglas Denon (1811–1897), lawyer and author, was born on 6 January 1811 in Chancery Lane, London, the second son of George Heath (1778–1852), serjeant-at-law, and his wife, Anne Raymond Dunbar. His father was a son of James *Heath [see under Heath family], the engraver, and half-brother of Charles Heath. Admiral Sir Leopold George *Heath and Dunbar Isidore *Heath, the notorious heterodox clergyman, were among his brothers. After education at Dr Burney's school in Greenwich, he spent the greater part of 1826–7 with friends of his father's in France; among the latter was his godfather, the savant Denon, master of the mint to Napoleon I. He matriculated at Trinity College, Cambridge, in Michaelmas term 1828, and read for a year with the well-known classical tutor, Henry Malden. With his brother John, Heath was one of the group styling themselves 'the Apostles', and among his intimates was James Spedding, in whose company he visited Wordsworth and Tennyson. Tennyson read him many scraps of his composition, which he recognized in poems published many years later. Heath obtained a scholarship at Trinity on 23 April 1830, and two years later graduated senior wrangler, and took the first Smith's prize. In the classical tripos of the same year (1832) he was placed ninth in the first class. He was elected to a fellowship on 2 October 1832.

Although strongly attached to Cambridge life, in deference to his father's wish Heath entered at the Inner Temple on 25 January 1830, and was called to the bar in January 1835. In 1838 his father succeeded in procuring him the reversion of his own lucrative post as county clerk of Middlesex. When in 1846 the courts of the county clerk were abolished, Heath took up the option conferred in the statute to become county court judge for the Bloomsbury district. He remained in that post until 1865, when he had to retire through deafness, and was at one time a member of the county court rule committee. During these years, at Spedding's request, Heath edited the legal writings of Bacon for the seventh volume of the great edition of the *Works of Francis Bacon* (1859). The various manuscripts of Bacon's professional writings were carefully collated, and many passages made intelligible for the first time.

Heath's emancipation from legal duties in 1865—though he remained a JP for Surrey—enabled him to give more time to his scholarly work. The first fruits were two elaborate papers on tides and sea levels in the *Philosophical Magazine* (1866 and 1867) and in 1874 he published *An Elementary Exposition of the Doctrine of Energy*, which was highly praised by Clerk Maxwell. His most characteristic work, however, was in connection with the Greek prose classics. He concentrated some acute, judicious, and closely reasoned work into his defence of Aristotle's doctrine of causation against misconception by Grote and others (*Journal of Philology*, vols. 7 and 8, 1877 and 1879), and produced papers entitled *On the So-called Arabicus Mons* and on Plato's *Cratylus* (ibid., vols. 5, 6 and 7, 1874, 1876, and 1877). Even more vigorous were his papers in defence of the honesty of Herodotus, his views greatly strengthened by a journey up the Nile as far as Dongola in 1874–5 (ibid., 15, 1886, 215).

On his father's death in 1852 Heath became owner of Kitlands, a small estate near Leith Hill, Dorking, Surrey. He resided there, continuing the reconstruction of the house begun by his father, and greatly benefited the parish of Coldharbour by his generosity. Tennyson, Spedding, and W. H. Thompson, master of Trinity, were fond of discussing poetry and philosophy in Heath's beautiful garden, in which Marianne North painted for the collection at Kew at least one flower she had missed in its native Himalaya. He was one of the founders and benefactors of the Surrey county school at Cranleigh. Heath was a broad-churchman and interested in (non-party) politics. He greatly admired Peel, but disliked and distrusted later party leaders. He died unmarried at Kitlands on 25 September 1897, and was buried in Coldharbour churchyard.

THOMAS SECCOMBE, rev. PATRICK POLDEN

Sources H. E. Malden, *Memoir of D. D. Heath* (1898) • Venn, *Alum. Cant.* • Boase, *Mod. Eng. biog.* • J. Foster, *Men-at-the-bar: a biographical hand-list of the members of the various inns of court*, 2nd edn (1885) • *Law Journal* (2 Oct 1897), 482 • *The Times* (27 Sept 1897) • *The letters of Alfred Lord Tennyson*, ed. C. Y. Lang and E. F. Shannon, 3 vols. (1982–90) • *VCH Surrey*, vols. 2–3 • 'Select committee on the Middlesex County Court Bill, 1838', *Parl. papers* (1843), 11.219, no. 10 • County Courts Act, 1846, c95 • *CGPLA Eng. & Wales* (1897) • Allibone, *Dict.*
Likenesses T. C. Wageman, watercolour sketch, 1836, Trinity Cam.

Wealth at death £7583 12s. 2d.: probate, 6 Nov 1897, *CGPLA Eng. & Wales*

Heath, Dunbar Isidore (1816–1888), Church of England clergyman, was born in London on 3 March 1816, the third son of George Heath, serjeant-at-law, of Kitlands, Surrey. He was educated at Westminster School and Greenwich, Kent, before matriculating at Trinity College, Cambridge, in 1835. He was elected to a scholarship in 1836 before graduating BA as fifth wrangler in 1838 and proceeding MA in 1841. In 1840 he was elected a fellow of Trinity. Ordained deacon (Ely) in 1843 and priest in 1844, he was presented to the college living of Brading in the Isle of Wight. On 22 February 1848 he married Emily Mary, daughter of James Harrison of Sandown, Isle of Wight. They had at least two sons.

In 1859 Heath preached a series of sermons, published as *Sermons on Important Subjects* (1860), which laid out his opinions, largely influenced by F. D. Maurice, concerning moral aspects of Christian teaching. Heath maintained that justification by faith is the putting of everyone in his right place by the Saviour's trust in the future, and that the faith by which man is justified is not his faith in Christ, but the faith of Christ himself; secondly, that Christ's blood was not poured out to propitiate his Father; thirdly, that forgiveness of sins has nothing at all to do with the gospel; and fourthly, that the ideas and phrases 'guilt of sin', 'satisfaction', 'merit', and 'necessary to salvation' 'have been foisted into modern theology without sanction from Scripture'.

In 1860 a suit was instituted against Heath in the court of arches by direction of his diocesan, Charles Richard Sumner, bishop of Winchester, through his secretary, John Burder, alleging that Heath was expressing views derogatory to the Thirty-Nine Articles. Judgment was delivered in the case of *Burder v. Heath* on 2 November 1861, when the defendant was declared to have forfeited his living under the statute of 13 Eliz. I, c. 12, an act requiring ministers of the church to be of sound religion. It was Lushington's judgment that Heath's exposition of doctrine could not be reconciled with the plain grammatical meaning of the gospel. An appeal was made to the judicial committee of the privy council, and the judgment, delivered on 6 June 1862, confirmed the decision of the lower court, and Heath was deprived of the vicarage of Brading after refusing to retract his opinions.

In retirement Heath wrote a *Defence of my Professional Character* (1862), in addition to works on ancient history and editing the *Journal of Anthropology*. He died at his home, Rochester House, Esher, Surrey, on 27 May 1888.

THOMPSON COOPER, rev. ELLIE CLEWLOW

Sources *The Athenaeum* (9 June 1888), 728 • *Cambridge Chronicle* (15 June 1888), 7 • *The Guardian* (6 June 1888), 825 • *Isle of Wight Observer* (9 June 1888), 5 • *Isle of Wight Observer* (16 June 1888), 6 • *The Times* (18 June 1861), 11 • *The Times* (19 June 1861), 11 • *The Times* (2 Aug 1861), 9 • *The Times* (4 Nov 1861), 9 • *The Times* (18 Nov 1861), 9 • *The Times* (9 June 1862), 9, 11 • Venn, *Alum. Cant.* • *Men of the time* (1884) • M. A. Crowther, *Church embattled: religious controversy in mid-Victorian England* (1970) • *CGPLA Eng. & Wales* (1888)
Wealth at death £1933 5s.: probate, 2 July 1888, *CGPLA Eng. & Wales*

Heath, Sir (Henry) Frank (1863–1946), academic and scientific administrator, was born on 11 December 1863 at 153 Regent Street, Westminster, London, the eldest son of Henry Charles *Heath (1829–1898) [see under Heath family], miniature portrait painter to Queen Victoria and a prolific exhibitor at the Royal Academy, and his wife, Georgina Woodcock. He was grandson and great-grandson of the engravers Charles *Heath (1785–1848) and James *Heath (1757–1834) [see under Heath family].

Heath was educated at Westminster School, at University College, London, where he won an exhibition in English, and subsequently at the then German University of Strasbourg. When he returned he was professor of English language and literature at Bedford College, London, from 1890 to 1895 and lecturer at King's College, London, from 1891 to 1895. On 6 August 1892 he married Antonie Johanna Sophie Therese Eckenstein (1868/9–1893), the daughter of Friedrich Gottlieb Eckenstein, a merchant, of Canonbury. Following her death he married, on 26 March 1898 Frances Elaine Sayer (1874/5–1939), the daughter of James Hawkins Sayer, a draper, of High Barnet and Hastings; they had two sons. From 1895 Heath was assistant registrar and librarian of London University. He edited *Modern Languages Quarterly* from 1897 to 1903, and was joint editor in 1898 of the *Globe Chaucer*. But he gave up an academic for an administrative career. In 1901 he became academic registrar and acting treasurer at London University at the time when it had just adopted a new constitution in an attempt to meet the pressures of contending interests, and Heath was seen as the best person to handle the position.

Heath's effectiveness and reputation soon led to his leaving the university for the Board of Education, where he was appointed director of special inquiries and reports. This post had been created by Arthur Acland, when in Gladstone's cabinet in 1894, to develop a new section within the education department to study systems, problems, and their solutions, and he had appointed Michael Sadler. Sadler's resignation in 1903 as a consequence of changed political circumstances and a clash with R. L. Morant—at one time his assistant but now permanent secretary—had led to an outcry. The board published a blue book in which it sought to justify its actions, and it needed to appoint as successor someone who was widely acceptable, expert, and well-informed on educational matters.

Within the broad field to which he had been appointed, Heath's interest in universities proved to be most opportune. The constitutional problems of the University of London led to the appointment of the royal commission in 1909, which reported in 1913, and which Heath served as joint secretary. Within the board Morant had done much to reorganize the administration of education since becoming permanent secretary in 1902, and he was anxious to extend its remit to cover grant aid to universities. Apart from the board's grants for teacher training and engineering, grants were made directly by the Treasury to university colleges on the recommendation of its advisory committee, of which Heath became a member in 1909. In 1910 Morant established a universities branch at the board

with the intention of taking over all financial assistance to universities. The chancellor of the exchequer, Lloyd George, was not attracted by this, and another year elapsed before the Treasury agreed. From 1910 Heath was principal assistant secretary at the head of the new branch as well as director of special inquiries and reports. An advisory committee was set up under the board with Sir William McCormick as chairman and Heath having administrative responsibility for its work. The bringing together of the separate forms of grant into block grants to universities and the extension of state aid to medical schools for the first time was accomplished by Heath with vision and efficiency; it came to form the basis which the University Grants Committee itself was to use to support the growth and expansion of universities, while fully respecting their autonomy, for much of the twentieth century. When in 1919 the University Grants Committee was established under the Treasury, McCormick continued as chairman.

The outbreak of war in 1914 made clear the dangerous dependence of Britain on Germany for supplies of many vital manufactured items including drugs and pharmaceutical products, magnetos, and even tungsten needed by the steel industry. By the end of 1914 Heath had submitted to the president of the Board of Education a memorandum on the failure of industry to develop an adequate scientific base and the consequent grave shortage of researchers in industry and universities. A small group was set up by the president under the chairmanship of McCormick with Heath as a member to consider in confidence the paper and the issues which it raised. Plans were prepared by this small group to create a permanent government office to deal with the organization of scientific and industrial research. The mechanism was to be a standing advisory council responsible to a committee of the privy council, and these arrangements were put into effect in July 1915. McCormick was chairman of the advisory council, seven distinguished scientists were members, and Heath was secretary. Initially no provision was made for any administrative machinery to serve the council; the white paper which was issued announced simply that the Board of Education would accommodate and service it.

The inadequacy of this arrangement soon became apparent, and in 1916 a separate Department of Scientific and Industrial Research was created with its own parliamentary vote, responsible to parliament through the lord president of the council. Heath was appointed in 1916 as the first permanent secretary of the new department and was made KCB in 1917.

The headquarters office remained small in size and absorbed very little of the total income. Heath's scheme for the establishment of research associations to encourage and foster co-operation began in 1917 with the foundation of the Fuel Research Board, followed by the Food Investigation Board in 1918 and the Building Research Board in 1920. The award of maintenance allowances for postgraduate students training in research began in 1916, and grants were also made to distinguished scientists to help them establish new projects. By 1920 the largest share of financial resources was going to individual research organizations which the department had taken over, such as the National Physical Laboratory and the Geological Survey.

In 1925 the Australian government invited Heath to advise on the organization and development of industrial and scientific research. Following an extensive visit and survey he recommended that the existing Commonwealth Institute of Science and Industry should be developed as the Council for Scientific and Industrial Research to meet the needs of science, agriculture, and industry. These recommendations were accepted and the necessary legislation was enacted in 1926. Subsequently he undertook a similar survey in New Zealand, where his recommendation to set up a department of scientific and industrial research was accepted by the government. Canada, South Africa, and India also set up similar organizations. These developments were all in their different ways consequences of Heath's earlier report to the British government.

Heath retired in 1927 and was appointed GBE, but his retirement proved to be a period of continuing activity and service since his talent and ability were widely recognized and sought. From 1924 to 1933 he was a member of the research committee of the Colonial Office. Also in 1924 he became a member of the Royal Commission for the Exhibition of 1851, and in 1931 became a governor of Imperial College, London, where his wide knowledge and experience of education and research were said to be of inestimable value. In 1929 he was asked to take on the secretaryship of the Universities Bureau of the British Empire and to give advice to a subcommittee on the whole question of the organization of the work of the bureau. Much needed to be done. Adequate premises and staff were required, but, above all, a new constitution was essential. In spite of some opposition these things were accomplished, and, in retrospect, Sir Eric Ashby in his *Community of Universities* (1963) wrote that Heath transformed the bureau from being a one-man show, not adapted for growth, into an organization which, though still small, could grow. In due course it grew into the Association of Commonwealth Universities. In 1946 Heath published (with A. L. Hetherington) a volume entitled *Industrial Research and Development in the United Kingdom*. He died at his home, 2 Morpeth Mansions, Westminster, on 5 October 1946.   PETER GOSDEN

Sources DNB · *Nature*, 158 (1946), 823–5 · *The Times* (7 Oct 1946) · H. Melville, *The department of scientific and industrial research* (1962) · R. O. Berdahl, *British universities and the state* (1959) · H. F. Heath and A. L. Hetherington, *Industrial research and development in the United Kingdom* (1946) · E. Ashby, *Community of universities* (1963) · E. Ashby and M. Anderson, *Portrait of Haldane* (1974) · P. H. J. H. Gosden, *The development of educational administration in England and Wales* (1966) · G. Sherington, *English education, social change and war, 1911–1920* (1981) · b. cert. · m. certs. · d. cert.
Archives PRO, ED and DSIR class documents | Bodl. Oxf., corresp. with Gilbert Murray
Likenesses W. Stoneman, photograph, 1915, NPG · D. Heath, oils, Department of Scientific and Industrial Research

Wealth at death £12,760 17s. 11d.: probate, 9 Jan 1947, CGPLA Eng. & Wales

Heath, Frederick Augustus (1810–1878). *See under* Heath family (*per. c.*1775–1898).

Heath, George Edward [Ted] (1902–1969), trombonist and band leader, was born at 76 Atheldene Road, Wandsworth, London, on 30 March 1902, the son of William George Heath, a journeyman carpenter, and his wife, Phoebe Mary Watling. He was taught to play the tenor horn by his father, who was the band master of the Wandsworth borough band; he was a member of that band and had played as featured soloist at the Crystal Palace brass band competitions by the time he was eight. His elder brother Harold played the trumpet. At fourteen he found a natural preference for the trombone, and he soon decided to be a professional musician. When his father was taken ill in 1919, he had to support the family and did so by working in a busking band until 1921. He was heard by Jack Hylton and asked to join his band, but found he was not yet ready for such work at that level and left after four days. He was with the Broadway Five in 1922 and for a short time with the Queen's Hall Roof Garden Orchestra, and was then recruited to play an engagement in Vienna with Will Marion Cook's Southern Syncopated Orchestra. On 31 July 1924 Heath married Audrey Hilda Keymer (*b.* 1897/8), daughter of William Keymer, a farmer. Heath subsequently played in Jack Hylton's Kit-Kat Club Band, directed by Al Starita (1925–7), then went on tour with Hylton's Metro-Gnomes led by Ennis Parkes (Mrs Jack Hylton). Meanwhile he worked on recording dates with Bert Firman and others.

Full recognition of Ted Heath's professional talents came during his important period with the Ambrose band from October 1928 to 1935, and he was now in regular demand for film, radio, and recording dates. His first wife, Audrey, died suddenly in 1932, and on 16 December 1933 he married Moira Tracey. He was with Sydney Lipton at the Grosvenor House Hotel (1936–9) and, after two brief engagements, with Maurice Winnick at the Dorchester. He joined the Geraldo orchestra in 1941 and played in hundreds of concerts and broadcasts with it during the war years, including a tour of the Middle East in 1944. He was regularly in the band's vocal group Three Boys and a Girl.

Heath was a quietly modest man and, though not often heard as a featured soloist, became known as one of the most proficient trombonists in the British dance-band world. But throughout his playing career he always nurtured the ambition to lead a band of his own. He had led a broadcasting band occasionally from 1941. His plans were given a final impetus when he met his idol Glenn Miller, who gave good advice, both encouraging and cautionary. It was at this time that a song, '(I haven't said) thanks for that lovely weekend' (1941), which he had written with his wife Moira, was recorded by Geraldo with the vocalist Dorothy Carless and became a great hit. With the accumulated royalties from this and 'I'm gonna love that guy' (1944) he was able to finance his ambitions and, with the

George Edward [Ted] **Heath** (1902–1969), by David Wedgbury, 1960

encouragement of the BBC dance band organizer Douglas Lawrence, began to recruit his own band in 1944. It was formed as an 'all star band' specifically for radio work and was first heard on the BBC that year, during which Heath had his own regular radio show. In 1945 he was commissioned to write music for the film *London Town*, in which the band appeared, and this helped it through struggling times. The band also appeared in the film *Dance Hall* (1950), and its subsequent song hits included 'Girls, Girls, Girls' and 'When you came along', both written in 1956.

Among Heath's first sidemen were the trumpeter Kenny Baker, the pianist Stanley Black, and the drummer Jack Parnell—who was the vocalist on two of the band's first Decca recordings—and others who followed later included Ronnie Scott, Tommy Whittle, Danny Moss, and Don Rendell. Heath's aim was not merely to be as good as his old employers in the British band world but to rival the big American bands led by Duke Ellington, Count Basie, and others. The immaculately organized and driving Heath sound began to attract attention, but he found it very difficult to keep a big band on the road in the lean post-war period; it took him some eleven years to get fully established. There were broadcasts and concerts, including the band's first royal command performance in 1948, and a recording contract with Decca, who assiduously and far-sightedly promoted the Heath sound. The Sunday swing sessions at the London Palladium (109 in all, lasting until 1955) attracted a big following. During the 1950s the band featured the vocalists Lita Roza, Dickie Valentine, and Denis Lotis. Among the arrangers Heath used were John Dankworth, Tadd Dameron, Kenny Graham, George Shearing, Robert Farnon, Johnny Keating, and Bill Russo. It has been neatly said that Heath 'preferred predictable excellence to unplanned excitement', and he certainly did much to raise the standards of dance-band musicianship.

Heath's band topped the bill at the Palladium and appeared in three royal command performances. It went on a world tour in March 1955 which took in Australia, followed by a first American tour in 1956 in an exchange, after the long Musicians' Union ban was lifted, for the Stan Kenton band. For the first time a British swing band was acknowledged to rival the best of the Americans like those of Woody Herman, Kenton, and the Dorseys. That first tour covered some 7000 miles and included forty-three appearances in thirty cities before culminating with a memorable appearance at Carnegie Hall, New York, on 1 May 1956. The band appeared in the films *It's a Wonderful World* (1956) and *Jazz Boat* (1960); and Heath wrote *The Ted Heath Story* (1954) and published his autobiography *Listen to my Music* in 1957, taking its title from the band's theme tune, which he composed. There were many recorded hits, from the band's first—aptly titled 'Opus 1' (1944)—through 'Bakerloo Non-Stop' (1946), 'Turn on the Heath' (1947), Ted Heath's own 'I'm gonna love that guy' (the band's first great success in the USA, 1948), 'Lyonia' (1949), and 'Seven Eleven' (1953), to 'Swingin' Shepherd Blues' (1958); and a number of fine LPs dominated the popular music scene in the 1960s. The LPs were always thoughtfully compiled, sometimes as tributes to famous songwriters and to the great American bands which the Heath band now so closely rivalled. *Big Band Percussion* was a top seller in 1962. In 1967 the BBC broadcast an hour-long documentary, also issued on record as *21st Anniversary Album*, with tributes from many famous admirers.

Heath directed until 1964, after which ill health precluded anything other than occasional public appearances. The band carried on under the leadership of Don Lusher, playing its final concert in 2000. In his last years Heath lived at Wentworth, Surrey; he died of pneumonia in Holloway Sanatorium, Egham, on 18 November 1969.

PETER GAMMOND

Sources T. Heath, *Listen to my music* (1957) · B. Kernfeld, ed., *The new Grove dictionary of jazz*, 2 vols. (1988) · A. McCarthy, *The dance band era* (1971) · D. Newlin, 'The music of Ted Heath' [online; Ted Heath Music Appreciation Society], 10 Dec 2000 · *The Times* (20 Nov 1969) · b. cert. · m. cert. [Audrey Hilda Keymer] · d. cert. · *CGPLA Eng. & Wales* (1970)
Likenesses photographs, 1949–55, Hult. Arch. · D. Wedgbury, photograph, 1960, NPG [*see illus.*]
Wealth at death £29,006: probate, 3 Aug 1970, *CGPLA Eng. & Wales*

Heath, (Seifield) Gordon (1918–1991), actor and folk-singer, was born on 20 September 1918 in New York city, the son of Cyril Gordon Heath, originally from Barbados, and his wife, Hattie, *née* Hopper. He was educated at the City College of New York. His early stage roles included Shakespeare's Hamlet for the Hampton Institute in 1945. Later that year he made his Broadway début in *Deep are the Roots*, the critically acclaimed drama by Arnaud d'Usseau and James Gow about racism in America's deep south. Heath played Brett Charles, an American army officer who returns home to the estate on which he has been raised. While serving in Europe during the war he has been treated as an equal, but at home he is forced to confront the virulent racism of the deep south again. In 1947 Heath visited London's West End with the production,

this appearance he had played leading roles in several BBC television dramas, including *Deep are the Roots* (1950) and Eugene O'Neill's *The Emperor Jones* (1953). In 1954 he narrated the award-winning animation film by Halas and Batchelor of George Orwell's *Animal Farm*, and the following year played the young priest in a BBC radio version of Alan Paton's *Cry, the Beloved Country*. In 1956 he took part in a reading of black poetry at the Royal Court with Cleo Laine. On film he played small roles in Orson Welles's *Confidential Report* (1955), Rudolph Cartier's *Passionate Summer* (1958), and Basil Dearden's *Sapphire* (1959). When Heath visited America it was always a shock for him because in his own country he was treated like a second-class citizen. As for his acting career, he was offered very few roles worthy of his attention and he eventually became a theatre director in Paris. He also directed occasional productions for the University of Massachusetts.

In America in the 1950s, when Heath was working in Britain and France, Sidney Poitier rose to fame in Hollywood. Perhaps if Heath had stayed in America after his success on Broadway in *Deep are the Roots*, he might have been offered the roles Poitier played. But his friend Leslie Schenck did not believe that Heath would have enjoyed that kind of international fame and popularity. Schenck recalled:

> Gordon preferred to remain a free agent … He loved the theatre, and a great cross he had to bear was that there were not enough roles for him to play, but he didn't make this a crutch as some people do, not at all. He just got on with his life and made the best of things. He didn't let it destroy him. (Bourne, 147–8)

Heath died in Paris on 28 August 1991 from an AIDS-related illness. He was undoubtedly one of the most talented and respected actors to emerge in the early post-war years.

STEPHEN BOURNE

Sources G. Heath, *Deep are the roots: memoirs of a black expatriate* (1992) · S. Bourne, 'Gordon Heath and Lionel Ngakane: extraordinary expatriates', *Black in the British frame: black people in British film and television, 1896–1996* (1998), 144–53 · J. Pines, ed., *Black and white in colour: black people in British television since 1936* (1992)

Likenesses photograph, 1955 (as Othello), BBC Picture Archive, London; repro. in Bourne, *Black in the British frame*, following p. 116 · photograph, BFI [*see illus.*]

(Seifield) **Gordon Heath** (1918–1991), by unknown photographer

and received more critical acclaim. After deciding to base himself in Europe, he lived with his lover, Lee Payant, mostly in Paris, where a more liberal attitude to homosexuality existed. From 1949 they ran a popular Left Bank café called L'Abbaye, and entertained customers with their folk singing. They remained together until Lee died in 1976.

In 1950 Heath made a record-breaking tour of Britain for the Arts Council in an innovative version of Shakespeare's *Othello*, staged by the theatre critic and producer Kenneth Tynan. Heath became the third black actor to play the role in Britain, after Ira Aldridge and Paul Robeson. With Heath on the Arts Council tour was a Jamaican-born actress called Pauline Henriques, who later recalled:

> Tynan wanted to take *Othello* to the theatreless towns of Britain. We toured for six months through the Midlands, North England, Scotland and Wales, playing in school halls, church halls and, if we were lucky, a full-size theatre! Tynan decided on a most original presentation of the play. … He cast Gordon Heath as Othello. He was a slim, sensitive American actor who was really a folk singer, but he had a lot to give the theatre. We were all amazed that he had the range to play the part but he was a very good and a very unusual Othello. (Pines, 30)

Five years later Heath played Othello again in Tony Richardson's celebrated BBC television production, with Paul Rogers as Iago and Rosemary Harris as Desdemona. Before

Heath, Henry [*name in religion* Paul of St Magdalen] (*bap.* **1599**, *d.* **1643**), Franciscan friar, the son of John Heath (*d.* 1652), was baptized at St John's Church, Peterborough, on 16 December 1599. His parents were protestants who sent him in 1617 to Corpus Christi College, Cambridge, to study for the ministry. Being appointed librarian of his college, he lived in the university for about five years, graduating BA in 1621. He began to study the writings of the fathers and works of controversy. He became more and more inclined towards Roman Catholicism and adopted a religious way of life, encouraging others to follow his example. Fearing that the college authorities might expel him or have him imprisoned he fled to London. He was introduced to George Fisher (alias Musket or Muscote), a priest who received him into communion with Rome. Through the good offices of the Spanish ambassador he

En quibus afflauit virtus diffusa decorem,
Quem Mors summe auctum reddidit,Ora vides.
Si simul austerum referat,doctumq piumq
vera Patris Pauli scilicet Icon erit

Henry Heath [Paul of St Magdalen] (*bap.* **1599,** *d.* **1643**), by unknown engraver, pubd 1649

obtained letters of recommendation to the English College at Douai and Dr Kellison, the president, admitted him as a convictor. Afterwards he entered the Franciscan convent of St Bonaventure at Douai and received the habit of St Francis in 1623, assuming the name of Paul of St Magdalen. At the end of that year he became a professed member of the order.

Heath remained in the convent for nearly nineteen years, leading a life of exceptional austerity. He was appointed vicar or vice-president of his house in December 1630 and master of the scholastics and lector in moral theology. He was elected guardian in October 1632 and in 1634 this was extended for another three years. He became *custos custodum* with the office of commissary of his English brethren and sisters in the Spanish Netherlands in 1637, and on 19 April 1640 he was again appointed guardian and also lector in scholastic theology.

In December 1641, on hearing of the arrest and condemnation of one of his intimate friends, Heath begged permission to go to England and take his place. He landed at Dover and travelled to London on foot disguised as a sailor. In the spirit of St Francis he begged for lodgings and one day a householder, finding him resting on the steps of his house, summoned a constable. The discovery of some catholic writings sewn into his cap revealed his identity.

He was indicted under the act of 27 Elizabeth for being a priest and entering the realm and was executed at Tyburn on 17 April 1643. He was beatified by John Paul II on 22 November 1987. His *Soliloquia, seu, Documenta Christianae perfectionis*, completed in 1634, was published at Douai in 1651, and (in English translation) as *Soliloquies, or, The Documents of Christian Perfection* at Douai in 1674.

His father, when a widower and nearly eighty years old, went to Douai, was reconciled to the Catholic church in St Bonaventure's Convent, and became a lay brother in the community; he died on 29 December 1652.

THOMPSON COOPER, *rev.* MICHAEL E. WILLIAMS

Sources *Soliloquies, or, The documents of Christian perfection of Father Paul of St Magdalen* (1912) · Gillow, *Lit. biog. hist.*, 3.239–42 · L. Wadding, *Annales minorum*, ed. J. M. Fonseca and others, 2nd edn, 29 (1948), 146–8 · Angelus à Sancto Francisco [R. Mason], *Certamen seraphicum provinciae Angliae pro sancta Dei ecclesia*, 2nd edn (Quaracchi, 1885) · *Meditations of a martyr being the Soliloquies, or, Documents of Christian perfection of the Venerable Francis Heath OSF 1674*, ed. J. Warren, London Catholic Truth Society (1912) · *The Tablet* (22 Jan 1887), 152
Likenesses line engraving, pubd 1649, BM, NPG [*see illus.*]

Heath, Henry (*fl.* 1822–1842). *See under* Heath, William (1794/5–1840).

Heath, Henry Charles (1829–1898). *See under* Heath family (*per. c.*1775–1898).

Heath, James (1629?–1664), historian, was the son of Robert Heath, of the Strand, Westminster, cutler to Charles I. Educated at Westminster School until 1646, he matriculated at Christ Church, Oxford, at the age of seventeen on 16 December 1646. He did not receive a degree as he was one of those ejected by the parliamentary visitors in 1648. During the Commonwealth he travelled with the court of Charles II to The Hague. At some point between 1649 and 1660 he returned to London, where he lived on his patrimony, married, and had several children. When his inheritance ran dry Heath earned a living by reading proofs and by writing on recent history.

Heath's most important works were *A brief chronicle of the late intestine war in the three kingdoms of England, Scotland, and Ireland* (1661) and the controversial *Flagellum, or, The life, death, birth and burial of Oliver Cromwell, the late usurper and pretended protector of England, truely collected and published for a warning to all tyrants and usurpers*, published in 1663 and reprinted several times. In the preface to *A Brief Chronicle* Heath noted that his sources were taken from 'whatsoever authentique accounts I could procure', and stated that his work was a 'perfect relation in this series of the War and succeeding affairs'. He obtained much of his information from several narratives taken directly from the contemporaries of Charles I and other witnesses to the period covered. He admitted that he was unable to verify all incidents surrounding the war, and purposely omitted 'the successful artifices of the usurpers' (Heath, *Brief Chronicle*, 10–14).

The *Brief Chronicle* gave great offence to the high-church party in England. Dibdin criticized the first edition as 'wretchedly printed, but by no means wholly useless, seems to have been put forth rather as a vehicle for cuts of the sorriest possible description' (J. Ames, *Typographical Antiquities*, enlarged by T. F. Dibdin, 4 vols., 1810–19, 1.191), and Wood was equally scathing:

> Some copies have in them the pictures of the most eminent soldiers in the said war, which makes the book the more valued by some novices. But this *Chronicle* being mostly compiled from lying pamphlets and all sorts of news-books, there are innumerable errors therein, especially as to name and time, things chiefly required in history. (Wood, *Ath. Oxon.*, 3.664)

The work was enlarged and republished in 1663, again in octavo, and after Heath's death was continued up to 1675 by John Philips, with another continuation to 1691, both in folio.

Heath's most controversial work, the *Flagellum*, a scathing account of Oliver Cromwell, brought him the most criticism. Heath, a fervent monarchist, despised Cromwell. His resentment towards the actions surrounding the execution of the king in 1649 was understandable given his father's relationship to Charles I, his own personal experience of having been denied his education by parliament, and Heath's own relationship to the court of Charles II. Besides his being termed 'Carrion Heath' by Cromwell's principal biographer, Thomas Carlyle, Heath's account of Cromwell has been considered slanderous, and his *Flagellum* was dismissed by one author as 'the chief fountain of all the foolish lies that had been circulated about Oliver' (Clark, 9, 23). As late as 1957 Heath was still described as a 'royal propagandist' who 'followed the Royalist party line' (Ashley, 14, 18).

Heath died of consumption and dropsy on 16 August 1664 at his house in Well Close Square, Smithfield, London, aged 'hardly 40' (*Brief Lives*), and was buried on 19 August at St Bartholomew-the-Less. He was intestate and left four or five children on the parish, two of whom were bound apprentice to weavers.   WENDY A. MAIER

Sources Wood, *Ath. Oxon.*, new edn, 3.663–4 · D. Trela, *A history of Carlyle's Oliver Cromwell's letters and speeches* (1992) · G. Clark, *Oliver Cromwell* (1893) · M. Ashley, *The greatness of Oliver Cromwell* (1957) · Foster, *Alum. Oxon.* · Allibone, *Dict.* · *Letters written by eminent persons in the seventeenth and eighteenth centuries … and lives of eminent men, by J. Aubrey*, ed. J. Walker, 2 vols. (1813)
Archives Harvard U., MSS · University of Illinois, Urbana-Champaign, MSS
Likenesses print, repro. in S. T. [J. Heath], *Flagellum*, 4th edn (1669)

Heath, James (1757–1834). *See under* Heath family (*per.* c.1775–1898).

Heath, John (b. c.1585), epigrammatist, was born in Bath, Somerset. His place of birth is often given as Stalls, perhaps because of a mistaken reading of Stall Street, in the old town of Bath. He may be the John Heath, son of William Heath, who was baptized at Bath Abbey on 7 February 1585. In 1600, said to be aged thirteen, he was entered at Winchester College, a school which produced many other epigrammatists during the English Renaissance, such as John Owen and Sir John Davies. He matriculated at New College, Oxford, on 11 October 1605, when his age is given as twenty, was admitted perpetual fellow in 1609, and proceeded BA on 2 May 1609, and MA on 16 January 1613. He

resigned his fellowship in 1616, at the time of a college scandal that had seen fellows alleged to be resigning in return for payments from scholars at Winchester who were waiting to join the fellowship of New College; Heath was not personally or specifically accused of corruption, however.

In 1610 Heath published *Two Centuries of Epigrammes*, inscribed to Thomas Bilson, the bishop of Winchester's son, vaunting the 'chastity' of his work and claiming that it was free from 'filthy and obscene jests'. Many of the epigrams are addressed to well-known literary men of the day. He contributed verses to *Iusta funebria Ptolemaei Oxoniensis* (1613), the volume issued on the death of Sir Thomas Bodley, and to other collections of the kind, such as that assembled to commemorate the visit of King Christian IV of Denmark to Oxford in 1606 (BL, Royal MS 12A LXIV). In 1613 he published *Accomplishment of the Prophecies of Daniel and the Revelation*, in defence of King James against Bellarmine, translated from the original by Peter du Moulin, and Wood says he translated some works out of Spanish. He was possibly the 'J. H. Gent' who published *The House of Correction, or, Certayne Satyrical Epigrams* (1619), which was republished with a different title-page in 1621, but it is very doubtful whether he is the 'I. H.' who wrote *The Divell of the Vault, or, The Unmasking of Murther* (1606). John Davies of Hereford has an epigram to Heath in the *Scourge of Folly* and Ben Jonson in his *Discoveries* (Jonson, *Works*, ed. C. H. Herford, P. Simpson, and E. Simpson, 8.582) says contemptuously, 'Heath's epigrams and the skuller's [John Taylor's] poems have their applause'.

N. D. F. PEARCE, rev. CHRISTOPHER BURLINSON

Sources STC, *1475–1640* · Foster, *Alum. Oxon.* · Wood, *Ath. Oxon.*, new edn · T. F. Kirby, *Winchester scholars: a list of the wardens, fellows, and scholars of … Winchester College* (1888) · J. Buxton and P. Williams, eds., *New College, Oxford, 1379–1979* (1979) · H. H. Hudson, *The epigram in the English Renaissance* (1947) · IGI

Heath, John (1736–1816), judge, was the only survivor of four sons of Thomas Heath (1704/5–1759) and his first wife, Ann Pyne (*bap.* 1701, *d.* 1736). The Heaths were Exeter merchants and fullers who forsook dissent for the established church. Thomas, author of *Essay on Job*, was twice mayor and his younger and wealthier brother Benjamin was well known as a critic and bookseller. John attended Westminster School from 1748 until 1754, when he went up to Christ Church, Oxford, graduating BA in 1758 and MA in 1762. Admitted to the Inner Temple in May 1759, he was called on 25 June 1762 but probably acquired no very extensive practice, for he was town clerk of Exeter from October 1766 to May 1775.

Heath became a close friend of Lord Chancellor Thurlow and not long after becoming recorder of Exeter (25 July 1779) he was raised to the bench on the first vacancy at Thurlow's disposal, succeeding Sir William Blackstone in the court of common pleas on 7 July 1780. He refused the customary knighthood, and though the cost may have been a factor (as alleged by R. W. Blencowe in *N&Q*, 3rd ser., 2, 1862, 11), it was also in keeping with the style he cultivated on the bench. He was 'plain John Heath' in his speech, harsh and indistinct, and his utterances, which were terse and unadorned, as well as his person. He had nevertheless acquired a store of legal and general knowledge (which later impressed John Scott, first earl of Eldon, who was lord chancellor at the time of Heath's death) and he combined it with shrewd judgement of character and intense concentration on the case in hand.

Heath paid scrupulous attention to evidence and argument but once he had formed an opinion he was not readily persuaded to depart from it. In his time the common pleas was overshadowed both in volume and importance of business by the king's bench and there was little scope for its puisnes to contribute to legal development, so Heath became chiefly known as a judge in criminal trials. He held the view that 'there is no regeneration for felons in this life, and for their own sake, as well as for the sake of society, I think it is better to hang' (James, 30) and put it consistently into practice, earning a lasting reputation for severity. According to Campbell he invariably hanged horse thieves, but Heath maintained that it was only settled depravity he was severe upon, and in *Jane Part* he followed the example of other judges in construing leniently the Murder of Bastard Children by Their Mothers Act. Old Heath, as he eventually became known, was opposed to Samuel Romilly's attempts to reduce capital offences, claiming that the deterrent effect of hanging was demonstrated by the salutary results of several which he had ordered shortly after an act of 1811 had made theft from bleaching grounds a capital crime. In private life he was reputed good natured and kind.

Heath was determined to die in harness, and in his later years tried to prepare himself for the rigours of the home circuit by regularly riding out from his country home, Hayes Park in Middlesex. He had been on the bench for more than thirty-five years when he died on 17 January 1816, either at Hayes or, more probably, of an apoplexy at his London house, 36 Bedford Square. He was buried in Hayes parish church. He had not married, and the sister with whom he had lived for many years predeceased him. He left most of his property to Edward Gattey, an Exeter friend who had married his niece.   PATRICK POLDEN

Sources W. R. Drake, *Heathiana: notes, genealogical and biographical, of the family of Heath* (privately printed, London, 1881) · [I. Espinasse], 'My contemporaries: from the notes of a retired barrister', *Fraser's Magazine*, 6 (1832), 423–31 · Foss, *Judges*, vol. 8 · H. W. Woolrych, *Lives of eminent serjeants-at-law of the English bar*, 2 vols. (1869) · R. W. Blencowe, *N&Q*, 3rd ser., 2 (1862), 11 · C. James, *Curiosities of law and lawyers* (1891) · R. Newton, *Eighteenth-century Exeter* (1984) · L. Radzinowicz, *A history of English criminal law and its administration from 1750*, 1: *The movement for reform* (1948) · Farington, *Diary*, vol. 14 · A. Polson, *Law and lawyers, or, Sketches and illustrations of legal history and biography*, 2 vols. (1840) · *Law Magazine*, 17 (1837), 43 · J. N. Brewer, *London and Middlesex*, 4 (1816) · will, PRO, PROB 11/1577, fol. 77 · PRO, death duty registers, IR 26/676, fol. 43 · Foster, *Alum. Oxon.*

Archives Lincoln's Inn, London, Dampier MSS, 'Buller paper books', corresp. with Sir Francis Buller

Likenesses Reinagle, portrait; exh. Exeter 1873; in possession of J. Gatley, 1875

Wealth at death approx. £8000 personalty: PRO, death duty registers, IR 26/676, fol. 43; will, PRO, PROB 11/1577, fol. 77

Heath, John Benjamin (1790–1879), merchant and banker, was born on 6 June 1790 at Genoa, Italy, the eldest son in a family of two sons and three daughters of John Heath (1749–1830), a merchant, and his wife, Jane Louise Pasteur (1736–1834). His father came from a nonconformist family which during the 1720s had been involved in the west-country wool trade. This Exeter family had religious and filial ties with continental Europe, and in 1764 John Heath was apprenticed to Doxat et Aubert of Genoa. In 1774 he became a partner in Robert Aubert et Cie of Geneva—his mother, Rose Mary Michelet, having connections with this city's Huguenot community. Charles Heath followed his brother John, and in 1781 went to Genoa, where he was joined in a business partnership by Lyle Gibbs of Antony Gibbs & Sons. In 1798 John Heath established the London house of Heath & Co. In consequence of all these trading and social links, Heath & Co. became one of the Anglo-European mercantile houses responsible for the transmission of funds from England to Austria during the revolutionary and Napoleonic wars.

John Benjamin Heath attended Harrow School (1798–1806) and for a time was fag to Lord Byron. He then entered his father's business, and in 1816 was appointed consul-general for the kingdom of Sardinia, a reflection of the firm's commercial ties with northern Italy. During the first half of the nineteenth century Heath & Co. became an established part of the City. This can be traced through the positions held by John Benjamin Heath, who was chairman of both the London Life Association and the Society of Merchants Trading to the Continent; most importantly, he was a director of the Bank of England for fifty years. A member of the bank's internal committee of 1838 which considered the restructuring of its business, he served as deputy governor between 1842 and 1845. No doubt because of his deep involvement in the preparation and first consequences of the 1844 Bank Charter Act, in 1845 Heath was appointed governor of the bank in succession to William Cotton.

A man of wide-ranging interests, Heath was master of the Grocers' Company in the City of London in 1829, and in the same year he published *Some Account of the Company of Grocers*. An accomplished musician and linguist, he was active in literary and archaeological circles. He was a member of the Roxburghe Club and also of the Dilettante Society.

In 1811 Heath married Sophia (1793–1863), the daughter of Robert Bland MD, of London. The couple had a large family, of whom four sons and three daughters survived their parents. Heath was elected a fellow of the Society of Antiquaries in 1832 and a fellow of the Royal Society in 1843. A barony in the kingdom of Italy was bestowed on him in 1867 (and later inherited by his eldest son). His wife predeceased him in 1863, and was buried in a vault at Highgate cemetery. He was laid to rest alongside her following his own death, on 16 January 1879 at 66 Russell Square, London.

Heath's eldest son, **Robert Amadeus Heath** (1818–1882), merchant and financier, was born in London on 12 December 1818. He was educated at Harrow School and shared a number of his father's interests: in 1879 he was elected a member of the Roxburghe Club. In 1847 he married Harriet (b. 1826), the daughter of Thomas Keen of Croydon and Coulsdon, Surrey; they had one son and two daughters.

Robert Amadeus Heath entered the family firm in 1837, where he was the junior partner until his father's death in 1879. During the mid-nineteenth century Heath & Co. remained important in Anglo-Italian trade, with Robert appointed vice-consul of Sardinia in 1844. The firm developed into a merchant bank through Heath's interest in Russian state finance and then Brazilian affairs, marked by his becoming chairman of the São Paulo Railway in 1861, three years after its establishment. Heath & Co. was located at 31 Old Jewry in the City, and it was there in May 1863 that the informal and private meetings were held that led to the creation of the International Financial Society (IFS), one of the first English corporate investment banks.

The first initiative came from a French merchant bank, Crédit Mobilier; however, a group of leading bankers and financiers from the City of London decided to establish their own independent concern. This was chaired by Heath, and involved the participation of a number of City firms, including Robert Benson & Co., Samuel Dobree & Sons, Fruhling and Goschen, Frederick Huth & Co., George Peabody & Co., Stern Brothers, and Heath & Co. An interest in art led Heath, together with Sir William Drake, a City solicitor, and Sir Austen Henry Layard, the archaeologist who, with Drake, had been responsible for the creation of the Ottoman Bank in 1856, to resuscitate the Venetian glass trade. This eventually resulted in the formation of the Venice and Murano Glass and Mosaic Company to safeguard future production.

Most of Heath's business life from 1863 was devoted to the affairs of the IFS, and from 1865 he became the linchpin of its permanent management committee. During 1863 he had overseen the society's reconstitution and reflotation of the Hudson's Bay Company. He conducted the society's ill-fated involvements in the Italian Land Company and the Italian Building Society, property companies which were to rebuild Turin as Italy's capital, and, similarly, he worked with the merchant bank Glyn Mills to float the loan that financed the emperor Maximillian's bid for a Mexican empire.

The IFS was a major force in the City during the boom of the mid-1860s, but the investment bank fell prey to the 1866 crisis, and for fourteen years thereafter Heath was largely responsible for its reconstruction, a task which at times, as in 1872, he found 'irksome'. He was thus obliged to run the English Erie Committee between 1869 and 1871. The objective of this association was both to protect British investors' interests and to dislodge Jay Gould from the management of the Erie Railroad Company in an episode that has been dubbed the 'Erie wars'. More positive was Heath's role as a founder of the Syndicate Union during the early 1870s, which institutionalized the relationships between the IFS, the Ottoman Bank, and the Anglo-Austrian Bank.

On the death of his father Robert Heath succeeded to the family's Italian barony. It would appear that he had lived largely under his father's shadow and the chairmanship of the IFS had been the only major outlet for his considerable energies, together with his chairmanship of the São Paulo Railway and a directorship of the Royal Exchange Assurance. There is every indication that Heath's business career over its last sixteen years was one of disappointment. The family firm never regained, during John Benjamin Heath's declining years, the status that it had held during the mid-century, and although Robert Amadeus Heath nursed the IFS back into liquidity, his early death prevented him from capitalizing on this considerable success.

Robert Heath died at 42 rue des Mathurins, Paris, on 5 June 1882, survived by his wife, and was buried at Highgate cemetery, Middlesex.   PHILLIP L. COTTRELL

Sources H. H. Gibbs, private letter-book to W. Gibbs, GL, A. Gibbs & Sons MSS, 11036/3, 1 May 1863, 2 May 1863 · W. R. Drake, *Heathiana: notes, genealogical and biographical, of the family of Heath* (privately printed, London, 1881) · Boase, *Mod. Eng. biog.* · *CGPLA Eng. & Wales* (1879) · *CGPLA Eng. & Wales* (1882) · D. Kynaston, *The City of London*, 1 (1994) · J. Clapham, *The Bank of England: a history*, 2 vols. (1944)

Archives BL, corresp. with Sir Robert Peel, Add. MSS 40524–40597 *passim*

Wealth at death under £250,000: probate, 21 Feb 1879, *CGPLA Eng. & Wales* · £161,916 4s. 7d.—Robert Heath: probate, 4 July 1882, *CGPLA Eng. & Wales*

Heath, Sir Leopold George (1817–1907), naval officer, a younger son of George Heath (1778–1852), barrister and serjeant-at-law, and his wife, Anne Raymond Dunbar, was born in London on 18 November 1817. Douglas Denon *Heath was his eldest brother. He entered the Royal Naval College, Portsmouth, in September 1830. He gained his first medal on passing out in 1831, and in December 1840 received a prize commission as lieutenant on passing his final examination. He served on the Mediterranean and East Indies stations and in the 1846 expedition against the sultan of Borneo. He was promoted commander on 3 August 1847, and in July 1850 was appointed to command the steam sloop *Niger*, and was sent to the west coast of Africa, where he served in the small squadron under Commodore Henry Bruce at the attack on Lagos in 1851.

At the end of 1852 the *Niger* was transferred to the Mediterranean, and Heath, remaining in her, was employed at the outbreak of the Russian war in blockading the Black Sea coasts. He accompanied the expedition to the Crimea, and from 14 September 1854 was beach-master at Eupatoria during the landing. At the bombardment of Sevastopol on 17 October 1854 the *Niger* was lashed alongside the line-of-battle ship *London*, and towed her into action. On 18 November Heath was appointed acting captain of the *Sans Pareil*, flagship of Sir Edmund Lyons (the appointment being subsequently confirmed by the Admiralty). A few days later he was made captain of the port (harbour master) of Balaklava. Criticism of the port under his management by *The Times* and other London newspapers was apparently ill-informed and prejudiced. Masters of vessels at the harbour stated their satisfaction with arrangements, and Sir Edmund Lyons himself was satisfied with Heath's work; in January 1855 Lyons recommended him to the Admiralty for the important post of principal agent of transports. Heath was appointed, and held the post until the war was practically over. In November 1855 he left for England, and in December was appointed to command the screw-mortar ship *Seahorse*, intended for the bombardment of Kronstadt, but not needed because of the peace. Heath returned to the Black Sea to help bring back the troops. Though almost the most junior captain in the Black Sea Fleet, he was among the first to be created CB (25 July 1855). He was also made a member of the Légion d'honneur and the Mejidiye (fourth class). He married in 1854 Mary Emma (d. 1902), daughter of Cuthbert Marsh, of Eastbury, Hertfordshire; they had five sons and two daughters.

Following the peace Heath commanded the coastguard ship in Southampton Water for a number of years, and in April 1862 became captain of the *Cambridge*, the gunnery-school ship at Devonport. A year later he was transferred to the Portsmouth gunnery school, where he remained until appointed, in July 1867, to the screw-frigate *Octavia* (39 guns) as commodore in command in the East Indies. He arrived on the station in time to help with preparations for the expedition from Bombay under Sir Robert Napier against King Theodore of Abyssinia, and afterwards he assisted in landing the troops, though for this duty Captain George Tryon was sent out from England as transport officer. Heath was created KCB and received the thanks of parliament. From his return to England in 1870 until his promotion rear-admiral on 20 December 1871 he was vice-president of the ordnance select committee. He was not actively employed as a flag officer, and retired on 12 February 1873. He rose on the retired list to vice-admiral on 16 September 1877, and admiral on 8 July 1884. In 1897 he published his *Letters from the Black Sea … during the Crimean War*, which included his vindication of his work at Balaklava, and his attack on correspondents who wrote 'downright untruths' (Heath, viii) and 'apparently considered that to interest and excite the readers of their newspapers was their only mission' (ibid., 140). He died on 7 May 1907 at his home, Anstie Grange, Holmwood, near Dorking, Surrey. His eldest son, Arthur Raymond Heath (1854–1943), was from 1886 to 1892 Conservative MP for the Louth division of Lincolnshire. Another son, Cuthbert Eden *Heath (1859–1939), founded the insurance brokers C. E. Heath & Co. Major-General Gerard Moore Heath DSO RE (1863–1929) was the youngest son.

L. G. C. LAUGHTON, rev. ROGER T. STEARN

Sources The Times (9 May 1907) · L. G. Heath, Letters from the Black sea (1897) · WWW · O'Byrne, Naval biog. dict. · W. E. F. Ward, The royal navy and the slavers (1969) · A. D. Lambert, The Crimean War: British grand strategy, 1853–56 (1990) · Boase, Mod. Eng. biog. · WWBMP
Likenesses W. M. H. Ward & Co., photograph, 1873, repro. in Heath, Letters from the Black sea, frontispiece
Wealth at death £50,065 14s.: resworn probate, 7 June 1907, CGPLA Eng. & Wales

Heath, Neville George Clevely (1917–1946), murderer, was born on 6 June 1917 at 15 Dudley Road, Ilford, Essex, the elder son of William George Heath, a soft goods traveller, and his wife, Bessie Louise, *née* Clevely. His father claimed descent from James Heath the engraver. After leaving his minor public school, Rutlish, at the age of seventeen, Heath worked as a packer in a City warehouse before enlisting in the Artists' Rifles in 1935. He received a short service commission in the RAF in 1936, but was court-martialled and dismissed the following year. The charges against him included embezzlement, being absent without leave, and borrowing a car without its owner's permission.

Heath was a bright, personable young man with charm and ability. Tall, broad, spruce, and fresh complexioned, with blue eyes and fair, wavy hair, he attracted many women. He used his gifts to woo a succession of middle-class young women with the intention of extracting money from their families. He was an incorrigible liar, braggart, cheat, and impostor. Although it is impossible to trace all his misdeeds some episodes reached the public domain. In November 1937 he was put on probation for two years after being convicted of fraudulently obtaining credit at a Nottingham hotel and of attempting to obtain a car by false pretences. Eight other offences were taken into consideration, including impersonation of the thirteenth Baron Dudley. In July 1938 he was sentenced to three years' borstal treatment after convictions for house-breaking, forging a banker's order, and stealing jewellery. He was released from the borstal at Hollesley Bay in Suffolk immediately after the outbreak of war, and was commissioned into the Royal Army Service Corps in March 1940. While serving in the Middle East he spent lavishly in the clubs and brothels of Cairo, where he liked to flagellate young women. In July 1941 he was court-martialled for being absent without leave, issuing dishonoured cheques, and fraudulently obtaining a second pay book. He absconded from a troopship returning him to England, and under the name of Armstrong enlisted in the South African Air Force, where he undertook transport and instructional duties. His operational duties amounted to one flight in October 1944 while seconded to the RAF. He stood his third court martial in South Africa in December 1945 on charges that included wearing decorations without authority. Wimbledon magistrates convicted him on a similar charge in February 1946.

In February 1942 in South Africa, Heath married Elizabeth Hardcastle Pitt-Rivers of Johannesburg, but she divorced him in October 1945. They had one son. His sexual aggression and dissolute habits were becoming more pronounced. After being deported from South Africa he returned to London. In February 1946 he took a married woman to a bedroom of the Strand Palace Hotel, where he had registered under his favourite alias, Captain James Cadogan Armstrong. He stunned and tied her, and was caning her when the hotel manager broke in. Neither the hotel nor the woman desired publicity. On the night of 20–21 June 1946, after a day of heavy drinking, he took Mrs Margery Aimée Brownell Gardner (b. 1915) to his room at

Neville George
Clevely Heath
(1917–1946), by
unknown
photographer, in
or before 1946

Accordingly he was executed by Albert Pierrepoint on 26 October 1946 at Pentonville prison, and was buried a few hours later in quicklime by the prison wall.

RICHARD DAVENPORT-HINES

Sources M. Critchley, *The trial of Neville George Clevely Heath* (1951) · F. Selwyn, *Rotten to the core: the life and death of Neville Heath* (1988) · S. Brock, *The life and death of Neville Heath* (1947) · G. Byrne, *Neville Heath* (1954) · C. Phillips, *Murderer's moon* (1956) · P. Hill, *Portrait of a sadist* (1960) · J. D. Casswell, *A lance for liberty* (1961) · I. Adamson, *The great detective* (1966) · K. Simpson, *Forty years of murder* (1970) · b. cert.

Archives FILM BFI NFTVA, documentary footage |SOUND BL NSA, 'Neville Heath', 1993, ICA 0024466 D234 BDA

Likenesses photograph, in or before 1946, repro. in Critchley, *The trial* [*see illus.*] · photograph, 1946, repro. in Casswell, *Lance for liberty*

the Pembridge Court Hotel at Notting Hill Gate. She was a masochist who had consented to sado-masochistic rites but (perhaps inflamed by drink) he lost control. After gagging her, he lashed her with a riding crop and subjected her to cruel and disgusting violence both externally and internally. During the attack she was suffocated. Afterwards he went to Worthing to meet his fiancée, Yvonne Symonds, to whom he spoke about the murder with a detailed accuracy that could not have been gleaned from newspapers. He also sent an ill-advised letter about the murder to the investigating officer at Scotland Yard, who initiated a nationwide search so that he could be questioned. On 23 June he arrived at Tollard Royal Hotel in Bournemouth staying under the name of Group Captain Rupert Brooke. In Bournemouth on 3 July he met a young convalescent rating in the Women's Royal Naval Service, Doreen Marshall, and, after getting drunk, cut her throat, leaving her naked body in Branksome Chine. Again he subjected her body to the most intrusive and repellent mutilations. Although her body was not found until 8 July, he was detained on 6 July by police investigating her disappearance, a detective constable having noticed the resemblance between Group Captain Brooke and Heath, whom Scotland Yard wanted for questioning in the Gardner murder. Evidence quickly accumulated tying him to both crimes.

Heath went for trial for the Gardner murder at the Old Bailey on 24 September 1946 before Sir John Morris (the Marshall murder charge was held back). Heath expressed no contrition, but made little effort to escape the gallows. His counsel, Joshua Casswell, was fascinated and charmed by him. The committal proceedings aroused a great sensation, while the trial was notable for its discussion by expert witnesses of the nature of sadism as a sexual perversion, and of the question of criminal responsibility in such a murder. This was the first time in British criminal justice that sadism was examined in such scrupulous detail in a murder trial. The jury on 26 September took under an hour to find him guilty; there was no appeal.

Heath, Nicholas (1501?–1578), administrator and archbishop of York, is of uncertain origins. His family is supposed to have come from Tamworth in Staffordshire, but a later tradition has him born in London, soon after the beginning of the sixteenth century. The names and status of his parents are unknown. He had a brother, William, but no other siblings are recorded. He is supposed to have been educated at the school attached to St Anthony's Hospital, which Stow describes as having been founded by the citizens of London as 'a free schoole for poore mens children' (Stow, 2.143). Stow also refers to the excellence of the teaching which had been provided earlier in the century. The tradition that attaches him to Corpus Christi College, Oxford, soon after its foundation in 1516 is unsubstantiated, as is his supposed nomination to Cardinal Wolsey's new foundation. He certainly attended Christ's College, Cambridge, and there graduated BA before the end of 1520. He was elected to a fellowship in 1521, and obtained his master's degree in 1522. In 1524 he was elected to a fellowship at Clare College, and was probably ordained priest at about that time on the college's title. When Cardinal Wolsey visited the university, Heath is supposed to have made such a good impression on him that he became one of his chaplains, but he did not leave Cambridge, where he was a university chaplain from 1529 to 1532.

Heath seems to have been personally known to Cranmer, and it may have been the future archbishop who introduced him to the clerical circle being patronized by the Boleyn family. In February 1532 he was provided to the vicarage of Hever in the deanery of Shoreham, and probably left the university at about that time. He has been tentatively identified as the chaplain who accompanied Cranmer on his German embassy later in 1532. He is noted to have preached 'wittily and learnedly' during the proceedings against Elizabeth Barton, the Nun of Kent, and her associates in 1533, and was at this time clearly a member of the evangelical circle around the archbishop. In 1534 he was appointed archdeacon of Stafford, and was commended by Cranmer to Cromwell, as a result of which in May of that year he accompanied Thomas Eliot on a mission to Germany. In 1535 he went with Edward Fox on his embassy to the Lutheran princes, and is said to have made a favourable impression both on Philip Melanchthon and on Martin Bucer. His conduct on that mission clearly

ATATIS 63.
1566

NICHOLAS HEATH   ARCH B. OF YORKE

Nicholas Heath (1501?–1578), by Hans Eworth, 1566

pleased the king, who appointed him an almoner to the royal household, and in 1537 he was instituted to the rectory of Bishopbourne and the deanery of South Malling, which he seems to have held in plurality with his existing benefices.

Heath acted closely with Cranmer over the biblical translations which resulted in the Great Bible of 1539, and it was probably with a view to strengthening the evangelical presence on the bench of bishops that he was nominated to the see of Rochester on 25 March 1540, no doubt with Cromwell's blessing. He was consecrated on 4 April. He was sworn of the king's council on 3 October 1540, specifically so that he could try cases in Star Chamber, and appointed a master of requests. Along with Cuthbert Tunstall of Durham he was then appointed by the king to 'oversee and peruse' the second edition of the Great Bible in 1541. In 1542 he supported Cranmer in the latter's attempts to modify the rigour of the Act of Six Articles, and in 1545 he was named to a commission for the suppression of 'superstitious practices'.

However, by this time Heath seems to have been having second thoughts about the extent of his evangelical commitment, and was one of those who benefited from the conservative reaction of the early 1540s. On 22 December 1543 he was elected bishop of Worcester, the see being vacant by the resignation of the advanced evangelical Hugh Latimer; the temporalities were restored on 22 March 1544, and he was enthroned by proxy on 10 April. Little is known of Heath as diocesan during his relatively brief incumbency at Rochester, but he seems to have been

both resident and conscientious. At Worcester, not being much in favour with the government for most of his episcopate, he was again able to spend time in his diocese. In 1548 he was pressed into an exchange of lands with the earl of Warwick, for which Warwick sought the duke of Somerset's support. Unusually, however, this was a reasonably fair exchange, and the temporalities suffered little, if at all. He carried out the usual local responsibilities of a diocesan, and was assessed to provide five great horses for military purposes, also in 1548. Heath's relations with his cathedral city were not always amicable, but there is little sign of overt hostility towards him. He was a good steward of his resources, although perhaps a little generous to his family when it came to leases, and it was only after he was deprived in 1551 that the diocese began to suffer financially.

Later in 1544 Heath was involved in preparing new statutes for those cathedrals which had been secularized after the dissolution of the monasteries, but he was not close enough to the court to be involved in the political struggles at the end of Henry's reign. Following the accession of Edward VI, Heath, unlike Gardiner, made no protest against either the royal injunctions or the homilies of the summer of 1547, but his position in respect of the changes seems to have been very similar. In December he responded in a conservative manner to Cranmer's questionnaire on the sacraments, and voted against the government in the House of Lords. By 1549 he was clearly identified as an opponent of change, but had committed no act of overt disobedience. In April 1549 he was included in a commission to investigate heresy, because the targets on that occasion were radical protestant dissenters, and he accepted the prayer book later that year with no recorded objection. There were, however, limits to his flexibility, and in 1550 he refused to sign the new ordinal, in spite of being one of those who had been appointed to devise it. He did not refuse to use it, but he had now overstepped the shadowy line which separated discontent from opposition. So far he had been protected, partly because of his long friendship with Cranmer, and partly because of his eirenic disposition. However, the earl of Warwick, the new president of the council, was less accommodating than Protector Somerset had been, and Cranmer's influence was being challenged by those more radical than himself. Early in 1551 Heath was brought before the council for his obstinacy over the ordinal, and when he refused to give way, on 4 March he was committed to the Fleet.

During the summer Heath came under pressure not only to sign the ordinal but also to accept the government's policy on the removal of altars and images. The latter course he found particularly obnoxious, and when he refused to yield, he was deprived of his see by royal commission on 10 October. Unlike the more abrasive dissidents such as Gardiner and Bonner, he did not remain in prison, but was released into the custody of Nicholas Ridley, bishop of London, in June 1552. At no time did Heath commit any clear statement of his position to paper, and it has to be reconstructed from his actions. He appears to have accepted the royal supremacy, the English Bible, and the English liturgy (with reservations); but to have defended the traditional sacraments, particularly the mass, and traditional ceremonies. By 1553 he had probably decided, like Gardiner, that the royal supremacy had been a mistake because of the manner in which it could be exploited by heretics, and was ready for a return to papal obedience.

Whatever the source of her information, Queen Mary had no doubts about Heath's reliability. Immediately after her accession he was recognized (6 August 1553) as bishop of Worcester, well in advance of any judicial review or decision; and at the same time appointed president of the council in the marches of Wales. He returned to the privy council on 4 September. When the papal jurisdiction was restored at the beginning of 1555 he was absolved and dispensed by Cardinal Pole, because neither his orders nor his appointment were recognized by Rome. As a councillor he was actively involved in the persecution of heresy, when that began in February 1555, and Foxe records his participation in a number of interrogations. Inevitably the martyrologist makes him appear bigoted and foolish, but not even Foxe claims that he was an enthusiastic persecutor. He was, however, one of Mary's more senior and experienced bishops, and when Robert Holgate was deprived of the archbishopric of York, Heath was translated there by papal provision on 21 June 1555. As *legatus natus* it was his responsibility to consecrate Pole to Canterbury after Cranmer's execution, on 22 March 1556.

Following his restoration to Worcester, Heath had applied himself to recovering losses suffered by his see during Hooper's episcopate, with at least a degree of success, although his duties as a member of Mary's privy council increasingly kept him away from his diocese after 1553. At York he was still more distracted by secular business, especially once he had become chancellor. As he attended over half the recorded council meetings of Mary's reign, he can have been only an occasional visitor to his province. However, he was now in an excellent position to defend the interests of his see, and he recovered many manors and advowsons which had been alienated by his predecessor, thereby restoring York to its position as one of England's wealthiest sees. These successes may have owed more to Mary's own policy of episcopal restoration than to any particular effort on the part of the archbishop, but the latter seems none the less to have conducted a competent management policy, albeit one very largely guided from a distance and carried out by agents. As at Worcester, Heath appears to have followed a leasing policy which favoured his own family, but with terms limited to twenty-one years.

When Stephen Gardiner died on 12 November 1555 the great seal was put into commission, and there seems to have been some disagreement between the king and queen over the appointment of his successor. Whether Heath was Philip's choice or Mary's is a matter of some controversy; perhaps he was a compromise. As chancellor, he had nothing like the panache or political influence of his predecessor, and his incumbency, from 1 January 1556 to 17 November 1558, has never been particularly

studied. When Mary died the great seal returned to the new queen, but Heath's political position was clearly revealed at once. His last act as chancellor was to proclaim Elizabeth in the House of Lords, and he was quite unequivocal (although not at all logical) in accepting her legitimacy. Briefly he remained a member of the council, and the new queen seems to have entertained hopes of his conformity to the religious settlement she was intending. Early in 1559 he collaborated with Sir Nicholas Bacon in setting up the Westminster disputation, and refused to support the Catholic participants when they objected to the procedure. However, these hopeful signs were deceptive. He voted against the settlement in the House of Lords, and refused the oath of supremacy, instead urging Elizabeth to continue her sister's policies. His integrity and outspokenness earned the queen's respect, but his deprivation inevitably followed, on 5 July 1559. For a time he was imprisoned with other deprived bishops in the Tower of London, but he clearly presented no political threat, and unlike Bonner had attracted no particular opprobrium. He was allowed to retire to his own estates at Chobham in Surrey in February 1561, on the condition that he abandon all public life.

Heath retained the queen's personal favour and lived in peaceful retirement for almost twenty years, dying in December 1578. For practical purposes he ended his days as a respected country gentleman, and was buried in the parish church at Chobham, neither his friends nor the authorities showing any objection to this accommodation. His brother William had predeceased him in 1569, and William's son Thomas was his executor and heir at Chobham. His will was proved in the prerogative court of Canterbury on 5 May 1579.   DAVID LOADES

Sources LP Henry VIII, vols. 7–17 • Foster, *Alum. Oxon.* • Venn, *Alum. Cant.*, 1/2.347 • *Fasti Angl., 1541–1857*, [Canterbury] • *Fasti Angl., 1541–1857*, [York] • *Fasti Angl., 1541–1857*, [Ely] • Gillow, *Lit. biog. hist.*, 3.242–51 • W. F. Carter, *Administrations in the prerogative court of Canterbury*, ed. R. M. Glencross, 2 vols. [1912–17] • *CPR, 1547–58* • J. Strype, *Annals of the Reformation and establishment of religion … during Queen Elizabeth's happy reign*, new edn, 4 vols. (1824) • *CSP dom., 1547–58* • *APC, 1542–70* • D. MacCulloch, *Thomas Cranmer: a life* (1996) • J. Stow, *A survay of London*, rev. edn (1603); repr. with introduction by C. L. Kingsford as *A survey of London*, 2 vols. (1908); repr. with addns (1971) • F. Heal, *Of prelates and princes: a study of the economic and social position of the Tudor episcopate* (1980) • L. B. Smith, *Tudor prelates and politics, 1536–1558* (1953)
Archives PRO, chancery, star chamber, and domestic state papers
Likenesses H. Eworth, oils, 1566, NPG [*see illus.*]

Heath, Sir Richard (*bap.* 1637, *d.* 1702), judge, was baptized on 22 October 1637 at Shalford, Surrey, the son of Roger Heath (*c.*1601–1661), recorder of Guildford, and Frances (*bap.* 1617, *d.* 1696), daughter of Simon Caryl of Surrey. Heath was admitted to the Inner Temple on 6 July 1652 and called to the bar on 24 November 1659. Still residing at the Inner Temple, he was licensed on 1 February 1665 to marry Katharine (*b.* 1644/5, *d.* in or before 1671), then aged twenty, daughter of Henry Weston MP of Ockham, Surrey. They had two daughters. This marriage must have ended with the early death of his wife because on 11 October 1671 at Guildford, Heath was licensed to marry Lettice (*b.*

*c.*1650, *d.* 1724x7), then aged about twenty-one, daughter of Sir George Woodroffe MP of Seale, Surrey. They had three sons and two daughters.

Heath's career seems to have proceeded quietly with his appointment to the bench of his inn in October 1677 and his appointment as a serjeant-at-law in January 1684. He was appointed a baron of exchequer on 21 April 1686 and was knighted on 22 October (the same day as Allibone, the Roman Catholic judge). He was in favour of the king's dispensing power, and seems to have been acting on court instructions to find the seven bishops guilty of a factious libel if Archbishop Sancroft's statement of 6 November is correct. Following the seven bishops' trial Heath went on circuit, in August 1688, and in his charge to the juries suggested that those lighting bonfires to celebrate the acquittal of the bishops should be indicted for riot. In October he wrote to the earl of Dartmouth for his assistance with Lord Chancellor Jeffreys to ensure that he did not lose his place. However, the invasion of William of Orange saw Heath's patent revoked, on 3 November 1688, and he was excepted from the Act of Indemnity passed in 1690 because of his support for the dispensing power.

Heath went into retirement at Hatchlands, East Clandon, Surrey, the manor he purchased in 1692, and on 28 July 1702 was reported to have died the previous week. He was buried at East Clandon. Following the death of his son, Sir Thomas, his grandsons conveyed the manor by private act to Sir Peter King in 1718. Heath's widow made her will in October 1724 and it was proved in September 1727. STUART HANDLEY

Sources Sainty, *Judges*, 126 · Baker, *Serjeants*, 448, 517 · *IGI* · J. E. Martin, ed., *Masters of the bench of the Hon. Society of the Inner Temple, 1450–1883, and masters of the Temple, 1540–1883* (1883), 35, 48 · J. L. Chester and J. Foster, eds., *London marriage licences, 1521–1869* (1887), 662 · O. Manning and W. Bray, *The history and antiquities of the county of Surrey*, 2 (1809), 109 · F. P. Verney and M. M. Verney, *Memoirs of the Verney family during the seventeenth century*, 2nd edn, 4 vols. in 2 (1907), vol. 2, p. 458 · *The manuscripts of the earl of Dartmouth*, 3 vols., HMC, 20 (1887–96), vol. 1, p. 118 · N. Luttrell, *A brief historical relation of state affairs from September 1678 to April 1714*, 5 (1857), 198 · HoP, *Commons, 1715–54*, 1.120 · Foss, *Judges*, 7.219–20 · *State trials*, 12.503–4 · will, PRO, PROB 11/617, sig. 210 [Lettice Heath]
Archives Folger, legal notes
Likenesses portrait; known to be at Hatchlands in 1814

Heath, Sir Robert (1575–1649), judge, was born in Brasted, Kent, on 20 May 1575, the son of Robert Heath (1535–1615) and his wife, Anne, formerly Posyer (1545–1626). Heath was descended from at least three generations of lawyers, and his father geared the boy's education to this career. Heath studied first at Tonbridge School (1582–9), then at St John's College, Cambridge. He left St John's in 1592 without taking a degree and entered Clifford's Inn. In May 1593 he moved on to the Inner Temple and on 19 May 1603 he gained the rank of utter (chief) barrister. Heath's association with the Temple was intimate. He served as summer reader there in 1619, as bencher (1617–31), and as treasurer (1626–8). These appointments, however, came only after he was established at court. He married on 10 December 1600 Margaret Miller (1578–1647).

As early as 1599 Robert Heath the elder brought his son

Sir Robert Heath (1575–1649), attrib. Cornelius Johnson

into the circle of Henry Brooke, Lord Cobham, but the younger Heath had no major patron until at least 1604, when he became a client of James Elphinstone, Lord Balmerino, president of the court of session. In 1607 Balmerino, seeking political allies as his position declined, sent Heath as a 'gifte' to Robert Carr, later the earl of Somerset, who was rising at court and would be the favourite of James I until his own fall in 1616. Like Heath's other early patrons, however, Carr did little to advance him. The situation changed dramatically in late 1616, when Heath entered the service of George Villiers, later duke of Buckingham.

Rise to power Owing to Buckingham's patronage, Heath began to gain major offices. In November 1618 Buckingham, supported by James, put pressure on the corporation of London to elect Heath as recorder. The Londoners had requested a free election, preferring a candidate who was not bound to the court, but Heath performed well from the perspective of the corporation. His most notable effort was to win London a new charter in 1619. So advantageous to the city was this charter that the court demanded its nullification, and Sir Henry Yelverton, who as attorney-general had drawn it, was stripped of his office and imprisoned by Star Chamber. Heath was charged with connivance in the preparation of the charter, but the case against him was weak, and this, probably coupled with Buckingham's support, secured him from punishment. Buckingham may also have been instrumental in obtaining for Heath his first major crown office, that of solicitor-general, on 22 January 1621; on 28 January Heath was knighted. When the attorney-generalship was vacated in autumn 1625 he obtained that office in turn, receiving his patent on 31 October.

The common practice of London was to elect the recorder to parliament, and therefore in November 1620 it returned Heath to the Commons, although when parliament met in January 1621 he sat as solicitor-general. He was returned for East Grinstead to the parliaments of 1624 and 1625. Since he had been elevated to the post of attorney-general by the time parliament met in 1625, his election was challenged on a precedent from 1614 that barred that officer from sitting in the Commons, but he was allowed to remain. East Grinstead elected him again in 1626, but this time the Commons did exclude him. While a member of the Commons Heath showed himself to be an active and able debater, and he chaired a number of major committees. In the parliaments of 1626 and 1628–9 he assisted the Lords, leading the prosecution of the earl of Bristol in 1626, and in April 1628, during a conference of both houses, confronting Sir Edward Coke in the celebrated debate 'on the liberty of the subject'. During the same years, as attorney-general, he played a key role in two cases that made him anathema to parliamentary radicals. In 1627 he successfully parried efforts by the 'five knights' to regain their freedom after having been gaoled for refusing to contribute to the forced loan of 1626. In late March 1628 John Selden accused Heath of having attempted to alter the records of the king's bench in such a way as to make the judges' ruling that the knights be remanded into a precedent establishing the king's authority to imprison indefinitely. It does appear that Heath had pressed the judges 'to have a judgment entered' (words of Sir James Whitelocke, Relf, 93), but not that the document provided the king with additional powers—powers that, in fact, Heath had not broached in court. Furthermore, it was clear that Heath had addressed the judges on the king's command. Possibly for this reason, parliament let the matter drop.

In early 1629, however, Heath came under attack in the Commons for having arranged the pardon of four churchmen whose views were condemned by many members and for having purposely mismanaged the prosecution of ten alleged Jesuits, so that all went free. Attempting to defend himself against the complaints, Heath revealed secret transactions. This prompted Charles I to confine him to his chambers (7 February), then, after several crown officials interceded on his behalf, to free him with the admonition to 'feare God and the Kinge and none els' (Sir Francis Nethersole to Elizabeth of Bohemia, 14 Feb 1629, Notestein and Relf, 250). Parliament was dissolved in March 1629, but only after the speaker was held in his chair while Sir John Eliot read a radical screed to the members. In the wake of this tumult, Heath successfully prosecuted Eliot and five other radicals.

Heath's time as a law officer coincided with extensive involvement in English colonization. In 1620 he became a charter member of the Council for New England and a councillor of the Virginia Company, simultaneously acquiring a tract from the latter. Although he co-authored the report that led to the dissolution of the Virginia Company in 1624, he remained actively involved in the affairs of the colony. In October 1629 Heath was granted a patent for 'Carolana', a tract in North America running from lat. 31° to 36° N and encompassing the Bahamas as well. Styled 'lord predominant', he did little to plant the vast region, and efforts by others to colonize there failed. Nevertheless, Heath retained an interest in colonial affairs. In 1637 he supported the formation of an English West India Company, arguing in a petition to the king that the projected company could serve national goals by attacking Spanish holdings in the Caribbean. Charles, however, refused to approve the plan.

Downturn in fortune The assassination of Buckingham in August 1628 deprived Heath of his main benefactor, and although he subsequently secured other patrons, notably James Hay, earl of Carlisle, he was never again as secure at court. In October 1631 he was raised to the bench as chief justice of the common pleas, but this may have marked a natural progression from the attorney's office rather than exceptional favour. On 13 September 1634 he was dismissed from the bench. The dismissal was probably engineered by William Laud, who may have been concerned that Heath was not friendly to him or his faction and might oppose from the bench certain policies that he advocated. To the end of his life Heath claimed that he did not know why he had been dismissed, and shortly before his death wrote in a memoir that no cause had then or since been given. It appears, however, that the reason for dismissal given out at the time was that, while attorney-general, Heath had engaged in speculative ventures that went against the king's interest. These activities were serious enough for him to be threatened with trial in Star Chamber, though he avoided this by a petition to Charles. While admitting no specific wrongdoing, he begged the king's 'gratious pardon for any errors past, which in soe many yeers service cann not but be many' (PRO, SP 16/274/22).

Heath quickly regained favour at court, and on 12 October 1637 he was appointed a king's serjeant. Nevertheless, the dismissal had done irreparable harm to his finances. Despite enjoying a considerable income during 1621–34 he had gone deeply into debt, using his wealth to purchase land and to invest in various highly speculative ventures, such as an effort to drain the Great Level and another to mine lead. Several of the schemes had tied him to Sir Cornelius Vermuyden, a Dutch engineer and his primary partner during these years. After the dismissal Heath was forced to sell much of his land to satisfy creditors, but he continued to speculate. Several of his enterprises involved him in extended litigation.

In March 1640 Heath stood as the court candidate for election to parliament in Reading, but failed to garner a single vote. On 23 January 1641 he was raised to the bench again, as a justice of king's bench, and consequent to this position he served as a messenger from the Lords to the Commons during the early months of the Long Parliament. Heath was not impeached at this time, as were the judges who had supported the crown in the ship-money decision of 1637. He was therefore free to follow the king and joined him at York in June 1642. The following 18 October he was raised to the position of chief justice of king's bench, replacing Sir John Bramston, who had been among those impeached and was bound to remain in London. Heath pursued his judicial duties so long as the royalist government remained viable. In November 1645, however, parliament impeached him and four other royalist judges and vacated their offices.

Loyalties Heath's perspectives and loyalties are well reflected in his personal letters and papers, in official correspondence, in legal opinions and statements in court, and in the speeches he made in association with his service in parliament. In most respects he was a moderate. He was high prerogative in that he believed that the monarch possessed extraordinary, virtually unlimited powers, which he could invoke in emergencies to augment his ordinary authority, and he left it to the king to decide when circumstances required that he use these powers. He also argued for the proposition that the king could do no wrong. Parliament clearly ranked lower in his constitutional scheme than did the monarch. During the series of conflicts between king and parliament that marked the 1620s, he generally argued that parliament should promote contentious issues by way of advice or petition, rather than confront the monarch through bills or pressure him by threatening to withhold supply until grievances were addressed. Nevertheless, he supported parliament's right to debate most matters, and during the three sessions when he sat in the Commons he joined the reformers on a number of issues, including the drive against monopolies in 1621. Although not surprisingly he was critical of parliamentary radicals and called on the king to bar them from crown service, he took a moderate stance toward the opposition at large. Even after the execution of Charles I in January 1649, he advised the court in exile to treat former rebels with moderation if it regained power, excepting only regicides from pardon.

Deeply religious himself, Heath saw the church as a unifying force and was intolerant of those who stood outside it. During the 1620s he was obliged, as a law officer, to administer campaigns to curtail the enforcement of anti-recusant legislation. Nevertheless, he supported the persecution of Catholics, even petitioning Charles to intensify it. But he was also fearful of radical protestants, and when addressing Star Chamber in the case of Alexander Leighton (June 1630) he stated that he was uncertain 'whether the Jesuits or the Protestants, frayed out of their witts, be the greatest enimys to a monarchical government' ('Speech of Sir Robert Heath', 7).

Heath's preoccupation with order was also evident in his social philosophy. He focused on the élite, whom he considered bound to promote unity. His attitude toward the lower classes was less consistent. The relationship that he had with tenants on his manors was often contentious, and his attempts to improve lands so that he might increase rent caused a series of riots. On the other hand, a judicial opinion that he prepared in 1633 showed marked sympathy for the poor and promoted a liberal interpretation of poor-law policy.

Exile and family Heath appears to have remained in Oxford until about the time of its surrender (June 1646). Although parliament did not move to apprehend him, he left England, later writing, 'I doe not call it an exile, because I made choice to desire it, rather than to live suspected' (Heath papers, Compton-Verney book, no. 65). Having embarked at Calais in December 1646 he moved on to Paris, and soon afterwards to St Germain, where he resided for more than two years before returning to Calais. His health began to decline in 1648, and after a lingering illness he died at Calais on 20 August 1649.

At his death Heath left behind six children: Mary (1608–1669); Edward (1612–1669); John (1614–1691), attorney of the duchy of Lancaster under Charles II; George (1617–1672), sometime rector of West Grinstead; Robert *Heath (*bap.* 1620), a royalist officer and the author of a collection of poems entitled *Clarastella*; and Francis (1622–1683), a civil lawyer. Heath appears to have been a devoted father, and he promoted the careers of his sons, sending all five to Cambridge and all but George on to legal studies at the Inner Temple. During the civil war he used his influence as chief justice to provide potentially lucrative offices for the four sons who had studied law. Heath's wife died at Brasted in December 1647, where she had remained during his exile, and a year later Heath wrote 'Anniversarium', a document that contained a tribute to her. On 7 September 1649 Heath's body was interred beside hers in the Heath chapel at Brasted church.

Heath never wrote for publication. During his lifetime, however, a work was published under his name, *A Machavillian Plot* (1642); this was the text of a document that Heath had prepared in 1629, condemning a memorial that called on the king 'to Bridle the Impertinence of Parliaments'. In 1694 William Brown, a clerk in common pleas, published two books that comprised Heath's law notes: *Praxis almae curiae cancellariae*, a collection of chancery precedents, and *Maxims and Rules of Pleading*. At least four editions of the former work were published, the last in 1725, while *Maxims and Rules of Pleading* was republished in an annotated edition in 1771.

In July 1626 Heath advised his two eldest sons, who were then students at Cambridge, 'remember that yee are the sonns of a father as is soe well known in the world that your faults will be more observed than of others' (Heath papers). He was indeed well known, both in his own time and for several generations beyond, but he was not consistently admired. Heath was often perceived along political lines: royalists admiring him; critics of the crown prerogatives and policies that he defended reviling him. More objectively, it may be said that he stood among the ablest crown officials of the early Stuart period.

PAUL E. KOPPERMAN

Sources P. E. Kopperman, *Sir Robert Heath, 1575–1649: window on an age* (1989) • P. E. Kopperman, 'Profile in failure: the Carolana project, 1629–1640', *North Carolina Historical Review*, 59 (1982), 1–23 •

PRO, State papers, SP 16 · University of Illinois, Heath papers · W. Notestein and F. H. Relf, eds., *Commons debates for 1629* (1921) · 'Anniversarium', ed. E. P. Shirley, *Philobiblon Society Publications*, 1 (1854) · P. E. Kopperman, 'Ambivalent allies: Anglo-Dutch relations and the struggle against the Spanish empire in the Caribbean, 1621–1641', *Journal of Caribbean History*, 21 (1987), 55–77 · I. H. C. Fraser, 'Sir Robert Heath: some considerations of his work and life', MA diss., 1954 · *DNB* · private information (2004) [J. H. Baker] · F. H. Relf, ed., *Notes of the debates in the House of Lords … AD 1621, 1625, 1628*, CS, 3rd ser., 42 (1929) · T. G. Barnes, 'Cropping the Heath: the fall of a chief justice, 1634', *Historical Research*, 64 (1991), 331–43 · W. A. Shaw, *The knights of England*, 1 (1906), 176 · 'Speech of Sir Robert Heath, attorney-general, in the case of Alexander Leighton, in the star chamber, June 4, 1630', *Camden miscellany, VII*, ed. J. Bruce and S. R. Gardiner, CS, new ser., 14 (1875) · J. H. Bloom, ed., 'Liber Edwardi Heath', *Miscellanea Genealogica et Heraldica*, 5th ser., 4 (1920–22), 156–7, 164
Archives BL, family and Verney Papers, Egerton MSS 2978–3008; Eg. Ch. 645-2116 · Society of Genealogists, London, letters and papers · University of Illinois, Urbana-Champaign, rare book room, commonplace book, diary, corresp., and papers | BL, letters, incl. to Sir William Trumbull · CKS, U55 · Northants. RO, 'NPL' collection · PRO, state papers and other collections · Shakespeare Birthplace Trust RO, Stratford upon Avon, Willoughby de Broke papers
Likenesses T. Rawlins?, silver medal, 1645, BM · W. Hollar, etching, 1664, BM, NPG; repro. in W. Dugdale, *Origines juridiciales* (1666) · C. Johnson, oils, Inner Temple, London · attrib. C. Johnson, portrait, priv. coll. [*see illus.*] · bust, Inner Temple, London · effigy, Heath chapel, Brasted · oils, Public Library, Nassau, Bahamas · oils, St John Cam.
Wealth at death most wealth and property distributed in family before death, or gone to creditors; small bequests, incl. books: Shakespeare Birthplace Trust RO, Stratford upon Avon, DR 98/1652; Kopperman, *Sir Robert*, 300

Heath, Robert (*bap.* 1620, *d.* in or after 1685), poet, was baptized at St Martin Ludgate on 22 October 1620, the fourth of five sons of Sir Robert *Heath (1575–1649), judge, and his wife, Margaret (1578–1647), daughter of John Miller, of Tunbridge Wells. He was admitted in 1634 as a fellow-commoner at Corpus Christi College, Cambridge, where he joined his elder brother George (*b.* 1617) and was in turn joined by his younger brother, Francis (*b.* 1622). He wrote a complimentary Latin tetrastich for the *Grammaticae Gallicae compendium* (1636) of Gabriel Dugres or Du Gres, a religious exile who taught French privately in the university. Some Greek verses that he contributed to the university volume on the birth of Princess Anne (*Synodia*, 1637, sigs. C3, C3v) are grouped there with Latin pieces by his brothers. His father's position at the Inner Temple gained him special admission there on 28 January 1638. After the outbreak of civil war the family moved to Oxford, where on 14 June 1643 Charles I appointed Heath one of the two auditors of the court of wards (BL, Egerton MSS 2978, fols. 133v, 139; 2979, fol. 26).

Some poems that Heath wrote during this period imply service in the field, though between March 1644 and September 1646 he seems to have found leisure to render into English all twelve books of the *Aeneid* (MS in the Clark Library; *N&Q*, 217, 1972, 19–20). In the same spirit his brother John (later Sir John) at some time rendered Martial's epigrams into English verse (BL, Add. MS 27343; Egerton MS

2982, fols. 175v–242v). *Clarastella; together with poems occasional, elegies, epigrams, satyrs. By Robert Heath, esquire* was entered in the Stationers' register by Humphrey Moseley on 24 October 1650; Thomason acquired his copy on 7 May following (BL, E.1364(1)). Moseley's address to the reader states that the volume was issued without its author's knowledge, and the prefatory verses by 'G. H.'—probably Heath's brother George—suggest that he was absent from England at the time. The earliest datable poem laments the death of Anne Kirke, *née* Killigrew, in July 1641, while the latest is that 'On the unusual cold and rainie weather in the Summer, 1648'. Despite obvious debts to Carew, Crashaw, and others, his poems have an assurance that shows him something more than a mere versifier with a competent command of metre and extended conceits. Seventeen pieces by 'R. H.' printed from a manuscript in the Rosenbach foundation in an appendix to L. C. Martin's edition of Herrick (pp. 423–39) are almost certainly the work of Heath (*N&Q*, 203, 1958, 249).

On 6 July 1652 Heath took up a call to the bar. In November 1653 the poet Fanshawe, writing to Edward Heath, sent his service to 'y^r Brother Robin' (BL, Egerton MS 2978, fol. 289v). He is evidently the 'R. H.' whose monogram is engraved on the two title-pages of *Paradoxical Assertions and Philosophical Problems* (1659), not least because a copy is listed, with a mark of distinction, among the books left by his brother Francis in 1683 (BL, Egerton MS, 2983, fol. 159). The work had been licensed on 26 November 1658 by Ralph Wood, who prefaced it with a letter to 'Thomas Norton in Blackfriars' that speaks of the 'great Friendship you have had and still preserve with the Author'. The brief prose pieces, 'long since written by the Author for his Youthful Pastime and Delight', consist of absurd, facetious, and sometimes indelicate propositions, followed by mock-scientific explanations for matters of common observation.

After the Restoration, although the Inner Templars appointed Heath auditor to their treasurer in November 1660, he and his brother John found themselves deprived of any hopes from their former grants when the abolition of the court of wards was confirmed (BL, Egerton MS 2979, fols. 26–33). In April 1661 he addressed an appeal for restoration of the court to an unnamed MP (ibid., fols. 41–4). John's petition for redress described Robert as related to Clarendon 'by his marriage wth one Mrs Goodfellow descended by the mother from one of y^r name & famyly' (ibid., fol. 33), and on these grounds in May he petitioned the chancellor to prefer his suit to the king for another place. Robert was then living at Otford, near Sevenoaks, in Kent, where he owned a moiety of the rectory left jointly to the three youngest brothers by their mother. In March 1667 the poet Sir John Mennes sought the reversion of an estate for Heath's sons John and Robert. In a covenant of 1672, where he is described as 'Maior Robert Heath of Otford' (BL, Egerton MS 2985, fol. 143), his second son, Robert, was named as residuary legatee of the estate of his uncle George. As administrator of the will Heath was arrested and briefly imprisoned in September 1673 for an unresolved debt of George's (ibid., fol. 153). His interest in

Otford rectory having lapsed in 1676, about June of the following year he petitioned on account of his sufferings in the late times to benefit from his discovery of a debt owed to the crown. Both he and his wife were still living in August 1681 when his brother Francis stipulated the bequest of rings to them. Heath made his final appearance on the Kentish grand jury panel in September 1685.

W. H. KELLIHER

Sources Venn, *Alum. Cant.* · *Synodia*, Cambridge University (1637) · F. A. Inderwick and R. A. Roberts, eds., *A calendar of the Inner Temple records*, 5 vols. (1896–1936) · *CSP dom.*, 1660–85 · will, PRO, PROB 11/375, sig. 5 [Francis Heath] · calendar of assize records, Kentish indictments, 1685, PRO, Charles II, 1676–8, no. 1186 · *N&Q*, 203 (1958), 249 · *N&Q*, 217 (1972), 19–20 · R. Herrick, *Works*, ed. L. C. Martin (1956)
Archives BL, Heath and Verney papers, Egerton MSS 2978–2985
Wealth at death see PRO, PROB 11/375, fol. 5

Heath, Robert (d. 1779), mathematician, was an army officer, described posthumously as a 'half-pay Captain of Invalids' (T. Leybourn, *The Mathematical Questions Proposed in the Ladies' Diary*, 4 vols., 1817, 1.ix). In 1736 he was seeking help with his studies from Thomas Simpson (1710–1761), whose rebuff may have engendered Heath's lifelong antipathy to him. In 1737 he was in Foulsham, 20 miles north-west of Norwich, and Simpson's pupil, John Turner (b. c.1717) 'of London', was reporting Heath's indignation over Simpson's alleged plagiarism. Heath served with his regiment in the Isles of Scilly, and wrote *A History of the Islands of Scilly* (1750), which included a new map of the isles, drawn by himself from a 1744 survey. He is best known as a frequent contributor from 1737 to the *Ladies' Diary*, posing many of the prize problems. He was soon assisting the editor, Henry Beighton (d. 1743), with the mathematical section. On Beighton's death the Stationers' Company allowed his widow, Elizabeth, to continue the publication with Heath as editor, the pair to share £15 per issue. Heath wrote on fluxions (calculus) in 1745 from Scilly, while the sequel, dated May 1746, was from Upnor Castle, near Rochester, Kent, an ordnance establishment. He still contributed problems and solutions under his own and assumed names, including Upnorensis, Newtoniensis, Critic Anser, and Hurlothundro.

Heath recommended the *Fluxions* of William Emerson (1701–1782), belittling, without identifying, Simpson's *New Treatise* (1737) for ignoring 'Increments, which include the very notion of what a Fluxion is' (*Ladies' Diary*, 1746, 44). Turner, in his periodical, *Mathematical Exercises* (1750–53), conducted a robust defence of Simpson, signed 'Honestus', against Heath's assertions. In the 1747 *Diary* Heath appealed for material for a new periodical; on the first appearance of this independent venture the 1749 *Diary* preface announced it as its own 'Appendix', under the title of *The Palladium*. The 1751 *Diary* preface advertised it as containing 'what Things we cou'd not find room for here', giving rise to the accusation that Heath purloined for it the best contributions.

Although the appropriation of *Ladies' Diary* material formed part of the case leading to Heath's dismissal by the Stationers' Company, his more damning offence appears

to have been the printing in the 1752 issue of two pseudonymous problems in doubtful taste, probably originated by Heath himself. He was replaced by his rival, Simpson, from the issue for 1754. He had his supporters, however; Mrs Beighton wrote to Simpson that Heath had been unfairly treated, and his collaborator, Thomas Cowper (*fl.* 1735–1774) of Wellingborough, continued to support *The Palladium*, where Heath concentrated his main energies. Here he vented his feelings against Simpson, Turner, the Stationers' Company, and the *Ladies' Diary*. His journal, which survived almost until his death, often changed title, always retaining the word *Palladium*; there were the *Gentleman and Lady's Palladium*, the *Palladium Enlarged*, and several others. Heath conducted his own paper with greater care than he had expended on the *Diary*, and suggested some useful schemes, such as reprinting the mathematical sections of the *Diary*, which through lack of subscribers he could not carry out.

While Heath continued his pungent criticism of others in minor publications, his most substantial work, *Astronomia accurata, or, The Royal Astronomer and Navigator* (1760), was delayed by a paucity of subscribers (eleven listed in the 1760 *Palladium*). In it Heath castigated James Ferguson (1710–1776) and Benjamin Martin (1704–1782) for errors, again lauding Emerson. His last publication, apart from the continuing *Palladium*, was *The Seaman's Guide to the Longitude* (1770) 'by the Author of the Royal Astronomer and Navigator'. Here he berated the astronomer royal, Nevil Maskelyne (1732–1811), for failing to publish Tobias Mayer's lunar tables on which the *Nautical Almanac* calculations depended, preventing public judgement of their worth. Heath insinuated that Maskelyne might be 'more of a Competitor for Emolument than Fame' (*The Seaman's Guide*, 4). The tables had actually been printed in 1767 and stored, probably awaiting Maskelyne's explanatory material; they were published in 1770. Heath suggested, as did James Cook (1728–1779), that the *Almanac* should be available well in advance so as to serve for long voyages, and the situation did improve. Following Heath's criticism of Maskelyne, the two agreed to seek adjudication over a mathematical point, referring it to George Coughron (1752–1774) of Newcastle, a young man with an exceptional reputation. The verdict, which favoured Heath, is confirmation of his mathematical ability.

Heath died in 1779, leaving a son, Robert Tyrrell Heath (*bap.* 1764), presumably the precocious author of *Practical Arithmetician, or, Art of Numbers Improved* (1774) 'by the Palladium-Author, junior'. It is not known whether Heath was married to Robert's mother, Ann Maria. Heath's intemperance, arrogance, and questionable honesty had made him enemies, but despite his failings, he was well read and perceptive, stirring the mathematical world and helping to popularize the study of mathematics.

RUTH WALLIS

Sources F. M. Clarke, *Thomas Simpson and his times* (1929) · R. V. Wallis and P. J. Wallis, eds., *Biobibliography of British mathematics and its applications*, 2 (1986), 61–2, 221, 298, 313–15, 318, 436 · E. G. R. Taylor, *The mathematical practitioners of Hanoverian England, 1714–1840* (1966), 180–81 · R. R. Bataille, 'Robert Heath, Thomas Cowper and

eighteenth century mathematical journalism', *Papers of the Bibliographical Society of America*, 81 (1987), 339–43 • E. Mackenzie, *An historical, topographical, and descriptive survey of the county of Northumberland*, 2nd edn, 1 (1825), 73 • PRO, PROB 11/1049, sig. 14
Archives BL, corresp. with Thomas Cowper, Add. MS 43741

Heath, Robert Amadeus (1818–1882). *See under* Heath, John Benjamin (1790–1879).

Heath [*née* Peirce-Evans; *other married name* Eliott-Lynn], **Sophie Catherine Theresa Mary**, Lady Heath (1896–1939), aviator, was born in Knockaderry, Newcastle West, co. Limerick, on 17 November 1896, the daughter of John Peirce-Evans, farmer, of Knockaderry, and Kate Dowling. She was cared for by her aunts, who disapproved of her passion for games, notably hockey. In search of an education that they thought fitting, and against which she would not rebel, they sent her to several different schools. She studied agriculture at Dublin University, where she took a degree in science.

About 1920 Peirce-Evans married William Davies Eliott-Lynn, but was soon widowed. It was as Mrs Sophie Eliott-Lynn that she came to public notice as the founder, in 1922, and vice-president of the Women's Amateur Athletic Association of Great Britain. A champion high-jumper, she attended the International Olympic Congress in Prague in the summer of 1925 as a member of the medical subcommission, giving evidence in support of the entry of women to world athletics. On her return to Britain she urged the government to increase its funding for youth sport, having earlier campaigned for more playing fields, particularly in deprived urban areas. Her *Athletics for Women and Girls* (1925) offered advice on training for the various track and field events, but also reviewed the arguments for women's participation in athletics. She particularly stressed the importance of medical and technical supervision to prevent damage to young women's childbearing capacity.

Sophie Eliott-Lynn first learned to fly at the age of twenty-two and first flew solo in 1925. She qualified for her A licence that year at the newly opened London Aeroplane School. Her route to the B licence, however, allowing her to work as a commercial pilot carrying passengers, was barred by the 1924 ruling of the International Commission for Air Navigation, which determined on grounds of physiology that such pilots must be male. In November 1925 Eliott-Lynn wrote to the commission offering herself as a guinea-pig in medical tests to challenge this ruling. And in the first three months of 1926 she put herself through the rigorous training required for the B licence, at the de Havilland works near Stag Lane aerodrome. Her efforts may have influenced the commission, which rescinded its ban on women in May 1926, allowing her to claim her prize.

A year later, on 18 May 1927, Eliott-Lynn took to the air with her fellow *aviatrice* and compatriot Lady Mary Bailey to attempt the world altitude record in a two-seater light aeroplane. She piloted their Avro Avian to 16,000 feet above Hamble, in Hampshire, setting the record. It was a remarkable achievement by amateurs in what had become a professionals' game, and by women in what was

regarded as a man's world. As the editor of *Flight* observed: 'It is still a common prejudice for women, as aviators, to be rather disdained. Mrs Eliott-Lynn has perhaps done more for her sex in the squashing of this prejudice than any other woman' (*Flight*, 19/21, 26 May 1927, no. 961, 336). In July she won the Grosvenor challenge cup, the main event at the Nottingham flying meeting; Lady Bailey, who came sixth, was the only other woman in the field of fourteen. That month Eliott-Lynn also undertook a tour of English airfields to highlight the needs of flying clubs, during which she made seventy-nine landings in a single day. In the autumn she promoted the Scottish air league and the Irish flying club, and even managed to fit in a display tour of central Europe.

Eliott-Lynn derived most of her income from flying and this financial pressure was eased by her marriage, on 11 October 1927, to Sir James Heath, bt (1852–1942), a wealthy ironmaster and colliery proprietor more than forty years her senior. She was his third wife; there were no children. He supported her flying expenses, provided her with a plane, and gave her a substantial additional income. When the couple travelled to South Africa in November, Lady Heath took with her a new Avro Avian III, intending to fly it back to London via Cairo. After spending time lecturing, giving flying exhibitions, and raising money for local flying clubs, she made her way from Cape Town to Pretoria, where her journey began in earnest on 25 February 1928. She travelled north in stages, hopping from one often makeshift aerodrome to another, before reaching Nairobi on 14 March and Khartoum on 31 March, where she delayed her departure in order to greet Lady Mary Bailey, who was flying south to the Cape. She reached Cairo on 4 April after a 700 mile final stage from Wadi Halfa.

Lady Heath's arrival in Cairo warranted only a brief note in *The Times*, where it prompted the former secretary of state for air, Frederick Guest, to ask 'if the average reader has the slightest idea what a tremendous individual feat has been accomplished … and by a woman' (*The Times*, 11 April 1928). He pointed out that much of the terrain over which Lady Heath had flown was jungle or bush: 'The chances of rescue if a forced landing occurred are little less hopeless than if it took place in the Atlantic' (ibid.). And Guest's 'gallant lady' now found herself prevented by local air authorities from proceeding alone across the Mediterranean. A speculative cable to 'Mussolini, Italy' procured the promise of an Italian seaplane escort, but after this became lost she proceeded up the coast of north Africa by herself, crossing to Sicily with an escort and visiting Rome, before finally arriving at Croydon via Le Bourget on 18 May 1928.

Lady Heath was welcomed home by her husband, a representative of A. V. Roe & Co., and a crowd of aerodrome workers. According to her own account, a reception had not been planned, but the editor of *Aeroplane* assumed otherwise, tartly observing that the 'large concourse of Advanced Feminists' had failed to materialize (*Aeroplane*, 34/21, 23 May 1928, 748). The journal's coolness towards her can be attributed to her active feminism and her flair for self-publicity, which paradoxically reinforced male prejudices. On arrival at Le Bourget she stepped from her plane wearing an elegant dress and hat rather than flying clothes, and announced:

> It is so safe that a woman can fly across Africa nowadays wearing a Parisian frock and keeping her nose powdered all the way … Really it was not hard. When my powder blew off I simply clamped the joystick between my knees, held my mirror with one hand, and powdered with the other, and I did it many a time with a lion, a giraffe, or a herd of elephants gazing up at me.   (ibid.)

She was said to have taken six dresses, a fur coat, and tennis rackets in the plane with her, and by her own account she ate chocolates and read a novel as she followed the course of the Nile towards Cairo.

But this picture of frivolity was for press consumption and obscured the reality of a careful aviator who methodically checked her engine before each day's flying, and whose medical supplies included morphine. She listed the clothes she had taken because, as she put it, 'so many people seem to consider this the most interesting part of flying!' (Heath and Murray, 202). Contrary to appearances, she did not. Her achievement in becoming the first woman to fly the Cape–Cairo–London route was honoured at a dinner given by the African Society and a later luncheon given by the Overseas League, and on these occasions she made clear her imperialist sympathies. Speaking 'as a Colonial', she hoped that her flight would strengthen the ties between the dominions and Britain, and suggested that by linking railheads the light aeroplane could be used to establish the 'all-red route' (*The Times*, 7 July 1928).

In July 1928 Lady Heath won the main event at the Rotterdam Aero Club meeting and soon after it was announced that she had been engaged as a second pilot by the Royal Dutch Air Lines (KLM). She undertook her first assignment on 27 July, when she flew from Amsterdam to Croydon and back in a twin-engine Fokker Jupiter. The considerable publicity attracted by this flight prompted the editor of *Aeroplane* to point out that her employment by KLM did not signal a change in airline policy, which was against hiring women: 'owing to the fact that few passengers would trust themselves in an air line machine piloted by a woman, the position should be made clear' (*Aeroplane*, 35/6, 8 Aug 1928, 284). To underline the point the journal observed that there were no passengers on Lady Heath's maiden flight, which it regarded as having been made purely for publicity purposes.

Lady Heath's reputation suffered a more serious reverse when on 4 October 1928 she claimed an altitude record for a light aeroplane of 23,000 feet, beating the record of 21,000 feet set by Geoffrey de Havilland on 27 July. The new record was 'subject to confirmation' but was quickly used to advertise the Cirrus-Moth plane in which it had been set. The Royal Aero Club, though, later announced that Lady Heath's sealed altitude meter had recorded only 18,800 feet. *Aeroplane* suspected another press stunt and ran a sharply critical editorial, advising Lady Heath in future 'to let her reputation rest on her undisputed ability

as a pilot—in which she is quite as good as the average male' (*Aeroplane*, 35/17, 24 Oct 1928, 706). The following month she travelled to America for a lecture tour amid the breakdown of her marriage. In August 1929 she was reported gravely injured in a crash in Cleveland, Ohio: she never completely recovered and it is not certain if she ever flew again. In January 1930, in Reno, Nevada, she filed for a divorce from her husband, which was granted that May. She later married an aviator called Williams. Lady Heath is reported to have died in a fall from a tramcar in 1939 in London. Her ashes were scattered over Newcastle West.

The publicity that she attracted, and sought, overshadowed Lady Heath's achievements as an aviator, and her work for women's rights both in this field and in athletics. She also suffered by comparison with Lady Mary Bailey, whose natural modesty won over press and public, and who was created DBE in 1930 for her services to aviation. Lady Heath arguably gave more, but received less. As Frederick Guest pointed out in April 1928 after her Cape–Cairo flight, aviation was the richer for her demonstration 'of what courage and a well-piloted light aeroplane can do' (*The Times*, 11 April 1928). In Ireland her 1928 Cape–Cairo flight was commemorated with a postage stamp, depicting her plane flying over the pyramids, as part of the 1998 Pioneers of Irish Aviation series.

MARK POTTLE

Sources V. Moolman, *Women aloft* (1981) · M. Cadogan, *Women with wings: female flyers in fact and fiction* (1992) · L. Yount, *Women aviators* (1995) · Lady Heath and S. Wolfe Murray, *Woman and flying* (1929) · *The Times* (15 April 1925) · *The Times* (12 June 1925) · *The Times* (12 Oct 1927) · *The Times* (April–July 1928) · *The Times* (11 Aug 1928) · *The Times* (5 Oct 1928) · *The Times* (3 Nov 1928) · *The Times* (30–31 Aug 1929) · *The Times* (26–7 Nov 1929) · *The Times* (21 Jan 1930) · *The Times* (5 May 1930) · *The Aeroplane* (23 May 1928) · *The Aeroplane* (1–8 Aug 1928) · *Lady Heath and S. Wolfe Murray* · *The Aeroplane* (24 Oct 1928) · *Flight* (26 May 1927) · *Flight* (24 May 1928) · *Flight* (9 Aug 1928) · *Flight* (11 Oct 1928) · *Flight* (11–25 Oct 1928) · *School Days*, 1/5 (1 Dec 1928), 21 · m. cert. [James Heath] · Burke, *Peerage* (1939) [Heath] · b. cert. [Eire]

Likenesses photographs, 1920–28, Hult. Arch. · photograph, repro. in S. Eliott-Lynn, *Athletics for women and girls* (1925)

Heath, Thomas. *See* Heth, Thomas (*fl.* 1563–1583).

Heath, Sir Thomas Little (1861–1940), civil servant and authority on ancient mathematics, was born on 5 October 1861 at Barnetby-le-Wold, Lincolnshire, the third and youngest son of Samuel Heath, of Thornton Curtis, Ulceby, Lincolnshire, a butcher whose hobby was the classics, and his wife, Mary, daughter of Thomas Little, of Hibaldstowe in the same county. He was one of six children, all musically as well as intellectually gifted; his elder brother Robert Samuel Heath (1858–1931) became professor of mathematics at Birmingham University. After a period at Caistor grammar school he went to Clifton College and thence, with a foundation scholarship, to Trinity College, Cambridge. He obtained a first class in both parts of the classical tripos (1881 and 1883); he was bracketed twelfth wrangler in 1882; and he was elected a fellow of Trinity in 1885 and an honorary fellow in 1920. He married on 2 June 1914 Ada Mary, daughter of Major Edward

Charles Thomas, of Wandsworth Common; they had a son and a daughter.

Heath passed first into the civil service in 1884 and entered the Treasury, where, after only three years' service, he became private secretary to Sir Reginald Earle, then permanent secretary. From 1891 to 1894 he was private secretary to successive financial secretaries and he became assistant secretary to the Treasury in 1907.

In 1913 Heath was appointed permanent secretary to the Treasury, jointly with Sir John Bradbury, and auditor of the civil list. Heath took control of the administrative side of the Treasury while finance work fell to Bradbury. In 1919, however, when Bradbury retired from the civil service and the government decided to reorganize the Treasury on a much larger scale than before the war, Heath became comptroller-general and secretary to the commissioners for the reduction of the national debt. His great knowledge of Irish land finance was valuable to the National Debt Office which dealt *inter alia* with this matter, for he had been closely concerned with the financial details of the various Irish land bills which guaranteed loans to Irish farmers in order to enable them to purchase their holdings. He was appointed CB in 1903, KCB in 1909, and KCVO in 1916. He retired from the civil service in 1926.

Heath was an excellent civil servant in the Victorian mould. He was quick, accurate, neat, painstaking, and thorough in all his written work, in which these qualities, together with his technical knowledge and his power of marshalling facts clearly and accurately for ministers, were of the greatest value. His courage and honesty were also beyond question. These strengths were, however, also his weaknesses because the climate of policy making and administration began to change after 1900. Heath was very much in the candle-saving school of Treasury officialdom. He used his considerable skills to pare down expenditure plans by other departments, but in a very negative fashion. His approach created strain between the Treasury and spending departments even before the great Edwardian expansion of social reform. Some departments regarded Heath as the special incarnation of all that was most angular and pedantic in Treasury traditions and practices. He also embodied the stuffy formality of the Treasury's internal organization, which was increasingly out of touch with the wider and changing administrative machine. Heath's emphasis on perfect prose prompted him to oppose the introduction of telephones to the Treasury on the ground that they would impair the ability of officials to write concisely. He also had deep-seated reservations about employing women in government departments. Heath did not adapt well to the demands of Lloyd George for oral briefings, and his rather ominous resistance to change convinced many politicians and administrators that fundamental reform of the civil service, proposed in 1914 but rendered essential by the chaotic expansion and dislocation of the wartime public service, implied major changes in the Treasury itself. Thus when administrative reform occurred in 1919, Heath was rather ignominiously pushed aside to an inferior position and

away from the task of recasting Treasury control in a more positive light.

After retiring in 1926 Heath, who had served as one of the Cambridge commissioners under the Universities of Oxford and Cambridge Act (1923), served from 1927 to 1929 on the royal commission on national museums and galleries. In 1927 he published an interesting and lucid monograph, *The Treasury*, in the Whitehall series, which contains a clear and accurate account of the British financial system. It was, however, to his unofficial work on Greek mathematics that Heath owed his earlier fellowship of the Royal Society (1912), on the council of which he served two terms; his presidency of the Mathematical Association (1922–3); and his fellowship of the British Academy (1932).

Heath was one of a small band of British public servants who have enriched scholarship by the judicious use of their limited leisure. His training at Cambridge in classics and mathematics had led him to take an interest in Greek mathematics, a subject explored by few at that time despite the unique place occupied by Euclid for generations in British education; and even Euclid was known only through imperfect versions of the simpler books of the *Elements*. Heath's labours in this field won for him the reputation of being one of the world's leading authorities on Greek mathematics; and he made accessible in a notation readily understood by all competent mathematicians the works of their leading Greek precursors.

Heath first gave his attention to Diophantus, whose *Arithmetica* had not previously been edited in England. His essay *Diophantus of Alexandria: a Study in the History of Greek Algebra*, published in 1885, was revised in 1910 so as to give not only a faithful rendering of the difficult Greek but a thorough history of Greek algebra; and he vindicated the high esteem in which the Alexandrian 'father of algebra' was held by Fermat and Euler. In 1896 he performed a similar service for Apollonius of Perga, whose masterly treatise on the conic sections was a book sealed even for good Greek scholars by the prolixity of its rigid geometrical proofs. Heath successfully produced a work which was 'Apollonius and nothing but Apollonius' but which, thanks to skilful compression and the substitution of modern notation for literary proofs, occupied less than half the space of the original. It was prefaced by valuable essays on the previous history of conic sections among the Greeks. In 1897 Heath applied the same methods to editing the works of Archimedes; and a savant chiefly known through the picturesque stories of his leap from the bath and his death at the hands of a Roman soldier was recognized as one of the supreme mathematical geniuses of all time. The work was supplemented in 1912 by a translation of the *Method* of Archimedes, discovered a few years earlier by J. L. Heiberg. In the meantime Heath had turned his attention to Euclid, publishing in 1908 a monumental three-volume edition of the *Elements* in which he followed the same principles. In this edition the notable tenth book on irrational magnitudes was for the first time rendered into English in an intelligible form; and Heath justified against modern 'improvements' Euclid's rigidly logical choice of axioms and postulates and his order of proof. A second edition appeared in 1926. He hoped to be able to re-establish the teaching of Euclid in schools, and to this end he produced in 1920 an edition of book 1 of the *Elements* in Greek.

In 1913 Heath published with a translation and commentary the Greek text of the tract of Aristarchus of Samos, *On the Sizes and Distances of the Sun and Moon*. He prefaced it with a thorough study of the history of Greek astronomy before Aristarchus, justifying the title of this author as the 'Copernicus of antiquity'. He also wrote short popular works on Aristarchus and Archimedes in 1920.

In 1921 Heath crowned his separate studies with *A History of Greek Mathematics* in two volumes. Arranged partly according to chronology and partly according to subject matter, it immediately became the standard work on the subject, and has remained so into the early years of the twenty-first century. Ten years later he condensed it into *A Manual of Greek Mathematics*, and in 1932 he published under the title *Greek Astronomy* a collection of translations covering the same ground as the prefatory matter of his edition of Aristarchus. He also gave much help to the ninth edition of Liddell's and Scott's *Greek–English Lexicon*, which had in earlier editions taken little notice of Greek mathematical terminology. At his death he was engaged on an edition (published in 1948) of the mathematical content of Aristotle's works.

Heath was a keen mountaineer and made ascents of most of the Dolomites; he was also an enthusiastic musician. He died at his home, Merry Hall, Agates Lane, Ashtead, Surrey, on 16 March 1940. Lady Heath, who survived him, was a musician of professional standing.

MAURICE HEADLAM and IVOR THOMAS, *rev.* ALAN BOOTH

Sources *The Times* (18 March 1940) · M. F. Headlam, 'Sir Thomas Little Heath, 1861–1940', *PBA*, 26 (1940), 424–38 · D. W. Thompson, *Obits. FRS*, 3 (1939–41), 409–26 · private information (1949) · personal knowledge (1949) · treasury registered files, PRO · E. O'Halpin, *Head of the civil service: a study of Sir Warren Fisher* (1989) · G. C. Peden, *The treasury and British public policy, 1906–1959* (2000) · Venn, *Alum. Cant.* · *CGPLA Eng. & Wales* (1940) · b. cert.
Archives TCD, corresp. with William Starkie
Likenesses T. M. Ronaldson, charcoal drawing, 1927, Trinity Cam. · W. Stoneman, photograph, 1931, NPG · photograph, repro. in Headlam, 'Sir Thomas Little Heath', 424
Wealth at death £18,427 9s. 2d.: resworn probate, 25 April 1940, *CGPLA Eng. & Wales*

Heath, William (1737–1814), revolutionary army officer in America, was born on 13 March 1737 in Roxbury, Massachusetts, the son of Samuel Heath, farmer, and his wife, Elizabeth Payson. He received little formal education, securing the rudiments from his parents. He chose farming as an occupation. On 19 April 1759 he married Sarah Lockwood; they had five children. From an early age he served in the Roxbury militia, evincing an avid interest in things military. He read works on military science and tactics, and rose to the rank of lieutenant. When he was refused promotion to captain, he resigned his commission. In 1765 he joined the Ancient and Honorable Artillery Company of Boston, and eventually became its captain. In 1761 he was elected to the Massachusetts legislature; in 1771 he was elected again, and served in that body until it was prorogued three years later. Under the pseudonym A Military Countryman he wrote two essays for the *Boston Gazette* in 1770, advocating military preparedness for America. Four years later, as tensions between Britain and America mounted, he was appointed colonel of the Suffolk county militia and was elected to the Massachusetts provincial congress, where he served on the committees of safety and supplies. On 9 February 1775 he was commissioned a brigadier-general of Massachusetts militia.

Heath commanded militia at Lexington and Concord on 19 April 1775, and was promoted major-general of Massachusetts militia on 20 June. Two days later he was commissioned a brigadier-general in the continental line. He spent the remainder of 1775 organizing American defences at Charlestown, and when the British evacuated Boston in the spring of 1776 he marched with his soldiers to New York. On 9 August 1776 he was promoted major-general of the continental army and given command of troops on the Hudson River above New York. In January 1777 he was ordered by General George Washington to attack Fort Independence. He handled an attempted assault on 29 January so badly that Washington privately scolded him for overcaution, and his fellow officers derided his poor performance. Afterwards Washington allowed him to serve only where no fighting was likely to occur. Dispatched to the eastern department, he commanded in Boston, doing such routine duties as watching over John Burgoyne's surrendered army until it was removed to Virginia, and trying to keep Bostonians from casting aspersions on America's French allies. On 11 June 1779 he returned to the Hudson River valley, and took command of the highlands. Offered a position on the congressional board of war, he declined to accept. On 16 June 1780 he was sent to Rhode Island to prepare for the reception of a French army, and he remained there for three months. In January 1781 he suppressed signs of mutiny among Massachusetts troops, and when Washington marched for Yorktown, Virginia, later in the year he was left in command of all troops in New York. He helped disband the army in the summer of 1783 and on 1 July returned to his home in Roxbury.

In 1788 Heath was a member of the Massachusetts convention that ratified the federal constitution, and he was a member of the state senate (1791–2). Also in 1792 he was appointed judge of probate for Norfolk county. Emerging a Jeffersonian in a largely federalist state, he expressed fears about the government's power to tax, and in 1793 resigned from the Society of the Cincinnati because he considered the organization too anti-democratic. He led public opposition to the federal government's arming of private vessels in 1797–8, and in the latter year stood unsuccessfully for congress against Harrison Gray Otis. In 1806 he was elected lieutenant-governor but declined to serve. He spoke out against the Anglo-American War (1812), even though it was declared by a Jeffersonian president, James Madison. He died on 24 January 1814 in Roxbury, in the house where he was born, the last of the major-generals of the revolutionary war.

PAUL DAVID NELSON

Sources *Memoirs of Major-General William Heath when in command of the eastern department*, ed. W. Abbatt (1900) • *Collections of the Massachusetts Historical Society*, 5th ser., 4 (1878) • *Collections of the Massachusetts Historical Society*, 7th ser., 4 (1904) • *Collections of the Massachusetts Historical Society*, 7th ser., 5 (1905) • G. P. Dolen, 'Major General William Heath and the first years of the American Revolution', PhD diss., Boston University, 1966 • *Daily Advertiser* [Boston, MA] (26 Jan 1814) • J. Bugbee, *Memorials of the Massachusetts Society of the Cincinnati* (1890), 237–41 • H. M. Ward, 'Heath, William', *ANB*
Archives Mass. Hist. Soc. | L. Cong., Washington MSS

Heath, William [*pseud.* Paul Pry] (**1794/5–1840**), caricaturist and illustrator, was born in Northumbria; it has been suggested that he was brought up in Spain (George, *English Political Caricature*, 207n.). There is little biographical information about this man, who was probably a soldier and certainly an accomplished artist, practising in caricature, military illustration, portraiture, and landscape. Dr John Brown called him 'poor Heath, the ex-Captain of Dragoons, facile and profuse, unscrupulous and clever' (Brown, 9). Since he cannot be identified in the *Army List* for the period, he may have been a captain in the yeomanry or possibly have assumed the title: 'Captain', said one of Farquhar's characters in *The Beaux' Stratagem*, 'is a good travelling name'.

Assuming that the particulars in his obituary notice in the *Gentleman's Magazine* are correct, Heath was only fourteen when his first satirical prints were published in 1809. Although he continued to etch occasional caricatures over the next fifteen years, he was principally occupied in illustrating books, mainly on military themes. The most notable are *The Martial Achievements of Great Britain and her Allies* (1815), for which he designed fifty-two plates, *The Wars of Wellington* by William Combe (1819), and his own *Life of a Soldier* (1823). During this time he also drew theatrical portraits or 'characters'. He described himself in 1819 as 'portrait and military painter' (George, *Catalogue*, 9.civ). When the demand for military prints declined in the 1820s Heath reverted to caricatures, published either as individual prints or as sets, and soon established himself in a leading position.

In 1825–6 Heath was in Scotland, writing and illustrating the first magazine in the world to be given over, predominantly, to caricatures. The *Glasgow Looking Glass*, later the *Northern Looking Glass*, was significant as presaging the transfer of caricature from prints to journals, but the artwork was scrappy and poorly printed. In 1827 Heath was in Newcastle upon Tyne, contributing works to the Northumberland Institution for the Promotion of the Fine Arts.

Heath returned to London in 1827 and for the next two years was the leading caricaturist, prolific alike in social and political satire. In 1827 he started to sign his prints with a little drawing of the actor Liston in the role of Paul Pry, a character who interfered in other peoples' business

in John Poole's eponymous comedy (1825). However the Paul Pry device attracted plagiarists on such a scale that in 1829, having complained on a caricature of a 'dirty rogue' who was 'robbing us of our ideas and just profit', he abandoned it. When on 1 January 1830 Thomas McLean, the leading purveyor of comic art, launched a monthly magazine of caricatures, available in plain and hand-coloured versions, called the *Looking Glass*, he advertised it as having been 'drawn and etched' by 'William Heath' for whom he acted as 'sole Publisher'. Clearly Heath's name was the selling point, yet after seven issues he was replaced by Robert Seymour. Perhaps McLean felt that Seymour's lithographs better expressed the new spirit of delicacy to which he was attuning himself. Or perhaps he had become exasperated by Heath's 'careless habits—drink, debts and unpunctuality' (a contemporary collector, quoted by George, *Catalogue*, 10.xciii). In any event, after 1830 Heath's output of caricatures declined rapidly. He concentrated instead on topographical illustration, such as his panorama of Dover (1836). The *Gentleman's Magazine* recorded that on 7 April 1840 'William Heath, artist' died at 'Hampstead, London, aged 45'.

Heath's *Northern Looking Glass* was a pioneering venture; his political caricatures demonstrated an insight that was sometimes remarkable; his social satires, especially those on extremes of fashion, were amusing; and his style was bold and attractive (examples of his work are held at the British Museum, the Victoria and Albert Museum, and the Laing Art Gallery, Newcastle upon Tyne). Altogether he was a talented artist, and his comparative neglect by writers on caricature and illustration can be explained only by the fact that so little is known about him as a person.

Henry Heath (*fl.* 1822–1842), caricaturist, is a shadowy figure. Because of a similarity in style between William and Henry Heath and their collaboration on three prints, it has been suggested that they were related, even as brothers (George, *Catalogue*, 9.liv). Henry Heath etched theatrical portraits from 1822 and both social and political caricatures from 1824, his work being published by Fores and Gans. In 1831 he started to imitate the political caricatures of HB, changing from etching to lithography and adopting the monogram HH. About this time various sets of his comic vignettes in the manner of George Cruikshank were issued and were collected in 1840 under the title of *The Caricaturist's Sketch Book*; in the 1830s he also drew cockney sportsmen, following the example of Robert Seymour. One cartoon by him was published in *Punch* in 1842. In the same year he drew some amusing caricatures of Queen Victoria's visit to Scotland, after which, according to M. H. Spielmann (*The History of Punch*, 1895, 452), he emigrated to Australia. Dorothy George called him 'a competent and versatile but very imitative caricaturist' (George, *Catalogue*, 10.xliv).   SIMON HENEAGE

Sources F. G. Stephens and M. D. George, eds., *Catalogue of political and personal satires preserved … in the British Museum*, 9–11 (1949–54) • M. Hall, *The artists of Northumbria*, 2nd edn (1982) • M. D. George, *English political caricature: a study of opinion and propaganda*, 2 vols. (1959) • M. Hardie, *English coloured books* (1906) • J. R. Abbey, *Life in England in aquatint and lithography, 1770–1860* (privately printed, London, 1953) • *GM*, 2nd ser., 14 (1840) • J. Brown, *John Leech and other*

papers (1882) • W. Feaver, *Masters of caricature: from Hogarth and Gillray to Scarfe and Levine*, ed. A. Green (1981)
Likenesses W. Heath, self-portrait, BM

Heathcoat, John (1783–1861), inventor of the bobbin net machine and lace manufacturer, was born at Duffield, near Derby, on 7 August 1783, the son of a farmer and grazier. The family moved to Long Whatton, Leicestershire, after his father became blind. There Heathcoat received a village-school education and was apprenticed to a maker of Derby ribbed stockings and framesmith. After completing his indentures he moved to Nottingham, the centre of the hosiery industry, to work for Leonard Elliott, a framesmith and builder of warp knitting frames. His mechanical skills soon brought Heathcoat the highest income earned by local artisans, for while common knitters earned 12s. to 15s. weekly, and men in the newest fashion branches up to 50s., Heathcoat received 3 guineas. About 1804 he married Ann Cauldwell of Hathern, Leicestershire.

Since the middle of the eighteenth century Nottingham framework knitters and framesmiths had striven to produce new meshes on the stocking frame in the hope of creating fashionable varieties that could bring them greater rewards. The merchant hosiers, the organizers of the domestic system, were keen to offer partnerships or licensing arrangements to inventors who could produce new fabrics which could be marketed as fashion varieties in London and through their provincial connection. The stocking frame proved capable of producing not only striped and zig-zag patterns, but also various fabrics resembling lace, which was the most profitable product of all. Heathcoat embarked on this well-trodden path to fortune and fame and, probably to pursue his experiments in greater secrecy, moved to Hathern, the next village to that where his family lived. He conceived the idea of imitating the motions of a pillow-lace worker with a machine, and in 1808 and 1809, at the age of twenty-five, achieved his first and greatest success with the invention of the bobbin net machine, which produced a fast hexagonal net by manual power. The originality of his patents for the machine was soon contested, for most of the components were used by rivals and other textile inventors, but as D. E. Varley expressed it with a striking simile:

> If the claims of Mozart to be the composer of Jupiter symphony are to be rejected on the grounds that he employed notes and instruments which were already well known, albeit in different orders and combinations, then we must equally reject those of Heathcoat to the invention of the bobbin net machine. (Varley, 8)

Jealousy and resentment of Heathcoat's success produced numerous patent infringers in Nottingham: 156 were discovered in 1816 and 200 in 1819. Two cases in the court of common pleas, *Bovill v. Moore* (1816) and *Heathcoat v. Grace & Co.* (1817), established the patentee's rights, after which he arranged a system of licensing which brought in some £10,000 royalties a year for the remaining period of the patent. An unusual feature of the licensing, which contrasts with that of some other successful patentees of the period such as Arkwright and Boulton and Watt, is

John Heathcoat (1783–1861), by William Holl

that it allowed the continuance of a considerable number of small producers, most of whom were Nottingham framework knitters, mechanics, and tradesmen, who had shifted their modest resources into the lucrative new business. Notwithstanding this generous policy, Heathcoat continued to be very unpopular in Nottingham, which no doubt was a major factor in the Luddite destruction of his machinery in his new Loughborough factory in 1816. It is not clear if the Luddites knew that he had already (December 1815) bought a large cotton mill in Tiverton, Devon, for conversion to lace-net production by power. Notwithstanding the offer of £10,000 compensation by the Leicestershire magistrates, Heathcoat took the whole of his business and many of his skilled workmen to Tiverton and seldom, if ever, returned to the midlands for any purpose.

The years of mechanical experiment, litigation, and factory building inevitably involved large costs, and not the least of Heathcoat's achievements lay in securing monied backers. W. J. Lockett, a Derby solicitor, lent him £20,000, after which he drew on the resources of Boden, Oliver and Cartwright, a firm of Loughborough hosiers, and when their confidence ran low, on Charles Lacy, a Nottingham point-net manufacturer closely connected with James Fisher, a London lace merchant, who was rising to leadership of the trade. He was also able to forge good banking connections, notably with Amorys of Tiverton (his daughter married one of their sons) and Glyn Mills in the City of London. The Tiverton mill had been built in 1791 by Heathfield, Denny & Co., London merchants, at the considerable cost of £24,000. Heathcoat had 147 bobbin net machines, worth up to £200 each, working there in 1819, £30,000 in all. He tried to create a fully integrated plant by starting a silk-reeling mill and a foundry to build machinery, but the former and his plans to take up sericulture do not seem to have succeeded. Nevertheless the business accounts record a capital of £120,000 in the 1820s and £100,000 in the 1830s. A warehouse was opened in London to market the nets, which were often hand-embroidered by girls working in their own homes in Tiverton and in the country areas round about. A second factory was opened at St Quentin, near Paris, in 1818, and £50,000 invested there.

From 1832 to 1859 Heathcoat was one of the two members of parliament for Tiverton, and so was drawn away from his business, which reached a plateau in the late 1820s. He liked to absorb his mind in mechanical problems and produced a stream of further inventions. His main endeavours were directed, like those of Nottingham mechanics, to machines inserting spots and then patterns in the net but, removed from the community of creative innovation, he soon fell behind and turned to more academic topics, such as inventing a steam plough. He died at Bolham House, Tiverton, Devon, on 18 January 1861, an honoured and patriarchal figure in the town, but one whose creative period as entrepreneur and inventor had passed away a generation earlier.   S. D. CHAPMAN

Sources W. Felkin, *A history of the machine-wrought hosiery and lace manufactures* (1867) · D. E. Varley, 'John Heathcoat (1783–1861): founder of the machine-made lace industry', *Textile History*, 1 (1968–70), 1–45 · *CGPLA Eng. & Wales* (1861) · d. cert. · *DNB*
Archives Devon RO, papers, 4302 B · Tiverton Museum, papers
Likenesses H. Holl, engraving, repro. in Felkin, *History of the machine-wrought hosiery* [*see illus.*]
Wealth at death £180,000: probate, 16 Feb 1861, *CGPLA Eng. & Wales*

Heathcoat-Amory. For this title name *see* Wethered, Joyce [Joyce Heathcoat-Amory, Lady Heathcoat-Amory] (1901–1997).

Heathcote, Sir Gilbert, first baronet (1652–1733), merchant and politician, was born on 2 January 1652, the eldest son of Gilbert Heathcote, ironmonger of Chesterfield, Derbyshire, and Anne, daughter of George Dickons of Chesterfield. Several generations of his family were interested in Derbyshire lead mining. Gilbert was the eldest of seven brothers, all of whom became merchants. Apprenticed at fifteen in London, he was sent overseas at nineteen and became a factor in Stockholm, but returned in a few years to set up in London as an independent merchant. On 30 March 1682 he married Hester (1659–1714), daughter and heir of Christopher Rayner, Eastland merchant of London, with whom he had three sons and four daughters. She died on 27 September 1714, and was buried on 6 October in Low Leyton church, Essex.

Early trading ventures An apprentice, freeman (1681), and ultimately master (1700) of the Vintners' Company, Heathcote is recorded (*c*.1690) as importing substantial quantities of wine and brandy from Catalonia in partnership with Arthur Shallett. Yet the wine trade was to be only a minor interest in his very varied and successful

Sir Gilbert Heathcote, first baronet (1652–1733), by Michael Dahl, *c*.1711

commercial career. By the 1680s his most important trade was that with the Baltic, eventually recognized by his election as the Eastland Company's treasurer (1697–9) and governor (1720). Four of his brothers also became freemen of that company, two of whom, Samuel and John, he helped settle as merchant factors in Danzig and Königsberg. When he returned to London in 1681 Gilbert was already a significant figure in the Eastland trade and by the mid-1680s was at or near the top. Although he traded in many commodities and to many ports, his Eastland imports came primarily from Stockholm (iron, copper, pitch, and tar), Riga (hemp, hemp-seed, and flax), and Danzig (potash, linen, and canvas). The strategic value of many of these commodities brought him very close to the post-revolution government. As early as 1689 he was part of a syndicate selling the navy £50,000 worth of hemp.

Heathcote also developed an important trade with the West Indies, where his brothers Josiah, John, and William were for some years settled in Jamaica. He was agent for that colony in London between 1692 and 1704 and received government contracts after 1689 to remit funds and to provision men-of-war there. Another brother, Caleb, settled as a merchant in New York. Although trade thither was not a major business for Gilbert, he had remittance and supply contracts there too, and was able to help Caleb to obtain appointment to the council and to several remunerative posts. Most probably in connection with his West Indian interests, Gilbert Heathcote as a licensed 'separate trader' sent out one vessel in 1702 in the west African slave trade. No further direct involvement in such trade is known, suggesting that he thought it too risky in war-time.

Financial dealings Heathcote was part of a coterie of energetic, committed whig merchants, who exerted themselves to help the government's finances during the difficult war of 1689–97. He was consulted by the Treasury on the great recoinage of 1695 and was later part of a syndicate that took in plate to help the new minting. He also lent money to the government in the early 1690s and was one of the inner group that promoted the chartering and flotation of the Bank of England. He contributed £8000 to the first subscription of 1694 and £6875 to the second of 1697, while his brother Samuel subscribed £7000 to the first and £2670 to the second. Gilbert became a member of the new institution's first court of directors in 1694 and remained there almost continuously until his death. He served twice as governor of the bank (1709–11; 1723–5)—an unusual honour. Legend has it that he made £60,000 when the bank's shares rose on the peace of 1697. Throughout his life Heathcote remained an important lender to his own government. In 1706 he was also one of the commissioners for raising a £250,000 loan in London for the Habsburg emperor, to which he personally subscribed £4000.

Heathcote was a key member of a group of whig merchants and financiers (including at least eight directors of the bank) who resented the domination of the East India Company in the 1680s by a tory, pro-court clique headed by Sir Josiah Child. In the 1690s he and his associates invested in interloping ventures to Borneo, the Red Sea, and elsewhere within the East India Company's privilege. When a vessel in which he was interested was seized by the company's agents in 1693, Heathcote testified before the House of Commons, influencing that body to adopt a resolution against the company's monopoly. Parliament tried to solve the problem by an act of 1698 opening the East Indies trade to those participating in a £2 million loan to the crown. Gilbert, who was a receiver for this operation, subscribed £17,000 and his brother Samuel £10,000. Gilbert became a director (1698–1704; 1705–9) of the resulting new East India Company and a manager (1702–4; 1705–9) of the joint trade of the new (or English) and old (or London) companies that lasted from 1702 until the two companies merged in 1709. (His brother Samuel was also a manager from 1704 to 1708.)

When Peter the Great visited England in 1698 Heathcote was one of a group of influential merchants (including directors of the bank and the new East India Company, and three of his brothers) who courted the tsar and obtained from him the exclusive privilege of importing tobacco into Russia. Heathcote initiated the necessary negotiations by a speech on tobacco delivered in German at a dinner given for the Russian visitors by the Eastland Company. Although this monopoly proved unenforceable in Russia, the 'adventurers' were powerful enough in English political life to obtain an act of parliament in 1699 opening up membership in the Russia Company to anyone paying an entry fine of £5, and influential enough to persuade the government to send the first English minister to Moscow in 1705.

London politics In the new century Heathcote became very active in London's corporate life. Having been a member of the court of common council for Walbrook ward from 1689 to 1702, he became an alderman for Walbrook in 1702, serving there until 1725, when he became an alderman for the ward of Bridge without, where he remained until his death. He was also sheriff, 1703–4. On the military (militia) side, he was colonel of the City's Blue regiment (1707–10; 1714–33), and was an active leader of the Honourable Artillery Company: treasurer (1708–11), vice-president (1711–20), and president (1720–33). On the eleemosynary side, he was an original commissioner for Greenwich Hospital in 1695 and president of St Thomas's Hospital from 1722 to 1733. In politics he was a controversial, partisan whig. He was unsuccessful when he first stood for parliament in the City of London in 1698, but was returned for that constituency in January 1701, only to be 'expelled' from the house in March because, as a trustee for circulating exchequer bills, he was ineligible to serve as an MP. This arbitrary extension of the scope of an act of 1693 excluding customs and excise officers from the house reflected the great tension in the Commons in 1701 between the friends of the old and new East India companies, a tension exacerbated by the return in the first election of 1701 of a majority opposed to the whig junto and to the new company. Heathcote's banishment was short-lived for he gave up exchequer bills and was returned for London in the election of November 1701. He continued to represent the City until he was defeated in the post-Sacheverell tory upsurge at the election of 1710, but he sat thereafter for Helston (1715–22), Lymington (1722–7), and St Germans (1727–33). He had announced his candidacy for the City again in 1727 but stood aside for the young Micajah Perry, preferring an effortless return for St Germans made available to him, as a friend of government, by the Eliots, the borough's patrons. In the Commons he spoke frequently on commercial matters, often in a protectionist vein, but was otherwise an orthodox junto and, later, Walpolean whig, voting for the impeachment of Dr Sacheverell (1710), the Septennial Act (1716), and the Peerage Bill (1719). He supported the foundation of Georgia in the house and helped to raise private funds for the venture. Elected FRS in 1705, he was knighted in October 1702 and created a baronet in January 1733, shortly before his death.

Heathcote's religious commitments are not clear. His grandfather was an officer in Cromwell's army and was forced out of the Chesterfield corporation when he failed to take the necessary oaths in 1663. However, Gilbert's father became alderman and mayor of Chesterfield. Both Gilbert and his father, as holders of public offices, would for the record have had to conform to the Church of England. In the House of Commons, Gilbert's strong stand against the Occasional Conformity and Schism Acts was clearly in the dissenting interest. He also had Quaker relatives who presumably would have been helped by the passage of the bill he introduced unsuccessfully in 1731 to restrict suits for tithes. His clear solicitude for non-conformity made him particularly unpopular with the high-church party which was so aggressive in the last years of Anne's reign.

Attacked by tories During these very years, Heathcote's private and public careers faced some very dangerous challenges. As governor of the Bank of England (1709–11), reputed spokesman for the junto, and known advocate of 'no peace without Spain', he was an object of particular antipathy to many tories. When Queen Anne, moving slowly towards a peace policy, dismissed the third earl of Sunderland as secretary of state in June 1710, Heathcote led a delegation of directors of the bank in an interview with the queen to urge her to make no further ministerial changes lest the government's credit be undermined. The queen was polite but noncommittal. When Heathcote repeated this advice via Lord Treasurer Godolphin in August, the queen responded by dismissing the latter. Implicit in this exchange was a warning that the leading London whig financiers, including Heathcote, might not wish to help a suspect ministry in remitting funds to the army in Europe. This contretemps was widely reported in the tory press as evidence of the arrogance of whig finance. The new tory ministers were, however, able to handle the remittance challenge and immediately reconstructed London's lieutenancy commission, leading to wide changes in the militia command, including the dismissal of Heathcote as colonel of the Blue regiment. But the whigs remained entrenched in the court of aldermen and in September that body chose Heathcote as lord mayor for the coming year, even though he had come in second in the preliminary voting by all freemen in Common Hall. In the parliamentary election in October, the aroused City voters responded by replacing with tories the City's four sitting whig members—including Heathcote. The animus of controversy continued to rise when, during Heathcote's mayoralty, the whig aldermen blocked the election of a new tory colleague. They also beat back Robert Harley's efforts to obtain the election of tory directors in the bank and United East India Company. Thus Heathcote could be re-elected a director of the bank when his term as governor expired in 1711. In the charged atmosphere of the queen's last years, the whigs valued all the more their control of the Honourable Artillery Company (of which Heathcote was then vice-president), which constituted their counterpoise to the tory-dominated lieutenancy commission in charge of the militia-trained bands. At the death of the queen Heathcote, as an active member of the Hanover Society, exerted himself to assure the peaceful accession of George I. A contemporary rumour had it that he was marked out for assassination in a planned, but aborted, tory riot.

Last years and death The years following the peace and the Hanoverian succession were much less demanding for Heathcote, once more a member of parliament. He now had friends in power and could in 1715 obtain for his brother Caleb the posts of surveyor-general of customs in the northern district of North America and Admiralty judge for New York, New Jersey, and Connecticut. Gilbert himself gradually withdrew from foreign trade and took no active part in the affairs of the East India Company after the merger in 1709, though his son John became a director of the united company in 1716. He was still, however, active as a director of the Bank of England and took a leading role in the negotiations between the government, the bank, and the South Sea Company when the 'Bubble' burst in September 1720. His insistence that, as a condition of his assistance, the South Sea Company keep its funds exclusively in the bank led to the collapse of the Sword Blade Company, whose banking activity had for a time threatened to rival that of the Bank of England itself. That failure further undermined the market's confidence in South Sea Company shares. The events of that dismal season signalled the complete triumph of Heathcote and whig finance over Harley's improvisations. The bank's shareholders probably had this in mind when they elected him governor a second time in 1723.

Heathcote died in St Swithin's Lane, London, on 25 January 1733. At his death he was reputed to be worth £700,000 and 'the richest commoner in England', but in his will he left barely £1000 to charities. He was succeeded as baronet by his eldest surviving son, John, also an MP and director of the Bank of England and the United East India Company. Their descendant, the fifth baronet, was created Baron Aveland in 1856, while the sixth baronet became earl of Ancaster in 1892. In his later years Sir Gilbert had moved his principal country residence from Low Leyton, Essex, to Normanton, Rutland, where he commenced the rebuilding of the manor house on a grand scale, and where he was buried. He seemed the most conspicuous embodiment of the rising commercial elements in society closely associated with whig finance. As such, he was particularly hated by many tories. The fact that he had also acquired a large landed estate in Lincolnshire and Rutland (as well as other holdings in Bedfordshire, Essex, Hertfordshire, and Middlesex) only made him more objectionable to Pope for whom:

> The grave Sir Gilbert holds it for a rule
> That every man in want is knave or fool.
> (*Epistle to Bathurst*, lines 103–4)

JACOB M. PRICE

Sources E. D. Heathcote, *An account of some of the families bearing the name of Heathcote … (1899)* • HoP, *Commons* • G. S. De Krey, *A fractured society: the politics of London in the first age of party, 1688–1715* (1985) • J. M. Price, *The tobacco adventure to Russia: enterprise, politics, and diplomacy in the quest for a northern market for English colonial tobacco, 1676–1722* (1961) • S. E. Åström, *From cloth to iron: the Anglo-Baltic trade in the late seventeenth century*, 1 (1963) • PRO, E 190/143/1 • J. Clapham, *The Bank of England: a history*, 2 vols. (1944) • A. Anderson, *An historical and chronological deduction of the origin of commerce from the earliest accounts to the present time, containing an history of the great commercial interests of the British empire*, 2 (1764), 219 • J. Carswell, *The South Sea Bubble* (1960) • D. R. Fox, *Caleb Heathcote, gentleman colonist … 1692–1721* (1926) • *VCH Rutland*, 2.295 • W. A. Shaw, ed., *Calendar of treasury books*, [33 vols. in 64], PRO (1904–69) • J. Redington, ed., *Calendar of Treasury papers*, 6 vols., PRO (1868–89) • state papers, domestic, PRO • will, PRO, PROB 11/656, sig. 45

Archives Lincs. Arch., papers relating to banking and commercial activities; papers relating to activities as lord mayor; provisional grant of arms | Hants. RO, Heathcote of Hursley MSS, Samuel Heathcote MSS
Likenesses M. Dahl, oils, *c*.1711; Sothebys, 9 Nov 1955, lot 110 [*see illus.*] · oils; at St Thomas's Hospital, Southwark, *c*.1900
Wealth at death approx. £700,000: *GM*, 3 (Jan 1733), 47

Heathcote, John Moyer (1834–1912), real tennis player, the eldest son of John Moyer Heathcote (1800–1892), of Conington Castle, near Peterborough, and his wife, the Hon. Emily Frances (*d.* 1849), third daughter of Nicholas William Ridley Colborne, first Baron Colborne, was born in London on 12 July 1834. He was educated at Eton College and at Trinity College, Cambridge, where he matriculated in 1852 and graduated MA in 1856. He was called to the bar at Lincoln's Inn (1859) and practised on the northern circuit before succeeding to the family estates in Huntingdonshire, which in 1883 amounted to over 7000 acres. He married on 18 December 1860 Louisa Cecilia (*d.* 1910), daughter of Norman Macleod of Macleod.

Heathcote was a man of many interests in sports and games, an amateur artist of some repute, and a graceful writer on sporting subjects. In middle life shooting, skating, and lawn tennis were among his hobbies, but he will always be best remembered as the finest amateur real tennis player of his generation.

Heathcote first played the game at Cambridge, and he played regularly at the court in James Street, Haymarket, London, from 1856 to 1866, when that famous court was finally closed. His chief professional teacher and opponent in those days was Edmund Tompkins, for some years world champion of the sport. In real tennis handicapping is commonplace, but gradually Heathcote reduced the odds between them until he could play his former master on level terms. About the year 1869 he was the equal of any player in the world, but after that George Lambert began to surpass him. However, there was still no amateur player who had any chance against Heathcote, and for over fifteen years he never lost to a fellow amateur on equal terms. Heathcote was generally first recognized as amateur champion about the year 1859, when C. G. Taylor retired from single match play. There was at that time no formal competition for the championship, but from 1867 the Marylebone Cricket Club annually offered prizes to its members for play in the court at Lord's, and the gold prize carried with it the blue riband of amateur tennis. Heathcote won this every year until 1882, when Alfred Lyttelton defeated him. Following this loss the MCC committee presented Heathcote with a replica of the trophy in the belief that his élite competitive career was over, but he regained the title the next summer. After this, however, Lyttelton outshone him, though Heathcote won the gold prize for the seventeenth time in 1886, at the age of fifty-two, when Lyttelton was unable to play. Heathcote kept up the game for many years and played in a number of courts after he had retired from competition play, and for the remainder of his life he was present at most of the great matches. He died at his seat, Conington Castle, on 3 August 1912, leaving two sons and two daughters.

Heathcote was a fine all-round player with a sound volley and an effective service, but his strongest point was his return. He contributed largely to *Tennis* (1890) in the Badminton Library series, and also wrote *Speed Skating* (1891) in the same series. Lawn tennis players owe him a debt of gratitude, for it was he who first suggested and tried the experiment of covering the ball with flannel.

E. B. NOEL, *rev.* WRAY VAMPLEW

Sources E. H. Thruston, *Athletic sports, tennis, rackets and other ball games* [1931] · Lord Aberdare [M. G. L. Bruce], *The Willis Faber book of tennis and rackets* (1980) · E. B. Noel and J. O. M. Clark, *A history of tennis*, 2 vols. (1924) · *The Times* (12 May 1915) · Burke, *Peerage* · Venn, *Alum. Cant.*
Likenesses photograph, repro. in Aberdare, *Willis Faber book of tennis*
Wealth at death £162,114 11s. 6d.: resworn probate, 3 Dec 1912, CGPLA Eng. & Wales

Heathcote, Ralph (1721–1795), Church of England clergyman and writer, was born on 19 December 1721 at Barrow upon Soar, Leicestershire, the son of Ralph Heathcote (*d.* 1765), curate there, and his wife, Mary. His mother was a daughter of Simon Ockley, the professor of Arabic at Cambridge. He was educated by his father at home in Derbyshire, and at Chesterfield grammar school, which he entered in 1736. He went up to Jesus College, Cambridge (his father's old college), as a sizar in 1741, graduated BA in January 1745, and proceeded MA in 1748; he was realistic about his slim chances of securing a fellowship, and left in 1748 to become curate at St Margaret's, Leicester, which was worth £50 a year. He continued to hold his curacy after becoming vicar of Barkby, near Leicester, the following year, and was early enjoying a comfortable living in the church. In August 1750 he married Margaret Mompesson of Nottinghamshire, who was the great-granddaughter of the vicar of Eyam during the plague.

Heathcote's first publication was a much admired treatise on astronomy, *Historiae astronomiae, sive, De ortu et progressu astronomiae* (1746). In his memoirs, which were later to be published in Nichols's *Literary Anecdotes*, Heathcote admitted that he had not been interested in classical learning at Cambridge, but he began to become so when he wrote two works relating to Conyers Middleton's *Inquiries into the Miraculous Powers of the Early Church*. He also claimed that he had originally found writing in English difficult, and blamed the classical curriculum of the schools and universities for this shortcoming. In his first major work in English, *Cursory Animadversions upon a Late Controversy Concerning the Miraculous Powers* (1752), Heathcote denounced polemical divinity as the source of persecution and abuse in learning, seeing it as his purpose to clear the grounds of such debate for the sake of clarity, common sense, and plain reason. Religion needed to be cleared of abstruse learning as well as superstition if it was to thrive. He defended the claim, derived from Middleton, that the miracles of the gospels were true, and that all claims for miraculous powers thereafter were, in all probability, false. He rejected the testimony of the fathers of the church, since they were credulous, and he insisted that his was a faith in the religion of the Bible alone, akin to that propounded by William Chillingworth. This argument was substantially repeated in his second engagement on the matter, *Remarks upon a Charge by Dr. Chapman* (1752). A similarly controversial work followed when he replied to a sermon of 30 January by Thomas Fothergill, and challenged the wisdom of delivering such commemoration sermons so long after the ferment of the civil war had died away. These pieces drew the admiring attention of William Warburton, who offered Heathcote the assistant preacher's place at Lincoln's Inn chapel.

Although the stipend was small, Heathcote was eager to take up the appointment since his ill health was not improved by the clerical duties required of him in the midlands. He was also keen to take up a literary life, and so he seized the opportunity of moving to London in June 1753, and quickly became part of an influential literary circle that included John Jortin and others. His marriage brought him comfortably independent means, which made residence in London possible. As a protégé of Warburton he took it upon himself to denounce the clerical enthusiasms of the age, and he attacked a sermon given by an Oxford Hutchinsonian, Thomas Patten, in a 1756 tract, *The use of reason asserted in matters of religion, or, Natural religion the foundation of revealed*. Heathcote argued that one needed to appeal to reason in order to discover Christianity to be a true revelation, and that miracles were not sufficient to confirm Christian revelation. Reason and common sense were the guarantors of the truth of the faith, and it was its misfortune to have been early mixed up with the mystifying philosophies of Plato and Aristotle, from whence arose only heresies and enthusiasms, of which Hutchinsonianism was but a recent and dangerous example.

Heathcote again attacked Patten in *A Reply to a Piece Intitled St. Peter's Christian Apology* (1756), in which he further repudiated the alleged proof offered by miracles, and denounced the polemical tone of Hutchinsonian apologists. He also replied to Warburton's personal *bête noire* in *A Sketch of Lord Bolingbroke's Philosophy* (1755). His appeals to reason were affirmed in the Boyle lectures which he delivered in 1763, and which he published that year as *A Discourse upon the Being of God: against Atheists*. He argued that knowledge of God was a form of intuitive knowledge, and that the systematic accounts developed by Descartes and Samuel Clarke were both illusory and needlessly complicating. He also denounced Spinozist pantheism alongside deistic critiques of religion as a form of political control. This rational apology for Christianity formed the substance of the address he delivered at Cambridge in 1759 when taking the degree of DD: *Fidei fundamentum ratio: concio ad clerum* (1759).

Despite the patronage of Warburton and the admiration of Middleton, Heathcote was to begin to regret the tone of these controversial writings, noting that:

> These were favourably received by the publick; yet, when the heat of controversy was over, I could not look into them myself without disgust and pain. The spleen of Middleton, and the petulancy of Warburton, who were then the writers in vogue, had too much infected me, as they had other young scribblers; though I never had the honour to be of what Hume, in his Life, calls the Warburtonian School.   (Nichols, 3.537–8)

This change in perception was aided by clerical preferment; he had acquired a prebend at Southwell in 1760, and succeeded his father in the Derbyshire living of Sileby in 1765, before becoming the rector of Sawtry All Saints in Huntingdonshire in 1766. He could not, however, leave off literary controversy, and anonymously produced *A Letter to the Honourable Mr. Horace Walpole, concerning the Dispute between Mr. Hume and Mr. Rousseau* in 1767. The language of this piece is still appreciably that of the circle from which he was beginning to distance himself, as he identified Rousseau as 'a Methodist in Philosophy' (p. 16), praising Hume as an amiable man, despite his unbelief (in this instance decidedly distancing himself from Warburton, who loathed Hume). He had become one of the chief writers on the *Biographical Dictionary* in 1761 at the recommendation of John Jortin, who had been impressed by the life of Thomas Burnet which he had provided at the request of William Whiston for a 1759 edition of Burnet's works.

Heathcote began to spend more time in the midlands at this point in his career, and became a JP at Southwell in 1772. An anonymous treatise on the law, *The Irenarch, or, Justice of the Peace's Manual*, first appeared in 1771, with a second edition in 1774, and a third in 1781. The second and third editions contained a dedication to Lord Mansfield, which some critics read as an attack on him, an accusation that Heathcote denied in the 'Miscellaneous reflections' which prefaced the 1781 edition. None the less, he pointed out his occasional agreement with the views of Junius and Edmund Burke, and his thinking was plainly close to that of the opposition at the time. The 1781 edition also contained an appropriate assize sermon, 'Morality and religion essential to society', which had first appeared in 1756. He provided a short and appreciative life of his old friend John Jortin for the *Biographical Dictionary* in 1784, which was then used to preface an edition of Jortin's sermons that appeared in 1787. In 1786 he produced the first of a projected series of anecdotes and dissertations which he called *Sylva, or, The Wood*. Only one volume appeared, in the course of which he laid out his reasons for citing a great deal of Latin and Greek (chiefly to encourage letters in an age that he felt to be in literary and moral decline), denounced Hume's 'unphilosophic attitude' when facing death (*Sylva, or, The Wood*, 90–91), and lamented the conduct of East India 'Adventurers'. He gave up London entirely for Sileby and Southwell in 1785, and became vicar-general of Southwell in 1788.

Heathcote died at the age of seventy-three on 28 May 1795, and was buried in the churchyard of Southwell Minster. He had two sons, both of whom were educated at Christ Church, Oxford. One served in the diplomatic service; the other was a clergyman.   B. W. YOUNG

Sources J. Gascoigne, *Cambridge in the age of the Enlightenment* (1989) • [W. Warburton], *Letters from a late eminent prelate to one of his friends*, ed. R. Hurd [1808] • Nichols, *Lit. anecdotes*, 3.531–44 • *IGI*

Heathcote, Sir William, fifth baronet (1801–1881), politician, was born on 17 May 1801, the only son of William

Sir William Heathcote, fifth baronet (1801–1881), by unknown engraver

Heathcote (1772–1802) and his wife, Elizabeth, daughter of Lovelace Bigg Wither of Manydown, near Basingstoke. His father was rector of Worting, near Basingstoke, and prebendary of Winchester. Heathcote was educated at Winchester College and Oriel College, Oxford, at which he graduated on 29 November 1821, with a first class in *literae humaniores*, John Keble being his tutor. He was a fellow of All Souls College, Oxford, from November 1822 to 1825 (having failed to be elected in 1821), becoming bachelor of civil law in 1824; he was, with Gladstone, one of its first honorary fellows in 1858. He prepared himself for the bar, but on 22 February 1825 he succeeded his uncle, Sir Thomas Heathcote, as fifth baronet and as owner of Hursley Park, Hampshire, a modest estate whose wealth came from supplying wood to the navy, a declining source as iron replaced oak in shipbuilding. On 8 November 1825 he married Caroline Perceval, youngest daughter of Lord Arden, and brother of Heathcote's schoolfriend, Arthur Perceval. She died, following a minor operation, in 1835, leaving him with three sons and a daughter. On 18 May 1841 he married Selina (d. 1901), eldest daughter of Evelyn Shirley of Eatington, Warwickshire; her good cheer and energy balanced her husband's pessimism and frequent illnesses; to Gladstone he 'always appeared unusually collected and ripe for death' ('Diaries', 10.113). They had four sons and four daughters.

From his undergraduate days, Heathcote was much influenced by Keble, whom he invited to become curate at Hursley in 1825; but Keble had to retire in 1826 for domestic reasons. In 1829 he unsuccessfully invited Keble to become vicar of Hursley and in 1836 secured his acceptance. Heathcote restored Hursley church on Tractarian principles and introduced a set of religious rules for his household. He shared Keble's loyalty to Anglicanism and his distrust of continental Catholicism. Keble somewhat moderated Heathcote's tendency to ultra-conservatism. As squire, Heathcote rather reluctantly entered politics; the only election he had to contest was that of 1865. In 1826, he was elected for Hampshire, the seat held by his uncle until 1820; he retired from the seat in 1832. In 1837 he was elected for North Hampshire, holding the seat until he resigned from it, through ill health, in 1849. He was 'in favour of all the aristocratic parts of our Constitution', with 'a horror of democracy … unbounded' and he was 'no partisan of Peel's, for centralization is a favourite hobby of his, and a paid French police'; he preferred 'the old Saxon plans'. R. H. Dana found him 'not a compromise man, but a decided Tory and Tractarian' (Awdry, 69–70, 115). He would not have dissenters as tenants, despite this principle's leading to substantial losses during the agricultural depression. In 1854, after a short period as a director of the South Western Railway, he succeeded Sir Robert Inglis as one of the MPs for Oxford University; as such he quietly represented conservative opinion in the university, in marked contrast to the constant controversy surrounding his fellow member, W. E. Gladstone (whose earlier election he had supported as chairman of his London committee). As MP he supported Gladstone's Oxford University Bill of 1854, though he had strongly disliked the royal commission to whose report the bill was a response; by his amendment, congregation included all resident members of the university. In the 1860s he strongly defended religious tests. Following an illness expected in 1868 to be fatal, Heathcote resigned his seat that year and devoted himself to the life of a country squire, managing his declining woods and estate, compiling a valuable library, and being active as chairman of quarter sessions, in diocesan affairs, and as guardian and subsequently friend of H. H. *Herbert, fourth earl of Carnarvon. He died at Hursley Park on 17 August 1881 and was buried in its mausoleum.

Heathcote was unusual as a Tractarian in remaining a staunch Conservative; he had little to offer national politics save his courteously expressed dislike of the tendencies of his age; but his role as 'Keble's Pupil, Squire and only Patron' (*Letters and Diaries of John Henry Newman*, 29.410) and his friendship with his neighbour, Charlotte M. Yonge, and other members of the Keble circle such as J. T. Coleridge, gained him an otherwise unwarranted significance.   H. C. G. MATTHEW

Sources F. Awdry, *A country gentleman of the nineteenth century: being a short memoir of the Right Honourable Sir William Heathcote* (1906) • J. Darling, *Catalogue of books … at Hursley Park*, 2nd edn (1865) • Gladstone, *Diaries* • *The letters and diaries of John Henry Newman*, ed. C. S. Dessain and others, [31 vols.] (1961–) • W. R. Ward, *Victorian Oxford* (1965) • J. B. Conacher, *The Aberdeen coalition, 1852–1855* (1968)
Archives Hants. RO, corresp. and papers; Hampshire shrievalty, corresp. and papers | BL, corresp. with Lord Carnarvon, Add. MSS

61066–61076 • BL, corresp. with W. E. Gladstone, Add. MSS 44208–44209 • BL, corresp. with Florence Nightingale, Add. MSS 45798–45801 [some copies] • priv. coll., corresp. with S. H. Walpole

Likenesses photograph, 1873, repro. in Awdry, *A country gentleman* • engraving, NPG [*see illus.*]

Wealth at death £46,023 2*s*. 8*d*.: resworn probate, Jan 1883, *CGPLA Eng. & Wales* (1881)

Heather, William (*c*.1563–1627), musician and benefactor, was apparently born at Harmondsworth, Middlesex. Nothing is known of his parentage, though he may have been related to the William Heather who was paid as a music copyist at Magdalen College, Oxford, in the early 1550s. His date of birth of about 1563 is calculated from his testamentary bequest that sixty-four mourning gowns be distributed to so many poor men at his funeral. Heather was a lay clerk at Westminster Abbey from Easter 1586 until 27 March 1615, when he was sworn in a gentleman of the Chapel Royal. On 24 June 1589 he married Margery Fryer (*d*. 1635) in St Margaret's, Westminster.

Heather was a close friend of William Camden, the antiquary and headmaster of Westminster School. They doubtless had common musical interests, for Camden sang in the abbey choir for a year while he was second master. Heather nursed him through a fever in 1601 and took him to his house in the almonry to avoid the plague during another illness in 1609. When Camden resolved to establish a chair of history at Oxford in 1622, he transferred all his right in the manor of Bexley in Kent to the university on the twofold condition that the manorial profits (valued at about £400 per annum) should be enjoyed by Heather, his heirs, and executors for ninety-nine years after Camden's death, and that during that period they should pay £140 annually to the professor of history. Heather delivered the deed of gift to convocation on 17 May 1622, on which day he was awarded by acclamation the degrees of bachelor and doctor of music, together with his friend and Chapel Royal colleague Orlando Gibbons. A proposed public disputation between Heather and Nathaniel Giles on musical questions came to nothing. Rumours first reported by Wood that Heather's MusD exercise was composed by Gibbons were later confirmed by William Gostling, who described the latter's eight-part anthem 'O clap your hands' as 'Dr Heather's Commencement Song'. On Camden's death eighteen months later, Heather, as his sole executor, received a warrant to preserve the king's game within the manor of Bexley. Heather later realized the value of the lease of the memorial profits by disposing of it (together with the obligation under the covenant) to Sir Francis Leigh of Addington, Surrey.

In 1626 Heather followed the example of his friend and took the first steps to founding the music lecture at Oxford which bears his name to this day. In a letter dated 5 May he proposed presenting the university with some instruments and music books to promote a weekly music practice. More precise ordinances, approved by convocation on 16 November, stipulated that the practice was to be held every Thursday afternoon in term (Lent excepted), and that a 'Master of the Musicke' was to be appointed to

care for the instruments and books and to bring to the weekly meeting two musical boys with whom he would rehearse pieces in three parts if nobody turned up to these sessions. His bequest to the music school included printed English and continental music by his contemporaries and one manuscript collection—the now famous Forrest–Heather partbooks containing sixteenth-century festal masses by English composers. Heather's endowment eventually provided instruction in both speculative and practical branches of the art. By an indenture dated 20 February 1627 he made over to the university an annuity, provided out of his Kent estates, of £16 6*s*. 8*d*. (increased to £17 6*s*. 8*d*. in his will) from which the music professor should draw a salary of £13 6*s*. 8*d*., the remaining £3 going to the reader of a lecture in English on music theory. The founder appointed Richard Nicholson, organist of Magdalen College, the first master; John Allibond MA, of the same college, was the first and only person to take up the position of lecturer, the latter's stipend being afterwards assigned to the speaker at Act time.

The state occasions at which Heather was present included the funerals of Elizabeth I, James I, and Queen Anne of Denmark, and the coronation of Charles I. He died at the almonry, Westminster Abbey, towards the end of July 1627, and was buried on 1 August in the broad aisle on the south side of the abbey. His widow was buried there on 6 September 1635. In his will, dated 21 July 1627, Heather made several charitable bequests, including £10 to the singing men and choristers of Westminster Abbey and £3 per annum for ever to Eton College. He left 40*s*. to the poor of Chislehurst and 40*s*. per annum to the scholars of the free school at Stanwell. The New Hospital in Tothill Fields, Westminster, to which he had donated £100 in his lifetime, now received £10 and the promise of another £100; £50 was also placed in the hands of the clerk of the cheque to be lent to such gentlemen of the Chapel Royal as suffered hardship through late payment of their wages.

In May 1926 a festival was held in Oxford in commemoration of the tercentenary of the foundation of the Heather chair, and on 18 June of that year a special service was held in Westminster Abbey at which the chancellor of the university, Viscount Cave, unveiled an inscribed stone close to Camden's monument to mark Heather's grave. In his lifetime, Heather was respected and honoured by his fellow musicians. The younger John Hilton, who was a beneficiary of his will, dedicated to him his *Ayres or Fa Las for Three Voyces* (1627), and Thomas Tomkins's six-part madrigal 'Music Divine' (*Songs*, 1622) bears the inscription 'To Mr Doctor Heather'.   DAVID MATEER

Sources H. W. Shaw, 'The Oxford University chair of music, 1627–1947, with some account of Oxford degrees in music from 1856', *Bodleian Library Record*, 16 (1997–9), 233–70 • wills of prerogative court of Canterbury, PRO, PROB 11/152, fols. 211–12 • Westminster Abbey muniments, treasurer's account book, 1585–6, MS 33643 • Westminster Abbey muniments, treasurer's account book, 1614–15, MS 33670 • [E. Hatton], *A new view of London*, 2 vols. (1708) • Wood, *Ath. Oxon.* • W. Camden, 'Memorabilia … de seipso', in T. Smith, *Gulielmi Camdeni … epistolae* (1691) • E. Gibson, 'The life of Mr Camden', in *Camden's Britannia*, ed. and trans. E. Gibson (1695),

11–21 • S. Gibson, ed., *Statuta antiqua universitatis Oxoniensis* (1931) • J. Westrup, 'Heyther, William', *New Grove* • E. F. Rimbault, ed., *The old cheque-book, or book of remembrance, of the Chapel Royal, from 1561 to 1744*, CS, new ser., 3 (1872) • M. Crum, 'Early lists of the Oxford music school collection', *Music and Letters*, 48 (1967), 23–34 • P. M. Gouk, 'Music', *Hist. U. Oxf.* 4: *17th-cent. Oxf.*, 621–40 • A. Ashbee, ed., *Records of English court music*, 9 vols. (1986–96) • *Reg. Oxf.*, vol. 2/1–4 • A. M. Burke, ed., *Memorials of St Margaret's Church, Westminster* (1914) • J. L. Chester, ed., *The marriage, baptismal, and burial registers of the collegiate church or abbey of St Peter, Westminster*, Harleian Society, 10 (1876) • libri computi, 1551–3, Magd. Oxf. • N. C. Carpenter, *Music in the medieval and Renaissance universities* (1958) • A. Wood, *The history and antiquities of the University of Oxford*, ed. J. Gutch, 2 vols. in 3 pts (1792–6) • A. H. King, *Some British collectors of music, c.1600–1960* (1963) • parish register (marriage), St Margaret's, Westminster, 24 June 1589

Archives Bodl. Oxf., music school collection, Forrest–Heather partbooks

Likenesses portrait, U. Oxf., faculty of music

Wealth at death £1300—excl. lands and tenements: will, PRO, PROB 11/152, fols. 211–12

Heatherington, Alexander (*d.* 1878), mining agent, is a figure whose early life is not documented. He was the founder in 1867 at Halifax, Nova Scotia, of the International Mining Agency, with which the Canadian Mines Bureau, at 30 Moorgate Street, London, was associated. He also started at Halifax a monthly paper entitled the *Mining Gazette*, the first number of which appeared on 10 January 1868. Heatherington was a fellow of the Geological Society, and a clever statistician. He wrote a number of statistical works on gold mining in Nova Scotia, as well as *A Practical Guide for Tourists, Miners, and Investors* (1868). He died at Toronto on 8 March 1878.

GORDON GOODWIN, rev. ROBERT BROWN

Sources *Geological Magazine*, new ser., 2nd decade, 5 (1878), 336

Heathfield. For this title name *see* Eliott, George Augustus, first Baron Heathfield of Gibraltar (1717–1790).

Heaton, Clement (1824–1882), joint founder of a firm of stained-glass makers and architectural decorators, was born on 21 August 1824 in Bradford-on-Avon, Wiltshire, and baptized there on 14 November, the only son of James Heaton (1782–1862), Methodist minister, and his wife, Sarah, *née* Walmsley. His co-founder **James Butler** (1830–1913) was born at The Butts, Warwick, the second son of James Butler (1786–1851?), publican, and his wife, Charlotte. Both men learnt their trade in Warwick where, until 1851, Clement Heaton was employed as a glass painter by the local stained-glass maker, William Holland, and James Butler worked as a lead glazier, very probably for the same firm.

In the early Victorian period the rising tide of the Gothic revival led to a rapid increase in the demand for stained glass. Aware, no doubt, that there were, as yet, few stained-glass makers in the capital, Clement Heaton left Warwick in 1851 or 1852 and travelled to London. Here he set up his own stained-glass studio in Albany Street, and married Mary Louisa Matthews (*b.* 1835), the daughter of a glass cutter, on 17 November 1853. They lived first at 94 Albany Street, later at 8 D'Aumale Villas, Twickenham, and Verulam House, Watford. Two years later James Butler followed Clement Heaton to London where, by 1857, the

two men had founded the firm of Heaton and Butler, with premises at 236 Marylebone Road. That year Butler married Kate Stultz (1830–1858), and they lived in Rutland Street, Hampstead. Kate died the following year. About 1865 Butler married, second, Eliza Bacon (1837–1896).

Although Clement Heaton and James Butler were sound craftsmen, and their business prospered, the artistic quality of the windows they produced in the early years of their partnership cannot be compared with that of the best designers in the field. Two far more accomplished artists, who were also engaged in establishing themselves as stained-glass makers at this date, were John Richard Clayton and Alfred Bell. But though they were skilled designers and draftsmen, their practical knowledge of the processes involved in the manufacture of stained glass was weak.

Clearly, the two firms must have seen advantage in working together for, in 1858, Heaton and Butler took additional premises at 24A Cardington Street, in the same building as Clayton and Bell. As a result, Heaton and Butler's designs drew closer to those of Clayton and Bell, who may on occasion have drawn the cartoons for the other firm's windows, while Clayton and Bell benefited from the technical expertise of Heaton and Butler who, according to one source, did much of their glass cutting, leading, painting, and fixing at this time.

The event which enabled the firm of Heaton and Butler to reach the top rank in terms of design, however, was the advent of **Robert Turnill Bayne** (1837–1915). He was born on 11 December 1837, at Starton in Stoneleigh, Warwickshire, the second son of Richard Roskell Bayne (1802–1878), architect and engineer, and his first wife, Ann Turnill. Bayne is said to have had a public school education and begun a career as a portrait painter before turning to stained glass. Initially he was apprenticed to Clayton and Bell but soon left to join Heaton and Butler, becoming a full partner on 26 March 1862. From then on the company was known as Heaton, Butler, and Bayne, the title it retained until it was dissolved in 1953. In 1869 Bayne married Marion Charlotte Hutchings, and they lived first at Ravensbourne Park, Lewisham, moving in 1896 to Wimbledon Park and then to Surbiton, Surrey. As part of his training with Clayton and Bell, Bayne learned to follow the principles of medieval design whereby the figurative elements of the composition are surrounded by a decorative architectural framework. But when he became chief designer of Heaton and Butler, a firm which had not as yet developed a distinctive style of its own, Bayne was free to experiment. Abandoning the strictly historicist approach advocated by Clayton and Bell, he began to heighten the drama of his work by exaggerating the gestures and 'medieval' facial features of the teeming figures that filled his windows. Fine examples of his work at this time are found at St Mary's, Brome, Suffolk (1863), Nordelph Church, Norfolk (1865), and St James's, Chilton Cantelow, Somerset (1865).

But just as striking as the improvement in design, was the firm's adoption of a much more vivid palette of colours. The production of stained glass is always a collaborative process carried out by a team of craftsmen, and this often makes it difficult to say who may have been responsible for what. However, it seems probable that Clement Heaton played an important part here since he was, throughout his life, particularly interested in the techniques involved in glass making and could, by this date, produce 130 different tints. But such things are also a matter of fashion. Heaton, Butler, and Bayne were not alone in changing their palette in the 1860s; although Clayton and Bell added only a few new colours at this time, Lavers and Barraud, the other major firm established in London during the previous decade, were much more adventurous. Following Pre-Raphaelite taste, both they and Heaton, Butler, and Bayne added lime greens, clear pinks, mauves, oranges, and various shades of blue to the more traditional range of colours—red, blue, amethyst, brown, and yellow—used in the medieval period.

The demand for stained glass reached a peak between 1860 and 1870, and it is no surprise, therefore, to find Heaton, Butler, and Bayne expanding at this time. In 1863 they moved to grand new premises at 14 Garrick Street in Covent Garden, a studio building specially designed for them by Arthur Blomfield, an architect with whom the firm had a long and successful relationship. Here there was sufficient space to experiment with other media and, by 1865, they had not only branched out into the field of painted decoration but were also carrying out designs using mosaic, inlaid stone, and incised mastic work. From 1870 until the beginning of the First World War they were the most prolific of all the firms producing large-scale decorative schemes for churches, public buildings, and private houses.

By the mid-1860s Heaton, Butler, and Bayne were probably employing upwards of a hundred men. Like all stained-glass firms of this date, they used production-line methods to keep the cost of their work within bounds. A few skilled cartoonists did nothing except figurework, while a second tier of draftsmen specialized in architectural decoration, drapery, or repetitive patterning. A further group of craftsmen carried out the more menial tasks of glass cutting, firing, leading, and fixing of the windows. And yet more men were employed to decorate walls and ceilings.

About 1870 taste changed again, and the jewel-like windows of the previous decade, formed by a kaleidoscope of different coloured pieces of glass, began to give way to something more sombre. From this time on until the beginning of the First World War, the colour range most frequently used by Heaton, Butler, and Bayne included brown, green, yellow, blue, and deep red. A typical design would also include plenty of contrasting white glass, with features such as yellow hair and gilded ornaments picked out in yellow stain. At the same time the firm abandoned their 'medieval' style, whereby faces and other features were merely drawn in outline, and began to use much more shading to make objects look three-dimensional. This also had the effect of reducing the luminosity of the glass and making the colours darker.

Some of the most outstanding stained glass made by the firm in the last three decades of the nineteenth century, however, was not designed by the 'in house' cartoonists but by specially commissioned freelance artists. This was the case at St Elisabeth, Reddish, in Manchester, where about 1883, the architect Alfred Waterhouse commissioned Frederick Shields to make the cartoons for the windows. Some years earlier, he also had Shields design glass for the chapel of the duke of Westminster's vast new mansion, Eaton Hall in Cheshire (house dem. 1961, chapel survives), where Henry Stacy Marks was employed to paint murals. Heaton, Butler, and Bayne made all the stained glass for the house and chapel windows, and were also asked to carry out much of the other decoration. They in turn called in Lewis F. Day, an artist who specialized in the design of wall coverings, tiles, and stained glass for domestic interiors, giving him a contract to help with this particular job.

On 24 February 1882 Clement Heaton died in Bournemouth and was succeeded by his son, Clement J. Heaton (1861–1940). Two years later, following a dispute with the other partners, Heaton resigned and set up his own company, Heaton's Cloisonné Mosaics Ltd, specializing in metalwork and enamelling. In 1893 he emigrated to Switzerland where he became a successful designer, eventually moving to America. Sadly, Robert Turnill Bayne had a stroke in 1885 and, although he lived until 1915, was no longer able to work. He died on 18 September 1915 at his home, Losely Hurst, in Surbiton, Surrey. After this the great years of the firm were over. James Butler died in London in 1913 and was succeeded by Clement James Butler (1859–1929). Richard Cato Bayne (1870–1940) joined the company in 1887, and his only son, Basil Richard Bayne (1897–1953) saw it through its final years.

TERESA SLADEN

Sources F. Skeat, 'Heaton, Butler and Bayne: a famous Victorian firm', *Family History*, 10 (1979), 69–70 · M. Harrison, *Victorian stained glass* (1980) · *Victorian & Edwardian stained glass* (1987) · B. Haward, *Nineteenth century Suffolk stained glass* (1989) · S. B. M. Bayne, *Heaton, Butler and Bayne: a hundred years of the art of stained glass* (1986) · *CGPLA Eng. & Wales* (1882) [Clement Heaton] · *CGPLA Eng. & Wales* (1915) [Robert Turnill Bayne]
Archives V&A NAL, accounts
Wealth at death £8513 5s. 2d.—Clement Bayne: probate, 13 April 1882, *CGPLA Eng. & Wales* · £23,340 10s. 1d.—Robert Turnill Bayne: probate, 16 Nov 1915, *CGPLA Eng. & Wales*

Heaton, Ellen (1816–1894), art collector and philanthropist, was born on 18 November 1816 at 7 Briggate, Leeds, the eldest of the two children of John Heaton (1769–1852), bookseller and printer, and his wife, Ann Deakin (1774–1841), who came from a family of West Riding farmers. Ellen Heaton and her younger brother, the physician John Deakin Heaton (1817–1880), received their earliest schooling from a Baptist minister, Mr Langdon, in Infirmary Street, Leeds. Both, however, became members of the Church of England as children. When she was ten years old, Ellen Heaton was sent to a school run by the Misses Plint in Wellington Street, Leeds; she remained there until 1833 when she became a boarder at Roe Head School, Mirfield.

Although Ellen Heaton was a brighter pupil than her brother, she was not encouraged to continue her studies because of the prevailing bias against advanced female education. She stimulated her intellect by joining the Leeds Literary and Philosophical Society, which was presided over by her brother and where she later delivered a paper entitled 'The care of health' (1875); she is also said to have been the proprietor of the Leeds Subscription Library. She also regularly attended meetings of the British Association throughout the British Isles and was a fellow of the Royal Botanical Gardens. After coming into an inheritance on the death of her father, Heaton was determined to lead an independent life. She indulged her love of travel with frequent visits to the continent, and in 1867 even ventured as far afield as Poland and Russia. She often travelled with Fanny Haworth, with whom she had formed a domestic relationship while abroad in 1853. Her spending and disregard of convention often exasperated her more conservative brother: Dr Heaton objected to her unchaperoned sojourn at the seaside with the married artist Thomas Richmond and, as her trustee, disapproved of her making a loan of £1200 to the artist, from whom in 1849 she had also commissioned her portrait. Her serene appearance belied her forceful and energetic personality.

Ellen Heaton cultivated literary and artistic relationships with some of the leading talents of her time, including Elizabeth Barrett Browning, Robert Browning, and John Ruskin. The Brownings were somewhat overwhelmed by her aggressive overtures of friendship and her insistence in 1859 that they sit for portraits by the artist Field Talfourd at her expense. That spring Elizabeth Barrett Browning confided to her sister Arabel:

> she comes here every day though not for long I must admit, just when people come. I find it trying sometimes. Only of course you won't repeat this—she has made herself famous in Rome by 'pushing' here & there & everywhere & people laugh—they laugh!—she gave twenty pounds for my picture—partly for me, & partly for the artist—& I am afraid we are both of us 'des ingrats'. (*Sublime and Instructive*, 261)

Heaton donated both portraits to the National Portrait Gallery in 1870.

Unlike the Brownings, Ruskin was not daunted by Heaton's unbridled enthusiasm for his friendship and relished the opportunity to be her mentor. She first approached him in 1855 after reading the early volumes of *Modern Painters* to seek advice about some sketches by J. M. W. Turner which she was interested in purchasing, having seen his work at the Royal Academy. Happy to oblige, Ruskin approved her selection of Turners and proceeded to guide her art collecting activities in the direction of the young Pre-Raphaelite artists. He suggested that she patronize Dante Gabriel Rossetti, Arthur Hughes, J. W. Inchbold, and Edward Burne-Jones. Heaton followed Ruskin's advice in each instance with the exception of Burne-Jones, whose art did not appeal to her. She far preferred that of Rossetti, from whom she purchased seven watercolours and one oil painting. That number would have been greater by one had Ruskin not intervened in her purchase of *Paolo and Francesca* (1855, Tate collection).

The pandit commandeered the watercolour for himself on the grounds that it represented the couple kissing, telling her that 'Prudish people might perhaps think it not quite a young lady's drawing' (Surtees, 37). In awe of Ruskin's reputation, and in the absence of more determined role models among women collectors, Heaton did not object to his interference.

Heaton remained loyal to Ruskin even after she stopped collecting art in the 1860s. Under his influence she turned her attention to philanthropy, working at Winnington Hall School for Octavia Hill and initiating charitable projects of her own in Leeds. She offered to pay the admission for Leeds working men to attend lectures on the university extension courses and planned teas for them in her home. She also collaborated with another Ruskin protégée, Lady Trevelyan, in promoting the products of poor lace makers in Devon and Cornwall. Ellen Heaton remained active in social causes until the last year of her life. After contracting bronchitis, she suffered a fatal heart attack at her home, 6 Woodhouse Square, Leeds, on Christmas day 1894. She was buried in St George's Church, Leeds. She left her estate to her nephew Beresford Rimington Heaton, who bequeathed her art collection to the Tate Gallery in 1940. DIANNE SACHKO MACLEOD

Sources *Extracts from the journals of John Deakin Heaton, M.D., of Claremont, Leeds*, ed. B. Payne and D. Payne, Thoresby Society, 53, pt 2 (1971), 93–153 • *Sublime and instructive: letters from John Ruskin to Louisa, marchioness of Waterford, Anna Blunden and Ellen Heaton*, ed. V. Surtees (1972), 141–51 • V. Surtees, *The paintings and drawings of Dante Gabriel Rossetti (1828–1882): a catalogue raisonné* (1971) • D. S. Macleod, *Art and the Victorian middle class: money and the making of cultural identity* (1996) • d. cert.
Archives V&A NAL, corresp. with A. Hughes • W. Yorks. AS, Leeds, Yorkshire Archaeological Society, John Deakin Heaton MSS • Yale U., corresp. with Rossetti
Likenesses M. Claxton, portrait, 1840 • J. Durham, bust, 1846–9 • T. Richmond, oils, 1849, repro. in Surtees, ed., *Sublime and instructive*; priv. coll. • F. Talfourd, portrait, exh. RA 1858
Wealth at death £15,203 0s. 2d.: probate, 11 Feb 1895, *CGPLA Eng. & Wales*

Heaton, Eric William (1920–1996), Church of England clergyman and biblical scholar, was born on 15 October 1920 at 3 Ellacroft Road, Horton, Bradford, the son of Robert William Heaton, a mechanical engineer, and his wife, Ella Mabel, *née* Brear. Heaton was educated at Ermysted's School, Skipton, from where he won an exhibition to Christ's College, Cambridge (1940–44). Its master, Charles Raven, enduringly influenced his religious outlook and values, while Heaton's study of English literature before theology in the tripos deeply marked his treatment of the Old Testament in his own books. In 1944 he was ordained straight to a joint post at Durham, as curate of St Oswald's and staff secretary of the Student Christian Movement. He returned to Cambridge in the following year, becoming chaplain and then dean, fellow, and tutor at Gonville and Caius College. On 26 March 1951 he married Rachel Mary (*b.* 1926/7), daughter of the New Testament scholar C. H. *Dodd. They had two sons and two daughters. He moved in 1953 to a residentiary canonry at Salisbury Cathedral, where he was chancellor from 1956 to 1960. In that year he became fellow, chaplain, and tutor in theology at

St John's College, Oxford, serving as its senior tutor from 1967 to 1973 and doing much to steady the nerves of the college deans' committee during the troubled years of student revolt. His appointment as dean of Durham in 1974 lasted only until 1979, when he returned to Oxford as dean of Christ Church. Pro-vice-chancellor of the university from 1984 to 1991, he retired in his seventy-first year, the occasion being marked by the award of the Lambeth DD and his appointment as *cavaliere ufficiale* of the Italian order of merit. He was made an honorary fellow of Christ's College, Cambridge, and of St John's and Christ Church, Oxford.

In his studies of the Old Testament, Heaton mostly followed his own agenda rather than addressing himself to technical issues of current scholarly debate. He was concerned with the needs of the intelligent non-specialist reader and addressed those needs not only in his earlier books—*His Servants the Prophets* (1949), revised and enlarged as *The Old Testament Prophets* (1958) and several times reprinted, together with his commentary on the book of Daniel (1956) and *The Hebrew Kingdoms* (1968)—but again in *A Short Introduction to the Old Testament Prophets* (1996). In academic circles, his best-known book remains *Solomon's New Men* (1974), in which he drew together a number of then fashionable lines of argument to suggest that there was an intellectual renaissance in Solomon's reign which was itself related to the rapid development of a civil service necessary for running his empire. This line of investigation was extended in Heaton's final book, *The School Tradition of the Old Testament* (1994)—his Bampton Lectures of that year, first proposed for 1980 and inevitably long delayed. Here he acknowledged and explained his continuing preoccupation with this topic: 'the school tradition characteristically found its authority in the capacity of human beings to discern moral norms by the light of nature' (p. 180). It was a fundamental conviction with Heaton that knowledge of God comes through a natural—if God-given—power of understanding what is good; the heart of his faith was the liberal axis which connected the goodness of the world with the moral interpretation of religion. Christology, redemption, and the mission of the church were not absent, but were comparatively under-elaborated in his preaching, which was orientated towards a common-sense moral responsibility and tended to have a domestic cast. He lived in perpetual reaction against what seemed to him to be excessive credal expectations and had little regard for much contemporary work in theology and biblical studies. A collection of his sermons, *For Questioning Christians*, was published in 1996.

Believing deeply with the prophets that 'it is in right human relations that God is known and served' (*The School Tradition*, 102), Heaton had a profound sense of the value of community, whether as embodied in the family—supremely—or in colleges and (potentially at least) cathedrals. At Durham he opened up and invigorated the life of the cathedral, seeking to make all and sundry feel welcome, whether they were the diocesan clergy, the cathedral's 'friends', or visitors generally. At Christ Church he

repeated this work, strengthened the cathedral's administration and finances, and achieved a new settlement with the university regarding the stipendiary arrangements for the canon–professors so as to ensure the stability of those posts. He set great store by the unique relationship at Christ Church between the cathedral and college aspects of a single institution, and displayed a most precise and well-judged understanding of its constitutional and social dynamics. Within the cathedral he showed himself conservative on liturgy, preserving the patterns he had inherited, committed to Anglican decorum, and viewing with equal disfavour what he saw as evangelical pressurizing and Anglo-Catholic ritualism. On various scores he much disliked Pusey. As regards the college, he characteristically played a decisive part in establishing both a new forum for academic planning and an old members' association.

Heaton approved of Solomon's scribes, or civil servants, for being men trained to know the ropes and even how to pull strings. He was himself a master of business and a superb chairman, clear and consistent, whether in chapter or in college committees. He was not, though, invariably serene. He could be combative, impatient, and prejudiced where he felt his primary loyalties challenged, and he could lose his temper, sometimes dramatically. But in the communities which he so notably served, his characteristic disposition was one of warmth and of friendly and cheerful openness. 'Bonhomie' was a favourite word of his; he practised and fostered it, rejoicing in conviviality as an expression of community. He valued and encouraged the many-sidedness of undergraduate life, on the river and the rugby pitch as well as in the library, and when Christ Church came head of the river, he entered into the celebrations with memorable enthusiasm. Heaton had an outstanding ability to motivate people of different kinds to do things and to give them a sense of being valued contributors to a shared endeavour. A unifying and enlivening presence, he earned confidence, invited co-operation, and elicited loyalty. He possessed in the highest degree personal authority, gladly acknowledged and accepted. He died in the John Radcliffe Hospital, Oxford, on 24 August 1996, and was buried in the cathedral garth of Christ Church.   R. W. TRUMAN

Sources D. H. Rice, *The Independent* (30 Aug 1996) · P. R. Baelz, *Christ's College Magazine*, 222 (1997), 71–2 · C. N. L. Brooke, *Christ Church Annual Report* (1996) [address given at memorial service in Christ Church Cathedral, 9 Nov 1996] · *Christ's College Boys' Home and Club*, 155 (1942), 13; 156 (1943), 45 · personal knowledge (2004) · private information (2004) · *The Times* (30 Aug 1996) · *Daily Telegraph* (30 Aug 1996) · b. cert. · m. cert. · d. cert. · Crockford (1990)
Likenesses M. Taylor, oils, 1986, Christ Church Oxf.
Wealth at death under £180,000: probate, 12 March 1997, *CGPLA Eng. & Wales*

Heaton, Sir (John) Frederick (1880–1949), road transport administrator, was born on 18 October 1880 in Bradford, Yorkshire, the son of a warehouseman in the woollen trade, and his wife, Mary Ellen, *née* Speight. He attended Bradford Technical College and studied accountancy, taking eighth place in the examinations of the Society of Incorporated Accountants and Auditors. In 1915 he was appointed accountant in the south London firm of Thomas Tilling. Originally 'jobmasters', with a fleet of horse-drawn omnibuses, Tillings had successfully motorized its services by 1912, when it entered into a pooling agreement with the London General Omnibus Company, which limited its motor bus fleet to 150. As a consequence it moved into provincial operation, and in 1916 began to develop a series of 'area agreements' to regulate competition between the Tilling subsidiary businesses and those of the British Electric Traction company (BET).

It was at this point that Heaton became Tillings' company secretary, being elected to the board in 1921. The family was persuaded to leave the management of the business in his hands, and when Richard Tilling, a son of the founder, died in 1929, Heaton succeeded to the chair a year later; thereafter he was effectively in sole command.

Richard Tilling had established the policy of collaboration with BET, and in 1928 a jointly owned holding company, Tilling and British Automobile Traction, was formed, in whose management Heaton was closely involved. This made him a key player in the struggle to prevent the four railway companies from acquiring control of the provincial bus companies. The BET board left him to confront Sir Ralph Wedgwood, general manager of the London and North Eastern, and to reach a settlement which, while giving the railways a share of the bus companies' profits, never gave them more than 49 per cent of the equity.

Under Heaton's direction, Tillings acquired a number of businesses which were not put into joint ownership with BET. He managed the group with attention to detail, in contrast with the hands-off attitude of the BET board to its own subsidiaries. Policy differences built up between them, and in 1942 the joint holding company was wound up and the businesses concerned were transferred to one or other of the parents. The divergence of policy may account for the voluntary sale of the Tilling group to the British Transport Commission in 1948, for £24 million, when BET turned down a comparable settlement.

Having seen the distribution to his shareholders of the greater part of the British Transport Commission 3 per cent stock, in which payment was made, Heaton retired. He had transformed the Tilling family business into one of the two ownership trusts that dominated the bus industry in England and Wales from 1916 to 1948, and left his mark in the management policies of the industry after nationalization.

Heaton served on the Inland Transport War Council from 1941 to 1944, and was unpaid chairman of Short Bros. (Rochester and Bedford), on behalf of the government, from 1942 to 1945. He was knighted in 1942. He had a reputation for ruthlessness, and a somewhat abrupt manner, but those who knew him personally saw a man with a sense of humour, and a range of kindnesses that were never publicized. His management style, centralized and authoritarian, remained evident in the industry up to the later days of the National Bus Company in the 1980s.

Heaton was twice married: in 1908, at St John the Baptist parish church, Kidderminster, to Ethel Irene Roberts, the daughter of a chemist; and in 1927, at Briskley Street parish church, Kent, to Mary Stewart Macleod, née Thomson, a widow. Of his three sons and two daughters, all but one daughter survived him. His main interest outside business, apart from his family, was his farm at Cam Court, Cirencester, Gloucestershire. He died of cancer of the prostate, on 27 April 1949, at his home at The Firs, Croxley Green, Hertfordshire.   JOHN HIBBS

Sources W. J. C. Taylor, 'Pioneers of the bus industry. No. 8. Sir Frederick Heaton', *Bus and Coach* (March 1966) · J. Elliot, 'Sir Frederick Heaton—an appreciation', *Railway Gazette* (27 May 1949) · C. F. Klapper, *Golden age of buses* (1978) · W. J. C. Taylor, *Crosville—the sowing and the harvest* (1948) · W. J. C. Taylor, *Crosville—state owned without tears* (1954) · 'Memorial service for Sir Frederick Heaton', *Railway Gazette* (13 May 1949) · J. Hibbs, 'Heaton, Sir John Frederick', *DBB* · *CGPLA Eng. & Wales* (1949)
Archives Kithead Trust, Droitwich Spa, Worcestershire, National Bus Company Archives
Wealth at death £233,013 13s. 1d.: probate, 28 Nov 1949, *CGPLA Eng. & Wales*

Heaton, Sir John Henniker, first baronet (1848–1914), postal reformer, was born at Rochester on 18 May 1848, the only son of Lieutenant-Colonel John Heaton, of Heaton, Lancashire, and his wife, Helen, daughter and coheir of John Henniker, of Rochester. Educated at Kent House School and King's College, London, Henniker Heaton went to Australia at the age of sixteen (1864), and spent some years in the bush. He subsequently moved to Parramatta, New South Wales, and joined the staff of the *Mercury* newspaper. He acted as town clerk of Parramatta from December 1869 until February 1870. Heaton then edited a paper in Goulburn with the prophetic title of the *Penny Post*, moving thence to Sydney, where he joined the staff of the *Australian and County Journal*, owned by Samuel Bennett, a writer on Australian history, described by Henniker Heaton as 'the best friend I ever had'. In 1873 he married Bennett's only daughter, Rose (she died on 23 March 1920). They had four sons and two daughters.

During the next ten years Henniker Heaton identified himself with the public life of Sydney, and wrote a pioneering standard work of reference, *The Australian Dictionary of Dates and Men of the Time* (1879). He bought much land in Australia. In 1882 he stood for parliament as a candidate for New South Wales, but was defeated by a small majority. He represented New South Wales as commissioner at the Amsterdam Exhibition of 1883, and Tasmania at the Berlin International Telegraphic Conference in 1885, when he succeeded in materially reducing the cost of cable messages to Australia; he was again commissioner for New South Wales at the Indian and Colonial Exhibition held in London in 1886. Throughout his life he so consistently forwarded Australian interests that he became known in Britain as 'the member for Australia'.

In 1884 Henniker Heaton settled with his family in London, and at the general election of 1885 he was returned as a Conservative for Canterbury, a corrupt but safe seat, which he held for twenty-five years. After the general election of 1892 he was offered a baronetcy in exchange for his seat, needed for a defeated former tory minister. He

(1985) · C. R. Perry, *The Victorian Post Office: the growth of a bureaucracy*, Royal Historical Society Studies in History, 64 (1992) · *Daily Telegraph* (21 Feb 1912) · *AusDB* · Burke, *Gen. GB*

Archives Bodl. Oxf., corresp. with Sir William Harcourt · CAC Cam., corresp. with Lord Randolph Churchill · HLRO, corresp. with Herbert Samuel · NL Scot., letters, incl. to Lord Rosebery · Richmond Local Studies Library, London, corresp. with Douglas Sladen

Likenesses photograph, 1895, AM Oxf. [*see illus.*] · B. Stone, print, 1897, NPG · W. Crane, pen-and-ink drawing, 1905, V&A · Spy [L. Ward], chromolithograph caricature, repro. in *VF* (17 Sept 1887), 528 · portrait, repro. in *ILN*, 113 (1898), 951

Wealth at death £363 7s. 0d.: probate, 31 March 1915, *CGPLA Eng. & Wales*

Sir John Henniker Heaton, first baronet (1848–1914), by unknown photographer, 1895

refused the exchange and, considerably irritated, subsequently three times rejected the offer of a KCMG. Henniker Heaton saw himself as a 'progressive conservative' and a fair-trader. During his parliamentary career he worked continuously and persistently at postal reform: owing to his exertions the cost of cabling to different parts of the world was much reduced, and imperial penny postage (except with Australia, New Zealand, and the Cape) came into force on 25 December 1898. In 1905 he founded a League for Universal Penny Postage, and a British–American penny post was introduced in 1908 (but not elsewhere: a letter to Calais still cost 2½d.). He strongly attacked the influence of unions in the Post Office in 'Wanted! An end to political patronage' in *Nineteenth Century and After* (59, 1906). After a problematic negotiation, a penny post to Australia was begun in 1911. In January 1910, Henniker Heaton only just held his seat against an independent Conservative and he did not contest it in the second general election that year. While in Australia in 1911, he finally accepted a baronetcy and on his return was formally welcomed by Lord Curzon and the British Empire League.

Henniker Heaton was a popular figure, a persistent campaigner and a keen clubman. In September 1914 he was taken ill while returning home from Karlsbad, and he died on the 8th in the National Hotel, Geneva.

H. C. G. MATTHEW

Sources R. H. H. Porter, *Life and letters of Sir John Henniker Heaton, bart.* (1916) · M. J. Daunton, *Royal Mail: the Post Office since 1840*

Heaton [*née* Keymer], **Mary Margaret** (1836–1883), art historian and critic, was born on 15 May 1836, the eldest daughter of James Keymer, a silk printer, and his wife, who was a sister of (Samuel) Laman Blanchard (1803–1845). Keymer was a familiar figure in the circle of writers with whom Blanchard was associated which included Douglas Jerrold and Charles Dickens. On 30 December 1862 Mary Keymer married Charles William Heaton (1835–1893), who became lecturer in chemistry at the Charing Cross Hospital in that year.

Encouraged by her lifelong friend Joseph Cundall, Mrs Heaton embarked on a literary career about the same time as her marriage. Her first published work appears to have been a series of nursery rhymes to accompany designs by Oscar Fletsch, published in 1862; this was followed by *The Great Works of Sir David Wilkie* (1868), for which she provided the descriptive catalogue and a memoir of the artist, and *Masterpieces of Flemish Art* (1869), to which she contributed the commentary. Her reputation was made, however, with the publication of *The History of the Life of Albrecht Dürer* (1870), neatly timed to appear the year before the 400th anniversary of the artist's birth. F. A. Eaton, the editor of Moriz Thausing's 1882 account of Dürer's life and works, noted that Heaton's biography was a 'useful and popular' summary of the results of recent German research (Eaton, 1.iv). Accordingly, it exhibited the nationalistic and protestant emphases of her Teutonic sources, as well as other biases characteristic of nineteenth-century accounts of Dürer: these included a tendency to vilify Dürer's wife, Agnes Frey, and to ignore the implications of the Venice letters, first fully published in 1828, which irreparably damaged Dürer's Romantic image as a Christ-like paragon of virtue. In the same year as Heaton's biography was published another popular life of Dürer, by William Bell Scott, also appeared; according to Mrs Heaton's memorialist Cosmo Monkhouse, a friendship between the two authors ensued, but Scott allegedly criticized her account as 'hysterical and prejudiced' (Sherman and Holcomb, 155) despite borrowing substantially from her translation of Dürer's journal, which she was the first to render into English.

The publication of Heaton's biography of Dürer also brought her to the attention of Charles Appleton, founder and editor of the cultural journal *The Academy*: she became one of the most active members of the staff of the journal, allegedly contributing a piece to every number for a period of nine years. In 1873 she published *A Concise History of Painting*, which ranged from ancient Egyptian art to the contemporary British school and exhibited her wide reading in the standard works of nineteenth-century art history. However, although she deplored the biographical and anecdotal emphasis of art history in her preface, her attempt to treat of schools and the artistic content of their works frequently produced a mere list of short biographies of painters. A critic savaged the work in the *Saturday Review*, perversely attacking it for just the qualities of concision and careful arrangement which Mrs Heaton considered necessary for such an elementary introduction to her large subject; with more justice, he criticized her 'gushing sentences' and tendency to speculation . Heaton also prepared a new edition of Allan Cunningham's *Lives of the most Eminent British Painters* (1879–80); wrote several important articles for a new edition of Michael Bryan's *Biographical and Critical Dictionary of Painters and Engravers* (3rd edn, 1884–9); translated *A. Allegri da Corregio* (1876), the biography of the painter by J. Meyer; and with C. C. Black wrote *Leonardo da Vinci and his Works* (1874). She died on 1 June 1883, after a long and painful illness. Mary Margaret Heaton was typical of the mid-Victorian woman writer on art: self-trained and wide-ranging in her interests, she acted essentially as a handmaiden to the new discipline of art history, serving as translator, popularizer, textbook writer, cataloguer, and researcher.

ROSEMARY MITCHELL

Sources C. Monkhouse, *The Academy* (9 June 1883), 408–9 · *DNB* · Boase, *Mod. Eng. biog.* [see also Charles William Heaton] · F. A. Eaton, 'Preface', in M. Thausing, *Albert Dürer, his life and works*, ed. F. A. Eaton, 2 vols. (1882), 1.iv · C. R. Sherman and A. M. Holcomb, eds., *Women as interpreters of the visual arts, 1820–1979* (1981), 13–14 · *Saturday Review*, 35 (1873), 459–61 · J. C. Hutchison, *Albert Dürer: a biography* (1990) · m. cert.

Heaton, (John) Wilfred (1918–2000), composer and music teacher, was born at 17 Blagden Street, Sheffield, on 2 December 1918, the younger of two children of John Heaton, a steelworker in a cutlery mill, then serving as a signaller with the Royal Field Artillery, and his wife, Marian Rawlins. The Heaton family were staunch members of the Sheffield Park corps of the Salvation Army: John Heaton was the bandmaster, and his wife had a fine singing voice. It was natural therefore for young Wilfred's unique musical talents to be nurtured through the Salvation Army. He began piano lessons at the age of eight and soon afterwards was learning the cornet and composing music of his own. His long life in music was underpinned by wide-ranging interests in the arts and in philosophy, and by his strong religious background and faith. At times, however, this creative impulse was often tested and questioned.

Wilfred Heaton left school at sixteen to become an apprentice in a small brass instrument manufacture and repair business in Sheffield, Cocking and Pace. He gained a diploma, the LRAM, for the piano at nineteen and worked at his compositions, mainly songs and brass band pieces, whenever he could. As he noted on a page of the score of his last work, the autobiographical *Variations*:

I got help initially from a crippled SA musician [George Marshall], who had a very sound harmonic instinct, but who stressed contrapuntal studies above all; then from a local music master who initiated me into the wider world of chamber and orchestral music; and finally, a lot later [the 1950s] Matyas Seiber, whose instruction on Bach studies was invaluable. These are three with whom I had personal contact, but along with other inspiring composers—the scores of the 18th century German giants and the 20th century masters.   (Heaton, MS, priv. coll.)

Heaton married a fellow salvationist, Olive Mary Fisher (1913/14–1986), on 13 October 1941. Three daughters were born to them in 1946, 1948, and 1958. After war service as a technician in the RAF, Heaton returned to Cocking and Pace and the Salvation Army in Sheffield, soon becoming deputy bandmaster to his father. He was determined to do his best for the Salvation Army creatively as well. The technical brilliance and musical complexities of his best works placed him firmly in the European classical mainstream, but his music was often thought to be too sophisticated for Salvation Army congregations. Those few pieces which were published in the 1940s, like the march *Praise* and the meditation *Just as I am*, have become classics of their kind, but several more adventurous pieces were rejected. Others, like the toccata *O the Blessed Lord* and the variations *Celestial Prospect*, found their way into print many years later.

In his twenties and thirties Heaton's musical ambitions extended beyond the brass band to orchestral, vocal, and chamber music. A substantial suite for orchestra dates from 1949. A concerto for oboe and string orchestra (1952) was performed in London in 1954 by Joy Boughton and the Boyd Neel String Orchestra, conducted by Norman del Mar. *Three Pieces for Piano* (1953), a substantial piano sonata, and a *Little Suite for Recorder and Piano* (1955) all reveal a composer searching for a modern musical language in which he could feel comfortable.

By the mid-1950s Heaton's life and work began to take a different course. The brass instrument business was proving unprofitable, and he had begun working as a professional french horn player and brass teacher in order to support his growing family. In 1963 the Heaton family moved to Harrogate, where Wilfred took up a full-time teaching post with the West Riding of Yorkshire county council. The Sheffield business closed the following year. Over the next twenty years Heaton became a much respected teacher and influential inspirer of young musicians throughout the Yorkshire dales. Between 1962 and 1969 he was musical director of the Leeds Symphony Orchestra, and in 1971 he spent some months as resident musical director of the Black Dyke Mills Band.

However, as his professional activities increased, Heaton's own creativity went into decline. Temperamentally resistant to all commercial aspects of musical composition, Heaton had been happy within the brass band world. If he could not break out of that world, he decided he would stop composing altogether. Another note on the score of *Variations* offers a further explanation:

all compositional ambitions were brought to a halt through my contact with Rudolf Steiner's Anthroposophical

Movement. Involvement in this seemed to dry me up at a tempo. I lost the impulse to compose. Such an activity seemed unimportant compared with the spiritual impulses provided by Steiner. (Heaton, MS, priv. coll.)

His discovery of anthroposophy, or the science of the spirit, provided him with the catalyst for a drastic personal reorientation.

Most of Heaton's spare time was now dedicated to systematically exploring the worlds of philosophy, of letters, and of spirituality. He became something of a recluse. From time to time, however, he was persuaded out of this creative semi-retirement, most notably in 1973, when he completed his masterpiece for brass band, *Contest Music*, from material sketched many years earlier, to a commission from the organizers of the national brass band championships. Because of its challenging musical idiom it was not used. Following the eventual success of this work in the 1980s, Heaton received frequent requests for new works and steadfastly turned most of them down.

Although he never regained his old fluency, Heaton was encouraged by family and friends to take up composing once again. After his retirement from teaching in 1983 and the death of his wife three years later, there was a welcome 'Indian summer'. He wrote two new concert marches, *Le tricot rouge* and *Glory! Glory!*, and reworked his three substantial orchestral works from the 1940s and 1950s into a symphonic partita for band (1986, using material from 1949), a virtuoso *Sinfonia concertante* for cornet and band (1990), and a lyrical trombone concerto (1992, using material from 1952). In his later years Heaton was pleased, but always appeared surprised—after many years of rejection—by the appreciative reception his music was gaining all over the brass band world. When he died in Harrogate District Hospital on 20 May 2000, he left a number of works in sketch form, including what amounts to his musical testament, *Variations* for brass band. A few weeks before his death Heaton recalled that as a young man all he wanted to be was a composer, adding that the urge never really goes away. He was cremated at Harrogate crematorium on 28 May 2000.

PAUL HINDMARSH

Sources personal knowledge (2004) · private information (2004) [Hilda Heaton, sister; Bryan Stobart, son-in-law] · J. W. Heaton, personal papers and MSS, priv. coll. · b. cert. · m. cert. · d. cert. · *The Salvationist* (10 June 2000) · *The Salvationist* (15 July 2000)
Wealth at death under £210,000—gross; under £210,000—net: probate, 9 Aug 2000, *CGPLA Eng. & Wales*

Heaviside, John (*bap.* 1748, *d.* 1828), surgeon and museum proprietor, the son of John Heaviside (*c.*1717–1787), surgeon, and his wife, Mary Elliott (*c.*1718–1792), was born in Hatfield, Hertfordshire, and was baptized on 18 April 1748. After being educated by Mr Garrow at Chipping Barnet he was apprenticed in 1764 to Charles Dance, a surgeon in the town. Heaviside ran away to London before completing his apprenticeship; on finding him his father took John to the eminent surgeon Percivall Pott, with whom he remained for four years.

From about 1770 to 1771 Heaviside was house surgeon at St Bartholomew's Hospital, London, and qualified for the diploma of the Company of Surgeons on 7 November 1771. On 29 November that year his father bought him a surgeon's commission in the 1st troop (horse) of the Grenadier Guards. He retired on full pay in 1788. Heaviside set up in practice in East Street, Red Lion Square, before moving to Oxford Street in 1777. Not long afterwards he married Mary (*d.* 1824), and they had a son, John (1780–1844). It is possible that the couple separated about 1804. Heaviside was twice unsuccessful (in 1784 and 1787) as a candidate for the post of assistant surgeon at St Bartholomew's.

After his father's death Heaviside came into a fortune and purchased 14 George Street, Hanover Square, where he lived for the rest of his life, and when the surgeon Henry Watson died in 1793, Heaviside bought his anatomical collection and formed a museum. The largest part of the collection, numbering more than 2500 items, was composed of parts of the human anatomy, in spirits, dried, or injected, and illustrating the body in both its natural and diseased states. Many of the specimens were taken from patients whom Heaviside had attended and his catalogue (1818) was punctuated with detailed, often gruesome, information about the cases. Heaviside's collection also included comparative anatomical material, minerals and coins, and a series of plaster casts of the faces of the famous and infamous. The museum, and especially its anatomical component, was one of the most extensive and valuable in Britain of its day.

Heaviside and his pupils John Burnall, John Dorratt, and John Howship added many preparations to the museum which became a popular attraction. According to some verse attributed to William Wadd,

With coffee, tea and buttered rolls,
He found an easy way to people's souls
(Peachey, 20)

The museum catalogue, said William Clift, showed that Heaviside was 'rather a collector than anatomist, his descriptions were generally vague and pompous and occasionally bordering on the marvellous, apparently unintentionally' (Peachey, 24). Among the curiosities of the museum was one of the testes of the late Chevalier D'Eon, whose body had been examined on his death in order to ascertain his true sex.

Heaviside was appointed surgeon-extraordinary to George III in 1790 and appointed to the court of assistants of the Company of Surgeons in 1793. He was elected FRS in 1797. Emma, Lady Hamilton, was among his patients. He was also a member of the Eumelian Club, founded by the surgeon John Ash and whose other members included Joshua Reynolds and James Boswell. Peachey claims that it was here that Heaviside 'made the acquaintance of many of those who, leaving England for France, took a conspicuous part in the French Revolution and were, nearly without exception, ultimately banished or guillotined' (Peachey, 27). Heaviside's own affairs took a serious turn in 1803 after he had attended a Captain Macnamara RN in his duel with Lieutenant-Colonel Montgomery of the 9th foot. Montgomery was killed and Heaviside found himself indicted with assisting in his murder. He was committed to Newgate for trial and spent a week there before the indictment was thrown out. The affair cost him £1000 and brought him unwelcome notoriety: Joseph Jekyll exclaimed 'Egad, we never have a homicide or a suicide without a Heaviside' (Peachey, 27).

Heaviside died in September 1828 at Hampstead, and was buried on 19 September at Hatfield church, where he is remembered by an inscription on the south wall. At the time of his death he had residences at Gower Street, London, and Geddons, near Hatfield. After his death Heaviside's collection was sold from its premises on George Street, Hanover Square, at an auction which lasted eight days.

P. E. KELL

Sources J. Heaviside, *Heaviside's museum: a catalogue of the anatomical museum* (1829) · *Catalogue of the museum of John Heaviside* (1818) · *GM*, 1st ser., 98/2 (1828), 380 · *The record of the Royal Society of London*, 3rd edn (1912) · N. Moore and S. Paget, *The Royal Medical and Chirurgical Society of London centenary, 1805–1905* (1905) · W. Sichel, *Emma, Lady Hamilton* (1905) · G. C. Peachey, *John Heaviside, surgeon* (1931) · P. J. Wallis and R. V. Wallis, *Eighteenth century medics*, 2nd edn (1988) **Likenesses** R. Earlom, two coloured mezzotints, 1803 (after J. Zoffany), Wellcome L. · W. Say, mezzotint, 1803 (after W. Beechey), Wellcome L. · J. Cochran, stipple, 1847 (after W. Beechey), Wellcome L. · W. Beechey, portrait, repro. in Peachey, *John Heaviside* · W. Daniell, soft-ground etching (after G. Dance), Wellcome L. · J. Zoffany, portrait **Wealth at death** under £6000: Peachey, *John Heaviside*

Heaviside, Oliver (1850–1925), physicist and electrical engineer, was born on 18 May 1850 at 55 King Street, Camden Town, London, the youngest of four sons of Thomas Heaviside (1813–1896), a wood-engraver from Stockton-on-Tees, and his wife, Rachel Elizabeth (1818–1894), the daughter of John Hook West of Taunton. In 1847 his mother's sister Emma had married Charles Wheatstone (1802–1875), one of the inventors of the telegraph, and through him both Oliver and his brother Arthur West Heaviside (1844–1923) were drawn into work on telegraphy. Although entirely self-taught, Heaviside became a leading authority on electromagnetic theory and its applications to telegraph and telephone transmission. He also acquired a reputation as an eccentric, particularly in his later years. One of his closest friends, the Cambridge physicist G. F. C. Searle (1864–1954), described Heaviside as 'a first rate oddity' though, he felt compelled to add, 'never, at any time, a mental invalid' (Searle, 'Sketch', 96).

Early years Heaviside's early years were pinched and difficult. His father, he later said, was 'a naturally passionate man, soured by disappointment, always whacking us, so it seemed'; his mother, formerly a governess, was 'similarly soured, by the worry of keeping a school' (Hunt, *Maxwellians*, 49–51). An early bout of scarlet fever left him nearly deaf and, though his hearing later improved, he developed a lifelong tendency to isolation and self-sufficiency. After starting at his mother's 'dame-school', he went to school in the High Street, St Pancras, and then to Camden House grammar school, where he came first in natural sciences in 1865. Further schooling was financially out of reach, however, and in 1867 he was sent north to Newcastle to join his brother Arthur in the telegraph business.

Oliver Heaviside (1850–1925), by Charles T. Heaviside, c.1893

In 1868 Heaviside took a job as an operator on the Anglo-Danish cable, first at Fredericia in Denmark and later back in Newcastle. The newly laid cable was part of the burgeoning global telegraph network, and Heaviside's work on it exposed him to the most advanced electrical technology of the day. In 1873 he sent the *Philosophical Magazine* an exhaustive mathematical analysis of the sensitivity of the Wheatstone bridge, or electrical balance, that drew praise from both William Thomson (later Lord Kelvin; 1824–1907) and James Clerk Maxwell (1831–1879), the leading electrical physicists of the day. Wishing to devote himself wholly to scientific work, Heaviside 'retired' from the cable company in 1874. He never again held a regular job, but spent the next fifteen years living with his parents in London, working full time and in almost total isolation on electrical theory. These were lean years but happy ones, for, as Heaviside later recalled in a 1908 letter to Joseph Larmor, 'I was making discoveries. It matters not what others may think of their importance. They were meat and drink and company to me' (Hunt, *Maxwellians*, 61).

Independent research Heaviside's main discoveries centred on telegraphic propagation and Maxwell's field theory. In 1854 Thomson had worked out a theory of signal transmission that treated the passage of a pulse of current as a case of simple diffusion. Although it gave a good account of how an initially sharp and clear signal was distorted en route by the joint action of resistance and capacitance, Thomson's theory was admittedly incomplete. In a series of highly mathematical papers published between 1874 and 1881, Heaviside revised and extended it, showing in particular that the action of self-induction or 'electromagnetic inertia' could cause a pulse of current not simply to diffuse along a wire but to surge back and forth in a series of waves.

In the mid-1870s Heaviside began to study Maxwell's *Treatise on Electricity and Magnetism* (1873). He spent the rest of his career teasing out the implications of Maxwell's theory, which focused not on charges and currents themselves but on stresses and strains in the electromagnetic field around them. Heaviside's greatest advance came in 1884 when he found that, on Maxwell's theory, energy flows through the field along paths perpendicular to the lines of both electric and magnetic force. Although he later learned that J. H. Poynting (1852–1914) had hit on this result a few months earlier—along with its surprising consequence that energy does not flow along within an electrical wire, as everyone had always thought, but enters it sideways from the surrounding field—it was Heaviside who made it the key to revolutionizing the way Maxwell's theory was understood and expressed. Once he had found the energy flow theorem, Heaviside later declared, 'I did more in a week than in all the previous years' (O'Hara and Pricha, 67). Working back from the flow formula, he recast Maxwell's long list of fundamental electromagnetic relations into a compact and symmetrical set of four vector equations, now universally known as 'Maxwell's equations'. He then used these equations to explicate the behaviour of electromagnetic waves, which had come to be recognized as the most distinctive feature of Maxwell's theory. Heaviside was by then publishing regularly in *The Electrician*, a weekly trade journal whose editor, C. H. W. Biggs, was his chief supporter. His new results appeared there in 1885 but initially drew little notice from other electrical theorists.

Heaviside's career reached a watershed in 1887, when he helped his brother Arthur, by then a prominent engineer in the Post Office telegraph system, write a paper on the new 'bridge system' of telephony. Applying his propagation theory to a circuit along which telephones were arranged in parallel, Heaviside found that the extra self-induction they introduced actually reduced the distortion signals suffered in passing along the line. Indeed, he showed that by loading a circuit with enough inductance and adjusting its other parameters, one could eliminate distortion altogether. Unfortunately, W. H. Preece (1834–1913), head of the Post Office telegraph engineers, had recently declared self-induction to be the great enemy of clear transmission. As Arthur's superior, Preece was able to block publication of the Heavisides' paper, and Oliver was convinced that Preece was also behind the abrupt removal of Biggs as editor of *The Electrician* in October 1887 and the subsequent cancellation of Heaviside's long-running series of articles. Heaviside developed an abiding bitterness towards Preece and peppered his later writings with sarcastic jibes at 'the eminent scienticulist'.

Rebuffed by the engineers (or at least by Preece), Heaviside turned to the physicists, whom he soon found to be remarkably receptive. Late in 1887 he sent the *Philosophical Magazine* the first of a series of articles on electromagnetic waves. Its publication in February 1888 gained the attention of the Liverpool physicist Oliver Lodge (1851–1940), whose experiments on lightning conductors would soon culminate in his detection of electromagnetic waves along wires. Struck by how thoroughly Heaviside had treated the theory of such waves, Lodge went out of his way in a London lecture to praise the 'singular insight' and 'masterly grasp of a most difficult theory' he had found in 'the eccentric, and in some respects repellent, writings of Mr Oliver Heaviside' (Hunt, *Maxwellians*, 149). The reservations about his style aside, Heaviside was delighted by the favourable notice Lodge's remarks stirred up. When the German physicist Heinrich Hertz's even more striking experiments on electromagnetic waves in air were announced to the British scientific public by G. F. FitzGerald (1851–1901) in September 1888, interest in Maxwell's theory, and particularly in Heaviside's writings, was raised to an even higher pitch. A final stamp of approval came in January 1889 when Thomson used his presidential address to the Institution of Electrical Engineers to praise Heaviside's transmission theory. After years on the fringes, Heaviside had suddenly been welcomed into the inner circle of electrical theorists. He soon struck up an active correspondence with Lodge and FitzGerald (both of whom visited him in London early in 1889), as well as with Hertz, and with them formed the core of the group known by contemporaries as the Maxwellians, who were to lead electrical theory over the next decade.

Mathematics and the 'Heaviside layer' Heaviside was a slim, short man with fair hair and an impish sense of humour. He never married, and in 1889 moved with his parents to Devon, where they lived above his brother Charles's music shop in the seaside town of Paignton. He remained there until after his mother's death in 1894 and his father's in 1896. By then his scientific reputation and influence had risen greatly: he was elected a fellow of the Royal Society of London in 1891, his collected *Electrical Papers* were published in two volumes in 1892, and the first of the three volumes of his *Electromagnetic Theory* (1893–1912) appeared in the following year. His system of vector algebra was becoming standard (though only after a nasty fight with advocates of the rival quaternion system), and his set of Maxwell's equations was finding its way into textbooks. His 'operational calculus' for solving differential equations attracted a following among physicists and engineers, but pure mathematicians criticized the method as unrigorous and blocked the Royal Society from publishing one of his papers on the subject in 1894. Incensed, Heaviside launched caustic attacks on 'mathematicians of the Cambridge or conservatory kind, who look the gift-horse in the mouth and shake their heads with solemn smile' (*Electromagnetic Theory*, 1894, 2.12).

The Electrician began publishing Heaviside's articles again in 1891 and, with a few gaps, carried one every few weeks until 1902. In an 1893 article he suggested that his idea of improving telephone transmission by loading lines with inductance might best be carried out by inserting coils at suitable intervals along the line. Such lumped loading eventually proved of enormous commercial value, but Heaviside never patented the idea and the profits went instead to Michael Pupin, who secured a United States patent in 1900, and to AT&T, which built an extensive network of loaded lines.

Heaviside's name became most widely known for an idea he mentioned as an aside in a 1902 *Encyclopaedia Britannica* article on telegraphy. The puzzling ability of radio waves to bend around the earth might be explained, he said, if there were a conducting layer in the upper atmosphere to act as a guide. After its existence was demonstrated experimentally in the 1920s, the 'Heaviside layer' became familiar to radio listeners around the world.

Declining years Although he long lived in near poverty, Heaviside was too proud to accept repeated offers of charity from the Royal Society and others. In 1896 FitzGerald and the London engineer John Perry secured a civil-list pension for him of £120 per year—and, what was harder, persuaded him to accept it. (It was increased to £220 in 1914.) In 1897 he left Paignton and rented a house in nearby Newton Abbot. 'Behold a transformation!', he wrote to FitzGerald. 'The man "Ollie" of Paignton, who lives in the garrets at the music shop, is transformed into Mr Heaviside, the gentleman who has taken Bradley View' (Hunt, *Maxwellians*, 234). However, the situation soon soured; local boys harassed him, calling him names and throwing stones at his windows. He had long suffered from dyspepsia and what he called 'hot and cold disease', and being now left to cook and keep house for himself, his health declined further. After Heaviside suffered an especially serious illness in 1908, his brother Charles arranged for him to board with Mary Way, Charles's sister-in-law, at her Torquay home. Miss Way eventually sold the house to Heaviside and moved out, and from about 1916 until just before his death in 1925 he lived there alone. A local policeman, Henry Brock, helped tend to his affairs and Searle and other scientific friends paid occasional visits, but Heaviside grew increasingly isolated and eccentric. He published little after 1905 and almost nothing after the third volume of *Electromagnetic Theory* finally appeared in 1912. Later reports that he continued to produce important new work in his last years appear to be unfounded.

In 1922 Heaviside agreed to accept the Institution of Electrical Engineers' newly instituted Faraday medal. When the president of the institution, J. S. Highfield, went to Torquay to present the award, he found Heaviside to be 'fully competent' and still wittily acerbic, though filled with 'homely grumbles at the many defects of his neighbours' (Nahin, 293). A fall from a ladder late in 1924 apparently precipitated Heaviside's final illness. On 4 January 1925 he was moved to Mount Stuart Nursing Home, Torquay, where he died on 3 February 1925. He was buried beside his parents in Paignton cemetery on 6 February 1925.   BRUCE J. HUNT

Sources P. J. Nahin, *Oliver Heaviside: sage in solitude* (1988) · B. J. Hunt, *The Maxwellians* (1991) · G. Lee, 'Oliver Heaviside—the man', *The Heaviside centenary volume* (1950), 10–17 · G. F. C. Searle, 'Oliver Heaviside: a personal sketch', *The Heaviside centenary volume* (1950), 93–6 · R. Appleyard, *Pioneers of electrical communication* (1930) · J. G. O'Hara and W. Pricha, *Hertz and the Maxwellians* (1987) · G. F. C. Searle, *Oliver Heaviside, the man*, ed. I. Catt (1987) · I. Yavetz, *From obscurity to enigma: the work of Oliver Heaviside, 1872–1889* (1995) · W. E. Sumpner, 'The work of Oliver Heaviside', *Journal of the Institution of Electrical Engineers*, 71 (1932), 837–51 · E. T. Whittaker, 'Oliver Heaviside', *Bulletin of the Calcutta Mathematical Society*, 20 (1928–9), 199–220 · D. W. Jordan, 'The adoption of self-induction by telephony, 1886–1889', *Annals of Science*, 39 (1982), 433–61 · B. J. Hunt, 'Rigorous discipline: Oliver Heaviside versus the mathematicians', *The literary structure of scientific argument: historical studies*, ed. P. Dear (1991), 72–95 · R. Appleyard, *The history of the Institution of Electrical Engineers, 1871–1931* (1939)
Archives Inst. EE, archives, corresp., and papers incl. notebooks · RS, MSS | CUL, corresp. with Lord Kelvin · Deutsches Museum, Munich, letters to Heinrich Hertz · ICL, corresp. with S. P. Thomson · Inst. EE, archives, corresp. with John Somerville Highfield · Royal Dublin Society, letters to G. F. Fitzgerald · RS, corresp. with Joseph Larmor · UCL, corresp. with Sir Oliver Lodge
Likenesses C. T. Heaviside, photographs, *c*.1893, Inst. EE [*see illus.*] · group portrait, photograph, *c*.1893 (with his family), Inst. EE; repro. in Appleyard, *Pioneers*, 225 · F. Hodge, oils, 1945 (after photograph by C. T. Heaviside), Inst. EE; repro. in Lee, 'Oliver Heaviside', frontispiece · photograph, Inst. EE
Wealth at death £1384 18s. 4d.: administration, 20 July 1925, CGPLA Eng. & Wales

Hebblethwaite, Peter (1930–1994), journalist and biographer, was born on 30 September 1930 at 91 Welbeck Street, Ashton under Lyne, Lancashire, the elder by five years of the two children, both boys, of Charles Hebblethwaite (*b*. 1903), an itinerant seller of crockery, and his wife, Elsie Ann, *née* McDonald (*b*. 1903), a winder in the cotton mills. He was baptized in the local Roman Catholic church of St Anne's and attended the primary school attached to the parish and then the Xaverian College in Manchester. In September 1948 Hebblethwaite joined the noviciate of the Society of Jesus at Manresa House, Roehampton. The decision of his superiors in 1951 to send him to study philosophy at the French Jesuit house of studies at Chantilly meant he came back in 1953 fluent not only in French, but more than adequately competent in German. After a year studying pedagogy, again at Roehampton (he was rewarded with a distinction in theory), he went to Campion Hall, Oxford, from which he emerged in 1958 with a first in modern languages. Two years of teaching at Mount St Mary's, Spinkhill, near Sheffield, were followed by four years of theology at Heythrop College, then in Oxfordshire. He was ordained priest in 1963.

Since Chantilly, Hebblethwaite's interests had been more philosophical than theological. Nor during his four years (1960–64) at Heythrop did he find the style of teaching much to his taste. He wrote *Bernanos: an Introduction* (1965) on the French Catholic writer (1888–1948) whose *Diary of a Country Priest* (1934) was at the time enjoying something of a revival, and he failed his final examinations. A career in lecturing was therefore judged to be closed to him, and after a final year of Jesuit training, the tertianship, spent at Paray-le-Monial in France, he was sent to use his literary skills on the Jesuit magazine *The Month*. The editor, Ronald Moffat SJ, sent Hebblethwaite to Rome to cover the final session (1965) of the second Vatican council. This marked a turning point in Hebblethwaite's career. Instead of an academic *manqué* he became a highly capable religious journalist, with a skill and perception which few of his secular colleagues could match, certainly none in the English-speaking world. He also came back to *The Month*'s office in the London headquarters of the English Jesuit province with a range of contacts among journalists, theologians, and prelates on which he drew for the rest of his career.

Hebblethwaite lived above the office, at 114 Mount Street, in the West End, for the remainder of his time as a Jesuit. In 1967 Moffat resigned as editor and let Hebblethwaite take over. In his charge, though the literary and spiritual traditions of the magazine were not wholly neglected, *The Month* provided informed commentary on Roman Catholic issues, and forged links with newspapers, radio, and television, to a degree uncommon among Jesuits elsewhere in the world. Hebblethwaite was of a rather unprepossessing appearance, balding, gazing myopically through thick glasses, and, though not shabby in dress, displayed a scholarly disregard for the quality of his suits. Though on first acquaintance rather brusque, and giving the impression (which was true) of not suffering fools gladly, Hebblethwaite had a gift for making friends, and many distinguished journalists, politicians, theologians, and others found themselves regaled—frequently, in Hebblethwaite's case, to excess—with drink in his Mount Street office. His writing style, under the tutelage of Patrick O'Donovan of *The Observer* newspaper, became sparse, direct, and humorous. Two feature-length articles for *The Observer* on Cardinal Benelli, the *éminence grise* of the pontificate of Pope Paul VI, were said to have undermined Benelli's candidacy for the papacy in 1978. Hebblethwaite had been flattered by the invitation to write on Benelli: the articles, he came to believe, had misrepresented one of the more liberal-minded of the papal civil servants.

In 1973 Hebblethwaite left the Society of Jesus. It has sometimes been suggested that he resigned because of problems over the Benelli articles, which had undoubtedly caused much embarrassment to Jesuit superiors in Rome, or because of a clamp-down on the liberal views espoused by himself, and by other contributors to *The Month*. Hebblethwaite was indeed liberal in outlook, but he was also—and remained to the end of his days—immensely loyal to the church and particularly to the Society of Jesus. He simply left the order to marry. On 21 July 1974 at the Roman Catholic chaplaincy of Oxford University he married Margaret Isabella Mary Speaight (*b.* 1951), a theologian and journalist. They set up house first in Bladon, Oxfordshire, and then in Earl Street, Oxford. Hebblethwaite was awarded a temporary fellowship in French at Wadham College; it was an enormous disappointment, which remained with him for the rest of his life, when Wadham failed to make the position permanent. By now he had published to acclaim *The Runaway Church* (1975, with a revised edition in 1978), an account of the changes within Roman Catholicism since the second Vatican council. The *National Catholic Reporter* of Kansas City hired him as their Vatican correspondent. In 1979 he moved to a flat in via della Pisana, Rome. He returned to Oxford, to 45 Marston Street, in 1981: this was to be the

family home—he had two sons and a daughter—for the rest of his life.

Hebblethwaite remained the *National Catholic Reporter*'s writer on Vatican affairs, and in 1984 published *In the Vatican*, an account of the inner workings of the papal curia. He contributed to many journals, particularly to the London *Tablet* for which, immediately after leaving the Jesuits, under the pseudonym of Robert Myddleton he had been the 'Broadcasting' columnist. He lectured around Britain and the United States and Canada, where his journalism was perhaps better known even than in Great Britain. He broadcast frequently. Two lengthy and meticulously researched biographies, *John XXIII: the Pope of the Council* (1984) and *Pope Paul VI: the First Modern Pope* (1992), established his reputation as a historian of the papacy, as well as a commentator on it. He was working on a study of John Paul II, specially his involvement with the collapse of communism, when he died at his Oxford home on 18 December 1994 of a gross enlargement of the heart, his death undoubtedly hastened by his heavy drinking. Hebblethwaite's funeral at St Aloysius' Church five days later was followed by a reception at Campion Hall, a sign of the close links he had always retained with his former confrères in the Society of Jesus. He was buried at Wolvercote cemetery on 23 December.   MICHAEL J. WALSH

Sources personal knowledge (2004) · private information (2004) [Margaret Hebblethwaite, widow] · *The Times* (19 Dec 1994) · *The Guardian* (19 Dec 1994) · *Daily Telegraph* (19 Dec 1994)
Wealth at death under £125,000: probate, 1 March 1995, *CGPLA Eng. & Wales*

Hebdon, Sir John (1612–1670), merchant and diplomat, was probably born in London or Oxfordshire, the elder son and eldest of three children of John Hebden (*b. c.*1583), merchant tailor of London, whose family came from Yorkshire, and his wife Elizabeth, daughter of Richard Pope of Oxfordshire. The first record of him in Russia is in 1640, and in 1651 he was a signatory for a loan from Tsar Alexis to Charles II of 20,000 roubles (£10,000), paid in furs and grain. Possibly as a result, Hebdon became a roving agent for Alexis from 1652, buying, to order, arms and many examples of western craftsmanship, recruiting military and other professional men to the tsar's service, and acting as partial translator at audiences with Oliver Cromwell's envoy to Russia in 1654. In 1656 he arranged ships to carry the tsar's embassy to Venice (from Archangel to Leghorn).

After the Restoration, Hebdon settled in Tooting, but remained Alexis's agent. He addressed two remonstrances to the king, urging him to send ambassadors to Russia, and arranged accommodation for Russian ambassadors in England. When Charles II repaid the Russian loan, in the presence of Russian envoys in May 1663, Hebdon was knighted and appointed a privy councillor. Soon afterwards he accompanied Charles Howard, earl of Carlisle, as envoy to Alexis, but was not admitted to the negotiations, the Russians probably suspecting him of changing masters. Carlisle's negotiations for the restoration of the long-standing English trading privileges, withdrawn on the execution of Charles I, were unsuccessful, as were

Hebdon's own efforts when he made his final visit to Russia in 1667, this time as envoy himself.

Hebdon and his wife, Phillippa, had four sons and two daughters. The eldest son, John, was envoy to Russia in 1676. The second son, Richard, a merchant, died in January 1668, and the third son, Thomas, died while accompanying Thomas Bryan (who also died), Sir John's son-in-law, on a mission to Persia in 1669 for Alexis. Sir John died in Tooting on 5 June 1670 and was buried in the old church; his will shows a debt due from the tsar and an amount still owed him for his allowance as ambassador.

J. R. HEBDEN, *rev.*

Sources Russia Company minutes · Calendars SP, PRO, SP 91/3, PC 2 · Thurloe State Papers · *Calendar of the Clarendon state papers preserved in the Bodleian Library*, ed. O. Ogle and others, 5 vols. (1869–1970) · S. Konovalov, 'England and Russia, 1666–1668', *Oxford Slavonic Papers*, 13 (1967), 47–71 · G. M. Phipps, 'Britons in 17th-century Russia', PhD diss., University of Pennsylvania, 1971 · P. Longworth, *Alexis, tsar of all the Russias* (1984) · will, PRO, PROB 11/333, sig. 77 · *LondG* (27–31 Jan 1669)
Likenesses F. Bol, portrait, 1659, Helen Campbell Blaffer Foundation, Houston, Texas
Wealth at death insolvent: will, PRO, PROB 11/333, sig. 77; inventory, PRO

Heber, Reginald (1783–1826), bishop of Calcutta, was born on 21 April 1783 at Malpas, Cheshire, the eldest of the three children of Reginald Heber, rector of Hodnet, Shropshire, and co-rector of Malpas, and his second wife, Mary, daughter of the Revd Cuthbert Allanson. Through his father's first marriage he had a half-brother, Richard *Heber, who became MP for Oxford University and an enthusiastic book collector. The Hebers were an old Yorkshire gentry family, lords of the manor of Marton; Reginald Heber senior had also inherited the manor of Hodnet.

At the age of eight the young Reginald went to Whitchurch grammar school and thence in 1796 to a small private boarding-school at Neasden in London. In 1800 he proceeded to Brasenose College, Oxford. He distinguished himself in 1803 by his recitation of *Palestine*, which marked his début as a minor Romantic poet: the work was received with great enthusiasm by the audience in the Sheldonian Theatre and was subsequently set to music by William Crotch. In 1804 Heber was elected a fellow of All Souls.

In July 1805 Heber and his friend John Thornton (son of Samuel Thornton, MP for Surrey, and nephew of Henry Thornton, banker and prominent evangelical) set out on what was, thanks to the Napoleonic wars, a somewhat unconventional grand tour. They travelled through Scandinavia and Russia as far as the approaches to the Caucasus, and on to the Crimea with its Muslim Tartar community—where Heber recorded his delight 'at being addressed for the first time by the oriental salam' (Heber, 1.267). This tour was Heber's introduction to the peoples of the East: he came to regard his experiences in south Russia as a foretaste of India. He returned home through central Europe and reached England in October 1806.

In 1807 Heber was ordained and, his father having died, became rector of Hodnet. He described his position as a

Reginald Heber (1783–1826), by Thomas Phillips, 1823

'half-way station, between a parson and a squire' (Heber, 1.392), but proved most conscientious as a parish priest. On 14 April 1809 he married Amelia Shipley, third daughter of William Davies *Shipley, dean of St Asaph. Through Shipley's influence Heber was appointed a prebendary of St Asaph Cathedral in 1817. In 1815 he had delivered the Bampton lectures at Oxford, and these were subsequently published under the title *The Personality and the Office of the Christian Comforter Asserted and Explained*. In 1822 he was appointed preacher to Lincoln's Inn.

Heber's ecclesiastical and theological position placed him in the centre of the Anglican spectrum, if anything inclining to the evangelical side, yet he was strongly critical of the factional rivalry between the evangelical and high-church parties. He felt some affinity with the seventeenth-century Anglican divine Jeremy Taylor, whose works he edited and published as *The whole works of Jeremy Taylor, with a life of the author, and a critical examination of his writings* (15 vols., 1822).

Of greater lasting significance was Heber's work as a pioneer of Anglican hymnography. Hymn singing was still suspect at the beginning of the nineteenth century, particularly in high-church circles, but Heber compiled a collection of ninety-nine hymns, including fifty-seven written by himself: they were published posthumously in 1827 as *Hymns Written and Adapted to the Weekly Church Service of the Year*. Some continued in regular use, including 'Brightest and best of the sons of the morning'; 'Holy, holy, holy, Lord God almighty'; and 'God that madest earth and heaven'. He considered that the Evangelical hymns then in use contained gross lapses of taste; his own were decorous, with a rather trite moralism combined with beauty of description (Watson, 321–3).

In 1823 Heber was appointed bishop of Calcutta, a post for which he was by then well qualified. He had taken an active interest in overseas missions, becoming a member of the Church Missionary Society (CMS), which was supported by the evangelical wing of the Church of England. Characteristically, however, he had made a proposal that the CMS should combine with the Society for the Propagation of the Gospel (SPG), associated with the high-church party. He had preached sermons on behalf of both the CMS and the Society for Promoting Christian Knowledge, as well as the British and Foreign Bible Society, which was supported by dissenters as well as Anglicans. In 1819 he had written the missionary hymn 'From Greenland's Icy Mountains' for a service in aid of the SPG at Wrexham. His interest in west and south Asia had developed after the initial stimulus provided by his travels in Russia and through his reading of works of literature and history, which provided some of the material for articles which he contributed to the *Quarterly Review*. His wife subsequently commented that by 1823 'those regions had a romantic charm in his mind' (Heber, 2.95).

Heber was the second bishop of Calcutta—a diocese which had been established in 1814 and which then included not only the whole of India but southern Africa and Australia too. The first bishop, Thomas Fanshawe Middleton, had found his role highly problematic and died a frustrated man in July 1822. Heber was offered the appointment by his friend Sir Charles Watkin Williams Wynn, president of the Board of Control for India. After some hesitation he accepted, in January 1823; he was consecrated on 1 June and arrived at Calcutta in October.

As bishop Heber's task was eased by a change in the law which enabled him to make the first Anglican ordinations of Indians; and he expedited the establishment of Bishop's College at Sibpur, whose main purpose was to be the training of clergy. Much of his time, however, was taken up with travel, to minister to the scattered Anglican communities which had come into existence throughout India and Ceylon. His most notable journey, of a length and difficulty unprecedented for a Church of England bishop, was the one which he undertook across northern India—up the Gangetic plain, through the mountains of Kumaon and the deserts of Rajputana, and finally visiting Ceylon on his way back to Calcutta by sea. His journal was published as the *Narrative of a journey through the upper provinces of India, from Calcutta to Bombay, 1824–1825, (with notes upon Ceylon); an account of a journey to Madras and the Southern Provinces, 1826; and letters written in India*. It was edited by his widow and appeared in 1828 in two volumes. Its popularity was attested by the fact that five editions had been published by 1844, and its exceptional value as a description of India was recognized by contemporaries and by modern historians alike.

Heber's interests encompassed the economy and administration, education and culture, and the predicament of Indian princes; he relished the architecture of palaces and the grandeur of the mountains. He shared the usual contemporary British distaste for Hinduism but not the prejudice against its adherents, whose moral character he was at pains to vindicate; in his judgements on British rule, he was sometimes critical while also giving credit where he felt it was due.

Heber was notable for his friendliness towards representatives of other churches, especially the non-Roman episcopal churches of the East, including the Armenians and Syrians. He came to be highly regarded by the English dissenting missionaries and the Church of Scotland ministers. In fact his charm, good sense, and humanity ensured him widespread popularity: Archdeacon Barnes of Bombay, who accompanied him through western India, commented on his 'unreserved frankness, his anxious and serious wish to do all the good in his power, his truly amiable and kindly feelings, his talents and piety, and his extraordinary powers of conversation, accompanied with so much cheerfulness and vivacity' (Heber, 2.299). Such qualities enabled him to make a significant contribution to the consolidation of the Anglican church in India despite the brevity of his episcopate.

In February 1826 Heber embarked upon a visitation of south India. A major problem which faced him there was that of the persistence of caste in the church, but before he could finally decide on how to deal with it he died suddenly, while taking a bath, at Trichinopoly on 3 April. He was buried there in St John's Church. His wife survived him, as did two daughters—Emily (*b.* 1821), and Harriet (*b.* 1824). Emily later married Algernon Percy, son of the bishop of Carlisle; and Harriet married John Thornton, the son of Heber's old friend. Collections of Heber's sermons, which he had preached in England and in India, were edited by his widow and published in 1829; his secular poetry was published in 1841.   MICHAEL LAIRD

Sources A. Heber, *The life of Reginald Heber, D.D., lord bishop of Calcutta; with selections from his correspondence, unpublished poems, and private papers; together with a journal of his tour in Norway, Sweden, Russia, Hungary and Germany, and a history of the Cossaks*, 2 vols. (1838) • D. Hughes, *Bishop Sahib: a life of Reginald Heber* (1986) • G. Smith, *Bishop Heber* (1895) • M. A. Laird, ed., *Bishop Heber in northern India: selections from Heber's journal* (1971) • M. E. Gibbs, *The Anglican church in India, 1600–1970* (1972) • G. D. Bearce, *British attitudes towards India, 1784–1858* (1961) • H. Cnattingius, *Bishops and societies: a study of Anglican colonial and missionary expansion, 1698–1850* (1952) • J. W. Kaye, *Christianity in India* (1859) • review, *QR*, 35 (1827), 445–81 • review, *QR*, 37 (1828), 100–147 • *EdinR*, 48 (1828), 312–35 • J. R. Watson, *The English hymn: a critical and historical study* (1997) • R. Cholmondeley, *The Heber letters, 1783–1832* (1950) • S. Neill, *A history of Christianity in India, 1707–1858* (1985)

Archives BL, analysis of Aristotle's *Ethics*, Add. MS 28322 • Bodl. Oxf., corresp. and papers • JRL, biblical quotations | BL OIOC, letters to Lady Amherst, MS Eur. F 140 • BL OIOC, Bengal ecclesiastical consultations • BL OIOC, Elphinstone MSS • BL OIOC, Munro MSS • Bodl. RH, USPG MSS • Derbys. RO, letters to Sir R. J. Wilmot-Horton • JRL, letters to E. D. Davenport • priv. coll. • Staffs. RO, Littleton MSS • U. Birm., CMS MSS

Likenesses T. Phillips, oils, 1823, All Souls Oxf. [*see illus.*] • F. Chantrey, marble statue, 1827–35, St Paul's Cathedral, London; clay model, V&A • Hoppner, portrait (after T. Phillips, 1823), Hodnet Hall, Shropshire • F. C. Lewis, stipple (after J. Slatter; *Grillion's Club* series) • E. Turner, pencil drawing, V&A

Heber, Richard (1774–1833), book collector, was born in Westminster on 5 January 1774, the eldest son of Reginald Heber, Church of England clergyman, and his first wife Mary Baylie. His half-brother, Reginald *Heber (1783–1826), poet and bishop of Calcutta, was the son of a second marriage. Heber studied under Samuel Glasse, classical scholar, and then went to Oxford where he was entered as a gentleman commoner at Brasenose College, graduating BA in 1796 and MA in 1797. Earlier, in 1790, at the age of sixteen, he had begun an edition of Thomas Brewster's translation of Persius's *Satires*, which he did not complete. His reading while he was at Oxford was largely in Greek and Latin authors, and his early views on book collecting were limited to the formation of a classical library, despite his father's objections to the sums he spent. He projected editions of those Latin poets not included in the printer J. Barbou's collection, publishing a two-volume edition of Silius Italicus in 1792 and printing part of an edition of Claudian, completed and published after his death by Henry Drury. While an undergraduate at Oxford he was greatly interested in politics and frequently travelled to London to listen to the parliamentary debates, often staying overnight.

When Heber's father died in 1804 he inherited the family properties in Yorkshire and Shropshire, and spent some time in improving them agriculturally. In 1806 he was an unsuccessful candidate for the representation in parliament of Oxford University, eventually being elected to that position in 1821. Between those years, among other pursuits, he visited France, Belgium, and the Netherlands in 1815 in the never-ceasing quest for rare books. During this period he was a member of a committee appointed in 1818 by the House of Commons to consider buying Dr Charles Burney's library. In 1821 he served as sheriff of Shropshire; on 19 June 1822 he was created DCL by Oxford University; and in 1825, while abroad, he resigned his seat in parliament, without having distinguished himself, although constant in attendance. During these years he continued to collect books, to lend books, and to assist friends and acquaintances in various ways. His direct help or influence was sought by Robert Southey, Sir Walter Scott, William Wordsworth, Charles Burney, Thomas Park, and Martin Routh, among others. Southey borrowed Heber's copy of *Amadis de Gaul*; Scott asked Heber, among other requests, to help his brother Tom by using his influence with Lord Palmerston; and Wordsworth asked him to assist in obtaining a fellowship at Merton College for his son. Burney sought Heber's support of his candidacy for the professorship of ancient literature in the Royal Academy; Routh asked if Heber thought it would be presumptuous of him to dedicate a work to the Scottish Episcopal church without first asking permission; and Heber transcribed some verses for Park's edition of Horace Walpole's *Royal and Noble Authors*. But if one contemporary account can be believed, Heber died without friends—Alexander Dyce, another recipient of his generosity, wrote to Sir Egerton Brydges about Heber's last day. 'Poor man' he wrote:

Richard Heber (1774–1833), by John Harris, *c*.1830

he expired at Pimlico, in the midst of his rare property, *without a friend to close his eyes*, and from all that I have heard I am led to believe he died broken-hearted: he had been ailing for some time, but took no care of himself, and seemed indeed to court death. Yet his ruling passion was strong to the last. The morning he died he wrote out some memoranda for Thorpe about books which he wished to be purchased for him. He was the most liberal of book-collectors: I never asked him for the loan of a volume, *which he could lay his hand on*, he did not immediately send me. (Fitzgerald, 230)

What is almost surely, however, the most extended acknowledgement of Heber's help is that of George Ellis in the advertisement to the third edition of his *Specimens of the Early English Poets* (3rd edn, 3 vols., 1803). There, after stating that the second edition had been 'found to contain very numerous, though not very important, typographical errors', he added:

For the detection and the removal of these; for the collation of nearly all the extracts contained in the work with the earliest and best copies of the originals, whether printed or manuscript; for the insertion of some new Specimens; and for much additional information in the notices prefixed to the several authors; the editor is indebted to the kindness of his friend Mr. Heber, and to the frequent assistance of Mr. Park.

There is, however, only one specific reference to Heber in the three volumes, and that is to his possession of an accurate transcript of John Skelton's 'Image of Ypocrycye', from which the poem is reprinted (G. Ellis, *Specimens of the Early English Poets*, 3rd edn, 1803, 2.8, 9–11).

The beginning of what was to be one of the largest collections of rare books in the areas of early English poetical and dramatic literature owned by an individual was said by Heber himself to have been his purchase of a copy of Henry Peacham's *Vallie of Varietee* (1638). He had earlier contemplated collecting the classic writers, having begun the uncompleted edition of Persius in 1790, but he was diverted by the purchase of the work by Peacham. Henceforth all else gave way to what has been quite properly called bibliomania. Indeed, his fame as a seeker-out and buyer of rare books became legendary in his own time. He scoured the great libraries of England, as well as many on the continent. His remark, variously phrased, depending on who quoted it, that 'No gentleman can be without three copies of a book, one for show, one for use, and one for borrowers', is both well known and true. He *was* a lender of books, as a number of his friends and acquaintances could attest and did acknowledge in one way or another. Although many, possibly most, of his books were bought at the great sales on the continent and at the libraries of such scholar–collectors as George Steevens, Richard Farmer, Isaac Reed, and Edmond Malone, he is reputed to have gone personally to considerable distances in pursuit of a rarity of whose remote existence he had learned. He also bought entire libraries, one such purchase being of 30,000 volumes in Paris.

Heber, did not confine himself, however, to collecting in certain limited areas. Besides the richness of his collection of early English literature, his library reflected his early love for the Greek and Latin classics, and his purchases abroad are similarly reflected in his library's coverage of the literature of Spain, Italy, France, and Portugal. He had, possibly uniquely among English collectors of his time, a considerable number of books printed in Mexico. As a collector he was not without his idiosyncrasies, chief of which would seem to have been his objection to large-paper books because they commanded so much shelf room—and yet, there must have been plenty of shelf room, given that he housed his books in some eight or more locations in England and on the continent. There have been various estimates as to the total number of volumes he possessed, one of the highest being that of Thomas Frognall Dibdin, who put the number of volumes stored in England at 127,500. Other estimates put the total, both in England and abroad, at between 145,000 and 150,000, and these figures are in addition to an indeterminate number of manuscripts, pamphlets, and letters.

Heber had inherited the large estate in Shropshire, and it was partly because of this and partly, possibly, because of some Latin verses addressed to him by a young man still at school that Heber became acquainted with Charles Henry Hartshorne (1802–1865) who was born in Shropshire. Heber was a man of great influence, and Hartshorne was advised by friends to cultivate him. In July 1821 the nineteen-year-old Hartshorne visited Heber, twenty-nine years his senior, for some four or five days. Thereafter he spent Christmas 1823 in Oxford with Heber and two months with him in London in 1824. As early as June 1824, when Heber introduced Hartshorne to the Roxburghe Club dinner, rumours were being spread about a homosexual relationship between the two. When Heber resigned as member of parliament for Oxford in 1825, there was a suspicion that the relationship was the reason for this totally unexpected action. The tory periodical *John Bull* wrote that 'Mr. Heber, the late Member for Oxford University, will not return to this country for some time—the backwardness of the season renders the Continent more congenial to some constitutions' (Munby, 187). The allusion to sodomy would not have gone unnoticed. Heber remained in Europe until 1831, despite much advice that he return and dispel the rumours. In a letter to a friend, dated 17 May 1826, Heber expressed surprise and annoyance at the gossip but declared that it would not force him to return to England. Hartshorne was evidently unaware of the rumours until August 1826, and in September of that year he wrote to Heber, then in Brussels, asking him to return to England and refute the charges. Heber refused, although he offered financial aid if Hartshorne wanted to sue *John Bull* for libel. Hartshorne chose instead to lodge a criminal charge against the periodical, a charge which he won, but at considerable financial expense to himself.

The reaction of one of Heber's dearest friends to the rumours was, ultimately, one of shock. Heber and Sir Walter Scott gave and lent books to one another and kept up a fairly regular correspondence, at least when Heber was in England, and one has but to read Scott's letters to Heber to realize how highly Sir Walter regarded him. Heber assisted Scott with his edition of Dryden's works and advised him on others of his projects. Scott, for his part, dedicated the sixth canto of *Marmion* to him, and concluded the introduction to that canto with the lines 'Adieu, dear Heber! life and health,/And store of literary wealth'. However, when Scott learned of the rumours of Heber's alleged homosexuality, he was evidently prepared to give them credence, for he recorded in his journal for 25 June 1826 that he had been told of Heber's 'having been detected in unnatural practices'. And while he hoped there were doubts about this, he concluded that it was true and wrote 'God, God whom shall we trust! Here is learning, wit, gaiety of temper, high station in society and compleat reception every where all at once debased and lost' (*Journal*, 162). On 10 July, in a letter to J. G. Lockhart, he wrote 'I think with horror that if he had asked me to let my son go on a trip to the continent with him or any other such expedition I should have considered it the most fortunate thing in the world' (*Letters*, 10.73). Despite Scott's reference to a warrant, one has not been discovered and Heber was never brought to trial. But on his return to England in 1831 he found that he was still under a cloud, although he was soon seen in the salerooms and was lending books to friends.

The writer of the obituary notice of Heber's death in the *Gentleman's Magazine* described Heber as tall and strong, able to walk from early morning until the advent of night. He was near-sighted, hardly an advantage to a collector of rare books, but was also indefatigable in their pursuit. He liked wine and music, and except in his declining years he was a cheerful companion and a memorable conversationalist with a store of anecdotes. Besides his knowledge of Greek and Latin, he had some acquaintance with Spanish and Portuguese. He never married, but at one time it was thought that he contemplated marrying a dear friend, Miss Frances Mary Richardson Currer (1785–1861), herself a book collector of some reputation, whose library was said to have contained some 15,000 to 20,000 volumes.

Heber was one member of a committee charged with most of the details for getting the newly founded Athenaeum organized. He was one of a distinguished group that included John Wilson Croker, Sir Humphry Davy, Thomas Moore, Samuel Rogers, and the earl of Aberdeen. Heber was also a trustee of the club from 1824, the year of its foundation, to 1828. He and his half-brother, the Revd Thomas Cuthbert Heber, were among those added to the membership of the newly formed Roxburghe Club, attending the inaugural dinner in June 1812. Three years later, Heber presented his edition of T. Cutwode's *Caltha poetarum, or, The Bumble Bee* to the club, the second work to be printed by it.

Heber died on 4 October 1833 at his home in Pimlico and was buried at Hodnet, Shropshire on 16 November. He is said to have died of an attack on the lungs accompanied by jaundice, but he also suffered from the gout. Although the funeral was private, many family members, tenants, and servants were present. Among them, also, was his old friend Thomas Frognall Dibdin, whose *Bibliomania* (1809), bore the words 'In an epistle addressed to Richard Heber'. It was Dibdin who described him therein as Atticus who 'unites all the activity of De Witt and Lomenie, with the retentiveness of Maglibecchi and the learning of Le Long' (1.131), linking him with other famous bibliophiles. Heber's will, dated 1 September 1827, was, characteristically, concealed on a bookshelf, until Dibdin found it. And while Heber had left instructions for the disposal of property valued at £200,000, he made no provision for the future of his vast library.

There were sixteen volumes of the sale catalogues of Heber's library, thirteen of them of the sales in England (covering the period from 10 April 1834 to 22 February 1837) and three dealing with European sales (in Paris, on 15 March and 7 October 1836, and in Ghent, on 26 March 1835). The English sales brought in £56,774, with those on the continent adding some £10,000, so that the total amount of all the sales came far short of the estimated £100,000 originally paid by Heber. The books in England were sold by Sotheby & Son and Evans and Wheatley, under the supervision of Payne and Foss. Most of the 1717 manuscripts in Heber's library were bought by the British Museum, the Bodleian Library, and Sir Thomas Phillips.

ARTHUR SHERBO

Sources *The Heber letters, 1783–1832*, ed. R. H. Cholmondeley (1950) • A. Hunt, 'A study in bibliomania: Charles Henry Hartshorne and Richard Hebar [pts 1–2]', *Book Collector*, 42 (1993), 25–43, 185–212 • *The letters of Sir Walter Scott*, ed. H. J. C. Grierson and others, centenary edn, 12 vols. (1932–79) • *The journal of Sir Walter Scott*, ed. W. E. K. Anderson (1972) • P. Fitzgerald, *The book fancier* (1887) • *DNB* • *GM*, 2nd ser., 1 (1834), 105–9 • A. N. L. Munby, *Essays and papers*, ed. N. Barber (1977)

Archives Bodl. Oxf., corresp. and papers | BL, letters to Philip Bliss, Add. MSS 34567–34568 • NL Scot., corresp. with James Morton • NL Scot., letters to Sir Walter Scott
Likenesses J. Harris, pencil drawing, c.1830, NPG [*see illus.*] • Copley, portrait (aged eight), repro. in Cholmondeley, ed., *Heber letters*, frontispiece
Wealth at death property valued at £200,000; English sale of books brought £56,774; continental sales approx. £10,000

Heberden, William (1710–1801), physician, was born on 13 August 1710 in the parish of St Saviour's, Southwark, London, the third child of Richard Heberden (1663–1717), an innkeeper, and his wife, Elizabeth Cooper (1672–1759). His father died when he was seven and in the same year he entered the parish grammar school; there his prowess in Greek, Latin, and divinity earned him at the age of fourteen a sizarship at St John's College, Cambridge. He received his BA in 1728 and in 1731 he was elected a fellow of his college; at that point he began the study of medicine. He was awarded his MD in 1738, one year earlier than the statutes prescribed.

Heberden was already planning an ambitious course of public lectures on materia medica—the many substances which were often credited with the power to heal; on 9 April 1740 he delivered the opening discourse of a series that was to be repeated annually at Cambridge until he moved to London in 1748. His notes for the introductory lecture demonstrate his ability to entertain as well as to instruct. The following year he completed a manuscript for his pupils entitled 'An introduction to the study of physic', which provided an up-to-date syllabus and a reading list of 114 titles. By this time plans were progressing at the Royal College of Physicians for a new edition of the *London Pharmacopoeia*, a volume containing numerous remedies which were at best useless if not dangerous. In 1746 Heberden printed a tract ridiculing two ancient recipes, theriac and mithridatium, both made up of mixtures of many drugs and authenticated only by long tradition but never challenged. In the new edition Heberden's influence was evident both in the introduction and in the many revisions that followed. In the same year he was elected fellow of the Royal College of Physicians.

In the autumn of 1748 Heberden moved to London and took a house in Cecil Street between Strand and the river. Within a year he was elected to the Royal Society, where he met not only other physicians but natural philosophers such as Cavendish and Priestley. At various times he read papers on rainfall, the effects of lightning, and other topics based on reports from his elder brother, Thomas, a surgeon who lived in Madeira and who sent him accounts of earthquakes and of his astronomical observations. In the Royal College of Physicians Heberden was active and influential. His first contribution was to deliver the Goulstonian lectures (1749) on the history, nature, and cure of poisons; even more important was his initiative that led to the college's agreement to publish *Medical Transactions*. To the first three volumes (1768–85) Heberden contributed a preface and sixteen papers, including his celebrated 'Account of a disorder of the breast' (angina pectoris), in which he gave the first description of this illness, identifying it as a hitherto unrecognized condition

William Heberden (1710–1801), studio of Sir William Beechey [original, *c*.1796]

and giving it a name. Other noteworthy papers concerned rheumatism, measles, chickenpox, and the hazards involved in drinking London pump-water.

In the meantime, having enhanced his social status by obtaining a grant of arms, Heberden married, on 1 June 1752, Elizabeth (1728–1754), daughter of the banker and MP John Martin; two years later she died following the birth of a son, Thomas, who was later ordained and became residentiary canon of Exeter. In January 1760 Heberden married Mary (1729–1813), daughter of Francis Wollaston, one of his friends in the Royal Society. Of their seven children three died in infancy; of the rest only two survived their father, Mary Heberden (*b*. 1763) and William *Heberden (1767–1845), later royal physician. In 1761 Heberden declined an invitation to become Queen Charlotte's physician, fearing that the appointment would be too time-consuming. In 1769 he and his family moved to Pall Mall, where he built a new house on the site of one formerly owned by Nell Gwynn. He kept in touch with his literary friends, and his devotion to classical learning led to his election to the Society of Antiquaries in 1770. Heberden favoured religious toleration and gave active support to two parliamentary petitions which reflected his own views.

On approaching the age of seventy-two Heberden purchased a house in Windsor near the castle as a summer retreat, and soon afterwards he completed the Latin version of his major work, *Commentaries on the History and Cure of Diseases*. He took no steps to publish it, but when his son William published the original version and an English translation in 1802 shortly after his father's death the

book was soon recognized as a medical classic. The raw material for the work was Heberden's individual case histories and his index of diseases; and because he relied on his own experiences the work was notable for its independence of outlook and absence of dogma.

Heberden continued to practise on a reduced scale and in 1783 he began his attendance on Dr Johnson, who referred to him as 'ultimus Romanorum, the last of our learned physicians' (Boswell). Probably Heberden's last patient before his final retirement was George III, to whose presence he was summoned in the autumn of 1788 to advise on the latter's mental derangement.

One of his many friends, the Revd William Cole, described Heberden as 'a tall, thin spare man' with 'a most clear and healthy countenance' and considered him very abstemious (Scott). Among the many contemporary tributes to Heberden's character and talents was one from another physician, Dr Wells, who wrote in 1799: 'No other person, I believe, either in this or any other country, has ever exercised the art of medicine with the same dignity or has contributed so much to raise it in the estimation of mankind' (Nichols). Heberden remained active until 1796, when he fell and broke his thigh. He died at his Pall Mall house in London on 17 May 1801 and was buried at the parish church in Windsor, where a tablet was erected to his memory.   ERNEST HEBERDEN

Sources R. F. Scott, ed., *Admissions to the College of St John the Evangelist in the University of Cambridge*, 3: *July 1715 – November 1767* (1903), appx, 377–9 · Munk, *Roll* · T. J. Pettigrew, 'Memoir of Dr W. Heberden', *Medical portrait gallery: biographical memoirs of the most celebrated physicians, surgeons … who have contributed to the advancement of medical science*, 4 vols. in 2 [1838–40], vol. 3 · W. Macmichael, *The gold-headed cane*, 2nd edn (1828), 169–73 · Nichols, *Lit. anecdotes*, 3.71–3 · R. Mann, *Modern drug use* (1984), 307–9 · *The last journals of Horace Walpole*, ed. Dr Doran, rev. A. F. Steuart, 1 (1910), 9–13 · Boswell, *Life*, 4.339 · will, proved, 6 June 1801, PRO, PROB 11/1359, sig. 390 · parish register (baptisms), St Saviours, Southwark, London · A. P. Burke, *Family records* (1897) · memorial tablet, Windsor parish church · W. Heberden, letter to senate, 1737, CUL, grace book · buttery books, St John Cam.

Archives Francis A. Countway Library, Boston, Massachusetts · RCP Lond., papers · RS, papers submitted to Royal Society · St John Cam. · Wellcome L. | BL, Add. MS 5720 fol. 90 · St Olave's and St Saviour's Grammar School Foundation, Orpington, Kent

Likenesses silhouette, *c*.1780, Francis A. Countway Library, Boston, Massachusetts · W. Beechey, oils, 1794, St John Cam. · studio of W. Beechey, portrait, RCP Lond. [*see illus.*] · J. Ward, mezzotint (after W. Beechey), repro. in E. Heberden, *William Heberden: physician of the age of reason* (1989)

Wealth at death probably over £60,000 incl. bequests of £12,500; also properties: will, PRO, PROB 11/1359, sig. 390

Heberden, William, the younger (1767–1845), physician, born on 23 March 1767 in Cecil Street, the Strand, London, was the only surviving son of William *Heberden (1710–1801), physician, and his second wife, Mary (1729–1813), daughter of Francis Wollaston. He was educated at the Charterhouse and at St John's College, Cambridge, where he distinguished himself both in classics and mathematics. On graduating BA in 1788 he became a fellow of his college. He proceeded MA in 1791, and was incorporated on this degree at Oxford, where he took his medical degrees of BM in 1792 and DM in 1795. Heberden studied in London at St George's Hospital, Hyde Park Corner, and was elected physician there on 15 November 1793, but he resigned his office in 1803. He was elected fellow of the Royal Society in 1791 and of the Royal College of Physicians in 1796. On 1 October 1795 he married Elizabeth Catherine (1776–1812), daughter and heir of Charles Miller of Oving, Sussex. In the same year he was appointed physician-extraordinary to the queen. By 1809 he had been appointed physician-in-ordinary to both the queen and the king. He declined more than once the offer of a baronetcy with a pension.

George III had been stricken on at least three previous occasions by an illness involving delusions and violent behaviour—now thought by some to have been the condition now known as acute intermittent porphyria—and when the symptoms recurred early in 1804 the royal physicians were ordered by the queen's council to leave the daily management to a 'specialist' mad-doctor with experience in treating mental disorders. For this task the council favoured the Revd Francis Willis (1718–1807), DM, owner of a private asylum, who had received the credit for the king's recovery in 1789. The regime was repressive and coercive, but despite this harsh treatment the king's recovery in 1804 was complete by the end of the year. For the next five years Heberden pursued his London practice, but in 1810 the king's illness reappeared and the repressive regime was renewed—a form of treatment that Heberden considered to be futile and inhumane. In September 1811 he wrote to the archbishop of Canterbury (the head of the queen's council), stressing the importance of:

> recalling the attention from the distractions of a disordered imagination to objects of reality and truth. It should be studied to soothe, to cherish, to comfort a mind worn by disease and disappointment, to encourage it by indulgence, by amusement, by conversation, by company, by reading, by the exertion of its own faculties. … But what has in fact been done? … The King has been kept in a state of unedifying confinement and seclusion … I cannot be insensible to the kindness and partiality with which his Majesty has honoured me for many years … I cannot forget that his Majesty had desired me not to leave him, not to desert him; … he always reposed his trust in me.   (BL, Add. MS 41735, fol. 33)

Heberden's protests were brushed aside and he and the other physicians found themselves virtually excluded from the sickroom. He was able to see his patient from time to time, but always in the presence of Willis or one of his associates. Heberden's letter was in line with the enlightened theories on psychiatry that had been gaining influence since the king's attack in 1788 (Macalpine and Hunter, 329), and it was his misfortune that his advice was rejected. On 21 May 1812 Heberden's wife died at their home in Pall Mall, after a brief illness, leaving him with nine children. He promptly abandoned his London practice, retired to Datchet, a village close to Windsor, and devoted himself to bringing up his family and trying to alleviate the king's distress. In July of the same year he was protesting once more: 'that the present medical treatment and management applied to His Majesty's case are fundamentally and practically wrong' (LPL, MS 2108).

In 1826 Heberden returned to London to act as mentor to one of his sons, a student at St George's Hospital. The death of this son in 1829 from a dissection wound, and of another son and a daughter shortly afterwards, induced him finally to retire from practice, and he devoted the rest of his life to study and authorship in theological subjects. His most influential medical work was probably as editor and translator of his father's classic text, which appeared in 1802 both in the original Latin, and in English as *Commentaries on the History and Cure of Diseases*. His two papers in the *Philosophical Transactions of the Royal Society* were concerned with the effect on health of the temperature of the atmosphere. Of his five papers in the *Medical Transactions of the Royal College of Physicians* the most interesting was 'The mortality of London', in which he was able to demonstrate the gradual improvement in life expectancy over the previous century. He was also the author of a monograph on pediatrics entitled *Morborum puerilium Epitome* (1804).

Heberden died at his home, 28 Cumberland Street, Marylebone, Middlesex, on 19 February 1845, and a few days later was buried in the family vault at Windsor parish church, where a memorial tablet was erected. His three surviving sons were by now settled in their careers: Charles had been called to the bar; Frederick had taken holy orders; and the eldest son, William (also ordained), had been presented to the living of Great Bookham, Surrey, by his father, who had bought the advowson for the considerable sum of £10,750 in 1818.

ERNEST HEBERDEN

Sources Munk, *Roll* · I. Macalpine and R. Hunter, *George III and the mad-business* (1969) · J. Q. Cantu and R. C. Cantu, 'The psychiatric efforts of William Heberden', *Bulletin of the History of Medicine*, 41 (1967), 132–9 · *Medical Transactions of the Royal College of Physicians*, 4 (1813), 103–18 · W. Heberden, 'Of the influence of cold upon the health of the inhabitants of London', *PTRS*, 86 (1796), 279–84 · W. Heberden, 'An account of the heat of July, 1825', *PTRS*, 116/2 (1826), 69–74 · d. cert. · BL, Add. MS 41735, fol. 33 · Archives of Great Bookham Church, Surrey · LPL, MS 2108 · Venn, *Alum. Cant.* · *DNB* · records for St Martin-in-the-Fields, 1767, City Westm. AC · parish register (marriages), 1 Oct 1795, London, St George's Hanover Square · memorial tablet, Windsor church

Archives BL, Add. MSS 35705, 41696, 41734 · Francis A. Countway Library of Medicine, Boston, Massachusetts · LPL · RCP Lond.

Likenesses R. Rothwell, oils, before 1843 · J. S. Templeton, drawing on stone, exh. RA 1843 (after painting by R. Rothwell), Wellcome L.

Wealth at death over £6850; plus property; bequests, incl. £6850 to daughter Emily and to her sister Mary an unspecified sum; to son William half of the rectory and tithes of Great Bookham, the advowson and right of presentation to the vicarage, also the freehold house with grounds adjoining the parsonage; to son Charles all the residue of real and personal estate: will, PRO

Hecht, Edward (1832–1887), conductor, was born on 28 November 1832 in Dürkheim, Bavaria, the son of Heinrich Hecht, a musician and singing teacher in Frankfurt. As a child he studied music with his father, and subsequently with Jacob Rosenhain, I. Christian Hauff, and F. Mosser. In November 1854 he emigrated to England and settled in Manchester as a piano teacher. Here he came into close association with Charles Hallé, and from 1870 served as chorus master for the Hallé concerts and deputy conductor of the orchestra. A first-rate pianist, he performed with Hallé in double concertos by Bach, Mozart, and

Dussek. He also had a large number of singing and piano pupils. He was conductor of the Manchester Liedertafel from 1859 to 1878, succeeded Hallé as conductor of the St Cecilia Choral Society in 1860, and conducted the Stretford Choral Society from 1879 and the Bradford and Halifax Musical Society. In 1875 he became a lecturer on harmony and composition at Owens College, Manchester.

Hecht's compositions were well known in their time, and include a symphony (played at Hallé's concerts), a cantata (*Eric the Dane*), two string quartets, songs, marches for military band, and piano pieces. He died suddenly at his home at Ravenswood, Spath Road, Didsbury, Manchester, on 6 March 1887.

ALBERT NICHOLSON, *rev.* DAVID J. GOLBY

Sources M. Kennedy, 'Hecht, Edward', *New Grove* · *Manchester Evening News* (7 March 1887)
Wealth at death £14,358 19s. 9d.: probate, 7 April 1887

Heckford [*née* Goff], **Sarah Maud** (1839–1903), philanthropist, writer, and traveller, was born at Blackrock, Dublin, on 30 June 1839, the youngest of the three daughters of William Goff (*d.* 1848), one time governor of the Bank of Ireland, and his wife, Mary Clibborn (*d.* 1845). The daughters were all educated at home. Pleasant-faced, though not pretty, with dark brown hair, Sarah contracted tuberculosis of the spine at the age of nine which left her with a hump on her right shoulder and slightly lame. A talented pianist, she also painted well and loved horses and riding.

William Goff left Ireland with his family in 1842, settling in Dresden. Mary Goff died in 1845 and her eldest daughter, Jane, soon afterwards. Their aunt Abigail Clibborn came out to look after Annie and Sarah. The family went to Switzerland, and in 1848 moved to Paris, where they were caught up in the revolution. From Paris they went to London where William Goff took rooms in Eaton Square, near his bachelor brother Robert. Shortly after Sarah's ninth birthday her father committed suicide. He had appointed his brother Robert (*d.* 1866) as the girls' guardian; they and Aunt Abigail moved in with him. Their father had insisted on regular lessons, but their uncle thought 'accomplishments' all that girls needed, and their sole duty to make a good marriage. Sarah Goff revelled in music lessons and went regularly to the National Gallery to copy pictures there.

In 1859, after the death of their aunt, the sisters took a house in Warwick Square, Pimlico, London. Each having inherited money from their parents, they were independent. Sarah Goff had become a serious, intense, strongminded young woman determined never to be handicapped by her lameness, but still under the influence of her elder sister. Fired by the women's movement she became a committed feminist. She wanted to train as a doctor but women could not matriculate at that time. Complaining bitterly about 'the barriers of young-ladydom', she abandoned churchgoing and visited the poorer streets near her home trying to help the women and children there. After an unhappy love affair she began to explore the East End and was appalled by what she saw.

It was the cholera epidemic of 1866 which set Sarah Goff free from having her 'life choked out' in respectable Belgravia. Both the Goff sisters answered Catherine Gladstone's appeal for nurses. Sarah, now twenty-six, was sent to the Wapping Fever Hospital, east of Tower Bridge, where Nathaniel Heckford was one of the doctors in charge. Born in Calcutta in April 1842, the son of Nathaniel Heckford, he was dark, good-looking, and easy-going, with a passion for children and animals. Finding Sarah poring over Gray's *Anatomy* on night duty, he encouraged her to study medicine, offering to tutor her for examinations. They were married at the Little Portland Street Unitarian Chapel on 28 January 1867.

With Sarah's money they founded the East London Hospital for Children and Dispensary for Women in two old warehouses in the Ratcliff Highway and lived on the premises. Sarah, who continued her medical studies, was the matron and attended women at home for their confinements. Dr Elizabeth Garrett (later Garrett Anderson) joined their staff the following year, a move strongly opposed in some quarters. Charles Dickens visited the hospital and the publicity he provided brought in funds that made possible a purpose-built hospital in Shadwell. In 1963 it was amalgamated with the Queen Elizabeth Hospital for Children in Hackney.

In 1870 Nathaniel Heckford fell ill, and he died of tuberculosis on 14 December that year. The couple had no children but had adopted a girl of twelve, Marian Matthews Heckford, an orphan who had been a patient at the East London Hospital. Sarah Heckford worked on the plans for the new hospital and as a lady visitor at the existing one. In 1873 she published *The Life of Christ and its Bearing on the Doctrines of Communism*, which applied Christian principles to contemporary social problems. She was a quiet revolutionary, an idealist who abhorred violence, cruelty, and injustice, and had the courage of her convictions.

When the new hospital was complete Sarah Heckford settled most of her remaining capital on it. She went to Naples with Marian, then aged seventeen, who met and married a young lawyer there. Sarah Heckford travelled to India and worked for the Zenana Mission, which gave medical help to women in purdah. For more than a year she was the resident medical adviser to the begum of Bhopal. In 1878, after a bout of malaria, she returned to England. Purchasing shares in the Transvaal Farming, Mining, and Trading Association, she set sail for South Africa, intending to make her living farming. She arrived at Durban in December 1878, and travelled to Pretoria with a party of new settlers. On arrival they found they had been hoaxed and the farms they had been promised were nonexistent. Short of money, she became a governess for two years on the farm Nooitgedacht. Then she bought a wagon, a team of oxen, and some trading goods and started for the Soutpansberg with only a driver and a small boy to lead the oxen. She did good trade and arrived back in Pretoria just before the outbreak of the First South African War in December 1880. During the siege of Pretoria she went to the commander of the British garrison and offered to ride through the Boer lines with dispatches for General Colley, who was trying to reach the town from

Natal. When he refused she retired to her wagon and passed the time writing her second book, *A Lady Trader in the Transvaal*, which was published in London in 1882. She was furious at the retrocession of the Transvaal after the end of the war in April 1881, and refused to remain under Boer rule. On her return to London she campaigned on behalf of the people she called the 'English Africanders', English-speaking farmers and traders who had been ruined and were being persecuted by the Boers.

In 1884 Sarah Heckford's novel *Excelsior* was published, which is thinly veiled autobiography. She also wrote *The Story of the East London Hospital* (1887) to raise funds, though she was no longer actively involved with it. She founded a co-operative store at Woolwich, based on the ideas of communism expressed in her book of 1873. She shared an interest in spiritualism and the occult with her friend Lady Sarah Nicholson, and took part in séances at the Nicholsons' home, where she went into trances and produced examples of automatic writing.

Before leaving South Africa, Sarah Heckford had bought a farm, Jackalsfontein, south of Pretoria. Hearing of the discovery of gold on the Witwatersrand, she returned to South Africa, where she spent most of the rest of her life. Finding there was no gold on Jackalsfontein, she tried to sell it to raise capital for a scheme for education and medical care among the farming community. Failing to find a buyer, she took a two-roomed shanty in Johannesburg and set up as a share broker, selling mining shares. With her greying hair cut in a short Eton crop, she became a well-known figure as she rode about town. Her timing was disastrous, and when the mines struck pyrites in March 1889 her business crashed, leaving her penniless. By the time the discovery of the cyanide process put the mines back into profitability she had sold out. She bought another wagon and span of oxen and rode transport again. This business thrived; she bought a farm, Ravenshill, in the Soutpansberg, and brought her friend Sarah Eland and her son out from England to settle on it. Sarah Heckford continued trading and transport riding. In the winter of 1891 she spent several months camping on the Klein Letaba goldfields. Using this experience she wrote and published *True Transvaal Tales*.

In 1893 Sarah Heckford rented another farm near Ravenshill and became friendly with Modjadje, the 'Rain Queen', being the only white person to penetrate her kraal. Once a house had been built on Ravenshill she and the Elands moved there in January 1894, but the area was disturbed by fights between the Boers and the Africans. Eventually she returned to Nooitgedacht where she became governess to the children of her former pupils. She was there when the Second South African War broke out in October 1899, and twice rode messages concerning the movements of the Boer forces to Lord Roberts. On the second occasion, aged sixty, alone and ill, she rode the 40 miles to Pretoria (which Roberts had taken in June 1900) in the course of one wintry day, warning the British at Commandonek on her way. She could not return to her farm, and remained in Pretoria to help reorganize and reopen the schools which had closed at the start of the war. She returned to her plans for farm schools and wrote a *Report on the educational needs of the Transvaal Colony from the Transvaal Women's Educational Union to the education department of the colony*. She finished it in March 1901, and it was sent to London.

Sarah Heckford then devised an adult-education programme for Boer women to be put in place after the war. In 1901 she went to London to buy a magic lantern and slides to illustrate the historical lectures she was writing for the scheme. She was violently opposed to Emily Hobhouse, who had protested against the British use of concentration camps during the Second South African War, and wrote to the papers with her own views. Requests to speak on South Africa poured in. Although an emotional speaker, she nevertheless had a firm grasp of facts and the ability to marshal them cogently. She also worked hard for the British Women's Emigration Society, urging teachers in particular to go out to South Africa after the war.

In spite of failing health and becoming blind in one eye Sarah Heckford continued to write and to travel the country on speaking engagements. By the end of 1902 she had completed her lectures and assembled the slides to illustrate them. Although clearly unwell she insisted on returning to Pretoria in February 1903, where she died on 17 April of the same year. She was buried in the old cemetery, Church Street East, Pretoria, on 19 April.

VIVIEN ALLEN

Sources V. Allen, *Lady trader: a biography of Mrs Sarah Heckford* (1979) • S. Heckford, *A lady trader in the Transvaal* (1882) • C. H. du Val, ed., *News of the camp* (1880–81) • S. Heckford, *The story of the East London Hospital* (1887) • private information (2004) • M. H. Sanders, *Glimpses of the past* (privately printed, *c*.1965) • S. Heckford, *True Transvaal tales* (1891?)
Likenesses photograph, *c*.1870; formerly at Queen Elizabeth Hospital for Children • S. Nicholson, pen-and-ink drawing, 1902, repro. in Allen, *Lady trader*; priv. coll

Hector [*née* French], **Annie** [*pseud*. Mrs Alexander] (1825–1902), novelist, born in Dublin on 23 June 1825, was the only daughter of Robert French, a Dublin solicitor who was a younger member of the family of French of Frenchpark, co. Roscommon, and his wife, Anne Malone (*d*. 1865), daughter of Edmund Malone of Cartrons. A son died in infancy. On her father's side she was a direct descendant of Jeremy Taylor (1613–1667) and was related to the poet Charles Wolfe (1791–1823); and on her mother's side she was related to the critic and author Edmund Malone (1741–1812). Educated under governesses at home, she read a great deal on her own. In 1844 her parents, owing to monetary losses, left Dublin for Liverpool, and after living at Chester, Jersey, and other places, settled in London. She visited Ireland only once more in her lifetime.

In London, Annie French made many literary acquaintances, including the novelist Anna Maria Hall. In 1856 she began lifelong friendships with the novelist Eliza Lynn (afterwards Eliza Lynn Linton) and W. H. Wills, sub-editor of *Household Words*, and his wife. She first attracted public attention in 1856 with 'Billeted in Boulogne', an article in *Household Words*. Her anonymously published novels *Agnes*

Waring (1854), *Kate Vernon* (1855), and *The Happy Cottage* (1856) were not successful.

On 15 April 1858 Annie French married, in London, Alexander Hector (1810–1875), a man of enterprise and ability who had joined Richard Lemon Lander in his exploration of the River Niger (1832) and General Francis Rawdon Chesney in the exploration of the Euphrates and Tigris rivers (1835–7). He then settled in Baghdad, opened up trade between Great Britain and the Persian Gulf, and carried out excavations. In 1857 he returned to England, having accumulated a large fortune.

The Hectors lived in Stanley Gardens, Notting Hill, and had a country house at Worcester Park, Surrey. However, the marriage was not very happy, due mainly to Hector's domineering attitude. His health was not good and he was often irritable; he insisted that Annie should account to him regularly for every penny of household expenditure, and he sometimes humiliated her in front of their servants. She found it necessary to give more money to her elderly father, who lived in lodgings nearby, and this stimulated her to write—without her husband's knowledge—*Look before you Leap* in 1865 and *Which shall it be?* in 1866. Despite these earnings in secret, she went into debt and had to pawn her jewels. Rows became more frequent, and matters came to a head when Hector discovered that she had borrowed money from the captain of one of his ships. At about the same time he formed a liaison with a Mrs Trevelyan. Finally, in 1870, the Hectors became legally separated.

Annie Hector kept a private diary, which reveals her likeable and affectionate personality, her integrity, her genuine compassion for the misfortunes of others, and her love for her children. Eliza Lynn Linton wrote of her: 'She is a woman in a thousand … she has not one petty feminine fault' (Anderson, 137). A witty, clever talker, of quick sympathies and social instincts, she was in many ways more able and broad-minded than her writings show. Her best-known novel, *The Wooing o't*, appeared as a serial in *Temple Bar* in 1873 and was reissued in three volumes at the end of that year. She adopted as a pseudonym her husband's Christian name, writing as Mrs Alexander.

After her husband's death in 1875, Annie Hector, left with a son and three daughters, and with smaller means than she had anticipated, began to write in good earnest. She spent six years with her family in Germany and France and then three years at St Andrews in Scotland. In 1885 she settled in London and from that time rarely left the city, as she was busily occupied with writing novels until her death.

In 1875 *Ralph Wilton's Weird* was published, and *Her Dearest Foe* in 1876. Forty-one novels followed, which were popular both in Britain and the United States. Eleven passed into a second edition; and *The Freres* (1882) was translated into Spanish, *By Woman's Wit* (1886) into Danish, and *Mona's Choice* (1887) into Polish. *Kitty Costello* (1904), a novel which presents an Irish girl's introduction to English life, and has autobiographical touches, was written when she was seventy-seven. Shortly after completing it, she died,

on 10 July 1902 following ten years' suffering from neuritis, at her London home at 10 Warrington Gardens, Maida Vale. She was buried in Kensal Green cemetery in London.   ELIZABETH LEE, *rev.* C. G. LEWIN

Sources H. C. Black, *Notable women authors of the day* (1893) • I. D. Hardy, 'Introduction', in Mrs Alexander, *Kitty Costello* (1904) • 'Mrs Hector's journal', 1871 [private diary, 1863–70; privately owned] • J. Sutherland, 'Alexander, Mrs [Annie] Hector (née French, 1825–1902)', *The Longman companion to Victorian fiction* (1988), 16–17 • private information (1912) • BL, MSS 46618, fols. 45, 267, 334; 46619, fols. 14, 192; 46620, fols. 114–16; 46621, fols. 243, 246; 46622, fols. 164–8; 46624, fol. 68; 46625, fol. 290 [agreements with publishers] • letter from A. Hector, 27 July 1863, BL, MS 39106, fol. 417 • PRO • P. Schlueter and J. Schlueter, eds., *An encyclopedia of British women writers* (1988) • N. F. Anderson, *Women against women in Victorian England* (1987), 137 • F. R. Chesney, *Narrative of the Euphrates expedition* (1868), 208, 229, 257–8, 552 • will, 29 June 1875, Principal Registry of the Family Division, London [Alexander Hector] • *CGPLA Eng. & Wales* (1902)

Likenesses Fitzgerald of Versailles, portrait, *c.*1858 • photograph, *c.*1890, repro. in Black, *Notable women authors of the day* • W. & D. Downey, woodburytype photograph, 1892, NPG • M. Hector, portrait, *c.*1902, repro. in *Today* (23 July 1902)

Wealth at death £1142 12s. 3d.: resworn probate, April 1903, *CGPLA Eng. & Wales* (1902)

Hector, Edmund (1708–1794), surgeon, was born on 30 January 1708 in Lichfield, Staffordshire, the eldest of the four children of Benjamin Hector (*bap.* 1682), sheriff of Lichfield, and his wife, Dorothy (*d.* 1726). It was natural for the young Edmund to take an interest in medicine as his uncle, George Hector, was the surgeon and man-midwife present at the difficult delivery of Johnson. His grandfather Edmund, his uncle Brooke Hector, and his cousin William Withering were physicians.

Hector and Samuel Johnson were schoolmates at Lichfield grammar school and close boyhood friends, and they corresponded throughout Johnson's life. After discussion with Johnson, Mrs Thrale turned to Hector for his 'kindly source of juvenile anecdotes' (Lobban and Hayward, 250–51), and much of the recorded early life of Johnson in the writings of Mrs Thrale, James Boswell, and Sir John Hawkins came from Hector. It was Hector who related that Sir John Floyer advised that Johnson be taken to receive the 'royal touch', a treatment for scrofula, a form of tuberculosis. Johnson told Hector of the problems this infection had caused him throughout life. When Johnson was fourteen or fifteen he wrote some poems, one of which, 'The Daffodil', survived through Hector and was passed to Boswell after Johnson's death, even though Hector said it was not very characteristic of the flower and that Johnson never much liked it. Johnson later said that Hector's sister Ann was his first real love; she, however, married the Revd Walter Carless. Hector's first wife, Elizabeth, daughter of A. Power of Kenilworth, died in 1741 without children. Edmund later married Mary Gibbons; this relationship was also childless.

In the autumn of 1732 Hector was becoming increasingly worried about Johnson's emotional state, as he seemed depressed after failing to secure a position as a teacher. Hector invited him to visit, and Johnson stayed more than a year. Hector was establishing himself as a surgeon in Lichfield and shared lodgings with the printer and bookseller Thomas Warren, in the High Street across from the Swan tavern. There was room for Johnson and the pair dined with the Warrens. Hector hoped that occupying Johnson would revive his spirits, and that his pride in his writing talents would improve his self-confidence. Warren was planning to start a weekly newspaper, and, without telling Johnson, Hector made plans to have the latter write articles for the new *Birmingham Journal*. There is a legend in Birmingham that Johnson was an assistant to Warren, but all that is known is that he wrote essays for the paper, though these have not survived. After six months Hector moved to another part of town, into a house owned by a man named Jarvis; Johnson felt he had relied on his friend enough, and decided to live without his daily company and support. Soon Johnson became depressed again and was verbally abusive to Hector, so much so that Hector ignored Johnson until coaxed back into their friendship. He remained concerned about Johnson's state of mind, but Johnson himself was reluctant to discuss this as he did not want his own concerns about a disordered mind confirmed.

Hector encouraged Johnson to translate Jerome Lobo's *Travels in Abyssinia*. Although he was able to send part of the work to the publisher, Johnson again fell into a deep depression and could not finish it. Hector felt he might respond to a humanitarian request and said the publisher had no other work and that he and his family would suffer if Johnson did not continue. Johnson felt barely able to move and lay in bed with the French text on his lap, dictating the translation to Hector, who acted as his scribe. Hector later made a clean copy, brought it to the publisher, and corrected the proofs. When the work was published in 1735 Johnson was paid the substantial sum of 5 guineas. Throughout the years Hector would help Johnson when he needed support, and he sent funds through Johnson's mother to pay expenses when he was working on his Shakespeare project.

In 1747 Hector purchased the house at 1 The Square, Birmingham, across the square from his cousin William Withering, a physician at the Birmingham General Hospital, where Hector was a consulting surgeon. On the recommendation of Johnson, both Mr and Mrs Thrale were seen as patients by Hector. He was to practise surgery in The Square from 1748 until his death. Johnson often visited Hector in Birmingham when he was travelling in the country, and in 1776 he brought Boswell to meet him. Boswell later wrote: 'It gave me pleasure to observe the joy which Johnson and he expressed on seeing each other again' (Smith-Dampier, 159).

On his last trip to Oxford, Lichfield, and Ashbourne, in November 1784, a month before he died, Johnson visited Hector. Referring to his friend of more than sixty years he said, 'We have always loved one another. Perhaps we may be made better by some serious conversation' (Boswell, *Life*, 1.526). They discussed the early days of their friendship, and the failing health of Johnson and his friends,

and then Johnson asked if Hector had observed a disordered mind some fifty years before, when they were living together. Hector said he had, and the matter was dropped. Two years later Boswell wrote to Hector, enquiring about the late Doctor Johnson's melancholy, but the physician responded vaguely to the prying questions about the emotional life of his friend; he later wrote to Boswell to thank him for the pleasure his *Life of Johnson* had afforded him and his friends.

Hector died at home on 2 September 1794, much respected and admired. He was buried in St Philip's Church, Birmingham, where there is a memorial to him. His will is detailed in *The Reades of Blackwood Hill* (1906). Hector's obituary in the *Gentleman's Magazine* noted that he was 'a gentleman eminent for skill and assiduity in his public character as a surgeon, and much deservedly esteemed in private life for his benevolence of disposition, liberality of sentiment and urbanity of manners' (*GM*, 866). Although respected in his community for his kindly nature and his skill as a surgeon, Edmund Hector is remembered as the lifelong friend of Samuel Johnson.   T. JOCK MURRAY

Sources W. J. Bate, *Samuel Johnson* (1977) · Boswell, *Life*, 1.526 · J. H. Lobban and A. Hayward, eds., *Doctor Johnson's Mrs. Thrale* (1910) · *GM*, 1st ser., 64 (1794), 866 · *European Magazine and London Review*, 26 (1794), 239 · *Scots Magazine*, 56 (1794), 655 · A. L. Reade, *The Reades of Blackwood Hill in the parish of Horton, Staffordshire: a record of their descendants* (privately printed, London, 1906), 154 · P. Rogers, *Samuel Johnson encyclopedia* (1996) · J. L. Smith-Dampier, *Who's who in Boswell* (1935)

Wealth at death see will, abstracted, Reade, *Reades of Blackwood Hill*

Hector, Sir James (1834–1907), colonial geologist and geological administrator, was born on 16 March 1834 in Edinburgh, the eldest son of Alexander Hector, lawyer and writer to the signet, and his second wife, Margaret Macrostie. He was educated at the Academy and at the high school in Edinburgh. In 1856 he graduated MD from Edinburgh University, medicine then being the only avenue for scientific study. Throughout his studies geology claimed a large proportion of his time, and in March 1857 Sir Roderick Murchison (1792–1871) nominated him as geologist to a government expedition, under John Palliser, for the exploration of western Canada. The Palliser expedition started from Detroit on 6 June 1857 and ended in Vancouver Island in January 1860. Acting as surgeon, cartographer, and geologist, and as Palliser's deputy, Hector made an outstanding contribution to the success of the enterprise. He has the distinction of being the first geologist and possibly the first medical doctor in western Canada. His personal story there is one of courage, hardship, and the pursuit of science under most adverse circumstances. Hector left his mark in the area in the geographical features that he named and those that were named for him by others. Kicking Horse Pass was named for a near-fatal accident which he suffered.

In 1861, again on the recommendation of Murchison, Hector was appointed geologist to the province of Otago. He arrived in New Zealand in April 1862, and for three years carried out exploration and geological reconnaissance of the province. In 1863 he made a pioneering

Sir James Hector (1834–1907), by unknown photographer, 1860s [right, with Captain John Palliser]

double crossing of the Southern Alps and reached Milford Sound. At the New Zealand Exhibition held in Dunedin in 1865, for which he acted as commissioner, Hector exhibited more than 5000 natural history specimens collected during his three years in Otago. It was his success in organizing this exhibition that brought him to the attention of central government. In March 1865 he was appointed director of the newly formed Geological Survey of New Zealand, and of the Colonial Museum. In August that year, together with his Otago staff, he moved to Wellington. As the only scientist of standing in government employment, Hector served in many capacities, holding posts as diverse as chancellor of the University of New Zealand, director of the meteorological department, and inspector of standard weights and measures. He was adviser to the government on all matters of science and higher education.

In 1867 the New Zealand Institute (later to become the Royal Society of New Zealand) was founded by act of parliament, and Hector became its manager and editor of its *Transactions*, posts which he held for thirty-six years. Soon after taking office he married, on 30 December 1868, Maria Georgiana Monro (1848–1930), elder daughter of Sir David Monro; they later had nine children. Despite the commitments of family and administration, Hector still found time for wide-ranging scientific research. In addition to catalogues and annual reports he was the author of more than 200 papers, on such diverse subjects as trilobites, seals, ferns, and tide gauges. However he remained first and foremost a geologist and, in the first

four or five years of the geological survey, he did most of the fieldwork himself.

Hector was an outstanding organizer and a considerate employer. Although his methods were autocratic he had the ability to develop the talents of his staff and he retained the loyalty of most of them for their entire careers.

Hector's sphere of influence was progressively curtailed from about 1886 onwards; this was due in part to a rationalization of government science, and in part to a decline in his powers of concentration as he grew older and his manifold responsibilities took their toll. Embittered and in poor health Hector took a leave of absence in July 1903, and travelled to Canada, where he received official appreciation for his work on the Palliser expedition. Following the sudden death in 1904 of his son Douglas, who had accompanied him to Canada, Hector returned to New Zealand. He died in Lower Hutt on 6 November 1907, and was buried there; his wife and six of his nine children survived him. Hector was of shorter than average stature—in middle age his figure was described as 'Pickwickian'. He was restless and fidgety by nature, and had a thin, husky voice. Self-conscious when young, he was later described as sentimental, emotional, and honest. He received many honours: he was elected a fellow of the Royal Society in 1866, received the Geological Society's Lyell medal in 1877, and was knighted in 1887. The New Zealand Institute commemorated him in 1911 when it established the Hector medal and prize as its major research award.

ALAN MASON

Sources P. Burton, *The New Zealand geological survey, 1865–1965* (1965), 11–16, 26–40 · C. A. Fleming, *Science, settlers, and scholars* (1987), 11–46, 124 · D. R. Oldroyd, 'Geology in New Zealand prior to 1900', MSc diss., U. Lond., 1967, 110–25, 263–70, 275–7 · J. Park, 'Centenary of Sir James Hector', *The New Zealand Journal of Science and Technology*, 18 (1937), 779–80 · W. O. Kupsch, 'Hector's geological explorations of the Canadian prairie west', *Proceedings of the Geological Association of Canada*, 23 (1971), 31–40 · R. E. Wright-St Clair, *Thoroughly a man of the world: a biography of Sir David Monro* (1971), 138–9 · W. C. Gussow, 'James Hector in Canada', *Newsletter of the Geological Society of New Zealand*, 30 (1971), 22–3 · I. M. Spry, ed., *The papers of the Palliser expedition, 1857–1860* (1968) · R. A. Stafford, *Scientist of empire: Sir Roderick Murchison, scientific exploration and Victorian imperialism* (1989) · G. L. Adkin and B. W. Collins, 'A bibliography of New Zealand geology to 1950', *New Zealand Geological Survey Bulletin*, new ser., 65 (1967) · *Transactions and proceedings of the New Zealand Institute and the Royal Society of New Zealand: author index, 1869–1971* (Wellington, 1978) · *DNB*

Archives GS Lond., maps and papers relating to Otago · National Museum of New Zealand, Wellington, archives, corresp. and papers · NL NZ, Turnbull L., journals, corresp. | Auckland Public Library, letters to Sir George Grey · National Museum of New Zealand, Wellington, Colonial Museum Archive · NHM, letters, corresp. with Richard Owen and William Clift · University of Otago, Dunedin, Hocken Library, Hector MSS

Likenesses photograph, 1860–69, Glenbow Archives, Calgary, Canada [*see illus.*] · L. H. Booth, portrait, 1903/4 (after photograph), Royal Society of New Zealand Science Centre, Wellington · photograph, Institute of Geological and Nuclear Sciences, Wellington · photograph, NL NZ, Turnbull L. · photograph, University of Otago, Dunedin, Hocken Library · photograph, National Museum of New Zealand, Wellington

Hedderwick, James (1814–1897), journalist and poet, was born on 18 January 1814 in Govan, Glasgow, the third son of James Hedderwick (d. 1864), letterpress printer, and Joanna McNeilage. His formative years were spent in Glasgow, but included a short spell in the USA at the age of eight in 1822, where his father had gone in search of work. On the family's return shortly thereafter, his father was appointed the queen's printer, and Hedderwick began an apprenticeship in his father's firm. His literary talents, which he cultivated through contributing to various local literary periodicals and newspapers in his late teens, soon led him to contemplate changing vocations, and in 1836 he began studies in English literature at London University, where he gained distinction in his first year by winning first prize in rhetoric. In 1837, however, he gave up academic study to return to Glasgow, where he started up the *Saltwater Gazette*, a short-lived literary periodical. Later that year he joined the staff of the Edinburgh *Scotsman*, becoming assistant editor under the direction of its editor, Charles MacLaren. It was a position he retained until 1842, when he returned to Glasgow to establish the *Glasgow Citizen*, a weekly paper run in conjunction with his elder brother Robert. The *Citizen* distinguished itself by featuring work of prominent Scottish authors such as Alexander Smith, David Gray, and William Black. Hedderwick also contributed original work to journals such as *Chambers's Journal*, and in 1844 published his first collection of poetry.

Now firmly established in a career as editor, poet, and newspaper proprietor, Hedderwick became engaged to Ellen Ness, a young woman from South Leith in Edinburgh. They were married on 11 January 1846 in Gorbals, Lanarkshire, and over the next seventeen years were to have seven children, including Thomas C. H. Hedderwick, lawyer and MP for Wickburghs in 1896. Ellen Ness died some time in the 1860s, and Hedderwick subsequently remarried.

Between 1850 and 1882 Hedderwick's career flourished. In addition to publishing further works of poetry (*Lays of Middle Age, and other Poems*, 1858; *The Villa by the Sea, and other Poems*, 1881) and running the *Glasgow Citizen*, in 1860 he founded *Hedderwick's Miscellany of Instructive and Entertaining Literature*, a compendium similar to *Chambers's Journal*. It was to last only two years, folding in 1862. Undaunted, Hedderwick started the *Glasgow Evening Citizen* in August 1864, a daily halfpenny evening newspaper that heralded and gave impetus to the subsequent expansion of cheap late-edition journalism in Britain. While not the pioneer of the first cheap evening paper in Scotland and Britain (that honour lay with the *Greenock Telegraph*), Hedderwick's *Glasgow Evening Citizen* was the best known and most successful of such enterprises, at one point claiming the largest circulation of any paper in the west of Scotland. Its success bred imitation south of the border, and Hedderwick was instrumental in aiding subsequent start-ups of other evening papers in England, including that of *The Echo* (London). Based on his initial success with the *Glasgow Evening Citizen*, Hedderwick also established the *Glasgow Weekly Citizen*, a weekly literary continuation

of the original daily broadsheet. He continued in his capacity as editor of both papers until 1882, when he retired to Helensburgh, near Glasgow. His literary and editorial work was recognized in 1878 by the award of an honorary degree of doctor of laws by the University of Glasgow, and he published a volume of memoirs entitled *Backward Glances* in 1891 which focused on the literary acquaintances he had made during his working career. He died from complications arising from a stroke on the morning of 1 December 1897 at his home in Rocklands, Helensburgh.   DAVID FINKELSTEIN

Sources *The Times* (2 Dec 1897), 9 · *The Scotsman* (2 Dec 1897), 7 · *Glasgow Herald* (2 Dec 1897), 4 · *Daily Record* (2 Dec 1897), 5 · *Scots Pictorial* (11 Dec 1897), 290 · *Evening Times* [Glasgow] (1 Dec 1897), 4 · J. Hedderwick, *Backward glances, or, Some personal recollections* (1891) · IGI
Archives NA Scot., family papers
Likenesses etching, repro. in *Evening Times* · photograph, repro. in *Scots Pictorial*
Wealth at death £6119 15s. 7d.: confirmation, 12 May 1898, CCI

Heddi. *See* Hædde (d. 705/6).

Heddle, Charles William Maxwell (1811/12–1889), merchant, was born in Goree, Senegal, the son of Dr John Heddle (1776–1812), an Orcadian medical officer in the Royal African Corps, and Sophy Boucher, a Senegalese, with whom he had several children. He was educated at the Dollar Academy, Clackmannanshire, at the expense of his uncle, Robert Heddle, who, having made a large fortune trading in Senegal, returned to Orkney in 1818 and bought the estate of Melsetter. Through his uncle's influence he was employed by the London firm of Forster and Smith, then the leading import and export firm in west Africa. After a brief period in the London office he returned about 1834 to west Africa where he spent the rest of his business career.

Heddle began as Forster and Smith's employee in the Gambia, but by 1838 had moved to Freetown, Sierra Leone. There he set up as an import and export trader, at first with locally recruited partners, but after about 1843, having inherited £2000 from an elder brother, a medical officer in India, on his own. He remained Sierra Leone agent for Forster and Smith, and could draw on their credit, while they acted as his agents in London. He traded from the most conspicuous commercial building in Freetown, a huge old store at the government wharf.

It was the start of a period of commercial prosperity in west Africa. By the middle of the nineteenth century many of the Sierra Leone recaptives (those liberated over previous decades from slave ships taking them illegally across the Atlantic) and their descendants had moved into the import–export trade. Freetown was becoming a prosperous commercial centre for the export of oil-bearing produce, increasingly in demand for processing in Europe for lubrication, cooking, and soap making.

Heddle had already begun exporting groundnuts (peanuts) from the Gambia, and is credited with being the first to export them from Sierra Leone. He was also the first entrepreneur to exploit the commercial potentialities of palm kernels, as distinct from palm oil. From the £4 worth he exported in 1846 exports grew until by the 1860s palm kernel exports outstripped the export of palm oil from Sierra Leone and, with groundnuts, had become the mainstay of the export trade.

It was a period when Heddle's African descent was of no serious disadvantage; indeed, during his years in Sierra Leone almost every senior official post, including governor, was at one time or another held by a man of part African descent. Hence he was not subjected to the discriminatory pressures that would have put him at a disadvantage later on during the period of racial imperialism. In 1845 he was appointed a member of the governor's council, and when the constitution was revised in 1863 he became a member of the legislative council.

Much of the export produce was grown along the rivers north of Sierra Leone, still unannexed by any European government. Heddle wanted them annexed to Sierra Leone and in 1845 persuaded the government to make treaties of friendship with the ruling chiefs. But policy in London at this period was against further acquisitions of territory in west Africa and, despite his continuing efforts, they were annexed by the French in 1867.

Heddle is reported as saying that once the first £10,000 has been made the second follows in half the time. But how he made his many thousands is not clear. The total annual import and export figures for Sierra Leone amounted to under £300,000 each at this period, so the profits from import–export trading, shared with many competitors, were limited. He invested extensively in Freetown house properties, but most were valued in hundreds rather than thousands. And although a shrewd property deal with the government netted him £16,000, this was a small sum for a 'merchant prince' (as he was called) who was able to write off unconcernedly a loss of between £20,000 and £30,000 when his uninsured warehouse burnt down. It seems likely to suppose that his largest gains were not made directly in west Africa but from investments on the London stock market.

In 1871 he left Sierra Leone, lame, and with impaired eyesight, and retired to France, where he purchased a former ducal mansion, the Château de Méréville, Seine-et-Oise, which he furnished opulently. He had never married, though with Emilie Caille (d. 1876), with whom he lived during his years in Freetown, he had an illegitimate son, John, whom he adopted legally. However, on 4 September 1888, aged then seventy-six, he married a twenty-two year old divorcée, Marie Léocadie Hortense Prume, née Leduc (c.1867–1898). He died at Cannes some eight months later on 29 April 1889. His will, leaving almost everything to his young widow, was contested in the courts, and eventually the estate was shared by settlement between her and his son. She died soon after, as the result of a car crash; he squandered his inheritance and died in debt. Neither left descendants.

Heddle's estate was valued for probate at £352,018 16s. 7d. Adding to this the money spent buying and maintaining his château, and his wife's marriage settlement, the fortune he had gained from his entrepreneurial activities is likely to be closer to half a million than quarter of a million pounds, a fortune far outstripping that of any contemporary in west Africa.   CHRISTOPHER FYFE

Sources C. Fyfe, 'Charles Heddle: an African "merchant prince"', *Entrepreneurs et entreprises en Afrique*, ed. A. Forest (1983), 1.235–47 · C. Fyfe, *A history of Sierra Leone* (1962)
Wealth at death £56,199 1s. 10d.: administration, 5 Oct 1889, *CGPLA Eng. & Wales* · £352,018 16s. 7d.: probate, 8 Jan 1890, *CGPLA Eng. & Wales*

Hedges, Sir Charles (*bap.* 1650, *d.* 1714), lawyer and politician, was baptized on 30 January 1650 at Wanborough, Wiltshire, the first son of Henry Hedges (*d.* after May 1673) of Wanborough and Margaret Pleydell (*b.* 1615) of Childrey, Berkshire. He was educated at Magdalen College, Oxford (BA, 1670; MA, 1673; DCL, 1675). Hedges embarked on a career in the civil law, receiving the assistance of the chancellor of Oxford University, the duke of Ormond, who in April 1675 excused him from further study provided that Hedges could perform the exercises required to gain his BCL and DCL. In October 1675 Hedges was admitted into the court of arches. Hedges married Eleanor (*d.* 1733), the daughter of George Smith, a London proctor, their first child being baptized at Richmond, Surrey, in May 1679. Altogether they had six sons and five daughters, only one of each sex surviving their parents.

By 1686, when he became chancellor of the diocese of Rochester, Hedges was resident in Doctors' Commons. His career as a civil lawyer was placed in jeopardy by James II's attitude towards the Anglican hierarchy. In September 1686 Hedges was an advocate of Bishop Compton of London, who faced the censure of the ecclesiastical commission for his lenient treatment of Dr John Sharp's preaching against Catholicism. Hedges was placed in a worse predicament in 1687 when James II sought to impose a master on the recalcitrant fellows of Magdalen College. Although an advocate of the king's cause, Hedges sought to moderate the actions of the more extreme members of the ecclesiastical commission.

Given his association with such strong Williamites as Compton, Hedges had no difficulty in transferring his allegiance to the new regime following the revolution of 1688. On 1 June 1689 Hedges was appointed a judge of the Admiralty, an office he held until his death, and he was knighted on the 4th. However, his attempt to exploit his governmental position at the 1690 general election ended in defeat at Dover, despite his use of letters of recommendation from the earls of Torrington and Shrewsbury. Between 1686 and 1691 Hedges appears to have lived in the parish of St Benet Paul's Wharf, where several of his children were baptized, but he became a Surrey JP in 1691. In 1695 Hedges attempted to secure election for Oxford University, but withdrew in favour of Sir William Trumbull. Hedges continued to be heavily involved in his work as an Admiralty judge, and his connections helped to secure his election to the 1698 parliament for the borough of Orford. His patron on this occasion was the earl of Orford, the head of the Admiralty. Hedges was regarded as a supporter of the court in the Commons, but he was unseated on petition on 2 February 1700.

Hedges was appointed secretary of state for the north and sworn of the privy council on 5 November 1700. Some commentators, including the French resident Bonet, saw him as an inconsiderable figure (BL, Add. MS 30000D, fol. 313), but he had important patrons such as the earl of Rochester. Although Hedges failed to win back his seat at Orford, he was returned for Dover at the February 1701 election. He was a leading figure of the government in the Commons, which was under attack from tories wishing to purge it of its remaining whig elements. Meanwhile Hedges was intent on purchasing a landed estate complete with a parliamentary interest. He fixed upon the manor of Compton Bassett, adjacent to the borough of Calne, Wiltshire, which he purchased in 1701, and in July of that year he became high steward of Malmesbury. Hedges does not seem to have enjoyed the full confidence of the king at this time, not being consulted over the timing of the dissolution of parliament in November 1701. Hedges was returned for Malmesbury at the ensuing election, and involved in a double-return at Calne. The splits which had riven the ministry came to a head over the election of a speaker in the new parliament. The king wished his ministers to support a whig, Sir Thomas Littleton, but Hedges was already engaged to Robert Harley, and as a consequence he resigned his secretaryship on 29 December 1701.

Queen Anne's accession altered Hedges's prospects, and he returned to the secretary's office on 2 May 1702, his fellow secretary, the earl of Nottingham, insisting on his reappointment. At the ensuing election he was returned for Calne and Malmesbury, choosing to sit for the former. Although a tory Hedges eschewed partisan measures, and as a committed Anglican he was useful to those ministers who wished to defeat such divisive measures as the second Occasional Conformity Bill in 1703–4. When Nottingham left office in April 1704, Hedges was sole secretary for a short period before assuming office as secretary of state for the south in May. Although Hedges had earned the sobriquet of 'keen Tory' (BL, Add. MS 29568, fol. 153) for his defence of Nottingham's conduct over the Jacobite activity in Scotland in 1703, his stance on other divisive issues such as the tack of the Occasional Conformity Bill in the 1704–5 session remained that of a moderate supporter of the court. Politically Hedges was now in a difficult position: his opposition to the tack had lost him tory friends, while the whigs no doubt agreed with Arthur Maynwaring that Hedges was a 'shrubster', a mean, inferior, insignificant person (*Poems on Affairs of State*, ed. G. de F. Lord, 1975, 7.13). He was defeated at both Calne and Wendover at the 1705 election, eventually finding a seat at West Looe in Cornwall. Furthermore, his ministerial position was under threat from the whigs, who were pressing for more places in the ministry, and he increased his vulnerability by siding with the tories on such partisan issues as election petitions, although on other matters he steadfastly followed the court line. In the event Hedges left office on 3 December 1706, only after being promised the office of judge of the prerogative court of Canterbury upon the death of Sir Richard Raines, which he had sought since 1693, as well as a pension of £1200 p.a. in the interim.

At the 1708 election Hedges was again returned for West Looe after failing to regain his seat at Calne. In May 1709 his appointment as a plenipotentiary at the expected peace negotiations was rumoured, and he was named in June as an administrator of Prince George's estate. A measure of his wealth can be gleaned from the reported portion of £10,000 that he gave to his daughter Anne upon her marriage in January 1710. The ministerial revolution of 1710 which brought Harley to power had no adverse effect on Hedges. He was returned again at West Looe in the election of that year, and following the death of Raines in December he became judge of the prerogative court of Canterbury. In 1711 Hedges was again mentioned as a possible peace plenipotentiary, but his new office had weakened his dependence upon the court, and the ministry's attack on Marlborough in January 1712 saw Hedges defend the duke against the charge of profiting from bread contracts. Hedges also failed to vote in several partisan divisions in the parliament, and was seen by some as a whig who would often vote with the tories. He was returned at the 1713 election for East Looe. Hedges died of 'an apoplexy' on 10 June 1714 at his house in Richmond, and was buried at Wanborough on the 15th. Hedges may have been the author of *Reasons for setling admiralty jurisdiction and giving encouragement to merchants, owners, masters of ships, material men, and mariners* (1690), but his main literary survivals consist of numerous volumes of his correspondence extant in the British Library.

STUART HANDLEY

Sources HoP, *Commons* [draft] · J. C. Sainty, ed., *Officials of the secretaries of state, 1660–1782* (1973) · J. C. Sainty, ed., *Admiralty officials, 1660–1870* (1975) · J. R. Bloxam, ed., *Magdalen College and James II, 1686–1688: a series of documents*, OHS, 6 (1886) · A. Macintyre, 'The college, King James II and the revolution, 1687–8', *Magdalen College and the crown: essays for the tercentenary of the restoration of the college, 1688*, ed. L. Brockliss, G. Harriss, and A. Macintyre (1988) · 'Grants and certificates of arms', *The Genealogist*, new ser., 17 (1900–01), 205–10, esp. 209 · *Miscellanea Genealogica et Heraldica*, 5th ser., 2 (1916–17), 84–8 · IGI · BL, Add. MS 24107, fols. 51–2, 166–79 · BL, Add. MS 7076, fols. 124, 130 · *Calendar of the manuscripts of the marquess of Ormonde*, new ser., 8 vols., HMC, 36 (1902–20), vol. 4, p. 599 · will, PRO, PROB 11/540, sig. 117 · DNB · Thomas Bateman to Sir William Trumbull, 11 June 1714, BL, Trumbull papers, Alphab. 52

Archives BL, corresp. and papers, Add. MSS 24102–24107, 28888–28948, *passim* · Cumbria AS, Carlisle, reports prepared as judge of admiralty court · Northants. RO, corresp. | BL, corresp. with duke of Marlborough, Add. MSS 70938–70946 · BL, letters to Lord Nottingham, Add. MSS 29568, 29588–29599 · BL, letters to Edward Southwell, Add. MS 38151 · BL, corresp. with C. Whitworth and G. Stepney, Add. MSS 7058–7059, 7064–7065, 37348–37354, 61118–61119, 61142 · CAC Cam., letters to Thomas Erle · CKS, corresp. with Alexander Stanhope · Longleat House, Wiltshire, corresp. with Earl Rivers · Magd. Oxf., papers relating to Magdalen College · Yale U., Beinecke L., letters to William Blathwayt

Hedges, Sir William (1632–1701), merchant, was born on 21 October 1632 at Coole, co. Cork, the eldest son of Robert Hedges (1604–70) of Youghal and his wife, Catharine (d. 1649), daughter of Edward Wakeman of Mythe, near Tewkesbury, Gloucestershire. Robert Hedges also held land in Stratton, Wiltshire, the county of the family's origin, where their surname was changed from Lacy.

The early career of William Hedges is obscure. He became a Turkey merchant, was sent to Smyrna as a Levant Company factor, and by 1668 had become the company's treasurer at Constantinople. He was succeeded in that position by Dudley North. He returned to England in 1670 and became a member of the London Mercers' Company and purchased £500 of the original share capital of the Royal African Company. In 1677 he resided in Basinghall Street, near Guildhall, in the heart of the city's commercial centre. He was a Levant Company assistant in 1675–9 and 1681–2, and a common councilman for his ward of Bassishaw in 1677–80. A close neighbour in Bassishaw was his merchant brother-in-law Jeremy Sambrooke. Hedges' first wife, Susanna, eldest daughter of Levant merchant Nicholas Vanacker of Erith, Kent, was a sister of Sambrooke's wife. Hedges' marriage to the daughter of a merchant of Dutch extraction associated him with London reformed and dissenting protestants. His brother-in-law Sambrooke would become a leading urban dissenter. Hedges himself subscribed to a public loan to Charles II that was promoted by London dissenters in 1670 in the hope of blunting the Conventicle Act of that year, but he eventually identified with the Church of England.

In April 1681 Hedges joined Sambrooke as a member of the court of committees, or directing board, of the East India Company. In September of that year he was chosen as the company's agent or administrator for its factories in the Bay of Bengal. He arrived there in July 1682, taking up residence in Hooghly. His instructions were to renegotiate the terms of the company's operations in Bengal with the regime of the Mughal emperor Aurangzeb, to curtail the trade of English interlopers in the company's monopoly, and to better manage the company's Bengal factors. Hedges' fluency in Arabic and Turkish and his familiarity with Islamic conventions earned him the respect of the nawab of Dacca, Shaista Khan. The increasing importance of the English trade to the local economy also provided him with important leverage. The nawab agreed to petition the emperor for a renewal of the company's exemption from Mughal customs, which Hedges reckoned would save some £20,000 in annual expenses.

Hedges was less successful with his more unruly countrymen in Bengal, whose behaviour left the nawab fuming that the English were a 'base, quarrelling people, and foul dealers' (*Diary*, 1.153). The company had ordered Hedges to apprehend Thomas Pitt, the ancestor of two prime ministers, and the most successful interloper in India. But this 'haughty, huffying, daring' entrepreneur eluded him (ibid., 3.x). Hedges was similarly outmanoeuvred by Job Charnock, a thirty-year veteran of India and the chief factor at Cossimbazar, who presided over a trade that profited the company while lining its servants' pockets. When Charnock defied every effort Hedges made to impose order, he lamented that 'It's absolutely necessary that one of us two be displaced', and Hedges promptly was (ibid., 1.146). Charnock and his cronies had

the ear of the sometime East India Company governor Sir Josiah Child, to whom they provided private intelligence. Hedges was sacked by the court of committees when he detained a letter directed to Child. In the meantime, his wife had died in childbirth at Hooghly in July 1683.

Hedges sailed from Bengal for the Persian Gulf in December 1684, with a cargo of Indian cloth. He arrived in Persia in May 1685. He travelled overland to Iskenderun with his goods, and apparently with his wife's remains, frequently negotiating with local officials and customs collectors and visiting English traders and other Europeans in Esfahan, Baghdad, Mosul, and Aleppo. He arrived in England in April 1687 and was interviewed by Lord Chancellor Sir George Jeffreys, who, according to Hedges, was sympathetic about his treatment by Child. Again taking up residence in Basinghall Street, where he kept at least one 'Black-more servant', Hedges also remarried, his second wife being Anne (d. 1724), daughter of Paul Nicholl and Anne Kendrick of Hendon, Middlesex, and the widow of Colonel John Searle of Finchley. They were married at St Michael Bassishaw in July 1687 by John Tillotson, dean of Canterbury.

Within months of his return Hedges was appointed by James II to the London lieutenancy commission; and in 1688 he was knighted by James and chosen master of the Mercers' Company. He was nevertheless an early subscriber to a January 1689 London loan to the prince of Orange. After the revolution of 1688 he remained on the London lieutenancy commission, also serving as colonel of a trained band regiment and on the Middlesex lieutenancy commission. Hedges re-entered civic politics in 1690. As the tory interest revived in London, he was unsuccessfully promoted by the 'church party' for the shrievalty (Luttrell, 2.47). In 1693 he was chosen for the London shrievalty with dissenting alderman Thomas Abney, apparently with whig support, against a tory candidate. Hedges was also chosen alderman for the ward of Portsoken, remaining in that office until his death. In 1694, when the subscription for the Bank of England was opened, he made an investment of £4000 and was chosen a director, continuing in that capacity until 1700. He had by that time also renewed his investments in the East India Company, from which he seems to have withdrawn after his Bengal experience.

Hedges' trading and investment interests, as well as his personal connections to both dissent and the church, placed him in the ambiguous middle of a whig–tory political divide being transformed by European warfare and the country's 'financial revolution'. As a shareholder in the Bank of England and the 'old' East India Company, he straddled the fence between the aggressive commercial capitalism promoted by William III's wartime whig ministry and the established world of tory investment. As a Bank of England director and as a Levant Company assistant (again in 1688–9 and 1694–9), Hedges rubbed shoulders with investors and traders who took a leading role in the whiggish bank and 'new' East India Company of 1698. Yet his continuing involvement in both the 'old' East India Company and the Royal African Company (of which he was an assistant in 1689–90, 1694, and 1696) kept him in association with merchants and investors who were hostile to whig commercial initiatives. Hedges' cross-grained politics matched those of his kinsman Sir Charles Hedges, a 'moderate tory' who became secretary of state in 1700.

When the two East India Companies made early efforts to co-operate in trade in 1699, Hedges was appointed by the 'old' company as one of its representatives for dealing with agents of its new counterpart. In 1700 Hedges was promoted by the whigs, again with the dissenting Abney (a fellow Bank of England director), for the London mayoralty in opposition to two strong church tory candidates, one of whom was also deputy governor of the 'old' East India Company. Abney was chosen. Hedges also served as master of the Mercers' Company for a second time in 1700.

Hedges died at Basinghall Street, London, on 5 August 1701 and was buried ten days later at St Margaret's, Stratton, in Wiltshire, where his first wife had previously been interred. He was survived by his second wife, by two sons from each marriage, and by a daughter from his first marriage. He still owned land in co. Cork at the time of his death. An inventory of his estate recorded his possession of ten family portraits, another eighty-eight paintings and prints, and household furnishings that reflected his Eastern travels. He had previously settled land on the Stratton parish as an augmentation to the vicarage and had directed that an annual charity sermon be preached on the anniversary of his first wife's death.

GARY S. DE KREY

Sources *The diary of William Hedges … during his agency in Bengal; as well as on his voyage out and return overland (1681–1687)*, ed. R. Barlow and H. Yule, 3 vols., Hakluyt Society, 74–5, 78 (1887–9) · J. R. Woodhead, *The rulers of London, 1660–1689* (1965), 88, 143–4 [Sir Jeremy Sambrooke] · *CSP dom.*, 1668–9, 477–8, 480, 525; 1687–9, 62; 1691–2, 164; 1694–5, 21 · A. B. Beaven, ed., *The aldermen of the City of London, temp. Henry III–[1912]*, 2 vols. (1908–13), vol. 2, p. 118 · J. Keay, *The honourable company: a history of the English East India Company* (1991), 149–53, 171–3 · S. P. Anderson, *An English consul in Turkey: Paul Rycaut at Smyrna, 1667–1678* (1989), 75, 82, 91, 97, 101, 165, 234 · *DNB* [Sir William Hedges, Sir Charles Hedges, Job Charnock, Thomas Pitt] · G. S. De Krey, 'Trade, religion and politics in London in the reign of William III', PhD diss., Princeton University, 1978, 266, 293 n. 55, 304, 314, 390, 393–4 · G. S. De Kray, *A fractured society: the politics of London in the first age of party, 1688–1715* (1985), 28, 88 · N. Luttrell, *A brief historical relation of state affairs from September 1678 to April 1714*, 6 vols. (1857), vol. 1, p. 433; vol. 2, p. 47; vol. 3, pp. 123, 131, 342; vol. 4, pp. 250, 448, 473, 689, 692; vol. 5, p. 81 · D. V. Glass, introduction, *London inhabitants within the walls, 1695*, ed. D. V. Glass, London RS, 2 (1966), 144, 257 · CLRO, MSS 40/30, 40/34–5 · will, PRO, PROB 11/461, sig. 113 · minutes of the court of committees of the Old East India Company, BL OIOC, B/41, fols. 359–60, 364 [13, 25 Jan 1699; 7 Feb 1699] · Old East India Company lists of adventurers, 1691–1702, BL OIOC, Home misc., vols. 1–3 · [S. Lee], *A collection of the names of the merchants living in and about the City of London* (1677); repr. as *The London directory of 1677* (1878) · W. M. Acres, 'Directors of the Bank of England', *N&Q*, 179 (1940), 39 · parish register, London, St Michael Bassishaw, 21 July 1687, GL [marriage] · *London Post* (30 Sept–2 Oct 1700) · *A list of the commissioners of lieutenancy of the City of London, as constituted in the year 1690* (1690) · *A list of the names of all the subscribers to the Bank of England* [n.d., c.1694], 2 · K. G. Davies, *The royal African company* (1957), 382 · D. W. Jones, 'London overseas merchant groups at the end of the seventeenth century, and the move against the East India Company', DPhil diss., U. Oxf., 1971,

401, 474, 486 · imports from overseas, Dec 1680–Dec 1681, PRO, London port books, E 190/102/1 · Royal African Company Journal, 1691–3, PRO, T 70/188, fols. 113–21 · H. Horwitz, *Parliament, policy and politics in the reign of William III* (1977), 278, 299–300, 348
Wealth at death £6500—in specified legacies and personal estate; land in co. Cork; ten family portraits, and eighty-eight additional paintings and prints: will, PRO, PROB 11/461, sig. 113; *Diary*, vol. 2, pp. xxxviii–ix; Anderson, *English consul*, 101, 165

Hedgewar, Keshavrao Baliram (1889–1940), Hindu nationalist, was born on 1 April 1889 at Nagpur, Maharashtra (then capital of Central Provinces in British India), the youngest of six children of Balirampant, a poor orthodox Deshastha Brahman priest, and Revatibai. He grew up in a high-caste Hindu milieu where traditions of Maharashtrian Hindu valour against pre-colonial Muslim rulers were being fostered to provide sustenance for an emergent nationalism, that could be both anti-British and anti-Muslim in shifting proportions. Expelled from Nilchiti high school, Nagpur, for anti-British activities inspired in Maharashtra by Bal Gangadhar Tilak, Hedgewar studied at Yeotmal national school and (1910–14) the National Medical College, Calcutta, where he is said to have had connections with the Anushilan revolutionary nationalist secret society. He returned to Nagpur permanently in 1914 with a medical degree, but never practised as a doctor. He remained a bachelor. Hedgewar was imprisoned for a year (1921) for participating in the Gandhian non-co-operation movement, but, like his early political mentor, Dr Moonje (principal associate of Tilak in Nagpur), became hostile towards Gandhi's methods and ideals: in particular, in the words of a biographer, for 'overemphasising the importance of Muslim participation in the freedom struggle'.

Hedgewar was influenced by the ideals of exclusivist, anti-Muslim Hindu nationalism propounded by V. D. Savarkar in his *Hindutva* (1923), and decided to give that ideology a firm organizational basis. The specific contexts for his foundation of the Rashtriya Swayamsevak Sangh (RSS), or National Volunteer Organization, in September 1925 were constituted by acute Hindu–Muslim tensions in Nagpur (where Moonje and Hedgewar had set up a Hindu Sabha and organized a big procession in October 1923 defying a government order not to play music before mosques), and the development of anti-Brahman movements among Hindu lower castes (of which, too, the Nagpur region became a principal centre in the 1920s). The meeting that set up the RSS felt that educated, high-caste Hindus should acquire combat skills themselves, and not depend any longer on lower-caste muscle-men.

The RSS displayed its street-fighting capacities in the September 1927 Nagpur Hindu–Muslim riots in which twenty-two were killed, but concentrated more on a long-term, unostentatious building up of organizational strength through what its founder liked to call 'man-making' and 'cultural' work. Its exclusively male membership was recruited very young (boys of twelve to fifteen being preferred, with minds like 'clean slates'), and organized into locality-based *shakhas* (branches) which met every day at fixed times for physical training, exposition of a simple Hindu nationalist ideology that was propagated also through rituals and occasional festivals, and the inculcation of the virtues of unquestioning loyalty and obedience. In November 1929 the RSS adopted the principle of 'following one leader', under which Hedgewar became *sarsang-chalak*, supreme director, on a lifetime basis, of a totally centralized, self-consciously undemocratic structure. In addition, he was given the power to appoint his own successor. The model, supposedly, was that of the patriarchal Hindu joint family, and RSS culture tried to blend martial discipline with familial ideology. Unlike any real family, women remained excluded from RSS membership, but in 1936 Hedgewar agreed to the formation of a subsidiary women's organization, the Rashtrasevika Samiti. Under Hedgewar's successor, M. S. Golwalkar, this system of affiliated organizations, floated and usually controlled by the RSS, proliferated into the 'RSS family', foremost among whose members in the 1990s were the Bharatiya Janata Party and the Viswa Hindu Parishad.

Hedgewar briefly gave up headship of the RSS when he courted arrest in 1930 as part of Gandhi's civil disobedience movement. His RSS biographer, C. P. Bhishikar, explains this in terms of Hedgewar's desire to propagate the ideals of his organization among nationalists in prison. The RSS itself kept consistently aloof from all anti-British movements, and so (except briefly in the Central Provinces in 1932–4, when government servants were banned from joining it) never became an object of colonial repression despite its paramilitary ways. Relations with the other major Hindu nationalist organization, the Hindu Mahasabha patronized by V. D. Savarkar (of which Moonje had become a leader) were initially close, but later became uncertain because of the RSS preference for long-term 'cultural', rather than directly political, work. In 1934, for instance, it lost a prominent organizer, Nathuram Godse, the future assassin of Gandhi, to the Mahasabha because of Hedgewar's refusal to make the RSS a more political body.

Initially confined mainly to Maharashtra, the RSS spread rapidly into northern India as Hindu–Muslim relations worsened there in the late 1930s, and organizers were also sent to the southern provinces by Hedgewar in 1938. There were about 500 *shakhas* with 60,000 members by 1939, and in 1940 the last 'officer's training camp' that Hedgewar was able to address was attended by trainees from every province except Assam, Orissa, and Kashmir. About half the branches, however, were still located in Maharashtra, and recruitment remained largely confined to high-caste, urban middle- and lower middle-class groups. Hedgewar had been in ill health since 1932, and died of high blood pressure in Nagpur on 21 June 1940, having had the satisfaction, as he had stated in his last speech to RSS trainees, of seeing before his eyes 'a miniature Hindu Rashtra [Nation]'.   SUMIT SARKAR

Sources C. P. Bhishikar, *Dr Hedgewar the master man-maker* (1989) · T. Basu and others, *Khaki shorts and saffron flags* (1993) · W. K. Anderson and S. D. Damle, *The brotherhood in saffron* (1987) · J. A. Curran, *Militant Hinduism in Indian politics: a study of the RSS* (1951) · N. H. Palkar, *Dr K. B. Hedgewar* (1964) [in Marathi] · C. P. Bhishikar, *Keshar Sanghriamata* (1979) [Marathi; 1980 Hindi]
Archives Nehru Memorial Library, New Delhi

Hedley, John Cuthbert (1837–1915), Roman Catholic bishop of Newport and Benedictine monk, was born on 15 April 1837 at Carlisle House, Morpeth, Northumberland, the son of Edward Astley Hedley, a physician, and Mary Ann Davison. He was educated at Mr Gibson's Grammar School in Morpeth and at Ampleforth College in Yorkshire, where he won numerous prizes and became an accomplished musician. In 1854 he joined the Benedictine community at Ampleforth, and studied philosophy and theology there under the direction of Dom Austin Bury, one of the first nineteenth-century English Benedictines to be sent abroad for theological studies. Hedley was ordained priest on 19 October 1862 and was then sent to Belmont, near Hereford, commonly the house of studies and noviciate for the English Benedictines, where he taught philosophy and theology and gained a reputation as 'an inspirer and guide in all studious pursuits' (Belmont Abbey Archives, MS 696, p. 5). He also set about the task of reforming the philosophy course in line with the recent continental revival of Thomism.

The 1860s, being the decade leading up to the First Vatican Council (1869–70), were years of controversy in the Catholic church, and it was during this period that Hedley made his first literary and theological contributions to the *Dublin Review*. His reputation as a preacher was considerable and he became the most sought-after speaker at almost every major English Benedictine event and every episcopal funeral. In 1873 he was consecrated auxiliary bishop of the see of Newport and in 1881 he succeeded to the see and moved the centre of the diocese from Hereford to Cardiff; he saw the Catholic population rise from 40,000 in 1881 to 80,000 in 1915. In 1895 he split the diocese, creating a northern see of Menevia. He advocated the elevation of Cardiff to the rank of archdiocese, with Menevia as the suffragan see, which took effect with the appointment, in 1916, of his successor, James Romanus Bilsborrow, as the first archbishop of Cardiff. Hedley was renowned for his care of his clergy and demonstrated particular concern to increase the number of diocesan priests and reduce dependence on the regular clergy; in 1881 there were only thirteen diocesan priests in Wales but by 1915 this number had risen to fifty-four.

Hedley was influential in reviving the practice of contemplative prayer, as taught by the seventeenth-century English Benedictine Father Augustine Baker, through an article entitled 'Prayer and contemplation', published in the *Dublin Review* in October 1876, which combined Baker's English Benedictine monastic spirituality with the pastoral spirituality of St Francis of Sales. The 1880s were turbulent years for the English Benedictines, with on the one hand a strong movement for monastic reform that sought greater emphasis on monastic life in the English houses, and on the other a desire for the continuation and consolidation of the missionary system, with monks continuing to live away from their monasteries in the Benedictine missions, many of which dated back to the seventeenth century. Hedley's work as a professor at Belmont in the 1860s had helped to provide intellectual breadth in the English Benedictine congregation and thereby sowed the seeds of a changed perception of the nature of English Benedictinism. He did not personally favour constitutional change, believing that the missions and the monasteries had different aims and should be kept apart. This view, however, was not shared by the Roman authorities, and in 1890 the missions were placed under the control of the monasteries, which, through the 1899 bull *Diu quidem*, became autonomous abbeys.

The 1880s and 1890s saw Hedley engaging with several major contemporary issues in the wider world. Articles he wrote for the *Dublin Review* on evolution, the authority of scripture, and faith were motivated by a determination to take seriously various developments in the modern world and their effect on religion. As editor of the *Dublin Review* he was credited for moving the journal away from the narrow, ultramontane concerns espoused by W. G. Ward; Bishop Ullathorne congratulated Hedley, commenting that 'it is high time it became a Catholic rather than a party review' (Wilson, 189). Wilfrid Ward, a later editor of the *Dublin Review*, noted that Hedley's gift was his 'great unity and great mellowness of intellect', which enabled him to be 'keenly alive to modern needs … yet seeing that human nature is ever the same, and that much that is modern is a recurrence of older ways of thinking' (Ward, 4–5). Hedley's pragmatic, steady judgement was also evident in his actions during the modernist crisis in the first decade of the twentieth century, when 'he kept his head … and was no doubt the cause for others keeping their heads too' (Beck, 221).

Hedley's determination to take the modern world seriously can also be seen in his involvement in the debate concerning Catholic higher education in the last two decades of the nineteenth century. He 'understood above all, the needs of education. He could grapple with the spirit of the age. Hence he was found the fittest to be chosen in 1896 as President of the Catholic University Board' (*The Tablet*, 13 Nov 1915). Despite the opposition of Cardinal Manning, Hedley advocated that Catholics be permitted to attend the ancient universities of Oxford and Cambridge; his efforts led to the ban's being lifted by Pope Leo XIII in 1895. It was therefore with some justification that one of Hedley's obituarists noted: 'in his long episcopate, he had immense influence on Catholicism in this country' (ibid.). His abilities did not go unrecognized in Rome, for in 1891 he was honoured by Pope Leo XIII with the title of assistant at the pontifical throne. Bishop Hedley died, of a heart attack, at Llanishen, near Cardiff, on 11 November 1915, and was buried on the 17th in Cardiff cemetery.

ALBAN HOOD

Sources J. A. Wilson, *The life of Bishop Hedley* (1930) · G. A. Beck, ed., *The English Catholics, 1850–1950* (1950), 217–22 · *The Tablet* (13 Nov 1915) · W. Ward, 'Bishop Hedley', *Dublin Review*, 158 (1916), 1–12 · I. Cummins, diaries, Belmont Abbey Archives, MS 696, 3 · G. Buisseret, history of Belmont, Belmont Abbey Archives, MS 673, 76 · G. Scott, 'The English Benedictine mission and missions', *Benedict's disciples*, ed. D. H. Farmer (1998) · B. Green, 'Cuthbert Hedley, 1837–1915', *EBC symposium papers*, 1987, 38–46 · J. E. Matthews, 'Bishop Hedley as editor', *Dublin Review*, 198 (1936), 253–66
Archives Ampleforth Abbey, Yorkshire, archives, MSS · Belmont Abbey, Hereford, archives, MSS · Douai Abbey, Woolhampton, Berkshire, archives, MSS · Downside Abbey, near Bath, archives, MSS · NL Wales, archives, corresp.
Likenesses oils, Ampleforth Abbey, Yorkshire

Hedley, William (1779–1843), designer and maker of steam locomotives, was born at Newburn, near Newcastle upon Tyne, on 13 July 1779, the second son in a family of eight children, of William Hedley, a grocer. He was educated at a school at Wylam, and when not yet twenty-two years of age was appointed viewer at Walbottle colliery in Northumberland. He afterwards held the same position at the Wylam colliery, taking charge, in addition, of the Blagill lead mine at Alston in Cumberland. Hedley married Frances Dodds (d. 1838) of Berwick upon Tweed on 2 June 1803; they had at least four children.

The expense of using horse-drawn wagons to carry coal along the 5 miles of railway between Wylam and the loading staithes on the River Tyne directed Hedley's attention to the possibilities of steam locomotive haulage. Careful experimentation convinced him that simple friction adhesion between the wheels of a locomotive and smooth-headed rails would be sufficient to haul considerable loads. The adhesion systems involving cogwheel and rack rails and other costly expedients, which earlier engineers such as Blenkinsop, Chapman, and Brunton had employed, were shown to be unnecessary. Hedley's simple friction adhesion system was patented on 13 March 1813 and became an essential factor in railway development.

Hedley was a designer and maker of locomotive engines, and his *Puffing Billy* of 1813, which ran for forty-eight years (and is now in the Science Museum), as well as two others built for Wylam colliery, possessed a final drive through gears which coupled the axles and minimized wheel slip, a principle widely applied to French electric locomotives 150 years later. Their power output was augmented by the double pass—instead of single pass—boiler flue, giving increased heat transfer and steam production, the latter assisted by passing exhaust steam from the cylinders through an intermediate chamber to an exhaust pipe in the chimney. This created a suction effect on the fire within the flue, increasing the intensity of combustion. This blast-pipe system, with contracted nozzle, was later greatly improved by Hackworth and became a fundamental factor in steam locomotive power capacity.

Hedley was a shipowner from 1808. In 1822, during a strike of the keelmen, he promptly placed one of his engines upon a barge, and, working it with paddles, towed the keels to the coal shoots without the men's assistance. Steamboats had been invented earlier, but were still little used, and the action was characteristic of Hedley's energy and resource.

In 1824 Hedley took the Crow Tees colliery, near Durham, and later that at Callerton, near Wylam. In 1828 he removed to Shield Row, where he rented for some time the South Moor colliery. While at Callerton he introduced an improved system of pumping the water out of collieries, which, though adversely criticized at the time, was soon in general use in the north of England.

Hedley died at his home, Burnhopeside Hall, near Lanchester, co. Durham, on 9 January 1843. Frances, his wife, died in 1838, and both were buried in the Hedley family grave at Newburn parish church. Four of his sons survived him: Oswald Dodd Hedley (d. 1882); Thomas Hedley (d. 1877), who left much money to endow the Northumberland bishopric; William Hedley; and George Hedley.

W. A. J. ARCHBOLD, rev. GEORGE W. CARPENTER

Sources M. Archer, *William Hedley, the inventor of railway locomotion on the present principle* (1882) · P. R. B. Brooks, *William Hedley, locomotive pioneer* (1980) · J. T. van Riemsdijk and K. Brown, *The pictorial history of steam power* (1980) · d. cert.
Likenesses portrait, 1808, repro. in Brooks, *William Hedley*, 3

Heelis, Stephen (1801–1871), lawyer, was born in Bolton. Articled to the firm of Sharpe, Eccles, and Cririe (antecedents of the present Slater Heelis solicitors) he was admitted as an attorney in the Hilary term of 1826. Heelis remained with the firm and became a partner in 1833. Credited as the founder of the Manchester Law Association, he became its president in 1843 and again in 1867. He was elected alderman for the Seedley ward of the borough of Salford. He is said to have been offered and refused a knighthood. He was mayor of Salford in 1855–6 and again in 1856–7. A strong Conservative supporter, he worked on several parliamentary election campaigns in Manchester and was a generous subscriber to the funds of the local Conservative association. He was also an early member of the Salford volunteer corps to which he also made generous financial contributions. As solicitor for John Owens, the Manchester industrialist, Heelis became one of the first trustees of Owens College (subsequently the Victoria University of Manchester). William Heelis, the husband of Beatrix Potter, was the great-grandson of a cousin of Stephen Heelis's father. Heelis died on Saturday 26 August 1871 at his house, Above Beck in Grasmere.

V. R. PARROTT

Sources V. R. Parrott, 'Pettyfogging to respectability: a history of the development of the profession of solicitor in the Manchester area, 1800–1814', PhD diss., University of Salford, 1992 · *Manchester Guardian* (29 Aug 1871) · *Salford Weekly News* (2 Sept 1871) · *CGPLA Eng. & Wales* (1871) · d. cert.
Archives Man. CL, Manchester Archives and Local Studies · Slater Heelis & Co., Princess Street, Manchester
Wealth at death under £40,000: probate, 30 Sept 1871, *CGPLA Eng. & Wales*

Heemskerk, Egbert Jasperszoon van (b. 1634), painter, was born in Haarlem in June or July 1634, and pursued a very successful career in Britain as a genre painter from c.1674. The precise identity of Heemskerk is unclear. The patronymic Jasperszoon indicates that he was probably not the son of the Dutch genre painter Egbert van Heemskerk (1610–1680). He is reputed to have had a painter/actor son who died in London in 1744; this may have been a grandson. Numerous references in contemporary auction catalogues to Old Heemskerk and Heemskerk indicate the work of two Heemskerks in England. It is possible that the man born in 1634 was the father of an unknown painter; possibly it was a son who died c.1704.

Heemskerk is said to have been a pupil of Peter de Grebber (1600–c.1652) and was a follower of Jan Miense Molenaer (c.1610–1668). He lived in Haarlem, and possibly in Amsterdam, and perhaps travelled to Italy. 1674 is the year he was last recorded in Holland, and the first he dated a painting in Britain. His contemporary reputation was that of a skilful and successful painter of 'drunken drolls, wakes, [and] quakers-meetings', establishing much-imitated precedents for the latter genre (Buckeridge, 430). He frequently introduced his own portrait into his pictures. Buckeridge's reference to Heemskerk's patronage 'by the late Earl Rochester' indicates he worked for John Wilmot, the infamous second earl (d. 1680) (and not Lawrence Hyde, first earl of the new creation, d. 1720), and it was noted that 'his … lewd pieces, have been in vogue among the waggish collectors, and the lower rank of virtuosi' (ibid.). He also executed a well-known painting of an election at Oxford (Oxford town hall) and was reputed to have lived there.

Heemskerk's output was prodigious, with over 887 paintings by Old Heemskerk or Heemskerk passing through auction houses between 1689 and 1692. His work was also reproduced in engravings, especially mezzotint, by R. Earlom, J. Smith, and others. An engraving by Francis Place after a portrait by Heemskerk of the printseller Pierce Tempest is in the British Museum. The Latin poet Vincent Bourne wrote poems on two of his pictures. After his death, possibly c.1704, his reputation endured, and his name was cited by poets such as John Gay as a byword for boorish behaviour.

L. H. CUST, rev. NICHOLAS GRINDLE

Sources H. Mount, 'Egbert van Heemskerk's Quaker meetings revisited', *Journal of the Warburg and Courtauld Institutes*, 56 (1993), 209–28 · [B. Buckeridge], 'An essay towards an English school of painters', in R. de Piles, *The art of painting, and the lives of the painters* (1706), 398–480 · E. K. Waterhouse, *The dictionary of British 16th and 17th century painters* (1988) · S. Slive, *Dutch painting, 1600–1800* (1995) · J. Turner, ed., *The dictionary of art*, 34 vols. (1996), vol. 14 · Vertue, *Note books*, vols. 1–2, 4–5
Likenesses J. Oliver, mezzotint (after E. Heemskerk), BM

Heenan, John Carmel (1905–1975), Roman Catholic archbishop of Westminster, was born in Ilford, Essex, on 26 January 1905, the youngest in a family of four sons and one daughter of James Carmel Heenan (d. 1937), a civil servant at the Patent Office, and his wife, Anne Pilkington (d. 1949). When he declared his youthful wish to become a priest this ambition was warmly fostered by his devout Irish Catholic parents and his parish priest, Paddy Palmer. He was educated at the Jesuit grammar school of St Ignatius, Stamford Hill, and began his studies for the priesthood at Ushaw College, near Durham, in 1922. While on a month's sick leave from the college he fell in love with a girl of his own age. For a while he wrestled with the choice between priesthood and marriage, but his sense of vocation proved stronger, and he was not troubled by further doubts during his student years. In 1924 he was sent to the English College in Rome and obtained the customary doctorates in philosophy and theology from the very traditional Gregorian University. The rector, Arthur Hinsley,

John Carmel Heenan (1905–1975), by Godfrey Argent, 1969

had created a tight-knit and happy community among the fifty-odd students who were there. While there Heenan made a close lifelong friendship with fellow student George Patrick Dwyer, later to become archbishop of Birmingham. Hinsley also found in Heenan a kindred spirit, clear thinking and quick to make decisions.

Heenan was ordained priest in 1930 and, when he had completed his course of studies in Rome, was appointed assistant priest at Barking in his home diocese of Brentwood in 1931. When Hinsley became archbishop of Westminster in 1935 he began to use Heenan to help him with drafting speeches and articles, although Heenan's bishop, Doubleday, refused Hinsley's request to have him as his personal secretary. Hinsley encouraged Heenan in his plan to visit the Soviet Union posing as a lecturer in psychology so as to study living conditions under an atheistic communist regime. The account of his visit, in the first volume of his autobiography, makes fascinating reading and shows him at his most fearless when shedding for a few weeks his clerical persona. On his return he presented a report to Cardinal Hinsley and to a special gathering at the Albert Hall. Heenan was a tall, smiling, if somewhat ascetic looking figure. He was an entertaining conversationalist, at ease with everyone. Beneath it all was an underlying piety; he remained a man of prayer until the end of his life.

In 1937 Heenan was appointed parish priest at Manor Park in East Ham where he remained throughout the war

years and until 1947. His life ambition was to be a parochial priest. Although he had great talents for writing, for public speaking, and for spiritual direction, all these were to be secondary concerns. With boundless energy he soon became a well-known speaker at Catholic functions and he wrote several expositions of the Catholic faith. He became a regular speaker on the BBC, known popularly as the Radio Priest. His increasing influence in Catholic circles provoked great resentment from his bishop who regarded him for many years as arrogant. Amid all these activities he found time to conduct a caring and imaginative ministry in his parish.

In 1947 Heenan was made superior of the newly re-established Catholic Missionary Society, a group of diocesan clergy who were to preach missions to Catholics and non-Catholics throughout England and Wales. One of his first acts was to travel to America to evaluate the new styles of such mission work there. He gathered around himself a team of brilliant preachers and speakers, some of them from his English College days, notably George Patrick Dwyer. It quickly made its impact throughout the country not only by missions but also by lectures in universities and colleges, hospitals, and public halls. It was a pyrotechnic display of the increasing self-confidence of the Catholic community, but it was also based on a regime of communal prayer and supportive mutual criticism. In 1949 his team organized a general mission throughout the country in preparation for the holy year of 1950. During these years he wrote a book of pastoral and practical advice for parochial clergy, *The People's Priest* (1951). It was his personal manifesto: the whole purpose of priesthood is to serve the people of God. He pursued this ideal in his own life at considerable personal cost.

On 12 March 1951 Heenan was consecrated fifth bishop of Leeds by Archbishop Godfrey. After some years under an ageing bishop followed by a long interregnum the diocese needed rejuvenation. He set about this task with typical impetuosity, making major changes and moving priests around very quickly in ways which he later admitted were mistaken. However, in his time the diocese seemed to come alive: the Catholic population grew by over 50,000, twenty-seven new churches were built, and conversions averaged 900 each year. In pursuit of his ideal of the parochial priesthood he took over the cathedral parish, said mass and heard confession there, and cycled around the parish visiting parishioners. He eventually had to acknowledge to himself with sadness that this was not a feasible model for a bishop in a large diocese. During this period he progressed from being 'the Radio Priest' to becoming an accomplished television personality.

In May 1957 Heenan was translated to Liverpool as its fifth archbishop. Although he no longer tried to fill the role of a parish priest he remained extremely active. Unlike his predecessors and successors he did not seek the services of an auxiliary bishop. On his visitations he always insisted on visiting all the housebound Catholics of the parish. His major achievement in Liverpool was to grasp the nettle of the diocesan cathedral. By 1957 only the crypt of the original design by Sir Edwin Lutyens had been completed and even the modified plans of Adrian Scott had become prohibitively expensive. He abandoned these and established a national competition with a panel of professional assessors under the terms of which the new design had to link with the existing crypt. There were 300 entrants and the revolutionary design of a conical cathedral in modern materials by Frederick Gibberd was chosen, with the glass work of the great lantern to be by John Piper and Patrick Reyntiens. By the time Heenan left Liverpool this was well on the way to completion and the old pro-cathedral of St Nicholas in which he had been installed was no longer in existence.

No one was surprised when, on the death of Cardinal Godfrey, Heenan was appointed eighth archbishop of Westminster on 2 September 1963. Until December 1966 most of his time was spent at the Second Vatican Council. English Catholicism had been ill-prepared for the council, and Heenan was out of tune with the liberal trends in European theology which were its driving force. This began a sad period in his life because he could not accept that the new men at the council, innovators in theology, apologetics, and catechists, were any more apostolic or capable exponents of Catholic doctrine than were their predecessors. At times he felt that they were undermining the faith, and he once launched a famous attack against the theological experts at the council, 'Timeo peritos et dona ferentes' ('I fear experts and those bearing gifts'). Nevertheless he too was responsive to the winds of change. Even before the council he had been appointed to the newly established secretariat for Christian unity. In August 1962 he organized a conference on ecumenism at Heythrop College with Cardinal Bea as principal speaker. His own ecumenism was practical rather than theoretical. He was happy occasionally sharing the non-eucharistic worship with Christians of other allegiances but it was not in his nature to lead or to follow along the paths to a more fundamental unity. Nor could he admit to himself that any of Rome's traditional positions could have been wrong. In some ways he found it easier to enter into a new relationship with the Jews where there was no commitment to shared belief or worship. He was particularly active in preparing the council's declaration on non-Christian faiths, and its decree on ecumenism.

Heenan was created cardinal in February 1965. Traditionally the archbishop of Westminster was president of the bishops' conference. Heenan petitioned Rome to make this an elective post with an annual term. The bishops had so much confidence in his leadership that they elected him to this post each year until his death. Many contemporary Catholic observers credited him with holding together the bishops' conference and the Catholic community of England and Wales. He could no longer act as an independent leader with a personal prophetic role, but learned to accept the discipline of collegial responsibility at least in matters of policy.

In 1968 the papal encyclical *Humanae vitae* rejected the strong advice of a commission appointed by the pope composed largely of lay experts, and repeated the traditional Vatican condemnation of the use of artificial means of contraception. This split the Catholic community, most of whom had expected a statement leaving the choice of the means of contraception to the individual conscience. Heenan personally accepted the authority of the encyclical (though few thought of it as infallible) but sought to mediate between the extremes of positions within the bishops' conference in order to preserve a unity of public utterance while at the same time respecting the private conscience of those who could not accept the papal ruling.

Heenan's last years were dogged with serious illness: encephalitis, heart attacks, and lack of sleep. He was deeply saddened by the number of priests who had left the active ministry. He could not comprehend how anyone could abandon the priestly role. Although he treated them kindly, his only explanation was that they were bad priests. In the second volume of his autobiography (*A Crown of Thorns*, 1974) he spoke of disintegration, of the neo-modernists and Catholic anarchists who were 'the enemy within'. He mourned the drift away from clerical and religious dress, the growing controversy over priestly celibacy, and the widespread loss of a habit of prayer and a belief in the supernatural. He found that his job at Westminster was getting beyond his strength and in September 1975 he offered his resignation to the pope but continued to undertake engagements. He died in Westminster Hospital on 7 November 1975 before his resignation was accepted. He was buried by the fourteenth station of the cross in Westminster Cathedral.

MICHAEL GAINE

Sources J. C. Heenan, *A crown of thorns* (1974) · J. C. Heenan, *Not the whole truth* (1971) · A. Hastings, *A history of English Christianity, 1920–1990*, 3rd edn (1991) · *The Tablet* (15 Nov 1975) · *DNB* · personal knowledge (2004)
Archives Liverpool archdiocesan archive, Skelmersdale, papers · Westm. DA | FILM BFI NFTVA, news footage | SOUND BL NSA, performance recording
Likenesses G. Argent, photograph, 1969, NPG [*see illus.*] · G. Thompson, oils, Upholland Northern Institute, near Wigan · photographs, Hult. Arch.
Wealth at death £3459: probate, 17 Dec 1975, *CGPLA Eng. & Wales*

Heenan, Patrick Stanley Vaughan (1910–1942), army officer and traitor, was born on 29 July 1910 at a small mining town, Reefton, South Island, New Zealand, the illegitimate son of Anne (Annie) Stanley (who was born on 8 December 1882 and outlived her son, dying after August 1946) and an unknown man. Possibly the father was George Charles Heenan (who was born on 13 September 1855 and died at Pauk, Upper Burma, on 24 October 1912), educated at Cheltenham College from 1869 to 1871, an Irish, and reportedly republican, mining engineer, with whom Stanley, posing as his wife, went to Burma. The boy was given the surname Heenan and passed as their son. He was baptized and brought up as a Roman Catholic. Following George Heenan's death, Stanley, posing as a widow, stayed in Burma, where presumably Heenan was educated at a mission school or schools. In 1922 or 1923 Stanley and her son moved to England, where in April 1929 she married Bernard Carroll, a widower and accountant.

Meanwhile, by unknown means, she had obtained sufficient money to buy her son a public-school education.

From 1923 to 1926 Heenan was a boarder at Sevenoaks School. He succeeded at games and boxing but not at school work; possibly he was expelled. He attended two crammers then in January 1927 entered Cheltenham College on the military side. Cheltenham was a leading army school and old Cheltonians won fourteen Victoria crosses. He again succeeded at games and boxing but not at school work: 'a dunderhead' (Elphick and Smith, 84), humiliatingly placed in a form of younger boys, he thrice failed the school certificate. He was in the OTC and passed certificate A in 1928. He was a gloomy, resentful misfit disliked by other pupils. He left the college, without academic qualifications, in July 1929. Almost immediately he joined, as a junior employee, the London offices of Steel Brothers, a trading company with extensive interests in the Far East. According to his later bragging, he frequented prostitutes.

Heenan decided to change to an army career. His lack of qualifications precluded normal entry as an officer, but there was a 'back door' route, the supplementary reserve of officers. In 1933, with a letter from his headmaster, he was commissioned into the supplementary reserve; he was 6 feet 1 inch tall, strongly built, and weighed 12½ stone. Placed on the unattached list of the Indian army, he sailed to India in 1935 with other new subalterns. They later remembered him as good looking—'reminded me a bit of Errol Flynn' (Elphick and Smith, 99)—but 'not quite a gentleman' (ibid.), unpopular, and friendless. New officers for the Indian army had to serve a year with a British battalion: Heenan was attached to the 1st battalion, the Royal Warwickshire regiment. He gained a reputation as an ill-mannered, uncouth sponger, who talked about fellow officers behind their backs and was a 'dirty' player at rugby. The commanding officer doubted his suitability and apparently refused to recommend him. So, exceptionally and humiliatingly, he had to undergo a further six months with another British unit, the 1st battalion, the Royal Norfolk regiment.

In 1936 Heenan joined the 16th Punjab regiment and became army heavyweight boxing champion of India. An officer later remembered, 'he had a huge grudge against society and was out to get his revenge' (Elphick and Smith, 104). Ill-mannered and a bully, he was again unpopular with his fellow officers and so from 1937 to 1939 was attached to the Royal Indian Army Service Corps, another humiliation. In 1936–7 he took six months' 'long leave' in Japan. There, possibly through a woman, he was presumably recruited by the Japanese intelligence service and trained as a spy. His motivation is unknown, but apparently it was personal and psychological—the 'chip on his shoulder' (Elphick, *Far Eastern File*, 306)—rather than ideological. Factors suggested by his biographers and others include his illegitimacy, a sallow complexion suggesting Asian blood, and his Irishness, but none of these in itself is sufficient explanation, and there is no evidence, only conjecture, that any of these motivated him.

In 1939, following an incident in September with military police, Heenan was returned to the 1st battalion, 16th Punjab regiment, and in 1940 saw active service on the north-west frontier. Some officers wanted him removed from the army and later in 1940 the new commanding officer had him transferred. Promoted temporary captain, he was moved to the 2nd battalion and in October went with it, part of the 6th Indian infantry brigade, to Malaya. The Malayan campaign of 1941–2, which culminated in the fall of Singapore (on 15 February 1942), was characterized by an almost incredible sequence of British bungling and bad luck. Heenan's role was part of this. As a junior regimental officer in India, especially on the north-west frontier, he would have been of limited use to the Japanese, yet Malaya was a key theatre. Early in 1941 the 6th Indian was stationed near the Thai border. Heenan had contact with Japanese agents—part of the complex Japanese network of espionage and subversion in Malaya—and disloyal Indians, and made clandestine journeys to Thailand. He was so unpopular and unsuitable that his commanding officer demanded he be transferred. In 1941 he was made an air intelligence liaison officer attached to the Royal Air Force. This was yet another British bungle, for in this capacity he had access to crucial RAF information at a time when the destruction of the already inadequate British air force in Malaya was a Japanese priority. He was stationed at Alor Star airfield in northern Malaya where he was disliked by RAF personnel, who nicknamed him Tom on account of his notorious womanizing. He supplied the Japanese with information on the air defence of northern Malaya and may have run a local network of Malay spies.

Some officers suspected that Heenan was a spy. Captain Harry Landray, second in command of the liaison section, reported his suspicions before or in October 1941: nothing was done. In October Landray was killed in a private-plane crash, possibly caused by Heenan's sabotage. In December 1941 the Japanese attacked Malaya and their warplanes had remarkable success in destroying RAF planes, many of them on the ground. Major James Cable France, commanding the liaison section, had found evidence of Heenan's espionage and believed that on the night of 9–10 December Heenan tried to murder him. On 10 December Heenan was arrested at Butterfield airfield near Penang. His quarters were searched: documents were found and two radios—one disguised as a typewriter, the other hidden in a fake chaplain's communion case. He was brought to Singapore, secretly court-martialled from 2 January 1942, and found guilty. On 8 February the Japanese invaded Singapore Island. On Friday 13 February 1942, in the fighting, destruction, and confusion, with the possibility that he might be rescued by the enemy, Heenan was taken by military police to the harbour and shot in the head; his body was pushed into the sea. On 15 February the British surrendered.

After the fall of Singapore it was widely known that there had been an officer traitor who was executed, and one book of an Australian officer's letters named Heenan. However, there was an official and unofficial cover-up, and some post-war history books gave inaccurate versions, claiming that the traitor was an RAF officer. In the early 1990s Peter Elphick and Michael Smith investigated the 'officer traitor affair', using official documents, interviews with survivors, and accounts written by participants. They published the first relatively full account in their *Odd Man Out: the Story of the Singapore Traitor* (1994). Later some additional information became available, which Elphick published in his subsequent books on Singapore and on the intelligence war in the Far East. Elphick claimed that Heenan's espionage was 'directly responsible for the virtual destruction of the RAF in northern Malaya' (Elphick, *Singapore: the pregnable Fortress*, 72). Possibly this exaggerated Heenan's role: the Japanese had many intelligence sources and the RAF was quantitatively and qualitatively decisively inferior to the enemy. Nevertheless, while the extent and results of Heenan's treachery cannot now be precisely known, possibly—as Elphick and Smith wrote—it 'played a significant part in that Japanese victory and perhaps, therefore, even in the end of the British Empire' (Elphick and Smith, 1).

ROGER T. STEARN

Sources P. Elphick and M. Smith, *Odd man out: the story of the Singapore traitor* (1994) · P. Elphick, *Singapore, the pregnable fortress: a study in deception, discord and desertion* (1995) · P. Elphick, *Far Eastern file: the intelligence war in the Far East, 1930–1945* (1997) · E. S. Skirving, ed., *Cheltenham College register, 1841–1927* (1928) · C. H. Pigg, ed., *Cheltenham College register, 1841–1919; additions and corrections, 1919–1951* (1953) · M. H. Murfett and others, *Between two oceans: a military history of Singapore from first settlement to final British withdrawal* (1999) · H. Probert, *The forgotten air force: the Royal Air Force in the war against Japan, 1941–1945* (1995) · CGPLA Eng. & Wales (1947)
Likenesses photographs, repro. in Elphick and Smith, *Odd man out*
Wealth at death £3216 7s. 1d.: administration, 26 Feb 1947, CGPLA Eng. & Wales

Heere, Lucas de (1534–1584), painter and poet, was born in Ghent, the second son of Jan de Heere, a sculptor, and Anna Smijters, a miniaturist. Having presumably received some training at home, he was apprenticed to Frans Floris. The painter and biographer Karel van Mander was subsequently de Heere's pupil and the biography written by the former provides much information. Only one signed work survives by de Heere: *Solomon and Sheba* (1559; cathedral church of St Bavo, Ghent), in which the face of Solomon is recognizably that of Philip II of Spain. Both de Heere and his father were employed in July 1559 on the decorations for the final chapter of the order of the Golden Fleece in Ghent Cathedral, with which this painting may be connected. A *View of the Estate of St Bavo* (Rijksuniversiteit, Ghent) and a *Crucifixion* (St Pauwels, near St Niklaas, Oost-Vlaanderen) have been ascribed to de Heere on the basis of documents. *The Liberal Arts Slumbering in Time of War* (Galleria Sabauda, Turin) has also been attributed to him, by comparison with the signed drawing of the *Three Virtues Asleep* (1564; Staatliche Graphische Sammlung, Munich), but this attribution remains inconclusive.

De Heere was a member of the chamber of rhetoric known as Jesus with the Balsam Flower and wrote numerous poems, of which the best known today are included in the anthology of his poetic works *De hof en boemgaerd der poesien* ('The Garden and Orchard of Poetry'), compiled in 1561. This volume refers to the status of art and artists and to the pre-eminence of painting among the liberal and mechanical arts, and includes a mythical contest in which Apollo decides in favour of art (then regarded as a manual and not an intellectual activity) over the accepted liberal art categories of the *trivium* and *quadrivium*, by reference to the book of Exodus. It also contains a defence of his old master, Floris, against an anonymous attack. Van Mander stated that during the iconoclasm that swept the Low Countries in 1566 de Heere hid some of Floris's works. Van Mander also recorded that de Heere wrote biographies of artists, but that he (van Mander) did not succeed in obtaining them; presumably they were inspirational to him. In a letter of September 1582 to the duc d'Anjou, de Heere referred to his employment by d'Anjou's mother, Catherine de' Medici, queen of France, in 1559–60. The designs for the Valois tapestries, 1582–5 (Uffizi, Florence), long considered to have been made by a Netherlandish artist with a connection to d'Anjou, have plausibly been attributed on stylistic grounds to de Heere, who is recorded by van Mander as travelling to France at an unspecified date, where he made tapestry designs. As members of the reformed religion, de Heere and his wife, Eleanora Carboniers, were proscribed by name in 1568, but may have fled to London as early as 1566. They are recorded there in 1571 and 1576. While in England, de Heere painted a gallery with the costumes of all nations for Edward Fiennes Clinton, earl of Lincoln (destr.). This included an Englishman unable to choose which clothes to wear, an image said to have amused Elizabeth I and to be typical of the nation. Drawings of costumes of the British Isles are also included in his *Beschriving der Britsche Eilanden* (1573–5; BL) and *Theatre de tous le peuples et nations de la terre* (1568 and later; Ghent University Library). The attribution to de Heere of *The Family of Henry VIII: an Allegory of the Tudor Succession* (c.1572; National Museum and Gallery, Cardiff), an image intended to reinforce Elizabeth I's right to the throne, is probably correct. This work belonged to Francis Walsingham whose contacts with de Heere are referred to in a letter dated July 1576 from William of Orange (*Proceedings of the Huguenot Society*, 4, 1891–3, 39). Portraits formerly attributed to de Heere on the basis of the monogram HE have been reattributed to Hans Eworth; consequently, the extent of de Heere's œuvre during his English period has been much reduced. He contributed drawings and poetry to the friendship books of his fellow exiles Abraham Ortelius (Pembroke College, Cambridge), Emanuel van Meteren (Bodl. Oxf.), and the merchant Jan Radermacher (Ghent University Library). The device of the *Siren Luring Sailors to their Doom*, which he drew in a fictive oval frame with accompanying verses on 2 August 1576 in the book belonging to the painter Joris Hoefnagel (Rijksmuseum, Amsterdam), bears his punning motto 'Schade Leer U' ('Misfortune teaches you') which van Mander stated that he adopted as an anagram of his name. While in London de Heere took John de Critz the elder, sergeant-painter 1605–42, as a pupil. De Heere and his wife returned to

Ghent after the pacification in 1576 and he was subsequently involved in the celebrations that took place on the announcement of an engagement between Elizabeth I and the duc d'Anjou in 1581, and the triumphal entries into Ghent of William of Orange in 1577 and the duc d'Anjou in 1582. De Heere died on 29 August 1584, possibly in Paris.   SUSAN BRACKEN

Sources K. van Mander, *The lives of the illustrious Netherlandish and German painters*, ed. H. Miedema, 1 (1994) · F. Yates, *The Valois tapestries*, 2nd edn (1975) · *Proceedings of the Huguenot Society*, 4 (1891–3), 36–9 · *Proceedings of the Huguenot Society*, 7 (1901–4), 46–52 · L. Cust, 'Notes on the inventory of paintings belonging to John, Lord Lumley, in 1590 and on the painter using the monogram HE', *Burlington Magazine*, 14 (1909), 366–8 · K. Hearn, ed., *Dynasties: painting in Tudor and Jacobean England, 1530–1630* (1995), esp. nos. 35 and 101 [exhibition catalogue, Tate Gallery, London, 12 Oct 1995 – 7 Jan 1996] · *Fiamminghi a Roma, 1508–1608: artisti dei Paesi Bassi e del Principato di Liegi a Roma* (Milano, 1995), no. 119 [exhibition catalogue, Palais des Beaux-Arts, Brussels, 24 Feb – 21 May, 1995 and Palazzo delle Esposizioni, Rome, 16 June – 10 Sep 1995] · E. Barker, N. Webb, and K. Woods, eds., *The changing status of the artist* (1999) · W. Waterschoot, 'De Heere', *Nationaal biografisch woordenboek*, ed. J. Duverger (1977)

Heete [Woodstock], **Robert** (d. 1433), canonist and chaplain, was presumably a native of Woodstock, Oxfordshire. He became a scholar of Winchester College in 1400 and in 1405 a scholar of New College, Oxford. He became a fellow in 1408 and was admitted bachelor of canon law about 1415. Heete was a pupil of William Barrowe, doctor of canon law and afterwards bishop of Bangor and Carlisle. In 1413, when Barrowe was chancellor, Heete delivered a lecture on the first book of the *Decretals*. He was appointed chaplain of the chantry of the Holy Trinity in All Saints' Church, Oxford, in 1418 but held this office for less than a fortnight before exchanging it to become rector of St Mildred's, Oxford. In 1421 he was admitted a fellow of Winchester College and was subwarden at the time of his death twelve years later.

Heete owned New College MS 192 and was the author of part of its contents ('Lectura super primum librum decretalium … extractum ex diversis doctoribus', fols. 9–82v; 'Lectura super decretalium librum quintum', fols. 83–99; 'Brocarda juris canonici et civilis secundum R. [Heete?]'). He may also have written some of the other articles, which include several anonymous orations and some legal 'adversaria'. The volume bears the inscription 'Lib' R. Heete precij xiii s. iiij d.' and a statement that it was bequeathed by him for the use of any law fellow of the college. It is almost certain that he was also the author of a short life of William Wykeham preserved in a manuscript at Winchester College: 'Libellus seu tractatus de prosapia, vita, et gestis venerabilis patris et domini, domini Willelmi de Wykeham, nuper episcopi Wynton'. This volume is dated 1424 and contains a dedication to the fellows of Winchester and New colleges. The life preserved in New College MS 288, art. 3, under the title 'Brevis chronica de ortu, vita, et gestis nobilibus reverendi domini Willelmi de Wykeham', is extracted from Heete's life. It was printed by Wharton in his *Anglia sacra* (2.355–6), where it is erroneously ascribed to Thomas Chaundeler, warden of New College.

Heete compiled registers of scholars and fellows of Winchester College. His sizeable personal library contained books on canon law and theology as well as sermon collections. He died in Winchester on 27 February 1433 and was buried in the entrance to Winchester College chapel, to which he bequeathed service books, vestments, and plate. He also left thirty-one books to Winchester College and three to New College.

C. L. KINGSFORD, *rev.* F. DONALD LOGAN

Sources Emden, *Oxf.* · A. F. Leach, *A history of Winchester College* (1899) · H. Chilty, *N&Q*, 11th ser., 9 (1914), 466 · H. O. Coxe, ed., *Catalogus codicum MSS qui in collegiis aulisque Oxoniensibus hodie adservantur*, 2 vols. (1852) · [H. Wharton], ed., *Anglia sacra*, 2 vols. (1691)
Archives New College, Oxford, MSS 192, 288 · Winchester College, life of William Wykeham

Heffer, Eric Samuel (1922–1991), politician, was born on 12 January 1922 in Hertford, the son of William George Heffer, a poor bootmaker and shoe repairer, and his wife, Annie, *née* Nicholls, who, in Heffer's words, 'cooked for the gentry' (personal knowledge). Since he was the grandson of a brickmaker and a railway signalman, he could boast 'I am completely proletarian in background' (ibid.). His early life was heavily influenced by churchgoing, three times every Sunday. As a choirboy, at eight he led a strike for better pay. He remained a high-church Anglican, whether his politics were communist, syndicalist, or hard-left Labour. He was educated at the Bengeo junior school and, until fourteen, at the Longmore senior school in Hertford. He was then apprenticed as a carpenter. He later studied with the Workers' Educational Association and the National Council of Labour Colleges. He became a serious reader, glorying in his collection of 12,000 books crowding his large house in Liverpool.

Heffer joined the Labour Party at sixteen in 1938, but left it for the Communist Party in 1941, where he met and, on 15 December 1945, married Doris Murray, daughter of Herbert Murray of Liverpool. She was also at that stage a communist. He was expelled from the Communist Party in 1946 for leading an unauthorized strike of shipboard carpenters. The Communist Party even tried to persuade his wife to leave him. He rejoined Labour in 1949, but left it to form a semi-syndicalist Socialist Workers' Federation with Harry McShane in 1954. This failed, and Heffer rejoined Labour in 1956. His early progress was in trade unions. He became vice-president of the Liverpool Trades Council in 1958, and its president in 1959. He caught the attention of a local MP, Harold Wilson, in 1960, when he settled an unofficial seamen's strike. He was runner-up for assistant general secretary of the Woodworkers' Union (later embraced in the Union of Construction, Allied Trades, and Technicians) in 1962. In 1960 he was elected to Liverpool city council.

In October 1964 Heffer captured Walton constituency from its Conservative MP, Sir Kenneth Thompson. Walton was the northernmost working-class seat in Liverpool, and housed two football grounds, Anfield and Goodison

Eric Samuel Heffer (1922–1991), by unknown photographer

Park. It was also the cradle of Militant Tendency, Liverpool's Trotskyist movement. From the beginning, warmhearted but truculent Heffer backed all left-wing causes as an MP: in 1966 he demonstrated against the use of napalm in Vietnam before the American embassy, and against the 'wage freeze' implicit in the Prices and Incomes Bill. In 1967 he urged the end of Polaris submarines. An animal lover, he repeatedly sought to ban hare coursing. His short fuse led him to threaten tories Nicholas Winterton and Norman Tebbit. He accurately warned against an impending Liverpool dockers' strike, but refused Harold Wilson's offer of a post as parliamentary secretary for technology in September 1967. He preferred opposition: voting against curbs on the entry of Kenyan Asians with British passports, urging reform or abolition of the Lords, and especially campaigning against Barbara Castle's 1969–70 'In Place of Strife' effort to curb unions. Although initially pro-EEC, by 1971 he had voted against Edward Heath's entry effort. The joint runner-up with Barbara Castle in the elections to the shadow cabinet, when a vacancy occurred he insisted on an election, which he lost in March 1972. A deputy spokesman on employment from 1970, he quit in disagreement with spokesman Reg Prentice, who later became a Conservative.

When Labour unexpectedly became the government in March 1974, Heffer agreed to become minister of state for industry, but was sacked by Wilson when he insisted on making an anti-EEC speech during the 1975 referendum, a privilege the prime minister had limited to cabinet ministers. On his eighth attempt in October 1975 he was elected to Labour's national executive committee (NEC), squeezing off Denis Healey. As chairman of its organization committee, he invited those who did not accept clause 4 to leave the party. He always opposed any action against Militant. He urged Commons reforms, including a freedom of information act. He opposed Scottish devolution. In January 1980 he boasted: 'I was the only [Labour] Opposition Member who attacked the Soviet Union for going into Afghanistan' (personal knowledge). He was also prominent in support of the solidarity movement in Poland. Egged on by his ego and the Militants in his constituency—who he feared might turn against him—he aimed higher. In 1980 he wanted to contest Labour's leadership

against James Callaghan, until Michael Foot became the left's accepted candidate. He came close to contesting the deputy leadership against Denis Healey in 1981, but did not want to cut into the vote of Tony Benn, who came close. That year Heffer came third in the constituency section of the NEC and was also elected to the shadow cabinet, becoming Michael Foot's spokesman on Europe. In 1983 he stood as the hard-left candidate for the leadership, winning 6.3 per cent of the vote, against 72.3 per cent for Neil Kinnock and 19.3 per cent for Roy Hattersley. His political decline began when, at Labour's 1985 annual conference, Kinnock launched his blitz against Liverpool's Militant Tendency. Heffer walked indignantly off the platform, prompting Kinnock to remark that 'he was looking for a walk-out part'. Next year he lost his seat on the NEC. The following year, complaining Labour was being 'sold to the public like soap powder', he was the third runner-up. Next year he teamed up under Tony Benn to challenge Labour's Kinnock–Hattersley leadership. Against Hattersley's 66.8 per cent and John Prescott's 23.7 per cent, he won 9.5 per cent.

In 1989 Heffer announced he would not stand again, letting friends know that he had terminal cancer. He made his peace with friends on the left he had alienated by becoming the puppet of Militant. But he died battling against Labour loyalists such as his successor as MP for Liverpool Walton, Peter Kilfoyle. In his last two years he wrote four books, including an autobiography, *Never a Yes Man* (1991). He died of cancer of the stomach at his London home, 704 Keyes House, Dolphin Square, Pimlico, on 27 May 1991. He was survived by his wife; there were no children of the marriage. A memorial service was held at St Margaret's Church, Westminster, on 10 July 1991.

ANDREW ROTH

Sources E. Heffer, *Never a yes man* (1991) · Parliamentary Profiles files · *WWW*, 1991–5 · personal knowledge (2004) · *The Times* (28 May 1991) · *The Independent* (28 May 1991) · m. cert. · d. cert.
Archives Labour History Archive and Study Centre, Manchester, corresp. and papers | SOUND BL NSA, current affairs recording · BL NSA, oral history interview · BL NSA, party political recordings
Likenesses photograph, repro. in *The Times* · photograph, repro. in *The Independent* (28 May 1991) · photograph, repro. in *The Independent* (6 June 1991) · photograph, News International Syndication, London [*see illus.*] · photographs, repro. in Heffer, *Never a yes man*
Wealth at death under £125,000: administration, 13 Sept 1991, *CGPLA Eng. & Wales*

Heffer, Reuben George (1908–1985), bookseller, was born on 29 January 1908 at 24 Chesterton Road, Chesterton, Cambridge, the younger son and third of three children of Ernest William Heffer, bookseller, of Cambridge, and his wife, Louisa Marion Beak, and grandson of the founder, William Heffer, of W. Heffer & Sons Ltd, booksellers, publishers, stationers, and printers. He was educated at the Perse School, Cambridge, where he acquired a lifelong interest in modern languages, especially French; that was the subject he read at Corpus Christi College, Cambridge, gaining a second class (division one) in part two of the modern and medieval languages tripos (1928) before completing his degree with a third in part two of the economics tripos (1929). He trained for a period at the London School of Printing.

Heffer then joined the family firm, with the intention that he should be involved with the printing side. But the untimely death in 1932 of his elder brother, Arthur, required his move to the bookshop in Petty Cury, where he worked with his father. On 25 June 1935 he married Nesta May (1911/12–1981), the daughter of Owen Thomas *Jones, professor of geology at Cambridge. In 1942 he joined the Royal Air Force, serving in flight control, Fighter Command, and then as a squadron leader at the Air Ministry, being demobilized in 1945. He took charge of the bookshop in 1948, became chairman of the firm in 1959, and continued thus until 1975, remaining a director after his retirement. A strong supporter of his trade, he was on the council of the Booksellers' Association, of the 1948 Book Trade Committee, of the Society of Bookmen, and of the Sette of Odd Volumes. Under his direction the family firm expanded to become international booksellers of high repute; and Heffer printed, published, and sold a wide range of books, particularly in medicine, oriental studies, and phonetics. He was not by nature a committee man; his shyness and his distrust of his natural speaking voice dictated his eschewing public office. He was one of the shrewdest and most balanced of booksellers never to be president of the Booksellers' Association.

A man of considerable charm, Heffer was unfailingly generous of his time and quiet advice. He was not at home with detail or administration or planning, but he was always meticulous in valuing and thanking those of his colleagues who undertook those chores on his behalf; he was a good master. A convivial man, he enjoyed good company as much as he contributed to it, and he enjoyed entertaining simply in the Norfolk country house that he had bought after the Second World War. He and his wife made many friends among booksellers and publishers. When his wife died in 1981 he was bereft of a lively and positive companion, and sadly he remained in many ways lost without her vivacity. Honest and caring, he was above all a liberal man. Though holding firm views, he never inflicted them on anyone. His great talent, giving him abiding pleasure, was to encourage success in those younger than himself.

Heffer kept his connections with his school and his college, presenting and maintaining there the splendid gown for schoolmaster fellow-commoners. He was also responsible in many ways for the continued existence of the *Cambridge Review*. Outside his career in the book trade he served as a JP for twenty-seven years, and with the Marriage Guidance Council, the Trustee Savings Bank, and the Cambridge Preservation Society. He helped to found the Bell School of Languages. All these activities were, typically for him, centred in Cambridge, for he had a strong sense of family and community. In recognition of his support, the Open University awarded him an honorary MA degree in 1979.

Heffer died on 17 July 1985 at his home, 89 Barton Road, in Cambridge. While swimming, as he loved to do, in the lake at the bottom of his garden, he suffered a heart attack. His son Nicholas became chairman of Heffers in 1984, third in direct line from its founder.

JOHN WELCH, rev.

Sources *The Bookseller* (27 July 1985), 396–8 · *The Times* (22 July 1985) · *The Times* (25 July 1985) · b. cert. · m. cert. · d. cert. · personal knowledge (1990) · private information (1990)
Wealth at death £157,574: probate, 2 Sept 1985, *CGPLA Eng. & Wales*

Hegat, William (*fl.* 1598–1621), humanist and academic, was born at Glasgow, the son most probably of William Hegat (*c.*1522–1591/2), burgess of Glasgow and notary, and his wife, Janet Graham (*d.* 1608). The elder William Hegat certainly had a son William, who in 1591 signed as brother of the former's eldest son, Archibald. The younger William was possibly the student who matriculated at Glasgow University in January 1591, then in 1592 graduated and was involved in a legal action.

Two works by Hegat were published at Poitiers in 1598 and 1599 respectively. The first, *Gallia victrix*, was a dramatic dialogue between the gods in Latin verse; its dedication to Walter Stewart, prior of Blantyre and treasurer of Scotland, applauds the recent edict of Nantes and the equal rights granted to Scots in France. In December 1599 Hegat matriculated at the University of Paris, in 1602 he was procurator of the German nation, and in 1600 and 1603 he had works published in Paris. It is unlikely that he was the William Hegat, Archibald's son, who assaulted a minister at Glasgow in August 1602.

Thomas Dempster, usually unreliable, provides the surest information on Hegat. In his *Historia ecclesiastica*, published posthumously in 1627, Dempster speaks of living with Hegat twenty years previously and outlines his career: first, teaching arts at Poitiers; then going to Paris; making a name for himself at Luxeuil or Lisieux ('Luxoveo'); teaching in a Jesuit college at Dijon; returning to Paris; and finally going to Bordeaux, to the Collège d'Aquitaine. The poem attributed to Hegat in Thomas Strachan's *Album amicorum*, dated Bordeaux, 1 January 1600, is not his. He did, however, publish a work at Nantes in 1604.

Hegat had presumably settled at Bordeaux by late 1616, when he delivered and published an oration there. Among the Scots at Bordeaux were Catholics, including other Hegats, and protestants, including the ministers John Cameron and Gilbert Primrose. Tension resulted, with Hegat openly hostile to Primrose. In 1620 the presbytery in Glasgow took action over devotional objects sent by Hegat, describing him as 'ane notorious and profest papist' (Durkan, 155). Indeed his father and his brother Archibald had been in conflict with the protestant authorities in Glasgow in the 1580s and 1590s. Archibald's sons were likewise committed Catholics: two were involved with the Jesuit John Ogilvie during his mission in Scotland in 1613–15; two others were ordained priest abroad and were connected with Bordeaux. Significantly Ogilvie's *Relatio incarcerationis*, smuggled out of prison piecemeal, was delivered to the Jesuit superior at Bordeaux.

The last known fact about Hegat is a publication at Bordeaux in 1621. Dempster, before his death in 1625, wrote that Hegat was alive and cultivating the muses with Robert Balfour, likewise an academic at Bordeaux. Hegat's publications, all in Latin, were slight and literary rather than scholarly, showing him in some demand for marking festive occasions with an oration or celebratory verse. Other writers included short poems by him in their published work, and Dempster also praised his personal qualities.   MARK DILWORTH

Sources *Thomae Dempsteri Historia ecclesiastica gentis Scotorum, sive, De scriptoribus Scotis*, ed. D. Irving, rev. edn, 2 vols., Bannatyne Club, 21 (1829) • A. G. Hepburn, 'A newly recorded book by William Hegate', *Innes Review*, 4 (1953), 118–19 • J. Durkan, 'John Ogilvie's Glasgow associates', *Innes Review*, 21 (1970), 153–6 • R. Renwick, ed., *Abstracts of protocols of town clerks of Glasgow*, 11 vols. (1894–1900) • W. A. McNeill, 'Scottish entries in the *Acta rectoria universitatis Parisiensis*, 1519 to c.1633', *SHR*, 43 (1964), 66–86 • C. Innes, ed., *Munimenta alme Universitatis Glasguensis / Records of the University of Glasgow from its foundation till 1727*, 3, Maitland Club, 72 (1854), 6, 60 • *Guglielmi Hegati Scoti Glasguensis Gallia victrix* (1598) • *Reg. PCS*, 1st ser., vols. 4, 6 • Francisque-Michel, *Les Ecossais en France*, 2 (1862), 194–6

Hegge, Robert (1597?–1629), antiquary and writer, was born in Durham, probably in the summer of 1597, apparently the eldest son of Stephen Hegge, notary public, and his wife, Anne, daughter of Robert Swyft, prebendary of Durham, and great-grandson of Thomas *Lever (1521–1577), master of Sherburn Hospital there. Admitted scholar of Corpus Christi College, Oxford, on 7 November 1614, he graduated BA on 13 February 1618 and proceeded MA on 17 March 1621. Befriended and encouraged by the mathematician and antiquary Thomas Allen of Gloucester Hall, Hegge was reckoned, according to Anthony Wood, 'the best in the University for the Mathematical faculty, History and Antiquities … as afterwards for his excellent knowledge in the Sacred Scriptures' (*Ath. Oxon.*, 2.457), and was elected a probationer fellow of his college on 27 December 1624.

At Corpus, Hegge engaged in a variety of college activities. He contributed Latin verses to collections assembled for presentation to its visitor Bishop James Montague of Winchester in March 1617, for presentation by the university to the king the same year and in commemoration of James's death (*Oxoniensis academiae parentalia*, 1625). He compiled a catalogue of men admitted to Corpus and not only produced a fine illustrated treatise on the theory and construction of sundials (Corpus Christi College, Oxford, MS 40) but also contributed practically to the restoration of the notable dial in the college's front quadrangle, of which there are drawings in his manuscript. He was tutor to Henry Oxenden, the future poet, who matriculated in 1626 and with whose family, the Oxendens of Maydekin, near Barham, Kent, he enjoyed good relations. One of his theological lectures, given in the college hall, was later published by his friend (and possibly kinsman) John Hall of Gray's Inn as *R. Heggi Dunelmensis in aliquot sacrae paginae lectiones* (1647).

Hegge was also interested in the history of his native county. His treatise on St Cuthbert and his churches at Lindisfarne, Cuncastre, and Dunholme, with an epistle to the reader dated 1 July 1626, published as *The Legend of St Cuthbert* first by Richard Baddeley, secretary to Bishop Thomas Morton of Durham, in 1663 and eventually by J. B. Taylor in 1816, is a work of local patriotism. However, although Hegge's grandmother Anne Lever Swyft had bequeathed among her jewellery a figure of St Cuthbert 'in jewels and ivory' (Hegge, vi), he himself was scornful of relics and by implication critical of the ecclesiastical domination of the Durham area. While he recounted the miracles following Cuthbert's death, he condemned subjection of the secular to the spiritual power: 'how could not the Monks but (like magicians when they meet together) laugh … to see royaltie so captivated under superstition, and majestie so dejected, when the end of their pretended sanctitie was only slothe, and fattnesse' (p. 33). Cuthbert, he considered, might be 'more beholden to the art of his monks, then to his own sanctity for his incorruption' (p. 51).

Hegge died of apoplexy on 11 June 1629, and was buried in the antechapel at Corpus. Some of his manuscripts passed to his younger brother Stephen Hegge (1599–1661), admitted to St John's College, Cambridge, in 1617 and ordained deacon at York in 1626, and his son Stephen (1645–1668), also of St John's, both of whom added to his collections of funerary inscriptions, before the papers finally returned to Corpus. Other manuscripts from Hegge's antiquarian collections remained in the college or passed to the Bodleian Library, the British Library, and Cambridge University Library.   VIVIENNE LARMINIE

Sources P. Pattenden, 'Robert Hegge: an Oxford antiquary', *Oxoniensia*, 45 (1980), 284–99 • Foster, *Alum. Oxon.* • Wood, *Ath. Oxon.*, new edn, 2.456–8 • Wood, *Ath. Oxon.: Fasti* (1815), 372, 393 • R. Hegge, *The legend of St Cuthbert*, ed. J. B. Taylor (1816) • *Hist. U. Oxf. 4: 17th-cent. Oxf.*, 386 • *BL cat.*
Archives BL, treatises and collections, Add. MS 27423 • BL, Legend of St Cuthbert, 1628, Sl MS 1322 • CCC Oxf., MSS 40, 430, 408, 28 | BL, Cotton MS Titus D.C. • BL, Cotton MS Vespasian D. VIII • BL, letters to Oxenden family, Add. MS 27999 • Bodl. Oxf., Rawl. MS poetry 171 • Bodl. Oxf., Top. Oxon. MS e 68 • CUL, MS kk.5.32

Heidegger, Johann Jakob (1666–1749), impresario, was born in Zürich on 19 June 1666, the son of a professor of theology from Nuremberg. He married in 1688, but otherwise his early career remains obscure. At an unknown date he abandoned his wife and four children and went to England. Anecdotes about his joining Queen Anne's life guards seem implausible.

By 1707 Heidegger was participating vigorously in the introduction of Italian opera to London. In April of that year he helped select arias for the pasticcio *Thomyris* at Drury Lane, and though credited in *A Critical Discourse upon Opera's in England* (1709) with *Clotilda*, performed at the Queen's Theatre in March 1709, he probably only translated the libretto. On 14 January 1710 *The Tatler* marvelled that 'such a Creature as Count Hideracre has been able to get 2 or 3000 guineas an Opera subscribed'—an extravagant sum, and the newspaper's remark was designed to critique the use of social graces to raise money for frivolous purposes. References in 'Colman's opera register' and the Coke papers show that Heidegger worked for the

Johann Jakob Heidegger (1666–1749), by John Faber junior, 1749 (after Jean Baptiste van Loo)

opera company at the Queen's Theatre in a secondary managerial capacity under various proprietors until Owen Swiney fled to the continent, bankrupt, in February 1713. For the balance of the season Heidegger managed on behalf of the singers. His long association with Handel began in these years.

An exchequer lawsuit shows that the exiled Swiney took Heidegger into partnership for the 1713/14 season. However, the inadequately underwritten enterprise lost still more money, and Heidegger was at risk of being ejected from the theatre and liable for large debts. The arrival in London of George I, a great opera lover, gave hope for the future, but 1714/15 was financially problematic despite the coronation festivities. Though Heidegger did succeed in disencumbering himself of Swiney, he had to fold the company in 1717. Operas with which Heidegger's name is linked as adapter, translator of the libretto, or simply manager include *Almahide* (1710), *Antiochus* (1711), *Ernelinda* (1713), *Arminio* (1714), *Lucio Vero* (1715), and Handel's *Amadigi* (1715). The lease Heidegger signed with Sir John Vanbrugh in 1716 at a rent of £400 per annum gave him control of the opera house, putting him at the centre of London's operatic ventures into the 1740s.

Advertisements for and references to masquerades in the capital start about 1711, and most authorities have assumed that Heidegger promoted the popular, later notorious, upper-class entertainments from the start. However, no evidence associates him with them until about 1715 or 1716. Heidegger's masquerades flourished into the 1730s; his last known advertisement for one was in February 1743, by which time they had fallen out of fashion. These fancy-dress parties were expensive to mount (food, drink, entertainment, and light were all lavish), but entry ran as high as a guinea and a half per ticket, and profits of £300–500 were possible. Anecdote credits Heidegger with an annual income of £5000, but so large a figure can hardly ever have been true.

From 1719 Heidegger was associated with the Royal Academy of Music as one of the 'directors' of the joint stock company, as landlord of the theatre, and evidently in a salaried capacity in management. When the feuding sopranos Faustina Bordoni and Francesca Cuzzoni disrupted the company in 1727, an anonymous pamphlet, *The Contretemps, or, Rival Queens*, satirized him as 'High-Priest to the Academy of Discord'. After the financial collapse of the opera in 1728, he joined forces with Handel and gained permission from the directors to use the academy's scenery and costumes for five years. Their new company opened on 2 December 1729 with Handel's *Lotario*. Though run on relatively economical lines, the venture failed to flourish. Their difficulties were compounded by the establishment of a rival company, the Opera of the Nobility at Lincoln's Inn Fields Theatre, to which the celebrated castrato Senesino immediately defected. After a season of competition in 1733/4, Handel and Heidegger ended their arrangement for the time being. While Heidegger rented his premises to the rival venture, Handel moved to Covent Garden. Two highly unprofitable seasons later, in 1737, following the demise of the Nobility experiment, they were back at the King's Theatre, Haymarket, this time with Handel working for Heidegger at a salary of £1000. Despite public acclaim for Handel, the subscription they offered for 1738/9 was rejected, forcing a retreat from opera, though Handel rented the theatre for oratorios. In the early 1740s an opera company run by Lord Middlesex occupied the theatre, but Heidegger is not known to have had any active part in its management.

Prominent in London society for more than thirty years, Heidegger became a celebrated figure. He was satirized (mostly good-humouredly) by John Hughes, Alexander Pope, Henry Fielding (as Count Ugly in *The Author's Farce*), and William Hogarth (particularly in *The Bad Taste of the Town*, 1724, and *Masquerade Ticket*, 1727), and he seems to have made a joke of the ugliness for which he was renowned. Pope refers to 'a monster of a fowl, / Something betwixt a Heideggre and owl' (*Dunciad*, book 1), and Heidegger reputedly won a wager with Lord Chesterfield that no uglier face could be found in London. In the early 1720s those who had moral objections to masquerades attacked Heidegger more virulently. On 12 February 1723 the grand jury for Middlesex petitioned the House of Commons to suppress Heidegger's entertainments 'as Nurseries of Lewdness, Extravagance, and Immorality, and also a Reproach and Scandal to Civil government' (Deutsch, 149). The bishop of London denounced the parties from the pulpit on 6 January 1724, and moralists campaigned against Heidegger in newspapers and pamphlets. The king's public declaration that he would continue to attend masquerades muted but did not silence the reformers.

Heidegger was nearly fifty years old when he began to appear in the public eye in England, but his flair for mounting masquerades quickly won the favour of George I, and his lease on the King's Theatre, Haymarket, made him an insider in the socially rarified if financially unprofitable world of Italian opera. He served for many years as a well-remunerated organizer of public and private festivities, including the October 1727 illumination of Westminster Hall for the coronation of George II, to whom Edward Croft-Murray reports Heidegger was appointed gentleman of the privy chamber on 13 June 1728. He evidently made quite a lot of money, some of which he spent on decorations to his house at 4 Maids of Honour Row in Richmond, Surrey. Though necessarily a gambler, he was reportedly also generous, especially to indigent Swiss immigrants.

Heidegger died at Richmond on 5 September 1749. His wife had died two years earlier, and their children had all predeceased him. In his will he left to his illegitimate daughter, Elizabeth Pappet (d. 1765), termed his 'goddaughter', whose mother was perhaps a box keeper of the same name at the King's Theatre, Haymarket, his tenant's interest in the theatre; her husband, Captain (later Vice-Admiral) Peter Denis, sold the interest in 1767. The *General Advertiser*, commenting on Heidegger's death, observed, 'Of him, it may be truly said, what one Hand received from the Rich, the other gave to the Poor'. As opera manager he seems to have been scrupulously fair and a man of his word. His honour and amiable character seem largely to have offset his association with masquerades in the public mind.   JUDITH MILHOUS

Sources Highfill, Burnim & Langhans, *BDA* · S. Sadie, ed., *The new Grove dictionary of opera*, 4 vols. (1992) · J. Milhous and R. D. Hume, eds., *Vice Chamberlain Coke's theatrical papers, 1706–1715* (1982) · O. E. Deutsch, *Handel: a documentary biography* (1955) · E. Gibson, *The Royal Academy of Music, 1719–1728: the institution and its directors* (1989) · T. Vetter, *Johann Jakob Heidegger, ein Mitarbeiter G. F. Händels* (1902) · J. Milhous and R. D. Hume, 'Heidegger and the management of the Haymarket opera, 1713–17', *Early Music*, 27 (1999), 65–84 · R. D. Hume, 'Handel and opera management in London in the 1730s', *Music and Letters*, 67 (1986), 347–62 · E. Croft-Murray, 'The painted hall in Heidegger's house at Richmond', *Burlington Magazine*, 78 (1941), 105–12, 155–9 · *A critical discourse upon opera's in England* (1709)

Likenesses M. Ricci, drawing, c.1720 · J. Groupy, engraving, 1728/9 (after M. Ricci) · M. Laroon, drawing, 1736, BM · J. Faber junior, mezzotint, 1749 (after J. B. van Loo), BM, NPG [*see illus.*] · Barlow, death mask?, line engraving, NPG · Barlow, line engraving, NPG · W. Sharp, two line engravings, NPG

Heigham, Sir Clement (b. in or before **1500**, d. **1571**), judge and speaker of the House of Commons, was born towards the end of the fifteenth century, being the eldest son of Clement Heigham (d. 1500) of Lavenham, Suffolk, and Maud, daughter of Lawrence Cooke of the same place. Several members of the family were connected with the law, most notably Richard Heigham (d. 1500), serjeant-at-law, who had been a bencher of Lincoln's Inn in the time of Edward IV. Clement was admitted to Lincoln's Inn in 1517 and called to the bar in 1525. By 1528 he was chief bailiff of the abbey of Bury St Edmunds, and from 1529 until his death a justice of the peace for Suffolk. He was a bencher of the Middle Temple by 1534 and in 1538 gave his first reading on the statute *De conjunctim feoffatis*; he served as treasurer in 1540–41 and gave a second reading in 1548.

About 1520 Heigham married Anne, daughter of John Munnings of Semer Hall (or perhaps of Thomas Munnings of Bury), with whom he had five surviving daughters. Heigham leased the manor of Semer from the abbey of Bury, and purchased it after the dissolution. His second wife was Anne (1505–1589), daughter of George Waldegrave of Smallbridge, and widow of Henry Bures of Acton. From Thomas Wentworth, first Baron Wentworth, to whom he was distantly related by this marriage, he acquired in 1539 the manor of Barrow in Suffolk and built Barrow Hall, which survived until the early eighteenth century. An adherent of the Roman church, he came suddenly to prominence on the accession of Mary I, when he rallied behind the new regime, becoming a member of parliament in October 1553 and a member of the privy council the following May. In five years he sat for the four constituencies of Rye, Ipswich, West Looe, and Lancaster, and was active on committees and commissions. As speaker of the Commons in 1554–5 he presided over the restoration of papal authority in England, and was rewarded with a knighthood on 27 January 1555. According to Foxe, he was particularly zealous in the persecution of protestants.

On 2 March 1558 Heigham was appointed chief baron of the exchequer, the last occupant of that position who was not a serjeant; but he held the office for little more than eight months, until the queen's death in November. Some sources say that he was continued in office briefly by Elizabeth, but no patent has been found and it seems likely that he was the only judge not reappointed in 1558; his successor (Sir Edward Saunders) was appointed on 22 January 1559. Heigham retired to his seat at Barrow and slid back into obscurity, though he was permitted to remain an active county magistrate and retained his office of *custos rotulorum*. He died on 9 March 1571, and was commemorated in Barrow church by a canopied monument with brass figures of himself in armour between his two wives, and a long inscription. His eldest son, Sir John *Heigham (1540–1626), was a member of parliament under Elizabeth I and James I.   J. H. BAKER

Sources HoP, *Commons, 1509–58*, 2.329–31 · W. Hervey, *The visitation of Suffolk, 1561*, ed. J. Corder, 2, Harleian Society, new ser., 3 (1984), 596–7 · W. P. Baildon, ed., *The records of the Honorable Society of Lincoln's Inn: the black books*, 1 (1897) · D. MacCulloch, *Suffolk and the Tudors: politics and religion in an English county, 1500–1600* (1986) · D. MacCulloch, 'The *Vita Mariae Angliae Reginae* of Robert Wingfield of Brantham', *Camden miscellany, XXVIII*, CS, 4th ser., 29 (1984), 181–301, esp. 206, 296 · Sainty, *Judges*, 95 · L. Abbott, 'Public office and private profit: the legal establishment in the reign of Mary Tudor', *The mid-Tudor polity, c.1540–1560*, ed. J. Loach and R. Tittler (1980), 137–58 · Norwich Consistory Court, 386 Flack · Barrow register, Suffolk RO, Bury St Edmunds, MS FL 525/4/1 · Baker, *Serjeants*, 170 · will, PRO, PROB 11/53, fols. 203–204v

Likenesses brass effigy on monument, c.1570, Barrow church, Suffolk

Heigham, Sir John (**1540–1626**), landowner, was born about July or August 1540, the first son of Sir Clement *Heigham (b. in or before 1500, d. 1571), judge and speaker of the House of Commons, and his second wife, Anne (1505–1589), daughter of George Waldegrave of Smallbridge, Suffolk, and widow of Henry Bures of Acton, Suffolk. Sir Clement Heigham increased the family estate through royal service, especially under Mary I. Following the accession of Elizabeth I, he retired from public life to the house that he built at Barrow, Suffolk, a move that reflected the strong Catholic convictions which he held to his death. Strong religious feelings passed from father to son, but with a twist. Unlike his father, John Heigham became a zealous protestant and, with his friend and neighbour Sir Robert Jermyn, the leading Suffolk gentleman of the cause of godly reformation.

Nothing is known of John Heigham's early education. He probably matriculated at Trinity Hall, Cambridge, in 1555 and is known to have entered Lincoln's Inn in 1558, where he was called to the bar in 1565. Heigham served at St Quentin in 1557. On 9 December 1562 he married Anne (d. 1619), daughter and coheir of Edmund Wright of Burnt Bradfield, Suffolk, and his second wife, Frances. The couple had four sons, including Sir Clement Heigham (d. 1634), and nine daughters. John Heigham appears to have succeeded to the family estates following his father's death in March 1571 and entertained Elizabeth at Barrow Hall on her progress through East Anglia in the summer of 1578. It was on this occasion that he was knighted.

Although Heigham's involvement in Suffolk politics preceded his father's death— he sat in the House of Commons as MP for the town of Sudbury in 1563—his standing in the county grew substantially in the 1570s. He was appointed JP for Suffolk in 1573, served as sheriff from 1576 to 1577, and was a deputy lieutenant of the shire from 1585. He also acted as a commissioner for piracy in 1577 and for grain in 1586, and held other local offices.

Heigham's religious convictions nearly proved his undoing as his zeal for further reformation in west Suffolk and particularly his support for the godly nonconformist preachers of the town of Bury St Edmunds, John Handson and James Gayton, brought him by the early 1580s into conflict with the attempts of the bishop of Norwich, Edmund Freke, to rein in clerical nonconformity. Freke's success in silencing Handson and Gayton seems to have goaded Heigham and other godly magistrates, such as Jermyn, to respond by attempting the removal of the non-preaching conformist curates from the town's churches. Pressure was brought to bear on these reading ministers to preach and, when they delivered their sermons, Heigham and his fellow magistrates charged the curates with preaching false doctrine. Or so Freke alleged. Heigham and Jermyn were charged with interfering in ecclesiastical matters and with countenancing separatist preachers at a time when the religious tensions in Bury had reached breaking point. Both men bore the brunt of the crown's determination to defend episcopal authority and conformity and in 1583, following the public execution of two separatists in Bury, both Heigham and Jermyn were removed from the commission of the peace. Whether or not Heigham was restored the following year

through the intervention of Robert Dudley, earl of Leicester, seems doubtful, but the earl did write in his favour in 1584. The best evidence would seem to indicate that although he remained active in county politics as a deputy lieutenant and enjoyed the support of the privy council, he appears to have been kept off the Suffolk bench until 1593. The anomaly of this position can only have been heightened when he was returned as MP for Ipswich in 1584 and as a knight of the shire for Suffolk in 1586 and 1604.

Heigham was an active parliamentarian, whose interests in both godly reformation and in Suffolk were reflected in the numerous committees to which he was appointed. In the parliament of 1586 he was one who spoke in favour of the speedy execution of Mary, queen of Scots, and the following year introduced a motion appealing for the release of Peter Wentworth and others held in the Tower of London. He appears to have moved from Barrow Hall to his house in Bury, perhaps by 1615, and maintained an active interest in county affairs until the end. Following his first wife's death in December 1619, Heigham married again. His second wife was Anne, the daughter of William Poley of Boxted, Suffolk, who predeceased him in June 1623. His will, which he drew up in Bury on 20 April 1626, 'being faynt and weak in body' and of the age of 'fower score and six yeares within a fewe monthes complete', reflects the strength of his protestant convictions. His soul bequest was a full statement of his trust in Christ's atonement and he requested that his 'good and lovinge freind' William Bedell, of the neighbouring parish of Horringer, deliver a funeral sermon 'to Gods glory and the edificacion of others' (Suffolk RO, MS IC 500/1/95 (148)). Heigham died between 20 April and 3 May, when he was buried at Barrow. A monument was erected to him in Barrow church at a cost of £40; the epitaph was later replaced by an inscription in memory of his eldest son, Clement.   JOHN CRAIG

Sources P. Collinson, 'The puritan classical movement in the reign of Elizabeth I', 2 vols., PhD diss., U. Lond., 1957 · J. Craig, *Reformation, politics and polemics: the growth of protestantism in East Anglian market towns, 1500–1610* (2001) · HoP, *Commons, 1558–1603*, 2.285–6 · D. MacCulloch, 'Catholic and puritan in Elizabethan Suffolk', *Archiv für Reformationsgeschichte*, 72 (1981), 232–89 · D. MacCulloch, *Suffolk and the Tudors: politics and religion in an English county, 1500–1600* (1986) · J. J. Muskett, *Suffolk manorial families*, 3 vols. (1900–10) · J. Gage, *The history and antiquities of Suffolk: Thingoe hundred* (1838) · W. A. Copinger, *The manors of Suffolk*, 7 vols. (1905–11) · Venn, *Alum. Cant.* · will, Suffolk RO, Bury St Edmunds, MS IC 500/1/95 (148)

Heigham, John [*alias* Roger Heigham] (*b. c.*1568, *d.* in or after 1634), bookseller, of whose life very little is known, in 1628 put his age at about sixty. He may at one time have worked for the London bookbinder William Wrench, whose secret Catholic press in Whitefriars was broken up in August 1597. Heigham himself was committed to the Gatehouse prison, London, in May 1597 and transferred to the Bridewell on 4 June. He may also be the Higham who was sent to the Bridewell in June 1599 after re-entering England illegally at Dover. In 1603 he left England, settling first in Douai, and in 1613 moved to St Omer, where he remained until at least 1632. After arriving in Flanders he initially went by the name Roger Heigham, perhaps to disguise his identity, or to distinguish himself from another John Heigham who had taken part in the northern uprising. He reverted to the use of the name John in 1610. Between 1603 and 1609, while living in Douai, he married Marie Boniface, a native of Arras, and they had at least one child before moving to St Omer, where seven more were baptized.

Heigham maintained himself as a merchant, specializing in the book trade and commissioning printing from Pierre Auroi, Charles Boscard, and Boscard's widow. His collaborations with these printers made him the most productive English Catholic publisher of the early seventeenth century after the English College press. He organized the printing of books, and also smuggled into England books published by himself and by others. He travelled to London with a cargo of books in 1608 and arranged the transport back of pupils for the English College at St Omer, and the following year his wife was apprehended smuggling Catholic books into England.

The great majority of books bearing Heigham's name as publisher were reprints of standard semi-liturgical texts such as the Tridentine primer, manual, breviary, and Jesus psalter, and of Counter-Reformation classics by such authors as Nicholas Sander, Thomas Stapleton, and Robert Southwell, or translations of continental writers, including Francis de Sales, Luis de Granada, Peter Canisius, and Robert Bellarmine. The emphasis was devotional, although Heigham did publish a few original controversial works, notably by Anthony Champney and Richard Broughton, and probably published more anonymously. He himself translated a number of devotional works and wrote an exposition of the mass (1622) and two controversial works, *The Gagge of the Reformed Gospell* (1623) and *Via vere tuta* (1631), which mentions his protestant background and discussions with protestant merchants and sightseers in Calais and St Omer.

Heigham's name was linked to more politically sensitive works, such as Thomas Fitzherbert's *Second Part of a Treatise Concerning Policy and Religion* (1610) and Matthew Kellison's *The Right and Jurisdiction of the Prelate and the Prince* (1617), but nothing was ever proved. Official inquiries by the Brussels authorities in 1613 at the request of the English ambassador did show Heigham to be the publisher of an unspecified book by Edward Weston. Heigham, his wife, and six of their children were apparently still living in 1634, when one son entered the English College at Rome; precise details of his death are unknown. PAUL ARBLASTER

Sources A. F. Allison, 'John Heigham of S. Omer (c.1568–c.1632)', *Recusant History*, 4 (1957–8), 226–42 • A. F. Allison and D. M. Rogers, eds., *The contemporary printed literature of the English Counter-Reformation between 1558 and 1640*, 2 (1994) • Brussels, Algemeen Rijksarchief Brussel, geheime raad spaanse periode, carton 1276/C, doc. 349; carton 1277/B, doc. 79 • J. Heigham, *Via vere tuta* (1631); repr. (1975)

Heighington, Musgrave (*bap.* 1680, *d.* 1764), composer, was one of the four recorded children of Ambrose Heighington of White Hurworth, Durham, and his wife, Catherine, daughter of Sir Edward Musgrave, first baronet, of Hayton Castle, Cumberland. He was baptized on 2 March 1680 at St Mary in the South Bailey, Durham. He described himself as 'of Queen's College, Oxford', but his connection to the university has not been traced. He was organist in Hull from 1717 to 1720, and gave concerts in Dublin between 1725 and 1728. His setting of Dryden's *Ode on St Cecilia's Day* (*Alexander's Feast*) was performed in Dublin on 22 October 1726, and later repeated elsewhere. The pantomime *The Enchanter, or, Harlequin Merlin* (now lost) possibly dated from this period. He was married twice, to Anne Conway and Mary Conner; one of them is described as 'an Irish lady'. In 1733 he and his family gave a concert in Great Yarmouth, and he was then chosen organist of that town. In 1736 he founded the Yarmouth Music Club, having become an honorary member of the Gentlemen's Society of Spalding, Lincolnshire, for whom he composed numerous works. In 1745 he took his family to live in Spalding when the Yarmouth city fathers cut his salary from £60 to £40, and in 1748 he was appointed organist at St Martin's, Leicester. About 1756 Heighington became organist at the Episcopalian church in Dundee; he founded the Dundee Musical Society, which was one of the earliest of its kind in Scotland. Very little of his music survives. He died in Dundee in June 1764.

A. H. MILLAR, rev. K. D. REYNOLDS

Sources C. Cudworth, 'Heighington, Musgrave', *New Grove* • 'Heighington, Musgrave', Grove, *Dict. mus.* (1927) • *IGI* • *N&Q*, 4th ser., 1 (1868), 435, 543

Heilbron, Sir Ian Morris [*formerly* Isidor Morris] (1886–1959), chemist, was born on 6 November 1886 in Glasgow, the younger son of David Heilbron, wine merchant, and his wife, Fanny Jessel. Originally named Isidor, he eventually adopted the name of Ian, by which he had been known for many years. He was educated at Glasgow high school, the Royal Technical College, Glasgow, and the University of Leipzig, where he took his PhD in 1909. Having come under the influence of the chemist G. G. Henderson at Glasgow and A. R. Hantzsch at Leipzig, Heilbron became a lecturer in chemistry at the Royal Technical College, Glasgow, in 1909. After an interruption due to the war and a brief period with the newly formed British Dyestuffs Corporation, he became professor of organic chemistry there in 1919–20. He subsequently held the chairs of organic chemistry at Liverpool (1920–33), Manchester (1933–5, in 1935–8 Sir Samuel Hall professor of chemistry), and the Imperial College of Science and Technology, London (1938–49). He resigned his chair in 1949 to become director of the newly formed Brewing Industry Research Foundation, Nutfield, Surrey, where he was mainly responsible for creating a centre of fundamental research into fermentation chemistry and biology. He retired in 1958.

Heilbron gained a worldwide reputation for his organizational skill and for his imagination in designing laboratories specifically fashioned to take advantage of new,

Sir Ian Morris Heilbron (1886–1959), by Howard Coster, 1940s

especially physical, techniques in organic chemical research. He was himself largely responsible for the general introduction of many of these into research work in Britain, notably the use of various forms of spectrometry, molecular distillation, microanalysis, and chromatography. He was a most inspiring teacher and a remarkable number of his students achieved eminence in either the academic or the industrial spheres at home or abroad. Especially in his later years he was widely sought as a consultant on scientific industrial problems.

Heilbron's scientific work began with a few years devoted mostly to questions of the detailed structures of various synthetic coloured substances. From 1919 onwards he was increasingly interested in miscellaneous naturally occurring materials, especially ones of pronounced biological activity. He determined the structure of squalene (from shark liver oil), and pioneered investigations on vitamins A and D as well as related carotenoid pigments and steroids, and over approximately thirty years became recognized as a world authority on the chemistry of these fields. This interest led to his opening up the broad topic of the general chemistry of acetylenic derivatives of diverse types to provide the foundation of much industrial development. Heilbron was in turn concerned with numerous other substances of actual or potential therapeutic interest and made important contributions to the chemistry of penicillin, particularly during the Second World War when the subject was of major national importance. He developed purification methods for the

small supplies of crude material that were initially available, and showed that penicillin exists in many forms. He wrote extensively in the scientific field as the author or part-author of about 300 publications dealing with original work. He was editor-in-chief for the *Dictionary of Organic Compounds*, and played an important part as chairman of the editorial board responsible at one time for Thorpe's *Dictionary of Pure and Applied Chemistry*, an important reference work of its time.

Heilbron received many academic honours including the fellowship (1931) and the Davy (1943) and Royal (1951) medals of the Royal Society, honorary degrees from Glasgow and Edinburgh, and membership and lectureships of the Chemical Society of London, of which he was president (1948–50), the American Chemical Society, the French Chemical Society, and the Royal Netherlands Academy of Sciences. In 1924 he married Elda Marguerite, daughter of Herbert J. Davis of Liverpool; they had two sons. He was deeply affected by her sudden death in 1954.

Heilbron saw active service in the First World War as lieutenant, later lieutenant-colonel, in the Army Service Corps, and as assistant director of supplies in Salonika, and was awarded the DSO. During the Second World War he was a scientific adviser successively to the ministries of Supply (1939–42) and Production (1942–5) and played a forceful part in the introduction of the insecticide DDT for military use in the south European and Far East regions.

During the course of a career which lasted for fifty years his experience of the growth of science and its increasing penetration into industry and the public service was probably unrivalled. Thus he took over many years a leading part, especially after 1945, in the organization of the International Union of Pure and Applied Chemistry and acted as chairman of various government committees and of the advisory councils of the Department of Scientific and Industrial Research (1950–54) and the Royal Military College of Science (1953–5). He was knighted in 1946, and received the American medal of freedom in 1947.

In a private capacity Heilbron was a man of fastidious taste, meticulous precision, and wide artistic interests. He died at St Mary's Hospital, Paddington, after a short illness, on 14 September 1959.

ALAN COOK, rev. K. D. WATSON

Sources A. H. Cook, *Memoirs FRS*, 6 (1960), 65–85 · E. R. H. Jones, *Proceedings of the Chemical Society* (1962), 242–5 · *The Times* (15 Sept 1959), 13a · *The Times* (21 Sept 1959), 19d · A. H. Cook and R. Robinson, *Nature*, 184 (1959), 767–8 · *CGPLA Eng. & Wales* (1959) · personal knowledge (1971) · private information (1971)
Archives ICL, professional and personal corresp.
Likenesses W. Stoneman, two photographs, 1931–53, NPG · H. Coster, photographs, 1940–49, NPG [*see illus.*]
Wealth at death £19,574 8s. 1d.: probate, 26 Nov 1959, *CGPLA Eng. & Wales*

Heilbronn, Hans Arnold (1908–1975), mathematician, was born on 8 October 1908 in Berlin, the son of Alfred Heilbronn, timber merchant, and his wife, Gertrud. No details of his ancestry are known, but the name (after a town in Baden-Württemberg) was not infrequent among Jews and suggests that the family was resident in Germany for a number of generations.

From 1914 to 1926 he attended the Heinrich von Kleist Realgymnasium, Berlin, and then entered university, reading first medicine, then mathematics and natural science in Berlin, Freiburg, and Göttingen. Mathematics soon became his main interest and in 1930 he became assistant to E. Landau at Göttingen. In 1931 he gained his DPhil for a thesis using function theory to improve prime number estimates. With his first few papers on prime numbers and analysis (some written jointly with Landau) he had begun to make a name for himself when Hitler's rise to power in 1933 effectively barred academic careers for Jews in Germany.

Landau, a man of high standards, had formed a good opinion of Heilbronn, and Harold Davenport, who had met Heilbronn in Germany, described him as 'one of the most promising German mathematicians' (Cassels and Fröhlich, 120). In November 1933 Heilbronn moved to Britain, supporting himself at first until, with the help of the Academic Assistance Council, he obtained a one-year position at Bristol University. At this time there was much interest in a conjecture made by Gauss in the early 1800s on the class number of definite binary quadratic forms, which was closely related to a problem on quadratic number fields. Some progress towards its proof had been made; building on this work, Heilbronn was able to prove Gauss's conjecture. His work represented important steps in an area of research that has remained active. In 1935 he was awarded a Bevan fellowship at Trinity College, Cambridge, and he spent the next five years there, during which time he wrote a dozen papers, some with Davenport, mainly on 'Waring's problem'. At this time he was able to help his parents and sister leave Germany and they made their home in Cambridge. When his fellowship expired in 1940, Trinity College council resolved to continue his position and salary, but, like many other refugees, he was interned. On his release he joined the Pioneer Corps and later the intelligence corps.

In 1946 Heilbronn returned to Bristol as reader; from 1949 he was professor and head of department. His research, interrupted by the war, resumed, as witness his elegant and decisive contributions on Euclid's algorithm, Zeta-functions, and the geometry of numbers. As a bachelor Heilbronn lived at Hawthorn's Hotel, across the road from the mathematics department, going to his family in Cambridge during vacations. Tall and athletic in appearance, he was keen on sports, especially rowing and tennis. His somewhat formal manner and the duelling scars he carried from his student days could be overpowering at first, but his friendly attitude, lacking all pomposity or aggressiveness, won him many friends. He was an excellent lecturer, always accessible to his students and taking an interest in their work, though his intellectual honesty did not allow him to pass over in politeness whatever he considered below standard. In all he exerted a major influence on mathematicians of the younger generation going well beyond what was recorded in print.

Towards the end of the 1950s, feeling concerned that government plans for university expansion would lead to a drop in standards, Heilbronn tried to convince policy makers of the dangers that lay ahead. This remained without effect so with characteristic directness he resigned his chair at Bristol and left the university in 1964. On 19 March of the same year he married Mrs Dorothy Greaves (1899/1900–1990), daughter of Philip Henry Shaw, a widow who lived in Cambridge and with whom he shared a keen interest in bridge. He also took up an invitation to spend some time in Caltech, and later that year he and his wife settled in Toronto, where he had accepted a chair at the university. Here he built up an active research school. Heilbronn was elected fellow of the Royal Society in 1951 and of the Royal Society of Canada in 1967. He was also a member (and during 1959–61 president) of the London Mathematical Society, the American Mathematical Society, and the Canadian Mathematical Congress. He was involved in planning the International Congress of Mathematicians in Vancouver in 1974, but at this time his previously robust health began to fail. He died on 28 April 1975 during an operation to implant a pacemaker. His widow on her death (13 September 1990) left a substantial sum to Trinity College, Cambridge, reportedly to fund scholarships for mathematics students from Europe.

P. M. Cohn

Sources J. W. S. Cassels and A. Fröhlich, *Memoirs FRS*, 22 (1976), 119–35 · E. J. Kani and R. A. Smith, *The collected papers of Hans Arnold Heilbronn* (1988) · Mrs Linfoot, *Mathematical Intelligencer*, 15 (1993), 39–43n · private information (2004) · m. cert.
Archives Bodl. Oxf., Society for Protection of Science and Learning MSS and home office files · Trinity Cam., corresp. with Harold Davenport
Likenesses photograph, repro. in Cassels and Fröhlich, *Memoirs FRS*, facing p. 119 · photograph, repro. in Kani and Smith, *Collected papers*, 1 · photograph, repro. in Linfoot, *Mathematical Intelligencer*, 39

Heimann, Carl Louis Bertram Reinhold (1896–1968), businessman, was born on 6 January 1896 in Copenhagen, Denmark, the second child in a family of three brothers and two sisters. His father, Carl Heimann (*d.* before 1920), was a cabinet-maker.

After running away from home Heimann moved to England in 1912, possessing only a few shillings and unable to speak English. In London he gained employment in the catering business, working his way up from waiter. His marriage to Jessie Cain (*b.* 1889/90), a restaurant proprietor, took place on 2 January 1919. In 1924 he was made catering manager for the People's Palace, east London, employed by a firm called Ye Mecca Cafes. Through his work for Mecca, Heimann soon became interested in the opportunities offered by dancing. In 1925 the firm, taking advantage of the boom for dancing, started to provide catering facilities for the popular dances held at the Royal Opera House, Covent Garden, then a dance-hall. Catering for the top nightclub the Café de Paris, in 1928, was a further source of inspiration. Heimann was quick to recognize the potential mass market open to dance-halls if they were properly organized and targeted the mass market decisively enough, believing that top-class facilities should be available to everyone. In 1928, while working as catering manager there, he persuaded Mecca Cafes to purchase Sherry's Dance Hall in Brighton with himself as general manager. He put his ideas to the test. Heimann was so successful that Sherry's was followed by the Ritz, Manchester, in 1930, the Locarno, Streatham, in 1931 and the Lido, Croydon, in 1932. He also persuaded Mecca to purchase a small band- and cabaret-booking agency run by Byron Davies, an entrepreneur he had first met at the Hammersmith Palais. By 1938 the Mecca Agency controlled 300 dance bands playing in some 2000 establishments, the largest in Britain.

By 1934 Heimann was general manager of Mecca Dancing, an offshoot of the original company. He had also begun to buy shares in the company, but was not yet in a controlling position. Stung by his only failure to date (a £50,000 loss at the Lido, Croydon), the Mecca board halted the dance-hall expansion. Heimann managed a compromise, however, persuading Mecca to allow him to branch out on his own. He was still general manager of the Mecca dance-halls, but was free to develop his own halls.

In 1935, therefore, Heimann started a joint venture with Alan Fairley, an important operator in the amusement and leisure industry in Scotland. This association proved his most fruitful. In 1936 they became joint managing directors of the Locarno, Glasgow. Their new circuit of dance-halls then grew rapidly and by 1938 had become the largest in the country, with halls in Edinburgh, Leeds, Sheffield, Nottingham, Bradford, and Birmingham. They also had several halls in London and by 1940 even controlled the Royal Opera House, Covent Garden, from where Heimann had first derived inspiration.

Heimann's formula for bringing social dancing to the masses was simple. Facilities were improved, prices lowered, and every attempt was made to get people dancing. Heimann's philosophy was 'to give Savoy Hotel standards at Palais prices'. His halls offered an unprecedented degree of luxury. Spectacular revolving bandstands were installed in the largest and elaborate cabarets with professional dancers were provided for the standard admission charge. Where previously one band had been employed, two, sometimes three, were taken on. Dancing competitions were also encouraged. Most importantly, however, Heimann commissioned his chief dance instructor, Adele England, to develop a series of simple, easy-to-dance group dances. The Palais Glide and the St Bernard's Waltz (1935) were followed by the Chestnut Tree and, the most successful, the Lambeth Walk (1938). This series of dances, promoted ruthlessly, lifted the fortunes of the dance business by countering the hesitation of potential dancers concerned about their ability to dance.

On the back of this independent success Heimann was invited in 1942 to join the board at Mecca, where he still managed their dance-halls. He was followed in 1945 by Fairley. In 1946 the two interests merged and Heimann and Fairley became joint chairmen of the new Mecca Ltd, taking 600,000 of the 700,000 shares issued.

Following the war Heimann's first big venture, in 1948, was to refurbish the Café de Paris, closed since 1941 when a bomb caused considerable damage. £7500 was spent on reopening it and it soon re-established itself as one of Europe's premier nightspots, attracting royalty and a host of cabaret stars from Grace Kelly to Noël Coward and Marlene Dietrich.

The 1950s saw further expansion, with more dance-halls and new projects, including ice- and roller-skating rinks. Moreover, Heimann introduced three of the post-war period's most popular entertainments. This he did in conjunction with Eric Morley, whom Heimann had first employed in 1946 as publicity sales manager for Mecca. First, in 1950, they introduced the ballroom dancing feature *Come Dancing*, BBC television's longest-running programme. Second, in 1951, they created the 'Miss World' competition as part of a publicity stunt for the Festival of Britain. Third, in 1961 they introduced commercial bingo to the UK. By this time Mecca was one of the biggest names in entertainment, valued at over £20 million, with a turnover of £5¼ million in 1960 and 7000 staff.

Heimann's first wife predeceased him, and on 12 January 1957 he married Brownie Elizabeth (b. 1925/6), daughter of John Scott Grimason, consulting engineer. Heimann never retired, and he was still working when he died at his home, Ashdown, 37 Hartfield Road, Bexhill, Sussex, on 11 November 1968. He was survived by his second wife and their two sons. A clever businessman, his work at Mecca brought dancing to the masses, making dance-halls comfortable, affordable, and respectable. Heimann's encouragement of ballroom dancing as a serious hobby also ensured that it would outlast the wider public demand for dance-halls and partner dancing.

JAMES J. NOTT

Sources R. Fairley, *Come dancing Miss World* (1966) · interviews with C. L. Heimann, 1938, U. Sussex, Mass-Observation Archive, topic collection: music, jazz and dancing, files 3/A and 3/E · P. J. S. Richardson, *A history of English ballroom dancing, 1910–1945* (1945) · *The Times* (13 Nov 1968) · C. Madge and T. Harrisson, *Britain by Mass-Observation*, 1939 · *Dancing Times* (Nov 1996) · H. S. Hampshire, 'Icons of the 20th C', *Dance News* (8 Feb 2001) · private information (2004) [correspondence with H. S. Hampshire, employee of Mecca] · m. certs. · d. cert. · CGPLA Eng. & Wales (1969)
Likenesses photograph, c.1960, repro. in Fairley, *Come dancing*
Wealth at death £106,378: probate, 31 Jan 1969, CGPLA Eng. & Wales

Heimann [*née* Klatzko], **Paula Gertrude** (1899–1982), psychoanalyst, was born on 3 February 1899 in Danzig, Poland, the fourth and youngest child of Russian Jewish parents. Heimann would later reflect that she was a replacement for a sister who had died; indeed this family background is significant in the context of her subsequent analytic experiences. Heimann's medical and psychiatric training, which was classically Freudian, was conducted at several German universities (she took her MD in 1928 in Berlin), during which time she married Franz Heimann, a specialist in internal medicine; in 1925 she gave birth to their only daughter Mirza. While living in Berlin, Heimann was analysed by Theodor Reik with a view to formally treating patients of her own, and she qualified in 1932 as associate member of the Berlin Psycho-Analytic Society.

Threatened under Nazism, Franz Heimann left for Switzerland while Paula and Mirza, denied the right to visit him, stayed in Germany. Mother and daughter left for

Britain in July 1933 with psychoanalyst Kate Friedlander, shortly after charges which had implicated Heimann in the Reichstag fire had been dropped; Heimann had been arrested following a party she had thrown on the night of the fire, an act which was taken to be a sign of her complicity. Heimann was first given a licence to practise in the East End of London cheek by jowl with prostitutes and criminals, but eventually she became part of a more conventional psychoanalytic circle in west central London. Supported by colleague Ernest Jones and friends such as the novelist Winifred Bryher, Heimann continued her training, obtained British medical qualifications at Edinburgh University in 1938, and was elected to associate membership of the British Psycho-Analytical Society in November 1933, leading to full membership in 1939; in 1944 she was recognized as a training analyst.

During her first few years in London, Heimann was assiduously courted by Melanie Klein as a confidant and disciple. Heimann had counselled Klein after the death of her son, but the roles were soon reversed when Heimann entered into a protracted analysis with Klein from approximately 1935 to 1953 (Heimann's marriage broke down in the early thirties). Colleagues saw the relationship between the two women as intense (replicating Heimann's relationship with her mother) and parasitical (Klein has been accused of stealing Heimann's ideas and passing them off as her own), and in the late 1940s Heimann staged a bid for independence. This was a courageous move given Klein's reputation and was to leave Heimann feeling 'traumatized'.

Taking a role in the British Psycho-Analytical Society's 'Controversial Discussions' of the validity of Klein's theories in the early 1940s Heimann was enlisted as her spokesperson and 'crown princess' (King, 6). Members of the society debated whether Klein's work was faithful to Freudian dogma or sufficiently divergent as to constitute a new school. Classic Freudians particularly took issue with Klein's reliance on psychiatry to theorize psychosis and her manipulation of Freud's concept of the death instinct. Heimann herself was already feeling her allegiance to Klein on the wane. She unofficially abdicated her position with the publication of her classic paper 'On counter-transference' (1950), which was later seen as a major contribution to psychoanalysis. The paper, arguing, against the tide of prevailing opinion, that the analyst's emotional responses to the patient could be a useful tool rather than an obstacle to analysis, enraged Klein, who saw it as a negation of her theories. Heimann's revolutionary idea was that counter-transference could be used to probe the patient's unconscious: the analyst's emotional attitude to the patient could be treated as clinical evidence because this response could be judged to be based on a correct analysis of the patient's motivations or intent. Heimann later took issue with Klein over her concept of innate envy, and in November 1955 officially resigned from the Melanie Klein Trust, becoming an independent for the rest of her career. In a sense Heimann had always been part of the independent, or Middle, group, a position which allowed her to maintain a balance between the more traditional Freudians and the Kleinians. Many feel her best work emanated from the divergence and rift from Klein, but she subsequently coupled Freudian theories with developments in ego psychology to develop original theories on narcissism and creativity, forming a close theoretical bond with Donald Winnicott. In 1947 Winnicott had voiced similar ideas regarding counter-transference, most notably that analysts must 'contain' the hatred evoked in them by their patients.

While Heimann is often portrayed as a passive pawn in Melanie Klein's power games this is to underestimate her own strong-mindedness, sense of humour, and charm. She died on 24 October 1982 at 42 Nottingham Place, Westminster, having continued to play a vital role in the society until her death. Her theories on counter-transference forever changed the relationship between analyst and analysand.   CLARE L. TAYLOR

Sources P. King, 'Paula Heimann's quest for her own identity as a psychoanalyst: an introductory memoir', in P. Heimann, *About children and children-no-longer: collected papers, 1942–1980*, ed. M. Tonnesman (1989), 1–25 • C. Geissmann and P. Geissmann, *A history of child psychoanalysis* (1992) • P. Grosskurth, *Melanie Klein: her world and her work* (1985) • J. Sayers, *Mothering psychoanalysis: Helene Deutsch, Karen Horney, Anna Freud and Melanie Klein* (1992) • E. Rayner, *The independent mind in British psychoanalysis* (1990) • *International Journal of Psycho-Analysis*, 64 (1983) • d. cert. • A. Limentani, *Between Freud and Klein: the psychoanalytic quest for knowledge and truth* (1989) • P. King and R. Steiner, eds., *The Freud–Klein controversies, 1941–1945* (1991)

Archives Melanie Klein Trust, London, corresp. with Melanie Klein

Likenesses photograph, repro. in Rayner, *The independent mind*, cover • photograph, repro. in *International Journal of Psycho-Analysis*, facing p. 1 • photographs, repro. in Grosskurth, *Melanie Klein*, 372–3

Wealth at death £92,830: probate, 11 July 1983, *CGPLA Eng. & Wales*

Heinemann, Margot Claire (1913–1992), writer and teacher, was born on 18 November 1913 at 89 Priory Road, Hampstead, London, the second daughter of Meyer Max Heinemann, a merchant banker, and Selma Schott, a non-Orthodox Jewish couple recently immigrated from Frankfurt, Germany. An only brother was born four years later. Margot Heinemann was educated at South Hampstead high school, King Alfred School, and, finally, Roedean, where in 1931 she won a major scholarship to read English at Newnham College, Cambridge. She gained a double first and was awarded a one-year research studentship.

During her undergraduate days, at the time of the depression and Hitler's rise to power, Heinemann first became intensely interested in politics and joined the socialist club and, after the passage of a contingent of hunger marchers through Cambridge in February 1934, the Communist Party. In its ranks she met and in 1935 started a relationship with (Rupert) John *Cornford (1915–1936), an energetic student leader and poet. Only three weeks after the outbreak of the Spanish Civil War in July 1936 Cornford travelled to Spain and enlisted in a republican militia, leaving behind an anguished Margot Heinemann, who wrote the first of several poems inspired by

Margot Claire
Heinemann (1913–
1992), by unknown
photographer

the Spanish Civil War, 'For R.J.C. (summer, 1936)'. Cornford returned safely on this occasion, but only to recruit more volunteers for the republican cause, with whom he set out again in October 1936, this time to join the newly formed International Brigades on what turned out to be a fatal mission. On the news of his death in action towards the end of 1936 Heinemann bravely responded with another poem, 'Grieve in a New Way for New Losses', which balances a reassuring refrain, 'All this is not more than we can deal with', against deeply pained verses:

> To think he lies out there, and changes
> In the process of the earth from what I knew,
> Decays and even there in the grave, shut close
> In the dark, away from me, speechless and cold.

Heinemann's 'For R.J.C.' had been reciprocated by Cornford in an untitled poem composed in the Aragon trenches, which begins 'Heart of the heartless world'. It was addressed to Margot Heinemann and for decades circulated, especially in the communist countries of eastern Europe, as 'To Margot Heinemann', following its publication under this title in *John Cornford: a Memoir* (1938). Heinemann's poems were first published alongside Cornford's dedicatory one in John Lehmann's magazine *New Writing* in autumn 1937.

Heinemann's first employment was as a teacher for factory girls in a day continuation school at Bourneville. She left in 1937 to join the staff of the Labour Research Department in London, where for the next twelve years she inquired into wage structures in the various industries, wartime production, and British trade policy. She also lectured to trade unionists, coalminers in particular. Among the journalistic work undertaken during this time and mostly published in *Labour Research* and *Labour Monthly*, sometimes under the pen-name Margaret Hudson, the frequent articles and books on the conditions in the

coalmining industry stand out. In *Britain's Coal* (1944), a Left Book Club choice prompted by the fuel shortage of the war years, she argued the case for pit nationalization, and in *Coal must Come First* (1948) she reviewed the progress made since the passing of the industry into public ownership. The mood of the country that put the Labour Party in power in 1945 and prepared the way for the nationalization of key industries is well captured in Heinemann's only novel, *The Adventurers* (1960), set in a fictitious 'mid-Welsh coalfield'.

Throughout the 1940s Heinemann contributed to the communist press, and towards the end of that decade moved closer to the centre of communist politics by working full-time for the party, among other things as a researcher and speech-writer for its general secretary Harry Pollitt. She served on the editorial board of the party's intellectual journal the *Modern Quarterly* (1945–53), and edited the weekly *World News and Views* from 1949 to 1951, and its literary supplement *Daylight* (1952–3), which promoted working-class writing. By standing as the Communist candidate for the Lambeth and Vauxhall division in the general election of 1950 and polling just over 500 votes (a mere 1.3 per cent of the votes cast) she experienced the hopeless isolation into which the Communist Party was drifting as a result of the developing cold war. However, this did not deter her from supporting the leadership's unquestioning adoption of Soviet cultural policies (Zhdanovism) in all the crucial inner-party debates of those years. In the 'Caudwell discussion', for example, conducted in the *Modern Quarterly* in 1950–51, she sided with Maurice Cornforth, who had launched the assault on Christopher Caudwell's unorthodox aesthetics. In this unwavering pro-Soviet stance and demand for orthodoxy she was at one with her partner (John) Desmond *Bernal (1901–1971), the eminent scientist and an international celebrity in the world communist movement owing to his indefatigable work for the World Peace Council and the World Federation of Scientific Workers.

The couple had begun a relationship in 1949. After the birth of their daughter Jane in 1953 Heinemann did not resume full-time party work. But even as a rank-and-file member she remained alert to the debates about the Stalinization of the party and was unsympathetic towards the intellectuals who left *en masse* in 1956–7 when the leadership defended the suppression of the Hungarian uprising, and belittled Khrushchov's 'revelations' of the mass repression and judicial murders habitual in the Soviet Union.

Heinemann's hardened stance relented only in the 1960s. By then she had returned to teaching (1959) and to academic life (1965), the latter when she became a lecturer in English at Goldsmiths' College, London. Her two main areas of research now were the 1930s and Renaissance drama, both periods marked for her by their fascinating relation between literature and politics. She collaborated with Noreen Branson, a friend since her Labour Research Department days, on *Britain in the Nineteen Thirties* (1971), and co-edited *Culture and Crisis in Britain in the Thirties* (1979), a major reappraisal of the left-wing cultural endeavours of the decade. This book had developed out of lectures at the Communist University, an annual summer school run in the 1970s and 1980s in which she taught a regenerated Marxism to a rejuvenated membership and to radicals from outside the party and the university.

But wider academic recognition came only with Heinemann's belated appointment as fellow of New Hall, Cambridge, in 1976 and the publication of her celebrated study *Puritanism and Theatre* (1980). In this book she portrayed Thomas Middleton as a playwright close to the growing number of critics of the court, and traced a thread of continuity between early Stuart theatre and the upsurge of popular pamphleteering in the 1640s. A vigorous lecturer combining lived political experience and a passion for literature and teaching, she was in her later years much in demand as a speaker and a contributor to essay collections, even after retirement.

Heinemann belonged to a generation of British Marxists whose formative years were during the anti-war and anti-fascist struggles of the first half of the 1930s. Loyalty to the Soviet Union, the country which embodied the hopes of millions of downtrodden people across the world, which alone had delivered arms to the beleaguered republican government of Spain, and which had borne the brunt of the German attack in the Second World War, came naturally. Conversion to communism was a total commitment, and devotion to the cause came before considerations of a career.

Heinemann always held dear the memory of John Cornford, to the point of becoming embattled against what she felt to be libellous statements about his behaviour. In scholarly debates she would, with sure touch, seize upon the weaknesses in an argument and could be both a formidable opponent and an equally indomitable ally. At the same time, former students and younger colleagues described her as a generous mentor, encouraging and supportive, critical but never evasive. Heinemann was small in stature, but a powerful personality with a piercing gaze which few who encountered her, political friend or foe, were ever likely to forget.

Heinemann died of bronchitis on 9 June 1992 in The Pines, a nursing home in Putney, London. After cremation her ashes were scattered on a mountain in Ross, Scotland. The Festschrift-to-be, *Heart of the Heartless World*, became a memorial volume.   H. GUSTAV KLAUS

Sources D. Margolies and M. Joannou, eds., *Heart of the heartless world* (1995) · P. Sloan, ed., *John Cornford: a memoir* (1938) · M. Straight, *After long silence* (1983) · J. Clark and others, eds., *Culture and crisis in Britain in the thirties* (1979) · private information (2004) [Jane Bernal, daughter] · b. cert.
Archives Goldsmiths' College, London
Likenesses photograph (in her thirties), communist party picture library; repro. in Pluto Press catalogue, 1995 · photograph, News International Syndication, London [*see illus.*]

Heinemann, William (1863–1920), publisher, was born on 18 May 1863 at Surbiton, Surrey, on the family farm, the eldest son of the four sons and two daughters of Louis Heinemann and his wife Jane Lavino. His mother was from Lancashire, but his father, a director of Parr's Bank,

William Heinemann (1863–1920), by George Charles Beresford, 1920

was a native of Hanover, Germany, and had become a naturalized British subject. Both parents were Jewish by descent, but the family had been Anglican for two generations. He received a cosmopolitan education, first with a tutor in England and later at Dresden Gymnasium and elsewhere in Germany. He became fluent in French and German and to a lesser extent in Italian. P. Chalmers Mitchell, who knew him from the age of twenty-one and who became one of his authors, recalled his appearance: 'He was rather short, with small hands and feet (of which he was very proud), a rather large, round head, sleek dark hair, getting thin on top and a small moustache. His mouth was small, with delicate firmly-held lips. He had a tendency to embonpoint, and especially when he was excited, the slightest of stutters gave a characteristic to his speech' (quoted in Whyte, 33–4).

Heinemann's earliest ambition was to be a professional musician, a pianist or possibly a composer, but he decided that he lacked the necessary talent to be a great artist and turned to his second love, literature. In 1879 he became an apprentice to Nicolas Trübner. At Trübners, Heinemann gained practical experience in every phase of publishing. After Trübner's death in 1884 Heinemann was largely responsible for the firm until it was sold to Charles Kegan Paul in 1889.

After leaving Trübners, Heinemann travelled on the continent and built connections with publishers in

France, Germany, Scandinavia, Russia, and Italy. In 1890 he opened his own publishing firm on the second floor at 21 Bedford Street, Covent Garden. Heinemann's staff consisted of W. Ham-Smith, who had followed him from Trübners and who became the business manager, and an office boy. One year later a secretary, Miss Pugh, joined the staff.

The first book published by the firm was Hall Caine's *The Bondman* (1890), which had been rejected by Cassell. This book had great popular success and put Heinemann on the road to fortune. Among the earliest publications was James McNeill Whistler's *The Gentle Art of Making Enemies* (1890). Heinemann, who was a friend of Whistler's, later published Mr and Mrs Joseph Pennell's *Life of Whistler*. The 1890–93 lists seem to be widely eclectic, but steadily a structure emerged, based on fiction aimed at subscription libraries, and book series such as The Great Educators, Heinemann's International Library, and Heinemann Scientific Books. Three authors contributed to the rapid establishment of Heinemanns: Frances McFall (Sarah Grand), Robert Hichens, and Thomas Beech (Henri Le Caron).

Two men in particular played substantial roles in the Heinemann firm: Edmund Gosse and Sydney Pawling. Gosse was a chief adviser, reader, editor, and author. Pawling joined the firm in 1893 as a full-time partner. In the 1890s Heinemann's fiction list included authors of the calibre of Robert Louis Stevenson, Rudyard Kipling, George Moore, Henry James, and H. G. Wells. The firm continued to attract a diverse group of skilled authors, among them E. F. Benson, John Masefield, D. H. Lawrence, Elizabeth Robbins, Mrs Dudney, Flora Annie Steel, Max Beerbohm, Joseph Conrad, William Frend de Morgan, and John Galsworthy. Between 1895 and 1897 Heinemann also published the *New Review*, under the editorship of W. E. Henley, and dramatic works including those of Sir Arthur Pinero, Somerset Maugham, Israel Zangwill, Henry Davies, and Charles Haddon Chambers. Heinemann's own plays—*The First Step* (1895), *Summer Moths* (1898), and *War* (1901)—were published by John Lane. On 22 February 1899 he married Magda Sindici, a young Italian author; he had published her first novel, *Via lucis* (1898), written under the pseudonym Kassandra Vivaria.

Although not all of Heinemann's authors were of the first rank, many became pillars of the firm's backlist, which was an essential ingredient for long-term prosperity. During his lifetime Heinemann's list came to include art books and books of exploration, medicine, and science. The Loeb Classical Library was published by the firm until 1988, when it was sold to Harvard University Press.

Heinemann's European connections, coupled with the advice and editorial expertise of Edmund Gosse, were reflected in the regular commissioning of translations of work by European authors. Stendhal, Victor Hugo, Flaubert, Daudet, Jules and Edmund de Goncourt, Goethe, Ibsen, and Björnstjerne Björnson were some of the authors included on the list. Another enduring contribution that Heinemann made to the British reading public was the commissioning of the translations of the Russian novelists Goncharov, Tolstoy, Turgenev, Dostoyevsky, and others by Constance Garnett, wife of the publisher's reader, Edward Garnett.

Throughout most of his professional life Heinemann had brushes with the Society of Authors, and he opposed the emergence of literary agents. Despite his opposition, however, Heinemann became one of London's most respected publishers, exerting considerable influence on the industry. He played a great part in founding the Publishers' Association of Great Britain and Ireland in 1896, and was president of the association from 1909 to 1911. From 1896 to 1913 he was the British representative on the international commission and executive committee of the International Congress of Publishers; it was largely due to his initiative that the congress came into existence. Through the congress, Heinemann played a leading role in the protection of international copyrights and he influenced the American Copyright Bill of 1909. After his resignation from the congress in 1913 and until his death in 1920 Heinemann was president of the Associated Booksellers of Great Britain and Ireland.

Heinemann's death was sudden and unexpected. On 5 October 1920, when his valet, George Payne, went to call him at half past eight in the morning at his home, 32 Lower Belgrave Street, London, he found him lying dead on the floor by his bed. At the inquest, his doctor said that he had been suffering from a chronic nervous disease, which eventually would have made him blind; the cause of death was a heart attack.

Heinemann's death provoked a crisis for his publishing firm. His marriage, which had ended in divorce in 1905, had produced no children, and his nephew John Heinemann, whom Heinemann had intended as his successor, had been killed in the First World War. Sydney Pawling, his business partner of twenty-seven years, could not afford to buy Heinemann's 55 per cent share of the firm. Liquidation of the company or its absorption by a rival was averted when the New York publisher F. N. Doubleday agreed to Pawling's plea that he buy a controlling interest in the firm and leave the company intact.

At his death Heinemann's estate was valued at £33,780 with a net worth of £32,578. He left £500 to the Publishers' Association as a reserve fund to meet any emergencies where the interests of British publishers were threatened; £500 went to the National Book Trade Benevolent Fund, of which he had been president. Sydney Pawling inherited his personal papers. Subject to the life of his mother and his two sisters, half of his residuary estate went to the Royal Society of Literature to establish the Heinemann Foundation of Literature, which was to give a prize of up to £200 for a work of worth. Although fiction was not excluded, Heinemann's intention was to reward classes of literature that were less remunerative—namely poetry, criticism, biography, and history. This prize continues to be awarded regularly.   LINDA MARIE FRITSCHNER

Sources 'Death of Mr Heinemann', *The Times* (6 Oct 1920), 13 · L. Griest, *Mudie's Circulating Library and the Victorian novel* (1970) · W. Heinemann, *The hardships of publishing* (1893) · A. Hill, *In pursuit of publishing* (1988) · M. S. Howard, *Jonathan Cape: publisher* (1974) ·

'International Publishers' Congress: the Copyright Convention', *The Times* (17 June 1913), 7 · 'Literature gifts endowment', *New York Times* (14 Oct 1920), 12 · J. London, 'London book talk', *New York Times Book Review* (20 Oct 1920), 19 [obit.] · V. Menkes, 'William Heinemann', *British Book News* (Oct 1989), 688–92 · 'Scholarship fund for literature', *The Times* (12 Oct 1920), 10 · J. St John, *William Heinemann: a century of publishing* (1990) · F. Warburg, *All authors are equal* (1973) · F. Whyte, *William Heinemann: a memoir* (1928) · *CGPLA Eng. & Wales* (1920)

Archives Heinemann Ltd, London, archive · Hunt. L., letters · Iowa University Libraries · National Library of Canada, Ottawa · Newcastle Central Library · Stanford University Library, California | BL, corresp. with Lord Northcliffe, Add. MS 62174 · NYPL, Berg collection · Richmond Local Studies Library, London, corresp. with Douglas Sladen

Likenesses G. C. Beresford, photograph, 1920, Heinemann Ltd, London [*see illus.*] · photographs, Heinemann Ltd, London

Wealth at death £33,780 19s. 4d.: probate, 12 Nov 1920, *CGPLA Eng. & Wales*

Heins, John (1732–1771). *See under* Heins, John Theodore (1697–1756).

Heins, John Theodore [*formerly* Dietrich] (1697–1756), portrait painter, was born in Germany, and probably settled in Norwich about 1720. By 1729 he was living in Hog Hill and receiving an uninterrupted flow of commissions for portraits of members of local county families and civic dignitaries. In 1726 he painted a small self-portrait (Norwich Castle Museum and Art Gallery), and in 1732 he received his first civic commission for a full-length portrait of the mayor of Norwich. He went on to portray a total of seventeen dignitaries, including Robert Walpole, earl of Orford (1743), all of which are in the Norwich Civic Portrait Collection. He also painted a small portrait of William Cowper's mother before her death in 1737, which some fifty years later inspired the poem 'On the Receipt of my Mother's Picture out of Norfolk'. The Astley family of Melton Constable, Norfolk, were important patrons; Heins was commissioned to paint several family portraits for them, including *A Musical Party at Melton Constable Hall* (1743), in which he included a portrait of himself among the gathering. As well as this departure into the conversation piece, he also attempted modern moral subjects, namely *Thomas Guy Counting his Money* and *The Death of Thomas Guy* (1737; Norwich Castle Museum and Art Gallery), the founder of Guy's Hospital, illustrating Guy's reputation as a miser, which circulated as prints. However, portraits and family groups predominate. The faces of his portraits are well modelled and portray character, but the poses of the figures tend to be somewhat wooden. During the first half of the 1720s he signed his work D. Heins, Dietrich being a German equivalent of Theodore; later his signature was simply Heins. He engraved some of his portraits, and was thus probably the first mezzotinter in Norwich. Heins died in Norwich on 10 August 1756 'after a painful illness' (*Ipswich Journal*, 14 Aug 1756). The following year a sale was held of the contents of his home in St Stephen's, Norwich. In his will, proved on 30 August 1756, he left everything to his wife, Abigail. At least one daughter is recorded and a son, **John Heins** (1732–1771), painter and engraver, who was presumably born in Norwich. His father apprenticed him to a textile

John Theodore Heins (1697–1756), self-portrait, 1726

manufacturer, but he preferred instead to become a painter. He married a Mrs Peacock of Enfield in 1765 and soon after probably moved to London. He worked as a portrait painter, miniaturist, and engraver, although little is known of his work, and he is often confused with his father. He exhibited once at the Free Society in 1767 and the Society of Artists in 1768, when his address was given as 211 St Clement's, the Strand, and again in 1770. He made detailed architectural drawings of views of Ely Cathedral and its monuments, which were engraved for James Bentham's *The History and Antiquities of the Conventual and Cathedral Church of Ely* (1771). He died in Chelsea in 1771.

NORMA WATT

Sources J. Strutt, *A biographical dictionary, containing an historical account of all the engravers, from the earliest period of the art of engraving to the present time*, 2 vols. (1785–6) · T. Fawcett, 'Eighteenth-century art in Norwich', *Walpole Society*, 46 (1976–8), 71–90 · priv. coll., Rajnai Norwich artists archive · J. C. Smith, *British mezzotinto portraits*, 4 vols. in 5 (1878–84) · *Norwich Gazette* (5–12 July 1729) · *Norwich Mercury* (26 Feb 1757) · will, Norwich archdeaconry · *DNB* · *Norwich Mercury* (26 Oct 1765) · exhibition catalogue [Society of Artists of Great Britain]

Likenesses self-portrait, oils, 1726, Norwich Castle Museum and Art Gallery [*see illus.*]

Wealth at death see will, Norwich archdeaconry

Heitland [*née* Bateson], **Margaret** (1860–1938), journalist and social activist, was born in Cambridge on 27 February 1860 in the master's lodge, St John's College. Daughter of William Henry *Bateson (1812–1881), master of the college, and his wife, Anna, *née* Aikin (1829–1918), she had three sisters and two brothers; among them were William *Bateson, a biologist, and Mary *Bateson, a historian. Margaret was educated at Highfield Finishing School in

Hendon, and at Heidelberg. She was fluent in French and German, and for a time coached pupils for the Cambridge higher local examinations. Inheriting her parents' concern for the advancement of women, in 1884 she became assistant secretary of the Cambridge Women's Suffrage Association, which her mother founded with Millicent Garrett Fawcett in that year. Finding in Cambridge inadequate scope for her energies, she took the unusual step of moving to London in 1886 to work as a journalist. In 1888 she began to write for *The Queen*, at that time a leading journal for women; she founded in 1889 its 'Women's employment department' feature, edited it until 1914, and made it a pioneering and powerful voice for the increase of opportunities for middle-class women. Gathering into a book, *Professional Women upon their Professions* (1895), her journal accounts of twenty-five interviews, she regretted that the choice given to young women was often 'between complete domestic obscurity on the one hand and the very highest distinctions that art and letters can offer on the other'; instead, she suggested 'the intense happiness that merely being and doing *something* yields'—a phrase typical of her writing in its enlightened yet practical helpfulness (M. Heitland, *Professional Women*, 1895, v–vi).

On her return to Cambridge after her marriage in 1901, Margaret was tireless in the suffragist cause, serving from 1905 until 1918 as chair of the Cambridge society, which at its height had 550 members; she was prominent with Mrs Fawcett and others in the National Union of Women's Suffrage Societies, founded in 1897 to co-ordinate the work of associations like Cambridge's in a non-violent and constitutionalist campaign. Her acuteness of mind, sense of humour, and capacity to work with others were further tested during the First World War; within a few months of its outbreak over 250 refugees from Belgium arrived in Cambridge, and as chair of the town's hospitality committee she had to arrange for their accommodation, support, and employment, and to do so in conjunction with two other committees representing the university and the county. Among the other societies with which she was involved was the Cambridge and District Women Citizens' Association, of which in 1918 she was one of the founders and the first chair; its aims were 'to stir up in women a sense of the community spirit' and to press for the removal of inequalities (*Annual Report of the Cambridge and District Women Citizens' Association: Jubilee Year 1919–1969*, 1969, 7).

A vigorous, self-confident, and forthright woman of independent mind, Margaret Bateson remarked that 'compassion acts like a strong poison upon those who have no need of it'. Thus 'the happiest and busiest spinster … if compassionated for her lot by a woman bound to a tedious husband and a family of troublesome children' was likely to feel on the margins of society. In contrast, she urged the joy and unselfishness of the spinster's home. 'It will be a school of training for your servants' and 'an oasis of peace to numbers of people in trouble and perplexity. The married woman cannot compete with you here, in her home distracted by family cares'. Admitting that 'all roads lead to the altar', she was glad (in 1895) that

the professional woman 'is often in no hurry to reach the bourne' (M. Heitland, *Professional Women*, 1895, 130–33). She herself was in no hurry, and it was not until 2 July 1901 that she married W. E. Heitland, a fellow of her late father's college.

William Emerton Heitland (1847–1935), classical scholar, was born on 21 December 1847 at Colkirk, Norfolk, the eldest child of Arthur Allan Heitland, an unsuccessful gentleman farmer, and his wife, Mary. They had two other sons and four daughters, of whom one son and three daughters reached full age. William was educated at Dedham grammar school and Shrewsbury School, where the classical teaching of the headmaster, Benjamin Hall Kennedy, was a lasting influence upon him. Relying on scholarships because of his family's straitened circumstances, he proceeded in 1867 to St John's College, Cambridge, and in 1871 graduated BA, being the most distinguished examinee (senior classic) in the classical tripos. He was immediately elected a fellow of St John's, which he remained until death. He was college lecturer in classics 1871–85 and tutor 1883–93.

Among Heitland's prolific writings on the classical world the most distinguished were *Agricola* (1921), on agricultural labour in antiquity, and the *History of the Roman Republic* (1909), which in its day was compared to Mommsen's great work. Heitland's scholarship was said to be 'consumed with a passionate desire to attain the truth' (Winstanley, 6–7). His judiciousness led, in his advancing years, to an excessive balancing of arguments in his speeches in the senate and his writings on issues of the day; despite his occasional prophetic voice, he was ineffective in essays on the menace of class war and the value of eugenicist planning, or the need to construct a league of peace after the First World War, or, within Cambridge, to transfer resources from colleges to the university. His most capable polemic was *A Letter to a Lady, or, A Word with the Female Anti-Suffragists* (1915), directed against a local audience in a cause to which Heitland was committed for many years.

Heitland was a stimulating and kindly, though pernickety, teacher, discerning and encouraging talents hidden from others. He was also renowned for his freakish and often mordant humour, his fidelity to close friends and the strength of his aversions, and his insistence on a changeless college routine. Departure from the expected led his 'irritable and sensitive' nature to take offence, and 'he found it difficult to forgive, and impossible to forget, wrongs which he thought he had suffered' (Winstanley).

Both Heitlands died at their home, Carmefield, Wordsworth Grove, Cambridge, William on 23 June 1935 and Margaret on 31 May 1938. He was buried in St Giles's cemetery, Cambridge, on 26 June 1935, she on 3 June 1938. Margaret Heitland's devotion to the cause of women manifested itself at the last in her will, under which she made Newnham College, Cambridge, her residuary legatee.

PETER SEARBY

Sources *Cambridge Independent Press* (16 Jan 1931), 4 • A. J. R., ed., *The suffrage annual and women's who's who* (1913) • *Cambridge Review* (9 June 1938), 492 • b. cert. • d. cert. • *Annual report of the Cambridge and*

District Women Citizens' Association: jubilee year, 1919–1969 (1969) • W. E. Heitland, *After many years: a tale of experiences and impressions gathered in the course of an obscure life* (1926) • *The Eagle*, 49 (1935–7), 119–22 • T. R. Glover, *Cambridge retrospect* (1943), 37–45 • *CGPLA Eng. & Wales* (1935) [William Emerton Heitland] • *CGPLA Eng. & Wales* (1938) • Venn, *Alum. Cant.* • *Cambridge Daily News* (4 June 1938) • *Cambridge Daily News* (27 June 1935) • m. cert. • D. A. Winstanley, *Cambridge Review* (11 Oct 1935), 6–7 [W. E. Heitland]

Archives St John Cam., T. R. Glover MSS

Likenesses two photographs, 1931 (William Emerton Heitland), St John Cam.

Wealth at death £16,515 5s. 9d.: probate, 30 Oct 1938, *CGPLA Eng. & Wales* • £26,519 4s. 4d.—William Heitland: probate, 1935, *CGPLA Eng. & Wales*

Heitland, William Emerton (1847–1935). *See under* Heitland, Margaret (1860–1938).

Heitler, Walter Heinrich (1904–1981), physicist, was born on 2 January 1904 in Karlsruhe, the second of three children and eldest son of Adolf Heitler, professor of engineering at the Technische Hochschule of Karlsruhe, and his wife, Ortilie Rudolf. He pursued a strong and independent interest in science in his youth, reading Einstein under the desk in spite of a teacher's disapproval of relativity, and installing a chemical laboratory in the family bath. In the first semesters of his tertiary studies in the Karlsruhe Technische Hochschule in 1922 his interests oscillated between chemistry and mathematics; he was not then aware that physics could be a career. Lectures from Bredig brought him into contact with quantum theory from the point of view of physical chemistry, thermodynamics, and statistics, giving the impression that quantum theory was at the borderlines of physics and chemistry. Heitler was soon to make decisive contributions through research focused on just this borderline.

Heitler travelled to Berlin to listen to the greats of physics and physical chemistry, Einstein, Planck, von Laue, Nernst, and Haber, but soon realized that he could not rely on the guidance of these figures for the preparation of a doctoral dissertation. Instead he went to Arnold Sommerfeld's department of theoretical physics in Munich and completed his dissertation on a study of concentrated solutions under Karl H. Herzfeld in 1926. He then took a Rockefeller studentship to Copenhagen to continue work in this field under the physical chemist Bjerrum. It was in order to change tack and assimilate the new work in quantum mechanics from one of its founders that he sought, mid-term, to transfer his studentship to Zürich and Erwin Schrödinger. There he met Fritz London, and the two young physicists set out to apply wave mechanics to the calculation of the interaction between two atoms.

In an interview for the Archives for the History of Quantum Physics, Heitler records that the decisive insight on the problem came to him after sleep induced by the hot south wind (the Föhn) which occasionally plagues Zürich. He telephoned Fritz London and before the following day was over they had mapped out the approach taken in their fundamental paper of 1927, 'Wechselwirkung neutraler Atome und homöopolaren Bindung nach der Quantenmechanik' (*Zeitschrift für Physik*, 44 1927, 455–72),

which provided a quantum mechanical explanation of the hydrogen molecule on the basis of electron exchange.

This work was well received, and led Max Born to offer Heitler an assistantship in Göttingen from 1929. Here Heitler assimilated matrix mechanics, the second major strand of quantum mechanics, and his next programme came to utilize the mathematical methods of group theory to explain chemistry on the basis of quantum mechanics. In 1933 he was forced to leave Germany on account of his Jewish ancestry and was appointed to a position in Nevill Mott's Institute of Theoretical Physics in Bristol. In Göttingen, Heitler had begun to regard quantum electrodynamics as the fundamentally unsolved problem and to focus on high energy phenomena (reasoning that it was here that the new theory might prove vulnerable). In Bristol he was able to take this programme further and in various collaborative papers (with, among others, Bethe, Bhabha, Fröhlich, Kemmer, and Powell), he developed a cascade theory of cosmic showers, showed that the heavy meson could be fitted into quantum field theory, and provided explanations of the magnetic moment of the neutron and proton. It was in part Heitler's interests which led Cecil Frank Powell to begin his Nobel prizewinning work on cosmic ray phenomena and the photographic emulsion method as a precision tool in particle physics. In this period Heitler's important textbook the *Quantum Theory of Radiation* was published, going into three editions in 1936, 1944, and 1954. Mott later described Heitler as a man with great charm and a natural courtesy.

In 1941, after a brief period of internment as an enemy alien in 1940, Heitler took up a position as assistant professor at the Dublin Institute of Advanced Studies, of which Schrödinger was director. In 1941 or 1942 he married Kathleen Winifred Nicholson, who had worked in biological research in Bristol; she was the daughter of John Winifred Nicholson and sister of John Henry Nicholson, later vice-chancellor of Hull University. Their son Eric was born in Dublin. In 1943 Heitler was granted a full professorship (and became a fellow of the Royal Irish Academy) and in 1946 succeeded Schrödinger to the institute directorship and took Irish citizenship. Here Heitler was responsible for the establishment of theoretical and experimental research groups on elementary particles. His 1945 book *Elementary Wave Mechanics* is illustrative of his lecturing style, presenting the essential physical facts without the encumbrance of sophisticated mathematics.

Heitler's final academic position allowed him to return to the German-speaking environment he most appreciated. In 1949 he assumed the directorship of the Institute for Theoretical Physics at the University of Zürich, from which he retired in 1974. In his later years, stimulated to take up publicly concerns which had originated in his student days by dismay at the direction physics had taken following the development of the atom bomb, Heitler wrote particularly on science, philosophy, and religion. In 1961 his well-received book *Man and Science* (published in both German and English editions) contended that the sciences were severely limited by their focus on causal and quantitative relations, which he argued were not incompatible with teleological principles. He felt that their presentation failed to recognize qualitative and holistic dimensions, and had led to an estrangement of science from life and man. In the 1970s he lectured and wrote a number of books (published in German only) on more specifically religious concerns, such as divinity and nature and proofs of God's existence. In this period he became a member of the Swiss Reformed church.

In 1948 Heitler had been made a fellow of the Royal Society. Among other honours he received the Max Planck medal in 1968, the Swiss Marcel Benoist prize in 1970, and the gold medal of the Humboldt Gesellschaft in 1979. He died in Zürich after a long illness on 15 November 1981. He was survived by his wife.   RICHARD STALEY

Sources J. L. Heilbron and W. Heitler, interview, 18–19 March 1963, Library of the American Philosophical Society, Philadelphia, Archives for the History of Quantum Physics [microfilm copy at various locations, including the Science Museum and ICL Library] · N. Mott, *Memoirs FRS*, 28 (1982), 141–51 · *DNB* · K. Gavroglu, *Fritz London: a scientific biography* (1995)

Archives University of Zürich, Switzerland, MSS | Bodl. Oxf., papers relating to Society for Protection of Science and Learning and Home Office · Duke U., Fritz London MSS · Library of the American Philosophical Society, Philadelphia, Archives for the History of Quantum Physics · University of Göttingen, faculty of mathematics, Ausarbeitungen of lecture courses · Copenhagen, Denmark, Bohr Collection | SOUND Library of the American Philosophical Society, Philadelphia, Archives for the History of Quantum Physics, interview with J. L. Heilbron, 18–19 March 1963, transcript

Likenesses W. Stoneman, photograph, 1948, repro. in *Memoirs FRS*, facing p. 141

Heke Pokai, Hone Wiremu (*c*.1807/8–1850), Maori war leader, was born at Pakaraka, inland from the Bay of Islands in the North Island of New Zealand. His birth probably took place shortly after the great battle between his people and Ngati Whatua, often known as Moremonui, which took place about 1807 or 1808. He was named Pokai for an uncle, Pokaia, killed in that battle, but was commonly known as Heke. He was the third child of Tupanapana and his wife, Te Kona, both of the Nga Puhi people; their various *hapu* ('clans or descent groups') were Ngati Rahiri, Te Uri-o-Hau, Ngati Tautahi, Ngai Tawake, and Te Matarahurahu, based around Kaikohe, Tautoro, and other districts of the inland Bay of Islands.

Brought up in Pokaia's *pa* ('fort'), Pateoro at Kaikohe, as a small child Heke was captured with his mother by Rewharewha of Ngati Whatua, but was saved by Te Hotete, father of Hongi Hika. As a young adult, Heke was obviously intelligent, but was initially regarded as wild and troublesome by missionaries, in whose Kerikeri mission school he was taught in 1824 and 1825. Some time during these years he married Ono, daughter of the renowned chief of Te Puna in the Bay of Islands, Te Pahi; at their baptism and formal marriage on 9 August 1835 she took the name Riria (a transliteration of Lydia), and he took the name by which (with Heke) he would become famous, Hone (John), and also Wiremu (William). They

Hone Wiremu Heke Pokai (*c*.1807/8–1850), by Benjamin Waterhouse Hawkins, pubd 1847 (after George French Angas) [left, with Eruera Maihi Patuone]

had two children but both died in childhood. Heke then married Rongo, a daughter of Hongi *Hika, on 30 March 1837; her baptismal name was Hariata (Harriet).

Although not of senior birth rank, Heke was descended from senior lineages and was respected as an emergent tribal leader. He fought in the northern war expedition against Tauranga in 1833, and took part in internal wars in the Bay of Islands in 1830 and 1837. But the events for which he is most remembered began with the signing of the treaty of Waitangi. The missionary William Colenso recorded that he signed as a chief of the *hapu* Te Matarahurahu. In the great debate of 5 February 1840 Heke supported the treaty, urged the governor to stay in New Zealand, and warned that without him his people would become slaves of the French or victims of rum sellers; he spoke of the missionaries and the governor as fathers to his people. On 6 February the former British resident, James Busby, knowing him to be mission-educated and one of the chiefs most in favour of the treaty, called his name first, and Hone Heke was the first to sign, as Hoani or, as it appears on the treaty sheet, Hoane Heke. (Hoani is an alternative transliteration of John.)

Soon after the establishment of the colony of New Zealand, the capital was shifted from Kororareka (Russell) to Auckland. Bay of Islands Maori lost markets, and were incensed when the nascent government imposed customs duties, banned trade in kauri timber and began to impose the European justice system. All these causes of local economic depression and offences against chiefly *rangatiratanga* ('paramount powers', the latter guaranteed to be retained in the Maori version of the treaty) took place against a background of Maori discontent over land sales in the Bay of Islands, whether because too much land had been sold to missionaries and settlers in some areas, leaving Maori with insufficient, or whether chiefs still wishing to sell land were prevented from doing so under the crown right of pre-emptive purchase established under the treaty of Waitangi. Hone Heke realized that Maori were now regarded as subject to the new European government. He focused on the British flag flying at Kororareka as a symbol of the degradation of chiefly independence; originally the timber for the flagstaff had been given to fly the Maori flag established in 1835. At dawn on 8 July 1844 his men, led by his lieutenant, Te Haratua, cut down the flagstaff for the first time; it was restored, but Heke cut it down again on the night of 9–10 January 1845, and again on 19 January. On 11 March 1845, although by this time it was heavily protected by the military, he had it cut down for the fourth time. At the same time the European town of Kororareka was sacked, partly by the forces of Heke and his ally, Kawiti, and partly by pro-government forces, including some of the British.

Heke withdrew inland to his *pa*, Te Ahuahu, and began the construction of a new, heavily fortified *pa* called Puketutu. There was some skirmishing with pro-government Maori forces led by Tamati Waka Nene, based at Okaihau. Colonel William Hulme arrived with troops in April 1845, but was heavily defeated by Heke on 8 May. Skirmishing with Maori forces continued, and Heke's *pa* at Te Ahuahu was taken by Maori pro-government forces when it was undefended; in a later battle Heke himself was severely wounded. By now his *mana* ('authority and prestige') was very high among large sections of Nga Puhi, and his opposition to the presence of the governor received significant support. He was regarded as so *tapu* ('sacred') that the offensive matter leaking from his wound could not be destroyed but was buried in a place fenced about and later walled as a *wahi tapu* ('sacred place'). While he was recovering Heke wrote to the governor that God had made New Zealand for the Maori; it could not be sliced up and shared like a whale; the governor should return to England. In subsequent correspondence he made it clear that he was not opposed to European settlement, trade, and missionaries, but to the powers of the colonial government over Maori.

British troops took Ruapekapeka, a *pa* belonging to Heke's ally, Kawiti, by bombardment on 10 January 1846. The *pa* had been virtually deserted at the time. Heke remained undefeated, and when Governor George Grey made peace Heke refused to make any gesture of submission. In 1848 he met the governor in Waimate North and presented him with a mere *pounamu* ('greenstone short club'), but intended the gift not as a token of submission, as the governor claimed, but as an acknowledgement of the governor's right to remain in New Zealand and a reaffirmation of the treaty of Waitangi. Heke's last years

were plagued by tuberculosis, and an attempt to achieve an heir by a short-lived, informal, third marriage was a failure. Heke died of tuberculosis on 6 August 1850 at Kaikohe, and was buried in secret at the Kaungarapa burial-ground at Pakaraka.

Hone Heke, as he was famously known, was the first of the great Maori leaders to struggle with the colonial government for Maori self-determination. Though militarily successful at the time, his effort was eventually swamped by settler migration, lack of wider Maori support, and changing circumstances, and by the adherence of many Nga Puhi to the government. But his dramatic destruction of the symbol of British power, the flagstaff bearing the union flag, not once but four times, lives on in the collective consciousness of New Zealanders.

ANGELA BALLARA

Sources *Extracts from a diary kept by the Rev. R. Burrows during Heke's war in the north in 1845* (1886) · W. Colenso, *The authentic and genuine history of the signing of the treaty of Waitangi* (1890) · H. Williams, letters and journals, Auckland Institute and Museum · *Ko Te Karere Nui o Nui Tireni (The Maori Messenger)* [contemporary government Maori newspaper] (1842–63) · F. Kawharu, 'Heke Pokai, Hone Wiremu', *DNZB*, vol. 1 · J. Rutherford, *Hone Heke's rebellion* (1947) · T. L. Buick, *New Zealand's first war* (1926) · J. Belich, *The New Zealand wars* (1936)
Likenesses B. W. Hawkins, engraving, pubd 1847 (after G. F. Angas), NL NZ, Turnbull L. [*see illus.*] · G. F. Angas, double portrait (with Eruera Patuone) · portraits, NL NZ, Turnbull L.

Hele, Sir John (1541/2–1608), barrister, was the fourth son of Nicholas Hele of Hele, Devon, and his second wife, Margaret, daughter of Richard Dune of Holesworthy. Admitted to the Inner Temple in 1564, he was called to the bar in 1574, made a bencher of the inn in 1589 and Lent reader in 1591. Hele consolidated his ties with the west country through appointments to the peace commission for Devon (1578) and Cornwall (c.1591), as recorder of Plympton (1584), Exeter (1585), and Plymouth (by 1604), and MP for Exeter in 1593, 1597, and 1601. His parliamentary career was unspectacular. In 1591 Hele acquired Wembury Manor near Plymouth, where he built an extensive house at the reputed cost of more than £20,000, and by the time of his death had purchased other properties in London and Warwickshire. Hele and his wife, Mary, daughter of Ellis Warwick of Holbeton, had two daughters and eight sons, only four of whom (Warwick, Nicholas, George, and Francis) appear to have outlived him.

From the 1570s Hele built up a lucrative legal practice in the central courts; by the 1590s he appeared regularly in Star Chamber, both as counsel and litigant. On 23 April 1594 he was created serjeant-at-law with the support of distinguished patrons including Henry Herbert, earl of Pembroke, Sir Christopher Hatton, and Sir John Popham, chief justice of the king's bench. On 6 May 1602 he was appointed queen's serjeant and rode the summer circuit as an assize judge. Hele was knighted in 1603, serving with Sir Edward Coke as prosecuting counsel at the trial of Sir Walter Ralegh.

Hele's desire to cement his professional standing

through appointment to the mastership of the rolls in chancery—in which he was initially seen as a likely successor to Sir Thomas Egerton—led him into complex financial and political waters after 1600, when he extended loans totalling £3500 to Henry Brooke, Lord Cobham, to press his claim, as well as a smaller loan of £400 to Egerton himself. The execution of the earl of Essex in February 1601 cost Hele more than £4000 in loans to Essex and removed a powerful ally at court, precipitating attempts by Egerton to discredit Hele in a 'vendetta' (Cockburn, 'Spoils', 341) almost certainly precipitated by Hele's attempts to recover Egerton's debt. Hele was left defending himself against allegations from Egerton's extensive clientele that he was an ambidexter of notorious reputation within his county—claims which must be viewed in light of an organized campaign to discredit him.

Accused of attempting to take unfair advantage of his legal office to secure money owed him by Cobham—who in another disaster of timing and association for him was attainted for treason on 25 November 1603—Hele's conduct became the subject of a 1604 privy council investigation, leading to his prosecution in Star Chamber. Hele was censured for breach of due process in attempting to secure Cobham's debt, resulting in a fine of £1000, imprisonment, and suspension from office. Attributing his troubles to the 'insatiable' malice of Sir Thomas Egerton (*Salisbury MSS*, 16.333), Hele was released after six weeks' imprisonment without sufficient spirit to resurrect his career or reputation. On 8 February 1608 he obtained dispensation from legal duties on account of his age. He died, aged sixty-six, on 4 June 1608—when, the Latin inscription to his monument at Wembury church records, he ceased 'to be miserable'.   D. X. POWELL

Sources J. S. Cockburn, 'The spoils of law: the trial of Sir John Hele, 1604', *Tudor rule and revolution: essays for G. R. Elton from his American friends*, ed. J. G. Delloyd and J. W. McKenna (1982), 309–43 · HoP, *Commons, 1558–1603*, 2.287–8 · Baker, *Serjeants*, 63, 65, 78, 83, 175, 313, 320, 435–6, 517 · *Les reportes del cases in camera stellata, 1593 to 1609, from the original ms. of John Hawarde*, ed. W. P. Baildon (privately printed, London, 1894), 171–6 · W. R. Prest, *The rise of the barristers: a social history of the English bar, 1590–1640* (1986), 368 · CSP dom., 1603–10 · *Calendar of the manuscripts of the most hon. the marquis of Salisbury*, 24 vols., HMC, 9 (1883–1976) · *The letters of John Chamberlain*, ed. N. E. McClure, 1 (1939), 92, 111, 117, 161, 319n. · J. S. Cockburn, *A history of English assizes, 1558–1714* (1972), 223–4, 268, 288 · L. A. Knafla, *Law and politics in Jacobean England: the tracts of Lord Chancellor Ellesmere* (1977), 62–3 · *The diary of Sir Richard Hutton, 1614–1639*, ed. W. R. Prest, SeldS, suppl. ser., 9 (1991), xv · W. Jones, 'Wembury church and Sir John Hele', *The Western Antiquary, or, Note-Book for Devon and Cornwall*, 10/1–2 (July–Aug 1890), 1–3 · H. W. Woolrych, *Lives of eminent serjeants-at-law of the English bar*, 2 vols. (1869), 1.172–3 · *Prince's cases*, 8 Coke Report 1a, 77 ER 481; 8 Coke Report 13b, 77 ER 496 [CD-ROM] · *Gomersall v. Gomersall*, 2 Leonard 194, 74 ER 472, 2 Bulstrode 326, 80 ER 1159, Godbolt 55, 78 ER 34 [CD-ROM] · *Sir Arthur George's case*, Moore KB 739, 72 ER 873 [CD-ROM] · monument, Wembury church · PRO, PROB 11/112, sig. 89 · W. H. Cooke, ed., *Students admitted to the Inner Temple, 1547–1660* [1878], 53

Archives BL, Add. MS 6704, fol. 142 · BL, Add. MS 34218, fol. 86 · BL, Add. MS 36767, fols. 58–9 · BL, Stowe MS 396, fols. 83–6 · CUL, Ms Gg. 2.31, fol. 474r · Hunt. L., Ellesmere MS 2699, 2702–4, 2706–9, 2710, 2712, 2713 · PRO, STAC 8/9/4

Wealth at death approx. £1640—plus goods and plate; est. £20,000 manor of Wembury; properties in London and Warwickshire: will, PRO, PROB 11/112, sig. 89

Helena [St Helena, Helen, Flavia Julia Helena] (*c.*248–328/9), mother of the Roman emperor Constantine I, has no historical connection with Britain, despite a widespread belief that she was of British origin. This myth, which stems from a strong medieval tradition resulting in numerous dedications to her, especially in Yorkshire and Lincolnshire, was revived as late as 1950, when Evelyn Waugh (1903–1966) published his novel *Helena*. More reliable historical evidence attests that Helena was born *c.*248 into a humble family in Asia Minor. The precise place is not known with absolute certainty, but a tradition stronger than that for her British origin places her birth in Drepanum, in the province of Bithynia (modern Herkes, Turkey). Constantine's refoundation of this town as Helenopolis does not prove concretely that it was her actual birthplace. About 270, apparently while working in an inn, Helena met Constantius Chlorus, a Dalmatian aristocrat who rose to become emperor *Constantius I in 305–6. Probably prevented from legal marriage by their different social statuses, the couple lived in concubinage until 289, when Constantius married Theodora, the daughter of the senior emperor Maximian. In 272 or 273 Helena and Constantius had a son, Constantine, who became the emperor *Constantine I: it is not known whether Helena bore Constantius any other children.

After Constantius's marriage to Theodora, Helena's life recedes into obscurity at least until her son was acclaimed as his father's successor by his troops at York in 306. It is generally assumed that from this time Helena lived at Constantine's court, first in Trier and then at Rome. Helena was given substantial lands in and around Rome, especially the Sessorian palace, in part of which the basilica later known as Santa Croce in Gerusalemme was built, and adjacent lands beyond the walls, on which was built the basilica of St Peter and St Marcellinus and its associated mausoleum. Constantine's biographer, Eusebius of Caesarea (d. 339), relates that Helena was converted to Christianity by her son, a plausible statement that dates the conversion to 312 or thereafter. The notion that she had been Jewish before her conversion, found first in the late fifth-century *Actus Silvestri*, is highly unlikely: the conversion of Jews was a popular motif in Christian literature of the period.

In the autumn of 324, immediately after he became sole emperor, Constantine honoured his mother by granting her the title of Augusta. Her status seems to have increased markedly: Eusebius relates that the imperial treasury was put at her disposal, and some sources even allege that she was Constantine's co-ruler. After her son's death (in 337), Helena's image was used to promote the claims to the imperial throne of Constantine's branch of the family over those of the branch descended from Constantius Chlorus's wife, Theodora. There is, however, no indication that Helena herself was behind Constantine's decision not to involve his half-brothers in the government during his lifetime.

In the last months of 326 or the first of 327, Helena set out from Rome to travel to the eastern provinces. Eusebius, who provides a near-contemporary account, presents her journey as a pilgrimage, motivated by faith. Part of her purpose certainly seems to have been to inspect the progress of the churches in the Holy Land, in Bethlehem and on the Mount of Olives, the construction of which her son had ordered. Her presence in the east, distributing largesse including donatives to army contingents, may also have been intended to assuage the discontent in those provinces provoked by Constantine's recent defeat of the eastern emperor Licinius and his concerted efforts to suppress heresies and pagan cults.

The journey took on new significance when later tradition claimed that it was then that Helena discovered the true cross. Although what was taken to be the true cross does seem to have been found during Constantine's reign, Helena does not appear in the earliest accounts of its discovery. Her name was first attached to the cross by a number of Christian writers of the late fourth century. The earliest are Gelasius of Caesarea, whose ecclesiastical history, written c.390, survives now only in the works of later authors, and St Ambrose, who relates the story in his funeral oration for the emperor Theodosius, delivered in 395. They derived their historical information from Eusebius who, however, does not mention the cross. That element of the story came, in all likelihood, from Jerusalem. It may have arisen partly in connection with the ultimately successful attempt to promote that city's claim to metropolitan status over that of Caesarea, and partly to provide a symbol of Christianity's victory over Judaism. It may have been for these reasons that a member of the imperial family—Helena—was associated with Jerusalem's holiest relic. Among many medieval retellings of the story is Cynewulf's ninth-century Old English poem *Elene*.

Circumstantial evidence, in particular the interruption in the issue of coins bearing her name, suggests that Helena died, aged about eighty, in 328 or the beginning of 329, perhaps in Trier. Eusebius remarks that Constantine was present at her death. She was buried in the mausoleum next to the basilica of St Peter and St Marcellinus, outside Rome. Her feast is celebrated on 18 August in the western church, on 21 May in the east. In the ninth century some of her remains were transferred to Rheims. Pope Innocent II (r. 1130–43) translated her bones to the church of Santa Maria in Aracoeli, on the Capitoline Hill.

Helena became a model of female Christian monarchy for later generations. Pope Gregory the Great (d. 604), for example, compared the role of Bertha (d. in or after 601), queen of Æthelbert I of Kent, in the conversion of the English with that of Helena in bringing Christianity to the Romans. At Trier, a life written c.850, and expanded in the second half of the eleventh century into a double life of Helena and Agricius, bishop of Trier from 314 to c.330, portrayed Helena as a native of that city as part of a protracted campaign to establish Trier's primacy in its ecclesiastical province. Although the claims of these lives are fiction, the remains of an imperial palace discovered in excavations since 1943 beneath Trier Cathedral have been securely dated to Constantine's reign. The reconstructed ceiling frescoes from one room may include a depiction of Helena in later life. While such a close identification is not certain, the existence of this palace suggests an origin for the medieval legends connecting Helena with Trier.

The notion that Helena was British, the daughter of King Coel, the legendary king of Colchester, appears first in Henry of Huntingdon's *Historia Anglorum*. Geoffrey of Monmouth drew on this work to relate that Constantius came to Britain as a legate of the Roman senate, seized the British kingship on Coel's death, and married Helena, with whom he had Constantine. It is probably through confusion with this story that medieval Welsh legends feature a Helena as the wife of the usurper emperor Magnus Maximus (r. 383–8), with whom she had a son named Constantine. Helena's cult was popular in the middle ages, with dedications to her attested as far back as 1010 (St Helen, Bishopsgate, London). The name of St Helens, Lancashire, however, may derive from a corruption of the name of the obscure St Elphin; while the island of St Helena in the south Atlantic was so called because it was discovered by Spanish sailors on her feast day.

MARIOS COSTAMBEYS

Sources J. W. Drijvers, *Helena Augusta* (1992) · P. M. Brunn, ed., *Constantine and Licinius, AD 313–337* (1966), vol. 7 of *The Roman imperial coinage*, ed. H. Mattingly and others (1923–94) · Geoffrey of Monmouth, *The history of the kings of Britain*, trans. L. Thorpe, pbk edn (1966) · F. Arnold-Foster, *Studies in church dedications*, 1 (1899) · Henry, archdeacon of Huntingdon, *Historia Anglorum*, ed. D. E. Greenway, OMT (1996) · D. H. Farmer, *The Oxford dictionary of saints*, 4th edn (1997)
Likenesses bust, Palazzo del Governatorato, Vatican City · portraits (on numerous coins), repro. in Mattingly and Sydenham, eds., *Roman imperial coinage*, 26 · sculpture, Museo Capitolino, Rome

Helena, Princess [married name Princess Christian of Schleswig-Holstein] (1846–1923), was born Helena Augusta Victoria in London at Buckingham Palace on 25 May 1846, the third daughter and fifth child of Queen *Victoria and Prince *Albert. Her pet name in the family throughout her life was Lenchen. A lively child, fearless and inclined to be a tomboy, she tended to quell any brotherly teasing with a swift punch on the nose and gained a reputation for being lively, outspoken, and awkward. Countess Blücher, a close friend of the family, once regretted that 'She is wanting in *charm*' (Battiscombe, 76). Like her sisters she was educated at home, and studied history, modern languages, and domestic arts.

On 5 July 1866 Helena married Prince (Frederick) Christian of Schleswig-Holstein-Sonderburg-Augustenburg (1831–1917), in the private royal chapel at Windsor, Berkshire. At first they made their home at Frogmore House, Windsor—a gift from Queen Victoria—and they then moved to Cumberland Lodge nearby, six years later. After the queen's death in 1901 they were also given a London residence, Schomberg House, in Pall Mall.

The eldest of their five children, Prince Christian Victor (1867–1900), was the first member of the royal family to attend school (Wellington College) instead of being educated privately by a tutor at home. He served with the army in the Asante kingdom and in the Second South African War, and died of enteric fever at Pretoria. Their second son, Prince Albert (1869–1931), was brought up in Germany as heir to the duchy of Schleswig-Holstein; he was obliged to enter the German army, though his refusal to fight against his mother's country during the First World War was respected. The third son, Harold, born in 1876, lived for only eight days. Their daughters Princess *Helena Victoria (1870–1948) and Princess *Marie Louise (1872–1956) both supported their parents tirelessly in their charity work in hospitals and the Young Women's Christian Association. Marie Louise was the only child to marry, but her childless union in 1891 with Prince Aribert of Anhalt was dissolved in 1900.

Helena devoted much time and effort to charitable causes. She set up and helped to supervise a holiday house for deprived and handicapped London children near Cumberland Lodge, and she was a founder member of the Red Cross. Her daughters helped to roll bandages for the wounded of the Russo-Turkish War in 1877, and she was active in voluntary work during the First World War. In 1872 she became founding president of the School of Art Needlework, later the Royal School of Needlework, set up to provide employment for women. For some years she was president of the Royal British Nurses' Association, in which capacity she was bold enough to go against the advice of Florence Nightingale. She actively supported the Society for the Prevention of Cruelty to Children; was for years a regular district visitor in the parish of Holy Trinity, Windsor; and took a keen interest in the Eton Mission at Hackney Wick, east London. On one occasion she enjoined a meeting of the Ladies' Association for the Care of Friendless Girls not to defer to her—'you must try not to mind me at all' (Prochaska, 115)—but she was far from being a background presence in her endeavours and presided over committee meetings with a sense of leadership that befitted Queen Victoria's daughter.

In 1884 Helena wrote a foreword to an edition of the letters to Queen Victoria of her late sister Alice, grand duchess of Hesse and by Rhine (1843–1878), prefaced with a biographical sketch by Dr Karl Sell. A revised edition was published in 1885 in which Sell's text was replaced by a memoir of Alice by Helena herself. Some three years later she translated and wrote an introduction to a new edition of the memoirs of Wilhelmina, margravine of Bayreuth, sister of Frederick the Great, and also in due course an edition of the margravine's correspondence with Voltaire. She loved music and was an accomplished pianist; as a girl she had played duets with the conductor and pianist Charles Hallé, and artists such as Jenny Lind and Clara Butt were among her personal friends.

In appearance Helena was plump and dowdy. Placid, level-headed, and businesslike in personality, her somewhat authoritarian spirit was tempered by sound common sense. During a national dock strike the archbishop of Canterbury composed a prayer of intercession, to be read in every church, that the dispute might be settled. At a service in Windsor Chapel one Sunday she picked up the leaflet from her pew, examined it carefully, and put it down, remarking—in what her daughter Marie Louise described as 'the penetrating Royal Family whisper, which carried farther than any megaphone'—'That prayer won't settle any strike' (Princess Marie Louise, 17).

Helena and Christian celebrated their golden wedding anniversary in July 1916—remarkably, in view of the fifteen years' age difference between them—and she was the only child of Queen Victoria to enjoy such an achievement. Although Britain and Germany had been at war for nearly two years, she was delighted to receive a congratulatory telegram from her nephew Kaiser Wilhelm II, passed to them through their niece Margaret, crown princess of Sweden. Christian died on 28 October 1917. Shortly after her seventy-seventh birthday Helena fell ill with influenza, and died at Schomberg House on 9 June 1923. She was buried in the Albert Memorial Chapel at Windsor on 15 June.   JOHN VAN DER KISTE

Sources *The Times* (11 June 1923) · J. Packard, *Victoria's daughters* (1998) · Princess Marie Louise, *My memories of six reigns* (1956) · J. Van der Kiste, *Queen Victoria's children* (1986) · M. Reid, *Ask Sir James* (1987) · G. Battiscombe, *Queen Alexandra* (1969) · N. Epton, *Victoria and her daughters* (1971) · F. Prochaska, *Royal bounty: the making of a welfare monarchy* (1995)

Archives Royal Arch., personal papers, incl. those of her children · Royal British Nurses' Association, London, letters as president of Royal British Nurses' Association | BL, corresp. with Florence Nightingale, Add. MS 45750 · Bodl. Oxf., letters to H. W. Acland and S. A. Acland · Bodl. Oxf., letters to Georgina Max Muller · Borth. Inst., letters to Emily Meynell-Ingram · ICL, letters to Lord Playfair · NAM, letters to General Mends · NL Scot., corresp. with fourth earl of Minto · NRA, priv. coll., letters to Dalrymple-Hamilton family · PRO NIre., letters to Lady Antrim, D/4091B/3/2 · Staffs. RO, letters to duchess of Sutherland · U. Durham L., corresp. with Charles Grey

Likenesses F. X. Winterhalter, group portrait, watercolour, 1847 (with Prince Alfred and Princess Alice), Royal Collection · F. X Winterhalter, drawing, 1849, Royal Collection · F. X. Winterhalter, group portrait, oils, 1849 (*The four royal princesses*), Royal Collection · F. X. Winterhalter, watercolour drawing, 1850, Royal Collection · L. Caldesi, albumen print, 1857, NPG · L. Caldesi, photograph, 1857, NPG · group portrait, oils, c.1865, NPG; on display at Bodelwyddan Castle, North Wales · portrait, 1865 (after F. X. Winterhalter), Osborne House, Isle of Wight · S. D. Durant, two metal medallions, 1866, NPG · C. Magnussen, group portrait, oils, 1866 (*The marriage of Princess Helena*), Royal Collection · A. Dixon, miniature, 1873, Royal Collection · H. von Angeli, oils, Royal Collection · Bassano, ten glass negatives, NPG · W. & D. Downey, woodburytype, NPG; repro. in W. Downey and D. Downey, *The cabinet portrait gallery*, 11 (1891) · S. Durant, medallions, NPG · F. W., group portrait, oils (*The opening of the Royal Albert Infirmary, 1865*), NPG · A. Hähnisch, miniature, Royal Collection · F. Holl, engraving (after R. Thorburn), Royal Collection · T. Prümm, cabinet photograph, NPG · M. Thornycroft, marble bust (as a child), Royal Collection · M. Thornycroft, marble bust, Royal Collection · Queen Victoria, drawings, Royal Collection · F. X. Winterhalter, oils, Royal Collection · cartes-de-visite, NPG · photographs, Royal Collection · prints, NPG

Helena Victoria, Princess (1870–1948), was born at Frogmore, Windsor Park, on 3 May 1870, the third child and elder daughter of Queen *Victoria's third daughter, Princess *Helena (1846–1923), and her husband, Prince Christian of Schleswig-Holstein (1831–1917); she was given the names Victoria Louise Sophia Augusta Amelia Helena, but was known to her family as Thora. Her early life was spent at Windsor, where her parents had a house in the park, of which her father was ranger. She saw a great deal of her grandmother: there are frequent references in the queen's journal to drives taken with Thora.

As a public figure Princess Helena Victoria grew up to follow the example of her mother and supported many and various philanthropic and benevolent causes, among them the Princess Christian Nursing Home at Windsor, of which she succeeded her mother as president. She particularly identified herself with the Young Men's Christian Association and took a close interest in every branch of its work, visiting France on its behalf during the First World War. It was she who obtained permission from Lord Kitchener to send musical and theatrical entertainments to the troops at the front. In 1917 George V accorded her the style of 'highness' and the territorial name of Schleswig-Holstein was dropped.

In contemporary social life the princess made a definite place for herself: she played lawn tennis, and also golf at a time when few women did so, and she maintained a lifelong zest for ballroom dancing. She had inherited the musical tastes of both of her maternal grandparents and, in the period between the two wars, she and her sister, Princess *Marie Louise, made their home into a musical centre; theirs was the last house in Pall Mall to be used as a private residence. This life of gentle, royal obscurity ended when she died, unmarried, in London on 13 March 1948 after some years of failing health.

H. E. WORTHAM, *rev.* K. D. REYNOLDS

Sources Princess Marie Louise, *My memories of six reigns* (1956) • private information (1959) • *The letters of Queen Victoria*, ed. A. C. Benson, Lord Esher [R. B. Brett], and G. E. Buckle, 9 vols. (1907–32) **Archives** FILM BFI NFTVA, news footage **Likenesses** Lenare, group portrait, photograph, 1945 (family group) • C. Beaton, photograph, NPG • H. Mann, portrait; in possession of Princess Marie Louise, 1959 • H. L. Oakley, silhouette, NPG

Helion family (*per. c.*1120–*c.*1450), gentry, held land in Essex in the twelfth and thirteenth centuries. The Helions are associated for most of the middle ages with the barony of Bumpstead, Essex. Their surname is believed to be derived from Helléan, a village about 6 miles north-east of Josselin, in the interior of Brittany. The Helion ancestor in England was apparently a follower or relation of Tihel Brito (Tihel the Breton) who was lord of Bumpstead in 1086. Once the *caput* of a considerable barony, Bumpstead, located about 8 miles east-north-east of Walden in Freshwell hundred, is today a hamlet known as Helions (and popularly as Helen's) Bumpstead.

The family is first represented by **William** [i] **Helion** (*fl.* 1123–1135), whose overlord was Aubrey (III) de Vere (*d.* 1194), one of the most powerful magnates of the day, who became the first earl of Oxford in 1141. William's son and heir, **Robert Helion** (*d.* 1175×86), owed 100 silver marks relief in 1155 and paid scutage (that is, the tax on his estate in place of military service) on ten knights' fees in 1165. Robert was succeeded by his son, another **William** [ii] **Helion** (*d.* 1212×18), who continued to pay this scutage.

This William married Mabel, daughter of Roger de *Clare, earl of Hertford (*d.* 1173). This alliance with the prestigious house of Clare suggests that the Helions' social status reached its apogee at about this time.

What happened next to cause the Helions to fall out of favour with the crown is problematical. However, there were already indications in the pipe rolls of King John that the estate was incurring large debts for scutage and by 1236 Jews exercised control in the barony. In that year **Andrew** [i] **Helion** (*fl.* 1224–1236) was unable to pay the scutage on the ten knights' fees in question, and paid thereafter for only one. Andrew, also mentioned in 1224 and 1232 with reference to scutage of these lands, appears to have been William's and Mabel's son and heir.

Andrew [ii] **Helion** (*d.* 1289), who was perhaps the aforementioned Andrew's son, married Rose. The couple jointly held lands at Haverhill, Suffolk, and a messuage at Helions Bumpstead. Summoned to serve against the Welsh in 1277, Andrew acknowledged having one knight's fee at Haverhill and Bumpstead to be served by two sergeants. He left a son and heir, **Henry** [i] **Helion** (*d.* 1303). (The fact that Henry was a minor at the time of his father's death suggests that the Andrew who died in 1289 is not identifiable with the person of that name living in 1224–36.) Henry married a certain Alice and served in Gascony in 1296. Leaving an heir who had not yet reached majority became a habit with the Helions: Henry [i]'s son, Henry [ii] Helion (*d.* 1332), was also a minor, as was the latter's son John [i] Helion (*d.* 1349). However, John was succeeded by his son Henry [iii] Helion (*d.* 1391), who was of age.

During the period between the second quarter of the thirteenth century, when the Helions suffered a serious reversal of fortune, and the late fourteenth century, no member of this family left behind sufficient evidence to support an outline of his or her life with anything approaching completeness. Such a dearth of documentation may be purely accidental, but the chances are that it accurately reflects the family's modest possessions and resources, or perhaps its desire to live in privacy.

Another family bears the name Helion, but its relationship to the Helions of Essex, if indeed there is one, has not been determined. Sir Walter Helion (*fl.* 1267–1300), of West Hyde, Bedfordshire, was a justice in 1267 and justice of the bench, Westminster, in 1278. He was a knight of the shire in Gloucestershire in 1295 and was summoned to serve against the Scots in 1298. His son and heir, Piers Helion, married Cecily, aunt and coheir of John Walerand (*d.* 1309), and was living in 1322.

One descendant of the Essex Helions, **John** [ii] **Helion** (*fl.* 1391), son and heir of Henry [iii] Helion, became a man of substance and improved his family's social standing considerably when he married Alice, wealthy daughter and coheir of Sir Robert Swynborne (*d.* 1391) of Belchamp-Otton and Little Horkesley, Essex, whose wife, Joane, was the only daughter and heir of John *Botetourt. The family's prominence was again short-lived: the son and heir of John and Alice, **John** [iii] **Helion** (*d.* 1449), married Edith, daughter and coheir of Thomas Rolfe of Gosfield,

Essex, but they left no male children and the Helion line ended.

After their initial prominence, and until nearly the end of the middle ages, when fortune smiled on them once again, the Helions were not great landed proprietors and, even less, movers and shakers of medieval England. They belonged rather to a type of lesser nobility who exerted very little influence and who, consequently, are rarely mentioned in history books. Nevertheless, such families are remembered to a varying degree in areas where they lived or held fiefs, and their names are at times perpetuated in local toponymy. According to the visitation of Essex by John Raven, Richmond herald, in 1612, the Helion arms were gules fretty argent, over all a fess or. The earliest record of this coat occurs in late medieval sources, and the genealogy provided by Raven traces the Helion family only back to John [ii]. The Helions of Bedfordshire have a far more ancient coat of arms: in heraldic records dating from the reign of Edward I, Sir Walter Helion bore Or, three stags' heads caboshed sable.   GERARD J. BRAULT

Sources I. J. Sanders, *English baronies: a study of their origin and descent, 1086–1327* (1960), 121–2 · P. Morant, *The history and antiquities of the county of Essex*, 2 (1768); repr. with introduction by G. H. Martin (1978), 292–3, 346, 440–41, 530–32, 540 · C. Moor, ed., *Knights of Edward I*, 2, Harleian Society, 81 (1929), 216–17 · J. H. Round, 'Helion of Helion's Bumpstead', *Transactions of the Essex Archaeological Society*, new ser., 8 (1900–02), 187–91 · L. C. Loyd, *The origins of some Anglo-Norman families*, ed. C. T. Clay and D. C. Douglas, Harleian Society, 103 (1951), 51 · G. J. Brault, ed., *Rolls of arms of Edward I (1272–1307)*, 2 vols. (1998) · P. Hide Reaney, *The place-names of Essex* (1935), 419–20, 509 · W. C. Metcalfe, ed., *The visitations of Essex*, 1, Harleian Society, 13 (1878), 203 · M. Altschul, *A baronial family in medieval England: the Clares, 1217–1314* (1965), table 1 · VCH Essex, 1.350, 541

Helion, Andrew (*fl.* 1224–1236). *See under* Helion family (*per. c.*1120–*c.*1450).

Helion, Andrew (*d.* 1289). *See under* Helion family (*per. c.*1120–*c.*1450).

Helion, Henry (*d.* 1303). *See under* Helion family (*per. c.*1120–*c.*1450).

Helion, John (*fl.* 1391). *See under* Helion family (*per. c.*1120–*c.*1450).

Helion, John (*d.* 1449). *See under* Helion family (*per. c.*1120–*c.*1450).

Helion, Robert (*d.* 1175x86). *See under* Helion family (*per. c.*1120–*c.*1450).

Helion, William (*fl.* 1123–1135). *See under* Helion family (*per. c.*1120–*c.*1450).

Helion, William (*d.* 1212x18). *See under* Helion family (*per. c.*1120–*c.*1450).

Heller, Thomas Edmund (1837–1901), teachers' union leader, was born on 15 May 1837 at Bishopsteignton, Devon. He was the son of Edmund Heller, a schoolmaster, who later moved to Cheam, Surrey. Heller attended the Cheam Schools as a pupil and then a pupil teacher, subsequently winning a queen's scholarship to the Cheltenham Training College, where he trained as a teacher from 1857

to 1858. He was then appointed master of the college's model school, and in 1862 became headmaster of the National Schools, Hercules Buildings, Lambeth. He rapidly became active in various Church of England teachers' associations, and was at the founding meeting of the National Union of Elementary Teachers (NUET) in 1870. In 1873 he became the second general secretary of the union, known from 1889 as the National Union of Teachers (NUT), and the first paid secretary. He served until 1891, when he became seriously ill and retired. In 1895, St Andrews University awarded him an LLD for services to education.

During Heller's period as general secretary the union's membership rose from under 7000 to over 18,000, and its finances became much more sound. He fought hard for a teachers' pension scheme, finally established soon after he retired, and campaigned against payment by results, the great *bête noire* of teachers of his period. For a long time progress on the latter was limited by the uncooperative attitude of the education department; the rapid decline of the system after 1890 was the result of pressure from a variety of groups, of which the NUT was one. Within the union, Heller seems to have been a moderate, opposing excessively militant demands which were likely to alienate the church school teachers, while pursuing a reasonably vigorous policy of attempting to ameliorate grievances. He was also a member of the London school board from 1874 to 1888 and of the royal commission on education (the Cross commission) between 1886 and 1888. On this latter he supported educational liberalization and opposed rate aid for voluntary schools.

Heller's career spans the transition from a largely church-dominated system of education to a much more secular one. He went to an Anglican evangelical training college, and was aligned with the church teachers' wing of the NUET in its early years. Subsequently his liberalism and his support for school boards seems to have caused some disaffection among church school teachers. He was also representative of the strong presence in the union of college-trained teachers: on the Cross commission, he supported the extension of college training and restrictions on untrained teachers. He symbolizes much that was characteristic of the NUET: church-influenced but also increasingly receptive to the pressures of secularization; educationally liberal but also concerned, in classic trade-union fashion, to limit entry to the teaching profession.

Heller was married twice: in his early twenties to Margaret Jane White (*d.* 1874); and in 1877 to Lydia C. Lee, a former headmistress, who also predeceased him. He had a daughter, who became a training-college tutor, and two sons, one a solicitor and the other an educational administrator. He was an enthusiastic musician and encourager of music in schools, and a freemason. He died on 17 February 1901 at his home, 51 Southside, Clapham Common, London, and was buried at Brompton cemetery, where also had been buried both his wives.   CHARLES MORE

Sources *The Schoolmaster* (23 Feb 1901) · A. Tropp, *The school teachers* (1957) · G. Sutherland, *Policy-making in elementary education, 1870–*

1895 (1973) • C. More, *The training of teachers, 1847–1947: a history of the church colleges at Cheltenham* (1992) • *CGPLA Eng. & Wales* (1901)
Archives UCL, letters to Sir Edwin Chadwick
Wealth at death £6315 5s. 9d.: administration with will, 2 April 1901, *CGPLA Eng. & Wales*

Hellier, Henry (1660/61–1697), Church of England clergyman, was born at Chew Dundry, Somerset, the son of John Hellier of Bristol, gentleman, and his wife, Elizabeth. He matriculated, aged fifteen, from Magdalen Hall, Oxford, on 5 May 1676, before becoming a scholar of Corpus Christi, Oxford, in April 1677. He graduated BA in 1680 and proceeded MA in 1683, BD in 1692, and DD in 1695. He was ordained deacon of Christ Church on 25 May 1684 and in 1687 was elected fellow of Corpus Christi, of which he was vice-president at the time of his death ten years later. In 1696 he was appointed rector of St Ebbe's Church, Oxford.

Hellier's posthumous notoriety came from a sermon, *Concerning the Obligation of Oaths* (1688), preached before the university on 4 December 1687, which the nonjuring antiquary Thomas Hearne claimed had accused James II of breaking his coronation oath. However, the sermon contains no explicit political content of this kind and only obliquely reproaches the king for using his dispensing power to free dissenters and Catholics from the obligation of the Test Acts.

Hellier committed suicide by cutting his throat at his home in Bicester, Oxfordshire, in early December 1697. Hearne later claimed that he had taken his own life as a result of a conscience troubled by his having taken the oaths of allegiance to William and Mary. Given that Hellier publicly defended King William as not merely *de facto* but also *de jure* monarch in his *A Treatise Concerning Schism and Schismaticks* (1697), this explanation is implausible. It is more likely that it was poverty (perhaps caused by the burden of debts inherited from his father) that brought Hellier to kill himself. His will reveals that he was so heavily in debt that he advised his sole legal executor, his sister Mary, to pay off one of his creditors with some 'fine needle work pictures' (Bodl. Oxf., OU Arch wills, He–Ho, fols. 7–9) in lieu of cash.   EDWARD VALLANCE

Sources Foster, *Alum. Oxon.* • *DNB* • *Remarks and collections of Thomas Hearne*, ed. C. E. Doble and others, 11 vols., OHS, 2, 7, 13, 34, 42–3, 48, 50, 65, 67, 72 (1885–1921), vol. 7, pp. 296–7; vol. 9, p. 156 • H. Hellier, *A sermon preached before the University of Oxford, December 4, 1687, concerning the obligation of oaths* (1688) • H. Hellier, *A treatise concerning schism and schismaticks; wherein the chief grounds and principles of a late seperation … are considered and answered* (1697) • Oxf. UA, OU Arch Wills, He–Ho, fols. 7–9 • Oxf. UA, OU Arch Inv., Eaton–Ta, fols. 109–109*v* • J. Griffiths, *An index to wills proved in the court of the chancellor of the University of Oxford* (1862) • Wood, *Ath. Oxon.*, new edn
Wealth at death possessions (excl. land) £56 18s.; cash £14 19s.: will, Oxf. UA, He–Ho, fols. 7–9; inventory, OU Arch Inv., Eaton–Ta, fols. 109–109*v*

Helliker [Hilliker], **Thomas** [called the Trowbridge Martyr] (1783–1803), woollen-cloth worker and machine breaker, was the sixth child of Thomas Hilliker (1745–1819) and Elizabeth Ebsworth (1749–1831); he was born at Horningsham, Wiltshire, and baptized there on 17 May 1783. Like his elder brothers John, William, and Robert, Thomas was apprenticed as a shearman in the woollen-cloth finishing trade in Trowbridge, Wiltshire. Known later as the Trowbridge Martyr, Helliker would be totally unknown, were it not for his involvement in the Wiltshire machine-breaking riots of 1802.

Shearmen were the labour aristocrats of the industry, responsible for 'dressing' the fulled cloth before sale. This involved first raising a nap, using a 'handle' set with teasel heads, and then shearing the nap with large hand-shears. It was a task which required both considerable skill and strength. It was said that shearmen could make a piece 20 per cent better or worse by due care and labour or the reverse. Their key role in production gave the shearmen a privileged status and a strong bargaining position. They were notoriously the best paid and most 'unruly' of all the cloth-making trades.

From the 1790s this position came under increasing threat from machinery. The gig mill, a simple system of revolving cylinders faced with teasel heads across which the fulled cloth was drawn, threatened to displace hand-raising. Wiltshire shearmen had successfully resisted its introduction into the fine-cloth trade throughout the eighteenth century. However, increasing use of the machine in Gloucestershire led several Wiltshire clothiers to follow suit. A still greater threat came from the shearing frame, invented in 1787 and substantially improved by a Sheffield clergyman, John Harmer, in 1794. Setting hand-shears into a travelling frame which ran along the cloth, shearing as it went, this device threatened to displace the shearmen completely . From the late 1790s Wiltshire clothiers attempted to set up shearing frames in their outlying shops.

The Wiltshire shearmen embarked on a determined resistance. A campaign of strikes, blacking, and incremental industrial violence developed, culminating in the notorious 'Wiltshire outrages' of 1802. Much of this violence was low-key and intimidatory, but the determined resolve of a handful of powerful clothiers to break the might of the shearmen by mechanization resulted in increasing attacks on their mills. In one incident on the night of 22 July 1802, a group of men, armed and allegedly with their faces blacked, burst into the isolated mill owned by Thomas Naish, a Trowbridge clothier, at Littleton, some 4 miles from the town. The mill certainly housed a gig mill. It may well also have contained a new shearing frame. Leaving one of their number to guard the manager, Ralph Heath, the men quickly set the mill on fire. The loss was said to amount to some £8000. The local authorities, under pressure from the government, made determined efforts to secure the perpetrators. On 3 August a nineteen-year-old shearman's 'colt' or apprentice, Thomas Helliker, working for Naish at his finishing shop in the Conigre at Trowbridge, was arrested by Naish and charged with having been the man who had held Heath prisoner. He was sent to Salisbury gaol under heavy military escort. That night Naish's Conigre workshops were burnt to the ground.

Helliker was brought to trial at the Salisbury assizes in March 1803. He was found guilty, solely on the evidence of

Heath, and sentenced to death. He was hanged outside the gaol on 22 March. Helliker was popularly believed to be innocent, and indeed there is good evidence to suggest that Heath's identification of his captor may have been induced by pressure from Naish or the prospect of the £500 reward. Helliker always protested his innocence but refused, despite constant inducements, to impeach any of his fellow shearmen. After the execution, Helliker's body was taken from the authorities, placed upon a cart, and pulled in solemn procession across Salisbury Plain back to Trowbridge. There, it was said, girls in white dresses led thousands of mourners who accompanied the body to the parish church where they forced the curate to bury Helliker in the churchyard with full rites. The burial place was marked by a fine tombstone erected by the woollen workers in his memory.   ADRIAN RANDALL

Sources A. J. Randall, *Before the Luddites* (1991) · K. G. Ponting, *The woollen industry of south-west England* (1971) · private information (2004)

Hellins, John (*d.* 1827), mathematician and astronomer, was born in or near North Tawton, Devon, into a poor family. His father worked as a labourer at Ashreigney, near Chulmleigh. Hellins was bound as a parish apprentice to a cooper at Chulmleigh and worked at that trade until he was about twenty, during which time he taught himself elementary mathematics. He then became master of a small school at Bishop's Tawton, and made the acquaintance of the astronomer Malachy Hitchins, vicar of St Hilary and Gwinear, Cornwall, through whose influence he was appointed an assistant in the Royal Observatory at Greenwich under Nevil Maskelyne. While so employed he studied Latin and Greek and qualified for holy orders. He was curate of Constantine in Cornwall (1779–83) and afterwards of Greens Norton, near Towcester, and in 1790 was presented to the vicarage of Potterspury in Northamptonshire. On 10 November 1794 he married Anne, *née* Brock of North Tawton, with whom he had one son. Admitted as a 'ten-year man' at Trinity College, Cambridge, in July 1789, he finally graduated BD in 1800.

Hellins published nine papers in the *Philosophical Transactions of the Royal Society* between 1780 and 1811. He was elected FRS in 1796 and two years later won the society's Copley medal for his 'improved solution of a problem in physical astronomy, by which swiftly converging series are obtained which are useful in computing the perturbations of the motions of the Earth, Mars, and Venus by their mutual attractions'. Comparing a paper by Hellins from the *Philosophical Transactions* ('On the rectification of the hyperbola') with one on the same subject by Robert Woodhouse, the *Gentleman's Magazine* contrasted the obscurity of the latter to the 'plain and perspicuous' style of Hellins's work.

In 1787 Hellins edited a new edition of Daniel Fenning's *Young Algebraist's Companion* and the following year published his own *Mathematical Essays on Several Subjects: Containing New Improvements and Discoveries*. In 1791 he wrote two of the tracts in Francis Maseres' *Scriptores logarithmici*;

between 1795 and 1814 he contributed a series of mathematical reviews for the *British Critic*; and in 1801 he superintended the publication of an English translation of Maria Agnesi's *Instituzioni analitiche ad uso della gioventù italiana* (1748). In 1806, when the then minister of war was projecting his new military system, Hellins furnished all the calculations and tables on which it was based.

Hellins died on 5 April 1827 at Potterspury and was buried there four days later. Paying tribute, Davies Gilbert, then president of the Royal Society, described him as 'one of those extraordinary men who, deprived of early advantages, have elevated themselves, by the force of genius and of industry, to a level above most persons blessed with regular education' (Nichols, 7.669–70) His wife survived him.   R. E. ANDERSON, *rev.* ADRIAN RICE

Sources Nichols, *Illustrations*, 6.40–43 · Nichols, *Illustrations*, 7.669–70 · R. Polwhele, *The history of Cornwall*, 7 vols. (1803–8); repr. with additions (1816), vol. 5, p. 107 · Boase & Courtney, *Bibl. Corn.*, 1.227 · Venn, *Alum. Cant.* · *GM*, 1st ser., 85/1 (1815), 18–22

Hellmuth, Isaac (1817–1901), bishop of Huron, Canada, born of Jewish parents near Warsaw, Poland, on 14 December 1817, attended rabbinical schools, and at the age of sixteen passed to the University of Breslau, where he was converted to Christianity. On coming to England in 1841, he was received into the Church of England at Liverpool. Trained for holy orders by Hugh McNeile and James Haldane Stewart, Liverpool clergymen of strong evangelical views, Hellmuth emigrated to Canada in 1844, bearing letters to George Jehoshaphat Mountain, bishop of Quebec, from Archbishop Sumner of Canterbury and other eminent men. Bishop Mountain ordained him deacon and priest in 1846 and appointed him to be professor of Hebrew and rabbinical literature at Bishop's College, Lennoxville, of which he soon became also vice-principal. At the same time he was made rector of St Peter's Church, in the neighbouring town of Sherbrooke, then the chief centre of English settlement in the province of Lower Canada. In 1847 he married Catherine (*d.* 1884), daughter of General Thomas Evans; they had two sons and one surviving daughter. Hellmuth's learning and zeal were widely recognized. He received the degree of DD from Lambeth in 1853 and from Lennoxville University in 1854, as well as the degree of DCL from Trinity College, Toronto, in the latter year.

Hellmuth subsequently resigned his posts in the province of Quebec to become superintendent of the Colonial and Continental Church Society in British North America. In this capacity he was very successful. He joined Dr Cronyn, bishop of Huron, in an endeavour to set up in the diocese an evangelical theological college as an alternative to Trinity College, Toronto. During a visit to England in 1861 Hellmuth collected a sum sufficient to endow the new Huron college in the diocese. It was established in London, Ontario, and when it was opened in 1863 Hellmuth became first principal and professor of divinity. He was also appointed archdeacon of Huron, dean of Huron, and rector of St Paul's Cathedral. His continued interest in education led him to institute at London, Ontario, in 1865

Hellmuth Boys' College and in 1869 Hellmuth Ladies' College. He published several works on the Bible, including *The Divine Dispensations and their Gradual Development* (1866) and *The Genuineness and Authenticity of the Pentateuch* (1867). In the 1860s he had a prolonged dispute with Francis Fulford, bishop of Montreal, about an interest-free loan for a church, Fulford denouncing Hellmuth's supposed extravagance in three pastoral letters.

On 19 July 1871 Hellmuth was made coadjutor-bishop of Huron to Dr Cronyn, with the title of bishop of Norfolk, and succeeded him as the second bishop of Huron on his death in September 1872. In his first charge to the diocesan synod, the bishop showed his strong evangelical views by recommending the canons of the Church of Ireland for use in his diocese, by way of preventing ritualism. In 1872 he opened a chapter house, which was intended to form part of a new cathedral. In 1878 he attended the Lambeth conference. The crowning achievement of his episcopate was the foundation of the Western University in connection with Huron College. The university was incorporated by an act of the Ontario legislature in 1878, and was inaugurated by Hellmuth at the chapter house on 6 October 1881. He contributed of his own means $10,000 (over £2000 sterling) to its endowment, and had visited England in 1880 to collect subscriptions.

On 29 March 1883 Hellmuth resigned the see of Huron owing to a misunderstanding. His friend Robert Bickersteth, bishop of Ripon, asked him to leave Canada to become his bishop-suffragan as bishop of Hull, an appointment to which Bickersteth publicly announced that the royal assent had been given. But, as an ordained bishop, Hellmuth was declared by the law officers of the crown ineligible for the post of suffragan. Thereupon Bickersteth installed him in the less satisfactory position of coadjutor-bishop, which lapsed with Bickersteth's death in 1884. Hellmuth became successively rector and rural dean of Bridlington (1885–91), chaplain of Trinity Church, Pau (1891–7), and rector of Compton Pauncefoot, Somerset (1897–9). In 1886 he married Mary Louisa, daughter of Admiral the Hon. Arthur Duncombe and widow of the Hon. Ashley Carr-Glynn; they had no children. Hellmuth died at Weston-super-Mare on 28 May 1901, and was buried there. His second wife survived him.

D. R. KEYS, *rev.* H. C. G. MATTHEW

Sources A. H. Crowfoot, *This dreamer: life of Isaac Hellmuth, second bishop of Huron* (1963) · H. J. Morgan, ed., *The Canadian men and women of the time* (1898) · *DCB*, vol. 13
Likenesses portrait, repro. in C. H. Mockridge, *Bishops of the Church of England in Canada* (1896) · wood-engraving (after photograph by W. Williamson), NPG; repro. in *ILN* (23 Nov 1878)
Wealth at death £597 10s.: administration, 19 Sept 1901, CGPLA Eng. & Wales

Hellowes, Edward (*fl.* 1574–1601), courtier and translator, was once thought to be a member of the Hallows family of Glapwell and Dethick, Derbyshire, although there is no documentary evidence to support this. He may be the Edward Hellowes who married Eleanor Showell at St Margaret's, Westminster, on 14 August 1592 or the Edward

Hellowes who baptized three sons in the same church between 1577 and 1580.

Hellowes translated three works from the Spanish of Antonio Guevara, bishop of Mondonnedo. *The familiar epistles of Sir Anthony of Guevara, preacher, chronicler and counsellor to Emperor Charles V* was first published in Spanish in Venice in 1546 or 1547. Hellowes's translation went into four editions, in 1574, 1575, 1577, and 1584. The letters, which are on various subjects, are based on models from Plutarch, Seneca, Plato, and others and are essays written in the form of sermons. Guevara was also the author of a work translated by Hellowes in 1577 as *A Chronicle Containing the Lives of Ten Emperors of Rome*. The work is an imitation of Plutarch and Suetonius and was based on texts which included Cassius Dio, Herodian, and the Scriptores historiae Augustae. It was dedicated to Queen Elizabeth as a subject fit for the perusal of princes. The third work by Guevara translated by Hellowes was *A Book of the Invention of the Art of Navigation* (1578), dedicated to Lord Charles Howard of Effingham, hero of the Armada, the queen's cousin, politician, and upholder of the protestant faith. The *Art of Navigation* was an appropriate subject for the lord high admiral of England, as it was designed for the intending sea voyager, giving practical advice for life on board ship. It draws on material from, among others, Pliny and Plutarch. The most up-to-date scholarship on Guevara does not mention Hellowes as his translator.

The Familiar Epistles of Sir Anthony of Guevara was dedicated to Sir Henry Lee, knight and master of the leash, who was Hellowes's patron. In the introduction Hellowes writes 'I begin to call to mind my God, my Prince, my country, and also your worship of whom I have received many good things'. One of the good things received was the appointment as groom of the leash, a position he resigned in January 1597 to become a groom of the chamber. On 27 January 1601 he was granted a pension of 12*d.* a day for life.

S. O. Addy suggests that Hellowes's translations are 'quaint, lively and clear' (*N&Q*, 485). The choice of the epistles as a text to translate shows an enquiring and eclectic mind. They cover subjects such as Solon's laws to the Athenians, discourses on ancient stamps of gold, ancient handwriting, advice on good lordship, and, in 'The epistle to Sir Peter of Acuna', advice on keeping order in the household, administering justice, being mild and of good governance (*Epistles*, 158). Other letters give advice on marriage, advising 'equality of blood and estate' and telling the woman 'to be very shamefaced and no babbler' (ibid., 309). Hellowes disappears from the records in 1601.

E. LORD

Sources E. Hellowes, trans., *The familiar epistles of Sir Anthony of Guevara* (1574) · *CSP dom.*, 1601, 387 · *N&Q*, 7th ser., 2 (1886), 485 · parish register, St Margaret's, Westminster · E. Hellowes, trans., *A chronicle containing the lives of ten emperors of Rome* (1577) · P. Coneso, *Antonio de Guevara: en essayista del siglo* (1985) · J. R. Jones, *Antonio de Guevara* (1975)
Archives CUL

Hellwis, Edward (*fl.* 1589). *See under* Helwys, Thomas (*c.*1575–*c.*1614).

Hellyer, Arthur George Lee (1902–1993), horticulturist, was born on 16 December 1902 at 15 Hartington Park, Redland, Bristol, the son of Arthur Lee Hellyer (*d.* 1921), a chartered accountant, and his wife, Maggie, *née* Parlett. His father was later state's auditor for Jersey, but initially kept the family home in London. Hellyer was educated at Dulwich College. As a result of a respiratory condition he left school in 1917, being advised on medical grounds to work out of doors. He worked first on a tomato farm in Guernsey before moving to Jersey to work as a farm labourer in order to be near his parents, who had now moved permanently to the island. After the death of his father in 1921, he moved back to Bristol to work as a nurseryman, specializing in propagation, herbaceous plants, and alpines. He moved briefly to Reading to work with herbaceous plants before returning to Bristol to work in a general nursery. Completely immersed in horticultural work, by the end of the decade he was a renowned plantsman.

In 1929 Hellyer moved from the potting shed to the printing shop, to become the assistant editor of *Commercial Horticulture* before rapidly moving on to become assistant editor of *Amateur Gardening*. On 18 January 1933 he married Grace Charlotte (Gay) Bolt (1907/8–1977), daughter of Ebenezer Zamora Bolt, a horticultural sundriesman. She was a botanist, who played an indispensable and integral role in all aspects of his life. Together they built a house, Orchard Cottage, and created a large garden at Rowfant in Sussex, on a 7 acre plot they purchased in the 1930s. They later also maintained a property with a large garden in Jersey, which Hellyer inherited from an uncle in 1956. They were a devoted couple, both keenly interested in gardening. They had three children: Edward, Peter, and Penelope Susan.

In 1946 Hellyer became editor of the *Amateur Gardener*, a position he retained until his retirement in 1967. Under his stewardship the magazine became one of the leading gardening publications, boasting a peak circulation of 300,000 copies a week. He also edited the monthly magazine *Gardening Illustrated* between 1947 and 1967, and was a director of the publishers W. H. and L. Collingridge Ltd from 1958 to 1967.

Hellyer was a prolific writer, being the principal author or editor of some sixty books. His first, *Practical Gardening for Amateurs* (1935), was followed by numerous others at regular intervals. All were written from the viewpoint of a dedicated horticulturist endeavouring to disseminate his ideas not only to the gardening fraternity but also to those who merely had a general interest in the subject. His *Popular Encyclopaedia of Flowering Plants*, first issued in 1957, had reached its twenty-third edition by the time of his death. His steady stream of texts continued until the late 1980s. He also contributed many articles to the Royal Horticultural Society's journal, *The Garden*, was a regular feature writer for *Country Life* and *Homes and Gardens*, and for many years was the Saturday gardening columnist for the *Financial Times*. He was particularly fond of writing about gardens that were open to the public, and was probably the first horticulturist of distinction to embark upon this activity. His long-term popularity derived from his open-minded approach to new techniques, and from his style of writing, which was invariably clear, informed, and accessible to a wide readership. His achievements were formally recognized when he was made a fellow of the Linnean Society (1948), appointed MBE (1967), and won the Royal Horticultural Society's most prestigious award, the Victoria medal of honour, in 1976.

Hellyer was one of the most respected and popular writers in British horticulture. Unlike some of his contemporaries he never allowed himself to become enmeshed in gardening dogma. He was not, however, afraid to disagree with fashionable theories. He remained throughout his life a practical horticulturist committed to giving his readers good sense coupled with a sound grounding in fact. He was a quiet, retiring man, a doyen of English gardening writers who was admired for his extensive knowledge of plants and gardens. The mainstay of his life was his wife Grace, who supported his endeavours and acted as an ideal sounding board for his literary contributions. After her death in 1977 their daughter Penelope took on this role.

Hellyer's domination of the gardening scene led to his ninetieth birthday being marked by a half-page spread in the *Financial Times*, and his photograph appearing on the front cover of *Country Life*. Unlike the younger generation of horticulturists, though, Hellyer had deliberately shied away from the broadcast media. By the end of his life he was the grand old man of what by this time was seen as the old school, depending on quiet professionalism without need of the embellishments cultivated by the new generation of horticultural media stars. Throughout his career Hellyer had been an active member (and for a number of years a member of the council) of the Gardeners' Royal Benevolent Society, a charity which cares for elderly gardeners and their wives. His final brief illness was spent in the society's home, Redoaks, Cagefoot Lane, Henfield, Sussex, where he died on 28 January 1993. He was survived by his three children.   JOHN MARTIN

Sources *Annual Obituary* (1994), 48–9 · *WWW, 1991–5* · *Financial Times* (29 Jan 1993) · *Financial Times* (30 Jan 1993) · *The Guardian* (30 Jan 1993) · *The Independent* (30 Jan 1993) · *Daily Telegraph* (30 Jan 1993) · *The Times* (1 Feb 1993) · *Financial Times* (16 Dec 1992) · b. cert. · m. cert. · d. cert.
Likenesses photograph, repro. in *The Times* · photograph, repro. in *Country Life* (Dec 1992)
Wealth at death £72,934: probate, 14 May 1993, *CGPLA Eng. & Wales*

Helmont, Franciscus Mercurius van, baron of Helmont and Merode in the nobility of the Holy Roman empire (**1614–1698**), physician and cabbalist, was born on 20 October 1614 at a house in the rue de Louvain, Vilvorde, near Brussels, the only surviving son of Jan Baptista van Helmont (1579–1644), Paracelsian medic and chemist, and Margerite van Ranst (*d.* 1654), daughter of a wealthy landowner. The forename Mercurius with which he was baptized proved to be apt as he was, by his own account, educated by his father 'in the select school of Hermes'. He himself later assumed the forename Franciscus which is always added to his name. Like and doubtless partly because of his father, he acquired an international reputation as a physician and even as a chemist, though only Jan Baptista was historically important in this respect. Both were unorthodox and both were persecuted by the Inquisition but, unlike his father, Mercurius renounced the settled but restricted life of a manorial lord in Catholic Brabant in favour of a freer itinerant life spent mostly in protestant states. He published his late father's collected works in 1648 and, in a preface—where he styled himself a 'wandering hermit'—he gave some account of his education and intellectual development. For some years he travelled in the service of various German courts and in 1658 the emperor Leopold conferred on him a patent of nobility in recognition of his peacemaking activities; he took the title baron of Helmont and Merode.

Van Helmont's first book, *Alphabeti vere naturalis Hebraici brevissima Delineatio* (1667), developed the cabbalistic idea of an original natural language spoken by Adam. His characteristic blend of the speculative and entirely practical was shown by his proposals arising from his theory for teaching those born deaf to speak and to understand speech. His interest in the cabbala—and that of Isaac Luria in particular—was developed through his association with Christian Knorr von Rosenruth. He obtained Hebrew manuscripts and helped Knorr in his grand project to make available an important set of cabbalistic texts, together with related literature. These were published, together with various related essays, as the *Kabbala denudata*, which appeared in two volumes, in 1677 and 1684. Van Helmont's own contributions included a dialogue in which he defended the cabbalistical theory of the origin of matter and an important summary of the Lurianic cabbala, the *Adumbratio Kabbalae Christianae*.

Van Helmont visited England initially on diplomatic missions, but he became resident physician to Anne, Viscountess Conway, from 1670 until 1679. They became closely associated as Christian cabbalists and they converted to Quakerism together. After Lady Conway's death van Helmont returned for a while to the continent, where he saw to the publication of her book. During a second extended stay in England (1681–5) he enjoyed the hospitality of Quakers, some of whom had been much influenced by him, and he published some of his expositions of the central doctrines of the Lurianic cabbala, such as his *Two hundred queries moderately propounded concerning the doctrine of the revolution of humane souls* (1684), in which he propounded the version of the transmigration of souls for which he became particularly known. In the late 1680s van Helmont was mostly in the Netherlands, where he befriended John Locke, with whom he stayed on his last visit to England in 1693–4, when he was no longer in favour with the Quaker leadership.

In 1696 van Helmont visited Hanover and revived two old friendships—one with the Electress Sophia, whose father, the elector of the Palatine, he had once served, and the other with the philosopher G. W. Leibniz. He persuaded Leibniz to draft and see to the publication of the *Quaedam praemeditatae & consideratae cogitationes super quatuor priora capita libri primi Moysis* (1697), a work that largely expounds van Helmont's cabbalistic reflections on the creation. He spent his last years as the guest of a female relative (named de Merode) at Ter Borg, where he died, unmarried, on 30 November 1698.

STUART BROWN

Sources Niedersächsische Landesbibliothek, Hanover, Leibniz/ van Helmont corresp., MSS LH, LBr. 389 • P. N. De Mévergnes, *Jean-Baptiste van Helmont: philosophe par le feu* (1935) • S. Brown, 'F. M. van Helmont: his philosophical connections and the reception of his later Cabbalistic philosophy', *Studies in seventeenth-century European philosophy*, ed. M. A. Stewart (1997), 97–116 • *The correspondence of John Locke*, ed. E. S. De Beer, 8 vols. (1976–89) [esp. vol. 6] • *The Conway letters: the correspondence of Anne, Viscountess Conway, Henry More, and their friends, 1642–1684*, ed. M. H. Nicolson (1930); rev. edn, ed. S. Hutton (1992) • A. P. Coudert, 'Francis Mercurius van Helmont: his life and thought', PhD diss., London, 1972 • F. M. van Helmont, 'Praefatio', in J. B. van Helmont, *Ortus medicinae* (1648) • *Correspondance de Leibniz avec l'électrice Sophie de Brunswick-Lunebourg*, ed. O. Klopp, 3 vols. (1874) • A. P. Coudert, *Leibniz and the Kabbalah* (1995) • F. M. van Helmont, 'Memoirs' and 'Observations', trans. D. Foote, BL, Sloane MS 530 • B. Orio de Miguel, 'Leibniz y la tradicion Teosofico-Kabbalistica: Francisco Mercurio van Helmont', PhD diss., University of Madrid, 1992 • G. B. Sherrer, 'Francis Mercury van Helmont: a study of his personality and influence', PhD diss., Case Western Reserve University, Ohio, 1937
Archives BL, alchemical and biographical notes and papers, Sloane MSS 508, 530, 617 | Case Western Reserve University, Ohio, Darrow manuscripts and collection, 'The life and works of F. M. van Helmont' • Niedersächsische Landesbibliothek, Hanover, Leibniz/van Helmont corresp., MSS LH, LBr. 389
Likenesses double portrait, engraving (with J. B. van Helmont), repro. in J. B. van Helmont, *Oriatricke, or, Physick refined* (1662), frontispiece • portrait, repro. in F. M. van Helmont, ed., *Alphabeti verè naturalis Hebraici brevissima delineatio* (Sulzbach, 1667)
Wealth at death over 12,000 francs: *Correspondence*, ed. De Beer, 721

Helmont and Merode. For this title name *see* Helmont, Franciscus Mercurius van, baron of Helmont and Merode in the nobility of the Holy Roman empire (1614–1698).

Helmore, Thomas (1811–1890), teacher and choirmaster, was born in Kidderminster on 7 May 1811, the son of a Congregational minister. Before going to Magdalen Hall, Oxford (BA, 1840; MA, 1845), he trained his father's choir and taught in his day school at Stratford upon Avon. He was ordained in the Church of England in 1840 and served for two years in Lichfield as curate of St Michael's; he was also appointed to a priest-vicar's stall in the cathedral. In 1842 he became vice-principal, and in 1846 precentor, of St Mark's College, Chelsea, established in 1841 as the first teacher training college for Church of England schools. In 1846 he succeeded William Hawes as master of the children of the Chapel Royal, to which in 1847 he was admitted as one of the priests-in-ordinary. He was presented by the crown in 1872 to the rectory of Beverstone, Gloucestershire, but he apparently resigned it immediately after his appointment. In 1877, after thirty-five years' service as clerical precentor of St Mark's College, he received a retiring pension from the National Society.

Helmore's publications reflect his belief that plainsong was the perfect form of congregational singing, and include the *Psalter Noted* (1849), the *Manual of Plainsong*

(1850), and the *Hymnal Noted* (1851–4), a collection of plain-song melodies with translations of the original texts by J. M. Neale (with whom Helmore also collaborated in two collections of carols). Helmore became the recognized authority on plainsong in Anglican circles, and his *Primer of Plainsong* (1877) was the standard English text (hence the phrase 'to sing your Helmore', which was widespread during his lifetime). Other publications include writings and other compositions associated with the church. Perhaps Helmore's most enduring contribution was towards establishing the English parochial choral tradition. In this he was assisted by his youngest brother, Frederick Helmore (1820–1899), who worked as a peripatetic choirmaster and became known as the Musical Missionary.

Thomas Helmore died at his home at 72 St George's Square, Pimlico, London, on 6 July 1890.

THOMPSON COOPER, *rev.* DAVID J. GOLBY

Sources B. Rainbow, 'Helmore, Thomas', *New Grove* • F. Helmore, *Memoir of the Rev. T. Helmore* (1891) • F. Helmore, 'Reminiscences of a musical missionary', *Organist and Choirmaster*, 5 (1898), 112, 120, 151, 172 • B. Rainbow, 'Thomas Helmore and the Anglican plainsong revival', *MT*, 100 (1959), 548–9 • B. Rainbow, 'Thomas Helmore and the revival of carol singing', *MT*, 100 (1959), 683 • B. Rainbow, *The choral revival in the Anglican church, 1839–1872* (1970)

Archives LPL, corresp. with A. C. Tait

Likenesses oils, College of St Mark and St John, Chelsea, London

Wealth at death £9894 5s. 5d.: probate, 15 Aug 1890, *CGPLA Eng. & Wales*

Helpmann, Sir Robert Murray (1909–1986), ballet dancer and actor, was born on 9 April 1909 at Kingsley House, Bay Road, Mount Gambier, South Australia, the eldest of the three children of James Murray Helpman (1881–1927), stock judge and auctioneer, and his wife, Mary (1883–1970), daughter of Robert Melville Gardiner and his wife, Catherine. His parents' origins were British (the extra 'n' in his surname was adopted for the theatre).

Helpmann's great-grandfather, Lieutenant Benjamin Helpman RN, served on HMS *Beagle* in 1840, contributing to the exploration of northern Australia. His maternal grandfather, Captain Robert Gardiner, born in Scotland in 1812, eventually owned sheep stations in South Australia. No connections with the theatre existed on either side but his maternal grandmother, according to her daughter Mary, was 'a good pianist, a good singer, and a devastating mimic, entertaining us with not always kind impersonations of visitors' (Helpman, 3). Mary grew up with a passion for plays and poetry, but professional acting was out of the question. Her frustration resulted in all three of her children—Robert, Max, and Sheila—making notable stage careers.

Robert was early indoctrinated into his mother's enthusiasms and, as an uninterested and recalcitrant scholar (at Prince Alfred College, Adelaide), he devoted his energies to dancing, piano, and theatregoing. In 1927, when Anna Pavlova toured Australia, she took him on as a student apprentice. Unable for family reasons (his father died in 1927) to go overseas with her, he accepted a contract with the theatre management J. C. Williamson Ltd as principal dancer for musicals, revues, and pantomimes.

Sir Robert Murray Helpmann (1909–1986), by Pamela Chandler, 1956

Prompted by the actress Margaret Rawlings, who was touring Australia, Helpmann went to England in 1932 with an introduction to Ninette de Valois, director of the Vic-Wells Ballet. De Valois recalled the meeting: 'This unknown young man impressed me with a strange sense of power; here, possibly, was an artist of infinite range' (Anthony, [7]). Although his experience was primarily in stage dancing, she took him on and never regretted it. He was one of a group of talented young men, but steadily outstripped them by reason of his versatility. Technically he was not a classical virtuoso, but ballet then largely required interpretative demi-character dance for which his skills were ideal. He had impeccable musicality, excellent *port de bras*, and an outstanding gift for partnering.

In April 1934 De Valois gave Helpmann his first created lead in *The Haunted Ballroom*. He partnered Alicia Markova in *Swan Lake*, and danced in operas and in open-air ballets at Regent's Park. In 1935 he was leading dancer in the revue *Stop Press*. Returning to the Wells, he danced the principal role in De Valois's latest ballet, *The Rake's Progress*, which, over many years, displayed his great histrionic power and depth. As part of the stimulating Vic-Wells organization he met people in drama, opera, and the visual arts as well as in ballet. One particular, and always acknowledged, mentor was Constant Lambert, the Vic-Wells Ballet's musical director.

In 1936 Frederick Ashton staged an intensely romantic work, *Apparitions*, featuring Helpmann and the teenaged Margot Fonteyn. Fonteyn recalled that this was when 'the harmony of dancing with Robert Helpmann began taking hold' of her: 'It is hard for me to explain the intensity of our involvement in that magical process of "theatre"' (M. Fonteyn, *Autobiography*, 1975, 61). An example of their perfectly matched partnership was their superb rendering of the Aurora *pas de deux* in *The Sleeping Beauty*.

Helpmann's inherited talent for comedy surfaced on stage in 1937, when Ashton's wittily eccentric *A Wedding Bouquet* proved his command of burlesque. As a comedian he understood how to differentiate between send-up fun, delicate wit, clever mimicry, and out-and-out clowning. Roles like his inventively crusty Dr Coppélius, and the endearingly inebriated Mr O'Reilly in De Valois's *The Prospect before Us*, won him staunch admirers. Ballet, however, would never be enough to satisfy Helpmann and in 1937, in a historic Old Vic production by Tyrone Guthrie of *A Midsummer Night's Dream*, he played Oberon to Vivien Leigh's Titania. It was at the Old Vic that he met the producer Michael Pickersgill *Benthall (1919–1974), with whom he had a lifelong homosexual partnership as well as many working collaborations.

During the Second World War, Sadler's Wells Ballet (as it was now known) alternated provincial tours with London seasons. It was accepted that drama, opera, and ballet had a vital part to play in supporting public morale. As an Australian, Helpmann was not liable to be called up, but his tireless wartime workload often involved dancing leads in three performances in one day. The appeal of his partnership with Fonteyn and of his own ballets resulted in the company being far better known and loved after the war than before.

Helpmann turned choreographer in 1942 after Ashton was called up. His first ballet, *Comus*, reflected Milton faithfully through lyrical and dramatic dancing, and two months later came a brilliantly condensed *Hamlet* set to Tchaikovsky's fantasy overture and stunningly designed by a discovery of Helpmann, Leslie Hurry. The kaleidoscopic action, representing Hamlet's dying memories, testified to Helpmann's thorough knowledge of the play; and in 1944 he acted the part in a Guthrie production for the Old Vic, giving a reading of keen intelligence and finely spoken verse. Later that year came another highly successful ballet, *Miracle in the Gorbals*. Theatrically compelling, this was a morality story of a Christlike stranger who raised a suicide and was killed by a gang of thugs. Classical dance, folk-dance, and popular social dances were smoothly intertwined.

Sadler's Wells Ballet transferred in 1946 to the Royal Opera House, Covent Garden, and at the gala première of *The Sleeping Beauty* Helpmann, although barely convalescent after a serious viral illness, doubled as Prince Florimund and an elegantly malevolent Carabosse. Healthwise he was in no way up to choreographing and dancing the lead in his complex *Adam Zero*, premièred in April. Although a memorably exciting production, it was uneven and over-ambitious, and as such was critically damned. Its failure alone did not alter Helpmann's relationship with the company, but another more important factor existed in Ashton's growing antipathy towards him. Temperamentally dependent on general admiration,

Ashton was fiercely envious of Helpmann's popularity with the public. Helpmann responded by turning more and more towards other activities.

Although Helpmann continued to dance and maintain connections with ballet—he choreographed the ballet in the film *The Red Shoes* (1948)—the next few years were primarily devoted to the dramatic theatre, for the most part in serious or tragic roles. In 1947 he and Benthall presented a triumphant revival of *The White Devil* in which he played Flamineo. In 1948 they joined Barry Jackson's company at Stratford upon Avon, and Helpmann added King John and Shylock to his repertory. In 1951 they were associated with the Olivier–Vivien Leigh season of Shaw's *Caesar and Cleopatra* and *Antony and Cleopatra*, when Helpmann played Apollodorus and Octavius Caesar. In 1952 he acted with Katharine Hepburn (who became a close friend) as the Doctor in *The Millionairess*. In 1954 he played Oberon at the Edinburgh festival, and was rightly acclaimed as The Devil in Günther Rennert's production of *The Soldier's Tale*. He returned to Australia in 1955 (after twenty-three years), with Hepburn and Benthall, in a stimulating trio of Shakespeare plays, acting Petruchio, Shylock, and Angelo in *Measure for Measure*. Three years later he danced for the first time in Australia with the Royal Ballet.

Helpmann was now directing plays, having staged a remarkable production of *Murder in the Cathedral*, starring Robert Donat, at the Old Vic in 1953. In opera, there was a spectacular and amusing production of *Le coq d'or*, starring Mattiwilda Dobbs, at Covent Garden in 1954. During Benthall's term as director of the Old Vic (1953–61), Helpmann regularly acted and directed there while at the same time appearing in West End plays such as Coward's *Nude with Violin* and Sartre's *Nekrassov* in 1957. Television plays included the solo performance *Box for One* in 1953, and his film roles included the terrifying Child-catcher in *Chitty Chitty Bang Bang* (1968).

Australian tours had tightened Helpmann's always strong family bonds, and in 1964 he choreographed *The Display* for the Australian Ballet. This related the lyrebird's mating dance to a group of young picnicking Australians, and was an immense local success. In the following year he became co-director of the company with Peggy van Praagh. Other ballets followed, and Helpmann's worldwide contacts and standards were also of great value to the Australian Ballet's development and its increasingly important overseas tours. His services to both British and Australian ballet were marked by a knighthood in 1968.

Helpmann's international reputation in the performing arts, and his mischievous delight in feeding the media with controversial material (he was wittily articulate), made him a household name in Australia. He was, however, often in conflict with the Australian Ballet board, and in 1976 they sacked him (his word) from his directorship. During the next ten years he continued acting and directing plays and operas. In May 1986, although suffering from emphysema, he appeared for the last time on stage as the Red King in an Australian Ballet revival of De

Valois's *Checkmate*, an impressive mime role he had created forty-seven years before. On 28 September 1986 he died at Sydney Royal North Shore Hospital.

Australia realized what it had lost. He was given a state funeral on 2 October at St Andrew's Cathedral, Sydney, before a private cremation, and tributes came from the senate and the house of representatives, where the prime minister (Bob Hawke) said: 'No one should underestimate Sir Robert Helpmann's role in the development of the growing maturity of Australia's art and culture'. De Valois summed up their long association more personally:

> To work with Robert Helpmann was always an inspiration. There was at work an alerted intelligence with an acute sense of perception … Bobby had a sense of humour that surmounted everything. Sometimes it was expressed by word of mouth, sometimes by an outburst of mime, at other times by just a look—and the latter could prove to be the most potent of all.   (*Daily Telegraph*, London, 29 Sept 1986)

Helpmann's achievements in the dramatic arts resulted from natural talents guided by a well-balanced and courageous character. He brought unremitting perfectionist application, as well as great zest, to everything he undertook. As a choreographer he created mime and movement dramas rather than plotless ballets, and always chose collaborating composers and designers of the highest calibre. Inevitably he had critics and denigrators, and people he upset either by his mimicry or by the incurable honesty with which he said what he thought. Great friendships, however, were a dominant feature of his life. Michael Somes of the Royal Ballet spoke for many who knew him when he wrote in *Uproar*, the Royal Ballet's house journal at Christmas 1986:

> Perhaps only those of us (from all branches of the theatre) who were fortunate enough and privileged enough to work and learn from him, can know how much we owe to his influence and example … [he] was not only a kind and generous human being who … was willing to share his talent for the benefit of others. Above all, on and off the stage, we owe him hours of laughter.

KATHRINE SORLEY WALKER

Sources M. Helpman, *The Helpman family story* (1967) • C. Brahms, *Robert Helpmann: choreographer* (1943) • G. Anthony, *Robert Helpmann: studies* (1946) [introduction by Ninette de Valois] • A. L. Haskell, *Miracle in the Gorbals* (1946) • M. Gibbon, *The red shoes ballet* [1948] • K. Sorley Walker, 'Robert Helpmann: dancer and choreographer', *Dance Chronicle*, 21/1 (1998), 1–72 [New York] • K. Sorley Walker, 'Robert Helpmann: dancer and choreographer', *Dance Chronicle*, 21/2 (1998), 229–83 [New York] • K. Sorley Walker, 'Robert Helpmann: dancer and choreographer', *Dance Chronicle*, 21/3 (1998), 411–80 [New York] • E. Salter, *Helpmann* (1978) • M. Clarke, *The Sadler's Wells Ballet* (1955) • E. H. Pask, *Ballet in Australia: the second act, 1940–80* (1982) • *CGPLA Eng. & Wales* (1988)

Archives NL Aus. | Helpmann Academy, Adelaide, Australia • Museum of the Performing Arts, Adelaide, Australia • Royal Opera House, London, archives • Sydney Opera House Archives, Australia • Theatre Museum, London

Likenesses P. Chandler, photograph, 1956, NPG [*see illus.*] • J. Cassab, portrait, Sydney Opera House • J. Dowie, bronze bust, Festival Theatre, Adelaide • N. Forrest, bronze bust • photographs, Hult. Arch.

Wealth at death £376,516: probate, 31 March 1988, *CGPLA Eng. & Wales*

Helps, Sir Arthur (1813–1875), public servant and author, was born in Balham Hill, Surrey, on 10 July 1813, the fourth and youngest son of Thomas Helps (1772–1842), a London merchant, alderman, and treasurer of St Bartholomew's Hospital. His mother was Ann Frisquet Plucknett (1777–1851), daughter of the Revd John Plucknett. He was educated at Eton College and at Trinity College, Cambridge, where he graduated BA in 1835 as thirty-first wrangler, taking his MA in 1839. On 27 October 1836 he married Elizabeth, youngest daughter of Captain Edward Fuller of co. Kerry, Ireland. Shortly after graduation he became private secretary to the chancellor of the exchequer in Melbourne's administration, Thomas Spring Rice (later Lord Monteagle), the father of one of Helps's Cambridge friends. From 1840 until the fall of the government in August 1841 he was private secretary to Lord Morpeth, chief secretary for Ireland; he was afterwards a commissioner of French, Danish, and Spanish claims. In 1843, partially through an inheritance from his father, Helps purchased a large estate of 3000 acres, Vernon Hill at Bishops Waltham, Hampshire, and devoted himself to literary work and social reform.

Helps's most successful works were two series of *Friends in Council*, published in 1847–9 and 1859, which took the form of discourses on social, political, and literary topics, each delivered by one of an imaginary coterie of congenial associates, followed by a discussion by members of the group. The format was inspired both by the Cambridge Conversazione Society (the Apostles), to which Helps had been elected in 1833, and by the conversations among distinguished visitors to Vernon Hill, who included Thomas Carlyle, John Ruskin, and Charles Kingsley. A compilation of contemporary commonplaces, written in a prolix style, *Friends in Council* was much admired at the time, especially by distinguished authors. Subsequently it lost its appeal, but more than a century after publication again gained favour among academic writers as a source of brief illustrative quotations. Helps's *The Life of Hernando Cortes* (1871) was dedicated to Carlyle, and a volume of *Conversations on War and General Culture* (1871) was dedicated to Ruskin, with whom Helps maintained a close literary and personal friendship. Helps used his familiar technique of an essay or narrative followed by a discussion among controversialists in his novel *Realmah* (1868), a *roman-à-clef*, in which he introduced under transparent disguises several prominent statesmen and set them to discuss popular questions of the day. One of the discussants, Leonard Milverton, is identifiable as Helps himself. A subsequent novel, *Casimir Maremma* (1870) considered the question of emigration. A tragedy, *Oulita the Serf* (1858), described the evils of serfdom. Helps's strong aversion to slavery led to his research on the Spanish conquest of America. First came *The Conquerors of the New World and their Bondsmen* (2 vols., 1848–52) and then *The Spanish Conquest in America and its Relation to the History of Slavery* (4 vols., 1855–61), which were the product of seven years' research, including visits to Madrid to consult original manuscripts. These works formed the basis of a number of biographies, which were more popular in their day than the complete histories. His

Sir Arthur Helps (1813–1875), by George Richmond, 1858

interest in writing history did not endure, and he declined Palmerston's offer in February 1860 of the regius professorship of modern history at Cambridge, which was later accepted by Charles Kingsley. It appears that in several of his published works Helps was striving to appeal to a mass audience because he needed the money. His finest writing was done in his letters, not intended for publication, in an era when letter writing was a fine art.

It was to social reform that Helps gave his deepest concern. In the 1840s he had taken an interest in the health of towns movement, and published in 1844 a paternalist essay on the relations between master and man, *The Claims of Labour*. He later (1872) wrote the biography of Thomas Brassey, the railway builder, who was noted for his innovative approach to labour questions. Helps had sympathies with the Christian socialists, contributing to *Politics for the People* (1848); but he also enrolled as a special constable to meet the Chartist threat. Influenced by the work of Sir John Simon, whom he much admired, he attempted in the winter of 1853–4 to establish a health fund for London. The object (which was not realized) was to raise £100,000 for sanitary improvements to avert an outbreak of cholera in the East End. Helps was active in the National Association for the Promotion of Social Science from its foundation in 1857, and his last published work *Social Pressure* (1875) was a plea for ameliorative social legislation.

On 9 June 1860, on the recommendation of Lord Granville, Helps was named clerk of the privy council, a post which he held until his death. This brought him into close association with the royal family as well as Gladstone and

Disraeli when prime ministers. He had known the prince consort sufficiently well to select and edit his *Speeches* (1862), to which he added an introductory appreciation. His most important royal assignment was to edit extracts from the queen's journal, published in 1868 as *Leaves from the Journal of our Life in the Highlands*. There was at times considerable tension between author and editor, especially over one note concerning John Brown, the queen's gillie. Helps's ordinary duties at the Privy Council Office came to involve him in the administration of the Cattle Disease Prevention Act (1866); his preoccupation with the transport of livestock inspired his *Some Talk of Animals and their Masters* (1873). On 20 June 1871 he was made CB; and on 12 July 1872 KCB. The honorary degree of DCL was conferred on him by Oxford University in 1864.

After 1867 Helps was severely embarrassed by financial problems. The discovery of china clay near Vernon Hill had encouraged him to develop it for the pottery industry. He invested heavily, and sought to provide welfare for his workers on the lines described in *The Claims of Labour*. The enterprise proved unable to compete with the Staffordshire potteries, and Helps, whose official duties prevented him from closely supervising the project, was defrauded by his agents. In 1869 he was forced to sell Vernon Hill, moving his family to a house at Kew provided by the queen.

Helps died of pleurisy at 13 Lower Berkeley Street, London, on 7 March 1875, having earlier contracted a chill during a levee of the prince of Wales. He was buried in Streatham cemetery on 12 March. On 4 May 1875 a civil-list pension of £200 a year was granted to his widow (who died in 1892) in consideration of her husband's public services. The eldest of his three sons and four daughters, Alice Plucknett Helps (1839–1924), remained unmarried and acted as Helps's literary assistant.   JOHN R. DEBRUYN

Sources *Correspondence of Sir Arthur Helps*, ed. E. A. Helps (1917) · J. R. DeBruyn, 'John Ruskin and Sir Arthur Helps [pts 1–2]', *Bulletin of the John Rylands University Library*, 59 (1976–7), 75–94, 298–322 · J. R. DeBruyn, 'Thomas Carlyle and Sir Arthur Helps [pts 1–2]', *Bulletin of the John Rylands University Library*, 64 (1981–2), 61–86, 407–32 · J. R. DeBruyn, 'Sir Arthur Helps and the royal connection [pts 1–2]', *Bulletin of the John Rylands University Library*, 66 (1983–4), 54–87, 141–76 · J. R. DeBruyn, 'Sir Arthur Helps, Gladstone and Disraeli', *Bulletin of the John Rylands University Library*, 68 (1985), 76–114 · J. R. DeBruyn, 'Journal of a plague year: Arthur Helps, Stephen Spring-Rice, John Simon and the Health Fund for London, 1853–54', *Bulletin of the John Rylands University Library*, 72 (1990), 171–86 · B. B. Schaffer, 'Sir Arthur Helps and the art of administration', *Public Administration*, 38 (1960), 35–47 · Helps family history · J. R. DeBruyn, 'Charles Dickens meets the queen: a new look', *The Dickensian*, 71 (1975), 85–90

Archives BL, letters, as sponsor, to the Royal Literary Fund, loan no. 96 · Duke U., Perkins L., corresp. and papers | BL, corresp. with W. E. Gladstone, Add. MSS 44397–44437 · BL, corresp. with Lord Ripon, Add. MSS 43539–43540 · Bodl. Oxf., letters to Benjamin Disraeli · Bodl. Oxf., Hughenden MSS · Castle Howard, letters to Charles Wentworth George Howard · JRL, letters to W. D. Christie · NL Ire., Spring-Rice MSS · NL Scot., letters to Thomas Carlyle · PRO, letters to Lord Granville, PRO 30/29 · U. Durham L., corresp. with Charles Grey · U. Southampton L., letters to Lord Palmerston · V&A NAL, letters to John Foster · corresp. with Sir Thomas Phillipps

Likenesses G. Richmond, chalk drawing, 1858, NPG [*see illus.*] · Ape [C. Pellegrini], chromolithograph caricature, NPG; repro. in *VF* (15 Aug 1874) · Alice Helps, terracotta bust · C. G. Lewis, line print (after F. Williams), BM · F. Williams, engraving · group portrait, oils (*The opening of the Royal Albert Infirmary, 1865*), NPG

Wealth at death under £1500: administration, 27 June 1876, *CGPLA Eng. & Wales*

Helsby, Laurence Norman, Baron Helsby (1908–1978), civil servant, was born at 14 Howard Drive, Garston, Liverpool, on 27 April 1908, the son of Wilfred Helsby (1870–1913), a sugar broker, and his wife, Marie Helena, *née* Bowen (*d.* 1953). He was educated at Sedbergh School and at Keble College, Oxford, where he played for the college rugby fifteen and graduated with a first in philosophy, politics, and economics in 1929. He went straight into academic life as a lecturer in economics at what was then the University College of the South-West (now Exeter University) from 1930 to 1931. He moved on as a lecturer in economics to Durham College in the University of Durham (1931–40). On 18 August 1938 he married Wilmett Mary Maddison (*b.* 1913/14), the daughter of William Grenville Maddison, a Durham solicitor. They had one son and one daughter.

In April 1940 Helsby became a clerk in the House of Commons, but he moved to the treasury, initially as a temporary appointment, a year later. In 1944 he was promoted to assistant secretary in the treasury and acquired his first responsibilities for the personnel and management questions which preoccupied him for most of his public service career. He was chosen from there to go to 10 Downing Street as principal private secretary to the prime minister (Clement Attlee), a post he held from 1947 to 1950; he was promoted to under-secretary while in that post.

Helsby was subsequently a deputy secretary in the Ministry of Food and then, in 1954, returned to dealing with civil service recruitment as first civil service commissioner. From there he was promoted in 1959 to be the permanent secretary of the Ministry of Labour. Edward Heath, as minister of labour, rated his work there highly.

In 1962 Norman Brook, who had been both secretary of the cabinet and head of the civil service, announced his retirement. There had been much discussion about what was the best role for being head of the civil service. The treasury had traditionally controlled civil service management and staffing issues—senior appointments, pay, grades, numbers, and so on. But inevitably the permanent secretary to the treasury would always be preoccupied by economic policy and not have time for the management issues which the role of head of the home civil service involved. The more recent combination (under Brook) of that position with the secretaryship to the cabinet also had its disadvantages, as the Cabinet Office role again took precedence.

As a result of these difficulties, on Norman Brook's retirement a decision was taken to have two joint permanent secretaries at the treasury, one being in charge of the management side as head of the home civil service with the other in charge of the economic side. The secretary of the cabinet became a third separate post. Harold Macmillan, as prime minister, was concerned to pick the right man for the job (no women were in the running) and interviewed several permanent secretaries. He was obviously impressed by Helsby, who had considerable experience of personnel issues and who came across as the strong, silent, reflective man of sound judgement. As the climax of his career Helsby became joint permanent secretary of the treasury and head of the home civil service, a post he held from 1963 to his retirement in 1968. Sir William Armstrong was the other joint permanent secretary, in charge of the finance and expenditure side, and Sir Burke Trend became secretary to the cabinet.

This period began with the aftermath of the Profumo affair, Macmillan's resignation, and the change of premier, and then covered the advent of the new Labour government in 1964. It was one of considerable turmoil in the civil service and increasing criticism of traditional civil service customs and practice. Helsby had not been well received in the treasury, and his rather distant personality and concern for detail made for some uneasy personal relations with colleagues. Thomas Balogh, Wilson's adviser on economic affairs, complained that Helsby tried to sideline him (Pimlott, 344); while Richard Crossman regretted Wilson's unwillingness to tackle Helsby (Crossman, *Diaries*, 1.332). He was not a natural innovator and perhaps struggled with the changes the Labour government brought. It was also a period of some spy scandals, with none of it made easier by Harold Wilson's paranoia on security issues.

Throughout this period Helsby concentrated on preserving traditional civil service standards when perhaps greater flexibility would sometimes have been desirable. The criticism of civil service practice culminated in the appointment in 1966 of the Fulton committee to examine the structure, recruitment, and management of the home civil service. Helsby supported the appointment of the committee and it fell to him to head the treasury evidence to that committee. Its report, heavily critical of the civil service, was not made until 1968, just after Helsby had retired.

On his retirement in May 1968 Helsby was made a life peer with the title Baron Helsby. He had been appointed CB in 1950, KBE in 1955, and advanced to GCB in 1963. He had always believed in and fostered connections between the business world and the civil service, and after his retirement he entered the business world with enthusiasm. He joined the boards of the Rank Organisation, the Imperial Tobacco Company, and the Midland Bank. From 1970 to 1978 he was chairman of the Midland Bank Trust Company. He was a director of the Industrial and Commercial Finance Corporation from 1972 to 1978.

Helsby was secretary of the Order of the British Empire 1963 to 1968, and honorary fellow of Keble College, Oxford, from 1959. In 1963 he received honorary doctorates from the universities of Exeter and Durham. He died, survived by his wife, at his home, Logmore Farm House, Westcott, Dorking, Surrey, on 5 December 1978.

TOM CAULCOTT

Sources The Times (23 Nov 1979) · WWW, 1971–80 · personal knowledge (2004) · B. St. G. Drennan, The Keble College centenary register, 1870–1920 (1970) · P. Hennessy, Whitehall (1989) · B. Pimlott, Harold Wilson (1992) · P. Ziegler, Wilson (1993) · W. D. Rubinstein, The biographical dictionary of life peers (1991) · R. H. S. Crossman, The diaries of a cabinet minister, 1 (1975) · b. cert. · m. cert. · d. cert.
Archives Bodl. Oxf., corresp. with Clement Attlee
Wealth at death £71,652: probate, 12 March 1979, CGPLA Eng. & Wales

Helsham, Richard (1683–1738), physician and natural philosopher, was probably born at Leggatsrath near the city of Kilkenny, the son of Joshua Helsham (d. c.1694), alderman and mayor of Kilkenny (1692–3), and Alicia Deane. He entered Kilkenny College on 20 January 1692 at the age of eight before matriculating at Trinity College, Dublin, on 18 June 1698. He obtained a scholarship in 1700 and a BA in 1702 before being elected a fellow of Trinity College, Dublin, in 1704. He was co-opted as a senior fellow in 1714 but resigned in 1730 owing to his marriage. Helsham was the first holder of the Erasmus Smith professorship of natural and experimental philosophy, from 1724 to 1738, having previously held a lectureship in mathematics. He was also regius professor of physic from 1733 to 1738. He had a good reputation as a doctor and was personal physician to Swift. Swift noted in a letter to Alexander Pope in 1729 that he was 'an ingenious and good-humoured physician, a fine gentleman, an excellent scholar' (Correspondence, 3.312). He was president of the King and Queen's College of Physicians in Ireland in 1716 and 1725. Through his friendship with Swift, Helsham was involved in Dublin's literary circle which also involved Stella and Patrick Delaney. He married Jane Putland (née Rolton), the widow of Thomas Putland, on 16 December 1730 and was awarded the freedom of the city of Dublin in 1737 for his assistance in the improvement of the piping of water into the city.

Helsham died on 25 August 1738 of a stomach tumour and was interred in the churchyard of St Mary's, Dublin. He was survived by his wife. His will instructed his executors that:

> before his coffin should be nailed up his head was to be severed from his body and that my corps be carried to the place of burial by the light of one taper only at the dead of night, without hearse or pomp, attended by my domestics only. (Irish Genealogist, April 1942)

Helsham's A Course of Lectures on Natural Philosophy, edited posthumously by a colleague and former student, Bryan Robinson, were published in 1739. It was one of the earliest textbooks to present the scientific discoveries of Bacon, Descartes, Boyle, and Newton to university students in an understandable manner. The book had an enduring popularity and was a compulsory text for students at Trinity College, Dublin, until 1849. A reprint of the fourth edition of Helsham's work to mark the millennium was part published by the physics department of Trinity College, Dublin, in 1999. H. T. WELCH

Sources T. P. C. Kirkpatrick, History of the medical teaching in Trinity College, Dublin, and of the School of Physic in Ireland (1912) · R. Helsham, A course of lectures in natural philosophy, 4th edn (1767) [repr. 1999, ed. D. A. Attis, P. Kelly, and D. Wearie] · 'The will of Richard Helsham, doctor of physic', Irish Genealogist, 1/11 (1942), 338–9 · R. B. McDowell and D. A. Webb, Trinity College, Dublin, 1592–1952: an academic history (1982) · E. O'Brien, A. Crookshank, and G. Wolstenholme, A portrait of Irish medicine (1984) · GM, 1st ser., 8 (1738), 491 · matriculation register of Trinity College, Dublin, TCD, MUN V/23/1, MUN V/23/2; repr. in Burtchaell & Sadleir, Alum. Dubl., 2nd edn · entrance and leaving book of Kilkenny College, TCD, MS 2019 [also in T. U. Sadleir, 'The register of Kilkenny School, 1685–1800', Journal of the Royal Society of Antiquaries of Ireland, 6th ser., 14 (1924), 152–69] · The correspondence of Jonathan Swift, ed. H. Williams, 3 (1963) · Thrift abstract, prerogative grant to Richard Helsham for his marriage to Jane Putland, 16 Dec 1730, NA Ire., Document Thrift Abs. 2869 · 'Notes concerning the will of Richard Helsham, dated 29 June 1737 (with codicil 16 Aug 1738), read 28 Aug 1738', Betham's abstracts of wills, NA Ire., Phillips MSS, Document Bet 1/32, H, 2/434/2 · 'Draft pedigree of descendants of Capt. Arthur Helsham of Leggatsrath, c.1680–1882', NL Ire., department of manuscripts, MS 803, part 5 [originally held at the Genealogical Office] · 'The will of Jane Helsham, of Jervis Street, in the city of Dublin, widow', Irish Genealogist, 1/11 (1942), 339 · B. M. Mansfield, 'The Helshams of Kilkenny', Old Kilkenny Review, 2/4 (1982), 319–27 · B. M. Mansfield, 'Dr. Richard Helsham "The most Eminent Physician of this city and Kingdom" (Dean Swift)', Old Kilkenny Review, 2nd ser., 3/1 (1984) · DNB
Likenesses T. Beard, engraving, Dr Steevens' Hospital, Dublin; repro. in O'Brien, Crookshank, and Wolstenholme, Portrait of Irish medicine
Wealth at death £300 to Dr Steevens' Hospital; also £50 books to William Ford: 'The will of Richard Helsham'

Helvius Pertinax, Publius. See Pertinax (126–193) under Roman emperors (act. 55 BC–AD 410).

Helwys, Sir Gervase. See Elwes, Sir Gervase (bap. 1561, d. 1615).

Helwys, Thomas (c.1575–c.1614), Baptist leader, was born into the Nottinghamshire gentry, the son of Edward Helwys (d. 1590), and grandson of William Helwys of Askham, Nottinghamshire (d. c.1557). It is possible that the otherwise unknown **Edward Hellwis** (fl. 1589), whose exposition of Revelation 12 was published in London in 1589 as A Marvell, Deciphered, with a dedication to Henry Carey, first Baron Hunsdon, was Thomas's brother. Admitted to Gray's Inn on 29 January 1593, in 1595 Thomas Helwys set up house at Broxtowe Hall, near Nottingham, signing the terrier that set out the bounds of its rectory. Broxtowe was part of the parish of Bilborough, and there, on 3 December, he married Joan Ashmore, probably of Little Eaton, Derbyshire. The first of their several children was baptized at Bilborough on 5 September 1596. Little else is known of them for several years, and there is no evidence that Helwys became a JP.

Shortly after 1600 Helwys began to develop radical religious views, possibly under the influence of his father or of his uncle, Sir Gervase Helwys. He became acquainted with Richard Bernard, a prominent local puritan, and also with the future separatist, John *Smyth, who was staying with Helwys at Broxtowe when he was taken ill about the end of 1606. However, although Smyth formally separated from the Church of England in the following February, Helwys does not appear to have followed him until about Michaelmas 1607.

Over the next few months the known separatists, led by Smyth, Richard Clifton, and John Robinson, left to join or found groups in Amsterdam and Leiden. It was reported that Helwys was a key figure in organizing the emigration: he 'above all either guides, or others, furthered this passage into strange countries: and if any brought oars, he brought sails'. Joan Helwys was arrested and imprisoned by the ecclesiastical commission, but attempts to have her husband arrested were unsuccessful, and Helwys sailed to Holland, writing to England from Amsterdam on 26 September 1608 to report a dispute with Francis Johnson's separatist 'Ancient Church'.

An even more dramatic development followed. About January 1609 Smyth rebaptized himself and then Helwys, and before autumn contact was made with the Waterlander congregation of Mennonites. This order of events is important: the English did not derive their baptism or, as Helwys later recalled, their [Baptist] faith, from the Mennonites. But some time in 1609 both he and Smyth adopted the doctrine of general redemption, at odds with hardline Calvinist doctrine, which limited salvation to the elect. In 1611 Helwys developed his views on this issue in *A Short and Plaine Proof*. Predestinarian theology was closely associated with the efforts of the Dutch Reformed leaders to establish themselves as the authoritative upholders of a religious orthodoxy, and consequently to restrict opportunities for religious freedom in Holland. This may in turn have encouraged the English emigrants to adopt theological views providing scope for freedom of thought.

By March 1610 John Smyth was seeking union with the Mennonites, having become convinced that his self-baptism had been disorderly. Helwys rejected the belief upon which this was predicated, that baptism should, in all cases possible, be received by succession from those duly ordained and baptized in a true church. In the ensuing split Smyth and the majority were excommunicated, by Helwys and a minority reported to number no more than ten. It was Smyth, they angrily charged, who had abandoned them, by embracing the priestly notion of succession. The experience heightened the new group's suspicion of intellectualism, strengthening its traditional separatist antipathy to the clergy. In Helwys's own words, 'the most simplest soul that seeks the truth in sincerity may attain unto the knowledge of salvation contained in the Word of God' (Helwys, preface, *Declaration of Faith* [1611]). And he himself provided an example of lay leadership in religion, attacking the impositions of church courts, and the use of the threat of excommunication to extract tithes and fees.

In Holland, Helwys's quarrel was at first solely with Smyth and his group, and he maintained cordial relations with the Mennonites. But as the underlying similarity between Smyth's positions and those of the Mennonites became clear, Helwys's hostility grew. He rejected the toleration within their ranks of Christological heresies that had already caused strife among English Baptists, and he criticized their leaders for making dangerous concessions to a profane 'popularity' which subverted the spiritual and civil order. Thus, he deplored the laxity of their sabbath observance, and he attacked their traditional Anabaptist exclusion of the magistrate from the church, which encouraged disrespect of lawful authorities. He

rejected attempts to appeal to broad layers of the people: 'gather together a holy people and build up pure churches' (Helwys, *An Advertisement* [1611], 81). His piety dovetailed with respect for the civil power.

And yet, for Helwys, the civil authorities ought themselves to be constrained, by law, reason, and Christian duty, to confine their jurisdiction to the civil sphere, and he opposed all compulsion, even of Roman Catholics and non-Christians, in matters of conscience. In this he went further than any other English thinker of the time; his radicalism stemmed partly from the rigour of Smyth's theoretical separation between the spiritual and material spheres. But Helwys interpreted this not as a denial of the godliness of magistracy, but as a call for the institutional separation of church and state. There is evidence that he had been impressed by the wide religious toleration allowed by the Dutch secular authorities.

Isolated in Holland, and desirous to further the cause of his newly discovered religious beliefs, Helwys and his group returned to England, probably in the winter of 1612–13, having organized the printing in Amsterdam of *The Mystery of Iniquity*. Its flyleaf, which Helwys signed from Spitalfields, bluntly warned King James that he was 'a mortal man and not God, and therefore hath no power over ye immortal souls of his subjects to make lawes and ordinances for them and to set spiritual lawes over them'. Helwys and his friends were soon arrested. In 1614 the House of Lords received from them a petition, which complained of long imprisonment and requested permission to take the oath of allegiance, imposed on recusants under the statute of 1610, through which Roman Catholics were able to claim their freedom. Helwys may have written this plea, which was 'rejected by the committee' (Burrage, 2.215–16), though another source relates that in 1613 John Murton was already leader of the group. However that may be, Thomas Helwys certainly died before 8 April 1616, when the will of his uncle Geoffrey, a prominent London merchant tailor, and sheriff in 1607, referred to Joan Helwys as his widow.

Thomas Helwys deserves recognition, as the lay organizer of the first Baptist church in England, and as a pioneer in the development of religious toleration: 'Let them be heretics, Turks, Jews, or whatsoever, it appertains not to the earthly power to punish them in the least measure' (Helwys, *Mystery of Iniquity*, 69). STEPHEN WRIGHT

Sources Helwys's Latin letter to Waterlanders, Amsterdam Gemeentearchief, Amsterdam, Mennonite archives, 'Wybrands Memorial B', MS 1349 • Helwys's English letter, Amsterdam Gemeentearchief, Amsterdam, Mennonite archives, 'Wybrands Memorial B', MS 1350 • Dutch correspondence concerning relations with the English, Amsterdam Gemeentearchief, Amsterdam, Mennonite archives, 'Wybrands Memorial B', MSS 1357–1363 [most of these trans. in Evans, *History*, or repr. in Dutch in Burrage, *Early English dissenters*] • B. H. Evans, *History of the English Baptists*, 2 vols. (1862) • C. Burrage, *The early English dissenters in the light of recent research, 1558–1641* [1912] • W. Burgess, *John Smyth, the se-baptist, Thomas Helwys and the first Baptist church in England* (1911) • B. R. White, *The English separatist tradition* (1971) • R. Marchant, *The puritans and the church courts in the diocese of York, 1560–1642* (1960) • W. K. Jordan, *The development of religious toleration in England*, 4 vols. (1932–40), vol. 2, pp. 278–84 • *The works of John Smyth*, ed. W. T. Whitley, 2 vols. (1915) · E. A. Payne, *Thomas Helwys and the first Baptist Church in England* (1966) · W. T. Whitley, 'Thomas Helwys of Broxtowe Hall', *Baptist Quarterly*, 7 (1934–5), 241–55; pubd separately as *Thomas Helwys of Gray's Inn and Broxtowe Hall* [1936] · W. H. Burgess, 'The family of Thomas Helwys', *Transactions of the Baptist Historical Society*, 3 (1912–13), 18–30 · T. Helwys, *A short and plaine proofe ... that Gods decree is not the cause off anye mans sinne or condemnation* (1611) · J. Robinson, *Of religious communion private, and publique* (1614) · J. Foster, *The register of admissions to Gray's Inn, 1521–1889, together with the register of marriages in Gray's Inn chapel, 1695–1754* (privately printed, London, 1889), 81

Helyar, John (1502/3–1541?), scholar, was born in Hampshire, probably at East Meon. He went to Corpus Christi College, Oxford, where he was admitted a scholar on 1 June 1522 at the age of nineteen. He graduated BA on 27 July 1524, MA on 3 April 1525, and BTh in April 1532. At Corpus he studied with Juan Luis Vives, to whom he wrote in 1524 and with whom he continued to correspond. Cardinal Wolsey probably patronized Helyar, perhaps through Edward Finch's recommendation, and Helyar may have been a member of Wolsey's household, perhaps along with Michael Throckmorton. He vacated the rectory of Milton, Berkshire, by February 1527, and the following year acquired East Meon, and on 24 April 1533 Warblington, by the countess of Salisbury's patronage (vacated by 8 December 1537). Helyar may have tutored some of her children, and was close to the family, especially Sir Geoffrey Pole.

In the summer of 1535 Helyar left England with his servant Henry Pyning and went to Paris to study, secure in the knowledge that Sir William Paulet and Sir Anthony Windsor would take care of his parish for him. His bishop, Stephen Gardiner, may have delayed reporting Helyar's departure; they were said to be close. Helyar's motive for leaving was not entirely scholarly, for he made clear his opposition to new religious policies in conversations with friends, and also began to translate from Greek John Chrysostom's *De incomprehensibili providentia ac potentia Dei*, which he meant to publish in England. Much of the work dealt with martyrs, although Helyar did not take the opportunity to embroider the translation. A preface, added later, argued that the work was more suited to present-day England than to the time in which it was written, given Henry VIII's cruelties in the wake of the supreme headship. A reference to the overthrow of the monasteries dates the preface to 1536 at the earliest. By adding it and other marginalia, Helyar converted the translation into a vehicle to attack English developments. For example, one note reads 'As now in England, where even more atrocious things are perpetrated' (reg. lat. 2004, fol. 44*r*), another underlined outrages to priests (ibid., fol. 46*v*), a third says 'So many in England constantly hold the faith in their hearts', another points to the sufferings of English Franciscans (ibid., fol. 51*r*), and Helyar did not omit the obligatory reference to John Fisher and Thomas More (ibid., fol. 51*v*). The notebook containing the translation also boasts the earliest copy of Ignatius of Loyola's *Spiritual Exercises*, and Helyar may have done them under Loyola's or Pierre Favre's direction, either in Paris or in Venice.

Helyar went to Louvain early in 1536, living initially with John Lobel, one of the canon law professors. Probably then he composed a daily timetable, beginning very early with legal study, and progressing through a full course of lectures, including more law, tutoring in Latin (for which he used Erasmus and Rudolf Agricola), and lectures on Greek and Horace. Within the year he had added the study of Hebrew, apparently with Andrew van Gennep. He knew Greek well and made a number of translations from it, besides Chrysostom, including several sermons of Basil the Great. In addition to a Latin epitaph of more than forty lines for Erasmus, originally published in a collection by one of his professors at Louvain and many times reprinted, he wrote another in Greek. This is the total of his known poetry, which may not seem to justify John Pits's judgement that he was one of the best poets of his time.

While at Louvain, Helyar probably met Reginald Pole, whom he may have known at Oxford, although Pole was never a student of Vives. Helyar was very likely the English student who wrote to Pole in 1537 proposing that both prayers for the reconversion of England and confutations of English attacks on papal primacy were needed. The letter showed particular concern with preaching, and accused English ministers of being wolves and poisoners of their flocks. The author calmly assured Pole that his reputation would easily restore England, especially its nobility, to the church, since the vast majority of English men and women still held the true faith; Helyar did not care whether Pole persuaded or coerced their leaders. He claimed to have recent evidence from a merchant of Southampton about the monstrous state of the English church. He further demonstrated his qualifications to write the proposed confutations in part through an extended passage in Greek. Helyar's letter almost reads as if he knew of Pole's *De unitate*, so closely does his analysis (and the terms in which he cast it) parallel Pole's. It is therefore unsurprising that he was included in the investigations into the Courtenay conspiracy, when his curate delivered several of his letters to Sir William Goring, one of Cromwell's most aggressive agents in Sussex. John Collins, chaplain to Sir Henry Pole, Lord Montague, received letters from Helyar about the disposition of some of his property and about Reginald Pole's promotion as cardinal, reinforcing Helyar's links to the Poles. Trips to Louvain by his brother-in-law John Fowle of Warblington suggest their further connivance in supporting Helyar.

Helyar was attainted along with Pole and many others on 19 May 1539. By then Helyar was in Rome. Already in March 1538 Pole had made him one of the chamberlains of the English hospice on his reorganization of it. Among the other brothers were Helyar's servant Pyning and old friend Throckmorton. Helyar held the post a short time, becoming instead the English penitentiary. He probably died in early December 1541, since Pole discussed his successor in a letter of 23 December.   T. F. MAYER

Sources H. de Vocht, *Monumenta humanistica Lovaniensa: texts and studies about Louvain humanists in the first half of the XVIth century* (1934), 14–16, 585–608 · Biblioteca Apostolica Vaticana, Vatican

City, Reg. lat. 2004 · Biblioteca Apostolica Vaticana, Vatican City, Vat. lat. 5826, fols. 39r–41v; 120r–121r · Emden, *Oxf.*, vol. 4 · *LP Henry VIII*, 7, appx 32; 9, no. 128; 13/2, nos. 695, 818, 829, 875, 986, 1017(1–3); 14/1, no. 867, cap. 15 · PRO, SP 1/121, fol. 91r, 1/135, fol. 105r, 1/136, fol. 181r, 1/138, fol. 191r · H. Chitty, ed., *Registrum Stephani Gardiner et Johannis Poynet* (1949) [introduction by H. E. Malden] · Bale, *Index* · J. Pits, *Relationum historicarum de rebus Anglicis*, ed. [W. Bishop] (Paris, 1619) · G. B. Parks, 'The Reformation and the hospice, 1514–1559', *The Venerabile*, 21 (1962), 193–217 [sexcentenary issue: *The English hospice in Rome*] · H. Thurston, 'The first Englishman to make the spiritual exercises', *The Month*, 142 (1923), 336–47

Archives Biblioteca Apostolica Vaticana, Vatican City, MSS, Reg. lat. 2004

Hemans, Charles Isidore (1817–1876), antiquary, was the youngest son of Captain Alfred Hemans and Felicia Dorothea *Hemans, poet. He accompanied his mother, whose special favourite he was, on a visit to Abbotsford in 1829, and was with her at the time of her death in 1835. He left England early in life, and after residing in various places on the continent, finally settled in Rome and made Roman history and archaeology his chief study. He was the originator in 1846 of the *Roman Advertiser*, the first English paper published in the city. He helped to establish the English Archaeological Society there in 1865, and afterwards became its honorary secretary and librarian. He wrote several books on the art and architecture of Rome in ancient and medieval times, including *A History of Ancient Christianity and Sacred Art in Italy* (1866) and its sequel *A history of medieval Christianity and sacred art in Italy, AD 900–1450; in Rome from 1350 to 1500* (1869–72). He briefly entered the Roman Catholic church and his historical and artistic judgement was frequently affected by his religious fervour. To English visitors in Rome and to English residents he was always a friendly guide, and his writings were useful to students of Italian ecclesiastical history and archaeology. After a serious illness at La Spezia in the summer of 1875 he moved to Bagni di Lucca where he died on 26 October 1876. He was buried in the protestant cemetery there.

G. C. BOASE, *rev.* RICHARD SMAIL

Sources *The Times* (3 Nov 1876) · *The Athenaeum* (4 Nov 1876) · Allibone, *Dict.* · Boase, *Mod. Eng. biog.*

Archives NL Scot., letters to Blackwoods

Hemans [*née* Browne], **Felicia Dorothea** (1793–1835), poet, was born on 25 September 1793, at 118 Duke Street, Liverpool, the daughter of George Browne and his wife, Felicity Dorothea, *née* Wagner (1766–1827). Her paternal grandfather was George Browne of Passage, co. Cork, Ireland; her maternal grandparents were Elizabeth Haydock Wagner (*d.* 1814) of Lancashire and Benedict Paul Wagner (1718–1806), wine importer at 9 Wolstenholme Square, Liverpool. Family legend gave the Wagners a Venetian origin; family heraldry an Austrian one. The Wagners' country address was North Hall near Wigan; they sent two sons to Eton College. Of three daughters only Felicity married; her husband George Browne joined his father-in-law's business and succeeded him as Tuscan and imperial consul in Liverpool.

Felicia Dorothea Browne was the fourth of six Browne children (three boys and three girls) to survive infancy. Of her two sisters, Elizabeth died about 1807 at the age of

Felicia Dorothea Hemans (1793–1835), by William Holl, pubd 1837 (after William Edward West, 1827)

eighteen, and Harriett Mary Browne (1798–1858) married first the Revd T. Hughes, then the Revd W. Hicks Owen. Harriett collaborated musically with Felicia and later edited her complete works (7 vols. with memoir, 1839). Her eldest brother, Lt-Gen. Sir Thomas Henry *Browne KCH (1787–1855), had a distinguished career in the army; her second brother, George Baxter CB, served in the Royal Welch Fusiliers 23rd foot, and became a magistrate at Kilkenny in 1830 and chief commissioner of police in Ireland in 1831; and her third brother, Claude Scott Browne (1795–1821), became deputy assistant commissary-general in Upper Canada.

Their business disrupted by war and wartime panic, the Brownes resettled at Gwrych near Abergele, north Wales, from 1800 to 1809. Felicia's father emigrated to Canada about 1806; he sent irregular remittances and died some time after April 1812. Felicia learned French, Italian, Spanish, Portuguese, German, drawing, and music at home; a 'gentleman' tutored her in Latin, lamenting '"that she was not a man to have borne away the highest honours at college!"' (Chorley, 1.20); her parents took her to London at the age of eleven and twelve, her only visits there. By 1807 she had written a book of poems whose 'simplicity', 'richness', and linguistic attainments 'quite surprised and delighted' William Roscoe, Liverpool's literary leader (Roscoe, 920 NIC 29/4). In 1808 her *Poems* appeared from Roscoe's publisher Cadell and Davies, with 978 subscribers and a dedication to the prince of Wales. One subscriber, Thomas Medwin, showed her work to Percy Shelley, who corresponded with her under a pseudonym, opposing the 'sanguinary' wartime enthusiasm of her second 1808 volume, *England and Spain, or, Valour and Patriotism*

(Barker-Benfield, 25). Felicia's mother intervened to discourage the correspondence.

In 1809 the Brownes moved to Bronwylfa in the cathedral town of St Asaph, Flintshire, gaining the patronage of Bishop Luxmoore and Dean Shipley. In 1812 Felicia published *The Domestic Affections*, and on 30 July of that year she married Captain Alfred Hemans (*b.* 1781), a wounded veteran of Peninsular and Low Country campaigns. The son of John and Alcey Morrison Hemans (pronounced Hemmons), Alfred had been schooled in north Wales in the care of the Wynnes, with whom he had family connections. As adjutant to the Northamptonshire local militia he took his wife to Daventry in 1812. On his release with no pay he returned to Bronwylfa early in 1814 with Felicia and their son Arthur Wynne (*bap.* 1813, *d.* 1837). Four more sons followed, George Willoughby (1814–1885), Claude Lewis (1815–1893), Henry William (1817–1871), and Charles Isidore *Hemans (1817–1876). The Hemans separated in 1818, perhaps because of the demands of her work, or the embarrassments of his finances, or through a combination of both factors. Captain Hemans appeared in London on business for his wife in 1819 and 1820, but settled permanently in Rome. In resuming her career, Felicia Hemans published in the *Edinburgh Annual Register* for 1815, and gained John Murray as a publisher for *The Restoration of the Works of Art to Italy* (2nd edn 1816) and *Modern Greece* (published anonymously, 1817). Byron admired the former (and echoed it in *Childe Harold*, 4), but criticized the latter, which opposed him on the issue of the Elgin marbles.

By 1820 Felicia Hemans was cautiously welcomed in tory circles, corresponding with William Gifford and H. H. Milman, and associating with Reginald Heber (Dean Shipley's son-in-law). Her work was praised in the October 1821 *Quarterly Review* by John Taylor Coleridge. To poems on the deaths of Princess Charlotte (*Blackwood's Edinburgh Magazine*, 1818) and King George (1820) she added prize poems and commissions: 'The Meeting of Bruce and Wallace on the Banks of the Carron' (*Wallace's Invocation to Bruce*, 1819), *Dartmoor* for the Royal Society of Literature (1821), and *A Selection of Welsh Melodies* for the Cymrodorion Society (with John Parry, 1822). Most noticed was her *The Sceptic* (1821): like *The Domestic Affections*, it defended domestic and religious values, though chillingly and from their 'necessity' (Coleridge, 135). In *Superstition and Revelation* she attempted a more liberal synthesis of paganism and Christianity, but after Heber's critique, this was abandoned as a fragment. Milman superintended her verse play *The Vespers of Palermo* through production at Covent Garden (12 December 1823); it failed, in part because an *ingénue* was miscast as its heroine. An Edinburgh performance on 5 April 1824 fared better, promoted by Joanna Baillie and Sir Walter Scott, and starring Harriet Siddons.

Hemans was more comfortable writing as an international liberal than as a British patriot, especially in her adaptations of Germaine de Staël and J. C. L. Sismondi in *Translations from Camoens* (1818), *Tales, and Historic Scenes* (1819), *The Siege of Valencia: the Last Constantine* (1823), and *The Vespers of Palermo* (1823). These works brought Staël's and Sismondi's interpretations of Italian destiny to bear on post-war developments, including the Mediterranean revolts of 1820–21. Other sources for this work were Plutarch, Petrarch, Gibbon, Schiller, Herder, Byron, Coleridge, and Baillie. By 1825 three prominent American Unitarians, Andrews Norton, William Ellery Channing, and George Bancroft, hailed Hemans's work as forwarding a liberal, disestablished protestantism. Norton superintended copyright publication for Hemans in Boston (1826–8), and offered her a magazine editorship, which she declined. Her last long poem, *The Forest Sanctuary* (1825), was inspired by the protestant conversion of the Anglo-Spanish émigré priest Joseph Blanco White. Two suppressed poems of this period oppose Benthamite reform ('Reform, a Poem' and *The Tale of the Secret Tribunal*), while lyrics in the *New Monthly Magazine* promote the Italian republicanism of Roscoe and Sismondi. Hemans published over 350 poems in magazines and verse annuals, many from sequences like *Records of Woman*, her most successful book (1828). She corresponded regularly with other women writers, especially Mary Howitt and Mary Russell Mitford, and entertained Maria Jane Jewsbury during the summer of 1828 at Rhyllon outside St Asaph and later in Wavertree.

On 11 January 1827 Hemans's mother died, and by autumn 1828 the extended Browne household had dispersed. Hemans sent her two elder sons to their father in Rome and took the others to suburban Liverpool, visiting first with Henry Park and his daughter Eliza at Wavertree Lodge, and renewing connections with Rose Lawrence of Wavertree Hall (the wife of Liverpool's whig mayor). Taking modest lodgings at a house later numbered 17 Wavertree High Street, Hemans contended with child care, contagious disease, autograph seekers, and constant literary business, her health plagued by mood swings and heart or lung complaints. Her renewed studies in German literature (Goethe, Tieck, Novalis, Körner, Oehlenschlaeger) and recent music (by Weber, Mozart, Pergolesi, and Paganini) fed the fevered production of *Songs of the Affections* (1830). Collaborating with Jewsbury and the Chorley family on verse annuals and with John Lodge on musical arrangements for her poetry, she also visited Roscoe, received the Nortons, and met John Bowring, free-trade advocate, among other travellers and linguists. Now the nation's most noted woman poet, she visited Scott at Abbotsford and Francis Jeffrey in Edinburgh in July 1829 (see Jeffrey, *Edinburgh Review*, 1829), and Wordsworth in the Lake District in the summer of 1830. She returned to Scotland in August of 1830 and visited Dublin later that year.

Advised by her doctors against another winter in Liverpool, Hemans moved to Dublin in 1831; her brother George was in Kilkenny, and she had made friends with the Graveses, a prominent family there. Young Robert Perceval Graves in particular, a clergyman-to-be, brought warmth to Hemans's religious faith and encouraged the interest in Wordsworth evident in her *Scenes and Hymns of Life* (1834) and 'Sonnets Devotional and Memorial' (Graves was to edit her sonnets posthumously for Blackwood's).

Graves tutored her youngest son, Charles, and Hemans enlisted Wordsworth in finding Graves a curacy in the Lake District. In Dublin she gained the friendship of William Rowan Hamilton and Maria Smith, and the support of Archbishop Whately and Colonel d'Aguilar, Rose Lawrence's brother and adjutant-general of Ireland. She continued, however, to reserve a non-sectarian sympathy for Ireland's Catholic martyrs. Early addresses for her in Dublin are 2 Upper Pembroke Street and 36 St Stephen's Green, but by 1833 she had moved to 20 Dawson Street, in Dublin.

Volumes of lyrics, songs, and hymns by Hemans appeared in Boston and Dublin (1827, 1833, 1834). Despite failing health she expressed ambitions 'to concentrate all my mental energy in the production of some more noble and complete work' worthy 'of a British poetess', namely 'The Christian Temple', to be introduced by her 1834 'Despondency and Aspiration' and modelled on Schiller's *Die Götter Griechenlands* (Chorley, 2.257–8, 343). She resumed translations and commentaries on foreign literature (*Edinburgh Magazine*, 1820–21; *New Monthly Magazine*, 1832, 1834), and planned a book of childhood reminiscences.

In the early autumn of 1834 Hemans contracted scarlet fever, which triggered a 'consumptive' decline. On 2 February 1835 Sir Robert Peel offered her son Henry a clerkship and granted her £100, referring to her 'embarrassing pecuniary circumstances' (Peel, BL, Add. MS 40413, fol. 291). (This is in contrast to P. R. Feldman's description of her 'comfortable income' (p. 149); it also conflicts with her family's claims of support (Leslie, 15.6).) Felicia Hemans died at 20 Dawson Street, Dublin, on 16 May 1835. She was buried on 29 May in the vault of St Ann's Church, Dawson Street, the place marked by a plaque and a stained-glass window featuring women of the scriptures, the latter commissioned by subscription in 1865. Her brothers provided a plaque (which mistakenly gives her age at death as forty) at St Asaph Cathedral, where a stained-glass window portrays the biblical Miriam and Deborah in war and peace. Another memorial is the annual Felicia Hemans poetry prize at the University of Liverpool.

Among Hemans's sons, Willoughby, a graduate of the military college at Sorèze, France, joined the Ordnance Survey in northern Ireland and later became a prominent civil engineer in Ireland and England. Claude joined the customs office in 1835, and went to America in 1836. Henry was appointed a clerk in the Admiralty in April 1835, just as Peel's ministry fell; thus he did not serve. He later clerked under the accountant-general at Somerset House and in 1864 became British consul at Buffalo, New York, where he contributed to the *North American Review* in 1870 and 1871. Charles Isidore became a historian of Rome and its archaeology.

Important literary portraits of and tributes to Hemans include Maria Jane Jewsbury's Egeria in *The Three Histories*, 'the Italy of human beings' (1830), and Letitia Elizabeth Landon's 'Stanzas on the Death of Mrs Hemans' (1835) and 'Felicia Hemans' (1838). L. E. L. was answered (in 'Stanzas …', 1835) by Elizabeth Barrett Browning, who remained ambivalent about Hemans. Wordsworth's 'Extempore Effusion' of 1835 portrays Hemans as an insubstantial 'Spirit' (Moorman, 2.519), while W. S. Landor's 'The heroines of England' and 'To the Author of Festus' (1849) capture the substance and heroism in Hemans's work. Landor mentions in particular 'Casabianca' (1826), Hemans's tribute to the boy martyr of the battle of the Nile, a popular and much parodied recitation piece (rehabilitated by Elizabeth Bishop in 1946). Musical settings of her work continued through the nineteenth century, and include 'The Swan and the Skylark: a Cantata' by Arthur Goring Thomas and C. V. Stanford. Noël Coward's high parody of her 'Stately Homes of England' appears in *Operette* (1938).

With twenty volumes and nearly four hundred poems published in magazines and annuals during her lifetime, Felicia Hemans was the most considerable woman poet of the Romantic period. Her work was republished frequently in Britain and America until the First World War, almost yearly through the mid-nineteenth century. Hemans's poetry ranged formally from sonnets and lyrics to narratives, dramas, and even polemics. Some readers find her floral and topographical language and frequent allusions to history and literature purely decorative, while others propose that these elements reflect a systematic and critical study of politics and gender. Hemans's characteristically insistent rhythm and insinuating tone appear to support the latter argument, as do her pointed revisions of sources such as the work of Gibbon or Byron.

Hemans's influence is traceable in nineteenth-century verse, especially in new forms of dramatic lyric in the Brownings, Tennyson, and Kipling in Britain; Sigourney, Longfellow, Whittier, and Harper in America; and Droste-Hülshoff in Germany. Even Wordsworth's 'Extempore Effusion' reflects Hemans, for in its draft title, 'The Graves of the Poets' (Moorman, 2.518), and catalogue form, it echoes her 'The Graves of a Household'. Most Victorian editions and reissues of her work omitted her learned notes and long poems, however, and helped to cast her as a 'parlour poet' and the very type of the 'sentimental poetess'. Oxford University Press included her in its Standard Authors series in 1914, but modernism, with its masculinist and anti-Romantic bent, put her into eclipse for over half a century. In the 1970s and especially the 1980s feminist critics began to find value in her studies of women's situations and women's creativity. In the 1990s historicist critics took up questions of style, poetics, and politics, arguing that these reveal Hemans as a critic of conventions such as patriotism and female self-sacrifice. Hemans is now recognized by many literary historians as the most notable British poet flourishing between the death of Byron and the rise of Tennyson and the Brownings.

NANORA SWEET

Sources H. F. Chorley, *Memorials of Mrs Hemans with illustrations of her literary character from her private correspondence*, 2 vols. (1836) · M. I. Leslie, 'Felicia Hemans: the basis of a biography', PhD diss., University of Dublin, 1943 · [H. B. H. Owen], 'Memoir of Mrs Hemans', *The works of Mrs Hemans*, 7 vols. (1839), 1.1–315 · R. Lawrence, 'Recollections of Mrs Hemans', *The last autumn at a favourite residence, with other poems and recollections of Mrs Hemans* (1836), 231–419 · W. L. Roscoe, note to Matthew Nicholson, 10 Jan 1807, Liverpool PRO, 920 NIC 29/4 · F. Nicholson, 'Correspondence between

Mrs Hemans and Matthew Nicholson, an early member of this society', *Memoirs of the Literary and Philosophical Society of Manchester*, 54/9 (1909–10), 1–40 • B. C. Barker-Benfield, 'Hogg–Shelley papers of 1810–12', *Bodleian Library Record*, 14 (1991–4), 14–29 • Sir Robert Peel, letter to Felicia Hemans, 7 Feb 1835, BL, Add. MS 40413, fol. 291 • P. R. Feldman, 'The poet and the profits: Felicia Hemans and the literary marketplace', *Keats–Shelley Journal*, 46 (1997), 148–76 • M. Moorman, *William Wordsworth, a biography*, 2: *The later years, 1803–1850* (1965), 518–20 • [J. T. Coleridge], review of *The restoration of the works of art to Italy*, QR, 24 (1820–21), 130–39 • B. D. Taylor, 'Felicia Hemans: professional poet', unpublished paper, 1995 • G. T. Shaw, 'The Liverpool homes of Mrs Hemans', *Transactions of the Historic Society of Lancashire and Cheshire*, 48 (1896), 123–34 • private information (2004) [M. Nott, E. Chitham] • *Extracts from the correspondence of Mrs Hemans with Mr Robert Perceval Graves*, Alexandra College, Milltown, Dublin

Archives Alexandra College, Milltown, Dublin, corresp. with Robert Perceval Graves • Lpool RO, corresp. and literary MSS; letters and literary MSS | BL, letters to Dr Samuel Butler, Add. MSS 34585–34589, fol. 275, etc. • Bodl. Oxf., corresp. and MSS • Boston PL, corresp. and MSS • Duke U., corresp. and MSS • Hist. Soc. Penn., corresp. and MSS • Hunt. L., letters; literary MSS • Mass. Hist. Soc., corresp. and MSS • McGill University, Montreal, corresp. and MSS • NL Ire., corresp. and MSS • NL Scot., corresp. and MSS • NL Scot., MS poems and letters to Blackwoods • NL Wales, corresp. and MSS • NYPL, Berg collection, corresp. and MSS • NYPL, Pforzheimer collection, corresp. and MSS • Princeton University, New Jersey, corresp. and MSS • TCD, commonplace book • TCD, corresp. with Robert Perceval Graves • U. Edin., corresp. and MSS • U. Lpool, special collections and archives, letters • Wordsworth Trust, Dove Cottage, Grasmere, letters; letters to Dorothy Wordsworth • Hamwood, Dunboyne, Meath, letters to Charles Hamilton of Hamwood

Likenesses W. E. West, portraits, 1827, priv. coll. • A. Fletcher, marble bust, 1830, NPG; plaster cast, NPG • E. Robertson, miniature, 1831, priv. coll. • E. Smith, line engraving, 1836 (after E. Robertson), BM; repro. in Chorley, *Memorials of Mrs Hemans* • collotype, 1837 (after medallion by E. W. Wyon), BM, NPG; repro. in H. F. Chorley, *Authors of England* (1837) • W. Holl, stipple (after W. E. West, 1827), BM, NPG; repro. in *Christian Keepsake* (1837) [*see illus.*]

Wealth at death no evidence of surviving wealth, but rather of need; in last months was occupied in situating youngest sons: Peel, letter to Hemans, BL, Add. MS 40413, fol. 291 • possessions distributed at death consisted mainly of books: C. Graves to Mr Graves, *Extracts*, 270

Heming, Edmund (*fl.* 1680–1699), street-lighting entrepreneur, who was living near the Steelyard in Thames Street, London, first came to notice in 1680 with a proposal that the government should raise £8 million by levying a tax of 2*d.* per week on householders' beds, claiming that this would not imperil the livelihood of any tradesmen. His proposal met with understandable derision.

About 1682 Heming became involved with the various projects for street lighting. Householders on London's throughways were required by law to hang lanterns outside their houses on dark nights, and the proprietors of the various new lights contracted with the householders for their erection and maintenance. These lanterns consisted of candles or oil lamps burning in glass boxes which were either backed with reflective foil, or had a convex lens on one face, so as to focus the light on to the footpath. In a document of 1687 where Heming pledged to set up and maintain a 'patent light' outside the premises of a shopkeeper in St Laurence Lane, there was a reference to

Edward Wyndus's Lights Royal, patented in 1684, which Heming was managing.

Heming's project met with opposition from John Vernatti, whose own Convex Lights, patented in 1683, were set up in Cornhill, and also from the tinsmiths and tallow chandlers, who saw their livelihood threatened. Heming's petition to the City aldermen to support the use of his lights reached the houses of parliament but was thrown out. Heming, fearing that his servants would be bribed to neglect his lights, maintained them himself, going round at midnight and again at four or five in the morning, which, he declared, made him ill. In 1686 want of funds obliged him to take partners, including two glass merchants, but these men brought him to the verge of bankruptcy by pirating his invention and refusing to contribute their share of the expenses. Heming resorted to law and as a first step published his grievances in his *Case* (1689). The partners responded by advertising in the *London Gazette* of 27–31 December 1688 that Heming was no longer authorized to negotiate leases and collect rents for the proprietors of the New Lights, this power being transferred to Ralph Greatorex, whom earlier documents show to have been Heming's clerk.

Heming's patent of September 1691 for a new way of making tinned iron plates was probably in connection with lamps; in November 1691 he applied for another patent, claiming that some five years previously he had made, and set up in the castle and city of Dublin, several lamps with convex glasses, intending to petition King James for a monopoly of his invention within Ireland, but 'the troubles within that kingdom soon coming on, the said grant was not obtained by him' (Petition entry book 2, 268, PRO, State papers domestic). Whatever the truth of this statement, in December 1692 Heming and Francis Jackson applied unsuccessfully for a patent for their 'new art or invention for light, differing and far exceeding all lights now extant, fit to be used in all churches, halls and such other large places as well as streets …' (Petition entry book 1, 425, PRO, State papers domestic). In 1692 Heming and Jackson sold their rights in the Lights Royal to a syndicate, after which Heming took no further interest. In 1699 he was granted another patent for 'sweeping streets, greens and walks; loading the dirt, dust or soil, also casks of all sorts, artillery carriages, waggons and carts, repairing the highways so as to throw ridges into the ruts'. How these feats were to be achieved is not disclosed. Heming thereafter disappears back into obscurity. The date of his death is not known.   ANITA MCCONNELL

Sources E. S. de Beer, 'Collections for the history of London street lighting', *N&Q*, 181 (1941), 4–8 • *LondG* (27–31 Dec 1688) • *Edmund Heming's proposal, humbly offered for raising eight millions of money* [1680] [broadsheet; duty on beds] • E. H. [E. Heming], *The case of E. H., who first set up the new lights in the City of London* (1689) • grant to Heming to make tinned plate, 17 Sept 1691, PRO, State papers domestic [H.O. warrant book 6, 180] • 7 Nov 1691, PRO, State papers domestic [Petition entry book 2, 268] • 13 Dec 1692, PRO, State papers domestic [Petition entry book 1, 425] • E. S. de Beer, 'The early history of London street lighting', *History*, new ser., 25 (1940–41), 311–24

Heming, John. *See* Heminges, John (*bap.* 1566, *d.* 1630).

Heming, William (*bap.* 1602, *d.* 1649×53), poet and playwright, was baptized on 3 October 1602 in St Mary Aldermanbury, London, the ninth child and third son of John Heming (*bap.* 1566, *d.* 1630), Shakespeare's acting colleague in the King's Men, and his wife, Rebecca Knell, *née* Edwards (*bap.* 1571, *d.* 1619). He attended Westminster School, and from there he was elected king's scholar to Christ Church, Oxford, in 1621. He did not matriculate at Christ Church until 24 July 1624, but graduated BA in 1625 and MA in 1628. He began writing poetry at Oxford, contributing a Latin poem to the collection *Carolus redux* (1623) and writing 'A Contemplation over the Duke [of Buckingham]'s Grave' (Bodl. Oxf., MS Malone 23, p. 130) in 1628. In December 1628 he was promised the next canon's place at Christ Church, but events soon led him instead to London and the theatre world in which he had grown up.

John Heming died in October 1630, and, as the eldest surviving son, William inherited his father's shares in the Blackfriars and Globe theatres. He apparently had nothing to do with running either theatre, merely collecting the income from the shares and following a profligate lifestyle which soon landed him in Ludgate prison for debt. These circumstances led Heming to sell part of his theatre shares to John Shank of the King's Men in 1633 for £156, and the remaining shares in 1634 for £350. However, he was also writing plays about this time, for his comedy, 'The Coursing of a Hare, or, The Madcap' (now lost) was produced at the Fortune Theatre in March 1633.

Two of Heming's poems were recorded by his fellow prisoner in Ludgate, Nicholas Burghe (now in AM Oxf., MS 38). The shorter of these (fol. 39) is a 28-line poem in which Heming laments his time in prison, calling it 'the sacrifice for sinn'. The longer poem (fol. 26) is a 248-line mock elegy for the finger of Heming's old Westminster schoolfriend Thomas Randolph, which had been cut off in a fray. This poem is dense with theatrical allusions, containing sketches of Shakespeare, Jonson, and many other poets and theatre people. A 59-line portion of it was printed anonymously in *Choyce Drollery* (1656) under the title 'On the Time-Poets'.

Two of Heming's plays have also survived, both of them very heavily indebted to Shakespeare. *The Fatal Contract* (printed 1653 but probably written *c.*1637) is based on Edward Grimeston's translation of Jean de Serres's *Inventaire general de l'histoire de France*, but it also borrows much language and many plot elements from *Hamlet*. These include a hero (Prince Clotair) modelled on Hamlet, a heroine named 'fair Aphelia' who is the daughter of the king's counsellor, a ghost, and a court masque staged for an ulterior motive. There are lesser parallels with other plays, particularly *Othello*. The play was adapted by Elkanah Settle as *Love and Revenge* (1675) and reprinted in 1687 under the title *The Eunuch*.

Heming's other surviving play, *The Jew's Tragedy*, was printed in 1662 but written much earlier, possibly at Oxford. Based on a story in Peter Morwyng's 1558 translation of Josephus, it tells the tragic tale of three seditious Jewish captains, Eleazer, Jehochanan, and Simeon, and their ultimately failed rebellion during the time of Nero

and Vespasian. Like Heming's other play, it contains many echoes of Shakespeare's works. Eleazer is closely modelled on Macbeth, and numerous passages recall *Hamlet*, *King Lear*, *The Merchant of Venice*, and several other plays.

At some point Heming married a woman named Rebecca, and their sons Edward (*b.* 1644) and William (*b.* 1647) were baptized in St James's, Clerkenwell, Middlesex. However, both boys were buried in St Giles-in-the-Fields in early 1649. Heming was dead by 1653, when the prologue to *The Fatal Contract* called him a 'worthy Gentleman' and said that 'at death he left greater Monuments of his worth and abilitie'.   DAVID KATHMAN

Sources G. E. Bentley, *The Jacobean and Caroline stage*, 7 vols. (1941–68), vol. 2, p. 470; vol. 4, pp. 539–47 · G. C. Moore Smith, 'Introduction', *William Hemminge's elegy on Randolph's finger* (1923), 1–9 · H. A. Cohn, 'Einleitung', *'The Jew's tragedy' von William Hemings* (1913), 1–103 · J. Q. Adams, 'William Heminge and Shakespeare', *Modern Philology*, 12 (1914–15), 51–64 · D. J. McGinn, *Shakespeare's influence on the drama of his age* (1938) · M. Eccles, *Shakespeare in Warwickshire* (1961), 82–3

Heminges, John (*bap.* 1566, *d.* 1630), editor of Shakespeare's first folio, was baptized on 25 November 1566 at St Peter de Witton, Droitwich, Worcestershire, the son of George Heminges. In 1578 his father sent him to London to serve an apprenticeship, and on 2 February, Candlemas, his master James Collins presented him for a nine-year term within the Grocers' Company, one of the major city livery companies. He lodged with the family in the parish of All Hallows, Honey Lane, near Guildhall, and when Collins died in 1585 he left a will bequeathing Heminges 40*s.*—a generous sum—'yf my wiffe shall thincke good' (PRO, PROB 11/69, sig. 4). Heminges completed his service, was made free on 24 April 1587, and became a freeman of the city (he describes himself as citizen and grocer in his will).

Heminges must have become stage-struck, for by 1593—while playing was still banned in London because of plague—he and Augustine Phillips were members of a small troupe employed by Ferdinando Stanley, Lord Strange (from September 1593, earl of Derby), before his death in 1594. On 6 May 1593 the privy council had granted Strange's actors a touring warrant allowing them to play anywhere free from plague and outside a 7 mile radius of the capital.

In 1594 the plague was over, and players from several small troupes became members of the new Chamberlain's Men, which opened to the public under the patronage of the queen's cousin Lord Hunsdon. Heminges is known to have acted in *Every Man in his Humour* and *Every Man out of his Humour*, written for the company by Ben Jonson, in 1598 and 1599; in 1603 James I acceded to the English throne and the Chamberlain's Men became the King's Men. Heminges's name appears immediately after those of Shakespeare, Burbage, and Phillips in their first licence, dated 19 May, and heads the list in the second, dated 27 March 1619. He was in four more plays by Jonson between 1603 and 1611, when he probably gave up acting; it is not known whether he ever appeared in any of

Shakespeare's plays. He seems always to have been mainly on the management side, and is believed to have succeeded as company manager and principal payee when Augustine Phillips died in 1605. Freemen of the Grocers' Company often became big businessmen, and his long apprenticeship would have fitted him well for the work. In his will Phillips named Heminges first of four executors and overseers and bequeathed him a silver bowl valued at £5.

Alexander Cooke, apprenticed to Heminges within the Grocers' Company, also later became a member of the King's Men; before his early death in 1614 he asked Heminges and Henry *Condell to deposit some of his money with the Grocers for the upbringing of his young children. Heminges acted as a trustee for Shakespeare when in 1613 he bought part of the Blackfriars gatehouse property; and in the retrospective list of twenty-six 'Principall Actors' in all Shakespeare's plays (the word 'actor' covering all theatre people, not just performers) Heminges comes third after Shakespeare and Burbage—principal playwright, player, and manager. In court records he is constantly referred to as 'presenter' of plays for command performances: in consultation with the master of the revels he would presumably have made the arrangements about places, times, dates, rehearsals, temporary seating in palaces, and transport.

On 5 March 1588, having come of age, Heminges, describing himself as a gentleman of St Michael Cornhill, had secured a licence to marry a young widow: Rebecca Knell, née Edwards (bap. 1571, d. 1619). Her first husband, the actor William Knell, had been killed in 1587 in an affray with John Towne, a fellow member of the Queen's Men, then on tour at Thame in Oxfordshire. Heminges and Rebecca Knell were married at St Mary Aldermanbury on 10 March 1588, and seem to have had fourteen children baptized there between 1590 and 1613, of whom probably about half survived to adulthood. Margaret (wrongly entered as Mary in the register) was baptized on 21 June 1611, and on 11 December 1627 she was married at St Mary Woolchurch in Lombard Street to a lawyer, Thomas Sheppard of Lincoln's Inn. In an imposing Latin entry she is described as 'filia Johannis Hemings generosus' ('gentleman')—further evidence of his status. Rebecca Heminges was buried at St Mary Aldermanbury on 2 September 1619, and John moved down to the Bankside parish of St Saviour, close to the Globe playhouse.

Shakespeare had become a very near neighbour of the Heminges and Condell families when in the early 1600s he lodged with the Huguenot couple Christopher and Marie Mountjoy in the parish of St Olave, Silver Street: playwright, theatre men, and skilled 'tyre' (attire) makers would have collaborated in productions for court and theatre, where audiences expected a 'good show' in both senses. In 1604–5 Heminges presented a play commissioned by James I's consort, Queen Anne of Denmark, who had her own household, and her accounts show that 'Marie Mountjoy Tyrewoman' was paid more than £50 for 'Roabes and other ornamentes'; she died in the following

year, and Shakespeare perhaps moved elsewhere, before finally retiring to Stratford upon Avon.

With Richard Burbage, Heminges and Condell are the only men from his London life whom Shakespeare mentions in his will: he left them two nobles each to buy a ring in his memory, a very common bequest at the time. In their epistle to 'the great Variety of Readers' they lay much stress on the 'care, and paine' with which they had collected the works, since the author had not 'liv'd to have set forth, and overseen his owne writings'. They declare that 'wee have scarce received from him a blot in his papers': if 'wee' and 'received' are to be taken literally, they seem to mean that Shakespeare actually gave them some manuscripts or transcripts to work on. The alleged scarcity of 'blots' may be taken as pardonable exaggeration.

Preparatory work on the folio began in 1620, and in that year the churchwardens' accounts of St Martin's, Carfax, in the centre of Oxford include a list of some seventy people who had contributed 'toward the Clocke & chimes': they are all parishioners with the exception of 'Mr John Hemmings of London', who contributed 10s. and whose name is tacked on at the end, presumably during a visit. The editor would have crossed Cornmarket to the wine tavern, still run by John and Jane Davenant who had often entertained Shakespeare in the past, seeking information and/or abandoned papers. Oxford is half-way between London and Stratford, where Heminges would probably have called at New Place in pursuit of papers in the late playwright's study, and perhaps useful information from his son-in-law Dr Hall.

After Heminges's death in October 1630, in the parish of St Saviour, Southwark, his body was taken back to St Mary Aldermanbury for burial on the 12th, no doubt as close to Rebecca as possible, as he had asked in his will; the funeral would have been conducted 'in decent and Comely manner … in the Evening without any vaine pompe or Cost' (terms similar to Condell's three years earlier) (Honigmann and Brock, 164–9). Funerals involving two churches were expensive, but both men could well afford it.

Probably 1000 copies of Heminges's and Condell's edition of the first folio had been printed, perhaps costing the solid sum of £1—a quarto of a single play usually cost 6d. In New York in October 2001 one of only five complete copies of the folio still in private hands was sold to an anonymous private bidder for £4.1 million.

MARY EDMOND

Sources GL, Grocers' Company MSS · parish register, London, St Mary Aldermanbury, 10 March 1588, GL, MS 3572/1 [marriage] · parish register, London, St Mary Aldermanbury, 12 Oct 1630, GL, MS 3572 [burial] · parish register, London, St Mary Woolchurch, Lombard Street, 11 Dec 1627 [marriage: Margaret ('Mary') Heminges, daughter] · parish register, Droitwich, St Peter de Witton, 25 Nov 1566, Worcs. RO [baptism] · churchwardens' accounts, St Martin's, Carfax, Oxon. RO, OA/Par 207/4/F/1, 129–30 · M. Eccles, 'Elizabethan actors, II: E–J', N&Q, 236 (1991), 454–61, esp. 457–9 · M. Eccles, 'Elizabethan actors, III: K—R', N&Q, 237 (1992), 293–303, esp. 296, 303 · M. Eccles, 'Elizabethan actors, IV: S to end', N&Q, 238 (1993), 165–76, esp. 174 · will, PRO, PROB 11/69, sig. 4 [James Collins] · will, PRO, PROB 11/158, sig. 86 · E. A. J. Honigmann and

S. Brock, eds., *Playhouse wills, 1558–1642: an edition of wills by Shakespeare and his contemporaries in the London theatre* (1993) · E. K. Chambers, *William Shakespeare*, 2 vols. (1930), vol. 2 · M. Edmond, 'In search of John Webster', *TLS* (24 Dec 1976), 1622

Wealth at death a man of property: Eccles, 'Elizabethan actors II', 457–9; will, 9 Oct 1630, PRO, PROB 11/158, sig. 86

Hemingford, Walter of. *See* Guisborough, Walter of (*fl. c.*1290–*c.*1305).

Hemming (*fl. c.*1095), monastic writer, was, to judge from his name, of Danish settler stock. He became a monk at Worcester Cathedral priory, where he rose to be sub-prior; he appears as Hemmingus in a list of Worcester monks entered in the *Liber vitae* of Durham. Hemming was long regarded as the compiler of both parts (Tib. I and Tib. II) of BL, Cotton MS Tiberius A.xiii, which as *Hemingi chartularium ecclesiæ Wigorniensis* was published by Thomas Hearne in 1723, and damaged in the Cotton fire of 1733; Hemming is the more accurate spelling of his name. This attribution rests on a statement of no special authority in a sixteenth-century hand at the beginning of the manuscript; but N. R. Ker's close analysis of the contents of Tib. I and II and of the hands (eight or more) in which they are written has shown that Tib. I, containing tenth-century Worcester charters and leases (BL, MS Cotton Tiberius A.xiii, fols. 1–118), dates from the first half of the eleventh century (perhaps from before 1016), and Tib. II (fols. 119–200) from about a century later. Thus only Tib. II is properly 'Hemming's cartulary': it contains Hemming's useful life of Bishop Wulfstan (*d.* 1095), and his important statements of the damage suffered by the cathedral priory's estates at the hands of neighbouring laymen (Danes *c.*1016 and Normans after 1066). In explaining those statements, Hemming describes himself as *monachus et sacerdos* and a colleague (*conservus*) of the brethren of the priory, and says that he copied them for the information of later ages from the sayings of many ancient men, and especially of Wulfstan himself, who ordered the compilation to be made. It was probably late in the time of Bishop Samson (1096–1112) that Tib. II was boldly rubricated and bound with Tib. I, which Hemming himself may never have seen. Hemming's parentage and likely dates of birth and death are all unknown.

Hemming recorded vital information on the impact of eleventh-century conquest and taxation on monastic property in a prosperous part of the west midlands. His statements can be compared with relevant entries in Domesday Book, which Hemming was the first to call the king's *carta* or *cartula*; he preserved copies of Worcester texts connected with Domesday, and of William Rufus's writ witnessed by Ranulf Flambard (*d.* 1128), demanding relief from Worcester tenants after Wulfstan's death. Hemming himself was an assiduous compiler, who has been fortunate in his first editor and in his modern analyst. A new edition by D. N. Dumville is announced.

J. F. A. MASON

Sources *Hemingi chartularium ecclesiæ Wigorniensis*, ed. T. Hearne, 2 vols. (1723) · N. R. Ker, 'Hemming's cartulary: a description of two Worcester cartularies in Cotton Tiberius A.xiii', *Studies in medieval history presented to Frederick Maurice Powicke*, ed. R. W. Hunt and

others (1948), 49–75 · V. H. Galbraith, 'Notes on the career of Samson, bishop of Worcester (1096–1112)', *EngHR*, 82 (1967), 86–101 · E. Mason, *St Wulfstan of Worcester, c.*1008–*1095* (1990) · J. Morris, ed., *Domesday Book: a survey of the counties of England*, 38 vols. (1983–92), vol. 16, appx 5 [Worcestershire] · [A. H. Thompson], ed., *Liber vitae ecclesiae Dunelmensis*, SurtS, 136 (1923) · *Hemingi chartularium ecclesiæ Wigorniensis*, ed. T. Hearne, rev. D. Dumville, facs. edn [forthcoming]

Archives BL, Cotton, MS Tiberius A.xiii

Hemming, George Wirgman (1821–1905), mathematician and law reporter, was born on 19 August 1821, the second son of Henry Keene Hemming of Grays, Essex, and of Upper Tooting, Surrey, and his wife, Sophia, daughter of Gabriel Wirgman of London. He was educated at Clapham grammar school and proceeded to St John's College, Cambridge, where in 1844 he was senior wrangler and first Smith's prizeman, and was elected to a fellowship. He entered as a member of Lincoln's Inn in the same year, but was not called to the bar until 3 May 1850, meanwhile continuing his mathematical studies. On 14 June 1855 Hemming married his second cousin Louisa Annie, second daughter of Samuel Hemming of Merrywood Hall, Bristol. They had four sons and four daughters, of whom the eldest son, Harry Baird (*b.* 1856), became a law reporter to the House of Lords, and a daughter, Fanny Henrietta (1863–1886), exhibited at the Royal Academy.

Hemming's work as a reporter in the chancery courts began in 1859 and continued without a break until 1894. From 1871 to 1875, when he was appointed QC, he was junior counsel to the Treasury—generally a stepping-stone to the bench. From 1875 to 1879 he was standing counsel to his university, and was appointed a commissioner under the Universities Act of 1877. As a QC he practised before vice-chancellor Bacon, and in 1887 was appointed an official referee. Elected a bencher in 1876, he rose through Lincoln's Inn to the position of treasurer in 1897.

Hemming wrote *An Elementary Treatise on the Differential and Integral Calculus* (1848; 2nd edn 1852); a book on plane trigonometry applied to surveying, published in 1851; and *Billiards Mathematically Treated* (1899; 2nd edn 1904). He published *Reports of Cases Adjudged in the High Court of Chancery, before Sir William Page Wood* for 1860–62 (2 vols., 1860–63, with Henry Robert Vaughan Johnson) and for 1862–5 (2 vols., 1863–6, with Alexander Edward Miller). On the establishment of the council of law reporting, Hemming acted from 1865 as an editor of *Equity Cases* and *Chancery Appeals*, subsequently merged in the Chancery Division series of the *Law Reports*. He discussed the possibility of *A Just Income Tax* (1852), and was a regular contributor to the irreverent *Saturday Review*, from which a pamphlet, *Thoughts on the Fusion of Law and Equity*, was reprinted in 1873. He died at his home, 2 Earl's Court Square, South Kensington, on 6 January 1905, and was buried in Old Hampstead Church. A watercolour sketch of Hemming when a young man, in fancy dress, was painted by his lifelong friend, Sir John Tenniel, and a miniature was exhibited at the Royal Academy by his niece, Edith Hemming.

C. E. A. BEDWELL, *rev.* ALAN YOSHIOKA

Sources *The Times* (7 Jan 1905) · *Law Journal* (14 Jan 1905), 38 · Venn, *Alum. Cant.* · *The records of the Honorable Society of Lincoln's Inn: the*

black books, 5, ed. R. Roxburgh (1968) · J. Foster, *Men-at-the-bar: a biographical hand-list of the members of the various inns of court*, 2nd edn (1885) · private information (1912) · *CGPLA Eng. & Wales* (1905)
Likenesses J. Tenniel, watercolour sketch, *c.*1840, priv. coll.; formerly in family possession, 1912 · E. Hemming, miniature, priv. coll.; formerly in family possession, 1912 · T. C. Wageman, watercolour, Trinity Cam.
Wealth at death £21,207 8s. 1d.: probate, 1 Feb 1905, *CGPLA Eng. & Wales*

Hempel, Charles Frederick (1811–1867), organist and composer, was born in Truro, Cornwall, on 7 September 1811, the eldest son of Charles William *Hempel (1777–1855), and his first wife, Katharine Grace Hempel (*née* Williams). Having received a sound musical education from his father, he became a teacher of music in Truro. In 1847 he began writing and publishing songs, the first being dedicated to the countess of Falmouth and entitled 'Heave one sigh for me at parting'. He also composed and printed piano and dance music. About 1844 he succeeded his father as organist of St Mary's Church. He was one of the first to introduce choral performances on a large scale into Cornwall. On 11 February 1855 he matriculated from Magdalen Hall, Oxford, and on the 15th of the same month took the degree of bachelor of music. On 19 March 1862 his oratorio *The Seventh Seal* was performed in the Sheldonian Theatre, Oxford, for the degree of doctor of music, and he received his degree the next day. Four pieces from this oratorio were published (1864–6), and the author was busy preparing the complete work for the press at the time of his death.

Hempel appears to have been a tireless student of music, but devoted himself more to the theory than to the practice of his art. In 1857 he became organist and choirmaster to St John's Episcopal Church in Perth. He was conductor of the Perth Choral Union and of the Euterpean Society, and also continued his teaching and composed many pieces of light music. He died at his home, 4 Rose Terrace, Perth, of apoplexy at midnight on 24 April 1867; his wife, Emely Grace Andrews, may have survived him.

G. C. BOASE, *rev.* DAVID J. GOLBY

Sources M. Kassler, 'Hempel, Charles William', *New Grove* · *Choir and Musical Record*, 5 (1867), 360 · Boase & Courtney, *Bibl. Corn.*, 1.227–8, 3.1226 [incl. work list] · G. C. Boase, *Collectanea Cornubiensia: a collection of biographical and topographical notes relating to the county of Cornwall* (1890), 349 · *Oxford University Herald* (22 March 1862), 8 · *West Briton* (10 May 1867), 4 · *West Briton* (17 May 1867), 5 · *Perthshire Courier* (30 April 1867), 2 · d. cert.

Hempel, Charles William (1777–1855), organist, was born in Chelsea, London, on 28 August 1777, the eldest child of the potters and crucible manufacturers Carl Friedrich Hempel and Johanna Hempel (*née* Ruel). Having shown early indications of musical talent, he was placed under the tuition of his uncle Augustus F. C. Kollmann, an organist and composer. He made rapid progress, and at the age of eight performed during the service at the Royal German Chapel in St James's. He later attended a boarding-school in Surrey, where all his leisure time was devoted to music and drawing. In 1793–4 he was on the

continent, chiefly in Leipzig and Dresden, where he cultivated his taste for music. Not finding employment in London, he moved to Truro in Cornwall, where in May 1804 he was elected organist of St Mary's Church and directed the choir. He held this post for forty years, supplementing his income by teaching music.

In 1805 Hempel composed and printed *Psalms from the New Version for the Use of the Congregation of St Mary's*, and in 1812 *Sacred Melodies* for the same congregation. These melodies became very popular, and some of them remained in musical collections until the end of the century. *A Morning and Evening Service, Twenty Original Melodies, and Two Anthems*, dedicated to the Hon. George Pelham, bishop of Lincoln, was published in 1820. For the use of his pupils in 1822 he printed an *Introduction to the pianoforte, comprising elementary instruction, with a series of select practical lessons*. He also became known as a poet in 1822 through a work entitled *The Commercial Tourist, or, Gentleman Traveller, a Satirical Poem in Four Cantos*. This book was embellished with coloured engravings designed and etched by J. R. Cruikshank, and in 1832 went into a third edition.

In his later life Hempel moved to Exeter, where he married for a second time. His eldest son, by his first wife, Katharine Grace Williams, was Charles (or Carl) Frederick *Hempel. His autobiographical letter of 2 February 1824 to the 'Proprietors of the "New Biographical Dictionary of Musicians"' is in the Ewing Collection at Glasgow University. Hempel died in the workhouse, Prince's Road, Lambeth, London, on 14 March 1855; his death certificate states his occupation as banker's clerk.

G. C. BOASE, *rev.* DAVID J. GOLBY

Sources M. Kassler, 'Hempel, Charles William', *New Grove* · Boase & Courtney, *Bibl. Corn.*, 1.227 [incl. work list] · G. C. Boase, *Collectanea Cornubiensia: a collection of biographical and topographical notes relating to the county of Cornwall* (1890), 349 · d. cert.

Hemphill [*née* Hare], **Barbara** (d. 1858), novelist, was the youngest daughter of Patrick Hare, rector of Golden, co. Tipperary, and vicar-general of the diocese of Cashel. Since her father was an absentee clergyman, it can be presumed that she did not reside in Golden for long periods of time. In 1807 she married John Hemphill (1777–1833) of Rathkenny, Cashel, and the couple had two sons and three daughters, of whom four survived their mother. The youngest son, Charles Hare *Hemphill QC (1822–1908), became the first Baron Hemphill in 1906.

Barbara Hemphill appears to have been writing for some time before she was encouraged to publish her works by Thomas Crofton Croker, a connection by marriage. Her first publication was a story called 'The Royal Confession, a Monastic Legend', which appeared in the *Dublin University Magazine* (vol. 12, September 1838). It dealt with Charles VIII and medieval France. Her first novel, *Lionel Deerhurst, or, Fashionable Life under the Regency*, was published in 1846, and edited by the countess of Blessington. *The Priest's Niece, or, The Heirship of Barnulph*, a historical novel taking place in Spain, Scotland, and Ireland, appeared in 1855. A reviewer of the *Irish Quarterly Review* described the novel as being 'full of incident, of invention, of bright flashes of genius, of descriptive power rarely excelled in those days', and believed that the author had 'the true talent of the genuine novelist' ('Novels and novelists', 108f.). Since Barbara Hemphill published her works anonymously, the reviewer thought the author to be a man. *The Priest's Niece* was very successful, and arrived at a second edition within five months of its publication. In 1857 *Freida the Jongleur*, another work dealing with medieval France, appeared. Again, it received praises from a reviewer of the *Irish Quarterly Review*, who by then was aware that the author was a woman, as the novel had been published under Barbara Hemphill's own name ('Rogues all?', 435). It is likely that she published more works than those attributed to her.

Barbara Hemphill died on 5 May 1858 at her son's residence, 6 Lower Fitzwilliam Street, Dublin. Her death went mostly unnoticed by the daily and weekly newspapers and by literary journals. In the twentieth century she has been remembered mainly as the mother of Charles Hare Hemphill. BRIGITTE ANTON

Sources *DNB* · Church of Ireland records of Relickmurry and Athassol (incl. the parish of Golden): births (1808–80), marriages (1809–45), deaths (1808–77), vestry entries, NA Ire., reel 11 · NL Ire., Sheehy Skeffington MSS, MS 22660 [incl. biography of Lord Hemphill, written in 1906] · Burke, *Peerage* (1856), 1080 · *CGPLA Ire.* (1858) · 'Art. IV - novels and novelists: *The priest's niece*', *Irish Quarterly Review*, 6/21 (March 1856), 94–109 (esp. 108f.) · 'Rogues all? Reality and romance', *Irish Quarterly Review*, 7/26 (July 1857), 385–439, esp. 415–39 [bk review of *Freida the jongleur*] · 'The royal confession, a monastic legend', *Dublin University Magazine*, 12 (1838), 287–328 · *GM*, 3rd ser., 4 (1858), 685 · *Freeman's Journal* [Dublin] (7 May 1858), 3 · S. J. Brown, *Ireland in fiction*, 2nd edn, 1 (1969), 134 · S. Halkett and J. Laing, *A dictionary of anonymous and pseudonymous publications in the English language*, ed. J. Horden, 3rd edn (1980–) · R. J. Hayes, ed., *Sources for the history of Irish civilisation: articles in Irish periodicals*, 2 (1970)

Archives Genealogical Office, Dublin, family MSS, MS 804 · NA Ire., family MSS, M 5612 and M 5621

Wealth at death £400: probate, 9 Sept 1858, *CGPLA Ire.*

Hemphill, Charles Hare, first Baron Hemphill (1822–1908), lawyer and politician, was born in August 1822 at his father's residence in Cashel. He was the youngest of the five children—two sons and three daughters—of John Hemphill (1777–1833) of Cashel and Rathkenny, co. Tipperary, and Barbara *Hemphill, *née* Hare (d. 1858), youngest daughter of Patrick Hare DD, rector of Golden and vicar-general of the diocese of Cashel. His great-grandfather was Samuel Hemphill, the Presbyterian divine and controversialist, while his paternal grandmother was Elisabeth Bacon of Rathkenny, a niece of Matthew Bacon, author of *Bacon's New Abridgment of the Law*. His elder brother, Edward, served as lieutenant in the 69th regiment, and died unmarried in October 1840. Hemphill, after his father's death in 1833, was placed at Dr Walls's school, Dublin. In 1839 he matriculated at Trinity College, Dublin, of which his maternal uncle and godfather, Charles Hare DD, was a distinguished fellow and tutor. Hemphill obtained a classical scholarship in 1842 and first classical moderatorship and the Large Gold Medal for classics in 1843, when he graduated BA. He was moreover auditor of the Trinity College Historical Society, in whose

debates he took a prominent part. His only known existing published work is a pamphlet containing his inaugural address to this society, delivered on 7 November 1844, in which he outlined his opinions on the merits of an academic education and the benefits to be derived from the existence of such a society. Among his friends and contemporaries in the society were William Magee, archbishop of York, and Sir Edward Sullivan, lord chancellor of Ireland. After serving his terms at the Middle Temple, London, and the King's Inns, Dublin, he was called to the Irish bar in midsummer term 1845, along with Charles Gavan Duffy and Lord Justice Barry. Hemphill joined the Leinster circuit, and rapidly acquired a large practice.

On 11 April 1849 Hemphill married Augusta Mary Stanhope (1821–1894), younger daughter of the Hon. Sir Francis Stanhope KH, and granddaughter of Charles Stanhope, third earl of Harrington. They had three sons and a daughter. Their second son, Francis, a major in the 1st Royal Berkshire regiment died in Malta on 7 June 1891 as the result of a polo accident. Augusta Hemphill died on 12 April 1899.

Hemphill's ambition from the first was for a political rather than a forensic career. In 1857 and again in 1859 he unsuccessfully contested Cashel, his birthplace, in the Liberal interest and was defeated, polling on the first occasion thirty-nine votes against fifty-four for Sir Timothy O'Brien. He took silk in 1860, and the following year declined an offer of a judgeship in the high court of Bengal. In 1863 he was appointed chairman of a county, the title at the time of a county court judge in Ireland. The office did not preclude him from practising at the bar, but rendered him ineligible for election to the House of Commons. He was successively chairman of the counties of Louth, Leitrim, and Kerry. The administration of the Irish Land Act of 1870 was entrusted to county court judges, and Hemphill strenuously endeavoured to carry out the intention of the legislature by securing for tenants capriciously evicted from their holdings compensation for improvements they had made. On the coming into operation of the County Courts (Ireland) Act of 1877, whereby county court judges were no longer permitted to practise at the bar, Hemphill elected to vacate his county court judgeship on a pension and to pursue his profession. In January 1882 he was appointed a bencher of the King's Inns, and in the same year was made one of three serjeants-at-law, in Ireland, who took precedence at the bar immediately after the law officers of the crown.

In 1886, on the split in the Liberal Party on the home-rule question, Hemphill threw in his lot with the Gladstonian Liberals. At the general election of that year, after nearly a generation, he was once more a parliamentary candidate, contesting unsuccessfully the West Derby division of Liverpool as a Liberal, and at the general election of 1892 he was defeated when standing for Hastings. On the fall of Lord Salisbury's administration in August 1892, Hemphill, although seventy years old, became Irish solicitor-general in Gladstone's fourth administration. He held the post until the fall of Lord Rosebery's administration in 1895, when he was sworn of the Irish privy council, an honour not previously accorded to an outgoing solicitor-general. At the general elections of 1895 and 1900 Hemphill was returned as a Liberal by majorities of ninety-nine and forty-four respectively as member for North Tyrone, and was the only member of the Liberal Party in the House of Commons representing an Irish constituency. Although in his seventies, his physical and mental alertness impressed his contemporaries, as did his enthusiasm for participation in parliamentary debate, where, while not renowned as a great orator, his knowledge of law and his personal amiability commanded respect.

On the formation of Sir Henry Campbell-Bannerman's administration in December 1905, Hemphill's age prevented his appointment to the Irish lord chancellorship. He was created Baron Hemphill, of Rathkenny and of Cashel, co. Tipperary, on 12 January 1906. He died on 4 March 1908 at his residence, 65 Merrion Square, Dublin, and was buried at Dean's Grange cemetery, Dublin, on 7 March. He was succeeded by his eldest son, Stanhope Charles John (1853–1919).

J. G. S. MACNEILL, *rev.* TERENCE A. M. DOOLEY

Sources *Irish Times* (5 March 1908) · *Freeman's Journal* [Dublin] (5 March 1908) · *Irish Law Times and Solicitors' Journal* (14 March 1908) · J. G. Swift MacNeil, 'Lord Hemphill: a sketch of a great and memorable career', *Irish Times* (7 March 1908) · Burke, *Gen. Ire.* · private information
Likenesses B. Stone, photographs, 1898, NPG · Morant, portrait; formerly priv. coll. · Spy [L. Ward], chromolithograph caricature, NPG; repro. in *VF* (11 Aug 1904)
Wealth at death £81,535 16s. 9d.: probate, 1 April 1908, *CGPLA Ire.* · £35,708 6s. 4d.—in England: Irish probate sealed in England, 13 May 1908, *CGPLA Eng. & Wales*

Hemphill, Samuel (*d.* 1741), minister of the Presbyterian General Synod of Ulster, was a native of Ulster, Ireland. Nothing is known about his parents or his place of upbringing, although the latter was probably co. Monaghan or co. Cavan. He appears to have entered Glasgow University on 5 March 1716 and to have received the degree of MA on 30 April. In 1718 he received a call from the new congregation of Castleblayney, co. Monaghan, and was ordained by Augher presbytery on 24 December.

Shortly after Hemphill entered the ministry the first subscription controversy broke out at the same time as the passing of the Irish Toleration Act (1719), which was without the condition of subscription. He voted with the subscribers and made his mark among them by issuing in 1722 *Some General Remarks, Argumentative and Historical, on the … Consistency of Subscribing.* It was an able work and a worthy match for the more polished productions of the non-subscribers. In June 1723 he was present at the meeting of the general synod in Dungannon, co. Tyrone, and was placed on the synod's committee. Soon afterwards he was at Edinburgh, where Charles Mastertown, the foremost man of his party, sent him a pamphlet bearing on the controversy for revision. Hemphill saw to its publication under the title of *Apology for the Northern Presbyterians,* and contributed a short preface to it. He was harshly criticized by John Abernethy for his pains, and he replied with

The Third Page of Mr Abernethy's Preface to the Defence of his Seasonable Advice Considered (1725). It was an inconsequential work concerned mainly with a few matters of personal dispute. In May 1726 he issued from Castleblayney his last publication, *A Letter to the Rev Mr Samuel Haliday*, in which with great skill he retorted upon Samuel Haliday one of the key arguments of the non-subscribers. If subscription be unscriptural, urged Hemphill, equally so is every method proposed by the non-subscribers for ascertaining the fitness of a minister. He blamed the non-subscribers for dividing the church and for failing to reassure subscribers concerning the orthodoxy of their doctrine. The publication was followed by the ejection of non-subscribers from the synod at the June meeting. Though he had deserved well of his party, he was left to struggle with the difficulties of a frontier congregation. In 1729 he was called to the new congregation at Antrim, formed by those who had withdrawn from the ministry of John Abernethy; the synod, however, would not permit him to move there. All through his ministry he struggled with pecuniary difficulties. He died in poverty on 28 March 1741 in Castleblayney, co. Monaghan, leaving a widow and family.

ALEXANDER GORDON, *rev.* A. W. GODFREY BROWN

Sources J. McConnell and others, eds., *Fasti of the Irish Presbyterian church, 1613–1840*, rev. S. G. McConnell, 2 vols. in 12 pts (1935–51) · T. Witherow, *Historical and literary memorials of presbyterianism in Ireland, 1623–1731* (1879), 250ff. · A. W. G. Brown, 'Irish Presbyterian theology in the early eighteenth century', PhD diss., University of Belfast, 1977, 400–04 · *Records of the General Synod of Ulster, from 1691 to 1820*, 3 vols. (1890–98), vols. 1, 2 · J. S. Reid and W. D. Killen, *History of the Presbyterian church in Ireland*, new edn, 3 (1867), 148, 168, 204 · S. Hemphill, letter to Principal Stirling, 16 Sept 1725, U. Glas., Stirling MSS, 4/128
Archives U. Glas., Stirling MSS, letter, 4/128
Wealth at death died in poverty: *Records of the general synod*, vol. 2, p. 291

Hempson, Denis (1694/5?–1807), harpist, was the son of Brian Darragher Hempson, and was born on his father's farm at Craigmore, near Garvagh, co. Londonderry. Hempson lost his sight due to smallpox at the age of three, and at twelve began to learn the harp from Bridget O'Cahan (Brighid Ní Chatháin), afterwards receiving instruction from John Garragher, Lochlann Fanning, and Patrick Connor, all Connaughtmen. When eighteen he lodged with the Canning family at Garvagh who, along with Squire Gage and Dr Bacon, bought him a harp. This harp was probably the one described as being made by Cormac Kelly in 1702 at Ballynascreen, co. Londonderry, of white willow, with a back of fir dug out of the bog. Hempson spent many years as an itinerant harper travelling through Ireland and Scotland, being entertained by many Scottish gentlemen. In 1745, during his second trip to Scotland, his popularity was confirmed when he played in front of Prince Charles Edward Stuart, the Young Pretender, at Holyrood.

Hempson subsequently travelled all over Ireland, playing in Dublin, Cork, and many other towns. Frederick Augustus Hervey, fourth earl of Bristol and bishop of Derry, bought him a house at Magilligan, where he spent

Denis Hempson (1694/5?–1807), by Edward Scriven, pubd 1809

the rest of his long life. Lord and Lady Bristol attended the house-warming, and their children danced to Hempson's harp. In 1781, at the reputed age of eighty-six, he married a woman (said to be lame) from Innisowen, and they had one daughter. In 1792 he attended the famous Belfast meeting of traditional harpers, where he met Edward Bunting, who transcribed much of Hempson's music and published a collection including these pieces. Hempson was a staunch traditionalist in terms of both performance technique and repertory, regarding the music of Turlough Carolan (1670–1738) as too modern. He was the only harper at the Belfast meeting to play with the traditional fingernail technique, by then abandoned by most other players.

The intricacy of Hempson's playing was said to amaze his listeners, and his staccato and legato passages, shakes, turns, and graces were executed with ease and clarity, and he often achieved better results than more modern harpers. He had a keen sense of humour, and often interspersed his playing with humorous anecdotes. He became temperate towards the end of his life and his favourite drink, once beer, became milk and water, and his diet consisted largely of potatoes. On the day before he died, Hempson was said to have sat up in bed and played a few notes on his harp to his carer, the Revd Sir Harvey Bruce. He died at Magilligan in 1807 having, according to popular folklore, reached the age of 112.

Lady Morgan, in her *Wild Irish Girl*, published a letter written in 1805 from George Sampson, a Londonderry historian and protestant clergyman, which described an interview with Hempson. It is in this letter that most of his biographical information can be found. Hempson won no prizes at the harpers' meetings, nor did Arthur O'Neill mention him in his famous memoirs. Whether this is a result of rivalry, or whether O'Neill merely considered Hempson as a musical anachronism, will probably never be known.　　NORMAN MOORE, *rev.* MARK HUMPHREYS

Sources S. Owenson, *The wild Irish girl*, 3rd edn, 3 vols. (1807) · E. Bunting, *The ancient music of Ireland* (1840) · G. Samson, 'The life of Denis Hempson', *Journal of the Irish Folk Song Society*, 1 (1904), 59 · G. Yeats, *The harp of Ireland* (1992) · *DNB* · *New Grove*
Likenesses E. Scriven, engraving, pubd 1809, NPG [*see illus.*] · engraving (after drawing by E. Scriven), repro. in Bunting, *Ancient music*

Henchman, Humphrey (*bap.* 1592, *d.* 1675), bishop of London, was born at Burton Latimer, Northamptonshire, in the house of the rector, Owen Owens, husband of his maternal aunt; he was baptized in the parish on 22 December 1592, the third son of Thomas Henchman, skinner of the city of London, and Anne, daughter of Robert Griffiths of Caernarfon, and grandson of Thomas Henchman of Wellingborough, Northamptonshire, whose family was well established in that county. The details of his early education have not been established, but on 18 December 1609 he matriculated from Christ's College, Cambridge. He graduated BA in 1612 or 1613 and proceeded MA in 1616, about which time he became one of the first two fellows on the Freeman foundation at Clare College, Cambridge, his grandmother being a close relation of the founder. He resigned his fellowship when appointed precentor and a prebend of Salisbury Cathedral in January 1623. On 4 May 1624 he became rector of St Peter's and All Saints', Rushton, Northamptonshire. In 1630 Henchman married Ellen, daughter of the former bishop of Salisbury, Robert *Townson (*bap.* 1576, *d.* 1621), cousin to Thomas Fuller, and perhaps most significantly the niece of the current bishop of Salisbury, John Davenant. Along with these connections to leading clerical dynasties Ellen brought considerable property with her to the partnership as a result of an earlier marriage to one J. Lowe. In 1631 on his own presentation in right of his precentorship Henchman became rector of Westbury, Wiltshire. In 1639 he became rector of Wyke Regis and Portland, Dorset, and Kingsteighton, Devon. Throughout the 1620s and 1630s Henchman devoted himself to his duties at Salisbury. His hospitality as a residentiary canon, his diligent attendance at cathedral services, and his careful attention to ceremonial and reverence were all noteworthy. He participated in the ordination of George Herbert and was a pallbearer at his funeral.

The civil wars threw Henchman's apparently quiet life into turmoil. He lost his benefices and some of his property. On 4 July 1643 the House of Commons admitted H. Way to the living of Portland because Henchman had allegedly gone to the royal army. Henchman later complained that his house and library at Portland were destroyed. His estate in Dorset was sequestrated but let again to him at a rent of £40 a year in 1645. In 1646 his wife was granted a fifth of the income from his former preferments

Humphrey Henchman (*bap.* 1592, *d.* 1675), by Sir Peter Lely, *c.*1665

for the support of herself and their family, but the following year some of these grants were revoked in view of Henchman's comfortable circumstances. In 1648 he compounded with the authorities for £200. It is clear from all this that Henchman was, and was recognized as, a committed royalist but was also a man of substance in the locality. He seems to have spent the 1640s and 1650s living privately and undisturbed in the cathedral close at Salisbury. He was in touch with royalist exiles, and after the battle of Worcester he met the fleeing Charles Stuart briefly at Hele House, near Salisbury. He maintained friendships with other excluded Anglican clergy such as Gilbert Sheldon, Henry Hammond, and Bishop Brian Duppa of Salisbury. In 1653 his name was mentioned as one of a group of clergymen meeting to consider the future for the Anglican communion. The same year he acted, at Duppa's behest, in gentry marriage negotiations in Hampshire.

Although he was probably involved in royalist intrigue there is no substantial evidence of Henchman's activities, bar a little correspondence, until 1659. In that year he became active in schemes promoted by Edward Hyde to fill vacant bishoprics in the proscribed Church of England. He was to approach likely candidates and to tell others that Charles would not bestow preferment on those who asked for it. His close relationship with Richard Allestree, another Anglican agent, at this time can be seen in the recommendation dated 27 October 1659 from Salisbury that Henchman supplied for *The Gentleman's Calling* (1660). He also provided the Latin epigraph for the monument to Henry Hammond, the leading Anglican theologian who died early in 1660, in the church of Hampton by

Westwood, Worcestershire. In 1659 Henchman spent some time in London where he met other lay and clerical Anglicans such as Henry Ferne, Peter Gunning, and John Evelyn. Evelyn records that he preached on Psalm 143 in the capital on 29 June and encouraged the followers of the Church of England to submit their wills to God and pray for deliverance from calamity.

After the Restoration, Henchman became a leading clerical figure. He preached on 'Christian circumspection' on 8 July 1660 when the prayer book was first used in public. Late in September he was nominated to succeed Duppa as bishop of Salisbury, a promotion which was undoubtedly due to his local connections, but which may also have owed something to his meeting with the king in 1651 or even to a lease of church lands which he had been arranging for the secretary of state Sir Edward Nicholas. Henchman was consecrated at Westminster Abbey on Sunday 28 October alongside Sheldon, Robert Sanderson, George Morley, and George Griffith, in the first consecration to be held since 1644. The sermon by John Sudbury was one of undiluted praise for episcopacy. In the same month Henchman attended the meeting at Worcester House which produced a declaration that sketched a broad-based national church. In 1661 he was one of the episcopalian representatives at the Savoy Conference. Although Richard Baxter was complimentary about his learning, demeanour, and calm contributions to the debate, there was no mistaking Henchman's resolve when it came to asserting the liturgy and episcopal government of the Church of England.

In his diocese Bishop Henchman was firm, moderate, and undoubtedly popular. He received a warm welcome, for example, when he conducted his first visitation in the late summer of 1662. When he visited Chippenham in September, he conducted a confirmation service; he dined with local gentry, clergy, churchwardens; and his choice of the Calvinist Thomas Tully as preacher for the occasion pleased the numerous local puritans. A letter of October 1661 to Secretary Nicholas indicates that he was at that stage identifying potential dissidents and sectaries among both the clergy and the laity of the diocese. Yet after the Act of Uniformity came into force in August 1662 he seems to have underestimated the number of diocesan clergy who would refuse to conform or to have charitably regarded them as negligent rather than determined nonconformists; subsequently local nonconformists like Thomas Taylor seemed to have enjoyed a degree of indulgence from their bishop. Henchman was more of a stickler when it came to the church's own affairs: in correspondence with Sir John Nicholas over a preferment for Nicholas's nephew, Henchman was adamant that only the king could dispense with the age requirement stipulated by statute, but he admitted that a legal expert, Dr Berkenhead, said, 'I am unnecessarily scrupulous in this' (BL, Egerton MS 2537, fol. 389). Henchman was an energetic restorer of Salisbury's cathedral and the bishop's palace, where he repaired and consecrated the domestic chapel.

Inevitably service in the House of Lords distracted

Henchman from his diocesan work. He was already serving Bishop Sheldon of London as an effective parliamentary ally over such matters as the Select Vestry Act and following Sheldon's appointment as archbishop in 1663, on 15 September Henchman succeeded him at London. The many and diverse duties which fell to the holder of the see (from policing the book trade to overseeing the pastoral provision of the tumultuous city) called for an energetic administrator rather than a theologian or spiritual leader. Accordingly Henchman's episcopate was marked by diligence and efficiency rather than brilliance. Yet even this is remarkable in view of his advanced age: when Pepys saw him give a blessing to a congregation at St Paul's in 1664 he described him as 'a comely old man' (Pepys, 5.67). Henchman was concerned that the parishes of the city were served during the great plague and took a leading role in organizing collections of money for distribution among the poor and the services of national humiliation and penance. He liaised with John Barwick and William Sancroft, successive deans of St Paul's, over the repair of that cathedral: he attended an inspection of the cathedral along with other commissioners on 27 August 1666, just days before it was reduced to a shell by the great fire. Thereafter he was energetic in the work of rebuilding: he made a personal annual subscription to the work and left a bequest towards its completion.

Bishop Henchman was never one to surrender the church's rights. He was concerned at the loss of rental income to the church as well as church buildings in the great fire, and was noted as a severe landlord to the mercers and booksellers of Paternoster Row in its aftermath. He was alert to the threat posed by parishioners' attempting to influence clerical appointments, as did those of St Martin Orgar in 1666. Yet he was a determined advocate for those who he judged were worthy of promotion. Along with Sheldon he did much to guide Sancroft's early career, lobbied hard for his appointment as dean of St Paul's, and tempted him in 1669 with the bishopric of Chichester. Henchman was far from confrontational. He threatened to make an example of one Essex minister who failed to conform fully, but another such incumbent, Ralph Josselin, noted at his death that Henchman was 'a quiet man to mee. God in mercy send us one that may be a comfort to us' (*Diary of Ralph Josselin*, 512, 587). Henchman understood the pastoral difficulties of his clergy. When, for example, Richard Kidder, the incumbent at St Helen, Bishopsgate, found that some of his parishioners would not receive communion while kneeling Henchman allowed him to give them the sacrament and advised that he 'should in private conversation endeavour their satisfaction' rather than preach against them (*Life of Richard Kidder*, 19–20). He drew a distinction between sectaries—crowing to Sancroft when a crackdown was ordered that 'I always sayd that the insolence of the sectaries would prove to our advantage'—and sober dissenters such as Dr Thomas Manton who 'deported himself civilly and prudently' when summoned before Henchman's consistory court (Bodl. Oxf., MS Tanner 44, fol. 101).

As lord almoner Henchman had duties at court, and these extended to washing the feet of the poor on Maundy Thursday when Charles II was otherwise disposed. Henchman was an effective preacher to judge by the occasional references in Evelyn's diary, but he published virtually nothing. None of this prevented him from enjoying a high reputation for his learning, his pious life, and the traditional episcopal virtues of charity and hospitality.

Henchman died at his episcopal palace in Aldersgate Street, London, on 7 October 1675 and was buried in the south aisle of Fulham parish church. Various broadside elegies were published for 'pious Henchman' claiming 'even schismaticks in Him could find no Blame' and offering execrable praise,

> and when the Lord shall come at the last Day,
> He'll be his Hench-man, and prepare the Way.

He left money to the rebuilding of St Paul's and of Clare College, Cambridge; he bequeathed his communion plate and altar furniture to the chapel (which he had rebuilt) in the restored episcopal palace in Aldersgate Street. His will mentions three sons: Thomas (father of Humphrey *Henchman (1668/9–1739)), Humphrey, and Charles, and a daughter, Mary, married to John Heath; reference to a son-in-law, Thomas Cooke, implies another daughter who had already died.   JOHN SPURR

Sources BL, Harley MSS 3784, 3785; Egerton MS 2537; Lansdowne MSS, Cole MSS • Bodl. Oxf., MSS Tanner • *An elegy on the right reverend father in God, the lord bishop of London* (1675) • *An elegy humbly offered to the memory of the reverend father in God, Doctor Humphrey Henchman* (1675) • T. Blount, *Boscobel* (1662) • *The life of Richard Kidder DD bishop of Bath and Wells, written by himself*, ed. A. E. Robinson, Somerset RS, 37 (1922) • Pepys, *Diary* • *The diary of Ralph Josselin*, ed. A. Macfarlane (1976) • I. M. Green, *The re-establishment of the Church of England, 1660–61* (1978) • R. S. Bosher, *The making of the Restoration settlement: the influence of the Laudians, 1649–1662* (1951) • *Calamy rev.* • *Walker rev.* • Wood, *Ath. Oxon.*, new edn • Wood, *Ath. Oxon.: Fasti*, new edn • Foster, *Alum. Oxon.* • Venn, *Alum. Cant.* • W. Kennett, *A register and chronicle ecclesiastical and civil* (1728) • *Fasti Angl.* (Hardy) • *The correspondence of Bishop Brian Duppa and Sir Justinian Isham, 1650–1660*, ed. G. Isham, Northamptonshire RS, 17 (1951)

Archives BL, letters to Sir Edward Nicholas, Egerton MSS 2537–2538 • Bodl. Oxf., Tanner MSS, corresp.

Likenesses P. Lely, portrait, *c*.1665, priv. coll.; on loan to Plymouth City Museum and Art Gallery [*see illus.*] • mezzotint (after Lely), BM, NPG • oils (after P. Lely); formerly Fulham Palace, London • oils (after P. Lely), Charterhouse, London

Henchman, Humphrey (1668/9–1739), lawyer, was the second son of Thomas Henchman (*b*. 1630) of Crutched Friars, London, and Fulham, Middlesex, and his wife, Mary, daughter of Thomas Howe of Abbots Langley, Hertfordshire. He was the grandson of Humphrey *Henchman (*d*. 1675), bishop of London. He entered Westminster School as a king's scholar in 1684, subsequently moving on to Christ Church, Oxford (aged eighteen at matriculation in July 1687), where he progressed BA in 1691, MA in 1694, and DCL in 1702. While at Oxford he contributed to the collection of verses celebrating William III's return from Ireland in 1690.

Henchman was admitted an advocate of Doctors' Commons on 23 October 1703 and began practising as a civil lawyer. In 1710 Dr Sacheverell petitioned for Henchman to be added to his defence team, which had suffered a series of resignations. Ingeniously, and contrary to the rest of the defence lawyers, Henchman argued in response to article one of the impeachment that Sacheverell had made the revolution of 1688 an exception to his doctrine of non-resistance. Apparently his legal skills were used in the drafting of the treaty of Utrecht and in the prosecution against William Whiston before the court of delegates. On 22 September 1713 he married Ann Wood (d. 1724), daughter of Thomas Wood of Littleton, Middlesex, the sister of his near contemporary at Doctors' Commons, Robert Wood (d. 1738). They had five children—three sons and two daughters—one son and one daughter dying young.

After the death of Sir Charles Hedges in June 1714 Dr William Stratford thought Henchman a strong candidate to succeed to some of his offices because 'there is no one of his profession who upon the test of merit can be a competitor with him' (*Portland MSS*, 7.188). On 22 June Henchman was duly constituted a judge of the high court of Admiralty. He was also named as chancellor of Rochester by Bishop Atterbury. He lost his Admiralty judgeship on 1 December 1714, but was advanced to the chancellorship of London by Bishop Compton in 1715. He served as a treasurer of Doctors' Commons (1723–4). His wife died on 15 July 1724. Henchman died at Hampton, Middlesex, on 15 August 1739, aged seventy. He was buried at Fulham. His will, written the previous year, bore testament to the influence of Anglicanism on his life: 'I die an unworthy member of the Church of England as by law established in which communion I was bred up and have always lived' (PRO, PROB 11/698/197). His executor was his wife's niece, Dame Elizabeth Isham (the wife of another advocate, Sir Edmund Isham, sixth baronet) to whom he left 'my best diamond ring and my snuff box in which is set a gold medal of Queen Anne' (ibid.), in acknowledgement of her friendship.   STUART HANDLEY

Sources J. Hutchins, *The history and antiquities of the county of Dorset*, 3rd edn, ed. W. Shipp and J. W. Hodson, 2 (1863), 831 • G. D. Squibb, *Doctors' Commons: a history of the College of Advocates and Doctors of Law* (1977), 186 • will, PRO, PROB 11/698, sig. 197 • IGI • G. S. Holmes, *The trial of Doctor Sacheverell* (1973), 118, 187–94 • A. Boyer, *The political state of Great Britain*, 28 (1724), 106; 58 (1739), 185 • *State trials*, 15.240–42, 304–8, 329–31, 357–9 • *The manuscripts of his grace the duke of Portland*, 10 vols., HMC, 29 (1891–1931), vol. 7, p. 188 • *Old Westminsters*, 1.446 • *N&Q*, 3rd ser., 3 (1863), 316 • *DNB* • Foster, *Alum. Oxon.*

Hende, John (d. 1418), royal financier and mayor of London, is of unknown origins, but by 1368 he was active in the drapery trade and had made the first of three prudent marriages. His first wife, Isabella, was the daughter of John Southcote; her mother, Margaret St Edmund, came from a family of rich drapers with city property. Hende may have been Southcote's apprentice. His marriage settlement in 1368 endowed him with a shop and solar in Candlewick Street, which he had previously rented from the Southcotes. In the 1370s he may have been finishing cloth and he had links with the Lucchese in London. Hende's role in his livery is obscure; early drapers' records are fragmentary. His unsuccessful attempt in 1384 to secure the future site of the Old Common Hall in St Swithin's Lane may have been on behalf of his first wife's

family, to whom he remained close for the rest of his life, rather than the livery.

An expanding network of rich clients marked his increasing success in the next decades; Hende bought real property and acted as banker as well as draper. Traces of his efficient business methods survive in a cancelled bond with John, Lord Cobham (d. 1408), in 1393, on security of plate. By 1392–4 Hende dominated the supply of cloth to Richard II's wardrobe. His sales of scarlet, long cloth dyed in grain, russet, and blanket, amounted to nearly £4150 in these years, more even than the value of the silks sold by his only near competitor, the mercer Richard Whittington (d. 1423). Hende continued to supply cloth on a smaller scale to Henry IV and Henry V, but by this time his real interests lay outside drapery.

Hende's rise in city government kept pace with his success as a draper. He served as a commissioner for the first time in 1369, as alderman of Candlewick ward in 1379, 1381, and 1384–92 and of Walbrook from 1394–1409. He was sheriff in 1381–2, during the mayoralty of the populist draper, John Northampton, and acquiesced in Northampton's condemnation in 1385. In October 1391 Hende was elected mayor. Conflict with Richard II over the city's refusal to lend money to the crown came to a head in May 1392. Richard moved the centres of government to York, and the city oligarchy was summoned to Nottingham before the king and council. On 25 June Hende and the sheriffs were stripped of office and imprisoned, Hende in Windsor Castle. The prisoners appeared before a commission of inquiry headed by the dukes of York and Gloucester at Aylesbury on 10 July, and at Eton eight days later, with the mayor and sheriffs of 1389–90. On 22 July the city was fined and lost its liberties, though the prisoners were freed on bail. The city conciliated Richard by a lavish civic reception and gifts of money and jewels. On 21 September Hende and the others were pardoned and the city liberties were provisionally restored on payment of a corporate fine of £10,000. It was not until 1397 that the liberties were fully confirmed. It is against this background that Hende's vast sales on credit to the royal wardrobe took place. Nearly £4350 for cloth supplied to Richard II's wardrobe remained unpaid until 1403 and 1404.

During Henry IV's reign Hende became the leading royal financier. Between 1402 and his death in 1418 he lent a total of £14,514 to the crown. As security he controlled the London wool customs between 1403–10; his fellow collector in 1407–10 was Richard Whittington, another major crown financier. Unlike Whittington, Hende does not seem to have exported wool. His only known agent was based in Bordeaux, but could have been a partner in a syndicate. He lent smaller but still substantial sums to Henry V. In 1426 his executors accepted partial repayment and returned crown jewels pawned to Hende.

Hende's second wife, by 1380, was Katherine, widow of Thomas Baynard, an Essex landowner; Katherine held a life interest in the inheritance of her son, the lawyer and MP, Richard Baynard. By 1407 Hende had married as his third wife, Elizabeth, perhaps daughter of Sir John Norbury. Besides her jointure, Elizabeth enjoyed in her own right city properties settled on her by Sir Adam Francis and a manor and lands in Essex. By 1419 she was the wife of Ralph Boteler, Lord Sudeley. The two sons of the third marriage were Hende's only surviving children. Both were called John and both were later sheriffs of Essex. At his death on 2 August 1418, besides property in London, Hende held twelve manors, and other lands, advowsons, and reversions in Essex and Kent. He had acquired the first of his eight Essex manors, Mascallsbury in White Roding, as early as 1370. In 1381 he began the disputed purchase of his chief manor, Bradwell-juxta-Coggeshall, securing title in 1383 and 1385. Geoffrey Chaucer and Ralph Strode, no doubt the common serjeant of the city and the 'philosophical Strode' (*Troilus and Cressida*) of the dedication of Chaucer's *Troilus*, acted as mainpernors over Bradwell, a possible indication that Hende had literary tastes. Hende consolidated his Essex holdings through his second marriage. Hende bought three further manors in Essex and his four in Kent from the estate of Maud de Vere, countess of Oxford. In 1412 the value of his own lands, excluding his wife's, was declared at approximately £200 p.a., in 1418 at over £250 p.a., both no doubt underestimates. Besides his real property, Hende left his widow and sons £4000 in cash, to be recovered from his debtors, plate, and jewels; he left a further sum of approximately £420 in pious bequests, to his *familia* and executors.

Hende's marble armorial monument in Holy Trinity Church, Bradwell, was lost before 1768, but fragments of armorial glass survive. According to John Stow, Hende rebuilt St Swithin's, the drapers' church, where his arms could be seen in glass. The stained glass arms at Drapers' Hall are modern. Thomas Middleton included Hende as one of the nine drapers' worthies in the civic pageant, *The Sun in Aries' Worlds*, written to honour the new draper mayor in 1621.   JENNY STRATFORD

Sources will, PRO, PROB 11/28, sig. 42 · *Chancery records* · F. Palgrave, ed., *The antient kalendars and inventories of the treasury of his majesty's exchequer*, 3 vols., RC (1836) · F. Devon, ed. and trans., *Issues of the exchequer: being payments made out of his majesty's revenue, from King Henry III to King Henry VI inclusive*, RC (1837) · N. H. Nicolas, ed., *Proceedings and ordinances of the privy council of England*, 7 vols., RC, 26 (1834–7) · J. L. Stahlschmidt, 'Lay subsidy in London, 1411–12', *Archaeological Journal*, 44 (1887) · BL, Add. MSS; Additional charters; Harley charters · CLRO · R. R. Sharpe, ed., *Calendar of letter-books preserved in the archives of the corporation of the City of London*, [12 vols.] (1899–1912), vols. F–I · A. H. Thomas and P. E. Jones, eds., *Calendar of plea and memoranda rolls preserved among the archives of the corporation of the City of London at the Guildhall*, 6 vols. (1926–61) · GL · HoP, *Commons, 1386–1421*, various articles, incl. Thomas Bataill, Richard Baynard, William Bourghier, John Doreward, John Shadworth, Robert Tey, and Henry Vanner · *The works of Thomas Middleton*, ed. A. H. Bullen, 7 (1886) · Drapers' Company records · J. Stow, *A survey of London*, rev. edn (1603); repr. with introduction by C. L. Kingsford as *A survey of London*, 2 vols. (1908); repr. with addns (1971) · A. B. Beaven, ed., *The aldermen of the City of London, temp. Henry III–[1912]*, 2 vols. (1908–13) · A. H. Johnson, *The history of the Worshipful Company of the Drapers of London*, 5 vols. (1914–22) · S. L. Thrupp, *The merchant class of medieval London, 1300–1500* (1948) · R. Bird, *The turbulent London of Richard II* (1949) · C. M. Barron, 'The quarrel of Richard II with London, 1392–7', *The reign of Richard II: essays in honour of May McKisack*, ed. F. R. H. Du Boulay and C. M. Barron (1971), 173–201 · L. C. Hector and B. F. Harvey, eds. and trans., *The Westminster chronicle,*

1381–1394, OMT (1982), 492–509 · C. M. Barron, 'Richard Whittington: the man behind the myth', *Studies in London history presented to Philip Edmund Jones*, ed. A. E. J. Hollaender and W. Kellaway (1969), 197–248 · A. Steel, *The receipt of the exchequer, 1377–1485* (1954) · P. Morant, *The history and antiquities of the county of Essex*, 2 vols. (1768) · T. Wright, *The history and topography of the county of Essex*, 2 vols. (1836) · R. C. Fowler, ed., *Feet of fines for Essex*, Essex Archaeological Society (1949), vol. 3 · M. M. Crow and C. C. Olsen, eds., *Chaucer life-records* (1966) · 'Oxford', GEC, *Peerage* · 'Sudeley', GEC, *Peerage* · S. J. Payling, 'Social mobility, demographic change, and landed society in late medieval England', *Economic History Review*, 2nd ser., 45 (1992) · W. J. Hardy and W. Page, eds., *Calendar of feet of fines for London and Middlesex* (1892) · D. Keane, ed., *Social and economic study of London: the Walbrook study* (1987)

Wealth at death approx. £4420 in cash bequests (incl. debts to be recovered); jewels and plate; real property worth (declared) £37 6s. 8d. (London), £41 (Kent), and £172 17s. 10d. (Essex), totalling £251 10s. 6d. p.a., incl. land held in right of third wife: will, PRO, PROB 11/28, sig. 42; inquisition post mortem

Henderland. For this title name *see* Murray, Alexander, Lord Henderland (1736–1795).

Henderson, Alexander (*c*.1583–1646), Church of Scotland minister and politician, was born about 1583 in Criech, Fife, probably in or near the village of Luthrie, since he left 2000 merks to the village school in his will. He was possibly the son of David Henderson, a tenant farmer who bought the small estate he worked from Seaton of Parbroath in 1601. According to tradition he was related to the Hendersons of Fordell.

Early years and parish ministry, 1583–1636 Very little is known about Henderson's early years. He matriculated at St Salvator's College, St Andrews, on 19 December 1599. He graduated MA in 1603 and was quickly appointed a regent, teaching logic and rhetoric. Between 1599 and 1606 Henderson witnessed the final stages of James VI's quarrel with Andrew Melville, the presbyterian leader who was based in St Andrews. At this stage Henderson was firmly aligned with the episcopal party, and he enjoyed the patronage of George Gladstanes, archbishop of St Andrews from 1605. Bishop Guthry alleged that at the laureation of one of his classes Henderson 'chose Archbishop Gladstanes for his patron, with a very flattering dedication, for which he had the kirk of Leuchars given him shortly after' (*Memoirs of Henry Guthry*, 21).

Henderson was licensed to preach in 1611 and settled at Leuchars in the spring of 1612. However, the parish was staunchly anti-episcopal and Henderson found the doors of the church barred to him, forcing him to enter by breaking one of the windows. It is not clear how Henderson reacted to presbyterian opposition, but according to one source, the turning point in Henderson's life came when he visited Forgan parish church to hear the charismatic presbyterian preacher Robert Bruce about 1615. Bruce preached on John, 10:1: 'He that entereth not by the door into the sheepfold, but climbeth up some other way, the same is a thief and a robber' (Fleming). This sermon convicted Henderson and converted him to the presbyterian cause. The story is plausible, though Guthry attributes Henderson's change of position to his 'intimate acquaintance' with the veteran presbyterian minister William Scot, who had once been a close associate of Melville

Alexander Henderson (*c*.1583–1646), by Sir Anthony Van Dyck, *c*.1641

(*Memoirs of Henry Guthry*, 21). Henderson's break with the episcopal party was also facilitated by the death of Gladstanes in 1615 and his replacement by John Spottiswoode. At the Perth general assembly in 1618 Spottiswoode engineered the passage of the controversial five articles, while Henderson and Scot led the opposition. Both during and after the Perth assembly the sympathetic town council of Edinburgh requested that the two ministers be translated to the capital, but without success. On 6 April 1619 Henderson was reported at the meeting of the provincial synod of Fife for not giving communion according to the prescribed order, 'because he is not as yet fully persuaded of the lawfulness thereof' (*Selections from Minutes of the Synods of Fife*, 88). In August he was called before the high commission at St Andrews, along with Scot and John Carmichael, and was charged with writing and publishing *Perth Assembly*, a tract actually written by David Calderwood. At a three-day conference in St Andrews in November, Henderson was the leading spokesman for the dissenting clergy in discussions with the bishops. Because of the strength of opposition to the five articles the king and the bishops decided to trouble Henderson no further.

Henderson remained in parish ministry at Leuchars, though attempts were made to lure him to Aberdeen (1623), Stirling (1631), and Dumbarton (1632). He seems to have been satisfied with a quiet country parish close to the ecclesiastical capital. Between 1626 and 1630 he attended conferences of clergy held in default of general assemblies. Surprisingly little is known about his activities from 1630 to 1636, but he maintained close links with other nonconformist clergy. In March 1637 Samuel Rutherford wrote to Henderson thanking him for his letters, which were 'as apples of gold to me', and telling him 'ye are the talk of the north and south; and so looked to, so as if ye were all crystal glass' (*Letters of Samuel Rutherford*, 233).

The covenanter revolution, 1637–1638 According to Guthry, Henderson met David Dickson, Lord Balmerino, and Sir Thomas Hope in Edinburgh in April 1637 to plan a campaign against the new Scottish prayer book. The two ministers later met with some godly Edinburgh matrons in a house in Cowgate and commissioned the women to organize a popular protest against the liturgy. On 6 July, Henderson met with a group of clergy including David Calderwood and Dickson, and they agreed to write down their objections to the book and send them to Henderson, and to encourage the 'weill affected' in Edinburgh to walk out of the first service where the prayer book was read. Their plans culminated in the famous prayer book riot on 23 July 1637. In August Henderson and two other clergy in the presbytery of St Andrews were ordered to introduce the new book to their parishes within fifteen days or face prosecution. They issued a petition complaining that the prayer book had been imposed on the kirk without the consent of the general assembly and that it promoted popish forms of worship. Before long a major petitioning movement was under way. Henderson was in Edinburgh on 17 October, when the petitioners were ordered to leave Edinburgh, and he supported the drawing up of the 'Supplication' which was signed on the following day. On 6 December the supplicants organized themselves into four tables representing the nobility, gentry, burgesses, and clergy, and set up a fifth table to act as an interim executive. Henderson and Dickson were the most prominent clergy on the fifth table, and were described by Baillie as 'the two archbishops' (*Letters … Baillie*, 1.42).

On 23 February, Henderson and Archibald Johnston of Wariston were given the task of drawing up a national covenant. The first section of the document reproduced the 1581 king's confession, the second section summarized various acts of parliament against popery, and the third section was the new covenant proper. Wariston was largely responsible for the second section, but the third section was more of a joint effort. Wariston records that on the evening of 23 February, 'I fell to the Band, quhairof we scrolled the narrative' (*Diary of Sir Archibald Johnston*, 319). Minor revisions to the whole document were then made by Rothes, Balmerino, and Loudoun. On 28 February the supplicants met in Greyfriars Kirk in Edinburgh, where following 'ane divine prayer most fit for the tyme and present purpose maid be Mr. Al. Henderson', the covenant was signed (*Diary of Sir Archibald Johnston*, 322).

In March, Henderson preached at St Andrews, urging his audience to turn their eyes away from 'Kings and their greatness' and recognize that magistrates and bishops were appointed 'for your good' (S. Rutherford, *Sermons, Prayers and Pulpit Addresses*, 1867, 9, 12). Although the town had been one of the few centres of opposition to the covenant, Henderson's visit was very successful and many signed up. At the end of the month he and Wariston drafted 'The least that can be asked to settle the church and kingdom in a solid and durable peace'. The paper demanded a free general assembly which could censure the bishops and the withdrawal of the prayer book, canons, high commission, and articles of Perth. In April these demands were reiterated in another paper jointly written by the two men entitled 'Articles for the present peace of the kirk and kingdom of Scotland'. In a sermon preached at this time Henderson declared that the whore of Babylon would be destroyed, even 'If all the kings and princes of the earth should turn (as they wrongfully call them), Catholick kings, and join all their powers and forces together for the holding up of Babel'. The implication was that Charles I was on the wrong side of the apocalyptic war between Christ and Antichrist, and Henderson prayed that the queen would be converted from popish blindness and become 'a hater of idolatry' (ibid., 153–4, 184). In June, Henderson was involved in the covenanters' negotiations with the king's commissioner, the marquess of Hamilton, drawing up reasons why they were quite unwilling to meet the royal demand that they surrender their subscribed covenants. In July he was a leading member of the deputation sent to dissuade the 'Aberdeen Doctors' from their opposition to the covenant. A series of papers were exchanged, but the doctors remained adamant in their refusal to sign the covenant, though the deputation did collect support from other quarters.

In August, Henderson was involved in further discussions with Hamilton over the conditions on which the general assembly could meet. On 20 September, as plans for a general assembly developed, he discussed the possibility of the complete abolition of episcopacy with Calderwood and Wariston. On the following day he and Wariston drafted a lengthy protestation against the king's covenant being proposed by Hamilton; Henderson contributed the paper's sixteen reasons why the covenanters could not subscribe the new covenant. In a sermon at St Andrews on 21 October he indicated the seriousness of the crisis when he said that the great question on men's minds was 'whether we sall have peace, or if we sall have war in it?' (S. Rutherford, *Sermons, Prayers and Pulpit Addresses*, 1867, 67).

The first general assembly since 1618 opened at Glasgow on 21 November. Two days earlier representatives of the nobles, lairds, burgesses, and ministers had decided that Henderson, 'incomparablie the ablest man of us all', should be elected moderator (*Letters … Baillie*, 1.121–2). During the first week of the assembly Henderson skilfully steered debates towards conclusions desired by the covenanters, despite the frequent interventions of Hamilton and Traquair. On 28 November, Hamilton left the assembly, declaring it dissolved, but Henderson argued that though Christian magistrates could convene assemblies, Christ 'hath given divine warrants to convocat assemblies whether Magistrats consent or not' (Peterkin, 147). In December the assembly declared null the general assemblies of 1606 to 1616, abjured the five articles of Perth, denounced Arminianism, abolished episcopacy, and deposed the bishops. Henderson directed proceedings with masterly gravitas, introducing each new item with a short speech indicating the official line and setting the tone for the debate. On 13 December he preached a sermon which was published in 1762 under the title *The Bishops' Doom*. After closing his sermon with prayer Henderson pronounced a sentence of excommunication upon eight of the bishops, warning that 'except their repentance be evident, the fearful wrath and vengeance of the God of Heaven shall overtake them even in this life, and, after this world, everlasting vengeance' (Peterkin, 180). When the assembly closed on 20 December, Henderson made a final speech, rejoicing that 'poore Scotland' was now 'rich in respect of the Gospell' (Peterkin, 190). When Laud heard about the assembly he complained that 'Mr Alexr. Henderson, who went all this while for a quiet and well-spirited man, hath showed himself a most violent and most passionate man and moderator without moderation' (C. H. Firth, ed., *Papers Relating to Thomas Wentworth, First Earl of Strafford*, 1890, 2.250).

From the bishops' wars to the solemn league and covenant, 1639–1643 In January 1639 Henderson left Leuchars to become minister of the high kirk in Edinburgh, having been elected by the town council in May 1638. The actions of the assembly had provoked the king into making preparations for war, and as the covenanters responded in kind Henderson played a key role in legitimizing their cause. In February he drafted 'The remonstrance of the nobility, barons, burgesses, ministers and commons, within the kingdom of Scotland', a short paper which was widely distributed in England and successfully generated a great deal of sympathy for the covenanters. Another manuscript tract by Henderson, 'Instructions for defensive arms' was widely circulated, and the text was liberally quoted in a pamphlet by the anti-covenanter minister John Corbet, in *The Ungirding of the Scottish Armour* (1639). It was finally published in England in 1642 as *Some speciall arguments which warranted the Scottish subjects lawfully to take up armes in defence of their religion and liberty*. Drawing on Althusius and other Calvinist resistance theorists Henderson argued that if the magistrate tried to break the terms of his covenant with the people they could justifiably resort to armed resistance led by inferior magistrates.

In June, Henderson was among the Scottish commissioners who negotiated the pacification of Berwick in the wake of the first bishops' war. On 13 June he and other covenanters met with Charles I, and Baillie recorded that 'the king was much delighted with Henderson's discourse' (1.217). Burnet later commented that 'it was strange to see a Churchman, who had acted so vigorously against Bishops for their meddling in civil affairs, made a commissioner for this treaty, and sign a paper so purely civil' (*Memoirs of the Dukes of Hamilton*, 1677, 143). The *Large Declaration* (1639) described him as 'the prime and most rigid Covenanter in the Kingdome' (p. 237). At the Edinburgh general assembly in August 1639 Henderson was once again proposed as moderator, but because permanent moderators had eventually become bishops in the Jacobean church, he declined. However, he preached the opening sermon and participated fully in the proceedings.

He also preached before the parliament which met on 31 August.

In January 1640 Henderson was elected rector of Edinburgh University, a position to which he was re-elected annually until his death. He was very successful at finding funds for the university: he raised a loan of £21,777 Scots, increased the number of benefactions, and persuaded the 1641 parliament to assign the rents of the bishoprics of Edinburgh and Orkney to the college. The building of a college library began in 1644, and Henderson purchased books for it during his visits to London. He also encouraged the appointment of a professor of Hebrew.

In 1640 a dispute arose in the church over private conventicles, and Henderson offended some of the radical ministers by taking a stand against all private meetings of the godly except family worship. However, Henderson drew up a paper on the subject and organized a conference with Dickson and Robert Blair, at which they all agreed to limits on private meetings. The controversy flared up once more during the Aberdeen general assembly in June. Henderson was absent from the assembly, having been asked to accompany the Scottish army on the eve of the second bishops' war. In the run-up to the Scottish invasion of northern England he defended the Scottish war preparations in two tracts, *The Intentions of the Army of the Kingdome of Scotland* (1640) and *A Remonstrance Concerning the Present Troubles* (1640). He also took part in the successful appeal to the city of Edinburgh for food and tents for the army. After the covenanter army had occupied Newcastle, Henderson participated in the peace negotiations of October which culminated in the signing of the treaty of Ripon.

On 6 November, Henderson and five other Scottish commissioners left Newcastle for London. He was to remain in the city until July 1641. Along with Baillie, Gillespie, and Blair, he preached in London churches to throngs of English puritans eager to hear the bold Scottish reformers. In January 1641 he wrote the final draft of the Scottish demand for war reparations. In the same month he also published *The Unlawfulnesse and Danger of Limited Prelacy, or Perpetual Presidency in the Church*. It argued that if the English persisted with the episcopal system they would 'cause continual jealousies, and heartburnings betwixt the two nations' (p. 12). In February he wrote a declaration which was circulated among sympathetic MPs, reassuring them that the covenanters were still determined to attack prelacy in England and exact justice on Laud and Strafford. Against the wishes of the Scots the declaration was published as *The Scots Commissioners Proclamation*, and it aroused the fury of the king. Because of its militant tone, however, it was labelled 'Johnston's paper'. The Scots were forced to issue a statement declaring that they had no wish to interfere in English affairs. On 10 March they submitted another document written by Henderson, entitled 'Our desires concerning unity in religion, and uniformity of church government'. It was printed in England as *Arguments given in by the commissioners of Scotland unto the lords of the treaty perswading conformitie of church government* (1641). Although he insisted that the Scots were

not demanding British uniformity in religion as a precondition of peace negotiations, Henderson did make it clear that he thought this the firmest basis for good relations between the kingdoms. The tract called for 'one Confession, one form of Catechism, one Directory for all the parts of public worship of God … and one form of Church government, in all the Churches of his majesty's dominions' (pp. 2–3). Henderson's final presbyterian pamphlet during this mission to England was entitled *The Government and Order of the Church of Scotland* (1641). It explained the Scottish system of Melvillian presbyterianism and defended it against various criticisms made by English advocates of episcopacy.

In July 1641 Henderson returned to Scotland. He was made moderator when the general assembly met at Edinburgh on 27 July, and had to deal once more with the dispute over private meetings. He also instigated a motion calling for a confession of faith, catechism, and *Directory for the Publique Worship of God* which would be acceptable to both England and Scotland. The motion was successful, and Henderson himself was asked to draw up these documents. Although this did not happen it revealed his continuing enthusiasm for British uniformity. Near the end of the assembly Henderson asked to be released from his parish in Edinburgh and return to Leuchars, on the grounds that his health was suffering in the capital and he needed a quieter parish. The city of Edinburgh was very reluctant to let him go, so it bought him a house located in a pleasant spot in the High School Yards south of the Cowgate and allowed him to take a break from preaching and the city whenever necessary.

On 14 August, Charles I arrived in Edinburgh. Henderson was appointed chaplain to the king and dean of the Chapel Royal at Holyrood with a substantial stipend of 4000 merks (£2670 Scots) to add to his income of £1200 as one of the ministers of Edinburgh. Between mid-August and mid-November he preached before the king on a number of occasions, and seems to have enjoyed good relations with Charles. This aroused suspicions among some covenanters, and there were 'many unpleasant whispers against him'. But at the general assembly in July 1642 he 'made a long and passionate apology for his actions' (*Letters … Baillie*, 2.48). In August 1642 Henderson visited his alma mater in St Andrews as part of an official commission to the university. They highlighted the need for a library, and Henderson himself donated £1000 Scots towards the necessary buildings.

In February 1643 Henderson was sent to Oxford to press for religious uniformity. He was openly mocked in the streets, and Clarendon suggests that he provoked the royalists by presenting a petition from the general assembly and displaying 'great insolence' in declining an invitation from the king's chaplain, Jeremy Taylor, to participate in a disputation with episcopalian divines. Although the king might have proceeded against him as someone who had no diplomatic immunity, he chose to be merciful (Clarendon, *Hist. rebellion*, 2.505–10). In May, Henderson returned to Scotland. In the middle of June he was dispatched to interview the earl of Montrose near Stirling. However, this last attempt to stop Montrose breaking with the covenanter movement was a failure. On 2 August, Henderson was elected moderator of the general assembly for the third time, his colleagues deciding that he was 'the only man fit for the tymes; yet it wes small credit to us, who so oft were necessitate to imploy one man' (*Letters ... Baillie*, 2.83). The assembly coincided with the visit of commissioners from the English parliament and the Westminster assembly. Henderson took part in negotiations over a covenanter–parliamentarian alliance. According to Baillie, 'the English were for a civil league, we for a religious covenant' (*Letters ... Baillie*, 2.90), but Henderson and Wariston tried to combine the two and drafted a solemn league and covenant. On 18 August, Henderson was named among the Scottish commissioners to be sent to the Westminster assembly, and he set sail for London twelve days later.

The Westminster assembly, 1643–1646 Henderson arrived in London on 14 September, and took up his seat in the Westminster assembly on the following day. The solemn league and covenant was signed by the Westminster divines on 25 September, with Henderson speaking of the great benefits Scotland had enjoyed from its covenants. In November, however, Baillie wrote that 'Mr Henderson's hopes are not great of their conformity to us before our army be in England' (*Letters ... Baillie*, 2.104). On 27 December, Henderson preached a fast sermon to the House of Commons, urging it to seize the opportunity for thorough reformation by ridding England of superstitious and idolatrous ceremonies, Sabbath-breaking, and the celebration of Christmas. In January 1644 the emergence of an outspoken group of Independent ministers within the assembly deepened the Scots' pessimism. Henderson wrote home to complain of the growth of the sects, noting that only a national assembly would cure the church in England of this problem. In the Westminster assembly itself he spoke only occasionally, but did respond vigorously to Independents like Philip Nye and Erastians like John Selden. He was the probable author of *Reformation of Church-Government in Scotland* (1644), a book issued in the name of the Scottish commissioners and distributed to the Westminster divines in January. In April, Baillie wrote that all the Scottish commissioners were agreed that 'Mr Henderson cannot be spared'; his contribution to drawing up the form of church government, the *Directory for the Publique Worship of God*, and the catechism was great, and if he was absent for even a short while things could go badly wrong (*Letters ... Baillie*, 2.172). On 18 July he preached to the Lords and the Commons about 'the reformation of religion', urging them to 'go about it more speedily' (McCrie, 98). In October, Henderson drew up 'a brave paper' against the Independents to be handed in to parliament and the assembly (*Letters ... Baillie*, 2.237). In December he drafted a directory on excommunication which won widespread support among the Westminster divines.

In January 1645 Henderson was appointed to assist the commissioners of the two parliaments in their negotiations with the king at Uxbridge. He debated the abolition of episcopacy with royalist divines, arguing that episcopacy was inexpedient, having led to war in both Scotland and England. However, the royalists were unwilling to accept the covenant or abolish episcopacy, and negotiations soon broke down. Henderson returned to Scotland for the general assembly in February, and reported on the progress of the Westminster assembly, which had approved a directory of worship and propositions concerning church government. He then returned to London, where, on 28 May, in his sermon to the Lords, he complained that 'such kings and kingdoms as are begun to hate the whore, and make her desolate and naked, do suffer themselves ... to be divided or retarded in accomplishing the work' (McCrie, 121). With work on the catechism and the confession still at a critical stage Henderson's colleagues were reluctant to let him leave the assembly. In July his health was poor, and he went with Rutherford to Epsom waters. In November he was due to return to Scotland to seek 'better union' among different parties in the kirk, but the London presbyterian divines were unwilling to lose him, and his journey was delayed. In January his plans to go home were once again frustrated by illness and bad weather.

When Charles gave himself up to the Scottish army in May 1646 Henderson was sent to Newcastle to persuade the king to embrace the solemn league and covenant. Charles told the Scots that he would be glad to have Henderson near him to discuss the question of religion, and between 29 May and 16 July Henderson and the king exchanged a number of papers about episcopacy, five written by Charles and three by Henderson. Henderson pleaded with Charles to accept the peace terms of the parliamentarian–covenanter alliance; one account suggests that he and Blair even fell 'upon their knees, with tears falling from their eyes, entreating and beseeching him, yet did he refuse' (*Life of Robert Blair*, 188). These fruitless negotiations placed great strain on Henderson's fragile health, and on 7 August Baillie wrote, 'Mr Henderson is dying, most of heartbreak, at Newcastle' (*Letters ... Baillie*, 2.387). A week later Henderson arrived back in Edinburgh. On 17 August he made his will. He had never married, and left his property to his nephew George. Among other items he bequeathed his share in a ship, his library, and some silver plate and gold pieces, altogether worth £4409. He also recorded that he was owed £23,821 in debts; his debtors ranged from the principal heritor of his first parish in Leuchars to the earl of Rothes. During the final years of his life he had enjoyed an income higher than that of any minister since the Reformation, including John Knox. He died in Edinburgh on 19 August 1646, and was buried on 21 August with the Hendersons of Fordell in Greyfriars churchyard.

In 1648 a pamphlet was published purporting to be Henderson's deathbed confession. It praised Charles I as 'the most intelligent man that ever I spoke with', and declared that Henderson had been one of those 'who out of imaginary tears and jealousies, were made real instruments to advance this unnatural war' (Aiton, 664). The general assembly quickly condemned the pamphlet as a forgery. It was probably produced by those who wished to raise support for the engagement.

Historical significance Henderson was a key figure at the heart of the Scottish revolution, and easily the most important covenanting minister. The deposed bishop of Ross, John Maxwell, described him as 'the Scottish pope' (*The Burden of Issachar*, n.d.); Clarendon referred to him as 'their metropolitan' (Clarendon, *Hist. rebellion*, 1.203); and Burnet called him 'by much the wisest and gravest of them all', though incapable of reining in the more militant covenanters (*Burnet's History*, 55). In a speech before the general assembly in 1647 Baillie declared that Henderson 'ought to be accounted by us and posterity, the fairest ornament, after John Knox, of incomparable memory, that ever the church of Scotland did enjoy' (*Letters … Baillie*, 3.12). We find his hand behind almost every important development between 1637 and 1646: orchestrating the initial protests against the prayer book, drafting the national covenant, guiding the Glasgow assembly to the abolition of episcopacy, defending armed resistance in the bishops' wars, negotiating the treaties of Berwick and Ripon, building an alliance with English parliamentarians, masterminding the solemn league and covenant, leading the Scottish commissioners in the Westminster assembly of divines, and helping to draw up the Westminster documents. His ability to appear moderate and dignified while pushing through drastic measures enabled the covenanters to retain broad support while pursuing a radical agenda. No other churchman could command the same respect, and the triumph of presbyterianism in the kirk owed much to his influence. Guthry believed that 'in Gravity, Learning, Wisdom and State-Policy, he far exceeded' the rest of the presbyterian faction; without him they would never have won the support of the bulk of the parish ministry (*Memoirs of Henry Guthry*, 21, 116). Henderson was irreplaceable, and it is significant that within a few years of his death the kirk was bitterly divided between protesters and resolutioners. Few individuals did more to lay the groundwork for the presbyterian church of Scotland.   JOHN COFFEY

Sources J. Aiton, *The life and times of Alexander Henderson* (1836) • T. McCrie, *Lives of Alexander Henderson and James Guthrie* (1836) • R. L. Orr, *Alexander Henderson: churchman and statesman* (1919) • *The letters and journals of Robert Baillie*, ed. D. Laing, 3 vols. (1841–2) • A. Peterkin, ed., *Records of the Kirk of Scotland* (1838) • *Memoirs of Henry Guthry, late bishop* (1702) • *Diary of Sir Archibald Johnston of Wariston*, 1, ed. G. M. Paul, Scottish History Society, 61 (1911) • R. Fleming, *The fulfilling of the scriptures* (1669) • *Fasti Scot.*, new edn • J. Row, *The history of the Kirk of Scotland, from the year 1558 to August 1637*, ed. D. Laing, Wodrow Society, 4 (1842) • A. F. Mitchell and J. Struthers, eds., *Minutes of the sessions of the Westminster assembly of divines* (1874) • *The life of Mr Robert Blair … containing his autobiography*, ed. T. M'Crie, Wodrow Society, 11 (1848) • Clarendon, *Hist. rebellion* • *Letters of Samuel Rutherford*, ed. A. A. Bonar (1891) • G. Kinloch, ed., *Selections from minutes of the synods of Fife, 1611–87* (1837) • *Burnet's History of my own time*, ed. O. Airy, new edn, 2 vols. (1897–1900) • Lord Hailes [D. Dalrymple], ed., *Memorials and letters relating to the history of Britain in the reign of Charles the First* (1766) • J. Kirkton, *The secret and true history of the Church of Scotland*, ed. C. K. Sharpe (1817) • *The diary of Mr John Lamont of Newton, 1649–1671*, ed. G. R. Kinloch, Maitland Club, 7 (1830) • R. Wodrow, *The history of the sufferings of the Church of Scotland from the Restoration to the revolution*, ed. R. Burns, 4 vols. (1828–30) • R. Wodrow, *Analecta, or, Materials for a history of remarkable providences, mostly relating to Scotch ministers and Christians*, ed. [M. Leishman], 4 vols., Maitland Club, 60 (1842–3) **Likenesses** W. Hollar, etching, 1641, BM, NPG; repro. in Orr, *Alexander Henderson* • A. Van Dyck, oils, c.1641, Scot. NPG [*see illus.*] • oils, Scot. NPG **Wealth at death** £4409 Scots—value of possessions; plus £23,821 owed by debtors: Aiton, *Life and times*

Henderson, Alexander, first Baron Faringdon (1850–1934), stockbroker and financier, was born at 25 Upper Winchester Street, Islington, London on 28 September 1850, the second son of the six sons and three daughters of George Henderson, printer, proof corrector, and Greek and Hebrew scholar, of London, and his wife, Eliza Cockshott, the daughter of a cabinet-maker. He was probably educated at a private day school in Ealing, where the family had moved, and in 1867 he became a clerk in the office of the leading City accountant, William Welch Deloitte.

In 1872, Henderson joined Deloitte's former partner, Thomas Greenwood, who had become a stockbroker specializing in railways. He became a member of the stock exchange in 1872 and in 1873 a partner in Greenwood & Co. The next year, he married Jane Ellen Davis (d. 1920), the daughter of Edward William Davis, gentleman of Ealing. Greenwood retired in 1884, to become an assistant to the preacher C. H. Spurgeon, and Henderson made his brother Henry (1862–1931) a partner in 1886. The firm became broker to most of the mainline British railway companies, as well as many lines in Spain and Latin America, including the Central Argentine Railway, Buenos Aires Great Southern Railway, and the Central Uruguay Railway. Henderson was also involved with port developments, telephones, electricity, and tramways throughout Latin America, where he was well placed as a result of family connections. His brother Frank (1858–1935) settled in Montevideo, but the most important link was his youngest brother, Brodie *Henderson (1869–1936), who was apprenticed to the engineer, James Livesey (1833–1925), the consultant on many of the railways with which Henderson was involved. In 1891 Alexander bought Brodie a partnership in Livesey's firm, which allowed him to co-ordinate the engineering and financial interests of the family in ventures such as the Trans-Andes Railway. Both Alexander and Henry acquired large personal investments in these concerns, as well as acting as brokers for the firms.

Henderson was also involved in domestic ventures. In 1887 he assumed responsibility for financing the Manchester Ship Canal, and he was a director from 1890 to 1897. He acquired an interest in the Shelton ironworks in Staffordshire at some point before 1891; and in 1894 he became director of the Manchester, Sheffield, and Lincolnshire Railway. The intention was to convert this local company into a trunk line between Manchester and London, and Henderson was crucial to providing the necessary finances. He created a rolling-stock trust, which bought equipment for the railway to use on hire purchase, and he raised finance in the City. In 1899, he became chairman of what had become the Great Central Railway. He had grandiose schemes. In 1900 he formed a company to build a dock at Immingham on the Humber, and the Great Central announced that it would take a lease; the new dock opened in 1912. However, the Great Central largely duplicated existing services and never lived up to its ambitions. By 1907 Henderson was planning an amalgamation with the Great Northern Railway. Terms were agreed in 1908–9, but the bill was rejected by the Commons. The Great Central was eventually absorbed into the London and North Eastern Railway in the reorganization of 1922, and Henderson was deputy chairman until his death. His last major achievement in international finance came in 1901, when he was responsible for the merger of the small British tobacco firms into the Imperial Tobacco Company in order to face American competition.

In 1889 Henderson bought a country house and estate of 3500 acres at Buscot Park, near Faringdon, in Berkshire. Most of the day-to-day business at Greenwoods was left to Henry, and Alexander was freed to spend more time on two pursuits: animal breeding and collecting works of art. (Ownership of Buscot, with its collections, passed to the National Trust.) He became president of the Shire Horse Society and the Hampshire Downs Sheepbreeder's Association. He purchased paintings both by old masters and by the Pre-Raphaelites, most strikingly Burne-Jones's sequence of *The Legend of the Briar Rose*. Increasingly, however, he became involved in politics, winning West Staffordshire in a by-election in 1898 as a Conservative, a seat which he held until 1906. He re-entered parliament in a by-election in 1913, for St George's, Hanover Square, which he held until he was made a peer in 1916. He was committed to imperial preference, and was both treasurer of the Tariff Reform League and a member of the tariff commission. He also acted as a conduit for Conservative Party funds to supportive newspapers, and it was in part for his services to central office that he obtained a baronetcy in 1902. He provided financial backing to the newspapers of C. Arthur Pearson, the chairman of the league; he acquired the *Standard* and *Evening Standard* in 1910, and was a shareholder in the *Daily Express*.

Henderson's business interests followed suit as he increasingly turned to the empire, and especially to the construction of railways in Africa in association with his brother Brodie. He acquired control of the Shire Highlands Railway around 1900, and built a major extension; he was also a creditor of the British Central Africa Company until 1912, when the debts were paid by a competing railway promoter in return for abandoning a further extension by the Shire Highlands Railway. His major business venture before the war was the creation of the National Bank of Turkey in 1909, in association with Sir Ernest Cassel and John Baring, Lord Revelstoke. The bank had been encouraged by the Foreign Office, as a response to the Imperial Ottoman Bank, which was dominated by French interests, but subsequent Foreign Office support was minimal. The hopes of developing railways, public works, and industry were disappointed, and the National Bank complained that the Foreign Office did not back its attempt to involve British capital, in co-operation with German banks, in extending railways. The problems were

exacerbated when the ships it financed for the Turkish navy were seized during construction by the British government at the outbreak of war. Furthermore, the bank was responsible, with Royal Dutch Shell and Calouste Gulbenkian, for the formation of the Turkish Petroleum Company in 1911, which held the exploration rights for large parts of the Middle East, with the significant exception of the concession to William Knox D'Arcy in Persia. This led to conflict with the Anglo-Persian Oil Company which, with backing from the British government, argued for the transfer of the bank's shares. Transfer was finally achieved in 1925, shortly before a huge oilfield was discovered in Iraq. Henderson's concerns for the future of British production, which had led him to support tariff reform, and his disappointment at the lack of government support for British business overseas in competition with the Germans, was to have a new urgency during the war.

During the First World War, Henderson visited Norway, Denmark, and the Netherlands to inquire into the blockade; he was deputy chairman of the shipping control committee; he chaired a committee to consider the relationship between the consular and diplomatic services in order to improve commercial intelligence; and he served on the Balfour committee on commercial and industrial policy. He argued on the Balfour committee that exports should be increased if the country were not to be bankrupted by surplus capacity after the war, and he submitted a minority report in favour of a 10 per cent *ad valorem* duty on imports. He took his case further as chairman of a committee appointed in 1916 to consider the financial facilities for trade. The committee recommended an industrial trading bank to overcome what was seen as the complacency of the City, and in 1917 the British Trade Corporation (BTC) was formed, of which he was governor until 1926. The proposal owed much to Dudley Docker, who believed that the main purpose of the political system was to expand foreign trade and develop British economic power, which were essential to survival as a nation. The venture arose from the feeling that German industry before the war, especially large firms such as AEG and Siemens in electrical engineering, were destroying their British rivals as a result of backing by the banks, and particularly in exports. Victory on the battlefields was not enough; measures had also to be taken to develop engineering to dominate world markets. The aim of the BTC was to assist industry in financing large overseas contracts, on more generous terms than were offered by banks; information offices were to be opened in cities throughout the world. It was also argued that the German firms achieved their dominance as a result of protection. Support for the scheme came from the large engineering, munitions and electrical exporters such as Vickers and Armstrong, which led to suspicion among smaller firms, which feared that policy was being dominated by monopolists; Henderson himself saw, quite correctly, that the main difficulty was in raising finance for small and medium concerns—the point made by the Macmillan committee in 1931. The BTC also met opposition from the merchant banks, which resented the suggestion that they had failed industry: the existing financial system was, they argued, perfectly adequate for British circumstances. The downfall of the BTC, however, was the tension, which was never resolved, between strategic and commercial considerations.

The government had been willing to support the BTC during the war as a means of countering German commercial dominance, especially in the Mediterranean and the Middle East, and in order to protect oil supplies. It was, in this sense, a continuation of the National Bank of Turkey, and in 1919 the BTC purchased the bank for £243,119. It also acquired the Levant Company and a merchant house trading in the eastern Mediterranean; it invested in the Portuguese Trade Company, formed the Anglo-Brazilian Commercial and Agency Company with the London and Brazilian Bank, and participated in the Inter-Allied Trade and Banking Corporation. It formed the South Russia Banking Agency to assist the allied support of White Russia, and attempted to develop a trade in manganese ore, before the victory of the Red Army. Like the National Bank, the BTC soon ran into difficulties, for its investments were not commercially viable and it received little support from the Foreign Office, which was wary of trade diplomacy. It did not pay any dividends after 1920 on an issued capital of £1 million, and went into voluntary liquidation in 1926. The assets were acquired by the Anglo-International Bank, of which Henderson became a director, and he bought back the assets of the National Bank of Turkey. Henderson felt that it was 'more than ever desirable to keep the flag flying' (Davenport-Hines, *Dudley Docker*, 148), an attempt which had cost him in all £643,500. His war-time efforts were, however, rewarded by a peerage in 1916, and the Companionship of Honour in 1917. He sat on one final committee, that on national expenditure in 1921–2.

The firm of Greenwood & Co. became less central to the activities of Henderson, and most of his wealth was outside the stockbroking business. There had been a reluctance to bring in outside partners, and it was clear that Alexander's two sons did not have sufficient dynamism. His elder son was Lieutenant-Colonel G. H. Henderson, who died in 1922, twelve years before his father. Alexander's brother Henry died in 1931, and his surviving son died in 1933, shortly after Greenwoods merged with Cazenove Ackroyd in 1932. The new firm became one of the most respectable brokers in the City; family members continued to be partners, and the office manager of Greenwoods, William Brabner, who handled Henderson's personal affairs, was given specific responsibility for the family investments. Apart from expertise in Latin America, Greenwoods brought a major asset to the merged firm—investment trusts. In 1909 Henderson created the Witan Investment Trust to handle his personal finances and to supervise the various family settlements; by 1924 its book value was £2,148,487.

Alexander Henderson died on 17 March 1934 at his home, 18 Arlington Street, Westminster, and was buried at Eaton Hastings church near Buscot. After his death Brabner created the Henderson Administration to handle the assets of the family, which included £1,117,408 left by Alexander in 1934, £423,327 left by his brother Henry in 1931, and a total of £936,532 left by his two sons in 1922 and 1933. Management of the investments was the responsibility of Charles Micklem, one of the senior partners in Cazenove. Micklem, with James Capel, dominated the trust market in the 1930s. By servicing investment trusts, both inside the firm and outside, Micklem secured a regular income from broking, and the family's assets benefited from the firm's best deals.

Henderson's name survived in the City through the activities of Henderson Administration, which proved more successful than many of the ventures with which he had been involved since the 1890s. By the time of his death, his campaign for imperial preference was being realized; but it cannot have been any consolation to the right-wing imperialist Henderson that his heir, his grandson Gavin Henderson, second Lord Faringdon (1902–1977), was closely involved with the Labour Party and an ardent anti-colonialist. What many of Gavin's colleagues in the Labour Party did accept was the need for improved financial and government support for production, but of a type with which Henderson and Docker would have had little sympathy.

MARTIN DAUNTON

Sources R. P. T. Davenport-Hines, 'Henderson, Alexander', *DBB* · D. Wainwright, *Henderson: a history of the life of Alexander Henderson, first Lord Faringdon, and of Henderson Administration* (1985) · D. Kynaston, *Cazenove & Co.: a history* (1991) · D. A. Farnie, *The Manchester Ship Canal and the rise of the port of Manchester, 1894–1975* (1980) · C. M. Lewis, *British railways in Argentina, 1857–1914* (1983) · A. Sykes, *Tariff reform in British politics, 1903–1913* (1979) · S. E. Koss, *The rise and fall of the political press in Britain*, 2 (1984) · R. P. T. Davenport-Hines, *Dudley Docker: the life and times of a trade warrior* (1984) · M. Kent, 'Agent of empire? The National Bank of Turkey and British foreign policy', *HJ*, 18 (1975), 367–389 · b. cert. · m. cert. · d. cert.
Archives Institute of Mechanical Engineers, London, corresp. and papers · St Ant. Oxf., Middle East Centre, papers relating to National Bank of Turkey
Likenesses W. Orpen, oils, *c*.1922, repro. in Wainwright, *Henderson*, frontispiece
Wealth at death £1,117,408: Wainwright, *Henderson*; Davenport-Hines, 'Henderson, Alexander' · £1,021,696 7*s*. 6*d*.: probate, 1934

Henderson, Alexander Farquharson (1779/80–1863), physician, was baptized on 6 June 1782 at St Paul's Church, Aberdeen, the son of John Henderson (1743–1814), and his first wife, Helen (*d*. 1788), eldest daughter of Harry Farquharson of Shiels and Whitehouse. John Henderson had studied at Marischal College, Aberdeen, between 1768 and 1772, and graduated MD from Edinburgh University in 1774. He migrated to Jamaica where he practised medicine and eventually bought a sugar plantation with a complement of black and mixed-race slaves. He returned to Scotland a wealthy man and in 1792 bought the estate and mansion house of Caskieben in the parish of Dyce, near Aberdeen. He became an improving landowner and benefactor in the community, and styled himself 'Esquire'. His black servant Thomas caused a sensation in the locality, but gained an annuity of £5 annually for his faithfulness.

Alexander Henderson was educated at Aberdeen grammar school, where he won several prizes for classics. He followed the arts course at Marischal College from 1794 to 1797 and concluded his studies at Edinburgh University, where he graduated MD in 1803 with a thesis on the response of brain and muscles to breathing. He became a licentiate of the Royal College of Physicians of London in 1808 and established his practice in the metropolis. He may have visited the family plantation in Jamaica in 1805; his library includes a small, annotated copy of the *New Jamaica Almanac and Register* for that year. His medical books, many personally inscribed by their authors, show his wide acquaintanceship with prominent medical men. He practised from his home in Mayfair and became well known for entertaining an extensive circle of artistic friends, including the poet Samuel Rogers, painters, botanists, and others. He was noted for his knowledge of wines, travelled widely on the continent, and was an accomplished linguist.

In 1806 Henderson published his translation of a French work by P. J. G. Cabanis, *Sketch of the Revolutions of Medical Science and Views Relating to its Reform*. In this the notes on Hippocrates' life and works reveal a detailed knowledge of the latter's medical writing. Hence Henderson disputed Cabanis's account of the manner in which syphilis was introduced into Europe and wrote enthusiastically of Erasmus Darwin's theory of fever as an example of the use of analytic method in the study of medicine. The work for which Henderson is best-known is his *History of Ancient and Modern Wines* (1824), an elegant book embellished by engravings of classical figures, grapes, and garlands. Henderson's account of wines and wine production was based on observations made during visits to the wine-growing districts of France, Italy, and Germany, to the sherry-producing districts of Spain, and to Portugal. His remarks about wine production in Madeira show that he had visited the island. His discussion of wines of the Cape includes comments on the methods used in production, and he remarked that the only exception to their execrable quality was found in wines from farms at the foot of Table Mountain. Henderson's copy of Edward Barry's *Observations Historical, Critical and Medical on the Wines of the Ancients* (1775) is extensively annotated and appears to form the basis for his own book.

Henderson spent his summers at Caskieben and his winters in London. He extended his Aberdeenshire estate by purchasing adjoining farms and he carried out extensive rebuilding of houses, farmsteads, and land drainage. He took an interest in crop rotation and experimented with different varieties of potatoes and other plants. Tree plantations were maintained and extended. Henderson supported railway construction in the locality by agreeing to convert half of his canal shares into preference shares in the Great North of Scotland Railway.

Henderson was a Liberal in politics and a local benefactor. He believed that the morals of the labouring classes would not improve unless they were provided with decent housing. To this end he left £1500 to build Henderson's Model Lodging House in Virginia Street, Aberdeen. He also supported industrial schools in the city. In 1857 he

endowed the chair of medical logic and medical jurisprudence at Marischal College, believing that many mistakes in medicine were caused by doctors' ignoring logical reasoning. The first holder of the chair was Dr Francis Ogston, who wrote a widely used textbook of medical jurisprudence. The part of the course on medical logic was never popular with students, and it was eventually dropped in favour of the study of public health.

Henderson never married, and on his death at Caskieben House on 16 September 1863 his surviving half-brother William inherited a life interest in Caskieben. On William's death in 1877 the estate was sold and the proceeds split between William's son and two daughters. The University of Aberdeen inherited Alexander Henderson's library of some three thousand volumes and his collection of paintings, sculpture, and antiquities. He was buried at Tullich, near Ballater.   CAROLYN PENNINGTON

Sources U. Aberdeen, Davidson and Garden collection, Henderson MSS · U. Aberdeen, Henderson MSS · A. A. Cormack, *The Hendersons of Caskieben* (1963) · P. J. G. Cabanis, *Sketch of the revolutions of medical science and views relating to its reform*, ed. and trans. A. F. Henderson (1806) · E. Barry, *Observations historical, critical and medical on the wines of the ancients* (1775) · A. F. Henderson, *The history of ancient and modern wines* (1824) · W. M. Ramsay, *Descriptive notes of the classical vases in the Henderson Collection, Marischal College, Aberdeen* (1881) · d. cert. · bap. reg. Scot., St Nicholas's parish, Aberdeen · Burke, *Gen. GB* (1850)
Archives U. Aberdeen, MSS · U. Aberdeen, Marischal College records, MSS | American Antiquarian Society, Worcester, Massachusetts, letters to J. Lancaster
Wealth at death £36,428: inventory, NA Scot.; Caskieben letter books, Davidson and Garden collection, U. Aberdeen

Henderson, Andrew (*fl.* **1731–1775**), writer and bookseller, was born in Roxburghshire, where he lived until the age of five, when he moved north with his father. He was at Marischal College, Aberdeen, from 1731 to 1735, receiving the degree of MA. He claimed to have studied also at the University of Edinburgh. For some time he taught at Edinburgh high school, and was private tutor in the families of the countess of Stair and Colonel Young, Lord Stair's aide-de-camp. During this period he travelled widely in Scotland, visiting all but three of the Scottish counties. He seems to have gone to London briefly and printed there an anonymous translation, *History of Charles XII of Sweden*, from the work by Voltaire. At the time of the Jacobite rising of 1745 he was in Scotland, and after he left Watts's academy, where he had taught mathematics, he returned to London, where he published *The History of the Rebellion, 1745 and 1746* in January 1748. This work was quite popular, being pirated twice and reprinted three times. Established as a bookseller in London, he published his anonymous *Life of John, Earl of Stair* (also in 1748) and in 1752 attached his name to a play, *Arsinoe, or, The Incestuous Marriage, a Tragedy*, which, however, was never performed.

Henderson published a large number of historical and biographical works, some of which involved him in controversy with other writers. His favourable account of the duke of Cumberland (1776) brought him into conflict with Tobias Smollett, for whom he conceived a permanent dislike. His *Dissertation on the Royal Line of Scotland* (1771) was to a large extent a similarly vigorous attack on Guthrie's *History of Scotland*. Henderson was extremely patriotic, and wrote a pamphlet in support of a Scottish militia (1760) as well as two attacks on Samuel Johnson's account of Scotland (1775) by which he had been offended. By his own account Henderson worked on a 'History of Scotland from 1748' and had a completed manuscript by 1771. However, this was never published. He also produced lives of King Frederick of Sweden, Count Daun, Marischal Keith, Archibald Cameron, and William the Conqueror. After 1760 most of Henderson's books were published in Westminster Hall, famous for a couple of centuries for booksellers' shops, although it is unlikely that Henderson himself had a shop there, and he probably sold books from an open stall. His life of William the Conqueror and some of the later publications were 'printed for the author and sold by J. Henderson in Westminster Hall'. This may have been his son, but there is no evidence of his ever marrying. The fact of his living or reading in the hall is alluded to in *The Pettyfoggers*, a parody on Thomas Gray's *Elegy* in which a group of Westminster boys playing at fives:

> Makes Henderson, the studious, damn their eyes
> When batt'ring down the plaster from the wall.

H. R. TEDDER, *rev.* ALEXANDER DU TOIT

Sources A. Henderson, 'Preface', *The life of William Augustus, duke of Cumberland* (1766) · A. Henderson, *A dissertation on the royal line and first settlers of Scotland* (1771) · A. Henderson, 'Preface', *The life of William the Conqueror* (1764) · *N&Q*, 3rd ser., 3 (1863), 216–17 · *Fasti academiae Mariscallanae Aberdonensis: selections from the records of the Marischal College and University, MDXCIII–MDCCCLX*, 2, ed. P. J. Anderson, New Spalding Club, 18 (1898), 308 · J. D. Reuss, *Alphabetical register of all the authors actually living in Great-Britain, Ireland, and in the United Provinces of North-America*, 1 (1791), 181–2
Archives BL, Birch collection

Henderson, Andrew (1783–1835), portrait painter, was born in the parish of Cleish, Kinross-shire, on 12 June 1783 and baptized there on 22 June, one of the sons of Thomas Henderson, gardener to William Adam (later chief commissioner of the Scottish jury court) at Blair Adam, and his wife, Jean Noble. At thirteen he was apprenticed to his brother, Thomas, gardener to General Scott of Bellevue, Edinburgh. Afterwards he was employed for a year in the earl of Kinnoull's gardens at Dupplin, Perthshire, and then worked for some months as a gardener to the earl of Hopetoun, near Edinburgh. Henderson's constitution was not strong, however, so he abandoned outdoor work. He obtained a position in a manufacturing house in Paisley and eventually rose to foreman for Messrs Hepburn and Watt in that town. An interest in art resulted in Henderson attending a local drawing school and in March 1809 he moved to London and studied at the Royal Academy, which he entered on 26 February 1811, for three to four years.

In 1813 Henderson returned to Scotland and established himself as a portrait painter in Glasgow. Henderson enjoyed considerable local success. He exhibited with the short-lived Glasgow Institution for the Encouragement of the Fine Arts from 1821 to 1822, and in 1825 was one of the founder members of its successor, the Glasgow Dilettanti

Society, with which he exhibited from 1828 onwards. In addition, Henderson exhibited three paintings at the Royal Scottish Academy between 1828 and 1830. Henderson's most successful portraits were painted in a precise manner yet enlivened with a freedom and vigour of colour, for example his undated *Portrait of William Motherwell* (Scot. NPG). His later works received less acclaim since, owing to failing eyesight, his colouring was weaker and his attention to detail more laborious.

Henderson's other main interest was the collecting and publishing of samples of the Scottish oral tradition. In 1832 he published *Scottish Proverbs*; this collection of pithy sayings had a preface written by his friend William Motherwell, and was illustrated with five etchings by Henderson. Using a light touch and a free line, these illustrations capture the humour and bizarre imagery of the proverbs. A second edition was published in 1876 without the illustrations. With Motherwell and another friend, John Donald Carrick, Henderson produced *The Laird of Logan: Anecdotes and Tales Illustrative of the Wit and Humour of Scotland*, which was published posthumously in 1835. As well as containing many anecdotes of Henderson's it also includes an account of his life. This book was also reprinted in 1889.

Andrew Henderson never married. He was large and ungainly in build but had a shrill, sharp voice. As a young man he suffered ridicule from his fellow students at the Royal Academy, but once back in Scotland his verbal eloquence and rich command of the vernacular brought him many friends and admirers. On 9 April 1835 he suffered an apoplectic fit and died a few hours later in Glasgow. He was buried in Glasgow necropolis.

L. H. CUST, *rev.* JOANNA SODEN

Sources A. Henderson, W. Motherwell, and J. D. Carrick, *The laird of Logan: anecdotes and tales illustrative of the wit and humour of Scotland* (1835) · G. Crayon, *A glance at the exhibitions of living artists under the patronage of the Glasgow Dilettanti Society* (1830), 43 · C. B. de Laperriere, ed., *The Royal Scottish Academy exhibitors, 1826–1990*, 4 vols. (1991), vol. 2, p. 260 · G. Fairfull Smith, 'The Glasgow Dilettanti Society', *Journal of the Scottish Society for Art History*, 3 (1998), 8–15 · bap. reg. Scot. · General Register Office for Scotland, Edinburgh · S. C. Hutchison, 'The Royal Academy Schools, 1768–1830', *Walpole Society*, 38 (1960–62), 123–91, esp. 166 · Royal Scot. Acad., RSA archives
Likenesses A. Henderson, self-portrait, oils, 1815, University of Strathclyde · A. Henderson, self-portrait, exh. 1835

Henderson, Arthur (1863–1935), politician, was born on 20 September 1863 at 10 Paterson Street, Anderston, Glasgow, the second son of Agnes Henderson (*b.* 1845/6), a domestic servant who made her mark on the birth certificate (and later on her marriage certificate). She was the daughter of a weaver, William Henderson. According to Arthur Henderson's family his father was a David Henderson, a cotton spinner, who died when Arthur was nine. It is likely, however, that both Agnes's sons were of a relationship which did not result in marriage. About 1872 Agnes Henderson and her sons moved to Newcastle upon Tyne, where she married on 9 May 1874 Robert Heath, a policeman; hence many of Henderson's formative years were

Arthur Henderson (1863–1935), by James Russell & Sons

spent in Newcastle. The family were nonconformist and attended a Congregational chapel.

Trade unionist and local politician Henderson left school at the age of twelve and was apprenticed as an iron-moulder in Newcastle, initially at Clarke's Foundry and later at the Forth Banks Locomotive and General Foundry Works of Messrs Robert Stephenson & Son. On completing his apprenticeship in 1880 Henderson worked for a year in Southampton before rejoining Stephensons. He was an eager trade unionist and soon became secretary of his branch of the Friendly Society of Iron Founders. When in 1892 his union restructured its organization, placing its 117 branches into eighteen districts, Henderson was the only candidate for the onerous, unpaid task of district delegate for his area, which covered not only Northumberland and Durham but also Lancashire. He was able to devote more time to union work when he left Stephensons for the board of the radical *Newcastle Evening News* in the summer of 1893. He came to prominence within his union as its local official during the major north-east iron-founders' dispute of March–September 1894. This wider standing was shown by his success in the union's annual ballot for three delegates for the 1894 Trades Union Congress.

Henderson, until after the turn of the century, was an archetypal Lib–Lab in politics. He was an admirer of Gladstone and a moderate in political and trade union affairs. His union, the Iron Founders, was predominantly Liberal, and the Newcastle branch was influentially moderate. Henderson's commitment to Christianity was strong, his

religious experience becoming more intense after hearing Gypsy Smith speak at a Salvation Army street meeting. He was a stalwart of the Wesleyan Methodist Mission chapel in Elswick Road, and on 11 March 1889 he married Eleanor Watson (*b*. 1861), one of his friends at the mission; she was the daughter of William Watson, painter. Henderson did not drink, smoke, or gamble. A tall, heavily-built man, in his younger years he was keen on sport, playing cricket and football. He was a founder of St Paul's Football Club, later one of the constituent parts of Newcastle United.

Henderson was a Lib–Lab councillor in Newcastle and later in Darlington. He was backed by the Tyneside National Labour Association when he won a by-election in 1892 for the Westgate North ward, Newcastle, in a high voter turnout. He advocated policies that were both radical and trade-union orientated, of the kind that John Burns and the Progressives pursued in London. He was an effective proponent of municipal measures to help the unemployed, having been out of work himself for six months in 1884, eight months in 1885, and for a shorter spell in 1894. When Robert Spence Watson and other leading Liberal figures sought a candidate likely to boost the working-class vote to run with John Morley for parliament for the two-member Newcastle seat at the 1895 general election Henderson was selected by the Liberal executive committee. However, the Liberal Thousand rejected his candidature and selected instead the wealthy James Craig, who had been unsuccessful in 1892. Henderson loyally accepted the decision. At the general election both Morley and Craig lost, an independent labour candidate polling 2302 votes, which probably ensured that they both were defeated.

Henderson, however, was offered and accepted the post of agent to Sir Joseph Pease, Liberal MP for Barnard Castle, beginning in December 1895. He was able to continue with his trade union and local political activities. He was elected as county councillor for Darlington in March 1898, won Darlington South ward in November 1898, and became mayor of Darlington in 1903. Pease died in June 1903, having already indicated from the previous December that he would not stand for parliament again. Henderson went from being Liberal agent to independent Labour candidate for the seat made vacant by Pease's death.

The Parliamentary Labour Party Henderson's move from Lib–Lab to Labour was due to trade union politics, not a major intellectual change. The Friendly Society of Iron Founders had been the fourth largest of those affiliating to the Labour Representation Committee (LRC) in the latter's first year. When the union had selected a parliamentary candidate in late 1902 Henderson had topped the list of six as the moderate Lib–Lab figure. The iron founders' executive and the LRC agreed that Henderson should fight Barnard Castle at the by-election held in July 1903. Henderson won by 3370 votes to the Conservative candidate's 3323 and the Liberal candidate's 2809, a famous early Labour victory. Henderson's success owed much to the declining popularity of Balfour's government. In addition the Liberal candidate was not sound on free trade and it was known that many leading Liberals had hoped that he would withdraw in favour of Henderson.

From the time of his election as the iron founders' parliamentary candidate until the state paid salaries to MPs in 1911 Henderson was funded by his union. This was a close relationship, with Henderson working as an organizer for the union, spearheading membership campaigns, and responding on behalf of the union to such issues as the introduction of premium bonus systems of pay. He became president of the union in 1910. Henderson in time became the long-serving Labour Party central bureaucrat, a stickler for upholding rules as chief whip of the Parliamentary Labour Party (1906–7, 1914, 1920–23, and 1925–7) and as secretary of the Labour Party (1912–34). He also served as the party's treasurer from 1904 to 1911 and from 1929 to 1936. Initially, before the 1906 general election, Henderson was reluctant to act independently, even having to be pressed to sign the LRC constitution in July 1904. However, with a Parliamentary Labour Party of thirty members after the 1906 general election his ambivalent attitudes towards independence evaporated.

Henderson was one of the ablest trade union figures in the Labour Party before 1914, along with David Shackleton and George Barnes. Though as moderate as them he surpassed them in his dedication to politics and his commitment to the mechanics of politics. The effective running of the party machine was his forte. Henderson not only represented a trade unionism that was dedicated to conciliation, rather than conflict, in industrial relations but he also was the embodiment of such sentiments in the wider social sphere. He was a major national figure in the Wesleyan Methodist Union for Social Service and in the Brotherhood Movement, being president of the latter in 1914–15. His commitment to temperance—in the 1890s he had travelled widely as a speaker for the North of England Temperance League—also contributed to his image as a solid, respectable, skilled trade unionist.

Henderson succeeded Keir Hardie as chairman of the Parliamentary Labour Party from 1908 to 1910 and in effect became party leader. By this time he was Labour's leading trade union figure and had conducted much of the detailed and time-consuming arrangements of parliamentary business with the Liberal whips in the House of Commons as chief whip. Henderson was both less charismatic and less erratic than Keir Hardie. As chairman he consulted his colleagues more than Hardie had done and he saw his role as that of their spokesperson rather than that of a dynamic leader. He pressed the Liberal government for action on unemployment but did so without the urgency and fervour of his predecessor. Henderson admired Lloyd George's 'people's budget' of 1909 and aligned Labour with the Liberal Party in the struggle with the House of Lords.

By 1911 Henderson felt strongly that Labour needed a charismatic leader, not a rotation of the abler worthies of the parliamentary party. After a year of George Barnes as chairman (1910–11) Henderson successfully pressed (James) Ramsay *MacDonald to succeed Barnes. He also arranged that MacDonald would become party treasurer and so continue to be ensured a place on the national executive committee, while he took over the post of party secretary. Hence for much of 1911–31 the two men were the hub of the party. As earlier, their relationship fluctuated from very bad to quite good; MacDonald relied much on the hardworking and methodical Henderson but was ungenerous in recognizing his services to the party and was prone to be highly touchy and egotistic. Henderson for his part could also be oversensitive as well as overbearing yet, unlike MacDonald, did not hold grudges for long.

The war cabinet Henderson, like Labour's other leaders, opposed Britain entering the European war in early August 1914 but once Britain was in the war he supported the war effort, wanting both a British victory and a democratic, just peace. He joined the Union of Democratic Control, the political pressure group committed to a democratic foreign policy and promoting such a non-annexationist peace, and resigned only when he took cabinet office. As Labour's chief whip he was a founder member of the parliamentary recruiting campaign and, like the other chief whips, he received a privy councillorship in the 1915 new year's honours list. His eldest son, David, was killed on 15 September 1916 on the Somme.

Henderson helped to make Labour effective in domestic politics through the War Emergency Workers' National Committee, which he chaired until he joined Asquith's coalition government when it was formed in May 1915. This committee took up many key issues affecting working people during the war, notably high food prices, lack of coal, poor separation allowances for the dependants of soldiers and sailors, and, at the outset of the war, unemployment due to wartime economic dislocations. Before he entered the government Henderson had also taken on government appointments; in January 1915 he became a commissioner with the task of finding work for Belgian refugees, and in February he joined a committee seeking to find employment for disabled servicemen.

When Asquith formed his coalition government Henderson took the one cabinet position given to the Labour Party—president of the Board of Education—while William Brace and George Roberts took lesser posts. Henderson wished for a post such as president of the Board of Trade, through which he could directly assist the mobilization of the economy for war. He had already been helping to increase munitions production, following the Treasury conference of 17–19 March 1915, serving as chairman of the national advisory committee, which was set up to help implement the agreements made then and a week later with the Amalgamated Society of Engineers. He was also a member of Lloyd George's munitions of war committee, which met from 12 April 1915. Throughout his twenty-seven months in office under Asquith and Lloyd George, Henderson's main task, whatever the title of his office, was to help maximize industrial output for war. He was the main forerunner of Ernest Bevin in the Second World War. Though the war effort took most of his attention while at the Board of Education Henderson did set up committees to review the teaching of science, the teaching of modern languages, and the education of the young after the war. He also improved relations between the board and local authorities, and paid more attention to the concerns of the teaching unions. However, in the face of criticism of the board from Ramsay MacDonald and others, Henderson requested to be moved from departmental responsibility. In August 1916 he insisted on resigning from education and became paymaster-general. He continued as the government's labour adviser until its fall in December 1916.

In the political crisis of that December Henderson made it clear that Labour would support any prime minister committed to winning the war, and so he did not join most of the former Liberal ministers in declining office other than under Asquith. Under Lloyd George Labour secured more substantial posts, with Henderson himself in the small war cabinet formed in December 1916. The particular areas assigned to him included manpower problems and national service in particular. However, while Henderson remained committed to British victory in the war he broke acrimoniously with Lloyd George's government in August 1917. Henderson went to Russia on behalf of the government and was a strong supporter of Kerensky's efforts to keep Russia in the war and to thwart the Bolsheviks. He came to believe that Labour Party participation in an International Socialist conference planned to take place in Stockholm would strengthen Kerensky's position. Henderson's ministerial colleagues, especially Conservatives, were outraged at such a proposal. Henderson was kept outside a war cabinet meeting ('on the doormat') while his position was discussed. He resigned in anger.

Secretary to the Labour Party Henderson's departure from the government heightened his political stature. He had stood up to Lloyd George and he had asserted Labour's independence. Although Labour remained in the coalition government Henderson was freed to devote his skills, as secretary of the Labour Party since 1912, to strengthening the party's organization and reformulating party policy, not least on war aims and social reconstruction. In the autumn of 1917 he stood down as chairman of the parliamentary party to work on the reorganization of the Labour Party, with provision for individual membership of the party (not only through affiliated trade unions or socialist organizations). As well as being much involved in the revision of the party constitution, with its socialist objective, he also played a major part in drawing up its new policy statement, *Labour and the New Social Order*, approved at the June 1918 conference.

Henderson's return to running the Labour Party machine, as well as his family being located in London, led to what proved to be a disastrous decision to leave his north-east political base. Following boundary changes he could have secured either the new Spennymoor seat or one of the Newcastle constituencies. Instead he accepted an invitation to stand at East Ham. This he failed to win at the 1918 general election, but he returned to parliament as the second of Labour's by-election victors in 1919, when he won Widnes in September. He won Newcastle East in January 1923 but lost it in the general election that

autumn. He won Burnley in February 1924 but lost it in 1931. He gained a safe seat only at the end of his career, Clay Cross in September 1933.

Like Labour's other major leaders Henderson vehemently opposed communism and the Third International. Henderson and MacDonald played major roles in attempting to rebuild the Second International as a focus for democratic socialism. For a while Henderson continued to support the exiled Kerensky and gave him a platform at the June 1918 Labour Party conference as well as at an inter-allied Labour and socialist conference in September 1918. Henderson represented the Second International's views on labour issues to the council of four major victor powers at the Paris peace conference in February 1919. Henderson was also a vigorous campaigner in support of a league of nations and appeared on a platform in his constituency, in 1920, with Lord Robert Cecil, a Conservative proponent of the league.

In opposition to the Lloyd George coalition government Henderson played a leading role in reformulating Labour's policy on Ireland. He was a strong home ruler and had worked with the Irish parliamentary party before 1914, presiding over the first joint Labour and Irish nationalist meeting in March 1909. In January 1920 Henderson and William Adamson led a Labour deputation to Ireland. After a period of illness and an operation for gallstones in June 1920 Henderson, in October 1920, offered his own solution for Ireland, and a few days later moved a motion of censure on the government and its policy of reprisals in Ireland. When Labour's call for an independent investigation into government-backed violence in Ireland was rejected Labour set up its own investigation under Henderson. This led to Henderson and the Labour Party moving beyond the old formulae of home rule politics. When Lloyd George did reach an Irish settlement, in December 1921, Henderson and Labour backed it against opposition from some of the coalition government's own supporters.

Henderson was also active in condemning the Lloyd George coalition government's responses to the unemployment that reached a high level from the time of the 1921–2 severe downturn in the economy. With Sidney Webb and others he revised Labour's proposals, which had been put forward in the war and to the National Industrial Conference in April 1919. The resulting policy statement, *Unemployment: a Labour Policy*, was endorsed at a special joint Labour-TUC conference in January 1921. Labour called for the lifting of restrictions on building and local government work, the carrying out of a list of 'necessary works', and for more to be done to improve international trade. However, when Lloyd George invited Labour to participate in an inquiry into unemployment Henderson declined on the grounds that the terms of reference were too narrow and that the government was trying to use Labour as a shield from the wrath of the unemployed.

The first Labour government When Labour formed its first government in January 1924 MacDonald combined being prime minister with the role of foreign secretary. After some prevarication by MacDonald, on the grounds that Henderson had lost his seat in the general election, Henderson became home secretary. This was a position which did not enhance his reputation. The Home Office reinforced his tendencies towards moderation and caution. He refused to countenance the reinstatement of men who had lost their jobs in the 1919 police strike, in spite of Labour Party and TUC pledges to do so. He was also very willing to operate the Emergency Powers Act of 1920, had major strikes not been settled. Henderson might well have been foreign secretary in 1924, having established himself as an alternative specialist in foreign affairs to the radical E. D. Morel. Henderson was closer to Labour Party sentiment over foreign issues than Home Office matters and more radical than MacDonald. Although stating what had hitherto been party policy Henderson caused controversy during his Burnley by-election in February 1924 by calling for a revision of the treaty of Versailles. Also, unlike MacDonald, he was a doughty advocate of the Geneva protocol for the pacific settlement of international disputes, urging a policy from 1917 onwards that was close to collective security. However, the protocol was not ratified by the first Labour government before it fell in November 1924, as MacDonald prevaricated at length.

After 1924 Henderson resisted attempts by Ernest Bevin and others to replace MacDonald as Labour Party leader. Henderson continued to see MacDonald as the necessary leader, combining charisma with moderate views. As the major alternative leader Henderson's support was decisive until 1931. After the fall of the 1924 government MacDonald found he needed to consult Henderson and a few other major figures more. Henderson also secured MacDonald's support for another major reformulation of Labour's policies, a new statement, *Labour and the Nation*, being ratified by the 1928 Labour Party conference.

During the 1926 general strike Henderson tried to mediate between the miners and the government. His whole career as a trade union leader and as Labour Party leader was marked by a belief in industrial co-operation rather than conflict. He had been instrumental in setting up a conciliation board in the iron industry in the north-east in 1894. He had backed other joint boards over the years and had been an initially keen participant in Lloyd George's 'parliament for industry', the National Industrial Conference set up in 1919. In the later 1920s he still hoped for the resurrection of the National Industrial Conference or the creation of a similar body. During the later 1920s he continued to be one of Labour's main speakers on foreign policy. Until the formation of MacDonald's second government in 1929 he remained the president of the Labour and Socialist International (the successor of the Second International). He also travelled extensively in 1926 and 1927, visiting Canada, the United States, Australia, and New Zealand. He made his claims for the Foreign Office quite explicit. Yet, in spite of his great political weight in the Labour Party, MacDonald's initial choice for foreign secretary was J. H. Thomas. However, when Henderson firmly pressed

his case, MacDonald reluctantly nominated him, thereby creating some resentment.

Foreign secretary Henderson took up his appointment on 8 June 1929; he was far more successful at the Foreign Office than he had been at the Home Office. Indeed at the time and subsequently he has often been judged to be the most successful minister of the second Labour government. Molly Hamilton, the Labour MP for Blackburn, later observed of Henderson at the Foreign Office: 'he knew what he wanted to do, and did it' (Hamilton, *Remembering my Good Friends*, 125). Hugh Dalton, Henderson's junior minister at the Foreign Office, later testified that he had 'learnt much from him, not only in his untiring pursuit of international peace but in his most competent handling of a great government department' (Cole, vii). Henderson, as foreign secretary, was admired for his careful and good judgement, his decisiveness, and his genial nature. His long experience as a trade union and Labour Party official, as well as that of cabinet office, gave him the confidence and the authority to manage the Foreign Office firmly.

As foreign secretary Henderson diligently carried out the party's policies as stated in *Labour and the Nation* (1928). He was very committed to disarmament by international agreement, rejecting calls for unilateral disarmament. This, according to Hugh Dalton, his parliamentary under-secretary, at the 1931 Labour Party conference, was the one foreign policy objective yet to be achieved when the government fell. Henderson was a much stronger supporter of the League of Nations than MacDonald, whose support on occasions was equivocal. Henderson played a substantial role in securing the removal of troops of occupation from the Rhineland. He also restored diplomatic relations with Russia and negotiated a trade agreement with the Soviet government in April 1930. Henderson improved Anglo-Iraqi relations by his promise of British support for Iraq's membership of the League of Nations 'without proviso or qualification', and Anglo-Egyptian relations by his withdrawal of troops from the cities to the Suez Canal area and by his replacement of the illiberal Lord Lloyd as British high commissioner.

Henderson was also active in trying to maintain Liberal support for the 1929–31 Labour government. He was willing to trade Labour support for the alternative vote (though he was against proportional representation) to obtain Liberal support for repeal of the 1927 Trades Disputes Act. Henderson was seen by many as the alternative Labour leader to MacDonald. In spite of MacDonald's many slights, not least in intervening without consulting in foreign affairs, Henderson continued to see MacDonald as the essential leader. Even after the formation of the National Government, Henderson tried to keep the door open for MacDonald to return, just as he had done after the split following Britain's entry into the European war in 1914. Henderson appears to have felt, by April 1931, that his career was nearing its end and he asked MacDonald if he could go to the House of Lords, thus freeing more time for his Foreign Office and Labour Party work.

However, Henderson was one of five ministers on the cabinet economy committee in August 1931 which was faced with the need to respond to Sir George May's report calling for substantial cuts in public expenditure to lessen the predicted huge budget deficit. In the committee and cabinet discussions on economies Henderson was agreeable to a £56 million package of cuts but resisted further reductions in levels of unemployment benefits. His loyalty to the wider labour movement proved stronger than to MacDonald and Philip Snowden, the chancellor of the exchequer. MacDonald, faced with dissent from half of his cabinet, went to see the king to resign, and advised the king not to send for Henderson but to see the opposition leaders instead. The king successfully suggested that MacDonald should form a national government, and on 24 August 1931 the Labour cabinet resigned.

Labour in opposition Henderson was shaken by MacDonald's departure. He was elected leader of the Labour Party on 27 August 1931. In attempting to ensure that Labour in opposition remained moderate, and in not wishing to be accused of aggravating the national economic crisis by vigorously attacking the new government, he failed to give vigorous leadership. He may also have been trying to avoid giving MacDonald a pretext for calling an early general election. If so, he failed. In the October 1931 general election Labour was reduced to fifty-two seats, most of its leaders, including Henderson, having been defeated. Henderson remained leader until October 1932 (with George Lansbury as leader of the Parliamentary Labour Party) but was out of sympathy with the more radical policies advocated by the TUC, let alone the Independent Labour Party. He was more interested in world peace.

While foreign secretary Henderson had been nominated to preside over the world disarmament conference at Geneva. In spite of poor health, due to a recurring gallstone complaint, Henderson opened the conference on 2 February 1932 and presided over it until it faded away in June 1935. Henderson's struggles to achieve disarmament in a world marked more by rearmament in Europe and the Far East earned him the Nobel peace prize in autumn 1934. Though returned to parliament in a by-election at Clay Cross in September 1933 his main concern remained the world disarmament conference. He set out his party's policy in *Labour's Way to Peace* (1935). Even though his health was deteriorating markedly he was nevertheless reluctant to stand down as Labour Party secretary and only did so at the end of 1934. He died in a London nursing home on 20 October 1935, survived by his wife, two of his sons, William and Arthur (who both were Labour MPs), and by his daughter Nellie. He was cremated at Golders Green on 24 October 1935; George Lansbury gave the address.

Widely nicknamed Uncle Arthur, Henderson was a much respected Labour Party figure. He was for Labour what Stanley Baldwin became for the Conservatives: the decent, solid, and respectable face of the party. In spite of his Scottish birth, like Baldwin, he also epitomized what many perceived to be moderate English characteristics. He was committed to his chapel and to his family. Within the Labour Party he was one of its most central and representative figures, a major trade unionist, a devoted central organizer and disciplinarian, a minister with much political weight, and a moderate in his views.

CHRIS WRIGLEY

Sources M. A. Hamilton, *Arthur Henderson: a biography* (1938) · C. J. Wrigley, *Arthur Henderson* (1990) · F. M. Leventhal, *Arthur Henderson* (1989) · E. A. Jenkins, *From foundry to foreign office* (1933) · J. Saville, 'Henderson, Arthur', *DLB*, vol. 1 · K. O. Morgan, *Labour people: leaders and lieutenants, Hardie to Kinnock* (1987) · M. A. Hamilton, *Remembering my good friends* (1944) · M. Cole, *Makers of the labour movement* (1948) · *The diary of Beatrice Webb*, ed. N. MacKenzie and J. MacKenzie, 4 vols. (1982–5) · *The political diary of Hugh Dalton, 1918–1940, 1945–1960*, ed. B. Pimlott (1986) · D. Carlton, *Macdonald versus Henderson: the foreign policy of the second labour government* (1970) · A. Thorpe, *The British general election of 1931* (1991) · A. Thorpe, 'Arthur Henderson and the British political crisis of 1931', *HJ*, 31 (1988), 117–39 · R. Skidelsky, *Politicians and the slump: the labour government of 1929–1931* (1967) · H. R. Winkler, *Paths not taken* (1994) · C. Wrigley, 'Arthur Henderson: from north-east industrial conciliation to international multilateral disarmament', *North East Labour History Bulletin*, 25 (1991), 5–24 · R. McKibbin, 'James Ramsay MacDonald and the problem of the independence of the labour party, 1910–1914', *Journal of Modern History*, 42 (1970), 216–35 · R. McKibbin, 'Arthur Henderson as labour leader', *International Review of Social History*, 23 (1978), 79–101

Archives People's History Museum, Manchester, corresp. and MSS | BL, corresp. with Lord Cecil, Add. MS 51081 · BLPES, corresp. with independent labour party · Bodl. Oxf., corresp. with Herbert Asquith · Bodl. Oxf., corresp. with Lord Ponsonby · CAC Cam., official corresp. with Lord Lloyd; corresp. with Sir Eric Phipps · HLRO, corresp. with Andrew Bonar Law; corresp. with David Lloyd George; letters to Herbert Samuel · Liverpool RO, Preston, corresp. with Lord Derby · London School of Economics, Dalton MSS; Webb MSS · NA Scot., corresp. with A. J. Balfour · NL Ire., corresp. with Thomas Johnson · People's History Museum, Manchester, labour party records · PRO, Cabinet papers · PRO, corresp., FO 800/280–284 · PRO, Foreign Office MSS · PRO, Ministry of Munitions MSS · PRO, Ramsay MacDonald MSS · PRO, corresp. with James Ramsay MacDonald, PRO 30/69/1/196 · U. Warwick Mod. RC, Friendly Society of Ironfounders records | FILM BFI NFTVA, current affairs footage; news footage · IWM FVA, actuality footage · IWM FVA, documentary footage · IWM FVA, news footage

Likenesses L. M. Mayer, miniature, *c.*1924, NPG · E. Kapp, lithograph, 1930–39, NPG · E. Kapp, drawing, 1935, Barber Institute of Fine Arts, Birmingham · J. Russell & Sons, photograph, NPG [*see illus.*]

Wealth at death £23,926 18s. 5d.: probate, 13 Dec 1935, CGPLA Eng. & Wales

Henderson, Sir Brodie Haldane (1869–1936), civil and military engineer, was born on 6 March 1869 at 24 Denmark Villas, Ealing, Middlesex, the sixth and youngest son of George Henderson, formerly of Langholm, Dumfries, a printer's reader, and his wife, Eliza, daughter of George Cockshutt of York. A brother of Alexander *Henderson MP, first Baron Faringdon, the railway promoter, financier, and newspaper proprietor, he was educated privately in Britain and Germany, and at King's College, London, and the Victoria University of Manchester. He began his career with Beyer, Peacock & Co., the great locomotive engineers, before joining in 1891 the consulting engineering firm James Livesey & Son as a partner, whereupon the business became Livesey, Son, and Henderson. Commissioned into the Royal Engineers in 1914, he became deputy director-general of transportation in Belgium and France, with responsibility for railways. Henderson had a distinguished war record, being mentioned in dispatches on four occasions, and rising to the rank of brigadier-general. In 1918 he became CMG, and a year later CB and KCMG. He was an officer of the Légion d'honneur, was awarded the Croix de Guerre, and was a commander of the Crown of Belgium. In 1928–9 he served as president of the Institution of Civil Engineers; he was also a governor of Imperial College of Science and Technology, a member of the delegation of the City and Guilds College, honorary consulting engineer to the Imperial War Graves Commission, sometime high sheriff of Hertfordshire and, at the time of his death, deputy lord lieutenant of the county.

A forceful character and capable administrator, for most of his working life Henderson was associated with Livesey and Henderson, one of the foremost consulting engineers of the period, specializing in railway projects. The firm received many commissions from railway companies financed by Alexander Henderson. Brodie Henderson became senior partner in 1893, on the retirement of James Livesey, when the firm became known as Livesey and Henderson; he travelled extensively in Africa and South America, supervising railway, docks, and harbour construction. Henderson was an engineer who believed that projects should be 'built to last' and was most closely involved with work commissioned by premier British-owned Argentinian railway companies such as the Buenos Ayres Great Southern and the Central Argentine. In Brazil he worked with the Great Western and the Leopoldina, and in Uruguay with the Central and North Western. The partnership also designed and built for the Antofagasta (Chile) and Bolivia Railway, the United Railways of Havana, the Midland Railway of Western Australia, and Nyasaland railways. Henderson also supervised the construction of the new docks in Buenos Aires and had business connections with various steelmakers and railway equipment manufacturers, such as Armstrong-Whitworth & Co., Dorman Long, the United Steel Company, the Birmingham Railway Wagon and Carriage Company, and Metropolitan-Cammell.

Henderson, is, however, most remembered for the Lower Zambezi Bridge on the Beira Railway. He claimed most of the credit for the project, much to the chagrin of rival firm Rendel, Palmer, and Tritton, responsible for the preliminary survey and contract drawings. Livesey and Henderson retained the business of site supervision, and Henderson was personally involved with the early earthworks, visiting the site during the course of construction. Built between Dona Ana and Sena in Mozambique, the lowest point at which the river could be crossed, the bridge is 2.24 miles long and has 33 main arched spans of 253 feet. Described as a triumph of British engineering, for many years it was the longest bridge in the world.

Henderson died of lung cancer, aged sixty-seven, on 28 September 1936 at his home, Upp Hall, Braughing, near Ware, Hertfordshire. His ashes were buried in the family grave at Braughing on 1 October, following cremation at Golders Green, Middlesex, on 30 September. A memorial service was held at St Michael, Cornhill, London, on 3 October. He was survived by Ella, Lady Henderson, daughter of James Jones of Lechdale, whom he married in 1901, sons Gerald Brodie, Neil Brodie, and Andrew Brodie, and daughter Joan. Neil and Andrew followed their father into Livesey and Henderson and became partners in the business, as did their cousin, the Hon. Philip Henderson, son of Lord Faringdon.   COLIN M. LEWIS

Sources DBB · M. R. Lane, *The Rendel connection: a dynasty of engineers* (1989) · G. Watson, *The civils: the story of the Institution of Civil Engineers* (1988) · *The Times* (29 Sept 1936) · *The Times* (1–3 Oct 1936) · *The Times* (31 Oct 1936) · DNB · WW · d. cert. · *CGPLA Eng. & Wales* (1936)
Archives Institution of Mechanical Engineers, London, letter-book
Wealth at death £263,716 6s.: probate, 29 Oct 1936, *CGPLA Eng. & Wales*

Henderson, Charles Cooper (1803–1877), equestrian painter, was born at the Abbey House, Chertsey, Surrey, on 14 January 1803, the younger son of John Henderson (1764–1843), an amateur artist, and his wife, Georgiana Jane *Henderson (1770–1850) [see under Keate, George], a painter, daughter of the author and painter George *Keate (1729–1797). His brother was John *Henderson (1797–1878), the art collector. Educated at Winchester College, he studied and qualified for the bar, but did not practise. Like John Ruskin, he took art lessons in his youth from Samuel Prout.

A prolific artist who painted in both oils and watercolour, Henderson specialized in equestrian and hunting subjects. He was best-known for his coaching scenes, a number of which were engraved and published by Messrs Fores of Piccadilly, Rudolph Ackermann, and other printsellers; some were etched by Henderson himself. He frequently used the monogram CH, with the 'C' reversed, and worked almost entirely for private patrons.

In 1828, against his father's wishes, Henderson married Charlotte, eldest daughter of Charles William By; they had seven sons and two daughters. He and his family lived at 3 Lamb's Conduit Place, London, from which address he sent his only two entries—both coaching scenes—to the Royal Academy exhibitions in 1840 and 1848. Following his mother's death in 1850, he was left financially independent and was able to paint simply as a hobby. He died at his home at Lower Halliford-on-Thames, Middlesex, on 21 August 1877 and was buried in Kensal Green cemetery, London. His children erected a brass tablet to his memory in St Nicholas's Church, Shepperton, Middlesex.

                                        L. H. CUST, *rev.* ROMITA RAY

Sources S. Mitchell, *The dictionary of British equestrian artists* (1985) · *CGPLA Eng. & Wales* (1877)
Wealth at death under £25,000: resworn probate, June 1879, *CGPLA Eng. & Wales* (1877)

Henderson, Sir David (1862–1921), army and air force officer, was born in Glasgow on 11 August 1862, the youngest son of David Henderson, shipbuilder, and his wife, Jane Pitcairn. He was educated at Glasgow University, where he studied engineering under Lord Kelvin, but he subsequently chose to enter the army. After passing through Sandhurst he joined the Argyll and Sutherland

Sir David Henderson (1862–1921), by Walter Stoneman, 1918

Highlanders in 1883 and served in South Africa, Ceylon, and China. In 1895 he married Henrietta Caroline (d. 1959), the second daughter of Henry Robert Dundas, and the granddaughter of the first Baron Napier of Magdala; they had a son and a daughter.

In 1898 Henderson served in the Sudan campaign as aide-de-camp to Brigadier-General Sir Neville Lyttelton, where he was mentioned in dispatches and promoted brevet major. On the outbreak of the Second South African War in October 1899 he became an intelligence officer on the staff of Sir George White, the commander at Natal, and was besieged at Ladysmith. Restless with the enforced inactivity he planned a night-time attack, in which he was wounded, to destroy two Boer guns that periodically bombarded the city from a hill to the east. After the relief of Ladysmith, Henderson moved with General Buller's force through Natal into Transvaal and was promoted brevet lieutenant-colonel in November 1900. From October 1900 to September 1902 he served as director of military intelligence under Lord Kitchener. Previously intelligence had been piecemeal with each local commander conducting his own reconnaissance. Henderson took a scientific approach, patiently collating intelligence at headquarters on a vast scale, allowing him to compile a daily map of the distribution of enemy forces. With the end of the war he was transferred to civil employment in the Transvaal and was awarded the DSO in 1902 in recognition of his wartime work.

In 1903 Henderson returned to staff work at the War Office. He set down the lessons he learned in Africa as a textbook, *Field Intelligence: its Principles and Practice* (1904), which greatly increased his military reputation. In 1907 he became staff officer to the inspector-general of the forces and wrote *The Art of Reconnaissance*, which was subsequently used as a training manual. The birth of aviation attracted Henderson's adventurous spirit. In 1911, at the age of forty-nine, he gained aviator certificate no. 118 at Brooklands, making him the oldest pilot in the world. Once an airman he became a passionate advocate for air power. In the third edition of *The Art of Reconnaissance* (1914) he acknowledged that aircraft were now an essential tool of reconnoitring. He was the natural choice to represent the army on a committee appointed by the committee of imperial defence to investigate the impact of aviation and draw up a scheme for air development.

The government was concerned that despite the formation of an army air battalion in 1911, Britain still lagged behind France and Germany in aviation for military purposes. The outcome of the committee was the establishment of the Royal Flying Corps (RFC) in April 1912. The RFC consisted of a military wing, a naval wing, the Central Flying School, and the Royal Aircraft Factory. In July 1912 Henderson became director of military training and took an interest in the expansion of the RFC. In September 1913 the War Office established a military aeronautics directorate to take charge of the military wing. Henderson was appointed director-general with control over recruitment, training, and equipment. Meanwhile the naval wing renamed itself the Royal Naval Air Service (RNAS) and developed its own independent organization and aspirations.

With the outbreak of war in 1914 Henderson went to France to command the RFC in the field. His early development of the corps had reflected his interest in reconnaissance. In the aerial tests of 1912, aeroplanes with good stability and downward visibility had been selected specifically for this purpose. The RFC was able to provide invaluable information to the British expeditionary force (BEF) on German troop movements during the early phase of the war. The air service was subsequently decentralized for tactical work to enhance the flow of information between the RFC and BEF. Squadrons were grouped as 'wings', which were then attached to army corps, but Henderson was careful to maintain the autonomy of the air service.

In October 1914 Henderson was promoted major-general and in November he returned to the infantry as commander of the 1st infantry division. It was possible he felt the RFC was not a big enough command for a general of his seniority. However, within a month Kitchener had ordered him back to the RFC. Henderson set about expanding the RFC's role. He encouraged his officers to experiment in anything that might assist the army, such as observation for the artillery using wireless telegraphy and aerial photography. He also requested aeroplanes capable of carrying machine-guns and bombs for offensive operations in their own right. The RFC enlarged in importance and strength but Henderson's dual role placed a strain on his health. In August 1915 he handed over command of the RFC in France to Brigadier-General Trenchard (although Henderson retained overall command until October 1917) and returned to the War Office to concentrate on the military aeronautics division. In February 1916 he was given a seat on the Army Council, from which he fought the corner of the fledgeling service with patient determination.

In 1917 Henderson was promoted lieutenant-general. By mid-1917 the government wanted a solution to settle the divisive inter-service rivalry between the RFC and the RNAS. Both branches competed for the same resources and neither was dealing adequately with air raids from German Gothas by day and Zeppelins by night. Haig wanted the air service to be incorporated into the army but Henderson argued masterfully for a separate, integrated air force that controlled all aspects of air war, including ground air defence. At the end of 1917 the cabinet agreed to such a plan. As General Smuts's adviser on the air organization committee, Henderson worked hard on plans for the amalgamation of the RFC and the RNAS into the Royal Air Force (RAF), which took place on 1 April 1918.

Henderson was vice-president of the newly formed Air Council from January 1918, but he resigned in April claiming he wished to avoid the atmosphere of intrigue permeating the Air Ministry. He was also annoyed at having been denied a top posting in the new service. He thus denied himself the chance to play an active role in the new organization he had worked so hard to create. In June personal tragedy struck when his son, Captain Ian Henderson, also an airman, was killed in a flying accident at Turnberry. Henderson went back to France as an area commandant until October 1918 and during the peace negotiations served as a military counsellor in Paris. Above all, Henderson was a natural soldier with a strong devotion to duty in whatever field he served. Kitchener had great confidence in his judgement throughout his career and he was once considered by Asquith as a candidate for chief of staff. With the signing of the Versailles treaty in June 1919, Henderson went to Geneva to organize and direct the league of Red Cross societies. This work was cut short by his death there on 17 August 1921. He was created KCB in 1914 and KCVO in 1919. His wife, who was created DBE in 1919, and daughter survived him.

The early history of the RAF is dominated by the figure of Sir Hugh Trenchard, who was responsible for developing its structure and doctrine. Yet Henderson, with his clear vision and well-disciplined mind, drove the development of air power from the early days of the air arm in 1911 to the formation of the combined service in 1918. Henderson had the personal prestige, technical knowledge, and practical wartime experience to accomplish this task.

Trenchard himself acknowledged Henderson as the 'father of the air force'. He wrote in 1954 that Henderson 'was well placed to use with effect his great powers of imagination, clear exposition and tact to persuade the Army Council that they could no longer afford to neglect this new weapon or starve its development' (Henderson papers, AC 71/12/196). However Henderson did not escape criticism, and his single-minded resolve led to charges of authoritarianism. Yet ultimately his endeavours left Britain, by 1918, with the largest and best-equipped air force in the world.   RICHARD A. SMITH

Sources RAF Museum, Hendon, London, Henderson papers · W. Raleigh and H. A. Jones, *The war in the air*, 1, 2, 3 (1922–37) · *DNB* · H. A. Jones, 'Sir David Henderson, father of the RAF', *Journal of the Royal Air Force College*, 11/1 (1931), 6–12 · M. Cooper, *The birth of independent air power* (1954) · E. Ash, *Sir Frederick Sykes and the air revolution* (1999)
Archives NL Scot., corresp. and press cuttings · RAF Museum, Hendon, department of research and information services, papers relating to Royal Flying Corps, etc. | FILM IWM FVA, actuality footage · IWM FVA, news footage
Likenesses F. Dodd, charcoal and watercolour drawing, 1917, IWM · W. Stoneman, photograph, 1918, NPG [*see illus.*] · M. Hoffman, bronze bust, 1919, Royal Air Force Museum, Hendon
Wealth at death £2992 4s. 1d.: confirmation, 24 Dec 1921, *CCI*

Henderson, Sir David Kennedy (1884–1965), psychiatrist, was born on 24 April 1884 in Dumfries, Scotland, the sixth child of John Henderson, a Dumfries solicitor, and his wife, Agnes Davidson. Henderson was educated at Dumfries Academy, Edinburgh high school, and Edinburgh University, where he gained his MD degree in 1907. About 1910, probably in New York, he married Margaret, daughter of William Mabon, a psychiatrist of New York; they had three daughters.

Henderson began his career at a time when asylum based psychiatry was perceived as a somewhat lowly, unrewarding specialism. Nevertheless, psychiatry was his first choice and he did much to secure an up-to-date training by working and studying with some of the leading international figures in this field. From 1907 to 1912 he held assistant posts under Sir Thomas Clouston at the Royal Edinburgh Asylum, Sir Frederick Mott at the pathological laboratories of the London county council, Claybury, three invaluable years under Adolf Meyer at the Psychiatric Institute, Manhattan State Hospital, New York, and six months with Emile Kraepelin and Alois Alzheimer at the Royal Psychiatric Clinic in Munich. In 1912 he was invited by Adolf Meyer to become senior resident physician at the newly opened Henry Phipps Clinic at Johns Hopkins Hospital, Baltimore; he returned to Britain in 1915 to serve in the Royal Army Medical Corps. Meyer's comprehensive or psychobiological approach to clinical practice had a lasting influence on Henderson and helped to shape the service he developed as physician superintendent at Glasgow's Royal Mental Hospital (1920–32). During his time at Glasgow, Henderson published his *Textbook of Psychiatry* (1927), co-written with R. D. Gillespie; this text went through nine editions by 1962, gained an international reputation, and came to be known simply as Henderson and Gillespie. This book was crucial to raising the status of psychiatry.

In 1932 Henderson became professor of psychiatry at Edinburgh University, a post which he held, along with that of physician superintendent at Edinburgh's Royal

Hospital, until his retirement in 1954. His energy was phenomenal, treating large numbers of patients in both hospitals and five nursing homes simultaneously. He was interested in the organic and social causes of mental illness and was a pioneer in employing psychiatric social workers and occupational therapists in clinics. Henderson gained many honours during his long career, and delivered the Morison lectures in 1931, the Norman Kerr memorial lectures in 1936, and the Salmon memorial lectures and Maudsley lecture in 1938. In 1946 he was elected to serve as president of the Royal Medico-Psychological Association, and in 1949 became president of the Royal College of Physicians, Edinburgh. He received honorary degrees from the universities of Edinburgh and McGill and from the National University of Ireland, and in 1947 he was knighted. Towards the end of his life Sir David was busy writing *The Evolution of Psychiatry in Scotland* (1964). The last grand old man of psychiatry, he died on 20 April 1965 at the City Hospital in Edinburgh, where he had lived latterly at 11 Braid Mount. He was survived by his wife.

K. LOUGHLIN

Sources D. K. Henderson, *The evolution of psychiatry in Scotland* (1964) · *The Lancet* (1 May 1965), 964–5 · *BMJ* (1 May 1965), 1194 · b. cert. · d. cert. · *WWW*
Archives Johns Hopkins University, Baltimore, Alan Mason Chesney medical archives, corresp. with Adolf Meyer
Likenesses D. Alison, oils, *c.*1949, Royal College of Physicians of Edinburgh
Wealth at death £60,945 10s.: confirmation, 23 July 1965, *CCI*

David Willis Wilson Henderson (1903–1968), by Walter Bird

Henderson, David Willis Wilson (1903–1968), immunologist and scientific administrator, was born on 23 July 1903 at Partick, Glasgow, the only child of John Henderson, accountant, and his wife, Mary Wilson. He was educated at Hamilton Academy where he enjoyed science and found ways to avoid working on subjects he disliked. On leaving school he chose a career in farming, but abandoned this abruptly because of his dismay at its unscientific methods. He instead enrolled for a degree in agricultural bacteriology at the West of Scotland Agricultural College and Glasgow University; he graduated BSc in 1926.

Henderson's first appointments were as adviser on dairy bacteriology to the Ministry of Agriculture and Fisheries, and lecturer in bacteriology at King's College, University of Durham. He began research on anaerobic bacterial infection in lambs (for which he received an MSc in 1930). In 1931 he joined the Lister Institute of Preventive Medicine, where he was Beit memorial research fellow between 1932 and 1935. (He gained a PhD from the University of London in 1934 and a DSc in 1941.) He moved to the institute's serum department at Elstree, where he worked until 1946 in routine testing of biological products and research. In 1930 Henderson married Beatrice Mary Davenport (*d.* 1952), daughter of Sir Westcott Abell, professor of naval architecture at Durham University.

In the 1930s Henderson published on a number of topics including viral diseases in sheep and the body's mechanisms for limiting infections of *Salmonella* and *Clostridium*

(gas gangrene). Early in 1940 Henderson demonstrated high fatality rates in mice exposed to gas gangrene toxins administered by the respiratory route. The potential of biological weapons was recognized by Sir John Ledingham and Paul Fildes, who lobbied successfully for the Chemical Defence Experimental Station, Porton Down (CDES), to investigate biological warfare. A biology department opened in October 1940 headed by Fildes and with Henderson the effective second in command among its eventual fifty staff. During the war Henderson was the driving force behind the department's research programme, on which he worked very closely with government laboratories in the United States. Work concentrated on the use of aerosols to spread bacterial toxins, spores, and the parent organisms themselves. To take ideas from bench to field trials Henderson created multidisciplinary teams drawing on expertise from within Porton Down and outside. His most famous project was the full-scale testing of anthrax bearing 'weapons' on sheep on Gruinard Island in Ross and Cromarty. The effectiveness of the methods led to plans, quickly shelved at the end of hostilities, for the large-scale production of anthrax spores for delivery in bombs and rockets. However, in Operation Vegetarian five million anthrax infected cattle cakes were stockpiled for use against an enemy's livestock industry. In recognition of his work in allied collaboration on biological warfare Henderson was awarded the US medal of freedom, bronze palm, in 1946.

Henderson remained at Porton Down after the war,

becoming chief superintendent of the new microbiological research department (MRD) in 1946. Although the development of nuclear weapons became the nation's main defence priority, the MRD was charged with maintaining an offensive biological weapons capability and establishing effective protective measures. Despite its military role Porton Down remained within the Ministry of Supply. With the support of an advisory board of eminent scientists and the generous resources afforded to military research, Henderson created a centre that enjoyed national, and in some areas international, renown in microbiological research. He also sought to prioritize long-range research into infection and immunity, which brought him into conflict with the defence chiefs who wanted more emphasis on field trials.

Henderson's approach to research management was seemingly simple: he sought to employ the best scientists from across a range of disciplines and to give them the freedom and resources to undertake fundamental research. However, Henderson played a key personal role, first in persuading often sceptical recruits to join such a controversial establishment, and then in welding their disparate talents together. In 1951, the department moved to new, purpose-built laboratories that Henderson had helped to design. Despite the classified nature of much of its work, the department enjoyed a university atmosphere and was able to offer facilities for visiting scientists from across the world. Apart from fostering a supportive research culture, Henderson's other great strength was his ability and willingness to protect staff from outside interference and bureaucracy. He was irascible and his famous temper was regularly exercised against what he saw as administrative interference. He did not suffer fools gladly and could be rude and offensive. As a benevolent autocrat he was treated with both affection and apprehension. He inspired loyalty, and many careers owed a debt to his nurturing. Yet he could also be overbearing and forthright in demanding high standards. Staff felt they worked for Henderson rather than the MRD or the ministry. Despite his increasing managerial duties Henderson maintained a close interest in day-to-day bench work and his technical judgements continued to be highly regarded.

Under Henderson's leadership the MRD developed recognized expertise on bacterial growth, the behaviour of bacteria in the air, the stages of bacterial infection, bacterial genetics, and immunology. The focus on disease prevention was quite distinctive as medical research elsewhere, due to the influence of the new antibiotics such as penicillin, was dominated by treatments. The MRD's investigations into the large-scale production of bacteria and the containment of biological hazards meant that it pioneered many of the techniques in what subsequently became known as biotechnology. Its success was formally recognized in 1957 when it became the Microbiological Research Establishment (MRE), at last gaining equal status with the older and more famous Chemical Defence Experimental Establishment (previously the CDES). However, problems were looming. In 1959 Henderson fought unsuccessfully against the decision to move both Porton establishments from the Ministry of Supply to the War Office. Yet dealing with the more rigid civil service attitudes of his new masters proved to be the least of his problems. Henderson was also confronted with the government's decision to abandon an offensive biological weapons capability and with the effects of cuts in the defence budget. Due to its scientific standing and the nature of its work the MRE was able to offset some of the cuts by attracting funding from other ministries, departments, and industry, but the wider political climate was moving towards the abandonment of biological weapons and hence their research base.

Henderson's duties as director left him little time for personal research. The apparatus he developed to deliver controlled aerosol doses to experimental animals, known as the piccolo because of its resemblance to the musical instrument, was adopted internationally. He retained a strong interest in aerosols and during a sabbatical year in 1955 he again took up the study of airborne infections and the effects of one infection on another, so-called mixed infections. A founding member of the Society for General Microbiology he served as president from 1963 to 1965. He was appointed CB in 1957 and a fellow of the Royal Society in 1959. The nature of Henderson's work and his commitment to multidisciplinary research is exemplified by the fact that he called himself an immunologist, though others regarded him as a microbiologist or experimental pathologist.

In 1953, following the death of his first wife, Henderson married Emily Helen, daughter of D. Theodore Kelly of New York, a prominent lawyer and vice-president of Manhattan Life. Pat, as she was known, was a bacteriologist and a fine scientific editor. Although Henderson was fond of children and they liked him, he had none of his own. He was renowned for his hospitality and entertaining, at which his combative style often produced vigorous discussions. He was a keen gardener and fisherman. He was able to combine these hobbies in his later years at the fifteenth-century cottage, Swayne's Living, which he bought at Great Durnford, Wiltshire, and which was bounded on one side by the River Avon.

Henderson, a heavy smoker who had long been troubled by high blood pressure, began to suffer chronic health problems in the early 1960s. Persistent respiratory infections in winter months took their toll and in 1964 he began to suffer from minor strokes. He resigned as director of MRE in August 1964 only to return to the bench to work part time on viral infections. After a more serious stroke in August 1967 he finally abandoned research. He died in his sleep at Swayne's Living on 16 August 1968. His second wife survived him.   MICHAEL WORBOYS

Sources L. H. Kent and W. T. J. Morgan, *Memoirs FRS*, 16 (1970), 331–41 · *Journal of General Microbiology*, 60 (1970), 145–9 · G. B. Carter, *Porton Down: 75 years of chemical and biological research* (1992) · *Nature*, 220 (1968), 101–2 · D. W. W. Henderson, 'The microbiological research department, ministry of supply, Porton, Wiltshire', *PRS*, 143B (1954–5), 192–202 · *CGPLA Eng. & Wales* (1968) · *DNB*
Likenesses W. Bird, photograph, RS [*see illus.*]
Wealth at death £18,199: probate, 22 Nov 1968, *CGPLA Eng. & Wales*

Henderson, Ebenezer, the elder (1784–1858), missionary, youngest son of George Henderson, agricultural labourer, and his wife Jean, *née* Buchanan or Buchannan, was born at The Linn, in the parish of Saline, Dunfermline, Fife, on 17 November 1784, and baptized in Queen Anne Street Church on 21 November. He received an elementary education at the school in Dunduff; he then went on to Dunfermline burgh school; but after a total of three and a half years' schooling he went, in 1796, to work with his brother John, making clocks and watches. A quarrel between the brothers over workmanship, however, led to his leaving after about eighteen months, and, after two or three months spent guarding sheep and cows, in 1799 he became a cobbler.

Henderson entered Robert Haldane's seminary in Edinburgh in 1803. On 27 August 1805, at the end of his studies, he was selected by the Revd John Paterson as a companion on a projected missionary journey to India, thus beginning a lifelong friendship with Paterson. At this time the East India Company did not permit the entrance of missionaries into India. Paterson and Henderson therefore sailed for Denmark, from where they could travel on to Serampore, then a Danish settlement. They found great difficulty in obtaining a passage to India, so they began on 15 September 1805 to preach in Copenhagen, thus starting an evangelistic ministry focused in northern Europe rather than in Asia, during the course of which they founded branches of the British and Foreign Bible Society in Denmark, Sweden, Norway, Iceland, and Russia. In January 1806 Henderson was settled as a minister at Helsingør (Elsinore), and began teaching English to young people. By 1807 he had learnt to preach in Danish, and had translated the *Memoir of Catharine Haldane*, which became very popular. The bombardment of Copenhagen, in September 1807, forced a move to Göteborg in Sweden, where he ministered to Danish prisoners and translated for their use a tract entitled *James Covey*. In 1808 he travelled in Sweden and Finland, where there was a great risk of his being captured by the Russian army.

Henderson had now become a competent scholar in Latin, Greek, Hebrew, French, German, Danish, and Swedish. After a visit to England in 1810 he returned to Sweden, and in the following year he published *An Exposition of the Prophecies of Daniel … by the Late Rev. Magnus Frederick Roos*, translated from German. On 6 October 1811 he formed the first Independent church in Sweden. The next two years (1812–13) he spent in Copenhagen, to superintend a translation of the New Testament into Icelandic, and in 1814 he helped to establish the Danish Bible Society. In June 1814 he went to Iceland, where he distributed the scriptures and travelled throughout the island. He published an account of his travels there in 1818. In 1816 he was elected a corresponding member of the Scandinavian Literary Society, and in June he received the diploma of doctor in philosophy from Kiel. In October he went to St Petersburg, where, under the patronage of Tsar Alexander, he printed the Bible in more than ten languages or dialects.

Henderson returned to England in 1817, and on 19 May 1818 he married Susannah, second daughter of John Kennion: they had at least one daughter, Thulia Susannah. On 28 September he set out on his third journey overseas, intending to end it in Persia, where he proposed to begin a new series of operations. He travelled via Hanover, Schleswig, Russia, and Astrakhan to Tiflis. Here the journey ended, in January 1822, after his and Paterson's resignation from the British and Foreign Bible Society, caused by a disagreement about a translation of the scriptures into Turkish which they felt to be erroneous and not in keeping with the society's principles on translation. Henderson then returned to Russia and lived in St Petersburg until 1825, when, through opposition from the Orthodox church, the Bible Society effectively ceased work; it was dissolved in Russia in 1826 by imperial ukase.

Henderson returned to England on 5 July 1825. In November he took charge of the London Missionary Society's seminary at Gosport. In 1826 he moved, with the seminary, to Hoxton College in London, to be resident and theological tutor until 1830. He then moved to Canonbury, and was tutor of Highbury College until 1850, when, on the amalgamation of Homerton, Coward, and Highbury colleges, he retired with a pension. He remained an honorary secretary of the Religious Tract Society and of the British Society for Propagating the Gospel among the Jews. From July 1852 to September 1853 Henderson was minister of Sheen Vale Independent Chapel at Mortlake, Surrey; he also undertook editorial work for the British and Foreign Bible Society, which made him an honorary life governor in 1854. Henderson died at his home, Argyle Cottage, Sheen Vale, Mortlake, on 16 May 1858, and was buried in Abney Park cemetery. He was survived by his wife.

Henderson wrote widely, though few of his sermons seem to have been printed. His major monographs were: *An appeal to the members of the British and Foreign Bible Society on the subject of the Turkish New Testament* (1824); and the further volume, *The Turkish New Testament incapable of defence, and the true principles of Biblical translation vindicated* (1825), in which he brought the controversy to the general public, and by which he encouraged the society to review its procedures on translation. In addition to accounts of his travels in Iceland (1818), Russia and the Crimea (1826), and the Vaudois (1845), he prepared an edition of the Icelandic Bible (1813) and an edition of Gutbirius's Syriac lexicon (1836), and he produced revised editions of some of the works of Albert Barnes. He contributed to a number of periodicals, but especially the *Missionary Magazine*, between 1796 and 1813; the *Congregational Magazine*, between 1825 and 1845; and the *Evangelical Magazine*, between 1793 and 1859. Largely forgotten in Britain, Henderson has remained a significant figure in Iceland and Denmark.

G. C. BOASE, *rev.* ALAN F. JESSON

Sources T. S. Henderson, *Memoir of the Rev. E. Henderson, Ph.D., D.D.* (1859) · J. H. Glassman, 'Ebenezer Henderson', PhD diss., U. Edin., 1957 · F. Olafsson, *Ebenezer Henderson Bibelselsskabets stifter* (1989) · *Annual Report* [British and Foreign Bible Society] (1854–8), 165–6 · *Congregational Year Book* (1859), 200 · J. Paterson, *A book for every land*

(1858) • *CGPLA Eng. & Wales* (1858) • parish records (birth and baptism), 21 Nov 1784, Queen Anne Street Church, Erskine
Archives DWL, letters and papers | CUL, British and Foreign Bible Society MSS • Kongelige Bibliothek, Copenhagen, archives • SOAS, London Missionary Society MSS
Likenesses W. T. Fry, stipple (after T. Wageman), NPG • H. Room, stipple (after J. Cochran), NPG • J. R. Wildman, oils, Dunfermline town council
Wealth at death under £2000: probate, 11 June 1858, *CGPLA Eng. & Wales*

Henderson, Ebenezer, the younger (1809–1879), author and historian, was born on 25 February 1809 at Bridge Street, Dunfermline, ninth of the ten children of John Henderson (1770–1854), clockmaker, and Janet Cooper (1766–1846). His uncle was Ebenezer Henderson, the elder (1784–1858), missionary and theologian. In his early years he learned his father's trade, but gave his real strength to scientific pursuits, producing by 1827 an orrery and an astronomical clock, both of which were much admired by his contemporaries. Between 1829 and 1863 he lived in England, mainly in Liverpool and London. His nominal post at first was clerk and assistant to his brother, William, who owned an extensive tannery at St Helens, but for much of the 1830s and 1840s he attempted to support himself by writing in popular scientific journals and by lecturing. In 1836 he issued a 'Prospectus for the establishment of a popular and practical astronomical observatory in Liverpool'. On 9 September 1839 he married Betsy Coldstream Brodie (1810–1888). Despite receiving a measure of recognition in 1850, when he was highly commended by Airy, Arago, and other European experts for an ingenious combination of wheels designed to show and check sidereal time, by 1851 he was experiencing serious financial difficulties. His brother gave him an appointment as superintendent at his tannery; this lasted until William's death in 1863, when Ebenezer received a small annuity from his brother's estate and he and his wife returned to live in Scotland. During this period he achieved recognition for his antiquarian researches and produced his major literary works. In 1858 he was granted the freedom of Dunfermline for his work in persuading the Ordnance Survey to accord Dunfermline the status of a city. He was also instrumental in restoring the old market cross there and 'Queen Margaret's stone' on the Dunfermline to Queensferry Road, for which he wrote the inscription.

In 1867 Henderson published his life of James Ferguson, the astronomer, a work that established the subject's reputation as a great popularizer of science and exemplar of self-education. This description would, of course, apply as well to Henderson himself. Throughout his life Henderson endured considerable pain and some mental distress caused by a head injury received in childhood. His affliction makes remarkable the sheer size of his output of scientific and historical publications; it may also serve to excuse some of his more dubious research methods and the lack of an adequately critical approach to his materials. His last work, *Annals of Dunfermline … 1069–1878*, published in the year of his death, was a lifetime's labour;

though not without instances of unsifted legend and specimens of archaeological credulity, it is on the whole a monument of patient industry and conspicuous ability.

In the autumn of 1879 the symptoms of Henderson's injury worsened and he died on 2 November at his home, Astral Villa, in Muckhart, Perthshire. He was buried five days later at a public funeral in his beloved Dunfermline.

T. W. BAYNE, rev. CHRIS NEALE

Sources [J. Currie], *A memoir of the late Ebenezer Henderson, by his niece* (1909) • *Dunfermline Saturday Press* (8 Nov 1879) • *Dunfermline Journal* (8 Nov 1879) • J. Norgate, M. Norgate, and F. Hudson, *Dunfermline clockmakers* (1982) • E. Beveridge, *A bibliography of works relating to Dunfermline and the west of Fife* (1901) • E. Henderson, MS notebooks, Central Library, Dunfermline • J. R. Millburn, *Wheelwright of the heavens: the life and work of James Ferguson* (1988) • H. H. Knie, 'Ebenezer Henderson and the Liverpool observatory', *Antiquarian Horology and the Proceedings of the Antiquarian Horological Society*, 10 (1976–8), 843–7 • P. Chalmers, *Historical and statistical account of Dunfermline*, 2 (1859) • private information • parish registers, Dunfermline
Archives Central Library, Dunfermline, MS notebooks relating to local history • District Museum, Dunfermline, incl. long-case clock | NL Scot., letters to Sir Joseph Patton • Royal Observatory, Edinburgh, Crawford collection, works of James Ferguson with MS annotations by Henderson • U. Edin. L., letters to David Laing
Likenesses photograph, c.1866, repro. in [Currie], *Memoir of the late Ebenezer Henderson* • H. Crickmore, engraving (after photograph, 1878), repro. in E. Henderson, *Annals of Dunfermline* (1879)
Wealth at death £792 10s. 6d.: confirmation, 19 Jan 1880, *CCI*

Henderson, Sir Edmund Yeamans Walcott (1821–1896), army officer and police officer, son of Vice-Admiral George Henderson, Royal Navy, of Middle Deal, Kent, and of his wife, Frances Elizabeth, daughter of Edmund Walcott-Sympson of Winkton, Hampshire, was born on 19 April 1821 at Muddiford, near Christchurch, Hampshire. Educated at a school at Bruton, Somerset, and at the Royal Military Academy at Woolwich, he received a commission as second lieutenant in the Royal Engineers on 16 June 1838. His further commissions were as first lieutenant (1841); second captain (1847); first captain (1854); brevet major (1858); lieutenant-colonel (1862).

After the usual course of professional instruction at Chatham, Henderson went to Canada in November 1839 and remained there for six years. After a year in Portsmouth, in June 1846 he was again sent to North America, with Captain Pipon of the Royal Engineers, as commissioner to make an exploratory survey in order to fix a boundary between Canada and New Brunswick in the territory ceded by the United States to Britain under the Ashburton treaty of 1842, and to determine the practicability of establishing a railway of some 700 miles between Halifax and Quebec to connect Canada, New Brunswick, and Nova Scotia.

The eastern half of the New Brunswick survey was allotted to Pipon, who died late in the autumn of 1846 in a canoe accident on the Restigouche River. The western half fell to Henderson, who, forty years after, wrote an account of his adventures for *Murray's Magazine* (March 1887). His official report was illustrated with his own panoramic sketches of the country, which attracted the attention of

Earl Grey, then secretary of state for the colonies. In 1848 Henderson married Mary Murphy at Halifax, Nova Scotia, and returned to England in November 1848, where he was quartered at Gravesend.

Early in 1850 Henderson accepted from Lord Grey the appointment of comptroller of convicts in Western Australia, where it had been decided to establish a penal settlement for the first time; the flourishing colonies of eastern and southern Australia were increasingly opposed to continuing to receive more convicts from Britain. Western Australia had not so far been a successful colony, and, as the government undertook to send out as many free emigrants as convicts, the increased supply of labour was welcomed. At the same time a new development of the convict system was to be tried. The prisoners were to be selected with reference to their fitness for colonial life, and, after passing a certain time in a public works prison, were to be sent out to private employment under police supervision, or else employed in public works in various parts of the colony.

Henderson arrived at Fremantle with the first party of convicts and a guard of sappers in June 1850. No preparations had been made for their arrival, and, after making temporary arrangements, he set to work to build a complete establishment. With the help of the 20th company Royal Engineers, commanded by Captain Henry Wray, with lieutenants William Crossman and Edmund Du Cane, not only the convict prison and quarters but a barrack and officers' quarters also were erected. Hiring depots were formed in different parts of the colony, while the ticket-of-leave men who could not obtain private employment were maintained by government and employed in making roads and building bridges.

At the end of 1855 Henderson lost his wife, and returned to England with his son. In 1857 he married Maria (*d.* 1896), daughter of the Revd J. Hindle of Higham, Kent, and returned to Western Australia early in 1858. He spent another five years there, during which time he took control of the colony's public works. 'Humane and liberal' (*AusDB*), he reduced corporal punishment and made educational provision for the convicts. He resigned the appointment in 1863.

On his return to England, Henderson gave evidence to Grey's royal commission on penal systems and transportation. On 29 July 1863 he succeeded Sir Joshua Jebb as chairman of directors and surveyor-general of prisons and inspector-general of military prisons. He sold his commission in the army on 1 October 1864. He carried out the changes in the administration of prisons made in consequence of the report of the royal commission, in which he was assisted by his former subaltern in Australia, Sir Edmund Du Cane, who succeeded him. Henderson was made a companion in the Order of the Bath, civil division, in 1868.

In 1869 Henderson reluctantly accepted the post of chief commissioner of Metropolitan Police on the death of Sir Richard Mayne. He found himself at the head of a public department, appointed over the heads of all serving in it, some of whom were not pleased by the appointment of an outsider. He succeeded in winning the confidence and respect of his subordinates through a combination of tact and competence. He increased the size of the force from 9000 to 13,000 men and the number of detectives from 15 to 260, and formed the criminal investigation department under Colonel Howard Vincent. In 1878 Henderson was promoted KCB. Following the 'black Monday' riots of a meeting of the unemployed in Trafalgar Square on 8 February 1886, criticisms of the police arrangements were made; without waiting for the report of the committee of inquiry, Henderson resigned. His honourable behaviour was rewarded by the recommendation of the home secretary, accepted by parliament, that he receive the highest possible pension. At a meeting held at Grosvenor House, Henderson was presented with his portrait painted by Edwin Long and a purse of £1000. The cab owners and drivers presented him with a model in silver of a hansom cab, Lord Wolseley acting as their spokesman, in recognition of the great interest he had taken in them, of the institution of cabmen's shelters, and of the support he had given to the Metropolitan Police Orphanage.

Henderson was a fluent speaker with an effective sense of humour, and excelled in anecdote. Quick in assimilating ideas, he expressed himself readily and clearly in official letters and reports. He died on 8 December 1896 at his residence, 4 Gledhow Gardens, London, and was survived by several daughters.   R. H. VETCH, *rev.* J. GILLILAND

Sources *The Times* (10 Dec 1896) · *Royal Engineers Journal*, 27/314 (1 Jan 1897) · *Royal Engineers Journal*, 27/315 (1 Feb 1897) · *AusDB* · Ward, *Men of the reign* · A. T. C. Pratt, ed., *People of the period: being a collection of the biographies of upwards of six thousand living celebrities*, 2 vols. (1897) · [E. H. Yates], ed., *Celebrities at home*, 3rd ser. (1879), 77–91 · *VF* (6 March 1875) · *The Period* (11 June 1870), 57 · *ILN* (13 March 1869) · *ILN* (4 Dec 1886), 600 · *ILN* (19 Dec 1896), 836 · *Murray's Magazine* (March 1887)

Archives Bodl. Oxf., corresp. with Sir William Harcourt · Norfolk RO, family and personal corresp. and papers

Likenesses Ape [C. Pellegrini], chromolithograph caricature, NPG; repro. in *VF* · E. Long, portrait · engraving, repro. in *The Period* · watercolour, repro. in *ILN* (4 Dec 1886) · wood-engraving (after photograph by Russell), NPG; repro. in *ILN* (19 Dec 1896)

Wealth at death £6360 13s. 3d.: resworn probate, Sept 1897, CGPLA Eng. & Wales

Henderson [*married name* Meier], **Eugénie Jane Andrina** (1914–1989), phonetician and linguistic scholar, was born on 2 October 1914 at Rose Villa, Archbold Terrace, Newcastle upon Tyne, the daughter of William Alexander Cruikshank Henderson, civil engineer, and his wife, Pansy Viola, *née* Schurer. The family moved in her early years to London where she went to school, though she continued to claim an ability to speak her original 'Geordie' English.

After school, Henderson read English at University College, London, and achieved first-class honours. Taking advantage of the provision of phonetics classes there, she attracted the attention of the professor of phonetics, Daniel Jones, who encouraged her to study the phonetics of south-east Asian languages, and appointed her to a junior teaching post in 1938. On 8 January 1941 she married

Eugénie Jane Andrina Henderson (1914–1989), by unknown photographer

George Meier (b. 1913). She was to go on consistently to balance the responsibilities of a family with the demands of her career as a scholar and university teacher with grace and aplomb, and once declared facetiously in an introduction to a public lecture series that her hobby was 'bringing up a family of four sons'. Throughout her lifetime she continued to use her maiden name for professional purposes.

Like a number of her contemporaries Henderson found the ultimate course of her career partly determined by the entry of Japan into the war at the end of 1941. In view of the urgent needs of the armed services for persons skilled in Japanese, and to a lesser extent in other Eastern languages, the School of Oriental and African Studies in the university became a major training centre in these languages for specific wartime purposes. Much of this work devolved on the department of phonetics and linguistics, headed by J. R. Firth, where Henderson remained until her retirement.

Henderson was appointed lecturer in phonetics in the department, and her principal work, along with others', was the intensive instruction of naval and air force personnel in service Japanese for various intelligence purposes. At the end of the war, research and teaching provision in oriental languages was greatly increased, following the recommendations of the Scarbrough commission, and she was made a senior lecturer, and subsequently appointed reader (1953) and professor of phonetics from 1964. At the 1982 International Congress of Linguists in Tokyo she read the plenary lecture on phonetics and phonology, subsequently published in the *Proceedings* (1983). In 1986 she was elected fellow of the British Academy. She did not shirk the administrative duties in scholarship: she was treasurer of the Philological Society from 1966 to 1974 and its president from 1984 to 1988, and she took the chairmanship of the Linguistic Association of Great Britain from 1977 to 1980.

Although Henderson continued her interest in Japanese she concentrated her attention, but not exclusively, on the languages of south-east Asia. She took responsibility within her own department for the initial training of newly appointed lecturers in specific south-east Asian languages (such as Thai, Vietnamese, and Cambodian) prior to these lecturers' transfer to the south-east Asia department following their initial year of study leave in the countries of their specialization. For a time she was acting head of that department, and later head of the department of phonetics and linguistics.

Henderson included within her competence experimental phonetics, and her 1970 article on the acoustic features of Kabardian (a central Asian language) has become one of the classics of that branch of phonetics. But the main thrust of her work in phonetics and phonology was made clear in her inaugural lecture, 'The domain of phonetics' (1965), in which she emphasized the importance of the subject, but always and necessarily within the wider context of linguistics as a whole discipline. At the time this stood in contrast to the approach of some traditional phoneticians, for whom syntax and morphology lay rather outside their terms of reference: 'The phonetician cannot close his eyes to grammatical considerations if he wishes to give the most helpful account of the use made of phonic features in a given language' (Henderson, *Domain*, 7). This attitude was exemplified in her work on Tiddim Chin. In 1964 she took part in a joint expedition to Tiddim in the Chin hills of Burma, in her case for fieldwork on the language. Her analysis covered the major levels of linguistics: sentence, phrase, 'figure' (intonation pattern), word classes, the morphological structure of words, and a brief stylistic analysis of two texts.

Henderson's more specifically phonological works involved the exposition and application of Firth's prosodic phonology to a number of languages. Notable among these are her 'Prosodies in Siamese' (Thai, 1949) and her contribution to the book *In Memory of J. R. Firth* (1966). Of the former article F. R. Palmer writes in his edited *Prosodic Phonology* that it is 'the neatest and, in some ways, the most convincing of all the articles written in the prosodic framework' (Palmer, 27). In it she offers an analytical presentation of the interaction of the phonetic features of Thai, segmental and intersegmental, as opposed to a serial phonemic account based on the needs of a broad transcription, itself ultimately based on the letters of the Roman and the Greek alphabets. A more detailed account of Henderson's Thai article appears in Robins (311–12). A full list of her publications may be found in Davidson (5–9). The *Buey Karen Dictionary*, on which she was working before her death, was later completed by Anna Allot and published in 1998. Finally, attention may be drawn to what has turned out to be her most widely read and best-known work, her edition of a volume of extracts from the writings of Henry Sweet, which she entitled *The Indispensable Foundation* (1971), following the claim by Sweet for his own subject in relation to the entire study of language (p. vii).

In addition to Henderson's academic achievement and her dedication to her family, she exhibited energy and ability in several fields: she was an accomplished amateur pianist, and for a time she ran a small dairy farm around her house and garden in Hertfordshire ('when I was a cow keeper'), to which her colleagues were regularly invited. This was a particular delight to her many students from south-east Asia who, fresh from reading Wordsworth in English literature classes, were thrilled actually to see in springtime 'A host of golden daffodils … Fluttering and dancing in the breeze'.

In politics and in social life Henderson maintained a fairly detached pragmatic posture, particularly with regard to the playtime revolutionaries of the 1960s and their more right-wing traditional critics. Challenged in a conversation once on 'principles', she replied 'I do so distrust people who act on principle'. No doubt it was her manifest common sense as well as her academic pre-eminence that led to her being approached by an Oxford college to be its head of house after her retirement, an invitation she declined as she wanted to retain her London home for visits by her sons and their families.

Eugénie Henderson died suddenly at her home, 9 Briardale Gardens, Camden, London, on 27 July 1989. Following her funeral in Hampstead on 31 July, a memorial service was held in a church near University College and the School of Oriental and African Studies.   R. H. ROBINS

Sources R. H. Robins, 'Eugénie Jane Andrina Henderson, 1914–1989', *PBA*, 80 (1993), 305–17 · J. H. C. G. Davidson, 'Biographical note', *Southeast Asian linguistics* (1989) · E. J. A. Henderson, *The domain of phonetics* (1965) · F. R. Palmer, ed., *Prosodic phonology* (1970) · *The indispensable foundation: a selection of the writings of Henry Sweet*, ed. E. J. A. Henderson (1971) · personal knowledge (2004) · private information (2004) [family] · b. cert. · d. cert.
Archives SOAS, papers
Likenesses photograph, British Academy [*see illus.*]

Henderson, (James) Ewen (1934–2000), ceramic artist, was born on 3 January 1934 at Cheddleton Hospital, Staffordshire, the second son and younger child of David Henderson (c.1900–1953), doctor of medicine, and (Beatrice) Mary Stewart (c.1905–1956), teacher and administrator, both of whom were Scottish. He was brought up, unconventionally and rather unhappily, in a large mental hospital near Leek, where his father was resident GP; he later described it as 'a frightening place designed to keep people mad' (Berthoud, 5). He then joined his brother, David, at Adams' Grammar School, Newport, Shropshire, which he attended from 1947 to 1952, excelling in cricket and rugby. He went on to complete his national service—in the RAF regiment in Germany. There he began to attend concerts, which resulted in a lifelong passion for music—

which for him was the first language of art and the emotions. Having been demobbed it was into industry and not further education that he initially went; he joined a chemical company based in Yorkshire and later managed a branch in Cardiff, specializing in timber preservation. While in Cardiff he met his future wife, (Shirley) Kay Rees (b. 1934), subsequently a college administrator. They married on 21 March 1958 and a daughter, Charlotte, was born in 1973.

In addition to his continuing musical interests Henderson began to read avidly and to explore the local Welsh museums and galleries. He was soon attending art classes and then, decisively, enrolled on the art course at Barry summer school. His teachers on the course included Kenneth Martin, Terry Frost, and—crucially—the painter Harry Thubron, a major influence. In 1964 he moved to London to join the foundation course at Goldsmiths' College. There he discovered clay and 'the vessel as a magical form' (Berthoud, 6) before transferring to Camberwell School of Arts and Crafts in 1965, to study ceramics, and taking his degree three years later. He was taught by the eminent potters Lucie Rie, Hans Coper, and Colin Pearson but the stubbornly individual Henderson was uninterested in the emphasis on throwing. He saw more potential in the expressive dynamic of hand-building, and so began a thirty-year odyssey of ceaseless experimentation in which his work became increasingly sculptural in its range and ambition.

The organic asymmetry of his construction reflected Henderson's passionate absorption of natural things, from the riches of the British landscape and coast to the *objets trouvés* discovered on a favourite beach in Turkey. Just as nature was constantly changing Henderson saw the elemental qualities of clay and its firing process as excitingly evocative of the earth's own flux and metamorphosis. He began to make a variety of vessels, which he was soon building up in layers, using clay bodies into which porcelain and bone china might be laminated. These astonishingly free objects owed much to the anonymous creations of ancient cultures (pre-Columbian, archaic Japanese, and Mediterranean art) but he was just as moved by the lyrical vision of modern painters such as Milton Avery, Peter Lanyon, and Richard Diebenkorn.

By using commercial stains and oxides to excess Henderson's pots became more rough and blistered, their fusing surfaces more integrated. By the late 1980s they were developing into more complex and intricate structures, investigating a world of intersecting volumes, spaces, and contours. He saw them as 'collages in Space', a kind of three-dimensional (and deeply romantic) reading of cubist concerns. Though he enjoyed many prestigious exhibitions his work seemed most at home in his Camden Town sculpture garden, where the clay forms combined with the trees and plants to create their own natural order. A mid-career retrospective was held at the British Crafts Centre in 1986, and a major show of new work was organized by Midlands Art Centre in 1995. This highlighted the importance of his parallel two-dimensional work—drawings, gouaches, and collages—which had grown inseparable from the abstract concerns of his sculpture. Additionally it focused on his new interest in British stone circles, resulting in an impressive series of monumental megaliths first shown at the Economist Plaza, London, a year earlier.

In 1995 Henderson curated *Pandora's Box*, a personal anthology of ceramics at the Crafts Council, which highlighted an important but little appreciated post-war tradition in British clay construction. This showed his polemical side. Warm, generous, and witty as a friend, his public persona was maverick and combative—railing against the arts establishment for neglecting clay as a medium of artistic import. Henderson's radical use of it seemed more appreciated abroad, where his ceramics could be seen in such major art museums as the Metropolitan Museum in New York, the Museum of Modern Art in Tokyo, and Amsterdam's Stedelijk Museum. In appearance he was a great bear of a man, with bushy beard and highly expressive eyes and hands, as animated and energized as his personality and his art.

In May 2000 Henderson was awarded an honorary fellowship of the London Institute, in recognition of his contribution to art and of his thirty years' distinguished teaching at Camberwell College of Arts (having joined the staff in 1970, when the school was still called Camberwell School of Arts and Crafts, his students included such notable ceramists as Jim Malone, Angus Suttie, and Sara Radstone). However, his health was already failing and in August he was diagnosed with cancer. He died on 6 October 2000 at the Middlesex Hospital, London, and was cremated at Golders Green on 13 October.

Ewen Henderson was one of the most important and influential ceramic artists of the late twentieth century. Going against the predominant interest in wheel-made forms, he helped to take clay into a new area of artistic and material expression. A restless explorer and risk-taker, his visceral art could be as delicate as it was powerful. Two steps ahead and always moving, this work seemed too unorthodox for many; however, his reputation, already considerable, seems likely to grow.

DAVID WHITING

Sources R. Berthoud, C. Reid, and D. Whiting, *Ewen Henderson* (1995) · *The Guardian* (9 Oct 2000) · D. Whiting, M. Robinson, and G. Clark, *Pandora's box* (1995) [exhibition catalogue, Crafts Council, London] · E. Williams and M. Hose, *Ewen Henderson: paintings* (2000) [exhibition catalogue, Portsmouth and London Institute] · C. Reid, *Ewen Henderson* (1986) [exhibition catalogue, British Crafts Centre, London] · private information (2004) [Kay Henderson, wife; David Henderson, brother] · b. cert. · d. cert.
Likenesses photograph, repro. in Berthoud, Reid, and Whiting, *Ewen Henderson* · photographs, repro. in *Crafts*

Henderson, (Alexander) Gavin, second Baron Faringdon (1902–1977), politician, was born at 52 Princes Gate, London, on 20 March 1902, the eldest of the four children of Lieutenant-Colonel Harold Greenwood Henderson (1875–1922), who was Conservative MP for Abingdon (1910–16) and secretary to the governor-general of Canada (1916–21), and his wife, Lady Violet Charlotte Dalzell (d. 1956), daughter of the fourteenth earl of Carnwath. He

was educated at Eton College, McGill University in Montreal, and Christ Church, Oxford, where he obtained a fourth class in modern history in 1924. As one of the 'Brideshead generation' at Oxford, he was prominent among the bright young things; at a dinner party held before his wedding, the guests poured gallons of petrol into the Thames near Henley to 'set the river on fire' (Wheen, 69). His marriage, on 2 June 1927, to Honor Chedworth Philipps (d. 1956), youngest daughter of Owen Cosby *Philipps, Baron Kylsant, the shipowner, was childless and was annulled in 1931. She married, in 1936, Charles Vere Pilkington; Henderson, referred to in various sources as homosexual, did not marry again.

In March 1934 Henderson succeeded his grandfather, the financier Alexander Henderson, as second Baron Faringdon and inherited Buscot Park. Rebelling against his family's Conservative politics, he joined the Labour Party and sat in the House of Lords as a Labour peer. He campaigned on behalf of Labour parliamentary candidates: Christopher Addison, standing for Swindon in October 1934; John Parker at Romford in 1935; and, later, in 1951 for his friend Tom Driberg at Maldon, where he addressed an election audience as 'My dears' (Wheen, 258). He belonged to the Parliamentary Pacificist Group, founded in 1936 with a policy of appeasement to avoid war. During the Spanish Civil War he supported the republican cause and found homes for Basque child refugees. His pacifist principles prevented him from serving in the Second World War but he joined the fire service and gave distinguished service during the blitz in London and Bristol, attending the House of Lords and Fabian Society committees in his fire brigade uniform. During the war years he was also treasurer of the National Council for Civil Liberties (1940–45). Hugh Dalton, unimpressed by the calibre of Labour's peers, dismissed him as 'a pansy pacifist of whose private tendencies it might be slander to speak freely' (*The Second World War Diary of Hugh Dalton, 1940–1945*, ed. B. Pimlott, 1986, 509). Faringdon was a member of a parliamentary goodwill mission to the USSR in January–February 1945, when he shocked the Russian interpreters by his outspoken criticisms of Churchill (*Labour and the Wartime Coalition: from the Diary of James Chuter Ede, 1941–1945*, ed. K. Jefferys, 1987, 210).

The closing years of the war saw Faringdon becoming increasingly active in the Fabian Society. From 1942 to 1966 he was on its executive committee, and was its vice-chairman (1959–60), chairman (1960–61), and vice-president (1970–77). His particular interest was in colonial and international affairs and he chaired the Fabian Colonial Bureau from 1952 to 1958. He frequently hosted specialist Fabian meetings at Buscot Park, including that chaired by Richard Crossman which produced the *New Fabian Essays* (1952). The last important conference held there was in 1970 after the fall of the Wilson government. During the early 1950s he became involved with the Bevanite Keep Left group, driving members of the group to meetings around the country in his green Rolls-Royce.

Faringdon also played an active part in London government, being a London county councillor (1958–61) and alderman (1961–5). After the creation of the Greater London Council, he joined its historic buildings committee. Other political activities included membership of the Colonial Economic and Development Council (1948–51). He chaired a committee to consider the appearance of local authority housing estates for the National Buildings Record (1942) and served on the Central Housing Advisory Committee (1946). He was a Lords member of the Parliamentary Labour Party's executive from 1957 to 1960 and served on the executive committee of the Fire Service Association, of which he was chairman from 1960 to 1969.

Faringdon devoted considerable time and money to restoring Buscot Park's eighteenth-century mansion. He earned a reputation as an authority on Georgian architecture and interiors, and did much to promote the preservation of Britain's country houses. He later made provision that Buscot Park and its contents should pass to the National Trust upon his death. Among his notable additions to its art collections was a fresco illustrating the history of international socialism. In 1936 he became a fellow of the Royal Society of Arts. He was a trustee of the Wallace Collection (1946–53 and 1966–73) and became president of the Theatres Advisory Council in 1946. He was a member of the Historic Buildings Council (1964–73) and president of the Friends of City Churches in 1943. He was an enthusiastic garden designer. In 1945 a visitor to Buscot described him as looking younger than his age and possessing 'all the aristocratic delicacy of feature and figure that you often find in the third generation parvenu … some would say he was rather cissy; certainly not clever, but cultivated and animated' (McFarlane, 48). Faringdon died at 28 Brompton Square, London, on 29 January 1977, and was buried at Buscot Park. The title passed to his nephew.   GAYNOR JOHNSON

Sources DNB · D. Wainwright, *Henderson: a history of the life of Alexander Henderson, first Lord Faringdon, and of Henderson Administration* (1985) · GEC, *Peerage* · Burke, *Peerage* (1999) · F. Wheen, *Tom Driberg: his life and indiscretions* (1990) · P. Hollis, *Jennie Lee: a life* (1997) · M. Caedel, *Pacifism in Britain, 1914–1945: the defining of a faith* (1980) · K. B. McFarlane, *Letters to friends, 1940–1966* (1997) · K. Morgan and J. Morgan, *Portrait of a progressive: the political career of Christopher, Viscount Addison* (1980) · *The backbench diaries of Richard Crossman*, ed. J. Morgan (1981) · b. cert.
Archives Bodl. RH, corresp. on colonial issues · Bodl. RH, private papers | St Ant. Oxf., papers relating to the National Bank of Turkey | FILM IWM FVA, actuality footage
Wealth at death £282,365: probate, 29 Dec 1977, CGPLA Eng. & Wales

Henderson, George (1783–1855), army officer and railway company director, son of Captain Henderson of the 4th regiment, was born on 4 June 1783 at Newton, his father's property, on the banks of the Dee, Aberdeenshire. After attending the Royal Military Academy, Woolwich, he was commissioned in the Royal Engineers as second lieutenant in March 1800. He was promoted lieutenant in 1801, and in 1803 was sent to Ceylon, where he served nine years. He returned to England in August 1812 with the rank of captain, and in September was sent to Spain to join Wellington's army in the Peninsula. He distinguished

himself at the siege of San Sebastian, for which he was mentioned in dispatches and received the gold medal; he also took part in the battles of the Nive, Nivelle, and Orthez. At the close of the war he was stationed in Ireland and, after his marriage, was in Canada until 1819, when he returned to England. He attained the rank of lieutenant-colonel on 30 December 1824, and retired on 9 April 1825.

In 1830 Henderson devoted himself to the formation of the London and South Western Railway Company, and was connected with it, first as general superintendent and subsequently as director, until his death. In May 1837 he was elected an associate of the Institution of Civil Engineers. In his later years he was chair both of the London Equitable Gas Company and of the Southampton Gas Company. Henderson died at 11 Anglesea Place, Southampton, on 21 April 1855.

                    R. H. VETCH, *rev.* JAMES FALKNER

Sources *Army List* · *Colburn's United Service Magazine*, 3 (1849), 141 · Royal Engineers Museum, Chatham · Boase, *Mod. Eng. biog.* · *PICE*, 15 (1855–6), 100–01

Henderson, George (1866–1912), Gaelic scholar, was born on 18 February 1866 at Heughden, Kiltarlity, Inverness-shire, the son of Elizabeth Fraser, daughter of a farmer; his reputed father was George Henderson, general merchant, of Inverness (d. cert.); he had a half-sister, Wilhelmina Fraser. He was educated at Raining's School, Inverness, under Dr Alexander Bain, the Gaelic lexicographer, whose *Outlines of Gaelic Etymology* Henderson was to edit in 1909, and at Edinburgh University, where he studied the arts curriculum in English literature, philosophy, and Celtic, the last under Professor Donald MacKinnon. He graduated in 1888. He was awarded the MacPherson scholarship in Celtic, and became examiner for the Celtic MA.

In 1892 Henderson spent some time in South Uist and made an important collection of oral Gaelic literature there, still mostly unpublished. He formed a friendship with Father Allan *McDonald, then parish priest at Daliburgh. Early in 1893 he went on a Dickson travelling scholarship to Vienna, where he acquired a PhD degree, and may have studied Old Irish under Julius Pokorny, who wrote articles on the subject for the *Celtic Review*. In 1893–6 Henderson collected and edited, with a memoir, John Morison's *Dain Iain Ghobha*, two volumes of religious verse very popular and influential in Gaelic circles. He returned from abroad in 1896 and went to Jesus College, Oxford, obtaining a BLitt degree for his work on Scottish Gaelic dialects, later published in the *Zeitschrift für Celtische Philologie*, volumes 4 and 5.

From 1892 to 1900 Henderson corresponded with Alexander *Carmichael over corrections and suggestions in *Carmina Gadelica* (1900), becoming a friend of Carmichael and his family. It is said that the Carmichaels had hoped that Henderson would marry their daughter Ella, and it came as a shock to them to hear that he had suddenly married a lady called Agnes Neighbour (on her marriage certificate) or Agnes D. Niebuhr (in Henderson's later entry in Scott's *Fasti ecclesiae Scoticanae*); they married in the parish church at Iffley near Oxford on 30 May 1901. In June 1901 he went to Edinburgh for ordination as a Church of Scotland minister, and subsequently to the remote parish of Eddrachillis in north-west Sutherland as assistant and successor to the Revd Kenneth MacKenzie, the parish minister.

In 1906, however, Henderson accepted an offer of the Kelly MacCallum lectureship in Celtic at Glasgow University. Between 1901 and 1906 he came into the possession of the valuable collection of Gaelic folksongs and their tunes collected on the Isle of Skye by Frances *Tolmie (1840–1926). In 1908 Henderson recommended publication of the collection by the Folksong Society, which was done in 1911; the delay allowed the appearance of the first volume of Marjorie Kennedy-Fraser's *Songs of the Hebrides* (1909), though Miss Tolmie had begun collecting as early as 1860. Henderson added notes to Tolmie's volume.

Henderson's output of published material was large, but at times erratic and inconsistent; his erudition seemed to get out of control. One of his most important works was an edition of *Fled Bricrend* ('The feast of Bricriu'), done for the Irish Texts Society as its second volume in 1899; a fourteen-page review in the *Zeitschrift für Celtische Philologie*, 3 (1901), by J. Strachan was mostly devoted to correcting errors in the translation. Other works of importance were *Leabhar nan Gleann* (1898); his work on Gaelic dialects in *Zeitschrift für Celtische Philologie*; and the Fionn Saga published in the *Celtic Review* (vols. 1, 2, and 3), beginning with a general discussion of the subject and concluding with a good version taken down on Eriskay with some assistance from Father Allan McDonald and never completed (the final part is in one of McDonald's notebooks). This was followed by *The Norse Influence on Celtic Scotland* (1910), an important early discussion of this subject, and *Survivals in Belief among the Celts* (1911). He also published *Arthurian Motifs in Gadhelic Literature* (1912). By this time Henderson's health was failing, and he died from nephritis and uraemia on 26 June 1912 at 28 Viewpark Drive, Rutherglen. His wife died on 19 September 1937.   J. L. CAMPBELL and H. C. G. MATTHEW

Sources D. MacKinnon, *Celtic Review*, 8 (Jan 1913), 245–51 · J. L. Campbell and T. H. Hall, *Strange things* (1968) · E. Bassin, *The old songs of Skye* (1977) · D. Beaton, *Bibliography of Gaelic books … for the counties of Caithness and Sutherland, with biographical notes* (1923) · *Fasti Scot.* · d. cert. · private information (2004)
Likenesses photograph, repro. in MacKinnon, *Celtic Review*, 246
Wealth at death £443 15s. 4d.: confirmation, 19 Nov 1912, CCI

Henderson, George David (1888–1957), Church of Scotland minister and historian, was born on 26 March 1888 in Flowerhill manse, Airdrie, Lanarkshire, the oldest of the four sons and two daughters of the Revd Robert Henderson (1855–1941), minister of the Church of Scotland, and his wife, Isabella Wright (1860–1935), daughter of Alexander Gibson, sometime town clerk of Kirkcaldy. He was educated at the high school, Glasgow, and then at the universities of Glasgow (MA with first-class honours in philosophy, 1910; BD, 1914; DLitt, 1931; hon. DD, 1935), Berlin (where he studied under Adolf Harnack), and Jena. Henderson was ordained, after assistantships in Glasgow, Edinburgh, and Hamilton, to the ministry of the Church of Scotland in the East Parish, Greenock, in 1916. From 1918 to 1920 he was seconded as chaplain to the forces in Mesopotamia. In 1922 he was translated to another industrial parish, St Mary's, Partick, Glasgow. In October 1924 he was appointed to the regius professorship of divinity and church history in the University of Aberdeen, a post he held for the rest of his life. On 5 August 1924 he had married Jenny Holmes McCulloch Smith of Greenock; they had two sons.

Henderson was through and through a Scottish Presbyterian. He was appointed professor of church history in a faculty of divinity where, at the time, his colleagues were, like himself, ministers of the Church of Scotland and his students were for the most part in training for its ministry. He participated fully in all the courts of the Church of Scotland from membership of the local kirk session in the parish of Old Machar to the moderatorial chair of the presbytery of Aberdeen, the synod of Aberdeen, and, finally, the general assembly itself in 1955–6. He was a member, and later convenor, of the colonial and continental committee of the general assembly and in that capacity travelled widely, from Iran to the West Indies. As a member of the union general assembly of October 1929 he participated in the historic uniting of the two main branches of Scottish Presbyterianism, the Church of Scotland and the United Free church. 'Auld Kirk' man though he was, when he was appointed master of the former United Free Church college in Aberdeen in 1947 he vigorously seized the opportunity thoroughly to remodel one of its buildings to create a chapel alongside its library and dining-room.

Generations of candidates for the ministry benefited not only from Henderson's highly effective teaching, which mingled academic rigour with practical sense and dry humour, but also from his care for their spiritual and professional formation. G. D., as he was universally known—if never so addressed, for, despite his lack of inches, he possessed a potent personality which commanded respect—was thus eminently suited by upbringing, education, aptitude, and experience to be in his day the voice of the mainstream Scottish reformed tradition. He was a prolific author, publishing numerous pamphlets, articles, sermons, and reviews, and in his lifetime several of his books attained classic status. These included *The Scottish Ruling Elder* (1935), *Religious Life in Seventeenth Century Scotland* (1937), *The Church of Scotland: a Short History* (1939), *Heritage: a Study of the Disruption* (1943), *Presbyterianism* (1954), and *The Burning Bush: Studies in Scottish Church History* (1957). By such works he came to be recognized as the world authority on Presbyterianism. His *The Claims of the Church of Scotland* (1951), a definitive statement of the Church of Scotland's estimate of its historical position, was neatly balanced by his sympathetic biography of the Jacobite and Catholic convert, *Chevalier Ramsay* (1952). His first book of all had been his edition of the correspondence of the *Mystics of the North-East* (1934).

A fellow of the Royal Historical Society, Henderson was thus no cloistered cleric or insular Scot. He participated fully in the wider life of his adopted university, being senatus assessor on the university court for eight years. Having acquired a fluent knowledge of Dutch (and Italian, in order to study the Waldensians), he was prominent in continental reformed circles and was one of the moving spirits behind the inaugural meeting of the World Council of Churches in Amsterdam in 1948. His international eminence was recognized by the award of the honorary degree of DTheol. by the Paris reformed theological faculty in 1954. In 1946 he had been appointed honorary professor at the Reformed Theological Academy in Budapest.

While attending the general assembly of the Church of Scotland in the year following his own tenure of the moderatorship, and while still at the height of his powers, Henderson died suddenly in Edinburgh on 28 May 1957.

WILLIAM JOHNSTONE

Sources *Fasti Scot.*, new edn · *WWW*, 1951–60 · J. M. Graham, 'G. D. Henderson, an appreciation', *Aberdeen University Review*, 37 (1957–8), 124–31 · *The Times* (30 May 1957) · A. O. Robertson, 'George David Henderson', *Aberdeen University Review*, 38 (1959–60), 391–2 · private information (2004) [Revd Peter M. Gordon, Very Revd W. B. R. Macmillan, son, G. D. S. Henderson]
Likenesses photograph, repro. in Graham, 'G. D. Henderson'
Wealth at death £14,160 19s. 1d.: confirmation, 13 Aug 1957, *CCI*

Henderson, George Francis Robert (1854–1903), army officer, historian, and military writer, was born on 2 June 1854 in St Helier, Jersey, the eldest of the fourteen children of William George *Henderson (1819–1905), from 1884 dean of Carlisle, and his wife, Jane Melville (*d.* 1901), daughter of John Dalyell of Lingo, Fife.

In 1862 the family moved to Yorkshire, and Henderson was educated at Leeds grammar school. In 1873 he won a history scholarship at St John's College, Oxford, and an exhibition from his school, but did not graduate. In 1876 he entered Sandhurst. On 1 May 1878 he was commissioned as second lieutenant in the York and Lancaster regiment, and joined the 1st battalion (65th) at Dinapore, India. On promotion to lieutenant on 24 June 1879, he passed to the 2nd battalion (84th), and after serving at Dover and in Ireland he went to Egypt, where his battalion formed part of Major-General Sir Gerald Graham's brigade. In 1882 he fought at the battles of Tell al-Mahuta, Qassasin, and Tell al-Kebir, and received the order of Mejidiye (fifth class).

In 1883 Henderson married Mary, daughter of Pierce Joyce of Galway, who survived him. They had no children. In the same year he went with his battalion to Bermuda, and then to Halifax, Nova Scotia. He visited the United States, especially Virginia and Maryland, to examine some of the Civil War battlefields. In January 1885 Henderson joined the ordnance store department, and served in it for five years, stationed at Woolwich, Edinburgh, Fort George (Scotland), and Gibraltar, and obtained a brevet majority on his promotion to captain on 2 June 1886. He did much research on the American Civil War and the Franco-Prussian War, and in 1886 he published *The Campaign of Fredericksburg*, which attracted the notice of Lord Wolseley, and led to Henderson's appointment in January 1890 as instructor at Sandhurst, at first in military topography, but afterwards in tactics, administration, and law. From 17

December 1892 to 22 December 1899 he was professor of military art and history at the Staff College, Camberley. On 10 November 1897 he was promoted substantive major.

At Sandhurst, and especially at the Staff College, Henderson could realize himself to the full. His ideas on tactics and strategy were highly regarded in military circles, and many officers who fought in the Second South African War (1899–1902) had studied under him. His published works also had much influence. *The Battle of Spicheren* (1891) was a masterly study in its breadth and detail. His greatest literary and historical triumph was *Stonewall Jackson and the American Civil War* (1898), a magnificent combination of biography, history, and military art that placed him in the first rank of military historians. Lord Roberts stated that this book helped to shape his plans for the war in South Africa.

In 1899 Henderson published a book on the battle of Wörth. He also wrote many articles, notably eight for the *Journal of the Royal United Service Institution* (1890–98) and six for the *Edinburgh Review* (1891–1900), and contributed articles on war, strategy, and tactics to the 10th edition of the *Encyclopaedia Britannica* (1902). He was a frequent lecturer at the United Service Institution and the military societies of Aldershot and Ireland. Some of these writings were reprinted in *The Science of War* (1905).

When Roberts embarked on 23 December 1899 to take up command of British forces in South Africa, he took Henderson with him on his staff, despite the latter's already poor health. He was made a substantive lieutenant-colonel, and on arrival in January 1900 was appointed director of military intelligence with the local rank of colonel. With characteristic enthusiasm he reorganized and expanded the intelligence department, discovered maps of the Transvaal intended for its Boer government, and prepared maps of the Orange Free State. As one of Roberts's confidants, he accompanied him to his operational base at the Modder River. On 11 February he saw the start of Roberts's great turning movement against General P. A. Cronjé, but just before Cronjé surrendered at Paardeberg on 27 February, Henderson's health failed due to malaria and exhaustion, and he returned home, being made CB on 29 November 1900.

Henderson's health had so improved that on 29 August 1900 he was placed on the staff of the War Office, as an assistant adjutant-general, to write the official history of the war. In the autumn of 1901 he went back to South Africa to examine the battlefields, but his health again broke down. He returned to England in February 1902, and at the end of 1902 was sent to Egypt for the winter. He continued his work on the history of the war, intending it to be a great picture, not a cold catalogue of facts. He completed the first volume, on the antecedents of the war, but died at Aswan, Egypt, on 5 March 1903, and was buried in the Roman Catholic cemetery in Cairo, where there is a memorial to him. After his death it was decided that the history of the war should be confined to the military contest, and his work was never published.

Henderson had rare gifts as a lecturer, historian, and

writer, and was also an able staff officer. He had a fascinating and pleasant personality. He has been described as the most scientific British strategist of his time; through his lectures and person he exerted a profound influence on young officers, and in that respect has been compared with Prussia's Helmuth von Moltke (1800–1891). By influencing Roberts's strategy in South Africa, Henderson helped shape the course of the war. He emphasized that the Boers were to be thoroughly defeated in the field, and that capturing their capitals would not end the war. After his return to England, this insight was lost, with detrimental effects for the British army in South Africa.

ANDRÉ WESSELS

Sources *The Times* (7 March 1903) · *The Times* (10 March 1903) · *The Spectator* (14 March 1903) · *The Leodiensian* (April 1903) · *Journal of the Royal United Service Institution*, 47 (1903) · PRO, WO 32/4755-4763 · PRO, WO 108/186 · PRO, WO 108/270 · *DNB* · A. Smirnoff, 'A tribute to the memory of Colonel G. F. R. Henderson', *Army Quarterly*, 17/2 (1929), 335–41 · J. Luvaas, 'The first British official historians', *Official histories: essays and bibliographies from around the world*, ed. R. Higham (1970), 488–505 · D. A. Fastabend, 'G. F. R. Henderson and the challenge of change', *Military Review*, 69/10 (1989), 66–77 · *The science of war: a collection of essays and lectures, 1892–1903*, ed. N. Malcolm (1905) · J. F. Maurice and M. H. Grant, eds., *History of the war in South Africa, 1899–1902*, 4 vols. (1906–10), vols. 1–2 · L. S. Amery, ed., *The Times history of the war in South Africa*, 3 (1905); 5 (1907) · *Army List* (1901) · G. F. R. Henderson, *Stonewall Jackson and the American Civil War*, 1–2 (1898) · G. F. R. Henderson, *The Civil War: a soldier's view*, ed. J. Luvaas (1958)
Archives University of the Witwatersrand, Johannesburg, Cullen Library | Hove Central Library, East Sussex, Wolseley MSS
Likenesses Hills & Saunders, photograph, 1896–1903?, repro. in Malcolm, ed., *The science of war* · A. Mountford, oils, 1905, Staff College, Camberley, Henderson room
Wealth at death £1469 6s. 5d.: probate, 8 May 1903, CGPLA Eng. & Wales

Henderson, George Gerald (1862–1942), chemist, was born on 30 January 1862 in Glasgow, the second son of George Henderson, merchant, and his wife, Alexandrina Kerr; the family was descended from a long line of Scottish country lairds. He was educated at a private school, then entered the University of Glasgow in 1877, where he diverged from school and home influences and read science in preference to the liberal arts. He graduated with first-class honours in chemistry in 1881, and published a meritorious original paper on the formation of serpentine from dolomite. Then, reversing the usual order of study, he read for an arts degree, acquiring lifelong scholarly tastes—there were few professors in his generation who were university prizemen in both chemistry and Greek. He was awarded an MA in 1884 and a DSc in 1890.

Having decided to pursue a career in chemistry, Henderson spent the winters as a lecturer in Glasgow teaching inorganic chemistry and mineralogy, and the summer semesters as a research pupil of Johannes Wislicenus in Leipzig. The value of this strenuous programme was soon apparent and in 1889 Henderson was appointed head of the chemistry department in Queen Margaret College, Glasgow. Here his successful teaching technique was perfected, and he was an obvious choice when in 1892 the

Freeland chair became vacant at the Glasgow and West of Scotland (later the Royal) Technical College. There his personality, his skill as a lecturer, and his appearance (tall, slim, athletic, and well tailored), commanded respect. Most of his students were preparing to become analysts or works chemists and their educational backgrounds varied greatly, but each was given Henderson's full attention.

Henderson built up close relationships with the manufacturing interests of the west of Scotland and took a leading part in providing the technical college with appropriate buildings. Soon after occupying his new laboratories, however, he was recalled in 1919 to the University of Glasgow as regius professor, and became involved for the second time in the creation of a new chemistry institute. It was a long struggle but once more Henderson 'found Rome brick and left it marble'. He acted as dean of the faculty of science and as an assessor on the university court, was elected president of the Society of Chemical Industry (1914), the Institute of Chemistry (1924–7), and the Chemical Society (1931). Other honours included fellowship of the Royal Society (1916), and honorary degrees from St Andrews (LLD, 1912), Belfast (DSc, 1934), and Glasgow (LLD, 1938).

From the late 1890s, for a period of about thirty years, Henderson's main field of research was the chemistry of the terpene hydrocarbons. He studied their reactions with some less powerful oxidizing agents, particularly chromyl chloride. About 1924 he began working on sesquiterpene chemistry. He was also interested in the chemistry of indiarubber, balata, and gutta-percha. His research was published mainly in the journals of the Chemical Society and the Society of Chemical Industry; in 1919 he published a book, *Catalysis in Industrial Chemistry*.

In 1895 Henderson married his cousin, Agnes Mackenzie, daughter of John Crawfurd Kerr, and although they had no children they were happily married for more than forty years. Her sudden death coincided with Henderson's resignation from his chair in 1937 and he retired, weary and broken-hearted, to the Isle of Harris, where they had spent many holidays together. He died on 28 September 1942 at his home in Horsaclett, Tarbert, Isle of Harris, closing a record of achievement which, taken in the aggregate, matched that of any chemist of his generation.

Henderson was a man of habit who never altered his appearance or his customs. He was probably the last of the professors of chemistry in the UK expected to represent all branches of a subject which was developing rapidly as the nineteenth merged into the twentieth century. His influence was far-reaching, and reflected the value of the contributions he made to science and to industry.

J. C. IRVINE, *rev.* K. D. WATSON

Sources J. C. Irvine and J. L. Simonsen, *Obits. FRS*, 4 (1942–4), 491–502 · T. S. Patterson, 'Prof. G. G. Henderson', *Nature*, 150 (1942), 485–6 · *The Times* (1 Oct 1942), 7e · W. I. Addison, *A roll of graduates of the University of Glasgow from 31st December 1727 to 31st December 1897* (1898)
Archives RS · U. Glas.
Likenesses photograph, repro. in *Obits. FRS*
Wealth at death £13,337 18s. 10d.: confirmation, 19 Feb 1943, CCI

Henderson, Georgiana Jane (1770–1850). *See under* Keate, George (1729–1797).

Henderson, Sir Hubert Douglas (1890–1952), economist, was born at Beckenham, Kent, on 20 October 1890, third son and sixth and youngest child of John Henderson, then London manager of the Clydesdale Bank, and his wife, Sarah, daughter of William Thomson, of an Edinburgh shipping family. The Hendersons moved back to Scotland when Hubert was eight, his father becoming manager of the North of Scotland Bank in Aberdeen and then general manager of the Clydesdale Bank in Glasgow. The family lived in a large Victorian house in Kelvinside and were wealthy enough to keep a carriage and pair.

Henderson was educated at Aberdeen grammar school and Rugby School; in the sixth form he switched from the classical side to mathematics. He went up to Emmanuel College, Cambridge, in 1909 with a mathematical exhibition, but his interest in mathematics waned as he acquired an enduring interest in politics and debate. After obtaining a third in part one of the mathematical tripos, he read economics, and gained first class honours in part two of the economics tripos in 1912, the year he was president of the union. In the heyday of Liberal reform he became a Liberal.

On graduating Henderson began to read for the bar, as his father wished, but stayed in Cambridge supporting himself by taking economics pupils for his college and for a time a Workers' Educational Association class. On the outbreak of war he volunteered for military service but was rejected on physical grounds. He entered the statistical section under Walter Layton at the Board of Trade, and lived at Toynbee Hall until his marriage, on 15 October 1915, to Faith Marion Jane Bagenal (*b.* 1889). She was the daughter of Philip Henry Bagenal, a barrister and political editor, of Dublin; they were to have two daughters and a son, and a singularly happy family life. In 1917 Henderson became secretary of the Cotton Control Board, on which he wrote a volume for the Carnegie Economic and Social History of the War (*The Cotton Control Board*, 1922).

At the end of the war Henderson had still to choose a career. The Board of Trade invited him to stay, his father offered to support him and his family while he established himself as a barrister, but he preferred to accept a fellowship at Clare College and a Cambridge University lectureship. He enjoyed the life and, according to Clay, 'had no wish to change it' (Clay, xv). His lectures were remembered as 'brilliantly discursive' and 'stimulating' ('Some British economists', 225). He wrote his famous textbook, *Supply and Demand* (1922), the first and one of the most successful of the Cambridge Economic Handbooks edited by J. M. Keynes, in the summer vacation of 1922.

Henderson was one of the Cambridge men in the group behind the Liberal summer schools, which began to meet regularly in 1922. When the opportunity arose to buy the weekly *Nation and Athenæum*, Keynes formed a company to purchase it and in February 1923 persuaded Henderson, his former pupil and now a colleague, to leave Cambridge and take on the editorship. According to Faith Henderson,

Sir Hubert Douglas Henderson (1890–1952), by Lafayette, 1932

he would spend all night writing his leaders to come up to the standard he set himself: in writing them he used

> the method of debate, in which he played the parts of both proposer and opposer of the motion, and of the chairman who sums up at the end. He liked to take a subject for discussion, give the arguments on both sides, and then decide at the end which side should win.   (Henderson, 8–9)

He came down in favour of the repeal of the McKenna duties on imported cars in 1924, against the return to gold in 1925, and for a policy of 'national development', government-aided capital investment, in 1927.

Henderson was a major contributor to the report of the Liberal industrial inquiry, *Britain's Industrial Future* (1928), which advocated a large-scale programme of national development. For the 1929 election he and Keynes produced a pamphlet, *Can Lloyd George do it?*, supporting the Liberal leader's claim to be able to conquer unemployment. Henderson stood unsuccessfully as a Liberal candidate for Cambridge University.

At the end of 1929 Henderson was offered a chair at the London School of Economics. He was seriously tempted but was persuaded, partly by Keynes, to accept in January 1930 the position of joint secretary to the Economic Advisory Council set up by the Labour prime minister, Ramsay MacDonald. With three assistants, including Colin Clark and Piers Debenham, the secretariat was a watered-down version of the 'economic general staff' advocated by the Liberal industrial inquiry. The council ceased to meet after the 1931 financial crisis and the fall of the second Labour government, but the secretariat and a standing committee on economic information remained in existence until the Second World War.

Henderson's earlier optimism about the possibilities of economic policy gave way under the impact of the world slump as it gathered momentum in 1930. He wrote in July:

> So far from our British difficulties having been aggravated during recent years by unfavourable world trade conditions, the truth, it is now clear, is rather that the full extent of those difficulties has been concealed by the fact that we have been passing through a favourable phase of the trade cycle. (Howson and Winch, 41)

This pessimistic assessment darkened his advice: he now doubted the viability of the Lloyd George schemes he had defended a year earlier, and deeply disagreed with Keynes on budgetary matters. He followed Keynes (a member of the council and several of its committees) in favouring a revenue tariff to help the budget and the balance of payments. After Britain left the gold standard (September 1931) he also parted company with Keynes on the desirable level of the exchange rate for sterling, but they came together again in a 'Keynes–Henderson plan' for an international note issue. Henderson originally put the idea forward as a proposal for the Lausanne conference on reparations in 1932, Keynes and the other members of the committee on economic information took it up, and the Treasury suggested a version of it to the USA for the World Economic Conference in 1933 (ibid., 114–21).

In 1934 Henderson left Whitehall for a research fellowship at All Souls College, Oxford, but remained an active member of the committee on economic information. He chaired a special subcommittee in 1935 to advise Sir William Beveridge, chairman of the Unemployment Insurance Statutory Committee, on the probable trend of unemployment, predicting an average unemployment percentage of 15½–16 for 1936–45. Henderson was particularly concerned about the deflationary consequences for Britain of the decline in the rate of population growth. At this time he also joined Lord Astor and Seebohm Rowntree in an inquiry into agricultural policy, and wrote their report, *The Agricultural Dilemma* (1935). In 1938–9 he was a member of the royal commission on the West Indies and spent six months there.

In Oxford, Henderson initiated and headed the Oxford Economists' Research Group, which interviewed businessmen as to the effect of interest rate changes and on their pricing policy over the cycle. He was the 'mainstay' of the group, 'not only because he could draw on a wide circle of acquaintances in business, but also because the patience, clarity and even temper with which he would always pursue an argument made him an ideal chairman' (Clay, xxii). The major findings were later published as *Oxford Studies in the Price Mechanism* (1951); Henderson contributed a notably sceptical assessment of the significance of the rate of interest. His contemporary criticisms of Keynes's *General Theory of Employment, Interest and Money* (1936) showed 'a change going on in his attitude to economic studies—a growing reliance on an historical

approach … and a growing preoccupation with the international element in British economic difficulties' (ibid., xxi). These tendencies came to the fore in his work during and after the Second World War.

Henderson was one of the 'three wise men' (the others being Josiah Stamp and Henry Clay) called on in June 1939 to advise the government on its economic plans for war. Their staff expanded into what became the economic section of the cabinet offices; Henderson himself, like Keynes and D. H. Robertson, moved into the Treasury for the duration. He was critical of Keynes's plan for an international clearing union and other post-war utopias: as one of his colleagues put it, his

> essential contribution [to post-war planning] was a firm and consistent determination not to ignore, or let the rest of us ignore, the great balance-of-payments difficulties with which [the UK] was bound to be faced after the war, and not to allow the Utopia-builders to promise more than we could reasonably expect to perform. (Waley, 47)

A lasting legacy of his time at the Treasury is his perceptive 'International economic history of the inter-war period', completed in 1943 (in Clay, 236–95).

In August 1942 Henderson suffered a coronary thrombosis, in his room at the Treasury. In December 1944 he returned to Oxford, and All Souls, and became Drummond professor of political economy in 1945. He led a very full life in Oxford: in addition to giving public lectures, he was chair of the committee of the Institute of Statistics, in whose founding in 1935 he had been involved; a member and for some time chair of the board of the faculty of social studies; a delegate of the university press; and active in college business. From 1946 to 1949 he chaired the royal commission on population, to which he had been appointed in 1944; he also chaired the Unemployment Insurance Statutory Committee in 1945-8. Knighted in 1942, he was elected president of the economic section of the British Association and a fellow of the British Academy in 1948, and president of the Royal Economic Society in 1950. The following year All Souls did him the honour of electing him, a Cambridge man, warden. But he had a third coronary thrombosis and had to resign the position, to which he was ideally suited, in January 1952. He died at his home, 5 South Parks Road, Oxford, on 22 February 1952, and was survived by his wife and children.   SUSAN HOWSON

Sources DNB · H. Clay, ed., *The inter-war years and other papers: a selection from the writings of Hubert Douglas Henderson* (1955) · S. Howson and D. Winch, *The economic advisory council, 1930-1939: a study in economic advice during depression and recovery* (1977) · F. Henderson, 'Editing the *Nation*', *Sir Hubert Henderson, 1890-1952*, ed. [T. Wilson] (1953), 7–27 [*Oxford Economic Papers* suppl.] · P. Debenham, 'The Economic Advisory Council and the great depression', *Sir Hubert Henderson, 1890-1952*, ed. [T. Wilson] (1953), 28–46 [*Oxford Economic Papers* suppl.] · 'Some British economists', *Banker*, 49 (Feb 1939), 216–26 · D. Waley, 'The treasury during World War II', *Sir Hubert Henderson, 1890-1952*, ed. [T. Wilson] (1953), 47–54 [*Oxford Economic Papers* suppl.] · D. E. Moggridge, *Maynard Keynes: an economist's biography* (1992) · I. Berlin, R. F. Harrod, and G. D. N. Worswick, 'Henderson at Oxford', *Sir Hubert Henderson, 1890-1952*, ed. [T. Wilson] (1953), 55–79 [*Oxford Economic Papers* suppl.] · T. Wilson and P. W. S. Andrews, eds., *Oxford studies in the price mechanism* (1951) ·

W. Young and F. S. Lee, *Oxford economics and Oxford economists* (1993) • Burke, *Gen. Ire.* (1958)

Archives BLPES, corresp. with the editors of the *Economic Journal* • Nuffield Oxf., corresp. and papers • PRO, Economic Advisory Council MSS, CAB 58 | BLPES, corresp. with Lord Beveridge • U. Cam., Marshall Library of Economics, corresp. with J. M. Keynes

Likenesses photograph, 1917, repro. in Clay, ed., *The inter-war years* • Lafayette, photograph, 1932, NPG [*see illus.*] • W. Stoneman, photograph, 1947, NPG • photograph, 1947, repro. in Clay, ed., *The inter-war years* • photographs, repro. in 'Some British economists'

Wealth at death £54,215 18s. 3d.: probate, 16 April 1952, CGPLA Eng. & Wales

Henderson, Ian (1910–1969), theologian, was born in Edinburgh on 13 April 1910, the son of Alexander Henderson and his wife, Elizabeth Gaudie. He was educated at George Watson's College, Edinburgh (1916–25), and Oban high school (1926–28), and graduated MA from Edinburgh University with first-class honours in mental philosophy in 1933. He received a BD with distinction in systematic theology in 1936, and was the recipient of an honorary DD in 1954. Henderson's senior Cunningham fellowship marked him as the leading divinity student of his year. He went abroad for his postgraduate studies, working in Zürich under Emil Brunner (1935) and in Basel under Karl Barth (1936–7). He was ordained to the charge of Fraserburgh South Church in 1938, and ministered there until 1942, when he was called to Kilmany, a charge once held by Thomas Chalmers, the leading figure in the disruption of 1843. In 1947 Henderson married Kathrine Margaret, daughter of William and Camilla Macartney, Edinburgh. In 1948 he was appointed to the chair of systematic theology in Glasgow, which he held until his death.

Following his continental studies Henderson was joint translator of Barth's *The Knowledge of God and the Service of God* (1938) and Walter Luthi's *In Time of Earthquake* (1939). His first major publication was *Can Two Walk together?* (1948), in which at one point he criticizes Barthians who thought that all they had to do was think Barth's thoughts after him—without doing any thinking for themselves. Later his chief concern was to be with the theology of Rudolf Bultmann in *Myth in the New Testament* (1952), a critical appraisal of Bultmann's demythologizing, and *Rudolph Bultmann* (1965). Bultmann at the time was suspect in the eyes of readers who were unfamiliar with the philosophical background of his work (and especially Heidegger's existentialism), and did not fully appreciate what he was trying to do. Henderson set himself to explain what Bultmann meant, to set things in proper context. He did not simply swallow Bultmann's ideas wholesale, like the Barthians he criticized in his earlier book, but subjected them to critical review. He was a man of independent mind who formed his own opinions. His experience of Swiss and German theology made him something of a radical among British theologians.

Henderson's best-known work was *Power without Glory: a Study in Ecumenical Politics* (1967), a critique of the fallacies of the ecumenical movement and the tactics employed by its adherents. He argued that they confused unity with uniformity in the effort to bring all the various traditions into one great church, which he saw as due to Anglican imperialism. Although the movement had made it possible for Christians from different denominations to meet on more friendly terms than formerly, within denominations it had led to hostility and division, since the ecumenicals denounced their opponents as enemies of the will of God, while themselves sinning against the divine law of love. However, the book was not merely a polemical pamphlet: it was a provocative and challenging survey of the history of Scotland's church and nation from the Union of 1707. The Union he regarded as an abject surrender; the treaty was already broken by the English parliament in 1712, when it imposed patronage on Scotland, the source of many divisions in the church for a century and a half. At times Henderson's book may seem nationalistic and anti-English, but that would be a superficial view.

A clue to understanding Henderson's attitude is provided in his last work, *Scotland: Kirk and People* (1969), and in particular the story of the invasion of the Isle of Tiree by the navy and a detachment of marines in support of a force of 700 police sent to quell an alleged crofters' revolt. They arrested just eight men, one of them Henderson's uncle, to whose memory the book was dedicated. It was not in fact a rebellion, but a protest against the conditions in which the crofters had to live and work: if a man made improvements to his farm, he reaped no benefit for himself; it only meant an increase in his rent for the following year. The injustices wrought by absentee landlords, the cruelties perpetrated by their agents (as in the highland clearances), the failure of a remote government to understand the needs of people in a different culture and tradition: these were the targets of his attack. This was the history of Scotland's church and nation as seen through the eyes of an Old Testament prophet such as Amos. Much of what he wrote has still a curious relevance. Henderson died on 8 April 1969 at Canniesburn Hospital, Bearsden.

R. McL. WILSON

Sources *Fasti Scot.*, new edn, vols. 9–10 • *WWW* • private information (2004) • *The Times* (12 April 1969) • d. cert.

Wealth at death £11,463 17s.: confirmation, 8 Aug 1969, CCI

Henderson, James (1782/3–1848), diplomat and writer, was a native of Cumberland or Westmorland. On 11 March 1819 he sailed from England to Rio de Janeiro. A letter of introduction from 'a nobleman', presumably Viscount Lowther, failed to secure him a post with Henry Chamberlaine, the British representative in Rio, and he joined a merchant house. He set about learning what he could about 'the vast regions of Brazil', and on his return to England published *A history of the Brazil: comprising its geography, commerce, colonization, aboriginal inhabitants, &c., illustrated with twenty-seven plates and two maps* (1821). Comparatively little of this work is Henderson's own. It is mostly a paraphrase or direct translation of Padre Manuel Aires de Casal's two-volume *Corografia Brazilica, ou, Relação historico-geografica do Brazil* (Rio de Janeiro, 1817). Henderson also wrote pamphlets on trade matters, including *An address to the South Americans and Mexicans: chiefly intended to dissuade them from conceding commercial privileges to other nations, in* *prejudice of Great Britain* (1822), and *Observations on the Great Benefit that will Result from the Warehousing Bill* (1823).

Henderson was appointed commissioner and consul-general in Bogota, Colombia. He resigned his post about 1836 and eventually settled in Madrid, where he wrote further pamphlets to the English and Spanish authorities concerning trade. These included *Letter Addressed to Richard Thornton, Esq., Chairman of the Spanish and Portuguese Bondholders* (1840), *A Review of the Commercial Code and Tariffs with Spain* (1842), and *Manifiesto al excmo. sr. d. José de Salamanca y a la nación Española relativa a la deuda estranjera* (1847). He died at Madrid on 18 September 1848, aged sixty-five.   GORDON GOODWIN, rev. JOHN DICKENSON

Sources F. A. Dutra, *A guide to the history of Brazil, 1500–1822* (1980) · P. Walne, *A guide to the manuscript sources for the history of Latin America and the Caribbean in the British Isles* (1973) · *GM*, 2nd ser., 30 (1848), 559
Archives Foreign Office · PRO, corresp., entry books, and papers

Henderson, Sir John [*alias* Peter von Berg] (*fl.* **1632–1658**), army officer and diplomat, was of Scottish descent, one of at least three sons of a soldier, and was brought up as a Roman Catholic. He may have begun his military service in the army of Denmark-Norway between 1625 and 1629; if so this must have been as an enlisted soldier, since he is not recorded in any of the muster rolls of officers. It is possible he was serving abroad some time earlier: the career in Swedish service of his brother-in-law Patrick *Ruthven, later first earl of Brentford (*d.* 1651), husband of his sister Jane (*d.* in or before 1633), stretched back to at least 1615. By 1632 Henderson was a lieutenant-colonel in the Swedish army under James Hamilton, third marquess of Hamilton, who had been sent to Germany in 1631 to assist the Swedes in an effort to recover the Palatinate. Henderson led a Scottish force at the battle of Lützen, where his regiment is reported to have destroyed eleven pieces of artillery and burnt several gun carriages.

It is unknown why or exactly when Henderson subsequently switched sides, although it is certain that he did. Between 1633 and 1638 he served as colonel of an imperial dragoon regiment then based in Bohemia. In his first year there Henderson signed the Pilsen agreement in support of General Wallenstein. As a result he received a command from Wallenstein to take guard of the town of Tabor. However, on the emperor's orders, he went to Vienna instead. On 6 March 1634, just two weeks after Wallenstein's assassination, he was given five companies of Count Ilow's dragoons. In the turmoil of the Swedish assault at Landshut he was shot in battle and fell into the hands of Swedes, but was released two months later. Henderson's dragoon regiment also fought at Nördlingen that September.

Soon afterwards Henderson undertook some minor diplomatic missions. He was sent to Augsburg in November 1634 by Emperor Ferdinand II, on a mission with letters from his son the king of Hungary, to hold discussions with Duke Bernard of Saxe-Weimar, with the object of bringing the duke back over to the imperial side. Henderson wrote from Gross-Heubach to General Piccolomini on 13 January 1635 regarding his negotiations there, but little is

known of their outcome. Henderson returned to his regiment and was once again taken prisoner by the Swedes, possibly at Regensburg. He spent some months as a hostage. On his release he helped in the attack on the town of Rathenow in May 1636 but the imperialists were defeated. His regiment spent most of 1636–7 in Pomerania and in February 1638 he fought at the battle of Rheinfelden, where the duke of Saxe-Weimar was victorious and General Savelli and a number of other imperialists were taken prisoner.

Henderson thereafter left imperial service to serve the house of Stuart, acting as the royalist governor of Dumbarton Castle during the bishops' wars in Scotland. He was knighted and by the early 1640s he had become a major Stuart diplomat in northern Europe, making many journeys to Denmark-Norway in particular. During the civil wars Colonel Henderson held another Stuart commission and acted as governor of Newark and as a field commander. He was defeated by forces of the solemn league and covenant at Winceby on 11 October 1643, but escaped to continue his diplomacy abroad. While on a mission from the Danish king to the English parliament, Henderson was imprisoned. He was eventually released, although the committee of both kingdoms cautioned Christian IV against employing diplomats who had raised arms against them. This deterred neither Henderson nor Christian IV. Charles I sent Henderson back to Denmark in 1645 and the Scot was back in Britain on a mission from Denmark in September the same year, although little is known of his remaining actions in England.

In 1649 Henderson returned to the Holy Roman empire to raise money and support for Charles II and was sent by Colonel John Cochrane to Frederick III of Denmark-Norway. These missions were part of the supply preparations required for the marquess of Montrose's ill-fated campaign of 1650. With the failure of that scheme, Henderson essentially pursued a private career in military service. In June 1651 the imperial war chancellery had cause to contact the imperial vice-chancellor on his account. That same month Emperor Ferdinand III also wrote to Charles II, stating that he had 'given such proof of his Imperial munificence to Colonel Henderson as the difficulties of his great expenses permit' (*Clarendon State Papers*, 2.103). Henderson moved on to Paris about that time, but the emperor's recommendations failed to impress Charles II. On 18 October 1652 Edward Hyde wrote to the Stuart agent John Taylor to tell him that the king was dissatisfied with Henderson for 'suggesting public employments for his friends and mentioning them as being persons of trust to the Emperor' (ibid., 2.835). The king obviously did not think Henderson equal to the tasks to which Taylor had assigned him. Henderson left Paris for Hamburg at the end of the year dissatisfied, since Charles II had neither provided a recommendation for him to the emperor, nor paid him the money he believed he was owed. At this point Lord Rochester summoned Henderson and sent him into Austria. This move surprised Hyde, who wrote to Rochester to complain 'he will do him [Charles II] no right wherever he goes' (ibid., 2, no.1085). His scepticism was perhaps due to the fact that Henderson had so many contacts elsewhere, especially among the former royalist community in Sweden whom Charles II had let down so badly during Montrose's campaign of 1640–50. In May 1653 Hyde wrote that he was surprised that Henderson retained sufficient influence with the Swedish court so 'as to procure a large sum of money for his own use' (ibid., 2.209). Yet given his family connections there, such support is not really surprising.

Henderson still sought to re-establish his influence with the exiled royalist regime. He was reported to have followed Rochester to the imperial diet at Regensburg, but did not meet with any success there. Hyde claimed that Henderson had failed in financial discussions with deputies from Bremen due to drunkenness. Yet within weeks he reported that Henderson had met Thomas Wentworth, Lord Wentworth, at Copenhagen and that Joseph Bampfield and Henderson 'held excellent councils' (*Clarendon State Papers*, 2, nos. 1314, 1323) together at Hamburg. Indeed by July, his opinion of Henderson appears to have reversed. Hyde wrote to Richard Bellings, the exiled former representative of the Irish confederation, on the subject of reports which hinted that the royalists were destined for defeat. Hyde suggested therefore that Henderson should be employed in receiving some moneys and 'returning it by bills of exchange upon his correspondents in Hamburgh or buying arms/ammunition in which he hath good skill' (ibid., 2.381).

The royalists were right to have their doubts about Henderson, however. He had already written to Oliver Cromwell from Hamburg, having brokered a bargain to supply arms and ammunition to Scotland. He mentioned to Cromwell that 'at Ratisbone I did break a bargain betwixt the Lord Willmot, ambassador, and one major-general Suigle, of armes, ammunition, victual, artillerie to the rate of 70,000 dollars to be presently sent to Scotland' (Thurloe, *State papers*, 4.467). Whether or not the royalists discovered Henderson's correspondence is unclear. He returned to work in imperial service once more but remained there for only one more year. On 10 January 1655 Edward Rolt wrote to the secretary of state John Thurloe, stating that Major-General Henderson had recently left the emperor's court and was offering his services to Charles II again. Rolt noted that if this offer was refused, Henderson intended to go to Sweden 'having refused a proper employment from the Emperor' (ibid., 4.407). Henderson wrote to Hyde from Cologne only weeks later to confirm that he had quit his imperial post. He also claimed to have lost his father and two brothers in imperial service, which they had undertaken, he wrote, in order to serve the interests of the house of Stuart. As a result, Henderson now recognized, he had consigned himself and his wife and eleven children (of whom nothing else is known) to a life of poverty, and of tireless work which had never been acknowledged by the king or his father, Charles I. Nevertheless, he still offered to serve Charles II on an expedition to Scotland. This request was denied.

Henderson then went to London and was given permission by Cromwell to raise levies, presumably for Swedish service. Throughout this unusual course of action he still claimed to want to serve the king and denied to Thurloe from Hamburg that he was simply after more money. The royalists were unconvinced and so Henderson took service in the Polish army, commanding a regiment of infantry. Although this force was defeated at Wirschau in 1656, he none the less received a recommendation from the king of Poland in 1657. That year he also entered Danish-Norwegian service. He commanded the Fyn infantry until he capitulated on 30 January 1658 at his men's desire and surrendered the garrison of Hindsgavl. At his court martial Henderson was pardoned in March due to British diplomatic intervention. It is not clear if this pressure came from the exiled Stuart court or from the Cromwellian government for whom he had served as an agent under the name of Peter von Berg. Thereafter Henderson disappears from public life. The date of his death is unknown.

STEVE MURDOCH and DAVID WORTHINGTON

Sources 'HHStA, Kriegsakten, Vienna, k.184, f.47/48', Vienna, Haus-Hof-und Staats Archiv and Kriegsarchiv · R. Munro, *Munro, his expedition with the worthy Scots regiment called MacKeyes* (1637) · *Calendar of the Clarendon state papers preserved in the Bodleian Library*, ed. W. D. Macray, 2: *1649–1654* (1869), 81, 103, 209, 220–21, 381, 835, 1085–9, 1126, 1314, 1323; 3: *1654–1657* (1869), 37 · *CSP dom.*, *1644–5*, 392–3 [Proceedings of the committee of both kingdoms, 8 April 1645] · *CSP Venice*, *1643–7*, 34; *1647–52*, 119 [Niccolo Sagredo to Venice, 25 Sept 1649] · Thurloe, *State papers*, 4.242, 407, 467 · Charles I to Christian IV, 6/9/1642 and 28/11/1644, Rigsarkivet, Copenhagen, TKUA England A II 15 · Charles I to Christian IV, 5/1644 and letter from the English parliament to Christian IV, 25/6/1645, Rigsarkivet, Copenhagen, TKUA England A I · C. F. Bricka and J. A. Fridericia, eds., *Kong Christian den fjerdes egenhaendige breve*, suppl. (Copenhagen, 1947), 352 · Bodl. Oxf., MSS Rawl. · A. Baker, *A battlefield atlas of the English civil war* (1986), 42–3 · J. C. W. Hirsch and K. Hirsch, eds., 'Fortegnelse over Dansu ou Norske officerer med flere fra 1648 til 1814', 12 vols., unpublished MS, 1888–1907, Rigsarkivet, Copenhagen, vol. 1 · GEC, *Peerage*, new edn · *Dansk Biografiskt Lexicon*, 6.344–5 · J. E. Hess, *Biographien und Autographien zu Schillers Wallenstein* (Jena, 1859), 142–8, 392–7, 399–419 · S. Murdoch, *Britain, Denmark-Norway and the house of Stuart, 1603–1660* (2000) · S. Murdoch, 'The search for northern allies: Stuart and Cromwellian propagandists and protagonists in Scandinavia, 1649–1660', *Propaganda: political rhetoric and identity, 1300–2000*, ed. B. Taithe and T. Thornton (1999), 79–90 · E. Schmidhofer, 'Das irische, schottische und englische Element im kaiserlichen Heer', PhD diss., University of Vienna, 1971 · E. Scott, *The king in exile: the wanderings of Charles II from June 1646 to July 1654* (1905) · J. Šula, 'Hospodarská korespondence Václava Králika, komendátora novomestského panství, s Walterem hrabetem z Leslie v letech, 1635–1643', *Stopami Dejin Náchodska*, 4 (Náchod, 1998), 177–210 · A. von Wrede, *Geschichte der k. und k. Wehrmacht*, 5 vols. (Vienna, 1898–1905), vol. 3, pt 2, p. 621

Archives Rigsarkivet, Copenhagen, foreign chancellery

Henderson, John (*bap.* 1747, *d.* 1785), actor, was born in Goldsmith Street, Cheapside, London, and was baptized on 8 March 1747. Little is known of his family, who were Irish but claimed descent from the Scots Hendersons of Fordell. His father, who was an Irish factor in London, died about a year after John was born. His mother then moved with her children to Newport Pagnell, Buckinghamshire. She appears to have been solely responsible for the early education of her two sons. John, who was the younger of the two, went to Dr Sterling's school at Hemel Hempstead,

John Henderson (*bap.* 1747, *d.* 1785), by Thomas Gainsborough, *c.*1773–5

Hertfordshire, for one year in 1758; from the age of twelve he studied drawing for five or six years in London with David Fournier (some etchings by Henderson were published in Fournier's *Theory and Practice of Perspective* (1764)). After this period of apprenticeship he went to live with a relative, a Mr Cripps, who was a silversmith in St James's Street. Whether he entertained any thoughts of learning this craft is unclear. What is clear is that by 1768—within a year of Cripps's death—he had set his sights on becoming an actor and making a career for himself in the theatre. However, he had to wait for a number of years before he was given his first professional engagement. An audition for George Garrick was unsuccessful, as was his approach to the playwright Paul Hiffernan for an introduction to David Garrick. In 1770, on his own initiative, he gave public recitations at the Old Parr's Head in Islington. He included in his programme an imitation of Garrick's ode delivered at the Shakespeare Jubilee in Stratford upon Avon the previous year. Eventually, when David Garrick did audition him, he recommended Henderson to the Bath businessman and postal reformer John Palmer the younger, who was the power behind the Theatre Royal in Bath.

Henderson became a member of the company that Palmer and his manager, William Keasberry, had been reorganizing with conspicuous success since the theatre in Orchard Street had been granted its royal patent in 1768. He made his first appearance on Tuesday 6 October 1772. The playbill for that night advertised that the role of Hamlet was to be performed 'by a young gentleman', and 'it was buzzed about in the Rooms, in the walks, and all over the city of Bath, that a new actor was arrived from London under the patronage of the great Roscius' (Davies, 9). Henderson performed, under the stage name Courtney, 'with so much ease, judgement and propriety in action as well as expression, as gained him the warmest plaudits of the whole audience' (Penley, 43). He repeated the role on the following Tuesday, and a week later, on Tuesday 20 October, he played the title role in *Richard III*. By the time he made his first appearance under his real name, on Saturday 26 December, as Hotspur in *I Henry IV*, he had added Benedick and Macbeth to his Shakespearian roles and played in Ben Jonson's *Every Man in his Humour*, the duke of Buckingham's *The Rehearsal*, Susannah Centlivre's *The Wonder*, and *The Earl of Essex*, by Henry Jones. A third of the way through his first season as an actor in the provinces he was the talk of a most fashionable town. On 5 January 1773 David Garrick wrote to Henderson congratulating him on his success, warning him of the dangers of being 'too much intoxicated with the applause' (*Letters*, 2.843), and inviting him to see him when he was next in London.

By the end of the season Henderson had played twenty major roles, added Lear to his Shakespearian repertory, and gained the nickname of the Bath Roscius. He had also made some influential friends, including Thomas Gainsborough and Richard Cumberland. In 1773, and again in 1774 and 1775, Cumberland tried to persuade Garrick to engage Henderson to play at Drury Lane. Henderson returned to London for the following two summers but was unable to secure engagements at any of the major theatres. He remained a full member of Palmer's company for the following four seasons and did not secure a London début before 11 June 1777, one year after Garrick's series of farewell performances. Whether Garrick's reluctance to engage Henderson was due to jealousy and fear of being overshadowed by a rival during the last years of his career, as Horace Walpole was to assert when Henderson finally established his reputation as Garrick's successor in London, or whether Garrick genuinely believed Henderson's skills were overrated, is uncertain.

During the following four seasons at Bath, Henderson performed many of the leading roles of the contemporary repertory, adding Othello, Posthumus, Shylock, King John, and Falstaff (in *The Merry Wives of Windsor*) to his portfolio and laying the foundations of his reputation as a Shakespearian actor at the very moment when the Bard's prominence in the theatrical repertory was being established (largely as a result of Garrick's efforts). In summer 1775 he performed in Bristol and was deemed 'the prince of country performers' (*Felix Farley's Bristol Journal*, 15 July 1775). During the summer of 1776 he acted in Birmingham, where he met the young Sarah Siddons and was so impressed by her acting that he pressed Palmer, unsuccessfully, to offer her an engagement at Bath. For the summer of 1777 he was engaged by George Colman at the Haymarket and made his long-delayed début in London in the role of Shylock. Fifteen days later, and after three further performances of Shylock, he played Hamlet—the role which initiated his success in Bath and which now rewarded Colman for his venture, as that summer 'no less a sum than £4,500 was taken during the thirty-four nights of Hamlet's performance' (Davies, 33). Among the other parts Henderson played at this time was Falstaff in both *Henry IV* and *The Merry Wives of Windsor*. He was engaged for the 1777-8 season at Drury Lane by Richard Brinsley Sheridan but first had to release himself from his contract with Palmer through a series of guest appearances at Bath. On 30 September 1777 he made his first appearance at Drury Lane in the role of Hamlet. Other Shakespearian interpretations that season were Richard III, Shylock, Falstaff, King John, Benedick, and Macbeth.

During summer 1778 Henderson performed in Dublin, Liverpool, and Bath, and then returned for a second season to Drury Lane, where for his benefit performance in March 1779 he first appeared in London as King Lear. It was during this second full season in London that Henderson married Jane Figgins (*c*.1752-1819) at St Paul's, Covent Garden, on 13 January 1779. They had one daughter, Harriet, baptized at St Martin-in-the-Fields on 18 November 1779. After summer appearances in Dublin, Limerick, and Cork, Henderson returned to London and rejoined the company at Covent Garden, where he remained for the next six seasons.

In the 1779-80 season Henderson added Jacques to his Shakespearian roles, and in the following years he acted, for the first time, the Duke in *Measure for Measure*, Cardinal Wolsey in *Henry VIII*, Iago in *Othello* (1781-2), and Malvolio and Leontes (1782-3). He appeared at Liverpool in the summers of 1780, 1782, and 1783, at Edinburgh in 1784, and returned to Dublin in 1785. In the same year he mounted a series of readings with Thomas Sheridan at the Freemasons Hall which proved very successful and led to a joint publication, *Sheridan's and Henderson's Practical Method of Reading and Writing English Poetry*, which was published, after his death, in 1796. Henderson was suddenly taken ill on 4 November 1785. He recovered enough to act the role of Horatius in William Whitehead's *The Roman Father* on 8 November, but this was to be his last stage appearance. He had a relapse and died of a heart attack on 25 November 1785, at the age of only thirty-eight.

> Scarce had we witness'd with admiring eyes
> His brilliant talents and his virtues bright
> Than cruel Heaven the valued boon denies
> Stops his career and tears him from our sight.
> (Harley, 8)

It is difficult to assess Henderson's achievements, given both the brevity of his London career and the delay caused to it, not to mention the shadow cast on it, by David Garrick. James Boaden, who would have seen Henderson in his late teens and early twenties is specific, though unrepresentative, in his praise:

> The power of Henderson was analytic. He was not contented with the mere light of common meaning—he showed it to you through a prism, and refracted all the delicate and mingling hues, that enter into the composition of any ray of human character. Besides the philosophic ingenuity of such

a design, he had a voice so flexible that its tones conveyed all that his meaning would insinuate. (Boaden, *Memoirs of the Life of John Philip Kemble*, 1.76)

This is a far cry from Garrick's alleged comment that he 'had in his mouth too much wool or worsted' (Highfill, Burnim & Langhans, *BDA*) or that as Hamlet he suffered either from a 'want of vivacity of passion, or a deficiency of power in the upper tones of his voice' (Pilon, 11). What is clear is that Henderson brought intelligence to his interpretations of Shakespearian roles. 'In the varieties of Shakespeare's soliloquy, where more is meant than meets the ear, he had no equal' (Ireland, 265). As Iago, for example, he was 'profoundly intellectual like the character' and turned 'the inside of design *outward* to the spectators, and yet externally seemed to be cordial and sincere and interesting among his victims' (Boaden, *Memoirs of Mrs Siddons*, 1.147). He was well-read—the catalogue relating to the sale of his library, published in 1786, lists 1059 books—and 'few men, even in his attractive profession, were ever surrounded by more learned and more brilliant companions' (ibid., 1.178). As contemporary descriptions and some forty known portraits show, Henderson's physique did not always help him as an actor. He was short, 'moulded with no extraordinary elegance or symmetry' (Pilon, 5), and 'his face, though rather handsome, was too fleshy to show all the muscular action, in which expression resides' (Boaden, *Memoirs of the Life of John Philip Kemble*, 1.75). It was as an interpreter of Shakespeare that he excelled and was admired—though all too briefly—as Garrick's successor. He was buried on Saturday 3 December 1785 in Poets' Corner, Westminster Abbey, close to Garrick's grave and to Shakespeare's monument. No will has been traced, but it is known that his widow was granted administration of his estate on 20 December 1785. As A. C. Sprague has observed, Garrick's successor was 'a gifted actor about whom we know all too little' (*Shakespeare and the Actors*, 1963, 137).

LESLIE DU S. READ

Sources Highfill, Burnim & Langhans, *BDA* · J. Davies, *A genuine narrative of the life of Mr John Henderson* (1778) · J. Boaden, *Memoirs of the life of John Philip Kemble*, 2 vols. (1825) · J. Boaden, *Memoirs of Mrs Siddons*, 2 vols. (1827) · J. Ireland, *Letters and poems by the late Mr John Henderson with anecdotes of his life* (1786) · G. D. Harley, *Monody on the death of Mr John Henderson* (1787) · F. Pilon, *Essay on the character of Hamlet as performed by Mr Henderson* (1777) · B. S. Penley, *The Bath stage: a history of dramatic representations in Bath* (1892) · *The letters of David Garrick*, ed. D. M. Little and G. M. Kahrl, 3 vols. (1963) · *Morning Herald* (5 Dec 1785)

Likenesses T. Beach, oils, 1773, Garr. Club · T. Gainsborough, oils, *c*.1773-1775, NPG [*see illus.*] · R. Dunkarton, chalk drawing, 1776, NPG · J. Kay, engraving, 1784, Harvard TC · J. Roberts, chalk drawing (as Falstaff), Garr. Club · attrib. G. Romney, oils (as Hamlet), Garr. Club · G. Romney, oils (as Macbeth), Garr. Club · T. Rowlandson, pencil drawing, Yale U. CBA · T. Rowlandson, watercolour, Ellen Terry Museum, Smallhythe · G. Stuart, portrait, V&A · oils, Garr. Club · prints, BM, NPG

Henderson, John (1757-1788), student and eccentric, was born on 27 March 1757 at Ballygarran, near Limerick, the only child of Richard Henderson (1736/7-1792), an Irishman, and his wife, Charlotte (*d*. 1775). The family came to England about 1762, and Richard became one of Wesley's best itinerant preachers, while John was sent to the school established by Wesley at Kingswood near Bristol. He was so precocious that at the age of eight he was able to teach Latin at Kingswood, and when only twelve he became a tutor at the countess of Huntingdon's newly founded evangelical seminary at Trefeca, where he taught Greek and Latin and incidentally argued against the predominant Calvinism of pupils twice his age. At fourteen he went to Oxford to be matriculated, but, after studying the university statutes overnight, he baulked at the oath required and returned home. About that time his father relinquished his itinerancy and established a boys' boarding-school at Hanham, close to Kingswood, where Henderson joined him and taught classics while pursuing his own studies. His mother died on 20 December 1775 and was buried at St George's, Kingswood.

Meanwhile Henderson was reading omnivorously in theology and metaphysics. He initiated a correspondence with the liberal theologian Joseph Priestley, who responded with advice and the loan of books, and he became a corresponding member of the religious discussion society established at Burnham, Somerset, as an offshoot from Trevecca College. He was drawn to astrology, geomancy, physiognomy, and the mysticism of Behmen and Swedenborg; he believed in spirits, apparitions, magic, and witchcraft; he thought the doctrines of original sin and everlasting punishment were absurd. With an extraordinary memory and a wonderful ear for accents and dialects he became a skilled linguist: before his early death he had reportedly mastered Persian, Arabic, Hebrew, Greek, Latin, Spanish, Italian, and German.

The accidental drowning of two of his pupils in the Avon so affected Richard Henderson's mind that he closed his school, and from January 1780 he kept a lunatic asylum in the same place. Wesley visited Hanham in 1781 and was convinced:

> there is not such another house for lunatics in the three kingdoms. [Henderson] has a peculiar art of governing his patients; not by fear, but by love. The consequence is, many of them speedily recover, and love him ever after. (*Journal of John Wesley*, 6.336, 29 Sept 1781)

One patient, 'Louisa, the celebrated maid of the haystack', was painted by William Palmer (1763–1790) and is described in Wesley's journal of 15 March 1782.

By this date John Henderson was in Oxford. He had come to the notice of the Bristol intelligentsia, notably Edmund Burke, Hannah More, Josiah Tucker, and Sir James Stonhouse; and, with a recommendation and loan of over £150 from Tucker, augmented by a subscription at Bristol, he was in residence at Pembroke College, whence he matriculated on 6 April 1781. A study of Bishop Sanderson's explanation of oaths had now removed his earlier doubts. In Oxford he attracted notice at once: partly for having unfashionably small shoe buckles, a schoolboy hair style, and no stock or neckcloth, but mainly for his wide, unconventional learning, quick discernment, and powers of reasoning which impressed his seniors as much as his contemporaries. Benjamin Kennicott, the eminent

Hebrew scholar, is quoted as saying 'The greatest men I ever knew were mere children compared with Henderson' (Macleane, 405). He was sociable, attentive, and entertaining, and his conversation bright and full of learning, so his company was sought by all.

Hannah More commissioned a portrait by William Palmer, which shows Henderson, aged twenty-five, looking boyishly up from a favourite volume of Scotus: it is now at Pembroke College, Oxford. When she visited the college with Johnson in June 1782 Henderson, who occupied Johnson's old rooms, was in their select dinner party, and when Johnson and Boswell visited the college again two years later Henderson, 'celebrated for his wonderful acquirements in Alchymy, Judicial Astrology, and other abstruse and curious learning', joined them for tea and supper. 'Dr Johnson surprised him not a little, by acknowledging with a look of horrour, that he was much oppressed by the fear of death' (Boswell, *Life*, 4.298–9, 12 June 1784). Henderson did not believe in everlasting punishment: Johnson did. It is said that the two men conversed in Latin for hours on end, but their only recorded conversation (in English) is about the reasoning of non-jurors and disappointingly casts Henderson in the Boswellian role of 'feed' (ibid., 286 n.3, 9 June 1784n.).

At Oxford, Henderson widened his studies yet further, especially in scholastic divinity and the physical sciences. He acquired a knowledge of medicine, which, with characteristic benevolence, he practised without payment among the poor of Oxford. During an epidemic of fever he spent all his spare money on drugs for the poor and sold his polyglot Bible to buy more. His physical experiments upon himself went beyond normal undergraduate affectation: he would sleep in a shirt he had just soaked with water from the college pump, he once starved himself for five days continuously, and he took mercury and opium. Less unconventionally, he went to bed at daybreak and rose in the afternoon, he smoked nearly all day long, he spoiled his sight by intensive night-long reading, and he impaired his constitution by heavy drinking. Tucker, Hannah More, and other friends and patrons were vexed by his contradictions. Kennicott's wife thought that if 'Dr Johnson had the shaking him about, he would shake out his nonsense, and set his sense a working' (Roberts, 1.220).

Henderson's residence in Oxford was irregular, but he eventually graduated BA on 27 February 1786. His habits and learning were famous enough to be discussed at length in the *Gentleman's Magazine* later that year; his patrons wanted him to become a lawyer, physician, or clergyman; William Wilberforce, it is said, offered him patronage and a living if he would reside in London; but, unambitious to enter any of the learned professions, he went home to pursue his studies and help his father in the lunatic asylum: in 1787 he was observed shepherding a famous inmate, William Gilbert, author of *The Hurricane*. Henderson died on 2 November 1788 while visiting Pembroke College, and was buried at Kingswood on 18 November. His father, who was so much affected by his death that he had the body exhumed a few days after interment, died on 14 February 1792, aged fifty-five, and was buried beside his wife and son.

Wesley's verdict that Henderson 'with as great talents as most men in England, had lived two-and-thirty years, and done just nothing' (*Journal of John Wesley*, 7.477, 13 March 1789) is fair. His friends hoped for scholarly writings from him, but, as Tucker confessed to Hannah More in 1782, 'Our little friend, I fear, is too volatile to fix to one point' (Roberts, 1.218). His posthumously published writings (in the *Gentleman's Magazine*, 59, 1789, 287–9, and 69, 1799, 752–3, in William Matthews's *The Miscellaneous Companions*, 1786, 3.111–15, and in the Burnham Society's *Pre-Existence of Souls and Universal Restitution*, 1798, 15–19), amount to only a dozen pages. However, an unpublished treatise on miracles written for a college contemporary, George Coleridge (1764–1828), brother of the poet, was in Southey's hands in 1797, and there is a story that when Henderson was at Oxford manuscripts stored in an unlocked trunk at Hanham were used for firelighting by a servant.

Henderson never married, though it is said that at least four ladies, including a daughter of Charles Wesley and Hannah More's sister Patty, hoped to marry him. He was of small stature and walked carefully—like an old man.

JAMES SAMBROOK

Sources Boswell, *Life*, 4.151 n.2, 286 n.3, 298–9 • D. Macleane, *A history of Pembroke College, Oxford*, OHS, 33 (1897), 345, 386, 397–405 • *The letters of the Rev. John Wesley*, ed. J. Telford, 8 vols. (1931), vol. 4, p. 311; vol. 8, pp. 87, 107, 230 • *The journal of the Rev. John Wesley*, ed. N. Curnock and others, 8 vols. (1909–16) • *GM*, 1st ser., 59 (1789), 287–9, 295–7, 503–7 • W. Roberts, *Memoirs of the life and correspondence of Mrs Hannah More*, 2nd edn, 4 vols. (1834), vol.1, pp.194, 216–20 • J. Cottle, 'Essay, 1, on the genius and character of John Henderson', *Malvern Hills, with minor poems, and essays*, 4th edn (1829), 349–71 • J. Tucker, letters to William Adams, master of Pembroke College, Oxford, 1780–83, Gloucester City Library, 17/633 • *GM*, 1st ser., 58 (1788), 1031 • *GM*, 1st ser., 56 (1786), 678, 739 • *European Magazine and London Review*, 22 (1792), 3–5, 96, 177–8, 337–8 • J. Cottle, *Reminiscences of Samuel Taylor Coleridge and Robert Southey*, 2nd edn (1848), 42–3 • Foster, *Alum. Oxon.* • J. Cottle, *Poems … with a monody to John Henderson and a sketch of his character* (1795) • *Pre-existence of souls and universal restitution considered as scripture doctrines*, Burnham Society (1798) • *The correspondence of Edmund Burke*, 5, ed. H. Furber and P. J. Marshall (1965), 112–13 • W. Agutter, *A sermon occasioned by the death of the celebrated Mr J. Henderson* (1788) • C. Atmore, *The Methodist memorial* (1801), 183–4 • L. Tyerman, *Wesley's designated successor: the life, letters, and literary labours of the Rev. John William Fletcher* (1882), 144–7 • *GM*, 2nd ser., 14 (1840), 17 • *DNB*

Archives Sheffield Central Library, Fitzwilliam MSS, letters to Edmund Burke

Likenesses W. Burgess, pencil drawing, 1771, BM • Ames, stipple and line engraving, BM • J. Condé, engraving (after miniature), BM, NPG; repro. in *European Magazine*, facing p. 3 • W. Palmer, oils, Pembroke College, Oxford • engraving (after W. Palmer), repro. in Cottle, *Malvern Hills*, frontispiece

Henderson, John (1780–1867), philanthropist, was born in Bo'ness, Linlithgowshire, the son of Robert Henderson, a merchant and shipowner in that town. With an elder brother, Robert, he started in business as a dry-salter in Glasgow, and later became an East India merchant in London. In May 1842 Robert was drowned, and the business was carried on by Henderson in partnership with several of his nephews.

From 1827 Henderson spent much of his income in promoting evangelical Christianity. During the last twenty years of his life he is said to have contributed from £30,000 to £40,000 a year to religious and charitable schemes. The maintenance of Sunday in Scotland as a day of rest and the support of missions in India and on the continent engrossed much of his time and effort. He maintained several religious newspapers, and on one occasion spent £4000 in sending a copy of a publication to all the railway servants in the country in the hope of convincing them of the sinfulness of Sabbath labour. He purchased a large proportion of the stock of the Edinburgh and Glasgow Railway and divided it among friends who he knew would oppose the running of Sunday trains. Railway travelling on Sunday between Glasgow and Edinburgh was thus interrupted until the amalgamation with the North British Company placed Henderson and his supporters in a minority.

Henderson gave an annual prize to the University of Glasgow for the best essay on the Decalogue. He also bought and maintained a number of mission churches in Glasgow, and built the Religious Institution rooms in St George's Place and the mission premises for the United Presbyterian church in Virginia Street. Although he was a member of the United Presbyterians and contributed generously to their extension in London, he helped every religious movement with which he felt any sympathy. It was mainly through his efforts that the Evangelical Alliance was established in 1845. The only public office that he held in Glasgow was that of chairman of the Royal Exchange.

Henderson married, on 24 November 1843, Mary, the daughter of John Macfie of Edinburgh, who survived him. They had no children. He died at Park, Inchinnan, Renfrewshire, on 1 May 1867.

GORDON GOODWIN, *rev.* MARK CLEMENT

Sources Boase, *Mod. Eng. biog.* • *GM*, 4th ser., 4 (1867), 115 • *Glasgow Herald* (2 May 1867) • m. cert.

Henderson, John (1797–1878), art collector, was born at Adelphi Terrace, London, and baptized on 23 May 1797, the son of John Henderson (1764–1843) and of Georgiana Jane *Henderson (1770–1850) [see under Keate, George], painter and only child of George *Keate FRS. His father was an amateur artist and early patron of Thomas Girtin and J. M. W. Turner, both of whom worked frequently in the house where Henderson grew up. These surroundings were perhaps instrumental in shaping the sensibilities of a young man who later became renowned for his discriminating taste. Certainly these artists left material traces: watercolour drawings by both remained in Henderson's collections and were mentioned in his bequests to the British Museum. Henderson matriculated on 7 April 1813 from Balliol College, Oxford, where his academic records indicate that he was a conscientious and successful student, graduating BA in 1817 and MA in 1820. He read for the bar, but did not practise. Henderson did not marry, and there is evidence in his will that his sister, Georgiana, lived with him at his house at 3 Montague Street, Bloomsbury, London. Charles Cooper *Henderson was his brother.

Henderson's considerable collections of decorative art, glass, and armour placed him in the orbit of London's learned societies. He was appointed honorary treasurer of the Archaeological Institute of Great Britain and Ireland in 1864. His contributions to the institute, and to the London Society of Antiquaries, of which he was elected a fellow in 1858, appear to have amounted to regular loans of a diverse range of objects. While significant items had come into his possession through Keate, his maternal grandfather, Henderson's treasures were largely amassed by himself during his lifetime, occasionally purchased from other collections, and sometimes acquired from more dubious sources. A note in the *Archaeological Journal* (30, 1873, 96) on an Indian ceremonial battleaxe exhibited by Henderson gives a telling example: the axe 'was obtained from the palace at Delhi by an officer of the Bengal Horse Artillery, from whom, through the kindness of Mr. Fortnum [Charles Drury Fortnum], it came into the possession of its present owner'.

On 16 November 1878 *The Athenaeum* regretfully reported Henderson's serious illness. He died at his home, 3 Montague Street, London, on 20 November 1878. Henderson bequeathed to the Ashmolean Museum, Oxford (in addition to significant gifts before his death), a large collection of Egyptian, Etruscan, Greek, and Roman antiquities. To the British Museum he left collections of decorative art, glass, and arms, as well as important watercolour drawings. He bequeathed to the British Library the correspondence of George Keate with Voltaire and Dr Edward Young. Watercolour drawings, two paintings by Canaletto, and any remaining old masters the trustees cared to choose were bequeathed to the National Gallery. Although the lasting significance of John Henderson lies undoubtedly in these great bequests, another, of £100 to the Female School of Design, Bloomsbury, whose finances had been uncertain since 1859, is equally expressive of the concerns of a man whose loss was genuinely regretted not only in the pages of specialized journals, but by the cultivated readers of *The Athenaeum*, and those of *The Times*.

R. S. CHECKETTS

Sources 'Preface', *Works of art in pottery, glass, and metal in the collection of John Henderson M.A. F.S.A. Photographed and printed by Messrs. Cundall and Fleming, for private use* (1868) [texts accompanying each pl. written by Henderson] · Burlington Fine Arts Club, *Drawings and sketches made by the late David Cox and the late Peter De Wint lent by John Henderson esq. M.A. F.S.A.* (1873) · G. Waagen, *Galleries and cabinets of art in Great Britain* (1857), 206–13 · *The Times* (22 Nov 1878) · *The Times* (17 Jan 1879) · *The Athenaeum* (16 Nov 1878) · *The Athenaeum* (23 Nov 1878) · *The Athenaeum* (11 Jan 1879) · *CGPLA Eng. & Wales* (1878) · will, 1 Nov 1877, Principal Registry of the Family Division, London · *Proceedings of the Society of Antiquaries of London*, 2nd ser., 8 (1879–81), 105 [see other references in 2nd ser., 1–8 (1859–81)] · *Archaeological Journal*, 10–36 (1853–79), esp. 36 (1879), p. 102 · Foster, *Alum. Oxon.* · D. Cherry, *Victorian women artists* (1993) · *DNB* · *IGI*
Wealth at death under £90,000: probate, 23 Dec 1878, *CGPLA Eng. & Wales*

Henderson, John (1804–1862), architect, was born on 1 March 1804 at Brechin, Forfarshire, the son of John Henderson, one of Lord Panmure's gardeners at Brechin Castle, and his wife, Agnes Thomson. Apprenticed as a carpenter, he studied building and construction before working as an assistant in the office of Thomas Hamilton in the early 1830s. He moved to Edinburgh, where he worked from various addresses and eventually lived at 7 Greenhill Park, which he designed. Early work in Brechin and Forfarshire bespeaks the influence of Lord Panmure. In 1831 he designed a new steeple for Arbroath parish church, followed by the Montrose Natural History Museum (1837), the tower and spire to Fettercairn parish church (1838), and the flamboyant and accomplished Jacobean Mechanics' Institute, Brechin (1838). Residual links with his home town comprised continuing alterations to Brechin Castle (1854–63), a bridge over Brechin's Den to the castle in 1856, and Tenements School, Brechin, three years later.

Henderson speedily developed an establishment clientele in Edinburgh. He designed the Highland Society's offices at 1–3 George IV Bridge (1836)—possibly through his association with Thomas Hamilton—and in one remarkable year, 1838, designed the striking Holy Trinity Episcopal Church, Dean Bridge (in lacy English Gothic), Newhaven parish church, and St Mary's, Dumfries, and refronted Lady Glenorchy's Chapel, Greenside Place, in plain swirling seventeenth-century Scottish style. His design for the Mariners' Church, Leith (1840), may have introduced him to Sir John Gladstone, for whom he designed St Thomas's Church, school, and manse, Leith, the same year. Gladstone was a substantial benefactor to the proposed Episcopalian public school of Trinity College, Glenalmond, for which Henderson was commissioned in 1843. That year he married Hannah Matilda Exley.

Beyond the suburb of Church Hill, laid out in 1842 for Thomas Chalmers, where he designed all the houses along one side, and the layout of Greenhill Park, Edinburgh, where he designed a number of houses, Henderson's residential projects other than manses were few: Carse Gray House, Forfar, a house in Newbattle, Midlothian, Borthwick Hall, Midlothian (1855), and at the time of his death possibly Carnwath, Lanarkshire. His forte was church architecture. His œuvre encompassed a few Church of Scotland buildings, such as the North Church, Stirling (1841; dem.), Holyrood Free Church (1848), St Luke's Free Church, Queen Street, Edinburgh (1852), and St Mungo's, West Linton (1857). After Glenalmond, however, he became the primary Scottish-born exponent of Tractarian–Early English Gothic in Scotland for the expanding Scottish Episcopal church. From 1844 to his death, save 1855–6, commissions came in at the rate of one or two a year. They included St Mary's, Montrose (1844), Barnton Place, Stirling (1845), St Mary's, Hamilton (1845), St Columba's, Edinburgh (1846), St Andrew's, Fasque (1847), St John's, Glasgow (1848; dem.), and St Philip's, Catterline (1848), Holy Trinity churches in Melrose and Dunoon (1849), St Mary's, Dalmahoy (1850),

Christ Church, Lochgilphead (1851), St Margaret's, Meigle (1852; dem.), Christ Church, Leith, and St Peter's, Galashiels (both 1853), St Mary's, Arbroath (1854), Holy Trinity, Lamington, St Saviour's, Bridge of Allan, and St Mary's, Port Glasgow (all 1857), St Peter's, Montrose, and Christ Church, Lanark (both 1858), and St Baldred's, North Berwick (1860). He also designed private chapels at Dalmahoy, Midlothian (1850), and Ardgowan, Renfrewshire (1854). At his death there were substantial unpaid fees, some for projects as yet seemingly uncompleted.

Between 1844 and 1846 Henderson had been joined as assistant by William Hay. On Henderson's death, his son George completed training with David Cousin, possibly working on India Buildings, Victoria Street, which Henderson had begun. After periods abroad (by Hay in Canada and George Henderson in Australia) the successor practice of Hay and Henderson was founded in 1878.

Externally, Henderson's earlier architecture was unpretentious, whatever the style, old-fashioned in plan—symmetrical entrance, Gothic tower and windows—and pleasing in form. He was the designer *par excellence* for the Scottish Episcopal church in the 1840s and 1850s. Of over sixty projects, the most prominent was Trinity College, Glenalmond, a worthy but uninspiring Gothic-fronted establishment. The interiors of his later churches, however, showed a developing austerity, and achieved their effects through plain form and the manipulation of light. Henderson died at his home, 7 Greenhill Park, Edinburgh, on 27 June 1862. He was survived by his wife.

BERTHA PORTER, *rev.* CHARLES McKEAN

Sources private information (2004) [D. Walker] · Colvin, *Archs.* · S. McKinstry, *Rowand Anderson* (1991) · [W. Papworth], ed., *The dictionary of architecture*, 11 vols. (1853–92) · J. Macaulay, *The Gothic revival, 1745–1845* (1975) · A. Maclean, 'The Scottish Episcopal church and the ecclesiastical movement, 1840–60', *Caledonia Gothica: architectural heritage*, 8 (1997), 47–59 · J. Grant, *Cassell's old and new Edinburgh*, 3 vols. [1880–83]; abridged edn (1979), vols. 1, 3 · Pevsner (1978–) [The buildings of Scotland series] · C. McKean, ed., *Illustrated architectural guides to Scotland* (1982–) · M. Glendinning, R. MacInnes, and A. MacKechnie, *A history of Scottish architecture* (1996) · NA Scot., SC 70/114, 575
Archives National Monuments Record of Scotland, MSS · Royal Commission on the Ancient and Historical Monuments of Scotland, Edinburgh, drawings, papers, etc.
Wealth at death £1459; excl. property: NA Scot., SC7/105/1D2

Henderson, John (1822–1867), circus performer and proprietor, was born in London, the son of John Henderson, an actor. He was advertised as a rider with Price and Powell's circus at Bristol in 1842. After a spell with Pablo Fanque in Lancashire, he was with Powell's circus at Hammersmith in 1843, performing as a trampolinist, clown, vaulter, and somersault thrower. He married Agnes Selina (*c*.1825–1879), the fifth daughter of Henry Michael Hengler, the circus rope-dancer, on 2 October 1843, at Canterbury. Their only child, a daughter, died at the age of twenty-one. In 1844 Charles Hengler (Mrs Henderson's brother) took over Powell's company; Henderson and William Powell were joint ringmasters in 1845. Henderson appeared as a leaper at Astley's Amphitheatre, London, in

1847, in William Batty's time, and returned in 1850 to perform on the iron wire. He continued with Hengler's company for many years, a brilliant all-round artiste, although he occasionally appeared in other arenas.

In October 1858 Henderson left Hengler to fulfil engagements in Moscow and St Petersburg, first selling his black mare Bess. By 1859 he had become involved in circus management, probably for Hengler, ostensibly of Frowde's Cirque Modele, at Sheffield, while at the same time appearing on the slack wire. The company was then transformed into Henderson's Grand Cirque, at Chester. Although he was always associated with Hengler, Henderson always strove towards success in his own right. During 1860 his circus toured England. For the next seven years he alternated between Hengler's, other circuses, and his own temporary companies. He was manager of the Christmas circus at the Agricultural Hall, Islington, London, for three seasons from 1863 to 1864, and ran the winter 1866–7 circus at the London Music Hall, Manchester. Henderson died of pleurisy on 10 May 1867 while his circus was at Ipswich, and was buried on 13 May in Ipswich cemetery. He was a fine tall man with curly hair and a bushy moustache.

JOHN M. TURNER

Sources J. M. Turner, 'The excitement and romance of circus history', *King Pole*, 71 (June 1986), 4ff. · T. McDonald Rendle, *Swings and roundabouts* (1919) · G. Van Hare, *Fifty years of a showman's life, or, The life and travels of Van Hare*, new edn (1893) · Boase, *Mod. Eng. biog.* · *The Era* (19 May 1867) · *Suffolk Mercury* (11 May 1867) · *Suffolk Mercury* (18 May 1867) · m. cert.
Likenesses engraving, repro. in *Illustrated Sporting and Theatrical News* (16 Dec 1865), cover · print, Harvard TC

Henderson, Joseph (1832–1908), portrait and marine painter, was born on 10 June 1832 at Stanley, Perthshire, the third and elder twin son of a builder and railway contractor, Joseph Henderson, and his wife, Marjory Slater. The family moved to Edinburgh, where the father died about 1840 in impoverished circumstances. All four boys were sent to work at a very early age: Joseph was apprenticed to a firm of drapers in George Street, and attended the 'trade' part-time design classes of the Trustees' Academy. On the recommendation of the sculptor Alexander Handyside Ritchie he enrolled as an art student on 2 February 1849. Here he studied alongside William Quiller Orchardson and Robert Herdman and, latterly, under Robert Scott Lauder. On 10 May 1853 he left the academy and settled in Glasgow. Henderson was married three times: first, on 8 January 1856, to Helen (1836/7–1866), daughter of James Cosh, with whom he had four children: a daughter, Marjory, who became the second wife of William McTaggart, and three sons, all of whom became artists; second on 30 September 1869, to Helen Young (1848/9–1871) of Strathaven, with whom he had one daughter; and third, in 1872, to Eliza Thomson, who survived him with two daughters.

From 1852 onward Henderson supported himself entirely by his art. His early work follows the earlier Scottish figurative tradition, developed by Thomas Duncan and Thomas Faed, but the genre subjects favoured by

Lauder and his pupils find echoes in Henderson's figurative interiors of the late 1850s. During a holiday on the Ayrshire coast about 1871 Henderson discovered sea painting. Although he was to continue to paint portraits into the 1890s, the sea henceforth was his prime inspiration. His early sea paintings, such as *Haul on the Sands* (1874; Glasgow Art Galleries and Museum), are essentially genre works set by the shore; in these, Henderson's palette is dark and his handling hard. Gradually, however, as in the work of William McTaggart, the figures became less important than the representation of the effects of raw nature, the colours clearer, and the brushwork freer. His best works, such as *The Flowing Tide* (1897; Glasgow Art Galleries and Museum) and *The Storm, Ballantrae* (City Art Centre, Edinburgh), were done during the last fifteen years of his life. Between 1871 and 1886 Henderson exhibited twenty pictures at the Royal Academy in London, but he showed principally at the Glasgow (later Royal Glasgow) Institute of the Fine Arts. He also painted in watercolour and was a member of the Royal Scottish Water-Colour Society. Henderson was a popular and respected artist in his day; the Glasgow Art Club, to mark his jubilee as a professional artist, organized an exhibition of his work in 1901, and the Royal Glasgow Institute of the Fine Arts, of which he was a vice-president, arranged a memorial exhibition. He died at Kintyre View in Ballantrae, Ayrshire, where for many years he had spent the summer, on 17 July 1908, and was buried in Sighthill cemetery, Glasgow. The main collections of his work are in Glasgow Art Galleries and Museum, and the City Art Centre, Edinburgh.   J. L. CAW, rev. ELIZABETH S. CUMMING

Sources P. Bate, *The art of Joseph Henderson* (1908) · *Glasgow Herald* (18 July 1908) · W. Hardie, *Scottish painting, 1837–1939* (1976) · D. Macmillan, *Scottish art, 1460–2000* (2000) · *Summary catalogue of British oil paintings*, Glasgow Art Gallery and Museum (1971) · J. L. Caw, *Scottish painting past and present, 1620–1908* (1908) · Graves, *RA exhibitors* · m. certs. · d. cert.

Likenesses W. McTaggart, oils, 1894, Glasgow Art Gallery and Museum · J. Henderson, oils; formerly in artist's possession, 1912 · J. Mossman, bronze medallion (with third wife)

Henderson, Sir Nevile Meyrick (1882–1942), diplomatist, was born on 10 June 1882 at Sedgwick Park, Horsham, Sussex, the second son in a family of three sons and one daughter of Robert Henderson (1851–1895), businessman, of Sedgwick Park, and his wife, Emma Caroline (*d.* 1931), younger daughter of Jonathan Hargreaves, justice of the peace, of Cuffnells, Lyndhurst, Hampshire. His father's family came from Leuchars in Fife; his grandfather Robert Henderson had founded a prosperous merchant business in Glasgow which enabled him to purchase three large estates. One of these was Sedgwick Park, which was inherited by his father, Robert. It was here that Henderson grew up, and Sedgwick played a central part in his life. Many years later he was to write that each time he returned to England from a diplomatic posting abroad, 'the white cliffs of Dover meant Sedgwick for me' (Henderson, *Water under the Bridges*, 10). His father was a director of the Bank of England, who managed the family business of R. and I. Henderson until his premature death

Sir Nevile Meyrick Henderson (1882–1942), by Walter Stoneman, 1935

when Henderson was thirteen, and about to enter Eton College. Thereafter Henderson was brought up by his formidable mother, Emma, who had travelled around the world at the tender age of twenty-four, and of whom her son remained in some awe.

It was his mother who decided that Henderson should enter the diplomatic service, when his preference would have been for the army. (He did in fact pass the entrance exam to the Royal Military College, Sandhurst.) He never married, although he had several close female friends including Princess Olga of Yugoslavia. He grew up to be a tall, elegant, good-looking man of whom the society diarist Chips Channon noted that he was always 'faultlessly dressed' (*The Diaries of Sir Henry Channon*, ed. R. Rhodes James, 1967, 219).

After leaving Eton, Henderson studied abroad, and in a series of crammers to improve his language skills. He entered the diplomatic service in February 1905, and was to spend most of the next thirty-four years abroad. His first posting was to St Petersburg, in November 1905, where he served under Sir Arthur Nicolson and was promoted third secretary in May 1907. He was then transferred to Tokyo in March 1909 (and promoted second secretary in November 1911), back to St Petersburg in January 1912, to Rome in March 1914, to Nish in September 1914, to Paris in January 1916, and to Constantinople in October 1920. He was promoted first secretary in November 1918. It was while serving in Paris that Henderson became convinced of the unfairness towards Germany of the treaty of Versailles and developed a suspicion of French diplomacy.

The Constantinople posting proved to be equally influential in Henderson's career. The ambassador was the robust Sir Horace Rumbold, whom Henderson much admired, and who also appreciated Henderson's capacity for 'jujitsu diplomacy' (Rumbold to Selby, 15 July 1927, PRO FO 794/10). Henderson was left in charge of the embassy for lengthy periods when Rumbold was attending the Lausanne conference, and was promoted to the rank of counsellor in May 1922. He was then posted to

Cairo in November 1924, where he had to deal with the pugnacious Viscount Allenby, arriving there after the dramatic murder of the sirdar, Sir Lee Stack. Henderson believed that the Egyptians should be given more autonomy, a view sharply at odds with that of the new high commissioner, Lord Lloyd, an old Eton schoolfriend who opposed a change in Egypt's constitutional status. Nevertheless, Lloyd appreciated Henderson's work, and his golden opinion was shared by the then foreign secretary, Austen Chamberlain. In April 1928 Henderson was transferred to Paris for the second time, though he remained a counsellor.

In November 1929 Henderson was given the most crucial posting of his diplomatic career to date, as minister to Belgrade. During his five-year period there Henderson made the closest male friendship of his life with King Alexander. When Alexander was assassinated in 1934, Henderson wrote that he felt more emotion at the king's funeral than 'at any other except my mother's' (Henderson to Vansittart, 28 Feb 1935, PRO FO 800/268). This close, and some thought obsessive, relationship allowed Henderson to exercise much influence, and the permanent under-secretary at the Foreign Office, Vansittart, recognized his achievement by promising him a post 'in the First Eleven' (Vansittart to Henderson, 13 Feb 1935, PRO FO 800/268). Henderson was therefore bitterly disappointed to be sent in October 1935 to distant Buenos Aires as minister, but his eventual appointment to Berlin in April 1937 was a reward for a long, and successful, diplomatic career. It was also recognition of Henderson's ability to hit it off with dictators, which the Foreign Office thought would be helpful in Berlin.

Henderson regretted the fact that he was only able to serve two short periods in the Foreign Office (in 1905 and 1915). This meant that when Sedgwick Park was sold by his sister-in-law following his mother's death in 1931, he had no real roots in Britain, although in appearance and manner he became the epitome of the polished British diplomat abroad. Some subordinates found him difficult, and he was a man of strong opinions whose tendency to cut corners in diplomatic practice, long evident before he went to Berlin, could irritate Foreign Office superiors. Henderson also had a tendency, most obvious in Belgrade and Berlin, to be too partial towards the host government. This was recognized by the Labour politician Hugh Dalton, whose comment on meeting him—'Ah, here's the pro-Yugoslav'—irritated Henderson considerably (Henderson, *Water under the Bridges*, 171).

Henderson had an interview with Neville Chamberlain in April 1937 (although no documentary record survives of this meeting), and became convinced that he was the personal representative of the prime minister's, rather than the Foreign Office's, policy in Berlin. He also had a fatalistic streak, writing in his memoirs that his Berlin appointment could 'only mean that I had been specially selected by Providence for the definite mission of, as I trusted, helping to preserve the peace of the world' (Henderson, *Failure of a Mission*, 13). This strong sense of personal mission, allied to his tendency to be unorthodox, and to place too much reliance on the value of personal friendship with individuals, opened Henderson up to Foreign Office accusations of disloyalty.

Henderson soon got into serious trouble with Sir Robert Vansittart for writing a lengthy memorandum in May 1937 which seemed to concede that eastern Europe was a natural sphere for German influence. He also insisted, unlike his predecessor Sir Eric Phipps, on attending the annual Nuremberg rally, and made a controversial speech to the Deutsche Englische Gesellschaft. But Henderson had been asked to follow a more sympathetic, emollient line towards the Nazis, which his two immediate predecessors had been unable to do, and seems to have been damned for doing what he had been asked to do.

Contrary to his reputation, Henderson was not pro-Nazi, and opposed the forcible incorporation of Austria and the Sudetenland into the Reich in 1938. Thus he wrote to the foreign secretary, Lord Halifax, on 16 March 1938 telling him that 'we now have to consider how to secure, if we can, the integrity of Czechoslovakia' (Henderson to Halifax, 16 March 1938, PRO). Neither, Henderson kept telling the Foreign Office, was Hitler ready to fight in 1938: he needed time to incorporate Austria into the Reich, and German military preparations were incomplete. Henderson thought that in March 1938 Britain and France had at least a year before Hitler would be ready to fight. This would provide time for both negotiation and rearmament.

Henderson's attitude changed after the so-called 'May scare' of 1938, when false rumours spread about a likely German attack on Czechoslovakia. Henderson was sure from the outset that these rumours were false, but became convinced that to prevent war the Czechs had to be pressured into ceding the Sudetenland, with its largely German-speaking population, to Hitler. So strong was this conviction that he sometimes erred on the side of prejudice against the Czechs and their president, Beneš. But he was not alone in this, for the former British minister in Prague, Sir Joseph Addison, was notoriously anti-Czech, and Henderson's superior, Sir Orme Sargent, likened Czechoslovakia to a Bolshevik aircraft-carrier in central Europe. In Prague, Henderson's colleague Basil Newton was even more convinced that the Czechoslovak state was unviable in its existing shape.

Henderson believed that the German claim to the Sudetenland in 1938 was a moral one, and he always reverted in his dispatches to his conviction that Versailles had been unfair to Germany. At the same time, he was unsympathetic to feelers from the German opposition to Hitler seeking to enlist British support. Henderson thought, not unreasonably, that it was not the job of the British government to subvert the German government, and this view was shared by Chamberlain and Halifax.

As the Czech crisis deepened in the autumn of 1938, there was much debate in the Foreign Office about whether Hitler should be given a formal warning about the consequences of an attack on the Czechs. Henderson believed very strongly that if such a warning were passed on to Hitler at the party rally at Nuremberg, the effect would be to enrage the Führer and make war more certain. He constantly referred back to the May scare, when Hitler had been wrongly accused of planning to attack the Czechs, and in an angry riposte had brought forward his military preparations against them. He warned the Foreign Office about the 'unpredictability of Hitler and his moods' and reported that 'his abnormality seemed to me greater than ever' (Henderson to Wilson, 9 Sept 1938, and Henderson to Halifax, 12 Sept 1938, PRO, FO 800/371/269). In the end, Henderson's advice was heeded, and no formal warning was presented at Nuremberg.

Henderson supported Neville Chamberlain's decision to intervene personally in the Czech crisis, and was one of the first people to be informed of his intention. He was present when Chamberlain met Hitler at both Berchtesgaden and Godesburg, and believed that Chamberlain's personal diplomacy had helped to prevent the outbreak of war. It followed therefore that Henderson was a strong supporter of the Munich agreement, which ceded the Sudetenland to the Reich. After the agreement was signed on 29 September, Henderson wrote to congratulate the prime minister in prescient terms. 'Millions of mothers', he told Chamberlain, 'will be blessing your name tonight for having saved their sons from the horrors of war. Oceans of ink will flow hereafter in criticism' (Henderson, *Failure of a Mission*, 168).

Henderson was an exhausted man after Munich, and his joy that war had been avoided was tempered by disillusionment. He wrote privately to Halifax asking him to 'move me to some other sphere. I never want to work with Germans again' (Henderson to Halifax, 6 Oct 1938, PRO, FO 800/314). His request for a transfer was refused, although by now cancer of the throat had been diagnosed by his doctors. He was then appointed to the international commission of ambassadors which was to adjudicate the details of the revised Czech–German frontier, and was disgusted by the bullying German tactics on it. At this point, in mid-October, Henderson was so seriously ill that he had to take four months' sick-leave, returning to his post only in February 1939.

In the light of Henderson's poor health, it was an extraordinary decision by the Foreign Office to send him back to Berlin. Halifax had lost faith in him, as had the new permanent under-secretary, Sir Alexander Cadogan, and the failure to recall him seemed even more bizarre after Hitler's occupation of Bohemia and Moravia on 15 March 1939. Henderson himself recognized in *Failure of a Mission* that it would have been wiser to have recalled him, because of his close association with the appeasement policy which had been dealt a fatal blow by Hitler's illegal act. The fact that Henderson, a seriously sick and deeply disillusioned man, who had little faith in the new policy of collective security, was kept in post can only be regarded as a serious executive failure by Halifax.

Blocked by Ribbentrop, whom he could not abide, and disdained by Hitler who referred to him as 'the man with the carnation', Henderson tried vainly to convince the Germans that an attack on Poland would mean war. In shouting matches with Hitler and Ribbentrop in late August, Henderson stuck to his guns but received little credit later for doing so. He continued to hope desperately that peace could be preserved and tried to use his personal friendship with Goering to achieve this object, but in vain. Ultimately, Hitler was determined to have his war, and Henderson's 'mission' proved to be an impossible one. This was fully recognized by Henderson's mentor, and predecessor in Berlin, Sir Horace Rumbold, who told him after reading *Failure of a Mission* that 'nobody could have succeeded in Berlin' (Rumbold to Henderson, 15 April 1940, PRO, FO 800/270).

On the day war broke out, 3 September 1939, it was Henderson's duty to present the British ultimatum at the Wilhelmstrasse, before finally returning to England a few days later. His offer to return as minister to Belgrade was declined, and his worsening health forced him to retire from the diplomatic service on health grounds in January 1940. He concentrated on writing his two diplomatic memoirs (the second of which, *Water under the Bridges*, was published posthumously in 1945) and an eccentric study of his dog Hippy, whom he had acquired during his stint in Belgrade.

Henderson remained a controversial figure, not least because in *Failure of a Mission* he showed no sign of repenting for his support of appeasement. Indeed, he remained convinced that appeasement had been the only realistic option. Other Foreign Office colleagues writing after the event were more circumspect, although they had been no less complicit in supporting appeasement at the time. Thus Henderson was frequently made a scapegoat for the overall failings of British policy when he was in no position to answer back. Moreover, he had been merely an agent of that policy, which had been formulated in Whitehall. He had been rightly horrified by the prospect of another war, and misguided only in his failure to perceive the messianic nature of Hitler's ambitions, and the ultimate evil behind Nazism. As his *Times* obituary recorded, he had 'striven hard, long and sincerely to bring about an understanding with Nazi Germany' (*The Times*, 31 Dec 1942).

Henderson died of the cancer which had afflicted him since 1938 on 30 December 1942, while staying at the Dorchester Hotel, London. He had been appointed CMG in 1923, KCMG in 1932, and GCMG in 1939.

PETER NEVILLE

Sources PRO, FO 794/10, 800/264–270 · N. Henderson, *Failure of a mission* (1940) · N. Henderson, *Water under the bridges* (1945) · DNB · *The diaries of Sir Alexander Cadogan*, ed. D. Dilks (1971) · *The diplomatic diaries of Oliver Harvey, 1937–40*, ed. J. Harvey (1970) · I. Kirkpatrick, *The inner circle: memoirs of Ivone Kirkpatrick* (1959) · A. Ryan, *The last of the dragomans* (1951) · J. Charmley, *Chamberlain and the lost peace* (1989) · V. B. Baker, 'Nevile Henderson in Berlin', *Red River Valley*, 2/4 (winter 1977) · R. Spitzy, *How we squandered the Reich* (1997) · P. Neville, 'The appointment of Sir Nevile Henderson, 1937: design or blunder?', *Journal of Contemporary History*, 33 (1998), 609–19 · P. Neville, *Appeasing Hitler: the diplomacy of Sir Nevile Henderson, 1937–9* (1999) · WWW · Burke, *Gen. GB* · *FO List* · *CGPLA Eng. & Wales* (1943) · *The Times* (31 Dec 1942)

Archives PRO, corresp. and MS autobiography, FO 800/264–270 · PRO, individual file, FO 794/10 | Bodl. Oxf., corresp. with Sir Horace Rumbold · Borth. Inst., corresp. with Lord Halifax · CAC Cam., letters to Lord Lloyd · CAC Cam., Phipps MSS · CAC Cam., Strang MSS · CAC Cam., Vansittart MSS · IWM, Mason Macfarlane MSS · Lpool RO, corresp. with seventeenth earl of Derby · NA Scot., corresp. with Lord Lothian · PRO, Cadogan MSS, FO 800 series · PRO, Halifax MSS · PRO, Orme Sargent MSS, FO 800 series · U. Aberdeen, Ogilvie Forbes MSS | FILM BFI NFTVA, documentary footage · BFI NFTVA, news footage · Pathé News | SOUND BL NSA

Likenesses W. Stoneman, photograph, 1935, NPG [*see illus.*] · photograph, 1938, Hult. Arch. · A. R. Thomson, portrait, priv. coll.

Wealth at death £60,651 16*s*. 11*d*.: probate, 9 July 1943, *CGPLA Eng. & Wales*

Henderson, Nigel Graeme (1917–1985), artist and photographer, was born on 1 April 1917 in St John's Wood, London, the second of three children, born in successive years, of Captain Kenneth Henderson, contracting engineer, son of Lord Farringdon, and Winifred (Wyn) Ellen Lester, a former music hall artiste, the illegitimate child of an illegitimate mother. Married in 1915, his parents were divorced in 1924. His mother, an unconventional and creative woman, was to remain an important influence on her son. Henderson attended Stowe School, which he hated, and left after only two years in 1933. His schools, and unhappy holidays at his paternal grandparents' house in Wimbledon, induced a lifelong distaste for upper-class conventionality, and a romantic identification with outsiders. Happier times were spent in his mother's artistic circle in Bloomsbury. Informally adopted by Adrian Stephen, a well-known psychoanalyst, brother of Virginia Woolf, and his wife, Karin Stephen, he stayed frequently with them in Gordon Square and at Landermere Quay in Essex.

In his late teens Henderson pursued an erratic and peripatetic self-education. He joined the Group Theatre, meeting Rupert Doone, Robert Medley, Louis MacNeice, W. H. Auden, Christopher Isherwood, and others. He spent time in the company of scientists, including J. D. Bernal and Solly Zuckermann, and in 1935 he enrolled at Chelsea Polytechnic to study biology. Restless and indecisive, in 1936 he became a junior picture restorer at the National Gallery. He experimented with collage, a sympathetic medium for an obsessive collector of ephemera and discarded objects, and recognized in the collages of John Piper and Julian Trevelyan, and the poetic surrealism of Humphrey Jennings, a sympathetic challenge to aesthetic orthodoxy. His mother's management of the Guggenheim Jeune gallery (1938–40) brought contacts with European artists, including Yves Tanguy, Laurence Vail, and Marcel Duchamp.

In 1939 Henderson joined Coastal Command as a pilot. Alternately exhilarated and terrified by flying, in 1942, after many sorties, he suffered a nervous breakdown and was moved to lighter duties. In 1943 he married (Karin) Judith Stephen (*d*. 1972), an anthropologist, daughter of Adrian and Karin, and moved with her to Bethnal Green, where they lived and worked (Judith as a social observer and teacher) until 1955, when they moved to Landermere Quay. They had four children. In 1945 Henderson enrolled

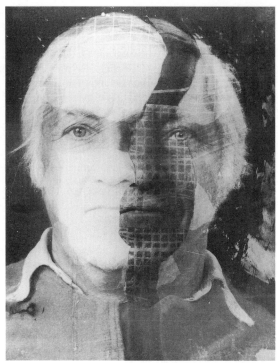

Nigel Graeme Henderson (1917–1985), self-portrait, 1980–82 [*Reforming*]

at the Slade School of Fine Art on a former serviceman's grant. His art studies were haphazard and inconclusive, but it was there he met Eduardo Paolozzi, a formidable friend and collaborator. They shared enthusiasms for science, unregarded ephemera, children's drawings, popular magazines, folk art, and cinema. When Paolozzi left for Paris in 1947, the artist Richard Hamilton became a close companion. The ground was prepared for future collaborations.

After leaving the Slade in 1949, Henderson at last began to find himself as an artist. He started taking the documentary photographs of street life in Bethnal Green that remain among his most enduring work. With Paolozzi he experimented with photograms, placing degraded and unconventional materials (for example, rubbish, coffee grounds, and gouache) directly on to the negative. These he recombined in photo-collages, with what he called 'stressed' photographs, to achieve chance expressive effects. From 1951 to 1954 he taught creative photography at the Central School of Arts and Crafts, undertaking at the same time commercial photography for *Vogue*, *Architectural Review*, and *Flair*. Through the 1950s he was an initiating participant in many influential Institute of Contemporary Arts (ICA) events. In 1951 he showed photograms at the ICA Festival of Britain exhibition 'Growth and form'; in 1953 he organized, with Paolozzi and the architects Alison and Peter Smithson, the exhibition 'Parallel of life and art', for which he made several 'stressed' photoworks; his contribution, with Paolozzi and the Smithsons, to the influential 'This is tomorrow' exhibition in 1955 was seen as a seminal contribution to the discussion of new brutalism; and he was a founder member, in 1952, of the Independent Group at the ICA, formed to promote interdisciplinary discussion. The relation of art to everyday life, and the environmental integration of architecture, design, technology, and art, were recurring themes in his work. In spite of his own aversion to formal education Henderson became a much admired teacher, at Colchester School of Art from 1957 to 1960, and at Norwich School of Art from 1965 to 1968, and from 1972 (the year of Judith's death) until 1982. His retirement in 1982 was marked by 'Heads eye Wyn', an exhibition of Dada-influenced photomontage images of his own head, an obsessive theme in his later work. In 1983 Henderson remarried; his new wife was Janet Allan (née Murray), a potter and noted amateur gardener. He died on 15 May 1985, survived by his second wife. MEL GOODING

Sources Heads eye Wyn (1982) [exhibition catalogue, Norwich School of Art] · Nigel Henderson (1977) [exhibition catalogue, Anthony d'Offay Gallery, London] · The Tate Gallery, 1974–6: illustrated catalogue of acquisitions (1978) · CGPLA Eng. & Wales (1985) · private information (2004) [family]
Archives Tate collection, corresp., notebooks, and illustrated exhibition catalogues | Tate collection, letters to Susan Watson [photocopies]
Likenesses N. G. Henderson, self-portrait, photomontage, 1980–82 (Reforming), priv. coll. [see illus.]
Wealth at death £13,271: administration, 5 July 1985, CGPLA Eng. & Wales

Henderson, Oscar (1891–1969), naval officer and television company executive, was born on 7 October 1891 at Oakley House, Windsor Park, Belfast, the third son of Sir James Henderson (1848–1914) and his wife, Martha Anne, daughter of David Pollock, architect. His father, the proprietor of the Belfast News-Letter, became the first lord mayor of Greater Belfast in 1898, and was knighted in 1899.

Henderson was educated at the Methodist college, Belfast, and Bradfield College, Berkshire, before entering the Royal Naval College at Osborne in 1904. He was gazetted midshipman in 1909. When the First World War broke out in 1914 he was serving on the destroyer HMS Ribble in the China squadron. He navigated his ship to the Mediterranean where he took part in sea action during the Dardanelles campaign. The Ribble, one of eight destroyers, assisted with the landing of allied troops in the face of desperate Turkish resistance at Gaba Tepe on the Gallipoli peninsula on 25 April 1915. Henderson, a lieutenant since January 1915, was commended for service in action in Vice-Admiral De Robeck's dispatch. Now in command of HMS Ribble, he later returned to the Dardanelles for the evacuation, for which he was again mentioned in dispatches. In April 1918 he took a leading part in one of the most daring exploits of the war—the raid on the German submarine base at Zeebrugge. German U-boats were based in Bruges docks, linked to the coast by a canal and protected by an impregnable, and heavily fortified, 1.5 mile long pier, the Zeebrugge mole. The British Admiralty decided the canal entrance had to be blocked. Lieutenant Henderson was second in command of HMS Iris II, one of

two Mersey ferryboats requisitioned to push HMS Vindictive, the main attacking ship, against the mole, and to carry additional troops. On St George's day, 23 April 1918, 132 men-of-war closed in on their rendezvous. Vindictive, Iris, and Daffodil created a diversion and landed storming parties on the seaward side of the mole, while the blocking ships made their way to the canal where they were successfully sunk. Iris came under German fire, which destroyed the port side of the bridge, causing serious fire and mortally wounding its commander. Lieutenant Henderson led a volunteer party to the upper deck to control the fire; seeing the condition of the bridge and finding Commander Valentine Gibbs dead, he took command of the Iris. Despite heavy casualties and severe damage Lieutenant Henderson succeeded in bringing Iris back to Dover. For his part in the Zeebrugge raid he was mentioned in the first dispatch from Vice-Admiral Sir Roger Keyes, of 9 May 1918. He received the Croix de Guerre and the Distinguished Service Order. For the remainder of the war he commanded destroyers in the Grand Fleet, and was present at the surrender of the German fleet, off Rosyth on the Firth of Forth, on 21 November 1918. He continued to command destroyers in the Atlantic until his retirement from the Royal Navy in July 1922.

In 1922, when the post of governor of Northern Ireland was created, Henderson was appointed private secretary and comptroller to the first governor, the third duke of Abercorn. He held the post until 1947, also serving the second governor, the fourth Earl Granville, from 1945 until his retirement. He was made a commander of the British empire in 1925 and commander in the Royal Victorian Order in 1935. On his retirement Henderson joined the family newspaper. The Belfast News-Letter, founded in 1737, had been connected with the Henderson family since 1795. He became managing director and played a leading role in launching Ulster's first Sunday newspaper, the Sunday News. He became president of the company, renamed Century Newspapers, in 1963.

Henderson had the foresight to realize the potential of commercial television, and first approached the Independent Television Authority in 1956, with the intention of applying for an ITV contract. He assembled an impressive applicant group, under the chairmanship of the earl of Antrim, which was successful. They took the name of Ulster Television (UTV), and went on air on 31 October 1959. UTV developed distinctive local programming with a popular news magazine, Roundabout, which became a model for other ITV regions, and a pioneering adult education series, Midnight Oil, praised as the first 'university of the air'. He retired as a director of UTV in 1961.

Henderson married Alicia Mary (Molly), only daughter of Mr and Mrs R. B. Henry of Laurel Lodge, Strandtown, on 4 August 1920. They had two sons: O. W. J. Henderson, who became chairman of Century Newspapers; and R. B. Henderson, who became the managing director, later chairman, of UTV. Henderson died at his home, Glenburn House, Dunmurry, co. Antrim, on 3 August 1969.

BARRIE MACDONALD

Sources *Belfast News-Letter* (4 Aug 1969) · *The Times* (4 Aug 1969) · *WWW* · 'Ostend and Zeebrugge: croix de guerre for British soldiers', *The Times* (20 May 1918) · citations for distinguished service order awards, *The Times* (24 July 1918) · *Ian Hamilton's despatches from the Dardanelles* (1917) · *Ostend and Zeebrugge, April 23 – May 10, 1918: the dispatches of Vice-Admiral Sir Roger Keyes … and other narratives of the operations*, ed. C. S. Terry (1919) · B. Pitt, *Zeebrugge: St George's Day, 1918* (1958) · *Navy List* (1909–22) · D. Griffiths, ed., *The encyclopedia of the British press, 1422–1992* (1992) · H. Shearman, *News Letter, 1737–1987* (1987) · B. Sendall, *Expansion and change, 1958–68* (1983), vol. 2 of *Independent television in Britain* (1982–90) · R. B. Henderson, *A musing on the lighter side of Ulster Television* (1989) · IBA archives · *CGPLA Eng. & Wales* (1970) · b. cert.

Archives PRO NIre., MSS · Ulster Television, Havelock House, Ormeau Road, Belfast | Century Newspapers Ltd, 46–56 Boucher Crescent, Belfast, *Belfast News-Letter* archives · Independent Television Commission, 33 Foley Street, London, Independent Broadcasting Authority archives

Likenesses M. F. Bell, portrait, priv. coll.

Wealth at death £3606 (effects in England): Irish probate sealed in London, 20 April 1970, *CGPLA Eng. & Wales* · £21,408 2s.: probate, 28 Feb 1970, *CGPLA Éire*.

Henderson, Sir Reginald Guy Hannam (1881–1939), naval officer, was born on 1 September 1881 at Trelew Mylor, near Falmouth, Cornwall, the second son of John Hannam Henderson, commander in the Royal Navy, and his wife, Elizabeth, niece and adopted daughter of Henry May of Honolulu, Hawaii. The Henderson family was originally Scottish but had settled in Kent. It had strong naval connections, all three of Reginald's uncles having been admirals, one, Sir William Hannam Henderson, having been a founder and long-standing editor of the *Naval Review* and another, Sir Reginald Friend Hannam Henderson, having helped found the Royal Australian Navy.

Henderson entered the Royal Naval College, Dartmouth, as a naval cadet on 15 July 1895 and did well enough to join *Mars* as an already promoted midshipman on 8 June 1897. The battleship was part of the channel squadron commanded by his uncle Reginald. He then transferred to the cruiser *Hermione* on the China station before returning to Britain in 1901 for the Greenwich sublieutenants' course. Although obtaining only second-class passes at Greenwich he obtained firsts in the more practical pilotage, gunnery, and torpedo work taught at the Portsmouth establishments. He was promoted lieutenant on 15 May 1902 and in November joined the battleship *Venerable*, flagship of the Mediterranean Fleet. Her captain reported that Henderson was a zealous officer of very good physique.

In September 1903 Henderson went to *Excellent*, the gunnery training establishment in Portsmouth. In 1906, after a successful long course, and almost a year on the junior staff, he joined the cruiser *Euryalus*, flagship of the North America and West Indies station. His commanding officers consistently described Henderson as a zealous officer, hard working, efficient, and capable. He returned home at the end of 1907 and early the following year was appointed gunnery officer in the battleship *Britannia* serving with the Channel Fleet. His reputation was such that in 1910 he was appointed to the staff at *Excellent* once more, being promoted commander on 30 June 1913. It was a sign of Henderson's stature that he was next sent to Greece as gunnery expert in Admiral Mark Kerr's mission to advise the Greek navy. He married in 1911 Islay Edith, daughter of Rhoderick McNeill Campbell of the Campbells of Dunstaffnage; they had two sons.

The day before the outbreak of the First World War in 1914 Henderson was appointed gunnery officer of the super-dreadnought *Erin*, just confiscated from the Turks to add to the Grand Fleet. He served in her at Jutland and impressed his captain, who considered him to possess quite exceptional ability and expected him to go very far in the service. He also impressed Admiral J. R. Jellicoe, who brought him to London on his elevation from fleet commander to first sea lord at the end of 1916. As the U-boat crisis reached its peak Henderson served in the vital anti-submarine division of the naval staff. He played a central role in the neutralization of the U-boat menace, notably by organizing a pioneer convoy scheme for the French coal trade and producing key statistics that proved the volume of shipping was not too great to escort. Henderson was thus instrumental in the general adoption of convoy which saved the whole allied cause.

The recognition of Henderson's achievement was appointment as naval assistant to the assistant chief of naval staff (ACNS) at the end of May 1917 and early promotion to captain on 18 October of the same year. In the summer of 1919 Vice-Admiral Sir A. L. Duff, former ACNS, took Henderson to China as flag captain in the cruiser *Hawkins*. Returning to Greenwich in 1922 for senior officers' technical and war courses, Henderson again distinguished himself and was immediately transferred to the war course staff, where he remained until 1926.

After brief duty at the Admiralty working on oil supplies, Henderson began his relationship with aircraft-carriers by becoming captain of HMS *Furious* from 1926 to 1928. He was promoted rear-admiral on 1 March 1929 and was sent on another advisory mission, this time in Romania. After more committee work at the Admiralty, Henderson was appointed the first rear-admiral, aircraft-carriers, in September 1931, flying his flag in *Courageous*. Henderson had direct responsibility for the operations of the carriers of the Atlantic Fleet and an advisory role to other fleets on all matters connected with the Fleet Air Arm (FAA). In the words of Stephen Roskill:

> Henderson was to prove an inspired selection for the new appointment, and much of the credit for the progress made in naval aviation in the 1930s and for improving the status and morale of the FAA should go to him. (Roskill, 200)

Henderson hauled down his flag at sea in September 1933. He was promoted vice-admiral on 10 October that year and on 23 April 1934 replaced Charles Forbes as third sea lord and controller. Thus began the high point of Henderson's career, with direct responsibility under the equally able first sea lord, Chatfield, for designing and building the fleet required by the rearmament programme. Sir Vincent Baddeley, a distinguished civil servant colleague, wrote later of this 'excellent opportunity to a man of Henderson's great administrative ability, infectious energy, and openness of mind. He took up his new post with buoyant enthusiasm' (*DNB*). Pressed by

Henderson, the normally cautious Admiralty took the most liberal view of Treasury controls to squeeze the maximum number and quality of ships into the building programmes. Henderson shared Chatfield's wish to prevent future warships suffering the catastrophic fate of their First World War predecessors and high levels of armoured protection were a feature of the vessels of this period. This required foreign sources of armour-plate and Henderson personally went to Czechoslovakia to secure supplies.

Henderson knew he was capable as no other of managing the hectic pace of naval rearmament and volunteered to continue in post as controller even at the cost of his future career. This may have reflected knowledge as to his health, which began to collapse in early 1938. He returned to duty after only four days sick at home but forcing himself was bound to exact its price. On 16 January 1939, two days after he was promoted admiral, illness again struck, this time terminally. Henderson was transferred from a London clinic to the Royal Naval Hospital, Haslar, Hampshire, on 19 April, a cerebral thrombosis being diagnosed. On 2 May he died, a major loss to the service. Henderson had been appointed CB in May 1919, KCB in February 1936, and was specially promoted GCB in 1939 by the king shortly before his death. He also received honours from the kings of those countries whose naval development he had assisted; he was appointed to the Greek order of St Saviour and received the grand cross of the order of the Crown of Romania.   ERIC J. GROVE

Sources PRO, ADM 196/46, fol. 76 · DNB · S. W. Roskill, *The period of reluctant rearmament, 1930–1939* (1976), vol. 2 of *Naval policy between the wars* · G. A. H. Gordon, *British seapower and procurement between the wars* (1988) · WWW · CGPLA Eng. & Wales (1939)
Archives NMM, corresp. with Julian S. Corbett · PRO, Admiralty MSS, ADM
Wealth at death £56,804 7s. 9d.: probate, 21 Aug 1939, CGPLA Eng. & Wales

Henderson, Roy Galbraith (1899–2000), singer and singing teacher, was born on 4 July 1899 at 12 Mansions House, Edinburgh, the son of Alexander Roy Henderson, Congregational minister, and his wife, Jane Boyd, *née* Galbraith. His father was soon afterwards appointed principal of Paton College, Nottingham, where Henderson was educated at the grammar school. After active service in the First World War, in the Artists' Rifles, Nottinghamshire and Derbyshire regiment, he studied singing at the Royal Academy of Music under Thomas Meux. As winner of the medal for the most distinguished student of his year and with a reputation for reliability and quick learning, he was soon in demand as a soloist in concert work and oratorio. On 27 March 1926 he married Bertha Collin Smyth (1901/2–1985), daughter of Thomas Wilson Smyth, shipowner. They had a son and two daughters.

In April 1925 Henderson gained a major success in taking over at short notice the baritone part in the first London performance of Delius's *Mass of Life* under the German conductor Paul von Klenau. He was heard altogether fourteen times in this rarely performed work, mostly under Sir Thomas Beecham and nearly always singing from memory. The composer himself admired Henderson greatly and asked for him as soloist in his *Sea Drift* and, in 1933, for the première of the *Idyll* at a Promenade Concert under Sir Henry Wood. Other works by British composers in which Henderson was soloist at the first performance include Dyson's *The Canterbury Pilgrims* (1931) and Vaughan Williams's *Five Tudor Portraits* (1935) and *Dona nobis pacem* (1936). He was also one of the sixteen soloists chosen for the *Serenade to Music*, written by Vaughan Williams as a tribute to Sir Henry Wood on his jubilee as a conductor in 1938.

Henderson's career in opera began with the British National Opera Company in 1926, when he appeared as Ford in Verdi's *Falstaff*. With little more stage experience and no orchestral rehearsal he was co-opted into the 1928 international season at Covent Garden as a last-minute replacement for the artist scheduled to sing Donner in Wagner's *Das Rheingold*. As a reward for his success he was engaged for later appearances in the season as Kothner in *Die Meistersinger von Nürnberg* and the herald in *Lohengrin*. Reviews were good, and the *Daily News* ran a headline 'Fame in a Night' (*Daily News*, 12 May 1928), but he never sang at Covent Garden again. Instead, Glyndebourne became the opera house with which he developed the closest associations. He sang Count Almaviva in Mozart's *Le nozze di Figaro* on the opening night of the company's first season, in 1934, and appeared every summer until the outbreak of war. His other roles were Guglielmo in *Così fan tutte*, Papageno in *Die Zauberflöte*, and Masetto in *Don Giovanni*. In 1940 the company went on tour with a production of *The Beggar's Opera* in which he played Peachum and would have taken over as Macheath had the fall of France and evacuation from Dunkirk not forced a cancellation.

Henderson retired from singing at the age of fifty-two, very much as he had planned to do from the start. Throughout his career he was regarded as one of the leading British soloists; it was, however, in an age when opportunities to sing abroad rarely arose, so his name was little known outside the United Kingdom. He had an extensive song repertory, but much of his best singing was done in large-scale choral works such as the Bach passions, Mendelssohn's *Elijah*, and Vaughan Williams's *Sea Symphony*. He was greatly admired in Elgar's *The Apostles*, of which *The Times* wrote, on a performance by the Royal Choral Society in 1951:

> Among the solo singers the most outstanding was Mr Roy Henderson, who delivered the words of Jesus with a gentle, firm conviction that tallied with his ability to sing the whole of the music without a score in his hand. He breathed the true atmosphere as by nature fitted to it. (*The Times*, 11 May 1951)

From 1940 to 1974 Henderson was one of the most sought-after of teachers at the Royal Academy of Music. His pupils, in addition to the contralto Kathleen Ferrier, included the soprano Jennifer Vyvyan, the contralto Norma Procter, and the baritone John Shirley-Quirk. In 1954 he contributed to Neville Cardus's *Memoir of Kathleen Ferrier*; she habitually referred to him as 'my prof'. He also conducted her in a recording of Pergolesi's *Stabat mater* made with the Nottingham Oriana Choir, which he founded and from 1937 to 1952 directed. He conducted the Huddersfield Glee and Madrigal Society from 1932 to 1939 and the Bournemouth Municipal Choir from 1942 to 1953. He was appointed CBE in 1970.

Henderson's solo recordings included Butterworth's *A Shropshire Lad*, and with the pre-war Glyndebourne company under Fritz Busch he took the roles of Almaviva and Masetto in the first complete recordings of *Le nozze di Figaro* and *Don Giovanni*. To celebrate his hundredth birthday a collection of his records was issued on compact disc, the earliest of them dating back to 1925 and the old pre-electrical recording process: he took some pride in being, as he said, 'one of the last people alive to have sung into a horn' (Potter). He liked also to say, in his final months, that he belonged to the still smaller number of singers who had lived in three centuries. He died at the Musicians' Benevolent Fund nursing home, Ivor Newton House, 10–12 Edward Road, Bromley, Kent, on 16 March 2000. He was survived by his son and a daughter, his wife and one daughter having predeceased him.   J. B. STEANE

Sources Royal Opera House, Covent Garden, London, archives · S. Hughes, *Glyndebourne: a history* (1981) · *The Times* (17 March 2000) · *Daily Telegraph* (17 March 2000) · *The Guardian* (17 March 2000) · *The Independent* (17 March 2000) · *The Scotsman* (20 March 2000) · *WWW* · T. Potter, disc notes, *Roy Henderson centenary recital* (1999) [Dutton 7038] · L. Carley, ed., *Delius: a life in letters*, 2 (1988) · *Musical Britain* (1951) · personal knowledge (2004) · private information (2004) · m. cert. · d. cert.
Likenesses photograph, 1940, repro. in *The Times* · N. Elder, photograph, 1998–9, repro. in *The Independent*
Wealth at death under £200,000—gross; under £200,000—net: probate, 1 June 2000, *CGPLA Eng. & Wales*

Henderson, Thomas (1798–1844), astronomer, was born in Dundee on 28 December 1798, the youngest of the family of two sons and three daughters of Thomas Henderson, a tradesman, and his wife, Isabell Rollo. When he was young his father died. He was sent first to Dundee grammar school, then in 1811 for two years to the high school, where, under the rector, Thomas Duncan (later professor of mathematics at St Andrews University), he distinguished himself in all his studies and received his first instruction in mathematics, natural philosophy, and chemistry. Like his elder brother, John, who became a noted advocate in Edinburgh but died at the age of only thirty-eight, Thomas was destined for a legal career, and when he was fifteen he entered the office of Mr Small, a Dundee solicitor, where his brother had been a partner. Six years later he moved to the office of a writer to the signet in Edinburgh, where his abilities earned the friendship and patronage of James Gibson Craig, on whose recommendation he was appointed secretary, first to the judge John Clerk, Lord Eldin, then to the earl of Lauderdale, and finally to Lord Advocate Jeffrey.

Astronomical interests Henderson's interests in astronomy undoubtedly began in early life, but in Edinburgh he had access to the observatory of the Astronomical Institution on Calton Hill, where he was encouraged by Captain Basil Hall, professors John Leslie and William Wallace, and others to make use of the modest equipment: the transit telescope and clock and the Troughton altazimuth

instrument. His official duties also took him to London for months at a time, where he made friends with several astronomers, notably Sir James South, who gave him full use of his Campden Hill observatory. However, since he had poor eyesight, perhaps a squint, Henderson's observing abilities were limited, so he set out to master the mathematics of practical astronomy—the reduction of observations and the computations of eclipses, occultations, and comet orbits. In 1824 he communicated to Dr Thomas Young, secretary to the board of longitude, an amended method of calculating the occultation of a fixed star by the moon. He received the thanks of the board, and his method was published in the *Quarterly Journal of Science, Literature and the Arts* (18, 1825, 343–7) and in the *Nautical Almanac* for the years 1827 to 1831. His paper to the Royal Society 'On the difference of meridians of the royal observatories of Greenwich and Paris' (*PTRS*, 117, 1827, 286) added to the reliability of Sir John Herschel's result by the detection and elimination of a small error and recalculation of the entire process. In a number of subsequent papers on the reduction of observations and on ephemerides he demonstrated the method of determining probable errors then in common use in Germany but not in Britain. A list of moon-culminating stars for Captain John Ross's Arctic expedition in 1830 earned him the gratitude of the Royal Astronomical Society (RAS), of which he became a fellow in 1832. Meanwhile he continued his legal duties and refused all payment for his astronomical calculations, although he was devoting much of his small income to supporting his mother and sisters.

In December 1828 Dr Robert Blair, the long-absent regius professor of practical astronomy at Edinburgh, died. Dr Young and Basil Hall supported Henderson as his successor, but Blair had for forty-three years treated the post as a sinecure, and the government was unwilling to appoint a new man until the effectiveness of the office was ascertained. In the following June Young himself died; he had earlier indicated in a document to Professor Rigaud of Oxford that he knew of no person more competent to succeed him as superintendent of the *Nautical Almanac* than Henderson. However, the post reverted to the astronomer royal, John Pond, who offered Henderson a share in the duties, with remuneration. He declined but continued to assist Pond with data.

Astronomer at the Cape On the death of Fearon Fallows in 1831 Henderson was regarded as one of the best candidates to direct the government observatory at the Cape of Good Hope. He was reluctant to leave Britain, and accepted only at the persuasion of his friends. He arrived at the Cape in April 1832 and with one assistant, Lieutenant Meadows, embarked upon a prodigious work programme including between 5000 and 6000 observations of the places of southern stars (later presented to the RAS as a catalogue of 172 stars); a marginally better estimate of the moon's parallax (57 minutes, 1.8 seconds of arc); the places of Encke's and Beila's comets; the transit of Mercury of 5 May 1832; Jupiter's satellites; lunar occultations; and a series of observations of Mars at opposition, by which he later deduced, by comparing data from Greenwich, Cambridge, and Altona, a solar parallax of 9.125 seconds of arc, higher than the then accepted 8.8. These observations were made with indifferent instruments—a 10 foot Dolland transit telescope and a mural circle by W. and S. Jones—which were both suffering from the ravages of the climate. Henderson, exhausted and ill, resigned in May 1833, having written to Thomas Maclear (his successor) that he had had enough of government neglect, Meadows's bickering, and the 'dismal swamp among slaves and savages'. He returned to Edinburgh to reduce his Cape observations, meanwhile subsisting on a £100 pension from his legal firm.

Henderson's most striking result was the series of observations of the bright double star α Centauri, whose large proper motion had been pointed out to him by Manuel Johnson at St Helena. A residual error of about 1 second of arc was, after further observations of its right ascension by Maclear at the Cape, concluded to be the star's parallax (later estimates gave 0.75 seconds of arc), but was not announced as such to the RAS until January 1839 (Henderson, 61–8). This, however, was two months after the announcement by Friedrich Wilhelm Bessel of Königsberg of the parallax of 61 Cygni, for which he was given the RAS gold medal. Henderson had been over-cautious because there had been spurious parallaxes before. Later he announced possible parallaxes for Sirius and other southern stars, most probably illusory. Despite this he and Bessel became firm friends and holidayed in Scotland together.

Astronomer royal for Scotland In 1834 an arrangement had taken place whereby the Astronomical Institution of Edinburgh's 'scientific observatory' on Calton Hill was made over to the university and to the government to be run as a public establishment under a principal observer who would be jointly regius professor and astronomer royal for Scotland. Henderson, with the support and encouragement of South, George Biddell Airy, Francis Baily, Sir Thomas Brisbane, and others was elected on 18 August 1834 to be the first holder of the post (at £300 per annum), which was no longer a sinecure. He lost no time in commencing to measure the positions of stars and planets with the Fraunhofer transit circle and the Troughton mural circle, and with the help of an assistant, Alexander Wallace, made some 60,000 observations in ten years. The board of visitors, which included the astronomer royal, Airy, was lavish in praise of Henderson's labours and insisted on a speedy publication of the results. The first five quarto volumes of the *Edinburgh Astronomical Observations* (for results 1835–9) were published by Henderson, and the rest appeared after his death, mostly produced by his successor, Charles Piazzi Smyth. Later investigations showed large systematic errors on account of the unexpectedly high coefficient of expansion of the sandstone transit piers. Henderson found little time for teaching, but sometimes deputized in mathematics or physics for ailing colleagues. He was elected fellow of the Royal Society of Edinburgh in 1834 and of London in 1840.

On 16 November 1836 Henderson had married Janet Mary (1807–1842), the eldest daughter of the well-known Edinburgh optician Alexander Adie, but her death in December 1842 only weeks after the birth of their only child, Janet Mary Jane, came as a great shock to a man already weakened by a worsening heart complaint. Worn out by the workload and by the daily climb up Calton Hill from his official residence at 1 Hillside Crescent, he died of heart failure on 23 November 1844 at 1 Hillside Crescent and was buried in Greyfriars churchyard. A commemorative tablet survives on the wall of Calton Hill observatory.

The author of seventy papers, Henderson had considerable mathematical ability but was not an innovator; he cultivated the methods of Bessel and Struve whom he admired. His weak constitution was aggravated by devotion to his work and his experience of typical government neglect of his two observatories.   DAVID GAVINE

Sources *Monthly Notices of the Astronomical Society of London*, 6 (1843–5), 157–80 · H. A. Brück, *The story of astronomy in Edinburgh from its beginnings until 1975* (1983), 14–21 · J. D. North, 'Henderson, Thomas', *DSB*, 6.263–4 · *Proceedings of the Royal Society of Edinburgh*, 2 (1844–50), 35–44 · R. Grant, *History of physical astronomy, from the earliest ages to the middle of the nineteenth century* (1852), 212–551 · A. M. Clerke, *A popular history of astronomy during the nineteenth century*, 4th edn (1902), 36 · Henderson MSS, Royal Observatory, Edinburgh · Airy MSS, Royal Observatory, Herstmonceux · papers and correspondence, RAS · U. St Andr. L., special collections department, J. D. Forbes MSS · D. Gill, *A history and description of the Royal Observatory, Cape of Good Hope* (1913) · B. Warner, *Astronomers at the Royal Observatory, Cape of Good Hope* (1979), 31–6 · parish register (baptism), Dundee · tombstone of Thomas Henderson, Greyfriars churchyard, Edinburgh · T. Henderson, 'On the parallax of α Centauri', *Memoirs of the Royal Astronomical Society*, 11 (1840), 61–8
Archives RAS, MSS, papers and corresp. · Royal Observatory, Edinburgh | Royal Observatory, Herstmonceux, Airy MSS · RS, corresp. with Sir John Herschel · U. St Andr. L., J. D. Forbes MSS · U. St Andr. L., corresp. with James Forbes
Likenesses A. McBride, sketch (of Henderson?; after sketch by C. Piazzi Smyth), repro. in Warner, *Astronomers at the royal observatory*, 33
Wealth at death £1173 3s. 2d.: will, Henderson MSS, Royal Observatory, Edinburgh

Henderson, William (1810–1872), homoeopathic physician, born at Thurso on 17 January 1810, was the fourth son of William Henderson, sheriff-substitute of Caithness, and his wife, Ann Brodie. After attending Edinburgh high school, he studied medicine at the university there. He graduated MD at Edinburgh in 1831, and continued his studies for two years longer in Paris, Berlin, and Vienna. In 1832 he was appointed, at an exceptionally early age, physician to the Fever Hospital in Edinburgh, and was subsequently made pathologist to the Royal Infirmary. His acuteness of observation very soon attracted attention. Between 1835 and 1837 he contributed a series of clinical studies to the *Edinburgh Medical and Surgical Journal*, on the heart and larger blood-vessels; his work included the first notice of the ejection murmur in a case of sacculated aortic aneurysm. In 1838 he was elected fellow of the Royal College of Physicians of Edinburgh, being already a member of the city's Medico-Chirurgical Society. As early as

1841 he employed the microscope in the anatomy of the lung in pneumonia, in the assessment of the skin disease *molluscum contagiosum*, and in other pathological studies. In 1842 he was appointed to the chair of general pathology in the University of Edinburgh, and in the following year, during a fever epidemic, he was the first to show, on irrefutable grounds, that typhus and relapsing fevers were distinct diseases and due to different causes.

In 1845, after conducting an investigation into homoeopathy in the wards of the Royal Infirmary at the instigation of John Abercrombie, the chief consulting physician in Edinburgh, Henderson adopted its methods. As a consequence, he resigned his appointment at the Royal Infirmary and lost most of his practice. The majority of his colleagues distanced themselves from him. The few who stood by him begged him to abandon what they regarded as a suicidal course at a time when the profession was looking upon him as a worthy successor to Abercrombie. Henderson stood firm, feeling that whatever the loss might be he could not tamper with what he regarded as the truth. Led by Professor Syme, an attempt was also made to oust him from his chair of pathology, but it failed because Henderson's appointment was for life. Next his colleagues tried, also unsuccessfully, to exclude pathology from the obligatory curriculum of study.

Henderson's first publication on homoeopathy, entitled *An Inquiry into the Homoeopathic Practice of Medicine* (1845) drew from John Forbes a plain-spoken article in the *British and Foreign Medical Review* for January 1846, called 'Homoeopathy, allopathy, and young physic'. Unfortunately for Forbes this was regarded by the medical establishment as too sympathetic to homoeopathy and contributed to the closure of the *Review*. Henderson's reply in a 'letter' to Forbes, which appeared in the *British Journal of Homoeopathy* for 1846, and also separately, raised him in public estimation, though it did not lessen the opposition of his former colleagues. In 1851 the College of Physicians called upon him to resign his fellowship or be expelled. The intimation was not followed up by any action though in December of the same year Henderson was expelled from the Medico-Chirurgical Society.

Over many years Henderson defended himself and homoeopathy against the virulent attacks of Professor Syme and Sir James Y. Simpson, publishing several letters and articles. His clinical acumen was always recognized and even Simpson is said to have advised patients to seek his opinion. Throughout this lengthened controversy Henderson showed tact and good temper, finally winning back the esteem of the more generous of his opponents. His pamphlets were models of acute reasoning, playful irony, and good-natured banter.

In private life Henderson's wit and accomplishments made him a delightful companion. He was very fond of field sports, particularly angling. In 1869, recognizing that he was suffering from an aortic aneurysm, which had been the subject of his earliest researches, he resigned his chair and gave up most of the consulting practice at his house. He died of the aneurysm at his home, 19 Ainslie

Place, Edinburgh, on 1 April 1872. His wife, Williamina, had predeceased him; his son, Alexander Henderson, became an advocate.

GORDON GOODWIN, *rev.* BERNARD LEARY

Sources *British Journal of Homoeopathy*, 30 (1872), 617–23 · *Homoeopathic World*, 7 (1872), 115–18 · *BMJ* (20 April 1872), 435 · *Medical Register* (1870) · *Medical Register* (1872) · *Medical Register* (1873) · *Cat. of printed books* in Advocates Library, 3, 721 · *CGPLA Eng. & Wales* (1872)
Archives Royal College of Physicians of Edinburgh, lecture notes · U. Edin. L., lecture notes
Likenesses F. Schenck, lithograph (after W. Crawford, 1845), Wellcome L.

Henderson, William George (1819–1905), dean of Carlisle, born at Harbridge, Hampshire, on 25 June 1819, was eldest son of the four sons and two daughters of Vice-Admiral George Henderson (1785/6–1864) of Harbridge and his wife, Frances Elizabeth, daughter of Edward Walcott-Sympson. Educated first at Laleham, and then at King's School, Bruton, Somerset, he matriculated from Wadham College, Oxford, on 30 June 1836, was elected to a demyship at Magdalen College in July, won the chancellor's prize for Latin verse in 1839, and graduated BA with a first class in classics and a second class in mathematics in 1840, proceeding MA in 1843, DCL in 1853, and DD in 1882. He won the prize for Latin essay in 1842 and the Ellerton theological prize the next year. In 1844 he was ordained deacon, but from some doctrinal hesitation did not take priest's orders until 1859.

In 1845 Henderson was appointed headmaster of Magdalen College School, but left it in the following year to become tutor in the University of Durham, returning to Oxford for a year in 1850 to serve as proctor. In 1851 he was appointed principal of Hatfield Hall, Durham. He held a fellowship at Magdalen from 1846 to 1853, when he vacated it following his marriage (on 4 August 1852) to Jane Melville (*d.* 1901), daughter of John Dalyell of Lingo, Fife. They had eight sons (the eldest of whom was George Francis Robert *Henderson) and six daughters.

In 1852 Henderson became headmaster of Victoria College, Jersey. His success there was pronounced, and in 1862 he was appointed headmaster of Leeds grammar school. A born teacher and good organizer, devoted to his school, he remained at Leeds until 1884. He was an active member of the Surtees Society, for which he edited a number of pre-Reformation service books including: *Missale ad usum insignis ecclesiae Eboracensis* (1874), for which he collated the extant manuscripts and the five printed editions; *Manuale et processionale ad usum insignis ecclesiae Eboracensis* (1875), to which he added in an appendix an abbreviated reprint of the Sarum manual and of such manual offices as occur in the Hereford missal or manual; and *Liber pontificalis Christophori Bainbridge archiepiscopi Eboracensis* (1875), the last surviving pontifical of the old English use. In 1882 he was awarded an honorary DD by Durham University.

In 1884, on Gladstone's recommendation, Henderson was appointed to the deanship of Carlisle. Though he did not take part in public controversies, he was a staunch high-churchman, signing the 1881 memorial in favour of the toleration of ritual. He sought to popularize the cathedral services, and interested himself in philanthropic work, but owing to weak health his later years were spent in comparative retirement. Henderson died suddenly at Rose Castle, Carlisle, on 24 September 1905.

A. R. BUCKLAND, *rev.* M. C. CURTHOYS

Sources *Yorkshire Post* (25 Sept 1905) · *The Guardian* (27 Sept 1905) · J. R. Bloxam, *A register of the presidents, fellows … of Saint Mary Magdalen College*, 8 vols. (1853–85), vol. 3, p. 273; vol. 4, pp. 342–4 · W. D. Macray, *A register of the members of St Mary Magdalen College, Oxford*, 8 vols. (1894–1915), vol. 6, pp. 149–50
Archives Bodl. Oxf., transcripts of English pontificals
Likenesses W. W. Ouless, oils, 1887; at Victoria College, Jersey, 1912 · W. G. Henderson, self-portrait, mezzotint, pubd 1888 (after W. W. Ouless), BM
Wealth at death £2537 17s. 4d.: probate, 7 Dec 1905, *CGPLA Eng. & Wales*

Henderson, Sir William MacGregor [Gregor] (1913–2000), veterinary virologist and scientific administrator, was born on 17 July 1913 at 14 Cameron Park, Edinburgh, the son of William Simpson Henderson (*b.* 1870), manager of a Christmas card works, and his wife, Catherine Alice Marcus (*b.* 1874), formerly Berry. He was educated in Edinburgh at George Watson's College, Edinburgh University, and the Royal (Dick) Veterinary College where he qualified in 1935. His first appointment was as assistant to the professor of pharmacy at his old college from 1936 to 1938. He joined the Pirbright, Surrey, laboratory to study foot-and-mouth disease in 1939 and on 24 April 1941 he married (Alys) Beryl (*b.* 1921/2), daughter of Owen Cyril Goodridge. They had four children.

Gregor Henderson, as he was generally known, and Dr John Brooksby were two of Dr Ian Galloway's new recruits at that time; the three of them did sterling work on foot-and-mouth and put Pirbright at the centre of the world map of research into the disease. They succeeded in establishing methods to quantify the amount of virus in infected materials, and on infectivity titration, vaccine production, and testing on the laboratory's large herd of Devon steers. In later years Henderson applied his method of quantifying another infectious virus in cattle, which earned him an Edinburgh DSc. The advice given by Henderson and his colleagues during the massive and prolonged outbreak of the disease in Mexico from 1946 to 1954 provided the Mexican and US governments (the latter at the time had no foot-and-mouth disease laboratory) with much expertise on its control. The massive outbreak of the disease in the UK in 1952 led to a great expansion of the Pirbright laboratory and in 1957 it became the world reference laboratory for foot-and-mouth disease. By that time, however, Henderson had departed to become director of the Pan-American Foot-and-Mouth Disease Center in Rio de Janeiro. In a situation where the disease was endemic with the inevitable consequence of low productivity, Henderson applied the techniques developed at Pirbright to introduce ring vaccination. This transformed the situation and eventually led to greater control of the disease in South America.

Henderson returned to the UK in 1966 essentially to

Sir William MacGregor Henderson (1913–2000), by unknown photographer

begin a new career as a scientific administrator with the Agricultural Research Council, as head of the microbiology department at the Institute for Research on Animal Diseases at Compton, Berkshire, becoming director a year later. This was followed in 1972 by his appointment as chief executive (secretary) of the Agricultural Research Council. In that position he sought to advance the work on any scientific topic that was being pursued. Among several areas of research he set up a committee to review and assess the work being done on scrapie, remarking to Professor Fred Brown, 'whatever happens I don't want to see a report which does *not* offer insight into the way we are proceeding' (personal knowledge). He had already seen that alterations were needed, and these were forthcoming a few years later when it was appreciated that scrapie and Creutzfeldt-Jakob disease should be studied in joint programmes with the Medical Research Council. He was knighted in 1976 and in the same year elected fellow of the Royal Society and of the Royal Society of Edinburgh.

On his retirement from the Agricultural Research Council in 1978 Henderson took up a variety of other responsibilities. Although he had no biochemical background, he readily appreciated its potential when biotechnology became a key growth point for developing entirely new products and he became chairman in 1979 of the new Genetic Manipulation Advisory Group. Henderson's *Personal History of the Testing of Foot-and-Mouth Disease Vaccines in Cattle* (1985) was published after he received the Massey-Ferguson national award in 1980 for services to UK agriculture. He became a consultant to the Wellcome Foundation and a board member of the newly formed Wellcome Biotechnology and Celltech. As an adviser on the control of viral diseases which were troubling the fish-farming industry he was able to travel to the Pacific coast of Canada where salmon was farmed on a large scale.

When Lord Zuckerman retired as president of the Zoological Society in 1984 Henderson was offered, and eagerly accepted, that position. It seemed to offer the opportunity of gene research on exotic species and he enjoyed the social side which it involved. London zoo's finances were, however, in a parlous state and although Henderson secured a grant to stave off closure, he was involved in so much political wrangling that he resigned after five years.

Henderson got on easily with people from all walks of life, and was always keen to chat with former colleagues. He received the Dalrymple-Champneys cup—the premier award of the British Veterinary Association—besides many other honorary degrees and fellowships. He died on 29 November 2000 at Cholsey, Oxfordshire, survived by his wife and children.   FRED BROWN

Sources personal knowledge (2004) · W. Plowright, *The Guardian* (19 Dec 2000) · A. Steven, *The Scotsman* (14 Dec 2000) · E. Boden, *The Independent* (21 Dec 2000) · W. Henderson, *A personal history of the testing of foot-and-mouth disease vaccines in cattle* (1985) · H. H. Skinner, 'The origins of virus research at Pirbright', *Veterinary History*, new ser., 6 (1989), 31–40 · b. cert. · m. cert.
Likenesses photograph, Universal Pictorial Press and Agency, London [*see illus.*]

Hendley, William (1690/91–1724), Church of England clergyman, was baptized on 11 April 1691 at Bearsted, Kent, the son of William Hendley and his wife, Elizabeth, of Otham, Kent. He was admitted sizar at Pembroke College, Cambridge, on 28 May 1708, aged seventeen. He gained his BA in 1712 and was ordained deacon of Ely on 21 December 1712. He became a priest in London on 12 June 1715 and the following year was given the lectureship of St James's, Clerkenwell. In 1717 Hendley took part in the Bangorian controversy and published *An Appeal to the Consciences and Common Sense of the Christian Laity*, in which he criticized Benjamin Hoadly for destroying the authority of the church and of its clergy. The following year he was elected to the lectureship of St Mary's, Islington, by a majority of sixty votes. He was also chaplain to Baron Willoughby and to Charles, Lord Fitzwalter.

On 24 August 1718 Hendley preached a sermon, which he later published, at the parish church of Chislehurst in Kent, entitled 'The rich man's proper barns'; it was on the subject of charity schools. During this service Mr Campman and Mr Prat, two of the trustees of the charity school of St Anne, Aldersgate, London, held a collection for the children. However while the collection was taking place a justice of the peace, Thomas Farrington, stopped the proceedings, declaring the collection to be illegal, as the children were vagrants, and accusing them of collecting funds for the pretender, James III (James Francis Edward Stuart). Hendley refused to stop the collection and read aloud to the congregation a number of rubrics which authorized collections for charity, and declared that he would complain about the JPs to the bishop of Rochester. Despite the attempt of the JPs to stop the collection the congregation were eager to give, and even threw their money into the plate when the crowds grew so great as to prevent their reaching the collectors.

Hendley took the collection plates to the altar and, when Farrington tried to seize them, he blocked his path. Farrington ordered the congregation to disperse but Hendley insisted that the service was not yet finished and

so continued his ministrations. After the service Hendley took the money to the bishop of Rochester, and later that afternoon the rector of Chislehurst, Mr Wilson, three of the children's trustees who had made the collection, and also Hendley were bound over to the quarter sessions that evening at Maidstone. They were all then tried on 15 July 1719 and convicted of being 'evilly and seditiously dispos'd to the Government' and of procuring 'unlawful gains, under Pretence of Collecting Charities, Alms and Gifts for the Sustenence and maintenance of Boys and Girls' (Defoe, 35). They were sentenced to pay 6s. 8d. each. Following this incident Hendley published *A Defence of Charity Schools* and the entire episode was recorded in a pamphlet by Daniel Defoe.

At some point Hendley married Bithiah, daughter of John Honeycott, who had been clerk and master of the charity school of St James's, Clerkenwell; they had a daughter, Mary. Hendley died in the early autumn of 1724. In his will he asked to be buried in Islington churchyard, near the grave of his former vicar, Archdeacon Cornelius Yeate.   REBECCA LOUISE WARNER

Sources Venn, *Alum. Cant.* · W. J. Pinks, *The history of Clerkenwell*, ed. E. J. Wood, 2nd edn (1881) · D. Defoe, *Charity still a Christian virtue, or, An impartial account of the tryal and conviction of the Reverend Mr. Hendley* (1719) · IGI · W. Hendley, will, PRO, PROB 11/599
Likenesses S. Nichols, group portrait, engraving (scene at parish church of Chislehurst), repro. in Defoe, *Charity still a Christian virtue*

Hendren, Elias Henry [Patsy] (1889–1962), cricketer, was born at 5 Jessop's Row, Turnham Green, Middlesex, on 5 February 1889, the fourth of five sons (there was also a daughter) of Denis Hendren (d. 1897), a plasterer, and his wife, Dinah Mary Cave (d. 1903). Because of his Irish ancestry (the family was originally named O'Hanrahan) he was referred to by the press as Patsy. A lifelong devout Roman Catholic, he attended St Mary's School, Acton, before becoming an engineering apprentice, which he loathed. His brother Denis Hendren (1882–1962) briefly played cricket for Middlesex and introduced him to the club. He joined the Middlesex ground staff at Lord's in 1905 and made his first appearance for the county in 1907, before becoming a regular first-team player in 1909. From 1908 he also played professional football, representing Manchester City, Queen's Park Rangers, and Coventry City before 1914.

Largely self-taught, Hendren became one of the finest batsmen of his day. Speed of foot, which made him a good footballer, served him well against slow bowling. He was renowned for his ability to hook, positioning himself just inside the line of the ball. A short, solidly built man, he possessed great strength, and stood at the wicket with a slight crouch. This was matched by the speed and excellence of his catching in the deep field. But he was initially afflicted with nerves, and did not establish himself as a batsman of the highest class until after the First World War. His ability to make big scores was, however, evident at an early age. In 1914 he made 221 not out against Nottinghamshire. Earlier that year, on 6 January 1914, he married Minnie Martha Crichton Dykes (b. 1884/5), a hospital nurse, daughter of Robert Dykes, of independent means. The marriage was childless. Following war service as an engineer with the 'sportsmen's battalion' of the Royal Fusiliers, he represented England at football in the 1919 victory international against Wales, and resumed his professional football career for Brentford City before retiring in 1927.

Hendren made his breakthrough as a cricketer in the 1919 season, when he finished second in the first-class batting averages. In the following season, when Middlesex were county champions, he scored 2520 runs. He was chosen for MCC's tour of Australia over the winter of 1920–21, in spite of having misgivings about leaving his wife in England as well as his commitments to Brentford. He had a poor series against Australia in England, in 1921, but in 1922 finished top of the first-class averages. In 1923, his best season to date, he scored thirteen centuries and in the following year he made his first test centuries (132 and 145) against the South African tourists. He struck 2601 runs in 1925 but, though well into in his thirties, was still not at his peak.

On MCC's tour of Australia in 1928–9 Hendren made 169 in the first test, and in the following winter tour, against the West Indies at Port of Spain, Trinidad, in February 1930, he achieved his highest test score, 205 not out. His achievement of four double centuries during the West Indies tour, and 1765 runs at an average of 135.76, is unsurpassed as a record for an English tourist. In 1933 he made his highest score, 301 not out, for Middlesex against Worcestershire. In that year, playing for MCC against West Indies at Lord's, he wore a special cap lined with rubber, with three peaks to protect his ears and temples in the face of some hostile bowling. His wife had made it for him, and it can be seen as a precursor of the modern helmet. After an absence of three years he was recalled for England in 1934, aged forty-five, to face the Australians, and scored 132 in the third test at Manchester. His county career ended with a duck against Surrey on 31 August 1937 (though the story, which he told against himself, that his career had also begun with a duck was an embellishment). Over his career he had progressed from being a good county professional to a cricketer who was almost as big a draw north of the Thames as his friend Jack Hobbs was south of it. Only Hobbs exceeded his achievement of scoring 170 centuries, and only that great batsman and Frank Woolley made more than his 57,611 runs (at an average of 50.80).

Hendren succeeded Wilfred Rhodes as cricket coach at Harrow School, where he remained for ten years before going on to coach Sussex (1947–51). He was among the first professionals given honorary membership by MCC in 1949. In 1952 he returned to Lord's as the Middlesex scorer, a post he held until 1959. He was renowned within the game for his friendliness and for his talents as a comic and mimic. He died at Tooting Bec Hospital, Tooting, London, on 4 October 1962. His wife survived him.

IVO TENNANT

Sources I. Peebles, 'Patsy' Hendren: the cricketer and his times (1969) • E. W. Swanton, The world of cricket (1966) • E. W. Swanton, As I said at the time (1983) • M. Golesworthy, The encyclopaedia of cricket (1962) • The Times (5 Oct 1962) • b. cert. • m. cert. • d. cert. • CGPLA Eng. & Wales (1962)
Archives FILM BFI NFTVA, documentary footage • BFI NFTVA, news footage • BFI NFTVA, sports footage
Likenesses photographs, 1936–8, Hult. Arch. • J. A. Hampton, photograph, 1950, Hult. Arch. • photographs, repro. in Peebles, 'Patsy' Hendren, 92
Wealth at death £2598 7s. 1d.: probate, 6 Dec 1962, CGPLA Eng. & Wales

Hendrick [Tiyanoga, Thoyanoguen] (c.1680–1755), leader of the Mohawk Indians, was born about 1680, the son of a Mohegan father and Mohawk mother. By 1710 he had risen to a position of prominence, holding the rank of sachem among the Mohawk and living in the village of Canajorharie. The Mohawk were a key member of the Iroquois confederation (also called Five or Six Nations), which was the leading American Indian power in northeastern North America at the time. By the early eighteenth century, the Iroquois had developed an intricate, but effective, system of diplomacy that played off the rival imperial powers of Britain and France, as well as the competing individual British colonies. Typically this would mean different member nations courting opposing sides at any given time. The most eastern of the Iroquois nations, the Mohawk led what was proved to be generally favourable relations with the British. To a large degree this success was owed to Hendrick.

Hendrick first appears in the British historical record in 1710, when he and three other Iroquois sachems accompanied Peter Schuyler to London in an effort to gain Queen Anne's support for an invasion of New France. Paraded through the court and around London, the 'four Indian kings', as they became known, were an enormous success. They inspected troops, toured Bedlam (Bethlem Hospital) and met Queen Anne. The visitors, dressed in robes and turbans, gifts of Queen Anne, were followed by throngs of Londoners wherever they went. Their portraits were painted in oils by J. Verelst, but the most popular souvenir marking their visit became the penny chapbooks that circulated throughout the nation for a further century. Whether through savvy diplomacy or genuine sentiment, the ambassadors pledged their loyalty to the queen and requested missionaries to establish themselves among the Iroquois. Missionaries were dispatched and translations of Bibles and hymnbooks soon appeared, all further strengthening Iroquois-British relations. Hendrick converted, a point celebrated in the ballad of the 'four Indian kings', and was later known for preaching (Hamilton, 46).

Upon his return to North America, Hendrick became the key Mohawk link to the British and consequently a leading sachem among the Iroquois. He played an important role in the conferences that steered Iroquois diplomacy and was a leader in the delegations that met with British and colonial American representatives. Known for his oratorical skills amid a people celebrated for their oral talents, Hendrick impressed both allies and opponents in these conferences. British and American colonists saw that Hendrick kept the Iroquois from siding with the French. In 1753 he chastised the governor of New York for not trying harder to keep the Iroquois from turning to the French; unsatisfied with the governor's response, he declared the alliance finished. British ministers, foreseeing a war with France, panicked and demanded that the alliance be restored. William Johnson, colonial trader, Indian agent for New York, and close friend of Hendrick, soothed the old sachem's anger and encouraged him to return to Albany in the following July for a general congress. Here too he chastised the British for their negligence. In a speech that was printed as far away as Ipswich, he declared:

> Brethren, you were desirous we should open our Minds and Hearts to you; look at the French, they are Men; they are fortifying every where; but, we are ashamed to say it, you are all like Women, bare and open, without Fortifications.
> (*Ipswich Journal*, 7 June 1755)

War between the British and French empires in America began in earnest in 1755—a conflict that came to span the globe as the Seven Years' War. The fatal consequences of a lack of American Indian allies became vividly apparent in the first major action of the conflict, when General Edward Braddock and his force of British regulars and Virginia militia were slaughtered in the Virginia wilderness in July 1755 by a much smaller force of French Canadians and their American Indian allies. The British nation thus depended upon William Johnson to gain a much-needed victory in that year's campaigning, and he in turn called upon Hendrick. True to his warnings, the Iroquois nation would not side wholeheartedly with the British, but nevertheless he assembled 300 warriors, mostly Mohawk, to support Johnson's campaign to take Crown Point. On 8 September the British and their Iroquois allies engaged the French and their American Indian allies at Lake George. Though victorious, the British suffered heavy losses that included Hendrick. According to Daniel Klaus, Hendrick's adopted white son, Hendrick was caught in an ambush. Despite being over seventy years old, the warrior met death boldly. When surrounded he declared 'We are the six confederate Indian nations the Heads & Superiors of all Indian nations of the Continent of America' (Hamilton, 160). His death on 8 September 1755 was mourned and noted throughout the British Atlantic world. Even the *Gentleman's Magazine* carried a brief description of Hendrick and his death (November 1755, p. 519). Without his influence, the British were unable to rally substantial numbers of Iroquois for four years.

TROY O. BICKHAM

Sources *The papers of Sir William Johnson*, ed. J. Sullivan and others, 14 vols. (1921–65) • M. W. Hamilton, *Sir William Johnson: colonial American, 1715–1763* (1976) • R. Aquila, 'Hendrick', *ANB* • D. Richter, *The ordeal of the longhouse: the peoples of the Iroquois league in the era of European colonization* (1992) • J. Merrell and D. Richter, *Beyond the covenant chain: the Iroquois and their neighbors in Indian North America, 1600–1800* (1987) • T. O. Bickham, 'Noble Savages? British discussions and representations of North American Indians, 1754–1783', DPhil diss., U. Oxf., 2001, chap. 3 • E. Hinderaker, 'The "four Indian kings" and the imaginative construction of the first British Empire', *William and Mary Quarterly*, 53 (1996), 487–526 • F. Jennings and others, *Iroquois Indians: a documentary history of the diplomacy of the Six Nations and their league* (1984) • *The history of the four Indian kings* (1710) • T. Shannon, 'Dressing for success on the Mohawk frontier', *William and Mary Quarterly*, 53 (1996), 13–42 • R. P. Bond, *Queen Anne's American kings* (1952) • J. G. Garratt, *The four Indian kings* (1985)
Likenesses J. Verelst, oils, 1710, Brown University, Providence, Rhode Island, John Carter Brown Library • engraving, 1755, Brown University, Providence, Rhode Island, John Carter Brown Library

Hendriks, Rose Ellen (*fl.* 1845–1856), novelist and poet, was of a Jewish family but raised as a Christian. Her early publications were historical novels, *The Astrologer's Daughter* (1845) and *Charlotte Corday* (1846), in both of which she included introductory comments drawing attention to her youthfulness and desire for literary fame. The partly autobiographical *The Young Authoress* (1847) offers insights into the state of mind of a young female author through the character Rosalie de Rochequillon, 'who seemed always in a wild fluttering ecstasy of literary hopes and fears—always talking of Dickens, or Bulwer, or Rose Ellen Hendriks'. *The Idler Reformed* (1846) mixes romance with the political question of the abolition of slavery, and *Political Fame* (1847) is a series of essays urging self-forgetfulness in favour of great causes. The title poem of *The Wild Rose and other Poems* (1847) allegorizes her life rather obscurely, and *Chit-Chat* (1849) which attempts social and literary satire in the manner of Byron reveals her disappointment at failing to become a 'Lioness'. She announced her impending marriage in 1849 and published her last novel, *Ella, the Ballet Girl*, in 1851 under the name of Temple. In 1856 appeared a collection of poems inspired by paintings, *The Poet's Souvenir of Amateur Artists*.

Rhapsodic, didactic, often clumsy in narrative, over-eager to please the reader and over-fond of describing women with 'luxuriant masses of dark hair waving in natural curls' who 'glide' in and out of rooms, Rose Ellen Hendriks nevertheless displays herself as a writer of

Rose Ellen Hendriks (*fl.* 1845–1856), by Lowes Cato Dickinson (after Alfred Tidey)

ambition, with ideas and passions, modelled on Mme de Staël's Corinne. Like other women writers of the time, she agreed that genius was 'a dangerous, a fatal gift, especially to a female' while doing everything in her power to earn the appellation for herself.   NORMA CLARKE

Sources R. E. Hendriks, *The astrologer's daughter, an historical novel* (1845) • R. E. Hendriks, *Charlotte Corday, an historical tale* (1846) • R. E. Hendriks, *The young authoress* (1847) • R. E. Hendriks, *The wild rose, with other poems* (1847) • R. E. Hendriks, *Chit-chat, a poem* (1849)
Likenesses L. C. Dickinson, engraving (after A. Tidey), NPG [*see illus.*] • engraving, repro. in R. E. Hendriks, *The poet's souvenir of amateur artists* (1856)

Hendrix, James Marshall [Jimi] **(1942–1970)**, rock musician and songwriter, was born on 27 November 1942 at the King County Hospital, Harbourville, Seattle, Washington, USA, the first child of James Allen Hendrix (*b.* 1919), landscape gardener, and his first wife, Lucille L. Jeter (1925–1958). He was originally named Johnny Allen Hendrix by his mother while his father was fighting in the Second World War, but the latter changed the child's name by affidavit on his return. Hendrix's parents separated and eventually divorced in December 1951.

The Seattle into which Hendrix was born was a racially mixed society, and Hendrix—who was of black, Mexican, and Cherokee heritage—never encountered racism until he enlisted in the US army in May 1961. He served in the 101st airborne division as a clerk, stationed in Fort Campbell, Kentucky, but was discharged on medical grounds in July 1962 after sustaining a broken ankle in a parachute jump. He had been given his first guitar by his father in June and belonged to many local Seattle bands during his teens; being left-handed, he played the instrument upside down. After leaving the army he toured (mainly in the southern states) as a backing musician for Little Richard, Ike and Tina Turner, the Isley brothers, Jackie Wilson, and Sam Cooke. In July 1964, having relocated to New York, he formed his own band, Jimmy James and the Blue Flames, who secured a residence at Café Wah in Greenwich Village. There he was spotted by Chas Chandler, bass player with the Animals, who recognized Hendrix's potential and convinced him to return with him to London.

The group arrived in London on 24 September 1966. Hendrix was initially refused entry to the country, but Chandler, who was now acting as his manager, eventually secured a temporary visitor's permit. Plans were immediately made to form a new band—the Jimi Hendrix Experience—featuring Noel Redding, formerly of the Lovin' Kind, on bass guitar and Mitch Mitchell, formerly with Georgie Fame's Blue Flames, on drums. The Experience embarked on a tour of France in October, which was used by Chandler to hone the group's act, though Jimi had already learned his stage tricks—playing the guitar behind his back, between his legs, or with his teeth—while touring in America. These became his visual trademarks, along with a guitar-smashing routine that began unintentionally at a show in Germany the following month.

The Experience recorded its first single, 'Hey Joe', in October 1966; the second, 'Purple Haze', recorded in the

James Marshall [Jimi] Hendrix (1942–1970), by unknown photographer, 1970 [at the Isle of Wight festival]

following January, became Hendrix's signature tune, with its lyrical references to drug culture and the experience of taking LSD. Both were top ten hits in the UK. After Hendrix was finally issued with a work permit, the band was at last able to tour the UK in early 1967. They achieved the status of an overnight sensation, aided by an ever more risqué, sexually provocative stage show. On occasions Hendrix would set his guitar on fire, which led the British press, with great racial insensitivity, to dub him 'the wild man of Borneo'.

Hendrix's first LP, *Are you Experienced?*, released in May 1967, showcased his extraordinary guitar-playing, and featured innovative studio techniques such as phasing and backwards guitar that gave this and subsequent recordings their distinctive sound. There was a raw quality to this record; his second LP, *Axis Bold as Love*, released in December, was more melodic and in tune with the psychedelic, drug-influenced music of the period. His lyrics had developed an outer-space connection—he sang of, among other subjects, UFOs—and his guitar virtuosity had become more polished and fluent. Hendrix had made Britain his home, but had to leave the country for a time in the summer of 1967 because his work permit expired. By the agency of Paul McCartney, the Experience made its American début at the Monterey festival, and made a successful two-month tour of the country. Another tour of the UK followed. The year 1968 saw the Experience play in Sweden, France, Italy, and Switzerland and another tour of America. In Britain Hendrix made a guest appearance in the Dusty Springfield show, in which he sang a duet of 'Mocking Bird' with the show's host.

In October 1968 the Experience released its third LP, *Electric Ladyland*. Again Hendrix courted controversy; the cover showed nineteen naked women, and many shops refused to display it. The music contained therein showed further developments in musical sophistication; the Hendrix composition '1983 a Merman I should Turn to Be' was compared to a sound painting. 'All Along the Watchtower', a Bob Dylan song which featured on the LP, became his only top twenty hit single in the USA. At this time Hendrix was based in London at 23 Brook Street, where he lived with his long-time British girlfriend Kathy Etchingham (*b.*

1946). The composer George Frideric Handel had lived next door at no. 25; the presence of a blue plaque commemorating this inspired Hendrix at the time, and he now has his own adjacent plaque, which was unveiled in September 1997.

Following two performances at the Royal Albert Hall in February 1969, the Experience again toured America. The group disbanded after a final performance at Denver in June, which ended in a riot. Hendrix then formed the short-lived Gypsy Sons and Rainbows, featuring Mitch Mitchell on drums and Billy Cox, an old army friend, on bass. They played at the historic Woodstock music and arts fair in August, and famously ended their set with an immense (and provocative) version of the 'Star-Spangled Banner'. In November Hendrix formed an all-black group, the Band of Gypsies, featuring Billy Cox and Buddy Miles on drums. After a handful of concerts and some recording sessions (an album was issued in early 1970), they too disbanded. Much of Hendrix's energy at this time went into private jam sessions with jazz musicians such as John McLaughlin, and it is clear that he was aiming to develop his own brand of fusion music.

Hendrix's new group, The Cry of Love (with Billy Cox and Mitch Mitchell), made its début in Los Angeles in April 1970, and played at the Isle of Wight pop festival in August. European gigs followed, but with the constant rigours of travelling and little sleep Hendrix collapsed on stage at Aarhus, in Denmark. He recovered enough to continue the tour, but his appearance at the Love and Peace festival in Germany on 6 September was, tragically, his last full performance. Back in London, he attended Ronnie Scott's jazz club to see former Animal Eric Burdon's new group, War, on 16 September. He was persuaded to join the group on stage for the final two songs, the last time he played in public. On 18 September an ambulance crew was called to the Samarkand Hotel, Notting Hill, where Hendrix was staying; he was dead on arrival at St Mary Abbots Hospital, Kensington. The coroner returned an open verdict, recording the causes of death as barbiturate intoxication and inhalation of vomit; accusations of incompetence and, still more dubiously, of racism were subsequently levelled against the ambulance crew who treated him. He was buried at the Dunlap Baptist Church, Seattle, on 1 October. With 'Voodoo Chile' Hendrix scored a posthumous number one single in the UK in late 1970, and there were several subsequent album releases of unreleased, live concert, and bootleg material. His influence was lasting and profound, and can be detected in many modern rock genres, including heavy metal and rap. A large collection of Hendrix memorabilia is on show at the Experience Music Project, Seattle, an interactive display museum designed by Frank O. Gehry.   TONY BROWN

Sources T. Brown, *Jimi Hendrix: a visual documentary* (1992) • T. Brown, *Jimi Hendrix: in his own words* (1994) • T. Brown, *Hendrix: final days* (1997) • T. Brown, *Jimi Hendrix: concert files* • T. Brown, www.hendrix-archives.demon.co.uk/contents.htm [Jimi Hendrix archives] • *The Times* (19 Sept 1970) • C. S. Murray, *Crosstown traffic: Jimi Hendrix and post war pop* (1989) • K. Etchingham, *Through Gypsy eyes* (1998) • J. Piccarella, 'Hendrix, Jimi', *New Grove dictionary of American music*; repr. in *The Jimi Hendrix companion*, ed. C. Potash (1996) • F. Owen and S. Reynolds, 'Why Hendrix still matters', *Spin* (April 1999); repr. in *The Jimi Hendrix companion*, ed. C. Potash (1996) • d. cert.

Archives priv. coll. | FILM BFI NFTVA, *The South Bank show*, ITV, 1 Oct 1989 • BFI NFTVA, *Mojo working*, 27 Nov 1992 • BFI NFTVA, *Reputations*, 5 June 1999 • BFI NFTVA, documentary footage • BFI NFTVA, performance footage | SOUND BL NSA, documentary recordings • BL NSA, oral history interviews • BL NSA, performance recordings

Likenesses photograph, 1970, Hult. Arch. [*see illus.*] • photographs, Hult. Arch.

Hendy, Sir Philip Anstiss (1900–1980), art administrator, was born at the Grammar School, Swifts Lane, Carlisle, on 27 September 1900, only son of Frederick James Robert Hendy, later director of the department of education, Oxford University (1919–28), and his wife, Caroline Isabelle, daughter of A. W. Potts, first headmaster of Fettes College. He was elected a king's scholar of Westminster School in 1914, and a Westminster exhibitioner of Christ Church, Oxford, in 1919. In 1923, after obtaining his BA degree with a third class in modern history (MA, 1937), he became assistant to the keeper and lecturer at the Wallace Collection, London, where he began work on a new edition of the catalogue. It was on the strength of his draft entries for this, shown by the keeper, S. J. Camp, to one of the trustees of the Isabella Stewart Gardner Museum, Boston, that Hendy was invited to catalogue the Gardner paintings; he was financed by the trustees to live in Italy for three years, preparing the catalogue, which was published in 1931.

With a growing reputation in Boston, in 1930 Hendy was appointed curator of paintings in the Museum of Fine Arts. With a budget of $10,000 to spend on modern paintings from Europe, he purchased works by Braque, Gino Severini, Eugene Berman, and Pavel Tchelitchew, among others. In addition, he chose works by contemporary British painters from the Camden Town and London groups, including W. R. Sickert, S. F. Gore, John Nash, and Robert Bevan. The trustees of the museum were alarmed by such radical acquisitions, and in 1933 Hendy resigned in the midst of a quarrel precipitated partially by his purchase of Matisse's *Carmelina* (1903), a controversial study of the nude.

A year after his return to England, Hendy accepted in 1934 the directorship of the Leeds City Art Gallery. The wartime evacuation of that gallery to Temple Newsam House near by gave Hendy scope for his undoubted talents, in rearranging the pictures in a fine eighteenth-century setting; and from 1936 until 1946 he combined his work for Leeds with the Slade professorship at Oxford. It was his success at Leeds and Temple Newsam that led to his appointment in 1946 to succeed Sir Kenneth Clark as director of the National Gallery. He held that post for twenty-one years; and he was knighted in 1950. He was president of the International Council of Museums (1959–65); and after retirement in 1967 he spent three years (1968–71) as adviser to the Israel Museum in Jerusalem.

At the National Gallery, Hendy's first task was to undertake the rehabilitation of the pictures returned from air-

Sir Philip Anstiss Hendy (1900–1980), by Howard Coster, 1950s

appointment such as Hendy's to the Wallace Collection in 1923, straight from Oxford with such limited experience, shortly became a thing of the past.

Hendy was handsome in a slightly exotic way, dark, tall, and thin, and had an undeniable charm of manner. He married twice: first, on 4 April 1925, Kythé Caroline (*b.* 1901/2), eldest daughter of Francis Ogilvy, a member of the London stock exchange; they had a daughter and a son. He married, second, Cicely, widow of (Charles) Christopher Martin, and daughter of Captain Thomas Lewis Prichard, of the Royal Welch Fusiliers. She cared for him after a severe stroke in 1975 left him in poor health, at their home at Great Haseley, near Oxford. Hendy died at the John Radcliffe Hospital in Oxford on 6 September 1980.

JAMES BYAM SHAW, *rev.*

Sources *The Times* (8 Sept 1980) · T. Cox, 'Sir Philip Hendy', *Burlington Magazine*, 123 (1981), 33 · H. D., 'Sir Philip Hendy', *Annual Obituary* (1980), 514–16 · H. Hall, 'Early twentieth-century British paintings in the Museum of Fine Arts, Boston', *Apollo*, 120 (1984), 195–200 · b. cert. · m. cert. [Kythé Caroline Ogilvy] · d. cert. · *CGPLA Eng. & Wales* (1980)

Archives National Gallery, London, corresp., diaries, and papers | Tate collection, corresp. with Lord Clark

Likenesses H. Coster, photograph, 1950–59, NPG [*see illus.*] · photograph, repro. in H. D., 'Sir Philip Hendy', 514

Wealth at death £29,615: probate, 17 Dec 1980, *CGPLA Eng. & Wales*

Heneage, George (1482/3–1549). *See under* Heneage, Sir Thomas (*b.* in or before 1532, *d.* 1595).

Heneage, Michael (1540–1600), antiquary, was born on 27 September 1540, the second son of Robert Heneage (*d.* 1556), esquire, of Lincoln and St Katherine Cree, London, and his first wife, Lucy (*d. c.*1554), daughter and coheir of Ralph Buckton of Hemswell, Lincolnshire. His father, an auditor of the duchy of Lancaster, later married Margaret, sister of Thomas Manners, earl of Rutland; his elder brother, Sir Thomas *Heneage (*d.* 1595), was a gentleman of the privy chamber by 1565, and subsequently vice-chamberlain of the household and chancellor of the duchy of Lancaster. Heneage matriculated at St John's College, Cambridge, in 1559, graduated BA in 1563, became a fellow in the same year, and proceeded MA in 1566. He was admitted to Gray's Inn in 1567. Heneage sat in four Elizabethan parliaments, representing Arundel (1571), East Grinstead (1572), Tavistock (1589), and Wigan (1593), although no evidence of his actions has come to light. In 1576 he and Thomas were appointed joint keepers of the records in the Tower of London, the principal depository for historical documents. The opposition of the master of the rolls, Sir William Cordell, who claimed the right to nominate to the keepership, was overcome by a compromise, whereby he appointed the Heneages, who were then confirmed in their position by the queen on 29 May 1581.

Michael Heneage enjoyed a distinguished career as an archivist, producing digests of charters, escheats, and related documents. The University of Cambridge acknowledged the assistance he gave to Robert Hare, the compiler of university records. Thomas Milles mentioned his help

conditioned storage in Wales during the war to the damaging atmosphere of London. His 1947 exhibition of pictures cleaned by the restorer Helmut Ruhemann occasioned criticism, much of it unjustified; letters to the press had alleged that Rubens's *Chapeau de paille*, Rembrandt's *Woman Bathing*, and Velázquez's *Philip IV* were spoilt. In 1961 Hendy was once again at the centre of controversy, when the theft of Goya's portrait of the duke of Wellington led to public criticism of the gallery's security systems. But Hendy rode both storms. He was naturally contentious and uncompromising, and his relationship with some of his trustees and senior staff was often turbulent. But he had loyal friends also, among his trustees and chairman—Henry Moore, Sir J. Alan N. Barlow, Lord Robbins, and Sir John Witt—and his achievement can be regarded as considerable in a difficult period.

Hendy's writings on art are full of original observations and ideas, even if sometimes marred by immature prejudices (his criticism of the Pre-Raphaelites, for instance, was intemperate). His publications included a general essay on Spanish art (1946), monographs on Giovanni Bellini (1945), Masaccio (1957), and Piero della Francesca (1968), and a small book on Matthew Smith (1944). His best achievement, probably, remains the Gardner catalogue, completed when he was less than thirty years old (republished 1974); his descriptions and appreciations of individual pictures there are more interesting than those of most modern catalogues. He belonged to a generation of museum officials who were still, strictly speaking, amateurs: interested in art, but self-taught in art history. An with the *Catalogue of Honor* (1610). Heneage was succeeded as keeper of the records by Peter Proby and William Lambarde, the latter his colleague in the Elizabethan society of antiquaries. Two papers delivered by Heneage to the society survive, on the topics of the antiquity of arms and sterling money. His only known surviving digest, on English noble families, was purchased from his widow by Sir Robert Cotton (BL, Cotton MS, Claudius C.i).

In 1577 Heneage had married Grace, daughter of Robert Honywood of Charing, Kent. At the time of his death all four of his surviving sons and two of his daughters were still minors. He died in modest circumstances on 30 December 1600 at his house at Hoxton, Essex; his widow was still living in 1601. Heneage had been a long-time resident of the London parish of St Katharine Coleman. His will, dated the day before his death, records leasehold property in Yorkshire and shows him taking particular care to dispose of his books. It also reveals a deeply devout protestant, for whom Christ was 'the verie love of my life, and life of my soule' (fol. 20v).　　　　　　J. D. ALSOP

Sources HoP, *Commons, 1558–1603*, 2.289–93 · will, PRO, PROB 11/97, fols. 20v–22v · T. Hearne, *A collection of curious discourses*, 2 vols. (1775) · J. Evans, *A history of the Society of Antiquaries* (1956) · *The diary of Henry Machyn, citizen and merchant-taylor of London, from AD 1550 to AD 1563*, ed. J. G. Nichols, CS, 42 (1848), 111, 403 · L. Fox, ed., *English historical scholarship in the sixteenth and seventeenth centuries* (1956), 18 · M. McKisack, *Medieval history in the Tudor age* (1971), 77–8 · R. G. Lang, ed., *Two Tudor subsidy assessment rolls for the city of London, 1541 and 1581*, London RS, 29 (1993), 133 · R. Cooke, *Visitation of London, 1568*, ed. H. Stanford London and S. W. Rawlins, [new edn], 2 vols. in one, Harleian Society, 109–10 (1963), 149 · L. Campbell and F. Steer, *A catalogue of manuscripts in the College of Arms collections*, 1 (1988), 299–300, 484 · Venn, *Alum. Cant.*, 1/2.354 · W. J. Jones, *The Elizabethan court of chancery* (1967)

Archives BL, Cotton MS Claudius C.i

Heneage, Sir Thomas (*b.* before **1482**, *d.* **1553**), courtier, was the eldest of the four sons of John Heneage (1452–1530) of Hainton, Lincolnshire, and his wife, Katherine, daughter of Thomas Wymbish of Nocton in the same county. The Heneages were a rising family in Lincolnshire. John, a lawyer, became prominent in local government there, as did his younger sons Robert (the father of another Sir Thomas *Heneage and of the antiquary Michael *Heneage) and John, who was returned as MP twice for Grimsby and once for Lincolnshire, while their brother George *Heneage [*see under* Heneage, Sir Thomas] became dean of Lincoln. The elder Sir Thomas strengthened his position in the county when he married Katherine (*d.* 1575), daughter of Sir John Skipwith of South Ormsby.

Heneage began his career in the household of Cardinal Wolsey. He was gentleman usher to Wolsey by March 1521, although he was already involved in the government of Lincolnshire, and held the post of customer of petty custom in the port of London. As a member of Wolsey's privy chamber he accompanied the cardinal on his embassy to Bruges in 1521 and Calais in 1527. He had taken over a large part of Wolsey's correspondence by the early 1520s.

In 1528 Wolsey transferred Heneage to Henry VIII's privy chamber as a response to the king's intention to marry Anne Boleyn. Her elevation in the royal affections had been accompanied by an increase in the political influence of her father, Sir Thomas Boleyn, and her uncle, the duke of Norfolk. The Howard/Boleyn faction was focused on the royal court, and so Wolsey, who needed his own clients close to the king, placed Heneage in the king's privy chamber. Heneage, who was thus effectively Wolsey's man with the king, sent Wolsey reports of the king's actions, and instructions from the king to his minister. As he was acceptable to Anne Boleyn, he also acted as intermediary between her and Wolsey. However, towards the end of 1528 Wolsey's instinctive distrust of anyone close to the king extended even towards his own client, and Wolsey relied instead on Sir John Russell to give him the news of the court.

Wolsey's instinct concerning Heneage proved correct, for when the minister fell from favour Heneage dissociated himself from his master. When Wolsey sought his help Heneage replied that Wolsey should 'content yourself with that you have' for 'the king will be good and gracious to your Grace' (*LP Henry VIII*, vol. 4, no. 6447). For the next few years Heneage quietly served the king and emerged as one of the leading gentlemen of the privy chamber. In an order of 10 April 1532 the gentlemen were divided in two groups headed by a noble and a commoner. The commoner in one group was Henry Norris, the groom of the stool, while Heneage headed the other with Lord Rochford, Anne Boleyn's brother. Heneage is reported to have been a member of the very small group present when Henry VIII married Anne on 25 January 1533.

The fall of the queen in 1536 resulted in the execution of both Rochford and Norris, and Heneage replaced Norris as groom of the stool and chief gentleman of the privy chamber, becoming a client of Thomas Cromwell, once his colleague in Wolsey's household. He once again took up his role as link between the king and his minister, although he was now Cromwell's man with the king. A system was developed in which Thomas Wriothesley acted as Cromwell's secretary, with Ralph Sadler as the messenger between Wriothesley and court and Heneage responsible for getting the king's signature on documents. Heneage was knighted on 18 October 1537.

Throughout the 1530s Heneage gained in influence, and it became common that anyone corresponding with a member of the court would ask to be commended to Heneage. By the 1540s he always headed the privy chamber at such official functions as the reception of Anne of Cleves, or the marriage of the king to Katherine Parr. He had survived the fall of Cromwell, but his presumed religious conservatism left him out of place in the growing evangelical atmosphere of the privy chamber in which Sir Anthony Denny, technically Heneage's junior, dominated. In the 1540s Heneage, though still very much involved in dealing with the king's privy accounts, became less influential in government, until in October 1546 he was replaced as chief gentleman of the privy chamber by Denny. Since he must have been about sixty he may have retired—whether voluntarily or not is unclear—on the grounds of age. Nevertheless at Henry

VIII's funeral Heneage was recorded as a gentleman of the privy chamber extra ordinary.

Heneage continued to serve as a gentleman of the privy chamber under Edward VI, but in a largely honorific capacity. He took little part in government and concentrated instead on his business dealings with William, Lord Willoughby of Parham, who had married Heneage's only child, Elizabeth. In 1553, according to Robert Wingfield, Heneage was slow to declare his support for Mary, but eventually made his way to the princess's camp at Ipswich and was permitted to congratulate Mary on her imminent victory. This done, 'he went back home, dying a few days later as if seized by a stroke thanks to this unexpected cause for joy' (MacCulloch, 270). He may well have acted thus in the interests of his son-in-law, who had signed the letters patent on behalf of Lady Jane Grey. Heneage died on 21 August 1553 and was buried in the chancel of Hainton parish church, as was his widow when she died in 1575.   MICHAEL RIORDAN

Sources LP Henry VIII · A. R. Maddison, ed., Lincolnshire pedigrees, 2, Harleian Society, 51 (1903) · D. R. Starkey, 'Intimacy and innovation', The English court, ed. D. Starkey (1987), 71–118 · D. R. Starkey, 'Court and government', Revolution reassessed, ed. C. Coleman and D. R. Starkey (1986), 29–58 · E. W. Ives, Anne Boleyn (1986) · J. G. Nichols, ed., The chronicle of Calais, CS, 35 (1846) · D. MacCulloch, 'The Vita Mariae Angliae Reginae of Robert Wingfield of Brantham', Camden miscellany, XXVIII, CS, 4th ser., 29 (1984), 181–301 · C. Haigh, English reformations (1993) · lord chamberlain's department, records of special events, PRO, LC 2/2 · J. C. Wedgwood and A. D. Holt, History of parliament … 1439–1509, 2 vols. (1936–8) · DNB · HoP, Commons, 1509–58, 2.334–5 · will, PRO, PROB 11/58, sig. 31 [Dame Katherine Heneage]

Heneage, Sir Thomas (b. in or before **1532**, d. **1595**), courtier, was the eldest son of Robert Heneage (d. 1556), landowner of Lincoln, and his first wife, Lucy (d. c.1554), daughter and heir of Ralph Buckton of Hemswell, Lincolnshire. Although the youngest of four brothers, including Sir Thomas *Heneage (d. 1553) and George Heneage [see below], Robert Heneage built up estates in Lincolnshire and Yorkshire through his career in royal service as auditor of the duchy of Lancaster, surveyor of forests, and customer of London. He settled Legbourne Priory, Yorkshire, on his heir, Thomas. His younger sons included Michael *Heneage (1540–1600). Thomas Heneage already had ambitions that extended well beyond Lincolnshire. In 1549 he matriculated at Queen's College, Oxford, though apparently without taking a degree; his MA of 1564 was honorary and his admission to Gray's Inn in 1565 does not indicate any legal study.

Heneage married Anne (c.1530–1593), daughter of Sir Nicholas Poyntz of Iron Acton, Gloucestershire, and his wife, Joan, on 5 November 1554. They had a daughter, Elizabeth (1556–1633), who married Moyle Finch and was created first countess of Winchilsea in 1628. In October 1553 Heneage was returned as MP for Stamford, Lincolnshire, possibly through his father's influence, but more probably through that of his cousin, the sheriff Sir William Skipwith, or through Sir William Cecil, whose seat Stamford normally was. Heneage may possibly have opposed Mary I's restoration of Catholicism: his will is

strikingly protestant. In 1559 he was MP for Arundel, Sussex, most probably through the influence of his friend and master, Henry FitzAlan, twelfth earl of Arundel.

The stewardship of Hatfield, Hertfordshire, in 1561 was the first fruit of Elizabeth I's favour. Heneage, so William Camden reported, was 'a man for his elegancy of life and pleasantness of discourse, born, as it were, for the court' (HoP, Commons, 1558–1603, 2.292)—where, indeed, he spent the rest of his life. He was in the privy chamber soon after Elizabeth's accession (as too, apparently, was his wife, an extraordinary gentlewoman of the privy chamber from 1559) and certainly before he was formally recorded as a gentleman of the privy chamber about 1565. By October 1565 his influence with her was already exciting the jealousy of Robert Dudley, earl of Leicester, the queen's favourite. Heneage received offices, lands, leases, and reversions almost every year, culminating in 1570, when he secured a major post, the treasurership of the queen's chamber, which disbursed about £15,000 per annum. He was knighted on 1 December 1577. In 1587 he succeeded the new lord chancellor, Sir Christopher Hatton, as vice-chamberlain of the household and became a privy councillor. He was appointed chancellor of the duchy of Lancaster in 1590: a post which he apparently regarded as the peak of his career, moving from his father's Heneage House or Bevis Marks in London to the Savoy in Westminster, where he entertained Elizabeth on 7 December 1594, and maximizing his duchy patronage.

Heneage's advancement depended not on his offices, though these indicated how far he had come, but on his influence with Elizabeth, which in turn stemmed from genuine friendship. They regularly exchanged new year's gifts. Hence he was a worthwhile intermediary for those in search of royal favours, rarely pressing them to the queen's displeasure, and quickly recovering her favour when he did. He was a mediator and fixer, the court insider par excellence, who generally got on with everybody. Whatever Leicester's initial fears, he was pushing Heneage's claims in 1571, and remembered his 'good old friend' with £40 in jewels and plate in his will in 1588 (HoP, Commons, 1558–1603, 2.292). There was no 'gentleman of the courte that lovythe you more dearlye', Leicester was reminded in 1586 (Bruce, 113). Heneage was friend also to Hatton, with whom he regularly corresponded, and in 1582 interceded for him with the queen when he was out of favour because of his rivalry with Sir Walter Ralegh. He even worked well with Ralegh, whom many regarded as difficult and untrustworthy. His friends and protégés included: Sir Philip Sidney, who bequeathed him a jewel worth £20; Sir William Pickering, whose monument at St Helen, Bishopsgate, London, he helped finance; his neighbour John Foxe, the martyrologist; the chancellor of the exchequer, Sir John Fortescue, who was his executor; Toby Matthew; and Francis Bacon, whom he supported in his unsuccessful bid to become solicitor-general in 1594. The fact that Heneage was in agreement with Robert Devereux, second earl of Essex, on this last occasion did not preclude good relations with Lord Burghley (Cecil) and Sir

Robert Cecil, who helped him gain appointment as chancellor of the duchy of Lancaster.

Heneage was an extremely active parliamentarian. He sat in at least eleven parliaments over forty years, between 1553 and 1593 (for Boston, Lincolnshire, in 1563; Lincolnshire in 1563, 1571 and 1572; and Essex in 1584, 1586, 1589, and 1593). He is recorded as speaking on several occasions and must have done so much more frequently, for he sat on a remarkable number of committees, sometimes reporting back, at a time when a committee stage was far from common. He was nominated to one committee in 1566, seven in 1571, to the principal committee on Mary, queen of Scots, in 1572, to seven in 1576, eleven in 1581, and nine in 1584–5. His only recorded intervention in 1586–7, concerning Peter Wentworth's defence of liberty of speech, was decisive: he 'so handled the matter that Mr Wentworth went to the Tower and the questions [were] not at all moved' (HoP, *Commons, 1558–1603*, 2.292). Heneage was yet more active in 1589, following his appointment to the privy council, steering through the purveyors' bill, relaying messages to and from the queen, sitting on at least sixteen committees and reporting on six. In 1593 he seconded the nomination of Edward Coke as speaker and sat on six committees, but his principal responsibility was securing the subsidy, which was not without trouble: a charge against him of misrepresenting the case of the House of Commons was withdrawn but may nevertheless have stuck.

Heneage evidently had a grasp of and views on a wide range of parliamentary and government business which extended far beyond his own limited experience and even into foreign policy. He wrote in 1592 to Sir Henry Unton of 'her Majesties likinge to be informed by me, as by other of her servants, of the state of thinges as they come and our understandynge both from abroade and at home' (*Correspondence of Sir Henry Unton*, 401). Hence Unton wrote seven times to him as well as sixty times to Burghley and seventeen times to Cecil. Only in 1586 was Heneage himself sent abroad, based on his abilities as a mediator, to overrule Leicester's acceptance of the governorship of the Netherlands. This mission ended in the earl's confirmation and Heneage overextended himself by promising that no peace would be made without consulting the Dutch rebels. Elizabeth angrily repudiated this commitment. 'Do that you are bidden' (Bruce, 243). Heneage's loss of favour was temporary, but he was not used as a diplomat again. In 1589 he advocated in the Commons that war be declared against Spain. From 1585 on he regularly sat on commissions to try traitors and in 1585, with Ralegh, reported on the ransom of English captives on the Barbary Coast; his interests extended even into speculative investment in Edward Fenton's 1581 voyage to Cathay (China), to the tune of £200. He was paymaster to the armies of Tilbury and under Henry Carey, first Baron Hunsdon, during the Armada campaign in 1588 and, as a privy councillor, was closely involved in strategic planning.

Heneage was initially an extremely assiduous privy councillor, attending up to a hundred council meetings a year, but his attendance fell to half that level during his later years. It was his more visible standing as a privy councillor that brought him the recordership of Colchester in 1590 and the high stewardships of Hull in 1590, Salisbury in 1591, and Winchester in 1592, which he attempted to use in 1593 to place clients in parliamentary seats. He was foiled at Salisbury but apparently successful at Hull. His efforts at Leicester were also rebuffed, but he seems to have placed his clients and kinsmen at Wigan and Clitheroe, Lancashire, Stockbridge, Hampshire, and Monmouth. Evidently the political skills of the household were ineffective when handling corporations.

Heneage started out with a modest estate, insufficient for a career at court, but fortunately he was a major beneficiary of his own influence and Elizabeth's largesse. He was an 'avid office-seeker' (HoP, *Commons, 1558–1603*, 2.291) and highly competitive about it, his pluralism unrivalled: the keepership of the records in the Tower, that he secured jointly with his brother Michael Heneage in 1576, was wrested from the master of the rolls, Sir William Cordell, in whose gift it properly belonged. The receivership and treasurership of the tenths on the profits of salt manufacture, to which Heneage was appointed in 1565, may have been lucrative and the treasurership of the chamber carried not only a fee and perquisites but also the opportunity to borrow liquid capital: he owed Elizabeth £1300 at his death. He repeatedly paid large sums for the leases he obtained. Moreover, he obtained more than his share of permanent endowments, including, about 1588, Ravenston and Stoke Goldington, Buckinghamshire, and the hospital of Horning, Norfolk, wrested from the bishopric of Norwich. Helfcolme in Yorkshire was bought from John Lumley, Baron Lumley.

These were exceptional outliers, for Heneage appears to have decided as early as 1561 to refocus his estate on Essex. In 1564 he was granted the reversion of Copthall in Epping, in that county, where he erected an elaborate mansion designed by John Thorpe and where he entertained the queen in 1568. The manor and rectory of Epping were added in 1573 and other manors in 1576, the year that Elizabeth induced the burgesses of Colchester to relinquish Kingswood Heath to him. He became recorder of Colchester in 1590 and ranger of Waltham Forest in 1593. His Epping estate was substantial by his death. From about 1573 he was JP and from about 1586 of the quorum for Essex and for Lindsey, Lincolnshire, and from 1584 he was returned to parliament for Essex rather than Lincolnshire. He became a deputy lieutenant for Essex in 1585.

Heneage complained repeatedly of ill health from the early 1580s, when he was much troubled both by the stone and by gout, and he had the perceived misfortune not to have a son. His estate was destined to pass to his only daughter, Elizabeth, 'the richest widow in present estate' (Stone, 110). Following his wife's death on 19 November 1593, on 2 May 1594 Heneage married Mary (d. 1607), widow of Henry Wriothesley, second earl of Southampton, and eldest daughter of Anthony Browne, first Viscount Montagu, and his first wife, Jane. The match indicates how much Heneage had come up in the world. The dowager countess was about ten years younger and had only a small dower, meaning that the couple married for companionship, not expecting children, and had probably been close friends for years. Heneage's final years were somewhat blighted by his quarrel with his daughter and her husband and with his denunciations of Sir Moyle Finch for ingratitude. He devoted much of his will, written at the Savoy on 20 July 1595, to protecting his widow's jointure against them. He died at the Savoy on 17 October that year and was buried in the lady chapel behind the choir of St Paul's Cathedral on 20 November.

George Heneage (1482/3–1549), clergyman, was born in 1482 or 1483, being twenty in 1503. He was the third son of John Heneage (1452–1530), landowner of Hainton, Lincolnshire, and his wife, Katherine, daughter of Thomas Wymbish of Nocton in the same county. He was a notable pluralist, who frequently changed livings to further his career. He graduated BCnL at Cambridge University in 1510–11, studied further at Bologna University in 1520, and was incorporated at Oxford University in 1522. He normally resided in Lincoln. The rectory of Benningworth, Lincolnshire, in 1503, five years before he was ordained deacon, was the first and last of his seven rectories, several of which he seems to have held concurrently. In 1503 he was dispensed to hold two incompatible livings for life. From 1518 Heneage worked his way up through four prebends and four dignities within the diocese of Lincoln, serving as dean of Lincoln from 1528 to 1539, when John Longland, bishop of Lincoln, secured him in preference to Cardinal Thomas Wolsey's son, Thomas Winter. Heneage was archdeacon of Lincoln from 1542 until his death. He was also a canon of York from 1533, of Salisbury from 1539, archdeacon of Taunton from 1540, and master of Tattersall College, Lincolnshire, from 1528 until its dissolution. He was devoted to 'good old father' and his siblings, to whom he left tokens 'in remembrance of natural disposition of kindness one brother and syster to another' (PRO, PROB 11/32, sig. 38). He died in September 1549, his will being proved on 19 September, and was buried in Lincoln Cathedral.   MICHAEL HICKS

Sources DNB · L. Stone, *The crisis of the aristocracy, 1558–1641* (1965); repr. (1966) · HoP, *Commons, 1558–1603*, 2.289–93 · HoP, *Commons, 1509–58*, 2.333–5 · wills, PRO, PROB 11/32, sig. 38 [George Heneage]; PRO, PROB 11/86, sig. 70 · GEC, *Peerage* · J. Bruce, ed., *Correspondence of Robert Dudley, earl of Leycester*, CS, 27 (1844) · VCH Essex, vol. 5 · B. I'Anson, *History of the Finch family* (1933) · S. Adams, ed., *Household accounts and disbursement books of Robert Dudley, earl of Leicester, 1558–1561, 1584–1586*, CS, 6 (1995) · R. Somerville, *History of the duchy of Lancaster, 1265–1603* (1953) · *The correspondence of Sir Henry Unton, knt: ambassador from Queen Elizabeth to Henry IV, king of France*, ed. J. Stevenson (1847) · CPR, *1550–82* · Emden, *Oxf.* · M. Bowker, *The Henrician reformation: the diocese of Lincoln under John Longford, 1521–1547* (1981)
Archives BL, corresp. and accounts, Harley MSS · Leics. RO, corresp. · PRO, private papers, E 192 | BL, letters to earl of Leicester, etc., Cotton MSS
Likenesses oils, *c*.1580, Ingatestone Hall, Essex

Henfrey, Arthur (*bap.* **1820**, *d.* **1859**), botanist, was reportedly born in Aberdeen on 1 November 1819 and recorded as baptized in that city on 1 November 1820. He was the son of Henry Bertram Henfrey, an English engineer and stone merchant, and his wife, Harriet, *née* Holenworth. He

studied medicine and surgery at St Bartholomew's Hospital, London, where his potential was recognized by Frederic Farre (1804–1866). Although admitted to the Royal College of Surgeons in 1843, Henfrey's asthma ruled out medical practice and he devoted his life to botany, becoming in 1847 a lecturer at the medical school affiliated to St George's Hospital, London. He was elected fellow of the Linnean Society in 1844 and of the Royal Society in 1852, and, in succession to Edward Forbes, became professor of botany at King's College, London, in 1854. He wrote some thirty-nine scientific articles and eleven books; his *Elementary Course of Botany* (1857–84), the leading botanical textbook of its time, went through four editions. He was a member and curator of the Botanical Society of London, a member of the council of the Horticultural Society, and examiner in natural science to the Royal Military Academy and the Society of Arts.

Henfrey married Elizabeth Anne, eldest daughter of the Hon. Jabez Henry, barrister, at the parish church of Tunbridge Wells on 26 August 1851. Their son was Henry William *Henfrey (1852–1881), a noted numismatist. Considered a gentle and kindly person, generous with his knowledge, Henfrey died of an 'effusion of the brain' after four days' illness, on 7 September 1859 at his home, 12 Heathfield Terrace, Turnham Green, Middlesex, where he had lived for many years.

Henfrey made few original scientific contributions but was influential as an editor. He founded and edited at his own expense the monthly *Botanical Gazette*, though it failed after its third year in 1851; he also edited the *Journal of the Photographic Society*. He was also influential as a translator and writer of textbooks, through which means he introduced to English readers the findings of continental plant science, the so-called 'new botany', which stressed physiological anatomy and comparative morphology rather than taxonomy. Henfrey did, however, hold a number of mistaken views: he sided with von Mohl's interpretation of cell division, which, as late as 1855, he believed did not occur in plants such as liverworts, and he seems never to have questioned the immutability of species, favouring 'centres of creation' in his *The Vegetation of Europe* (1852). Nevertheless, he was right to be against those who held that the pollen grain contained the embryo and that the ovule was merely a brood chamber for the young plant. He was commemorated by John Lindley in the plant genus name, *Henfreya* Lindley, of the Acanthaceae family.

D. J. MABBERLEY

Sources F. W. Oliver, 'Arthur Henfrey', *Makers of British botany*, ed. F. W. Oliver (1913), 192–203 · Desmond, *Botanists*, rev. edn, 334 · CGPLA Eng. & Wales (1860) · m. cert. · parish register (baptism), Aberdeen, Scotland, 1 Nov 1820
Archives RBG Kew, letters | Manchester Museum, plant specimens
Likenesses Maull & Polyblank, photograph, 1855, NPG · engraving, RBG Kew
Wealth at death under £600: administration, 1 Feb 1860, CGPLA Eng. & Wales

Henfrey, Henry William (**1852–1881**), numismatist, born in London on 5 July 1852, was the eldest son of the botanist Arthur *Henfrey (*bap.* 1820, *d.* 1859) and his wife, Elizabeth

Anne, *née* Henry. He was educated at Brighton College, but was prevented by an accident from proceeding to Oxford University. He was encouraged in his natural bent for archaeological and numismatic studies by Peter Cunningham (1816–1869), Joseph Bonomi (1796–1878), and William Henry Smyth (1788–1865). One of his first numismatic writings was a paper in the *English Mechanic* on the Queen Anne farthings. He joined the Numismatic Society of London on 19 November 1868, became a member of the council, and contributed to its proceedings twelve papers, chiefly on English coins and medals, which were printed in the *Numismatic Chronicle*. He was a foreign member of the Belgian and French numismatic societies, and of several American societies. He was elected a member of the British Archaeological Association in 1870, and contributed papers to its proceedings, especially on the medals of Cromwell, and on the coins of Bristol and Norwich. At the time of his death he was arranging for the press a history of English country mints, for which he had been for many years collecting material; it was never published. In 1870 he published *A Guide to the Study and Arrangement of English Coins* (2nd edn, ed. C. F. Keary, 1885), a useful little handbook; and in 1877 his principal work, the *Numismata Cromwelliana*, giving a full account of the coins, medals, and seals of the protectorate. Henfrey died, after returning from a visit to Italy, on 31 July 1881 at Widmore Cottage, his mother's house at Bromley, Kent.

W. W. WROTH, *rev.* H. C. G. MATTHEW

Sources *Numismatic Chronicle*, 3rd ser., 2 (1882), 21–2

Hengham, Ralph (*b.* in or before **1235**, *d.* **1311**), justice, was long believed to have been a member of a Norfolk gentry family which took its name from Hingham in that county, but there are good reasons for supposing that his surname is in reality derived from Sible Hedingham in Essex. Hengham may have been born there. He had certainly become rector of Sible Hedingham by 1274. When he acquired lands jointly with his sister Clemencia in 1289 it was at Toppesfield, only 3 miles north-west, and he acquired by himself a number of other properties in the same area of Essex. There is also evidence for a link between Sible Hedingham and Ralph's first known employer, Giles of Erdington.

Hengham probably entered Erdington's service as a clerk while Erdington was still serving as one of the justices of the common bench before 1255. Erdington presented Hengham to the church of Yardley (near Birmingham) in 1264. His predecessor in that living was one William of Hengham, presumably a relative and possibly his father. By 1260 he had become one of the clerks of king's bench and was later to reminisce about Hugh Bigod's activity as justiciar, probably while presiding in the court, between 1258 and 1260. From there he passed into the service of Richard of Middleton and may have served with him in the eyre circuit of 1262 led by Martin of Littlebury. He certainly served with Middleton on the eyre circuit Middleton himself led in 1268–9.

In July 1269 Middleton became chancellor. The presence of this patron at the heart of the royal administration, as

well as Hengham's own undoubted abilities, may help to explain the rapidity with which Hengham then achieved judicial office and promotion. He was appointed one of the junior justices of the eyre circuit led by Master Roger of Seaton in April 1271 (when he was still perhaps only in his mid-thirties) and in May 1272 was made senior justice of an eyre circuit of his own. When Henry III's death brought the eyres to an end he passed straight into his first central court appointment, as a junior justice of the common bench (in Hilary term 1273). During the next year and a half he also served as an assize justice with Walter de Heliun in five west midland counties. When he left the common bench it was again on promotion, this time to become chief justice of the court of king's bench (from Michaelmas term 1274). He served as its chief justice for fifteen years. This period coincides with that of the great Edwardian statutes. Hengham probably took a part in the drafting of those statutes with his fellow justices and others, but it is doubtful whether he should be seen as the directing intelligence behind them. When, in an early fourteenth-century case, Hengham said 'Do not gloss the statute. We know it better than you because we made it', he seems not to have been claiming individual authorship for himself, but rather collective authorship and authority for himself and for his fellow justices. There is certainly no sign, in other cases involving the interpretation of statutes, of his fellow justices' deferring to Hengham's view of a statute, as might have been expected if Hengham had generally been known as the prime author of the legislation concerned.

Hengham was among the royal justices dismissed from office and disgraced in 1289–90. In his case dismissal did not come until after the end of Hilary term 1290. He was convicted of misconduct in only a single case, and then on what looks like a technicality. The technicality cost him dear. The price of his release from prison and subsequent pardon was probably 10,000 marks (the highest fine paid by any of the disgraced justices) paid over the next five years; part of the money had to be borrowed from Lucchese merchants. The size of the fine reflects not the degree of his guilt but Hengham's perceived ability to pay. A clerk in major orders, Hengham is known to have held three cathedral canonries (at Hereford, Lichfield, and St Paul's), prebends in five collegiate churches, and livings in ten counties. He was also in receipt of annual pensions from seven major religious corporations and had acquired significant land holdings in four counties (Cambridgeshire, Essex, Kent, and Warwickshire). The story that the fine went to pay for a clock tower at Westminster has no contemporary warrant. Although his judgment was quashed in one further case he provided a spirited defence against other allegations of wrongdoing, and had his judgments upheld in at least four other cases.

In November 1292 Hengham was living in St Thomas's Hospital in Southwark, and in February 1294 was present in the chapter house at Blackfriars in London for an arbitration between the abbot of Ramsey and the bishop of Coventry. The first evidence of his having recovered the king's favour is his appointment in September 1299 to a commission for perambulating forest boundaries. In September 1300 he was appointed as an assize justice by Bishop Antony (I) Bek in co. Durham, and by the end of 1300 was again a member of the king's council.

When John of Mettingham, the chief justice of the common bench, died in the summer of 1301, Hengham was appointed to replace him. Hengham was reappointed at the beginning of Edward II's reign in 1307, but was replaced as chief justice by William Bereford in March 1309. The reports indicate that he was absent from the court during only a single term (Trinity term 1302), when he and two of his colleagues were in London for a session of parliament while the court was in session at York. Hengham was not too proud to ask for William Bereford's advice on a procedural matter, and in another case deferred to Elias Beckingham's thirty years of experience in the court. His own reminiscences of cases he had seen or heard went back as far as the mid-1250s, and he clearly enjoyed telling stories, like that about a man assigning dower to a widow, whom he tricked into accepting only a small part by feigning a headache while out in the fields and promising to return the following day to finish the job.

Hengham is the first chief justice known to have taken time at the end of a case to explain the general point of law involved for the law students (apprentices) present in the court. He is also the probable author of *Hengham parva*, written between 1285 and 1290, and possibly based on a course of lectures he had given for the benefit of an earlier generation of law students. Contemporaries also credited him with the authorship of *Hengham magna*, another short but unfinished legal treatise, but this is unlikely on stylistic and other grounds. There are better grounds for ascribing to him authorship of two consultations, one on points of *quo warranto* law written in 1285 for the justices of the Northamptonshire eyre, the second written some time after 1285 in response to a question from justices in Ireland.

Hengham lived for only a little over two years after his retirement from the common bench. He died on 18 May 1311 and was buried in the north-east of the choir of St Paul's Cathedral in London.   PAUL BRAND

Sources *Chancery records* · court of common pleas, feet of fines, PRO, CP 25/1 · Common Bench plea rolls, PRO, CP 40 · Curia Regis rolls, PRO, KB 26 · King's Bench plea rolls, PRO, KB 27 · A. J. Horwood, ed. and trans., *Year books of the reign of King Edward the First*, 5 vols., Rolls Series, 31 (1863–79) · law reports of the reign of Edward I, BL · [R. De Hengham], *Radulphi de Hengham summae*, ed. W. H. Dunham (1932) · P. A. Brand, *The earliest English law reports*, 1, SeldS, 111 (1995) · P. Brand, *The making of the common law* (1992) · W. Stubbs, ed., *Chronicles of the reigns of Edward I and Edward II*, 1, Rolls Series, 76 (1882), 270

Likenesses caricature, PRO, CP 40/55, m. 61

Hengist (d. 488?). *See under* Kent, kings of (*act. c.*450–*c.*590).

Hengler, (Frederick) Charles (1820–1887), circus proprietor, was the second of the four sons of Henry Michael Hengler (1784–1861), a circus rope-dancer, and his wife, Jane, *née* Pilsworth (*c.*1790–1869). He came from an established family of circus performers: his grandfather, (John)

(Frederick) Charles Hengler (1820–1887), by unknown photographer, *c.*1880

Michael Hengler (d. 1802), was a Hanoverian rider and pyrotechnist who emigrated to England, while his brothers, Edward Henry (1819–1865) and John Michael *Hengler (1831–1919), formed a celebrated double tightrope act. Charles, as he was invariably known, was too tall to be suited to the family profession of acrobatics, and he played in the band of Old Wild's portable theatre in the 1840s. But he proved a highly effective and successful circus proprietor. He took over a circus from his elder brother, Edward, in 1846, which was soon closed down; but in the next year he started a new circus, and 1847 has generally been regarded as the date of the founding of the Hengler circus.

For some ten years the circus tented during the summer and played in temporary structures in towns during the winter, but in 1857 Hengler opened a permanent circus building in Liverpool as his headquarters. Similar permanent structures followed in Glasgow and Dublin (1863), Hull (1864), Birmingham and Bristol (1866), and London (the Palais Royal, Argyll Street, 1871). This last was rebuilt as the Palladium Theatre in 1910 and retained part of the façade of the original building. Some of Hengler's circuses were rebuilt during his management: the Grand Cirque in Liverpool, for instance, constructed in 1876, was a splendid building after the style of the Cirque Napoléon (or d'Hiver) in Paris, with a ceiling covered with folds of chintz and the pillars supporting the roof neatly papered and embellished with flags and shields.

Hengler maintained companies that moved from one to another of his circuses; at Christmas he had three different companies performing simultaneously, and he established a reputation for providing good entertainment. Among his regular performers were the genial ringmaster Felix Rivolti and the clowns 'Whimsical Walker' (who also played at Drury Lane) and 'Little Sandy', who was a great favourite of the princess of Wales. The equestrian acts were always of the highest quality, and the pantomimes were magnificently staged.

Hengler was remembered by 'Whimsical Walker' as

a good straight man, somewhat severe—would have his business done to his liking—and that was his success through life. I have seen him go round the stables with his white handkerchief in his hand smoothing down the horses' backs to see if they were clean. He was a terror with the grooms—the least dirty spot on a horse—the groom had to go. (McCarthy, 8)

He asked a clergyman to officiate in the circus whenever it was performing, and required every member of his troupe to attend Sunday services.

In 1846 Hengler married Mary Anne Frances Sprake (c.1828–1902) at Portsea; among their children were Frederick Charles (1855–1889) and his younger brother Albert Henry, who together carried on their father's circus activities. Their innovations included the installation of 'sinking rings', which could be filled with water to provide facilities for aquatic displays. Hengler's daughter, Jenny Louise *Hengler (b. 1849), was a noted equestrian performer before her marriage to Count Waldemar Kamienski in 1874.

Hengler died at his residence, Cambridge House, Fitzjohns Avenue, Hampstead, on 28 September 1887, having made a fortune of over £60,000 from his circuses. He was buried in Hampstead cemetery. GEORGE SPEAIGHT

Sources J. M. Turner, *Victorian arena: the performers* (1995), vol. 1 of *A dictionary of British circus biography* · G. Speaight, *A history of the circus* (1980) · T. Frost, *Circus life and circus celebrities* (1875) · S. McCarthy, *Hengler's Circus* (1981) · *CGPLA Eng. & Wales* (1889) · J. M. Turner, 'Historical Hengler's Circus', *Liverpool Family Historian*, 4/3 (1982), 48–54

Likenesses photograph, c.1880, Theatre Museum, London [*see illus.*] · photograph, priv. coll.

Wealth at death £60,520 2s. 3d.: resworn probate, Jan 1889, *CGPLA Eng. & Wales* (1887)

Hengler, Jenny Louise (b. 1849), equestrian performer, was born on 23 March 1849, at Lewes, Sussex, the second daughter of the circus proprietor (Frederick) Charles *Hengler (1820–1887) and his wife, Mary Ann Frances Sprake (c.1828–1902). She performed as a juvenile artiste in her father's arenas from an early age, her first recorded appearance being in the 1856–7 winter season at Bradford, in the pantomime. A great beauty, she became one of the most celebrated *haute école* riders of her day, setting the standard against which others were judged. In November 1865 the *Liverpool Daily Post* called her 'the most remarkable feminine attraction of the day', and at the end of the season observed that, 'It is feared that when we see her

Jenny Louise Hengler (b. 1849), by unknown photographer, c.1870

next she will be much grown, but the flower will be expanded and more beautiful'.

On 6 May 1874 Hengler married the putative Polish count Waldemar Alexander Oscar Kamienski, a rider who had been billed as Alexander Oscar at Hengler's since 1869. The wedding was not widely reported, and she never rode in any of her father's arenas again; however, as Jenny Louise Hengler-Oscar, she appeared in her husband's International circus, being noted at Newcastle upon Tyne in 1882. The Kamienskis later went to the United States, where Count Kamienski ran a horse training and riding school at Beretta College. They lived in Astoria, Long Island, with their three children, Philip, Charles, and Beatrice. She visited Britain in 1892, on the occasion of her sister Lydia's marriage, but nothing is known of her after this date. JOHN M. TURNER

Sources J. M. Turner, *King Pole*, 76 (Sept 1989), 9 · *Liverpool Daily Post* (20 Nov 1865) · *Liverpool Daily Post* (17 Feb 1866) · m. cert. · IGI · census returns for Bradford, 1851

Likenesses photograph, c.1870, Theatre Museum, London, Guy Little collection [*see illus.*] · photographs, Theatre Museum, London, Guy Little collection

---

Hengler, John Michael (1831–1919), tightrope walker and circus manager, was born on 10 July 1831 at Lambeth, London, the fourth son of Henry Michael Hengler (1784–1861) and his wife, Jane, née Pilsworth (c.1790–1869), of Dublin. (Frederick) Charles *Hengler was his brother. The son of a famous circus rope-dancer, Hengler first appeared on the rope, without the aid of a balance pole, at the age of six. He also became an accomplished rider, and took part in hippodramatic sketches and spectacles. He was noted with Price and Powell's circus at Camden Town in 1843 performing backward and forward somersaults on the tightrope. In 1850 'Young Hengler' was turning somersaults on the rope while playing Louis Jullien's *Drum Polka* on a side drum or an overture on the violin. By 1851 he was billed as the 'Prince of Tight Rope Artistes', his sobriquet for the next twenty years. In 1852 he first performed the dramatic role of Hamlet: acting and dramatic recitations became part of his stock-in-trade. During a visit to Denmark in 1855 he performed before Frederick VII at Copenhagen. Hengler spent twelve months in the United States in 1856–7, when he was based in New York. On his return he joined the new circus in Liverpool run by his brother Charles Hengler. He visited Copenhagen again in 1858, and later went on to Paris.

Hengler married Hannah Frances (1843–1920), the daughter of Thomas Lloyd, a horse dealer, at St Silas's Church, Liverpool, on 6 August 1865. They had a son and five daughters, none of whom were to be associated with the circus. On the death of his eldest brother Edward Henry Hengler in January 1865, Hengler became sole proprietor of the Liverpool Riding School in Elizabeth Street, although he continued to perform in the arena. His last performance on the tightrope was in 1872 at Sheffield, when he also recited 'The Charge of the Light Brigade', accompanied by orchestral effects.

During the 1880s Hengler became a Liverpool shipowner and went into local politics: he was a member of the West Derby (Liverpool) local board from 1881 to 1890, serving as chairman for the year from April 1886. He was the last manager (1889–95) of Hengler's circus in Argyll Street, London. He died at his residence, Airlie House, Meols Drive, Hoylake, Chester, on 17 November 1919, and was buried at Flaybrick Hill cemetery, Hoylake, on 19 November. JOHN M. TURNER

Sources T. Frost, *Circus life and circus celebrities* (1875) · T. M. Rendle, *Swings and roundabouts: a yokel in London* (1919) · *The Era* (4 April 1847) · *Doncaster, Nottingham and Lincoln Gazette* (20 Sept 1850) · *Liverpool Citizen* (12 Sept 1888) · *Liverpool Citizen* (26 Sept 1888) · *Liverpool Mercury* (23 May 1851) · *The Era* (12 May 1855) · *The Era* (3 June 1855) · J. N. Ireland, *Records of the New York stage, from 1750 to 1860*, 2 vols. (1866–7) · *Liverpool Daily Post* (13 June 1857) · *Liverpool Daily Post* (22 June 1857) · *Sheffield and Rotherham Independent* (19 Nov 1872) · D. Howard, *London theatres and music halls, 1850–1950* (1970) · *Gore's Directory of Liverpool* (1862–1920) · census returns, 1881 · parish register (marriage), St Silas's, Liverpool · indexes, General Register Office for England · *CGPLA Eng. & Wales* (1920) · cemetery records
Likenesses photograph, Theatre Collection, London, Guy Little collection
Wealth at death £21,747 6s. 10d.: probate, 2 Jan 1920, *CGPLA Eng. & Wales*

Hengler, Sarah (c.1765–1845), artist in fireworks, was born in Surrey and became the second wife of John Michael Hengler (d. 1802), circus performer. There were two sons and a daughter of this marriage, the eldest of whom, Henry Michael Hengler (b. 1784), who probably trained in Paris, became a rope walker.

Madame Hengler, as she was known, supplied fireworks for displays at Astley's Royal Amphitheatre, at the Royal Circus or Surrey Theatre, and especially at Vauxhall Gardens, Surrey, where her husband performed until the year before his perhaps untimely death. She married William Feild (or Field) on 6 December 1808 but retained her former husband's name, by which she was best-known. The open space at Vauxhall, long established as a fashionable resort, lent itself to grand displays of fireworks, celebrating or commemorating national events or simply rendering dramatic spectacles. Thomas Hood's 'Ode to Madame Hengler', written in 1839 and running to 103 lines, acknowledges her skill and her fame as creator of these events:

> Oh, Mrs Hengler!—Madame,—I beg pardon.
> Starry Enchantress of the Surrey garden!
> Accept an ode not meant as any scoff—
> The Bard were bold indeed at thee to quiz.
> Whose squibs are far more popular than his:
> Whose works are far more certain to go off.
> (Hood, 257)

From 1795 Sarah Hengler occupied 4 Asylum Buildings, a three-storey house in Westminster Road, on the Surrey side of Westminster Bridge. She lived above the ground-floor show-room, the other rooms being used for several purposes: to store the fireworks manufactured in Kennington; to finish them off, by covering roman candles and binding up catherine wheels; and to sort and tie them in readiness for the displays. In this she employed several staff and was assisted, at least latterly, by her married daughter Magdalen Elizabeth Jones and one of her grandsons.

When the business started up at Asylum Buildings the area was largely open ground but it had since become densely built up, creating both a nuisance and a hazard. In August 1818 the house was damaged by an explosion in which three people died. Sarah Hengler met her own end in a similar and perhaps appropriate manner. On 9 October 1845, with the approach of the busy winter season and the house full of men, women, and children about their various tasks, an accident with an oil lamp showered sparks onto a stock of fireworks and triggered an explosion. The fire spread rapidly into Sarah Hengler's room. Though disabled (she had been for many years), she managed to make her way to the window but she was too stout to get out, even with the help of the firemen and the people with ladders who gathered below to assist the escape of the other occupants. After the fire was quenched her body was recovered and taken in a coffin to the workhouse. At the inquest two days later the jury returned a verdict of accidental death. ANITA McCONNELL

Sources S. McCarthy, *Hengler's circus: a history and celebration, 1847–1924* (1981) · *GM*, 2nd ser., 24 (1845), 545 · *The Times* (21 Aug 1818), 3 · *The Observer* (13 Oct 1845), 4 · *The complete poetical works of Thomas Hood*, ed. W. Jerrold (1906) · census returns, 1841 · parish register, St Andrew by the Wardrobe, 6 Dec 1808 [marriage] · d. cert.

Henley. For this title name *see* individual entries under Henley; *see also* Eden, Morton, first Baron Henley (1752–1830).

Henley, Alice (d. 1470), abbess of Godstow, occurs as a senior nun of the Oxfordshire house in 1445, was elected abbess between July and September 1446, and ruled until her death about August 1470. Her name is chiefly linked with the so-called English register of Godstow Abbey, an innovative work of administration. In 1403–4 a cartulary of the Latin charters of Godstow (PRO, E 164/20) had been compiled at the costs and labour of Alice of Gatton, prioress of the house. Under Henley, a royal confirmation of Godstow's foundation charters was obtained in 1462 and the cartulary was translated into English at an unknown date. This English register (Bodl. Oxf., MS Rawl. B. 408) contains a preface observing that religious women, lacking great knowledge of Latin, depend on learned men to interpret their records and have trouble in keeping their business secret. Accordingly, 'a poor brother and well-wisher' to Abbess Henley has summarized the charters in English, so that the nuns might better understand their muniments and instruct their servants. The summary is preceded by an alphabet and paraphrases of basic prayers in English, in the manner of a school book. The register is paralleled by a similar English text of about the same date from the nearby abbey of Osney, and is an example of administrative development caused by the needs of women. It is also significant in the history of the use of the English language for keeping and understanding records.

NICHOLAS ORME

Sources CPR, 1441–6, 454; 1446–52, 2; 1461–7, 235; 1467–77, 212 • A. Clark, ed., *The English register of Godstow Nunnery, near Oxford*, EETS, original ser., 129, 130, 142 (1905–11) • A. H. Thompson, ed., *Visitations of religious houses in the diocese of Lincoln*, 2, Lincoln RS, 14 (1918) • PRO, E 164/20 [Godstow Latin cartulary] • Godstow English register, Bodl. Oxf., MS Rawl. B. 408

Henley, Anthony (1666/7–1711), wit and politician, was the eldest son of Sir Robert Henley (c.1624–1692), MP and chief protonotary of the king's bench court, and Catherine (1642–c.1673), daughter of Anthony *Hungerford (d. 1657) the royalist. A daughter and two more sons, one of whom died in infancy, were born to this marriage before Catherine died, probably in 1673. In 1674 Sir Robert, whose office was worth £4000 p.a., increased his wealth by marrying Barbara Every (d. 1727), heir to a large fortune and estates in Somerset, Dorset, and Devon. Two sons and three daughters of this second marriage survived to adulthood.

Anthony entered Oxford: he matriculated from Christ Church on 3 March 1682, aged fifteen, but took no degree. He was admitted as a student of the Middle Temple on 3 May 1684. It has been claimed that he was the Oxford entrant who, according to a famous story in *The Spectator* no. 494, was so terrified by his interview with Thomas Goodwin (1600–1680), that he did not dare present himself for examination again, but the ages and whereabouts of the two men make this impossible. On the death of his father in December 1692 Anthony inherited The Grange, Northington, Hampshire, with other landed properties, to which, on the death of his brother Henry about a week later, were added six valuable houses in North Row, Lincoln's Inn Fields. He now spent much of his time in political and literary circles in London; his fortune was said to be £3000 a year at this time (Le Neve, 532).

Henley was acquainted with Sir William Temple,

Anthony Henley (1666/7–1711), by John Smith, 1694 (after Sir Godfrey Kneller, c.1690)

through whom he became a lifelong friend of Temple's sister, Lady Martha Giffard, and Jonathan Swift. He was a skilled musician on several instruments and wrote words for settings by the Purcell brothers, Henry and Daniel. He became a protégé of Charles Sackville, earl of Dorset, and in his turn befriended other men of letters. Daniel Purcell, Thomas Southerne, Samuel Garth, and John Dennis were among those who dedicated work to him, and it was said in 1712 that 'There is hardly an Author living who has not tasted of his Bounty' (Le Neve, 532). He wrote songs for two of Southerne's plays and gave Dennis the hint for his Canadian tragedy, *Liberty Asserted* (1704). His own few poems appeared anonymously in compilations by his friend John Oldmixon and in other collections. He perhaps contributed to the collective satire against Sir Richard Blackmore, *Commendatory Verses, on the Author of the Two Arthurs and the Satyr Against Wit* (1700). He wrote a life, now lost, of his music master Tom Durfey which was amusing enough for Pope to consider incorporating it into the *Memoirs of Martinus Scriblerus* (Spence, 1.56).

On 8 February 1700 Henley married Mary Bertie (*bap.* 1669), sister to Countess Paulet and granddaughter of the second earl of Lindsey; she brought a fortune of £30,000. They had four sons and three daughters between 1702 and 1710.

Henley's political patron was the whig grandee Robert Spencer, earl of Sunderland, and he was personally known to William III. On 3 March 1697 he was granted government pensions totalling £2000 p.a. which he enjoyed until his death. According to the prejudiced tory William

Legge, earl of Dartmouth, Henley was 'a professed atheist, a zealous Republican, and a most obsequious follower of the Earl of Sunderland in all his notions as well as vices' (*Burnet's History*, 2.464n.). One of a political family (Henley's father, uncle, cousin, two half-brothers, and two brothers-in-law became members of parliament), Henley was MP for Andover, the seat formerly held by his father, from 1698 to 1701, and for the conjoint boroughs of Weymouth and Melcombe Regis from 1702 to his death. He was a member of the whiggish Kit-Cat Club and, as a strong whig in the House of Commons, he moved on 14 December 1709 that the queen should bestow some church dignity on the notoriously controversial Benjamin Hoadly on account of his writings in defence of liberty and the protestant religion.

Even so, Henley seems to have been as much the dilettante in politics as in literature. In 1709 he was involved by Swift and Lady Giffard in their dispute over the publication of Temple's *Memoirs*, but was tactful enough to retain the friendship of both. There are references to Henley's witticisms and jokes in Swift's *Journal to Stella*, and a letter from Henley to Swift dated 2 November 1708 includes the story of the farmer dying of asthma which found its way into *The Tatler*, 11 (5 May 1709), by Steele. Henley wrote several (unspecified) papers for the continuation of *The Tatler* (January to May 1711), conducted by Swift's protégé William Harrison (1685–1713). Some scholars have attributed parts of the original *Tatler* nos. 26 and 193 to him on uncertain evidence. A letter in the whig journal *The Medley*, 32 (7 May 1711), is also attributed to him.

Henley died of apoplexy in August 1711; administration was granted to his widow on 5 September. At some time in the next nine years she married her kinsman the Hon. Henry Bertie (1675–1735), third son of James, first earl of Abingdon. Of her children with Henley the two eldest sons, Anthony (1704–1748) and Robert *Henley (*c*.1708–1772), followed their father into parliament; the third, Bertie (*d*. 1760), became a prebendary of Bristol.

JAMES SAMBROOK

Sources J. Le Neve, *Memoirs British and foreign of the lives and families of the most illustrious persons who dy'd in the year 1711* (1712), 531–7 · *Burnet's History of my own time*, ed. O. Airy, new edn, 2 (1900), 464n. · J. Swift, *Journal to Stella*, ed. H. Williams, 1 (1948) · *The correspondence of Jonathan Swift: in four volumes*, ed. D. Woolley, 1 (1999), 209–12, 260–65, 273–4 · P. Rogers, 'Anthony Henley and Swift', *American Notes and Queries*, 8 (1970), 99–102, 116–20 · Foster, *Alum. Oxon.* · H. A. C. Sturgess, ed., *Register of admissions to the Honourable Society of the Middle Temple, from the fifteenth century to the year 1944*, 3 vols. (1949) · *VCH Hampshire and the Isle of Wight*, 3.395–6; 4.154, 196, 204, 374 · J. Hutchins, *The history and antiquities of the county of Dorset*, 3rd edn, ed. W. Shipp and J. W. Hodson, 3 (1868), 742–3, 747–8 · J. G. Longe, *Martha, Lady Giffard, her life and correspondence, 1664–1722* (1911), 198, 209, 234, 239–43 · *An act to enable trustees to cut and sell timber on the estate of the late Anthony Henley, esq.* (1711) · J. Spence, *Observations, anecdotes, and characters, of books and men*, ed. J. M. Osborn, new edn, 1 (1966), 56, 58 · will of Sir Robert Henley, proved 4 Jan 1693, PRO, PROB 11/413, sig. 9 · W. A. Shaw, ed., *Calendar of treasury books*, 11, PRO (1933), 418; 17/1 (1947), 240; 25/2 (1961), 212, 382 · *CSP dom.*, 1702–3, 393 · F. B. Zimmerman, *Henry Purcell, 1659–1695: his life and times*, rev. edn (1983) · C. L. Day and E. B. Murrie, *English song-books, 1651–1702: a bibliography with a first-line index of songs* (1940) · J. D. Stewart, *Sir Godfrey Kneller and the English baroque*

portrait (1983), pl. 32b · N. Luttrell, *A brief historical relation of state affairs from September 1678 to April 1714*, 2 (1857), 641 · *The lucubrations of Isaac Bickerstaff*, 5 (1712), title-page, preface · *The critical works of John Dennis*, ed. E. N. Hooker, 2 vols. (1939–43) · *The works of Thomas Southerne*, ed. R. Jordan and H. Love, 1 (1988), 418; 2 (1988), 207, 428–9, 466, 483 · A. C. Elias, *Swift at Moor Park: problems in biography and criticism* (1982), 105–7, 262–3 n. 154 · W. L. W. Eyre, *A brief history of the parishes of Swarraton and Northington* (1890), 28–32 · *Members of parliament: return to two orders of the honorable the House of Commons*, House of Commons, 2 vols. (1878), vol. 1, pp. 582, 594, 601; vol. 2, pp. 2, 10, 20 · T. H. B. Oldfield, *The representative history of Great Britain and Ireland*, 6 vols. (1816), vol. 3, pp. 379–80 · HoP, *Commons, 1660–90* · N. M. Shawyer and J. Hayward, *The Rothschild Library: a catalogue of the collection of eighteenth-century printed books and manuscripts formed by Lord Rothschild*, 2 vols. (1954), nos. 1009, 2319 · F. H. Ellis, *Swift vs Mainwaring: The Examiner and The Medley* (1985), 408–11, 429 · R. C. Boys, *Sir Richard Blackmore and the wits* (1949), 138–9 · F. H. Suckling, 'George Henley of Bradley, Hants', *N&Q*, 10th ser., 9 (1908), 143 · parish register, Swarraton · Burke, *Peerage* (1837)
Archives BL, letters to Jonathan Swift, Add. MS 4804, fols. 5–10 · BL, letters to the duke of Marlborough, Add. MS 61284, fols. 71–746 · Trinity Cam., Rothschild collection, letters to Lady Giffard
Likenesses J. Smith, mezzotint, 1688 (after G. Kneller), BM, NPG; repro. in Stewart, *Sir Godfrey Kneller* · J. Smith, mezzotint, 1694 (after G. Kneller, *c*.1690), NPG [*see illus.*] · W. C. Edwards, portrait (after G. Kneller), BM, NPG; repro. in Eyre, *Brief history* · G. Kneller, oils
Wealth at death left substantial landed property in trust to seven children: *An act to enable trustees*; administrations, Sept 1711 and June 1720, PRO, PROB 6/87, fol. 164*v*; PRO, PROB 6/96, fol. 119*v*

Henley, John [*known as* Orator Henley] (**1692–1756**), dissenting minister and eccentric, was born on 3 August 1692, probably at St Mary's vicarage, Melton Mowbray, coming from a line of eminently respectable clerical forebears. His father, the Revd Simon Henley (1665–1731), vicar of St Mary's from 1690 to 1731, was the son of the Revd John Henley, vicar of Towcester, and his mother, Arabella Dowell (1664–1734), was the daughter of the previous incumbent at St Mary's, the Revd John Dowell.

Henley attended the local free school at Melton Mowbray, a medieval grammar school where he learned the rudiments of Latin and Greek, and, according to his own report, 'His Passion for Learning, his Desire of excelling others, and his unweary'd Attachment to Study, shew'd themselves in him very early' (Henley, 'Narrative'). In his last year his father moved him to Oakham School, no doubt mindful of the sixteen exhibitions available there to Cambridge for boys who had been 'one whole yeare at the least'. After a happy year at Oakham, Henley was awarded a place and an exhibition of 40s. a year at St John's College, and was admitted pensioner on 15 June 1709.

Henley's experience of Cambridge was not entirely happy. Though he admired his tutors, he found the methods of teaching intellectually restricting and excluding freedom of discussion. His later opposition to authority and his love of contention were already apparent, though he prudently expressed them only in formal disputations. Years later he admitted that 'He was always impatient under these Fetters of the free-born Mind, and privately resolv'd some Time or Other, to enter his Protest against any Persons being bred like a Slave' (Henley, 'Narrative', 3), and bitterly recalled 'St. John's, (the College where I had the Stupidity to be educated' (Henley, 'Discourse', 24 June 1753). Despite all this he exercised his wit in two letters to *The Spectator* (nos. 396 and 518) on punning and the physiognomy of Cambridge undergraduates, and a not altogether worthless poem, 'On a LADY that could not Help Laughing at Nothing', later printed in 1719 by the notorious Edmund Curll of Grub Street. He persevered in his studies and passed his exercises for the bachelor's degree in 1712, when he claimed he 'bested *Ten Examiners* & was thanked by the University and College' (Henley, 'Discourse', 1 March 1752).

On returning home Henley became an assistant teacher in his former school and in 1716 a master, liberalizing the teaching methods, introducing daily elocution lessons, and abolishing physical punishment. Ordained deacon in 1716 after an examination which he condemned as 'very short and superficial', he added the routine work of a curate at St Mary's to his scholastic labours and reforms, still finding time and energy to write and publish in 1714 *The History of Queen Esther: A Poem in Four Books*, which, compared with many of the unread epics of the century, is not a mean attempt. Early in 1719 he conceived the idea of producing a universal grammar and later in the year published the first volume, *A Grammar of the Spanish Tongue*, followed in quick succession by Italian, French, Greek, Latin, and Hebrew. These typical Grub Street examples of copying and compilation of previous grammars, imperfectly understood, received general ridicule and abuse, which followed him through the years. The time had arrived when the narrow compass of Melton Mowbray, even with all this activity, confined his energies, and he resolved to go to London, where he might fulfil his high ambitions, and set his foot on the ladder of preferment, perhaps 'with the aerial perspective lighted by a visionary mitre' (Disraeli, *Calamities of Authors*, 1.165).

Henley arrived in November 1720 and, armed with testimonials and letters of introduction, established himself in a house in Millman Street. In 1725 he married Mary Philips (*d.* 1737), widow of William Clifford. Henley's first attempt to climb the ladder seemed successful, as he was appointed assistant preacher at St John's Chapel near Bedford Square, and reader at St George the Martyr in Queen Square, and preached often in City pulpits. Viscount Molesworth appointed him his chaplain, a coveted prize, and the following year he was instituted rector of Chelmondiston in Suffolk by the patron, the lord chancellor, the earl of Macclesfield. The tide turned when Macclesfield resigned the seals of office in 1725 and with them his patronal influence. Henley was rejected as a candidate for a lectureship at Blomsbury Chapel, to his great fury, but was appointed to a similar post at St Mary Abchurch.

There were other labours to divert Henley from this ecclesiastical struggle. Early after his arrival in London he had met Edmund Curll and, under his wing, produced between 1720 and 1725 no fewer than nine books and dedications to books, translations, compilations, and even an edition of the works of Sir Philip Sidney, all of them typical examples of Grub Street at work and the sort of demand its hack masters strove to satisfy. Curll also introduced Henley into the murkier world of Robert Walpole's secret service, a huge body of spies and informers willing to supply the prime minister with information to aid the control of the press and discover seditious libels in return for money and favour. Henley had by now politically thrown in his lot with the whigs and was in personal contact with Walpole himself.

For all this labour spent in hack work, preaching many sermons in many pulpits, and the mean work of spying and informing, the one chief prize of a rich and influential City living now seemed beyond reach. Henley believed that William Gibson, bishop of London, was determined to prevent his advancement. He would not endure the life at his quiet Suffolk rectory, which was all he could hope for, and he resolved on a completely new and drastic course. Resigning his living at Chelmondiston and his lectureship at St Mary Abchurch in 1725, he planned something entirely his own, independent of patronage and the establishment. He founded the Oratory, his own chapel, and assumed his lasting title, the Orator. The next thirty years are the story of the bizarre and tumultuous history of that foundation.

Henley first made certain that by openly separating from the Church of England he would not incur ecclesiastical or civil penalties, and that his priestly orders would not be invalidated. Assured on these points he registered himself as a dissenter permitted to conduct public worship in a meeting-house registered with the archdeacon's court. The legal ground cleared, he moved in 1726 into a large room at the top of the Market house in the busy meat centre of Newport Market, London, which had a long history as a dissenting house, already fitted with benches, pulpit, and a communion table. In 1729 he removed to finer quarters in Clare Market, a lofty room with large windows, a two-decker pulpit with a rich frontal at its centre, and an altar at its side, all fenced off with a spiked rail. In front was an enclosed area with seats, an area for those standing, and a gallery along one wall. Both locations carried entry charges for, without tithes and endowment stipend, Henley had to make a living. In the pay-box at the head of the stairs his servant collected the shillings and sixpences from those who were not paid-up subscribers, with gold, silver, or bath-metal medals. With these takings, the sale of his books, and some government payments Henley managed to survive.

In the first years the proceedings of the Oratory were comparatively sober and orthodox. On Sundays Henley preached a morning sermon, with his peculiar elocution and exaggerated use of bodily and facial gesture which earned him the title Restorer of Antient Eloquence. Once a month he celebrated the primitive liturgy, which he had modelled on the liturgy in the apostolic constitutions of Clement. In the afternoon there was a theological lecture, and on Wednesday evenings an academical oration. The times and subjects of these meetings were advertised in the Saturday papers, and, as the years went by, the subjects became more political and satirical commentaries on contemporary affairs, and the advertisements so increasingly eccentric and incomprehensible that one had to attend to hear the Orator unravel their confusion. In later years he also advertised his Gentlemen's Own University, offering lectures and private tutorials in such a fantastic range of subjects and fees, that it is difficult to discover the reality of Henley's attempt at further education behind his extreme claims and puffs.

All this activity continued with few breaks until Henley's death, in the face of a constant assault by the press and the satirists, and in uproar, heckling, and riot in the Oratory itself. In 1730 he found a wider audience when he started his weekly newspaper, the *Hyp Doctor*, in opposition to the tory *The Craftsman* and a useful organ to respond to the continuous stream of satirical attacks on him in the *Grub Street Journal*, inspired by Pope and his circle. Week after week until the fall of Walpole in 1742 Henley never failed to produce his 2*d.* sheet, filled with discussion of the burning political topics of the day, sometimes solemn and dull, sometimes lively and amusing, and often witty and inventive.

After 1742 Henley and his preaching became more and more politically biased as he inveighed with increased violence at what he saw as a growing political degeneracy, until by 1754 he described England as a 'Hanoverian Pigstye' (BL, Add. MS 11794). After the defeat of the Young Pretender in 1746 the savage reprisals which followed Culloden outraged Henley, and the violence of his orations led to his arrest and custody on the charge of 'tending to alienate his Majesty's Subjects from their Duty and Allegiance'; but after his examination before the Lords of the privy council and a fortnight in custody, he was released on bail and discharged after his appearance at the court of king's bench in 1747.

Henley's closing years were sad and lonely. His wife died in November 1737 and he lived in the house attached to the Oratory with only a female servant to care for him. His family had all but disowned him. When his father died in 1731 he cut off his eldest son with a shilling, and his sisters all predeceased him. He increasingly sought company in taverns and public houses, and soon gained the reputation of being the heavy and often boisterous drinker whom Pope immortalized in the couplet:

How Henley lay inspir'd beside a sink,
And to mere mortals seem'd a Priest in drink.
(*Dunciad* ii.425–6)

He found other social solace in the Ancient Society of Freemasons and even in the rough and tumble debates of the Robin Hood Society, but returned to his lonely house still to produce books and to write his sermons, which now propounded a doctrine far removed from his earlier orthodoxy, interpreting the scriptures by right reason as little more than a record on which man might base his moral and political life and rejecting most of the supernatural tenets of the faith. These were sermons heard by increasingly small congregations at the Oratory, and the resulting diminishing of his income added penury to his loneliness, now cheered a little by a mysterious Sarah Brown, to whom he was to leave everything he possessed.

Henley became increasingly ill from 1754, seeking help from Dr William Stukeley, but still forcing himself to preach and joke until the summer of 1756, when the uncommon form of jaundice from which he suffered finally silenced him, and he died at his home on 13 October 1756. The whereabouts of his grave is unknown and, a fortnight after his death, the *Evening Advertiser* offered an inscription for it, if it were ever found:

Here
Rots unregretted
The Residium of J. Henley
A Man
Below all Character.

GRAHAM MIDGLEY

Sources G. Midgley, *The life of Orator Henley* (1973) • *DNB* • J. Henley, *A guide to the Oratory* (1726) • J. Henley, 'A narrative', *Oratory Transactions*, 1 (1728) • D. Lysons, ed., 'Collectanea, or, A collection of advertisements and paragraphs', BL, C. 103.k.12 [cuttings from newspapers dated 1726–56 chiefly relating to J. Henley] • *Collections towards the history and antiquities of the town and county of Leicester* (1790), pt 50 [7/3] of *Bibliotheca topographica Britannica*, ed. J. Nichols (1780–1800) • Nichols, *Lit. anecdotes* • Nichols, *Illustrations* • [I. D'Israeli], *Calamities of authors*, 2 vols. (1812) • I. Disraeli, *The quarrels of authors* (1814) • T. F. Dibdin, *Bibliomania, or, Book madness: a bibliographical romance*, 2nd edn, [2 vols.] (1811) • A. Pope, *The Dunciad*, ed. J. Sutherland (1943), vol. 5 of *The Twickenham edition of the poems of Alexander Pope*, ed. J. Butt (1939–69); 3rd edn [in 1 vol.] (1963); repr. (1965) • J. Henley, 'Discourse', 24 June 1753, BL, Add. MS 11790 • J. Henley, 'Discourse', 1 March 1752, BL, Add. MS 11782 • private information (2004) • BL, Add. MS 11794

Archives Bath Central Library • BL, notes for sermons and lectures, Add. MSS 4336–4345; 10346–10349; 11768–11801; 12199–12200; 19919–19925; 22168; 22586; 22938–22946; 23200; 23743; 24668 • BL, Egmont MSS • Bodl. Oxf., discourses and letters • GL, notes for lectures delivered in London, on political, religious, and historical subjects, with a sermon • PRO, letters, SP Domestic 36 vol. 5.101/vol 7.23 • U. Aberdeen, King's College, notes for sermons • U. Birm. L., notes

Likenesses S. Ireland, etching, pubd 1786 (after W. Hogarth), BM, NPG • line engraving, 1818, NPG • E. Finden, stipple, NPG • W. Hogarth, oils, BM • J. Stow, line engraving, BM, NPG • engraving, NPG • silver medal, BM

Wealth at death house and contents: will, PRO, PROB 11/825, sig. 274

Henley, Joseph (1766–1832). *See under* Henley, Michael (*c.*1742–1813).

Henley, Joseph Warner (1793–1884), politician, born on 3 March 1793, probably at Putney, was the only son of Joseph *Henley (1766–1832) [*see under* Henley, Michael], an eminent London merchant, and his wife, Anne, daughter of C. Rooke of Wandsworth. His father, having leased the estate of Waterperry in Oxfordshire of a Mr Curzon in 1814, settled there and was high sheriff in 1817; he purchased the estate in 1830. After schooling in Fulham, Henley entered Magdalen College, Oxford, as a gentleman commoner on 27 April 1812, and graduated BA 1815 and MA 1834. He spent two years (1815–17) in his father's office in London, and in after life often referred to the advantage this training proved to him. On 9 December 1817 he married Georgiana, fourth daughter of John Fane MP, and his wife, Lady Elizabeth. She died on 15 June 1864 having borne him four sons and six daughters. Henley succeeded in due course to the position of a country gentleman at Waterperry, soon taking a leading part in county and magisterial business. In 1846 he became chairman of the quarter sessions.

In 1841 Henley was unopposed as one of the Conservative candidates for Oxfordshire and held the seat until his retirement from public life in 1878. That year he published *A Conservative's Opinion on the Contagious Diseases Act*. Henley was nearly fifty years old when he entered parliament, but his plain common sense, salty sayings, and clear insight into business soon made him conspicuous. In 1852 he took office as Lord Derby's president of the Board of Trade (having been earlier considered for the Home Office), and became a privy councillor. His tenure of office was brief, for the government lasted only nine months. In 1854 the University of Oxford conferred on him the honorary degree of DCL. When Derby, in March 1858, formed a second Conservative ministry, Henley once more joined the cabinet as president of the Board of Trade; but in the following February, differing from his colleagues on their policy of introducing parliamentary reform, especially as affecting the county franchise, he, together with Spencer Walpole, resigned from the government. As president, he was a strong opponent of government 'interference'.

Henley never held office again, though in July 1866 he was offered the home secretaryship by Lord Derby, which he declined on account of partial deafness. He frequently sat on royal commissions, contributing with especial effect to that for the reform of the court of chancery. He was sometimes an apologist for the drink trade and opposed governmental intervention in merchant shipping safety questions. In January 1878, increasingly infirm, he retired from parliament at the age of eighty-five. Henley died at Waterperry House on 8 or 9 December 1884. His eldest son, Joseph John Henley CB, of Waterperry House, JP and deputy lieutenant for Oxfordshire, was general inspector of the Local Government Board from 1867 to 1892.

RICHARD HOOPER, rev. H. C. G. MATTHEW

Sources *The Times* (10 Dec 1884) · *Disraeli, Derby and the conservative party: journals and memoirs of Edward Henry, Lord Stanley, 1849–1869*, ed. J. R. Vincent (1978) · P. Smith, *Disraelian Conservatism and social reform* (1967) · Boase, *Mod. Eng. biog.*
Archives Lpool RO, letters to the fourteenth earl of Derby · NRA, priv. coll., letters to S. H. Walpole
Likenesses F. Grant, oils, 1860, county hall, Oxford · H. C. Balding, stipple and line print (after photograph by H. Barraud), NPG · Hills & Saunders, carte-de-visite, NPG · D. J. Pound, engraving, repro. in D. J. Pound, *The drawing room portrait gallery of eminent personages* (1859) · D. J. Pound, stipple and line print (after photograph by Mayall), NPG; repro. in D. J. Pound, *The statesmen of England* (1862) · portrait, repro. in *St James's Magazine* (1870), 771
Wealth at death £11,411 19s. 5d.: probate, 30 Jan 1885, CGPLA Eng. & Wales

Henley, Michael (*c*.1742–1813), merchant and shipowner, was probably born at Rotherhithe. His origins are obscure though he may well have been the son of a Francis Henley from Ireland, who lived in Rotherhithe before being buried at Bermondsey in February 1785. Michael Henley married Mary Tonks on 4 August 1765 at St Clement Danes in the parish of Westminster. The marriage produced three daughters and two sons, the eldest, Joseph [*see below*], playing an active part in his father's business. In December 1790 or January 1791 Mary died, and was buried in the family's vault at St John-at-Wapping. Michael married his second wife, Ann Lacey, in 1792. The marriage probably took place in Derby, and she appears to have been an educated woman of independent means.

Henley began his working life by serving an apprenticeship as a Thames waterman and lighterman. He was apprenticed to William Barrett of Bermondsey from 13 May 1757 to 12 July 1764. In the course of the following decade he appears to have made a success of his occupation as a London waterman, and then a coal merchant at Shadwell and Wapping. By 1775 he had expanded his operations through the purchase of a couple of old collier vessels, which were used to transport coal from Newcastle to London. In the following years he dabbled in related activities, including ship breaking and ship stores. However, Henley's shrewd entrepreneurial talents, and his experience of the mercantile and maritime sectors, alerted him to the cyclical influence of warfare upon the shipping industry. Thus the 1790s were a watershed in the evolution of the firm, when coal merchanting and most ancillary activities were abandoned, in order to specialize in shipowning, and thereby take advantage of the wartime booms in the shipping industry. By 1790 he owned nine vessels, a figure which had increased to fifteen by 1805. In 1810 the fleet reached its maximum size of twenty-two vessels with an aggregate tonnage of 5934. Henley's innovative nature also led him to deploy his vessels flexibly and widely across many trade routes including in the Baltic, the Mediterranean, and the Atlantic. Employment as government transport vessels provided further opportunities for Henley's fleet.

By decoupling mercantile and shipping operations, Henley appears to have been one of the pioneers of specialist professional shipowning, which became more common in the first half of the nineteenth century. Another important feature of his approach was the emphasis upon sole ownership of almost all of the vessels, in contrast to the more common contemporary practice of fractional ownership. On the few occasions where Henley shared ownership this was with a master of long standing, who took on greater managerial discretion in operating the vessel. In spite of these considerable entrepreneurial achievements, Henley's level of educational attainment appears to have been quite modest, and his business papers suggest only a low level of literacy. Although he developed some accounting skills, probably through his apprenticeship, his second wife wrote most of his letters for him.

The Henleys' eldest son, **Joseph Henley** (1766–1832), appears to have become interested in his father's business from a relatively young age, and by the early 1780s he was playing an active role in it. He was bound as an apprentice waterman to his father in 1780, and as an apprentice farrier in 1784. In 1791 he married Anne Rooke (Nancy) at Wandsworth. They had two children, Anna Maria Rooke, who later died in childbirth, and Joseph Warner *Henley, a Conservative politician. Like his father, Joseph Henley was a perceptive entrepreneur, and he played a prominent part in the further expansion of the firm in the first decade of the nineteenth century. Lacking his father's specialized interest in the coal trade, he was probably an important influence in the family's movement away from this activity. As the business expanded his father appears to have taken primary responsibility for the vessels, and Joseph for chartering and insurance. Additionally, Joseph appears to have improved the firm's system of accounting.

By 1805 Michael Henley had retired to Derby, and left Joseph with primary responsibility for the business, although the two communicated regularly on policy matters with the father offering frequent advice. In 1811 Joseph was elected a member of Lloyds, following its reorganization into a formal institution. With Michael Henley's death on 11 September 1813 at Friargate, Derby, Joseph was left to run the business on his own. Michael Henley was buried in a vault at St Werburgh's, Derby, where he had been a churchwarden, and left £125,000 excluding freeholds. After his father's death Joseph leased Waterperry House, near Wheatley, a few miles from Oxford; and he purchased it in 1830. Anne Henley died in Derby in 1833.

Joseph received temporary support from his own son, Joseph Warner, before the latter went into politics. Although Joseph had served the office of high sheriff in 1817, his main commitment was to his business enterprise, but this was not the case for his son. Joseph Henley also received assistance from Edward Rule, a shipbroker, and several managing clerks including Thomas Dennis and W. Williams. However, lack of entrepreneurial continuity within the family, and the prolonged shipping depression of the 1820s, convinced the ageing Joseph of the need to contract his active shipping operations. A number of vessels were sold during the temporary economic upturn in the mid-1820s and by 1831 the firm appears to have ceased trading. Joseph died in 1832 in the middle of a commercial depression, and left £60,000 excluding freeholds.   SIMON VILLE

Sources S. P. Ville, 'Michael Henley and son, London shipowners, 1770–1830', in S. P. Ville, *English shipowning during the industrial revolution* (1987) · A. Currie, *Henleys of Wapping* (1988) · S. Ville, 'Michael Henley and son, London shipowners, 1775–1830: with special reference to the war experience, 1775–1830', PhD diss., U. Lond., 1984 · S. Ville, 'Size and profitability of English colliers in the eighteenth century: a reappraisal', *Business History Review*, 58 (1984), 103–52 · S. Ville, 'James Kirton, shipping agent', *Mariner's Mirror*, 67 (1981), 149–62 · PRO, IR 26/582/697 · PRO, PROB/11/1802, fol. 443; IR 26/1292, fol. 380
Archives NMM
Wealth at death £125,000: PRO, death duty registers, IR 26/582/697 · £60,000—Joseph Henley: will, PRO, PROB 11/1802, fol. 443; PRO, death duty registers, IR 26/1292, fol. 380

Henley, Orator. *See* Henley, John (1692–1756).

Henley, Phocion (1727/8–1764), composer, was one of the three sons of John Henley (1677–1732), of Wootton Abbots, Dorset, MP for Lyme Regis, and his wife, Hester, *née* Bagwell. Robert Henley, first earl of Northington, was his cousin. John Henley died while his son was an infant, leaving his property and family to the care of his brother, Robert Henley of Glanville Wootton. Phocion Henley matriculated at Wadham College, Oxford, on 7 May 1746, at the age of eighteen, and graduated BA on 14 February 1749. As an undergraduate, he spent much time studying music, and was to compose several chants and anthems. He apparently published a collection of six hymns, *The Cure of Saul* (not traced), and, some years after his death, his *Divine Harmony, being a Collection of Psalm and Hymn Tunes in Score* appeared; it was republished by John Page, with four psalm tunes by Thomas Sharp, in 1798. From 1759 until his death Henley was rector of two London churches, St Andrew by the Wardrobe and St Ann Blackfriars. He died on 29 August 1764.   R. F. SHARP, *rev.* K. D. REYNOLDS

Sources W. H. Husk, 'Henley, Phocion', Grove, *Dict. mus.* (1878–90) · *GM*, 1st ser., 34 (1764), 399 · Foster, *Alum. Oxon.* · HoP, *Commons* · Venn, *Alum. Cant.*

Henley, Robert (1591–1656), legal official, was born in Taunton, Somerset, the eldest son of Andrew Henley, a minor Somerset landowner, and his wife, Dorothy Sandford. He was educated in Taunton, at Lincoln College, Oxford, from 1605, and then at the Middle Temple, being called to the bar in 1615 (confirmed the next year). He was also, most unusually for someone pursuing a legal career, a member of the Leathersellers' Company of London, of which he became free by redemption (also in 1615). In 1618 Henley bought one of the six clerkships in chancery, it was said for £6000; estimates of the annual value of these offices vary between £2000 and £1200, the lower figure being due to the clerks' losses from the fire which destroyed their premises in 1621. How he raised the money to buy this office is perhaps the biggest mystery of his career; no evidence survives of his borrowing on bond or by mortgage, but he could scarcely have saved this much after only two or three years in law practice, or three years as a master leatherseller. In 1629 he and his future deputy, Samuel Wightwick, acquired the chief clerkship of king's bench. One of the most lucrative offices in the entire administration, it had attracted the attention of successive royal favourites—Robert Carr, earl of Somerset, and George Villiers, duke of Buckingham; the latter's trustees sold it (after the duke's assassination) to Henley and Wightwick. Henley sold his chancery office in 1632, perhaps to help pay off the outlay on this richer prize. But by then the six clerks had come under unwelcome scrutiny from the commissioners on exacted fees; and in 1635 Henley obtained a retrospective pardon for any offences which he might have committed in that capacity. Investigation of the king's bench office was, however, reserved to a special committee of the privy council.

In 1640 Henley lent the king £3000 for the campaign against the Scots, and after the outbreak of civil war in England he joined the royal court at Oxford, leaving his deputy in London to execute the office. By the 1650s Wightwick had actually become chief clerk, and Henley had paid penal fines for his royalism, possibly totalling as much as £9000. After having been inactive in his trade for many years, Henley was elected third warden of the

Leathersellers in 1650 and then, on being elected as an alderman of the City, master of the company for 1650–51. In December 1650 he was cited before the indemnity committee for being an alderman contrary to the parliamentary ordinances of 1647. The case dragged on until March 1652, by which time he had been discharged and heavily fined by the City, the committee adding a notional penalty of another 40s. He was also dispensed from serving as sheriff of London and Middlesex later that year. Besides increasing their landholdings in Somerset, he and his family had been acquiring property in Dorset, Wiltshire, and Hampshire, their main base shifting to the latter county. When he made his will at the end of 1655 Henley also had interests in Kent and in the fens. Besides annuities to his second wife Anne Eldred and daughters, he left £10,000 to each of his two younger sons. The eldest son's line was ruined by extravagance; his second son resumed the king's bench office at the Restoration, and seems to have held it until his death over thirty years later, also acting by deputy. His great-grandson, also Robert *Henley (c.1708–1772), was to become lord chancellor and earl of Northington. Robert Henley is one of the clearest examples of someone from a modest gentry family whose wealth depended on the tenure of office, and where the family's subsequent fortunes remained at risk from individual failings and demographic mischance. He died in 1656, possibly at Temple Bar, London, and was buried on 29 February in the Temple Church. G. E. AYLMER

Sources G. E. Aylmer, *The king's servants: the civil service of Charles I, 1625–1642*, rev. edn (1974), 214–15, 305–8 · M. W. Helms and P. Watson, 'Henley, Andrew', HoP, *Commons, 1660–90* · P. Watson, 'Henley, Sir Robert', HoP, *Commons, 1660–90* · J. P. Ferris, 'Henley, Sir Robert', HoP, *Commons, 1660–90* · HoP, *Commons, 1690–1715* [draft] · J. S. Wilson, 'The administrative work of the lord chancellor in the early seventeenth century', PhD diss., U. Lond., 1927, esp. appx 3 · M. Blatcher, 'The working of the court of king's bench in the fifteenth century', PhD diss., U. Lond., 1936 · 'Henley', GEC, *Baronetage* · 'Northington', GEC, *Peerage* · F. T. Colby, ed., *The visitation of the county of Somerset in the year 1623*, Harleian Society, 11 (1876) · G. D. Squibb, ed., *The visitation of Somerset and the city of Bristol, 1672*, Harleian Society, new ser., 11 (1992) · *VCH Somerset*, vol. 4 · A. B. Beaven, ed., *The aldermen of the City of London, temp. Henry III–[1912]*, 2 vols. (1908–13) · W. H. Black, *History and antiquities of the Worshipful Company of Leathersellers, of the City of London* (privately printed, London, 1871) · *CSP dom.* · M. A. E. Green, ed., *Calendar of the proceedings of the committee for advance of money, 1642–1656*, 3 vols., PRO (1888) · M. A. E. Green, ed., *Calendar of the proceedings of the committee for compounding … 1643–1660*, 5 vols., PRO (1889–92) · *JHC*, 7 (1651–9) · deeds (bargains and sales, mortgages; leases), Som. ARS · deeds, Dorset RO [bargains and sales, mortgages; leases] · deeds, Hants. RO [bargains and sales, mortgages; leases] · F. A. Inderwick and R. A. Roberts, eds., *A calendar of the Inner Temple records*, 2 (1898), 365 · will, PRO, PROB 11/254, sig. 129
Archives Leathersellers' Company, London, records · PRO, state papers

Henley, Robert, first earl of Northington (c.1708–1772), lord chancellor, was the second son of Anthony *Henley (1666/7–1711), landowner and whig MP, of The Grange, Hampshire, and Mary, daughter of the Hon. Peregrine Bertie and granddaughter of the second earl of Lindsey. He was educated at Westminster School, and entered St John's College, Oxford, in 1724; he graduated BA in 1729

Robert Henley, first earl of Northington (c.1708–1772), by Thomas Hudson, 1760–61

and MA in 1733, having been elected a fellow of All Souls in November 1727. He was admitted to the Inner Temple in 1728, and called to the bar in 1732. As a young man he developed an addiction to port, about which he is reputed to have muttered when older and finding difficulty in walking in the House of Lords, 'If I had only known that these legs were one day to carry a Lord Chancellor, I'd have taken better care of them when I was a lad' (Campbell, 5.178). His notoriously bad temper in later life was attributed to gout. He passed his vacations at Bath, where he met a young lady in a wheelchair taking the waters. He courted her, she was cured, and they married on 19 November 1743. His bride was Jane (*bap.* 1716, *d.* 1787), daughter and coheiress of Sir John Huband, second baronet, and Rhoda Broughton; they had three sons and five daughters. Their only surviving son, Robert *Henley, followed his father into politics. Henley's practice at king's bench and on the western circuit was slow to flourish, but his conviviality made him so popular at Bath, a borough where the parliamentary franchise was confined to the corporation, that he was returned as one of its MPs at the 1747 general election. In 1748 he succeeded his elder brother Anthony in the family estates, but chose to adhere to his legal career rather than opt for the life of a country squire.

In parliament Henley, of an old whig family, was expected to be a ministerial supporter, but he joined the opposition Leicester House party of Frederick, prince of Wales, and in the ministry planned for that prince's accession he was put down for attorney-general. All such hopes were dashed by the sudden death of the prince in 1751.

The princess dowager abandoned political opposition, and Henley was made solicitor-general to the new prince, the future George III. Horace Walpole described Henley as then 'a lawyer in vogue, but his abilities did not figure in proportion to the impudence of his ill-nature' (Walpole, *Memoirs*, 1.96). In 1754 he was promoted to be the prince's attorney-general. Henley became a frequent speaker in parliament, supporting Lord Hardwicke's Marriage Act of 1753, and the ministerial treaty with Russia in a famous debate of 10 December 1755. His legal practice blossomed after his appointment as a KC in 1751. He took the lead on the western circuit, and a prominent role at the court of king's bench. He was offered but declined a judgeship in 1753.

The turning point of Henley's career came with the political crisis of the mid-1750s, when the disastrous start to the Seven Years' War led to the resignation of the duke of Newcastle as prime minister. Henley was knighted on 29 October 1756 and then appointed attorney-general in the new Pitt–Devonshire ministry, without having held the junior post of solicitor-general. Leicester House support of the administration may have explained this surprise promotion, and Horace Walpole could be mistaken in his oft-cited attribution of it to Henry Fox, an opponent of the ministry. When George II dismissed this administration in April 1757, the prolonged negotiations that led to the formation of a Pitt–Newcastle coalition seemed likely to founder on the legal appointments. Pitt did not want Newcastle's ally Lord Hardwicke to return as lord chancellor, and George II was unwilling to grant the peerage other candidates demanded. Henley was not one of those first under consideration. He lacked experience, and the king disliked him for his previous attachment to Prince Frederick. But he left the way open by not insisting on a peerage, and in a last-minute decision he was made lord keeper of the great seal on 30 June 1757, with appointment to the privy council and cabinet. This was a post with virtually the same burdens of office as lord chancellor, even the role of speaker in the House of Lords, but without the prestige of that office, or even a peerage. It was the last time the office was ever created. Pitt favoured Henley, who had no connection with either himself or Newcastle, since he would create no problems in cabinet.

Lord Keeper Henley now had to resign his Commons seat, and was precluded from taking part in Lords debates. Since his attendance at cabinet was a formality, politics did not distract him from his judicial duty in the court of chancery. He was not a man whose conduct on the bench aroused admiration, and his dislike of humbug sometimes led him to violate the rules of decency by his sharp tongue. But he was reckoned as impartial and upright as his predecessor Lord Hardwicke, and conscientiously took notes of precedents and the arguments of learned counsel. His opinions were deemed sound, but lacking in the logic and caution of Hardwicke. It was said that in nine years only six of his judgments were reversed or altered on appeal to the House of Lords. His elevation to a peerage, on 27 March 1760, as Baron Henley, was fortuitous. Lord Ferrers had killed a servant, and for the trial of a peer

a lord high steward was appointed to preside, who must himself be a peer, and was customarily the holder of the great seal. Horace Walpole thought Henley behaved badly at the trial, where Lord Ferrers was unanimously found guilty. 'He neither had any dignity, nor affected any. Nay, he held it all so cheap, that he said at his own table t'other day, "I will not send for Garrick and learn to act a part"' (*Letters of Horace Walpole*, 4.370).

The accession of George III in 1760 brought Henley nearer to political centre stage. The new king favoured him as having been a steady adherent of Leicester House, and saw him as an ally for his favourite Lord Bute. On 16 January 1761 Henley became lord chancellor, a post he retained through four ministries until 1766. He was soon emboldened to obtain another favour from his sovereign, namely permission to discontinue the evening sittings of the court of chancery, on Wednesdays and Fridays, frankly explaining that he liked his bottle of port at dinner: the reason amused the king, who often told the story afterwards. The new lord chancellor at first maintained a low political profile. During the Bute ministry he failed to speak in the Lords on such controversial matters as the peace terms of 1762 and the cider tax of 1763. In the Grenville ministry he avoided direct involvement in the *North Briton* case, leaving it to the attorney-general and solicitor-general. But he did have to act as lord high steward again in 1765, for the trial of Lord Byron over a death in a tavern duel: Lord Byron was found guilty of manslaughter, but discharged after pleading privilege of peerage. Meanwhile on 19 May 1764 Henley had been created earl of Northington, taking his title from a Hampshire hamlet near the family estate of Grange: and he was also appointed lord lieutenant of his native county. These were marks of royal favour, and his role of being the king's man in the cabinet became significant during the Rockingham ministry of 1765–6. George III sometimes then confided to Northington his private conversations with the prime minister, and in January 1766 even conceived of an administration headed by Northington that would free him from the clutches of politicians like Grenville, Rockingham, and Pitt. That was a pipe dream, but Northington was to play a key political role that year. His colleagues were men of natural reserve and strict propriety, and the robust lord chancellor thought as little of their characters as he did of their abilities: 'a damned silly system' he had deemed it from the first, and this opinion was strengthened by disapproval of the conciliatory American policy the ministry came to adopt (Langford, 4).

When news of colonial resistance to Grenville's Stamp Act reached Britain, Northington was among those who called it rebellion. At a projected cabinet meeting of 31 October 1765 he intended to propose the enforcement of the Stamp Act, by use of the army if necessary. But the death that same day of the duke of Cumberland, the other hardliner in the cabinet, killed that possibility, and the ministry began to consider concessions. Northington considered irregular Rockingham's practice of informal cabinet discussions, and on 11 December asked whether the king would be informed: on receiving a negative answer, he himself told George III of the apparent decision not to enforce the Stamp Act. Northington did not yet break with the ministry in parliament. He spoke for the address on 17 December 1765, and against opposition demands concerning American papers on 14 and 20 January 1766. When the Lords on 3 February debated the ministerial resolution asserting parliamentary supremacy over the colonies, preparatory to the Declaratory Act, Northington denounced as unconstitutional Lord Camden's contention that taxation must be linked to representation. But by then the cabinet had finally decided on repeal of the Stamp Act, and the lord chancellor's hostility was demonstrated when he voted on 4 and 6 February for successful opposition motions on such indirect topics as compensation for victims of colonial riots. These were among the parliamentary setbacks that caused Rockingham to secure open royal support for repeal, which passed the Commons by early March. But the ministry feared that the lord chancellor's opposition might well prove fatal to the measure in the Lords. The prime minister therefore persuaded the king to put pressure on Northington, whose role in the crucial Lords debate of 11 March was probably decisive. Northington began by stating that the colonial behaviour was equivalent to rebellion; but he then nevertheless urged the Lords to accept repeal, not on the merits of the case, but so as to avoid a dispute between the two houses of parliament: for only the Commons could vote taxation. The repeal was then carried by 73 votes to 61.

The lord chancellor was obliging his sovereign rather than his colleagues, and he was to be the instrument of their dismissal a few months later. By the spring of 1766 George III had decided that the Rockingham ministry was too incompetent to continue, and successfully sounded Pitt on his willingness to head a new administration. Northington's role was to provide the opportunity. His motives were both personal and political. His poor health and irascible temper meant that he was feeling the strain of the triple task of his office: presiding over both the House of Lords and the court of chancery, as well as attendance at cabinet. He may also have been aware of a promise made to Attorney-General Charles Yorke in August 1765 that he would become lord chancellor in a year's time. Certainly he was on the look-out for a more comfortable billet. But the lord chancellor was motivated by principle, or at least prejudice, as well as self-interest, for the political issue at stake was one on which he held strong views. In June the cabinet considered a Board of Trade report on Canada that recommended the limited use of French law, lawyers, and language. Northington took a particular interest in Canada, and clearly had the small British minority there in mind when he told Rockingham on 22 May his opinion of the report. 'Should it pass into a law, it would be the most oppressive to the subject that ever was enacted' (Keppel, 1.343–4). He also raised a constitutional objection to the ministry's intention of enacting the policy by royal instructions to the governor of Quebec, stating that such an important matter should be decided by parliament, not the crown. At the cabinet on 27 June Northington sought to block the measure by

announcing his refusal to attend further meetings on the subject. When the ministry decided to ignore him and implement the policy, Northington's fury knew no bounds. 'By God! They shall never meet again', he was reputed to have declared (Campbell, 5.209). On 6 July, as lord chancellor, by prior arrangement he formally advised the king that the ministry was too weak to continue, and Pitt, as earl of Chatham, now formed a new one. Northington acted as the link between him and George III, who told Pitt in a letter of 7 July, 'there is no man in my service on whom I so thoroughly rely' (ibid., 210). Northington carefully safeguarded his own position, stating in a letter of 20 July to Pitt that 'I found His Majesty very desirous that I should take a great office in his administration' (ibid., 212). On 30 July he gladly surrendered the great seal to Pitt's nominee Lord Camden in exchange for the prestigious but less onerous post of lord president of the council. In addition to his salary he obtained an immediate pension of £2000, to be raised to £4000 on resignation of his office.

There was a sequel to the Canada episode. When the report was resurrected in 1767 Northington finally killed its implementation by insisting that any plan for Quebec needed 'the sanction of Parliament' (Thomas, 336). Northington was a slender man of middle height, with an overbright complexion. Whether or not his early drinking led to his later bad health, this now so deteriorated that his political twilight came early. Although he took part in Lords debates of early 1767, he spent much of that year at home in Hampshire. 'I barely walk, and am without strength or appetite', he wrote on 9 July to the duke of Grafton, then acting head of the ministry (Campbell, 5.219). His continuous request to resign was finally granted on 23 December. During 1768 his health recovered enough for him to be offered the post of lord privy seal when Chatham resigned it in October, but he refused, and his gradual physical decline ended in his death at The Grange on 14 January 1772. He was buried at Northington church. A balanced obituary may be found in Grafton's recollection that he was 'a man full of honour, a disinterested gentleman, and though much devoted to the King, with great zeal for the constitution. As a lawyer, his knowledge and ability were great, but his manner and speech were ungracious' (ibid., 220n.).

PETER D. G. THOMAS

Sources J. Campbell, *Lives of the lord chancellors*, 7 vols. (1845–7) • P. D. G. Thomas, *British politics and the Stamp Act crisis: the first phase of the American revolution, 1763–1767* (1975) • H. Walpole, *Memoirs of the reign of King George the Second*, ed. Lord Holland, 2nd edn, 3 vols. (1847) • *The letters of Horace Walpole, fourth earl of Orford*, ed. P. Toynbee, 16 vols. (1903–5) • P. Langford, *The first Rockingham administration, 1765–1766* (1973) • G. Thomas, earl of Albemarle [G. T. Keppel], *Memoirs of the marquis of Rockingham and his contemporaries*, 2 vols. (1852) • R. R. Sedgwick, 'Henley, Robert', HoP, *Commons, 1715–54* • R. A. Humphreys and S. M. Scott, 'Lord Northington and the laws of Canada', *Canadian Historical Review*, 14 (1933), 42–61 • J. C. D. Clark, *The dynamics of change: the crisis of the 1750s and English party systems* (1982) • J. Brooke, *The Chatham administration, 1766–1768* (1956) • DNB • GEC, *Peerage* • IGI • HoP, *Commons, 1690–1715* [draft]
Archives BL, commonplace book and legal notebooks, Add. MSS 26060–26066 • Northants. RO, papers | BL, corresp. with George

Grenville, Add. MS 57812 · BL, corresp. with duke of Newcastle, Add. MSS 32871–33069 *passim* · BL, corresp. with Charles Yorke and earls of Hardwicke, Add. MSS 35592–35639, 36223 *passim* · Linn. Soc., letters to John Ellis · Suffolk RO, Bury St Edmunds, letters to duke of Grafton
Likenesses T. Hudson, oils, 1760–61, All Souls Oxf. [*see illus.*] · studio of T. Hudson, oils, NPG

Henley, Robert, **second earl of Northington** (1747–1786), politician, was born on 3 January 1747 in the parish of St Andrew's, Holborn, London, the second and only surviving son of Robert *Henley, first earl of Northington (*c.*1708–1772), lord chancellor, and his wife, Jane Huband (*bap.* 1716, *d.* 1787). He was educated at Westminster School and at Christ Church, Oxford, whence he matriculated on 24 October 1763, and received an MA on 30 April 1766. In April 1763 he was appointed a teller of the exchequer, and at the general election of March 1768 he was returned to parliament uncontested for Hampshire. He appears to have spoken only once in the Commons, on 8 November 1768, when he moved the address. He was created LLD of Cambridge on 3 July 1769 and became master of the hanaper office in chancery on 28 November 1771. On his father's death on 14 January 1772 he succeeded as second earl of Northington, and he took his seat in the Lords on 17 February. On 18 August 1773 he became a knight of the Thistle, and on 6 March 1777 he was elected a fellow of the Society of Antiquaries.

On the formation of the coalition ministry of Charles James Fox and Lord North, Northington, a close friend of Fox, was appointed lord lieutenant of Ireland, after the post had been declined by the duke of Devonshire, Lord Fitzwilliam, and Lord Althorp. He was sworn of the privy council on the same day as he took office, 30 April 1783. Having been sworn in at Dublin on 3 June 1783, he opened the first session of the new Irish parliament on 14 October 1783. Northington's six-month term of office was not successful. At an early stage his only venture into policy making, an attempt to introduce annual sessions for the Irish parliament, had to be abandoned in the face of Lord North's disapproval. Before long Northington had allowed the Irish privy council to press him into placing Irish commercial interests above those of Britain and the empire. Only the united opposition of cabinet ministers in London prevented an attempt by Irish politicians to have imperial peace treaties laid before the Irish parliament, a move that would have sundered the unity of the two kingdoms. Northington failed also to manage the ill-assorted alliance of patriots and former government supporters who made up the new 'broad bottom' privy council. His first secretary, William Windham, quit his post after a few weeks, defeated by Northington's willingness to believe malicious gossip from Dublin Castle about him. Even his new secretary, Thomas Pelham, recognized that his apparent success in orchestrating the Irish Commons had more to do with the disorganized state of his political opponents than with the strength and ability of the castle party. More dangerous still was Northington's failure to deal effectively with the twin challenge of parliamentary

reform, which was debated in the house, and the volunteers, who met in open convention in November 1783. Within parliament he was unable to prevent the Commons from voting to himself and Pelham salary rises which he believed would place him under an obligation to the house.

Northington resigned with the coalition ministry and, after awaiting the arrival of his successor, left Dublin on 26 February 1784. He died at Paris, aged thirty-nine, on 5 July 1786, on his return from Italy, where he attempted to regain his health; he was buried at Northington church, Hampshire. As he was unmarried his titles became extinct, and his estate, The Grange, near Alresford in Hampshire, was sold to Henry Drummond. Wraxall wrote of him that he was unwieldy in person, wanting in grace, and not brilliant, but that he made himself beloved in Ireland in spite of his infirmities.

G. F. R. BARKER, *rev.* GERARD O'BRIEN

Sources G. O'Brien, *Anglo-Irish politics in the age of Grattan and Pitt* (1987) · Northington letter-book, BL, Add. MS 38716 · BL, Thomas Pelham papers, Add. MS 33100 · PRO, HO 100/9, HO 100/10 · BL, William Windham papers, Add. MS 37873 · *Memorials and correspondence of Charles James Fox*, ed. J. Russell, 4 vols. (1853–7), vol. 2 · *The Windham papers* (1913) · *The manuscripts and correspondence of James, first earl of Charlemont*, 1, HMC, 28 (1891) · H. Grattan, *Memoirs of the life and times of the Rt Hon. Henry Grattan*, 5 vols. (1839–46), vol. 3 · *The correspondence of the Right Hon. John Beresford, illustrative of the last thirty years of the Irish parliament*, ed. W. Beresford, 2 vols. (1854), vol. 1 · J. Porter, P. Byrne, and W. Porter, eds., *The parliamentary register, or, History of the proceedings and debates of the House of Commons of Ireland, 1781–1797*, 17 vols. (1784–1801), vol. 2 · GEC, *Peerage* · M. M. Drummond, 'Henley, Robert', HoP, *Commons, 1754–90* · Bucks. RLSS, Spencer-Bernard Papers, OI/8/11 · *Correspondence of Emily, duchess of Leinster (1731–1814)*, ed. B. Fitzgerald, 3 vols., IMC (1949–57), vol. 3 · *The papers of George Wyatt, esquire, of Boxley Abbey in the county of Kent*, ed. D. M. Loades, CS, 4th ser., 5 (1968) · DNB · *The historical and the posthumous memoirs of Sir Nathaniel William Wraxall, 1772–1784*, ed. H. B. Wheatley, 5 vols. (1884) · B. Burke, *A genealogical history of the dormant, abeyant, forfeited and extinct peerages of the British empire*, new edn (1883), 270 · Foster, *Alum. Oxon., 1715–1886*, 2.645
Archives BL, letter-book as viceroy of Ireland, Add. MS 38716 · Yale U., Beinecke L., letter-book | BL, corresp. with C. J. Fox, Add. MS 47567 · BL, letters, mainly to Thomas Pelham, second Earl Chichester, Add. MS 47567 · BL, Thomas Pelham papers, Add. MS 33100 · BL, William Windham papers, Add. MS 37873 · NL Ire., letters to Sir Ralph Payne · PRO, HO 100/9, HO 100/10
Likenesses J. Reynolds, oils, exh. RA 1785, NG Ire. · W. C. Edwards, engraving (after J. Reynolds), repro. in R. Henley, earl of Northington, *Memoir of Lord Chancellor Northington* (1831) · J. Reynolds, oils, NPG

Henley, Robert [*formerly* Robert Henley Eden], **second Baron Henley** (1789–1841), lawyer, was born on 3 September 1789 at Dresden, the eldest surviving son of the first baron, Morton *Eden (1752–1830), and his wife, Elizabeth (*d.* 1821), daughter of Robert *Henley, first earl of Northington. He was educated at Eton College from about 1801 to 1806 and matriculated at Christ Church, Oxford, on 24 October 1807; he graduated BA with a third class in classics in 1811 and proceeded MA in 1814. He was called to the bar at Lincoln's Inn, London, in 1814, a commissioner of bankrupts from 1820 to 1826, was king's serjeant for the duchy of Lancaster from 1825 to 1826, and was a master in chancery from 1826 to 1840, when a mental disorder incapacitated him. He was tory MP for Fowey, Cornwall, from 1826 to 1830. On 11 March 1824 he had married, at Drayton Basset, Stafford, Harriet Eleanora (d. 1869), third daughter of Sir Robert *Peel (1750–1830), and sister to the statesman Sir Robert Peel (1788–1850). They had four sons, and Eden succeeded his father in the peerage on 6 December 1830. On 31 March 1831 he assumed by royal licence the name Robert Henley in commemoration of his maternal ancestors.

In 1818 Henley published two volumes of the decisions, in the court of chancery, of his grandfather Lord Northington, and he published a memoir of him in 1831. As a lawyer Henley distinguished himself for the special attention he paid to the laws of bankruptcy and injunctions, his works on these subjects running to several editions. His *Treatise on the Law of Injunctions* (1821) enjoyed wide circulation.

An evangelical, Henley also devoted much attention to reform of the English church, and he was pre-eminent among writers on church reform in the early 1830s. His *Plan of Church Reform* (1832) received wide circulation, and went to eight editions. Two years later he wrote *A Plan for a New Arrangement and Increase in the Number of Dioceses of England and Wales*. Henley urged reduction of cathedral and collegiate establishments, the redistribution of property, and the maintenance of a resident minister in every parish. However, his most original proposal was that certain church properties should be taken over by a body of commissioners. The ecclesiastical commissioners of 1835–40 adopted a number of his ideas, notably those dealing with the redistribution of income.

Henley died insane, after a long illness, at his home in Whitehall Place, London, on 1 or 3 February 1841. He was buried at Watford, Northamptonshire, on 10 February. His eldest son, Anthony Henley, succeeded him in the barony. G. B. SMITH, rev. V. MARKHAM LESTER

Sources Foster, *Alum. Oxon.* · *GM*, 2nd ser., 15 (1841), 425 · G. F. A. Best, *Temporal pillars: Queen Anne's bounty, the ecclesiastical commissioners, and the Church of England* (1964) · O. Chadwick, *The Victorian church*, 1 (1966) · GEC, *Peerage*, new edn, vol. 6
Archives BL, corresp. with Sir Robert Peel, Add. MSS 40269–40606, *passim*

Henley, Samuel (1740–1815), Church of England clergyman and writer, was a native of Devon, and was admitted sizar at Queens' College, Cambridge, on 28 November 1770, as a 'ten-year man', a status which did not involve residence at the university. He was ordained a priest in the Church of England, and recruited by Dr Burton to act as a professor of moral philosophy at William and Mary College in Williamsburg, Virginia. During his tenure there he won the friendship of such men as George Wythe, Peyton Randolph, and Thomas Jefferson, and was an admired teacher of James Madison, Edmund Randolph, James Monroe, and Jefferson's younger brother Randolph Jefferson. His sermons, three of which were published at Williamsburg, show him to have been a liberal and enlightened man. His views made him some enemies,

including the more religiously conservative treasurer of Virginia, Robert Carter Nicholas (1728–1780), whose fiercely vocal opposition to Henley's candidacy for the rectorship of Bruton parish church may well have cost him the position.

Henley returned to England in May 1775 because of the increasing tension of the political situation in Virginia just before the American War of Independence. He obtained an assistant mastership at Harrow School, and soon afterwards received a curacy at Northall in Middlesex. In 1778 he was elected a fellow of the Society of Antiquaries, and four years later he was presented to the living of Rendlesham in Suffolk. His letters show that he continued to spend the greater part of his time at Harrow. Henley engaged largely in literary work, and maintained an extensive correspondence on antiquarian and classical subjects with Michael Tyson, Richard Gough, Dawson Turner, Bishop Percy, and other scholars of the time. In 1779 he edited *Travels in the Two Sicilies* by Henry Swinburne, the well-known court chronicler. On 10 June 1780 Henley married Susanna, daughter of Thomas Figgins, of Chippenham, Wiltshire. In 1784 he published with notes an admirable English translation of *Vathek*, the French romance written (but then still unpublished) by William Beckford (1760–1844). The French original was not published until 1787. Stephen Weston stated in the *Gentleman's Magazine* in 1784 that *Vathek* had been composed by Henley himself as a text 'for the purpose of giving to the public the information contained in the notes'. Henley replied that his book was merely a translation from an unpublished French manuscript. Beckford, in the preface to the French version of 1815, mentions that the appearance of the English translation before his original was not his intention, and mysteriously attributes it to circumstances 'peu intéressantes pour le public'. Henley was a frequent contributor to the *Monthly Magazine*. He also occasionally wrote short poems for private circulation among his friends.

Henley's religious works included *A Candid Refutation of the Heresy Imputed by R. C. Nicholas to the Revd. Samuel Henley* (1774) and a *Dissertation on the controverted passages of St. Peter and St. Jude concerning the angels that sinned* (1778). His other publications included *Observations on the subject of the fourth eclogue, the allegory in the third Georgic, and the primary design of the Aeneid of Virgil, with incidental remarks on some coins of the Jews* (1788) and an *Essay towards a New Edition of the Elegies of Tibullus, with Translation and Notes* (1792).

On 1 June 1805 Henley was readmitted to Queens' College, Cambridge, as a fellow-commoner, and in the same year was appointed principal of the newly established East India College at Haileybury. He was awarded a DD (Lambeth) in 1806. He died on 29 December 1815, having resigned as principal in January of that year. His son Cuthbert succeeded him as rector of Rendlesham (1816–30).

G. P. MORIARTY, rev. JOHN D. HAIGH

Sources *GM*, 1st ser., 86/1 (1816), 182 · *GM*, 1st ser., 57 (1787), 120 · Venn, *Alum. Cant.* · *IGI* · Nichols, *Lit. anecdotes*, 8.15–16 · Nichols, *Illustrations*, 3.759–65 · BL, Add. MS 19197, fol. 202 · C. E. Buckland,

Dictionary of Indian biography (1906) · Colonial Williamsburg Foundation, www.history.org/almanack/almanack.cfm [online historical almanack], 1997 · T. W. Tate, 'Nicholas, Robert Carter', *ANB* **Archives** Boston PL, corresp. | Bodl. Oxf., corresp. with William Beckford

Henley [Hanley], **Walter of** (*fl. c.*1260), writer on agriculture, was the author of a treatise known from more than thirty manuscripts; written in French, in most versions it is entitled *Husbandry* (*Hosbondrye*, and so on) but only about ten of them give the author's name, which was apparently not included in the original work but added by copyists. The text at one point refers to 'au tens qe ieo fu baillif' ('the time when I was bailiff'; *Walter of Henley*, ed. Oschinsky, 338) and one early fourteenth-century copy adds to the author's name 'qui primes fu chivalier e puis se rendist frere precheur' ('who was originally a knight and then became a Friar Preacher'; ibid., 344). No more is known of the author's life, and even this much is open to doubt: it was perhaps not the treatise's author who had been a bailiff but its presumably fictitious narrator—the father instructing the son, and his becoming a friar preacher, a Dominican, may conceivably be no more than a jocular reference to its style and structure.

Contemporary records refer to at least two persons named Walter of Henley (or Hanley). One, from Great Kimble, Buckinghamshire, was in the service of the earl of Gloucester and held lands of the earl's brother, Thomas de Clare; references to him occur between 1266 and 1275, and he may well be the same as the Walter of Henley who was given a horse by Isabella de Forz, countess of Aumale, in 1267 and who visited her (temporarily alienated) manor of Borley, Essex. Another Walter, from Henley near Buckland Newton, Dorset, had surrendered all his lands there to the abbot of Glastonbury before 1265. There is nothing but the name to associate these men with the treatise; its author may be any or none of them. Nor can the treatise and its author be convincingly linked with a particular region: a supposed association with Canterbury, from the provenance of certain manuscripts, cannot be sustained, and suggested similarities with later agricultural practice in Gloucestershire and Herefordshire are too slight.

However, from what the treatise says of estate administration at a time when methods were changing, it seems likely that it was written in the 1250s or 1260s. It is one of six treatises on managing agricultural properties that survive from mid- or late thirteenth-century England. Only one of the others has a named author—Robert Grosseteste, bishop of Lincoln (*d.* 1253)—and Walter of Henley's treatise was the most widely read of them all, as shown by the number of surviving manuscripts and by the degree of variation between them, pointing to frequent copying and glossing. Its popularity is understandable, for it is written with great charm and verve. Its structure is that of a contemporary sermon, with prologue and epilogue related to the main theme but looking beyond its technical content. This theme was a commentary on a slightly earlier treatise, the *Seneschaucy*; it enlarges on the techniques involved in, successively, manorial management,

corn growing, and livestock. It is written from the viewpoint of the owner of a small estate, who managed it in person, and it bears many marks of the author's individuality, among them an emphasis on profit, honestly and honourably gained, the occasional proverb in English, and digressions to calculate, for instance, the relative cost of oxen and horses in plough-teams. The author seems to have produced two versions of the text and it has been suggested that the first was for oral delivery, the second for reading. Although the treatise was soon out of date in some details of management, its agricultural precepts continued to be valid, and in the fifteenth century it was still being copied, apparently as of practical value. A much revised version in English was composed in the fifteenth century and printed by Wynkyn de Worde in 1510.

P. D. A. HARVEY

Sources *Walter of Henley, and other treatises on estate management and accounting*, ed. D. Oschinsky (1971) · G. R. Elvey, 'Walter of Henley reconsidered', *Records of Buckinghamshire*, 20 (1977–80), 470–77 · N. Denholm-Young, 'Walter of Henley', *Collected papers of N. Denholm-Young* (1969), 227–35 · P. D. A. Harvey, 'Agricultural treatises and manorial accounting in medieval England', *Agricultural History Review*, 20 (1972), 170–82 · *Walter of Henley's Husbandry together with Robert Grosseteste's Rules*, ed. and trans. E. Lamond (1890) · A. Vere Woodman, 'A note on Sir Walter de Hanley', *Records of Buckinghamshire*, 16 (1953–60), 216–18 · F. G. Gurney, 'An agricultural agreement of the year 1345 at Mursley and Dunton, with a note upon Walter of "Henley"', *Records of Buckinghamshire*, 14 (1941–6), 245–64 · T. H. Aston, review, *EngHR*, 72 (1957), 528–30

Henley, William. *See* Henly, William (*d.* 1779).

Henley, William Ernest (1849–1903), writer, was born on 23 August 1849 at 47 Eastgate Street, St Michael, Gloucester, the eldest of the five sons of William Henley (1826–1868), an unsuccessful stationer, bookseller, and printer, and his wife, Emma Morgan (1828–1888), who was descended from the critic Joseph Warton. Little is known about W. E. Henley's early years. He was educated at the Crypt Grammar School, Gloucester, and never forgot the kindness and encouragement he received from its headmaster, the Manx poet T. E. Brown, who became a friend for life. From the age of twelve Henley was never wholly free from pain and ill health caused by a tuberculous disease and on that account, and possibly because of his father's poverty, there were long breaks in his education. He left school in 1867, the year in which he passed the Oxford local examination as a senior candidate.

Friendship with Stevenson and literary work Henley moved to London in 1867 and for the next few years, in conditions of great poverty, he earned a precarious living through hack journalism, interrupted for nine months in 1868–9 by treatment in St Bartholomew's Hospital. This was probably when his left leg was amputated a few inches below the knee; thereafter he had a wooden leg and walked painfully with the aid of crutches. The disease next threatened his right foot; he moved to Margate in Kent and became for several months in 1873 a patient at the Royal Sea-Bathing Infirmary. He refused to accept the doctors' advice that amputation was the only remedy and in August 1873 he travelled to Edinburgh to seek treatment

William Ernest
Henley (1849–
1903), by Auguste
Rodin, 1884–6

at the Royal Infirmary from Joseph Lister, the great pioneer of antiseptic surgery. Lister managed to save his foot but Henley had to spend nearly two years in hospital receiving treatment and convalescing. He had always been a great reader and the enforced leisure of his sickbed gave him the opportunity to study literature, to learn languages, and to write poetry.

Two meetings in hospital were to change Henley's life: one with Robert Louis Stevenson and the other with his future wife. On 13 February 1875 Stevenson described, in a letter to his friend Frances Sitwell, how Leslie Stephen, in Edinburgh on a lecture visit, had taken him the day before 'to see … a bit of a poet who writes for him':

> Stephen and I sat on a couple of chairs and the poor fellow sat up in his bed, with his hair and beard all tangled, and talked as cheerfully as if he had been in a King's Palace, or the great King's Palace of the blue air.   (*Letters of Robert Louis Stevenson*, 2.117)

The friendship between Stevenson and Henley became a very special one and for the next twelve years they poured out letters to each other full of private jokes and comments on their literary work. Their relationship had an emotional, rather adolescent character and Henley never reconciled himself to the more mature person that Stevenson became.

Henley was discharged from hospital in April 1875 and found work on the staff of the *Encyclopaedia Britannica*, dealing with French authors. Eighteen months later he was back in London writing for the short-lived magazine *London*. It was founded by Robert Glasgow Brown, a friend of Stevenson's, but Henley soon took over from him as editor: it ran from 1877 to 1879. Henley contributed anonymously many verses and articles but it is now remembered only because it published Stevenson's *New Arabian Nights*.

The financial security achieved from his editorship of *London* enabled Henley to marry the young woman he had met in hospital when she was visiting her brother, a captain in the merchant navy and a fellow patient of Henley's. She was Hannah (Anna) Johnson Boyle (1855–1925), the youngest daughter of Edward Boyle, mechanical engineer, of Edinburgh and his wife, Mary Ann Mackie. They were married in Edinburgh on 22 January 1878 and set up home in rented rooms in Shepherd's Bush, the first of many they were to occupy in this area of London over the next ten years. One of Henley's brothers described the marriage as a 'bold action for a lame man with a family on his back' (Connell, 83). Henley's widowed mother and his four brothers were living in London and, poor as he was, looked to him for financial support. On 4 September 1888 their daughter Margaret Emma was born and became the focus of all Henley's hopes; she died of cerebral meningitis on 11 February 1894 and the light went out of his life. She appears briefly as Reddy in J. M. Barrie's novel *Sentimental Tommy* (1896) and her childish attempt to call him 'Friendy' was Barrie's inspiration for Wendy in *Peter Pan* (1904).

Henley became a prolific contributor of articles and reviews to *The Athenaeum*, the *Saturday Review*, the *St James's Gazette*, and other journals and wrote dramatic criticism for the *Pall Mall Gazette*. From November 1881 to October 1886 he was editor of the monthly *Magazine of Art*. In its pages he championed the work of Rodin, then hardly known in England, and Whistler. Rodin became a personal friend and executed at least two fine busts of him. Henley started his friend R. A. M. Stevenson (Robert Louis Stevenson's cousin Bob) off on his distinguished career as an art critic by persuading him to contribute to the magazine. Henley later acted for a time as adviser to the *Art Journal*.

Henley was a tall, powerfully built man, with a large head and a shock of yellowish-red hair frequently ruffled and standing up all over his head, and a short irregular red beard (later to turn grey and then white); his eyes were light blue and he was extremely short-sighted. It was as a forceful personality and brilliant talker that he impressed his contemporaries and achieved an influence which at the time of his death was likened to that of Samuel Johnson. Stevenson put him into his essay 'Talk and talkers' (in *Memories and Portraits*, 1887) as Burly, one of the 'loud, copious, intolerant talkers', describing him as a man whose 'presence could be felt in a room you entered blindfold': 'There is something boisterous and piratic in Burly's manner of talk. … He will roar you down, he will bury his face in his hands, he will undergo passions of revolt and agony.' This accords with Oscar Wilde's comment: 'His personality is insistent. To converse with him is a physical no less than an intellectual recreation' (Rothenstein, 312). His friends remembered Henley's tremendous energy and vitality, his 'wild flood and storm of talk' (Pennell, 134), his vehemently expressed likes and dislikes, his loud laughter and lively sense of fun, and the courage with which he faced the pain of his ill health. Stevenson famously based Long John Silver on certain aspects of his character, confessing: 'It was the sight of your maimed strength and masterfulness that begot John Silver in *Treasure Island* … the idea of the maimed man, ruling and dreaded by the sound was entirely taken from you' (*Letters of Robert Louis Stevenson*, 4.129). In his later years, with increasing ill health, Henley grew more waspish and irritable. He quarrelled at one time or another with many of his friends, and yet W. B. Yeats wrote: 'I disagreed with him about everything, but I admired him beyond words' (Yeats, 124).

Quarrel with Stevenson Convinced that the theatre was a sure way to make their fortunes, Henley and Stevenson collaborated with enthusiasm in the writing of four plays: *Deacon Brodie* (privately printed, 1880; in revised form, 1888), *Beau Austin* and *Admiral Guinea* (both privately printed, 1884), and *Macaire* (privately printed, 1885)—a new adaptation of the popular French farce done at the invitation of Herbert Beerbohm Tree but rejected for performance. The first three were published as *Three Plays* (1892); *Macaire* was added in 1896. Although they were eventually all produced on the stage, sometimes for a single performance only, they failed to achieve lasting success. Under the pseudonym Byron McGuiness, Henley wrote a burlesque called *Mephisto*, making fun of Henry Irving in *Faust*. It was performed at the Royalty Theatre, London, on 14 June 1886 with Henley's ne'er-do-well brother, Edward John Henley (who also took the name part in *Deacon Brodie*), playing the lead. It was condemned by the critics and ran for only two weeks.

The main reason for the quarrel which arose between Stevenson and Henley appears to have been Henley's dislike of Stevenson's American wife, Fanny. In March 1888, when Stevenson was in the United States, Henley accused her of plagiarism in publishing under her own name alone a short story based on one written earlier (and abandoned) by Stevenson's cousin, Katharine de Mattos. Stevenson reacted furiously. The main issue for him was that Henley had been disloyal in making such an accusation against his wife and he saw it as the latest example of Henley's penchant for stirring up trouble behind his back and speaking ill of him to his friends. Henley apologized but the old cordial relations were never restored. The final straw for Stevenson came in December 1890 in Samoa when he learned that Henley, living in Edinburgh, had failed to call on his widowed mother.

Henley's 'revenge' eventually came in his notorious review in the *Pall Mall Magazine* in December 1901 of the authorized biography of Stevenson by Graham Balfour. It was a savage attack on what he saw as Fanny Stevenson's attempt to present an idealized picture of her husband, but his famous gibe about 'this Seraph in Chocolate, this barley-sugar effigy of a real man' (Henley, 'R. L. S.', 508) was not really true of the portrait presented in Balfour's biography, despite the reticences inevitable so soon after Stevenson's death. Henley went on to write patronizingly

and contemptuously about Stevenson's personal qualities and to belittle his work, and the article caused a sensation in the literary world.

Editorship of *Scots Observer* and poetry In January 1889 Henley took over the editorship of the *Scots Observer*, a weekly journal founded in Edinburgh a few weeks earlier in the interests of the Conservative Party. The main proprietor was Robert Fitzroy Bell, but Henley's friends Robert Hamilton Bruce and W. B. Blaikie (of T. and A. Constable who printed the paper) were also involved. In an attempt to widen its appeal the title was changed in November 1890 to the *National Observer*. Henley, his wife, and young daughter lived in Edinburgh for three and a half years—the happiest of his life—but moved south again in September 1892; from that year the paper was edited from London.

Henley's editorship has become something of a legend. He had a gift for finding and encouraging new talent and gathered round him a group of what were called his Young Men—nicknamed the 'Henley regatta' by Max Beerbohm (Rothenstein, 285)—who were a little in awe of him. He maintained firm editorial control and imposed his own style and opinions throughout by ruthlessly revising contributions. Yeats recalled that he 'made us feel always our importance, and no man among us could do good work, or show the promise of it, and lack his praise' (Yeats, 128). In addition to Yeats and Henley himself, the contributors included such famous names as Stevenson, G. B. Shaw, J. M. Barrie, Thomas Hardy, Rudyard Kipling ('Barrack Room Ballads'), Kenneth Grahame, Alice Meynell, and H. G. Wells, along with such almost forgotten names as Gilbert Parker, G. S. Street, and H. B. Marriot Watson. Charles Whibley, the assistant editor, who was responsible for some of the wittiest and most savage of the articles, became a close friend and partly filled the gap in Henley's affections left by the break with Stevenson.

The dominant note of the paper's politics was its militant Conservatism and advocacy of imperialism. This did not always fit well with the provocative and iconoclastic articles with their scorn for conventional ideas. The links with the Conservative Party led Henley into close friendships with George Wyndham and Harry Cust. The circulation of the *National Observer* was less than 2000 and in March 1894 his heavy losses forced Fitzroy Bell to sell the journal; Henley, already shattered by the loss of his daughter, was without a job. One was found for him at the end of the year by making him editor of William Heinemann's *New Review*; this too was a financial failure and came to an end in December 1897. Many of his old contributors appeared in its pages and the same high standards were maintained, though without the zest and distinctive character of the *National Observer*. Among the memorable serials were *The Time Machine* by H. G. Wells and Joseph Conrad's *The Nigger of the 'Narcissus'*.

Henley first came into prominence as a poet with *A Book of Verses* (1888), which was favourably reviewed; it was followed by *The Song of the Sword and other Verses* (1892), which in its second edition was retitled *London Voluntaries and other Verses* (1893). These two collections were combined (with revisions and omissions) as *Poems* (1898). In 1898 he wrote a series of quatorzains to accompany coloured drawings by William Nicholson for an attractive volume of *London Types*. The Second South African War inspired a small book of patriotic poems under the title *For England's Sake: Verses and Songs in Time of War* (1900). A year later came *Hawthorn and Lavender with other Verses*. His first experience of being driven in a fast car led to his final work, *A Song of Speed* (1903).

Henley's poetry shows his originality, his skill in the use of a variety of metrical techniques, and his gift for choosing an appropriate phrase to convey a mood or an emotion. The In Hospital poems—grim, realistic impressions of his experiences in Edinburgh—with their pioneering use of irregular rhymeless verse, are considered to be his most effective work. Heine seems to have been an influence here and also in the London Voluntaries, vivid, impressionistic studies of London by day and night.

Henley is often derided for his defiant poem 'Out of the night that covers me', with its declaration that he is 'the master of my fate … the captain of my soul', but the poem has a different ring when it is known that it was written when he was fighting against a painful disease. He wrote some delicate lyrical poems of love and death and was a dexterous maker of the formal, artificial ballades and rondeaus as popularized by his friend Austin Dobson. Some of his later poems in celebration of war and imperialism show him at his embarrassing worst, but his 'Pro rege nostro'

What have I done for you
England my England

expressed popular sentiments in a striking way. The poem 'The Song of the Sword', with its references to the sword 'making death beautiful' managed to out-Kipling Kipling, to whom it was dedicated.

Final years In 1890 Henley published *Views and Reviews*, described in his preface as 'a mosaic of scraps and shreds recovered from the shot rubbish of some fourteen years of journalism'. It mainly consists of short critical studies of English and French authors, both classical and modern. His critical writings were extravagantly praised by his contemporaries but they have not worn well. They show his wide reading but are marred by his mannered and jaunty style with its fondness for epigrams and archaic words; they are brilliant table talk and witty journalism rather than considered or original criticism.

Henley provided introductory essays, biographical notes, and comments on the paintings for three sumptuously produced catalogues of art exhibitions (two of them of French and Dutch paintings) in 1888–9, and for a volume of reproductions of portraits by Sir Henry Raeburn (1890). An edited selection from this material, plus three later essays, was published as *Views and Reviews II* (1902).

Henley did other editorial work of distinction. In collaboration with T. F. Henderson he edited the Centenary Edition of *The Poetry of Robert Burns* (4 vols., 1896–7), to which he contributed a major essay on Burns which gave great offence to the sentimentalists. With J. S. Farmer he enjoyed over many years the task of compiling a *Dictionary of Slang and its Analogues* (1890–1904). He published in 1897 the first volume of an edition of *Byron's Letters* with detailed biographical sketches; the project was abandoned, however, because of copyright difficulties. He contributed introductions to collected editions of the works of Smollett (1899), Hazlitt (1902), and Fielding (1902). He was one of the editors of the collected poems of T. E. Brown (1900) and he began in 1901 to edit the Edinburgh Folio Shakespeare, which was completed in 1904 by Walter Raleigh. Among a number of anthologies the most famous was *Lyra heroica* (1892). A valuable project was his supervision of the splendid series of *Tudor Translations* (1892–1903), each work with an introduction by a leading scholar, and finely printed and bound. The series began with Florio's *Montaigne* and ended with the *Tudor Bible*, publication of which was in progress at the time of his death.

Henley received the degree of LLD from the University of St Andrews in 1893. There were two disappointments in 1895: he lost to George Saintsbury the opportunity to become professor of English literature at the University of Edinburgh and his friends failed in their efforts to secure for him the poet laureateship. After his editorship of the *New Review* ended he had no assured source of income; his financial worries were eased by the grant of a civil-list pension of £225 in 1898. After he came back from Edinburgh in 1892 he had homes in various London suburbs at Croydon, Barnes, and Muswell Hill; in 1899 he moved to Worthing in Sussex and in 1901 to Woking, Surrey. His last years were plagued by chronic illness and increasing pain and he had several operations. William Ernest Henley died on 11 July 1903 at his home, Heather Brae, Maybury Hill, Woking; he was survived by his wife. His body was cremated at Woking on 14 July and his ashes interred in his daughter's grave in the churchyard in the village of Cockayne Hatley, Bedfordshire, the home of his friend Harry Cust.

ERNEST MEHEW

Sources J. Connell [J. H. Robertson], *W. E. Henley* (1949) · K. Williamson, *W. E. Henley* (1930) · *DNB* · J. H. Buckley, *William Ernest Henley* (1945) · E. Mehew, 'The main correspondents: Stevenson's family and friends', in *The letters of Robert Louis Stevenson*, ed. B. A. Booth and E. Mehew, 1 (1994), 44–62 [esp. pp. 54–63] · *Selected letters of W. E. Henley*, ed. D. Atkinson (1999) · E. R. Pennell, *Nights* (1916), 125–55, 213–14 · W. B. Yeats, *Autobiographies* (1955), 124–9, 131–2, 295–9 · *Some letters of William Ernest Henley* (1933) [privately printed] · H. Stephen, 'William Ernest Henley as a contemporary and an editor', *London Mercury*, 13 (1925–6), 387–400 · S. Low, 'William Ernest Henley: some memories and impressions', *Cornhill Magazine*, [3rd] ser., 15 (1903), 411–12 · L. C. Cornford, *William Ernest Henley* (1913) · W. Rothenstein, *Men and memories: recollections of William Rothenstein*, 2 vols. (1931–2), vol 1, pp. 285–6, 296–7, 312–13 · W. E. Henley, 'R. L. S.', *Pall Mall Magazine*, 25 (Sept–Dec 1901) · R. L. Stevenson, 'Talk and talkers', *Memories and portraits* (1887) · b. cert. · m. cert. · d. cert. · d. cert. [Emma Henley] · grave, Cockayne Hatley churchyard, Cockayne Hatley, Bedfordshire

Archives Harvard U., Houghton L., letters · Hunt. L., letters and literary MSS · Morgan L., corresp. and papers · University of British Columbia Library, letters and literary MSS · Yale U., Beinecke L., letters and MSS | BL, corresp. with William Archer and letters to Macmillans, Add. MS 45292 · LUL, letters to Austin Dobson · LUL, letters to W. P. Ker · Musée Rodin, Paris, letters to A. Rodin · NL Scot., corresp. incl. with Sir Graham Balfour, Lord

Rosebery, Robert Louis Stevenson • NL Scot., letters to Black-woods • U. Leeds, Brotherton L., letters to C. K. Shorter and E. Gosse • University of Illinois, letters to H. G. Wells

Likenesses A. Rodin, bronze bust, 1884–6, NPG [*see illus.*] • A. G. Dew-Smith, photographs, *c.*1885–1886, NPG • A. Rodin, bronze bust, 1886, NG Scot.; copy, St Paul's Cathedral, London • H. S. Mendelssohn, portrait, 1888, repro. in *Art Journal* (Jan 1906), 35; copy, NPG • F. Hollyer, photograph, 1893, V&A; copy, NPG • photograph, 1893?, National Museum of Photography, Film and Television, Bradford, Royal Photographic Society collection; repro. in *Literature* (11 May 1901) • J. Whistler, lithograph sketch, 1896, BM • W. Rothenstein, lithograph, 1897 • F. Dodd, pastel drawing, 1900, NPG • Elliott & Fry, photograph, *c.*1901, NPG • W. Nicholson, oils, 1901, Tate collection • S. Bussy, pastel drawing, 1902 • G. C. Beresford, photograph, NPG • H. Furniss, pen-and-ink sketch for a caricature, NPG • W. Nicholson, lithograph, repro. in M. Steen, *William Nicholson* (1943), facing p. 19; copy, BM • Spy [L. Ward], chromolithograph, NPG; repro. in *VF* (26 Nov 1892)

Wealth at death £840 1*s.* 2*d.*: probate, 19 Aug 1903, *CGPLA Eng. & Wales*

Henley, William Thomas (1813?–1882), electrical engineer and manufacturer, was born at Midhurst, Sussex, and from the age of four was brought up by his grandparents. From the ages of six to eleven he received elementary education in Midhurst. Aged sixteen, he moved to London, fired with the ambition of one day possessing a large factory with machines and wheels in motion. He worked first as a light porter for a silk mercer in Cheapside, and then as a dock labourer. For six years he used his spare time to teach himself the trade of a philosophical instrument maker.

About 1837 J. P. Gassiot, a keen amateur scientist, and one of Henley's early customers, recommended him to Professor Wheatstone of King's College, for whom he made telegraph equipment and electric motors. Henley found that cheap insulated wire was not readily available for making electromagnets, so he developed a wire-covering machine that insulated six wires in cotton or silk simultaneously. By 1839 he was supplying insulated wire in quantity to other instrument makers and experimentalists at about half the price of his rivals, and he used the profits to strengthen his business and to fund electrical experiments.

The Electric Telegraph Company acquired the Cooke and Wheatstone telegraph patents in 1846 and placed significant manufacturing orders with Henley, but failed to pay him. Henley responded by inventing an improved telegraph, in which pulses of electric current were produced by a combination of moving coils and permanent magnets, rather than from batteries (patent no. 12236, 1848). He won a gold medal for his equipment at the 1851 Great Exhibition. In 1852 he sold his patent rights to the English and Irish Magnetic Telegraph Company for £68,000. Because the rival Electric Telegraph had a monopoly of railway way-leaves, Henley, working as a subcontractor to the Magnetic, laid his wires underground, confounding his critics by digging trenches from London to Carlisle and from Dublin to Belfast.

Having mastered the art of laying underground cables, Henley set up as submarine cablemaker in Greenwich in 1857, and moved to a new factory in north Woolwich in

William Thomas Henley (1813?–1882), by Basil Holmes, 1870

1859. Here he manufactured the Persian Gulf cable 1651 miles long, which was the first submarine cable to be exhaustively tested during manufacture, transport, and laying. This success enabled him to win the contract for the armoured shore sections of the successful 1865 and 1866 Atlantic cables. His profits between April 1868 and December 1873, during the submarine cable boom, were £560,000. His works had by then expanded to 16 acres, and his workforce to more than 2000; he owned three cable-laying ships and a wireworks in Wales. Altogether he manufactured over 14,000 miles of cable.

In 1874 Henley failed to win a number of cable contracts. Unwisely, he continued to diversify, thereby rapidly increasing his debt. Problems in laying the Majorca–Minorca cable, the loss of his cable ship, the *La Plata* in the Bay of Biscay in November 1874, and mounting losses in his Welsh wireworks compounded his problems. In March 1875 he was bankrupted with debts of £500,000, his debt having increased from £200,000 in less than a year.

In 1876 a limited company was formed to carry on work under the title of W. T. Henley & Co. Ltd. When this was wound up, most of the works became the property of the Telegraph Maintenance and Construction Company, who then closed it. A small portion of the works was formed into W. T. Henley's Telegraph Works Company (Limited) in 1880, of which Henley was a director.

Henley was an early member of the Society of Telegraph Engineers. He was also always interested in the application of electric power. He built motors to his own design in the 1840s, and in 1849 built electrical generators for the Alliance Company of France. In later years his interest was rekindled, and between 1880 and 1882 he registered five patents on electric power.

Early hardship enabled him to understand his workmen who, for the most part, were devoted to him, respecting him for his expertise, physical strength, and generosity. However, some foremen took advantage of him by taking second jobs and neglecting their responsibilities to the company. The spirited independence which enabled Henley to build up a successful business single-handed and to make a notable contribution to the telegraph and the development of electrical engineering, also made it difficult for him to take advice or delegate when a competitive climate required the introduction of sound management. Henley lived simply, and never married. He died at his home, Chesterton House, Plaistow, Essex, on 13 December 1882, aged sixty-eight or sixty-nine, and was buried in Kensal Green cemetery.   ANTONY ANDERSON

Sources A. F. Anderson, 'William Henley, pioneer electrical instrument maker and cable manufacturer, 1813 to 1882', *IEE Proceedings*, A132 (1985), 249–61 · W. T. Henley, 'The early life of W. T. Henley by himself', *Henley Telegraph* (June 1924), 4–10 · W. T. Henley, 'The early life of W. T. Henley by himself', *Henley Telegraph* (Sept 1924), 3–10 · *The Electrician* (23 Dec 1882), 136 · *The Engineer* (22 Dec 1882), 471 · S. A. Garnham and R. L. Hadfield, *The submarine cable* (1934), 218–20 · *CGPLA Eng. & Wales* (1883) · d. cert.
Archives Sci. Mus.
Likenesses B. Holmes, oils, 1870, Inst. EE [*see illus.*]
Wealth at death £12,750 13s. 6d.: probate, 2 March 1883, *CGPLA Eng. & Wales*

Henly, William (d. **1779**), linen draper and electrical experimenter, lived in the Borough, Southwark, London. He was a co-partner of the wife of Thomas Masham, their drapery being in the parish of St Vedast, Foster Lane, in the City of London. He probably began experimenting in the 1760s, but he came to prominence in 1772, when Joseph Priestley communicated Henly's design for an electrometer to the Royal Society. Similar in design to that of Georg Wilhem Richmann, it was more sensitive in registering electrical charges than previous designs and it became standard. This and other experiments led to his election to the Royal Society in 1773. His proposers included Priestley and Benjamin Franklin.

Henly was a firm adherent to Franklin's theories about the nature of electricity—he was 'momentarily the Royal Society's most prolific Franklinist' (Heilbron, 421). Franklin was in England between 1757 and 1775, and Henly was in contact with him and other 'Franklinist' experimenters such as John Canton and Edward Nairne. Much of Henly's research aimed to prove Franklin's theories: in 1774 he carried out experiments to show that pointed lightning conductors were the most effective form, as claimed by Franklin in opposition to the claims being made for blunt rods by Benjamin Wilson and others. Similarly his demonstrations on the flow of electricity were based on Franklin's beliefs. In 1776 Henly was involved in getting the works of the Italian experimenter Tiberius Cavallo published, and he also addressed the (later, Royal) Humane Society, of which he was briefly a director, about using electricity to revive victims of drowning.

Henly was well aware that the true nature, properties, and potential of electricity had not yet been realized. In the same year he wrote that 'much remains to be done, and the field for future labourers seems daily to enlarge … I cannot but be of the opinion … that, compared with the facts still undiscovered [discoveries already made] bear but a very small proportion' (Henly, 17–18). In 1779, having written his will on 1 May, Henly committed suicide. According to Benjamin Vaughan, who informed Franklin of Henly's death, Henly cut his throat with a penknife, despite the efforts of family to calm him. He was buried at St Saviour's, Southwark, on 7 June 1779.

TIM PROCTER

Sources J. L. Heilbron, *Electricity in the 17th and 18th centuries: a study of early modern physics* (1979) · *PTRS*, 62–68 (1772–8) · RS, Canton MSS · election certificate, RS · *The writings of Benjamin Franklin*, ed. A. H. Smyth, 7: 1777–1779 (1907) · W. Hawes, ed., *The transactions of the Royal Humane Society*, 1 (1774–84) · *Reports of the Humane Society* (1777) · will of William Henly, PRO, PROB 11/1055, sig. 305 · W. Henly, *Experiments and observations in electricity* (1776), 17–18 · parish register (burial), 7 June 1779, Southwark, St Saviour
Archives RS, letters to John Canton and William Canton

Henman, Philip Sydney (1899–1986), transport entrepreneur, was born on 21 December 1899 at Haddon Villas, Yalding, near Maidstone, Kent, the second son and third child of seven children of the Revd Sydney James Henman, Baptist minister at Yalding, and his wife, Ellen Gertrude, née Brine. Philip attended several schools, including Caterham School and later Shoreham grammar school. Rheumatic fever thwarted his early ambition to go to college and into the Christian ministry. At seventeen he joined a firm of Lloyd's insurance brokers, Alexander Howden & Co. Conscripted in 1917, he joined the King's Royal Rifle Corps and was demobilized as a sergeant in 1921. Having studied some accounting, in 1922 he got a job as accountant to the General Lighterage Company, operating two barges from Hay's wharf. He became managing director in 1929, and began acquiring companies in wharfage, warehousing, road haulage, and other ancillary services, as well as barges and tugs. By 1939 he was chairman of the General Lighterage Company, and bought out Colonel Edgar Richard Hatfield, the firm's founder.

Henman survived the nationalization of the road haulage industry in 1947 by confining his business to short distance work. In 1950 he formed a public holding company, General Lighterage (Holdings) Ltd, to run sixteen subsidiaries, which together offered a 'package' service, from ship to inland customer. Troubled labour relations in the docks and new methods of conveying commodities from ship to shore (such as pipelines and, later, containers) pointed to new directions, especially after the denationalization of long distance road services in 1953. He expanded his business by buying out smaller, often family, firms. Henman's success came from his rigorous cost-accounting, and from his style of management, which allowed his companies to retain their individual characters. When he retired in 1969 his group comprised over eighty operating subsidiaries in Britain, three in South Africa and Rhodesia, three in Australia, and seven in Europe. Turnover of the whole group stood at £50 million, compared to under £1 million in 1950. The group, renamed the Transport Development Group when it became a public company in 1957, operated over 4500 lorries, compared to 150 in 1950. Henman's other major business enterprise was the Square Grip Reinforcement Company, formed in 1934 by his elder brother, Frank Espinett Henman, to make twisted high tensile steel for the construction industry.

Henman married Jessie Mary *née* Nairn (1898–1976), daughter of the manager of the London branch of the Scottish Provident Life Association, in 1931. They had one daughter, Mary Jessie. Among the many Christian causes Henman supported were the London Bible College (which John William Laing and he were instrumental in founding), Inter Varsity Fellowship (of which he became chairman), the British and Foreign Bible Society, and the Africa Inland Mission (whose home council he chaired). He was elected a patron of the Royal College of Surgeons and a benefactor of the Royal Society of Medicine in recognition of his large gifts to them. He became chairman, and later vice-president, of the council of the London chamber of commerce; vice-president of the Institute of Transport; member of the grand council of the CBI, and chairman of its transport committee; member of three city livery companies, the Paviors, Farmers, and Watermen and Lightermen; honorary doctor of the University of Surrey; high sheriff of Surrey (1971–2), and deputy lieutenant of Surrey. For relaxation he took up farming in Surrey and in Scotland. He died on 8 November 1986, at Sundridge Hospital, Sundridge, Kent.   DAVID J. JEREMY

Sources D. J. Jeremy, 'Henman, Philip Sydney', *DBB* · *CGPLA Eng. & Wales* (1987) · b. cert. · m. cert. · d. cert.
Likenesses photograph, repro. in Jeremy, 'Philip Sydney Henman'
Wealth at death £1,291,462: probate, 17 March 1987, *CGPLA Eng. & Wales*

Henn, Thomas Rice (1849–1880), army officer, third son of Thomas Rice Henn (1814–1901) of Paradise Hill, co. Clare, JP and deputy lieutenant, recorder of Galway, and his wife, Jane Isabella (*d.* 29 April 1902), daughter of the Rt Hon. Francis Blackburne, lord chancellor of Ireland, was born in Dublin on 2 November 1849. He was educated at Windermere College, and entered the Royal Military Academy, Woolwich, second of the successful candidates, aged seventeen. On 7 July 1869 he was commissioned into the Royal Engineers, and after the usual Chatham course was sent to India. He was posted to the Bombay sappers and miners at Kirkee, the 2nd company of which he commanded in the Anglo-Afghan War in 1880. He was present in the Bolan Pass, and also at Kandahar, when he was appointed brigade major of Royal Engineers. In July 1880 he took part in the advance of General G. S. R. Burrows's brigade to the Helmand, and fought in the disastrous battle of Maiwand (27 July). When the battle became a rout Henn and his half-company of sappers were with the battery of horse artillery. Its commander, Major G. F. Blackwood, had been mortally wounded, and Captain J. R. Slade, who succeeded him, ordered the battery to limber

up and retire. Henn, already wounded in the arm, successfully covered the operation with his few men, firing volleys at the crowd of Ghazis pouring down upon them. Henn then fell steadily back, carrying the wounded Blackwood, and following the line of retreat of the 66th regiment across the nullah to a garden on the other side, in the village of Khig. Behind the garden wall Henn, the remnant of his sappers, a party of the 66th regiment, and some Bombay grenadiers made their stand. They held the enemy at bay, fighting to cover the retreat of their comrades. When only Henn and ten others remained alive, he led them in a final charge: all were killed. Around the spot were afterwards found, lightly buried, the bodies of Henn and 14 sappers, 46 men of the 66th regiment, and 23 grenadiers. General Primrose's dispatch of 1 October 1880 described, on the authority of an eyewitness—an Afghan artillery colonel—their stand. Wolseley wrote, 'No hero ever died more nobly than he did—I envy the manner of his death' (*Royal Engineers Journal*). Henn was unmarried. A memorial tablet was placed in St Patrick's Cathedral, Dublin, and a memorial window in Rochester Cathedral.

R. H. VETCH, *rev.* ROGER T. STEARN

Sources *LondG* (1880) · Institution of Royal Engineers, Chatham, records · S. H. Shadbolt, ed., *The Afghan campaigns of 1878–1880*, 2 vols. (1882) · B. Robson, *The road to Kabul: the Second Afghan War, 1878–1881* (1986) · E. W. C. Sandes, *The military engineer in India*, 1 (1933) · *Royal Engineers Journal*, 12 (1882), 171 · Burke, *Gen. Ire.* (1958) · Boase, *Mod. Eng. biog.* · T. A. Heathcote, *The military in British India: the development of British land forces in south Asia, 1600–1947* (1995) · B. Mollo, *The Indian army* (1986) · *CGPLA Eng. & Wales* (1881)
Wealth at death under £600: administration, 25 May 1881, *CGPLA Eng. & Wales*

Henn, Thomas Rice (1901–1974), literary scholar and writer, was born on 10 November 1901 at the family home, Paradise, Ennis, co. Clare, Ireland, the fifth and youngest child of Francis Blackburne Henn (1845–1915), barrister, and resident magistrate at Bellina and later at Sligo, and his wife, Helen (1857–1936), daughter of Colonel Gore, master of foxhounds, of Woodlawn, co. Clare. He was named after his grandfather Thomas Rice *Henn (1849–1880), a lieutenant of the Royal Engineers. Henn had an absorbing boyhood: a member of an old Anglo-Irish family, which had lived in the district since the seventeenth century, he was much occupied with field sports. Coached by his father, he was an excellent shot by the age of eight. None of this was done solely for sport, but also to provide food: everything he or his father brought down was either used by the household or given away. He enjoyed shooting throughout his life, but later became a noted angler. One of his lifelong interests, fly-tying, arose from this; he wrote a manual, *Practical Fly-Tying* (1950), which emphasised the aesthetic appeal of the craft. Among other sports, rowing and sailing especially claimed his interest.

Much of Henn's youth was overshadowed by the 'troubles', which originated long before the Easter rising of 1916. Yet he bore no enmity towards his republican neighbours, and recalled that as a boy he went snipe-shooting with one who was a known murderer. This did not exempt the Henn family from unwelcome attentions and death threats, and there were also rick- and stack-burnings, and the destruction of trees and plantations, and of Anglo-Irish buildings. Henn, aged fourteen at the time of the rising, remembered a potentially ugly incident from his boyhood. An execution squad arrived early one morning, having heard that he possessed a bomb. The 'bomb' turned out to be the sound-box of a gramophone in a box. When he played part of a record with it, all ended happily, with the republicans entertained to breakfast, followed by a snapshot by Henn of the firing party with rifles at the ready. Indeed the Irish countryside was menacing. There were seventeen raids on Paradise, by republicans and the British, both of whom looted anything that took their fancy. To all of this, however, Henn endeavoured to maintain a tolerant attitude. Well-read in Irish history, he was fully aware of the deep divisions of Irish life.

Francis Henn died on 10 November 1915 (Henn's fourteenth birthday), leaving his wife and family almost penniless: none of his tenants had paid rent for years, and his pension terminated with his death. Consequently Helen Henn was unable to support her son in his ambition to follow the same career as his father at the Irish bar. He was, however, fortunate enough to win at his Fermoy preparatory school a mathematical scholarship for Aldenham School, Hertfordshire, where his sporting proficiency led him in time to the school captaincy. He worked well in class, and in due course obtained a scholarship to read modern languages at St Catharine's College, Cambridge. In itself this was insufficient to support him, so Aldenham added an exhibition for three years. There still remained a formidable shortfall, but the bishop of Burnley, Henn's uncle, made up most of this, and he was able to become an undergraduate in 1919.

Among Cambridge dons who strongly influenced Henn was Sir Arthur Quiller-Couch ('Q'). Even greater was the influence of E. M. W. Tillyard, lecturer in English from 1926 to 1950, and later master of Jesus College, who was Henn's supervisor and director of studies for his first two years, and eventually became a close friend. Cambridge had many first-class humanistic dons in the 1920s and 1930s, among whom were the medievalist G. G. Coulton, the literary historian Sir Herbert Grierson, the author and scholar F. L. Lucas, the eccentric Mansfield Forbes, creator of Finella, an art deco house in Queen's Road, and S. C. Roberts, Johnsonian, Shakespearian, and wit. It was a rich background, and Henn made the most of it, accumulating much scholarly benefit and friendship. He also made good use of the sport provided at Cambridge, above all becoming an enthusiastic oarsman during his undergraduate years. In rowing he enjoyed and appreciated above all the intermittently attainable perfection of rhythm.

Henn left Cambridge in 1923, after one extra term, having in 1922 obtained a first in modern languages, and various prizes. After some disappointments he accepted a job as an assistant in the Burmah Oil Company at Calcutta. Apart from some rowing and shooting, and despite becoming fluent in Urdu and learning much about big business, he was bored and unhappy, suffered intermittent attacks of dengue and malaria, and lost weight. Also

the company rules forbade marriage until after three years of service. Thus, when he was given an opportunity to return home, he accepted immediately, not least because during his last months in Cambridge he had met his future wife, (Mary) Enid Roberts (b. 1900/01), daughter of Edward Augustus Roberts MD of London, who was at Newnham College, reading modern languages, literature, and history. They married on 25 September 1926, some seventeen months after his return.

Having come back to St Catharine's in April 1925, Henn at once began to teach and examine, and to coach oarsmen. He also became director of studies for several other colleges. On Monday evenings his attic rooms at St Catharine's became a centre where his pupils and others met for discussion, argument, coffee, and tobacco. These gatherings became so popular that it became necessary to restrict them to members of colleges where Henn had an official position. In 1926 he became a fellow of St Catharine's, was prelector in 1927–35, tutor in 1934, and senior tutor in 1946–56. Former undergraduates claimed that Henn never taught in a conventional manner, but used their enthusiasm to guide them along suitable academic paths, while quoting freely from his capacious memory line after line of pertinent poetry and prose. Above all he encouraged his pupils to think creatively, and not to allow mere facts to dominate their thought. At times brusque and formidable, he invariably returned quickly to half-shy calm.

In 1936 Henn visited the south of France to recuperate from surgery for the removal of a fibroma, caused by an earlier appendectomy. Here the sight of peasant children driving the herds and flocks to the hills to graze, and to rest later beside the waters, gave him the feeling that for the first time he was seeing the true background of pastoral poetry. Henn's output as a poet was never extensive, but from this time it began to mature.

During the 1930s Henn suffered from outbreaks of almost suicidal depression. He was helped through these by the noted psychiatrist Leonard Foster Browne. In one of his early consultations he broke down, weeping uncontrollably. He had never come to terms with his father's death, the ensuing poverty at Paradise, the rebellion, and his own unsuccessful attempts to do his duty to his mother and to the family estate. All this had preyed on his mind for nine years, finally reducing him to neurosis. With Browne's guidance, and by reading widely in the most important works in psychiatry and psychology, especially Jung's, he recovered. These experiences, disturbing though they were, enabled him to identify and help and advise undergraduates similarly afflicted.

In 1939, at the outbreak of war, Henn continued with his lectures, but felt dissatisfied with doing nothing (as he thought) towards the prosecution of the war, and tried, at first unsuccessfully, to join the armed forces. His call finally came at the time of Dunkirk, when the War Office commissioned him as a subaltern in the intelligence corps. After several short postings, he was sent to southern command, which provided him with a room (he was then its only intelligence officer who knew German) at Wilton House, near Salisbury. He was instructed to learn and note all he could about the German army. It was thought that a German invasion was imminent, probably not later than September or October 1940, and the Henns decided that they ought to take advantage of an offer made by Yale University to take in children of Oxford and Cambridge dons, and to assume responsibility for them for the duration of the war, and for their education if their fathers were killed. So Enid and their two children, Rosalind (b. 1927) and Desmond (1929–1964) were shipped off to America, Henn remaining to perform his military duties. Enid later returned to join the WAAF; like her husband, she was fluent in German, and was sent to Bletchley Park, where she later took charge of intelligence concerning German night-fighters.

After various postings Henn was sent in August 1944 on a mission to Italy, where he was appointed deputy assistant chief of staff at allied forces headquarters. He was later promoted to brigadier, working under Lieutenant-General Sir Brian Robertson and General Sir John Harding: as such he had to deal with refugees and displaced persons, and to investigate Nazi atrocities. In some of his activities he found use for his classical knowledge, as when he sought to ease the way for a Yugoslav prelate to visit the pope, by writing a note in Latin to the Holy See. With the ending of hostilities things became more arduous: he had to supervise distribution of food and other supplies, to investigate partisans paying off old scores, and to deal with the lines of refugees, and with Nazi loot found in caves. Amid such mounting problems he was not sorry when in August 1945 he left Italy, and after demobilization was able to return to St Catharine's as senior tutor. He had been twice mentioned in dispatches, and was appointed CBE and the US Legion of Merit.

At St Catharine's, Henn worked with characteristic application, modernizing his section of the college administration and expanding the annual undergraduate intake. He was also appointed to the faculty board of English, later becoming its chairman. Soon after his return to Cambridge he began to study the life and work of W. B. Yeats, at that time neglected and even denigrated by Dublin society. Spurred by this, Henn decided to take action to reverse the trend. He was probably the only man in England who knew intimately the Yeats country in Sligo and Clare, and as a beginning made a point in 1948 of revisiting Sligo, which he had not seen since 1913. At the same time he visited Yeats's widow in Dublin. He found Sligo little changed, but was sad to find Paradise neglected, almost in ruins; even the soil was being ruined by the invasion of the sea through a breached sea wall, leaving everywhere dead trees and grey mud. Much encouraged by his former supervisor, Tillyard, Henn wrote his magisterial book on Yeats's work, *The Lonely Tower* (1950; rev. edn, 1965), which contributed more than any other single study to the revival of Yeats's reputation.

A Yeats Society had been founded in Sligo, out of which grew the Yeats International Summer School, which met for two weeks each August. Henn became its director until his retirement in 1969; even after that he occasionally lectured. Scholars from all over the world travelled there to lecture and take seminars, and there was large student attendance, indicating the growing international interest in Yeats, an interest largely attributable to Henn's indefatigable scholarship and enthusiasm.

On 29 December 1964 Henn's only son committed suicide. In many ways a brilliant young man, Desmond nevertheless found difficulty in having meaningful relationships with others. He was homosexual and Tom detested homosexuality. If he suspected it in any student he would pass him over without comment to an assistant supervisor. The discovery that his son was so inclined must have been traumatic. Soon another blow fell: the destruction by fire of Paradise on 6 October 1970. The official explanation of the cause of the fire was a fault in the central-heating system installed by its new German owner, but suspicions remain that it was the work of republicans. Whatever its cause, the fire marked the end of a family era as surely as had the death of Desmond.

Henn retired from his Cambridge appointments in 1969, when he became an emeritus fellow of St Catharine's. He had been president (deputy head of house) of St Catharine's in 1959–62, and university reader in Anglo-Irish literature in 1968–69, and had undertaken much work elsewhere, including a brief visiting professorship at Trinity College, Dublin. His wide-ranging scholarship is reflected in his books, especially, as author, *The Lonely Tower*, *The Harvest of Tragedy* (1956), *The Bible as Literature* (1970), *Last Essays* (1963), and, as editor, *The Plays and Poems of J. M. Synge* (1963). He had the gift of communicating enthusiasm to his readers, although his writing was not without imperfections: he sometimes quoted other writers inaccurately, and sometimes used tabulations and diagrams instead of relying on his excellent prose, which exemplified the best English usage. He tried especially to persuade scientific writers to express themselves in good, clear, jargon-free prose. For such writers he wrote *The Apple and the Spectroscope* (1951), and *Science in Writing* (1960).

Apart from quoting it here and there in his other writings, and despite its undoubted quality, Henn published little poetry. There are two small collections: *Shooting a Bat* (1962), and *Philoctetes and other Poems*, published posthumously as a section in his autobiography, *Five Arches* (1980). Despite its sometimes pessimistic note, Henn's poetry confirms his deep religious mysticism, which is present even in his threnody on the death of Desmond: '29 December 1964'.

Henn was a heavily built yet athletic man, but in his later years had poor health. An arthritic hip, legacy of a rough landing in an aircraft during the war, limited his mobility. Some time before he died he suffered a major stroke, during which his heart stopped. After regaining partial health, he expressed disappointment that in his experience there was only oblivion, nothing of what he called 'the grandeur of death'. He died at 12 Barrow Road,

Cambridge, from coronary thrombosis on 10 December 1974, and his funeral was held on the 16th at St Mark's Church, Barton Road, Cambridge. **RAYMOND LISTER**

Sources personal knowledge (2004) · private information (2004) · T. R. Henn, *Five arches: a sketch for an autobiography, and Philoctetes and other poems* (1980) · T. R. Henn, *Last essays* (1976) · d. cert.
Likenesses P. Townshend, oils, St Catharine's College, Cambridge
Wealth at death £23,962: probate, 15 March 1975, *CGPLA Eng. & Wales*

Hennedy, Roger (1809–1876), botanist, was born in August 1809 at Carrickfergus, near Belfast. His father was from Ayrshire and his mother from Paisley. He was apprenticed about 1825 as a block cutter to a calico printer in Belfast, but felt oppressed by a master of Methodist observance but tyrannical behaviour. He ran away to Glasgow, where he managed to complete his apprenticeship with a Rutherglen firm of calico printers.

In 1832 Hennedy took up a post with the Liverpool customs, but, disliking the duties, he soon returned to Glasgow to pursue his trade. In 1834, the year he married Miss Cross of Rutherglen, the new process of lithography was being introduced into the Glasgow textile industry and block cutting was soon rendered obsolete. Hennedy adapted to this change of circumstances by teaching himself the technique of tracing designs on paper for transfer to stone. He quickly acquired great skill in drawing, establishing himself as a fabric designer, and it seems to have been this interest in design which led him toward the study of flowers.

By 1838 Hennedy had embarked upon a comprehensive study of botany, developing microscopical skills to investigate algae and diatoms, and when the Glasgow Athenaeum opened in 1848, Hennedy began to teach botany under its auspices. The following year he was similarly engaged at the mechanics' institute. During this period Scotland's textile industry was experiencing economic uncertainties and Hennedy's business ventures were not successful. From the late 1850s his principal occupation was botanical teaching. In 1863 he was appointed professor of botany at the Andersonian Institute in Glasgow, a post which he occupied until his death on 22 October 1876, at Whitehall, Lanarkshire. His wife survived him.

Hennedy's modest manner, facility at blackboard sketching, and assiduousness in the field, made him an excellent teacher. The manual which he wrote for his botanical class, *The Clydesdale Flora*, first appeared in 1865; a fourth, memorial, edition was published in 1878. This little work was a classic of its genre, forming the basis for later publications on the field botany of west central Scotland, notably those of King and Lee. Hennedy's herbarium and slide collection of diatoms were later owned by Strathclyde University. The algal genus *Hennedya* is named for him. **MALCOLM NICOLSON**

Sources W. Simpson, 'Biographical sketch of Roger Hennedy', in R. Hennedy, *The Clydesdale flora*, 4th edn (1878), xi–xxiii · Desmond, *Botanists*, rev. edn · *Glasgow Herald* (23 Oct 1876) · *Journal of Botany, British and Foreign*, 15 (1877), 96 · D. H. Kent and D. E. Allen, *British and Irish herbaria*, 2nd edn (1984) · B. Lloyd, 'Algal herbaria', *British Phycological Bulletin* (1964), 385–6
Archives University of Strathclyde, Glasgow, Herbarium
Likenesses W. Simpson, engraving, 1878, repro. in Hennedy, *Clydesdale flora* [frontispiece]
Wealth at death £433 5s. 10d.: inventory given up, 5 Dec 1876, CCI

Hennell, Charles Christian (1809–1850), religious writer, was born in Manchester on 30 March 1809, the fifth of a family of eight children of James Hennell (or Hennel) (1782–1816) and his wife, Elizabeth Marshall (1778–1858). His sisters included the writers Mary *Hennell, Sara Sophia *Hennell, and Caroline *Bray. His father, a Unitarian and a commercial traveller, based first in Manchester and then in London, died in 1816. The Hennells attended the famous Gravel Pit Chapel in Hackney where Charles received his earliest education. Later he was sent to his uncle's, the Revd Edward Higginson's, school attached to Friar Gate Chapel, Derby. Here, between 1823 and 1824 he enjoyed an intensive grounding in languages, ancient and modern, and in the sciences. In 1824 he became a clerk in the London mercantile house of Morris, Prévost & Co.; in 1836 he began his own business as a silk and drug merchant in Threadneedle Street, London, and in 1843 became manager of an iron works, continuing there until his retirement in 1847 to Woodford, Essex.

In 1835 Charles Bray, a brash and outspoken sceptic, had married Hennell's sensitive and refined sister Caroline (Cara). Troubled by her husband's atheism she suggested her brother write a book confirming to their mutual satisfaction the family's inherited Unitarian beliefs. Charles at once began his researches, but the resultant volume, *An Inquiry Concerning the Origins of Christianity* (1838; 2nd edn, 1841), proved a surprise even to advanced Unitarians. Hennell's sharp intellect and his mastery of languages led him to the conclusion that the Bible should be studied by the same criteria as any other human compilation: the prophets were presented as men of their own times; the synoptic problem was identified; Jesus was seen alternating between a gentle and high-souled ethicism and political involvement (this interpretation may well have served as George Eliot's model for Savonarola in her novel *Romola*); the early church was described as creating a picture of its founder in terms of its own needs. The tenor of the work was reverent, not sceptical. Christianity was defined as 'the purest form yet existing of natural religion' and, as such, Hennell argued in his *Christian Theism* (1839), would continue to appeal to future generations. In 1840 the *Inquiry* was translated into German by Ludwig Georgii, with a preface by David Friedrich Strauss himself, congratulating the Englishman, albeit in condescending terms, on reaching, alone and unaided, conclusions at which a whole bevy of German scholars had arrived only after a generation of painful effort. Later Albert Schweitzer was to be far less laudatory of Hennell's work.

This same year Hennell became engaged to Elizabeth Rebecca (or Rufa, the nickname given her by Coleridge) Brabant, daughter of Dr R. H. Brabant of Devizes. The match was opposed by Dr Brabant, who did not consent to their being married until March 1843, when the ceremony was held in W. J. Fox's advanced Unitarian church in Finsbury Place, London. By now Hennell had become a frequent visitor, with Rufa and his sisters Mary and Sara, to Rosehill, the Coventry home of Charles and Cara Bray. Here they were introduced to Mary Ann Evans (George Eliot), who became a lifelong friend of the family. In August 1841 Joseph Parkes, the radical politician, had asked Hennell to arrange a translation of Strauss's *Das Leben Jesu* and promised financial help. Sara refused the task, but Rufa undertook it until 1844, when the project was handed over to Mary Ann Evans, who agonized over it for two years; in the spring of 1846 it was Sara and Charles who checked and emended the text, published that year under the name George Eliot.

Hennell's final years were unhappy. Increasingly consumptive, he had been from 1840 involved with Barber Beaumont in the substantially humanist New Philosophical Institution, Beaumont Square, Mile End, London, writing two hymns for its service book. But this project ended in acrimony and a costly chancery suit over finances. He also lost heavily in the railway mania of the late 1840s. He died at Woodford, Essex, on 2 September 1850. In 1857 his wife married W. M. W. Call. The Hennells should be considered in their own right and not merely as an episode in the intellectual development of George Eliot. This provincial family's mastery of the German language and of German 'neology' stands in sharp contrast to the English establishment's deep ignorance of both.

IAN SELLERS

Sources S. S. Hennell, *A memoir of C. C. Hennell* (1899) · J. W. Cross, ed., *George Eliot's life as related in her letters and journals*, 3 vols. (1885) · G. S. Haight, *George Eliot: a biography* (1968) · B. Willey, *Nineteenth century studies: Coleridge to Matthew Arnold* (1949) · J. C. Knoepflacher, *Religious humanism in the Victorian novel* (1965)

Hennell, Mary (1802–1843), author, was born in Manchester on 23 May 1802, one of eight children and the eldest of several daughters of James Hennell or Hennel (1782–1816), a Unitarian and a merchant, first in Manchester and then in London, and Elizabeth Marshall (1778–1858) of Loughborough. These daughters, educated at home, were very close to one another and are thought to have been the originals of the Meyrick family in George Eliot's *Daniel Deronda* (1876). Mary's sisters included Sara Sophia *Hennell and Caroline *Bray, and her brother was Charles Christian *Hennell. After her father's death, the family moved to Hackney, Middlesex. Mary Hennell was the author of *An outline of the various social systems and communities which have been founded on the principle of co-operation*, first published in 1841 as an appendix to *The Philosophy of Necessity*, by her brother-in-law the Owenite social reformer Charles *Bray, with whom she had a close relationship. It was afterwards printed separately, in 1844, with the addition of a substantial introduction dealing with the existing conditions of industrial Britain. Her family was associated with the manufacture of ribbon, and she wrote the article 'Ribbons' for Charles Knight's *Penny Cyclopaedia*. She died from tuberculosis in Hackney on 16 March 1843.

J. M. SCOTT, *rev.* C. A. CREFFIELD

Sources *GM*, 2nd ser., 19 (1843), 547 · private information (1888) · C. Bray, *Phases of opinion and experience during a long life, an autobiography* (1884), 77 · G. S. Haight, *George Eliot: a biography* (1968), 48, 146

Hennell, Sara Sophia (1812–1899), author, the seventh and penultimate child of James Hennell (1782–1816), traveller and partner in the mercantile firm of Fazy & Co. (Manchester), and Elizabeth Marshall (1778–1858), of Loughborough, Leicestershire, was born on 23 November 1812 at 2 St Thomas's Square, Hackney, Middlesex. Her sisters included Mary *Hennell and Caroline *Bray. On her father's death the family moved to 5 Pleasant Row, moving again in 1826 to 7 Hackney Terrace. The girls of this close-knit family, thought to have provided the original upon which the Meyrick family of George Eliot's *Daniel Deronda* (1876) was modelled, were educated at home where Sara learned German, Latin, music, and painting and drawing. The family worshipped at Robert Aspland's Unitarian congregation at Gravel Pit Chapel, Hackney, though Sara Hennell was to repudiate Unitarianism as taking too little account of the darker side of human nature. Between 1832 and 1841 she worked as a governess: the lasting friendships she forged while working, between 1837 and 1842, in the home of the Bonham family of Ditcham, near Petersfield, resulted in holiday invitations and acquaintance with their cousin, Florence Nightingale.

When her adored brother Charles Christian *Hennell married 'Rufa' Brabant in 1843 Sara Hennell and her mother moved to Clapton, near Hackney. In 1851 they moved to Ivy Cottage, St Nicholas Street, Coventry, next door to Rosehill, the home of her younger sister 'Cara' and her husband, the freethinker Charles Bray. By 1855 she had become governess to Charles Bray's adopted, illegitimate daughter and her nephew, Frank Hennell.

It was at Rosehill, in 1842, that Mary Ann Evans (George Eliot) met Sara Hennell. The range of endearments from 'Beloved Achates' to 'Cara Sposa' employed by Evans in the ensuing twelve years of constant correspondence charts their intimacy. Declining to translate David Friedrich Strauss's *Das Leben Jesu*, Hennell agreed instead to revise the work of her sister-in-law Rufa, and then of Mary Ann Evans, to whom the task of translation was passed in 1844. That summer, travelling with the Brabants in Germany, Hennell met Strauss. In 1854 Evans consulted her over her translation of Feuerbach. At the end of their 'German period' their theological and political paths diverged (Hennell was an active campaigner for women's rights) until by 1869 Evans noted herself 'irritated' during her friend's increasingly rare visits (*George Eliot Letters*, 5.47).

Sara Hennell espoused the natural theism of her brother Charles. Her mythical tale *Heliados* (written in 1846, published 1884) testifies as much to sisterly devotion as admiration for martyrdom consequent upon unorthodox religious beliefs. She won first prize and praise from both the orthodox and freethinking press in a competition for laypeople sponsored by the Glaswegian George Baillie, with *Christianity and Infidelity: an Exposition of the*

Sara Sophia Hennell (1812–1899), by unknown photographer, c.1850

Arguments on both Sides (1857). Her next entry won second prize. In 1895 W. E. Gladstone still regarded her *Essay on the Sceptical Tendency of Butler's 'Analogy'* (1859) as meriting refutation and paid tribute to her 'palpably serious and earnest' criticism (Gladstone, 723). *Thoughts in Aid of Faith* (1860) aimed to salvage feeling and moral duty from a critique of contemporary theology and philosophy, but its convoluted, qualificatory style formed a lukewarm recommendation for 'theistical pantheism'. Even her sixpenny tract *On the Need of Dogmas in Religion* (1874) sacrificed clarity to longwinded scrupulosity. A three-volume work entitled *Present Religion as a Faith Owning Fellowship with Thought* (1865, 1873, 1887) sought to outline her comparativist repudiation of positivism. Its method of giving 'a faithful delineation of my own mental process' places it in the classic mode of nineteenth-century spiritual autobiography, though the total absence of personal material makes it dry reading. The portion of her brother's memoir she completed before senility overcame her supplies an interesting glimpse of her intellectual and artistic milieu and offers evidence of a crisper style and more approachable personality.

Her unwise investment in John Chapman's publishing company, combined with the Brays' straightened circumstances, resulted in their combining forces at Ivy Cottage from 1857 to 1861, and then, for a time, at 3 Barr's Hill Terrace. This 'small-featured delicate-faced' woman (*George Eliot Letters*, 4.90), died at Ivy Cottage on 7 March 1899 and was buried in Coventry cemetery. ELISABETH JAY

Sources S. S. Hennell, *A memoir of Charles Christian Hennell* (1899) · *The George Eliot letters*, ed. G. S. Haight, 9 vols. (1954–78) · G. S. Haight, *George Eliot: a biography* (1968) · G. S. Haight, *George Eliot's originals and contemporaries: essays in Victorian literary history and biography* (1992) · W. E. Gladstone, 'Bishop Butler and his censors', *Nineteenth Century*, 38 (1895), 715–39 · *Coventry Herald* (10 March 1899)
Archives Nuneaton Museum and Art Gallery, Warwickshire | NL Scot., letters to George Combe
Likenesses C. Bray, watercolour, 1833, Nuneaton Museum and Art Gallery; repro. in J. Uglow, *George Eliot* (1987) · daguerreotype, c.1850, Nuneaton Museum and Art Gallery [*see illus.*] · Stanley of Hertford Street, Coventry, two sepia photographs, 1875, Nuneaton Museum and Art Gallery · Maull & Co., photograph, 1897, repro. in Hennell, *Memoir of Charles Christian Hennell* · C. Bray, two pencil sketches, Nuneaton Museum and Art Gallery · C. Bray, watercolour, Nuneaton Museum and Art Gallery · S. S. Hennell, self-portrait, watercolour, Nuneaton Museum and Art Gallery · sepia photograph (the Hennell sisters in old age), Nuneaton Museum and Art Gallery
Wealth at death £4496 11s. 5d.: probate, 28 April 1899, CGPLA Eng. & Wales

Hennen, John (1779–1828), army officer and military surgeon, born on 21 April 1779, at Castlebar, co. Mayo, was the younger son of James Hennen, a medical practitioner, and was descended from a family who had held land near Castlebar since the Cromwellian occupation. After school at Limerick, he became a medical apprentice to a near relative (perhaps his father) at Castlebar. In 1796 he entered the medical school at Edinburgh, was more sociable than studious, and married, aged seventeen, Miss Malcolm of Dumfries. He qualified at the Edinburgh College of Surgeons in 1798, joined the Shropshire militia as assistant surgeon, in 1800 was appointed to the 40th (2nd Somersetshire) regiment, and went with it to the Mediterranean. He served throughout the Peninsular War in various regiments, and became staff surgeon in 1812. A skilful operator and energetic officer, he was noted for being never without a cigar in his mouth.

Hennen retired on half pay in 1814, but had hardly settled at Dumfries, when he was recalled to active service in Flanders. For his services after Waterloo, he was promoted deputy inspector of hospitals, and placed on the home staff at Portsmouth. There he utilized his abundant notes of cases to begin his *Observations on some important points in the practice of military surgery, and in the arrangement and police of hospitals*, which he finished and published in 1818 at Edinburgh, having been transferred there in 1817 as principal medical officer for Scotland. A second edition was published in 1820 with the title *Principles of Military Surgery*, and a third edition with a biography by his son in 1829. At Edinburgh he attended classes for a second time, and graduated MD in 1819. In 1820 he was appointed principal medical officer in the Mediterranean, residing at Malta and Corfu. His *Medical Topography* of these islands and of Gibraltar, in the form of reports to the army medical department, was brought out by his son in 1830. In 1826 he became principal medical officer at Gibraltar, and died there on 3 November 1828 of a fever (probably yellow fever) contracted while combating the disastrous epidemic which had broken out in the garrison in September of that year. A monument to him was erected by subscription at Gibraltar. He was twice married and left five children.   CHARLES CREIGHTON, *rev.* DAVID GATES

Sources D. O. Edwards, *The Lancet* (11 April 1829), 44–6 · *Edinburgh Medical and Surgical Journal*, 31 (1829), 225–8 · J. Hennen, 'Life', in J. Hennen, *Principles of military surgery*, 3rd edn (1829) · D. Gates, *The Spanish ulcer: a history of the Peninsular War* (1986) · N. Cantlie, *A history of the army medical department*, 1 (1974)

Hennessey, John Baboneau Nickterlien (1829–1910), surveyor, born at Fatehpur, in northern India, on 1 August 1829, was the son of Michael Henry Hennessey and an Indian mother of whom nothing more is known. After being educated locally, he joined the junior branch of the great trigonometrical survey on 14 April 1844. For some years he worked in the marshy jungle of Bengal and the areas bordering the Nepal *terai*. Of the party of 140 officers and assistants which he joined, forty died from fever in a few days and Hennessey himself was often ill. None the less, his enthusiasm and thoroughness attracted notice. He was transferred to the Punjab in 1850, where he fixed the longitudinal position of Lahore, Amritsar, Wazirabad, and other places. Attached to the superintendent's field office in 1851, he helped the astronomical assistant collate computations of latitude observations and in other work. In October 1853 he was put in charge of the branch computing office, and in the following year helped the surveyor-general at the Chach base line. Promoted to the senior branch on 25 April 1854, he was employed at headquarters at Dehra Dun in reducing the measurements of the Chach base line, and preparing a report on the northeast longitudinal series. During the Indian mutiny he was at Mussooree, a hill-station 10 miles outside Dehra Dun, where for nearly five months he was under arms, serving in difficult conditions.

After service with the base line at Vizagapatam, in the south, Hennessey took two years' leave to England in March 1863. He entered Jesus College, Cambridge, on 31 October as a fellow commoner, and showed considerable talent for mathematics. He learned the new process of photozincography at the Ordnance Survey offices in Southampton, and when he returned to duty in India in April 1865 took out equipment with which he established the process at Dehra Dun. This equipment, and the men he trained, made possible the rapid reproduction of maps and survey sheets, an achievement of considerable importance in India where the need was for a ready supply of rough but accurate maps, rather than highly finished ones.

As head of the amalgamated computing office and calculating branch, in 1866 Hennessey was engaged in verification of the standards of length and determined the 10 ft standard bar of the trigonometrical survey. He also took in hand the huge quantity of material from William Lambton, Sir George Everest, and Sir Andrew Scott Waugh, and with the help of a large staff reduced it to order. He married at Calcutta in March 1868 Elizabeth Golden, only daughter of R. Malcolm Ashman; they had a daughter and a son, Lieutenant J. A. C. Hennessey, of the 45th (Rattray)

Sikhs, who was killed in action at Jandola, Waziristan, in October 1900.

Hennessey helped General James Thomas Walker edit the *Account of the Operations of the Great Trigonometrical Survey of India* (19 vols., 1870–1910). He made significant contributions to some volumes, fourteen of which were issued during his tenure of office. He also wrote the report on *Explorations in Great Tibet and Mongolia* (1884) and supervised the drawing of its maps. He was designated deputy superintendent of the trigonometrical survey in September 1869, officiated as its superintendent in 1874, and after the three branches of survey operations had been amalgamated under the title of the Survey of India, he was appointed in February 1883 deputy surveyor-general. On 9 December 1874, with the equatorial telescope of the Royal Society, he observed from Mussooree the transit of Venus. This won him the fellowship of the society (1875), to whose *Proceedings* he contributed twelve papers. Cambridge conferred on him an honorary MA degree in 1876, and after his retirement on 1 October 1884 on a special pension granted by government, he was made a CIE (6 June 1885).

At Mussooree, where he at first lived after retirement, he was an active member of the municipality, captain of the local volunteer corps, and discoverer of the spring from which the water supply was obtained. Later he moved to London and lived at 18 Alleyn Park, West Dulwich, where he died on 23 May 1910 of a strangulated ventral hernia; he was buried at Elmers End cemetery.

    F. H. BROWN, *rev.* ELIZABETH BAIGENT

Sources C. R. Markham, *A memoir on the Indian surveys*, 2nd edn (1878) · List of officers in survey dept to Jan 1884, Calcutta · *The Times* (26 May 1910) · Venn, *Alum. Cant.* · personal knowledge (1912) · *CGPLA Eng. & Wales* (1910) · Indian survey report for 1884–5 · d. cert.

Wealth at death £4,307 0s. 7d.: probate, 17 June 1910, *CGPLA Eng. & Wales*

Hennessy, Henry (1826–1901), physicist and inventor, was born on 19 March 1826 at Cork, the second son of John Hennessy (*d.* 1867) of Ballyhennessy, co. Kerry, and his wife, Elizabeth, daughter of Henry Casey of Cork. Sir John Pope-*Hennessy was a younger brother. Educated at Cork under Michael Healy, Hennessy received an excellent training in classics, modern languages, and mathematics, but, as a Roman Catholic, was deprived of a university education, and adopted the profession of an engineer. His leisure was from early youth devoted to mathematical research, in which he engaged quite spontaneously. From an early period he made original and valuable contributions to British and foreign scientific journals, which he continued through life.

In 1849 Hennessy was made librarian of the nondenominational Queen's College, Cork, and in 1855, on the invitation of Cardinal Newman, he became professor of physics at the newly established Catholic University of Ireland in Dublin. In 1874 he transferred his services to the Royal College of Science, Dublin, where he was appointed professor of applied mathematics. His work there was of exceptional merit, and he was dean of the college in 1880 and again in 1888. He was made a member of the Royal Irish Academy in 1851, and was its vice-president from 1870 to 1873. He was elected FRS in 1858. He married Rosa, youngest daughter of Hayden Corri, and had children.

In 1890 Hennessy resigned his chair under the then recent compulsory rules for superannuation in the civil service at the age of sixty-five. A memorandum to the government protesting against his retirement attracted influential signatories but was without effect.

Hennessy was remarkable for his versatile interests and scientific ingenuity. In his earliest paper, published in 1845, when he was only nineteen, in the *Philosophical Magazine*, he proposed the use of photography for the registration of barometric and thermometric readings. In 'Researches in terrestrial physics' (*Philosophical Transactions of the Royal Society of London*, 141, 1851, 511–47) he argued from the figure and structure of the earth and planets, that they were of fluid origin, and that a fluid nucleus at a high temperature was enclosed within their crust. He also wrote on meteorology and on climatology (*Notes and Abstracts of … the British Association for the Advancement of Science*, 1857, 2), deducing laws which regulate the distribution of temperature in islands. The excellence of a paper on the influence of the Gulf Stream (*Proceedings of the Royal Society*, 9, 1857–9) led to a request to report on the temperature of the seas surrounding the British Isles for the committee on Irish fisheries in 1870.

Among Hennessy's other proposals was one for a decimal system of weights and measures founded on the length of the polar axis of the earth, a quantity capable of more accurate determination than the earth's quadrant on which the metric system is based. Standards such as the polar foot and the polar pound, and a complete set of weights and measures on the polar system, constructed under Hennessy's supervision, are in the museum of the Royal College of Science, Dublin. In the same museum are many models of his mechanical inventions, one of them illustrating the structure of sewers best adapted to obtain the greatest scour with due provision for a great influx of storm water.

Besides his papers in scientific periodicals Hennessy published separately: *On the Study of Science in its Relation to Individuals and Society* (1858; 2nd edn, 1859); *On the Freedom of Education* (a paper delivered at the Social Science Congress, Liverpool, in 1858, published in 1859; and *The Relation of Science to Modern Civilisation* (1862). After his retirement he spent much time abroad, due to the inadequacy of his pension. Towards the end of his life he returned to Ireland on medical advice, and died at Bray, co. Wicklow, on 8 March 1901.   [ANON.], *rev.* ISOBEL FALCONER

Sources W. N. H., *PRS*, 75 (1905), 140–42 · *Men and women of the time* (1899) · *WW* · A. T. C. Pratt, ed., *People of the period: being a collection of the biographies of upwards of six thousand living celebrities*, 2 vols. (1897) · election certificate, RS

Hennessy, (Richard) James Arthur Pope- (1916–1974), writer, was born in London on 20 November 1916, the younger son (there was no daughter) of Major-General (Ladislaus Herbert) Richard Pope-Hennessy (1875–1942) and his wife, Dame Una Constance (d. 1949), daughter of

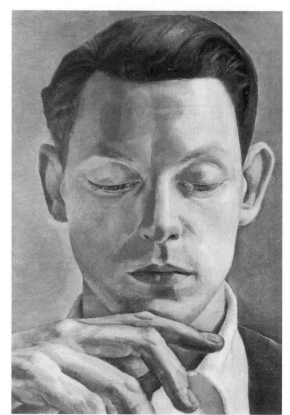

(Richard) James Arthur Pope-Hennessy (1916–1974), by Lucian Freud, 1955 [*A Writer*]

Sir Arthur Birch, lieutenant-governor of Ceylon. With his elder brother John Wyndham Pope-*Hennessy, James was brought up in an exclusively intellectual, closely knit Catholic family. The father was a tolerant, cultivated soldier, the mother a highly educated writer and woman of formidable personality. She exercised a strong hold upon her sons and inculcated in both the desire to work. Pope-Hennessy was educated at Downside School and Balliol College, Oxford, but at neither of these institutions was he wholly happy. He did not take a degree. He had no respect for organized games or the accepted diversions of youth. While remaining devoted to his family, he developed a questing, questioning spirit which induced him never to take for granted the shibboleths of his class and upbringing. A natural rebelliousness was accentuated by his unremitting homosexuality. By mixing with people of every sort he became totally un-class conscious. Indeed he detested all forms of injustice and snobbishness. His strong compassion for the underdog sometimes induced him to express intemperate opinions. Although physically attracted to his own sex he loved the companionship of women, to whom most of his enchanting correspondence was addressed. They were fascinated by his understanding and sensitivity. All his life he was much sought after by hostesses for his sparkling conversation.

Thanks to his mother's influence Pope-Hennessy knew from an early age that he was destined to be a writer; and writing always had first call upon his time and energies. In consequence by relentless discipline he developed a natural gift into a fluent, witty, beautifully descriptive, and often poetic prose style. His parents were never well off and Pope-Hennessy had to earn a living. On leaving Oxford he worked in 1937–8 as an editorial assistant for Sheed and Ward, the Catholic publishers in Paternoster Row. There he got to know intimately the churches and Dickensian alleys of the City of London. They were lovingly described in his first book, *London Fabric* (1939), for which he was awarded the Hawthornden prize. The publishing of religious books, however, bored him and just before the Second World War broke out his mother got him a job as private secretary to Sir Hubert Young, governor of Trinidad. He hated the flag-waving formality of Government House protocol, making his views plain in *West Indian Summer* (1943), an account of the experiences of nine English visitors to the West Indies. On the outbreak of war he returned to England and enlisted as a private in an aircraft battery. Commissioned in 1940 to military intelligence, he was sent in 1943 as a member of the British army staff to Washington. When the war was over he returned to London.

On demobilization Pope-Hennessy lived on his writings, if that is an accurate account of an author so profligate of his earnings that he underwent recurrent financial crises, from which he was constantly relieved by the bounty of friends. Only from 1947 to 1949 did he have regular employment—as literary editor of *The Spectator*. He continued to produce books between bouts of travelling. *America is an Atmosphere* (1947) was an engaging travel book inspired by affection for Washington, just as *Aspects of Provence* (1952) echoed his delight in the song and sunburnt mirth of the warm south. But the two books which established his reputation as an outstanding biographer were parts 1 and 2 of *Monckton Milnes* (1949), namely *The Years of Promise* and *The Flight of Youth*. These volumes epitomized the Victorian patrician, political, and literary milieu. They were followed by the less inspired *Lord Crewe, the Likeness of a Liberal* (1955). After an interval came *Queen Mary* (1959), for which he was appointed CVO (1960). With the possible exception of *George V* (1952) by his friend Harold Nicolson, no other royal biography of the century has so successfully combined sympathetic character study with social history in such brilliant narrative form.

After preparatory visits to Ireland, Malaysia, Hong Kong, Africa, and Mauritius appeared what may be his best book, *Verandah* (1964), about scenes in the life of his grandfather, Sir John Pope Hennessy, an impulsive and provocative colonial governor who hailed from co. Kerry and was immortalized by Anthony Trollope as Phineas Finn. The portrait Pope-Hennessy drew of his Irish progenitor's character bears no small resemblance to his own.

As a break in the catalogue of Pope-Hennessy's biographies *Sins of the Fathers* (1967) was an angry indictment of the Atlantic slave traffickers. *Anthony Trollope* (1971) and the posthumous *Robert Louis Stevenson* (1974) marked a resumption of his literary biographies. These books were written mostly in Banagher, co. Offaly, where in 1970 he

had gone to live, quixotically adopting Irish citizenship. Trollope's was a character to which Pope-Hennessy had long been attached although so staid and unlike his own. With Stevenson's he was not in total sympathy. Besides, he did not live to correct the proofs. The book is the least convincing of his literary studies and suggests too hasty composition. Pope-Hennessy was in truth in a hurry to embark upon the life of Sir Noël Coward, for which he received a handsome advance. Alas, it was owing to indiscreet mentions of this welcome fortune that he met his death. On 25 January 1974 he was slaughtered by some ruffianly associates of the unscrupulous youths with whom he chose to consort, and died of his injuries at the St Charles Hospital, Kensington. For during his last years an addiction to alcohol and what Peter Quennell called the 'denizens of back-street bars and pubs' (*A Lonely Business*, ed. Quennell) led him to take appalling risks of blackmail and violence. Sad though these habits were, they did not intrude upon his writings or lose him the affection of his friends, even though they curtailed some old relationships. That charm, which in his youth was so irresistible, never entirely deserted him. To the last he remained the brilliant raconteur with a mischievous sense of humour and a sense of the ludicrous.

His good looks were striking. Slender and well built, he carried his head proudly. He had a pale alabaster complexion, strangely hooded eyes, and thick raven-black hair, features which he liked to attribute to the Malaysian blood of his grandmother, Lady Pope Hennessy. All his movements, like his mind, were rapid and darting. In walking he would outpace a companion in a sort of bounding gait.   JAMES LEES-MILNE, *rev.*

Sources *A lonely business: a self-portrait of James Pope-Hennessy*, ed. P. Quennell (1981) · personal knowledge (1986)
Archives Getty Research Institute for the History of Art and the Humanities, Los Angeles, papers
Likenesses L. Freud, oils, 1955 (*A writer*), priv. coll. [*see illus.*] · C. Beaton, photograph
Wealth at death £26,498: probate, 30 May 1974, *CGPLA Eng. & Wales*

Hennessy, Sir John Pope (1834–1891), politician and colonial governor, was born on 8 August 1834 in Cork, the third of five sons of John Hennessy (*d.* 26 April 1867), hide merchant, of Cork, and his wife, Elizabeth, daughter of Henry Casey, butter merchant, of Cork. Hennessy's parents were Roman Catholic and anti-British. His father's family claimed descent from the indigenous Irish landed gentry and styled themselves Hennessy of Ballyhennessy, co. Kerry. As a boy Hennessy suffered from chronic bronchitis, and was educated by a private tutor. His family intended him for a medical career and for five years he attended Queen's College, Cork, gaining first-class honours in surgery and medicine. In May 1855 he went to London, where he continued his medical training at Charing Cross Hospital, but later that year he procured a clerkship in the Privy Council Office. Small, pushy, arrogant, ambitious, manipulative, and an accomplished charmer and bluffer, he was part of the migration of 'middle-class or *petit bourgeois* careerists … micks on the make' (Foster,

Paddy and Mr Punch, 283-4). He started to read for the bar, in preparation for a political career.

Like some other Irish Catholics then, angered by the Liberals' policies on the Queen's Colleges and the Ecclesiastical Titles Bill, Hennessy became a Conservative, and he especially admired Disraeli. In the general election of 1859 he stood as 'Irish Nationalist Conservative' candidate for King's county, generally supporting Disraeli but independent on Irish issues. Surprisingly, with no money or powerful patrons, he was elected, the first Roman Catholic Conservative MP. Surviving on arrogance, bluff, and possibly a clandestine subsidy from Conservative Party funds, he publicized himself, intrigued, cultivated Disraeli and others likely to be useful to him, and baited the Liberal leaders. He advocated amendment of Irish land laws and the reclamation of bogs to counter emigration, and criticized the government system of education. He supported the causes of Poland and Italy, and contributed to some minor reforms: amendment of the Irish poor law (1861-2), the Prison Ministers Act (1863), and amendment of the Mines Regulation Acts. In November 1861 he was called to the bar at the Inner Temple. His rise had been meteoric and some contemporaries considered him the model for Trollope's Phineas Finn. However, at the general election of 1865 he was defeated by seven votes, through not paying his debts from the previous election to the King's county jaunting-car owners; they refused to work for him, so he could not transport rural voters to the polls. He was involved in business speculation, and acquired a mistress, Miss A. M. Conyngham, with whom he had two illegitimate daughters. In 1866, with £2000 borrowed from a moneylender, he attempted to gain wealth by snaring a rich heiress, a Miss Canning, into marriage, but failed. In debt, he lived in hiding in the country. In 1866 the Conservatives returned to office and, through Disraeli's patronage, Hennessy procured a colonial governorship, of Labuan, a small island off Borneo. With typical arrogance he accepted under protest, wanting Queensland—which was not even vacant—and complained of being given 'such a small place' (Pope-Hennessy, 51). In fact it was only because of lingering 'old corruption' and jobbery, and mid-Victorian metropolitan irresponsibility towards the lesser tropical dependencies that so dubious a failed politician—without colonial, naval, military, or administrative experience—was given a position he so little deserved. In September 1867 he sailed for Labuan.

Hennessy was governor of Labuan from 1867 to 1871. It was swampy, unhealthy, backward, and impoverished, and he achieved little there. He freed prisoners (a favourite gesture of his), increased taxes, quarrelled with other officials, and was reproved by the Colonial Office. On 4 February 1868 he married a beautiful but dowryless Eurasian girl, educated in England and Switzerland, Katherine (Kitty) Elizabeth (1850-1923), second child and only daughter of Hugh Low, colonial treasurer at Labuan and botanist, and his wife Catherine (d. 1851), herself half Scottish and half Malay. They had three sons, but reportedly their marriage was not happy. In 1871 Hennessy was designated to the governorship of the Bahamas. He left Labuan in September 1871 and reached London in December.

From February 1872 to February 1873 Hennessy, temporarily seconded from his Bahamas appointment, was governor-in-chief of the British west African settlements—Sierra Leone, the Gambia, the Gold Coast, and Lagos—with his headquarters at Freetown, Sierra Leone. Against Colonial Office advice he insisted on taking his first born, three-year-old son, John Patrick (Johnnie). Soon after arrival at Freetown the child died of dysentery: that year over a quarter of the Europeans died. Hennessy tried to curry favour with the local people and, despite corruption scandals—the creole Treasury cashier stole over £800—wanted the appointment of Creoles to more senior positions: the Colonial Office refused. He criticized missionaries and missionary education (presumably because of his anti-protestant prejudice), praised the Muslims of the interior, and supported Edward Wilmot Blyden's proposal for the establishment of a west African university. He introduced limited sanitary reform in Freetown, and abolished Sierra Leone land and other direct taxes, leaving specific duties the mainstay of the local budget. His tariff chiefly benefited French traders. He also abolished timber duties, removing the only check on deforestation. He was popular with Freetown Africans, and for years afterwards 'Pope Hennessy day' was celebrated annually. Before leaving, Hennessy announced a £5000 surplus: later the auditor found he had omitted a month's expenditure. Hennessy claimed that customs revenue would rise, but it fell. By the end of 1873 there was a colonial deficit, the first for nearly twenty-five years. Following the Anglo-Dutch treaty of 1872, Hennessy in April 1872 received from the Dutch their Gold Coast forts. He was made CMG. However, as so often during his colonial career, trouble followed policies. His unpopular appointment of a new civil commissioner at Elmina led to riot and murder there.

At Lagos, annexed by Palmerston in 1861, the British administrator from 1866 was Captain John Hawley Glover RN (1829–1885), a dynamic 'man on the spot' who favoured British expansion and had a vigorous, interventionist, anti-Egba and pro-Ibadan policy. In 1872 the colonial secretary, Lord Kimberley, instructed Hennessy to caution Glover. Hennessy went to Lagos in April 1872 and quickly formed an antipathy to Glover. The newly arrived Hennessy told Glover, who had fifteen years' west African experience and spoke Yoruba, 'you know nothing of the country, the place or the people' (Pope-Hennessy, 135). Exceeding Kimberley's instructions, in June he sent Glover home. Kimberley disapproved but did not reverse this. Hennessy quickly and with evident animus reversed Glover's anti-Egba policy. Hennessy's pro-Egba policy soon failed. Glover criticized to Kimberley Hennessy's 'vanity and culpable weakness' (Newbury, 372). On the Gold Coast Hennessy was hostile to the Fante confederation and contributed to its failure. He negotiated with the Asante and as usual thought he was doing well. The Asante invasion of 1873 surprised him, and he initially denied that there was an invasion. However, he left the problem to his successor, as he sailed for Liverpool in February 1873. Back in Britain some blamed him for the Second Anglo-Asante War: he blamed others. Controversy continued between him and the officials with whom he had quarrelled. Sir George Barrow, head of the Colonial Office African department, wrote in February 1873: 'one of the "pope's" failings is to endeavour to establish infallibility & at the same time to obtain supremacy—hence his liability to anathematise all around him … but … he may be the victim of his own selfish policy' (Pope-Hennessy, 145). He continued to hope to re-enter Irish politics.

The Colonial Office insisted that Hennessy next be governor of the Bahamas, a post which he had earlier accepted. He demanded a superior governorship and, with mendacious effrontery, claimed he had been insufficiently rewarded after he 'abandoned another career to enter the Colonial service' (Pope-Hennessy, 150). In fact when he procured his first colonial appointment he had been a careerless, disreputable adventurer, in debt and in hiding. He arrived in the Bahamas in May 1873. He introduced some minor reforms and demanded that the crown agents buy a £300 carpet from a shop in Cork. He again mismanaged colonial finances and made false claims about them. A Colonial Office official noted that 'when Mr Hennessy leaves a Colony the state of the Finances are not found to be in so satisfactory a state as he has led us to believe' (ibid., 153). He stayed for only eight months, a tranquil interlude he enjoyed, then in June 1874 was called home on leave and never returned.

In 1874 Hennessy's patron Disraeli again became prime minister, and in 1875 Hennessy was promoted to the governorship (salary £4000) of the Windward Islands, with his capital in Barbados, where he arrived on 1 November. The Colonial Office favoured federation of the Windward Islands, and this Hennessy tried to implement. Always more sympathetic to criminals than to their victims, he released convicts and abolished flogging. He encouraged emigration to other West Indian islands. In Barbados the planters still dominated the assembly, and they opposed federation. Some formed the Barbados Defence Association and, with their allies in London, pressed for Hennessy's recall. At Easter (April) 1876 labourers, their hopes raised by Hennessy, rioted (the federation riots). Hennessy suppressed them. In May the assembly voted for his recall. The imperial government defended him, but in November moved him to Hong Kong.

Appointed governor of Hong Kong in November 1876, Hennessy arrived there in April 1877. The traveller Isabella Bird (Mrs Bishop) described him as 'a little man much overdressed in white kid gloves and patent leather boots with a mouth which smiles perpetually and sinister eyes which never smile' (Pope-Hennessy, 188). An inefficient administrator, he favoured the Chinese and in 1880 appointed the first Chinese member of the legislative council, and increased the revenue from opium. British residents criticized his 'Chinomania' and 'native race craze' (Lowe and McLaughlin, 228). Prejudiced against the protestant Scots and English there, he promoted his Catholic favourites. He quarrelled with the merchants, the

military commander, and the governor of Macao, and was censured by the Colonial Office. In 1878 an official told the new colonial secretary, Sir Michael Hicks Beach, that Hennessy 'cannot ever gain the confidence of those over whom he is placed' (Pope-Hennessy, 195). Despite a disastrous fire and demands from the residents, he failed to establish an effective fire service. He again freed convicts. His pro-criminal sympathies and failure to act effectively against increased violent crime alienated the British population, who called for his dismissal and boycotted Government House. Nevertheless in April 1880 the outgoing Conservative government, to his delight, made him a KCMG. Finally, following a scandal—in April 1881 Hennessy publicly assaulted with an umbrella a former favourite, Thomas Child Hayllar QC, member of the legislative council, apparently because of Hayllar's relationship with Hennessy's wife—Hennessy was removed from Hong Kong. He left in March 1882 ostensibly on leave. When it was rumoured that he might return, the leading British merchants sent 'the strongest remonstrances' (Eitel, 567) to the British government.

In December 1882 Hennessy was appointed governor of Mauritius, and he arrived on 1 June 1883. He favoured the Francophone Creoles—who demanded 'Mauritius for the Mauritians'—and Indian immigrants, openly and extravagantly condemned British rule, and quarrelled with Charles Dalton Clifford Lloyd, the lieutenant-governor, and other British officials. In September 1886 a royal commission was issued to Sir Hercules Robinson, governor of Cape Colony and high commissioner in South Africa, to inquire into Hennessy's administration: an unprecedented situation. The subjects for special inquiry were Hennessy's relations with Lloyd, pro-Creole partisanship, financial maladministration, 'persecution' of English officials, and pro-criminal bias. Robinson arrived in early November 1886, and on 16 December suspended Hennessy. In January 1887 the colonial secretary, Sir Henry Thurstan Holland (from 1888 Lord Knutsford), ordered Hennessy back to England. In July, Holland decided, after a long inquiry, that sufficient cause had not been shown for Hennessy's removal, though he had been guilty of 'want of temper and judgment', 'vexatious and unjustifiable interference' with the magistrates, and undue partisanship. Accordingly he returned to Mauritius and served out his time, retiring on a pension in December 1889.

When Hennessy left Mauritius he was suffering from tropical anaemia, and Holland had made it clear that he would be offered no further governorship. He had become a governor only by default, and returned to his true métier of politician. He hoped Gladstone would later make him a peer, and in 1890 bought a large house, Rostellan Castle, near Cork. In December 1890 he contested the by-election at North Kilkenny—described by The Times as a 'priest-ridden agricultural constituency' (Callanan, 69) as anti-Parnellite home rule candidate. Tim Healy and Michael Davitt organized the anti-Parnellite campaign, Parnell campaigned for Vincent Scully, Fenians supported Parnell, and Catholic clergy and farmers opposed him. The contest was bitter and violent. Hennessy, who campaigned despite the winter cold, was apparently almost incidental: the election was fought for and against Parnell. Hennessy was elected by a majority of 1165: a disaster for Parnell, shattering his mystique of electoral invincibility.

Hennessy died of heart failure on 7 October 1891 at his residence, Rostellan Castle, near Cork, and was buried in his father's grave, with no separate headstone or monument, in Cork city cemetery. A statue by M. Loumeau (1908) was erected in Port Louis, Mauritius. Hennessy's widow in 1894 married a much younger man, Edward Francis Thackwell JP (b. 1868, only son of Major-General W. de W. R. Thackwell of Aghada Hall, co. Cork). She was superstitious and a spiritualist and, following supposed messages through a ouija board, she sold Hennessy's books and destroyed most of his private papers. His grandson (Richard) James Arthur Pope-*Hennessy (1916–1974) wrote a sympathetic but not entirely accurate or impartial biography of Hennessy, *Verandah: some Episodes in the Crown Colonies, 1867–1889* (1964).

Hennessy was controversial and, according to his biographer, 'essentially a man who produced the most violent reactions in all those with whom he came in contact' (Pope-Hennessy, 23). To his admirers he was the champion of the underdog and of racial equality. Others saw him as prejudiced, perverse, deceitful, arrogant, autocratic, and quarrelsome. Ernst Johann Eitel, his private secretary in Hong Kong, wrote that 'the centre of his world was he himself' (Eitel, 573). *The Times* obituary stated: 'he ought never have been placed in charge of such colonies' (Pope-Hennessy, 22). More recently Frank Welsh has written that he had 'an almost complete lack of common sense, method, reliability, tact or management skills' (Welsh, 255), and H. J. Lethbridge that he 'would have been analysed by Adler as suffering from an inferiority complex, as someone who "overcompensated" for physical miniaturization … an egomaniac who imposed his will regardless' (Eitel, vii). As C. A. Harris wrote: 'he never acquired the habit of making definite and accurate statements' (*DNB*).

ROGER T. STEARN

Sources J. Pope-Hennessy, *Verandah: some episodes in the crown colonies, 1867–1889* (1964) · *DNB* · *The Times* (8 Oct 1891) · private information (1896) · Boase, *Mod. Eng. biog.* · C. W. Newbury, ed., *British policy towards West Africa: select documents, 1786–1874* (1992) · C. Fyfe, *A history of Sierra Leone* (1962) · W. D. McIntyre, *The imperial frontier in the tropics, 1865–75* (1967) · D. Kimble, *A political history of Ghana: the rise of Gold Coast nationalism, 1850–1928* (1963) · E. J. Eitel, *Europe in China* (1983) [with an introduction by H. J. Lethbridge] · W. P. Morrell, *British colonial policy in the mid-Victorian age* (1969) · K. Lowe and E. McLaughlin, 'Sir John Pope Hennessy and the "native race craze": colonial government in Hong Kong, 1877–1882', *Journal of Imperial and Commonwealth History*, 20 (1992), 223–47 · F. Welsh, *A history of Hong Kong* (1993) · F. Callanan, *The Parnell split, 1890–1* (1992) · B. O'Brien, *The life of Charles Stewart Parnell, 1846–1891*, 2 (1898) · F. S. L. Lyons, *Charles Stewart Parnell* (1977) · G. B. Endocott, *A history of Hong Kong* (1973) · T. W. Moody and others, eds., *A new history of Ireland*, 6: *Ireland under the Union, 1870–1921* (1996) · R. F. Foster, *Paddy and Mr Punch: connections in Irish and English history* (1995) · R. F. Foster, *Modern Ireland, 1600–1972* (1989) · Gladstone, *Diaries*,

vol. 12 · *WWBMP* · Kelly, *Handbk* (1914) · E. Lodge, *Peerage, baronetage, knightage and companionage of the British empire*, 81st edn, 3 vols. (1912)
Archives Bodl. Oxf., corresp. and papers · J. Paul Getty Museum, California, corresp. and papers | BL, letters to W. E. Gladstone, Add. MSS 44443–44483, *passim* · Bodl. Oxf., letters to Benjamin Disraeli · Bodl. Oxf., letters to Lord Kimberley · CUL, corresp. with Lord Kimberley · LPL, corresp. with Edward Benson
Likenesses Ape [C. Pellegrini], caricature, watercolour, NPG; repro. in *VF* (27 March 1875) · wood-engraving (after photograph by Elliott & Fry), NPG; repro. in *ILN* (3 Jan 1891)
Wealth at death £10,504 14s. 10d.: administration with will, 1 Dec 1891, CGPLA Eng. & Wales · £4152 6s. 4d.: administration, 7 Jan 1892, CGPLA Ire.

Hennessy, Sir John Wyndham Pope- (1913–1994), museum director and art historian, was born on 13 December 1913 at 29 Grosvenor Place, Belgravia, London, the elder son (there were no daughters) of Major-General (Ladislaus Herbert) Richard Pope-Hennessy (1875–1942), colonial official and army officer, and his wife, Dame Una Constance Pope-Hennessy (d. 1949), only daughter of Sir Arthur Birch (1837–1914), colonial official. On his father's side he came from poor farming stock in co. Cork, but his grandfather Sir John Pope *Hennessy (1834–1891) succeeded through hard work, talent, and ambition in winning a parliamentary seat. This was a rarity for a Roman Catholic in the middle of the nineteenth century. He went on to be governor of a number of British crown colonies, including Barbados, the Bahamas, Hong Kong, and Mauritius. His governorships had the reputation of being both benign and liberal. One of Pope-Hennessy's godfathers became a general and another an air vice-marshal, but he never showed any interest in the military life, nor did he ever wish to retrace his grandfather's footsteps to the places that formed some of the stories of his childhood. He left that to his younger brother, (Richard) James Arthur Pope-*Hennessy (1916–1974), a writer of exceptional talent, some of whose books drew on the family legacy.

During a peripatetic childhood both in Britain and abroad, that was controlled by his father's postings, Pope-Hennessy was dominated by his formidable mother (who was made DBE in 1920 for her work for the Red Cross, on behalf of prisoners of war). Her antecedents were substantial upper-middle class and her family began by opposing her marriage to a man who was a Catholic and, at the time, a mere colonial officer; but her strength of will overcame this and during her life she converted to the Catholic faith. In his autobiography, *Learning to Look* (1990), Pope-Hennessy mentioned that his mother—who was in the habit of dashing into the playroom and galvanizing everyone into action—was known by the two brothers as Mummy Tiger. One of her first presents to her elder son was a battered typewriter when he was six years old. On this he wrote his first playlets, which were sent to Lady Gregory, a family friend, for inspection, but his mother also saw that he was usefully employed in typing her own manuscripts. She began by writing for the *Edinburgh Review* and ended with very respectable biographies of Dickens and Meredith. This marked the start of Pope-Hennessy's lifelong love affair with the typewriter. During

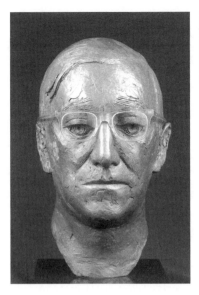

Sir John Wyndham Pope-Hennessy (1913–1994), by Dame Elisabeth Frink, 1975

his six-year tenureship as director of the Victoria and Albert Museum one of the most familiar sounds to be heard was the clacking away of the Pope-Hennessy machine behind firmly closed doors. From his mother he began to learn the art of scholarship, aided by a substantial library; from his father he inherited the principle of public service. Although throughout his life he produced a steady stream of books, all noted for their scholarship, precision, and accuracy, he remained a public servant. He only ever worked for major art institutions.

A conventional Catholic education at Downside School did not bring very many rewards. Pope-Hennessy abhorred all team games and he spent much time in the school library. He had already became an inveterate collector, starting with sea shells and butterflies; towards the end of his life he admitted, a little ruefully, that he always had preferred objects to people. However, one of the teachers there helped to open his ears to music with the help of a wind-up gramophone. It was the start of a lifelong passion for opera in particular, which eventually led to a seat on the board of the Royal Opera House, Covent Garden, where he became a coruscating, if not always constructive, critic of artistic standards, especially visual ones.

An exhibition to Balliol College, Oxford, to read modern history in 1932 opened up new vistas. There was the Ashmolean Museum, but there was also a vibrant cultural life, with many of the world's finest musicians and actors coming to the city. It was there too that Pope-Hennessy was to form some of the connections that were later to serve him well. Among them was an introduction to Kenneth Clark, effected by a family friend, Logan Pearsall Smith. Clark was already one of the brightest stars in the fine arts world. The two men could not have been more different: Clark was suave and polished, with the good looks and charm of the matinée idols of the day, anxious to draw in the public to the things he admired most; Pope-Hennessy was aloof to the point of chilliness, and self-contained.

But Clark became a mentor and close friend. Against expectations Pope-Hennessy only managed a second-class degree in 1935. Contrary to his parents' wishes he decided to spend the mid-1930s travelling in Europe, helped by a legacy from an uncle. He could not have made a wiser decision. He called that period his *Wanderjahre*, although the time spent was very far from aimless. He used it to visit many of the major museums of western Europe and, with suitable introductions, a number of private collections as well. In the evenings there was the opera, notably in Berlin, Dresden, and finally Salzburg. It was to provide him with a deep international experience, not only of singing but of production and design. But most important of all was the cementing of his love of Italian art and his devotion to two cities, Siena and Florence. It was the latter that he chose for his final home, and where he died.

On return to London, Pope-Hennessy joined the staff, once again with the help of family connections, of the Victoria and Albert Museum, in the prints and drawings department. His study of Giovanni di Paiolo (1937) was followed by *Sassetta* (1939), but the war put an end for the time being to any other books. Pope-Hennessy worked in RAF intelligence and was rewarded with an MBE in 1944. On return to civilian life he was faced with three career choices: he could use his administrative skills, proven in his RAF career and well established by the family genes; he could return to the prints and drawings department; or he could explore a new avenue of scholarship. He opted for the last, and returned to the Victoria and Albert Museum on condition that he joined the sculpture department. By 1954 he was appointed keeper, with responsibility for architecture as well, a post that he held for the next twelve years. Pope-Hennessy wrote a steady stream of books during this time, including monographs on Paolo Uccello (1950) and Fra Angelico (1952). There were excursions into British art, including a *Lecture on Nicholas Hilliard* (1949), but Italy remained the core of his interests, and in 1964 came the massive *Catalogue of Italian Sculpture in the Victoria and Albert Museum*. Simultaneously Pope-Hennessy was polishing his skills as a lecturer, so successfully that his international reputation began to grow, notably in America. At home he became Slade professor of fine arts at Oxford (1956) and he occupied a similar position at Cambridge (1964), a rare double distinction. Peterhouse, Cambridge, made him a fellow, as did his old Oxford college, Balliol.

The Pope-Hennessy star rose so quickly that there was some talk of him gaining the directorship of the Victoria and Albert Museum when Sir Leigh Ashton retired in 1955. But the post went to an older man, Sir (George) Trenchard Cox, and Pope-Hennessy had to wait a further twelve years before taking over at the helm. Pope-Hennessy's directorship of the Victoria and Albert Museum (1967–73) was authoritarian, even autocratic, but it was extremely efficient. He was knighted in 1971. He bought wisely, occasionally making the odd acquisition for himself and his house in Kensington, which was not far from the museum. With caution he extended the previously limited range of special exhibitions, casting the net wide from Chinese ceramics to English sixteenth- and seventeenth-century silver from the Kremlin. But to Pope-Hennessy the Victoria and Albert was a place for meticulous scholarship and equally meticulous labelling. It was not necessarily an educative institution, but one that provided the wherewithal for self-education. He was openly critical of the attempts of his successor, Sir Roy Strong, to popularize the museum, and was positively vitriolic about Elisabeth Estève-Coll, who followed Strong. To many of his staff he was a chilly figure as he patrolled the corridors of the museum. Inevitably he was known as the Pope, in part a reflection of his deeply held Catholic beliefs, but mainly because of his habit of making pronouncements that were to be received as definitive. These were delivered in a high-pitched voice which came strangely from so tall and imposing a man, and it was much imitated by friends and colleagues alike—some of the more frivolous among the latter were seen to genuflect behind his back as he passed by.

In 1972 the first feelers were put out to Pope-Hennessy suggesting that he take over the directorship of the British Museum as successor to Sir John Wolfenden. The trustees sought a director who could give the museum clear and professional direction. Pope-Hennessy's immediate reaction was a firm refusal. But under pressure, notably from Lord Trevelyan, he eventually succumbed. One of the reasons, as he was to write himself, was that the shortlist of other candidates was so poor that he felt obliged to accept. He did not much like what he found when he arrived in 1973: muddle, much time wasted in writing inter-office memoranda, and very poor working conditions for many of the staff. There were other major drawbacks to the job, not least of which were the quite large areas of the museum that held little interest for him, and even worse was time spent in wrestling with committees, including the trustees, instead of being his own master. More disagreeable still was the required attendance at white-tie dinners in the City and elsewhere. At the beginning of this uneasy period there occurred an incident that changed the course of Pope-Hennessy's life. One January evening he was told that his brother, James, had been found murdered at home in brutal and sordid circumstances. James had the charm and intelligence to move in high circles—his study of Queen Mary (1959) was one of his best books—but he also had an unquenchable appetite for low life and he eventually paid the penalty. Pope-Hennessy, resilient and self-contained though he was, never really got over the shock. It was a crucial reason for his deciding to leave London and the museum after only three years as director.

Pope-Hennessy's first instinct was to return to Tuscany and a life of pure scholarship. However invitations started to arrive, notably from America, to which his links had become stronger and stronger over the years. One of the most attractive was to take over the department of European paintings at the Metropolitan Museum in New York. He decided to link this with a professorship at the Institute of Fine Arts at New York University. This last decade of his working life was both rewarding and agreeable. It

was a relief, he said, to stop being an administrator and become a curator again. He had always got on well in the cultivated circles of the city's high society. He liked them and they liked him. In contrast to the penny-pinching atmosphere of London there was money to spend, and he made best use of it with many notable acquisitions. As seventy-five approached he thought that the time had come to retire, which he did to his favourite city, Florence, living within walking distance of many of the sculptures and paintings to which he had devoted his life. He died at his home, via de' Bardi 28, Florence, on 31 October 1994. He was unmarried. Much of his personal collection was the subject of a Christies sale in early 1996, which raised some $1.5 million. A requiem mass was held at the Brompton Oratory in London on 1 June 1995.   JOHN HIGGINS

Sources J. W. Pope-Hennessy, *Learning to look* (1991) · *The Times* (2 Nov 1994) · *The Independent* (2 Nov 1994) · *The Independent* (1 Dec 1994) · *Daily Telegraph* (2 Nov 1994) · *The Guardian* (2 Nov 1994) · personal knowledge (2004) · private information (2004) · b. cert. · d. cert. · *WWW*, 1991–5
Archives Harvard University Center for Italian Renaissance Studies, near Florence, Italy, letters to Bernard Berenson · Tate collection, corresp. with Lord Clark | SOUND BL NSA, interview, B8297/02 · BL NSA, performance recording
Likenesses E. Frink, sculpture, 1975, NPG [*see illus.*] · photograph, repro. in *The Guardian* · photograph, repro. in *Independent on Sunday* (7 Jan 1996)

Hennessy, Sir Patrick (1898–1981), motor vehicle manufacturer, was born on 18 March 1898 in Midleton, co. Cork. His father, also named Patrick, was an estate foreman and a Catholic; his mother, Mary Benn, was the daughter of the protestant estate owner and was disowned at her marriage. Hennessy was educated at Christ Church School, Cork, until the outbreak of the First World War, when he falsified his age and enlisted in the Royal Inniskilling Fusiliers. He was later commissioned, and taken prisoner by the Germans in April 1918. After his release he convalesced at an agricultural college and then in 1920 went to work in the Ford tractor plant at Cork. He started in the foundry, a particularly taxing environment, later claiming that he had joined Ford to build up his muscles for rugby. A series of routine jobs (he described himself as 'a navvy at times') took him via the blacksmith's shop and assembly line to become a tractor demonstrator and then, after little more than a year, to the British Ford plant at Old Trafford, Manchester. There he was picked out as a promising young man, and appointed Ford's travelling representative in Ireland; he returned to Cork as sales representative, and was promoted to sales manager in 1924. In 1923 he married Dorothy Margaret Davis (d. 1949) of Boardmills, co. Down. They had two sons and a daughter.

Ford's decision in 1928 to concentrate worldwide tractor production at Cork gave Hennessy his opening. An American expert failed to solve the difficulties of supplying spare parts for 25,000 Ford tractors in the USSR and left Hennessy with the problem. By subcontracting and tightening prices he completed the contract early and caught the eye of an American efficiency team which was assessing the European plants. Hennessy was chosen to be purchasing manager when Ford opened its new British plant at Dagenham in 1931. There he repeated the pattern. Although Dagenham had been purpose-built, with the demise of the Model T, Ford had no competitive car model and concentrated on trucks. At the insistence of British management, a small 8 hp car, the Model Y, was rapidly designed in Detroit and rushed into production. Hennessy played a key part in co-ordinating the supply of components and machinery.

But success was short-lived. Although the Model Y took over 50 per cent of the market for its class of small car by 1934, it gave ground to the new Morris 8 before making substantial profits. Hennessy then ran a thorough purchasing review, costing every bought-in component and forcing suppliers' prices lower. As a result in 1933 the Ford Y became the first fully equipped car to be sold for only £100, a major sales incentive. Hennessy's view was: 'I don't think we could have done it otherwise. It increased the efficiency, the tightness of the organisation perhaps like nothing else would have done at the time.'

Ford of Britain was indeed a tight organization under Hennessy as he became successively general manager (1939), a director (1945), managing director (1948), deputy chairman (1950), and chairman (1956–68). His knighthood in 1941 followed a wartime secondment to the Ministry of Aircraft Production where he was in charge of material supplies from April 1940. His plan to increase deliveries of key materials helped double the output of fighter aircraft by the autumn of that battle of Britain year.

Within Ford, Hennessy was known for his hard driving—'the biggest dictator I have ever met' (Adeney, 224)—and for his challenging approach—'he was very tough and rough with people. If they didn't respond in like manner, he assumed they didn't have a case. If you fought back he seemed to like it.' At the same time he was respected for his wide understanding. One former colleague described 'an exceptional intellectual grasp. He would sit down with engineers and make suggestions; later the tax manager would come in to discuss a complicated corporation tax matter and he would grasp that' (private information). In the plant he was nicknamed 'the chief stylist' for his regular visits to that department. During his time, Ford of Britain overtook its rivals to become the most successful motor company in the country. It had a well-balanced manufacturing base (aided by his prescient purchase of Briggs, the firm which supplied its bodies, only narrowly before Chrysler took over its parent in the USA), and well-designed products for which he could take much of the credit. In 1963 it opened a second major manufacturing plant, at Halewood in Lancashire.

In 1945 Ford's share of the UK market stood at 14 per cent, rising to 19 per cent by 1950 without the introduction of a single new model. That had to wait for the Consul and Zephyr range of 1950, followed by the Prefect and Anglia. Engineered in Britain, they were styled in the USA because, Hennessy argued, the key export markets preferred American styling. Market share rose to 27 per cent and the cars provided Ford with a quality image to combat its old reputation of selling on price. 'What is the time

when one Ford passes another?' ran an old joke. 'Tin past tin' (Adeney, 14).

Hennessy shrewdly managed Ford politics. Keenly aware of growing competition from the renascent Ford of Germany in the early 1960s, he insisted on developing his own rival to the German Cardinal project to build a medium car for both the German and American market. Combatively the British baptized their project 'Archbishop', even though they knew that 'Cardinal' referred to an American bird. The project, which produced the Cortina, the most successful post-war British car, started as an attempt to rival the BMC Mini whose rapid sales were alarming the American management. But when Ford engineers concluded, correctly, that the Mini was priced uneconomically, Hennessy backed their switch to a larger and more traditionally engined vehicle without the fashionable front wheel drive. Detroit and British dealers were almost incredulous but the Cortina became the car that all other British manufacturers tried, and failed, to emulate for the next twenty years. Hennessy and his project manager, Terry (later Sir Terence) Beckett, had the pleasure of watching their car outstrip the Cardinal at a test-drive watched by Henry Ford II.

Hennessy claimed that Ford of Britain had become the most powerful both of Ford's overseas companies and of British motor companies. Aware that this status depended on the goodwill of the American company and the controlling Ford family, he spent weeks on end lobbying for his projects at Ford's Dearborn headquarters and forged close relations, first with Edsel Ford, Henry Ford's son, and then after his early death with his son Henry Ford II. Edsel's widow was sure of careful squiring from Hennessy on visits to Britain. Henry II, himself an Anglophile, appreciated it: 'We always had one friend in Detroit' (private information), was the judgement of one of Hennessy's long-serving managers.

However, even a shrewd and successful autocrat like Hennessy could not stand against the tide of internationalization of the industry. In 1961 Ford of America assumed total control of Ford of Britain when it bought out the minority shareholders for the then enormous sum of £119 million on the grounds of 'greater operational efficiency'. Henry Ford pledged that it would continue 'without change in its employment policy or in its development programme', but significantly no chairman after Hennessy was allowed the same power. In 1967, the year before his retirement as non-executive chairman, a new company, Ford of Europe, was created to oversee all Ford's European operations. Hennessy's successor, Sir Terence Beckett, was responsible for sales in the UK and dealings with its government, but not for manufacturing, and as British labour relations deteriorated, power shifted more and more towards Germany.

Hennessy had fused himself with Ford in a remarkable total of sixty-one years' service. He remained a director of the Irish Ford company and a consultant until his death from pneumonia on 13 March 1981 at his home, Larkmead, Abridge Road, Theydon Bois.

MARTIN ADENEY

Sources Ford Motor Co. archives, Warley, Essex • l'Estrange Faw-cett, Wheels of fortune, Ford Motor Co. archives, Warley, Essex • private information (2004) • M. Adeney, *The motormakers* (1988) • *The Times* (16 March 1981), 14f • d. cert. • WWW
Archives Warley, Essex, Ford archives • Dearborn, Michigan, Ford archives | HLRO, corresp. with Lord Beaverbrook | SOUND private source, CR's own source
Likenesses photograph, 1960, Hult. Arch. • photographs, Ford Motor Co., Warley, Essex
Wealth at death £202,307: probate, 10 July 1981, *CGPLA Eng. & Wales*

Hennessy, Prudence Loveday, Lady Windlesham. *See* Glynn, Prudence Loveday (1935–1986).

Hennessy, Richard (1729?–1800), brandy distiller, was born at Ballymacmoy, near Mallow, co. Cork, the second son of at least six children of James Hennessy (*d.* 1768), one of a close-knit group of minor Catholic gentry in the Blackwater valley, and his wife, Catherine Barrett (*d.* 1770). His early education was probably with the Catholic schoolmaster in the parish of Monanimy. In 1748 he joined the French army, enlisting in the Irish regiment of Viscount Clare in which his kinsman, an earlier Richard Hennessy, had served with distinction. His army record describes him as 6 feet tall, auburn-haired, and blue-eyed, with a handsome, freckled, oval face. Warm-hearted, kind, and convivial in personality, in later life he was a freemason. His military career was brief, and he saw no active service. Commissioned *sous-lieutenant* in 1753, he was by then already absent from his unit and attempting to start a business career in Ostend, with the consequence that the following year his service was terminated. He remained on good terms with Hiberno-French army officers, however, and in 1757 secured a certificate from Lord Clare falsely stretching his military service to ten years to qualify him for *de facto* French nationality. In 1759 he volunteered his services for Choiseul's projected invasion of the British Isles, but his offer was rejected.

Hennessy's early abandonment of the army was almost certainly prompted by the lack of prospects. Ostend was the location of the brandy-exporting business of his uncle, Charles Hennessy, but no partnership in the firm was offered to Richard, and he can have enjoyed only a precarious living there until his marriage in January 1765 to Ellen (Nelly) Hennessy, *née* Barrett (*d.* 1781), the widow of his Ostend cousin, James, and a kinswoman of his mother. She was also a cousin of Edmund Burke, a childhood friend and schoolmate of Hennessy with whom he remained in periodic contact. The expectation of his wife's dowry (paid only belatedly, if at all) persuaded him to leave Ostend and acquire premises and an adjoining warehouse at Cognac, the centre of the brandy trade in which a number of Irishmen were involved. His wife and infant son, James (*b.* October 1765), joined him in May 1766. A daughter, Bridget (Biddy), was born in 1767. The volatility of the brandy trade, his lack of capital, and his deficient commercial and accountancy skills made much of Hennessy's career in business very difficult. He visited Ireland briefly in 1755 and again in the summer of 1768 during his father's final illness, but his hope at that time of exploiting his Cork connections to develop his trade was

frustrated by competition from cheap American rum. Although he never returned again to Ireland, his correspondence shows that he always maintained an avid interest in the happenings and personalities of the district of his birth. A partnership with the Irish firm of Connelly and Arthur in Dunkirk did not provide the access to the London market for which he had hoped. He seriously contemplated emigration to the West Indies, but instead in 1776 he moved to Bordeaux. There he formed a partnership with George Boyd at a premises in the Chartrons district of the city where he developed an impressive sixteen-still capacity. The trade was chiefly with Ireland, much of it carried by smugglers.

In 1781 Hennessy experienced great personal tragedy with the death in September of his wife, whose health was always frail, followed in October by the deaths of his two youngest sons from scarlet fever. Mounting losses undermined his relationship with Boyd, and in 1787 he was driven out of distilling, becoming for a time a brandy jobber and broker. His surviving son, James (Jemmy), after education at Douai, had eschewed the offer of a military career in the Franco-Irish regiment of General Arthur Dillon to enter business, first in Dunkirk and from 1785 in the Cognac house of his father's friend and fellow Irishman, John Saule. On Saule's death in 1788 the Hennessys, father and son, took over his business, and the following year the partnership was expanded by the addition of Samuel Turner, nephew of the Hiberno-Huguenot brandy merchant James Delmain. Having re-established himself in Cognac, Richard Hennessy travelled to London to promote the brandy trade in the winter of 1791–2, visiting Edmund Burke during his stay. James Hennessy and Turner proved capable and hard-headed businessmen who developed their house into the largest brandy business in Cognac during the revolutionary era. The Hennessys had no difficulty in accommodating themselves to the political changes of the time. Richard was appointed lieutenant of the *garde nationale* in Cognac, and James in time became its *commandant*, leading 150 men to join in the suppression of the La Vendée royalists in 1793. Following the outbreak of war the Hennessys benefited enormously from government contracts to supply the expanding French army and navy, while Turner developed a lucrative export trade through Hamburg. In 1795 James further consolidated his position by marriage to a daughter of the rival Martell house. An estate was acquired at La Billarderie, near Cognac, and it was here, in the role of country squire, that Richard Hennessy spent his declining years until his death, after a short illness, on 8 October 1800.

HARMAN MURTAGH

Sources L. M. Cullen, *Irish brandy houses of eighteenth-century France* (Dublin, 2000) • L. M. Cullen, 'The Blackwater Catholics and county Cork society and politics in the eighteenth century', *Cork: history and society—interdisciplinary essays on the history of an Irish county*, ed. P. O'Flanagan and C. G. Buttimer (1993) • Burke, *Gen. Ire.* (1976), 574–5
Archives Archives, Cognac, France | Archives Départementales du Morbihan, Vannes, France, Warren papers
Likenesses oils, *c.*1790–1799, Hennessy collection, Cognac, France; repro. in Cullen, *Irish brandy houses*

Wealth at death probably quite extensive due to success of brandy house, acquisition of property, etc.

Hennessy, William Maunsell [Uilliam Ua hAonghusa] (1828/9–1889), linguistic scholar, was born at Castlegregory, co. Kerry, and was educated privately, passing his early youth with a maternal uncle, Dr Finn. A native speaker of Irish and English, he received a grounding in the classics, and later exhibited knowledge of German and French. He spent some years in the United States and, on his return, took up journalism; he wrote for the revived nationalist newspaper *The Nation* from 1853 to 1856. He had a post in the office of inspectors of lunatic asylums from 1856 to 1868 when, on the establishment of the Public Record Office (PRO) in Dublin, he was appointed to the senior staff as a first-class clerk. Pressure of official duties during more than twenty years in the PRO limited his scholarly output. He was elected a member of the Royal Irish Academy and was Todd professor in the academy for 1882–4. Hennessy was strongly interested in promoting the Irish language: it was largely on his advice that a knowledge of the language became a requirement for PRO staff, and in 1876 he was among the principal founders of the Society for the Preservation of the Irish Language. In April 1887 he was promoted to assistant deputy keeper in the PRO. However, the death of his wife, apparently in tragic circumstances, in 1885, followed shortly afterwards by that of a married daughter, caused his health to decline. Hennessy died, aged sixty, on Sunday 13 January 1889, at his home, 71 Pembroke Road, Ballsbridge, Dublin. This had been his residence for the previous decade or so; before that he had lived for many years at 8 Islington Avenue, Dún Laoghaire (then known as Kingstown). He was buried in Glasnevin cemetery in a grave which remains unmarked by a memorial. His extensive library was sold by auction in June 1890. Hennessy was survived by a son, William Charles, a member of the Irish bar and contributor to various Dublin newspapers who also wrote, *inter alia*, comic verses, pantomimes, a one-act comedy, and a Parnellite pamphlet; he died at the age of thirty-eight in 1898.

Hennessy was one of the leading scholars in the field of native Irish learning in the decades immediately following the deaths of John O'Donovan and Eugene O'Curry (1861 and 1862 respectively). The great German Celtic scholar Kuno Meyer declared that he was 'one of the few native scholars who did not shut his eyes to the progress of Celtic research on the Continent' (Ó Lúing, 99) and even the ever critical Whitley Stokes deemed him 'the best native Irish scholar then living' (Ó Lúing, 106). Among his most significant publications were his edition of two important collections of Irish annals, *Chronicum Scotorum* (1866), ending at AD 1150, and the *Annals of Loch Cé* (2 vols., 1871), covering the period from AD 1014 to the end of the sixteenth century. Both editions, published in the Rolls Series of *Chronicles and Memorials of Great Britain and Ireland*, contain lengthy and still valuable introductions. Although far from impeccable, neither edition had been superseded at the end of the twentieth century. Hennessy's edition of the *Book of Fenagh*, an interesting late

medieval work from co. Leitrim, appeared in 1875 (only fifty copies were printed), and in 1887 he produced an edition of the early portion (down to AD 1056) of the most important of all Irish annalistic collections, the annals of Ulster. The work was completed after Hennessy's death, in three further volumes, by Bartholomew MacCarthy. The work of both editors was severely criticized by the leading Irish scholar of the day, the formidable Whitley Stokes. Other notable publications include a translation of the ninth-century tripartite life of St Patrick (1870), an annotated translation of the famous Middle Irish tale *Aislinge Meic Conglinne* (1873), a revision of a portion of *The Ancient Laws of Ireland* (1879), an edition of the Ulster tale *Mesca Ulad* (1889), and numerous smaller items such as an essay on the history and antiquities of the Curragh of Kildare in the *Proceedings of the Royal Irish Academy* (1864–6), an article on 'The ancient Irish goddess of war' in the first volume of *Revue Celtique* (1870–72), and an edition of the tale *Cath Cnucha* in the second volume of the same journal (1873–5). Hennessy was also noted for his ready generosity in providing assistance to other authors—for instance, to W. F. Skene during the preparation of the latter's monumental three-volume *Celtic Scotland* (1877–80).

NOLLAIG Ó MURAÍLE

Sources S. Ó Lúing, 'William Maunsell Hennessy, Celtic scholar, 1829–1889', *Journal of the Kerry Archaeological and Historical Society*, 19 (1986), 80–120 [including comprehensive list of sources] · DNB
Archives NL Ire. · Royal Irish Acad. · TCD
Likenesses photograph, Royal Irish Acad.; repro. in Ó Lúing, 'William Maunsell Hennessy', 81
Wealth at death £1327 0s. 5d.: probate, 1889, CGPLA Ire.

Henniker. For this title name *see* Major, John Henniker-, second Baron Henniker (1752–1821).

Henniker, Sir Frederick, second baronet (1793–1825), traveller, eldest son of Sir Brydges Trecothick Henniker, first baronet (1767–1816), of Newton Hall, Essex, and his wife, Mary (d. 1840), eldest daughter of William Press, and grandson of John, first Baron Henniker, was born on 1 November 1793. He had three younger brothers and two younger sisters. He was educated at Eton College and from 1811 at St John's College, Cambridge, where he graduated BA in 1815. He was admitted at Lincoln's Inn in 1815. He succeeded his father as second baronet on 3 July 1816.

Henniker turned his attention to travel and, after passing through Europe, visited Egypt and Palestine in 1820, and accompanied George Francis Grey to Upper Egypt. Henniker was the first known person to climb to the apex of the Second Pyramid, then a difficult task since the smooth casing stones were still in place near the summit. In 1821 he acquired the coffin of Soter. He gave it to Henry Salt, from whom the British Museum acquired it. From Egypt he went to Mount Sinai and Jerusalem, returning home by Smyrna, Athens, Constantinople, and Vienna. While on his way from Jerusalem to Jericho he was severely wounded by bandits and left stark naked. In 1834 he published a lively and amusing account of his travels under the title *Notes during a Visit to Egypt, Nubia, the Oasis, Mount Sinai, and Jerusalem*. In the spring of 1825 he canvassed Reading with a view to contesting that borough in the event of a dissolution, but withdrew his candidature because of the unpopularity of his opposition to Catholic emancipation. He died at his chambers in the Albany, Piccadilly, London, on 6 August 1825 after a short but painful illness. He was buried on 13 August in the family vault at Great Dunmow, Essex. He was unmarried, and was succeeded in the baronetcy by his brother Augustus Brydges Henniker. Frederick Henniker's early death made his influence on Egyptology more limited than his early travels had suggested.

G. F. R. BARKER, *rev.* ELIZABETH BAIGENT

Sources W. R. Dawson and E. P. Uphill, *Who was who in Egyptology*, 3rd edn, rev. M. L. Bierbrier (1995) · Burke, *Peerage* · Venn, *Alum. Cant.* · *GM*, 1st ser., 95/2 (1825), 185–6 · H. E. C. Stapylton, *The Eton school lists, from 1791 to 1850*, 2nd edn (1864) · Allibone, *Dict.* · J. J. Halls, *The life and correspondence of Henry Salt*, 2nd edn, 2 vols. (1834) **Archives** Inst. EE, corresp. with Sir Francis Ronalds

Henniker, Sir Mark Chandos Auberon, eighth baronet (1906–1991), army officer and author, was born at Northmoor, Minehead, Somerset, on 23 January 1906, the only son and older of the two children of Frederick Chandos Henniker (1866–1953) of the Indian Civil Service, and his wife, Ada Russell (*d.* 1958), daughter of Arthur Pearce Howell, also of the Indian Civil Service. He was educated at Marlborough College, the Royal Military Academy, Woolwich, and King's College, Cambridge, and was commissioned into the Royal Engineers in 1926. He was in India from 1928 to 1934 and was awarded an MC in the campaign against the Mohmands in 1933 when serving with the Bengal Sappers and Miners, for his skill and courage while supervising the building of a road up the Karappa Pass from the Vale of Peshawar, a distance of some 20 miles in conditions of considerable danger. In 1939 he went to France as adjutant of 2nd divisional engineers. In the retreat to Dunkirk he was given command of a field company in 3rd division and defended a sector of the perimeter of the port. With the evacuation virtually completed he set off back to England with the remainder of his company in two rowing boats. On the way they encountered an abandoned, damaged naval pinnace which they boarded and from which they were picked up by a British gunboat, which landed them at Dover.

Back in Britain, Henniker was selected to command the sapper element in the 1st airborne division, which was in the process of formation. In this capacity he trained the sappers and took part in the Bruneval raid. Bruneval, near Le Havre, was known to be the site of a radar unit which was using new equipment and thus causing heavy losses among British bombers. A force of 120 from the parachute regiment of Royal Engineers parachuted in, escorting a radar expert who knew what to take out; the raid was successful, as were also the resultant counter-measures the RAF adopted. Henniker subsequently served in north Africa and then took part in the invasion of Sicily in July 1943. He crash-landed by glider near Syracuse, but was unhurt. Later he was wounded in seven places and also sustained a broken arm, but he managed to take part in the capture of the important bridges at Ponte Grande and Primasole, though swathed in bandages. He was with 1st

airborne in their landing and occupation of Taranto, which he subsequently organized into a base for the future campaign in Italy. He was appointed OBE in 1944.

In 1944 Henniker was appointed commander, Royal Engineers, in 43rd (Welsh) division and distinguished himself in the aftermath of the Arnhem disaster of September 1944, when he rescued many of the survivors of 1st airborne division by ferrying them across the Rhine in assault boats, a process that the Germans were doing their best to prevent. He was immediately appointed DSO. Subsequently he fought through the remainder of the northwest Europe campaign, including the Rhine crossing, the Ardennes, and the capture of Bremen and Cuxhaven. At Nijmegen he drove over a bridge five minutes before it was blown up by German frogmen. On 5 September 1945, three days after the formal conclusion of hostilities in the Far East, Henniker married Kathleen Denys Anderson (*b.* 1909/10), second daughter of John Cousmaker Anderson, barrister, of Pilgrim's Way, Farnham, Surrey. They had two children, Adrian Chandos (*b.* 1946) and Fiona Jane (*b.* 1951).

In 1946 Henniker returned to India and in 1947 he was engaged in trying to preserve lives in the turbulence which followed partition. He was then posted to Malaya as commander of 63rd Gurkha infantry brigade, a period about which he subsequently wrote a book entitled *Red Shadow over Malaya* (1955), in which he described the brigade's successful operations against elusive communist terrorists. He was appointed CBE in 1955. In the same year he returned to Europe to be commander, Royal Engineers in 1st (British) corps, and was involved in the Suez operation, for which he was mentioned in dispatches. He retired from the army in 1958, and on 19 February became eighth baronet on the death of his cousin Sir Robert John Aldborough Henniker.

Honker was no ordinary soldier. A brisk, enquiring mind, and a tendency to reject the first or obvious solution to a problem, enabled him to tackle numerous problems successfully, often to the irritation of his contemporaries, who thought along more orthodox lines. With red hair and a piercing gaze he was not a person to suffer fools gladly, but he had a philosophic sense of humour. He published four volumes of autobiography. *Memoirs of a Junior Officer* (1951) was followed by *Red Shadow over Malaya* in 1955. *Life in the Army Today* came in 1957, and *An Image of War* in 1987. He also contributed regularly to *Blackwood's Magazine*.

After retiring from the army Henniker founded a private oil company, from which he retired in 1977. He was honorary colonel of the parachute engineer regiment (Territorial Army) from 1939 to 1968, and honorary colonel of the Corps of Royal Electrical and Mechanical Engineers (Territorial Army) from 1964 to 1968. He was deputy lieutenant, Monmouthshire, in 1963. He died of a cerebrovascular haemorrhage at the Avenue Road Nursing Home, Avenue Road, Abergavenny, Monmouthshire, on 18 October 1991. He was survived by his wife and two children, and was succeeded as baronet by his son.

PHILIP WARNER

Sources *The Times* (22 Oct 1991) · *WWW*, 1991–5 · Burke, *Peerage* · private information (2004) · M. Henniker, *Memoirs of a junior officer* (1951) · M. Henniker, *Red shadow over Malaya* (1955) · M. Henniker, *Life in the army today* (1957) · M. Henniker, *An image of war* (1987) · Chatham, Kent, royal engineers' records · D. Boyd, *Royal engineers* (1975) · T. Gander, *The royal engineers* (1985) · *CGPLA Eng. & Wales* (1992) · b. cert. · m. cert. · d. cert. · *Debrett's Peerage*
Archives King's Lond., Liddell Hart C., papers · Royal Engineers, Brompton barracks, Chatham, Kent, records
Likenesses photograph, repro. in *The Times*
Wealth at death £4085: probate, 12 March 1992, *CGPLA Eng. & Wales*

Henning, John (1771–1851), sculptor, was born 'a little after sunrise' on 2 May 1771 at the rear of 56 High Street, Paisley, Renfrewshire, the eldest of the eleven children of Samuel Henning (d. 1809), a wright and architect, and his wife, Agnes Robertson. Originally from the Netherlands, the family moved from Ireland to Dumfries, where Samuel Henning's father, Alexander Henning, married Jean Harberson in 1747. After attending the commercial school in Meeting-House Lane, Paisley, under the writing master Ebenezer Macome, 'the man of whom I learned the value of application' (inscriptions on portrait medallions, Paisley Museum and Art Galleries, and Scottish National Portrait Gallery, Edinburgh), John Henning joined his father in 1784, when he 'began to seriously handle the hatchet, saw, plane and other implements of carpentry' (Bodl. Oxf., MS Pigott d. 8).

Having read about the voyages of James Cook, George Anson, and John Byron he decided, in 1787, to run away to sea, but this plan was thwarted by his mother's illness. He grew to maturity during a period of severe political unrest: his neighbour, Alexander Wilson, known as 'the father of American ornithology', was an ardent supporter of Thomas Paine. Following a fire in 1818 which destroyed the building that had housed his father's workshop, a hiding place was uncovered containing the minute book of the Paisley branch of the British Convention, of which Samuel was secretary. In a manuscript letter sent to his brother-in-law, John Henning states that, in 1794, he was on a list of 185 proscribed persons in Paisley who were to be imprisoned for their political views. In later life, when he was in London, he continued to help the radical cause by selling the *Weavers' Magazine*, published in Paisley, and he also attempted to interest Princess Charlotte, daughter of George IV, in books on Scottish dissent while she was sitting for her portrait. These she read, later remarking, 'Mr. Henning, I am not indulged with that kind of reading' (Pyke, 66).

On 7 September 1799 Henning married Katharine Sunter, and of their eight children Agnes Henning (*bap.* 19 Aug 1800), the eldest, married the artist Kenny Meadows (1790–1874), who later designed the fifth cover for *Punch*; Samuel Henning (d. 1832) assisted his father but concentrated on gem-engraving, receiving the silver palette in 1818 from the Society of Artists and exhibiting at the Royal Academy from 1823 to 1831 and the British Institution in 1825–6; Archibald Henning (c.1805–1864) designed the cover for the first issue of *Punch* (17 July 1841) and a number of illustrations for Henry Mayhew's *London Labour and the London Poor* (1851); and John Henning (1802–1857) assisted his father on the replicas of the Parthenon friezes (see below) and their application as building decoration, producing the classical reliefs on Decimus Burton's triple screen at Hyde Park Corner and the reliefs for the front of the Manchester City Art Gallery.

In 1799 Aubin's 'Royal Museum', a small collection of curiosities which included wax busts, visited Paisley. Henning was critical of them and a friend suggested that he try and do better himself. Shortly afterwards, on a visit to Edinburgh, he had the opportunity to visit the studio of Sir Henry Raeburn where he saw a portrait of General Macdowall, after which he 'resolved to attempt a portrait myself, and try and model a head in wax' (National Library of Scotland, MS 4946, fols. 9–10). First he modelled profile portraits in wax from life, but later worked from life-size sketches, completing medallions in his workshop. From wax originals he produced copies in plaster, bronze, or vitreous enamel. Under the patronage of Mrs Anne Grant of Laggan, Inverness-shire, he obtained a wide range of sitters, including James Watt, Sir Walter Scott, and Princess Charlotte. Josiah Wedgwood produced six of Henning's medallions—the duke of Wellington, Sir Samuel Romilly, Dugald Stewart, Sir Henry Brougham, the Revd James Graham, and Sir Walter Scott—as pottery cameos. In 1801 Henning moved to Glasgow, and by 1806 to Rose Street, Edinburgh. Here he attended life classes at the Trustees' Academy, where his fellow pupils included David Wilkie. In 1811 he moved to London, where he saw the newly arrived Elgin marbles and thereafter obtained permission to draw them, in spite of strong opposition from Benjamin West, the president of the Royal Academy. He spent over twelve years copying the Parthenon friezes and those from the temple at Bassai, introducing his own restoration for missing parts. He also copied nine of Raphael's tapestry cartoons depicting scenes from the Acts of the Apostles. Princess Charlotte requested him to prepare a miniature of the Parthenon frieze in ivory; at the suggestion of his son John he carved moulds of the friezes in slate at a height of 76.2 mm and produced plaster replicas at £31 10s. a set. As these were unprotected by copyright, they were pirated, and one dealer in Paris claimed in 1835 to have sold 12,000 copies. A larger version of the Parthenon frieze was used to decorate buildings such as the exterior of the Athenaeum in Pall Mall, London, and a medium-sized version for interiors such as the College of Surgeons in Lincoln's Inn Fields, London, and Eastwood House in east Renfrewshire. During the last ten years of Henning's life he worked with the engraver A. R. Freebairn to produce copies of his medallions and the Parthenon friezes by using a 'curious machine', invented by a Mr Bates, which produced a remarkable three-dimensional effect. However, Freebairn died suddenly, and the scheme failed.

Henning executed memorials to John Heaton (1818, St John the Evangelist, Havering atte Bower, Essex) and John Ellis (1836, St Giles, Wyddial, Hertfordshire), and occasionally did metalwork, producing a seal matrix for the Independent Gas, Light, and Coke Company (1829) and medals of the duke of Wellington (1828) and the duke of Clarence, later William IV (1829). He was a founder member of the Society of British Artists and a member of the Royal Scottish Academy (1827) and the Glasgow Dilettanti Society (1832); in 1846 he became a freeman of Paisley. Despite all his success, he died in poverty. His death occurred on 8 April 1851 at his home, 8 Thorn Hill, Bridge Place, Caledonian Road, London; he was buried on the 11th in St Pancras churchyard, Finchley, Middlesex.   JOHN MALDEN

Sources R. J. Malden, *John Henning … a very ingenious modeller* (1977) • b. reg. Scot. • bap. reg. Scot. • m. reg. Scot. [S. Henning and A. Robertson] • m. reg. Scot. • parish register, Glasgow • parish register (death), London, St Pancras • Bodl. Oxf., MSS Pigott • E. J. Pyke, *A biographical dictionary of wax modellers* (1973) • R. Gunnis, *Dictionary of British sculptors, 1660–1851* (1953) • J. Morrison, *Tait's Edinburgh Magazine*, new ser., 11 (1844), 19 • committee minutes, 1829, Athenaeum, London • building committee minutes, 1835 and 1838, RCS Eng. • R. Brown, *History of Paisley grammar school* (1875) • *Art Journal*, 13 (1851), 212 • *The Builder*, 9 (1851), 297 • NL Scot., MS 4946

Archives BL, Add. MSS 43245, 46140 • NA Scot., GD 51/9/342, 51/9/346, NG 1/1/31 • NL Scot., MSS 3895, 3915, 3989, 4944, 4946, 4949, 4950, 11147 • Paisley Museum and Art Galleries, collection of drawings, corresp., portrait medallions, etc. • Royal Arch., MSS 26724–26726 • U. Edin., Gen 1801/5; La II 93/3–93/15, 93/357 • UCL, letters to the Society for the Diffusion of Useful Knowledge • University of Keele, Etruria MSS 2617–2619, 12025, 12035 | Bodl. Oxf., Pigott MSS

Likenesses R. Scott-Lauder, oils, *c.*1840, NG Scot. • J. Henning, self-portrait, medallion, 1843, Paisley Museum and Art Galleries • O. Hill, photographs, *c.*1850, NG Scot. • sculpture, cement replica (after a self-portrait), NG Scot. • sculpture, plaster medallion (after a self-portrait), NG Scot.

Henri, Adrian Maurice (1932–2000), poet and painter, was born on 10 April 1932 in the maternity hospital at Tranmere, Birkenhead, Cheshire, the eldest child of Arthur Maurice Henri (1898–1970), a dancing instructor and war department clerk, and Emma Johnson (d. 1970). His paternal grandfather, Louis Ernest Henri Celine (b. 1856), was a Mauritian sailor who arrived in Liverpool in 1888 and established a seaman's mission in Birkenhead. Adrian Henri had five much younger siblings. In 1938 the family moved to Rhyl where Henri attended St Asaph grammar school before going on to King's College, Newcastle, to study art with Lawrence Gowing, Roger de Grey, and Richard Hamilton. On graduating BA honours in 1955, Henri spent his summers working as a scene painter at Rhyl fairground and his term time teaching art at a local secondary school. On 28 October 1957 he married Joyce Wilson (1934/5–1987); the marriage was dissolved in 1974. Henri moved to Liverpool to work as a scenic artist at the Playhouse. Creative and energetic, he became an enthusiastic member of the Liverpool scene and the 1960s were his most important years. His painting *Christ's Entry into Liverpool* (1961), a homage to James Ensor's *Entry of Christ into Brussels*, is an exuberant composition featuring many of Liverpool's most celebrated figures, including the Beatles and George Melly, accompanied by Henri's own personal icons—among them William Burroughs, Charlie Parker, and Alfred Jarry. He exhibited at the Walker Gallery and Bluecoat Chambers in Liverpool, and the Institute of Contemporary Arts (ICA) in London in 1968.

Henri had been writing since the age of seventeen and also nurtured poetic ambitions. These were realized when he met Roger McGough and Brian Patten in 1961. Henri wanted poetry to be less élitist and his early writing was influenced by jazz and American beat poetry; he replaced traditional, classical poetic references with allusions to contemporary television series, such as *Batman*, and advertising slogans. His poems were full of bitter-sweet humour and affection for what he saw as ordinary, working-class life—he described his approach as 'more to do with pram wheels than chrome hubcaps' (Milner, 10). He was a self-confessed romantic and the overriding themes of his writing, as of his life, were love and sex. Henri used emotions generated from his many love affairs to create an intimacy with his readers. He brought his work to a wider audience through performance, an experience that Henri saw as an antidote to the painter's solitary life. Henri, Patten, and McGough, known as the Liverpool poets, read to packed houses around Liverpool in events that also included music and comedy. Henri was a huge man, dominating the stage by sheer physical presence, his soft and well-modulated voice perfectly capturing the various characters and emotions expressed in his poetry. The formation in 1967 of the poetry/rock group the Liverpool Scene was a natural progression. The group toured with Led Zeppelin and performed at the Bath and Isle of Wight festivals before disbanding in 1970. Henri's fame culminated in the publication of *The Mersey Sound* in 1967, a poetry collection by Henri, Patten, and McGough. The book was an immediate success and exceeded its 20,000 print run within a month. It is a remarkable volume—vibrant, emotive, and humorous—and became a classic and a fixture on school reading lists.

Henri's frenetic work schedule was cut short in 1970 when he suffered a heart attack following the deaths in the same year of his parents and grandparents. He remained typically productive, submitting two volumes of poetry, *Six Landscapes for Susan* and *Poems for Wales*, and exhibiting at the ICA in London. However, his poetry became more reflective in tone and focused on pastoral rather than urban themes, as evinced by his *Autobiography* (1971), a poetic trawl through his Welsh childhood. Henri continued to perform his poetry through the next three decades, touring theatres and schools, sometimes accompanied by his fellow Liverpool poets. He produced several notable volumes, including *Collected Poems* (1986), *Wish you Were Here* (1990), and *Not Fade Away* (1994), as well as a follow-up volume to *The Mersey Sound* in 1983. He also applied his wry humour and surreal outlook to several works for children, *Eric the Punk Cat* (1980), *Eric and Frankie in Las Vegas* (1987), and *The World's your Lobster* (1998). He wrote a version of the *Wakefield Mysteries* in 1988 (published 1992) which was performed at the Wakefield 100 festival, while *Yesterday's Girl* (1973) and *The Husband, the Wife and the Stranger* (1986) were performed on television.

Although Henri is best known as a poet, he continued to paint throughout his life. He experimented with a range of different styles, from urban collages to detailed Pre-Raphaelite studies and primitive Latin American style depictions of Liverpool. He won the prestigious John Moores prize in 1972, and a retrospective exhibition of his paintings was held at the Walker Gallery in 2000. In 1999 he had a multiple heart bypass operation followed by two strokes. He later developed cancer. He was nursed by his long-term partner Catherine Marcangeli, a French academic.

Henri was awarded honorary degrees from Liverpool Polytechnic in 1990 and Liverpool University in December 2000. He was proud to be a provincial poet and artist, and continued to live in Liverpool, a city he loved, long after fellow 1960s luminaries had moved away. He was made a freeman of the city on 19 December 2000. A day later he died from heart failure at his home, 21 Mount Street, Liverpool.   CATRIONA HAIG

Sources F. Milner, *Adrian Henri paintings, 1953–1998* (2000) · *The Independent* (22 Dec 2000) · *Daily Telegraph* (22 Dec 2000) · *The Times* (22 Dec 2000) · *The Guardian* (22 Dec 2000) · A. Henri, *Autobiography* (1971) · A. Henri, B. Patten, and R. McGough, *The Mersey sound* (1967) · b. cert. · m. cert. · d. cert. · 'Words on the run', 1995 [tour]
Archives U. Lpool L., Sydney Jones Library, corresp. and literary papers
Likenesses P. Edwards, oils, 1985, NPG · J. Connolly, photograph · P. Jones Griffiths, photograph · D. McCullin, photograph

Henrici, Olaus Magnus Friedrich Erdmann (1840–1918), mathematician, was born in Meldorf, Danish Holstein, the son of Theodor Henrici. Between the ages of nine and sixteen he attended the *Gymnasium* in Meldorf, before working for three years as an apprentice engineer at Flensburg. When he was nineteen he went to the Karlsruhe *Polytechnicum*, where, following the advice of Rudolf Clebsch, he studied mathematics. From the age of twenty-two he was a student of Ludwig Otto Hesse at Heidelberg, where he obtained his doctorate, and then moved to Berlin, where he studied under Karl Weierstrass and Leopold Kronecker, leading mathematicians there. He then became a *Privatdozent* at Kiel University but, being unable to support himself, moved to London in 1865.

Struggling to earn a living, Henrici provided for himself by teaching elementary mathematics to schoolboys, an experience that was to prove invaluable to his subsequent career by developing his power of expression. He obtained an introduction from Hesse to James Joseph Sylvester which enabled him to become acquainted with many of the foremost British mathematicians of the day, including Arthur Cayley, William Kingdon Clifford, and Thomas Archer Hirst, then professor of pure mathematics at University College, London. Henrici became Hirst's assistant and, in 1869, was appointed mathematics professor at Bedford College for Women.

At Easter 1870 Henrici stood in for Hirst who had fallen ill; a few months later he was appointed the new professor at University College, following Hirst's resignation. He held the chair of pure mathematics for ten years. In 1879 Clifford, the professor of applied mathematics and mechanics, died, and Henrici acted as a temporary replacement before transferring to the applied chair the following year. He introduced projective geometry, vector analysis,

Olaus Magnus Friedrich Erdmann Henrici (1840–1918), by unknown photographer

and graphical statics into the University College mathematics syllabus—a radical departure from the analytically biased Cambridge-style course previously taught.

In 1884 Henrici left University College to become professor of mechanics and mathematics at the newly founded Central Technical College (later part of Imperial College) in South Kensington. There he set up an innovative laboratory of mechanics upon which many others were later based. Being highly proficient in the construction of models and apparatus, Henrici soon filled it with a myriad of machines and devices, including his 'harmonic analyser'. This modified version of a machine originally invented by Lord Kelvin to obtain Fourier coefficients mechanically was perhaps his most original piece of work.

Henrici was a great perfectionist and would publish only when he was entirely convinced the work was satisfactory. Consequently, his publications are not voluminous, but the quality is very high. Among the most significant, a short book, *Congruent Figures* (1878), attempted to familiarize students with the new projective methods he was introducing. A second volume dealing with similar figures was planned but never written. Similarly, another small book, *Vectors and Rotors* (1903), based on his lectures to first-year students, dwelt only on the elementary part of the subject, being intended as the first part of a more comprehensive work which was never completed. Nevertheless, Henrici can be given the credit for introducing vectorial analysis into English mathematical teaching, making much use of it in his classes, where his success is confirmed by student accounts of 'the singular lucidity of his teaching' (Hill, xlix) and the 'masterly ease and freedom' (Bellot, 322) of his exposition.

Other notable works are two papers read before the London Mathematical Society on the theory of discriminants and singularities of envelopes of series of curves (*Proceedings of the London Mathematical Society*, 1st ser., 2, 1869). He also contributed lengthy and perceptive articles to the eleventh edition (1910–11) of the *Encyclopaedia Britannica* on calculating machines, Euclidean geometry, projective geometry, and projection, as well as shorter pieces on descriptive geometry and perspective.

In 1874, Henrici was elected a fellow of the Royal Society, and he served on its council in 1882–3. He was also president of the London Mathematical Society from 1882 to 1884. On 15 August 1877 he married Helen Stodart Kennedy of Stepney Green, daughter of John Kennedy, a Congregational minister. Their son, Major Ernst Olaf Henrici of the Royal Engineers, collaborated on Henrici's final published work in 1912, a paper on the theory of measurement by metal tapes and wires in catenary, in which formulae were given to facilitate accurate measurements when using a catenary on any sizeable slope. Henrici retired in 1911 and moved to Chandler's Ford, Hampshire, where he died at his home, Hiltingbury Lodge, on 10 August 1918. He was survived by his wife.

ADRIAN RICE

Sources M. J. M. Hill, *Proceedings of the London Mathematical Society*, 2nd ser., 17 (1918), xlii–xlix · H. H. Bellot, *University College, London, 1826–1926* (1929), 322 · A. R. Hall, *Science for industry: a short history of the Imperial College of Science and Technology and its antecedents* (1982) · W. P. Ker, ed., *Notes and materials for the history of University College, London: faculties of arts and science* (1898) · M. J. M. Hill, 'Some account of the holders of the chair of pure mathematics from 1828 to the present time', 1924, UCL, materials for the history of UCL, Mem. 2A/19, fols. 5–6 · M. J. Tuke, *A history of Bedford College for Women, 1849–1937* (1939), 344 · *WWW*, 1916–28 · d. cert. · m. cert. · election certificate, RS

Archives Sci. Mus.

Likenesses photograph, UCL [*see illus.*] · photograph, Sci. Mus., Robert Tucker collection

Wealth at death £2716 8s. 3d.: probate, 25 Oct 1918, *CGPLA Eng. & Wales*

Henrietta. *See* Henriette Anne, duchess of Orléans (1644–1670).

Henrietta Maria [Princess Henrietta Maria of France] (**1609–1669**), queen of England, Scotland, and Ireland, consort of Charles I, was born at the Louvre Palace in Paris on 16/26 November 1609, the fifth surviving child and youngest daughter of Henri IV, king of France and Navarre (1553–1610), and his second wife, Maria de' Medici [Marie de Medicis] (1573–1642), daughter of Francesco I, grand duke of Tuscany, and his wife, Archduchess Johanna of Austria. Her names in French were Henriette Marie.

Early years and education Henrietta Maria's early years were a period of great political instability in the French kingdom, marked by the assassination of her father on 14 May 1610 and the contested regency of her mother. She

Henrietta Maria (1609–1669), by Sir Anthony Van Dyck, 1632

went with the royal family on a ten-month expedition to Bordeaux in 1615 for the double marriage exchange of Spain and France, watching her sister Elizabeth leave for Madrid and her new sister-in-law Anne arrive in France. Frequent other celebrations and ceremonials, all magnificent and expensive, drew her and the other younger children to the court. Otherwise she lived mainly at St Germain, the palace and its gardens engraving themselves on her heart as models of rural pleasure that she would try to replicate in England.

Henrietta Maria was educated like her sisters in riding, dancing, and singing, and was a frequent participant in court theatricals. Although she had a tutor, she does not seem to have progressed much beyond reading and writing. But she was carefully shaped by the Carmelites in the *dévot* piety that reigned at the French court, an aesthetic and moral code that she would translate to the English scene. Although several possible marriage alliances were canvassed for her, including one with the count of Soissons, the English project was alive as early as 1619. Prince Charles (later *Charles I) (1600–1649) paid little heed to her when he stopped in Paris on his way to woo the infanta in 1623, but the French negotiation was rapidly and vigorously pursued on both sides after the Anglo-Spanish match fell through.

Marriage and early life in England, 1625–1630 It was unprecedented for a Catholic princess to be sent in marriage to a protestant court, and this was reflected in the promises that Pope Urban VIII extracted from France in exchange for a papal dispensation. Accordingly, France insisted that the marriage treaty signed in November 1624 include commitments about religious rights of the queen, her children, and her household; while in a separate secret document Charles promised to suspend operation of the penal laws against Catholics. Some religious concessions in the treaty, such as the provision of chapels for the queen in every royal house, were scrupulously fulfilled; others, such as her claim to be served by an exclusively Catholic household, were not. The promise of general relief for the English Catholics was a dead letter, in the face of parliamentary intransigence. There were disappointed expectations on both sides and these, combined with continuing conflict over England's role as protector of the French Huguenots, clouded the marriage in the early years.

Despite the sudden death of James I at the end of March, the wedding went ahead with little delay, Charles de Lorraine, duke of Chevreuse, taking the place of George Villiers, first duke of Buckingham, as the proxy for Charles I. An elaborate betrothal ceremony was followed by an even more elaborate wedding, celebrated on 1/11 May 1625 at the church door of Nôtre Dame, after which the bride and the French left the English protestant ambassadors and Chevreuse at the door, and entered to attend the nuptial mass. The week of sumptuous banquets, balls, and festivities that followed, the rich trousseau and furnishings with which she had been provided, and the slow journey to Boulogne with her large retinue must have left a lasting impression of the splendour of the homeland she was leaving. Hundreds of French appointed to serve in her household, and dignitaries accompanying her to the marital court, crossed the channel with her in early June. The English courtiers closely involved in the match, such as Henry Jermyn, remained close to the queen for many years.

The English with their king who came to meet Henrietta Maria at Dover saw a short and slight but vivacious girl of fifteen, with brown hair and black eyes and a combination of sweetness and wit remarked on by almost every observer. When Charles looked down at her feet, seeming to wonder if she had high-heeled shoes, she quickly raised the hem of her skirt to show him: 'Sire, I stand upon mine own feet. I have no help by art. This high am I, and neither higher nor lower' (Ellis, 1st series, 3.197). That she had not only her father's wit but also his temper became quickly evident in a dispute over seating in the royal carriage when her lady of honour was excluded. None the less, the queen's initial reception in England by king and court was warm, and several tiffs between competing chaplains were brushed over. Chevreuse and his wife stayed on as guests for months and were popular with king and queen alike.

The larger French objectives of exerting influence over the English court and building a party of friends among English Catholics made little headway in the early years, but it was more intimate issues that disturbed the marriage. The demands by Henrietta Maria's Oratorian confessors that she rigidly observe Catholic practices of abstinence from sexual relations at certain days and seasons, and the disruptions caused by her French attendants, soured relations between the 16-year-old girl and her inexperienced 25-year-old husband.

Charles was locked in struggles with his boisterously anti-Catholic parliaments, and dependent on the advice of the duke of Buckingham, whose relations he wished to place in positions of dignity around the queen. Buckingham saw in the young queen a potential rival for influence and attempted to bully or manipulate her. Henrietta's refusal to be crowned by a protestant prelate early in 1626 (or even to attend the coronation ceremony, although a special screened place had been prepared for her) was deeply offensive to the king. The French government's instructions to its ambassadors in 1625 had anticipated some form of coronation, not surprisingly given the traditional view that the ritual legitimized the children of the royal marriage. The outcome is especially paradoxical in view of the long French experience of regencies since the mid-sixteenth century, and her own mother's insistence on being crowned in 1610.

Continued wrangles over the queen's jointure and the finances of her household, and over her public religious practice, culminated in the expulsion of most of her French attendants from the country in early August 1626. Although the episode was unusually dramatic, the exchange of original attendants for those from the marital court was standard; and the experienced French ambassador François de Bassompierre, sent over later in the year, might well have smoothed things over had war not broken out on other grounds. A comparative estrangement between the royal couple lasted until Buckingham's assassination in June 1628, after which their intimacy was complete and lasting.

During this early period Henrietta Maria's psychological isolation from those closest to her—she was attached to a few key figures among her remaining French attendants, and to her Scottish Oratorian confessor Father Robert Philip—threw her back on her religious loyalties, and shaped lifelong personal loyalties. She was far from reclusive at this time, for she supervised at least three court entertainments in 1626 and 1627, already evincing an independent and highly developed taste in the arts. Here she followed in the footsteps of her mother, an ambitious and extravagant patron of artists and artisans. The painter Orazio Gentileschi came to England from her mother's court in 1626, and in the next decade much of his production came into her possession, including a *Finding of Moses* that seems to signify her own sense of mission about bringing true religion to England, and was later taken by her to France to the house in which she died. In the 1630s the controversial exchange of agents with the papal court was sweetened for the king by the access it provided to artists under Barberini patronage.

At Buckingham's death Henrietta Maria took the king in her arms both literally and figuratively; he thenceforth had no other favourite, and, as all observers remarked, when she chose to exert her influence she had a great deal. Their intimacy led to a pregnancy and the premature birth of a son, who lived only two hours in May 1629. The eldest surviving child, later *Charles II (1630–1685), was born on 29 May 1630; she bore six more children from then until 1644, including *Mary, afterwards princess of Orange (1631–1660), James, later *James II and VII (1633–1701); and Henrietta, future duchess of Orléans (1644–1670) [see Henriette Anne]. The fecundity and serenity of the royal family was commemorated by Anthony Van Dyck in a series of famous portraits which have come to typify the age of Charles I.

Peace, parenthood, and patronage, 1630–1637 The close relationship with the king after Buckingham's death brought Henrietta Maria into contact with the great lords of the court, and she found their company pleasant; they appreciated her as a potential ally who had the king's ear, and who ensured that no second Buckingham would rule the king's affections and patronage. Already in 1627 she had grown close to James and Lucy Hay, earl and countess of Carlisle; now she associated also with Thomas Howard, fourteenth earl of Arundel, and his countess, Alathea—both noted patrons of the arts—Algernon Percy, tenth earl of Northumberland, and Robert Sidney, second earl of Leicester.

For seven years after the birth of her first child the queen's life was spent in happy activity that revolved around her family, her palaces, the regular routine of a peacetime court, and securing and extending the position of her Catholic faith. She bore four more children before the middle of 1637, and was seldom apart from the king; when he had a mild case of smallpox in 1632 she refused to leave his side. His visit to Scotland without her for a belated coronation in his other kingdom in 1633 saw him making the last of the return journey in great haste to surprise her. Together they went hunting, went out to the theatre or saw plays at Whitehall, and entertained ambassadors from foreign courts. Most summers they embarked on progresses: whether quite close to London, further afield (Salisbury, Portsmouth, East Anglia), or, as once in 1634, well north as far as Derbyshire. She enjoyed being outdoors, and stories of her informal expeditions in the countryside reveal that she did not stand on ceremony, but could enjoy games and jokes. The impulsiveness and occasional mischief making of her first years in England, as when she and her French ladies rudely interrupted a protestant service in her palace, seem subdued after 1630, although the underlying obstinacy re-emerged in the 1640s. This was the period, as she later told Madame de Motteville, when she was 'the happiest of women' (Motteville, 1.184).

Henrietta Maria had French tastes, and had brought with her a vast trousseau of clothes, jewellery, and furnishings suitable for a French princess about to become a queen. In England she lost no time in identifying artisans already on the scene who could supplement the French servants she lost in 1626; the French kitchen servants were never dismissed. Her bills for dress and textiles were high; Gentile (or Genty) the embroiderer and Grynder the upholsterer appear regularly on her pension and payment records, and her perfumer and various London jewel merchants profited greatly. From an early date she set about remodelling and redecorating her palaces, redesigning their gardens, and stocking them with fruit trees and plants sent for from France. Six royal palaces had been added to her jointure by 1630, of which four (Somerset House, Greenwich, Nonesuch, and Oatlands) had been held by Queen Anne, and two (Richmond and Holdenby) had been held by Charles as prince of Wales; in 1639 the king bought Wimbledon Manor to give to her. Somerset House and Greenwich Palace, in particular, were remodelled and furnished with great elegance and luxury. Inigo Jones had already worked on both palaces for Queen Anne; now he started again at Greenwich for the second stage of the 'Queen's House', and by the mid-1630s the queen was commissioning paintings for the interior by Gentileschi and other artists. Henrietta Maria was the subject as well as the patron of important commissions; in 1632 Van Dyck came to work at the English court, and it has been estimated that the queen sat for him a total of twenty-five times in the next eight years.

More ephemeral but much more expensive than commissioned portraits were the court entertainments in which Henrietta Maria so delighted, a taste she had brought with her from France and highly developed at the English court. Almost yearly from the winter of 1630–31 the king and queen presented masques to each other at twelfth night and Shrovetide, representing in words, music, dance, and scenic effect the themes of order and harmony that were so fully realized in their own marriage. All these masques were staged by Inigo Jones, and they embodied ideals of Platonic love in a Christian context that was much influenced by the queen's French Catholic spirituality and devotional practice, particularly the Marian cult that she was sponsoring at the court. These allusions were not lost on puritan critics, some of whom were also scandalized by the queen's appearing on stage herself. The production of a pastorale composed by the courtier Walter Montagu in early 1633, in which the queen had the central role, coincided with William Prynne's publication *Histriomatrix*, in which he described actresses as whores. For this he suffered a Star Chamber sentence of the pillory and mutilation.

Political and religious activity, 1630–1637 Henrietta Maria's approach to international politics was personal, dynastic, or cultural rather than nationalistic. The Anglo-French war that ended in spring 1629 had made her unhappy; she did not rejoice at the Anglo-Spanish peace of 1630. But the 'day of dupes' in November 1630, when Maria de' Medici decisively and permanently lost her position in the French government, left Henrietta with loyalties as divided as the French royal family. Her mother left France for good in the summer of 1631, thereafter living in exile mainly in Brussels as a guest of the Habsburg court there. Others of the queen's family and friends—her brother Gaston, Marie, duchesse de Chevreuse, the chevalier de Jars—were in more or less perennial opposition to Cardinal Richelieu by 1630. It is scarcely surprising, therefore, that French ambassadors in the early 1630s were complaining of how little the queen supported their efforts to influence English policy in the direction favoured by the cardinal's government. On the contrary, she became caught up in an international conspiracy, centred on the marquis de Chateauneuf, who had been ambassador to England in 1629–30, and promoted by Montagu, who had close acquaintance among Richelieu's enemies. The queen's closest French servant, Mme de Vantelet, was also implicated. This plot had the double objective of toppling Richelieu in France and Lord Treasurer Richard Weston in England. Henrietta thought the latter kept her on a short financial tether, while his peace policy could be smeared as Hispanophile by domestic rivals such as Henry Rich, earl of Holland. The plot collapsed in 1633, but remained fresh in Richelieu's memory.

In the course of these intrigues Henrietta Maria became associated with the party at court that supported a vigorous protestant foreign policy on behalf of the king's exiled sister *Elizabeth of Bohemia, widow of the elector palatine Frederick V, and her eldest son, Charles Louis. This prince and his brother Rupert made a visit to England in 1635–7 to drum up support; they were well entertained by king and queen, visited Oxford in summer 1636, and were encouraged by an apparent *rapprochement* with France that might lead to military action on their behalf. The outbreak of direct hostilities between France and Spain in 1635 had led Richelieu to court the queen and her circle; the Percy family connection (the earls of Northumberland and Leicester, Henry Percy, and Lucy, countess of Carlisle) were also proponents of this design. Although the projected alliance fell through by mid-1637, the queen had experienced her first serious essay at foreign policy making.

By contrast, the advancement of the Catholic religion and protection of English Catholics had been a consistent concern of Henrietta Maria from the moment of her arrival in England; and her days and seasons were framed around religious observance. The marriage treaty had provided for a Catholic chapel and priests to staff it; even during the late 1620s her practice was never under threat, although she then had only two Oratorians in her service. None of her musicians, who served in both chapel and court, had been sent away in 1626; indeed this part of her household was enhanced in 1627–9 by the addition of at least half a dozen players, including the Irish harpist Daniel Cahill and the organist Richard Dering. After the Anglo-French peace the only important change in her household (and the only one she had sought) was the addition of the new complement of priests who were sent to serve her—a dozen Capuchins this time, as Richelieu's new adviser was the Capuchin Père Joseph.

The Capuchin order was in the vanguard of the French Catholic reform, distinguished for proselytizing activity on the borders of protestantism. Those sent to serve Henrietta Maria never succeeded in displacing her confessor Father Philip, but they provided a vigorous evangelizing presence, especially after the construction by Inigo Jones of a new chapel for the queen at Somerset House, her chief residence. This chapel, begun in September 1632 with a dedication service that attracted many hundreds of observers, opened in December 1635 with a sung pontifical mass. A spectacular 40 foot high architectural setting to surround the holy sacrament (an 'apparato', or stage set, of the kind newly fashionable in Italian churches) had been constructed by the sculptor François Dieussart. The festivities lasted three days, and attracted the attention and visits of numerous non-Catholics, including the king. The queen's almoner James du Perron, nephew to the noted anti-protestant controversialist Jacques Davy du Perron, was made bishop of Angoulême with the king's tacit consent.

The overt and implicit Catholicism at court had already for several years been evident to protestant observers and critics, who were particularly alarmed by the exchange of diplomatic agents with the papal court that got under way in 1633. Optimistic reports from Catholics in England about the possibility of the king's conversion and reunion of the churches induced Urban VIII to send a series of agents, whose activities in England wrought damage that far outweighed the partial and temporary relaxation of anti-Catholic measures that they achieved. The Oratorian priest Gregorio Panzani, who arrived late in 1634 and stayed two years, associated with British Catholics and crypto-Catholics at the court. His activities, and the presence at court of reunionists such as the Franciscan Christopher Davenport, lent colour to those who suspected Archbishop William Laud of plotting to take the Church of England back to Rome. Panzani's successor in the late 1630s was the Scot George Con, an agile courtier fluent in English whose ambitions for a cardinal's hat were supported by the queen, and who spent much time in the company of the royal couple. Con repeated to Rome what he observed and what Father Philip reported on the queen's faith and character: 'the actions of her majesty are full of incredible innocence … she has no sin, except those of omission' (*Letters*, ed. Green, 32). Through Con the king was able to acquire works of art from Rome, including Bernini's head of the king done from a three-way portrait by Van Dyck.

The British wars of religion, 1638–1641 Egged on by Con and her Catholic courtiers, notably Walter Montagu, whose conversion in 1635 was a *cause célèbre*, Henrietta Maria not only intervened to protect English Catholics, and kept her chapel open to them, but also proselytized energetically among the court women. By 1638 her successes led one observer to lament, 'Our great women fall away every day' (*Earl of Strafford's Letters and Dispatches*, 2.194). In 1638 as well, two grand intriguers arrived at the English court with numerous Catholic hangers-on: first the duchesse de Chevreuse, then the queen's own mother, Maria de' Medici, unwelcome to the king but not in the end rejected. Maria stayed until the middle of 1641, an expensive and disruptive embarrassment to an increasingly besieged king.

Against this backdrop of court Catholic revival, it was easy for the king's critics to portray the prayer book crisis in Scotland and the covenanting revolt in terms of religious war. This reading of the situation was reinforced by the queen's attempt to rally Catholics from all three kingdoms behind her husband's two northern campaigns in 1639 and 1640. In particular, the contribution she organized in 1639 among the English Catholics proved a great deal more politically damaging than financially useful. It was also at this time that the queen made her first secret effort to secure a papal loan to support the king's military efforts, an initiative that was repeated several times in the 1640s. By the time George Con left England in mid-1639, he was near death and his hopes to become a cardinal were dashed, but he had helped the queen create a militant Catholic party whose activities were continued by his successor, Carlo Rossetti, from 1639 to 1641.

Even before Con had left England, the protestant backlash had begun in sermons, placards, and pamphleteering attacks on the court. When financial necessity forced the king to call his first parliament in eleven years, in April 1640, the leaders of the House of Commons picked up the attack on court Catholicism. The queen, her mother, the papal nuncio, the Capuchins and their chapel, and the Catholic contribution were all pinpointed. The early dissolution of this parliament was followed by intense disquiet in London with petitions, graffiti, riots, and extravagant rumours; and, as its members dispersed back into the counties, they carried with them a newly urgent sense of danger emanating from the heart of the court.

The Long Parliament and the Popish Plot, 1640–1642 The activities of Henrietta Maria and court Catholics provided a thematic focus for the opposition in the Long Parliament; claims that the king had been either a party to or a victim of a 'popish plot' throughout his reign were central to the arguments and publications of the parliamentary party from the grand remonstrance of 1641 through to 1648. The resulting atmosphere of fear and suspicion on both sides contributed to the more radical decisions that led to hostilities between the king and parliament. One after another of the queen's friends and servants was summoned to be questioned in the House of Commons in the session of 1640–41, several fled to the continent, there were repeated demands that no Catholics be allowed to serve her, and she was forced to apologize for her efforts to raise money from English Catholics to support the Scottish campaign of 1639. She began to speak of going to France for a year of rest, but was discouraged by the French court.

London was a centre of international intrigue at this time, with the imperial and Spanish ambassadors there actively fomenting the rebellion of French exiles against Richelieu; this presented a model for political conflict that almost certainly influenced Henrietta Maria's views. The so-called army plot to use or threaten force against parliament was conjured up by young hotheads among her protestant courtiers, including Henry Percy, Sir George Goring, and Henry Jermyn, the last already identified as one of her closest confidants. Its exposure in May marked the queen irrevocably in public opinion as a proponent of violent measures. Only half known to her critics were the queen's continuing efforts to procure aid for her family from outside England: from France, Ireland, and especially Rome. From the beginning of the Scottish troubles she had encouraged the extravagant projects of Randal MacDonnell, second earl of Antrim, to raise men in Ireland for the king's service, and had urged Rome to seize the opportunity the crisis presented to benefit Catholics throughout the British Isles. In vain she argued that a papal subsidy for Irish and foreign troops would bring concessions from the king.

The spring of 1641 saw Henrietta Maria absorbed by two very different dramas. Her husband's chief counsellor, Thomas Wentworth, earl of Strafford, was on trial for his life in parliament, and she was almost daily attending the trial in March and April. She later claimed to have attempted to assist Strafford in secret meetings with various parliamentary leaders; she was almost certainly in negotiation with parliamentarians in January and February 1641, although the content of these discussions can only be conjectured. Concurrently, arrangements for the marriage of Princess Mary to William, son of Frederick Henry, prince of Orange, were being finalized. The queen had been toying with ideas of a Spanish match, but the United Provinces seemed willing to promise assistance to the king in exchange for the marital capture of the eldest daughter. The young prince made a happy impression on both king and queen, and the wedding was performed on 2 May 1641, but days away from Strafford's execution. The princess at nine was too young for more than a token 'consummation', and her young husband returned home alone.

Henrietta Maria was terribly alarmed by the riots in London in the last days of Strafford's trial, and these accelerated with the exposé of the army plot. Both in parliament and by the crowds she was accused as a chief evil counsellor of her husband, and her confessor Father Philip was arrested in late June 1641. The papal agent Rossetti, long under attack by parliament, left before the month was out. After the trial and execution of Strafford the queen seems to have believed it was only a matter of time before she met a similar fate, and she made contingency plans for a flight to the continent. Ambassadors variously reported that she might settle in Holland, in Brussels, or in France. A planned trip to The Hague with Princess Mary, when she would also carry jewels to pawn for the king's support, was forestalled in July by protests of the House of Commons.

In August 1641 Maria de' Medici left for the continent, and the king departed for Scotland to attempt to secure support there; he left Henrietta Maria in a position of considerable influence with the councillors left behind, who reported to her weekly. Her frequent letters to him, full of advice, reveal how closely she was following political winds in London. But she was very fearful of violence against herself, and had moved out to Oatlands. Her letters to her sister Christine lamented that she was like a prisoner, and that the king had lost all his power. Nor were her fears groundless; alarmed at the king's initial political success in Scotland, the parliamentary leaders floated a rumour that they intended to seize the queen and the prince as hostages. Even so, then and later, she retained a resilient hopefulness and a confidence that beyond the capital city the king's support was overwhelming.

In November, the king still absent, the queen had to relinquish custody of the prince of Wales to a governor named by parliament, who claimed that the prince was endangered by the presence and influence of Catholics around his mother. The king's triumphant return from Scotland and entry into London later that month were a short-lived victory, for the outbreak of the Irish rising had persuaded the parliamentary opposition that all they had feared about Catholic plotting was true, and that the queen was at the centre of it. The grand remonstrance detailed this conspiracy at length, starting at the beginning of the reign and connecting 'popery' at every stage with alleged royal 'tyranny'. Parliament's decision in mid-December to print this document marked the beginning of a long pamphlet campaign that demonized the queen and discredited the king; both official and unofficial publications about her swelled the flood of print that was unleashed in 1641–2. A rising level of real and threatened violence in London, and the repeated suggestions that the queen was the author of the Irish rising and might be impeached for treason, hardened her completely against compromise. She renewed her attempts to obtain papal funds to support Irish troops. It is very probable that she encouraged the king in the attempted arrest of the five members in early January 1642; certainly she was widely believed to have done so. Thereafter, rumours of her intended impeachment multiplied, and she feared imprisonment or even death.

The queen in Holland, 1642–1643 The king and queen left London on 10 January 1642, he not to return until the eve of his execution, and she only after the Restoration. Their fear for the queen's safety doubtless contributed to the decision to go; from Hampton Court they moved to Windsor. The older princes and princess went with them, but *Henry (1640–1660) and *Elizabeth (1635–1650) were fatally left behind. George, Baron Digby of Sherborne, one of the king's most fervent supporters, had fled to Holland, and from there wrote advising the queen (and king) to take firm measures; this was the first of many intercepted letters to or from the queen that were printed by parliament. On 19 February 1642 parliament issued a 'declaration of causes and remedies' that focused on the queen, her household, and her role as adviser; this evolved into the nineteen propositions presented to the king in June. She departed with Princess Mary for Holland on 23 February from Dover, the king riding along the shore miserably watching her ship disappear. She left instructions for her Capuchins left behind in London to keep the chapel at Somerset House for her remaining household. In her company were the earl of Arundel, Lord Goring, Mary Stuart (née Villiers), duchess of Richmond, Susan Feilding (née Villiers), countess of Denbigh, and Jean Ker (née Drummond), countess of Roxburghe, Father Philip and two Capuchins, the dwarf Hudson, and her faithful dog Mitte. It was the first of several difficult channel passages;

before she touched shore, a storm sank one boat carrying her chapel plate.

Henrietta Maria's letters to the king are full of her frustrations in summer 1642. She was welcomed by the prince of Orange and Prince William, and by Elizabeth of Bohemia, whom she was meeting for the first time, and was installed in a refurbished palace in The Hague. But she found it difficult to pawn the jewels, was impatient with the stadholder's attempts to entertain her, and was outraged that the states general received an envoy from parliament. For the first time she mentioned the toothaches, headaches, and other physical ailments that were a refrain of all her future letters. Absence from her husband, the perennial problems of communication, and the prevalence of rumours all damaged her nerves. Henry Jermyn and Lord Digby were soon at her side planning the purchase of arms to send back to England, and others such as John Finch and Henry Percy who had been named 'delinquent' by parliament began to frequent her court. In Cologne her mother died; the queen had been refused permission by the Dutch to go to her.

Throughout the autumn Henrietta Maria tried to return to England, but was foiled by contrary winds, and was exasperated by the king's failure to take her advice to move vigorously against the munitions centre and port of Hull. During 1642 she was handling her own correspondence, not only with Charles but also with Sir Thomas Culpeper, John Ashburnham, and William Cavendish, earl of Newcastle; she did not hesitate to advise the king on appointments even of privy councillors. Elizabeth of Bohemia, whose eldest son Charles Louis, the prince palatine, had been in England since April 1641, believed that the queen ruled the king, and that she always counselled the use of force. It is impossible to put reliable figures on the amount of money the queen raised in her trip to Holland in 1642–3, or the amount of ordnance and supplies, or the exact numbers of English soldiers drawn out of continental armies for the king's service. Some of this aid was waylaid by parliamentarian ships or otherwise diverted before it reached the royal army. But her efforts were unremitting, and substantial resources reached the king, some of it brought over by his palatine nephews Rupert and Maurice when they reached England in September 1642. Her intercepted letters, detailing as they did her continued negotiations with the French and Danish crowns, further alarmed parliament about the extent of foreign aid that might become available to the king, prompting the sending of parliamentary agents to Holland and the French court. Rumours of invasion from Denmark or France, or both, were rife; and agents in Holland, where parliament had many sympathizers, were able to report her efforts there in some detail. There were alarms along the coast at Yarmouth and other suspected landing places. At the end of 1642 she was buoyed by the death of Richelieu, whom she had regarded as an enemy of her husband; her hopes of French assistance revived, she sent Walter Montagu to plead her cause with his old friend Cardinal Mazarin.

The 'popish army' of the north, 1643 In mid-January 1643 the earl of Newcastle, commanding the king's forces in the north, retook the city of York, and Henrietta Maria finally set off for England. The trip was dangerous; John Pym was alleged to have said that if they could capture her they would be able to set their own conditions with the king. In stormy weather it took her two tries and the loss of a boat carrying her horses, carriages, and grooms to get across to Bridlington Bay in Yorkshire, bombarded by parliamentary ships during and after the landing. She was summoned by parliament to appear, but instead spent three months in York, during which time she met Scottish supporters of the king, among whom James Graham, fifth earl of Montrose, made a lastingly good impression. She once again sent off her old protégé the earl of Antrim to raise forces in Ireland, but he was captured with incriminating letters that only fed the swelling propaganda campaign.

The political reverberations of the queen's efforts were at least as important as any contribution to the royalist military effort that they made. Her image as the leader of a Catholic crusade was bolstered by her enthusiasm for posing at the head of the forces that would march south from Yorkshire to Oxford in June and July 1643. Writing to the king, she described herself as 'her she-majesty generalissima' (*Letters*, ed. Green, 222). In Newcastle's army a large minority of senior officers were Catholic, and this had already evoked references to an 'army of Papists'; these allegations now multiplied, the London newsbooks picking up the theme. The war became seen by many, especially below the gentry class, as a religious struggle; and there developed an English version of the 'black legend' formerly aimed at Spain, which linked brutality with Catholics; this provided a link in the chain of accusations that culminated in the cry, later in the decade, that Charles I was a 'man of blood'.

The queen's warlike acts were explicitly connected to a series of symbolic depredations by which, in spring 1643, the House of Commons 'purified' London of 'popish' symbols. Early in April a group of MPs led by Sir John Clotworthy and Henry Marten pillaged and desecrated her chapel and Capuchin convent at Somerset House. On 3 June, Marten was also a leader among those who broke into the chapel at Westminster Abbey where the crown regalia were stored, and made a mockery of the items before taking an inventory. On 23 May the House of Commons drew up a resolution of impeachment for high treason against the queen, on the grounds that she had levied war against the parliament and kingdom. Their demand that she appear before them was of course a dead letter, but on 21 June 1643 the Commons passed the articles of impeachment, which then languished in the Lords.

On 3 June 1643 Henrietta Maria had left York with a large force that she estimated at 3000 foot, some 1800–2000 horse and dragoons, six cannon, and two mortars, Jermyn serving as colonel of her guards. Having moved on to Newark, she waited two weeks in vain hopes for the surrender of Hull before continuing southwards. In later life she spoke nostalgically to Mme de Motteville of this early summer of 'campaigning', in which she had lived with the troops; her brother King Louis XIII had died on 14 May, and perhaps she was thinking of the father she had hardly known and recalling his military exploits. Early July saw her on the road to Oxford, where the king had made his headquarters; Prince Rupert met her at Stratford upon Avon. At her joyous reunion with Charles near Edgehill on 13 July he yielded to a request for a peerage for her courtier Henry Jermyn; a few days later the king and queen were in Oxford.

The 'Indian summer' of the reign, 1643–1644 Henrietta Maria's presence in the wartime 'Oxford court' lasted only from July 1643 to April 1644. The royal couple entered the city in a festive and noisy procession, culminating in a mayoral welcoming speech at Carfax, and a volume of poetry in her honour was presented to the queen by scholars of the university. These were personally happy months; the king was at Christ Church and she was installed at Merton College, using the college chapel for her Catholic services, with elegant musical performances. She was the centre of a glittering if sometimes rowdy group of courtiers. But the Oxford court was full of rivalries and conflicting views about policy, in which the queen and her circle became deeply engaged. She suffered a blow to her hopes of French aid by the capture of her favourite Walter Montagu, who attempted in October to sneak into England with the new French ambassador; he remained imprisoned for four years. The parliamentary *Perfect Diurnal* of 2–9 October 1643 alleged that his return was 'clear evidence to all the world of the great design in this kingdom for the Catholic cause, when such grand Jesuited Papists as this shall be brought over hither to have intercourse with both their Majesties'. Montrose was entertained at court and given the commission he had long sought with her backing, but her chief hopes still lay in Ireland. The cessation with the Irish confederacy in September, soon followed by parliament's alliance with the Scots, opened the door to a new phase of royal negotiations for Irish soldiers and papal subsidy. Antrim, escaped from captivity, reappeared at court with new plans to unite Ireland behind the king; with the queen's blessing, he set off for Ireland with James Butler, first marquess of Ormond, at the beginning of 1644 on yet another mission that would be shipwrecked on personal animosities and papal intransigence.

Finding that she was pregnant in the early spring of 1644, the queen wanted to give birth in a safer place than Oxford and left the city on 17 April, little realizing she would never see her husband again. With but a few attendants, she travelled to Bath and then to Exeter, the parliamentary army under Robert Devereux, third earl of Essex, still trying to catch her as she escaped westward. She was ill and miserable, and her desperate husband begged the elderly physician Theodore Mayerne to travel from London to attend her; 'Mayerne, for the love of me, go to my wife, C.R.' (*Letters*, ed. Green, 243). In Exeter on 16 June she gave birth to her last child, a girl. Having escaped from the besieged city soon after giving birth, and having left the infant in the care of Anne Villiers, Lady Dalkeith, the queen moved through Cornwall. She finally took sail out of Falmouth Bay about 14 July with Jermyn, Father Philip, one lady, a physician, and her dwarf and dog. Her bishop du Perron had been sent to France late in 1643 to test the possibility of a retreat there, and there she now headed. In her last letter to the king before she left, she wrote:

> I hope yet to serve you. I am giving you the strongest proof of love that I can give; I am hazarding my life, that I may not incommode your affairs. Adieu, my dear heart. If I die, believe that you will lose a person who has never been other than entirely yours, and who by her affection has deserved that you should not forget her. (ibid., 249)

Initiatives in France, 1644–1646 The crossing to France marked the end of an era, although Henrietta Maria may not have realized it; she referred frequently and longingly to a future reunion with her husband. But now she was thrown into dependence on Jermyn, who handled much of her private and public correspondence and negotiations with the French court. Nor did she ever regain good health; modern analysis of her symptoms suggests she was suffering from tuberculosis. After landing in Brittany on 16 July after a stormy and contested passage, she sent Jermyn to Paris for help, then travelled slowly through the French countryside during the summer heat. She was met by doctors and messages from Anne of Austria, whose help for her person, if not for her cause, never thereafter failed her; she was immediately awarded a pension of 30,000 livres a month. She travelled inland with Father Philip and her ladies Richmond and Denbigh, finally arriving at the spa city of Bourbon on 25 August, where she stayed through September. She had grown sicker during the trip, an abcess in her breast having to be lanced; Mme de Motteville, a lady-in-waiting sent by Anne of Austria to bring her to Paris, found her in terrible condition, able to think and speak of nothing but the situation in England. She set out painfully for Paris, and was met at Nevers by her brother Gaston, duke of Orléans, and her girlhood friend Anne-Genevieve de Bourbon-Condé, duchess of Longueville, neither of whom had she seen since 1625, and by delayed bad news from England of the king's defeat at Marston Moor. Only after that battle had the king reached his infant daughter in Exeter and baptized her Henrietta.

Henrietta Maria reached Paris by early November, and was met by Anne of Austria, who settled her at the Louvre with a generous allowance, and by Gaston's daughter Anne Marie Louise, duchess of Montpensier (Mademoiselle de Montpensier), who figured in her dynastic plans for years to come. At court she found some of her friends who had been exiled while Richelieu lived; and around her, at the Louvre and at her summer residence in St Germain, gathered a court of royalists in exile. After the defeats in northern England late in 1644, first Newcastle and Henry, second Viscount Wilmot, then Percy made their way to Paris. They did not form a happy or united group; Jermyn was self-indulgent and a focus for resentment, while the queen's stinting to save money from her allowance to send to Charles I meant few crumbs for her courtiers, and

constant squabbling over them. For the next two years there was a steady stream of letters back and forth across the channel, the queen urging her husband to resolution, detailing her efforts on his behalf, pleading for news from him, advising him on appointments.

Despite continued ill health, Henrietta Maria immediately renewed her struggle for men, money, and diplomatic support for her husband. Over the next few years she turned ceaselessly from Mazarin and the duke of Lorraine to Ireland, Scotland, Denmark, Norway, Sweden, and Pope Innocent X. She revived overtures to the prince of Orange about a second marriage alliance between their houses linked to aid for her husband; this project limped on despite the stadholder's obvious lack of interest until mid-1646. Observers in London reported the various rumours of her plans for invasions, and noted the 'no small anxiety and apprehension' they aroused. Her activities were reported by the London newsbooks, and more direct evidence would be provided by her captured correspondence. In France she presented her cause in the guise of defence of Catholicism, as she said in one letter to Charles reprinted in *King's Cabinet Opened*: 'All the assistance that I get from France to send you, is from the Catholics, as a sort of bribe to assist the Catholics of England' (*Letters*, ed. Green, 290–91). Early in 1646 her old almoner the bishop of Angoulême urged the French clergy to raise funds to help save the Catholics of England; his speech to the assembly was picked up and later (1647) printed in translation by parliament. This did not misrepresent what the king had expressed himself willing to offer a year earlier in 1645, to 'take away all the penal laws' against the Catholics in England in exchange for sufficient help (ibid., 291). At the time of the Uxbridge negotiations she counselled her husband to stand to his principles, not abandon those who had served him, and above all not to venture unguarded into the hands of his enemies. Very revealing of her state of mind was a passage, later mocked by parliamentary commentators, in which she expressed her fears for his (and her) safety. 'I do not see how you can be in safety without a regiment of guard; for myself, I think I cannot be, seeing the malice which they have against me and my religion, of which I hope you will have a care of both …' (ibid., 279). Like Angoulême, she was able to contemplate the slaughter of the royal family. After the king's defeat at Naseby in June 1645 his cabinet of correspondence was captured, and a few months later Digby also lost revealing letters. It was neither the first nor the last time her letters were caught by her enemies and printed, to the grave detriment of her husband's cause.

Although Henrietta Maria's efforts yielded some arms and money, the continental war absorbed French resources, and Dutch sympathy for the English parliament forestalled the prince of Orange. Mazarin, as sceptical about the Stuarts as Richelieu had been, was happy enough to let her think the duke of Lorraine could furnish 10,000 men, which would conveniently relieve the pressure this troublemaker exerted on France. The royalist defeats of 1645 reduced the likelihood of French aid, and the loss of Bristol and then Plymouth in that year eliminated the possibility of it. When the king went to join the Scots in May 1646, entering into negotiations brokered by the French, who found they preferred a weakened king to a republic in England, she entered into this new project with some enthusiasm, vainly urging him to come to terms with the Scots over the episcopacy but not take the covenant: 'You should no more impose the covenant upon other people than you should take it yourself, for all those who take it swear to punish all delinquents, that is all of your party, myself the first' (*Letters*, ed. Green, 329).

In 1645 and 1646 both king and queen still had high hopes from Ireland. Since 1643 she had been trying to persuade the Irish Catholic confederates to accept the limited religious concessions that Ormond was authorized to offer; how much she knew of the more expansive offers made via her old courtier friend Edward Somerset, Lord Herbert of Raglan, now raised to the earldom of Glamorgan, is unclear; she almost certainly would have approved of them. Certainly in Paris in 1644-5 she lent a too ready ear to the grandiose schemes proposed by the Jesuit O'Hartagan for what amounted to an Irish invasion of England. She had constantly since the later 1630s linked her hopes from Ireland with papal aid, but her reiterated efforts were in vain. The new pope, Innocent X, was surrounded by Spanish influences and unimpressed by her agent Sir Kenelm Digby. Digby returned with a little money for Ireland, and very high demands for religious concessions in both England and Ireland as the price for anything more substantial. Papal agents in Ireland were positively hostile to the Stuart cause; first Scarampi then the nuncio Rinuccini (1645-8) obstructed Ormond's efforts to unite the Catholics behind a royalist standard.

It is easy in retrospect to label the queen unprincipled, considering the various strands of her projects and suggestions in these years; but she belonged to a world of dynasties, not of nation states, and her own father had famously thought that Paris was worth a mass. Her loyalties were not the less firm for later seeming archaic; from the outset of the war she was more frightened than the king of his enemies and what they might do.

The royal family and the end game, 1646–1648 The disappointments and irresolution of mid-1646 were lightened for Henrietta Maria by the company of her eldest son and her youngest daughter, both recently arrived from England. Prince Charles had moved from the west of England to the Scilly Isles, then to Jersey, in spring 1646, the queen pursuing him and his ministers with letters begging that he join her in France, to which she had obtained the king's concurrence. She assured him that he would remain free in his movements and free from her attempts on his conscience, and did not fail to send a picture of France's wealthiest potential match, her niece and Gaston's daughter, Mlle de Montpensier. Finally he agreed. Princess Henrietta, captive for several months after the fall of Exeter, was spirited out of England in disguise by her governess Anne Douglas (*née* Keith), countess of Morton, arriving within a month of her brother. Henriette Anne, as she was

now named out of regard for the queen regent (or Minette, as Prince Charles nicknamed her), was the constant companion of her mother from the day of their reunion until the girl's marriage in 1661. Minette was brought up to be French and also Catholic, in not so vague anticipation of a Catholic royal marriage. The arrival of her son in July enabled Henrietta Maria to develop new marriage plans for him to replace the long-moribund negotiations with the prince of Orange. She spent the winter of 1646-7 introducing a not particularly willing teenage son to the court life of Paris and to his cousin and potential partner. Henrietta Maria seems to have set her heart on this match; and Queen Anne, Mazarin, and Gaston showed some interest, perhaps to avoid offending her. The young woman was older than the prince, sharp-tongued, and considered a snob even by her royal aunts, but she was the richest heiress in France, if not in all Europe; the logic of Henrietta's ambitions was very sound. Unfortunately, Mlle de Montpensier was unimpressed by her cousin, who seemed awkward and was strangely unable to speak French.

During the two years when Charles I was in the hands of the Scots, the English parliament, and then the army, Henrietta Maria tried to maintain contact with him under increasing difficulties. She despaired of his apparent willingness to compromise on issues such as the militia that she thought fundamental. She still hoped for aid from Ireland, sending a secular priest, George Leyburn (codenamed Winter Grant), to the duke of Ormond in June 1647, and talking of going there herself. She sent Sir Kenelm Digby to Rome one last time, receiving after the usual delays a final rejection in March 1648. Hoping to take advantage of the rumoured sympathy of some in the army in late 1647, she sent Sir John Berkeley and two others to attempt mediation with the Independents. Nothing worked.

Passing through Paris in summer 1647, Montrose reported with dismay on the demoralized character of the exiled court; there were endless quarrels and threats of duels. In the autumn the queen lost her old Scottish confessor Father Philip; he was replaced by Walter Montagu, who was released from an English prison, joined her in Paris in mid-1649, and took orders in 1651. If all about her was crumbling, the queen none the less kept her resolution and grasped at every straw of good news. To the end she encouraged the king to believe in the possibility of aid from across the channel and tried to organize it; and to the end the intercepted letters between king and queen detailing these projects for foreign troops were fatal. The declaration on the vote of no addresses in February 1648 rehearsed, as had the grand remonstrance, all the past history and present currency of 'plots' to bring in foreign and Irish troops. When the second civil war was launched in the spring and summer of 1648, she supported the decision to send Prince Charles to Scotland, and raised £30,000 with her last jewels to help finance this effort.

Late in 1648 the queen made a final effort to go to her husband, sending letters to the houses of parliament and to General Thomas Fairfax that were laid aside unopened until long after the Restoration. That winter she was living in such poverty that she was unable to heat her rooms; Cardinal de Retz had felt compelled to intervene with the parlement of Paris on her behalf for a grant of money.

The regicide, 1649 Henrietta Maria was at the Louvre when Charles I was executed; she did not hear about her husband's death for over a week because of the poor communications between central Paris and the French court, which was then at St Germain because of the Fronde uprisings. Upon being told by Jermyn, she was thunderstruck, in such shock that her sister-in-law Françoise, duchess of Vendôme, was summoned to help revive her. Leaving Henriette Anne with her governess Lady Morton and Father Cyprien, Henrietta retired to the Carmelite convent at the rue St Jacques in which she had spent happy days as a girl. There she read the last letter sent her by her husband.

Henrietta Maria never really recovered from this event, and her personality seems to have permanently changed. She was thirty-nine, and devoted the rest of her years to promoting her son's claim to the throne, bringing up her youngest daughter, and her own religious practice. She emerged from the convent, at the urging of Father Cyprien, who said her family needed her, in the simple black dress that she wore for the rest of her life. In the sad months after her husband's death, when her son's future either through Ireland or through Scotland seemed to hang in the balance, she turned to her sister Christine, duchess of Savoy, and streams of letters in both directions testify to their affection.

Although Henrietta Maria kept her hopes up in 1649–50, advising her son to look to Ireland and Scotland for aid, she faced successive personal blows. Her old almoner du Perron died, it was said of shock, soon after hearing of the regicide; her daughter Elizabeth died in captivity at Carisbrooke Castle in September 1650, and the husband of her daughter Mary, William II, prince of Orange, died suddenly in November. The last was the harshest blow, it seems, as she said 'in him were placed all my hopes for my son's restoration' (*Lettres de Henriette-Marie*, 405). Her second son, James, duke of York, having escaped from England, came to France in spring 1649, but he was restless and within a year departed on the first of several periods of military service under foreign princes.

Politics of the post-regicide court From the regicide until Charles II's return from Scotland, late in 1651 Henrietta Maria and her associates (most importantly Jermyn, also Percy, Wilmot, and Lord Digby) formed a party labelled 'the Louvre' by Sir Edward Hyde and Sir Edward Nicholas, who were often at odds with them. As former army plotters, these courtiers were indeed inauspicious as a group thought to be guiding the young king. Moreover, they were perceived because of the queen's support for the Scottish initiative as favouring compromise with the presbyterians. The poverty of the exiled court much exacerbated all these rivalries; the queen was unfailingly generous with her own reduced assets, offering in March 1649 to sell her pawned jewels to support her son's projected trip

to Ireland. But the perception that Jermyn utterly controlled and misused her funds is a constant theme in the correspondence of Hyde, Nicholas, and Christopher, first Baron Hatton.

After Charles's return from Scotland Henrietta Maria's role as an adviser was measurably diminished; but since the young king's support—he was granted a French pension in May 1652—was funnelled through her household, the appearance and fear of her influence remained strong. By spring 1654 Charles was consulting her so little that Jermyn remonstrated with him, evoking a defensive letter from the king. The queen's role in the accusations against Hyde which convulsed the exiled court in the winter of 1653–4 may have been only a supporting one—it was her old courtier George Digby, now earl of Bristol, who did the main work—but it doubtless added distance between her and the king.

The queen had always taken an international perspective on England's politics, and she remained hopeful in the early 1650s that Ireland or Scotland, or any of a number of foreign powers, would intervene decisively on behalf of Charles II. She supported an embassy to Madrid in 1650–51 to try for a loan or for Spanish assistance with the pope, or to reconcile Spain and France; it bore no fruit. As Walter Montagu was an old friend of Cardinal Mazarin, she hoped yet again to persuade that minister to aid her son; but even had Mazarin been so inclined, the Fronde precluded any such initiative until the rise of Oliver Cromwell tipped the international political balance firmly against the royalists. Both religious politics and her contacts with Irish nobility inclined her still to hope more from Ireland than from Scotland. At one point in mid-1649 there was even renewed talk of her going to Ireland with her son. She trusted Ormond—as did the rival party among her son's advisers—but he proved unable to bring together the warring Irish factions in the face of determined papal opposition. Pope Innocent X would provide neither funds nor his blessing, and Cromwell's victories in Ireland by the end of 1649 forestalled a royal visit there. A project for the duke of Lorraine to rally support in Ireland would be floated on and off from 1650 to 1652. Henrietta made a fresh effort with the new pope in 1655, but to no avail. Rome for once had correctly assessed the situation in the British Isles; the need for Scottish support repeatedly compromised any efforts to win concessions for Irish Catholics.

Of all these possibilities, the most promising was the young king's trip to Scotland, and Henrietta Maria encouraged it. After negotiations at Breda, during which he promised to take the covenant, he sailed for Scotland in May 1650. She was horrified by his concessions, which she thought dishonourable, involving as they did disowning his Catholic relatives and followers. The familiar story of his adventures there—his coronation, the defeat at Dunbar, the daring escape from Worcester in September 1651—became known to his anxious mother in dribs and drabs, with few letters but many rumours. He returned a sterner man, even more withdrawn from his mother's influence, and increasingly anxious to be free of the dependence on a French pension which kept him at her side. Mlle de Montpensier found him more interesting than he had seemed in 1646 or 1649, but still a timid courtier, handicapped in his tentative suit by his religion, and more decisively by his lack of a kingdom. 'Given the state England was in I wouldn't have been happy to be queen of it' (Montpensier, 1.236–7). He never forgot her aspersions on his poverty and dependence. The renewal of the Fronde distanced both Mlle de Montpensier and her father, both Frondeurs, from the English royal family; and although Henrietta Maria chided her in 1656 for having lost an opportunity to gain independence and perhaps a crown through marriage, little more was said about this project.

Far from getting help from continental powers, the royal family lost ground with both France and the United Provinces between 1651 and 1655 because of the continuing Franco-Spanish war and growing naval power of the Cromwellian regime. The Anglo-Dutch wars of 1652–4 had served the exiles well; but first Holland (April 1654) then France (October 1655) made peace with the new regime in England. Mazarin found that one price of peace with England was formal recognition of its government, to which he had yielded in December 1652. In each peace treaty Cromwell exacted promises to stop aid to the Stuart cause; the Dutch had to cease hosting the exiled court and to keep royalist privateers from their ports, while France promised to expel both Charles and James. The queen thus lost contact with both her elder sons from the mid-1650s onwards; after Charles's departure from France in July 1654, and especially after her attempt at his brother Henry's conversion, she lost what little influence she had with him.

A 'holy court', 1651–1654 Henrietta's piety deepened after the loss of her husband, and she had lost the moderating influence of her old confessor Father Philip. Unlike Philip, Walter Montagu was not a moderating influence on the queen's proselytizing instincts. She wrote to Christine in December 1650 that God obviously wanted her to attend to non-worldly things. Her sister-in-law Anne of Austria had a similar reaction to political misfortune, and was given to interpreting the Fronde as a divine judgment. Possibly egged on by Montagu, Anne pressed Henrietta Maria to restrict protestant practice at her court, and the queen partially submitted, against the protests of her son. She had permission for John Cosin, chaplain to her English servants, to hold services in the Louvre, but he was now forced out and into the residence of the English ambassador, Sir Richard Browne. By the end of 1651 she was threatening to stop support to those of her servants who would not convert; several, such as Lady Denbigh, had already done so.

Henrietta Maria's regular retreats into the Carmelite convent since her arrival in Paris in 1644 no longer satisfied her need for a life half in and half out of the world, and she was drawn to the aristocratic Sisters of the Visitation, or Filles de Sainte Marie, at the rue St Antoine, introduced to her by Mme de Motteville. Her visits in 1651 developed into a plan to found a convent of the order, and

she purchased a house at Chaillot formerly owned by Marshal Bassompierre, whom she had entertained as her brother's ambassador in 1626. The money to accomplish her endowment was raised by contributions from Anne of Austria and devout aristocratic friends. In June 1651 she installed a dozen nuns at Chaillot, several of whom became close friends; the queen regent attended the first high mass said at the convent. The queen soon began to spend weeks at a time at Chaillot, where she was visited by Anne and other courtiers. She discharged Lady Morton, Henriette Anne's protestant governess, and effectively moved the girl into the convent. She was given suitable courtly skills, but also a thorough Catholic instruction under the guidance of Father Cyprien.

The release from English captivity of Henrietta Maria's youngest son, Henry, duke of Gloucester, early in 1653 created a joyful anticipation in his mother, to whom he was rather reluctantly sent in June for what was intended to be a short visit. The apprehension felt by Princess Mary and by Charles II's councillors at the prospect of this visit was fully justified, as the queen did attempt to convert her son despite the prohibitions that had been reiterated by both her husband and her eldest son. There was a successful precedent for her effort; for in May 1645 she had helped engineer the marriage of her palatine nephew Edward to a Catholic heiress of Mantua, and his conversion to her religion. After a year in the company of her charming and attractive boy she resolved to win him over by the promise of preferment within the Catholic hierarchy such as was enjoyed by Lord Ludovick Stuart d'Aubigny, the king's (third) cousin and her future almoner. She began shortly after Charles left, encouraged by Anne of Austria and with the connivance of Percy and Jermyn. She tried to buy off the boy's protestant tutor, and enlisted Abbé Montagu to argue her son into submission and into entering the Jesuit college at Clermont. The abbé put it to the boy that a conversion would enable him to help his brother with the Catholic princes of Europe, while the king's councillors felt sure that all would be lost in England if this ploy succeeded.

Henry stubbornly resisted, and English protestants in Paris rushed to his support. The marquess of Ormond was sent to Paris by Charles with the king's letters to his brother, to his mother, and to her intimates, and with orders to remove Henry from France. This ended the episode, for neither the French court nor the queen mother could withstand his authority. Her final parting with her youngest son was bitter, she refusing him a word or a blessing as he prepared to leave with Ormond. She may have been sincere in protesting to Jermyn that he and his friends had assured her that the prince's conversion would do no political damage to the king. It was the end of any possible influence she might have wielded on Charles II.

A slow retreat from politics, 1655–1659 Alone in Paris in 1655, Henrietta Maria spent a good deal of the year in unhappy defensive manoeuvres. She had soured relations not only with Charles but also with most of her other relatives; she was in particularly poor health and remained so for the next few years despite annual trips to Bourbon. Although she, like her son, continued to seek Catholic aid, most of the avenues he explored bypassed the queen. Her agent would have been Montagu, and both he and Jermyn were distrusted as tools of Mazarin by Charles's advisers. So when the accession of a new pope, Alexander VII, in February 1655 revived hopes of a papal loan to finance Irish troops under the leadership of the duke of Lorraine, the desultory negotiations set on foot went through Spain, the duke of Neuburg, the priest Peter Talbot, or via Cardinal de Retz, with whom Charles could freely converse in Brussels.

It had been rumoured that the peace between Mazarin and Cromwell would require even Henrietta Maria and Henriette Anne to leave France, but in the end it was James who had to leave French service in summer 1656—his mother hoped vainly he might be employed by her sister Christine—for various places in the Low Countries, where he finally entered the Spanish service for the campaign of 1657. The reception of an English ambassador at the French court in May 1656 wounded her deeply. The only bright spot in these years was an extended visit from Princess Mary in 1656. Mary brought an array of jewellery with her, dazzled the French court with those and her good looks, and was splendidly entertained. She also brought with her Anne Hyde, who met the duke of York and instantly conquered him. Henrietta and Mary paid a visit in July to Mlle de Montpensier at her château of Chilly, and Mary, who hated Holland, was loath to leave Paris; only news of her son's illness finally forced her to return to The Hague in September.

Henrietta Maria had used the occasion of the Anglo-French accord to make Mazarin request the return of her dowry and personal possessions from England, but it is unlikely that anything was received. Instead she was granted some funds by the French clergy in 1657. Anne of Austria augmented her sister-in-law's pension from her own funds, enabling her to purchase a small château in Colombes, a village on the Seine 7 miles north-west of Paris. She decorated elegantly, as the nuns had not permitted her to array Chaillot; and from the latter part of 1657 she divided her time between the two houses. Early in 1658 she welcomed to Chaillot her niece Princess Louise of the Palatinate, a fugitive convert who had been invited to Paris by her Catholic brother Edward. Henrietta Maria helped Louise on to a Cistercian convent near Pontoise, where she became abbess. Her relations with Elizabeth of Bohemia, never very warm, became even chillier.

The death of Cromwell in September 1658, whom the queen referred to as 'ce selerat' ('that villain'; *Lettres de Henriette-Marie*, 430), did not seemingly arouse her to much emotion. Her daughter Mary's conflicts with her mother-in-law and with the Dutch anti-royalist party seem to have preoccupied her more, as did the plans of the French court to marry Louis XIV to Marguerite, daughter of her sister Christine of Savoy, rather than to her own

Henriette Anne. Charles II settled in Brussels over the winter of 1658–9 to watch events across the channel. Sir John Reresby, visiting Paris, reported how Henrietta Maria (unlike her resentful daughter) defended her adopted land, praising the people of England for 'their courage, generosity, good nature; and would excuse all their miscarriages in relation to unfortunate effects of the late war, as if it were a convulsion of some desperate and infatuated persons' (*Memoirs*, ed. J. Cartwright, 1875, 43).

The Restoration Henrietta Maria's projects seemed to be foundering in 1658 and 1659, and she was very much on the sidelines. Successive royalist risings in England failed, and the death of Cromwell made no immediate difference; her continuing efforts via Jermyn and Montagu to press Mazarin for assistance were fruitless. The prospects of her daughter Henriette Anne for a royal marriage, a pet idea with the two widowed queens, seemed crossed. But the long-sought Franco-Spanish peace was finally achieved, and the Savoy marriage project was abandoned for a match between Louis XIV and the Spanish infanta. The court left for the Spanish border, and Henrietta went into seclusion at Colombes for the rest of 1659. There her son Charles visited her for the first time in six years, wary of his mother's political initiatives but captivated by his much grown sister Henriette Anne. He yielded to a request for Jermyn, who was made earl of St Albans. The death of the queen's brother Gaston in February 1660 was a mixed sorrow; since the Fronde she had not been close to him, and his successor in the title of duke of Orléans, with its massive revenues, was Louis XIV's brother Philippe, whom she now wanted to marry Henriette Anne.

The rapid developments of 1660 took Henrietta Maria by surprise. She viewed the Restoration, for which she had so tirelessly worked and prayed, with amazed joy, scattering letters at her son as he made his way back to England in May and June 1660. To her sister she wrote, 'I hope yet to see before I die my whole family together and no longer vagabonds' (*Lettres de Henriette-Marie*, 433). She had a Te Deum said at Chaillot, and put on bonfires and a ball in Paris. Her own return to England was delayed by her plans for Henriette Anne; it was only when the French court returned from the long trip to Spain that it was possible to formalize Henriette Anne's betrothal to the new 'Monsieur'. Henriette Anne's dowry would come from England. The girl had been educated by Father Cyprien, who published before her marriage a three-volume work, *Exercises d'une ame royale*, to prove her suitability for a Catholic royal marriage. The trip to England would permit the formal approval of the king of England for Henriette Anne's marriage, and the restoration of Henrietta Maria's own English revenues; it was propelled also by her concern over the marriage of her son James to Anne Hyde. Before she arrived in London at the end of October, she lost her youngest son, Henry, who had accompanied Charles to England, and whom she had not seen since their quarrel over his religion in 1654. He was taken by smallpox in September, and died aged twenty. Princess Mary died, probably of the same cause, on Christmas eve 1660, her mother having been kept from her deathbed by anxious physicians.

The first stay in England was short, full of emotional reunions; Henrietta Maria was met by her old friend Charlotte Stanley, *née* de la Trémouille, dowager countess of Derby, and stayed at Whitehall, as Somerset House was still too dilapidated. Samuel Pepys saw her at court, 'a very little plain old woman, and nothing more in her presence in any respect nor garb than any ordinary woman' (*Diary*, ed. Wheatley, 2 vols., 1946, 1.196). She left very soon after Mary's funeral, having at the last moment been reluctantly reconciled with James. Mazarin had urged her to conciliate the father of the new duchess of York, the same chancellor Hyde who would be managing the dowry and her own newly granted pension and jointure. Henriette Anne's wedding, a little delayed by Mazarin's death, took place on 21/31 March 1661 in the queen's chapel in the Palais Royal. Henrietta prepared slowly to move herself out of that palace and make a final return to England; in her absence her son was crowned (in April 1661) and married (in May 1662) to Catherine of Braganza. In spring 1662 she felt needed in France to oversee Henriette Anne's first pregnancy, and to mediate in what was quickly developing into a turbulent marriage. Henriette Anne had successive flirtations at court, a very jealous husband, and in the course of her short life numerous mainly unsuccessful pregnancies, only two girls living to adulthood. She died less than a year after Henrietta Maria.

In August 1662 Henrietta Maria returned to London with Charles's natural son James, later duke of Monmouth, for whom she had cared. She settled in Somerset House, with much of the same household that had been with her before the war and stayed with her through her exile: Jermyn, the Vantelet family, Sir Kenelm Digby, Sir John Wintour, the duchess of Richmond, Abbé Montagu, and a new complement of Capuchin chaplains. This began a three-year period of real happiness. She got along very well with her new daughter-in-law, Catherine of Braganza, whose agreeable and devout nature pleased her, the king, her son, was kind to her, and she enjoyed the ballets and other court entertainments. Pepys reported that her court was full of 'laughing and mirth' (Pepys, *Diary*, 1.538) and more frequented than that of the more austere Catherine. Her contemporaries continued to leave the scene; her sister Christine died in 1663, and her old friend Charlotte de la Trémouille the following year.

Henrietta Maria restored both the fabric of Somerset House—a new gallery was constructed after an earlier design by Inigo Jones—and its role as a centre for London Catholicism. The Capuchins once again presided over numerous and crowded masses, catechizing in both French and English, public lectures, marriages, and baptisms; the confraternity of the rosary was revived with processions and other pious exercises. One of the Capuchins provided the high altar with 'rare pieces of workmanship' (Gamaches, 458–9), arranging new chapel plate given her to replace what she had been forced to sell in 1649. Pepys was one of those who admired her new construction at Somerset House, calling it 'most stately and nobly furnished' (Pepys, *Diary*, 1.990); others directed hostile attention to her chapel activities: as in the 1630s, placards calling for the 'extirpation of popery' were posted at her palace.

Final years in France, 1665–1669 The Engĺish climate continued to give Henrietta Maria problems, possibly either bronchitis or a recurrence of tuberculosis, and she missed her daughter. In spring 1665, as the plague year was beginning, she left for France with Father Cyprien, the other Capuchins staying behind as had been done in 1642 with the injunction to continue Catholic proselytizing. In Paris she was granted a palace in the city, but Anne of Austria's death in 1665 lessened the appeal of the court. She spent her remaining years mainly at Chaillot and at Colombes, which she fitted with furnishings from Somerset House; the inventory taken after her death details the rich surroundings of these later years. Mme de Motteville was in frequent attendance on her, constructing the memoir of her life; she tells us that in her later years the queen read daily from *De imitatione Christi*, and when at Chaillot went to morning and evening prayers. She lived in these years as she had been raised, a queen but also a *dévote*.

After hostilities began between France and England early in 1666, Henrietta Maria was mentioned only infrequently in public sources, usually in connection with an attempt at mediation through her ministers. But Louis XIV seems to have consulted her more than once about the peace that was concluded in mid-1667. Her revenues from England had been hard to collect since this war began, and were formally reduced at the end of 1668; her last letters to Charles II were expostulations on this subject. She was ill throughout 1669, suffering from fevers and insomnia that the royal doctors could not mend; she died at Colombes early in the morning of 10 September 1669 NS, most probably of an opiate pressed upon the reluctant patient by a doctor several days before, and which she had finally agreed to take during that night. Her Capuchin Cyprien de Gamaches and St Albans were both at her deathbed; the household was full of servants who had served her for decades, including five of her bedchamber women who had been with her for forty years. The duchess of Richmond, her chief lady, had grown up at the queen's court in the 1630s and followed her back and forth across the channel ever since.

The settlement of the late queen's estate was tricky; no will was found, and her son-in-law Orléans had to be restrained from taking possession on behalf of his wife according to French law. Charles II prevailed but was generous; possessions at Chaillot were left to the convent, Colombes and its lands were given to Henriette Anne, the contents of Colombes were divided among Charles, Henriette Anne, and the queen's serving women. Louis XIV paid for the state funeral at St Denis, which followed the lying in state at Chaillot.

The queen's heart was interred on 16 November NS in the chapel of the Convent of the Visitation at Chaillot, where was preached the best-known of her funeral sermons, by Bishop Jacques Bossuet (*Oraison funebre*, Paris, 1669). He based it on a memoir specially written for his guidance by Mme de Motteville at the request of Henriette Anne. This sermon was translated into English by the secular priest Miles Pinckney (pseudonym Thomas Carre) and printed at Paris in 1670. Two other eulogies were printed: that delivered at the state funeral and interment in the abbey of St Denis on 20 November 1669 NS by François Faure, bishop of Amiens (*Oraison funebre*, Paris, 1670); and one delivered at Nôtre Dame on her birthday, 25 November, in the following year by the Oratorian Jean François Senault (*Oraison funebre*, Paris, 1670).

Reputation The vicious and sustained parliamentary attacks on the queen in the 1640s had a lasting effect on her reputation. Her personal integrity and fidelity were questioned, first with rumours in 1641 that Henry Jermyn was her lover, and later with rumours that she had married him after the king's death. These were fed by Jermyn's unpopularity among royalist exiles in the 1650s and his influence after the Restoration, but had no basis in evidence or in her own character. Other elements of the parliamentary attacks, portraying her as a sinister, foreign, Catholic influence on the king, stuck more firmly. These views were reinforced by the royalist and post-Restoration need for a scapegoat, by the force of anti-Catholicism well into the modern era, and by an even more tenacious conservatism about the appropriate role of women in the political sphere. Thus, the king's supporters lamented with Clarendon that the king 'saw with her eyes and determined by her judgment' (E. Hyde, first earl of Clarendon, *The Life of Edward, Earl of Clarendon … Written by Himself*, new edn, 3 vols., 1827, 1.185). The nineteenth-century biographer of Prince Rupert, with whom she had often been at odds, regarded her as fatal to the war effort, and described her influence as excluding 'all that was wise, or good, or truly noble, in the Court' (B. E. G. Warburton, *Memoirs of Prince Rupert and the Cavaliers*, 3 vols., 1849, 2.300). A twentieth-century historiographical tradition focusing on public institutions, and in particular on parliament, deflected attention from the *ancien régime* courts and from the serious analysis of politics in courtly, dynastic cultures. This made it difficult to assess the life and role of Henrietta Maria, or indeed of any queen consort.

A relatively sympathetic tradition began in the Restoration, a first biography in English by John Dauncey appearing in 1660, and a French biography by C. Cotolendi in 1690. The funeral sermons by Senault (1670) and Bossuet (1669) were published, the latter based on material provided by Mme de Motteville. All these works emphasized her piety and heroism, and the courage with which Henrietta Maria faced the tragedy of the king's execution. The tragic view of her life predominated when interest revived in the nineteenth century, epitomized in I. A. Taylor's *The Life of Queen Henrietta Maria* (1905) and continuing in a 'queen of tears' tradition well into the twentieth century. But the finely edited collection of her letters by M. A. E. Green (1857), together with the publication of the memoirs of Motteville and many other sources for the period, had laid the basis for modern biography. This began with the volume devoted to her in Agnes Strickland's *Lives of the Queens of England* (1857), and reached a high point in the sympathetic but balanced and deeply researched life by Carola Oman (1936).

Direct evidence about the queen's character and influence on the king is very meagre for the period before the war; but the flood of correspondence that passed between king and queen in the 1640s reveals a strong-minded, assertive, and focused political actor. Assertions about her frivolity in the preceding period should therefore be carefully weighed; this traditional picture derives largely from the reports of successive French ambassadors who were unable to enlist her full support for Richelieu's projects. Yet her very Frenchness gave added life to the impression of frivolity, and it was endorsed by most modern biographers in English. Alongside the references to her being reckless and intriguing, however, there has been increasing recognition of her courage and tenacity.

CAROLINE M. HIBBARD

Sources *Letters of Queen Henrietta Maria*, ed. M. A. E. Green (1857) • *CSP dom.*, 1625–49 • *CSP Venice*, 1625–70 • C. de Gamaches, 'Memoirs of the mission in England of the Capuchin friars', *Court and times of Charles I*, ed. T. Birch, 2 (1848) • *The Nicholas papers*, ed. G. F. Warner, 4 vols., CS, new ser., 40, 50, 57, 3rd ser., 31 (1886–1920) • *Calendar of the Clarendon state papers preserved in the Bodleian Library*, ed. O. Ogle and others, 1–4 (1869–1932) • S. R. Gardiner, *History of England from the accession of James I to the outbreak of the civil war, 1603–1642*, 10 vols. (1896–9) • C. Oman, *Henrietta Maria* (1936) • C. M. Hibbard, *Charles I and the Popish Plot* (1983) [incl. detailed bibliography on 1637–42] • *JHC*, 2–3 (1640–44) • G. Groen van Prinsterer, ed., *Archives … de la maison d'Orange-Nassau*, series 2, 1584–1688 (1857–61), vols. 3, 4 • *The manuscripts of Henry Duncan Skrine, esq. Salvetti correspondence*, HMC, 16 (1887) • H. Ellis, ed., *Original letters illustrative of English history*, 1st ser., 3 (1824); 2nd ser., 3 (1827); 3rd ser., 4 (1846) • *The manuscripts of his grace the duke of Buccleuch and Queensberry … preserved at Drumlanrig Castle*, 2 vols., HMC, 44 (1897–1903), vol. 1, pp. 438–40 • 'Memoir by Madame de Motteville on the life of Henrietta Maria', ed. M. G. Hanotaux, *Camden miscellany, VIII*, CS, new ser., 31 (1880), 1–31 • E. Veevers, *Images of love and religion: Queen Henrietta Maria and court entertainments* (1989) • Clarendon, *Hist. rebellion* • G. Albion, *Charles I and the court of Rome* (1935) • F. Bertaut de Motteville, *Mémoires … sur Anne d'Autriche et sa cour*, ed. M. F. Riaut, 1–4 (1904) • H. Haynes, *Henrietta Maria* (1912) [material from Chaillot and other French sources for the 1650s not used by other biographers] • *Life and death of Henrietta Maria de Bourbon* (1685) • A.-M.-L. d'Orléans, duchesse de Montpensier, *Mémoires*, ed. A. Cheruel, 4 vols. (Paris, 1858–9), vols. 1, 2 • *Letters of Elizabeth, queen of Bohemia*, ed. L. M. Baker (1953) • F. de Bassompierre, *Journal de ma vie: mémoires … de Bassompierre*, ed. de Chanterac, 1 (1870); 3 (1875); Société de l'Histoire de France, 153, 173 • G. Radcliffe, *The earl of Strafforde's letters and dispatches, with an essay towards his life*, ed. W. Knowler, 2 vols. (1739) • *Report on Franciscan manuscripts preserved at the convent, Merchants' Quay, Dublin*, HMC, 65 (1906) • *King's cabinet opened* (1645) • *Lettres de Henriette-Marie de France … a sa soeur Christine, duchesse de Savoie*, ed. H. Ferrero (1881) • *Diary and correspondence of John Evelyn*, ed. W. Bray, 4 vols. (1883–7), vols. 1, 2, and 4 • *Charles I in 1646: letters of King Charles the first to Queen Henrietta Maria*, ed. J. Bruce, CS, 63 (1856) • C. de Baillon, *Henriette-Marie de France … étude historique … suivie de ses lettres inédites* (1877)

Archives Archives du Ministère des Relations Extérieures, Quai d'Orsay, Paris • Bibliothèque Nationale, Paris, childhood letters, fonds français, MS 3818 • BL, Harley MS 7879 • BL, letters to Charles I, Egerton MS 2691 • BL, letters to marquess of Newcastle, Harley MS 6988 • BL, letters to Silius Titus, Egerton MS 1533 • Bodl. Oxf., letters to Charles I • LPL, letters to Charles II, MS 645 • NA Scot., letters to marquess of Montrose • NL Wales, Wynnstay MSS, household records • PRO, state papers, France, SP 78 • PRO, signed establishment books for her household, LR 5/57, 63 · Sheff. Arch., letters to earl of Strafford

Likenesses F. Pourbus the younger, oils, *c*.1611, Uffizi Gallery, Florence; repro. in R. K. Marshall, *Henrietta Maria: the intrepid queen* (1990), 10 · G. van Honthorst, oils, 1628, Royal Collection; repro. in Veevers, *Images*, 151 · W. J. Delff, line engraving, 1630 (after D. Mytens), BM, NPG · D. Mytens, oils, *c*.1630–1632, Royal Collection; repro. in O. Millar, *The Tudor, Stuart and early Georgian pictures in the collection of her majesty the queen* (1963), pl. 59 · J. Hoskins the elder, miniature, watercolour on vellum, *c*.1632, Royal Collection; repro. in O. Millar, *Age of Charles I: painting in England, 1620–1649* (1972), cover [exhibition catalogue, Tate Gallery, London, 15 Nov 1972 – 14 Jan 1975] · D. Mytens, oils, 1632, Royal Collection; repro. in O. Millar, *The Tudor, Stuart and early Georgian pictures in the collection of her majesty the queen* (1963), pl. 58 · D. Mytens, or studio of Van Dyck, oils, 1632, State House, Annapolis, Maryland · H. G. Pot, group portrait, oils, 1632, Royal Collection; repro. in O. Millar, *Age of Charles I: painting in England, 1620–1649* (1972), no. 83 [exhibition catalogue, Tate Gallery, London, 15 Nov 1972 – 14 Jan 1975] · A. Van Dyck, group portrait, oils, *c*.1632, Royal Collection; repro. in O. Millar, *The Tudor, Stuart and early Georgian pictures in the collection of her majesty the queen* (1963), pl. 66 · A. Van Dyck, oils, 1632, Royal Collection [*see illus.*] · A. Van Dyck, oils, 1633, National Gallery of Art, Washington, DC; repro. in C. Brown and others, *Van Dyck, 1599–1641* (1999), pl. 67 [exhibition catalogue, Antwerp and London, 15 May – 10 Dec 1999] · J. Hoskins the elder, miniature watercolour on vellum, 1635, Walters Art Gallery, Baltimore, Maryland · oils, *c*.1635, NPG · A. Van Dyck, oils, 1636, Wrightsman Collection, New York; repro. in O. Millar, *Age of Charles I: painting in England, 1620–1649* (1972), 62 [exhibition catalogue, Tate Gallery, London, 15 Nov 1972 – 14 Jan 1975] · studio of A. Van Dyck, oils, *c*.1636, Royal Collection · A. Van Dyck, oils, *c*.1637–1638, The Hermitage, St Petersburg, Russia · A. Van Dyck, oils, *c*.1638, Royal Collection; repro. in O. Millar, *The Tudor, Stuart and early Georgian pictures in the collection of her majesty the queen* (1963), pl. 68 · A. Van Dyck, oils, *c*.1638, Brooks Memorial Art Gallery, Memphis, Tennessee; repro. in C. Brown and others, *Van Dyck, 1599–1641* (1999), pl. 92 [exhibition catalogue, Antwerp and London, 15 May – 10 Dec 1999] · F. Dieussart, marble bust, 1640, Rosenborg Slot, Copenhagen; repro. in O. Millar, *Age of Charles I: painting in England, 1620–1649* (1972), 126 [exhibition catalogue, Tate Gallery, London, 15 Nov 1972 – 14 Jan 1975] · C. le Febvre, oils, after 1649 (*The widow of the martyr*), repro. in Oman, *Henrietta Maria*, 307 · P. Lely, oils, 1660, Musée Condé, Chantilly · H. David, line engraving, BM, NPG · W. Hollar, print (after A. Van Dyck), NPG · H. Le Sueur, bronze statue, St John's College, Oxford · F. Pourbus the younger, oils (*Henrietta, aged about eight*), Uffizi Gallery, Florence; repro. in R. K. Marshall, *Henrietta Maria: the intrepid queen* (1990), 18 · A. Van Dyck, oils, Audley End House, Essex · medals, BM · mezzotint (after A. Van Dyck), BM, NPG · oils (after A. Van Dyck), Marble Hill House, London · pastel drawing, Audley End House, Essex · print (*Henrietta Maria as a widow*), BM; repro. in A. Plowden, *Henrietta Maria* (2001)

Wealth at death goods and furnishings (many valuable): PRO, SP 78/128, fols. 190–206

Henriette Anne [*formerly* Henrietta], **Princess, duchess of Orléans** (1644–1670), was born at Bedford House, Exeter, on 16 June 1644, the sixth and youngest of the children of *Charles I (1600–1649) and Queen *Henrietta Maria (1609–1669) to survive infancy and the eighth in all. By her father's command she was baptized into the Church of England in Exeter Cathedral on 21 July. Shortly after Henrietta's birth her mother left for France, leaving her in the care of her governess, Lady Dalkeith. Late in 1645 Exeter was besieged by a parliamentarian army, surrendering in April 1646. Lady Dalkeith took Henrietta to Oatlands,

Princess Henriette Anne, duchess of Orléans (1644–1670), by Sir Peter Lely, *c*.1662

where she remained, despite orders from the Commons that she should join her brother Henry and sister Elizabeth at St James's Palace. Instead of complying, Lady Dalkeith slipped away from Oatlands in disguise with her young charge on 25 July, crossing to France, where Henrietta was reunited with her mother, who resolved to have her raised as a Catholic: she claimed later that the king had agreed to this, but as he was now in the custody of the Scots, he was powerless to prevent it. It was in Paris that the name Anne was added to that of Henrietta, with which she had been christened, as a compliment to Anne of Austria, the widowed queen of Louis XIII and mother to the young Louis XIV: she was now known as Henriette Anne.

Having survived the Fronde, when she and her mother suffered considerable penury and hardship, Henriette began to make her mark at the French court, making her first appearance in a ballet early in 1654. She became something of a favourite at court, Anne of Austria being particularly fond of her, but her mother's hopes that she might marry Louis XIV foundered on his lack of interest. When Sir John Reresby visited Paris in 1659 he was charmed by her. She made him dance while she played the harpsichord and later had him push her on a swing in the garden; she danced very well, he added. In December of that year Charles II saw her for the first time for several years. She had grown up rapidly and he did not recognize her at first. They spent ten days together, during which time the pair formed a deep and lasting friendship: there was to be no doubt thereafter that, even though they rarely saw one another, she occupied a special place in his affections.

At the end of 1659 Henriette's marriage prospects were limited, but they improved dramatically as her brother's restoration to the English throne became first possible and then certain. She already had an admirer in Louis's younger brother Philippe, duke of Anjou (1640–1701). His mother, mindful that Louis XIII's younger brother Gaston, duke of Orléans, had been a constant thorn in his side, had done her utmost to ensure that Philippe would pose no such threat to his elder brother. She had brought him up as far as possible in the company of girls and women, so that he developed a fondness for make-up and dressing in women's clothes. Nevertheless, he declared that he had fallen in love with Henriette. Louis, Anne of Austria, and Cardinal Mazarin were all ready to approve the marriage now that Charles II was truly king of England. For Henrietta Maria it was as fine a match as she could hope for and Henriette herself seemed willing enough to agree: after all, Philippe was still only twenty, he claimed to be in love with her, and marriage to a lovely young wife could be expected to cure him of his effeminacy. The marriage was delayed until March 1661 by the need to secure a papal dispensation to allow the marriage of first cousins. By now Louis had given his brother the title of duke of Orléans; the new duke was more generally known as Monsieur, as was the norm for the younger brother of a king of France. His wife came therefore to be known generally as Madame. (In some of Charles's letters he called her by his personal pet name of Minette, but nobody else appears to have called her this.)

At the end of 1660 Henriette came to England with her mother, who was determined to break the marriage of James, duke of York, to Anne Hyde. Pepys was disappointed by her: she was very pretty, but not the great beauty he had expected, and he did not like 'her dressing of herself with her hair frized short up to her ears' (Pepys, 1.299). Others commented favourably on her blue eyes, her chestnut hair, and above all her dazzling smile. Her natural slimness was exaggerated by ill health: Louis once compared her unkindly to the bones of the holy innocents. She also suffered from a slight deformity, in that one shoulder was a little higher than the other, but this she generally managed to conceal. While opinions differed about her looks, it was generally agreed that she possessed great charm and a sweet disposition.

Henriette's sweetness was to be severely tested by her husband. His alleged passion soon cooled and he became jealous, initially of his brother, who began to find his new sister-in-law charming company. The French court was full of sexual intrigues and gallantries, some innocent, some not. Madame, who was still in her teens, was flattered by the attentions she received, naïvely unaware how they would be misinterpreted by her husband or a censorious public. The brutal realities behind the flirtations at court became clear when the king sent away her admirer, the comte de Guiche, and clearer still as Monsieur deprived her of one confidant (or confidante) after another, leaving her isolated and lonely. To make matters worse, Monsieur became besotted with the chevalier de Lorraine, who wasted no opportunity to turn him against his wife. Successive pregnancies took their toll on her health—at least Monsieur played the part of a husband in that respect. The two daughters who survived, Marie Louise and Marie, became queen of Spain and duchess of Savoy respectively. But meanwhile Madame became thinner and frailer, with a tendency to faint after even the slightest exertion.

Madame's importance in the history of international relations stemmed from her unique position as a personal link between the French and English courts, and between Louis XIV and Charles II. Henriette had other correspondents in England, including James, duke of York, George Villiers, duke of Buckingham, Henry Bennet, earl of Arlington, and the king's mistress, Barbara Palmer, countess of Castlemaine. But it was her correspondence with Charles which was the most important and she was able to discuss its contents frequently and confidentially with Louis, who enjoyed her company but also respected her intelligence and valued her undoubted influence with her brother; in the early months of 1670 he worked with her every afternoon. From the time of his return Charles had wanted an alliance with Louis: he saw the two of them as natural allies against the Dutch republic. Louis, however, saw the Dutch as more capable than the English of thwarting his ambitions in the Spanish Netherlands and so signed a defensive treaty with the Dutch in 1662. Meanwhile, his relations with Charles were soured by disputes over money, protocol, and sovereignty over the narrow seas. When Charles went to war with the Dutch in 1665, Louis was eventually forced (under the 1662 treaty) to declare war on England. In 1668 Louis was furious when England, the Dutch republic, and Sweden signed the triple alliance, designed in part to limit French gains in the Spanish Netherlands—and doubly furious because Charles had promised less than a year before to conclude no treaties in the next twelve months without informing him.

When, in 1668, Charles again expressed a wish for an alliance with France, with a view to making war on the Dutch, Louis was understandably reluctant to trust him, especially as Charles insisted on beginning with a commercial treaty and declared that he neither liked nor trusted Colbert de Croissy, recently appointed French ambassador in London. Louis, however, insisted that Croissy was the best man for the job, so by October 1668 Charles and Madame were discussing in their letters the terms of a possible alliance. In December, Charles sent Henriette a cipher so that their correspondence could be more secure, and in January 1669 there took place the famous private meeting at which Charles declared his intention to announce his conversion to Roman Catholicism and that he judged that to facilitate this an alliance with France was essential. Neither Croissy nor the English ambassador in Paris, Ralph Montagu, was informed of this. Instead a draft treaty was taken over by an unofficial envoy, Henry, Lord Arundell of Wardour, a Catholic who was master of the horse to Henrietta Maria and who had been one of the four at the meeting; he was ordered to consult Madame frequently. Early in November, at Louis's insistence, Croissy was informed of the full English proposals, including Charles's intention to announce his conversion, but Montagu was not, so the most important English negotiator in Paris remained Madame. It has been argued, on the basis of her letter to the king dated 11/21 September 1669, that she was concerned more for Charles's interests than for Louis's (Hartmann, 277–81). The letter could equally be read as an attempt to persuade Charles that his anxiety about French naval and commercial power was unfounded and that he could safely agree to the terms which Louis proposed. This is not to suggest that she was biased towards France, but rather that she saw the treaty as a means to unite her brother and brother-in-law, the kingdom of her birth and the kingdom that had become her home (she almost always wrote in French because her written English was so bad), while at the same time advancing Catholicism. It was not a matter of favouring one side or the other, as she saw the two kings' interests as entirely compatible.

As the treaty neared completion, Henriette Anne had one last part to play. Louis wanted war against the Dutch to precede Charles's announcement of his conversion, while Charles (ostensibly) wished his announcement to come first. Louis decided that the best way to clear this impasse was for Madame to appeal to her brother in person. Monsieur, more spiteful than ever and furious that Louis had sent away the chevalier de Lorraine, at first refused to let her go and then insisted that she could go for only a few days and travel no further than Dover. After an emotional reunion Charles seemingly allowed himself to be persuaded that war with the Dutch had to come first, and so the secret treaty of Dover was signed on 22 May 1670. In fact, he had almost certainly decided this anyway, but he wished his sister to have the credit for changing his mind, which would enhance her standing at the French court and strengthen her hand in her ongoing struggle with her husband. On her return Monsieur was as cruel as ever and Madame was noted to be pale and very weak. On 19/29 June she complained of a violent pain in her side, immediately after drinking iced chicory water, and cried that she had been poisoned. She died at St Cloud in the small hours of the following day. Louis, anxious to dispel the rumours of poison, ordered a very public autopsy, after which a number of doctors, French and English, declared that she had died of natural causes; more modern research suggests that the cause was acute peritonitis following the perforation of a duodenal ulcer. She was buried, alongside her mother and many kings and queens of France, at St Denis on 11/21 August.   JOHN MILLER

Sources C. H. Hartmann, *Charles II and Madame* (1934) • *Report on the manuscripts of his grace the duke of Buccleuch and Queensberry … preserved at Montagu House*, 3 vols. in 4, HMC, 45 (1899–1926), vol. 1 • M. de la Vergne [Madame de la Fayette], *Histoire de Madame Henriette d'Angleterre* (Amsterdam, 1720); repr. (Paris, 1925) • J. Miller, *Charles II* (1991) • *The life of James the Second, king of England*, ed. J. S. Clarke, 2 vols. (1816) • Pepys, *Diary* • F. A. M. Mignet, *Négociations relatives à la succession d'Espagne*, 4 vols. (1835–42) • *Memoirs of Sir John Reresby*, ed.

A. Browning, 2nd edn, ed. M. K. Geiter and W. A. Speck (1991) • correspondence of the French ambassadors in London, Archives du Ministère des Relations Extérieures, Quai d'Orsay, Paris [incomplete transcription in PRO, PRO 31/3] • correspondance politique, Angleterre, Archives du Ministère des Relations Extérieures, Quai d'Orsay, Paris
Archives Archives du Ministère des Relations Extérieures, Quai d'Orsay, Paris, mémoires et documents, France, vol. 26 • LPL, MS 645 • PRO, state papers, France
Likenesses C. Mellan, drawing, c.1655, BM; repro. in R. Norrington, ed., *My dearest Minette: the letters between Charles II and his sister Henrietta, duchesse d'Orléans* (1996) • P. Lely, oils, c.1660, Goodwood House, West Sussex • J. M. Wright, oils, c.1660–1670, Royal Collection • P. Mignard, oils, after 1661, Versailles, France; version, NPG • H. Gascar, oils, c.1661–1670, Goodwood House, West Sussex • A. Mathieu, oils, c.1661–1670, Versailles, France • P. Lely, portrait, c.1662, NPG [*see illus.*] • P. Mignard, oils, Scot. NPG • oils (as Minerva), Royal Collection • portrait (after P. Lely), Goodwood House, West Sussex • portrait (after S. Cooper), Exeter Guildhall; presented by Charles II, 1672 • portrait (after Mignard), NPG

Henrion, (Frederick) Henri Kay [*formerly* Heinrich Fritz Kohn] (1914–1990), graphic designer, was born on 18 April 1914 at Nuremberg, Germany, the son of Max Kohn, a solicitor, and his wife, Paula, *née* Rosenau (d. 1965). His parents were Franco-German.

After leaving the Melanchthon Gymnasium in 1933 Henrion chose neither to follow his father's profession nor to remain in antisemitic Germany. Instead he went to Paris, where he slaved away for a while in a textile-design sweatshop and then studied in the studio of the well-known poster designer Paul Colin. Another important influence was A. J.-M. M. Cassandre, to whose studio he was about to transfer when in 1936 his plans changed and he came instead to England, aged twenty-two, already with a vitality, a taste for the avant-garde, and a whiff of cosmopolitanism foreign to the placid British design world of the 1930s. He was one of the immigrant designers and typographers like George Him, Hans Schleger, Jan Tschichold, and Berthold Wolpe who settled here and between them radically changed British ideas about design.

Henrion set to work in this country making posters and designing a notable exhibition for the Modern Architectural Research (MARS) Group of architects, learning how as he went along. During the war, after a spell of internment, he worked for the Ministry of Information (his admirably simple and telling photomontage posters, 'Dig for Victory', 'Aid the Wounded', and 'Grow More Food', were pinned up at this writer's school; others warned about poison gas and VD). Later in the war he also worked for the US office of war information and in advertising, designing pastiche surrealist press ads for the fashion firm Harella and magazine covers for Harpers. After the war he turned briefly to publishing, as art director of George Weidenfeld's Contact Books with panache, and again to exhibitions, designing two striking pavilions—Agriculture and The Country—for the Festival of Britain, that optimistic and un-dumbed-down celebration of the resurgent national identity. He had another go at advertising, with the American agency Erwin Wasey, but eventually turned to the pioneering work in the burgeoning sphere of corporate identity with which he became most

(Frederick) Henri Kay Henrion (1914–1990), by Wolfgang Suschitzky, 1955

closely identified: co-ordinating every visual aspect of corporate existence from letterheads to lorries and from airliners to boarding cards. He was confident and enthusiastic for change and for making new connections; and the time was right. His clients included British European Airways (BEA), KLM, London Electricity, Girobank, Fisons, the Festival Hall, the National Theatre, and the Post Office. His best logos and symbols for these organizations became classics; those for BEA and British Airways look better than any of their successors. But the symbols were only signals of a task whose scale was so vast that he had to build up his studio until, as Henrion Design Associates and Henrion Design International, he eventually employed some twenty-five people. And compared with his earlier posters, much of the work of corporate identity was impersonal and anonymous.

But there were other sides to Henrion. He was also a tireless and idealistic promoter of the respectability and seriousness of design, through the Artists' International Association, the Society of Industrial Artists and Designers (later the Chartered Society of Designers), and the Council of Industrial Design; in 1952 he became one of the earliest members of AGI (Alliance Graphique Internationale), in which designers from all over the world could make common cause; he was elected a royal designer for industry in 1959 and later became the faculty's master. In all these quasi-public roles he was genial but incisive. He also taught, with *élan* and charm, at the Royal College of Art and the London College of Printing. He was kind, encouraging, and cultivated, though he could be sharply

exacting if anyone was being sloppy or lazy. And he had wide interests—he experimented with product and three-dimensional design and jewellery, and he painted. And he had an interesting circle—his work had brought him into contact with an odd assortment of people including Julian Huxley, Nigel Nicolson, Walter Neurath, Tony Benn, Richard Rogers—and he in turn widened many young designers' horizons by setting up the Icograda student seminars at which distinguished European and American designers could show and explain their work to cinema-capacity student audiences.

Henrion had started off as a solitary and alien poster artist in a now-vanished tradition, but he had the flair to adapt to a changing and increasingly commercial world. His early achievements lay in surviving, adapting, and even flourishing in a sceptical and insular country still more at home with words than images, and also in stabilizing and gaining respect for the then fledgeling design profession, never especially keen to organize itself. Later, having mastered the technique of creating corporate identities for large organizations, and becoming in the process a businessman as well as an artist, he inevitably had to suppress some of his initial graphic adventurousness and individuality; yet he retained a faith, even into the market-driven eighties when to many such a conviction seemed incomprehensible, that design had a social role and a purpose beyond money-making. But perhaps his most enduring achievement lay in teaching and helping students and young designers, by setting up useful institutions for them, by his own example, and by his friendliness and humanity. Henrion was appointed MBE in 1951, OBE in 1985.

In appearance Henrion was informal but elegant, of medium height; his face aquiline, his expression wry and amused, his style more Gallic than Teutonic—warm, vigorous, and with a hint of self-mockery. He was firm when he had to be, but not assertive; intellectually curious, as a non-practising Jew without religious belief; without apparent hang-ups, and with a lightness of touch that prevented him from being pretentious or complacent. He said he found his permanent feeling of insecurity a useful spur.

Henrion was married twice. His first marriage, from April 1947 to 1980, was to the distinguished sculptor Daphne Hardy (*b.* 1917); her spirit is echoed in his more graphic posters and in the confident modelling of the plaster trees in his festival pavilions. They had two sons, Max and Paul, and a daughter, Emma, to whom he was a good and affectionate father. His second marriage, from 18 January 1990 until his death, was to Marion Wesel (*b.* 1936), already for many years his close companion, who brought youth and great personal warmth, as well as a clear-headed European outlook, into his later life. Marion and Henri were warm hosts to many parties of artists and designers, often from abroad, in the metal and glass studio behind their Georgian brick house in Hampstead. This writer remembers him also during his last illness, in his bedroom by the garden window, by now dying but courageous and wry as ever, and still interested in work, his family, and his friends. Henrion died of cancer of the liver at his house at 35 Pond Street, Hampstead, on 5 July 1990. He was cremated at Golders Green crematorium a few days later.   DAVID GENTLEMAN

Sources personal knowledge (2004) · private information (2004) [Marion Henrion] · F. H. K. Henrion, *AGI annals: Alliance graphique internationale, 1952–1987* (Zürich and Tokyo, 1989) · F. H. K. Henrion, *Five decades a designer* (1989) [exhibition catalogue, Flakman Gallery, Staffordshire Polytechnic, Stoke-on-Trent]
Archives University of Brighton, archive | RSA, royal designer for industry boxes
Likenesses W. Suschitzky, photograph, 1955, NPG [*see illus.*] · photograph, Hult. Arch. · photograph, repro. in *RSA Journal* (Oct 1990)
Wealth at death £928,231: probate, 29 Nov 1990, *CGPLA Eng. & Wales*

Henriques, Sir Basil Lucas Quixano (1890–1961), founder of youth clubs and magistrate, was born in London on 17 October 1890, the youngest of the five children of David Quixano Henriques, who had an import and export company in Manchester and London, and his wife, Agnes C. Lucas, who was a great-niece of Sir Moses H. Montefiore. The family of Quixano Henriques, originally Sephardi Jews from Portugal, settled in Jamaica. They achieved some prominence, holding minor office in the legal and military establishment of the island. In the nineteenth century one branch of the family transferred its considerable import and export business to England. There was, therefore, ample wealth to sustain the family of David Henriques in a lifestyle of comfort and elegance and to provide for Basil and his wife a modest investment income throughout their lives.

Like his elder brothers, Henriques was sent to Harrow School (1904–7), but he was not a great scholar and he left before obtaining a place at Oxford. Careful tuition at home and abroad did, however, produce the desired result and he entered University College, Oxford, in 1909. Once again he found difficulty in facing the world of books and barely managed to get a degree, obtaining a third class in history in 1913. The other side of Oxford, however—its wealth of personalities, of ideas, and of social theories—was the formative influence in his life. Two people in particular contributed to his development and to the shape of his future: one was Alexander H. Paterson and the other Claude J. G. Montefiore. Paterson and his social theories were fairly new to Henriques but the writings of Montefiore and his work for the liberalization of Jewish ritual and practice in England was part of his family background. His mother was related to the Montefiores and was herself immersed in the liberal tradition. But British Jews in the early part of the twentieth century were deeply divided in the matter of their religious practices. The strict orthodoxy of some, particularly those more recently arrived from Europe, was seen by liberal intellectuals as a barrier to the Anglicization which they wished to achieve for all Jews who found a home in England. Moreover, many members of old-established Jewish families had come to admire the Anglican tradition and to appreciate the social cohesion brought about by the use of

a rich living language in the everyday liturgy of the English church. Claude Montefiore was the chief spokesman for those who held these views. One of his books, *The Bible for Home Reading* (2 pts, 1896 and 1899), came into the hands of Henriques while he was still at Harrow; it impressed him deeply. At Oxford he threw himself into the liberal Jewish movement, organizing English–Hebrew services and rousing sluggish and uninterested undergraduates to co-operate with him. He showed his capacity for persuasion by joining with Claude Montefiore and the chief rabbi to promote the establishment of an academic post in rabbinical studies. The first holder of this post was Herbert M. J. Loewe, who became Henriques's brother-in-law.

This lifelong interest in the religious life of British Jews was the Mount Sion of Henriques's intellectual and emotional perspective. His Parnassus was the study and practice of club work among underprivileged boys and young men. The source of this enthusiasm was the work of Alec Paterson, who, although he was living in the East End of London, maintained his links with Oxford and came up frequently to talk to undergraduates about his club and its members. Henriques, convinced that such social intervention was necessary and indeed admirable, went to stay at the Oxford and Bermondsey Mission, and decided, as a result of this experience, that social work, and particularly club work, was to be his profession. His family at first opposed him. He persuaded them, however, that he had no other ambition and they agreed to support him, suggesting at the same time that he should concentrate his energies on work among East End Jews whom he might help to 'Anglicize' by the provision of the kind of social service he had in mind. Thus his two interests became one and he spent the rest of his life among the Jewish people of Commercial Road and Berner Street (later renamed Henriques Street) as club leader and magistrate.

Henriques had no easy task; the boys to whom he first offered club membership were mostly the sons of first-generation Jewish immigrants from Russia, Latvia, Poland, and parts of eastern Europe. Some of them were resolutely Jewish, speaking no English and refusing to give up their strict orthodoxy. Others, particularly the Russian Jews, already possessed, or were easily converted to, the revolutionary views that had been preached in the political and industrial organizations which flourished at the turn of the century in the Jewish East End. To both these groups the religious component of Henriques's social programme must have seemed unwelcome. He himself was aware of the conflict between the religious orthodoxy of the immigrant and the liberal practices he taught in his club. He does not seem to have appreciated the irony that the very street where his settlement was founded and which was later to bear his name had been the centre of the activities of the Russian Jewish anarchists. His first club, the Oxford and St George's in the East Jewish Boys Club, was opened in March 1914—an inauspicious time for innovations. Henriques joined the army (the 3rd battalion of the East Kent regiment) in 1915 but exercised a kind of remote control over his club through his wife,

Rose Louise, daughter of James H. Loewe, a linguist and at one time secretary of the Jewish Colonial Trust, and granddaughter of Louis Loewe, linguist. They were married in 1916. Since she had founded the girls' club, at whose centre she remained for more than thirty years, she was already part of the organization. There were no children of the marriage.

In the First World War, Henriques's first commission was held in the Buffs, but he was seconded in 1916 to the newly formed tank corps (the heavy branch of the machine-gun corps). He was wounded in the first tank attack on the Somme in 1916 and returned to England. Later, as reconnaissance officer, he showed great skill and bravery, was twice mentioned in dispatches, and gained the Italian silver medal.

When the war was over Henriques returned to the Oxford and St George's Club, but the original buildings were too small to house the new activities he had in mind. With courage and determination he set out to find money for premises in which there could be a meeting-place for older club members, a luncheon club for social workers and teachers, a room for religious services, and the various club rooms for the boys and girls for whom this whole enterprise had been undertaken. The Jewish community, particularly the liberals of the older British families, supported him generously. Having founded his settlement Henriques remained there for more than thirty years, stimulating its development and directing its gradual moves from the original cramped premises to the spacious Bernhard Baron St George's Jewish settlement in Berner Street. He retired as warden in 1947.

Although Henriques always fostered self-government in his boys' and girls' clubs, he was by nature something of an autocrat, with firm opinions, which he expressed with great force. With his usual skill he had himself made a magistrate in 1924 and served faithfully on the bench until he retired in 1955. Since his club work was primarily with young people, he had some share in the discussions that preceded the setting up of the new 'welfare' juvenile courts in 1933. It is arguable that Henriques found his greatest enjoyment in sitting as chairman of the east London juvenile court, to which he was elected in 1936. There was, of course, a difference between those who came to the settlement (well-intentioned and aspiring Jewish families) and those who appeared in the juvenile court. Henriques himself was fond of saying that the strength of Jewish family life, its habits of prayer and sobriety, helped to prevent delinquency. Those who knew him as a magistrate, therefore, while admiring his firm kindliness, noted that his understanding of some of the problems of young offenders and their families, and, in particular, of young girls and women, was limited by his experience and his imagination. Nevertheless, as magistrate, settlement warden, and social worker, he remained an important figure in the world of the London East End poor.

The final human judgement upon Henriques must be made in the two areas of his endeavour. As social worker, club leader, and magistrate he gave himself entirely to those whom he sought to serve, striving at the same time to impose his own standards of self-control and moral rectitude upon people who had no share in the kind of upbringing which produced them. To all his practical work, however, there was another dimension, his Liberal Judaism. He was tireless in his efforts to modernize and simplify the Jewish rituals. If this were done, he believed, not only would the Jewish faith survive among later generations of British Jews, but the Anglicizing of immigrant Jews would be easier to achieve. Since his own identification with the British state was complete, he was doubtful about the establishment of a Jewish state, fearing that nationality would take the place of religion among members of the Jewish community. Thus the foundation of the state of Israel was not, for him, an undiluted blessing, nor did he think it should be for any British Jew who was already a citizen of a proud empire. With these simple but strong beliefs in righteousness, religious practice, civic duty, and national pride Henriques attempted the kind of social work which was characteristic of the first part of the twentieth century. Such ideas and style of social work did not survive into the second part.

In appearance Henriques was majestic—6 feet 3 inches in height and broad-shouldered. In his early years he had a shock of fair hair, which thinned and silvered fairly rapidly, but he was an upright, strong figure until just before his death.

His written work was considerable, although much of it is merely of historical interest. Among his books were *Club Leadership* (1933, reprinted thrice), *The Indiscretions of a Warden* (1937), *The Religion of the Jew* (with A. Marmorstein, 1946), *The Indiscretions of a Magistrate* (1950), *Fratres, Club Boys in Uniform* (1951), *Club Leadership Today* (1951), *The Home-Menders: the Prevention of Unhappiness in Children* (1955), and pamphlets on Judaism, juvenile delinquency, boys' clubs, and printed sermons and prayers.

Henriques was appointed CBE in 1948 and knighted on his retirement from the east London juvenile court in 1955. He died in the Prince of Wales General Hospital, Tottenham, Middlesex, on 2 December 1961.

SARAH McCABE, *rev.*

Sources L. Loewe, *Basil Henriques: a portrait* (1976) · *The Times* (4 Dec 1961) · *The Magistrate*, 18 (1962) · W. J. Fishman, *East End Jewish radicals, 1875–1914* (1975) · private information (1981) · personal knowledge (1981) · CGPLA Eng. & Wales (1962) · WWW

Archives U. Southampton L., corresp., papers; articles, memorial lectures, notebook, photographs

Likenesses J. Mendoza, oils, 1955, East London juvenile court, Bow Road, London

Wealth at death £65,630 11s. 9d.: probate, 5 March 1962, CGPLA Eng. & Wales

Henriques, Pauline Clothilde (1914–1998), actress and broadcaster, was born on 1 April 1914 in Half Way Tree, Kingston, Jamaica, one of the six children of Cyril Charles Henriques, an import and export merchant, and his wife, Edith Emily. Her father wanted his children to have an English education and moved his family to London, settling in St John's Wood in 1919 when Pauline was five. One of her brothers, Sir Cyril George Xavier Henriques (1908–1982), became lord chief justice of Jamaica; he was knighted in 1963. Another, (Louis) Fernando Henriques

(1916–1976), was president of the Oxford Union in 1944 and became professor of social anthropology at Sussex University.

The Henriques family were passionately interested in theatre, and Pauline gained early acting experience when her family gathered together to read plays at home. In 1932, encouraged by her parents, she joined a drama course at the London Academy of Music and Dramatic Art. She later recalled:

> I had an English accent which was perfect for 'classic' roles. The course lasted for one year, and I appeared in many school productions, but I had to play my parts in white face, including Lady Bracknell and Lady Macbeth! I went along with it because I was very anxious to learn my craft, and to be taken seriously as a dramatic actress … However, after leaving drama school, I finished up with comic black maids and one line—'Yessum. I'sa coming!'—which I learned to express about eighteen different ways! (Bourne, 127)

On 4 June 1936 she married Geoffrey William Henebery (b. 1908/9), an insurance clerk, son of Patrick Henebery, a postal clerk. They had one daughter.

During the Second World War Henriques worked as an actress and producer with the Carlisle Little Theatre, and began a long association with the radio series *Caribbean Voices*, broadcast on the BBC's West Indian Service. In 1946 she became one of the first black actresses to appear on British television when she played Hattie in Eugene O'Neill's *All God's Chillun Got Wings*. The BBC's television service was still in its infancy when she made this historic live broadcast from Alexandra Palace; she later recalled:

> It was wonderful because theatre came into the sitting rooms of television viewers, but for an actor it was tremendously difficult to do because everything was transmitted live … Also, we only had one television camera and it was static. It was fixed to the studio floor and didn't move. So the actors had to remember to keep in shot all the time, and yet a sort of magic came out of this chaos. (Bourne, 126)

Ten years later she acted in another ground-breaking BBC drama, *A Man from the Sun*, television's first look at Caribbean settlers in post-war Britain.

Away from the BBC, Henriques pursued her first love, theatre. In 1947 *Anna Lucasta*, an American play with a black cast, successfully transferred from Broadway to London. Running for almost two years, it offered understudy work to several British black actors, including Henriques. She formed the understudies into the Negro Theatre Company, which staged several productions of its own. Her biggest break in the theatre came in 1950 when Kenneth Tynan cast her as Emilia in an Arts Council tour of Shakespeare's *Othello* with the African-American actor Gordon Heath playing the Moor. Meanwhile, her first marriage having ended in divorce in 1948, she married, on 25 October that year, the actor Neville Cobblah Crabbe (b. 1922/3), son of Andrew Nyaku Kwesi Crabbe, a barrister. They had one son.

In the mid-1950s Henriques began a new career in social work. She later explained 'I grew tired of playing American maids and I needed to have a full-time career' (Bourne, 129). She worked first for the London Council of Social Service, then for the National Council for the Unmarried Mother and her Child. Her second marriage ended in divorce in 1960, and on 26 November 1969 she married Joseph Benjamin (1920/21–1995), a social worker, and son of Samuel Benjamin. She became secretary of the London Brook Advisory Centre in 1971. In 1969 abortion had become legal, and she insisted that anyone requesting an abortion should have counselling, previously a medical decision. She also insisted that any expectant mother under sixteen should be counselled to find out, for instance, whether they had been abused. From then on counselling became an integral part of Brook Advisory work.

In 1966 Henriques became Britain's first black woman magistrate, and in 1969 she was appointed OBE. After retiring, she took part in several television documentaries, and ran a playwriting group for the University of the Third Age near her home in Brighton. She died at the Royal Sussex County Hospital, Brighton, on 1 November 1998, of heart failure. She was survived by the daughter of her first marriage and the son of her second, her third husband, Joseph Benjamin, having predeceased her.

STEPHEN BOURNE

Sources S. Bourne, *Black in the British frame: black people in British film and television, 1896–1996* (1998) • J. Pines, ed., *Black and white in colour: black people in British television since 1936* (1992) • *The Independent* (21 Nov 1998) • personal knowledge (2004) • m. certs. • d. cert.
Likenesses photograph, 1950, repro. in Bourne, *Black in the British frame*, following p. 116 • photograph, 1952, repro. in *The Independent*

Henrisoun, James (d. before 1570), merchant and propagandist, was apparently a native of Edinburgh and by 1527 owned land on the south side of the High Street. He made his living principally by trading to the Low Countries, where he bought military supplies for the crown. In this he co-operated with Francis Aikman, another Edinburgh burgess who was also a protestant, and he came to share Aikman's religious beliefs. He made repeated efforts to secure the position of conservator of Scottish privileges in the Netherlands, and eventually did so on 16 January 1543 from the second earl of Arran, the governor of Scotland, who was then inclined towards protestantism, but he lost it again the following year; in May 1544, as the regime became increasingly Catholic, Henrisoun presented himself to Edward Seymour, earl of Hertford, during the earl's assault on Edinburgh (when Henrisoun's own house was burnt) and asked to be taken into the service of Henry VIII. Consequently he went to London with the English army as it returned home, and as 'James Harryson, Scottishman' was recorded in March 1546 as 'received to the King's service with a gift of 200 crowns by year', which was then twelve months in arrears (*LP Henry VIII*, vol. 21, pt 1, no. 462).

After three years in obscurity Henrisoun's time came following the old king's death, when Seymour, now duke of Somerset and lord protector, adopted a much more forward Scottish policy. Henry had made little use of propaganda, but under Somerset five significant pieces were printed and circulated, and Henrisoun had a major hand in at least three of them. The most important was the first, *An exhortacion to the Scottes to conforme them selfes to the honorable, expedient, and godly union betwene the twoo realmes of Englande and Scotlande* (ESTC, 12857), probably written in summer 1547 to accompany the English campaign which culminated in Somerset's great victory at Pinkie on 10 September. Dedicated to the protector, it formed part of an English attempt to persuade the Scots to agree to the provisions of the treaty of Greenwich of 1543, which had stipulated that Queen Mary was to marry Prince Edward (now Edward VI) in 1553. In an argument which makes massive use of the word 'Britain' (about 100 appearances) Henrisoun argues that the island had once formed a political unity and urges that for its inhabitants the single word 'Briton' should be substituted for the 'hatefull termes of Scottes and Englishmen' (*Exhortacion*, 228). There is heavy stress on the material benefits which will flow from union and emphasis too on how such a marriage can help the two countries to 'agre in the concorde & unite of one religion, & the same the pure, syncere & incorrupt religion of christ' (ibid., 231).

Two further treatises followed soon afterwards. In September 1547 came a *Proclamation* (ESTC, 7811) and in February 1548 *An epistle or exhortacion, to unite & peace* (ESTC, 9181). Both urge the Scots to commit themselves to union with England through the marriage of Mary and Edward while simultaneously rejecting links with France and the papacy, and each stresses English magnanimity and the likely gains for the Scots. No author is named, but it seems certain that Henrisoun was closely involved in their production. Then in July 1548 he submitted to the king 'The godly and golden booke for concorde of England and Scotland' (PRO, SP 50/4, fols. 128–37), an even more radical manifesto of the benefits which Scotland will enjoy through union with England. As well as swifter justice, a revitalization of the personnel and structure of the church, and security of tenure for 'poor labourers of the grounde', Henrisoun advocates instruction for the Scots in a range of modern skills, such as mining, draining marshlands, and making sawmills, and the provision of 100 ships, along with an equal number of instructors, to revive the fishing industry in the Scottish ports. There was even to be a canal 'to drawe the weste and easte sees together so that partable vessles shall goo between' (Merriman, *Rough Wooings*, 284). By now, however, continued Scottish resistance was causing Somerset to lose interest in proposals for peaceful union. Henrisoun, by contrast, appears to have believed in the cause he was promoting and in 1549 remonstrated at length with the protector over the counter-productive ravages now being inflicted by English armies on lowland Scotland.

Following Somerset's fall from power in October 1549 Henrisoun found himself without either patron or employment and complained to the privy council of the government's ingratitude and neglect, threatening to detail his misfortunes in print. He had lost his burgess status in Edinburgh by 1546 and his property in the town in 1549. Approaches to fellow Scots, and even to Mary of Guise, brought no result. Restoration and rehabilitation

finally came from an unforeseeable direction. In April 1551 Robert Stewart, a member of the king of France's Scots guard, arrived in London and sought out the duke of Northumberland, now head of the English government, with a plot so extraordinary that at first he would not divulge the details to Northumberland, but revealed them to Henrisoun instead, thinking him to be 'un bon Anglois' (Merriman, 'James Henrisoun', 100). A kinsman of her cook, Stewart had easy access to Queen Mary's kitchen, and he proposed to put poison in the young queen's food. Henrisoun promptly revealed Stewart's scheming, the would-be assassin was arrested and transported to France and execution, and the whistle-blower reaped his reward.

By January 1553 Henrisoun was back in Scotland, enjoying a pension from Mary of Guise, and on 21 May 1554 he was once more made conservator of Scottish privileges in the Low Countries. Failing health meant that he had to employ a deputy, but on 30 October 1555 he was made overseer of the crown's mines and fishings, for his services 'in conservatioun of hir hienes persoun the tyme he was in Ingland' (*Register of the Privy Seal*, 1548–56, no. 3068). Meanwhile he remained intellectually vigorous. On 7 October 1552 he presented a set of strikingly original proposals for the regeneration of Edinburgh, including a school, a playground, a covered market, piped water to four fountains, and a new town hall, or tollbooth. Many of these suggestions progressed from Henrisoun's drawing-board into reality, none so dramatically as his remarkable vision of a new hospital with 'ane priest, ane surrigiane, ane meddicinar, and 40 beddis' (Merriman, 'James Henrisoun', 102). By 1562 contributions were being collected (Henrisoun himself gave money) and construction began in 1567, to be completed in 1578. Henrisoun lived to see only the beginning of the work, since he appears to have been dead by 1570.   MARCUS MERRIMAN

Sources M. H. Merriman, 'James Henrisoun and "Great Britain": British union and the Scottish commonweal', *Scotland and England, 1286–1815*, ed. R. A. Mason (1987), 85–112 • M. Merriman, *The rough wooings: Mary queen of Scots, 1542–1551* (2000) • *LP Henry VIII*, vol. 21/1 • M. Livingstone, D. Hay Fleming, and others, eds., *Registrum secreti sigilli regum Scotorum / The register of the privy seal of Scotland*, 4 (1952) • *CSP Scot.*, 1547–63 • ESTC

Henry [Henry of Huntingdon] (*c*.1088–*c*.1157), historian and poet, was the son of an unnamed Englishwoman and a Norman clerk, Nicholas, who was archdeacon of Huntingdon and canon of Lincoln from the late 1070s to his death in 1110. Although Henry is commonly called Henry of Huntingdon, there is no authority for the toponymic: Huntingdon was the title of the archdeaconry in which he succeeded his father in 1110. As he was a kinsman of William de Glanville, the founder of Broomholm Priory, Norfolk, his father, Nicholas, was perhaps a son of Robert de Glanville, a Norfolk subtenant in 1086, whose origin was the Norman village of Glanville (Seine-Maritime). Henry's early childhood was spent in the fenland, probably at Little Stukeley, Huntingdonshire, which was a tenancy of the abbot of Ramsey. Little Stukeley was to be Henry's home and that of three generations of his descendants.

The name of Henry's wife is unknown. His son, Master Adam of Stukeley, a clerk, succeeded him as tenant of Little Stukeley, and was in turn succeeded by the elder of his two sons, Master Aristotle, also a clerk, whose own son Nicholas of Stukeley, another clerk, surrendered Little Stukeley to the abbot of Ramsey c.1230.

In the 1090s Henry was taken to Lincoln by his father and became acquainted with members of the cathedral chapter, including Master Albinus of Angers, probably master of the schools at Lincoln, who taught him grammar and rhetoric. He was brought up in the household of Bishop Robert Bloet (d. 1123), and in 1110 was promoted by him to his father's archdeaconry, which he held until his death some time between October 1156 and 1165, probably c.1157. As archdeacon of Huntingdonshire and Hertfordshire he was active in ecclesiastical affairs, both locally and nationally, and was well placed to gain information on political events.

Alexander the Magnificent (d. 1148), who succeeded Bloet as bishop of Lincoln in 1123, was claimed by Henry as the patron of his major work, the Historia Anglorum ('The history of the English people'). By 1130 Henry had completed a first version, comprising seven books, which covered the period between the invasions of Julius Caesar and the year 1129. He continued to write, revising and adding to the work until just before his death. The final version consisted of ten books, taking the historical narrative down to the coronation of Henry II in 1154.

The Historia Anglorum has a moral purpose, presenting a strongly thematic narrative in which the five invasions of Britain—by the Romans, the Picts and Scots, the Angles and Saxons, the Danes, and the Normans—are seen as five punishments or plagues inflicted by God on a faithless people. The account of the Anglo-Saxon invasions is focused on the setting up of seven kingdoms, a concept—the heptarchy—which was adopted by later historians, and survived until it was discredited in the 1980s.

The chief source for the early sections of the Historia, down to 731, was Bede's Historia ecclesiastica, which Henry used in substantial verbatim quotations and in précis. This was supplemented by material taken from the Historia Brittonum (in the 'Vatican recension'), by quotations on the Roman emperors from Paul the Deacon's Historia Romana, and, in book 9 on 'The miracles of the English', by notes from saints' lives. The other major written source was the Anglo-Saxon Chronicle, Henry's translation of which, though not without errors, shows considerable skill: in his Latin version of the poem on Brunanburh he imitated the stress patterns, alliteration, and rhyme of the original. He had access to at least two versions—one very close to the surviving Peterborough version, E, and another linked to the Abingdon version, C. Other material was drawn from a lost version of the chronicle which was also available to John of Worcester, another historian of the early twelfth century. On six occasions in the narrative Henry incorporated his translations from lost Old English poetry. English oral tradition provided dramatic stories for the first half of the eleventh century, such as the legend of Cnut and the waves and anecdotes about Earl Siward. French vernacular chansons seem to lie behind stories about early Normandy and about Taillefer at the battle of Hastings. For his account of the first crusade, Henry used the Gesta Francorum, probably in an epitome.

Book 8 contains three pieces in epistolary form. Two of these expand the chronological scope of the Historia. The first is addressed to Henry I, though it was not completed until four years after the king's death. The subject is 'the succession of the most powerful kings who have flourished throughout the whole world from the beginning of history to this present time' (Historia Anglorum, ed. Greenway, 503). The line of kings is traced from Peleg, the fifth generation from Noah, down to the emperor of Henry's own day, Conrad III (r. 1138–52). The chief source is Bede's Chronica maiora (a universal chronicle contained in his De temporibus), supplemented by extracts from the chronicle of Marianus Scottus. The second letter, addressed to a certain Warin the Breton, concerns 'the origin of the British kings who reigned in this country down to the coming of Julius Caesar, or else of the English people' (Historia Anglorum, 503). Its source is Geoffrey of Monmouth's Historia regum Britanniae, which Henry was shown at Bec in 1139 by the historian Robert de Torigni, when Henry stopped there on the way to Rome with Archbishop Theobald (d. 1161).

For events in his own lifetime Henry used an E-type version of the Anglo-Saxon Chronicle down to 1133, adding his own observations and information drawn from his contemporaries. He was particularly well informed on events in the royal court in 1122–3, 1127–8, and 1130–33: he may have been present in the company of the bishop of Lincoln. Vivid personal recollections of some of the leading personalities of Henry I's reign form the core of the letter De contemptu mundi, one of the components of book 8, composed between 1135 and c.1138. To conclude his summary of the miracles of English saints, written no later than c.1140, Henry gave an account of Wulfric of Haselbury, who lived until 1155: this predated John of Forde's Life of Wulfric by more than forty years. From 1133 to the end of the Historia, in 1154, the material is all in some sense 'original', though Henry's rhetorical preoccupations tend to put a coloured filter over his eyewitness observations. His report of the battle of Lincoln in 1141, for example, is largely taken up with fictitious speeches put into the mouths of the leading combatants. Henry's poems, which form an important element in the Historia Anglorum, being inserted to heighten the drama at twenty-four points in the narrative, occupy more space in book 10, covering the reign of King Stephen (1135–54), than in any of the earlier books.

In addition to the poems written for inclusion in the Historia, Henry composed eight books of epigrams (six jocunda and two seria). Only the two books of serious epigrams survive, and appear in some manuscripts as books 11 and 12 of the Historia Anglorum. They were influenced by Martial, and also by the Loire poets Marbod and Hildebert, to whose work Henry had probably been introduced by his Angevin master at Lincoln. His poems are of special interest for their use of varied and unusual metres. His poem on herbs, to which he alludes in *De contemptu mundi* and from which Leland quotes four lines, consists of four books, with more than 160 poems in over 6000 lines; many poems are based on Macer, but others demonstrate Henry's literary imagination. According to Leland, Henry was the author of books, now lost, presumably in verse, on spices and gems. Leland also records lost prose works: on the law of God, on Psalm 118 (probably a sermon), and a little book on weights and measures.

The *Historia Anglorum* enjoyed a wide circulation in the middle ages. About forty medieval manuscripts survive, chiefly from English centres and a few from Normandy, with isolated copies from Ireland, Wales, and Scotland. They reveal a complex textual tradition of six authorial versions, two of which were twice further redacted. The work exercised a powerful influence on English historiography. Already before Henry's completion of his final version, a text extending to 1146, perhaps taken to France by Bishop Alexander, was absorbed by Robert de Torigni into his own chronicle, and passed thence into the annals of Waverley. A version ending in 1148 was used, before 1161, in the northern *Historia post obitum Bedae*, and from there was taken into Roger of Howden's chronicle and also later into the chronicle of Walter of Guisborough. A Crowland continuation of John of Worcester's chronicle incorporated a section of text of the final version of the *Historia Anglorum* from 1131 to 1154: this compilation received further continuations and came later to be known as the chronicle of Walter of Coventry. Other English historians who made major borrowings from the *Historia Anglorum* between the twelfth century and the fourteenth include William of Newburgh, Gervase of Canterbury, the Meaux chronicler, Roger of Wendover, Matthew Paris, the Norwich chronicler, and Ranulf Higden. But Henry's influence on later histories went deeper than a mere catalogue of 'borrowings' might suggest. Through his emphasis on the development of the kingdom of Wessex and the emergence of its rulers as sole kings of England, Henry gave English history an enduring shape and unity.   D. E. GREENWAY

Sources Henry, archdeacon of Huntingdon, *Historia Anglorum*, ed. D. E. Greenway, OMT (1996) · D. E. Greenway, 'Henry of Huntingdon and the manuscripts of his *Historia Anglorum*', *Anglo-Norman Studies*, 9 (1986), 103–26 · D. E. Greenway, 'Henry of Huntingdon and Bede', *L'historiographie médiévale en Europe*, ed. J. P. Genet (1991), 43–50 · D. E. Greenway, 'Authority, convention and observation in Henry of Huntingdon's *Historia Anglorum*', *Anglo-Norman Studies*, 18 (1995), 105–21 · *Henrici archidiaconi Huntendunensis historia Anglorum / The history of the English … from AD 55 to AD 1154*, ed. T. Arnold, Rolls Series, 74 (1879) · F. Liebermann, 'Heinrich von Huntingdon', *Forschungen zur Deutschen Geschichte*, 18 (1878), 265–95 · A. G. Rigg, 'Henry of Huntingdon's metrical experiments', *Journal of Medieval Latin*, 1 (1991), 60–72 · private information (2004) [A. G. Rigg, who is preparing a study of the poems on herbs, which he has identified in Prague MS Knihovni, Metr. Kap. 1359, and BL, Sloane MS 3468] **Archives** BL, Egerton MS 3668 · CCC Cam., MS 280

Henry, earl of Northumberland (*c.*1115–1152), prince, was the only surviving adult son of *David I (*c.*1085–1153), king of Scots, and his queen, *Maud (or Matilda) (*d.* 1131) [*see under* David I], widow of Simon (I) de Senlis. From *c.*1128 his name was linked with his father's in governance, and in

1144 he appears as *rex designatus* ('king-designate'). Although the exact significance of this style is unclear, it seems certain that he had formally been proclaimed as future king; and in practice from the 1130s 'David's was a dual reign … with joint or at least coadjutorial royal government' (Barrow, 'Charters', 34). This partnership—though Henry was self-evidently the junior partner—had momentous consequences for the Scots monarchy's power and prestige. Henry shared fully in David's policies of modernization by which Scotland began to be transformed into a European-style kingdom, and above all he was inseparably associated with his father in furthering historic Scottish claims to 'northern England'. Leading vast armies against King Stephen, they made extensive gains at his expense.

By the first treaty of Durham (February 1136) Henry was given Doncaster and the lordship of Carlisle, together with his mother's inheritance, the honour and earldom of Huntingdon, which had previously been held by David. However, he never seems to have styled himself earl of Huntingdon. Having done homage to Stephen at York, Henry took the place of honour at the king's right hand during the Easter court of 1136, whereupon Earl Ranulf (II) of Chester (who wanted Carlisle for himself) and possibly Henry's step-brother Simon (II) de Senlis (who nursed rival claims to the Huntingdon honour) withdrew from court in disgust. In January 1138, after Henry had vainly demanded from Stephen the earldom of Northumberland, Scottish assaults were renewed, and at the battle of the Standard (22 August 1138), despite the Scots' defeat, his bravery in leading a cavalry charge against the flank of the Yorkshire army was widely admired. By the second treaty of Durham (9 April 1139) Stephen confirmed or restored Henry's gains of 1136 and gave him Northumberland, albeit under strict safeguards to protect English sovereignty.

Almost immediately Henry married *Ada de Warenne (*c.*1123–1178), no doubt at Stephen's request, and then fought throughout the summer in his service. While besieging Ludlow Castle, Stephen rescued Henry from capture after he had been unhorsed, and in 1140 the king supplied an escort to thwart the earl of Chester's plans to entrap Henry on his way to Scotland. But the Scots deserted Stephen for good in the summer of 1141, when Henry's midland honour and earldom passed permanently to Simon (II) de Senlis. Thereafter Henry gave indispensable support to David in annexing the 'English' north to the Ribble and the Tees, or at least the Tyne, and ruling it in peace as an integral part of a greater Scoto-Northumbrian realm. He issued coins in his own name at Bamburgh, Carlisle, and Corbridge, and showed his sensitivity to local interests by endowing numerous religious houses. At Carlisle on 22 May 1149 he stood sponsor to Henry Plantagenet for his knighting, and offered to marry one of his own daughters to Chester's son in order finally to settle their differences. His last major act was to join with David in 1150 in founding a Cistercian house at Holmcultram, Cumberland, for monks from Melrose Abbey.

Northern English chroniclers acclaimed his kingly qualities and it was said that both English and Scots mourned his passing.

Henry's untimely death at the age of about thirty-seven—on which the earldom of Northumberland was assigned to the second of his three sons, the future King *William I (the Lion)—was a major blow for Scotland. When David died a year later, in 1153, his successor was not a mature, experienced heir, but a twelve-year-old boy-king, William's elder brother, *Malcolm IV; and in 1157 the Scots meekly withdrew to the Tweed–Solway line. Nevertheless, Scotland itself was a stronger kingdom, not least because vigorous exploitation of Cumberland silver had regenerated the Scottish economy, and any assessment of its emergence as a well-founded medieval state must recognize the key importance of Henry's legacy. Perhaps never robust in health, he almost succumbed to a serious illness in 1140, when his recovery was attributed to the miraculous intervention of a revered visitor to the Scottish court, the great Irish reformer St Malachy. Henry died on 12 June 1152, probably at Peebles, and was buried in Kelso Abbey. His youngest son *David was born in this same year. KEITH STRINGER

Sources A. O. Anderson, ed., *Scottish annals from English chroniclers, AD 500 to 1286* (1908); repr. (1991) • A. O. Anderson, ed. and trans., *Early sources of Scottish history, AD 500 to 1286*, 2 (1922); repr. with corrections (1990) • G. W. S. Barrow, ed., *The charters of King David I: the written acts of David I king of Scots, 1124–53, and of his son Henry earl of Northumberland, 1139–52* (1999) • G. W. S. Barrow, ed., *Regesta regum Scottorum*, 1 (1960) • G. W. S. Barrow, 'The charters of David I', *Anglo-Norman Studies*, 14 (1991), 25–37 • K. J. Stringer, 'State-building in twelfth-century Britain: David I, king of Scots, and northern England', *Government, religion and society in northern England, 1000–1700*, ed. J. C. Appleby and P. Dalton (1997), 40–62 • G. W. S. Barrow, 'The Scots and the north of England', *The anarchy of King Stephen's reign*, ed. E. King (1994), 231–53 • G. W. S. Barrow, 'King David I, Earl Henry and Cumbria', *Transactions of the Cumberland and Westmorland Antiquarian and Archaeological Society*, [new ser.], 99 (1999), 117–27 • I. Blanchard, 'Lothian and beyond: the economy of the "English empire" of David I', *Progress and problems in medieval England: essays in honour of Edward Miller*, ed. R. Britnell and J. Hatcher (1996), 23–45 • H. Summerson, *Medieval Carlisle: the city and the borders from the late eleventh to the mid-sixteenth century*, 1, Cumberland and Westmorland Antiquarian and Archaeological Society, extra ser., 25 (1993)
Likenesses coins, AM Oxf. • coins, BM • coins, National Museum of Antiquities of Scotland, Edinburgh • coins, NMG Wales • coins, Stavanger Museum, Norway • seals, U. Durham L., archives and special collections; repro. in Barrow, ed., *The charters of King David I*, pls. 16, 19–20

Henry [St Henry] (*fl.* 1156×60), bishop of Uppsala and missionary, was an Englishman by birth, who became bishop of Uppsala when St Erik was king of the Swedes (*r. c.*1156–1160). That Henry went to Sweden in the train of his fellow countryman, Nicholas Breakspear (the future Pope Adrian IV), whom Pope Eugenius III sent as legate to Scandinavia in 1152, and that he was consecrated by Nicholas, seems to be mere conjecture. Other connections could have led Henry to follow in the footsteps of those English churchmen who had been active among the peoples of Sweden, the Svear and the Götar, from at least the early eleventh century. Henry's earliest (thirteenth-century) biographer gives no details of his subject's English background. He

simply says that Henry and the king were the two great lights who illuminated their people in the way of true religion; that Henry assisted Erik in his reforms, both secular and ecclesiastical; that he accompanied him in an expedition against the heathen Finns, which resulted in the total defeat and subjection of the latter, the baptism of many converts, and the foundation of churches; and that when the king returned home in triumph, the bishop remained in Finland, until his zeal in enforcing the church's penitential discipline won him the crown of martyrdom at the hands of a disaffected convert. Archaeological evidence, however, suggests the presence of Christians in Finland before the mid-twelfth century and a more gradual exposure and transition to the new religion than the swift mass conversion of the population presented by this hagiographical tradition. Further, the partnership of King Erik and Bishop Henry in the so-called 'first crusade' to south-west Finland has been questioned, on the grounds that propaganda to that effect may have been manufactured to consolidate Swedish supremacy in the thirteenth century. Bishop Henry's position in Sweden and his ministrations among the Finns are not, however, challenged by this revisionist view.

No authority is known for the statement of the seventeenth-century Swedish Catholic writer Vastovius that Henry was canonized by Adrian IV in 1158 (Vastovius); but he was undoubtedly recognized in the fourteenth century, if not earlier, as the apostle of Finland and one of the patron saints of Sweden. Two festivals were kept in his honour: that of his martyrdom on 20 January (19 January in Sweden) and that of his translation on 18 June. The latter commemorated the removal in 1300 of his relics from their original burial place at Nousis, near Åbo, to the new cathedral church at Åbo itself, which was dedicated to him. L. ABRAMS

Sources 'Vita et miraculi S. Henrici', *Scriptores rerum Suecicarum medii aevi*, ed. E. M. Fant and others, 3 vols. in 6 (Uppsala, 1818–76), vol. 2, pt 1, pp. 331–5 • C. J. A. Oppermann, *The English missionaries in Sweden and Finland* (1937) • P. L. Lehtosalo-Hilander, 'The conversion of the Finns in western Finland', *The Christianization of Scandinavia*, ed. B. Sawyer and others (1987), 31–5 • J. Vastovius, *Vitis aquilonia, seu, Vitae sanctorum que Scandinauiam*, ed. E. Benzelius (Uppsala, 1708), 65

Henry [Henry the Young King] (1155–1183), prince, was the second son of *Henry II and *Eleanor of Aquitaine. Born in London on 28 February 1155, he became heir to the throne of England in December 1156, when his elder brother, William, died. He had three younger brothers: the future *Richard I (1157–1199), *Geoffrey, duke of Brittany (1158–1186), and *John (1167–1216); and three sisters: *Matilda (1156–1189), Eleanor (*b.* 1161), and *Joanna (1165–1199). In 1158, when four years old, Henry was betrothed to Margaret, the six-month-old daughter of Louis VII of France and Constanza of Castile. The marriage was ratified in October 1160 and rushed through in November by Henry II, who wished to acquire control over the Norman Vexin, her dowry. The union produced one child, who was born and died in 1177.

In 1162 the young Henry was sent to be educated in the

household of Thomas *Becket, at that time chancellor of England. Becket became fond of the boy and spoke of him as his adoptive son, but by the end of 1163 Henry had been removed from his care: appointed archbishop of Canterbury in 1162, Becket had already fallen foul of the king over the right to try criminous clerks. Despite his subsequent reputation for impiety Henry was consistently to protest his affection for and loyalty to his former tutor. Henry II had by this time taken the momentous decision that the young Henry should be crowned as his successor to the throne of England: in 1162 Becket had taken young Henry to England to receive the fealty of the English barons and instructions had been issued for a crown to be made for him. No doubt it was in furtherance of this policy that in July 1163 the Scottish king and the princes of Wales did homage at Woodstock 'to the king of England and to Henry his son' (*Diceto … opera historica*, 1.311). It was a policy intended to secure the succession, but it was to prove a major source of discord between father, son, and brothers throughout the Young King's life. Its execution was delayed by the dispute between the king and Becket, culminating in Becket's exile from 1164.

The right to crown the king of England was vested in the archbishop of Canterbury, but eventually, on 14 June 1170, the young Henry was crowned at Westminster by Roger, archbishop of York (*d.* 1181), to the fury of the pope, Alexander III, the monks of Canterbury, and many of the English bishops, not to mention Becket himself. His second coronation at Winchester on 27 August 1172, with Margaret, was arranged to satisfy Louis VII, and was carried out by Rotrou, archbishop of Rouen. The Young King had done homage to Louis VII in 1169 for his father's lands of Anjou and Maine and for Brittany, which his brother Geoffrey was to hold from him. Their brother Richard was in 1170 invested with the duchy of Aquitaine and the county of Poitou, the patrimony of their mother, Eleanor of Aquitaine, for which he too did homage to the French king. This excited the anger and resentment of the Young King. Other sources of tension between father and son were the death of Thomas Becket in 1170, and the Young King's rising tide of debt. According to Robert de Torigni, at Christmas 1172 the young Henry held a banquet so lavish that one room alone was filled with 110 knights all named William. In February 1173—the year when the Young King was knighted by his lifelong friend William (I) Marshal—Henry II announced his intention to hand over to John, his youngest son, three important fiefs in Anjou: Chinon, Loudun, and Mirebeau. This slight was compounded by the older king's refusal to allow the Young King any real power in the lands for which he did homage in 1169 or in England; authority remained with Henry II's officers.

In March 1173, the young Henry slipped secretly away from his father's court by night and fled to the court of his father-in-law, Louis VII, in Paris; here he was joined in open rebellion by his brothers Richard and Geoffrey. When Henry II's envoys arrived in Paris to negotiate, they were refused entry to court on the grounds that the Young King rather than his father was the legitimate ruler of the Plantagenet dominions. The coalition was reinforced by a number of powerful and high-ranking enemies of Henry II from within his lands and by Philip, count of Flanders (*d.* 1191). In the face of this critical threat Henry II acted decisively, crushing the armies of Louis and his allies in Normandy in 1173, but it was not until 30 September 1174, at Montlouis, that he and his sons finally made peace. The grant of lands to John was upheld, but in return for a pledge of good conduct the Young King was formally assigned two castles in Normandy, to be chosen by his father, and 15,000 Angevin pounds for his upkeep.

1175 saw the Young King involved with his father in royal duties, such as attendance at the Council of Northampton. Refused permission to go on pilgrimage to Santiago de Compostela in 1176, he went instead to the court of the manipulative Philip, count of Flanders, who exercised a strong influence over him. At Philip's court in 1176–7 and 1178–9 he honed his martial skills in lavish tournaments and built up, largely at Philip's expense, a reputation for chivalrous largesse and a major following of landless young men. In 1179 Philip transferred his attentions to Philip Augustus, who became king of France in 1180. The Young King and his father then, unusually, combined forces to thwart the count of Flanders in his efforts to dominate the young French king, with whom they allied themselves.

In 1182 the Young King renewed his demands for more power, and once again fled to the French court in defiance of his father. Henry II responded by increasing his allowance by an extra 110 Angevin pounds a day for himself and his wife—and this generosity averted the threat of further warfare between them. However, the Young King was open in his support of the rebellious barons of Aquitaine against Richard, and claimed that this was justified by Richard's seizure and fortification of Clairvaux, which arguably lay within the borders of Anjou rather than Poitou. Henry II called a peace conference of the barons and his sons in January 1183, and demanded—perhaps in response to the Young King's demands—that Richard should perform homage to the Young King for Aquitaine. Richard withdrew in anger to his duchy, and the Young King, accompanied by his brother Geoffrey, followed him, ostensibly to mediate, but in reality to foment discord against Richard among his barons. At first the young Henry was received enthusiastically in Richard's lands as a liberator from Richard's political and military domination; his reputation for largesse was confirmed by his gift of a banner embroidered *Henricus Rex* to the shrine of St Martial at Limoges.

But soon the tide turned against the Young King. Besieged in Limoges by Richard and Henry II, during April 1183 he played a number of ruses against his father while he fortified the city and sent out for mercenary troops, paying for all this by plundering the townsfolk and the shrine of St Martial. Returning from a raid on Angoulême, however, he was refused entry to Limoges by its exasperated citizens, and set off on a haphazard expedition around southern Aquitaine, despoiling the monastery of Grandmont and the shrines of Rocamadour. He fell seriously ill at Martel in Quercy and sent a letter to his father begging for his forgiveness, but Henry II, suspecting another trick, kept his distance, merely sending a ring as a token. On 11 June 1183 the Young King died of dysentery, allegedly after repenting on his deathbed. He had asked for his body to be buried at Rouen and his entrails at Limoges, but while his cortège was on its way to Normandy the people of Le Mans seized his body and buried it in their cathedral. The citizens of Rouen threatened force against Le Mans, and Henry II insisted that his son's wishes be observed by his reburial at Rouen.

This bizarre incident demonstrates the popularity of the Young King during his lifetime. Tall, blond, charming, and attractive, he was a persuasive talker and extravagantly generous. Henry II's critics, such as Gerald of Wales, praised him as a contrast to his father, but more detached contemporaries highlighted his failings: his arrogance, greed, frivolity, incompetence, and inconsistency. William of Newburgh saw his popularity as evidence of people's gullibility, while Ralph of Diceto commented that the world was a much better place without him. ELIZABETH HALLAM

Sources O. H. Moore, *The Young King Henry Plantagenet, 1155–83, in history, literature and tradition* (1925) • W. L. Warren, *Henry II* (1973) • R. W. Eyton, *Court, household, and itinerary of King Henry II* (1878) • *Radulfi de Diceto ... opera historica*, ed. W. Stubbs, 2 vols., Rolls Series, 68 (1876) • *Chronica magistri Rogeri de Hovedene*, ed. W. Stubbs, 4 vols., Rolls Series, 51 (1868–71) • W. Stubbs, ed., *Gesta regis Henrici secundi Benedicti abbatis: the chronicle of the reigns of Henry II and Richard I, AD 1169–1192*, 2 vols., Rolls Series, 49 (1867) • *Gir. Camb. opera* • R. Howlett, ed., *Chronicles of the reigns of Stephen, Henry II, and Richard I*, 4, Rolls Series, 82 (1889) • R. Howlett, ed., *Chronicles of the reigns of Stephen, Henry II, and Richard I*, 1, Rolls Series, 82 (1884) • P. Meyer, ed., *L'histoire de Guillaume le Maréchal*, 3 vols. (Paris, 1891–1901) • *The historical works of Gervase of Canterbury*, ed. W. Stubbs, 2 vols., Rolls Series, 73 (1879–80) • T. Agnellus, 'De morte ... Henrici Regis Junioris', in *Radulphi de Coggeshall chronicon Anglicanum*, ed. J. Stevenson, Rolls Series, 66 (1875) • A. L. Poole, *From Domesday Book to Magna Carta, 1087–1216*, 2nd edn (1955) • E. B. Fryde and others, eds., *Handbook of British chronology*, 3rd edn, Royal Historical Society Guides and Handbooks, 2 (1986)

Henry [Henry de Reyns; *called* Master Henry] (*fl.* 1243–1253), master mason, was invariably called 'Henry' or 'Master Henry' during his lifetime. However, a charter issued by his son Hugh in 1261 refers to him as 'de Reyns'; and following much discussion it is now generally agreed that this refers to Rheims in Champagne, whose cathedral was a major influence on Henry's most important work, the rebuilding of the abbey church of Westminster. Despite that church's many French-derived features, it seems clear that it is the design of an architect trained in the English Gothic tradition. The most likely significance of Henry's sobriquet is therefore that it commemorates a period of work at Rheims, perhaps as a journeyman in the 1220s or 1230s. He disappears from the records after June 1253 and the brevity of his *floruit* suggests that he may have died young.

The earliest mention of Henry occurs in 1243, when he was granted a robe of office as master mason at Windsor Castle. The work in hand was a complex of buildings in the lower ward which had been begun in 1240. These comprised chambers for the king and queen, a large chapel dedicated to St Edward, and a cloister linking the chambers and chapel. Only the north wall and west porch of the chapel survive, the former sufficient to indicate that the chapel proper was rectangular in plan and divided into five bays. In a letter of August 1243 Henry III ordered that the vault was to be of timber simulating stonework. Clearly, a chapel which lacked a stone vault and an apse was no slavish copy of any French prototype; however, the treatment of the bases in the arcading on the external face of the north wall derives specifically from Rheims Cathedral. A hint that the windows of the chapel anticipated those of Westminster Abbey in containing Rheims-derived bar tracery is the reference in a 1295 schedule of glazing repairs to at least one circular cusped opening.

In March 1245 Henry was sent to York to inspect the castle defences. The outcome was the building from 1246 of the existing keep on the motte (Clifford's Tower). Its quatrefoil plan, which has no English precedent but resembles the hundred-year-old towers at Étampes and Amblény, presumably reflects Henry's knowledge of French architecture. Its detailing includes English Gothic ornaments not found in Henry's documented works and was doubtless due to a locally recruited master. Apart from acting as 'viewer' (inspector) of a tower built at the Tower of London in 1250, the remainder of Henry's career seems to have been devoted entirely to the greatest enterprise of Henry III's reign, the rebuilding of Westminster Abbey.

Demolition of the eastern parts of the Romanesque abbey church began in July 1245, by which time Henry must have produced a design for the king's approval. The progression to the more space-demanding activity of drawing the full-size details needed for the execution of the masonry is probably reflected in the king's grants of May and June 1246 of two houses in Westminster to be used for Henry's work. Since Henry III did not see for himself any of the Gothic cathedrals of northern France until 1254, he may well have imagined that he was about to become the patron of a great church in the French style. If so, he was mistaken. Admittedly, the basic format and many of Westminster's details were fairly authentically French and would have registered as novel to someone familiar with only English architecture, but Henry, whether at his royal master's prompting or not, was clearly attempting a synthesis of the two national traditions. The great height, the elongated proportions of the bays, the apsidal plan of the east end, the tracery—especially that of the rose windows in the transepts—and the cavernous portals of the north transept façade all bespeak a determination to emulate French prototypes; yet their effect is transformed by Henry's adherence to the key characteristics of English Gothic, namely thick-wall structure and its concomitant ornamental complexity. The one feature of the abbey which suggests that Henry III had an informed knowledge of French Gothic is the use throughout the upper and lower levels of the lateral elevations of two-light-and-oculus windows. Their purpose was evidently to evoke the French church functionally analogous to Westminster, the coronation cathedral of Rheims (begun 1211), a building which was out of date in stylistic terms. Left to himself, it is likely that Master Henry would have made more prominent use of recent Parisian tracery patterns, which the chapter house and the north part of the east cloister walk show that he knew. Although Henry's work was impossible to imitate wholesale, by virtue of its exceptional size and sumptuousness, its influence proved sufficient to end the insularity hitherto characteristic of thirteenth-century English Gothic architecture.   CHRISTOPHER WILSON

Sources J. Harvey and A. Oswald, *English mediaeval architects: a biographical dictionary down to 1550*, 2nd edn (1984), 251–3 · H. M. Colvin and others, eds., *The history of the king's works*, 6 vols. (1963–82), vol. 1, pp. 98 and n., 104–5, 130–57; vol. 2 · C. Wilson and others, *Westminster Abbey* (1986), 22–30, 37–48, 52–67 · C. Wilson, 'The English response to French Gothic architecture, c.1200–1350', in J. Alexander and P. Binski, *Age of chivalry: art in Plantagenet England, 1200–1400* (1987), 75–7 [exhibition catalogue, RA] · P. Binski, *Westminster Abbey and the Plantagenets: kingship and the representation of power, 1200–1400* (1995), 13–28, 33–43

Henry, Prince, duke of Gloucester (1640–1660), was born on 8 July 1640 at Oatlands, Surrey, and baptized there on 22 July, the fourth, but third surviving, son of *Charles I, king of England, Scotland, and Ireland (1600–1649), and Queen *Henrietta Maria (1609–1669). He was declared duke of Gloucester soon after his birth, although no patent was issued. From his birthplace he has sometimes been called Henry of Oatlands, in the fashion of medieval English royal children. When Charles I left the capital in January 1642, Henry was left behind at St James's Palace with his sister Princess *Elizabeth, and so fell under the control of parliament. Initially he was placed in the charge of Jane Ker (*née* Drummond), countess of Roxburghe (*d.* 1643). After being joined by their brother James, duke of York, later *James II and VII, in November 1642, the royal children were moved into the city under the 'pretext of securing them against injury from the armies' (*CSP Venice, 1642–3*, 192–3), but in reality to ensure their retention as bargaining chips should the king triumph militarily. In June 1643 (Mary Vere (*née* Tracy), Lady Vere, was entrusted with Henry's care by the House of Commons, but the Lords insisted on consulting her first and she did not take on the role. In July both houses committed him to the care of Mary Sackville (*née* Curzon), countess of Dorset. In March 1645 he was committed to the care of Algernon Percy, tenth earl of Northumberland, but the order took effect only after the death of the countess of Dorset in May 1645. Following Charles I's capture by parliament in June 1647, Henry was reunited with his father on 16 July 1647 at the Greyhound Inn in Maidenhead. He now saw more of his father, often at Northumberland's Syon House or Hampton Court, where his father was held prisoner. In April 1648 Henry was part of the game of hide-and-seek which provided the cover for his brother James to escape from St James's Palace into exile.

Henry and his sister were able to bid Charles I farewell on the eve of his execution. During this interview Charles I impressed upon Henry that 'you must not be a king, so long as your brothers Charles and James so live, for they will cut off your brothers' heads (when they catch them),

and cut off thy head too at last'. Henry promised, saying 'I will be torn to pieces first' (Carlton, 356). Northumberland ensured that Henry and Elizabeth were absent from the capital on the day of their father's execution. Following Northumberland's resignation, Henry came under the charge of Northumberland's sister, Dorothy Sidney, countess of Leicester, and was taken to Penshurst in Kent, 'that they might not be the objects of respect, to draw the eyes and application of people towards them' (*Clarendon State Papers*, 4.334–5). At this time Richard Lovell was appointed his tutor. Following the landing of Charles II in Scotland, Henry was removed to Carisbrooke Castle, on the Isle of Wight, under the charge of Anthony Mildmay. It was here that his sister Princess Elizabeth died on 8 September 1650.

From the middle of 1652 Henry was agitating for more freedom, not least on health grounds, and at the end of 1652 it was decided to allow him to leave the country. On 12 February 1653 he sailed from Cowes into exile. He went first to Holland to visit his sister *Mary, princess of Orange, and while he was at The Hague, Charles nominated him a knight of the Garter. In May he arrived in Paris to visit his mother. When Charles II went to the Spanish Netherlands in July 1654, Henry remained behind in Paris, where his wild behaviour began to evince some concern from royalists such as Christopher, first Baron Hatton, who wrote of his fears that Gloucester 'will contract so great a rudeness (besides other vices) as may be very troublesome and incorrigible another day' (*Nicholas Papers*, 2.90), and remarked that his tutor, Lovell, was unable to restrain him. In October 1654 Henrietta Maria removed Henry to the care of her almoner, Abbé Walter Montagu, head of the rich abbey of St Martin at Pointoise, where he was regaled with the advantages to his soul and material circumstances of converting to Catholicism. Gloucester resisted the entreaties of his mother and the arguments of Montagu and wrote to Charles about his predicament. A furious Charles II, alert to the damage to his cause should such a conversion succeed, wrote to his brother to remain steadfast or 'you must never think to see England or me again' (Ollard, 104), and dispatched James Butler, marquess of Ormond, to collect Henry from Paris and bring him into the royal presence in Cologne.

The Cromwellian regime's *rapprochement* with France saw Charles II ally with Spain, in the hope of launching an invasion from the Spanish Netherlands. Henry now joined his brother the duke of York in being appointed, in December 1656, a colonel of an Irish regiment in Spanish service. With an offensive alliance between the Cromwellian regime and France in operation from March 1657, Henry served in the campaigns of the next two summers, attending the siege of Ardres and in June 1658 the battle of the Dunes. He narrowly avoided capture when Dunkirk fell. On 27 October Charles II made him a privy councillor, and on 13 May 1660 he was created earl of Cambridge and duke of Gloucester, although he had used the latter title from birth.

Gloucester landed with Charles II at Dover on 25 May 1660, apparently 'while the rest were shouting God Save the King, the duke of Gloucester threw up his hat and cried "God bless General Monck"' (*Le Fleming MSS*, 25). He took his seat in the House of Lords on 31 May 1660 and attended regularly thereafter; he 'has made many speeches with great applause' (*Hastings MSS*, 2.141), including one at a conference with the House of Commons on the Indemnity Bill. In June he was made high steward of Gloucester, and in July he was made ranger of Hyde Park.

Gloucester last attended the Lords on 29 August 1660. Shortly afterwards he fell ill with the smallpox, and, although his recovery was confidently reported on the 8th, he died at Whitehall Palace on 13 September. 'Next day he was opened, and his lungs were found as full of blood as they possibly could hold' (*Fifth Report*, HMC, 156). He was buried in Westminster Abbey on the 21st. Charles II was much aggrieved by his brother's death, not least because he 'had all the natural qualities requisite to make a great prince' (Clarke, 1.386). Edward Hyde, first earl of Clarendon, concurred with this sense of loss, having described him once 'as a prince of extraordinary hopes, both from the comeliness and gracefulness of his person and the vivacity and vigour of his wit and understanding' (Clarendon, *Hist. rebellion*, 5.336). STUART HANDLEY

Sources GEC, *Peerage* · J. Dobson, *The children of Charles I* (1975) · *CSP Venice*, 1640–61 · *CSP dom.*, 1640–53 · C. Carlton, *Charles I: the personal monarch* (1983) · R. Ollard, *The image of the king: Charles I and Charles II* (1979) · *Calendar of the Clarendon state papers preserved in the Bodleian Library*, ed. O. Ogle and others, 5 vols. (1869–1970), vols. 4–5 · Clarendon, *Hist. rebellion*, vols. 4–5 · *The life of James the Second, king of England*, ed. J. S. Clarke, 1 (1816) · Pepys, *Diary* (1970–83), vol. 1 · *The Nicholas papers*, ed. G. F. Warner, 2, CS, new ser., 50 (1892) · *JHL*, 11 (1660–66) · *The manuscripts of S. H. Le Fleming*, HMC, 25 (1890), 24–6 · *Report on the manuscripts of the late Reginald Rawdon Hastings*, 4 vols., HMC, 78 (1928–47), vol. 2, p. 141 · *Fifth report*, HMC, 4 (1876), 156 [Sutherland MSS]

Likenesses P. Lely, oils, 1647 (children of Charles I), Petworth House, Sussex · attrib. A. Hanneman, oils, *c*.1653–1654, National Gallery of Art, Washington, DC · J. Boeckhorst, oils, *c*.1659, Groothuis, Bruges, Belgium; copy, NPG · P. Thyssens, oils, *c*.1660, Knole, Kent · studio of P. Lely, oils (probably posthumous), Euston Hall, Suffolk · C. Van Dalen, line engraving (after S. Luttichuys, *c*.1660), BM, NPG · line engraving (as an infant), BM, NPG

Henry, Prince, first duke of Gloucester (1900–1974), was born Henry William Frederick Albert at York Cottage, Sandringham, on 31 March 1900, the fourth of six children and third of five sons of Prince George, duke of York, later *George V (1865–1936), and Princess (Victoria) *Mary (May) of Teck (1867–1953). The prince's oppressive upbringing, in which disparagement played a more prominent role than affection, inspired him with feelings of inadequacy. In 1910, the year his father became king, Prince Henry was sent to St Peter's Court, a preparatory school at Broadstairs. Three years later he went to Eton College, where his housemaster, S. G. Lubbock, found him cheerful and unassuming but lacking in self-confidence. He was the first son of a reigning monarch to attend a regular public school. In 1918 he entered Sandhurst and was commissioned the following summer. His formal education ended with a year's course at Trinity College, Cambridge (1919–20).

Prince Henry, an outstanding horseman and shot, was attracted by the life of a cavalry officer. His inclinations and talents were those of a country gentleman, and he felt completely at home in the 10th Royal Hussars to which he was posted in 1921. Nothing irritated him more than to discover that as a king's son he was repeatedly prevented from joining his regiment overseas on active duty.

In 1928 Prince Henry was created duke of Gloucester and began undertaking official engagements, such as his mission to Japan in 1929 to confer the Garter on the emperor Hirohito, to Ethiopia in 1930 to attend the coronation of Haile Selassie, and to Australia and New Zealand in 1934–5.

On 6 November 1935 the duke of Gloucester married Lady Alice Christabel (*b*. 1901), the third daughter of John Charles Montagu-Douglas-Scott, seventh duke of Buccleuch. The Gloucesters moved into York House, and in 1938 bought Barnwell Manor, Northamptonshire. They had two sons: Prince William, born in 1941, and Prince Richard, born in 1944. The duke's family life was supremely happy, and Princess Alice gave him the support and confidence he had hitherto lacked.

The death of George V and the abdication of Edward VIII in 1936 left the duke third in line to the throne. Moreover, until Princess Elizabeth came of age in 1944, he was also regent designate. Under these circumstances he was reluctantly obliged to abandon peacetime soldiering.

Soon after the outbreak of war in 1939 the duke was appointed chief liaison officer between the British and French armies in Europe. In May 1940 he was slightly wounded after his staff car was dive-bombed. In 1941 he was appointed second in command of the 20th armoured brigade. During the war he visited troops throughout the United Kingdom, north Africa, the Middle East, and as far afield as India and Ceylon.

Early in 1945 the duke succeeded the first earl of Gowrie as governor-general of Australia, where he wielded greater powers than those of the king in Britain. The country was ravaged by strikes, and several members of the new Labour government proved eager to advertise their disenchantment with royalty. To make matters worse, the duke was infectiously shy and lacked the winning charm and fluent small talk of his eldest brother (the duke of Windsor). Nevertheless, he won the hearts of many Australians by his forthright simplicity, his informed interest in farming, and his willingness to visit scattered communities in the remotest parts of their continent. During his two years of office he travelled over 75,000 miles. In 1947 he was summoned back to England to act as senior counsellor of state, while the king, queen, and two princesses visited South Africa.

The accession of Elizabeth II in 1952 did nothing to diminish her uncle's duties, nor to shorten the list of institutions to which he gave considerably more than his name: prominent among which were those concerned with hospitals, youth, and farming. In 1953 the duke represented the queen at the inauguration of King Faisal II at Baghdad, and of King Hussain in Amman, and in 1957 he conferred independence within the Commonwealth upon the Malayan Federation. The following year he revisited Ethiopia where he was cordially entertained by the emperor. He returned to Africa in 1959 to represent the queen at the proclamation of Nigeria's independence.

Early in 1965, while returning to Barnwell from Sir Winston Churchill's funeral, the duke overturned the Rolls-Royce he was driving. He was not seriously injured in the accident, but his health gradually deteriorated from then onwards. Later that year he revisited Australia to mark the fiftieth anniversary of Anzac day, and in 1966 he returned to Malaysia. His strength, however, was failing, and in 1968 he was rendered helpless by two severe strokes. Princess Alice nursed him solicitously, struggling the while to fulfil his public engagements. The duke died at Barnwell Manor 10 June 1974 and was buried at Frogmore. He was succeeded in the dukedom by his younger son, Prince Richard Alexander Walter George (b. 26 Aug 1944).

During his career the duke of Gloucester acquired the usual dazzling array of orders. He was sworn of the privy council in 1925, and received a host of foreign decorations, ranging from the Ethiopian order of the Seal of Solomon (1930) to the order of Mohamed Ali (1948). He served in virtually every rank of the army, from lieutenant (1919) to field marshal (1955). The regiments of which he was colonel-in-chief included the 10th Royal Hussars, the Gloucestershire regiment, the Gordon Highlanders, and the Scots Guards.

The duke's volatile temper, crisp invective, and penetrating stare could be momentarily terrifying, but his wrath was short-lived and soon dispelled by his shrill, staccato laugh. Probably he would have preferred the life of a country gentleman to that of a public figure, but he was sustained in his royal role by the peremptory sense of duty instilled in him by his parents.

Prince William of Gloucester (1941–1972), the elder son of the duke and duchess of Gloucester, was born on 18 December 1941 in Lady Carnarvon's Home, Barnet, a Hertfordshire nursing home, and named William Henry Andrew Frederick. His schooling began in 1950 at Wellesley House, Broadstairs. Four years later he passed high into Eton College, where he proved gregarious, enterprising, and intelligent. Prince William's student days were spent at Magdalene College, Cambridge (1960–63), where he obtained a third class in part one and a second class (second division) in part two of the historical tripos. With his parents' full approval he shared the unsheltered life of his fellow undergraduates. Indeed, the unprecedented freedom with which he chose his companions, male and female, was seen as a challenging novelty. In 1963–4 he spent a postgraduate year studying economics and political science at Stanford University, California.

The prince was a born explorer and in the summer vacation of 1963 made a film for the BBC of a 12,000 mile safari in Africa. Those who accompanied him on such journeys praised his resource, humour, integrity, and courage. He never wearied of travel, partly because of the opportunities it gave him to fly, drive, climb, ski, shoot, and skin dive. But he was no mere playboy.

Suspecting that the army might treat him as a mascot,

Prince William sought a career elsewhere. Possibly the deepest need of his nature was to achieve greatness and not have it thrust upon him. In 1965 he joined the Commonwealth Relations Office as third secretary on the staff of the British high commission at Lagos, from which vantage point he witnessed the Nigerian civil war. Three years later he was transferred to the British embassy in Tokyo as second (commercial) secretary. During his tour of duty he vigorously promoted Anglo-Japanese trade, travelled all over the country, and helped restore friendly relations with the imperial family. His charm, good looks, and informality won Britain many friends.

Prince William returned to England in 1970 to undertake some of his father's public duties. In that year he represented the queen at the celebrations marking Tonga's independence, and in 1971 at the state funeral of President Tubman of Liberia. The prince was killed in a flying accident at Halfpenny Green, Staffordshire, on 28 August 1972, while competing in an air race.

Prince William was something of a nonconformist, torn between the demands of his inheritance and his love of independence. In struggling to resolve this conflict he pioneered a new style of royalty. He was unmarried.

GILES ST AUBYN, rev.

Sources N. Frankland, *Prince Henry, duke of Gloucester* (1980) · Duchess of Gloucester, *Memoirs* (1983) · G. St Aubyn, ed., *William of Gloucester* (1977) · personal knowledge (1986) · *The Times* (29 Aug 1972) · *The Times* (11 June 1974)
Archives FILM BFI NFTVA, documentary footage · BFI NFTVA, news footage
Wealth at death £734,262: probate, 9 Sept 1974, *CGPLA Eng. & Wales*

Henry I (1068/9–1135), king of England and lord of Normandy, was the fourth and youngest son of *William I (the Conqueror), king of England and duke of Normandy, and *Matilda of Flanders.

Family, childhood, and adolescence Henry was born in England, possibly at Selby, between either mid-May and early September 1068 or early February and early May 1069. He was reared in England and remained there, apart from occasional trips to Normandy, until after receiving knighthood from his father at Westminster on 24 May 1086. William of Malmesbury and Orderic Vitalis testify independently that Henry was literate and, indeed, well educated in the liberal arts. Writers between the fourteenth and nineteenth centuries much exaggerated the extent of his learning, asserting that he had a mastery of Greek, was a gifted poet, and had earned a degree from the University of Cambridge—which, of course, did not yet exist (his epithet Beauclerc appears to have originated in the fourteenth century). These amusing exaggerations must not obscure the fact that Henry was indeed literate, and probably better educated than any previous English king except Alfred. Moreover, as V. H. Galbraith aptly observed, Henry's education marked a permanent change in the rearing of royal heirs: with the likely exception of Stephen, kings of England from Henry I's time onward were normally trained in letters.

Henry's tutor or *magister* cannot be identified with any

Henry I (1068/9–1135), manuscript drawing [sleeping, threatened by peasants (above) and knights]

certainty. The person was most likely a learned prelate of the English church, perhaps someone of the type of Osmund, bishop of Salisbury, a former royal chancellor and an avid bibliophile who enormously expanded his cathedral library, built the earliest Norman Romanesque cathedral at Old Sarum, and probably assisted in making the Domesday survey. By order of William the Conqueror from Normandy, the young Henry, accompanied by Bishop Osmund, visited Abingdon Abbey for several days during the Easter season of 1084, and Henry's attestations are to be found along with Bishop Osmund's on a number of the Conqueror's charters. But this evidence is obviously inconclusive.

Early manhood, 1086–1088 After being knighted Henry accompanied his father on the latter's final trip to the continent in 1086. He was present at the Conqueror's deathbed at St Gervais outside Rouen in September 1087, and at his entombment at Caen shortly afterwards. William I, having left the duchy of Normandy to his eldest son, *Robert Curthose, and the kingdom of England to his second surviving son, *William II (Rufus) (another son, Richard, had died in a hunting accident), bequeathed to Henry no lands but a large treasure—£5000 according to the most reliable reports. Henry had also been granted by his mother (who died in 1083) her lands in England, which are recorded in Domesday Book as being worth something in excess of £300 a year. The evidence suggests, however, that he never enjoyed the revenues from these lands. They were in fact granted by William Rufus to the royal

familiaris Robert fitz Hamon and later passed, through Robert's daughter Mabel (or Maud), to her husband, Henry's eldest natural son, *Robert, whom Henry created earl of Gloucester.

Henry did, however, acquire a large territorial base when, in the spring of 1088, Duke Robert Curthose sold (or possibly pawned) most of western Normandy to him for the sum of £3000, which Robert squandered that same year on a fruitless attempt to conquer England from Rufus. Along with these territories, which included at least the Cotentin and Avranchin with the abbey of Mont-St Michel, Henry acquired the title 'count of the Cotentin'. His rule there earned him a number of powerful friends among the barons of western Normandy, including Hugh, vicomte d'Avranches and earl of Chester, and Richard de Revières, who acquired vast lands in southern England on Henry's accession to the throne, and whose descendants were earls of Devon.

Henry had joined Robert Curthose's court in Normandy after his father's death and, although not yet twenty, evidently rose quickly to become a leading ducal counsellor—judging by the appearance of his name and new comital title alongside Robert Curthose's in ducal charters: 'Signum Rotberti comitis Normanniae + Signum Hen+rici comitis, fratris ejus …' and 'Si+gnum Rotberti comitis … Si+gnum Henrici comitis' (Haskins, 291). After Rufus had defeated the combined rebellion and invasion of 1088 that had aimed unsuccessfully at placing Robert Curthose on the throne of England, Henry journeyed to Rufus's court in the summer of 1088, to request possession of his mother's English lands. Henry had delayed his visit until such a time as he could make an appearance in the kingdom without seeming to take sides in the armed struggle between his older brothers for the English crown. Orderic's report that his visit with Rufus was cordial is supported by Henry's attestation of a royal charter in the late summer or early autumn of 1088. But, as has been said, there is no clear evidence that Henry ever received his mother's lands, and as Orderic makes clear, he did not possess them in 1091.

Relations with Robert Curthose, 1088–1089 Henry crossed back to Normandy in the autumn of 1088, in the company of a person who would later become one of his foremost adversaries, Robert de *Bellême, whom contemporaries described as a brilliant military architect but sadistically cruel. Robert was the eldest son of the Conqueror's companion and kinsman, Roger de Montgomery, lord of Arundel and earl of Shrewsbury, one of the three or four wealthiest lords in both Normandy and England. Robert de Bellême's mother, Mabel, was heir to the immense lands of the ancient family of Bellême (or Talvas), whose holdings stretched across the southern frontier of Normandy towards Maine. At her death in the late 1070s Mabel's lands had passed to Robert de Bellême, and he would soon inherit the great Montgomery holdings in Normandy from his aged father. He subsequently acquired, on the death of his younger brother Hugh, his father's lands in England: the earldom of Shrewsbury and the rape of Arundel.

When Count Henry and Robert de Bellême arrived in Normandy, they received a most unpleasant surprise. Robert Curthose took them both captive, on the advice of his disgruntled uncle, Odo, bishop of Bayeux, who alleged that they had been plotting with Rufus against the duke. The king had just disseised Odo of his immensely wealthy earldom of Kent and banished him from England for his leadership of the recent rebellion, and the bishop had returned to Normandy in an ugly mood. Robert Curthose revoked Henry's comital title and consigned both captives to the custody of Bishop Odo, who imprisoned Henry in his episcopal city of Bayeux.

The inconstant Curthose first launched a military campaign against the Montgomery–Bellême castles, then came to terms with Robert de Bellême's father, Roger de Montgomery, and good-heartedly released Robert de Bellême from captivity. Subsequently, some time in spring 1089, Curthose released Henry as well, having yielded, so Orderic explains, to the supplications of Norman *optimates*—presumably Henry's friends in western Normandy. A ducal charter of 24 April 1089, attested by Henry's supporter Richard de Revières, along with Ranulf, vicomte de Bayeux, and his son, and an unusual number of other western Normans, may mark the event.

Count in the Cotentin, 1089–1091 On his release Henry seems to have returned to western Normandy, where Curthose's authority was evidently non-existent. Henry resumed his comital title, probably without reference to Curthose. The sources suggest that he remained there, exercising his comital authority without challenge and eschewing the ducal court, until late October or early November 1090, when he responded to Robert Curthose's plea for help against a rebellion planned by citizens in the ducal capital of Rouen, acting in league with William Rufus. King William, while remaining in England, had been striving to win Normandy from his brother by buying the allegiance of major barons in the north-eastern part of the duchy. Rufus had also won over to his cause the richest merchant in Rouen, a certain Conan son of Gilbert Pilatus, whose numerous followers among the townspeople, known as 'Pilatenses', were prepared to rebel on Rufus's behalf and open the gates of Rouen to Rufus's Norman allies. Having yielded western Normandy to Henry, and forfeited most of north-eastern Normandy to Rufus, Curthose stood to lose his ducal authority altogether if he lost Rouen. He therefore begged the assistance of several Norman magnates, including his two victims of 1088, Count Henry and Robert de Bellême. Surprisingly, both responded, perhaps hoping for the ransoms of wealthy burghers whom they might take captive (although Henry is not known to have taken any captives for ransom).

When fighting broke out within the city, on 3 November, Curthose himself took refuge in the church of Notre-Dame-du-Pré, a priory affiliated to Bec just outside Rouen, while Henry and other ducal supporters engaged the rebels and their royalist allies in the city's streets and, after much bloodshed, defeated them. Conan son of Gilbert fell into the hands of Henry himself, who led him atop the tower of Rouen Castle and then pushed him out

to his death, declaring that his betrayal of his lord, Duke Robert, was unforgivable. Some modern historians have condemned Henry for gratuitous cruelty. Contemporary observers, on the other hand, seem generally to have viewed the event as a righteous act of summary execution by a high-spirited prince against a treacherous burgess. Supporters of Curthose on the ground below, who obviously shared that view, tied Conan's lifeless body to a horse's tail and had it dragged through the city streets, like Hector, as an example to other traitorous townsmen, and long afterwards the tower bore the striking name 'Conan's Leap'. Altogether, Henry emerged from the rebellion with a considerably better reputation than Curthose, who left his refuge at Notre-Dame-du-Pré only after peace had been restored to the city. Afterwards Henry returned to western Normandy.

On 2 February 1091 Rufus personally led an army into north-eastern Normandy against Curthose. Thoroughly intimidated, the duke quickly negotiated a peace on terms highly favourable to Rufus. In essence, their treaty provided for the division of Normandy between them, to the total exclusion and disinheritance of Henry. Rufus and Curthose thereupon marched westward against their brother, forcing Henry to withdraw from the Avranchin and Cotentin and to make a last stand in the mountain-top abbey of Mont-St Michel. There, in March and April 1091, Rufus and Curthose besieged their younger brother until at length, with water running short, Henry agreed to relinquish the abbey and departed Normandy under a safe conduct, accompanied by his remaining companions and his baggage.

The young Henry and his brothers, 1091–1100 For more than a year thereafter Henry wandered through the French Vexin in a state of relative poverty, accompanied by only a handful of companions. His luck changed when, in 1092, the townsmen of the hilltop citadel of Domfront to the south of Normandy repudiated their lord, Robert de Bellême, and invited Henry to rule them. Henry, reconsidering his attitude towards townsmen who betrayed their lords, accepted gladly. He pledged to the citizens never to change their customs or to abandon his lordship of their town. For the next several years Domfront remained his primary power base.

Meanwhile, Curthose and Rufus had fallen out again, and Rufus, continuing his effort to extend his authority over Normandy, reached an accommodation with Henry. With Rufus's encouragement and support Henry led raids from his hilltop citadel at Domfront against the forces of both Robert Curthose and Robert de Bellême. These raids were highly effective, and before long, with Rufus's consent, Henry had re-established his authority over much of western Normandy. From at least 1094 until Rufus's death in August 1100, he and Henry remained friends and allies. They met at London around the end of 1094, and in the spring of 1095 Henry 'crossed back to Normandy with great treasures, in fealty to the king against their brother' (*ASC*, s.a. 1095).

Normandy fell into Rufus's hands at last in 1096, when Robert Curthose resolved to pawn the duchy to his royal brother and join the first crusade, accompanied by Odo of Bayeux and many others. On Curthose's departure Rufus, recognizing Henry's former comital status, ceded to him all of western Normandy—Cotentin, Avranchin, and Bessin—except the episcopal city of Bayeux and the ducal centre at Caen. Historians have assumed that this grant expanded Henry's original comital holdings, but it may simply have restored them. Henry now spent much of his time at the king's court. He is reported to have been a commander in Rufus's campaigns of 1097–8 in the French Vexin, but his exploits, if any, have gone unrecorded. His participation in the campaign may well have been less than enthusiastic in view of the fact that Rufus's chief military leader was Robert de Bellême. Henry attested two surviving charters of Rufus issued from England during the final fifteen months of the reign, and was a member of Rufus's ill-starred hunting party in the New Forest on 2 August 1100.

The accession of Henry I Although some historians once suspected Henry of having plotted Rufus's killing, that notion is unsupported by historical evidence and is no longer taken seriously. Nevertheless, as any ambitious person would have done in his position, possessed of intelligence and sagacious advisers, Henry responded to the news of Rufus's death with alacrity. At the crucial moment his foremost advisers were the Beaumont brothers—Henry, earl of Warwick, and Robert, count of Meulan—whose vast holdings in England, Normandy, and the French Vexin placed them at the pinnacle of the Anglo-Norman aristocracy. Both had been close friends of Rufus and Henry alike, and Robert of Meulan, the more assertive of the brothers, was reputed to possess the most powerful intelligence among the Anglo-Norman baronage.

It was probably in the company of the Beaumonts that Henry made his dash to Winchester to seize control of the royal treasure and win the 'election' of a rump group of barons. Against the objections of some, his cause was successfully upheld by Henry of Warwick (whom William of Malmesbury describes as an old friend), and once he had the treasure and the election in hand, the newly elected king immediately undertook the journey to Westminster for his coronation, accompanied by Robert of Meulan. It could well have been in the course of the journey that Robert of Meulan and the future Henry I hammered out the clauses of Henry's coronation charter, based on the tradition of previous royal coronation oaths but the first to be committed to writing. In it he undertook to reform specific abuses of William Rufus's regime, particularly as regards the exercise of royal lordship over tenants-in-chief, and to restore 'the law of King Edward together with such emendations to it as my father made with the counsel of his barons' (*English Historical Documents*, 2, ed. D. C. Douglas and W. Greenaway, 1953, 434).

Henry promised, for example, to exact just and lawful reliefs rather than the arbitrarily high reliefs that Rufus had presumably imposed. He also promised to take nothing from the demesnes of churches during vacancies, to refrain from charging for the marriages of heiresses, and

to permit widows to marry or not, as they chose. Some of these promises Henry broke, others he kept, and still others seem ambiguous. Henry's regime did, for example, collect the annual revenues from church demesnes during vacancies, but it differed from Rufus's in refraining from selling off capital assets such as timber or church ornaments, and from mistreating the monks or clergy. From what one can tell, Henry's reliefs were not excessive, but he did run a brisk traffic in marriageable heiresses and widows. Most information on these matters comes from the pipe roll of 1130, from which distant perspective it was perhaps difficult to recall promises made a long generation earlier under very different circumstances. The coronation charter became famous in the annals of English constitutional history and served as a precedent for Magna Carta, but for Henry it was simply one of several expedients to secure a precarious succession.

It would be anachronistic to describe the succession as a usurpation—as has been done. Although Robert Curthose was the older brother, and was returning home from the crusade just then, there was as yet no firm tradition of primogeniture in English royal succession custom, and William Rufus, at the instigation of William I and Archbishop Lanfranc, had taken precedence over his elder brother in succeeding to the English throne in 1087. Had William Rufus left a son, the latter's claim would have indeed been strong, perhaps decisively so if the son had been more than an infant, but Rufus left no heirs. And although primogeniture was taking hold in Normandy, in England the succession of an eldest son to the throne had been uncommon ever since the time of King Alfred, whose own succession had violated the rule of primogeniture. Henry's problem was not that his accession was illegal but that it was disputed. He and his friends arranged a swift coronation at Westminster Abbey, on 5 August 1100, by Bishop Maurice of London in the absence of Archbishop Anselm, who was in exile, and Thomas of York, who had not yet arrived. Having once received the all-important royal consecration, Henry undertook to circulate the coronation charter to shire courts and bishoprics. Continuing to act quickly, he arrested Rufus's unpopular chief minister, Ranulf Flambard, bishop of Durham, consigning him to the Tower of London as its first political prisoner. Henry also wrote to Anselm urging his return and apologizing profusely to him for proceeding with the coronation without the customary archiepiscopal anointment. In the days and weeks that followed, Henry received the homage of most English barons (including Robert de Bellême, earl of Shrewsbury), all of whom were anxious to perform the ritual that enabled them to retain title to their estates under the new regime.

The new king With Rufus's death from a stray arrow, and Henry's accession to the throne, the character of the English monarchy changed significantly. For although in recent years Rufus and Henry had been friends and companions, and although both were far more competent rulers than their elder brother, they were nevertheless very different in character and temperament. First and most obviously to contemporaries, Henry was avidly heterosexual. With a bevy of mistresses (most of whom were of sufficient social distinction to be identifiable) he had some twenty-two to twenty-four known bastards, more than any other English king, whereas Rufus had none. Whether this was a result of Henry's willingness to accord formal recognition to his bastards and Rufus's preference for more casual relations with women of low status, or perhaps a result of Rufus's homosexuality or (as a recent biographer suggests) bisexuality, it left Henry with natural sons to support his cause, and a plethora of natural daughters wherewith to forge marriage alliances with neighbouring princes, whereas Rufus enjoyed no such family ties.

The contemporary historian William of Malmesbury, who excelled in the art of personal description, portrayed Henry as of medium height, with black, receding hair, a broad chest, and a tendency to gain weight with advancing years. He was sociable and witty, temperate in eating and drinking, casual and informal in speech. He slept soundly and had a most regrettable tendency to snore. Unlike Rufus, he preferred diplomacy to battle: 'He would rather contend by counsel than the sword; he conquered without bloodshed if he could, and if not, with as little as possible' (Malmesbury, *Gesta regum*, 2.488).

In political affairs, Henry was more cautious than Rufus, more thoughtful (or calculating), and by all indications more intelligent. He was unique among medieval monarchs in maintaining strict peace throughout his kingdom of England during his final thirty-three years—an achievement that was widely and deeply appreciated by his subjects. He maintained this peace through a policy that combined strict justice, high taxes (particularly in times of war in Normandy), severe punishment for wrongdoing, and the adroit use of royal patronage to attract talented new men to his court while at the same time keeping most of the old conquest families loyal to his regime.

Henry's foreign policy was radically different, too. Whereas Rufus's territorial ambitions seemed virtually limitless (at his death he was on the verge of taking Aquitaine in pawn), Henry, having once reunited his father's dominions, sought to safeguard their frontiers rather than extend them. As king of the English, and as his father's son, he was strongly committed to retain or recover all the lands and privileges that the Conqueror had possessed, but Henry's ambitions do not appear to have extended beyond that commonplace ideal of royal stewardship. After the first six turbulent years of his reign, when he was preoccupied with saving his throne and reuniting England and Normandy, his policies were primarily defensive.

Ecclesiastical policy: early relations with Anselm Henry's relations with the church were much better than Rufus's, and he enjoyed a far more favourable treatment at the hands of contemporary monk–historians such as William of Malmesbury, John of Worcester, Robert de Torigni, Orderic Vitalis, and even Eadmer of Canterbury—whose advocacy of Archbishop *Anselm caused him to dislike

both kings, though in differing degrees. Henry was generous in his benefactions to churches, including the great Burgundian abbey of Cluny for which he underwrote a major rebuilding programme of the immense church known as Cluny III. He had a friendly correspondence with Bernard of Clairvaux, and major figures in his court and administration supported the establishment of the first English Cistercian houses: Waverley, Fountains, and Rievaulx. He collaborated in the elevation of the abbey of Ely (1108) and the priory of Carlisle (1133) into bishoprics— the last English bishoprics to be created until the Reformation.

Of Henry's own religious foundations, which included priories at Cirencester, Dunstable, and Mortemer in eastern Normandy, by far the greatest was Reading Abbey, which he established on a lavish scale in the early 1120s shortly after the death of his son William, and surely in his memory, and which became the site of Henry's own burial. And whereas Rufus's ruthless sequestration of the revenues and properties of vacant churches had evoked an anguished and quite justifiable chorus of complaints from contemporary ecclesiastical writers, Henry's exercise of 'regalian right' was relatively restrained and generally accepted. Moreover, Henry fully supported his archbishops of Canterbury in their summoning of kingdom-wide primatial councils, which they regarded as essential instruments in their governance of the English church and had summoned frequently under William the Conqueror, but which Rufus had absolutely forbidden.

Following Henry's agreement to eschew Rufus's severe policies towards the church, Anselm returned from exile, but almost immediately the archbishop raised the novel and unexpected issues of lay investiture of prelates and clerical homage to lay lords, both of which he had tolerated under Rufus, but which Pope Urban II's Council of Rome in 1099 had banned in Anselm's presence. Anselm, who seems to have had no personal objection to these rituals, felt absolutely constrained to obey a direct papal and conciliar decree affirmed in his presence. He therefore refused to accept investiture from Henry, to render him homage, or to permit any other English prelate to do either. This issue created a grave dilemma, for in rendering due obedience to a solemn papal decree, Anselm was challenging Henry's own deeply felt determination to rule as his father had done, retaining all customary prerogatives and rituals of his royal predecessors. Henry and Anselm, both of whom possessed sufficient practical intelligence to understand the other's dilemma, remained accommodating despite their differences. They agreed to postpone the issue, while sending a joint delegation to the papal court to seek advice and perhaps a dispensation.

Marriage Meanwhile Henry sought to buttress his political position further by marrying the Scottish princess Edith, who had adopted the Norman name *Matilda (1080–1118). Reared at Romsey Abbey in Hampshire but never having taken religious vows, Matilda was the orphaned daughter of Malcolm III (Canmore), king of Scots (*d.* 1093), and his celebrated queen, the saintly Margaret (*d.*

1093), and, through Margaret, a direct descendant of Edmund Ironside and the West Saxon kings. Matilda's marriage to Henry would thus have pleased both Scots and Anglo-Saxons. More importantly, however, it reinforced Henry's claim to the throne by providing his children with a direct hereditary link to the old English royal line. The blood of both Alfred and William the Conqueror would flow through them. By an odd chain of circumstances, Matilda was also the god-daughter of Henry's brother, Duke Robert Curthose.

Some contemporary critics alleged that the fact of Matilda's having been reared in a convent while wearing a nun's habit made her a *de facto* nun and barred her from marriage, regardless of whether she had taken religious vows. Many years later, after Henry's death, advocates supporting King Stephen's claim to the English throne raised the same objection in order to stigmatize the Empress *Matilda, daughter of Queen Matilda and Henry I, as a bastard. But in November 1100 a tribunal of friendly Anglo-Norman prelates decided otherwise, and Archbishop Anselm, always at pains to co-operate with Henry whenever he could do so without serious moral compromise, officiated at both the marriage ceremony and Matilda's subsequent coronation on 11 November. She became a widely admired queen, presiding competently as regent over England during Henry's frequent sojourns in Normandy and, through her patronage, making the English royal court a centre for writers and musicians. She commissioned the writing of a history of England by the monks of Malmesbury Abbey, for example, and thus became a benefactor of the great historian William of Malmesbury. She may also have given her patronage to the unknown writer who produced the first major poem to be written in Anglo-Norman French, the *Voyage of St Brendan*. Moreover, as a spiritual disciple of Anselm, Matilda used her close relationships with both the archbishop and her royal husband to intervene with some effect in the complex negotiations over lay investiture. The impression conveyed by her letters is that while her love of Anselm was deep and genuine, it was exceeded by her devotion to her husband and his policies.

Establishing the new regime, 1100–1102 Robert Curthose, on his return from crusade in the autumn of 1100, resumed his lordship over Normandy and, as in 1088, began planning a campaign to conquer England. He received invaluable help from Ranulf Flambard, who made a daring escape from the Tower of London by climbing down a rope that had been smuggled into his room in a wine cask. The portly prelate skinned his hands badly on the way down, but he nevertheless managed with the help of confederates to ride to the coast, sail to Normandy, and join Curthose's court. Flambard's mother, a sorceress who was said to converse regularly with the devil, followed her son across the channel with his treasure. Henry responded to Flambard's escape by summoning an army to Pevensey on the channel coast, sending ships into the channel to defend the English shore, and levying a heavy fine on the keeper of the Tower, William de Mandeville. But Curthose, under the astute guidance of Ranulf Flambard, won

over the ships' crews, avoided Pevensey, and landed with an army at Portsmouth on 20 July 1101. A considerable number of magnates, including Robert de Bellême, betrayed Henry and defected to Curthose, while others, undecided in their allegiance, were persuaded to remain in Henry's camp only by the persuasive preaching of Archbishop Anselm and his suffragan Gundulf, bishop of Rochester. Only the Beaumont brothers, along with Richard de Revières, Robert fitz Hamon, and a small handful of other magnates gave Henry their unstinted support.

The two armies met at Alton in Hampshire, not far from Winchester, where the barons on both sides helped mediate a peace between the brothers. Curthose relinquished his claim to the English throne, and Henry in return granted him custody of the Cotentin and all his other holdings across the channel except Domfront, along with an annuity of 3000 marks—which Curthose relinquished two years later on the petition of his god-daughter Queen Matilda. The brothers further agreed that barons on both sides should be permitted to keep or recover their lands. But to preserve the peace of the cross-channel condominium, they agreed that any baron who in the future was charged with treason by one brother should be regarded as a traitor by the other.

In the years immediately following Henry sought to win the majority of the Anglo-Norman barons to his cause, and to drive the incorrigibles from England. In 1102, adroitly isolating Robert de Bellême and his kinsmen from their potential supporters, he charged Robert with forty-five separate acts of malfeasance, seized his castles one by one—Tickhill, Arundel, Bridgnorth, and Shrewsbury—and banished him from England. Robert de Bellême, whose penchant for violence and cruelty was widely abhorred, could claim few sympathizers. Indeed, his departure for Normandy was greeted with joy. When, in the following year, Robert Curthose came to terms with Robert de Bellême, Henry charged Curthose with violating their treaty of 1101.

Meanwhile, Henry and Robert of Meulan were winning supporters among the Norman baronage through acts of patronage, consisting chiefly of generous landed endowments or marriages to aristocratic women, including both close relatives of Henry and his bastard daughters. Through such means, for example, great magnates—including the counts of Perche and Boulogne, and the lords of L'Aigle, Tosny, and Breteuil—became Henry's allies. Breteuil, one of the wealthiest honours in Normandy, was especially important. It had been left without an undisputed heir by the death of its childless lord, Guillaume de Breteuil, in 1102. After a considerable struggle between rival claimants, Robert of Meulan manipulated the conflict in such a way that the honour passed to Guillaume de Breteuil's bastard son Eustace, who had married Henry I's bastard daughter Juliana and thereafter became a staunch ally of the English monarchy.

Anselm, investitures, and the conquest of Normandy, 1102–1106 While winning friends in Normandy, Henry was continuing to resist Anselm's demand that he relinquish the royal custom of investing prelates and receiving their homage. In other respects Henry's behaviour towards the church was relatively benign. In particular he permitted Archbishop Anselm to preside at a large primatial council at Westminster Abbey at about Michaelmas 1102, which passed important legislation against clerical marriage and other abuses and deposed a number of simoniacal or otherwise unworthy abbots. And he was also prepared to fill the numerous ecclesiastical vacancies left over from Rufus's reign (or created by the depositions of 1102). However, this process was impeded by Henry's insistence on investing new prelates, and by Anselm's refusal to condone the ceremony on the grounds of the papal prohibition of 1099. After the failure of successive joint delegations to Rome, Anselm himself in 1103 undertook to petition the pope to waive the investiture ban for England. Pope Paschal II granted Anselm important primatial privileges for Canterbury but refused his petition to permit royal investiture in England, and, with Henry remaining adamant, Anselm returned to exile in the French archiepiscopal city of Lyons, where he had spent much of his previous exile under Rufus. Henry wrote affably to Anselm but also confiscated the Canterbury estates. Anselm objected firmly to this confiscation. At Queen Matilda's urging, Henry restored half the Canterbury revenues, but Anselm refused to be placated until the king had restored them all.

In the meantime Henry's courtship of the Anglo-Norman baronage was achieving remarkable success. Crossing to Normandy in 1104 he found himself joined by a plethora of Norman nobles, who accompanied the king in a kind of festive cavalcade through his brother's duchy. Henry's entourage even undertook to adjudicate Robert Curthose's competence to govern the duchy in a kind of court proceeding, with Curthose himself evidently present. The luckless duke was able to forestall the judgment only by granting Henry the allegiance and homage of still another powerful Norman magnate, Guillaume, count of Évreux.

Henry's Norman campaign of the following year, 1105, began even more promisingly but ended in disarray. Crossing with a large force to the port of Barfleur in the Cotentin, he marched unopposed to Bayeux, reduced the city by burning it to the ground, and intimidated the townspeople of Caen into surrendering, but then found his army stalled before the ducal castle of Falaise. The difficulty was unquestionably Anselm, who had seized the opportunity of Henry's climactic Norman campaign to resolve the investiture controversy and make possible his own return to Canterbury. Henry had justified his Norman campaign by the argument, by no means implausible, that his purpose was to rescue the Norman church from the violence resulting from Curthose's anarchic rule and Robert de Bellême's depredations. Henry's image as God's avenger was fatally weakened, however, when Anselm moved northward from Lyons with the publicly announced intention of excommunicating him. News of the venture of this internationally celebrated holy man is said to have given pause to many of Henry's baronial supporters. His ally Elias, count of Maine, a friend and correspondent of Anselm, defected before the walls of Falaise and returned home with his Manceau troops, and Henry's siege failed. Having negotiated fruitlessly with Curthose shortly thereafter at Cintheaux (between Caen and Falaise), Henry evidently concluded that he had no choice but to come to terms with Anselm. The archbishop, in the meantime, had broken his northward journey at the castle of Adela, countess of Blois, his spiritual daughter and Henry's favourite sister, who arranged a meeting between the king and archbishop at the castle of L'Aigle in south-eastern Normandy. There Anselm and Henry worked out a compromise, which verged on a royal capitulation. The king could continue to require the homage of his prelates—which the pope had originally banned but had later passed over in silence—but Henry relinquished the right to investiture with pastoral staff and ring. After a fruitless effort at delay on Henry's part, the compromise was sent to Rome, Paschal accepted it, and Henry and Anselm came to terms at last.

Henry returned to Normandy in force in summer 1106. He met with Anselm at Bec to confirm the agreement on investitures, and then proceeded to the castle of Tinchebrai in south-western Normandy. There, on 28 September, Henry cleverly employed mounted and dismounted knights, infantry, and a hidden Manceau reserve force (led once again by Count Elias) to win a decisive victory over Robert Curthose. Robert de Bellême managed to flee, but Duke Robert and most of his other followers fell into Henry's hands. Curthose remained his brother's prisoner, well treated but closely guarded, until his death twenty-eight years later. Henry's lifelong imprisonment of Curthose has been seen as a major stain on the king's character. But to have set Curthose free would very likely have resulted in a major upsurge in civil strife and violence within the Anglo-Norman dominions.

The battle of Tinchebrai therefore brought Normandy firmly under Henry's rule, and the continued incarceration of Robert Curthose was doubtless a significant factor in the maintenance of peace throughout Henry's dominions. After a long effort, and at the cost of investitures, he had reforged his father's Anglo-Norman state.

Henry's reorganization of government In the months and years immediately following Tinchebrai, Henry undertook to reinstitute strong rule in Normandy and to reform the government of England. In late 1106 and early 1107, at Lisieux, he asserted firm ducal lordship over Normandy, receiving the homage of the Norman baronage, affirming the peace of the duchy, and re-establishing tenures as they existed under William the Conqueror. But by his own volition, he avoided (unlike his Angevin successors) any ceremony of installation as duke of Normandy, and his chancery usually avoided giving him the title of *dux Normannorum* in charters, styling him only *rex Anglorum*.

In August 1107 Henry's concession of investitures received the assent of a great council of magnates and prelates meeting in the king's presence at the palace of Westminster. With the settlement ratified, Henry undertook immediately to break the logjam of abbatial and episcopal consecrations, installing new prelates in many leaderless abbeys and in five bishoprics that had lain vacant because of the investiture impasse (some of these were already filled by bishops-elect). Because Henry no longer insisted on investing them, Anselm was now free to consecrate the new prelates. Henry appears to have followed Anselm's advice in appointing to abbacies men with serious spiritual vocations, and often with Bec connections. The newly consecrated bishops, on the other hand, were more notable for their administrative skills than their holy zeal. Anselm must have found them acceptable, but it is clear that he had not nominated them. The most notable of the new episcopal appointees, Roger of *Salisbury, bishop of Salisbury, had formerly been Henry's chancellor, and had managed Henry's affairs during the years before his coronation. Roger of Salisbury directed the royal administration throughout Henry's reign and served as English regent after 1123. An administrator of extraordinary skill and originality, he was responsible for notable advances in the financial and judicial institutions of the kingdom.

In the following year, on the advice of Anselm and others, Henry undertook a series of reforms in the operation of his household and administration. He earned general praise by instituting severe punishments for various acts of lawbreaking, false coining in particular, which resulted, fifteen years later, in the mutilation of most of the minters in England. And he reformed his own itinerant court by forbidding pillaging of the localities through which it passed—a practice that had evidently reached horrendous proportions under William Rufus and Robert Curthose and continued through Henry's opening years. The reform included strictly enforced regulations regarding the requisitioning of local goods, and set fixed prices for their purchase. Henry also established specific allowances for his household officers and stipends for magnates attending his court, thus arranging that everyone in his entourage should receive fixed payments for their subsistence. His new arrangements for the royal household seem to be reflected (with a few emendations) in a unique document of c.1136, the *Constitutio domus regis*, which was probably drawn up by Henry's administrators for the guidance of King Stephen's household.

By 1109 Henry had negotiated the marriage of his daughter Matilda to Heinrich V, emperor and king of Germany (r. 1106–25). It was a dazzling alliance for the Anglo-Norman house, and Henry proudly reported the successful conclusion of the negotiations in a letter of 1109 to Anselm, written shortly before the archbishop's death. It may well have been in connection with the raising of Matilda's immense marriage gift of 10,000 marks of silver (c.1110) that Henry and his chief administrator, Roger of Salisbury, redesigned the royal accounting system, known thereafter as the exchequer (*scaccarium*), and instituted the records of its annual audits known as pipe rolls.

The exchequer system was a fundamental step forward in English administrative history.

The defence of Normandy, 1106–1119 The state of peace and stability resulting from Tinchebrai began to crumble with the accession in 1108 of an assertive new king of France, Louis VI, and in 1109 of a vigorous young count of Anjou, Foulques (V), who became count of Maine in the right of his wife in 1110. The Angevin annexation of Maine constituted a severe diplomatic challenge to Henry I, whose father had ruled Maine during much of his reign; Henry could not relinquish it altogether without betraying his commitment to the stewardship of his father's possessions. Foulques and Louis VI were now joined by Robert (II), count of Flanders, in a hostile coalition that sought to replace Henry's rule of Normandy and perhaps England with that of his nephew, *William Clito, the only legitimate son of the captive Robert Curthose. William Clito had fled Normandy c.1110, and in the following year open warfare broke out between Henry and his enemies. Almost miraculously, Henry managed to keep his Anglo-Norman dominions free of conflict during these years by identifying and arresting potential rebels—Guillaume, count of Évreux, William Crispin, Philip de Briouze, William Malet, and William Bainard—and by stirring up rebellions within his enemies' lands. Luck intervened on Henry's behalf when Robert of Flanders was mortally injured while campaigning in 1111. The following year Henry arrested Robert de Bellême (who had once again joined Henry's foes) and consigned him to lifelong imprisonment. And throughout the conflict Henry kept Louis VI off balance by encouraging uprisings by such French magnates as Hugues du Puiset and Thibaud, count of Blois. Henry was thus able to conclude an altogether favourable peace settlement early in 1113. He betrothed his son and heir, *William Ætheling (1103–1120), to Matilda, daughter of Foulques (V), count of Anjou, who in return did homage to Henry for Maine. Louis came to terms shortly afterwards, conceding to Henry the overlordships of Bellême, Maine, and Brittany.

Two or three years later, however, hostilities resumed. Once again Henry found himself pitted against Louis VI, Foulques (V), and the new count of Flanders, Baudouin (VII), all fighting on behalf of William Clito's succession. The crisis deepened when the aged Guillaume, count of Évreux, died in 1118 without a son and heir, leaving his wealthy and strategic county to a powerful French magnate and potential enemy of Henry I, Amaury de Montfort, who had fought against Henry in the war of 1111–13. Amaury enjoyed close relations with both France and Anjou. His sister, the celebrated, and indeed notorious, Bertrada de Montfort, had married, successively, Foulques (IV) of Anjou and Philippe I of France, as a result of which Amaury was both the uncle of Foulques (V) and an associate of the French royal family. Henry tried to block Amaury's succession to the county, but the castle garrison of Évreux, defying the king, put Amaury in possession of the citadel. For nearly a decade Amaury remained Henry's chief adversary in Normandy, replacing the long incarcerated Robert de Bellême. Indeed, with his strong international connections and a much more amiable disposition, Amaury was a more dangerous enemy than Robert de Bellême had been.

In 1118 the fighting became intense when Louis VI brought a large army by stealth into the Norman Vexin and was supported by a number of rebellious barons throughout Normandy. Henry's cause was weakened by the death on 1 May 1118 of his wife, Matilda, who had served regularly and effectively as English regent during his absences in Normandy. Henry suffered the further loss of his stalwart baronial supporter Robert, count of Meulan, who died at his monastery of Préaux a few weeks later. For a time major Norman magnates defected right and left. Even Henry's own daughter Juliana and her husband, Eustace de Breteuil, turned against him and cast their support behind William Clito. Although Henry received staunch backing from his natural son Richard, from the young Richard, earl of Chester, and from members of the king's military *família* such as Ralph de Pont-Èchanfray (Ralph the Red), there seemed few other Norman barons whom Henry could trust completely. About Christmas 1118 Foulques (V) defeated the Anglo-Norman forces in an important though ill-recorded battle at Alençon in southern Normandy, and Henry's life was endangered at about this time in an assassination attempt by a treasurer of his own household—the low-born court official Herbert the Chamberlain. Thereafter Henry slept with a sword and shield near his bed, and it is said that he did not sleep soundly.

Henry's fortunes revived the following year. In May 1119 he persuaded Foulques (V) of Anjou to break his alliance with Louis and conduct a separate peace. Then in the following month his son William married Matilda of Anjou and received as his dowry the lordship of Maine. At about the same time Count Baudouin of Flanders died of a battle-wound received the previous autumn. Moving more firmly onto the offensive, Henry's forces laid siege to Évreux and set fire to the town, having obtained permission to do so from Audoin, bishop of Évreux, on the king's promise to rebuild the cathedral on a grander scale than before. (Much of this post-1119 rebuilding has survived in the nave of the present cathedral.) The keep of Évreux Castle continued to hold out for a time, defended by Amaury's friends and kinsmen, but Henry was clearly regaining control of the duchy. On 20 August 1119 he and his army, using highly sophisticated tactics, routed the forces of Louis VI at Brémule in eastern Normandy. Henry's men took some 140 prisoners and the French royal banner, and drove the French from the duchy. In the weeks that followed the king worked out amicable settlements with rebellious Norman barons, one after the other. He restored Eustace and Juliana de Breteuil to his good graces, although not to the honour of Breteuil. Before the year's end Amaury de Montfort had surrendered the citadel of Évreux and, on his promise of peace and loyalty, Henry granted him the comital title with jurisdiction over the county of Évreux itself, apart from the

citadel which would remain garrisoned by Henry's knights. Finally in mid-1120, with the help of papal mediation, Henry entered into a definitive peace with France. Louis accepted young William's homage for Normandy, thus formally repudiating Clito's claim to the duchy, and on 25 November 1120, with a durable peace at last achieved, Henry I set off for England in triumph.

The *White Ship* and the problem of the succession, 1120–1121
On that same evening Henry's plans were brought to ruin when William Ætheling and a flock of his aristocratic companions drowned in the wreck of the *White Ship* as it departed the harbour of Barfleur. Both the passengers and crew had evidently been celebrating to excess, and many were said to have been intoxicated, when the pilot carelessly permitted the ship to strike an underwater rock a short distance offshore. Everyone aboard was lost except, it is said, a butcher of Rouen. The disaster altered the lines of succession of several major Anglo-Norman families and cost the lives of some of Henry's most stalwart supporters in the recent war—including his natural son Richard, his natural daughter Matilda of Perche, Richard, earl of Chester, and Ralph the Red. No one dared inform Henry of the catastrophe for some time after he had landed in England. His grief at the death of his only legitimate son was exacerbated by the unravelling of the peace agreements with France and Anjou that he had achieved after such prolonged effort. Both agreements had hinged on William: his marriage to Matilda of Anjou and his homage to Louis VI. Worst of all, the loss of Henry's one legitimate son, to whom the barons of Normandy and England had all rendered homage, threw the royal succession into total disarray.

On the advice of his counsellors Henry remarried almost immediately. On 29 January 1121, at Windsor Castle, he wed *Adeliza (or Alice) (c.1103–1151), daughter of Godfrey, count of Louvain and duke of Lower Lorraine, and she was crowned queen the following day. Like Matilda, Adeliza of Louvain was landless but of distinguished birth and keen literary interests. Perhaps more importantly, in the light of Henry's need for an heir, she was young and, so it was said, beautiful. She did not serve as English regent, as Matilda had done, because Henry kept her constantly at his side. Yet in the course of their fifteen-year marriage she gave birth to no children. Henry was in his early fifties at the time of the marriage, and notwithstanding his prowess in fathering illegitimate offspring, the failure was clearly his. After Henry's death Adeliza married William d'Aubigny, son of the royal butler, and bore several children.

War and diplomacy, 1123–1125 In time both Louis VI and Foulques (V) resumed their support of William Clito. Foulques arranged for Clito to marry his second daughter, Sibylla, and dowered her with Maine. A rebellion on Clito's behalf broke out in Normandy in 1123, backed by the French and Angevins and led by their friend and kinsman Amaury de Montfort, count of Évreux. To Henry's chagrin one of the chief Norman rebels was the young Waleran, count of Meulan, son and continental heir of

Henry's intimate friend, the late Robert de Beaumont, count of Meulan, and lord of a string of Beaumont family castles dominating the Risle valley in central Normandy. The rebellion collapsed the following spring when, on 26 March 1124, a well-led troop of Henry I's household knights surprised and defeated virtually the entire rebel force as it emerged from the Forest of Brotonne *en route* from the Beaumont stronghold of Vatteville for the castle of Beaumont (Beaumont-le-Roger). The battle is variously described as having been fought near the town of Bourgthéroulde, about a dozen miles south-west of Rouen, and (perhaps more accurately) at Rougemontier, a village some 10 miles west-north-west of Bourgthéroulde near the present edge of the forest and directly on what would probably have been the rebels' route from Vatteville to Beaumont.

The battle was brief but decisive. The royal troops, using mounted archers on the only known occasion in Anglo-Norman history, took most of the rebel leaders prisoner, including Waleran of Meulan who spent the next five years in captivity. (Henry released him, and returned his estates to him, in 1129 on the death of William Clito.) Amaury de Montfort escaped by a hair's breadth. In the meantime Henry managed to keep French forces out of Normandy by persuading his son-in-law, the emperor Henry V, to invade France from the east. The German invasion occurred in summer 1124, well after the collapse of the Norman rebellion, but advance rumours of the emperor's project would probably have kept Louis from involving himself directly in the Norman hostilities. The imperial expedition turned out to be an utter failure. The German army approached Rheims but then withdrew, overawed by the size of the army Louis had managed to assemble, perhaps intimidated by the oriflamme of St Denis, and possibly terrified by a partial eclipse of the sun.

Meanwhile, through complex negotiations between Henry I and the Roman curia, papal legates annulled Clito's marriage to Sibylla of Anjou on the grounds of consanguinity, narrowly interpreted. Foulques (V) was furious and is reported to have singed the whiskers of the legate who brought him the news. Henry rewarded the papacy for its good services by permitting a papal legate to exercise full legatine powers in England for the first time in his reign. In September 1125 Cardinal Giovanni da Crema presided at a legatine council in London that once again forbade clerical marriage and enforced ecclesiastical discipline in a variety of ways. The council manifested papal authority to a degree that Henry had not previously permitted in England, much to the chagrin of William de Corbeil, archbishop of Canterbury, whose customary precedence at kingdom-wide councils Cardinal Giovanni had pre-empted. English churchmen retaliated by concocting scandalous stories about the cardinal's womanizing during his sojourn in England. But to Henry, the concession to the legate was a cheap price to pay for the quashing of Clito's Angevin marriage.

William Clito and the Flemish crisis, 1125–1128 As the years passed by without Adeliza bearing a child, it became necessary for Henry to look elsewhere for an heir. 'In grief that the woman did not conceive,' William of Malmesbury wrote (Malmesbury, *Historia novella*, 3), 'and in fear that she would always be barren', the king turned to his daughter Matilda, whose own childless marriage to Heinrich V had ended with the emperor's death in 1125. The following year Henry I summoned her to join him in Normandy, and in autumn 1126 they crossed to England in the company of a distinguished assemblage of magnates, prelates, high royal officials, and neighbouring princes. Since the king and his daughter had not met face to face since she had left for Germany at the age of eight, Henry would surely have taken the time to consider her qualifications and discuss them with his counsellors. Such consultation occurred that autumn, with the result that the empress's succession was opposed by some but supported strongly by her half-brother, Henry's natural son Robert, earl of Gloucester (d. 1147), by Earl Robert's good friend, the Breton Brian fitz Count, lord of Wallingford, and by Matilda's uncle, David, king of Scots, brother of the late Queen Matilda. Their advice prevailed, and on 1 January 1127 King Henry had his court swear to support his daughter as his heir to England and Normandy. Roger, bishop of Salisbury, presided at the oath taking, and Robert of Gloucester vied for the honour of swearing first with Henry's nephew *Stephen, younger son of Adela, countess of Blois, and, thanks to Henry's generosity, a major Anglo-Norman landholder.

It was doubtless Henry's decision in favour of the empress that prompted Louis VI to give all-out support to William Clito's rival claim. Before the end of January 1127 Louis had married his wife's half-sister, Jeanne de Montferrat, to Clito, and had endowed him with the lordship of the French Vexin. Shortly afterwards Clito led an armed force to Henry's frontier castle of Gisors, where he issued a formal claim to Normandy. Clito's fortunes rose still higher when, on 2 March 1127, political enemies of the childless Charles the Good, count of Flanders, murdered him at mass. In less than two weeks Louis VI was at Arras to help punish the murderers and participate in the selection of a new count, and on his advice and command the Flemings chose William Clito, grandson of Henry I's mother, Matilda of Flanders, over several other candidates with various claims of kinship to the comital house. But even as count of Flanders, Clito was by no means ready to abandon his designs on Normandy. On the contrary, he was in a position to advance them more forcefully than ever before. Henry could now expect a renewal of the Franco-Flemish-Angevin coalition that had nearly toppled his regime in 1118–19.

Henry responded by devoting money, energy, and all his diplomatic ingenuity to forestalling the impending coalition and shaking Clito's hold on Flanders. He secretly provided financial support to the several unsuccessful claimants to Flanders, placing himself nominally at their head by asserting his own claim to the countship (as son of Matilda of Flanders), and encouraging them all until he could discern which one might win sufficient support to unseat Clito. By 1128, through Henry's machinations and

Clito's inept handling of Flemish townspeople, the county was in a state of general rebellion. Louis returned to Flanders briefly in May to support Clito in his need, but was forced to withdraw when Henry launched a military threat against the Île-de-France. Shortly before the Flemish crisis broke, Louis VI and Amaury de Montfort had quarrelled and broken off their friendship; their dissension made it possible for Henry I to lead an army unopposed to Amaury's castle of Épernon, between Chartres and Paris, and to remain there peacefully as Amaury's guest for over a week, forcing Louis to withdraw from Flanders to defend Paris. When he did, Henry returned to Normandy.

By then Thierry, count of Alsace, had emerged, with Henry's aid, as Clito's chief rival to the Flemish countship. Hostilities continued in Flanders until late in July, when Clito was mortally wounded in an assault on Thierry's castle of Aalst. Clito's death brought the crisis, and Henry's troubles, to a sudden end, and the Anglo-Norman state remained at peace with Flanders and France for the remaining years of the reign. But before Clito met his end, Henry, in the heat of the crisis, had once again negotiated a marriage alliance with Anjou.

The alliance with Anjou, 1127–1128 As at previous moments of military crisis, Henry saw the critical importance of separating Anjou from France, and while he was undermining Clito's regime in Flanders, he was also negotiating with Foulques (V) the marriage of Foulques's son and heir, Geoffrey Plantagenet, with the Empress Matilda. Henry had probably never intended to leave Matilda unmarried, for his great hope would have been a grandson to succeed him—a male heir who, like the long-lost William, would unite the Norman and Anglo-Saxon royal lines. The grave threat arising from the crisis of 1127 had the effect of hastening Henry's search for a consort for Matilda and determining its direction. The royal succession was of enormous importance to him, but the immediate threat to his Anglo-Norman dominions was more important still. And the marriage of Matilda and Geoffrey might well answer both these urgent needs: an Anglo-Norman heir and peace with Anjou.

The marriage was negotiated in the spring of 1127, and the betrothal occurred late in the same year, at Sées or possibly Rouen. On Whitsunday (10 June) 1128 Henry knighted Geoffrey in Rouen, and a week later Geoffrey and Matilda were married at Le Mans in the presence of King Henry and Count Fulk. At the time of their marriage Matilda was a widow of twenty-five and her bridegroom a boy of fourteen. But despite Geoffrey's youth Foulques immediately associated him in the governance of Anjou. In 1129 Geoffrey became sole count when Foulques departed for the Holy Land to marry the heiress of the kingdom of Jerusalem. Meanwhile, less than six weeks after Matilda's marriage to Geoffrey, its chief motivation was suddenly and unexpectedly removed with Clito's death in battle. The international crisis ended, but the marriage endured.

Anglo-Norman governance and culture Henry I's reign witnessed notable developments in administration, patronage, and culture. In all three areas, the changes are clearly products of a far more general cultural upsurge that was transforming contemporary western Europe and has been termed the renaissance of the twelfth century. It is marked by a novel impulse to explain the cosmos and the everyday world in rational terms, viewing nature not as a theatre of miracles, but as a natural order operating on principles intelligible to the human mind and susceptible to logical enquiry. This new approach had a profound impact on the disciplines of theology, law, and history. During Henry I's reign, the best centres of higher learning were in France—at Paris, Chartres, Laon, and elsewhere—but the Anglo-Norman world was by no means isolated from these new intellectual currents. Archbishop Anselm was the most gifted theologian of his generation, while William of Malmesbury and Orderic Vitalis were among the foremost historians of their time. Indeed, a most remarkable configuration of historians was at work in Henry I's dominions, including such notable figures as Eadmer of Canterbury, Robert de Torigni, Henry of Huntingdon, Simeon of Durham, John of Worcester, and the Peterborough chronicler, along with a host of lesser writers of annals and annotated cartularies—all of whom cast welcome illumination on King Henry and his reign.

The new currents and cross-currents of thought had a significant effect as well on the operations and records of Henry I's government. The relationship between the new learning and advances in Anglo-Norman administration is suggested by the close links between the scholarly centre of Laon in northern France and the court of Henry I. Ranulf, Henry's chancellor between 1107 and c.1122, sent both his sons to Laon for their education, and Roger of Salisbury, the head of Henry's government in England, sent his nephews, Alexander and Nigel, to study there as well. After their return Alexander was advanced to the wealthy bishopric of Lincoln and also played a major role in the royal entourage and administration. Nigel became the first royal treasurer for both England and Normandy, and although he was elevated to the bishopric of Ely in 1133, he remained active in royal governance. Another Laon student, Gui d'Étampes, became master of Bishop Roger's school at Salisbury. Not surprisingly, when a group of canons from Laon Cathedral arrived at Salisbury in the course of a fund-raising tour of England in 1113, they received the warmest of welcomes from Bishop Roger.

A highly literate government such as Henry I's, directed by officials who were in close touch with one of Europe's foremost centres of learning, could well be expected to produce administrative records unprecedented in their abundance and originality. Henry's government more than met such expectations with a great flood of governmental documents. They included an unprecedented outpouring of royal charters (using the term in its broad and contemporary sense to include all royal written orders, including writs), of which about 1500—a small fraction of the original avalanche—have survived, as compared with less than 500 surviving charters of William the Conqueror and William Rufus, whose two reigns spanned an equivalent period. The charters of Henry I furnish, as in no previous reign, an abundance of information on the activities and personnel of the royal government.

The systematization of government Another product of Henry I's precocious administration was the first record of the newly constituted exchequer, the pipe roll of 1130, the sole surviving exemplar of an annual series of such accounts, and by far the earliest surviving kingdom-wide financial survey in the history of Europe. The exchequer, meeting at Winchester, very likely originated under Henry I and his great minister Roger of Salisbury. It was a monument in the evolution of medieval government from itinerant household administration to administrative kingship based on sedentary departments.

Henry I's regime also produced an elaborate record, again the first of its kind, of the organization, rank, and emoluments of the royal household, the aforementioned *Constitutio domus regis*. An anonymous administrator in Henry I's government wrote the first treatise on English law, the *Leges Henrici primi*, and was also very probably the author of a very significant companion treatise, the *Quadripartitus*. The two treatises are best seen as products of a single interconnected enterprise to make explicit the unwritten 'Laws of Edward the Confessor' which Henry, in his coronation charter, had undertaken to restore. Henry further recognized the authority of pre-conquest legal practices in a writ mandating the continued functioning of shire and hundred courts, to meet 'as they were wont to do in the time of King Edward, and not otherwise' (*Reg. RAN*, 2, no. 892). It is characteristic of twelfth-century intellectual developments that the *Leges Henrici primi* and *Quadripartitus* both rest on deep historical foundations, penetrating far into the past, yet analyse these foundations with a self-awareness and coherence that is altogether new.

Henry I himself appears to have participated fully in this newly systematic approach to governance. He surrounded himself with systematizers, but none was more systematic than Henry himself. According to Orderic:

> He inquired into everything, and retained all he heard in his tenacious memory. He wished to know all the business of officials and dignitaries; and, since he was an assiduous ruler, he kept an eye on all the happenings in England and Normandy. (Ordericus Vitalis, *Eccl. hist.*, 6.100)

Royal patronage The two aspects of Henry I's government in which the emergence of new ideas of reason and order is most apparent are, first, royal patronage and, second, administrative machinery. Southern has described patronage as perhaps Henry I's most fundamental contribution to English history. It was Henry, Southern writes, 'who first controlled the whole range of government patronage with which we are later familiar; and it was under him that we can first observe the effects of this patronage at all closely' (Southern, *Medieval Humanism*, 209). Whether Henry I's contribution to the development of royal patronage is actual, or an illusion created by the vast increase in surviving sources, will perhaps never be determined. But Henry was indeed notably successful in drawing into

his regime some of the wealthiest persons in the Anglo-Norman world, and some of the most intelligent: new men 'raised from the dust' such as Roger, bishop of Salisbury, and his swiftly ascending clerical kinsmen Alexander of Lincoln and Nigel of Ely, along with such laymen as William and Nigel d'Aubigny and Geoffrey of Clinton. One must also include those men neither old nor new—high-born, non-inheriting cadets and bastards, such as Robert of Gloucester, Stephen of Blois, Stephen's brother Henry, bishop of Winchester, and Brian fitz Count. And there were also members of the great old families: Beaumont, Warenne, Boulogne, Clare, Chester. As Southern cogently argues, Henry I drew these diverse people into his net through means well known to later kings in later times: marriages to heiresses, forgiveness or delay of debts, exemptions from taxes or fines, the granting of wardships, shrievalties or other ministries, leniency in regard to collateral inheritances, and an endless variety of other royal favours made available to the king's friends—or, occasionally, to their clients.

The whole vast system of Henry I's patronage is recorded in detail in the pipe roll of 1130, which might well be described as a record of royal benefactions no less than of royal income. Since no earlier pipe roll has survived, nor any later one until 1155, the antiquity of the system that the pipe roll of 1130 displays is not certain. But Walter Map, writing under Henry II, credits Henry I with initiating a highly systematic approach to rewarding his magnates: he had a survey prepared of all his earls and barons, so Map asserts, and, as has been seen earlier, provided them with fixed *per diem* allowances of bread, wine, and candles when they were present at his court. And the lists of exemptions from geld and *auxilium burgi* (levies on boroughs) listed county by county in the pipe roll of 1130 suggest, once again, the development of highly systematic arrangements for allotting and recording favours to royal servants and friends.

Justice and finance The same systematizing tendency induced the government of Henry I to develop into what several historians have aptly described as an administrative 'machine'. As a response to his conquest of Normandy, Henry established viceregency governments in both the kingdom and the duchy, the members of which operated the royal courts and administration either in the king's presence or, if he was across the channel, on their own. These officials—Roger of Salisbury, Robert Bloet, bishop of Lincoln, and others in England, Jean de Lisieux, Robert de la Haie, and others in Normandy—also presided at the semi-annual English and Norman exchequer audits. It was in the 1120s that Nigel, nephew of Roger of Salisbury and future bishop of Ely, became the first truly Anglo-Norman treasurer, exercising responsibility over the revenues of both England and Normandy.

By that time Henry had reorganized the English judicial system by instituting a novel and comprehensive system of itinerant royal justices in place of the shire justiciars of earlier times (whose names and activities fade from the records about midway through Henry I's reign). The new itinerant justices now administered the bulk of royal judicial business in the shires. In the years between about 1125 and 1130 they were visiting all or nearly all the shires of England. This system of what would later be called 'justices on eyre' is disclosed to us only by the fortuitous survival of the pipe roll of 1130. No such arrangements are known to have operated in contemporary Normandy, but since no exchequer record survives for Normandy until the late twelfth century, confident conclusions one way or the other are not possible. Whatever the case, the surviving evidence does disclose a remarkable and evidently self-conscious administrative reorganization that had the effect of centralizing and systematizing the governance of both England and the entire Anglo-Norman *regnum*.

Henry's final years, 1128–1135 After William Clito's death and the marriage of Matilda and Geoffrey, Henry ruled his dominions in relative peace. He protected his frontiers with a great arc of stone castles, and by an encircling ring of friendly princes bound to Henry by vassalage, or marriage alliances, or both. Henry had married his natural daughters at one time or another to princes all along the Anglo-Norman periphery—to Rotrou, count of Perche, Guillaume Gouet, lord of Montmirail (Perche), Bouchard de Montmorency (with interests in the French Vexin, Eustace de Breteuil, Roscelin de Beaumont-le-Vicomte (Maine), Conan (III), duke of Brittany, Fergus of Galloway, Alexander, king of Scots, and, quite possibly, Gui (IV), lord of Laval (Maine).

Henry's relations with Louis VI were now placid. He remained a friend of Thierry of Alsace, count of Flanders, and had the pleasure of seeing Thierry wed to the same Sibylla of Anjou who had once alarmed Henry by marrying William Clito. The county of Anjou was now in the family, although tensions continued owing to the Empress Matilda's stormy relations first with her husband, then with her father. Wales and Scotland had never posed serious problems for Henry: the latter was ruled by a succession of Henry's brothers-in-law—Edgar, Alexander, David—all siblings of Queen Matilda and friends of Henry. Alexander, indeed, had been wed to one of Henry's bastard daughters (although it was said that he had not been overly fond of her), and David was virtually a member of Henry's court. The Welsh had posed more difficulties, and Henry had responded by leading military expeditions into Wales in 1114 and 1121, settling a colony of Flemings in Pembrokeshire, and endowing trusted Anglo-Norman magnates with strategic holdings within Wales— Gilbert fitz Richard de Clare in Ceredigion, Robert, earl of Gloucester, in Glamorgan and Gwynllŵg, Brian fitz Count in Abergavenny, Henry, earl of Warwick, in Gower.

Unfortunately for Henry, the marriage of Geoffrey and Matilda did not stabilize his relationship with Anjou as he had hoped. In mid-1129 Matilda quarrelled with Geoffrey and returned to Henry's dominions, thus delaying the conception of the all-important heir. She was with her father in England in summer 1131 when Henry received a message from Count Geoffrey asking that his wife return to him. At a great council on 8 September in Northampton, Henry and his magnates determined that Matilda should go back to Anjou, and the magnates once again swore fealty to the empress and to any son she might bear. Returning to Geoffrey, Matilda at last gave birth to a son, the future Henry II, on 5 March 1133. In August, despite the alarming portents of a solar eclipse and an earthquake, Henry set off for Normandy for the last time. Matilda joined him in Rouen the following year, where she bore a second son, Geoffrey. Henry is said to have taken great pleasure in his grandsons, whose births seemed to resolve the Anglo-Norman succession issue at last.

In mid-1135, however, Matilda and Geoffrey quarrelled with King Henry, demanding to be put in possession of castles that Geoffrey claimed Henry had promised him at the time of the wedding. The Angevin couple also demanded that Henry reinstate Guillaume Talvas, son and heir of Robert de Bellême, in his lands. Henry refused both requests, and undertook a minor military expedition along the Norman–Angevin border during the summer and autumn of 1135; he occupied several of Guillaume Talvas's castles, and afterwards retired to Normandy. Having journeyed to his lodge at Lyons-la-Forêt to indulge in his favourite pastime of hunting, he fell mortally ill on about 25 November after feasting on lampreys—a delicacy that his physician had forbidden him. The legend that Henry died of 'a surfeit of lampreys' has no basis in the historical record. It was not that he ate too many lampreys, but that his physician had advised him not to eat any at all.

Death and burial As he lay ill Henry summoned to his side his good friend, the churchman Hugh of Amiens, whom he had made first abbot of his great foundation at Reading and then had advanced to the archbishopric of Rouen. On Archbishop Hugh's advice Henry revoked all sentences of forfeiture that had been pronounced by his courts, allowed exiles to return and the disinherited to recover their inheritances. He ordered his son Robert of Gloucester, who had charge of his treasure at Falaise Castle, to pay out £60,000 in wages and gifts to his household and military retinue, and he asked that his body be taken to Reading Abbey for burial. Finally, he asked all in his hearing to devote themselves, as he had, to the preservation of peace and the protection of the poor. Then, after making his last confession and receiving absolution and last rites, Henry I died on the evening of 1 December 1135, after a reign of more than thirty-five years.

The crowd at Henry's deathbed included Archbishop Hugh, Bishop Audoin of Évreux, many magnates, and five counts or earls, among them Robert, earl of Gloucester, and Waleran, count of Meulan. As a group they bore Henry's body from Lyons-la-Forêt to Rouen Cathedral, where it was embalmed. His entrails were buried at the Bec priory of Notre-Dame-du-Pré where, forty-five years earlier, Robert Curthose had taken refuge while the young Henry had struggled to put down a rebellion in the streets of the ducal capital. From Rouen royal officials escorted the king's bier to Caen and, after a long wait for suitable winds, to Reading where it was buried at the abbey on 4 January 1136. Among those present at the burial was the new king of the English, whom Henry had never intended to succeed him, Stephen of Blois.

Historical interpretations Henry I has been seen as contributing very significantly to the rise of administrative kingship in England, and also to the development of royal patronage. In his time he was the most respected of kings. Orderic Vitalis and William of Malmesbury (neither of them court historians) admired him greatly. Walter Map, in the following generation, compared him favourably with his grandson Henry II. Later historians praised him as England's first learned king, and eminent historians of the nineteenth century, for instance William Stubbs and E. A. Freeman, saw him as an important 'constitutional' monarch and (in Freeman's case) a stalwart, native-born representative of the English after their humiliation in 1066. Henry I fared less well in the twentieth century. Distinguished British historians such as Sir Frank Stenton, Sir Richard Southern, and Christopher Brooke have viewed Henry I's regime as oppressive and his rule as savage and cruel. Others, such as Marjorie Chibnall, Judith Green, and the present writer, have seen Henry as a well-intentioned king who, while seeing to his own interests, nevertheless sought to live up to the standards and aspirations of medieval kingship—to rule in peace, to protect the church and the poor, and to safeguard and carry on the rights and privileges of his royal predecessors.

In pursuit of his goals Henry could be ruthless and at times, out of necessity, even cruel. He has been accused by twentieth-century historians of presiding over a regime that mutilated prisoners and persecuted persons who betrayed their lord king or publicly ridiculed him. But such crimes and punishments had been condemned for many generations in English law. Mutilation, for example (as Suger of St Denis stated in Henry's own time), was viewed as less severe than execution, and publicly ridiculing the king was a felony in Old English law. Judgements on Henry I differ, but if he is judged by contemporary standards rather than by those of the twentieth century, Orderic Vitalis's judgement, that although Henry was lascivious, he was, nevertheless, 'the greatest of kings' may serve as his epitaph. Or as Hugh of Amiens said at Henry's deathbed, 'God grant him peace, for peace he loved' (Malmesbury, *Historia novella*, 14).

Aftermath Henry's seemingly trivial quarrel with Matilda and Geoffrey in 1135 proved to be of decisive importance, for at his death he had not been on speaking terms with them for several months. Their separation from Henry made it possible for his nephew Stephen of Blois, now count of Boulogne in the right of his wife, to seize the English throne. The long and tragic civil war between Stephen and Matilda was the result not of a fundamental error in policy on Henry's part, but of an egregious miscalculation by Matilda and Geoffrey. Had Matilda been with Henry at the time of his death, there is little question but that she would have acquired England immediately afterwards, with the backing of the magnates and prelates at the royal deathbed. But as it was, the peace that Henry struggled so hard to maintain throughout his Anglo-Norman dominions died with him. Eventually, in 1154, Henry's grand design for the royal succession did bear fruit, and his precocious administrative advances resumed, when Henry II, his grandson and namesake, and a descendant of the ruling houses of Normandy, Wessex, and Anjou, became the first of the Angevin kings.   C. WARREN HOLLISTER

Sources *Reg. RAN*, vols. 1–2 • W. Farrer, *An outline itinerary of King Henry I* (1920) • Ordericus Vitalis, *Eccl. hist.* • William of Malmesbury, *Gesta regum Anglorum / The history of the English kings*, ed. and trans. R. A. B. Mynors, R. M. Thomson, and M. Winterbottom, 2 vols., OMT (1998–9) • William of Malmesbury, *The Historia novella*, ed. and trans. K. R. Potter (1955) • *Willelmi Malmesbiriensis monachi de gestis pontificum Anglorum libri quinque*, ed. N. E. S. A. Hamilton, Rolls Series, 52 (1870) • *Eadmeri Historia novorum in Anglia*, ed. M. Rule, Rolls Series, 81 (1884) • Henry, archdeacon of Huntingdon, *Historia Anglorum*, ed. D. E. Greenway, OMT (1996) • *The chronicle of John of Worcester, 1118–1140*, ed. J. R. H. Weaver (1908) • *Florentii Wigorniensis monachi chronicon ex chronicis*, ed. B. Thorpe, 2 vols., EHS, 10 (1848–9) • *ASC* • 'Historia regum', Symeon of Durham, *Opera*, vol. 2 • William of Jumièges, *Gesta Normannorum ducum*, ed. J. Marx (Rouen and Paris, 1914) • R. Fitz Nigel [R. Fitzneale], *Dialogus de scaccario / The course of the exchequer*, ed. and trans. C. Johnson, rev. edn, rev. F. E. L. Carter and D. E. Greenway, OMT (1983) • *S. Anselmi Cantuariensis archiepiscopi opera omnia*, ed. F. S. Schmitt, 6 vols. (1938–61); repr. with *Prolegomena, seu, Ratio editionis* (1968) • *The letters of Saint Anselm of Canterbury*, ed. and trans. W. Fröhlich, 3 vols. (1990–94) • S. N. Vaughn, *Anselm of Bec and Robert of Meulan: the innocence of the dove and the wisdom of the serpent* (1987) • R. W. Southern, *Medieval humanism and other studies* (1970) • R. W. Southern, *Saint Anselm: a portrait in a landscape* (1990) • J. A. Green, *The government of England under Henry I* (1986) • C. W. Hollister, *Monarchy, magnates, and institutions in the Anglo-Norman world* (1986) • D. Knowles, *The monastic order in England*, 2nd edn (1963) • F. Barlow, *The English church, 1066–1154: a history of the Anglo-Norman church* (1979) • F. Barlow, *William Rufus* (1983) • M. Brett, *The English church under Henry I* (1975) • D. Whitelock, M. Brett, and C. N. L. Brooke, eds., *Councils and synods with other documents relating to the English church, 871–1204*, 2 (1981) • M. Chibnall, *Anglo-Norman England, 1066–1166* (1986) • M. Chibnall, *The world of Orderic Vitalis* (1984) • F. M. Stenton, *The first century of English feudalism, 1066–1166*, 2nd edn (1961) • C. H. Haskins, *Norman institutions* (1918) • I. J. Sanders, *English baronies: a study of their origin and descent, 1086–1327* (1960) • D. Crouch, *The Beaumont twins: the roots and branches of power in the twelfth century*, Cambridge Studies in Medieval Life and Thought, 4th ser., 1 (1986) • J. Hudson, *Land, law, and lordship in Anglo-Norman England* (1994) • P. Dalton, *Conquest, anarchy, and lordship: Yorkshire, 1066–1154*, Cambridge Studies in Medieval Life and Thought, 4th ser., 27 (1994) • C. A. Newman, *The Anglo-Norman nobility in the reign of Henry I: the second generation* (1988) • S. Morillo, *Warfare under the Anglo-Norman kings, 1066–1135* (1994) • A. Luchaire, *Louis VI le Gros: annales de sa vie et de son regne (1081–1137)* (1890) • *Hugh the Chanter: the history of the church of York, 1066–1127*, ed. and trans. C. Johnson (1961) • Suger, abbot of St Denis, *Vie de Louis VI le Gros*, ed. and trans. H. Waquet (1929); repr. (Paris, 1964) • W. Farrer and others, eds., *Early Yorkshire charters*, 12 vols. (1914–65), vol. 1

Likenesses coins, BM • manuscript drawing, CCC Oxf., MS 157, fol. 383 [*see illus.*] • portrait, repro. in John of Worcester, *Chron.* • war seals, BM

Henry II (1133–1189), king of England, duke of Normandy and of Aquitaine, and count of Anjou, was the eldest of three sons born to Empress *Matilda, daughter of *Henry I, and Geoffrey Plantagenet, count of Anjou. Geoffrey's sobriquet, which is attested by several contemporary sources, has been plausibly but not certainly ascribed to his wearing a sprig of broom, *Planta genista*, in his helmet.

But its attribution as a surname to all the kings of England descended from him until 1485, though undeniably a genealogical convenience, is factually unwarranted. That Richard II adopted the broomcod as one of his personal emblems was purely coincidental—he borrowed it from the French monarchy. Only in the mid-fifteenth century did the name Plantagenet appear as a royal surname, when *Richard, duke of York, claimed the throne in 1460 as 'Richard Plantaginet, commonly called Duc of York' (*RotP*, 5.375). The name was also borne by illegitimate sons of Edward IV and Richard III. In the following century it was known to Shakespeare, thus in *King John* the Bastard Falconbridge, who has been identified as the illegitimate son of Richard I, proclaims that 'I come one way of the Plantagenets' (*King John*, V.vi.12). But not until the late seventeenth century did it pass into common usage among historians. In their time the kings between Henry II and Richard III were usually identified by reference to their parentage or their places of birth—Henry II himself was commonly referred to as Henry FitzEmpress.

An Anglo-Norman inheritance Henry's birth on 5 March 1133 at Le Mans brought to fruition the plan of his grandfather and namesake, Henry I, for the English and Norman successions set in motion by the marriage in 1128 of the widowed empress and the young Count Geoffrey. Henry I had made all his barons swear oaths of fealty to his daughter and his grandson. However, the family's estrangement at the time of Henry I's death in December 1135 allowed those within the Anglo-Norman court who opposed both female and Angevin rule, or either one of these, to forswear their oaths and accept another member of the ducal–royal house, Henry I's nephew Stephen, count of Mortain and Boulogne, as their king. This momentous turn of events, followed by the inability of the empress and the count to regain the birthright of the child Henry, either through diplomacy or force of arms, led to years of war and civil unrest. In 1139 Matilda went to England, where she spent nine years before giving up the attempt to wrest control of the throne from Stephen in person. Meanwhile Geoffrey began a slow sweep of Norman defences in 1141, which ended with the fall of Rouen and the count's investiture as duke in 1144. The conquest of Normandy gave the Angevin party in England the necessary resolve to hold out until Henry came of age, assumed the duchy's leadership himself, and launched the ultimate campaign to reunite Normandy and England. True to this vision, in December 1149, within a year of his knighting at the age of sixteen by his uncle David, king of Scots, Henry became duke. Now the spectre confronting Stephen and his allies was not one of a woman trying to rule in a man's world, nor of an alien Angevin trying to conquer the Anglo-Norman world, but of a reigning Norman duke of Norman blood, a man boundless in energy and the excitement of youth.

Desperate, Stephen sought a renewal of his old alliance with Louis VII of France, who had just returned from the second crusade. The French king was at odds with Count Geoffrey over his treatment of their vassal Giraud Berlai, the seneschal of Poitou. Throughout 1150 diplomatic missions were sent by the English, Normans, and Angevins to Paris, each vying for Louis's support. The death of Abbot Suger, Louis's chief adviser, who favoured holding with the Angevins, and Geoffrey's pressing of the siege of Berlai's castle of Montreuil-Bellay, led the French king in 1151 to join with his brother-in-law Eustace, Stephen's son and count of Boulogne, in an attack on Normandy. Momentarily the Angevin cause was in jeopardy. Louis had yet to recognize Henry as duke. If Normandy were

Henry II (1133–1189), tomb effigy

overrun, perhaps Eustace might claim the title. In any event, attacking Normandy kept Henry out of England. It was a good strategy.

Count Geoffrey remained in Anjou during the crisis just long enough to bring about a successful conclusion to his three-year siege of Montreuil-Bellay (a feat that much impressed contemporaries), and then moved with an Angevin army up into Normandy where he joined his son. Few in the French camp were comfortable with the thought of an attack on the combined Norman–Angevin armies, least of all Louis VII himself who, feeling ill, withdrew to Paris. There in August 1151 a complex process of disengagement followed in which Eustace's interests proved expendable. Geoffrey, Henry, and Louis VII met for a peace conference under the guidance of Bernard of Clairvaux. In the outcome Geoffrey made amends for his harsh treatment of the Berlai family, while Louis accepted Henry's homage as duke of Normandy—the price for which was the duke's agreement to the surrender of the Norman Vexin. Norman–Angevin arms, skilled diplomacy, and luck, ably assisted by the Cistercians, had carried the day. Son and father finally were freed to concentrate their energies on helping the Angevin party in England without compromising the security of Normandy or Anjou.

Whatever frustrations Eustace felt with his brother-in-law's about-face are not recorded; the Normans on the other hand were elated. Within days of the peace conference a war council was called to come together at Lisieux on 14 September 1151 to prepare the invasion of England. Then the unexpected happened. Count Geoffrey died after a brief illness. The catch on fortune's wheel was released. At the age of eighteen Duke Henry became count of Anjou, Maine, and Touraine, though he had not wished it so. The English invasion would have to wait while he took control of his father's county. It was precious time to lose.

Even with Henry on the continent Stephen's position in England was becoming more uneasy. Lately magnates on both sides in the civil war had adopted a policy of 'wait and see'. They entered into private agreements among one another, intent on limiting the scope of war and protecting their territorial interests. The son and heir of Robert, earl of Gloucester (d. 1147), for example, married the daughter of Robert, earl of Leicester (d. 1168), joining in some degree of friendship the two principal rival baronial houses in the kingdom. Stephen's scope for action against the Angevin party was becoming increasingly limited. The idea that Stephen was rightfully king, but that Henry, not Eustace, was rightfully heir, had gained ground among the magnates, as it had within the church. That Stephen never tried to have the magnates swear fealty to Eustace as heir, or perform homage, shows how little store he put in the mechanism Henry I used to ensure his succession plan. After all, Stephen himself had shown how chancy a mechanism it could be. Stephen had only one recourse left, force. Rebuffed by Pope Eugenius III on the question of his son's anointing, the king gathered together all the English bishops in March 1152 in London

and demanded their blessing and acquiescence in Eustace's anointing. To a man the bishops refused. Stephen had gained the throne through perjury, they said, so the son could not inherit. These were Eugenius's words, but they were Angevin sentiments, planted in their minds long ago. Frustrated and outraged Stephen imprisoned his bishops, but Archbishop Theobald of Canterbury escaped to the continent. Faced with the hopelessness of trying to bully a united English episcopate the king released the others.

Marriage to Eleanor of Aquitaine, 1152, and confrontation with Stephen Henry, on the other hand, had a decisively better spring. In March 1152 Louis VII divorced his wife, *Eleanor of Aquitaine (d. 1204), and foolishly allowed the former queen to return alone to Poitou. On 18 May in the same year, 'either suddenly or by design', Eleanor married Henry, whom she had met the previous August in Paris (*Chronica Roberti de Torigneio* in *Chronicles*, ed. Howlett, 4.165). These events, which in a matter of months had made Henry overlord of virtually all of western France, left observers astonished. Within weeks of the marriage he was at Barfleur ready to sail for England.

Louis VII's response to Eleanor's marriage to Henry, however, ended any chance for an English expedition in the summer of 1152. Instead Henry found himself faced the other way fighting for all his possessions, including Normandy and Anjou. Louis wanted to ruin his vassal, to confiscate his lands and redistribute them among a coalition expressly formed for this purpose. The coalition was made up of Eustace, count of Boulogne, who had rushed over from England with renewed hopes, Henri, count of Champagne, the betrothed of the eldest daughter of Louis and Eleanor, who had been declared legitimate before the divorce and promised part of Aquitaine as her inheritance, Robert, count of Perche, Louis's brother, and Geoffrey of Anjou, Duke Henry's brother. Robert de Torigni gives the details of the fighting, and reports that the duke's masterful defence of his possessions won him praise, even from his enemies. In a little more than two months, by early September, Henry had secured the Norman frontier from attack and crushed his brother's rebellion in Anjou. This was the first of many similar victories to come wherein Henry fought great coalitions over long distances in protecting his Angevin dominions. The year 1152 not only brought the duke–count great resources, it fixed his reputation. Here was a man who would be king. Finally, in January 1153, Henry, braving winter seas, sailed for England—a new endgame had begun.

On a bitter January morning Duke Henry and King Stephen, each at the head of his troops, met face to face near Malmesbury separated only by the River Avon, swollen by winter rains. Torrents of rain and sleet poured down upon the two armies. Yet it was not adverse weather conditions that prevented the all-out battle the duke and king sought as the moment of final reckoning. Barons on both sides, like the church, desired peace, not wanting to engage further in the risks of war. Stephen lost confidence in the magnates serving him, agreed to a truce, and withdrew to London. For the next six months it seemed as if both men intentionally avoided one another in their campaigns. Stephen still held the loyalty of the major towns, like London, with their vast resources of money and manpower. Henry moved about making grants and concessions to churches and magnates. Rewards were given to longtime supporters, such as the Fitzhardings of Bristol, while enticements for defection were offered to royalists. When the dominant magnate in the midlands, the earl of Leicester, openly declared for the duke, the strength of the king's cause suffered measurably. And when, in late July or early August, Henry finally marched to relieve the Angevin outpost of Wallingford, holding out under siege even after the death of its lord Brian fitz Count, Stephen had to react. However, their confrontation at Wallingford ended in the same fashion as it had at Malmesbury: the opposing armies refused to fight.

Peace negotiations, which had been progressing behind the scenes throughout the year, now were conducted in the open. Archbishop Theobald took part with Bishop Henry of Winchester and others in fixing the terms. The basic idea went back to the early 1140s; Stephen was to remain king as long as he lived, Henry would inherit after his death. Feeling betrayed, Eustace left his father's court for East Anglia in a destructive rage. Eustace's sudden death on 17 August 1153 ended any hesitation Stephen might have had about concluding the negotiations. He seemed most concerned with securing and enlarging the inheritance of his youngest son, William. In the first weeks of November, Stephen and Henry met at Winchester where the king adopted Henry as his heir. William was well provided for by being ensured of his mother's extensive lands in England (she had died in May 1152), the Anglo-Norman estates conferred on his father by Henry I, the cross-channel lands of the earls of Warenne which were to come to him through marriage, and other significant properties, towns, and castles in England. If William was not to inherit the kingdom, he would be its greatest magnate and rule independently, as his brother had, in Boulogne. By this arrangement Stephen preserved his family's honour and future power as best he could under the circumstances. From Winchester king and duke went on to London, where during the Christmas holidays a notification executing the treaty was prepared and witnessed at Westminster.

Henry's succession to the English throne, 1154 No one at the outset of 1154 could easily have predicted how long the treaty would hold, whether the civil war in England was truly finished. Powerful forces had combined to put a stop to the war, not the least of which was pressure from the papacy skilfully manipulated by the Angevins. But Bernard of Clairvaux and Eugenius III had died in the summer of 1153 along with Count Eustace, whose coronation they had helped prevent. The Angevin victory, if it was to be maintained, would have to depend after all upon Stephen's continued co-operation and the goodwill of the barons themselves. And when Duke Henry hastily quit England for the continent in April after a plot against his life by Flemish mercenaries had been uncovered, it could not have been foreseen that Stephen, even at the age of

sixty, would die only months later in October, and that Duke Henry would become king within a year of the treaty, unopposed, as happened on 19 December 1154.

In retrospect the events of 1151–4 were extraordinary. They brought into being an Angevin dominion scarcely imaginable in the 1140s, centred on the older Anglo-Norman state, but including much of central and southern France. It would take four more years, however, for the young King Henry to secure this vast dominion. As it happened, no cleric, no magnate, no family stood for long against the new king–duke, and in this he, who as a child had felt denied his rightful place, took great satisfaction. Later, reflecting on the early accomplishments of his reign, Henry II proudly boasted that he had attained the authority of his grandfather, Henry I, who 'was king in his own land, papal legate, patriarch, emperor, and everything he wished' (*Letters of John of Salisbury*, 2.581).

Personality, habits, and appearance of Henry II Contemporaries have left a vivid portrait of this first Angevin king, who at once was an immovable and moving force. Henry was of medium height, with a strong square chest, and legs slightly bowed from endless days on horseback. His hair was reddish, lightening somewhat in later years, and his head was kept closely shaved—a picture to which the image on his tomb at Fontevrault is very true. His blue-grey eyes were his most distinctive features, described by Peter of Blois as 'dove-like when he [was] at peace', but 'gleaming like fire when his temper [was] aroused', and flashing 'like lightning' in bursts of passion (*Patrologia Latina*, 207.48–9). Ever restless and ever travelling, Henry, to Herbert of Bosham, was like a 'human chariot dragging all after him' (*Patrologia Latina*, 190.1322). Famous for his rapid movements, he often seemed to appear out of nowhere as if 'he must fly rather than travel by horse or ship' (Diceto, 1.351). And as he hurried through the Angevin provinces he investigated what was being done everywhere, and was 'especially strict in his judgement of those whom he has appointed as judges of others' (*Patrologia Latina*, 207.48–9).

Gentle and friendly, Henry nevertheless displayed a ferocious temper common to his Angevin ancestors, which struck terror into those around him. A misplaced word of praise for the king of Scotland one morning threw him into a fit of rage in which he 'fell out of bed screaming, tore up his coverlet, and threshed around the floor, cramming his mouth with the stuffing of his mattress' (Robertson and Sheppard, 6.71–2). Tireless, he preferred to stand rather than to sit, which caused great discomfort among his courtiers. Always approachable, he took care to listen with patience to petitioners, and his memory was unusually sharp. He was generous to those who experienced misfortune, once paying for the losses of sailors hit by a violent storm during one of his numerous channel crossings. His leisure hours were divided between hunting, hawking, reading, and intellectual debates with a circle of clerks or visiting monks. At moments of tumult at court he fled in silence to his beloved forests, seeking a solitary peace in the wild. Once he loved someone the bond was unbreakable; those whom he hated remained unforgiven.

And, although from many points of view he was liberal with his family, he denied them the one thing they cherished the most and only he could give, unrestricted power.

Geoffrey fitz Count's revolt, 1155–1156, and Henry's ascendancy In the autumn of 1155 Henry de Blois, the bishop of Winchester, fled into self-imposed exile at Cluny, clearly signalling that no resistance to Henry II's rule in England was possible after the king's methodically decisive actions in breaking the power of the few barons who defied him following his coronation. If anything, Henry II's most serious challenge in his first year as king arose on the continent, not in England, and came from his own brother, Geoffrey. In December 1155 Geoffrey raised a revolt in Anjou calling for the fulfilment of their father's will—that when and if Henry gained England, he should turn over the Touraine, Anjou, and Maine to Geoffrey in completion of his inheritance, which in 1151 had included the strategically located castles of Chinon, Loudun, and Mirebeau.

At word of the revolt Henry II crossed from Dover to Wissant on the coast of Boulogne in January 1156, and reached Rouen by 2 February. In the next weeks a family conference was held in the Norman capital to discuss the fraternal dispute. Several Angevin family members directly or indirectly affected gathered there: Henry II, *William FitzEmpress, his youngest brother, Matilda, his mother, Sibylla, countess of Flanders (his aunt), and Geoffrey. Henry saw to Geoffrey's diplomatic isolation by securing papal and Capetian assent to his retention of Anjou. Indeed, Henry performed homage to Louis VII for Normandy, Anjou, and Aquitaine the very week before the conference began, and had sent an embassy to the English pope Adrian IV months earlier, with a request to be released from the oath he had sworn, to uphold the will, because he had done so under duress. Perhaps this isolation, or the promise of a fair hearing by the family in Empress Matilda's presence, is what drew Geoffrey away from his Angevin strongholds to Rouen. Whatever the case, a peaceful resolution of the conflict could not be agreed upon. When Geoffrey withdrew from Rouen into Anjou, Henry followed.

Not until the summer of 1156 did Henry finally coerce his brother into submission. Later in that same year, after Geoffrey had renounced his claims to their father's lands in favour of an annuity and possession of a single castle (Loudun), Henry helped him to become the new count of Nantes, extending Angevin power along the Loire into Brittany. With Anjou firmly in hand, Henry, joined now by Eleanor, journeyed to Aquitaine, where he punished the vicomte of Thouars for supporting his brother's revolt. And if any lingering doubt over the propriety of Henry's overlordship of Anjou remained, it was removed with Geoffrey's unexpected death a short time later in 1158. By this date England, Normandy, Anjou, and Aquitaine were all under control, and Henry II, at the age of twenty-five, stood foremost among the princes of Western Christendom.

Henry II's success in governing his vast dominions with their varied populations and frontiers rested, in part, on his boundless energy and pragmatism. His energy is seen in his constant travels, his pragmatism in his selection of advisers. Among a group of ten or so of the king's most influential advisers during the late 1150s and 1160s were: his uncle Reginald, earl of Cornwall; his mother, Empress Matilda; William d'Aubigny, earl of Arundel, Queen Adeliza's widower; the justiciars Robert, earl of Leicester, and Richard de Lucy; the king's youngest brother, William FitzEmpress; the English chancellor Thomas Becket; the Norman constable Richard du Hommet; the archbishops Theobald of Canterbury, Roger of York, and Rotrou of Rouen; Arnulf, bishop of Lisieux; and the archdeacons of Poitiers and Canterbury, Richard of Ilchester and Geoffrey Ridel. These individuals, with few exceptions, came from an older generation, one once divided by civil war, yet now working largely in harmony with their king–duke. Of this group, only Becket would prove a major disappointment. Too late Henry recognized the mistake of advancing his once faithful chancellor to be primate of all England. The lesson was harsh.

The quarrel with Becket, 1163–1169 In July 1163 at the Council of Woodstock, Thomas Becket, archbishop of Canterbury, infuriated Henry by attacking a crown project to turn the annual aid paid to sheriffs into royal revenue. Henry shouted, 'By the eyes of God, it shall be given as revenue and entered in the royal rolls: and it is not fit that you should gainsay it, for no one would oppose your men against your will'. To which Becket is said to have responded, 'By the reverence of the eyes by which you have sworn, my lord king, there shall be given from all my land or from the property of the church not a penny' (Robertson and Sheppard, 2.373–4).

Becket's behaviour in 1163 and in the coming years, as his quarrel with Henry II intensified, was conditioned in part by his choice of a role model—Anselm of Bec, archbishop of Canterbury and defiant opponent of William II and Henry I. A month or so before the Woodstock confrontation Becket had lobbied, albeit unsuccessfully, for Anselm's canonization at the Council of Tours. A biography of Anselm, now lost, had been prepared by John of Salisbury in support of canonization. As R. W. Southern remarked, 'Henry II might have noted an ominous significance in his [Becket's] admiration for Anselm' (Southern, 337).

When Henry promoted Becket to the see of Canterbury in May 1162, he was expecting a Lanfranc, a Roger of Salisbury. What he got instead was a reincarnated Anselm, and an imperfect copy at that. Becket, unlike Anselm, proved to be an inept politician whose defiance, justified or not, hopelessly alienated the king and his counsellors. The series of miscalculations started in 1163 with Becket's attempt to restore, as Anselm had done, tenures lost by the archiepiscopal see, reached a climax in January 1164 with the death of Henry II's brother, William FitzEmpress, and ended with the archbishop's own murder in 1170 at the hands of a former member of the prince's entourage. It is a story of struggle for castles, baronies, and political influence, a story of two individuals, Thomas Becket and William FitzEmpress, tied together by fate in death, deaths which left their imprint on the remainder of Henry II's reign.

Soon after Woodstock the king and archbishop quarrelled again, this time over church–state issues: the archbishop's right to excommunicate tenants-in-chief without first consulting the king, the king's rights with regard to clerks charged with serious crimes. Alarmed by Becket's behaviour and compelled by his own need for systematization, Henry in the autumn of 1163 pressed the English bishops to recognize certain customs regulating the interaction of church and state. Predictably Becket refused to assent to any customs that would weaken church prerogatives. Henry responded decisively, stripping the archbishop of the castles and baronies of Berkhamsted and Eye, which he had retained from his days as chancellor. All that was left to Becket now was Canterbury itself.

Stung by the king's move, Becket lost little time in repaying in kind. He used his office to ruin Henry's plans for the marriage of William FitzEmpress. After the death of King Stephen's son, William of Blois, Earl Warenne, in 1159 Henry sought his brother's marriage to Isabella, the earl's highly connected and wealthy widow. This Becket now prohibited on the grounds of consanguinity, and it was within his right to do so since the two were distant cousins. For the moment Becket had his revenge. Henry kept the game and the rivalry alive by selecting Berkhamsted as the site for his Christmas court. Here, in apartments the archbishop had had built for his own pleasure, planning for the Council of Clarendon took place. Revenge begot revenge.

William, angry, sought consolation and advice in Normandy from his mother, Empress Matilda. What soothing words she had for her youngest son are unknown. William died on 30 January 1164, just two days after the conclusion of Clarendon. Henry was distraught over the news of his brother's death. More than that, he held Becket directly responsible. The quarrel was now more than a fight over payment of aids, castles, or church independence; it was personal.

Becket, and other members of the English episcopate, had taken oaths at Clarendon to uphold sixteen ancient customs governing relations between the king, his courts, and the church, set down for the first time now in writing in the celebrated constitutions of Clarendon. One of the principal constitutions, or clauses (no. 4), dealt with appeals to Rome—they were not to proceed without the king's approval—and another (no. 3) with the disposition of criminous clerks—they were to be tried in an ecclesiastical court and, if found guilty, defrocked and remanded for sentencing as a layman by a secular court. With close to one-sixth of the adult population in clerical orders, this last innovation was as pervasive and invasive as the prohibition of direct appeal to the Roman curia. The majority of the remaining fourteen clauses outlined limits on ecclesiastical jurisdiction, and one in particular (no. 7) sought direct control over the church's use of its spiritual weapons by requiring that before any baron or royal officer was excommunicated, or their lands placed under interdict, an appeal must be made to the king himself. In all ten of the constitutions were later condemned by the pope, and even Henry's sagacious mother disapproved of the innovation of having the English bishops swear to them in writing. But Henry, acting out his vision of his grandfather, who had been 'everything he wished' in his land, evidently wanted little to be left to ambiguity. Following Clarendon king and archbishop kept their distance: Henry by choice, Becket on the advice of Pope Alexander III, an exile in France. Alexander was a former papal chancellor and as such an experienced canon lawyer. Whatever sympathies he harboured with the archbishop's challenge of so-called 'evil customs' fostered by the English king, political pragmatism kept him from seeking a confrontation with the sovereign of fifty Anglo-French bishops. Alexander's pre-eminent concern was Frederick I 'Barbarossa', the German emperor, whose Italian policy and support for two successive antipopes, Victor IV and Pascal III, had forced him to France and the protection of Louis VII. This was not the moment to disturb the balance in which matters were suspended. Becket, however, could not be restrained, and Henry could not forgive.

In late 1164, after Becket had imprudently tried to leave the kingdom without permission, he was summoned first to London and then to Northampton to answer a series of suits, the most problematic of which related to his tenure as royal chancellor. A few days into the Council of Northampton it was evident to everyone that Henry, encouraged by his advisers, intended to break the archbishop of Canterbury, with incalculable financial repercussions for those who might support him. The trigger was the demand for an accounting for more than £30,000 in revenues that had passed through Becket's hands as chancellor—an impossible request, the more so since the accounting was demanded of him on the spot. Rather than humble himself and ask for Henry's mercy, the archbishop chose defiance. Brandishing his cross he strode out of the castle hall and miraculously escaped a throng of angry courtiers through an open gate. The flight from Northampton ended in Flanders; Henry did not see the archbishop again for five years. Eventually Becket found refuge at the Cistercian abbey of Pontigny, protected, as was Alexander III, by the French king. From this point the quarrel became 'a side issue in the papal schism and Henry II's relationship with Louis VII' (Barlow, *Becket*, 134). Henry II let Alexander and Louis know that any extreme action against the English crown or church would be met with a complete repudiation of allegiance and a counter-alliance with Frederick I. This message took on a more certain reality in 1165, when the emperor's chancellor, Rainald, archbishop of Cologne, was welcomed in Rouen and London on a mission to join the houses of Anjou, Hohenstaufen, and Saxony through a series of marriages, and at the continuation of these negotiations at the Diet of Würzburg, where Henry's ambassadors, carried away, perhaps, by the excitement of the moment, are said to have participated in an oath swearing never to recognize Alexander as pope.

The murder of Becket and its consequences, 1169–1172 Becket seemed to thrive emotionally on the turmoil and intrigue surrounding his exile, as if it were some great diplomatic dance. The roads through France and the channel ports were alive with envoys and secret messengers to and from the papal curia, English, French, German, and Sicilian courts, and the archbishop's own expanding international nexus of confidants and supporters. What Henry II disliked most of all, beyond his former friend's sheer ingratitude, was this revelry in self-importance and intrigue—the personality of the anti-authoritarian, incapable of working within established hierarchies, claiming always the principled ground of a higher authority. In an interval of several months during 1169–70, when Alexander III, Frederick I, Louis VII, and Henry II all sought solutions for their own differences, which in the end enabled Becket to regain his primacy, the archbishop put revenge ahead of peace and excommunicated his English 'enemies' upon landing in England. And yet Becket's action was not taken without provocation; Henry himself must be assigned a fair share of blame for the uncertainty of their *rapprochement* reached at Fréteval in July 1170 and its disastrous collapse. He failed to make effective provision for the restoration of confiscated lands and revenues, and, equally important, he avoided giving a public expression of his settlement with the archbishop by exchanging a kiss of peace with him.

When Becket landed in Kent on 1 December 1170, he landed alone without the king, who had promised to make the journey with him. For reasons of his own, Henry had broken this promise and others. The return of lands and revenues taken from the see of Canterbury during the exile had not been wholly effected, nor had expected restitutions been made to members of the archbishop's household. And, while the citizens of Canterbury and London seemed genuinely happy to have their archbishop with them once again, royal officers displayed an open hostility, going so far as refusing to allow Becket to visit the young Henry, his former ward, who at that moment was residing in England, and whose coronation by the archbishop of York on 14 June 1170 had greatly exacerbated relations between Becket and the English bishops who had continued to support Henry II. Had the king accompanied Becket as planned, the excommunications might have been forestalled and the affronts to archiepiscopal dignity blunted; and events might not then have spun so easily out of control. Certainly, Henry knew how volatile Becket could be; even so, when he heard the news of the recent excommunications, he let his own fury explode with words hung with a challenge: 'What miserable drones and traitors have I nourished and promoted in my household, who let their lord be treated with such shameful contempt by a low-born clerk!' (Robertson and Sheppard, 1.121–3; 2.429; 3.127–9, 487), later rendered in oral tradition: 'Who will rid me of this turbulent priest?' (Lyttelton, pt 4, 353). Four knights took up the challenge, sped from Normandy to England, and later in the afternoon of 29 December confronted Becket in Canterbury Cathedral. Whether their original intent was murderous remains unclear. But at least one of the knights, Richard Brito, had personal cause to see Becket dead, for he cried out as he struck the archbishop with his sword: 'Take this for the love of my lord William, the king's brother!' (Robertson and Sheppard, 3.142).

When he heard the terrible news, Henry went into seclusion for three days and then employed all his diplomatic skills and resourcefulness to distance himself from the murder. Clergy all over Europe were outraged. Pope Alexander even refused to speak to an Englishman for more than a week upon learning of Becket's martyrdom. Pressure arose on all sides; an interdict was threatened, then proclaimed. Henry feared excommunication, and took measures to prevent papal legates from entering his lands, closing the channel ports behind him when he left the continent for Ireland—a journey with momentous consequences for that island, and its involvement with the Anglo-Norman world. Only in 1172, when Henry had reappeared from Ireland, did the storm finally end. The king met Alexander III's legates at Avranches in May and submitted to their judgment. In what became known as 'the compromise of Avranches', Henry admitted that, although he never desired the killing of Becket, his words may have prompted the murderers. Kneeling at the door of the cathedral in a full and abject display of penance, the king accepted the legates' terms for reconciliation: to maintain his obedience to Alexander III as long as he treated Henry as a 'Christian king'; to take the cross and set out for Jerusalem, or, if he wished, to fight the Moors in Spain; never again to impede lawful appeals to the pope in ecclesiastical suits; to abolish all customs introduced by him injurious to the church and no longer to require bishops to observe them; to restore all its possessions to Canterbury; and to bestow his peace on all Becket's followers. With this, Henry was absolved and the quarrel, at last, resolved. Made wiser by experience, Henry made no further overt efforts to impede appeals to Rome (though he was sometimes able to exert a degree of control over them), and he increased his donations to religious houses, though not to the point of lavishness. His reward for his new flexibility was control of the English church in all important respects as complete as his grandfather's had been, given perfect expression in the famous writ addressed to the monks of Winchester Cathedral priory in 1173, 'I order you to hold a free election, but nevertheless, I forbid you to elect anyone except Richard my clerk, the archdeacon of Poitiers' (Poole, 220).

Still, these unsettling times brought on a new problem Henry II never quite proved able to manage: the disaffection of his queen, Eleanor, and their sons. The death in 1167 of the Empress Matilda had removed an experienced voice whose wise counsel might have prevented the coming perpetual family crisis. Where before Henry had seemed the master of his success, he now became its uncertain prisoner. And, not without irony, he found the salvation of his kingdom in St Thomas.

Family problems Queen Eleanor and Henry II had eight children, all but one of whom survived infancy. In 1170 their four sons and three daughters ranged in age from fifteen to three years old. The eldest daughter, *Matilda, was wed to Henry the Lion, duke of Saxony. Her sister Eleanor was betrothed to Alfonso, king of Castile. The eldest surviving son, *Henry, was married to Margaret, daughter of Louis VII of France and his second wife, Constanza of Castile, while another son, *Richard, was betrothed to her uterine sister, Alice. Their brother, *Geoffrey, was betrothed to the heir of Brittany, Constance, in whose name Henry II had taken over governance of the duchy from her father, leaving the youngest children, *Joanna and *John, as yet without provision. Henry also had an illegitimate son, William [see Longespée, William (I)]. After two marriages and four daughters, Louis VII finally had had a son and heir, Philip, with his third wife, Adèle de Blois. Adèle's own brothers, the counts of Champagne and Blois, had been married to the eldest daughters of Louis's marriage to Eleanor in the early 1160s. The French king may well have looked to the day when his son and heir would rule over a kingdom whose prominent barons were his brothers-in-law. Certainly it was in Louis VII's mind that the Angevin dominions be broken into their constituent parts in the next generation. Under the treaty of Montmirail of 1169 Henry II had agreed to as much, by formally designating Henry as the heir to England, Normandy, and Anjou, Geoffrey as the heir to Brittany, and Richard as the heir to his mother's Aquitaine. Again in 1170, a few months before Thomas Becket's murder, while Henry II lay seriously ill at a small castle near Domfront on the Norman frontier with Maine, he made out a will reaffirming that inheritance scheme. More importantly, Henry II had engineered the anointing of his son and namesake as co-king of England that summer, fixing the English portion of the inheritance in a fashion that had eluded Stephen. But there were two absences from the anointing—the archbishop of Canterbury, whose right it was to crown the kings of England, and the younger Henry's wife, Margaret, who should have been made a queen. No doubt Henry II calculated the effect of the anointing on Louis VII and Becket as influencing the French king into pressuring the archbishop to quit his exile, return to England, and redeem both their honours by a second crowning—one that included the French princess. The calculation worked. Becket did return, but the consequences were tragic. In his manipulations Henry II snared himself, giving Louis VII the advantage of playing off the sons against the father.

In May 1172 Henry II returned to Normandy, having spent seven months in Ireland, to receive absolution from the papal legates awaiting him there concerning complicity in Thomas Becket's murder. Once reconciled with the church he was willing to accede to Louis VII's wish for a recrowning of young Henry with Margaret's inclusion as his queen. This was done at Winchester in August. Earlier that summer Richard had been formally installed as duke of Aquitaine in separate ceremonies at Poitiers and Limoges in the presence of his mother, Eleanor. So the inheritance scheme worked out in 1169 was taking on a greater reality, although Henry II never intended to give

up any of his authority soon. If anything he was intent on maintaining his 'old path of family politics and territorial expansion' (Gillingham, *Richard the Lion Heart*, 62). He had been working on a marriage proposal with Humbert, count of Maurienne, since 1171. The count's lands controlled all the passes through the western Alps. Since Humbert had two daughters but no sons, Henry II was willing to pay a vast sum of money to secure the marriage of his youngest son, John, to the count's heir, whichever daughter she might turn out to be. A meeting took place at Montferrat in the Auvergne in early February 1173 to draw up an agreement. Later in the month the court moved to Limoges where Raymond, count of Toulouse, with the kings of Navarre and Aragon looking on, performed homage in turn to Henry II, Henry, the Young King, and Richard.

It was a splendid display, one far removed from the necessary humiliation of Henry's scourging by the papal legates as part of his absolution months before. The young king had watched that scene, and well may have wondered where he fitted into this one. When his father, at Count Humbert's urging, agreed to give the Angevin castles of Chinon, Loudun, and Mirebeau to the five-year-old John to finalize the marriage arrangement, young Henry exploded in anger. Louis VII already had pointed out to his son-in-law that he was twice crowned, but not lord, in any real sense, of anything. He now demanded that his father hand over any one of his inheritances: England, Normandy, or Anjou. He was after all within days of his eighteenth birthday, about the same age as Henry II was when Count Geoffrey released Normandy. The demand was promptly refused. It is hard to imagine that what occurred next was completely spontaneous. Eleanor, Henry II discovered, was plotting against him with their sons. And, behind the plotting, stood his overlord, the king of France.

The 'great rebellion', 1173–1174, and its aftermath In the civil war that consumed the next two years Henry II once again proved himself the luckiest and most resourceful of princes. With the kings of France and Scotland, the counts of Boulogne, Flanders, Dreux, and Blois all arrayed against him, with his wife and sons in rebellion, with their rebellion supported by numerous barons throughout the Angevin dominions, he triumphed. And he triumphed from a distance. The count of Boulogne's death from a chance crossbow shot in the summer of 1173 ended the campaign of his brother, the count of Flanders, deep into Norman territory that year, while Eleanor's capture and imprisonment, as she tried to leave Poitou to join her sons in Paris, prevented her involvement in the war. Similarly, the capture by the king's men first of the earl of Leicester, son of the former justiciar, in the autumn of 1173, and then of the king of Scotland in the summer of 1174, broke the back of the rebellion in England. On each of these occasions Henry was elsewhere. He effectively managed his men and resources from afar, trusted his subordinates to perform their jobs, and chose the right moments to intervene in person. The size of the Angevin dominions was never an important factor in their defence. What was important was the sheer talent of the administrators and barons upon whom Henry relied: their capacity to take charge, the protection and control of transportation routes, on both land and sea, the loyalty of churchmen and townsmen, the ready wealth used to hire mercenaries, and Henry II's own renowned defensive genius and capacity for instant attack. Even so, many of the problems that had brought about the civil war remained.

First, the estrangement of Henry and Eleanor offered no ready resolution. Whatever the motives for Eleanor's rebellion—anger at her husband's affair with Rosamund *Clifford, a longing for real political power away from her husband's shadow, fear of the permanent vassalage of Aquitaine to the English kings have all been suggested—Henry blamed her for the civil war and never again either trusted her or forgave her. In 1175 he tried to persuade a papal legate, visiting England on other business, to annul their marriage. After the annulment Eleanor was to be placed in seclusion at the convent of Fontevrault. Later in 1176 the younger Henry, Richard, and Geoffrey vigorously protested against their father's intentions. Even Rotrou, archbishop of Rouen, one of Henry's closest confidants, refused to sanction such an idea. Family and court opinion aside, Alexander III's rejection of the proposal ended the initiative. What Henry decided upon instead was Eleanor's continued imprisonment, keeping open the wound occasioned by her rebellion.

Second, Henry was unable, or unwilling, to accommodate the reasonable expectations of his eldest son. Where after 1174 Richard was allowed a certain freedom as duke of Aquitaine, and Geoffrey, following his marriage to Constance of Brittany (1181), much the same in that province, Henry III, as the younger king was sometimes called, was never given outright a territory of his own to rule. He died in 1183, aged twenty-eight, once again in rebellion against his father.

Problems of succession, 1183–1186 The Young King's death, far from settling matters, threw the Angevin dominions into yet another succession crisis. It had been easy for the kingdom of France. When Louis VII became incapacitated in 1179, his only son Philip, a youth of fifteen, succeeded him. Henry II's misfortune was to have too many sons. And the hostility of the Angevin males towards one another had become a common feature of political interaction by the 1180s. Even if Henry had, in fact, resigned one or more of his territories, there is little reason to believe that Richard, Geoffrey, or John ever could have coexisted peacefully. Before Henry would name Richard as his heir to England, Normandy, and Anjou, he wanted Aquitaine for John. Richard saw no usefulness in giving up real power over his duchy for the empty mantle of his elder brother, so he baulked. Henry could have gone ahead and declared Richard his heir anyway. The spectre of a permanent union of Aquitaine with Anjou, Normandy, and England, though, might have proved too much a threat for the French monarchy to ignore, and would certainly have alienated Geoffrey and John. Everything was tangled. John had been promised the county of Mortain and the earldoms of Cornwall and Gloucester.

Geoffrey was earl of Richmond by right of his wife, and had designs on Normandy. Making Richard heir to England and Normandy without just compensation for the other sons would only lead to further trouble. Not designating Richard heir would lead to trouble too. Besides this, there was the issue of Richard's betrothal to Alice, the half-sister of Philip Augustus. On several occasions the French king pressed for the marriage to take place. She had been with the Angevin court since 1169; the delay was scandalous. Yet, beyond Henry's own rumoured affection for Alice, he had justification for putting off this marriage. He did not want Richard falling in with Capetian in-laws as Henry, the Young King, had done. Some immutable law seemed at work. The effect of keeping Philip and Richard apart was to bring Philip and Geoffrey closer together. Just before Geoffrey's accidental death at a Parisian tournament in August 1186 he had been boasting that he and the French king were going to devastate Normandy. And although death removed another son from the equation, the year ended with the succession question unsolved.

Philip Augustus and Count Richard, 1186–1187 While Geoffrey's departure from the stage of Angevin family politics closed one door for King Philip, another was opened to him. He claimed the wardship of the eldest of Geoffrey's two daughters and, with her, custody of the whole of the duchy of Brittany. Henry II was not about to compromise the Angevin lordship of Brittany in any way, especially since he knew Geoffrey's widow, Constance, was in the early stages of pregnancy (she gave birth to a son, Arthur, in March 1187). The future of the Breton inheritance too was uncertain. The English king employed a favourite tactic of medieval politics—the delay—to put Philip off. In early October 1186 a royal embassy headed by William de Mandeville, earl of Essex and count of Aumale, the English justiciar Ranulf de Glanville, and the former vice-chancellor Walter de Coutances, archbishop of Rouen, was dispatched to the French court to request a truce regarding this matter. They asked for the truce to last until mid-January. After successfully completing their mission, two of the ambassadors, William and Walter, were sent back again to ask for an extension of the truce until Easter, about the time Constance was due to give birth. This second request met with a cool reception. Earl William was in charge of castle defences in upper Normandy. It seems that a kinsman of his, Henry de Vere, constable of Gisors, had found the French building a castle in the vicinity and had attacked the workers, killing the son of an important nobleman. Outraged, Philip had arrested all the king of England's subjects on the French side of the border. In retaliation French subjects found on the Norman side of the border also had been arrested. Although all those who had been arrested were released shortly afterwards, tensions remained high.

Henry expected a full-scale war. In December, Ranulf de Glanville went into Wales to recruit mercenaries for a campaign in Normandy. Welsh mercenaries had been used with great effect in the civil war of 1173–4 and Henry had come to rely upon them. By January 1187 Philip was attacking in the area of Gisors and Henry had begun to collect his forces for a massive movement of supplies and personnel from England to the continent. One group that attempted the winter crossing from Shoreham in Sussex to Dieppe was lost at sea with a large part of the king's treasure. Henry himself crossed from Dover to Wissant in late February, and was met by the counts of Flanders and Blois, who escorted him to Normandy. The French barons, it appears, were not seeking the battle King Philip apparently wanted. A meeting in April between the two kings ended without any reconciliation. Henry then divided his army into five groups: one under his command, the others under the commands of William de Mandeville, the king's sons Richard and John, and Henry's natural son *Geoffrey, since 1182 chancellor of England. Richard and John took their groups into Berry where in June they came under siege by Philip's forces at Châteauroux. Upon learning this Henry marched with a great army to their relief. Philip was caught, his prestige at risk. This was his first open attack on the Angevins. His father had tried on numerous occasions to defeat his Angevin counterpart, and had faltered. Philip decided to risk all in a pitched battle. Henry showed himself equally determined.

Every morning for the next fortnight the two opposing armies, separated by the Indre River, arrayed themselves in battle formation, while individuals from both sides, well acquainted with the dangers of pitched battle, sought a settlement. Rumours flowed back and forth. Troops from the county of Champagne were said to have been bought off by the English, causing much concern among the French. Henry became worried when he found out that Richard, swayed by the count of Flanders, was meeting in secret with Philip. Somehow Richard persuaded Henry to agree to a truce, and promptly left with Philip for Paris. The armies rejoiced in the peace. Alarmed, Henry sent messengers to recall Richard; he had been down this path before.

Final years and death, 1187–1189 Henry and Richard were reconciled in time, though the succession issue still divided them. Philip kept up the pressure by massing an army on the Norman border and threatening an invasion if Henry, among other things, did not proceed with Richard's marriage to Alice. At this point international events further complicated the problem. In the summer of 1187 news of the losses at the battle of Hattin in the Holy Land shocked and depressed Westerners. The fall of Jerusalem to Saladin in October of the same year made the need for a crusade all the more urgent. At a conference on 21 January 1188 the kings of England and France, and a host of French barons, Richard included, took the cross. Later that month the famous 'Saladin tithe' was proclaimed at a conference in Le Mans. While Henry II went into England from the conference to oversee the collection of the tithe, Richard was drawn to Aquitaine to suppress a revolt. After this he became embroiled in a fierce war with the count of Toulouse. His successes in this war caused King Philip to invade Berry, hoping to attract Richard's attention away from Toulouse. The fighting

brought Henry II out of England. He landed back in Normandy in July with a large force of Welsh and English troops. Battles erupted all along the frontiers of the Angevin and French dominions; towns were burnt, villages destroyed. With no end to the fighting in sight, and pressure for a crusade continuing to build, a preliminary peace was agreed upon in November, but only after the counts of Flanders, Blois, and others had refused to participate any further in the hostilities. As details of peace were being worked out in a meeting between the two kings, Philip asked for Richard's marriage to Alice, and that the barons of England and the rest of the Angevin dominions swear an oath of fealty to Richard as Henry's heir. More importantly, in front of those present, Richard asked if his father would recognize him as heir. Henry, trapped by the legacy of Henry, the Young King, kept silent. In a startling move, Richard then knelt before Philip and rendered him homage for Normandy, Anjou, and Aquitaine. All that Henry had sought to avoid came to be.

There was little room for negotiations this time. While truces were agreed upon, the first lasting through Christmas, another extending through March, then Easter, nothing could bring Richard to depart on crusade now without having secured his inheritance, and nothing could bring Henry to recognize Richard publicly as his heir. King Philip was the pivot; his interests lay in causing the Angevins as much trouble as possible, although he might be turned if a suitable arrangement were devised for his sister, Alice. In a parley at La Ferté-Bernard on the Maine–Blois border Henry tested Philip's attachment to Richard by offering to settle a long-standing dispute over the Vexin with Alice's marriage to John. The offer also played against Richard's fears of losing the major part of the Angevin dominions to his younger brother. The parley took place in the last week of May 1189. Behind the scenes Henry had been preparing for war. Mercenaries had been recruited again from among the Welsh, troops brought over from England, and an army readied in Normandy at Alençon. Instead of leaving the area after the parley, Philip and Richard caught Henry unawares by overrunning local castles and marching on Le Mans. On 12 June, with the city on fire, Henry was forced to flee for his life, narrowly escaping capture by Richard. Inexplicably he stopped only hours short of the safety of Alençon, where his army awaited him, and slipped back into Anjou, going on some 200 miles to Chinon. The king's health had been failing for several months, and this last exertion in the summer's heat caused his illness to become all the more intense. Unable to prevent the continuing collapse of Anjou's defences, Henry was persuaded by the counts of Flanders and Burgundy to reach a settlement. On 4 July near Azay-le-Rideau, Henry II, visibly ill, listened as conditions were read out to him in the presence of Richard and Philip. Added to the old demands for Alice's marriage and Richard's recognition were an indemnity of £20,000, the surrender of key castles, and a willingness to follow Philip's pleasure in all things. Henry agreed, but defiantly whispered in Richard's ear, 'God grant that I may not die until I have my revenge on you' (*Gir. Camb. opera*, 8.296).

Too weak to ride back to Chinon, Henry was borne thither on a litter; he died there two days later, on Thursday 6 July 1189, his heart finally broken by the discovery that his youngest son, John, too, had joined his adversaries. He was buried at the abbey of Fontevrault. With this the family quarrels ceased, and the Angevin dominions passed intact to the next generation. Ironically, despite all Philip's machinations, Richard carefully stepped into a position of power as great as, perhaps even greater than, that of his father.

Henry II and the politics of success During the years of family tumult Henry II seems to have found his most gratifying moments of affirmation in Canterbury at the shrine of Thomas Becket. Before 1170 the king is known to have visited Canterbury only twice, once briefly in 1156 and then again in 1163. Starting in 1174, however, Henry made at least ten, perhaps thirteen, visits to Canterbury, and had intended another. Indeed, the king went so often to Becket's shrine that the author of the *Gesta Henrici secundi* described his visits as 'customary' (*Gesta ... Benedicti*, 1.207). Henry's obvious devotion to the shrine came from the mythologized fact he himself promoted: at the very minute of the very hour in July 1174 that the embattled king had emerged from Canterbury Cathedral, ending an all-night vigil, William the Lion of Scotland was captured far off in northern England. Contemporary hagiographers and historians alike drew from these events the lesson Henry wished. God, to many minds, in recognition of the king's reconciliation in spirit with St Thomas, had intervened in the affairs of men; Henry's enemies were vanquished, his rule validated. Joining Henry at the shrine on various occasions were his sons Henry, the Young King, and Richard, Louis VII of France, Philip, count of Flanders, Theobald, count of Blois, and William, archbishop of Rheims—all losers in the great war, all now courting saint and king. If Henry, as it is said, hated pomp, surely he loved theatre. And nowhere was Angevin theatre more pronounced than at Canterbury.

The control of England and Normandy Given the totality of Henry's victory over his enemies in the war, it is remarkable that he did not indulge in wholesale confiscations of baronies. Rebel families on both sides of the channel regained most of their lands over time, although their castles were summarily destroyed or occupied by the king's men. But if Henry's sons had disappointed him, their allies and sympathizers had disappointed him more. Never again would any of his barons be allowed to challenge him. The tightened grip touched friend and foe. Bristol, the former Angevin stronghold long coveted by the crown, was simply taken from William, earl of Gloucester, while the earldom itself was promised by marriage to the king's son John. When Reginald, earl of Cornwall, died in 1175, leaving three daughters as heirs, this earldom too was set aside for John. The son of William d'Aubigny, earl of Sussex, gave up Arundel Castle on his father's death. Even the justiciar Richard de Lucy returned Ongar Castle on his retirement. In Normandy Bishop Arnulf of Lisieux, implicated in Henry III's rebellion, was

later hounded from office. When William le Gros, count of Aumale, died in 1179, his daughter married William de Mandeville, earl of Essex, one of the king's best friends and the man in charge of the Norman defensive network of castles based on Gisors. Earl William headed a newly prominent group of courtier–managers in Normandy with English interests or experience. The older dominance of Beaumont, Tancarville, Montfort, Tosny, Gournay, and others was eclipsed by the elevation of Stuteville, du Hommet, St Jean-le-Thomas, Verdun, Cressy, Bardolf, Pipard, Paynel, St Martin, Fitzralph, and Mandeville.

This Anglicization of Norman administration during the 1170s and 1180s took place in both personnel and practice. In 1176 Richard of Ilchester, bishop of Winchester, was given the job of reshaping the duchy's finances along the lines of the English exchequer. After completing this task, the bishop turned over the seneschalcy and government to William fitz Radulf, sheriff of Nottingham and Derby, who relocated to Caen. The bailiff of Exemes in 1180, Gilbert Pipard, was at times in his career sheriff of Gloucester, Hampshire, and Lancaster, a justice in England on the great eyres of 1176 and 1178, and a member of John's household during his unfortunate Irish expedition. The same year another sometime English justice, Hugh de Cressy, acted as constable of Rouen, while the Stutevilles, who held royal castles and shrievalties in northern England, were entrusted with Arques and Lyons-la-Forêt. Alfred de St Martin, castellan of Driencourt, formerly castellan of Hastings and Eu, began his career as a household knight of John, count of Eu, and through the king's grace married the count's widow, Alice, daughter of William d'Aubigny, earl of Arundel, about 1176. He controlled her considerable *maritagium* and dower in England, worth 23 knights' fees and £143 sterling in annual rents, making him as wealthy as any English baron beneath the magnate class. The king–duke's Anglicization policy placed Normandy solidly under Henry's domination and effectively ended any chance of Norman disloyalty sparking another revolt, as it had in 1173. In the end, however, his unwillingness to name Richard as heir to Anjou, Normandy, and England, as the count of Poitou wished, undermined Henry's mastery of international politics, and he died in 1189 a broken man.

Visible expressions of power Henry II clearly understood power, its uses, its trappings. To awe his contemporaries he consciously employed any combination of the features of impressive size and quality of construction and finishing in the structures he built. The historian Robert de Torigni reacted in 'astonishment' when first viewing the leper house the king had constructed in 1161 at Caen, and he was equally astounded by the scale of royal or ducal building projects undertaken that same year throughout Normandy, Aquitaine, Maine, Anjou, the Touraine, and England. He tells of castles, parks, royal residences, manor houses, hunting lodges, and more, all under repair or in new construction. This display of taste and wealth, on a scale as vast as the Angevin dominion itself, was meant to project an aura of strength and prosperity, and was connected, perhaps, with a perceived need to refashion a reputation diminished by the failure of the Toulouse campaign of 1159. Later, when Henry built the famous Everswell at Woodstock for his mistress Rosamund Clifford—a great house centred on a spring, with rectangular pools and a cloister, similar to the marvellous palaces of Norman Sicily and to fictional palaces like those depicted in the romance of *Tristan*—he added a useful element of mystery and romance to his subjects' image of the 'old king' triumphant over the 'young king' and his brothers. During the course of his reign Henry came to understand well the power of architectural statement. The magnificent square keep at Dover, with its surrounding mural towers raised majestically above the white cliffs in sight of an old Roman lighthouse (largely complete by 1184 at a cost of over £6500), might have been fashioned to deter the odd invader, yet daily spoke with eloquence 'this is my kingdom' to the more numerous pilgrims and princes intent only on going as far as the shrine of St Thomas at Canterbury. Other massive building projects initiated by Henry II—hospitals at Bayeux, Rouen, Le Mans, Angers, and Fontevrault; churches at Witham, Waltham, Cherbourg, Mortemer, and Grandmont; an embankment 30 miles long beside the Loire between Saumur and Tours; bridges at Rouen, Angers, Saumur, and Chinon; castles at Scarborough, Newcastle, Nottingham, Orford, Osmanville, Gisors, Ancenis, and Chinon; and palaces at Windsor, Clarendon, Quévilly, and Saumur—attest to the king-duke's pervasive interest in architecture. The famous octagonal kitchen at Fontevrault with its radiating apses and pyramidal stone roof, also attributable to Henry's patronage, resembles monastic kitchens found elsewhere in the Loire region (Vendôme, Saumur, and Marmoutier), and kitchens as far away as Normandy (Caen) and England (Canterbury). A dominion bound by few institutional commonalities was evolving, under Henry II's guidance, a common culture in stone.

Courts and counsellors in Henry's reign But Henry II's real power, despite the greater size of the Angevin dominion, derived from his stewardship of the older Anglo-Norman state, from its wealth, its manpower, its institutions. In the period from December 1154 to July 1189, 37 per cent of Henry's time was spent in the British Isles, 43 per cent in Normandy, and only 20 per cent elsewhere in France beyond the duchy's borders. Thus for 80 per cent of his reign as king–duke Henry II travelled or resided in the realm of his mother's Norman ancestors. In England he stayed most often in an area marked by a line drawn from Portchester up to Salisbury and on to Gloucester and Worcester, across to Northampton, down to London, and down again to Portchester: for the most part the Thames valley and central Wessex. In Normandy, Henry was found most often in the upper Cotentin peninsula, the region of the Orne River valley, the Roumois, and the Norman Vexin. His main administrative centres, on the evidence of charter issues, were Westminster–London, Winchester, Woodstock, Rouen–Quévilly, Caen–Bur, and Argentan. If one of these centres stood above the rest, it was Rouen,

where courtiers from the Angevin dominion came in larger numbers than to any other site.

From the outset of his reign Norman and English advisers dominated Henry II's court. Although the witnesses to his charters tend to be fewer on average than those of previous king–dukes, attestation statistics from over 2500 acts present a reasonably accurate portrait of Henry's inner court. Notably lacking from this select group are men whose origins derived from the county of Anjou. The inner court, the first twenty-five of whom are ranked here according to their attestations, included: Richard du Hommet, the constable of Normandy (371); Manasser Biset (298); Thomas Becket, chancellor of England, later archbishop of Canterbury (296); Richard de Lucy, the English justiciar (249); Reginald de Dunstanville, earl of Cornwall (240); Geoffrey Ridel, archdeacon of Canterbury, later bishop of Ely (165); Richard of Ilchester, archdeacon of Poitou, later bishop of Winchester (163); Ranulf de Glanville, the English justiciar (136); Hugh de Cressy, constable of Rouen (135); Arnulf, bishop of Lisieux (130); John of Oxford, dean of Salisbury, later bishop of Norwich (130); Reginald de Courtenay, lord of Okehampton (123); Robert, earl of Leicester, justiciar of England (120); Rotrou de Newburgh, bishop of Évreux, later archbishop of Rouen (111); Theobald, archbishop of Canterbury (107); Richard de Camville (107); Walter de Coutances, archdeacon of Oxford, later bishop of Lincoln and archbishop of Rouen (100); Roger, archbishop of York (99); Philip de Harcourt, bishop of Bayeux, former chancellor of King Stephen (97); Hugh du Puiset, bishop of Durham (95); William de Mandeville, earl of Essex and count of Aumale (91); William Fitzaudelin, marshal and royal steward (91); Warin Fitzgerald, chamberlain of the English exchequer (90); Robert de Chesney, bishop of Lincoln (89); and William fitz Radulf, the Norman seneschal (79). The English pipe rolls provide other indicators of the level of the inner court's involvement in Anglo-Norman governance. For example, William de Mandeville, Walter de Coutances, and Richard du Hommet and his sons are reported to have crossed from England to Normandy no less than twenty-one times on the king's business between 1174 and 1189.

Angevin governance Like Henry II's court the surviving evidence for Angevin governance in general is predominantly Anglo-Norman, and more completely English. No financial accounts from this period similar to the English pipe rolls remain at all from lands outside the Anglo-Norman state, while those for Normandy regrettably cover only two years (a partial roll from 1180 and a fragmentary roll from 1184). Although much detail of government can be found in various histories of Henry's reign, only the Norman historian Robert de Torigni, abbot of Mont-St Michel, provides a significant chronicle from the perspective of a western French author. Curiously no Angevin was inspired to write a *geste* of the count who became king. But from an English court perspective the works of Ralph de Diceto, Roger of Howden, Jordan Fantosme, Gerald of Wales, Gervase of Canterbury, and William of Newburgh provide a collection of histories unrivalled by those for any other twelfth-century king. These histories set beside the pipe rolls (1155–89), the *Dialogus de Scaccario*, and the legal treatise known as *Glanvill*, testify to the achievement of English government under Henry II—a government of which the king and his advisers were duly proud. The practice of regular country-wide visitations by justices, together with the maintenance of central royal courts for managing finances and hearing civil litigation, in place by the mid-1170s, allowed for the creation of a coherent body of national custom which in the thirteenth century evolved into the English 'common law'. Historians, always curious as to origins, need look no further than Richard of Ilchester, Geoffrey Ridel, John of Oxford, Richard de Lucy, Ranulf de Glanville, and, of course, Henry II himself, for the fathers of this law.

Walter Map's account of a conversation with Ranulf de Glanville relating to royal justice highlights the importance of Henry's presence, or near presence, to the smooth functioning of a national system. After hearing a case Glanville adjudicated in favour of a poor man, Map remarked with some wonderment, 'Although the poor man's judgement might have been put off by many quirks, you arrived at it by a happy and quick decision.' To which Glanville replied with some pride, 'Certainly we decide causes here much quicker than your bishops do in their churches.' 'True,' countered Map, 'but if your king were as far off from you as the pope is from the bishops, I think you would be quite as slow as they.' With these words both men laughed knowingly (Map, 509). Henry II may have distanced himself often from his tumultuous, whirling court for the solitude of forest and hills, or lost himself in the pleasures of the hunt, but he paid attention. According to Gerald of Wales, the king 'had at his fingertips a ready knowledge of nearly the whole of history and also the practical experience of daily affairs' (*English Historical Documents*, 2.417–18). The men with whom Henry surrounded himself and to whom he entrusted the governance and defence of his dominion loved the active life, the excitement of ruling, as he did. William Fitzaudelin, the Irish marshal and a frequent attestor of the king's charters, is said to have been 'ambitious for power at court', and, although acquisitive, 'loved the court no less than he did gold' (Gerald of Wales, *Expugnatio*, 173). Henry understood these men. He managed them; they managed the dominion. And to contemporaries this king–duke stood above his predecessors.

Law and judicial administration under Henry II Although sometimes distant from England, Henry II was never an uninterested manager. He is reported to have lain awake at nights working through in his mind the proper judicial language to give form to his ideas of government (*De legibus*, 3.25). Through a series of inquests and assizes (royal edicts acceded to by the barons in council) a coherent and centralized bureaucratic system, built on foundations laid by the Saxon and Norman kings, evolved. Sheriffs, other local officials, and even local landholders, were brought under scrutiny in 1170 to demonstrate that corruption on any level would no longer be tolerated while the king was absent on the continent. The assize of Northampton (1176) increased the powers of itinerant justices at the expense of the sheriffs, while the assize of the forest (1184) brought the regulation of forest offences, previously based largely on the king's whim, into the realm of customary law.

The possessory assizes made it easier for all the king's subjects, not just élites, to prosecute claims to lands and inheritances, lost, or withheld, within recorded memory or the memory of the local community. There were in the beginning four writs initiating actions under these assizes: novel disseisin, designed to answer the question of whether a plaintiff had been unjustly and without cause ejected from his freehold; mort d'ancestor, asking whether a plaintiff's ancestor had been possessed of disputed land, and whether the plaintiff was his heir; darrein presentment, which applied the principle of mort d'ancestor to ecclesiastical benefices, to ask who had last presented to a disputed living; and utrum, which sought to establish whether land was held by secular or spiritual services. These writs—which were the monopoly of the king's courts—and the quick proceedings they fostered allowed jurors to determine whether individuals had been in possession of a property (seisin) and unjustly dispossessed (disseisin), but not the actual legal property right in the matter. If the thornier issue of right was raised in court, as an alternative to the duel as the means of proof, there could be recourse (after 1179) to the 'grand assize' in which twelve knights of the shire carefully looked at descent as far back in time as possible to resolve the question of property rights, as opposed to who had recently had possession.

The inquest of knight service of 1166, recorded in documents as the *Cartae baronum*, was the first country-wide listing of knights' fees, and was used by Henry's exchequer to increase the potential yield from military taxation by a quarter to one-third. The 'Saladin tithe' (1188) represented an innovative attempt to raise money by taxing personal property. The assize of Arms (1181) revived the ancient Anglo-Saxon *fyrd* by fixing the level of military preparedness demanded of freeholders, not on the amount of land they had, but on their annual income. And the most momentous development of the reign, perhaps, can be found in the assize of Clarendon (1166) by which the principle of jury-inquest in criminal cases first came to be applied on a national level. According to this assize (which was reinforced at some points by that of Northampton ten years later) four lawful men brought together from every township, and twelve from every county hundred, were compelled to denounce before their sheriff, or the king's justices, all malefactors within their jurisdictions. The names of those who may have fled these jurisdictions were also recorded, and provisions outlined for their apprehension and trial. Suspects of particularly evil repute were to abjure the realm even if they succeeded in clearing themselves by the ordeal, which was still the normal means of proof in criminal cases. No special franchises were immune from the newly established presenting jury, later called the grand jury. Thus the kingdom's myriad competing feudal jurisdictions fell before a uniform royal judicial administration, which owed much of its effectiveness to the increasingly frequent and well-organized activities of the king's justices itinerant. Henry's thinking in this regard, only anti-baronial as far as it was pro-royal, may, ironically, have been influenced by the successes of a centralizing papal monarchy, knowledge of which the king had intimately, if painfully, acquired through his quarrel with Becket. But, while the papacy was busily erecting an imperial-like church bureaucracy, Henry II's managerial policy of involving juries at the local level in English affairs led more beneficially to what A. B. White has called 'self-government at the king's command'.

Henry II and Magna Carta Given these innovations, it is perhaps surprising that the later resentment of the Angevin system implicit in Magna Carta might have been fostered by Henry II's mastery of men and government. Certainly many of the barons at Runnymede in 1215 saw John's excesses as expansions of those of his father. Both the Waverley annalist and Ralph of Coggeshall link Henry with John in propagating the host of 'evil customs' addressed in the great charter. William of Newburgh, however, offers a somewhat more objective truth on this score. To William, the complaints about Henry's government in the king's own lifetime, warranted perhaps in the cases of forest fines and unduly long episcopal vacancies, understandably softened in later years, following exposure to the rule of his successors. Indeed, the predatory nature of English government in the fifty or sixty years on either side of the year 1200, as viewed by modern historians, is more illusionary than real, at least with regard to the upper classes. Recent analyses of military taxes and of scutages, under the Angevin kings, indicate that the wealthiest landowners were either forgiven their assessments or never assessed at all. A similar study of fines offered the crown for the control of heirs' estates in the period 1180–1212 shows procedures in place to protect the investment of custodians through favourable terms of mortgage with low or no annual payments. The nature of the financial burden placed on people lower down the social scale is less clear, though the sum of £12,305 collected by the exchequer from the forest assizes of 1175, an enormous amount for the time, was paid by smaller landholders, not magnates. Comparable evidence for the 'Saladin tithe' of 1188, the carucatage of 1198, and the seventh of 1203 is missing, but the thirteenth on incomes and moveables of 1207 brought in some £57,431, again mostly from churches and non-élites. It may well be, then, that the negotiators of Magna Carta tapped a collective anger in many who believed that Henry II was as culpable as John in driving the monarchy towards excess, whether or not the burden of the Angevin system actually fell equally on all English subjects.

Henry II's historical reputation and identity Gerald of Wales, annalist of the Anglo-Angevin intervention in Ireland, regarded Henry II as 'our Alexander of the West' (Gerald of Wales, *Topography of Ireland*, 124). The author of the *Dialogus de Scaccario*, Richard fitz Nigel, bishop of London, wrote in his youth a history of Henry, now lost, titled *Tricolumnis*, wherein one of three columns chronicled his lord's noble deeds, 'which are beyond belief' (*Dialogus*, 27). Gerald of Wales, again, best gives perspective to contemporaries' perception of Henry's martial exploits:

> he not only brought strong peace with the aid of God's grace to his hereditary dominions, but also triumphed victoriously in remote and foreign lands, a thing of which none of his predecessors since the coming of the Normans, not even the Saxon kings, had proved capable. (*English Historical Documents*, 2.410)

Gerald goes on to list these triumphs, beginning with the subjection of Ireland and the domination of Scotland through the capture of William the Lion, 'contrary to anything that had ever happened before'. Gerald continues his account by noting the king–duke's vast French inheritances of Maine, Anjou, Touraine, Poitou, and Gascony, to which Henry had added the Vexin, the Auvergne, and Berry. The good-natured Louis VII, in Gerald's eyes, was no match for Henry II, who 'even desired to extend into the Roman Empire, taking advantage of Frederick Barbarossa's troubles' with his Italian subjects. The opening for expansion through the alpine valley of Maurienne almost came off with the ill-fated marriage contracted with Count Humbert for John. This proposed marriage, viewed against the background of the king–duke's marrying his daughters to the heirs of the duchy of Saxony, and the kingdoms of Castile and Sicily, suggests an imperialist bent to Henry II's outlook captured in a boast attributed to him by Gerald, that 'the whole world was too small a prize for a single courageous and powerful ruler' (*English Historical Documents*, 2.410). Henry's dreams of empire, present perhaps from early childhood, fired the imagination of courtiers like John, count of Eu, who went so far as to date a charter of 1155 'at Winchester in the year in which the conquest of Ireland was discussed' (Flanagan, 305). And indeed, what William II had only boasted he would perform, Henry II achieved, as the first king of England both to visit and to claim authority in Ireland. At Henry's court nothing was beyond discussion for ambitious knights and clerics; with Henry II Plantagenet as their lord, all the world was within reach.

But who was Henry II? Richard the Poitevin derisively referred to him as the 'King of the North Wind' (Meade, 279). Less poetic, but more accurately, Ailred of Rievaulx called Henry the 'cornerstone of the English and Norman races' (*Patrologia Latina*, 195.711–38). Yet for modern historians Henry's identity—perhaps ethnicity is the better word—is problematic. He was 'king of the English' but spoke only French and Latin. To many modern legalists he is the father of the English common law, yet he is buried at the nunnery of Fontevrault in France, a land more influenced by Roman law. He spent the majority of his reign in Normandy, was schooled as a youth by William de Conches, the greatest Norman philosopher of his day, but is labelled 'Henry of Anjou' by twentieth-century writers.

Early in life he adopted the title 'Henry son of the Empress' for worthwhile political reasons—his claim to the Anglo-Norman inheritance of Matilda, his mother—and rarely employed the name of his father, Geoffrey Plantagenet. Whereas William, Henry's youngest brother, changed the inscription on his seal after 1154 from 'William son of Empress Matilda', to 'William brother of Henry King of England', Henry remained known to the end of his life as 'FitzEmpress'. The chronicler Roger of Howden, a member of Henry II's entourage, always refers to his lord king as 'son of the Empress' when describing the celebration of a Christmas court—December marking the beginning of Henry's regnal year as well as the traditional new year (*Chronica … Hovedene*, 1, 213 ff.). Even the distant annalist of Inisfallen, in recording the momentous events of 1171, wrote, 'The son of the Empress came to Ireland and landed at Waterford' (Flanagan, 174). Indeed, Henry II encouraged this identification with his mother, her ancestors, her former imperial station. Only later did his father Geoffrey's epithet 'Plantagenet' come to define the family and, with this definition, its first English king.

Modern English historians' thoughts on Henry II's reputation vary. To the Victorian William Stubbs, Henry stood with Alfred, Cnut, William the Conqueror, and Edward I as the 'conscious creators of English greatness' (*Gesta … Benedicti*, 2.xxxiii). Stepping back for a wider view of the stage on which Henry played, Stubbs lamented that the king's chance to lead a grand crusade, which 'might have presented Europe to Asia in a guise which she has never yet assumed', was ruined by a thankless wife, loveless children, and a pernicious French overlord (*Gesta … Benedicti*, 2.xix–xx)—a scenario given vivid visual expression for twentieth-century cinema-goers in Anthony Harvey's film *The Lion in Winter* (1968), in which Peter O'Toole plays King Henry with panache. A similarly wistful reflection on Henry's lost promise surfaces in W. L. Warren's sympathetic biography:

> The course of history might have been radically different if Henry II, instead of devoting himself principally to the pursuit and exploitation of the rights of lordships which fell to him fortuitously, had turned his energies to forging the unity of the British Isles. (Warren, *Henry II*, 627–8)

That Henry could have done something more to change history, the history of the Middle East, the history of Ireland, had he been allowed and had he wished, shows the uncompromising faith of Stubbs and Warren in his greatness, his potential to be, as Gerald of Wales expressed it, truly the 'Alexander of the West'. And behind this vision and these feelings lies a belief in the ability of the individual to determine history, a belief in great men. Historians such as Christopher Brooke and Frank Barlow agree, and yet there is dissent from those who disavow the 'great man' theory. For Bryce Lyon, the legal strides made in England during Henry's reign owed more to his choice of advisers than to Henry's own interest in or mastery of the law, while Michael Clanchy credits English constitutional development in this period to the impersonal force of the spreading use of the written word, a technological advance, the product not of English genius, but of a 'brilliant time in Western Europe' (Clanchy, 154, 158, 161). In the end, wherever historians focus their attention—on individuals or impersonal forces—the scope of Henry II's life and the records of his reign provide a tantalizing wealth of material to which they are sure to return again and again. Perhaps this is legacy enough.

THOMAS K. KEEFE

Sources L. Delisle and others, eds., *Recueil des actes de Henri II, roi d'Angleterre et duc de Normandie, concernant les provinces françaises et les affaires de France*, 4 vols. (Paris, 1909–27) · *The letters of John of Salisbury*, ed. and trans. H. E. Butler and W. J. Millor, rev. C. N. L. Brooke, 2 vols., OMT (1979–86) [Lat. orig. with parallel Eng. text] · R. W. Eyton, *Court, household, and itinerary of King Henry II* (1878) · K. R. Potter and R. H. C. Davis, eds., *Gesta Stephani*, OMT (1976) · E. Searle, ed., *The chronicle of Battle Abbey*, OMT (1980) · Pipe rolls, 2–4 Henry II · R. Howlett, ed., *Chronicles of the reigns of Stephen, Henry II, and Richard I*, 4 vols., Rolls Series, 82 (1884–9) · *Chronique de Robert de Torigni*, ed. L. Delisle, 2 vols. (Rouen, 1872–3) · *Reg. RAN*, vol. 3 · *English historical documents*, 2, ed. D. C. Douglas and G. W. Greenaway (1953) · H. Hall, ed., *The Red Book of the Exchequer*, 3 vols., Rolls Series, 99 (1896) · *The historical works of Gervase of Canterbury*, ed. W. Stubbs, 2 vols., Rolls Series, 73 (1879–80) · Henry, archdeacon of Huntingdon, *Historia Anglorum*, ed. D. E. Greenway, OMT (1996) · William of Newburgh, *The history of English affairs*, ed. P. G. Walsh and M. J. Kennedy, bk 1 (1988) · J. C. Robertson and J. B. Sheppard, eds., *Materials for the history of Thomas Becket, archbishop of Canterbury*, 7 vols., Rolls Series, 67 (1875–85) · John of Salisbury, *Historia pontificalis: John of Salisbury's memoirs of the papal court*, ed. and trans. M. Chibnall (1956) · M. Bouquet and others, eds., *Recueil de historiens des Gaules et de la France / Rerum Gallicarum et Francicarum scriptores*, 24 vols. (1738–1904) · L. Halphen and R. Poupardin, eds., *Chroniques des comtes d'Anjou et des seigneurs d'Amboise* (Paris, 1913) · G. de Vigeois, 'Chronica', *Novae bibliothecae manuscriptorum*, ed. P. Labbe, 2 (Paris, 1657) · *Chronique de Geoffrey, prieur de Vigeois*, ed. F. Bonnelye (1864) · P. Marchegay and E. Mabille, eds., *Chroniques des églises d'Anjou* (Paris, 1869) · L. Halphen, ed., *Recueil d'annales angevines et vendômoises* (Paris, 1903) · A. Salmon, ed., *Chroniques de Touraine*, 1 vol. and supplement (1854–7) · W. Stubbs, ed., *Gesta regis Henrici secundi Benedicti abbatis: the chronicle of the reigns of Henry II and Richard I, AD 1169–1192*, 2 vols., Rolls Series, 49 (1867) · Ralph de Diceto, 'Ymagines historiarum', *Radulfi de Diceto … opera historica*, ed. W. Stubbs, 2 vols., Rolls Series, 68 (1876) · *Chronica magistri Rogeri de Hovedene*, ed. W. Stubbs, 4 vols., Rolls Series, 51 (1868–71) · R. Fitz Nigel [R. Fitzneale], *Dialogus de scaccario / The course of the exchequer*, ed. and trans. C. Johnson, rev. edn, rev. F. E. L. Carter and D. E. Greenaway, OMT (1983) · G. D. Hall, ed., *Tractatus de legibus et consuetudinibus regni Anglie qui Glanvilla vocatur*, 2nd edn, OMT (1993) · T. Stapleton, ed., *Magni rotuli scaccarii Normanniae sub regibus Angliae*, 2 vols., Society of Antiquaries of London Occasional Papers (1840–44) · Pipe rolls, 5–34 Henry II · *The great roll of the pipe for the first year of the reign of King Richard the first, AD 1189–1190*, Great Britain Exchequer, ed. J. Hunter, RC, 32 (1844) · J. C. Holt and R. Mortimer, eds., *Acta of Henry II and Richard I* (1986) · W. Map, *De nugis curialium / Courtiers' trifles*, ed. and trans. M. R. James, rev. C. N. L. Brooke and R. A. B. Mynors, OMT (1983) · Giraldus Cambrensis, *Expugnatio Hibernica / The conquest of Ireland*, ed. and trans. A. B. Scott and F. X. Martin (1978) · Gerald of Wales, *The history and topography of Ireland*, trans. J. J. O'Meara, rev. edn (1982) · W. L. Warren, *The governance of Norman and Angevin England* (1987) · W. L. Warren, *Henry II* (1973) · E. Amt, *The accession of Henry II in England* (1993) · T. K. Keefe, 'Place-date distribution of royal charters and the historical geography of patronage strategies at the court of King Henry II', *Haskins Society Journal*, 2 (1990), 179–88 · T. K. Keefe, 'Counting those who count: a computer-assisted analysis of charter witness-lists and the itinerant court in the first year of the reign of King Richard I', *Haskins Society Journal*, 1 (1989), 135–45 · T. K. Keefe, 'Geoffrey Plantagenet's will and the Angevin succession', *Albion*, 6 (1974), 266–74 · T. K. Keefe and C. W. Hollister, 'The making of the Angevin empire', *Journal of British Studies*, 12/2 (1972–3), 1–25 • T. K. Keefe, 'Proffers for heirs and heiresses in the pipe rolls: some observations on indebtedness in the years before Magna Carta (1180–1212)', *Haskins Society Journal*, 5 (1993), 99–109 • T. K. Keefe, *Feudal assessments and the political community under Henry II and his sons* (1983) • J. Boussard, 'Les mercenaires au XIIe siècle: Henri II Plantagenêt et les origines de l'armée de métier', *Bibliothèque de l'Ecole de Chartes*, 106 (1945–6), 189–224 • J. Boussard, 'Les influences anglaises sur le développement des grandes charges de l'empire d'Henri II Plantagenêt', *Annales de Normandie*, 5 (1955), 215–31 • J. Boussard, *Le gouvernement d'Henri II Plantegenêt* (1956) • P. A. Brand, '*Multis vigiliis excogitatam et inventam*; Henry II and the creation of the English common law', *Haskins Society Journal*, 2 (1990), 197–222 • C. N. L. Brooke, 'The marriage of Henry II and Eleanor of Aquitaine', *The Historian*, 20 (1988), 3–8 • R. H. C. Davis, *King Stephen*, 3rd edn (1990) • M. Chibnall, *The Empress Matilda* (1991) • G. J. White, 'The end of Stephen's reign', *History*, new ser., 75 (1990), 3–22 • E. King, ed., *The anarchy of King Stephen's reign* (1994) • P. Brand, *The making of the common law* (1992) • J. Gillingham, 'Conquering kings: some twelfth-century reflections on Henry II and Richard I', *Warriors and churchmen in the high middle ages*, ed. T. Reuter (1992), 163–78 • B. Bachrach, 'The Angevin tradition of family hostility', *Albion*, 16 (1984), 111–30 • J. Baldwin, *Philip II Augustus: foundations of French royal power in the middle ages* (1986) • F. Barlow, *Thomas Becket* (1986) • R. Benjamin, 'A forty years war: Toulouse and the Plantagenets, 1156–1196', *Historical Research*, 61 (1988), 270–85 • M. Pacaut, *Louis VII et son royaume* (1964) • M. Chibnall, *Anglo-Norman England, 1066–1166* (1986) • D. Crouch, *William Marshal: court, career and chivalry in the Angevin empire* (1990) • M. T. Flanagan, *Irish society, Anglo-Norman settlers, Angevin kingship: interactions in Ireland in the late twelfth century* (1989) • J. Gillingham, *The Angevin empire* (1984) • J. A. Green, 'Unity and disunity in the Anglo-Norman state', *Historical Research*, 62 (1989), 115–34 • C. H. Haskins, *Norman institutions* (1918) • C. W. Hollister, *Monarchy, magnates, and institutions in the Anglo-Norman world* (1986) • J. C. Holt, 'The end of the Anglo-Norman realm', *PBA*, 61 (1975), 223–65 • J. C. Holt, 'The Acta of Henry II and Richard I of England, 1154–1199: the archive and its historical implications', *Fotografische Sammlungen mittelalterlicher Urkunden in Europa*, ed. P. Ruck (1989), 137–40 • A. Kelly, *Eleanor of Aquitaine and the four kings* (1952) • J. E. Lally, 'Secular patronage at the court of King Henry II', *BIHR*, 49 (1976), 159–84 • P. Latimer, 'Henry II's campaign against the Welsh in 1165', *Welsh History Review / Cylchgrawn Hanes Cymru*, 14 (1988–9), 523–52 • R. Mortimer, 'The charters of Henry II: what are the criteria for authenticity?', *Anglo-Norman Studies*, 12 (1989), 119–34 • B. Lyon, 'Henry II: a non-Victorian interpretation', *Documenting the past: essays in medieval history presented to George Peddy Cuttino*, ed. J. S. Hamilton and P. J. Bradley (1989), 21–31 • J. Le Patourel, *Feudal empires: Norman and Plantagenet* (1984) • K. Norgate, *England under the Angevin kings*, 2 vols. (1887) • R. Pernoud, *Eleanor of Aquitaine* (1967) • F. M. Powicke, *The loss of Normandy, 1189–1204: studies in the history of the Angevin empire*, 2nd edn (1961) • C. Schriber, *Arnulf of Lisieux: the dilemmas of a twelfth-century Norman bishop* (1990) • R. B. Patterson, 'Bristol: an Angevin baronial capital under royal siege', *Haskins Society Journal*, 3 (1991), 171–81 • E. Mason, '"Rocamadour in Quercy above all other churches": the healing of Henry II', *The church and healing*, ed. W. J. Sheils, SCH, 19 (1982), 39–54 • M. Meade, *Eleanor of Aquitaine: a biography*, 2nd edn (1991) • L. Grant, 'Le patronage architectural d'Henri II et de son entourage', *Cahiers de Civilisation Médiévale*, 37 (1994), 73–84 • R. Mortimer, *Angevin England, 1154–1258* (1994) • J. Hudson, *Land, law and lordship in Anglo-Norman England* (1994) • R. Brown, H. M. Colvin, and A. J. Taylor, eds., *The history of the king's works*, 1–2 (1963) • V. Moss, 'England and Normandy in 1180: the pipe roll evidence', *England and Normandy in the middle ages*, ed. D. Bates and A. Curry (1994), 185–96 • L. Grant, 'Architectural relationships between England and Normandy, 1100–1204', *England and Normandy in the middle ages*, ed. D. Bates and A. Curry (1994), 117–30 • D. Bates, 'The rise and fall of Normandy, c. 911–1204', *England and Normandy in the middle ages*, ed. D. Bates and A. Curry (1994), 19–36 • P. Dalton, *Conquest, anarchy, and lordship: Yorkshire, 1066–1154*, Cambridge Studies in Medieval Life and Thought, 4th ser., 27 (1994) • J. Gillingham, *Richard the Lion Heart*, 2nd edn (1989) • R. W. Southern, *Saint Anselm and his biographer: a study of monastic life and thought, 1059–c.1130* (1963) • C. N. L. Brooke, *From Alfred to Henry III, 871–1272* (1961) • F. Barlow, *Feudal kingdom of England, 1042–1216*, 4th edn (1987) • M. T. Clanchy, *England and its rulers, 1066–1272* (1983) • A. B. White, *Self-government at the king's command* (1933) • Henricus de Bracton, *De legibus et consuetudinibus Angliae*, 3 • G. Lyttelton, *The history of the life of King Henry the Second*, 2nd edn, 4 vols. (1767–71) • J. G. Nicholls, 'Observations on the heraldic devices discovered on the effigies of Richard II and his queen in Westminster Abbey', *Archaeologia*, 29 (1842), 32–59 • *RotP*, 5.375 • Petrus Blesensis, *Patrologia Latina*, 207 (1855) • *Gir. Camb. opera*, vol. 8 • A. L. Poole, *From Domesday Book to Magna Carta, 1087–1216*, 2nd edn (1955)

Archives U. Cam., Angevin family *Acta* project

Likenesses penny coin, BM • seals, BL • seals, PRO • tomb effigy, Fontevrault Abbey, France [*see illus.*] • tomb effigy, replica, V&A • wax seals, BM

Henry III (1207–1272), king of England and lord of Ireland, and duke of Aquitaine, called Henry of Winchester from his birthplace, was the eldest of the five children of King *John (1167–1216) and his second wife, Queen *Isabella of Angoulême (*d*. 1246). He was born on 1 October 1207 and named after his grandfather *Henry II. His fifty-six year reign, the third longest in English history, may be conveniently divided into four periods. The first, of some sixteen years, was largely that of the king's minority, during which policy was to a considerable extent directed by others. It was followed by a brief period of turbulence, from 1232 to 1234, which was formerly regarded as one in which the king began to take control of affairs, but is better seen as one in which Henry was still the tool of faction, but in different hands. The years from 1234 to 1258 were those of Henry's personal rule: it was a period of political peace, albeit with intermittent difficulties arising from rivalries within the royal family, finance, and foreign policy. In 1258, however, factional struggles at court, combined with wider discontents in the country at large, launched an extended period of instability which lasted almost until the end of the reign. At first a sudden but peaceful coup by what is often mistakenly referred to as a 'baronial reform movement' produced three years of conciliar government, not unlike that of the minority; however this developed, in response to the king's recovery of power in 1261, into a period of civil war from 1263 to 1267. Henry emerged victorious and in his last years resumed his personal rule, over a kingdom shakily at peace when he died. Unable to reverse the disasters of 1204–5, he maintained the continental claims of his forebears until forced by pressures at home to surrender most of them in 1259. In England his reign was at its best characterized by peace and prosperity for most of propertied society; it also saw important institutional, legal, and social developments. Hardly a stereotypically ideal king, Henry none the less restored the fortunes of the Angevin dynasty in England after the disasters of his father's reign.

Childhood and early reign, 1207–1219 Not much is known about Henry's childhood. He saw little of his father, but was close to his mother. He later pensioned his wet-

Henry III (1207–1272), by William Torel [tomb effigy]

nurse—Ellen, wife of William Dun—comfortably at Havering. In 1209 John ordered a general oath to Henry, and about 1212 handed him over to the guardianship of his Touraingeau henchman Peter des Roches, bishop of Winchester. Des Roches supervised Henry's education until he was fourteen. He commissioned for him a 2200-line grammar from Master Henry of Avranches. By the age of nine Henry spoke with unusual 'gravity and dignity' (Paris, *Historia Anglorum*, 2.196); years later he could still recite lists of barons and sainted kings of England, perhaps from early lessons. Des Roches probably influenced Henry's reverence for his Angevin ancestors (especially Richard I and Eleanor of Aquitaine), his taste for art, and his devotion to Anglo-Saxon saints. Henry's knightly training under des Roches's Breton retainer Philip d'Aubigny was less successful. Ralph of St Samson, Henry's bodyguard, may have taught him to ride.

The civil war of 1215–17 following John's repudiation of Magna Carta left a lasting impression on Henry, detectable in documents of fifty years later. John died unexpectedly on 19 October 1216. Nine months later, Isabella deserted her children and returned to France to remarry. Henry did not see her again until 1230. Not surprisingly, he became dependent on father figures until well into his twenties.

Against the background of civil war the throne was an uncertain legacy. But John had secured the pope's protection, personified by the legate Guala, and nearly all the higher clergy were loyal, permitting the royalists to arrange Henry's coronation at Gloucester Abbey on 28 October. It was poorly attended. Henry came over from Devizes and William Marshal, earl of Pembroke, knighted

him on 27 October. During the coronation Guala tactfully permitted the bishops of Winchester, Worcester, and Exeter to anoint Henry and crown him with a lady's chaplet. Henry immediately performed homage to Guala and, four days later, took the cross. William Marshal assumed regency of the realm, and it was decided on 12 November to issue a modified form of Magna Carta in order to enhance the royal cause's popularity.

The rebels imported as their leader Louis, son of King Philip Augustus of France, who had a claim to the throne. Few defected, and stalemate was broken only by military victory, at Lincoln on 20 May 1217, when the regent captured many rebels, and on 24 August when Louis's supply fleet was defeated by Hubert de Burgh's navy near Sandwich. Louis lost heart and was bribed to depart, while his supporters were treated leniently. Magna Carta, further modified, was reissued in a great council held at Westminster in October and November, with a new charter of the forest. Alexander II of Scots came to peace but Llywelyn ab Iorwerth (Llywelyn the Great) of Gwynedd kept most of his recent conquests.

Guala discretely deferred to the regent, whose prestige and diplomatic skills slowly restored order to government. In November 1218 Henry was given a great seal, entrusted by common consent to Ralph Neville; no perpetual grants could be made, however, until the king came of age. Progress was slowed, though not halted, by the Marshal's last illness. On 9 April 1219 he resigned Henry to the protection of a new legate, Pandulf. He also warned him not to follow the example of a 'criminal ancestor' (King John) or else God would deny him a long life, advice which Henry heeded. At a council in Reading next day des Roches reasserted his rights as tutor, boldly seizing the boy-king by the head, but was rebuked by the bystanders. The Marshal died a month later.

The minority and its problems, 1219–1227 A great council at Oxford in April sanctioned a triumvirate, confirming Pandulf as 'first counsellor and chief of the kingdom' (Carpenter, *Minority*, 128), with Hubert de Burgh as justiciar and Peter des Roches as Henry's tutor. This lasted until 1221. From the start Pandulf permitted the justiciar to dominate. In spite of its continuing impoverishment the regime performed Henry's second coronation with pomp in Westminster Abbey on 17 May 1220, and in the years which followed continued its work of rebuilding the administrative machinery disrupted by civil war, a process which advanced as much through bribery as force. The leading figure in its manoeuvrings and machinations was increasingly Hubert de Burgh. Pandulf resigned in July 1221 and des Roches's tutorship of the king was terminated in the autumn, and in the next three years Hubert steadily consolidated his position. Des Roches's influence was marginalized. At a council held in London in June 1222, after concessions including suspension of a forest eyre, a measure to resume the royal demesne was agreed, nearly doubling the king's income. While at Oxford with the king after Christmas, Hubert ensured that Henry confirmed the charters before a council at Westminster in January 1223, offsetting opposition to another inquiry into royal rights. In the following months war broke out in Wales where Hubert's ally, the earl of Pembroke, conquered most of the south-west, undermining Llywelyn's dominance. Hubert brought the king, decked in his first suit of armour adorned with the royal coat of arms, to relieve Builth on 23 September and then found a new castle at Montgomery, where on 7 October he received Llywelyn's submission.

On 10 December at Westminster, Archbishop Langton connived with Hubert to give Henry nominal control over his own seal. The government then demonstrated its domestic strength, at least, by forcing the remaining supporters of Peter des Roches to resign their shrievalties and royal castles. In summer 1224 the revolt of another former loyalist to King John, the dangerous Falkes de Bréauté, was suppressed. Falkes's castle of Bedford was captured after an eight-week siege (20 June – 15 August). The young Henry was present when it fell. He may himself have ordered, or more probably was induced by Hubert to order, that the entire garrison, over eighty knights, should be hanged.

These power struggles were exploited by Philip Augustus's successor, Louis VIII (r. 1223–6). In July 1224 he overran Poitou, capturing La Rochelle. Henry secretly blamed the justiciar for this. However, Hubert planned for its recovery. In a council at London in February 1225 he exploited rumours of another French invasion to obtain £40,000 through a fifteenth on movables, the first major tax of the reign, in return for what proved to be a definitive reissue of the charters. The success of the 1225 tax (and of other taxes until 1237), in contrast to the failure of the 1217 scutage and 1220 carucage, helped to establish the principle of political concessions in return for taxation. In the end it hamstrung Henry III's government, making the king financially dependent for major undertakings on the consent of great councils and later of parliaments. But although the charters imposed constraints on the crown's exploitation of feudal incidents and local government, notably the forest, their repeated confirmation constituted in the short term a series of timely concessions to gain acceptance for the re-establishment of royal government in the localities, for instance through a general eyre in 1218 and a forest eyre in 1221.

In the longer term the reissues established the charters and the principles they represented in the public imagination and gave them the force of law. Increasingly regarded as the yardstick for acceptable standards of royal government, they were especially highly regarded by knights and gentry, a development which helped stimulate a rapid increase in recourse to the increasingly professionalized royal courts. Henry III later committed himself publicly to the principles of the charters, often exhorting the barons to uphold them in their dealings with their own men. In 1255 he ordered the sheriffs to have them proclaimed in the county courts and to see that they were observed by all, on pain of punishment. But at the same time royal lawyers and local officials worked hard to find and exploit ambiguities and loopholes.

In August 1225 the king's sixteen-year-old brother *Richard (d. 1272), now styled count of Poitou, who was knighted and created earl of Cornwall in February, nominally headed an expedition which recovered Gascony by the end of the year, perhaps the high water mark of Henry III's minority. 1226, by contrast, was probably a year of disillusion, thanks to disagreements with the papacy over ecclesiastical taxation and frustrated hopes of campaigning in France. In November, following the death of Louis VIII, Henry sent embassies to Normandy, Anjou, Brittany, and Poitou, plotting against the Capetians. Then on 8 January 1227, now in his nineteenth year, he held a council at Oxford at which 'by common counsel' he declared himself of full age, thereby ending the minority.

The dominance of Hubert de Burgh, 1227–1232 Henry did not really begin to rule in 1227, he merely assumed the power to make charters to buttress Hubert's justiciarship. He created Hubert earl of Kent and over the next year enriched him and his family, culminating in Hubert's barefaced elevation on 27 April 1228, ostensibly 'on the advice of the magnates', to the justiciarship of England for life. After this, Hubert's popularity declined, while between 1227 and 1231 Henry built up an independent household of nearly seventy knights and began to interfere in government, bringing him into periodic conflict with Hubert. However, he long lacked the resolve to part with his fatherlike justiciar.

In 1227 Henry's declaration of majority was turned into profit by forcing the confirmation of earlier royal charters, and the holding of general and forest eyres; several areas were reafforested. This produced a reaction, exploited by the king's brother Richard, who had only been invested earl of Cornwall during pleasure in May and resented Hubert's tutelage. Supported by seven earls, he threatened civil war, but was easily bought off. But Hubert continued to lose ground, his authority decisively dented first by his failure to strengthen Montgomery Castle, threatened by Llywelyn in September 1228, despite the levying of a scutage of 2 marks per fee, and then by his lukewarm attitude towards the recovery of the Angevin continental lands. Henry celebrated Christmas at Oxford in 1228 and received invitations from the nobility of Normandy and Poitou to invade. 1229 was spent ostensibly preparing for this. However, despite much warlike talk, a scutage of 3 marks per fee, and a tallage of the royal demesne, plans were bungled. There was no muster at Portsmouth before 13 October, the principal feast day of Henry's patron St Edward, too late for any fighting, and the fleet proved too small. Departure had to be postponed; only an alliance with Brittany was achieved. Henry is said to have blamed Hubert and to have attacked him with a sword. He had reason for suspicion: in secret negotiations with the French regent in 1229, Hubert had envisaged renunciation of Normandy, in order to concentrate on recovering Poitou. Nevertheless, after Henry spent Christmas 1229 at York with the king of Scots, another scutage was raised, and on 3 May 1230 Henry, decked in crown, sceptre, and a white silk mantle, landed at St Malo with a substantial force. But although Normandy was poised to revolt, Hubert is said to have advised against attacking

Normandy, and there was little fighting, discouraging allies from rebellion. Subsequent efforts concentrated on Poitou, and there was an expedition as far as Bordeaux, but few permanent gains resulted. By the autumn Henry and Richard were ill, tired, and short of money. They retreated to Brittany. Leaving a token force, Henry sailed home to Portsmouth on 28 October. The campaign, arguably the last opportunity to recover Normandy, was a costly fiasco.

Upon his return, in a petty bid for independence, Henry began to use a privy seal in communicating with the chancellor. Even in Brittany in June 1230 he overrode justiciar and council and requested a papal legate (none arrived until 1237). None the less, Hubert continued his domination for more than another year. He entertained Henry for Christmas at Lambeth and received important wardships, including the lands and heirs of the earl of Gloucester. On 15 April 1231 to his grief, Henry's brother-in-law, William (II) Marshal, earl of Pembroke, died. Henry's exclamation at the Temple Church funeral, 'Woe is me! Is not the blood of the blessed martyr Thomas fully avenged yet?' (Paris, *Chron.*, 3.201), reflected gratitude to William (I) Marshal, and perhaps also wider frustrations. Once more government languished as faction-fighting broke out at its centre. Hubert persuaded Henry to prevent the younger William Marshal's estranged brother Richard from succeeding to the earldom of Pembroke, claiming that his Norman lands made him a liegeman of the king of France. Richard Marshal's subsequent revolt, abetted by Richard of Cornwall, prevented Henry making any headway against Llywelyn in an early autumn campaign. Then Peter des Roches, Hubert's bitter enemy, returning heroically from the crusade, was received back to court with his supporters and gradually gained an ascendancy over the king. In an acrimonious council held at Westminster at the end of October, Henry was persuaded by Richard Marshal and the duke of Brittany to abandon plans to marry the youngest sister of the king of Scots in favour of the duke of Brittany's daughter Yolande, reviving prospects of another French campaign. According to Matthew Paris, Hubert had for years been blocking other marriage proposals by spreading rumours that Henry was malformed and impotent. Henry now snubbed Hubert, his customary host since 1224, by spending Christmas at Winchester, lavishly entertained by Peter des Roches.

Hubert's final decline started in January 1232 when des Roches was appointed a baron of the exchequer and began promised financial reforms. In truth few of these achieved much, but they generated wild expectations in the king, who was running into debt. Henry's recent failure in France had exposed his financial weakness, now compounded by the expense of campaigning in Wales and maintaining foreign subsidies, for instance to the duke of Brittany. Thanks to Hubert's patient restoration of government, the king's ordinary annual revenue by 1230 was about £24,000, a great improvement on the mere £8000 of 1218, but even without allowance for inflation only two-thirds of average income in the early years of John's reign. The limitations placed on royal finance by concessions

resulting from civil war and the reissues of the charters meant that Henry's freedom to manoeuvre depended largely on his ability to bargain for subsidies from great councils. He could not even enjoy his remaining revenues to the full, as corrupt bailiffs pocketed the profits of office, well-connected 'curial' sheriffs kept the exchequer's receipts from the counties, the shire 'farms', at traditionally low rates while themselves harvesting most of the true profits, and royal manors were leased on unduly generous terms. Schemes to reverse this situation greatly exercised the king in the 1230s and 1240s. But until the mid-1240s they brought only temporary improvements, the curtailment of royal patronage implicit in fiscal reform generating more political tension than any moderate increase in revenue warranted. As was repeatedly demonstrated, only a long period of peace could produce the savings necessary for the king to live of his own—an admission of his limitations not to Henry's taste. Consequently his resources were never sufficient for his ambitions, and inadequate finance remained a fatal weakness of Henry's rule, one that dogged him throughout his reign.

On 7 March 1232, at a council held at Westminster, Hubert's enemies ensured rejection of a major tax on movables, greatly weakening the regime and forcing Henry into negotiations with Llywelyn. In May, Henry and Hubert left for the marches; on the 19th they stopped at Worcester to see the body of King John translated to a splendid new tomb, and on the 23rd met inconclusively with Llywelyn at Shrewsbury. During their return, on 11 June, des Roches's kinsman Peter de Rivallis was granted the treasurership of the king's household for life. Even now Henry was still balanced between factions. Seeking inspiration, he went on pilgrimage to the Holy Rood at Bromholm, Norfolk, and was entertained by Hubert de Burgh on 2 July, where he confirmed Hubert and his followers in all their offices for life; the justiciar, on the king's orders, swore to coerce Henry into keeping his oath.

During July, however, Henry turned decisively against Hubert. Des Roches reported (probably correctly) that Hubert had plotted riots against Italian clerics appointed by the pope to English benefices. Mindful of old obligations to the papacy, Henry ordered the arrest of several of Hubert's men. Finally, Hubert himself precipitated a breach, if Matthew Paris can be believed. For a king now aged twenty-four their violent quarrel at Woodstock was one liberty too many, and he dismissed Hubert as justiciar.

The regime of Peter des Roches, 1232–1234 The fall of Hubert de Burgh merely permitted the rise of Peter des Roches, another father figure, as well as initiating two years of almost continuous political tension. At first des Roches shared power with Richard Marshal and the stewards of the household. Hubert was quickly stripped of his offices and lands, and fled into sanctuary. His eventual trial in London in November before his peers may have been Henry's idea, reflecting either his leniency towards courtiers or his preference for baronial consent, following

Magna Carta, chapter 39. Nevertheless, sentence was severe: indefinite detention at Devizes and confiscation of his treasure, albeit retaining his title and hereditary lands. This met with general approval. In September the council at Lambeth voted the fortieth on movables refused in March, the only time a grant was made without conditions throughout Henry's reign; but thanks to the poor harvests, it raised only £16,500.

Des Roches quickly took control of government. Despite posing as a financial reformer, he purged opponents and enriched followers with shrievalties and royal castles. Some of his party were foreigners, and his regime was generous to the Angevins' continental allies. However, he was less interested in Henry's continental ambitions than in his own accumulation of patronage. In January 1233 Gregory IX renewed Henry's authority to recover crown rights, permitting cancellation of charters to de Burgh's supporters; over fifty were overturned 'by royal will' alone. The beneficiaries were des Roches's men. This provoked opposition. In particular the regime quarrelled with Richard Marshal, who resented the advancement of des Roches's men at the expense of his own retainers. In February 1233 Richard retired to Wales and Ireland; by August he was in revolt.

For some six months or so there was a sharp, but limited, civil war. Richard Marshal was the only insurgent magnate. Although he courted popularity as a champion of Englishmen against foreign favourites—winning the chroniclers' sympathy—he was never supported by more than sixty knights, and King Henry, directing forces supplemented by foreign mercenaries, was able to reduce his castles of Hay, Ewyas, and Usk between 28 August and 8 September. Henry then characteristically offered negotiations, at a council summoned to Westminster for 2 October. This was delayed a week by Hubert de Burgh's escape into sanctuary. However, talks broke down. Goaded by his affinity the Marshal rebelled again, now allied with Llywelyn, while his retainer Richard Siward snatched Hubert de Burgh from Devizes. By 12 November, much to his discomfort, Henry resumed campaigning in the marches. While at Grosmont he suffered the humiliating capture of his baggage train in a night raid. After that the campaign ground to a halt during the winter. In the following February further fighting was averted only by the Marshal's sudden withdrawal to Ireland. Llywelyn then opened negotiations.

There was a stalemate. Henry was short of funds. In a council at Westminster on 2 February 1234 Edmund, the archbishop-elect of Canterbury, and several bishops denounced the regime. As baronial irritation at des Roches's autocratic rule increased, Henry promised to follow Edmund's advice as soon as he could. He then escaped on a tour of East Anglian shrines as the strain took its toll. He fell ill, and after gathering relics for his private chapel he ordered a silver votive-statue of himself to be deposited at Bromholm commemorating his recovery. On 8 March a council in Northampton authorized the bishops to treat with Llywelyn. Henry attended Edmund's consecration at Canterbury on 2 April; des Roches still sat next to him, but the other bishops theatrically faced them across the choir. At a council at Westminster on 9 May, Edmund threatened excommunication unless there was a change of regime. Henry thereupon ordered des Roches to retire to his diocese, while de Rivallis and other henchmen were dismissed. Thereafter the rebels were appeased by concessions, while des Roches's disseisins *per voluntatem* were reversed. Henry displayed grief on receiving news of Richard Marshal's death, possibly by assassination, in Ireland. However, his fortuitous demise curtained the most embarrassing process whereby Henry truly learned his lesson in kingship.

Marriage and the achievement of stability, 1234–1242 Henry III's personal rule began well, establishing a political stability which not only remained largely unbroken for over fifteen years, but was also resilient enough to persist for several years more after tensions began to revive in the early 1250s, finally succumbing only to the coup of 1258. Henry cultivated courtiers who were largely indifferent to the old factions, men like John Mansel, Robert Passelewe, Henry of Wingham, Bertram de Criol, William de Cantilupe, John of Lexinton, Paulinus Piper, and Robert Waleran; these men and their clans formed a tightly knit community. There were favourites, but none achieved the hegemony of the ministers of the minority. A new generation of magnates was wooed into peaceful political activity in parliament. Under the influence of Archbishop Edmund, Henry made his peace with Peter des Roches and Hubert de Burgh, both of whom received pardons before their deaths in 1238 and 1243 respectively. Their followers had almost all been restored to office by 1236. Henry could not afford further warfare. In June 1234 the archbishop secured a two-year truce with Llywelyn, extended until the latter's death in 1240. Another truce with the king of Navarre in January 1235 protected Gascony. In the following August a four-year truce was agreed with Louis IX, following the collapse in November 1234 of Henry's alliance with the duke of Brittany.

1235 was largely devoted to family matters. Henry's sister *Isabella (1214–1241) married the emperor Frederick II in May, producing an ally against Louis IX, albeit at a cost of a dowry of £20,000. Himself almost into middle age, early in 1235 Henry proposed to Jeanne, heir to Ponthieu, but Louis IX persuaded the pope to prohibit the match. Nothing daunted, Henry turned to Raymond Berengar, count of Provence, for the hand of his eleven-year-old daughter *Eleanor (d. 1291). She was not a rich match: Henry proposed a dowry ranging from 20,000 to only 3000 marks and was at one stage prepared to take her for nothing; the 10,000 marks eventually agreed was never fully paid. However, she was excellently connected; her elder sister had recently married Louis IX, while her mother's family, the counts of Savoy, controlled the passes into north Italy and were courted by both pope and emperor in their wars against each other. Thus Henry both gained leverage in the papal curia and significantly improved his relations with Louis IX, now his brother-in-law.

Betrothed at Canterbury on 14 January 1236, Eleanor and Henry were married at Westminster on the 20th by

Archbishop Edmund, her coronation setting new standards of lavish ceremonial. Beautiful and clever, Eleanor
quickly monopolized Henry's affections, helping him to
break fully with earlier influences, though she favoured
policies of moderation and reconciliation. She had been
accompanied by one of her brilliant uncles, William of
Savoy, bishop-elect of Valence, and early in April, Henry
suddenly reconstructed his council at Windsor as a sworn
body of twelve headed by William. Financial reforms—
resumptions of demesne, exploitation of royal manors,
increments on the shire farms—which increased the
king's revenues by about 10 per cent were made tolerable
in the shires by the dismissal of courtiers as sheriffs, to be
replaced by local men on oaths of good conduct. Moreover, William was no Peter des Roches, for he cultivated
men from all factions, supported the jurist and administrative reformer William of Raleigh, and promoted few
foreigners. He also maintained peaceful relations with
Scotland and France.

Richard of Cornwall resented his demotion after
Henry's marriage. He boycotted the court for the next two
years and to boost his position took the cross at Winchester in June 1236. But the discontent he hoped to foment
was deftly offset by William of Savoy and Raleigh at a great
council at Westminster in January 1237, a large assembly
which may also have been attended by representatives of
burgesses and knights: Magna Carta was reissued, and
recent resumptions of royal demesne were abandoned;
three magnate victims of resumptions were even
co-opted on to the king's council. In return, Henry III was
granted a thirtieth on movables; the last major parliamentary tax for over thirty years, it raised some £22,500. William of Savoy was so secure that he could even go abroad
from February to April, while in June the newly arrived
papal legate Otto (another moderating influence) publicly
reconciled Hubert de Burgh with Peter des Roches. In September Alexander II relinquished ancient claims to the
northern counties of England in return for lands worth
£200 p.a. William of Savoy's brother, Thomas, married the
countess of Flanders in the autumn, bringing Henry further allies.

The reissue of the charters in 1237 marked the culmination of a period of important legal development: ordinances enacted in great councils regulated watch and ward
in 1233, and the holding of and attendance at local courts
in 1234, while 1236 saw wide-ranging legislation in the
form of the Statute of Merton, which dealt with such
issues as the rights of widows, access to common pasture,
and the payment of dead men's debts. The final separation of the court *coram rege* from the common bench,
probably in 1234, marked the continued development and
sophistication of royal justice, itself celebrated about that
time in the famous legal treatise known as *Bracton*. The initiative in these processes, however, came less from Henry
III himself, who except in artistic concerns was rarely
(unlike his royal predecessors) the initiator of significant
developments, than from his ministers and from the legal
profession. Indeed, apart from a provision of 1253 concerning Jews, which though much to Henry's taste was

essentially ecclesiastical in origin, there was little further
legislation before the enactments of the period after 1258.
Unlike King John, Henry interfered little in the workings
of the courts, except in a handful of notorious cases to
delay proceedings against favourites. The principal complaint which emerged against royal justice seems to have
been its growing complexity, remoteness, and expense,
which tended to favour richer litigants who could afford
the means to influence its workings. This attitude may
help to explain the appeal in some quarters during the
1240s and 1250s of a call to reform via a return to old ways:
the revival of the lapsed offices of justiciar and chancellor,
both subject to public scrutiny.

William of Savoy was again abroad when Simon de
Montfort, a rising star at court, began a liaison with Henry
III's widowed sister, *Eleanor. To hush up the scandal,
Henry planned their secret marriage in his chamber
chapel at Westminster on 7 January 1238. This provoked
Richard of Cornwall into rebellion supported by Gilbert
Marshal, earl of Pembroke, and the earl of Winchester;
they denounced Montfort and other favourites and condemned the marriage as contracted without magnate con-
sent, winning much sympathy. On 23 February they met
Henry in arms at Stratford-le-Bow, but he retreated to the
Tower until 2 March. This was Henry's sharpest crisis until
the 1260s. It was resolved by William of Savoy. Richard
was bought off with 16,000 marks for his crusade, about
half the proceeds of the thirtieth, and remained loyal for
the remainder of the reign. On 4 March, now reconciled,
Richard and Henry attended the deathbed of their sister
*Joan, queen of Scots, at Havering.

In May 1238 William of Savoy left to assist Frederick II in
Italy and never returned. In June, Henry proposed William
for the bishopric of Winchester, but lacking his counsel,
bungled the election. The usually co-operative monks first
proposed William of Raleigh and then, despite Henry's
intervention, elected Ralph de Neville; enraged, Henry
appealed to Rome and deprived Ralph of the chancellorship on 28 August. He soon relented, returning the title
and emoluments of office to Ralph until his death in 1244.
Soon afterwards, on the night of 9 September, Henry narrowly escaped assassination at Woodstock by a deranged
clerk associated with William de Marisco and the pirates
of Lundy. In November Henry was at Kenilworth for the
baptism of Eleanor and Simon de Montfort's eldest son,
Henry, a sign of Montfort's continuing advancement,
which culminated in February 1239 when Henry created
him earl of Leicester. William of Raleigh retired in April
and a more relaxed policy towards the exploitation of the
shires and the royal manors followed. Henry did have
other resources at his disposal, and his finances remained
reasonably healthy for several years. As well as feudal incidents, tallages, and the profits of justice, his right to the
revenues of vacant bishoprics was important, and
between 1240 and 1244 he derived 10 per cent of his
income from them, thanks to the coincidence of vacancies at Winchester (exploited with unusual thoroughness), Canterbury, and London. Henry's officers often
pushed his rights to the utmost, particularly through the

general and forest eyres, but they still had to contend with the constraints imposed by the charters. To offset the resultant drop in income Henry adopted a new policy of tallaging the Jews, which exhausted their resources during the 1240s.

On the night of 17 June 1239, confounding rumours of sterility, Queen Eleanor gave birth at Westminster to a boy. While the Londoners celebrated by torchlight, Henry's clerks sang the 'Christus vincit'. The infant was baptized by the legate at Westminster Abbey three days later; Richard of Cornwall and Simon de Montfort were the godparents. Henry's choice of *Edward as a name for his heir (a departure from Angevin tradition) proclaimed his devotion to Edward the Confessor. Edward's birth ensured that Eleanor would henceforth be Henry's principal adviser. The number of Savoyards and Provençals at court began to grow, while Henry suddenly quarrelled with Simon de Montfort at the queen's churching and drove him into exile with his wife. King and earl were reconciled in the following April, but Simon's influence was never the same again.

Although Henry III was greatly grieved by the news of William of Savoy's death at Viterbo in November 1239 (Matthew Paris reports that he tore his clothes and threw them into the fire), 1240 and 1241 were good years for the English king. He took advantage of the death in April 1240 of Llywelyn ab Iorwerth of Gwynedd to exploit a succession dispute. He threw his weight behind Llywelyn's son Dafydd against his half-brother Gruffudd, and in a theatrical ceremony at Gloucester on 15 May knighted Dafydd and received his homage, reducing him to a client ruler. On 10 June at Dover, Henry and the legate saw Richard of Cornwall off to crusade; then, after a reconciliation with Henry possibly effected by the queen, who could now afford to be generous, Simon de Montfort departed on his own crusade. On 29 September, to further public joy, Eleanor produced a daughter who was baptized *Margaret, probably after Eleanor's sister, the queen of France.

Henry III spent Christmas at Westminster, fêting the legate before his departure in January 1241. This left Henry even more dependent on Eleanor's family. Another of her uncles, Peter of Savoy, arrived and was knighted on 5 January, the feast of St Edward's deposition, in a great ceremony at Westminster Abbey. Soon dominant in Henry's council, where he favoured a continuation of moderate policies, Peter was granted the honour of Richmond in April, while in February another of Eleanor's uncles, Boniface, was elected archbishop of Canterbury. Tension rose briefly early in 1242 when it was thought that Richard of Cornwall might oppose the rise of the Savoyards when he returned from the east, but the court's fears came to nothing. When Richard landed at Dover on 7 January he was met by both the king and queen. Feasted on the 28th in London, which was decorated in his honour, he was immediately won over to the new regime by the flattery of Peter of Savoy, who offered to resign but was recalled by the king. Richard was probably too impoverished after his crusade to cause much trouble. Moreover Peter may have

persuaded him that he could profit from an expedition to Poitou, of which he was still nominally count.

The expedition to Poitou, 1242–1243 Henry III had continued to hope to recover his father's lost continental lands. In August 1241 he had surprisingly halted an attempted rebellion by Dafydd of Gwynedd after only a fortnight's bloodless campaign, assisted by Welsh defections and unusually clement weather. At Gwerneigron Dafydd readily accepted a compromise, surrendering Gruffudd and his son Owain as hostages. For Wales was far less interesting to Henry than Louis IX's investiture of his brother Alphonse as count of Poitou in June 1241, a calculated snub to Angevin claims and one which immediately gave rise to plans for revenge. His eventual intervention in Poitou was, however, an ill-considered piece of opportunism, one that he threw himself into before he was ready, when Hugues de Lusignan, count of La Marche, and his wife, Isabella of Angoulême, Henry's own mother, rebelled against Louis IX at the end of 1241, shortly after making an alliance with the English king. Henry lacked effective allies, while his income, at this time about £40,000 per annum, was dwarfed by that of the French king, whose resources, worth over £70,000 per annum, made him a truly formidable adversary. Parliament was summoned to Westminster in January 1242 but whether from realism (having regard to Henry's lack of generalship and money) or from selfishness (few of them claimed lands in Poitou) the magnates refused taxation besides a scutage because there was a truce in force with King Louis. However, Henry was in religious mood and not easily deflected, and after a tour of his favourite East Anglian shrines, he sailed for Poitou in May in his ship fitted with panelled chambers, leaving the archbishop of York as regent. He ordered fifteen man-sized candles to burn perpetually around the shrine of St Edward at Westminster throughout his absence abroad. In the event of his father's death Edward would be protected by Queen Eleanor and her uncles, an interesting reflection on the position of Richard of Cornwall. Henry brought about £35,000, scraped together from a 20,000 mark Jewish tallage and other resources. Although seven earls accompanied him his forces were inadequate—hardly 200 knights, half of them from the household—and this doomed the expedition from the start.

Henry landed on 12 May, but did not reach Pons in Saintonge until the 20th. At first he characteristically delayed, preferring negotiations. He may have hoped that Louis would buy him off, or he may have sought a cause to generate more support in England. He recruited allies, betrothing Richard of Cornwall to Sanchia, another daughter of the count of Provence, and so freeing the count of Toulouse, who was engaged to her, to make a marriage alliance with the Lusignans. Then on 8 June he ended his truce with Louis and advanced first to Saintes (11–19 June) and then to Taillebourg on the Charente (30 June). But the additional troops he had summoned from England and Gascony failed to appear, and by 19 July he was back in Saintes. Louis now began reducing Lusignan castles; whereupon Henry suddenly dashed to secure

Taillebourg, only to fall into a trap. Louis moved up on 20 July and surrounded him, heavily outnumbering his forces. Henry escaped only thanks to Richard of Cornwall, whose services on crusade led to the English army being given a day's grace by the French knights. Richard advised Henry to 'get out of here quickly' (Paris, *Chron.*, 4.212) and they fled, Henry losing a coronet in the rush. Some English knights and Simon de Montfort were able to distinguish themselves on 22 July, beating off a French night ambush, but Saintes was abandoned. Only Louis IX's illness halted the French. Hugues and Isabella defected back to Louis on 1 August, destroying the Poitevin revolt. Only the isles of Oléron and Ré remained in Henry's hands in Poitou.

The failure was caused largely by inadequate finance. In the autumn Henry was forced to borrow at Bordeaux; a further £20,000 reached him from England and Ireland only after several months. In a letter to the emperor in September 1242 Henry castigated Poitevin treachery, a line followed by Matthew Paris. But his own inadequate generalship was also to blame: his indecision, inactivity, and tendency to fall into traps meant that allies lost confidence, as they had in 1230. Well might Simon de Montfort declare at Saintes that Henry, like Charles the Simple, should be locked up by his subjects—an insult the king remembered twenty years later.

Henry remained at Bordeaux for a year, making no further forays, and on 5 April he came to terms with Louis, renewing the truce for five years. Concern for the queen delayed him: she had been pregnant at the start of the campaign and at Bordeaux on 25 June 1242 gave birth to a daughter, Beatrice, named after Henry's mother-in-law, Beatrice of Provence, who visited them in the following May. In August 1243 Henry made a new and more ample dowry settlement for his wife. Failure in Poitou had made him even more dependent on her, causing another quarrel with Richard of Cornwall, who returned to England in September 1242. Henry had probably granted Gascony to Richard in gratitude for saving him at Taillebourg, only to change his mind a few weeks later on the advice of Eleanor who wanted Gascony for the Lord Edward. Richard was bought off with wedding gifts from his brother. Henry's expedition to Poitou cost him a clear £80,000, leaving debts of £15,000. Limited fighting had kept costs low, and his debts were cleared by the end of 1244, while Henry stubbornly maintained his claims to Normandy and Poitou for another fifteen years. Nevertheless, he found this fiasco difficult to live down.

The aftermath of Poitou, 1243–1245 After Poitou, Henry avoided major confrontation for many years. He continued to be much influenced by the queen and her kinsmen, and by ministers like John Mansel. Thanks mainly to heavy taxation of the Jews, and to a decade of almost unbroken peace, his finances gradually recovered. It is significant that there was no rebellion against him on his return like the one that had confronted John after Bouvines. Fortuitous minorities in the ruling dynasties of Scotland and Wales, and among the English magnates, assisted him. Henry deliberately cultivated good relations

with the baronage, to whom he was lavish with hospitality and generous with patronage. He was indulgent towards their debts to the crown, and relaxed in his approach to their liberties; although his justices periodically investigated these, Henry took no action to reduce them and sometimes even added to them. He paraded his unity with the aristocracy in major artistic commissions, for example for Westminster Abbey and Dublin Castle. For several years sustained criticism of his rule came only from those ranks of society which were excluded from court: merchants, county knights, and lesser clergy. Henry's government did at times show itself responsive to the grievances of these men. But as long as he kept the magnates on his side any opposition could be controlled.

Ceremonial repaired Henry's dented image somewhat. He sailed back to Portsmouth on 9 October 1243, to be received at Westminster four days later with a religious procession lit by innumerable tapers. Eleanor's sister, Sanchia, with their mother, Beatrice of Provence, arrived at Westminster on the 18th, and on 23 November Richard of Cornwall married Sanchia in Westminster Abbey. To mark the occasion Henry gave the abbey a gold-worked banner with his arms interwoven with those of the count of Provence. Richard renounced his claims to Gascony and was promised lands worth £500 p.a. Eleanor's vigilance over Edward's interests explains why Richard simultaneously waived claims to Ireland. Beatrice of Provence finally reconciled Henry to Simon and Eleanor de Montfort and Henry granted them 500 marks p.a. and Kenilworth Castle. Beatrice departed in the new year and Henry gave her an enormous jewelled eagle in gold and a loan of 4000 marks, and ordered that all the churches between London and Dover be lit up in her honour.

Finance remained a problem, one exacerbated by temporarily strained relations with Scotland, whose king was showing unwelcome signs of independence—in 1239 Alexander II had married Marie de Coucy, a French noblewoman. In the summer of 1244 Henry raised an army consisting largely of mercenaries supplied by Thomas of Savoy, but the differences were resolved without fighting, and on 15 August, Alexander agreed that his son and heir, another Alexander, aged three, should marry Henry's three-year-old daughter Margaret. A fresh Welsh rebellion, too, was cause for expense. Efforts to raise money prompted resentment, and in November, Henry faced criticism at a parliament of magnates and prelates (the latter objecting to recent challenges to monastic liberties and episcopal elections) in the refectory of Westminster Abbey.

Henry appealed in person for a major subsidy, foolishly emphasizing his need to settle debts arising from Poitou. Nobles and clergy elected a committee of twelve, mainly courtiers, to negotiate their response. They suggested a mild concession, modelled on that of 1237, in return for taxation: on their advice, Henry should appoint a justiciar and a chancellor, presumably in the belief that great officials would make Henry more popular with lesser subjects. Even when Henry refused, disliking the element of compulsion involved, they mildly replied that if he would voluntarily appoint these officials and take the committee's advice on expenditure, they would secure him an aid. It is most unlikely (despite a rubric stating the contrary) that a more radical 'paper constitution' (preserved by Matthew Paris), which would have effectively recreated the minority regime, was actually presented or approved by the king; it cannot have met with magnate approval and probably emanated from a radical minority of the clergy. Henry then attempted to negotiate a separate grant of clerical taxation, but in vain. What ultimately kept him afloat financially was perhaps the enormous Jewish tallage of 60,000 marks proclaimed in 1244; gradually collected, it had raised about 40,000 marks by 1249.

When parliament reassembled at London in February 1245, a compromise was agreed underlining Henry's warm relations with the magnates. The birth of his second son on 16 January, after concerns for Eleanor's health, won him sympathy; amid celebration, the infant was named *Edmund after the great East Anglian saint. Henry was also committed to intervention in Wales. Consequently parliament agreed to an aid for the marriage of Henry's eldest daughter, while Henry promised to uphold the charters, and the bishops renewed the excommunication of those infringing them. Henry thus requested magnate consent even to prerogative taxation: it was levied at an old rate with low yield, but it cleared his debts as intended. In March, Henry made a thanksgiving pilgrimage to St Albans and Bromholm. He began his greatest work, the rebuilding of Westminster Abbey, and, perhaps in a bid for popularity, snubbed an attempt by the pope to tax the English clergy.

Westminster Abbey provides the main visual evidence for Henry's artistic tastes, a field in which his close personal interest, extending to the colours of vestments and the shape of windows, is recorded in scores of detailed written commissions. The abbey's lofty French-derived architecture, lavish use of statuary and coloured glass, and exotic decoration in Italian Cosmati marble were intended to project an image of the majesty of monarchy; Henry was deliberately copying Louis IX and Frederick II, mighty rulers whom he hoped to rival in magnificence even if he could not defeat them on the battlefield. Similarly intended to impress were his great palace complex at Westminster, which became the focus for a court life in whose ceremonial piety was as much in evidence as pageantry, and the numerous other commissions—wall and panel paintings full of symbolic figures and images of favoured saints like Edward the Confessor, statues, stained-glass windows, gold-worked embroidery—which transformed the appearance of over three-quarters of the royal residences, even those he never visited. Notable works included a processional gateway into the Tower of London (which collapsed in 1241) and a great hall at Winchester which still survives. Henry also lavished extravagant offerings, particularly statues of precious metal, on his favourite shrines at Westminster, Canterbury, and Walsingham. Like Charles I, Henry was a distinguished collector as well as patron. He amassed jewels (of which he was particularly fond), regalia, precious objects, and

clothes, the latter of both English and foreign workmanship, intending them both for his personal use and for distribution as munificent gifts. Much of his collection had to be pawned in the 1260s.

It is sometimes argued that Henry's taste for splendour was intended to reinforce an absolutist ideology of kingship. He certainly enjoyed the company of kings, and was jealous of his prerogatives throughout his reign, from the 1240s onwards repeatedly rejecting proposals which might have limited them. He was no less determined in asserting his rights, especially that of choosing his own councillors, as he showed in the 1260s. But in practice Henry was a ruler who usually accepted some restraints, not least those imposed by the charters. This was in keeping with current legal doctrine, as expressed in *Bracton*, that the king was under the law. Henry did not coerce parliaments into submission, and even co-operated with conciliar measures from the 1240s onwards which were intended to preserve the interests of 'the crown' at the expense of the man who wore it. None the less, the fact that his councillors were among those who rebelled against him in 1258 suggests that he was far from consistent in accepting these limits, and that it is this inconsistency which provides an important key to the political tensions of his personal rule.

Family, France, and finance, 1245–1249 In June 1245 Welsh aggression finally caused Henry to summon the feudal host. He arrived at Chester on 13 August, dawdled there a week, and by the end of the month had reached the Conwy river. Here he characteristically got bogged down for two months, constructing Deganwy (or Gannoc) Castle. Amid demoralizing shortages and Welsh raids he may have lost control of his troops, who expressed their anger in savage sorties. He finally withdrew at the end of October, having accomplished little. Richard of Cornwall gave considerable assistance to the campaign in the form of loans, but his attempt to gain the earldom of Chester from Henry was thwarted by Queen Eleanor and Peter of Savoy, once more defending the claims of Henry's sons. Welsh resistance was effectively broken by Dafydd's sudden death, without a direct heir, early in 1246.

Henry continued to look abroad. In January 1246 he accepted the homage of the count of Savoy for key castles and transalpine routes in return for 1000 marks and an annual pension of 200 marks. This deal, concocted by the Savoyards, was approved by the council, in the hope that it would give Henry leverage in the succession to Provence. But in spite of murmurings in parliament, and Henry's own attempts at further resistance, papal taxation of the English clergy could no longer be prevented. Perhaps Henry was too pious, or grateful, to withstand the pope for long; he may, too, have feared excommunication, remembering King John or the recently deposed Emperor Frederick II. But he was also alarmed by Innocent IV's rapprochement with Louis IX, which soon enabled Louis to occupy Provence. In May he ordered his chaplains at Dover to pray day and night that death might be averted from the king and his household.

Against this background the death of his mother, Isabella, at Fontevrault on 4 June must have reminded Henry of past sorrows. He mourned her with grants of alms, especially to the scholars of Oxford and Cambridge. Henry's fortunes improved in 1247, however. He was entertained for Christmas at Winchester by William of Raleigh, now restored to favour, and a parliament held at Oxford in April approved a great recoinage covering England, Ireland, and Wales, a lucrative addition to royal finances. Henry immediately farmed this out to Richard of Cornwall, thereby acquiring the means to settle many debts. Henry also seemed completely triumphant in Wales: undermined by minorities and disunity, and sapped by a trade embargo, the native princes all came to heel. At Woodstock on 30 April, Henry was accepted as feudal overlord of Wales. The crown also absorbed Chester and vast tracts of the marches, more than reversing territorial losses under King John.

But Henry's greatest triumph lay in the expansion of his family. In May, Edmund de Lacy, earl of Lincoln, and Richard de Burgh, lord of Connaught, both royal wards, were married to two of Eleanor's kinswomen, underlining the importance of marriage in linking the king with the magnates. Later that month Henry received four of his half-brothers and a half-sister of the house of Lusignan at Westminster. He had invited them over, and immediately settled three of them in England: Aymer, promised a bishopric, studied at Oxford, and became bishop-elect of Winchester in 1250; William de Valence was established in the Welsh marches in August, marrying Joan de Munchensi, a Marshal coheiress, which brought him the lordship of Pembroke; in the same month Alice married John de Warenne, earl of Surrey, another royal ward. There were fears of French expansion into Gascony at this time, so closer links with the Lusignans made political sense.

Then on 13 October, the feast of the translation of St Edward, Henry staged a propaganda set piece at Westminster in the presence of all lay and ecclesiastical magnates. He had obtained from the community of Outremer a great relic: a phial of Christ's blood. After a vigil fasting on bread and water he received the relic at St Paul's the next day and in person carried it in liturgical procession 1 mile to Westminster, even through the palace, in a show of piety influenced by the new Corpus Christi devotion. He presented the holy blood to the abbey, and the bishops of Norwich and Lincoln preached that the relic was superior even to Louis IX's holy cross. The day ended with a mass knighting in Westminster Hall, when those dubbed included William de Valence and several Poitevins and Gascons. Henry, presiding in coronet and robes of gold, ordered Matthew Paris to record everything. Such typically grand ceremonial bound Henry still closer to his magnates. Nevertheless, by the end of the year many English knights were considering joining Louis's crusade.

Henry attempted to maintain pressure on Louis in 1248, but wavered between policies. He wished to participate in Louis's crusade; indeed, he amassed a gold treasure for it and requested papal permission for a contingent under the captaincy of Gui de Lusignan. This plan failed thanks to the French king's opposition. But Henry also plotted to recover the Angevin lands once Louis had departed, and cultivated more allies for the purpose. However, all his resources were soon diverted towards Gascony, threatened by rebellion and the ambitions of Alphonse of Poitiers and the king of Navarre. Henry's failure to exploit this opportunity to turn the tables on the Capetians might seem a major mistake, but its unpopularity at home never made it a realistic option. In February he approached a very well-attended parliament (possibly including knights) for money, but failed to obtain a grant of taxation. Instead, there were complaints, especially from merchants and clergy, and demands for the election of three great officers. Henry prorogued parliament, but further sessions at Westminster in July, and in the following January and April, were equally obdurate. After the Poitou fiasco, another major war was probably rated a waste of money.

The king's advisers thought a limited expedition to Gascony would sidestep demands for change. After a pilgrimage to Walsingham and Bromholm, Henry managed in May 1248 to persuade Simon de Montfort to abandon another crusade for the lieutenancy of Gascony, with a seven-year contract so generous to be almost a bribe. Queen Eleanor pressed Montfort's appointment. Financed by sales of royal silver plate, Jewish tallages, and further loans from Richard of Cornwall (completely mortgaging the recoinage), a small army set sail in August, ironically the same month in which Louis embarked for the east. For about a year Montfort enjoyed considerable success. Yet even such a modest force strained the royal finances, prompting Henry to try to raise a loan from the principal English abbots in December, and to step up the fiscal pressure on sheriffs and royal bailiffs, a development which did little for the popularity of his rule in the localities and Wales.

Indeed, from this point the conduct of Henry's government strained his observance of the charters. His refusal to burden the magnates meant that the weight of his rule fell instead on his lesser subjects. Judicial and forest eyres became much more exacting, and there were attempts at reafforestations. The exchequer demanded increments on the shire farms that were sometimes treble or quadruple those imposed in the 1230s, driving the sheriffs—often of the harshest professional type and strangers in their counties—into introducing new obligations or reviving old ones, and imposing a whole host of petty exactions. Merchants complained about the abuses of royal purveyance, goods taken for the king's household but not paid for. Alan de la Zouche extorted double the sums raised by his predecessors from Henry's 'new conquest' of the Four Cantrefs in north-east Wales. The oppressions of government were if anything made worse by the wide variety in its intensity (it was relatively lenient in some counties), as well as by high levels of corruption. The king sold hundreds of franchises in this period, many of them involving exemption from the burdens of knighthood and local administration; these prolonged the acceptability of his rule in some quarters but exacerbated social divisions in general. But though there were grumblings Henry did not hear them, and his mood remained assured and relaxed. In September 1249, on the advice of Queen Eleanor and Peter of Savoy, he bestowed Gascony on the Lord Edward, and two months later was so confident of success in the duchy that he pardoned the rebel Gaston de Béarn.

Crusading plans and Gascon crisis: the beginnings of decline, 1250–1254 Louis IX's defeat at Mansourah in February 1250 spurred Henry, flushed with his apparent success in Gascony, into taking the cross in a grand public ceremony presided over by the archbishop of Canterbury at Westminster on 6 March. He planned to take the queen, who supported the plan, and most courtiers with him. Henry's crusading is now considered sincere; he undertook to embark in 1256 and meanwhile earnestly began to collect funds. The pope granted a crusading tenth of clerical revenues for three years. From now on, Henry prevented English crusaders, even his half-brother William de Valence, from sailing independently. Meanwhile, imitating Louis IX's crusading preparations, he ordered the reduction of expenses of the royal households and inquiries into alienations from his demesne, demanded further taxation of the Jews, and made promises of better government. Even Henry's artistic commissions had a crusading theme, with Antioch chambers ordered at Winchester, Clarendon, and Westminster. After witnessing the dedication of Richard of Cornwall's Cistercian foundation at Hailes, Gloucestershire, in November 1251, the king spent Christmas at York, where, in further preparations for the crusade, the alliance with Scotland was renewed, with her new king, Alexander III, marrying Henry's eldest daughter, Margaret, amid scenes of great pageantry. Henry knighted Alexander, who performed homage for his English lordship (in accordance with the 1237 treaty) but not for Scotland itself.

However, as with so many of his schemes, Henry's crusade came to nothing, greatly to his disappointment, due to the eruption of rebellion in Gascony against Montfort's harsh rule. While at York, Henry forbade Montfort to return to Gascony; concerned to protect Edward's interest, Eleanor narrowly prevented a quarrel. But when Henry sent envoys to investigate Montfort's rule, a harvest of complaints resulted. On 28 April 1252, on Peter of Savoy's advice, he attempted to mollify opposition by regranting Gascony to Edward, while from May to June Montfort was forced to answer charges put by leading Gascons before the king in parliament. Henry took the Gascons' side and had some sharp exchanges with Montfort, who claimed that the king had undermined his lieutenancy. Thanks to the support of Eleanor, Richard of Cornwall, and other powerful magnates, Montfort escaped condemnation, but he refused to resign, and the only way to prevent further rebellion was for Henry to announce on 13 June that he would pacify Gascony in person before the following February. He planned to arrive in October but could not complete his preparations in time. Montfort

returned to Gascony and started up another fierce conflict, forcing Henry to dismiss him in October, and ultimately to buy him out of his contract at a humiliatingly high price.

Unfortunately the Gascon rebellion continued to escalate, to the extent that Gaston de Béarn, its leader despite his recent pardon, invited Alfonso X of Castile to revive his ancestral claims to Gascony. Henry's failure to obtain taxation from parliament in October forced delay. The clergy, led by Robert Grosseteste, opposed the papal crusading tenth because it was to be levied at a new rate, and the laity refused taxation without the participation of the clergy. There also seems to have been confusion over Henry's ambitions in France. Even now he still hoped for a cheap victory while the French were weak: in June he wrote blusteringly to Louis IX at Acre offering to sail sooner than 1256 if Louis restored the Angevin lands.

However, Henry now encountered serious domestic political difficulties, ominously foreshadowing later developments. In his frustration over Gascony he quarrelled with Eleanor, their first public breach since 1236. Eleanor had sympathized with Montfort; their differences persisted throughout the year. But after Geoffrey de Lusignan intervened in Gascony in February and negotiated a truce, his success encouraged Henry to rely on the military contacts of his half-brothers. The political influence of the Lusignans began to grow and their arrogance made them unpopular. On 3 November, relying on Henry's support, they even raided the palaces of Eleanor's uncle, Archbishop Boniface of Canterbury. The tension grew into a sharp crisis reminiscent of that of twenty years earlier: the court divided into factions, and four earls threatened armed support for one side or the other.

Such was the Gascon emergency that Henry and Eleanor hastened to resolve their differences; in January 1253, assisted by the bishops, they pacified the baronial factions. Significantly, Eleanor became pregnant in the spring—perhaps her first successful pregnancy for eight years. The well-attended parliament which met in May proved more amenable. Alfonso of Castile's threat to Gascony strengthened Henry's case. Henry characteristically bargained again for prerogative taxation, but the magnates and knights only granted him an aid for the knighting of Edward, in return for reissuing Magna Carta. On 3 May the charters were confirmed in Henry's presence in Westminster Hall. But the aid met a bare fraction of the costs of the campaign, which was financed only by the exploitation of all available resources, including Irish revenues and a tallage on Jews and the demesne. Still intent on his crusade, in January Henry imposed restrictions on the Jews. In May the clergy consented to a crusading tenth for three years, provided that the magnates oversaw expenditure.

Henry drew up his only extant will on 1 July 1253. He made Eleanor sole custodian of his children and realm until Edward's majority, binding her and his executors to implement his crusade. She was given an enlarged dower and appointed regent during her husband's absence, assisted by Richard of Cornwall and a council. Henry probably hoped that Gascony could be speedily pacified. In May he negotiated for Edward to marry Alfonso's half-sister Eleanor, but too late to prevent a campaign. Eventually he set sail from Portsmouth on 6 August, to the last delayed by tardy preparations and contrary winds. He was reluctant to leave Eleanor when she was pregnant, and in July asked Alexander of Scots to let Margaret return to keep her mother company.

Henry arrived at Bordeaux on about 24 August. His Gascon campaign was unpopular: the feudal summons was poorly supported, and some of the magnates, notably the earl of Gloucester, arrived late; there were many quarrels, even desertions. Henry brought about 300 knights, many from the royal household. He also had his crusading treasure, approximately £20,000, which partly explains why this was his only successful overseas campaign. He was soon assisted by over 100 Poitevin knights recruited by the Lusignans. As ever, Henry's strategy was cautious. Fortunately potential enemies like the kings of France and Castile did not intervene. Bordeaux and Bayonne remained loyal, and the Dordogne valley was quickly secured. Only in the valley of the Garonne was there a serious resistance, needing a full year to overcome, albeit with a break in the winter. Bergerac was taken at the beginning of July 1254, La Réole in August, after which Henry could return to Bordeaux.

As usual Henry was generous with the aim of winning supporters. Gascons received pensions, concessions, and a new seneschal. Rebels who submitted were pardoned and restored to their lands. By February, Henry even offered to mediate between Simon de Montfort and Gaston de Béarn, but Gaston refused. Montfort, who had received overtures from the French, was enticed back to Henry at Benauges in October 1253 by a financial settlement which was not only generous in itself, but which even gave Montfort a claim on the revenues of several counties ahead of the royal exchequer. Alphonse of Poitiers's complaints received immediate compensation of £3000. Henry lavished grants on the Lusignans and others. Not surprisingly, by Christmas he was impoverished and had to borrow at Bordeaux before Queen Eleanor sent fresh supplies of money.

Essential to Henry's position in Gascony was peace with Alfonso of Castile. In February 1254 John Mansel and the Savoyard bishop of Hereford negotiated the marriage of Edward and Alfonso's half-sister Eleanor. Edward was in the same month put in possession of a huge appanage, including Gascony, Ireland, Chester, and the Channel Islands, nominally worth £10,000 p.a., but in fact worth £6000, while his future wife was offered a substantial dowry. Late in March, Henry heard rumours of a planned Castilian invasion, and wrote for assistance from England. Queen Eleanor had in February summoned a parliament for 26 April, its membership to include two knights from each shire and representatives of the parish clergy. Henry might have been voted a tax, albeit under most stringent conditions, had Montfort not returned with news that the emergency was over: on 31 March, Alfonso proposed peace, renouncing claims to Gascony in return for the marriage alliance and Henry's assistance in a crusade to north Africa, conditions only partly met. On 11 June, Eleanor, well recovered from giving birth to Princess Katherine on 25 November 1253, arrived at Bordeaux, accompanied by Edward, Edmund, and the archbishop of Canterbury. Richard of Cornwall tactfully remained in England. Edward, with a fairly modest retinue, was sent to Burgos. To Henry's disappointment, since he had planned a grand ceremony for him in England, Edward was to be knighted by Alfonso. The marriage took place on 1 November in the abbey of Las Huelgas. Three weeks later Edward and his consort returned, but Henry did not see them for nearly a year, for Edward remained in Gascony as ruler until the following summer.

As he waited for La Réole to fall in 1254, Henry dabbled in further and grander schemes. On 12 February 1254, now that Richard of Cornwall and Charles of Anjou had withdrawn their candidatures, he sent proctors to receive the crown of Sicily for Edmund from the pope. Confirmation from Innocent IV was received in May. In March he had prepared to dedicate Westminster Abbey in October 1255 before he departed for the Holy Land. Now he hoped to crusade from Sicily.

After three months (August–October) in Bordeaux settling Gascony, Henry set off home. He requested permission from Louis IX to cross France, partly because he disliked the long sea-crossing, but principally so that he could befriend Louis, thereby ensuring the security of Edward and Gascony when he departed on crusade. He is also said to have admired this recently returned crusader, and wished to meet him. Accompanied by Eleanor, Edmund, Archbishop Boniface, William de Valence, and others, Henry progressed through Poitou and Anjou in November. He reached Fontevrault on the 15th where with typical filial piety (which also pleased the Lusignans) he ordered his mother's tomb to be moved inside the abbey. He then made a pilgrimage to the shrine of St Edmund at Pontigny. At Chartres he admired the cathedral with a connoisseur's eye and finally met King Louis. He paid a week-long state visit to Paris at the start of December, staying first at the Old Temple and then at the royal palace. Henry was reputedly eager to see all the city's churches and buildings, especially Louis's Sainte Chapelle. He won admiration from the Parisians for feeding crowds of poor at the Old Temple, for his spectacular state banquet for Louis and the king of Navarre, and for gifts to the French nobility. The occasion cemented the links between the two kings created by their marriages. Queens Marguerite and Eleanor, and Beatrice of Provence and her daughter, Beatrice, attended; Sanchia of Cornwall travelled over to complete the family party. Henry and Louis established a lasting understanding which set in motion an eventual peace-settlement. At the same time the presence of Thomas of Savoy, putative captain of Henry's expeditionary force, probably meant that Louis gave his blessing to the Sicilian plan. Henry had hoped to spend Christmas in England, but was delayed at Boulogne by bad weather. But he was able to cross on the 27th, and by 5 January, the feast of St Edward, he was back at Westminster. A few months later Louis sent him the impressive present of an elephant, the first seen in England, which was kept in his menagerie at the Tower.

The growth of political opposition, 1255–1258 Henry returned from Gascony in debt, having spent his crusader's gold treasure and incurred obligations to Edward, the Savoyards, the Lusignans, and Simon de Montfort, in vain efforts to calm tensions within the royal family. His finances were in disarray. His resources were shrinking: indulgence towards too many of his family in a period when escheats and great wardships were scarce reduced his supply of patronage; the English Jews, formerly such a good source of revenue, were drained dry, and in 1255 Henry made them over to Richard of Cornwall; the market for sales of liberties was shrinking. Yet he made no economies, and did not try to call in long-standing debts from the magnates. Instead he tried to live of his own, further intensifying the pressure on the localities (which served to increase the corruption of his officials) and resorting to occasional levies like tallages, for instance one of £2000 on London in February 1255. He also borrowed from his family: in the same month Richard of Cornwall advanced £5000 for his household expenses. As he sank further out of his depth in the Sicilian project, Henry's increasing dependence on his family and leading courtiers had the effect of making him ever more indulgent towards them, ignoring their arbitrary behaviour and permitting them a whole host of liberties, while simultaneously reducing his capacity to respond to the grievances which his exactions and their misconduct provoked. Thus the fuse was lit for the 1258 explosion.

Henry hardly changed policy. He again collected gold for the crusade, and by 1257 had £4000. In April 1255 his request to a large parliament of prelates and magnates, and perhaps wider representation, for help in settling his debts was refused. There were demands for three great officials responsible to parliament, perhaps signalling discontent in the localities, but Henry was still able to refuse. His trump card was the crusade and Sicily, which he thought the clergy and magnates could not obstruct. In April, using crusading funds, he bought up Frederick II's pawned crown jewels. An extension of the truce with Louis IX was negotiated in June. Pope Alexander IV, desperate for Henry's aid against the Hohenstaufen, committed himself to Edmund, and in May permitted Henry to substitute the Sicilian scheme for his crusading vow. In October the deal with Pope Alexander, which Henry and his council had already accepted, was published in parliament. Henry's undertaking to pay the papacy 135,000 marks by Michaelmas 1256, on pain of excommunication, and his vision of leading an army overland to Sicily through France, alike met with a frosty reception. Yet there was no effective opposition, and Edmund was invested as king of Sicily by the bishop of Bologna.

Many English ecclesiastics did not regard Sicily as a worthy destination for a crusade, illustrating the ambivalence of Henry's relations with the church. Unlike John, he was himself conspicuously pious. He and his wife were personally interested in ecclesiastical reform and gave generous support to friars and poor scholars. He was also grateful for the support of the papacy and its legates during his minority. But royal policy inevitably brought clashes with sections of the church. The potential grounds for disagreement were numerous. The English church expected the king to protect it against papal taxation and papal provisions to benefices (hence the riots of 1231–2 against the latter), but Henry found it difficult to do this and retain the pope's support. The first clause of Magna Carta declared that the church was to be free, but the king always needed to be able to reward his servants with bishoprics and to maintain his regalian rights over vacant sees; he also needed to be able to tax the clergy. From the 1240s, moreover, royal lawyers had a reputation for challenging ecclesiastical liberties, which made him many enemies and especially among the monks—this is reflected in the hostile image of Henry's rule projected in the writings of Matthew Paris of St Albans. Henry usually had his way, though not without occasional confrontations, but he was much more hesitant in imposing his will than his predecessors had been. The fact that he ruled in a period of ecclesiastical reform, personified by bishops like Robert Grosseteste of Lincoln, in which the church aspired to greater independence and higher standards, was a further cause of friction. Although Henry usually retained the backing of the papacy, ecclesiastics formed some of his most implacable—and also articulate—opponents in the 1260s.

During 1256 Henry remained committed to the crusade. He added his Dominican confessor, John of Darlington, to his council, and considered an expedition to north Africa with Alfonso of Castile; his order in April that landholders with estates worth £15 p.a. should take up knighthood or pay a fine, which deepened his unpopularity among the gentry, was probably designed to swell his campaigning fund. But the parliament which met at the end of April was unco-operative, and magnates who lacked confidence in his generalship tried to dissuade him from going. Ever optimistic—his querulously ineffective speech at the exchequer in October, ordering all sheriffs and bailiffs to account regularly in person, perfectly encapsulates his overconfidence at this time—Henry countered with another plan, to install Richard of Cornwall on the throne of Germany. After months of negotiations, the archbishop of Cologne came to Westminster at Christmas, and announced Richard's election to the crown of Germany. Encouraged by Henry and the Lusignans, Richard accepted. Henry could now impress magnates with his royal relations.

Within months Henry's plans collapsed. Llywelyn ap Gruffudd, master of Gwynedd after the battle of Bryn Derwin (June 1255), launched a widespread Welsh revolt in November 1256 and overran the Four Cantrefs. Meanwhile, Richard's election backfired: Alfonso of Castile was a rival candidate, and again threatened Gascony. An Anglo-German alliance alarmed Louis IX, and Henry had to begin negotiations to detach him from Alfonso. Above all, Henry's crusading hopes floundered, following the defeat and capture of Thomas of Savoy in Italy. The lack of enthusiasm of the English magnates proved decisive. In January 1257 Henry was refused aid by an assembly of Cistercian abbots, while in March, Richard of Cornwall's election as German emperor was greeted with dismay by parliament because of his reputation for moderate counsel and for keeping Henry solvent (in February the latter had planned to accompany Richard to his coronation). When Henry and the bishop of Messina theatrically presented Edmund in Apulian dress and again requested taxation, there was uproar. Magnates and prelates composed a dossier of objections exposing the expedition's impracticality and complaining of lack of consultation; the clergy made the gesture of conditionally offering £52,000 to pay Henry's debts to the pope, but also began to organize opposition. Henry started to capitulate, and asked the pope for an extension of his terms.

Richard was crowned at Aachen on 17 May. Before his departure Henry's council, hoping to counteract opposition, took a new oath of good conduct which was envisaged as embracing other officials of central and local government and generating reform. On 10 April, desperate to keep his household solvent, Henry ordered that payment of fees should cease; the treasurer could disregard even Henry's personal orders to the contrary. These schemes were ineffective, but they helped inspire the reforming ideas of the following year. Meanwhile, Henry mourned the death on 3 May of his sickly three-year-old daughter, Katherine. Eleanor fell ill with grief at Windsor, and Henry suffered a long fever at Westminster. Katherine received a lavish funeral and monument in the abbey.

There were further disappointments in Wales. The disastrous defeat of Stephen Bauzan in the Tywi valley in June led to an escalation of the Welsh revolt. Very belatedly a two-pronged English riposte was prepared, but although the earl of Gloucester made headway in the south, Henry himself, operating from Chester, made little progress, and on 4 September, already fearing the onset of winter, he called off the campaign. It seems he was already in financial trouble. A better-prepared attack was planned for May 1258. In the meantime north Wales was left entirely in Llywelyn's hands, while in Scotland the magnates threw off the English tutelage established two years earlier and made a treaty with Llywelyn. The Londoners complained to the king's face of Henry's overvalued and impractical gold coinage, introduced in August 1257, while Archbishop Boniface ignored a royal ban and convened the first English convocation of prelates and lower clergy, which remonstrated against royal and papal exactions. Hopes of a settlement with Louis IX, including the return of Angevin territories, came to nothing.

Henry's wayward policies in the years 1254–8, like the problems of the close of the minority, can be explained by the breakdown of his court into factions. The Lusignan ascendancy, which began after the Gascon emergency which Henry believed they had helped him resolve, stung Eleanor and the Savoyards into action. They opposed this challenge to their long monopoly over Henry: Edmund's candidature for Sicily, and Henry's rapprochement with Louis IX, represented their bid to reassert themselves. By 1257 its perceived failure played into the hands of the Lusignans. They were celebrated warriors, and may well have encouraged Henry and Edward to reassert Angevin claims against the Capetians. After Richard of Cornwall's departure Henry found it difficult to hold the balance between factions, especially as he needed loans from the Lusignans, who were the principal beneficiaries of his order of about November 1256, forbidding writs in chancery against favourites. They quarrelled with Simon de Montfort and the earls of Gloucester, Norfolk, and Hereford, and were unpopular with courtiers who generally co-operated with the moderate Savoyards, not least because their claims on royal patronage were often thwarted by Henry's generosity to his half-brothers. The Lusignans' harsh estate officials, too, were hated. Their arrogance only intensified with the Welsh emergency, which made them indispensable. Most importantly, perhaps, late in 1257 they forged an alliance with the Lord Edward, who had hitherto been nurtured exclusively by Savoyards but now, anxious to assert his political independence, blamed Eleanor and the king's older councillors for Henry's inability to contain Llywelyn. He began to borrow from the Lusignans, completing the ascendancy of the latter in a new alignment which precipitated the 1258 revolution.

Crisis, 1258 Against a background of harvest failure and famine, defeat in Wales, and worsening relations with the church over his debt to the pope, Henry summoned a parliament to Westminster for early April 1258. But his hopes of financial relief were disappointed when the magnates split into factions, a development precipitated by Aymer de Lusignan's attack of 1 April on John fitz Geoffrey, a veteran royal servant and confidant of the queen, at Shere in Surrey. When John demanded justice, Henry refused. On the 12th, probably with the queen's blessing, a group of magnates led by Peter of Savoy, Simon de Montfort, and the earls of Gloucester and Norfolk swore to support one another against the Lusignans; on the 28th, finally provoked into action by Henry's request for aid against Llywelyn, they stormed into the palace, armed, with an ultimatum.

Faced with opposition within his own court, Henry capitulated, and on 2 May swore to accept a committee of twenty-four to reform the realm by Christmas, in return for a vague promise that the magnates would request taxation from the community of the realm, provided in turn that Alexander IV improved the terms for the Sicilian business. The twenty-four would settle Henry's debts and outstanding claims for patronage, and war against Llywelyn was to continue. This compromise was doomed to failure. Entitled to nominate half the committee, Henry mainly chose Lusignans and their adherents, but was so isolated that he could not find twelve suitable men. Another parliament was fixed for June, but in the meantime Henry's objections to peace with Louis IX were at last overruled, and on 8 May emissaries who included Simon de Mont-fort, Peter of Savoy, and—in a futile attempt to delay mat-ters—the Lusignans began negotiating the renunciation of Normandy; they quickly drew up articles for peace.

Parliament reconvened at Oxford about 11 June, while a large assembly of knights mustered for a land and sea campaign in Wales. However the Lusignans' enemies had worked on Henry to negotiate with Llywelyn, whose emis-saries were therefore present. Against a background of disputes over patronage, the magnates realized that the Lusignans must be removed. Since Henry and Edward had foiled their previous attempt in April, they canvassed the support of the 'community of the realm', promising a general reform which would embrace the localities and making the Lusignans scapegoats for Henry's misrule. A collection of grievances, the 'petition of the barons', was drawn up, and a common oath taken in the Dominican church against 'mortal enemies'. Henry III's rule disinte-grated, as the magnates resurrected the justiciarship, appointing Hugh Bigod to bring justice to high and low, while the war against Llywelyn was abandoned. On 22 June, Henry consigned the principal royal castles to magnate-appointed castellans, and on the same day four electors chose fifteen magnates, mostly courtiers, to form a royal council. The transfer of power from Henry to that council was quickly enacted under the so-called provi-sions of Oxford. About 28 June, in a foolhardy gesture of defiance, the Lusignans and the Lord Edward fled from Oxford to Aymer de Lusignan's castle at Winchester. The magnates pursued them and their resistance collapsed. Edward took his oath to the provisions on 10 July, and four days later the Lusignans left the realm, completing Henry's defeat.

The rise and fall of the magnate regime, 1258–1262 The new regime lasted three years. Although Henry complained in 1261 that he had hated his initial demotion he was slow to act, even when the magnate council fell into disarray, per-haps because he feared civil war—unlike his father in 1215. He was kept in honour and comfort, his beloved pal-aces and building projects well maintained. The council, by contrast, quickly consolidated its authority to prevent the Lusignans' return, and dominated the thrice-yearly parliaments, undermining the king's position. By 4 August four knights from each county had been ordered to collect grievances against officials, royal and seigneur-ial, and report to parliament by October. In addition the new justiciar toured some half-dozen counties, hearing complaints against officials and gaining much popularity. Envoys finalized a truce with Llywelyn and restored rela-tions with the Scottish council; papal support was sought for the provisions, for renegotiating the Sicilian business, and for the deposition of Aymer de Lusignan from Win-chester. When parliament met in October, Henry endorsed the council's actions and ordered all his subjects to swear obedience to its statutes. A further ordinance denounced the misdeeds of sheriffs and promised improvements. These proclamations went out in Latin, French, and English, a novelty and also effective propa-ganda. Baronial retainers were installed as treasurer and

as a co-steward of the king's household. In November, Simon de Montfort's attempts to dominate the Anglo-French negotiations at Cambrai were foiled only because Louis IX refused to recognize Simon's emissaries.

During these months Henry was isolated. As Matthew Paris noted, he was acutely afraid of Montfort. Between July and October 1258 he accompanied the justiciar, but thereafter Bigod acted independently, and Henry retreated into religion. On 30 September he attended the dedication of Salisbury Cathedral; and in November and December, still mourning Katherine, paid visits succes-sively to St Albans, Bury St Edmunds, and Waltham abbeys. Richard of Cornwall's return from Germany in January 1259 may have aroused Henry's hopes of reinstat-ing the Lusignans, but it seems he was too impoverished to help his brother and immediately took the oath to the provisions.

It is a measure of Henry's persisting weakness that for much of 1259 he was almost entirely inactive, even though serious divisions opened up within the baronial regime, over the pace of reform and also over the Anglo-French peace negotiations. But the council was still strong enough in August to foil his attempt to admit a papal nun-cio, sent to demand Aymer de Lusignan's restoration to Winchester—a rare gesture of royal independence, and a futile one. Nor could Henry prevent a rapprochement between Montfort and the Lord Edward, both of whom objected to the renunciations proposed in the negoti-ations with France. In October, following a protest against the council by the 'community of the bachelors of Eng-land', the provisions of Westminster enacted long-awaited reforms in law and government, and decreed a well-planned general eyre to hear complaints against royal and seigneurial officials. Nevertheless, at the same time the council retreated from the provisions of Oxford by allowing newly appointed sheriffs to farm their offices.

Only in November did Henry begin to recover some free-dom of manoeuvre, when with Eleanor, Peter of Savoy, the earl of Gloucester, and some of the council he crossed to France to conclude the treaty with Louis, leaving Bigod and the remaining councillors in charge of the realm. By 26 November the party had reached Paris, to be warmly entertained by Louis and his queen. It was later said that because Henry tried to hear mass in every Parisian church he passed, Louis jocularly had them all closed to prevent him delaying business. On 4 December peace was pro-claimed. Henry formally surrendered all the lost Angevin territory and received Gascony as a vassal with border con-cessions and a pledge to finance 500 knights for two years, probably for a crusade. In the apple orchard of Louis's pal-ace Henry knelt, swore homage, and became a peer of France, with the title duke of Aquitaine. Although Louis reserved 15,000 marks due under the treaty until the claims of the Montforts had been met, the latter had lost their leverage. Montfort offensively deserted Henry later in December, to join Edward in plots against their enemies on the council.

After Christmas in Paris, Henry delayed another four

months in France. He spent much of January 1260 in religious exercises at St Denis. He was much affected by the sudden death of Prince Louis, the French king's heir, and on 14 January acted as a pall bearer at his funeral at Royaumont. On the 22nd Louis and his queen reciprocated by attending the marriage at St Denis of Henry's daughter Beatrice to Jean, son of the duke of Brittany. Shortly afterwards, news came that Llywelyn had broken the truce and was now besieging Builth Castle. Instead of returning home Henry moved to St Omer, on the coast, for another three months. In vivid letters to the justiciar and council he explained his delay as resulting from further diplomatic negotiations; then went down with tertian fever in March and was visited by Louis IX during Holy Week. His delay cannot be seen as a deliberate tactic to postpone parliament, in defiance of the provisions. Rather Henry was controlled by faction. The queen and the earl of Gloucester sought time to raise mercenaries to crush Edward and Montfort's rebellion: the latter plotted to manipulate parliament, depose Peter of Savoy from the council, and restore the Lusignans. Late in March, Gloucester returned and both sides mustered around London where Henry summoned a handpicked armed parliament. It was rumoured that Edward planned to dethrone his father. Richard of Cornwall and the justiciar intervened to prevent this, with little fighting. Financed by a loan from Louis, 100 mercenaries escorted Henry and Eleanor home.

Henry landed at Dover on 23 April and entered London on the 30th. The rebellion largely collapsed. Some of Montfort's associates were removed from their castles and posts in the royal household, but Henry did not overthrow the provisions, and early in May he was reconciled to Edward by Richard of Cornwall and the archbishop of Canterbury. Moderation was necessary because Henry lacked the money to keep his mercenaries beyond July. Edward and Montfort had much support, partly because the treaty of Paris was widely unpopular. Their alliance lasted another year. On 5 June, perhaps acting on Gloucester's advice to bid for wider support, Henry cancelled the general eyre. Then, urged on by Eleanor and Gloucester, he arranged a public investigation of Montfort's recent actions before parliament in July. This was aborted after Builth Castle fell to Llywelyn. However, Gloucester prevented war by engineering a truce, waiving Llywelyn's proffered payment for a settlement, a disgraceful arrangement which Henry refused to ratify for several months.

Montfort and Edward were still working together in parliament in October, and were able to establish a grip on government, their supporters being elected to the great offices, so that even Gloucester came to terms. They prevented the revival of Montfort's trial, menacing the king's proctors, but at the same time the provisions were modified, so that no new sheriffs were appointed and the magnates were licensed to discipline their own officials. Henry knighted the duke of Brittany's son Jean, but he too defected to Edward, and the two young men departed with two of Montfort's sons for tournaments in France. A newly elected council remained in session until the end of

the year and began to undermine the position of Peter of Savoy. Henry's only consolation for his continuing powerlessness was the visit at the end of October of his daughter Margaret, who was now pregnant, with her husband Alexander III of Scots. In December, Henry learned to his grief that Aymer de Lusignan had died at Paris, still plotting to return.

Aymer's death allowed Eleanor and Peter of Savoy to persuade Henry during Christmas at Windsor to move against the provisions. In January 1261 John Mansel's nephew and namesake, one of Eleanor's closest confidants, was sent to Rome to secure papal annulment of Henry's oath to the provisions. Help was also requested from Louis IX. But Henry's mood was far from confident and on 9 February, in an apparent moment of panic, he dashed into the Tower of London. He proceeded to bid for baronial support while exploiting Eleanor's contacts to recruit mercenaries in Flanders. He also compiled a manifesto of grievances while pretending to support the provisions. During the parliament of February–March he negotiated from the Tower until on 14 March the council, unwilling to risk civil war, agreed to an arbitration over his grievances while the Montforts undertook to appeal to Louis IX over their disputes with the king. Although arbitration failed late in April, Henry could now present himself as a moderate. Early in May he sallied from the Tower, catching his opponents off guard, and seized Dover Castle and the Cinque Ports. This enabled papal bulls to be landed, and also about a hundred mercenary knights whom Henry retained until August. Late in May he moved to Winchester where about 12 June he published the papal annulment of the provisions and then appointed his own supporters as justiciar and chancellor. Soon afterwards he named new sheriffs and castellans as well.

The result was confusion and disorder, as Gloucester, Montfort, and their followers appealed to Louis IX and the pope, and also tried to appoint sheriffs of their own in several counties. There was also something of a propaganda war. On 16 August, Henry issued a general manifesto, stressing the peaceful benefits of his long reign, and promising to deliver the shires from magnate domination, and followed this up in October, by summoning all who owed military service to London and requesting help from 'friends' abroad. But by the start of November, before foreign assistance could arrive, the opposition collapsed. Gloucester and his supporters came to negotiate at Kingston, and on 28 November terms were finalized, with a compromise over shrievalties and agreement that points of variance would be adjudicated by a committee from both sides, with Richard of Cornwall mediating in the event of disagreement, and the possibility of a final appeal to Louis IX. Henry left the Tower, where he had been since October, and was back at Westminster for Christmas. Full pardons were offered to all sealing this 'treaty of Kingston'. Early in 1262 its benefits to Henry matured. Richard of Cornwall's arbitration was invoked in February; by the end of May he inevitably awarded Henry full power to appoint sheriffs. In March the new pope, Urban IV, confirmed his predecessor's annulment of the provisions, whereupon Henry revived the profitable general eyre. His victory seemed so complete that Richard of Cornwall returned to Germany in June, while Henry himself visited France in July.

Recovery and relapse, 1262–1264 Henry owed his victory in 1261 principally to the advice of Eleanor, Peter of Savoy, and Richard of Cornwall, along with his old ministers John Mansel and Robert Waleran. He had avoided war and appeased opponents with arbitrations and grants, even allowing earls to retain some castles gained in 1258–61. He kept the justiciarship, the more willingly because Philip Basset, its new holder, was Richard of Cornwall's retainer, and unlikely to be independent. The magnates, remembering John's reign, were reluctant to cause civil war, and soon lost any chance of a legitimate figurehead when Edward returned from France and was won over by Eleanor late in May; in August he departed for Gascony. Eleanor even allowed Henry to recall William de Valence and the remaining Lusignans in April. Montfort was often abroad, pleading his disputes with Henry before Louis IX, and Gloucester, now a sick man, had less military ability. The majority of the barons, tired of instability, supported Henry's recovery of power as they had after 1234. His sheriffs, often loyalist local barons, held their offices under advantageous financial terms. The famine of the late 1250s was over and the shires gave little trouble, while Henry was careful not to abandon London to his opponents. The provisions also lacked international support. Henry craftily ratified the truce with Llywelyn in March. Louis IX's subsidies underpinned his success. With the pope and the kings of Scots and Germany also supporting him, Henry's coup in 1261 constituted his greatest political triumph.

Over the next two years, however, Henry made several miscalculations. In May 1262 he ordered his absolution from observing the provisions to be proclaimed in the shires and commanded the arrest of all preaching against him. For a while he even revived the Sicilian business, only for Urban IV to revoke it in July 1263. He also blundered into disastrous quarrels which further divided his court by mishandling his patronage. Early in 1262 Queen Eleanor secured the disgrace of Roger of Leybourne and other leading knights of Edward's household, sowing trouble for the future. In July the earl of Gloucester died, and Henry hamfistedly delayed admitting his son, Gilbert de Clare, to his inheritance, even though Clare was supported by William de Valence. In November he wooed Valence from Gilbert by granting him part of the latter's lands consequently driving the new earl of Gloucester into rebellion in 1263.

Most importantly Henry failed to reconcile Montfort. On 14 July 1262, in a remarkable gesture, he sailed with Eleanor from Dover, leaving the justiciar in charge, to resolve differences with Montfort through the queen of France's adjudication. Anticipating victory, Henry raked up every grudge since the start of Montfort's career, but when proceedings began in Paris in August they proved inconclusive. In September, moreover, Louis's court was hit by an epidemic, killing about sixty of Henry's entourage. Henry himself nearly died. On 30 September he wrote to Richard of Cornwall that he was still so weak that he could only leave his bed for short walks. He sent reassuring messages concerning his condition, but on 8 October also warned the justiciar that the arbitration had failed and that Montfort might cause trouble. It would appear that in October, Montfort did indeed return briefly to England, where he attempted to persuade parliament to observe the provisions. But still enfeebled, Henry delayed in France, travelling on pilgrimage to Rheims in November despite news of a new Welsh insurrection. Only on 20 December did he return to England. After Christmas at Canterbury, he was back at Westminster early in January.

Henry lay ill at Westminster for three months. Part of his palace was destroyed by fire in January, to his distress. In January he republished the provisions of Westminster, with additions, 'of the mere and free will of the king and in his full and free power' (*CPR, 1258–66*, 253). At the same time he wrote to Louis IX urging another effort to conciliate Montfort; on 22 February, Louis reported his failure. On 22 March, Henry ordered all to swear to maintain Edward as his heir. Tewkesbury monks mistook this to mean that Henry had died. Disorder followed, fanned by rumours about a succession struggle.

About 25 April, Montfort finally returned to England to co-ordinate an uprising around Leybourne and the other knights who had been ousted from Edward's retinue in favour of foreign mercenaries. The conspirators met Montfort at Oxford where they were joined by the earl of Gloucester, Richard of Cornwall's son Henry, and other malcontents, forming a narrow, but powerful, coalition which rallied around renewed oaths to the provisions of Oxford, and gained popularity by denouncing aliens. At the same time Henry, responding to Edward's initiatives, attempted to rally support through efforts to relieve Llywelyn's pressure on the Welsh marchers. Edward began an alliance with Roger Mortimer, and on 25 May Henry summoned the feudal host to Worcester. This was foiled by the opposition's sharp campaign of violence directed primarily against Eleanor, her kinsmen and associates, and against Edward; rebels imprisoned the bishop of Hereford, and ravaged the estates of Peter of Savoy and the archbishop of Canterbury. Outmanoeuvred and short of money, Henry retreated to the Tower on 19 June, whereupon Montfort dashed from the midlands and secured the Cinque Ports, cutting off the possibility of help from Louis IX. By 12 July, moreover, Montfort had secured the support of the Londoners, after a radical faction overthrew the city oligarchy. Henry vainly offered concessions, perhaps advised by Richard of Cornwall. Edward raided the New Temple and retreated with mercenaries to Windsor; other courtiers and aliens fled abroad. Eleanor, who had lost faith in Henry, attempted to leave the Tower to join Edward on 13 July, but was driven back with insults by the London mob. Two days later the rebels entered the city, and on the 16th, bottled up in the Tower, Henry had to accept their terms: restoration of the provisions, all offices and castles consigned to natives, and the banishment of all aliens except for those specifically excepted. Then, joined by Eleanor, he returned to Westminster.

Baronial nominees took control of government both at the centre and in the shires, but the new regime had little baronial and only modest knightly support; its main supporters were the clergy. It was quick to make a truce with Llywelyn, and even offered him peace in August, but it had no programme of reform and soon disintegrated. Montfort, acting as hereditary steward of England, alienated his allies by granting offices principally to his personal supporters, and by failing to implement the promise to restore plundered estates which he made to parliament early in September. He even allowed Henry to appeal to Louis IX in person, possibly a tactic suggested by Eleanor.

On 23 September, therefore, Henry, Eleanor, and their two sons crossed to Boulogne, along with Montfort and his supporters, for Louis's adjudication, promising to return immediately. Perhaps Henry muddled his case, for Louis surprisingly endorsed the July settlement, provided that the despoiled received restitution. Eleanor and Prince Edmund broke their oath and remained in France, plotting revenge, but Henry and Edward returned to Westminster for parliament in October. Amid recriminations over restitutions and Henry's demands to appoint his own officials, Montfort's regime collapsed, allowing Edward to take the initiative. From this point a strong 'royalist' party began to crystallize. Henry became increasingly dependent on Edward's advice and military skills, and consequently became ever more intransigent towards the Montfortians. Regardless of his mother's feelings, Edward was reconciled to Leybourne and the other knights expelled from his household eighteen months earlier, and on about 16 October he seized Windsor Castle, where Henry joined him. Most of Montfort's baronial supporters deserted him, forcing him to accept a truce negotiated on 1 November by Richard of Cornwall: Henry would maintain the provisions, pending Louis IX's further arbitration. Nevertheless, Henry marched on Oxford soon afterwards and there dismissed the 'baronial' treasurer and chancellor. Winchester Castle too was recovered and early in December, Henry attempted to seize Dover. Montfort himself was nearly cornered at Southwark, but was rescued by the Londoners. Across the channel Queen Eleanor raised support. On 22 November, Urban IV appointed Gui Foulquois as legate with instructions to restore the king's authority.

By now Montfort's supporters had woven together a persuasive propaganda case against Henry, portraying him as no longer fit to rule without the supervision of a council: he had consistently attempted to put himself above the law and had broken his oaths to the charters and to the provisions (it is from this period that the provisions of Westminster, which were acceptable to Henry, begin to be confused with those of Oxford, which were not); he had initiated disastrous and unpopular policies like the Sicilian project; he had violated the liberties of the church; he had abused the crusade; he had filled his court with aliens

and squandered his resources; he had allowed the oppressions of his officials and his favourites in the provinces to go uncorrected. Henry answered his critics with a general proclamation reiterating his commitment to the provisions and promising to defend his people's liberties; he denied that he was planning to bring aliens into the country, as was widely preached.

On 28 December, Henry crossed to France and met baronial emissaries before Louis IX at Amiens. Both sides presented elaborate depositions setting out their claims. This time Louis's award, or 'mise', quashed the provisions entirely, asserting Henry's right to appoint ministers at will. Eleanor's diplomacy, papal support, irrefutable evidence that most of the magnates supported Henry, Louis's outrage over Montfortian attacks on royalist clergy, all prevailed. Montfort's absence after a riding accident could not have affected the outcome. The die seemed cast for Henry's victory.

War and peace, 1264–1267 That no easy victory ensued is explained by Henry's blunders in 1264 and Montfort's brilliant generalship. No sooner had Louis's award been published than Montfort gave the signal for rebellion, sending his sons early in February 1264 to attack enemies on the Welsh marches, probably with Llywelyn's connivance. Edward left France and managed to relieve Gloucester. Henry returned to England on 14 February, and within three weeks summoned an army. He had finally plucked up the courage to inaugurate the second civil war of his reign. He set up his headquarters at Oxford, but remained characteristically static during Lent (8 March to 3 April), though he rejected Montfort's offers to accept the mise of Amiens, provided that Henry only appoint natives to office: he again refused restraints on his prerogative. Meanwhile, the earls of Derby and Gloucester, who both hated Edward, rallied to Montfort, along with a group of younger barons, many of them formerly exploited as royal wards, to form the core of a narrowly based but still powerful rebellion.

Henry hoped to divide his enemies in the midlands. Ignoring attacks on royalists in the London area, he sallied north, and after making offerings in Oxford (thereby uncharacteristically defying the curse associated with St Frideswide on kings who entered the town) on 5 April he surprised and captured the castle and town of Northampton with its large rebel garrison, including Simon de Montfort the younger, which nearly won him victory at a stroke. These clever tactics should almost certainly be attributed to Richard and Edward. The capture of Nottingham and Leicester followed. In the meantime Montfort had besieged Rochester, whereupon Henry immediately swept south in a series of forced marches, even more uncharacteristically setting out on Easter day. He failed to surprise Montfort but relieved Rochester and captured Gloucester's castle at Tonbridge. Rebels in the Weald attempted an ambush: Henry, acting with unwonted brutality on Richard of Cornwall's advice, had 315 peasant archers beheaded in his presence at Ticehurst on 2 May, echoing the treatment of the garrison of Bedford in 1224. He reduced the Cinque Ports, and prepared to blockade

London. Forced to evacuate the capital, Montfort moved south to offer battle. Alarmed, Henry began to wear armour every day. He reached Lewes by 11 May, and lodged in comfort at St Pancras's priory rather than in John de Warenne's castle. Montfort closed in and, for two days, offered terms: a diluted form of the provisions, mainly that Henry rule through Englishmen, and £30,000 damages for royalists. Henry might have accepted, rather than risk battle, but he was overruled by Edward and Richard, who refused any compromise. On the 13th the Montfortians finally renounced their allegiance.

The battle of Lewes, on 14 May, was a disaster for Henry. Although greatly outnumbered, Montfort routed him in just a few hours. Henry's error was to advance up a sharp hill along a broad front in three columns. His control over his army, often insecure, quickly broke down. Edward scattered the lightly armed London infantry, but his undisciplined pursuit left Richard, in the centre, and Henry, on the left, exposed to Montfort's charges. In fierce fighting Henry was much beaten by swords and lances and two horses were killed under him. Richard fled to a windmill; Henry's bodyguard got him back to Lewes Priory. When Edward reappeared everything was over; part of his force fled to the coast and he too retreated to the priory. Although they could have offered further resistance, the next day the royalists accepted Montfort's 'mise of Lewes': restoration of the provisions with contentious clauses renegotiated (terms Montfort failed to honour) and release for the marchers in Henry's entourage. Henry pointedly surrendered to Gloucester; Edward and Henry of Almain became hostages.

After nearly fifty years on the throne, Henry retained only 'the shadow of a name' (*Flores historiarum*, 2.505). He was now eclipsed by Simon de Montfort. Nominally he was supervised by a council of nine, but these and his household officers were Montfort's appointees, and he remained mainly with his captor, in relative comfort, but humiliated by having to endorse Montfort's acts. He consoled himself by repeatedly hearing the mass of Edward the Confessor. Delayed by negotiations conducted through the papal legate, Eleanor missed her chance to invade England with a mercenary army, and confined herself to securing Gascony for her husband.

Montfort's government failed to secure general acceptance. The writ summoning his 'model parliament' of Hilary 1265, with its 'novel' representation of knights and burgesses, reveals that he could count on only a handful of magnates, although over a hundred bishops and abbots were summoned. His regime was compromised by its collaboration with Llywelyn of Wales, which the marchers would never accept. Instead Montfort sought security by hiring a huge retinue of knights. While Henry spent a grim Christmas at Woodstock, Montfort feasted in splendour at Kenilworth. But his ever more exacting rule alienated his leading supporters. In February he quarrelled with Derby and ordered his arrest. Shortly afterwards Gloucester went into opposition, and on 28 May engineered Edward's escape from Hereford. Rebellion broke out in the Welsh marches, and Montfort marched west to

suppress it, but was cornered by the royalists led by Edward, and routed and slain at Evesham on 4 August. Dragged along in the earl's entourage, Henry could not escape involvement in the battle. Dressed in a suit of Montfort's armour, he was wounded in the shoulder and would have perished had he not shouted, 'I am Henry of Winchester your king, do not kill me' (*Chronicle of Walter of Guisborough*, 200–02). Roger of Leybourne rescued him. Had Montfort won, Henry could not have long escaped deposition and death.

It is unlikely that Henry ordered the slaughter of the Montfortians that accompanied the battle of Evesham, or the mutilation of Simon's body; some say he ordered it an honourable burial. His own instincts were conciliatory—witness his unusual concern even for the welfare of widows and orphans of his slain enemies—but his control over the triumphant royalists was weak, and his own family, especially Edward, wanted revenge. Consequently the civil war lasted another two years. After a few weeks' recuperation, Henry summoned parliament to Winchester in September. Already, royalists had seized Montfortian property. Henry belatedly took control of the situation when parliament met by seizing these lands into his own hands before distributing them to his supporters on the advice of his secretary Robert Waleran. Few joined Richard of Cornwall in dissenting. The estates of 254 rebels were officially granted to 71 favoured royalists, the lion's share going to members of Henry's family, household knights, and officials. Faced with ruin, hundreds took to guerrilla warfare.

Over the next two years the remaining pockets of rebellion were nevertheless relentlessly reduced, a process orchestrated mainly by Edward. Henry was happy to leave the work to him: it involved hard campaigning, not to his taste. Early in October he entered London, and on the 13th celebrated the feast of St Edward again at Westminster, wearing his crown in thanks for victory. The city's punishment included a fine of 20,000 marks. Then at the end of the month, Henry greeted Queen Eleanor at Canterbury, returning with her kinsman Cardinal Ottobuono Fieschi, the new papal legate. Henry celebrated by then and there creating his son Edmund earl of Leicester and steward of England, granting him all Simon de Montfort's lands. But he also treated his widowed sister, Countess Eleanor, with magnanimity, permitting her to evacuate Dover Castle and retire to a nunnery in France. Four Montfortian bishops were suspended and exiled.

The task of breaking down Montfortian resistance went slowly on, and late in June 1266 Henry himself commenced besieging Kenilworth Castle, the last rebel stronghold. It was not easily taken. Several blundering attacks were repulsed, and Henry soon opted for a blockade. Ultimately its resistance, along with a revolt based on the Isle of Ely, forced a reconsideration of policy. At the end of August, Henry empowered a committee of magnates and bishops to recommend peace measures. The result of their deliberations, the dictum of Kenilworth, with its unprecedented declaration of royal authority, was issued on 31 October. Total forfeiture was rejected in favour of redemption of estates at fixed terms, and many lesser rebels submitted. However, specified exemptions victimized leaders, and only appalling privation forced Kenilworth's surrender in mid-December.

Henry spent Christmas at Oxford. But in February 1267 he went to Bury St Edmunds for a campaign against the Isle of Ely. He was now so impoverished that he had to pawn even the jewels adorning St Edward's shrine at Westminster Abbey. Then in April, his campaign was interrupted by the earl of Gloucester. Indignant at being insufficiently rewarded for his services in the civil war, and determined to win better terms for disinherited rebels, he marched on London which rose in his support. He blockaded Ottobuono and another civil war looked possible, as Henry and Edward prepared to besiege London and Eleanor summoned Flemish mercenaries. Fortunately Gloucester's nerve failed, and after negotiations he submitted on 16 June, having obtained a vital concession. The dictum of Kenilworth was modified: rebels could recover their estates in order to raise the fines with which to redeem them; Ottobuono even promised financial assistance from the clergy. Henry re-entered London on 18 June and on 1 July the remaining rebels submitted. In August, Henry proceeded to the Welsh marches for negotiations with Llywelyn. Although it was Ottobuono who on 29 September concluded the treaty of Montgomery recognizing Llywelyn as prince of Wales (he had taken the title in 1258 against Henry's will), and confirming his recent gains in return for his homage and a yearly payment of 3000 marks, it embodied a compromise which showed that Henry had no further stomach for war. The Statute of Marlborough, issued on 18 November by a parliament possibly attended by representatives of the commons, reaffirmed the charters, the dictum, and, in a modified form, the provisions of Westminster. Thus the civil war ended on a note of moderation, in keeping with the best qualities of Henry's long reign.

The end of the reign, 1268–1272 Henry's last years were clouded by family tensions, illness, and bereavement. Most Montfortians quickly re-entered public life, and no tenurial revolution resulted from the civil war, but much discontent remained, exacerbated by debt. Royal officers were often as unpopular as ever, while public order was menaced by outlaws and magnate feuds. The royal finances were perilously weak; clerical taxation granted by the pope in 1266 barely paid off Henry's debts.

Henry's problems were compounded by Edward's decision in June 1268 to join Louis IX's new crusade. Early in 1269 his father gave him custody of London, seven royal castles, and eight shires, revenues he could hardly spare, to increase his income. Edward's crusade also forced Henry to appeal to parliament for taxation, a process which began in the autumn of 1268 and was not concluded until April 1270, when a grant of taxation was finally made. During the interval Henry bargained with his subjects in successive parliaments, and added to the strain on his finances by Edmund's marriage to Aveline, heir to the earldoms of Aumâle and Devon, and Henry of Almain's to Constance de Béarn, both in the spring of

1269. But as the year advanced his fortunes improved. In August, Richard of Cornwall returned with his new bride, Beatrix von Falkenburg. And two months later Henry realized his dearest dream, the translation of the body of St Edward to Westminster Abbey and the shrine in it that he had been constructing over many years, even during the recent troubles. Although the church was unfinished, Henry feared further postponement might rob him of his triumph; he may also have been moved by the consideration that the calendar of this year exactly matched that of the Confessor's first translation in 1163. On 13 October, Henry, princes Edward and Edmund, and Richard of Cornwall bore St Edward's relics on their shoulders to the shrine. The pomp was tarnished, however, by disputes over precedence between citizens of Winchester and London, and between the archbishops of Canterbury and York. Nor did Henry and Eleanor wear their coronation crowns, as originally planned, owing to last-minute misgivings.

Even so the ceremony was a splendid one, witnessed by knights, burgesses, and lesser clergy, but it did not sway the parliament which met at this time. Only on 27 April 1270 was the crusading twentieth finally approved by the laity in parliament, in return for confirmation of the charters and the excommunication of those who infringed them, while clerical opposition to the tax continued for several months. The full restoration of the liberties of London on 1 June may have been a necessary concession by the king.

On 4 August, Edward took leave of Henry at Winchester and departed on crusade. He left his children and affairs in the custody of councillors loyal to both Henry and himself, headed by Richard of Cornwall. Queen Eleanor was omitted, perhaps for fear of anti-alien sentiment. From now on, it is difficult to gauge what control Henry retained over government. He may already have been ill, hence his failure to mark the death of Louis IX in the autumn of 1270. He fell so ill in March 1271 that on the 7th Richard of Cornwall was appointed to protect the realm, and the council summoned Edward to return. Henry suddenly recovered in April, however, and himself vowed to go on crusade: on 16 April the council ordered severe economies, ostensibly to begin a crusading fund. But it is significant that early in 1272 it was ordered that revenues should be paid directly into the treasury in order to prevent Henry intercepting them, echoing the provisions of Oxford. Clearly his advisers had concluded he had learned no financial prudence from the barons' war. It seems that Henry's health was never really restored: he hardly moved from Westminster for the rest of his life and missed the funerals of his nephew Henry of Almain at Hailes on 21 May, and of his grandson John, Edward's five-year-old heir, in Westminster Abbey on 8 August. These bereavements, particularly Henry's murder by his cousins Guy and Simon de Montfort at Viterbo in March, must have deeply distressed him. Another blow was Richard of Cornwall's complete incapacitation by a stroke on 12 December; he died on 2 April following.

Henry was ill again at Winchester at Christmastide 1271,

and could not depart until after Epiphany. In May 1272 he wrote to the new French king, Philippe III, excusing himself from performing homage in person for Aquitaine because of sickness. In August he rallied and reconsidered a visit to France, even raising loans for it. But he was prevented by a riot in Norwich during which the cathedral was burnt down; parliament met there in September and he punished the rioters harshly. Perhaps this strain hastened his end. After a final pilgrimage to Walsingham and Ely, Henry returned to Westminster in October for the feast of St Edward. On 4 November he ordered preparations for another Christmas at Winchester. He collapsed, and while London was convulsed with riots over a mayoral election, he died at Westminster on 16 November, aged just over sixty-five, having reigned fifty-six years and twenty days. It is likely, but not certain, that Queen Eleanor was with him at the last.

Henry had left his body to Westminster, but his heart to Fontevrault, showing that he remained an Angevin to the last. On 20 November his corpse was laid in the Confessor's old coffin, dressed in full regalia, and given a magnificent funeral attended by all the magnates, headed by the earls of Gloucester, Surrey, and Hereford. For some years a cult developed around his temporary tomb, near the high altar at Westminster. The Furness chronicle noted 'frequent' miracles in 1275, as did the Westminster-based *Flores historiarum* in 1276; the bishop of Bath and Wells issued indulgences to all visiting the tomb, as did other English, Irish, and French bishops until as late as 1287. The cult was supported from the start by Eleanor of Provence. In 1274 she hoped his miraculous power would save Edward I's mortally ill son Alfonso, but was disappointed. Edward himself was openly sceptical in 1281 when a knight claimed restoration of sight through Henry's merits, but Eleanor reproved him. Construction of a tomb with niches, typical of a shrine, and adorned with Italian Cosmati work, was probably under way when Edward purchased jasper from France for it in 1279. On 11 May 1290, shortly before Eleanor's death, Edward arranged for Henry's translation to the new tomb. It took place at night, with little ceremony. According to the *Annals of London*, Henry's body was intact with a luxuriant beard. Edward had hoped to upstage the developing cult of Louis IX by delaying the translation, but was disappointed: the cult of Henry III had lost its appeal. Not until 10 December 1291, after Eleanor's death, was Henry's heart surrendered to the nuns of Fontevrault, in a ceremony which took place without Edward I's presence. The heart may have survived the French Revolution, finally coming to the Ursuline convent at Edinburgh. Henry's majestic tomb, flanking Edward the Confessor's shrine, remains in Westminster Abbey, topped with his magnificent stylized crowned effigy in gilded bronze, completed by William Torel on Edward I's orders in 1291.

Henry III: appearance, personality, assessment No contemporary description of Henry's appearance survives, suggesting that it was unremarkable. Nicholas Trevet, son of a royal justice, later recorded that Henry was of medium height and strong build, with a drooping eyelid covering part of the pupil. His health was sound until late middle age but deteriorated thereafter. His tomb was opened in November 1871 but no detailed investigation followed; his coffin measurement indicates that he was only about 5 feet 6 inches tall, the same height as his father but much shorter than Edward I.

Contemporaries agreed that Henry was a *vir simplex*, an uncomplicated, almost naïve man, pious, and a lover of peace. His unworldliness was noted by fourteenth-century chroniclers, and also by Dante and the gossipy Franciscan Salimbene. Such a characterization is in most respects accurate. Henry preferred a quiet life at Westminster or in one of his palaces in the Thames valley (on the beautifying and domesticating of which, especially with lavatories, he had spent so much money). In contrast to John he travelled little, either in England or abroad, until the 1260s. His personal demeanour was open and accessible, and he was easily moved to tears. His bouts of anger, which were relatively rare, were short and easily appeased. Unlike his son he was a generous patron of scholars and artists, but he was certainly no intellectual—his possession of 'a great book of romances' probably indicates his literary tastes (*Calendar of the Liberate Rolls*, 1226–40, 288). He was easily dominated by advisers, hence his reputation for inconsistency. He did, however, cling to certain policies, such as the crusade, but lacked the ability to foresee their consequences. He was served by able officials, but in politics these were always subordinated to his family.

From the 1230s Henry replaced the father figures who had acted as his justiciars with an influential family circle, albeit one within which the power of its individual members varied at different periods. His marriage was happy; there were difficulties in the 1250s and 1260s, but Eleanor of Provence preserved her power over him at least until 1263. He and Eleanor were also devoted to their five children, though Edward ultimately resisted their attempts to control him, and after 1263 emerged as a power in his own right. Henry also indulged his brother, his sister and brother-in-law, his wife's relations, and his own half-brothers. Ironically, it was rivalries within the royal family, of which Henry eventually lost control, that more than anything else created the turmoil of 1258 onwards.

Henry was genuinely pious, and he was considerably influenced by friars, especially his Dominican confessors. He heard mass at least every day and ordered tabernacles for the exposition of the eucharist. He loved personal luxury and clearly regarded it—unlike Louis IX—as vital to kingship, but though he liked to have his religion, too, celebrated with pomp, glittering vestments, and music (he heard the 'Christus vincit' sung eight times a year), it would be unjust to regard it as shallow. He ensured that his chapels were equipped with books as well as richly decorated. He naïvely believed that piety brought good fortune, but was also moved by sermons. He set a high moral tone at his court—unlike his father and grandfather he was unfailingly faithful to his wife. Matthew Paris relates that Henry customarily prepared himself for the feasts of St Edward by fasting on bread and water, dressed in plain woollen garments. Joinville later recorded his belief that Henry washed the feet of lepers and kissed them. His lavish charity is amply documented: his feeding 500 paupers a day in the 1240s; his help for orphans; his donations, often of building materials, to innumerable religious houses, hospitals, and houses for converted Jews; his gifts of vestments to bishops. He must have been the greatest patron in his day of the friars in England. The houses of the Dominicans at Canterbury, the Carmelites at Oxford, and the Franciscans at Reading, York, Shrewsbury, and Norwich were largely built at Henry's expense. He did not actually found any others (although he took over patronage of Peter des Roches's Netley Abbey, Hampshire, claiming to be its founder, in the 1250s). His great work was the rebuilding from 1245 at his own expense of Westminster Abbey, a new royal mausoleum to replace Fontevrault, at a staggering cost not far short of £50,000. Henry's love of pilgrimage (especially at moments of crisis), for example to Bromholm, Walsingham, and St Albans, is also well-attested, as is his devotion to numerous saints. St Edward the Confessor, like Henry an orphan and reputedly a man of peace, was both his patron, his role-model, and his 'friend'. Significantly, he chose the imagery of the Confessor for his 1257 gold penny.

Henry was essentially a man of peace, kind and merciful. Unlike Edward I he was chivalrous to his foes, their children and womenfolk, and generous to state prisoners like his cousin Eleanor of Brittany and Gruffudd ap Llywelyn of Gwynedd (who grew enormously fat during his incarceration in the Tower). Although he ordered important improvements to many royal castles, he had no military ability, hated campaigning, and took little interest in tournaments and hunting. His peacefulness was both a strength and a weakness. He tried to avoid another civil war of the kind which had nearly destroyed his dynasty during his childhood. Until the 1260s he was remarkably successful in consolidating his dynasty and maintaining peace. He fostered peaceful conduct among the magnates; indeed, he can take some of the credit for the limited scope and successful aftermath of the barons' war. However, peace was often achieved by appeasing his family, courtiers, and magnates; under Henry their power and those of their bastard feudal affinities grew in the localities at the expense of lesser men, generating many of the tensions which arose in the 1260s. His government was on the whole lax and weak. This suited his relative poverty: the charters restricted his revenues, and he lacked the will to force parliament to grant supply. Nor could he persuade parliament to fund him in the hope of successful war. In the 1230s his yearly income rose to over £20,000, while by the early 1240s more vigorous management may have doubled it to over £40,000; but by the mid-1250s, it had dropped back to under £20,000, hence his inability to respond to political difficulties. His reign made it inevitable that the crown's freedom of manoeuvre would be limited without access to parliamentary taxation.

It is sometimes argued that Henry's difficulties after 1258, which have greatly damaged his reputation, stemmed from his autocratic rule, especially his favouritism towards aliens in disregard of growing national sentiment. However, this view is anachronistic, coloured by rebel propaganda disseminated in the localities during the barons' war. His Savoyard and Lusignan favourites and their followers—nearly 200 of the former and 100 of the latter—were well rewarded but only a small proportion were resident in England, and their role in public affairs was limited; they never supplanted native Englishmen in office. Henry competed with the Capetians in buying up international support and talent, especially to further his interests in Gascony and the papal curia. He hoped to learn from John's diplomatic mistakes. He also hoped naïvely to imitate the chivalry of Louis IX. But the mystique of monarchy to which Henry aspired was an outward show designed to bind him to his magnates: neither in theory nor in practice did he challenge their liberties. Indeed, he helped to set the fashions for aristocratic luxury for the rest of the century.

Historiography The most valuable narrative sources for the reign of Henry III are the St Albans chroniclers, Roger of Wendover and Matthew Paris. The latter, in particular, is indispensable for the years before his death in 1259 thanks to his contacts with the court, though his biases against aliens, and indeed against foreigners generally, and suspicion of anything smacking of a threat to liberties, especially ecclesiastical ones, always need to be taken into account when evaluating his writings. Other thirteenth-century monastic chronicles are less useful, being provincially focused until the 1260s and usually violently anti-royalist during the barons' wars (though a few royalist accounts were attempted under Edward I, for instance the Westminster *Flores* and the chronicle of Thomas Wykes). The shortcomings of these sources, however, were precisely those which gave them considerable appeal in the sixteenth and seventeenth centuries, when the causes at issue during Henry's reign, and especially in the decade after 1258—kingship, nationalism, and anti-papal sentiment—were such as to stimulate research and the publication of sources. Archbishop Matthew Parker edited Matthew Paris under Elizabeth, and in the following century religious and political partisanship caused scholars and polemicists like Sir Robert Cotton (whose *Short View of the Long Life and Raigne of Henry the Third* appeared in 1627), William Prynne, and Sir William Dugdale to rescue and publish many valuable documents. Prynne's investigations of parliamentary antiquities and Dugdale's of the English baronage have by no means lost their value, but present-day scholarship is still most heavily influenced by the liberal-nationalist constitutionalist historians of the second half of the nineteenth century, for whom Henry's reign was relevant particularly in their quest for the origins of parliament. They edited most of the chronicles, above all in the Rolls Series, and though they used some documents it was upon the narrative sources that they mainly relied. Given their dependence upon chronicles, it is not surprising that the accounts of Henry III by historians like Bishop William Stubbs, Sir

James Ramsay, and William Hunt (author of the article on Henry in the *Dictionary of National Biography*) should have tended to be nationalistic in focus, accepting uncritically the complaints of the king's opponents. Their views continued to carry weight well into the twentieth century.

The means to rectify the historiographical balance started to become available in the years after 1900, as the Public Record Office published the records of central government, and above all of the chancery. This was an enterprise which not only made an immense amount of factual information easily available for the first time, but also made it possible to scrutinize the workings of government from the point of view of those who controlled it. It was against this background that in the 1920s T. F. Tout and his followers began a reappraisal of Henry's government. Tout's view of Henry was not in fact particularly favourable—'a thriftless, easy-going temperament, desiring chiefly to be surrounded by personal friends and dependents' (Tout, *Admin hist.*, 2.10)—but his work brought new perspectives, and also stimulated further research among financial and judicial records which remained unprinted. One of its first fruits was E. F. Jacob's exploration of the impact of the barons' wars on the localities, published in 1925. R. F. Treharne's account of the baronial movement (1932, revised edition 1971) was old-fashioned by comparison; though well-grounded in the record sources, it perpetuated a constitutionalist interpretation of Henry's reign.

In the years immediately after 1945 Treharne's assumptions came under challenge, through biographical studies of Richard of Cornwall by N. Denholm-Young (1947) and of Hubert de Burgh by Clarence Ellis (1952), and above all in the writings of Sir Maurice Powicke, whose two-volume *King Henry III and the Lord Edward* (1947) immediately acquired classic status. A many-layered analysis of thirteenth-century political culture, and of the forces which moved its development, written in a somewhat romantic style, *Henry III*—along with Powicke's *The Thirteenth Century* (1953, second edition 1962), which gave proportionately more space to administrative history—created an image of Henry's reign of such weight that it went almost unchallenged for some thirty years, while the thirteenth century, which had formerly been regarded as the high point of the English middle ages, was neglected in favour of other periods. In the early 1980s, however, a revival of interest in the thirteenth century (spearheaded by biennial conferences held at Newcastle and later at Durham) began to shed new light on Henry III, as on much else. Much valuable work remains accessible only in academic journals and unpublished dissertations, yet the last fifteen years of the twentieth century saw the appearance of major studies of Edward I (Michael Prestwich, 1988), Simon de Montfort (John Maddicott, 1994), Peter des Roches (Nicholas Vincent, 1996), and Eleanor of Provence (Margaret Howell, 1998), along with David Carpenter's reinterpretation of the minority (1990) and R. C. Stacey's of royal finance (1987). The complex relationship between Henry III and the church awaits modern treatment, but at the opening of the twenty-first century the principal desideratum remains a reappraisal of the king himself, to do for a new generation what Powicke did for his.

H. W. RIDGEWAY

Sources Chancery records · Rymer, *Foedera*, new edn, 1/1 · W. W. Shirley, ed., *Royal and other historical letters illustrative of the reign of Henry III*, 2 vols., Rolls Series, 27 (1862–6) · A. Luders and others, eds., *Statutes of the realm*, 11 vols. in 12, RC (1810–28), vol. 1 · *Memoriale fratris Walteri de Coventria / The historical collections of Walter of Coventry*, ed. W. Stubbs, 2 vols., Rolls Series, 58 (1872–3) · *Radulphi de Coggeshall chronicon Anglicanum*, ed. J. Stevenson, Rolls Series, 66 (1875) · *Rogeri de Wendover chronica, sive, Flores historiarum*, ed. H. O. Coxe, EHS, 4–5 (1841–4) · Paris, *Chron.* · *Matthaei Parisiensis, monachi Sancti Albani, Historia Anglorum, sive … Historia minor*, ed. F. Madden, 3 vols., Rolls Series, 44 (1886–9) · H. R. Luard, ed., *Flores historiarum*, 3 vols., Rolls Series, 95 (1890) · *Ann. mon.*, vols. 1–4 · W. Stubbs, ed., *Chronicles of the reigns of Edward I and Edward II*, 1, Rolls Series, 76 (1882) · R. Howlett, ed., *Chronicles of the reigns of Stephen, Henry II, and Richard I*, 2, Rolls Series, 82 (1885) · *The historical works of Gervase of Canterbury*, ed. W. Stubbs, 2: *The minor works comprising the Gesta regum with its continuation, the Actus pontificum and the Mappa mundi*, Rolls Series, 73 (1880) · *The metrical chronicle of Robert of Gloucester*, ed. W. A. Wright, 2 vols., Rolls Series, 86 (1887) · *Willelmi Rishanger … chronica et annales*, ed. H. T. Riley, pt 2 of *Chronica monasterii S. Albani*, Rolls Series, 28 (1865) · *F. Nicholai Triveti, de ordine frat. praedicatorum, annales sex regum Angliae*, ed. T. Hog, EHS, 6 (1845) · T. Stapleton, ed., *De antiquis legibus liber: cronica majorum et vicecomitum Londoniarum*, CS, 34 (1846) · *The chronicle of Walter of Guisborough*, ed. H. Rothwell, CS, 3rd ser., 89 (1957) · E. A. Bond, ed., 'Historiola de pietate Regis Henrici III', *Archaeological Journal*, 17 (1860), 317–19 · *Matthaei Paris, monachi Albanensis, Angli, historia maior*, ed. M. Parker (1571) · R. Cotton, *A short view of the long life and raigne of Henry the Third, king of England* (1627) · W. Prynne, *The history of King John, Henry III and Edward I* (1670) · W. Dugdale, *A short view of the late troubles in England … also some parallels thereof with the barons-wars in the time of King Henry III* (1681) · W. Stubbs, *The constitutional history of England*, 2 (1876) · J. Ramsay, *The dawn of the constitution* (1908) · K. Norgate, *The minority of Henry III* (1912) · Tout, *Admin. hist.*, vols. 1–2 · H. Johnstone, 'Poor relief in the royal households of thirteenth century England', *Speculum*, 4 (1929), 149–67 · M. A. Hennings, *England under Henry III illustrated from contemporary sources* (1924) · E. F. Jacob, *Studies in the period of baronial reform and rebellion, 1258–67* (1925) · E. F. Jacob, 'The reign of Henry III, some suggestions', *TRHS*, 4th ser., 10 (1927), 21–53 · R. F. Treharne, *The baronial plan of reform, 1258–63* (1932) · R. F. Treharne and I. J. Sanders, eds., *Documents of the baronial movement of reform and rebellion, 1258–1267* (1973) · F. M. Powicke, *King Henry III and the Lord Edward: the community of the realm in the thirteenth century*, 2 vols. (1947) · F. M. Powicke, *The thirteenth century* (1953) · N. Denholm-Young, *Richard of Cornwall* (1947) · N. Denholm-Young, *Collected papers* (1969) · M. R. Powicke, 'Distraint of knighthood and military obligation under Henry III', *Speculum*, 25 (1950), 457–70 · C. Ellis, *Hubert de Burgh* (1952) · C. H. Knowles, 'The disinherited, 1265–89', PhD diss., U. Wales, Aberystwyth, 1959 · C. H. Knowles, *Simon de Montfort, 1265–1965* (1965) · C. H. Knowles, 'The justiciarship in England, 1258–65', *British government and administration: studies presented to S. B. Chrimes*, ed. H. Hearder and H. R. Loyn (1974) · C. H. Knowles, 'The resettlement of England after the barons' war, 1264–67', *TRHS*, 5th ser., 32 (1982), 25–41 · C. H. Knowles, 'Provision for the families of Montfortians disinherited after the battle of Evesham', *Thirteenth-Century England*, 1 (1986), 124–7 · M. T. Clanchy, 'Did Henry III have a policy?', *History*, 53 (1968), 203–16 · G. O. Sayles, *The king's parliament of England* (1975) · G. L. Harriss, *King, parliament and public finance in medieval England to 1369* (1975) · C. A. F. Meekings, *Studies in thirteenth century justice and administration* (1981) · R. Vaughan, *Matthew Paris*, Cambridge Studies in Medieval Life and Thought, new ser., 6 (1958) · A. Gransden, *Historical writing in England*, 1 (1974) · T. Borenius, 'The cycle of images in the palaces and castles of Henry III', *Journal of the Warburg and Courtauld*

Institute, 6 (1943), 40–50 • R. Brown, H. M. Colvin, and A. J. Taylor, eds., *The history of the king's works*, 1–2 (1963) • H. M. Colvin, *Building accounts of King Henry III* (1971) • D. A. Carpenter, *The battles of Lewes and Evesham* (1987) • D. A. Carpenter, *The minority of Henry III* (1990) • D. A. Carpenter, *The reign of Henry III* (1996) • N. R. Vincent, *Peter des Roches* (1996) • R. C. Stacey, *Politics, policy and finance under Henry III, 1216–45* (1987) • R. C. Stacey, '1240–60: a watershed in Anglo-Jewish relations?', *BIHR*, 61 (1988), 135–50 • H. W. Ridgeway, 'The politics of the English royal court, 1247–65, with special reference to the role of aliens', DPhil diss., U. Oxf., 1983 • H. W. Ridgeway, 'The Lord Edward and the provisions of Oxford, a study in faction', *Thirteenth-Century England*, 1 (1986), 89–99 • H. W. Ridgeway, 'King Henry III and the aliens, 1236–72', *Thirteenth-Century England*, 2 (1988), 81–92 • H. W. Ridgeway, 'Foreign favourites and Henry III's problems of patronage, 1247–58', *EngHR*, 104 (1989), 590–610 • H. W. Ridgeway, 'King Henry III's grievances against the council in 1261', *BIHR*, 61 (1988), 227–42 • H. W. Ridgeway, 'The sheriffs of the baronial movement, 1258–61', *Regionalism and revision: the crown and its provinces in England, 1250–1650*, ed. P. Fleming, A. Gross, and J. R. Lander (1999), 59–86 • M. Howell, *Eleanor of Provence* (1998) • M. Howell, 'The children of Henry III and Eleanor of Provence', *Thirteenth-Century England*, 4 (1992), 57–72 • J. R. Maddicott, 'Magna Carta and the local community, 1215–1259', *Past and Present*, 102 (1984), 25–65 • J. R. Maddicott, 'Edward I and the lessons of baronial reform: local government, 1258–80', *Thirteenth-Century England*, 1 (1986), 1–30 • J. R. Maddicott, 'The crusade taxation of 1268–70 and the development of parliament', *Thirteenth-Century England*, 2 (1988), 93–117 • J. R. Maddicott, *Simon de Montfort* (1994) • S. D. Lloyd, *English society and the crusade, 1216–1307* (1988) • P. Brand, 'The contribution of the period of baronial reform, 1258–67, to the development of the common law in England', DPhil diss., U. Oxf., 1974 • P. Brand, 'The drafting of legislation in mid-thirteenth century England', *Parliamentary History*, 9 (1990), 243–85 • P. Brand, *The origins of the English legal profession* (1992) • P. Brand, *The making of the common law* (1992) • S. L. Waugh, 'Reluctant knights and jurors: respites, exemptions and public obligations in the reign of Henry III', *Speculum*, 58 (1983), 937–86 • S. L. Waugh, 'Marriage, class and royal lordship under Henry III', *Viator*, 16 (1985), 181–207 • S. L. Waugh, *The lordship of England, royal wardships in society and politics, 1217–1327* (1988) • J. R. Studd, 'The Lord Edward and King Henry III', *BIHR*, 50 (1977), 4–19 • J. B. Smith, *Llywelyn ap Gruffudd, prince of Wales* (1998) • R. R. Davies, *Conquest, coexistence and change: Wales, 1063–1415* (1987) • R. F. Frame, *The political development of the British Isles, 1100–1400* (1990) • R. F. Frame, 'King Henry III and Ireland', *Thirteenth-Century England*, 4 (1992), 179–202 • M. Prestwich, *English politics in the thirteenth century* (1990) • P. R. Coss, *Lordship, knighthood and locality: English society, c.1180–1280* (1991) • P. R. Coss, 'Bastard feudalism revised', *Past and Present*, 125 (1989), 27–64 • D. Crouch and D. A. Carpenter, 'Bastard feudalism revised: debate', *Past and Present*, 131 (1991), 165–203 • P. Binski, *Westminster Abbey and the Plantagenets: kingship and the representation of power, 1200–1400* (1995) • J. C. Holt, *Magna Carta*, 2nd edn (1992) • N. Coldstream, *The decorated style: architecture and ornament, 1240–1360* (1994) • J. R. Maddicott, 'An infinite multitude of nobles: quality, quantity and politics in the pre-reform parliaments of Henry III', *Thirteenth-Century England*, 7 (1999), 17–46

Likenesses W. Torel, bronze tomb effigy, Westminster Abbey, London [*see illus.*] • W. Torel, tomb effigy, electrotype, NPG • coins, BM • manuscript drawing, CCC Cam., MS 16, fol. 56r; *see illus. in* Langton, Stephen (*c*.1150–1228) • wax seals, BM

Henry IV [*known as* Henry Bolingbroke] (**1366–1413**), king of England and lord of Ireland, and duke of Aquitaine, was the only son of *John of Gaunt, duke of Lancaster (1340–1399), fourth son of *Edward III, and his first wife, *Blanche (1346?–1368) [*see under* John of Gaunt], the younger daughter but sole heir of *Henry, first duke of

Henry IV (1366–1413), tomb effigy, *c*.1408–27

Lancaster. He was born in Gaunt's castle at Bolingbroke in Lincolnshire, almost certainly in 1366 and perhaps on 7 April.

Young Henry, 1366–1386 Blanche died of plague on 12 September 1369, but by then Henry and his sisters *Philippa and *Elizabeth had been in the care of their great-aunt Blanche, Lady Wake, for at least a year. They remained with her until 1372 and then joined the household of Gaunt's second wife, Constanza of Castile, and later that of Katherine Swynford, Gaunt's mistress who became his third duchess in 1396 [*see* Katherine, duchess of Lancaster]. In December 1374, when Henry was eight, Thomas Burton, a mature esquire of Gaunt, was appointed his 'governor' and in 1376 Sir William Montendre, a Gascon, became his military 'master'. It was probably Hugh Herle, his long-serving chaplain, who taught Henry to read and write in English and French and gave him at least a working knowledge of Latin.

In the months immediately before Edward III's death on 21 June 1377 Gaunt brought together Henry and the heir to the throne, his slightly younger cousin *Richard, and on St George's day (23 April) both were knighted and admitted to the Order of the Garter. Henry carried the sword *Curtana* for his father during part of Richard's coronation ceremony on 16 July. Henry now began to use the courtesy title of earl of Derby, which his maternal grandfather had borne. His first surviving receiver's account, for September 1381–2, shows him riding, hunting, and travelling with Gaunt, jousting and beginning to be an onlooker at state events. He only just escaped death during the peasants' revolt in June 1381. A prime target of the rebels, Gaunt took refuge in Scotland but Henry, perhaps a fugitive from his father's castle at Hertford, was besieged with King Richard and others in the Tower of London. On 14 June, Richard tried to draw off the rebels by going to meet them at Mile End, but some entered the Tower, and Archbishop Sudbury and several others were dragged out and murdered. All that is known of Henry is that his life was saved 'in a wonderful and kind manner' by one John Ferrour of Southwark (PRO, E 37/28). The experience was clearly a terrible one, for this was recorded in a pardon given to Ferrour by Henry for taking part in the January rebellion of 1400, nearly twenty years later.

In July 1380 Gaunt paid King Richard 5000 marks for the marriage of Mary Bohun (c.1369–1394), the younger daughter and coheir of Humphrey de Bohun, eleventh earl of Hereford, who had died in 1373. Henry and Mary were married at her home, Rochford Hall in Essex, probably on 5 February 1381. Mary's elder sister, Eleanor, was already married to Henry's uncle, *Thomas of Woodstock, who according to Froissart tried to persuade Mary to become a Poor Clare in order to secure the whole Bohun inheritance in his own wife's right. The story may be invention, but there is no doubt that Thomas and Henry disputed the division of the Bohun estates. Henry and Mary probably consummated their marriage in late 1384 when she was fourteen. Their first child, Henry, the future king *Henry V, was most likely born in September 1386, and they had five more children, *Thomas, *John, *Humphrey, Blanche, and Philippa. Mary died giving birth to Philippa in 1394, perhaps on 4 July, the date her anniversary was celebrated in 1406, and she was buried in Our Lady's chapel in St Mary of the Newarke, Leicester, a Lancastrian collegiate foundation.

Henry was always close to his mighty father and sole heir to his great duchy of Lancaster. In 1382 he took part in the jousting that formed part of the celebrations of Richard II's marriage to Anne of Bohemia, and he subsequently became one of the most assiduous and accomplished English jousters of his generation. But he took strikingly little part in public affairs when Gaunt was in England. He accompanied Gaunt to treat with French envoys at Calais in November 1383; he may have served in Gaunt's raid into Scotland in 1384, and he was certainly a member of his father's contingent in Richard's campaign there in 1385. He was summoned to parliament for the first time in October 1385, but his prime ambition was to win honour in the lists and in battle.

Henry and King Richard, 1386–1398 Henry was at Plymouth in July 1386 to see his father sail in an attempt to give effect to his claim to the throne of Castile. Gaunt did not return until November 1389 and it was during his absence that Henry incurred King Richard's lasting hatred. Henry was present in the parliament of October 1386 when Richard was forced to dismiss some of his officials and accept a commission with authority for a year to investigate and reform government. The commission was due to expire on 19 November 1387, and as Richard prepared to resume power and take revenge, the duke of Gloucester and the earls of Arundel and Warwick assembled men to resist a force raised in Richard's name in Cheshire by Robert de Vere, duke of Ireland, and accused ('appealed') a number of Richard's friends of treason. In the first days of December two young lords, Henry and Thomas Mowbray, earl of Nottingham and earl marshal, joined the three older lords in their appeal [see Lords appellant]. Why Henry did so is unclear. He may have been angered by the way de Vere, as justice of Chester, had exploited his authority in the north-west at the duchy of Lancaster's expense. He may also have resented the coolness, sometimes even hostility, with which the king and his entourage had often treated Gaunt earlier in the decade.

Henry's decision to join Gloucester was a fateful one, ensuring that Richard's distrust of Gaunt was henceforth also directed at himself. As de Vere came through the Cotswolds he was confronted by Gloucester near Moreton in Marsh. His army broke up and he led a remnant by Burford to cross the Thames at Radcot Bridge and join the king at Windsor. Henry was defending the bridge and had broken the heads of its arches. On 20 December there was a brief engagement in which the constable of Chester was killed and de Vere's men scattered. Henry was the hero of the campaign, though his household accounts describe it as only a foray, an *equitatio*. The victors marched to London, Henry and Warwick in the van, and confronted Richard in the Tower. The king may have been deposed for a few days on the initiative of Gloucester, who hoped to succeed him, but Henry is said to have resisted this drastic step in the interests of his absent father and showed Richard some goodwill.

When parliament met on 3 February 1388 the five appellants, dressed in cloth of gold, entered arm in arm to pursue charges against Richard's friends. There were several executions and all five shared a grant of £20,000 for their actions, but Henry and Nottingham tried to save the life of Sir Simon Burley, Richard's tutor and confidant, and it was effectively Gloucester, Arundel, and Warwick who governed until Richard resumed royal authority in May 1389. Richard, however, intended to take revenge on all five appellants.

Gaunt's return to England in November 1389 brought stability to Richard's government and allowed Henry to eschew politics. In March–April 1390, with other English knights, Henry took part in a great international feat of arms at St Inglevert near Calais and was held to have gained great credit. He planned to go on to crusade in Tunisia, leading a force of some 120 men, but this proved impossible because the French (possibly at Richard II's request) refused him a safe conduct. Instead he resolved to join the Teutonic knights in a *reyse*, a crusading campaign into pagan Lithuania. Two ships were hired and he sailed from Boston in July 1390 with thirty-two knights and esquires and a large household. They reached Danzig by 10 August 1390 and joined the knights and others advancing up the River Niemen. They were at Vilnius by 4 September; a fort was captured but a five-week siege of the principal castle was fruitless and the crusaders returned to Königsberg, the headquarters of the knights, by 22 October. It was too late in the year to return by sea and Henry chose to enjoy the knights' lavish hospitality through the winter. He and his party sailed from Danzig on 31 March and reached Hull by 30 April 1391. The expedition had cost almost £4000, most of it provided by Gaunt. All Henry received from his German hosts was thanks, but he had clearly enjoyed the experience, and as late as 1407 spoke warmly of the Teutonic knights.

On 24 July 1392 Henry sailed for Prussia again and reached Danzig by 10 August. But at Königsberg he found that there would be no *reyse* that year and quickly decided to make a pilgrimage to Jerusalem. On 22 September, with a travelling household of about fifty, Henry set out from Danzig across eastern Europe. He took care to proclaim his rank as he went, sending heralds ahead to announce his coming and to put up escutcheons of his arms above his various lodgings. They rode by Frankfurt-an-der-Oder to Prague where Henry was entertained by King Wenzel of Bohemia, brother of King Richard's queen, Anne; to Vienna to be fêted by Duke Albrecht of Austria and meet King Sigismund of Hungary, the future emperor; then by Leoban, Villach, and Treviso to Venice on 1 or 2 December. Forewarned, the Venetian senate had granted Henry a galley hull for the voyage, and on 23 December 1392 he set sail with a reduced household.

They celebrated Christmas at Zara and sailed by Corfu, Rhodes, and Cyprus and reached Jaffa in late January 1393. Henry spent more than a week in Palestine visiting the holy places and making offerings. He then returned to Cyprus, made a longer halt in Rhodes, and reached Venice by 21 March where 2000 marks transferred by Gaunt were awaiting him. On 28 April he set out again with the goods and animals he had acquired, going by Padua and Verona to Milan, where its ruler Giangaleazzo Visconti entertained him for several days, then by the Col du Mont Cenis and western Burgundy to Paris, and then Calais, finally reaching Dover by 30 June and London by 5 July. His second *viagium* had cost at least £4849.

Exile, 1398–1399 Now a man with an international reputation, Henry undoubtedly expected to travel and fight abroad again, but in the event he was out of England only once more before his exile in 1398, and then only for a few days in October 1396, with Gaunt and others escorting King Richard's French bride, Isabella, from Ardres to Calais. He came to court, witnessing fourteen of the forty-two royal charters granted between 1393 and 1398 and attending parliaments and great councils. He lived well but his life was first saddened and then once more threatened. In 1394 his wife, Mary, died in childbirth and Henry was in mourning for a year. By now Richard had another circle of favoured lords and Gaunt's influence was waning. He and Henry became anxious about the inheritance of the great Lancaster estate and their concern was greatly increased in July 1397 when the senior appellants of 1387, Gloucester, Warwick, and Arundel, were arrested and appealed of

treason. Proclamations announced that this was done with the approval of both Gaunt and Henry. Gaunt presided over the trials in parliament and Henry is said to have spoken out against Arundel. Both condemned the three accused. Arundel was executed, Gloucester was probably murdered at Calais, and Warwick was imprisoned. On 29 September, Henry was created duke of Hereford, but he remained apprehensive and sought to please Richard by coming to court more often and giving him a great feast and entertainment during the September parliament.

In mid-December 1397, as Henry was riding to London from Windsor, he was overtaken by Thomas Mowbray, now duke of Norfolk. Their conversation is known only from the written account given by Henry to Richard in January 1398, stating that Norfolk had said that 'We are on the point of being undone', in revenge for 'what was done at Radcot Bridge' in 1387, and that there had been a plan to seize or kill Gaunt and Henry at Windsor in September 1397 and disinherit Henry, Norfolk, and others (Given-Wilson, *Chronicles*, 86–7). Although by his own account Henry said little, he was clearly frightened. He made a rapid pilgrimage north to the shrines of Beverley and Bridlington before reporting the conversation to his father, who then told Richard. On 31 January 1398 Henry begged for pardon and Richard granted it in full. In fact he and Norfolk had already obtained pardons for their role in the events of 1387–8, on the ground that they had moderated the actions of the other appellants. But in February 1398 Henry and his father found it necessary to secure a promise from Richard that he would not exploit the judgment given on Thomas of Lancaster in 1322 in order to claim any of the Lancastrian lands. There is also evidence from this time of a plot against Gaunt and his family among the king's entourage. Meanwhile Norfolk was deprived of the offices of marshal of England and captain of Calais. He behaved wildly and was imprisoned. The council considered the accusation several times, and on 29 April decided that it must be determined by battle. In early August, Henry was told that the combat would be at Coventry on 16 September.

Henry trained and made expensive preparations, employing armourers from Milan. But as the two dukes advanced to fight Richard took the quarrel into his own hands and sent both combatants into exile—Henry for ten years, Norfolk for life, to leave England by 20 October. Richard appeared to show Henry goodwill, gave him 1000 marks towards his costs and, most important, letters permitting him to obtain livery of any succession or inheritance that came to him during his exile. Gaunt died on 3 February 1399 and on 18 March, two days after his funeral in St Paul's, the letters were revoked on the ground that they had been granted by 'inadvertence' (*RotP*, 3.372).

Return and usurpation, 1399 Henry left London about 13 October 1398 and went to Paris, where he was welcomed by King Charles and the royal dukes and given the Hôtel de Clisson as his residence. Even after the forfeiture of his inheritance he continued to receive money from the duchy of Lancaster's receiver-general, forwarded to him by Italian merchants. He attended university debates and showed that he was looking to the future by contemplating matrimony, first to Lucia Visconti, Giangaleazzo's daughter, and then to Marie, comtesse d'Eu, a niece of the French king—the prospect of the latter match so alarmed Richard II that he sent the earl of Salisbury to Paris to scotch it. Henry also contemplated going on crusade, but his father suggested that he should visit the courts of Castile and Portugal, where his sisters *Katherine and Philippa reigned. In the event Gaunt's death, and Henry's own disinheritance, prevented his travelling south.

At the time of Henry's exile the effective government of France was in the hands of the duke of Burgundy, who favoured peace with England. There can be little doubt that the duke was expected to keep an eye on Henry, and to prevent him acting in any way contrary to the interests of Richard II, now married to a French princess. In May 1399, however, an outbreak of plague kept Burgundy out of the French capital, and enabled his rival, the king's brother Louis, duc d'Orléans, to take over the government. Anglo-French relations had recently become tense, and Orléans was himself the leader of the French war party. On 17 June he made a formal alliance with Henry, in which each man undertook to be 'the friend of the other's friends and well-wishers, and the enemy of the other's enemies' (Given-Wilson, *Chronicles*, 114). Orléans seems to have been entirely cynical. In effectively giving Henry *carte blanche* to return to England it is unlikely that he expected him to enjoy much success against an apparently secure ruler. He may only have hoped to stir up trouble for Richard, and so perhaps weaken the latter's grip on Aquitaine, where Orléans himself had ambitions. The replacement of the pacific Richard by the militarily experienced Henry was probably the last thing Orléans wanted.

For Henry, however, the treaty was vital in giving him the chance of a *revanche*, one that might never recur. On 1 June 1399 Richard landed in Ireland, and in the last week of that month Henry secretly left Paris and sailed from Boulogne with Thomas Arundel, the exiled archbishop of Canterbury, and a small number of his own retainers and servants. He was relying on the support he would find in England and on the absence of the king, who was accompanied to Ireland by nearly all his most loyal lords and retainers. Whether Henry set off with the intention of deposing his cousin or only of recovering his inheritance can never be known for certain, but the likelihood is that by now Henry knew Richard well enough, and particularly his suspicious and vindictive qualities, to understand that, once back in England, he could never be secure unless he replaced Richard entirely or assumed an effectively viceregal authority over him. The stress he placed at this time on his position as steward of England, which forms part of his style in the treaty with Orléans, may indicate that he kept the latter possibility in mind. But to be only duke of Lancaster, and perhaps heir presumptive to a king decidedly brittle on the subject of the succession, was hardly likely to be protection enough against future vengeance.

It appeared at first as if Henry might land in Sussex, but he sailed up the east coast and landed at Ravenspur on the northern tip of the Humber estuary in early July—the 4th is given in several sources. He then went by his own castles at Pickering, Knaresborough, and Pontefract, through areas with many Lancaster lands and retainers, to Doncaster where Henry Percy, earl of Northumberland, his son Henry (Hotspur), Ralph Neville, earl of Westmorland, Lord Willoughby, and other northern lords joined him with their men. Chroniclers exaggerate the numbers but Henry clearly had a substantial force, led by men who had been forewarned. He is reliably reported to have declared in public that he had come only to recover his inheritance, but Northumberland and other leading supporters must have realized that he was likely to claim the throne. They too knew the revenge Richard took on those who opposed him.

Late in June, *Edmund, duke of York, uncle of both Richard and Henry, and keeper of the kingdom while Richard was in Ireland, received reports of men gathering across the channel and assembled over 3000 men at Ware in Hertfordshire, but it was only on 11–12 July that he learned that Henry had landed in Yorkshire. York slowly withdrew west, his forces dwindling, to join Richard on his return from Ireland. Henry was able to advance unopposed by way of a series of mostly Lancastrian strongholds—Derby, Leicester, Coventry, Warwick (where he had the royal arms over the castle gate knocked down), Evesham, and Gloucester—and on the 27th he met York at Berkeley Castle. The duke was sent to join the queen at Wallingford and Henry went on to Bristol on the 28th. The castle and Richard's remaining forces surrendered and three of his leading councillors, the earl of Wiltshire, Sir John Bussy, and Henry Green, were captured, summarily tried, and executed. Henry made no attempt to dissociate himself from the deaths of Richard's friends, underlining the likelihood that he had resolved to take the crown. His grant of the wardenship of the west march to the earl of Northumberland on 2 August, made under the duchy of Lancaster seal, points to the same conclusion. He had met no significant resistance since his return to England.

Delayed by indecision and lack of ships Richard returned to Milford Haven on 24–25 July with several thousand men, intending to join York. About six days later he learned that resistance to Henry was collapsing and rode at once with only a small group of friends to Conwy Castle in north Wales, arriving there on 12 August. No doubt he hoped to rally support in the duchy of Chester, his personal stronghold, but Henry had read his intentions and was too quick for him, leading his growing army back north by Hereford and Shrewsbury to Chester, which he reached on the 9th. He also took possession of Richard's treasure stored at Holt. With no options but flight or surrender, Richard sent the duke of Exeter and the earl of Surrey to Henry but they were arrested at once. Northumberland was then sent to Conwy. Exactly what was agreed remains unknown, but it seems certain that the earl promised Richard that his life would be secure, and he may have repeated Henry's assertion that he had only come to claim his Lancastrian inheritance. His undertakings were sufficient to persuade Richard to leave the castle, and Northumberland escorted him virtually under guard to Flint Castle. On the 16th Henry came to Flint, fully armed and carrying the steward's rod, waited while Richard dined and then probably spoke politely about assisting him to govern. In no position to do anything but agree, Richard was taken to Chester and thence to Westminster; on 2 September he was lodged as a prisoner in the Tower. Henry rode to St Paul's to pray at Gaunt's tomb.

At first Henry continued to issue letters in Richard's name under the latter's great seal. It was thus that on 19 August a parliament was summoned for 30 September. But from 10 September, Henry was dating duchy of Lancaster letters by years Anno Domini rather than Richard's regnal years, a clear sign that the latter had run their course. The problem of replacing Richard with Henry as king was a practical rather than a constitutional issue. Henry did not want to advertise the fact that he had taken the throne by an act of *force majeure*, accompanied by a good deal of perjury and prevarication; rather he was anxious to stress that he represented continuity with earlier monarchs and with the traditions of good government that they represented. Removing Richard from the throne was relatively straightforward—before parliament could meet, to be faced with the awkward task of deposing the king who had summoned it, he was terrorized into resigning his crown. None of those who assembled on 30 September can have been deceived by the formal record that on the previous day Richard had 'with a cheerful expression' stepped down in his cousin's favour (Given-Wilson, *Chronicles*, 170), but nobody at this stage was prepared to stand up for the deposed ruler.

The problem of finding adequate grounds to replace Richard by Henry was resolved through the adoption of a multifaceted formula, stressing simultaneously Henry's Plantagenet descent, the divine grace and powerful friends underpinning his claim, and the misgovernment from which his accession would rescue England. On the day that Richard's resignation was announced, and after a mass of the Holy Spirit in Westminster Abbey, Henry crossed to Westminster Hall and took the seat Gaunt had occupied. The archbishop of York explained to parliament the reasons for Richard's resignation, and Lords and Commons accepted it. Henry then rose and said:

> In the name of Fadir, Son, and Holy Gost, I Henry of Lancastre chalenge this rewme of Yngland, and the corone with all the membres and the appurtenances, als I that am disendit be right lyne of the Blode comyng fro the gude lorde Kyng Henry therde, and thorgh that ryght that God of his grace hath sent me, with helpe of my Kyn and of my Frendes to recover it: the whiche Rewme was in poynt to be undone for defaut of Governance and undoyng of the gode Lawes. (*RotP*, 3.422–3)

It was a disingenuous statement but good enough in the circumstances. One by one, the lords spiritual and temporal gave their assent and Henry was led to the throne. His reign had begun.

Securing the throne, 1399–1400 On 6 October 1399 the members who had sat on 30 September met again as Henry's first parliament. Archbishop Arundel spoke of the reasons for Henry's accession and his intention to rule well. Parliament was then adjourned for the coronation. Henry was crowned on the 13th in the traditional manner, though he was also the first English king to be anointed with a sacred oil reputedly given by the Virgin Mary to Thomas Becket, and perhaps the first to be enthroned on the 'stone of Scone' taken by Edward I from Scotland. The traditional coronation banquet and the challenge by the king's champion then followed in Westminster Hall. When the champion defied all and sundry to gainsay Henry's title, the new king is reported to have declared that if necessary he would defend his crown himself.

Parliament met again on the following day. The decisions of the parliament of 1397–8 were revoked and those of 1386 restored. On the 15th Henry took a first step towards securing the throne for his descendants when he had his eldest son, now aged twelve or thirteen, invested in parliament as prince of Wales. On the following day trials of Richard's friends began. Henry was generally forgiving. Sir William Bagot, a retainer of both Gaunt and Henry, had become Richard's councillor and harassed them both in 1398. He now testified against his recent friends and was imprisoned for a year—then given a £100 annuity by Henry. He resumed his career and sat in parliament again in 1402. The five surviving lords appellant of 1397 lost the titles, lands, and grants given to them then by Richard, but they were not punished further and by December some were at court and council again. But the earl of Salisbury, who feared Henry's vengeance for having prevented his French marriage, was with the king's support accused of connivance in the duke of Gloucester's murder, while John Hall, a valet who admitted being present when Gloucester was killed, was barbarously executed. The Commons asked that Richard be punished for his crimes, the Lords that he be held secretly and securely. He was taken under strict guard to Leeds Castle in Kent and then to Pontefract Castle in Yorkshire.

Henry may have felt strong enough to be merciful in many cases, but his position had severe weaknesses, stemming from the paradoxical nature of his kingship. As if his succession had been entirely regular, he repeatedly stressed throughout his reign that he expected to rule as his predecessors had done, with no diminution in the prerogatives he had inherited from them. But in order to gain the throne he had to promise concessions. Some were no more than pledges to uphold the conventional trappings of good governance, for example his promise to maintain the inheritance laws. But one was to have a most serious effect on his ability to rule. Just as he had apparently sworn at Doncaster only to pursue his rights as duke of Lancaster, so he seems also to have given promises of reductions in taxation, promises that quickly came to be understood—as perhaps they were meant to be understood—that no taxes would be levied at all. When the Canterbury convocation met in autumn 1399, it was told by the earl of Northumberland, acting as Henry's spokesman, that it was not the new king's intention to exact money from his realm, except when the urgent needs of war had to be met. Such undertakings inevitably raised expectations that Henry could not possibly meet, even though by adding the Lancastrian patrimony (worth an estimated £12,500 per annum) and his share of the Bohun lands to the crown estate he commanded far greater resources than any of his immediate predecessors—as his subjects doubtless appreciated.

Henry lacked detailed administrative experience, and before 1398 he had relied for money largely on subventions from his father. From the beginning of his reign he continued to treat his Lancastrian and Bohun lands as personal property, to be kept administratively separate from those of the crown, and used their revenues primarily to fund substantial and very expensive retaining fees. In the early months of his reign he also gave large numbers of grants of land and annuities, both to buy the loyalty of Richard's retainers and to reward that of his own. The result was a massive increase in the cost of the royal household, a cost which was hardly ever brought under control during his reign. The problem was compounded by the reluctance of the Commons to grant taxes. They did not renew a tenth and fifteenth granted to Richard and due to be collected on 30 September, and though they confirmed the customs duties, Henry benefited less than he must have hoped because of a considerable fall in wool exports. A shortage of specie may also have contributed to his financial difficulties—it was eventually remedied in 1412 with a reduction in the weight of the gold and silver currencies. Henry's retaining policy was not without its successes. By bringing men from the northern shires into the royal affinity he was to some extent able to rectify a regional imbalance, while his ability to rely on loyal and experienced Lancastrian followers, such men as Sir Hugh Waterton, Sir Thomas Erpingham, and Sir Thomas Rempston, both helped to make up for his own relative ignorance of government and provided him with a hard core of support which did much to preserve his throne. But he paid a very high price, literally as well as figuratively, for that support, one that effectively blighted his reign.

Henry spent Christmas 1399 at Windsor, but on 4 January 1400 he learned that there was a plot by lords loyal to Richard to kill him and his sons and restore the deposed king. Henry rode at once to the safety of London; the plotters fled and were killed by local people, who showed no nostalgia for the deposed monarch. Henry presided over trials of lesser rebels on 12 January at Oxford. Two of Richard's chamber knights and twenty others were executed but thirty-seven were pardoned.

On 9 February, Henry met thirty-three bishops and lay lords in a great council at Westminster to review the major issues now facing him. There was retrospective concern that so many nobles had been lynched, and Henry decreed that in future men should not be killed without trial; the Scots were raiding across the border; and negotiations had begun with the French king, again called *nostre adversaire*, for the return of Richard's queen, Isabella. But

already Henry was short of money. Significantly the lords advised against summoning a parliament and offered only small sums of their own money or their services in kind. He also approached the Londoners for a loan, only to be referred to his own promise to refrain from such demands.

By mid-February 1400 King Richard was dead. There is no evidence that he was murdered and his skeleton showed no sign of violence. He could have been starved to death or even starved himself. His body was brought to London with its face exposed, a precaution which did not prevent later claims that he was still alive. Henry attended Richard's funeral service in St Paul's but not his modest burial in the Dominican friary at Kings Langley. It was Henry V who in December 1413 reburied Richard in Westminster Abbey.

Scotland and Wales At the very beginning of his reign Henry hoped to maintain peaceful relations with the Scots, but raids into northern England, and Robert III's refusal to acknowledge his title, led on 10 November 1399 to Henry's announcing in parliament that he would make war on Scotland. His hand was strengthened early in 1400 by the disaffection of George Dunbar, earl of March, who had quarrelled with the Douglases, and at Newcastle upon Tyne on 6–7 August, Henry wrote formally to King Robert and his lords demanding their homage. On the 14th he crossed into Scotland, in a campaign that gave a striking demonstration of the military value of the royal household—in an unusually large army of over 15,000 men, the household contingent contributed 800 men-at-arms and 2000 archers. He met almost no resistance and did not waste the countryside. He was in Leith beside Edinburgh on the 17th, and there was an exchange of letters with King Robert's lieutenant, the duke of Rothesay, and a meeting of envoys. But Henry and his army were back in England by the 29th. A Scottish chronicler summed up the campaign fairly: 'nothing worthy of remembrance was done' (Bower, 8.36–7). Henry never returned to Scotland. Border raids, meetings of envoys, and short-term truces continued, however, as did intermittent war, which in 1402 went decisively against the Scots. On 14 September a strong Scottish force returning from raiding across the east march was defeated at Homildon Hill by the earl of Northumberland, and four earls and the flower of the Scots' fighting men were killed or captured.

On his way back from Scotland in 1400 Henry learned at Northampton that a Welsh esquire, Owain Glyn Dŵr, had proclaimed himself prince of Wales and raided English towns in north Wales and Shropshire. Henry immediately ordered able-bodied men from midland counties and the Welsh marches to join him at Shrewsbury. He was there by 26 September, and though the immediate danger was over, he led a rapid raid by Bangor, Caernarfon, Harlech, and back to Shrewsbury by 15 October. None the less by June 1401 there were incidents of rebellion throughout much of north and central Wales. The last major uprising in Wales against English lordship was economically and politically an event of major importance, though neither

Henry himself nor his advisers seem at first to have appreciated its significance. Henry was a very considerable Welsh landowner—it has been calculated that he and his son exercised lordship over more than half the surface area of Wales, and he could normally expect his estates there to provide him with an annual income of at least £8500, often much more. As the revolt spread not only were those revenues lost, but its suppression became the cause of immense additional expenditure, not least because the rising could not be ended by pitched battles. It needed castle garrisons and attrition until 1407 to contain it. Henry himself mounted five further expeditions into Wales: in May and October 1401; in September 1402, when he led a large force from Shrewsbury as part of a plan of encirclement but was thwarted by bad weather (on 7 September his tent was blown down—fortunately he was wearing armour); in September 1403; and (briefly) in September 1405. But the brunt of the war in Wales was borne by others, at first by the Percys, later by Henry, prince of Wales, and his captains and castellans.

The Percys The Percys and in particular Henry Percy, created earl of Northumberland in 1377, had been Henry's principal supporters and advisers throughout the usurpation. They were well rewarded but, like many kingmakers, they were not easy to satisfy. The earl was appointed constable of England for life, warden of the west march and Carlisle, given hereditary possession of the Isle of Man, and he continued to be Henry's principal adviser. The earl's brother Thomas Percy, earl of Worcester, became a councillor, admiral of England, a senior member of the commission negotiating with France, and in 1401 steward of Henry's household. And Northumberland's only son, Henry (Hotspur), became justice of Chester and north Wales, keeper of a number of their castles, warden of the east march, captain of Berwick and Roxburgh, and in 1401 governor of Prince Henry.

It was a dangerous concentration of authority in one family and by 1402 Henry must have become aware of this, for Ralph Neville, earl of Westmorland, the other great northern lord, was given custody of Roxburgh Castle in the east march and Hotspur was refused permission to ransom either Scottish prisoners taken at the battle of Homildon Hill or his own brother-in-law, Edmund Mortimer, captured by the Welsh in June 1402. Henry appears to have tried to divert Percy ambitions by granting the earl and his heirs on 2 March 1403 a great stretch of land north of the Scottish border, with a promise of financial support to conquer it. In May 1403 Hotspur led a force there and laid siege to Cocklaws, a small tower near Hawick, and he and his father then appealed to Henry for support and the money he owed them. On 26 June, Northumberland added in his own hand on a letter to Henry: 'Your Mathathias who begs you to take his estate and labour to heart in this matter. H[enry]' (*Proceedings … of the Privy Council*, 1386–1410, 204–5). Though Henry set out quickly from Kennington, on 12 July, when he was near Nottingham, he learned that Hotspur was calling out men in Cheshire and Wales, and claiming that Richard II was alive.

Henry was fortunate to have a retinue with him and be able to summon his retainers and levies, particularly from the duchy of Lancaster lordships in the north midlands. Urged by the earl of Dunbar to strike at the Percys before they could be reinforced by Glyn Dŵr, on 20 July Henry occupied the town and castle of Shrewsbury ahead of Hotspur, and after an attempt at negotiations had failed they fought a severe battle near the town on the 21st—the only true battle in which Henry fought. Casualties were heavy, and according to Adam Usk included two men protecting the king by wearing armour identical with his. At first Hotspur's Cheshire archers drove back the royal vanguard and Prince Henry was wounded in the face by an arrow. But in the ensuing mêlée Hotspur was killed, effectively deciding the battle. The earl of Worcester was captured and executed. Northumberland, who arrived too late to fight, surrendered. He was tried by the lords in parliament in February 1404, found guilty of trespass but not treason, and pardoned. Henry, typically, did not treat Northumberland harshly. He lost his constableship and other offices, but continued to attend the council and witness royal charters, though much less often than before.

Parliament and finance, 1401–1402 Henry had overcome his rebels, but he was unable to live within his means. However, a reassessment of his early years as king suggests that he retained the support of the landowning classes in parliament. Finance was certainly a perpetual problem, but it is arguably a mistake to see him as also intermittently locked in conflict with the Commons over his choice of councillors. Like previous rulers he took advice as he chose, by no means only from members of a formal council, and the size and composition of the latter fluctuated according to the needs of the moment. When Sir Arnold Savage, the speaker in Henry's second parliament in 1401, requested the king not only to appoint men of 'honourable estatz' as his great officers and councillors and 'charge' them to advise him, but also to have the names and responsibilities of his councillors publicized (Chrimes and Brown, 205–6), he and his fellow MPs may have been principally concerned to enhance the accountability of the king's government by identifying the men in charge of it, rather than to determine the king's choice of such men. Whatever their aims, there is no clear evidence that they achieved them. The chancellor and treasurer were indeed dismissed at the end of the parliament, to be replaced by more considerable men, but perhaps Henry would have acted thus anyway, hoping that experienced administrators would help him manage his finances more successfully.

Henry's greatest problem was not lack of counsel but shortage of money. On 16 August 1401 letters were sent to bishops, earls, barons, and a large number of knights and esquires in the counties to come to Westminster on 16 August to advise 'on certain very pressing matters concerning the well-being of us and of you and the common good of our realm'—that is, on money (*Proceedings … of the Privy Council*, 1386–1410, 165). There were so many letters written by the treasurer to Henry that there was not even enough money in the treasury to pay the messengers delivering them. And in March 1402 Henry sent out letters asking for loans to pay for the marriage of his daughter Blanche. It was not easy to be Henry IV's treasurer—and there were six of them between 1399 and the end of 1404. A growing disillusion with Henry's kingship is vividly suggested by a letter to the king apparently from Philip Repyndon, bishop of Lincoln, in 1401, comparing the jubilation that greeted Henry's accession with present lamentation: 'joy has turned to bitterness, while evils multiply themselves everywhere, and hope of relief fades from the grieving hearts of men' (*Chronicle of Adam of Usk*, 139).

Foreign policy: the pursuit of recognition Securing his throne entailed obtaining recognition abroad. Henry's prowess as a jouster and his widespread travels had brought him considerable fame by 1399; nevertheless his usurpation caused outrage at the French court, which refused to acknowledge his title to the English throne, and precipitated a crisis in Anglo-French relations. The prime mover in these developments was the belligerent duc d'Orléans, now confronting the results of his own spoiling tactics. He could exploit the problems that now arose over the return of Richard II's widow, Queen Isabella, who should have been sent back to France along with her substantial dowry; after acrimonious negotiations she finally went home, dowerless, in 1401. Still more promising as a *casus belli* was the running sore of the status of the duchy of Aquitaine, which must have seemed particularly apt for Orléans's purposes because Richard II had been popular there (he was born in Bordeaux), whereas Henry was regarded with suspicion by the Gascons, who had resented the grant of the duchy to his father, John of Gaunt, in 1390. In January 1401 Charles VI bestowed Aquitaine upon his heir, the dauphin Louis, and later in the year order was given for the interception of an English fleet sailing to the duchy. Meanwhile large-scale piracy broke out in the channel, unrestrained by the governments of either England or France.

In 1402 a Franco-Scottish alliance extended the maritime conflict. Orléans kept up the pressure, giving hostilities a personal dimension when in August 1402 and March 1403 he challenged Henry to combat; Henry responded in kind by declining to fight a man of lesser dignity than himself. In 1403 French armies threatened Calais and invaded Aquitaine, where the frontiers of English rule retreated steadily during the next four years. The heartland of Gascony remained loyal, in part thanks to Henry's conciliatory dealings with the local nobility, but in 1404 there were French naval attacks on the English south coast, and in 1405 some 2500 French troops arrived in Wales to reinforce Glyn Dŵr.

The ramifications of the Anglo-French conflict were extensive, both at home and abroad. The hostilities added considerably to Henry's financial difficulties—the defence of Aquitaine is estimated to have cost some £1300 per annum between 1400 and 1403—as did the impact of piracy on trade, not least by exacerbating difficulties in relations with the German Hansa. In 1405 a diet at Lübeck placed heavy restrictions on English commerce in the Baltic. Henry responded with efforts to raise his personal

standing and find continental allies. It may have been purely for reasons of prestige that in 1402 he received envoys from the Byzantine emperor, but the marriages of his daughters were diplomatic initiatives. In 1401 he negotiated the marriage of Princess Blanche to Ludwig, eldest son of Rupert, count palatine of the Rhine and king of the Romans. He had to raise a dowry of £13,333 6s. 8d., but the union gave him an ally in the French rear. No less expensive was the marriage of Princess Philippa to Erik IX, king of Norway, Sweden, and Denmark, which took place in 1406 and was at least partly intended to secure Scandinavian support in dealings with the Hansa. Henry provided his daughter with a sumptuous trousseau of clothes, plate, and a magnificent bed. Other European rulers were linked to the English crown through appointment to the Order of the Garter—the king of Portugal in 1400, the king of Castile c.1402.

Henry's own second marriage was certainly dictated by diplomatic and strategic considerations. On 3 April 1402 he was married by proxy to *Joan (1368–1437), widow of John de Montfort, duke of Brittany, and daughter of Charles II of Navarre. She arrived in England early in 1403, and the marriage ceremony took place on 7 February in Winchester Cathedral. The effective independence of Brittany gave Henry hopes of Breton support in his dealings with the French monarchy. Those hopes were unfulfilled, but the marriage seems to have been successful in personal terms, although they had no children. Joan is rarely mentioned in chronicles, but she continued to live in England after Henry's death and was buried beside him in Canterbury Cathedral in 1437.

Continued financial problems Henry met his third parliament at Westminster on 30 September 1402. The victory of the Percys at Homildon Hill on 14 September and the display of some of the Scottish prisoners made it a relatively positive assembly. The customs duties were continued and a subsidy of a tenth and a fifteenth was granted, to be collected over a whole year. By the time parliament met again, in January 1404, the Percy rising had been crushed, but the king's victory did nothing to improve his finances. There were still conspiracies to guard against, the Welsh revolt continued to gather strength, and French pressure on Aquitaine and Calais was intensifying. Sir Arnold Savage, who was again the speaker, complained about the inadequate defence of the realm and the mismanagement of royal finance, the latter evident in the excessive cost of the king's household. In the previous six months there had been two French landings on the south coast, and John *Beaufort, earl of Somerset, one of Henry's three half-brothers, claimed to be owed almost two years' wages for his service as captain of Calais. Henry agreed to appoint councillors who would ensure 'good and just governance' and remedy for the many complaints, grievances, and mischiefs shown to him (*RotP*, 3.530). The three great officers remained unchanged, however, and all but two of the nineteen appointed to the council were already serving members. Henry could not easily dispense with tried and trusted servants.

A second parliament, called the Unlearned Parliament

because the writs of summons forbade the return of lawyers to the Commons, met at Coventry on 6 October 1404. Household finance remained a problem, and the Commons now proposed radical remedies for the king's difficulties, a resumption of all grants which were part of the inheritance of the crown before 40 Edward III (1366–7), and (apparently) the temporary expropriation of the temporalities of the church. Henry responded that such measures were neither honest nor expedient, but grants would be investigated and their revenues during the current year diverted to the crown. Two tenths and fifteenths were granted, together with a novel land tax, but on condition that two named treasurers of wars received the issues and accounted for them in the next parliament, to ensure that the money was spent on defence rather than the royal household. It was a generous grant, altogether the highest direct taxation of the reign, and Henry was prepared to accept the restrictive conditions attached.

Archbishop Scrope's rising 1405 was a critical year for Henry. He was at Windsor for the Garter ceremony on 23 April and then set out to campaign in south Wales. About 23 May, however, he heard from the council at Westminster that Lord Bardolf, who had been expected to serve with him, was on his way north. Henry at once returned to Worcester, and by the time he reached Derby on the 28th he knew that the earl of Northumberland, the earl marshal Thomas Mowbray, and Bardolf were in revolt. He spent several days at Nottingham assembling an army and by 6 June he was at Bishopthorpe, the archbishop of York's manor south of the city, and was joined by the earl of Westmorland and Prince John, the wardens of the Scottish marches. The king's haste may have been in part due to the involvement in the rising of Archbishop Richard Scrope of York. Scrope's motives for allying himself with the rebels are unclear, for his recorded utterances suggest he was primarily associating himself with the complaints against the king's government voiced in parliament, and no doubt elsewhere. Yet again, finance and especially the cost of the royal household bulked large. Scrope preached in his cathedral against taxation and purveyance, and issued a manifesto to the same effect.

Scrope and the earl marshal raised a force of several thousand men, but not far from York they met Westmorland, who promised that their grievances would be remedied. Scrope discharged his men, whereupon he and Mowbray were arrested. Henry had probably decided to remove Scrope as archbishop by 1 June, when he granted away a pension which 'he who is next created archbishop of York' would be required to pay to a royal clerk (Storey, 18). He may also have decided to do so by executing Scrope, with whom he was so furious that he led the archbishop out before the citizens of York as they begged for pardon and berated him as a traitor who had brought misery on his flock. If Henry had qualms about killing a prelate, they were overcome by his household, who demanded Scrope's head in revenge for his attacks on themselves. Chief Justice Gascoigne declined to act, whereupon Scrope and his associates were condemned by an *ad hoc* commission on 8 June and beheaded outside York the

same day, in spite of an appeal by Archbishop Arundel who had hurried north.

Hitherto Henry had usually been merciful, and in having Scrope put to death he may have showed the overwhelming strain of recent events. That strain, together with feelings of guilt, whether over the execution or from having deceived Arundel, whom he had reassured immediately before it took place, perhaps contributed to a temporary breakdown of health, which immobilized Henry at Ripon for a week. He recovered and continued north, first to Durham and then through the Percy heartland to Berwick, where the surrender of the castle early in July completed his victory. By mid-August he was back in Leicester on his way to Hereford, to resume the campaign in Wales, where a large French force had recently arrived to assist Glyn Dŵr. In late September he led a force to relieve Coety Castle in Glamorgan, though some of his baggage was looted by Welsh rebels afterwards. He then spent three weeks at Kenilworth before returning to London in mid-November.

The Long Parliament of 1406: breakdown in health At the beginning of 1406 the defeat of the English rebels may have led Henry to believe that his prospects were brightening, but there was little improvement in Wales, and a continuing danger of French attacks, on both sides of the channel. Consequently finance remained a very serious problem, and dominated the sixth parliament of the reign. It met at Westminster on 1 March 1406, and sat until 22 December with a three-week break for Easter in April and a harvest break from mid-June to mid-October. Henry probably expected trouble, and there is some evidence that the ranks of the knights of the shires were packed by crown servants, while the speaker, Sir John Tiptoft, had been in Henry's household before 1399. There were vociferous complaints of financial maladministration and failure to provide adequate defence, but Tiptoft kept opposition within bounds, and as far as possible led it in constructive directions. His task was made harder, however, by a sudden breakdown in the king's health; in the short term this hampered the progress of deliberations in parliament, while ultimately its repercussions were felt in every development involving the exercise of royal authority for the rest of the reign.

Contemporary moralists described Henry's illness as leprosy, and attributed it to divine vengeance for the execution of Scrope, but the examination of Henry's physical remains in the nineteenth century revealed no sign of skin disease. The king had certainly suffered a brief illness after the archbishop was beheaded, but the evidence suggests that he made a full recovery, and that his sickness in 1405 was unconnected with his subsequent affliction. Indeed, until 1406 he seems usually to have enjoyed good health, enabling him to withstand great pressure while leading a very mobile life. He employed a French physician, who was granted letters of denization on 28 March 1405, but this is probably more an indication that he took proper care of himself, than that he needed particular attention. On 28 April 1406, in his first reference to his failure of health, Henry himself spoke of a leg injury and perhaps ague (*une grande accesse*); the former, at least, could point to circulatory problems. Whatever its nature, it was a condition that quickly worsened, making it impossible for him to attend parliament, and ultimately placing heavy restrictions on his ability to govern. Its severity may also be reflected in the consideration that in May began to be given to the succession to the throne, a process concluded in a formal settlement at the end of the year.

Parliament's first session had ended on 3 April, and after several deferments because of the king's sickness its second began on the 30th. But Henry's health did not mend, and finally it was agreed on 22 May, on the king's own initiative, that his breakdown in health was such as to make it necessary for him to be assisted in the task of government by a council nominated in parliament. Seventeen councillors were accordingly appointed to support him. They had all served before, however, and perhaps partly for that reason the Commons demanded guarantees of future financial responsibility before they would grant further taxation. Further debate followed, sometimes acrimonious—at one point Henry rallied sufficiently to declare angrily that it was not for kings to account to their subjects—and eventually parliament was prorogued from 19 June until 13 October. The autumn session is poorly recorded, and either because Henry resisted further reform, or because further bouts of ill health created uncertainty and hampered discussion, only in mid-November did agreement begin to be reached.

The final programme of financial reform had two essential components: a list of thirty-one articles laying down detailed rules for the control of expenditure; and the appointment of a new, smaller, and more substantial council, headed by Prince Henry and consisting of the three great officers (chancellor, treasurer, and keeper of the privy seal), Archbishop Arundel—who became chancellor on 30 January 1408—the bishops of Winchester and London, Edward, duke of York, and John Beaufort, earl of Somerset. It was a small executive body governing in the king's name, and its membership changed little until late 1409. Its character is shown in the record of a meeting, probably its first, at Westminster in the afternoon of 8 December 1406. Prince Henry, Archbishop Arundel, Chancellor Thomas Langley, the duke of York, the earl of Somerset, and the treasurer, Lord Furnival, reviewed the 'governance' of the royal household with three of its officers, one of them Sir John Tiptoft, now treasurer of the household. One of their first decisions was that the king and his household should withdraw after Christmas to a place where costs were less.

In retirement The new government achieved a considerable measure of success, particularly in matters of finance. Operating principally through the exchequer, the council was able to ensure that revenue was directed towards defence rather than to the household, whose costs fell sharply. When parliament met again, at Gloucester in the autumn of 1407, one session sufficed to obtain a grant of taxation, along with an easing of the restrictions

placed on royal expenditure a year earlier. The council could claim the credit for its own competence. It also benefited from a number of developments that reduced the pressure on England's defences. Already in March 1406 the capture *en route* for France of Prince James, the heir to the Scottish throne, closely followed by the death of his father, Robert III, had given the English government a valuable card in its dealings with its northern neighbour. And by the end of 1407 the tide of war had at last turned in Wales to England's advantage. Glyn Dŵr's rising was not yet suppressed, but it never again threatened to destabilize the whole realm. Even more important, the murder of the duc d'Orléans on 23 November 1407 brought an immediate reduction in the pressure on Gascony and Calais, gave a central place in the government of France to the duke of Burgundy, by tradition and interest an ally of England, and soon led to a French civil war which offered inviting prospects for English intervention. At the beginning of 1408 the earl of Northumberland and Lord Bardolf launched a desperate invasion from Scotland into Yorkshire. Their defeat and deaths at Bramham Moor on 19 February finally secured the north of England for the king, in whose name the region was thereafter governed by Prince John and the earl of Westmorland.

Henry was not deprived of all his royal authority, but his participation in government was limited both by intermittent ill health and by the increasing prominence of the prince. In time this led to tensions, not just between the king and his eldest son but also between their followers, for the prince came to Westminster with an entourage he had gathered while serving in Wales, headed by the young earls of Arundel and Warwick, and subsequently augmented by men who had hitherto been his father's retainers, above all the Beauforts. Such men looked to the heir to the throne, rather than to its present occupant, for leadership and advancement. Henry relied increasingly on Archbishop Arundel, whose friendship did much to sustain him. They exchanged warm personal letters. For example a letter from Henry at Birdsnest Lodge in Windsor Forest to Arundel in May 1409 ends: 'I thank yow hertely of the great besinesse that ye do for me and for m(y) reaume … hopynge to God to spek to you hastely, and thank you with good herte, Yowre true frend and chyld in God, H. R.' (Hingeston, 2.27). This close connection endured. Henry visited Canterbury several times and it was in Arundel's cathedral that he chose to be buried.

King Henry and the church Henry's reliance on Arundel was at all times both personal and political. The archbishop had given vital support during the usurpation, and carried almost all the other bishops with him. In return Arundel required royal support for religious orthodoxy against heresy. He was able to force the withdrawal of Sir John Cheyne, a suspected Lollard, as speaker of the parliament of 1399, and in 1401 he was the driving force behind the statute of *De haeretico comburendo*, which for the first time made heresy a capital offence in England. The burning of William Sawtre, carried out on Henry's orders on 2 March (the statute had not then been formally enacted), underlined the king's willingness to endorse the church's policy. But as so often, Henry's freedom of manoeuvre was restricted by his insecurity. He needed the church's backing, but he could not afford to antagonize supporters with Lollard sympathies, least of all those among his Lancastrian retainers. Proposals for the disendowment of the church in order to improve the royal finances made by some knights of the shires in the Coventry parliament of 1404, and repeated at the parliament of 1410, may have stemmed from anti-clericalism rather than heresy as such, but there certainly seem to have been reputed Lollards in Henry's household: in 1404 some of them were rebuked by Arundel for failing to show due reverence to the consecrated host as it was borne through the Coventry streets.

The danger to the church from heresy was probably a useful bargaining counter for Henry when his financial needs obliged him to tap ecclesiastical resources, as they often did. During his reign he levied some forty subsidies from the two English provinces, and was also able to demand frequent and substantial loans—in 1403 he borrowed over £11,000 from the church. That Henry was personally devout no doubt helped him retain the loyalty of nearly all the church hierarchy. He was also careful and responsible in filling vacancies on the episcopal bench. His control of appointments was as complete as that of his predecessors, but unlike Richard II he elevated few members of his own household. The trend towards a university-educated episcopate continued. Some of Henry's bishops were theologians, and still more were canon or civil lawyers. Henry and his advisers chose able men, whether royal servants like Thomas Langley and Henry Bowet (who succeeded Scrope at York) or a personal friend like Philip Repyndon, who became bishop of Lincoln, or the ecclesiastical administrator and future archbishop of Canterbury Henry Chichele. None neglected his diocese, most became conscientious resident pastors.

The execution of Archbishop Scrope in 1405 could have been disastrous for Henry's relations with the church, but in fact it had remarkably little discernible impact. The primate's burgeoning cult was as far as possible repressed, and Innocent VII's excommunication of all involved in Scrope's death was effectively ignored. Henry was exculpated in 1407, on terms said to have included the foundation of three religious houses, but only the Bridgettine house of Syon gave effect to this vow, and that was founded by Henry V; two years later he felt confident enough to lift the ban on Scrope's cult. No doubt it was largely the weakness of the papacy during the schism which had begun in 1378 that enabled Henry to ignore its strictures. Like his predecessor he had been loyal to the Roman popes, but now his growing security at home permitted his involvement in efforts to bring the schism to an end. In 1408, following a court sermon in which the cardinal-archbishop of Bordeaux urged action against the scandal of a double papacy, an English embassy went to the church council summoned to Pisa, which in 1409 deposed the Roman and Avignon popes and elected Alexander V to succeed both.

Although Henry's role in domestic government was restricted by this time, the initiative behind English participation at Pisa appears to have been largely his. Two years later, when effective government was in the prince's hands, Henry again showed his residual authority when he backed Archbishop Arundel in his drive against heresy at Oxford. Opposition to the primate was led by Richard Courtenay, a close associate of the prince, who invoked a bull of Boniface IX exempting the university from such visitation, but Henry not only rejected this privilege himself but also persuaded John XXIII, Alexander V's successor, to revoke it. Arundel duly conducted a visitation, whose principal effect was to reassert his own authority over the university, but also went some way towards affirming Henry's continued kingship.

Further breakdown The dispute over Arundel's jurisdiction at Oxford constituted a relatively indirect pointer to the strains that could arise from the division of authority resulting from King Henry's sickness. But such strains were slow to appear. Government continued to be conducted in the king's name, even though important matters, particularly those concerning finance, were determined by the prince and the council. For example privy-seal warrants to the exchequer ordering payments were now almost always said to be approved by the council. Henry came to Westminster for great occasions, as when Arundel replaced Thomas Langley as chancellor on 30 January 1407. But he spent the next few months at Hertford, a favourite royal castle, while the prince held council meetings at Westminster. Henry attended the Garter service at Windsor on St George's day, as he had always done, and then made an extended visit to the midlands and the north from June to September, before attending the opening of parliament at Gloucester on 20 October 1407. Henry's retention of at least a nominal authority at this time is shown by the numerous letters under the great seal which were still warranted *per ipsum regem*—'by the king himself'. These may sometimes or even often have been a formality, but when Henry was in the north in August and September he had a great seal and clerks with him to write and enrol his letters. But now very few grants were made that diminished the king's resources.

Early in March 1408 Henry chose to go north to oversee the punishment of rebels. He was then in and around London from mid-May, but in mid-June 1408 he had a seizure at Archbishop Arundel's manor at Mortlake on the Thames. He is said to have been unconscious for some hours and even appeared to be dead. He remained at Mortlake for a month before going to his own castle at Hertford, but although he seemed to have made a good recovery he was ill again at the end of the year, and on 21 January 1409 he made a hasty will in English at Greenwich (Nichols, 203–5). His references to himself as 'sinful wretch' and to his 'lyffe I have mispendyd' have led to his will being characterized as 'unusually abject' and associated with feelings of guilt over his usurpation (McFarlane, 103). But other devout men in this period made wills hardly less anguished, and the tone of Henry's may only reflect physical distress and a pious fear of death and judgement. As far as his kingship was concerned he reviewed his whole reign, requesting payment of his debts, forgiving his enemies and thanking those who had done him 'trewe service'. Prominent among the latter must have been the Lancastrian retainers who had stood by him throughout—three of them were named as witnesses. It was in keeping with this apparently retrospective state of mind that in March 1409, and again in February 1410, Henry was concerned to found or extend a chapel on the battlefield at Shrewsbury. His health improved, however, and he became reasonably active, even planning to go on campaign again. But his hopes were invariably disappointed, and his itinerary suggests that he was slowing down. In 1409, essentially a year of convalescence, he probably remained in or near London save for short visits to Canterbury in July, and to Northampton and Leicester in November and early December.

Crisis in government Shortly before Christmas 1409 there were changes in the two great offices. On 20 December the treasurer, Sir John Tiptoft, was dismissed but his successor, Lord Scrope of Masham, was not appointed until 6 January. On the 21st Archbishop Arundel resigned as chancellor and returned the great seal to the king. King Henry held it himself until 19 January 1410, releasing it to seal writs and letters, and the keeper of the rolls then held it until Sir Thomas *Beaufort was appointed chancellor on 31 January 1410, shortly after parliament had assembled. Long voids were unusual, and it is significant that both Scrope and Beaufort were Prince Henry's men. These developments point to a crisis at the heart of the government. Its precise nature is elusive, but it clearly turned on the relations between the king and his eldest son, probably above all as they were affected by the position of Archbishop Arundel and the recurrent problem of finance. The latter was less severe than in 1406, but money was still scarce, and in 1410 there was another almost total stop on the payment of annuities to royal retainers. There was also growing concern about law and order, an issue hitherto overshadowed by the threat of rebellion and civil war, but now prompting petitions to parliament, especially from the north and the Welsh marches. Arundel had proved unable to deal effectively with such matters, and with the prince and his young followers ambitious to take control of government his position became untenable, even though the king would doubtless have liked to retain his services.

The establishment of a new regime created a potentially fraught situation, with the king still ostensibly possessed of all his powers, while the prince became the effective head of the government. Restraint and tact would be needed on both sides if the experiment was to work, and in the end the impatience of the prince's followers, led by the Beauforts, did much to bring it to an end. But at first all went well, assisted by the king's personal trust in his eldest son at this time—in 1409 Henry had named the prince as executor of his will. During the January parliament a council headed by the prince with four bishops, Lord Burnell, and 'other lords and officers' was 'assigned', nominally by the king himself (*RotP*, 3.649). As far as finance was concerned they resumed what was essentially the policy of retrenchment adopted at the end of 1406, with a fair degree of effectiveness and with the king's co-operation.

King and prince were also in agreement, at least at first, over foreign policy, above all in their dealings with France, where the civil war resulting from the murder of Orléans led to an appeal from both sides for English assistance. The king and his son alike favoured Burgundy, to the extent that in summer 1411 the former planned to cross the channel to join Duke John with a force under his own command, and had armour and tents prepared, along with 'an old streamer of worsted worked with the arms of the king, St Edward and St George for the king's ship for his voyage to Calais' (PRO, E 101/405/25). Henry then changed his mind, not just about going himself but also about any English involvement in France, whereas the prince remained committed to intervention; in September 1411 a small force led by his friend and ally the earl of Arundel went to support the duke of Burgundy, and on 9 November shared his victory over the Armagnacs (Orléanists) at St Cloud.

To King Henry his son's show of independence was probably unwelcome in itself. It became intolerable in the light of suggestions apparently voiced by Henry *Beaufort that the king should resign his throne in the prince's favour. The king's move to reassert himself became apparent in his support for Arundel against Richard Courtenay and Oxford University in autumn 1411, and was made obvious in the parliament that assembled on 3 November. Henry was unable to attend on the first day, but when the speaker, Sir Thomas Chaucer, made his customary protestation on the 5th Henry accepted it but then said forcefully that he wished for no sort of novelty—*nulle manere de novellerie*—in the parliament (*RotP*, 3.648). And on 20–21 December, after the dissolution, he further reasserted his authority. Sir Thomas Beaufort and Lord Scrope were dismissed, while Archbishop Arundel became chancellor once more and Sir John Pelham, Henry's retainer since the 1390s and the sword-bearer at his coronation, became treasurer.

The end of the reign Henry's kingship was not challenged again. Presumably in order to maintain control over government he now lived in or near London, save for a last visit to Archbishop Arundel at Canterbury between late February and mid-April 1412. However, the last fifteen months of his reign were troubled by continuing disagreements over foreign policy, which spilled over into differences between the king and the prince, and between the prince and his brother Thomas. On 18 May 1412 the treaty of Bourges signalled a reversal of the previous year's Burgundian alliance, with King Henry pledging support for Burgundy's Armagnac enemies, in return for an expanded duchy of Aquitaine. At first he himself again intended to cross the channel at the head of an army, albeit with the prince leading a smaller force, but when this once more proved beyond his strength the main command was entrusted not to Prince Henry but to Prince Thomas, probably their father's favourite son, whose relations were uneasy with his elder brother, and decidedly strained with the latter's Beaufort supporters. Resenting his father's lack of trust, late in June the prince brought a large retinue to London by way of parading his strength and following, but to no avail. The army left under Thomas (now duke of Clarence), though a shift in the French balance of power led to its being bought off in November. By then Prince Henry's anxiety and frustration had led him in September to make a second demonstration in London, after which he is said to have confronted his father in Westminster Hall, where he swore his continued loyalty and even asked the king to kill him. Henry, greatly moved, forgave his son. The interview brought the latter no more authority, but seems to have cleared the air and improved relations between the two men. Even so, at the end of his reign, as at its beginning, Henry placed his trust principally in his Lancastrian retainers.

Writs dated 1 December summoned a parliament to meet at Westminster on 3 February 1413. It met but there is no roll of proceedings because Henry, who had been seriously ill shortly before Christmas, collapsed in Westminster Abbey and died on 20 March in the Jerusalem Chamber in the abbot's house nearby. His dying advice to Prince Henry was widely circulated, but seems to have been quickly contaminated by improbable expressions of remorse for his usurpation; the earliest version, preserved by Thomas Elmham, contains only recommendations to righteousness and piety, a comparison of Henry's former strength with his present weakness and misery, and a plea for the settlement of his debts. The dead king's body was taken by water to Gravesend and buried, as he wished, in Canterbury Cathedral, near the tomb of Edward, the Black Prince, in Becket's chapel, on 18 June. Queen Joan had a fine alabaster life-size effigy of Henry placed on his tomb. His leaden coffin was opened in 1832, largely in order to disprove Clement Maidstone's story that it had been thrown into the Thames, and for an instant before the air took effect, 'the face of the deceased King was seen in complete preservation' (Spry, 444).

Personality Henry IV presents an opaque image to posterity. It may owe something to a policy of deliberate self-concealment—not surprising, perhaps, in a man who was nearly killed in 1381 and subsequently had to negotiate the political shoals of Richard II's last years. His public image was that of a man who excelled in all the activities most valued in knightly circles, and he was certainly at home in the world of aristocratic chivalry in a way that Richard was not. This ideal image was in some respects truthful. There are no scandals recorded of his private life (unlike his father's), with no known mistresses or bastards. He was also indisputably pious. The first English king known to have possessed a vernacular Bible, he supported the canonization of John of Bridlington, gave a pension to the anchoress Margaret Pensax, and maintained close relations with several Westminster recluses. His household accounts as king record conventional payments to large numbers of paupers (no less than 12,000 on Easter day 1406), and the maintenance of twenty-four *oratores domini regis* at 2*d*. a day each to make intercession for him. After 1399 he seems to have maintained his court in appropriate style, and appeared in fine clothes when

occasion demanded; for St George's day 1408 his tailor made him a gown, kirtle, and hood of blue cloth, all furred with minever, while the hood was also lined with scarlet.

With this show of conventional virtues went qualities that may have been less common. Henry had been carefully educated by his father, and was no less concerned for the intellectual training of his own sons. When in exile in Paris he attended the schools there, and is reported to have had a taste for casuistry—the application of general moral principles to particular problems. He enjoyed reading, and owned books in Latin and English which included works of history, poetry, and theology as well as bibles and psalters, and had a two-tier desk made for his books at Eltham Palace. Henry was also highly musical. In the 1390s he travelled abroad with a small body of musicians, and as king maintained a group of royal minstrels. Indeed, he almost certainly went beyond enjoying music to composing it: the 'Roy Henry' whose 'Gloria' and 'Sanctus' are preserved in the Old Hall manuscript is most probably to be identified with Henry IV. He patronized poets too. As earl of Derby he gave an annuity to Chaucer, and later owned at least one book by John Gower (who never ceased to admire him); as king he tried in vain to persuade Christine de Pisan to join his court.

Intellectual and artistic interests are no guarantee of moral rectitude. Henry's conduct in 1399 alone shows that he was capable of considerable deviousness, even outright dishonesty, as well as demonstrating his capacity for decisive action. But he was also a good judge of men, and though the size of his household was criticized, its composition was not—he was never said to have undesirable favourites. He does not seem to have been cruel, though in 1399 the earl of Salisbury feared his vindictiveness, and he was capable of outbursts of devastating anger—twice in 1402 the exasperated king is said to have sent treasonous Franciscans to the gallows with the words 'By this my head you shall lose your own' (*Eulogium historiarum*, 3.390–92). Archbishop Scrope may also have been the victim of royal fury. Such outbursts were rare, however, and Henry usually seems to have kept his temper under control. He showed during the parliament of 1406 that he could accept criticism of his regime and make concessions without resentment against those who forced them on him. A sense of humour may have provided release from self-imposed constraints: Walsingham reports that when the Scottish Prince James was captured on his way to France, to be educated there, Henry joked that the Scots could have sent the boy to him for tuition, since he knew French himself. Physically he was of moderate height and sturdy in build, becoming corpulent in later life, perhaps due to lack of exercise after his health failed. The representation on his tomb may be an accurate likeness, not least in its prominent beard—when the tomb was opened in 1832 it was seen to be 'thick and matted, and of a deep russet colour' (Spry, 444). His military prowess and far-ranging travels suggest considerable bodily strength; ironically, it was this innate quality that failed him after 1406, while his largely acquired attributes of patience and perseverance were what best enabled him to face and overcome the problems of his reign.

Historiography The reign and character of Henry IV prompted conflicting opinions from the moment of his death. The opposing standpoints of his contemporaries are encapsulated in the differing verdicts of Adam Usk, for whom Henry ruled powerfully but none the less died in misery and squalor, and Thomas Walsingham, who saw him as having reigned, quite simply, gloriously. It was Usk's vision that prevailed, reinforced by the elaborated accounts of Henry's death and last advice to his son. All emphasize the strain and effort of the reign, and the sorrow this brought upon the king. Even so, Henry IV remained a king worthy of respect, and this was still the case for Edward Hall in the 1540s. An overtly hostile note, however, is struck by John Foxe, who follows earlier chroniclers in seeing Henry's reign as 'full of trouble, of blood and misery', but differs from them in linking this with Henry's role as a persecutor of Lollards—he was 'the first of all English kings that began the unmerciful burning of Christ's saints for standing against the pope' (*Acts and Monuments*, 3.229). This new element may explain why Holinshed, in his *Chronicles*, having quoted Hall's ultimately favourable verdict almost verbatim, none the less concludes by attacking Henry as a usurper whose subjects deserved the miseries of his reign.

William Shakespeare's anecdotal debt to Holinshed was great, but his portrait of Henry IV is closer to Hall's. Henry is hardly the hero of the two plays that carry his name—he is overshadowed by Falstaff and Prince Hal throughout—but by consistently striking a note of responsibility, dignity, and courage he contributes an essential element to the analysis of kingship which is fundamental to Shakespeare's great sequence of history plays. Aspects of Henry's rule that might have detracted from this image are omitted or played down—the execution of Archbishop Scrope, for instance, is attributed entirely to John of Lancaster—but at the same time his human qualities are brought out in recurrent expressions of paternal anxiety and above all of remorse, two strands unforgettably worked together at the end of the second play. It is not his enemies but the dying Henry himself who remembers:

> By what by-paths and indirect crookt ways
> I met this crown, and I myself know well
> How troublesome it sate upon my head.
> (2 *Henry IV*, IV. v, ll. 184–6)

The two plays do not constitute a tragedy, but Shakespeare's Henry IV is close to being a tragic figure.

Shakespeare's plays have encapsulated for posterity an image of Henry IV both moral and political, the usurper whose actions brought misery on both his country and himself. Onto this later writers grafted some very different elements, arising from their perceptions of Henry's exercise of his authority. Starting perhaps with David Hume (1762), they placed increasing stress on the role of parliament in the events of Henry's reign, and gave particular emphasis to what they saw as foreshadowings of the constitutional principles of their own times. Henry Hallam went so far as to claim, 'of this revolution of 1399',

that 'there was as remarkable an attention shown to the formalities of the constitution, allowance made for the men and the times, as in that of 1688' (Hallam, 55–6).

This tendency culminated in the writings of William Stubbs, where, however, Henry IV is not seen only as a mere catalyst of constitutional development. Despite a characteristically Victorian taste for moralizing colour, Stubbs painted a subtle and credible picture of a man whose character changed over time (usually for the worse) under the pressure of events and a guilty conscience:

> he seems to us a man whose life was embittered by the knowledge that he had taken on a task for which he was unequal, whose conscience, ill-informed as it may have been, had soured him, and who felt that the judgments of men, at least, would deal hardly with him when he was dead.
> (Stubbs, 3.9)

Stubbs's portrait was in turn praised by K. B. McFarlane (1953, printed 1970), who then proceeded to bury it, primarily by pouring scorn on that 'constitutionalism' which Stubbs saw as the principal feature of Henry's reign, presenting the king instead as 'not a man of constitutional principle at all but an opportunist and a *politique*' (McFarlane, 24). In terms of factual resource McFarlane enjoyed the advantage over Stubbs in having access to J. H. Wylie's four-volume monograph *The History of England under Henry IV* (1884–98), even though no clear picture of Henry IV emerges from its welter of facts. Twentieth-century historians have exploited Wylie's labours, but McFarlane's reprinted lectures aside, only the useful study by J. L. Kirby (1970) has attempted a detailed analysis of Henry's life.

Assessment In the parliament that followed the accession of Henry V the speaker reminded the new king how in his father's time 'good governance was several times asked for by the Commons and their request granted. But how that was done and performed afterwards, our lord the king knows well' (*RotP*, 4.4). Henry had also died so much in debt that his executors at first declined to undertake the administration of his will, and his debts do not appear ever to have been fully paid. It would be easy to deduce from this evidence for disillusion and bankruptcy that those two qualities characterized the whole of Henry IV's reign, and to conclude that survival represented the sum of his achievement. By comparison with both his father and his eldest son Henry IV undoubtedly presents an uncharismatic image to posterity, and it is tempting to perceive him as an unremarkable, even weak, man, unable to foresee problems, still less to forestall them, and so always at the mercy of events. In such a perspective the success of his usurpation was exceptional, his struggles to deal with its consequences only what might have been expected of a ruler with his personal limitations.

It is certainly impossible to dissociate the difficulties of Henry IV's reign from the circumstances of its beginning, not least because they aroused unrealistic expectations among those who did most to make him king, and also made the support of his Lancastrian retainers indispensable to the maintenance of his regime, with drastic repercussions for the latter's cost. What seems remarkable is not, in fact, that Henry faced difficulties but the extent to which he overcame them. The greatest mistake of his reign was arguably his failure to offer the concessions needed to settle the Welsh revolt before it grew out of control, a missed opportunity that did more than anything else to multiply his difficulties with warfare and finance. But neither there nor anywhere else did he abandon the struggle to maintain his position, even after ill health overwhelmed him physically, while he clung to his royal prerogative with a tenacity that could reasonably have earned him the gratitude of his heir.

Henry's reign also had positive achievements to its credit. The challenge of heresy to religious orthodoxy was firmly resisted; although Ireland was neglected Wales was eventually secured; both Calais and Gascony, having come under serious threat, remained under English rule. In his involvement in efforts to resolve the papal schism and his intervention in French domestic politics Henry IV led the way for the more spectacular successes of his son. Thanks principally to Shakespeare, Henry's reign is commonly seen under the twin shadow cast by his usurpation of the throne and by the perception that in it lay the seeds of the Wars of the Roses. The attention given by more recent historians to the shortcomings of Henry VI should go a long way towards clearing Henry IV of responsibility for England's misfortunes under his grandson.

Once placed firmly in the context of his own reign Henry IV can be seen as a considerable figure, a humane and cultivated ruler, politically skilled but by no means invariably unprincipled. It is possible to argue that McFarlane dismissed too readily the 'constitutionalism' found in Henry's rule by Stubbs, that the latter's anachronistic phraseology masked an understanding that Henry's rule was characterized by a consensual style of politics which aspired to the same sort of rapport with magnates and gentry, in parliament and elsewhere, that had marked the highly successful kingship of Edward III. Unlike Richard II, Henry IV retained to the end of his reign the loyalty of the bulk of the political nation. That loyalty may sometimes have been grudgingly given, and Henry's reign may not have been as glorious as Walsingham claimed, but it ultimately saw much more success than failure, while the triumphs of Henry V, usually regarded as even more brilliant through comparisons with the effortful gloom of his father's reign, owed more than is often appreciated to the legacy of Henry IV.

A. L. BROWN and HENRY SUMMERSON

Sources duchy of Lancaster, accounts various, PRO, DL 28 · chancery, charter rolls, PRO, C 53/164–7 · exchequer, treasury of receipt, court of the Marshalsea, PRO, E 37/28 · exchequer, king's remembrancer, accounts various, PRO, E 101/404/21, 405/14, 22, 25 · BL, MS Harley 319 · N. H. Nicolas, ed., *Proceedings and ordinances of the privy council of England*, 7 vols., RC, 26 (1834–7), 1386–1410, 1411–22 · *RotP*, vols. 3–4 · *RotS*, vol. 2 · *Chancery records* · H. Ellis, ed., *Original letters illustrative of English history*, 2nd ser., 4 vols. (1827) · Rymer, *Foedera*, 1st edn, vols. 7, 8 · J. L. Kirby, ed., *Calendar of signet letters of Henry IV and Henry V* (1978) · F. C. Hingeston, ed., *Royal and historical letters during the reign of Henry the Fourth*, 1, Rolls Series, 18 (1860) · M. D. Legge, ed., *Anglo-Norman petitions and letters*, Anglo-Norman Text Society, 11 (1941) · S. B. Chrimes and A. L. Brown, eds., *Select documents of English constitutional history, 1307–1485* (1961) · J. Nichols, ed., *A collection of all the wills now known to be extant of the kings and queens of England* (1780) · D. Wilkins, ed., *Concilia* (1737), 3.238–9 · L. T. Smith, ed., *Expeditions to Prussia and the Holy Land made by Henry, earl of Derby*, CS, new ser., 52 (1894) · *John of Gaunt's register, 1379–1383*, ed. E. C. Lodge and R. Somerville, 2 vols., CS, 3rd ser., 56–7 (1937) · G. F. Beltz, *Memorials of the most noble order of the Garter* (1841) · W. P. Baildon, 'The trousseaux of Princess Philippa, wife of Eric, king of Denmark, Norway, and Sweden', *Archaeologia*, 67 (1916), 163–88 · M. H. Keen and M. Warner, eds., 'Morley vs Montagu (1399): a case in the court of chivalry', *Camden miscellany, XXXIV*, CS, 5th ser., 10 (1997), 141–95 · C. L. Kingsford, ed., *Chronicles of London* (1905) · C. Given-Wilson, ed., *Chronicles of the revolution, 1397–1400* (1993) · *Johannis de Trokelowe et Henrici de Blaneforde ... chronica et annales*, ed. H. T. Riley, pt 3 of *Chronica monasterii S. Albani*, Rolls Series, 28 (1866) · *Thomae Walsingham, quondam monachi S. Albani, historia Anglicana*, ed. H. T. Riley, 2 vols., pt 1 of *Chronica monasterii S. Albani*, Rolls Series, 28 (1863–4), vol. 2 · *The chronicle of England by John Capgrave*, ed. F. C. Hingeston, Rolls Series, 1 (1858) · *Johannis Capgrave Liber de illustribus Henricis*, ed. F. C. Hingeston, Rolls Series, 7 (1858) · F. S. Haydon, ed., *Eulogium historiarum sive temporis*, 3 vols., Rolls Series, 9 (1858), vol. 3 · J. Raine, ed., *The historians of the church of York and its archbishops*, 3, Rolls Series, 71 (1894) · T. Wright, ed., *Political poems and songs relating to English history*, 2, Rolls Series, 14 (1861) [incl. Elmham's version of Henry IV's last words] · *The chronicle of Adam Usk, 1377–1421*, ed. and trans. C. Given-Wilson, OMT (1997) · *Knighton's chronicle, 1337–1396*, ed. and trans. G. H. Martin, OMT (1995) [Lat. orig., *Chronica de eventibus Angliae a tempore regis Edgari usque mortem regis Ricardi Secundi*, with parallel Eng. text] · T. Walsingham, *The St Albans chronicle, 1406–1420*, ed. V. H. Galbraith (1937) · *The chronicle of John Hardyng*, ed. H. Ellis (1812) · W. Bower, *Scotichronicon*, ed. D. E. R. Watt and others, new edn, 9 vols. (1987–98), vol. 8 · B. Williams, ed., *Chronicque de la traïson et mort de Richart Deux, roy Dengleterre*, EHS, 9 (1846) · M. L. Bellaguet, ed., *Chronique du religieux de Saint-Denys*, 6 vols. (1839–52) [Collection des Documents Inédits sur l'Histoire de France] · J. Boucicaut, *Livre des faits du bon messire Jean le Maigre, dit Boucicaut*, ed. J. A. C. Buchon (1835) · J. Froissart, *Chroniques*, ed. K. de Lettenhove, 25 vols. (1866–77) · J. Froissart, *Chronicles*, trans. T. Johnes, 5 vols. (1803–10) · *Hall's chronicle*, ed. H. Ellis (1809) · *Holinshed's chronicles of England, Scotland and Ireland*, ed. H. Ellis, 3 (1808) · *The acts and monuments of John Foxe*, ed. S. R. Cattley, 8 vols. (1837–41), vol. 3 · C. Allmand, *Henry V* (1992) · J. F. Baldwin, *The king's council in England during the middle ages* (1913) · S. I. Boardman, *The early Stewart kings: Robert II and Robert III, 1371–1406* (1996) · R. Brown, H. M. Colvin, and A. J. Taylor, eds., *The history of the king's works*, 1–2 (1963) · H. Castor, *The king, the crown and the duchy of Lancaster: public authority and private power, 1399–1461* (2000) · H. E. L. Collins, *The order of the Garter, 1348–1461* (2000) · R. R. Davies, *The revolt of Owain Glyn Dŵr* (1995) · G. Dodd and D. Biggs, eds., *Henry IV: the establishment of the regime, 1399–1406* [forthcoming] · GEC, *Peerage* · C. Given-Wilson, *The royal household and the king's affinity: service, politics and finance in England, 1360–1413* (1986) · A. Goodman, *John of Gaunt: the exercise of princely power in fourteenth-century Europe* (1992) · R. A. Griffiths, *King and country: England and Wales in the fifteenth century* (1991) · H. Hallam, *The constitutional history of England from Edward I to Henry VII*, 4th edn (1869) · G. L. Harriss, *Henry V: the practice of kingship* (1985) · G. L. Harriss, *Cardinal Beaufort: a study of Lancastrian ascendancy and decline* (1988) · P. Heath, *Church and realm, 1272–1461* (1988) · HoP, *Commons, 1386–1421* · J. Hughes, *Pastors and visionaries: religion and secular life in late medieval Yorkshire* (1988) · D. Hume, *The history of England from the invasion of Julius Caesar till the accession of Henry VII*, 2 (1762) · M. H. Keen, *England in the later middle ages* (1973) · J. L. Kirby, *Henry IV of England* (1970) · E. F. Jacob, *The fifteenth century, 1399–1485* (1961) · J. E. Lloyd, *Owen Glendower* (1931) · K. B. McFarlane, *Lancastrian kings and Lollard knights* (1970) · P. McNiven, *Heresy and politics in the reign of Henry IV* (1987) · N. Orme, *From childhood to chivalry* (1984) · S. J. Payling, *Political society in Lancastrian England* (1991) · J. Sherborne, *War, politics and culture in fourteenth-century England* (1994) · R. L. Storey, *Thomas Langley and the bishopric of Durham, 1406–1437* (1961) · W. Stubbs, *The constitutional history of England*, 2nd edn, 3 (1878) · A. Tuck, *Richard II and the*

English nobility (1973) · C. J. Tyerman, *England and the crusades, 1095–1588* (1988) · M. G. A. Vale, *English Gascony, 1399–1453* (1970) · B. P. Wolffe, *The royal demesne in English history* (1971) · J. H. Wylie, *History of England under Henry the Fourth*, 4 vols. (1884–98) · J. M. W. Bean, 'Henry IV and the Percies', *History*, 44 (1959), 212–27 · D. Biggs, 'The reign of Henry IV: the revolution of 1399 and the establishment of the Lancastrian regime', *Fourteenth century England*, ed. N. Saul, 1 (2000), 195–210 · A. L. Brown, 'The Commons and the council in the reign of Henry IV', *EngHR*, 79 (1964), 1–30 · A. L. Brown, 'The reign of Henry IV', *Fifteenth century England*, ed. S. B. Chrimes, C. D. Ross, and R. A. Griffiths (1972), 1–28 · D. Crook, 'Central England and the revolt of the earls, January 1400', *BIHR*, 64 (1991), 403–10 · R. G. Davies, 'Thomas Arundel as archbishop of Canterbury, 1396–1414', *Journal of Ecclesiastical History*, 24 (1973), 9–21 · R. G. Davies, 'The episcopate', *Profession, vocation and culture in later medieval England*, ed. C. H. Clough (1982), 51–89 · F. R. H. du Boulay, 'Henry of Derby's expeditions to Prussia, 1390–91 and 1392', *The reign of Richard II*, ed. F. R. H. du Boulay and C. M. Barron (1971), 153–72 · C. J. Ford, 'Piracy or policy: crisis in the channel, 1400–1403', *TRHS*, 5th ser., 29 (1979), 63–78 · P. McNiven, 'The Cheshire rising of 1400', *Bulletin of the John Rylands Library*, 52 (1969–70), 375–96 · P. McNiven, 'The betrayal of Archbishop Scrope', *Bulletin of the John Rylands Library*, 54 (1971), 172–213 · P. McNiven, 'Prince Henry and the constitutional crisis of 1412', *History*, 65 (1980), 1–16 · P. McNiven, 'The problem of Henry IV's health, 1405–1413', *EngHR*, 100 (1985), 747–72 · A. J. Pollard, 'The Lancastrian constitutional experiment revisited: Henry IV, Sir John Tiptoft and the parliament of 1406', *Parliamentary History*, 14 (1995), 103–19 · A. Rogers, 'The political crisis of 1401', *Nottingham Medieval Studies*, 12 (1968), 85–96 · A. Rogers, 'Henry IV: the commons and taxation', *Medieval Studies*, 31 (1969), 44–70 · T. A. Sandquist, 'The holy oil of St Thomas of Canterbury', *Essays in medieval history presented to Bertie Wilkinson*, ed. T. A. Sandquist and M. R. Powicke, 330–44 · H. Summerson, 'An English Bible and other books belonging to Henry IV', *Bulletin of the John Rylands Library*, 79 (1997), 109–15 · A. Tuck, 'Henry IV and Europe: a dynasty's search for recognition', *The McFarlane legacy*, ed. R. H. Britnell and A. J. Pollard (1995), 107–25 · S. Walker, 'Political saints in late medieval England', *The McFarlane legacy*, ed. R. H. Britnell and A. J. Pollard (1995), 77–106 · E. Wright, 'Henry IV, the commons and the recovery of royal finance in 1407', *Rulers and ruled in late medieval England*, ed. R. E. Archer and S. Walker (1995), 65–81 · J. H. Spry, 'A brief account of the examination of the tomb of King Henry IV in the cathedral of Canterbury, August 21 1832', *Archaeologia*, 26 (1836), 440–45

Archives PRO, C 53/164–167; DL 28; E 37/28; E 101/404/21, 405/14, 22, 25

Likenesses alabaster tomb effigy, c.1408–1427, Canterbury Cathedral [*see illus.*] · Worthington, line engraving, pubd 1823 (after unknown artist), NPG · coins, BM · illuminated initial, PRO, DL42/1; repro. in Kirby, *Henry IV*, frontispiece · tomb effigy, electrotype, NPG · wax seals, BM

Henry V

Henry V (1386/7–1422), king of England and lord of Ireland, and duke of Aquitaine, eldest son of *Henry IV (1366–1413) and his first wife, Mary, second daughter and coheir of Humphrey (IX) de Bohun, seventh earl of Hereford (*d.* 1373), was born in the chamber of the gatehouse tower of Monmouth Castle, an association which gave him the name Henry of Monmouth by which he was sometimes known.

Childhood to 1400 Two dates for Henry's birth, 9 August or 16 September, in either 1386 or 1387, can plausibly be put forward (Allmand, 1992, 7). The name of his nurse (*nutrix*), Joan Waryn, is recorded in the sum of 40s. a year paid for her services, and is confirmed by the grant of £20 for life paid to her after Henry had become king. Henry's early years were marked by two factors: the frequent absences

Henry V (1386/7–1422), by unknown artist

abroad of his father (then known as Henry of Derby), and the death of his mother in June 1394 when he was but six or seven years old. Since he was not born to be king, little is known of his childhood: an illness in 1395 is recorded, as is talk, in the same year, of a possible espousal to Marie, daughter of Jean (IV), duke of Brittany. The name of his governess, Mary Hervy, is also recorded. With his brothers, *Thomas of Lancaster, duke of Clarence, *John of Lancaster, duke of Bedford, and *Humphrey, duke of Gloucester, and possibly his two sisters, Blanche and Philippa, Henry spent time in the care of Joan, countess of Hereford, their maternal grandmother, and on their father's estates (part of the lands belonging to the duchy of Lancaster). A late fifteenth-century tradition that, in 1398, he resided at Queen's College, Oxford, in the care of his uncle Henry *Beaufort (*d.* 1447), second of John of Gaunt's illegitimate sons by Katherine Swynford (and thereby a half-brother to his own father), at the time chancellor of the university, is unsupported. However, the year was important for the young man, for it marked the banishment of his father by Richard II, who nevertheless treated Henry well, granting him £500 a year for his maintenance. In February 1399 John of Gaunt died, his death soon being followed by the forfeiture to the king of the rich inheritance of the duchy of Lancaster. In May Richard went on a voyage of pacification to Ireland and took Henry with him, dubbing him knight soon afterwards. When Henry's own father landed at Ravenspur in Yorkshire, around the beginning of July, with the avowed intention of reclaiming his inheritance, his son was placed in a difficult position, but he persuaded Richard that he had nothing to do with the course of events now rapidly developing. None the less, whether for his security or, perhaps more likely, as an honourable hostage, Henry was kept in the castle of Trim, north-west of Dublin. However, once his father had secured the throne, he returned to England, now heir to a new inheritance.

Events moved quickly. It was as a member of the newly created Order of the Bath that Henry carried the sheathed and blunted sword representing justice at his father's coronation in Westminster Abbey on 13 October 1399, a year to the day since the new king had gone into exile. Two days later parliament agreed that Henry should be created prince of Wales, duke of Cornwall, and earl of Chester; later in the month he was named duke of Aquitaine and, on 10 November, he was awarded the title of duke of Lancaster, along with its liberties and franchises, but not the duchy itself. Yet not all was as well as it may have seemed. At Epiphany 1400 a conspiracy against the king, hatched by certain high-ranking nobility, was uncovered. Both he and his eldest son survived, but it set the tone for some of the main problems which the coming years were to reveal.

Early service in Wales, 1400–1410 These years were to be dominated by events in Wales, where a major rebellion, led by Owain Glyn Dŵr, a landowner with estates in north Wales and more widely based political support, began in September 1400. As prince of Wales Henry was responsible for the suppression of the rebellion; much of the cost had to be borne from his (by now) considerably diminished Welsh revenues supplemented by contributions from Cornwall, Chester, and the central exchequer. Still a youth at the beginning of the troubles, Henry began to serve under Henry Percy, history's Hotspur, who had been named justiciar of Chester and north Wales in October 1399, and who took charge of carrying out policy. Considerable military activity, some undertaken by the prince himself, brought very mixed results in 1401 and 1402; the rebellion was spreading within Wales, since it was proving difficult, in mountainous terrain, to bring the enemy to battle, while raids into rebel-held territory were expensive and achieved little. In July 1403 Henry and his father faced a new and serious threat: rebellion by the now disaffected Percy family, whose force, coming from the north and advancing through Cheshire, was confronted by a royal army 2 miles north of Shrewsbury on 21 July. In the ensuing battle Henry was wounded in the face, but fought on; he was probably not personally responsible for Hotspur's death (as Shakespeare was to have it), but that event led quickly to the collapse of the rebel army.

English fortunes in Wales reached their low point in 1404–5. As was reported in parliament, Henry was active against rebel forces, but successes did not come easily, while the financing of the war was proving increasingly

difficult. Then, early in 1406, full command was placed in Henry's hands. Matters now began to take a turn for the better; possibly because of better financial provision, most probably because the Welsh failed to maintain their military activity—in particular after the capture of Aberystwyth by the English under Henry late in 1408. The rebellion was dying out, and by 1410 was all but over. As a practical experience in early manhood, its effects upon Henry were considerable. It was at this time that he learned what a soldier's work was; that he formed friendships which were to last all his life; and that he came to appreciate how effective command and proper organization, together with the regular provision of money and equipment, could bring success in war.

Apprenticeship in government, 1407–1413 Henry was also learning about government. By the end of 1406 it was already clear that an improving situation in Wales meant that his presence in the principality was no longer so necessary, a fact which enabled him to become a much more regular member of his father's council. Very soon, along with Archbishop Thomas Arundel (d. 1414), appointed chancellor in January 1407, he became a leading member of the group which, with clear parliamentary approval, tackled problems of government, the chief of which was the reordering of his father's finances. Between October 1407 and January 1410 no parliament was called; increasingly the council ruled in the place of the king, whose difficulties were accentuated by serious ill health in 1408–9. A group of men, notably John (d. 1410), Henry, and Thomas Beaufort (d. 1427), who had been legitimized in February 1407, and Thomas Chaucer (d. 1434), son of the poet and their cousin, speaker of the Commons in 1407, 1410, and 1411, slowly gained the ascendancy over Arundel who resigned the chancellorship in December 1409. Henry now took over more than formal charge of the council. During the two-year period from December 1409 to November 1411 he and its members—men such as Henry and Thomas Beaufort, Thomas Langley (d. 1437), already bishop of Durham and to be Henry's chancellor in 1417, Henry Chichele (d. 1443), to be appointed archbishop of Canterbury in 1414, and Richard Beauchamp (d. 1439), a former companion-in-arms—effectively ruled England. As a group they strove to follow a political programme (although it was not spoken of as such) best expressed by Henry Beaufort, whose aim was the achievement of order, justice, and efficiency in government, notably in the proper regulation of the king's finances.

However, on 30 November 1411, perhaps stung into action by Henry's open support for the Burgundians in their struggle for power against the Armagnac party in the civil troubles occupying France, perhaps roused by a call allegedly made by Henry Beaufort that he should abdicate in favour of his son, the king reasserted himself. Announcing that he wanted 'nulle manere de novellerie' (RotP, 3.648), he dismissed Henry and the council. In January 1412 Archbishop Arundel was recalled, and the king now turned to his second son, Thomas, who was made duke of Clarence, for help and advice. For the next fifteen months

Henry was a political exile in his own country. The possibility of a marriage with Anne, daughter of John the Fearless, duke of Burgundy, was discussed, but came to nothing. The period was characterized by considerable political and personal tensions. Henry may have been seriously at odds with his father and brother. There were attempts to undermine his position in England. Stories about him circulated at court and, perhaps, outside it. Henry was disillusioned by his very public exclusion from government, by the way the country was being governed, and by the pro-Armagnac policy being actively pursued in France, to the point that he felt obliged to defend his apparent isolation publicly. If true, Monstrelet's story, that Henry took his father's crown from his bedside to see how it fitted, applies to this time. For the prince, a young man of energy and ideas, the death of his father on 20 March 1413 can have come scarcely a moment too soon.

Beginnings of kingship and the Lollard revolt, 1413–1414
Henry was crowned at Westminster on Passion Sunday, 9 April 1413. The snow which fell that day was taken by some to mean that a period of austerity lay ahead, by others that the austerity was over, and that better days were to come. The many stories, not all contemporary, which underline the change which came over the king as he assumed his responsibilities had as their purpose to show how it was hoped that his rule would form a contrast to that of his father (what was already known of Henry gave rise to high hopes that this would, indeed, happen), and that whereas he had in the past sometimes mocked the law and its officers, he would now rule firmly and fairly according to that law. In 1412, when still prince of Wales, Henry had received from Thomas Hoccleve (*d.* 1426) the dedication of his *Regement of Princes*, with its emphasis on a king's obligation to see the rule of law obeyed. In the first parliament of the new reign Henry Beaufort, recently appointed chancellor, was to urge upon the king the need to seek advice before taking decisions; Henry had a duty, Beaufort argued, to provide good rule ('bon governance'; *RotP*, 4.3), something which, the speaker of the same parliament reminded Henry, had not been provided in his father's time. The reign was being launched with a sense of expectation in the air. The alleged change in the new king's lifestyle, along with his rejection of his past, suggested that the times marked a new beginning.

Attempts were soon made to reconcile differences between Henry and those who had been at odds with his father. At the end of 1413 the body of Richard II, exhumed from its burial-place at Kings Langley, was brought with appropriate ceremony for reburial next to his first wife, Anne of Bohemia (*d.* 1394), at Westminster Abbey. In the parliaments of 1414 the heirs to the titles of Huntingdon and Salisbury, involved in the conspiracy of 1400, and Henry Percy, who had rebelled in 1403, were encouraged to seek publicly their restoration to favour and estates. When, in September 1413, another companion-in-arms, the Herefordshire knight John Oldcastle, was condemned for his heterodox views by an ecclesiastical court presided over by Archbishop Arundel, Henry, who had already

tried to get him to see the error of his ways, still seemed willing to give him an opportunity to reflect upon his position by granting him a respite of forty days which he would spend in the Tower of London. Perhaps because he felt that Henry would give no assistance towards furthering what he and his Lollard supporters regarded as necessary changes within the church (evidence for Henry's unsympathetic attitude had already been provided by the petition against Lollard-inspired practices and beliefs presented by the prince and others in parliament late in 1406, and again by his attendance at the execution of the heretic John Badby in March 1410), Oldcastle rebuffed the offer thus extended, by escaping from imprisonment late in October, and then by planning a conspiracy against the king and members of his family, who had been celebrating Christmas at the royal manor of Eltham, outside London. On the night of 9 January 1414 Lollard supporters from several parts of the country converged on St Giles's Fields, to the north outside the city's walls. Forewarned of the plot, Henry sent men to apprehend the rebels, and although many escaped in the confusion and darkness, a certain number were arrested, to be tried and executed on the 'lollers galowes'. Oldcastle, however, was not among them, and he was to remain at large until finally captured in mid-Wales late in November 1417 when, condemned as a traitor before the parliament which met in December, he was executed soon afterwards. Although the events of early 1414 were regarded by largely hostile contemporaries as an attempt by rebels to upset both the spiritual and temporal orders, modern research has cast doubts on the actual danger they posed to law-abiding society. Neither the evidence of surviving legal records concerning the numbers alleged to have taken part nor, more difficult to evaluate, that concerning their motives fully sustains the picture of events found in some chronicles. Although it led to a number of executions, the rising was a less dramatic episode than many wished to make out.

Yet the rebellion led to the enactment of new legislation against Lollardy by the 'law and order' parliament which met at Leicester at the end of April. This was soon followed by further action against those responsible for the wider problem of local disorder when a superior eyre, undertaken by members of the court of king's bench exercising jurisdiction in both civil and criminal matters, travelled from Leicester into Staffordshire and Shropshire, and then to Wolverhampton, hearing complaints and dealing with a large backlog of cases. The active application of justice was a social necessity, an aspect of a king's obligation to his subjects which Henry took very seriously.

Wales and Scotland Henry's policies in regard to two other areas of trouble demonstrate his awareness of problems at home. The conflict in Wales over, Henry worked to deal with the effects of war in the former rebel territories in ways reflecting his determination to act firmly but in a spirit of reconciliation. Pardons were issued (they had to be paid for); inquiries into acts of oppression by royal officers were initiated; and attempts were also made to restore the social order and economic prosperity of Wales. These were the acts of a man who wanted the Welsh on his side. That many fought for him, and even more for his son, in the French wars was a mark of the success which his efforts brought him.

Henry aimed, too, at securing peace in another area which threatened the order of his kingdom—the Scottish border. Here, by pursuing a policy which could not be dissociated from the conflict in France, Henry played a pragmatic game of diplomacy and war whose aim was to secure the return of the young Henry Percy (d. 1455), Hotspur's son and the heir to the earldom of Northumberland, a prisoner–hostage in Scotland, to fulfil the traditional family role of keeping the border against the Scots; this was a move that made excellent sense in view of Henry's personal commitment to waging war against the French. In February 1416 Percy was finally exchanged for Murdoch Stewart, earl of Fife, a prisoner in England since 1402. In the person of James I, king of Scots, captured in 1406, Henry held another strong card, as the possible release of the king divided the Scottish aristocracy and forced its more bellicose members to control their military activities on the border for some while. In the late summer of 1417 a raid, termed the 'foul raid' by the Scots themselves, failed miserably, and the military advantage now turned to the English, in whose hands it was to remain. From 1419 onwards the main Scottish effort against the English would be expressed through assistance given directly to the 'auld' French ally on the soil of France itself. In the meanwhile, the castles of the border lands, garrisoned by local troops led by Henry Percy, kept the peace in the area, leaving the king to concentrate his attention on military activity elsewhere.

Increasingly involved in a continental war, Henry was to depend upon others to carry out the day-to-day government of England. In addition to his three brothers, and those already mentioned who had helped him during his father's reign, Henry came to rely upon a group whose membership was drawn from those serving in the royal household (Sir Thomas Erpingham and Sir Walter Hungerford, for example), former companions-in-arms in Wales (Hugh Mortimer), and employees of the duchies of Cornwall and Lancaster (such as John Waterton and John Leventhorpe). These were the men loyal both to the king and to the dynasty who helped to constitute the administrative groups upon whom Henry was to count. The resulting continuity among the personnel who served during the reign, itself a reflection of their devotion to their monarch, underpinned the stability of government upon which the good of the country, whose king was abroad for more than half his reign, depended. Yet, as his surviving correspondence indicates, Henry never lost touch with events and affairs in England, and his direct influence was often felt by those acting there on his behalf.

The start of the French war, 1414–1415 It was in France, however, that Henry was to earn his lasting reputation, and in the spring of 1414 that there appeared the first public references to the claims to France which were to constitute the driving theme of his reign. The French king, Charles VI (d. 1422), who had ruled since 1380, had long suffered from a mental disorder which frequently incapacitated

him. His power, and that of the crown, was exercised by royal princes whose rivalries, as Henry well recognized, caused deep divisions within the country. While the court was at Leicester, ambassadors from Burgundy were received, and Henry accredited envoys to make their first visit to the French king to stake his claim, if not to the crown of France, at least to territories which were either regarded as historically English, or as more recently ceded to Edward III in 1360 by the terms of the treaty of Brétigny; they were also to demand the hand of *Catherine of Valois (1401–1437), Charles VI's youngest daughter, in marriage, as well as a substantial dowry. These attempts to secure what he sought having failed, Henry was obliged to think of war, the likelihood of which was announced to parliament in November 1414, and preparations for which began not long afterwards. Neither last minute attempts to head off an invasion made by French ambassadors, who brought Henry and his nobility the dauphin's gift of a box of tennis balls 'be-cause he schulde have sumwhat to play with-alle, for hym & for his lordes' (Brut, 2.374), nor an alleged plot against his life (said to have been backed by French gold) by Richard, earl of Cambridge, Henry, Lord Scrope, and Sir Thomas Grey of Heaton, by which Edmund (V) Mortimer, earl of March (d. 1425), would be made king, prevented Henry from sailing for France, where he and his army came ashore on 14 August near the well-defended town of Harfleur, on the northern shore of the Seine estuary.

Henry's army, transported in a fleet of some 1500 vessels, probably consisted of about 10,500 fighting men, with a large attendant force. Within a few days Harfleur was surrounded by the army and blockaded from the sea. The use of artillery, prominent in the eyewitness account left by the anonymous author of the *Gesta Henrici quinti*, undoubtedly made its mark; the dauphin's tennis balls, metamorphosed into 'harde & grete gune-stonys, for the Dolfyn to play with-alle' (*Brut*, 2.375) were now being used against his own people, who were to regret deeply the insult thrown at the king of England. In spite of strong resistance, Harfleur finally agreed to surrender on 22 September. Faced with the problem of what to do next, Henry decided to leave a large garrison to defend his recent conquest, ship home the considerable numbers who had fallen sick, and march with the remainder to Calais. It is likely that the army which set out with him on 8 October numbered some 6000 or so fighting men.

The battle of Agincourt, 1415 The story of their 'long march' is one of an already weary force, courageously yet fearfully advancing in a generally north-easterly direction, harassed by the enemy and in constant need of having its morale raised, being urged to greater effort by the exhortation and example of Henry himself. After a little over two weeks it became apparent that an encounter with a French army, long threatened and feared, could not be avoided. On 25 October, the feast day of Sts Crispin and Crispinian, the battle took place close to the village of Agincourt, where the French army had grouped itself. On the basis of superior numbers alone the French should have been the easy victors; their confidence, according to

English sources, contrasted with the want of it in the English army. The French, however, lacked cohesion, self-discipline, and a single command, while the English had the advantage of an inspired leader in the person of their king, and superiority in the weapon which was to count, the longbow. Furthermore, luck was with them. On the night before the battle rain fell, making the recently ploughed field that separated the two armies very soft. When, on the next day, Henry, having reminded his men that they fought for a just cause and that England was at that moment praying for them, enticed the enemy into an attack, the French were hindered by the softness of the ground underfoot. Their numbers, far from presenting them with an advantage, worked against them when they came under the heavy and disciplined fire of the English archers. Wounded or killed, certainly scared by the hail of arrows, the men in the French ranks tried to turn or break out, causing disorder among those who followed. Confidence soon turned to panic, and large numbers of French were killed by the English archers, who, having run out of arrows, joined in the hand-to-hand fighting against an enemy rapidly becoming demoralized by the turn of events. For only a brief while did it seem that a relieving force (if it was that) might deny the English their hard-earned victory. At that moment, Henry appears to have ordered that the French prisoners, who now constituted a threat, should be killed. Many undoubtedly suffered death; but whether the massacre was as complete as has been claimed is open to doubt.

Henry and his army continued the next day, and arrived in Calais on 29 October. On 16 November the king crossed to Dover and then proceeded to the city of London, which he entered on 23 November to much rejoicing and a formal reception which bore resemblance to contemporary French royal *entrées*, and which was clearly intended as a major publicity exercise. Entering into the spirit of the moment, parliament had recently awarded Henry a vote of tunnage and poundage for life, along with other taxes. Having ruled for little more than two and a half years, the king was already very much master of his kingdom.

Diplomatic activity, 1415–1417 Outwardly the next eighteen months, until the summer of 1417, appear to have constituted a period of relative calm. They none the less witnessed considerable activity. It was important that the military (and psychological) success achieved in 1415 be built upon, so that the initiative gained would not be lost. Three parliaments met between November 1415 and October 1416, to be confronted by increasingly heavy demands for financial support. In spite of this, the provision thus made appears to have been insufficient, as first the practice of bringing forward the date at which a tax was due was tried, and then, as this measure proved increasingly unpopular, the alternative one of seeking loans (thereby obtaining extra money quickly), guaranteed by a specific proportion of a future subsidy, was developed. At the start of April 1416, Sigismund, king of the Romans (d. 1437), began a visit to England, hoping both to enlist Henry's support for measures to end the schism then dividing the church, and to help achieve peace between England and France. In these months Harfleur lay at the centre of the dispute between the two countries. Militarily its position was becoming increasingly difficult to maintain, due to a land and sea blockade imposed by the French and their allies, including the Genoese, whose ships were being made available to the French. Diplomatically, too, Harfleur was at the centre of negotiations which were taking place throughout the summer and early autumn. To help him, Henry needed the support of his 'superillustrious' guest whom, along with a sizeable retinue, he entertained for several months, and upon whom he conferred membership of the Order of the Garter at a ceremony held at Windsor towards the end of May. On 15 August, at Canterbury, Henry sealed a treaty of mutual assistance with Sigismund—in all appearance a success for English powers of persuasion; in reality the general nature of the treaty's terms would make it very difficult to enforce. On the same day Henry's brother, John, duke of Bedford, in charge of a fleet, successfully broke the enemy's stranglehold upon Harfleur by either destroying or capturing the Franco-Genoese ships blockading the port. Another major success against the French, this time a victory at sea, had been recorded.

Shortly afterwards, on 4 September, Henry sailed to Calais, where Sigismund had already gone, for a final attempt to reach a settlement with the French ambassadors who had come there. If little came out of these discussions, the occasion gave Henry the chance to meet John the Fearless, duke of Burgundy, for a number of secret meetings. In the end, however, the talks only increased the sense of suspicion, among both French and English, that Burgundy, whatever he said or did, 'would be found a double-dealer, one person in public and another in private' (*Gesta Henrici quinti*, 175) and, therefore, not to be trusted. It is clear that, whether he had or had not made any secret plans with Burgundy for war against France, it was in the latter country that Henry was now determined to pursue England's destiny. In October 1416 he told parliament that, since negotiations had failed, he would resort to war, for which he was granted a double subsidy. Preparations now went ahead for another expedition which would be launched in the coming summer.

The conquest of Normandy, 1417–1419 On what came to be known in France as 'la journée de Touques', 1 August 1417, Henry landed on the southern shore of the Seine estuary, opposite Harfleur. He had with him an army of some 10,500 men, including rather more archers, in relation to the total size of the army, than had been the case two years earlier. In 1418 a further 2000 or so men were dispatched to supplement those already in France. Henry's new plan, while it could build upon earlier achievements, differed from them in a fundamental sense. The failure to secure his aims by means of diplomatic pressure had led inexorably to the decision to use the only available alternative, physical conquest, to win and secure the lands to which he laid claim. His methods had to live up his aims. Ever since the English had attacked France in the previous century, towns had built walls to defend themselves. Such a one was Caen, the second town of the duchy of Normandy, where William I was buried in the abbey he had founded there. It was no coincidence that Henry should have brought with him several cannon with which to beat down the walls and other defences of those places which, because they were fortified and might resist him, he would have to capture in order to make his conquest effective and permanent.

Upon landing Henry advanced directly to begin the siege of Caen which, heavily invested, fell on 4 September, although the castle defied him for about a fortnight longer. Then, striking south, he was soon on the frontier of Normandy, seeking to capture those places controlling the area through which help against him might come. During the winter and the spring which followed, the army, under either Henry's command or that of one of his most able lieutenants, Richard Beauchamp, earl of Warwick, was at work capturing towns such as Alençon, Falaise, and Domfront, while the king's youngest brother, Humphrey, duke of Gloucester, was left to starve Cherbourg into surrender, a task finally completed, after a five-month siege, at Michaelmas 1418. In the meantime, having spent much of the spring in Caen setting up the administration of his newly won territory, Henry once again took charge of the army, leading it in an easterly direction. On 20 July Pont-de-l'Arche, a few miles above Rouen on the River Seine, was taken; in this way the Norman capital was effectively cut off from any help coming downriver from the direction of Paris, a point emphasized when a great iron chain was drawn across the river to prevent boats from approaching Rouen. On 31 July the siege began.

It was to last five and a half months. By cutting off access by river to the beleaguered city Henry made the task of successful resistance virtually impossible. By Christmas 1418 conditions within Rouen were becoming desperate; the largely civilian population was suffering from every form of deprivation, and the ditch harboured many who, to save food, had been driven outside the city's walls. Such action was bound to cause divisions among the besieged. At the new year (1419) the majority called upon Henry to treat; after much difficulty his negotiators agreed terms. Rouen was to pay a huge fine of 300,000 crowns (the equivalent of £50,000, it was still being paid off a dozen years later), and a new, fortified, palace was to be built by the Seine. In return, those who recognized Henry as their liege lord were to have their property rights and commercial privileges restored. On 19 January the city formally surrendered, and on the next day Henry entered to give thanks in the cathedral. He also took possession of the castle, the holder of whose keep was traditionally regarded as duke of Normandy.

The alliance with Burgundy and the treaty of Troyes, 1419–1420

The end had finally occurred because no rescue came (taken as evidence of the divisions among the French), and because Henry had had the time, the determination, and the resources to bring about the city's fall. During the late autumn he had been in negotiation with both French parties—the Burgundians and their rivals, the dauphinists; if he had secured no immediate advantage, he had none the less maintained the divisions between them. Working from his new capital Henry now concentrated his attention on two matters: administration and the furthering of his political aims through diplomacy. It was in these months that he continued the process, already begun less than a year earlier in Caen, of rebuilding the structures of Norman government and of appointing new personnel who would be loyal to him. Later, as he had already done in Caen, he was to make many grants of estates both to his English followers and to Normans whom he wished to reward and encourage, a policy which stamped something of the character of a political settlement upon the lands which he had conquered. Looking ahead he also pursued his aim of dividing the opposition yet further by diplomatic means, attempting to negotiate first with one party, then with the other. Having failed to make contact with the dauphin at Évreux in late March 1419, two months later Henry and the leading members of his court came together with the duke of Burgundy, Isabella, queen of France, and her daughter, Catherine (King Charles being absent on account of his disorder) near Meulan, for a series of eight formal meetings which extended well into June. Henry restated his demand for Catherine's hand, along with his territorial claims to the lands ceded at Brétigny, the duchy of Normandy, and the lands so far conquered, all to be held in full sovereignty; his claim to the French crown could rest. The negotiations, however, were doomed to failure when the French had second thoughts about the concessions which Henry was demanding. Furthermore, a *rapprochement* between Burgundy and the dauphinists was in the making, an agreement to unite to expel the English invader (thereby, among other things, saving the capital, Paris, from the dangers of the enemy army now working its way up the Seine valley towards it) being made at Pouilly on 11 July. On 30 July Henry sent Gaston de Foix and the earl of Huntingdon to capture Pontoise, a strategic town on the road from Rouen to Paris close to where the River Oise converges with the Seine. The daring dawn raid was successful, and a few days later Henry's brother the duke of Clarence was on a reconnoitre at the gates of Paris itself. The French capital was now directly threatened.

From the French viewpoint, the future would clearly be difficult. One reason was the evident lack of trust existing among the French themselves. This was made plain when, on 10 September, John of Burgundy was murdered in the very presence, and possibly with the full connivance, of the dauphin, Charles, at Montereau. If John had played a double game with Henry, his heir, Philip the Good, duke of Burgundy, drew the Burgundians towards the English side, a move of which Henry was to take full advantage. On 27 September his ambassadors informed the French royal council of his intention to seek the crown and kingdom of France, as well as the hand of Catherine in marriage. By 2 December, following negotiations, Duke Philip was ready to accept a peace to be made between England and France, a marriage between Henry and Catherine, and the eventual succession of their children to the French throne. On Christmas eve a general truce, excluding the dauphin, was sealed at Rouen. Over the coming months the text of a broad agreement was gradually put together, and on 5 May Henry pronounced himself satisfied. What would become the treaty of Troyes was ready to be ratified. By this time Henry was already on his way from Rouen to Troyes, travelling by way of Pontoise, St Denis, Charenton, and Provins. He reached Troyes on 20 May, and on the next day the treaty was formally sealed before a distinguished gathering. Henry was to marry Catherine and be recognized as heir to the French throne until the death of his father-in-law, Charles VI, when he would inherit the crown of France. In the meanwhile, he was to act as regent, helped by a council of Frenchmen and observing existing French laws and customs. A number of clauses dealt with problems arising from the recent years of conflict. Normandy, now separate, was to be united to form part of the French kingdom when Henry became king, while other problems arising out of disputed landholding were also to be resolved. Henry undertook to use every possible means to bring all parts of France to recognize the treaty which had thus been forged. It was hoped that his marriage to Catherine, solemnized at Troyes on 2 June, would help to further that process.

Renewed warfare in France, 1420–1422 Yet the fighting was still far from over. Many would not accept the treaty's basic clauses regarding the succession, a fact which increased the determination of the supporters of the dauphin, now disinherited in favour of his brother-in-law, the king of England, to fight on as the supporters of the 'legitimate' France. Henry saw the urgent need to move against them, in particular against the hold which they exercised over a number of well-fortified towns in the upper reaches of the Seine and its tributaries. Two days after his marriage, accompanied by Burgundy, Henry set out to besiege Sens, which fell by 10 June. Montereau opposed him rather longer, but it capitulated on 1 July. Next was Melun where the resistance, encouraged by some Scots, lasted for about four months, until mid-November. On 1 December Henry entered Paris to a show of public rejoicing. A week later, at a meeting of the estates of France (those parts outside Normandy which accepted the legality of English rule), the terms of the treaty of Troyes were ratified and urgent currency reforms were enacted. On 23 December, at a *lit de justice*, the dauphin, having failed to appear to answer the charges against him arising from the murder of John of Burgundy, was declared incapable of inheriting the throne. By due process of law, it could be argued, Henry's position as heir, gained by treaty, had been confirmed by legal decision. It was as heir, although with something of the look of a conqueror, that he spent Christmas in Paris. It was now he, not the king of France, who claimed public attention.

A few days later Henry and Catherine left Paris for Rouen, where they spent a short time before setting out for England, which Henry had last seen at the end of July 1417, some three and a half years earlier. He landed at Dover on 1 February 1421 and went ahead to London to supervise arrangements for the coming coronation of his queen. Catherine herself arrived on 21 February, to be greeted with a fine reception, and was formally crowned at Westminster, probably two days later. Soon afterwards the royal couple set out on separate tours of England: Henry visited Bristol, Hereford, and Shrewsbury, then Kenilworth (a favourite residence of his early years), Coventry and Leicester (where his mother was buried), at which point Catherine rejoined him. Together they visited Nottingham and York, after which Henry made pilgrimages to the shrines at Beverley and Bridlington. Shortly afterwards, news was brought to him that his brother Thomas, duke of Clarence, whom he had left in charge of affairs in France, had been killed on 22 March at Baugé, in Anjou, in an encounter with a Franco-Scottish force. Contemporaries recorded Henry's grief on hearing the news, which he was later said to have borne manfully. While the defeat can now be seen not to have been a serious military setback, it was none the less the first defeat suffered by the English since Henry had invaded France. It tends to show how much English successes depended upon the leadership of the king himself.

Henry met parliament (the last time, as it turned out, that he would do so) at the beginning of May, but was sensible enough, in the difficult economic conditions then prevailing, not to seek a subsidy, although the clergy of the southern province, meeting in convocation, voted him a tenth. In the meantime he had to make do with loans—two separate ones amounting to £17,666 from Henry Beaufort, bishop of Winchester, and many very much smaller ones from both individuals and corporations. At the same time he met representatives of the Benedictine order to urge reform upon them. Then, returning to France, he landed at Calais on 10 June, with an army of some 4000–5000 men who had been recruited during the past weeks. Making his way southwards he visited Paris, which he had left in the charge of his uncle Thomas Beaufort, before leading much of his force towards Chartres (to whose cathedral he went on pilgrimage) and then on to the line of the Loire. From there he returned in a north-easterly direction, through the Gâtinais, towards the River Yonne, and thence back to Paris. He had made up his mind that the heavily fortified town of Meaux, some 30 miles due east of Paris, then held by the dauphinist enemy, should be made to submit; the well-being and security of Paris and its region demanded this. Henry took charge of the operation himself, assisted by some notable English commanders and an army of about 2500 men. Since the siege began about 6 October 1421, Henry must have been ready to experience the rigours of warfare in winter, as he had done before at Falaise and Rouen. Yet he may not have foreseen the degree of resistance which he would meet. It was not until seven months later, on 11 May 1422, that the garrison of the Marché at Meaux finally surrendered. This may have been a considerable success for Henry, but the appalling conditions which he endured made him and his army pay heavily for their success. In terms of manpower, declining morale, and money, it was proving increasingly costly to bring France to recognize the legitimacy of the treaty of Troyes.

Illness and death, 1421–1422 At the end of May Henry was joined by his queen who did not, however, bring with her the baby, also called *Henry, to whom she had given birth at Windsor on 6 December 1421. Henry would never see his son and heir who, unlike his father, would one day bear the title 'king of France'. Together with the French court, the royal couple went to rest at Senlis. It was while they were there that the first signs of illness came over Henry. Called upon by Philip of Burgundy to give him assistance before Cosne, on the upper Loire, Henry set out, but did not get far. It soon became evident that he could not ride, and he was taken in a litter to the royal castle of Vincennes, south-east of Paris. There his illness, perhaps dysentery, more likely one of fluid loss, began to overcome him. He had already made a will on 24 July 1415, and had added a codicil (sometimes called a will) on 21 July 1417, and perhaps a further one on 9 June 1421. On 10 June he had drawn up his second will in which he expressed his wishes regarding his burial and the monument he wanted erected, his funeral, and the masses to be said for his soul. Legacies were made to his monastic foundations, to his queen, his brothers, uncles, and to many others. His executors were also named. On 26 August 1422, realizing that he was now very near to death, he added a final codicil making further legacies to his queen and leaving the guardianship and protection (*tutela et defensio*) of his son to his brother Humphrey, while to Thomas Beaufort was given the personal care (*regimen et gubernatio*) of the boy and the choice of his servants. Arrangements were also made for the rule of France to be bequeathed to Philip of Burgundy, or, should he decline the responsibility, to John, duke of Bedford.

On 31 August 1422, in a room at the royal castle at Vincennes, near Paris, Henry died a pious and edifying death, a reflection of the deeply religious man that he was. After his death Henry's body, accompanied by his widow, was taken by river to Rouen, then overland to Calais, before being conveyed to Dover and, finally, to London. On 7 November he was buried at Westminster Abbey 'with grete solempnite' in a ceremony of rich symbolism. His tomb, made of Purbeck marble, was to be sited at the east end of the chapel of St Edward the Confessor, and it was here that a wooden figure, covered in silver gilt, with head and hands of solid silver, was placed, at the expense of his queen, by 1431. Later, probably about 1450, a large chantry chapel was erected and completed on the orders of his executors. The figure was robbed of its metal in 1545, and was not restored until 1971, and even then not fully. The remains of Queen Catherine, who married Owen Tudor and died in 1437, were placed in Henry's chantry chapel in 1878.

Overall achievements Military heroes no longer enjoy the popularity they once did; there exists a reluctance to acclaim what many see as an attempt to satisfy personal ambition vindicated under the guise of the 'just war' theory. Not unnaturally recent scholarship has tended to move the emphasis away from the war against France. Even among his contemporaries Henry's reputation rested on something else—the benefits of firm rule that his countrymen felt they had lacked for many years. So it has come about that, in the late twentieth century, it is the study of what Henry accomplished as king of England that has commanded increasing interest, thus making it possible to form a more widely based judgement of his achievement.

Henry impressed his contemporaries not only by his victory in 1415 and the consequent campaigns of conquest; the speed of his achievement was also regarded as out of the ordinary. Traditionally his success has been attributed in large measure to his skill as a strategist and to his undoubted qualities as a leader in facing both the immediate dangers of the battlefield and, more frequently, the difficulties of a commander besieging a town or castle. His gifts of decisiveness and firm action, his love of order, and his unwillingness to show favour to anyone, earned him the highest respect. Here was a man who knew what he was doing and could inspire others to follow him. So much can be gleaned from the chronicles; the study of administrative records often confirms what the chronicles only hint at. For example, both sources stress how Henry relied upon careful preparations for his campaigns, an enormous task without which he would probably not have achieved the successes which eventually came his way. Furthermore, like none before, he understood the role that the sea might play in his wars. The thirty-six or so ships which he came to own played no decisive part in the conflict; but his recognition of the importance of patrolling the channel, thus securing for himself almost unimpeded access, by sea and then by river, deep into Normandy for the siege of Rouen, was the result of his clear appreciation of the enabling and supportive role that ships could play, even when the action was taking place some distance from the sea itself.

Religious policy In what constitutes something of a political manifesto, the author of the *Gesta Henrici quinti* set out Henry's aims as king thus: 'to promote the honour of God, the extension of the Church, the deliverance of his country and the peace and tranquility of kingdoms' (*Gesta Henrici quinti*, 3). In all these the personal role of Henry as king was to be of the greatest significance. God was to be honoured and his church extended through royal action. It was to God that victories in war, notably that at Agincourt, were attributed, and to him that thanks were given. It was for God's greater glory that Henry founded three monasteries, one each for the Carthusian, the Bridgettine, and the Celestine orders, on the Thames above London, of which only the first two, however, were to prove successful. It was to the same end that he met representatives of the Benedictine order in May 1421 to urge reform upon them. In all these the deeply religious nature of the king's character and his concern for current ecclesiastical issues become evident. The steps which Henry took against the Lollards showed him as the champion of God's church against heretics, the defender, too, of the established social order and the rule of law. At the international level Henry contributed towards freeing the church from the shackles of division and schism, through the role that the English delegation and Bishop Henry Beaufort played at the Council of Constance in bringing about the election of Pope Martin V in November 1417. But in his dealings with the new pope Henry was to be firm, resisting papal attempts to reassert its authority over the church in England. By the end of the reign, it may be argued, it was the crown which exercised the greatest single influence over the ecclesiastical affairs of England.

Political agenda Peace and stability at home were a high priority, as the statements made to parliament by Henry's two chancellors, Henry Beaufort and Thomas Langley, make clear. Peace could mean a number of different things. It could include the settling of differences between the king's subjects. The tale is told of two north-country gentry, whose quarrels were causing breaches of the peace, who were summoned into the royal presence as the king was going to dinner, to be told that if they were not reconciled 'be that tyme that he had etyn his owystrys, they shulde be hangyd bothe two [bef]or evyr he sopyt'. Faced with this ultimatum the two responded at once, 'and so, aftyr that, ther durst no lorde make no party nor stryf; and thus he beganne to kepe his lawis and Iustise, & therfor he was belouyd & bedred' (*Brut*, 2.595–6). In addition, new laws, such as the statute against Lollards (1414), were enacted to guard the country against the perceived dangers of that sect, while the Statute of Treasons (1414) was planned with a view to protecting commerce at sea and encouraging trade. This last measure, it must be admitted, was generally far from successful. Stability, too, might be achieved through the attempts made to restore a currency which, in spite of a revaluation carried out in 1411, was not maintained at a proper level. In England, and even more so in Normandy, Henry was successful in restoring a coinage which won confidence, even if the remedy was at times painful to bear.

Henry's intention of providing effective government depended, in no small measure, upon his ability to unite the country behind him. His success in achieving this derived from a number of factors. He knew how to appeal to popular opinion, and how to win it. A study of the addresses made to parliament by his chancellors, particularly the influential Henry Beaufort, indicates the skilful approach of the court to the matter of mixing information and exhortation when relations with the king's subjects required it. Henry's entry into London, after the success won at Agincourt (the occasion when those at home had prayed for England while the king and his soldiers had fought for her) was an attempt to involve the city, which had made generous financial provision, in the celebration of victory. In 1417, and again in 1421, Henry visited London and other parts of his kingdom to rally support for his plans. The need for harmony between those holding responsibilities in government is underlined by the fact that Henry kept on the best of terms with those who worked close to him, changes of personnel at court being relatively infrequent. Past differences between himself and his brother Thomas never seem to have overtly resurfaced after Henry's accession to the throne. His relations with his other brothers, John and Humphrey, both of whom enjoyed his trust to a high degree, were excellent.

Henry Beaufort's one misjudgement, that of accepting a cardinal's hat in 1417, was dealt with so discreetly that the episode remained a secret until modern times, while Thomas Beaufort was among Henry's most constantly loyal supporters. The assistance he received from the nobility, especially those whose fathers had quarrelled with his father, is a notable mark of the spirit of reconciliation which Henry encouraged and inspired. The result was that, by contrast with France, England could face her enemy united behind her king.

Henry's invasions of France have been termed 'unprovoked and unjustifiable' (*DNB*, 9.505). If the first judgement may stand (although it should not be forgotten that the capture of Harfleur was planned to end its use as a base by those who attacked English commerce at sea), the second should not. Henry was not alone in his generation to use history to justify or encourage a particular policy, such as an attack upon a neighbour's territory. Moreover, since the French had not fulfilled the obligations which they had entered into at Brétigny in 1360, Henry had a claim which, it was argued, he should pursue. It was incumbent upon him to do what was necessary to fulfil it. Yet what his exact aim was is debatable. He certainly modified his claim as time went on, and in September 1419 he might have been satisfied with Normandy and the surrounding *pays de conquête*. However, the murder of John of Burgundy changed all that: the chance to win the crown of France was too good to miss. The result would be the treaty of Troyes and the political settlement which it incorporated. In spite of the difficulties that arose in the last two years of the reign and later, it should not be assumed that the treaty constituted a political arrangement which had little or no hope of lasting. Nor was it simply optimism or arrogance that made the English call it the 'final' peace. The settlement of Englishmen in France, a settlement based upon grants of lands and titles and, in some cases, corresponding military obligations, as well as the establishment of reasonably effective rule in Normandy (reflected, albeit grudgingly, by the anonymous author of the 'Parisian journal' and the so-called Religieux de St Denis) accorded a certain sense of stability to the English presence in France, in spite of Henry's difficulties in raising sufficient soldiers to fight for him. Neither in 1422 nor for some years to come would there be serious doubts whether the settlement sealed at Troyes would last. It needed the exploits of Jeanne d'Arc to begin the long process that would finally destroy it.

Personal characteristics The image of the king who achieved this has survived in a portrait, attributed to about 1520, a copy of an earlier work showing a man in his middle to late twenties, with thick brown hair, a long, straight nose, his eyes oval-shaped, and with distinctive lips and ears. Two other small portraits give prominence to Henry's lean face and long nose. His physical characteristics are described in three Latin texts, one probably written by a member of his court, two some years later. Even while making allowance for the element of idealism inherent in such descriptions, the main elements complement what is found in the portraits: the thick hair, the smooth brow, the straight nose, the long face, the sparkling eyes which, when angry, could instil fear as might those of a lion, together with the well-proportioned body. The later descriptions, particularly that by Tito Livio dei Frulovisi, emphasized the king's above average height, his long neck, and graceful body, and his ability to outrun all others, a characteristic befitting one who loved hunting.

Although his career was dominated by action, Henry was driven by other factors, too. To a French observer in 1415 he resembled more a priest than a soldier, perhaps a reference to his well-known piety, perhaps to the sense of calm and order which he radiated. It is noticeable that, in times of crises, even when angry, he would not be panicked; confidence in God and in his own cause motivated him strongly. The chronicles convey his deep sense of justice, his insistence on the correctness of his course of action. As was appropriate for the elder brother of two notable collectors and patrons, John and Humphrey, Henry was also a person with a sympathetic understanding of artists and scholars, a well-read man of traditional literary tastes, who read, wrote, and spoke both French and Latin. He encouraged Thomas Hoccleve and John Lydgate (d. 1451) to make translations into English for him. Furthermore he himself wrote good English, which he used in his signet letters to convey his personal wishes, the language being that of a man of decisive character accustomed to having his instructions carried out. These letters have an added significance in the encouragement they gave to the development of the English language during Henry's reign. The acceptance of a 'King's English' must rank as a major cultural advance, in which the king himself played an important personal part.

Posthumous reputation Generally speaking, Henry's reputation has suffered very much less than that of many other kings, since it was deliberately created within his own lifetime and fostered by those who came soon after him. Contemporaries were presented with a figure who did great things because he acted as God's agent, refusing any personal credit for himself. The success won against the odds at Agincourt marked Henry out as an outstanding inspirer of men; it also reflected the fact that the king's cause was a good cause—that of justice. Thus launched, the tradition was to be developed, the emphasis being placed upon his military successes which, in 1437, were given full emphasis by Tito Livio dei Frulovisi whose *Vita Henrici quinti regis Angliae*, written at the request of Henry's youngest brother, Humphrey, was to be used to encourage the policy of continued military intervention in France that he then favoured. From then on Henry became the great soldier, 'the myghty and puissaunt conquerour' whose achievements against the French, transformed into the Catholic enemy, Shakespeare was to praise in 1599 in his *Henry V*.

Change came in the early eighteenth century when, in 1704, Thomas Goodwin published a long life that, while eschewing neither tradition nor a tendency to moralize, made good use of documents of which many have since disappeared. The history of Henry's modern historical

reputation may be said to have originated in 1878 with William Stubbs, who praised him as 'by far the greatest king in Christendom', in whom 'the dying energies of medieval life kindle[d] for a short moment into flame' (Stubbs, 3.95–6), a view reflected in the subtitle, 'the typical medieval hero', given to the biography of him written by C. L. Kingsford, but borrowed directly from Stubbs (p. 77). Of the co-authors of the three-volume study of Henry's reign published between 1914 and 1929, the elder, J. H. Wylie, was less an interpretative historian than a gentleman–scholar, turned inspector of schools, who loved to collect historical material, it being left to the younger, W. T. Waugh, a representative of the new breed of academic historian whose judgements and opinions still merit very close consideration today, to complete the work on Wylie's death. After the Second World War, it was hardly surprising that the French historian Édouard Perroy, although a good friend of England, should have judged Henry's 'achievement' to be inimical to the interests of his country. In England historical judgements continued to differ or, at least, to reflect different nuances. K. B. McFarlane, in a lecture delivered in 1954, expressed the carefully worded opinion that Henry was 'the greatest man that ever ruled England' (McFarlane, 133), while in 1961 E. F. Jacob, who also admired much of Henry's personality and achievement, none the less wrote that 'in the last analysis [he] was an adventurer, not a statesman' (Jacob, *Fifteenth Century*, 202). Today the academic emphasis is more on the breadth and totality of Henry V's achievement, the record of which 'is sufficient to establish him as a great king' (Harriss, *Henry V*, 1985, 201). More generally, however, Henry remains best known through the two film versions of Shakespeare's play: the first, made by Laurence Olivier (1944), in which the king appears as a virile man of action; the second, that of Kenneth Branagh (1991), which places greater emphasis on the physical exertions of those who fought in the war that Henry had begun to further his cause.

The overriding impression left by Henry V is of a man of order, toughness, determination, and tireless energy, firm (sometimes even harsh) in his dealings with others, perhaps a man of relatively few words. Admired even by his enemies for his public virtues of honour and chivalry, and not least for the effectiveness of the discipline that he exercised over his soldiers, he was a man whom all could respect. Those who worked closely with him were inspired by something more—real devotion and loyalty, and a feeling that they were serving a remarkable man. Such was Henry's legacy, destined to become part of his legend which still has a powerful influence in our own day.

C. T. ALLMAND

Sources F. Taylor and J. S. Roskell, eds. and trans., *Gesta Henrici quinti / The deeds of Henry the Fifth*, OMT (1975) • F. W. D. Brie, ed., *The Brut, or, The chronicles of England*, 2 vols., EETS, 131, 136 (1906–8), vol. 2 • *First English life of Henry the Fifth*, ed. C. L. Kingsford (1911) • T. Walsingham, *The St Albans chronicle, 1406–1420*, ed. V. H. Galbraith (1937) • C. A. Cole, ed., *Memorials of Henry the Fifth, king of England*, Rolls Series, 11 (1858) • *Titi Livii Foro–Juliensis vita Henrici quinti*, ed. T. Hearne (1716) • *Thomae de Elmham Vita et gesta Henrici Quinti*,

Anglorum regis, ed. T. Hearne (1727) · 'The chronicle of John Strecche for the reign of Henry V, 1414–1422', ed. F. Taylor, *Bulletin of the John Rylands University Library*, 16 (1932), 137–87 · L. Bellaguet, ed. and trans., *Chronique du religieux de Saint-Denys*, 2 (Paris, 1840) · *A Parisian journal, 1405–1449*, trans. J. Shirley (1968) · J. H. Fisher, M. Richardson, and J. L. Fisher, eds., *Anthology of chancery English* (1984) · *Hoccleve's works*, ed. F. J. Furnivall, 3: *The regement of princes*, EETS, extra ser. 72 (1897) · [T. Goodwin], *The history of the reign of Henry the Fifth* (1704) · C. T. Allmand, *Henry V* (1968) · C. Allmand, *Henry V* (1992); new edn (1997) · G. L. Harriss, ed., *Henry V: the practice of kingship* (1985); pbk edn (1993) · G. L. Harriss, *Cardinal Beaufort: a study of Lancastrian ascendancy and decline* (1988) · K. B. McFarlane, *Lancastrian kings and Lollard knights* (1972) · E. F. Jacob, *Henry V and the invasion of France* (1947) · E. F. Jacob, *The fifteenth century, 1399–1485* (1961) · *DNB* · C. L. Kingsford, *Henry V: the typical medieval hero* (1901) · J. H. Wylie and W. T. Waugh, eds., *The reign of Henry the Fifth*, 3 vols. (1914–29) · E. Powell, *Kingship, law, and society: criminal justice in the reign of Henry V* (1989) · R. A. Newhall, *The English conquest of Normandy, 1416–1424: a study in fifteenth-century warfare* (1924) · E. Perroy, *The Hundred Years War*, trans. W. B. Wells (1951) [Fr. orig., *La guerre de cent ans* (1945)] · P. Strong and F. Strong, 'The last will and codicils of Henry V', *EngHR*, 96 (1981), 79–102 · A. Curry, 'Lancastrian Normandy: the jewel in the crown?', *England and Normandy in the middle ages*, ed. D. Bates and A. Curry (1994), 234–52 · A. Gransden, *Historical writing in England*, 2 (1982) · P. J. Bradley, 'Henry V's Scottish policy: a study in realpolitik', *Documenting the past: essays in medieval history presented to George Peddy Cuttino*, ed. J. S. Hamilton and P. J. Bradley (1989), 177–95 · R. A. Griffiths, 'Wales and the marches', *Fifteenth-century England, 1399–1509*, ed. S. B. Chrimes, C. D. Ross, and R. A. Griffiths (1972), 145–72 · J. L. Kirby, *Henry IV of England* (1970) · R. Vaughan, *John the Fearless* (1966) · R. Vaughan, *Philip the Good: the apogee of Burgundy* (1970) · K. H. Vickers, *Humphrey duke of Gloucester: a biography* (1907) · E. C. Williams, *My lord of Bedford, 1389–1435* (1963) · W. Stubbs, *The constitutional history of England in its origin and development*, 3 (1878) · *RotP* · P. Strohm, *England's empty throne: usurpation and the language of legitimation, 1399–1422* (1998)

Archives Archives Nationales, Paris · Bibliothèque Nationale, Paris · BL, Cotton MS Vespasian F.iii, fol. 8 · BL · PRO **Likenesses** stone statue, 15th cent. (choir screen), York Minster; repro. in *Henry V: the practice of Kingship*, 1985 edn only, ed. Harriss, cover · portrait, *c*.1421, CCC Cam., MS 213; for John de Galopes, trans. of Cardinal Bonaventura, 'Vita Christi', 1421? · portrait, *c*.1430, BL, Cotton MS Julius E.iv, fol. 17v; repro. in S. B. Chrimes, *Lancastrians, Yorkists and Henry VII* (1964) · stained-glass window, *c*.1440–1450, All Souls Oxf. · oils, *c*.1600, NPG · manuscript illumination, Bodl. Oxf., MS Digby 232, fol. 1; *see illus. in* Lydgate, John (*c*.1370–1449/50?) · oils, Royal Collection [*see illus.*] · oils, Eton; repro. in M. W. Labarge, *Henry V* (1975) · oils, Queen's College, Oxford · portrait, BL, Arundel MS 38, fol. 37; repro. in F. Hepburn, *Portraits of the later Plantagenets* (1986)

Henry VI (1421–1471), king of England and lord of Ireland, and duke of Aquitaine, was born at Windsor Castle on the feast of St Nicholas (6 December) 1421, the only child of *Henry V (1386/7–1422) and *Catherine of Valois (1401–1437).

Infancy and accession, 1422 Henry's godfathers were two senior members of the house of Lancaster: the baby's great-uncle, Henry *Beaufort, bishop of Winchester, and Henry V's brother *John, duke of Bedford. Henry V never saw his only son, and his 21-year-old queen, Catherine of Valois, joined her husband in France five months after the birth. When she next saw her son, he was king of England, for Henry V died at Vincennes, near Paris, on 31 August 1422, leaving as his heir the nine-month-old baby. As he lay dying he added a codicil to his will which referred to his

Henry VI (1421–1471), by unknown artist, *c*.1540 (after earlier portrait)

son as prince of Wales, though no formal ceremony of creation was held. In accordance with the treaty of Troyes (1420), Henry VI was also heir to the kingdom of his mother's father, the elderly and insane Charles VI of France, who died two months later, on 21 October 1422. Within a generation of Henry IV's usurpation in 1399, a baby succeeded to the English throne and inherited awesome claims in France, without any suggestion that an adult prince should be preferred.

Henry IV's arrangements for the succession, declared in parliament in 1406, were followed to the letter, and Henry V's achievements, and the loyalty of his subjects, ensured that his son faced no rival. The new king's reign began on 1 September, the day after the day on which Henry V was alive and dead, a common practice (other than in 1327 and 1399) since Edward I's death that underlined the continuity of English kingship. Not since 1199 had a king of England died outside his realm, but Henry V's youngest brother, *Humphrey, duke of Gloucester, had been nominated keeper of the realm in May 1422 during the king's absence, and three senior ecclesiastics were on hand: Bishop Beaufort; Henry Chichele, archbishop of Canterbury, who ordered prayers on 25 September for Henry V's soul and for the health and prosperity of his successor; and Thomas Langley, bishop of Durham and chancellor of England, who arrived at Windsor from Yorkshire by 28 September. Within a month of Henry V's death decisions could be taken to inaugurate the new reign, despite the uncertain and tragic circumstances.

The accession of a baby created major problems: how

and by whom should Henry be brought up; and by whom should England and Lancastrian France be ruled during his long minority? Furthermore, Henry V's conquests in France were incomplete, and the 'dual monarchy' created by the treaty of Troyes placed unprecedented obligations on his successor. Practical responsibilities had to be shouldered by others in the king's name. Yet the dynasty and realm were stable enough to weather the longest minority in English history and historians (notably K. B. McFarlane) have been impressed by the loyalty and unity of the English noble and ecclesiastical élites after 1422.

The codicils of Henry V's will, dictated on 26 August 1422, outlined his preferred arrangements for his son's upbringing and custody. Gloucester, who was already in charge of England, was nominated as Henry VI's custodian and protector. According to those at Henry V's deathbed, he gave responsibility for English France to Bedford. These wishes were taken into account, but so too were Richard II's and Henry III's minorities in 1377 and 1216, and the expectations of the Lancastrian royal family. Royal relatives and respected soldiers, especially Thomas *Beaufort, duke of Exeter, Henry V's uncle, had care of the baby's welfare, with authority to appoint his servants, while nurses saw to his personal needs. Queen Catherine was at his side, and she held him when he attended parliament in 1423. As to the two realms, a compromise was reached which was generally acceptable, though Bedford and Gloucester had serious, but different, misgivings. At a meeting at Windsor on 28 September 1422 a small group of bishops and nobles left in England by Henry V did homage and swore fealty to Henry of Windsor (as the infant king was known), and reappointed royal officials. Further progress required wider consultation and parliament was summoned at the earliest opportunity. Intensive discussions followed the arrival, on 5 November, of nobles and bishops with Henry V's body, and on 9 November parliament opened. It was a further month before the compromise, which departed from Henry V's wishes, was ready.

Bedford and Gloucester and their two uncles, Exeter and Bishop Beaufort, were loyal but suspicious of one another and very ambitious, and each expected a place in the new regime. The outcome of discussions was a regency of English France for Bedford, and the novel constitutional device of a protectorate for England, with Gloucester as 'protector and defender of the realm and chief councillor for the king' (*RotP*, 4.174), so long as Bedford was abroad, and with a formally appointed council to serve during the king's minority. This may have been an appropriate division of responsibilities, but it did not avoid disputes between Bedford and Gloucester, or between Gloucester and Bishop Beaufort, who was assigned no special role other than that of councillor.

Childhood and the protectorate, 1423–1429 Henry VI lived with his mother during the 1420s. He was rarely taken far from the royal residences in the Thames valley—Windsor Castle, Hertford Castle, and Eltham—though occasionally he visited Woodstock, Kennington, and even Kenilworth, and he went on pilgrimage to Waltham Abbey and Bury St

Edmunds. On 23 April 1424 his nurses were joined by a senior governess, Dame Alice Boteler, who was charged with his early education in 'courtesy and nurture' (*Proceedings … of the Privy Council*, 3.143); she also had authority to chastise him without fearing the consequences. He was brought up in the company of noble royal wards, and a master was appointed to school them, according to Sir John Fortescue, in 'physical activity, behaviour and manners' (Fortescue, 110–11, 193).

A new phase in Henry's education opened in 1428 with the appointment of Richard Beauchamp, earl of Warwick, as his governor, tutor, and master, with a small establishment of knights and esquires of the body to provide a more structured training for the king. Warwick's role was to teach Henry 'good manners, letters and languages', as well as the nurture and courtesy that Dame Alice had instilled in him, all in the context of Christian virtue (*CPR, 1422–9*, 491–2). Warwick had authority to regulate access to the young king as the needs of state and the royal family dictated.

Henry seemed a healthy boy. In May 1423 it was reported to Bedford in France that he was in perfect health, and by March 1428 he was described as 'ser goon and growen in persone, in wit and understandyng' (*RotP*, 4.326–7). There is nothing to suggest that he was other than a normal, healthy child whose upbringing and education took place in an environment dominated by former members of Henry V's establishment who sought to nurture in his son the requisite kingly qualities.

In Henry's early years formal acts were performed in his presence and he was shown to his people on ceremonial occasions, for instance in London before the opening of parliament at Westminster in 1423. The rivalries among his uncles, especially Gloucester and Bishop Beaufort, can hardly have affected him personally, though in 1425–6 he was at their centre in a formal sense. He was brought to London in state in April 1425 for the opening of parliament and rode through the city on a horse; in November he was paraded through the city again, on his way back to Eltham, this time by the triumphant Gloucester after an ugly confrontation with the bishop's supporters. At Leicester Castle, where parliament met in February 1426, the feud in the royal family might have been more apparent to the boy, especially because Bedford returned from France to compose differences. Moreover, towards the end of the session, the authority of the king was emphasized when Bedford knighted his nephew, who then himself dubbed thirty-eight new knights. Yet the protectorate government had fair success in providing stable government and preserving order. Across the channel Henry V's war continued under Bedford's generalship, and several battles were won. Only in 1429, when Jeanne d'Arc's appearance sparked a revival of French morale and revived Charles VII's fortunes, did the tide turn against the English.

Henry's world changed dramatically in 1429. His mother had developed a relationship with Edmund Beaufort, count of Mortain, the bishop's nephew, and then with the Welsh squire, Owen Tudor, despite a statute of

1428–9 governing the future marriage of a queen dowager. By 1430 the king ceased to reside regularly with his mother. In France the French adopted a bolder strategy whose centrepiece was Charles VII's coronation at Rheims on 17 July 1429. This precipitated Henry's visit to France for his own coronation as king of the realm bequeathed to him by the treaty of Troyes. This meant that he should be crowned king of England first, and this was arranged at Westminster on 5 November 1429 when he was barely eight. This ceremony formally vested him with the powers of kingship which had been exercised in his name since 1 September 1422. The English monarchy had emerged from a difficult phase: despite personal tensions and disagreements among the élite, stability had been maintained at home and the military effort in France had been sustained.

English and French coronations, 1429–1432 The king's English coronation emphasized Henry VI's dual heritage as monarch of two realms. On the eve of the coronation he lodged in the Tower of London, where he followed tradition and created new knights, more than thirty of them. Next day his guardian and governor, Warwick, took him to Westminster Abbey where Bishop Beaufort, a cardinal since March 1426, sat on his right and Queen Catherine sat nearby. Archbishop Chichele anointed the young king with holy oil. Henry seems to have appreciated the significance of the occasion, for he reportedly looked round 'saddely and wysely' as the heavy crown was placed on his head ('Gregory's chronicle', 165). The coronation *ordo* was modified in the light of French practice, underlining the theocratic nature of Henry's kingship of both realms. Hurried though the arrangements had been, this coronation also marked the formal end of the protectorate, though others perforce continued to rule for him.

The English position in France was causing anxiety, especially after the failure before Orléans (1429) and Charles VII's coronation at Rheims, which owed much to Jeanne d'Arc's inspiration. Bedford responded with propaganda and military campaigns centred on the young King Henry and his dual monarchy, combined with blackening Jeanne's reputation before and after her execution at Rouen on 30 May 1431. The aim was to encourage the English forces in northern France, maintain the Anglo-Burgundian alliance, and reassert the agreements made at Troyes. More immediately, hard-pressed cities like Paris and Rouen had to be relieved. The results were less effective than was anticipated.

Henry's journey to France was his first outside his English realm. It required much planning: in April 1430, the royal entourage, more than 300 strong, crossed the channel with a large army; the king was accompanied by senior nobles, and the cost was prodigious. The exodus had implications for English government as well as for Lancastrian France. The company crossed to Calais in the last week of April, but the military situation in the Seine valley delayed Henry's arrival at Rouen until the last week of July. There he remained for over a year. Both Warwick, his governor, and Master John Somerset, his doctor and tutor, went with him.

French kings, including Charles VII, were traditionally crowned at Rheims, but despite the capture of Jeanne d'Arc in May 1430, and her subsequent burning, the military situation and expense prevented Henry from journeying to Paris, let alone Rheims, until December 1431. His coronation therefore took place in Notre-Dame on 16 December; it had a strong English flavour, with Cardinal Beaufort crowning the ten-year-old monarch. It was marred by a dispute between the canons of Notre-Dame and English courtiers, an invasion of the banqueting hall by Parisians, and the failure of 'Henri II' to distribute largesse. This French ceremony was hardly the propaganda coup that had been envisaged, for Henry and his entourage returned to the safety of Rouen in haste, and then on to Calais in the first week of January 1432. Henry VI never again visited France after returning to England at the beginning of February.

Some Lancastrian advisers remained worried about the future of English rule in France, and about the reliability of Burgundy; and Bedford showed signs of exhaustion and disillusion. Three days before Henry landed at Dover, the Burgundians concluded a truce with Charles VII which reflected the hollowness of the coronation spectacle. It was a turning point in the fortunes of Lancastrian France. Nevertheless, Henry VI made a solemn entry into London on 21 February, amid festivities and services of thanksgiving in St Paul's Cathedral and Westminster Abbey that celebrated his two crowns. The impression on the king himself may be imagined: contemporaries observed how well he endured the long and gruelling ceremonies, and he can hardly have failed to note the significance of the rituals and his part in them.

The king's adolescence, 1432–1436 The two coronations delayed a radical reappraisal of the situation in France. Most royal advisers were not ready to make peace with the French, and did not believe that anything more than a truce could properly be negotiated while Henry was a minor. In these circumstances, differences of view emerged about future strategy: Bedford wanted to defend Normandy, while Gloucester was committed to Calais, and Cardinal Beaufort inclined to peace. Negotiations were inconclusive, even at the Congress of Arras in the summer of 1435, when Beaufort was mediator. The English were unrealistic in their demands and concessions, and a few days after the congress ended in September, the duke of Burgundy deserted to Charles VII. This was a mortal blow to English sovereignty in France and Henry VI wept when given the news, evidently understanding its implications: years later, in 1456, he told Burgundian envoys that the duke had 'abandoned me in my boyhood, despite all his oaths to me, when I had never done him any wrong' (Wolffe, 83). Bedford, Henry V's effective successor in France, had died shortly before, on 15 September.

The end of the protectorate in November 1429 had few immediate consequences in England: although the status of Bedford and Gloucester was affected, the latter was designated the king's lieutenant while Henry was in France. These changes, and the situation in France, sharpened the tension between Gloucester and Cardinal Beaufort, and in the 1430s their differences over French policy, and their rivalry in the government of England before Henry's coming of age, were accentuated. Only Bedford, who returned to England in June 1433, seemed able to contain their mutual hostility when he acted temporarily as the king's chief councillor. Bedford's own handling of the war was criticized by Gloucester in the parliament of 1433, and the twelve-year-old king, with a child's innocence, intervened in the council personally, begging his uncles to become friends again, before Bedford's departure for France in July 1434. The failure of the Congress of Arras and Bedford's death left Gloucester in an advantageous position at home and his policy in France in the ascendant, culminating in the raising of the siege of Calais and the defeat of Burgundy in August 1436.

Changes in the king's household after his return to England in 1432 bear the stamp of Gloucester, though they made Warwick, the king's governor, uneasy. Several clerics who were engaged in the household were firmly orthodox in religion and may have influenced the king's Christian upbringing. Warwick noted in 1432 that Henry was 'growen in years in stature of his persone and also in conceyte and knowleche of his hiegh and royale auctoritee and estate' (*Proceedings … of the Privy Council*, 4.134) and may have become less easy to direct. There was also a danger that he would be distracted from his studies and influenced by others when Warwick and the household knights were absent. Accordingly, on 29 November 1432 Warwick received detailed guidelines for the king's upbringing to safeguard the earl's position and protect the king: at least one knight should be present at all interviews with Henry.

By August 1433 William de la Pole, earl of Suffolk, who was married to Beaufort's kinswoman, became steward of Henry VI's household. In July 1434, before Bedford left for France, the council confirmed the authority of Warwick, Suffolk, and other household officials to arrange the king's movements as seemed appropriate; the council was aware that 'mocions and sturinges' of which Warwick had complained might re-emerge once Bedford was gone (*Proceedings … of the Privy Council*, 4.259–61, 287). In November 1434 it was necessary to tell the king that, despite 'greet understandyng and felyng, as evere thei sawe or knewe in eny Prince, or other persone of his age', he still lacked sufficient experience of government to dispense with his councillors; he was advised not to change his officers or policies without consulting them, and to be wary of those who urged him to do so (ibid., 4.287–9). Warwick eventually resigned as Henry's guardian on 19 May 1436 and no successor was appointed. He may have felt that his influence with the teenage king was ebbing and that political changes made his position increasingly untenable.

As for Queen Catherine, she does not appear to have lived with the king following his return to England, or to have associated with him much except at ceremonies or special occasions, such as new year festivities at Gloucester in 1435. She married Owen *Tudor c.1430 and had four children with him thereafter; by 1436 she had fallen into serious illness which caused her death on 3 January 1437.

Joan of Navarre, the widow of *Henry IV, had long lived in seclusion, and apart from presenting her with new year gifts, Henry's relations with her were distant, though he formed a close friendship with her grandson, Gilles of Brittany, after he arrived in England in 1432.

Contemporaries who observed Henry VI as a young teenager thought him personable, educated, even precocious. However, his closest relatives created about him an atmosphere of political bitterness, even personal hatred, and after Bedford's death Gloucester and Beaufort strove to dominate him in private and public. These pressures accustomed Henry VI to dependence: most commentators agree that his ability to assert his own will consistently was stunted. To go so far as to say (as, for instance, John Watts has done) that he had no independent will is to contradict councillors' reports, like those cited above, of his early self-awareness and youthful powers of perception. Observers in France and England in the 1430s noted an elegant, dignified, good-looking, and well-mannered boy who spoke French as well as English. On 1 October 1435, apparently for the first time, Henry attended a council meeting that was not merely ceremonial, and he was personally involved in making appointments and grants in the first half of 1436. In May Warwick resigned as his governor. It is not realistic to suppose that a fourteen-year-old could initiate personal rule alone or suddenly, but henceforward the king and his developing attitudes would need to be taken into account by those who had governed for him, and especially by Gloucester and Beaufort.

The ending of the minority, 1436–1437 Henry VI took an active part in decision making just when the future of the dual monarchy was beginning to divide English political opinion as never before. Gloucester and Beaufort had not only to fight for their respective policies, but also to pay attention to, and to mould, the young king's attitudes. Beaufort's position was undermined by the collapse of the Congress of Arras and the defection of Burgundy. England's policy thereafter concentrated on defending Calais and prosecuting the war in Normandy. After Gloucester departed to relieve Calais in July 1436, Beaufort had the king's ear: on 28 July he induced Henry to make him a grant, under his sign manual (or signature), of Canford manor and the town of Poole, in Dorset, free of charge and for the cardinal's life. However, Gloucester's success at Calais made him popular: when parliament met early in 1437 he was warmly thanked and on 25 February he knelt before his nephew seeking reinforcements for Calais. Gloucester was determined to pursue his French policy and preserve his political influence.

A measure of Henry's emergence in government was his personal authorization of warrants by his signet seal and sign manual; before February 1438 his signet was being kept by a secretary, Thomas Beckington, who was previously in Gloucester's household. The king rewarded members of his household, headed by Suffolk, and he sometimes expressed political views, such as on the conditions under which Warwick took command in France (20 May

1437). Without formal announcement, Henry was exercising his prerogative, though with guidance from his councillors, especially Gloucester and Beaufort.

Two particular issues attracted the king's attention and determined on whom he would most heavily rely for advice. The first was the tussle between Pope Eugenius IV and the Council of Basel; this dispute was of great interest to a young king whose piety was nurtured by chaplains (and by a lengthy stay at Bury St Edmunds in 1433–4, when he asked to be admitted to the abbey's fraternity) and whose coronation oaths enjoined him to uphold the faith and protect the church. Henry supported Eugenius, whose agent, Piero da Monte, personally appealed to the king. Though exaggerated for public effect, Monte's report lauded Henry's intelligence, wisdom, and kindliness, his royal dignity, and Christian morality. The young king's attitude to Eugenius accorded with Beaufort's. The second issue was the French war. It became apparent that Henry was inclined to share Beaufort's preference for peace. Gloucester resigned the captaincy of Calais on 8 January 1438, and in November the king authorized negotiations, under Beaufort's leadership, at Gravelines, even though Henry was aware that several of his relatives and of his great council were hostile.

Thus, as Henry VI emerged from his minority, Gloucester was losing his influence. In the summer of 1437 Henry VI visited the midlands and west country. On his return a great council met at Sheen on 21 October. An adjustment of the roles of king and council took place on 12 November, ending Gloucester's formal position as chief councillor, at a time when Beaufort was becoming Henry's most influential adviser. The king's public crown-wearing at Merton Priory in Surrey on 1 November may have marked the change that was taking place. This peaceful adjustment reserved all matters of grace to the king and referred all matters of 'grete weght and charge' to him (*Proceedings … of the Privy Council*, 6.312). The initiative may have sprung from councillors like Beaufort, from the king himself, and, of course, from the English and French custom whereby kings in their mid-teens began to shoulder their royal responsibilities. It happened gradually probably because it happened peacefully and without crisis. Control of affairs shifted gradually from the formal council of the minority to the king. A group of councillors, without a nominated chief councillor, assisted the young and inexperienced monarch, with no formal control over him but stressing the wisdom of his taking advice on important matters.

Early personal rule: the problem of France, 1437–1444 By 1437 Henry VI was ruling in fact as well as in name; his confidence grew with the years. He seems to have been repelled by war—its misery, waste, and expense—to judge by the declaration to which he lent his name in October 1440; and he believed that it prevented Christendom from ending the scandalous division between pope and council. It was probably his personal decision, fortified by Beaufort and others, to release the highest-ranking prisoner captured by Henry V at Agincourt (1415), Charles, duke of Orléans, to advance the cause of peace by influencing Charles VII and his nobles. Yet Henry did not contemplate surrendering hard-won territory at this stage, still less his title of king of France. His dilemmas were highlighted by the fierce clash between Beaufort and the militant Gloucester, who was the king's presumptive heir from Bedford's death in 1435 until Gloucester's own demise in 1447. They flung insults at each other whenever France was discussed, and the peace conference at Gravelines, near Calais, in the summer of 1439 collapsed. Its only outcome was the release of Orléans, whose political value in peacemaking was exaggerated in England. Gloucester skilfully denounced the release as unwise and a betrayal of the past. In 1440 a ransom was agreed for the duke: 40,000 nobles down and 80,000 more in six months' time; if Orléans arranged a peace then the ransom would be cancelled. As Orléans swore his oath in Westminster Abbey on 18 October 1440, Gloucester stalked out. Orléans crossed the channel early in November, was greeted by the duchess of Burgundy, and married a niece of the duke, but failed to gain even an interview with Charles VII.

It soon became clear that to consolidate Lancastrian rule in northern France and Gascony was beyond English resources, and confused arrangements for military command after Bedford's death poisoned relations among the English nobles, especially the Beaufort family, the duke of York, and Gloucester. By 1442 Henry VI was studying marriage proposals from a southern French noble, the count of Armagnac, and he commissioned portraits of the count's daughters so that he could choose the more appealing. Such an alliance would protect Gascony and wean some French nobles to the English side, and it is not reasonable to doubt Henry's personal interest in his own nuptials. The prospect of such an alliance outraged Charles VII, and it was abandoned. After the failure of the expedition of John Beaufort, duke of Somerset, to northern France in 1443, the most far-reaching step in the search for an honourable peace was conceived: Henry's marriage to a princess of the French royal house, with Charles VII's blessing; by early 1444 the name of *Margaret (1430–1482), daughter of René, duke of Anjou, and niece of the French queen, was canvassed.

A Christian prince The king's other passion at this time was the planning of two educational and religious foundations, Eton College and King's College, Cambridge. Henry's education had not been neglected, and his habit of reading chronicles and books is attested; he developed an interest in King Alfred, for whom he sought canonization in 1442. This admiration for a king who was a notable promoter of education and literacy in a Christian context may reflect Henry's convictions. Moreover, several councillors and officials had similar interests, and some of them participated in Henry's schemes. There is no reason to doubt that the inspiration for Eton, in the lee of his birthplace, Windsor Castle, was the king's; similar motives were expressed in his authorization in March 1445 of a new library at Salisbury Cathedral, 'for the keping of the bookes to the said Churche belanging and also for thencrece of connyng and of vertu of such as wol loke and studie in the same' (PRO, E28/75/11–13). Henry's devotion to Eton and King's was sustained with lavish endowments and privileges during the 1440s; he laid foundation stones and personally supervised (and modified) the building details. According to Eton's foundation charter of 11 October 1440:

> having now taken into our hands the government of both our kingdoms, [we] have from the very beginning of our riper age carefully revolved in our mind how, or in what manner, or by what royal gift, according to the measure of our devotion and the example of our ancestors, we could do fitting honour to that our same Mistress and most Holy Mother [that is, the church], to the pleasure of that Great Spouse [that is, God].   (Maxwell Lyte, 6–7)

The new college's size was remarkable: no previous king of England had endowed such a public grammar school, even though it was not completed at the time of Henry's deposition in 1461. The plans for King's were formulated a little later, and in August 1443 an even larger site was designated; in 1448 architectural specifications were approved by Henry. An enlarged Eton could appropriately serve an augmented university college, for by August 1446 Eton's scholarly community was increased to seventy. Henry's pride in his new 'general school' was undisguised: 'the lady mother and mistress of all other grammar schools' (*English Historical Documents*, 4.918–19). John Blacman, who was at Eton in the 1440s, recalled the king's interest in the boys of Eton whom he met at Windsor and what he proudly said to them: 'be you good boys, gentle and teachable, and servants of the Lord' (Blacman, 34).

Henry showed unwavering interest in these foundations, and the colleges' statutes and constitutions demonstrate that his aims were educational and devotional; his pride in them need not be mistaken for vainglory, and to claim that their inspiration and execution stemmed from courtiers alone is unwarranted. Educational and religious motives were closely entwined in such foundations. Henry's encouragement of university reform and clerkly education, and his promotion of scholars and his religious advisers and confessors to the episcopate from 1436, suggest a concern for the quality of the church and its leadership, and probably an active piety in the king. One consequence was that the theologically trained presence on the bench of bishops was strengthened: most of the dozen bishops elected between 1437 and 1445 were capable men with an interest in spiritual matters.

Henry practised Christian virtues. His piety was orthodox, and he took seriously his oath to protect the faith and church. Less conventional in a king were the compassionate, humane, and sensitive traits of character that became well known to his subjects, and which led him to pardon lawbreakers too readily. He was shy of women in his youth (according to John Blacman who knew him); he was shocked to see women and men bathing naked when he visited Bath in 1449, and concerned to shield the boys of Eton from corrupting influences of courtiers in the nearby castle. He enjoyed hunting and gaming, and he dressed well, especially on formal and festive occasions. He was generous to a fault.

The king's household and advisers   Henry rewarded friends, servants, and courtiers to such a degree that the crown was impoverished and his control in the localities was weakened. Analyses of the king's household and councillors, his appointments to offices in England and Wales, and his grants of favours and rewards lend substance to these observations. After Henry came of age, it was natural that his household should expand and be a focus for his activities and decisions. At the same time his relationship with his councillors was adjusted, though not always easily; the king attended council meetings frequently after 1437, and there seems to have been greater flexibility as to whom he consulted. Additions to the ranks of councillors may reflect the king's interventions, and household officials were soon nominated, as well as the earl of Salisbury, Beaufort's nephew recently returned from France. Gloucester's eclipse became more obvious from 1439 as the peace policy gained momentum; correspondingly, Cardinal Beaufort's influence grew, along with that of household officials led by the steward of the household, Suffolk, who was appointed a councillor himself in 1441. Sir Ralph Boteler, the chamberlain of the household, joined the council in 1441 and was created Lord Sudeley by the king; two years later he became treasurer of England. Adam Moleyns, clerk of the council since 1436, became a councillor in February 1443 and remained close to Suffolk; in 1445 he was appointed bishop of Chichester. And Edmund Beaufort, marquess of Dorset and the cardinal's nephew, also joined them as a councillor in February 1444. It was Suffolk, above all others, who was the most constant, intimate, and influential of Henry VI's advisers by the mid-1440s, exercising authority through government departments and the royal household, and also by dint of his personal relations with the king, Cardinal Beaufort, and several nobles. When Beaufort withdrew from affairs at the end of 1446 (his death followed on 11 April 1447), Suffolk had no effective rival as the king's mentor. He also had large ambitions of his own.

Disquiet appears to have been expressed among the councillors as to the handling of important business and the exercise of the king's authority. During 1444 formal arrangements were made to ensure efficiency and clarity in decision making and managing the king's patronage; Henry did not demur, and may have welcomed relief from routine duties. These arrangements in no way prejudiced Suffolk's role; indeed, his masterminding of Margaret's journey to England for her wedding in 1445 strengthened it. Such power tempted him to abuse his position in his own interests and those of his associates, servants, and dependants, at court, in East Anglia (where his estates were mainly situated), and elsewhere in the realm. Suffolk and his circle—which included Lord Sudeley, Suffolk's successor as steward of the household from 1447, Sir Roger Fiennes, treasurer of the household in 1439–46, Roger's brother James, who became chamberlain of the household in 1447 and was created Lord Saye and Sele, and Sir Thomas Tuddenham, keeper of the great wardrobe from 1446—became deeply unpopular, and their unpopularity inevitably tarnished the reputation of the household and of the king himself.

An associated source of criticism was the burgeoning size and cost of the household under Suffolk's stewardship. The numbers of servants in the king's employ increased to such an extent that it was found necessary to limit them to 420 in 1445, when a new establishment was created for the queen. Henry also accommodated his closest friends in the household, notably Henry Beauchamp, the young earl of Warwick, and Gilles of Brittany; after 1442 he seems to have taken a close interest in the upbringing of his two half-brothers, Edmund *Tudor and Jasper *Tudor, the children of Catherine of Valois and Owen Tudor. The residences which Henry used most often—Westminster Palace, Windsor Castle, and manor houses in the Thames valley like Sheen and Eltham—were repaired at considerable expense, especially in preparation for his marriage. By the later 1440s the debts of the household were spiralling.

Household servants were foremost among those who received lands, cash, offices, and other favours from Henry VI after 1436: they had a unique opportunity to attract his attention. In June 1444 Suffolk secured the wardship and marriage of the richest heiress in England, Margaret Beaufort, daughter of the duke of Somerset and therefore Henry's kinswoman; and a number of household officials benefited in 1446 when Henry Beauchamp, whom the king had created a duke the year before, died leaving his young heiress and estates in Henry VI's charge. Henry was even prepared to make life grants, and to do so without asking for payment in return. Such prodigality ran the risk of depleting the king's resources, and also of undermining accountability on the part of officers who frequently relied on deputies to discharge their duties. Thus Sir Robert Roos, a household knight who regularly attended on the king, was nevertheless granted the offices of chamberlain and customer of Berwick, on the Anglo-Scottish border, for life in 1443. Henry was even ready to pardon their misdemeanours. These ill-conceived actions caused misgivings and damaged effective royal government, both in the English shires and in royal dominions like the principality of Wales, where Suffolk was justiciar of north Wales from 1440. Such lack of foresight produced conflicting grants that could be embarrassing or even cause disputes. Most famously, the royal stewardship in Cornwall which had been assigned to Lord Bonville in 1438 was granted in similar terms to his rival, the earl of Devon, three years later, and this worsened relations between them.

Henry mistrusted those who attacked him personally. He took a close interest in the prosecution of Gloucester's second wife, Eleanor Cobham, in 1441 because he believed her to be plotting his death by magic. The duchess's disgrace was a measure of her husband's declining influence during the years when the king placed his confidence in Beaufort and Suffolk. Duke Humphrey bitterly resented the way in which he and other of the king's relatives were ignored, and he was implacably opposed to policies designed to reach a peace with France, and especially to withdraw from hard-won territory. By 1447 Henry VI may have believed rumours that his uncle was plotting, and he condoned the duke's arrest at the parliament held at Bury St Edmunds. Gloucester's sudden death in custody on 23 February inevitably, but almost certainly mistakenly, gave rise to reports that he had been murdered.

At the time of his death Gloucester, though a political opponent, was still the king's heir. Dynastic insecurity explains Henry's elevation of his closest relatives, the Beauforts, Hollands, and Staffords, in the peerage in 1443–8, culminating in the creation of his two half-brothers, Edmund and Jasper Tudor, as premier earls in November 1452, and the advantageous marriages that were arranged for some of these kinsmen.

The traditional view that Henry was the epitome of Christian virtue is myopic. At the other extreme, K. B. McFarlane's view that he never acquired the mental equipment of an adult is contradicted by evidence. Nor is it easy to endorse B. P. Wolffe's verdict of a wilful and untrustworthy incompetent. Rather does he seem well intentioned with laudable qualities, especially in relation to war, education, and religion, but with other qualities that were obstacles to effective kingship—extravagance, generosity, compassion, and suspicion. He disappointed many of his subjects by failing to provide fair and effective justice. He lacked foresight and discrimination; instead, simplicity was the abiding characteristic that contemporaries ascribed to him. He was neither uneducated nor unintelligent, but he remained inexpert in government and politics, and found it difficult to assert his independence and to concentrate on kingly matters in which he had little interest.

Henry's marriage, 1444–1449 Henry V's marriage to Catherine of Valois in 1420 had symbolized England's victory over the French. The significance of Henry VI's marriage was quite different. Following the disastrous expedition of 1443 and the failure of peace negotiations, England was now the suppliant: Henry's marriage might do no more than stop the fighting, leaving the matters of English sovereignty and occupied territory in France unresolved. Charles VII offered negotiations in 1443 and a new marriage proposal may have been conveyed to Henry VI by the duke of Brittany's envoys as early as August; the friendship between Henry and Gilles of Brittany, the younger brother of Duke François II, may have helped. Yet Charles VII did not offer one of his own daughters, which might buttress the English claim to his throne. The queen's niece, Margaret of Anjou, seemed more suitable. From the English point of view, Margaret was not ideal: she was not her father's heir, and Duke René was not a wealthy noble. Nevertheless, by the end of January 1444, Henry's council resolved to pursue the match with Margaret. By 1 February it was decided to send the earl of Suffolk to France to negotiate a marriage and an end to the war, though he left with misgivings, not least about his own exposed position. The king's role was central in this decision and more than formal. In the 1430s the council had declined to entertain marriage proposals so long as Henry was young; now that a firm proposal had emerged with important political implications affecting his French realm, it was inconceivable that he should play little part; he had certainly investigated the count of Armagnac's daughters in 1442. The marriage with Margaret was arranged during Suffolk's embassy, and on 24 May a ceremony of betrothal was held at Tours Cathedral, with Suffolk taking the king's place. On his return, Henry VI rewarded him with a marquessate, a rare distinction, on 14 September.

Suffolk's second mission to France in 1444 was to bring Margaret (who was already referred to as queen) to England and to advance the peace negotiations. A large embassy crossed the channel in November at considerable cost. Margaret was received by an English delegation at Nancy in February 1445, and on 2 March the party began its journey to England via Paris and Rouen. The wedding of Henry and Margaret in person took place at Titchfield Abbey in the New Forest on 22 April. Margaret's entry to London on 28 May and her coronation two days later were lavish celebrations: the queen was portrayed in the accompanying pageants as the dove of concord. Gloucester, York, and Cardinal Beaufort had been present at her reception, but this could not conceal the caution—even scepticism—of some about the prospective peace arrangements; Suffolk assured parliament that he had made no embarrassing commitments. This did not end rumours that concessions had been made, and within a year talk was heard of Margaret's lack of dowry, and accusations that the surrender of Maine and Anjou had been promised to Duke René.

The dynastic significance of Henry's marriage was another matter. It took place when the king badly needed an heir to give security to his crown, for Gloucester was fifty-five years old, and had a disgraced wife and no legitimate children. However, the failure of Henry and Margaret to produce an heir for eight and a half years, Margaret's association with the fraught issue of negotiating peace, and the recurrence of war and English defeats in 1449–50, made her unpopular. As Henry later acknowledged, she intervened, in a minor way, in December 1445, to exert pressure on her husband, at the request of Charles VII and Duke René, to surrender Maine as an aid to peace. As a peace agreement proved elusive, despite the surrender of Maine, and the war recommenced in July 1449, with her own father serving in the French army that invaded Normandy, Margaret's stock plummeted.

There is no reason to doubt that Henry and Margaret were close after their marriage. They spent much time in each other's company, and until the crises of 1450–51 they were together for most of each year. As befitted a queen, she was endowed handsomely with land and income, and Margaret took an active interest in affairs, and specifically followed her husband's example at King's by founding another Cambridge college nearby, appropriately named Queen's, in 1447. Her household was staffed by many servants who also served the king.

Unrest and rebellion, 1449–1450 Judgements on Henry VI in fifteenth-century chronicles are mostly distorted by the propaganda of civil war, and Yorkist or Tudor views of recent history. Even those few chronicles completed in Henry's reign may be distorted by a reluctance to criticize the monarch; but when they do offer criticisms these are telling ones. One anonymous writer noted Henry's habitual dilatoriness; John Hardyng, in the first version of his chronicle, while acknowledging that Henry ruled well enough, obliquely criticized him by drawing attention to civil unrest and local injustice. John Capgrave's eulogy of the king in 1446 also reported that the navy and sea-keeping were neglected. And Abbot John Whethamstede of St Albans tempered his praise of the king c.1456 by saying that Henry could not resist those who led him to unwise decisions and prodigality. These strictly contemporary estimates hint at a monarch who, though possessed of worthy personal qualities, neglected some of his kingly duties.

Nor did he cut a dash in war. Henry VI was the first English king never to command an army against an external foe, despite the occasional plans to lead an army to France. He never visited France after 1432: the projected visit in 1445–7 to discuss peace with Charles VII never took place. He never fought in Scotland or crossed to Ireland, and he rarely set foot in Wales—perhaps only once, in August 1452, when he visited Monmouth. The only occasion when his subjects saw him in battle array before the civil war were in 1450 and 1452 when he rode through London with his nobles against his own subjects. Henry's interest in the Order of the Garter was genuine, and he rarely missed the festivities at Windsor on St George's day, but in the 1440s the order began to lose its exclusively military character as the king conferred membership on European princes and knights, and on members of his household.

By 1449 England faced political, military, and commercial crises that distressed many of his subjects and were an indictment of Henry's rule. In the summer of 1449 parliament was critical of Suffolk, the handling of Normandy's defence, and the king's impoverishment. Henry refused to resume all grants made from his resources, and parliament was soon dissolved, on 16 July. The next parliament, which assembled in November 1449, faced mounting crisis: the French war had resumed in May and military defeats followed, culminating in the duke of Somerset's expulsion from Rouen just before parliament opened. Naval protection was so defective that it could not deter French raids on coastal towns, and trade with France collapsed as Burgundy took measures against England's cloth trade with the Low Countries. During this parliament, Suffolk, the king's chief adviser and steward of his household, and other counsellors and servants were denounced; the keeper of the privy seal, Bishop Adam Moleyns, was murdered at Portsmouth on 9 January 1450. Suffolk defended himself in parliament in January 1450, but he was sent to the Tower and formally impeached on 7 February, accused of treason and plotting to kill the king, and of abusing his trust and exploiting Henry's favour, to the crown's impoverishment. Henry sought to protect him, and Suffolk placed himself in the king's hands. On 7

March Henry summoned a large group of lords and offi-cials to his private chamber at Westminster and inter-viewed Suffolk, who again protested his innocence of any charge and threw himself on the king's mercy. The chan-cellor read out Henry's decision: Suffolk was banished for five years, from 1 May, but Henry declined to make a deci-sion on the substantive charges. Suffolk fled, so exposing Henry directly to his regime's critics. The duke was appre-hended and executed on 2 May, as he was taking ship abroad.

Henry withdrew from London as soon as he had announ-ced his decision, and on 29 March made his way to the midlands, a favourite retreat during the next few years. Parliament was adjourned to the relative calm of Leices-ter. While it was still sitting, the south-eastern shires clos-est to events across the channel rose under John Cade, and other parts of the south followed suit, partly for economic reasons. Having earlier rejected demands for resumption of grants, Henry now capitulated and accepted a bill of resumption, but with a large number of exemptions which he signed himself. News of the popular rising brought the king back to London, to St John's, Clerken-well, by 13 June. Stubbornly refusing to consider the rebels' petitions, he moved to confront them with a force. Claiming to be loyal subjects, on 17 June they withdrew from Blackheath temporarily. Firmness with restraint might have saved the day for the king. Instead, he refused concessions and his men rampaged in pursuit of the rebels: he and his courtiers were badly jolted when a royal contingent was ambushed near Sevenoaks in Kent. Signs of mutiny among his own supporters, and the spectacle of defeated soldiers returning from Normandy, made the situation worse: Henry responded by arresting leading members of his household whom the rebels had denoun-ced. He moved to Greenwich, then to London on 20 June, and on to Westminster; he resisted pleas from the mayor to stay in the city. By 26 June he retired further west to Berkhamsted and then to Kenilworth Castle in the mid-lands; many of the rebels returned to Blackheath on 29 June, their morale high, and they broke into London. The queen remained at Greenwich and was instrumental in offering pardon to persuade the rebels to disperse on 6–7 July. Henry had been obstinate, then vacillated, and finally lost his nerve.

New 'captains of Kent' appeared following the capture and death of Cade in mid-July, and disturbances con-tinued in southern England after the duke of York returned from Ireland in September 1450 and the duke of Somerset's forces slunk back from Normandy. Henry recovered his nerve to some extent: he tried to restore order in London and toured disaffected areas, garnering 'a harvest of heads' in 1451 ('Gregory's chronicle', 197). Yet in spurning the rebels Henry also spurned those in parlia-ment and elsewhere who shared their grievances.

Political divisions, 1450–1453 *Richard, duke of York, who returned from Ireland without authority in the autumn of 1450, had a good claim to be the king's heir presumptive after Gloucester's death in 1447, although Henry VI may

have regarded other kinsmen, especially Edmund *Beau-fort, duke of Somerset (d. 1455), as more acceptable. Dyn-astic uncertainties, along with York's resentment at his treatment by the government while he served in France, and popular shock at the loss of Normandy in 1449–50, were a dangerous combination. To the near revolutionary atmosphere caused by popular revolt, parliamentary out-bursts, and the murder of Suffolk and others, York added his protest and claimed a central role in affairs. Henry, ten years the duke's junior, resented him and distrusted his presumption. Their first known contact was at Henry's coronation in 1429; York accompanied the king to France and attended the coronation in Paris. Between 1436 and 1445 he was mostly in France and hardly knew the king as the latter embarked on personal rule: they were never close. Critics of the government in 1450 urged York's recall. Towards the end of April, when the king was at Stony Stratford on his way to the Leicester parliament, he was confronted by John Harries, a Yorkshire shipman, who wielded a flail in front of Henry and declared that York would do the same to traitors when he returned from Ireland. The king took such things seriously (Harries was executed for treason), and, as he later explained to York, he resented threats and prognostications. Cade's uprising was a further sign of York's popularity, not least because Cade took the name of Mortimer which had unmistakable dynastic overtones: Duke Richard himself had a Mortimer mother, and would eventually claim the throne on the grounds of his descent from Edward III through succes-sive Mortimer earls of March.

When York landed in north Wales in September, Henry and his servants were alarmed. The king may have author-ized the duke's arrest, but he eluded the royal servants and spent two months in eastern England, attracting sup-port before the parliament of November 1450, and capital-izing on the hostility in London towards Somerset and the Lancastrian court. On 3 December the king asserted him-self, and with his nobles tried to overawe the city. Yet par-liament introduced a bill demanding the dismissal of Henry's entourage, headed by Somerset and the dowager duchess of Suffolk. Henry eventually gave way and granted the Commons' petition, but inserted so many exemptions that its purpose was defeated. Henry refused a bill of attainder against the dead Suffolk and in the last session in May 1451 he was offended by a proposal that York be acknowledged as his heir. York had withdrawn to Ludlow by Christmas 1451.

By the beginning of 1452 York resolved on another polit-ical challenge, focused on the duke of Somerset, the neg-lect of France, and his own victimization—while carefully stressing loyalty to Henry VI. Henry and his advisers resolved to confront the duke and hold a council at Coven-try. With a retinue in the royal livery of white and blue, the king and his nobles left London on 16 February, but news of the duke's advance caused them to return to the capital. On 24 February the king ordered London to bar York's entry; when York arrived he was denied entry to the city and made for his estate at Dartford in Kent. The king arrived in the capital soon after, on 27 February, and on 1

March advanced to Blackheath with a large force. A delegation of lords was sent to interview the duke, and fighting was avoided. Henry and York met peaceably and the duke made his protests against Somerset. But he was deceived and Somerset was not placed under restraint. York was disarmed and escorted to London by the king's men: on 10 March, at St Paul's Cathedral, he was induced to swear in the king's presence never to rebel again.

Henry joined some of the judicial commissions that sat in the summer and autumn of 1452 in areas where York had estates, including the Welsh marches and the midlands. He and his court had again recovered their nerve. On 23 November 1452 Henry ennobled his Tudor half-brothers, Edmund and Jasper, thereby buttressing the royal house; they were also given wardship of the Beaufort heir, Margaret, in March 1453—a grant of dynastic significance. Henry is unlikely to have made these arrangements 'without some expectation that the collateral lines [of the house of Lancaster] would be entwined' (Chrimes, 13). The Reading parliament of 1453 consolidated the king's political recovery, for it was one of the most royalist parliaments of his reign. Henry may have lacked finesse, but he was not without imagination in fortifying himself dynastically and quelling opposition; he had not, however, removed the sources of criticism.

The king's illness, 1453–1454 York's third opportunity came unexpectedly. About the beginning of August 1453 Henry VI suffered severe mental collapse, accompanied by crippling physical disablement. He appeared in the parliament chamber at Westminster on the last day of parliament, 2 July; days later he began a tour to the west country. By the end of July news arrived of the final English defeat at Castillon in Gascony: it may have been a bitter blow for the king, since the duchy had been English since 1154. The onset of his illness was accompanied by a frenzy, and it seemed as if 'his wit and reson [were] withdrawen' (Flenley, 140), and that he had 'no natural sense nor reasoning power' (*Incerti scriptoris Chronicon Angliae*, 4.44). He was prostrate for seventeen months, spent in seclusion at Windsor. He was in the care of a committee of doctors and surgeons, under the council's oversight. The precise cause of Henry's illness is unclear and speculation as to its nature—catatonic schizophrenia is favoured by some, a depressive stupor by another—is less worthwhile than estimating its effect upon him and his capacity to rule. He was left helpless, and several pages and grooms stayed with him day and night so long as the illness lasted; he was fed by them and supported by two of them when he moved from room to room. He was mentally unresponsive: he recognized nobody and understood nothing, and after he recovered he could not recall what had happened in the meanwhile. No English monarch since 1066 had been in such an impotent state. The dynastic implications were serious: his father's brothers were dead and he himself had no children, though the queen was pregnant. More immediate was the problem of who should rule the realm.

Henry VI was oblivious of the birth of his son, *Edward, on 13 October 1453, and when the baby was presented to

him after new year's day 1454, he gave no sign of recognition. Edward's birth eased the dynastic uncertainty but it made the political problem of who should govern the realm during the king's incapacity and while his heir was a minor—or, if the king should die, during the long minority—a more sensitive one. Arrangements made now would have implications for the succession, since it was unclear who the next heir was after Prince Edward. Efforts were made to exclude York from the discussions in the autumn of 1453, and parliament was delayed until February 1454. There was bitter dispute between Somerset and York, who could hardly be ignored. In the new year Queen Margaret staked a claim to the regency, and tensions in London increased. York opened parliament at Westminster on 14 February and the death on 22 March of the chancellor, Archbishop John Kemp, precipitated matters: York was appointed protector and defender of the king and realm, after councillors visited Windsor on 25 March to verify that Henry was still incapacitated.

When the king recovered at Christmas 1454, there was widespread joy: 'Blessed be God, the Kyng is wel amended', reported John Paston's correspondent on 9 January (*Paston Letters*, 3.13). There was no formal announcement, and the illness ended as suddenly as it began. Henry recognized his son for the first time when Margaret presented the baby to him: his elation at the birth and naming of the child was genuine. Before his illness Henry expressed delight when the queen became pregnant, and stories in the later 1450s that Edward was not his son were unfounded. Whether Henry recovered fully his powers may be doubted: it was reported on 28 October 1455 that 'summe men ar a-ferd that he is seek ageyn' (ibid., 3.50), and the measures taken to establish a protectorate in 1455–6 were identical with those of 1453–4, when he certainly had collapsed.

The approach of civil war, 1454–1456 York's first protectorate was different from that of 1422. Henry VI might recover at any time and his household remained in existence; the queen was frustrated yet vigilant; and Prince Edward's rights were safeguarded. Henry VI's secretary, Master Richard Andrew, continued to keep the signet seal, though it was little used during the king's illness. In the summer of 1454 York and the council limited the size and cost of the royal establishments, but political control was beyond their reach. The protectorate was challenged by Henry Holland, duke of Exeter, whose royal blood gave him a plausible claim to influence during the king's incapacity; he was captured on 23 July and imprisoned.

The king's recovery removed the reason for the protectorate and Henry VI, Margaret, and certain nobles sought Somerset's release from prison, where he was held without charge. His release on 26 January was confirmed at a council meeting, in York's presence, on 5 February. York resigned as protector soon afterwards. Henry presided at the council on 4 March when the conditions were nullified that secured freedom for Somerset, who two days later was reinstated as captain of Calais in York's place.

Exeter was freed from prison on 19 March. The Lancastrian royal family was thus reassembled in the spring of 1455 to buttress the king's throne. In mid-April the Yorkist lords abruptly and without permission left the court, probably for Yorkshire.

On 21 April the king summoned a great council to meet at Leicester, well out of range of the Londoners. The Yorkists feared punitive measures: they declared their loyalty but expressed resentment especially of Somerset, and with an army they advanced towards London. Mediation failed, and so did efforts to avoid confrontation. The king took no discernible part in these negotiations on 21 May on the way to St Albans, where the duke of Buckingham acted for him with full authority. Even if Henry had not fully recovered from his illness it is likely that he approved the royal negotiating position and the protection of Somerset. In the fighting that followed in St Albans on 22 May, Henry was deserted beneath his banner and wounded in the neck; Somerset was killed and Buckingham struck in the face more than once. The king took refuge in the tanners' house, whence York escorted him to the abbey; there the duke and his Neville allies submitted to Henry on their knees. Henry besought them 'to cesse there peple, and that there shulde no more harme be doon' (*Paston Letters*, 3.29). Most of the dead were servants of the king's household or the duchy of Lancaster. This was the first battle in which Henry VI had been personally involved, and he had lost.

York's objectives—to resume political life with himself as the king's chief councillor—were more difficult to achieve after the battle than before. He formally made his peace with Henry, and the two men entered London together; at a solemn crown-wearing at St Paul's Cathedral on 25 May, Henry received the crown from York's hands. The queen and many nobles were not reconciled so easily. Parliament met on 9 July: it established York's control, and on 24 July a great council received declarations of loyalty to the king from sixty spiritual and lay lords. When parliament adjourned a week later, Henry thanked its members in person. For six months York tried to rule the realm. His second protectorate was established on 19 November because Henry was said to be unable to discharge his responsibilities personally. There are hints that he was not fully restored to health, but no incontrovertible evidence of a major relapse. York's hold on power was uncertain in the second half of 1455 and it could be ended at the king's pleasure, though with the Lords' advice—a significant difference from his commission in 1454. York's relations with several nobles were strained; moreover, Prince Edward's position as his father's eventual heir was emphasized, and that of the queen, who resented York's dominance, was safeguarded. An Act of Resumption protected Margaret and the king's Tudor half-brothers, and Henry VI was enabled to make further exemptions at his pleasure, though with advice. Henry's uncertain health, the existence of an heir, and the queen's determination created an impossible situation for a man with York's grievances, dynastic claims, and political objectives. Lack of support from the Lords led him to resign the protectorship on 25 February 1456, in the king's presence.

Failing kingship, 1456–1459 The weakness of the English monarchy, in the hands of a listless king and with the succession hanging by a thread, produced governmental paralysis and conflicting personal ambitions. In March 1456 there was rioting in London against Italian merchants; Henry wanted to intervene and on 30 April was rowed from Westminster to the bishop of London's palace where he established a commission of inquiry next day; but then he withdrew on 5 May, leaving the city tense. From the end of August Henry, Margaret, and their son, their courtiers, and advisers, spent much time away from the capital, usually in the midlands, where many of Margaret's and the prince's estates, as well as a substantial number of those of the duchy of Lancaster, were concentrated. Government did not collapse, but it was ineffective and weakened by political faction; regular communication with London was maintained by the king's messenger service. Relations with York disintegrated: he did not attend a great council at Coventry after the winter of 1456–7, and several nobles urged Henry to treat him and his allies firmly. Consultation with the king's councillors and lords was not easy, but the court returned to the south-east in November 1457 and stayed until April 1459. At a great council at Westminster on 28 November 1457 Bishop Reginald Pecock was brought before the king and Archbishop Bourchier to recant his heresy. In these years Henry seems to have been actively well-meaning, and a 'compelling desire to pardon became a pious obsession' (Griffiths, 775). He may have devised the 'loveday' of March 1458 which sought to reconcile his nobles, despite large royalist forces in London. On 24 March an arbitration award was accepted by the Yorkists and the young Lancastrians whose fathers had been slain at St Albans. Henry stayed in the capital for much of the following year, attending jousts and tournaments at the Tower and the queen's manor of Greenwich. His personal initiation of warrants was rare, though he cherished his foundations of Eton and King's. Henry appeared passive in public, which contemporaries interpreted as simplicity. Yet he went to Westminster Abbey in the late 1450s to discuss at length his tomb. In May 1459 he and Margaret returned to Coventry.

Helpless in a political world from which he could not escape (and perhaps mentally enfeebled), Henry VI abandoned his responsibilities, and his actions were dictated largely by his wife. One later chronicler even claimed that she tried to persuade him to abdicate in favour of Prince Edward, though this is probably a Yorkist slander. She increasingly dominated the king's and prince's households, and, in so far as it was possible from the midlands, the government too. A crucial great council was held at Coventry in late June 1459: the queen and prince seem to have been present, but York, the Nevilles, and other lords were not. At Margaret's insistence, charges were laid against York and his allies, with the result that the accused and their retinues planned to converge on Worcester to appeal as loyal subjects directly to the king. When the earl of Salisbury's men were intercepted in an indecisive engagement at Bloreheath on 23 September, Henry was not present but the queen awaited the outcome a few miles off. Henry and his force arrived from Nottingham to join Margaret, and they made their way to Worcester and then to Ludlow in pursuit of the retreating Yorkists. At Ludford Bridge, his pardon was offered to the Yorkists, who were reluctant to face Henry personally in battle; some of Warwick's men from Calais deserted, despite rumours that the king had died. The confrontation on 12 October saw the Yorkists surrender or flee.

In parliament at Coventry on 20 November the Yorkist leaders were attainted. Towards the end of the meeting, on 11 December, those present swore an oath to Henry in his presence, acknowledging him as king, and undertaking to preserve the queen and honour the prince as his heir. It was a military triumph, but the enemy had fled and were still at liberty.

Henry's downfall and captivity, 1460–1470 Warwick, York's son Edward, earl of March [see Edward IV], and the Yorkist lords who had fled to Calais returned to Sandwich on 26 June 1460; they swore loyalty to Henry VI but demanded radical changes in government. The king's army, outnumbered, confronted them at Northampton on 10 July. Henry and his advisers rejected a parley on three occasions; in the battle that followed, the king was taken in his tent, deserted by some supporters while others were killed. The victors recoiled from deposition and maintained their loyalty to the captive monarch; he was taken in some state to London on 16 July and installed in the bishop's palace. Thenceforward he was their creature, 'more timorous than a woman, utterly devoid of wit or spirit', recorded Pope Pius II, who was kept informed of events in England in 1460–61 (Wolffe, 20). Whatever his mental state, Henry was presumably dejected by recent events. His household was purged, and his servants were replaced by keepers rather than by congenial companions.

The duke of York arrived from Ireland on about 8 September 1460. On his way he engaged retainers in the Welsh marches by contracts that omitted expressions of loyalty to the king. Arriving in London in regal state he made as if to take Henry's place in parliament on 10 October. He disdained to meet the king, who strove to avoid him in the Palace of Westminster. The customary ceremonies on St Edward's day, 13 October, when Henry could be expected to wear his crown in Westminster Abbey, were cancelled. On 31 October he was brought to accept a compromise settlement, whereby York would succeed to his throne after his death. To demonstrate his acceptance, Henry went crowned in procession to St Paul's the next day, accompanied by available nobles.

In the months that followed, Queen Margaret and the young Prince Edward rallied support in Wales and Scotland to challenge the Yorkist settlement, even promising in Henry's name to cede Berwick to the Scots. At Wakefield, near Sandal in Yorkshire, on 30 December, the duke of York was killed and his army defeated. The way was open for Margaret and her northern forces to advance on London and recover possession of her husband. Henry

supposedly spent the battle of St Albans on 17 February 1461 under a tree a mile or so off. The king was so overjoyed by the success of his wife's army and his own release that he blessed and knighted their son on the spot. It was a decisive battle that ensured that civil war would continue. Henry was accused by the Yorkists of breaking his oath to the accord of 31 October, though he may have been as passive a figure then as he subsequently was at St Albans. When Edward, earl of March, at last entered London, after defeating the western Lancastrian army at Mortimer's Cross on 3 February 1461, he declared Henry unfit to rule and was crowned himself (4 March). And Henry, Margaret, and Prince Edward waited at York while their army was destroyed by the new Yorkist king, Edward IV, at Towton, on 29 March. All three fled to Scotland.

After Towton, Henry and his queen were received by the queen regent of Scotland, Mary of Gueldres, who on 25 April 1461 agreed to aid them in return for the surrender of Berwick. Henry seems to have accompanied Lancastrian raids in northern England, perhaps to express a determination to recover his throne, while Margaret turned to negotiate French aid from her father and Louis XI. But on 9 December 1463 an Anglo-Scottish truce, following soon after an Anglo-French truce, meant that the Scots ceased to support the fugitives, and Henry crossed into northern England, where he installed himself in Bamburgh Castle for a season. He was not at the encounter with a Yorkist force on Hedgeley Moor on 25 April 1464, nor at the Lancastrian defeat at Hexham on 15 May, when he awaited the outcome at Bywell Castle some distance away. Thereafter, he was on the run until he was captured in Ribblesdale in July 1465. He was taken to the Tower of London, securely bound to his saddle, and there kept for five years, until division within the Yorkist ranks enabled his supporters to release him. His captivity was strict but honourable: members of Edward IV's household were his attendants and he was allowed visitors. But on his release in October 1470 it was observed that he was 'not worschipfully arayed as a prince, and not so clenly kepte as schuld seme such a Prynce' (Warkworth, 11).

The restoration and death of Henry VI, 1470–1471 In May 1470 Warwick and Edward IV's brother, Clarence, arrived in France as rebels against Edward IV. Their reconciliation with Margaret of Anjou at Louis XI's court was the beginning of a campaign to restore Henry VI to his throne, with essential help from Yorkist dissidents. After Warwick's invasion caused Edward IV to flee abroad, Henry was enthroned a second time, on 3 October 1470; but his second reign (described by contemporaries as his 'readeption', or reattainment, of his throne) did not last long. Returning from Flanders, Edward IV approached London in the first week of April 1471: Warwick's brother, Archbishop George Neville, accompanied Henry VI through the streets, presumably to rally support for his cause. But the fifty-year-old monarch, who may not have understood the significance of events and was dressed shabbily in a long blue gown, aroused little enthusiasm among the citizens. When Edward arrived on 11 April, he took Henry from the bishop of London's palace and returned him to the Tower. Two days later Henry was forced to join Edward to confront the approaching Lancastrian army at Barnet, presumably in order to induce its surrender. After Edward's victory back to the Tower he went.

Following the battle of Tewkesbury on 4 May, when Margaret was captured and Prince Edward killed, Henry was put to death in the Tower on 21 May, within hours of Edward's return to the capital. There is little doubt that he died violently, and on Edward's authority, since no less a person than King Edward's brother, Richard, duke of Gloucester, and other lords were then in the building. The next evening the body was escorted to St Paul's, where it bled on the pavement and lay overnight, 'opyn vysagid, that he mygth be knowyn' (*Great Chronicle of London*, 220). The following morning it was conveyed up river to Chertsey Abbey for a modest burial. 'And so no-one from that stock remained among the living who could now claim the crown', in the words of a contemporary notice (Kingsford, *English Historical Literature*, 375).

The ending of the dynasty and the manner of Henry VI's death explain why he was venerated as a martyr in several parts of England by 1472–3. His statue on the rood screen of York Minster was removed in 1479 to stop the veneration. Richard III, on the other hand, in 1484 transferred the body from Chertsey to a new shrine at St George's Chapel, Windsor, in a symbolic act of reconciliation; he was wise to harness the dead king's reputation rather than try to suppress it as his brother had done, in view of the growing popular veneration and the miracles associated with Henry's name which are recorded from 1481.

Henry VI's rehabilitation continued under Henry VII, his nephew. The statue in York Minster was restored, and John Blacman penned *A Compilation of the Meakness and Good Life of King Henry VI* which was part of an official campaign to secure Henry's canonization. From 1494 Henry VII petitioned several popes, ordered the compilation of a book of miracles allegedly worked by the king (BL, Royal MS 13 C. viii), and proposed to rebury the body in Westminster Abbey as Henry VI had wished. Pilgrims flocked to Henry's tomb at Windsor, even Henry VIII, and Tudor writers like Polydore Vergil attributed the stylized qualities of sainthood to him. The Reformation cut short the canonization campaign, though even at the end of the twentieth century the Henry VI Society kept his memory bright. Historians take a less charitable view.

Estimate No king who loses his crown and dies in prison, and whose reign ends in civil war, can be counted a success. Henry VI's inheritance as king was daunting, and the legacy of his reign disastrous for the realm, though assessments of his personality and abilities have varied widely since the fifteenth century. He was the youngest monarch ever to mount the English throne; his minority came to an end earlier than that of all other young English kings since 1066; and he inherited not only a realm and dominions that extended throughout the British Isles (excepting Scotland), but also large territories and claims in France, where he was the only English monarch to be acknowledged by French authorities as the rightful French king,

and to be crowned as such. The early death of his father, Henry V, at the height of his European-wide fame left a military and political void which a baby could not fill. Nevertheless, his reign was the third longest since the Norman conquest—almost thirty-nine years—and not all of it was a catalogue of blunders and failures.

Care is needed lest Henry as a ruler be judged in the light exclusively of the last eight years of his reign, after his mental collapse. He faced a uniquely daunting inheritance in England and France, a long minority, dynastic fragility, exceptional military commitments, and vaunting noble ambitions and rivalries, without, however, the requisite character, intellectual capacity, and powers of judgement. Ruling the 'dual monarchy' overstrained his capacities. His peace policy was bold, but he lacked subtlety and foresight in executing it. His choice of advisers and servants was not always sound, and in patronizing them and others he could be careless and profligate. The foundation of Eton and King's are enduring monuments to his piety and concern for education. His qualities and inclinations, admirable in a private person, did not make him a successful ruler. Gathering crises by 1453 broke him.

The last decade of his reign saw political upheaval and the beginnings of a civil war during which (for only the second time since 1066) the monarch and his rightful heir were discarded in favour of another claimant. In the ensuing dynastic struggle, the Wars of the Roses, Henry was restored briefly in 1470—the only English king to date to have a second reign. His murder in 1471 began a rehabilitation that brought him a reputation approaching sanctity under the early Tudors. Opinions of fifteenth- and sixteenth-century writers about Henry VI were therefore frequently distorted, either by partisanship, fear, or propaganda generated by civil war, or by the reflections of those who wrote after 1485. Chroniclers writing after 1461 disparaged the king and official Yorkist writings denounced his rule. After 1471 John Warkworth was less harsh about Henry's character but judged him an unsuitable ruler. Veneration of the dead king from the 1470s, and the accession in 1485 of his nephew, Henry Tudor, produced verdicts that suggested a man of remarkable personal virtue and piety who was the victim of malign forces at home and abroad. The early Tudor campaign for his canonization had an echo in the twentieth century.

Historians of the twentieth century reduced his reputation and stressed his inability to provide effective rule and so prevent the descent of England and its dominions into civil war. Yet they differed sharply in their conclusions about Henry VI himself, about the depths of his inadequacy and 'inanity' (underlined by McFarlane and by Watts), the complexity of his personality and attitudes before they were undermined by a breakdown in 1453 (Griffiths), and the extent of his active role in government (stressed by Wolffe). The reasons for these differences of opinion are not far to seek. Henry VI was not a robust ruler who left a consistent stamp on the workings of government, though to dismiss recorded expressions of his opinions and will as mere administrative convention goes too far. Henry was not a successful soldier, but to judge his (and Cardinal Beaufort's) policy of reaching an accommodation with France as defeatism, and the loss of Normandy and Gascony as entirely the king's fault, is too simplistic. Henry lost his crown at the outset of a dynastic, civil war, but to regard him (as many writers have done) as directly and solely responsible for the Wars of the Roses fails to take fully into account the circumstances of Henry's own life and of the age in which he lived.

R. A. GRIFFITHS

Sources PRO · *Chancery records* · N. H. Nicolas, ed., *Proceedings and ordinances of the privy council of England*, 7 vols., RC, 26 (1834–7) · *RotP*, vols. 4–5 · 'John Benet's chronicle for the years 1400 to 1462', ed. G. L. Harriss, *Camden miscellany, XXIV*, CS, 4th ser., 9 (1972) · J. A. Giles, ed., *Incerti scriptoris chronicon Angliae de regnis trium regum Lancastrensium*, pt 4 (1848) · J. S. Davies, ed., *An English chronicle of the reigns of Richard II, Henry IV, Henry V, and Henry VI*, CS, 64 (1856) · 'William Gregory's chronicle of London', *The historical collections of a citizen of London in the fifteenth century*, ed. J. Gairdner, CS, new ser., 17 (1876), 55–239 · J. Blacman, 'Henry the Sixth': a reprint of John Blacman's memoir, ed. and trans. M. R. James (1919) · Rymer, *Foedera*, 3rd edn · *The Paston letters, AD 1422–1509*, ed. J. Gairdner, new edn, 6 vols. (1904) · J. Stevenson, ed., *Letters and papers illustrative of the wars of the English in France during the reign of Henry VI, king of England*, 2 vols. in 3 pts, Rolls Series, 22 (1861–4) · R. A. Griffiths, *The reign of King Henry VI: the exercise of royal authority, 1422–1461* (1981) · B. P. Wolffe, *Henry VI* (1981) · K. B. McFarlane, 'The Wars of the Roses', *England in the fifteenth century: collected essays* (1981), 231–61 · J. Fortescue, *De laudibus legum Anglie*, ed. and trans. S. B. Chrimes (1942) · J. Watts, *Henry VI and the politics of kingship* (1996) · H. C. Maxwell Lyte, *A history of Eton College, 1440–1875*, 2nd edn (1889) · *English historical documents*, 4, ed. A. R. Myers (1969) · C. L. Kingsford, 'The first version of Hardyng's chronicle', *EngHR*, 27 (1912), 462–82, 740–53 · *Johannis Capgrave Liber de illustribus Henricis*, ed. F. C. Hingeston, Rolls Series, 7 (1858) · H. T. Riley, ed., *Registra quorundam abbatum monasterii S. Albani*, 2 vols., Rolls Series, 28/6 (1872–3) · S. B. Chrimes, *Henry VII* (1972) · R. Flenley, ed., *Six town chronicles of England* (1911) · J. Warkworth, *A chronicle of the first thirteen years of the reign of King Edward the Fourth*, ed. J. O. Halliwell, CS, old ser., 10 (1839) · A. H. Thomas and I. D. Thornley, eds., *The great chronicle of London* (1938) · C. L. Kingsford, *English historical literature in the fifteenth century* (1913) · G. L. Harriss, *Cardinal Beaufort: a study of Lancastrian ascendancy and decline* (1988)

Archives PRO, E28/74/11–13 · PRO

Likenesses stained-glass window, *c*.1440–1450, All Souls Oxf. · oils, *c*.1480–1500, Royal Collection; versions, NPG · statue, 1500–40, All Souls Oxf. · statue on lectern, 1509–28, King's Cam. · oils, *c*.1518–1523?, Royal Collection · oils, *c*.1540, NPG [*see illus.*] · groat, BM · manuscript illumination, repro. in J. Lydgate, *Poems*, BL Harleian MS 2278 · manuscript illumination, repro. in Psalter, BL Cotton MS Domitian XVII · manuscript illumination, repro. in *Poems and romances*, *c*.1445, BL MS Royal 15 E VI · manuscript illumination, repro. in 'Pageants of Richard Beauchamp, Earl of Warwick', BL Cotton MS Julius E IV · wax seal, BM

Henry VII (1457–1509), by unknown artist, 1505

Henry VII (1457–1509), king of England and lord of Ireland, was the son of Edmund *Tudor, first earl of Richmond (*c*.1430–1456)—half-brother of *Henry VI through their mother, *Catherine of Valois—and his wife, Margaret *Beaufort (1443–1509), only daughter of John *Beaufort, duke of Somerset, and great-great-granddaughter of *Edward III through the liaison of *John of Gaunt, duke of Lancaster, with Katherine Swynford [*see* Katherine, duchess of Lancaster].

Early life Henry's parents' marriage, arranged by Henry VI in 1453 to strengthen his loyal Tudor kin, was brief. When

Henry was born at Pembroke Castle on 28 January 1457, his father had been dead, probably of plague, for almost three months. Soon Henry was also separated from his mother, as the triumphant *Edward IV granted his wardship to William, Lord Herbert, his leading supporter in Wales, in February 1462. Herbert brought Henry up at Raglan Castle, intending to marry him to his eldest daughter, and doubtless counting on the eventual restoration of his father's estates and title. Henry was tutored by two clerics, Edward Haseley and Andrew Scot, and perhaps trained in gentlemanly pursuits by Sir Hugh Johnys; he had certainly learned some archery by 1469. In July of that year, however, Herbert was executed after the battle of Edgcote, to which Henry had accompanied him. Through the political convulsions of the next fifteen months Henry stayed at Weobley with Herbert's widow, while his mother and her husband, Henry Stafford, engaged in anxious negotiations over his future.

The Lancastrian readeption of 1470–71 brought Henry an audience with the restored Henry VI on 27 October 1470, an occasion on which it was later claimed that the saintly king prophesied his nephew's future reign. Henry seems to have spent most of the readeption period with his uncle, Jasper *Tudor, the restored earl of Pembroke. They were in south Wales when Edward won back the throne in 1471, and by September they were besieged in Pembroke Castle. From there they escaped to Tenby and took ship, heading for France but landing in Brittany late in the month after a stormy voyage. François (II), duke of Brittany, offered them an asylum that steadily, under Edward's diplomatic pressure, turned into house arrest in a succession of castles and palaces. In 1474 they were separated and deprived of their English servants, and for the next two years Henry stayed with Jean de Rieux, marshal of Brittany, at Largoët. Late in 1476 François agreed to surrender Henry to Edward's envoys, but at St Malo Henry's embarkation was delayed by illness until François countermanded his orders; in the ensuing confusion Henry took sanctuary and Edward's men returned empty-handed. Edward and Louis XI each made other efforts to secure custody of Henry and Jasper Tudor, but from 1476 they seem to have lived at the Breton court, in receipt of generous expenses from the duke, but under the supervision of Breton noblemen.

Henry's return to England need not have been as a prisoner. Margaret Beaufort's last marriage to Thomas *Stanley, second Baron Stanley and later first earl of Derby, lent her influence at the Yorkist court, and by 1482 arrangements were well advanced for Henry to return. He would be pardoned and granted rights of succession to his mother's estates, probably be restored to his father's title and possessions, and possibly even marry Edward IV's eldest daughter, *Elizabeth of York (1466–1503). In 1483 Edward's death, Richard III's usurpation, and the presumed death of Edward's sons in the Tower of London, opened more dramatic possibilities. The direct Lancastrian line had been extinct since 1471, and other potential claimants to the throne had died in the intervening years, leaving Henry as a credible candidate by his Beaufort blood, despite Henry IV's declaration of 1407 that the Beauforts, though legitimized, should not be allowed to inherit the crown. Margaret began plotting with various other opponents of Richard, including the dowager queen Elizabeth Woodville, to place her son on the throne, duly married to Elizabeth of York. In October 1483 a series of rebellions broke out across southern England, loosely co-ordinated with the revolt in Wales of Henry Stafford, duke of Buckingham, who had himself been in contact with Henry. All collapsed within a month. Henry was proclaimed king at Bodmin on 3 November, but did not leave Brittany with the ships and money lent him by Duke François until after 30 October. His fleet was scattered by a storm, he found the coasts of Dorset and Devon occupied by Richard's soldiers, and further storms blew him back to Normandy, whence he returned overland to Brittany. There he met those of the rebels who had escaped from England, some 400 in number, most of the leaders being relatives of the Woodvilles or veterans of Edward IV's household. At Christmas 1483 he vowed to marry Elizabeth of York, and they swore homage to him as king.

Winning the throne A new assault on England was planned for spring 1484 with French encouragement, but never got under way. Instead the exiles spent the year at Vannes while Richard treated with Duke François's treasurer, Pierre Landais, for their surrender, promising him English archers for use against his noble opponents and their French allies. Landais was about to strike in late September or early October when Henry, forewarned, slipped in disguise over the border into France. François, perhaps ashamed of what had been done in his name, let the other exiles join him. Henry was welcomed to the French court at Montargis and followed its travels to Paris, Évreux, and Rouen in the first half of 1485. His party was swollen by the arrival of supporters such as John de Vere, earl of Oxford, who had escaped from Hammes Castle in the Calais pale, but weakened by the attempted defection of Thomas Grey, marquess of Dorset. At length, as the regents for the young king, Charles VIII, managed to pacify their domestic opponents and saw the advantage in challenging the bellicose Richard III, Henry secured sufficient support in money, ships, and men to seek the crown once again.

Henry's fleet sailed from the mouth of the Seine on 1 August, carrying perhaps 400 English exiles, and similar or rather larger numbers of French and Scottish troops. Letters had been circulated since at least December 1484 encouraging his friends to prepare men to fight Richard, and valuable promises of support seem to have come from Wales, where some bards would hail Henry with his red dragon standard as a native redeemer king. Thus Henry headed for Milford Sound, landing on 7 August, probably in Mill Bay. For more than a week he marched across Wales, slowly gathering support until Shrewsbury opened its gates to his army. Some Englishmen joined him at Newport, Stafford, Lichfield, and Tamworth, which he reached on the 20th. But much stronger forces were converging on Nottingham, where Richard had been awaiting invasion since June, and on Leicester, where the king met his southern levies, also on 20 August. Next day the two armies marched towards each other, and on Monday 22 August battle was joined near Market Bosworth. The details of the encounter are hard to reconstruct, but the stout fighting of Henry's vanguard under the earl of Oxford seems to have laid the foundation for his success, aided by the failure to engage—perhaps deliberate—of the earl of Northumberland and other of Richard's followers. At the moment of decision the Stanleys, who had been shadowing the rival armies throughout the campaign without as yet committing themselves, intervened on Henry's side and Richard was struck down in a last desperate attack on Henry and his entourage. Henry, crowned on the battlefield with Richard's crown, marched into Leicester and then, slowly, onwards to London. On 3 September he entered the capital in triumph.

Some Ricardians fought on, notably at Harlech Castle, on Jersey, and in the Furness Fells. A few were executed, more imprisoned, and some fled into sanctuary. But most hastened to make their peace with the new king, at least for the moment. Henry had little choice but to accept their service, especially in the north, where few of his own adherents might claim any influence. His supporters did not go unrewarded, however, and the greatest received new dignities, foremost among them Jasper Tudor as duke of Bedford. Henry was crowned on 30 October and parliament sat from 7 November to 10 December, attainting

Richard's closest followers and petitioning Henry to marry Elizabeth of York. Papal support, probably secured in advance by Bishop John Morton on a trip to Rome early in 1485, facilitated the match with a dispensation from the impediment to their union provided by their shared descent from John of Gaunt, and on 18 January 1486 they were married.

The Simnel conspiracy Henry and his successors made much of the theme that this match between Lancaster and York had healed the dynastic wounds of past generations. Some of those who became Henry's most influential counsellors were veteran Lancastrians, such as Bedford or Oxford. Others were servants of his mother such as Sir Reynold Bray, chancellor of the duchy of Lancaster, whose promotion was an early sign of the influential role Lady Margaret would play throughout her son's reign. Others again were recruits from Henry's time of French exile, such as Richard Fox, the king's secretary and later keeper of the privy seal. But more were old servants of Edward IV. Thus John Morton was soon promoted archbishop of Canterbury and chancellor, and John, Lord Dynham, treasurer of the exchequer; Thomas Stanley was made earl of Derby and his brother Sir William chamberlain of the household; and the exiles of 1483, Sir Giles Daubeney and Sir Robert Willoughby, were made barons in 1486 and about 1489. Even those who had fought for Richard at Bosworth were allowed to work their way gradually back into favour, most notably Thomas Howard, earl of Surrey, who eventually succeeded Dynham as treasurer. The image of united red and white roses, prominent in the pageantry and court poetry of the reign, reflected a political reality.

Yet Henry was never able to free himself from Yorkist plots against his throne. The blend of insecurity and magnificence characteristic of his reign was typified by his rapid establishment of an armed bodyguard, the lineal ancestor of the present yeomen of the guard. On his first progress in 1486, north to Cambridge, Huntingdon, Lincoln, Nottingham, and York and west to Worcester, Hereford, Gloucester, and Bristol, he had to face not only loyal pageants laid on by one corporation after another, but also risings in Yorkshire, Warwickshire, and Worcestershire stirred by Francis, Viscount Lovell, and Humphrey Stafford of Grafton. Worse was soon to follow, despite the dynastic stability brought to the new order by the birth of Henry and Elizabeth's first son Prince *Arthur at Winchester on 19 September. By February 1487 Lambert Simnel had appeared in Ireland, claiming to be Edward, earl of Warwick, the young son of Edward IV's brother George, duke of Clarence. Henry had placed Warwick securely in the Tower at the start of his reign, and now he had him exhibited in London, while Queen Elizabeth Woodville and Robert Stillington, bishop of Bath and Wells, suspected of involvement in the plot, were placed under arrest. John de la Pole, earl of Lincoln, nephew of the Yorkist kings, fled to the Netherlands to join his aunt Margaret of York, dowager duchess of Burgundy, and take up the reins of the conspiracy together with Viscount Lovell.

Henry consulted with his leading subjects in a great council at Sheen, strengthened his defences in East Anglia, and then moved to Coventry and Kenilworth to await invasion.

Lincoln sailed from the Netherlands to Dublin, with some 2000 mercenaries supplied by Margaret. Whether out of fond memory of the Irish administration of Richard, duke of York, resentment at Henry's restoration of the Butler earls of Ormond, or sheer opportunism, most of the Irish political community had recognized Simnel as king. At Dublin on 24 May, led by Gerald Fitzgerald, earl of Kildare, the lord deputy recently confirmed in office by Henry, they crowned him as Edward VI. Backed by several thousand Irish troops in addition to Margaret's mercenaries, Simnel and his patrons landed at Foulney Island on the Cumbrian coast on 4 June and marched across northern Lancashire, over the Pennines and rapidly southwards, gathering support from Ricardian die-hards. Henry moved through Leicester to Nottingham, steadily assembling a large army—probably twice the size of his rivals'—from the retinues of loyal peers and household knights. At East Stoke, near Newark, on 16 June, Henry's archers decimated the unarmoured Irish levies, and after hard fighting his vanguard, again under Oxford, put the rebels to flight. Complete though his victory was, Henry spent the next four months moving cautiously through the midlands and north, venturing as far as Newcastle upon Tyne to secure the region's loyalty.

Consolidation continued into the autumn, as parliament met on 9 November and the queen was at last crowned on 25 November. Of the leading rebels, Lincoln and Kildare's brother, Thomas, had been killed in the field, Lovell may have fled to Scotland but afterwards disappeared, and Simnel was taken into the royal household as a menial. Comparatively few of their supporters were executed or attainted, but a number were heavily fined or bound over to keep allegiance to Henry in future, a characteristic procedure of the king's already used in the wake of the rebellions of 1486. Henry's commissioner Sir Richard Edgcumbe was instructed to take similar bonds from Kildare and other Irish noblemen in summer 1488, though in practice all they would offer was a solemn oath of allegiance. Henry was not entirely free from concerns about his safety at home—in December 1487 an obscure plot was discovered within his own household—but for the moment he could turn to events in neighbouring realms.

Scotland, Brittany, and France From the start of the reign Henry had sought good relations with James III of Scotland, but James's responsiveness alarmed some of his border nobles. James's death in battle against the rebel lords at Sauchieburn in June 1488 led Henry, while concluding truces with the Scots in 1488, 1491, and 1492, to patronize opposition to the new regime, just as *James IV soon began to dabble in Yorkist plots. Meanwhile François (II) of Brittany found the effective independence of his duchy under increasing pressure from Charles VIII of France. English volunteers under Edward Woodville, Lord Scales, served in François's army in summer 1488, but Henry tried to arbitrate a settlement between his two former hosts. By autumn the defeat, capitulation, and death of François, leaving as his heir his twelve-year-old daughter Anne, forced Henry out of his neutrality. He called a great council of peers and burgesses to Westminster and, having secured their advice, sent ambassadors to France and Brittany but also to potential allies against France: Ferdinand of Aragon and Isabella of Castile, and Maximilian, king of the Romans.

Parliament met in January 1489 and voted an unprecedented subsidy, directly assessed on wealth and incomes and continuing in succeeding years without further consultation should the war continue. It was to be collected in addition to the more traditional fifteenth and tenth also levied in that year, and in rapid succession to two fifteenths and tenths granted in 1487. On 14 February 1489 the treaty of Redon promised 6000 English troops to defend Brittany at the duchess's expense, but also provided for Breton assistance should Henry reassert English rights in France. Parallel alliances were concluded with Maximilian at Dordrecht in February and with Ferdinand and Isabella at Medina del Campo in March. For Maximilian this brought English military assistance under Giles, Lord Daubeney, against the rebel Flemish cities, notably at the battle of Dixmude in June; for the Spanish monarchs, the promise of a marriage between their daughter *Katherine of Aragon and Prince Arthur. In March and April, Henry's troops, some 7400 strong under Robert, Lord Willoughby de Broke, crossed to Brittany. Most were home by Christmas 1489, but in July 1490 Willoughby led a second expedition, fewer in men but stronger in ships. That year and the next brought English raids on the French coast and French attacks on Dorset. The war was complicated by Breton civil strife, in which Henry tended to support his old host Jean de Rieux, by popular revolt and by attempted papal mediation. Henry's alliance with Maximilian was broken when the latter settled with the French at Frankfurt in July 1489, but renewed at Woking in September 1490, a reconciliation marked by Maximilian's acceptance of investiture with the Order of the Garter in December. The final crisis of Breton independence came in 1491, as the French captured Nantes in March. Henry called a great council and levied a benevolence in July, funding a third, smaller expedition. But their task was forlorn. The French invasion ended in the marriage of Duchess Anne to Charles VIII on 6 December 1491. Henry had spent some £124,000 for nothing.

These foreign adventures did at least demonstrate the expansion in naval strength Henry had ordered early in his reign, exemplified by the heavily armed carracks *The Regent* and *The Sovereign*, larger than any ships built by his immediate predecessors. Navigation acts passed in 1485 and 1489, restricting the carriage of Gascon wine and woad to English ships, strengthened the merchant shipping available as a naval reserve and also kept trading interests happy. Yet in other ways the wars gave rise to domestic difficulties. The novel subsidy of 1489 raised only a third of what was expected, but prompted first calls for relief and then rebellion in Yorkshire. In April 1489 Henry Percy, earl of Northumberland, was killed by rioters. In response Henry marched north from Hertford through Leicester and Nottingham, gathering an impressive army before entering York on 23 May. The rebels had already dispersed, but trials and executions followed. When Henry returned south in June, he compensated for Northumberland's loss by leaving Thomas Howard, earl of Surrey, as his lieutenant in the north, a role the rehabilitated Ricardian performed with distinction, for example in his rapid suppression of another tax revolt in 1492.

Henry's dynasty received further reinforcements in these years, as Princess *Margaret was born on 29 November 1489, Arthur was ceremoniously created prince of Wales on the following day, and a second prince, Henry (the future *Henry VIII), was added on 28 June 1491. Yet Yorkist conspiracy, often under French patronage, revived repeatedly. Plots in favour of the earl of Warwick late in 1489 resulted in three executions and the imposition of a large fine on the abbot of Abingdon. The next plot to be revealed involved Sir Robert Chamberlain, who was caught at Hartlepool in January 1491 while attempting to leave for France. Most threatening was the conspiracy gathering in Ireland at the end of that year around a new pretender, Perkin Warbeck, presented as Richard, duke of York, the younger of Edward IV's sons. His appearance, then his transfer to Charles VIII's court in March 1492, stimulated Henry's preparations for a full-blown war against France.

Parliament, assembling on 17 October 1491, was induced to vote two fifteenths and tenths for collection in 1492, the first such double levy since 1429, all the more remarkable as its collection would follow that of a 'loving contribution' or benevolence, yielding some £50,000, approved by a great council in July 1491. A conspiracy to liberate Brittany with English assistance faltered, and Henry's fleet was at length repulsed from Normandy after devastating raids in June and July. He sent troops under Sir Edward Poynings to assist Maximilian's siege of the rebel stronghold of Sluys, but, despite what seem to have been good intentions on Maximilian's part, received no immediate help in return. Yet he continued to gather an army of 15,000 men, with which he crossed to Calais in October, rejecting the advice of his councillors to postpone the campaign again as he had done three times since June. On the 18th he besieged Boulogne, and on 3 November at Étaples he obtained perhaps the best he could now hope for, a peace providing for a generous annual payment in compensation for his expenses in the Breton war, and a French promise to expel Warbeck and his supporters. As his father had done when making the similar treaty of Picquigny with Edward IV in 1475, Charles VIII also granted pensions to eight of Henry's councillors, an additional incentive to English quiescence while he pursued his ambitions in Italy.

The Warbeck conspiracy Unfortunately for Henry, Warbeck moved next to the court of Margaret of York, who welcomed him as her nephew and gave fresh impetus to his cause. This increased the urgency of pacifying Warbeck's starting point and future hope, Ireland. After 1491 English troops were sent out on several occasions and the influence of the Butlers was further increased to countervail that of the Fitzgeralds, who had done little to stop Warbeck. Stability was impossible, however, without the loyalty of Kildare. He was dismissed as deputy in June 1492, responded by feuding with the king's new agents, came to court in November 1493 to discuss matters with Henry in person, and within months of his return was arrested and attainted for treasonable contact with the Gaelic chiefs of Ulster.

Kildare's removal only complicated matters for the new regime led by Sir Edward Poynings, who was named deputy in September 1494, and was expensively equipped with English troops and administrators to pursue war against the Gaels and security against the Yorkists. By the time of his recall in December 1495, Poynings had achieved little against the first enemy but sufficient against the second. More famously, he and his colleagues had presided over a strengthening of royal control in Ireland epitomized by the enactment of Poynings' law, which limited the Irish parliament to legislation approved in advance by the king and his English council. Their success made feasible the restoration of Kildare; their dependence on English subsidies made it desirable. In October 1495 Kildare's attainder was reversed, and in August 1496 he was restored as deputy. He retained that position for the remainder of the reign, combining his unparalleled local influence with the wide powers granted him by the king to provide effective, if largely unsupervised, governance. Once, in 1506, Henry did consider personal intervention in his Irish lordship with an army large enough to subdue the Gaels, but after discussion with his council he resolved to leave Kildare to continue his successful holding operation.

Meanwhile Henry faced threats closer to home. From early 1493 such senior figures at the English court as John Radcliffe, Lord Fitzwalter, and even Sir William Stanley were apparently drawn into plots in favour of Warbeck. Though these were not yet revealed, Henry spent the summer of that year at Warwick, Kenilworth, and Northampton, poised to meet an invasion, his trusted supporters holding troops ready to march at one day's notice. At about this time he also increased his personal security, and perhaps also his freedom from importunate suitors, by creating a privy chamber staffed by servants of humble origin into which he could withdraw from the pressures of the court. In May commissioners were appointed to investigate treasons across fifteen counties and some plotters were arrested, but in June Sir Robert Clifford and others slipped away to Margaret's court. In July Sir Edward Poynings and Dr William Warham arrived in the Netherlands to denounce Warbeck's imposture, but they could not persuade the councillors of the young Philip the Fair of Burgundy, recently emerged from the regency of his father Maximilian, to restrain the dowager duchess's support for the pretender. Henry resolved to follow persuasion with coercion, suspending all direct trade to the Netherlands, the staple market for English cloth exports, in September. The ban hurt London, where unemployed

workers rioted on 15 October against the Steelyard, home to the privileged Hanseatic merchants; but it did not yet hurt Warbeck, who with Margaret's help was rapidly becoming an intimate of Maximilian.

Early in 1494 more plotters were arrested, executed, or fled to sanctuary. Henry's spies and double agents were hard at work, but so were Yorkist recruiters. To distract attention from the soi-disant duke of York, Henry on 31 October 1494 gave that title to his second son, Prince Henry, a creation he proceeded to celebrate with a splendid round of tournaments. Then, in mid-November, a series of arrests began which by late January had brought in the leading suspects accused by Sir Robert Clifford, who fled Margaret's court to turn king's evidence. The knights, gentlemen, and clerics—including the dean of St Paul's and the provincial of the Dominicans—were tried for treason by the end of the month and executed or imprisoned within a week. Sir William Stanley was tried on 6–7 February and executed on the 16th, Lord Fitzwalter convicted on 23 February but imprisoned at Guînes in the Calais pale, only to be executed in 1496 after trying to escape.

Undaunted, Warbeck and his backers prepared to raise revolt in Ireland and invade England by sea in 1495, while Margaret petitioned Pope Alexander VI to remove his predecessor's excommunication, issued in 1486, of any challenging Henry's title to the throne. Again Henry moved through his kingdom watching for invasion; when he was in the west with his eyes on Ireland, Cardinal Morton stayed in London to co-ordinate defence of the southern coasts. Naval defences were strengthened by the construction at Portsmouth of a fortified harbour, dock, and storehouse. Warbeck's men landed at Deal on 3 July but were attacked on the beach by local levies: 163 were captured and perhaps 150 killed. Henry's vengeance was implacable: fifty-one Englishmen among the prisoners were tried for treason and subsequently executed at various sites around the country, while the foreigners were tried as pirates and many of them likewise put to death. Warbeck sailed on to Ireland while Henry toured the Welsh marches and the Stanley heartlands of Cheshire and Lancashire, doubtless with Sir William Stanley's recent treason in mind. In Ireland Warbeck joined Maurice Fitzgerald, earl of Desmond, who had rebelled on his behalf, in besieging Waterford until Poynings relieved the city on 3 August. Thwarted in Ireland, the pretender moved on to Scotland, as the welcome guest of James IV. Meanwhile parliament, assembling on 14 October, testified to the insecurities of king and subjects alike by passing what was to become known as the De facto Act: not, as later misinterpretation made it, a grand statement distinguishing between rightful and merely *de facto* rulers, but an assurance that those fighting for Henry could not be charged with treason by some future king, just as he would not henceforth count traitorous those who had fought for Richard III when he was generally recognized as king.

Scottish war and Cornish revolt Warbeck's transfer to Ireland, then Scotland, enabled Henry to improve relations with the continental powers. Trade with the Netherlands was restored in February 1496 by the treaty later known as the Intercursus Magnus. Meanwhile Henry negotiated both with the French and with the members of the Holy League who sought their expulsion from Italy; in July he joined the league, but without committing himself to fight the French. As James prepared for war in support of Warbeck, Henry repeatedly offered him peace and the hand of his daughter Margaret, but James pressed ahead. In September he invaded, but Warbeck soon left him, perhaps disillusioned by the failure of his manifesto to raise revolt by its denunciations of Henry's harsh taxes and low-born ministers. James demolished a few small fortifications and then also withdrew, but Henry was bent on retaliation. While Surrey raided across the border, the king secured consent from a great council in October–November for a forced loan of over £50,000 and then from parliament, assembling on 16 January 1497, for £120,000 in taxation, half of it in directly assessed levies like those of 1489, though with fixed county quotas. This was the heaviest taxation of the century, raised to fund a large fleet carrying 5000 men, an army of which the vanguard alone numbered about 10,000, and an imposing artillery train for a stunning blow against the Scots.

The blow never fell. In mid-May 1497 the Cornish rose in revolt against Henry's taxes and marched east, drawing on the support or acquiescence of militant clergy and Somerset gentlemen, themselves inspired either by residual Yorkist loyalty or resentment at Henry's favour to his few local intimates. Led by James Tuchet, Lord Audley, Thomas Flamank, a man of property in Bodmin, for which he was MP in 1492, and Michael Joseph an Gof, a blacksmith of St Keverne, they headed for London; but at Blackheath, on 17 June, Henry and his loyal nobility and gentry defeated them. The leaders were executed by the end of the month and in the ensuing years thousands of their followers would be fined after painstaking investigations. Attention turned to the north, where Bishop Fox defended Norham Castle against James's siege and Surrey led a brief counter-invasion. But the south-west was not yet quiet. The rebels had called Warbeck to lead them, and on 7 September he landed near Land's End. Though he assembled perhaps 8000 men to besiege Exeter, Henry was far too strong for him, and his army dissolved in the face of forces under Daubeney and Willoughby de Broke after only a fortnight's campaign. Henry marched westwards in triumph, to Bath, Wells, Taunton, and Exeter. At Taunton he received Warbeck, who had left sanctuary on promise that his life would be spared. A truce was made with the Scots on 30 September, and collection of the outstanding quarter of the year's parliamentary taxes was cancelled. Having survived perhaps the greatest crisis of his reign, Henry was proceeding with caution.

Marriages and deaths Even amid the convulsions of 1496–7, arrangements had been proceeding for the marriage of Prince Arthur to Katherine of Aragon. They were solemnly betrothed in August 1497 and married by proxy in May 1499 and again in autumn 1500 when Arthur was aged fourteen. Alliance with Spain did not draw Henry into hostility towards France, and in July 1498 he renewed the

treaty of Étaples with Charles VIII's successor Louis XII. From 1499 he again sought a secure peace with the Scots through the marriage of James IV to his daughter Margaret, finally agreed upon by treaties of 24 January 1502. In May and June 1500 he visited Calais for a meeting with Philip the Fair of Burgundy, to confirm the resolution of disputes between English merchants and the authorities in the Netherlands arrived at in 1497–9, and to discuss possible marriages for Prince Henry and his younger sister, *Mary, born in 1496. This dynastic and diplomatic consolidation found its architectural counterpart in Richmond Palace, a development of the old royal palace of Sheen which was partially destroyed by fire at Christmas 1497. At a cost of some £20,000, and echoing the style of Burgundian ducal palaces, it was a grand setting for Arthur's and Katherine's marriage festivities. These took place in November 1501, marked by tournaments, disguisings, and abstrusely allegorical London pageants, the authors of which did not blush to identify Henry with God the Father and Arthur with Christ his Son.

Yet this Tudor apotheosis had a darker side. In February 1499 a pretender, Ralph Wilford, who claimed to be the earl of Warwick, was arrested, tried, and executed. In July 1499 Edmund de la Pole, earl of Suffolk, nephew of the Yorkist kings through his mother, fled to the Netherlands when facing indictment for the murder of a man engaged in litigation before the king's council. In August 1499 Warwick himself became caught up in a plot with Perkin Warbeck, who had been in the Tower since fleeing the court and being recaptured in June 1498; sympathizers were to free them both and place one upon the throne. On 12 November a council meeting more than sixty strong advised the king to do justice on the conspirators. Warbeck and Warwick were convicted and dead by the end of the month. The Yorkist threat seemed to have died with them: Suffolk had been persuaded to return home, and John Taylor, the co-ordinator of much of the plotting of the past decade, was in the Tower having been surrendered by the French in September. In January 1500 the Spanish ambassador wrote home that 'England has never before been so tranquil and obedient as at present' (*CSP Spain, 1485–1509*, 213). But in August 1501 Suffolk left the country again, assuming the Yorkist title of White Rose, demanding the restoration of the ducal title to which he had not been allowed to succeed on the death of his father, and seeking the support of Warbeck's old patron Maximilian. Within six months leading figures at court and in the garrisons of the Calais pale—Lord William Courtenay, Sir James Tyrell, and Sir Robert Curson—were under suspicion of plotting with him against the king. Another round of arrests, executions, and declarations of ecclesiastical censure upon those beyond Henry's reach was the result. Meanwhile Henry, having consulted a great council early in 1502, began again the weary diplomatic round of neutralizing all possible support for a pretender. In June and July he bought Maximilian's withdrawal of assistance from any English rebels for £10,000, and asked Louis XII to use his influence in Germany to arrange the purchase of Suffolk from whichever potentate managed to secure him next.

The political insecurities of the period were heightened by the deaths of a number of Henry's leading councillors and supporters: John, Lord Cheyne and John, Viscount Welles, in 1499, Cardinal Morton in 1500, John, Lord Dynham, in 1501, Robert, Lord Willoughby de Broke, in 1502, Sir Reynold Bray and George Stanley, Lord Strange, in 1503, and finally Thomas Stanley, earl of Derby, in 1504. Far worse for the king were the bereavements he suffered among his family. On 19 June 1500 his youngest son, Edmund, born on 21 or 22 February 1499, died at Hatfield. On 2 April 1502 Prince Arthur, holding court in the Welsh borders with his new wife, suddenly died at Ludlow. Henry and Elizabeth were each distraught, recorded one witness, but comforted one another, not least with the prospect that they might yet have more children. A daughter, Catherine, was indeed born on 2 February 1503, but lived only a few days. Elizabeth herself died nine days after the birth. Henry's deep but lonely grief was as characteristic of his later years as the readiness with which he secured the Spanish alliance and Katherine of Aragon's dowry, by agreeing to Ferdinand's proposal to betroth her to his younger son, Prince Henry. The papal dispensation necessary for Katherine's remarriage was slow in coming, but in August 1503 another link in Henry's chain of dynastic alliances was at length secured by the marriage of Margaret to James IV in Edinburgh, Henry having escorted her from Richmond to his mother's house at Collyweston before bidding her farewell. The book of hours that he gave her, inscribed with a request to pray for him, still survives at Chatsworth House.

Diplomatic turmoil The death of Isabella of Castile in November 1504 shattered the framework of Henry's European alliances by making her widower, Ferdinand of Aragon, the rival of Philip the Fair, husband of their elder daughter, Joanna, for control of Castile. In 1505 each tried to woo Henry with a candidate for his own remarriage, paired with a match for Prince Henry. Ferdinand's accompaniment to his daughter Katherine was his niece Joanna, dowager queen of Naples. Philip offered his sister, Margaret of Austria, dowager duchess of Savoy, for Henry, and his daughter Eleanor for the prince. Meanwhile Louis XII tried to tempt either Henry or the prince with his cousin Marguerite of Angoulême. Philip sought additional leverage by obtaining custody in July 1505 from the duke of Gueldres of Edmund de la Pole. Louis appealed to Henry's knightly piety with the gift of the silver-encased leg of St George, with which the king processed in state through London on 22 April that year.

Matters were brought to a head in January 1506 when Philip and Joanna, on their way to Castile, were driven by storms onto the Dorset coast. Henry welcomed his involuntary guests to Windsor, where they were provided with lavish entertainment and encouraged to enter into a number of agreements. Renewed commercial disputes which had led to another suspension of the cloth trade were resolved on terms very favourable to the English merchants; Suffolk would be delivered to Henry, who undertook

to spare his life; and Philip would press his sister to marry Henry. In return Henry would sustain Philip in his campaign for the Castilian throne, as he had already begun to do with generous loans, the first of a series to the Habsburgs which were to total between £226,000 and £342,000 by Henry's death. The amity was sealed by the exchange of chivalrous orders, Henry's Garter for Philip's Golden Fleece, the latter granted to the prince of Wales since Henry himself had already been chosen a companion of the Burgundian order in 1491.

Philip sailed onwards in April, but his undertakings were soon being unravelled by others. Margaret determined to stay a widow, and the authorities in the Netherlands dragged their feet over implementing the commercial treaty until Philip's sudden death in September threw affairs into turmoil once again. For his part Henry, who had steered between Philip and Louis in the summer by offering his arbitration over the latter's support for the duke of Gueldres, a thorn in the side of the Netherlands, now began simultaneous wooing of the ever reluctant Margaret of Austria, the equally reluctant Marguerite of Angoulême, and Philip's widow, Joanna. Though the last was already busy acquiring the sobriquet 'the Mad', it was suggested that a sensible husband such as Henry would do wonders for her. Henry, suspicious that her madness was a fiction convenient to Ferdinand, sought her hand on and off until his death, just as he did that of Margaret of Austria.

None of these matches came to fruition, but from Henry's continuing contacts with Margaret and Maximilian came another marriage agreement of enormous potential significance in the coming generation. This plan, tentatively broached by Philip and Henry in 1506 but firmly agreed in December 1507, was for Henry's daughter Mary to marry Charles of Ghent, son of Philip and Joanna, lord of the Netherlands in succession to his father, and heir apparent to his mother as king of Castile, his maternal grandfather, Ferdinand, as king of Aragon, and his paternal grandfather, Maximilian von Habsburg, as the most eligible candidate to be Holy Roman emperor. For the vistas opened up by this marriage, Henry's final abandonment of the commercial terms of 1506 and his expanding loans to the insatiable Maximilian looked a small price to pay. Henry ordered his subjects to celebrate the treaty, and towns from Shrewsbury to Dover lit bonfires of joy. In December 1508 the young couple were betrothed by proxy at London amid further celebrations. Equally remarkably, Henry had managed to draw near to the Habsburgs without finally alienating Ferdinand or the French. European politics now focused increasingly on Italy, as the powers combined in the League of Cambrai to dismember Venice's mainland empire, leaving Henry to ponder in peace his successful passage through a turbulent five years.

Avarice and wealth The years after 1502 were marked by a decline in Henry's health and, some contemporaries felt, in the character of his kingship. His eyesight began to fail and he found writing difficult. At one point—the source, a report of treasonable talk, does not give the exact date—

he lay seriously ill at Wanstead, reportedly ill enough for the great men outside his room to start to speculate on the succession to his throne. From 1507 he fell sick in the early part of each year, rallying in the summer. Meanwhile the deaths among his trusted councillors brought new men to the fore. Most notorious among them was Edmund Dudley, an able common lawyer who served as speaker of the last parliament of the reign in January 1504. This seems to have been a troubled assembly. Numerous attainders were passed, chiefly against minor followers of Warbeck or Suffolk, but other legislation met with more resistance. An act against retaining, stricter than that of 1468, was limited to the king's lifetime. Henry's request for feudal aids for knighting his eldest son and marrying his eldest daughter was deflected by the grant of what was in effect a peacetime subsidy, apparently so as to avoid the compilation of a register of tenancies-in-chief which might then have been used to extract further feudal incidents from those who held land from the king.

This opposition, in which the young Thomas More reputedly took part, was symptomatic of a feeling growing during Henry's last decade that he was becoming unduly rapacious towards his subjects. The notoriety of Dudley, who became president of the king's council by 1506, sprang from his role as a chief agent of those exactions, but how new, unjustified, or counter-productive they were is a matter of dispute. Henry had always been keen to maximize royal income. He steadily expanded his landed estate and improved its administration until it yielded an income of approximately £40,000 a year, nearly double that of Richard III. By the diplomatic encouragement of trade, the fervent prosecution of smugglers, and the introduction of a book of rates setting official values for taxable merchandise, he capitalized on a revival of European commerce to raise his annual customs income likewise to £40,000 or more, one-third above the level of the mid-fifteenth-century depression. Although until 1504 he levied parliamentary taxation only to fund wars, that taxation was, as already discussed, heavy in incidence and innovative in assessment. The clergy, too, were taxed more heavily than under his predecessors. Throughout the reign he exploited intensively his feudal rights over those who held land directly from him, selling the wardships of under-aged heirs and the marriages of his tenants' widows, charging livery fees to those inheriting estates, and investigating and fining heavily those who seemed to be evading these liabilities. Penal statutes for economic regulation, outlawries, and fines for negligent prison-keepers were all likewise turned to profit. Royal commissioners toured the shires with increasing frequency, uncovering potential victims for such fiscalism, while pressure was put on the county escheators to secure verdicts favourable to the king's rights. By Henry's last years all these sources of income were being squeezed hard, and others less reputable, such as the sale of office and even the sale of the king's favour in lawsuits, were being added to them.

The impression that Henry was driven more by avarice than statecraft was heightened by the administration of his finances. As the reign progressed he moved control over ever more areas of income from the exchequer to the chamber, a more flexible institution, more intimately under his own control, less transparent to his subjects in its operations, and more apt for dealing in the large sums of cash flowing in from his estates. Beyond the chamber stood a network of king's coffers for cash deposits so shadowy that it still remains unclear whether Henry left vast or merely modest reserves to his son. The resultant image of a king personally in control of important matters, and rich enough to meet all contingencies, was politically valuable, but readily became distorted into that of a ruler bent on amassing wealth for its own sake. After Bray's death in 1503, moreover, individual ministers or bodies with responsibility for the pursuit of different classes of income began to proliferate. Some were specific in their duties: the master of the wards, the surveyor of the king's prerogative, the general surveyors of crown lands. Others ranged more widely to take profit for the king wherever it might be found, as did Dudley and the king's council learned in the law, led by Sir Richard Empson. Thus was the impression of relentlessness and ingenuity added to that of avarice, while failures of co-ordination among these agencies lent an edge of arbitrariness.

King and nobility Henry's exactions fell most visibly on his greatest subjects, noblemen, prelates, gentlemen, and London merchants. This was not only because they had more money for the king to take, but also because he used debt as a means of political control. As Dudley put it, Henry was 'much sett to have many persons in his danger at his pleasure' (Harrison, 86). Those fined for offences or made to enter bonds for their good behaviour had to commit themselves to pay large sums, of which Henry graciously demanded only a little each year so long as they retained his favour. Their friends and relations were drawn in as sureties for their debts, thus tying up much of the political nation in a web of obligation to the king. Bonds had been used by Henry to restrain those under suspicion from the earliest years of his reign, but their use seems to have accelerated sharply from about 1502.

The policy was of a piece with other aspects of the king's relationship with the nobility. Though quite prepared to give responsibility and reward to noblemen he trusted, he gave less wholeheartedly than most previous kings. Those he trusted from the start, such as Oxford and Derby, never gained untrammelled regional power. Those he grew to trust as they proved themselves, such as Thomas Howard, earl of Surrey, and George Talbot, earl of Shrewsbury, grew in influence only little by little. Those he never trusted, such as Edward Stafford, duke of Buckingham, and Henry Percy, fifth earl of Northumberland, he seemed to frustrate at every turn. These last were also prominent victims of his financial exactions. Meanwhile great offices which might have been vehicles for noble ambition were often kept in the king's hands, or were granted to his sons and exercised by deputies of knightly rank. The king's council, ever more influential in co-ordinating the work of government, was dominated not by great nobles but by clerics, lawyers, and household men. Henry's parsimony in making grants of land or annuities after the earliest years of his reign doubtless frustrated even these intimates, but they could use their political influence and the wealth it brought them to buy land as the wider nobility could not.

Although Henry relied heavily on his peers and greater gentry to recruit for his armies, he was also from the earliest years of his reign quick to prosecute those who retained followers illegally. From 1504 retaining licences were used to confine military force still more closely into the hands of the king's intimates, and councillors such as Sir Thomas Lovell constructed extensive retinues largely on the basis of the offices they held on crown and ecclesiastical estates. The king's lands served more widely to reinforce the local influence of the knights, esquires, and gentlemen who acted as Henry's stewards and receivers, who were in turn often personally tied to the king as office-holders in the expanding court. Conversely, many of the new crown estates had been confiscated from noble families, who resented their retention in the king's hands or had to pay large sums for their return. In national as in local politics, when confronted with the king's intrusive councillors and courtiers, many noblemen felt their rightful power constrained by Henry's rule, above all in his latter years.

Henry's financial concerns and suspicions of noble power were felt even in those areas of the kingdom where noblemen's freedom of action had been best guaranteed by distance from the capital, military necessity, and franchisal jurisdiction. In the far north he cut the wages of the wardens of the marches and captains of border fortresses, and tried to substitute southerners or lesser peers for the great border families in those offices, though the result seems to have been a decay of locally effective governance rather than any decisive strengthening of royal control. In Yorkshire he established a council to oversee local justice and government led by Thomas Savage, archbishop of York from 1501, but Savage fell out dangerously with the earl of Northumberland. In Wales, though considerable responsibility was given to Jasper Tudor, Sir Rhys ap Thomas and, latterly, Charles Somerset, Lord Herbert, Prince Arthur's council oversaw local government from 1489 and royal commissioners continued to do so after his death. Marcher lords were bound in recognizances to maintain good order in their lordships, but, as elsewhere, the king's fiscalism itself became a threat to stability. The inhabitants of the northern shires of the principality and some northerly marcher lordships were freed from their disabilities under English law by charters of 1504–8, but at the cost of heavy communal fines, while the attempt to make profit out of princely jurisdiction in Meirionydd prompted revolt there in 1498.

Everywhere the expanding judicial activities of Henry's council, the forerunner of the later courts of Star Chamber and requests, threatened to cramp noble freedom of action. At least one in three of Henry's peers, probably more, appeared before the council courts, and on occasion the king took notes of the evidence against them in his own hand. The commissions of the peace were enlarged to give more of the gentry a role in local government, and especially at moments of crisis Henry's most trusted councillors were added to the commissions to oversee their operations. Experimental conciliar tribunals and new statutes, some permitting prosecution by information rather than indictment before a jury, were introduced to punish local perversions of justice. In the midlands the king's mother's council operated as a regional equity court. At sea strict measures were taken against piracy, whether English or foreign. Disorder did erupt on occasion, sometimes indeed at the hands of Henry's aggressive courtiers, sometimes in ways that might have been contained by the hand of a locally dominant lord. Yet while it is hazardous to render any verdict on the state of law and order in Henry's England, it appears, from what indications exist, that at least by the end of the reign it was improving. Credit is due to Henry's councillors, among whom common lawyers were more influential than in the counsels of any previous king, and to Henry himself. But once again the achievement was marred not only by the rapacity of councillors such as Empson and Savage, who seem to have perverted justice to their own advantage, but also by the rapacity of the king, who found himself promising on his deathbed that, if God would spare his life, he would reform his ministers so that justice would be impartially done and would pardon his subjects for the old (and often technical) offences for which he continued to mulct them.

That Henry's noblemen continued to fight for him, indeed did so in ever larger numbers as the crises of 1487, 1489, and 1497 succeeded one another, was not solely attributable to intimidation. His reluctance to create new peers or promote individuals within the peerage, which allowed the number of peers to decline from fifty-five to forty-two over the reign, mostly by natural wastage, allowed more prominence to those who survived; his use of the great council as a consultative body, at least until his last decade, gave the wider peerage a formal role in government; and loyal peers even outside the king's inner circle drew some rewards and favours from the king. Noblemen, even those under fiscal pressure or political suspicion, were welcome at court, and many took part in the splendid tournaments and dances with which Henry celebrated great diplomatic and dynastic events. Here they featured both as part of the cast in a magnificent drama designed to impress foreign observers and English subjects alike, and as a key element in that domestic audience.

Courtly magnificence The magnificence of Henry's court was calculated and expensive. He dressed richly, though latterly all too often in sophisticated but mournful black. His physical appearance as contemporaries described it—somewhat over the average in height, slender, strong, and blue-eyed—lent itself to a regal bearing, though late in life his hair turned white and his teeth were few and black. Formal crown-wearing ceremonies and regular touchings to heal his scrofulous subjects of the king's evil reinforced his majesty. Widespread use of his dynastic badges on buildings, charters, and the liveries of his servants proclaimed his inherited right to rule. An ultimately unsuccessful campaign for the canonization of Henry VI aimed to sanctify his Lancastrian lineage. Court poets glorified his achievements whether in the Latin of Pietro Carmeliano, the French of Bernard André, or the English of Stephen Hawes. Polydore Vergil of Urbino, deputy papal tax collector in England, was commissioned to write a history of England from the earliest times to the glorious Tudor present in the new humanist mode. Netherlandish and Italian artists such as Maynard Werwick and Guido Mazzoni came to work for the king. Royal residences were improved, sometimes beyond recognition. In addition to Richmond, Henry built new towers with more comfortable royal lodgings at Windsor Castle and the Tower of London from 1500, rebuilt Baynard's Castle, London, about 1501, and constructed from 1498 a completely new house at Greenwich, even closer in design than Richmond to the brick urban palaces of the Burgundian Netherlands. Tapestries, some depicting the great events of the reign, and several hundred thousand pounds' worth of jewels and plate were bought from the continent to adorn these royal palaces. Henry doubtless enjoyed the life of his court, playing tennis, gambling, shooting longbows and crossbows, and above all hunting and hawking day after day; but he also knew the advantages of visible greatness.

Henry's splendour was not confined to the capital and its environs. His earliest domestic building works were at Woodstock and Kings Langley from 1494—Woodstock may have cost more than Greenwich—and later he worked on houses at Woking and Hanworth. Though he became less peripatetic with age, his progresses still took him to such towns as Nottingham in 1503, Winchester in 1504, Salisbury in 1505, Cambridge in 1506, and Ely and Reading in 1507. In 1489 he issued the first gold sovereign, at 20s. the largest denomination yet issued by an English king. It depicted him enthroned and wearing a closed imperial crown rather than an open royal one. From 1504 his coins bore a profile portrait more individualized than that of any predecessor. His proclamations justified his policies in persuasive detail and he used printed propaganda of increasing sophistication, from a translation of the papal bull permitting his marriage in 1486, to the Latin and English tracts praising the marriage alliance made for his daughter Mary in 1508.

Henry's piety blended with his magnificence. Richmond and Greenwich housed friaries for the austere Franciscan Observants, his favourite religious order. His ecclesiastical building projects were conceived on a splendid scale, stressed his Lancastrian heritage, and were covered in Tudor badges. The continuation of the chapel of Henry VI's King's College, Cambridge, the lady chapel at Windsor in which Henry originally planned to be buried together with his sainted uncle, the Savoy Hospital, the Westminster almshouses, and the king's own lavish burial chapel at Westminster Abbey cost some £34,000 in the king's lifetime, and his executors added at least £22,000 more. Henry's flamboyant royal religion, echoing

that he had seen at the courts of Brittany and France, came dear.

The morality of kingship Henry's piety blended uneasily with his rapacity; indeed, much of the money he spent on his devotions was drawn from the church. His financial dealings with newly appointed clerical dignitaries came sufficiently close to simony for him to secure in 1504 a special clause in the papal licence for his confessor confirming whatever absolution he had been given for illicit receipts from the sale of spiritual office. He tended to choose administrators and diplomats trained in the law for his bishops, and to move them regularly from see to see to maximize his profits. He offered the church little protection against the assaults that common lawyers, led by some of his own councillors, made against the jurisdiction of the ecclesiastical courts, benefit of clergy, and the rights of sanctuaries. He expressed sufficient enthusiasm for the crusade to be named protector of the knights of St John at Rhodes in 1506, but never did much more. He was loyal enough to the papacy to be presented with the blessed sword and cap—gifts sent by the pope to specially favoured rulers—by three successive pontiffs, in 1488, 1496, and 1505. This was a unique feat for any ruler in Christendom, yet he was not loyal enough to see the English church taxed for the pope's benefit rather than his own until 1502, when two-thirds of the money raised was sent not to Rome but to Henry's ally Maximilian for crusade expenses. Henry's dedication to the God of battles was intense—he regularly offered up his banners in worship after victory—but his devotion to the church was more measured.

Henry's relationship with urban élites was as ambivalent as that with the nobility and the prelates. He invited burgesses on a generous scale to his great councils, and granted 'close corporation' charters consolidating the powers of the leading citizens of boroughs such as Bristol and Exeter. Many towns established a mutually beneficial relationship with one of the king's leading councillors: for instance, Bray at Bedford, Empson at Coventry, Lovell at Nottingham, and Sir James Hobart, the attorney-general, at Norwich. In commercial diplomacy Henry generally favoured the interests of English merchants against those of foreigners, or at least tried to secure reciprocal privileges for Englishmen abroad when conceding special terms to foreigners in England. He supported English traders to the Mediterranean and fishers off Iceland, and from 1496 patronized Bristol-based voyages of Atlantic exploration by the Genoese Cabot family. Yet his fierce attacks on customs evasion and other offences, leaving three former mayors in prison, were resented in London, as were his attempts to manipulate city politics in favour of the Tailors' Company against the Drapers, and the large fine he charged in 1505 for a new charter which failed to confirm rights granted in 1478. Once again his concern with control and profit soured his commitment to good government.

It seems that moral decline and political consolidation were inseparable. Repeated threats to the Tudor succession, from pretenders abroad and deaths at home, left

Henry more concerned to be obeyed than loved. Rapacity gave him handholds for political manipulation, funded the magnificence that might inspire awe, backed the loans to the Habsburgs that bought him peace and security. What passed for avarice was not an adventitious moral failing but an aspect of his always intensely personal monarchy. The Henry who obsessively checked his accounts was the same Henry who in August 1488 went for a sail on Southampton Water in *The Sovereign* before she set out to the Breton wars; the same Henry who in April 1498 at Canterbury personally persuaded a heretic priest to recant his errors; the same Henry who in August 1501 at Richmond checked the design for the collars of Prince Arthur's trumpeters; the same Henry who, in September 1507, struck out the term 'for life' in a grant of local offices to Sir Richard Empson and inserted 'during pleasure'. To his English contemporaries, the foreign character of Henry's political experience before he took the throne can only have amplified the impenetrability of purpose that accompanied such personal control. 'He would like to govern England in the French fashion, but he cannot' reported the Spanish ambassador in 1498 (*CSP Spain*, *1485–1509*, 178).

Death and reputation The tensions of Henry's later years were reflected in turbulence at court. Charges of corruption, of illegal retaining, and of old Yorkist loyalties, stresses between clerics and lawyers brought variously demotion, disgrace, fines, imprisonment, and even the threat of execution to such leading councillors and courtiers as Giles, Lord Daubeney, George Neville, Lord Bergavenny, Sir Richard Guildford, Sir James Hobart, Lord William Courtenay, and Thomas Grey, marquess of Dorset. None the less, Henry's inner circle held together well enough to ensure his son's peaceful succession when at last the old king's recurrent, though now unidentifiable, illness got the better of him. By 24 March 1509 he was regarded as beyond hope of recovery, on 31 March he made his last will, yet he lingered at Richmond until 11 p.m. on Saturday 21 April, in an agony of pain and penitence vividly described by Bishop John Fisher in his funeral sermon. Those around him kept his death secret until the afternoon of the 23rd to smooth his son's path. Edmund Dudley and Sir Richard Empson were arrested next morning and rapidly cast as scapegoats for Henry's more unpalatable policies as the battle over the king's reputation commenced.

Most of Henry's provisions for his own immediate commemoration were carried out to spectacular effect. Thousands of pounds were spent on masses for his soul and alms to the poor and on 11 May, after grand funeral processions from Richmond to St Paul's and then on to Westminster, he was interred in his new chapel. In 1512 his executors commissioned Pietro Torrigiano, who had probably made the head for the effigy used during the king's funeral, to make a tomb with recumbent effigies of Henry and Elizabeth. By 1518 it was complete, its Italianate putti, saints, and angels making it one of the first great monuments of Renaissance art in England. Yet one striking memorial Henry envisaged was never put in place: a gold-plated statue of the king, kneeling in full armour, holding

the crown as he had received it at Bosworth by the judgement of God, which his will ordered to be placed atop the shrine of Edward the Confessor, holy of holies of English monarchy.

Henry's contemporaries soon began to pass their verdicts upon him. Two verse epitaphs, one perhaps by Hawes, were printed, lamenting his death and praising him in rather vague or standardized terms. Fisher, preaching in St Paul's on 10 May, praised Henry's 'polytyque wysedome in governaunce' and the respect, peace, and prosperity it brought him at home and abroad, before describing at length his pious end. In lauding Henry's prudence and its benefits he echoed the comments of foreign ambassadors and others in the king's lifetime. Yet even he had to remind his auditors that if Henry were alive again 'many one that is here present now wolde pretende a full grete pyte & tendernesse' towards him (*English Works*, 269, 280). Such tenderness was conspicuously lacking in Thomas More's verse greeting the advent of Henry VIII, bitterly critical of the old king's treatment of noblemen and Londoners alike. Polydore Vergil, completing his history in manuscript about 1513, praised Henry's skills and achievements but charged him unequivocally with avarice in his last years, a charge toned down but not eliminated in his printed edition of 1534. For Edward Hall and later Tudor chroniclers, Henry's pacification of civil strife obscured the tension between wisdom and avarice, but the question was reopened by Francis Bacon in his account of the reign, written in 1621–2 as an exercise in the new 'politic history' inspired by Tacitus and Machiavelli. His depiction was conditioned not only by the need to shape an entertaining and instructive tale but also by his own concerns at the court of James I. Bacon found Henry skilful in the short term but somewhat lacking in foresight except with regard to his legislation, which he thought second in significance only to that of Edward I. Bacon especially valued the various statutes reforming judicial procedure, the Navigation Acts, and the (rarely enforced) statute against enclosure of 1489—this last for its defence of the yeomanry against aggressive landlordship. He also, however, found Henry obsessively and consistently avaricious.

Bacon's portrait of Henry held the field for two and a half centuries. The publications of record material from the 1850s by scholars such as James Gairdner and William Campbell did not much dent it, and curiously even Wilhelm Busch's demolition of its status as a primary source in 1892 left its judgements on the king's character largely intact. By this stage the moral argument was being bypassed by the assimilation of Henry's reign to a longer period of 'new monarchy', in which assertive rulers restored stability after the Wars of the Roses by repressing self-interested and over-mighty noblemen, and allying themselves with middle-class interests represented by gentlemen justices of the peace, merchants, and bureaucrats. In the mid-twentieth century detailed investigations of the machinery of government by J. R. Lander and B. P. Wolffe reinforced the impression of continuity between Henry and his Yorkist predecessors, as did G. R.

Elton's stress on the 1530s as the great period of modernization of English government. Meanwhile a swing away from administrative and traditional constitutional history towards a social history of politics, led by K. B. McFarlane, questioned the need for Henry to tame the magnates, and made him look nothing more special than one of a number of later medieval kings successful in managing the political nation. Avarice returned briefly to the fore in a sharp debate between Elton and J. P. Cooper about Henry's last years, but now debate turned less on Henry's morals than on whether his exactions constituted a politically stabilizing reassertion of royal authority or a politically destabilizing tyranny. Since then wide-ranging research on local politics, Henry's court, council, and judicial machinery, his relations with the church, and other topics, has delivered a mixed verdict both on his novelty and on the success of his rule. Often inscrutable to his contemporaries, Henry seems destined to remain so. Though much of Bacon's history has thus been dethroned from its once authoritative position, the biblical motto on the frontispiece of his first edition still stands: *Cor regis inscrutabile*—'Unsearchable is the heart of a king'.

S. J. GUNN

Sources A. F. Pollard, ed., *The reign of Henry VII from contemporary sources*, 3 vols. (1913–14) · *Three books of Polydore Vergil's 'English history'*, ed. H. Ellis, CS, 29 (1844) · *The Anglica historia of Polydore Vergil, AD 1485–1537*, ed. and trans. D. Hay, CS, 3rd ser., 74 (1950) · *CSP Spain* · *The English works of John Fisher, bishop of Rochester … part 1*, ed. J. E. B. Mayor, EETS, extra ser. 27 (1876) · C. J. Harrison, 'The petition of Edmund Dudley', *EngHR*, 87 (1972), 82–99 · *The will of King Henry VII*, ed. T. Astle (privately printed, London, 1775) · G. V. Scammell and H. L. Rogers, 'An elegy on the death of Henry VII', *Review of English Studies*, new ser., 8 (1957), 167–70 · C. E. Sayle, ed., *Cambridge fragments* (1913) · St Thomas More, *Latin poems*, ed. C. H. Miller and others (1984), vol. 3/2 of *The Yale edition of the complete works of St Thomas More*, 101–13 · F. Bacon, *The history of the reign of King Henry VII, and selected works*, ed. B. Vickers (1998) · W. Busch, *King Henry VII (1485–1509)* (1895), vol. 1 of *England under the Tudors* [first pubd in Ger., 1892] · R. L. Storey, *The reign of Henry VII* (1968) · S. B. Chrimes, *Henry VII* (1972) · M. M. Condon, 'Ruling elites in the reign of Henry VII', *Patronage, pedigree and power in later medieval England*, ed. C. D. Ross (1979), 109–42 · R. A. Griffiths and R. S. Thomas, *The making of the Tudor dynasty* (1985) · M. K. Jones and M. G. Underwood, *The king's mother: Lady Margaret Beaufort, countess of Richmond and Derby* (1992) · A. V. Antonovics, 'Henry VII, king of England, "By the grace of Charles VIII of France"', *Kings and nobles in the later middle ages*, ed. R. A. Griffiths and J. Sherborne (1986), 169–84 · C. S. L. Davies, 'Bishop John Morton, the Holy See, and the accession of Henry VII', *EngHR*, 102 (1987), 2–30 · M. J. Bennett, *The battle of Bosworth* (1985) · S. Anglo, *Spectacle, pageantry, and early Tudor policy* (1969); repr. (1989) · M. Bennett, *Lambert Simnel and the battle of Stoke* (1987) · S. Cunningham, 'Henry VII and rebellion in north-eastern England, 1485–1492: bonds of allegiance and the establishment of Tudor authority', *Northern History*, 32 (1996), 42–74 · S. G. Ellis, *Tudor Ireland: crown, community, and the conflict of cultures, 1470–1603* (1985) · R. B. Wernham, *Before the Armada: the growth of English foreign policy, 1485–1588* (1966) · J. M. Currin, 'Henry VII and the treaty of Redon', *History*, new ser., 81 (1996), 343–58 · J. M. Currin, '"The king's army into the partes of Bretaigne": Henry VII and the Breton wars, 1489–1491', *War in History*, 7 (2000), 379–412 · M. J. Bennett, 'Henry VII and the northern rising of 1489', *EngHR*, 105 (1990), 34–59 · D. A. Luckett, 'The Thames valley conspiracies against Henry VII', *Historical Research*, 68 (1995), 164–72 · I. Arthurson, *The Perkin Warbeck conspiracy, 1491–1499* (1994) · I. Arthurson, 'The rising of 1497: a revolt of the peasantry?', *People, politics, and community in the later middle ages*,

ed. J. T. Rosenthal and C. F. Richmond (1987), 1–18 · G. Mattingly, *Catherine of Aragon* (1942) · R. Wellens, 'Un épisode des relations entre l'Angleterre et les Pays-Bas au début du XVIe siècle: le projet de mariage entre Marguerite d'Autriche et Henri VII', *Revue d'Histoire Moderne et Contemporaine*, 29 (1982), 267–90 · G. R. Elton, 'Henry VII: rapacity and remorse', *Studies in Tudor and Stuart politics and government*, 1 (1974), 45–65 · G. R. Elton, 'Henry VII: a restatement', *Studies in Tudor and Stuart politics and government*, 1 (1974), 66–99 · J. P. Cooper, 'Henry VII's last years reconsidered', *HJ*, 2 (1959), 103–29 · S. J. Gunn, 'The accession of Henry VIII', *Historical Research*, 64 (1991), 278–88 · B. P. Wolffe, *The royal demesne in English history: the crown estate in the governance of the realm from the conquest to 1509* (1971) · P. Ramsey, 'Overseas trade in the reign of Henry VII: the evidence of customs accounts', *Economic History Review*, 2nd ser., 6 (1953–4), 173–82 · S. J. Gunn, *Early Tudor government, 1485–1558* (1995) · M. R. Horowitz, 'Richard Empson, minister of Henry VII', *BIHR*, 55 (1982), 35–49 · K. B. McFarlane, *The nobility of later medieval England* (1973) · J. R. Lander, *Crown and nobility, 1450–1509* (1976) · T. B. Pugh, 'Henry VII and the English nobility', *The Tudor nobility*, ed. G. W. Bernard (1992), 49–110 · A. Cameron, 'The giving of livery and retaining in Henry VII's reign', *Renaissance and Modern Studies*, 18 (1974), 17–35 · D. A. Luckett, 'Crown office and licensed retinues in the reign of Henry VII', *Rulers and ruled in late medieval England: essays presented to Gerald Harriss*, ed. R. E. Archer and S. Walker (1995), 223–38 · S. J. Gunn, 'Sir Thomas Lovell (c.1449–1524): a new man in a new monarchy?', *The end of the middle ages? England in the fifteenth and sixteenth centuries*, ed. J. L. Watts (1998), 117–53 · S. G. Ellis, *Tudor frontiers and noble power: the making of the British state* (1995) · R. W. Hoyle, 'The earl, the archbishop and the council: the affray at Fulford, May 1504', *Rulers and ruled in late medieval England: essays presented to Gerald Harriss*, ed. R. E. Archer and S. Walker (1995), 239–56 · J. B. Smith, 'Crown and community in the principality of north Wales in the reign of Henry Tudor', *Welsh History Review / Cylchgrawn Hanes Cymru*, 3 (1966–7), 145–71 · C. Carpenter, *Locality and polity: a study of Warwickshire landed society, 1401–1499* (1992) · P. Holmes, 'The great council in the reign of Henry VII', *EngHR*, 101 (1986), 840–62 · S. J. Gunn, 'The courtiers of Henry VII', *EngHR*, 108 (1993), 23–49 · A. F. Sutton, 'Order and fashion in clothes: the king, his household, and the city of London at the end of the fifteenth century', *Textile History*, 22 (1991), 253–76 · S. Anglo, 'The court festivals of Henry VII: a study based upon the account books of John Heron, treasurer of the chamber', *Bulletin of the John Rylands University Library*, 43 (1960–61), 12–45 · B. Thompson, ed., *The reign of Henry VII* [Harlaxton 1993] (1995) · D. Starkey, ed., *Henry VIII: a European court in England* (1991) · G. Kipling, *The triumph of honour: Burgundian origins of the Elizabethan Renaissance* (1977) · S. Thurley, *The royal palaces of Tudor England* (1993) · H. M. Colvin and others, eds., *The history of the king's works*, 3–4 (1975–82) · A. Goodman, 'Henry VII and Christian renewal', *Religion and humanism*, ed. K. Robbins, SCH, 17 (1981), 115–25 · C. Burns, 'Papal gifts and honours for the earlier Tudors', *Miscellanea Historiae Pontificae*, 50 (1983), 173–97 · H. Miller, 'London and parliament in the reign of Henry VIII', *BIHR*, 35 (1962), 128–49; repr. in *Historical studies of the English parliament*, ed. E. B. Fryde and E. Miller, 2 (1970), 125–46 · P. G. Lindley, *Gothic to Renaissance: essays on sculpture in England* (1995) · S. Anglo, 'Ill of the dead: the posthumous reputation of Henry VII', *Renaissance Studies*, 1 (1987), 27–47

Archives BL, letters, Add. MS 46454 · PRO

Likenesses coins, c.1500, BM · A. Bruchsal, silver coin, 1504 · oils on panel, 1505, NPG [*see illus.*] · attrib. M. Werwick, panel painting, c.1505–1509 (*The family of Henry VII with St George and the dragon*), Royal Collection · wax funeral effigy, 1509, Westminster Abbey · P. Torrigiano, bronze effigy, 1509–18, Westminster Abbey; electrotype, NPG · attrib. P. Torrigiano, plaster head, 1509–18 (for funeral effigy terracotta bust), Westminster Abbey · attrib. P. Torrigiano, terracotta bust, 1509–18, V&A · J. Le Boucq, drawing, 1530–70 (after presumably lost and contemporary painting), Bibliothèque d'Arras, Recueil d'Arras, MS 266 · H. Holbein the younger, ink and watercolour drawing, 1536–7, NPG; *see illus.* in *Henry VIII (1491–*

1547) • P. Vanderbank, line engraving, pubd 1706, BM, NPG • copy (after lost panel painting of *c.*1500), S. Antiquaries, Lond. • wax seal, BM

Henry VIII (1491–1547), king of England and Ireland, was the second surviving son of *Henry VII (1457–1509) and his wife, *Elizabeth (1466–1503), eldest child of Edward IV. He was born at Greenwich on 28 June 1491 and baptized in the church of the Observant friars there, by Richard Fox, then bishop of Exeter. Although created duke of York on 31 October 1494, Henry's childhood was overshadowed by his brother *Arthur (1486–1502), prince of Wales and five years his senior. Indeed, Henry's first known public appearance was at the marriage of Arthur and his Spanish bride, *Katherine (1485–1536), daughter of Ferdinand of Aragon, on 14 November 1501, when the ten-year-old led their wedding procession through London. Twenty weeks later Henry's status and expectations were transformed by the death of Arthur on 2 April 1502. In October he was created duke of Cornwall and in February 1503 prince of Wales and earl of Chester.

Upbringing Details of Henry's education are sparse, but it probably resembled that of his brother, Prince Arthur. This was based on the classics and covered grammar, poetry, rhetoric and ethics, and a good deal of history. Henry's first tutor was the poet John Skelton. Lord Herbert of Cherbury claimed that Henry was initially destined for the see of Canterbury but cited no evidence, and since he became heir to the throne at the age he did, any such intention would have had little effect on his training. That a career in the church was ever thought of seems unlikely, given the lands and offices granted to Henry at the age of three to support the dukedom of York. Herbert's suggestion was probably an attempt to account for the very considerable interest in and knowledge of theology which the adult Henry showed, before as well as after his dispute with Rome.

A remark of Thomas More that Henry was nourished on philosophy and the Nine Muses suggests that his education had a humanist cast, and comments by Erasmus (who met the boy and corresponded with him) confirm this. Henry spoke French and Latin well, understood Italian and learned some Spanish. He was very well read and had real, if not profound, intellectual interests. Genuine curiosity made him fascinated with scientific instruments, maps, and astronomy. The adult Henry resembled his grandfather Edward IV, reaching a height of 6 feet 2 inches; at twenty-one his waist was 32 inches. He had a fair complexion and his hair inclined to ginger. He could dominate any gathering and was extrovert, affable, and charming. Full of energy and proud of his athleticism, Henry cast himself above all in a military role and had a passion for weapons and fortifications. A fine horseman and an excellent archer, he was an enthusiast for those two substitutes for war: hunting and the tournament. In 1511 he took the first steps which led in 1515 to the organization of the royal armouries at Greenwich to equip himself and his courtiers to fight at the barriers and to joust.

This was Henry as his subjects saw him, but the years would reveal that behind this apparent extroversion and

Henry VIII (1491–1547), by Hans Holbein the younger, *c.*1536–7 [left, with Henry VII]

good humour was a highly complex individual. How much of the royal psychology was the product of upbringing it is possible only to speculate. Erasmus was much taken with the eight-year-old Henry and a portrait bust attributed to Guido Mazzoni which probably represents him at the same age shows a happy child, engaged and responsive. Arthur's death possibly affected Henry's status more than his emotions, but his mother's death early the next year left a wound which he recalled years later, though it is impossible to tell whether that was a genuine memory from the age of eleven, or merely a Renaissance trope. There have been suggestions that Henry's grandmother Lady Margaret Beaufort had some influence on his upbringing, but precisely how is unclear and she was to die only two months after his accession.

Information on Henry's relations with his somewhat withdrawn and controlled father is mixed. His cousin

Reginald Pole claimed that Henry VII showed no affection to his heir and it is true that all hopes had been focused on Prince Arthur. In contrast to his elder brother, Henry was given no public authority and the Spanish diplomat Fuensalida wrote of a boy kept under a minute supervision more suited to a girl, and 'so subjected that he does not speak a word except in response to what the King asks him' (*Correspondencia de … Fuensalida*, 449). Yet with only one of Henry VII's sons left alive, this might well be simple protectiveness (which could well explain other reports of teenage rebellion). That it was less than excessive is clear from reports in these same diplomatic sources of the prince spending much of his last summer of freedom in the tilt-yard at Richmond, on at least one occasion performing for his father.

Personal monarchy Henry VIII succeeded to a monarchy in which the ruler was directly responsible for policy and directly involved in the business of government. An agenda for his attention might include fifty items and his signature would be needed several times a day. Monarchy was personal. Everything, therefore, depended on the king's willingness to devote himself to business. Henry VII had been a model in this respect, but not his son. Henry VIII frequently behaved as though he wanted government to take care of itself. His favourite hours for business were during morning mass and before bed. Most state papers were read to or summarized for him and he did almost all his work by word of mouth. Only on issues which engaged him personally was he willing to become fully committed. On the other hand, Henry was not willing to delegate consistently. He always reserved to himself the freedom to intervene as and when he wanted. The consequence was not only that decisions might have to wait for the king to return from hunting or to be in the mood for work, but that Henry might decide to initiate action independently and even contradict steps already put in hand. These habits of work also exacerbated a problem inherent in personal monarchy: that the physical locus of policy and government was necessarily the royal household, but that this household was peripatetic. Henry's court moved (as did other great households in the days of poor sanitation), from palace to palace, or, in somewhat reduced numbers, accompanied him in summer and autumn on a progress through southern England which could last as much as five months. The result was a separation between the king and the royal administrative institutions which depended on his decisions and were effectively static in Westminster and London. For example, how during the law terms could counsellors be present to advise the ruler when they were required to sit in star chamber, or again, what were counsellors at Westminster to do when instructed to spend money they knew they did not have?

The need to accommodate Henry VIII's particular version of personal monarchy explains much in the story of his reign. In essence there were two options. The first was that the royal council should attempt to provide some regularity and the second that a minister should take over as chief executive, leaving the king as overall director. Neither met the difficulties fully and the story of the reign

is of oscillation as the options were tried in turn and successively broke down.

The conciliar option, 1509–1514 At the start of the reign the conciliar option was in place, effectively inherited from Henry's father. The grey heads in royal service were happy to see their inexperienced new master busy with first his marriage on 11 June to his brother's widow, Katherine of Aragon, and then a magnificent joint coronation on 24 June. Behind the scenes, however, there had been a coup. Henry VII's death had been kept a close secret for forty-eight hours to allow aristocratic counsellors to put a stop to the old king's mechanism of financial terror, arrest his principal agents, Richard Empson and Edmund Dudley, and secure a general pardon to wipe out past vulnerabilities. It was the first of the factional confrontations which would become so characteristic of the reign.

Henry's priority in these early years was to establish his European status and reputation by war against the traditional enemy, France. A majority of the council, however, adhered to his father's preference for peace and there was also a need to find allies, so that it was not until 1512 that war was declared. A year of failed expeditions followed (not least because of treachery by his father-in-law and supposed ally, Ferdinand), but in 1513 Henry himself led an army into the Low Countries. There, with minimum support from another ally, Maximilian I, the holy Roman emperor, the English won the scrambling cavalry action known as the battle of the Spurs and captured Thérouanne and Tournai from the French. Henry lived on the fame of this success for the rest of his life but in his absence a far more significant victory was won by the earl of Surrey over the Scots at Flodden which left their king dead in the field. Further campaigning in 1514 was, however, brought to a halt following the desertion of his allies, and under pressure from the pope Henry himself made peace with France and sealed it by marrying his sister *Mary (1496–1533) to the decrepit French king, Louis XII.

Developments at court After five years on the throne, conciliar administration was beginning to wear thin. Henry felt more able to decide for himself and round him was growing up a circle of courtiers and advisers who were his own. Several of the men whom he had looked up to as a young king had been casualties during the war, and Henry now began to prefer the company of younger men who looked up to him. And the change was in more than personnel. In each royal residence Henry, like his father, occupied a private suite insulated from the ceremonial side of the court. However, while Henry VII had been perfectly prepared to be attended in this 'privy chamber' by servants, his son wanted the company of these new companions, and by the time the first decade of his reign was over a new staffing pattern had emerged which surrounded him with 'gentlemen' and 'grooms of the privy chamber' who, as well as attending to his needs, provided him with a social life. They were headed by 'the groom of the close stool', his most intimate attendant, who doubled in the post of chief gentleman of the privy chamber. This availability of a private staff of gentlemen directly dependent on him allowed a king who wished to do so to bypass the usual channels and take direct action, as, for example, when arresting both the duke of Buckingham and Cardinal Wolsey. The reverse, however, was that closeness to the king gave the privy chamber the potential for real political importance, with the staff able to meddle in the exercise of patronage and to attempt to sway royal thinking. The groom of the stool, in particular, could be influential in assisting or discouraging access to the king.

Wolsey as minister, 1514–1526 The French war of 1512–14 saw Thomas *Wolsey emerge from the pack of royal counsellors as someone who could offer Henry the option of ruling through a principal minister rather than at first hand through a council. It was not only because of his boundless energy and undoubted ability, but because Wolsey saw it as his function (and guarantee of his continued enjoyment of success and power) to give the king what he wanted, or could be persuaded that he did want. Collectively the other royal counsellors were reduced to giving advice only when Henry and Wolsey wished and to discharging the council's judicial work, although individually they continued to manage particular activities as they had under Henry VII. Wolsey reported to Henry in person, usually at least once a week, and also by letter. A small group of counsellors Wolsey could trust was also always in attendance at court.

For a decade and more, working through Wolsey allowed Henry to rule in the way he wanted. It led some contemporaries (and later historians) to the illusion that the minister was in charge—hence talk of him as 'the person who rules both the king and the kingdom' (*CSP Venice, 1509–19*, 569). In reality, however, the collaboration ensured that Henry was consulted on everything important and, should he wish, could initiate, but was left free of detail and day-to-day routine. George Cavendish, Wolsey's gentleman usher, described the system from firsthand observation. The minister:

> wold first make the king privye of all suche matters (as shold passe throughe [the council's] handes) byfore he wold procede to the fynyssheng or determynyng of the same, whos mynd and pleasure he wold fullfyll and followe to the uttermost wherewith the king was wonderly pleased. (Cavendish, 12)

Judging from the state papers which have survived from Wolsey's ministry, Henry's principal interest in these years was diplomacy—how to place England in relation to the shifting context of the Italian wars. The policy pursued by the minister (at Henry's instigation he was elected archbishop of York in 1514, then appointed cardinal in 1515, and in 1518 papal legate a latere) has been interpreted variously as support for the Holy See in the hope of himself becoming pope, pursuit of a balance of power, searching for peace (in part for reasons of principle), and personal self-advancement. A simpler explanation is suggested by the situation in Europe. There Charles V, Katherine's nephew, had united the Habsburg lands and the holy Roman empire with the kingdoms of Spain and its American empire, and he was engaged in great-power rivalry with François I of France. In comparison England

was significantly inferior—the population of France was six times greater and Charles V's income was seven times larger than Henry's. Wolsey's object, therefore, was to manoeuvre in such a way as to achieve equivalent status for Henry, in effect to enable England to punch far above its weight. The cardinal's greatest triumph was the treaty signed in London in 1518 which brought together the major European powers and twenty smaller ones in an alliance for 'universal peace'. Subsequently Charles V accepted an invitation to discussions in London in May 1520, and the next month Henry met François I at Ardres, on the border between France and English-occupied Calais. Both summits were made occasions for magnificence and especially the latter, known thereafter, because of the finery worn for the occasion, as the Field of Cloth of Gold.

Underneath the ostensible harmony 'concluded in England' (*CSP Venice, 1509–19*, 458) there were, however, increasing signs of the return of Franco-imperial rivalry over Italy, a development which left Henry 'the arbiter of Europe' on the sidelines. He therefore followed the 1520 meeting with François I with a second and more businesslike meeting with Charles which eventually led to England going to war with France in 1522 as an ally of the emperor. What followed exposed the hollowness of Henry's pretensions to big-power status. Raids into northern France in 1522 and 1523 achieved nothing, money ran out, and when Charles captured François on 23 February 1525 at the battle of Pavia, the emperor refused to countenance a wild proposal by Henry to divide France between them. Unable to gain any kudos as Charles's ally, England thereupon made peace with France and when the pope put together the Holy League of Cognac to try to contain imperial power, Henry became its 'protector'. Shortage of funds ruled out any more positive involvement.

Against what may to later minds appear the charade of this foreign posturing, the collaboration of Henry and Wolsey in domestic affairs did have long-term significance. The coup against Henry VII's methods which had opened the reign had significantly weakened royal finances, notably by reducing the income of the crown estates. This was made worse by the expense of foreign war—the war with France in 1512–14 cost about £1,000,000, perhaps ten times Henry's normal revenue. The sequel was a determined and partially successful campaign to increase royal revenues from taxation. In 1515 progress was made on developing the parliamentary subsidy, a tax assessed on real wealth in place of the older system of fixed levies. In 1522 a 'general proscription' or survey was carried out, allegedly to measure military preparedness, and the data collected was used to assess and levy a non-parliamentary forced loan. The survey was also used to assess the subsidy of 1523–5 and succeeded in taxing perhaps 90 per cent of rural households and up to two-thirds of townsmen. It became the model for future years. The country grumbled, but it was only when the crown added a call for a 'benevolence' in 1525, the so-called 'amicable grant', that it encountered serious resistance where it mattered, in London, the home counties and East

Anglia. Thanks to his system of ruling at one remove, Henry was able to claim ignorance of the demand, make tactful concessions, and leave Wolsey to take the blame publicly.

Another consequence of the palace coup on Henry VII's death had been the partial relaxation of his stern disciplining of élite misconduct. In 1516, therefore, his son presided at a special council meeting where Wolsey announced a return to the policy of 'indifferent justice' and the king himself provided an object lesson by sending the fifth earl of Northumberland to the Fleet prison. The following year saw riots in London against immigrant Flemish workers, the 'Evil May Day', with some fourteen or so offenders being hanged and the remainder paraded in Westminster Hall before the king and queen, the lords, and the council. Wolsey berated both the city government and the rioters and called for more executions but on Queen Katherine's petition (clearly arranged in advance) Henry exercised the prerogative of mercy. Two years later the king appeared in council to deal with Sir William Bulmer who despite being a royal officer had nevertheless accepted a retainer from the third duke of Buckingham.

The royal endorsement of the 'law and order' policy given by Henry's appearance at these set pieces was followed up by Wolsey in a large number of less high-profile cases pursued through the routine legal machinery. Landowners fell foul of him particularly over breaches of the statutes prohibiting the enclosure and conversion of arable land for pasture. It would, however, be wrong to suggest that Henry had sanctioned an assault on the country's élite, a supposition frequently labelled as 'the attack on over-mighty subjects'. Royal power depended on the men of power using their social authority to serve the state, most especially the military potential of their tenants and 'well-wishers'—their *manred*. In particular a peerage was essential to monarchy. It provided a majority of counsellors, was the bedrock of royal influence in parliament and created the setting for royal magnificence, and was a reservoir of higher commanders in war. Henry 'inherited' forty-two peers and in his first twenty years created a further thirteen and promoted six more. This was followed in 1529 by seven more creations and three promotions. Thereafter creations and/or promotions took place almost every year. Certainly individuals were prosecuted, liberties and rights questioned, but always in relation to personal conduct or perceived unreliability. The most famous example of this was the duke of Buckingham, whose unwise behaviour suggested disaffection and led to his execution in 1521.

The king's 'Great Matter' The danger which Buckingham represented was undoubtedly exaggerated in Henry's mind by a concern which was beginning to worry him more and more—the lack of a son to succeed him. Katherine's first child miscarried and the second, Prince Henry (born on new year's day 1511) survived only a matter of days. Only one of four further conceptions was successful—the birth of Princess Mary [see Mary I] in 1516—and in 1519 (the year of her last pregnancy) the king was anxious enough to bring physicians over from Spain to examine his wife, who at thirty-four was approaching her last years of fertility.

Katherine clearly had problems in bringing pregnancies to full term but six pregnancies in ten years of marriage show that the couple also had difficulty in achieving conception. Henry must then have taken comfort from the birth to Elizabeth Blount, also in 1519, of an illegitimate son, Henry *Fitzroy. The king had no qualms in acknowledging the boy and in 1525 he was created duke of Richmond and Somerset. These peerages were closely associated with the Tudor family and some at the time (and since) have believed that Henry was toying with the idea of legitimating Richmond as heir apparent; Katherine allegedly took the news very badly. Henry's more immediate motive was probably the desire to make use of his son as a surrogate—a month after the investiture Richmond was made warden-general of the Scottish marches—but if the possibility of the boy succeeding him was in the king's mind at all, the risk that would involve is only further evidence of anxiety about the future. Time was now not on Henry's side. He was thirty-four. His grandfathers had died aged twenty-six and forty-one. His father had died aged fifty-two. In 1524 the king had abandoned intercourse with Katherine, and England, for the first time since the early twelfth century, was heading for a female on the throne. The only escape would be by a son of a second marriage—and this required either the death of Katherine or the ending of her marriage to Henry. Moreover, unless that son was born in the near future he would succeed as a minor, and the success record of royal minors was bleak.

Katherine, though childless, was in good health, but breaking a marriage for dynastic reasons was by no means an impossibility. 'Divorce' in its modern meaning was not allowed under canon law, but 'annulment'—a declaration that no valid marriage had been contracted—was a real option, generally on the ground of consanguinity which was construed much more strictly than today. Katherine's marriage to Henry had certainly fallen into the prohibited category, since by her union with his brother Arthur she was held to have become Henry's sister and so quite out of the question as a wife. However, the church also claimed the power to condone potential defects revealed in advance, and Pope Julius II had issued a papal bull allowing Katherine and Henry to marry despite their relationship. For his marriage to Katherine to be annulled, that dispensation had to be impugned.

There is evidence that Henry had long had niggling doubts about the lawfulness of his marriage but, with Wolsey's connivance, the first secret steps towards an annulment were not taken until May 1527. It was later claimed that the king's doubts had been aroused by questions asked during the previous winter in the negotiations for a marriage between Princess Mary and François I's second son, but though that may have been so, it was just what was needed to crystallize Henry's innermost anxieties. He was meticulous in his religious duties—God must be on his side—yet his children continued to die in the womb or in infancy. And did not Leviticus 20: 21 say that if a man had sexual relations with his brother's wife, they would be childless?

What part did *Anne Boleyn (c.1500–1536) play in Henry's decision? He seems to have been pursuing her from the early part of 1526, but the first sign that she had agreed to marry him was an application to Pope Clement V for the two of them to be dispensed which was sent off in August 1527. The letters the king wrote to Anne in 1527 and 1528 can be variously interpreted, but the probable resolution is that his original object had been to secure her as his mistress in succession to her sister Mary, with whom he had enjoyed a childless relationship in the early 1520s. Not until after he had decided to seek an annulment did Anne's refusal of what seems to have been his invitation to become *maîtresse en titre* suggest that she would be the ideal second wife instead of a French princess as Wolsey had assumed.

Henry and Anne clearly expected to wed within months, but five and a half years' frustration lay ahead. The delay was in part caused by the international situation. The victory of Charles V at Pavia in 1525 and the sack of Rome two years later had put Katherine of Aragon's nephew on the way to a mastery of Italy. The pope still had hopes of the league of Cognac but caution removed all incentive to burn his boats by accommodating Henry. He therefore deliberately deceived the king, making a series of apparent concessions while secretly doing everything possible to hold matters up. In all fairness to Clement it must also be said that he was ill-informed. The opinion in Europe was that all Henry wanted was a new bedmate in place of his ageing, barren, and increasingly lachrymose wife. Time, therefore, would solve the problem: Anne would pass into the royal bed and later out of it to a suitably discreet marriage, or Katherine would solve the problem by dying. Henry's obstinate morality was something which a pope in Renaissance Rome found hard to understand.

The pope's reluctance was, moreover, also prompted by the real legal difficulties which annulment presented. To Henry, God's commands might be blindingly obvious. His marriage to Katherine was contrary to divine law as stated in the Bible and therefore could not be set aside. It was said that 'an angel descending from Heaven would be unable to persuade him otherwise' (*LP Henry VIII*, 4/2, no. 4858). But not only did Henry's conviction require the pope to accept that Julius II had exceeded his authority in issuing the original dispensation, Clement had good reason to believe that the king had got hold of the wrong biblical text. The passage Henry relied on appeared to refer not to a brother's widow but to a brother's wife and so be a prohibition on adultery. Moreover, verse 5 of Deuteronomy 25 specifically instructed a brother to marry his widowed sister-in-law if she had had no sons in order to provide a surrogate heir for his dead sibling. Henry's obstinate fixation on Leviticus and the explanation it provided for his childlessness drove him deeper and deeper into a legal and exegetical cul-de-sac from which the only escape would be to break down the barrier of papal authority.

The failure of Wolsey, 1527–1529 The struggle for the annulment falls into three phases, 1527 to 1529, 1529 to 1530, and 1530 to 1533. In the first, royal policy was directed by Wolsey and ended with the minister becoming the first casualty of the King's Great Matter. The cardinal had to fight on three fronts. In international affairs he strove to free the pope from the emperor's domination by reducing the imperial position in Italy. At Rome he negotiated tirelessly for the decision Henry wanted. At home he struggled to retain royal favour and the control of policy despite continuing set-backs which gave opportunity to his enemies at court.

Wolsey's diplomatic options were restricted by royal financial weakness and the fact that England's economic ties with the Low Countries made significant direct action against Charles impracticable—the war declared early in 1528 had to be abandoned within weeks. Initial French moves did raise some hope that the pope would evade dependence on Charles but these were followed in 1528 by reverses in the south of Italy, and in June 1529 by defeat at the battle of Landriano and expulsion from the north. On 29 June Clement VII signed the treaty of Barcelona with Charles which recognized the emperor's position in Italy and, by implication, his own future as an imperial satellite. Five days afterwards the efforts of François I's mother, Louise of Savoy, and Charles's aunt, Margaret of Austria, brought about the 'Ladies Peace' (treaty of Cambrai) by which France agreed to abandon its claims to Italy. England was effectively ignored and Wolsey was left without diplomatic leverage.

In the meantime, at Rome Henry's agents had been pursuing his suit. Initial attempts to keep Katherine in ignorance failed, and in July 1527 the queen alerted both emperor and pope to her side of the story which was that her marriage with Arthur was void because never consummated. Everything thereafter would depend on where the case would be decided and in December 1527 Henry sent a mission to Rome requesting a legatine commission empowering Wolsey and Lorenzo Campeggi or Campeggio, cardinal protector of England and bishop of Salisbury *in commendam*, to hear and settle the case in England. Successive papal commissions were issued throughout 1528, but none with power to make the final binding decision which Henry had to have to be secure. In October 1528 Campeggi eventually arrived in England and with a convincing commission, but also with orders that it should not be used (he later destroyed it) and a secret mandate to procrastinate. Eventually a legatine court did open at Blackfriars in June 1529. Katherine formally appealed to Rome and on 21 June the confrontation took place between king and queen later made famous by Shakespeare. Katherine appealed to Henry to admit that she was a virgin when she married him, and torn between the fatal truth and the lie no one would believe, Henry said nothing and the queen walked out. The one-sided hearing dragged on until Campeggi announced that the court must keep Roman law terms and on 31 July adjourned business until October.

Through all these delays, and especially during 1529,

Wolsey had also been fighting to maintain his position. The personal nature of the annulment suit encouraged Henry into one of his periodic bouts of activity and he also began to listen to other advisers as well. When, in January 1529, there was still no progress despite Campeggi's arriving three months before, Anne Boleyn decided that Wolsey was complicit and she abandoned her previous reliance on him. Her new hostility put Henry's continuing confidence in the cardinal under question and a mixed bag of public figures began to come together united by dislike of the minister, but only a few of them positive Boleyn supporters. A dossier of complaints against Wolsey was prepared, and on the collapse of the Blackfriars court this was submitted to the king. Henry, however, was unable to break free of fifteen years of dependence on the cardinal and took no action. It was only at the end of August when Wolsey began to advise against the alliance with France which Henry saw as crucial to breaking the impasse over the marriage that the cardinal really lost favour. He recovered somewhat after a positive meeting with Henry at Grafton on 19 September, but three weeks later the king yielded to the cardinal's critics and allowed him to be charged in the court of king's bench with the offence of *praemunire*—that is, breaching the fourteenth-century statutes restricting papal authority in England. Even that decision may, paradoxically, have been motivated by Henry's desire to protect Wolsey; parliament had been summoned for November and this threatened an alternative and far worse danger—an act of attainder. Wolsey pleaded guilty, was dismissed as chancellor, and sent into comfortable house arrest.

A return to conciliar government, 1529–1531 With the fall of Wolsey the problem of the annulment passed to Henry and to the cardinal's replacements headed by Anne Boleyn's uncle, Thomas Howard, third duke of Norfolk. No one had much idea what to do, and the real concern of the new advisers was to prevent Wolsey returning to the side of a king who had already been heard to mutter 'every day I miss the cardinal of York more and more' (*CSP Milan*, 530). Fortunately for them, death removed that danger on 29 November 1530. The king's own reaction to Blackfriars had been to bluster. According to the imperial ambassador, Henry threatened that if Clement VII did not accommodate him, he 'would denounce the pope as a heretic and marry whom he pleased' (*CSP Spain*, 1529–30, 224). Although parliament, the accepted forum for national consensus, had been called, nothing relevant to the annulment suit could be found for it to do. As for the Roman curia, the royal cause dragged on there with minimal progress; indeed, since Henry could count no trial outside England a certainty, his agents actively encouraged delay. The only positive step was implementing a casual suggestion by Thomas Cranmer that the universities of Europe should be consulted, a venture which cost Henry a good deal in bribes but produced eight favourable opinions and a mass of potentially relevant documents. Very clearly neither the king nor his post-Wolsey counsellors had a coherent strategy, still less had decided to 'go it alone'. Henry's only notion was to turn his threats into action; bullying the English church would make the pope realize that Henry was serious! In June 1530 a meeting of English notables, clerical and lay, was called to support a national petition to Rome pleading for an immediate verdict in the king's favour and uttering further dire but vague menaces. In the autumn fifteen leading members of the church hierarchy were charged with complicity in Wolsey's offences.

The final phase, 1530–1533: new ideas In the latter part of 1530 there comes a dramatic change in tone. For example, in October the king instructed his agents at Rome to deny the right of the pope to consider Katherine's appeal because 'in [our kingdom] we are supreme and so rule that we recognise no superior … and he who acknowledges no superior has the power to prohibit all appeals by his subjects' (*State Papers, Henry VIII*, 7.262). In January 1531 words became action. Henry declared that in exercising the jurisdiction of the church courts the English clergy had fallen 'into divers dangers of his laws' and demanded that convocation should raise £100,000 to purchase a pardon. The church agreed to pay, but the king then made further demands, insisting that the church should admit three principles: that he was 'the only protector and supreme head of the English church and clergy', that God had committed to him a 'cure' ('care') of souls (in other words that he possessed a spiritual character and function), and that the church could only enjoy powers 'which do not disparage the regal authority and laws' (Wilkins, 3.257). This time convocation did not give way and the king had to compromise. On the first point the crown offered the ambiguous qualification 'as far as the law of Christ allows' and the king's claim to a quasi-spiritual 'cure of souls' was watered down (Scarisbrick, 'The pardon of the clergy', 34). The issue of church authority was fudged. Even so there was considerable local opposition in the dioceses, with protests of loyalty to Rome, which the crown met with further *praemunire* charges.

Where had the king's new assertiveness come from? Not from his own thinking. When his interest was engaged, Henry was capable of intellectual effort. In 1521 he had published the *Assertio septem sacramentorum*, a rebuttal of Martin Luther's anti-papal diatribe *De captivitate Babylonica*, which earned him the title 'Defender of the Faith'. Yet although effective at one level, the book does not suggest that the king had an original mind. Its affirmation of papal supremacy and condemnation of schism is quite conventional. It is also clear that the king had relied on help. Very probably a team did the preliminary work, leaving Henry to give the final touches to a book made unusual only by reason of the identity of the author. It was the same subsequently, when he was wrestling with his matrimonial dilemma. He told Anne Boleyn in 1528 how four hours work on 'his book' had given him a headache (Stemmler, xiv).

What had given Henry this new confidence was again the work of other men. The study of canon law, theology, and the opinions of the European universities had not stopped with the collapse of the Blackfriars trial. In November 1531 Thomas Cranmer was able to publish *The*

Determinations of the Most Famous and Excellent Universities, an elaboration of the case put to the legatine court which achieved a new stage in menace by asserting that 'the duty of a loving and a devout bishop [was] to withstand the Pope openly to his face' for failing to enforce obedience to God in matrimonial cases such as Henry's (Sturtz and Murphy, 265). At the same time researchers had been ransacking biblical, patristic, and later evidence on the issue of papal jurisdiction. The scholars involved here were led by the king's future almoner, Edward Fox, and probably again included Cranmer. By August 1530 their report was in Henry's hands, under the inconvenient label, *Collectanea satis copiosa*. This demonstrated—or claimed to demonstrate—that there was simply no warrant for the centuries-old assumption that the pope was supreme in spiritual matters. The king possessed by divine gift, imperial authority (*imperium*), so that instead of the old theory of 'two swords'—temporal and spiritual authority in the hands of king and pope respectively—both swords belonged to the king. He was the true 'Vicar of God'.

Fox and Cranmer were very much under Boleyn patronage, but Anne herself introduced Henry to further revolutionary ideas which were circulating in Germany about the true place and role of the ruler in God's scheme of things. These had been given currency in England in *The Obedience of the Christian Man*, published in October 1528 by the reformist exile and Bible translator, William Tyndale. Anne had obtained a copy soon after publication and she lent it to Henry with the relevant passages already marked. Tyndale asserted that for princes to submit to the power of the church was not only 'a shame above all shames and a notorious thing' but an inversion of the divine order. 'One king, one law is God's ordinance in every realm' (*Tyndale's Works*, 1.206–7, 240). Henry's response was, 'This is a book for me, and all kings to read' (Nichols, 57).

That such radical ideas rang a bell with the author of something as orthodox as *Assertio septem sacramentorum* was not merely because they suggested a novel way to get what he wanted. In 1515, as his response to the affair of Richard Hunne shows, Henry was already highly sensitized on the matter of his God-given authority, particularly encroachments by the church. In 1519 he declared ecclesiastical rights of sanctuary to be an encroachment on royal authority which he would reform unilaterally. Thus far he may merely have been asserting the traditional right of the temporal to delimit the spiritual, but the difficulties of the King's Great Matter inevitably forced Henry to ask, 'what does it mean to be a king under God?' If he was, as he described himself in a letter of 1520 'Soveraigne Lorde and Prince' and 'of our absolute power … above the lawes', and if it:

> so moche toucheth our honour to conserve our rightfull inheritaunce that We neither may ne woll suffre any Prince, of what soever preheminence he bee, to usurpe or detaigne any parte therof, but, by our puysaunce, to represse suche usurpacion and detencion

it was incongruous in the extreme to find himself a rejected suppliant at Rome (*State Papers, Henry VIII*, 3.53).

The headship of the church Despite the attractiveness of the radical option and his willingness to use it as a threat, Henry was reluctant to go all the way with the programme of Anne and her supporters—hence his failure to press home the attack in the pardon of the clergy. Behind him was a lifetime of posing as a loyal son of the church. His comments on the margins of the *Collectanea* show that its thesis seemed too good to be true, and he immediately sent agents abroad to ransack foreign libraries for further evidence to establish that this imperial authority was a reality and was truly independent of the pope. There was also the question of what procedure would legitimate a resumption of such authority. Christopher St German of the Middle Temple was advising Henry that statute did provide a valid basis for legislating on ecclesiastical matters because 'the king in parliament [is] the high sovereign over the people which hath not only charge on the bodies but also on the souls of his subjects' (*St German's Doctor and Student*, 327). Yet was parliament really competent to overturn the objection that the supreme government of the church 'may no temporal prince presume by any law to take upon him, as rightfully belonging to the See of Rome, a spiritual pre-eminence [granted] by the mouth of our Saviour himself personally present upon earth?' (Roper, ed. Sylvester and Harding, 248).

The international situation also suggested caution. Charles, for once at peace with France, was a potential threat. François I promised support, but since he was bidding for papal favour on his own account, that help might not extend to an open breach with Clement. François, indeed, might be in a position to achieve an alternative solution by persuading the pope to compromise, and a papally endorsed annulment would give Anne and her expected offspring the great advantage of acceptance Europe-wide. English opposition was also becoming more vocal. At first this came from the clergy, particularly Katherine's champions, but more and more there were signs of unease in the country at large. Hostile placards appeared in London and the king's problems became a matter of popular debate. Earlier soundings had made clear that a unilateral English solution to the impasse was unacceptable to the nobility. The court became polarized and before the year was out, so too the royal council, with Sir Thomas More doing all he could to frustrate the radicals.

The growing confidence of the conservatives was evident in the third session of parliament which assembled in January 1532. The second session, which had met in January 1531, had done nothing for the king's problem except to enact the pardon of the clergy, and Norfolk and the other counsellors now realized matters could wait no longer. Might financial pressure on the pope do the trick? A bill was drafted to put an end to the pope's principal source of revenue from England, the payment of annates, in theory the first year's income of newly appointed members of the hierarchy. The Lords refused to entertain the idea and the crown offered to compromise by suspending operation of the bill for an unstated period. Even so, to get that emasculated version through the house, Henry had to appear in person on three occasions. The Commons was equally difficult, forcing the crown to specify that the period of suspension would be a full year and to sanction the continued payment to Rome of five shillings in the pound 'for the pains and labours taken' there. Moreover, the bill was approved only after the king had again arrived in person—he engineered a division, the earliest example of the procedure. Conservatives also blocked other moves by Norfolk. Archbishop William Warham refused to defy the pope, and when the duke tried out the arguments of the *Collectanea* on a group of his supporters he was turned down flat.

The emergence of a new minister If the king and his counsellors were frustrated, so too was Anne Boleyn. Only the radical solution would save the day, but how could royal doubts and conservative resistance be overcome? It is here that another key player entered the scene, Thomas *Cromwell. A protégé of Wolsey, Cromwell had been in touch with Anne since 1529 and had quickly absorbed radical ideas. By the opening of 1531 he had been sworn a member of the royal council—indeed, the Trojan Horse formula 'as far as the law of Christ allows' may have been his. He was not yet the supreme policy maker he was to become, but he was a parliamentary expert and a first rate political tactician.

The issue which Cromwell saw he could exploit was agitation in the Commons about church officers abusing their authority over lay people. This had been an issue in the first session, and since then Thomas More's campaign against so-called 'heretics' had raised the temperature. Cromwell responded to this concern by drafting for the Commons a petition cataloguing the faults of the ecclesiastical judges, the so-called 'supplication against the ordinaries'. The opening complaint was a direct challenge to the independent legal status of the church and the supplication ended with an appeal to the king as 'the only head, sovereign lord, protector and defender of both the said parties, in whom and by whom the only sole redress, reformation and remedy herein absolutely rests and remains', in other words a thinly veiled reference to his supreme headship (Bray, 56).

It is unlikely that Henry recognized the supplication as a subtle way to test the meaning of a supreme headship 'as far as the law of Christ allowed'. To Henry the matter was plain; after all, as he told Bishop Tunstal, 'words were ordained to signify things, and cannot therefore by sinister interpretation alter the truth of them' (Wilkins, 3.762). He therefore simply informed the delegation of the Commons which presented the supplication that he would send it to convocation for comment. Instead, the MPs discovered that what was then uppermost in the king's mind was another issue, the loss which his feudal rights of wardship and livery were sustaining from a legal device, 'the use', which enabled tenants-in-chief to escape by putting land in trust. The Lords had accepted a compromise Henry had offered in 1529 but when a bill was put to the Commons in 1532, the king suffered a blank refusal. The warning the members were given was entirely in character: 'I assure you, if you wyll not take some reasonable ende now when it is offered, I wyll serche out the

extremitie of the lawe, and then wyll I not offre you so moche agayne' (Hall, 785).

If Henry did not recognize the time bomb in the supplication, neither did convocation. It called on Henry's favourite bishop, Stephen Gardiner, to reply and he walked straight into the trap. He wrote:

> We take our authority of making of laws to be grounded upon the Scripture of God and the determination of Holy Church, which must also be a rule and square to try the justice and righteousness of all laws, as well spiritual as temporal.

If friction occurred, the church would conform its law 'to the determination of Scripture and Holy Church' and it looked to Henry to 'temper your grace's law accordingly'. As for the demand to submit canon law to Henry's approval, 'we, your most humble subjects, may not submit the execution of our charges and duty, certainly prescribed by God, to your Highness's assent' (Bray, 59). The reply produced the royal reaction which Cromwell had counted on. Henry passed the answer to the speaker with a thinly veiled instruction to continue agitation against the church. Then he sent Edward Fox to demand that convocation surrender all claim to legislative independence. When that was resisted he summoned a Commons delegation, denounced the bishops as 'but half our subjects, yea, and scarce our subjects', and, flourishing copies of the incompatible oaths which the bishops took to the king and the pope, sent the MPs away 'to invent some order that we be not thus deluded of our spiritual subjects' (Hall, 788). Faced with the draft of a parliamentary bill which made the clergy 'lower than shoemakers' (*LP Henry VIII*, 5, no. 1013) the church retreated. Henry called off the Commons by proroguing parliament and the upper house of convocation accepted the royal demands in full.

Marriage and the breach with Rome Thanks in part to the eyewitness account of Edward Hall, the history of what became known as the 'submission of the clergy' provides to later generations a striking vignette of Henry VIII when fully engaged. To contemporaries, it represented the triumph of the radical solution to the Great Matter. The following day More resigned. Henry's problems could now be settled in England. There followed, however, a strange hesitation. Despite having the enabling legislation ready, parliament was postponed and negotiations at Rome continued. Was Henry concerned about rumbles of aristocratic unhappiness? Was he frustrated by Warham's longevity at Canterbury? Did he need the face-to-face meeting he and Anne had with François I at Calais in October before being able to rely on existing French promises of support? Possibly, but the likeliest explanation is that the king's thinking was not yet free of the chains of convention. The archbishop died at last on 22 August, but when Henry created Anne Boleyn marchioness of Pembroke ten days later, he still thought it wise to provide that the title would descend to her son whether or not born in lawful wedlock. Despite everything, he was not certain that any second marriage while Katherine was alive could be valid.

If Henry was not yet able to break free psychologically, it

was very probably Anne who took decisive action. During the visit to Calais or shortly afterwards, she began at long last to sleep with Henry. By the end of the year she could suspect that she was pregnant and in January 1533, probably on the 25th, the two were married in a secret ceremony before dawn in the new Whitehall Palace. Anne was accorded royal status at court from Holy Saturday and given a magnificent coronation seven weeks later. It spread over four days and deliberately manoeuvred the upper classes into endorsing Anne and so showing *hoi polloi* that their betters were fully behind the king's second marriage. Anne gave birth to her daughter Princess Elizabeth [*see* Elizabeth I] on 7 September. There is no doubt that Henry had wanted and expected a boy, but no evidence suggests that the arrival of a girl was the crushing psychological blow which some have supposed. By the following spring Anne was pregnant again and Henry was quite sure that this time it would be a son.

While Henry was at last making public his relationship with Anne, the required formalities were put through by others: Thomas Cromwell, the man whose tactics had undermined the independence of the church, and that other Boleyn protégé, Thomas Cranmer, who was installed as archbishop of Canterbury on 30 March 1533. Parliament passed an Act in Restraint of Appeals which enunciated the *Collectanea* ideology and required ecclesiastical suits to be heard in England. This empowered Cranmer to try the Great Matter and pronounce on 23 May that the marriage with Katherine had been null and void, so making the marriage with Anne fully valid and Princess Mary illegitimate. Katherine of Aragon was reduced to the status of dowager princess of Wales. Rome responded with forceful action at last, condemning the Boleyn match and ordering Henry to take Katherine back. The king responded by formally refusing papal jurisdiction and appealing to a general council of the church, a blatantly schismatic move which implied that the pope was not, under God, the ultimate authority in the church. Further legislation broke all ties with Rome and although Paul III, who succeeded Clement in September 1534, made overtures to win Henry back (which it suited the king to echo), the die had been cast. Henry VIII was 'the only Supreme Head on earth of the Church of England' (Bray, 114).

The royal supremacy defended: foreign danger For the remainder of the decade English policy abroad and at home was dominated by the need to defend the supremacy Henry had asserted, and the implications this had for the succession to his throne. The potential for international danger was obvious. Henry's attack on the unity of western Christendom positively challenged the pope to retaliate, while the insult to Katherine and Mary, the emperor's relatives, offered Charles V every incentive to take up the cross on behalf of the holy father. François I had indeed promised Henry some support, but his own agenda was now to win the support of the newly elected Pope Paul III and to promote the reunion of the western church by a general council, an assembly hardly likely to endorse Henry's claims to supremacy. A papally engineered *rapprochement* between France and the empire

would be even more dangerous, facing England with overwhelming odds.

Relations with his 'brother' rulers was very much a king's personal province and initially Henry felt these threats were remote. The pope was restrained by François from declaring Henry deposed. Charles, facing Turkish pressure on his Habsburg lands in south-eastern Europe and trouble with the German Lutheran princes, showed no wish to add England to his troubles. He confined his protest to words, and blocked the pope's wish to place England under an interdict. Then over the winter of 1535–6 France and the empire came to blows over the duchy of Milan, and the death of Katherine of Aragon on 8 January let Henry announce: 'God be praised that we are free from all suspicion of war now that the real cause of our enmity no longer exists' (*CSP Spain, 1536–8*, 19). The execution of Anne Boleyn which followed in May opened the way to an uncontestable third marriage—to Jane Seymour the same month—and offspring of impeccable legitimacy. In July the king felt strong enough to have convocation rule that no general council of the church could be legal without the consent of all Christian princes—an impossible condition.

At this point the sky began to darken. Following the death of James IV at Flodden, Henry had hoped for friendlier relations with Scotland under its minor heir James V, whose mother was Henry's sister *Margaret (1489–1541). However, James refused to break with Rome and in September 1536, with no word to Henry, sailed to France where he married François I's daughter Madeleine on new year's day. Although Madeleine died after a few months, James confirmed his adherence to the 'auld alliance' by a second marriage (June 1538) to Mary of Guise, the daughter of one of François's leading counsellors. In the same month the unthinkable happened. François and Charles accepted papal mediation, ended a war which had brought advantage to neither side, and signed a ten-year truce at Nice. In July the two rulers met at Aigues-Mortes. The pope published the bull deposing Henry and sent agents to both monarchs and to James V pressing for an invasion.

The king of England was less agitated by this diplomatic blizzard than were his ministers. Not only did the emperor have his hands full with a rebellion in Ghent, but Henry knew François and Charles well enough to believe that no reconciliation could last long. Nevertheless, he did take diplomatic measures to counter England's isolation. A peace treaty was signed with Scotland and James V was wooed with gifts. The half-hearted negotiations which Henry had initiated with the Lutheran princes in 1533–4 were revived, and he also made overtures to any state in dispute with Charles or the pope. The king also decided to seek his fourth wife from the anti-imperial camp, and fixed on *Anne (1515–1557), the sister of the duke of Cleves, though only after a good deal of wavering. What finalized his decision was possibly Charles's exceptional gesture of trust in François when in the autumn of 1539 he began an imperial progress through France to the Low

Countries, with the two monarchs spending Christmas together at Fontainebleau.

Henry backed diplomacy with military preparedness, which continued even after the signs of a split between François and Charles became evident during 1540. As the duke of Suffolk then remarked to Cromwell, 'these bruits be well laid [to rest], but the king does well to provide for the worst' (*LP Henry VIII*, 14/1, no. 749). Henry had inherited a very few ships from his father, but by 1539 he could put over 150 ships to sea including some forty specialized warships. These varied from the *Great Harry*, displacing 1000 tons, to specialized row-barges of 20 tons. Ordnance was revolutionized. Guns had always been one of Henry's enthusiasms—he had set up his own experimental foundry in 1511—and by then had already equipped two of his ships with heavy cannon, firing broadside through gunports, as well as the older lighter pieces mounted on the upper decks. By the time of the crisis, a warship such as the *Mary Rose* might have a broadside of ten heavy guns, many of them now bronze muzzle-loaders, not iron breech-loaders.

Naval preparations were matched by a massive programme of fortifications from the Humber to Milford Haven. Described as 'the most extensive scheme of work of its kind undertaken in England until the last or even the present century', the programme exploited the ability of efficient large cannon to inhibit sea-borne landings (O'Neil, 49). Henry again was the driving force. The overall scheme, entitled the 'device by the king' and dating from February 1539 (*LP Henry VIII*, 14/1, no. 398), was drawn up after a survey of 'all the Portes and daungiers on the coastes where any meete or convenient landing place might be supposed', with the king doing part of the inspecting himself (Hall, 828–9). Much of the immediate design was Henry's too. He produced 'plats' and determined details down to the shape of gun embrasures. The resulting style of fortification based on the circular 'gun-tower' has few European counterparts, was short-lived and is frequently dismissed as obsolete in comparison with the angled-bastions of contemporary Italy. However, Henry may have consciously rejected continental models, since a bastion at Camber Castle in the early Italian round form with orillons and attributable to a visiting Moravian 'deviser', was begun and abandoned. Coastal defence did not require buildings to resist a formal siege but protected gun-platforms producing maximum fire power against ships and troops when at the most vulnerable stage of disembarkation.

The royal supremacy defended: the home front The external dangers which Henry faced were self-evident. The case was otherwise at home. Henry's claim to the supreme headship introduced England for the first time to the question of conformity in belief. To the age-old requirement to be loyal was added the requirement to think as the king did. Ideology had arrived. Men henceforth would face the choice implicit in Thomas More's last reported words: 'he died the King's good servant but God's first' (Harpsfield, 266). Given the principles of the common law,

measures to enforce the changes domestically and to punish opponents had to be put through parliament, and a comprehensive series of measures was placed on the statute book. The person largely responsible, and now regularly relied on by Henry, was Thomas Cromwell and he also oversaw a nation-wide policy of day-to-day vigilance. A number of instances suggest, however, that Henry was no mere bystander in this, although interested in results rather than method. The king's order, as transmitted by Cromwell, was that 'wheresoever any such cankered malice shall either chance to break out or any to be accused thereof, his highness would have the same tried and thoroughly pursued with great dexterity and as little favour as their demerits shall require' (*LP Henry VIII*, 13/1, no. 107). The king was certainly personally involved in the attempt to force Thomas More to endorse the supremacy, and the parliamentary bill of attainder which in November 1534 followed his obdurate silence. Six months later royal fury at the award of a cardinal's hat to Katherine's champion, Bishop John Fisher, determined Henry to get rid of both this turbulent priest and a former chancellor whose silence shouted from the housetops. For Henry, convinced beyond reasoning that his status was God given, wilful blindness deserved no mercy.

Alongside legislation went propaganda, derived from the *Collectanea* and the work on papal jurisdiction. The highly successful *A Glasse of Truthe* (1531) was partly the king's own work; intended for a popular audience, it ran to three editions and translations into Latin and French. Henry was present at the council meeting of December 1533 which considered how to promulgate the new ideas and probably authorized publication of *Articles Devised by the Whole Consent of the King's Honourable Council*. It also decided to publish the text of the Act in Restraint of Appeals to Rome in proclamation form to be posted up in market places and the like, and the preambles of other key enactments were used to spread the *Collectanea* ideas. Defenders of the church who had personally felt the king's wrath wrote fulsome retractions, works like Cuthbert Tunstal's *Pro ecclesiasticae unitatis defensione* and Stephen Gardiner's *De vera obedientia*, particularly effective with a clerical readership.

Doctrinal revolution To contemporaries who, unlike Thomas More, did not appreciate the rationale of the break with Rome, Henry VIII's behaviour appeared schismatic, merely the latest instance of a monarch falling out with a pope. The reality was quite different. Henry had redefined kingship. A supreme headship over the church had been discovered to be integral to the identity of the 'king of England by the grace of God'. All that convocation had done was to recognize fact, and all parliament had done was to provide statutory instruments to enforce the king's God-given personal title. Yet what did it mean for Henry VIII to be head of the church in England?

A common assumption is that Henry maintained orthodoxy except in respect of Rome—the often repeated 'catholicism without the pope'. Others have argued that he followed a middle course, between traditional religion and reform. However, what neither explanation takes proper account of is the king's determination to take charge and direct the church. In 1535 he appointed Thomas Cromwell to the new post of vicar-general and vicegerent in spirituals and in 1536 injunctions were issued specifying the doctrines to be taught, as well as the way the clergy were to behave and the substantial charitable donations they were to make. What is also not recognized is the extent of the religious change Henry licensed. Certainly this change can often appear inconsistent and erratic, a response to the political realities at home and particularly abroad. For example, during the threats of 1539 Henry gave royal assent to an apparently draconian statement of orthodoxy, the Act of Six Articles. This allowed Cromwell to tell the 1540 parliament that 'the king leaned neither to the right nor to the left' (Lehmberg, *Later Parliaments*, 90). Or again, the king was warned in January 1545 that the imperial alliance he then wanted would be set back unless he checked impending religious changes, so he instructed Cranmer to 'take patience herein and forbear until we espy a more apt and convenient time for the purpose' (*Acts and Monuments*, 5.562). Yet even when external pressures are allowed for, it becomes evident that from the break with Rome onwards, Henry VIII moved progressively towards a personal formulation of Christianity which was as distinct from Rome as it was from Luther.

In making these changes Henry was undoubtedly influenced by those around him. Yet it is important to stress the king's direct input. He worked personally on the antecedents of the Ten Articles of 1536, the first of his definitions of religion, and then instructed Edward Fox to elaborate this into a more substantial statement of faith. When this was issued in 1537 it became known as the Bishops' Book precisely because the king had not had time to vet it, though very soon after publication he sent Cranmer 250 corrections and additions. In 1543 a revision was published, known as the King's Book, with a preface by Henry in the first person. The final innovation in worship was the King's Primer of 1545 which advanced reform within the externals of tradition, with again a commendatory preface by Henry.

In the story of progressive religious change initiated by Henry, one of his doctrinal formulations may appear to go against the grain. This was the Six Articles of June 1539. Henry himself drew up the final text, and instead of publishing it like the other formularies of the reign on episcopal or royal authority alone, he chose the form of a penal statute. As has been suggested, the statute's ringing endorsement of transubstantiation and five other orthodox doctrines with the dreadful penalties attached did reflect the need to display orthodoxy at a time when the diplomatic situation was dark and the Pilgrimage of Grace had shown how much hostility there was in England to recent religious changes. However, the importance Henry attached to the bill (he came down to the Lords himself to ensure that it passed), the vigorous opposition which the bill met from the evangelical bishops (two subsequently resigned), and the reaction of reformers in Europe have convinced most historians that the act was a watershed, a substantive turn by Henry away from the reform of recent years towards conservative reaction.

The problem with this interpretation is that the reformers in the Lords did not question transubstantiation, merely the way Henry himself had chosen to define the real presence; most of their fire was directed at article three, the prohibition on clerical marriage. What is more, when it came to vote, the majority of critics supported the bill. Transubstantiation, indeed, was not the Rubicon between orthodoxy and reform it became in later years. Cranmer and Cromwell did not doubt the miracle of the altar, any more than Anne Boleyn had. Little use was made of the Six Articles Act. When juries of enthusiastic London conservatives seized on the new measure and indicted two (or possibly five) hundred reformers, the king himself intervened. All in all only six people suffered under its provisions. Nor did royal assent to the bill mark the end of reform. During the passage of the measure through parliament, Henry had approved the issuing of the Great Bible, the most significant of his religious reforms, and in 1541 a fine was instituted for parishes which failed to buy a copy. Later that year further feast days were abolished and the order was given to destroy all remaining shrines. The relaxation of the rules for Lent was continued until further notice (an announcement repeated in 1542), and so it went on. Where transubstantiation was important was as a litmus test for Anabaptists, and a more satisfactory explanation for the statute is as the climax of a campaign (no doubt triggered by horror stories from Münster) which since 1535 had seen two proclamations expelling the sect and the burning of over twenty 'twice-baptisers'. The campaign was continued the next year when the advocating of adult baptism and a whole raft of Anabaptist beliefs were excluded from the statutory general pardon, as well as denial of transubstantiation. Henry was not repudiating respectable reformers but religious fanatics.

Significant doctrinal shift (or, as Henry would say, reform) was, of course, implicit in the break with Rome. By claiming that he was rescuing the English church from the evil of papal usurpation, Henry was consciously asserting what had previously been heresy. In its place came Caesaro-papalism, the king as pope in all but name. Henry was the Old Testament King David, come again. Bishops in consequence found themselves holding office during the king's pleasure and being styled 'by royal authority'. As well as this denial of the apostolic succession as it had previously been understood, Henry denied the traditional catholicity of the church. Instead of a visible unity transcending all frontiers and focused on the bishop of Rome as Christ's representative on earth, he understood the church universal to be a metaphysical unity of national churches. Henry never claimed that he was a priest, but he certainly saw himself as the vicar of Christ for England, responsible for what his subjects believed. When he declared in the creed, 'I believe in one Holy Catholic and Apostolic Church' he meant what nobody had meant before.

Henry had no qualms about interfering with belief.

True, the king's adamant refusal to countenance justification by faith can suggest strict orthodoxy and so too his adherence to the doctrine of transubstantiation. However, he insisted on each because they were integral to his mechanistic and inadequate understanding of salvation. He did accept the need for faith, but understood this as assent to the creeds, not—as the reformers, Catholic and non-Catholic, understood—a lively personal commitment to God. As for the need for good works, that was equally vital because otherwise there was no incentive to virtue. The supreme good work was the mass, yet what Henry understood the mass to be was distinctly shallow. It was the mechanics of the miracle of transubstantiation which mattered, far more than the mass as the offering of Christ to God. In the will which he drafted in 1544 he described the mass as given 'for our better Remembrance' of the passion of the Lord (Rymer, *Foedera*, 15.110).

Ambiguous on the eucharist, Henry was heretical on the nature of the priesthood. He denied that holy orders were of divine origin and always deleted the adjective when he had the opportunity. He saw no difference between bishops and priests, spoke of the primary function of the clergy as teaching and preaching, and treated them as administrators, not channels of divine grace. Henry also undermined belief in the efficacy of prayers for the dead, a central preoccupation of late medieval western Christendom. His father disposed directly or though his executors of in excess of £50,000 in pious works for the repose of his soul. Henry VIII gave assets worth £600 a year to St George's, Windsor. By 1537 he already accepted that prayers for the dead were only justified by ancient precedent and charity and that their value was only to reduce 'some part' of the pain of the dead of whose condition nothing is known. In 1538 he rejected the word 'purgatory' on the ground that neither purgatory nor the purgation of souls appears in scripture. He did, certainly, take vestigial comfort in knowing that Windsor would pray for him *post mortem*, but his last will is a confused attempt to have it all ways, beseeching the Virgin and saints to pray for:

> Us and with Us whiles We lyve in this World, and in the Time of passing out of the same, so that We may the soner atteyn everlasting Lief after our Departure out of this transitory Lief, which We do both hope and clayme by Christes Passion and Woord. (Rymer, *Foedera*, 15.110)

The King's Primer of 1545 (which Henry claimed as his own) was blunt to a point: 'There is nothing in the dirige [the office of the dead] taken out of scripture that maketh any mention of the souls departed than doth the tale of Robin Hood'.

Henry also made drastic changes in traditional religious practice. From 1536 the clergy were required to preach against superstitious images, relics, miracles, and pilgrimages while injunctions in 1538 ordered the removal of all 'feigned' images and decreed that candles must only be burnt before the rood, the tabernacle (for the host), and the (Easter) sepulchre. Shrines were destroyed—most notably that of St Thomas at Canterbury—and relics were held up to public ridicule. His promotion of the vernacular Bible defied generations of the English episcopate. In 1543 the king assented to the reform of the service books and in 1545 the King's Primer, in addition to its notable frankness about purgatory, made no mention of the saints. The litany was by then in English (preserving only 5 per cent of the traditional invocations to the saints) and the king had Cranmer working on a communion rite. By the time of Henry's death, Catholic practice had been drastically curtailed. Robert Parkyn, a conservative Yorkshire cleric wrote, 'thus in Kyng Henrie days began holly churche in Englande to be in greatt ruyne as it appearide daly' (Dickens, 295).

The most evident of Henry VIII's destructions was the ruin of English monasticism. That there was a need for reform was widely agreed. Every king for more than a century had dissolved religious houses and applied the income to charitable purposes thought more relevant, and a strong body of opinion now saw the opportunity for a major redistribution of monastic wealth into education and charity. On the other hand, given that the total income of religious houses equalled or even exceeded that of the crown, the temptation to secularize the wealth of the monasteries was dazzling. In 1533, as the Act in Restraint of Appeals to Rome was passing through the Commons, Henry was already talking of reuniting 'to the crown the goods which Churchmen held of it, which his predecessors could not alienate to his prejudice' (*LP Henry VIII*, 6, no. 235). In the end the argument for immediate limited secularization prevailed, but without commitment for the future, and in 1536 about 250 of the smaller religious houses were dissolved by act of parliament, bringing the crown in excess of £70,000 gross over the next thirty months. Subsequently the greater houses fell in to the crown, generally by surrender; last, Waltham Abbey, did so in April 1540. The detail of all this was handled by Thomas Cromwell, but there is no doubt that secularization was fully supported by Henry. Indeed, he may have appeared in the Commons in person to promote the 1536 Dissolution Bill and in 1543 he specifically condemned 'the superstitious works of men's own invention … in which … them that were lately called religious (as monks, friars, nuns, and such other), have in times past put their great trust and confidence' (Lacey, 158).

Opposition For Henry VIII, recovering royal supremacy over the church and exploiting it to produce reform was the achievement of his reign. Beneath the great family portrait which Holbein painted for the wall of the privy chamber in Whitehall Palace was the assertion that Henry:

> drives the unworthy from the altars and brings in men of integrity. The presumption of popes has yielded to unerring virtue and with Henry VIII bearing the sceptre in his hand, religion has been restored and with him on the throne the truths of God have begun to be held in due reverence.

Yet the more the extent of Henry's Reformation is appreciated, the more difficult it becomes to account for the limited reaction which it produced. To a degree this can be explained by Henry moving progressively and spas-modically. He had no initial agenda beyond vindicating his kingly identity, but the logic of Caesaro-papalism drove towards heterodoxy. It is also true that engrained loyalty to the crown was a huge disincentive to protest. Nevertheless, the populous south of England rebelled against excessive taxation, and its failure to rise in sup-port of the traditional church suggests that the changes Henry introduced were greeted with enough support or apathy to disable concerted challenge. It is noteworthy that the latter part of his reign saw a spontaneous reduc-tion in provision for prayers for the dead as endowed chantries were voluntarily surrendered in large num-bers.

The partial exception to the picture of acquiescence, whether grudging or positive, was the country north of the Wash. On 1 October 1536 the county of Lincoln broke out in unrest, followed a week later by large areas of York-shire and beyond. The Lincolnshire rising lasted about a fortnight, but nine well-armed and organized 'hosts', numbering 30,000 in all, retained control of the northern counties for several months. Henry VIII called the pro-testers 'rebels' but they saw themselves acting 'for the commonwealth' on a 'pilgrimage for grace' from the king, and their object was:

> the preservacyon of Crystes churche, of thys realme of England, the kynge our soverayne lord, the nobylytie and comyns of the same, and to the entent to macke petycion to the kynges highnes for the reformacyon of that whyche is amysse within thys realme and for the punnyshement of the herytykes and subverters of the lawes.   (Dodds and Dodds, 1.176)

Although this manifesto indicates a complex of general discontents, there can be little doubt that religion was the catalyst, not only the start of monastic dissolution but a sense of threat to the church overall. The pilgrims marched under the banner of the five wounds of Christ and the banner of St Cuthbert.

Henry's response to the Lincolnshire rising was to blus-ter and to threaten, but the Tudor system of support for the civil power worked well. Several noblemen put their retainers in readiness, so providing the king with a force in short order, and this was sufficient to persuade the gentlemen of the county that it was better to represent their own involvement as a responsible attempt to pre-vent violence and to let a leaderless peasantry slink home. Forty-six executions followed. The Pilgrimage of Grace was a different order of problem and caught the king out badly. He had disbanded the forces gathered for Lincoln-shire and the principal reason the situation did not get worse was because the pilgrims had no intention of marching south. New royal forces which had to be raised arrived piecemeal and were hopelessly outnumbered, thus forcing the duke of Norfolk to parley. However, as he wrote to the king, 'I beseche you to take in gode part what so ever promes I shall make unto the rebells, for sewerly I shall observe no part thereof' (Dodds and Dodds, 1.260). A truce followed, during which Henry continued to insist

that he would punish Robert Aske, the captain of the pil-grims and the other ringleaders, but eventually he had to concede a general pardon and the promise of a parlia-ment. Before the pilgrims agreed to disband, Norfolk was forced to agree in addition that the abbeys should be restored until the parliament met, but he was able to avoid promising a further dangerous concession which Henry was prepared to make, that parliament should meet wherever they wished it.

The king's next move was not what the trusting north-erners expected. He had been outmanoeuvred in the field, but not in guile. He never had any intention of honouring promises made, and so remained silent, though he did get Norfolk to woo the gentry. Sir Francis Bigod of Settrington in the East Riding, a former MP, realized the king's dishon-esty and called out the East Riding men in January, but he was unpopular with his neighbours, had no gentry back-ing, and the rising collapsed. The next month the com-moners of Cumberland decided to go it alone, only to be defeated in an attack on Carlisle. These outbreaks of dis-order were what Henry had been counting on to provide the excuse to wipe out in blood the disgrace of his surren-der. The gentry leaders were rounded up for trial and Nor-folk declared martial law on the north. Henry's endorse-ment was enthusiastic:

> You shal in any wise cause suche dredfull execution to be doon upon a good nombre of thinhabitauntes of every towne, village and hamlet that have offended in this rebellion, aswell by hanging of them uppe in trees, as by the quartering of them and the setting of their heddes and quarters in every towne, greate and small, and in al suche other places as they may be a ferefull spectacle to all other herafter that wold practise any like matter whiche we requyre you to doo, without pitie or respecte.   (State Papers, Henry VIII, 2.538)

In all upwards of 200 died.

The 1536 risings were contained geographically because of the loyalty to the crown of the majority of the nobility of the south and the midlands, and the willingness of the servants, tenants, and 'well-wishers' who comprised their 'powers' to side with them. This was true even of the group of supporters erstwhile of Katherine of Aragon, now of Princess Mary, who were fully in sympathy with the aims of the northerners. The most notable, Henry Courtenay, marquess of Exeter, was the king's cousin, had been brought up by Henry, and served in the privy cham-ber staff; Lord Montagu and Sir Geoffrey Pole were sons of Margaret Pole, countess of Salisbury, the king's cousin once removed. Yet their loyalty was palpably grudging. Unwilling to challenge Henry's changes but also unwill-ing to accept them, Exeter and the Poles continued to use their standing at court to express criticism. Their support for Katherine and Mary had significantly alienated Henry, but he became paranoiac over the behaviour of Margar-et's other son, the cleric Reginald Pole, whose education he had also fostered. In 1536, from the safety of the contin-ent, Reginald addressed a swingeing public criticism of his former patron:

> You have squandered a huge treasure; you have made a laughing-stock of the nobility; you have never loved the

people; you have pestered and robbed the clergy in every possible way; and lately you have destroyed the best men in your kingdom [Fisher and More], not like a human being, but like a wild beast. (Schenk, 71)

Pole was then created a cardinal and sent to Flanders in February 1537 to try to implement the bull excommunicating the king. Henry replied by vowing the destruction of the Poles. Geoffrey was forced to provide evidence of treasonable intent against his brother and Exeter, who were executed in January 1539 along with Montagu's brother-in-law Sir Edward Neville, a long-serving gentleman of the privy chamber; a gentleman of even longer service, Sir Nicholas Carew, followed in March 1539. Exeter's wife and son and Montagu's son were incarcerated in the Tower along with the countess of Salisbury; the countess was beheaded in May 1541, leaving Reginald and his disgraced brother Geoffrey as the sole survivors of the blood royal outside the immediate Tudor family.

Henry and kingship The greatest challenge to Henry VIII's rule was the risings of 1536—indeed they were the largest peacetime revolt in English history. His response is very revealing of his attitude to kingship. Egoism dominated. This may be understandable in the case of the Great Matter, but for Henry, the right to rule was innate and uncircumscribed. His response to the Lincolnshire protesters had been abuse:

> How presumptuous then are ye, the rude commons of one shire, and that one of the most brute and beastly of the whole realm, and of least experience, to find fault with your prince … whom ye are bound by all laws to obey and serve, with both your lives, lands and goods, and for no worldly cause to withstand.

And he had demanded one hundred selected scapegoats (*LP Henry VIII*, 11, no. 780(2)). And this response Henry described as 'conceived as of itself to make them repent their follies and ask mercy without any tarrying!' (ibid., no. 780(1)). Nor was this uncharacteristic. When he discovered that the council had written to France on his accession offering amity and peace (that is, the continuation of his father's policy) he burst out: 'Who wrote this letter? I ask peace of the King of France who dares not look me in the face, still less make war on me?' (*CSP Venice, 1509–19*, 11). A month before his death he rejected requests to include Stephen Gardiner among the council for the next reign saying: 'You should never rule him, he is of so troublesome a nature. Marry …, I myself could use him and rule him to all manner of purposes, as seemed good unto me; but so shall you never do' (*Acts and Monuments*, 5.691–2). Henry's rooted conviction was that he possessed superior wisdom and that it was unforgivable presumption to challenge him, an impertinence towards the Lord's anointed which was conclusive evidence of fixed malevolence. The vindictiveness he displayed in the aftermath of the Pilgrimage was duplicated in the attack on the Scots in 1544, when he ordered men, women, and children in and around Edinburgh to be put to fire and sword for Scottish 'falsehood and disloyalty' (Bain, 2.326).

Egoism was compounded by falsity and deceit. During the Pilgrimage of Grace the king invited Aske to meet him secretly 'to here of your mouthe the hole circumstance and begynning of that matier' (*State Papers, Henry VIII*, 2.523) and he later wrote to thank him for his efforts to calm the north. The erstwhile captain of the pilgrims was then tricked into returning to London so that the king could 'wade with him with fair words as though he had great trust in him' and once that disguised interrogation was over, arrest him (*LP Henry VIII*, 12/1, no. 698(1)). Henry was very much the *faux bonhomme*; after Thomas More had been seen walking with the royal arm round his shoulders, the future martyr commented that the king would behead him without a qualm if it 'could win him a castle in France' (Roper, ed. Hitchcock, 21). Indeed to free Henry to invade France, Edmund de la Pole, Edward IV's nephew, had been beheaded in 1513, despite assurances which Henry VII had given that he would be spared. Henry VIII executed more English notables than any other monarch before or since. The victims comprised two wives, one cardinal, over twenty members of peerage families, four prominent public servants, and six of the king's close attendants and friends. And this takes no account of the three mitred abbots and various heads of major monastic houses who were executed, nor of Cardinal Wolsey and the three members of aristocratic stock who died in prison or on the way there. As Thomas Wyatt wrote, 'circa Regna tonat' ('round the throne the thunder rolls'; Wyatt, 185).

Linked to this was the king's ability to deny reality, an obstinate conviction that facts were as he understood or wanted to understand them and not as they were. Among armchair strategists Henry had few equals. At the height of the Pilgrimage he wrote to the embattled Norfolk:

> it is moche to our mervayl to receyve soo many desperate letters from yow, and in the same no remedyes. We might thinke that either thinges be not so wel loked on as they might bee, whenne youe canne loke but only to thone side, or elles that youe be soo perplexed with the brutes of the oon parte that ye doo omytt to write the good of thother. (*State Papers, Henry VIII*, 2.517)

This refusal to face facts could at times lead to remarkable political blindness. Henry knew he depended on 'men of power and worship' and during his reign steadily built up the number of important landowners who were sworn to his service. Yet when Norfolk was at his wit's end to find the men of the substance and reputation vital to restore normality to areas which had supported the Pilgrimage, Henry responded in his own handwriting: 'We woll not be bound of a necessitie to be served with lordes. But we woll be served with such menn of what degree soever as we shall appoint to the same' (*LP Henry VIII*, 12/1, no. 636).

Egoistical self-righteousness made Henry both the most forgiving and the most unforgiving of men. An alleged offender who could reach him in person, abjectly confess himself guilty of what the king suspected, whether true or not, and throw himself on royal mercy, would in so doing confirm Henry's perspicacity and could expect mercy. As the king is reported to have said after Stephen Gardiner had confessed to popish leanings, 'you know what my nature and custom hath been in such matters, evermore to pardon them that will not dissemble, but confess their fault' (*Acts and Monuments*, 5.690). On the other hand, if the king detected dissembling, 'stiffness', or ingratitude he would be brutal and harsh in the extreme, as the attack on Courtenay and the Poles demonstrates. The French ambassador Charles de Marillac identified other traits. Writing to the duc de Montmorency in 1540 he pointed to three major vices. 'The first is that he is so covetous that all the riches in the world would not satisfy him'. The second was suspicion and fear so that 'he dares not trust a single man', and the third 'lightness and inconstancy' (*LP Henry VIII*, 15, no. 954).

Henry's passion for money is well attested and supremely seen in the rape of the church, not only the secularization of the monasteries but the start of 'voluntary' land exchanges with the bishops. As for unpredictability and suspicion (for which he was notorious) Henry represented this as policy: 'if I thought that my cap knew my counsel, I would cast it into the fire and burn it' (Cavendish, 184). Some scholars accept this as evidence of the king's decisiveness and independence. For them Henry is an authoritative individual determining the conduct of affairs. Nothing got by him and he behaved as he wished, when he wished. The alternative view is that the mistrust and the variability reflected a fundamental insecurity. Later generations have known Henry overwhelmingly through the paintings of Hans Holbein the younger but this image of the dominant hero was the creation of the artist. Earlier likenesses of Henry VIII suggest nothing of the kind. Precisely why Henry suffered from insecurity can only be conjectured. Perhaps he learned watchfulness and extreme caution from his father, and his continued failure to have a male heir meant that until middle age he was always vulnerable as the sole male Tudor. However, his son's birth in 1537 only switched anxiety to the boy. Henry's habits of mind were fixed and his sense of insecurity reached its peak in the last decade of the reign.

Henrician politics How did Henry VIII's approach to kingship affect politics? His personality was certainly determinative, as must be the case with any single individual heading a pyramid of power. Furthermore, in such a power structure, gaining and keeping the confidence of the head is crucial to success, with the result that the organic form of interaction is faction and a competition for favour and reward. Those scholars who see Henry in the Holbein mould, strong and confident, argue that he exploited faction within the royal entourage to his own advantage, in particular to free himself from dependence on any group or individual and make himself the lodestar of officials and courtiers. Against this, scholars who see the public persona as a mask for inner uncertainty argue that the king was vulnerable to persuasion and that factions set out to influence the king's mind on both matters of patronage and of policy. The pressure on Henry to abandon Wolsey and the king's reluctance to do so certainly indicate that on that occasion the king was responding, not leading. The radical solution to his matrimonial dilemma was similarly sold to him in the teeth of traditionalists who advised otherwise. In both cases Anne

Boleyn was central, and on her and the influence she could wield focused all those who supported change, not only the royal supremacy but the more evangelical stance in religion which she represented. Moderate reform progressed in the 1530s because initially Anne and subsequently Cranmer and Cromwell had command of the king's ear. Anne Boleyn patronized and promoted clergy of a reforming turn of mind. Cromwell was a convinced reformer—he even lost money on the printing of the Great Bible. Cranmer, who had an intimacy with Henry which nothing could shake, moved steadily towards doctrinal change. As John Foxe wrote: 'so long as Queen Anne, Thomas Cromwell, Archbishop Cranmer, Master Denny, Doctor Butts with such like were about him and could prevail with him, what organ of Christ's glory did more good in the church than he [Henry VIII]?' (*Acts and Monuments*, 5.605). There is no incompatibility between a Henry whose will was law and a Henry who was capable of being influenced. Indeed his suspicious nature precisely exposed him to suggestion. Wolsey said: 'be well advysed and assured what matter ye put in his hed, for ye shall neuer pull it owt agayn' (Cavendish, 179).

Royal marriages, 1509–1537 Henry VIII of course did not leave egoism, pig-headedness, and distrust behind when he entered his private apartments. Evidence about his relations with his first wife, Katherine of Aragon, is sparse. Initially Henry behaved as the perfect courtly lover, but the suspicion is that once more egoism was the real motive. Katherine was a beautiful object, an audience for his chivalric posturing. In the early years—while her international connections were useful—he appears to have relied on her for help and advice in diplomacy, and she was an effective 'governor of the realm' during the first French war. How intimate their relation was is another matter. In 1511 he held a tournament in honour of his wife on the birth of their first son, only for the child to die a week later. Undoubtedly Henry was disappointed, but his response was to go in for a bout of gambling and then to order another tournament, action which certainly does not suggest real closeness between him and his sorrowing wife. There are a few stories and hints of extramarital flirtations. For example Jeanne Poppingcourt, a Frenchwoman in Katherine's household, had a lively reputation and Henry gave her £100 on her return to France in 1516. However the king's only definite liaisons during the Aragon marriage were with Elizabeth *Blount and Mary Carey, *née* Boleyn [see Stafford, Mary]. Elizabeth was one of the queen's ladies, cousin to her chamberlain. The *affaire* with her, which gave Henry his only known bastard child, possibly began in 1518 and may have lasted as little as a year. The relationship with Mary Carey is known only by Henry's own admission years later (there were no acknowledged children) but it must have taken place in the early 1520s. By the standards of contemporary popes and monarchs that record was sexually modest, but scholars differ as to the reason. Was it fidelity, morality, or lack of interest? Another possibility is increasing anxiety, possibly leading to impotence, the consequence of his inability to produce offspring which survived. In the 1530s he was certainly having psychosexual problems.

Henry's relationship with Anne Boleyn began, as already noted, in 1526. At first a typically selfish effort by Henry to possess the most exciting woman at court, it soon turned into genuine passion, what Henry called his 'so-great folly' (Savage, 30). However, his decision to substitute a love match for the intended liaison with Anne led Henry into uncharted waters, to a royal marriage based on emotion, in place of the norm of an arranged union with a foreign princess based on diplomatic advantage. The result was almost unique in royal circles, a story of sunshine and storm in which a feisty Anne alternately entranced and infuriated a besotted Henry. Anne, however, also exerted real influence. Her positive input during the divorce crisis continued, not only in the promotion of evangelical change but in patronage issues, in exploiting her French connections for diplomatic advantage, and as the leader of the predominant faction at court.

The unique closeness between Henry and Anne throughout their marriage gives the lie to the popular belief that the king rapidly tired of this second wife and hence had her arrested on Tuesday 2 May 1536. True, to Henry's great distress, the queen (who had miscarried in the summer of 1534) miscarried again on 29 January 1536. Fanciful explanations for Anne's rejection have been built on the supposition that the foetus on this occasion was deformed. They have no merit. The story about deformity emerges only in the 1580s in recusant black propaganda, along with the allegation that Anne was Henry's daughter. The 1536 miscarriage was, nevertheless, important because it stirred Henry's doubts, not about Anne, but about God. God had not permitted him sons by Katherine. Was he frowning on this marriage too? Henry was also suffering from the aftermath of a crashing fall in the tiltyard five days earlier which left him unconscious for two hours. With Anne out of circulation after childbirth, the traditionalist faction at court allied with the king's new protégé, Edward Seymour, to organize a claque against Anne and entice Henry with the milk and water charms of Edward's sister *Jane (1508/9–1537). Yet as long as the king continued firmly committed to his marriage to Anne, all this was mere dalliance, and only a fortnight before she was arrested Henry was going to great lengths to force the representative of Charles V to recognize her as his queen.

The campaign of the conservative faction became dangerous only when it was joined by Thomas Cromwell. Hitherto he had been Anne's faithful supporter, but in late March they fell out, principally over the decision to secularize rather than redirect the assets of the smaller monasteries. Anne's attempt to block secularization failed, but it had resulted in a very public breach with the minister, and he knew that no more than Wolsey could he survive for long with Anne as his enemy. Cromwell therefore made peace with the traditionalist faction at court, misrepresented the liveliness of the queen's admirers as evidence of sexual misconduct by Anne and the leading members of her faction (particularly Henry Norris, groom

of the stool), and used that to provoke the king's suspicions. Henry, taken unawares, challenged Norris (the nearest he had to a friend), offering pardon if he would confess his offence. Norris refused to lie in order to save his neck and went to the block along with Anne's brother and some smaller fry, with Anne following two days later. The king broke down in maudlin self-pity from which the traditionalist faction saved him (and from any opportunity to change his mind) by dangling the bait of Jane Seymour. His only gesture to Anne was the 'kindness' of a French headsman to execute her in the continental fashion. Henry married Jane eleven days later.

Henry's seventeen-month marriage to Jane Seymour was too short to leave traces of much influence. The memory of Anne was never far away and when Jane pleaded for the abbeys during the Pilgrimage, Henry reminded her 'that the last queen had died in consequence of meddling too much with state affairs' (LP Henry VIII, 11, no. 1250). However, the motto Jane adopted—'Bound to obey and serve'—suggests that she understood this very well and styled herself in deliberate contrast to her predecessor. Colourless she may appear, but Jane Seymour achieved something which neither Katherine nor Anne had managed, a healthy male child who grew to adolescence. Henry was genuinely broken when his wife died twelve days after the birth and to his death Henry represented Jane as his 'true and loving wife' (Rymer, Foedera, 15.111). It is, however, impossible to evaluate this emotion; was it deep personal bereavement or regret at the loss of the first partner whose marriage was undeniably valid and had been endorsed by God giving the son he had withheld for so long?

The royal parent, 1537–1553 The birth of Edward [see Edward VI] in September 1537 settled the final shape of the king's family—Henry's bastard son, the duke of Richmond, had died in July 1536. In the fashion of the time, Henry, not the mother, took responsibility for care and upbringing—in Edward's case he wrote out the regimen in his own hand. However, against the fashion of the time Henry displayed real fondness for his infant offspring, willing to spend a considerable time playing with them. At appropriate ages they were each given a separate household and arrangements made for an excellent education. Children were also valuable pieces on the chessboard of European diplomacy and Henry exploited the possibility of making marriages for them from an early age. Mary was betrothed at the age of two, Elizabeth's marriage was under discussion before her first birthday, and Edward's marriage—the greatest prize—was fixed when he was five and a half.

As the children grew, their relationship with their father changed. He expected absolute obedience and deference and their letters to him display 'half fearful delight'. The turmoil of his first two marriages had, of course, a major impact on his daughters. Elizabeth was declared illegitimate by the second Succession Act of July 1536. The precocious 2½-year-old noticed the change—'how hap it yesterday Lady Princess and today but Lady Elizabeth'—and the king had to be reminded to provide for her (*Rutland MSS*, 1.310). Nevertheless, her age and the fact that her attendants remained unchanged cushioned the impact of her mother's death and her change of fortune. Not so her elder sister. Mary experienced what can only be described as long-term parental abuse which probably accounts for some of her later obsessions and possibly for her recurrent ill health. By 1531, when she was sixteen, she had become a bone of contention between her parents and when, following her mother's reduction to the rank of princess dowager in the summer of 1533, Mary insisted on still being styled 'Princess', Henry closed her establishment and sent her to reside as the poor relation of the new heir, Elizabeth. Mary behaved impossibly and rejected Anne Boleyn's overtures with insult, but it has been suggested that Henry was not so much angry with his daughter as jealous of her relationship with Katherine. He allowed her to see Mary only once more. What is certainly true is that he was determined to enforce obedience to his will.

That determination produced a second political crisis in 1536. Following the fall of Anne Boleyn, Mary, and her traditionalist allies at court, had expected that, with 'that woman' out of the way, she would be restored to favour and recognized as heir presumptive. Cromwell, however, knew better and exploited his certainty that Henry was determined that Mary should first admit her illegitimacy. The father put intense psychological pressure on his daughter, and a number of her supporters were either sent to the Tower or interrogated. Faced with the choice between her own integrity and their liberty—and perhaps lives—Mary cracked, and she, like her sister, was formally declared illegitimate by the 1536 Succession Act. Mary's surrender saved her friends, but, as Cromwell had calculated, he was now free of his erstwhile traditionalist allies. The cost to the princess was incalculable.

With his elder daughter returned, as Henry saw it, to proper filial obedience, the family settled to a kind of normality. Only *Katherine Parr (1512–1548) of his later wives had much of an impact, particularly in respect of Elizabeth and Edward. The most important consideration in this final decade was the king's increasing age and ill health. Henry was putting on an enormous amount of weight: his chest measurement reached 57 inches and his waist 54 and eventually he had to be moved around his palaces in a 'trauewe', a sort of carrying chair. He also suffered enormous pain from a chronic leg ulcer which produced dangerous attacks of fever. The cause was not syphilis (voluminous medical evidence proves that his doctors never diagnosed this well-recognized condition) but either varicose veins or osteomyelitis, and the ulcer was made much worse by Henry's insistence on riding. He could become black in the face with pain. Given this context, the prospect of the next reign loomed even larger. One key decision was Henry's choice of moderate reformers to staff the prince's household once, as Edward later wrote, he ceased to be brought up 'among the wemen' (*Literary Remains*, ed. Jordan, 2.209). Another arose from the king's lack of other legitimate heirs. Henry's conviction that neither of their mothers had been married to

him ruled out the obvious answer—legitimating his two daughters. Instead, the 1536 Succession Act empowered Henry to bequeath the crown by will and he hinted to François I that he intended Mary to be next in line. In 1543 that was enacted by statute, along with a remainder to Elizabeth, and was repeated in the king's last will. This attempt to defy the common law of inheritance by placing bastards in the line of succession before his legitimate nieces and nephews was a characteristic piece of Henrician hubris. It caused his daughters considerable difficulty when they came to the throne in their turn and was totally ignored when his great-great-nephew became king in 1603.

Henry VIII and Cromwell Henry VIII owed the successful assertion of his royal supremacy to the political skills of Thomas Cromwell. It is, however, more difficult to separate king and minister in the secular affairs of the 1530s. One of the most important developments concerned parliament. In the first place it was called more frequently. From 1509 to 1531 there were eleven sessions; from 1532 to 1540 there were ten. More than that, the legislation after 1532 asserted the novel competence of statute to enforce the religious authority of the supreme head of the church and the ability of parliament to override property rights, most notably in the dissolution of the monasteries. Government departments were created from scratch. Law reform became a frequent item, accelerating after 1540 and signalling a swing from judicial construction to enactment. The succession to the crown was settled. In all, the last twelve parliamentary sessions of Henry's reign, average duration ten weeks, produced upwards of 500 bills which received the royal assent and others which did not.

This growth of parliament's authority, capacity, and legislative output in no way trenched on the standing of the monarchy. Royal supremacy over the church was implemented through, not granted by, parliament, and was not in conflict with a headship inherent in Henry's person. In 1542 he declared 'we, at no time stand so highly in our estate royal as in the time of parliament, wherein we as head and you as members are conjoined and knit together into one body politic' (Elton, 277). Parliament was the supreme expression of kingly power, and Henry treated it as such. He was meticulous in monitoring and managing the two houses either through Cromwell and his fellow counsellors or, if need be, by his personal appearances. The Commons was not 'packed' but from 1529 the king added fourteen English borough seats in part to facilitate the attendance of men he wanted in the Commons. The crown also took care to manage by-elections (a requirement of lengthier parliaments) and to advise unhelpful peers to stay away. Once parliament was in session the king never allowed himself to be far away from Westminster. Henry also used parliament as a forum through which to address the political nation. The most famous instance was in 1545 when he wept when commenting on the lack of charity which religious dissension was producing between those 'to styff in the old

Mumpsimus' and those 'to busy and curious in their new Sumpsimus' (Hall, 866).

A. F. Pollard argued that by using parliament to effect the Reformation, Henry took the nation into partnership. A more realistic comment would be that whatever the king claimed or wanted, only parliament could provide teeth sharp enough to enforce his will. It was essentially a tool of royal power. This is amply demonstrated in the treason legislation which gave Henry's reign such a bloody harvest. The treason statute of 1352 he inherited covered only an overt attempt to kill or dethrone the prince. From 1531 to 1544 twelve statutes enacted that a spectrum of offences were high treason. The most notorious, passed in 1534, 'made words treason' but in fact only expressed in statute what was already judge-made law. However the others ranged from the protection against criticism of Henry's various marriages (including criticism in print) to punishing mass poisoning, forging the king's privy seal, signet, or sign manual, and refusing to swear the oath renouncing papal authority.

Pollard also saw Henry VIII as the great architect of parliament. On occasion the king's initiative is beyond doubt. The refusal of the Commons to accept the compromise on the subject of uses which he had offered in 1532 convinced Henry that the MPs deserved no mercy. He exploited his influence in the law courts to win a test case in 1535 which undermined all property titles based on a use. Disaster thus faced landowners, but instead of compromise Henry now insisted that the 1536 session grant him his full pound of flesh. The social disruption which followed figured among the grievances of the Lincolnshire and Yorkshire rebels. In the second session of 1536 he retrospectively justified the Boleyn divorce by a general enactment that illicit sexual intercourse created degrees of consanguinity and affinity which could not be dispensed. His last-minute discovery that Norfolk's half-brother had contracted himself to marry his niece, led to an act of attainder being rushed through all stages on the final morning of that same session, along with a general enactment that marrying into the royal family without permission was a treasonable offence. In 1542 a clause was attached to the act of attainder against *Katherine Howard (1518x24–1542) which declared that any unchaste woman who married the king was a traitor.

On the other hand, it has been vigorously argued that in general policy originated more with Thomas Cromwell than with Henry. There can be no doubt that as well as being principally responsible for the drafting and the passage of legislation, the minister provided the initiative in many measures. He clearly always had a preference for statute as an instrument of government where Henry's instinct was to stand on prerogative. Cromwell must be credited with the legislation which provided administrative machinery to deal with church wealth (the provision for a treasurer and general receiver of first fruits and tenths in 1534 and the court of augmentations in 1536) as well as the 1539 Statute of Proclamations which provided him as vicegerent with better ways to enforce religious change. He was, too, almost certainly behind the large number of statutes which addressed social and economic problems. The first 1536 session, for example, legislated on fishing, leather, horses, pirates, enclosures, cloth manufacture, maximum prices, harbours, and town improvement, issues hardly likely to have been proposed by Henry any more than the 1536 poor-law statute which can certainly be credited to Cromwell. Indeed, thanks to the comprehensiveness of Cromwellian legislation directed to 'the common weal', parliament became established in the eyes of Englishmen as the mechanism through which desired change, nationally, locally, and individually, could be achieved.

But all this said, Henry VIII was certainly more involved in government in the 1530s and after than during Wolsey's ministry. Cromwell's own briefing notes for his meetings with the king show how careful the minister was to keep him informed even on the most minor matters. It is, therefore, best to see Henry recreating with Cromwell the chairman–managing director relationship which he had had with the cardinal (perhaps with himself playing a somewhat more hands-on role), but sanctioning more government action than he initiated.

Wales, Calais, and the north Thanks to the authority of parliament, significant changes were made in the structure of Henry's dominions. The first to benefit was Wales. In 1509 the principality consisted of some forty-five quasi-independent marcher lordships, the legacy of the piecemeal conquest of earlier centuries, plus the six coastal counties set up by Edward I. The chronic problem was lawlessness since the crown had very little authority in either counties or lordships, and effective power was in local hands. A council in the marches of Wales had existed under different guises off and on since 1476, but to limited effect, even after Wolsey strengthened its authority and machinery in 1525 when Princess Mary was sent to Ludlow as its nominal head. There were no better results from the other measures periodically tried by Henry VII and Henry himself: aggregating local offices in the hands of a royal nominee to create an artificial 'proconsul', or imposing indentures on the marcher lords. In January 1534 a final attempt at discipline began with the appointment of Rowland Lee, a Cromwell protégé, as bishop of Chester (that is, Coventry and Lichfield) and as president of the council in the marches, a man 'stowte of nature, redie witted, roughe in speeche, not affable to any of the Walshrie, an extreme severe ponisher of offenders, desirous to gayne credit with the king and comendacion for his service' (Williams, 82). The appointment was followed at the autumn session of parliament by legislation which, *inter alia*, gave marcher lords a financial interest in doing justice, placed their officers under the supervision of the council, and allowed prosecution for lawlessness in Wales to take place in the nearest English shire.

Two years later there was a remarkable volte-face. Bills were put into parliament to integrate Wales and England, introduce English law and institutions into the principality, and divide it into counties on the English model with twenty-seven MPs, a policy completed by a statute of 1543. A further act of 1536 abolished local franchises and rights of jurisdiction in England. In the same session, too, the government of Calais was dealt with comprehensively in the lengthiest of all Henrician enactments, which included granting it two seats in parliament like any English borough. Taken together, this 1536 legislation can be seen as powerful evidence of a deliberate crown policy to move towards a sovereign unitary state. Moreover, since these moves substantially coincide with Cromwell's period as chief minister and are congruent with the legislation he carried through asserting national independence against the pope, with the preambles to statutes which he drafted, the policies advocated by writers in his employ, and the language of his own letters, it is obvious to allow him much of the credit.

On the other hand there must be real doubts about the depth of the king's interest in the Cromwellian agenda. He undoubtedly endorsed anything which expressed what he saw as proper to his authority, but Henry himself appears to have been motivated more by pragmatism than ideas. In Wales he had been personally involved in preparing the 1534 legislation and early in 1536 he asked Rowland Lee to devise 'further articles for the helping of Wales' (*LP Henry VIII*, 10, no. 330). However, Lee was given no inkling that policy was about to change and it was a month into the parliament before news of the U-turn reached him—to his utter horror. The 1536 act was also drafted with a provision for the king to suspend it which had to be invoked in the following February. Two years later matters were still held up and the crown admitted that the reorganization of Wales had run into trouble because the king had been too busy. All this suggests that the act was introduced with inadequate forethought and smacks very much of an impulsive change of mind by Henry. Admittedly, in requesting Cromwell to 'considre and kepe the fomer statutes provided for the saide Countreye of Wales' Lee could be implying that the legislation was down to the minister, but the news which had reached him was that 'the Kinges Graces pleasure was to make Wales Shiregrounde' (*State Papers, Henry VIII*, 1.454–5).

Similarly, the source of the interest which eventually produced the Calais legislation of 1536 was an inspection of the town which the king made in person during his visit in 1532. He then produced a comprehensive 'Devyse' for remodelling the defences according to his own interpretation of modern warfare, but when after two and a half years little had been done, Henry ordered William Fitzwilliam and the duke of Norfolk to survey the defences again as they visited Calais on embassy. Their report led to a special commission of inquiry being sent out in the autumn of 1535, headed by Fitzwilliam, which 'founde this towne and marches farre out of order' and in part needing to be remedied by an act of parliament (Lehmberg, *Reformation Parliament*, 239).

Events rather than principles certainly determined the degree of royal interest in Calais at other times during Henry's reign. Holding the town was important to all English kings, and especially to Henry, because it proclaimed the right to the French crown and provided a ready base for intervening on the continent. On the other hand, of itself, Calais was a municipality in economic decline and with a falling English population, a fortified town with a poor harbour, built in a drained marsh in defiance of nature. Its strength lay in its water defences, but as Wolsey was told in 1527, 'watyr works be straunge & mervelus to kepe in ordyr but yff they may be contynually oversene & also holpyn in tyme' (*History of the King's Works*, 3.344). However, instead of a steady investment in maintenance and repair, the policy was one of emergency patching-up. Action was forthcoming only when external circumstances drew attention to the town.

In 1512 the declaration of war with France was accompanied by a ruling that the offspring of the increasing number of mixed marriages in Calais should henceforth be counted as English. The Calais conferences of 1520 and 1522 were followed by the release of considerable sums for repairs and fortifications. In 1527 Wolsey inspected the evidence of major sea damage, after which the sea wall was replaced and the king issued proclamations ordering the town to be repaired and offering customs privileges in the hope of revived trading at Calais (and hence funds available). After the 1536 act Calais again went on the back burner but the diplomatic crisis of 1539 gave it the highest priority and the resulting modernization produced, as Norfolk boasted, 'the strongest town in Christendom' (*LP Henry VIII*, 16, no. 850). The three outer defences of Calais—at Newneham Bridge, Guînes, and Hammes—were also updated and six new 'bulwarks' were built. The overall cost of the fortification programme between 1538 and 1547 was £120,700.

Pragmatic considerations rather than grand theory may also account for the statute of 1536 abolishing palatinates and franchises. The principal impact of the measure was on the rights of the church, especially the monasteries, and it solved the immediate problem of what would become of the jurisdictional powers of a dissolved abbey. The act was also less comprehensive than its preamble suggests. It effectively preserved the authority of the palatine bishopric of Durham and the archbishop of York's control of Hexhamshire. Even more important, it preserved the palatine identity of the county of Lancaster. The only palatinate to go was Chester—redundant now that Wales was to be shired.

It must also be noted that where uniformity was promoted, it was not necessarily in the nation's interest. As has been seen, Henry depended heavily on a peerage which through much of the country had become a service-nobility. Instances where particular aristocrats fell foul of the king were in no way part of any deliberate anti-aristocratic policy. Yet on the border an older breed of noble was needed, possessed of and willing to use *manred* to maintain order and fend off the Scots. Henry failed to see this different requirement and treated some of the leading northern families with grave suspicion precisely because they were not on the service-noblemen model. Thomas, third Baron Dacre, who was warden of the west marches for forty years, was made warden-general by Henry VIII and built his 'power' into an effective bulwark against the Scots, but was nevertheless sacked and heavily fined in 1525 because he had not imposed order of the quality expected in a southern county. His son and successor William was tried for treason in 1534 on account of the cross-border ties he had built up, to the benefit of both England and Scotland. In 1537 the sixth earl of Northumberland gave up and abandoned the Percy estates to the crown.

Thanks to doubts about northern nobles and an unwillingness to fund them properly, Henry was forced to turn to 'mean men' such as Sir Thomas Wharton, but they did not possess the requisite local clout and had frequently to be supported by royal lieutenants from the south. As Edward Seymour, earl of Hertford, pointed out when trying to evade a commission as warden-general, 'he that shall serve here had neide to be both kyn and alied emong them of thies parties and suche oon as hathe and dothe bere rule in the countreye by reason of his landes or otherwise' (Bain, 1.lxii–lxiii). The result of the king's refusal to collaborate with suitable local magnates was that when he died border defence was more expensive and less effective and English officials began to write of 'the decay of the borders'. Wharton had to be replaced by Lord Dacre in 1549.

One development which did less for law and order in the border than might appear was the emergence of the council of the north. As with Wales there were earlier precedents for this, but its continuous history began only in 1525 with the organization by Wolsey of a standing council to support the duke of Richmond's appointment as the king's lieutenant in the north, and with authority over the marches as well as Yorkshire. In 1530 Richmond and his estates were hived off and Cuthbert Tunstal, bishop of Durham, became president with authority only over Yorkshire. When this council was tested by the Pilgrimage of Grace it failed entirely (many of its members were involved with the pilgrims), so in 1537 a further reform produced a properly organized bureaucratic body. Its initial remit extended beyond Yorkshire but its responsibilities for the border fluctuated and the system of wardens of the marches remained unchanged.

The Irish problem Whether or not Henry consciously pursued ideas of the unitary state, Cromwell's legislation did integrate the border regions and the rest of England. In the lordship of Ireland the situation was far more complex, as a report to the king c.1515 explained. 'Folke dayly subgett to the Kinges lawes' occupied Dublin and its hinterland known as the pale, between 20 and 40 miles deep. The 'Kinges Iryshe enymyes' held Ulster and Connaught plus important enclaves in the mountainous areas south of Dublin and in the far west. Here society was Gaelic-speaking, pastoral, clan-based, and according to the report 'lyveyth onely by the swerde'. The rest of Ireland was occupied by the king's 'Englyshe rebelles', holders of marcher franchises carved out by medieval English colonists where obedience to the king's overlordship was decidedly flexible. The report envisaged the disciplining of the 'wylde Iryshe' through a wholesale militarization of the loyalist population plus renewed immigration.

Military expeditions on their own were useless. 'An armye that is moveing temperall for a season and not perpetuall, shalle never profyt the King in Ireland withoute the Kinges subgettes of the land be put in ordre, for assone as the army is agoo, the Kinges obeysaunce is' (State Papers, Henry VIII, 3.1–31). It was an opinion which Henry's father had shared: 'little advantage or profit hath grown of such armies and captains as have been sent for the reduction of Ireland' (Bayne and Dunham, 46–7).

For the first decade of his reign Henry followed his father in leaving the greatest of the marchers, the Fitzgerald earls of Kildare, to provide the deputy and enhance the king's power by enhancing their own. Then, possibly inspired by the report of c.1515, Henry began to take a personal and novel interest in Irish affairs. He summoned Gerald Fitzgerald, the ninth earl, to the royal court in 1519, detained him, and in 1520 sent over the earl of Surrey as lord lieutenant. What was novel about this was that Henry entertained the possibility of drawing Gaelic Ireland into the Tudor state by 'sober waies, politique driftes and amiable persuasions founded in lawe and reason', although characteristically he also envisaged the crown recovering its long defunct feudal rights (State Papers, Henry VIII, 3.52). Surrey, however, advocated the traditional policy of compulsion and Henry rapidly lost interest in the call for men and money, particularly as his interest shifted to war with France. He recalled the earl to England saying:

> We and our Counsaill, taking regard aswell to the mervalouse great charges that we yerely susteyne, by enterteignement of you, our Lieutenaunte, with the retynue under you there, as also the litle effecte that succedeth therof have clerely perceyved and in maner determyned that to employe … any other English Lieutenaunte with lyke retynue as ye have nowe, shulde be frustratorie and consumpcion of treasour in vayne.   (ibid., 3.90–91)

He had come up against the rock which would obstruct all Tudor ambition for Ireland.

This recognition of realities marks the point at which the king's first personal initiative came to a halt. The letter was drafted by Wolsey, but the minister's short-term alternatives turned out no more successfully. Two years of Piers Butler, earl of Ormond, as deputy was followed by four years of his rival, Kildare, and despite a commission sent to compromise their quarrel, Kildare–Ormond rivalry continued (backed by partisans at the English court). In 1528 came the settlement between Piers Butler and Anne Boleyn's father of their competing claims to the Butler peerage (with Butler becoming earl of Ossory) and Henry, believing that Kildare was trying to force himself back into office, overrode Wolsey and sent Ossory back as deputy. The situation deteriorated further and in June 1529 the duke of Richmond was made lieutenant with a council in support—the expedient which had been tried in Wales and the north in 1525.

Sir William Skeffington went with a small body of troops to represent Richmond, but within the year the king cut his funds—money again. The element of court faction became even more important and in 1532 led to the return of Kildare as deputy. Cromwell also entered the picture, but the new minister came with no preconceived policy except suspicion of Kildare, and he built up the Butlers and the pale administrators against the earl. In February 1534 Kildare eventually complied with yet another order to come to London and Skeffington took his place in July, but with no new policies and predictably weak forces. A new complication also emerged, the need to have Ireland repudiate papal authority. Then, in a massive miscalculation of Geraldine indispensability, Kildare's son, 'Silken Thomas', publicly denounced royal policies and besieged Dublin Castle. Kildare himself was sent to the Tower where he died, and Silken Thomas, now earl of Kildare, presented the rising as a crusade against heresy, even though no religious change had occurred. There was widespread support from the clergy and many palesmen and the king's own officials joined in too. Charles V did not respond to pleas to intervene, but by the autumn only Dublin, Kilkenny, and Waterford stood out for Henry. However, Skeffington arrived in October with 2300 men and brought the pale gentry back into line; and when Kildare's main stronghold surrendered in March 1535, he massacred the garrison ('the pardon of Maynooth'). Kildare surrendered in August on promise of his life and was sent to London. He and his five uncles were executed in February 1537 in the aftermath of the Pilgrimage of Grace, and the destruction of the Kildare ascendancy forced Henry to find another way to rule the lordship, and Gaelic lords to reorder their alliances likewise.

Henry abandoned once and for all the attempt to achieve satisfactory government by aristocratic delegation; henceforward the deputy would have to be English and backed by a standing army and a council under English control. Skeffington died in December 1535 and was followed by Lord Leonard Grey who called the Irish 'Reformation' parliament in May. The first session passed the appropriate reformation statutes but royal money bills were rejected in September and the king had to do a deal with the gentry over monastic dissolution. The Irish council called for conquest but Henry decided that policy should be limited to what the revenue from Ireland would pay for. Reforming commissioners who kept close contact with Cromwell were sent in September 1537. They cut down the army (and hence limited operations in the marches) and instead fortified the pale as an English enclave. There was to be no more interference in Gaelic Ireland; within the Englishry, Cromwellian administrative reform was to lay a firm base for the future. Financial inquiries showed a rise in the nominal revenue, thanks to the religious dissolutions which were possible in areas of English influence, but the actual income declined and the administration fell into debt. Not that financial stringency was all bad. It did put a stop to the more extravagant notions about integration.

This policy of treating the pale as a fortified bastion like the pale of Calais proved unsustainable because it was impossible to ignore the vacuum of authority in the marches and Gaelic Ireland which the fall of the Geraldines had produced. There, something like a Hobbesian state of nature prevailed with no Leviathan to discipline individual magnates and clan overlords. Grey therefore reverted to the Kildare policy of putting pressure on and doing deals with the Gaelic chiefs, only to be recalled to England, tried, and executed. However Cromwell, too, had fallen and the next deputy, Sir Anthony St Leger, therefore had considerably more freedom. He was an administrator, not a soldier, and a major success. He pursued a policy of inducing the Gaelic chiefs to accept Henry as sovereign in return for a recognition of their title to land and significant reductions in the king's theoretical feudal claims. In June 1541 the Irish parliament facilitated this by recognizing Henry as 'king' of Ireland, a change (greeted by public celebrations in Dublin) which incidentally also extinguished papal claims to Ireland. Henceforward the 'Kinges Iryshe enymyes' would be his subjects and English policy would be an 'all-Ireland' policy. The affinity to the settlement in Wales is clear but Henry was anything but pleased. 'Considre whither it be either honor or wisdom for Us to take upon Us that title of a King, and not to have revenues there, suffycyent to maynteyn the state of the same' (*State Papers, Henry VIII*, 3.331). Revenue had to be found and since deals with the Gaelic chiefs involved the surrender of what he still believed were valuable royal rights, they must be stopped immediately. In future, a contribution to the revenue must be agreed in advance.

Despite royal annoyance the policy which became known as 'surrender and regrant' did produce results. The Gaelic chieftains came to court, made a submission to Henry, and were invested with their lands, and with titles. The deputy was able to arbitrate in a number of long-running Gaelic feuds and practical benefit came to the English crown in 1544 when Henry was able to enlist Irish troops, the first recourse for centuries to what would be a major recruiting ground for the English crown. Admittedly there were problems. Change came too slowly, some of the English administrators hankered after expropriation (a pressure which would grow), and Gaelic power structures were hard to disentangle. And there was always the problem of money. The kingdom's debt reached £12,000 sterling and yearly subsidies were still needed—in part to make up for official peculation.

Henry VIII's reign nevertheless ended with Ireland relatively settled. It had also been fundamentally changed. The old policy of maintaining an English bridgehead into a culturally divided Ireland had been replaced by a commitment to the reduction and Anglicization of the whole island. To a degree that reflected the king's thinking when he sent Surrey in 1520, but it would be too much to say that he had arrived at this by planning and intention. Nor were matters stable. The commitment to Anglicization was open-ended and would require further progress in the imposition of religious reform which had yet to touch Gaelic Ireland. What is more, the obstacle he faced in 1520 was still there. The effective government of Ireland involved a continuous drain on the English exchequer.

The Cleves marriage While king and minister were busy with legislation and initiatives which, for good or ill, had long-term effects for the British Isles, Henry's private life continued to create problems. Despite any grief he may have had at the death of Jane Seymour on 24 October 1537, the search for a fourth royal consort began within days. At least nine European partners were considered—and the consequent diplomatic implications of each—before, as has been seen, Henry's choice eventually lighted on Anne, the sister of the duke of Cleves, a decision determined by a dangerous *rapprochement* between the emperor and the king of France.

The marriage took place on 6 January 1540 and it lasted six months and a day. Henry took an instant dislike to the 24-year-old Anne. Despite tradition, this can scarcely have been because of her looks. Portraits suggest that she was hardly less pleasing than Henry's other wives and the 'Flanders mare' sneer is an eighteenth-century invention. The more probable explanation is again Henry's egoism. At their first meeting Anne thoroughly punctured his self-esteem. He had swept into her room at Rochester, disguised and bearing gifts, a 48-year-old trying to recapture chivalric youth, but instead of an elegant sophisticate who would recognize this courtly trope, Henry found himself embracing a dowdy provincial, with neither personality, wit, nor knowledge of English, who then turned away to continue watching a bull being baited in the courtyard below. And he had only himself to blame, having been warned that in conformity with German court culture, Anne neither sang nor played and had been brought up to eschew 'good cheer' (*LP Henry VIII*, 14/2, no. 33). A deflated Henry tried to cancel the marriage plans but diplomatic inevitability prevailed. However, as Wolsey had said, an idea once planted in Henry's head was almost impossible to eradicate and nothing that Anne was or did changed the king's mind. Not that she did much, since she was innocent of the arts of seduction and despite sleeping with the king for several months remained a virgin. They were divorced in July 1540 on grounds of non-consummation and the evidence Henry gave to his doctors suggests that during this marriage he was impotent. Anne Boleyn had reported similar inadequacy from time to time.

The fall of Cromwell On 28 July, three weeks after the annulment of the Cleves marriage, Thomas Cromwell was beheaded and the common supposition has been that the two events were the joint consequence of Cromwell's misjudgement in making the Cleves marriage. In fact the initiative had been as much Henry's, if not more. The failure of the Cleves marriage was, nevertheless, ominous for the minister. Henry's eye fell on Katherine Howard, the frisky niece of the duke of Norfolk, so allowing the duke and the rest of the faction opposed to the minister to dangle Katherine before the king, much as Jane Seymour had been offered for sale. The prospect of a Howard in the royal bed was abhorrent to Cromwell and although Henry had told him in late March that there was an 'obstacle' to consummating the marriage, Cromwell chose to encourage Anne to be more vivacious, rather than taking prompt action to free Henry from a union which made increasingly less diplomatic sense as Charles V and François I drifted apart. Perhaps Cromwell relied too much on the favour implicit in Henry's final promotions, elevation in April 1540 to the earldom of Essex and appointment as lord great chamberlain. If so, he was wrong. Howard and his allies increasingly had the royal ear and poisoned it with the story that Cromwell's reforms cloaked Anabaptist opinions—a charge bolstered by reports of the number of 'sacramentarians' (those who denied transubstantiation) who had infiltrated the ranks of the reformers at Calais. Cromwell counter-attacked with allegations of crypto-popery but he was arrested, condemned by act of attainder, and executed.

The emergence of a privy council The fall of Cromwell in June 1540 put an end to the second period of kingly rule via a chief minister and ushered in a further, and this time enduring, period of government via a council. It was, however, not the council which Cromwell had sidelined before the break with Rome. The risings of 1536 had strongly criticized the minister and other counsellors 'of low byrth and small reputation' (*LP Henry VIII*, 11, no. 705(1)). What is more, the risings had been too much to be handled by king and minister alone. Leading magnates had therefore been called in to join a war cabinet to issue instructions and pronouncements during the risings, making as little mention as possible of the hated Cromwell, Cranmer, and Cromwell's ally Sir Thomas Audley. The body proved its worth and quickly became a permanent 'privy council' of notables and office holders. On the other hand, Cromwell was not immediately ousted. Henry was not ready to give up the use of a principal minister, nor was Cromwell ready to share power with other counsellors, particularly because many of them were bitterly hostile to the religious changes Henry was promoting under his and Cranmer's influence. The consequence was a period of some three and a half years when Cromwell was dominant, but always having to guard his back, and when the privy council was denied bureaucratic machinery of its own, that would have allowed it to operate as an executive.

Nevertheless, the existence of a majority on the council hostile to Cromwell had had its effect on Henry, as the traditionalists exploited the access which his interest in Katherine Howard gave them. Cromwell's arrest actually took place at a council meeting. Some months later Marillac reported Henry as saying that his counsellors 'upon light pretext, by false accusations, had made him put to death the most faithful servants he ever had' (*LP Henry VIII*, 16, no. 590). Nevertheless, Henry continued with the privy council format, although in the final months of the reign there are signs that Sir William Paget was on the way to becoming his third chief minister.

Royal marriages, 1540–1547 Henry's marriage to Katherine Howard, his fifth, took place on 28 July 1540, the day of Cromwell's execution, and the king was rejuvenated, 'so amorous of her that he knows not how to make sufficient demonstrations of his affection, and caresses her more than he did the others'. Katherine played up to her sugar daddy. Gossip told how 'the king had no wife who made him spend so much money in dresses and jewels as she did, and every day some fresh caprice' (Hume, 77). He allowed an influx of Howard relatives on to her staff and conservatives dominated the court. In the following June, Henry set off with Katherine on a huge progress via Lincoln to the city of York, exhibiting all his royal magnificence to seal the pacification of the north. There was a setback when James V, who had been invited to meet his uncle at York, did not turn up, but the king continued on his triumphant way, finding time *en route* to plan new fortifications for Hull. On his return he ordered public thanksgiving for his marriage to be made on All Saints' day, only to receive a letter in his pew next day telling him that when he married her, the queen had not been a virgin. Henry broke down and Katherine was placed under house arrest. Interrogation revealed not only pre-nuptial misconduct but improper behaviour after her marriage and at least the intent to commit adultery with a royal favourite, Thomas Culpeper. In December the men involved were executed and Katherine and her confidante Lady Rochford, the widow of George Boleyn, followed on 13 February 1542. The Howards who had known about her early misconduct were sent to the Tower. Norfolk retired to his house in Suffolk and wrote bewailing 'the most abhomynable dedes done by 2 of my niesys agaynst Your Highnes' (*State Papers, Henry VIII*, 2.721).

Henry remained a widower until 12 July 1543 when he married the childless, twice-widowed Katherine Parr. Although Katherine was pleasing and graceful, this time Henry was choosing on grounds of companionship, not looks. Katherine was well-educated for a woman of her time and rank, of reformist opinions but judiciously expressed, a good conversationalist who knew how to handle the king and knew her duty, even though she had been hoping to marry the younger and more exciting Thomas Seymour, Prince Edward's uncle. Her motto, 'To be useful in all I do', says it all. If Henry's final years had some element of tranquillity, he owed it to Katherine.

A return to war In the 1530s domestic priorities governed royal policy. After the Katherine Howard débâcle—perhaps partly in compensation—external concerns came once more to occupy the king's mind. The Scottish border certainly called for action. Theoretically England was at peace with Scotland—a treaty had been signed in 1534 following an outburst of raids and counter-raids on the borders in late 1532 and 1533. However, disorder was endemic and in July 1542 Henry decided to give the Scottish border reivers 'oon shrewd turn for an other' (*State Papers, Henry VIII*, 4.206). When the resulting punitive raid was defeated at Haddon Rig, Henry ordered a bigger incursion in November. Tit for tat ended dramatically on 23 November when the Scottish riposte was heavily defeated at Solway Moss and a number of significant prisoners captured, and even more decisively when James V died suddenly on 14 December, leaving the Scottish crown to his week-old daughter, Mary. Europe, however, was also beginning to present diplomatic and military opportunities. Open hostilities between Charles V and François I had resumed in June 1542 and this gave Henry possibilities to manoeuvre and strut on the international stage which he had not enjoyed since the 1520s. In February 1543, despite the

potential of the Scottish situation, Henry agreed with Charles V on joint invasions of France, and he dispatched 5000 men in June.

In the following month the war with Scotland was ended by the treaties of Greenwich, but Henry had not got all he wanted and five months later he resumed hostilities. In the following spring a combined operation involving 14,000 troops wreaked havoc on the Scottish lowlands. But a month later Henry invaded France with almost 40,000 men and he joined them in person in mid-July. Montreuil and Boulogne were invested and the latter surrendered on 14 September, four days before Charles and François concluded the bilateral peace of Crépy. Through 1545 England fought on alone, defeating invasion attempts and attacks on Boulogne, and answering the arrival of French reinforcements in Scotland with a massive counter-raid. Eventually stalemate and lack of funds forced the belligerents to make peace at Camp (otherwise Ardres) in June 1546.

The sense to be made of all this has been the subject of considerable debate. One theory is that Henry's policies towards France and Scotland were distinct in origin and affected each other only because the two countries were old allies. An explanation more frequently heard is that the king's principal objective was the unification of Britain. With legislation in 1536 ending the distinctiveness of Wales and the 1541 declaration that Henry was king of Ireland, attempting to annex Scotland can appear to be the last piece in the jigsaw. On this hypothesis, France was attacked in an attempt to neutralize 'the auld alliance'. However, judged by the respective levels of military commitment, France not Scotland appears to have been the major target, and as has been seen neither the shiring of Wales nor the upgrading of the Irish title was inspired by constitutional aspirations.

An alternative interpretation of foreign policy sees Henry's cross-channel assault in 1544 as a return to his earlier desire to reopen the Hundred Years' War and achieve military glory at the expense of France, with the raids across the border merely attempts to pre-empt Scottish intervention in support of an ally. That military glory certainly was a motive in Henry's policy to France is evident. It was inevitable that 'a hero king' would make attempts to recover land which the English crown had held as recently as his grandfather's youth. Along with honour went profit. The significant pension which France had paid the English king since 1475 had not been honoured for several years and by 1542 the arrears were more than £200,000. Overall, however, the best explanation of Henry's motivation is dynasticism. Early modern rulers saw it as a moral duty to acquire and retain what belonged to them by legal right, with the related obligation to advance the future interests and standing of their families. Such concerns motivated Charles and François. So too Henry. When it suited him, or when he was in no position to take action, he could make light of his claim to the crown of France, but this was not so at other times. Towards Scotland in the 1540s dynastic considerations were paramount. James was the next legitimate heir to the English crown after Prince Edward. As James committed Scotland more and more to links with France and to Catholic orthodoxy, the potential threat he presented to a dubious English succession was obvious. His replacement by Mary, queen of Scots, raised issues that were different but still dynastic. Was this not a golden opportunity to add Scotland to the English crown through marriage, the technique which had brought about Charles V's world empire? Did not the contrary to this—the danger that another European power would use marriage with Mary to annex Scotland—provide an even greater reason to intervene? Alternatively, should Scottish weakness be exploited to reassert England's claim to suzerainty north of the border or 'at the leaste the domynion on thisside the Frethe [Forth]?' (*State Papers, Henry VIII*, 4.319).

Honour and dynastic tradition drew Henry to attack France; dynastic opportunity and dynastic danger drew him to give Scotland priority. In typical fashion he attempted to have the best of all worlds. Some of the Scottish nobles captured at Solway Moss were persuaded to support him ('the assured lords') and with their help Henry secured the apparent triumph of a provision in the treaties of Greenwich that Edward and Mary should marry. However, his immediate intention was clearly to dominate Scotland. The negotiations might talk about a union and a single kingdom called 'Britain', but that was shorthand for Tudor family expansion. The Scots stalled and, angry at the delay, Henry had recourse to the big stick. Given Scottish weakness, that might have succeeded if he had deployed the biggest stick he had, but the king reserved that for France. As a result he fell between two stools. The attempt to compel Scotland to allow the marriage was reduced to spasmodic punitive expeditions and the attack on France yielded Boulogne. In 1545 not only did France reply with an attack on the south coast—which cost Henry his flagship, the *Mary Rose*—but it also put troops into Scotland! The peace made in 1546 gave the king nothing north of the border, and although he was to retain Boulogne for eight years, the town was, as his advisers had told him, the whitest of white elephants. Henry, attempting a grand slam, had ended with one minor trick.

An evil legacy Historians in the twentieth century have often written as though, in contrast to the dramatic changes of the thirteen years which preceded them, the last seven years of Henry's reign have little importance. This is a mistake. From 1540 onwards not only were the earlier changes 'road tested', but the legacy of these last years substantially determined the agenda of the next twenty. And an evil legacy it was. After the break with Rome the king had become an active supreme head who developed his own very self-confident, eclectic, and at times highly idiosyncratic theology. This, however, was no recipe for stability once he was gone. His young son was left in mid-stream between positions which can now, without anachronism, be characterized as Catholic and protestant, and Mary would find that her wish to turn the clock back would be frustrated less by recent changes

associated with her brother than by the destruction and anti-traditionalism of her father's reign.

The foreign adventuring of Henry VIII's last years was an equally poisonous bequest. Nor was this simply his folly in allowing the potential dynastic danger from Scotland to become entangled with French resentment at the insult which was Boulogne. The war had been massively expensive—£1,600,000 plus the costs of garrisons and fortifications. Government expenditure on this scale gave a huge boost to an already perceptible inflation produced by population change. The rate of price increase may, it seems, actually have been easing in the 1530s but by 1544 the index had risen nineteen points. In order to fund the war the king first imposed the highest level of parliamentary and non-parliamentary taxation since the fourteenth century. That provided a quarter of the cost. Perhaps as much again was made from the sale of former church lands, with important long-term social consequences. The remainder, except for limited borrowing in London and abroad, was obtained through coinage manipulation—the so-called 'great debasement' which began in 1544 and saw coins being made smaller and their fineness reduced by 16 per cent for gold and 64 per cent for silver. Fortunately much of the debased money which Henry struck—in effect 'printed'—was spent abroad, but English economic stability was affected and by the time he died the index had risen a further twenty-three points, to nearly twice its level of 1509. Debasement also damaged overseas trade. Between January 1544 and January 1547 the pound lost nearly 13 per cent of its international value.

Henry's evil legacy also extended to politics and government. The privy council had replaced Thomas Cromwell, but it was deeply divided. At one level the division was over religion, to influence the king towards maintaining tradition or towards protecting and advancing reform. However, at another level the issue was positioning for the next reign and a royal minority which could not long be delayed. From time to time the factions attempted coups of the sort which had been successful in the past. Cranmer was the target of determined scheming throughout 1543 in which Bishop Gardiner, Sir John Baker, another conservative privy councillor, and the duke of Norfolk sought to exploit complaints by traditionalists at Windsor and in Kent. The climax came, probably in November, when Henry did give way to pressure and sanction action against the archbishop. Within hours he had changed his mind, fetched Cranmer out of bed, and given him a ring to produce—the token Henry customarily used to signal that he was taking personal charge of a case. He also read Cranmer a lesson on what would have happened otherwise:

> Doo you not thincke that yf thei have you ones in prison, iii or iiij false knaves wilbe procured to witnes againste you and to condemne you, whiche els now being at your libertie dare not ones open thair lipps or appere before your face. Noo, not so, my lorde, I have better regarde unto you than to permitte your enemyes so to overthrowe you.   (Nichols, 255)

A few weeks later there was a counter-attack which took

the life of Germain Gardiner, Winchester's nephew and secretary and his agent against Cranmer, but the bishop was warned and saved himself by getting to the king before he could be arrested.

As the 1540s proceeded, new figures emerged to lead the political élite, notably Prince Edward's uncle Edward Seymour, earl of Hertford, and John Dudley, Viscount Lisle. They were cautious reformers but their influence on the privy council was limited because from 1542 they were busy on military matters, Hertford as the king's principal general and Lisle at the admiralty, both high in favour. As peace in 1546 became certain, the prospect of their return tilting the balance of influence, forced the traditionalists to make another attempt to discredit reform in Henry's eyes. In April a popular preacher, Dr Edward Crome, denied the existence of purgatory and the ensuing inquiry dragged in others, including Hugh Latimer. Burnings were followed by the arrest of an outspoken reformist gentlewoman, Anne Askew, who was known to have links with the like-minded ladies around Queen Katherine, including Hertford's wife and the wife of Sir Antony Denny, the reformist chief gentleman of the privy chamber. Despite being racked by the hands of Sir Thomas Wriothesley, the lord chancellor, Anne implicated nobody, but following an occasion when the king was unwell and Katherine had bested him in theological argument, Gardiner persuaded the annoyed husband that she too should be investigated for heresy. Timely warning allowed the queen to make her peace with Henry before the guard arrived to arrest her. With the return of his commanders the traditionalists steadily lost ground as the king spent much time in their company. Either by maladroitness or misrepresentation Gardiner fell from favour, Wriothesley changed sides, and Norfolk's injudicious son, Henry Howard, earl of Surrey, said enough to be arrested in December for treason, followed by his father. The earl was executed on 21 January but his father survived because the bill attainting him received the royal assent only a few hours before the king's own death.

The king's will It was in the context of this final factional battle that Henry revised his last will and testament on 30 December 1546. It was authenticated by the dry stamp, a form of signature by proxy which Henry had introduced in 1545 to save himself trouble. This system was in theory open to abuse, but the will is undoubtedly genuine. Arguments that it was stamped only after the king became incapacitated, or even after he was dead, do not stand up to analysis. The king designated Edward as heir and after Edward, Mary and Elizabeth, though the girls were to lose their places in the succession if they married without the written permission of a majority of privy councillors. Next in line he put the Grey and Clifford families, descendants of Mary, his younger sister. The granddaughter of Henry's elder sister, Margaret—Mary, queen of Scots—was not mentioned, though presumably she qualified in the final remainder to the next rightful heirs. To govern the country during his son's minority, Henry nominated sixteen executors who were to function as Edward's privy council, and since sixteen might be too few for day-to-day

business, he named a further twelve to be counsellors to the sixteen as and when required.

Henry's will provoked discussion in the reigns of Mary and Elizabeth and also in modern times. Some historians have argued that because traditionalist and anti-traditionalist councillors were roughly equal in numbers, Henry's intention was to rule from the grave and preserve his individual religious policy. This, however, ignores the fact that political weight and leadership were all on the side of the reformers. Others have made the improbable suggestion that Henry did not know of, or was not concerned with, religious affinities. Nor is it convincing that the will simply froze the political *status quo* of late December 1546, or that it was imposed by the reformist faction on a fast-failing king. All the evidence suggests that, though seriously unwell, Henry was in control. In December he annotated the charges against Surrey with his own hand and as late as 17 January he was fully in command when receiving the French and imperial ambassadors. All in all, the conclusion has to be that, in deciding on his son's counsellors, his intention was to limit the influence of religious conservatism. And the reason is not hard to seek. Recovering the supreme headship of the church in England had been his greatest achievement, and conservatives could not be trusted to preserve that in its full force. It was a conviction of which Henry had given sign several years earlier when he decided to appoint the moderate reformers Richard Cox and John Cheke as Edward's tutors.

Henry did not name a protector. The office had unhappy overtones. However, councils of regency also had a poor history and were easily vitiated by faction. To guard against this Henry was careful to provide that the named membership of the privy council could not be changed and that decisions had to be taken by simple majority vote of 'such of them as shall then be alive' (Rymer, *Foedera*, 15.115). In other words his designated counsellors were locked into a need to collaborate. Given that, the king made it quite clear that this restricted body had full plenary power to act as it thought best. Henry clearly expected Hertford to lead—he gave the stamped will to him for safe keeping and he created him earl marshal and treasurer. However, fettered by the majority rule and with no opportunity to pack the council with their own nominees, neither Hertford nor any other regent would, he hoped, be able to abuse royal authority.

Henry died at Whitehall Palace in the early hours of Friday 28 January 1547. His body was embalmed and lay in state in the presence chamber at Whitehall. On 14 February it was moved by stages to Windsor where it was buried in the morning of the 16th in the vault of St George's Chapel, next to the grave of Jane Seymour.

The royal magnificence In 1546 Henry did not go bankrupt as Charles V and François I did on more than one occasion, but he died in debt. However, against this had to be set his enormous accumulated wealth. The remarkable inventory made after his death lists nearly 20,000 items. The tone is set by the first, his gold crown weighing nearly 7 lb and adorned with some 340 precious stones. His gold and silver candlesticks alone weighed a quarter of a ton; he had hundreds of tapestries; thousands of yards of cloth of gold were in store, ready to make into his elaborately ornamented costumes. Beside this fortune in chattels must be set his houses: he inherited thirteen; when he died he owned over fifty, most of which he acquired after 1530.

Not only did he acquire property, but from the time of Wolsey's fall Henry developed a passion for construction and reconstruction. In consequence, for much of his reign he lived in a series of building sites. His underlying determination was to display his status as one of Europe's 'big three'. That, in particular, required continual development at his three greatest palaces: Greenwich, perhaps his favourite, built by his father; Hampton Court, which Wolsey gave him and on which Henry spent £62,000 in ten years; and Whitehall, which he extended over 23 acres from a nucleus of the London house of the archdiocese of York which Wolsey had rebuilt. And as soon as Henry had designed, he wanted the finished result, with the consequence that what he constructed was often impressively disguised jerry-building. Not that better quality work would necessarily have been wiser; Henry regularly wanted to change what had been built, immediately he saw it.

Henry's most remarkable venture followed his decision in 1537 to create Hampton Court Chase, an enormous hunting-ground upstream of the palace on the opposite bank of the Thames. A preserve of this size required a subsidiary hunting-lodge, so Henry swept away the village, church, and manor house of Cuddington near Esher and built Nonsuch, as its name indicates the palace to eclipse all others, in particular the famous châteaux of François I. What justified its name was the exterior of plaster-stucco panels bearing classical scenes and motifs in high relief, between borders of carved and gilded slate. Most of the craftsmen on Henry's buildings were Flemish but the Nonsuch exterior was worked on by Nicholas Bellin of Modena whom he had purloined from working for François I on Fontainebleau. A design by Bellin, possibly for the interior of Nonsuch, is clearly related to the Galerie François Ier at Fontainebleau, so the Italian artistic influence on the palace via France may have been considerable.

Henry's own tastes in fine art are hard to pin down. He was possibly something of a squirrel, collecting what took his fancy. Whitehall was decorated with history paintings of his triumphs, and Henry owned hundreds of pictures, principally portraits and religious paintings on largely predictable themes. However, he was undoubtedly attracted by the new Renaissance fashions of which Wolsey had been the great ambassador. The royal plate was often decorated in the antique style and so too the jewellery designed for him, although nothing is known of the designs the king himself produced. He employed intaglio cutters and possessed the earliest portrait medals known in England, although here Italian influence was mediated via Germany. Renaissance motifs were used in decorating the walls and windows of his palaces although they were balanced by a riot of traditional heraldic badges and symbols.

Henry engaged a number of foreign artists. The most successful Italian in his service was Antonio Toto who became sergeant-painter, though Henry employed half-a-dozen others including Pietro Torrigiani who designed a tomb and highly Italianate altarpiece at Westminster commemorating the king's father. The tomb commissioned by Wolsey from Benedetto da Rovezzano was appropriated by Henry and substantially (but not completely) finished by Giovanni da Maiano. For miniatures, the king used the Horenbout family from Flanders, but it was Anne Boleyn who introduced Hans Holbein the younger into the royal circle. After the latter's death in 1543 Henry recruited Guillim Scrotes who had worked for Mary of Hungary, the regent of the Habsburg Netherlands. Much of the time of the royal Cartists was devoted to ephemeral court entertainments, while Holbein appears never to have been fully appreciated and to have been regarded as the equivalent of a superior photographer.

Holbein nevertheless created the definitive image of Henry in heroic classical pose. The original semi-profile face mask survives as the half-length portrait of 1536 in the Thyssen collection and in the full-length cartoon of the figure of Henry for the privy chamber wall painting of the following year, showing Henry with his father and mother and Jane Seymour. The realized fresco was destroyed by fire in 1698 but surviving small-scale copies show that Holbein switched to a direct frontal image for the finished work. Numerous later versions of this image survive, head and shoulders, three-quarter length, and full length. Holbein used it himself for the cartoon of Henry and the barber–surgeons and for the associated (but unfinished) painting. Appearances of Henry in groups by anonymous artists include *The Family of Henry VIII* (Royal Collection) and *Charles V and Henry VIII* (priv. coll.), while Lambert Barnard's panel paintings in Chichester Cathedral include a scene of Henry restoring the privileges of the see to Bishop Robert Sherborn. Henry also appears in a number of history paintings, such as the *Field of Cloth of Gold* (Royal Collection). There are two earlier anonymous half-length portraits (c.1520 and c.1527) and one of c.1535 by Joos van Cleeve (Royal Collection). There are also two post-Holbein patterns, one full-length, possibly by Lucas Horenbout. Horenbout also produced a miniature dated 1526–7. A miniature by Holbein shows Henry as Solomon and so too a window in the chapel of King's College, Cambridge. He appears in a number of illuminated manuscripts: the great tournament roll of Westminster, the procession of the peers in the 1512 parliament, the king's own psalter (playing the part of King David), the Wriothesley Garter book and the black book of the Garter, and on various legal and diplomatic documents. A drawing survives of Henry as an infant and another showing the adult Henry in the privy chamber; an engraving by Cornelis Matsys depicts Henry in the last years of his life. In print, Henry appears on the frontispiece in both the Coverdale Bible and the Great Bible. A terracotta bust by Guido Mazzoni is possibly of Henry as a child. Two portrait medals of Henry exist and where the king's head appears on coins, it was clearly intended as a portrait. The sculptured relief of Henry at the Field of Cloth of Gold on the Hotel du Bourgthéroulde in Rouen was damaged in 1944.

Erasmus and Thomas More enthused that the younger Henry was a patron of good letters. He certainly employed humanists at court and in government, both foreigners and Englishmen such as More and Pace. Henry was also a target for aspiring authors: many of the contemporary works he owned were presentation copies. Although there is evidence that he often preferred being read to rather than to read himself, and that Anne Boleyn marked selected passages for him, the king liked to picture himself as a *littérateur*. He had long and enjoyable conversations with visiting scholars and many of his books carry annotations by him. He was also the first English king to write, publish, and print a book, even with help, and, as has been seen, he did work on many of his government's pronouncements on religion. Henry had a library at Hampton Court and at least two at Greenwich, while the main collection was at Whitehall. In all he possessed some 1500 titles in both manuscript and print. Some he had inherited, others were religious works published abroad (a number confiscated from Anne Boleyn), there were numerous classical texts, and many of the non-print items had belonged to the monasteries.

Henry's greatest artistic interest was in music. At death he possessed over three hundred instruments of his own. No mean performer himself on the lute and the virginals, the king studied the organ, then a notoriously difficult instrument. Henry was also a keen singer and a more than competent sight-reader. Unusually for a time when ensemble work was generally left to professionals, Henry played the recorder and he and his courtiers sang together. He also composed. Neither of the masses he wrote has survived but thirty-three of his other pieces are known, all but one secular. He was much applauded, but modern research has established that many of his compositions are, effectively, arrangements of continental originals. Henry also employed about sixty professional musicians, a minority of whom worked in the privy chamber while the rest provided music outdoors or in large gatherings. As the reign progressed the king began to employ instrumental groups to perform the new polyphonic music. Most came from abroad, where the making and care of the newer sort of instrument was more advanced. One family, the Bassanos, served the court until the civil war. Henry also cherished the choir of the chapels royal and sought talent for it everywhere, even poaching from Wolsey. Not that the duties of the five men and ten boys were exclusively liturgical, since they acted as extras in royal pageants and disguisings.

Henry VIII—an assessment That the reign of Henry VIII was enormously significant is beyond question. His rejection of western Christendom in favour of a national church, the mortal wound he gave to traditional Christian life in England, his effective toleration and even promotion of moderate religious reform, his plundering and subsequent liquidation of the accumulated wealth of the church, the innovative use of statute and the resulting change in the qualitative role and importance of parliament, all these left a deeper mark on English history than any monarch since the Norman conquest and any who have followed him. Even more profound has been the consequence of Henry's decision to require, for the first time ever, that subjects should accept belief as defined by the state. From that point on it ceased to be sufficient any longer to offer the crown loyalty and ability; the monarch needed to search hearts. Ideological conformity and nonconformity became substantial and permanent features of English life.

Many historians from the Victorian period and later have wanted to go beyond this factual record. J. A. Froude's monumental *History of England from the Fall of Wolsey to the Defeat of the Spanish Armada* (1858–70) cast Henry as a hero, a statesman of destiny, the father of his people who led them out of medieval darkness towards their worldwide (and Victorian) destiny as 'top nation'. S. R. Gardiner was less effusive but just as convinced of Henry's distinctiveness. He claimed that with no army to back him, Henry's power necessarily 'rested entirely upon public opinion'; 'his strength was in the main the result of his representative character' (Gardiner, 1.6, 11). A. F. Pollard's monumental biography took much the same line. Henry was not only a man of courage in the right place at the right time, but someone who had a deep symbiotic relationship with the people of England and an astute, perhaps instinctive, identification with the contemporary *zeitgeist*. He embodied the national will. That in making omelettes Henry smashed a large number of valuable eggs was beside the point; the alternative would have been civil strife and bloodshed on a huge scale. Other writers have gone even further, claiming that Henry changed the mindset of the nation by embodying in his person 'a self-contained, self-sufficing sovereign *imperium*' which produced 'in the minds of his subjects a new conception of the state', and touched 'their imaginations in a way that no English king had done before' (Morris, 102–3).

Over the years, however, the voices in favour of Henry VIII have not been in a majority. Herbert of Cherbury, writing in the reign of Charles I, emphasized Henry's paranoia—'impressions privately given him by any court-whisperer were hardly or never effaced'—and he remarked that respect for Henry, both on the continent and at home, disappeared so rapidly 'that it may truly be said, all his pomp died with him' (Herbert, 747). Seventeenth- and eighteenth-century religious controversy focused particularly on Henry's motives in breaking with Rome and dissolving the monasteries, a delicate area for defenders of the protestant establishment. Bishop Gilbert Burnet argued that defective though Henry was, God used him to achieve his will. This was hardly a good enough response when, following the Relief Acts, Roman Catholic publicists sought to advance their claim for complete emancipation by representing the Reformation as a wrong to be righted. Henry's actions brought no spiritual benefits to the country; they were driven by lust and greed. Non-Catholics too accepted the charge. William Cobbett declared 'It was not a reformation but a devastation of England' (Cobbett, 19). The advent of the Tractarian movement produced writers from within the Church of England who also wanted to disavow the past. Thus Canon R. W. Dixon was a competent historian but nevertheless explained the Reformation as the work of:

> a man of force without grandeur: of great ability, but not of lofty intellect: punctilious yet unscrupulous: centred in himself: greedy and profuse: cunning rather than sagacious: of fearful passion and intolerable pride, but destitute of ambition in the nobler sense of the word: a character of degraded magnificence.   (Dixon, 1.4)

More recent scholarship has not been flattering either. Scarisbrick emphasized the negative: 'rarely, if ever, have the unawareness and irresponsibility of a king proved more costly of the material benefit of his people' (Scarisbrick, *Henry VIII*, 526). L. B. Smith stressed the king's lack of consistency. A view that sees Henry as undoubtedly in personal charge of his kingdom but heavily dependent on others and frequently influenced by the balance of factions at court has received strong support. G. R. Elton concluded that the king was far from masterfully competent or invariably in charge. True, a minority including L. B. Smith has tried to argue that Henry genuinely dominated both court and government and that factions, in so far as they existed, followed his lead. However, it is a fallacy to imagine that dominance and malleability cannot co-exist. The object of a faction was to influence the king as he was making his decision. Henry's subjects had no doubt that this was a real possibility and many lived, and some even died, by that belief. Instead of Henry VIII governing according to his autonomous will, government action emerged from the shifting political and personal context around him.

All this is very evident in the central issues of the reign, the divorce, the breach with Rome, and the royal supremacy. Henry certainly worked at his Great Matter, but to get anywhere he had to rely on others. The theory of royal supremacy was developed by a think-tank of scholars, exploiting these ideas through the medium of parliament required the political skills of Thomas Cromwell, and for courage the king relied on Anne Boleyn.

As this example shows, Henry VIII's policies were essentially personal and not, *pace* his admirers, conceived of in the national interest. Pollard's picture of a king galvanizing the national will needs to be upended: the nation was galvanized to express the king's will. In foreign affairs, where Henry was most continuously and most personally active, he again followed the devices and desires of his own heart. Before 1527 the object was to establish his credentials as a monarch of European standing. From 1527 policy became dominated by the king's Great Matter and the need to protect the action he had taken. There was no other reason for a break with Rome. Having no male heir was dangerous, but Henry's myopic efforts to displace Mary and ignore James of Scotland simply made matters worse. Henry's promotion of religious reform may have had the effect of preventing religious war in England, but whatever Froude and Pollard imagined, this was never in the king's mind. As for the 1540s, the revival of Henry's personal obsession with winning territory in France led him to mishandle the opportunity presented by the victory at Solway Moss and the accession of the infant Mary to the Scottish throne, and so throw away a chance to bring about a peaceful union of Great Britain.

Henry VIII's monumental selfishness was disguised by highly effective propaganda. Holbein's great painting in the privy chamber at Whitehall extolled Henry's achievement in driving out the unworthy and restoring true religion. The frontispiece to the Great Bible, set up in each parish church, is dominated by a Henry declaring 'I make decree that in every dominion of my kingdom men tremble and fear before the living God' (who peeps into the frame to say 'I have found a man after my own heart who will do my will'). The proclamation of May 1544 which set in hand the swindle of debasement was announced as a move to protect the supply of bullion, made by a king 'tendering above all things the wealth and enriching of this his realm and people' (Hughes and Larkin, 1.328). In 1545, the bill to enact what was the heaviest tax demand of the reign was disguised as 'a poor token of our true and faithful hearts' towards a king who 'has preserved us for almost these forty years' (37 Hen. VIII c. 25).

Henry VIII to his contemporaries This modern critical assessment would not, however, have been endorsed by Henry VIII's loyal subjects. For them, whatever they might like or loathe in his policies, Henry was everything a king should be; he had all the monarchical virtues in full measure. The first was magnificence, immediately obvious in his personal appearance, whether excelling in the joust before a crowd of courtiers and commoners or grandly robed to dominate a diplomatic set piece. The reputation of the Field of Cloth of Gold spread throughout Europe, not simply as a vastly expensive exercise in image building, but as regal glory in action. Then there were his palaces. The *pièce de résistance* of Henry's Nonsuch challenge to François I was a great statue of Henry himself, with Edward beside him.

A second contemporary royal virtue was military power and success; apostles of peace like Colet, Erasmus, and Zwingli were very much in the minority. Henry's fascination with military technology, most notably heavy guns on board ship and the consequent need to encourage cannon-founding, was entirely in the kingly tradition. So was war. No one was allowed to forget Henry's triumph at the battle of the Spurs, even though it was a skirmish fought in his absence. His armies not only won massive victories which culled two generations of Scottish nobles; in 1544 they savaged the lives of ordinary Scots and ruined the lowland economy. Supremely, with the capture of Boulogne, Henry became the only king to win territory in France for more than a century. A taste for building and a taste for war came together in his huge programme of coastal fortification after 1539, and the creation of the best navy in Atlantic waters. If Henry was not the first warrior of Europe, it was not for want of trying.

The third thing which impressed Henry's people was his personality. More than fifty years after his death, London's Fortune Theatre could put on a play with the simple title *When you See me you Know me* and be sure that the public would know who was meant, and even that an audience would recognize Henry's mannerisms on stage. The performance was such a hit that Shakespeare's company had to reply with *Henry VIII*. Thanks to printing, and particularly the Great Bible, Henry was almost certainly the first English monarch whose likeness his subjects could recognize. Popular ballads celebrated Henry's fame, while in political circles he was a byword for how a king should be obeyed. His daughter Mary, faced with the tendency of her masculine courtiers to treat the orders of a queen regnant as an invitation to debate, declared that 'she only wished [her father] might come to life again for a month' (*CSP Spain*, 1554, 167).

Subsequent images Henry's personality has continued to impress to the present day, even inspiring a popular Victorian music-hall song. One reason for this was his continuing relevance to ongoing religious controversy. Another factor was the theatre, in particular Shakespeare's *Henry VIII*. Continuously popular in the seventeenth and eighteenth centuries and also frequently performed in the nineteenth, the play attracted all the great actors, though more for the role of Wolsey than for Henry himself. This, in turn, led to scenes from the play becoming popular subjects for painters, and Victorian book illustrators followed. The illustrations by Joseph Nash to his four-volume *The Mansions of England in the Olden Time* (1839–49) are a notable example; the set was reissued three times, the last as late as 1912. Historical novelists also focused on Henry, such as William Harrison Ainsworth in *Windsor Castle* (1843) and Ford Madox Ford in *The Fifth Queen* (1906–8) and many more subsequently.

Shakespeare's *Henry VIII* with its emphasis on pageantry went out of fashion in the twentieth century, but pageantry and costume coupled with the drama of Henry's private life made the king an obvious subject for the cinema. Pride of place must go to *The Private Life of Henry VIII* (1933) which won an Oscar for Charles Laughton as the king, though at the cost of implanting in the mind of every viewer a fallacious conception of Tudor table manners. Richard Burton's playing of Henry in *Anne of the Thousand Days* (1969) was colourless and there is little to be said for James Robertson Justice in *The Sword and the Rose* (1953) or for the various versions of the *Prince and the Pauper*. The farcical *Carry on Henry* (1971), with Sidney James, is notable only as the most widely seen treatment of Henry VIII. Henry has been better served by television, probably because more time is available. The BBC series, *The Six Wives of Henry VIII* (1972), was a brilliant evocation of the claustrophobia of the Tudor court and Keith Michell portrayed a Henry who developed and aged in ways entirely credible. The transfer to the cinema, *Henry VIII and his Six Wives* (1972) was not successful. However, all these pieces concentrate on the domestic Henry. Robert Bolt's play about Sir Thomas More, *A Man for All Seasons* (1960, filmed

1969) is of quite another order, setting out to face the issues of the 1530s head on. The result is a brilliant study of conscience in an amoral world, yet one which not only underplays More's own moral ambivalence, but also the complexity of the character of Henry VIII (played in the film by Robert Shaw), the reality of the royal conscience, and the fact that the divorce was an issue of huge national significance.

Judged for more than his private life and by the contemporary values of magnificence, military prowess, and 'force' or personality, Henry VIII's great achievement was to uncover the power of the English crown. Thomas More had advised Thomas Cromwell to 'ever tell [the king] what he ought to doe but never what he is able to doe ... for if [a] Lion knew his owne strength, harde were it for any man to rule him' (Roper, ed. Hitchcock, 56–7). Under Henry VIII parliament did his will; the great of the land walked wary of him; he laid the ghost of Thomas Becket; local franchises were brought to heel; he had wealth greater than any previous monarch. Most significant of all, Henry annexed to himself a theocratic kingship which was distinctive and personal. What the break with Rome established in England was not 'catholicism without the pope' but the king as pope. Not that Henry claimed the sacramental powers of the pontiff, but what he did claim was absolute spiritual sovereignty in England, even to the point of defining what the English must believe.

That this exalting of the status of the English monarchy was Henry's own achievement there can be no doubt. It was probably a product of instinct more than thought, and it certainly needed other minds to rationalize and develop it. Nevertheless, the driving force was Henry's personal awareness of his own unique status, of what it meant to be king. Nor was this the product of his quarrel with Rome, although the opposition he met then did force him to push back the limitations on his identity even further. As early as 1515 he had declared in *Hunne's Case*: 'By the ordinance of God we are King of England, and kings of England in time past have never had any superior but God only' (Ogle, 153). Three years later he dismissed the ancient claim of Westminster Abbey to be a permanent sanctuary for offenders as a travesty of what the Anglo-Saxon kings and 'holy popes' had intended, and announced that he would unilaterally sweep away 'the abuses which have encroached and have the matter reduced to the true intent of the original makers' (72 ER 369). In his first attempt to stabilize English rule in Ireland he reminded his lieutenant, the earl of Surrey, that as 'sovereign lord and prince ... of our absolute power we be above the laws' (*State Papers, Henry VIII*, 3.53).

Henry VIII's achievement was, thus, to aggregate to his person—and to exercise directly—more authority than any previous English king. After him—in some ways because of him—government would become steadily bigger, more bureaucratic, and unavoidably less personal. In politics, royal initiative would retreat before the need to sustain consensus among an élite which could exploit parliament to assert an increasing voice. 'The supreme head of the church of England' would shrink to a 'supreme governor of this realm as well in all spiritual or ecclesiastical causes as temporal'. Henry VIII's reign, in other words, saw the apogee of personal monarchy in England.

E. W. IVES

Sources W. Harrison Ainsworth, *Windsor Castle* (1843) · C. G. Bayne and W. H. Dunham, eds., *Select cases in the council of Henry VII*, SeldS, 75 (1958) · R. Bolt, *A man for all seasons* (1960) · G. Burnet, *The history of the Reformation of the Church of England*, ed. N. Pocock, 7 vols. (1865) · *CSP Spain, 1509–54* · *CSP Milan* · *CSP Venice, 1509–54* · G. Cavendish, *The life and death of Cardinal Wolsey*, ed. R. S. Sylvester, EETS, original ser., 243 (1959) · M. A. S. Hume, ed., *Chronicle of King Henry VIII* (1889) · W. Cobbett, *A history of the protestant Reformation* (1850) · H. M. Colvin and others, eds., *The history of the king's works*, 3–4 (1975–82) · *Correspondencia de Gutierre Gómez de Fuensalida*, ed. duque de Berwick y de Alba (Madrid, 1907) · *Writings and disputations of Thomas Cranmer*, ed. J. E. Cox, Parker Society, [17] (1844) · A. G. Dickens, *Reformation studies* (1982) · E. Sturtz and V. Murphy, eds., *Divorce tracts of Henry VIII* (Angers, 1988) · R. W. Dixon, *History of the Church of England* (1878–1902) · G. Bray, ed., *Documents of the English Reformation* (1994) · M. H. Dodds and R. Dodds, *The Pilgrimage of Grace, 1536–1537, and the Exeter conspiracy*, 2 vols. (1915) · *Literary remains of King Edward the Sixth*, ed. J. G. Nichols, 2 vols., Roxburghe Club, 75 (1857) · G. R. Elton, *The Tudor constitution*, 2nd edn (1982) · *English historical documents*, 5, ed. C. H. Williams (1967) · ER · F. Madox Ford, *The fifth queen* (1906–8) · *The acts and monuments of John Foxe*, ed. S. R. Cattley, 8 vols. (1837–41) · J. A. Froude, *History of England*, 12 vols. (1856–70) · S. R. Gardiner, *Students' history of England*, 3 vols. (1895) · *Great Bible* (1539) · E. Hall, *The union of the two noble and illustre fameliles of Lancastre & Yorke*, ed. H. Ellis (1809) · J. Bain, ed., *Hamilton papers*, 2 vols. (1890–92) · E. Herbert, *The history of England under Henry VIII*, ed. White Kennett (1870) · *The manuscripts of his grace the duke of Rutland*, 4 vols., HMC, 24 (1888–1905) · D. Starkey, ed., *The inventory of King Henry VIII: the transcript* (1998) · T. A. Lacey, ed., *The King's Book*, Church Historical Society, new ser. (1932) · *The King's Primer* (1545) · *LP Henry VIII*, vols. 1–21 · S. E. Lehmberg, *Reformation parliament* (1970) · S. E. Lehmberg, *The later parliaments of Henry VIII* (1977) · H. Savage, ed., *Love letters of Henry VIII* (1949) · D. MacCulloch, *Thomas Cranmer: a life* (1996) · C. Morris, *The Tudors* (1955) · J. G. Nichols, ed., *Narratives of the days of the Reformation*, CS, old ser., 77 (1859) · J. Nash, *The mansions of England in the olden time*, 4 vols. (1839–49) · B. H. St J. O'Neil, *Castles and cannon* (1960) · A. Ogle, *The tragedy of the Lollards' Tower* (1959) · N. Harpsfield, *The life and death of Sr Thomas Moore, knight*, ed. E. V. Hitchcock, EETS, original ser., 186 (1932) · R. Pole, *De unitate ecclesiasticae defensione* (1555) · A. F. Pollard, *Henry VIII* (1902) · J. J. Scarisbrick, 'The pardon of the clergy', *Cambridge Historical Journal*, 12 (1956), 22–39 · W. Roper, *The life of Sir Thomas More*, ed. E. V. Hitchcock, EETS, 197 (1935) · W. Roper, 'The life of Sir Thomas More', *Two early Tudor lives*, ed. R. S. Sylvester and D. P. Harding (New Haven, 1962) · Rymer, *Foedera*, 2nd edn · J. J. Scarisbrick, *Henry VIII* (1968) · W. H. Schenk, *Reginald Pole* (1950) · W. Shakespeare, *Henry VIII* · L. B. Smith, *A Tudor tragedy … Catherine Howard* (1961) · L. B. Smith, *Henry VIII* (1971) · *St German's Doctor and student*, ed. T. F. T. Plucknett and J. Barton, SeldS, 91 (1974) · *State papers published under … Henry VIII*, 11 vols. (1830–52) · A. Luders and others, eds., *Statutes of the realm*, 11 vols. in 12, RC (1810–28) · T. Stemmler, *Die Liebesbriefe Heinrichs VIII an Anna Boleyn* (Zürich, 1988) · R. Strong, *Holbein and Henry VIII* (1967) · P. L. Hughes and J. F. Larkin, eds., *Tudor royal proclamations*, 1 (1964) · *Tyndale's works*, ed. H. Walter, 3 vols., Parker Society (1848–50) · D. Wilkins, *Concilia Magnae Britanniae* (1737) · W. L. Williams, 'The union of England and Wales', *Transactions of the Honourable Society of Cymmrodorion* (1907–8), 47–117 · T. Wyatt, *Collected poems*, ed. J. Daalder (1975)

Archives BL, corresp. and papers relating to Scotland, Add. MSS 32646–32656 · BL, household book, Add. MS 45716 · BL, letters, Add. MS 46454 · BL, letters, Lansdowne MS 1236 · BL, wardrobe accounts, Egerton MS 3025 · CUL, letters and papers · PRO · Vatican | BL, corresp. and instruction sent by him and by Wolsey to various ambassadors in Europe [copies] · Harrowby Manuscript Trust, Sandon Hall, Staffordshire, letters to Anne Boleyn [copies]

Likenesses oils, *c.*1520, Anglesey Abbey, Cambridgeshire · L. Hornebolte, miniature, *c.*1526–1527, Royal Collection · attrib. J. Van Cleeve, oils, *c.*1535, Royal Collection · two oil paintings, *c.*1535–1547, NPG · H. Holbein the younger, portrait, 1536, Thyssen-Bornemizza Collection, Madrid · H. Holbein the younger, ink and watercolour drawing, *c.*1536–1537 (with Henry VII), NPG [*see illus.*] · H. Holbein, group portrait, cartoon drawing, 1540–43 (*Henry VIII and the barber surgeons*), RCS Eng. · H. Holbein, group portrait, oils, 1540–43 (*Henry VIII and the barber surgeons*), Barbers' Company, London · attrib. H. Holbein, oils, *c.*1542, Castle Howard, North Yorkshire · C. Matsys, line engraving, 1544, BM · group portrait, oils, 1545 (*The family of Henry VIII*), Royal Collection · H. Eworth, oils, 1567 (after H. Holbein), Trinity Cam.; version, Walker Art Gallery, Liverpool · R. van Leemput, group portrait, oils, *c.*1669 (after H. Holbein), Royal Collection · coins, BM · manuscript, BL, Royal MS 2A, XVI, fol. 63 · wax seals, BM · window (as Solomon), King's Cam., chapel

Wealth at death see Starkey, ed., *Inventory*

Henry VIII, privy chamber of (*act.* 1509–1547), body of personal servants to the king, was an institution whose importance has only recently been fully appreciated. Developments at the royal court from the mid-fifteenth century put in place new living arrangements for the king—a private suite known (from its most important room) as 'the privy chamber'. In turn this led by the end of the first decade of the reign of Henry VIII to the appearance of a new category of gentle-born courtiers who alone attended the sovereign there and provided the social milieu in which he spent much of his time when away from the public eye. The benefits of belonging to the privy chamber circle meant that there was a constant pressure for growth in numbers; the ten of 1526 had more than doubled by the time of the king's death on 28 January 1547.

The principal member of the privy chamber staff was the groom of the stool, the king's most intimate body servant: Sir William Compton from 1509 to 1526, Henry Norris from 1526 to 1536, Sir Thomas Heneage from 1536 to 1546, and Sir Anthony Denny from 1546 to 1547. There were generally also one or two noblemen of the privy chamber, including George Boleyn, Viscount Rochford, from 1530 to 1536, and Edward Seymour, earl of Hertford, from 1536 to 1547. Most of the remaining staff were divided into gentlemen of the privy chamber and grooms, although over time the difference tended to elide. Nominal rank, however, was not the most important factor; indeed a number of men (whose numbers tended to grow) were appointed additionally, unpaid, while others in the charmed circle such as Sir Thomas Wyatt the elder enjoyed no official status at all. What mattered was royal favour, and a number of men were able to build major public careers on their privy chamber service. Among the most successful of these were Sir John Russell, later first earl of Bedford, and Sir William Herbert, later first earl of Pembroke.

The complete index of Henry's privy chamber circle has yet to be established, but its importance is not only to be measured in the effect on individual careers where, as the

Sir Henry Neville (c.1520–1593), by unknown artist, 1592

case of Sir William Brereton shows, an income equivalent to that of an aristocrat was a possibility. The privy chamber was of enormous importance politically. In the first place, not only might there be the opportunity to influence the king personally; court parties also operated with objectives both mercenary and political—something which explains the disasters that befell, among others, Brereton, Sir Nicholas Carew, and Norris. Henry, though, was not the prisoner of his courtiers and employed them in a direct executive role to give him independence against his leading royal servants, Cardinal Thomas Wolsey and Sir Thomas Cromwell. He used his intimates to carry out confidential missions. It was Russell and Norris who conducted the private communication that the king maintained with Wolsey after the cardinal's fall. The credence commanded by privy chamber status also made it possible for Henry to send many instructions by word of mouth. Privy chamber staff even possessed a surrogate royal authority. When Henry Percy, sixth earl of Northumberland, tried to arrest Wolsey the cardinal demanded to see his warrant. However, Wolsey surrendered to Walter Walsh [see below], a groom of the privy chamber, saying:

Ye be oon of the kynges privye chamber your name I suppose is [Walsh] I ame content to yeld unto you but not to my lord of Northumberland without I se his commyssion And you are a sufficyent commyssion your self in that behalfe in as myche as ye be oon of the kynges privy chamber Ffor the worst person there is a sufficient warraunt to arrest the greattest peere of this realme. (G. Cavendish, The Life and Death of Cardinal Wolsey, ed. R. S. Sylvester, 1959, 156)

An identity as a royal alternate meant that privy chamber staff were prominent in military operations. From 1536 to 1547 the lord high admiral was always a member of the privy chamber. The representative character of privy chamber service also meant that the gentlemen were heavily employed in diplomacy. Four or five ambassadors to France between 1520 and 1526 held the rank.

It would, however, be wrong to assume that everyone in the privy chamber circle was high-profile. **Sir John Welsbourne** (c.1498–1548), son of Thomas Welsbourne, possibly of Chipping Wycombe in Buckinghamshire, landowner, and his wife, Margery, daughter of Thomas Poure of Bletchingdon, Oxfordshire, was in many ways a typical courtier. Little is known of him before he entered the privy chamber in June 1519, the year in which Wolsey expelled the 'minions', Henry's group of favourites that included Carew and William Carey, and installed his own men there. Welsbourne was perhaps introduced to provide the menial service that Wolsey's group of distinguished careerists could not be expected to give. He was first appointed to the post of page of the privy chamber with an annuity of £10 a year. By 1521 he was a groom, and by 1523 he was so firmly established in the privy chamber that he was allowed to exercise his office of controller of custom in Bristol by deputy as 'he has been retained as one of the grooms of the Privy Chamber' (LP Henry VIII, 3.3214, no. 17).

However, in 1526 Welsbourne was expelled from the privy chamber. The minions had returned to the privy chamber in the early 1520s, and with Wolsey's appointees also serving there, its size had started to grow out of control. Wolsey therefore set about reforming the court, and in 1526 he issued the Eltham ordinances. This reduced the staff of the privy chamber, and Welsbourne was one of those to go. However, he did not leave empty-handed, for he was made an esquire of the stable. Two years later he was brought back to intimate royal service as an esquire for the body. From 14 March to 19 December 1530 he was sent as special ambassador to François I, the French king, receiving a diet of £1 6s. 8d. per day. There is no evidence that the mission was of great importance, but Welsbourne received his reward none the less, for by July 1531 he was restored to the privy chamber, now as a gentleman.

Welsbourne continued to serve as a gentleman for the remainder of Henry's reign, attending the great occasions of state, such as the baptism of Edward, prince of Wales, in 1537, and the reception of Anne of Cleves in 1540. Throughout the 1530s he tried to win Cromwell's favour, and the principal secretary does seem to have found him useful, particularly in the dissolution of Abingdon Abbey, from which Welsbourne wrote many letters begging to be allowed to return to the royal presence. Welsbourne did, however, settle near the abbey with the help of several grants of land, and served as JP not only in Oxfordshire, but also Berkshire and Northamptonshire. In October 1537 Welsbourne wrote to Cromwell asking for help in obtaining land, trusting 'in the goodness of the King to all those who are daily waiting on him' (LP Henry VIII, 12/2). He was knight of the shire for Oxfordshire in 1539, probably through Cromwell's influence. Welsbourne survived Cromwell's fall and was knighted on 30 September 1544.

On 1 February 1546 he obtained a licence to marry Elizabeth (*d.* in or after 1548), daughter of one Lawrence of Fulwell, co. Durham. They had two sons. He also had an illegitimate son. Despite his complaints, Welsbourne seems to have been a wealthy man when he died on 11 April 1548.

Walter Walsh (*d.* 1538) was the son of John Walsh and his wife, Elizabeth Blount, and was another courtier who was able to profit from his position as a member of the privy chamber. Unlike Welsbourne, Walsh seems to have entered the privy chamber as a result of the Eltham ordinances, probably becoming salaried at the same time. There is some confusion about his role in the privy chamber, for he is referred to as yeoman, page, and groom at different times during 1526–7. However, in December 1528 he is listed in the accounts of Sir Brian Tuke, the treasurer of the chamber, as a groom, and after this the title remains consistent.

The best documented episode of Walsh's career is his mission, with Northumberland, to arrest Wolsey on 4 November 1530. On 22 November 1529 Walsh married Elizabeth or Werburga (*d.* in or after 1538), widow of Sir William Compton. This brought Walsh not only great riches, but also the life sheriffwick of Worcestershire, his own county. He seems to have lived out the remaining decade of his life away from court as a leading gentleman of Worcestershire and local agent for the government. The extent of Walsh's wealth is evident from the fact that Henry stayed three nights with him in 1535. Walsh died in March 1538, and even as he lay dying the fighting to obtain his offices had already begun.

Sir Richard Long (*c.*1494–1546) was the third son of Sir Thomas Long (1449–1508), landowner, of Draycot Cerne in Wiltshire, and his wife, Margery (*d.* in or after 1508), daughter of Sir George Darrell of Littlecote in Berkshire. He also gave long service to the crown from within the privy chamber. In 1512 Long was among the retinue of Sir Gilbert Talbot, who went as deputy to Calais. By 1515 he was one of the spears of Calais, a post that he seems to have retained for the remainder of his life. It is not clear how he came to be appointed to the court, but in December 1528 Long was listed by the treasurer of the chamber as working in the stables, and by 1533 he was certainly an esquire of the stable. By this time he had come to the attention of Cromwell, who arranged for him to be non-resident in Calais, except in times of war. In 1532 Long's brother, Sir Henry Long (*b.* in or before 1487, *d.* 1556), had already written to Cromwell to thank him for his favour to Richard.

In 1535 Long gained a position in the privy chamber as gentleman usher, possibly through Cromwell. He quickly gained the favour of the king and rose in prominence. In 1537 he was one of those who held the canopy over Edward at his baptism, and he was knighted on 18 October in the celebrations following, the same day that his kinsman Sir Edward *Seymour (*c.*1500–1552) was created earl of Hertford. In 1538 Long was appointed master of the buckhounds and master of the hawks, and by 1539 he was

a gentleman of the privy chamber. He was MP for Southwark in 1539. Long survived the fall of his patron, Cromwell, and became a prominent servant of the government throughout the 1540s.

During these years Long was one of the most senior members of the privy chamber and his intimacy with the king made him a useful agent for secret and covert affairs. In January 1541 he was sent to Calais to put its affairs in order, being described by the French ambassador, Charles de Marillac, bishop of Vienne, as 'a person of authority and conduct' (*LP Henry VIII*, 16.466). On his return he was instructed to arrest Sir John Wallop, a diplomat suspected of colluding with Cardinal Reginald Pole. This was a mission that required him to be discreet and wise, and its failure was blamed not on Long, but on his kinsman Hertford. He was still trusted enough later that year to work on various commissions and juries dealing with the treason of Catherine Howard. On 10 November 1541 he obtained the marriage settlement of Margaret (1508/9–1561), only daughter of John Donington of Stoke Newington in Middlesex and widow of Sir Thomas Kitson of London and Hengrave in Suffolk. They had one son and three daughters. The government also made use of Long's military experience. He was made governor of Guernsey, Alderney, and Sark in 1541, a post that he held until sickness forced him to retire in 1545, and in 1542 he was appointed captain of Kingston upon Hull, with a place on the king's council of the north. His marriage, together with many land grants, meant that like his fellow courtiers Welsbourne and Walsh, he was a rich man at his death on 30 September 1546. His widow married John Bourchier, second earl of Bath, on 11 December 1548. She died on 20 December 1561 at Stoke Newington and was buried at Hengrave on 12 January 1562.

Sir Maurice Berkeley (*c.*1514–1581) was the second son of Richard Berkeley, landowner, of Stoke, and his wife, Elizabeth (*d.* in or after 1538), daughter of Sir Humphrey *Coningsby (*d.* 1535). He had also been a client of Cromwell. The earliest that is known of Berkeley is that he was trained for a legal profession in the office of the protonotary of the common pleas. His stepfather, Sir John *Fitzjames (*c.*1470–1538?), was chief justice of the court of king's bench, and in January 1535 he wrote to Cromwell asking that Berkeley might be appointed clerk to the assize. Berkeley never gained this office, but it seems that Cromwell recognized his abilities, for by 1537 he was a member of his household. There is no certain evidence that Berkeley was appointed to the court until being referred to as a gentleman usher of the privy chamber in 1539, but it is likely that he was the Mr Bark who ran at the tilt at Lord William Howard's wedding in June 1536, and that he was therefore familiar at court before his appointment. Berkeley's appointment may have been aimed at strengthening Cromwell's hold on the court, particularly once he had given up the secretaryship. Unlike Wolsey, who tried to undermine the privy chamber, Cromwell aimed to control it by packing it with his own appointments.

Berkeley survived his patron's fall, and continued to

serve as gentleman usher for the remainder of Henry's reign. Unlike Welsbourne, Walsh, and Long, Berkeley's activities were centred entirely on the court, for it was the gentlemen ushers who were responsible for the daily organization of the privy chamber, and many of the menial tasks. He was rewarded for this service in 1543 when he was given licence to hold a prebend at Ripon, despite the fact that he was married and a layman. His wife was Katherine (d. 1560), daughter of William *Blount, fourth Baron Mountjoy (c.1478–1534), and widow of John Champernowne of Modbury in Devon. Berkeley accompanied the king to France for war in 1544 where he was knighted on 30 September, and in 1545 he succeeded his brother as chief banner-bearer of England. His service throughout the 1540s was rewarded by Henry, in whose will he received £133 6s. 8d. He continued to serve in the privy chamber under Edward VI, becoming a gentleman by 1550, and was MP four times between 1547 and 1572. Under Mary I he was excluded, though he notably arrested the rebel Sir Thomas Wyatt the younger; however, he was restored to the court under Elizabeth I when in 1562 he married one of the queen's gentlewomen, Elizabeth (d. after 1581), daughter of Anthony Sands. With his first wife he had three sons, including Sir Edward Berkeley (d. 1596) and Sir Henry Berkeley (c.1547–1601), and five daughters, and with his second wife two sons, including Robert Berkeley (1566–1614), and one daughter. Berkeley died on 11 August 1581.

Sir Thomas Paston (c.1517–1550) was the fourth but third surviving son of Sir William *Paston (1479?–1554), landowner, of Caister and Oxnead in Norfolk, and his wife, Bridget (d. in or before 1554), daughter of Sir Henry Heydon of Baconsthorpe in Norfolk. He seems to have owed his career at court to his family's standing. The Pastons were a noted Norfolk gentry family, and Thomas Paston's brothers Clement *Paston (c.1515–1598) and John *Paston (c.1510–1575/6) were also able to find employment in the court. Thomas Paston first appears in the records as a gentleman of the privy chamber in February 1538, an office that he retained until his death in 1550. In December 1541 he was also appointed to the post of keeper of the gallery at Greenwich Palace, which contained the armoury. By 1544 he was married to Agnes (d. before 1590), daughter of Sir John Leigh of Stockwell in Surrey. They had two sons and a daughter. Paston may have had some experience as a soldier, for he accompanied the king to France in 1544 where he was knighted with his fellow courtier Berkeley on 30 September. He was knight of the shire for Norfolk in 1545. Like Berkeley he received 200 marks under the king's will, and continued to serve in Edward's privy chamber. He also continued to serve as a soldier, fighting under William Parr, marquess of Northampton, against Thomas Kett and his rebels in summer 1549. Paston died on 4 September 1550.

Sir Henry Neville (c.1520–1593) was the second son of Sir Edward *Neville (d. 1538), alleged conspirator, of Addington Park in Kent, and his wife, Eleanor, daughter of Andrew Windsor, first Baron Windsor, and his wife, Elizabeth. He came from noble stock, and it can be said that his appointment to the privy chamber was not because of this, but rather despite it. His father was the brother of George *Neville, third Baron Bergavenny, and had been at one time a favourite of the king. However, he was executed on 9 January 1539 as a consequence of the Courtenay conspiracy. His children, though, did not suffer. Henry Neville, the younger son, was the king's godson and an annuity of £20 was granted to him in October 1539, only nine months after his father's execution. It is possible that he had been destined for a diplomatic career, for in March 1542 he was with the French ambassador. However, by 1546 he was a groom of the privy chamber—a considerable prize for the son of an alleged traitor.

Neville seems to have been favoured by his royal godfather, for he was one of the grooms who witnessed Henry's will, and received £100 under its terms, and was also able to state at the trial of Stephen Gardiner, bishop of Winchester, in 1551 that the king had felt a great hatred towards the bishop. Neville gained even more favour under Edward, particularly from John Dudley, earl of Warwick, who made him a gentleman of the privy chamber in 1550, along with his friend Henry Sidney. They were both knighted on 11 October 1551. Between 1551 and 1555 he married Winifred (d. in or before 1561), daughter of Hugh Loss of Whitchurch in Middlesex. They appear to have had no children. By 1561 Neville had married Elizabeth (d. 1573), daughter of Sir John Gresham of Titsey in Surrey. The couple had four sons, including the MPs Sir Henry Neville (1562–1615) and Edward Neville (b. 1567), and two daughters. In May 1578 Neville married his third wife, Elizabeth (d. 1621), daughter of Sir Nicholas *Bacon, first baronet (c.1543–1624), and his wife, Anne, and widow of Sir Richard Doyley of Greenlands in Buckinghamshire. They had no children. Neville was knight of the shire for Berkshire five times between March 1553 and 1584. Under Mary he found it necessary to travel abroad because of his protestantism, but he returned under Elizabeth to spend the last thirty-five years of his life living as a prominent gentleman in Berkshire, holding various local offices. He died on 13 January 1593 and was buried in the church at Waltham St Lawrence in Berkshire.

Sir William Fitzwilliam (c.1506–1559) was the second son of Thomas Fitzwilliam of Baggotrath, co. Dublin, and his wife, Eleanor, daughter of John Dowdall and his wife, Margaret. He never served in Henry's privy chamber but throughout the 1540s was being groomed to serve Edward. Fitzwilliam's father was at one time sheriff of Dublin, and his family had a long history of serving in the Irish administration. He was possibly admitted to Gray's Inn in 1531. Fitzwilliam first came to prominence by his service to his namesake Sir William Fitzwilliam, later earl of Southampton. There is no evidence as to how he entered service with Sir William though it is possible that they were kinsmen. By 1536 Sir William Fitzwilliam was referring to him as his 'trusty servant', and he was his principal servant by 1539 (LP Henry VIII, 11.128). He may have sat as MP for Guildford in 1539 and certainly did so in 1542, through the patronage of his master. He was MP again three times between 1547 and 1559. By 1539 he had married Jane (*d.* after 1559), daughter and coheir of John Roberts of Cranbrook in Kent. They had four daughters.

Southampton died in 1543, and the following year Fitzwilliam was appointed to be a gentleman in Prince Edward's privy chamber. By November 1545 he was the chief gentleman, and when Edward succeeded to the throne in 1547, Fitzwilliam followed him into his privy chamber as a gentleman, where he continued to serve for the rest of the reign. He was knighted between September 1551 and May 1552. He died on 3 October 1559 and was buried in St George's Chapel, Windsor.

MICHAEL RIORDAN

Sources *LP Henry VIII*, vols. 3–4, 11–13, 16 • D. R. Starkey, 'The king's privy chamber, 1485–1547', PhD diss., U. Cam., 1973 • HoP, *Commons, 1509–58*, 1.418–19; 2.141–2, 545–6; 3.7–8, 68–9, 575–8 • HoP, *Commons, 1558–1603*, 1.432; 2.129–30; 3.124–5 • D. R. Starkey, 'Intimacy and innovation: the rise of the privy chamber, 1485–1547', *The English court from the Wars of the Roses to the civil war*, ed. D. Starkey and others (1987), 71–118 • S. Brigden, *New worlds, lost worlds: the rule of the Tudors, 1485–1603* (2001) • *CSP dom.*, 1547–53 • PRO, PROB 11/27, sig. 18; 11/31, sig. 18; 11/32, sig. 16; 11/33, sig. 25; 11/42B, sig. 53; 11/63, sig. 40; 11/81, sig. 1 • W. P. W. Phillimore, ed., *The visitation of the county of Worcester made in the year 1569*, Harleian Society, 27 (1888)
Archives PRO, state papers
Likenesses portrait, 1592 (Sir Henry Neville), priv. coll. [*see illus.*]

Henry Benedict [Henry Benedict Stuart; styled Henry IX; *known as* Cardinal York] (**1725–1807**), cardinal and Jacobite claimant to the English, Scottish, and Irish thrones, was born Henry Benedict Thomas Edward Maria Clement Francis Xavier in the Palazzo Muti in Rome on 6 March 1725, and baptized there some hours later by Pope Benedict XIII. He was the second son of *James Francis Edward (1688–1766), king of England and Wales, Scotland, and Ireland in the Jacobite succession, and his wife, the Polish princess *Clementina, *née* Sobieska (1702–1735). His father claimed to be James VIII and III, the rightful king of England, Scotland, and Ireland; his elder brother, *Charles Edward (1720–1788), was known to the Jacobites as prince of Wales, and Henry bore the title of duke of York. The atmosphere within the family was turbulent. Clementina, immature, vivacious, and hot-tempered, was impatient with James's gloomy reserve, and when Henry was eight months old she became convinced that her husband was having an affair and fled to the Ursuline convent of St Cecilia. Her family did not see her again until the summer of 1727, when she emerged, appointed Winifred, fifth countess of Nithsdale as Henry's governess, and threw herself in to a life of piety and good works.

Early years and the Jacobite rising A small, pretty, dark-haired boy, Henry impressed everyone who saw him with his charm of manner, and in 1729 his father proudly declared himself to be 'really in love with the little duke, for he is the finest child can be seen' (Fothergill, 23). Henry had his mother's quick temper though, and when, at nine, he was refused permission to accompany his adored elder brother to the siege of Gaeta, he flung his sword across the room in a tantrum, and had his Order of the Garter

Henry Benedict [Henry Benedict Stuart] (**1725–1807**), by Louis-Gabriel Blanchet, 1748

removed by their father as a punishment. In 1735 Clementina died, worn out caring for the poor of Rome, leaving her sons sick with grief. That same year the Englishman Samuel Crisp saw the Stuart princes in Rome and reported that Henry had 'more beauty and dignity in him than ever one can form to oneself in idea. He danced miraculously, as they say he does all exercises, singing, I am told, most sweetly' (Vaughan, 14).

Henry had inherited not only his mother's love of music, but the asthma which had plagued her, and her piety. In 1742 his tutor James Murray, earl of Dunbar, described how he spent much of his time in agitated prayer, sometimes hearing as many as four masses a day and seemed in a constant state of anxiety, his watch always in his hand, lest he miss any of his religious observances. He appeared to be 'unable to take pleasure in anything', said Dunbar, and by the evening often had 'a blackness about his eyes, his head quite fatigued and his hands hot' (Tayler and Tayler, 108). Henry was not told when, in 1744, his elder brother slipped away to France to lead a Jacobite invasion of Great Britain, for fear that he might inadvertently betray the secret. Once he did know he was eager to help, and his father told Louis XV, 'He cannot endure the idea of having to remain in Rome while his brother is in Scotland' (Fothergill, 43).

Finally Henry, too, was allowed to go to France, setting off secretly on 29 August 1745. Given nominal command of a naval expedition being prepared by the duke of Richelieu to invade England, Henry spent that winter at Dunkirk, but when news came of his brother's retreat from Derby the French lost interest and the proposed invasion was abandoned. Henry remained on the coast until the disastrous defeat of the Jacobites at Culloden on 16 April 1746. Desperately anxious about Charles's fate, he instigated various naval rescue attempts and served bravely with the French army at the siege of Antwerp, later visiting his cousin the duc de Bouillon at the Château de Navarre. Louis XV then gave him a house at Clichy, near Paris, and it was there that he learned of Charles's safe arrival at Roscoff in October 1746. He set out at once to meet him, and after a glad reunion they travelled together to Paris.

Cardinal York The brothers' formerly close and affectionate relationship now came under considerable strain. Humiliated, tortured by the knowledge of his followers' sufferings, and unable to accept defeat, Charles was drinking heavily and only too ready to lash out at the person closest to him. Hurt and embarrassed, Henry became more and more convinced that his own vocation lay within the Roman Catholic church and he felt that the collapse of the 1745 rising had absolved him of any obligation to take part in political or military affairs. He was aware that his father had always gone to great lengths to play down the family's Catholicism, knowing it to be unacceptable to the protestant British whom he regarded as his subjects, but James was sympathetic to his younger son's needs and advised Henry to return to Rome without disclosing his intentions to Charles, who would be sure to be angry.

In a state of nervous apprehension, Henry handled the matter clumsily, inviting his brother to dinner on 29 April 1747 and then disappearing without a word before they could meet. Several weeks later Charles received a letter from their father, explaining, 'I know not whether you will be surprised, my dearest Carluccio, when I tell you that your brother will be made a cardinal the first days of next month'. Appalled, Charles declared the news to be 'a dager throw my heart' (Tayler and Tayler, 209) and refused to have Henry's name mentioned in his presence. The Jacobite cause was undoubtedly damaged by Henry's career choice, but he himself was content. On 30 June 1747 he received the tonsure from his godfather, Pope Benedict XIV, and on 3 July was given the red hat at a ceremony in the Sistine Chapel. Appointed cardinal-deacon with the title of Santa Maria in Campitelli, one of the parish churches in Rome, he had his scarlet garments trimmed with regal ermine, was addressed as 'royal highness and eminence', and was known as Cardinal York. At his own request he was ordained as a priest on 1 September 1748 and twelve days later was elevated to the office of cardinal-priest.

Twenty-two years old now, slender and elegant, with a long, oval face and large, dark eyes, Henry soon became a leading figure in Roman literary and artistic circles, organizing concerts and commissioning new masses. Presented with benefices by the kings of France and Spain he enjoyed considerable wealth, and his appointment as archpriest of the Vatican basilica in 1751 brought him an official residence in the piazza della Sagrestia. However, he preferred to go on living in the Palazzo Muti, helping his increasingly frail father with his voluminous paperwork and bickering with him interminably. A month before his death in May 1758 the pope made Henry Cardinal Camerlingo, head of the papal treasury and organizer of the next papal conclave.

Middle years The new pope, Clement XIII, created Henry archbishop of Corinth in November 1758, and when George II died in 1760 and there was no public support for the Jacobite claimant, Henry remained immersed in his chosen career. The following year he resigned his titular archbishopric of Corinth to become bishop of Tusculum, moving to Frascati, where his enthronement took place in the cathedral on 13 July 1761. His episcopal palace of La Rocca now became his preferred residence and there he entertained lavishly, continued to patronize the arts, built up a fine library, and at the same time was diligent in his ecclesiastical duties. 'His charities were without bounds: poverty and distress were unknown to his see', the English Cardinal Wiseman was later to remark (Fothergill, 85). When Henry became vice-chancellor of the holy Roman church in 1763, he acquired the magnificent Palazzo della Cancellaria in Rome, but he continued to live in his beloved Frascati, dashing at great speed between his two residences in his coach and six.

His brother, meanwhile, had been expelled from France and was leading a strange life, wandering incognito through Belgium, Germany, and Switzerland, sustained by Henry's own pension of 12,000 crowns from the apostolic chamber. In the autumn of 1765 it became evident that their father was nearing the end of his life and Henry tried in vain to persuade Charles to return to Rome. James died on 1 January 1766 and Henry was chief mourner at the funeral six days later, when his father was buried in St Peter's. Charles arrived at the end of the month and the brothers' long estrangement ended in an affectionate reunion. The pope refused to recognize Charles as King Charles III, however, and Henry was soon shamed once more by his brother's drinking and embarrassing behaviour.

In 1769 Pope Clement XIV gave Henry charge of the former Jesuit seminary at Frascati, and he began an energetic programme of reorganization. He extended the premises, reformed the curriculum, installed a printing press and a stage for the student theatrical performances which he so enjoyed, and moved his own priceless collection of books into the library. His peaceful routine was abruptly shattered in March 1772 when he heard without warning that Charles had entered into a proxy marriage with an attractive, impoverished, nineteen-year-old German princess, *Louisa, daughter of Prince Gustav Adolf of Stolberg-Gedern. Louisa soon charmed Henry, but a further complication arose the following year when Charles's former mistress Clementine *Walkinshaw appeared in Rome with their daughter, Charlotte, seeking an increase in the allowance long paid to her by Henry. When Charles refused to see them, it was left to Henry to fend off their demands.

It was probably a relief to Henry when Charles and his new wife moved to Florence in 1774, but six years later he was appalled to receive a letter from Louisa saying that she had been forced to leave her husband after he had attacked her. All too familiar with Charles's unfortunate propensity for 'the nasty bottle' (Vaughan, 126), Henry was sympathetic, inviting Louisa to take up residence in the Ursuline convent in Rome, where his mother had found shelter. He did not realize that she was having an affair with the dramatic poet Count Vittorio Alfieri. Louisa came to Rome, but did not rest until she had persuaded Henry to let her move from the convent to the Palazzo della Cancellaria, where she held court with Alfieri as a frequent visitor.

Everyone in Rome knew about the relationship except Henry. He remained innocently unaware of the liaison until Charles fell seriously ill in 1783, sent for him, and poured out his side of the story. Appalled at Louisa's deceitfulness, Henry forbade her to receive Alfieri and eventually agreed, reluctantly, to the legal separation of Charles and his wife in the spring of 1784. Louisa promptly went off to live with her lover in Colmar on the Rhine, and in October of that same year Charles sent for his daughter Charlotte and created her duchess of Albany. This dukedom rightfully belonged to the younger son of the king of Scots and Henry was indignant, composing a long protest about what he saw as a threat to his position as heir presumptive. Charlotte, however, adopted a conciliatory attitude to him and he was won over when he saw at first hand the care she took of her frail, increasingly difficult father when Charles returned with her to live in the Palazzo Muti in December 1785.

Henry IX Charles finally died there on 31 December 1788. Refused permission to have him buried in St Peter's with their father, Henry conducted the funeral service in the cathedral at Frascati, the tears running down his cheeks. Whatever the differences between the two brothers, they had remained deeply attached to one another. The cardinal now considered himself to be the rightful King Henry IX, adjusted his coat of arms accordingly, styled himself 'Cardinal *called* duke of York', and upon occasion touched for the king's evil. He was deeply hurt when, in 1789, against the background of the French Revolution, the pope decided to recognize George III as king of Britain. Henry issued an indignant protest, but to no avail.

Louis XVI went to the guillotine in 1793 and Henry held a mass for him at Frascati. Three years later, Napoleon Bonaparte invaded Italy. The pope was twice forced to come to terms and on the second occasion, in 1797, Henry generously placed almost his entire fortune at the pope's disposal, including the fabulous Sobieski ruby which had belonged to his mother. Despite these efforts at appeasement, the French marched on Rome in 1798, captured the city, imprisoned the pope, and declared a republic. Taking some of his valuable plate, Henry fled to Naples with his faithful secretary, Monsignor Angelo Cesarini, and valet, Eugenio Ridolfi. In his absence the French plundered his paintings, books, and manuscripts, putting some of them up for sale at public auction.

Several other cardinals also sought refuge in Naples, but the advance of the revolutionary forces compelled them to move on. Having hired a small vessel, Henry sailed through terrible storms to Messina, his epic voyage lasting twenty-three days. He could not stay there long, for Pope Pius VI was dying and the cardinals would have to assemble in Venice for the conclave to elect his successor. In February 1799 Henry crossed to Reggio, on the coast of Calabria, and along with two other cardinals hired a Greek merchant vessel to complete the journey. Another dreadful storm forced them to put in at Corfu, but they finally reached Venice and found lodgings in a house near the Rialto. Henry then sold his remaining plate and sought shelter in a nearby monastery, that autumn attending the conclave which elected Pope Pius VII.

Later years Henry was now seventy-five years old and not only destitute but in poor health. Somewhat surprisingly, he had made friends with Sir John Coxe Hippisley, George III's envoy in Rome, and Sir John now came to the rescue. The British government owed Henry £1,500,000, the arrears of the jointure of his grandmother, Mary of Modena. Such an astronomical sum would never be paid, but Sir John asked Henry's old friend Cardinal Stefano Borgia to write a letter describing Henry's plight, and this was placed before the prime minister, William Pitt. With any Jacobite threat to the Hanoverian succession long since extinguished, the British government ministers could afford to be charitable. On 22 November 1799 Sir John was able to arrange for a preliminary letter of credit for £500 sterling to be sent to Cardinal York, and on 7 February 1800 the earl of Minto, British ambassador in Vienna, wrote him a tactful letter informing him that George III was granting him an annual pension of £4000. Henry was touched and delighted.

Not long afterwards Napoleon sought better relations with the Holy See, and Henry was able to return to Frascati. His residence was refurbished in preparation for his arrival, his suite of rooms in the Palazzo della Cancellaria was renovated, and he reached Rome on 25 June 1800 amid great rejoicing. Pausing only to take some refreshment, he left at once for Frascati, where crowds lined the streets, brass bands played, and the cathedral bells rang out in welcome. In no time at all he had settled back into his lavish lifestyle, despite his depleted resources. With the death of Cardinal Albani in 1803 Henry became senior cardinal, succeeding automatically to the position of dean of the Sacred College and bishop of Ostia and Velletri. This meant that he had to resign the see of Tusculum, but he was allowed to live on at La Rocca.

Although now very frail, Henry insisted on attending ecclesiastical ceremonies in Rome until, after a special mass in 1804, he felt so weak that he had to be carried from St Peter's in a litter. By 1806 his memory was failing, and in the following summer he caught a feverish chill. He died after a fortnight's illness, on 13 July 1807, the forty-sixth anniversary of his enthronement in Frascati Cathedral. Three days later his body was taken to lie in state in the

Palazzo della Cancellaria, and his funeral was held in the nearby church of Sant' Andrea delle Valle, probably on 16 July. He was then buried beside his father in the crypt of St Peter's, and his brother's body was brought from Frascati and placed in the same vault. Most of his resources gone, his pensions spent, and his Mexican properties lost in South American revolutions, he left the remaining royal jewels in his possession to George III, in a gesture of gratitude, and the Stuart archives eventually passed to the Royal Library at Windsor. When in 1819 Pope Pius VII commissioned the white marble monument by Canova which stands above the Stuart tomb, the future George IV contributed £50 towards the cost.

Henry had found great satisfaction as a prince of the church, and his contemporaries saw nothing strange in the contrast between his lavish lifestyle and his genuine piety and philanthropy. Affectionate, sensitive, and intelligent, he was not a scholar but he was rightly admired as a bibliophile and patron of the arts. With his intense religiosity, he had in adolescence seemed to many to compare unfavourably with his more dashing brother, and Jacobites criticized him bitterly for entering the church instead of producing male heirs. Others alleged, however, that he would have had no children, being homosexual. The historian Andrew Lang alluded cryptically to James's comment that his younger son would never marry although many marriages had been planned for him (Shield, x), but there seems to be no conclusive evidence as to Henry's sexual orientation. What is more significant is that while Charles never could accept that the Jacobite cause was lost, Henry had the courage and realism to pursue the career for which he was best fitted.

ROSALIND K. MARSHALL

Sources DNB · B. Fothergill, *The cardinal king* (1958) · H. M. Vaughan, *The last of the royal Stuarts* (1906) · A. Shield, *Henry Stuart, cardinal of York and his times* (1908) · A. Tayler and H. Tayler, eds., *The Stuart papers at Windsor* (1939) · L. L. Bongie, *The love of a prince: Bonnie Prince Charlie in France, 1744–1748* (1986) · B. W. Kelly, *Life of Henry Benedict Stuart, cardinal duke of York* (1899) · S. Borgia, *Letters from the Cardinal Borgia and the cardinal of York, MDCCXCIX* (1899) · M. Mastrofini, *Orazione per la morte di Errico, cardinale duca denominato duca di York* (Rome, 1807) · G. Lockhart, *The Lockhart papers: containing memoirs and commentaries upon the affairs of Scotland from 1702 to 1715*, 2 vols. (1817) · H. Tayler, *Bonnie Prince Charlie's daughter* (1950) · M. de Ruvigny and Raineval, ed., *The legitimist kalendar for the year of Our Lord 1895* (1895) · *The manuscripts of the marquess of Abergavenny, Lord Braye*, G. F. Luttrell, HMC, 15 (1887), 234, 246, 257, 265 · *Scots peerage*, 1.35

Archives BL, corresp., official diaries, and papers, Add. MSS 30428–30477, 34634–34647 · Royal Arch., corresp., mainly business; papers, account books, and diary; papers, mainly domestic · Royal Library, Windsor Castle, Berkshire, Stuart papers | NL Scot., corresp. with Sir John Hippisley · Westm. DA, corresp. with Lady Harriet Webb

Likenesses O. Hamerani, bronze medal, 1729, Scot. NPG · O. Hamerani, silver medal, 1729, Scot. NPG · A. David, oils, 1732, Scot. NPG; version, NPG · L.-G. Blanchet, oils, 1738, priv. coll.; [registered with RA, 1960] · L.-G. Blanchet, oils, 1738, Royal Collection · J. J. Parrocel, oils, 1742, Duchess of Alba's Collection, Madrid · V. Stern, miniature, 1743, priv. coll.; [registered with Scot. NPG, B/5448] · L.-G. Blanchet, portrait, 1748, priv. coll. [*see illus.*] · oils, c.1748 (after D. Corvi), Scot. NPG · D. Allan, drawing, 1773, NG Scot. · attrib. H. D. Hamilton, pastels, c.1786, NPG · G. Hamerani, copper medal, 1788, Scot. NPG · G. Hamerani, silver medal, 1788, NPG · L.-G. Blanchet, oils, repro. in R. K. Marshall, *Bonnie Prince Charlie* (1988); priv. coll. [registered with Scot. NPG B/3051] · D. Corvi, oils, priv. coll.; [registered with Scot. NPG, B/3060] · attrib. G. Gattelli, miniature, watercolour on ivory, Scot. NPG · O. Hamerani, silver medal, Scot. NPG · attrib. V. Stern, miniature, watercolour on ivory, Scot. NPG · attrib. R. Strange, wash drawing, Scot. NPG · M. Q. de la Tour, pastels, Townley Hall, Ireland · oils (after P. Batoni?), NPG · oils (after L.-G. Blanchet), Scot. NPG · oils (after L.-G. Blanchet), priv. coll. · oils (after D. Corvi), priv. coll.; [registered with Courtauld Inst.] · oils, priv. coll.; [registered with Courtauld Inst.] · pen-and-ink drawing, Scot. NPG

Wealth at death 'comparatively poor': Vaughan, *Last of the royal Stuarts*, 268 · assets 'swallowed up'; property in Mexico lost in South American revolutions: Shield, *Henry Stuart*, 302

Henry de Bray. *See* Bray, Henry (*b.* before 1248, *d.* 1311×13).

Henry de Wakefield. *See* Wakefield, Henry (*c.*1335–1395).

Henry fitz Ailwin (*d.* 1212), first mayor of London, was of English descent, as may be seen in the names of his father Ailwin, or Æthelwine, and grandfather Leofstan. The latter, who was later believed to have been the reeve of London associated with the royal foundation (1108) of Holy Trinity Priory, Aldgate, may have been the domesman who died in 1115 and was buried in Bermondsey Priory. It was in the house of Ailwin son of Leofstan that the London husting court was meeting before 1130, the year in which Robert son of Leofstan accounted for the London weavers' guild. Henry fitz Ailwin and his brother Alan succeeded to their father's land, probably at Watton-at-Stone, Hertfordshire, in 1164/5. Like many wealthy citizens Henry had estates strategically situated around London. His chief country seat was at Watton, and his land at Edmonton, Middlesex, probably served as a staging post. He also had lands in Surrey and by the Thames in Kent. His headquarters in the city occupied a large site on the north side of Candlewick (now Cannon) Street, adjoining the church of St Swithin, whose patron he was, and extended into the parish of St Mary Bothaw. Apart from his dwelling it included a horse mill and tenters for stretching cloth. He also held many properties in the eastern half of the city, including a quay next to London Bridge. The distribution of his holdings suggests that as well as drawing rent he was active in trade, including the distribution of rural produce. Candlewick Street was the focus of London's woollen textile industry, and there were many dubbers (in this context possibly dyers) among his neighbours. That circumstance, together with his tenters and his presumed uncle's association with weavers, suggests that he and his family had a direct interest in making, finishing, and selling cloth.

Henry fitz Ailwin was an alderman of London by 1168, and from then on appears frequently as a witness with other chief citizens. His equestrian seal, resembling that of the influential William Bucuinte, is expressive of claims to status and ancestry. He had a close connection with the sheriff Richard fitz Reiner, a key figure in the emergence of the commune in the early 1190s. Henry's appearance at the head of a group of four men of rank—*nobiles* of the city—who included Richard, indicates his role as civic leader. He is first certainly identified as mayor in 1194. Initially that position may have been informal, for even after that year he sometimes witnessed in an official capacity without being styled mayor. But no other person is named as holding the mayoralty during his life time, and there can be no doubt that Henry held it until his death. No other mayor of London has held office on a life term. As mayor Henry fitz Ailwin embodied the interests of the leading citizens, sometimes in opposition to the majority—who found a vociferous spokesman in William fitz Osbert (d. 1196)—but he was also the king's man, as is evident from his frequent association with the justice Roger fitz Reinfrey. Throughout his mayoralty he was regularly accompanied by Roger fitz Alan, his successor as mayor and probably his nephew. On a few occasions about 1205 he was designated *dominus*, a style not generally accorded to mayors of London until a later date.

Henry fitz Ailwin's recorded actions illuminate his public role rather than his personal character. In 1193 he was one of those entrusted with the money collected for the king's ransom, and in 1194 he arrested a foolish messenger from the king's brother. In 1208 he negotiated for the use of ground outside the walls as a burial-ground for Londoners during the interdict. After the great fire of 1212 he and other barons of London issued a code governing rebuilding. He was a pious benefactor to the church and, probably after 1199, endowed obits at Holy Trinity Priory, St Bartholomew's Hospital, Westminster Abbey, London Bridge Chapel, and the nunneries of Clerkenwell and Godstow. He also contributed to the foundation of St Mary Spital, and was remembered as the founder of a chapel at Watton. Appropriately, he was buried in the entry to the chapter house at Holy Trinity Priory.

Henry fitz Ailwin died on 19 September 1212, probably in London. Henry's wife, Margaret, who survived him, was probably the mother of his four sons. The eldest of these, Peter, married Isabel, daughter of Bartholomew de Chennay and heir to estates in Surrey and Sussex; she predeceased her husband and was buried in Bermondsey Priory. But Peter himself died before his father, who about a year before his own death divided his lands between his surviving sons, Alan, Thomas, and Richard. Peter's surviving daughter, Joan, inherited her parents' properties and then those of her uncles. Her second marriage brought the Candlewick Street site into the knightly Aguillon family, whose members used it as their London base until *c*.1286. In the meantime her grandfather's reputation remained high. By 1274 the complex body of city customs known as the assize of buildings had come to be attributed to the beginning of Henry fitz Ailwin's mayoralty, then dated to 1189. His obit continued to be observed, and his tomb was still recognizable in the sixteenth century. A later observer noted monuments to him at St Mary Bothaw.   DEREK KEENE

Sources T. Stapleton, ed., *De antiquis legibus liber: cronica majorum et vicecomitum Londoniarum*, CS, 34 (1846) · *Chronica magistri Rogeri de Hovedene*, ed. W. Stubbs, 4 vols., Rolls Series, 51 (1868–71) · S. Reynolds, 'The rulers of London in the 12th century', *History*, new ser., 57 (1972), 337–57 · C. N. L. Brooke and G. Keir, *London, 800–1216: the shaping of a city* (1975) · W. Page, *London: its origin and early development* (1929) · J. H. Round, 'The first mayor of London', *The Antiquary*, 15 (1887), 107–11 · G. A. J. Hodgett, ed. and trans., *The cartulary of Holy Trinity Aldgate*, London RS, 7 (1971) · W. O. Hassall, ed., *Cartulary of St Mary Clerkenwell*, CS, 3rd ser., 71 (1949) · B. R. Kemp, ed., *Reading Abbey cartularies*, 1, CS, 4th ser., 31 (1986) · B. R. Kemp, ed., *Reading Abbey cartularies*, 2, CS, 4th ser., 33 (1987) · E. Mason, J. Bray, and D. J. Murphy, eds., *Westminster Abbey charters, 1066–c.1214*, London RS, 25 (1988) · patent rolls, 1212, PRO, C 66/9

Archives CLRO, Bridge House deeds · PRO, ancient deeds · St Bartholomew's Hospital, London, deeds

Likenesses seal, repro. in F. Palgrave, ed., *Rotuli Curiae Regis* (1835), cxv

Henry fitz Count (*b*. in or before **1175**, *d*. **1221**?), baron, sole but illegitimate son of Reginald de Dunstanville, earl of Cornwall, and Beatrice de Vannes, was born in or before 1175, when his father died. Since Henry was illegitimate, the earldom reverted to the crown, and Cornwall was one of the counties and lordships granted by Richard I to his brother Count John in 1189. Henry was not left destitute, however. In 1194 the king granted him the manors of Kerswell and Diptford, Devon, previously granted to Earl Reginald by Henry II, along with the manor of Liskeard, Cornwall. King John was altogether more generous. In particular he granted Henry the barony and castle of Totnes in 1209 at pleasure (after depriving his fallen favourite, William (III) de Briouze, of the honour), the escheated barony of Bradninch, Devon, which Henry secured in 1204–5, and the manors of Ipplepen, Cornworthy, Loddiswell, Devon, and Kingston Lacy, Dorset, all of which were in his possession by 1212 at the latest. Other marks of royal favour indicate that the king had confidence in Henry and that the two enjoyed a close relationship. In 1205 he was pardoned 400 marks of the fine of 1200 marks that he had made with the king for Bradninch, and little of the outstanding sum was paid in the following years. Henry also received robes, gift of the king, in 1206 and 1207, and probably at other times. These and other instances of royal patronage suggest that Henry may well have been a member of John's household after *c*.1204. Much, certainly, of the king's munificence stemmed from actions that Henry took on John's behalf as a military captain and administrator. These include his participation in the expedition to Poitou in 1206, prests taken on the king's behalf in 1209, measures to help raise shipping and sailors for the expedition to Ireland in 1210, and actions in connection with the king's campaigns in Wales in 1211. In 1214 he was summoned along with four other knights to accompany the expedition to Poitou—John's final attempt to regain his lost inheritance in France—and was duly acquitted of his scutage.

Henry's greatest aspiration was undoubtedly to secure the earldom of Cornwall, despite his illegitimacy, and the dominant position that he had come to enjoy in the southwest, largely through royal favour, provided him with some considerable leverage once civil war loomed after the granting of Magna Carta in June 1215. John was well aware that it was important to his cause to retain Henry's loyalty, not least because of the influence that Henry could be expected to exert upon local freemen and knights. Already, in May 1215, he had granted Henry the lands of the rebels William de Mandeville and Giles, bishop of Hereford, in Devon and Gloucestershire. Then, in September 1215, he declared that Henry's rights to the earldom would be judged once peace in the realm was secured. At the same time he appointed Henry sheriff of Cornwall and granted him the lucrative stannaries in the county. Although he was replaced as sheriff in November, the regency council of the infant Henry III plainly felt it was not in a position to do anything but appease Henry when the county was granted to him again in February 1217, a perilous moment in the struggle against Prince Louis of France and the English rebels. The grant was made expressly that he hold the county as his father had held it. Such a grant cannot be seen as implying (or, indeed, confirming) that the earldom of Cornwall had been conferred upon Henry, and in the royal records he is never referred to as earl. Nevertheless he termed himself earl in a number of the charters he issued at this time, and revealed that he had every intention of exploiting the problems of the young Henry III's regency government in these critical years. His hopes of establishing the sort of position of quasi-autonomy that his father had held are clear. He demanded that the men of Cornwall do homage to him as their lord; he sought to eject Robert de Courtenay as sheriff of Devon, even besieging him in Exeter Castle in late 1217; and he also refused persistently to deliver Totnes to Reginald de Briouze, the rightful heir. More significantly, it was brought to the regency's attention in September 1219 that he had ordered that an assize mort d'ancestor be taken in Cornwall on his own authority and had appointed justices to hear petty assizes. The men of Cornwall were accordingly commanded not to allow anyone to be put on any assize in the county without special royal precept. Later, in November 1220, it also became apparent, through royal inquisition, that Henry had been granting royal demesne land in Cornwall to his knights and other followers as patronage.

Such presumptive actions made it certain that Henry would face the full wrath of the regency government once circumstances allowed. That point was finally reached in April 1220, following Henry's continued disobedience and then his unilateral withdrawal from court without licence. He was deprived of the shrievalty of Cornwall and the king's subjects in the county were commanded to obey him no longer. In July Robert de Cardinan nominally replaced him as sheriff, but it must have soon become apparent that tougher and more direct action was necessary if Henry were to be brought to heel. The question of Cornwall, and Henry's alarming indications of his aspirations towards it, was rendered all the more urgent at this time following the arrival in England of envoys of Guy, vicomte of Limoges, and his brother, who now sought grant of the earldom. They were the grandsons of Reginald, earl of Cornwall, by his eldest daughter, Sarah, and Aymer, vicomte of Limoges, but their claim was dismissed in September 1220 when they were informed that Henry III was barred from making any permanent alienations until he came of age, in accordance with the oath taken by the English magnates to that effect in November 1218.

Their very claim, however, naturally sharpened the anxiety of the regency council concerning the fate of Cornwall as a result of Henry's actions. The issue was discussed at the council held at Oxford in August 1220, following which the justiciar, Hubert de Burgh, and the papal legate, Pandulf, decided to march against Henry. On 1 September, joined by Peter des Roches, bishop of Winchester, they reached Exeter and summoned the knights of the western shires to join them there in arms. But their services were not required; alarmed by the prospect of force, Henry quietly submitted and agreed to terms. An agreement was drawn up by which Henry surrendered the county of Cornwall and Launceston Castle to the king on condition that the king, when he came of age, would do full justice to Henry concerning his claims. In effect, this promise was meaningless, given Henry's illegitimacy, and he surely knew that. But he did not come away empty-handed, since he received 500 marks in compensation immediately and was promised a further 600 marks in the future, that sum being duly paid in May 1221. This is a measure of the seriousness with which the regency council, given its chronic impecuniosity, regarded his challenge. After this agreement Henry caused no further problems to the government but, as previously, he was reluctant to cede Totnes to its rightful holder, Reginald de Briouze. Only after prolonged litigation in 1220–21 was he prevailed upon to return it in or shortly before July 1221. By then his preparations to go on the fifth crusade to Egypt were well advanced, and he must have departed shortly afterwards. It is unknown if he reached Egypt, but he certainly died abroad on his crusade, presumably at some point in late 1221. On 31 January 1222 the sheriff of Cornwall was instructed to take into royal hands his lands and chattels in the bailiwick, and a later writ of October 1222, on behalf of Henry's executors, states that he had died on his pilgrimage and grants that they were to have his chattels and rents in Cornwall up to the crusaders' term.

SIMON LLOYD

Sources Chancery records · Pipe rolls · Curia regis rolls preserved in the Public Record Office (1922–) · T. D. Hardy, ed., Rotuli de liberate ac de misis et praestitis, regnante Johanne, RC (1844) · D. A. Carpenter, The minority of Henry III (1990)

Henry Frederick, prince of Wales (1594–1612), was born early on 19 February 1594 at Stirling Castle. He was the eldest child of King *James VI of Scotland (1566–1625) and *Anne (1574–1619), second daughter of Frederick II, king of Denmark, and Sophia, and older sister of Christian IV. Although Henry's birth was celebrated immediately in Scotland, his baptism awaited the arrival of the earl of Sussex, proxy of Queen Elizabeth, the child's sole godparent. The ceremony finally took place on 30 August 1594 in the Chapel Royal at Stirling Castle. Henry's birth and baptism were marked by myriad festivities: nativity poems, banquets, tilts, and masques.

Childhood, 1594–1603 Two days after Henry's birth arrangements were made for his fostering with James's confidante, John Erskine, second earl of Mar, and his mother, Annabel Murray. Stirling Castle was then Mar's residence and there the prince was to live, legally

Henry Frederick, prince of Wales (1594–1612), by Isaac Oliver, *c.*1610–12

removed from his reputedly Roman Catholic mother, who kept her primary residences at Edinburgh Castle and Buccleuch. The separation from her infant caused Anne great pain and in March 1595 she began vigorously to fight these arrangements, attracting powerful allies such as Chancellor Maitland to her cause of familial reunion. Her angry machinations were directed primarily against Mar, but James too fell victim to her well-considered efforts. Nevertheless, the king was steadfast in his choice of Mar: in July 1595 he wrote to his friend, 'not to deliver [Henry] out of your hands except I command you with my own mouth' (Barroll, 23). At the behest of her own mother, Anne gave up her bid for Henry and was reconciled with her husband and Mar in August 1595. Although signs of her displeasure continued to surface, Henry remained at Stirling until the spring of 1603.

In 1598 James clarified his educational programme for Henry in his *Basilicon doron*. Though originally written in Middle Scots it was reworked by James in English the following year; only a few copies of this 1599 version were printed, suggesting that the king intended it primarily for the edification of his heir and those near to him. In July 1599 James named the scholar Adam Newton as the prince's tutor, and placed the learned Sir David Murray in the youth's bedchamber. Along with Mar, these two men were charged with Henry's education. The courageous, resilient youth proved especially adept at sports and physical exercises, demonstrating early a penchant for endeavours

equine and matters military. His promise was already recognized far beyond Scotland. Early in 1603 James received an offer from Pope Clement VIII of financial support for his bid for the English throne if he would transfer Henry to Rome for further education. Unsurprisingly, James refused.

When Elizabeth I died in late March 1603, James VI of Scotland was immediately recognized as King James I of England, and Henry acquired the title duke of Cornwall. James left Edinburgh for London on 4 April 1603, accompanied by numerous nobles including Mar. Despite being four months pregnant, Anne was to follow James in mid-May, leaving Henry and her other two children, Princess *Elizabeth (1596–1662) and Prince *Charles (1600–1649), behind to continue their Scottish fostering. This is not what transpired, however, for Anne seized the opportunity to assert control over Henry's upbringing. She travelled to Stirling on 4 May and insisted that the prince be handed over. Initially rebuffed by Mar's mother and younger brother, Anne experienced a fury and despair so intense that she miscarried on 10 May; despite her illness, she steadfastly refused to leave Stirling without Henry. News of this situation reached James in England, and he commissioned Mar to return to Scotland and bring Anne to England. Mar failed: Anne declined to see him or to leave unless Henry was with her. Towards the end of May, James relented, officially transferring Mar's responsibilities for Henry to the duke of Lennox. Lennox then gave Henry up to the privy council, which, at the king's urging, delivered the prince to Anne. She returned to Edinburgh accompanied by Henry on 27 May, and together they departed for England on 1 June 1603. Due to Anne's fortitude, the new duke of Cornwall arrived in England much sooner than James intended.

English adolescence, 1603–1610 On their journey into England, Anne and Henry were hosted from 25–27 June at Althorpe (Northamptonshire) by the Spencers, who regaled them with entertainments scripted by Ben Jonson. The two were soon reunited with James and they proceeded toward Windsor Castle, arriving on 30 June. On 2 July Henry was invested as a knight of the Garter. His august bearing and lively intelligence during this ceremony impressed the English privy councillors the earls of Northampton and Nottingham. Due to concerns about the plague Henry was then removed to Oatlands Palace, Surrey, where James constituted Henry's first household, perhaps again trying to isolate the youth from his mother. He made Sir Thomas Chaloner governor, kept on Newton and Murray as tutors, and surrounded Henry with other trusted men and youths, numbering 141 by the year's end. Anne rose valiantly to this new challenge: in 1604 she forced the dissolution of Oatlands. As a result Henry took up a peripatetic life, moving between Nonsuch, Richmond, St James's, and other palaces, with Anne now enjoying near-constant access to him.

In August 1603 Henry was visited at Oatlands by Scaramelli, the Venetian ambassador, who (like Northampton and Nottingham) was struck by his wit and carriage: 'He is ceremonious beyond his years', remarked Scaramelli, 'and with great gravity he covered and bade me be covered. Through an interpreter he gave me a long discourse on his exercises, dancing, tennis, the chase' (Wilson, 18–19). The first two of Henry's many portraits, painted at Oatlands by Robert Peake the elder that autumn, accord well with the Venetian's report: both depict the heir as an athletic young huntsman triumphing over a slain deer.

These references to Prince Henry at Oatlands, both verbal and visual, proved indicative of his future behaviour and interests. His ceremoniousness surfaced often. Anne and her ladies regaled him with a masque at Winchester in mid-October 1603 and he probably attended her twelfth night masques of 1604, 1605, and 1608; he expressed great interest in Anne's 1609 show, *The Masque of Queens*; he danced brilliantly at the conclusion of Jonson's 1606 marriage spectacle, *Hymenaei*; and he attended entertainments hosted by Robert Cecil, earl of Salisbury, in 1606, 1607, and 1609. Henry also appeared in venues beyond the court milieu. On 15 March 1604, accompanying his parents, he entered London amid great fanfare, and on 16 July 1607 he was initiated into the company of the Merchant Taylors at their guildhall. Henry's comportment at Oxford in July 1605, when he visited for four days and symbolically matriculated at Magdalen College, similarly reassured learned men of his determined (if not bookish) wisdom.

Prince Henry often displayed a preference for sports over learning. Newton and others encouraged him in his studies but his enthusiasm and energy were otherwise directed. An apocryphal tale has James scolding Henry for his lack of diligence in studies compared to his younger brother Charles, and Henry retorting, then 'we'll make him archbishop of Canterbury' (Strong, 15). Henry's inclinations were noticed by many outside his immediate family. Sir Charles Cornwallis, treasurer of Henry's household and his biographer, remarked that the prince 'pl[ied] his book hard for two or three years, continuing all his princely sports, hawking, hunting, running at the ring, leaping, riding of great horses, dancing, fencing, tossing of the pike' (Wilson, 19–20). And the French ambassador, La Boderie, writing on 31 October 1606, reported that:

> none of his pleasures savour the least of a child. He is a particular lover of horses ... He studies two hours a day, and employs the rest of his time in tossing the pike, or leaping, or shooting with the bow, or throwing the bar, or vaulting. (Strong, 66)

Increasingly Henry displayed ebullience in military, chivalric, and naval endeavours. He encouraged friends to send him secret reports on French fortifications, and he received suits of armour from several well-wishers. Gifts of horses were frequent, and during 1607–9 Henry sponsored the erection of a riding school at St James's Palace. When his uncle Christian IV of Denmark visited England in July–August 1606 the prince tilted before him. And from 6 March 1604, when Lord Admiral Nottingham presented him with a small ship—the *Disdain*—designed by Phineas Pett, Henry's passion for maritime pursuit was unflagging. Pett later crafted the mammoth *Prince Royal*

(1608–10) for the heir, who returned the favour by successfully, if blindly, protecting Pett from well-founded charges of corruption in May 1608. Henry was also a supporter of Sir Walter Ralegh, who though imprisoned in the Tower of London by James remained a valued correspondent and adviser on naval, colonial, and matrimonial matters. As the prince, often compared to Sir Philip Sidney and the second earl of Essex, promoted Elizabethan-style rites of knighthood and sea voyages of exploration, he electrified a resurgent war party frustrated by James's pacific policies. Likenesses of Henry from these teenage years repeatedly capture these martial interests. Marcus Gheeraerts the younger portrays him in his Garter robes and sporting a ship jewel upon his headdress (1608); an anonymous artist paints Henry in the suit of armour received from Henri IV (after 1607); Rowland Lockey fashions a miniature depicting the prince in armour from the prince de Joinville (1607); and Robert Peake depicts the heir as a dashing young conqueror about to unsheathe his sword in a canvas for the duke of Savoy (1604–10).

In religion Henry was unambiguously protestant, and in manners abstemious. Having survived the Gunpowder Plot of November 1605, his fervent commitment to reformed causes, both in England and on the continent, increased. Cornwallis recalls that he was 'a reverent and attentive hearer of sermons', that he had 'boxes kept at … St James, Richmond, and Nonsuch', and that he demanded 'all those who did swear in his hearing, to pay moneys to the same, which were after duly given to the poor' (Wilson, 41–2). A proclaimed enemy of Roman Catholicism, Henry worked zealously to root out recusants and bring them to justice. Books of all kinds were dedicated to Henry throughout his life, but the sermons, commentaries, and religious epistles of protestant clerics and reformers were especially plentiful.

Henry's burgeoning household included the godly, the learned, and the militant. Chaloner complained in 1607 of the expenses of this 'courtly college or … collegiate court' (Birch, 97) and Cornwallis claimed that nearly 500 men were attached to Henry by 1610. Chief among the prince's contemporaries were John Harington of Exton, the third earl of Essex, and William Cecil, Lord Cranborne. Henry's older friends included Edward Cecil and the earls of Southampton and Arundel. Outside of this immediate circle Prince Henry was widely noted, and the king's privy council paid him great respect. In fact, Salisbury seems to have encouraged the prince's inquiries into foreign affairs, and even sought his opinion on matters such as the Julich–Cleves succession crisis of 1609–10.

Prince Henry's scrutiny of events abroad was answered by great continental interest in the ambitious English heir apparent, especially as a potential marriage partner. Catholic proposals were more frequent than protestant offers. The grand duke of Tuscany looked into such possibilities as early as 1601. The potential of a match with the Spanish infanta was first broached in November 1603 and resurfaced again in 1605; the alliance was still being mooted as late as 1610, when Philip III secretly matched the infanta with the French dauphin following the assassination of

Henri IV. To placate James, Philip encouraged the duke of Savoy to effect a double match between his children and Henry and Elizabeth, a proposal that caused great stir in London. The prince and many of his circle, such as Ralegh, were violently opposed to the Savoyard proposals, and following his investiture as prince of Wales, Henry took the lead in discovering a suitable protestant prince for Elizabeth, and searched too for a reformed bride for himself. Henry's earnestness in looking for a proper wife—he supposedly rejected the Catholic matches tendered by James with the rejoinder that 'two religions should never lie in [my] bed' (Williamson, 135)—gives the lie to his reputed dalliance with Frances Howard.

Prince of Wales, 1610–1612 Henry's installation as prince of Wales in June 1610 conferred financial and political independence and increased prestige. In February 1609 a special tax for his knighting had been levied. Although the privy council urged James, for monetary reasons, to delay the creation for two years, the heir refused to wait. Late in 1609 Henry commissioned research on previous installations of princes of Wales; arguing from historical precedent his servant Connock reported that Henry should be created in parliament as soon as possible. By 1609 Salisbury had accepted Henry's and Connock's position, and he commissioned William Camden and Robert Cotton to conduct further research to articulate the prince of Wales's prerogatives *vis-à-vis* parliament and the monarch. Armed with their opinions in December, Salisbury was able to convince James and his fellow privy councillors that the installation should occur quickly, perhaps even in February 1610, on or near Henry's sixteenth birthday. Due to lack of money the event was delayed until London agreed to a loan of £100,000.

On 4 June 1610 Henry was created prince of Wales and earl of Chester by his father in an elaborate ritual scripted by Salisbury. The installation took place in the court of requests at Westminster Palace before both houses of parliament and numerous guests; everyone compared the ceremony to a coronation. Trappings of solemnity were ubiquitous: the chamber had been hung with arras; all participants were lavishly robed and carefully seated; the prince donned an ermine-lined gown costing more than £1300; symbolic tokens—a sword, ring, verge, and coronet—were bestowed upon Henry; and an illuminated patent was proclaimed by Salisbury in both Latin and English.

This extraordinary quasi-sacramental parliamentary installation was surrounded by a whole year of court festivities that further demarcate 1610 as the signal year in Henry's short life: on 6 January he tilted and performed in Ben Jonson's and Inigo Jones's neo-Arthurian show, *The Barriers*; on 31 May he enjoyed a water pageant on the Thames at Chelsea performed by a fleet of City boats and barges; on 3 June he witnessed the creation of twenty-five knights of the Bath he had personally selected; on the evening of his installation, Henry and his father attended *Tethys Festival*, a masque written by Samuel Daniel and designed by Jones; on 5 June he tilted again; and finally, on 1 January 1611, he witnessed Jonson's and Jones's famous show, *Oberon*, along with the *Barriers* his most important masque commission.

At the time of his investiture Henry maintained the appearance of a healthy, sturdy teenager. One of his biographers, probably his bedchamberer William Haydon, recalls that:

> he was tall and … strong and well proportioned … his eyes quick and pleasant, his forehead broad, his nose big, his chin broad and cloven, his hair inclining to black … his whole face and visage comely and beautiful … with a sweet, smiling, and amiable countenance … full of gravity. (Strong, 12)

Haydon claimed Henry resembled his uncle Christian IV. In the autumn of 1611 his physiognomy altered to favour his mother. Hawkins, another biographer, wrote that 'his visage began to appear somewhat paler, longer and thinner than before' (Strong, 12), and Francis Bacon remembered 'his face long and inclining to leanness … his look grave … the motion of his eyes composed' and expressing 'marks of severity' (Strong, 12). This adult countenance, focused and stern, is marvellously depicted in Isaac Oliver's miniature of about 1610x12: Henry, clad in gilt armour, gazes confidently outward; a cannon and several armed soldiers before an encampment appear in the background.

Officially ensconced in St James's Palace, Henry developed into a major patron of the arts. He commissioned the Florentine architect de Servi and the Huguenot hydraulic engineer and garden designer de Caus to plan major renovations (never realized) at Richmond Palace, and he launched Inigo Jones's career. He avidly collected mannerist paintings from northern Italian and Netherlandish artists (although he never acquired a much-desired Michelangelo), Florentine bronzes (a remarkable set of fifteen arrived in May 1612), antique coins, medals, and cameos, and curiosities of every variety. He sponsored musicians and scientific inquiry at St James's. He inspired the praise of numerous authors, including George Chapman, John Davies, Michael Drayton, and Henry Peacham, and Francis Bacon dedicated the second edition of the *Essays* (1612) to Henry. After the prince acquired Lord Lumley's library in October 1609 he continued eagerly to collect books until his untimely death.

During the busy summer and autumn of 1612 Henry's arrangements for the visit of Frederick, the elector palatine, his chosen match for Elizabeth, particularly occupied him. Then, without warning, he fell desperately ill with fever (now thought to be typhoid) in mid-October; despite the best efforts of a bevy of doctors, including Theodore de Mayerne, the king's physician, he died on 6 November 1612. St James's was draped in black, and there was widespread grief across the nation, shared by many abroad. He lay in state for more than a month until his funeral on 7 December at Westminster Abbey; he was buried within an abbey chapel twelve days later. Among those who memorialized the prince were Thomas Campion, John Donne, Joseph Hall, and George Herbert. Ralegh perhaps best captured the gloomy mood, claiming his *History* (1614) was 'left to the world without a master' (Wilson, 143).

Despite the jolt caused by Henry's death, estimations of what was lost have been greatly inflated, then and now. Clearly the prince of Wales was ambitious and bright, dedicated to protestant reform and artistic renewal. However, his death probably purchased six years of additional peace for protestant England and Catholic Europe before the misfortunes of his sister Elizabeth and brother-in-law Frederick in 1618 led to thirty years of religious wars. Moreover, given the flowering of *al' antica* culture in later Jacobean and Caroline England, the notion that England lost a renaissance with his demise seems inflated. Future research on this fascinating individual might wisely emphasize cultural continuity instead of rupture, and further investigate Roman Catholic relief at his passing in addition to protestant mourning. JAMES M. SUTTON

Sources R. Strong, *Henry prince of Wales and England's lost renaissance* (1986) · J. W. Williamson, *The myth of the conqueror: Prince Henry Stuart, a study of 17th century personation* (1978) · E. C. Wilson, *Prince Henry and English literature* (1946) · T. Birch, ed., *The life of Henry, prince of Wales* (1760) · J. L. Barroll, *Anna of Denmark, queen of England: a cultural biography* (2001) · W. W. Seton, 'The early years of Henry Frederick, prince of Wales, and Charles, duke of Albany [Charles I], 1593–1605', *SHR*, 13 (1915–16), 366–79 · *DNB* · P. Croft, 'The parliamentary installation of Henry, prince of Wales', *BIHR*, 65 (1992), 177–93 · C. A. Patrides, '"The greatest of the kingly race": the death of Henry Stuart', *The Historian*, 47 (1985), 402–8 · R. Badenhausen, 'Disarming the infant warrior: Prince Henry, King James, and the chivalric revival', *Papers on Language and Literature*, 31/1 (1995), 20–37 · M. C. Williams, 'Merlin and the prince: the speeches at Prince Henry's *Barriers*', *Renaissance Drama*, 7 (1977), 221–30 · J. Pitcher, '"In those figures which they seem": Samuel Daniel's *Tethys' festival*', *The court masque*, ed. D. Lindley (1984), 33–46 · R. Lockyer, *James VI and I* (1998) · P. C. Herman, '"Is this winning?": Prince Henry's death and the problem of chivalry in *The two noble kinsmen*', *South Atlantic Review*, 62/1 (winter 1997), 1–32 · R. H. Wells, '"Manhood and chevalrie": *Coriolanus*, Prince Henry, and the chivalric revival', *Review of English Studies*, 51 (2000), 395–422 · A. R. Beer, '"Left to the world without a maister": Sir Walter Ralegh's *The history of the world* as a public text', *Studies in Philology*, 91/4 (autumn 1994), 432–63 · J. R. Mulryne, '"Here's unfortunate revels": war and chivalry in plays and shows at the time of Prince Henry Stuart', *War, literature and the arts in sixteenth-century Europe*, ed. J. R. Mulryne and M. Shewring (1989), 165–96 · E. Y. L. Ho, 'Author and reader in renaissance texts: Fulke Greville, Sidney, and Prince Henry', *Connotations*, 5/1 (1995–6), 34–48 · R. Soellner, 'Chapman's *Caesar and Pompey* and the fortunes of Prince Henry', *Medieval and Renaissance Drama in England*, 2 (1985), 135–51 · S. Gossett, 'A new history for Ralegh's *Notes on the navy*', *Modern Philology*, 85 (1987), 12–26

Archives BL, papers and corresp., Harley MSS 7002, 7007, 7008, 7009 | Archivio di Stato, Florence, MS 4189 · Archivio di Stato, Florence, ASF Mediceo 1348, 1349, 1350 · PRO, audit office and state papers

Likenesses M. Gheeraerts the younger, oils, *c*.1603, NPG · R. Peake the elder, double portrait, oils, 1603 (with J. Harington), Metropolitan Museum of Art, New York; version, Royal Collection · R. Peake the elder, oils, 1604–10, Palazzo Chiablese, Turin, Italy · R. Peake, oils, *c*.1605, Museum of London · N. Hilliard, miniature, watercolour, 1607, Royal Collection · attrib. R. Lockey, miniature, watercolour, 1607, Royal Collection · oils, *c*.1607, Dunster Castle, Minehead, Somerset · N. Hilliard, miniature, watercolour, *c*.1607–1610, Royal Collection · studio of I. Oliver, miniature, watercolour, *c*.1610, NPG · R. Peake, oils, *c*.1610, Magd. Oxf. · R. Peake the elder, oils, 1610, Parham Park, Pulborough, Sussex · R. Peake the elder, oils, *c*.1610, NPG · I. Oliver, miniature, oils, *c*.1610–1611, FM Cam. · I. Oliver, miniature, watercolour, *c*.1610– 1612, Royal Collection [*see illus.*] · S. de Passe, line engraving, 1610?–1612?, BM · I. Jones, drawing, 1611, Chatsworth, Derbyshire, Devonshire collections · C. Boel, line engraving, 1612, BM · H. Peacham, emblem, 1612, repro. in H. Peacham, *Minerva Britanna* (1612) · W. Hole, line engraving, BM; repro. in G. Chapman, *An epicede* (1612) · W. Hole, line engraving, BM, NPG; repro. in M. Drayton, *Poly-Olbion* (1612) · C. de Passe, line engraving, BM; repro. in C. de Passe, *Regiae Angliae … pictura* (Cologne, 1604) · attrib. R. Peake the elder, oils, priv. coll.; on loan to Scot. NPG · medals, BM · portraits, repro. in Strong, *Henry* · portraits, repro. in Williamson, *Myth of the conqueror*

Henry Frederick, Prince, duke of Cumberland and Strathearn (1745–1790), was born on 26 October 1745 at Leicester House, London, the sixth child and fourth son of *Frederick Lewis, prince of Wales (1707–1751), and his wife, *Augusta (1719–1772), daughter of Friedrich II, duke of Saxe-Gotha-Altenburg. He shared in the sheltered upbringing of his brothers and sisters. His formal education was still in progress in November 1765 when a dispute broke out within the royal family and household over who should act as his tutor, his usual reader of modern languages having been diverted to supervise the dying Prince Frederick William at Kensington. He was never regarded as intelligent and it was probably partly on this account that his career was held back compared to those of his older brothers. In July 1766 *George III appointed him ranger of Windsor Forest and Great Park in succession to his late uncle William Augustus, duke of Cumberland; on 22 October that year he was created duke of Cumberland and Strathearn in the British peerage, and earl of Dublin in the Irish. In 1767 parliament granted him £17,000 per annum.

Cumberland entered the navy as a midshipman at the late age of twenty-two in 1768. That year he was sent to the Mediterranean in an attempt to demonstrate British commitment to Corsica, but the conquest of the island by France came unexpectedly and his ship, *Venus*, was hastily recalled that September. He was promoted to rear-admiral in 1769 and vice-admiral in 1770.

Cumberland had been intended by his brother for a sober career as a naval officer but it was becoming clear that he was to be remembered for less reputable exploits. In early 1769 he began a sexual relationship with Harriet, *née* Vernon (*d.* 1828), wife of Richard, first Baron Grosvenor. They were often seen in public together and attracted speculation and the fury of Lord Grosvenor. A little before 2 a.m. on 22 December 1769 Grosvenor's servants discovered Cumberland and Lady Grosvenor in bed together at the White Hart inn, St Albans. Grosvenor pursued the matter in the courts and on 5 July 1770 Cumberland was tried for criminal conversation with Lady Grosvenor. Despite the best efforts of his counsel, John Dunning, to show that the testimony of Grosvenor's agents was doubtful and supporting evidence circumstantial, the court found against Cumberland and he was ordered to pay damages of £10,000 to Grosvenor. This damaged the duke's already precarious financial position and he borrowed £12,000 from a grudging king. A rash of books and pamphlets was

Prince Henry Frederick, duke of Cumberland and Strathearn (1745–1790), by Thomas Gainsborough, *c.*1783–5 [with Anne, duchess of Cumberland, and her sister, Lady Elizabeth Luttrell]

farming families he met at Berwick upon Tweed, unconcerned at their ignorance of court etiquette. After returning to London, Cumberland married Anne Horton on 2 October 1771. The duke broke the news to George III on 2 November by presenting him with a letter announcing the marriage; the couple then departed for Calais. The marriage horrified George III, not only because of the duchess's politically controversial family, but also because a marriage between a prince and a commoner was unequal in imperial law, barring any children from inheriting the electorate of Hanover. In Britain:

> where the Crown is too little respected it must be big with the greatest mischiefs. Civil Wars would by such measures again be common in this Country, those of the Yorks and Lancasters were greatly giving to intermarriages with the Nobility.   (George III to the duke of Gloucester, 9 Nov 1771, RA GEO/15938)

Cumberland refused to disavow the marriage and in consequence was barred from the king's presence. His mother, who was by now terminally ill, also refused to see him and they remained unreconciled at her death. Cumberland's failure to seek the king's permission for his marriage led to the king's forcing the Royal Marriages Act through parliament. It stipulated that no descendant of George II, other than the descendants of princesses who married into foreign families, could marry without the sovereign's consent. The measure also forced Cumberland's older brother *William Henry, duke of Gloucester and Edinburgh, to admit that for six years he had been married to the dowager Countess Waldegrave.

Horace Walpole described the duchess to Sir Horace Mann as 'Coquette beyond measure, artful as Cleopatra, and completely mistress of all her passions and projects' (Walpole, *Corr.*, 23.345). It was probably her determination to be recognized as a princess that drove the couple forward, whereas the duke was more relaxed about his social status. Excluded from the court of George III, the Cumberlands established a rival centre at Cumberland House in Pall Mall, which Cumberland acquired from the duke of Gloucester in 1772. They staged lavish entertainments, patronized musicians, had a succession of portraits painted, and travelled conspicuously in their state coach. Cumberland was still living on his original financial settlement and, beset by debts, the couple spent the period from summer 1773 to summer 1774 travelling in France and Italy. To the frustration of British diplomats attempting to execute George III's instructions that the Cumberlands should be allowed no precedence, the duchess's claims to royal status were enhanced when she was received privately by Empress Maria Theresa at Vienna.

On their return to Britain the duke and duchess renewed their attempt to provide a livelier alternative to the court of George III. In 1775 Cumberland became patron of a boat club, the Cumberland Fleet, giving the duke and duchess the opportunity to sail down the Thames in a barge flying the royal standard at the centre of a well-attended social occasion. The society evolved into the

published to exploit the affair, including a collection of the couple's correspondence which exposed Cumberland's adolescent expressions of emotion and his uncertain grammar to ridicule.

For a little while after the trial Cumberland renewed his relationship with Lady Grosvenor but he was then distracted by a Mrs Maria Bailey, until, on 25 July 1771, at his Garter investiture at Windsor, he met Anne Horton.

Anne [*née* Anne Luttrell; *other married name* Anne Horton], duchess of Cumberland and Strathearn (1743–1808), was born in Marylebone on 24 January 1743, the daughter of Simon Luttrell, Baron Irnham (1713–1787), and his wife, Judith Maria Lawes (*d.* 1798). Her family were notorious political opportunists who had attracted great opprobrium after Anne's eldest brother, Henry Lawes *Luttrell, stood as the court candidate against John Wilkes at the Middlesex election in 1769 and was then placed in the seat by parliament despite the debarred Wilkes's overwhelming victory. Anne Luttrell's first husband was Christopher Horton (*bap.* 1741), the son of Christopher Horton and his wife, Frances, of Catton Hall, Derbyshire. They married on 4 August 1765, but Horton died on 5 August 1769.

Cumberland did not prosecute his suit with great vigour. In August he toured Northumberland (the furthest north any member of the eighteenth-century royal family travelled for a social purpose) where he was reported by Bishop Thomas Percy to be at ease in the company of the

Royal Thames Yacht Club. In the navy, the duke was promoted to admiral in 1778, but was forbidden to assume a command. In summer 1779, suffering from ulcers on his lungs, he moved to Brighthelmstone (Brighton), Sussex, which he had first visited in September 1771. Cumberland was the first member of the royal family seriously to patronize the emerging spa and he later introduced the place to his nephew George, prince of Wales.

Like his brother the duke of Gloucester, Cumberland was reconciled to George III in 1780 after offering his services to the king in the face of the Gordon riots. However, the relationship between George III and his youngest surviving brother remained uneasy, substantially as a result of the growing friendship between the Cumberlands and the prince of Wales. The prince always insisted that Cumberland was a restraining influence on his impulsive character. Cumberland's health continued its gentle decline, and it was as much because of this as their poor finances that the duke and duchess spent almost all the period from November 1783 to October 1786 on the continent. They returned to London for about six weeks in October and November 1785 to advise the prince of Wales, whose invalid marriage to Maria Fitzherbert they subsequently supported. They made a more permanent return in autumn 1786 on the advice of the prince of Wales's surgeon, Sir Gilbert Blane, who had travelled to Spa to treat Cumberland. The duke retained the role of a favourite uncle for the prince of Wales, and in 1787 served as an emissary from the prince to Pitt's ministry during negotiations to clear the prince's debts. Both the Cumberlands were active supporters of the prince of Wales during the regency crisis, Cumberland writing to his nephew Prince William (later William IV) in the West Indies to ensure his support, and the duchess attending Commons debates on the Regency Bill. Cumberland died outside Cumberland House, Pall Mall, after alighting from his coach, on 18 September 1790; a post-mortem found his right lung 'universally diseased' (*Correspondence of George, Prince of Wales*, 2.92) and the back of the roof of his mouth occupied by an ulcer that had entirely destroyed his uvula. He was buried in Westminster Abbey on 28 September 1790. He and the duchess had no children, and the claims of Olivia Serres to be his daughter can probably be discounted.

The duchess of Cumberland was granted an annual allowance of £4000, which the prince of Wales thought 'shabby' (*Correspondence of George, Prince of Wales*, 2.103). She raised additional funds by auctioning the duke's music library—including manuscripts by Handel and Haydn—musical instruments, and books at Christies during February 1791. She at first remained on close terms with the prince of Wales, but distance grew between them after it was reported in December 1794 that while a guest at Brighton Pavilion she had criticized the prince for breaking with Maria Fitzherbert. Mounting debts led her to move out of Cumberland House in 1793. She transferred the lease to her bankers in 1800 and went into exile on the continent. She died at Gorizia, near Trieste, Venetia, on 28 December 1808.

The success of Cumberland House as a focus for fashionable society may in part have been attributable to the duchess's almost constant companion and sister, **Lady Elizabeth Luttrell** (*d.* 1799). Luttrell witnessed the Cumberlands' marriage and was installed in a new west wing of Cumberland House, designed by Robert Adam and completed in 1773. She accompanied the Cumberlands on their continental tours and was nicknamed Princess Elizabeth. She managed the gaming tables at Cumberland House by which the Cumberlands helped sustain their finances. Her fortunes declined after she and the duchess left Cumberland House in 1793; she was fined £50 for illegal gambling in March 1797 and was sued and confined to prison for debts of £7000 in November, but soon left, allegedly after persuading a hairdresser to marry her for £50, by which her debts became his. She died in poverty in Germany in 1799: according to the nineteenth-century memoirist Sir Robert Heron, she had been working as a street-sweeper in Augsburg and committed suicide by poison.   MATTHEW KILBURN

Sources C. N. Gattey, *Farmer George's black sheep* (1985) • J. Brooke, *King George III* (1972) • Royal Arch., RA GEO/54424–54506; RA GEO/15938 • GEC, *Peerage*, new edn, 3.573; 6.209–10 • *The correspondence of George, prince of Wales, 1770–1812*, ed. A. Aspinall, 8 vols. (1963–71) • *The correspondence of King George the Third from 1760 to December 1783*, ed. J. Fortescue, 6 vols. (1927–8) • *The later correspondence of George III*, ed. A. Aspinall, 5 vols. (1962–70) • Walpole, *Corr.* • T. Percy, 'An account of the duke of Cumberland's visit to Alnwick Castle in 1771. The brother of King George the 3d', BL, Add. MS 39547, fols. 7–12 • J. Ingamells, ed., *A dictionary of British and Irish travellers in Italy, 1701–1800* (1997) • *The letters and journals of Lady Mary Coke*, ed. J. A. Home, 4 vols. (1889–96) • journals of Lady Mary Coke, priv. coll. • *The trial of His r. h. the d. of C., July 5th 1770, for criminal conversation with Lady Harriet G—r* (1770) • A. Bourke, ed., *The history of White's*, 2 vols. (1892), 1.136 • will, PRO, PROB 11/1196 • *A full and complete history of his r—l h— the d— of C—d and Lady G—r, the fair adultress* (1770) • *GM*, 1st ser., 35 (1765), 395 • *GM*, 1st ser., 39 (1769), 415 • *GM*, 1st ser., 69 (1799), 998–9

Archives Royal Arch., Georgian archive and additional Georgian archive

Likenesses B. du Pan, group portrait, oils, 1746 (*The children of Frederick, prince of Wales*), Royal Collection • G. Knapton, group portrait, pastels, 1748 (*The children of Frederick, prince of Wales*), Royal Collection • G. Knapton, pastel drawing, *c.*1748, Royal Collection • G. Knapton, group portrait, oils, 1751 (*The family of Frederick, prince of Wales*), Royal Collection • J. Reynolds, oils, exh. RA 1773, Royal Collection • T. Gainsborough, oils, exh. RA 1777, Royal Collection • T. Gainsborough, oils, 1783, Royal Collection • T. Gainsborough, group portrait, oils, *c.*1783–1785, Royal Collection [*see illus.*] • J. S. Copley, group portrait, oils (*The collapse of the earl of Chatham in the House of Lords, 7 July 1778*), Tate Collection; on loan to NPG • J. E. Liotard, pastel drawing, Royal Collection

Henry Hotspur. *See* Percy, Sir Henry (1364–1403).

Henry Maurice, Prince, of Battenberg (1858–1896). *See under* Beatrice, Princess (1857–1944).

Henry of Abendon. *See* Abingdon, Henry (*d.* 1437).

Henry of Almain [Henry of Cornwall] (1235–1271), courtier, was the second and eldest surviving son of *Richard, first earl of Cornwall (1209–1272), and of Richard's first wife, Isabella (*d.* 1240), daughter of William (I) *Marshal, earl of Pembroke, and widow of Gilbert de Clare, earl of

Gloucester. Through his father, Henry was a grandson of King *John and nephew of *Henry III.

Early years Henry was born on 2 November 1235 and baptized shortly afterwards at his father's manor of Hailes by the bishop of Hereford. Following the death of his mother and his father's departure for crusade in June 1240, he was left in the care of the king. In December 1240 he is recorded at Windsor, in the company of other young noblemen who included the king's son, the Lord Edward. He may also have spent at least part of his childhood in France, since at a later date, his kinswoman, Queen Marguerite, wife of Louis IX, offered him hospitality during a convalescence from illness, claiming that Henry would prefer to stay at the French court than in some unknown and foreign place. In 1247 he returned to England following an embassy by his father to the French king, and in the same year, aged eleven, was promised the choice of any heiress in England or Ireland as a bride, although no betrothal appears to have resulted. He accompanied his father on a further embassy to the French court in 1250, and in December 1254, at Boulogne, was instrumental in obtaining a royal pardon for a notorious robber. By 1256 he was in receipt of occasional gifts of venison from the king in England. In 1257, shortly before departing for Germany to accept his election as king of the Romans and claimant to the Holy Roman empire, Richard of Cornwall is said to have granted Henry the honour of Knaresborough in Yorkshire. Henry himself accompanied his father to Aachen, where he was knighted on 18 May 1257 in a splendid ceremony, intended to impress Richard's new German subjects. Thereafter he followed the opening stages of Richard's royal progress southwards along the Rhine, returning to England in late September.

Henry and the baronial movement In June 1258 Henry attended the Oxford parliament where he opposed baronial demands for reform, but failed to join his kinsmen, the Lusignans, and the young Earl Warenne, in fleeing from Oxford to Winchester. He was nominated one of the twelve royalist members of the council of twenty-four, although initially he refused to swear an oath which the barons had demanded, to uphold the provisions made at Oxford, claiming that he held no lands in England save through his father, Richard of Cornwall, and that he would therefore require Richard's consent before swearing. The barons reluctantly allowed him forty days in which to obtain his father's approval. In the spring of 1259 he was allowed to borrow £100 from the confiscated rents of his cousin, William de *Valence (d. 1296), and it is possible that for several years to come he was plagued by financial problems, compounded by his father's vast expenses in Germany. Throughout this period, his closest allegiance appears to have been to his cousin and contemporary, the Lord *Edward, son of Henry III, on whose behalf in March 1259 he sealed a treaty, allowing for mutual counsel and support between Edward and Richard de Clare, earl of Gloucester, Henry's maternal kinsman. With the collapse of this arrangement, in October 1259 he went on to seal a similar treaty between Edward and

Simon de Montfort, earl of Leicester, who at this time was attracting considerable support from the younger members of the royal family, including both Edward and Henry, in his disputes with the crown.

Over the next three years Henry was to shuttle uncertainly between the rival Montfortian and royalist camps. In April 1260 he was sent as a royal proctor to the barons in London, and in June he was granted an annual pension of £100 by the king. In October 1260, however, he appeared at court, claiming to act as proxy for Simon de Montfort in the latter's hereditary position as royal steward, a position that Montfort was keen to exploit as a political lever. From 1262 onwards he sided with Montfort against the Lord Edward in the opening stages of civil disturbance, and although he attended negotiations at Paris in February 1263 at the summons of the king, by May he was openly in the Montfortian camp. In June or July 1263 he crossed to France as an adherent of Montfort, perhaps to harass the exiled royalist, John Mansel. However at Wissant or Boulogne he was taken prisoner by Ingram de Fiennes, a kinsman of Queen Eleanor, wife of Henry III. His release, which had been obtained by 10 July, was a matter of grave concern to his father, Richard of Cornwall, and had been included by the Montfortians among the conditions demanded from the king and the Lord Edward for the making of peace. Despite this, within a month Henry once again defected, abandoning Simon de Montfort to rejoin the royalist camp, probably by 26 July when he was granted custody of the castles of Corfe and Sherborne. His defection is said to have been influenced by a substantial bribe from the Lord Edward, including a promise of the honour of Tickhill. According to the chronicler William Rishanger, in notifying Montfort of his defection, Henry promised never to take up arms against him. Montfort replied, with a sneer, that it was Henry's constancy, not his arms, that had been wanting.

The Montfortian rebellion In August 1263 Henry was one of the royalists sent to make peace with the Welsh and later that year he accompanied the court to Amiens, where the French king, Louis IX, effectively quashed the entire Montfortian programme of governmental reform, provoking Montfort into a campaign of civil war. In the spring of 1264 Henry joined the Lord Edward in a military expedition to the west country, which included an attempt to raise the baronial siege of Gloucester. However, on 14 May, following the baronial victory at the battle of Lewes, he was taken prisoner, together with Richard of Cornwall and the king. Thereafter, with the Lord Edward, he was held hostage by Montfort and the barons, his release being made conditional upon a full implementation of baronial demands. Since this in turn required a firm peace between the Montfortians and the king's allies in France, Henry was sent on several occasions to the court of Louis IX, in an attempt to secure the baronial demands. Twice in September 1264 he was allowed out of prison at Dover, to carry peace proposals into France, with the English bishops pledging 20,000 marks if Henry should fail to surrender himself into custody on his return. On the second of these missions he was attacked and his letters of credence were confiscated by the men of Boulogne. In November 1264, still a prisoner, he was removed from custody at Wallingford to the greater security of Montfort's castle at Kenilworth. On 10 March 1265, together with the Lord Edward, he was transferred from the custody of Henry de Montfort, Simon's son, to that of Henry III, but immediately agreed, or more likely was compelled, to suffer further imprisonment until August, as a security for the good conduct of the newly released Lord Edward. Despite this, in April 1265 he was once again sent overseas to present baronial terms to the French, and he was still overseas in mid-May when the barons wrote to demand that he speed his return. As a result, he was absent during the closing stages of Montfort's regime, and seems to have played no part in the Lord Edward's military campaign, which culminated in the defeat and death of Montfort at the battle of Evesham.

In the aftermath Henry received various grants of rebel land, including the entire honour of Gilbert de Gant. He also seems to have made good his claim to the honour of Tickhill promised to him by the Lord Edward, to the honour of Peak, another custody bestowed by Edward, and to the castle of Corfe, first granted to him as a royal custody in 1263. In February 1266 he was sent as royalist commander to keep the peace in the north of England, and on 15 May 1266 inflicted a crushing defeat upon the rebel baron Robert de Ferrers in battle at Chesterfield, as a result of which Ferrers was taken prisoner. In August that year he was named, together with the legate Ottobuono, as arbiter in the dictum of Kenilworth, and it is apparent that, despite his own previous gains, he was instrumental in obtaining relatively lenient terms for the rebels to redeem their former lands, perhaps acting under advice from his father. In February 1267 he was sent to Rome as an envoy of his father Richard, who was titular king of the Romans, and in the following year, in one of the final acts of the baronial war, played a part in the surrender and reconciliation of his kinsman, the earl of Gloucester, at one time being appointed by the pope to take custody of the earl's castle at Tonbridge. Throughout this period, in company with the Lord Edward, he is said to have been instrumental in reviving the tradition of knightly tournaments, dormant since the civil war.

Henry and the Lord Edward's crusade On 24 June 1268, together with Edward, he took the cross at Northampton, and in the following month he was sent to Ireland, as Edward's representative, to resume control of Edward's lands and rights. In the same year the two men are said to have acted in concert to persuade the king's council to issue an ordinance, restricting the level of interest that the Jews could charge on their loans, one of the first signs of the future Edward I's hostility to the Jews. Having remained unmarried well beyond the customary age, in 1269 Henry was at last betrothed, to Constance, daughter of Gaston de Béarn. The marriage, which had been subject to negotiations since at least 1265, was completed in a splendid ceremony at Windsor on 21 May 1269. It was intended both to strengthen Plantagenet power in Gascony, on the eve of the Lord Edward's departure for crusade, and also to extinguish the claim advanced by the surviving sons of Simon de Montfort, now exiled from England, to inherit Montfort's claim to the Gascon county of Bigorre. As such it may have contributed significantly to the future enmity between Henry and Montfort's sons. In the same month, in payment of arrears of his annual pension and in compensation for the expenses he had incurred at Corfe, Henry was granted the castle of Rockingham and custody of the forests between Oxford and Stamford, to hold until his expected accession as earl of Cornwall. Also in 1269, he participated in a distinctly underhand arrangement by which Robert Ferrers, held in captivity since 1266, was released from prison and persuaded to transfer the vast bulk of his estate to Edmund, the king's younger son, in theory pending the payment of a ransom of £50,000, in practice in perpetuity, with Henry standing pledge to the terms of ransom.

Between May and August 1269 Henry was engaged at Paris in the negotiation of terms with Louis IX for the Lord Edward's participation in the forthcoming crusade, and in August 1270 he duly sailed with Edward's crusading army. From Sicily, early in 1271, he was sent north by Edward, to accompany the funeral cortège of King Louis, who had died at Tunis that winter, and in an attempt to negotiate a peace with the surviving sons of Simon de Montfort, who since 1265 had established themselves in leading positions within the administration of Charles of Anjou, Louis IX's brother, ruler of Sicily and much of central Italy.

Murder at Viterbo At Viterbo, during the season of Lent, the party in which Henry was travelling encountered Guy and the younger Simon de Montfort, who arrived in the city on 12 March 1271. On the following morning, Friday 13 March, as Henry was attending mass in the church of San Silvestro, now the Chiesa di Gesù, he was set upon by Guy de *Montfort, stabbed and dragged from the church. Henry is said to have cried out for mercy, only to be answered by Guy, 'You had no mercy on my father and brothers'—Earl Simon de Montfort and his sons slain at Evesham (Maddicott, 371). At least one bystander is said to have shouted 'Remember Evesham', as Henry was killed. Following the murder, Guy and his accomplices may have mutilated Henry's body in much the way that Earl Simon had been castrated and mutilated on the field of Evesham.

The act itself was probably unpremeditated: a spontaneous explosion of anger, in revenge for Henry's desertion of Simon de Montfort in 1263, the subsequent misfortunes that had befallen Montfort's family, and, perhaps, for the part played by Henry's marriage in denying Montfort's sons their inheritance in Gascony and Bigorre. The pursuit of Guy de Montfort was hindered by the support he obtained from his allies in Italy and by the fact that the papal see was vacant at the time of the murder. Nonetheless, for the next ten years Guy de Montfort and his supporters were to be hounded by papal excommunication and demands for retribution. Henry's viscera were buried in the cathedral church of Viterbo. His body was carried back to England, where on 21 May his bones were interred before the high altar of Hailes Abbey in Gloucestershire, Richard of Cornwall's principal religious foundation. His heart was buried separately at Westminster Abbey in, or close to, the newly rebuilt shrine of St Edward the Confessor. His widow, Constance de Béarn, vicomtesse de Marsan, with whom he had no children, was immediately granted a pension of £100 from Henry's former honours of Tickhill and the Peak, held from Queen Eleanor on behalf of the Lord Edward. She later claimed part of the customs revenue of Bordeaux and the honour of Tickhill as her dower and obtained partial possession of Tickhill from 1274 until 1279, again from 1284 until 1291, when she sided with the French in the Anglo-French war, and finally from 1304 until June 1312. Henry's claim to his father's earldom of Cornwall passed to his younger stepbrother Edmund, Richard's son from his second marriage.

Henry's one act of religious patronage, a grant of property in Westminster held from his father to the monks of Westminster Abbey, to finance lights before the shrine of St Edward, suggests a keen devotion to the cult of the Confessor and a desire to obtain divine protection on the eve of his sailing for the crusade. His arms, a lion rampant recorded on his seal, are identical to those of his father, Richard of Cornwall, and in the same way, his activities as peacemaker and his prevarication in matters of personal loyalty suggest that he was very much his father's son. His violent and unheroic death at Viterbo shocked contemporaries in England, France, and Italy, and lent tragedy to the last months of the lives of both Richard of Cornwall and Henry III. For his part in the murder Guy de Montfort is placed in the seventh circle of Dante's *Inferno*, immersed in a river of boiling blood, while the gruesome events of 1271 were further commemorated by a cycle of wall-paintings commissioned by the men of Viterbo.

NICHOLAS VINCENT

Sources Chancery records · Ann. mon. · Paris, Chron., vols. 4–6 · P. Chaplais, ed., *Diplomatic documents preserved in the Public Record Office*, 1 (1964) · G. Villani, *Cronica*, ed. F. G. Dragomanni (1844) · *Sir Christopher Hatton's Book of seals*, ed. L. C. Loyd and D. M. Stenton, Northamptonshire RS, 15 (1950) · *The historical works of Gervase of Canterbury*, ed. W. Stubbs, 2 vols., Rolls Series, 73 (1879–80) · F. M. Powicke, *King Henry III and the Lord Edward: the community of the realm in the thirteenth century*, 2 vols. (1947) · J. R. Maddicott, *Simon de Montfort* (1994) · N. Denholm-Young, *Richard of Cornwall* (1947) · R. Studd, 'The marriage of Henry of Almain and Constance of Béarn', *Thirteenth century England: proceedings of the Newcastle upon Tyne conference* [Newcastle upon Tyne 1989], ed. P. R. Coss and S. D. Lloyd, 3 (1991), 161–77 · R. F. Hunnisett and J. B. Post, eds., *Medieval legal records edited in memory of C. A. F. Meekings* (1978) · Westminster Abbey muniments, MS Domesday, fol. 355v
Archives Westminster Abbey, MS Domesday, fol. 355v

Henry of Avranches. See Avranches, Henry d' (d. 1262/3).

Henry of Blois. See Blois, Henry de (c.1096–1171).

Henry of Cornwall. See Henry of Almain (1235–1271).

Henry of Eastry. See Eastry, Henry (d. 1331).

Henry of Grosmont. See Henry of Lancaster, first duke of Lancaster (c.1310–1361).

Henry of Lancaster, third earl of Lancaster and third earl of Leicester (c.1280–1345), magnate, was the second son of *Edmund (Crouchback), earl of Lancaster (1245–1296), the youngest son of *Henry III, and Blanche (d. 1302), daughter of Robert, count of Artois, and widow of Henri, king of Navarre and count of Champagne (d. 1274). Henry's birth placed him in the highest political circles of England and France: nephew to *Edward I, cousin of *Edward II and *Edward III, half-blood cousin through his mother's daughter Jeanne to the French royal family, and younger brother of *Thomas of Lancaster, the most powerful nobleman under Edward II.

Early career Henry was probably born about 1280–81 and spent his early years with his brother Thomas in the company of John, duke of Brabant, who was married to Edward I's daughter Margaret. Henry participated with Thomas in tournaments, and served in the royal army in Flanders in 1297–8 and at the siege of Caerlaverock in 1300. He was summoned to parliament for the first time in February 1299. Two years later he had been knighted, and in the barons' letter to the pope of 1301 he was described as Henry of Lancaster, lord of Monmouth.

Monmouth was the head of the estate settled on Henry by his father. Edmund had surrendered the castles of Grosmont, Skenfrith, and Whitecastle, two Gloucestershire manors, and Monmouth to the king. Edward regranted them to Edmund and Henry jointly, with Edmund to hold them for life, so that they passed to Henry when Edmund died in 1296. Earlier, in a similar settlement, Henry's grandmother, Queen *Eleanor, granted her county of Provence in equal portions to Thomas and Henry. Marriage greatly augmented Henry's estate. Patrick of Chaworth died in 1283 leaving a daughter and heir, Maud [see Chaworth family]. Since she was only a year old, she became the king's ward, and in 1291 Edward I granted her marriage to Edmund, so that she could marry Henry, or if Henry were to die, Henry's brother John. Henry and Maud had married before 2 March 1297, when he would have been sixteen or seventeen and she was fifteen. Through Maud, Henry acquired property in Hampshire, Gloucestershire, Wiltshire, Northamptonshire, and Wales.

Henry was regularly summoned to perform military service in Scotland from 1300 onwards. In 1309–10, 1317, and 1323, the king ordered him to raise troops from his Welsh lands to fight the Scots. When Llywelyn Bren revolted in Glamorgan in 1316, Edward sent the earl of Hereford and a number of other marcher lords, including Henry, to subdue the uprising. In recognition of Henry's service, the king granted him the forfeitures of Henry's tenants who had participated in the insurrection.

Relations with Edward II Politics also occupied Henry's attention during Edward II's reign. He was summoned to meet Edward and Queen Isabella when they arrived at Dover in 1308. Shortly afterwards, he took part in the coronation ceremony, bearing the royal staff surmounted with a dove. Within two years, however, he was among those barons who forced Edward to appoint the lords ordainers to draw up ordinances for the reform of the realm. His precise role in the events of these years is not known, but like many others he received a pardon in 1313 for the killing of Edward II's favourite, Piers Gaveston. Henry was summoned to France in 1317 to do homage for the lands in Champagne and Brie that he had inherited from his father, but Edward II wrote to Philippe V asking him to postpone the homage. Henry nevertheless travelled overseas, and was out of England from 1318 to at least 1320, perhaps attending to his French lands. Henry had never been close to his brother Thomas, and when Thomas and his allies rebelled against Edward II in 1321–2, Henry was notably absent from their ranks. As Thomas's heir, however, Henry quickly petitioned Edward for the earldoms of Lancaster and Leicester, along with the lands his brother had forfeited, but he only recovered his family property and titles piecemeal. He was styled earl of Leicester in 1324 and was given some, but not all, of the Lancastrian lands in 1324 and 1326.

As the Despensers, father and son, rose to dominance at Edward II's court in the aftermath of the baronial rebellion of 1322, Henry became a leading opponent of Edward II and his favourites. Henry, in fact, was an in-law of the Despensers, since Hugh *Despenser the elder had married Isabel, widow of Patrick of Chaworth and mother of Maud, Henry's wife. Despite this connection, Henry soon fell out of the king's graces. Adam Orleton, the bishop of Hereford, had been accused of supporting the king's enemies and then of plotting against the king. Orleton asked Henry to intervene on his behalf to be restored to the king's favour. Henry agreed. When Edward II discovered their communication, he accused Henry of treason, and amplified the charge by stating that Henry had begun to use the heraldic arms of his brother Thomas, and had erected a cross at Leicester in Thomas's honour. The matter was to be brought before parliament, but was set aside as the king and Lords debated the issue of whether Edward should go to France to perform homage for Gascony. Henry was then summoned to serve with Edward in France, but the expedition never set out, because Edward was afraid that if he left the country the English would rebel against the Despensers. In the waning days of the reign the king appointed Henry one of the justices to inquire into the murder in 1326 of the justice Roger Beler, and named him captain and chief surveyor of the array in the midlands.

The deposition of Edward II By then, however, Henry had turned against the regime. He joined Queen Isabella, Roger Mortimer, and their army shortly after they landed at Orwell in September 1326. In early October John Vaux came to Leicester with Hugh Despenser the elder's treasure, arms, and horses, hoping to bring them to Despenser to support his opposition to the queen. Lancaster's men besieged Vaux in Leicester Abbey and when he fled to Henry's protection in Leicester Castle, they seized the wealth and delivered it all to Henry. Within three days Henry gathered all the forces he could and rejoined the queen at Dunstable. On 26 October Henry, now styled earl of Lancaster and Leicester, attended the special baronial council in Bristol that declared that Prince Edward would be keeper of the realm in his father's absence. The following day Henry participated in the trial of the elder Despenser, which condemned him to death. Soon after Henry pursued Edward into Wales and captured him at Neath, along with the younger Despenser and other favourites. Henry was given custody of the king and conducted Edward to Monmouth, where on 20 November he surrendered the great seal. From there, Henry led Edward to Kenilworth, where he was imprisoned in Henry's custody until the following April. In December the new government named Henry keeper of the honour and castle of Lancaster, as well as of the other castles, manors, and lands which had formed the bulk of Thomas's estate.

Henry stepped forward to help establish the new government. He attended the parliament in January 1327 that was responsible for deposing Edward II and raising Prince Edward to the throne. He was in the delegation that required Edward II to abdicate and, along with the bishop of Winchester, lifted Edward from the floor, where he had collapsed, half dead with grief, on hearing the demand. Henry led the magnates at Edward's coronation, and was appointed chief guardian of the young king by common assent of the entire realm. He presided over a regency council of prelates and magnates, including the king's uncles, Edmund of Woodstock, earl of Kent, and Thomas of Brotherton, earl of Norfolk, as well as Lancaster's son-in-law, Thomas *Wake (d. 1349), who was married to Henry's daughter Blanche. Henry also knighted Edward. Aside from its constitutional work, the January parliament heard and approved Lancaster's petition to recover the lands that his brother had forfeited, and to reverse the judgment on Thomas of Lancaster. In March the process against Thomas was fully annulled, and in April Henry finally recovered the bulk of his brother's patrimony. The king appointed Henry in July 1327 to serve on a panel of magnates and justices to put into effect the statute passed in parliament annulling the grants, gifts, and recognizances of debts that the Despensers had forced landholders into making with them.

As soon as Edward had taken the throne, the Scots invaded the north of England, penetrating as far south as co. Durham. An army was summoned to repel the invasion, and Henry was directed to lead forces mustered in Wales to Newcastle. In June Edward named Henry and his own uncle, the earl of Kent, as captains of the royal army in the marches of Scotland, and a month later appointed Henry captain of the army without mentioning Edmund. However, when the English finally confronted their enemy at Stanhope Park, they baulked at attacking and allowed the Scots to slip away, to Edward's great shame. Chroniclers claimed that Mortimer had prevented the attack, against the advice of Lancaster and others. This humiliating episode was followed by the treaty of Edinburgh on 17 March 1328, which provided for peace with Scotland. Many considered the terms of the treaty, which conceded Scottish independence, to be dishonourable, and blamed Mortimer for surrendering English claims for the sake of peace. The treaty was particularly resented by the 'disinherited', English lords who had lost lands in Scotland, including Lancaster's son-in-law, Thomas Wake.

The crisis of 1328 By the spring and summer of 1328 disaffection with Isabella and Mortimer was growing, and Lancaster gradually emerged as the leader of the opposition. But although Henry was nominally head of the government, real power lay with Isabella and Mortimer. Discontent focused on several issues: Stanhope and the treaty of Edinburgh, the depletion of the royal treasury through gifts to Mortimer and Isabella, the fact that the regency council had never been allowed to do its work, and the failure to maintain the peace of the realm. As one chronicler put it, the love that had greeted Isabella when she landed in England to overthrow the Despensers had turned to hate. She also took into her circle Sir Robert Holland, who had betrayed Thomas of Lancaster at Boroughbridge. He was thoroughly despised by the Lancastrians, and one of their number, Thomas Wither, on 15 October murdered him on his way to London to meet with the queen and sent his head to Henry. Matters reached a crisis point at the parliament that met at Salisbury in October. Lancaster had been estranged from the court, and had refused earlier in the year to attend a meeting of the royal council at York to discuss relations with Gascony. He now declined to attend the parliament, and stayed a short distance away in Winchester, despite entreaties from the king. Lancaster reiterated popular complaints about the court and the failures of the government. Bishop John Stratford also reported that Lancaster did not attend parliament because of his quarrel with Mortimer, who Henry claimed was intent on destroying him. Mortimer, who was created earl of March during the parliament, swore not to do any harm to Lancaster, but Henry stayed away none the less.

After parliament broke up, Lancaster headed towards Leicester, the centre of his patrimony, while the court moved first to Westminster and then to Gloucester and Worcester. Armed conflict seemed inevitable, despite negotiations throughout December. Lancaster arrived in London at the beginning of January, and was supported by followers such as Thomas Wake, and by other magnates who included the king's uncles, the earls of Kent and Norfolk. In the meantime royal forces under the direction of Isabella and Mortimer moved towards Leicester, where they plundered Lancaster's estates. Henry marched to Bedford with a large force of Londoners. At this critical juncture the earls of Kent and Norfolk went over to Mortimer, forcing Lancaster to surrender. His submission was made before Archbishop Mepham of Canterbury and other prelates and magnates, and the accord stipulated that the next parliament would amend the grievances that had spurred rebellion.

The government ordered the seizure of Lancaster's lands along with those of his followers on 16 January, and Henry was fined £11,000. On making a bond of recognizance for £30,000 on 6 February, he recovered his lands, but four of his adherents, Henry Beaumont, Thomas Roscelin, William Trussell, and Thomas Wither, were banished from the realm for their part in the murder of Sir Robert Holland. The rest of his followers received fines of varying amounts. During this period Henry became blind as well as old and weak.

Exclusion and recovery Mortimer would certainly have liked to have Lancaster out of the way, and in September 1329 Henry received protection to travel to France in the company of a number of his knights, yeomen, and clerks. The protection lasted until Christmas, but on 3 December the king dispatched the bishop of Norwich, William Airmyn, to join Lancaster in an embassy to Philippe VI, king of France, to negotiate various issues arising out of Edward's homage to Philippe on 6 June 1329. Henry's stay abroad was extended in January, when the king commissioned his envoys to negotiate for a marriage between Edward's sister Eleanor and Philippe's eldest son, Jean, which never occurred. On 28 February, moreover, the king wrote to his envoys instructing them to resume negotiations for peace between England and France.

It is not certain when Henry returned to England. On 2 April 1330 Edward gave him permission to grant lands in mortmain to found a hospital in Leicester Castle in honour of God and the Virgin, with dwellings for a master, chaplains, and the poor, but he was clearly out of favour in these years. Though he frequently attested royal charters between the coronation and 1331, his name was notably absent from royal charters between July 1328 and October 1330, a period when his opposition to Mortimer and his departure overseas kept him far outside the court circle. Nor did Henry take an active part in the coup against Mortimer at Nottingham on 15 October. According to one account, Henry was to have lodged in town at a house next to the queen's, but when Mortimer heard of this he exploded and ordered Henry, an enemy of the queen, to stay a mile outside town. When the blind Lancaster heard of the coup he shouted for joy. At the next parliament at Westminster the Lords assented to pardons for Lancaster and his adherents, and on 12 December the king formally pardoned their fines.

Despite his infirmities Henry served on a number of royal commissions in the following years and was summoned to parliament and councils. In 1331 he sat on a judicial commission, and he was among those magnates and prelates ordered to assist John of Eltham, whom the king had appointed keeper of the realm when he went overseas. The following year Lancaster acted as one of the keepers of the peace in Leicestershire. He was summoned to perform military service in Scotland in 1333, but the general summons of 1335 excused him from serving personally. The king also appointed Henry to survey and collect wool in Lincolnshire in 1339. In that same year, he was one of several earls representing the king in a treaty between England and Brabant. Henry also enjoyed various marks of royal favour in these years, in the form of both money and privileges.

Last years, death, and reputation Increasingly during these years it was Lancaster's son, *Henry of Grosmont, who came to the fore, fighting in Scotland and representing his father in parliament. He was knighted in 1330, but did not have any independent means of support until 1333, when Henry granted him family lands in south Wales and Yorkshire properties. Henry's first wife, Maud of Chaworth, had died c.1317x22, and he married as his second wife, Alix, daughter of Jean de Joinville and widow of Jean, sieur d'Arcies sur Aube et de Chacenay. Henry had at least seven children—his son Henry and six daughters—all of whom he provided with good marriages, in some cases to children of his own followers and friends such as Wake and Beaumont. Henry died on 22 September 1345 and was buried in the Hospital of the Annunciation, which he had founded in Leicester Castle (later expanded to form the college of St Mary in the Newarke). The king and queen along with a large company of magnates and prelates attended the funeral, befitting a lord who had been instrumental in establishing Edward's rule and keeping it on course.

Lancaster occupied the political stage for less than a decade during the tumultuous period between his brother's execution in 1322 and Mortimer's in 1330. Though not close to Thomas, Henry displayed some of his brother's qualities when he came into his own after 1322. He argued tenaciously for his right to the Lancastrian inheritance, struggled to keep the large Lancastrian retinue and administration intact, and developed a reputation for fighting on behalf of the community of the realm in the face of a grasping, acquisitive court faction, whether the Despensers or Mortimer and Isabella. His landed wealth, which in the early 1330s produced an annual income of about £5500, made him a dominant figure among the nobles. As a veteran of wars in Scotland and Wales he also appreciated the use of force, and seems to have been prepared to fight against the Despensers in 1326, the Scots at Stanhope Park in 1327, and Mortimer in 1328. The *Brut* calls him good and noble, and emphasizes his commitment to the king and to good counsel, all strong Lancastrian qualities. Froissart says Henry was nicknamed Tortcol ('Wryneck'), which could refer either to a physical deformity, or to the stiff-necked pride that he displayed in his family's political and territorial heritage. The blindness and debility that cut short his active public life in middle age was probably more than a personal misfortune.   SCOTT L. WAUGH

Sources GEC, *Peerage*, new edn, 7.396–401 · F. Palgrave, ed., *The parliamentary writs and writs of military summons*, 2 vols. in 4 (1827–34) · *RotP*, vols. 1–2 · *Chancery records* · Rymer, *Foedera*, new edn · *Chronicon Henrici Knighton, vel Cnitthon, monachi Leycestrensis*, ed. J. R. Lumby, 2 vols., Rolls Series, 92 (1889–95), vol. 1, pp. 434–7, 447–51, 460 · *Adae Murimuth continuatio chronicarum. Robertus de Avesbury de gestis mirabilibus regis Edwardi tertii*, ed. E. M. Thompson, Rolls Series, 93 (1889), 46, 49, 58 · W. Stubbs, ed., *Chronicles of the reigns of Edward I and Edward II*, 1, Rolls Series, 76 (1882), cxv–cxxiii, 122, 162, 170, 242, 306, 317, 319, 332, 342–4, 348, 366; 2, Rolls Series, 76 (1883), 87, 99, 129, 217, 280–82, 284, 292, 308, 311, 313, 315 · N. Fryde, *The tyranny and fall of Edward II, 1321–1326* (1979), 18, 20, 30, 72–3, 183, 188, 191, 192, 204, 207, 217–22, 272 · G. A. Holmes, 'The rebellion of the earl of Lancaster, 1328–9', *BIHR*, 28 (1955), 84–9 · J. R. Maddicott, *Thomas of Lancaster, 1307–1322: a study in the reign of Edward II* (1970), 4, 9, 48, 59–60, 62–3, 68, 184, 319 · K. Fowler, *The king's lieutenant: Henry of Grosmont, first duke of Lancaster, 1310–1361* (1969), 23–8, 72, 172, 176–8, 185–6, 188, 191, 194, 213, 218, 225–6 · R. Nicholson, *Edward III and the Scots: the formative years of a military career, 1327–1335* (1965), 22–3, 26, 56, 61–2 · R. Somerville, *History of the duchy of Lancaster, 1265–1603* (1953), 31–8

Henry of Lancaster [Henry of Grosmont], **first duke of Lancaster** (c.1310–1361), soldier and diplomat, was the son of *Henry, third earl of Lancaster (c.1280–1345), and Maud Chaworth (d. 1317x22).

Youth, family, and connections Henry was born not, as stated in older works, in 1299–1300, but c.1310, probably at his father's castle of Grosmont in the honour of Monmouth; he was often referred to as Henry of Grosmont in order to distinguish him from his father. In 1322 Grosmont's uncle *Thomas, earl of Lancaster, was deprived of his title and put to death after having rebelled against Edward II. However, Thomas's heir, his brother Henry, was successful in re-establishing the family's rights to some of its ancestral lands, and after supporting Queen Isabella in the coup of 1326–7 was restored to the title of earl of Lancaster. Nevertheless, the elder Henry's relationship with the minority regime of Edward III proved uneasy, and Grosmont cannot necessarily be assumed to have had close contact with the royal court until Edward had seized power from his mother and her lover, Roger (V) Mortimer, and declared his majority in 1330: his first recorded involvement in a royal tournament was at Cheapside in September 1331.

According to his own memoir, the *Livre de seyntz medicines*, Henry of Grosmont was in his youth tall, blond, and lean, strong in the arts of the chase and at the lists, though weaker in bookish matters: he claimed that he learned to write only later in life, and remained ill at ease with French. His possession of two gold statues, one of Tristan and Isolde and the other of the god of love, suggests that he took an interest in the romance literature of courtly love. Apart from these sparse details, nothing is known of Henry's early years: there is no evidence to support the later tradition that he spent his adolescence as a crusader. Already during 1330, however, he was emerging as a political figure in his own right within England: he was knighted and represented his father (who became blind about this time) in parliament. It was in the same year that he married: his wife, Isabella, daughter of Henry, Lord Beaumont, brought him into contact with a powerful family with political interests in both England and Scotland. She was probably considerably younger than Henry, for their only recorded children—two daughters—were born some time after the marriage: Maud (b. 1341) was first betrothed to Ralph, son of Ralph, first earl of Stafford, but later married the duke of Bavaria; *Blanche of Lancaster (1346?–1368) [see under John of Gaunt] was originally intended for the son of Lord Seagrave, but married *John of Gaunt.

The first indications of Grosmont's intimacy with Edward III came in 1331, when he accompanied the king on a secret mission to France. The fact that he was so close in age to Edward III (who was born in 1312) presumably helped to foster a close relationship between the two men. He served on the king's Scottish campaign of 1333, which had been precipitated by the intervention of Grosmont's

Henry of Lancaster, first duke of Lancaster (*c*.1310–1361), manuscript painting, *c*.1430

own father-in-law and other 'disinherited' English magnates determined to win back their lands in Scotland; although it is uncertain that he fought in Edward's army at Halidon Hill, he was present at the subsequent surrender of Berwick into English hands. He served in Scotland again during the winter campaign of 1334–5 and was summoned to parliament in his own right in 1335. In April 1336 Grosmont was appointed, in effect, as the king's lieutenant in Scotland with far-reaching authority over royal ministers in the border region; at the end of the year, however, he was dispatched back to England to make preparations for the defence of the south coast, whose security was now threatened by the French.

Favour and service The impending war with France encouraged Edward III to raise some of his most trusted friends to the titled nobility and thus restock the ranks of the English military command. Grosmont was one of six men given the title of earl during the parliament of March 1337, and was granted the style of earl of Derby, one of his father's lesser titles. Grosmont's high status and military distinction probably did much to persuade the political community that the king's actions were timely and wise. Although he played no part in the diplomatic missions preparatory to the outbreak of the Hundred Years' War in 1337, he did lead an expedition to the Low Countries in August and conducted a raid on Cadzand. He accompanied the king to the continent in July 1338 and was with him throughout the long months of negotiation and stalemate

that ensued, leading a detachment in the brief Thiérache campaign of 1339.

Early in 1340 Henry took his first recorded part in English diplomacy as one of the English ambassadors appointed to treat with the pope's representatives at Valenciennes; after returning to England in February, he went back to the continent in June and was present at the naval battle of Sluys. He was one of the negotiators of the truce of Esplechin in September, but was then required to submit to imprisonment as one of the hostages for Edward III's debts in the Low Countries. Although he secured a number of temporary releases to take part in sieges and jousts, Henry remained bound to his sentence throughout the winter of 1340–41, and had to undertake considerable financial commitments to secure his own release. He travelled back to England and was appointed as the king's lieutenant in the north on 7 October 1341 preparatory to an inconclusive campaign against the Scots: he spent much of the winter of 1341–2 at Roxburgh, organizing jousts and treating for a truce.

The outbreak of the succession crisis in Brittany in 1341 drew Edward III's attention back to the war in France, and in October 1342 Henry again departed for the continent in the company of the king. Early in 1343 he was negotiating in the Low Countries. He was then dispatched to Spain to treat with the king of Castile, and took part, along with the earl of Salisbury, in the siege of Algeciras. In March 1344 Henry and the earl of Arundel were appointed joint lieutenants in Aquitaine with authority to continue the diplomatic negotiations with Alfonso XI of Castile. After attending the peace negotiations being held under papal presidency at Avignon, Henry returned to England to report to king and council. It was proposed to send him back to Avignon early in 1345; but military planning took precedence, and Henry was put in charge of an army mustering at Southampton in preparation for an expedition to Gascony.

Lieutenant of Aquitaine With peace negotiations stalled, the king devised a three-pronged attack against his enemy, with English armies converging from Brittany (led by the earl of Northampton), Flanders (led by the king), and Aquitaine (led by Henry) to make a combined attack on Philippe VI. On 13 March 1345 Henry was made lieutenant of Aquitaine with extensive authority, and in June he disembarked with his army at Bordeaux. He at once set out via St Macaire to Bergerac, which rapidly surrendered to his forces. Having garrisoned the town, he then moved on to Périgueux, defeating the comte de l'Isle at Auberoche on 21 October in what has been described as 'the greatest single achievement of Lancaster's entire military career' (Fowler, 58–9). As a result of this victory, the Agenais and much of Périgord and Quercy, lost since the outbreak of the war, were brought back into Plantagenet control. The earl of Lancaster (as he now was, his father having died in September) also took considerable personal advantage from the battle. It was rumoured that the ransoms collected by the English after Auberoche amounted to £50,000 and more, and it is hardly surprising that Lancaster's great palace of the Savoy in London, begun in the late 1340s, was said to have been constructed on the profits of this campaign. The winter of 1345–6 was spent at La Réole, consolidating the re-established English regime in the region.

Early in 1346 Jean, the dauphin of France, who had already been campaigning in the south during 1345, returned to Aquitaine and laid siege to the English position at Aiguillon. It was this long siege, together with the collapse of the Flemish alliance and delays in Edward III's own departure from England, that put a stop to the original plan of English armies advancing on Philippe VI from three corners of his own realm. In July Edward eventually landed in Normandy, and although Jean moved off quickly to try to save his father, Lancaster made no attempt to march north to assist his own king in the victory at Crécy. Instead, freed from immediate danger, Lancaster prepared a new campaign, moving first into the Agenais and then northwards into Saintonge (where he rescued Sir Walter Mauny and others from imprisonment in St Jean-d'Angély) and thence to Poitiers, which he took by force on 4 October. The campaign had much in common with Edward III's own *chevauchée* through Normandy: Froissart was convinced that the troops in Lancaster's expedition of 1346 had returned to Bordeaux 'altogether rich and burdened with good things' (*Chroniques*, 4.16).

Duke of Lancaster Early in 1347 Lancaster returned to England, where he was relieved of his lieutenancy of Aquitaine on 1 February in order that he might devote his energies to the siege of Calais. He arrived there by 1 June, and remained with the English army until the surrender of Calais on 4 August and the sealing of an Anglo-French truce (which he helped to negotiate) on 28 September. It was during and immediately after the siege of Calais that the king made various generous grants to Lancaster in recognition of his outstanding services to the crown and the need to reorganize his titles and honours now that he was no longer earl of Derby but earl of Lancaster, the senior nobleman in England. Grants of the lordship of Bergerac (with the very special right to mint his own coins) and the former Lancastrian honour of Pontefract in 1347–8 signified Lancaster's importance to Edward III's regime on both sides of the channel; his inclusion among the founder members of the Order of the Garter at its inception in 1348 demonstrated the king's very personal favour to his kinsman and confidant. At the next available parliament, held early in 1351, Edward affirmed this personal bond by raising Lancaster to the rank of duke and granting his county of Lancaster the status of a palatinate for the term of his life. Only one duke had been created in England before this date (Edward the Black Prince, had been made duke of Cornwall in 1337), and the grant of palatine powers was without parallel in recent history, establishing the county on the same privileged basis as the ancient palatinates of Cheshire and Durham. It may be that Edward III felt it safe to make his cousin king in all but name within the county of Lancaster because Henry had no son to inherit. It was only the subsequent marriage of John of Gaunt to Henry's daughter Blanche and the desire of the king to build up a powerful apanage for his third

son that led Edward to revive and perpetuate both the ducal title and its palatine powers. Above all, however, the grant of 1351 exemplified publicly the highly productive alliance now established between the houses of Plantagenet and Lancaster: the contrast with the situation in the previous reign is not likely to have been lost on contemporaries.

Lancaster's landed estates and political interests spread widely across England and Wales, with particular areas of concentration in the north, the midlands, and the Welsh borders. His permanent affinity, though it cannot be reconstructed definitively, seems to have been inherited from his father and reinforced with newly available annuities on estates inherited from his mother; the strong sense of continuity in the Lancastrian retinue is evident in the number of Henry's men who went on to serve John of Gaunt. The duke's heavy involvement in war and diplomacy left him little time for domestic administration, and he was not a particularly active presence in the provinces: when he was in England, he seems to have spent most of his time either in London or at what he regarded as his principal seat, Leicester Castle.

Throughout the period of his political promotion Lancaster had continued a busy round of responsibilities. He was one of the English deputation to treat with the count of Flanders at Boulogne and Dunkirk late in 1348, as a result of which a further series of co-ordinated campaigns was planned in France. Lancaster was again appointed lieutenant of Aquitaine on 28 August 1349 and left for the duchy in September; after a brief but effective *chevauchée* southwards from Bordeaux as far as Toulouse (which he reached at Christmas), Lancaster agreed to papal requests for a truce. His experiences during the campaign of 1349 made him aware of the threat posed, especially at sea, by the Castilians, who had abandoned sympathies for the English and made an alliance with Philippe VI. He was back in London by May 1350, and was one of the English commanders at the naval victory over the Castilian fleet which took place off Winchelsea on 29 August. Lancaster is said to have saved the lives of the Black Prince and John of Gaunt in this affray by boarding the Castilian ship that was threatening their own vessel.

Throughout 1351 Lancaster was occupied in English diplomacy, shuttling back and forth between London and Calais on various missions to treat with the Flemish and the French; none of the proposals for alliances (with Flanders) or peace (with France) proved successful. Perhaps frustrated by this stalemate, or else genuinely fired by his commitment to the ideal of crusade, Lancaster now determined to campaign with the order of Teutonic Knights and to fight for the forces of Christendom in that last bastion of European heathenism, Prussia. His expedition there, which began late in 1351 and was over by 11 April 1352 (when he arrived at Koblenz), is difficult to piece together, though it is known that he reached Stettin and intended to journey into Poland. At Cologne, he publicly challenged Otto, duke of Brunswick, claiming that the latter had planned to ambush him during his crusade; Lancaster returned briefly to England in the summer and in

September travelled to Paris, where the parties had agreed to put their suit before the court of the French king, Jean II. The arbitration process foundered, and plans were made for an individual combat between Henry and Otto; the two rivals were armed, mounted, and ready for combat when, at the last moment, the king took the matter into his hands and insisted that the grounds of the quarrel were insufficient to justify fighting. Lancaster returned home with a precious gift, a thorn from Christ's crown of thorns, selected from the French royal collection of relics.

The search for peace In 1353–4 Lancaster was intermittently involved in the Anglo-French peace negotiations staged at Guînes. At the end of 1353, however, he moved to the Low Countries to negotiate an English *détente* with his own son-in-law, Wilhelm, duke of Bavaria and count of Holland and Zeeland. The timing proved unfortunate: during the winter Edward III was in discussion with his kinsman Charles of Navarre over a possible alliance against Jean II; when Charles wrote to Lancaster requesting military support (as the English king had promised), Henry told him that he was too busy to assist. This rebuff may have contributed to Charles's defection, in February 1354, to the French camp; and it was as a result of this reversal that Edward III was constrained to revive the peace process at Guînes. The English king seems not to have laid any blame for this set-back on Lancaster, however: Charles of Navarre was already known as a highly fickle politician, and in fact he quarrelled with Jean II and reverted to the English cause at the end of the year, just in time to allow Edward to call off the ratification of the treaty of Guînes and to make preparation for the renewal of war. That Lancaster remained in favour throughout this period is demonstrated by his commission, with the earl of Arundel, to represent Edward at what was at least publicly understood to be the confirmation of the Anglo-French peace at Avignon late in 1354. Lancaster remained at the papal palace at Avignon from November 1354 to March 1355, where he was treated with the regard and splendour appropriate to a royal plenipotentiary visiting the most ostentatious court of Europe.

In 1355, as a decade earlier, Edward III planned his new attack on the Valois regime in France as a pincer movement, originally intending that the Black Prince would operate in Aquitaine and the duke of Lancaster in Normandy. Both expeditions were delayed by problems with the weather and—in Lancaster's case—the return of his proposed co-commander, Charles of Navarre, to the French cause; as a result, it was proposed to divert Lancaster's expedition to Brittany, and in this expectation he was appointed as the king's lieutenant for Brittany on 14 September. When Jean II suddenly arrested Charles in April 1356, however, the Navarrese party in Normandy, led by Charles's brother, Philippe, and Godfrey Harcourt, indicated their eagerness to make common cause with the English. Lancaster accordingly disembarked at La Hogue, on the Cotentin peninsula, in early June 1356. Over the following month, his army—which, with the detachments provided by Charles of Navarre and others, amounted to about 1000 men-at-arms and 1400 mounted archers—made a lightning raid through the duchy, advancing via Carentan and Lisieux to Pont-Audemer, then moving south as far as Verneuil before retreating back to the Cotentin via Argentan: an account of the campaign survives, written apparently by one of Lancaster's knights or clerks (*Robertus de Avesbury de gestis mirabilibus*, ed. Thompson, 462–8). Although the force was too small to undertake a major siege or battle, this *chevauchée* was of sufficient concern to the French to cause Jean II, who had already reached Chartres in pursuit of the Black Prince's army, to re-route his army northwards into Normandy. This may have prevented Lancaster's forces from penetrating the Île-de-France, but it otherwise did little to undermine the Anglo-Navarrese regime in Normandy. In September Philippe of Navarre recognized Edward III as 'king of France and duke of Normandy' and was appointed as his lieutenant in the duchy. Although Lancaster had already moved off into Brittany at this point to assume his lieutenancy there, he seems to have regarded it as his privilege over the following two years to intervene directly, if sporadically, in military affairs in Normandy.

Lancaster was to remain in Brittany until early 1358, the longest sustained period that he spent in any of his military commands. It was not, however, the most eventful of his lieutenancies. From October 1356 to July 1357 he was occupied in the siege of Rennes, the last major town in Brittany to remain hostile to the English-backed duke, John de Montfort. The siege ought to have been lifted under the terms of the Anglo-French truce effected at Bordeaux in March 1357, and Edward III wrote twice to remonstrate with his cousin over his failure to observe orders on this matter. Lancaster's side of the argument was not stated, though one English chronicler suggested that he was conducting the siege on behalf of John de Montfort, and was therefore not, on this occasion, under the direct instruction of the king of England (*Anonimalle Chronicle*, 40). He was also doubtless motivated by pride and a gritty determination to see the job finished to his own satisfaction.

Lancaster's return from Brittany to England in 1358 freed him to participate, the following year, in the last of Edward III's great *chevauchées* through France. Lancaster's own detailed itinerary during the Rheims campaign of 1359–60 is not well charted, though it is likely that he remained in the main vanguard of the army during most of the expedition. As soon as it ended, he was appointed the principal English negotiator to sue for peace in the talks held at Brétigny, near Chartres, in early May 1360. Froissart believed that Lancaster genuinely wanted an end to the war and advised the king to accept the terms that he, the Black Prince, and others negotiated in the treaty of Brétigny (*Chroniques*, 6.4). In the event, however, Lancaster lived to see neither the preliminary fulfilment nor the subsequent collapse of this treaty: he returned to England in November, and by early 1361 was seriously ill. He made his will on 15 March and died at Leicester Castle on 23 March. It is possible that he had fallen victim to the plague, which was then making its second visitation through England. His wife outlived him, but for how long is not known; she was, and remains, a shadowy figure who took little part in Lancaster's public life.

Piety, personality, and posthumous fame The survival of the *Livre de seyntz medicines*, a prose text in Anglo-Norman French composed by Lancaster in 1354, means that rather more can be discerned about his personality, and particularly his piety, than is usual for men of his era and status. The book (which survives at Stonyhurst College and in Cambridge, Corpus Christi College, MS 218) is an elaborate allegory in which the author draws parallels between the sicknesses of the body and those of the soul: Christ is the physician whose ministrations heal the five senses from infection by the seven deadly sins. The historical interest of the text tends to lie in the incidental detail. Henry reveals his taste for courtly pastimes in youth and his middle-aged predilection for good food and wine: the *Livre* indicates that he was suffering from gout when he wrote it. The medical detail in the text has also been associated with the contemporary practices of military surgeons, with whom he would have come into close contact on campaign. His motives for writing the text (which he evidently intended to be read by others) were, however, self-consciously penitential: it ends with a plea for divine mercy. His piety is also attested by his patronage of the cult of his murdered uncle, Thomas.

It is interesting in light of the theme of the *Livre de seyntz medicines* that Henry's principal religious foundation, the college of the Annunciation of St Mary in the Newarke at Leicester, was a hospital for fifty poor men and women, originally set up by his father in 1331. In the mid-1350s, when he was writing the *Livre*, Lancaster made arrangements to refound this establishment, with a lavish new endowment, as a properly constituted secular college. It was here that he was buried, in accordance with his instructions, on 14 April 1361, on the south side of the high altar, opposite his father; the tomb was still in this position when it was observed by Leland in the early sixteenth century.

Lancaster enjoyed some posthumous fame: chroniclers and poets of the late fourteenth century looked back to Edward III, the Black Prince, and Henry of Grosmont as the three great heroes of the opening phase of the Hundred Years' War. It has often been suggested that he was the model for the 'parfit gentil knyght' in Chaucer's *Canterbury Tales*, as a result of certain coincidences between his own and the Knight's crusading careers. It was in the fifteenth century, however, that his reputation achieved its greatest heights. As the grandfather and namesake of Henry Bolingbroke, later *Henry IV, he was identified as one of the worthy ancestors of the Lancastrian regime, figuring prominently in Capgrave's account of the illustrious Henrys of England; and his devotional treatise continued to circulate, one copy finding its way into the library of Humphrey, duke of Gloucester. The dynastic changes of the later fifteenth century seem to have quelled this historiographical interest, however, and it

was not until 1969 that Henry of Grosmont became the subject of a full-scale historical biography by Kenneth Fowler. W. M. ORMROD

Sources K. Fowler, *The king's lieutenant: Henry of Grosmont, first duke of Lancaster, 1310–1361* (1969) · GEC, *Peerage* · DNB · J. Sumption, *The Hundred Years War*, 1 (1990) · K. B. McFarlane, *The nobility of later medieval England* (1973) · W. M. Ormrod, *The reign of Edward III* (1990) · [Henry of Lancaster], *Le livre de seyntz medicines*, ed. E. J. Arnould, Anglo-Norman Texts, 2 (1940) · *Chroniques de J. Froissart*, ed. S. Luce and others, 15 vols. (Paris, 1869–1975) · A. Hamilton Thompson, *The history of the hospital and new college of the Annunciation of Saint Mary in the Newarke, Leicester* (1937) · J. Vale, *Edward III and chivalry: chivalric society and its context, 1270–1350* (1982) · S. Walker, *The Lancastrian affinity, 1361–1399* (1990) · *Chronicon Galfridi le Baker de Swynebroke*, ed. E. M. Thompson (1889) · *Adae Murimuth continuatio chronicarum. Robertus de Avesbury de gestis mirabilibus regis Edwardi tertii*, ed. E. M. Thompson, Rolls Series, 93 (1889) · V. H. Galbraith, ed., *The Anonimalle chronicle, 1333 to 1381* (1927) · [J. Nichols], ed., *A collection of … wills … of … every branch of the blood royal* (1780) · *Johannis Capgrave Liber de illustribus Henricis*, ed. F. C. Hingeston, Rolls Series, 7 (1858) · M. Wade Labarge, 'Henry of Lancaster and *Le livre de seyntz medicines*', *Florilegium*, 2 (1980), 183–91 · E. R. D. Elias, 'The coinage of Bergerac, 1347–1361', *British Numismatic Journal*, 49 (1979), 56–73 · W. M. Ormrod, 'England, Normandy and the beginnings of the Hundred Years War', *England and Normandy in the middle ages*, ed. D. Bates and A. Curry (1994), 197–213 · T. Jones, *Chaucer's Knight: the portrait of a medieval mercenary*, rev. edn (1985)
Archives PRO, DL
Likenesses manuscript painting, *c*.1430, BL, Bruges's Garter book, Stowe MS 594, fol. 8 [*see illus.*] · Geremia, stipple, pubd 1806, NPG · J. Faber senior, mezzotint, BM, NPG · Hastings brass, Elsing, Norfolk
Wealth at death approx. £8380 for English and Welsh estates: Fowler, *The king's lieutenant*, 172

Henry of Marlborough. *See* Marlborough, Henry (*d.* in or after 1421).

Henry of Saltrey. *See* Saltrey, H. of (*fl. c*.1184).

Henry the Young King. *See* Henry (1155–1183).

Henry, Augustine (1857–1930), botanical collector and dendrologist, was born on 2 July 1857 in Dundee, the first of six children of Bernard Henry (*c*.1825–1891) and Mary MacNamee. His father, at one time a gold-prospector in California and Australia, was a native of the townland of Tyanee on the west bank of the River Bann in co. Londonderry. Soon after Austin (as Augustine was called within his family) was born, the family moved to Cookstown, co. Tyrone, where his father was in business as a flax dealer and owned a grocery shop.

Henry was educated at Cookstown Academy and in Queen's College, Galway. He studied natural sciences and philosophy, graduating with a first-class bachelor of arts degree and a gold medal in 1877. Henry then studied medicine at Queen's College, Belfast, where he obtained his master of arts degree in 1878. For a year he was in the London Hospital, and during a visit to Belfast in 1879, at the suggestion of one of his professors, he applied for a medical post in the Chinese imperial maritime customs service. Henry completed his medical studies as rapidly as he could, became a licentiate from the Royal College of Physicians in Edinburgh, passed the Chinese customs service examinations (for which he required a working knowledge of Chinese), and left for China in the summer of 1881.

Henry's first posting was in Shanghai, but in March 1882 he was assigned to Ichang (Yichang), a port on the Yangtze (Yangzi) River more than 900 miles inland in Hupeh (Hubei) province. There he served as the assistant medical officer and also performed customs duties. Bored by the routine of life within the small European community, Henry began collecting plants in the vicinity of Ichang in November 1884. Four months later he contacted the Royal Botanic Gardens, Kew, offering to collect specimens and seeking assistance with identification. As a result, Henry became one of the most important botanical collectors to have worked in central China, although he regarded this work as a hobby. He undertook two long field trips in the Hupeh–Szechwan (Sichuan) region, and also paid native collectors for specimens. During the next four years he accumulated a vast collection of pressed, dried specimens; the first set is preserved at Kew. In April 1889 he was transferred to Hainan where he stayed four months.

At the end of a year's home leave, on 20 June 1891, Henry married Caroline Orridge (c.1860–1894), daughter of a London jeweller, at St George's, Bloomsbury, London. They travelled to China, and were based in Shanghai before transferring to Taiwan. Henry wrote *Notes on Economic Botany of China* (1893) during this period. The tropical climate did not suit Caroline, who became progressively more ill with tuberculosis. She sought respite elsewhere, and in January 1894 left for Denver, Colorado, USA, where she died in September 1894; the couple had no children. A genus of tropical Chinese primroses was named *Carolinella* in her memory; because the few species are indistinguishable from *Primula* it is no longer regarded as distinct. After his wife's death, Henry decided to remain in China and was transferred to the isolated southern cities of Mengzi and thence Simao, where he continued his duties within the customs service as well as continuing to collect plants and to publish notes about the Chinese flora. He resigned and left for Europe on 31 December 1900.

By 1901 Henry was famous as a botanical collector; the Royal Horticultural Society of London recognized this by awarding him the Veitch memorial medal in 1902 and the Victoria medal of honour in 1906. He stayed in London from the spring of 1901 until the autumn of 1902, sorting his botanical collections at Kew. During this period he helped to finance the establishment by his friend Miss Evelyn Gleeson of a craft centre at Dun Emer in Dublin; this centre made a most important contribution to the Celtic revival. Henry gradually decided to make a career in forestry, and persuaded the Irish authorities to secure a place for him in the School of Forestry, Nancy, France. While Henry was studying there, Henry John Elwes (1846–1922), a wealthy arboriculturist, asked him to collaborate on a monograph about trees cultivated in Ireland and Britain, so he left France and set to work visiting estates, plantations, and gardens throughout Britain and Ireland to record, identify, and measure trees. *Trees of Great Britain and Ireland* was printed privately by Elwes in seven volumes with an index volume between November 1906 and July 1913.

Early in 1907 Henry became reader in forestry at the University of Cambridge; he remained there until January 1913 when he became the first professor of forestry in the Royal College of Science, Dublin (later part of University College, Dublin). He retired in 1926 and died at his home, 5 Sandford Terrace, Clonskeagh, co. Dublin, on 23 March 1930. A lapsed Roman Catholic, Henry was buried with the rites of that church in Dean's Grange cemetery, Dublin.

Henry had married Alice Helen (Elsie; 1882–1956), daughter of the physician Sir Lauder Brunton, on 17 March 1908; they had no children. Elsie Henry was herself a keen amateur botanist and dendrologist, and she organized her husband's herbarium of voucher specimens for *Trees of Great Britain and Ireland* and presented it to the National Botanic Gardens, Glasnevin, along with some of his profusely annotated books. The Henrys had a wide circle of friends and acquaintances including the Yeats family, George Russell (pseudonym A. E.), and George Bernard Shaw and his wife.

As an expert with unequalled knowledge of the exotic trees cultivated in Ireland (and their performance in Irish conditions) Henry gave evidence to the committee of inquiry into Irish forestry established in 1907. He advocated commercially viable plantations of more than 500 acres, planted with conifers from the north-western coastal region of North America. This recommendation was largely accepted, and Henry is highly regarded as the 'father' of Irish commercial forestry. There is a memorial stone at Avondale in co. Wicklow, and a memorial plaque in Portglenone Forest, co. Antrim.

Henry's accomplishments in China were recognized when a wing of the Fan Memorial Institute of Botany in Peking (Beijing) was named in his honour (although this no longer exists), and fascicle II of *Icones plantarum Sinicarum* was dedicated to him. An uncounted number of plants bear names that mark Henry's exploration of the Chinese flora; examples include *Acer henryi*, *Parthenocissus henryana*, and *Rhododendron augustinii*. Henry himself introduced an orange-blossomed lily, *Lilium henryi*, and of this plant, Ernest Wilson, Henry's successor as a botanical explorer in China, wrote: 'It is particularly fitting that such a notable addition to our gardens should bear the honoured name of a pioneer who has done so much to acquaint a sceptical world of the floral wealth of interior China' (Wilson, 80).   E. CHARLES NELSON

Sources S. Pim, *The wood and the trees: Augustine Henry, a biography*, 2nd edn (1994) • B. D. Morley, 'Augustine Henry: his botanical activities in China, 1882–1890', *Glasra*, 3 (1979), 21–81 • E. C. Nelson, 'Augustine Henry and the exploration of the Chinese flora', *Arnoldia*, 43 (1983), 21–38 • A. Henry, *Notes on economic botany of China*, ed. E. C. Nelson (1986) • E. C. Nelson, '"The joys and the riches of o' Kathay": Augustine Henry and the trees of China', *Irish Forestry*, 52 (1995), 75–87 • E. C. Nelson and S. Andrews, 'Augustine Henry's plants in Kew Gardens', *Kew Magazine*, 3 (1986), 136–40 • E. H. Wilson, *The lilies of eastern Asia* (1925) • *CGPLA Éire* (1930)
Archives Archbishop Marsh's Library, diaries and papers • Henry Library, J. F. Kennedy Park, New Ross, co. Wexford • National

Botanic Gardens, Glasnevin, Dublin · National Botanic Gardens, Glasnevin, Dublin, Henry Forestry Herbarium · RBG Kew, botanical corresp. and papers relating to China | Hants. RO, corresp. with E. L. Hillier · NL Ire., letters to Evelyn Gleeson

Likenesses C. Harrison, oils, 1929, National Botanic Gardens, Glasnevin

Wealth at death £704 6s. 1d.: probate, 11 June 1930, CGPLA Éire

Henry, (William) Charles (1804–1892). *See under* Henry, William (1774–1836).

Henry, David (1709–1792), printer, was born on 26 December 1709 and baptized the following day at Foveran, 12 miles north of Aberdeen, the son of Alexander Henry; his mother's name is unrecorded. It is thought that the father of the American hero Patrick Henry (1736–1799) was his cousin (Timperley, 776). David Henry's father intended him for the church and sent him to the College of Aberdeen, but before the age of fourteen he decamped to London, where he was employed by the printer Edward Cave (1691–1754) at St John's Gate.

Henry married Cave's sister Mary (*bap.* 1699, *d.* 1756) in 1736 and set up his own printing office in Reading, where he founded the *Reading Journal and Weekly Review* (distributed also in Winchester), compiled a simplified abridgement of Tillotson's sermons in *Twenty Discourses* (1743), and sold patent medicines. Among the books he published at Reading were historical compilations (1747–8) for which he paid the unfortunate Samuel Boyse (1703?–1749) at a very low rate. By January 1754 Henry was back at St John's Gate as joint publisher, with Richard Cave (Edward Cave's nephew), of the *Gentleman's Magazine*. This was a valuable property: a one-twelfth share in the magazine sold for £333 6s. 8d. in 1755. Henry also had a financial interest in the successful porcelain factory established in Worcester in 1751.

Henry's wife died on 20 January 1756. In March 1762 he married Hephzibah Newell, *née* Appletree (1726–1808), widow of a part-owner of St John's Gate. It was perhaps through this marriage that Henry also acquired a farm at Clayhill, Lewisham, Kent: his *The Complete English Farmer* (1771) is 'by a practical farmer' (title-page). Richard Cave died on 8 December 1766, after which Henry became sole publisher of the *Gentleman's Magazine*. In addition to numerous articles on antiquities, history, economics, and agriculture in the *Gentleman's Magazine*, Henry wrote popular guidebooks to the Tower of London, St Paul's Cathedral, and Westminster Abbey (1753 and often revised and reissued). He also edited the first two volumes of *An Historical Account of All the Voyages around the World* (4 vols., 1773–4, originally published in 48 parts) and accounts of Cook's second and third circumnavigations (1775 and 1786). He took John Nichols (1745–1826) into partnership in 1778 and from January 1781 to Henry's death the title-page of the *Gentleman's Magazine* announced that it was printed by Nichols for Henry 'late of St. John's Gate'. Nichols took over the entire management and salary in 1791, when growing infirmities kept Henry away from London.

Henry died at Lewisham on 5 June 1792 and was buried there on 13 June. He was survived by his second wife, who died on 2 February 1808, aged eighty-two, and by their only son, Richard (*d.* 1807), and only daughter, Hephzibah. A daughter by Henry's first wife and a natural daughter named Caroline predeceased him.

JAMES SAMBROOK

Sources Nichols, *Lit. anecdotes*, 3.423–6 · H. R. Plomer and others, *A dictionary of the printers and booksellers who were at work in England, Scotland, and Ireland from 1726 to 1775* (1932) · will, PRO, PROB 11/1221, fols. 49r–50v · IGI · *Minor lives, a collection of biographies by John Nichols*, ed. E. L. Hart (1971), 232–6 · E. L. de Montluzin, 'Attributions of authorship in the *Gentleman's Magazine*, 1731–77', *Studies in Bibliography*, 44 (1991), 271–302 · C. H. Timperley, *A dictionary of printers and printing* (1839), 775–6 · T. Ram, *Magnitude in marginality: Edward Cave and the Gentleman's Magazine, 1731–1754* (1999) · *London Magazine*, 25 (1756), 43 · VCH Berkshire, 1.401 · F. A. Edwards, 'Hampshire booksellers and printers', *N&Q*, 10th ser., 5 (1906), 482 · C. Welsh, *A bookseller of the last century, being some account of the life of John Newbery* (1885), 84n.

Archives BL, corresp. with Thomas Birch, Add. MS 4310 · Col. U., letters to John Nichols

Wealth at death freehold estate of Clayhill in Lewisham, Kent; freehold and leasehold estates in St John's parish, Clerkenwell; share of the Worcester porcelain works; share in printing house and many copyrights, incl. *Gentleman's Magazine*; annuities totalling £80 p.a.; lump sums totalling £850; rentals totalling over £160 p.a.: will, PRO, PROB 11/1221, fols. 49r–50v

Henry, Sir Denis Stanislaus, first baronet (1864–1925), lawyer and politician, was born on 7 March 1864 in Draperstown, co. Londonderry, the sixth son of James Henry, farmer, of Cahore, Draperstown, co. Londonderry, and his wife, Ellen Kelly. He was educated at Marist College, Dundalk, Mount St Mary's College, Chesterfield, and Queen's College, Belfast, where he won every law scholarship open to a student. In 1885 Henry was called to the Irish bar, where his strong physical appearance and voice helped make him a respected figure. He became a king's counsel for Ireland in 1896 and a bencher of King's Inns in 1898. During his career at the bar Henry was engaged in a number of notable trials. When acting as crown prosecutor at the Belfast winter assizes in December 1898 he conducted, with the attorney-general, Lord Atkinson, an extraordinary series of murder trials. In a matter of nine days he dealt with three murder cases, the defendant being found guilty in each case. Two were later executed and the third sentenced to life imprisonment.

Although he was a Catholic, Henry was a confirmed Unionist in politics, and spoke frequently at Unionist meetings. Henry's religious beliefs were nevertheless important to him: he himself was a generous contributor to many Catholic charities, while two of his brothers and two sisters were members of religious orders. He declined a number of invitations to stand for parliament in Ulster constituencies but in 1906 was persuaded to stand as the Unionist candidate for North Tyrone. At that time the constituency was almost evenly divided between Catholic and protestant voters but although there was a small protestant majority, it was estimated that there were between 150 and 200 Presbyterian farmers who supported the Liberals. Although these Liberals would not vote for a Unionist candidate, they would not vote for a nationalist either. As a result, in 1906 the Catholic Unionist Henry opposed a protestant Liberal candidate, William Heuston Dodd, who supported home rule. Henry was defeated by nine votes.

In March 1907, after Dodd was elevated to the bench, Henry again contested North Tyrone. In a tense atmosphere, Henry was defeated by Redmond Barry KC by seven votes. The turnout was 97 per cent. The fact that a major sectarian confrontation did not occur, as the police expected, was at least partly the result of the friendly manner in which Henry and Barry (who were in any event personal friends) behaved toward each other after the result was declared. On 1 October 1910 Henry married Violet (1879–1966), third daughter of Hugh Holmes, lord justice of appeal in Ireland. They had two sons and three daughters. In August 1912 he was made a commissioner of charitable donations and bequests. In 1916 he was selected by Londonderry South Unionists to contest the seat vacated by John Gordon on his appointment to the high courts. Henry easily won the by-election, polling 3808 votes to the independent Unionist Arthur Turnbull's 214. He held the seat until 1921.

In December 1918 Henry was appointed solicitor-general for Ireland on the death of James Chambers. He had earlier refused the position, saying that to accept the post would imply his acquiescence in the policy of home rule. In July 1919, after Arthur Samuels was appointed a High Court judge, Henry became attorney-general for Ireland, and was the last person to hold the post before partition. In the same year he was also made a privy councillor for Ireland. He was appointed lord chief justice of Northern Ireland in August 1921, and as such was responsible for setting up the judicial machinery of the new jurisdiction. He was created a baronet in November 1922.

Henry was a member of the senate of the Queen's University of Belfast from which he received the honorary degree of LLD in July 1921, and was deputy lieutenant for co. Londonderry. During 1925 he began suffering from headaches and, after the rising of the High Court for the summer, on the advice of his doctors, he went to Harrogate for a holiday. Shortly after his return to Belfast he suffered a seizure and died two days later at his home, Lisvarna, Windsor Avenue, Belfast, on 1 October 1925. He was buried two days later in the family burial-ground at Draperstown. He was succeeded to the baronetcy by his son James Holmes Henry (1911–1997). Tributes to Sir Denis Henry illustrated that he was widely respected and admired. Typical of the sentiments expressed were those of the *Belfast News-Letter* of 2 October 1925 which said: 'He proved an excellent judge—patient, courteous, sagacious and intensely human in his sympathies'.

GORDON GILLESPIE

Sources A. D. McDonnell, 'The 1918 general election in Ulster and the biography of a candidate, Denis Henry', PhD diss., Queen's University of Belfast, 1983 · *Belfast News-Letter* (2–5 Oct 1925) · *Belfast Telegraph* (1–3 Oct 1925) · *Northern Whig and Belfast Post* (2–5 Oct 1925) · *Irish News and Belfast Morning News* (2–5 Oct 1925) · *Belfast Gazette* (1921–5) · *Dublin Gazette* (1912–21) · Burke, *Peerage* (1967)
Wealth at death £9385 6s. 9d.: probate, 1925, Northern Ireland

Henry, Sir Edward Richard, baronet (1850–1931), police officer, was born at Shadwell, Middlesex, on 26 July 1850,

the only surviving son of Alexander Henry MD (d. 1890), of Lagaturn, co. Mayo, and his wife, Maria McDonnell. He was educated at home and, briefly, at St Edmund's College, Ware, Hertfordshire, a Roman Catholic institution. At sixteen he commenced work as a clerk at Lloyds in London. He also took evening classes at University College, London, to prepare for the Indian Civil Service entrance examination. On passing the examination in 1873 he was posted to the Bengal taxation service. By 1888 he was a magistrate collector, and by 1890 secretary to the board of revenue. On 24 November 1890 he married Louisa Langrishe, daughter of the Revd John Lewis Moore, vice-president of Trinity College, Dublin. Three children of the marriage survived infancy.

Henry might have remained in the Indian Civil Service until retirement but for the stimulus to his intellectual curiosity and practical interests in administration provided by seeing the use of fingerprints, in rural Bengal, for identifying illiterate government contractors and pensioners on official documents. In India the system had been pioneered by Sir William James Herschel, a magistrate in Bengal. Henry met Herschel in 1879 and Herschel encouraged Henry to develop the classificatory system and its applications. In so doing, Henry corresponded with Francis Galton, the author of *Finger Prints* (1892). Henry's contribution lay in the development of a simple, fast, and reliable method of fingerprint classification that would be acceptable in courts for identification purposes.

Henry's appointment as inspector-general of police for Lower Bengal in 1891 gave him access to a data base of print records from which to develop a new classificatory system. In this work, based upon numerical indices of the characteristics of the lines on all the digits, Henry was ably assisted by sub-inspectors Aziz-ul-Haque and Hem Chandra Bose. An Indian government committee in 1897, selected Henry's fingerprint system as a superior identification system to the Bertillon body measurement system. The 1899 Indian Evidence Act recognized court use of fingerprint experts. In the same year Henry gave evidence to the Home Office Belper committee on the identification of criminals, which selected his system for use by the British police. By 1899 Henry was seeking employment away from India, as two of his children had died there. No suitable British post was then available, but in 1900 he was seconded to help with police reorganization in the Transvaal and in the same year he published his book *Classification and Uses of Fingerprints*. The book went through eight editions up to 1937 and sold 40,000 copies.

In 1901 Henry resigned from the Indian Civil Service on his appointment as assistant commissioner 'C' in the Metropolitan Police with responsibility for the Criminal Investigation Department. His first priority was the establishment of the central fingerprint bureau, followed by the development of the habitual criminals register to incorporate fingerprints and the criminal records office. With these improvements in tracing and identifying offenders and his introduction of a detective training school in 1902, he demonstrated his commitment to developing professional policing. By 1905 a total of 5155 fingerprint identifications were held and he reported that this was 'ten times larger than the highest figures recorded in the anthropometric system' (Ascoli, 184). The first conviction secured by the fingerprint evidence was that of a burglar, Henry Jackson, in 1902.

The Home Office had seen Henry as a natural successor, as commissioner, to Sir Edward Bradford and he duly moved to that office in 1903, on Bradford's retirement. It is generally acknowledged that Henry served the force well as commissioner from 1903 to 1918. His strengths lay in his general management abilities, concern for police pay and conditions, and attention to operational matters. He quickly secured Home Office approval to raise the establishment by 1600 and to build new section houses and married quarters. He also introduced the first uniformed police training school in 1907. He was pleased that the 1906 royal commission inquiry into allegations of police misconduct found the vast majority of allegations to be unfounded.

Public order problems between 1903 and 1914 found the Metropolitan Police called upon to handle labour disputes and the new challenges of the women's suffrage movement. In these difficult circumstances Henry was attentive to the full range of a commissioner's responsibilities from the legal arrangements for military aid to the civil power, to the allowances for his officers on detached service in south Wales. The parsimony of the Home Office and Treasury towards police remuneration was an early and continuing problem. In 1911 he challenged the Home Office on its interpretation of lodging allowances, writing: 'I think the fact that a man occupied a fourth share of a bed on any particular day would afford insufficient grounds for depriving him of the lodging allowance to which he would otherwise be entitled' (Williams, 78).

Henry's health in office as commissioner was somewhat affected by a gunshot wound inflicted in 1912 by Alfred Bowes, an unsuccessful applicant for a cab driver's licence. His management of the force was also affected by his inability to persuade the government to address the poor morale, particularly in the war years, caused by the relatively low pay and allowances that the police received. In 1913 he had to remind his officers formally that standing orders forbade any involvement in the National Union of Police and Prison Officers, founded by a dismissed inspector, John Syme. So serious did unrest become that Henry warned the home secretary, Sir George Cave, in 1917 of the dangers of a strike. A strike by the police did occur on 30 August 1918, but it was swiftly ended on 31 August, when Lloyd George promised pay rises. Henry's resignation on the same day is generally held to have met the need for a scapegoat for political failures. He was created a baronet on 6 November 1918, having been knighted (KCVO) in 1906, appointed KCB in 1910, and advanced to GCVO in 1911 after attending the king and queen at the imperial durbar at Delhi. Among his foreign honours he was appointed a knight grand cross of the Dannebrog of Denmark and a commander of the Légion d'honneur of France.

In retirement Henry divided his time between keeping up to date with developments in fingerprint recognition techniques and voluntary work as chairman of the Athenaeum committee, member of the central committee of the National Society for the Prevention of Cruelty to Children, and member of the Berkshire magistrates' bench. Henry died at his home, Cissbury, Ascot, Berkshire, on 19 February 1931, and was buried in All Souls' cemetery, south Ascot. His wife survived him. Their only son, Edward John Grey, predeceased him in 1930 and the baronetcy became extinct. F. E. C. GREGORY

Sources J. Rowland, *The finger-print man: the story of Sir Edward Henry* (1959) · G. R. Williams, *The hidden world of Scotland Yard* (1972) · D. Ascoli, *The queen's peace: the origins and development of the metropolitan police* (1979) · P. Griffiths, *To guard my people: the history of the Indian police* (1971) · D. G. Browne, *The rise of Scotland Yard* (1956) · *DNB* · *The Times*

Archives BL, letters to Lord Gladstone, Add. MSS 46064–46074 · New Scotland Yard, London, metropolitan police archives

Likenesses Spy [L. Ward], chromolithograph caricature, NPG; repro. in *VF* (5 Oct 1905) · photograph, repro. in J. R. Nash, *Encyclopedia of world crime*, 1519

Wealth at death £11,281 1s. 3d.: resworn probate, 29 April 1931, CGPLA Eng. & Wales

Henry, George (1858–1943). *See under* Glasgow Boys (*act.* 1875–1895).

Henry, James (1798–1876), classical scholar and physician, was born in Dublin on 13 December 1798, the eldest child in a family of two sons and three daughters of Robert Henry, woollen draper, of College Green, Dublin, and his wife, Katherine Olivia, *née* Elder (1769–1845). Henry was educated by Joseph Hutton, a Unitarian minister, and George Downes, before entering Trinity College, Dublin, in 1814. He became a scholar there in 1817, classical gold medallist in 1818, BA in 1819, MA and MB in 1822, and MD in November 1832. He practised with considerable success as a physician in Dublin from 1823 to 1845, and in 1832 was elected vice-president of the King and Queen's College of Physicians in Ireland, although he charged his patients only a 5s. fee instead of the orthodox guinea and supplied them medicines free of charge. On the receipt of a large legacy after his mother's death in 1845 he ceased to practise.

Already on his eleventh birthday Henry had selected an edition of Virgil as a present, and from about 1841 he devoted his attention to the translation of the *Aeneid*. Translation led him to interpretation, and interpretation to textual study. From 1846 to 1849 with his wife, Ann(e) Jane (*née* Patton), whom he married in 1826, and their sole surviving daughter, Katharine Olivia—two older daughters died in infancy—he visited German, Italian, and other libraries to collate Virgilian manuscripts and meet eminent foreign scholars. His wife died at Arco, north of Lake Garda, in March 1849, but he continued to travel with his daughter, who shared his tastes and literary labours. They wandered on foot through many parts of Europe, crossing the Alps seventeen times, sometimes in deep snow. They finally returned in 1869 to Ireland, where they spent the last few years of their lives and continued to work on Henry's massive commentary, entitled *Aeneidea*. Henry's daughter (*b.* 20 November 1830) died suddenly on 11

December 1872, to his great grief. He himself died at his brother's residence, Dalkey Lodge, Dalkey, near Dublin, on 14 July 1876 after a lifetime of good health until a stroke of paralysis three months before his death. He was buried at the Barrington family burial-ground, Glendruid, co. Dublin, and interred with him in his coffin were the ashes of his wife, whose body he had been compelled, against his wish, secretly to cremate near Arco.

A portrait of Henry at the age of fifty-six bears out J. P. Mahaffy's description of him in old age: 'his long white locks and somewhat fantastic fur dress … were combined with great beauty and vivacity of countenance, and a rare geniality and vigour of discourse. There was a curious combination of rudeness and kindness … of severity and softness in him' (Mahaffy, 163). Despite his singularity or eccentricity, he was widely respected for his knowledge, kindness, and integrity.

One of the greatest of Virgilian commentators, Henry sought the truth with uncompromising independence and very extensive learning. He and his daughter examined manuscripts, devoted great care to exegesis, and avoided emendation. In 1873 he published volume 1 (pt 1) of his *Aeneidea, or, Critical, exegetical, and aesthetical remarks on the Aeneis, with a personal collation of all the first class Mss., upwards of one hundred second class Mss., and all the principal editions*, which superseded earlier work, privately printed or published in journals. Volume 1 (continued), 1877, and volume 2, 1878–9, were published by his literary executor, Professor J. F. Davies; volumes 3–5 were issued (1889–92) by Arthur Palmer and L. C. Purser, fellows of Trinity College, Dublin. The style of this great work is diffuse but vivacious, demanding but rewarding, serious but entertaining, and gives full play to the idiosyncrasies of the author. He wrote much verse, direct in style, rather rough in rhythm, and colloquial in diction, that vividly mirrors his passing moods, experiences, and musings; although his poems have been described as 'more curious than beautiful', and as 'rather pedestrian', they have recently been championed by C. Ricks in his *Select Poems of James Henry* (2002). His travel poems are graphic and interesting.

Henry was also the author of numerous vigorous and racy pamphlets, attacking what he considered abuses, or defending the religious scepticism which replaced his early presbyterianism. Among his extensive writings may be mentioned: *The Eneis, Books i. and ii. Rendered into English Blank Iambic, with New Interpretations and Illustrations*, 1845; *The Unripe Windfalls in Prose and Verse*, 1851; *My Book*, 1853; *Thalia petasata, or, A Foot Journey from Carlsruhe to Bassano, Described on the Way in Verse*, 1859; *Thalia petasata iterum, or, A Foot Journey from Dresden to Venice, Described on the Way in Verse*, 1877. Many of Henry's writings were privately printed: the fullest bibliography (not quite complete) is in J. B. Lyons's *Scholar and Sceptic* (1985).   J. A. RICHMOND

Sources J. P. Mahaffy, *The Academy* (12 Aug 1876), 162–3 · J. Richmond, *James Henry of Dublin: physician, versifier, pamphleteer, wanderer, and classical scholar* (1976) · J. B. Lyons, *Scholar and sceptic: the career of James Henry M.D., 1798–1876* (1985) [bibliography] · J. S. Starkey, 'James Henry and the "Aeneidea"', *Hermathena*, 64 (1944), 19–31 [bibliography] · J. Henry, *My book* (privately printed, Dresden, 1853), 3

Archives TCD, MSS 2507–2509
Likenesses E. C. Schmidt, engraving, repro. in J. Henry, *Poematia* (1866) [frontispiece]
Wealth at death under £25,000: probate, 7 Aug 1876, *CGPLA Ire.*

Henry, John (1746?–1794), actor and theatre manager, is usually stated to have been born in Dublin in 1746, although this claim, like William Dunlap's that he was 'liberally educated' (Dunlap), has never been substantiated. His initial stage outings were most likely in 1761 in Belfast and Dublin. He apparently joined the Charles Storer theatrical family when they departed from Ireland in 1762 for Jamaica, where Henry married one of the Storer's seven daughters, Jane. Five years later, in August 1767, while travelling to join the American Company of Comedians in the colonies, Henry and the remaining Storer family were involved in a ship accident off the coast of Rhode Island that claimed Henry's wife and two young children.

Henry made his American début in Philadelphia on 5 October 1767 as Publius Horatius in William Whitehead's *The Roman Father* with the American Company, led by Lewis Hallam the younger and David Douglass. For his New York début, on 7 December 1767, he played Aimwell in George Farquhar's *The Beaux' Stratagem* opposite Hallam's Archer. With the American Company he appeared in Philadelphia again, from 4 October 1768 to 6 January 1769; at New York from 9 January to 19 June; at Albany, New York, in July; and at Philadelphia, from 8 November to 24 May 1770. In March 1770 Ann Storer was listed as Mrs Henry, though there is no evidence of a legal marriage. After Philadelphia the American Company appeared in Annapolis, Maryland, and Williamsburg, Virginia; it then returned to Philadelphia in 1772–3 and played in New York for the final season (April) until after the American War of Independence. They followed this with appearances in Charles Town, South Carolina, after which, in 1774, they departed for Jamaica in order to evade the prohibition of theatrical events during hostilities between the colonies and Britain.

In Jamaica Henry assumed the management of the American Company and led them at three locations, including a new venue in Kingston, from July 1775 until 10 May 1777, after which he apparently sailed for England, where he appeared during the summer at the small China Hall theatre in Rotherhithe. Henry's activities for the next two years are unverified, although it has been suggested that he was an officer in the British army during this period. It is known that on 16 October 1779 he made his London début at Drury Lane as Othello; on the same evening 'A Young Lady' (very likely another Storer sister, Maria) made her début at Covent Garden. By 1788 Maria was known as Mrs Henry, her sister Ann having returned to Ireland rather than go to Jamaica with Henry in 1774. Records of this Henry–Storer marriage have not been located, yet the union proved successful.

By June 1781 Henry, back in Jamaica, was joined by Hallam in the management of the American Company. On 25 August Henry's play *School for Soldiers, or, The Deserters* was presented. He later wrote and staged *The Convention, or,*

HENRY, MATTHEW 582

The Columbian Father, performed in New York on 7 April 1787. During the 1780s Henry returned to the United States, where he helped to re-establish professional theatre, following the end of hostilities; he also spent time in Jamaica and London, and on 21 November 1785 rejoined efforts with Hallam in New York in what was now known as the Old American Company. Despite a volatile relationship they dominated American theatre for the next seven years. With the threat of competition from former company member Thomas Wignell, in 1792 Henry went to London to recruit actors, including John Hodgkinson, who, with the support of Hallam, drove Henry and his wife out of the company. At the end of the 1794 season Henry sold his shares to Hallam for $10,000.

Henry died at sea near Fisher's Island, off the New England coast, 'very suddenly of gout of the stomach' on 16 October 1794 (*Columbian Centinel*, 1 Nov 1794); he was buried either at Bristol, Rhode Island, or, according to Dunlap, under the sand of an island in the sound. Maria, who reportedly had the body returned to her, died on 25 April 1795 at Philadelphia.

Tall and handsome and effective in Irish comic roles, Henry was also a respectable musician who sang musical roles and often played with the theatre orchestra when not needed on stage. His parsimonious behaviour and arrogant manners, however, made him many enemies throughout his career.   DON B. WILMETH

Sources Highfill, Burnim & Langhans, *BDA* · W. Dunlap, *A history of the American theatre* (1832) · J. S. Bost, *Monarchs of the mimic world* (1977) · E. Hill, *The Jamaican stage, 1655–1900: profile of a colonial theatre* (1992) · *Columbian Centinel* (1 Nov 1794) · indenture of share transferral belonging to John Henry, 1794, Hunt. L. · D. B. Wilmeth and T. Miller, eds., *Cambridge guide to American theatre*, new edn (1996) · E. Willis, *The Charleston stage in the XVIII century: with social settings of the time* (1933)

Likenesses C. Tiebout, engraving (after 'C. B.'), repro. in J. O'Keeffe, *Wild oats* (1793)

Wealth at death received $10,000 for shares in Old American Company

Henry, Matthew (1662–1714), Presbyterian minister, was born prematurely on 18 October 1662 at Broadoak, Flintshire, which was in the chapelry of Iscoed in the parish of Malpas (Cheshire), the second and only surviving son of Philip *Henry (1631–1696), ejected minister, and Katherine (1629–1707), only daughter and heir of Daniel Matthews of Broadoak. Though a sickly child, he was intended for the ministry from an early age, and was educated privately at home. He was taught grammar first by William Turner, a student with his father, and then by his father, and gained considerable proficiency in the learned languages, especially Hebrew. In 1680 he was sent to London to study under Thomas Doolittle, who conducted an important academy at Islington. His studies in London were interrupted by intensified persecution of dissenters, and when Doolittle was forced to move his academy to Battersea in 1683 Henry returned home to Broadoak. In April 1685 he returned to London, but (with the encouragement of Rowland Hunt of Boreatton) to study law at Gray's Inn. The reasons for this change in his studies were clearly related to the difficult political situation. Though a

Matthew Henry (1662–1714), by George Vertue, pubd 1710

'knowledge of the Law would not only be convenient for one that was Heir to an handsome Estate', it had a further advantage because of 'the forensick Terms so much used in the Holy Scriptures' (Tong, 34). According to his sister Sarah *Savage he 'kept Terms with other Students yet stil with a secret purpose for Divinity' (diary of Sarah Savage, 6). Henry kept up his divinity studies by attending a weekly disputation of ministerial students conducted by Francis Glascock. He also attempted to hear the best preachers of the day, though because of the persecution they were all conformists.

In June 1686, during the law vacation, Matthew Henry left London to visit his father at Broadoak for four months. He 'now began to preach pretty often as a Candidate' for the ministry, 'and every where met with great Acceptance and Encouragement' (Tong, 43). He preached at Chester at the house of Anthony Henthorne, a wealthy sugar-baker, though very discreetly because 'the liberty not being yet granted' (ibid., 44). As a result he was earnestly pressed to become their minister. After consulting his father, Henry agreed, but first returned to London to complete his studies. On 9 May 1687 he was ordained by six ejected ministers, but in 'great Privacy' (ibid., 70) because of the difficulty of the times, and returned home to Broadoak. On 1 June he was brought to Chester where, the following day being the lecture-day, he preached his first sermon publicly. The congregation met originally in some converted stables in the Whitefriars belonging to Henthorne. As a result of a change in ownership and the growing size and importance of the congregation, it was decided in September 1699 to build a meeting-house in Crook Lane, which was completed in July 1700 at a cost of £532 16s. In September 1706 a gallery was added to accommodate the members of the Independent meeting which had dissolved.

Henry married first, on 19 July 1687, Katherine (1664–1690), the only daughter of Samuel Hardware of Bromborough Court, Wirral; she died in childbed of smallpox on 14 February 1690, aged twenty-five, leaving a daughter, Katherine. He married secondly, on 8 July 1690, Mary (d. 1731), the youngest daughter of Robert Warburton of Helperstone Grange. He and his second wife had eight daughters, three of whom died in infancy, and one son, Philip, who assumed the surname of Warburton on becoming heir to Helperstone Grange. He was MP for the city of Chester from 1742, and died unmarried on 16 August 1760.

Henry's reputation as a leading minister of his generation was founded on extraordinarily active evangelical ministry both in the pulpit and in the study. His talent for preaching was matched by willingness to preach whenever requested. In addition to his work with his own congregation, both public and private,

> The Towns and Villages that lay near to Chester enjoyed a great share of his Labours, … there was scarce a Week but he was at one or more of these Places preaching the Gospel (besides his constant Work at home).   (Tong, 184–5)

He also used to take an annual preaching excursion into Staffordshire and latterly into Lancashire as well. He was a strong supporter of the Cheshire classis founded at Macclesfield in March 1691, and a major influence on its affairs after the death of his father. He was much called upon to take part in ordinations. Nevertheless, he was subject to a considerable amount of intimidation and abuse from those hostile to dissent. An attempt was made to burn down his meeting-place in October 1692, and he and his congregation were publicly abused by high-churchmen and subject to petty slanders, particularly in Queen Anne's reign.

Henry's most celebrated and enduring work was his *Exposition of the Old and New Testament*, 'distinguished, not for the depth of its learning, or the originality of its views; but for the sound practical piety, and large measure of good sense, which it discovers' (W. Orme, *Bibliotheca biblica*, 1824, 240–41). Begun in November 1704, the first volume covering the five books of Moses was published in folio in 1707; a further three volumes published in 1708, 1710, and 1712 brought the commentary to the end of the Old Testament. Henry had completed a fifth volume on the New Testament as far as the Acts, which was in the press when he died. After his death thirteen nonconformist ministers, not all of whom were equal to Henry, undertook the work on the Epistles and Revelation. Henry's

commentary gained great popularity, and by 1855 twenty-five editions had been published, with further editions in the modern period, including an electronic version on the world wide web. Henry published a further thirty works principally concerned with family religion, instructing youth, and religious faith, but his earliest work was also his most controversial, an immature effort entitled *Nature of Schism* (1689). He was answered by Alderman Thomas Wilcocks and others, whose charges were effectively refuted only by Henry's friend William Tong in 1693. With the exception of his father's funeral sermon, a volume of family hymns issued in 1695, and his *Discourse Concerning Meekness* (1699), Henry published nothing further until 1702. His *Scripture Catechism* (1703) had reached a third edition by 1714; his *Communicants Companion* (1704) a sixth by 1715; and his *Method of Prayer* (1710) a fourth by 1715. Over half his published works appeared during the final five years of his life. Many of his published sermons were originally delivered in London and printed at the request of those that heard them delivered.

With his growing reputation Henry received calls from other congregations. He refused invitations from Hackney in 1699; from Salters' Hall, London, in 1702; from Manchester in 1705; and from Silver Street and Old Jewry, London, in 1708. In 1710 he was again invited to Mare Street, Hackney, one of the most important congregations near London. He at first declined, then, after further application and much irresolution on his part, was persuaded to accept on the basis of being more generally serviceable at Hackney. He eventually left Chester in May 1712 with many tears. In London he quickly took his place among the leading ministers. He remained in considerable demand as a preacher, and was frequently invited to preach and catechize at other meetings and consulted on the issues of the day. He was elected a manager of the Presbyterian Fund in January 1712, before he had left Chester. He was also named by Dr Daniel Williams as one of the original twenty-three trustees of his charity, though because of his premature death he never acted.

Henry died on 22 June 1714 at the home of the Revd Joseph Mottershead, near Nantwich, as a result of a fall from his horse while on a visit to Cheshire. Too much time spent in his study had made him corpulent. The sorrow at his death was universal, 'there was hardly a Pulpit of the Dissenters in London but what gave Notice of the great Breach that was made upon the Church of God' (Tong, 282). He was buried on 25 June in the chancel of Holy Trinity Church, Chester, attended by eight of the city clergy. Funeral sermons were preached at Chester by Peter Withington and John Gardner, and in London by Daniel Williams, William Tong, John Bates, and John Reynolds; the last four were published. Tong also published a biography, which, drawing upon Henry's manuscript diaries and correspondence, provides many valuable details. Because of the honour in which Henry was held both during his life and subsequently, his correspondence and sermons were preserved by his descendants and also collected by his contemporaries. Henry kept a diary from

1690, but only the portion from January 1705 to December 1713 survives. After his death the Hackney congregation divided in two. DAVID L. WYKES

Sources DNB · W. Tong, *An account of the life and death of Mr. Matthew Henry, minister of the gospel at Hackney, who dy'd June 22, 1714 in the 52d year of his age* (1716) · M. Henry, 'A short account of the beginning and progress of our congregation', chapel book, 1710, Ches. & Chester ALSS, records of the Matthew Henry Chapel, D/MH/1 · H. D. Roberts, *Matthew Henry and his chapel, 1662–1900* [n.d.] · S. Savage, diary, 31 May 1714–25 Dec 1723, Bodl. Oxf., MS Eng. misc. e. 331 · A. Gordon, ed., *Freedom after ejection: a review (1690–1692) of presbyterian and congregational nonconformity in England and Wales* (1917), 16, 282 · A. Gordon, ed., *Cheshire classis: minutes, 1691–1745* (1919), 178–9 · J. Hunter, *Familiae minorum gentium*, ed. J. W. Clay, 4 vols., Harleian Society, 37–40 (1894–6), 1.359 · W. D. Jeremy, *The Presbyterian Fund and Dr Daniel Williams's Trust* (1885), 106–8 · parish register, Holy Trinity, Chester, 25 June 1714 [burials] · parish register, Holy Trinity, Chester, 14 Aug 1731 [burials; Mary Henry, wife] · C. M. Farrall, ed., *Parish register of the Holy and Undivided Trinity in the city of Chester, 1532–1837* (1914)

Archives BL, letters to his father, mother, and wife, fragments of sermons, Add. MSS 42849, 45538 · Bodl. Oxf., corresp. · Bodl. Oxf., diary, MS Eng misc e 330 · Evangelical Library, London, sermon notes · Flintshire RO, Hawarden, sermons · University of Leicester Library, sermons | DWL, corresp. and papers · W. Yorks. AS, Leeds, Yorkshire Archaeological Society, letters to Ralph Thoresby

Likenesses G. Vertue, line engraving, pubd 1710, BM, NPG [*see illus.*] · oils, DWL · oils (probably a copy), Congregational Centre, Castle Gate, Nottingham

Henry, Michael (1830–1875), patent agent and newspaper editor, was born on 19 February 1830 at Eltham House, Kennington, south London, the youngest son of Abraham Henry (c.1790–1840), merchant, and his wife, Emma, daughter of Solomon Lyon of Cambridge. Both his parents were Jewish. A noted scholar, Solomon Lyon was Hebrew tutor to the philosemitic duke of Sussex; in 1812 his talented daughter Emma became, it seems, the first Anglo-Jewish woman to have a literary work published when a volume of poems she had written appeared. When Michael Henry was three he moved with his family to Ramsgate, where his own poetic and literary inclinations, evident from an early age, were encouraged by his mother. Upon his father's death in April 1840 the family returned to the capital, and he spent the ensuing four years at the City of London School, where he achieved a praiseworthy academic record. He left school in June 1844 and was employed for a short time as a trainee bookkeeper in Paris, where his sister lived. But the rigid commercial environment proved uncongenial and he obtained work with James Robertson, patent agent and editor (1823–52) of Britain's earliest inexpensive scientifically oriented periodical, the *Mechanics' Magazine*. He turned his hand to both sides of the business. Following Robertson's death in 1857 he set up successfully on his own as a patent agent at 68 Fleet Street, becoming a sought-after expert on patent law. He wrote a highly regarded pamphlet on that subject, which was used by members of a relevant committee of the House of Commons. He edited the *Investors' Almanac*, wrote for the *Mining Journal*, and belonged to several learned bodies, including the Society of Civil Engineers. In 1847 he founded a charitable organization, the General Benevolent Association, serving as its honorary secretary until his death. He represented Sheffield Hebrew congregation on the London-based board of deputies of British Jews.

An enthusiastic supporter of the Society for the Diffusion of Religious Knowledge, Henry was devoted to the cause of Jewish education. He sat for many years on the council of Jews' College and was deeply involved in the work of the Committee for Providing Free Lectures to Jewish Working Men and their Families. Especially close to his heart was the Stepney Jewish school system; he was honorary secretary of its committee and worked tirelessly on its behalf. He was never happier than when visiting the pupils, lecturing to them, and encouraging them academically with treats and prizes.

During the 1860s Dr Abraham Benisch, proprietor and editor of the *Jewish Chronicle*, appointed Henry assistant editor. Benisch was impressed by Henry's literary abilities, journalistic skills, Jewish awareness, and incisive grasp of wider issues. In 1869 the consortium which took charge of the paper when Benisch stepped down owing to financial difficulties appointed Henry editor. Under his industrious and successful editorship the paper veered for the first time towards support for the Conservative Party. Henry deplored the creeping state interventionism of W. E. Gladstone's administration (1868–74), which he believed threatened Jewish exclusiveness in certain spheres. Faced with Forster's Education Act of 1870, which introduced compulsory state education for all children, he argued that Anglo-Jews must 'manage and support their own schools, just as they manage and support their own synagogues and their own burial grounds' (*Jewish Chronicle*, 15 April 1870). He feared that Jewish schools would be placed under state supervision and described the prospect of lower- and lower-middle-class Jewish children being educated alongside their non-Jewish counterparts as 'frightfully, fatally dangerous' (ibid., 18 Nov 1870). He used scripture to reinforce his contention that Judaism opposed political radicalism, denied Gladstone's claim during the election campaign of 1874 that Jews in the City of London endorsed the Liberal Party, and rebutted the concept of a Jewish vote. Despite his partisanship he was well respected and admired within the Jewish community generally. He helped to create the important and enduring United Synagogue organization of Anglo-Jewish congregations, first advocating the formation of such a body in a leading article during 1866 and vigorously campaigning for it once he became editor.

Possibly owing to chronic 'delicate' health Henry never married. He died on the evening of 16 June 1875 at his home—6 Argyle Square, St Pancras, London—his clothing having been ignited by a candle flame while at his office in Fleet Street the previous day. His death was officially ascribed to 'collapse following severe burns on the body' (d. cert.), a finding noted soon afterwards in *The Lancet* under the heading 'Death from shock'. He was buried in Willesden cemetery, London, on 21 June following a funeral attended by numerous mourners representing a wide swathe of Anglo-Jewry. Evidently he never forgot the perils facing seafarers witnessed during his Ramsgate childhood. Shortly before his death some Jewish schoolboys, at his suggestion, had begun saving towards a new lifeboat for the Royal National Lifeboat Institution. With his passing, this initiative became the Jewish Scholars' Life Boat Fund, formally opened in his memory; the resultant vessel, launched at Newhaven, was named the *Michael Henry*. HILARY L. RUBINSTEIN

Sources R. Henry, *The late Michael Henry* (1875) · *Jewish Chronicle* (18 June 1875) · *Jewish Chronicle* (25 June 1875) · *Jewish Chronicle* (2 July 1875) · *Jewish Chronicle* (13 Nov 1891) · D. Berger, ed., *The Jewish Victorian: genealogical information from the Jewish newspapers, 1871–1880* (1999) · D. Cesarani, *The Jewish Chronicle and Anglo-Jewry, 1841–1991* (1994) · *The Jewish Chronicle, 1841–1941: a century of newspaper history*, Jewish Chronicle (1949) · Michael Henry's last will and testament, 26 Nov 1874 · D. Cesarani, 'The importance of being editor: the *Jewish Chronicle*, 1841–1991', *Transactions of the Jewish Historical Society of England*, 32 (1990–92), 259–87 · d. cert. · CGPLA Eng. & Wales (1875)
Wealth at death under £450: probate, 1875, CGPLA Eng. & Wales

Henry, Mitchell (1826–1910), politician and businessman, was born into a nonconformist family at Ardwick Green, Manchester, the younger son of Alexander Henry, Liberal MP for South Lancashire (1847–52), who died on 4 October 1862, and his wife, Elizabeth, daughter of Henry Brush of Dromore, co. Down. Having been educated privately and at University College School, London, Henry joined the Pine Street medical school in Manchester, which was subsequently incorporated into the medical department of Owens College. He became a member of the Royal College of Surgeons in 1847 and practised as a consulting surgeon in Harley Street, London, and then as surgeon to the North London Infirmary for Diseases of the Eye before being appointed, in 1857, assistant surgeon to the Middlesex Hospital. In the following year he became surgeon in the same hospital, where he remained until 1862, when he abandoned medicine to become a partner in the family mercantile and general warehouse firm of A. and S. Henry of Manchester, Huddersfield, Leeds, and elsewhere. While at the Middlesex Hospital he lectured on morbid anatomy and later on surgical jurisprudence. In 1850 Henry married Margaret, daughter of George Vaughan of Dromore, co. Down. They had three sons and three daughters. In 1854 he was elected a fellow of the Royal College of Surgeons. During his years as a surgeon he authored significant medical papers.

In Manchester, Henry became involved in the Liberal Party and soon developed political ambitions. He stood unsuccessfully as a Liberal in a by-election at Woodstock in 1865. He then fought the Manchester by-election on 27 November 1867 as a Liberal and stood in that constituency again at the general election in 1868, when he finished at the bottom of the poll. As part of his election bid he established the *Evening News*, but sold it after his defeat. His older brother, John Snowdon Henry (d. 30 Oct 1896), also a partner in the family firm, sat for South East Lancashire as a Conservative between 1868 and 1874.

Both of Henry's parents were born in Ulster, as was his wife. He visited Ireland regularly and, attracted by the possibilities of good angling, purchased a large estate of about 14,000 acres of poor-quality land in the western part of co. Galway, where he built the visually impressive Kylemore Castle in mock baronial style. He soon found himself immersed in politics: he joined the new Home Government Association founded in 1870 and became a member of its council. Elected unopposed on 21 February 1871 as a home-ruler at the by-election for county Galway, he represented this constituency until the dissolution in 1885. His first major speech came in 1872, during the parliamentary debate on the offensive comments on clerical intimidation made by Judge Keogh when giving his verdict on the successful Galway election petition. Although a protestant and generally a supporter of Gladstone, in 1873 Henry voted against the Irish University Bill, which had been condemned by Ireland's Catholic bishops. He was a prominent participant in the national conference in November 1873 which founded the Home Rule League. He also played a major role in the new Home Rule Party formed in March 1874 and sometimes deputized for Isaac Butt during the leader's increasingly frequent absences. His expertise was valuable, especially on financial questions, and he also had a reputation as an expert on tenant-right. He was a friend and confidant of Butt, and remained loyal to him during the dispute with Charles Stewart Parnell and Joseph Biggar over parliamentary 'obstruction'. Although never comfortable with Parnell's style of parliamentarianism, Henry was equally critical of the Conservative government's lack of legislative proposals for Ireland. In 1880 he voted for William Shaw in the contest for the chairmanship of the Irish party. Like the other 'nominal home-rulers', he took no part in the Land League agitation and distanced himself from the militants led by Parnell, though he remained an advocate of tenant-right legislation. Despite previously good relations with his tenants, Henry found that his own estate was not immune from Land League agitation. This added to his disenchantment with the militants who followed Parnell. Along with Shaw and others, he ended his membership of the party in January 1881, voted for the Land Bill, and thereafter supported Gladstone during the parliament of 1880–85.

At the general election of 1885 Henry successfully contested the new division of Glasgow Blackfriars and Hutchesontown. Experience of the land war and with the Parnellites disillusioned him. He was often the target of vitriolic attacks in the nationalist press. Henry maintained that the home rule he had advocated would bring Ireland and Britain together, whereas the Parnellites meant to secure it to break the connection between the two countries. Thus he voted against the Government of Ireland Bill on its second reading in June 1886. He stood as a Liberal Unionist for Glasgow Blackfriars and Hutchesontown in July 1886 but was defeated, and his parliamentary career came to an end. A man of very considerable financial means, he afterwards concentrated on business. His firm A. and S. Henry was converted into a limited liability company in 1889, and he remained its chairman until 1893. His wife died in 1874 and was buried in a magnificent mausoleum on the Kylemore estate. After the early 1880s Henry spent little time in Ireland and eventually disposed of the estate to the duke of Manchester. He lived for many years at Leamington Spa, where he died on 22 November 1910.   ROBERT DUNLOP, *rev.* ALAN O'DAY

Sources *Manchester Guardian* (24 Nov 1910) • *The Times* (23–4 Nov 1910) • V. G. Plarr, *Plarr's Lives of the fellows of the Royal College of Surgeons of England*, rev. D'A. Power, 1 (1930) • *Annual Register* (1910) • *WWBMP* • D. Thornley, *Isaac Butt and home rule* (1964) • C. C. O'Brien, *Parnell and his party, 1880–90* (1957) • H. W. Lucy, *A diary of two parliaments*, 2 vols. (1885–6) • *Dod's Parliamentary Companion* • J. L. Hammond, *Gladstone and the Irish nation* (1938) • A. M. Sullivan, *New Ireland*, [new edn] (1882) • M. MacDonagh, *The home rule movement* (1920)
Archives NL Ire., Isaac Butt and O'Neill Daunt MSS
Likenesses Spy [L. Ward], chromolithograph caricature, NPG; repro. in *VF* (19 April 1879)
Wealth at death £401 17s. 11d.: probate, 25 May 1911, *CGPLA Eng. & Wales*

Henry, Patrick (1736–1799), revolutionary politician in America, was born on 29 May 1736 in Hanover county, Virginia, to Colonel John Henry (*c*.1705–1773), Scottish-born tobacco planter, and his wife, Sarah Winston Syme (*c*.1710–1784). He was raised in the established Church of England and held orthodox views; he once derided deism as 'another name for vice and depravity' (Meade, 2.443). After attending a local school until age ten, he received a classical education from tutors and his father, a former student at King's College, University of Aberdeen; he owned a library of 219 volumes at his death. In 1754 he married Sarah Shelton (1738–1775), whose dowry included a 300 acre farm and six slaves; they had six children. Having tried storekeeping, tobacco planting, and managing an inn, Henry studied law by himself and qualified for the bar in Hanover county in 1760. So thriving was his practice that in its first three years he handled 1185 cases (and won most of them).

Public acclaim suddenly came to Henry after he defended the taxpayers' interests in the 'parsons' cause'. This controversy stemmed from the Anglican clergy's attempt to reap a financial windfall from the tobacco crop's failure in 1755, when a tripling of that commodity's price induced the legislature to alter the manner of compensating parish rectors, from paying them with 17,280 pounds of tobacco—which they then sold on the market—to a cash salary equalling that much leaf valued at 2d. per pound (slightly above recent prices). Once Whitehall disallowed this measure, clergymen began suing for arrearages equal to twice their usual stipend. Henry represented Louisa county against one such suit in December 1763, during which his impassioned denunciation of clerical avarice proved so compelling that the jury awarded token damages of just 1d. for the minister. This case won him colony-wide acclaim at age twenty-seven, and led to his election two years later as assemblyman from Louisa county, where he owned land but did not reside.

Recognition as one of Virginia's foremost orators quickly came to Henry, whose voice reportedly could carry almost half a mile. Whereas contemporary fashion called for well-rehearsed, highly formal orations embellished with allusions to classical literature or constitutional history, Henry was the master of swaying audiences with an extemporaneous, direct, and highly dramatic style. Edmund Randolph, later Virginia's attorney-general, wrote:

> In Henry's exordium there was a simplicity … His pauses, which for their length might sometimes be feared to dispel the attention, riveted it the more by raising the expectation … His style … was vehement, without transporting him beyond the power of self-command … His figures of speech … were often borrowed from the Scriptures … His lightning consisted in quick successive flashes, which rested only to alarm the more.   (Randolph, 179–81)

Henry's gifts were perfectly suited for arousing the sense of emergency, indignation, and moral fervour necessary to turn complacent subjects into rebels.

Henry entered the legislature simultaneously with news about the Stamp Act (1765), parliament's first attempt at raising revenue from internal trade in America. On his own initiative, he proposed seven resolutions explicitly denying parliament's authority to levy taxes in the colonies and implicitly endorsing non-compliance with their collection. After an emotionally charged speech that intemperately admonished George III to respect English liberties—lest some modern-day Brutus imagine him to be another Caesar—he persuaded his colleagues to endorse five of them on 30 May 1765. The Virginia Resolves set Britain's largest overseas province squarely in opposition to parliamentary taxation; more importantly, their example was critical in arousing other assemblies to adopt similar declarations soon after.

Eight years passed before Henry again took a central role in the imperial crisis. Co-authoring the Virginia Resolutions of 12 March 1773, Henry helped lay the basis for co-ordinating American opposition to British policies through a network of legislative committees of correspondence. The ensuing call for American unity culminated eighteen months later in the first continental congress, at which Henry, as a Virginia delegate, sat on the most important committees: those investigating parliamentary abuses of American rights, summarizing the colonies' constitutional position within the empire, and drafting a declaration of rights and grievances.

Back in Virginia after congress's adjournment in October 1774, Henry emerged as the most outspoken advocate of placing its militia on a footing for war during an extra-legal convention of elected delegates at Richmond. His resolutions for military preparedness were carried shortly after the delegates heard his most famous oration, which he reputedly ended with the celebrated phrase: 'Give me liberty or give me death', on 23 March 1775. After Royal Marines seized Virginia's military arsenal at Williamsburg a month later, Henry led an armed force that menaced the capital until the government paid £330 as restitution for the commandeered munitions. When the governor issued a proclamation that essentially outlawed Henry, a succession of volunteer companies escorted the firebrand through each of Virginia's counties to shield him from arrest on his way to the continental congress in May. Henry arrived late at the continental congress, received no committee assignments until a month passed, and took a secondary role at that session. He left congress in August 1775, well before the issue of independence was debated. Having no national ambitions, he never again held office outside Virginia.

Eager for military glory, Henry became colonel of a Virginia regiment in August 1775, but he chafed under the close (and sometimes inept) supervision of civilian superiors and resigned his command in February 1776 without having seen any action. Henry represented Hanover county at the extra-legal Virginia convention that met from 6 May to 5 July 1776. He initially hesitated to support American independence if declared prior to securing assistance from France and other powers hostile to Britain, but quickly relented when this strategy appeared impractical. Henry was the first delegate to the Virginia convention to propose instructing its delegates at the continental congress to offer motions for renouncing allegiance to George III. The convention's endorsement of this policy marked the earliest instance in which any colony officially committed itself to separation from Britain, and was the decisive event that shifted the continental congress's official agenda from defending American rights within the empire to debating the merits of independence.

At this time, after the death of his first wife, Henry married on 9 October 1777 Dorothea Dandridge (1757–1831), who added twelve slaves to their household and was a second cousin of George Washington's wife, Martha; they had ten children. The Virginia convention elected Henry as the state's first wartime governor. Besides supervising the mobilization of soldiers and supplies, of which Virginia's contribution was second only to that of Massachusetts, he influenced the war's outcome decisively in 1778 by financing and equipping (without any orders or assistance from congress) the troops who consolidated American military control over the Ohio Valley. The resulting campaign helped deter Britain from retaining any territory south of the Great Lakes through the Treaty of Paris.

Virginia's constitution precluded Henry's holding the governorship continually beyond 1779. He then exercised enormous influence in the legislature and again served as governor from 1784 to 1786. He strongly objected to the national constitution written in 1787, but his oratory and prestige failed to keep Virginia's narrowly divided convention from ratifying the new federal government a year later.

Increasingly enervated by failing health, he resigned from the legislature in 1790, and later declined offers of high national office. A thriving legal practice had brought him great wealth, including 66 slaves and 27,690 acres by 1788, when he was Virginia's ninetieth wealthiest taxpayer. In a desperate attempt to relieve an acute intestinal inflammation, his doctor persuaded Henry to swallow a vial of liquid mercury, which killed him on 6 June 1799 at his plantation of Red Hill in Charlotte county, where he was later buried.　THOMAS L. PURVIS

Sources D. Meade, *Patrick Henry*, 2 vols. (Philadelphia, 1957–69) · R. R. Beeman, *Patrick Henry: a biography* (New York, 1974) · E. Randolph, *History of Virginia*, ed. A. H. Schaffer (1970) · W. W. Henry, *Patrick Henry: life, correspondence, and speeches*, 3 vols. (New York, 1891) · A. M. Burke, *The prominent families of the United States* (1908), 449 · J. T. Main, 'The one hundred', *William and Mary Quarterly*, 11 (1954), 354–84, esp. 364, n. 19
Likenesses clay bust, 1788, L. Cong. · T. Sully, oils, 1815 (posthumous), L. Cong.
Wealth at death £5727 in Virginia's currency [£4000] in personal property, incl. approx. 100 slaves and 250 head of cattle: Meade, *Henry*, 2.437, 459 · by 1788 ranked as ninetieth wealthiest taxpayer in Virginia; possessed sixty-six slaves, 22,190 acres in Virginia, and 5500 acres in Kentucky: Meade, *Henry*, 2.421; *William and Mary Quarterly*, 364, n. 19

Henry, Philip (1631–1696), clergyman and ejected minister, was born on 24 August 1631 at Whitehall, Westminster, the fourth of the eight children of John Henry (1590–1652), keeper of the orchard at Whitehall and later page of the back stairs to James, duke of York, and of his wife, Magdalen Rochdale (*bap.* 1599, *d.* 1645), the pious daughter of Henry Rochdale. Henry's godparents—the earls of Pembroke and Carlisle and the countess of Salisbury—reflected his father's status as a courtier. As a boy his playmates were princes Charles and James, and from the latter he received a prized book and two pictures. The family's loyalty to the court was manifest when Henry's father took him to visit Archbishop William Laud in the Tower of London.

Education and early ministerial career After learning Latin at a school in St Martin-in-the-Fields and, for a summer, at Battersea, in 1643 Henry entered Westminster School, where he studied under Thomas Vincent and later Richard Busby. As the latter's student he helped collect material for a Greek grammar. Attending daily lectures at the abbey, he heard such noted puritans as Stephen Marshall and Philip Nye, and he also frequented the Thursday lectures at St Martin-in-the-Fields to hear Thomas Case. Often he was present during trials in the courts at Westminster. Partly owing to Pembroke's influence, he was appointed a king's scholar in October 1645. On 15 December 1647 he entered Christ Church, Oxford, as a commoner, aided by a gift of £10 from Pembroke to help with his expenses. Henry Hammond formally admitted him as a student on 24 March 1648. During his student days his political sympathies were royalist, and he was dismayed when he witnessed Charles I's execution, but his religious views were shaped by puritans such as Cage and Marshall. He graduated BA on 7 February 1651 and proceeded MA on 10 December 1652; a month later, on 9 January 1653, he preached his first sermon at South Hinksey, Oxfordshire.

At the recommendation of John Owen, dean of Christ Church, Henry was appointed tutor to the sons of John Puleston, judge of the common pleas, and his wife, at Emral Hall, Flintshire, where he took up residence on 30 September 1653. He also preached daily at Worthenbury chapel in the parish of Bangor Is-coed. After fulfilling his six months' commitment he returned to Oxford, accepting the Pulestons' eldest two sons as his charges in June 1654. The same year his short poem 'Noli timere musa!'

Philip Henry (1631–1696), by Robert White, pubd 1712 (after R. Holland)

was published in *Musarum Oxoniensium Elaiophoria*, the only work he would ever commit to print. Although he retained his place at Oxford another two or three years he accepted an invitation from Judge Puleston, who gave him a stipend of £100 per annum, to return to Worthenbury during the winter of 1654–5. With Ambrose Lewis of Wrexham he launched a monthly conference of ministers on 11 September 1655. After applying for ordination on 6 July 1657, he underwent his trials, including examinations in Hebrew, Greek, and logic, before being ordained as a presbyterian at Prees, Shropshire, on 16 September, 'a Day never to bee Forgotten' (*Diaries and Letters*, 58). In the same year the judge built a parsonage for him in Worthenbury, offering a sixty-year lease if he agreed to stay. At this point Henry's congregation comprised only forty-one, mostly poor, communicants. The previous year he had begun the practice of donating 10 per cent of his income to aid the needy. A gifted preacher, he attracted people from other areas, though he disliked this because of his commitment to the parish system. In 1658 he played a major role in helping to organize episcopalian, presbyterian, and Independent clergy from the region into a north Wales association, drafting that part of its agreement that

dealt with worship. He and his colleagues were inspired by accounts of the Worcestershire and Cumberland associations. The same year he took a month off to visit Oxford, preaching at St Mary the Virgin and at Christ Church and Corpus Christi College, and London, where he preached at Westminster Abbey.

Henry's rising stature as a preacher was apparent in March 1659 when he was offered the vicarage of Wrexham. He declined this opportunity as well as a substantial (but unspecified) position near London, preferring to remain at Worthenbury, to whose living Puleston formally presented him on 6 April 1659. Quakers challenged him to a debate the same year, but he refused. When Henry learned of Sir George Booth and Sir Thomas Myddelton's insurrection in August, he evinced no disapproval, and eight months later he was, in the words of his son Matthew *Henry, 'a hearty well-wisher to the return of the King' (M. Henry, 58). While the eyes of the nation were focused on the imminent Restoration, Henry married Katherine (1629–1707), the only daughter and heir of Daniel Matthews (d. 1667) of Broad Oak and Bronington, Flintshire, at Whitewell chapel on 26 April 1660. They were to have six children, all but the eldest of whom were born at Broad Oak: John (3 May 1661–12 April 1667), who was born at Worthenbury, Matthew (18 Oct 1662–22 June 1714), Sarah (7 Aug 1664–1752) [see Savage, Sarah], Katherine (7 Dec 1665–1747), Eleanor (23 July 1667–1 Aug 1697), and Ann (25 Nov 1668–6 Sept 1697).

The Restoration and Henry's ejection, 1660–1663 For refusing to use the Book of Common Prayer, Henry, Robert Fogg of Bangor, and Richard Steele of Hanmer, Flintshire, were presented at the Flint assizes in September 1660, but no punishment was imposed. In the aftermath of Thomas Venner's Fifth Monarchist uprising, Henry's house was searched for weapons on 8 February 1661, but none were found. A week later he was in Oxford to consult with John Fell, dean of Christ Church, about conforming, but Henry left unpersuaded. He deemed reordination neither justifiable nor necessary, he had reservations about elements of the liturgy, and he favoured Archbishop James Ussher's 'reduction of episcopacy'. Although Fogg conformed, Henry and Steele refused to do so, and on 28–9 March 1661 they were again presented at the assizes. During the spring and summer of 1661 Henry struggled as he tried to square his belief in a protestant state church with his nonconformist scruples. In his judgement the administration of the Lord's supper in the Anglican service to virtually all comers was promiscuous and amounted to pandering to the 'rabble'. At funerals he stayed only for the sermon. Pressured to conform, he wrote in his diary on 16 June 1661: 'Common-prayer-book tendred again, why, I know not—lord, they devise devices against mee' (*Diaries and Letters*, 89).

Although he regarded the interregnum regime as usurpers and the Restoration as a manifestation of divine mercy, Henry removed the order to burn the solemn league and covenant after it was posted in his church. For declining to publish an order prohibiting strangers from attending his church, he was cited to appear before the bishop's court on 17 October 1661, but he refused to attend. Five days later, Henry Bridgeman, rector of Bangor, ejected him from his curacy. By this point the Pulestons had ceased to pay his stipend, partly because his relationship with the family had deteriorated following the deaths of Lady Puleston in September 1658 and her husband a year later, and partly because he refused to use the Book of Common Prayer.

When Henry and Edward Lawrence, vicar of Baschurch, Shropshire, preached to a ministerial conference at Wem, Shropshire, in November 1661, the deputy lieutenants summoned the participating clergy to Shrewsbury and imprisoned them, but Henry avoided punishment by returning to Flintshire. In the same month he took the oath of allegiance at Overton-on-Dee. During this period he followed the discussions in London dealing with the possible comprehension of presbyterians in the Church of England, and he mostly concurred with the nonconformists' critique of the Book of Common Prayer. Continuing to struggle with the implications of nonconformity, he chose not to attend a private baptism because it implied an endorsement of separatism, and he was present for a conformist baptism despite his opposition to the sign of the cross, 'not daring to turn my back upon Gods Ordinance, while the essentials of it are retayn'd, though corrupted circumstantially in the Administration of it' (Diaries and Letters, 102–3). Although he had been ejected the previous October, he attached special significance to 24 August 1662, the day the Act of Uniformity, which legally silenced noncomplying clergy, took effect. 'I dyed', he wrote a year later, 'that fatal day to the Godly painful Ministers of England' (ibid., 145). Responding to a suit filed by Roger Puleston, Henry vacated the parsonage at Worthenbury in September 1662, and moved his family to Broad Oak. He attended worship services at Whitewell Chapel, or, if no minister was present, at Tilstock or Whitchurch, but during inclement weather he occasionally preached to family and friends in his house. He had his son Matthew baptized at Whitewell but he refused to assist because the sign of the cross was used. He soon regretted not having baptized Matthew himself after Richard Steele baptized his own son in March 1663, although this was illegal; when Henry later baptized his daughter Sarah in March 1665 the rector of Malpas, Cheshire, cited him in the church court for his offence. In 1663 Henry was chosen constable for neighbouring Tybroughton, but the justices permitted him to find a substitute.

Adjusting to nonconformity, 1663–1680 In the crackdown triggered by the northern rebellion Henry, Steele, and others were arrested in October 1663, taken to Hanmer for interrogation, and dismissed after four days upon providing security. Despite his own travails Henry followed reports of the fighting between imperial and Turkish forces, thinking this could lead to major changes in the Christian world, and in 1665 he noted the outbreak of the Second Anglo-Dutch War, which although an offensive war he deemed a just one. On 31 March 1665 the Flintshire commissioners nominated him to collect the royal aid at

Bangor, apparently to underscore his status as a layman in their eyes, but he oversaw others who collected the money. When magistrates seized Steele's diary in April, Henry determined to be more cautious with respect to the entries in his own diary. In September he was again arrested, taken to Hanmer, and questioned about conventicles. Admitting that he had attended private meetings in Shropshire but not administered the Lord's supper, he was released on a recognizance of £20. When the Five Mile Act was passed, he carefully measured the distance between Worthenbury and Broad Oak, finding that the distance barely exceeded the statutory minimum. Although he continued to attend Anglican services, he refused to partake of the Lord's supper because he objected to kneeling, finding it contrary to the notion of a supper and in keeping with the idolatrous practice of Catholics. For his refusal he was again in trouble in the spring of 1666, though he was discharged after his wife paid his fees.

Henry was again appointed to collect the royal aid in June 1666, but when summoned to Hanmer in August and told to subscribe to a loan for prosecuting the war, he refused, insisting he did not have the minimum £20. That autumn he distributed 120 copies of a Welsh translation of Richard Baxter's Call to the Unconverted in north Wales, a gift from the author. To quiet criticism that he was in violation of the Five Mile Act and to provide a better education for his children, he moved to Whitchurch in Shropshire in March 1667. His son Matthew recalled that it was here his father began to administer the Lord's supper privately, a significant step given his aversion to separatism, but also an indication of the spiritual need he felt to renew observance of the sacrament. An outbreak of smallpox at Whitchurch, the need to harvest crops, and his wife's wishes prompted him to return to Broad Oak in July, staying three months before going back to Whitchurch. After he and Lawrence preached at Betley, Staffordshire, in February 1668, an MP falsely accused them in the House of Commons of trampling on the surplice and pulling the minister out of the pulpit. When the Commons complained, the crown issued a proclamation ordering enforcement of the penal laws. In May Henry returned to Broad Oak, where he lived the rest of his life. Henceforth he taught young scholars in his home, both before and during their university years. According to the episcopal returns of 1669 he was one of four preachers ministering to eighty people at Whitchurch.

During a visit to London in late August and early September 1671 Henry observed a fast at the countess of Exeter's house, preached to the congregations of Thomas Doolittle and Steele, met with other dissenting ministers, including Samuel Annesley and Robert Chambers, and attended the funeral of the nonconformist John Burgess with more than 100 other clergy. His discussions with Annesley and others may have concerned renewed efforts for comprehension of nonconformists in the state church and the alternative of toleration for those whose principles precluded compromise. When Charles II issued the declaration of indulgence in 1672, Henry was critical of it on the grounds that it encouraged separatism at the expense of 'our Parish-order which God hath own'd' (*Diaries and Letters*, 250). Instead he wanted 'sober' nonconformists to have access to pulpits in parish churches as a means of fostering protestant unity. Nevertheless, through Steele's efforts he was licensed on 30 April as a presbyterian to preach at his house in Broad Oak. He had done some preaching at Stafford and elsewhere in 1671, but after he was licensed he was more active, ministering at various places in Shropshire, Cheshire, and Denbighshire, and gathering a congregation at Broad Oak to which he administered the Lord's supper once a month. Although the indulgence was withdrawn in March 1673, the Flintshire magistrates were tolerant, enabling him to continue preaching.

In addition to following major developments in foreign affairs, Henry evinced an interest in domestic events. In January 1680, for instance, he read accounts of the alleged Popish and Meal-Tub plots by Thomas Dangerfield and Rodney Mansell. As the succession crisis unfolded he seems to have been neutral, hoping God would 'secure the Interest that is thine own' (*Diaries and Letters*, 284). With Matthew he visited London in July, preaching to the congregations of Doolittle, Steele, and Lawrence. In August he spent twelve days as the guest of Lord and Lady Paget at Boreatton, reading John Rushworth's collection of material about Strafford's trial and the civil war as well as a hostile biography of Stephen Marshall, whom he admired. He conversed with two other guests, the MPs Philip Foley and John Swynfen, both prominent friends of dissenters. On an earlier visit to Boreatton, in 1670, he had conferred with Swynfen and Richard Hampden, another MP supportive of nonconformists. Through his friend Rowland Hunt of Boreatton, whose wife was the daughter of Lord Paget, Henry also had links to Sir Henry Ashurst MP and Sir Anthony Irby MP, both of whom supported nonconformists in parliament. Once more Henry was appointed to a civil office, this time as a high constable in 1680, and, though he found a substitute, he was responsible for managing the finances.

From persecution to toleration, 1680–1696 Henry again tasted persecution in the early 1680s. For preaching a funeral sermon at Weston in the parish of Hodnet, Shropshire, he was fined £40 in June 1681, but he refused to pay. When magistrates sought to distrain his goods he resisted by locking up his livestock as well as his house, though ultimately they seized coal, barley, a cart, and a sled. He was presented at the Flint assizes on 19 September for holding an illegal meeting at his house and urging defiance against the Conventicle Act, but George Jeffreys, chief justice of Chester, whom he had examined when the latter was a schoolboy, was uninterested in prosecuting him. Eight days later Henry and two other nonconformists engaged in a five-hour public debate with William Lloyd, bishop of St Asaph, at Oswestry, Shropshire, about the legitimacy of ordination by presbyters. The bishop subsequently sent for Henry to discuss a plan for improving discipline in his diocese. The two men remained on friendly terms, and in March 1682 Henry sent the bishop a

letter appealing for leniency toward dissenters. As conditions worsened he went to Paget's house in July to discuss the plight of nonconformists with him and Swynfen. During the tory reaction he had to confine his ministry largely to his family. At the time of Monmouth's rebellion he was incarcerated for approximately three weeks in Chester Castle, but he accepted his condition stoically, convinced that a guilty conscience was a much worse prison.

By 1687 conditions were improving, and on 9 May Henry and five colleagues were able to ordain Matthew Henry at Broad Oak. That summer Henry joined others in thanking James II for his declaration of indulgence. In 1687–8 he saw all five of his surviving children marry, his four daughters in Whitewell Chapel; after each wedding he preached to his family. In the two years following James's indulgence Henry worshipped at Whitewell unless there was no sermon, in which case he preached in his own house. Nominated as a justice of the peace for Flintshire in May 1688, he successfully requested to be excused from serving.

Although Henry welcomed the liberty provided by the Act of Toleration the following year and favoured comprehension, he opposed the sacramental test, whereby nonconformists could take Anglican communion once a year to qualify for public office. For a time he continued to worship at Whitewell, but so many people came to hear him preach that he regularly did so at Broad Oak for the rest of his life, administering the sacraments as well. He also observed the public fasts proclaimed by the government. Sensing impending death, in 1694 he dated his letters in his 'dying year'. In fact, he lived until 24 June 1696, when he died at Broad Oak after recurring bouts with colic and possibly the stone. Francis Tallents of Shrewsbury preached a funeral sermon at Broad Oak and Henry was buried at Whitchurch church on 27 June. His son Matthew and James Owen of Oswestry also preached funeral sermons. In his will, dated 24 August 1695, Henry bequeathed each daughter a copy of Matthew Poole's biblical annotations, a psalter, and a specified religious book. With these exceptions, his wife was allowed to retain whatever books and manuscripts she wanted, with the remainder going to Matthew. Modest bequests were provided for other members of his family and his servants, with the rest of the estate going to his wife, who died on 25 May 1707.

Historical assessment Although Henry vacillated with respect to some of the finer points of dissent, particularly concerning the sacraments, he remained firm in his hostility to traditional prelacy. His refusal to conform to the liturgy as a minister was grounded in his dislike of prelacy, but as a private person he attended services in the established church as a testimony against separatism, which, he argued, unchurches the nation, 'pluck[s] up the hedge of Parish order', and allows unordained people to preach. Although he admired the Independents for maintaining discipline and loving one another, he objected to their repudiation of the parochial system:

If I were an Independent, I must be an Anabaptist, for if Baptism bee the door into the Christian-church & I am no church-Member till I embody in that way, then I must come in by that door. (*Diaries and Letters*, 277)

In fact, he rejected both positions. He found prelacy objectionable because the decrees of excommunication and absolution were administered by lay chancellors and lay rural deans. As the fundamental reasons for his dissent he cited his refusal to be reordained, to renounce the solemn league and covenant, and to embrace the unreformed liturgy. Those aspects of the liturgy he found especially objectionable were the sign of the cross in baptism and kneeling at communion, neither of which had scriptural warrant and both of which offended his conscience. 'The Presbyterian Interest', he averred, was the most appropriate as 'the middle between two extreames' (ibid., 132).

Beginning in 1657 Henry kept a diary, which by the time of his death filled perhaps thirty-nine volumes. The entries are typically brief and deal with such subjects as his family, news, and the weather. He was particularly interested in recording events that could be interpreted as examples of divine providence. His diary is especially valuable because it manifests how he regarded his family as his congregation, the provisions he made for its worship, his unique calendar highlighting special days of both a public and a private nature, and the application of his dissenting values to family life. Above all, the diary provides an invaluable record of what it felt like to be a dissenting minister. Diaries for the following years are known to be extant: 1657, 1661–3, 1665–7, 1669–74, 1676, and 1678–84. He also left many unpublished sermons, an exposition of the first eleven chapters of the book of Genesis, commonplace books, and assorted other manuscripts. Despite his association with prominent supporters of dissent in parliament, his vision of nonseparating nonconformity ultimately failed in 1689, but his reputation for holy living and resolute commitment to his ideals became almost legendary.

RICHARD L. GREAVES

Sources *Diaries and letters of Philip Henry*, ed. M. H. Lee (1882) · M. Henry, *The lives of Philip and Matthew Henry*, ed. J. B. Williams, 2 vols. in 1 (1974) · *Eighteen sermons, by the Rev. Philip Henry, A.M.*, ed. J. B. Williams (1816) · G. F. Nuttall, 'The nurture of nonconformity: Philip Henry's diaries', *Transactions of the Honourable Society of Cymmrodorion*, new ser., 4 (1998), 5–27 · G. F. Nuttall, 'Philip Henry and London', *Journal of the United Reformed Church History Society*, 5 (1992–7), 259–66 · D. R. Lacey, *Dissent and parliamentary politics in England, 1661–1689* (1969) · *CSP dom.*, 1671–2, 326, 342, 413 · *Calamy rev.* · BL, Add. MS 42849 · Foster, *Alum. Oxon.* · P. Crawford, 'Katharine and Philip Henry and their children: a case study in family ideology', *Transactions of the Historic Society of Lancashire and Cheshire*, 134 (1984), 39–73 · A. Gordon, ed., *Freedom after ejection: a review (1690–1692) of presbyterian and congregational nonconformity in England and Wales* (1917) · T. Richards, *Wales under the penal code, 1662–1687* (1925)
Archives BL, corresp. and papers, Add. MSS 24629, 42849, 43688, 44056, 45534–45538 · Bodl. Oxf., papers, MSS Eng. lett. e 29; misc. e 330–331, d 311, c 293–294 · CUL, commentary on Genesis, Add. MS 7338 · DWL, corresp., MSS 90.5–7 · DWL, diary, cash book, and sermon notes, MSS 90.1, 90.10 · DWL, sermon notes and commonplace books, MSS L197–207 · Flintshire RO, Hawarden, sermons, MSS D/DM/86 · Harris Man. Oxf., sermons · priv. coll., diaries · Shrewsbury School Library, diary | BL, Add. MS 4275, fols. 314–25 · DWL, corresp. with Matthew Henry

Likenesses R. Grave, engraving (after oils, c.1696), repro. in Henry, *Lives of Philip and Matthew Henry* · R. White, line engraving (after R. Holland), BM, NPG; repro. in M. Henry, *An account of the life and death of Mr Philip Henry* (1712) [*see illus.*] · portrait, priv. coll.

Henry, Robert (1718–1790), Church of Scotland minister and historian, was born on 1 March 1718, the son of James Henry, a farmer in Muirton, St Ninians, Stirlingshire, and Jean Galloway, also from Stirlingshire. He attended the parish school and subsequently the grammar school at Stirling, and then studied arts and divinity at the University of Edinburgh. For a time during the mid-1740s he was master of the grammar school at Annan, in southern Dumfriesshire, and he obtained his licence to preach from the presbytery of Annan on 27 March 1746. Two years later he accepted a call from the Presbyterian congregation at Carlisle, where he was ordained on 4 November 1748. He moved to the high meeting in Berwick upon Tweed on 13 August 1760, and a sermon that he preached there on 2 March 1762 became his first publication when it appeared in London soon afterwards as *The Christian Evangelist*. On 26 June 1763 he married Ann Balderston (d. 1800), daughter of Thomas Balderston, a Berwick surgeon. The marriage was a happy one, though it produced no children. Through the influence of his brother-in-law Gilbert Laurie, the lord provost of Edinburgh, Henry moved to New Greyfriars Church, Edinburgh, on 24 May 1768 and on 19 December 1776 he was translated to the second charge in the Old Kirk, where he remained for the rest of his life. In 1774 he had the unprecedented honour of being elected moderator of the general assembly of the Church of Scotland on his first appearance as a member of that body. Unlike most Scottish clergymen of letters of his day, he generally sided with the popular party against the ascendant moderates. Nevertheless he remained on good terms with the moderates, and received an honorary DD degree from the University of Edinburgh on 24 July 1770, during the tenure of Principal William Robertson, the moderate party leader. He mixed comfortably with the Edinburgh literati as a member of the Society of Antiquaries of Scotland and, from 17 November 1783, a fellow of the Royal Society of Edinburgh.

The move to Edinburgh in 1768 gave Henry access to excellent libraries and encouraged him to pursue in earnest a work of history he had begun in Berwick, *The History of Great Britain, from the First Invasion of it by the Romans under Julius Caesar*. It appeared in five large quarto volumes between April 1771 and December 1785; a sixth quarto volume, published posthumously in 1793, was partly the work of Malcolm Laing and was edited by Sir Henry Moncreiff Wellwood. Henry's so-called 'new plan' was adapted from Goguet's *De l'origine des loix, des arts, et des sciences et leurs progrès chez les anciens peuples* (1758) and proposed separate coverage of seven different topics in each of the historical periods he treated: civil and military history, religious history, political and legal history, the history of learning and the learned, the history of arts, economic history, and the history of manners and customs. Henry is believed to have translated at least the first volume of the three-volume English edition of Goguet's work which appeared in Edinburgh in 1761, and since the imprint of that edition stated that it was printed 'for the translator', he may have been its publisher as well. Yet the 'General preface' to the first volume of the *History* obscured this French debt by asserting that Henry's method was completely different from any other, and unsuspecting commentators, such as Lord Cockburn, reiterated that Henry's work demonstrated 'complete originality in the plan' (*Memorials … by Lord Cockburn*, 53).

Henry's *History* faced four considerable obstacles. First, the enormous scale of the undertaking was perhaps too ambitious for one man, who was also engaged in a full-time career as a clergyman. Starting in the age of the Roman occupation of Britain, Henry intended to carry the study up to the present in a work of ten large volumes, but he got only as far as the accession of Henry VII in volume 5 and the death of Henry VIII in the posthumous sixth volume. Second, when Henry approached the leading London booksellers with his first volume in 1770, he received 'little or no encouragement' (John Douglas to Alexander Carlyle, 6 April 1771, Edinburgh University, Dc.4.41, no. 19), and rather than accept less than he believed it was worth, he opted for self-publication, an expensive and risky undertaking. The ledgers of William Strahan reveal that it cost approximately £85 to print one thousand copies of the first volume alone, in addition to paper, advertising, and the printing of 1500 subscription proposals; the retail price was 1 guinea. Writing to David Hume on 1 March 1771, when the first volume was about to appear, Strahan cited two reasons for refusing to purchase the copyright: 'the Extent of the Plan, which cannot possibly be completed in any reasonable Time', and the author's inflated asking price (NL Scot., Hume MSS, MS 23157, no. 62), which prompted him to query to the same correspondent three years later, on 9 April 1774: 'is not his work an exception to your own general rule, that no good book was ever wrote for money?' (*Letters of David Hume*, 285). To the author himself, however, Strahan wrote on 18 December 1772 that 'we decline the Purchase purely from the nature and length of the Work' (NA Scot., RH 9/17/195). In conversation with Boswell and Johnson in April 1778, William Robertson criticized Henry both for failing to define his topic more manageably and for 'not selling his first volume at a moderate price to the booksellers, that they might have pushed him on till he had got reputation' (Boswell, *Life*, 3.333–4). Nevertheless the work eventually gained a following and brought its author handsome remuneration. In April 1786 Andrew Strahan and Thomas Cadell of London, whose respective firms had handled the printing and selling of the book from the beginning, contracted to pay Henry £1000 for the rights to a second edition of the completed portion of the work, with the additional opportunity to purchase future volumes at the same rate. This second edition appeared in 1788 in ten octavo volumes (augmented by two posthumous octavo volumes in 1795) and was dedicated to the author's patron, Lord Mansfield, who had secured him a government

pension of £100 per annum for life in the spring of 1781. A Dublin reprint followed immediately. Although Henry fretted that the sale of the quarto edition was slowed by 'the carelessness of Booksellers as it is not their property' (R. Henry to R. Harrison, 17 Jan 1783, priv. coll.), the work apparently sold well enough, and in 1786 he sold Strahan and Cadell 140 sets of the five published volumes for £455. Henry claimed that the *History* earned him a total of £3300, and it continued to generate income for his estate after his death.

Yet the strain of self-publishing on this scale took its toll on the author and probably increased his vulnerability to a third difficulty: the incessant attacks of Gilbert Stuart. Stuart had favourably reviewed the first volume of Henry's *History* in the *Monthly Review* for July 1771, but in his own periodical, the *Edinburgh Magazine and Review*, damned one of Henry's published sermons in 1773 and subsequently blasted the second volume of his *History* in a two-part review that appeared early in 1774. In the course of what steadily became a smear campaign against Henry, Stuart also abused David Hume by first altering, and then suppressing, a favourable review of Henry's work which Hume had prepared for his magazine. In the spring of 1777 Henry visited Stuart's London publisher and friend, John Murray, in an unsuccessful effort to learn the source of Stuart's hostility and smooth over the reception of his third volume, which was dedicated to the king.

The fourth obstacle facing Henry was declining health. From about the early 1780s he was too weak to preach, and his debilitating condition, along with a tremor in his hand, made historical composition increasingly difficult. In a notice headed 'To the public', prefixed to the fifth volume in 1785, he mentioned among the reasons for the tardiness of that work 'several interruptions from want of health' (p. iv). 'I sincerely think you have made a good bargain', Henry wrote to Cadell on 8 April 1786 in regard to the rights to his second edition and projected volumes. 'But you must remember to pray powerfully for my life' (BL, Add. MS 48901, fols. 29–30). As his condition deteriorated, he passed more of his time at his country home, Millfield, near Polmont in south-east Stirlingshire, where he had built a separate room to house his library. One day in November 1790 he invited Moncreiff Wellwood to Millfield, allegedly in a letter that read: 'Come out here directly. I have got something to do this week, I have got to die' (*Memorials … by Lord Cockburn*, 51). In these final days he executed a deed bequeathing his books to Linlithgow, for the establishment of a public library there. He also dictated detailed directions for the management of his affairs, including a list of friends whom he wanted to attend his funeral. Henry died at Millfield that week, on 24 November 1790, and was buried in the churchyard at Polmont, where a monument was erected in his honour. He was survived by his wife and his *History*, which was reprinted as a twelve-volume octavo edition by Cadell and Davies and Andrew Strahan in 1799–1800, 1805–6, and 1814, and finally reached a sixth edition for different publishers in 1823 and 1824. A French translation which had begun to appear in the year before Henry's death was completed in 1796. In the same year Cadell and Davies published a continuation of the *History* by James Pettit Andrews. Although the title-page identified the book as volume 1, the death of Andrews in 1797 put an end to his efforts, and Henry's 'new plan' was never carried beyond the year 1603.   RICHARD B. SHER

Sources W. Adam, *Sequel to the gift of a grandfather* (1836) · D. Allan, *Virtue, learning and the Scottish Enlightenment: ideas of scholarship in early modern history* (1993) · Allibone, *Dict.* · Boswell, *Life* · Chambers, *Scots.* (1835) · *Memorials of his time, by Lord Cockburn*, rev. edn, ed. W. Forbes Gray (1946); repr. (1989) · J. Gary, *The Royal Society of Edinburgh: literary fellows, 1783–1812*, ed. S. Devlin-Thorp (1981), vol. 2 of *Scotland's cultural heritage* (1981–4), 44 · [I. D'Israeli], *Calamities of authors*, 2 vols. (1812) · *Edinburgh Evening Courant* (22 May 1784) · M. S. Phillips, *Society and sentiment: genres of historical writing in Britain, 1740–1820* (2000) · *Letters of David Hume to William Strahan*, ed. G. B. Hill (1888) · C. Kidd, *Subverting Scotland's past: Scottish whig historians and the creation of an Anglo-British identity, 1689–c.1830* (1993) · [H. M. Wellwood], 'The life of Robert Henry, D.D.', *History of Great Britain*, ed. R. Henry, 6 (1793), vii–xx · R. L. Meek, *Social science and the ignoble savage* (1976) · E. C. Mossner, 'Hume as a literary patron: a suppressed review of Robert Henry's *History of Great Britain*, 1773', *Modern Philology*, 39 (1941–2), 361–82 · T. P. Peardon, *The transition in English historical writing* (1933), 34–8 · *Scots Magazine*, 36 (1774), 269 · *Scots Magazine*, 37 (1775), 279 · *Scots Magazine*, 42 (1780), 273–9 · *Scots Magazine*, 53 (1791), 365–70 · 'Account of the life of Robert Henry, extracted from vol. VI of his *History of Great Britain*', *Scots Magazine*, 58 (1796), 293–6 · *Fasti Scot.*, new edn, 1.34, 76–7 · R. B. Sher, *Church and university in the Scottish Enlightenment: the moderate literati of Edinburgh* (1985) · W. Zachs, *Without regard to good manners: a biography of Gilbert Stuart, 1743–1786* (1992) · J. Douglas, letter to A. Carlyle, 6 April 1771, U. Edin. L., MS Dc.4.41, no. 19 · W. Strahan, letter to D. Hume, 1 March 1771, NL Scot., Hume MS 23157, no. 62 · R. Henry, letter to R. Harrison, 17 Jan 1783, priv. coll. · R. Henry, letter to T. Cadell, 8 April 1786, BL, Add. MS 48901

Archives NA Scot., lecture given to Society of Antiquaries on the standing stone of Stainhouse, Orkney · NRA, priv. coll., corresp. relating to *History of Great Britain* | BL, corresp. with Thomas Cadell and Andrew Strahan, Add. MS 48901, fols. 27–36 · BL, Strahan MSS, Add. MS 48801, fol. 59 · BL, Add. MS 48814A, fol. 13 · BL, Add. MS 48815, fol. 116 · NL Scot., MS 948, no. 3; MS 962, fol. 109; MS 9657, fol. 30; Acc 11693 · U. Edin., La. II. 219, nos 23 and 24

Likenesses J. Caldwall, engraving, 1771 (after D. Martin), BM · D. Martin, portrait (in clerical dress), Scot. NPG

Henry, Robert Mitchell (1873–1950), classical scholar, was born on 11 February 1873 in Belfast, the eldest of the four sons of the Revd Robert Mitchell Henry (1824–1891), of 61 Botanic View (later University Road), Belfast, and his wife, Kate Anne (1838–1928), eldest daughter of the Revd Thomas Berry, a Baptist minister, of Athlone, co. Westmeath. The Berrys were said to be descended from Jean, duc de Berry (1340–1416). Henry's father had been a Presbyterian minister and then a Baptist minister, but after a preaching tour of the United States had left the Baptists in the early 1870s to start his own mission in Belfast, later joining the Plymouth Brethren.

Mitchell and his brothers, one of whom was the painter Paul Henry (1876–1958), had a strict and isolated upbringing. He was educated at the Methodist College, Belfast, and read classics at Queen's College, Belfast, part of the Royal University of Ireland, where he was awarded a first

in 1893. He took another first in classics from London University in 1896, and in 1898 was awarded an MA and a studentship at the Royal University of Ireland, which was followed by a junior fellowship in 1900 and a readership in 1906. At the same time he was senior classics master at the Royal Belfast Academical Institution from 1899 to 1905. In 1907 he was appointed professor of Latin at the Royal University of Ireland, and when this was abolished in 1908 and Queen's College became Queen's University, Belfast, he occupied the chair of Latin.

Although Henry was a protestant, he was also an Irish nationalist, and disliked the Unionist politics of Ulster and the extremism of the Orange order. In sympathy with the aims of the Gaelic League, with its emphasis on Irish language and culture, he was the main champion of a proposal put forward by the Gaelic League in 1911 to raise the recently established lectureship in Celtic at Queen's University to the status of a chair, a move which was approved but later dropped by the senate. He supported home rule for Ireland, but in *The Evolution of Sinn Féin* (1920), while agreeing that Ireland was a nation and as such had a right to independence, he concluded that full independence for Ireland would be impossible in the foreseeable future. Later in his life he was unwilling to join any political pressure groups, and refused to support the Ulsterman Major-General Hugh Montgomery in his efforts to set up the Irish Association (founded in 1938), a society which was promoting conciliation between the Catholic and protestant communities in Northern and southern Ireland. But his interest in Irish civilization continued, and when the Ulster Society for Irish Historical Studies was founded at Queen's University in 1936 he was the first president, and he helped to found the journal *Irish Historical Studies* in 1938, jointly with the Irish Historical Society in Dublin.

At Queen's University Henry was at the centre of academic politics and administration. According to the new constitution of the university, the senate, made up predominantly of non-academics, was the governing body, while internal academic affairs were run by the academic council of professors. Henry was elected secretary of the academic council at its first meeting in November 1909, and remained in this post until his resignation in 1936, making it one of the most important offices in the university. In addition he managed to be appointed to the first professorial vacancy on the senate in January 1911, and although the members of the senate and the academic council were mainly Unionists, he was able to play an important part in determining the policy of the new university. In 1933, when the vice-chancellor, Sir Richard Winn Livingstone, resigned, there was some suggestion that Henry might be appointed as his successor, but at this point his political views told against him, and he was passed over, although he was appointed pro-vice-chancellor until the position was filled. From then on it became established practice for the secretary of the academic council to deputize for the vice-chancellor and to step in during a vacancy, and Henry did so again in November 1938. When he was approaching his sixty-fifth birthday the senate voted against extending his tenure of the chair of Latin, although he would have liked to stay on, and it was thought that this was also because of his political views. In 1929 Henry donated over 1000 volumes of Irish history and civilization from his own very fine library to the library of Queen's University, and these formed the nucleus of the R. M. Henry collection, to which he added during the 1930s. In 1951 the university bought most of his remaining library to add to the collection. On his retirement he was appointed to an honorary chair of classical literature at Trinity College, Dublin, and in 1939 he accepted the chair of humanity at the University of St Andrews, which he held until 1947. From 1947 until his death he lectured and taught in Dublin.

Henry's most important academic publication was his completion of T. W. Dougan's edition of Cicero's *Tusculan Disputations* (1934), and his other works include an edition of Livy's Book 26 (1905), *An Irish Corpus astronomiae* (1915), and *Virgil and the Roman Epic* (1938). He was president of the Classical Association of Ireland in 1920, and of the Classical Association of Northern Ireland from 1929 to 1938, and president of the Classical Association of England and Wales in 1936. He believed in the importance of adult education, and from 1919 to 1938 served as chairman of the Belfast (later Northern Ireland) branch of the Workers' Educational Association. It was largely as a result of his efforts that the senate of Queen's University created the new post of lecturer and director of extramural studies in 1928.

Henry was awarded honorary degrees by Queen's University, Trinity College, Dublin, and the University of St Andrews. He died on 21 December 1950 at his home, 17 Herbert Road, Bray, co. Wicklow, and was buried at St Patrick's Church, Enniskerry. He was twice married: first to Margaret Jane, youngest daughter of John MacFarlane, of Omagh, co. Tyrone, and second to Kathleen Elizabeth Raleigh, eldest daughter of Herbert Watson, engineer, of Belfast. A copy of the portrait painted by Paul Henry for Queen's University in 1933 hangs in the university library.　ANNE PIMLOTT BAKER

Sources T. W. Moody and J. C. Beckett, *Queen's, Belfast, 1845–1949: the history of a university*, 2 vols. (1959) · S. B. Kennedy, *Paul Henry* (2000) · P. Henry, *Further reminiscences* (1973) · J. W. Henderson, *Methodist College, Belfast, 1868–1938* (1939), vol. 1, pp. 84–5 · T. W. Moody and D. E. W. W., 'R. M. Henry: an appreciation', *Irish Times* (23 Dec 1950) · *The Times* (16 Jan 1951) · *Queen's University Association Annual Record* (1950), 40–41 · WW
Archives Queen's University, Belfast, unpublished papers
Likenesses P. Henry, portrait, 1933, Queen's University Library, Belfast; repro. in Kennedy, *Paul Henry*, 112 · photograph, *c*.1938, repro. in Moody and Beckett, *Queen's, Belfast*, vol. 1, fig. 24 · photograph, repro. in Henderson, *Methodist College, Belfast*, 84
Wealth at death £5210 7s. 8d.—in England: probate, 31 May 1952, CGPLA Eng. & Wales

Henry, Sarah. *See* Savage, Sarah (1664–1752).

Henry, Thomas (1734–1816), apothecary and chemist, was born on 28 September 1734 at Wrexham, Wales, the third of five children and the second of three sons of William Henry. His parents kept a school but his father was best known as a dancing-master. Of his elder brother, James (*b.* 1729), little is recorded, but his younger brother, Ellis

(1743–1815), eventually went to Brasenose College, Oxford, and entered the church. Thomas was educated by his mother and at Wrexham grammar school. He had hopes of going to Oxford and into the church but the family means fell short of this and he became apprenticed to a Richard Jones, apothecary of Wrexham. Jones died in 1752 and Henry completed his apprenticeship at Knutsford. During this time he taught himself chemistry (the theory for the most part from Boerhaave's *Elementa chemiae*, 1724; Eng. trans., 1727). Towards the end of his apprenticeship he did go to Oxford—as an apothecary (assistant to a Mr Malbon), not to the university. There he made social acquaintances who encouraged his ambitions, and he added to his scientific knowledge by attending lectures on anatomy.

On completing his apprenticeship Henry set up on his own in 1759 in Knutsford. He prospered, was married in 1760 to Mary Kinsey (*d.* 1805), and, in 1764, moved to Manchester, to prosper even further. He and Mary had six children, of whom his third son, William *Henry, acquired scientific distinction. The expansion of Manchester in industry and population made it a centre for religious and political activity, and for intellectual development. Henry remained a member of the established church until all his children had been baptized (the last in 1775), but he then became a Unitarian, joining the community based at the Cross Street Chapel. He worked with fellow dissenters, some associated with the Lunar Society, so meeting James Watt, Matthew Boulton, and Joseph Priestley. In Manchester a close friend was the physician Thomas Percival who stimulated Henry to engage in his own experimental science. With him and Thomas Barnes he helped to found the Manchester Literary and Philosophical Society in 1781. Its emphasis on natural philosophy was soon established and it became a leading scientific society, held for some time to be second in England only to the Royal Society; Henry was one of its first joint secretaries and later its president. He co-operated in the foundation of two educational establishments: a College of Arts and Sciences (1784–7) and, in 1786, the Manchester Academy, or 'New College', which moved to York in 1800. The college was short-lived but the Manchester Academy was effective enough for it to be worthwhile Henry's bringing John Dalton to Manchester to teach at it. Henry himself taught chemistry at both institutions.

Henry actively concerned himself with some of the industries that were growing up in Manchester. In the phenomenal expansion of the cotton industry, he saw opportunities in the study of the essential process of bleaching, and applied the newly discovered substance chlorine to good effect. Theoretically he offered a correct explanation of the function of mordants in dyeing. He acquired rights in a process for the manufacture of magnesia. At first he imitated the work of Samuel Glass (1709–1786), who had already developed a trade in magnesium carbonate, but later he improved on it to make a more effective and palatable magnesium oxide. After some years of controversy over rights he was able to establish

'Henry's Magnesia' as a source of income for the family for more than a century.

Henry was president of the Manchester Literary and Philosophical Society, with one brief interval, from 1805 to 1816. Of his few papers, none of great weight, most were published in the *Manchester Memoirs*. He co-operated with Percival in studying the cause and control of putrefaction, and, after experiments on the interaction of air and green plants, eventually adhered to the new antiphlogiston theory of chemistry. He made what remained the only English translation (1776) of Lavoisier's *Opuscules* (1774). He became a fellow of the Royal Society in 1775 but his provincial position and his limited scientific originality meant that he had no great influence in it. His great merit was in his insistence on a knowledge of science as a basis for effective industrial enterprise. His lectures at the Manchester society, and also at the College of Arts and Sciences, were given in the evening so that they could be heard by persons gainfully occupied during the day. They were based on his view that 'the arts' were to be taken to mean the practical and profitable arts, chemistry being one of them. This attitude was expressed as early as 1781 in his first lecture to the society, when he complained 'that few dyers are chemists, and few chemists dyers'.

Henry lived in times of political unrest. He was sympathetic to a radicalism he took care not to preach openly, possibly for concern lest his business suffer at the hands of those who burned Priestley's house in 1791. After 1764 he lived in Manchester for the rest of his life, first at his place of business in St Ann's Square, and then in a better house in King Street. He died at Manchester on 18 June 1816 and was buried at Cross Street Chapel.

FRANK GREENAWAY

Sources W. V. Farrar, K. Farrar, and E. L. Scott, 'The Henrys of Manchester [pt 1]', *Ambix*, 20 (1973), 183–208 • W. Henry, 'A tribute to the memory of the late president of the Literary and Philosophical Society of Manchester', *Memoirs of the Literary and Philosophical Society of Manchester*, 2nd ser., 3 (1819), 204–40 • W. Henry, 'A tribute to the memory of the late Thomas Henry, F.R.S., … president of the Literary and Philosophical Society of Manchester', *Annals of Philosophy*, 14 (1819), 161–76 • W. V. Farrar and K. Farrar, 'The Henrys of Manchester', *Royal Institute of Chemistry Reviews*, 4 (1971)
Archives Manchester Literary and Philosophical Society
Likenesses portrait, repro. in Farrar and Farrar, 'The Henrys of Manchester', 37

Henry, Sir Thomas (1807–1876), police magistrate, was born in Dublin, the eldest son of David Henry of St Stephen's Green, Dublin, head of the firm of Henry, Mullins, and MacMahon, government contractors. He was educated in Dublin first at Von Feinagle's school and then at Trinity College where he graduated BA in 1824 and MA in 1827. Called to the bar at the Middle Temple on 23 January 1829, he practised on the northern circuit, and attended the West Riding of Yorkshire sessions. He was magistrate at the Lambeth Street police court, Whitechapel, from April 1840 until 1846, when he was transferred to Bow Street. He became chief magistrate there on 6 July 1864, and was knighted on 30 November 1864. It is said that he discharged his duties with general approval. He took a leading role in the development of the law of extradition

of his time. The Extradition Act and the various treaties connected with it between Britain and foreign powers were in each case drawn by him. He was for many years the chief adviser to the government on policing questions, and his opinion was acted upon in various licensing bills, betting acts, Sunday trading legislation, and similar measures. He gave evidence before the committee on theatrical licenses, and advised on the appropriate level of regulation of music halls and casinos. He died at his residence, 23 Hanover Square, London, on 16 June 1876, and was buried in the grounds of St Thomas's Roman Catholic Church, Fulham, on 21 June.

G. C. BOASE, rev. ERIC METCALFE

Sources *The Times* (17 June 1876), 10 • *The Times* (22 June 1876), 5 • *Law Times* (1 July 1876), 167 • *The Graphic* (24 June 1876), 614 • *ILN* (14 March 1846), 174 • *ILN* (24 June 1876), 623 • *ILN* (1 July 1876), 3–4
Likenesses portrait, repro. in *Graphic* • portrait, repro. in *ILN* (14 March 1846), 172 • wood-engraving, NPG; repro. in *ILN* (1 July 1876), 3–4
Wealth at death under £14,000: probate, 29 June 1876, *CGPLA Eng. & Wales*

Henry, William [*pseud.* Britanno-Hibernus] (*d.* 1768), dean of Killaloe and writer, was possibly born in co. Donegal or co. Fermanagh to a branch of a Gloucestershire family; he was educated in Dublin. Nothing is known for certain of his early life or his parents, and his first recorded contact with Dublin University was not until the awarding of his MA in 1748. He proceeded BD and DD in 1750. The details of his wife and marriage are equally obscure, although it is known that his wife survived him and went on to remarry. In October 1731 Henry was presented to the benefice of Killesher, co. Fermanagh, by Josiah Hort, bishop of Kilmore, to whom Henry had acted as chaplain, and whose will he was later to witness. Three years later Henry became rector of Urney, co. Tyrone, apparently holding the parish until his death, despite his appointment as dean of Killaloe on 29 November 1761.

Henry is most notable for his various writings, both published and private, rather than for his ecclesiastical career. While at Killesher he wrote a natural history of the parish, and a description of counties Antrim and Down, both of which survive in their original manuscript form (respectively in BL, Add. MS 4435, and Armagh Public Library). While at Urney he appears to have travelled widely in the north and west of Ireland, and he compiled a short natural and topographical history of the counties adjacent to Lough Erne. This was later edited and published by Sir Charles King as *Henry's Upper Lough Erne in 1739* (1892). Contemporarily he published three scientific papers in the *Philosophical Transactions of the Royal Society*, being elected a fellow of the Royal Society in February 1755. He was also a member of the Physico-Historical Society, the predecessor of the Royal Irish Academy. He published at least a dozen sermons and political pamphlets, including an anonymous attack on the Dublin radical Charles Lucas in 1749, and *A Philippic Oration Against the Pretender's Son and his Adherents* in 1745. Alarmed by the consequences of the heavy whiskey drinking he witnessed in Ireland, Henry became an early advocate of temperance. He produced a series of pamphlets to support his ideas, and corresponded in the Irish press on the matter. His letters to a number of influential figures in the Irish and British administrations touch on this issue, and many others, including a plea for arms to equip his Tyrone parishioners for a projected colonization of Connaught.

Taken together, Henry's historical and scientific writings reveal him as a keen and astute observer of his surroundings. The accumulative impression of his sermons is of a gradual shift from low- to high-church principles. Although he remained a supporter of protestant unity, his tolerance did not extend to Catholics. Politically he remained a whig, although he had no time for radicals, and he avoided the Irish protestant patriotic movement of his day. He was a sincere advocate of temperance, but his correspondence reveals him to have been a somewhat authoritarian and unsympathetic man. In 1763 a proclamation by the Oakboys, a group of militant anti-tithe agitators, referred to him as 'that covetous man'. In essence, Henry was perhaps a not untypical member of the Church of Ireland clergy of his day—socially conservative, but committed to the moral and economic improvement of his adopted homeland. He died in Dublin on 13 February 1768, and was buried three days later in St Anne's Church there.   NEAL GARNHAM

Sources BL, Newcastle MSS, Add. MSS 32930, fol. 114; 32967, fol. 280; 32968, fol. 202; 32970, fol. 25; 32980, fol. 58; 32988, fol. 56 · BL, Hardwicke MSS, 1761–3, Add. MSS 35396, fols. 391, 400, 452; 35597, fols. 268, 275 · BL, Hardwicke MSS, letter to Archbishop Herring of Canterbury (1753), Add. MS 35592, fol. 225 · BL, Hardwicke MSS, letter to Lord Cadogan (1752), Add. MS 4440, fols. 123–5 · *Pue's Occurrences* (20 Feb 1768) · *Belfast News-Letter* (7 Jan 1757) · 'Calendar of miscellaneous letters and papers prior to 1760', NA Ire. · PRO NI, letter to duke of Northumberland (1763), T/2872/5 · *London Magazine*, 32 (Aug 1763) · *GM*, 1st ser., 33 (1763)

Archives BL, Hardwicke MS · BL, Newcastle MS

Henry, William (1774–1836), chemist, was born at St Ann's Square, Manchester, on 12 December 1774. He was the third son of Thomas *Henry (1734–1816), apothecary and chemist, and his wife, Mary, *née* Kinsey (d. 1805). His older brothers were Thomas (1767–1798) and Peter (1769–1808). Henry was educated at a private school run by the Revd Ralph Harrison (1748–1810), a minister at the Cross Street Chapel, which was then an influential centre of dissent. When he was about ten he was injured by a falling beam, and suffered for the rest of his life from neurological pain. The consequent restraint turned him from normal boyish activity to study, which formed his character for life.

In 1786 Henry went to the Manchester Academy that his father had helped to found. In 1790 he became secretary-companion to the leading physician in Manchester, his father's medical colleague Thomas Percival (1740–1804), pioneer of medical statistics and epidemiology. With him, Henry began to study medicine and in 1795 he entered Edinburgh University. Although this led to many friendships (such as that with Henry Brougham) he left after only a year to help in his father's apothecary practice and magnesia manufacturing business, which had become the mainstay of the family fortune. Neither of the other two sons had the character or aptitude to help, so Henry

William Henry (1774–1836), by Henry Cousins, pubd 1838 (after James Lonsdale, c.1836)

found himself at the centre of family affairs. He now also began to take an increasingly important part in the intellectual life of Manchester, and particularly in the Manchester Literary and Philosophical Society, which his father had helped to found. He became increasingly attracted to chemistry and published several papers. In June 1803 he married Mary Bayley (1775–1837), daughter of Thomas Bayley of Booth Hall. They had nine children, of whom only five survived to adult life. His eldest son was (William) Charles Henry [see below]. Henry returned to formal study in Edinburgh in 1805 and was admitted MD in 1807, on the strength of a thesis on uric acid, the first of several studies of urinary disease. He was elected to the Royal Society in 1809 and was soon awarded the Copley medal in recognition of his existing record of research, notably on the solubility of gases.

By the time Henry returned to Manchester, conditions in the city were changing radically. Increasing industrialization meant that many Manchester citizens, like the Henrys, were becoming rich. However, many more of a rapidly expanding population sank into extreme poverty, generating violent protest, culminating in the Peterloo massacre of 1819, close to Henry's home. Henry saw all this social change but kept aloof from religious friction, political conflict, or organized action; a similar detachment is seen in his avoidance of scientific controversy. However, he was widely influential as a recorder of experimental results, and as an exponent of the state of chemical science, in the long-lived and important *Epitome of Chemistry* (1801). This work sprang from a set of lectures delivered in 1798–9. Successive editions kept its content up to date, and the title was changed with the sixth to *Elements of Chemistry*. Henry also engaged in the construction and sale of chemical apparatus. The book acted as an illustrated catalogue of the many types of laboratory apparatus, for research and commercial use. In later editions the reader was referred to a commercial supplier; Henry felt he was unable to engage personally in such a growing trade.

Although not entering actively into the debate, Henry, like his father, was eventually convinced by the work of Lavoisier on the system of chemical elements and the nomenclature of compounds. His major experimental work was on the physical and chemical behaviour of gases, his most personal and original contribution being that now known as Henry's law, enunciated in 1804: 'At a given temperature water dissolves the same volume of a compressed gas as of that gas under normal pressure.' In the theoretical basis of this work his friendship with Dalton was beneficial to both men, since their results were seen to be interrelated. Much of Henry's gas work had a great commercial and social significance, particularly his analysis of coal gas and several other kinds of illuminating gas, the use of which was being tested on a considerable scale.

Henry was forced for most of his life to strike a balance between the desire for the pursuit of theoretical and experimental science and the need to manage industrial processes. He had to refuse the offer of the regius professorship of chemistry at Glasgow because he recognized that its duties would conflict with his responsibility to the family's apothecary's practice and magnesia factory. His fellowship of the Royal Society was a sufficient guarantee of recognition but it was the Manchester Literary and Philosophical Society which provided him with a stage for his wider scientific activities. When his father died he was offered its presidency but declined the honour. However, he actively supported the formation of the British Association for the Advancement of Science.

Henry studied the transmission of disease, notably cholera, and worked for some years on a theory that disease was transmitted by material substances which could be destroyed by heat. At the height of the cholera epidemics of the 1830s he carried out experiments on the heating of infected clothing, successful enough to support his theory, although (as became apparent long after his death) for the wrong reason.

Henry lived comfortably, and in his later years, splendidly. He moved from house to house many times as his wealth increased, the last, Pendlebury House, having its own private chapel. As he grew older and suffered greater pain he left to others as much of his active gainful business as he could. He was ceremonious and cold in manner, but this was said to conceal a generous and hospitable disposition. He showed variations in mood which have been attributed to the possibility that he took opium for the relief of his neurological pain. By 1824 Henry had to give up any experimental work needing skilled manipulation. Eventually the pain became too much for him and on 2

September 1836 he withdrew to his chapel and shot himself. He was buried on 7 September in the cemetery of the Cross Street Chapel.

(William) Charles Henry (1804–1892), physician and chemist, who was born in Manchester on 31 March 1804, was William Henry's eldest son, and the only one to survive infancy. He was educated at William Johns' Unitarian Seminary (with some private tuition from John Dalton) and at Edinburgh University. He graduated MD, unimpressively, and spent short periods in other universities in Britain and Europe. In 1828 he took up an honorary post in the Manchester Infirmary (observing, *inter alia*, the cholera epidemic of 1832). He joined the Manchester Literary and Philosophical Society but published little of consequence in its *Memoirs*. He did some physiological research for the British Association, which helped his election to fellowship of the Royal Society in 1834. The need to support his ailing father in chemical manufacture turned him to chemistry, in which he did some work on the reactions of gases, and went to several laboratories in Germany. In 1832 he married Margaret Allan (*d*. 1890), daughter of Thomas Allan (Edinburgh mineralogist, 1777–1833). They had two sons, both of whom became army officers; two daughters married army officers.

Following his father's tragic death Henry gradually withdrew from Manchester and thereafter lived as a country gentleman at Haffield, near Ledbury in Herefordshire. He also withdrew from practical science but kept many scientific friendships, notably one with Liebig. Dalton had named him as his literary executor but it was not until Dalton had been dead for ten years that Henry produced a biography, a mediocre book of little scholarly value. Henry died at Haffield on 7 January 1892.

FRANK GREENAWAY

Sources W. V. Farrar, K. Farrar, and E. L. Scott, 'The Henrys of Manchester [pts 1–5]', *Ambix*, 20 (1973), 183–208; 21 (1974), 179–228; 22 (1975), 186–204; 23 (1976), 27–52; 24 (1977), 1–26 · J. R. Partington, *A history of chemistry*, 3 (1962), 822–6

Archives JRL, notes · RS, papers | BL, letters to Charles Babbage, Add. MSS 27184–27200

Likenesses H. Cousins, mezzotint, pubd 1838 (after J. Lonsdale, *c*.1836), BM, NPG [*see illus.*] · J. F. Skill, J. Gilbert, W. and E. Walker, group portrait, pencil and wash (*Men of science living in 1807–08*), NPG

Henryson, Edward [*known as* Henry Édouard] (1522–*c*.1590), lawyer, was born in Edinburgh on 27 December 1522; according to the nineteenth-century publisher Joseph Swan he was probably the grandson of the poet Robert *Henryson. No details are known about his early life, but he first studied at the University of Paris, where he incepted between 16 December 1543 and 24 March 1544 under the name of Henricius Eduardus of the diocese of St Andrews. He retained the surname Édouard while he was on the continent. He left Paris for Bourges in 1544 to study civil law under the tuition of Éguinaire Baron. In January 1547, as 'Henry Edouard Ecossais', he was chosen to give young Ulrich Fugger, then a student in the faculty of law, lessons in Greek, and in October he was employed on a two-year contract at a salary of 100 livres tournois by the Fuggers, who took him to the Tyrol, near Augsburg. There he remained until 1552, translating and collecting classical texts for Ulrich Fugger. He translated Plutarch's *Septem sapientum convivium* (1551). The following year he returned briefly to Scotland, where he found a new patron in Henry Sinclair, president of the college of justice. He is said to have planned a Latin edition of the *Enchiridion* of Epictetus with Arrian's commentaries upon it.

By 1553 Henryson was back in Bourges, now professor of Roman law at the university, though with the very low salary of 45 livres a year. A treatise by Baron on the law of jurisdiction was attacked by Gouveia, and in October 1554 Henryson wrote a Latin reply in defence of his former tutor: *Pro Eg. Barone adversus Antonium Goveanum de jurisdictione* (1555) was dedicated to Fugger and is likely to have pleased him by demonstrating how Roman legal texts could be used in a contemporary context. The same year Henryson published another work on Roman law, *Commentatio in tit. x libri secundi institutionum de testamentis ordinandis*, dedicated to Michel de l'Hôpital, chancellor of France. It was republished in 1556 by Vascosan, himself editor of Giovanni Ferrerio, the continuator of Hector Boece. Ferrerio in turn recommended Henryson to Robert Reid, bishop of Orkney, who called him back to Edinburgh in 1556. Nothing certain is known about Henryson's teaching in Bourges, but according to Patrick Tytler, writing early in the nineteenth century, he followed his masters, mainly Alciato and Cujas.

Henryson left Bourges in 1556 and on 9 June was appointed royal lecturer in law, Greek, and Latin in Edinburgh. On 22 February 1557 he was admitted advocate. Nominated to the office of commissary in 1563, he replaced Lethington as an extraordinary lord of session on 14 January 1566. During that year he worked for a commission assembled to revise, correct, and print the laws and acts of parliament from 1424 to 1564. Henryson was the editor of the text and wrote the preface to it. His religious position is unclear. His dedicating a book to l'Hôpital could indicate that he was a Catholic moderate, like the French chancellor, but he certainly had the opportunity during his years at Bourges to meet protestants and learn from them, and once he was back in Scotland he seems to have adapted easily to a protestant environment. Indeed, in 1573 he was one of the procurators for the church. He married Helen Swinton (*d.* 1584), eldest daughter of John Swinton of Swinton. They had two sons, one of whom, Thomas *Henryson, also became a lawyer, and a daughter, Helen, who married Sir Thomas Craig of Riccarton, a famous lawyer and jurist. Edward Henryson died about 1590 in Edinburgh; Thomas is said to have erected a monument to his memory in the churchyard of Greyfriars, Edinburgh, where he may have been buried.

MARIE-CLAUDE TUCKER

Sources M.-C. Bellot-Tucker, 'Maîtres et étudiants écossais à la faculté de droit de l'Université de Bourges aux XVIe et XVIIe siècles', PhD diss., University of Clermont-Ferrand, 1997, 1.268–70, 337, 346–8; 2.434–7 · J. Durkan, 'Henry Scrimgeour, Renaissance bookman', *Edinburgh Bibliographical Society Transactions*, 5/1 (1971–87), 1–31, esp. 2–4 · G. Brunton and D. Haig, *An historical account of the senators of the college of justice, from its institution in MDXXXII* (1832), 132–3 · *DNB* · T. M'Crie, *The life of Andrew Melville*, new edn (1856), 365 · J. Swan, *Views of Fife*, 3 (1840), 229 · W. Maitland, *The history of Edinburgh* (1753), 198 · G. Meerman, *Thesaurus juris civilis et canonici* (1752), 3.451 · A. P. T. Eyssel, *Doneau, sa vie et ses œuvres* (Dijon, 1860), 57–8 · P. F. Tytler, *An account of the life and writings of Sir Thomas Craig of Riccarton* (1823), 269 · Sr Catherinot, *Le calvinisme de Berry* (1684), 4 · J. Durkan, 'The royal lectureships under Mary of Lorraine', *SHR*, 62 (1983), 73–8, esp. 74 · W. A. McNeill, 'Scottish entries in the *Acta rectoria universitatis Parisiensis*, 1519 to c.1633', *SHR*, 43 (1964), 66–86, esp. 80 · F. J. Grant, ed., *The Faculty of Advocates in Scotland, 1532–1943*, Scottish RS, 145 (1944), 200 · Vatican Library, MS pal. lat. 1425, fol. 165 · Bibliothèque Nationale, Paris, MS Lat. 9953, fols. 213v, 217v

Henryson, James, of Fordell (*d.* 1513), lawyer, was a younger son of the Edinburgh burgess Robert Henryson. He had two elder brothers, John and George, and a sister who married Henry Foulis and became the mother of the lawyer James Foulis. Henryson studied arts at the University of Paris; first recorded there in January 1484, he was elected procurator of the German nation the following year. His name appears on the matriculation roll of the University of St Andrews in 1488, and it is possible he spent time there on his return from Paris. By 1490 he was acting as a procurator before the lords of council on behalf of a number of prominent clients. He also appears in May 1493 designated as a notary. Before April 1494 he had married Helen Baty or Beattie, the daughter of another Edinburgh burgess. They were to have three sons, Patrick, George, and James, and three daughters, Margaret, Agnes, and Isabella.

In October 1493 Henryson appeared before the lords of council on the king's behalf for the first time, and thereafter he appeared regularly for the king, becoming the first holder of the office of king's advocate. During the reign of James III, Sir John Ross of Montgrennan had occasionally used the title, but in a limited context; unlike Montgrennan, Henryson in 1495 received a fee for his services, and this became regularized as an annual pension of £10 from 1498. A list of the lords of council in 1496 includes him with the designation *advocatus* and he acted consistently as a lord of council except where debarred by his activities as king's advocate or as an advocate for private parties. In 1502 he appeared in a case as 'advocat til [to] the pure folkis', though there is no indication that he fulfilled the separate office of advocate for the poor, which became a feature of later sixteenth-century practice. That same year he was acting as town clerk of Edinburgh, an office he appears to have retained until 1512. In 1504 and 1506 Henryson was a commissioner to parliament. In 1507 he succeeded Richard Lawson as justice-clerk-general, and during the exchequer in July 1508 he was made bailie to the king's treasurer. In 1509 he is mentioned as being justice-clerk of the regality of Glasgow. Prior to Flodden, Henryson was peripherally involved in the diplomatic manoeuvring between James IV and Henry VIII; safe conducts were issued for him to go to England on several occasions but remained unused, though he did confer with English agents in Scotland.

Henryson drew considerable income from his attendance at justice ayres and chamberlain ayres, as well as from fees and pensions paid to him by private clients and ecclesiastical corporations who retained him to act as their man of law. He bought the barony of Fordell in Fife, an estate with which his family may have had a long-standing connection. Early in 1511 Henryson systematically purchased lands in Fordell, and in May of that year the king erected them into a free barony. Thereafter Henryson continued to purchase land in the area, creating the estate from which his family afterwards took its designation. He also acquired lands in the borders. Henryson made his last appearance before the lords of council on 27 July 1513 and died during the Flodden campaign, possibly killed in the battle. His reputation suffered from his activities on the king's behalf, and he was blamed for James IV's fiscal policies, particularly his rigorous pursuit of the crown's feudal rights. Sir Richard Maitland of Lethington, writing about 1560, by implication accused him of inventing ways of disinheriting the barons of Scotland. Henryson was succeeded by his son George, who died with his own son William at the battle of Pinkie in 1547.

JOHN FINLAY

Sources NA Scot., muniments, Henderson of Fordell: GD 172 · NA Scot., Acts of the lords of council, CS 5 · J. Finlay, 'James Henryson and the office of king's advocate', *SHR*, 79 (2000), 17–38 · W. Stephen, *History of Inverkeithing and Rosyth* (1921) · [T. Thomson], ed., *The acts of the lords auditors of causes and complaints*, AD 1466–AD 1494, RC, 40 (1839) · [T. Thomson], ed., *The acts of the lords of council in civil causes, 1478–1495*, 1, RC, 41 (1839) · G. Neilson and H. Paton, eds., *Acts of the lords of council in civil causes, 1496–1501*, 2 (1918) · A. B. Calderwood, ed., *Acts of the lords of council, 1501–1503*, 3 (1993) · *APS*, 1424–1567 · C. B. B. Watson, ed., *Roll of Edinburgh burgesses and guildbrethren, 1406–1700*, Scottish RS, 59 (1929) · J. D. Marwick, ed., *Extracts from the records of the burgh of Edinburgh*, AD 1403–1528, [1], Scottish Burgh RS, 2 (1869) · M. Livingstone, D. Hay Fleming, and others, eds., *Registrum secreti sigilli regum Scotorum / The register of the privy seal of Scotland*, 1 (1908) · J. M. Thomson and others, eds., *Registrum magni sigilli regum Scotorum / The register of the great seal of Scotland*, 11 vols. (1882–1914), vol. 2 · T. M. Chalmers, 'The king's council, patronage, and governance of Scotland, 1460–1513', PhD diss., U. Aberdeen, 1982 · *The protocol book of John Foular*, ed. W. Macleod and M. Wood, 1–3, Scottish RS, 64, 72, 75 (1930–53) · N. Macdougall, *James IV* (1989) · R. Maitland of Lethington, *The history of the house of Seytoun to the year MDLIX*, ed. J. Fullarton, Maitland Club, 1 (1829)

Archives NA Scot., Henderson of Fordell muniments

Henryson, Robert (d. c.1490), poet, is first recorded in the muniments of Glasgow University, where he was incorporated on 10 September 1462. Incorporation usually meant matriculation as a student; Henryson, however, is described as *vir venerabilis* ('venerable man'), as *magister* (master, of arts, that is to say), and as 'licentiate in arts and bachelor of decrees'. This implies that he was already of some age and standing and that he had studied at a university, as yet unidentified but perhaps on the continent, where after four years he had gained the licentiate and mastership in arts, and after another two years the bachelorship in canon law. At Glasgow it is possible that he was incorporated as *legens* ('reader'), lecturing in canon law. Almost certainly he was also a priest. In March 1463 David Cadzow, first rector of the university, who had himself given lectures in canon law in 1460, founded a chaplaincy of 12 merks (£8 Scots) yearly, the clerk of which was to celebrate a daily mass for the donor's soul and to lecture publicly in the faculty of canon law. Henryson may have

been the first incumbent. His narrative poem *Orpheus and Eurydice* is based on Boethius's *De consolatione philosophiae*, III, *metrum* xii, together with the commentary of Nicholas Trevet (d. 1328). During the fifteenth century the library of Glasgow Cathedral contained a copy of this work—a possible indication that the poem is a product of Henryson's residence in Glasgow.

Henryson's academic qualifications were soon outshone, in particular by Master Thomas Lauderdale, doctor of canon law and licentiate in civil law, whose name first appears in university muniments in 1468. Henryson is usually connected with Dunfermline and often described as schoolmaster there; he may have made the move in or about 1468 at the invitation of Richard Bothwell, abbot of Dunfermline, who had Glasgow connections, and who in that year provided a house and land for the town schoolmaster, together with yearly rents of the value of 11 merks (£7 6s. 8d. Scots) and more, for the maintenance of poor scholars, whom the master was to teach free of charge. Henryson's interests may have suited him more for a grammar school than a law faculty. He was certainly resident in Dunfermline during the 1470s and probably the 1480s. One of his *Morall fabillis*, 'The Trial of the Fox', may be interpreted as referring to the increased secularization of monastic life during the reign of James III (r. 1460–88), exemplified, according to John Leslie, bishop of Ross (d. 1596), by the royal intrusion in 1472 of Henry Crichton as abbot of Dunfermline in place of Alexander Thomson, whom the monks had duly elected. On 18 and 19 March and 6 July 1478 Henryson, described as notary public, witnessed three grants made by Crichton of lands near Dunfermline. Another fable, 'The Lion and the Mouse', may plausibly be interpreted as containing some reference to the Lauder Bridge incident of July 1482, in which James III was made prisoner, but afterwards released, partly through the efforts of the burgesses of Edinburgh. Two fables, 'The Fox and the Wolf' and 'The Fox, the Wolf and the Husbandman', may show the influence of Caxton's *History of Reynard the Fox* (1481), and another, 'The Wolf and the Wether', is almost certainly based on a similar episode in Caxton's *Aesop* (1484). *The Testament of Cresseid* is probably referred to in *The Spektakle of Luf*, a prose treatise completed by G. Myll in St Andrews on 10 July 1492.

The earliest text of any of Henryson's poems appears in additions made to the Makculloch manuscript (Edinburgh University Library, MS La.III.149), additions probably made c.1500, a *terminus ad quem* for the composition of the two poems included, namely, the 'Prolog' and its sequel, 'The Cock and the Jasp'. If the unique text of 'The Annunciation' in the Gray manuscript (NL Scot., Adv. MS 34.7.3) was in fact written by James Gray (d. c.1505), it belongs to the same period and carries similar implications for date of composition.

The earliest of Henryson's poems to be issued in printed form were 'The Praise of Age', *Orpheus*, and 'The Want of Wise Men', which appeared in tracts printed by Chepman and Myllar in or about 1508. 'The Praise of Age' is the second item in the seventh tract; the other two make up the eighth with the colophon: 'Heir begynnis the traitie of

Orpheus kyng and how he yeid to hewyn & to hel to seik his quene And ane othir ballad in the lattir end' (Beattie, 149). Neither tract mentions Henryson's name as author. Indeed, none of the shorter poems is to be regarded as certainly his work.

Henryson's death in Dunfermline is mentioned by William Dunbar in his poem 'Timor mortis conturbat me', a printed text of which appears in a black-letter tract of undetermined provenance and date, but approximately contemporary with the Chepman and Myllar prints. Dunbar commemorates a number of dead poets, the latest of whom are 'gud gentill Stobo and Quintyne Schaw' (line 86). Stobo is known to have died in 1505; Schaw was still alive in 1504. Henryson's death must therefore have been earlier than 1505. His poetry contains no obvious reference to events in the reign of James IV, who succeeded in 1488; Henryson may therefore have died between 1484 and 1488 or very shortly thereafter. In 1519 a priest, Sir John Moffat, is first mentioned as schoolmaster in Dunfermline; he is recorded in the burgh as early as 1493 and it is possible that by then he had already succeeded to Henryson's post. Sir Francis Kinaston (d. 1642) preserves an entertaining anecdote of Henryson's death as a very old man, but impossibly makes his *floruit* towards the end of the reign of Henry VIII, in the 1540s.

Other evidence confirms that in the first quarter of the sixteenth century Henryson's poetry had achieved some reputation. In its present condition the imperfectly preserved Asloan manuscript (NL Scot., MS Accession 4233), dated *c.*1520, contains only two of his poems, *Orpheus* and 'The Two Mice', but when complete it also included six other fables, in an order different from that found in later prints and manuscripts, together with the *Testament* and the lost 'master Robert hendersonnis Dreme On fut by forth' (Craigie, 1.xiv). Parts of the manuscript appear to have been copied from earlier prints. In a note to the first book of his own translation of the *Aeneid* Gavin Douglas (d. 1522) makes a complimentary reference to Henryson and *Orpheus*. The poetry of Sir David Lindsay (d. 1555), in particular *The Dreme* (1528), contains many Henrysonian reminiscences.

In the later sixteenth and early seventeenth centuries the number of surviving prints and manuscript versions multiplies. Only the more important need be noted. *The Testament of Cresseid* was included as Chaucer's work in William Thynne's London edition of Chaucer of 1532 and often subsequently. The Bannatyne manuscript (NL Scot., Adv. MS 1.1.6.), completed in 1568, contains all but three of the *Fabillis*, not in the order now generally accepted, as well as *Orpheus* and two of the twelve shorter poems. The Charteris print of the *Fabillis*, first to give the order now generally accepted, appeared in 1569, the Bassandyne in 1571, and the Hart in 1621. The Charteris print of the *Testament* appeared in 1593. All were printed in Edinburgh. In England too there was some interest. An Anglicized version of the *Fabillis*, 'translated' and printed by Richard Smith, appeared at London in 1577. In 1639 the Englishman Sir Francis Kinaston produced, as an appendix to his

Latin translation of Chaucer's *Troilus and Criseyde*, an annotated version of the *Testament*. This is preserved in a single manuscript (Bodl. Oxf., MS Add. C.287, pp. 475–509).

The apparent direct simplicity of Henryson's poetry conceals many difficulties of both text and interpretation. A major, if largely unrecognized, problem with the *Fabillis* is the order and internal relationship of the individual tales, which may not have been intended to form a unified collection.

As a narrative poet Henryson's chief characteristics are his brevity and moral force—'In breif sermone ane pregnant sentence wryte' (Fox, 119)—with which he combines human sympathy, an ironic sense of humour, sometimes embracing the grotesque, and a subtle use of allegory. Courts of law, together with legal pleas and decisions, figure extensively. His numerical composition is based partly on biblical sources, partly on medieval and early Renaissance Platonism. In terms of his favourite rhyme-royal stanza and other more lyrical forms, Henryson is a metrical virtuoso, melding elements of the earlier Chaucerian and alliterative traditions. His tendency is to base his poems on older material—Chaucer, for instance, Boethius, or the verse *Romulus*, a twelfth-century collection of Latin fables attributed to Gualterus Anglicus—but to develop it in ways which are highly individual. *Orpheus and Eurydice* best illustrates his method of Platonic numerical composition. *The Testament of Cresseid* heightens the tragedy of Chaucer's *Troilus and Criseyde*, on which at the same time it makes an oblique comment. Its 616 lines contrast with Chaucer's 8239. Cresseid's suffering is subjected to profound but sympathetic moral analysis, some, as in her trial before the planetary gods, at once allegorical and vivid. The planetary portraits, especially that of Saturn, illustrate Henryson's use of the grotesque. His humour also is felt here, as in the ironic presentation of the narrator in the proem. The 85 stanzas (plus 1 for the epilogue) naturally fall into 3 divisions, each of 203 lines, two containing 29 stanzas, the other 27. Every number and its factor has its own significance. The variety of effects compassed by the stanza forms, rhyme-royal, and the nine-line structure of 'The Complaint of Cresseid' demonstrate Henryson's metrical virtuosity.

Tragedy and pathos are present in individual fables, 'The Preaching of the Swallow', for instance, or 'The Paddock and the Mouse'. Comedy, however, is more characteristic, whether of the gentle variety found in 'The Two Mice', the more serious kind found in 'The Lion and the Mouse', or the savage farce found in the three episodes of 'The Talking of the Tod'. A trial features prominently in the last two. Most have a numerical structure, illustrated by the forty stanzas of another fable, the Lenten comedy, 'The Fox, the Wolf and the Cadger'. Henryson's greatness is most plainly to be seen in the range of general principles and ideas which informs his poetry and which allows it to encompass tragedy and comedy alike. He is the most Shakespearian of the early Scottish poets.

JOHN MACQUEEN

Sources C. Innes, ed., *Munimenta alme Universitatis Glasguensis / Records of the University of Glasgow from its foundation till 1727*, 4 vols.,

Maitland Club, 72 (1854) • Register of Dunfermline Abbey, NL Scot., Adv. MS 34.1.3A, nos. 478–80 • *CEPR letters*, vol. 12 • E. Beveridge, ed., *Burgh records of Dunfermline* (1917) • D. Laing, ed., *The poems and fables of Robert Henryson* (1865) • D. Fox, ed., *The poems of Robert Henryson* (1981) • J. MacQueen, 'Poetry: James I to Henryson', *The history of Scottish literature*, ed. C. Craig, 1: *Origins to 1660*, ed. R. D. S. Jack (1988) • J. Durkan, *William Turnbull bishop of Glasgow* (1951) • J. D. Mackie, *The University of Glasgow, 1451–1951: a short history* (1954) • W. Beattie, ed., *The Chepman and Myllar prints: a facsimile* (1980) • *The Asloan manuscript*, ed. W. A. Craigie, 2 vols., STS, new ser., 14, 16 (1923–5), vol. 1

Archives Bodl. Oxf., MS Add. C.287, pp. 475–509 • NL Scot., Accession MS 4233 • NL Scot., Adv. MS 1.1.6 • NRA, priv. coll., literary papers • U. Edin. L., MS La.III.149

Henryson, Sir Thomas, Lord Chesters (*d.* **1638**), judge, was a son of Edward *Henryson (1522–*c.*1590), lawyer, and possibly Helen Swinton (*d.* 1584). He may possibly be identified with a student of the same name at the University of Glasgow in 1585. At an unknown date he married Rebecca Weir (*d.* 1637), and they had a daughter, Elizabeth (*d.* 1643). He was one of the commissaries of Edinburgh from at least June 1598 and he acted as advocate-depute in certain processes of forfeiture before parliament in 1606. In 1609 he was commendator of Pittenweem. A staunch Episcopalian, the following year he was appointed judge when two courts of high commission were created under the royal prerogative. In 1618 Henryson acted as advocate on behalf of the kirk against the heritors of Cranston parish in a case concerning the modification of teinds (tithes).

An ordinary lord in the court of session from 6 June 1622, when he succeeded Sir Lewis Craig of Wrightslands, Henryson took the title Lord Chesters and was knighted. He became a member of the privy council in March 1625 but resigned in order to retain office as a judge when, in 1626, Charles I restructured the privy council and prevented councillors from simultaneously holding ordinary judgeships. In an undated letter, probably from 1637, Henryson wrote to the king wishing to resign from the office of advocate-depute of the kirk because of his 'great aage [*sic*] and last seiknes'. His wife died on 30 November 1637, and he survived her only by weeks, dying on 9 February 1638; he left a modest estate valued at £3269.

JOHN FINLAY

Sources NA Scot., CC 8/8/32; GD 135, Stair Muniments; GD 406/1, Hailten corresp.; CC8/8/60; CC8/8/59 • J. M. Thomson and others, eds., *Registrum magni sigilli regum Scotorum / The register of the great seal of Scotland*, 11 vols. (1882–1914); facs. repr. (1984) • *Reg. PCS*, 1st ser., vols. 1–3 • M. Livingstone, D. Hay Fleming, and others, eds., *Registrum secreti sigilli regum Scotorum / The register of the privy seal of Scotland*, 8 vols. (1908–82) • C. Innes, ed., *Munimenta alme Universitatis Glasguensis / Records of the University of Glasgow from its foundation till 1727*, 4 vols., Maitland Club, 72 (1854) • G. Brunton and D. Haig, *An historical account of the senators of the college of justice, from its institution in MDXXXII* (1832)

Wealth at death £3269: NA Scot., CC 8/8/60, fol. 70

Henschel, Sir George [*formerly* Isidor Georg] (**1850–1934**), singer and conductor, was born on 18 February 1850 in Breslau, Silesia, the only son of Polish Jews, Moritz Jacob Henschel, a wool and coal merchant, and his second wife,

Sir George Henschel (1850–1934), by Sir Lawrence Alma-Tadema, 1879

Henriette, the daughter of Joseph Frankenstein, of Landshut, Silesia. His father had two sons and one daughter from his previous marriage. Henschel converted to Christianity when young, and never used the first of his two original names, Isidor Georg. He was educated in Breslau at Magdalen College and the Wandelt Institute. In 1859 he sang the treble solo in Mendelssohn's 'Hear my prayer' with the Breslau University choral society, and in 1862 made his début as a pianist in Berlin. He entered the Leipzig conservatory in 1867 and the Berlin conservatory in 1870. He developed a fine baritone voice and in 1874 had his first important engagement, in Cologne, when he sang at the lower Rhine festival. He became a close friend of Brahms after singing under him in the St Matthew passion in 1875. He first performed in England in 1877, where he had great success, and was the only living musician to earn an entry in the first edition of Grove's *Dictionary of Music and Musicians* (1879).

Henschel then went to the United States, where he was the first conductor of the Boston Symphony Orchestra, from its foundation in 1881 until 1884, when he returned to London. In 1881 he married an American singer, Lillian June (1860–1901), the only daughter of Lucien Champlin Bailey of Columbus, Ohio. He had sung at her London début in 1879. They had one daughter, who also became a singer. Their marriage opened a long and successful series of duet recitals in Europe and the United States, in which Henschel acted as accompanist as well as singer. In 1884 the Henschels returned to England, where they settled. He founded the London symphony concerts in 1886, and continued to conduct them until 1897. He was a professor of singing at the Royal College of Music from 1886 to 1888, and sang in the Birmingham festivals of 1891 and 1894, performing the parts of Satan in Stanford's *Eden* and the King in Parry's *Saul*.

Henschel was the first conductor of the Glasgow-based Scottish Orchestra from 1893 to 1895, and conducted a royal command performance for Queen Victoria at Windsor Castle in 1895, the first such occasion since the death of Prince Albert in 1861. After his wife's death in 1901, Henschel retired to Scotland. In 1907 he married Amy, the eldest daughter of Alexander Louis of New York; they had one daughter. In 1909 he returned to the concert platform as a conductor and a concert singer, and continued to perform until his retirement in 1914, although even then he continued to direct the Handel Society of London. He returned to broadcast during the Schubert centenary celebrations in 1928. As a singer, Henschel was probably the most successful and widely appreciated performer of his era, celebrated for the vitality and excitement of his singing, his sense of rhythm, and the authority of his style in classical lieder.

Henschel was also a composer. His *Stabat mater* was performed at the 1894 Birmingham festival, and his opera, *Nubia*, was staged in Dresden in 1899. His other works included the popular songs 'Morning Hymn' and 'Young Dietrich', a requiem mass, *Missa pro defunctis* (1916), written in memory of his first wife, and two masses written for All Saints' Church, Margaret Street, London.

Henschel, who was naturalized as a British subject in 1890, was knighted in 1914 and received an honorary MusDoc from Edinburgh University in 1910. He died at his residence, Alltnacriche, Aviemore, Inverness, on 10 September 1934. His second wife survived him.

ANNE PIMLOTT BAKER

Sources G. Henschel, *Musings and memories of a musician* (1918) · *New Grove* · H. Henschel, *When soft voices die* (1944) · private information (1949) · personal knowledge (1949) [*DNB*] · *DNB* · *CGPLA Eng. & Wales* (1934)
Archives NL Scot., corresp. and music MSS | BL, corresp. with Macmillans, Add. MS 55239 · BL, letters to Mr and Mrs Edward Speyer, Add. MS 42233
Likenesses L. Alma-Tadema, portrait, 1879; Christies, 22 Nov 1990 [*see illus.*] · J. S. Sargent, portrait, 1889 · E. O. Ford, bronze bust, 1895, NG Scot. · P. A. de Laszlo, oils, 1917, NPG · Barraud, photograph (with his wife), NPG; repro. in *Men and Women of the Day*, 14 (1891) · V. & D. Downey, woodburytype photograph, NPG; repro. in W. Downey and D. Downey, *The cabinet portrait gallery*, 2 (1891) · P. A. de Laszlo, portrait, priv. coll.
Wealth at death £3,943 18s. 10d.: probate, 14 Dec 1934, *CGPLA Eng. & Wales*

Hensey, Florence (*fl.* 1748–1760), physician and spy, was born in co. Kildare, the son of Florence Hensey (*d.* 1757) of Ballycumeen, and his wife, Mary (*d.* 1748). Brought up as a Catholic, he moved to England when very young; he then apparently was educated at the English College at St Omer, and, from October 1748, at the University of Leiden, where he studied medicine and graduated MD. He travelled in Switzerland, Italy, Portugal, and Spain before settling in Paris, where he practised as a physician for some years. On the outbreak of the Seven Years' War he returned to England and offered his services as a spy to the French foreign office. In return for a payment of 500 livres (about £25) per quarter he promised to supply information about the movements of the British fleet, on troop numbers, and the location of regiments. As the quality of his information improved, so his payments rose to 500 livres per month. At first he sent his reports to a contact in Cologne, who forwarded them to Paris via another contact in Bern, but later he was directed to send his letters to his brother, who was chaplain and secretary to the Spanish ambassador at The Hague.

By summer 1757 Hensey's frequent foreign correspondence had aroused the suspicions of a postman, who told his superiors; his mail was intercepted, his letters were opened, and Hensey was arrested on a charge of high treason on 21 August. He was found guilty at his trial before Lord Mansfield on 12 June 1758 and was sentenced to death two days later. On 12 July, the day appointed for his execution, he received a respite, and after several more stays of execution he was admitted to bail and released from Newgate on 7 September 1759. Shortly after George III's accession in 1760 he received a free pardon and returned to France. Nothing further is known of his life.

C. L. KINGSFORD, *rev.* M. J. MERCER

Sources *GM*, 1st ser., 28 (1758), 240, 287–8, 337–8, 378 · *GM*, 1st ser., 29 (1759), 438 · *A genuine account of the proceedings on the trial of Florence Hensey, MD* (1758) · *Authentic memoirs of the life and treasonable practices of Doctor Florence Hensey* (1758) · *Annual Register* (1758), 97–8 · J. Caulfield, *Portraits, memoirs, and characters, of remarkable persons, from the revolution in 1688 to the end of the reign of George II*, 4 vols. (1819–20) · A. Knapp and W. Baldwin, *The new Newgate calendar, being interesting memoirs of notorious characters*, 5 vols. [n.d., 1826?]
Likenesses line engraving, pubd 1820, BM; repro. in Caulfield, *Portraits*; version, NG Ire.

Henshall, Samuel (1764/5–1807), philologist, was baptized on 8 February 1765 at Sandbach, Cheshire, the son of George Henshall, grocer. He attended Manchester grammar school, then Brasenose College, Oxford, as one of Hulme's exhibitioners, matriculating on 11 October 1782. He graduated BA on 14 June 1786, MA on 12 May 1789, and after ordination was elected to a college fellowship. In 1792, being then curate of Christ Church, Spitalfields, he was an unsuccessful candidate for the lectureship of St Peter-le-Poer.

Henshall's first scholarly publication, *Specimens and parts; containing a history of the county of Kent and a dissertation on the laws* … (1798), was to have been completed in six quarterly parts, but only part 1 was published. He first came to wider notice with *The Saxon and English Languages Reciprocally Illustrative of Each Other* (1798). His stated purpose was confrontational:

> To assert that no correct ideas can be collected from the laborious exertions of a Hickes, a Gibson, or a Wilkins; to affirm that their Latin interpretations are of little authority, unintelligible, and delusory; argues certainly a daring

Challenger, or a Champion conscious of the merits of his cause, and therefore not easily intimidated. (p. 1)

Henshall's methodology was fundamentally flawed, as was quickly pointed out in reviews by John Horne Tooke in the *Analytical Review*, and Richard Gough and Charles Mayo in the *Gentleman's Magazine*. Henshall's disparagement of George Hickes, Edmund Gibson, and David Wilkins was controversial, and his denigration of several contemporary scholars, including John Horne Tooke ('we pity his fiend-like mind'; p. 53), resulted in a severe reaction. Gough and Mayo noted that:

If we were not apprized of the motive's for Mr. H's publication, we should be tempted to say he had undertaken what he does not understand … Mr. H's literal version … appears to be founded on nothing but an imaginary resemblance of sound. (*GM*, 68.861)

'To call Dr. Hickes' inaccurate versions and unfaithful translations, every judicious critick must deem the height of ignorance and presumption' (ibid., 863). 'We know Mr. H. and respected his talents; but ill manners (we had almost given it a harder name) is not an apology for imprudence' (ibid., 865).

As a 'champion … not easily intimidated' Henshall persevered. He believed he was the object of a plot to discredit him ('Preface', *Etymological Organic Reasoner*, 1807, 15). He recounted that in September 1798 John Reeves, editor of the *Anti-Jacobin Review* (to which Henshall frequently contributed), had been approached by William Beloe to write a review which would expose Henshall's 'total ignorance of the Saxon language'. Further, similar reviews to be published in October in the *Gentleman's Magazine* and the *Analytical Review* had been arranged for the same purpose. The latter two appeared with devastating results, but for Henshall this proved his assertion.

Henshall's next publication was *Strictures on the late motions of the duke of Leinster, … Richd. Brinsley Sheridan, … and a paragraph in the semi-official chronicle of opposition* (1798), which was dismissed in the *Gentleman's Magazine* (*GM*, 70.645) as 'uninteresting'. In the following year he published *Domesday, or, An Actual Survey of South Britain* (1799), the first of ten projected volumes, but the project was discontinued owing to its errors. On 12 November 1800 he stood for election as professor of Anglo-Saxon at Oxford, losing to Thomas Hardcastle, 71 to 148 (ibid., 1097). In 1801 Henshall was appointed a public examiner in the university, and on 22 January 1802 he was presented by his college to the rectory of St Mary, Stratford Bow, Middlesex. He married in May 1802.

Henshall was not without his supporters, as the dedication of his final work, the *Etymological Organic Reasoner*, to Richard Heber, who had allowed Henshall access to his library, illustrates. In that work, which appeared in monthly numbers (the fifth, due on 30 September 1807, was stopped by Henshall's last illness), was included an 'occasional preface'. Here he turned on his critics and threatened to expose 'this mystery of iniquity', in which 'many Antiquaries, Blackstonians, Electioneering Oxonians, Reviewers, Low Churchmen, Presbyterians, Methodists, and other herds of animals that follow their leader's tail

are concerned'. Soon after, on 17 November 1807, he died aged forty-two and was buried at St Mary, Stratford Bow, Middlesex.   RICHARD W. CLEMENT

Sources J. Petheram, *An historical sketch of the progress and present state of Anglo-Saxon literature in England* (1840), 114–15, 121–3 · Foster, *Alum. Oxon.* · J. F. Smith, ed., *The admission register of the Manchester School, with some notes of the more distinguished scholars*, 2, Chetham Society, 73 (1868), 8–10; 3/2, Chetham Society, 94 (1874), 322 · 'The Saxon and English languages reciprocally illustrative of each other', *GM*, 1st ser., 68 (1798), 861–5 · *GM*, 1st ser., 77 (1807), 1176 · *IGI*

Henshaw, Joseph (1603–1679), bishop of Peterborough, was born possibly in Cripplegate, London, or in Sompting, Sussex, the son of Thomas Henshaw, solicitor-general of Ireland, and his wife, Joan, only daughter of Richard Wistow, surgeon to Elizabeth I. In July 1614 he was among the first scholars admitted by Thomas Sutton on grounds of kinship to the new foundation of Charterhouse, from where he proceeded to Magdalen Hall, Oxford, in 1621. He graduated BA in 1624 and was incorporated as MA at Pembroke College, Cambridge, in 1628.

Henshaw was ordained and soon attracted the patronage of John Digby, earl of Bristol, who appointed him as chaplain. He was also chaplain to Buckingham at the time of the favourite's assassination in 1628, whereupon he was appointed to the prebend of Bishopscourt at Chichester Cathedral by Charles I before the consecration on 24 August of the new bishop, Richard Montague. Henshaw was preacher at the Charterhouse in the early 1630s and instituted to the vicarage of St Bartholomew-the-Less, London, on 13 July 1631. In 1633 he married Jane (*d.* 1639), daughter of John May of Rawmarsh, Sussex, and in 1634 was instituted to the living of Stedham with Hayshott, in the same county. In 1636 he resigned St Bartholomew but kept Stedham in plurality on his appointment as rector of East Lavant, Sussex, on the presentation of Archbishop Laud. He proceeded BD in 1635 and DD in 1639, his theses, on the latter occasion, being all concerned with questions of obedience to church authorities and the evils of separation.

Henshaw published, in 1631, a book of meditations, *Horae succisivae, or, Spare Houres of Meditations upon our Dutie to God, Others, Ourselves*, which achieved a reputation for its pastoral wisdom and went through five enlarged editions in the following decade. To this he added another compilation, *Meditations Miscellaneous, Holy and Humane*, in 1637. His comment in the second edition of 1639 that 'it would conduce much to the peace of the church, if books of this nature were more in use' and that 'they shall finde on the last day that it is holiness, not knowledge (I do not say holinesse without knowledge) that must bring them to heaven' ('Letter to the reader'), placed Henshaw firmly in the pastoral tradition of Anglican churchmanship.

At the outbreak of the civil wars Henshaw was deprived of his prebendal stall and ejected from his livings for his support of Charles, and he removed to Exeter, a royalist garrison. After the capture of Exeter by Fairfax, Henshaw was declared a delinquent by parliament and his livings were sequestered in 1645. He compounded for his delinquency, paying a fine of £177 in all, and remained at East Lavant for a year or two, but his movements thereafter are hard to trace, though he seems to have spent some time at Lady Paulet's house at Chiswick, and may have received some support from Lady Anne Cotington, to whom he dedicated the 1650 edition of *Horae succisivae*.

In 1658 a mandate to install Henshaw as precentor of Chichester was issued and this took effect at the Restoration, he being installed on 12 July 1660. Later that year, on 29 November, Henshaw was installed as dean of Chichester, but was allowed to retain both the precentorship and his prebendal stall, to which he had also been restored. Henshaw continued to live in the precentor's house, the deanery having been destroyed during the civil wars, and was also permitted to retain the income from one of the residentiary canons' portions because of the poverty of the deanery and the expenses he would incur in restoring its fortunes. In the event he played a prominent part in the recovery of the cathedral and close.

On 10 May 1663 Henshaw was consecrated bishop of Peterborough. Once again he entered an impoverished post, claiming within a year of arriving that he was '£400 poorer then when I came' (Bodl. Oxf., MS Tanner 147, fol. 56), and he was later said by Browne Willis to have lived not very hospitably in his diocese. He also fell foul of the more vigorous Anglican gentry of the county who blamed him for not enforcing the Clarendon code sufficiently. Matters came to a head in 1669 over the appointment of a schoolmaster at Wellingborough whose views were not orthodox enough for the leading Anglican layman, Sir Henry Yelverton, who sought the master's ejection. This was refused by Henshaw who, claimed Yelverton, wrote to him 'in a very lofty style, not as if he had been Bishop of Peterborough and might want the assistance of gentlemen, but as if he had been the Pope himself' (Spurr, 60). Thereafter things settled down, but Henshaw's episcopate was noted neither for vigour nor popularity in the diocese.

Henshaw died in London on 9 March 1679, and was buried at East Lavant beside his wife and his son Thomas, a former fellow of All Souls College, Oxford. His surviving daughter, Mary, wife of Sir Andrew Hacket of Mixhull, Warwickshire, was the chief beneficiary of his will.

WILLIAM JOSEPH SHEILS

Sources H. I. Longden, *Northamptonshire and Rutland clergy from 1500*, ed. P. I. King and others, 16 vols. in 6, Northamptonshire RS (1938–52) • *Walker rev.* • J. Henshaw, *Horae succisivae*, 6th edn (1650) • J. Henshaw, *Meditations miscellaneous, holy and humane* (1637) • J. Spurr, *The Restoration Church of England, 1646–1689* (1991) • will, 1679, PRO, PROB 11/361, sig. 171 • *Fasti Angl., 1541–1857*, [Chichester] • Henshaw's Oxford Act theses, 1639, PRO, SP 16/425/28
Archives BL, corresp. with John Palmer, archdeacon of Northampton, Add. MS 22576 • Bodl. Oxf., Tanner MSS, stray letters
Wealth at death over £1000: will, PRO, PROB 11/361, sig. 171

Henshaw, Nathaniel (*bap.* 1628, *d.* 1673), physician, the younger son of Benjamin Henshaw (*d.* 1631), 'one of the captains of the city of London', and his wife, Anne, daughter of William Bonham, citizen of London, was baptized at St Mary Abbots, Kensington, on 31 July 1628. He studied first at Padua, which he entered in 1649; he then entered at Leiden on 4 November 1653 in order to study medicine; he graduated MD at Leiden and was admitted to the same degree at Dublin in the summer term of 1664.

On 20 May 1663 Henshaw was elected FRS as one of the first members of the newly established Royal Society. He practised in Dublin, but spent much time in London, where he was an acquaintance of John Evelyn and Robert Boyle in the 1650s, and active in the Gresham Society from 1660 to 1662 (Frank, 162).

Henshaw was the author of a treatise entitled *Aerochalinos, or, A Register for the Air* (1664). The second edition, published posthumously in 1677, was printed by order of the Royal Society at a meeting held on 1 March 1677, having been prepared for the press by the author's elder brother, Thomas *Henshaw (1618–1700). It was reviewed in the society's *Philosophical Transactions* (12.834–5) by Henry Oldenburg.

Henshaw died in London in September 1673, and was buried on the 13th of that month in Kensington church. His will, dated 6 August 1673, was proved at London on the following 11 September by his sister Anne Grevys.

GORDON GOODWIN, *rev.* PATRICK WALLIS

Sources R. W. Innes Smith, *English-speaking students of medicine at the University of Leyden* (1932), 48 • R. G. Frank, *Harvey and the Oxford physiologists* (1980), 162 • T. Thomson, *History of the Royal Society from its institution to the end of the eighteenth century* (1812) • M. Hunter, *The Royal Society and its fellows, 1660–1700: the morphology of an early scientific institution* (1982) • Wood, *Ath. Oxon.* • Burtchaell & Sadleir, *Alum. Dubl.*, 2nd edn • will, proved, 11 Sept 1673, PRO, PROB 11/342, sig. 113 • *IGI* • parish register (death), London, Kensington

Henshaw, Thomas (1618–1700), alchemist and writer, was born on 15 June 1618 at Milk Street, London, the eldest son of Benjamin Henshaw (*d.* 1631) and Anne Bonham (*d.* after 1650). Both father and mother were later described by Hartlib as 'great chemists'—a fact that may have influenced the interests of Thomas and his brother Nathaniel *Henshaw. After education at Barnet and at Thomas Farnaby's Cripplegate school, Henshaw matriculated as a commoner at University College, Oxford, on 17 October 1634. After two years he was sent to study mathematics with the respected mathematician William Oughtred, parson of Aldbury, Surrey. He was then admitted to the Middle Temple on 21 April 1638, and was called to the bar on 24 November 1654, by which time he was discouraged by political circumstances from any desire to practise.

At the onset of the civil war Henshaw, with his mother's brother, joined Charles I at York. His active participation in the royalist cause was cut short when he was arrested on a foray to London to supply himself with funds and horses. Having been released only on his promise not to rejoin the king's forces, he soon afterwards obtained a pass to go overseas. A brief spell in the army of the prince of Orange followed, then travels in France, Spain, and Italy. The last were largely in the company of his friend John Evelyn: they met in Pisa on 20 October 1644 and travelled together for more than a year, visiting Rome, Naples, Padua, and Venice.

Henshaw was back in England by early January 1649.

The hostile political climate militated against active public or professional life, so during the 1650s he devoted himself to intellectual pursuits at his house in Kensington. (The Thomas Henshaw who was implicated in the 1654 royalist plot to assassinate Cromwell and wrote *A Vindication*, 1654, was a cousin.) In addition to Evelyn, Henshaw's circle at this time included the alchemists Thomas Vaughan and Robert Child. In 1650 Child informed Hartlib that Henshaw was trying to form a 'model of Christian learned society'. Henshaw's connection with Thomas Vaughan is memorialized in Vaughan's dedication of *Magia Adamica* (1650). Another friendship, which, like the one with Evelyn, would last many years, was with Elias Ashmole, who drew on Henshaw's alchemical library for both *Theatrum chemicum* (1652) and *The Way to Bliss* (1658); the 'very intimate Friend (one extraordinary Learned and a Great Ornament to our Nation)' who supplied Ashmole with the manuscript from which *The Way to Bliss* was printed is identified as Henshaw in Ashmole's own annotated copy (Bodl. Oxf., MS Ashmole 537, preface, MS note).

By the sale of his Middle Temple chamber to Ashmole in November 1658, Henshaw relinquished any intention of practising law, but at the Restoration he emerged into a more public role. In September 1662 he presented his paper on saltpetre to the Royal Society, of which he was an early member. He served for many years on its council and was vice-president from 1677. About this time Evelyn helped him obtain the post of French secretary to Charles II, which post he continued to hold under James II and William III; he was also gentleman-in-ordinary of the privy chamber to Charles and James. In 1671 he was appointed secretary to the duke of Richmond on an extraordinary embassy to Christian V of Denmark, and he remained in Denmark until 1674 as envoy after Richmond's death.

Henshaw published short chemical treatises in the Royal Society's *Philosophical Transactions*, and prepared for publication Stephen Skinner's *Etymologicum linguae Anglicanae* (1671) and the second edition of his brother Nathaniel's *Aero-chalinos* (1677). He is the 'Person of quality' who translated, from the Italian, *The History of that Great and Renowned Monarchy of China* (1655), by the Portuguese Jesuit F. Alvarez Semedo.

Henshaw married Anne, *née* Kipping, widow of James Darell, at Kensington on 23 April 1657. They had six sons and two daughters, and Anne died on 4 October 1671. Only one daughter, Anne, who married Thomas Halsey of Gaddesden, Hertfordshire, survived her parents; she and her children were the principal beneficiaries under Henshaw's will dated 7 July 1697. Henshaw died in Kensington on 2 January 1700 and was buried on 6 January in Kensington parish church.   JENNIFER SPEAKE

Sources will, PRO, PROB 11/454, sig. 8 · Wood, *Ath. Oxon.*, new edn, 3.794; 4.444 · *The diary of John Evelyn*, ed. E. S. De Beer (1959) · S. Hartlib, *Ephemerides* (1650) · *Elias Ashmole (1617–1692): his autobiographical and historical notes*, ed. C. H. Josten, 5 vols. (1966 [i.e. 1967]) · 'A true account of the late bloody and inhumane conspiracy … London', 1654, Bodl. Oxf., MS Wood 367(9), sig. B1 · J. Aubrey, Bodl. Oxf., MS Aubrey 6, fol. 42 · E. Ashmole, *The way to bliss*, 1658, Bodl. Oxf., Ashmole MS 537 [Ashmole's interleaved annotated copy] ·

E. Ashmole, *Theatrum chemicum Britannicum*, 1652, Bodl. Oxf., MSS Ashmole [Ashmole's interleaved annotated copy], 971–2 · F. A. Semedo, *History of … China* (1655) · T. Vaughan, *Magia Adamica* (1650), foreword · S. Pasmore, 'Thomas Henshaw (1618–1700)', *Notes and Records of the Royal Society*, 36 (1981–2), 177–88

Archives Bodl. Oxf., Wood MS SC 25216, fol. 181 (autobiography) · Bodl. Oxf., Ashmole MSS · RS, letters to Henry Oldenburg

Likenesses T. Athow, watercolour drawing, *c*.1645, AM Oxf. · T. Flatman, miniature, 1677, repro. in G. G. Williamson, *How to identify portrait miniatures* (1909)

Wealth at death extensive bequests: will, PRO, PROB 11/454, sig. 8

Henslow, George (1835–1925). *See under* Henslow, John Stevens (1796–1861).

Henslow, John Stevens (1796–1861), botanist and Church of England clergyman, was born on 6 February 1796 at Rochester, Kent. He was the eldest of eleven children; his father was John Prentis Henslow, a solicitor, and his mother, Frances, was daughter of Thomas Stevens, a wealthy Rochester brewer. Surrounded by many books on natural history and greatly encouraged by both his parents, the young Henslow began his education at home, continuing at day schools in Rochester and then, as a boarder, at a school in Camberwell. Here the drawing-master, George Samuel, a keen entomologist, introduced Henslow to eminent zoologists and entomologists.

In October 1814 Henslow entered St John's College, Cambridge. At that time there was little choice of subject available, and his study was principally mathematical. He obtained a reasonable BA degree in January 1818 and became a fellow of the Linnean Society on 9 February 1818. Henslow added geology to his interests by accompanying the newly appointed Woodwardian professor of geology, Adam Sedgwick, on a tour of the Isle of Wight in 1819. Their idea to found a 'corresponding society' to promote science in Cambridge came to fruition in November 1819, when they established the Cambridge Philosophical Society. Henslow was, it may be assumed, judged too young to be an officer, but he became one of the secretaries in 1821 and held the office for eighteen years.

On the death of Clarke, in 1822, the chair of mineralogy became vacant, and Henslow was elected. This election was a complex and acrimonious affair, but Henslow's part in it seems to have been entirely honourable. In succeeding Clarke, who was a popular lecturer and brilliant showman, he had taken on a difficult challenge. Henslow's style of lecturing, to quote Leonard Jenyns, his brother-in-law and biographer, 'was not what would be called eloquent, but he had a good voice and a remarkably clear way of expressing himself'. Being now assured of an academic career, Henslow married Harriet (1797–1857), daughter of Revd George Leonard Jenyns of Bottisham Hall, on 16 December 1823 and set up house in Cambridge. Two years later, on the death of Thomas Martyn, the professor of botany, he succeeded to this chair also and began his rejuvenation of botanical science in Cambridge. Shortly afterwards he resigned his professorship of mineralogy.

In 1824 Henslow was ordained and obtained a curacy in Cambridge. Whatever struggle took place in his mind

John Stevens Henslow (1796–1861), by unknown artist

about the relative merits of a church or a university career, there is some evidence that the resolution of doctrinal difficulties affecting his Christian belief was important in shaping his future career. There is little difficulty in understanding his acceptance of the chair of botany, however. The aged Martyn had treated his professorship as a sinecure, and had ceased to live in Cambridge, or even visit it, for nearly thirty years. What survived of Cambridge botany was a small, traditional botanical garden unsuited, to use Henslow's own words, 'to the demands of modern science'; in it there was little or no botanical teaching or research. This was a real challenge to a gifted and enthusiastic young man, and he set about rescuing what he could from the old museum, planning a course of botanical lectures and practical 'demonstrations', and setting in motion the plans for the new Cambridge Botanic Garden on the present site of nearly 40 acres. Disarmingly, Henslow himself is quoted as saying of his election to the chair of botany: 'when appointed, I knew very little indeed about botany … but I probably knew as much of the subject as any other resident in Cambridge' (J. S. Henslow, *Address to the members of the University of Cambridge on … the botanic garden*, 1846).

From 1825 to 1832 seems to have been a golden age for botanical science in Cambridge. Not only were Henslow's lectures well attended, but the more gifted pupils found the young professor charming, friendly, accessible, and very knowledgeable over the whole field of natural science. The field classes run by Henslow became very popular, partly because they took in zoology and geology as freely as botany, and the Friday evening soirées at the

Henslow home overlooking Parker's Piece were brilliantly successful. The young Charles Darwin, who went up to Christ's College in 1828, fell under his spell, with important consequences for modern biological science. Darwin assessed his teacher thus:

> He had a remarkable power of making the young feel completely at ease with him, though we were all awe-struck with the amount of his knowledge … When I reflect how immediately we felt at ease … I think it was as much owing to the transparent sincerity of his character, as to his kindness of heart; and, perhaps even still more to the highly remarkable absence in him of all self-consciousness. (Jenyns, 51)

Thus began a lifelong friendship, which survived even the strain of the publication of *The Origin of Species* in 1859. Ironically, Henslow, who had first recommended Darwin as naturalist for the *Beagle*, was in the chair for the famous meeting of the British Association in Oxford in 1860 when Thomas Henry Huxley clashed with Bishop Wilberforce over man's descent from the apes.

Henslow's only substantial work, entitled *The Principles of Descriptive and Physiological Botany*, published in 1835, made widely available to British scientists the important work of De Candolle and other, mainly French, botanists. The book reveals how effectively Henslow had equipped himself with an all-round picture of botany as an important science, but already, by 1832, when he obtained the living of Cholsey-cum-Moulsford in Berkshire, the Cambridge halcyon days were nearly over. The new vicar of Cholsey resided in the village during the long vacation, but continued to live in Cambridge until 1839. In 1837 he accepted the lucrative living of Hitcham in Suffolk, but soon decided that he could not conscientiously discharge his duties there without leaving Cambridge. From 1839 onwards he attended to his minimum commitments in Cambridge, which included a lecture course in the Easter term, and an interest in the new botanic garden, which was officially opened in 1846, and which retains today many marks of Henslow's ideas. The far-sighted design of planting hardy trees in systematic groups was specifically chosen by Henslow for its educational value, and the whole purpose of the garden was explained by him in his *Address to the members of the University of Cambridge on the expediency of improving, and on the funds required for remodelling and supporting the botanic garden*. This twenty-page pamphlet, dated 1846, sets out with admirable clarity what a botanical garden should do, in providing facilities for growing plants for teaching and research. Published at a time when there was still no regular teaching in the individual sciences in Cambridge, this document reads prophetically, and it is good to recall that, the year before he died, Henslow was able to examine the first tripos candidates for botany.

A new career began for Henslow when the family left Cambridge for the rectory at Hitcham. He had already displayed in Cambridge an active interest in local politics, and had indeed incurred a good deal of criticism for his willingness to act as 'common informer' in a court case involving election bribery. (As an extraordinary witness to this affair there remained visible for more than a century afterwards an inscription in thick black paint on the wall of Corpus Christi College stating 'Henslow—common informer'.) This wider concern for the good of 'the common people' Henslow increasingly exercised in and around his Suffolk parish. In spite of opposition, sometimes quite violent, among the local farmers, who saw in any education of the labouring classes a dangerous, even revolutionary step, he established schools, benefit and sports clubs, allotments, horticultural shows, and parish excursions. One of these excursions, held on 27 July 1854, took more than 200 parishioners by the newly constructed railway for a day visit to Cambridge, where, on a carefully planned itinerary, they were shown the new botanic garden and several colleges and university buildings, and taken to dinner at 2 p.m. in the hall of Downing College where, according to a pamphlet he had printed about the visit, 'the Vice-Chancellor and his Lady have kindly added to our ordinary frugal fare by the present of a Barrel of Beer, and Plum-puddings enough for the whole party'.

The fame of Henslow's experiments in popular education reached far beyond Hitcham, and he was even invited by Prince Albert to give a short course of botanical lectures to the royal children. He made an important contribution to the development of scientific teaching in the University of London, where he acted as an examiner for twenty-two years, and pioneered the introduction of a practical examination. Henslow was also involved with the early years of the Ipswich Museum, acting as president of the managing committee from 1850.

Henslow and his wife had three daughters, and three sons of whom one died in infancy. The eldest daughter, Frances, married the botanist J. D. Hooker (1817–1911) and the younger son, George Henslow, became a popular botanical lecturer. Harriet Henslow died on 20 November 1857. Henslow died at the rectory, Hitcham, on 16 May 1861, and of his funeral at Hitcham on 22 May, Jenyns records that 'church and churchyard alike [were] filled with the parishioners'.

George Henslow (1835–1925), botanist, was born on 23 March 1835 in Cambridge. He was educated privately at the vicarage at Sawston, near Cambridge, then at King Edward VI's Grammar School, Bury St Edmunds. He entered Christ's College, Cambridge, in 1854 and graduated in 1858 with a first class in the natural sciences tripos together with a second class in both mathematics and divinity. After ordination his first curacy was at Steyning, Sussex, from 1859 to 1861, followed by two consecutive appointments as headmaster of grammar schools at Warwick and London (Store Street). From 1886 to 1890 he held the lectureship in botany at St Bartholomew's medical school, and was honorary professor of botany to the Royal Horticultural Society from 1880 to 1918. Henslow was married three times. In October 1859 he married Ellen Weekley (d. 1871); the couple had five children, but only one (also George), survived infancy. In 1872 he married Georgina Brook Bailey (1842/3–1876); following her death he married, in 1881, Katherine (1845/6–1919), widow of Richard Yeo.

A large man with an impressive bearing, Henslow was an excellent lecturer, very popular with amateur gardeners and naturalists. His lectures were illustrated with large coloured wall-diagrams, many of which came to him from his father, who had used them in his own lectures in Cambridge. Though accepting the general idea of organic evolution, George Henslow found Darwinian natural selection unconvincing as a mechanism, preferring Lamarckian explanations as in his books *The Origin of Floral Structures* (1888) and *The Origin of Plant Structures* (1895). These views, combined with a somewhat authoritarian manner, made him less universally acceptable in scientific bodies such as the Linnean Society of London, of which he was a fellow. Henslow died at his home in Bournemouth on 23 December 1925.

S. MAX WALTERS

Sources S. M. Walters and E. A. Snow, *Darwin's mentor: John Stevens Henslow, 1796–1861* (2001) · L. Jenyns, *Memoir of the Rev. John Stevens Henslow* (1862) · J. Russell-Gebbett, *Henslow of Hitcham* (1977) · N. Barlow, *Darwin and Henslow: the growth of an idea (edited letters)* (1967) · M. M. Garland, *Cambridge before Darwin: the idea of a liberal education, 1800–1860* (1980) · J. S. Henslow, *The principles of descriptive and physiological botany* (1835) · J. Browne, *Charles Darwin* (1995) · *The Times* (2 Jan 1926) [George Henslow] · *Proceedings of the Linnean Society of London*, 138th session (1925–6), 82–3 [obit. of George Henslow] · *Journal of Botany, British and Foreign*, 64 (1926), 55–6 [George Henslow] · *The Garden*, 59 (1901), 226 [George Henslow] · J. Peile, *Biographical register of Christ's College, 1505–1905, and of the earlier foundation, God's House, 1448–1505*, ed. [J. A. Venn], 2 (1913) · parish register, Cambridge, Great St Andrew's Church, Cambs. AS [marriage, George Henslow, Oct. 1859]

Archives Christ's College, Cambridge, geological papers · RBG Kew, corresp. and diaries · Suffolk RO, Bury St Edmunds, corresp. and papers · Suffolk RO, Ipswich, corresp. and papers · U. Cam., department of plant sciences, corresp. and papers | Bath Central Library, corresp. with Jenyns · Bath Royal Literary and Scientific Institution, Bath, letters to Leonard Blomefield · CUL, corresp. with Sir George Airy · CUL, corresp. with Charles Darwin · CUL, letters to Sir J. D. Hooker · Ipswich Museum, letters to George Knights · NHM [George Henslow] · NHM, corresp. with Sir Richard Owen and William Clift · Oxf. U. Mus. NH, letters to J. O. Westwood · RBG Kew, letters to Sir William Hooker · Trinity Cam., letters to William Whewell · Tyne and Wear Archives Service, Newcastle upon Tyne, letters to William Hutton · U. Newcastle, letters to Sir Walter Trevelyan

Likenesses T. H. Maguire, lithograph, pubd 1851, BM, NPG · T. H. Maguire, portrait, Ipswich; copy, Cambridge · T. Woolner, marble bust, RBG Kew; version, FM Cam. · photograph, Botanic Garden, Cambridge · portrait, Ipswich Museum [*see illus.*]

Wealth at death £25,000: probate, 18 June 1861, *CGPLA Eng. & Wales*

Henslowe, Philip (*c*.1555–1616), theatre financier, was the son of Edmond Henslowe of Lindfield, Sussex, who served as master of the game in Ashdown Forest and Broil Park, and Margaret Ridge who seems to have come from a local family. The family name was originally Hensley and they were from Devon. When the name changed from Hensley to Henslowe is unknown; the men of the family identified themselves frequently as Hensley, as did many of their contemporaries. The family coat of arms, described in the 1623 visitation of Surrey, consisted of 'gules, a lion of England, and a chief of France Ancient'. For years the Henslowe family resided near Lindfield, Sussex. They also had connections to Buxted, Sussex. The family was associated with the Sussex nobility and conservative factions at court through the appointment of Edmond Henslowe, and also through members of the extended family as well. Edmond's son-in-law Ralph Hogge operated one of the most important iron foundries in England, supplying both advice and practical know-how to the royal armoury on the making of cannon. Philip's older brother Edmond was a servant to the lord chamberlain. Throughout his political career—which began most obviously with his appointment as groom of the chamber in 1593 and ended with his death—Philip Henslowe was consistently a member of the court circle. Moreover, there is every indication that he used his privilege both to protect and to promote his commercial interests, including the ownership of several London playhouses.

Early life Although Henslowe was probably born in Sussex he migrated to London at an indeterminate date and gained his freedom in the Dyers' Company under the supervision of Henry (Harry) Woodward who was reputed to have been bailiff to Viscount Montague. Woodward subsequently died and was buried in St Saviour's parish on 8 December 1579. On 14 February 1580, a mere two months later, Philip Henslowe married Woodward's widow, Agnes (d. 1617), who was somewhat older than he. Although the couple never had children of their own Henslowe became a stepfather to two daughters (Joan and Elizabeth) from Agnes's previous marriage. Traditionally, historians have posited that Henslowe had much to gain financially from the marriage; however, there is every indication that Henslowe had his own family money (Cerasano, 'Biography', 66–71).

Records of Henslowe's early years in London are sparse. There is no indication that he practised the dyer's trade; yet never missing an opportunity to turn a penny he apparently engaged in a variety of business investments including starch making, pawnbroking, and property investment. For a decade (1576–86) he negotiated the sale of wood in Ashdown Forest. In June 1584 he was involved in buying and dressing goatskins, and in 1593 Henslowe purchased property in Buxted, Sussex, near to the land owned by Ralph Hogge. This pattern—taking on whatever investment would provide a financial return—seems, to modern eyes, indiscriminate. However, it was typical of investors, large and small, during Henslowe's day, and it was a pattern that Henslowe followed throughout his life, frequently investing in several enterprises simultaneously.

Building the Rose and Fortune playhouses By 1587 Henslowe had accumulated enough money to make his first large-scale investment, that of the Rose Playhouse in Southwark, near to the southern end of what is now Southwark Bridge. (The property had been purchased in March 1585, and was called 'the little Rose' because of its distinctive rose gardens.) The original arrangements for the playhouse were made by Henslowe in partnership with John Cholmley, a grocer, but by the time that the Rose opened its doors Cholmley had disappeared from the partnership. What became of him is unclear. By 1592 the Rose was apparently such a successful venture that Henslowe renovated the structure, enlarging it to accommodate a sizeable audience. In February of the same year Henslowe also began to keep an account book of the debts owed him by the Lord Strange's Men (who were then performing at the Rose) and the profits earned on individual performances of plays, along with sundry notes of other financial and legal dealings. This memorandum book—which has become known as his 'diary'—remains one of the most revealing theatrical documents of the 1590s. Its pages illustrate the many tasks in which Henslowe engaged as a theatre financier, lending money for playbooks and costumes, paying for performance licences, and keeping the playhouse in good repair. But although Henslowe came to know some of the actors intimately he was so absolutely a businessman that he required them to sign bonds agreeing to specific terms for performance, and he held the players, both individually and as a group, sharply to the terms of repayment for the loans he extended. Despite the fact that the interpretation of various sums recorded in the *Diary* is open to debate, it is clear that Henslowe invested large sums in his theatrical endeavours. Periodically he would 'cast up' his accounts, arriving at a total of outstanding debt that was not infrequently as large a sum as the Rose Playhouse cost to build.

In October 1592 Henslowe's stepdaughter Joan married the prominent actor Edward Alleyn who was performing with Strange's Men. From this time onward the two men formed a familial and financial partnership, operating the most lucrative theatre business of the period that came to include several playhouses and the bear-baiting arena in Southwark. Letters from Henslowe to Alleyn, written in 1593 while the latter was on tour in the country, refer to 'well beloved son Edward Alleyn', suggesting that the relationship between the two was extremely close (Greg, 35–6, 38–9). Moreover, it seems to have remained so throughout the many years of their association. Here again Henslowe's *Diary* is instructive, preserving notations through which theatre historians can trace the specific ways in which Henslowe and Alleyn together owned and operated the Rose Playhouse.

In 1600, when the Rose was thirteen years old, Henslowe and Alleyn decided to construct a new playhouse, to be known as the Fortune, north of London Wall in the parish of St Giles Cripplegate. The area was well known to Alleyn, who had been raised east of this district, in Bishopsgate. (Alleyn had also, for some time, been donating to the poor relief in St Giles which boosted his political sway when the local justices attempted, later on, to stay the construction of the theatre.) The owners contacted Peter Street, a former master of the Carpenters' Company and builder of the Globe Playhouse, with whom they signed a formal contract on 8 January 1600. Construction began almost immediately, with the completed playhouse costing £520 in addition to the lease for the property on which the theatre was constructed (Chambers,

2.436–9). Henslowe played a major role in the financial execution of the theatre, recording detailed payments for materials and workmen's wages on the reverse of the contract. But however smoothly the project may have begun, the situation apparently became very strained as it neared its conclusion. Henslowe met with the master carpenter on several occasions in order to ply him with money. At one time Henslowe paid Street so that the carpenter could fetch his horse out of pawn, and at another time money changed hands simply, as Henslowe noted, 'to pacify him [Street]'. The playhouse seems to have been completed some time in August, and the Fortune's doors were opened in the autumn with Alleyn's company, the Lord Admiral's Men, in residence (*Henslowe's Diary*, 137, 306–10). Henslowe and Alleyn continued to own the theatre jointly until Henslowe's death when it appears that plans were in process to turn the theatre over to the players. Nevertheless, these never materialized and in 1618 Alleyn, who maintained ownership of the playhouse, was leasing the playhouse to the acting company for £200 per annum (Warner, 242–3).

Interests in bear-baiting After the Rose had been vacated by the Admiral's Men several acting companies rented the space, including Worcester's Men. By this time theatre ownership seems to have been lucrative enough for Henslowe and Alleyn to contemplate the construction of a combination baiting arena and playhouse on Bankside, near to the Rose and Globe. The owners' interest in baiting, which had begun in the 1590s, peaked in 1598 when the mastership of the royal game—a court office still in the purview of the crown—fell vacant. However, much to their disappointment it had already been promised to a pensioner who received the patent and vacated the office on his death in 1604. A second time Henslowe and Alleyn tried to gain the privilege, but they were again unsuccessful, and the patent passed instead to one of King James's Scottish friends. Finally, a few months later, the men decided simply to purchase the office, which they did, retaining the patent until Henslowe's death when the entire office passed to Alleyn. In order better to accommodate the baiting, which produced a sizeable income, Henslowe and Jacob Meade (one of Henslowe's former business partners in the bear-baiting) contracted with Gilbert Katherens, a carpenter, to build the Hope Playhouse, a structure with a moveable stage that could be adapted to both baiting and dramatic performance. For unexplained reasons the construction seems to have been delayed until the following year; however, by October 1614 the playhouse was being used by Lady Elizabeth's Men who performed Ben Jonson's *Bartholomew Fair* there. According to the 'Induction' the locality suited the play because it was 'as dirty as Smithfield, and as stinking every whit'. But soon thereafter disputes erupted between Henslowe and the players who had agreed initially to allow the space to 'lie still' one day per fortnight in order to accommodate the baiting. Subsequently, Prince Charles's Men used the space, and although there is some indication that Meade actually took charge of managing the playhouse, Henslowe retained a share that eventually passed to Alleyn.

Court connections Henslowe accumulated much property during his lifetime, mostly in and around Southwark. His holdings included several inns, a variety of houses, and the Pike Garden. Like many landlords he was periodically denounced by one of his tenants for being overly harsh. Nevertheless, Henslowe's dealings with the players, tenants, London businessmen, and members of the court circle seem to have been overwhelmingly successful. Nor did his involvement with the theatres—always suspect by some—impair his progress at court. After his initial appointment as groom of the chamber he went on to become gentleman sewer of the chamber under James I in 1603. And despite the fact that he and Alleyn had purchased the mastership of the bears Henslowe took this position seriously. Henslowe held on to his half of the mastership to his last days when he commented that he was a servant of the king and would be buried as such. Moreover, throughout his lengthy career he was in favour with a broad spectrum of statesmen and London officials. The list of distinguished personages was large and included Sir Julius Caesar (master of the rolls), Thomas Howard (earl of Suffolk), Charles Howard (lord high admiral), and Thomas Sackville (Lord Buckhurst). Additionally, Henslowe consulted the legendary astrologer Simon Forman once on medical ailments and at another time in order to purchase a magic spell that was supposed to discover which of his household servants was stealing from him. It is from a reference in one of Forman's notebooks—noting that Henslowe was 'of 42 years' (in 1597)—that his date of birth can be calculated (Cerasano, 'Philip Henslowe', 153).

Henslowe's extended family Henslowe's family was extensive and omnipresent, especially when they were short of money. His nephew Francis Henslowe—who appears to have been a prodigal young man—was connected, for short periods of time, to the Duke of Lennox's Men and the Queen's Men, perhaps as an actor. On both occasions Henslowe lent Francis money to invest in these companies. On two occasions the nephew pleaded with his uncle for more money in order that he could be released from prison. (He was apparently arrested for debt.) Other entries in Henslowe's *Diary* record additional loans to Francis, as well as many entries from the pawn accounts of 1593–4, during which time Francis served as an intermediary for his uncle and also sold some of his wife's jewellery to make ends meet. Sadly, in 1606 Henslowe ended his relationship with his nephew when he paid funeral expenses for Francis and his wife, and laid out additional funds to settle with Francis's creditors. The causes of death are unknown but might well have been plague-related.

Edmond Henslowe, Philip's brother, died before 1593 leaving three children who initially lived with their mother, Margery (who was supported by her brother-in-law); when Margery Henslowe died a few years later, Philip Henslowe provided for the children. And some money changed hands on happier occasions. When Henslowe's sister Mary married John Walters, Henslowe provided her marriage portion, perhaps under the will of her father.

Henslowe lived all his adult life in Clink Liberty, in a house located somewhere between the Clink prison and an inn called the Bell. The location offered proximity to the Bankside playhouses and the local baiting arenas. For several years Henslowe served as a collector for the lay subsidy taxes in that district, and when he was not resident at court he paid £10 per collection in taxes there. Henslowe also took an active interest in local church politics and shouldered the responsibilities of several administrative positions, serving as vestryman (1607), churchwarden (1608), and overseer of the poor of St Saviour's parish, the parish in which the players who lived nearby Shakespeare's Globe, and Shakespeare himself, would have worshipped. Later, he served as one of the governors of the free grammar school in that parish (1612) and was chosen, with four others, in 1613 to purchase the rectory of St Saviour's 'for the general good of posterity as good cheap as they might' (Warner, 30–31, 139, 266).

Henslowe's death and ensuing litigation On 6 January 1616 Henslowe died, and on 10 January he was buried in the chancel of St Saviour's Church 'with an afternoon knell of the great bell'. In his will he stated that forty poor men should receive mourning gowns so that they could accompany his body to the burial, and, in addition, he left a bequest to the poor of the parish. Henslowe left a sizeable estate, estimated in one inventory to include £1700 in property alone. Much of his income seems to have been earned through the bear-baiting and theatrical investments (in addition to rents from various properties). In his will Henslowe clearly left his wife, Agnes, sole executor, and designated several others (including Edward Alleyn) to serve as overseers of the estate (PRO, PROB 11/127, fol. 45r). Nevertheless, a lawsuit was filed by Henslowe's nephew John, who argued that Alleyn, in collusion with Agnes Henslowe and Roger Cole, interfered with the drawing-up of the will and the subsequent valuation of the estate so as to hold back certain leases (including that of the Fortune playhouses). The depositions that were filed in the course of the litigation recount the story of Henslowe's last days in some detail. Apparently, because Henslowe was suffering from a 'palsy' (probably a paralytic stroke) a will was drawn up hastily by Roger Cole, the bishop of Winchester's registrar, on 5 January, which Henslowe signed in his own hand. On the following day Cole was recalled to put the will into a better form; however, by this time Henslowe's palsy was so profound that he could only make his mark on the will, despite the fact that he was 'then of good & perfect memory and of a disposing mind' (according to James Archer, one of the deponents). According to another deponent (Joan Horton, domestic servant to the Henslowe family), by the time that Cole finished his task Henslowe appeared to be failing badly; and, according to a third deponent, by the end of the day he had died. Generally speaking, the deponents agreed that Alleyn was innocent of any malice in dealing

with Henslowe's will; but the thicket of suits that ensued after Henslowe's death represents, at best, a confused mass of claims, some of them contradictory.

Agnes Henslowe, who was old at the time of her husband's death (though not necessarily one hundred, as some contemporaries claimed) inherited his estate. She died a year later, in 1617, and was buried in Dulwich College chapel on 9 April 1617. (Her will was written during the previous year and witnessed by Matthias Alleyn, first warden of Dulwich College. It was proved on 3 July 1617 and a note written on it indicates that an inventory had been exhibited previously, on 3 June.) In her will Agnes requested that she be buried 'without vain pomp or show' and that £20 be set aside for 'eighty poor widows and women' living in the liberty of the Clink, along with the annual proceeds from a lease to be given also to 'eighty poor widows and women' in St Saviour's parish (PRO, PROB 10/344). Her daughter Joan (Alleyn's wife) was also buried in the chapel of Dulwich College, on 1 July 1623, as was Joan's husband, Edward Alleyn, in November 1626.

The Henslowe–Alleyn papers The Henslowe papers are primarily housed in the Wodehouse Library at Dulwich College, which was founded by Edward Alleyn in 1619 as a 'hospital' for orphans and homeless pensioners. Henslowe's *Diary* provides a unique picture of the operation of an Elizabethan playhouse. The book offers crucial evidence that allows historians to understand how dramatists, players, and playhouse owners functioned together within an enterprise that was at once an artistic endeavour and a product of the new capitalism. The legacy of the Henslowe papers has been fraught with perils, however. The *Diary* and certain other theatrical documents were borrowed from the college about 1790 by Edmund Malone. By the time they were returned by James Boswell the younger (Malone's executor) in 1812, some of the papers had gone missing. Subsequently, an unidentified person cut selected signatures from the *Diary*, several of which are now in the British Library manuscript collection. Later, another individual (probably J. P. Collier) forged entries in the *Diary*, as well as in several entire manuscripts in the collection; and Collier perhaps also lost other manuscripts as well (Warner, i–xii).

S. P. CERASANO

Sources *Henslowe's diary*, ed. R. A. Foakes and R. T. Rickert (1961) • R. A. Foakes, ed., *The Henslowe papers* (1977) • W. W. Greg, ed., *The Henslowe papers* (1907) • E. K. Chambers, *The Elizabethan stage*, 4 vols. (1923) • G. E. Bentley, *The Jacobean and Caroline stage*, 7 vols. (1941–68) • G. F. Warner, ed., *Catalogue of the manuscripts and muniments of Alleyn's College of God's Gift at Dulwich* (1881) • W. Rendle, *The Genealogist*, new ser., 4 (1887), 149–59 • S. P. Cerasano, 'Cheerful givers: Henslowe, Alleyn, and the 1612 loan book to the crown', *Shakespeare Studies*, 28 (2000), 215–19 • M. B. Rose, 'Where are the mothers in Shakespeare? Options for gender representation in the English Renaissance', *Shakespeare Quarterly*, 42 (1991), 291–314 • S. P. Cerasano, 'Revising Philip Henslowe's biography', *N&Q*, 230 (1985), 66–71 • *DNB* • will, PRO, PROB 11/127, fol. 45r • will, PRO, PROB 10/344 [Agnes Henslowe] • E. Turner, 'Ashdown Forest', *Sussex Archaeological Collections*, 14 (1862), 35–64 • E. Straker, *Wealden iron* (1931) • parish register, Southwark, St Saviour's, 10 Jan 1616 [burial]

Archives Dulwich College, London, corresp., diary, and account book

Wealth at death approx. £1700: Rendle, 'Philip Henslowe'

Hensman, John (1780–1864), Church of England clergyman, was born at Bedford on 22 September 1780, the son of Thomas and Anne Hensman. He was educated at Bedford grammar school, after which he matriculated as an exhibitioner at Corpus Christi College, Cambridge, in 1797. After graduating BA as ninth wrangler in 1801, he was elected a fellow. Ordained deacon in 1802, he assisted the Revd Charles Simeon at Cambridge before being ordained priest in 1803. In the same year he became curate to James Vaughan, rector of Wraxall, Somerset, and married his rector's sister, Elizabeth (*d.* 1860), on 16 September 1808. They had one child, a daughter, Harriet.

In 1809 Hensman went to Clifton, near Bristol, as curate in charge of the parish church, the living being at that time under sequestration. He played a large part in replacing the seventeenth-century church with a new parish church, which was consecrated on 12 August 1822. When in 1822 the sequestration was removed and the incumbent returned, Hensman, at the bishop's request, took charge of Dowry Chapel as curate. In 1830 his friends built Trinity Church, Hotwells, for him; it was consecrated on 10 November 1830 and he held the incumbency from 10 January 1831 until 8 October 1844, when he accepted the perpetual curacy of Christ Church, Clifton, where, once again, the church was built for him. In March 1847 he was instituted to the living of Clifton on the nomination of the Simeon trustees. He was instrumental in building St Paul's Church, consecrated on 8 November 1853, and St Peter's, consecrated on 10 August 1855. He was made an honorary canon of Bristol Cathedral by Dr Baring, bishop of Bristol, in 1858. On the completion of fifty years of his Clifton ministry, a chapel of ease was built as a memorial to him, and was consecrated in December 1862. By then he was considered to be one of the wisest and oldest members of the evangelical party. He did not engage in party controversy, and was a plain preacher, whose sermons were persuasive rather than eloquent. He died at Clifton on 23 April 1864, his wife having predeceased him in November 1860. He was buried at Wraxall.

WILLIAM HUNT, *rev.* ELLIE CLEWLOW

Sources private information (1891) · personal knowledge (1891) · Venn, *Alum. Cant.* · Boase, *Mod. Eng. biog.* · *GM*, 3rd ser., 16 (1864), 803–4

Likenesses W. O. Geller, mezzotint (after S. West), NPG

Wealth at death under £5000: probate, 20 May 1864, *CGPLA Eng. & Wales*

Henson, Gravener (1785–1852), workers' leader and author, was born in Nottingham in 1785 but nothing else is known about his origins. He may well have received some education at a local Wesleyan Sunday school, but he became familiar with popular contemporary writers, British and European, through hard study in his leisure time. He married Martha Farnsworth (who predeceased him) at St Mary's, Nottingham, in 1813; they are not known to have had children. Henson became a journeyman framework knitter, but subsequently worked with

the local point net lace industry. He had 'a short neck, keen small eyes, and a head very broad at the base, rising angularly to an unusual height' (Thompson, ch. 14).

In 1809 Henson became involved in his first strike and probably spent some time in prison in 1810 as a result of the part he played. In 1811 he attempted, unsuccessfully, to prosecute four hosiers under the Combination Acts, which were intended to cover employers as well as workers, and in 1812 made the first of many attempts to secure parliamentary regulation of the hosiery and lace trades and the organization and co-operation of their workers throughout Britain. These activities, coinciding with the machine breaking of the Luddites, caused Henson to be identified by some as General Ned *Ludd, the (probably mythical) organizer of machine breaking, though his public statements were hostile to Luddism and his attempts to create trade union organizations and to work though parliament were the very antithesis of industrial sabotage.

To this day historians have experienced lingering doubts and Henson has retained his enigmatic quality in his varied activities. In 1816 he acted successfully against two truck-paying hosiers, and in 1817 spent eight months in Cold Bath Fields Prison in London, having been arrested on suspicion of treasonable practices as local and central authorities found difficulty in distinguishing between the constitutionalism of the Hampden clubs and the insurrection of the Pentrich rebels. Henson expressed amusement at the continuing accusations, despite the alibi supplied by his majesty (in virtue of his being in prison), but he experienced further misfortunes in 1818, when he spent some time in St Mary's workhouse, Nottingham. Afterwards he resumed his industrial campaigns, assisting in the organization of a strike of midlands framework knitters in 1821, and in 1823 undertook another ambitious campaign to secure the parliamentary regulation of the hosiery and lace trades. Working closely with George White, a House of Commons clerk, he produced a history of the workings of the Combination Acts, which he sought to have repealed and replaced by a virtual charter of workers' rights. This visionary scheme had no prospect of success, but Henson was at least able to present evidence to the committee on artisans and machinery and help to secure repeal.

By this time Henson was assuming a more detached role, offering himself as an intermediary in disputes between masters and men, stressing the need for both sides to work together for the good of the trade, practising co-operation rather than confrontation. He sought the help of Francis Place in his campaign for the reform of the patent laws which he believed were inhibiting invention and technical advance, to which Henson had himself made some useful contributions as an ingenious mechanic. In 1831 he published his *History of the Framework Knitters*, his greatest practical achievement, and in December of that year returned briefly to the political arena, as treasurer of a local committee that sought a pardon for convicted Reform Bill rioters. He was highly critical of the conduct of both the local magistracy and the special commission.

More characteristic of the new Henson were his trade articles in the local press and his leading role in local committees to promote invention, popularize local products, and persuade the authorities to enforce the laws against the export of lace machinery. He collected evidence against offending exporters in 1833 but was left without support. What he called the cruel system of free trade would, he believed, work to the detriment of Britain's artisans if competitors secured access to British technology, and he condemned the new poor law of 1834 as another manifestation of *laissez-faire* that would abandon the working classes to a harsh fate. He nevertheless rejected both general unionism, for its oppressiveness, and Chartism, for its remoteness from economic issues, as viable options for the working classes.

Adherence to class co-operation in the promotion of local trades was a suitably mature position to be adopted by a former trade union organizer. However, Henson's earlier militancy confirmed him in E. P. Thompson's judgement as one of three truly impressive English working-class leaders in the period 1780–1832. When giving evidence to the select committee on postage in 1838 he was clearly disillusioned in many of his earlier aspirations, but still inclined to pontificate with what Cobbett called offensive conceit. In the 1840s, when local directories were variously describing Henson as a writer and an accountant, he continued to press for government legislation on the hosiery and lace trades but was disappointed at the outcome of the 1844 inquiry. Henson died on 15 November 1852 at Broad Street, Nottingham, of asthma and paralysis, with his hopes unfulfilled.

MALCOLM I. THOMIS

Sources R. A. Church and S. D. Chapman, 'Gravener Henson and the making of the English working class', *Land, labour and population in the industrial revolution: essays presented to J. D. Chamber*, ed. E. L. Jones and G. E. Mingay (1967), 131–61 · G. Henson, *History of the framework knitters* (1831) · W. Felkin, *A history of the machine-wrought hosiery and lace manufactures* (1867) · G. Henson and G. White, *A few remarks on the state of the laws at present in existence for regulating masters and work people* (1823) · E. P. Thompson, *The making of the English working class* (1963) · J. L. Hammond and B. Hammond, *The skilled labourer, 1760–1832* (1919) · M. I. Thomis, *Politics and society in Nottingham, 1785–1835* (1969) · d. cert.
Archives PRO, Home Office MSS | BL, Place MSS · U. Nott., Newcastle MSS

Henson, Herbert Hensley

Henson, Herbert Hensley (1863–1947), bishop of Durham, was born in London on 8 November 1863, the son of Thomas Henson (1812–1896), a businessman, and his second wife, Martha Fear (d. 1870). When Henson was two the family moved to Broadstairs.

Early life and education Henson's Kentish childhood, which could have come straight out of the pages of Charles Dickens, was extremely unhappy, and he was afterwards reluctant to discuss it; his otherwise exhaustive memoirs, *Retrospect of an Unimportant Life*, contain only three pages on the first eighteen years of his life. His mother died when he was six, and, he later remarked, 'with her died our happiness' (Henson, *Retrospect*, 1.3). Henson's father was an evangelical who had repudiated

Herbert Hensley Henson (1863–1947), by Walter Stoneman, 1918

the Church of England and become involved with the Plymouth Brethren. He refused to allow his son either to be baptized or to attend school until in his teens, and his bigotry left Henson with an enduring hatred of protestant fanaticism. What little happiness there was in the Henson household seems to have come from Emma Theodora Parker, the German widow whom his father took as his third wife (it is not clear that they were ever formally married) three years after Henson's mother's death. She helped develop Henson's literary style by introducing him to the works of Walter Scott and translations of classical authors, and ensured that he received an education. He remained devoted to her, calling her Carissima and caring for her until her death in 1924.

Henson was destined by his father for a career in business, and when he was thirteen one of his brothers secured a clerkship for him in the City. But as Henson was about to leave for London his brother sent a telegram to say that the position no longer existed. At his stepmother's prompting, Henson was instead sent to Broadstairs collegiate school in 1877; here he became head boy, but after being falsely accused of lying by the headmaster he absconded. He managed to secure a position as an assistant master at Brigg grammar school in Lincolnshire. Spotting his ambition and ability, the headmaster suggested he apply to Oxford. Henson's father opposed this course, but relented under pressure from his stepmother, and Henson matriculated in 1881. Unable to afford affiliation to any college—his father was by now badly in debt, and eventually went bankrupt—Henson eked out a lonely and precarious existence as an unattached student. His isolated childhood, lack of schooling, and exclusion from normal university life all gave him the powerful sense of being an outsider which dominated the rest of his career.

In 1884 Henson was rescued from poverty and obscurity when, having taken a first in the modern history school, he was elected to a fellowship at All Souls. Here he found the companionship, security, and status which he had hitherto lacked. Among his friends were A. V. Dicey, Charles Oman, and A. C. Headlam. In the warden, Sir William Anson, he found a father figure; he later edited a *Memoir* (1920) of Anson. Henson was at this time a high-churchman and was much influenced by Charles Gore, though he was already critical of the excesses of ritualists. He was also a devoted supporter of the principle of establishment, and in 1886 he set up the Laymen's League to counter the threat of disestablishment.

Priest and bishop Ever since his family had discovered him preaching impromptu sermons in his nightshirt as a young boy, Henson had wanted to be ordained. He was briefly tempted by Dicey's suggestion that he should instead deploy his oratorical mastery at the bar. But Gore convinced him of his priestly vocation, and he was ordained priest in 1888. Henson felt called to minister to the poor, having been deeply affected by the poverty which he had seen in Birkenhead in 1885 while working as private tutor to the son of a merchant. In 1887, while still a deacon, he became head of the Oxford House Settlement in Bethnal Green. But he did not stay long because in 1888 he was appointed vicar of Barking. At twenty-five, and having been ordained priest only six months, he was the youngest vicar in the Church of England. He proved a brilliant success, restoring the church, establishing clubs for parishioners, and holding open-air services. Cosmo Gordon Lang estimated that in six months Henson had increased the congregation from 250 to 1100 (Lockhart, 76). But this relentless work overtaxed his health. Help came in 1895 from Lord Salisbury, who had admired his work in the Laymen's League, and who offered him the less onerous chaplaincy of St Mary's Hospital, Ilford, which was in his personal gift. In 1900 it was again Salisbury—this time in his prime-ministerial capacity—who promoted Henson vicar of St Margaret's, Westminster, and a canon of Westminster Abbey. In 1902 Henson married Isabella (Ella) Caroline (1870–1949), only daughter of James Wallis Dennistoun of Dennistoun, Scotland, and niece of Sir Robert Peel's biographer, C. S. Parker. With characteristic impulsiveness, he proposed four days after first meeting her.

Henson had by now acquired a national reputation as a brilliant preacher and polemicist. He had moved away from the high-churchmanship of his youth towards latitudinarianism. His 1898 book *Cui bono* accused the ritualists of undermining establishment. He also wrote a series of books and pamphlets advocating reunion with the nonconformists. When his old mentor Gore, as bishop of Birmingham, prohibited him from preaching in the institute of Carr's Lane Congregational Church in 1909 Henson

defied him, hanging a framed copy of Gore's inhibition on his study wall. This confrontational style led Asquith to change his original plan of making Henson dean of Lincoln, concluding that this would be 'like sending a destroyer into a land-locked pool' (*The Times*). Instead, in 1912 Henson became dean of Durham.

Henson was at this time the foremost defender of the principle of establishment and most vehement critic of moves towards church self-government. He opposed both William Temple's Life and Liberty campaign and the creation of the church assembly in 1919. Such an assembly, he warned, would be unrepresentative, dominated by Anglo-Catholics, and would inevitably lead to disestablishment. Only parliament could guarantee the tolerant traditions of Anglicanism.

In 1917 Lloyd George made Henson bishop of Hereford, against the advice of the archbishop of Canterbury, Randall Davidson. In *The Creed in the Pulpit* (1912) Henson had defended the right of clergy to express doubts about the virgin birth and bodily resurrection, and many prominent Anglo-Catholics, led by Gore, believed that he shared these doubts and argued that he was unfit to be a bishop. Davidson was satisfied by Henson's orthodoxy but, feeling that the controversy left him in an impossible position, briefly considered resigning as archbishop. Eventually, Davidson drafted a statement of faith to which Henson reluctantly gave his assent; Henson denied that he had retracted his earlier views. Gore called off his protests but boycotted Henson's consecration, as did a number of other bishops. Henson was greatly distressed by this episode, and in particular by the decision of Cosmo Lang, archbishop of York, not to attend the consecration. He had been ostracized by his fellow bishops; more than ever, he felt, he was an outsider.

Social and theological concerns Henson had been at Hereford only just over two years when, in 1920, Lloyd George made him bishop of Durham. He returned to a diocese where the coal industry had collapsed and the miners were on strike. Henson believed that strikes were wrong because they harmed innocent parties, and he had a violent, almost obsessional, dislike of trade unions; as vicar of Barking he had suffered recurrent premonitions that he would die in a street battle with strikers. In 1920s Durham he was fearless to the point of recklessness in condemning union militancy. In 1921 he accused miners of shirking, and was jeered when he went to preach in a mining village. In 1925, after Henson had attacked the strikers in the *Evening Standard*, the dean of Durham, J. E. C. Welldon, who had probably been mistaken for Henson, was beaten and kicked at the Durham miners' gala and almost thrown into the River Wear.

Henson's aversion to trade unions was an aspect of his wider anti-socialism. An individualist, he abhorred class-consciousness as un-Christian and disapproved of government spending on welfare. He was a vehement critic of Christian socialism, attacking both the Conference on Christian Politics, Economics and Citizenship, presided over by William Temple in 1924, and the latter's ill-fated attempts at intervening in the coal strike in 1926. Henson revered his friend Stanley Baldwin as a great Christian leader—he was moved to tears by his speech on the abdication—but feared that Baldwin was not firm enough with the unions. After the general strike he visited the prime minister in Worcestershire to try to persuade him to introduce tough anti-union measures.

There was a tension between Henson's conservatism and the instinctive sympathy for the underdog which he had shown as a young slum parson. In 1912 his concern for social justice had impelled him to use the pulpit of Westminster Abbey to condemn the atrocities of the Putumayo Rubber Company in Peru, which had been exposed by Roger Casement. Though he despised their union leadership, Henson was sympathetic to the plight of the unemployed Durham miners, promoting charitable efforts to assist them. He liked to think of himself as a radical, and often quoted William Anson's judgment on him, that he was 'a Jacobin lacquered over to look like a Tory' (Henson, *Retrospect*, 1.30).

The House of Commons' rejection of the revised prayer book in 1927, and again in 1928, brought about the greatest crisis of Henson's career. Henson had supported the revision of the prayer book, loudly denouncing its evangelical opponents as 'the Protestant underworld' and 'an army of illiterates generalled by octogenarians', a reference to the elderly evangelical leader, Bishop Knox (Henson, *Retrospect*, 1.164). He was devastated when the book was unexpectedly defeated. Parliament's action had destroyed his main argument for establishment—that only parliament could defend the church's freedom.

Disestablishment and other campaigns Henson now undertook a complete volte-face. Repudiating the belief in establishment which had been the cornerstone of his churchmanship, he began to agitate loudly for disestablishment. The church, he argued in *Disestablishment* (1929), could not enjoy its rightful spiritual freedom if it was shackled to a state whose citizens and institutions were no longer professedly Christian. Henson now became a fervent supporter of the church's right to govern itself through the church assembly, which he had previously denounced.

Henson had, in fact, been considering disestablishment for some time before the bill's first defeat because he feared that a Labour government would misuse ecclesiastical patronage. Nevertheless, his conversion seemed to most church people too abrupt to be credible. The disestablishment campaign was an abject failure, and, as so often in his career, Henson was aware of his total isolation. He continued to advocate disestablishment in books such as *The Church of England* (1939), but his cries became more muted. The events of the later 1930s also forced him to reassess his conclusion that the English people were no longer Christian. He was impressed by the contrast between the latent Christianity of the English (which he discerned in public ceremonies like the 1937 coronation) and the paganism of Nazi Germany. In his Gifford lectures, published as *Christian Morality* (1936), Henson argued that the survival of civilization depended on nations retaining their corporate Christianity.

Henson's campaign for disestablishment brought him into public conflict with many of his old supporters in the modernist wing of the church, including his close friend Ralph Inge. Henson had since the early 1920s been at pains to distance himself from what he saw as the extreme modernism of the Modern Churchmen's Union. The breach was exacerbated in 1933–4, when Henson was among the bishops who criticized the modernist dean of Liverpool, F. W. Dwelly, and his bishop, A. A. David, for allowing Unitarians to preach in Liverpool Cathedral.

After the failure of his disestablishment agitation, Henson turned to other campaigns. *The Oxford Groups* (1933) was a forceful critique of the fervid emotionalism of the American evangelist Frank Buchman. He supported divorce law reform, speaking in favour of A. P. Herbert's Matrimonial Causes Bill in the Lords in 1937. He also successfully campaigned for the preservation of Durham Castle. Most important of all, he publicized the plight of German Jews and Christians. Henson was a prominent critic of Nazi antisemitism, and contributed an introduction to Victor Gollancz's celebrated exposé *The Yellow Spot* (1936). His support for the German Confessing Church and for the imprisoned Martin Niemöller brought him into public conflict with his old friend Arthur Headlam, bishop of Gloucester. Henson was also critical of British foreign policy in the 1930s. In speeches to the House of Lords, and in his pamphlet *Abyssinia* (1936), he condemned Britain's passivity in the face of Mussolini's invasion of Abyssinia. He was one of the few senior churchmen who did not rush to support the Munich agreement, which he regarded as a 'grievous injury' to the Czechs and a shameful capitulation to Germany (Henson diaries, vol. 73, 2 Oct 1938).

Personal characteristics Henson retired from Durham at the age of seventy-five, eight months before the Second World War began, and went to live at Hintlesham in Suffolk. He supported what he saw as a 'holy war' against pagan barbarism, insisting that 'there can be no compromise or patched up peace' (Braley, *Letters*, 123). This rhetoric was strikingly similar to that of Winston Churchill, to whom Henson fulsomely dedicated the third volume of his memoirs. There were other similarities between the two men; both had spent much of the interwar years as isolated and reviled mavericks before being vindicated by their resolute opposition to Hitler. Churchill decided that Henson's preaching could make a useful contribution to wartime morale, and in 1940 he persuaded him out of retirement to become a canon of Westminster Abbey. But this proved to be an unhappy appointment. Henson's failing eyesight, combined with the wartime black-out in the abbey, meant that he was unable to read his sermons, and he resigned in 1941.

Henson was a small, slender but pugnacious man with beetling eyebrows. He was obsessed with fresh air and would regularly interrupt services to upbraid members of his congregation for coughing. He combined an abrupt manner with an acerbic wit, and his 'Hensonisms' were legendary. The most famous of these arose in 1924, when Archbishop Cosmo Gordon Lang complained that his new portrait by Sir William Orpen made him look 'proud, prelatical, and pompous'. 'And may I ask Your Grace to which of these epithets Your Grace takes exception?' Henson allegedly asked in reply (Lockhart, 290). But each of these epithets could equally justly have been applied to Henson, who was inclined to stand on his palatine dignity, sometimes seeming to forget that Durham was no longer a prince-bishopric.

As a bishop, Henson reserved his mornings for reading and writing, doing episcopal business only in the afternoons. He disliked administration and refused to install a telephone in Auckland Castle because he could not operate it. But his literary output was prodigious. Besides publishing numerous collections of speeches, sermons, and charges, he maintained copious diaries, writing a page of exercise book with a quill pen every day from 1885 until shortly before his death. These diaries contained waspish appraisals of his clerical and political contemporaries, together with frequent passages of self-examination.

Memoirs and death Extracts from these diaries appeared in Henson's three volumes of memoirs, *Retrospect of an Unimportant Life* (1942–50), which he produced in retirement. The title, with its unintentional echo of G. Grossmith's *Diary of a Nobody*, was indicative of the content; the memoirs were by turns snobbish, self-regarding, and self-dramatizing, and Ralph Inge was one of many friends who felt that Henson should not have published them. The memoirs were also exasperating to readers because of Henson's stubborn and disingenuous refusal to admit to the manifest inconsistencies of his career; throughout, he insisted that it was others who had changed, while he remained steadfast. Another of Henson's literary activities was *The Bishoprick*, a quarterly journal which he wrote himself and distributed to the clergy of his diocese; he later published selected essays, indicative of his penchant for archaic spelling, as *Bishoprick Papers* (1946). Henson's brilliance as a writer is perhaps best displayed in the two volumes of his letters which were edited by E. F. Braley after his death.

In his writings Henson repeatedly owned to two great regrets about his life. The first was that he had not been to public school. To this he attributed his sense of being a perpetual outsider. The second regret was that he and his wife had been unable to have children. In 1905 his wife gave birth to a stillborn son; she later suffered a miscarriage. Henson sought to compensate for this loss by unofficially adopting a series of poor boys and paying for their education. He called them his 'sons'; his favourite, Dick Elliott, was later ordained by Henson and died in an Italian prisoner of war camp during the Second World War.

Henson never overcame the loneliness which had begun in childhood. Indeed, it grew more acute in later years as his wife's deafness made it hard for him to talk to her. Instead he sought out conversation with the unemployed miners whom he met on his daily walks in Auckland Park or with his wife's companion, Fearne Booker, who lived with the Hensons for over thirty years. Henson's relationship with Miss Booker formed the basis of a best-selling novel by Susan Howatch, *Glittering Images*

(1987), in which Henson appeared as Alex Jardine. But, as the author herself made clear, there was no evidence whatsoever for her racy fictional depiction of a sexual relationship between the two.

Henson died at Hyntle Place, Hintlesham, Suffolk, on 27 September 1947. His wife survived him by two years. His ashes were interred in Durham Cathedral.

MATTHEW GRIMLEY

Sources H. H. Henson, *Retrospect of an unimportant life*, 3 vols. (1942–50) · O. Chadwick, *Hensley Henson: a study in the friction between church and state* (1983) · E. F. Braley, ed., *Letters of Herbert Hensley Henson* (1950) · E. F. Braley, ed., *More letters of Herbert Hensley Henson* (1954) · Durham Cath. CL, Henson MSS · H. H. Henson, *Bishoprick papers* (1946) · G. K. A. Bell, *Randall Davidson, archbishop of Canterbury*, 2 vols. (1935) · J. G. Lockhart, *Cosmo Gordon Lang* (1949) · *The Times* (29 Sept 1947) · *DNB* · *CGPLA Eng. & Wales* (1948)
Archives Durham Cath. CL, corresp., papers, journals, and letterbooks | All Souls Oxf., letters to Sir William Anson · BL, letters to E. H. Blakeney, Add. MS 63089 · BLPES, letters to Violet Markham · Bodl. Oxf., letters to Geoffrey Dawson · Bodl. Oxf., letters to Sir James Marchant · Bodl. Oxf., corresp. with Lord Selborne · LPL, corresp. with R. T. Davidson · LPL, letters to A. L. Morrison · PRO NIre., corresp. with Lord Londonderry · U. Durham L., letters to H. C. Ferens · Westminster Abbey, letters to J. Boden-Worsley | FILM BFI NFTVA, news footage
Likenesses W. Stoneman, photograph, 1918, NPG [*see illus.*] · W. H. [W. Hester], caricature, NPG; repro. in *VF* (24 April 1912) · H. Speed, oils, Auckland Castle, Bishop Auckland · photograph, St Hild and St Bede College, Durham · portrait, repro. in Braley, ed., *More letters* · portraits, repro. in Henson, *Retrospect* · portraits, repro. in Braley, ed., *Letters*
Wealth at death £38,441 11s. 5d.: probate, 30 Jan 1948, *CGPLA Eng. & Wales*

Henson, Josiah (1789–1883), escaped slave, slavery abolitionist, and Methodist minister, was born on 15 June 1789 in Charles county, Maryland, USA, one of six children of slave parents. He experienced the harsh realities of slavery early in life. He saw his father receive 100 lashes and then have his ear cut off as punishment for defending his mother from the plantation overseer. His father was then sold south and was never heard from again. Henson also witnessed the sale of his brothers and sisters, and was himself sold several times. Much of his young adulthood was spent on a plantation in Montgomery county, Maryland, where he became a trusted supervisor. When his owner, Isaac Riley, fell into debt he sold Josiah and Josiah's mother to his brother, Amos Riley, who lived in Kentucky. During an argument between his new master and the overseer of a neighbouring plantation, Henson protected his master. Several days later the overseer and three other men beat him so severely that he was never again able to lift his arms to his head. Henson received training from a Methodist preacher and became a self-proclaimed minister; he was formally admitted into the ministry of the Methodist Episcopal church in 1828. Two years later his owner, reneging on an arrangement by which Henson was to purchase his own freedom, secretly arranged to sell him. Fearing their separation, Josiah and his wife Charlotte (d. 1852), whom he had married about 1811, fled to Canada with their four children.

The Henson family settled in the Waterloo area of Lower Canada where Josiah worked as a farm labourer, before moving on to Colchester. He showed his loyalty to his adopted homeland during the Canadian uprising of 1837 when, as part of a regiment of black soldiers known as the Essex company of coloured volunteers, he fought in defence of Fort Malden. He also helped to bring an unknown number of slaves to freedom.

In 1842 Henson, along with the white abolitionist Hiram Wilson and James Fuller, a Quaker philanthropist, founded the British American Institute near Dresden, a manual school for blacks. The goal was to create a self-supporting black settlement that would give blacks their own land, self-employment, and education. Henson performed numerous functions at the Dawn Settlement, the name by which it was usually known. He continually sought financial assistance for the institute and the settlement, conducting fund-raising tours throughout the northern United States and England. Henson worked to bring industrial endeavours, including a sawmill, to the settlement. He also served as pastor of the British Methodist Episcopal church at Dawn. But despite the efforts of Henson and others, the institute's debts increased, as did internal dissension, and in 1868 it was abandoned and the land sold.

Henson became an abolitionist reformer, lecturing in Canada, England, and the United States. Having been taught to read and write by his eldest son Tom, Henson put his life's story in writing: *The Life of Josiah Henson, Formally a Slave, now an Inhabitant of Canada* (1849). Within this narrative Henson described in agonizing detail the harshness of slavery from the point of view of a slave. *The Life of Josiah Henson* quickly became one of the best-known slave narratives, selling more than 100,000 copies. It was rewritten and reissued, under slightly different titles, in 1858 and 1879. Three years after the book's initial printing Harriet Beecher Stowe wrote what became the most powerful piece of anti-slavery propaganda ever written, *Uncle Tom's Cabin*. Stowe had met Henson, and he was widely presumed to be the model on whom she based her main character, Uncle Tom, though historians continue to dispute this.

Josiah Henson was the sole black exhibitor at the Great Exhibition of 1851. There, as a member of the Canadian delegation, he displayed four huge planks of black walnut which he planed and polished until they shone like mirrors for the exhibition's six million visitors. He took home a bronze medal from the exhibition. While he was in Britain, Henson received numerous invitations to speak on the cruelties of slavery. He also met leading British figures including the prime minister, Lord John Russell, and the archbishop of Canterbury. In 1876—at eighty-seven—Henson made his last fund-raising tour to Britain. He and his second wife Nancy, *née* Gamble, a free-born widow whom he had married about 1856, were summoned to Windsor Castle to meet the queen, an event commemorated in a watercolour by Francis Walker. A year later Henson was an honoured guest of President Rutherford B. Hayes at the White House. He died at Dresden, Ontario, on 5 May 1883, and was buried there.

Henson's life and memory have been honoured in many ways. In 1965 his grave site was declared a historic site and his home near Dresden, Ontario, is now a museum which portrays the life of black people in that part of nineteenth-century Canada. In 1983 the Canadian government honoured Josiah Henson for his many notable achievements by depicting his image on a postage stamp, the first African-American to receive this honour. His achievements place him among the leading African-American leaders of the mid-nineteenth century.

SHARON A. ROGER HEPBURN

Sources J. Henson, *Uncle Tom's story of his life: an autobiography of the Rev. Josiah Henson*, ed. J. Lobb (1876) • W. B. Hargrove, 'The story of Josiah Henson', *Journal of Negro History*, 3 (Jan 1918), 1–21 • W. Pease and J. Pease, *Black utopia: negro communal experiments in America* (1963) • R. Winks, *Blacks in Canada: a history* (1971) • J. Marsh, 'The real Uncle Tom', *The Guardian* (21 April 2001) • J. L. Beattie, *Black Moses: the real Uncle Tom* (1957) • *New York Times* (17 May 1990) • *DCB*, vol. 11 • E. Z. Vicary, 'Henson, Josiah', *ANB*

Likenesses F. Walker, watercolour • bust, American Museum, Bath • portraits, NYPL, Schomburg Center for Research in Black Culture, portraits, photographs, and print division

Henson, Leslie Lincoln (1891–1957), actor and theatre manager, was born at Notting Hill, London, on 3 August 1891, the eldest son of three children of Joseph Lincoln Henson, tallow chandler, of Smithfield, and his wife, Alice Mary, daughter of William Squire, of Glastonbury. At Cliftonville College, Margate, and Emanuel School, Wandsworth, he was a stage-struck schoolboy. With the encouragement of the younger masters he wrote and presented theatrical pieces at both schools. 'What's doing on Sunday, Troutie?' (an allusion to the boy's piscatorial features), a teacher would ask. 'We're getting up a bit of a show, sir', was the invariable answer (Henson, 15).

During an eighteen-month struggle to come to terms with the family business young Henson seized all his spare time to train himself for the stage. If he was not making faces in a mirror until he had mastery over every facial muscle, he was studiously wiggling his ears or acting in amateur shows. Suspecting him to have a real gift for comedy, his mother proposed he should quit the family firm and go to drama school. The Cairns–James School of Musical and Dramatic Art 'taught me almost everything I know about stage technique. Unconsciously I am employing his methods and remembering his sound advice every time I face an audience', Henson wrote half a century later (Henson, 19).

He first appeared on the public stage in 1910 at Bath with The Tatlers' concert party; and a few months later in an East End pantomime as Binbad in *Sinbad the Sailor*. After touring as Jeremiah in *The Quaker Girl* he made his West End début in 1912 in *Nicely Thanks*; and after a year with The Scamps' concert party played on Broadway in the musical comedy *Tonight's the Night*. When that show transferred to the Gaiety Theatre, London, in 1915 he had a triumph at a theatre already famous for its comedians. Henson added to that fame.

With his croaky voice, bulging eyes, india-rubber features, and jerky eyebrows, Henson knew how to turn the broad map of his face into a constant source of comedy.

Leslie Lincoln Henson (1891–1957), by Lenare, 1942

Cockney alertness and bubbling humour underlined or embroidered his speech; and in the development of stage business through mime and choreography the young actor showed a highly imaginative and inventive instinct as well as precision of timing. Henson's mind was always dwelling on some way of working up a short, slightly amusing sketch into something he could elaborate into sustained absurdity. His command of an audience's attention did not depend so much on patter or personality as on the expressive skill with which he changed his countenance. Was this a monkey contemplating the folly and ugliness of its keeper? Was this a tortoise imprudently come out of its shell and accused of being born yesterday? Or was it rather an angry goldfish ousted from its bowl? Or a moth which has eaten too much tapestry? Or a crumpled trout, even a squeezed lemon, or (the only time he seems to have been likened to a human being) a mandarin about to sneeze? Whatever phrases critics sought in trying to sum up Henson's buffoonery they fastened on his face. The critic James Agate used also to quote Charles Lamb on the nineteenth-century actor Munden: 'When you think he has exhausted his battery of looks, in unaccountable warfare with your gravity, suddenly he will sprout out an entirely new set of features, like Hydra' (Agate, 55).

Henson's career was long, prosperous, and highly patriotic in two world wars in which he entertained the troops with unsurpassed popularity. During the First World War he sowed the seed for what was to be called, over two decades later, ENSA. One night in 1916 he and a group of performers from the Gaiety, including Stanley Holloway and

half a dozen chorus girls, left the West End after their Saturday evening performance and together took the night mail to Chester. On the train they compiled a revue. The next morning they rehearsed it at the garrison theatre, Park Hall army camp, Oswestry, which had been built from regimental funds. That Sunday evening (in vain Henson strove years later for Sunday opening of London theatres) they performed the revue twice to the troops. Henson revelled in the chaos and spontaneity of composing an entertainment off the cuff.

After such West End hits as *Theodore and Company* (Gaiety) and *Yes, Uncle* (Prince of Wales, 1917), Henson joined the Royal Flying Corps and was sent to northern France to organize more shows for the troops. At Lille opera house he gathered round him a little company of amateurs and professionals, which called itself the Gaieties. Back in London in 1919 he returned to the West End in such shows as *Kissing Time*, *A Night Out*, *The Cabaret Girl*, *The Beauty Prize*, and two particular hits at the Winter Garden, *Sally* (1921) and *Kid Boots* (1926).

Henson also went into management and presentation, co-producing all kinds of show, including many he appeared in. Among these were *Lady Luck*, *Funny Face*, *Follow Through*, *Nice Goings On*, and *Lucky Break*. He joined Tom Walls to present the first of the so-called Aldwych farces, *Tons of Money* (Shaftesbury, 1922)—the rest with the same team were acted at the Aldwych—and they subsequently co-produced the whole series. In 1935, with Firth Shephard, Henson took control of the Gaiety Theatre where he had had most of his successes and had four more in a row: *Seeing Stars*, *Swing Along*, *Going Greek*, and *Running Riot* (1938) in which he played Cornelius Crumpet. During the run the old theatre was officially condemned, and had to be closed.

Although he made films from the 1930s, including *The Sport of Kings*, *It's a Boy*, *A Warm Corner*, *Oh Daddy*, *The Demi-Paradise* (1943), and *Home and Away* (1956), Henson's art required the co-operation and inspiration of an audience. Like all great comedians Henson took his work seriously but never himself; and just before the outbreak of the Second World War he founded with Basil Dean at Drury Lane Theatre the government-sponsored organization which he named Entertainments National Service Association. As ENSA it was known to the troops as 'Every night something awful'. Its object was to provide entertainment of all kinds for the troops at home and abroad, and it led to state subsidy for the arts.

When Henson entertained the troops during the Second World War in Europe, the Middle East, and the Far East he was welcomed in every mess and canteen, raising laughter and spirits wherever he went. He also appeared in West End revues such as *Up and Doing* (1940–41), *Fine and Dandy* (1942), and *The Gaieties* (1945). One of the most persuasive testimonials to his hold over an audience remains a widely published photograph of George VI and others taken during a performance for the fleet at Scapa Flow in 1943.

After the war Henson found less theatrical scope for his ebullient brand of humour, partly because he accepted 'straight' roles. He was always pleasing but he was never a 'straight' actor and it showed—as Elwood P. Dowd in *Harvey* (1950), in which he toured; as Samuel Pepys with full-bottomed wig in a musical version by Vivian Ellis of J. B. Fagan's *And So to Bed* (1951); as Mr Pooter in *The Diary of a Nobody* (Duchess, 1955); and as Old Eccles in a musical version of *Tom Robertson's Caste* (1955). Where Henson came into his own at last again was in the title role of Austin Melford's musical farce, *Bob's your Uncle* (1948). Connoisseurs treasured a scene in which he swallowed a Seidlitz powder. Over the bulbous Hensonian visage swept a series of expressions. First, that of distaste; then of relief that the potion had gone down without amiss; and lastly of horror as the realization dawned that perhaps after all it had not. The facial cataclysm that expressed the final fear set the house roaring as Henson had been doing to observers since boyhood.

Indefatigable in his defence of charitable causes, Henson became president of the Royal Theatrical Fund in 1938. He was married three times: first on 9 December 1919 to Marjorie Kate Farewell (Madge) Saunders (*b.* 1891/2), actress, daughter of Edward Saunders, gentleman. They were divorced in 1925. Second he married on 8 July 1926 Gladys Hilda Barbara Katie Gunn (*b.* 1897/8), daughter of John Francis Gunn. This marriage also ended in divorce. His third wife, whom he married on 6 May 1944, was Harriet Martha Day (*b.* 1909/10), a widow, daughter of Edward Alfred Collins, general merchant. They had two sons, one of whom, Nicky Henson, himself achieved some distinction as an actor. Leslie Henson died at Harrow Weald, Middlesex, on 2 December 1957.

ERIC SHORTER

Sources J. Parker, ed., *Who's who in the theatre*, 12th edn (1957) · L. Henson, *Yours faithfully* (1948) · J. Agate, *Immoment toys* (1945) · *The Guinness who's who of stage musicals* (1994) · *DNB* · m. certs. · CGPLA *Eng. & Wales* (1958)
Archives FILM BFI NFTVA, home footage · BFI NFTVA, news footage · BFI NFTVA, performance footage |SOUND BL NSA, performance recordings
Likenesses J. H. K., watercolour, 1891 · E. Kapp, drawing, 1930, Barber Institute of Fine Arts, Birmingham · Lenare, photographs, 1942, NPG [*see illus.*] · caricature, Garr. Club · photographs, repro. in Henson, *Yours faithfully*, 65, 86
Wealth at death £17,067 13*s.* 8*d.*: probate, 7 March 1958, CGPLA *Eng. & Wales*

Henstridge, Daniel (*c.*1646–1736), organist and composer, has until recently been assumed to be the son of a man of the same name who was organist at Gloucester Cathedral from December 1666. It is now thought that they were one person. Henstridge was married at Gloucester Cathedral in 1669. In 1673 he became organist of Rochester Cathedral, where he remained until 1698, when he succeeded Nicholas Wootton as organist of Canterbury Cathedral. In December 1718 he gave up his mastership of the choristers, remaining organist in name only until his death. Henstridge was a very minor composer, who also transcribed into score the compositions of others, and made a copy of John Coprario's 'Rules for composition', wrongly attributed to John Blow. Some of these manuscripts are in the British Library. He was buried in Canterbury Cathedral on 4 June 1736. L. M. MIDDLETON, *rev.* K. D. REYNOLDS

Sources W. Shaw, 'Henstridge, Daniel', *New Grove* · W. H. Cummings, 'Henstridge, Daniel', Grove, *Dict. mus.* (1927)

Henton, Simon. *See* Hinton, Simon of (*fl. c.*1248–1262).

Henty, Edward (1810–1878), pioneer colonist in Australia, and his brother **Stephen Henty** (1811–1872) were born respectively, on 28 March 1810 and 3 November 1811, the fourth and fifth surviving sons of Thomas Henty (1775–1839), a farmer and latterly a banker from West Tarring, near Worthing, Sussex, and Frances Elizabeth Hopkins (*c.*1776–1847) of Poling, near Arundel, Sussex. They were educated locally before working on the family farm. Thinking their prospects better in Australia than in agriculturally depressed Sussex, the family decided to emigrate, and sent the eldest son James (1800–1882) with Stephen and their younger brother John to Western Australia in 1829 to establish a farm.

Finding Western Australia unpropitious farming country, James recommended they relinquish the land granted to them, in the hope of receiving in exchange a smaller grant in Van Diemen's Land. Although the Colonial Office had already refused this request, in November 1831, his father, mother, Edward, and two other brothers sailed for Launceston, Van Diemen's Land, where they landed in April 1832. The colonial government naturally followed the Colonial Office in refusing a land grant, but the father bought a 2000 acre farm on the Tamar, where the brothers worked and the family settled. However, grazing land was expensive, so Edward began to think of other activities and other places. In April 1833 he joined a whaling ship, but soon transferred to the family's schooner, *Thistle* (58 tons); when she called at Portland Bay on the Australian mainland in July he was impressed by its possibilities for settlement. In March 1834 James sailed for London to seek permission to buy 20,000 acres at Portland Bay to be paid for over ten years, but Edward persuaded his father to allow him to 'squat' at Portland without waiting for an answer to their request. This was a formal 'no' but it was made known unofficially that the Hentys would not be ejected.

On 13 October 1834 Edward left Launceston in the *Thistle*, and after an extremely stormy voyage in which much of the livestock was lost he landed at Portland Bay on 19 November with four indentured servants, thirteen heifers, two working bullocks, six dogs, plants, provisions, building materials, and farm implements. Edward began to build his house and to plant his fruit, vegetables, and wheat; a month later he welcomed his youngest brother, Francis (1815–1889), who arrived with more livestock (including the first thoroughbred merino sheep in Victoria), plants, and stores. In September 1836 Stephen arrived, having finally left Western Australia, with his bride, Jane (1817–1906), the daughter of an East India Company captain, Walter Pace, whom he had married on 14 April 1836 at Fremantle. In 1837 Francis and Stephen

Edward Henty (1810–1878), by Batchelder & Co., c.1870

moved inland, but Edward preferred to continue farming and trading at Portland. On 15 October 1840 he bought 20 acres of suburban land. The following day he married Anne Maria, the daughter of Hugh Gallie of Plymouth, whom he had met when he was in Melbourne on business; the couple had no children.

By then Edward was an established citizen and magistrate, but he soon began to suffer from the prevailing economic depression. When the family businesses were reorganized in 1842, Francis took the 14,000 acre Merino Downs and Edward moved to Muntham, a sheep station of 57,300 acres on the Wannon River, which in 1849 carried 3520 cattle and 24,000 sheep. This made him a prosperous squatter, but in 1856 he moved back to live in Portland. He sat in the legislative assembly as a conservative until 1861 and became actively involved in the Western Victorian Separation League, which advocated breaking away from 'the intolerable yoke of Melbourne'. Unfortunately his stock gradually deteriorated, and when sold after his death none was fit to breed from. Like Stephen, Edward had moved permanently to a large town house in Melbourne. He died at Offington, St Kilda Road, Melbourne, on 14 August 1878 and was buried the next day in Boroondara cemetery. Stephen, a merchant and magistrate at Portland and an MP from 1856 to 1870, had died on 18 December 1872 at Hamilton, leaving four sons and six daughters. He was buried in the cemetery there.

Edward was the first permanent settler at Portland. At first capable and energetic, he became somewhat extravagant and socially pretentious as he played the part of the country squire, but though Francis at Merino Downs and

Stephen as Portland's leading merchant may have done more for the district's progress, Edward's distinction of 'being the first' remains.   A. G. L. SHAW

Sources M. Bassett, *The Hentys: an Australian colonial tapestry* (1954) · M. Kiddle, *Men of yesterday: a social history of the western district of Victoria, 1834–1890* (1961) · G. Forth, *The Winters on the Wannon* (1991) · N. F. Learmonth, *The Portland bay settlement* (1934) · D. Garden, *Hamilton, a western district history* (1984) · *Portland Guardian* (1842–3) · *Gipps–La Trobe correspondence, 1839–1846*, ed. A. G. L. Shaw (1989) · M. Bassett, 'Henty, Edward', *AusDB*, vol. 1 · R. Spreadborough and H. Anderson, eds., *Victorian squatters* (Melbourne, 1983) · M. Syme, *Shipping arrivals and departures: Victorian ports*, 2 vols. (1984–7) · d. cert. · *The Argus* [Melbourne] (19 Dec 1872) [S. Henty] · 'Henty, Stephen', *AusDB*, vol. 1

Archives Mitchell L., NSW · State Library of Victoria, Melbourne

Likenesses Batchelder & Co., photograph, *c.*1870, State Library of Victoria, Melbourne, La Trobe collection [*see illus.*] · J. Flett, oils, 1877, Portland town council · J. Kemp, oils, 1886, State Library of Victoria, Melbourne, La Trobe collection · photograph (Stephen Henty), State Library of Victoria, Melbourne, La Trobe collection

Henty, George Alfred (1832–1902), journalist and children's writer, was born at Trumpington, near Cambridge, on 8 December 1832, the second son of the four children of James Henty (*bap.* 1799, *d.* 1872), stockbroker, manager of coal and iron mines, and Mary Bovill (1808–1887), daughter of Dr Edwards of Putney, Surrey. At Westminster School and at Gonville and Caius College, Cambridge, he studied classics. A delicate child, at school he took up rowing and boxing with enthusiasm, continuing those interests at university. He went down for a year after matriculating because of illness, but helped his father to manage a Welsh colliery. He left Cambridge in 1854, prematurely, when he and his younger brother, Frederick, were commissioned in the army commissariat department on the outbreak of the Crimean War. Henty's letters home were shown by his father to the editor of the *Morning Advertiser*, who published a number as from 'A Military Correspondent', including his description of Florence Nightingale's arrival at Scutari. While there, Henty's brother died of cholera. Henty was invalided home, receiving the Turkish order of the Mejidiye, and promoted to purveyor, as a captain. He was sent to organize Italian hospitals during the war with Austria, and briefly, without relinquishing his commission, worked as a mining surveyor in Sardinia.

Later Henty had charge of commissariat departments, in Belfast and then in Portsmouth districts. On 1 July 1857 he married Elizabeth Finucane (1836–1865) in Dublin. After his marriage he found army office routine wearisome and insufficiently lucrative to support a family, and resigned his commission. Two sons and two daughters were born, but in 1865 his wife died of tuberculosis, aged only twenty-nine. Henty was devastated. He sought active life as a war correspondent, was accepted by *The Standard* on the strength of his military experience and published reports from the Crimea. Leaving his children in his mother's care, he went in 1866 to join Garibaldi advancing on Milan, and later the Italian fleet at Brescia. Arrested *en route* as a spy, with his journalist's pass confiscated, he managed by brave subterfuge to board a frigate, and made a detailed report of the naval battle of Lissa.

George Alfred Henty (1832–1902), by Harry Furniss

In the Tyrol, Garibaldi, hearing of boxing skills Henty had used to defend himself from aggressive *soldati*, requested a demonstration. George Meredith, then *Morning Post* correspondent, volunteered as sparring partner, and a three-round contest was arranged. A year later Henty published a three-decker novel, *A Search for a Secret* (1867). In the following spring *The Standard* assigned him to Sir Robert Napier's expeditionary force to Abyssinia, and some of his reports were copied by the weekly *Illustrated London News*. Henty sent them more, with his own drawings, which were engraved and reproduced. An edition of his dispatches, *The March to Magdala*, and a second three-decker, *All but Lost*, both appeared in 1868.

In 1869 Henty attended the inauguration of the Suez Canal. On the outbreak of the Franco-Prussian War, the following July, he set off in a very British, pro-German, frame of mind. But he applied vainly, in Berlin, Frankfurt, and Mannheim, for a correspondent's pass. And when permission finally arrived, to accompany the German armies, there were new forebodings and horror, shared by such as Matthew Arnold and George Meredith, which Henty expressed to his readers: 'For more than a quarter of a century Europe was convulsed by the ambition of France: is it to be that we are doomed to a quarter of a century's war … because of the ambitions of Germany?' (*The Standard*, 1870, quoted in Arnold, 8). He moved from the German troops to the French, and switched twice more, spending the last weeks heartily sickened by events in the siege of Paris.

In 1871 Henty published *Out on the Pampas*, written in 1868 for his children, their names given to the main characters. Soon followed *The Young Franc-tireurs* (1872), based on recent experiences: it was the first of a new sort of boys' book that would set a pattern for future work. But first he was sent to report from Wales on mining disturbances; to Russia in the wake of Colonel Fred Burnaby; and

in 1873 with Sir Garnet Wolseley to west Africa. During that campaign Henty's reports again appeared in the *Illustrated London News*, which on 28 February 1874 published an atmospheric drawing by its special artist, Melton Prior, of Henty in camp with his fellow correspondent and friend H. M. Stanley. Henty also established a lasting friendship with Wolseley, and in 1885, when editor of the *United Service Gazette*, strongly supported his actions in the Sudan. Henty's dispatches from the Second Anglo-Asante War were the basis of *The March to Coomassie* (1874). In 1874 Henty was sent to Bilbao for the Spanish Civil War, and in 1875–6 to accompany the prince of Wales on his royal tour of India. Henty did not relish his assignment in 1876 to the Turco-Serbian War, and returned, when peace came, again a sick man. Although burly and physically strong in middle life, now he felt too weary for the fatigue of a campaign and was ready to settle down.

To follow *The Young Franc-tireurs* Henty began a great series of historical adventure stories for boys, devising a plot formula that would serve him for life, through several changes of publisher. The early stories were serialized in periodicals; all were published as books. He had intended to cover the history of England, but soon also set stories in other countries. Unaccountably selective of both period and subject matter, with the exception of *Under Drake's Flag* (1883), he passed over sixteenth-century England, and, strangely for a seafaring man, avoided great naval engagements. But the range was wide: from ancient Egypt to the Second South African War, with stories of the Americas, Africa, and India. Forty of the eighty novels were set in the nineteenth century: *With Buller in Natal* (1901), *With Roberts to Pretoria* (1902), and *With Kitchener in the Soudan* (1903) were the best-sellers, with Henty's confident style perhaps more that of a war reporter than a history teacher. Several pure adventure stories, with no more history than their period settings, include *Redskin and Cowboy* (1892), possibly the very first 'western'. Its intricate, skilfully organized plot certainly predates Zane Grey and Harold Bell Wright in the USA.

Henty repeatedly proclaimed his ambition to edit a boys' magazine, and in April 1880 took on the *Union Jack* from W. H. G. Kingston, whose health had failed six months after appointment. In that venture, and again later, Henty showed himself not cut out for editorial management. After passing as a lame duck through the hands of three publishers, the *Union Jack*, to his enormous dismay, finally closed in 1883. By then the success of his boys' books drew him to Blackies of Glasgow, whose success in publishing such work remained assured in his lifetime, and for decades later. For them he wrote three, often four, books each year, finding the work congenial, and frequently dictating 6500 words a day. He insisted on historical accuracy, and relied on leading historians for background material, not always eschewing plagiarism. Blackies rapidly became leading publishers of fine children's books, both content and production acclaimed by reviewers and educationists alike. Henty himself became an institution, for prep-school boys and their generous uncles: A. J. P. Taylor and others later declared they would not have become historians but for Henty. During his last decades he spent six months of each year writing, and six yachting.

In the 1890s, among the last three-deckers to appear in Britain, Chatto and Windus published four novels by Henty. The first, *Rujub, the Juggler*, was the most popular, 11,000 copies being sold, practically all within three years. It was the eighth of his eleven adult novels: though selling fewer copies than his best boys' books, the later titles were, contrary to often expressed belief, remarkably popular. Altogether Henty wrote over 120 books, and contributed stories and articles to nearly as many more, apart from prolific work in newspapers and periodicals. His authorized American editions were far exceeded in number by those that were pirated, and he became more widely read in the USA and Canada than in Britain. His books were translated or issued as school readers in nine European countries.

Henty had had long, sad years of loneliness following the untimely death of his first wife, and suffered several bouts of ill health. He married his second wife, Elizabeth Keylock (1854–1926), twenty-two years his junior, on 21 December 1889. She was the daughter of John Keylock, a farmer, and had kept house for him and his sister over some years, and he remained devoted to her. She was with him when he died aboard his yacht, the *Egret*, in Weymouth harbour on 16 November 1902. He was buried five days later in the family grave in Brompton cemetery, London.

Henty's friend Sir Henry Lucy considered him 'one of the warmest-hearted shortest-tempered men in the world' (Lucy, 89). Edward Marston, friend and publisher, called him 'a rough diamond of the first water, sometimes boisterous, genial, generous, sympathetic, and simple-minded as a child' (Marston, 260): Henty told him he had 'for some years been a great sufferer from gouty diabetes' (ibid., 262), perhaps explaining his noted outbursts of irritability. His daughters had both died young of tuberculosis, as their mother had done. His elder son, Charles Gerald Henty, an army captain, survived him.

PETER NEWBOLT

Sources G. M. Fenn, *George Alfred Henty: the story of an active life* (1907) · P. Newbolt, *G. A. Henty (1832–1902): a bibliographical study* (1996) · G. Arnold, *Held fast for England: G. A. Henty, imperialist boys' writer* (1980) · H. W. Lucy, *Sixty years in the wilderness*, new edn, 1 (1911) · E. Marston, *After work* (1904) · Henty Society Archives · private information (2004) [A. J. King, Henty Society] · *The Captain*, 1 (1899), 3–8 · m. cert. [G. A. Henty and Elizabeth Keylock] · burials book, Brompton cemetery · grave inscriptions, Brompton cemetery [James Henty and Mary Bovill Henty]

Likenesses pencil drawing, 1897, NPG · W. H. Bartlett, group portrait, oils (*Saturday night at the Savage Club*), Savage Club, London · H. Furniss, pen-and-ink sketch for a caricature, NPG [*see illus.*] · photograph, repro. in Newbolt, *G. A. Henty* · photograph, NPG

Wealth at death £6035 19*s*. 7*d*.: probate, 12 Dec 1902, *CGPLA Eng. & Wales*

Henty, Stephen (1811–1872). *See under* Henty, Edward (1810–1878).

Henwood, (William) Jory (1805–1875), mining surveyor, was the eldest son of John Henwood, a clerk at the iron foundry of G. C. Fox & Co., and his wife, Mary, daughter of William Jory. He was born at Perran Wharf in Cornwall on 16 January 1805. Little is known about his early education, but at a later age he did receive some tuition in science at the home of Charles Fox while employed as a clerk in that family's iron foundry at Perran Wharf (from about 1822). His ability having been noticed by the Fox family, about 1827–8 he was given financial help and encouragement to embark on a survey of the mines of Cornwall and Devon. The survey was later continued with the assistance of subscriptions raised from Cornish gentry, and was published in 1843 as volume five of the *Transactions of the Royal Geological Society of Cornwall*. Although of value as a historical record of Cornish mining, it attracted little attention at the time, being based on a theory which lacked support from most geologists: Henwood wrote that vein formation was coeval with the formation of the surrounding rocks. He also engaged in controversy with R. W. Fox, whom he accused of plagiarizing his theory of formation of mineral veins.

Henwood was elected a fellow of the Geological Society in 1828 and FRS in 1840. In 1838 he was awarded the Telford gold medal of the Institution of Civil Engineers for his researches into Cornish pumping engines. In 1832 he was appointed deputy assay master to the duchy of Cornwall and in 1836 he was promoted to assay master of tin; this post was abolished when tin coinages ended in 1838, but after appeals were made on his behalf by various eminent men Henwood was appointed assistant underground surveyor of mines for the duchy in 1839. He left that employment in 1842, after being accused of withholding some rents and because he had left his post for about four months in 1841 to look at mining in Canada and the United States of America.

In 1843 Henwood went to Brazil to undertake a survey for the imperial Brazilian mines and afterwards became manager of the Gongo Soco goldmines. While in South America he became concerned about the conditions of slaves there, especially those working in mines, and he published a pamphlet on the subject in 1864 (repeated in volume eight of the *Transactions of the Royal Geological Society of Cornwall*, 1871). He later undertook mining investigations in Ireland and India and detailed accounts of these were also published in the same volume. Henwood, who never married, returned to Penzance in 1858 because of ill health, and died there at his home, 3 Clarence Place, on 5 August 1875. He was buried on 7 August at Perranworthal parish church.

DENISE CROOK

Sources Boase & Courtney, *Bibl. Corn.* · W. J. Henwood, 'On the metalliferous deposits of Cornwall', *Transactions of the Royal Geological Society of Cornwall*, 5 (1843), 1–386 · W. J. Henwood, 'Observations on metalliferous deposits', *Transactions of the Royal Geological Society of Cornwall*, 8 (1871) [whole issue] · D. A. Crook, 'The early history of the Royal Geological Society of Cornwall, 1814–1850', PhD diss., Open University, 1990, 212–34 · private information (2004) · 'President's address', *Transactions of the Royal Geological Society of Cornwall*, 10 (1879), xi–xxv, esp. xiii [65th annual report] · d. cert.

Archives Cornwall RO, letters relating to stannaries | Cornwall RO, letters to John Hawkins

Wealth at death under £6000: probate, 10 Sept 1875, *CGPLA Eng. & Wales*

Hepburn, Audrey [*real name* Edda Kathleen Hepburn-Ruston] **(1929–1993)**, film actress, was born on 4 May 1929, at 48 rue Keyenveld, Ixelles, Brussels, the only child of Joseph Victor Anton Ruston (also known as (Joseph) Anthony Hepburn or Hepburn-Ruston; 1889–1980), one-time honorary British consul in the Dutch East Indies, and his Dutch second wife, Baroness Ella Van Heemstra (1900–1984), third child of Baron Aarnoud Van Heemstra, colonial governor and first mayor of Arnhem in the Netherlands, and his wife, Elbrig. Her father, a British subject born in Austria, adopted Hepburn for its aristocratic resonance (James Hepburn, earl of Bothwell, was the third husband of Mary, queen of Scots). The marriage began to fail from 1935, when the family moved to Belgium, owing to Ruston's infidelities and 'adventurer' temperament. An active supporter of Leon Degrelle's Nazi party, Ruston settled in London following his divorce. His fascist activities there caught the attention of the British security services. Audrey—as Edda had become known in the family—was thus reared largely by her mother and educated in Arnhem, where they moved in 1939, and at periods at a local school in Elham, Kent, where her mother's new romance had taken the family. Caught in the Netherlands by the war, they suffered severe privations, despite which, Hepburn, at some personal risk, performed minor services for the Dutch resistance as an innocent-looking child courier. Her father had been interned in England in 1939 as a suspected enemy agent under regulation 18B. He spent the war years in a concentration camp on the Isle of Man, and upon release in May 1945 went to the Irish republic. Hepburn did not see her father, or even learn his whereabouts, for nearly twenty years. Her emotional and physical traumas, plus the ingrained optimism of her mother's Christian Science faith, had a positive effect on the child, rather than the reverse, contributing to a lifelong practical concern for those less fortunate than herself.

In childhood Hepburn had shown an aptitude in ballet lessons—maintained with difficulty under the occupation—which helps explain the grace of movement and natural serenity that distinguished her film stardom. Her career-in-waiting was hinted at just before mother and daughter left the Netherlands for London about 1947. Then seventeen or eighteen, she secured a role as an air stewardess in a tourist film, *Dutch in Seven Lessons* (1948), produced for the Dutch airline KLM. Her charming smile was the first of many on screen. In London she was accepted into the Ballet Rambert but her self-critical sense told her she lacked the precision (and possibly the physique) to succeed in that art. After trying other short-term outlets—as a fashion model, and as a travel clerk—she was hired for the chorus line of Jack Hylton's musical *High Button Shoes*, gaining promotion to solo spots in intimate revue. Her radiant personality won her minor roles in several British films (including *Laughter in Paradise*, 1951, and *The Lavender Hill Mob*, 1951). Though these were somewhat decorative parts, her photographic charm earned her a

Audrey Hepburn (1929–1993), by Bassano, 1950

three-year contract (at £12 a week) with a major studio, Associated British Picture Corporation. Ironically, she never made a film for her employers. Throughout her career, they profited from lucrative 'loan-outs' for roles in other films, British and American, the first of which was *The Secret People* (1952), a political thriller set in London, directed by Thorold Dickinson. Her vivacity as a young dancer ensnared in a bomb plot showed her to advantage: she stays alert even when doing nothing, poised like a bird ready to flit off its branch.

While making her next film, an Anglo-French comedy called *Nous irons à Monte Carlo* (*Monte Carlo Baby*, 1951), Hepburn was spotted by Colette, the French author who was then seeking an actress suitable to play Gigi in the non-musical adaptation of her autobiographical novel on Broadway. Hepburn was 'borrowed' from Associated British, but before the play opened, in 1951, she was screen tested by Paramount for William Wyler's romantic comedy, *Roman Holiday* (1952), to be filmed immediately after *Gigi* had ended its successful run. The princess who discovers the simple joys of living like ordinary folk while incognito in the company of Gregory Peck's newspaperman, but who returns to her royal duties, was the role that defined Hepburn's personality and talents for the rest of her life: innocence and good sense, wide-eyed eagerness for life, a gift for happiness, a vulnerability that invited protection, but also an air of natural independence. Her liberated princess had her hair cut by a barber in the film, and the androgynous gamine style was set as the Hepburn look for a generation or more of female filmgoers. An even bolder visual signature was her encounter in 1953 with the French couturier Hubert de Givenchy, who had been engaged to design some of her dresses for her next film, Billy Wilder's modern Cinderella story, *Sabrina* (1954). Givenchy's minimalist simplicity, worn on a figure that had no protuberances to interfere with his classical concept, conferred a dateless elegance on the film star on and off screen. Hepburn's engagement to James Hansom, the future property magnate, was broken off owing to the conflicting claims of her new fame. She appeared on the cover of *Time*'s 7 September 1953 issue, even before *Roman Holiday* had opened in America—a rare tribute.

Hepburn met Melchior (Mel) Gaston Ferrer (b. 1917) when both were starring in her next stage venture, Jean Giraudoux's *Ondine* (1954), a medieval fable in which she played the eponymous water nymph. They were married in a civil ceremony on 24 September 1954, with a church wedding in Burgenstock, Switzerland, the next day; the marriage produced one son, Sean (b. 1960). Ferrer is usually credited with using his knowledge of the film industry's bargaining politics to shape Hepburn's career and considerably enhance her fees. For *Sabrina* she received only $15,000; for her next film, *War and Peace* (1956), she received at least $350,000. Cast as Tolstoy's heroine, she excelled as the young, exuberant Natasha, but had not quite acquired the maturity to personify the post-Napoleonic survivor. *Funny Face* (1957), a musical with Fred Astaire, directed by Stanley Donen, showed her again as the youthful innocent on which she now almost owned the screen patent. Then came another comedy, *Love in the Afternoon* (1957), which made a cheekily Wilderesque virtue of the thirty-year age gap between her pert and truant girl and Gary Cooper's amorous millionaire. Hepburn's gifts responded to the coaching of directors such as Wyler and Wilder, who shared her own European inheritance and tastes. Though she worked mostly in American films, she never belonged to the Hollywood 'system', and spent the periods between films in domestic seclusion in Europe. She and her husband had settled in Switzerland, where the discreet mode of living offered by small village life was more to her taste than cosmopolitan lifestyles; it was not so helpful to her husband's career, however.

After Fred Zinnemann's *The Nun's Story* (1959), Hepburn's most popular film was probably Blake Edwards's *Breakfast at Tiffany's* (1961). As Holly Golightly, the up-scale call-girl in Truman Capote's metropolitan fairy tale, the first shot of her wandering up Fifth Avenue at dawn, a sophisticated apparition wearing pearls and a black Givenchy sheath and munching a breakfast pastry while advancing on the baubles in the eponymous jeweller's window, created one of the great iconic images of cinema. It easily competed in her fans' affections with the prestigious title role in *My Fair Lady* (1964) opposite Rex Harrison, for which she received a million-dollar fee. She gave a precise but not transcendent rendering of Shaw's heroine, the flower-girl Eliza Doolittle who learns to be a lady by speaking 'proper'. Paradoxically, if understandably, Hepburn's character seemed already more at home in high society

than on her Covent Garden pavement pitch. Her performance suffered a slight loss of spontaneity by being partially dubbed by a professional singer, Marni Nixon. About this time, through a Belgian cousin, Walter Ruston, she discovered her father living in Dublin, where he had married again, and a reconciliation took place.

Hepburn's problems of finding mature roles—Stanley Donen's time-juggling comedy, *Two for the Road* (1967), contained love scenes in line with the new candour of the 'Swinging Sixties'—were compounded by a collapsing marriage, which was dissolved amicably in 1968. On 18 January 1969 she married Dr Andrea Dotti (b. 1938), an Italian psychiatrist, with whom she had a son, Luca (b. 1970). This marriage was dissolved in 1982. Though she occasionally returned to the screen—her last appearance was a cameo role as a heavenly angel in Steven Spielberg's *Always* (1989)—Hepburn found a second and more emotionally fulfilling career from 1988 on as a special ambassador for UNICEF, the United Nations humanitarian mission for children. She used her celebrity intelligently and unselfishly to draw attention to the need for economic and medical aid in lands ravaged by disease, famine, and civil war. She made more than fifty exhausting and sometimes dangerous field trips for UNICEF to Sudan, El Salvador, Bangladesh, Kenya, and Somalia. Her indefatigable efforts may have contributed to the cancer that caused her death on 20 January 1993, surrounded by her family and her new companion, the former actor Robert Wolders, at La Paisible, the manor house at Tolochenaz-sur-Morges, near Lausanne, Switzerland, which she had made her home since the mid-1960s. She was buried on 24 January under a simple wooden cross in the village graveyard. Famous, beautiful, and dutiful, Hepburn was one of the few stars who lived for others besides themselves—and, many were left thinking, died for others, too.

ALEXANDER WALKER

Sources A. Walker, *Audrey: her real story* (1994) · *The Times* (21–2 Jan 1993) · *The Times* (25 Jan 1993) · *The Independent* (22 Jan 1993) · *The Independent* (27 Jan 1993) · WWW, 1991–5
Likenesses Bassano, photograph, 1950, NPG [*see illus.*] · A. McBean, photograph, 1951, NPG · photograph, repro. in *The Times* (22 Jan 1993) · photograph, repro. in *The Times* (25 Jan 1993) · photograph, repro. in *The Independent* (22 Jan 1993) · photographs, repro. in Walker, *Audrey*, following pp. 126, 270, and 271 · photographs, Hult. Arch.

Hepburn [*née* Harper]**, Edith Alice Mary** [*pseuds.* Anna Wickham, John Oland] (1883–1947), poet, was born on 7 May 1883 at 5 The Ridgeway, Wimbledon, Surrey, the second and only surviving child of (William) Geoffrey Crutchley Harper (1859–1929), piano shop keeper and tuner, and his wife, Alice Martha, *née* Whelan (1857–1937?), teacher, hypnotist, and 'character reader'. Her father's family was a mix of lapsed and practising Methodists originally from Shropshire. Her mother's family, of Irish, English, Belgian, and Italian stock, were Anglican. Her own affiliation was variously listed as Wesleyan or Anglican. Her autobiographical 'Prelude to a Spring Clean' (published in *The Writings of Anna Wickham, Free Woman and Poet*, 1984), describes an early conversion experience at a chapel Sunday school. She moved often during childhood: her parents' marriage was disrupted when her unconventional mother suddenly embarked for Australia with her infant daughter. The venture lasted a year, until her mother contracted pneumonia and Edith was placed in an institution. Her father arranged their return to England about 1885, and encouraged Edith to write from an early age. About 1890 the family emigrated to Australia. Her mother's teaching and character-reading career as a clairvoyant, Madame Reprah ('Harper' spelt in reverse), and her father's various positions led to an unsettled life. In Maryborough, Queensland, she attended the local convent school, where she was praised for her singing. She later attended All Hallows' School, Brisbane (1894–6) and Sydney Girls' High School (1897–9); according to her own account she was outstanding at neither. But she learned much from the philosophical arguments which her father loved and vowed to him that she would become a poet. Drilled in grammar and elocution by her mother, Edith developed a commandingly resonant, pleasing speaking manner. Later the mother and daughter taught elocution and dramatic-reading classes, and Edith wrote two plays for children: *The Seasons: a Speaking Tableau for Girls* (1902) and *Wonder Eyes: a Journey to Slumbertown* (1903).

When she returned to England in August 1904, Edith Harper studied acting at Beerbohm Tree's academy, London, and singing technique and operatic repertory with Alberto Randegger in London, and Jean de Reszke in Paris. However, a promising professional career was checked when she married Patrick Henry Hepburn (1873–1929), a solicitor and amateur astronomer, on 9 February 1906. She accompanied her husband on strenuous treks and sailing trips until they interfered with her pregnancies. After a sailing accident she gave birth to a premature daughter, born at their flat, 22 Tavistock Square, London, who lived only a few minutes. She also suffered a miscarriage but by 1909, when the family moved to 49 Downshire Hill, Hampstead, she had borne two sons, James (1907) and John (1909).

In Hampstead, Edith Hepburn befriended David Garnett and D. H. Lawrence (she wrote an essay on him called 'The spirit of the Lawrence women'). She was active in such causes as women's suffrage and improved health for poor women and children through the School for Mothers; these causes and her own experiences as wife, mother, and woman, formed the basis for her first mature poetry. Writing under the pen name John Oland, she privately published *Songs* (1911?) with the Women's Printing Society; this brought her attention, some of it personal. Her husband, angry at this, had her placed in a private asylum for the summer of 1913. Despite her feelings of betrayal, they later were reconciled and had two more sons, Richard (b. 1917) and George (b. 1919), conceived while Patrick was home on leave from war service in the Royal Naval Air Service and RAF.

Edith's incarceration in the asylum actually hardened her resolve to commit herself to poetry, and during and just after the First World War she found acclaim as Anna Wickham, naming herself after Wickham Terrace, Brisbane, where she had vowed to be a poet. She published poems, which aired her feminist concerns, in journals such as Harold Monro's and Alida Klementaski's *Poetry and Drama*. Further poems and books followed in quick succession. *The Contemplative Quarry* (1915), published by Monro, created a stir, some reviewers referring to her poetry as 'fresh', 'unconventional', 'piquant' (The Poetry Bookshop's booklets of verse, unsigned, BL). Grant Richards published her third book, *The Man with a Hammer* (1916), but with her next book of verse, *The Little Old House* (1921), she returned to Monro. However, she thought this book a 'domestic exhibit' (letter, 21 Sept 1921, Untermeyer MSS, Indiana University), complaining that her friend Monro, with whom she was increasingly dissatisfied, printed her too 'innocently' (Jones, 70). In America, Louis Untermeyer, the distinguished critic who once referred to her as 'this magnificent gypsy of a woman', arranged publication in 1921 of a combined American edition of *The Contemplative Quarry* and *The Little Old House* (*From Another World*, 340). It was enormously popular. In 1922, after the death of her son Richard from scarlet fever, Edith stopped trying to publish her work and took herself and her eldest son to Paris, where she continued to write. Here she mingled with various American expatriates, among them the wealthy lesbian writer and arts patron Natalie Clifford Barney, who referred to her as 'dear and incorrigible Anna' (Jones, 244). She and Barney maintained a lifelong correspondence.

Edith's husband legally separated from her in 1926. She and her children rented Harold Monro's house for a while. She was briefly reunited with her husband before he died as a result of a hiking accident on Christmas day 1929. She had predicted his death in her poem 'The Homecoming' in 1921. In the 1930s she welcomed an exciting and sophisticated circle of friends to her London home at 68 Parliament Hill, Hampstead. Writers such as Malcolm Lowry date their lasting friendship with her from this period when, as one visitor wrote on the wall devoted to poetry, a visit to her home was 'Better than a Continental holiday' (*Writings of Anna Wickham*, xx). Her precise, imaginative descriptions and aphoristic sayings were often quoted in her wide circle of those in the arts, dance, and theatre. During this period her eldest sons became a well-known tap-dancing duo known as the Hepburn Brothers.

In 1936 John Gawsworth persuaded Edith to publish *Thirty-Six New Poems*. Her relationships with Gawsworth and others were full of laughter, but on occasion could be confrontational. During her last ten years she threw Dylan Thomas out of her house over a disagreement and threatened others with both her fists and her curses. However, memoirs of the times abound with remarks about her kindness and her personal interest in her friends. In 1938 she helped organize a group of feminists called the League for the Protection of the Imagination of Women. During the Second World War she gave her support to her sons in the army and RAF. Her house was bombed and she lost several manuscripts and all of her correspondence.

In stature, Edith Hepburn was striking and imposing.

With a noble head, and long arms and legs, she stood almost 6 feet tall. She was willowy and beautiful in her youth, statuesque in middle age, but in later years had a somewhat dishevelled appearance. Throat and lung problems plagued her. A strong believer in self-sufficiency, she had said she never wanted to die under the care of others. On 30 April 1947 she hanged herself at the door leading into the garden at 68 Parliament Hill and, characteristically, left a poem instead of an explanation. In mid-life she had looked into spiritualism, and wittily found failings and deficiencies in religion (she said in a poem that she 'built god a breast'). She was buried on 6 May in the churchyard extension of the Hampstead parish church, Church Row, Hampstead, London. Wickham left behind more than a thousand unpublished poems. Some of these were published in a selection of her poems edited by David Garnett in 1971, and her writings were collected in 1984. Forgotten for decades, her work now receives renewed attention. JENNIFER VAUGHAN JONES

Sources The writings of Anna Wickham, free woman and poet, ed. R. D. Smith (1984) · A. Wickham, 'I & my genius', Women's Review, 5 (March 1986), 16–20 · J. V. Jones, 'The poetry and place of Anna Wickham, 1910–1930', PhD diss., University of Wisconsin-Madison, 1994 · private information (2004) · BL, Anna Wickham papers, Add. MSS 71877–71896 · J. Hepburn, 'Anna Wickham', Women's Review, 7 (May 1986), 41 · A. Wickham, 'The spirit of the Lawrence women: a posthumous memoir', ed. D. Garnett, Texas Quarterly, 9/3 (autumn 1966), 33–50 [ed. with introduction by D. Garnett] · L. Birch, 'Anna Wickham: a poetess landlady', Picture Post (27 April 1946) · N. Barney, Adventures of the mind, trans. J. S. Gatton (1992), 144–50 [trans. with annotations] · A. Mitchell, 'Anna on Anna' [unpublished play (opened 15 Aug 1988)] · From another world: the autobiography of Louis Untermeyer (1939) · b. cert. · m. cert. · d. cert.

Archives BL, papers, Add. MSS 71877–71896 · priv. coll., papers · priv. coll., collection · Ransom HRC, MSS collection · State University of New York, Buffalo | Bibliothèque Ste Geneviève, Paris, Fonds Littéraire Jacques Doucet, Natalie C. Barney papers · BL, Harold Edward Monro corresp., diaries, literary papers, MSS 57734–57768 · Indiana University, Bloomington, American Literature Collection, Louis Untermeyer MSS · priv. coll., John Kershaw collection · U. Reading, T. I. F. Armstrong (John Gawsworth) collection · University of Chicago, Poetry Magazine papers

Likenesses B. Abbott, photograph, 1926, priv. coll. · pencil or charcoal drawing on paper, 1938, U. Reading · K. Hutton, photographs, 1946, Hult. Arch. · P. Hepburn, photographs, priv. coll. · C. Morris, portrait, priv. coll. · photograph, Bibliothèque Ste Geneviève, Paris, Fonds Littéraire Jacques Doucet, Natalie C. Barney papers · plaster life mask, priv. coll.

Wealth at death £1334 4s.: administration, 18 Sept 1947, CGPLA Eng. & Wales

Hepburn, Francis (1779–1835), army officer, born on 19 August 1779, was the second son of Colonel David Hepburn of the 39th foot and 105th highlanders and his wife, Bertha Graham, of Inchbrakie, Perthshire. His grandfather, James Hepburn of Rickarton and Keith Marshall, spent his fortune in the Stuart cause. Hepburn was appointed ensign in the 3rd foot guards (later the Scots Guards) on 17 December 1794; became lieutenant and captain on 23 April 1798; captain and lieutenant-colonel on 23 July 1807; brevet colonel on 4 June 1814; major on 25 July 1814; and major-general on 19 July 1821. He served with his regiment in Ireland in 1798, and in the Netherlands in

1799; was aide-de-camp to General W. P. Acland at Colchester, and in Malta and Sicily, but was laid up with fever and ophthalmia during the descent on Calabria and the battle of Maida.

Hepburn joined his battalion at Cadiz in 1809, and his leg was shattered at the battle of Barrosa on 5 March 1811. He refused to submit to amputation, and by the autumn of 1812 had recovered sufficiently to rejoin his battalion, although his wound remained open and caused frequent and severe suffering during the subsequent campaigns. He was placed in command of the detached light companies of the 2nd (Coldstream) and 3rd foot guards in 1812; was present at Vitoria, the Nivelle, and the Nive; and at the end of 1813 was ordered home to command the 2nd battalion of his regiment in the expedition to the Netherlands. Delayed by contrary winds, he arrived after the expedition had sailed, but followed the battalion to the Low Countries and commanded it there during the winter of 1814–15. He joined Wellington's army in April 1815.

Hepburn was in temporary command of the 2nd brigade of guards until the arrival of Sir John Byng in May. He commanded his battalion at Quatre-Bras and Waterloo, where the light company of the battalion was sent with other troops to occupy Hougoumont on the night of 17 June. The rest of the battalion reinforced them during the battle of the next day, Hepburn taking command of the troops posted in the orchard of the château. The credit for this important contribution was erroneously given to a junior officer, Colonel Hume. The mistake was explained officially, but never notified publicly, and, allegedly, was the means of depriving Hepburn of the higher honours awarded to other senior officers of the guards division. Hepburn was made CB, and received Netherlands and Russian decorations. In 1821 he married Henrietta, eldest daughter and coheir of Sir Henry Poole, fifth and last baronet, of Poole Hall, Cheshire, and Hook, Sussex; they had two sons and a daughter, and she survived him. His wound and gout undermined his health and he died at Tunbridge Wells on 7 June 1835, aged fifty-five.

H. M. CHICHESTER, rev. DAVID GATES

Sources GM, 2nd ser., 4 (1835), 101, 650 · United Service Journal, 3 (1835), 383–4 · F. W. Hamilton, The origin and history of the first or grenadier guards, 3 vols. (1874) · Army List (1791–1838) · D. Gates, The Spanish ulcer: a history of the Peninsular War (1986) · A. B. Rodger, The war of the second coalition: 1798–1801, a strategic commentary (1964)

Hepburn, Francis Stewart. See Stewart, Francis, first earl of Bothwell (1562–1612).

Hepburn, Sir George Buchan, first baronet (1739–1819), judge, was born in March 1739, son of John Buchan (d. 1792) of Letham, Haddingtonshire, and Elizabeth (d. 1742), daughter of Patrick Hepburn of Smeaton (1685–1726) and Marion Suttie of Balgonie. He was educated at the University of Edinburgh, where Henry Dundas (afterwards Viscount Melville) was among his intimate friends. He succeeded to the barony of Smeaton-Hepburn in 1764, and thereupon assumed the name and arms of Hepburn of Smeaton. In January 1763 he had been admitted a member of the Faculty of Advocates, Edinburgh, and he was solicitor to the lords of session from 1767 to 1790, when he was appointed judge of the high court of Admiralty in Scotland. On 31 December 1791 he was made baron of the exchequer. He was the author of *The general view of the agriculture and rural economy of East Lothian, with observations on the means of their improvement* (1796). He retired in 1814, and on 6 May 1815 was created a baronet. He died on 3 July 1819. He was twice married. His first wife was Jane, eldest daughter of Alexander Leith of Glenkindy and Freefield. On 19 April 1781 he married Margaretta Henrietta (*d.* 1823), daughter of John Zacharias Beck, and widow of Brigadier-General Simon Fraser. With his first wife he had an only son, John (1776–1833), who succeeded him in the baronetcy.   T. F. HENDERSON, *rev.* MICHAEL FRY

Sources Burke, *Peerage* (1970) · F. J. Grant, ed., *The Faculty of Advocates in Scotland, 1532–1943*, Scottish RS, 145 (1944) · M. Fry, *The Dundas despotism* (1992) · Irving, *Scots.* · *GM*, 1st ser., 89/2 (1819), 91 **Archives** NL Scot., legal corresp. · U. Newcastle, household account book | BL, letters to G. Chalmers, Add. MSS 22900–22902 · Falkirk Museums History Research Centre, letters to William Forbes · NA Scot., letters to Lord Melville, John Macleod, and J. Leith

Hepburn, James, fourth earl of Bothwell and duke of Orkney

(1534/5–1578), magnate and third consort of Mary, queen of Scots, was the only son of Patrick *Hepburn, third earl of Bothwell (*d.* 1556), and his wife, Agnes Sinclair (*d.* in or after 1572). His mother was the daughter of Henry Sinclair, third Lord Sinclair (*d.* 1513), and his wife, Margaret Hepburn (*d.* 1542), sister of Patrick Hepburn, first earl of Bothwell.

Early career James Hepburn's parents divorced before 16 October 1543 and he was brought up at Spynie Castle, Moray, by his notorious great-uncle, Patrick *Hepburn, bishop of Moray. Continuing his studies in Paris, where he learned to speak fluent French, he read military history and theory in French translations from the Latin and wrote in an elegant, italic hand. He was twenty-one when in 1556 he inherited his father's titles along with the hereditary offices of lord high admiral of Scotland, sheriff of Berwick, Haddington, and Edinburgh, and bailie of Lauderdale, and also the castles of Hailes and Crichton. Contemporaries described him as being short, muscular, and simian in appearance. The only authentic likeness of him, a miniature painted in 1566, shows a dark-haired, weather-beaten man with a long moustache and what looks like a broken nose.

Although a committed protestant Bothwell strongly supported the Catholic queen regent, Mary of Guise. He signed the act of 14 December 1557 appointing commissioners to negotiate the marriage contract of *Mary, queen of Scots (1542–1587), and the future François II of France, and was made keeper of Hermitage Castle, Roxburghshire. Having repelled a raid by the earl of Northumberland, he was in October 1558 appointed lieutenant of the border. While busy ransoming Scottish prisoners taken by the English, he found time in 1559 to begin a passionate affair with Janet Beton (*b.* 1516), the Wizard Lady of Branxholm, a mature beauty who was forty-three years

James Hepburn, fourth earl of Bothwell and duke of Orkney (1534/5–1578), by unknown artist, 1566

old to his twenty-four, three times married, and the mother of seven children. Always willing to promise marriage to the women he seduced, he was rumoured to have made her his wife, but if they were irregularly married they soon discarded her to concentrate on his pursuit of power.

In October 1559 Elizabeth I sent £3000 north for the protestant lords of the congregation. Bothwell seized John Cockburn, laird of Ormiston, who was carrying the silver, and passed it to Mary of Guise. Furious, the protestant leaders James Hamilton, third earl of Arran, and Lord James Stewart captured Crichton Castle, taking away not only the furnishings but also Bothwell's family charters. Bothwell refused to hand back the money and challenged Arran to single combat. 'When you may recover the name of an honest man, I shall answer you as I ought', Arran retorted (Gore-Browne, 85). Bothwell did not accompany Arran and Lord James to Fife at the end of 1559, but he was in Leith when the English besieged it early the following year, slipping out regularly to harass their supply columns. With Mary of Guise's approval he then set off for the French court to seek further military assistance, moving on to Denmark, where he hoped to persuade Frederick II to lend him his fleet. Mary of Guise died on 11 June, however, and on 6 July the French and English signed the treaty of Edinburgh, agreeing to withdraw all their forces from Scotland.

Bothwell had by now met Anna, daughter of Christopher Throndsen, a wealthy Norwegian noble and retired admiral living in Copenhagen. A contemporary described seeing her at a fashionable wedding, dark and exotic, dripping with pearls and precious stones, clad in a red damask tunic, a gold chain round her head. She fell desperately in love with Bothwell; he promised to marry her, and when he set off for Paris she insisted on going too. Contrary to later accounts he does not seem to have deserted her in

Flanders, but left her there while he continued his journey. Mary, queen of Scots, and François II rewarded him for past services with 600 crowns and the post of gentleman of the king's chamber. In November Bothwell suddenly left Paris, causing Nicholas Throckmorton, the English ambassador, to warn Elizabeth I against this '[vain] glorious, rash and hazardous young man' whose 'adversaries should have an eye to him' (*CSP for.*, *1560–61*, 409). Bothwell seems to have spent the next three months in Flanders with Anna, who may have been pregnant and could have been the mother of his one illegitimate son, William. Perhaps he even took her back to Scotland, where he received the queen's orders to convoke a meeting of parliament. François II had died on 5 December, and the protestant lords now invited Queen Mary to return to Scotland; Bothwell, as lord high admiral, went to France to escort her home.

The reign of Queen Mary On 6 September 1561 Bothwell became a member of Mary's new privy council. Mary tried to end his feud with Arran by obliging them to keep the peace, but trouble flared up again when Bothwell and his brother-in-law, Lord John Stewart, forced their way into the house where Arran's mistress lived. After a street fight between the Hamiltons and the Hepburns, Bothwell was ordered to leave Edinburgh. John Knox managed to effect a reconciliation between the two men, but Arran now claimed that Bothwell had urged him to kidnap the queen. This might have been so, but Arran had obviously suffered a mental breakdown. Both were arrested and imprisoned, first at Falkland, then at St Andrews, and finally in Edinburgh Castle. Bothwell managed to escape on 28 August and Anna Throndsen received a passport to sail to Norway that autumn. By the end of December, Bothwell was aboard a merchant ship bound for France but storms drove his vessel to Holy Island off the coast of Northumberland; taken by the English, he was held at Tynemouth before being consigned to the Tower of London.

Following the intervention of Queen Mary and the French, Bothwell was released on parole in May 1563. After a summer spent in the north of England he was allowed to go to France, bearing a letter from Queen Mary recommending him for a vacant position as captain of the Scottish archers. He was back in Edinburgh again by 5 March 1565, however, perhaps having heard that Queen Mary's latest suitor, Lord Darnley, had arrived in Scotland a fortnight earlier, but his stay was brief. His enemy Lord James Stewart, now earl of Moray, was determined that he should be outlawed and although the queen resisted this, when she was told that Bothwell had said that she and Elizabeth I 'could not make one honest woman' (*CSP for.*, *1564–5*, 325), she summoned him for *lèse majesté*. He failed to appear, and fled back to France. However, well aware of Moray's opposition to her intended marriage to Darnley, Mary decided that she needed Bothwell's support and recalled him on 16 July. He sailed from Flushing, narrowly avoided capture by the English, and took part in the chaseabout raid, driving the rebellious Moray out of Scotland. Early the following year, possibly at the queen's suggestion, Bothwell decided to marry one of her ladies-in-waiting, Lady Jane (Jean) Gordon [*see* Gordon, Jean, countess of Bothwell and Sutherland (*c.*1546–1629)], sister of his friend the fifth earl of Huntly. A dispensation was obtained, for they were within the forbidden degrees. Bothwell insisted on a protestant marriage and the ceremony took place at Holyrood on 22 February 1566.

Less than three weeks after his wedding, on the night of 9 March 1566, Bothwell was in the palace of Holyroodhouse when the queen's secretary David Riccio was murdered. Bothwell and his brother-in-law Huntly had also been intended victims, but they got away through a back window. Mary managed to win over Darnley and escape to Dunbar, where Bothwell was one of those who joined her. She later credited him with her survival. She entered Edinburgh once more on 18 March, and on 19 June 1566 gave birth to the future James VI. Her marriage by now was in deep trouble and her reliance on Bothwell was arousing suspicion. Henry Killigrew noted on 24 June, 'Bothwell's credit with the Queen is greater than all the rest together' (*CSP for.*, *1566–8*, 93), and the earl of Bedford confirmed this on 27 July, adding that Bothwell was 'the most hated man among the noblemen in Scotland' (ibid., 110). That autumn Bothwell was seriously wounded in a fracas while carrying out his duties as lieutenant on the border. Recovering at Hermitage Castle he received a visit from Mary on 16 October, presumably to discuss the perennial problem of peacekeeping along the frontier with England. Their enemies put it about that this had been some kind of illicit assignation, but in reality the queen had been accompanied by a large number of courtiers; they included Moray, by now returned and restored following Riccio's death.

The Darnley murder Bothwell was among those lords who met Mary at Craigmillar Castle in November 1566 to discuss what should be done about Darnley, and, according to the earl of Morton, it was he who suggested that they should murder the queen's troublesome husband, presumably with the intention of supplanting him. Early the following January, Darnley fell gravely ill in Glasgow. Mary effected some sort of reconciliation with him and arranged to bring him to Kirk o' Field, on the outskirts of Edinburgh, to complete his convalescence. Bothwell met them outside the capital and escorted them the rest of the way. At 2 a.m. on Monday 10 February the house where Darnley was staying was demolished in a massive explosion, and he and his servant were discovered dead in a garden on the other side of the town wall. They had been either strangled or asphyxiated.

Bothwell was in his apartments at Holyrood when the explosion shook the town, ready to leap from his bed to investigate the crime in his capacity as sheriff of Edinburgh. He had actually just returned from Kirk o' Field. According to the depositions of four of his retainers, he had been responsible for placing the gunpowder in Darnley's lodgings and had returned at the last moment with characteristic rashness to make sure that the fuse was lit.

The version of events given by the four men, who were later executed, includes some highly improbable detail, but there is little doubt that Bothwell played a principal part in the murder. A week later the queen moved from Holyroodhouse to Seton, leaving Bothwell and Huntly in charge of her baby son. Bothwell visited her at Seton and Tranent, and by 29 March there were reports that they would marry.

Within a week of the murder placards had begun appearing in Edinburgh, accusing both Mary and Bothwell of Darnley's death. On one, Bothwell was depicted as a hare, from his coat of arms, while the queen featured as a mermaid, the symbol for a prostitute. Whatever the sexual attraction between them, she looked to him more than ever as her powerful and reliable protector. She left it to her father-in-law to prosecute him for the murder of Darnley, but Lennox did not attend the trial on 12 April, for Edinburgh was packed with his enemies and he had been forbidden to bring more than six followers with him. Bothwell was acquitted, and on 14 April parliament confirmed his rights to his various lands and lordships. On 19 or 20 April he persuaded a group of leading lords and ecclesiastics to sign the so-called Ainslie bond, urging the queen to marry him. She refused to do so but he persisted, and on 24 April, apparently at his request, his wife raised an action for divorce in the protestant commissary court of Edinburgh on the grounds of his adultery with one of her maidservants.

Marriage to the queen That same day Bothwell seized Queen Mary on her way back to Edinburgh from Linlithgow and carried her off to Dunbar Castle, where he raped her. He is unlikely to have had any romantic feelings for her, but he was willing to go to any lengths to achieve his ends and had presumably persuaded her to agree to the abduction. Mary would not have expected it to culminate in rape, but she told the bishop of Dunblane two weeks later, 'Albeit we found his doings rude, yet his words were gentle' (*Lettres*, 2.31). James Melville, who was in Dunbar Castle at the time, pertinently remarked, 'The queen could not but marry him, seeing he had ravished her and lain with her against her will' (*Memoirs*, 149). On 3 May 1567 Lady Bothwell was granted her divorce, and three days later Bothwell and Mary returned to Edinburgh, he leading her horse by the bridle as if she were his captive; on the 7th Archbishop Hamilton's recently reinstated consistory court annulled his marriage on the pretext that it had taken place without the necessary dispensation for consanguinity. On 12 May Bothwell was created duke of Orkney by the queen and their marriage banns were proclaimed. The contract was signed on 14 May and the following day Bothwell and Mary became husband and wife in a protestant ceremony in the great hall at Holyroodhouse.

Regardless of the Ainslie bond the lords were now consumed with jealousy and exploited rumours that the queen was bitterly unhappy, repelled by her new husband's boorish behaviour, and overcome with remorse at having contracted a protestant marriage. According to James Melville, Bothwell was so suspicious that he reduced the queen to tears every day, while Maitland commented that not only was Bothwell jealous if Mary looked at anyone but himself, but his language was appalling, and he accused her of being like all women, preoccupied with frivolity. On 16 June the lords signed a new bond, complaining that they were unable to see the queen without Bothwell being present, and alleging that he was virtually keeping her prisoner. Forewarned of an attempt to capture them, the couple fled to Borthwick Castle. When Morton and Lord Home surrounded it with their men Bothwell managed to slip away to Dunbar, where he gathered a powerful force. Mary escaped, and joined him, and they marched towards Edinburgh, confronting the lords at Carberry Hill near Musselburgh on 15 June. A spokesman for the enemy challenged him to single combat and Bothwell was eager to agree, but the queen would not allow it and in the end she sent him away and surrendered. Imprisoned in Lochleven Castle, she miscarried his twins towards the end of July and was forced by her captors to abdicate.

Exile, imprisonment, and death Bothwell rode for Dunbar, where he remained until 26 June, when the lords announced that they had proof that he had been 'principall author' of Darnley's murder (*Reg. PCS*, 1.524). They now had in their possession a silver casket taken from one of Bothwell's followers containing, it would be alleged, letters proving that the queen, passionately in love with Bothwell, had lured Darnley to his death. With a price on his head Bothwell rode north to Strathbogie, where Huntly refused to assist him, and then to Spynie. He intended to assemble a naval force to help the queen but was forced to move on when his great-uncle's illegitimate sons plotted to murder him. He sailed to Orkney and then Shetland, and when the privy council sent a naval expedition against him, he left for Norway.

Stopped and taken to Bergen by a Danish warship, Bothwell was questioned by the authorities. He declared that he was supreme ruler of Scotland and confidently awaited his release. However, unknown to him Anna Throndsen was living in the town, and she immediately sued him for money she had lent him during their time in Flanders. His papers were searched and were found to include not only a letter in the handwriting of Queen Mary deploring her situation, but proclamations against him for treason and murder. Bothwell nevertheless managed to buy Anna off with the promise of an annuity and convinced the authorities that he should be allowed to sail on to Copenhagen, where he hoped to enlist the help of Frederick II. The Danish king, who was in north Jutland, gave orders that he was to be held in Copenhagen Castle until his return. Regarding Bothwell as a useful pawn, Frederick refused Moray's requests for his extradition, but had him moved to the much more secure Malmö Castle on what is now the Swedish mainland. Desperate to obtain his freedom, Bothwell claimed to have the authority to offer the return of Orkney and Shetland to Denmark, and possibly as a result Frederick continued to refuse Moray's repeated demands.

In 1568 Mary escaped from Lochleven, was defeated at

Langside, and fled to England, where she was to spend the rest of her life in captivity. Seeing marriage to a respectable protestant English nobleman as her best hope of release, she decided to divorce Bothwell; however, contrary to the comments of the English ambassador in Paris, she did not secure an annulment of her marriage in 1570 and, according to a report sent to William Cecil on 19 January 1571, was still in 'daily' correspondence with her husband (*CSP Scot.*, *1509–89*, 310). She did send Bishop John Lesley to Rome in 1576 to seek an annulment, but, though the pope clearly regarded her as being free to marry again, no decree of nullity has ever been found. When it became obvious that Mary's cause in Scotland was lost Frederick treated Bothwell more severely, and in June 1573 had him removed to Dragsholm in Zeeland, where he was kept in solitary confinement, allegedly chained to a pillar half his height, so that he could never stand erect. He died there, insane, on 14 April 1578, and his mummified remains were displayed in Faarevejle church until finally buried in the late twentieth century.

A daring, reckless opportunist, Bothwell had revelled in his early adventures, but when with his customary ruthless disregard for everyone else he aimed for supreme power, he underestimated the jealousy of his fellow noblemen and precipitated the downfall not only of himself but also of Mary, queen of Scots.

ROSALIND K. MARSHALL

Sources A. Fraser, *Mary, queen of Scots* (1969) • G. Donaldson, *The first trial of Mary, queen of Scots* (1969) • R. F. Gore-Brown, *Lord Bothwell* (1937) • *Les affaires du conte de Boduel*, ed. [T. G. Repp], Bannatyne Club, 29 (1829) • M. H. Armstrong, *The casket letters* (1965) • R. K. Marshall, 'Mary, queen of Scots and Bothwell's bracelets', *Proceedings of the Society of Antiquaries of Scotland*, 127 (1997), 889–98 • R. S. Ellis, *Latter years of James Hepburn, earl of Bothwell* (1861) • *CSP for.*, *1558–62*; *1564–8* • *Memoirs of Sir James Melville of Halhill*, *1535–1617*, ed. A. F. Steuart (1929), 149 • *Lettres de Marie Stuart*, ed. and trans. A. Teulet (Paris, 1859) • *Lettres, instructions et mémoires de Marie Stuart, reine d'Écosse*, ed. A. Labanoff, 7 vols. (1844), vol. 2, p. 31 • *Reg. PCS*, 1st ser., 1.524 • *Scots peerage*, 2.159–67; 4.534–9 • *CSP Scot. ser.*, *1509–89* • G. Donaldson and R. S. Morpeth, *A dictionary of Scottish history* (1977)
Likenesses miniature, oil on copper, 1566, Scot. NPG [*see illus.*] • O. Bache, oils, Scot. NPG; repro. in Fraser, *Mary, queen of Scots*

Hepburn, James [*name in religion* Bonaventure] (*b.* **1573**, *d.* in or after **1623**), orientalist, is identified with the fourth son of Thomas Hepburn (*d.* 1585), the well-connected parish minister of Oldhamstocks in Haddingtonshire, born on 14 July 1573 (Mackenzie, 3.513). Chambers (*Scots.*, 3.39–42) gives a witty and sceptical survey of the partial, contradictory, and often improbable evidence available to him. No record survives of his education at St Andrews, but a James Hepburn graduated from Edinburgh in 1592. Wodrow says Hepburn's father's insecure conversion to the kirk provoked the son's reversion to Catholicism. He may have travelled in the East (Mackenzie, 3.314); he may have prepared an Arabic primer published in Rome in 1592. Dempster (p. 364) writes that he entered the order of the Minims at Avignon in 'MLXIX' (for 1609?); he took Bonaventure as his name in religion and assisted the general of the order in France. After five years retired in

the French monastery of Santa Trinità dei Monti in Rome, he took charge of oriental collections in the Vatican. Dempster says he died at Venice in October 1620, but Hepburn writes from Santa Trinità an imprimatur for a volume with a dedication to Philip IV dated Madrid, 11 May 1623. Here he describes himself appointed by Cardinal Fabrizio Verallo as professor of oriental languages. Mackenzie says portraits survive in the Vatican and Venice. Hepburn is commended by Vincenzo Bianchi in his *Parere* on the inscriptions on St Peter's knife and by Conn; and John Leech, in *Musae priores* (1620), acknowledges a gift of Hepburn's *Virga aurea* from one Robert Dobbs.

Of twenty-nine works listed by Dempster (pp. 363–4) two certainly by Hepburn are published: the *Lexicon sanctae linguae succinctum* [1620?] and the *Virga aurea* (1616). The *Virga* survives in five double-folio plates, the first two praising the Virgin in more or less fantastic transliterations of her biblical types, the latter three supplying a calendar of the names of God. Additionally, by *Grammatica arabica* Dempster may intend the anonymous *Alphabetum arabicum* (1592). Hepburn's version of Solomon ibn Gabirol's *Keter malkhut*, said by Mackenzie to be printed in Venice, is lost; one survives by Francesco Donati (1618). For the rest, among unidentifiable texts, Dempster lists versions (now lost) of: Abraham ibn Ezra on numerology and on sevenfold interpretation; Jehoseph ben Hanan's *Ka'arat kesef* (already translated by Reuchlin); Abraham ben David's *Sefer ha-kabbalah* (taken over from Gilbert Genebrard) and his *Sefer yetsirah*; David Kimhi on the Psalms; the cabbalistic *Shimmush Tehillim*; the *Rashba*; Joseph ben Abraham Gikatilla's *Sha'are tsedek*; the books of Tobias and Enoch; and the *Book of Eldad*.

ROBERT CUMMINGS

Sources J. B. Hepburn, *La virga aurea*, ed. F. de Mély (Paris, 1922) • *Thomae Dempsteri Historia ecclesiastica gentis Scotorum, sive, De scriptoribus Scotis*, ed. D. Irving, 2 vols. (1627), rev. edn, Bannatyne Club, 21 (1829) [ed. and rev. D. Irving (1829)] • G. Mackenzie, *The lives and characters of the most eminent writers of the Scots nation*, 3 vols. (1708–22) • M. R. James, *A descriptive catalogue of the manuscripts in the library of Corpus Christi College, Cambridge*, 2 vols. (1912) • Chambers, *Scots.* (1835) • G. Conn, *De duplici statu religionis apud Scotos*, 2 pts in 1 (Rome, 1628) • R. Wodrow, 'Biographical collections', 1731, U. Glas., Gen. MS 1207, item 25 • J. Durkan, 'The Scottish Minims', *Innes Review*, 2 (1951), 77–81 • D. Laing, ed., *A catalogue of the graduates … of the University of Edinburgh*, Bannatyne Club, 106 (1858) • C. G. Imbonati, *Bibliotheca Latino-Hebraica* (Rome, 1694) • A. F. Allison and D. M. Rogers, eds., *The contemporary printed literature of the English Counter-Reformation between 1558 and 1640*, 2 vols. (1989–94) • J. Leech, *Musae priores* (1620)

Hepburn [Hebron], James (*d.* **1637**), army officer in the Swedish and French services, was the son and heir of Hepburn of Waughton, Haddingtonshire. His earliest recorded military service was in the Swedish army in the late 1620s, as a lieutenant in Von Thurn's regiment, and then as a captain in the regiment of James Ramsay until 1629 when he was transferred to a captaincy with the Scottish troops serving in the élite 'Green brigade' of the Swedish army. Later he served in William Baillie's regiment and was promoted lieutenant-colonel in 1631.

James Hepburn may well have taken the side of his kinsman Sir John *Hepburn in his refusal to remain in the service of Gustavus Adolphus after a slighting remark supposedly made by the Swedish king about Charles I. Certainly when Sir John took service with the French crown in 1633 James Hepburn was serving as one of the captains in his Scottish regiment of 2000 soldiers. In the cases of both men their French employers wrote and pronounced the name 'Hebron', and it appears in this form in all French correspondence. Sir John Hepburn's promotion to *maréchal de camp* on 26 September 1633 gave him the status of divisional commander, and effective command of his infantry regiment passed to James Hepburn, now the lieutenant-colonel.

In January 1635 the regiment was assigned to the army corps of Bernhard of Saxe-Weimar, supporting the duke's actions in defence of Heilbronn and the capture of Speyer. Subsequently the regiment was transferred to the army commanded by Cardinal Richelieu's *fidèle* Louis de Nogaret, cardinal de La Valette, third son of the duc d'Épernon, and suffered badly, like all the other units in the army, in the disastrous campaign to relieve Mainz during the summer of 1635. The regiment remained in the army of La Valette during the 1636 campaign, and officers and men distinguished themselves campaigning against imperial forces in May and June 1636. As a result the *maréchal de camp* Hepburn was rewarded with the right to the 4000 écus of ransom attributed to the captured imperial Colonel Metternich. But before Sir John could claim the ransom he met his death reconnoitring the defences of Saverne.

Although the proceeds of Metternich's ransom were transferred without demur to James Hepburn there was fierce competition for command of the regiment. Richelieu attempted to stir up the issue of religious affiliation by suggesting that it would be more appropriate to appoint the Catholic first captain of the regiment, James Douglas, to the colonelcy. This was in line with ministerial policy of trying to ensure that foreign regiments serving near the king contained Catholic officers, and the particular wish that the regiment of Hepburn should serve as a 'retraitte en France' for Scottish Catholics (Aubery, 1.660). However, the cardinal de La Valette proved an indefatigable supporter of James Hepburn, and though the dispute dragged on for two months, it was resolved with Hepburn's appointment to the colonelcy in September 1636.

Hepburn's first campaign at the head of his regiment was his last. He was assigned to the army corps of Maréchal Châtillon, whose orders were to cover the substantially larger army of La Valette while it conducted the siege of La Capelle in Champagne. Only after the successful end of this siege in mid-September was Châtillon allowed to undertake an independent operation, the siege of the small place of Damvilliers, in Lorraine. It was at this siege on 16 October 1637 that James Hepburn was killed by a musket shot through the chest. With no heirs or close relatives of Hepburn in the regiment, command was transferred to Lord James Douglas. Despite the high regard of the French crown for the services of the Hepburn family there seem to have been some outstanding questions concerning James Hepburn's service, at least judging by a request in March 1640 to the lieutenant civil of Paris to acquire the papers of the late Colonel Hebron, held by a Scottish doctor in the city. DAVID PARROTT

Sources Service historique de l'Armée de Terre, Vincennes, Paris, Archives de la guerre, A 1 32, fol. 218; A 1 58, fol. 118 · *Lettres, instructions diplomatiques et papiers d'état du cardinal de Richelieu*, ed. D. L. M. Avenel, 8 vols. (Paris, 1853–77), vol. 4, pp. 710, 754; vol. 5, pp. 295, 479, 486, 980 · Archives du Ministère des Affaires Étrangères, Paris, Correspondence Politique, Lorraine 26, fol. 153 · Archives du Ministère des Affaires Étrangères, Paris, Mémoires et documents, vol. 842, fol. 228v · J. Grant, ed., *Memoirs and adventures of Sir John Hepburn* (1851), 205–11 · A. Aubery, *Mémoires pour l'histoire du cardinal duc de Richelieu*, 1 (Paris, 1660), 653–4, 660, 681, 694 · Vicomte de Noailles [A. R. M. A. Noailles], *Épisodes de la guerre de trente ans*, 3 vols. (Paris, 1906–13), vol. 1, p. 28; vol. 2, pp. 159, 165; vol. 3, pp. 32, 48, 50, 54, 136, 143, 157, 178, 257, 263 · S. Murdoch and A. Grosjean, 'Scotland, Scandinavia and Northern Europe, 1580–1707', www.abdn.ac.uk/ssne/ · F. Michel, *Les écossais en France, les français en Écosse*, 2 vols. (1862), vol. 2, pp. 291–318 · Pinard, *Chronologie historique-militaire*, 8 vols. (Paris, 1760–78), vol. 6, p. 100

Hepburn, John (*c.*1460–1525), prior of St Andrews and administrator, was the fourth son of Patrick Hepburn, first Lord Hailes (*c.*1412–1482/3), and possibly his second wife, Ellen Wallace (*fl.* 1440–1480). He may have been born at the family home of Hailes Castle, Haddingtonshire, and was probably about nineteen when he graduated MA at St Andrews in 1479. (There is no evidence for Dempster's statement that Hepburn studied in Paris.) In 1483, as crown nominee, he had papal provision as prior of St Andrews, with permission to hold office before receiving the habit as an Augustinian canon. For over forty years he was prominent in the ecclesiastical and academic life of St Andrews. Belonging to a leading baronial family, however, he was also politically active. The Hepburns and the Humes, allied by marriage, were decisively involved in the 1488 rebellion against James III and in the regime established after it. John Hepburn—perhaps the faction's *éminence grise*—became keeper of the privy seal, with control over royal patronage. In 1492, Hepburn–Hume dominance now less secure, he resigned; but his official career continued, notably in the judiciary.

By the turn of the century Hepburn had acted once, and would soon act again, as vicar-general of St Andrews during archiepiscopal vacancies (1497, 1504). As prior he was responsible for substantial building work on the cathedral and its precinct. Liturgically, he showed particular concern for the cathedral music. He was also active in academic affairs, most notably in the foundation in 1512 of St Leonard's College, where he chose as his model the austere Parisian Collège de Montaigu. His co-founder, the young Archbishop Alexander Stewart (James IV's illegitimate son), had studied with Erasmus in Siena: the 'new learning' was combined with scholastic theology in the new college. Hepburn's chief concern seems to have been that this 'college of poor clerks' should improve the quality of the priesthood.

Alexander Stewart died with his father at Flodden on 9 September 1513. One element in the crisis following that military disaster was thus a vacancy in the primatial see. Hepburn, vicar-general for a third time, was soon himself a candidate for the archbishopric in an unstable political situation. After the death on 25 October 1514 of the octogenarian William Elphinstone, the candidate backed by both chapter and government, Hepburn, elected by the chapter and supported by opponents of the queen dowager, Margaret Tudor, and her new husband, the eighteenth earl of Angus, prosecuted his claim vigorously, seizing St Andrews Castle from Angus's favoured candidate, Gavin Douglas. Eventually, however, he lost the factional struggle and incurred a papal interdict (October 1515) for obstinately opposing the ultimate appointee, Andrew Forman. Hepburn nevertheless held out successfully for substantial material compensation. When Forman died on 11 March 1521 Hepburn became vicar-general yet again, and continued in office until James Beaton's translation from Glasgow to St Andrews became belatedly effective in 1523.

Hepburn's political position during his last ten or twelve years may perhaps be described as flexible. After supporting, and benefiting from, the opposition to Angus and Queen Margaret, he 'grew great in the Court' (*History of Scotland*, 124) in the early years of the duke of Albany's regency. Deserted (as he saw it) by the third Lord Hume in the archiepiscopal contest with Forman, he contributed to Hume's downfall in 1516. His influence with the regent and his prominence seemingly declined later, though he remained politically active to the end. In the confused situation after Albany's final withdrawal in 1524 Hepburn is found with Archbishop Beaton and Bishop Gavin Dunbar of Aberdeen in unlikely alliance with the earls of Angus and Lennox early in 1525. He was still alive on 7 October, but had died before the end of the year; he was probably buried in St Andrews Cathedral.

Hepburn's career obviously exemplifies the way in which late medieval churchmanship could be combined with political (and indeed military) involvement, and how all these could be used to serve personal and family advancement. He may well have been, in Buchanan's words, 'powerful, factious … cunning … profoundly avaricious' (Buchanan, 12.xliv, xlviii). His achievements certainly fell short of his ambitions; but at least his academic foundation suggests that those ambitions were not exclusively selfish.   J. H. BURNS

Sources A. I. Dunlop, ed., *Acta facultatis artium universitatis Sanctiandree, 1413–1588*, 2 vols., Scottish History Society, 3rd ser., 54–5 (1964) · J. Herkless and R. K. Hannay, *The archbishops of St Andrews*, 5 vols. (1907–15), vol. 1 · D. E. R. Watt, ed., *Fasti ecclesiae Scoticanae medii aevi ad annum 1638*, [2nd edn], Scottish RS, new ser., 1 (1969) · J. Lauder, G. Donaldson, and C. Macrae, eds., *St Andrews formulare, 1514–1546*, 1, Stair Society, 7 (1942) · N. Macdougall, *James III: a political study* (1982) · N. Macdougall, *James IV* (1989) · J. Herkless and R. K. Hannay, *The College of St Leonard* (1905) · A. B. Calderwood, ed., *Acts of the lords of council, 1501–1503*, 3 (1993) · *CEPR letters*, vol. 13 · *LP Henry VIII*, vol. 4 · *The history of Scotland, from 21 February 1436 to March 1565 … by Robert Lindesay*, ed. R. Freebairn (1728) · G. Buchanan, *Rerum Scoticarum historia* (1762) · *Scots peerage*, 2.141–52 · records, U. St Andr.

Hepburn, John [*known as* Sir John Hepburn] (*c*.1598–1636), army officer in the Swedish and French service, was the second son of George Hepburn of Athelstaneford, near Haddington, East Lothian; his mother's name is not known. He probably studied at the University of St Andrews in 1615, and then travelled to France with his friend Robert Monro (later like Hepburn a colonel in the Swedish service), visiting Paris and Poitiers.

Following the outbreak of the Bohemian revolt and the election by the rebels of the elector palatine, Frederick V, as their king, in 1620 Sir Andrew Gray began levying forces in Scotland for the support of Frederick and his wife, Elizabeth, daughter of James VI and I, setting up a camp on Hepburn family property at Monkrig. Hepburn joined Gray's forces, leaving Scotland in May 1620, and commanded a company of pikemen who guarded the elector palatine. After the defeat at the battle of the White Mountain (8 November 1620) Gray's forces combined with those of Count Ernst Mansfeldt. By 1622 Hepburn held the rank of captain, fighting that year at the battles of Bergen op Zoom in July and Fleurus in August.

When Mansfeldt's army was disbanded in 1623 Hepburn and his men entered Swedish service, and in 1625 he became colonel of his own infantry troop at a salary of £380 per annum. Hepburn and his troops served with honour in Sweden's Prussian campaigns, particularly in the defence of Mewe against a Polish army of 30,000 in 1625. He served with Colonel Alexander Leslie (later earl of Leven) near Danzig in 1626. During further operations in 1627 Hepburn captured the castle of Marienburg. He was also active in Poland in 1628. In preparation for Gustavus Adolphus's entry into the German campaigns of the Thirty Years' War, Hepburn was commissioned to negotiate with Danzig, a vital independent Baltic port, for its support of the Swedish cause. The Swedish chancellor, Axel Oxenstierna, told the king that he simply did not know anyone more suited to the task than Hepburn. Shortly thereafter he again represented Swedish interests when negotiating with the state of Brandenburg. Hepburn also developed a close working relationship with the Swedish king, meeting him on his arrival in Pomerania in June 1630. Hepburn's relationship with Gustavus Adolphus was such that other Scottish officers relied on him to introduce them to the king. Monro observed that Hepburn's men were usually called upon when troops were needed for particularly dangerous operations. In addition, Oxenstierna noted several times that he never received complaints about Hepburn's well disciplined troops.

During those first two years of Swedish involvement Hepburn and his troops, known as the Green brigade, were engaged in most of the Swedish campaigns as Gustavus Adolphus's forces marched southwards into the German territories of the Habsburg empire. Hepburn was in joint command with Colonel Maximillian Teuffel at Colberg, which surrendered to the Swedes in 1630. That year Colonel John Hepburn was placed as governor of the nearby castle of Rügenwald, after five years in Swedish service. This proved to be one of the first strongholds gained by the Swedes in the German campaigns, and this was only the first of several occasions on which Hepburn was given the post of governor. Hepburn and his men particularly distinguished themselves at Frankfurt an der

Oder in 1631 and again at Breitenfeld, near Leipzig. The timely intervention of the Green brigade was noted as decisive for the Swedish victory there. On the death of Colonel Teuffel, Gustavus Adolphus ordered Hepburn to lead the centre, alongside Sir James Lumsden and Lord Reay, who were under Colonel Robert Monro's command.

In 1632 Hepburn was in charge of the infantry at Werben, and when the Swedish king divided the army into two sections he left Hepburn in charge of one half. During a seven-day campaigning spree he captured six German towns, including Erfurt, and was present at the storming of Marienburg. The capitulation to Hepburn's troops of Oppenheim, where Swedish forces took their first Spanish colours, allowed Gustavus Adolphus to cross the Rhine unhindered as he continued his march southwards through Germany. Hepburn successfully gained Mentz, Donauworth, and Oberndorff which meant that Bavaria, a heartland of the Holy Roman empire, was largely under Swedish control. Hepburn became the interim governor at Landshut until Gustavus Adolphus took up the position in person. In reward for this, Hepburn became the governor of Munich.

Some time between 28 July and 18 August 1632 Hepburn and Gustavus Adolphus had a disagreement which led to Hepburn's resignation from Swedish service. The source of contention may have been Hepburn's adherence to the Catholic faith, or his alleged flamboyant personal style. Hepburn was not the only high-ranking officer to leave Swedish service at this time, as he was accompanied by James, marquess of Hamilton, and Colonel James Hamilton of Priestfield. The Green brigade then became the responsibility of Colonel Robert Monro. Hepburn returned to Britain, spending some time in London where it has been claimed he met Charles I and was knighted; by 1633 contemporary texts refer to him as Sir John, but this may reflect his ennoblement in Sweden, which is also uncertain.

After 1632 France formed an alliance with Sweden, and as Hepburn still desired to fight for the Bohemian cause he then joined the French army (where he was known as Hebron). His first commission was dated 26 January 1633 and he became a *maréchal de camp* with a regiment of over 1000 men. One source states that he led a corps of 2000 Scots who formed a special guard for the French king. In April 1633 Hepburn came to London to undertake a levy of 3000 Scots. After Charles I's initial refusal, resulting in the detention of some of Hepburn's officers in England, he was permitted to levy 1200 men in November 1634. Hepburn was again victorious in his campaigns, capturing Briche and La Mothe from imperial troops in Alsace and Lorraine. He also relieved former comrades in arms in Swedish service from the siege at Heidelberg. Sir Henry Vane, comptroller of the household, was in debt to Hepburn to the amount of £1189 sterling (equivalent to £14,268 Scots) at this time, but when he attempted to settle the debt Hepburn replied that he had no use for money in Scotland and that the bond had been passed to another person in London. Hepburn appeared to have no intention of returning to his native country. On his imprisonment

by German soldiers he convincingly feigned being a German officer and was released. In November 1635 captains Alexander Gordon and Robert Towers obtained two warrants from Charles I to recruit sixty men each in Scotland for Hepburn's regiment. That year his regiment joined forces with the Duke Bernhard of Weimar's army, and then served under Louis de Nogaret, cardinal de la Vallette, in the Mainz campaign.

In June 1636 Hepburn requested the release of 4000 écus of ransom money received for the imperialist general Metternich, but before he could collect it he was killed in July by a gunshot wound to the neck at the siege of Saverne. Sources conflict as to his exact date of death, offering variously 8 July, before 20 July, or 21 July. Before the month was out a man called Andrew Hepburn, who claimed to be John Hepburn's 'brother german', petitioned the privy council of Scotland to inherit whatever property and foods Hepburn and his kinsman Lieutenant-Colonel James *Hepburn, who had died around the same time, had left in France. John Hepburn was buried with his sword, helmet, and spurs in the cathedral at Toul in France, and a monument, since destroyed, was erected there on the western side of the left transept. He appears neither to have married nor to have had any children. Hepburn's regiment remained active and in February and March 1637 a warrant for a levy of 1000 men was given to Captain Robert Hume for transport to France. In 1639 Hepburn's siblings still sought £20,000 from a factor in Paris named Beaton which they claimed was owed to their deceased brother.

A. N. L. GROSJEAN

Sources S. Murdoch and A. Grosjean, 'Scotland, Scandinavia and Northern Europe, 1580–1707', www.abdn.ac.uk/ssne/ · military muster rolls, Krigsarkivet, Stockholm, 1630/22–33 · *Rikskansleren Axel Oxenstiernas skrifter och brefvexling*, 1/5 (Stockholm, 1915) · R. Monro, *Monro his expedition with the worthy Scots regiment (called Mac-Keyes regiment) levied in August 1626* (1637) · *The Swedish discipline* (1632) · *Reg. PCS*, 2nd ser., vol. 6 · *CSP dom.*, 1633–4 · *CSP Venice*, 1632–6 · *Lettres, instructions diplomatiques et papiers d'état du cardinal de Richelieu*, ed. D. L. M. Avenel, 8 vols. (Paris, 1853–77), vol. 5 · J. Grant, *Memoirs of Sir James Hepburn* (1890) · B. Steckzén, *Svenskt och brittiskt* (Stockholm, 1960) · N. F. Holm, ed., *Det svenska svärdet* (Helsingfors, 1948) · *DNB*
Archives NA Scot., corresp. and papers
Wealth at death ransom of 4000 écus paid by the French; £20,000 owed by a factor in Paris: Grant, *Memoirs*

Hepburn, John (*d.* 1723), Church of Scotland minister, was the son of Major James Hepburn of Balnageith, Moray. He was educated at King's College, Aberdeen, graduating as master of arts in 1669. Hepburn became a preacher to presbyterian dissidents in Scotland, being ordained by exiled Scots ministers in London in 1678. After working in Ross-shire, in 1680 he was called to become preacher to the parish of Urr, Kirkcudbrightshire, though he continued also to preach widely in both the north and the south-west. His arrest was ordered in 1680, and in 1683 he was captured in London and sent back to Scotland for trial.

After the restoration of presbyterianism in 1690 he was accepted as parish minister of Urr by the church, though with reluctance as he was strongly influenced by the 'society people', the presbyterian groups who refused to recognize the legitimacy of the Church of Scotland through its abandonment of the covenants. Hepburn combined his work as parish minister with encouraging the formation of prayer societies among his supporters, avoiding giving either wholehearted recognition to the Church of Scotland, or rejecting it completely like the more extreme dissidents of the Cameronian societies. Hepburn was suspended from the ministry in 1696 and, on refusing to take the oath of allegiance, he was briefly imprisoned before being exiled to Brechin.

Hepburn was allowed back to his parish in 1699. By 1700 his first wife, a Leslie from the 'North' (McMillan, 230–31), had died, and on 20 April 1701 he married Emilia, daughter of Alexander Nisbet of Craigentinny in Urr. Although the rest of Hepburn's personal life is obscure, he is known to have had two children. Hepburn was again suspended in 1704, and was deposed on 9 April 1705. Though he fiercely attacked the union of parliaments of 1707 he opposed armed resistance to it, and this may have contributed to the decision to restore him to Urr on 12 August 1707, at the desire of his parishioners.

In 1715 Hepburn, seeing the Jacobite rebels as a greater threat to the truly godly than the existing regime, raised his supporters in arms to oppose them. Though he died on 20 March 1723 the strength of the dissident tradition he and others had established helped to inspire the 'Levellers of Galloway', whose forcible resistance in 1724 to agricultural improvements involving evictions was suppressed by the army. The Hebronites never numbered more than a few thousand people, and most joined the Secession church after 1733.   DAVID STEVENSON

Sources *Fasti Scot.*, new edn, vol. 2 · W. McMillan, *John Hepburn and the Hebronites* (1934) · *The diary of Alexander Brodie of Brodie … and of his son James Brodie*, ed. D. Laing, Spalding Club, 33 (1863) · W. Ferguson, *Scotland: 1689 to the present* (1968)

Hepburn, Margaret (*bap.* 1726, *d.* in or after 1758), shopkeeper, was baptized on 4 September 1726 at St Giles, Edinburgh, the second daughter of the four children of John Hepburn (*d.* 1771), minister of Old Greyfriars Church, Edinburgh, and of Margaret Fenton, daughter of Thomas Fenton, merchant and bailie of Edinburgh. In company with her business partner, Lilias Christie, Margaret sold and hired funeral provisions of all kinds before this kind of supply became part of the undertaker's business. The term of undertaker did not come into use in Scotland until the second half of the eighteenth century. What is particularly interesting about Margaret Hepburn is that, although her father came from a professional background, through her mother she was part of a well-established family network of Edinburgh burgesses, all of whom were operating in similar businesses. Her mother's two sisters, Emelia and Isobel, married merchants; Isobel's husband, Paul Husband, was a well-known wholesale supplier of funeral provisions to other shopkeepers and their daughter Emelia married Thomas Elder, a well-known wine merchant, who could also supply wine for funerals. The wives in this family network were involved

in the businesses, personally receipting customers' bills. The fact that Margaret Hepburn's grandmother was Emelia Christie suggests that Margaret and her business partner were related, probably as cousins. The two women not only supplied plum cake and biscuit but also had to provide mourning draperies for the house and the church, and to contact a 'master household', who made all the practical arrangements on the day of the funeral. Margaret's bills show that items such as sugar-tongs, glasses, and sconces for the candles were hired and that the customer had to pay for any glasses that were broken.

The fact that Margaret's father was a minister probably helped the two women to gain contacts. These personal contacts were vital in the business world of eighteenth-century Scotland, where word of mouth was more important in building up a clientele than reliance on advertising. Margaret Hepburn, with Lilias Christie, supplied clients both in the burgh community and in the country, including landed families. Surviving bills show that she was in business from 1749 to 1758 but she may well have been in business before and after these dates. The 1749 bill was due by the countess of Roxburghe, who would have been unlikely to employ someone who had only recently set up in business. By 1758 Margaret (who never married) appears to have been trading on her own, her business partner having died. Margaret Hepburn did not leave a will and the date of her death is not known.

ELIZABETH C. SANDERSON

Sources E. C. Sanderson, *Women and work in eighteenth-century Edinburgh* (1996) · Edinburgh commissary court processes, NA Scot., CC8/4/484; CC8/4/485; CC8/4/490; CC8/4/501; CC/8/4/503; CC/8/4/510 · NA Scot., Hay of Haystoun muniments, GD 34/559a · bap. reg. Scot., Edinburgh, 1726

Hepburn, Patrick, first earl of Bothwell (*c.*1455–1508), magnate and administrator, was the eldest son of Adam Hepburn (*d.* 1479), master of Hailes, and Ellen, younger daughter of Sir Alexander Hume, first Lord Hume. His family's base lay at Hailes, east of Haddington, and he himself came to hold substantial estates in south and south-east Scotland. By birth he had close ties with another major south-east magnate family with political aspirations, the Humes; by inheritance he acquired, first, the barony of Dunsyre in Lanarkshire on his father's death in 1479, and, second, the title of second Lord Hailes, succeeding his grandfather, Sir Patrick, between 1482 and 1483. He was to use both these advantages to acquire for himself and his family not only the most important offices of state in the kingdom, but also the enduring trust of James IV.

Patrick's father, Adam, had sinned in supporting the Boyd coup of July 1466; Patrick made ample amends to James III in the summer of 1482, however, defending Berwick Castle against a huge invading English army. Although the burgh of Berwick was tamely surrendered, he held the castle until the seizure of James III by his own magnates at Lauder, after which the king's incarceration in Edinburgh Castle removed the Berwick paymaster and made further defence of the castle impossible.

In the mid-1480s Hailes continued to enjoy royal trust.

He was one of the conservators of the truce with Richard III of England (r. 1483–5), negotiated at Nottingham in September 1484, and by August 1487 he had been elected provost of Edinburgh. Yet James III's assault on Hailes's Hume kinsmen, in the long-running Coldingham dispute, forced him to head one of the rebel factions of 1488. Initially a moderate who had been prepared to negotiate with the king in April that year, he rapidly became a hard-liner when James III failed to honour written agreements. The Hepburns were certainly present at Sauchieburn (11 June 1488), supporting the future James IV against his father; and Hailes and his kin moved with remarkable speed to consolidate their power at the head of the new government before calling a parliament. Thus the day after Sauchieburn the first grant of the new reign was to William Hepburn, who became clerk register, and there followed a spate of royal patronage—to Alexander Hepburn as sheriff of Fife, Adam Hepburn of Ogston as master of the king's stable, John Hepburn of Rollandston as steward of the household, Patrick Hepburn as master of the royal larder, and George Hepburn as director of chancery. Hailes's uncle John Hepburn, prior of St Andrews, became keeper of the privy seal, giving him effective control of crown patronage, while Hailes himself made the greatest gains: the keepership of Edinburgh Castle and sheriffdom of Edinburgh, with custody of the king and his younger brother; the title earl of Bothwell, made up of the lordships of Bothwell and Crichton, both forfeited by James III's familiar John Ramsay in 1488; and the office of admiral of Scotland.

In the past other magnate families, most notably the Livingstons and Boyds, had played the dangerous game of advancing their interests through control of the king during a royal minority, and ultimately suffered for it. The Hepburns, however, were shrewd and careful politicians whose relations with James IV were good. They survived a major rising against their government in 1489, and thereafter they gradually relinquished control of major offices—above all the privy seal in 1492—while retaining their positions on the royal council, thus avoiding a political backlash against them when the king took control of government in 1494–5.

Bothwell's principal rival, Archibald Douglas, fifth earl of Angus (d. 1514), lost out to Bothwell on the borders. Earl Patrick had become warden of the west and middle marches by July 1489 and had forced Angus out of his lordship of Liddesdale and castle of Hermitage by the end of 1491; he may also have been responsible for Angus's imprisonment in Dumbarton Castle (1501) and on the Isle of Bute (1502–9). Meanwhile Bothwell continued to conduct an even-handed foreign policy for James IV, first negotiating the French alliance of 1492, then standing proxy for the king at the ceremony of betrothal to James's English bride, Margaret Tudor, in January 1502.

The first earl of Bothwell was married twice. His first wife was Janet Douglas (d. before 24 Feb 1491), daughter of James *Douglas, first earl of Morton, with whom he had one daughter, Joanna. Between February and April 1491 he

married Margaret, elder daughter of George Gordon, second earl of Huntly (d. 1501), and they had four sons and one daughter: Adam, who succeeded as second earl of Bothwell, Patrick, William, and John, who became bishop of Brechin, and Margaret. Bothwell died, probably in Edinburgh, on 18 October 1508.   NORMAN MACDOUGALL

Sources APS, 1424–1567 · J. M. Thomson and others, eds., *Registrum magni sigilli regum Scotorum / The register of the great seal of Scotland*, 11 vols. (1882–1914), vol. 2 · G. Burnett and others, eds., *The exchequer rolls of Scotland*, 9 (1886) · [T. Thomson], ed., *The acts of the lords of council in civil causes, 1478–1495*, 1, RC, 41 (1839) · T. Dickson, ed., *Compota thesaurariorum regum Scotorum / Accounts of the lord high treasurer of Scotland*, 1 (1877) · D. Laing, ed., *The Bannatyne miscellany*, 3, Bannatyne Club, 19b (1855) · *Scots peerage*, vol. 4 · N. Macdougall, *James III: a political study* (1982) · N. Macdougall, *James IV* (1989)

Hepburn, Patrick (c.1487–1573), bishop of Moray, was the son of Patrick Hepburn of Beinstoun and Christian Ogilvie. He seems to have been born c.1487, for he was said to have been eighty years of age in July 1567. He matriculated at St Andrews University in 1509, entering the Pedagogy (replaced by St Mary's College in 1538); and after graduating he pursued an ecclesiastical career as parson of Whitsome in Berwickshire from 1521, and as coadjutor to his paternal uncle John, who was prior of St Andrews, from 1524. He took his seat in parliament in 1525, and served as secretary to James V from March 1525 until June 1526.

On his uncle's death in January 1526, Patrick Hepburn became prior of St Andrews where one of his own canons, the reforming Alexander Alane (Alesius), in 1529 preached against the prior's irascible nature and dissolute life. In March 1538 he was presented by James V to the bishopric of Moray and commendatorship of Scone Abbey, as a reward for service to the crown. Papal provision followed in June. He proved a conspicuous dilapidator of his benefices. In parliament, he was elected to the committee of the articles in 1540 and was a member of Governor Arran's privy council in March 1543. But he gave his support to Cardinal David Beaton against Arran in July that year in opposing English efforts to gain custody of the infant Mary, queen of Scots. In 1547 he leased Scone Abbey for nineteen years to John Erskine of Dun, an early protestant sympathizer. He attended the provincial council of the Scottish church, summoned in 1549 to effect internal reform, and witnessed the burnings for heresy of Adam Wallace in 1550 and Walter Milne in 1558. When the final provincial council of 1559 reiterated earlier decrees against concubinage, the bishop of Moray, who 'ever was ane hure maister all his dayis and committit huredome and adullterie baitht with meadins and mens wyffis', protested, it was said, that 'he wald nocht put away his hure noe mor nor the bischope of Sanctandrois wald put his away ffor it was as lesum to him to haue ane hure as hie', arguing that it was in accord with the decretals that 'he might haue ane hure in absence of his wyffe' (*Historie and Cronicles*, 2.141).

With the approach of the Reformation, the protestant lords of the congregation warned Hepburn that unless he co-operated they could not protect his abbey at Scone. He promised to do as they wished, to provide them with force, to vote against the clerical estate in parliament, and even to join the congregation. The earl of Argyll and Lord James Stewart, acting on behalf of the congregation, duly saved his abbey, palace, and church from attack on 25 June 1559, but Hepburn quickly withdrew his promise, whereupon reformers from Dundee sacked the abbey. He failed to attend the Reformation Parliament of 1560, but in 1569 agreed to repair Elgin Cathedral for protestant worship, despite his continued dilapidation of the bishopric. In 1561 he supported the earl of Huntly's advice to Mary that she land at Aberdeen, rather than Leith, on returning home from France, in the hope of thereby restoring the fortunes of Catholicism in Scotland. Charged as an accessory in Darnley's murder, he was acquitted in November 1567. Curiously, Mary's third husband, James Hepburn, fourth earl of Bothwell, whom she married by protestant rites in May 1567, had earlier been brought up by the bishop at Spynie Castle; then in 1567 the bishop was accused of sheltering the earl as he fled for safety northwards to Scandinavia. During the civil war Bishop Patrick promised to serve Mary with the Hamiltons. With the ascendancy of King James's party, however, he was forfeited by parliament in August 1571. He died at Spynie Castle in Moray on 20 June 1573 and was buried in the choir of the cathedral in Elgin. No fewer than ten of his illegitimate children were legitimated. With his mistress Isabell Liddell he had four sons and a daughter—Patrick, Adam, George, John, and Jane; three sons were legitimated in 1545. With Marion Strang he had a son, William; with Janet Urquhart he had three sons, Patrick, David, and Thomas, and a daughter, Joanna; with Elizabeth Innes, a son Alexander; two other daughters, Janet and Agnes, born of his liaison with an unnamed woman, were legitimated in 1550.

JAMES KIRK

Sources A. I. Dunlop, ed., *Acta facultatis artium universitatis Sanctiandree, 1413–1588*, 2 vols., Scottish History Society, 3rd ser., 54–5 (1964) • J. M. Anderson, ed., *Early records of the University of St Andrews*, Scottish History Society, 3rd ser., 8 (1926) • J. M. Thomson and others, eds., *Registrum magni sigilli regum Scotorum / The register of the great seal of Scotland*, 11 vols. (1882–1914), vols. 3–4 • M. Livingstone, D. Hay Fleming, and others, eds., *Registrum secreti sigilli regum Scotorum / The register of the privy seal of Scotland*, 1–6 (1908–63) • *Reg. PCS*, 1st ser., vols. 1–2 • *APS*, 1424–1592 • C. Innes, ed., *Registrum episcopatus Moraviensis*, Bannatyne Club, 58 (1837) • *CSP Scot.*, 1547–74 • *John Knox's History of the Reformation in Scotland*, ed. W. C. Dickinson, 2 vols. (1949) • *The historie and cronicles of Scotland … by Robert Lindesay of Pitscottie*, ed. A. J. G. Mackay, 3 vols., STS, 42–3, 60 (1899–1911) • D. Patrick, ed., *Statutes of the Scottish church, 1225–1559*, Scottish History Society, 54 (1907) • *Scots peerage*, vol. 2 • D. Calderwood, *The history of the Kirk of Scotland*, ed. T. Thomson and D. Laing, 8 vols., Wodrow Society, 7 (1842–9) • D. E. R. Watt, ed., *Fasti ecclesiae Scoticanae medii aevi ad annum 1638*, [2nd edn], Scottish RS, new ser., 1 (1969)

Hepburn, Patrick, third earl of Bothwell (c.1512–1556), magnate, was the only son of Adam Hepburn, second earl of Bothwell (d. 1513), and Agnes Stewart (d. 1557), the illegitimate daughter of James *Stewart, earl of Buchan, half-brother of James II. The Hepburns first became prominent in the late fourteenth century; initially followers of the Dunbar earls of March, they switched first to the Douglases and then to the crown. They were originally associated with the south-east, where they rose into the nobility first as lords Hailes (from 1452–3) and then as earls of Bothwell (from 1488), but became a power on the west march when the first earl was made keeper of Liddesdale about 1491. By then he was also admiral of Scotland, a position usually occupied by his descendants too—a curious combination.

Patrick Hepburn became earl of Bothwell as a babe in arms following the death of his father at Flodden on 9 September 1513 and thus did not enter into the personal administration of his estates until the conclusion of his wardship, which was entrusted to members of his extended family, headed by his uncle Patrick, master of Hailes, and his great-uncle Patrick, prior of St Andrews and later bishop of Moray. When James V took control of government in 1528 from his detested stepfather, Archibald Douglas, sixth earl of Angus, Bothwell, though still under age, was summoned to council meetings and given responsibilities in the borders, involving action against the Douglases in the east and brigands in the west. Early in 1529 he was made lieutenant of the east march, and by way of encouragement was granted the lands of Tantallon, Angus's principal fortress. But he failed to capture it, and the king eventually granted Tantallon elsewhere.

James seems to have become dissatisfied with the earl's performance, while Bothwell certainly became discontented with his treatment by the king, for by the end of 1531 he was in touch with the sixth earl of Northumberland, promising to assist Henry VIII with 1000 gentlemen and 6000 foot soldiers in the event of an English invasion of Scotland. To justify his treason he complained of being dealt with as if still under age, of having been imprisoned for six months in 1529 for failing to pacify Liddesdale, and of the king's harsh treatment of Angus and other nobles. His youth may in fact have saved the earl's life, but by June 1532 he was none the less a prisoner in Edinburgh Castle, where he stayed until 1535, when he was moved to Inverness. Licensed in 1539 to go from Aberdeen to the continent, he went to Denmark at some point, while by summer 1541 he was in Venice. He offered his services without success to both Charles V and François I.

Following the death of James V on 14 December 1542 Bothwell hastened home via England, having signed articles with Henry VIII pledging to advance the marriage of Queen Mary to the prince of Wales. He also swore to induce others to become Assured lords. Back in Scotland, he attended the packed parliament in March 1543 which confirmed the second earl of Arran as governor and allowed the scriptures in the vernacular. His patrimony had remained intact during his imprisonment and exile, except that Liddesdale was annexed to the crown in 1540. This was now recovered, as were his various offices—lord admiral and sheriff of Edinburgh and of Haddington. Re-established at home, Bothwell quickly forgot his pledge to Henry VIII, seduced, it was alleged, by the prospect of marriage to the queen dowager, Mary of Guise. He had married Agnes Sinclair (d. 1572) in 1533 or 1534. She may have been his first cousin, making it easy for him to have their marriage annulled (by 16 October 1543) on the grounds of consanguinity. They had two children who lived to maturity: James *Hepburn, the third husband of Mary, queen of Scots, and Janet, who married first John Stewart, an illegitimate son of James V, and was mother to the fifth earl. If he ended the marriage in order to wed the queen dowager, Bothwell's dreams were unfulfilled. But first he entered into a lively competition with the fourth earl of Lennox, who may have had similar aspirations. Until his funds ran out he spent considerable sums on masques and feasts in order to impress the royal widow.

Politically, Bothwell remained true Scots for a while, standing surety for Cardinal David Beaton on the latter's release by Arran in March 1543, then joining with the cardinal in July at Linlithgow to effect the removal of the child queen thence to Stirling, and appearing at Leith with his retainers when the English assaulted the town in May 1544. He also used this period of advancement to enrich himself as lord admiral. Not only did he control the admiralty court, thus denying the Dutch justice for Scots pirates, but he outfitted ships which raided vessels from the Low Countries passing Scotland to the North Sea and Icelandic fishing grounds. As befitted Beaton's ally, he played the Catholic card with vigour. He sought to deprive Arran of his governorship on the grounds that he promoted protestants; he also attempted to censor Wishart's preaching at Haddington and then saw to the arrest of the reformer. The story is famous, although Bothwell's infamy is not as clear-cut as was once thought. When he arrested Wishart at Ormiston in early January 1546, he pledged to keep him out of the clutches of his enemies and tried to honour his promise, warding the preacher in his castle of Hailes. The privy council had to threaten him with severe punishment before he surrendered his charge to the government, probably on 31 January 1546, to be burnt as a heretic on 1 March. Knox and his followers never forgave Bothwell for his failure.

During the 1540s Bothwell was increasingly playing a double game: showing loyalty to Mary of Guise (he had supported her attempt to become regent in June 1544), while simultaneously negotiating with the English (probably in the hope of safeguarding his position as a border baron). Late in 1544 he was charged with treason, and in particular with receiving English money, but was soon remitted. However, when the occupation of St Andrews by the assassins of Cardinal Beaton ended in August 1547, Bothwell's name was discovered on a list of English supporters: if Protector Somerset could arrange his marriage to the dowager duchess of Suffolk, he pledged to aid England in the war. Although French assistance was beginning to turn the military balance in Scotland's favour, the earl continued to consort with the English and as a result was once more taken into custody. He was released the day after the battle of Pinkie (10 September 1547) and returned to Hermitage, but as late as August 1549 undertook to be an English subject and on 3 September signed a bond with Edward VI. This assured him a pension of 1000 crowns along with the protection of 100 horsemen; should he be forfeited of his lands in Scotland, equivalent possessions in England would be given him. The first

down-payment was apparently made, but within a year he was complaining from Newcastle that he was severely out of pocket due to lack of funds. Bothwell clearly lived in England until November 1553, when (perhaps persuaded by Mary of Guise) he returned home. In March 1554 he was pardoned for his blatant treasons and between February and April took part in the negotiations whereby Arran, now duke of Châtelherault, finally surrendered his governorship to the queen dowager. He was thus once again part of the Scottish aristocratic polity which ruled the kingdom.

In 1556 Mary of Guise made Bothwell warden of the west march and lieutenant of the borders, but he died in September shortly after his appointment, probably at Dumfries. He aroused widely differing emotions among his contemporaries. In 1531 Northumberland had been much taken with him, but over a decade later Sir Ralph Sadler found him insolent and vain. Knox loathed him; Pitscottie (though a protestant) rather liked him, describing the earl as 'fair and quhittlie and sumthing hingand schoulderit and zeid [yet] sumthing fordwart witht ane gentil and human continance' (*Historie and Cronicles*, 2.17). In an English account of Somerset's Pinkie campaign he was sketched as a 'gentleman of right cumly porte and stature, and heretofore of right honourable and just meaning and dealing' (Patten, 77). Bothwell was seldom either honourable or just in his dealings, and his inexplicable adherence to the English cause in 1549, when his allies were manifestly losing the war, was a major blunder. But his charms were such as to win him the favour, though not the hand, of Mary of Guise, and by the time he died, in his bed, he had restored his family to a position of esteem in Scotland.   MARCUS MERRIMAN

Sources J. M. Thomson and others, eds., *Registrum magni sigilli regum Scotorum / The register of the great seal of Scotland*, 11 vols. (1882–1914), vols. 3–4 · M. Livingstone, D. Hay Fleming, and others, eds., *Registrum secreti sigilli regum Scotorum / The register of the privy seal of Scotland*, 3–6 (1936–57) · *LP Henry VIII*, vols. 5–21 · D. Laing, ed., *The Bannatyne miscellany*, 3, Bannatyne Club, 19b (1855) · W. Patten, *The expedicion into Scotlande* (1548) · *The historie and cronicles of Scotland … by Robert Lindesay of Pitscottie*, ed. A. J. G. Mackay, 3 vols., STS, 42–3, 60 (1899–1911) · *John Knox's History of the Reformation in Scotland*, ed. W. C. Dickinson, 2 vols. (1949) · *Scots peerage*, 2.156–61 · GEC, *Peerage*, 2.238–9 · J. Cameron, *James V: the personal rule, 1528–1542*, ed. N. Macdougall (1998) · M. Merriman, *The rough wooings: Mary queen of Scots, 1542–1551* (2000) · R. K. Marshall, *Mary of Guise* (1977) · M. H. B. Sanderson, *Cardinal of Scotland: David Beaton, c.1494–1546* (1986) · DNB

Hepburn, Patrick George Thomas Buchan-, Baron **Hailes** (1901–1974), politician and governor-general of the Federation of the West Indies, was born on 2 April 1901 at Smeaton Hepburn, East Lothian, the third son (there was also a daughter) of Sir Archibald Buchan-Hepburn, fourth baronet (1852–1929), a barrister, and his wife, Edith Agnes (*d.* 1923), daughter of Edward Kent Karslake KC. The Buchan-Hepburns were descended from Patrick Hepburn, who was ennobled as Lord Hailes in 1452. Buchan-Hepburn was educated at Harrow School (1915–19) and at Trinity College, Cambridge (1919–22). By his own later account, his schooldays were not happy and his academic

Patrick George Thomas Buchan-Hepburn, Baron Hailes (1901–1974), by Bassano

record was 'quite undistinguished' (Hailes MSS, 5.29). He left Cambridge with no clear ideas for his future. A talented amateur painter and a connoisseur of historic buildings, he proceeded to travel widely.

From January 1926 to February 1927 Buchan-Hepburn served as an honorary attaché at the British embassy in Constantinople. After returning to Britain with political ambitions, he secured appointment as unpaid private secretary to Winston Churchill. Other steps in his political apprenticeship were a foredoomed contest as Conservative candidate for Wolverhampton East in the 1929 general election, and a spell as an elected member for North Kensington on the London county council in 1930–31. At the 1931 general election the Conservative landslide carried him into parliament as member for the East Toxteth division of Liverpool. 'I owe my good fortune very largely to you', he wrote to Churchill (Hailes MSS, 4/2).

Buchan-Hepburn was no orator and seldom took part in Commons debates; rather, his talent was for organizational work. Importantly for his career, Oliver Stanley, who was widely seen as a future prime minister, took him on as parliamentary private secretary. Between 1931 and 1939 Stanley held ministerial appointments in the Home Office, transport, labour, education, and trade. By remaining with him as parliamentary private secretary throughout these years, Buchan-Hepburn acquired detailed knowledge of the workings of government. In June 1939 he became an assistant government whip and in November he was appointed a junior lord of the Treasury. He retired

from this post in June 1940 in order to join the 11th (City of London yeomanry) light anti-aircraft regiment of the Royal Artillery, in which he became a brigade major on staff and served until 1943. Summoned by Churchill back to the Commons, he resumed his appointment as a junior whip in 1944. On 7 June 1945 he married Diana Mary (d. 1980), daughter of Brigadier-General the Hon. Charles Lambton and a descendant of Lord Durham. Her first husband, Major William Hedworth Williamson, had been killed at Alamein in 1942.

When the Conservatives went into opposition in July 1945 Buchan-Hepburn became deputy to James Stuart, the party's chief whip. In 1947 Stuart decided for personal reasons to retire from his post, with Buchan-Hepburn his obvious successor. Churchill was slow to authorize the transition, and Buchan-Hepburn effectively served as *de facto* chief whip until his promotion was formalized in July 1948. In the same year boundary changes left him without a safe seat to contest at the next election. Churchill failed to persuade the Liverpool tories to endorse him for Garston. Soon afterwards, however, he won endorsement for Beckenham, which he went on to hold from 1950 until his retirement from politics in 1957.

During the 1950–51 parliament Buchan-Hepburn was centrally involved in the Conservatives' systematic campaign to harry the Attlee administration from office. In government after October 1951 he continued as chief whip, becoming parliamentary secretary to the Treasury and a privy councillor. His effectiveness could be reckoned from the fact that in the years 1951–4 the government's average majority in divisions was twenty-nine, almost double its paper majority. 'A prodigy!' was Churchill's tribute (Hailes MSS, 4/2).

Buchan-Hepburn was credited by his contemporaries with inaugurating a new style in his office. Typically, tory chief whips had been military men who took a bluntly disciplinarian approach to their responsibilities. Buchan-Hepburn was subtler, more inclined to seek his objectives by turning to account his intuitive perception of the traits and motivations of others. He was articulate, charming, and persuasive, and also had the advantage of looking the part, being tall and notably elegant. He was known in parliament as 'Mr Efficiency'—but also as 'the Gorgeous Peacock' (*Yorkshire Post*, 10 May 1957; *Sunday Times*, 12 May 1957). Behind the charm he was rather vain and sensitive to criticism, and at times his composure gave way to bursts of anger. 'I am not "pussyfoot" by nature', he once remarked (Hailes MSS, 4/20). But he made few political enemies, and as a chief whip who delivered the desired results, he enjoyed the full confidence of the party's leaders.

Though Buchan-Hepburn remained personally loyal to Churchill, he was anxious to see Anthony Eden succeed to the premiership, and from 1952 he was among those seeking to persuade Churchill to retire. On attaining the premiership at last in April 1955, Eden kept him on as chief whip until the reshuffle of December 1955, when he promoted him to the post of minister of works with a seat in cabinet. It was an office in which he could apply his architectural interests, but as things turned out he had little time to make an impact. He spent the later months of 1956 embroiled in the Suez crisis, as one of the few in cabinet who from first to last opposed the use of force. Yet in the aftermath of the abortive invasion he took a leading role in cabinet in urging Eden to stay on as prime minister. At the cabinet meeting of 17 December he argued that party unity was at stake and that Eden's departure would be seen as an admission of failure; an argument supported by every other minister who spoke except his old chief Stuart, who had never been an Edenite.

When on 9 January 1957 Eden did resign, Buchan-Hepburn was the sole minister to give unequivocal support to R. A. Butler for the succession. In a subsequently published letter to the victor, Harold Macmillan, he asked not to be considered for the new ministry. On 15 February Macmillan elevated him to the Lords; reviving the family title, he became Baron Hailes of Prestonkirk.

A governor-general was needed for the Federation of the West Indies, a newly devised grouping of ten Caribbean islands which the Colonial Office (CO) hoped might become, in time, a viable independent state. Both the CO and the leading Caribbean politicians felt that the governor-generalship should go to a sympathetic colonial administrator such as Sir Hugh Foot, governor of Jamaica. Indeed the colonial secretary, Alan Lennox-Boyd, had already discussed the position with Foot. But Macmillan had other plans. He informed the CO that he proposed to appoint someone with British parliamentary, ministerial, and cabinet experience, as being more appropriate for a territory close to self-government. Hailes's appointment was announced in May. The appointment as GBE followed in September.

Hailes arrived in the Caribbean in January 1958. To an interviewing journalist he seemed both 'sensitive' and 'practical' (Hailes MSS, 5/29). As governor-general and commander-in-chief he had responsibility for external affairs, defence, and the maintenance of financial stability, along with appointive powers and a veto power over legislation. He also chaired the federal council of ministers—'a pretty formidable task', in the CO's judgment (Hailes MSS, 5/3). But within the federal structure the central government was weak vis-à-vis the island governments, and this limited Hailes's ability to maintain the federal momentum in the face of strong inter-island rivalries. Further, leading politicians such as Norman Manley and Eric Williams chose to hold office at island rather than federal level, which placed them outside his sphere of direct authority. His poor relationship with the governor of Trinidad (Sir Edward Beetham) did not help.

A federal review conference in 1959 foundered upon Jamaica–Trinidad recriminations, and Trinidad in particular began pressing for a separate independence. Hailes sought reinforcement, in the shape of a visit by the colonial secretary, Iain Macleod. The Macleod visit in June 1960 was followed two months later by full internal self-government at the federal level. Hailes approved, but in April 1961, with further constitutional talks approaching,

confided to Macmillan that he was 'not very sanguine' (Hailes MSS, 4/16). Late in 1961 the anti-federation outcome of a Jamaican referendum signalled the end of the experiment. The federation was dissolved in May 1962. It was all a 'bitter disappointment' to Hailes (Hailes MSS, 5/77). He had been a conscientious and energetic governor-general, but one whose institutional position was never very strong. His real problem, however, was that he was the agent of a misjudged overall policy. Federation made administrative sense in London, but not much political sense in the Caribbean.

Following the dissolution of the federation Hailes was appointed a Companion of Honour (1962) and retired once more. In retirement he took on the chairmanship of the Historic Buildings Council for England, a post which he held from 1963 to 1973 and in which his love of art and architecture could find practical expression. He died at his home, 1 Pelham Place, London, on 5 November 1974. There being no children from the marriage, the barony became extinct.   DAVID GOLDSWORTHY

Sources CAC Cam., Hailes MSS • *DNB* • *The Times* (6 Nov 1974) • *The West Indies. Appointment of governor general, 1957–8*, PRO, CO 1031/2870 • J. Ramsden, *The age of Churchill and Eden, 1940–1957* (1995) • R. R. James, *Anthony Eden* (1986) • *FO List* (1926–7) • Burke, *Peerage* (1967) • college register, Trinity Cam. • *WW*
Archives CAC Cam., corresp. and papers | U. Birm. L., corresp. with Lord and Lady Avon
Likenesses Bassano, photograph, NPG [*see illus.*]
Wealth at death £47,565: probate, 25 April 1975, *CGPLA Eng. & Wales*

Hepburn, Robert (1690?–1716), advocate and essayist, was born at Bearford, near Haddington, Haddingtonshire, the son of Robert Hepburn. Like many Scots at the time he studied law in the Netherlands, probably at the University of Leiden, returning in 1710 to pursue a legal career in Edinburgh. He was enrolled in the Faculty of Advocates on 15 June 1714.

Shortly after arriving in Edinburgh, Hepburn began publishing *The Tatler, by Donald MacStaff of the North*, a periodical essay in the manner of Steele and Addison. He produced some forty numbers between January and May 1711, of which only fifteen appear to survive. They are competent enough imitations of their model, addressing 'the softer, the politer, the wittier part of Mankind' (*The Tatler*, no. 10). Alexander Tytler saw in them 'vigorous native powers' (Tytler, *Memoirs*) and some learning, and certainly an essay defending the right of fighting even in an unjust war (*The Tatler*, no. 5) shows considerable skill in advocacy. Unfortunately the extant numbers are otherwise undistinguished. Tytler said that the venture failed because the essays caused offence by describing known characters, both in church and state, 'with no gentle or delicate hand' (Tytler, 1.165n.). Although perfunctory, the character sketches certainly seem to have been recognized: Hepburn was warned 'that there are such Things as *Swords* and *Pistols* to be feared, if I continue to be as particular as I have been hitherto' (*The Tatler*, no. 14).

Hepburn's later publications are more decorous. Later in 1711 he published *An Idea of the Modern Eloquence of the Bar*, a translation from Sir George Mackenzie's Latin text, evidently finding congenial Mackenzie's thesis that legal oratory was intrinsically superior to any other. Hepburn developed this position in a work of his own in 1715, *A Discourse Concerning the Character of a Man of Genius*, arguing that genius found its supreme manifestation in oratory. Other writings include a demonstration, in elegant Latin, of the existence of God (1714), and a brief account, also in Latin, of the writings of Dr Archibald Pitcairn (1715). This he dedicated to Joseph Addison. His last work was *A Discourse Concerning Fews and Superiorities* (1716), arguing that the Scottish mode of land ownership was a relic of the feudal system, which had 'tended to inflame and foment the late unnatural *Rebellion* among us against the best of Kings' (p. 31). Hepburn evidently might have become an accomplished historian, but this publication was probably posthumous. He died in Edinburgh on 18 October 1716.   GEOFFREY CARNALL

Sources A. F. Tytler, *Memoirs of the life and writings of the Honourable Henry Home of Kames*, 2 vols. (1807), vol. 1 · *The Tatler, by Donald MacStaff of the North* (1711) · F. J. Grant, ed., *The Faculty of Advocates in Scotland, 1532–1943*, Scottish RS, 145 (1944) · Chambers, *Scots.*, rev. T. Thomson (1875)

Hepburn, Thomas (1796–1864), miners' leader, was born in February 1796 in the Durham pit village of Pelton. His father was killed in a mining accident, leaving a widow and three children, of whom Thomas was the eldest. Hepburn received a scanty education at the village school, and could read the Bible when he began work at Urpeth colliery at the age of eight; he soon moved to another local pit, at Fatfield. He took every opportunity to extend his education by private study and by attending classes after work. He joined the Primitive Methodists, becoming an active local preacher, which developed his powers of persuasion, public speaking, and organization. Hepburn married in 1820 and soon afterwards moved to a colliery at Jarrow and then to the recently opened Hetton colliery. This pattern of moves within a small area was typical of the lives of skilled hewers, and Hepburn thereby gained experience of a variety of mining communities. Hetton was a large new colliery, with a newly gathered workforce ripe for the establishment of its own leadership.

Although miners had often shown a capacity for effective collective action, formal trade unionism among them had never achieved long-term success. In 1830 Hepburn became involved in attempts to resuscitate a mining union, encouraged by the existence of a number of grievances, including the long hours worked by colliery boys and the existence of the annual 'bond' or written contract of employment which tied miners to a coal-owner's service for a year. Early in 1831 Hepburn took a leading role in mass meetings at which these grievances were expressed and steps taken to form a revived union. In early April, when the annual bond was due for renewal, thousands of pitmen refused to sign and the northern coalfield was crippled by a major lock-out which lasted more than two months. The coal-owners were unable to maintain united resistance and by the summer the miners had won a major victory, which included the concession of shorter working hours for boys. Throughout the campaign, Hepburn worked hard to keep the men together and present a moderate and law-abiding public front. Some of the other 1831 leaders, including other Primitive Methodist lay preachers, were cast in the same mould; their obvious honesty, moderation, and respectability helped to confer a favourable public image on the union. It was said that Hepburn 'many times prevented the men from running into excess and extravagance' (*Newcastle Weekly Chronicle*). The effect of these tactics on the authorities, and on uncommitted public opinion, was crucial in the miners' victory.

The union remained in existence following the 1831 settlement, and in August 1831 Hepburn was elected as its paid organizer, after a short period in which he had tried to support his family by founding a small school. Thereafter things began to go awry for the union and its leader. Many employers were alarmed at the way in which the coal-owners had been coerced into concessions, fears shared in some influential quarters in local and central government. Hepburn was unable to maintain control of all of his followers. There was a continuing rash of local colliery disputes which imperilled the continuance of the 1831 settlement, since the concessions made had not ensured industrial peace on the coalfield. Another widespread dispute brought most of the northern pitmen out again in 1832, in an atmosphere that turned ugly. There were outbreaks of violence, including attacks on collieries and at least two murders, which played a part in turning the authorities and uncommitted public opinion against the miners. The union's unity proved fragile, and in face of the coal-owners' greater determination to resist coercion, and the threat presented by the import of many blackleg miners, 'Hepburn's Union' was broken by the end of the summer of 1832, leaving its leader in serious difficulties. Hepburn tried teaching again, without success, and then selling tea door-to-door in the pit villages. After years of hardship, he made a desperate appeal for employment to T. E. Forster, the manager of Felling colliery. Forster agreed to take him on, but apparently exacted a promise of abstention from union activities. For the rest of Hepburn's life, Forster supported and befriended him. Successive employments as a deputy overman, inspector of safety lamps, and master wasteman, enabled Hepburn to support his family respectably.

Hepburn's public activities did not end with the union catastrophe of 1832. Although they coincided with the political crisis over parliamentary reform, there was little broader political inspiration behind the 1831–2 strikes, and the miners' case was mostly confined to immediate mining grievances. There were sound tactical reasons for this, though Hepburn himself was a keen supporter of political reform. After he had secured his Felling employment, he was prominent in the 1839 Chartist agitation on Tyneside. When the great mining strike of 1844 began, some miners begged Hepburn to join its leadership. His memories of 1832 remained sharp and he steadily refused 'as he had been forsaken by them and taken care of by Mr.

Forster' (*Newcastle Weekly Chronicle*). In his last years, when Hepburn had been forced to give up work and his mental state had deteriorated, Forster continued to treat him kindly. He lived at Office Row, Hebburn, until he was taken to his daughter's home three months before his death in Newcastle upon Tyne on 9 December 1864. His funeral at Heworth was attended by few mourners, his part in the events of 1831–2 being by then largely forgotten. A few years later the publication of Richard Fynes's *The Miners of Northumberland and Durham* (1873) revived interest in Hepburn's achievements. In November 1875 a headstone was erected on Hepburn's grave, extolling the way in which he had striven for 'shorter hours and better education for miners'. His significance as an early pioneer of trade unionism in that movement's heroic age has since been widely accepted. In 1974 Hepburn was included in a small group of early labour leaders selected for an issue of commemorative postage stamps.

NORMAN MCCORD

Sources J. Oxberry, *Thomas Hepburn of Felling: what he did for miners* (c.1938) • R. Fynes, *The miners of Northumberland and Durham* (1873) • *Newcastle Weekly Chronicle* (17 Dec 1864)
Likenesses engraving, repro. in Fynes, *Miners of Northumberland and Durham*, 36 • engraving, repro. in *The Guardian* (15 April 1976) • group portrait, engraving (*The pitmen's union 1832*), repro. in W. A. Moyes, *The banner book* (1974), 25

Hepplewhite, George (1727?–1786), cabinet-maker and furniture designer, of whose origins firm evidence is lacking, was almost certainly born in 1727, the son of George Hepplewhite (1678–1733) of Ryton, a prosperous Tyneside village in co. Durham, and Sarah, *née* Rootlish (d. 1729), his wife. If this identification is correct, both Hepplewhite and his successor in the standard canon of English furniture designers, Thomas Sheraton, were natives of co. Durham, albeit from opposite ends of the county. Hepplewhite was first mentioned when his fourth son, Benjamin William, was baptized at St James's, Clerkenwell, in 1768. Clerkenwell was then an important centre of the furniture trade, the seat of such celebrated firms as those of Giles Grendey and of William and Richard Gomm. Hepplewhite is next mentioned, again in Clerkenwell, in 1776, when his first son, George, was apprenticed to John Bowyer, citizen and turner, of Clerkenwell Close. In November 1784, when George achieved his freedom, the family were still in Clerkenwell. At Christmas 1785, however, Hepplewhite and his son George insured premises at 48 Redcross Street, Cripplegate, with the Sun Insurance Company. 'Utensils and stock' were valued at £500. Hepplewhite had died intestate at Redcross Street by 27 June 1786, when administration was granted to his widow, Alice. In 1786 'Kepplewhite & Son' were listed in Lowndes's London directory at 48 Redcross Street. The auction of 'the valuable stock on trade and household furniture of Mr. Hepplewhite, cabinet manufacturer deceased' was announced in the *Public Ledger* (10 October 1786). That Hepplewhite's third son, John, subscribed to the *Treatise on the Five Orders of Architecture* (1787) by George Richardson, a former draughtsman for the Adam firm, and that his second son, Andrew, was listed as a drawing master at 6 Oxendon Street, Haymarket, in 1811, suggests connections with the book trade and with architectural and design circles.

In 1788 Isaac and Josiah Taylor published *The cabinet-maker and upholsterer's guide, or, Repository of designs for every article of household furniture, in the newest and most approved taste … the whole exhibiting near three hundred different designs, engraved on one hundred and twenty-six plates: from drawings by A. Hepplewhite and Co. cabinet-makers* from their architectural library at 56 Holborn. No compendium of furniture designs had appeared since 1762, when Thomas Chippendale issued the third edition of his *Gentleman and Cabinet-Maker's Director*. In publishing the Hepplewhite *Guide* the Taylors were filling a yawning gap. The plates were issued in batches at the beginning of July, September, and October 1787. In January and February 1788 a subscription was promoted in such papers as the *Lincoln, Rutland and Stamford Mercury* and *Williamson's Liverpool Advertiser*. The price was 2 guineas. The preface adopts a modest tone: 'To unite elegance and utility, and blend the useful with the agreeable, has ever been considered a difficult but an honourable task.' It stressed the *Guide*'s utility to 'the mechanic', to 'young workmen in general, and occasionally to more experienced ones'. A successful subscription 'enabled us to exceed the number of plates originally proposed'.

The designs, covering many furniture types, are either plain and functional or in a competent but unadventurous neo-classical manner, which seems indebted to the example of James Wyatt. Given their backward character and the fact that they appeared scarcely a year after George Hepplewhite's death, the traditional suggestion that Alice, his widow, was capitalizing on his designs seems plausible. However, the appearance in 1789 of a second edition with an extra plate, and of six plates signed 'Hepplewhite' or 'Heppelwhite' and dated October, November, and December 1792 and May 1793 in *The Cabinet-Makers' London Book of Prices* edition of 1793 suggests that the firm designed after his death. This was proven when, in reaction to criticism from Thomas Sheraton, who stated in his *Cabinet-Maker and Upholsterer's Drawing Book* (1793) that the Hepplewhite *Guide* had already 'caught the decline' in design standards, a third edition was issued in 1794 containing new or altered plates, in which many curvilinear or shield-back chairs of 1788 are replaced by neat rectilinear forms in the French style, which Sheraton had derived from Henry Holland at Carlton House. Perhaps John and/or Andrew Hepplewhite may have been responsible for these 'posthumous' productions. The *Guide*'s text, containing information on nomenclature, fashion, materials, finishes, and upholstery, was changed in 1794 to take account of the altered plates, only two of which bear that date, but, curiously, comments of 1788 on a chair 'executed with a good effect for his Royal Highness the Prince of Wales' apply, in 1794, to a completely different design.

The Hepplewhite *Guide* was influential beyond England, in America, in Denmark, where J. C. Lillie used it for designing chairs for Liselund in 1793, and in Germany, where F. G. Hoffmann pirated Hepplewhite designs in his *Meubles-Magazin* (1795). A late nineteenth-century Hepplewhite revival led to an 1897 reprint of the *Guide* by Batsford, and a modest myth grew up around George Hepplewhite, who was stated to have been apprenticed to Gillows of Lancaster and London: this seems unlikely as, in 1801, they wrote: 'We have not Hebbelthwaite's Publication' (Westminster Reference Library, Gillow Records).

SIMON JERVIS

Sources G. Beard and C. Gilbert, eds., *Dictionary of English furniture makers, 1660–1840* (1986) · private information (2004) [E. I. Hill, A. Janes]

Hepworth [*married names* Skeaping, Nicholson]**, Dame (Jocelyn) Barbara** (1903–1975), sculptor, was born on 10 January 1903 at Wakefield, Yorkshire, the eldest in the family of three daughters and one son of Herbert Raikes Hepworth (1881–1958), civil engineer to the West Riding of Yorkshire, and his wife, Gertrude Allison Johnson (1879?–1972).

Early years Hepworth was educated at Wakefield Girls' High School. She entered Leeds School of Art in September 1920, and a year later moved to the Royal College of Art, in London, to study sculpture. A fellow student in the sculpture departments at both Leeds and London was Henry Moore, who remained a friend and colleague for the whole of her working life. Hepworth completed her course at the Royal College of Art and was awarded the diploma of associateship in July 1923, at the unusually early age of twenty. She returned for a post-graduate year and was short-listed for the prix de Rome in sculpture. The award went to John Rattenbury *Skeaping (1901–1980), but Hepworth was commended and awarded a scholarship for a year's travel abroad. She left for Florence in September 1924, and on a short visit to Rome in November met Skeaping, whom she married at the Palazzo Vecchio in Florence on 13 May 1925. His father was Kenneth Mathieson Skeaping, painter, of Woodford, Essex. John and Barbara Skeaping had one child, Paul, born in 1929, who was killed while serving in the RAF in Malaya in 1953.

The Skeapings spent the academic year 1925–6 at the British School in Rome, then under the enlightened direction of the classical archaeologist Bernard Ashmole. While in Rome, Hepworth learned how to carve stone—not part of the sculptor's normal training at that time but considered the work of a stonemason. The Skeapings' continued study was interrupted by John's poor health, and they returned to London late in 1926. During 1927 they lived at 24 St Ann's Terrace, St John's Wood, London, and at the end of the year moved to a studio residence, 7 The Mall, Parkhill Road, in Hampstead. In June 1928 they had their first important exhibition, at the Beaux Arts Gallery in London, showing mainly stone carvings of figures and animals. A second joint exhibition followed at the gallery of Arthur Tooth & Son, London, in October 1930.

Hepworth had by this stage built up a circle of influential admirers of her work, including George Hill and Laurence Binyon (who both worked at the British Museum),

Dame (Jocelyn) Barbara Hepworth (1903–1975), self-portrait, 1950

the great collector of Asian art George Eumorfopoulos, and the zoologist Solly Zuckerman, then prosecutor at the London Zoo. Hepworth's early carvings were well received and sold for substantial sums. However, the marriage to Skeaping was not happy, and was dissolved in 1933.

Abstraction In 1931 Hepworth had met the painter Ben *Nicholson (1894–1982), and they began to work in very close association, living together at 7 The Mall from summer 1932. The forms in Hepworth's sculptures became more and more simplified. In 1931–2 she had made a small, near-abstract sculpture, *Pierced Form*, in alabaster (destroyed in the Second World War), the dominant feature of which was a large hole in the centre. This idea was at once taken up by her friend Henry Moore, and together they enriched the language of sculpture by seeking a balance of concavities and convexities in their work. *Pierced Form* was shown under the title *Abstraction* in the exhibition at Tooth's gallery in November 1932 that Hepworth shared with Nicholson. Another joint exhibition followed in October 1933 at the Lefevre Gallery, where Hepworth showed her work regularly until 1952.

By the end of 1934 Hepworth was making totally abstract sculpture—not simplifications (or abstractions) of human or organic forms, as was the case with her contemporaries Brancusi and Arp. These works by Hepworth can be regarded as the first completely abstract sculptures made anywhere in the world, the equivalent of the carved White Reliefs that Ben Nicholson was making simultaneously. In the next five years, up to 1939, Hepworth developed a repertory of very simple abstract shapes with such titles as *Single Form*, *Two Forms*, *Pierced Hemisphere*, *Helicoids in Sphere*, *Conoid*, *Sphere and Hollow*.

The commitment to abstraction brought Hepworth to

the forefront of modern art. Visits to Paris with Ben Nicholson in 1933–5 had put them in personal contact with an international avant-garde, in particular Braque, Brancusi, Arp, Miró, and Mondrian. They were members of the Paris-based group Abstraction-Création in 1933–4; in England, Hepworth was a member of the Seven and Five exhibiting society from 1932 to 1935, and of Unit One in 1933–4.

By the late 1930s Hepworth's studio in Parkhill Road, shared with Ben Nicholson, had become the centre of the abstract art movement in Britain. Living nearby were Henry and Irina Moore; the poet and writer on art Herbert Read; the Russian-born constructivist sculptor Naum Gabo; and, from 1938, the Dutch painter Piet Mondrian. The circle of friends also included the painter and critic Adrian Stokes, the anthropologist Henri Frankfort, the scientist J. Desmond Bernal, and architects such as Serge Chermayeff, Walter Gropius, and Leslie Martin and his wife, Sadie. Hepworth made an important contribution to the exhibition *Abstract and Concrete* arranged by Nicolete Gray in 1936, and to the publication on modern art and architecture *Circle* (1937) edited by Nicholson, Gabo, and Martin; she was active in anti-fascist exhibitions. Her sister Elizabeth (1910–1991) had in March 1938 married the architectural historian John Summerson.

On 17 November 1938 Hepworth was able to marry Ben Nicholson, newly divorced by his first wife, Winifred. He was the son of Sir William Newzam Prior *Nicholson. In August 1939, with war in Europe imminent, the Nicholsons and their five-year-old triplet children (a son and two daughters) left London for St Ives, in Cornwall, at the invitation of Adrian Stokes. This small Cornish fishing port and tourist centre, long a magnet for artists, was to become Hepworth's home until her death in 1975.

Hepworth's abstract sculpture had had little commercial success, and abandoning the Hampstead studio precipitately meant leaving behind work that did not survive the German bombing of London. Inadequate accommodation in St Ives, the demands of a husband and a young family, lack of materials—all made sculpture almost impossible. What time she had was devoted to drawing, and from 1940 onwards she made many studies for abstract sculptures that show an affinity to the work of Gabo, who had also taken refuge in St Ives and stayed until 1946. The Nicholsons tried to persuade their friend Mondrian to join them but when his London studio was bombed in September 1940 he preferred to flee to New York, where he died four years later.

Cornwall In July 1942 the Hepworth–Nicholson family moved into a larger house, Chy-an-Kerris, Headland Road, in the Carbis Bay suburb of St Ives, and in 1943 Hepworth began making sculpture again. Her work had changed. The influence of the Cornish landscape immediately made itself felt. Her sculpture was no longer austerely abstract but now contained references to landscape forms and to the patterns of nature. The movement of tides, pebble and rock formations, and the Cornish moorland landscape all enriched her work. The ancient standing stones,

dolmens, and quoits of west Cornwall provided an analogy for her own sculpture, which became increasingly a paradigm for the figure in a landscape and an expression in abstract terms of man's harmonious relationship to his fellows and to the world in which he lives. The inherent classicism of all Hepworth's work comes to the fore; her art always aspires to a timeless, universal concept of abstract beauty.

A first retrospective exhibition, in April–June 1943, with Paul Nash at Temple Newsam, Leeds, arranged by its director, Philip Hendy, was a stimulus to this new beginning, though the illness of Hepworth's daughter Sarah, her own suspected tuberculosis, and general debility as a result of war-time conditions held her back. Despite this the carving *Wave* (1943–4; National Gallery of Scotland, Edinburgh), in which the concavities of the plane wood are painted white and strings are stretched across the aperture, is an unquestioned masterpiece, as is *Pelagos* (1946; Tate collection)—both inspired by her feeling for the curve of St Ives Bay, viewed from her house.

With the end of war in summer 1945 matters improved only marginally, particularly for abstract artists such as Hepworth and Nicholson, whose work remained very unpopular in a climate that preferred realist and neo-Romantic art. Hepworth began making figure drawings with colour in 1947, and through her friendship with the surgeon Norman Capener, who had operated on her daughter, she began a series of about sixty hospital scenes of surgeons operating or getting ready. These brought her some success when shown in London and New York in 1948 and 1949, and they remain the most accessible part of her work.

A figurative element also enters into Hepworth's sculpture of the later 1940s, resulting in such work as the blue marble *Cosdon Head* (Birmingham Museum and Art Gallery) of 1949. Hepworth's public profile rose when she was commissioned to design sculptures for the new Waterloo Bridge, London (never executed) in 1947, and to show at the Venice Biennale in 1950. This was immediately followed by two important commissions for the Festival of Britain in 1951: *Contrapuntal Forms* was commissioned by the Arts Council and consists of two over-life-size figures carved in blue Irish limestone, symbolizing the spirit of discovery; *Turning Forms*, in reinforced concrete, painted white, was a direct contract from the festival authorities. An abstract sculpture, it was placed by the Thames-side Restaurant, designed by another distinguished woman, Jane Drew, of the architectural firm Fry, Drew & Partners. In 1953 the Arts Council presented *Contrapuntal Forms* to the new town of Harlow, in Essex; *Turning Forms* is sited at Marlborough School, St Albans.

Contrapuntal Forms was much the largest sculpture that Hepworth had made to date. It was possible only because in 1949 she had purchased Trewyn Studio, in the centre of St Ives, where she lived permanently from 1950 until her death in 1975. She now had a garden in which to work and display her sculptures, as well as simple living and working accommodation on two floors. From the late 1950s three other major commissions followed in quick succession. *Meridian* was a large, transparent, abstract sculpture made for the now demolished office block State House, in High Holborn, in 1958 (*Meridian* is now owned by the Pepsi Cola Corporation and sited in the sculpture garden of their New York headquarters). *Winged Figure* (1962) was an enlargement of a sculpture of 1957 made from sheet aluminium and commissioned by the John Lewis Partnership for their Oxford Street flagship store. *Single Form* (1961–4), an abstract bronze sculpture twenty feet high and Hepworth's largest work, stands in the United Nations Plaza in New York. Hepworth was a friend of the United Nations secretary general Dag Hammarskjöld, who admired and collected her work. On his tragic death in 1961 the sculpture was commissioned as his memorial.

Hepworth had begun to work in bronze and other metals in 1956. She had just completed a group of monumental carvings using a warm-coloured African wood, guarea: *Corinthos* (1954–5; Tate collection), *Curved Form (Delphi)* (1955; Ulster Museum, Belfast), and *Oval Sculpture (Delos)* (1955; National Museum and Gallery of Wales, Cardiff). Up to this date she had worked almost exclusively on wood and stone carvings, making unique pieces with no more than a single assistant to help at certain times. The move to bronze was a liberating experience; it allowed her to invent a new vocabulary of sculptural forms, more open and transparent than hitherto. This new language was anticipated by a group of very free, abstract paintings and drawings made in 1957. Using bronze as a material allowed Hepworth to cast small editions of her work, with between three and nine copies of each sculpture. This helped her to meet the now considerable international demand for her work, particularly from the United States.

Though Hepworth's marriage to Ben Nicholson was dissolved in 1951 he remained in St Ives until 1958, and the mutually beneficial influence of painter and sculptor on each other's work persisted. They gradually regained their international reputation after the hiatus of the Second World War and its aftermath. Hepworth had important retrospective exhibitions at the Whitechapel Art Gallery in 1954 and 1962, at the São Paulo bienal, Brazil, in 1959 (where she was awarded the grand prix), and at the Tate Gallery in 1968. She exhibited regularly in London, New York, and Zürich, and was shown throughout Europe and the United States, in Japan, and in Australia.

A lover of poetry, dance, theatre, and music, Hepworth made illustrations for Kathleen Raine's first book of poems, *Stone and Flower*, in 1943; sets and costumes for Michel Saint-Denis's production of Sophocles' *Electra* at the Old Vic in 1951 with Peggy Ashcroft; and sets and costumes for the first performance of Michael Tippett's opera *The Midsummer Marriage* at the Royal Opera House, Covent Garden, in 1955. She might have undertaken more work of this kind had she not lived in the relative isolation of St Ives, totally dedicated to sculpture and drawing. It was for this reason that she travelled little, and then mainly to attend the openings of her exhibitions in New York, Paris, Zürich, and Copenhagen. Her only true holidays were short trips to the Isles of Scilly, from which she drew much inspiration for the remainder of her life. She returned to Italy only for the biennale in 1950. She retained a lively interest in scientific matters, and was a lifelong friend of Lord (Solly) Zuckerman and Professor J. D. Bernal. Her political views were radical, and she supported the Labour Party and knew some of its leading members.

Later years Hepworth won widespread public recognition in the last years of her life, when she was regarded as the world's greatest woman sculptor. In her obituary in *The Guardian* she was described as 'probably the most significant woman artist in the history of art to this day'. No militant feminist herself, she asked simply to be treated as a sculptor (never a sculptress), irrespective of sex. She was appointed CBE in 1958 and DBE in 1965. Honorary degrees were awarded to her by the universities of Birmingham (1960), Leeds (1961), Exeter (1966), Oxford (1968), London (1970), and Manchester (1971), and by the Royal College of Art (1964), where she was also senior fellow (1970). She was made a bard of Cornwall in 1968, and in 1973 an honorary member of the American Academy of Arts and Letters. She served as a trustee of the Tate Gallery from 1965 until 1972.

Hepworth was small and intense in appearance, deeply reserved in character. It was always surprising that an apparently frail woman could undertake such demanding physical work but she had great toughness and integrity. She remained proud of her Yorkshire roots, though devoted to St Ives and the west Cornish landscape that provided her with enduring inspiration. In the last years of her life she took no more commissions and preferred to follow her own path. She had long been interested in two-part sculptures, representing in abstract language the relationship of one person to another, and now was increasingly occupied with multi-part sculptures, in both bronze and marble. She could afford to make large bronze sculptures, such as the nine-part *Family of Man* (1970; a set is in the Yorkshire Sculpture Park, near Wakefield) and the six-part *Conversation with Magic Stones* (1973; casts in the Scottish National Gallery of Modern Art, Edinburgh, and the Hepworth Museum, St Ives). The marble carvings *Assembly of Sea Forms* (1972; Norton Simon Art Foundation, Pasadena, California), and her final artistic statement, *Fallen Images* (1973–5; Hepworth Museum, St Ives), offer a similar paradigm for man's role in society and relationship to nature—issues that concerned Hepworth throughout her entire career. Nor was she afraid to surprise her admirers; the *Construction (Crucifixion)* in bronze (1963; there is a cast in the close of Winchester Cathedral) signalled a wish for a more constructivist sculpture, as well as a return to the high-church Anglican faith of her childhood.

Barbara Hepworth died in a fire in her studio at St Ives on 20 May 1975 after suffering serious illness for some years. She was buried in Longstone cemetery in St Ives. As she herself had hoped Trewyn Studio, where she had lived and worked from 1949, was opened to the public by her family in 1976; it was presented to the nation by her family and executors in 1980, together with a representative collection of her work. It is now an outstation of the Tate Gallery, which also has a very considerable Hepworth collection. Hepworth's work is represented in more than a hundred public collections throughout the world, with particularly fine work in the Leeds and Wakefield city art galleries; in the Scottish National Gallery of Modern Art, Edinburgh; in the Art Gallery of Ontario, Toronto; and in the Rijksmuseum Kröller-Müller, at Otterlo, in the Netherlands. ALAN BOWNESS

Sources personal knowledge (2004) · J. P. Hodin and A. Bowness, *Barbara Hepworth* (1961) · A. Bowness, *The complete sculpture of Barbara Hepworth, 1960–69* (1971) · B. Hepworth, *A pictorial autobiography* (1970); 2nd edn (1978) · H. Read, *Barbara Hepworth* (1952) · A. M. Hammacher, *Barbara Hepworth* (1968); 2nd edn (1987) · M. Gardiner, *Barbara Hepworth* (1982) · S. Festing, *Barbara Hepworth* (1995) · P. Curtis and A. G. Wilkinson, *Barbara Hepworth: a retrospective* (1994) · D. Thistlewood, ed., *Barbara Hepworth reconsidered* (1996) · P. Curtis, *Barbara Hepworth* (1998) · M. Gale and C. Stephens, *Barbara Hepworth: works in the Tate Gallery collection and the Barbara Hepworth Museum, St Ives* (1999) · CGPLA Eng. & Wales (1975)
Archives priv. coll., family MSS · Tate collection, corresp. and MSS · Tate collection, MSS · Tate collection, sculpture notebooks | Tate collection, letters to Margot Eates and E. H. Ramsden · Tate collection, corresp. with Curt Valentin [copies] · Tate collection, corresp. with Sir John Summerson, etc. · U. Sussex, corresp. and MSS · V&A, questionnaire completed for Kineton Parkes | FILM BFI · Tate collection | SOUND BL NSA · Tate collection
Likenesses B. Nicholson, oils, 1933, NPG · B. Hepworth, self-portrait, oil and pencil, 1950, NPG [see illus.] · photographs, Hult. Arch.
Wealth at death £2,970,049: probate, 1975

Cecil Milton Hepworth (1874–1953), by unknown photographer, c.1900

Hepworth, Cecil Milton [formerly Herbert Milton] (1874–1953), film-maker, was born Herbert Milton Hepworth on 19 March 1874 at 12 Beaufort Gardens, Lewisham, London, one of three children of Thomas Craddock Hepworth (1834–1905), hospital secretary, and his wife, Sarah Margaret Stevens. Thomas Hepworth provided his son with an ideal background as he was an eminent late Victorian magic lanternist, who published a number of popular and successful books on the subject. His publications included *The Book of the Lantern* (1888). As a boy, Cecil (as he was always known) accompanied his father on his lantern tours and learned how to operate the biunial lantern, a double-lensed projector designed to produce a 'dissolving view'. In 1896, at the age of twenty-two, Hepworth was very aware of the arrival of film for commercial use in theatres and music-halls but, as his articles in the *Amateur Photographer* reveal, he was sceptical of the new medium's ability to produce a flicker-free image that could rival the beauty and colour of the lantern image. Within a year these doubts were replaced by real enthusiasm for the moving image, a fact demonstrated by his first book, *Animated photography: the ABC of the cinematograph, a simple and thorough guide to the projection of living photographs, with notes on the production of cinematograph negatives* (1897). It was the first on the subject to be published in England. The rest of Hepworth's life would be involved with the moving image.

For the next two years, 1898 and 1899, Hepworth was employed as a film processor and camera operator by the Warwick Trading Company in London, then the largest film production company in the country. Here he designed and patented the first film processing machine (patent no. 13315, 1898). All future machines designed for this purpose would descend from Hepworth's invention. Dismissal from Warwick led Hepworth and his cousin Monty Wicks to acquire a house on Hurst Grove in Walton-on-Thames in 1899. For almost twenty-five years this site would be the home of the Hepworth Manufacturing Company. On 11 February 1902 Hepworth married Margaret Hope (b. 1873/4), daughter of Andrew McGuffie, a manufacturer.

At Walton films were first made out of doors and then processed within the detached house which served as the laboratory. By 1905 a purpose-built glass house studio with electric-arc lighting was erected. The 1903 Hepworth catalogue marked the company's rapid rise and expressed Hepworth's commercial understanding of the popular and the topical. It listed film subjects under such headings as 'Animated portraits' (the king, the queen, Lord Kitchener), 'Comics' (facial expressions, jokes on policemen, motor cars), 'Pageants', 'Processions', 'Railway scenes', 'Military subjects', and 'Street Scenes'. Hepworth was now a leader of this new entertainment industry.

In 1905, under the direction of Lewin Fitzhamon, the most famous Hepworth film was made, *Rescued by Rover*. It was Hepworth's first international success. He described it as:

> a particularly family affair. My wife wrote the story, my baby—eight months old—was the heroine, my dog the hero, my wife the bereaved mother and myself the harassed father … we had to make it all over again a second time and then even a third, because we wore out the negative in the making of the four hundred prints to satisfy the demand. (Hepworth, *Came the Dawn*, 66–7)

The total cost of the first production was £7 13s. 9d. The film moved fluently from studio shots to locations and was an important example of an effective early film rescue narrative. Over the next fifteen years the Hepworth

Company's films evolved from short comedies and dramas of only a few minutes in length to multi-reel works of over one hour. The company chose a path that reflected a particularly English sense of pictorialism, theatricality, and the national literary heritage. It made *Hamlet* (1913) in Devon and Walton, with Forbes-Robertson as the prince, as well as adaptations of *Oliver Twist* (1912) and *David Copperfield* (1913). Underpinning this work was the Hepworth Stock Company, which operated along the lines of a traditional theatre company. Its leading players, including Alma Taylor, Chrissie White, and Henry Edwards, would become the first British movie stars.

Hepworth's sense of his company's direction after the First World War was very clear. 'I was to make English pictures, with all the English countryside for background and with English atmosphere and English idiom throughout' (*Came the Dawn*, 144). However, in a market now dominated by new American work this strategy was not successful. Hepworth's films began to lose their appeal. The collapse of his company in 1924, the direct result of an under-subscribed share issue, was devastating and made only the more painful by the necessary sale of the company's most important asset—its original film negatives. Tragically, this invaluable film heritage of over 2000 works of fiction and non-fiction was not preserved, but melted down for 'dope' for aeroplane wings (ibid., 196). Over the next twenty years Hepworth found some employment at the national screen service making film trailers. Official recognition of his significant place in British film history finally came with the fiftieth anniversary of cinema in 1946. Hepworth became an honorary fellow of the Royal Photographic Society, the British Kinematographic Society, and the British Film Academy, and was chairman of the British Film Institute's history committee. He wrote his second book, *Came the Dawn: Memories of a Film Pioneer* (1951), in these last years. Accompanied by his own illustrations, it is a charming anecdotal account. Hepworth died at his home at 211 Eastcote Road, Ruislip, on 9 February 1953, survived by his daughter Valerie.   FRANK GRAY

Sources C. Hepworth, *Animated photography: the ABC of the cinematograph* (1897) • C. Hepworth, *Came the dawn: memories of a film pioneer* (1951) • T. C. Hepworth, *The book of the lantern: being a practical guide to the working of the optical (or magic) lantern* (1888) • J. Barnes, *The rise of the cinema in Great Britain: Jubilee year, 1897* (1983), vol. 2 of *The beginnings of the cinema in England, 1894–1901* • R. Low, *The history of the British film*, 7 vols. (1948–85) • *CGPLA Eng. & Wales* (1953) • b. cert. • d. cert. • m. cert.
Archives BFI • Elmbridge Museum, Weybridge, Surrey | FILM BFI NFTVA, 'Came the dawn', 1985
Likenesses photograph, c.1900, Elmbridge Museum, Weybridge [*see illus.*] • photograph, repro. in Barnes, *The rise of the cinema*, 173 • photograph, repro. in C. Hepworth, *Came the dawn* [frontispiece]
Wealth at death £2397 4s. 10d.: probate, 7 Aug 1953, *CGPLA Eng. & Wales*

Hepworth, Joseph (1834–1911), clothing manufacturer and retailer, was born on 12 May 1834 at Lindley, Huddersfield, the son of George Hepworth, shoemaker. He left school and entered the textile trade at the age of ten, working at Joseph Walker's woollen mill in Lindley as a half-timer, converting to full-time work two years later. In 1850 he was engaged as a teasel setter in George Walker's Wellington mill, a job that disappeared in 1860 as the Walkers went out of business. He then acquired an overlooker's position in another local mill, before spending twelve arduous months as a travelling salesman for a woollen manufacturer. In 1855 he married Sarah Rhodes; they had three sons and four daughters.

Hepworth's career assumed a new and significant direction in 1864 as he and James Rhodes, his wife's brother, established a small woollen drapers' business in Briggate in central Leeds. The partners were also practical tailors, owning nine sewing machines, and their business included the making-up of garments for the wholesale clothing trade. Small though the enterprise was, it provided the basis on which after twelve months both men, separately, moved into wholesale clothing manufacture. They both achieved long term success, but Hepworth's progress was particularly impressive.

In 1865, in the context of the early period of expansion of the Leeds clothing industry, Hepworth's first sole tailoring enterprise, located in Bishopsgate Street, employed twelve people. Several changes of premises accompanied regular and sound expansion through the 1870s. By 1881 Hepworth's Wellington Street factory employed 500 and, as Joseph was joined by his son Norris, a strategic change was made to the business, which became a retail as well as a manufacturing enterprise. The Hepworths, wishing to distance themselves from the financial vagaries of those retailers with whom they conducted business, decided to sell their clothes direct to the public. While this was a significant departure from the normal practices of the Leeds trade, it was not only a striking and immediate success, but it became a practice developed by other clothing manufacturers in the town and elsewhere. Although Hepworth is typically credited with the idea, which is seen as his particular contribution to the Leeds industry, William Blackburn, also a prominent Leeds clothing manufacturer, simultaneously, and quite possibly independently, set up shops for the sale of his factory manufactured goods.

The 1880s saw the most expansive period in the history of the Leeds clothing industry, the largest proportion of which was assigned to the making of men's tailored garments, to which Hepworth made a significant contribution. It was common practice among Leeds wholesale clothiers for the factories to make trousers and vests while subcontracting to Jewish workshops the making of coats and jackets. Hepworth, however, deviated from this pattern and rarely engaged the services of Jewish subcontractors. The firm also depended more heavily than many Leeds clothing manufacturers on the export trade. By the end of the decade Joseph Hepworth & Son employed 2000 operatives producing garments for the company's 107 retail outlets, and for the South African and Australian export markets where Hepworth's subsidiary plants were located. By this stage Hepworth was sufficiently wealthy to purchase the grand Headingley House, vacated by the

Marshall family in 1888. The firm continued to add to productive and retailing capacity. The conversion to private company status in 1891, with a capital of £360,000, coincided with the erection of a new factory in Claypit Lane. By 1907, when a further factory was added, and with 145 shops, Joseph Hepworth & Son had become one of the largest concerns in the clothing industry. Ten years later with 160 retail outlets, it headed the list of British companies engaged in the sale of men's clothing and headwear.

Joseph Hepworth was a paternalistic employer, introducing paid holiday entitlement, an eight-hour day, and a clean working environment before these became standard. His political and religious activities, however, gradually overshadowed his work for the company. Hepworth became a Liberal councillor in 1888, and alderman and magistrate in 1892; and his work for party and community was rewarded by his appointment as lord mayor in 1906. During this year his nonconformist leanings and teetotalism influenced civic life, as he banned alcohol from all municipal functions. As a leading member of the Methodist New Connexion he provided financial support for the United Methodist church founded in 1907. The value he placed on technical education was reflected in his involvement in the Leeds Mechanics' Institute, the Yorkshire College, and as governor of Leeds University.

Joseph Hepworth died at Comber House, 19 Park Drive, Harrogate, on 17 October 1911, survived by his wife. The business was initially carried on by Norris who himself died in 1914, and thereafter by later generations of the family.   KATRINA HONEYMAN

Sources J. Thomas, *A history of the Leeds clothing industry* (1952) · W. Yorks. AS, Leeds, Joseph Hepworth business records · A. J. Kershen, *Uniting the tailors: trade unionism among the tailoring workers of London and Leeds, 1870–1939* (1995) · D. Fraser, ed., *A history of modern Leeds* (1980) · M. F. Ward, 'Industrial development and location in Leeds north of the River Aire, 1775–1914', PhD diss., U. Leeds, 1972 · *Menswear* (10 Nov 1906) · *Menswear* (21 Oct 1911) · *Yorkshire Evening Post* (17 Oct 1911) · *Menswear* (27 April 1918) · *Menswear* (17 March 1928) · E. P. Hennock, *Fit and proper persons: ideal and reality in nineteenth-century urban government* (1973) · *CGPLA Eng. & Wales* (1911) · d. cert. · E. J. Connell, 'Hepworth, Joseph', *DBB*

Wealth at death £168,218 2s. 10d.: probate, 22 Dec 1911, *CGPLA Eng. & Wales*

Herapath, John (1790–1868), mathematical physicist and journalist, was born on 30 May 1790 at Bristol, the son of a maltster. He initially took up his father's trade, but later began teaching mathematics, first at Knowle Hill, Bristol, then from 1820 at Cranford, Middlesex, until 1832 when he moved to London. About 1836 he became part owner and manager of the *Railway Magazine*, later fully owned. Under his ownership this journal was variously entitled: *The Railway Magazine, and Annals of Science*, *The Railway Magazine and Commercial Journal*, and *Herapath's Railway Journal*. He was married in 1815 and had at least eleven children. His first cousin, William Herapath, became an eminent chemist.

In his own day Herapath was known for his journalism and for the controversy surrounding his scientific work, but the details of that work were not well known. For later generations his main claim to attention lay in those details, from which he emerges as an early advocate of the kinetic theory of gases.

Largely self-taught, Herapath had acquired a knowledge of French and of Newton, coupled with an enthusiasm for French mathematical physics. In his early twenties he observed some discrepancies between observed and calculated motions of the moon, and came to suspect that Newton's law of gravitation was in need of minor correction, perhaps to accommodate temperature differences. This led him to investigate the suspected cause of gravity—density variations in an ethereal fluid filling all of space; this in turn suggested exploring the relationship between temperature, density, and pressure in gases generally.

Following Newton's lead Herapath's contemporaries envisaged gases as static arrays of molecules, mutually repelling each other. The pressure a gas exerted on its container was generated by this repulsion. Herapath proposed something quite different, viewing gases kinetically, as 'composed of a number of very minute, perfectly hard particles … flying about in all directions' which 'by their collisions on each other and the sides of the containing vessel, maintain a constant pressure against the sides, as if endeavouring to press them outwards' (*Mathematical Physics*, 1.237). From this hypothesis he sought to infer links between pressure, density, and temperature, suggesting for instance that the pressure of a gas was proportional to the product of its density and the square of its temperature. Unsure whether his work was original he published this result, without proof, in the *Annals of Philosophy* of 1816.

Herapath's hypothesis was not entirely new: a similar view of gases had been explored by Daniel Bernoulli a century earlier. Herapath's model differs from modern kinetic theory for it links temperature to the momentum (rather than energy) of the gas particles, and thus leads to unusual predictions about the temperatures achieved in mixtures, which, he claimed, were supported by experiment. It is also not clear if he envisaged his particles as wandering through the gas: as Mendoza observes, they may well have been vibrating in a static array.

In mid-1820 Herapath submitted a fuller account of his theory to the Royal Society for consideration for the *Philosophical Transactions*. This discussion not only derived the temperature–density–pressure relationship announced in 1816, but applied the theory to a variety of other phenomena, such as latent heat, sound propagation, and the diffusion of gases. After consulting Humphry Davy, soon to be president of the society, and others, Davies Gilbert, to whom the paper had originally been submitted, rejected it, and thus precipitated a prolonged controversy between Herapath and the Royal Society. Much offended Herapath published his paper (with a sequel, plus some protesting correspondence) in the 1821 *Annals of Philosophy*, and later (1826–8) sent a series of complaints to *The Times*, challenging mathematicians to prove some theorems he announced. His polemics against the Royal Society attracted some attention, and he believed (almost certainly falsely) that this forced Davy's resignation. The argument was later carried on in his own journal.

Our records of this controversy reach us mainly through Herapath himself, yet we can readily understand why his work was rejected: the discussion is not clear and makes dubious assumptions (for example, the perfectly hard, yet perfectly elastic, atoms rebound from each other instantaneously); it is set out deductively rather than inductively; it is connected with experiment only indirectly and inconclusively; finally it presents itself as speculation on a cosmic scale, rather than as careful analysis of a few properties of gases. Readers of *Annals* also objected to the theory, and a few criticisms of it were published, together with replies (and other papers) by Herapath.

By the mid-1840s, however, new experimental evidence was appearing, giving additional support to Herapath's speculations, notably Regnault's measurements of the pressure of hydrogen, Graham's experiments on gas diffusion, and Joule's measurements of the thermal effects of gaseous expansion. Herapath was able to cite this new evidence in a further reworking of the theory, published at length in two volumes as *Mathematical Physics* in 1847 (a projected third volume never appeared). This book reproduced his estimation of the velocity of the particles in a gas (said to be the first known evaluation of this parameter) together with an important discussion of the speed of sound in air, both following his 1832 report to the British Association, which was recorded in his own magazine.

Herapath's *Mathematical Physics* was read by Joule, who was keen to find allies for his approach to the theory of heat. Joule was strongly committed to the idea that heat was caused by microscopic motions, and had been inclined to follow Davy in envisaging these as rotations; now, however, he decided to adopt Herapath's rectilinear model (as being simpler) and also followed him in estimating the particle velocity. Though Joule was significantly influenced by Herapath, it seems that others involved in developing the kinetic theory, who also adopted a rectilinear model, such as Clausius, Krönig, and Maxwell, were not influenced in this preference by Herapath—though he indeed sought to claim priority over the idea in a letter of 1860 to *The Athenaeum*.

About 1827 Herapath had dealings with Henry Brougham, for whom he was to write a book on the calculus. The proposal involved a possible appointment as professor of mathematics at University College, London, but the two fell out, and the project collapsed.

In addition to the works mentioned above Herapath also published a number of memoirs in the *Philosophical Magazine*, including some translations of French works, an 1829 pamphlet on the advantages of steam transport, various notes in the *Mechanics Magazine*, and many contributions to his own journal.

Herapath's journalism was far more successful than his scientific work, though still accompanied by vigorous public dispute and lawsuits. His magazine generally involved itself with the commercial side of the thriving new industry, and was also often used to continue his

scientific publications. Many of his articles took up the important and none too easy task of applying relatively abstract scientific theory to the day-to-day tasks of the engineer. For example, he attempted to use his kinetic theory to calculate the way air resistance changes with speed, since the empirical data on this question was very confusing. He withdrew from active involvement in publishing some years before his death, and his son Edwin took over the magazine, which survived well into the twentieth century.

Herapath died at Catford Bridge, Lewisham, London, on 24 February 1868. He was survived by his wife.

KEITH HUTCHISON

Sources *Herapath's Railway Journal*, 30 (1868), 234, 275–8, 309 · S. Brush, 'Herapath'. *The kind of motion we call heat: a history of the kinetic theory of gases in the 19th century*, 2 vols. (1976) · J. Herapath, *Mathematical physics and selected papers*, ed. S. Brush (1972) [with introductory essay and bibliography] · E. Mendoza, 'The surprising history of the kinetic theory of gases', *Memoirs of the Literary and Philosophical Society of Manchester*, 105 (1962–3), 15–28 · G. R. Talbot and A. J. Pacey, 'Some early kinetic theories of gases: Herapath and his predecessors', *British Journal for the History of Science*, 3 (1966–7), 133–49 · S. Brush, 'The Royal Society's first rejection of the kinetic theory of gases (1821), John Herapath versus Humphry Davy', *Notes and Records of the Royal Society*, 18 (1963), 161–80 · E. Mendoza, 'A critical examination of Herapath's dynamical theory of gases', *British Journal for the History of Science*, 8 (1975), 155–65 · GM, 4th ser., 5 (1868), 544–5 · S. G. Brush, 'The development of the kinetic theory of gases: I. Herapath', *Annals of Science*, 13 (1957), 188–98 · C. Lee, 'Herapath's *Railway Magazine*', *Railway Gazette* (17 Sept 1943), 278 · S. Mason, 'Herapath's *Railway Magazine*', *Railway Gazette*, 79 (10 Sept 1943), 250 · E. Mendoza, 'A sketch for a history of the kinetic theory of gases', *Physics Today*, 14 (March 1961), 36–9 · *The Times* (26 Feb 1868), 1 · *The Times* (27 Feb 1868), 1, 10 · C. Truesdell, 'Early kinetic theories of gases', *Essays in the history of mechanics* (1968), 272–304 **Archives** RS · Stanford University, California, Hopkins railway library | RS, corresp. with Sir John Herschel **Likenesses** portrait, repro. in Mendoza, 'The surprising history of the kinetic theory of gases', facing p. 18 **Wealth at death** under £16,000: probate, 14 March 1868, CGPLA Eng. & Wales

Herapath, William (1796–1868), analytical chemist, was born on 26 May 1796 in Bristol, the son of William Herapath (*d. c.*1815), who conducted an extensive business as maltster and brewer in St Philip's out-parish. The younger Herapath exhibited an early interest in science and the mechanical arts, and was known in his family as 'the little philosopher'. He received his formal education at a school in Bristol kept by a Mr Pocock, but was otherwise largely self-taught. At the age of fourteen he took up the study of chemistry, and was led by necessity to construct much of his own apparatus. On leaving school in 1812 he entered the Bristol City Bank, where he worked for three years, pursuing scientific studies in his leisure time. After his father's death in an accident Herapath took over the running of the business, initially in partnership with his cousin John *Herapath (1790–1868), who soon left to open a mathematical academy. Herapath proceeded to devote all of his leisure time to the study of chemistry and, increasingly, toxicology, until he developed so great a reputation that he began to be consulted as a professional analyst. In 1834 he gave up the malt trade completely in order to devote himself to his career as a chemist.

As a result of his local prominence as an analyst, Herapath was retained by the prosecution at the 1835 trial of Mary Ann Burdock in Bristol, who was accused of having poisoned her lodger, Clara Ann Smith, over a year earlier. Herapath exhumed the body of the victim, which had been buried for fourteen months, and successfully demonstrated the presence of arsenic in it. Burdock was convicted. This was the first time that exhumation for the purpose of chemical analysis had been carried out in England; as a result, Herapath's reputation grew to the extent that he was frequently called upon to give evidence in criminal and civil cases. The most notorious of these was the trial of William Palmer in 1856, when Herapath testified unsuccessfully for the defence, in opposition to Alfred Swaine Taylor (1806–1880), the most famous English forensic toxicologist of the day.

Herapath was married; his wife's name is not known. He was one of the founders of the Bristol medical school, which opened in 1832 and in which he lectured on chemistry and toxicology until 1867. He was an original member of the Chemical Society of London, of which he became a fellow, but published only occasionally, mainly on arsenical poisons and elemental analyses. He contributed his 'Instructions for the prevention and cure of cholera' to Clifton Cleve's *Hints on Domestic Sanitation* (1848), and an analysis of the spa waters for *The Hand Book for Visitors to the Bristol and Clifton Hotwells* (1853).

In addition to his professional work as a chemist, Herapath, who lived throughout his life in Bristol, was active in public office. As a young man he was an ardent radical, and was president of the Bristol Political Union at the time of the Reform Bill of 1832. During the riots of October 1831 he was appointed under-sheriff and worked to quell the disturbances. After the passing of the Municipal Reform Act he was elected to the town council, and eventually became a justice of the peace. In later years his politics became less liberal, and he lost his seat on the council. At the time of his death he was the senior magistrate for Bristol. He died at his home, Manor House, in Old Park, Bristol, on 13 February 1868 from complications arising from diabetes.

Two of Herapath's sons became chemists. The youngest, Thornton John Herapath (1830–1858), published more than sixty papers before his death in a drowning accident. The eldest, **William Bird Herapath** (1820–1868), physician and chemist, was born on 28 February 1820 in Bristol, and acted as laboratory assistant to his father before studying at the Bristol medical school and the London Hospital. He took his MB degree at London University in 1844, and graduated MD in 1851; he was elected FRS in 1859. His medical practice became extensive, but he devoted much of his time to chemical and other scientific studies. He was known chiefly for his discovery of the optical properties of the crystals of iodoquinine sulphate (called herapathite), which he suggested be used as artificial tourmalines (*Philosophical Magazine*, 1852). His broad

range of interests was indicative of his belief that chemistry, medicine, and medical research should be closely allied, a view expressed in his *On Chemistry in its Relations to Medicine and its Collateral Sciences* (1863). He died at his home, 32 Old Market Street, Bristol, on 12 October 1868 from jaundice, leaving a widow, Lucy, and six children.

K. D. WATSON

Sources J. F. Waller, ed., *The imperial dictionary of universal biography*, 3 vols. (1857–63) · C. Knight, ed., *The English cyclopaedia: biography*, 6 vols. (1856–8) [suppl. (1872)] · *JCS*, 21 (1868), xxiv–v · *JCS*, 22 (1869), vi–vii [obit. of William Bird Herapath] · *Quarterly Journal of the Chemical Society*, 12 (1860), 171–2 · J. Latimer, *The annals of Bristol, 1600–1900*, 5 (1906) · A. Prichard, *The early history of the British Medical School* (1892) · M. R. Neve, 'Natural philosophy, medicine and the culture of science in provincial England', PhD diss., U. Lond., 1984 · *Chemical News* (21 Feb 1868), 97 · *Chemical News* (30 Oct 1868), 213 · *Report of the British Association for the Advancement of Science* (1836) · C. K. Deischer, 'Herapath, William Bird', *DSB* · *The Times* (15 Oct 1868), 5 · Boase, *Mod. Eng. biog.* [William Bird Herapath] · census returns, 1881

Archives CUL, Stokes MSS · JRL, Moulton collection · University of Bristol, British Medical School records

Likenesses pencil sketch, 1840, University of Bristol · photograph, *c*.1860, repro. in Latimer, *Annals of Bristol*, vol. 5

Wealth at death under £4000: resworn administration, 21 Dec 1868, *CGPLA Eng. & Wales*

Herapath, William Bird (1820–1868). *See under* Herapath, William (1796–1868).

Heraud, John Abraham (1799–1887), writer, was born on 5 July 1799 in Holborn, London, the son of James Abraham Heraud (*d.* 1846), a law stationer of Carey Street, Lincoln's Inn Fields (later 25 Bell Yard, Temple Bar), and his wife, Jane (*d.* 1850), daughter of John and Elizabeth Hicks. His father, of Huguenot descent, compiled handbooks on the stamp laws in 1798, 1801, and 1824. Privately educated and originally earmarked for business, Heraud began writing for the journal market, in which his knowledge of German, then a rare accomplishment, gave him an advantage. An early interest was the philosophy of Schelling, which he attempted to popularize in Britain, although his contributions to the weightier journals began only in 1827, with the *Quarterly*. In 1820 his first poems appeared: *Tottenham*, after the district where he lived, and *Legends of St Loy*, with other poems. On 15 May 1823 at old Lambeth church Heraud married Ann Elizabeth (*d.* 1867), daughter of Henry Baddams.

Heraud had grand and lofty aims in poetry. Especially ambitious were the epics *The Descent into Hell* (1830, expanded 1835) and *The Judgement of the Flood* (1834) in twelve books. He was keen to cultivate literary luminaries in the hope of benefiting from their critical acumen, in which respect his assistant editorship on the newly founded *Fraser's Magazine*, from 1830 to 1833, was useful. Wordsworth was approached and tactfully described the 1830 poem as 'vigorous', if 'in some places diffuse, [and] in others somewhat rugged, from the originality of your mind' (*Letters of the Wordsworth Family*, 2.439); but he refused the detailed critique Heraud sought. Heraud's relationship with Carlyle was even more importunate, yet he was tolerated for his irrepressible good humour. Of his intellect, despite his idolization of Coleridgean metaphysics, Carlyle had a low opinion. To Jane Welsh Carlyle he characterized Heraud in 1831 as 'the most insignificant *haddock* in nature; a dirty greasy Cockney apprentice; altogether empty and non-extant except for one or two metaphysical quibbles' (*Collected Letters*, 5.378). Through sheer persistence, Heraud became a frequent visitor to the Carlyle household over more than a decade, yet Carlyle's assessment of him, although mellowed by time, never really changed. On enquiry from Emerson (who was intrigued by Heraud's reviews), he described him in 1840 as:

> a loquacious scribacious little man, of middle age, of parboiled greasy aspect … chiefly remarkable as being still with his entirely enormous vanity and very small stock of faculty,—out of Bedlam. He picked up a notion or two from Coleridge many years ago; and has ever since been rattling them in his head, like peas in an empty bladder. (ibid., 12.92–3)

William Charles Macready, who was unremittingly pestered in the mid 1830s for judgements on what he privately regarded as Heraud's unactable tragedies, saw only the inflated vanity.

Heraud wrote essays on, among other topics, poetic genius (1837) and the profession of education (1839) and he even edited a book of Mediterranean voyages (1837); but his main effort went into editing journals and to reviewing, including the works of Byron, Shelley, Landor, Southey, Wordsworth (whom he noticed twice), and Sheridan Knowles. Of special note is his unsigned review of Coleridge's *Aids to Reflection* (1832), which was selected for reprinting in *Coleridge: the Critical Heritage* (1970). In 1838 he was founder editor of *The Sunbeam*, a weekly devoted to 'polite literature and music' (which lasted ninety-two issues), and from 1839 to 1842 he edited the *Monthly Magazine*, to which he also contributed. Subsequently he was associated with (perhaps edited) the *Christian's Monthly Magazine and Universal Review*, part religious, part literary, published from 1844 to 1846. In 1843 he began contributing to *The Athenaeum*, later becoming its theatre critic; and from 1849 he occupied the same post at the *Illustrated London News*, where he remained until his retirement about 1873. He built up a considerable theatrical knowledge, which he drew on to edit Henry Butler's *Theatrical Directory* (1860 and thereafter). But he was on shakier ground with *Shakspere: his Inner Life as Intimated in his Works* (1865).

Heraud's public career as a playwright was as unspectacular as it was short, being effectively confined to the late 1850s (although the *Era Almanack* for 1868 still described him as an active dramatist). There were at least two early unacted tragedies: *The Death of Nero* (rejected in 1836 by Macready as 'an impossible subject' (*Diaries*, 1.340), and not printed) and *The Roman Brother* (2nd edn, 1840). A five-act dramatic poem *Salvator* (privately circulated, 1845) included remarks on the parlous state of the theatre. His verse tragedy *Videna*, 'a legend of Early Britain', was staged with modest success in 1854; two later plays, *Wife or No Wife* (1855) and *Medea in Corinth* (1857), were performed but not printed.

If Heraud's poetry was too elevated in sentiment for its own good and his dramas lacked theatricality, as critic he was a ubiquitous presence in the world of Victorian letters. Small in stature, gregarious, and opinionated, he was invariably more impressive on paper than in person or conversation. He craved other people's regard but seemed not to notice when they were being rude to him. In spite of himself Carlyle had a soft spot for Heraud, even in his vaingloriousness, and Heraud seems to have had similar effects on others, including John Stuart Mill, who commented that he might be excused his full-flight interpretations of the universe when one discovered that he could not pronounce his aitches.

By nomination of Gladstone (with whom he had been in intermittent correspondence since 1858), Heraud was made a brother of the Charterhouse, London, on 21 July 1873, and continued writing verse almost up to his death there on 20 April 1887. He was survived by his two children: Claudius William (of Woodford, Essex) and Edith, an actress, who nursed him in his final illness, and published a volume of memoirs in 1898.

JOHN RUSSELL STEPHENS

Sources *The Athenaeum* (23 April 1887), 554 · *The Athenaeum* (30 April 1887), 577 · *ILN* (30 April 1887) · *DNB* · private information (1891) [C. R. Heraud] · *The collected letters of Thomas and Jane Welsh Carlyle*, ed. C. R. Sanders, K. J. Fielding, and others, [30 vols.] (1970–) · *Letters of the Wordsworth family from 1787 to 1855*, ed. W. Knight, 3 vols. (1907) · *The diaries of William Charles Macready, 1833–1851*, ed. W. Toynbee, 2 vols. (1912) · A. Nicoll, *Early nineteenth century drama, 1800–1850*, 2nd edn (1955), vol. 4 of *A history of English drama, 1660–1900* (1952–9) · E. Heraud, *Memoirs of John A. Heraud* (1898) · *Wellesley index* · J. R. de J. Jackson, ed., *Coleridge: the critical heritage* (1970), 585–606 · *Era Almanack and Annual* (1868) · *IGI*

Archives BL, letters, as sponsor, to Royal Literary Fund, in loan no. 96 | BL, publisher's agreement between John A. Heraud and Henry Colburn and Richard Bentley, Add. MS 46611, fol. 209 · NL Scot., letters to William Blackwood & Sons · NL Scot., letters to John Hill Burton · NL Scot., letters to J. G. Lockhart

Likenesses H. Watkins, albumen print, *c*.1856–1859, NPG

Wealth at death £225 15*s*.: probate, 9 May 1887, *CGPLA Eng. & Wales*

Herault, Jean (1569–1626), judge and civil administrator, was born in the parish of St Saviour, Jersey, the eldest son of Thomas Herault of the parish of St Clement on the island, and his wife, Mabel, the daughter of John Nicolle, seigneur of Longueville, and sister of the bailiff, Hostes Nicolle. In 1597 he matriculated from All Souls at Oxford, but he does not appear to have taken a degree. In 1607 Sir Robert Gardiner and Dr James Hussey, who had been sent to Jersey as royal commissioners, were given Herault to attend them on account of his experience in the language and customs of the islands.

On 28 July 1611 Herault obtained by royal patent the reversion of the office of bailiff of Jersey, but in order to take possession he had to persuade George Poulet to resign, which involved him in 'great charges' (*CSP dom.*, addenda, 1580–1625, no. 89). The governor of Jersey, John Peyton, claimed to have himself the right to choose the bailiff, there being a clause in his own letters patent to this effect. This was the beginning of protracted animosity between the bailiff and the governor. The case was referred by the privy council to Sir Randolph Crewe and Sir Henry Yelverton. Herault was sworn in as bailiff on 28 July 1615, but formal settlement in his favour came by an order in council of 9 August that year, in which it was declared that the right to appoint to the office had been inserted in the governor's patent contrary to the king's intent and meaning.

The wrangling continued as Peyton charged Herault with usurping the office of governor. Not only had he declared himself the king's lieutenant, but he had also willed the ministers on the island to change the form of prayer to name the bailiff before the governor, pretended to the power of assembling the states, or legislative assembly, and displaced Philippe Maret from the office of attorney-general to which Peyton had appointed him. This case was heard before the council and a verdict given in February 1617, in which was laid down the rule that has since been of great importance for the constitutional history of Jersey, that 'the charge of military forces be wholly in the governor, and the care of justice and civil affairs in the bailiff' (order in council, 18 Feb 1617; *CSP dom.*, addenda, 1580–1625, 564). The bailiff was acquitted of all undutifulness towards the king's majesty, indeed of everything except heat of words. Following this dispute, Herault called for a royal commission. The commissioners Sir Edward Conway and Sir William Bird arrived in Jersey in April 1617. By decision of this commission, the bailiff was granted precedence over the governor in court and states.

In 1620 Herault became embroiled in controversy again when he opposed and stalled the election of churchwardens, contending that the oath to them should be administered by the temporal power, represented by the bailiff, and not the spiritual power, represented by Dean Bandinel. He was summoned to Westminster, and his impudent answers to the lord chancellor earned him imprisonment in the Marshalsea and suspension from office. On 27 September 1621 Herault was released but he was required to remain in London until August 1624. That year Herault was confirmed in the charge of bailiff by the king: the office of bailiff was no longer to depend on the governor but on the crown, in accordance with the Ordonnances of Henry VII and the patent of 1615. In October Herault returned to Jersey but, trying unsuccessfully to reclaim his arrears of salary, returned to London for a few months soon after.

Herault styled himself the seigneur of St Saviour, on account of a small property he owned in that parish, but there was no precedent for the use of the title, and it was widely contested by his contemporaries. He died, unmarried, in St Helier on 10 March 1626 and was buried in St Saviour's Church.   HELEN M. E. EVANS

Sources G. R. Balleine, *A biographical dictionary of Jersey*, [1] [1948] • J. A. Messervy, 'Liste des baillis, lieut.-baillis et juges-délégués de l'île de Jersey', *Annual Bulletin* [Société Jersiaise], 4 (1897–1901), 92–116 • *Reg. Oxf.*, vol. 2/2 • *CSP dom.*, addenda, 1580–1625 • *APC, 1613–16* • Balleine's 'History of Jersey', revised and enlarged by M. Syret and J. Stevens (1998)

Herbert (*d.* 1164), bishop of Glasgow, was probably one of the first monks brought by Earl David from Tiron in France to found Selkirk Abbey about 1114, for he became its third abbot in 1119 and must have presided over its shift to Kelso about 1127. He failed in his hopes to become bishop of Durham when William Comyn was rejected there in 1142, but was elected to succeed John (another Tironensian monk) as bishop of Glasgow early in 1147. He was consecrated by Eugenius III at Auxerre on 24 August 1147, but during his episcopate ignored repeated papal injunctions to promise obedience to York. He is found witnessing royal charters, including no fewer than twenty-six of Malcolm IV.

Herbert certainly worked energetically for his cathedral, increasing the endowment of at least three of its prebends and adding a seventh to the existing six; named canons first appear in his time. His introduction of customs of Salisbury probably marked the formal constitution of the chapter as a *collegium*. He commissioned a life of Kentigern of which only the early chapters survive, but the preface shows that this work was an important recasting of an ancient life, and it was probably the main source for the life written after 1176 by Jocelin of Furness.

Perhaps in early 1164 Somerled so ravaged around Glasgow that its clergy and people fled. According to the *Carmen de morte Somerledi*, Herbert was absent, and Kentigern's failure to respond to his prayers led the bishop to disparage the saint. But Kentigern eventually awoke to his duty, persuading the bishop to leave his bed and set out for Glasgow without knowing that Somerled had returned. When he heard, and despite misgivings, Herbert rallied his forces and attacked Somerled at Renfrew, killing him and destroying his force.

> A priest cut off the head of the miserable leader Somerled, and gave it into the bishop's hands. As his custom was, he wept piously on seeing the head of his enemy, saying, 'the Scottish saints are truly to be praised'. And he attributed the victory to the blessed Kentigern, whose memory keep ye always. (Anderson, *Early Sources*, 2.258)

In the same year, 1164, Herbert died, at some time before 13 September and probably in Glasgow.

Herbert continued the work of his episcopal predecessor John, and these two are eloquent testimony to the effectiveness of monk-bishops in a rapidly developing church. Herbert's encouragement to the institutions of Glasgow Cathedral probably explain revived interest in the cult of Kentigern, which was perhaps popularized by the defeat and death of Somerled. It is difficult to believe that Herbert, now old, led the men of Glasgow; but he certainly seems to have inspired them.

A. A. M. DUNCAN

Sources J. Dowden, *The bishops of Scotland … prior to the Reformation*, ed. J. M. Thomson (1912), 296–7 • O. Engels and others, eds., *Series episcoporum ecclesiae Catholicae occidentalis*, 6th ser., 1, ed. D. E. R. Watt (1991), 58–9 • N. F. Shead, 'Origins of the medieval diocese of Glasgow', *SHR*, 48 (1969), 220–25 • N. F. Shead, 'The administration of the diocese of Glasgow in the twelfth and thirteenth centuries', *SHR*, 55 (1976), 127–50 • A. P. Forbes, ed., *Lives of S. Ninian and S. Kentigern* (1874), 121–33 • A. O. Anderson, ed. and trans., *Early sources of Scottish history, AD 500 to 1286*, 2 (1922) • A. O. Anderson and M. O. Anderson, eds., *The chronicle of Melrose* (1936)

Herbert of Bosham. *See* Bosham, Herbert of (*d. c.*1194).

Herbert, Sir Alan Patrick (1890–1971), author and politician, was born on 24 September 1890 at Ashtead Lodge, Ashtead, Leatherhead, Surrey, the eldest of the three sons of Patrick Coghlan Herbert Herbert of Ashtead Lodge, an Irish civil servant at the India Office, and his wife, Beatrice Eugénie Selwyn (1865–1898), daughter of Sir Charles Jasper *Selwyn, a lord justice of appeal. His mother died when he was seven.

From about 1903 Herbert was educated at Winchester College, where he won the king's medals for public speaking and verse composition and published the first of his many volumes of light verse, a genre that became one of the several main strands in his versatile writing career. In his final year at school he began to contribute to *Punch*. He went to New College, Oxford, in 1910, where in 1914 he gained first-class honours in jurisprudence. Career considerations went into abeyance at the outbreak of war in August 1914, and he enlisted as an ordinary seaman in the Royal Naval Volunteer Reserve.

On 31 December 1914 Herbert married Gwendolen Harriet Quilter (*b. c.*1894), daughter of Harry *Quilter, an artist and newspaper art critic whose nephew was the composer Roger Quilter. Three months after his marriage Herbert was commissioned sub-lieutenant in the Royal Naval Volunteer Reserve and was on active service with the Royal Naval division at Gallipoli and in France. He was wounded on the western front in 1917 and invalided home. During his convalescence he wrote *The Secret Battle*, the story of a Gallipoli soldier's nervous breakdown and execution for cowardice. Published in 1919, the novel launched his writing career and enjoyed lasting public acclaim. The *Times Literary Supplement* immediately compared Herbert to Thomas Hardy and John Galsworthy, remarking that 'One's discomfort in reading the book is enhanced by the certainty that something very like it must have happened over and over again' (3 July 1919), and as late as 1970 it was recalled as 'a masterpiece of realistic fiction' (Pound, 65). Field Marshal Lord Montgomery called it 'the best story of front-line war I have read', and Winston Churchill wrote a reverent introduction to a later edition (*The Times*, 12 Nov 1971). The novel was credited with bringing about much needed reforms in the court martial procedure.

Herbert was called to the bar from the Inner Temple in 1918 but did not practise. After two years as private secretary to Sir Leslie Scott he joined the staff of *Punch* in 1924, representing the magazine at the Third Imperial Press Conference a year later. *Punch* was both stage and platform for his role as literary entertainer, and it was here that the crusading spirit that animated much of his life and work first found expression. In *Punch*, Herbert foreshadowed social and political causes that he subsequently championed in parliament and elsewhere. His long-running 'Misleading cases' series of articles satirized the law and its anomalies, bringing him celebrity in legal circles throughout the English-speaking world. The series was published as a hugely popular book in 1927, running to many editions and three sequels.

Until his forties Herbert's reputation rested on his *Punch* connection, the fame of *The Secret Battle*, and his series of comic operas and musicals shown at the Lyric, Hammersmith, London, during its inter-war heyday. His *Riverside Nights* (1926) revue was followed by a sequence of operettas, the best-known being *La vie parisienne* (1929), *Tantivy Towers* (1931), and *Derby Day* (1932). A regular correspondent with *The Times*, his letters were often the talk of the West End clubs. His novel about the canal people, *The Water Gypsies* (1930), brought him a new public. *Holy Deadlock* (1934) was an unashamedly propagandist novel which exposed crudities of the English divorce laws and helped to create a more favourable attitude to reform.

Herbert's fame increased when he stood as an independent candidate at the general election of 1935 and was elected to the Oxford University seat. Within a year he steered the Matrimonial Causes Act (1936) through the Commons, writing up the experience in *The Ayes have it: the Story of the Marriage Bill* (1937).

When the Second World War broke out, Herbert joined the River Emergency Service which operated on the Thames as part of the London defences. When the service was merged in the Royal Naval Auxiliary Patrol he was given the rank of petty officer RN and the right to fly the white ensign on his converted canal boat, *Water Gipsy*. He gave an account of his wartime years on the Thames in *A. P. H.: his Life and Times* (1970). In June 1940 he went ashore to do battle in the House of Commons with the chancellor of the exchequer, who was proposing to subject books to purchase tax. His speech was a philippic of outraged sensibility, and three weeks later books were exempted from tax. He received a knighthood in Churchill's resignation honours list of 1945. The abolition of the university franchise in 1950 deprived him of his place in parliament after fifteen years: 'an independent Member *par excellence*' (*The Times*, 12 Nov 1971). His political autobiography, *Independent Member* (1950), reaffirmed the worth of the private member in a parliamentary democracy.

After the war Herbert deployed his talent to amuse in a number of spectacular musical plays for the West End stage, of which the conspicuous success was *Bless the Bride* (1950). Neither the bright lights nor the loss of his parliamentary seat distracted him from continuing his many campaigns. Over the next twenty years he was an ardent and colourful spokesman for a number of diverse causes: he was in favour of a water bus service for the Thames, a public lending right for authors, and a betting tax, but was against a spelling reform bill, the law of obscenity, an entertainments tax, and bureaucratic jargon. He was a particularly enthusiastic campaigner for the rights of authorship, on one occasion tearing up and setting alight the Copyright Bill on television. He was president of the Society of Authors while simultaneously president of the London Corinthian Sailing Club and the Inland Waterways Association, vice-president of the Performing Right Society, and a trustee of the National Maritime Museum,

Greenwich. In 1957 Queen's University, Kingston, Ontario, Canada, recognized his reforming zeal and contribution to public life by making him an honorary doctor of laws, and Oxford University followed suit in awarding him a DCL in 1958.

Herbert was tall, loose-limbed, and little concerned with his appearance in terms of fashion or style. He suffered from a nervous reflex of the head and neck when talking. He died on 11 November 1971 at 12 Hammersmith Terrace, London, his home and working base for the previous fifty-four years. His death occurred shortly after the publication of his autobiography to commemorate his eightieth birthday. He was survived by his wife, three daughters, and son, and speeches of condolence were made in the house of representatives in Washington, DC, USA.   REGINALD POUND, rev. KATHERINE MULLIN

Sources R. Pound, *A. P. Herbert, a biography* (1976) · *The Times* (12 Nov 1971) · A. Herbert, *A. P. H.: his life and times* (1970) · G. H. Fabes, *The first editions of A. E. Coppard, A. P. Herbert and Charles Morgan* (1933) · *TLS* (29 May 1919)
Archives NRA, priv. coll., papers · Ransom HRC, letters and papers · U. Birm. L. | BL, corresp. with League of Dramatists, Add. MS 63396 · NRA, priv. coll., corresp. and papers relating to Public Lending Right Society · University of Cape Town Library, corresp. with C. J. Sibbett | SOUND BL NSA, talks by A. P. Herbert, 1966–70
Likenesses H. Coster, photographs, c.1930, NPG · E. G. Faber, pen and ink and wash, 1933, NPG · M. Gerson, photograph, 1965, NPG · N. Vogel, three photographs, c.1969, NPG · G. Argent, photograph, 1970, NPG · H. Coster, photograph, NPG · H. L. Oakley, silhouette, NPG · R. Spear, oils, NPG · photographs, repro. in Pound, *A. P. Herbert* · photographs, repro. in Herbert, *A. P. H.* · photographs, Hult. Arch.
Wealth at death £25,746: probate, 25 Jan 1972, CGPLA Eng. & Wales

Herbert, Alfred (c.1820–1861), watercolour painter, was born in Southend, Essex, son of Thomas Herbert, a Thames waterman. He was apprenticed to a boat builder but decided to become an artist. He exhibited coastal and fishing scenes, mainly of Suffolk and the Netherlands, and Thames views, including *Schevening Beach, Coast of Holland* (exh. Society of British Artists, 1854), with the Society of British Artists from 1844 to 1855 and at the Royal Academy from 1847 to 1860. His paintings were not very popular, and he could only sell them at very low prices. Herbert died suddenly in January 1861, in Southend, leaving a widow and seven children. His *Wreck off Appledore, North Devon* and *Man-of-War, off Dover* are in the Victoria and Albert Museum. The National Maritime Museum, Greenwich, also has two of his watercolour drawings, one of which—*A Schooner and a Dutch Vessel Close Hauled in a Fresh Breeze in St Helier's Bay* (1846)—was exhibited in the 'Masters of the sea' exhibition at the museum in 1987.
ANNE PIMLOTT BAKER

Sources Mallalieu, *Watercolour artists*, vols. 1–2 · J. Johnson, ed., *Works exhibited at the Royal Society of British Artists, 1824–1893, and the New English Art Club, 1888–1917*, 2 vols. (1975) · Wood, *Vic. painters*, 3rd edn · L. Lambourne and J. Hamilton, eds., *British watercolours in the Victoria and Albert Museum* (1980) · Graves, *RA exhibitors* · Boase, *Mod. Eng. biog.* · *Art Journal*, 23 (1861), 56 · 'Catalogue of prints and drawings', www.nmm.ac.uk, 7 Dec 1998

Wealth at death left widow and children 'in distressed circumstances': DNB

Herbert, Sir Alfred Edward (1866–1957), machine tool manufacturer, was born on 5 September 1866 in West Street, Leicester, the second son of William Herbert, building contractor and farmer, and his wife, Sarah Anne, née Thompson. Following an elementary education at Stoneygate House School in Leicester, he became a premium apprentice at the late age of eighteen in the firm of Joseph Jessop & Sons, crane and hoist builders, for three years and trained as a turner, fitter, and draughtsman.

Immediately prior to the completion of his apprenticeship in 1887, Herbert migrated to Coventry to take up the post of manager in the small engineering firm of Coles and Matthews, a post secured for him by his elder brother, William, one of the firm's directors, at a salary of £2 per week. After only a year the firm was offered to Herbert for the relatively low price of £2375 and he immediately entered into partnership with a former school friend and fellow apprentice, William Hubbard, under the name of Herbert and Hubbard, making boilers and general engineering equipment. This was an equal partnership, in which the father of each of the two principals provided their sons with a capital of £2000 each. Initially, production concentrated on ploughing tackle and steam rollers but moved very swiftly to making machine tools and tubing directed at the cycle trade, a move facilitated by the acquisition of an agency from the French firm La Compagnie Française des Métaux for producing weldless steel tubing, again acquired through the good offices of his elder brother. This undoubtedly helped the firm in its early days, but by 1891 the emphasis was firmly on machine tools.

By 1894 Herbert had bought out Hubbard, who left the business, which was turned into a limited liability company with a capital of £25,000, split into £5000 shares. Seeing the growing worldwide importance of machine tools, Herbert quickly became an agent for overseas machine tool manufacturers, especially American, and set up branches in numerous parts of the world including Paris and Lille in France, before venturing into Spain, Italy, India, Japan, Belgium, Canada, and Australia. In Britain agencies were established in virtually all major industrial cities. Besides working as an agent Herbert ploughed back profits and quickly established himself as a prominent machine tool manufacturer in his own right. Rising output necessitated an expansion of his original premises in Coventry's Butts area, with the premises growing from 1360 square feet in 1888 to over 70,000 square feet a decade later; further expansion was inhibited by surrounding buildings and the railway. In 1899 a foundry was built at Edgwick and it was there that ultimately all production was to be concentrated.

Though managing director of the company, with his elder brother as chairman, Herbert realized the importance of surrounding himself with able people, and to this end recruited an American, Oscar Harmer, from Churchills of America, who brought with him a wealth of experience. Similarly, the talented draughtsman Arthur

Marston joined the team. Under this triumvirate the firm flourished and established a reputation for the quality of its products, a willingness to adopt American technology, mirrored in the development of turret lathes, and its good after-sales service. By the turn of the century, Alfred Herberts was the largest machine tool company in Coventry, employing over 800 men, a figure that moved to 1500 in 1910, before increasing to 2400 in 1920, 3500 in 1930, and finally to 3800 in 1938, making Herberts the largest machine tool firm in the world by volume of employment. Similarly, in 1908 the firm accounted for 8 per cent of total UK output of machine tools, a figure that had swollen to 18 per cent in 1937.

With the death of his brother in 1910, Herbert assumed the position of chairman. During the First World War he was prominent in government service, becoming controller of machine tools at the Ministry of Munitions. Indeed he was an obvious choice and had control not only of production but for the whole logistical exercise of ensuring tools were allocated to appropriate factories. In 1917 he received a knighthood for his services and was also accorded the French Légion d'honneur. A year later the order of St Stanislas (second class) and the Belgian order of Leopold were also bestowed on him. He married three times: first, in 1889, Ellen Adela, daughter of Thomas Ryley of Coventry, with whom he had four daughters; second, in 1913, Florence (d. 1930), widow of Lieutenant-Colonel H. E. E. Lucas; and finally in 1933, Marian, née Arundel (1881–1969), widow of Lieutenant-Colonel Pugh.

The inter-war years were difficult for British industry, yet Alfred Herberts proved to be a success story in that troubled era and continued to expand. Herbert continued the policy of innovation through incremental improvements such as the introduction of tungsten carbide to his tools, which caused a considerable amount of redesign work at Edgwick. Alongside this was the introduction of pre-selected spindle speeds and the overall introduction of electricity, with almost every machine being driven by an individual electric motor by 1931. Besides forging ahead with innovations, Herbert continued with his policy of marketing machines on behalf of other concerns and this became a substantial part of the overall business, particularly in overseas markets. A third strand of business at this time, especially in the 1920s, was the policy of reconditioning older machinery bought from bankrupt or near bankrupt firms such as Beardsmores of Glasgow and Clyno of Wolverhampton and selling this both at home and abroad.

During the thirties Herbert expressed his anxiety about the state of the British machine tool industry in the event of war and was invited to participate in the shadow factory scheme. During the ensuing hostilities of the Second World War, the firm produced over 65,000 powered machine tools, including innovations such as the combination turret lathe and the chip steam box. In the post-war years he continued to innovate and expand, acquiring Sigma Instruments in 1948, and four years later obtained a patent for tape control systems. Indeed even into his eighties he showed a willingness to listen, take advice, and implement it when necessary.

Herbert was a firm believer in managerial rights and defended them resolutely. Towards his workers he had a tough-minded attitude that promoted the idea of high quality apprenticeships to the extent that to have been a Herberts apprentice was a hallmark of quality training. Combined with this was a high degree of paternalism that was born of pragmatism rather than convenience. He was an early pioneer of industrial safety and welfare programmes, establishing a works canteen and a fully equipped surgery at Edgwick to deal with industrial accidents. He wrote with sympathy and compassion to the families of workers killed or wounded in combat and often aided workers with donations of food in times of hardship or illness.

In his public life Herbert was active in the Machine Tool Association, becoming its president in 1912, a position held for twenty years until his resignation over policy disagreements in 1934. Locally he was a founder member of a Coventry District Engineering Employers Association in 1907. He was president of the Institution of Production Engineers and an honorary life member of the Institution of Mechanical Engineers and a fellow of the Society of Arts. He was made an honorary freeman of London and in 1933 also of Coventry. Politically he was of a strong Conservative persuasion and a champion of free enterprise, but he campaigned heavily for protection from imports during the 1930s.

To his adopted city Herbert exercised considerable generosity. He was both chairman and a committee member of the Coventry and Warwickshire Hospital and in 1915 donated £1000 for a ward for wounded servicemen; later he donated another £10,000. In 1935 he built six almshouses for elderly women and a further six two years later, backing that with a total endowment of £11,000. Additionally, he paid for decorating the lady chapel of St Barbara's Church in memory of his second wife and presented Town Thorns, a large country house near Brinklow, as a camp for Coventry's poor children. His generosity extended to funding a covenant of £25,000 for the rebuilding of Coventry Cathedral, and he donated £200,000 for the construction of a new art gallery and museum, named after him.

In later life Herbert purchased Dunley Manor in Whitchurch, Hampshire, where he enjoyed hunting and fishing. However, he did not retire and still retained the titles of chairman and managing director at the time of his death on 26 May 1957, at Compton Manor, King's Somborne, Hampshire. He was buried in Litchfield, Hampshire.   THOMAS DONNELLY

Sources R. R. Brittain, 'The development of the machine tool industry in Coventry', MPhil diss., Coventry University, 1989 · J. M. G. David, 'Social relations in an engineering factory: Alfred Herbert Ltd', MA diss., Warwick University, 1983 · J. Lane, 'Herbert, Sir Alfred', *DBB* · R. Floud, *The British machine tool industry, 1880–1914* (1976) · d. cert. · d. cert. [Marian Fraser Herbert]
Archives Coventry City RO, Alfred Herbert Company records · Leics. RO, corresp. with Pick, Everard, Keay, and Gimson, civil

engineers · Shakespeare Birthplace Trust RO, Stratford upon Avon, papers
Likenesses photograph, repro. in Lane, 'Herbert, Sir Alfred'
Wealth at death £5,336,051: Lane, 'Herbert, Sir Alfred'

Herbert, Algernon (1792–1855), antiquary, was born on 12 July 1792, the fourth son of Henry Herbert, first earl of Carnarvon (1741–1811), and his wife, Elizabeth Alicia Maria (d. 1826), elder daughter of Charles Wyndham, second earl of Egremont. He was educated at Eton College from 1805, and then went to Christ Church, Oxford, where he matriculated on 23 October 1810. He afterwards migrated to Exeter College, where he graduated BA in 1813 and proceeded MA in 1825. He was elected a fellow of Merton College in 1814, and became sub-warden in 1826 and dean in 1828. On 27 November 1818 he was called to the bar at the Inner Temple. He married, on 2 August 1830, Marianne (d. 1870), sixth daughter of Thomas Lemprière of La Motte, Jersey; they had one son, Sir Robert George Wyndham *Herbert, and two daughters.

Between 1826 and 1849 Herbert produced a variety of publications which were abstruse and often inconclusive. The earliest of these, *Nimrod: a Discourse upon Certain Passages of History and Fable*, was published in 1826 and reprinted in a revised edition in 1828, with a third and fourth volume following in 1828 and 1829–30 respectively. Other works included *Britannia after the Romans* (1836–41), *The Irish Version of the 'Historia Brittonum'* (1848), and *Cyclops Christianus, or, The Supposed Antiquity of Stonehenge* (1849). He also wrote 'On the poems of the poor of Lyons' and three other articles in the appendix of J. H. Todd's *Book of the Vaudois* (1865), as well as an article on 'Werewolves' published in the Roxburghe Club's edition of *The Ancient English Romance of William and the Werewolf* (1832), edited by Frederic Madden. Herbert died at Ickleton, Cambridgeshire, on 11 June 1855.

G. C. BOASE, rev. JOANNE POTIER

Sources GM, 2nd ser., 44 (1855), 649–50 · Boase, *Mod. Eng. biog.* · *Annual Register* (1855), 280 · Foster, *Alum. Oxon.* · *A catalogue of all graduates … in the University of Oxford, between … 1659 and … 1850* (1851) · Allibone, *Dict.* · Burke, *Peerage*
Archives CUL

Herbert, Anne, countess of Pembroke (b. before 1514, d. 1552). *See under* Herbert, William, first earl of Pembroke (1506/7–1570).

Herbert, Arthur, earl of Torrington (1648–1716), naval officer and politician, was born between July and October 1648, the third son of Sir Edward *Herbert (c.1591–1657), attorney-general to Charles I, and Margaret Carey, the widow of Thomas Carey (d. 9 April 1634), second son of Robert Carey, earl of Monmouth, and only daughter of Sir Thomas Smith, master of requests under James I.

During Herbert's early years his parents were royalist exiles living abroad in Brussels and in Paris, where the young boy had his early education. By 1661 the family had returned to England and settled at Weybridge, Surrey, where Arthur Herbert developed an early desire to serve in the navy. Probably through his mother's connections Sir William Coventry, secretary to James, duke of York, recommended to Sir Robert Holmes that Holmes take

Arthur Herbert, earl of Torrington (1648–1716), by John Closterman, c.1689–90

Arthur Herbert with him on his voyage to Guinea in 1664. Discharged from his first ship on 3 January 1665, Herbert probably followed Holmes in joining *Revenge* a month later at the opening of the Second Anglo-Dutch War, and may have been with him during the battle of Lowestoft in June 1665.

Naval service Less than a year later, on 28 March 1666, Herbert was appointed a lieutenant in the 66-gun *Defiance* under Holmes, who had taken command of her two days previously. He was in her during the four days' battle early in June, when the ship was heavily damaged and suffered many killed and wounded. Later that month, on leaving *Defiance*, Holmes recommended Herbert to the duke of York, who in turn recommended him to the joint admirals, Prince Rupert and Albemarle. No immediate appointment was made for Herbert, and when another of the ship's lieutenants was discharged wounded Herbert was apparently left to supervise repairs to the ship at Great Yarmouth. Captain John Kempthorne succeeded Holmes in command and Herbert remained in the ship, being present during the St James's day fight on 25 July 1666, when the ship again had many killed and wounded. In the autumn, when *Defiance* returned to Portsmouth, Herbert was discharged on 8 September.

On 8 November 1666 Herbert received his promised preferment and was appointed to command the 28-gun *Pembroke*. Early in 1667 he was in action against a much larger Dutch privateer, earning praise for his gallantry. Discharged from *Pembroke* on 2 April he took command of the 42-gun *Constant Warwick* on the following day and remained in her for seventeen months until September 1668. Remaining ashore during the following winter he took command of the 38-gun *Dragon* on 6 March 1669; he served with Sir Thomas Allin's squadron in the Mediterranean and remained there after Sir Edward Spragge replaced Allin in 1670.

In April 1671, during an engagement with two heavily armed Algerian corsairs, Herbert was wounded when a pistol bullet struck him below the right eye and lodged in his head. Despite his injury he was able to participate in the attack on ten Algerian ships in Bugia Bay, between 8 and 13 May 1671. A year later Herbert returned to England with Spragge's squadron and was discharged from *Dragon* on 20 May 1672. In April or May he married Ann, widow of Walter Phesant (who had died in September or October 1668) and daughter of George Hadley of Southgate, Middlesex.

On 25 May 1672 Herbert took command of the 62-gun *Dreadnought*, and a week later he participated in the battle of Solebay, where his ship had two men killed and fourteen wounded. On returning to port Herbert left *Dreadnought* on 9 June and immediately took command of the 70-gun *Cambridge* in the place of Sir Freschville Holles, who had been killed at Solebay. In *Cambridge* during the following year Herbert took part in the two battles of Schooneveld in May and June 1673. During the battle of the Texel in August 1673 *Cambridge* was immediately astern of Spragge's flagship and was so heavily damaged that the ship was sent to Chatham for repair. Discharged from *Cambridge* on 11 October Herbert took command of her again seven weeks later, on 30 November. Early in 1674 Herbert was ordered to sail for the Shetland Islands in company with *Crown* (Captain Robert Carter) to search for a disabled Dutch merchant ship, which they took as a prize. In April Herbert sailed for the Mediterranean, first landing troops at Tangier and then joining Sir John Narbrough at Algiers. On his return to England in June Herbert was reportedly imprisoned briefly in the Tower and then, on 12 June 1675, dismissed from his command for failing to force two French warships to strike their flags in recognition of England's sovereignty over the British seas.

In 1676 Herbert was among a group—including Charles II, James, duke of York, and Samuel Pepys—who contributed funds for the *Prosperous Pink* (Captain William Flawes) to accompany the *Speedwell Sloop* on an ill-fated attempt to find a north-east passage to the Far East. During summer 1677 the Admiralty consulted him and other captains on the new establishment of men and guns. On 26 November 1677 he returned to sea in command of *Rupert*, and appearing personally before the king and duke of York persuaded them not to sheathe the vessel's underwater hull in lead. While fitting out his command at Portsmouth he was called again to the Admiralty on 8 December to participate in a discussion on whether to institute an examination for promotion to lieutenant.

Mediterranean command While commanding *Rupert* Herbert was appointed vice-admiral under Sir John Narbrough in the Mediterranean, on 15 February 1678. On the report of a large fleet of French warships in the channel the Admiralty diverted Herbert to join Sir John Holmes's squadron in the Downs. When the reports turned out to be false Herbert sailed for Tangier on 6 March, in company with *Mary*, commanded by Narbrough's rear-admiral, Sir Roger Strickland, and *Phoenix* (Captain Thomas Roomcoyle). Off Cape St Vincent they encountered the Algerian corsair *Tiger* on 20 March. In the action that followed, the English ships took the Algerine. Among the casualties Herbert temporarily lost his eyesight when a bandolier exploded in his face. By early May he had recovered his sight, and remained in command. A year later, in April 1679, Narbrough returned to England and left Herbert with a squadron of nine vessels, initially as acting commander-in-chief in the Mediterranean. Still in the Mediterranean a year later Herbert shifted from command of *Rupert* on 6 April 1680, and on the following day took command of *Bristol*. In July 1680, despite Samuel Pepys's dislike of giving a flag to officers with small squadrons, the Admiralty appointed Herbert as admiral and commander-in-chief, a position he retained for three more years. Herbert shifted from the *Bristol* on 8 May 1682 to the 46-gun *Tiger*, and returned to England in her in June 1683. While serving in the Mediterranean, Herbert had been invited, in December 1679, by his cousin Lord Herbert of Cherbury to stand for parliament at Montgomery Boroughs, but had declined.

Pepys disliked Herbert and was highly critical of his conduct in the Mediterranean, noting that his clerk

> W. Hewer tells me of captains submitting themselves to the meanest degree of servility to Herbert when he was at Tangier, waiting at his rising and going to bed, combing his peruque, brushing him, putting on his coat for him, as the king is served, he keeping a house on shore and his mistresses visited and attended one after another as the king's are. (*Tangier Papers*, 138)

Despite Pepys's negative opinion of his character modern scholarship has tended to justify Herbert's professional conduct, looking favourably on his defence of Tangier and his squadron's successes against Algerine corsairs leading to his negotiation of peace with Algiers in April 1682. In addition Herbert's years in the Mediterranean were seminal through the patronage and leadership he provided to young officers such as Matthew Aylmer, George Byng, John Graydon, Thomas Hopson, David Mitchell, George Rooke, Cloudesley Shovell, Woolfran Cornwall, and Francis Wheeler, who later provided the dedicated nucleus of like-minded conspirators who carried the navy through the revolution of 1688–9, many of them becoming leaders of the navy afterwards. At odds with Pepys over Tangier, Herbert found its mole unsatisfactory for fleet use and pioneered English interest in and use of Gibraltar as an alternative repair base in 1680–82.

On his return to England in June 1683 Herbert remained in command of *Tiger* until 16 August 1683. Less than a week later, on 22 August, he was appointed a supernumerary commissioner of the Admiralty, a post he held until 17 April 1684, when he was appointed an ordinary commissioner until the Admiralty board was dissolved on 19 May

1684. In the meantime Charles II appointed him rear-admiral of England on 22 January 1684 and James, duke of York, appointed him groom of the bedchamber. Herbert's marriage was apparently breaking down at this time, but on James II's accession to the throne the new king commanded him 'to take his wife again' (Sir Charles Lytleton to Hatton, 6 March 1685, Thompson, 2.55). Herbert became master of the robes in the king's household on 30 May 1685 and publicly exercised that role in the coronation procession. Early in 1685 the king, as warden, nominated Herbert as MP for Dover, and he took his seat on 4 April, probably unopposed in the election. On reports of Monmouth's landing at Lyme Regis in June Herbert was ordered to sea in command of a squadron of ten ships. Following Monmouth's defeat at Sedgemoor, Herbert returned to London to resume his duties at the Admiralty, in the royal household, and in parliament. On 12 March 1686 he was additionally appointed colonel of the 15th regiment of foot.

Changing allegiance In March 1687, when James II began his campaign to repeal the Test Act of 1673, the king sought full support from MPs in a series of personal interviews. The king pressed Herbert to agree to his proposal. Herbert

> answered the king very plainly that he could not do it either in honour nor conscience. The king said he was a man of honour, but the rest of his life did not look like a man that had great regard to conscience. (*Burnet's History*, 1.428)

To this Herbert responded, 'every man has his failing' (Speck, 64–5 n. 49).

Dismissed from his offices Herbert initially considered going to Venice to volunteer his services in the naval war against the Turks and his initial request, as a naval officer, to leave England was approved but shortly afterwards revoked. In the months that followed he became increasingly involved with those who opposed James's policies. In May 1688 the prince of Orange used Edward Russell as an intermediary to send Herbert an invitation to come to the Netherlands. In July Herbert sailed to join him, disguised as a common sailor, and carried with him the invitation for William to come to England as well as the news that the seven bishops had just been acquitted. Late in September William appointed Herbert as luitenant-admiraal-generaal of Rotterdam, and he became one of William's closest advisers in planning the invasion of England. In October 1688 William astutely appointed Herbert as the nominal commander-in-chief of the expedition, utilizing his popularity in the English navy to weaken James II's first line of defence and helping to signal the transformation of a Dutch invasion into a popular English movement. William ordered Herbert to work closely with his flag officers and placed two Dutch admirals, luitenant-admiraal of Zeeland, Cornelis Evertsen, and luitenant-admiraal of Holland, Phillips van Almonde, to manage the mainly Dutch force. The Dutch admirals resented William's appointment of Herbert over them, but this was to become a pattern in Anglo-Dutch naval operations over the next quarter-century.

After the landing at Torbay in November 1688 Herbert solicited support for William among the nearby gentry, and when *Newcastle* (Captain George Churchill) became the first English warship to defect to William, Herbert saw to it that William immediately paid the officers and men their wages. In December 1688 Herbert was elected MP for Plymouth. After returning to London to take his seat in parliament on 17 January 1689 he began to organize the new regime's naval affairs, leaving briefly early in February to command the small squadron that took Queen Mary II to England from the Netherlands. On 26 February the king named him a privy councillor, and two days later he was appointed to head the new Board of Admiralty commissioners and authorized to act on his own authority until they could gather for the first time on 8 March.

Commander-in-chief In addition to appointing him to the Admiralty, William III appointed Herbert admiral and commander-in-chief of the fleet on 11 March. Early in April he sailed from Portsmouth with the fleet to cruise off the coast of Ireland, where on 1 May 1689 he intercepted the French fleet under Châteaurenault in Bantry Bay after French troops had landed. In the first fleet action of the Nine Years' War, Herbert kept his fleet intact, although it was heavily damaged and forced to retire. Although it was no decisive victory the hard fought battle created an occasion for the king to encourage the navy and its adherence to his cause. On Herbert's return to Portsmouth with the fleet William visited and congratulated it on 15 May. On 21 May the House of Commons voted the thanks of the house to Herbert for his victory. In his response he moved for the establishment of a home for sailors 'for support of such as are maimed in the service and defence of their country' (*JHC*, 10, 142), anticipating the establishment of Greenwich Hospital five years later. On 29 May 1689 he was created Baron Herbert of Torbay and earl of Torrington; he took his seat in the Lords on 1 June. About the same time he became an elder brother of Trinity House, serving as master in 1689–90.

In July and August 1689 Torrington returned to sea with the fleet, cruising off Brest to blockade the French fleet. In October he resumed his seat as first lord at the Admiralty, but resigned on 20 January 1690 as a protest against mismanagement of its affairs and left his cousin, Thomas Herbert, eighth earl of Pembroke, to be named to succeed him. In lieu of his Admiralty seat Torrington was granted a pension of £1000 a year and then, on 28 April 1690, was named admiral and commander-in-chief of the Anglo-Dutch fleet. In further recognition of his services, on 14 May 1690 he was granted an area of 10,000 acres in the fens, called the Peterborough or Bedford level, valued at some £3000 p.a.

Torrington rejoined the fleet, then fitting out at Portsmouth, on 31 May 1690. Late in June he began to receive reports of the French fleet proceeding up the channel from Brest. Even with fifty-six allied Anglo-Dutch ships Torrington's fleet was still not up to full strength and his council of war estimated that the French outnumbered it by twenty-five ships. On 23 June Torrington wrote to Secretary of State Lord Nottingham, 'the ods are great and you know it is not my fault … Let them tremble at the consequence whose fault it was the fleet is noe stronger' (*Finch MSS*, 2.307–8). With the relative strength in mind Torrington's council of war recommended on 25 June that the Anglo-Dutch fleet retreat to the eastward and take shelter at the Gunfleet to await reinforcements from Sir Cloudesley Shovell, whose squadron had recently escorted the king and troops to Ireland, and Vice-Admiral Killigrew's squadron, due back shortly from convoying a fleet from the Mediterranean, before Torrington's force attempted to engage the French. When the war council's opinion was received in London, Queen Mary and the lords of the council were deeply concerned about the possibility of a French attack on the south coast or in the Thames and Medway areas. Torrington's rival at the Admiralty, Admiral Edward Russell, judged that the French were not as strong as Torrington believed. In addition there were suspicions about Torrington's health, judgement, and motivations. With these thoughts in mind the queen overruled the fleet war council's decision and ordered Torrington into battle. Informed of her order Torrington and the Anglo-Dutch flag officers discussed the issues at great length in a fleet council of war on 29 June.

A disastrous action Off Beachy Head early on the morning of 30 June 1690 the Anglo-Dutch fleet sighted the French ships under the comte de Tourville. Torrington, flying his flag in *Royal Sovereign*, ordered his fleet to engage in what quickly became a highly confused action lasting a full day. The Dutch in the van engaged first and took the brunt of the French response as they became surrounded. Seeing them on the verge of being overpowered in the early afternoon Torrington manoeuvred to support them and thwart a French manoeuvre to cut off his own rear squadron, but his attempt failed when the wind dropped. As the tide ebbed Torrington and his squadron anchored between the French and the Dutch. The English ships suffered relatively light damage, but the Dutch had many casualties in officers and men, losing thirteen of their twenty-two ships. Under the circumstances Torrington's Anglo-Dutch council of war decided that their best course of action was to retreat towards the east, burning three of their most heavily damaged ships to prevent their capture. On reaching the Nore, Torrington set about repairing the damage and refitting the ships. Meanwhile the French fleet, having a severe shortage of supplies, did not attempt to exploit fully its command of the channel and returned to France.

Reporting the events to the king in Ireland, Secretary of State Lord Nottingham wrote from London on 3 July that this defeat 'was occasioned by the base treachery or cowardice of my Lord Torrington, as there is great reason to believe' (*Finch MSS*, 2.333–5). The government feared that Torrington's conduct might have been motivated by Jacobite sympathies and judged it more dangerous to leave him in command than to face the practical problems associated with removing a fleet commander at that critical moment. On 8 July Torrington left the fleet for London, where on 10 July he was imprisoned in the Tower. Meanwhile the press attacked Torrington in print and

the Dutch ambassador demanded his trial and execution. The queen commissioned the earl of Pembroke, the earl of Macclesfield, Sir Robert Howard, Sir Henry Goodricke, and Sir Thomas Lee to investigate and to make a report on the battle. Their investigation failed to indict Torrington, and on 4 October he petitioned the House of Lords that his imprisonment was an unjustified breach of privilege. After much debate the Lords eventually agreed in a resolution on 20 October, but decided that he could be tried by court martial under the articles of war.

On 12 November Torrington addressed the House of Commons and explained the events in the battle, criticizing the conduct of the Dutch in the process. Granted permission to write a detailed account of the battle Torrington completed it several days later and included in it a much quoted phrase that two centuries later became an important concept for the theory of naval deterrence: 'I always said that whilst we had a fleet in being, they would not dare make an attempt' (*The Earl of Torrington's Speech to the House of Commons in November 1690*, 1710, 29).

Torrington's court martial convened on board *Kent* at Chatham on 10 December. Presided over by Admiral Ralph Delavall it was made up of twenty-seven officers, eight of whom owed their careers to Torrington's patronage. The court martial board heard a variety of witnesses, including twelve English and three Dutchmen, who offered evidence against Torrington, as well as Torrington's own defence of his actions. In his report to the Admiralty Delavall commented that the Dutch 'gave their opinions, but with too much heat, and indeed, the evidence against my lord was but of letle waight' (*Finch MSS*, 2.495). Acquitted by the court Torrington was cheered and saluted as he returned up the river to London. His commission as vice-admiral of England revoked on 12 December, Torrington retired to his home at Walton-on-Thames.

Torrington remained a member of the privy council until 23 June 1692 and was an active member of the House of Lords up to August 1714. He served on a large number of committees and retained an active interest in naval affairs, always voting with the court during the reign of Anne. In 1702 he played a prominent part in the attacks on Sir George Rooke's conduct at the failure of the Cadiz operation. He participated in major whig political conferences between 1703 and 1711 and was mentioned as a possible commander of the fleet in 1701 and again after Rooke's resignation in 1705. In 1710 his name emerged again as a possible candidate to succeed the earl of Orford at the Admiralty.

On 20 July 1696 Torrington was awarded Oatlands, near Weybridge, Surrey, and the lease of eight chambers in Serjeants' Inn, the confiscated property of his brother Sir Edward *Herbert (1645–1698), whom, in exile at his court at St Germain, James had created earl of Portland in 1689. Torrington's first marriage having ended, he married, about 1 August 1704, Anne, *née* Airmine (d. 2 April 1719), the widow of Thomas Crew, second Baron Crew of Steane (d. 30 Nov 1699). On hearing the news Abigail, Lady Pye, wrote to Anne Harley on 23 August 1704 that the unexpected marriage had created 'much chat in these parts. …

Having both a good spirit and purse, she is more likely to deal with his lordship better than the last poor lady' (*Portland MSS*, 4.112–13). The outcome of this marriage is however uncertain, as Anne was not mentioned in his will. In 1708 Torrington left Walton-on-Thames and moved to Oatlands. He died on 13 April 1716 and was buried on 22 April in the south aisle of Westminster Abbey, but no monument or memorial tablet was raised to him.

Torrington was described towards the end of his life as 'very fat' (Macky, 78), and was regarded as 'a man abandoned to luxury and vice' (*Burnet's History*, 1.428). His two marriages produced no children, though he is known to have had at least one illegitimate son. Apart from some small annuities and bequests to others he left his property to Henry Clinton, earl of Lincoln (1684–1728).

JOHN B. HATTENDORF

Sources P. Le Fevre, 'Arthur Herbert, earl of Torrington', *Precursors of Nelson: British admirals of the eighteenth century*, ed. P. Le Fevre and R. Harding (2000), 18–41 • P. Le Fevre, 'Arthur Herbert's early career in the navy', *Mariner's Mirror*, 69 (1983), 91 • P. Le Fevre, 'Arthur Herbert and his scheme for establishing convoys in the Mediterranean', *Mariner's Mirror*, 64 (1978), 134 • P. Le Fevre, '"Meer laziness" or incompetence: the earl of Torrington and the battle of Beachy Head', *Mariner's Mirror*, 80 (1994), 290–97 • P. Le Fevre, 'The battle of Bantry Bay', *Irish Sword*, 18 (1990) • *The manuscripts of his grace the duke of Portland*, 10 vols., HMC, 29 (1891–1931), vol. 4 • *Report on the manuscripts of Allan George Finch*, 5 vols., HMC, 71 (1913–2003), vol. 2 • *Bishop Burnet's History of his own time*, new edn (1857) • J. Macky, *Memoir of the secret service of John Macky* (1733) • *JHC*, 10 (1688–93), 138, 142 • E. M. Thompson, ed., *Correspondence of the family of Hatton*, 2, CS, new ser., 23 (1878) • *VCH Surrey*, 2.786–8 • *Tangier papers of Samuel Pepys*, ed. E. Chappell, Navy RS (1935) • register of all commission officers, 1660–85, PRO, ADM 10/15 • W. A. Speck, *Reluctant revolutionaries: Englishmen and the revolution of 1688* (1988) • will, PRO, PROB 11/553, sig. 134

Archives BL, corresp. and papers, Egerton MS 2621 • CKS, speech 1710 • Yale U., Beinecke L., letter-book | CKS, report to Commons, W 515 • Leics. RO, corresp. with earl of Nottingham and related material, DG7

Likenesses J. Closterman, oils, *c*.1689–1690, Normanby Hall Country Park, Scunthorpe [*see illus.*] • R. White, line engraving (after J. Riley), BL

Wealth at death property at Oatlands, Weybridge, Surrey; left approx. £3000 in bequests, plus £450 in annuities: will, PRO, PROB 11/55/3, sig. 134, fols. 7v–9r

Herbert, Arthur John (1834–1856). *See under* Herbert, John Rogers (1810–1890).

Herbert, Auberon Edward William Molyneux (1838–1906), politician and author, born at Highclere on 18 June 1838, was the third son of Henry John George *Herbert, third earl of Carnarvon (1800–1849), and his wife, Henrietta Anne Howard (1804–1876), a niece of the twelfth duke of Norfolk. His eldest brother, Henry Howard Molyneux *Herbert (1831–1890), became the fourth earl of Carnarvon when Herbert was eleven years old. Herbert was educated at Eton College and St John's College, Oxford, where he held a founder's kin fellowship. His early Oxford career was marked more by sporting prowess than academic achievement, and this seems to have prompted his family to purchase a commission for him in the 7th hussars, where his service took him to India in the immediate aftermath of the mutiny. Having returned to Oxford in

Auberon Edward William Molyneux Herbert (1838–1906), by Frederick Hollyer

1862 he graduated BCL followed by DCL three years later. While at Oxford, Herbert was president of the Union and was responsible for founding the Chatham and Canning clubs, Conservative dining societies. After graduation he briefly lectured on history and jurisprudence at St John's, resigning his fellowship in 1869.

Herbert's early political beliefs were Conservative, in line with family custom. In July 1865 he stood unsuccessfully as Conservative candidate for Newport, Isle of Wight, and subsequently served as private secretary to Sir Stafford Northcote, president of the Board of Trade in Lord Derby's ministry. However, even at this stage of his political career Herbert described himself as a 'liberal conservative', stressing that he wished to harmonize the new and old orders rather than opposing all attempts at reform. His growing sympathy for Liberalism was signalled by his membership of the Dominicans, a Sunday dining club founded by John Stuart Mill in 1865. However, the decisive turning point in his political allegiance appears to have been Disraeli's decision to oppose disestablishment of the Irish church, a measure for which his brother spoke in favour in the House of Lords. Lord Carnarvon drew a distinction between disestablishment in Ireland, where a majority of the population professed Catholicism, and in England, where they did not. Thus he could see no conflict with remaining true to the Conservative support for an established church in England. For Auberon Herbert, however, the issue was to result in a more fundamental shift of political allegiance, and at Goldwin Smith's instigation he contested Berkshire as a Liberal in 1868, stressing the justice of the case for Irish disestablishment in his election address. Although he was unsuccessful in this election, he was returned as member of parliament for Nottingham in a by-election held in February 1870, with the support of A. J. Mundella, one of the leaders of advanced radicalism. During his brief parliamentary career Herbert was aligned with the radicals, criticizing the House of Lords' veto, arguing for secular national education, supporting a bill for proportional representation, and making a strongly republican speech in support of Sir Charles Dilke's motion for an inquiry into the civil list. He was later to describe himself at this stage of his career as believing that he 'might do much for the people by a bolder and more unsparing use of the powers that belonged to the great law-making machine'.

At the dissolution of 1874 Herbert retired from parliamentary life, having concluded that he was temperamentally unsuited for party politics. At about this time he also encountered the intellectual influence that was to have the most profound impact on the rest of his life. A chance encounter at the Athenaeum with Herbert Spencer prompted him to begin a study of his writings, resulting in a conversion which, in the words of Herbert's biographer, resembled that of 'one of the medieval saints' (Harris, *Doctrine of Personal Right*, 204). Under Spencer's influence, Herbert repudiated his earlier belief in the efficacy of state action, becoming instead what Beatrice Webb described as 'a Don Quixote of the nineteenth century' who had 'left the real battle of life to fight a strange ogre of his own imagination—*an always immoral state interference*' (Webb, 189). Webb has left an insightful pen portrait of both Herbert himself and of life at the Old House in the New Forest, where the Herbert family lived a somewhat bohemian existence far from the grooves of aristocratic custom.

Despite Herbert's conversion experience on reading Spencer, his political thought in fact owes comparatively little to the most distinctive aspects of the synthetic philosophy. Herbert's writings lack the emphasis that Spencer placed on evolutionary processes, in particular his attempt to demonstrate that freedom of contract and a minimalist state were the natural outcome of invariable sociological laws. Herbert instead based his defence of a limited state on the proposition that individuals possess certain natural rights, something which he treats as intuitively obvious rather than as the corollary of biological or sociological theory. In this sense his political theory is closer to that of a late eighteenth-century thinker such as Joseph Priestley than it is to the mainstream of ideas at the end of the Victorian era. In virtue of individuals' possession of natural rights, Herbert argued, it followed that the only legitimate social arrangements were those into which they had voluntarily entered. He called this form of extreme individualism voluntaryism, and considered it to have demonstrated the illegitimacy of state action over a wide range of social and economic activities. The state might enforce contracts and protect property rights, but it had no right to redistribute property, provide education

from public funds, or to prohibit contracts being freely made. Indeed, Herbert pushed his voluntaryism to the point at which he considered it illegitimate for the state to tax individuals even to support its legitimate policing functions. Instead he argued for a form of 'voluntary taxation' in which each individual contributed to the state only that which they were prepared freely to give. His uncompromising opposition to coercion and neo-anarchist beliefs led a number of contemporary commentators to liken his views to those of Tolstoy, a comparison Herbert himself always rejected.

Herbert outlined his theory in a variety of publications, including the pamphlet *The Right and Wrong of Compulsion by the State* (1885), and a newspaper, the *Free Life*, which he edited from 1890 to its demise in 1901. In 1884 he published *A Politician in Trouble about his Soul*, a series of semi-autobiographical political dialogues which feature a thinly disguised portrait of Herbert Spencer as the artisan Markham. A number of his articles and papers were collected posthumously and published as *The Voluntaryist Creed* (1908). This volume also contains the text of the first Herbert Spencer lecture which Herbert gave at Oxford University shortly before his death in 1906. In it Herbert both outlined his own creed and spoke movingly about the impact on his mind of Spencer's writings. He was named as one of Spencer's three trustees on the latter's death in 1903.

Following his 'conversion' to Spencer's thought Herbert made comparatively few forays into public life. He did however return briefly to take part in the 1876 agitation caused by the Bulgarian atrocities and the 1878 'anti-Jingo' demonstrations against the prospect of war with Russia, as well as to speak in support of Charles Bradlaugh at a mass meeting in Hyde Park in 1880. He also was briefly associated with the Liberty and Property Defence League, a loose coalition of landed and commercial interests opposed to further extensions of state activity. Although Herbert contributed to several league publications, including its riposte to the *Fabian Essays in Socialism*, entitled *A Plea for Liberty* (1891), he never formally joined the league, considering its constitution 'coercive' (Bristow, 773).

Throughout his life Herbert exhibited great moral and physical courage. Not only prepared to take a stand for ideas which were deeply unfashionable, he also distinguished himself by rescuing the wounded from Danish redoubts during the Prussian-Danish War of 1864. For this action he was made a knight of the order of the Dannebrog. He was present as an observer during both the American Civil War and the Franco-Prussian War, becoming one of the first to enter Paris after the siege, and remaining there during the commune. In later life he received the Austrian order of the iron crown for his role in rescuing the crew of an Austrian vessel wrecked off Westward Ho!, Devon. Herbert was also an active sailor and a keen mountain climber, and a member of the Alpine Club. In 1894 he published a volume of poetry, *Windfall and Waterdrift*, which draws on his experiences of climbing and sailing.

Herbert married Lady Florence Amabel Cowper (d. 1886), daughter of the sixth Earl Cowper, on 9 August 1871. They had four children, two sons and two daughters, of whom only the younger son and younger daughter survived to adulthood. The younger son, Auberon Thomas *Herbert, succeeded his uncle, the seventh earl of Cowper, as Lord Lucas of Crudwell and Lord Dingwall in 1905. Herbert died at the Old House on 5 November 1906, and was buried at his request in a grave in its grounds on 8 November.   M. W. TAYLOR

Sources S. H. Harris, *Auberon Herbert: crusader for liberty* (1943) · *DNB* · B. Webb, *My apprenticeship* (1926); repr. (1979) · M. W. Taylor, *Men versus the state* (1992) · S. H. Harris, *The doctrine of personal right* (1935) · E. Bristow, 'The Liberty and Property Defence League and individualism', *HJ*, 18 (1975), 761–89 · Burke, *Peerage* (1999)
Archives Highclere Castle, Highclere, Oxford notebooks | Bishopsgate Institute, London, letters to George Howell · BL, letters to Sir Charles Dilke, Add. MS 43898 · CAC Cam., letters to W. T. Stead · Herts. ALS, corresp. with Henry Frederick Cowper · HLRO, letters to Herbert Samuel
Likenesses F. Hollyer, photograph, National Museum of Photograph, Film and Television, Bradford [*see illus.*] · photograph, repro. in A. E. W. M. Herbert, *The right and wrong of compulsion by the state and other essays*, ed. E. Mack (1978)
Wealth at death £19,654 17s. 6d.: resworn administration with will, *CGPLA Eng. & Wales* (1907)

Herbert, Auberon Mark Yvo Henry Molyneux (1922–1974), landowner and campaigner for eastern European causes, born in Egham on 25 April 1922, was the only son of Aubrey Nigel Henry Molyneux *Herbert (1880–1923), MP, of Pixton Park, Dulverton, and his wife, Mary Gertrude Vesey (b. 1889), only child of the fourth Viscount de Vesci. His grandfather was Henry *Herbert, the fourth earl of Carnarvon (1831–1890). He had three sisters, one of whom married Evelyn Waugh. From his father, who died shortly after his birth, he inherited an interest in national causes. His militant Catholicism came from his mother, a strong character converted by Hilaire Belloc. An unorthodox pupil at Ampleforth College (1934–40), Herbert's career at Balliol College, Oxford (1940–42), was academically undistinguished. Already at Oxford his mannered charm and the variety—indeed eccentricity—of his intellectual interests brought him a circle of friends that was to extend from Taiwan to Alberta. It included Roy Harrod, whose intercession helped to save him from disciplinary disaster at Balliol.

On leaving Oxford, Herbert was rejected for service not only in the British army but also by the Free French and Dutch forces. Undeterred he applied and was accepted as a private by the Polish army in the 14th Jazlowiecki lancers; transferred to the 1st Polish armoured division, he became the only British born officer in the Polish army. He fought through the Normandy campaign of 1944 and was awarded the Polish order of merit with swords. In 1944, when on a personal mission from Winston Churchill to the Polish armoured division, he was arrested by Canadian military police in a Ghent bar; his striking appearance, an absence of identity papers combined with an abundance of money, and fluency in both Polish and English led his captors to suspect him as a spy, beating him up so severely that his face remained scarred.

Poland and its fate became Herbert's passionate concern: a Catholic country had been allowed to slip under a monstrous tyranny by what he regarded as a cowardly betrayal by the West at Yalta. He devoted his energy to the organization of the Polish Resettlement Organization and to the Anglo-Polish Society. Individual acts of kindness gave the London Poles the sense that they were not without friends in their darkest hours of isolation and despair. He founded and financed the Dulverton Textile Mills to give less fortunate Poles employment. He was awarded the civil decoration Polonia Restituta by the government in exile.

Herbert saw in what he was to call in a letter to *The Times* (30 August 1957) the 'ethnic revolution' a hope for the oppressed in the Soviet Union. He became vice-president of the Anglo-Ukrainian Society, visiting Ukrainians in Canada and returning with renewed enthusiasm. He was founder president of the Anglo-Byelorussian Society, his championship of that nation deepened by its attachment to an age-old liturgy untouched by reforming hands that destroyed his own Latin mass.

Herbert's devotion to these causes derived from a sense that it was the duty of his class, in return for the advantages it received, to support unfashionable causes, however remote their chance of success, simply because few others cared. Pixton, his large house near Dulverton in Somerset, where he kept up the open house tradition of his Acland forebears, was a refuge for exiles: Anatoly Kuznetsov, the Chinese pianist Fou Tsong, and indeed anyone in trouble. He also inherited property at Portofino where he enjoyed and entered into the feuds of local politics with the gusto of an English *grand seigneur*.

Herbert's efforts to follow his father into British politics were a predictable failure. He stood as a National Liberal candidate in two post-war elections; the electors of Aberafan and Sunderland revelled in his vivid oratory in a hopeless contest. His great disappointment was that the Conservative Party never gave him a safe seat in the west country. The mastery of tongues, which was his special gift, and his awkward sympathies for the oppressed, appeared to respectable Conservatives disqualifications for public office and proof of some incurable eccentricity—an impression heightened by his unreliability in mundane matters.

After a painful legal action to recover a large sum of money which the carelessness of a London bank and Herbert's own incapacity for business had allowed a Polish 'friend' to appropriate by forging cheques—it was characteristic of his unfailing generosity of mind that he continued helping the friend to survive after the disaster—Herbert's health suffered and he retired to Pixton, finding in the local life in which he had always taken an active interest and the care of his estate some compensation for the disappointment of his larger ambitions. Without his Catholic faith and his family he would have been rudderless. Like his brother-in-law Evelyn Waugh he despaired at the reforms of the Second Vatican Council, particularly the abandonment of the Latin mass.

Herbert displayed an old-fashioned courtesy in his relations with women but his closest friendships were with men. To his mother's distress and incomprehension he never married. He died suddenly at Pixton Park, Dulverton, on 21 July 1974. RAYMOND CARR

Sources J. Joliffe, ed., *Auberon Herbert* (1976) • *West Somerset Free Press* (2 Aug 1977) • Mrs Herbert, correspondence with the master of Balliol, 1940, Balliol Oxf., archives • Burke, *Peerage* (1980) • *The Times* (30 Aug 1957) [letter] • private information (1986) • *Ampleforth Journal*, 79 (1974), 109–11 • d. cert.
Wealth at death £895,772: probate, 6 Feb 1975, *CGPLA Eng. & Wales*

Herbert, Auberon Thomas [Bron], **eighth Baron Lucas of Crudwell and fifth Lord Dingwall** (1876–1916), politician and airman, was born at Ashley, Hampshire, on 25 May 1876, second of the two sons and third of the four children of the Hon. Auberon Edward William Molyneux *Herbert (1838–1906), political philosopher, and his wife, Lady Florence Amabell (d. 1886), sister of Francis Thomas de Grey Cowper, seventh and last Earl Cowper. His elder brother died as a child in 1882 and his mother four years later, leaving him heir-general to his uncle Earl Cowper. On the earl's death without issue in 1905 the baronies of Lucas of Crudwell and Dingwall devolved upon his nephew, who also became a coheir to the barony of Butler.

Herbert was educated at Bedford grammar school and at Balliol College, Oxford (1895–9). In 1898 and 1899 he rowed at number 7 in the university boat race against Cambridge. In the Second South African War he acted as correspondent to *The Times* and was wounded in the foot. The injury eventually led to the amputation of his leg below the knee. After he became Lord Lucas he was private secretary for a year to the secretary of state for war, R. B. Haldane. As one of the few Liberal peers he quickly gained office under the new Liberal government, and in 1908 he was appointed under-secretary of state for war; he held this position until 1911, when he was transferred to the Colonial Office as under-secretary. A few months later he was again moved, having been appointed parliamentary secretary to the Board of Agriculture and Fisheries. He was nominated a member of the privy council in 1912. In 1914 he became president of the Board of Agriculture and Fisheries, though without a seat in the cabinet; he remained president until the coalition government was formed in 1915, under which he did not gain office. Charles Hobhouse, a cabinet colleague, described Lucas's character as 'a good example of a Liberal peer, by conviction and training. Industrious after 11 a.m., courageous, rather advanced, hating the Germans and the Yankees' (*Inside Asquith's Cabinet*, 231).

G. K. Chesterton said of Lucas that his courage was 'casual and ... in a quiet way, crazy' (*Letters to Venetia Stanley*, 54). Having already served in South Africa, and in spite of his physical disability and the fact that he had passed the standard age, Lucas joined the Royal Flying Corps and proved himself a skilful pilot. He served in Egypt and then returned to England in 1916 as an instructor; on one occasion he was involved in a training accident in which his pupil was killed but he escaped. Lucas was offered the command of a squadron but preferred to go on active service in France. He had been at the front only for a short time when, on 3 November 1916, he made a flight over the German lines and did not return. He was reported missing, and on 4 December his death was officially announced by the War Office.

Lucas had made Wrest Park, his house at Ampthill in Bedfordshire, a hospital for the wounded and had offered it as a home for disabled soldiers. He was a close friend of Asquith, who devoted a section of his *Memories and Reflections* (1928) to him. John Buchan said he was 'a gypsy to the core' (*Letters to Venetia Stanley*, 54) and although he had been considered for vice-regal office Asquith noted that he 'hated the ceremonial side of things' (ibid., 541). Those who knew him suggested that he was perhaps happiest in the air. Bron, as he was always known, never married and his only surviving sibling, the Hon. Nan Ino Herbert, succeeded to his titles at his death.

ALFRED COCHRANE, rev. MARC BRODIE

Sources *The Times* (10 Nov 1916) • *The Times* (4 Dec 1916) • *Balliol College war memorial book, 1914–1919*, 2 (1924) • Burke, *Peerage* • H. H. Asquith, *Memories and reflections, 1852–1927*, ed. A. Mackintosh, 2 vols. (1928), vol. 2 • *H. H. Asquith: letters to Venetia Stanley*, ed. M. Brock and E. Brock (1982) • *Inside Asquith's cabinet: from the diaries of Charles Hobhouse*, ed. E. David (1977) • I. Elliott, ed., *The Balliol College register, 1833–1933*, 2nd edn (privately printed, Oxford, 1934) • *Raymond Asquith: life and letters*, ed. J. Jolliffe (1980)
Archives Herts. ALS, letters to Lady Desborough, etc.
Wealth at death under £100,000: probate, 5 Jan 1917, *CGPLA Eng. & Wales*

Herbert, Aubrey Nigel Henry Molyneux (1880–1923), diplomatist and traveller, was born on 3 April 1880 at Highclere Castle, Hampshire, the son of Henry Howard Molyneux *Herbert, fourth earl of Carnarvon (1831–1890), secretary of state for the colonies under Lord Derby (1866–7) and Disraeli (1874–8), and lord lieutenant of Ireland under Lord Salisbury (1885–6), and his second wife, Elizabeth or Elisabeth Catharine (Elsie; d. 1929), daughter of Henry Howard of Greystoke Castle, Cumberland, his first cousin. Aubrey was the elder son (there were no daughters) from the second marriage, Lord Carnarvon already having had a son and three daughters from his first. Although born into a family of great wealth and influence, Herbert suffered an affliction of the eyes from an early age which made him in effect blind for much of his life. He scraped through the Eton College of Dr Edmond Warre, under the particular care of Arthur Benson, his housemaster, without distinction, but in 1902 gained a first class in modern history at Balliol College, Oxford, where he also made a reputation for himself as a roof-climber, despite his blindness.

On leaving Oxford, Herbert was secured the position of honorary attaché at the embassy in Tokyo in 1902, but never allowed himself to become much interested in Far Eastern affairs. It was his next appointment in March 1904, to the embassy in Constantinople, which fired his enthusiasm for the Middle East and settled the subsequent course of his brief but eventful life. He was the

Aubrey Nigel Henry Molyneux Herbert (1880–1923), by unknown photographer, c.1916

model for the eponymous hero of *Greenmantle* (1916) by John Buchan, first Baron Tweedsmuir.

On his marriage on 20 October 1910 to Mary Gertrude (1889–1970), only child of John Robert William Vesey, fourth Viscount de Vesci, and his wife, Lady Evelyn Charteris, daughter of the eighth earl of Wemyss, Herbert's mother gave him Pixton Park, in Somerset, with 5000 acres, and a substantial family property in Portofino, Italy. Lady de Vesci gave them her splendid London house at 28 Bruton Street, and it was thought he should have a seat in parliament. After twice contesting South Somerset in the Conservative interest in 1910 he won in the 'coupon' election of 1918 and remained an MP for the rest of his life, for South Somerset until 1918, and then for Yeovil.

Membership of the House of Commons did not interrupt Herbert's extensive travelling in the Middle East. Throughout 1911 his attention was focused almost exclusively on the Balkans, to which he travelled frequently, having many friends among remote inland brigands as well as among the cream of Kemal Atatürk's reformist movement in Constantinople. His tireless work for the cause of Albanian nationalism was rewarded in 1913 with the first of two enquiries on the point of whether he would be prepared to accept the throne of Albania, if it was formally offered to him. On this occasion Herbert was quite keen to accept, but H. H. Asquith (a close family friend) was not encouraging and Sir Edward Grey, the foreign secretary, was against any British involvement in the Balkan tangle. The prize this time went to Prince William

of Wied, representing the Austrian faction. He did not last six months. Herbert was largely responsible for the creation of the modern, independent state of Albania after the First World War, championing the rights of the Albanians against the other Balkan states.

On the outbreak of the First World War, Herbert joined the Irish Guards, despite his near blindness, by the simple method of buying himself a second lieutenant's uniform and falling in as the regiment boarded ship for France in August 1914. After being wounded and briefly taken prisoner during the retreat from Mons, he joined the intelligence bureau in Cairo, later known as the Arab bureau, in December 1914 with T. E. Lawrence, who became a close friend and ally. As liaison officer and interpreter he took part in the Gallipoli campaign in 1915. He found that his ready command of French, Italian, German, Turkish, Arabic, Greek, and Albanian, and his personal friendship with many of the key figures in the area, made his presence invaluable to the commander-in-chief, although eyebrows were sometimes raised at his unremittingly pro-Turkish stance. He spent the rest of the war in intelligence work in Mesopotamia, Salonika, and Italy.

By 1920, although still receiving the Conservative whip in parliament, Herbert regarded himself as an independent, formally crossing the floor on the Irish vote on 20 November and thereafter sitting on whichever side he felt inclined. Effectively he was immersed in Albanian politics, although in February 1921, at the request of Sir Basil Thomson of Scotland Yard's special branch, he travelled to Germany for a secret meeting with Talaat, the Turk generally held responsible for the post-war Armenian massacres. Later that year, in Constantinople, he found himself put under surveillance by British military intelligence, the task being entrusted to his nephew, Henry Herbert, Lord Porchester.

Herbert's eccentricity was to dress as a tramp, and his appearance was further affected by his blindness and by a piebald hair coloration, the result of an early attack of alopecia. Herbert and his wife had one son, Auberon Mark Yvo Henry Molyneux *Herbert, and three daughters, the youngest of whom, Laura, became the wife of Evelyn Waugh. In the last year of his life Herbert was revisited by the total blindness which had afflicted his earlier years. In 1923, at a Balliol gaudy, he met his old tutor, A. L. Smith, now the master, who advised him that the best cure for blindness was to have the teeth extracted. Following this advice, Herbert developed blood poisoning and died on 26 September 1923 at 12 Beaumont Street, Portland Place, London. AUBERON WAUGH, rev.

Sources D. MacCarthy, *A memoir* (1924) • A. Herbert, *Mons, Anzac, and Kut* (1919) [repr. 1930 with an introduction by D. MacCarthy] • A. Herbert, *Ben Kendim: a record of eastern travel* (1924) • M. FitzHerbert, *The man who was Greenmantle* (1983) [a biography of Aubrey Herbert] • personal knowledge (1993) • Burke, *Peerage* (1999) • d. cert. • *CGPLA Eng. & Wales* (1924)

Archives Som. ARS, corresp., diaries, and papers | CUL, letters to Sir Samuel Hoare

Likenesses photograph, c.1916, priv. coll. [*see illus.*]

Wealth at death £49,970 15s. 4d.: probate, 31 March 1924, *CGPLA Eng. & Wales*

Herbert, Cyril Wiseman (1847–1882), painter, was born on 30 September 1847 at 1 Gloucester Road, Old Brompton, London, the youngest son of John Rogers *Herbert (1810–1890), painter and convert to Roman Catholicism, and his wife, Kezia Mary Dedman. He was the godson of Cardinal Wiseman and was educated at St Mary's College, Oscott, near Birmingham, and King's College, London. Like his brothers Arthur John *Herbert (1834–1856) [see under Herbert, John Rogers] and Wilfrid Vincent Herbert (d. 1891) he trained in his father's studio, and in 1868 he visited Italy, where he made many sketches, chiefly among the mountains around Olevano. He exhibited five paintings at the Royal Academy, including *Homeward after Labour: Cattle Driven Home* (exh. 1870) and *Returning to the Fold: Welsh Sheep Driven Home* (exh. 1874), which was purchased by Sir Andrew Walker and presented to the Walker Art Gallery, Liverpool. He exhibited at the Royal Academy for the last time in 1875, when he sent *Escaped Home*, portraying a collie dog returning to its mistress at a cottage door. Early in 1882 he was appointed curator of the antique school in the Royal Academy, but he died on 2 July 1882 at his home, The Chimes, in Kilburn, London. He was buried in the catacombs of Kensal Green Roman Catholic cemetery, London.

R. E. GRAVES, *rev.* ANNE PIMLOTT BAKER

Sources *Art Journal*, new ser., 2 (1882), 256 · *The exhibition of the Royal Academy* (1870–75) [exhibition catalogues] · Wood, *Vic. painters*, 3rd edn · Boase, *Mod. Eng. biog.* · private information (1891) · b. cert.

Herbert, Edward, first Baron Herbert of Cherbury and first Baron Herbert of Castle Island (1582?–1648), diplomat and philosopher, the eldest son of Richard (d. 1596) and Magdalen Herbert (d. 1627) of Montgomery Castle, was born on 3 March, probably in 1582, at the home of his maternal grandparents, Sir Richard (d. 1570) and Lady Margaret Newport at Eyton-on-Severn, Shropshire, where he lived until he was nine.

Family, early years, and marriage Edward's grandfather Sir Edward Herbert (d. 1593), who served as member of parliament for Montgomeryshire in 1553 and 1556–7, to a significant extent established the family fortune and was famed for his hospitality. Among the manors he acquired was that of Cherbury (or Chirbury), not far from Montgomery where he was constable of the castle. He was succeeded by Richard Herbert, who is said to have been handsome, brave, and accomplished in Latin and in history. Richard Herbert had been sheriff of Montgomeryshire in 1576 and 1584 and, probably, member of parliament for the county in 1585–6. His wife, Magdalen, was considered to be a lady of considerable virtue, charm, and piety who was esteemed by John Donne (with whom she developed a deep friendship, and who preached at her funeral) and Izaak Walton. In 1608 she married Sir John *Danvers, who was much younger than she.

Edward Herbert had six younger brothers and three sisters. The brothers were Richard (d. 1622), a soldier who fought in the Low Countries; William, also a soldier who died young, having fought in both Denmark and the Low Countries; Charles (d. 1617), a fellow of New College, Oxford; George *Herbert, poet and divine; Henry *Herbert, a strong royalist who was appointed master of the revels by James I and who was knighted in 1623; and Thomas *Herbert, who served at sea with some distinction. His sisters were Elizabeth, who married Sir Henry Jones of Abermarlais, Carmarthenshire; Margaret (d. 1623), whose marriage to John Vaughan of Llwydiarth marked the end of a prolonged conflict between their families; and, Frances, who married Sir John Brown of Lincolnshire.

Edward Herbert had a sickly infancy, suffering from discharges from his ears, and it was a long time before he started to speak. He reports, however, that he understood what others were saying and only refrained from speaking out of fear of saying something impertinent or imperfect. He also alleges that one of his first questions was to enquire how he came to be in the world—a question that caused some mirth among those looking after him. In 1591 he stayed nine months with Edward Thelwall of Plas-y-Ward in Denbighshire in order to learn Welsh, but gained little because he was ill all the time that he was there. When his health improved, he was sent to 'one Mr Newton at Diddlebury in Shropshire' (*Life*, 15) to learn Greek and logic, so as to make up what had been lost of his education because of his illness. His progress was such that in May 1596 he matriculated at University College, Oxford. A few months later he was called home by his mother because his father was seriously ill. After his father's death, he returned to his studies in Oxford. His relatives then arranged for him to wed Mary Herbert (1578?–1634), one of his relatives, who was four years older than he and whose inheritance as the heir to her father, Sir William *Herbert (d. 1593), was on condition that she marry someone whose surname was Herbert. The wedding took place at Eyton on 28 February 1599, after which Herbert returned to Oxford with his wife and also his mother. The couple had two sons, Richard [see below] and Edward, and two daughters, Beatrice and Florence (who died in infancy). Herbert claims that he studied hard at the university, teaching himself French, Italian, Spanish, and music in order, as he puts it, 'to make my selfe a Citizen of the world as farr as it were possible' and to avoid needing 'the company of younge men in whome I obserued … much ill example and deboist [debauchery]' (ibid., 17). He also developed his skills in riding and fencing.

In 1600 Herbert moved to London, but continued his studies. On presenting himself at court, the ageing Queen Elizabeth noticed him and, after being told who he was, remarked that 'It is pitty he was married soe young!' (*Life*, 37). He travelled to Burleigh House, Stamford, in April 1603 to meet the new king, James, who was on his way to London, and in July he was made a knight of the Bath. Herbert's autobiography professes that he took the chivalrous duties of knighthood very earnestly; although this was a time when honour was taken seriously, and while he was brave as well as gallant and very ready to take part in duels, there sometimes seems to be an underlying touch of wry comment in his descriptions of his involvement in such matters that perhaps reflects the sense of an older person recalling the more extravagant episodes in his youth. In 1605 Herbert's family persuaded him to move to Montgomery Castle to continue his studies, rather than accompany the earl of Nottingham's mission to Spain. That year he served as sheriff of Montgomeryshire and was elected member of parliament for the county; thereafter his name is regularly on the role of magistrates for the county. In 1607 James I gave Montgomery Castle to Philip Herbert, who had been made earl of Montgomery in 1605. Edward Herbert reacquired it from his cousin in July 1613 on paying £500; in 1616 it was then granted to Sir William Herbert to administer on behalf of the crown, but once again Edward Herbert soon regained its possession.

Soldier and traveller In 1608 Herbert went abroad with Aurelian Townsend. Through Sir George Carew, the English ambassador to the French court, he was introduced to French society. He developed a close acquaintance with Henri de Montmorency, the constable of France, and spent considerable time at his estates, where he rode and hunted. On his return to Paris he lodged with Isaac

Casaubon. According to his autobiography he 'much benefited' from 'learned Conversation' with 'that Incomparable scholler' (*Life*, 49), but he provides no information about the topics discussed. He also attended the court. In January 1610, after a stormy passage from Dieppe in which he was nearly shipwrecked, he returned to England. After spending some time in London at court and with his family, Herbert returned to the continent in late June with Grey Brydges, Lord Chandos, to take part in the siege of Juliers, where the English forces were commanded by Sir Edward Cecil. Here he behaved bravely, if sometimes foolhardily, and is claimed to have been the first to enter the town on its fall. During the siege a quarrel with Lord Howard of Walden (later the second earl of Suffolk) led to a challenge, but while Herbert was determined to fight a duel, he was prevented by the interventions of Sir Edward Cecil and later, in England, the matter was investigated by the privy council. On leaving Juliers he returned to England by way of Düsseldorf, along the Rhine to Antwerp, Brussels, and Calais.

In London, Herbert claims that he was 'in great Esteeme both in Court and Citty' and that people had copies of his portrait made (*Life*, 60). Sir John Ayres became

Edward Herbert, first Baron Herbert of Cherbury and first Baron Herbert of Castle Island (1582?–1648), by Isaac Oliver

jealous of his wife's interest in Herbert (although the latter says that 'litle more then common Civility ever past betwixt us' (ibid.)) and, aided by four others, attacked him. Herbert was stabbed but fought off his assailants. In February 1614 the register indicates that Herbert was admitted to Gray's Inn, but he does not seem to have thought this important. Later that year Herbert, with other English volunteers, joined the Dutch army under Maurice of Nassau that was involved in renewed conflict with Spanish forces. He was well received and on one occasion, outside Wezel, offered to accept a challenge from a Spanish officer to end the conflict by single combat. The Spanish commander, Spinola, forbade the duel; when Herbert went over to the Spanish camp to discover why, Spinola honoured Herbert at his table. On leaving him Herbert told Spinola that if the latter ever fought 'against the Infidels', he would join him.

Herbert then left the forces and travelled to Cologne and Heidelberg where he met the elector palatine and his wife, the daughter of James I. Travelling through Ulm and Augsburg, he visited the English ambassador at Venice before seeing the sights in Florence and Siena. When he arrived in Rome, he went to the English College and told the person who came to the door that he had not come 'to study Controversies but to see the Antiquityes of the Place' and closed the conversation by remarking that he was not seeking a quarrel since,

> I conceived the Points agreed upon on both sides were greater Bonds of Amity betwixt us Then that the Points disagreed could break them, that for my part I loved euery body that was of a pious and vertuous life, and thought the Errors on what side soever, were more worthy Pitty then Hate. (*Life*, 74)

He does not record any reply being made to his theologically liberal sentiments, but reports that he spent about a month touring Rome. He describes Rome as the centre of first a political empire and then, later, of an even more powerful religious empire, since the power of absolution gave greater control over people than political force could ever achieve. He left Rome in some haste. Having gone to see 'the Pope in Consistory', he aroused the suspicion of the Inquisition by departing suddenly when the Pope was about 'to give his Blessing' (ibid., 75). Among the places that he then visited were Florence, where he was entertained by Sir Robert Dudley; Padua where he attended lectures, in particular by Cesare Cremonini; and Venice where the English ambassador, Sir Dudley Carleton, invited Herbert to accompany him to Turin. In Turin the duke of Savoy invited Herbert to serve him by going 'to Languidoc in France to conduct 4000 men of the reformed Religion … unto Piedmont', where they were to assist the duke in his war against the Spanish (ibid., 77). After a hard and adventurous journey Herbert reached Lyons, where he was arrested by the governor. Although he did not behave tactfully in this situation (and eventually challenged the governor to a duel), he was soon released by the interventions of Sir Edward Sackville, who was visiting the town, and the duc de Montmorency. Continuing his travels, he stopped in Geneva before visiting the elector

palatine and his wife in Heidelberg; he then moved on to the Low Countries, where he was favourably entertained by Maurice of Nassau. After several attempts to cross the channel, he made a difficult winter passage. Reaching London early in 1617, he fell ill with 'a Quartuan Ague' from which he suffered 'without intermission' for a year and a half, and then intermittently for another such period (ibid., 87ff.). At those times that he was healthy, Herbert attended to his studies, got into scrapes (the privy council telling him after one episode that he should appreciate that his state of health was too poor for fighting), and developed friendships with John Donne, Ben Jonson, John Selden, and Thomas Carew. Five letters that he wrote in 1617–18 to Sir Robert Harley about religion have survived. In them Herbert affirms that 'God's Church is all mankind' and that 'God makes no man whom hee gives not means to come to him' and to receive 'eternall Happines' by loving him (BL, Add. MS 70001). These liberal views were later to be developed in his works on philosophy and religion. The correspondence indicates that Harley was not happy with them.

Diplomacy In 1619 George Villiers, earl of Buckingham, was introduced to Herbert. Following this Herbert was appointed to be the English ambassador to France, which he did not expect; he reports that he thought he was in trouble again when the privy council summoned him to tell him of the appointment. Herbert left London on 13 May, the day on which Queen Anne was buried, and crossed the channel 'with a Train of an hundred and odd persons' (*Life*, 92), although without his wife, who refused to accompany him to France. His instructions were 'to renew the Oath of Alliance' between the kings of England and of France (ibid., 89) and to ensure peaceful relations between their countries. Setting himself up with some style in Paris, he soon showed himself to be an able but somewhat independently minded diplomat and succeeded in securing precedence at the French court over the Spanish ambassador. While in France he attempted to frustrate Spanish Habsburg plans, recommended to Buckingham a marriage between Prince Charles and Henrietta Maria of France, sought to aid protestants both in France and elsewhere, and supported the attempts of the elector palatine to hold the Bohemian throne. In the last of these matters especially, he went beyond the wishes of James I—who, he comments, was 'that pacifike Prince all the world knew' (ibid., 102)—for the king would not take action to help the elector palatine, although he was his son-in-law. Herbert as a result was reprimanded, but it should be noted that, as with other ambassadors of James I, he was handicapped by not receiving clear instructions from the king about English diplomatic policy. In 1621, however, he was told to try to prevent planned military attacks on French protestants. His endeavours led to a quarrel with the duc de Luynes, the favourite of Louis XIII, and the threat of a duel. The French complained and Herbert was summoned back to England in July. De Luynes died in December and in February 1622 Herbert was sent back to France with no clearer general instructions than to use his own discretion as to what was best. To aid him in this he collected information from correspondents throughout western Europe. After the abortive attempt to marry Prince Charles to the Spanish infanta, Herbert was given the delicate task of seeking to arrange a marriage with the French princess, Henrietta Maria. Herbert's advice on the matter, however, offended both James I and the French; he was curtly recalled in a letter dated April 1624 and returned to England in July. His autobiography ends at this point. The crown failed to reimburse considerable debts that he had incurred during his time as ambassador, but sought in December to fob him off with the Irish barony of Castle Island, co. Kerry, and, in April 1629, with the English barony of Cherbury.

Philosophy Before Herbert left Paris he had found time to complete and—after gaining the approval of Grotius and Tielenus—to have privately printed his major philosophical work, *De veritate, prout distinguitur a revelatione, a verisimili, a possibili, et a falso* ('On truth, in distinction from revelation, probability, possibility and error'). An English translation of the work was eventually made by Meyrick H. Carré (1937). The first edition of 1624 is dedicated to 'the whole human race', but the second edition of 1633 and final edition of 1645 are dedicated, perhaps less grandly, to 'every reader of sound and unprejudiced judgement'. In this work Herbert attempts, sometimes in rather obscure Latin and with cloudy reasoning, to determine how people may and do identify what is true. Eschewing the appeal to supposed authorities, he maintains that the use of 'right reason' ('recta ratio') provides a reliable way between the errors of scepticism and bigotry. While, however, he presupposes that reason is the final arbiter of what is true, he is aware that people come to different judgements and so, paradoxically, holds that individuals should test their judgements against the standard of universal consent.

Herbert's epistemology is based on his doctrine of what he calls the 'faculties' ('facultates'). According to this doctrine there is in each person a huge number of faculties, each of which corresponds to a distinguishable object, whether physical or intellectual. Truth is grasped when an object is perceived in terms of the pre-established faculty that conforms to it, and it is known to be so grasped by an inner sense of satisfaction. In this way Herbert presents what may be regarded as a common-sense view of truth that recognizes that the mind is not a passive tabula rasa on which objects make impressions but is active in knowing them. At the same time, contrary to Locke's criticism, he holds that what are innate are not actual propositions, but latent modes of thought that have to be actualized by appropriate experiences. Herbert also holds that among the intellectual objects latent in the faculties are certain 'common notions' ('notitiae communes'). These are implanted by God in every person. When raised to consciousness through appropriate stimulation, they are recognized by all reasonable people to provide the normative principles for distinguishing what is true and good from what is false and bad.

Probably the most famous (and controversial) part of Herbert's thought is his application of his doctrine of common notions to religious belief. He maintains that the criterion for true belief and the authentic way to salvation are not given in alleged revelations, but in the five common notions of religion. These are that: God exists; God ought to be worshipped; the heart of religion is found in virtue joined with piety; evils must and can be expiated by means of repentance; and people face reward or punishment after this life. While, finally, Herbert allows that some truths may have been divinely revealed, he suggests stringent tests for authenticating supposed revelations and maintains that no alleged revelation can be from God if it contradicts (as opposed to reaffirming or adding to) what is established in the five common notions of religion. In spite, however, of his remarks about revelation, the last pages of his autobiography intriguingly report that he finally determined to have *De veritate* printed after receiving, in answer to prayer, what he interpreted as a divine sign to publish it.

In 1645 Herbert published a third, enlarged edition of *De veritate*, some copies of which included *De causis errorum: una cum tractatu de religione laici, et appendice ad sacerdotes; nec non quibusdam poematibus* ('Concerning the causes of errors, with a treatise concerning religion for the laity, and an appendix to priests; with certain poems'), a collection of writings that was also issued separately. The first of these pieces deals with fallacies that arise through failure to meet the appropriate conditions for perceiving the truth as laid down in *De veritate*. The second (an English translation of which was published by H. R. Hutcheson in New Haven in 1944) maintains that lay people can and should decide between rival systems of belief and avoid the errors introduced into religion by priestcraft. This is by applying the criterion of the common notions of religion that God has planted in the mind ('in ipsa mente coelitus descriptae') to judge what is to be believed and practised. The religious significance of what the Bible reports is also to be determined by this criterion.

History On returning to England in 1624 Herbert divided his time between London and Montgomeryshire. Although he was a member of the council of war and, as such, drew up proposals about a private militia for the king, he was without a significant official position. In an attempt to gain royal approval, he wrote two histories. The first, *Expeditio in Ream insulam* ('The expedition to the Île de Ré'), using notes made by Buckingham, was an attempt to vindicate Buckingham's conduct in leading the English forces sent to the Île de Ré in 1627 to aid the Huguenots in La Rochelle. Written in response to criticisms made in French pamphlets, particularly one by Jacques Isnard, Herbert's defence of Buckingham was not very successful—but the mission was such a fiasco that it is impossible to envisage how he could have succeeded. The Latin manuscript, dedicated to Charles I and dated 10 August 1630, was not published until 1656. The major response that it gained from the king was a request to write a history of Henry VIII. Consequently, following the death of his wife in October 1634, Herbert began work on *The Life and Raigne of King Henry the Eighth*. In writing it he made use of materials in official archives and in the Cotton Library, which had been closed to the public since 1629. To help his researches, in which he was assisted by Thomas Master of New College, Oxford, Herbert was provided with apartments in Hampton Court Palace. In a petition in January 1635 he asked permission to move to Whitehall or St James's in order to be more conveniently placed to use the records in the former and the library in the latter. As a good historian he was prepared to contrast what was widely said to have happened with what is stated in the documents, but on occasion he was also prepared to insert remarks that give voice to his own point of view—as when, in reporting a debate of the House of Commons in 1529, he interpolates a speech advocating the canon of the 'Common, Authentick, and universal Truths' that are recognized throughout humankind due to the benevolent providence of God. While the work was completed in 1639, it was not published until 1649. Although it too failed to gain any significant mark of royal approval, it was long regarded as a standard, authoritative study of the reign.

In another fruitless effort to win royal favour, Herbert had in March 1635 submitted to Charles I a paper on royal supremacy in which he argued that the king should be the sole head of the church. In sending the paper to Laud, the king did not help Herbert's relationship with the archbishop, with whom he had previously enjoyed good relations. A little later that year the papal envoy, Panzani, reported to the pope that conversations with Herbert indicated that he was not hostile to the Church of Rome and that he was prepared to submit his *De veritate* to papal criticism. It is not improbable, however, that the report may reflect a misunderstanding of a combination of Herbert's desire for appreciation with his conviction that all sensible people, even the pope, would acknowledge the yardstick of the five common notions of religion.

Civil war and final years As a member of the council of war, Herbert was summoned in 1639 to attend the king at York in connection with the expedition against the Scots. After initially drawing attention to his grievances over failure to pay debts that he had incurred in serving the crown, he eventually joined the court, accompanied by his younger brother, Henry. At Alnwick he wrote a poem, 'The Idea', whose musings on the contrast between Platonic perfections and earthly reality suggest that his mind was not focused on the threatened conflict. Returning to London at the end of the year, he took up his intellectual pursuits, in particular on the question of the 'religio laici' ('religion for the laity') and on *De causis errorum* ('Concerning the cause of errors'). In March 1640, however, he wrote to F. Liceti that he did not expect to be able to finish the latter because of the noise of warfare. In April he took his seat in the House of Lords and in September joined the king at York where, on 6 October, he spoke in the council against making a treaty with the Scots, who had now invaded England. His advice rejected, Herbert, whose health was not good, retired to Montgomery Castle. In 1641 he was in London and was one of the peers who voted for the bill of attainder against Strafford. During May the following

year, however, he was committed to the Tower of London by the Commons for suggesting that the king should only be held to have broken his coronation oath if he made war on parliament 'without cause'. He was released after apologizing and he retired again to his studies in Montgomery. From then on, although his sons were active in the royalist forces, he himself attempted so far as was possible to avoid being involved in the civil war. Pleading ill health he declined to join the king at Oxford and, on two occasions in 1644, he declined to join Prince Rupert at Shrewsbury. He also told the prince that the presence of his son's troops at Montgomery meant that there was no need to send more soldiers to garrison the castle. On 3 September Sir Thomas Middleton's parliamentary force reached Montgomery and summoned Herbert to surrender the castle. In February 1644 parliament had resolved on the confiscation and sale of Herbert's property in London, but officials postponed the sale of his valuable library in London that was planned for 30 August to learn what Herbert would do about surrendering the castle. Herbert, who was accompanied in the castle by his daughter Beatrice, was unwell, in no mood to fight, and valued his books. He surrendered the castle, having had a sentence included in the articles of agreement laying down that none of the occupying troops should 'enter into the library or study of the said Edward Lord Herbert, or the two next roomes or chambers adjoyning to the said study or library' (the text of the articles of surrender, printed in *Autobiography*, 284–6n.). As a result, parliament's threat to his property was then lifted.

Having watched a royalist attempt to capture Montgomery Castle being fought off, Herbert moved to London. He affirmed his allegiance to parliament and on 2 November petitioned for financial support. In February 1645 he was granted £20 per week and no restrictions were placed upon his liberty. He primarily devoted himself to his studies, although in October 1646 he was appointed steward of the duchy of Cornwall and warden of the stannaries. In March 1647 he was permitted to appoint a governor for Montgomery Castle but a few weeks later, on 12 May, he was summoned to the House of Lords to explain why his governor had not resisted a royalist assault. During the autumn he visited Gassendi in Paris and may have gone to Holland to meet Gerard Vos (Gerardus Vossius) and his son Isaak, who had offered to have Herbert's *De religione gentilium* published in Holland. On 9 November he was fined for absenting himself from the House of Lords, but he pleaded ill health and the fine was remitted. Continuing to be troubled by money matters, on 4 May 1648 he reminded parliament that his pension was much in arrears. His health was now poor and on 1 August he made his will, designating his grandson Edward (the son of his elder son, Richard) as the main beneficiary of his unencumbered possessions, while leaving his numerous books in Latin and Greek to Jesus College, Oxford. According to John Aubrey's *Brief Lives*, on his deathbed Herbert asked his old friend James Ussher, archbishop of Armagh, to bring him the sacrament but then added, in typically robust fashion, that it would do him no harm even if it did not do him any good. Ussher was offended and refused. Herbert died on 20 August 1648 (according to his monument but the date has been queried since the burial register and the *Calendar of State Papers Domestic, 1648–1649* give the date as 5 August: see Evelyn Rogers, *N&Q*, new ser., 28, 1981, 524). He was buried, as he directed, 'without pomp or other ceremony than is usual' and without 'shew of mourning' at midnight in St Giles-in-the-Fields, London.

Posthumous publications and reputation At his death Herbert left several unpublished manuscripts. The *Expeditio in Ream insulam* and *The Life and Raigne of King Henry the Eighth* have already been mentioned. His *De religione gentilium* was published in 1663, when Isaak Vos saw it through the press in Amsterdam. An English translation by William Lewis (*The Antient Religion of the Gentiles and Causes of their Errors Consider'd*) was printed in 1705. In this work Herbert attempts to show that the evidence of actual religions, which he takes mainly from classical authors, confirms his thesis that the five common notions of religion are universally acknowledged. Data that seem to contradict this thesis are dismissed as arising either from priestly corruptions or from a failure to recognize symbolic usage. He ends the treatise by submitting it to the 'Judgement of the *Catholick* and *Orthodox* Church; but not to the impetuous Enemies of Universal Divine Providence and the Publick Peace' (*The Antient Religion*, 388). In 1768 W. Bathoe published *A Dialogue between a Tutor and his Pupil*. Although there are some doubters, and although the manuscript evidence indicates that the printed version needs editorial revision, this text as a whole is generally considered to be correctly ascribed to Herbert. In it he develops the thesis advanced in *De religione gentilium* by paying particular attention to the recognition of the third and fourth common notions of religion (virtue as piety, and expiation by means of repentance) in all faiths. Priestly corruptions are again denounced. The work stops before the fifth common notion (post-mortem judgment) is discussed. Four years earlier *The Life of Edward Lord Herbert of Cherbury Written by Himself* had been published with a dedication and introduction by Horace Walpole. Again there are problems with the original published text, and a revised edition by J. M. Shuttleworth was published by Oxford University Press in 1976. In it, in a lively and somewhat tongue-in-cheek fashion, Herbert tells the story of his life and ideas up to the time of his recall from France in 1624. In the course of his story he throws light on his views on such matters as duelling and education, herbal remedies and religion. A continuation of the life, but in a properly sober, academic manner, was provided by Sidney Lee in a usefully annotated edition of the autobiography published in 1886. An edition of Herbert's poems in English and in Latin (but not including the three that appeared in 1645) was published by Sir Henry Herbert, his brother, in 1665. While the poems show the influence of John Donne and Giambattista Marino, the later ones in particular show qualities that suggest that Herbert may be considered to be an unwarrantably neglected poet.

Finally, a comment needs to be made about Herbert's reputation as a 'deist' and 'the father of deism in England'.

The latter ascription has been so long and so commonly made that it has become almost a second title for Herbert. Its justification is, however, open to question. On the one hand, it is not clear that—apart from being one of the sources used by Charles Blount (an eclectic and at times plagiarizing writer)—Herbert's views had any notable influence on those later writers commonly called deists, itself an unclear designation of doubtful value. On the other hand, Herbert's own statements indicate that he is to be regarded as a theologian of liberal convictions who sought to establish a rationally warranted understanding of religious belief that avoided the pitfalls of scepticism and bigotry; properly acknowledged the actuality of God as a universal providence whose gracious activity influences the lives of individuals; recognized that divine salvation is available to all humankind through repentance; affirmed the efficacy of prayer and the reality of personal immortality; was suspicious of the pretensions of priestcraft; and sought through the common notions to identify ways by which any reasonable person can justifiably choose between the competing claims of rival systems of faith. Herbert claimed to be an independent thinker and, although he was more of a provocative gentleman thinker than a rigorous scholar, he deserves to be respected as such—and, so far as modern English (or perhaps it should be said Anglo-Welsh) writers are concerned, as one who presented in *De veritate* the first metaphysical treatise and in *De religione gentilium* the first study of comparative religion.

Richard Herbert, second Baron Herbert of Cherbury and second Baron Herbert of Castle Island (1600?–1655), the elder son of Edward Herbert, was a magistrate in Shrewsbury, Shropshire, in 1634 and was involved in relieving the poor there during an attack of the plague. He married Lady Mary, the daughter of John *Egerton, the first earl of Bridgewater, in November 1627. They had four sons, Edward Herbert [*see below*], John (who died young), Henry *Herbert, and Thomas, and four daughters, Frances, Florence (or Florentia), Arabella, and Alicia. Like his younger brother, Henry, Richard had somewhat extravagant tastes for his means. Correspondence from December 1635 and January 1636 concerns a quarrel with his father about his debts. In 1639 he commanded a troop of horse in the expedition against the Scots, while on the outbreak of the civil war he was commissioned in September 1642 to raise a regiment of foot and was appointed governor of Bridgnorth. In the following month he received a commission to be captain of a troop of horse; when the queen landed from Holland at Bridlington, Yorkshire, in 1643, he accompanied her to the court at Oxford. Later, in September, he was made governor of Ludlow. Attending the assembly of royalist members of the houses of parliament at Oxford in 1644, he signed the letter that was sent to the earl of Essex, the parliamentary general, seeking an end to the conflict. In that same year he was with Prince Rupert at Shrewsbury and was made governor of Aberystwyth Castle. On the death of his father in August 1648 he succeeded to the title and was bequeathed his father's horses while his wife received his father's viols and lutes.

Having been active on the royalist side in the civil war, parliament imposed on Herbert a large fine. It also required him to demolish Montgomery Castle while permitting him to keep whatever he could realize from its materials. He died on 13 May 1655 and was buried in the church at Montgomery. His son **Edward Herbert**, third Baron Herbert of Cherbury and third Baron Herbert of Castle Island (1630–1678), was born in February or March 1630, the favourite grandchild of the first Baron Herbert of Cherbury. According to the latter's will, money in a trunk and plate in his house in London were to be used for his grandson's education at university or in overseas travel. He was also left the contents of Montgomery Castle with the instruction that he was not to sell, or even to lend, the books and furniture there, and only to allow his father use of them on his giving good surety for their return 'with safety and without diminution'. Like his father and uncle he supported the royalist side throughout the civil war and he was imprisoned for a short time after joining Sir George Booth, Lord Delamere, in declaring for Charles II in Cheshire in 1659. He married first Anne, daughter of Sir Thomas Middleton (who had captured Montgomery Castle from his grandfather), and then Elizabeth Brydges, daughter of Lord Chandos, a granddaughter of his grandfather's friend. There were no children from either marriage. After the Restoration he was appointed *custos rotulorum* for Montgomeryshire in 1660 and for Denbighshire in 1666. In 1663 he built a house near the site of the former Montgomery Castle. Richard Davies, a Quaker from Welshpool, often interceded with Edward Herbert on behalf of imprisoned Quakers and was treated with consideration. Edward himself complained that his great-uncle, Sir Henry Herbert, with whom he corresponded, did not respect him properly, although it should also be noted that when in 1665 Sir Henry published a collection of the first Lord Herbert of Cherbury's poems, he dedicated them to Edward. Edward Herbert died on 9 December 1678 and was buried in St Edmund's Chapel in Westminster Abbey.   DAVID A. PAILIN

Sources *The autobiography of Edward, Lord Herbert of Cherbury*, ed. S. L. Lee (1886) · *The life of Edward, first Lord Herbert of Cherbury written by himself*, ed. J. M. Shuttleworth (1976) · J. D. Griffin, 'Studies in the literary life of Edward, Lord Herbert of Cherbury', DPhil diss., U. Oxf., 1993 [incl. extensive bibliography] · M. M. Rossi, *La vita, le opere, i tempi di Eduardo di Cherbury* (1947) · D. A. Pailin, 'Should Herbert of Cherbury be regarded as a "deist"?', *Journal of Theological Studies*, new ser., 51 (2000), 113–49 · D. A. Pailin, 'Herbert von Cherbury', *Die Philosophie des 17. Jahrhunderts*, ed. J. P. Schobinger, 3 (Basel, 1988) · R. D. Bedford, *The defence of truth: Herbert of Cherbury and the seventeenth century* (1979) · E. D. Hill, *Edward Lord Herbert of Cherbury* (1987) · G. Gawlick, 'Einleitungen', in E. Herbert, *De veritate* (1966) [facs. edn] · G. Gawlick, 'Einleitungen', in E. Herbert, *De religione gentilium* (1967) [facs. edn] · G. Gawlick, 'Einleitungen', in E. Herbert, *A dialogue between a tutor and his pupil* (1971) [facs. edn] · *Montgomeryshire Collections* · J. Leland, *A view of the principal deistical writers*, 1 (1754) · *Brief lives, chiefly of contemporaries, set down by John Aubrey, between the years 1669 and 1696*, ed. A. Clark, 2 vols. (1898) · R. Warner, *Epistolary curiosities* (1818) · G. V. Lechler, *Geschichte des Englischen Deismus* (1841) · C. Guttler, *Edward Lord Herbert von Cherbury* (1897) · C. F. M. Rémusat, *Lord Herbert de Cherbury: sa vie et ses oeuvres* (1874) · C. C. J. Webb, *Studies in the history of natural theology* (1915) · *DNB* · E. Herbert, letters to Sir R. Harley, 1617–18, BL, Add. MS 70001

Archives BL, letter-book and Tractatus De Veritate, Add. MSS 7081–7082 · NL Wales, corresp., papers, and literary MSS · NL Wales, library catalogue and papers · NRA, letters and literary MSS · PRO, corresp., diaries, and papers, PRO 30/53

Likenesses oils, c.1600–1605, NPG · W. Larkin, oils, c.1609–1610, Charlecote Park, Warwickshire · W. Hollar, etching, c.1635–1640, BM · A. Walker, line engraving, pubd 1764 (after I. Oliver), BM, NPG · I. Oliver, miniature, Powis Castle, Powys [*see illus.*] · R. Peake, oils, Powis Castle, Powys · oils, Powis Castle, Powys

Herbert, Sir Edward (c.1591–1657), judge, was the son of Charles Herbert of Aston, Montgomeryshire, uncle of Edward, Lord Herbert of Cherbury, and Jane, daughter of Hugh ab Owen. He was educated at Queen's College, Oxford, and was admitted to the Inner Temple in 1609. Nine years later he was called to the bar and started what was to become a distinguished legal career as well as playing a leading role in the Virginia Company. In 1621 he was elected to parliament as MP for Montgomery, probably through family influence. This also accounts for his subsequent service in the House of Commons (1625, 1626, 1628) as one of the members for Downton, Wiltshire. In the 1626 parliament he helped manage the impeachment of George Villiers, first duke of Buckingham, and in 1629 he acted as one of the counsel for John Selden who was prosecuted for his actions in the Commons in the 1628 parliament.

During the 1630s, however, Herbert increasingly moved towards the court and became an avid supporter of royal policy. On 1 July 1630 he was appointed steward of the Marshalsea and in October 1633 he served as a member of the committee which arranged a masque presented by the inns of court against the recent publication of William Prynne's *Histrio-Mastix*. His legal prowess impressed the crown sufficiently for him to be appointed attorney-general to Queen Henrietta Maria in 1635, and two years later he assisted in the prosecution for seditious libel of Prynne, Henry Burton, and John Bastwick. His standing also continued to rise at the Inner Temple where he was named as autumn reader in 1636 and treasurer in 1638. Perhaps his only blemish in wholehearted support for government policy during the 1630s was when in 1633 he acted as one of the counsel for John Williams, bishop of Lincoln, who was being prosecuted by William Laud, archbishop of Canterbury, for his views on the placement of the altar table.

Clearly any differences Herbert and Laud may have had were patched up by 1640. On 25 January 1640 Herbert was appointed solicitor-general and shortly afterwards Laud nominated him for a seat at Old Sarum in the Short Parliament. Duly elected, he also served as MP for Old Sarum in the Long Parliament until 29 January 1641 when he was elevated to the position of attorney-general, and, as was customary, vacated his seat in the Commons to attend as a legal assistant in the House of Lords. He was knighted on 28 January 1641. Clarendon later noted that, in the Commons, Herbert had been 'so awed and terrified with their temper' that he had 'longed infinitely to be out of that fire' (Clarendon, *Hist. rebellion*, 1.279). However, due to his intense dislike of Herbert, Clarendon's remarks should be viewed with some caution.

As attorney-general Herbert exhibited the articles against those who had led the debates on the grand remonstrance who became known as the five members (John Hampden, Sir Arthur Hesilrige, Denzil Holles, John Pym, and Sir William Strode) and Lord Kimbolton. He charged them on 3 January 1642 before the House of Lords with traitorously conspiring to subvert the fundamental laws and other offences of high treason. Affronted at his actions, the Commons started impeachment proceedings against him on 14 February. He stoutly defended himself, claiming that he had only acted at the express command of the king. Charles also gave him support and wrote to the Commons on 8 March stating that he had drafted the articles against the five members, not Herbert. Nevertheless, he was declared guilty by the Commons although it declined to order any punishment. When the lower house informed the Lords of its decision, in deference to its wishes, the Lords committed Herbert to the Fleet and declared him ineligible to sit in either house of parliament or to hold any other office than that of attorney-general. He was released from prison on 11 May although he was ordered to reside within a day's ride of London and forbidden from entering London or Westminster without the permission of the Lords.

At the outbreak of the civil war Herbert joined the king at Oxford, although when he drafted a proclamation dissolving the parliament, Charles commented that 'he no more understood what the meaning of it was than if it were in Welsh' (*Life of … Clarendon*, 1.212). He did not lose Charles's favour, however, until 1645 when he declined the office of lord keeper. Thereupon on 1 November 1645 he was removed as attorney-general. Parliament sequestered his property in the following year and he was one of those royalists described as 'incapable of pardon'. In 1648 he fled to sea with Prince Rupert. He moved quickly to seek preferment from the new king after the execution of Charles I. He travelled to The Hague and was appointed attorney-general by Charles II. However, he did not remain long with Charles, as he journeyed to Brussels where he established himself as a confidant and adviser to James, duke of York. He increasingly became identified with a court faction known as the Swordsmen. Under the guidance of Prince Rupert, and led by Herbert and Lord Gerard, the Swordsmen opposed the policy of aligning the royalists with both the Scots and English presbyterians—a policy propounded by the Louvre group, the leading faction on the privy council. This stance, combined with his intrigues with the duke of York, incurred the wrath of the queen mother, Henrietta Maria. He returned to Paris with James in 1651 and took up residence at the Luxembourg. He continued to play a role in court politics and with the other Swordsmen attacked Clarendon's policy of supporting conspiracies among the royalists remaining in England. Herbert, however, seems to have retained the king's confidence and he was appointed lord keeper of the great seal in April 1653.

Herbert's elevation to the lord keepership did not stifle his desire to undermine Clarendon, especially by opposing the latter's support for the Sealed Knot. The culmination of this was the organization by the Swordsmen of the ill-conceived Ship tavern plot which led to the arrest of a number of royalists in London. Herbert's intrigues and hostility towards Hyde resulted in his downfall in 1654. The king refused to take Herbert with him to Germany and he resigned as lord keeper. He died in Paris in December 1657.

Herbert married, between 1635 and 1647, Margaret, daughter of Sir Thomas *Smith, master of requests, and widow of Thomas Carey, second son of Robert, first earl of Monmouth. Because of Herbert's losses during the war, at the Restoration she received a grant of the king's new year presents, less £1000, for three years. Their three surviving sons all achieved some measure of fame. The eldest, Arthur *Herbert (1648–1716), admiral, was created earl of Torrington; Charles lost his life serving William III during the battle of Aughrim (1691); and Edward *Herbert (1645–1698) was made lord chief justice by James II.

CHRIS R. KYLE

Sources Keeler, *Long Parliament* · HoP, *Commons, 1640–60* [draft] · D. Underdown, *Royalist conspiracy in England, 1649–1660* (1960) · *The life of Edward, earl of Clarendon … written by himself*, new edn, 3 vols. (1827) · Clarendon, *Hist. rebellion* · R. Scrope and T. Monkhouse, eds., *State papers collected by Edward, earl of Clarendon*, 3 vols. (1767–86) · R. Hutton, *Charles the Second: king of England, Scotland and Ireland* (1989) · Foss, *Judges* · *The autobiography of Edward, Lord Herbert of Cherbury*, ed. S. L. Lee (1886) · *JHC* · *JHL* · T. C. Dale, ed., *The inhabitants of London in 1638*, 2 vols. (1931)

Herbert, Edward, third Baron Herbert of Cherbury and third Baron Herbert of Castle Island (1630–1678). *See under* Herbert, Edward, first Baron Herbert of Cherbury and first Baron Herbert of Castle Island (1582?–1648).

Herbert, Edward [styled Sir Edward Herbert], **Jacobite earl of Portland** (1645–1698), judge and politician, was born on 10 June 1645, the younger son of Sir Edward *Herbert (c.1591–1657) and Margaret Carey, widow of Thomas Carey, and daughter of Sir Thomas *Smith, master of requests. His brother was the future Admiral Arthur *Herbert, the earl of Torrington. The elder Edward Herbert, while attorney-general, had impeached the 'five members' of the Long Parliament and later served as lord keeper during the exile of Charles II. Herbert and his mother remained in England during the interregnum and apparently suffered considerable poverty after the elder Herbert's death in 1657. Their fortunes improved after the Restoration. Herbert entered Winchester School in 1661 and matriculated from New College, Oxford, in August 1665. After taking his BA on 21 April 1669, he entered the Middle Temple. He soon looked to Ireland for a career. He was appointed as chief justice of Tipperary and as the king's attorney-general of Ireland in 1677, but a contemporary reported that Herbert was soon 'resolved to settle at Westminster Hall, for which he hath encouragement from some grandees there' (Cruickshanks, 529). Herbert returned to England and a series of royal appointments followed. In October 1683 he was appointed chief justice of Chester and solicitor-general to the duchess of York. On

10 February 1684 he was knighted. During the early months of 1685, Herbert acted as attorney-general to the duke of York.

In April 1685 Herbert secured election to parliament as the member for Ludlow. His parliamentary career was brief and undistinguished. He sat on committees to provide carriages for the royal progresses and to repair Bangor Cathedral. Eventually the Herbert family's long and loyal service to the Stuarts paid off handsomely during the reign of James II. In October 1685 Herbert was appointed to the privy council. When Justice George Jeffreys was made lord chancellor on 23 October, Herbert replaced him as chief justice of the king's bench. Jeffreys marked the occasion by urging Herbert to 'execute the law to the utmost of its vengeance upon those that are now known … by the name of whigs' and 'likewise to remember the snivelling trimmers' (*DNB*). Herbert later remembered these as ('difficult times' E. Herbert, *A Short Account of the Authorities in Law upon which Judgement was Given in Sir Edward Hales his Case*, 1688, 3) and claimed that he initially tried to decline the post. Contemporary rumours seem to confirm this reticence (*Fifth Report*, HMC, 499). But Jeffreys and the king, anxious to secure a pliable chief justice, prevailed upon Herbert to accept.

The 'new very young Lord Chief Justice' was soon thrown into the maelstrom of controversy (Evelyn, 4.517). At the Rochester assizes in March 1686 Sir Edward Hales was convicted for violating the provisions of the Test Act. A Roman Catholic, Hales had been appointed lieutenant of the Tower of London, and his coachman, Arthur Godden, had brought a collusive action against him. Hales appealed to the king's bench, arguing that James II had granted him a dispensation under the great seal, freeing him from the test. *Godden* v. *Hales* was immediately recognized as a critical case, one that would render judgment on the king's claimed power to 'dispense' with parliamentary statute. The case was heard before all twelve judges of the king's bench, the common pleas, and the exchequer. Infamously, James purged four judges hostile to his cause before the trial, a power entirely within his prerogative at the time. Herbert presided over the trial. 'The coachman's cause', Burnet remembered, was 'argued with a most indecent coldness, by those who were made use of on design to expose and betray it' (*Burnet's History*, 427). The case was heard on 16 June, and the next day, having consulted with the entire bench, Herbert delivered a verdict of eleven to one in favour of Hales and the crown. He spoke for about fifteen minutes, and held: 'tis an inseparable prerogative in the Kings of England to dispense with penal laws in particular cases, and upon particular necessary reasons'; 'that of those reasons and those necessities the King himself is sole judge'; and 'that this is not a trust invested in or granted to the King by the people, but the ancient remains of the sovereign power and prerogative of the Kings of England' (*State trials*, 11.1195). The decision, according to Evelyn, 'astounded all' (Evelyn, 4.517), and Burnet remembered that it was held in 'little regard' by even Herbert's 'nearest friends' (*Burnet's History*, 438). Angry denunciations of the decision were published,

including one that fumed that it was 'the reproach of our times to have men advanc'd to courts of judicature for other merits besides integrity and learning' (W. Atwood, *The Lord Chief Justice Herbert's Account Examined*, 1689, 1). Having fallen under 'the greatest infamy and reproach', Herbert published an able defence of his decision. He argued that the court had ruled only in favour of the king's power to dispense with laws in individual cases, not to suspend laws entirely. The latter suspending power must 'stand or fall on its own bottom, I am sure the case I am now speaking of has nothing to do with it', he wrote (E. Herbert, *A Short Account of the Authorities in Law upon which Judgement was Given in Sir Edward Hales his Case*, 1688, 3, 7). For generations whiggish historians have condemned Herbert's ruling in *Godden* v. *Hales* as perverse. Certainly James had been heavy-handed in rigging the courts to decide in his favour. Yet Herbert's distinction between the dispensing and the suspending power was critical. The latter was a traditional feature of the royal prerogative until it was outlawed by the Declaration of Rights.

In any case Herbert found himself riding high. There were soon rumours that he might replace Jeffreys as chancellor. Herbert had reportedly 'exposed' Jeffreys by 'laying open his bribes and corruption' during the bloody assizes, and Sunderland was using this information in an effort to topple Jeffreys (*Correspondence of Henry Hyde, Earl of Clarendon and Laurence Hyde, Earl of Rochester*, ed. S. Singer, 2 vols., 1828, 1.486). But as it transpired, Herbert himself soon fell from favour. As if to confirm that his decision in *Godden* v. *Hales* was one of conviction and not of expediency, he began to render decisions against the king. Appointed as a member of the king's ecclesiastical commission, he voted for the acquittal of Bishop Compton and against the effort to incapacitate the expelled fellows of Magdalen College. In a decision of 1687 over whether the king enjoyed the authority to execute deserters from his army during peacetime, Herbert demurred. For this decision he was demoted to the court of common pleas. Out of favour, he spent much of his time remodelling Oatlands, an estate in Surrey granted him by the king. Rumours that he had 'declared himself a Roman Catholic' were false (*CSP dom.*, James II, 2.345).

Herbert played little role in the great events of the coming year, but the collapse of James's reign left him dangerously exposed. By 11 December 1688 it was reported that he had fled London and was seen in Calais. He had never married, and so had no immediate family to concern him. He was exempted from William's Act of Indemnity, and his estate of Oatlands was seized. Herbert spent the remainder of his life at James's exiled court at St Germain-en-Laye, and was created earl of Portland in the Jacobite peerage in 1690. He was appointed James's chancellor, but his protestantism effectively disqualified him from the council. He was popular with the English Jacobites, but James kept him at arm's length. Herbert died of apoplexy at St Germain on 5 November 1698. He was buried next to the grave of his father in Paris.   JEFFREY R. COLLINS

Sources John, Lord Campbell, *The lives of the chief justices of England from the Norman conquest till the death of Lord Mansfield*, 2 vols. (1849); repr. (1997) · Foss, *Judges* · *State trials* · Foster, *Alum. Oxon.* · T. B. Macaulay, *The history of England from the accession of James II*, new edn, ed. C. H. Firth, 6 vols. (1913–15) · Holdsworth, *Eng. law*, vol. 6 · Wood, *Ath. Oxon.*, 1st edn · *CSP dom.*, 1689–95 · *Bishop Burnet's History of his own time*, new edn, 2 vols. (1838) · Evelyn, *Diary* · G. Agar-Ellis, ed., *The Ellis correspondence: letters written during the years 1686, 1687, 1688, and addressed to John Ellis*, 2 vols. (1829) · W. A. Speck, *Reluctant revolutionaries* (New York, 1972) · E. Cruickshanks, 'Herbert, Sir Edward', HoP, *Commons, 1660–90* · *DNB* · *Fifth report*, HMC, 4 (1876)

Herbert [*formerly* Clive], **Edward**, **second earl of Powis** (**1785–1848**), politician, born on 22 March 1785, was the eldest son of Edward *Clive, who was created earl of Powis in 1804, and his wife, Lady Henrietta Antonia Herbert (1758–1830), only surviving daughter of Henry (*c*.1703–1772), first earl of Powis (created 1748), and was grandson of Robert *Clive, first Baron Clive of Plassey. He was educated at Eton and St John's College, Cambridge, 1803 to 1806, when he took his MA. At the general election in November 1806 he was elected MP for Ludlow, holding the seat, mostly unopposed, until he succeeded to the peerage in 1839. He was a frequent though usually silent attender of the Commons, but moved the address in 1812 and 1829. He was a persistent conservative, opposing parliamentary reform, Catholic emancipation, and the abolition of slavery. He took the arms and surname of Herbert only in lieu of Clive by royal licence on 9 March 1807 in accordance with the will of his maternal uncle, George Edward Henry Arthur (1755–1801), second earl of Powis by the 1748 creation (*London Gazette*, 1807, 379). On 9 February 1818 he married Lady Lucy Graham, third daughter of James *Graham, third duke of Montrose, and his second wife, Caroline Maria. They had five sons, including the politician Sir Percy Egerton *Herbert, and two daughters; she died on 16 September 1875. In 1828 he was elected a member of the Roxburghe Club, of which he became president on 16 May 1835. In that year he contributed to the club *The Lyvys of Seyntys; Translatyd into Englys be a Doctour of Dyuynite Clepyd Osbern Bokenam*.

On 7 April 1830 Herbert succeeded his father as lord lieutenant of Montgomeryshire. He was thanked by the whig government for the active part which he took in suppressing the Chartist riots in that county (*The Times*, 10 May 1839). On the death of his father, on 16 May 1839, he succeeded to the earldom, and took his seat in the Lords on 14 June following. He was created LLD of Cambridge in 1835, DCL of Oxford in 1844, and KG in 1844. He strenuously opposed the scheme for the creation of a bishopric of Manchester by the union of the sees of Bangor and St Asaph, which, after a struggle lasting over four sessions (1843–6), and the appointment in January 1847 of a royal commission on the state of bishoprics in England and Wales, of which he was a member (*Parl. papers*, 1847, 33), he succeeded in defeating. This gained him great popularity with the clergy and at the universities. A subscription, amounting to over £5000, was collected as a testimonial to him, which was expended in the institution of 'Powis exhibitions' for the maintenance at Oxford or Cambridge of Welsh students acquainted with the Welsh language,

Edward Herbert, second earl of Powis (1785–1848), by Sir Francis Grant, 1843

and intending to enter holy orders (Herbert). On the death of the duke of Northumberland, Powis, at the invitation of the master and fellows of St John's College, was a candidate for the chancellorship of the University of Cambridge in opposition to Prince Albert. The prince, after a contest arousing considerable ill feeling, was elected by 953 votes to 837 on 27 February 1847. Powis died on 17 January 1848 at Powis Castle, Montgomeryshire, after being accidentally shot in the leg ten days earlier by one of his sons while pheasant shooting; he was buried in Welshpool church. He was succeeded by his eldest son, Edward James, third earl of Powis (1818–91).

G. F. R. BARKER, *rev.* H. C. G. MATTHEW

Sources GEC, *Peerage* · HoP, *Commons* · *GM*, 2nd ser., 29 (1848), 428–32 · *The Times* (19 Jan 1848) · Burke, *Peerage* · E. Herbert, *A narrative of the foundation of the Powis exhibitions to commemorate the maintenance of the sees of St Asaph and Bangor* (1847)

Archives NL Wales, corresp. and papers on chartist riots; corresp. and papers relating to union of dioceses of St Asaph and Bangor | BL, corresp. with Sir Robert Peel, Add. MSS 40485–40575, *passim* · LUL, letters to James Loch · U. Southampton L., letters to first duke of Wellington

Likenesses F. Grant, oils, 1843, Powis Castle [*see illus.*]

Herbert, Edwin Savory, **Baron Tangley** (**1899–1973**), lawyer and public servant, was born on 29 June 1899 in Egham, Surrey, the eldest child of Henry William Herbert (1860–1933), chemist, and his wife, Harriett Lizzie Elmes (*d.* 1953). He was one of a closely knit family of five children (four boys and one girl), brought up in a Methodist household under the kindly but strict influence of his God-fearing parents. This influence had a lasting effect on his character throughout his life. It was initially reflected in the fact that, after finishing his schooling at Queen's College, Taunton, in 1916, he was articled as a solicitor's clerk to George Macdonald, son of the Revd F. W. Macdonald, president of the Methodist conference.

In 1917 Herbert joined the Royal Naval Volunteer Reserve as a signalman, serving at sea, and after two years in the navy he returned home to complete his articles of clerkship. A London University law scholar, he studied in the Law Society's School of Law and gained first-class honours in the LLB examination in 1919, qualifying as a solicitor in the following year. From 1921 to 1924 he practised alone in Egham, after which he became a partner in the well-known City firm Sydney Morse, in which he eventually rose to be senior partner, having proved himself a practitioner of exceptional ability. On 29 December 1932 he married Gwendolen Hilda, daughter of Thomas Langley Judd CBE, an accountant, of London. They had one son and three daughters.

For nearly thirty years after 1935 Herbert was a member of the Law Society council and in 1956 he was elected the society's president. In 1967 he was the moving spirit in the foundation of the solicitors' European group of the Law Society, with the object of promoting better understanding in the profession throughout the continent. He served as the group's first president, a position he held until his death when the group numbered nearly 20,000 members.

Herbert also served on many government departmental and interdepartmental committees, beginning on the outbreak of war in 1939 with the aliens' tribunal and the regional price regulation committee, of which later he was chairman. In 1940 he was appointed director-general of the postal and telegraph censorship department at a time when it was barely emerging from its early teething troubles. Within eighteen months Herbert's energy and organizing powers had converted it into a highly efficient machine, spreading a worldwide net over both enemy and neutral mail and other means of communication, particularly at the imperial censorship stations in Bermuda and Vancouver. Convinced that the United States would eventually be forced into the conflict, he fostered and trained a shadow organization there, with the assistance of his censorship colleague Charles des Graz, director of the western area, to ensure that an integrated operation could immediately start up in the USA on similar lines when required. As soon as he heard the news of Pearl Harbor, with characteristic personal courage Herbert had himself flown across the Atlantic in a bomber so as to be at hand to offer the American director-designate of censorship in Washington his advice and encouragement. From that moment until the end of the war the two departments functioned as one in a remarkable display of co-operation and harmony. For his wartime services Herbert was knighted in 1943. He was subsequently awarded the American medal for merit and the Norwegian King Haakon's liberty cross.

After the war, while he remained a partner in his law firm, Herbert acquired a wide range of commercial interests in concerns where his expertise proved of great value.

In 1946 he became chairman of the oil company Ultramar, and was likewise chairman, deputy chairman, or director of the Industrial and General Trust, the Trustees Corporation, Imperial and Continental Gas, Yorkshire Insurance, Rediffusion, and other companies. In addition he served on the interdepartmental committees on matrimonial causes and on leaseholds in 1947 and 1948, respectively. He chaired the departmental committees on intermediaries (1949), and on the inquiry into the electricity supply industry (1954). In 1956 he was promoted KBE. A year later he was appointed chairman of the royal commission on local government in Greater London, which reported in 1960. For his work in this connection he was created a life peer on 22 January 1964, taking the title Baron Tangley of Blackheath, Surrey. Another royal commission on which he sat at this period was that on reform of the trade unions and employers' associations, 1965–8. In 1970 he became president of the court of arbitration of the international chamber of commerce.

In the House of Lords, Tangley sat on the cross-benches, where he proved a lucid and persuasive speaker, although he usually confined himself to subjects of which he possessed expert knowledge such as local government, the legal profession, law and order, and law reform, including the measure to abolish the death penalty for murder, which he supported.

Tangley was a modest man of great determination and energy, with an unlimited capacity for hard work. His recreations were sailing and mountaineering: he was an enthusiastic climber in his younger days, being honorary secretary (1935–40) of the Alpine Club, of which he later became president from 1953 to 1955. Also in 1953 he chaired the Everest committee when the world's highest peak was scaled for the first time. He had previously been chairman of the finance committee of the Commonwealth Trans-Antarctic Expedition led by Vivian Fuchs. He held honorary LLD degrees from Montreal (1956) and Leeds (1960). In 1969 he became an honorary fellow of Darwin College, Cambridge, and an honorary LLD of the university. He died at St George's Hospital, London, on 5 June 1973. H. MONTGOMERY HYDE, *rev.*

Sources *The Times* (7 June 1973) · *The Times* (11 June 1973) · *The Times* (14 June 1973) · H. Montgomery Hyde, *Secret intelligence agent* (1982) · private information (2004) · personal knowledge (2004) · b. cert. · Burke, *Peerage* (1967) · *CGPLA Eng. & Wales* (1973)
Archives Alpine Club, London, letters and papers
Likenesses W. Narraway, portrait, Law Society, London · W. Narraway, portrait, priv. coll.
Wealth at death £313,239: probate, 10 Aug 1973, *CGPLA Eng. & Wales*

Herbert [*née* Spencer], **Elizabeth, countess of Pembroke and Montgomery** (1737–1831), courtier, was born on 29 December 1737, the second of five children of Charles *Spencer, third duke of Marlborough (1706–1758), colonel and lord of the bedchamber, and his wife, Elizabeth (*d.* 1761), daughter of Thomas, second Baron Trevor of Bromham. Generally known in her youth as Lady Betty Spencer, she was described by Walpole as having 'the face of a

Elizabeth Herbert, countess of Pembroke and Montgomery (1737–1831), by Sir Joshua Reynolds, c.1765–7

Madonna' (Walpole, *Corr.*, 22.9) and was also known for 'her serenity and dignified conduct' (Long, 171). On 23 March 1756 she married Henry *Herbert, tenth earl of Pembroke and seventh earl of Montgomery (1734–1794), general and lord of the bedchamber, and thus became countess of Pembroke and Montgomery. The couple had probably first met in the 1740s when Lady Betty's brothers attended Eton College with Lord Pembroke. A child delivered on 9 June 1758 was stillborn, but on 10 September 1759 their first surviving child, George Augustus *Herbert, Lord Herbert (1759–1827), subsequently eleventh earl of Pembroke and eighth earl of Montgomery, was born.

Lady Pembroke's marriage did not turn out well. Lord Pembroke enjoyed foreign travel and was 'away on military duty for months at a time' (Long, 41), and in 1762 he eloped with Elizabeth Catherine (Kitty) Hunter, daughter of Thomas Orby Hunter MP, who was then one of the lords of the Admiralty. Evidently, he was bored with Lady Pembroke's 'goodness and sweetness' (Rowse, 93), although he left behind a letter 'to witness to the virtue of Lady Pembroke, whom he says he has long tried in vain to make hate and dislike him' (Walpole, *Corr.*, 22.10). Lady Pembroke and her husband were reconciled in March 1763, but the earl was followed by his illegitimate son with Kitty Hunter, Augustus Reebkomp. Lady Pembroke raised the child as a member of the family.

Lady Pembroke's main preoccupation became the education of her son, which she supervised at her homes—Pembroke House in London, Wilton House in Wiltshire, and Pembroke Lodge in Richmond Park—until he entered Harrow in 1770. She and Lord Pembroke had a further child, Charlotte (1773–1784). She ensured that she approved the choice of companions for her son's grand tour, the clergyman and historian William Coxe and Captain John Floyd. Her letters kept her son informed of political affairs, urging him to maintain his study of ancient and modern history, while Lord Pembroke emphasized more fashionable manly accomplishments such as fencing and dancing. Following Lord Herbert's return after four years abroad in June 1780, and his election as MP for

Wilton, she advised him to avoid becoming an active opposition supporter like his father. This far-sighted advice probably helped the Pembroke interest survive the political turmoil of the early 1780s, as the family avoided being closely identified with any of the political leaders mistrusted by George III. In October 1780 Lady Pembroke sent her son to the secretary to the Admiralty in order to prevent Augustus Reebkomp being commissioned a lieutenant as Augustus Herbert, as his father wished; the action hurt Lord Pembroke, but she succeeded in determining that only her children should bear the family name.

In November 1782 Lady Pembroke became a lady of the bedchamber to Queen Charlotte, a position which she retained until the queen's death in February 1818. This role put her in direct contact with George III. During his periods of 'madness', George III imagined that he was married to Lady Pembroke. Apparently, 'his infatuation went back to the days when he was only seventeen and she, of the same age, was Elizabeth Spencer' (Long, 312). The king went so far as to make 'her handsome offers if she would be his mistress. One of the ministry said that his pursuit of [her] was renewed "with so much ardor and such splendid offers that I tremble for her virtue"' (ibid., 317). The king referred to her variously as Queen Esther, Queen Elizabeth, and Minerva. Following his recovery from the illness of 1788–9, he wrote to her, and she responded on 8 April 1789:

> Your majesty has always acted by me as the kindest brother as well as the most gracious of sovereigns … if I might presume to say that I felt like the most affectionate sister towards an indulgent brother it would exactly express my sentiments. (Brooke, 335)

The countess continued to be above reproach in all her dealings with the royal family, although it was said that 'the Prince of Wales had hoped that if she became his father's mistress he would be able to "govern the King through her"' (Somerset, 247).

Despite the embarrassment that the king's infatuation had caused Queen Charlotte, Lady Pembroke still accompanied the royal family on a summer holiday to Weymouth in 1789. The queen's 'self-denial was rewarded' (Somerset, 247) since the 'visit, which was much dreaded, proved most serviceable' (ibid.), as Lady Pembroke behaved throughout the visit with such exquisite tact that it was not long before her hosts were put at their ease. In 1804 the king suffered another attack of dementia and again announced his desire for Lady Pembroke. This situation aroused some amusement among younger courtiers since she was by this time almost seventy years old. Her discretion, coupled with the fact that she did nothing to encourage the king's attentions, helped relieve a potentially hazardous and embarrassing situation.

Lady Pembroke died at Pembroke Lodge on 30 April 1831. Her role as object of the deranged George III's affections gave her a place in the mythology of the reign. The character of Lady Pembroke was portrayed in Alan Bennett's screenplay *The Madness of King George* (1995) as a seductive court intriguer, much younger than the historical Lady Pembroke was in 1788; this interpretation of her role would have alarmed her and baffled her contemporaries.   LISA HARTSELL JACKSON

Sources *Henry, Elizabeth and George, 1734–1780: letters and diaries of Henry, tenth earl of Pembroke and his circle*, ed. S. Herbert (1939) · *The Pembroke papers, 1780–1794: letters and diaries of Henry, tenth earl of Pembroke and his circle*, ed. S. Herbert (1950) · J. C. Long, *George III: the story of a complex man* (1960) · A. L. Rowse, *The Churchills: from the death of Marlborough to the present* (New York, 1958) · *DNB* · A. Somerset, *Ladies in waiting: from the Tudors to the present day* (1984) · C. Spencer, *The Spencers: a personal history of an English family* (1999) · J. Brooke, *King George III* (1972) · I. Macalpine and R. Hunter, *George III and the mad-business* (1969) · Walpole, *Corr.* · A. Bennett, *The madness of King George* (1995) · T. Lever, *The Herberts of Wilton* (1967)
Likenesses J. Reynolds, oils, *c.*1765–1767, Wilton House, Wiltshire [*see illus.*] · C. Turner, mezzotint, pubd 1824 (after G. Hayter), BM, NPG · F. Bromley, mezzotint (after J. Reynolds), BM, NPG · D. Gardner, pastel drawing, Wilton House, Wiltshire; repro. in *Pembroke papers* · J. Reynolds, double portrait, oils (with her son, George, Lord Herbert), Wilton House, Wiltshire · G. Romney, portrait, repro. in Long, *George III* · A. N. Sanders, mezzotint (after J. Reynolds), NPG

Herbert, (Mary) Elizabeth, Lady Herbert of Lea (1822–1911), Roman Catholic convert and philanthropist, was born on 21 July 1822, the only daughter of General Charles Ashe À Court Repington (1785–1861), sometime MP for Heytesbury, and his wife, Mary Elizabeth Gibbs (*d.* 1878), daughter of a West Indies planter. Elizabeth à Court Repington was a highly gifted young woman of considerable beauty, whose family moved in widely influential circles. She numbered among her friends Lady Dufferin and Lady Canning (both wives of future viceroys of India), and this circle was widened further after her marriage. On 12 August 1846, when she was twenty-four, she married Sidney *Herbert (1810–1861), half-brother to the twelfth earl of Pembroke, whom she had known since childhood. They had four sons: George Robert Charles *Herbert, who became thirteenth earl of Pembroke; Sidney, who succeeded him as fourteenth earl; Reginald, who became a naval officer and was drowned at sea in 1870; and Michael, who became ambassador in Washington in 1902. Their daughters were Mary, who married Baron Friedrich von *Hügel, philosopher and mystic; Elizabeth Maude, who married Sir Hubert *Parry, the composer; and Constance Gladys, who married firstly the fourth earl of Lonsdale, and, following his untimely death, Lord de Grey, who later became second marquess of Ripon.

Following her marriage Elizabeth Herbert took a keen interest in politics and did much of her husband's secretarial work. During the winter of 1847, while on their delayed wedding tour in Rome, the Herberts met Florence Nightingale for the first time. That meeting resulted in the close friendship which later assisted Florence Nightingale in her efforts to send nurses to Scutari during the Crimean War. The early days of Elizabeth Herbert's marriage saw the formation of other important friendships, notably with Henry Manning, whom she met while he was an Anglican. An old schoolfriend of Sidney Herbert, Manning was introduced to Elizabeth as 'the holiest man I have ever met'. The friendship blossomed and he assumed the role

(Mary) Elizabeth Herbert, Lady Herbert of Lea (1822–1911), by Richard James Lane, 1850 (after James Rannie Swinton, 1850)

of her spiritual director until he left the Church of England in 1851.

Elizabeth Herbert was very concerned about the plight of the poor, especially unemployed domestic servants who were considered to be in grave moral danger. For such women, often the only alternative to the workhouse was to resort to petty crime or prostitution. Early attempts at rescue work on behalf of the Church of England, such as the Clewer House of Mercy founded near Windsor by Mariquita Tennant in 1849, received the enthusiastic support of both Elizabeth Herbert and her friend and near neighbour W. E. Gladstone. Her letters to Mrs Tennant reflect a genuine concern for the underprivileged, which was both practical and down-to-earth. The Herberts also enthusiastically supported a number of state-assisted emigration schemes for the poor.

Elizabeth Herbert's social concern was born of her firm religious convictions. She was brought up in the Church of England and later recalled her early experience of religion as 'utterly and entirely distasteful', but with the coming of the Oxford Movement she found 'all that my heart and mind had longed for and hungered after for years—I found life, and warmth and practice'. The secession of Archdeacon Henry Manning to the Roman Catholic church was a blow which was widely felt, indeed Gladstone commented, 'It was not a parting: it was a death.' On a personal level it meant the severance of the friendship and spiritual counsel which had been so important to Elizabeth Herbert. She later described it as a 'sort of a religious shipwreck' and from this time onwards she began to have serious doubts about Anglicanism. At first she discussed this with her husband but, finding that it worried him, ceased doing so. If she had followed Manning at that time there would have been serious repercussions for her husband politically—the country was embroiled in the Crimean War and Sidney Herbert was secretary of state for war—and as the heir to his half-brother, the twelfth earl of Pembroke. Elizabeth laid aside her 'wracking doubts' and channelled her energies into supporting her husband and assisting Florence Nightingale in her scheme to send a task force of female nurses to the battle front.

Sidney Herbert never recovered from the stress his high office had placed on him: he died on 2 August 1861, just eight months after being created a baron, with the title Lord Herbert of Lea. During her mourning Lady Herbert retired at first to the south of France and subsequently to Rome. Her religious doubts increased and she once more sought counsel from Manning. Meantime, it was widely rumoured in English society that she had joined the Roman Catholic church. Her husband's family gave notice that if she took such a step they would make her children wards in chancery, her eldest son now being the heir to the earl of Pembroke. This threat greatly added to her confusion in addition to the grief of widowhood. And there were other matters to be considered too: Sidney Herbert had been a loyal Anglican and had built a magnificent church in Wilton, costing £30,000, where he was buried. Elizabeth went there daily to pray while at Wilton, and was organist in the chapel in the house which she and her husband had restored. She also knew she would be exchanging a respected position in society for 'the contempt and distrust of all those whose good opinion I most valued'. Not least among these was Gladstone, and when, after much turmoil, she finally took the step, it marked the end of a long and valued friendship, though he continued to involve himself in her children's education.

On 5 January 1866 Lady Herbert was received into the Roman Catholic church in a private ceremony at Palermo in Sicily. Having returned to England she was advised by Archbishop Manning to visit Father (later Cardinal) Herbert Vaughan who was establishing a missionary brotherhood at Mill Hill. From their first meeting in October 1866 an extraordinary spiritual friendship developed which has been compared with that of St Francis of Sales and St Jane Frances de Chantal: it lasted until Vaughan's death in 1903. Lady Herbert's conversion had resulted in her estrangement from family and friends and severance from her Anglican charities. She now embraced the missionary cause embodied in the work of the Mill Hill Fathers, as they became known. Through her financial help, and that of her new Catholic friends, Vaughan was able to realize his vision. From its beginnings at Holcombe House, the buildings expanded down the hill with the construction of St Joseph's College, the foundation stone of which was laid on 29 June 1869.

The college at Mill Hill took several years to complete, during which time missionary priests were being trained and sent abroad. The college chapel was consecrated in March 1875, one of the celebrants being Vaughan, by now a bishop. Vaughan's letters to Lady Herbert (her letters to him have not survived) reveal the depth of trust between them; there was also a great bond of mutual affection and a wide range of interests, as well as humour. It was a friendship of mutual need and encouragement: he consulted her widely on all his projects and respected her advice; she listened to his spiritual counsel and took comfort from it in her loss of family ties. Elizabeth Herbert's conversion to Roman Catholicism was total, her only regret being that, of her seven children, only Mary, wife of the mystic Baron Friedrich von Hügel, shared her Catholic faith (her husband's friends went to considerable lengths to see that this was so).

As in her Anglican days, Lady Herbert's influence covered a wide spectrum. For many years she acted as honorary treasurer of St Joseph's Foreign Missionary Society, Mill Hill, and hosted its meetings at Herbert House, 38 Chesham Place, Belgrave Square. She gave considerable sums from her own resources to this work and extracted further donations from her circle. The Sisters of Charity were also closely associated with the Mill Hill mission, and Lady Herbert founded and maintained a girl's orphanage at Salisbury which the sisters ran. Another project which Lady Herbert enthusiastically embraced and financially assisted was that of Westminster Cathedral. Cardinal Manning had not favoured the idea, but his successor, Cardinal Vaughan, did so and laid the foundation-stone in 1895, although he did not live to see the project come to fruition. After her conversion Lady Herbert wrote a number of religious booklets aimed at attracting converts, one of which, *How I Came Home* (1894), told the story of her own conversion.

Lady Herbert died at Herbert House on Monday 30 October 1911 after a long illness. Her body lay in state at Herbert House until Friday 3 November, when a solemn requiem was celebrated at Westminster Cathedral, the absolution being pronounced by Archbishop Bourne. She was buried in the cemetery at St Joseph's College, Mill Hill, near the grave of Cardinal Vaughan. Her surviving children attended, despite the earlier difficulties. Lady Herbert had been known at Mill Hill as 'The Mother of the Mill' because of her generosity: the epithet in life became her epitaph in death.

VALERIE BONHAM

Sources *The Times* (31 Oct 1911) • *The Tablet* (4 Nov 1911) • *St Joseph's Foreign Missionary Advocate*, 25 (winter 1911) • *The Times* (4 Nov 1911) [funeral] • *The Tablet* (11 Nov 1911) [account of funeral] • M. E. Herbert, *How I came home* [1894] • *Letters of Herbert Cardinal Vaughan to Lady Herbert of Lea, 1867–1903*, ed. S. Leslie (1942) • A. McCormack, *Cardinal Vaughan* (1966) • V. Bonham, *A place in life: the Clewer House of Mercy, 1849–83* (1992) • C. Woodham-Smith, *Florence Nightingale, 1820–1910* (1950) • Gladstone, *Diaries*

Archives BL, family corresp., Add. MS 59671 • Wilts. & Swindon RO, family and general corresp. | BL, corresp. with W. E. Gladstone, Add. MS 44212 • BL, letters to Sir Edward Walter Hamilton, Add. MS 48620 • BL, corresp. with Florence Nightingale, Add. MS 43396 • Bodl. Oxf., letters to H. E. Manning • Community of St John the Baptist, Clewer, 'Letters of the penitents' • U. Southampton L., letters to Lord Palmerston

Likenesses R. J. Lane, engraving, 1850 (after J. R. Swinton, 1850), NPG [*see illus.*] • J. R. Swinton, sketch, St Joseph's College, Mill Hill •

R. Thorburn, group portrait, oils? (*Lady Herbert of Lea and family*), Wilton House, Wiltshire

Wealth at death £33,809 19s. 10d.: probate, 30 Dec 1911, *CGPLA Eng. & Wales*

Herbert, George (1593–1633), Church of England clergyman and poet, was born on 3 April 1593 at Montgomery, seventh of the ten children of Richard Herbert (*d.* 1596) and his wife, Magdalen or Magdalene Newport (*d.* 1627). Herbert was (as his early biographer, Barnabas Oley, asserted) '*extracted out of a Generous*, Noble, *and Ancient Family*' (*Herbert's Remains*, sig. b6r); his paternal grandfather was Sir Edward Herbert, constable of Montgomery Castle and, from 1553, lord of Cherbury, while his maternal grandfather, Sir Richard Newport, was descended from Gwenwynwyn, ruler of southern Powys. Herbert's father was MP, JP, sheriff and deputy lieutenant of the county of Montgomery, and his first son, Edward, George's eldest brother, became the philosopher, diplomat, and poet Edward *Herbert, first Baron Herbert of Cherbury. George's younger brothers were Henry, born in the summer of 1594, who became Sir Henry *Herbert, master of the revels from 1623, and Thomas *Herbert, who became a naval officer.

George Herbert's place of birth was probably not Montgomery Castle, despite the claim of his seventeenth-century biographer, Izaak Walton; it is more likely that Herbert's parents were living in Black Hall in the valley below the castle (Charles, *Life*, 26–7). There is no extant record of Herbert's baptism, and the Montgomery period of his life was relatively short and overcast by mortality. When George was about six weeks old, his Herbert grandfather died, and some three and a half years later George's own father—described by Edward Herbert as a 'black haired and bearded' figure with 'a manly or somewhat stern look'—died of a 'Lethargie … which continued long upon him' (*Life*, ed. Shuttleworth, 2, 15). Magdalene Herbert was two months pregnant with their tenth child at the time of her husband's death. After the birth of this last son, Thomas, in May 1597, she moved with her large young family to the home of her mother, Margaret Newport, in Eyton-on-Severn in Shropshire. By early 1599, however, George's maternal grandmother had died and his family was on the move once again.

In 1599 Herbert's 'good and godly' mother (*Herbert's Remains*, sig. b6v) took her household to Oxford, where her eldest son, Edward, was already studying at University College. According to Walton it was during this Oxford period that Magdalene Herbert, and presumably George, met John Donne, though the earliest firm evidence of this friendship is a letter from Donne to Magdalene Herbert in July 1607. Meanwhile, however, the unsettled nature of George's early years had again reasserted itself: within two years of moving to Oxford, the family had left for London, taking a house in the Charing Cross area of the city early in 1601, at the very time of the Essex rebellion. While political frustrations were expressed on the streets of London, life within the walls of the Herbert home is vividly suggested by the extant *Kitchin Booke*, begun on 11 April 1601, from which is learned that there were twenty-six

George Herbert (1593–1633), by Robert White [posthumous]

members of the 'ordinary Howshold' (family and staff) in total. As George's brother Edward later tartly observed:

> My Mother together with my selfe and wife removed up to London where wee tooke house and kept a greater Family then became either my Mothers widdows estate or such young beginners as we were especially since six brothers and three sisters were to bee provided for. (*Life*, ed. Shuttleworth, 36)

The *Kitchin Booke* also records the livestock kept in the grounds of the house at Charing Cross, the meals served, the many visitors entertained and the resources expended on them. Among the guests for supper in 1601 were the composers John Bull and William Byrd, and the historian William Camden, whose company George may also have had during the summer of 1601 when he and his brother Richard stayed at the house shared by Camden with Will Heather, a lay vicar of Westminster Abbey. By this time the eight-year-old George was hard at work on his private study, including Latin; a number of tutors' names appear in the list of those attending the household, and the *Kitchin Booke* records that in August 1601 George needed paper for a 'Coppie and Phrase booke'. He also regularly heard sermons by Thomas Mountfort, a close friend of Donne, at the nearby parish church of St Martin-in-the-Fields.

Formal education George Herbert's eldest brother, Edward, acknowledged that their widowed mother 'brought up her Children carefully'; in the case of the boys of the family, this entailed not only the religious and moral discipline of the home, but a formal commitment to be 'brought up in Learning' (*Life*, ed. Shuttleworth, 8).

George entered Westminster School as a day pupil in 1604, while the renowned scholar and preacher Lancelot Andrewes was dean of Westminster. Andrewes was said to allow the pupils 'not an hour of Loitering-time from morning to night' and to check their 'Exercises in Prose and Verse' strictly for 'Style and Proficiency' (Hacket, *Scrinia reserata*, 1.44). Soon afterwards, Andrewes became bishop of Chichester and was succeeded as dean by Richard Neile, upon whose recommendation Herbert was elected a scholar at Westminster and thus became a residential pupil in 1605. The chief master was Richard Ireland, who oversaw a syllabus of classical rhetoric, logic, and grammar, including an unusual amount of Greek in addition to Latin, combined with a particular emphasis on liturgical music because of the close association of the school with Westminster Abbey.

Herbert's first months as a pupil in residence coincided with the danger and political turmoil caused by the unsuccessful Gunpowder Plot against the king at the Palace of Westminster in November 1605. Despite this uneasy setting, Herbert soon showed himself to be an 'excellent' scholar (*Life*, ed. Shuttleworth, 8). He and his contemporary John Hacket, the future bishop of Lichfield and Coventry, were together regarded as two of the brightest and most scholarly young men of their generation. When they were both elected as Westminster scholars to Trinity College, Cambridge, their chief master was reported to have said that:

> he need give them no counsel to follow their Books, but rather to study moderately, and use exercise; their parts being so good, that if they were careful not to impair their health with too much study, they would not fail to arrive at the top of learning in any *Art* or *Science*. (Hacket, *Century of Sermons*, v)

Herbert did indeed arrive at the 'top of learning' in Cambridge, where he was admitted to Trinity College on 5 May 1609. He became a bachelor of arts in 1613 (ranked second of the 193 graduates in the year), proceeded to become a minor fellow of Trinity College in 1614, and was promoted to major fellow and master of arts in 1616. In 1617 he was employed as *sublector quartae classis* (assistant lecturer) at Trinity, after which he became *praelector* in rhetoric in 1618, deputy to the university orator, Sir Francis Nethersole, in 1619, and university orator in 1620. His Cambridge years were marred, however, by persistent bouts of ill health and a continuing shortage of money for books, both of which are mentioned in the surviving letters written from Cambridge by Herbert to, among others, his stepfather. In 1608, just before George went up to Cambridge, Magdalene Herbert had ended her twelve years of widowhood and single-handed raising of ten children (all of whom survived into adulthood) by marrying Sir John *Danvers, a man less than half her age. Danvers came from a distinguished Wiltshire family and was said by contemporaries to be a man whom 'People would run after in the street' in order to see and admire (Charles, *Life*, 56). Magdalene Herbert's marriage to this striking young man led to the establishment of a second family home—Danvers's house by the Thames in Chelsea—which was frequently visited by Sir Francis Bacon and John Donne as well as, presumably, by Herbert in his vacations from Cambridge.

During his Cambridge years Herbert also began the activity for which he is now most famous: writing poetry. As early as 1610, if Walton's dating is to be trusted, Herbert sent two sonnets in English to his mother, lamenting the fact that poetry always wears '*Venus* livery' and, in the accompanying letter, resolving 'that my poor Abilities in *Poetry*, shall be all, and ever consecrated to Gods glory' (*Works*, 206, 363). Although no firm dates can be assigned to his poems in manuscript, he probably wrote devotional poetry in English throughout his time at Cambridge; Herbert's late twentieth-century biographer suggests a date as early as 1614 for 'The Church-Porch' (Charles, *Life*, 80–84). Meanwhile, in 1612, Herbert contributed two Latin poems—his first publication—to a Cambridge collection of elegies on the death of Prince Henry, heir to James I, who died of typhoid fever aged eighteen (he was just a year younger than the poet); in 1619 he similarly published a Latin elegy for James I's queen, Anne of Denmark (in *Lacrymae Cantabrigienses*, 1619). While in Cambridge, Herbert also wrote an unpublished set of Latin epigrams, *Musae responsoriae*, satirizing the puritan extremism of the Scottish church reformer, Andrew Melville. Melville's poem attacking the ceremonies of the Church of England, *Anti-tami-cami-categoria* (written in 1603–4), was first published in 1620, and Herbert's response was probably written in that year, though it remained unpublished until 1662 when it appeared in *Ecclesiastes Solomonis* by James Duport, fellow and vice-master of Trinity College, Cambridge. Herbert's devotional poems in Latin, *Passio discerpta* and *Lucus*, were both appended to the early manuscript of his English poems and are also likely to date from his last years in Cambridge, the early 1620s. They explore in epigrammatic baroque style the sufferings of Christ and the paradoxes of faith. They were not published as a group until Alexander Grosart's edition of Herbert's works in 1874. Among a small number of miscellaneous English poems attributed to 'G. H.' in the seventeenth century, one—'To the Queene of Bohemia' with its associated 'L'Envoy' (*Works*, 211–13)—seems to be genuinely by Herbert, judged on stylistic grounds, and dates from 1621–2 when the poem's subject, Elizabeth, daughter of James I and queen to the elector palatine, was in exile in Holland.

'Court-hopes'? Much debate centres around George Herbert's plans and hopes after 1620. Did he become Cambridge University orator as part of a longer-term plan to move into the public world of court and politics? In letters to his stepfather in 1619, Herbert had sought to convince Sir John Danvers of the worth of the position, describing it as 'the finest place in the University' and a 'dignity' that 'hath no such earthiness in it, but it may very well be joined with Heaven' (*Works*, 369, 370). As orator, Herbert came into contact with the highest in the land, addressing letters and speeches to King James I, Charles, prince of Wales, and the earl of Buckingham, as well as to visiting ambassadors and dignitaries. On 12 March 1623 Herbert gave an oration in the presence of the king, and a contemporary observed that 'his majesty was pleased to stay there, while the orator Mr Herbert did make a short Farewell Speech unto him' after which the king called for a copy of 'an epigram the orator made' (BL, Harley MS 7041, fol. 38*v*). According to Walton, James regarded Herbert at the time as 'the Jewel of that University' (Walton, 23).

It is quite possible that Herbert saw the position of public orator as the means to a career at court, since his two predecessors in the post, Sir Robert Naunton and Sir Francis Nethersole, both went on to become secretaries of state. The role of orator required not only rhetorical skill, but also adroit manoeuvrings in the complexities of current policy, especially England's difficult relations with Spain. Herbert's third oration, *Reditum Caroli*, delivered on 8 October 1623 on Prince Charles's return from Spain without the infanta as his bride, carefully but bravely upheld the principle of peace despite the prince's known warlike intentions. It is, however, difficult to discern whether Herbert took any more than linguistic delight in his negotiation of such political labyrinths.

In 1624 Herbert stood for parliament and was elected to represent the borough of Montgomery, a traditional function for male members of the Herbert family. Again it is unclear whether he took on the role of MP as a duty or a career move, but its temporary nature is at any rate indicated by the mere six months of leave granted to their orator by the Cambridge University senate. The 1624 parliamentary session in which Herbert participated was stormy, dominated not only by the continuing diplomatic drama with Spain, but also by the crisis in the Virginia Company (with which his stepfather was closely involved). Herbert would have observed the political fortunes of factions and individuals—including his stepfather, his distant cousin and patron, the earl of Pembroke, and his friend John Williams, bishop of Lincoln—rising and falling around him. For whatever reason, Herbert's parliamentary career was short-lived; by the 1626 session of parliament, the MP for Montgomery was no longer George but his brother Henry.

Several of Herbert's early biographers suggested that he entertained courtly or political ambitions which failed in the mid-1620s. Barnabas Oley cited 'sober men' who censured Herbert as 'a man that did not manage his brave parts to his best advantage and preferment' (*Herbert's Remains*, sig. b11*v*–b12*r*), and in his 1670 *Life of Mr George Herbert* Izaak Walton suggested that Herbert's 'Court-hopes' were dashed by the deaths of his likely patrons, the duke of Lennox, the marquess of Hamilton, and the king himself, by 1625 (Walton, 30). However, the evidence that Herbert had set his sights on a courtly future is more circumstantial than convincing; Walton, for instance, took Herbert's phrase 'my friends die' in the lyric 'Affliction' (I) to imply that Herbert gave up his secular ambitions because his patrons died. The term 'friends' was used in the seventeenth century to refer to relatives, and Herbert had suffered a number of severe losses in his family, including the deaths of four of his siblings between 1617 and 1623, two of his brothers (William and Richard) dying as a result

of the war in the Low Countries. It is therefore possible that 'Affliction' (I), clearly an autobiographical poem, outlines a general sense of depression and uncertainty in 'a world of strife' rather than the failure of specific secular hopes.

'Setting foot into Divinity' While public orator and member of parliament, Herbert was already thinking of a career in a different direction, namely the church. As early as 1618, in a letter to his stepfather requesting money to buy more theological books, Herbert explained that he was 'setting foot into Divinity, to lay the platform of my future life', and he was busily reading 'infinite Volumes of Divinity' throughout the time that he was employed as fellow and orator in Cambridge (*Works*, 364–5). Another letter written from Cambridge reveals that Herbert assumed he would at some date have 'enter'd into a Benefice' (ibid., 367). Indeed, by accepting a major fellowship at Trinity, he had committed himself to being ordained within seven years (that is, by 1623), though he would have known that this rule was not always strictly enforced.

Evidence brought to light relatively recently (Charles, 'Deacon', 272–6) confirms that, while he was the member of parliament for Montgomery, Herbert was envisaging his immediate future in a less secular sphere. In autumn 1624 he applied to the archbishop of Canterbury for permission to be ordained deacon at any time (and not after the normal waiting period of a year) by John Williams, lord keeper, dean of Westminster, and bishop of Lincoln. The permission was granted on 3 November 1624. Unfortunately there is (as yet) no evidence of the date of Herbert's actual ordination as deacon, but it probably took place soon after the permission was given, since on 6 December 1624 Bishop Williams presented Herbert to a portion of the rectory of Llandinam in Montgomeryshire, a preferment (with no residential duties) which Herbert held until he died. The ordination must certainly have taken place by 5 July 1626 when Herbert was installed as canon of Lincoln Cathedral and prebendary of Leighton Ecclesia in Huntingdonshire. The installation had to take place by proxy since Herbert was involved in the same month with his last public duties as orator of Cambridge University, addressing the duke of Buckingham at York House on 13 July 1626 on behalf of the university to welcome him as its new chancellor.

In his new role as deacon and non-residentiary canon of Lincoln Cathedral, Herbert was required to deliver an annual sermon, and although it was possible to put in a deputy, there is evidence that Herbert himself fulfilled the duty at least once, at Whitsuntide 1629 (Charles, *Life*, 124). As for his commitment to Leighton Ecclesia, Herbert is said by Walton to have vowed to rebuild the then disused church, and he continued to plan and raise money for the refurbishment of the building during the remainder of his life. It is still possible to see within the church (at Leighton Bromswold) the pulpit and reading desk of equal height, signifying that the words of the preacher should not be regarded as higher than the words of scripture. Herbert's connection with Leighton also took him close to

Little Gidding, home of the religious community established by his friend Nicholas Ferrar, who was later to play a major role in the posthumous publication of Herbert's English poems. Ferrar and members of his family withdrew into a life of devotion which eventually led their puritan critics to denounce the household as an 'Arminian nunnery' (the title of a 1641 pamphlet); in the twentieth century T. S. Eliot named one of his *Four Quartets* (1942) after Little Gidding and regarded it, by contrast, as a place 'where prayer has been valid'.

After his ordination as deacon Herbert continued to spend at least some of his time living at the home of his mother and stepfather in Chelsea. For the second half of 1625 Donne was in residence with them, taking refuge from the plague in London, and in a letter written in December 1625 Donne confirmed that 'Mr. *George Herbert* is here' (Bald, 276). In 1626 Herbert 'betook himself to a Retreat from *London*' (Walton, 30), first to the home of a friend in Kent and later to his brother Henry's house at Woodford in Essex. By May 1627, Herbert is known to have been back in Chelsea, since he wrote a letter of advice (in Latin) from there on 6 May to his deputy orator in Cambridge, Robert Creighton. The following month, June 1627, Magdalene Herbert, Lady Danvers, pillar of the Herbert family and the single most important influence in George's formative years, died, probably in her mid-sixties; she had been intermittently unwell since at least May 1622, when Herbert had written a long letter 'To his Mother, in her sickness' (*Works*, 372–4). She was buried in Chelsea parish church on 8 June 1627, and on 1 July Donne preached a commemorative sermon there, creating a vivid image of a woman of passion and principle who successfully stewarded the resources of her two husbands and led her large family with 'holy cheerfulnesse', summoning them to their daily devotions with the cry, '*For God's sake let's go*' (*Sermons*, 7.88, 86). The sermon was registered for publication by Philemon Stephens on 7 July 1627, along with Herbert's elegiac verses in Latin and Greek entitled *Memoriae matris sacrum*. This collection, Herbert's first published poems on a personal rather than a public subject, celebrates his mother's 'wit / And wisdom' and her 'spirit bright' which illuminated the whole house. The poet argues that 'you taught me how to write', and therefore 'That skill owes you praise' (*Latin Poetry*, 127, 125, 129).

Although there is no evidence that Herbert had lived in Cambridge or functioned fully as public orator since his request for leave of absence in 1624, it was not until 28 January 1628 that the senate of Cambridge University elected a new orator—Herbert's deputy, Robert Creighton. The year 1628 was thus a decisive turning point for Herbert, marking the end of both his long connection with Cambridge and his extended association with his mother and her homes in London. Herbert went to Dauntesey in Wiltshire to stay with Henry Danvers, earl of Danby, the elder brother of his stepfather, and came into contact with their cousin, Jane Danvers (*d.* 1661). This led to another decisive move for Herbert, into matrimony: on

5 March 1629 he and Jane were married in Edington Priory, the parish church of her home at Baynton House, Wiltshire. Walton claimed (no doubt with greater romance than accuracy) that Herbert had met his wife only three days before their wedding, having conducted the courtship by proxy. Although this story is unlikely to be true, there was certainly something unusual about the timing of their marriage, with the drawing up of the bond (dated 26 February 1629) and the ceremony itself both occurring in Lent, and the period before the wedding being too short for banns to be called. Whatever the circumstances of their courtship and marriage, Herbert chose as his wife a 'loving *and* vertuous Lady' according to Oley (*Herbert's Remains*, sig. c5v), though Jane's relative John Aubrey characterized her more colourfully as 'a handsome *bona roba* and ingeniose' (*Brief Lives*, 295), suggesting that she combined a well-rounded body with a keen mind. The newly married couple continued to live with Jane's widowed mother at Baynton, near Dauntesey, until Herbert was presented as rector to the living of Fugglestone-with-Bemerton, near Salisbury, Wiltshire, in April 1630. He had thus finally committed himself fully to the path of 'Divinity', though not perhaps in the way that had been expected; he remained the rector of Bemerton until his death.

Bemerton Although Herbert only lived and worked in Bemerton for just under three years, it is the place with which he has come to be most frequently associated. The small fourteenth-century church of St Andrew's, and the modest stone rectory across the road from it, are taken to typify the humble choice made by Herbert to serve as a parish priest in a rural setting; as some of his contemporaries put it, he '*lost himself* in an humble way' (*Herbert's Remains*, sig. a12r). However, it is misleading to overlook the courtly connections which led Herbert and his wife to Bemerton. The parish boundaries took in Wilton House, the seat of his relations, the earls of Pembroke, and it was at their request that King Charles I presented George to the vacant living in Bemerton on 16 April 1630. (As William Herbert, the third earl, died on 10 April 1630, it is not clear whether it was he or his brother Philip, the fourth earl—or both—who used his influence on George's behalf. A few years earlier, William Herbert had been instrumental in gaining a knighthood for George's brother Henry.) Although Herbert's appointment at Bemerton did not include the position of chaplain to Wilton House, it is likely that he kept in close contact with his aristocratic relations, since a letter dated December 1631 reveals that he had become a friend and spiritual adviser to the fourth earl's wife, the diarist Lady Anne Clifford. Among Herbert's English poems is a lyric entitled 'A Parodie' which is a sacred version of a secular love song, 'Soules joy, when I am gone', written by the third earl of Pembroke.

A detailed account of Herbert's induction to Bemerton church on 26 April 1630 is given in Walton's *Life* on the basis of information supplied to the biographer by Herbert's friend, Arthur Woodnoth, the cousin of Nicholas

Ferrar; Woodnoth was said to have recalled the unusually long time spent by the new rector prostrate with humility before the altar of his church. At the time of this significant move into the service of the church, Herbert was still a deacon; his ordination to the priesthood took place at Salisbury Cathedral on 19 September 1630. It is not easy to discern why Herbert's ordination had been so long delayed, particularly as it now seems clear that he had been a deacon since 1624; possible reasons for his late entry into the priesthood may include long-term financial uncertainty, a sense of unworthiness (attested to in the poem 'The Priesthood'), continuing interest in a secular career—academic or courtly—and his chronic ill health. Even after he had become rector of Bemerton, however, Herbert did not take the earliest opportunity to be ordained priest; twelve men, including his curate Nathanael Bostocke, were made priests at Salisbury Cathedral on Trinity Sunday, 23 May 1630, a month after Herbert's installation at Bemerton. Herbert's biographer Amy Charles suggests that Herbert was unable to be present for ordination in Salisbury at that time as he would have been discharging his final duty as canon of Lincoln Cathedral before committing himself wholly to a ministry in Wiltshire. The ceremony at Salisbury in September 1630 was in fact the next opportunity in his diocese for Herbert to be ordained.

The duties carried out by Herbert in the Bemerton parish are likely to have matched those described in his prose handbook, *A Priest to the Temple* (otherwise known as *The Country Parson his Character and Rule of Holy Life*), written in the early 1630s and published with Barnabas Oley's prefatory biography of Herbert in 1652. In this work Herbert particularly emphasized the parson's humility, charity, patience, and 'grave livelinesse' in prayer, but also recommended a proper restraint (he should not exceed 'an hour in preaching', for example) and the appropriate liturgical 'middle way between superstition, and slovenlinesse' (*Works*, 231, 235, 246). Despite his immense learning, evident rhetorical skills, and lifelong attachment to books, Herbert defined 'The Countrey Parson's Library' not as a Cambridge-style collection of volumes but 'a holy Life' (ibid., 278). He saw the function of a priest in a community in practical terms: primarily spiritual, of course, through teaching, preaching, charity, and the celebration of the sacraments, but extending also to the giving of legal advice and the provision of health care. It is not known whether Jane Herbert possessed 'the skill of healing a wound, or helping the sick' recommended in a parson's wife (ibid., 260), but it is certainly clear that she was willing to welcome into her household Herbert's nieces (daughters of his elder sister, Margaret, widow of John Vaughan) who were orphaned in 1623 and came to join the Herberts at Bemerton rectory in 1630.

In addition to his work as rector and his intense poetic activities in this period, Herbert was also afforded the opportunity to enjoy what he termed (in his lyric 'Church Music') 'the sweetest of sweets'—liturgical music—and to practise his own considerable skills as a musician. Twice a week, according to Walton, Herbert walked from Bemerton to Salisbury to attend evensong at the cathedral, followed by a 'private Musick meeting' at which he would 'sing and play his part' (Walton, 60). One of Walton's most memorable (though no doubt apocryphal) anecdotes about Herbert concerns a musical evening at which the rector arrived in a dishevelled state, having helped a 'poor man, with a poorer horse' while on his way there. Unruffled by the critical reactions of his fellow musicians, Herbert is said to have defended his charitable act (which *'would prove Musick to him at Midnight'*) and, without any further ado, concluded, 'And now, let's tune our instruments' (ibid., 62–3). According to Aubrey, Herbert 'had a very good hand on the lute' (*Brief Lives*, 295) and was thought to have set some of his own poems to music, and Walton recounted that Herbert rose from his deathbed to sing verses from 'Sunday' and 'The Thanksgiving' (Walton, 77). The frequent use of musical forms and metaphors in his English lyrics certainly bears witness to a creative partnership between poetry and music.

Illness and death   Throughout his life Herbert had endured bouts of poor health, referred to openly in his letters as well as indirectly in his poems. As early as 1610 he had reported suffering from an 'Ague' while in Cambridge (*Works*, 363), and in 1617 and 1622 he had undergone periods of a particularly serious illness which would now be called tuberculosis; in 1629 this became what Walton termed 'a sharp *Quotidian Ague*' (Walton, 35). In a letter to his mother in May 1622, when she herself was unwell, Herbert had commented: 'I alwaies fear'd sickness more then death, because sickness hath made me unable to perform those Offices for which I came into the world, and must yet be kept in it' (*Works*, 373). Presumably this sense of frustration must have afflicted Herbert when he became terminally ill after about two years as a priest, even though he saw death itself as 'fair and full of grace' rather than an 'uncouth hideous thing' ('Death'). On 19 October 1632 he found it necessary to employ a second curate to assist him in carrying out his duties, and by the early weeks of 1633 he was on his deathbed, suffering from the last stages of consumption. On 25 February 1633 he dictated his will to his first curate, Nathanael Bostocke, naming Arthur Woodnoth as executor and Sir John Danvers, his stepfather, as overseer of the will. Less than a week later, on 1 March 1633, he died in the presence of Bostocke and Woodnoth, while (according to Walton) his wife and nieces wept and prayed in an adjoining room. Herbert's funeral service was sung by the 'singing men of Sarum' (*Brief Lives*, 295) at St Andrew's, Bemerton, on 3 March 1633, exactly a month before his fortieth birthday; his body was buried in an unmarked grave near the altar of the church of which he had been rector.

According to his elder brother Edward, George Herbert made such an impression with his 'holy and exemplary' life at Bemerton that he was 'litle less than Sainted' in the area around Salisbury. Edward added, however, that George 'was not exempt from passion and Choler, being infirmities to which all our Race is subject, but that excepted, without reproach in his Actions' (*Life*, ed. Shuttleworth, 8–9). This potentially contradictory portrait of George Herbert is a reminder of the complexity of his career and the difficulty of interpreting the known facts of his life history. While some biographers (notably Charles) are keen to stress the continuity of his life, seeing him as consistently devoted to religion, others (particularly Walton) suggest a dramatic change of heart in response to the apparent failure of his courtly ambitions. The range encompassed by his relatively short adult life is indeed striking: the university orator who addressed King James I became the priest who asserted that preachers should not be 'witty, or learned, or eloquent, but Holy' (*Works*, 233). However, whether this signifies a continuing line of development towards a higher calling, or a shift of purpose (for whatever reason) remains open to interpretation. What may further strike the modern interpreter is the restlessness of Herbert's life, lacking both a father and a stable place of residence in his early years, and uneasily seeking the right 'employment' (as often referred to in his verse) in his adulthood. Ironically, he appears to have found both domestic security and a clear vocation only in his last few years, at which stage he could boldly advise, in *The Country Parson*, 'Do well, and right, and let the world sinke' (ibid., 270).

There is one extant visual image of George Herbert, a pencil drawing by Robert White (1645–1703) taken from an unidentified portrait (possibly by Sir Anthony van Dyck or Cornelius Janssen), made by White as preparation for an engraving which appeared in Walton's *Life* (1670) and the tenth edition of *The Temple* (1674); it is now in the Houghton Library, Harvard. All other known likenesses of Herbert are based on this drawing, which depicts the head and shoulders of a sober churchman with sharply defined, sensitive features and shoulder-length wavy hair. Herbert had no direct descendants: he and his wife had no children, though Jane Herbert later married Sir Robert Cook of Highnam in Gloucestershire, with whom she had one daughter.

The Temple (1633) The most profound and lasting impression of George Herbert is to be found in his poetry, on which his high reputation to this present day is largely based. During his lifetime, however, none of his English poems was published, nor is there any evidence that they were circulated among his friends or family, with the exception of the early sonnets sent to his mother. There are two surviving manuscripts of the devotional poems eventually published as *The Temple*, held respectively at Dr Williams's Library in London (MS Jones B62, known as *W*) and the Bodleian Library, Oxford (MS Tanner 307, known as *B*). The earlier of the two manuscripts, *W*, contains seventy-nine English poems (as well as the Latin sequences *Passio discerpta* and *Lucus*) and reveals that, at an early stage, Herbert had already organized his collection of English poetry into three sections, 'The Church-Porch', 'The Church', and 'The Church Militant'. The manuscript includes revisions in Herbert's own hand and was almost certainly completed well before he moved to Bemerton in 1630. The later manuscript, *B*, contains 165 English poems, many of which are further revised versions of those in *W*, though more than half of them are new lyrics probably written towards the end of his life. *B* is not in Herbert's hand but was copied out at Little Gidding, probably by Nicholas Ferrar's nieces, Anna and Mary Collett. Walton recounted how, not long before he died, Herbert had given a '*little Book*' to Ferrar's friend Edmund Duncon, instructing him to pass it on to Ferrar since it contained '*a picture of the many spiritual Conflicts that have past betwixt God and my Soul, before I could subject mine to the will of Jesus my Master*' (Walton, 74). Ferrar was advised by Herbert, according to Walton, to publish the work '*if he can think it may turn to the advantage of any dejected poor Soul*', but otherwise the instruction was, '*let him burn it*' (ibid.). Fortunately for posterity, Ferrar chose the first of the two options, though it is clear that *B* is not the original '*little Book*' brought to him by Duncon, but a folio fair copy made for presentation to the press.

Ferrar chose to publish the poems in Cambridge rather than London, and the first edition, expertly set by the university printer, Thomas Buck, was ready by September 1633. The process was not without its problems: in private, there were tensions between Ferrar and Herbert's executor, Woodnoth, over where the poems should be published, and in Cambridge the vice-chancellor delayed the publication since lines 235–6 of 'The Church Militant' were thought to be potentially dangerous in their reference to 'religion' passing over to the '*American* strand' (*Works*, 196). However, the poems were eventually published in an unaltered state and their impact was enormous: by 1641 there had already been six editions of *The Temple: Sacred Poems and Private Ejaculations* by 'Mr. George Herbert, late Oratour of the Universitie of Cambridge' (title-page as reset later in 1633). The idea of naming the volume *The Temple* probably came not from Herbert but from Ferrar, in whose hand the title and supporting epigraph ('In his Temple doth every man speak of his honour', Psalm 29, verse 8) were inserted into *B*. Ferrar also added a preface, 'The printers to the reader', which constitutes the earliest biographical sketch of Herbert and led to the reading of the poems as the work of one who, 'Quitting both his deserts and all the opportunities that he had for worldly preferment, … betook himself to the Sanctuarie and Temple of God, choosing rather to serve at Gods Altar, then to seek the honour of State-employments' (*Works*, 3).

As admirers of the 'late Oratour' might have expected, Herbert's English poems are notable for their controlled and inventive use of form: the central section of *The Temple*, 'The Church', contains over 160 lyrics in a striking variety of poetic structures, from sonnets and hymns to hieroglyphic lyrics with stanza forms unique to their composition and subject. In tone and narrative mode, too, Herbert demonstrated his versatility, writing lyric conversations, allegories, fables, monologues, epigrams, meditations, and prayers. More surprising in a classical rhetorician, however, was Herbert's conscious simplicity of purpose and manner, given expression in lyrics such as 'A True Hymn' and the 'Jordan' poems with their desire to 'plainly say, *My God, My King*', and finding perhaps his most poised triumphs in 'The Flower', 'Virtue', and 'Love' (III). In his attention to formal variety as well as to the subject of writing itself, Herbert was working in the poetic tradition of Philip Sidney and his sister Mary (wife of Herbert's distant relative the second earl of Pembroke), whose translation of the psalms into English lyric verse was the clearest poetic influence on *The Temple*. In fact, in the number of lyrics and the range of moods they represent, as well as in their scriptural tone and borrowings, Herbert's English poems most closely resemble the biblical book of the Psalms; this was presumably the reason for Ferrar's choice of title and Oley's description of Herbert as 'The sweet singer of the Temple' (*Herbert's Remains*, sig. a11v). Like the psalms, too, the lyrics construct many different voices: the self-confident narrator of the sonnet 'Redemption', the troubled believer in 'Deniall', the rebellious speaker of 'The Collar', and the accepting voice in 'The Forerunners'. From the despair of the 'Affliction' poems through the intensity of a lyric such as 'Longing' to the joy celebrated in 'Easter' and 'The Odour', *The Temple* vividly encompasses the complete spectrum of devotional experience.

Other writings In addition to his collections of Latin and Greek verse, Herbert wrote four occasional Latin poems in honour of Francis Bacon and his works, and one in reply to Donne's Latin verse sent to Herbert with one of Donne's seals 'of the Anchor and Christ'. Herbert's Latin response, 'In sacram anchoram piscatoris', with two English versions, was appended to Donne's *Poems* (1650); it praises the 'eloquence' of the older poet and preacher as well as the appropriateness of the anchor and cross together as 'the symbole' of 'certainty' (*Works*, 439). His extant Latin prose consists of three of his public orations (two of which, addressed to the Spanish ambassadors and to the prince of Wales, were published separately in 1623) and eighteen epistles (all but two of which come from a manuscript collection in Cambridge entitled *The Orator's Book*). Of the two epistles written by Herbert in his private capacity, rather than as orator, one was addressed to his teacher, Lancelot Andrewes, bishop of Winchester, confirming continuing contact with this distinguished 'Father in God' (ibid., 473) after his appointment to the see of Winchester in 1619.

The most significant of Herbert's prose writing in English is *A Priest to the Temple* (or *The Country Parson*), the priestly conduct book written in his last years which not only puts forward Herbert's model churchman but also reveals the fundamental principles of faith, human relationships, and religious rhetoric which underlie his poems. He advised, for instance, that 'things of ordinary use' such as ploughs, leaven, or dances, could be made to 'serve for lights even of Heavenly Truths' (*Works*, 257). Further insight into Herbert's poetic principles is afforded by his enormous collection of proverbial sayings, first published in 1640 as *Outlandish Proverbs, Selected by Mr G. H.* (containing 1032 sayings) and enlarged with a further sixty-eight proverbs in *Jacula prudentum* (1651). The homely wit

of these wise observations is frequently echoed in *The Temple*, and is particularly present in poems such as 'The Church-Porch' and 'Charms and Knots'. *A Priest to the Temple* and *Jacula prudentum* were published together as *Herbert's Remains* (1652), prefaced by Oley's 'View of the life and vertues of the authour'.

Nineteen of Herbert's English letters survive, several of which have been individually cited as biographical evidence but which together deserve further consideration. His most frequent correspondent was his stepfather, and other members of his family to whom letters are extant include his mother, his brother Henry, and his eldest sister, Elizabeth. Among the friends to whom he wrote were Nicholas Ferrar and Lady Anne Clifford. His elegant letters reveal a recurring concern for others in sickness or difficulty, frequent anxiety about his own poor health, a love of books and fine language, his need for security of employment, and a constant awareness that, as he wrote to his mother, 'the thred of Life' is 'like other threds or skenes of silk, full of snarles and incumbrances' (*Works*, 373).

Herbert also played an active part in a number of translation projects. He was one of the scholars who translated Bacon's *Advancement of Learning* into Latin, published as *De augmentis scientiae* in 1623, and, in recognition of these 'paines' taken by Herbert 'about some of my Writings', Bacon dedicated his *Translation of Certaine Psalmes into English Verse* to Herbert in 1625 (Bacon, sig. A3r). Nearer the end of Herbert's life, his friend Nicholas Ferrar prepared an English translation, as *The Divine Considerations*, of a work by the sixteenth-century Castilian humanist, Juan de Valdes, and sent it to Herbert in 1632 for his comments. Herbert's resulting 'Brief notes on Valdesso's *Considerations*' were published with the translation in 1638, after the deaths of both translator and commentator. Herbert identified the original (Catholic) author as a 'true servant of God' but was persistently critical of Valdesso for showing insufficient respect for the scriptures (*Works*, 304–20). It was also in connection with Ferrar's Little Gidding community that Herbert himself undertook the translation, under the title *Treatise of Temperance and Sobriety*, of a mid-sixteenth-century Italian work by Luigi Cornaro. Although Herbert apparently knew Italian, as well as Spanish and French (Walton, 27), his translation was largely based on a Latin version of the text and was published in 1634 with a preface explaining that:

> Master *George Herbert* of blessed memorie, having at the request of a Noble Personage translated it [Cornaro's treatise] into English, sent a copie thereof, not many moneths before his death, unto some friends of his, who a good while before had given an attempt of regulating themselves in matter of Diet. (*Works*, 565)

It is likely that the 'Noble Personage' who commissioned the translation was Bacon and the 'friends' were the Ferrars.

These humanist literary activities of Herbert are a reminder that he was far more than a major lyric poet in English: he was a busy writer in many spheres of practical theology, received wisdom and folklore, politics, ecclesiastical satire, public and private elegy, devotional epigram, and rhetorical prose for all occasions.

Reputation and influence The pattern of Herbert's career, and the works published during his lifetime, suggest that he was respected by his contemporaries as an 'esteemed Master in the *Roman* eloquence' (*Works*, xl) and one in whom 'Divinitie, and Poesie, met' (Bacon, sig. A3v), but was probably not known as a writer of English verse. Even after his death and the publication of *The Temple*, his fame as a classicist continued to predominate in some quarters. His brother Edward, for example, wrote that George's English works, though 'rare', were 'far short of expressing those perfections which he had in the Greek and Latin Tongue, and all divine and human Literature' (*Life*, ed. Shuttleworth, 8). Other commentators disagreed, arguing as Oley did that although the *Musae responsoriae* were 'very good', yet they were 'dull or dead in comparison of his Temple Poems' (*Herbert's Remains*, sig. b7r). Another important element began to shape Herbert's reputation soon after his death, and that was the holiness of his last years. Oley described Herbert as 'A Peer to the primitive Saints, and more then a pattern to his own age' (ibid., sig. b8v), while in the Little Gidding 'family' Herbert's life and work were seen as a model for those who 'feared God, and loved the Church of England' (Blackstone, 59). Walton's 1670 *Life* confirmed this emphasis on Herbert's personal holiness—'thus he liv'd, and thus he dy'd like a Saint' (Walton, 79)—and, moreover, detailed the poet's commitment to the established church. The second half of Walton's biography turns into a celebration of the liturgy found in the Book of Common Prayer, as well as of Herbert's diligent upholding of its practice. Some of Herbert's poems (particularly 'The 23d Psalme', 'Antiphon' (I), 'Praise' (II), and 'The Elixir') continue to be sung regularly as hymns, and so pervasive is the continuing respect for this Anglican 'saint' that in 1980 the Church of England designated 27 February as the commemorative day of 'George Herbert, priest, pastor, poet'.

Without calling Herbert's holiness into question, it is important to perceive his posthumous reputation in context, since it was inevitably coloured by the political revolutions which followed within a decade of his death; the biographical sketches of him which appeared during the seventeenth century tell as much about the ecclesiastical loyalties (and cultural nostalgia) of their authors as about Herbert's own life. Meanwhile, Herbert's English poetry, despite its entanglement with his more partisan personal reputation, was enormously popular. *The Temple* went through thirteen editions by 1709 and appealed to a readership spanning the political and ecclesiastical spectrum: Charles I read Herbert's poems when imprisoned in Carisbrooke Castle before his execution, while at the same time *The Temple* was undoubtedly admired by at least one of the regicides (Herbert's own stepfather) and recommended as devotional reading by the chaplain to Oliver Cromwell, Peter Sterry. Herbert's verses were put to an

extraordinary variety of uses: *The Temple* was cited in treatises against Quakers and to reform 'drunkards and tipplers'; parts of it were translated into scholarly Latin while other verses were turned into a devotional alphabet for children; lyrics were set to music by Lawes, Purcell, and Blow, and in 1697 a volume of *Select Hymns Taken out of Mr Herbert's 'Temple'* was published for congregational use (Wilcox, 153–68). The moderate nonconformist Richard Baxter spoke for many seventeenth-century readers when he praised *The Temple* as a text in which 'Heart-work and Heaven-work' were combined (Baxter, sig. A7r).

In addition to his posthumous fame as a holy individual and a writer whose work gave spiritual comfort to readers from all traditions, Herbert also had a considerable influence on the development of English poetry—so much so, that it is more accurate to speak of a school of Herbert than a school of Donne. From its first publication *The Temple* had attracted imitators such as Christopher Harvey, whose sequence entitled *The Synagogue* was bound with Herbert's poems from the sixth edition of *The Temple* (1641) onwards, and Ralph Knevet, who supplied a poetic *Gallery to the Temple* in the late 1640s. Among Herbert's more imaginative seventeenth-century poetic admirers were Cardell Goodman, Richard Crashaw, and, above all, Henry Vaughan, who declared in the preface to the second edition of his sacred poems, *Silex scintillans* (1655), that he owed his inspiration to 'the blessed man, Mr. *George Herbert*, whose holy *life* and *verse* gained many pious converts (of whom I am the least)'. Herbert's fame and influence spread abroad, too, as is indicated by the Herbertian style of the early American poets Edward Taylor and Philip Pain. The very popularity of sequences of English devotional lyrics in the seventeenth century may be attributed to the influence of *The Temple*.

The decline of Herbert's reputation, at least as a poet, began in the classical period of the later seventeenth century and was typified by Dryden's mockery in *Mac Flecknoe* (1682) of poets who inhabit 'Acrostick Land' and display poems in the shapes of 'wings' and 'altars', obviously alluding to Herbert's 'Easter-wings' and 'The Altar'. No new editions of *The Temple* appeared between 1709 and 1799, while Dr Johnson's attack on the 'race of writers that may be termed the metaphysical poets' in his life of Cowley (*Lives of the Poets*, 1781) confirmed that Herbert's mode of wit continued to be out of fashion. The revival of interest in *The Temple* began in the early nineteenth century with Coleridge's admiration recorded in *Biographia literaria*, followed by the editions of Herbert's collected poetry and prose brought out by William Pickering (1835–6) and Alexander Grosart (1874). In the twentieth century the first landmark was George Herbert Palmer's edition (1905), in which he made a bold though ultimately doomed attempt to arrange the English lyrics in chronological order. One of Herbert's most influential admirers of the century was T. S. Eliot, and the most significant textual publication was F. E. Hutchinson's 1941 edition of the complete *Works*. Herbert continues to be a major influence on poets writing in English, including—among those in the twentieth century—the American writer Elizabeth Bishop and the Irish poet and critic Seamus Heaney.

Herbert's devotional poetry still fascinates, inspires, and intrigues a range of readers, and, though the quality of his work has been accepted without question since the publication of Joseph Summers's pioneering study, *George Herbert, his Religion and Art* (1954), the critical debates about *The Temple* are unceasing. Recent discussions have focused on issues such as the nature of Herbert's church allegiance (for which all positions from pro-Catholic via moderate Anglican to extreme Calvinist have been claimed) and the relationship of Herbert's sacred writing to secular matters, including sexual desire and political controversy. Particular features of the lyrics—their achieved and graceful simplicity, their musical and biblical echoes, the careful process of their revision, their emblematic titles, the subtle arrangement of the sequence in 'The Church'—continue to generate critical analysis and appreciation. Herbert has undoubtedly achieved an assured place in literary history as the greatest of English devotional poets.

HELEN WILCOX

Sources A. M. Charles, *A life of George Herbert* (1977) · *The works of George Herbert*, ed. F. E. Hutchinson (1941) · *Herbert's remains* (1652) · I. Walton, *The life of Mr George Herbert* (1670) · *The Latin poetry of George Herbert*, ed. M. McCloskey and P. R. Murphy (1965) · DWL, Jones MS B62 [W] · Bodl. Oxf., MS Tanner 307 [B] · G. Herbert, *The temple* (1633) · *The life of Edward, first Lord Herbert of Cherbury written by himself*, ed. J. M. Shuttleworth (1976) · *Aubrey's Brief lives*, ed. O. L. Dick (1949); repr. (1972) · *The sermons of John Donne*, ed. G. R. Potter and E. M. Simpson, 10 vols. (c.1953–1962) · B. Blackstone, ed., *The Ferrar papers: containing a life of Nicolas Ferrar … a selection of family letters* (1938) · A. M. Charles, 'George Herbert, deacon', *Modern Philology*, 72 (1974–5), 272–6 · D. Benet, 'Herbert's experience of politics and patronage in 1624', *George Herbert Journal*, 10 (1986–7), 33–45 · J. Hacket, *Scrinia reserata: a memorial offer'd to the great deservings of John Williams*, 2 pts (1693) · J. Hacket, *A century of sermons upon several remarkable subjects* (1675) · H. Vaughan, *Silex scintillans* (1655) · R. C. Bald, *John Donne: a life*, ed. W. Milgate (1970) · H. Wilcox, 'Herbert's *Temple* and seventeenth-century devotion', *Images of belief in literature*, ed. D. Jasper (1984), 153–68 · T. S. Eliot, *George Herbert* (1962) · J. H. Summers, *George Herbert, his religion and art* (1954) · R. Baxter, *Poetical fragments* (1681) · D. W. Doerksen, 'Nicholas Ferrar, Arthur Woodnoth, and the publication of George Herbert's *The temple*, 1633', *George Herbert Journal*, 3 (1979–80), 22–44 · F. Bacon, *Translation of certaine psalmes into English verse* (1625) · *The alternative service book* (1980) · J. D. K. Lloyd, 'Where was George Herbert born?', *Archaeologia Cambrensis*, 119 (1970), 139–43 · A. Charles, 'Mrs Herbert's *Kitchin booke*', *English Literary Renaissance*, 4 (1974), 164–73 · J. Powers-Buck, *The Herbert family dialogue* (1998)
Archives NRA, letters and literary papers
Likenesses R. White, line engraving (after R. White), BM, NPG; repro. in G. Herbert, *The temple*, 10th edn (1674) · R. White, pencil drawing (after portrait), Harvard U., Houghton L., MS Eng. 1405 [see illus.]
Wealth at death £750; plus money, books, and furniture bequeathed to wife: *Works*, ed. Hutchinson, 1633

Herbert, George Augustus, eleventh earl of Pembroke and eighth earl of Montgomery (1759–1827), army officer and landowner, was born on 10 September 1759 at Wilton House, Wiltshire, and was baptized there on 29 October, the only son of Henry *Herbert, tenth earl of Pembroke and seventh earl of Montgomery (1734–1794), an army officer, and his wife, Lady Elizabeth Spencer (1737–1831) [see Herbert, Elizabeth, countess of Pembroke and Montgomery], a lady of the royal household and the daughter of Charles *Spencer, third duke of Marlborough. Styled Lord Herbert, he was educated at home and at Harrow School from 1770 to 1775. He was appointed ensign in the 12th foot in 1775 and for the following five years undertook extensive travels to France, Austria, eastern Europe, Russia, and Italy with the Revd William Coxe, later archdeacon of Winchester, and Captain John Floyd. Having been promoted lieutenant in 1777 he became captain in the 75th foot in January 1778 and held the same rank in the 1st (Royal) Dragoons from December that year. He secured a majority in the 22nd light dragoons in 1781 and late the following year was made lieutenant-colonel in the 2nd dragoon guards.

At the general election of 1780, having just come of age, Herbert was returned to parliament for the family borough of Wilton, and in the Commons he sided reluctantly and silently with the whig opposition. He held the seat until November 1784, when he was appointed vice-chamberlain of the household and was sworn of the privy council (17 November), and again from January 1788. On 8 April 1787 he married his first cousin Elizabeth (d. 1793), the daughter of Topham *Beauclerk and Lady Diana Spencer [see Beauclerk, Lady Diana]. They had three sons and one daughter. At the start of the French revolutionary wars he showed considerable gallantry in skirmishing actions in Flanders, where he commanded the 2nd and 3rd dragoon guards and liaised with the Prussian and Austrian forces. He played an important part in the siege of Valenciennes in 1793, and at Dunkirk later that year he distinguished himself by capturing an enemy post at Hundssluyt. On his father's death on 26 January 1794 he inherited his titles, as well as Wilton House, the north and west fronts of which were later rebuilt by James Wyatt. His management of the Wilton estates saw the rent roll increase from £35,000 to over £100,000; he also possessed the electoral patronage of the borough. Having relinquished his household position, Pembroke succeeded his father as lord lieutenant of Wiltshire, where he exercised a steady and benign influence in local affairs for the rest of his life. He took his seat in the House of Lords on 20 February 1794, and thereafter was a staunch, but largely inactive, supporter of the ministry of William Pitt the younger and subsequent tory administrations.

Pembroke was promoted major-general in 1795 and became colonel of the 6th (Inniskilling) dragoons in 1797, after which he held responsibility for the south-western district of England. Having obtained the rank of lieutenant-general in 1802, he was awarded the KG in 1805. In 1807, when he served as plenipotentiary on a special mission to Austria, he was appointed governor of Guernsey. On 25 January 1808 he married Catherine (1783–1856), the daughter of the long-serving Russian ambassador to London, Semyon Romanovich, Count Vorontsov. They had one son and five daughters, including Catherine *Murray, promoter of the Harris tweed industry. An honourable and retiring man of amiable disposition, Pembroke, who was made a general in 1812, died at his London residence, Pembroke House, Privy Gardens, Whitehall, on

26 October 1827 and was buried at Wilton on 12 November. As he had quarrelled with Robert Henry, the sole surviving son of his first marriage, who succeeded to his titles, over an unfortunate marriage to an Italian princess, he left the bulk of his unentailed and personal estate, which included personalty sworn under £600,000, to his only son by his second wife, Sidney *Herbert, later Lord Herbert of Lea.   S. M. FARRELL

Sources *The Pembroke papers: letters and diaries of Henry, tenth earl of Pembroke and his circle*, ed. S. Herbert, 2 vols. (1939–50) · Sidney, sixteenth earl of Pembroke, *A catalogue of the paintings and drawings in the collection at Wilton House, Salisbury, Wiltshire* (1968) · T. J. P. Lever, *The Herberts of Wilton* (1967) · *The Times* (3 Nov 1827) · *GM*, 1st ser., 97/2 (1827), 557–8 · L. B. Namier, 'Herbert, George Augustus', HoP, *Commons, 1754–90* · GEC, *Peerage* · Colvin, *Archs.*, 1119 · J. Ingamells, ed., *A dictionary of British and Irish travellers in Italy, 1701–1800* (1997)

Archives Wilts. & Swindon RO, accounts, corresp., papers, and travel journals, etc. | BL, corresp. with Lord Hardwicke, Add. MSS 35643–35652, *passim* · BL, corresp. with Sir Robert Keith, Add. MSS 35514–35536, *passim* · BL, corresp. with Sir Robert Peel, Add. MSS 40356–40386, *passim* · BL, letters to second Earl Spencer · Hants. RO, letters to James Harris, first earl of Malmesbury · Hungerton Hall, Grantham, letters to John Le Marchant · NL Wales, corresp. with first Marquess Townshend · Wilts. & Swindon RO, corresp. with Baskerville

Likenesses J. Reynolds, two oil paintings, 1762–5, Wilton House, Wiltshire · D. Morier, oils, 1764–5, Wilton House, Wiltshire · P. Batoni, oils, 1779, Wilton House, Wiltshire · W. Owen, oils, 1821, Wilton House, Wiltshire · R. Westmacott, relief bust on marble monument, 1827, Wilton church, Wiltshire · D. Gardner, group portrait, pastel drawing, Clandon Park, Surrey

Wealth at death under £600,000 personal wealth: PRO, death duty registers, IR 26/1141/1251

Herbert, George Edward Stanhope Molyneux, fifth earl of Carnarvon (1866–1923), sportsman and Egyptologist, was born at Highclere Castle, near Newbury, Berkshire, on 26 June 1866, the only son of Henry Howard Molyneux *Herbert, fourth earl of Carnarvon (1831–1890), Conservative politician, and his first wife, Lady Evelyn (d. 1875), only daughter of George Augustus Frederick Stanhope, sixth earl of Chesterfield. He was a first cousin of Auberon Thomas Herbert, eighth Baron Lucas of Crudwell and fifth Lord Dingwall. His mother succeeded to the Bretby and other Stanhope estates on the death of her brother, the seventh earl of Chesterfield. Herbert inherited them on his mother's death in 1875. Viscount Porchester—as Herbert was styled during his father's lifetime—was educated at Eton College, but left early in order to study modern subjects with private tutors at home and abroad, with a view to joining the army. He changed his plans and went up to Trinity College, Cambridge, in 1886. Cambridge gave him his two main interests in life—archaeology and sport. He went down from Cambridge after two years without taking a degree and embarked on a leisurely yachting trip around the world. He never completed the circumnavigation, but later visited South Africa, Australia, and Japan. In 1890 he succeeded his father as fifth earl of Carnarvon.

Carnarvon now indulged his passion for travel, leading the life of an aristocratic pleasure seeker to the full. His father had been serious and scholarly, but little of this rubbed off on the son. Horse-racing was his major passion.

George Edward Stanhope Molyneux Herbert, fifth earl of Carnarvon (1866–1923), by unknown photographer

He built up a famous stud farm and became a member of the Jockey Club, winning many important races, among them the Ascot Stakes, and Stewards' Cup at Goodwood, and the Doncaster Cup. On 26 June 1895 he married Almina Victoria Maria Alexandra (d. 1969), the only daughter of Frederick Charles Wombwell. They had a son, Henry, Viscount Porchester, in 1898, and a daughter, Lady Evelyn Herbert, in 1901.

After his marriage Carnarvon continued to pursue his many interests, becoming an accomplished photographer and an expert golfer. He was also an early, and apparently somewhat reckless, motoring enthusiast, owning a car in France before they were permitted in England. In 1903 he was nearly killed in a serious motor accident in Germany. His doctors advised him that he should spend the winters out of England's damp climate. From 1903 he spent every winter for the rest of his life in Egypt.

At the time Cairo was a fashionable winter resort, crowded with wealthy tourists. Carnarvon could have spent his time on social pursuits, but instead he turned to archaeology. On his own testimony, he had been interested in excavation since 1889, but the opportunity did not present itself until 1906, when he began excavating at Luxor, with a permit supplied by the Egyptologist Gaston Maspero. The first six-week season yielded only an empty burial pit and a mummified cat, but Carnarvon's enthusiasm was undiminished. On the advice of Maspero he teamed up with the archaeologist and artist Howard Carter, former inspector-in-chief of antiquities in Luxor. Their partnership endured for sixteen years. Between 1907 and 1912 the two men excavated at or near Deir el Bahari on the west bank of the Nile opposite Luxor. The excavations were often frustrating and bore witness to the universal activities of looters. Nevertheless, they made important discoveries, helped by Carter's intimate knowledge of the area, among them the tomb of a king's son of the eighteenth dynasty (1908); a small funerary temple of Queen Hatshepsut (1909), and a richly decorated twelfth-dynasty sepulchre. At times they employed as many as 270 men. Their finds, which included an important tablet commemorating the expulsion of the Hyksos kings of the delta by the pharaoh Kamose in 1532 BC, were published by them in *Five Years' Exploration at Thebes* (1912). Meanwhile Carnarvon built up a magnificent collection of Egyptian antiquities with Carter's expert assistance, using his faultless sense of taste.

Carnarvon had his eyes on the Valley of Kings, the burial place of Egypt's New Kingdom pharaohs, but the concession was held by the American Theodore Davis. Carter was convinced that the tomb of the obscure pharaoh Tutankhamun awaited discovery in the valley, and Carnarvon wanted to search for it. Davis relinquished the concession only in 1913. Carnarvon applied for it at once, but the permit was not forthcoming until 1914, just before the outbreak of the First World War. Carnarvon's health prevented him from undertaking military service. He and Lady Carnarvon converted their residence, Highclere Castle, into an officers' hospital, and later moved to London. Carter stayed in Egypt, doing sporadic work at general headquarters in Cairo, which left him considerable time to prepare for future excavations at Luxor.

Excavations in the Valley of Kings began in 1917 and continued annually without result until 1922. Predecessors had searched for tombs by sinking pits through the huge accumulation of rubble on the valley floor; Carnarvon and Carter adopted a more radical strategy and decided to clear the overburden left by their predecessors to reach bedrock over a large area. This task involved shifting between 150,000 and 200,000 tons of near-sterile debris. Five years of arduous excavation produced no tombs. By 1922 Carnarvon was hesitant to commit more funds without tangible results. Carter persuaded him to embark on a final season. On 4 November 1922, at the very beginning of the new excavations, Carter's men unearthed a set of seventeen rock-cut steps and a sealed doorway in the valley floor. He promptly cabled Carnarvon, who arrived at Luxor with his daughter, Lady Evelyn Herbert, on 23 November. An entrance passage blocked with rubble led to a second doorway bearing Tutankhamun's seal. This led to an antechamber filled with magnificent furnishings, among them funerary beds, the pharaoh's chariots, his thrones, and his personal possessions stored in chests and boxes. Many of the jumbled artefacts bore the name of King Tutankhamun of the eighteenth dynasty, establishing the identity of the tomb's owner beyond doubt. A sealed doorway leading to the burial chamber was guarded by two wooden statues of the pharaoh. In the small hours of the following night Carter and Carnarvon are alleged to have secretly entered the burial chamber, then sealed it again, having verified that the king's sarcophagus and burial shrines were intact—but there are no reliable records of this event.

The discovery of Tutankhamun's tomb was an international sensation. While Carter made preparations for clearance, Carnarvon returned to England. He was received in audience by George V, who listened 'with great interest' to his account of the tomb. As Carter cleared the packed antechamber, his patron negotiated a controversial arrangement with *The Times* for exclusive coverage of the investigation. On 16 February Carnarvon was present as Carter and his assistant, A. C. Mace, broke open the sealed doorway of the burial chamber in the presence of official representatives. They revealed a great shrine built of wood covered with sheet gold and inset with blue faience plaques—the outermost of the pharaoh's shrines. Two days later the king and queen of the Belgians came to see what had been found. The strain of the international searchlight which blazed on Carnarvon and Carter caused them to quarrel, despite years of friendship. So serious were their disputes that Carter sealed the tomb in February 1923, deciding that he would spend the rest of the season in conserving and transporting the fragile artefacts from the antechamber. On 6 March Carnarvon was bitten on the cheek by a mosquito while at the village of Qurna on the west bank of the Nile near the Valley of Kings. While shaving in his hotel room in Luxor, he scraped the bite, which turned septic. He soon became seriously ill with erysipelas and blood poisoning, followed by pneumonia, and was transported to Cairo, where he died at the Continental Hotel on 5 April 1923. His body was returned to England, and he was buried, as he had wished, on the summit of Beacon Hill overlooking Highclere Castle. Inevitably there were press stories of the curse of the pharaohs felling him before the tomb was completely cleared.

Howard Carter completed the clearance of Tutankhamun's tomb after his friend's death, the two men having been reconciled at Carnarvon's bedside. After prolonged negotiations the Egyptian government paid Carnarvon's heirs £35,979 for the expenses incurred in finding and clearing the tomb between 1922 and 1929. In exchange the estate relinquished claims to the objects from the sepulchre. The Metropolitan Museum of Fine Arts in New York purchased Carnarvon's magnificent collection of Egyptian antiquities for $145,000 in 1927. The discovery assured Lord Carnarvon an archaeological immortality beyond his own professional competence, for he was a patron with good taste rather than a working Egyptologist. Amateur archaeologist he may have been, but Carnarvon was a man of great versatility, social graces, and personal charm, whose place in history is assured by Tutankhamun's tomb. His only son, Henry George Alfred Marius Victor Francis Herbert (1898–1987), succeeded him as sixth earl.

BRIAN FAGAN

Sources *The Times* (6 April 1923) · Lady Burghclere, introduction, in H. Carter and A. C. Mace, *The tomb of Tut-Ankh-Amen*, 1 (1923) · *DNB* · W. R. Dawson and E. P. Uphill, *Who was who in Egyptology*, 3rd edn, rev. M. L. Bierbrier (1995) · H. V. F. Winstone, *Howard Carter* (1991) · Burke, *Peerage* (2000) · Venn, *Alum. Cant.*

Archives BL, account of discovery of Tutankhamun's tomb, RP 1799 [copy] · Highclere Castle, Hampshire · U. Oxf., Griffith Institute | FILM BFI NFTVA, news footage

Likenesses H. Burton, photographs, AM Oxf. · photograph, U. Oxf., Griffith Institute [*see illus.*]

Wealth at death £398,925 7s. 11d.: probate, 14 May 1923, *CGPLA Eng. & Wales*

Herbert, George Robert Charles, thirteenth earl of Pembroke and tenth earl of Montgomery (1850–1895), travel writer, the eldest son of Sidney *Herbert, first Baron Herbert of Lea, and Elizabeth *Herbert, daughter of Lieutenant-General Charles Ashe À Court Repington, was born in Carlton Gardens, London, on 6 July 1850, and succeeded his father as second Baron Herbert of Lea on 2 August 1861, and his uncle as earl of Pembroke and Montgomery on 25 April 1862. He was educated at Eton College, but because of poor health spent much time in Italy, Sicily, Spain, Egypt, and Palestine. He made two voyages to the south Pacific before the age of twenty-one, accompanied by Dr George Henry *Kingsley. The second voyage ended in shipwreck and the loss of their yacht on a coral reef in the Ringgold Islands, Fiji, all on board making their escape to an uninhabited, uncharted island. After ten days the weather improved, the party set sail in three of the yacht's boats, and, while endeavouring to make the Nanuku passage, south of the Ringgold Islands, were picked up by a Swedish schooner. The voyages were described in Lord Pembroke and Dr Kingsley's *South Sea Bubbles, by the Earl and the Doctor* (1872).

Lord Pembroke married, at Westminster Abbey, on 19 August 1874, Lady Gertrude Frances Talbot (*d.* 1906), the third daughter of Henry John Chetwynd Talbot, eighteenth earl of Shrewsbury. In 1874 Disraeli appointed him under-secretary for war (his father had earlier been war secretary), but ill health led him to resign his post in 1875. He never accepted office again, and rarely spoke in the House of Lords, although he was still interested in public affairs. He took an active part in the volunteer movement and commanded the South Wilts battalion until within a few months of his death. He built and endowed the Pembroke Technical School near Dublin, where children learned industrial crafts. He died childless at Bad Neuheim, Hesse, on 3 May 1895 and was buried at his seat, Wilton House, near Salisbury. He was succeeded by his brother Sidney Herbert.

H. E. MAXWELL, *rev.* ELIZABETH BAIGENT

Sources Burke, *Peerage* · private information (1901) · *CGPLA Eng. & Wales* (1895)

Archives NL NZ, travel journal · Wilts. & Swindon RO, corresp. and papers | BL, corresp. with Lord Carnarvon, Add. MS 60774 · BL, letters to Mary Gladstone, Add. MS 46251 · BL, corresp. with W. E. Gladstone, Add. MSS 44438–44461 · BL, letters to Sir Edward Walter Hamilton, Add. MS 48620 · Bodl. Oxf., letters to Lady Edward Cecil · Herts. ALS, letters to Lady Desborough · U. Hull, Brynmor Jones L., Lawley MSS, letters to Lady Wenlock

Likenesses A. Gilbert, bronze statue, 1900, Wilton House, Wiltshire · Ape [C. Pellegrini], chromolithograph, NPG; repro. in *VF* (14 July 1888) · W. B. Richmond, oils, Wilton House, Wiltshire

Wealth at death £268,296 6*s.* 0*d.*: probate, 14 Sept 1895, *CGPLA Eng. & Wales*

Herbert, Henry, **second earl of Pembroke** (*b.* in or after 1538, *d.* 1601), nobleman and administrator, was the elder son of William *Herbert, first earl of Pembroke (1506/7–1570), and his first wife, Anne *Herbert (*b.* before 1514, *d.* 1552) [*see under* Herbert, William (1506/7–1570)], daughter of Sir Thomas Parr and sister of Queen Katherine Parr [*see* Katherine (1512–1548)]. Lord Herbert, as he was known

Henry Herbert, second earl of Pembroke (*b.* in or after 1538, *d.* 1601), by unknown artist, *c.*1590

after his father's elevation to the earldom in 1551, first married, on 25 May 1553 when still a boy, Katherine Grey (1540–1568) [*see* Seymour, Katherine]. This marriage was planned by John Dudley, duke of Northumberland, to gain Pembroke's support for the succession of his own daughter-in-law, Lady Jane Grey, Katherine's elder sister. After the failure of the plot and the accession of Mary, the marriage was annulled on the ground of non-consummation. Herbert in no way suffered as a result of his links with Dudley's plans. He was made a knight of the Bath at Mary's coronation on 29 September 1553 and later became a gentleman of the bedchamber to King Philip. When his father was appointed to lead the English forces to France in 1557, Herbert accompanied him and was present at the siege of St Quentin. In February 1563 he married for the second time; his new wife was Katherine (*d.* 1576), daughter of George *Talbot, sixth earl of Shrewsbury; they had no children. She died in May 1576. Eleven months later on 21 April 1577 he married Mary *Herbert, *née* Sidney (1561–1621), daughter of Sir Henry *Sidney and sister to Sir Philip *Sidney. They had three children who survived infancy: William *Herbert (1580–1630), Philip *Herbert (1584–1650), and Anne.

In 1570 Herbert succeeded his father in the earldom and was appointed lord lieutenant of Wiltshire, intermittently to begin with and permanently from 1586. The first earl had been granted large estates in Wiltshire and Glamorgan as a reward for services to the crown under Edward VI, and the principal family home was at Wilton, near Salisbury. With the decline of the older Wiltshire peers, Stourton and Hungerford, and the temporary eclipse of the Seymours, Pembroke was very much the dominant figure in the county, striving successfully to build up influence over parliamentary elections, but mostly standing aloof from the faction-fighting in the shire. He played a larger part in the political contests in Glamorgan, where he could count upon the support of his numerous Herbert cousins. Here, too, he wielded considerable influence over the return of men to parliament: his brother-in-law Sir Robert Sidney was knight of the shire in 1584 and 1593. The vigorous feuds in the county often revolved around the hostility of the major gentry towards Pembroke himself and his Herbert allies. His dominance was confirmed and extended when Pembroke was appointed to succeed his father-in-law, Sir Henry Sidney, as lord president of the council in the marches of Wales in 1586.

Pembroke had some advantages for the post over his predecessor. He could speak Welsh, had much experience of Wales, and was, indeed, described by a Welsh contemporary as *llygad holl Cymru* ('the eye of all Wales'; *DWB*, 351). On the other hand he had already made enemies. One of them, William Mathew of Radur, Glamorgan, bitterly attacked the appointment: 'I never harde it thought agreeable with the law of this or of any country whatsoever … that such a one should hear … our capital causes of whom … all our lands, especially within Monmouth and Glamorgan shires are holden' (Williams, *Council in the Marches*, 276). Pembroke was quick to make more enemies yet. He rightly saw that many abuses had crept into the council during Sidney's last years and set out to remedy them. Within a short time he had united against himself almost all the officers of the council, who had until then been quarrelling among themselves for years. By the middle of the 1590s Pembroke had also alienated the judges on the council, who successfully reduced his authority. From about 1595 he engaged in a bitter feud with Robert Devereux, earl of Essex, who was building up a rival faction in Wales: Pembroke's tactlessness equalled or even exceeded that of Essex himself, and it was soon reported from court that he 'hath very few friends or none left here, himself so careless of them when he hath them' (Collins, 1.382). In the 1570s and 1580s Pembroke had been an influential figure at court, Leicester and he referring to one another as father and son. But by the end of his life he had antagonized most of his friends, while his attempts to reform the council had ended in failure.

Pembroke's life at Wilton, however, was more positive, thanks largely to his wife. 'In her time', wrote Aubrey, 'Wilton House was like a college, there were so many and ingenious persons. She was the greatest patroness of wit and learning of any lady in her time' (*Brief Lives*, 1.312–13). Principal among her guests was her brother Philip Sidney, who wrote much of the *Old Arcadia* there. But Pembroke himself played a role as patron, appointing Fulke Greville as secretary to the council in the marches and Abraham France as queen's solicitor there. His chaplain, Gervase Babington, probably owed his preferment to the see of

Llandaff to Pembroke. In the theatre he patronized Burbage's company, known as Pembroke's men. During the last five years of his life his health declined: 'I dream of nothing but death, I hear of little but death, and … I desire nothing but death,' he wrote to Sir Francis Hastings on Christmas eve 1595 (Brennan, 101). There were signs of dissension in the family. His son William asked Robert Cecil to secure for him the queen's permission to stay at Wilton with his father, otherwise the latter would give away all his money. Pembroke died at Wilton on 19 January 1601, 'leaving his lady as bare as he could and bestowing all on the young lord, even to her jewels', according to John Chamberlain (*Letters of John Chamberlain*, 1.116). This is not, however, borne out by his will, in which he left the countess jewels and plate to the value of 3000 marks and substantial rents, both for her life or until she married again. He was buried in Salisbury Cathedral.

Pembroke emerges as intelligent, forceful, perceptive, but disastrously lacking in tact. He once sent a letter to the queen which his secretary refused to deliver, thinking it dangerous to have 'so passionate a letter delivered unto the Queen' (*De L'Isle and Dudley MSS*, 2.200). His persistent ill health seriously hampered his attempts to reform the council in the marches.   PENRY WILLIAMS

Sources DNB · GEC, *Peerage* · P. Williams, *The council in the marches of Wales under Elizabeth I* (1958) · P. Williams, 'The political and administrative history of Glamorgan, 1536–1642', *Glamorgan county history*, ed. G. Williams, 4: *Early modern Glamorgan* (1974), 143–201 · H. Sydney and others, *Letters and memorials of state*, ed. A. Collins, 2 vols. (1746) · *Report on the manuscripts of Lord De L'Isle and Dudley*, 2, HMC, 77 (1933) · VCH *Wiltshire*, vol. 5 · A. Wall, 'Faction in local politics, 1580–1620', *Wiltshire Archaeological Magazine*, 72–3 (1977–8), 119–33 · H. H. [H. Holland], *Herōologia Anglica* (Arnhem, 1620), 115–16 · M. Brennan, *Literary patronage in the English Renaissance: the Pembroke family* (1988) · *Brief lives, chiefly of contemporaries, set down by John Aubrey, between the years 1669 and 1696*, ed. A. Clark, 1 (1898), 310–13 · will, 1601, PRO, PROB 11/98, sig. 39 · DWB · report on the council in the marches of Wales, BL, Lansdowne MS 51, fols. 103–14 · *The letters of John Chamberlain*, ed. N. E. McClure, 2 vols. (1939)

Archives BL, corresp.

Likenesses oils, *c*.1590, NMG Wales [*see illus.*] · Passe, line engraving, BM, NPG; repro. in Holland, *Herōologia Anglica*, 115–16

Wealth at death £3600–£5399—rental p.a.: L. Stone, *The crisis of the aristocracy* (1965), 760; E. Kerridge, 'The movement of rent', *Econ. Hist. Rev.*, 2nd ser. (1953)

Herbert, Sir Henry (*bap.* 1594, *d.* 1673), master of the revels, was baptized on 7 July 1594 at St Nicholas's Church, Montgomery, the sixth of seven sons (and three daughters) of Richard Herbert (*d.* 1596) and Magdalen or Magdalene, *née* Newport (*d.* 1627), of Montgomery. The family were Anglo-Welsh gentry, connected to the Herbert earls of Pembroke. Herbert's mother was later patron of John Donne, and two of his brothers were notable poets: the eldest, Edward *Herbert (later Lord Herbert of Cherbury), and George *Herbert. His younger brother Thomas *Herbert was a naval officer.

Education and diplomatic career Magdalene moved to Oxford in 1599 to supervise the education of her sons

Sir Henry Herbert (*bap.* 1594, *d.* 1673), by unknown artist, 1639

(there is no record of Henry attending school or university, and he was probably privately tutored), and to London in 1601, taking a house in Drury Lane. In 1609 she married the much younger Sir John Danvers, who took an interest in his step-children.

By 1615 Herbert was in France, acquiring a command of the language and acting as a diplomatic courier. In April 1619 he was sent to Paris to prepare for his brother Edward's appointment as British ambassador, and was involved in important business, including abortive negotiations for the marriage of Prince Charles to the Princess Henrietta Maria. He began to be noticed at court and determined to make a separate career for himself; in March 1622 he became a gentleman of the privy chamber, a largely ceremonial post, but with some access to the king. When Edward returned to Paris, Henry did not go with him, but continued to act as his agent from London. In his autobiography Edward noted that the whole family was prone to be passionately angry and quarrelsome, 'infirmities to which all our Race is subject', and that Henry (who acted as second when Sir Robert Vaughan challenged Edward to a duel in 1619) 'gave several proofs of his courage in duels, and otherwise being no less dexterous in the ways of the court as having gotten much by it' (*Life*, ed. Shuttleworth, 9).

Master of the revels On 24 July 1623 Henry Herbert came to a business understanding with Sir John Astley, the master of the revels. Technically Astley appointed him as his deputy but for practical purposes he sold Herbert the post in return for £150 per annum. Herbert enjoyed the full dignity of the office from the outset, but had Astley died

before Ben Jonson, who held the next reversion, he would have lost it. In fact Jonson died in 1637, and Astley in 1640; only then did Herbert's own reversion (acquired jointly with Simon Thelwall in 1629) become operative. The revels office was primarily responsible for overseeing theatrical entertainment at court, mainly hiring in the leading acting companies in the festive season between November and Lent and on other special occasions. It also attended to some practical aspects of court masques, especially the lighting.

Earlier masters of the revels had also carried a special commission, which gave them wide-ranging powers over the acting community. In fact, Herbert never received this commission, presumably because of his arrangement with Astley, which may explain why he had such difficulty reasserting this authority after the Restoration. But prior to the civil war he behaved as if he had, controlling the major acting companies (usually four in number) privileged to perform in London and at court. He also licensed touring players, at least in principle throughout the country, and all manner of other entertainments—exotic animals, puppet shows, 'monsters' (people with malformations, including Siamese twins, bearded ladies, children with multiple heads, or no arms), and so on. Most important, from the perspective of later ages, this involved him in the censorship and licensing of all plays, both for performance and for print. Since few records of his principal predecessors, Edmund Tilney and Sir George Buc, have survived, his office records comprise by far the most revealing documents we possess about the censorship of late Elizabethan and early Stuart plays. Neglected for many years after his death, they have now disappeared. But partial transcripts were made by Edmund Malone, George Chalmers, Rebecca Warner, and Craven Ord, and passed into print by various means. The tale of these documents and their transmission is best told in N. W. Bawcutt's authoritative edition of 1996.

Herbert's work and 'wisdom' On 7 August 1623 King James knighted Herbert and 'was pleased likewise to bestow many good words upon me & to receive mee as M.r of his Revells' (*Control and Censorship*, 4–5). This was at Wilton, home of William, earl of Pembroke, lord chamberlain and Herbert's kinsman and patron; Pembroke's involvement prompts speculation that the arrangement with Astley was not purely a commercial business, and may have been related to wider accommodations at court. But the evidence is inconclusive. Herbert certainly took up office, however, when the political situation was unusually fraught. The unprecedented influence of the duke of Buckingham and a proposed marriage between Prince Charles and the Spanish infanta were both highly contentious issues. Something of this doubtless affected his view, for example, of Thomas Drue's *The Duchess of Suffolk*, which 'being full of dangerous matter was much reformed' before he licensed it in January 1624 (ibid., 148). Conversely, he licensed Thomas Middleton's *A Game at Chess* on 12 June despite its transparent discussion of the Spanish match, presumably because it accorded with official policy at the time; the privy council suggested that he should account for this, when the play was an unprecedented success and the Spanish ambassador protested to the king (ibid., 154). We do not know if Herbert was actually called to account, but Pembroke played a lord chamberlain's part in smoothing matters over, ensuring that the actors suffered no more than a brief suspension of business. The King's Men again exploited anti-Spanish sentiment in December with *The Spanish Viceroy*, circumventing Herbert's authority by failing to license the play at all. He was furious, and got the principal members of the company to admit their fault in writing.

These were exceptional incidents in what was normally a cordial relationship of mutual self-interest between the actors and the masters of the revels. More typical was Herbert's decision to 'allow' *The Winter's Tale* for the King's Men, without even a fee, on the word of the actor John Heminge 'that there was nothing profane added or reformed' even though the copy licensed by Buc was missing (*Control and Censorship*, 142). They relied upon Herbert's licence to be allowed to perform and for a form of copyright over their plays; he relied upon their commercial success for quality drama at court and for a steady income. In the early years Herbert earned a pound for each play he licensed for the stage, and 10s. for a licence to print; the sums later doubled. He also received fees for licensing the companies and their theatres, for waiving restrictions on playing in Lent, and at various times the proceeds of benefit performances, or flat rate payments in lieu of these, or presents such as books. From the court he was due an allowance for each day or night in attendance, and an annual allowance of £50 for rent and lodging, though some of this went to house the revels office. His office probably earned him overall at least twice what he was paying Astley every year. By the 1630s, moreover, he had shares in four of the theatres, and in the Restoration claimed these had brought him £400 per annum. The extensive property we know Herbert owned establishes that he was a wealthy man at the height of his career.

In the summer of 1625 Herbert married Susan, *née* Slyford (d. 1649/50), widow of Edmond Plumer, who had bequeathed her significant land and property, especially in Woodford, Essex, and £5000 in cash. They settled in Woodford, where their three children were born: William (May 1626) and the daughters Vere (August 1627) and Frances (1628). In 1627 they bought what was to be their principal property, Ribbesford, a country manor house in Worcestershire. Herbert carried a bannerol in the funeral procession of King James in 1625, and the following year was elected MP for Montgomery. His brother George was seriously ill at this time and lived for a year at Woodford, apparently on good terms. The brothers shared an interest in restoring churches, Henry making a number of gifts to Ribbesford and helping George with Leighton in Huntingdonshire. Another houseguest (1633) was Richard Baxter, later a noted preacher, then aged eighteen. Correspondence shows Herbert attached to a web of patronage and influence, including Philip, earl of Pembroke (who succeeded his brother as lord chamberlain in 1626) and John, Viscount Scudamore, to whom Herbert sent regular newsletters between 1624 and 1671.

Isaac Walton observed that Herbert's place as master of the revels 'required a diligent wisdom with which God hath blessed him' (Walton, 262). This was tested to the full in the 1630s. He briefly experimented with licensing nontheatrical works, for one of which (Donne's, *Paradoxes*) he had to answer in November 1632 before the court of Star Chamber. At about that time Jonson's play *The Magnetic Lady* was investigated by the court of high commission; the King's Men argued that they had only performed what Herbert allowed. The issue was not resolved until October 1633, when 'the players … did mee right in my care to purge their plays of all offence, my lords Grace of Canterbury [that is, Archbishop Laud] bestowed many words upon mee, and discharged mee of any blame' (*Control and Censorship*, 184). In the same week Herbert had another altercation with that company over their revival of an old play, *The Tamer Tamed*. Such revivals were normally permitted without hindrance if the 'allowed' text was unchanged. Here he stopped the performance at short notice, and insisted henceforth that old plays must be relicensed, for which he would charge a half-fee. This 'raysed some discourse in the players, thogh no disobedience' (ibid., 182). A number of his entries in his office-book from this time are unusually, perhaps prudentially, detailed. Two instances involved King Charles himself. In January 1634 Davenant objected that Herbert had dealt over-zealously with profanities in his play, *The Wits*, and the king was 'pleasd to take *faith, death, slight*, for asseverations, and no oaths, to which I doe humbly submit as my masters judgement'; but in June 1638 Charles ruled that a passage in a play by Massinger was 'too insolent, and to bee changed' (ibid., 186, 204).

The royalist Herbert was a royalist, but not as uncritical as some accounts suggest; assertions that he fought for the king are based on misidentifications. In 1639 he joined the king's entourage at Berwick in the expedition against the Scots, but commented on the incompetence and over-confidence of his army. In 1640 he was elected MP for Bewdley in both the Short and Long parliaments, being involved in deliberations over several disputed elections, and coming to blows with the parliamentarian lawyer Serjeant (John) Wilde. In 1642 he was one of the royalists debarred from the Commons, and in August wrote in his office-book: 'Here ended my allowance of plaies, for the war began' (*Control and Censorship*, 211). The following year he joined the king's parliament at Oxford. From the beginning, however, he was concerned about the consequences for his estates, which were sequestrated, and his plate, which was later seized. He took deep offence when his brother, Edward, refused to keep his horses safe in Montgomery Castle. By late 1645 he began negotiations to come to terms with parliament, taking the solemn league and covenant in February of the following year, and the negative oath that August. In March 1648 the Commons agreed to accept £1330 10s. as a third of his property, to pardon his delinquency and remove the sequestration of his estate.

By November Herbert's son William and daughter Frances were both dead; Lady Herbert died, and was buried at St Mary Bothaw in London on 5 January 1650. Relations with his surviving daughter, Vere, were soured by a chancery suit taken out against Herbert to recover money entrusted by his mother to Sir John Danvers for her dowry. A year after the death of his first wife, he married Elizabeth (d. 1698), daughter of Sir Robert Offley of Dalby in Leicestershire, thereby linking with the family of the diarist John Evelyn. They had seven children, of whom only three survived their father. These included the elder son, Henry *Herbert, who in 1694 was created Lord Herbert of Cherbury.

During the interregnum Herbert lived quietly in London and on his estates. On the restoration of Charles II he resumed some of his former offices, being sworn in as a gentleman of the privy chamber on 31 May 1660 and master of the revels on 20 June. But he never re-established his old authority. Most critically Thomas Killigrew and William Davenant persuaded the king to give them a monopoly of London playing; that August Charles granted licences authorizing each to erect a theatre in London, create an acting company and license their own plays, without reference to Herbert. He went to law to assert his rights, and two years of litigation, negotiation, and arbitration ensued. He finally came to accommodations with both men, under which he was to license and censor plays but have no other influence in London theatrical affairs. His authority to license plays for the press also seems to have been curtailed. Even his authority outside London was not unchallenged. The mayor of Maidstone (9 October 1660) denied his right to license actors in the provinces, and officials in Norwich later also resisted his authority. Some travelling actors and other entertainers simply ignored his office, despite his efforts to prosecute them. As a result, when he deputized Edward Hayward in 1663 and the flamboyant John Poyntz joined the revels office under a pre-war agreement, there was insufficient income for either of them. They were dismissed in 1665. Yet Herbert himself retained considerable holdings in land and property, and remained active in business affairs.

Herbert was returned to parliament for Bewdley in May 1661 and served for the remainder of his life. In 1665 he prepared his brother Edward's poems for the press. His own translation of two parts of Jean de Silhon's The Minister of State, a treatise on the principles of statesmanship, appeared in 1658 and 1663. Other works by Herbert, including two series of prose meditations, The Broken Heart (1620/21, Bodl. Oxf., MS Don. fol. 26) and Herberts Golden Harpe (1624, Bodl. Oxf., MS Don. fol. 27 and Huntingdon MS HM 85), and a verse play, The Emperor Otho (NL Wales, MS 5302B), have never been printed but survive in manuscript. Herbert was still actively engaged in business affairs until a month or so before his death (probably at his home in James Street, Covent Garden) on 27 April 1673; he

was buried in St Paul's, Covent Garden, on 6 May. Elizabeth survived her husband by twenty-five years, dying on 7 July 1698.   RICHARD DUTTON

Sources The control and censorship of Caroline drama: the records of Sir Henry Herbert, master of the revels, 1623–73, ed. N. W. Bawcutt (1996) · A. M. Charles, 'Sir Henry Herbert: the master of the revels as man of letters', Modern Philology, 80 (1982–3), 1–12 · A. M. Charles, A life of George Herbert (1977) · The life of Edward, first Lord Herbert of Cherbury written by himself, ed. J. M. Shuttleworth (1976) · I. Walton, The lives of John Donne, Sir Henry Wotton, Richard Hooker, George Herbert, and Robert Sanderson, [new edn] (1927) · R. Dutton, Mastering the revels: the regulation and censorship of English Renaissance drama (1991) · R. Dutton, '"Discourse in the players, but no disobedience": Sir Henry Herbert's problems with the players and Archbishop Laud, 1632–34', Ben Jonson Journal, 5 (1999), 1–25 · E. Rowlands, 'Herbert, Sir Henry', HoP, Commons, 1660–90 · R. C. Bald, John Donne: a life, ed. W. Milgate (1970)

Archives BL, papers, Add. MS 74244 · Bodl. Oxf., devotions · NL Wales, personal and family papers

Likenesses oils, 1639, Powis Castle, Montgomeryshire [see illus.] · oils (after portrait, 1639), St Leonard's Church, Ribbesford, Worcestershire, vestry

Wealth at death property in Essex and Worcestershire: will, PRO, PROB 11/342, fol. 59v; outlined in Charles, 'Sir Henry Herbert', Control and censorship, ed. Bawcutt, 38–41

Herbert, Henry, fourth Baron Herbert of Cherbury and fourth Baron Herbert of Castle Island (c.1640–1691), politician, was one of the sons of Richard *Herbert, second Baron Herbert of Cherbury and of Castle Island (1600?–1655) [see under Herbert, Edward, first Baron Herbert of Cherbury], and his wife, Lady Mary Egerton (d. 1659), daughter of John *Egerton, first earl of Bridgewater (1579–1649), and his wife, Lady Frances Stanley, daughter and coheir of Ferdinando, fifth earl of Derby. He was probably born about 1640, though the age of thirty-eight given on his marriage licence in December 1681 (a not necessarily reliable source) would suggest a slightly later date of birth, probably in 1643. Henry was a prominent whig and a supporter of the campaign (1679–82) to exclude the Catholic duke of York from the succession, though the Herbert family had traditionally been very loyal supporters of the crown. The barony was created in 1629 to reward Henry's grandfather Edward *Herbert (1582?–1648), traveller, scholar, and soldier, for his diplomatic services to James I; and Edward's six brothers included distinguished soldiers and politicians, as well as the poet George *Herbert. Because of his advanced age Edward remained ostensibly neutral during the civil war, but his son Richard Herbert, second baron from 1648 to 1655, commanded a troop of horse in the Scottish war of 1639, raised a regiment of 12,000 foot for the king in 1642, and was heavily fined by parliament when he succeeded to the title in 1648. Richard's eldest son, Edward *Herbert (1630–1678) [see under Herbert, Edward, first Baron Herbert of Cherbury], succeeded as third baron in 1655, and four years later he in turn took part in Sir George Booth's unsuccessful royalist rising in Cheshire.

Henry Herbert also joined the rebellion and then entered the army shortly after the Restoration, serving abroad under the duke of Monmouth with the French in 1672. He succeeded to the barony in 1678, on the death of his brother Edward, and next year followed his brother as *custos rotulorum* for Montgomeryshire. This was, however, the limit of royal favour toward him, for in 1678, when he took his seat in the Lords, the Popish Plot alarm was near its height, and this, together perhaps with his acquaintance with the duke of Monmouth, drew him into opposition to the court. He voted in favour of putting the five Catholic lords allegedly implicated in the plot on trial, and voted too for the impeachment of the earl of Danby, Charles II's principal minister for many years. He was one of the half-dozen opposition peers who in November 1679 joined the earl of Shaftesbury in giving countenance to Titus Oates by attending the trial of two men accused of defaming him. Unsurprisingly the king now ordered Herbert to give up his army commission. Undeterred, Herbert was active in the petitioning campaign of 1679–80 to persuade Charles to meet the parliament elected in 1679 and repeatedly prorogued, and attended the public dinners given by exclusionists in the City. When the struggle shifted in 1681 to control of the government of the City of London, Herbert was one of three leading whigs (with Shaftesbury and Francis Charlton) to be given the freedom of a major London livery company. By November 1681 Herbert had become so identified with the duke of Monmouth's exclusionist faction as to join with the duke, and his close crony Ford, Lord Grey of Wark, in issuing a public declaration that, while the three avowed their intention to exclude the duke of York, they were nevertheless completely loyal to the king and had no intention of subverting the monarchy. When a copy of their declaration was torn down in Covent Garden, Herbert at once replaced it, swearing to fight with pistol and sword any who touched it again. In March 1682 his prominence among the exclusionists was shown once again when the king banned the City of London from entertaining in any way Monmouth, Shaftesbury, Grey, or Herbert. When Monmouth went on procession in the midlands in September of that year to raise popular support, Herbert was prominent among the notables who accompanied him.

But while Herbert was undoubtedly close to Monmouth he also maintained good relations with Shaftesbury's wing of the whigs. Lord Howard of Escrick testified, during investigations into the Rye House plot in 1683, that in October of the previous year the earl of Shaftesbury (then desperate and trying to raise an insurrection) had told him that Herbert was one of those who would raise several thousand of the earl's 'brisk boys' in London. This link with treason was too slight for a prosecution, and the same was true too of the testimony of another plotter, James Holloway. Captured, tried, and executed in 1684, Holloway could swear to no more than having heard Herbert's name mentioned in connection with the Rye House plot. Nevertheless, after coming to town to support Algernon Sidney at his trial for treason in 1683 Herbert, like most other whigs, lived quietly, avoiding any public notice. Under James II, however, he once again moved into parliamentary opposition to the crown. In particular, Herbert's name appeared on a shortlist of opponents of the king throughout the country, men of 'real position and influence, who might countenance a movement against

James II' (Browning, 3.158), and he was almost certainly involved in the secret contacts with William of Orange which preceded the prince's descent on England in 1688. He took arms for William, and with Sir Edward Harley raised his part of the Welsh marches in support of the revolution. William subsequently rewarded him, Herbert becoming cofferer of the royal household in 1689, and in the same year colonel of the 23rd regiment of foot, later the Royal Welch Fusiliers. He died on 21 April 1691, and was buried in St Giles-in-the-Fields, London, on 28 April, with no heir from his marriage by licence dated 14 December 1681 to Lady Catherine Newport (*c*.1653–1716), daughter of Francis *Newport, first earl of Bradford. The barony died with him, but was recreated for Henry *Herbert (1654–1709), another whig.   ROBIN CLIFTON

Sources GEC, *Peerage* · K. H. D. Haley, *The first earl of Shaftesbury* (1968) · *CSP dom.*, 1672–91 · *State trials*, vols. 9–10 · *Diary of the times of Charles the Second by the Honourable Henry Sidney (afterwards earl of Romney)*, ed. R. W. Blencowe, 2 vols. (1843) · R. Clifton, *The last popular rebellion: the western rising of 1685* (1984) · J. R. Jones, *The first whigs* (1961) · *DNB* · A. Browning, *Thomas Osborne, earl of Danby and duke of Leeds, 1632–1712*, 3 vols. (1944–51) · W. A. Speck, 'The Orangist conspiracy against James II', *HJ*, 30 (1987), 453–62 · PRO, PROB 11/405, quire 127 (fols. 267r–268r)
Archives NL Wales, corresp. and military journal · Powis Castle
Likenesses G. Soest, portrait, Powis Castle, Powys

Herbert, Henry, first Baron Herbert of Cherbury (1654–1709), politician, was born on 24 July 1654 at the house of his uncle George Evelyn (brother of the diarist John Evelyn) in King Street, Covent Garden, London. He was the eldest son of Sir Henry *Herbert (*bap.* 1594, *d.* 1673), politician and royal household official, and his second wife, Elizabeth (*d.* 1698), daughter of Sir Robert Offley of Dalby, Leicestershire. He was educated at Trinity College, Oxford, in 1670, at the Inner Temple in 1671 and Lincoln's Inn in 1672. On 12 February 1678 he married Anne (*c*.1661–1716), daughter of the London alderman John Ramsey, who brought him a dowry of £8000. In addition to inheriting estates at Ribbesford, Worcestershire, and Dowles (then in Shropshire) from his father, Herbert maintained a residence at Leicester Fields, in Soho, London.

Obeying his father's dying wish Herbert contested the parliamentary seat for the borough of Bewdley, Worcestershire, left vacant by his father's death in April 1673, but lost the vote to Thomas Foley, the Stourbridge ironmaster. The defeat may well have reflected local resentment at an inexperienced nineteen-year-old presuming to sit in parliament as a matter of inheritance. He successfully petitioned parliament in March 1676 to have the result overturned, complaining that 'exceptions were taken to most of Mr. Foley's electors, but the Deputy Recorder being Mr. Foley's friend admitted them anyway' (*The Case of Henry Herbert*). Curiously, and despite the warnings from his London agent that 'some will make no good construction of your absence' (Warner, *Epistolary Curiousities, Series the First*, 112), he avoided attending parliament in October and November 1678 during the time that Titus Oates was 'revealing' the Popish Plot. Herbert was defeated by Philip Foley, Thomas's son, in the first general election of 1679 but obtained a seat for the city of Worcester in the third Exclusion Parliament of 1681. Later that year he sat on the Middlesex grand jury which indicted the earl of Danby for complicity in the Popish Plot.

Herbert's differences with his political rivals at Bewdley seem at first to have been personal rather than ideological, but later took on the contours of a whig–tory struggle. Salwey Winnington, the heir to the Foley interest in Bewdley, became a protégé of Robert Harley. Herbert, meanwhile, developed into a staunch whig whose 'actions and opinions', as his son put it, 'have always showed against passive obedience' (Warner, *Epistolary Curiousities, Series the Second*, 36). He participated actively in the revolution of 1688, going over to the Netherlands and returning with William's invasion force, and being appointed one of William's commissioners for managing the revenues while in Exeter. He was elected to the Convention and then again to parliament in 1690. As a member of the House of Commons and, after 1694, the House of Lords, Herbert rarely spoke but served as teller many times and chaired numerous committees, showing a particular interest in matters of naval preparedness and the prevention of commercial fraud.

On constitutional matters Herbert was sufficiently committed to English liberties to support the Triennial Bill with the pithy declaration, 'I would rather have a standing army than a standing parliament' (Grey, 10.301). On the other hand he obstructed 'country' efforts to extract from the king a more explicit promise to respect the constitution after his veto of the place bill in 1694 (Grey, 10.384). He further expressed his loyalty to the crown in an address of 11 October 1701 from the county of Worcester declaring that 'if their representatives do not comply with his [William's] just desires they will upon calling a new parliament elect such as shall' (Luttrell, 5.99). His unwavering support of William's government was the subject of an impassioned letter to Lord Chancellor Somers in 1700, wherein he described himself as having 'continued in the same warmth for this government as I brought over at the P[rince] of O[range's] landing, without any personal profit' (Warner, *Epistolary Curiousities, Series the Second*, 1–2).

None the less Herbert felt his services were under appreciated; as he told William in 1691, 'I fear I've labored under some misrepresentations to your majesty' (Warner, *Epistolary Curiousities, Series the First*, 147). The letter to Somers was in fact a plea 'if Lord Montagu lays down the treasury to recommend me there', and Herbert made many such requests for office during the reigns of William and Anne. Although he was created Baron Herbert of Cherbury in 1694 (the title having fallen vacant upon the death of his cousin the fourth Baron Herbert of Cherbury in 1691), Herbert's place seeking was generally unsuccessful. Only in 1707 was he made one of the commissioners of trade and plantations. The post carried a salary of £1000 per annum and was desirable enough that Sidney Godolphin told the duke of Marlborough at Herbert's death, 'I could send you a list, I dare say, of about fifty people that have asked for the vacancy in the council of Trade' (Snyder, 3.1212).

Despite his commitment to preserving the revolution of 1688 Herbert's career exemplifies the less democratic aspects of unreformed politics. He is best remembered for his cynical attempts to control Bewdley's parliamentary representation by manipulating the composition of its tiny electorate. Having complained in his petition of 1676 that Bewdley had too many voters, he complained to parliament in 1679 (after losing to Philip Foley) that Bewdley had too few; his about face had little to do with a newfound commitment to wider suffrage but to the hope of drowning out Foley's majority by the addition of new voters. In 1699 Herbert initiated a legal campaign to invalidate the charter that Bewdley had been given during Charles II's 1684–5 *quo warranto* campaign and (most controversially) to allow the crown to choose a new corporation (rather than recognize the tory dominated body already sitting). Herbert's efforts harnessed popular resentment of a narrow oligarchy, but also (as tory critics loudly made plain) represented an outrageous instance of ministerial tyranny, giving the crown in effect the right to pick an MP. Herbert won the fight in 1707, when Bewdley was given a new charter and in an election the same year the new corporation duly elected Herbert's son, Henry Herbert [*see below*]; in 1710, however, that result was invalidated by a now tory dominated parliament. By that time Herbert was dead, having succumbed to a fever on 22 January 1709. He was buried on 25 January at St Paul's Church, Covent Garden. His wife survived him and died on 24 April 1716.

Herbert's only child, **Henry Herbert**, second Baron Herbert of Cherbury (*d.* 1738), nobleman, was educated at Westminster School in 1696 by Thomas Knipe, who was unimpressed by his 'insufferable negligence' (*Old Westminsters*, 1.449). He was tutored by Abel Boyer in 1699, who also found him an unwilling student. In 1705 Herbert stood unsuccessfully for his father's seat at Bewdley but was returned at a by-election in May 1707, being again defeated at the 1708 elections. Having succeeded his father as Lord Herbert in January 1709, on 12 December 1709 Herbert married Mary (*d.* 1770), daughter of John Wallop of Farley, Southampton, and sister of John *Wallop, first earl of Portsmouth. They had no children. Herbert followed his father's whig politics, but was not appointed to any government office. He died, his debts greatly increased, at Ribbesford on 19 April 1738, possibly by suicide. His main property at Ribbesford was inherited by a cousin, Henry Morley. His widow became lady of the bedchamber to Princess Anne, daughter of George II, and died on 19 October 1770.

RACHEL WEIL

Sources P. Styles, 'The corporation of Bewdley under the later Stuarts', *Studies in seventeenth century west midlands history* (1978), 42–70, 271–7 · A. Collins, *The peerage of England: containing a genealogical and historical account of all the peers of England* · E. Rowlands, 'Herbert, Henry', HoP, *Commons, 1660–90* · 'Herbert, Henry', HoP, *Commons, 1690–1715* [draft] · R. Warner, ed., *Epistolary curiousities, series the first: consisting of unpublished letters of the seventeenth century illustrative of the Herbert family* (1818) · R. Warner, ed., *Epistolary curiousities, series the second: consisting of unpublished letters of the eighteenth century illustrative of the Herbert family* (1818) · A. Grey, ed., *Debates of the House of Commons, from the year 1667 to the year 1694*, 10 vols.

(1763) • Herbert family letters, BL, Add. MS 37157 • Bewdley charter, BL, Harley MS 6274, fols. 192–226 • *A speech made in the House of Commons upon the late ministry's forcing a new charter upon the town of Bewdly* (1710) • *A list of all the conspirators that have been seized, 1683–4*, BL, Egerton MS 2543, fol. 251 • *The case of Henry Herbert esq; in the election for the town of Bewdley in the county of Worcester* [1676] • *The case of Thomas Foley, esq; concerning his election for the town of Bewdley* [1676] • N. Luttrell, *A brief historical relation of state affairs from September 1678 to April 1714*, 6 vols. (1857) • D. Gilbert, 'Bewdley: the political and religious background', in *Bewdley in its golden age: life in Bewdley, 1660–1760*, Bewdley Historical Research Group (1991) • *CSP dom.* • *CSP col.* • *Journal of the commissioners for trade and plantations*, [vol. 1]: *From April 1704 to February 1708/9* (1920) • *The manuscripts of the House of Lords*, new ser., 12 vols. (1900–77), vols. 1–7 • *The Marlborough–Godolphin correspondence*, ed. H. L. Snyder, 3 vols. (1975) • GEC, *Peerage*, new edn • *Old Westminsters*, vol. 1

Archives BL, Add. MS 37157 • NL Wales, MSS 5303E–5305E

Herbert, Henry, second Baron Herbert of Cherbury (*d.* **1738**). *See under* Herbert, Henry, first Baron Herbert of Cherbury (1654–1709).

Herbert, Henry, ninth earl of Pembroke and sixth earl of Montgomery (*c.*1689–1750), architect and patron, was the eldest son of Thomas *Herbert, eighth earl of Pembroke and fifth earl of Montgomery (1656/7–1733), and his first wife, Margaret (*d.* 1706), daughter of Sir Robert Sawyer of Highclere, Hampshire. He matriculated at Christ Church, Oxford, in 1705, at the time when the dean, Henry Aldrich, was working on his 'Elementa architecturae' (printed *c.*1708), and the precociously Palladian Peckwater quadrangle was being built. On his grand tour in 1712 he visited Venice, Rome (where he met William Kent), and Naples (where he met Lord Shaftesbury). With the accession of George I he was appointed lord of the bedchamber to the prince of Wales and, as first lord of the bedchamber and from 1735 groom of the stole, he remained a close associate of George II after he became king.

Son of a famous antiquary and collector, Herbert shared these tastes but was most distinguished for his interest in architecture. This was acknowledged by Jonathan Swift, and George Vertue; according to Horace Walpole, 'no man had a purer taste in building' (*Works*, 3.486), even if to a sour critic such as Sarah, duchess of Marlborough, Herbert's attention to architectural decorum was ridiculed as no more than a talent to 'imitate ill whatever was useless' (Scott Thomson, 54) in the buildings of Jones and Palladio. While still a bachelor, he built a house in Whitehall to the design of Colen Campbell. This was completed by 1724, when he began a long connection with that architect's junior associate Roger Morris. The connection is tantalizingly imprecise: Morris, whose own Palladian ideas were developing at this time, seems to have been content to act as the builder for an aristocrat who left few traces of professional involvement, although for one commission he demanded substantial payment for 'explanations of [Lord Herbert's] directions' to the workmen involved (BL, Add. MS. 61477, fol. 34). Architectural drawings by William Townsend for the Column of Victory at Blenheim Park, Oxfordshire, had to be submitted to Lord Herbert's examination in 1727. Horace Walpole recorded that the water tower on his father's estate at Houghton (*c.*1730) was

designed by him. At this level, Herbert could be seen as typical of several dilettanti, but specific architectural details were left to his decision at Castle Hill, Devon (1729), and he played a part in the design of Wimbledon House, Surrey (1730–33).

More significantly, Marble Hill, Twickenham, Middlesex (1724–9), and Westcombe House, Blackheath, Kent (1727–8), where Herbert was closely involved, mark important and widely imitated developments in the evolution of the English Palladian villa. Their façades are divided in three parts both horizontally and vertically; details of door and window proportions demonstrate the fastidious restraint which characterizes the English adoption of Palladian ideas; and their pyramidal roofs emphasize the handling of mass which makes these buildings more than mere two-dimensional patterns copied from engravings. At Marble Hill, Herbert acted the intermediary between the owner, Henrietta Howard, mistress of the prince of Wales, and Morris; at Westcombe he was himself patron. Their close partnership is also apparent at Wilton, Wiltshire where, after Herbert had succeeded his father as ninth earl in 1733, the Palladian bridge was built in the grounds of the house. George Vertue stated that it was 'the design of the present Earl and built by his direction' (Vertue, *Note books*, 5.130), but other sources suggest that the design was Morris's. In 1734 this ten-year architectural collaboration was marked by the gift of a silver cup, bearing the head of Inigo Jones, to Morris from his patron.

Pembroke's most important architectural activity involved neither his own estates nor the houses of his friends, but a major transport artery, in London: here he acted not as architect, but as tireless promoter. Amid much pamphlet controversy, an act of parliament sanctioning the building of a bridge at Westminster was passed in 1738; Lord Pembroke laid the first stone in January 1739 and the last one (of the main structure) in 1747. The last of his 120 attendances at meetings of the bridge commissioners was on the morning of his death. He was the consistent supporter of the engineer Charles Labelye, whose original idea for construction by the use of caissons faced continuous opposition from other contestants for the arduous commission, as spiteful as they were inexpert. When a pier subsided in 1747, Pembroke was lampooned in *The Downfall of Westminster Bridge, or, My Lord in the Suds*. Besides architecture, Pembroke put more of his famed energy into litigation than into politics. At court, although a long-standing and close servant, he was not particularly intimate with the king; he gained little from attempts to mediate in the bitter disputes between George II and Frederick, prince of Wales. Despite a powerful role in the parliamentary constituency of Wilton, his participation in wider politics was slight. In the great family house, he promoted the cataloguing, under the supervision of Sir Andrew Fountaine, of the extensive collections built up by his father, and redecorated some of the rooms of the south front.

Lord Pembroke married Mary (1707–1769), eldest daughter of Richard, Viscount Fitzwilliam, in August 1733; their only child, Henry *Herbert, later tenth earl of Pembroke and seventh earl of Montgomery, was born in July 1734. Constantly active, playing tennis daily and enjoying swimming, he is shown in the portrait bust by Roubiliac at Wilton to have been powerfully built and strong. But in the winter of 1743 he spent weeks at Bath and had experienced difficulty in breathing; Walpole mentions asthma in his detailed account of Pembroke's collapse and death on 9 January 1750 at Pembroke House, Privy Gardens, Whitehall. Another report suggests that the fatal seizure was occasioned by anger at disagreeable business at the bridge commission. Horace Walpole summed up Pembroke's contradictory character as 'public-spirited and inflexibly honest, though prejudice and passion were so predominant in him, that honesty had not fair play' (Walpole, *Corr.*, 20.108–9); Queen Caroline felt 'he wishes well, but he is as odd as his father was, not so tractable, and full as mad' (Hervey, 3.828). He was buried on 16 January 1750 at Wilton.   T. P. CONNOR

Sources Colvin, *Archs.* · J. Lees-Milne, *Earls of creation: five great patrons of eighteenth-century art* (1962) · *Letters of a grandmother: being the correspondence of Sarah, duchess of Marlborough, with her granddaughter Diana, duchess of Bedford*, ed. G. Scott Thomson (1943) · A. Green, 'Letters of Sarah Churchill, duchess of Marlborough, on the column of Victory at Blenheim', *Oxoniensia*, 31 (1966), 139–45 · Vertue, *Note books* · Walpole, *Corr.*, vol. 20 · *The works of Horatio Walpole, earl of Orford*, ed. R. Walpole and M. Berry, 5 vols. (1798) · R. J. B. Walker, *Old Westminster Bridge: the bridge of fools* (c.1979) · J. Bold, *Wilton House and English Palladianism* (1988) · *The downfall of Westminster Bridge, or, My lord in the suds: a new ballad, to the tune of 'King John, and the abbot of Canterbury'* (1747) · John, Lord Hervey, *Some materials towards memoirs of the reign of King George II*, ed. R. Sedgwick, 3 vols. (1931) · GEC, *Peerage* · *GM*, 1st ser., 20 (1750), 43
Archives Wilts. & Swindon RO, corresp. and papers
Likenesses J. Richardson, oils, c.1709–1710, Wilton House, Wiltshire · C. Jervas, oils, c.1714, Wilton House, Wiltshire · W. Hoare, chalks, 1744, Wilton House, Wiltshire · J. Reynolds, double portrait, red chalk, 1749–50 (with wife), Wilton House, Wiltshire · L. Roubiliac, marble bust, 1750, Wilton House, Wiltshire; replica, Birmingham Museums and Art Gallery

Herbert, Henry, **tenth earl of Pembroke and seventh earl of Montgomery** (1734–1794), army officer, was born on 3 July 1734 at Pembroke House, Privy Garden, Whitehall, London, the only child of Henry *Herbert, ninth earl of Pembroke and sixth earl of Montgomery (c.1689–1750), and his wife, Mary Fitzwilliam (1707–1769), the daughter of Richard Fitzwilliam, fifth Viscount Fitzwilliam, and his wife, Frances Shelley. By 1743 he was boarding at a school in Wandsworth and by 1746 at Eton College, which he left after succeeding to his father's title in 1750. From late 1751 until December 1754 he travelled on the grand tour in France, Germany, Austria, and Italy.

On 13 March 1756 Pembroke married Lady Elizabeth Spencer (1737–1831) [see Herbert, Elizabeth, countess of Pembroke and Montgomery], the second daughter of Charles *Spencer, third duke of Marlborough, and Elizabeth Trevor. Their son, George Augustus *Herbert, Lord Herbert (later eleventh earl of Pembroke), was born on 10 September 1759; they also had a daughter, Charlotte (1773–1784). Pembroke first sat in the House of Lords on 13 November 1755. On 3 April 1756 he was appointed lord lieutenant of Wiltshire, where the family seat of Wilton

House, near Salisbury, was situated. In November 1756 he became a lord of the bedchamber to the prince of Wales, a position he retained after the prince's accession as George III, but he resigned it in 1762 when he eloped abroad with Elizabeth Catherine (Kitty) Hunter (d. 1795), the daughter of Thomas Orby Hunter MP. Society was scandalized. The affair resulted in a son, Augustus Retnuh Reebkomp (1762–1797), whose strange names reflected Hunter and Pembroke; later, as Augustus Montgomery, he became a captain in the Royal Navy. Lady Pembroke took her husband back in March 1763, although later in the marriage they lived much apart and he was often abroad. He had other affairs and certainly one illegitimate daughter. Pembroke's second, and final, appointment as lord of the bedchamber from 1769 to 1780 marked his restoration to favour. His unpredictable character remained. In 1784 his son Lord Herbert described him as 'perhaps ... the most unaccountable of all human beings' (*Pembroke Papers*, 2.260), while Horace Walpole was 'not surprised at any extravagance in his Lordship's morals' (Walpole, 25.497).

Since youth Pembroke had been, in his own words, 'horse mad' (Pembroke to Newcastle, 23 Sept 1754) and he had attended riding academies during his grand tour. Service in the cavalry ensued naturally, and he was appointed a cornet in the 1st King's dragoon guards on 12 October 1752. Two years later he became a captain, but in 1756 he transferred to the 1st foot guards. He was made aide-de-camp to George II on 8 May 1758; the rank of colonel followed. Having been appointed lieutenant-colonel in the newly raised 15th light dragoons on 10 March 1759, he joined them in July 1760 in Germany, where they formed part of the British contingent during the Seven Years' War. He left regimental service the same month to command a cavalry brigade. He was promoted major-general on 10 March 1761 and put on the staff in Germany. This was rapid advancement, even for a rich aristocrat. Pembroke was present at the battles of Warburg (31 July 1760) and Vellinghausen (15–16 July 1761) and acquired a good reputation.

In 1761 Pembroke published *A Method of Breaking Horses, and Teaching Soldiers to Ride* (2nd edn 1762; 3rd and 4th edns 1778 and 1793 entitled *Military Equitation*). This influential book provided sensible and much-needed advice. The author emphasized the need for officers to superintend the management of horses, advocated riding with a natural seat, and opposed the docking of horses' tails. On 9 May 1764 he was appointed colonel of the 1st (Royal) Dragoons, a position he described as 'the most pleasant & eligible object in the military of this country' (*Pembroke Papers*, 2.227), and which he retained until his death. Although seldom present with his regiment, he was a good example of the conscientious colonel, then common, who carefully attended to regimental efficiency. He was promoted lieutenant-general on 30 April 1770 and general on 20 November 1782. Other appointments were as colonel of the Wiltshire militia from 1770 to 1778 and governor of Portsmouth from June 1782.

In October 1778 Pembroke entertained George III and

Queen Charlotte in splendour at Wilton, and in 1782 Lady Pembroke became a lady of the bedchamber to Queen Charlotte. Pembroke increasingly hated Lord North and his policies and voted on 8 February 1780 for a motion of inquiry into public expenditure and the granting of contracts. A consequence of opposition was deprivation of his lord lieutenancy; it was restored to him on 8 April 1782. His forthright ideas and argumentative character led to family quarrels over his son's army career and financial matters. He was devoted to horses, dogs, and beautiful women, enjoyed travelling and shooting, had some interest in music and the arts, rebuilt his London residence, Pembroke House, in 1754–6, and was a lively correspondent. His portraits show a plumpish but not unpleasing face, with a prominent nose.

Pembroke died, after several months' illness, probably of a stroke, at Wilton on 26 January 1794 and was buried there on 3 February.　　　　　　J. E. O. Screen

Sources *The Pembroke papers: letters and diaries of Henry, tenth earl of Pembroke and his circle*, ed. S. Herbert, 2 vols. (1939–50) • GEC, *Peerage* • C. T. Atkinson, *History of the royal dragoons, 1661–1934* (1934) • H. C. Wylly, *XVth (the king's) hussars, 1759 to 1913* (1914) • Cobbett, *Parl. hist.*, vols. 20–21 • I. R. Christie, *The end of North's ministry, 1780–82* (1958) • *The manuscripts and correspondence of James, first earl of Charlemont*, 1, HMC, 28 (1891), 257–62 • Lord Pembroke to duke of Newcastle, 23 Sept 1754, BL, Add. MS 32736, fol. 571 • Walpole, *Corr.*, vols. 25, 27 • *Annual Register* (1778) • *JHL*, 28 (1753–6), 426b

Archives Wilts. & Swindon RO, family and estate MSS • Wilts. & Swindon RO, corresp. and papers, incl. accounts of illegitimate children | BL, corresp. with duke of Newcastle, Add. MSS 32730–32924, *passim* • NRA, priv. coll., letters to Lord Lansdowne • priv. coll., NRA Scotland, letters to Lord Southesk • U. Hull, Brynmor Jones L., letters to Sir Charles Hotham-Thompson • Wilts. & Swindon RO, letters to Lord Bruce • Yale U., Beinecke L., corresp. with James Boswell

Likenesses W. Hoare, chalk drawing, 1744, Wilton House, Wiltshire • P. Batoni, oils, 1754, Wilton House, Wiltshire • J. Reynolds, oils, 1763 (with Lord Herbert), Wilton House, Wiltshire • D. Morier, group portrait, oils, 1765, Wilton House, Wiltshire • D. Morier, oils, 1765 (with Domenico Angelo), Wilton House, Wiltshire • J. Reynolds, oils, 1767, Wilton House, Wiltshire • D. Morier, group portrait, oils (with his regiment, royal dragoon guards), Wilton House, Wiltshire; copy, Royal Collection

Wealth at death Wilton House and estate and Pembroke House to son; pecuniary bequests and annuities; administration to son: will, PRO, PROB 11/1243

Herbert, Henry Howard Molyneux, fourth earl of Carnarvon (1831–1890), politician, was born in Grosvenor Square, London, on 24 June 1831, the eldest son of Henry John George *Herbert, third earl of Carnarvon (1800–1849), and his wife, Henrietta Anne (1804–1876), eldest daughter of Lord Henry Molyneux Howard, a brother of Bernard Edward Howard, twelfth duke of Norfolk. Auberon *Herbert (1838–1906) was his brother. Herbert, who bore the courtesy title Viscount Porchester until 1849, inherited many of his father's characteristics, being literary rather than practical, cultured, and with a remarkable facility for words. Both, too, shared a love of travel. From an early age, Porchester enjoyed family visits abroad. The last of these journeys, undertaken when he was eight years of age, was intended to include parts of

Henry Howard Molyneux Herbert, fourth earl of Carnarvon (1831–1890), by Lock & Whitfield, pubd 1880

Asia Minor; but at Constantinople, he was taken seriously ill with fever and the family was obliged to return urgently to England. At Athens on the homeward journey his sister contracted fever, and in Italy his governess and nurse both died.

Academically very able from an early age, Porchester entered Eton College in April 1844 conversant with the works of many Latin and Greek authors. His four years at the school were followed by study at Oxford, where he matriculated from Christ Church on 17 October 1849. His father died on 10 December 1849 and he succeeded to the earldom. At Oxford, where Carnarvon was awarded a first class in *literae humaniores* in 1852, Henry Mansel, later Waynflete professor of moral philosophy and dean of St Paul's, exercised a powerful intellectual influence on him. While at Oxford, Carnarvon formed a lifelong friendship with Lord Sandon, later third earl of Harrowby. Shortly after graduating, the two men made an adventurous journey to Asia Minor, reaching Babylon, then relatively little visited. From his observations in Damascus, Carnarvon later published *Recollections of the Druses and Notes on their Religion* (1860).

Early political life Carnarvon had become interested in politics during his time at Oxford and was early marked out for a political career. He was asked by Aberdeen, then head of a coalition government, to move the address in answer to the queen's speech in the Lords on 31 January 1854. In his maiden speech, Carnarvon expounded his belief in a strong British empire, with the colonies living in harmony with their mother country. The Crimean War had broken out and the colonies had made financial contributions to the conduct of the campaign. On 1 March 1855 Carnarvon suggested in the Lords that the government should move a vote of thanks in recognition of their help. Shortly after the end of the war, he toured the battlefields in the Crimea with his old friend, Admiral Lord Lyons.

With the fall of the Palmerston government in February 1858, Lord Derby became prime minister. Carnarvon was offered, at the age of twenty-six, the office of undersecretary for the colonies. It was typical of his firm adherence to principles that he at first hesitated to accept because of the cabinet's refusal to continue with Palmerston's Conspiracy Bill. He gained valuable experience under first Lord Stanley and then Sir Edward Bulwer-Lytton during the eighteen months of the Derby ministry, which fell in June 1859.

Out of office, Carnarvon devoted his time to travel and closely observing the political scene. He strongly disliked the new reform bill which was threatened by the incoming Palmerston government and he expressed his concerns over imperial defence after a visit to Malta. As a country gentleman and landowner, he attended to the estate at Highclere, the family home in Hampshire, and carried out his duties in the county. Carnarvon's first efforts at penal reform with offenders had begun in 1854 and he became chairman of the judicial committee of the Hampshire quarter sessions in 1860. His paper *Prison Discipline* (1864) formed the basis of a Prisons Bill which was enacted by parliament the following year. He was appointed high steward of Oxford University in 1859 and created DCL. On 5 September 1861 Carnarvon married Lady Evelyn Stanhope (*d.* 1875), only daughter of the sixth earl of Chesterfield, at Westminster Abbey. They had a son, George Edward Stanhope Molyneux *Herbert, who succeeded as fifth earl, and three daughters.

Colonial secretary, 1866–1867

On the death of Palmerston, Lord Derby once more formed an administration, and Carnarvon was appointed colonial secretary in June 1866. One outstanding issue was the future of Canada. In 1858 Sir Edmund Head, governor-in-chief of British North America, had announced the policy of confederation to the Canadian parliament. No immediate action was taken though Carnarvon had followed developments in Canada while out of office. A formal meeting of North American delegates met in London in January 1867 under Carnarvon's chairmanship to discuss the British North America Bill which had been drafted. The main object was to unite Canada, Nova Scotia, and New Brunswick in one federal dominion under the crown with its own parliament, divided into upper and lower houses, with a seat of government, ultimately agreed, at Ottawa. The dominion of Canada came into existence on 1 July following the royal assent to the British North America Bill.

Carnarvon had early in office favoured federation to annexation. He was later to attempt the same solution in South Africa and in Ireland with less success. He had previously expounded his philosophy in a speech at a banquet for delegates from Nova Scotia and New Brunswick in September 1867:

> Changes in the course of time may come, which may vary our relationship with our distant Colonies, but changes depend very much in their nature on the spirit in which they are conceived, and also the spirit in which they are met … Once in the history of England it so happened that we parted from some of our great Colonies with a bad spirit and in a misunderstanding, the evil effects of which were felt for many a long year … this has taught us a useful lesson, and we need not be ashamed to own it. It taught us that conciliation is better than coercion: that if we give our confidence, it will be repaid us a hundredfold. It taught us and it taught the Colonies also—that their interests properly understood are not separate and distinct; but that the more prosperous the Colonies are, the greater will be the strength they confer on the Mother Country.   (Hardinge, 1.300–01)

Resignation over the franchise, 1867

In February 1867, a few days before Carnarvon introduced the second reading of the bill in the Lords, Lord Derby again raised the household suffrage question in cabinet. At first there was hostility towards the proposals though Disraeli, in charge of the bill in the Commons, made concessions. Carnarvon disliked the notion of the working classes' predominating among the electorate. Lord Cranborne (later the third marquess of Salisbury), then secretary for India, agreed with Carnarvon's misgivings on Disraeli's action and they determined to act in concert. At a cabinet on 23 February the business was hurried through, with Carnarvon objecting to important changes' being proposed only two days before the scheme was to be put to Conservative supporters. At a further meeting on 25 February only Carnarvon, Cranborne, and General Jonathan Peel, secretary for war, were not prepared to accept the reform plan. All three resigned at the cabinet meeting on 2 March. Carnarvon wrote in his journal, 'Lord Derby closed a red box with a heavy sigh and said, "The Party is ruined", and Disraeli added rather cynically, "Poor Tory Party"' (BL, Add. MS 60899). Carnarvon made a personal explanation in the Lords on 4 March and handed in his seals of office to the queen four days later. The Representation of the People Bill became law on 15 August.

Out of office, 1867–1874

Although he was often characterized as a high-churchman, Carnarvon's early contact with the Puseys and the Tractarian movement made him an intermediary between the conflicting schools of evangelical and high-church opinion.

When the relations between church and state in Ireland were being discussed in parliament in June 1868, Carnarvon told his friend Canon Liddon: 'I believe disestablishment to be inevitable, though I admit the conclusion possibly may not be so immediate as many suppose' (Hardinge, 2.2). In a speech in the Lords on the second reading of the Irish Church Bill on 26 June 1868, much to the delight of the Liberals, Carnarvon refused to assist in rejecting Gladstone's bill to suspend the creation of fresh interests in the Irish church (*Hansard 3*, 193, 1868, cols. 2–16). With the general election in November 1868 and the return of a Liberal ministry, led by Gladstone, an Irish Church Bill was introduced in March 1869. Before the bill reached the

Lords, a private meeting of Conservative peers was held at Lord Derby's house in St James's Square. Carnarvon, unlike the majority of the meeting, was unable to support opposition to the bill and once more expressed his personal views in a Lords debate on 14 June.

Having resigned from the government two years previously and subsequently accepted the principle of Irish disestablishment, Carnarvon was for a time unpopular with both his fellow peers and churchmen. Nor did he oppose the Irish Land Bill of 1870, believing that it would assist in the pacification of Ireland. However, the resignation of Lord Cairns as leader of the Conservatives in the Lords and the need to find a strong successor brought Carnarvon back into the picture. He acted as a negotiator with Salisbury and Stanley, neither of whom would accept the post while Disraeli led in the Commons. In a conversation with Gathorne Hardy, it was suggested that Carnarvon would be the best leader. He noted in his journal:

> I told him that the Party in the House of Lords had behaved to me with so much injustice and unkindness that though I had forgiven it I should not forget it and that … I was not inclined to take the lead. (journal, 22 Feb 1870, BL, Add. MS 60902)

Finally, the duke of Richmond was persuaded to take the post.

A great personal blow to Carnarvon occurred shortly afterwards with the murder in Greece of his favourite cousin, Edward Herbert. Herbert, then secretary to the British legation in Athens, was captured by brigands, along with three companions, on an expedition to Marathon. The party were held to ransom for £25,000 with amnesty and on receiving the news on 14 April, Carnarvon raised the money and telegraphed it to the Greek government. Unfortunately, the call for amnesty was refused, and, although the brigands were captured, the four men had been murdered on 21 April. The news shocked the nation, and Carnarvon, who was overwhelmed at the loss, heavily criticized the Greek government in the Lords for their action.

Early in 1872 Carnarvon suffered a serious breakdown and illness which was followed by a long convalescence. It was during this time that he wrote a book, published anonymously the following year, *The Shadows of a Sick Room*, which expressed his religious beliefs. A keen yachtsman, Carnarvon embarked on one of his frequent cruises with friends and colleagues and later toured the Franco-Prussian battlefields in January 1873.

Carnarvon's responsibilities as a landowner had increased with the death of his brother-in-law, Lord Chesterfield. The extensive Bretby estate and collieries in Nottinghamshire—over 13,000 acres—were left to his mother and himself. Carnarvon had already inherited 22,000 acres in Somerset and Hampshire, the family seat at Highclere, and Pixton Hall, Somerset, on the death of his father in 1849. The total property amounted to 35,583 acres. Carnarvon was a conscientious steward of the properties, paying frequent visits, maintaining close contact with tenants and villagers, and staying at one of his three country houses on the estates.

The political situation also caused Carnarvon some anxiety. Gladstone's ministry was becoming increasingly unpopular and the prospect of a government led by Disraeli was a real possibility. As Salisbury was, in this eventuality, unlikely to take office, Carnarvon felt bound to share his view. However, in July 1873 Disraeli and Carnarvon united to oppose Selborne's Judicature Bill, though in vain. In October, Disraeli visited Bretby and had a long and amicable conversation with Carnarvon. 'His mind has a much more *classical* culture than I had supposed', Carnarvon noted (journal, 10 Oct 1873, BL, Add. MS 60905). On political matters, 'One of the most remarkable features of this remarkable man [Disraeli] is the apparently total absence of personal rancour. He seems to have no feeling against those who have shown the greatest feeling against him' (journal, 7 Oct 1873, BL, Add. MS 60905). With the Conservative victory at the general election in February 1874, Salisbury and Carnarvon were both publicly and privately urged to join Disraeli's government. After an interview with the prime minister on 19 February, Carnarvon once more accepted the post of secretary of state for the colonies.

Colonial secretary, 1874–1878 Disraeli was happy to leave matters of colonial policy largely to Carnarvon. One vexed problem facing the new colonial secretary was the future of South Africa. The situation there was a delicate one. The recent discovery and annexation of the diamond fields of Griqualand West had accentuated the rivalry between the English and Dutch settlers. Sir Richard Southey, the lieutenant-governor, failed to keep order in the colony: Carnarvon was obliged to telegraph for troops from Cape Town to quell a serious disturbance in April 1875. The governor at the Cape and high commissioner of South Africa, Sir Henry Barkly, gave little guidance to his ministers when difficult diplomatic dealings with the Orange Free State and the South African Republic were taking place. Further, the English colonies of Cape Colony, Natal, and Griqualand West were pursuing a policy of harshness towards the native peoples, as were the Dutch Boers. Carnarvon determined to pacify the natives, reversing a sentence of high treason on a chief, Langalibalele, and recalled the governor, Sir Benjamin Pine.

Carnarvon believed that a South African federation, on the lines of his Canadian scheme, was necessary, especially in the eventuality of war with the native people. In 1874 he dispatched his friend, James Anthony Froude, the historian, to South Africa to urge federation; the mission was unsuccessful. Undeterred, Carnarvon received cabinet agreement in April 1875 to invite the Dutch states, Orange Free State and the Transvaal, to meet with the three English colonies to discuss the matter. The proposal, sent to Barkly for immediate publicity, was received by the Cape assembly with great hostility, not helped by a further visit by Froude in June.

In the face of such opposition Carnarvon withdrew his scheme in October 1875, but suggested a conference in London. In negotiations with John Henry Brand, president of the Orange Free State, in July 1876, it was agreed that for a sum of £90,000 Griqualand West should be united with ot left out of a partition ofope.

Carnarvon supported a policy of strict neutrality: on 30 April 1877 he announced in the Lords that such a policy would be followed in eastern Europe. Towards the end of the year, as Russian advances continued, Russophobe feelings rose to a new height. Carnarvon made a speech to a deputation on 2 January 1878 which received widespread coverage in the national press. In it he declared, 'I apprehend that there are very few people now who look back upon that war [the Crimean War] with satisfaction, and I am confident that there is nobody insane enough in this country to desire a repetition of it.'

Carnarvon was rebuked by Disraeli when the cabinet met the following day, and Carnarvon indicated that he might resign. Efforts were made to persuade him not to do so. Meanwhile he wrote to Salisbury:

> I not only do not wish you to leave with me—if it comes to this—but I doubt whether it is wise for you to do so. The point is quite sufficient for one person to stand upon; but perhaps not large enough for three. (3 Jan 1878, Hatfield House MS 3M/F)

On 7 January Carnarvon apologized at the cabinet meeting amid great relief from his colleagues. However, with the report on 23 January that the Russians were advancing on Gallipoli, Disraeli ordered the fleet to the Dardanelles. At the cabinet meeting that day, Carnarvon, along with Derby, resigned. In a detailed speech in the Lords on 25 January Carnarvon justified his conduct, at the same time publicly regretting leaving many issues relating to his office incomplete and unsettled.

During the course of his public life that year Carnarvon travelled to Edinburgh to address the Edinburgh Philosophical Institute on imperial administration (5 November). On the way he revisited his mother's former home at Greystoke Castle, Cumberland. There he met his cousin, Elizabeth Catharine (d. 1929), eldest daughter of Henry Howard; he married her six weeks later at Greystoke on 26 December 1878. The union, which produced two sons, one of whom was the diplomatist and traveller Aubrey Nigel Henry Molyneux *Herbert, brought Carnarvon great happiness.

Parliamentary reform, 1884–1885 To some extent, Carnarvon was now an isolated figure. In his journal at the end of 1879, he wrote, 'There has been extreme bitterness during the last two years towards me and many of the cabinet and their supporters. All intercourse has ceased and hardly a letter ever passes'. He composed his position if, as seemed likely, the Liberals took office. As for Gladstone: 'I have far more in common with him than most living statesmen' and socially and intellectually Carnarvon admitted to sharing many views with him. 'Morally I feel quite free to act, as I may think best; politically I believe there is a road open to me in either direction' (journal, 29 Dec 1879, BL, Add. MS 60913). Three years after Gladstone formed his second ministry, Edward Hamilton, then Gladstone's principal private secretary, reported a conversation with Lord Bath: 'He tells me he knows for certain that Lord Carnarvon was disappointed at not being asked to join the

Government when it was formed ... His disappointment, however, has subsequently turned into very open bitterness against the Government' (diary, 3 Feb 1883, BL, Add. MS 48633, fol. 43).

For a time, less conspicuous in politics, Carnarvon was called on to be chairman of the secret royal commission for the defence of British possessions and commerce abroad (1878–81) which undertook a comprehensive review of imperial defence. Carnarvon was irritated at Gladstone's failure two years later to follow up its recommendations, observing in the Lords his suspicion that the report had been 'consigned to the pigeon-hole' (*Hansard 3*, 278, 1883, cols. 1831–5). Reconciliation with Disraeli took place in May 1881, when Carnarvon returned to the front opposition bench. On the third reading of the Irish Land Bill in August, Carnarvon expressed his reservations on the experiment which, if it failed, could lead to repressive measures or civil war (*Hansard 3*, 264, 1881, cols. 1180–86).

Carnarvon played a prominent role in Gladstone's Franchise Bill of 1884 which would give the vote to 2 million more people. In a speech in the Lords on 8 July, Carnarvon opposed the bill, arguing that parliament would become 'less and less a true mirror and true representation of the people'. The bill was rejected by the Lords: Gladstone withdrew the bill on 10 July, promising to reintroduce it in the autumn session. Carnarvon, along with other Conservative leaders, organized mass meetings throughout the country which they addressed. The highpoint was at Nostell Priory, Yorkshire, where he and Northcote addressed an enthusiastic audience of 40,000–50,000 people. Salisbury's handling of the crisis drew criticisms from Carnarvon, demonstrating how far the two men had drifted apart. 'One thing is very clear to me', wrote Carnarvon in his journal:

> Salisbury has not the confidence of those who follow him or who are supposed to be his colleagues and advisers. The first he alarms by his supposed rashness. The latter he alienates by seeming to distrust them ... Time will show but I am afraid that with all his great gifts he will be a failure and may even do mischief   (18 July 1884, BL, Add. MS 60923)

At a meeting in October, Carnarvon suggested that the redistribution question be referred to three or four impartial men who had the confidence of both parties. Both Gladstone and the queen were favourable to this suggestion and Carnarvon was involved as the broker between the parties, despite Salisbury's initial opposition to compromise and conciliation. When it was announced on 17 November that the government was to make an announcement of its intentions on the matter, Carnarvon was one of twelve Conservative peers called by Salisbury to meet at his house the following day. Subsequently, Salisbury entered into direct negotiations with Gladstone: on 4 December the bill passed through the committee stage in the Lords with little discussion. A pleasing aspect of the outcome for Carnarvon was the recognition by the queen of his part in the proceedings in the form of an invitation to Windsor. 'It is evidence', he recorded in his journal, 'of a reconciliation on her part after nearly six years of absolute silence' (journal, 8 Dec 1884, BL, Add. MS 60923).

Lord lieutenant of Ireland, 1885–1886   One of the major decisions facing the minority Conservative government when it was returned, headed by Salisbury, in June 1885 was the future of the Crimes Act in Ireland. The need to search for a compromise solution rather than the use of coercion in dealing with Parnell was paramount. On 15 June Salisbury offered Carnarvon the lord lieutenancy of Ireland with a seat in the cabinet: Carnarvon reluctantly accepted, stipulating that he would resign after the coming general election. Armed with the knowledge that the majority of his cabinet colleagues believed that Ireland could be ruled without coercion, Carnarvon visited that country in early July. On his return, he announced in a conciliatory speech in the Lords on 6 July that the Crimes Act would not be renewed and that a land purchase bill would be introduced. Salisbury was aware of Carnarvon's advocacy of a federal solution to Anglo-Irish relations.

That morning Carnarvon had a conversation with Justin McCarthy, the Parnellite leader, at the home of Howard Vincent, where it was suggested that Carnarvon might meet Parnell on Irish matters. Salisbury was informed of the proposal and, with his approval and that of Ashbourne, lord chancellor of Ireland, a secret meeting was arranged (Hardinge, 3.174–6). The interview took place, without witnesses, on 1 August in an empty house at 15 Hill Street, Mayfair. The exploratory discussion gave rise to optimism that agreement on a range of outstanding issues could be settled and Carnarvon drew up a memorandum of the meeting which he showed Salisbury the same day. As the lord lieutenant was acting on his own initiative, the cabinet was not informed of the meeting even though it was known to at least two of its members.

Carnarvon's regime in Ireland was a pacific one. He made a tour of the west in August, visiting remote districts where he was well received. The proper and efficient organization of the police was considered as well as the creation of industrial schools, the promotion of technical education, and an expansion of higher education, though he complained of the reluctance of colleagues to devote expenditure to these causes. There was a decline in agrarian crime. Salisbury, whose attitude towards Ireland differed considerably from Carnarvon's, made only vague references to the question in his Newport speech of 7 October. Later that month, Carnarvon threatened Salisbury with resignation unless home rule was considered but at length withdrew the threat. With increasing dissatisfaction at Salisbury's attitude towards Ireland, however, at a meeting at Hatfield on 13 December Carnarvon expressed his wish to resign. At a cabinet the following day when Ireland was discussed—'the result of which was that the Cabinet would do nothing and announce no policy' (journal, 4 Jan 1886, BL, Add. MS 60926), the matter of Carnarvon's resignation was raised. He was persuaded to defer his decision until after a vote of confidence was disposed of. On returning from Ireland on 13 January 1886, however, he read in that day's *Standard* the announcement of his retirement at the end of the month. Carnarvon attended his last cabinet meeting on 16 January, shortly before the Conservatives were defeated by Gladstone.

It was only on 7 June 1886 that the meeting of the previous year between Carnarvon and Parnell was revealed during a Commons debate. Parnell claimed he had been promised that a tory majority would have granted home rule. In his reply in the Lords, Carnarvon emphatically denied having given such a pledge, making no reference to Salisbury's implication in setting up the meeting (*Hansard 3*, 306, 1886, cols. 1256–60). Carnarvon also expressed his belief in a limited form of self-government for Ireland: this statement was badly received by his party and when the new ministry was formed in July 1886 Carnarvon was not offered a post and his political career came to an end. He had already contemplated whether to accept a post if it were offered him. Noting the coldness of his former colleagues, he wrote, 'To accept would cure the seeming differences of opinion for the time: but if a break were afterwards to come it would be impossible ever again to mend the broken china' (journal, 5 July 1886, BL, Add. MS 60927).

Final years and death Carnarvon visited South Africa and Australia (August 1887 to February 1888), still taking a close interest in many aspects of colonial affairs. His health, which was never strong, began to fail and he died at his London house, 43 Portman Square, on 28 June 1890. He was buried on 3 July in the chapel which he had erected at Highclere.

Political and scholarly reputation Carnarvon was a man of great sensibility and gentleness, though handicapped by an oversensitive nature. As Lord George Hamilton wrote of him, 'Possessed as he was by a great charm of manner, of eloquence and industry, yet he had a microbe of incurable fidgetiness in his composition. Three times in twenty years did he resign from office' (G. Hamilton, *Parliamentary Reminiscences and Reflections, 1886–1906*, 1922, 10). He was more of an aristocratic whig than a party man, attracting enemies among his colleagues for his independence of thought. Carnarvon told Salisbury in 1878 at the height of the Turco-Russian crisis, 'You know me of old and that when once I have made up my mind on a question like this I am what my friends will call obstinate and my opponents perhaps something worse' (26 Jan 1878, Hatfield House MS 3M/E). His greatest accomplishment was the establishment of a federal constitution for Canada, though he was unsuccessful in South Africa and Ireland. Carnarvon's distrust of Disraeli was manifest at the time of the second Reform Act in 1867 and the Russo-Turkish conflict in 1876–8. On both occasions, he preferred resignation to compromise. Carnarvon played a significant part in the negotiations leading to the passing of the Franchise Bill in 1884. His period as lord lieutenant of Ireland roused suspicions that he was more eager for home rule than many of his colleagues.

As a classical scholar, Carnarvon published a translation of Aeschylus's *Agamemnon* (1879) and of the first twelve books of Homer's *Odyssey* (1886); a posthumous work of his Oxford tutor, Dean Mansel, *The Gnostic Heresies of the First and Second Centuries* (1881); the unpublished letters of Lord Chesterfield (1890); and *The Herberts of Highclere* (1890). He was greatly interested in history and archaeology, writing a history of ancient Hampshire and on the archaeology of Berkshire. Carnarvon was elected a fellow of the Society of Antiquaries on 15 March 1877 and was president from April 1878 to April 1885. His first action was to direct the society's protest against the destruction of parts of St Albans Abbey during its restoration. Carnarvon was also an active member of the Historical Manuscripts Commission from 1882 and a trustee of the British Museum. He was a firm believer in education based on the principles of the Church of England. At the same time, he held a true scientific education to be of the highest importance. Carnarvon gave many addresses on education to a variety of audiences, including the National Association for the Promotion of Social Science. He was also a prominent freemason. Carnarvon became lord lieutenant of Hampshire on 21 March 1887 and accepted a seat on the new county council after its formation on 20 November 1888.

PETER GORDON

Sources A. Hardinge, *The life of Henry Howard Molyneaux Herbert, fourth earl of Carnarvon, 1831–1890*, ed. Elisabeth, countess of Carnarvon, 3 vols. (1925) · G. E. Buckle, *The life of Benjamin Disraeli*, 6 (1920) · R. Milman, *Britain and the Eastern question* (1979) · A. B. Cooke and J. Vincent, *The governing passion: cabinet government and party politics in Britain, 1885–6* (1974) · M. Cowling, *1867: Disraeli, Gladstone and revolution* (1967) · L. P. Curtis, *Coercion and conciliation in Ireland* (1963) · R. Blake, *Disraeli* (1966) · A. Jones, *The politics of reform, 1884* (1972) · J. D. Fair, 'The Carnarvon diaries and royal mediation in 1884', *EngHR*, 106 (1991), 97–116 · A. Adonis, 'The survival of the great estates: Henry, 4th earl of Carnarvon and his dispositions in the eighteen-eighties', *Historical Research*, 64 (1991), 54–62 · *The Times* (30 June 1890), 10 · d. cert. · H. Herbert, journal, BL, Carnarvon MSS

Archives BL, corresp. and papers, Add. MSS 60757–61100 · Highclere Castle, corresp. and papers · PRO, corresp. and papers, PRO 30/6 · Som. ARS, corresp. and papers | BL, corresp. with Lord Aberdeen, Add. MSS 43252–43253 · BL, Carnavon MSS · BL, corresp. with Lord Cross, Add. MS 51268 · BL, corresp. with W. E. Gladstone, Add. MSS 44378–44608, *passim* · BL, corresp. with Sir Stafford Northcote, Add. MS 50022 · Bodl. Oxf., letters to H. W. Acland · Bodl. Oxf., letters to Lord Clarendon · Bodl. Oxf., letters to Benjamin Disraeli · Bodl. Oxf., corresp. with Lord Kimberley · CAC Cam., corresp. with Lord Randolph Churchill · CKS, letters to Edward Stanhope · Glos. RO, letters to Sir Michael Hicks Beach · Herts. ALS, corresp. with Lord Lytton · HLRO, letters to Lord Ashbourne · Hove Central Library, Sussex, letters to Viscount Wolseley · ING Barings, London, corresp. with earl of Northbrook · LPL, letters to A. C. Tait · Lpool RO, letters to fourteenth earl of Derby · Lpool RO, letters to fifteenth earl of Derby · New Brunswick Museum, corresp. with Sir W. F. Williams · NL Ire., letters to Lord Monck · NL Wales, letters to Lord Rendel · priv. coll., letters to Augusta, Lady Vincent · PRO, letters to Lord Cairns, PRO 30/51 · PRO NIre., corresp. with Lord Dufferin · Sandon Hall, Staffordshire, Harrowby Manuscript Trust, letters to Lord Harrowby · Suffolk RO, Ipswich, letters to Lord Cranbrook · Trinity Cam., letters to Lord Houghton · U. Durham L., letters to third Earl Grey · W. Sussex RO, letters to duke of Richmond · Yale U., Beinecke L., letters to T. J. Pettigrew

Likenesses portraits, 1860–85, repro. in Hardinge, *Life of Henry Howard Molyneaux* · Ape [C. Pellegrini], chromolithograph caricature, NPG; repro. in *VF* (11 Sept 1869) · W. Holl, stipple (after G. Richmond), BM · Judd & Co., lithograph, NPG; repro. in *Whitehall*

Review (16 Feb 1878) • Lock & Whitfield, woodburytype photograph, NPG; repro. in T. Cooper, *Men of mark: a gallery of contemporary portraits* (1880) [*see illus.*] • P. Morris, oils, United Grand Lodge of England, London • E. Stodart, stipple and line print (after a photograph by London Stereoscopic Co.), NPG • portrait, Highclere Castle, Hampshire • print, NPG

Wealth at death £328,809 0s. 11d.: resworn probate, Jan 1892, *CGPLA Eng. & Wales* (1890)

Herbert, Henry John George, third earl of Carnarvon (1800–1849), travel writer, born on 8 June 1800 in Grosvenor Square, London, was the eldest son of Henry George Herbert (1772–1833), the second earl, and Elizabeth Kitty (1772–1813), daughter of Colonel John Dyke *Acland of Pixton, Somerset. He was at first known as Viscount Porchester, was educated at Eton College, and matriculated from Christ Church, Oxford, on 22 October 1817, but did not take a degree. A love of adventure led him from an early age to spend much time abroad. He travelled in north Africa, and subsequently for many years in Portugal and in Spain, where he was imprisoned by the Christinos for displaying active sympathy with the Carlists. An intelligent observer and an excellent linguist, he was attracted by Spanish history and literature, and in 1825 published *The Moor*, a poem in six cantos, and in 1828 *Don Pedro, King of Castile*, a tragedy, which was successfully produced at Drury Lane during his absence abroad, on 10 March 1828, when Macready and Ellen Tree filled the chief parts. On returning home he published the results of his observations in *The Last Days of the Portuguese Constitution* (1830), and in *Portugal and Galicia* (1830).

Portchester married, on 4 August 1830, Henrietta Anne (1804–1876), the eldest daughter of Lord Henry Molyneux Howard. They had five children: Henry Howard Molyneux *Herbert, fourth earl (1831–1890); Alan Percy Harty Molyneux Herbert MD (1836–1907); Auberon Edward William Molyneux *Herbert (1838–1906), Eveline (d. 1906), who married Isaac Newton Wallop, fifth earl of Portsmouth; and Gwendoline Ondine. In 1831 he was elected MP for Wootton Basset, Wiltshire, and spoke eloquently against the Reform Bill which abolished his constituency. On 16 April 1833 he succeeded his father as third earl and continued his opposition to Liberal measures, including municipal reform, in the House of Lords.

In 1839 Carnarvon travelled through Greece, then suffering from the effects of war and civil disturbances—his notes of the tour were published in 1869 by his son Henry under the title *Reminiscences of Athens and the Morea*. Between 1839 and 1842 Carnarvon undertook restoration of the family seat, Highclere, Hampshire, on a very elaborate scale. He engaged Sir Charles Barry who encased the existing classical mansion in an Elizabethan façade, based loosely on Woollaton, but with Gothic influences. The exuberant style reflected Carnarvon's liking for the exotic, which he had indulged in his travels, and for the theatrical—and his dislike for styles he thought whiggish. He was jealous of his rights and in 1844 established in the courts his claims to free-warren over the manors of Highclere and Burghclere, giving him the exclusive right to kill game on those estates; but in private life he was kind and unassuming.

Carnarvon's health was never very good, and he died at Pusey House, Berkshire, the home of his brother-in-law, Philip Pusey MP, on 10 December 1849. His funeral chapel was by Thomas Allom, in Highclere Park, north of the house.   [ANON.], *rev.* ELIZABETH BAIGENT

Sources Burke, *Peerage* • Ward, *Men of the reign* • R. B. Mosse, *The parliamentary guide* (1836) • *Annual Register* (1849), 249 • *GM*, 2nd ser., 33 (1850), 205–6 • *Hampshire and the Isle of Wight*, Pevsner (1967) • M. Girouard, *The Victorian country house*, rev. edn (1979) • d. cert. • GEC, *Peerage*
Archives BL, corresp., literary MSS, and papers, Add. MSS 60984–61019 • Som. ARS, corresp., literary MSS, and papers | BL, letters to Lord Holland, Add. MSS 51633, 51831–51832 • CKS, letters to Lord Mahon • Highclere, Barry MSS • U. Southampton L., letters to first duke of Wellington
Likenesses T. Kirkby, oils, Eton • H. Robinson, stipple and line engraving (after W. Walker), BM, NPG • E. Walker, portrait
Wealth at death under £10,000: will, GEC, *Peerage*

Herbert, Henry William [*pseud.* Frank Forester] (1807–1858), sportsman and writer, was born on 7 April 1807 at 10 Poland Street, London, the eldest son of the Revd William *Herbert (1778–1847), dean of Manchester, and the Hon. Letitia Emily Dorothea, daughter of Joshua, fifth Viscount Allen. He was educated privately until 1819 and afterwards at a school in Rottingdean kept by the Revd Dr Hooker, and at Eton College from 1820 to 1825. It is likely that he was destined for a career in holy orders, and in 1830 he graduated BA from Gonville and Caius College, Cambridge, where, as a *bon viveur* and member of the Cambridge yeomanry cavalry, he early showed a taste for dissipation, scholarship, outdoor sports, and writing. Upon graduation, prompted perhaps by personal and financial indiscretions, he fled somewhat suddenly to France and, in 1831, to New York. None of his biographers satisfactorily explains the reasons for self-exile, but his family refused thereafter to acknowledge his existence.

Having abandoned plans to settle in Canada, Herbert accepted employment in New York as a classics master at the Revd R. Townsend Huddart's Classical Institute. He remained there for eight years, during which his engagingly eccentric manner and outlandish dress brought him a social cachet among sportsmen, literary men, and educated merchant leaders. Since boyhood an ardent participant in country pursuits, nevertheless as a classical scholar he had few equals in North America, and his translations from Greek, Roman, and French originals received high praise. To his extensive knowledge of English history and literature he added a marked ability as a pen-and-ink artist. Finding his British citizenship was a barrier to a legal career, he was to become one of the first professional writers in the United States. The extent of his writings is revealed in William Van Winkle's *Bibliography* (1936), covering 1832–58, supplemented by Stephen Meats in *Papers of the Bibliographical Society of America* (67, 1973, 69–73). Herbert's North American literary début coincided with a burgeoning mass-market magazine industry and initially he co-edited with James G. Bennett the *Courier and Inquirer*.

Stung by rebuffs from the *Knickerbocker Magazine* and *Parlour Journal*, Herbert began publication in 1833 with A. D.

Patterson of the *American Monthly Magazine*, whose prospectus promised poetry, biography, theatre reviews, and travel. In the belief that literature influenced public morality and mass education, symbolically the first issue began with an introduction on the value of periodical literature. In pursuit of this ideal, practical economic matters were ignored and with Patterson's resignation in 1834 the magazine collapsed in early 1835. Having become a truculent fop and roadhouse brawler by the mid-1830s, the floridly moustachioed author achieved modest recognition in leading contemporary periodicals, and some of his fugitive poetry was well received by Edgar Allan Poe. The same luminary, however, mightily trashed much of Herbert's other works. An attempt to edit *The Era*, the first American Sunday family-oriented journal, fell foul of both sabbath inhibitions and unauthorized reproduction of its contents by regional newspapers. The launch of a sports magazine also collapsed but the momentum this generated helped to identify Herbert 'as an important figure in the prehistory of general circulation sports magazines in the United States' (Riley, 182).

Before a break-up with Charles Fenno Hoffman, co-editor of the *Monthly*, whom he suspected of political leanings, Herbert's first serial novel, *The Brothers: a Tale of the Fronde*, appeared anonymously in 1834 along with a series of sporting sketches for the *Spirit of the Times*. Of his several romances, *Marmaduke Wyvil* (1843) was foremost in popularity. The others were carefully written but prolix and unimaginative, more akin to historical recitals than romances. Although he retained his real name for the series of sentimental romances which he hoped would establish a 'literary' reputation, a readership beneath his perceived dignity prompted him to adopt the pseudonym Frank Forester, under which between 1839 and 1841 he wrote humorous sporting and wildlife articles for the *American Turf Register and Sporting Magazine*. These were later collected as *The Warwick Woodlands* (1845; rev. edn, 1851). Other works, on closely related themes in a sub-Surtees vein, were *My Shooting Box* and *The Deerstalkers* (1849) for *Graham's American Monthly Magazine* (1846). With *Field Sports in the United States* (1849), coupled with burlesque wearing of hunting attire, he took on the role of the father of American sporting and hunting literature.

The publication in three volumes of *Frank Forester and his Friends, or, Woodland Adventures in the Middle States of North America* by Richard Bentley in London (1849), featuring amusing characterization and vulgar dialect, prepared an overseas readership for similar genial treatment of British hunting scenes as depicted in *The Quorndon Hounds, or, A Virginian at Melton Mowbray* (1852). A thread of poetic imagination runs through Herbert's rural literature, enhanced and enlivened by his drawings. The twin volumes of *Frank Forester's Fish and Fishing in the United States and British Provinces of North America* (1849–50) and the similarly titled *Horse and Horsemanship* (1857) head his non-humour category and are authoritative works to which devotees still turn. In later years he turned to purely historical writings such as *The Captains of the Roman Republic*

(1854), but his most profitable literary work was the translation of Eugène Sue and several of Alexandre Dumas's shorter novels.

Buffeted by implacable and possibly dishonest creditors, Herbert relinquished his chosen 'image' of cavalier boots, spurs, and Scottish plaid shawl and preferred a semi-reclusive literary retreat at The Cedars on the Passaic River outside Newark, New Jersey. On 31 December 1839 he married Sarah, daughter of John Barker, mayor of Bangor, Maine, whom he met on a hunting excursion. She died in 1844, leaving a son, William George, who later went to England and stayed there. The failure of his second marriage in February 1858 to Adela R. Budlong of Providence, Rhode Island (the divorced wife of an actor), after only a few weeks' duration caused the emotionally mercurial and heart-broken author on 17 May 1858 to shoot himself in the Stevens House Hotel on Broadway, New York. He was buried in Mount Pleasant cemetery, Newark, where eighteen years later the Newark Herbert Association erected a simple gravestone bearing the word 'Infelicissimus'. In 1920 a memorial to him by the sportsmen of America was unveiled at Warwick, Orange county, New York, the background scenario to much of his most colourful and affectionate work.   GORDON PHILLIPS

Sources H. E. Starr, 'Herbert, Henry William', *DAB* • S. G. Riley, ed., *American magazine journalists, 1741–1850* (1988) • *DNB* • W. M. Van Winkle, *Henry William Herbert: a bibliography of his writings, 1832–1858* (1936) • J. Myerson, ed., *Antebellum writers in New York and the south*, DLitB, 3 (1979) • S. H. Gale, ed., *Encyclopedia of American humorists* (1988) • D. W. Judd, *Life and writings of Frank Forester*, 2 vols. (1882) • D. Griffiths, ed., *The encyclopedia of the British press, 1422–1992* (1992) • A. H. Higginson, *British and American sporting authors* (1949) • W. S. Hunt, *Frank Forester: a tragedy in exile* (1933) • F. L. Mott, *A history of American magazines, 1741–1850*, 1 (1957), 480–81, 618–19 • T. M. Rees, *Notable Welshmen* (1908) • L. White, *Henry William Herbert and the American publishing scene, 1831–1858* (1943)

Archives Boston PL, corresp. and papers • Hist. Soc. Penn. • New York Historical Society • NYPL, MSS • Yale U., MSS | BL, agreement with R. Bentley, MS 46615, fol. 150

Likenesses photograph, repro. in Riley, ed., *American magazine journalists*, 175

Herbert, Sir John (c.1540–1617), civil lawyer, was the second son of Matthew Herbert of Swansea, gentleman, and Mary, daughter of Sir Thomas Gamage of Coety in Glamorgan. Educated at Christ Church, Oxford, he graduated BA (5 July 1558), MA (12 December 1561), and BCL (9 February 1565). Despite the ruling (6 May 1570) that only advocates of the court of arches should be admitted to Doctors' Commons, Herbert was admitted exceptionally at Archbishop Parker's request (28 November 1573). Noted for his linguistic proficiency, he was employed to interrogate foreign prisoners (1574), was joint commissioner of the admiralty with David Lewis (1575–84), and was master of requests from 1586 to 1601, with William Aubrey (1590–95).

Herbert's linguistic gifts were also utilized on diplomatic missions to Denmark (1583, 1600, September 1602 to March 1603), Poland (between 1583 and 1585), Brandenburg (1585), and the Netherlands (1587). He sat in every parliament for a quarter of a century, representing Grampound, Cornwall (1586), Gatton, Surrey (1588–9), Christchurch, Hampshire (1593), Bodmin, Cornwall (1597–8), Glamorgan and Wallingford, Berkshire (1601), and Monmouthshire (1604–11). A DCL (23 June 1587), he was chosen to dispute before Elizabeth I on her visit to Oxford of 1592. He was a JP for Glamorgan (1595), Hampshire (1604), and Montgomeryshire under James I.

Increasingly associated with the Cecils at court, Herbert accompanied Robert Cecil in 1598 on a mission to induce Henri IV of France not to conclude a separate peace with Spain. Although his role was supportive, on his return he became Cecil's secretary and confidant. A clerk to the privy council since 1590, he became a privy councillor in 1600, and obtained the novel position of second secretary of state, earning the jibe 'Mr. Secretary Herbert'. From May to August 1600 he assisted the ambassador to France in negotiations with the Spaniards at Boulogne. He was nominally on the council of the north (1601–4), and, having been knighted (31 January 1602), served on the council of Wales and the marches until his death. He participated in the trial of Sir Gelly Meyrick and others following the earl of Essex's revolt (1601).

On Elizabeth I's death Herbert was kept in office by James I and served as a commissioner for the Scottish union and for various ecclesiastical causes (1603–6). With Cecil's elevation to the Lords, Herbert was left to defend royal policy in the Commons, for instance defending the king's financial needs in 1606, but he lacked the political acumen for the role. When Cecil died in 1610 his hopes of succeeding him as principal secretary of state were disappointed and he withdrew from public life, nominally retaining his positions.

Fluent in Welsh, Herbert kept his associations with Wales, marrying in 1591 Margaret, daughter of William Morgan of Pen-clawdd, Glamorgan, and leasing Neath Abbey from 1591 before purchasing it in 1599. They had one child, Mary, who married Sir William Doddington and had ten children. A devoted father, Herbert left court abruptly in 1602 to be with his seriously ill daughter. He inherited family property in Cardiff and Swansea on the death of his elder brother, William, without issue in 1609, and he owned land in fifteen different parts of Wales, as well as being involved in various commercial enterprises.

Appointed dean of Wells in 1590, Herbert sought to have a fellow civilian appointed chancellor, leading to a dispute with the canons. Like others of his family, he was at times unruly, once being reported to have broken the window of Thomas Basset's Cardiff house in retaliation for the latter having threatened him with a pistol. He is said to have gone abroad to fight a duel with Sir Lewis Tresham in May 1617 shortly before his death at Cardiff on 9 July, which may have resulted from the exertion or from injuries suffered. He was buried in the church of St John the Baptist, Cardiff, in a handsome tomb erected by his wife with full effigies of himself, in his lawyer's gown, and his brother William.   T. G. WATKIN

Sources G. Williams, 'The Herberts of Swansea and Sir John Herbert', *Glamorgan Historian*, 12 [1976], 47–58 • *DWB* • B. P. Levack, *The civil lawyers in England, 1603–1641* (1973) • Foster, *Alum. Oxon.* • [C. Coote], *Sketches of the lives and characters of eminent English civilians, with an historical introduction relative to the College of Advocates* (1804) • P. Williams, *The council in the marches of Wales under Elizabeth I* (1958) • D. H. Willson, *The privy councillors in the House of Commons, 1604–1629* (1940) • W. R. Williams, *The parliamentary history of the principality of Wales* (privately printed, Brecknock, 1895) • HoP, *Commons, 1558–1603*
Archives NL Wales, Penllergaer MSS
Likenesses monument, St John the Baptist, Cardiff
Wealth at death see will, proved 12 Dec 1617, PRO, PROB 11/130, sigs. 117 and 107

Herbert, John Rogers (1810–1890), painter, was born on 23 January 1810 in Maldon, Essex, the son of a controller of customs. Little is known about his early life. In 1826 he went to London, sent by his family, to train as an artist in the Royal Academy Schools, which he entered on 15 December. But after nearly two years, in 1828, upon the death of his father, he abandoned his course of study and took up paid work, specifically portraiture and book illustration. While living at an address in York Place, near Portman Square, he first exhibited at the Royal Academy in 1830 with *Portrait of a Country Boy*, presumably a 'fancy picture'. He exhibited further portraits at the academy over the next few years, and small-scale subject paintings at the British Institution. Herbert's first recorded portrait, of a Scottish family in 1831, indicates conventional beginnings in the manner of Sir Thomas Lawrence. In 1834 he drew Princess Victoria. About this time he married Kezia Mary Dedman (1809/10–1890). Arthur John [*see below*], probably their first child, became an artist.

In the late 1830s Herbert's illustrative work on a small scale gave him a penchant for illustrating Romantic literature, with exotic, Eastern, and Italian settings; two such works derived from the poetry of Byron. Italian subjects became his speciality, as in his landmark work, *The Brides of Venice* (exh. RA, 1839, and at Liverpool, where it won a prize of £50). This large painting nearly 7 feet across (version, ex Sothebys, London, 17 June 1992), set in the early sixteenth century, caught the fashion for Italianate scenes, as did Herbert's vivid set of illustrations (mostly executed in 1840) for Thomas Roscoe's *Legends of Venice* (1841). It is uncertain whether he travelled to Italy in the mid-1830s, but for a young husband and father this seems unlikely. Nevertheless, the imminent change in Herbert's style at this time suggests the influence of the Nazarenes, who worked in Rome.

Herbert's personal life and career changed direction as he was drawn to Roman Catholicism; at the same time he developed a close friendship with Augustus Welby Pugin. The actual date of Herbert's conversion is not known; most sources indicate that it took place in 1836 when he was twenty-six. By 1838 he had already contributed to Pugin's decorative scheme for the chapel of St Mary's College, Oscott, near Birmingham, by painting the figures on the reredos. Herbert's obsession with religion is evident in his art from 1840 onwards when he exhibited *The monastery in the fourteenth century: boar-hunters refreshed at St Augustine's monastery, Canterbury* (Forbes Magazine collection,

John Rogers Herbert (1810–1890), by unknown engraver, pubd 1890

New York). The painting evoked pre-Reformation England, still wholly Catholic, with the church as benevolent provider for all. The focus on St Augustine's monastery, a holy place of pilgrimage that had fallen into ruins, illustrates Herbert's adoption of the beliefs of his friend Pugin, whose book *Contrasts* defends the beauty and nobility of medieval architecture.

By November 1841 Herbert had been elected an associate member of the Royal Academy; his *Pirates of Istria Bearing off the Brides of Venice* (exh. RA, 1841) marked the culmination of his interest in Italian subjects. He became master of the figure in the newly formed Government School of Design at Somerset House, where his students included Walter Howell Deverell, who later became a Pre-Raphaelite painter. Herbert set up home at 1 Gloucester Road, Old Brompton, London, with his growing family; he had at least five children by 1847.

Herbert continued to paint religious subjects; *The First Introduction of Christianity into Britain* (exh. RA, 1842; ex Sothebys, London, 29 March 1995) celebrates the conversion of native Britons against the backdrop of Stonehenge, a pagan site. With a new and more serious attitude, he wrote in 1845, 'thank God the age of splash and dash is nearly over' (Hamlyn, 47–8). The new style of his work, lighter in tone and clearer in outline, set Herbert apart from many of his artist contemporaries such as Benjamin Robert Haydon, who considered that his art was 'German and affected' (*Diary*, ed. Pope, Nov 1845). He continued to depict religious themes in *Sir Thomas More and his Daughter* (exh. RA, 1844; Tate collection), *The Trial of the Seven Bishops* (exh. RA, 1844), and *Our Saviour Subject to his Parents at Nazareth* (exh. RA, 1847; Guildhall Art Gallery, London). Such works attracted critical praise, and in February 1846 he was elected Royal Academician, submitting as his diploma work *St. Gregory the Great Teaching the Roman Boys to Sing the Chant* (exh. RA, 1845; RA). Herbert's appearance in these years reinforced his serious view of himself and his art: C. R. Leslie noted his 'hair, red, long and very smoothly brushed straight down. [He had] a mediaeval look both in appearance and dress' (Leslie, 176).

Herbert's impressive portrait of Cardinal Wiseman (exh. RA, 1842; St Mary's College, Oscott) indicates the high Catholic circles in which he moved, which also included Lady Herbert of Lea, wife of Sidney Herbert (no relation). He painted A. W. N. Pugin's portrait in a Holbeinesque style (1845; Palace of Westminster, London). With his family Herbert regularly visited Pugin's home, The Grange, Ramsgate, in Kent, during the creation and building of the designer's great work, the new Palace of Westminster. Pugin's early death in 1852 was a blow to Herbert.

The Pre-Raphaelite Brotherhood looked to Herbert as an example. He supported its journal *The Germ* when it was founded in 1849, but William Michael Rossetti did not feel that the younger artists could go much further in enlisting his approval since, as he wrote to F. G. Stephens, in effect they were trying to 'out-Herbert Herbert' (*Selected Letters*, 6). Herbert advocated painting in the open air, a central tenet of Pre-Raphaelitism. Indeed the older artist's curious monogram, which incorporated a cross, may also indicate an influence on the Pre-Raphaelites' famous monogram PRB. A family connection resulted when Kezia's sister married James Collinson, a Pre-Raphaelite painter and staunch Catholic.

In 1846 Herbert was commissioned to paint frescoes in the new houses of parliament, even though he had submitted only one entry to the competitions in 1844—an entry which had been disqualified because too late for consideration. But Herbert's connection with William Dyce, head of the Government School of Design, and his friendship with Pugin ensured his participation in this important scheme. Originally commissioned to paint nine Old Testament subjects illustrating Human Justice in the peers' robing room, he eventually produced a massive painting, *Moses' Descent from Mount Sinai* (completed 1864; House of Lords), which took fourteen years to complete, and *Lear Disinheriting Cordelia* (now fully restored), for the upper waiting hall, called the Poets' Hall. For all the artists involved fresco proved a difficult medium; Herbert eventually turned to the water-glass technique for *Moses*, for which he spent much time researching details of costume as well as technique.

Herbert received £5000 for his houses of parliament work, thanks to his own hard bargaining. By this time he had left the School of Design, since he did not find favour with Henry Cole, director from 1857 of the South Kensington Schools of Art, the successor to the Government School of Design. Yet his fortunes improved, as indicated by a move to Church Row, Hampstead. In 1853 and/or 1854 he travelled to France, where he painted a portrait of the eminent artist Horace Vernet (exh. RA, 1855) and exhibited in Paris at the Universal Exhibition in 1855. He became a corresponding member of the Institut de France (Académie des Beaux Arts) in 1869. He 'developed the odd habit of speaking English with a strong French accent' (*The Times*, 20 March 1890, 10), a report that reveals his distinctly eccentric personality. He was, however, a committed family man and painted a portrait of his two young daughters in 1851 (on loan to the Tate). After studying with his father and in the Royal Academy Schools, exhibiting two well-received historical scenes, his eldest son, **Arthur John Herbert** (1834–1856), baptized on 28 June 1837, died aged twenty-two after falling ill with typhoid fever at Mauriac, in the Auvergne.

During the 1850s Herbert became well acquainted with W. E. Gladstone, who greatly respected the artist for his strength of character, commenting, 'What a lofty spirit' on hearing how Herbert destroyed most of his fresco of *Moses* in 1861 when the technique had failed (Gladstone, *Diaries*, 6.26). Herbert exhibited a portrait of Gladstone in 1883. His religious art also attracted the attention of the royal family; Queen Victoria visited his studio in 1858 and, impressed with his work on *Moses*, commissioned *The Virgin's Flight into Hill Country* (exh. RA, 1860; later given to Princess Louise; ex Sothebys, 16 April 1986, lot 216), in which the landscape (as in his other religious works) was based on Herbert's alleged travels to Egypt and Mount Sinai in 1856 or 1857.

Herbert moved to Grove End Place in St John's Wood in 1856 and remained there until 1869; here he formed a close friendship with Sir Edwin Landseer, his neighbour and billiards partner. *Laborare est orare* (exh. RA, 1862; Tate collection) varied the pattern of his work with a splendid landscape of the area around St Bernard's Abbey, Leicestershire, the monastery for which it was painted, in which Herbert included himself in the foreground. C. R. Leslie noted that he was a confirmed smoker who 'stated that he could not work well without a cigar in his mouth' (Leslie, 176), so the Royal Academy council had to allow him to smoke on varnishing day, with the result that Herbert generally found himself positioned near a window for ventilation and therefore a good light for his paintings. His academic reputation withstood such eccentricity, and in 1865 he even received two votes in the ballot for the election of president of the Royal Academy. In 1869 he moved with his family to his newly built London residence, The Chimes, West End Lane, in Kilburn, designed by Pugin's son Edward.

Herbert's later style hardened, and his subject matter proved unremittingly serious. By the 1860s he appeared old-fashioned to a younger generation; in testifying at the commission into the Royal Academy, in 1863, he denounced the use of the female nude model at the academy's life school. He also took advantage of his position as Royal Academician, always sending in the full complement of paintings, and insisting that they be exhibited 'on the line'. In his later years his distinctive appearance, 'his short, sturdy figure, with his olive complexion, white beard, and steely, piercing eyes' seemed to reflect his fierce religious convictions (*Magazine of Art*, April 1890, xxviii). He staged his own exhibition at the Hanover Gallery in New Bond Street, London, in 1881 to mixed reactions. Of his other sons, Cyril Wiseman *Herbert, a painter, died, aged thirty-four, in 1882, shortly after receiving an appointment as curator of sculpture at the Royal Academy; Wilfrid Vincent Herbert (*d.* 1891), also an artist, painted his father's portrait (exh. RA, 1881). By 1886 Herbert had retired as an active member of the Royal Academy, his poor eyesight having long adversely affected his

art. He died at his home, The Chimes, on 17 March 1890, a month after his wife's death. Both were interred (Herbert on 22 March) in the upper catacombs of Kensal Green Roman Catholic cemetery, London. The lack of a substantial posthumous biography has hindered a full assessment of Herbert's career, leaving many gaps regarding his life and work.   BARBARA COFFEY BRYANT

Sources Bryan, *Painters* (1903–5) · W. Sandby, *The history of the Royal Academy of Arts*, 3 (1862) · *Magazine of Art* (April 1890), xxviii · *The Athenaeum* (22 March 1890), 377 · *The Times* (20 March 1890), 10 · T. S. R. Boase, 'The decoration of the new Palace of Westminster, 1841–1863', *Journal of the Warburg and Courtauld Institutes*, 17 (1954), 319–58 · *DNB* · C. R. Leslie, *The inner life of the Royal Academy* (1914) · R. Redgrave and S. Redgrave, *A century of British painters* (1890) · L. Errington, 'Social and religious themes in English art, 1840–1860', PhD diss., Courtauld Inst., 1973; pubd (1984) · Gladstone, *Diaries* · R. Hamlyn, *Robert Vernon's gift: British art for the nation, 1847* (1993) [exhibition catalogue, Tate Gallery, London, 16 March – 31 Oct 1993] · A. Wedgwood, *Catalogue of the drawings collection of the Royal Institute of British Architects: the Pugin family* (1977) · A. Staley, ed., *The Royal Academy (1837–1901) revisited: Victorian paintings from the Forbes Magazine collection* (New York, 1975), 64–5 · P. Atterbury and C. Wainwright, eds., *Pugin: a Gothic passion* (1994) [exhibition catalogue, V&A] · *The diary of Benjamin Robert Haydon*, ed. W. B. Pope, 5 vols. (1960–63), vol. 5 · B. Ferrey, *Recollections of A. W. N. Pugin* (1861), C. Wainwright, ed. (1978) · *Selected letters of William Michael Rossetti*, ed. R. Peattie (1990) · O. Millar, *The Victorian pictures in the collection of her majesty the queen*, 2 vols. (1992), xxxii–xxxiii, no. 52 and fig. X · *IGI* · E. Morris and F. Milner, *And when did you last see your father?* (1992) [exhibition catalogue, Walker Art Gallery, Liverpool, 13 Nov 1992 – 10 Jan 1993] · Graves, *RA exhibitors* · d. cert.
Archives V&A NAL, letters | BL, letters to W. E. Gladstone, Add. MSS 44379–44786, *passim*
Likenesses C. H. Lear, chalk drawing, c.1845, NPG · L. Wyon, portrait, exh. RA 1845 · J. R. Herbert, self-portrait, oils, exh. 1862, Tate collection · W. V. Herbert, oils?, exh. RA 1881 · wood-engraving, NPG; repro. in *ILN* (29 March 1890) [*see illus.*] · wood-engraving, second version, NPG

Herbert, Lady Lucy (1669–1744), prioress of St Augustine, Bruges, and devotional writer, was born in Redcastle or Powis Castle in Montgomeryshire, the fourth daughter of William *Herbert, first marquess and titular duke of Powis (*d.* 1696), politician, and his wife, Elizabeth Somerset (*c*.1634–1691), younger daughter of Edward Somerset, second marquess of Worcester, and governess to James II's children.

Born into a Roman Catholic family, Lady Lucy decided that she wanted to become a nun, and she spent some time touring English convents on the continent. In February 1692 she visited the priory of the English canonesses of St Augustine at Bruges and, struck by their simplicity, she decided to enter their order. She was admitted the following month and was professed on 1 June 1693, taking the name in religion of Sister Teresa Joseph.

Lady Lucy had a long and successful life in the convent. Having been elected prioress on 5 March 1709 she made many improvements, increasing convent membership, erecting a new chaplain's house, and rebuilding the convent church. In 1738 she also installed a fine marble altar imported from Rome. After the Jacobite rising in 1715 her sisters, Lady Montagu and Lady Nithsdale [*see* Maxwell, Winifred, countess of Nithsdale], paid her a long visit at the convent.

Lady Lucy published two devotional works, *Several Excellent Methods of Hearing Mass* (1722) and *Several Methods and Practises of Devotion* (1743), which were reprinted throughout the eighteenth and nineteenth centuries. She died in Bruges on 19 January 1744 and was buried, probably in the convent, on 23 January.

THOMPSON COOPER, *rev.* EMMA MAJOR

Sources Gillow, *Lit. biog. hist.* · GEC, *Peerage*, new edn · C. Dodd [H. Tootell], *The church history of England, from the year 1500, to the year 1688*, 3 (1742), 447 · ESTC · *The devotions of the Lady Lucy Herbert of Powis*, ed. J. Morris (1873), preface

Likenesses oils, Powis Castle, Montgomeryshire

Herbert [*née* Sidney], **Mary, countess of Pembroke** (1561–1621), writer and literary patron, was born on 27 October 1561 at Tickenhall, near Bewdley, Worcestershire, the third daughter of Sir Henry *Sidney (1529–1586) and Lady Mary *Sidney (1530x35–1586), who was the daughter of John *Dudley, duke of Northumberland, and his wife, Jane *Dudley [*see under* Dudley, John]. Her eldest brother was Philip *Sidney (1554–1586); her two younger brothers were Robert *Sidney, later earl of Leicester (1563–1626), and Thomas (1569–1595). She had three sisters: Mary (Margaret), who died in infancy at Penshurst in 1558; an elder sister, Elizabeth, who died at Dublin in 1567; and a younger sister, Ambrosia, who died at Ludlow in 1575.

Sidney's father was lord president of the council in the marches of Wales (1559–86); he also served as lord deputy of Ireland from 1565 to 1571 and from 1575 to 1578. Because Henry Sidney's father had been chamberlain to young Edward, he himself had been educated with the prince, and Edward died in his arms. Her mother was a close friend of Queen Elizabeth and took an active role in court politics until she contracted smallpox after nursing the queen; she was badly scarred by the disease and thereafter rarely appeared at court. The Dudley connections established Mary Sidney's social position: she was the niece of Guildford Dudley, who was executed with his wife, Lady Jane Grey; of Henry Hastings and Katherine Dudley Hastings, earl and countess of Huntingdon; of Ambrose Dudley and Anne Russell Dudley, earl and countess of Warwick; and of Robert Dudley, earl of Leicester, Queen Elizabeth's favourite.

Education and marriage At home Sidney received an education in the humanist curriculum analogous to that of Queen Elizabeth, the learned Cooke sisters, and her own mother. She was schooled in scripture and the classics, trained in rhetoric, and was fluent in French, Italian, and Latin; she may also have known some Greek and Hebrew. She was well trained in the conventional female skills of music (both as singer and as lute player), and in needlework, so that her name was later used as a celebratory endorsement for needlework patterns and for books of music. John Taylor, the water poet, for example, says that her needlework will make her fame live for ever, and puns:

A Patterne, and a Patronesse she was
Of vertuous industry, and studious learning.
(J. Taylor, *The Needles Excellency*, 1634, sig. A3v)

Similarly Thomas Morley says that she is famous for her

Mary Herbert [Sidney], **countess of Pembroke** (1561–1621), by Nicholas Hilliard, *c.*1590

singing (*Canzonets*, BL, Add. MS 23625). Like other aristocratic women she was also trained in household medicine and administration.

After the death of her sister Ambrosia, Sidney was invited to court by Elizabeth in 1575. That summer she was present at the magnificent entertainment for the queen at Kenilworth and was praised in a posy presented to her at Woodstock. Her uncle Leicester arranged her marriage, on 21 April 1577, to the recently widowed Henry *Herbert, second earl of Pembroke (*b.* in or after 1538, *d.* 1601), one of the wealthiest landowners in Britain. Leicester arranged a dowry of £3000, a serious financial problem for the Sidneys. Henry Sidney asked Leicester to 'bear with my poverty for if I had it, lyttell would I regard any sum of money' to achieve this match for young Mary (De L'Isle MS U1475 C7/3). Mary Sidney was Pembroke's third wife. In 1553 his father and the duke of Northumberland had arranged his marriage to Lady Katherine Grey, as part of their effort to put Lady Jane on the throne; he harshly repudiated that marriage. In 1563 he had married Katherine Talbot, who died childless in 1576.

Mary Herbert bore four recorded children between 1580 and 1584: William *Herbert (1580), later third earl of Pembroke; Katherine (1581); Anne (1583); and Philip *Herbert (1584), later earl of Montgomery and fourth earl of Pembroke. At William's birth Pembroke was so elated by finally having an heir that he put up a celebratory tablet in St Mary's Church in Wilton. Katherine died on the day that Philip was born; Anne died, unmarried, in her early twenties. In addition there was at least one child who was stillborn or died in infancy.

The Pembrokes lived primarily at Wilton, their country estate near Salisbury, and at Baynards Castle, their London home; their other residences included the smaller estates of Ramsbury and Ivychurch, both in Wiltshire. When Mary was a young bride her parents, her brother

Philip, and other family members frequently visited Wilton. Philip Sidney began to write *The Countess of Pembroke's Arcadia* (1593) there, saying in his dedication that he wrote because 'you desired me to doo it' and that it was written 'in loose sheetes of paper, most of it in your presence' (sig. A3). His sonnet sequence *Astrophil and Stella* was also circulated at Wilton, and he may have begun paraphrasing the Psalms there as well. Sidney seems to have entrusted several of his manuscripts to his sister, including those of *Certain Sonnets*, *Astrophil and Stella*, and the *Lady of May*, which she later had printed in the 1598 edition of the *Arcadia*, which served almost as Sidney's collected secular works.

Philip Sidney died on 17 October 1586, from wounds received in Zutphen, where he was fighting with the English forces that hoped to rescue the Netherlands from the rule of Catholic Spain. As a woman Mary was barred from participating in his elaborate funeral and from publishing in any of the volumes of elegies put out by the universities of Oxford, Cambridge, and Leiden. Her father (on 5 May) and her mother (on 9 August) had both died that same year. In her grief Mary retired to Wilton for two years of mourning. There, during the attack of the Spanish Armada, she provided a safe haven for her sister-in-law Barbara Sidney (*née* Gamage) and her infant daughter Mary, later Mary Wroth. After the armada was dispersed Mary returned to London, in November 1588, for the accession day celebrations. That return marked the beginning of her public literary activities.

Literary patronage Mary Herbert honoured her brother's memory by serving as a literary patron to those who honoured him, by supervising the 1593 and 1598 editions of his *Arcadia*, by translating works that he would have approved, by completing the metric paraphrase of the Psalms that he had begun, and by writing poems to praise him. These efforts on his behalf also permitted her to achieve a literary career herself, despite cultural injunctions to female silence. Her self-description as 'Sister of Sir Philip Sidney' appears self-abnegating but it is part of an autograph postscript on a business letter that also asserts her own worth: 'it is the Sister of Sir Philip Sidney who yow ar to right and who will worthely deserve the same' (BL, Add. MS 12503, fol. 151). Similarly her deference to her brother in 'To the Angell Spirit of the most Excellent Sir Philip Sidney' needs to be placed in the context of other elegies of Sidney that praise him in extravagant terms. Sir Walter Ralegh, for example, called him the '*Scipio, Cicero*, and *Petrarch* of our time' (E. Spenser, *Astrophel*, 1595, sig. K2). All the poets, Edmund Spenser said:

> did weep and waile, and mone,
> And meanes deviz'd to shew his sorrow best.
> (ibid., F4)

Poets who had sought Philip Sidney's patronage now sought Mary's, making her the first non-royal woman in England to receive a significant number of dedications (F. Williams, 'The literary patronesses of Renaissance England', *N&Q*, 207, 1962, 364–6). She particularly encouraged writers in her own family and household. Not only did Philip Sidney dedicate his *Arcadia* to her but also their younger brother Robert wrote a manuscript of poems and

addressed it 'For the Countess of Pembroke' (BL, Add. MS 58435). Except for her husband, who provided the financial and political backing that constituted her patronage, most of the family wrote poetry: her son William; possibly her daughter Anne; and, most importantly, Mary Sidney, Lady Wroth, her niece, namesake, and goddaughter. But it seems that everyone at Wilton was writing, including her children's tutors, the secretaries, the family physician, and even old family retainers like Thomas Howell, so that Nicholas Breton can claim that she has more 'servants' writing poetry to her than did Elizabetta Gonzaga, celebrated in Castiglione's *Courtier* (N. Breton, *Pilgrimage to Paradise*, 1592, sig. A2). Samuel Daniel credits her with encouraging his poetry, saying that he had received 'the first notion for the formall ordering of those compositions at Wilton, which I must ever acknowledge to have beene my best Schoole' (S. Daniel, *A Panegyrike … with a Defence of Ryme*, 1603, sig. G3). Thomas Churchyard, in *A Pleasant Conceite*, says that she 'sets to schoole, our Poets ev'ry where' (sig. B1v) and John Aubrey later describes Wilton as a 'College' (*Brief Lives*, 138). The inevitable squabbling among those who sought her patronage is evident in the works of Nicholas Breton, Thomas Nashe, and even Abraham Fraunce (M. Lamb, *Gender and Authorship in the Sidney Circle*, 1990, 28–71), who incorporated her name into the titles of several works that he presented to her, including *The Countesse of Pembrodkes Emmanuel* (1591) and the three parts of *The Countesse of Pembrokes Ivychurch* (1591–2). Nicholas Breton similarly entitled poems 'The Countesse of Penbrookes Love' and 'The Countess of Pembrokes Passion'.

Mary Herbert seems to have participated in the exchange of poems at Wilton. An early draft of her 'Angell Spirit' was found among Daniel's papers, and Thomas Moffet mentions her Petrarch translation and her *Psalmes* before they were complete. Learned aristocratic women had usually confined their work to the family circle but Mary's works also circulated outside the household, since she asks Edward Wotton to return a poem that she had sent him about 1594 (*Collected Works*, 1.286–7), and Spenser, in 'The Ruines of Time', claims to have read an unpublished elegy that she had written, probably 'The Dolefull Lay of Clorinda', later published in his *Astrophel* (1595). She achieved public recognition as a literary figure, demonstrated not only by the eagerness with which poets sought to be members of her literary coterie but also by the extent of the circulation of her works. Daniel, instead of promising his patron that he would immortalize her through his verse, prophesied that she would achieve fame through her own metric psalms:

> Those *Hymnes* that thou doost consecrate to heaven …
> Unto thy voyce eternitie hath given.
> (S. Daniel, *Delia & Cleopatra*, 1594, sig. H6)

Mary Herbert's duties included assisting her husband with some political correspondence (in which she attempted to smooth over problems caused by his tactless remarks), supporting public works, seeking justice for her servants, and interceding for friends and family at court, particularly her brother Robert, in his repeated efforts to obtain leave to return home from his position in Flushing. Like other aristocratic women she oversaw household administration for the family estates; because of the scale of the Pembroke wealth she served primarily as hostess and as titular head of an organization of servants with its own hierarchical bureaucratic structure. After her husband succeeded her father as lord president of the council in the marches of Wales in 1586 she also performed the tasks that had been her mother's at Ludlow Castle and other official residences. Her duties also included encouraging the spiritual instruction of her family and retainers. Gervase Babington, chaplain at Wilton, praises her support of religious education even as he admonishes her to persevere in 'the studie of his worde, and all other good learning' (G. Babington, *A brief conference betwixt Mans frailtie and faith*, 1584, sig. A5). Nicholas Breton goes even farther when he asks her to turn from the classics to patronize only religious works: 'thinke not of the ruines of Troie, but helpe to builde up the walles of Jerusalem' (N. Breton, *Pilgrimage*, sig. A2). So identified had she become with devout learning that in an epitaph William Browne declares that there was 'so much divinity' in her that her loss would injure 'Our Age, too prone to Irreligion' (BL, Lansdowne MS 777, fol. 44).

Writings Such praise has led some scholars to portray Mary Herbert as a dour religious figure; however, her niece Mary Wroth shadows her in *Urania* and *Love's Victory* as a lover and as a writer of secular verse. Undoubtedly some of her writing has been lost but the works that have survived appear to fit approved categories for women—elegy, encomium, and translation—thereby allowing her to stretch the boundaries for women even while she appeared to remain within them. She never apologizes for, or even mentions, her role as a woman writer, unlike the many early modern women writers who strewed their work with apology. Her surviving works demonstrate not only her protestant faith but also her erudition, her skill with rhetorical figures, and her witty wordplay. Her primary literary debt is to the works of her brother Philip, including a similar choice of rhetorical devices (particularly alliteration, polyptoton, chiasmus, and compound epithets), numerous scattered allusions to his verse, and the recasting of sonnet 5 of *Astrophil and Stella* in her paraphrase of Psalm 73. She is also indebted to Spenser, as signalled by her diction and poetic style, her use of Spenserian characters in 'Astrea', and specific allusions to *The Faerie Queene* in Psalms 77, 104, and 107.

Mary Herbert's psalm paraphrases are based on extensive scholarship in the multiple versions and commentaries available to her in English, French, and Latin. She is so indebted to the phrasing of the Book of Common Prayer, the Geneva Bible of 1560, the *Psaumes* of Clément Marot and Theodore Beza, and the psalm translations and commentaries of John Calvin and of Beza (both in Latin and in English translation) that she must frequently have worked with them open before her. She consulted many additional sources, including the commentaries of Victorinus Strigelius, Franciscus Vatablus, George Buchanan, and Immanuel Tremellius. Where these sources differ she

typically chooses the version closest to the Hebrew, so she may have had some access to the Hebrew text and scholarship (T. Steinberg, 'The Sidneys and the Psalms', *Studies in Philology*, 92, 1995, 1–17). She also occasionally echoes phrases from earlier English metric psalms, including those by Anne Lock, Matthew Parker, Robert Crowley, Thomas Sternhold and John Hopkins, and George Gascoigne. Her phrasing sometimes derives from her own experience, with expansions of metaphors that allude to life at court, to the experiences of an aristocratic wife, and to motherhood. She employed a dazzling array of some 126 different verse forms, including ottava rima, rime royal, terza rima, two sonnet forms, and some highly original stanzaic forms. Samuel Woodforde's transcription of her working papers (Bodl. Oxf., MS Rawl. poet. 25) gives a glimpse of her process of poetic composition. She typically began with a paraphrase of the Book of Common Prayer or the Geneva Bible, and then consulted other psalters and scholarly commentaries, expanded metaphors, added rhetorical flourishes, and improved the rhyme, metre, and phrasing.

The *Psalmes*, Mary Herbert's most significant achievement, were widely circulated in manuscript; eighteen manuscripts are now known to be extant, only one of which includes her two dedicatory poems, 'To the Angell Spirit of the most Excellent Sir Philip Sidney' and 'Even now that care', addressed to Queen Elizabeth. Two manuscripts (BL, Add. MSS 12047 and 46372) were rubricated for morning and evening prayer, indicating that they were thought suitable for worship. Others of her psalms were set to music; two penitential psalms (51 and 130) were set for treble voice and lute (in the fragmentary BL, Add. MS 15117), and portions of Psalm 97 (ll. 10, 15, 32, 38) in *All the French Psalm Tunes with English Words* (1632). Individual psalms also circulated in private correspondence, including three (51, 104, and 137) included with *The Triumph of Death* in transcriptions that John Harington of Kelston sent to Lucy, countess of Bedford (Library of the Inner Temple, Petyt MS 538.43.14, fols. 284–6).

Two of Mary Herbert's translations from French, *A Discourse of Life and Death*, dated 'The 13 of May 1590. At Wilton', and *Antonius*, dated 'At Ramsburie. 26. of November 1590', were published together by William Ponsonby in 1592. Both works include Senecan themes, emphasizing reason over emotion and public duty over private relationships. *A Discourse of Life and Death*, her translation from the French of Philippe de Mornay, attracted little attention in print but was widely read; it was reprinted three times and reissued once. An example of how the work was reshaped for individual use is seen in Elizabeth Richardson's early-seventeenth-century précis of, and meditation on, Mary Herbert's translation (Washington, Folger Shakespeare Library, MS V.a.511).

Antonius, Mary Herbert's translation of Robert Garnier's *Marc Antoine*, was far more influential. Such neo-Senecan drama, widely popular in France, deliberately emphasizes rhetoric and didacticism, and develops characters through soliloquy rather than dramatic action. The first dramatization of the story of Antony and Cleopatra in

England, and one of the first English dramas in blank verse, it also helped to introduce the continental vogue for using historical drama to comment on contemporary politics. Daniel wrote *Cleopatra* as a companion to her play, and Shakespeare borrows elements of her phrasing and characterization in *Antony and Cleopatra*. *Antonius* also seems to have inspired a vogue for drama primarily intended to be read or performed in private.

Two other works printed in Mary Herbert's lifetime are her pastoral dialogue praising Elizabeth, 'A dialogue between two shepherds, *Thenot* and *Piers*, in praise of *Astrea*', evidently written for the queen's intended visit to Wilton in 1599 and printed in Francis Davison's *Poetical Rapsody* (1602); and, almost certainly, 'A Dolefull Lay of Clorinda', an elegy for Sidney published with Spenser's *Astrophel* (1595), although it is sometimes attributed to Spenser himself (*Collected Works*, 1.119–32).

Mary Herbert's husband died on 19 January 1601, after a long illness, leaving her some £3000 in plate, jewels, and household goods, and life interest in numerous properties so long as she remained 'solo and unmaryed'. She subsequently helped to arrange the marriages of her children, continued her literary patronage on a much reduced scale, travelled on the continent, brought lawsuits against jewel thieves, pirates, and murderers, and built a country home, Houghton House, in Bedfordshire. King James visited her there in July 1621. The letters of Dudley Carleton and John Chamberlain describe her life in Spa, where she conducted a literary salon, wrote, danced, played cards, took tobacco, shot pistols, and carried on a flirtation with her handsome and learned doctor, Matthew Lister. Correspondence printed as hers by John Donne the younger in *A Collection of Letters Made by Sir Tobie Matthew, Knight* (1660) mentions additional writings and translations from this period but none written after 1600 are known to be extant.

Death and reputation Mary Herbert died, of smallpox, at her home in Aldersgate Street, London, on 25 September 1621. After a magnificent torchlight procession and a funeral befitting her rank she was buried next to her husband under the choir steps of Salisbury Cathedral. She died without having made a will; her son Philip was given responsibility for her estate on 3 October 1621 (PRO, PROB 6/10, fol. 140*r*).

Mary Herbert had a reputation for beauty and was said to resemble her brother Philip, particularly by those who wrote poems honouring him in order to attract her patronage and that of her wealthy husband. A miniature by Nicholas Hilliard is now at the National Portrait Gallery; two oil portraits, not yet fully verified, include one in private hands in Geneva and another in private hands, now on display in the Fitzwilliam Museum, Cambridge. The most famous portrait is the 1618 engraving by Simon de Passe, which appears to be her self-presentation. Dressed in embroidered silk, lace, ermine, and extravagant ropes of pearls, she holds out to the viewer a volume clearly labelled 'Davids Psalms'—that is, the Sidneian psalm paraphrase. The cartouche identifies her as 'Mary Sidney, Countess of Pembroke', asserts her rank by a coronet,

includes the Sidney pheon, and establishes her position as a writer by a laurel wreath and a design of quill pens in ink wells.

Mary Herbert was renowned as a writer in her own day. Contemporaries who celebrated her works and / or borrowed from them include Samuel Daniel, John Davies, John Donne, Michael Drayton, Gabriel Harvey, George Herbert, Aemilia Lanyer, Henry Parry, William Shakespeare, Edmund Spenser, and Mary Wroth. Although Sir Edward Denny praised her translation of 'the holly psalmes of David' in order to rebuke her niece for her secular works (*The Poems of Lady Mary Wroth*, ed. J. A. Roberts, 1983; repr. 1992, 239), in the semi-autobiographical fiction of *Urania* Wroth shadows Mary Herbert as the queen of Naples, who writes secular verse and is described 'as perfect in Poetry, and all other Princely vertues as any woman that ever liv'd, to bee esteemed excellent in any one, [but] shee was stor'd with all, and so the more admirable' (M. Wroth, *Urania*, 1621, sig. R3*v*).

Mary Herbert was also praised by John Donne for her joint authorship of the Sidneian psalm paraphrases. Calling Philip and Mary Sidney 'this Moses and this Mariam' he says that, while once the Psalms were 'So well attyr'd abroad, so ill at home', the Sidneys have equalled continental psalters such as that by Marot and Beza:

> They shew us Ilanders our joy, our King,
> They tell us *why*, and teach us *how* to sing

thus providing a model for English religious verse. Now that God 'hath translated those translators', Donne says, 'We thy Sydnean Psalms shall celebrate' (J. Donne, *Divine Poems*, ed. H. Gardner, 1978, 34–5). Daniel had promised her that her *Psalmes* would keep her 'fresh in fame' even after '*Wilton* lyes low levell'd with the ground', and that is exactly what happened (S. Daniel, *Delia & Cleopatra*, sig. H6*v*). Wilton burnt in 1647; only the east front and the Holbein porch survive from her time.

Mary Herbert's most famous epitaph is William Browne's description of her as 'Sidneys sister, Pembroke's mother' (BL, Lansdowne MS 777, fol. 43*v*) but Thomas Archer reverses that identification in 1760, calling Sidney 'Brother to the Countesse of Pembroke' (BL, MS Add. 5830, fol. 179*v*). The most notorious posthumous account is John Aubrey's entirely unsubstantiated statement, a century after Philip Sidney's death, that a royalist friend had told him that he had heard old men say that 'there was so great love' between Sir Philip Sidney and 'his fair sister that … they lay together, and it was thought the first Philip Earl of Pembroke was begot by him' (*Brief Lives*, 139). Though Aubrey wrote in the middle of a political battle with the Herberts and though there is no evidence to support his assertion it has continued to intrigue readers, provoking several Freudian readings of Mary's works. Like most other early modern women writers her reputation was eclipsed in the nineteenth and early twentieth centuries; relegated to the margins in accounts of Philip Sidney, she was accused of bowdlerizing his *Arcadia* and of attacking the popular stage. Her own writing was largely ignored, yet large sections of *Antony and Cleopatra* were improbably attributed to her (G. Slater, *Seven Shakespeares*, 1931).

No longer in her brother's shadow, Mary Herbert is currently recognized as one of the first significant women writers in English. The influence of *Antonius* on English drama and of *Psalmes* on seventeenth-century religious verse is widely acknowledged. She is frequently portrayed as a role model for subsequent women writers, including Aemilia Lanyer, Elizabeth Cary, and, most notably, her niece Mary Wroth. The literary merit of her writings has gained increasing attention, so that she is now accepted as a canonical writer; her works have been collected in a modern edition and individual writings are routinely included in anthologies.

MARGARET PATTERSON HANNAY

Sources M. P. Hannay, *Philip's phoenix: Mary Sidney, countess of Pembroke* (1990) · *The collected works of Mary Sidney Herbert*, ed. M. P. Hannay, N. J. Kinnamon, and M. G. Brennan, 2 vols. (1998) · Sidney family psalter, Trinity Cam., R.17.2 · esp. corresp. of Robert Sidney, priv. coll., De L'Isle and Dudley papers, De L'Isle and Dudley MS U1475, ser. C12, C81 [property of the Viscount de L'Isle] · G. F. Waller, *Mary Sidney, countess of Pembroke: a critical study of her writings and literary milieu* (1979) · F. Young, *Mary Sidney, countess of Pembroke* (1912) · *Aubrey's Brief lives*, ed. O. L. Dick (1949) · K. Duncan-Jones, *Sir Philip Sidney: courtier poet* (New Haven, 1991)
Archives BL, corresp. · Hatfield House, Hertfordshire, corresp. · Longleat House, Wiltshire, corresp. · LPL, corresp. · Princeton University, New Jersey, corresp. · PRO, corresp. | priv. coll., De L'Isle and Dudley papers, esp. corresp. of Robert Sidney, De L'Isle and Dudley MS U1475 ser. C12 and C81
Likenesses N. Hilliard, miniature, *c*.1590, NPG [*see illus.*] · S. de Passe, engraving, 1618, NPG · Bocquet, stipple, pubd 1806, NPG · J. de Courbet, line engraving, BM, NPG
Wealth at death considerable; Houghton House, Bedfordshire, and properties: 'Lands for the ioynture of Marye nowe Comtess of Pembroke …', Harvard U., Houghton L., fMS 725 · contents of husband's will, incl. plate, jewels, and household goods worth £3000; plus series of rents from property: will of Henry Herbert, earl of Pembroke, PRO, PROB 6/10, fol. 140r, 1621

Herbert, Lady Mary (1686–1775), speculator and mining entrepreneur, was the eldest of the six children born to William *Herbert, second marquess of Powis (1657×61–1745), and his wife, Mary (*b*. after 1664, *d*. 1724), elder daughter and coheir of Sir Thomas Preston, baronet, of Furness, Lancashire. At the revolution of 1688 she went into exile with her mother. Her father, a leading Jacobite, eventually joined them in Flanders, where Mary was educated at the English Benedictine convent at Ghent. Her father succeeded to the titular (Jacobite) dukedom of Powis in 1696. As a young woman, Mary became the companion of her paternal aunt Anne, Lady Carrington, the widow of Francis, second Viscount Carrington. After 1715 they travelled between Paris and London, carrying messages from the earl of Mar to English Jacobites. In 1718, when the match between James Stuart and Clementina Sobieska was in jeopardy, Lord Panmure proposed Lady Mary, probably at her own suggestion, as a possible alternative bride for the Pretender.

Soon after the launch of the Louisiana, or Mississippi, Company by John Law in 1717 Lady Mary became a leading speculator and reputed millionaire. Her wealth and status as the daughter of a duke attracted some eminent suitors, including Philippe de Bourbon, chevalier de Vendôme and grand prior of France, and the duc d'Albret, but she rejected their overtures. She had by now linked her fortunes with those of the gambler and speculator Joseph *Gage, younger son of Joseph Gage (1652–1700), of Firle, Sussex, and (from about 1682) of Shirburn Castle, Oxfordshire. In 1719–20 Gage and Herbert played the stock and money markets with spectacular results, banking on a continuing rise in the value of Mississippi shares, and relying on the infallibility of Law's 'system'. By the spring of 1720 Lady Mary's equity stake amounted to some 6.5 million livres, and she had drawn her father, her two brothers, and Lady Carrington into her web as co-guarantors of massive loans drawn on the Irish banker Richard Cantillon, in Paris, and on Samuel Edwin, in London. When Law's paper empire collapsed in May 1720, the whole Herbert family was involved in her ruin, with total debts estimated at £170,000. To recoup their losses, Gage and the Herberts sued Cantillon for usury, and Mary's two brothers sued her for deceit and fraud. Gage went into hiding, and Lady Mary and Lady Carrington were briefly confined in a debtors' prison in Paris. The Herberts' properties were mortgaged, and their lucrative lead mines at Llangynog were handed over to trustees.

In 1726 Lady Mary relaunched herself as a mining entrepreneur, exploiting her family's reputation for mining to seek a concession to reopen and work disused silver and copper mines in Andalusia. In 1727 she signed a contract with the Española Company in Madrid whereby she undertook to drain and work the silver mine at Guadalcanal, in the province of Seville. She and Lady Carrington moved to Seville that year, accompanied by Gage, who acted as works manager. The mine was successfully drained by September 1732, but the Española Company reneged on the contract and prolonged litigation ensued while Gage prospected elsewhere. In 1732 Gage and Herbert were satirized in Alexander Pope's *Epistle to Bathurst* (lines 129–34) as avaricious gold-diggers. Pope incorrectly located their mining operations in Asturias. On the basis of services rendered, Gage made several attempts to obtain Lady Mary's hand in marriage, but she eluded him by procrastination.

In 1740 Lady Mary's litigation reached a successful conclusion, and she was granted the rights for thirty years to the five mines of Guadalcanal, Cazalla, Galaroza, Rio Tinto (potentially the most valuable), and Aracena. In 1743 she returned to Paris in order to raise capital for their exploitation, but her credit was now exhausted—as were the Herberts' resources. Though mining proceeded spasmodically in her absence, little progress was made, and she finally forfeited the concession in 1767.

Lady Mary's later years were devoted to further speculation, intrigue, and matchmaking. At his death in 1748 her brother, the third marquess of Powis, bequeathed his estate to his distant cousin Henry Arthur, Lord Herbert of Cherbury, a protestant and a whig. To secure the succession in perpetuity, Lord Herbert (created earl of Powis in 1748) was eager to arrange a marriage with Barbara Herbert, the third marquess's only child, and Lady Mary offered her services in delivering the young heiress to her fate. In return she was to receive an annuity, but the earl reneged on their unwritten agreement. She sued him for breach of promise, and obtained a generous settlement from the House of Lords in 1766.

In 1750 Lady Mary had accepted the prince de Conti's offer of an apartment in the Hôtel de Boisbodron, Temple, Paris, where she spent her declining years—an object of curiosity to visitors, such as Horace Walpole, who were acquainted with her legend. False reports of her clandestine marriage to Joseph Gage were still current at her death, which occurred at the Hôtel de Boisbodron in September 1775. She was buried in Paris. Joseph Gage predeceased her in 1766.   G. MARTIN MURPHY

Sources M. Murphy, 'Maria's dreams: Lady Mary Herbert, 1685–1775', *Montgomeryshire Collections*, 85 (1997), 87–100 · M. Murphy, 'Maria's dreams: the reckoning', *Montgomeryshire Collections*, 86 (1998), 65–80 · A. E. Murphy, *Richard Cantillon: entrepreneur and economist* (1986) · A. Pope, *Epistles to several persons*, ed. F. W. Bateson (1961) · M. Murphy, 'Pope's "congenial souls": Joseph Gage and Lady Mary Herbert', *N&Q*, 237 (1992), 470–73 · H. Tayler, *Lady Nithsdale and her family* (1939) · D. Avery, *Not on Queen Victoria's birthday: the story of the Rio Tinto mines* (1974) · NL Wales, Powis Castle papers, PC 15598
Archives NL Wales, Powis Castle archive | BL, Caryll MSS
Likenesses painting (as Minerva), Powis Castle

Herbert, Mary Katherine (1903–1983). *See under* Women agents on active service in France (*act.* 1942–1945).

Herbert, Percy, **second Baron Powis** (1598–1667), politician and writer, was the son of William Herbert, first Baron Powis (1573?–1655), and Lucy Eleanor (*d*. 1650), daughter of Henry Percy, the 'wizard earl' of Northumberland. Percy was named in honour of his mother's illustrious family. He belonged to a recusant branch of the Herbert family that lived at Powis Castle, a medieval fortress in the Welsh marches, which was built of striking red sandstone and consequently known as the 'red castle'. On 19 November 1622 Herbert married Elizabeth (*bap*. 1600, *d*. 1662), first surviving daughter of Sir William *Craven (*c*.1545–1618), an extremely wealthy alderman of the City of London. Writing to his wife, Herbert counted among his blessings 'that your fortune made upp my estate & my conversation resolv'd you a Catholick' (PRO 30/53/7, no. 33). Herbert was knighted on 7 November 1622, and created baronet on 16 November 1622.

Herbert began public life as MP for Shaftesbury in 1620 and for Wilton in 1624–5. However, Powis owed what notoriety he achieved in national affairs to his entanglement in the 'Welsh army plot' scare. He was alleged in the Long Parliament to have made use of his powers as deputy lieutenant of Montgomeryshire to transfer arms from the county magazine to Powis Castle at the instigation of the marquess of Worcester, who was widely believed to have a commission from the king to receive into Wales an army raised in Ireland for the suppression of parliament (*Commons Journal*, 2.463; *Journal*, ed. Notestein, 349). After a vote in the Commons, Powis was summoned to London, where he was held under restraint for about eighteen months, before being released on bail. He is said by his wife to have

fortified Powis Castle at his own charge, and raised and trained soldiers for the king's army in Wales. However, Lord Powis, Powis's father, usurped his command, alleging that he had forfeited his commission. The king summoned Herbert to Oxford, where articles were preferred against him. He was then commanded to follow the king on his march to besiege Gloucester, and he took advantage of the distraction caused by the arrival of Essex's army at Gloucester to slip away from the king's camp. There is no evidence that Herbert was a traitor (parliament continued to treat him as a papist and a malignant) but he certainly had reservations about the involvement of Catholics in the civil war, 'not that I can doubt the cause (though I doe not like this cause of fighting for the True protestant religion)' (PRO, 30/53/7, no. 33).

In September 1644 Powis crossed the sea to the Low Countries, taking his son William *Herbert (*c*.1626–1696) with him. He continued abroad until 1649, travelling in Italy, France, and the Netherlands. He was in Italy in 1645. Powis and young William spent the summer of 1646 in Rome, occasionally dining at the English College. In September, 'as soon as the heats began to decline', they travelled to Naples in the company of Thomas Whetenhall, Maurice and Charles Berkeley, and their tutor Hugh Cressy (Chaney, 74–5, 368–9). From 1647 to 1648 Herbert was in Paris, where William attended an academy, and his uncle Lord Craven trained him 'in manly exercises'.

The county committee for Montgomeryshire resumed the case against Powis as a delinquent, and the Commons voted to summon him from the continent. He returned to England before the end of May 1649, the deadline stipulated by parliament. Powis vigorously defended his case, but he was unsuccessful, and his estates were forfeited and sold in 1652–3. These included Hendon manor in Middlesex and several manors in Montgomeryshire. His wife kept Pipewell manor and abbey, Northamptonshire, but the estate was partially sequestered. Nothing is known about Powis's whereabouts in the 1650s, except for two licences issued in the summer of 1658 that gave Powis and his family permission to leave London for their country house (*CSP dom.*, 1658–9, 576–7). In 1656 he became second Baron Powis in succession to his father.

Powis's first publication was *Certaine Conceptions* (1650), a book of pietistic and moralistic essays written for his son. Powis apparently paid for the paper and printing of the first edition (Stationers' Company court book D, fol. 62), but the book proved popular, and there were several subsequent editions. Powis is important in early modern prose fiction as the author of *Cloria and Narcissus*, a massive political *roman à clef* published in five instalments from 1653 to 1661, which encompasses the Bourbon–Habsburg wars, the English civil wars, the war of the covenant in Scotland, the confederate war in Ireland, and the Fronde in France. The fourth instalment was completed by summer 1656 (Stationers' register, 5 June 1656). Powis died on 19 January 1667. He was succeeded by his son William.

IAN WILLIAM M^cLELLAN

Sources P. Herbert, 'The state of the cause of Sir Percy Herbert submitted to the House of Parliament' (1651?), NL Wales [printed

sheet] • E. Herbert, Lady Elizabeth's petition to the king (1647?), NL Wales, Herbert papers, parcel 12, no. 39 • W. J. Smith, ed., *Herbert correspondence. The sixteenth and seventeenth century letters of the Herberts of Chirbury, Powis Castle and Dolguog, formerly at Powis Castle in Montgomeryshire* (1963) • E. Chaney, *The grand tour and the great rebellion: Richard Lassels and 'The voyage of Italy' in the seventeenth century* (Geneva, 1985), 74–5, 368–9 • letter from Sir Percy Herbert to his wife, PRO, 30/53/7, no. 33 • Lady Herbert, letter to P. Herbert, NL Wales, Herbert papers, parcel 23, letter no. 78 • letter from Sir Percy Herbert to his wife, PRO, 30/53/7, no. 41 • S. Griffin, preface, in P. Herbert, *Cloria and Narcissus: a delightfull and new romance, imbellished with divers politicall notions, and singular remarks of moderne transactions* (1653) • P. Herbert, *Certaine conceptions, or, Considerations of Sir Percy Herbert upon the strange change of peoples dispositions and actions in these latter times* [1650] • GEC, *Peerage* • M. A. E. Green, ed., *Calendar of the proceedings of the committee for compounding … 1643–1660*, 5 vols., PRO (1889–92), 1375–8 • *Powis Castle: catalogue of pictures* [n.d.] • R. F., *Powis Castle* [n.d.] • Stationers' Company, court book D, fol. 62, 21 Jan 1661; see R. Myers, ed., *Records of the Worshipful Company of Stationers (1554–1920s)*, 1987, reel 56 [microfilm] • C. M. Hubbard, *Charles I and the Popish Plot* (1983) • *The journal of Sir Simonds D'Ewes from the beginning of the Long Parliament to the opening of the trial of the earl of Strafford*, ed. W. Notestein (1923)
Archives NL Wales, manuscripts and documents of Edward Herbert, first Baron of Cherbury • PRO, 30/53/7
Likenesses oils, Powis Castle, Montgomeryshire

Herbert, Sir Percy Egerton

Herbert, Sir Percy Egerton (1822–1876), army officer and politician, was born at Powis Castle, near Welshpool, on 15 April 1822, the second son of Edward *Herbert, second earl of Powis (1785–1848), and his wife, Lady Lucy Graham (d. 1875), third daughter of James *Graham, the third duke of Montrose. Herbert's father was the grandson of Robert Clive, first Baron Clive of Plassey. Herbert was educated at Eton and the Royal Military College, Sandhurst. In January 1840 he was appointed ensign 43rd (Monmouthshire) light infantry, in which he became lieutenant on 7 September 1841 and captain on 19 June 1846.

Herbert saw much hard service with his regiment in the war against the Xhosa of 1851–3, and was present with it in the expedition against the Orange River Boers and at the battle of Berea. He was promoted major on 27 May and lieutenant-colonel on 28 May 1853.

In February 1854 Herbert entered parliament as Conservative MP for Ludlow, after an uncontested election. He sat as MP until September 1860. Soon after his election, he was appointed assistant quartermaster-general of Sir De Lacy Evans's division of the army of the East, with which he landed in the Crimea. He was dangerously wounded at the Alma, but was present with his division at Inkerman and at the siege and fall of Sevastopol (when he was again wounded). He was one of the most active and indefatigable staff officers in the whole army. After the return home of Sir Richard Airey, Herbert was quartermaster-general of the army up to the evacuation of the Crimea. For his Crimean services he was made aide-de-camp to the queen and CB, and received the brevet rank of colonel (28 November 1854), as well as French, Sardinian, and Turkish orders.

On 19 February 1858 Herbert was appointed lieutenant-colonel 82nd (Prince of Wales's) foot. He joined the regiment at Cawnpore on 21 April 1858, and commanded the left wing in the campaign in Rohilkhand, including the capture of Bareilly and Shahjahanpur. He then commanded the Cawnpore and Fatehpur districts until the spring of 1859. In December 1858 he was sent in pursuit of Firuz Shah and a body of rebels on the banks of the Jumna.

In September 1860 Herbert resigned his parliamentary seat and became deputy quartermaster-general at the Horse Guards. On 4 October the same year he married Lady Mary Caroline Louisa Petty-Fitzmaurice, daughter of the third marquess of Lansdowne; she survived him. They had two sons and two daughters: the elder son, George, became fourth earl of Powis.

From April 1865 Herbert was Conservative MP for South Shropshire. He successfully contested elections in July 1865 and November 1868, and was returned unopposed in March 1867 and February 1874. He served as assistant quartermaster-general at Aldershot 1865–7 and treasurer of the queen's household 1867–8. He became a privy councillor in March 1867, major-general in January 1868, KCB in 1869, and lieutenant-general in September 1875. Herbert died at his residence, The Styche, Market Drayton, Shropshire, on 7 October 1876, aged fifty-four, and was buried at Moreton Say.

H. M. CHICHESTER, *rev.* ALEX MAY

Sources *Army List* • *Hart's Army List* • Burke, *Peerage* (1869) • Burke, *Peerage* [Powis] • R. G. A. Levinge, *Historical records of the forty-third regiment, Monmouthshire light infantry* (1868) • S. P. Jarvis, *Historical record of the 82nd regiment or prince of Wales's volunteers* (1866) • A. W. Kinglake, *The invasion of the Crimea*, 8 vols. (1863–87) • J. W. Kaye, *A history of the Sepoy War in India, 1857–1858*, 9th edn, 3 vols. (1880) • G. B. Malleson, *History of the Indian mutiny, 1857–1858: commencing from the close of the second volume of Sir John Kaye's History of the Sepoy War*, 3 vols. (1878–80) • E. H. Nolan, *The illustrated history of the war against Russia*, 2 vols. (1857) • H. T. Weyman, *Shropshire members of parliament* (1928) • H. T. Weyman, 'The members of parliament for Ludlow', *Transactions of the Shropshire Archaeological and Natural History Society*, 2nd ser., 7 (1895), 1–54 • H. T. Weyman, 'The members of parliament for Bridgnorth', *Transactions of the Shropshire Archaeological and Natural History Society*, 4th ser., 5 (1915), 1–76 • H. T. Weyman, 'The members of parliament for Wenlock', *Transactions of the Shropshire Archaeological and Natural History Society*, 3rd ser., 2 (1902), 297–358 • H. T. Weyman, 'The members of parliament for Bishop's Castle', *Transactions of the Shropshire Archaeological and Natural History Society*, 2nd ser., 10 (1898), 33–68 • *CGPLA Eng. & Wales* (1876)
Likenesses T. L. Atkinson, mezzotint, *c.*1856, NAM • F. Grant, oils, 1857, Powis Castle, Welshpool
Wealth at death under £10,000: probate, 3 Nov 1876, *CGPLA Eng. & Wales*

Herbert, Philip, first earl of Montgomery and fourth earl of Pembroke

Herbert, Philip, first earl of Montgomery and fourth earl of Pembroke (1584–1650), courtier and politician, was born on 10 October 1584 at Wilton House, Wiltshire, the younger son of Henry *Herbert, second earl of Pembroke (d. 1601), and his third wife, Mary *Herbert, *née* Sidney (1561–1621), and younger brother of William *Herbert, third earl of Pembroke (1580–1630). He was named Philip after his mother's brother, Sir Philip Sidney. He matriculated at New College, Oxford, on 9 March 1593, but only stayed at the university for three or four months. He first visited court in April 1600; on 27 December 1604 he married Lady Susan De Vere (1587–1629), daughter of Edward De Vere, seventeenth earl of Oxford. James I

Philip Herbert, first earl of Montgomery and fourth earl of
Pembroke (1584–1650), by Sir Anthony Van Dyck, 1635–8

played a prominent part in the elaborate ceremony, and
gave the bride £500 in land and the bridegroom lands to
the value of £1000 a year.

Court favourite, 1603–1630 Edward Hyde, earl of Clarendon, later wrote that the young Philip Herbert:

> had the good fortune, by the comeliness of his person, his
> skill, and indefatigable industry in hunting, to be the first
> who drew the King's eyes towards him with affection … He
> pretended to no other qualifications than to understand
> horses and dogs very well, which his master loved him the
> better for.   (Clarendon, *Hist. rebellion*, 1.74)

As John Aubrey later wrote, 'His Lordship's chiefe delight
was in hunting and hawking, both of which he had to the
greatest perfection of any peer in the realm' (*Brief Lives*,
304). Honours followed in quick succession: gentleman of
the privy chamber (May 1603), knight of the Bath (23 July
1603), gentleman of the bedchamber (1605), Baron Herbert of Shurland, and first earl of Montgomery (4 May
1605). He accompanied James to Oxford in August 1605
and was created MA. He was a prominent participant in
court tournaments and masques, and was passionately
interested in both hunting and gambling: the king's

favour was evident in James's reported willingness in
1606–7 to pay Montgomery's extensive debts.

This royal favour continued despite Montgomery's
growing reputation for rough, foul-mouthed, and even
violent behaviour. In 1607 at Croydon races he so provoked William Ramsay, a page of the king's bedchamber,
that Ramsay hit 'him on the face'. In 1610 Montgomery
had a quarrel with the earl of Southampton at a game of
tennis, but the king mediated a reconciliation. While
accompanying James on his journey to Scotland in 1617,
Montgomery had a violent altercation with Lord Howard
de Walden. Yet the king continued to bestow titles and
offices upon him: knight of the Garter (23 April 1608), high
steward of Oxford University (10 June 1615), keeper of
Westminster Palace, Spring Gardens, and St James's Park
(4 December 1617), lord lieutenant of Kent (17 March 1624),
and privy councillor (December 1624). According to Clarendon, James recommended Montgomery to Charles 'as a
man to be relied on in point of honesty and fidelity' (Clarendon, *Hist. rebellion*, 1.74–5) and in 1625 the new king
appointed him one of the embassy to accompany Henrietta Maria from Paris to England. He carried the spurs at
Charles I's coronation on 2 February 1626, and the following August succeeded his elder brother as lord chamberlain of the king's household. In 1628 he was appointed
lord lieutenant of Buckinghamshire.

Montgomery was on friendly terms with Buckingham,
who shared his interests in hunting and gambling, and
their relationship was made easier by the fact that Montgomery lacked his elder brother's political interest and
ambition. In September 1619 Buckingham became godfather to his son, Lord Charles Herbert (1619–1636). The
marriage agreement of 3 August 1626, whereby this boy
was betrothed to Buckingham's four-year-old daughter,
Mary, cemented a rapprochement between the duke and
the Pembroke interest which helps to explain why Pembroke and his allies took a relatively moderate line during
the 1628 parliament. Montgomery was at Portsmouth in
August 1628 when Buckingham was assassinated.

Montgomery's first wife died in January 1629, and on 3
June 1630 he married Anne (1590–1676) [*see* Clifford,
Anne], widow of Richard Sackville, third earl of Dorset,
and daughter of George Clifford, third earl of Cumberland. On 10 April 1630 Montgomery became fourth earl of
Pembroke on the death of his elder brother. This led to a
series of further official appointments in which he succeeded his brother: he became lord lieutenant of Wiltshire, an office which he held from 1630 until his death,
and he also served as lord lieutenant of Somerset (1630–
43) and Cornwall (1630–42). On 12 August 1630 he was
appointed high steward of the duchy of Cornwall and lord
warden of the Stanneries in succession to his brother. In
addition, his inheritance of the earldom of Pembroke
brought him an extra income of £14,000 a year, together
with a further £6000 a year belonging to his brother's
deranged widow during her lifetime (she lived on until
early 1650, the year of Pembroke's own death). John Aubrey estimated that his total income was about £30,000 a
year.

Wilton House and patronage of the arts Such revenue enabled Pembroke to live in lavish style, and he allegedly spent £18,000 a year on hunting. He maintained a household of eighty in London, and another twice as large at his country seat at Wilton House, where he entertained the king every summer during the personal rule. Charles took a great interest in the earl's building operations as well as in his burgeoning art collection. In Aubrey's words, Pembroke:

> did not delight in books, or poetry: but exceedingly loved painting and building, in which he had singular judgement, and had the best collection of any peer in England, and was the great patron to Sir Anthony Van Dyck: and had most of his painting. (*Brief Lives*, 304)

When in January 1637 a consignment of pictures arrived in London as a present from the pope to the king, Pembroke was among a select group (also comprising Henrietta Maria, the earl of Holland, and Inigo Jones) whom Charles invited to join him in opening the cases. From the early 1630s Pembroke employed Solomon De Caus to design a new palace at Wilton on a grandiose scale, surrounded by a variety of formal and informal gardens planned by his brother Isaac De Caus. The king had initially recommended that Pembroke employ Inigo Jones, and although Jones was too busy at Greenwich to accept the commission, he did provide the De Caus brothers with many suggestions. In 1647 a disastrous fire destroyed most of the house, and shortly afterwards Inigo Jones and John Webb designed a new house, in the Palladian style: this building incorporated those portions that had survived the fire and was completed in 1654.

Although not a man of books, Pembroke was active as a literary patron. During his lifetime he received the dedications of over forty separate publications, and of a further ten jointly with his elder brother. As early as 1619 he was the dedicatee of an English edition of the medieval romance *The Ancient, Famous and Honourable History of Amadis de Gaule*. He and his elder brother were the 'incomparable pair of brethren' to whom the first folio of Shakespeare's works was dedicated in 1623. Three further examples, chosen almost at random, serve to indicate the remarkably wide range of works that were dedicated to him: Alice Sutcliffe's *Meditations of Man's Mortalitie* (1634); Sir Thomas Herbert's *A Relation of some Yeares Travaile, Begunne anno 1626. Into Afrique and the Greater Asia* (1634); and Alexander Read's *A Treatise of the First Part of Chirurgerie* (1638). He was a patron of his kinsman, the poet and divine George Herbert, and in 1630 he requested Charles I to present Herbert to the rectory of Fugglestone with Bemerton in Wiltshire. Like his mother and brother he was also a loyal patron of Philip Massinger, and after the dramatist's death in 1640 he continued to provide a pension for his widow. That same year he paid for a translation of Gilbert Saulnier's *The Love and Armes of the Greeke Princes*.

Relationship with Charles I Although they shared artistic and architectural interests, in other ways Charles and Pembroke were less in tune. Henrietta Maria disliked him, and in his religious beliefs the earl inclined towards godly protestantism. This was connected with his long-standing interest in colonial enterprises. A member of the council of the Virginia Company from 1612, he became one of the incorporators of the North-West Passage Company on 26 July 1612, and of the Guiana Company on 19 May 1626. He also became a member of the East India Company (1614), and later (February 1628) received a grant of the islands of Trinidad, Tobago, Barbados, and Fonseca. He was not well disposed towards Archbishop Laud, especially after the latter was elected in 1630, by a majority of only nine votes, to the third earl's old office of chancellor of Oxford University. Pembroke's position at court was further complicated by his incorrigibly rough manners: in February 1634, for example, he broke his staff over the back of Thomas May.

Pembroke's ambivalent relationship with the court, together with his religious sympathies, helps to explain why he strongly favoured peace during the campaigns against the Scots in 1639–40. He was a commissioner for the negotiations at both Berwick and Ripon, and some of the Scottish covenanters, such as the earl of Rothes, regarded him as secretly sympathetic to them, a charge which he vigorously denied. Together with the earls of Holland and Salisbury, he urged Charles to accept the Scots' terms in October 1640, whereupon the king ordered him to return to London and to raise £200,000 towards the costs of the campaign.

Thereafter Pembroke became rapidly more alienated from the court. By virtue of his many offices and his extensive estates, especially in Wiltshire and in central and southern Wales, he wielded considerable electoral influence. In the Short and Long parliaments the Commons probably contained about a dozen members who owed their seats directly to his patronage. Perhaps the most prominent member of the Pembroke interest was Sir Benjamin Rudyerd, and other notable figures included the earl's secretary, Michael Oldisworth, Samuel Turner, Sir Robert Pye, Thomas Pury, Sir Richard Wynne, and several of his own relatives. Politically the Pembroke network was rather disparate and never really formed a coherent group, although there is some evidence that in the Long Parliament elections Pembroke tended to support candidates known to be hostile to the exponents of 'Thorough'. He subsequently voted in favour of Strafford's attainder, and on 3 May 1641 he greatly offended Charles by telling the anti-Straffordian demonstrators milling outside Westminster Hall that 'His Majesty had promised they should have speedy execution of justice to their desires' (*A Perfect Journal of the Daily Proceedings and Transactions in that Memorable Parliament, Begun at Westminster, 3 November, 1640*, 1641, 90).

The queen recommended that Pembroke be dismissed as lord chamberlain, and an opportunity soon presented itself. On 19 July he became involved in one of his periodic quarrels, this time with Lord Maltravers in a committee of the Lords: there was a violent altercation which culminated in his striking Maltravers twice with his staff. This episode provided the king with an excuse to demand Pembroke's resignation from his post, and shortly afterwards the earl of Essex was appointed to succeed him. This marked Pembroke's final breach with the court, but at the same time he won growing support from among the king's critics in the Commons. In August 1641 the Commons recommended that he be appointed lord steward when the king departed for Scotland. However, on 29 November Pembroke assured Sir Edward Nicholas, newly appointed as secretary of state, that he would never accept any office 'but by his Ma[jes]t[ie]s grace and nominacion' (Christ Church Muniment Room, Oxford, Evelyn collection, Nicholas letters, unfoliated, Pembroke to Nicholas, 29 Nov 1641), and Charles refused the Commons' request the following month.

Allegiance to parliament, 1642–1648 Pembroke's subsequent allegiance to parliament was probably grounded on a mixture of personal alienation from the court and an underlying attachment to godly protestantism. Another consideration may well have been the fact that the Herbert family's ancient rivals for local dominance in Wiltshire, the Seymours, chose to become royalists. Clarendon also identified a further motive—Pembroke's:

> fear, which was the passion always predominant in him above all his choler and rage, prevailed so far over him, that he gave himself up into the hands of the Lord Say to dispose of him as he thought fit.   (Clarendon, *Hist. rebellion*, 2.540)

Pembroke was always a very moderate parliamentarian, and he was one of the peers most regularly involved as a messenger or negotiator between the houses and the king. On 9 March 1642 he and Holland met Charles at Royston where they presented him with a declaration from the houses detailing his misgovernment. In June he ignored the king's summons to York, yet he remained in touch with Edward Hyde and sent assurances of his loyalty to Charles. On 4 July he was one of five peers appointed to the committee of safety comprising members of both houses. Meanwhile, secret contacts between Hyde and Pembroke, with the latter's eldest son, Lord Herbert, acting as go-between, continued until early August. But on 8 August the houses appointed Pembroke governor of the Isle of Wight, and Clarendon later wrote that he 'kindly accepted it, as a testimony of their favour; and so got into actual rebellion, which he never intended to do' (ibid., 2.541). He was among the members of both houses who presented a petition to the king at Colnbrook on 11 November, and in January 1643 he was one of the commissioners sent to Charles at Oxford with peace propositions. He was present at the treaty of Uxbridge (January–February 1645), and one night had a conversation with Hyde in which he allegedly 'told him that there was never such a pack of knaves and villains as they who now governed in the Parliament' (ibid., 3.494). Hyde felt that his adherence to parliament was guided principally by fear of losing Wilton and a desire to be on the winning side.

Certainly throughout the years of civil war Pembroke's political affiliations were highly changeable. He was intermittently associated with the Saye–Northumberland group in the Lords which also included peers such as the earls of Kent, Nottingham, and Salisbury, and Lord Howard of Escrick, Lord North, and Lord Wharton. Like them he supported the self-denying ordinance and the creation

of the New Model Army in 1645. In March 1646, along with Saye, Northumberland, Wharton, and Salisbury, he was appointed to the committee of revenue, and thereafter this group wielded considerable influence over the exchequer. Yet from August 1646 he started to distance himself from the Saye–Northumberland group, and by May 1647 he had emerged as one of the army's most outspoken critics and a vigorous advocate of its speedy disbandment. On 3 May he delivered a speech to the common council of the City of London in which he allegedly asserted that the army was 'no longer the New Modle for there were 7000 Cavaliers in it' (DWL, MS 24.50, diary of Thomas Juxon, fol. 107), and that 'hee conceived it were high time they were disbanded' (C. H. Firth, ed., *The Clarke Papers*, 4 vols., CS, new ser., 49, 54, 61–2, 1891–1901, 1.26).

Pembroke's speech to the London common council may well have helped to strengthen the growing hostility towards the army felt within the capital. When on 26 July rioters besieged the houses of parliament in support of the presbyterian leaders and their attempts to disband the army, Sir John Maynard alleged that Pembroke 'was all for the apprentices, and incouraged them' (Beinecke Library, Yale University, Osborn MS Fb 155, commonplace book of John Browne, fol. 239). Unlike other peers associated with the Saye–Northumberland group he did not flee to the army and instead continued to attend the house. But when, early in August, the army entered London and reinstated the members of both houses who had fled, Pembroke claimed that he had been acting under duress. He now once again insisted that he was a friend to the army and tried to identify himself with the proposed settlement promoted that summer by such peers as Saye, Northumberland, Wharton, and Salisbury. James Howell attributed this change of heart to Saye's continuing influence over the earl (*A Letter to the Earle of Pembrooke Concerning the Times, and the Sad Condition both of Prince and People*, 1647, 12). Pembroke's manoeuvres prompted the royalist earl of Dorset, in a letter to his son-in-law, the parliamentarian earl of Middlesex, to observe with heavy sarcasm that: 'You cannott suffer, while you have soe sure and constant a man amongst you … Paraselsus himselfe cowld never have fixed the mercuriall spirit thatt predominates in his breast: if hee weere alive to practise on him' (Dorset to second earl of Middlesex, 1 Aug 1647, Centre for Kentish Studies, Sackville MS, U 269/C248, unfoliated). Likewise, a contemporary satire bitingly applied the phrase 'life of loyalty' to Pembroke (Bodl. Oxf., MS Douce 357, political satires, fol. 37r).

Pembroke's religious attitudes were similarly complex. He was clearly unsympathetic towards Laudianism and inclined towards godly protestantism. From 1643 he served as a member of the Westminster assembly. As the 1640s progressed, he emerged as a supporter of moderate episcopacy whose most consistent priority was an Erastian hostility to the more radical demands of both the high presbyterians and the Independents. In November 1644 he and the earl of Warwick went to the Westminster assembly and 'chide the Independ[en]ts for retardeinge the worke of Reformation[n]' (DWL, MS 24.50, fol. 27). He supported Laud's attainder in January 1645, but in March 1646 he voted to reject the high presbyterian petition submitted by the City of London. Evidence of his moderate episcopalianism may be found in his choice of the future bishop of Winchester, George Morley, as his domestic chaplain, as well as in the nature of his ecclesiastical patronage within the parish of St Martin-in-the-Fields, of which he was a resident.

Notwithstanding his changeable political associations, Pembroke remained sufficiently trusted within the houses to be appointed to a range of further offices. In July 1644 he became lord lieutenant of Somerset, and on 1 December 1645 the houses voted him a dukedom. On 27 July 1648 the Lords sought the Commons' agreement to his appointment as constable of Windsor Castle and keeper of Windsor Great Park, although the consent of the lower house was not forthcoming until 19 December. Perhaps most notably, on 6 July 1641, following Laud's imprisonment, he had been elected to the chancellorship of Oxford University. It was indicative of his political alignments that Pembroke nominated Saye to succeed him as high steward of the university. When Oxford became the king's headquarters, the marquess of Hertford displaced Pembroke as chancellor, but on 3 August 1647 the houses issued an ordinance for his restoration. This followed an earlier ordinance (1 May 1647) 'for the visitation and reformation of the University of Oxford' and the 'due correction of offences, abuses, and disorders, especially of late times, committed there' (C. H. Firth and R. S. Rait, eds., *Acts and Ordinances of the Interregnum, 1642–1660*, 3 vols., 1911, 1.925–7).

The visitors, led by Sir Nathaniel Brent, began work at Oxford in September 1647, directed by a committee of both houses in London under the chairmanship of Pembroke. Their instruction that all university officers should take the solemn league and covenant encountered so much resistance that the heads of houses were summoned before the committee in November, where Pembroke soundly berated them. In February 1648 he nominated a new vice-chancellor, Dr Reynolds, together with many new heads of houses. A parliamentary order of 8 March instructed him to take possession of his place as chancellor, and the following month he entered Oxford in person and presided in convocation. Thereafter the visitors encountered little resistance and harsh measures were imposed on the recalcitrant. No fewer than eight royalist satires were published in London and Oxford, mercilessly lampooning Pembroke's lack of scholarly pretensions. Among the most mordant was *Newes from Pembroke and Mongomery, or, Oxford Manchester'd* (1648), attributed to Sir John Berkenhead, which presented a mock speech by Pembroke as chancellor containing such choice phrases as: 'I love the Bible, though I seldome use it; I say I love it … I can love it though I cannot read it'; and 'my name may be French, for I cannot spell English' (pp. 2, 5). Anthony Wood later wrote that Pembroke was 'so foulmouthed and so eloquent in swearing that he was thought more fit to preside over a Bedlam than a learned academy' (Burrows, lxx).

Pembroke's response to the crisis of 1648–1649 Events on the national scene were meanwhile moving ever more rapidly. In January 1648, believing the king to be indispensable to any settlement, Pembroke opposed the vote of no addresses and resolutely refused to leave Wilton in order to attend the Lords' debates upon it. The fire at Wilton in 1647, together with the depredations of civil war, eroded his finances, and his total income in 1648 was estimated at £20,203, a sum which exceeded his total expenses by only £1064 (Elmhirst MS, Pye deposit, EM 1356, EM 1359). In July 1648 he voted that the duke of Hamilton, who had led the recent Scottish intervention into England, be declared a traitor, and the following month he wished to see those English royalists who had assisted the Scottish invasion declared traitors: he entered his dissent when this proposal was defeated. In the autumn he was among the parliamentarian commissioners appointed to negotiate with the king at the treaty of Newport, and at the beginning of December he accepted the king's concessions as a basis for further talks. After Pride's Purge brought the treaty to an abrupt halt Pembroke, together with Denbigh, Mulgrave, and Lord Grey of Warke, formed a deputation to Fairfax on about 10 December, the main purpose of which appears to have been 'to assure him of their support of the Army's position with respect to the House of Lords' (I. Gentles, *The New Model Army in England, Ireland and Scotland, 1645–1653*, 1992, 298). Then, on 19 December, he joined Salisbury and Northumberland in the delegation which Denbigh led to the council of officers in an eleventh-hour attempt to secure a possible compromise by which Charles would abandon his negative voice, consent to the perpetual alienation of bishops' lands, and abjure the Scots.

Although the Denbigh initiative failed, Cromwell and other leading army officers seem to have been keen to cultivate Pembroke's support. On that same day, 19 December, the earl's secretary, Michael Oldisworth, conveyed to the Lords the Commons' consent to an ordinance appointing Pembroke as constable of Windsor Castle, thus making him in effect the king's gaoler. Pembroke promptly appointed as his deputy Bulstrode Whitelocke, whom he appears to have regarded as an ally. On 2 January 1649 Pembroke was appointed to the high court of justice to try the king. However, he reportedly 'swore he loved not to meddle with businesses of life and death and (for his part) hee would neither speake against the ordinance nor consent to it' (*Mercurius Pragmaticus*, nos. 40–41, 26 Dec 1648–9 Jan 1649, 2 Jan 1649).

Pembroke's death Despite such prevarication the Rump still wished to secure Pembroke's support, and on 14 February 1649 he was appointed a member of the newly established council of state. The fact that he was one of five peers so nominated, only a week after the abolition of the Lords, is indicative 'of the boundaries of the Rump's revolutionary zeal' (B. Worden, *The Rump Parliament, 1648–1653*, 1974, 178). When the Rump decided to permit the election of peers as commoners, Pembroke (like Salisbury and Howard of Escrick, but unlike Saye and Wharton) was among those who stood for election; he was returned on

16 April 1649 as member for Berkshire. However, he appears to have played little further part in public affairs, and the evidence of apothecaries' bills suggests that he began to suffer from his final illness during May. He died at his lodgings in The Cockpit, Westminster, on 23 January 1650. His body was embalmed at a cost of £118 17s. 4d., and he was buried in Salisbury Cathedral on 9 February. The council of state ordered all members of parliament to accompany his cortège for 2 or 3 miles on the journey out of London.

The fifth earl Pembroke's fourth, and eldest surviving, son from his first marriage, **Philip Herbert** (bap. 1621, d. 1669), succeeded him as fifth earl of Pembroke. He was baptized at Enfield on 21 February 1621 and educated at Westminster School and at Exeter College, Oxford, where he matriculated on 20 April 1632. From 1636 onwards he was styled Lord Herbert, and between 1635 and 1637 he travelled in France and Italy. On 28 March 1639 he married Sir Robert Naunton's daughter Penelope (b. 1620), the widow of Viscount Bayning. That year he also served with the king as a captain during the first bishops' war.

The fifth earl sat for Wiltshire in the Short Parliament, and for Glamorgan in the Long Parliament. Like his father he sided with the parliamentarians in the civil wars, and on his father's death he took over his seat for Berkshire in the Rump Parliament. His first wife had died by 1647 and in or before 1649 he married Katherine Villiers (d. 1678), daughter of Sir William Villiers and Rebecca Roper. Pembroke was elected a member of the council of state on 1 December 1651, and briefly served as president of the council from 3 June to 13 July 1652. In 1655 he was appointed a militia commissioner for south Wales, and in 1659 the council of state accepted his offer to raise a regiment of horse at his own charge.

At the Restoration, Pembroke made his peace with Charles II and was appointed a councillor for trade and navigation on 7 November 1660. He bore the spurs and acted as cupbearer at Charles II's coronation on 23 April 1661. According to Aubrey, the fifth earl 'had an admirable witt, and was contemplative but did not much care for reading. His chiefest diversion was Chymistrie, which his Lordship did understand very well and he made Medicines, that did great cures' (Brief Lives, 304). He died on 11 December 1669 and was buried in Salisbury Cathedral on 24 December.

The only son of his first marriage, William Herbert (1640–1674), succeeded him as sixth earl of Pembroke. He was granted a pass to travel overseas in September 1658. He was member for Glamorgan between 1661 and 1669, and he died unmarried on 8 July 1674. He was buried in Salisbury Cathedral on 1 August 1674.

The infamous seventh earl of Pembroke, 1653–1683 The eldest son of the fifth earl's second marriage, **Philip Herbert** (1653–1683), succeeded William Herbert as seventh earl of Pembroke. In character, he was in many ways a throwback to his paternal grandfather and namesake, only in a more extreme form. Aubrey observed in 1680 that Pembroke had 'at Wilton 52 mastives and 30 grey-hounds, some

beares, and a lyon, and a matter of 60 fellowes more bestial then they' (Brief Lives, 305). The earl quickly acquired an unenviable reputation for barbarous and violent behaviour. He nearly killed a man in a duel in November 1677. On 28 January 1678 the lord chancellor informed the House of Lords that the king had committed Pembroke to the Tower 'for uttering such horrid and blasphemous words, and other actions proved upon oath, as are not fit to be repeated in any Christian assembly'. Pembroke submitted a petition to his fellow peers, claiming to 'detest and abhor' the words of which he stood accused, and hoping that, as he was accused by only one witness, the peers 'will not believe the accusation, or your petitioner capable of so horrid a crime' (JHL, 13.131–2). The house thereupon resolved (with seven bishops, Lord Berkeley, and the duke of York entering their dissents) to petition the king for Pembroke's release, which Charles granted on 30 January.

However, only a few days later, on 5 February 1678, Philip Rycaut complained to the Lords that Pembroke had assaulted him in the Strand on 2 February. The Lords responded by ordering the earl to give security by a recognizance of £2000 to keep the peace towards Rycaut and all the king's other subjects. Meanwhile, on 4 February Pembroke had killed Nathaniel Cony in a drunken scuffle in a Haymarket tavern; one week later the Middlesex grand jury convicted him of murder. He submitted another petition to the Lords, and was tried by his peers on 4 April: six found him guilty of murder, eighteen not guilty, and forty guilty of manslaughter. He then 'prayed that he might have his privilege of peerage': this was granted and he was discharged upon payment of his fees (JHL, 13.200).

The rake's progress continued thereafter, and on 18 August 1680 Pembroke killed an officer of the watch, William Smeeth, while returning from a drinking binge at Turnham Green. The Middlesex grand jury tried him on 21 June 1681 and found him guilty of murder. He could not claim privilege of peerage a second time, but on this occasion, following a petition on his behalf to the king signed by twenty-four peers, he was granted a royal pardon and discharged. He died on 29 August 1683, aged only thirty, and was buried in Salisbury Cathedral on 10 September. On 17 December 1674 he had married Henrietta de Kéroualle (d. 1728), sister of Charles II's mistress, Louise de Kéroualle, duchess of Portsmouth. They had no children, and he was succeeded by his younger brother Thomas *Herbert (1656/7–1733), who became eighth earl of Pembroke. DAVID L. SMITH

Sources Clarendon, Hist. rebellion • JHL, 3–13 (1620–81) • Pye deposit, Sheff. Arch., Elmhirst MSS • PRO, SP 14 [state papers domestic, James I] • PRO, SP 16 [state papers domestic, Charles I] • PRO, SP 18 [state papers domestic, interregnum] • PRO, SP 25 [council of state papers] • PRO, SP 29 [state papers domestic, Charles II] • GEC, Peerage, new edn, 10.410–25 • Aubrey's Brief lives, ed. O. L. Dick (1949); repr. (1972) • M. Burrows, ed., The register of the visitors of the University of Oxford, from AD 1647 to AD 1658, CS, new ser., 29 (1881) • J. B. Crummett, 'The lay peers in parliament, 1640–4', PhD diss., University of Manchester, 1972 • J. S. A. Adamson, 'The peerage in politics, 1645–1649', PhD diss., U. Cam., 1986 • V. A. Rowe, 'The influence of the earls of Pembroke on parliamentary elections, 1625–41', *EngHR*, 50 (1935), 242–56 · accounts general, Hatfield House, 12/19 · bills, Hatfield House, 247, 670 · *DNB*

Archives BL, letters and papers | Sheff. Arch., Elmhirst MS, financial and executorship papers, Pye deposit

Likenesses attrib. W. Larkin, oils, *c*.1615, Gov. Art Coll. · oils, *c*.1615–1625, NPG · D. Mytens, oils, 1624, Hardwick Hall, Derbyshire · D. Mytens, oils, *c*.1625, Wilton House, Wiltshire · R. van Voerst, line engraving, 1630 (after D. Mytens), BM, NPG · A. Van Dyck, group portrait, oils, *c*.1634–1635, Wilton House, Wiltshire · A. Van Dyck, oils, 1635–8, Wilton House, Wiltshire [*see illus.*] · A. Van Dyck, oils, *c*.1635–1640, Longleat House, Wiltshire; version, NPG · attrib. A. Cooper, miniature, NPG · attrib. D. Mytens, oils, Hatfield House, Hertfordshire · S. de Passe, line engraving (when earl of Montgomery), BM, NPG · mezzotint (after unknown artist), NPG

Wealth at death £20,203 16*s*. 2*d*.—income in 1648: Sheff. Arch., Elmhirst MS, Pye deposit, EM 1356; EM 1359

Herbert, Philip, second earl of Montgomery and fifth earl of Pembroke (*bap.* **1621**, *d.* **1669**). *See under* Herbert, Philip, first earl of Montgomery and fourth earl of Pembroke (1584–1650).

Herbert, Philip, fourth earl of Montgomery and seventh earl of Pembroke (**1653–1683**). *See under* Herbert, Philip, first earl of Montgomery and fourth earl of Pembroke (1584–1650).

Herbert, Richard, second Baron Herbert of Cherbury and second Baron Herbert of Castle Island (**1600?–1655**). *See under* Herbert, Edward, first Baron Herbert of Cherbury and first Baron Herbert of Castle Island (1582?–1648).

Herbert, Sir Robert George Wyndham (**1831–1905**), colonial administrator and civil servant, was born on 12 June 1831 at his father's house at Brighton, the son of Marianne Lemprière (*d.* 1870) of Jersey and her husband, Algernon *Herbert (1792–1855), an antiquary, himself the youngest son of Henry Herbert, first earl of Carnarvon. After preparation by private tutors and at Mr Daniel's school in Sawston, he attended Eton College, where he was in Edward Coleridge's house. His generation of Etonians was to capture the civil service 'by storm' (West, 52). A particular friend was his cousin Henry Herbert, who was to become fourth earl of Carnarvon in 1849.

At Balliol College, Oxford, Herbert won a series of prizes; he graduated BA in 1854 and the same year became a fellow of All Souls College. He started his administrative career as a private secretary to W. E. Gladstone (1854–5), at the same time pursuing his legal studies; he took his BCL in 1856 and DCL in 1862. In 1858 Carnarvon became parliamentary under-secretary at the Colonial Office. A new colony in Australia, to be called Queensland, was about to be established, and Herbert was chosen to be private secretary to the governor, Sir George Bowen, and colonial secretary. He arrived in Queensland in December 1859 and immediately became premier; he led the colonial parliament until 1866. He had little experience, but learned from, and worked with, Bowen. Herbert found Queensland trying: the hot wind 'roaring loudly, the blinding white fog, the deep red sun, the despair of animals and birds, the utter prostration of man, all combine to make a picture of the end of the world' (Knox, 139). None the less

Sir Robert George Wyndham Herbert (1831–1905), by Henry Tanworth Wells, 1897

he enjoyed the life, the friendships (particularly that of his Balliol contemporary John Bramston, who had accompanied him), his 50 acre property near Brisbane, and his public activities. His capacity for administration was admired, his political skills less so. Herbert alienated the large Queensland working class by his proposals on the franchise, masters and servants legislation, and immigration. He resigned in February 1866 but was recalled for three weeks by Bowen in July in the midst of a financial and constitutional crisis, which brought further conflict with those whom he described as 'the drunken and unwashed' (ibid., 35). His departure from Queensland was accompanied by the hope of the leading metropolitan newspaper that he would never return.

Herbert's homecoming was preceded by Carnarvon's appointment as colonial secretary, which Herbert welcomed as of 'a cousin and a conservative' (Knox, 246). After a period from 1868 to 1870 as assistant undersecretary at the Board of Trade, where he supervised expanding commercial activities, such as railways, Herbert was appointed by the Liberal government to an assistant under-secretaryship at the Colonial Office. His Queensland experience had served him well, and in 1871 he became permanent under-secretary, a position he held until 1892. He was made KCB in 1882.

Herbert was to provide the acceptable face of the Colonial Office to those in the white colonies who had criticized the office. One of his particular achievements was to cultivate good relations with some prominent people in those colonies. He was tactful and pleasant to such visitors and to their representatives in London. This was a personal contribution to his goal of the closer union of what was to be in the twentieth century the white Commonwealth. The instrument of this union was to be the federation of the colonial groups; Canada provided a model in 1867, and Herbert was involved in Carnarvon's attempt in the 1870s to secure the federation of South Africa. That was a clear failure, and South African union was to be obtained only in 1910. Still, Herbert cautiously advanced the same nostrum in the Australian case until his retirement in 1892. He had explained to Carnarvon that

> the solidarity of the Empire will be improved by Australian federation, which will get rid of the now dangerous nuisance of 7 ministries getting up quarrels with Downing Street in order to draw off attention from their corrupt and bad home policy. (Herbert to Carnarvon, 30 Oct 1889, BL, Add. MS 60795)

At his retirement banquet in 1892 Herbert spoke of the rich territories brought under the influence of the imperial government during his time. He was, however, speaking of a system oppressive to many of the poorer people who came under its sway, of a closer union of the empire which involved the loss of land, resources, and standing, especially for indigenous peoples in both the self-governing colonies and the dependencies. The justification was in part the intense racial prejudice which Herbert shared with his contemporaries, although in his case it was sometimes modified by a scepticism of the motives of colonial inhabitants whose skin colour was similar to his own but whose social class was different.

In retirement Herbert headed the British Empire Society, which gave some play to his tariff protectionism, which he had earlier tended to conceal from the view of a predominantly free-trade public. This fitted well with the agenda of Joseph Chamberlain, colonial secretary from 1895 to 1903, who recalled him in 1900 to act as head of the office during Australian federation. Chamberlain, leaving office in 1903, appointed him to head the commission established to assist his tariff reform agitation.

Herbert mixed easily with his frequently aristocratic political chiefs and was, in the clubs which he visited, an embodiment of the classical education. He was just over 5 feet in height, with interests in music and natural history, happy with his gardens both near Brisbane as a young man and at Ickleton in Cambridgeshire, the small estate he inherited from his father. He was comfortably off with a salary of £2000 and investments and directorships in the empire which he helped rule: his readiness to work in co-operation with private commercial interests may have been part of the 'genial cynicism' noted by a colleague, H. E. Dale. He was troubled by gout, which interrupted his work at times, but generally maintained a steady pace despite the great increase over twenty years in the flow of documents, which he drafted with considerable skill. Herbert died at his home, The Caldreen, Ickleton, on 6 May 1905; he had never married.   LUKE TRAINOR

Sources B. Knox, ed., *The Queensland years of Robert Herbert, premier* (1977) • D. M. L. Farr, *The colonial office and Canada, 1867–1887* (1955) • A. West, *Recollections, 1832–1886* (1899) • B. Jones, 'The role of Robert Herbert in the colonial office, with particular reference to his influence on policies towards New Zealand and Fiji', DPhil diss., U. Oxf., 1980 • B. Blakeley, *The colonial office, 1872–1892* (1972) • R. B. Pugh, 'The colonial office, 1801–1925', *The empire-commonwealth, 1870–1919*, ed. E. A. Benians, J. Butler, and C. E. Carrington (1959), vol. 3 of *The Cambridge history of the British empire* (1929–59), 711–29 • *Proceedings of the Royal Colonial Institute*, 23 (1891–2), 354–8 • *The Spectator* (13 May 1905), 711 • *The Spectator* (20 May 1905), 746 • L. Trainor, *British imperialism and Australian nationalism: manipulation, conflict, and compromise in the late nineteenth century* (1994) • D. Murphy, R. Joyce, and M. Cribb, eds., *The premiers of Queensland* (1990) • T. H. S. Escott, *Pillars of the empire* (1879) • d. cert. • *DNB*

Archives PRO, corresp., CO 959/4 • Queensland Women's Historical Association, Brisbane, letters to his family • Royal Anthropological Institute, London, letters to his family • State Library of Queensland, South Brisbane, John Oxley Library, letters to his family | All Souls Oxf., letters to Sir William Anson • Balliol Oxf., corresp. with Sir Robert Morier • BL, corresp. with Lord Carnarvon, Add. MSS 60791–60795 • Bodl. Oxf., corresp. with Lord Kimberley • CUL, letters to Sir John Glover • Glos. RO, corresp. with Sir Michael Hicks Beach • PRO, Colonial Office series • PRO NIre., Meade MSS

Likenesses H. T. Wells, calotype, 1897, NPG [*see illus.*] • G. Frampton, bust, repro. in Farr, *Colonial office*, 313

Wealth at death £39,897 13s.: probate, 8 June 1905, *CGPLA Eng. & Wales*

Herbert, St Leger Algernon (1850–1885), journalist, was the son of Frederick Charles Herbert (1819–1868), commander RN (grandson of Henry Herbert, first earl of Carnarvon), who married, at Glanmire, co. Cork, Bessie Newenham Stuart, daughter of Captain Henry Stuart of the 69th regiment. He was born at Kingston, Ontario, Canada, on 16 August 1850, and attended the Royal Naval School, New Cross, Kent. He was a scholar of Wadham College, Oxford, from 1869 to 1874, taking a first class in classical moderations (1872), and a third class in *literae humaniores* (1874). From 1875 to 1878 he was in the Canadian civil service, and occasionally served as private secretary to Lord Dufferin, the governor-general. Herbert acted as private secretary to Sir Garnet Wolseley during the occupation of Cyprus in 1878, and when Wolseley was high commissioner in South Africa. He was attached to Ferreira's Horse at the storming of Sekokoeni's mountain, and was made a CMG (1880). While in Cyprus and South Africa he acted as correspondent for *The Times*, and on returning to England was employed during the autumn and winter of 1880 in writing leading articles for it. In February 1881 he went to Africa as secretary to Sir Frederick Roberts, and on the latter's immediate return he was appointed in the same capacity to the Transvaal commission. He wrote on a variety of subjects in papers and magazines.

From September to December 1883, and from February to June 1884 Herbert served in Egypt as special correspondent of the *Morning Post*. He was at the battles of al-Teb and Tamai, and was shot through the leg, above the knee, at Tamai. In September 1884 he returned to Egypt, and was attached to the staff of General Sir Herbert Stewart, on the Gordon relief expedition in the Sudan. He escaped, unwounded, at Abu Klea. At the battle of Gubat, near Metemmah, on 19 January 1885, Herbert was conspicuous in a soldier's red coat—the troops themselves wore grey and khaki—and drew enemy fire. Frederic Villiers told him to take off the coat, but Herbert was shot between the eyes and killed. Wolseley wrote in his journal that Herbert was 'as brave as a lion … and [was] admitted to the intimacy of the best in the Army … because he was socially their equal' (Preston, 202). According to Wolseley, Herbert was an unbeliever in revealed religion. A monument was placed in St Paul's Cathedral crypt to Herbert and the six other correspondents who died on the Sudan campaigns of 1883–5.   JAMES WILLIAMS, rev. ROGER T. STEARN

Sources *Morning Post* (29 Jan 1885) · private information (1890) · *In relief of Gordon: Lord Wolseley's campaign journal of the Khartoum relief expedition, 1884–1885*, ed. A. Preston (1967) · R. Furneaux, *News of war* (1964) · O'Byrne, *Naval biog. dict.* · Boase, *Mod. Eng. biog.* · Foster, *Alum. Oxon.* · M. Barthorp, *The British army on campaign, 1816–1902*, 4: *1882–1902* (1988) · G. Arthur, ed., *The letters of Lord and Lady Wolseley, 1870–1911* (1922) · J. Symons, *England's pride: the story of the Gordon relief expedition* (1965) · R. B. Gardiner, ed., *The registers of Wadham College, Oxford*, 2 (1895)
Archives Bodl. Oxf., corresp. with Lord Kimberley
Likenesses Hills & Saunders, carte-de-visite, NPG

Herbert, Sidney, first Baron Herbert of Lea (1810–1861), politician, was born at Richmond, Surrey, on 16 September 1810; he was the only son of George Augustus *Herbert, eleventh earl of Pembroke (1759–1827), and his second wife, the Countess Catherine (*d.* 1856), only daughter of Semyon, Count Vorontsov, formerly Russian ambassador at the court of St James, and long resident in England. He was educated at a preparatory school, Hall Place, Beaconsfield, and at Harrow School. He matriculated from Oriel College, Oxford, on 17 May 1828. There he proved himself an elegant scholar, and was admired as a speaker at the Union Debating Society even by the side of W. E. Gladstone, Roundell Palmer, and others. In his final schools in November 1831 he went in for a pass degree. He was invited by the examiners after his first papers to seek honours, but declined, and received an honorary fourth class.

Early political career As a youth Herbert was known for a marked grace of character and an elegant appearance which much impressed his contemporaries. His elder half-brother, Lord Pembroke, had married a Sicilian and lived abroad; so Sidney Herbert ran Wilton House, the family seat in Wiltshire, as if he was the earl, but was also able to stand for the Commons. In December 1832 he was elected for South Wiltshire as a tory and held the seat until ennobled in 1861 (he was twice opposed at general elections, in 1852 and 1857, leading the poll on both occasions). He confirmed his party credentials in his maiden speech on 20 June 1834 which opposed the removal of restrictions excluding dissenters from Oxford. He declined Sir Robert Peel's offer of becoming a government whip in December 1834, but accepted a secretaryship at the Board of Control in January 1835, holding the post until April 1835, when the government fell. In opposition between 1835 and 1841 Herbert established himself as an able speaker from the tory point of view, opposing, for example, the new system of penny postage. In 1841 Peel made him secretary to the Admiralty. Lord Haddington, the first lord, was in the Lords and Herbert was thus

Sidney Herbert, first Baron Herbert of Lea (1810–1861), by Sir Francis Grant, 1847

responsible for naval business in the Commons. He reformed the naval school at Greenwich and was preparing extensive changes—including the retirement of 300 captains—when Gladstone's resignation early in 1845 triggered a reshuffle. Herbert shrewdly declined the poisoned chalice of the Irish secretaryship and on 4 February was made secretary at war with a seat in the cabinet. Herbert was seen as a protectionist and when on 12 March 1845 Richard Cobden was making his motion for a select committee to inquire into the effect of protection upon the landed interest, Peel, who was sitting next to Herbert, said, 'You must answer this, for I cannot.' In his reply Herbert expressed dislike of members coming to parliament 'whining for protection'. Disraeli afterwards said that Peel had 'sent down his valet, a well-behaved person, to make it known that we are to have no whining here' (Morley, 1.318). When in November 1845 Peel first asked his cabinet to support suspension of the corn laws, Herbert was one of only three to support him. He did so believing that 'the fact is, the present law has failed' (Stanmore, 1.46). He was widely—and inaccurately—believed to have leaked news of the change of policy to the press through his close friend Caroline Norton. The calumny was repeated in George Meredith's *Diana of the Crossways* (1884). He defended Peel's policy in the Commons in the early months of 1846 and voted for repeal in June 1846. At the War Office he began the educational reforms which he was able later to continue and instituted an inquiry into reforming the militia. When Peel's government resigned on 29 June 1846, Herbert was marked as the leader of the younger Peelites, more reliable if also less able than his close contemporary, W. E. Gladstone.

Marriage and life in Wiltshire Out of office, on 12 August 1846 Herbert married Mary Elizabeth (1822–1911) [see Herbert, (Mary) Elizabeth], daughter of General Charles Ashe À Court (later À Court Repington) of Amington Hall, Warwickshire, and his wife, Mary Elizabeth, née Gibbs. He had known his future wife as a child. When they married she was regarded as one of the most striking of society beauties. They had four sons and three daughters. At Wilton in the opposition years from 1846 to 1852 Herbert was an energetic reformer. He had already rebuilt the parish church (consecrated on 9 October 1845). He played a prominent role in the county, provided charitable assistance to the clergy and their families, and founded the Herbert Cottage Hospital at Charmouth (later moved to Bournemouth) under the care of a German protestant sisterhood. In this he and his wife were helped by Florence Nightingale, whose acquaintance they had made on a visit to Rome. The area of Donnybrook, on the outskirts of Dublin, was left him by Lord Fitzwilliam, and he expanded the estate, modernized the lease structure, and doubled the rent roll. Like Gladstone, with whom his friendship intensified in the 1840s, Herbert was much influenced by the Tractarian movement, and encouraged cathedral reform. He and his wife founded in 1849 the Female Emigration Fund, to promote assisted female emigration (Disraeli wrote of it: '35,000 needle-women to be deported at £5 a-piece'; Stanmore, 1.199).

The Aberdeen coalition and the Crimean War Herbert and other Peelites attempted to promote their views by purchasing in 1848 the *Morning Chronicle*; it was expensive to run and was sold to William Glover in 1854. Herbert also played some part in the establishment of the *Saturday Review* in 1855.

After Peel's death in 1850, Herbert and Gladstone, more than other leading Peelites, showed some signs of a *rapprochement* with the tory party, but this came to nothing. On the formation of the Peelite-led Aberdeen coalition in December 1852, Herbert again became secretary at war. The death of the duke of Wellington that year made army reform easier and Herbert anticipated continuing the moderately reforming pattern of his earlier tenure of the office. France, not Russia, was seen as Britain's most likely enemy. While in 1853 Britain drifted towards war with Russia in defence of the Ottoman empire, Herbert, with the other Peelites, urged caution. His semi-Russian parentage led to accusations of lack of patriotism.

The Crimean War, which began in March 1854, placed Herbert in a very difficult position. The secretary at war was subordinate to the secretary of state for war and the colonies (the duke of Newcastle) and was chiefly responsible for military finance. Herbert and others had enlarged these responsibilities in an *ad hoc* way to promote reform, and the absorption of the secretary of state in colonial duties meant that in peacetime the secretary at war often stood in for him. Herbert and Newcastle were both in the cabinet. Neither was a dominating politician, but Herbert was more so than Newcastle. The war quickly exposed the falsity of this arrangement. In the prolonged wrangle over the character of a new structure, Herbert defended the usefulness of his secretaryship but, eventually, proposed to the cabinet on 21 January 1855 a board (similar to the Admiralty board) to be presided over by the secretary of state. This was accepted by the cabinet but the government fell before any action was taken. Herbert's post was not filled when he left it and from that time was subsumed into the secretaryship for war, until its abolition in 1863.

Herbert had, therefore, little formal executive responsibility for the military conduct of the war, but, with Newcastle in the Lords, he was *de facto* spokesman for the army in the Commons and he was to an extent responsible for the supply of food, clothing, and shelter, and of medical services: precisely those areas most notorious for failure. Though Herbert ordered materials, the commissariat which supplied them was controlled by the Treasury, whose priority was the prevention of waste. An important reform achieved in part by Herbert was the transfer of the commissariat to the War Office, but this came too late. Herbert was aware of the defects of the medical support for the army and from the start of the war made strenuous and in part effective efforts to improve it. His boldest move was to send female nurses to assist in what were traditionally all-male hospitals.

On 15 October 1854 Herbert wrote to Florence Nightingale (already preparing an unofficial initiative) to ask her to take charge of a small group of female nurses sent to Scutari. She agreed and a legendary expedition was launched, Herbert exhorting the party in a farewell speech in his dining-room. In December he sent out a second party, led by Mary Stanley. This provoked a furious reaction from Florence Nightingale, and she offered her resignation. Herbert's cool and subtle handling of Miss Nightingale led to a satisfactory agreement, and both parties of nurses worked in the hospitals. Herbert was one of the few people Florence Nightingale respected; she kept his death day annually until her own.

Criticism of the government's handling of the war, and consequently of Herbert, came to a head in J. A. Roebuck's motion for a committee of inquiry into the state of the army before Sevastopol. Newcastle intended resignation and Aberdeen intended to replace him with Herbert, when Lord John Russell's resignation precipitated a crisis only ended by the passing of Roebuck's motion and the resignation of the cabinet on 30 January 1855. In Palmerston's succeeding government, Herbert was briefly, for a few days in February, colonial secretary (in the new arrangements of secretaryships); he resigned with Gladstone and Sir James Graham when Palmerston failed in his assurance that he would prevent the Roebuck inquiry. Herbert gave evidence to the inquiry on 9 May 1855 and favourably impressed it, later being exempted by Roebuck from its severest censures. Herbert's qualities of even-handed fairness and a determination that was quiet rather than dramatic equipped him well for peacetime office, but, as he himself sometimes sensed, equipped him insufficiently for the administrative complexities of the Crimean War.

Final years in politics and early death Herbert now considered himself 'a member of the liberal party' (Stanmore, 2.81) and favoured, much more than Gladstone, accommodation between the Peelites and the whig-Liberals. While in opposition, from 1855 to 1859, he wrote quite frequent public letters, and a signed article on army reform for the *Westminster Review* (January 1859). When Palmerston formed his second government in June 1859, Herbert became secretary of state for war, with the task of consolidating that new office, of transferring the Indian army to the crown, of developing the volunteer movement, and of introducing rifled ordnance. A war with France was thought likely by some and, doubtless mindful of his experience in 1853–4, Herbert planned not merely army reform but military expansion, with increased estimates and a programme of fortifications along the south coast of England and elsewhere. Though supported by Palmerston, he quickly found himself in sharp confrontation with Gladstone, now chancellor of the exchequer and intent on a reduction of government expenditure. The balance in cabinet swung away from Herbert, who offered his resignation in April 1860, and then away from Gladstone, who considered offering his. A compromise was found by financing through a loan. In addition to these disputes, Herbert organized the highly contentious war against China in 1859–60.

By the autumn of 1860 Herbert's health had begun to break down; he was suffering from Bright's disease and diabetes, and perhaps renal disease. On 1 January 1861 he resigned his seat in the Commons (but not his secretaryship) and went to the Lords as Baron Herbert of Lea. Suffering also from pleurisy, he went with his family to Spa, resigning office on 16 July. He returned to Wilton House and died there on 2 August 1861 and was buried at Wilton. He was succeeded by his son George Robert Charles *Herbert, who in 1862 also succeeded as earl of Pembroke, the title of Herbert of Lea thus ceasing to be used. Herbert's widow converted to Roman Catholicism, to the consternation of her husband's Peelite friends.

Unusually, the whole of Herbert's official career had been spent in military offices. His policy in them had been that of common sense rather than systematic reform and in the confused politics of his time he had some success. He was sometimes regarded as a possible prime minister but it is unlikely that his gentlemanly nature equipped him for success in that office. Lord Houghton's view of his qualities—'that birth, wealth, grace, tact, and not too much principle' equipped him 'to rule England' (Reid, 2.72)—attributed to Herbert just that tough cunning which he in fact lacked. H. C. G. MATTHEW

Sources Lord Stanmore, *Sidney Herbert, Lord Herbert of Lea: a memoir*, 2 vols. (1906) · J. B. Conacher, *The Peelites and the party system* (1972) · J. B. Conacher, *The Aberdeen coalition, 1852–1855* (1968) · Gladstone, *Diaries* · J. Sweetman, *War and administration: the significance of the Crimean War for the British army* (1984) · *The Times* (3 Aug 1861) · J. Morley, *The life of Richard Cobden*, 2 vols. (1881) · E. T. Cook, *The life of Florence Nightingale*, 2 vols. (1913) · F. B. Smith, *Florence Nightingale* (1982) · T. W. Reid, *The life, letters, and friendships of Richard Monckton Milnes, first Lord Houghton*, 2 vols. (1890) · GEC, *Peerage*

Archives BL, family corresp., Add. MS 59671 · Hunt. L., corresp. relating to cathedral institutions · Wilts. & Swindon RO, corresp. and papers | BL, corresp. with Lord Aberdeen, Add. MS 43197 · BL, letters to T. G. Balfour, Add. MS 50134 · BL, corresp. with W. E. Gladstone, Add. MSS 44210–44211 · BL, Nightingale MSS, Add. MSS 43393–43395 · BL, corresp. with Sir Robert Peel, Add. MSS 46407–46603 · BL, letters to G. D. Ramsay, Add. MS 46448 · BL, corresp. with Lord Ripon, Add. MS 43533 · Bodl. Oxf., corresp. with Doyle family · Bodl. Oxf., Graham MSS, film · Bodl. Oxf., corresp. with Lord Kimberley · Bodl. Oxf., corresp. with H. E. Manning · Bodl. Oxf., corresp. with Florence Nightingale · Bucks. RLSS, letters to duke of Somerset · Devon RO, letters to duke of Somerset · LMA, letters to S. C. Hall · Lpool RO, letters to fourteenth earl of Derby · NA Scot., letters to Lord Panmure · NAM, corresp. with Lord Raglan · NL Scot., Panmure MSS · NRA, priv. coll., corresp. with Lord Wemyss · PRO, corresp. with Lord John Russell, PRO 30/22 · St Deiniol's Library, Hawarden, corresp. with Catherine Gladstone · St Deiniol's Library, Hawarden, corresp. with duke of Newcastle · Surrey HC, letters to Henry Goulburn · U. Durham L., archives and special collections, corresp. with third Earl Grey · U. Nott., letters to duke of Newcastle · U. Southampton L., corresp. with Lord Palmerston · W. Sussex RO, letters to duke of Richmond · Wellcome L., corresp. with Thomas Longmore · Wellcome L., corresp. with E. A. Parkes

Likenesses F. Grant, oils, 1847, NPG; related portrait, posthumous, Wilton House, Wilts. [*see illus.*] · woodcut, pubd 1858 (after photograph by J. J. E. Mayall), NPG · C. Marochetti, bronze statue, *c*.1863, Salisbury · J. B. Philip, marble effigy, 1864, Wilton church, Wiltshire · J. H. Foley, marble bust, 1865, Harrow School, Middlesex · J. H. Foley, bronze statue, 1867, Waterloo Place, London · Disderi, carte-de-visite, NPG · J. H. Foley, statue, Haymarket, London · J. Gilbert, group portrait, pencil and wash (*The coalition ministry, 1854*), NPG · G. Hayter, group portrait, oils (*The House of Commons, 1833*), NPG · W. Holl, stipple (after Grillion's Club series by G. Richmond), BM · chalk drawing, Oriel College, Oxford · oils, Admiralty, London

Wealth at death £160,000: probate, 21 Nov 1861, *CGPLA Eng. & Wales*

Herbert, Thomas (*b.* 1597, *d.* before 1643), naval officer, was born at Montgomery on 15 May 1597, the seventh and posthumous son of Richard Herbert (*c*.1557–1596) of Montgomery Castle and his wife, Magdalen (*d.* 1627), daughter of Sir Richard and Dame Margaret Newport of High Ercall, Shropshire. In 1608 Magdalen Herbert made a second and happy marriage to Sir John Danvers, the regicide, who was half her age. Thomas's brothers included Edward *Herbert, first Baron Herbert of Cherbury (1582?–1648), the poet George *Herbert (1593–1633), and Sir Henry *Herbert (*bap.* 1594, *d.* 1673), master of the revels.

Thomas must have accompanied his mother when she went to live in Oxford in 1599–1600 while her son Edward was studying there after his marriage. When he left school Thomas became page to Sir Edward Cecil in Germany, distinguished himself at the siege of Juliers in 1610, and took service with Benjamin Joseph, commander of an East India Company voyage in 1616. Sir Thomas Smyth, governor of the company, told Edward Herbert that after Joseph was killed in battle with a Portuguese ship Thomas rallied the men and renewed the fight. Edward Terry, chaplain, tells a different story. According to him, Thomas was sent to the east because of his unruliness at home and although engaged as a companion to Joseph, was soon sent before the mast with the common men. Terry asserts that the master took charge after Joseph was killed, and makes no mention of Herbert's role in the fight. He also says that once in India, Herbert beat and shot at a native servant and was 'the most hasty and cholerick young man that ever I knew' (Terry, 177). Terry was prejudiced but other, admittedly brief, accounts of the battle do not mention Herbert, although he may well have distinguished himself. Once attached to Sir Thomas Roe, the English ambassador to the Mughal emperor, Herbert behaved creditably, although Roe had had reservations beforehand.

Herbert soon returned to England and did well as captain of the *Marmaduke* in the Algiers expedition of 1620–21 and of the *Seven Stars* in the fleet which brought home Prince Charles and the duke of Buckingham from their escapade to Spain in pursuit of a bride for Charles. Edward Herbert asserts that Thomas Herbert tried to save the ship in which he was conducting Count Mansfelt to the Low Countries, when she was cast away. The shipwreck, however, occurred in November 1624 when Mansfelt was on his way to England, and the captain of the ship, the *Speedwell*, makes no mention of Herbert. On 25 September 1625 Buckingham appointed Herbert as captain of the *Dreadnought*, with orders to serve against the Dunkirkers. The *Dreadnought* was, however, assigned to the Cadiz expedition under another captain, though Herbert commanded the *Assurance* from December 1625 until June 1626. There is no further mention of him, apart from his being listed as a possible captain in 1627 and 1629.

Some trifles which were published in the early 1640s have been attributed to Herbert, implausibly, since the pamphleteer states that he was Kentish born, whereas Herbert's birthplace was Montgomery. Herbert probably was, however, the author of a poem, 'The Storm'. Edward Herbert, writing about 1643, states that disappointment of promotion had led Thomas Herbert to withdraw into a private and melancholy life until his death and burial in St Martin-in-the-Fields, London. There is no entry in the parish register.   G. G. HARRIS

Sources *The autobiography of Edward, Lord Herbert of Cherbury*, ed. S. Lee, 2nd edn [1906], 12 · *The life of Edward, first Lord Herbert of Cherbury written by himself*, ed. J. M. Shuttleworth (1976), xi, 5–7, 9–10, 16, 36 · E. Terry, *A voyage to East-India* (1655), 35–49, 176–8 · *The embassy of Sir Thomas Roe to India, 1615–19*, ed. W. Foster, rev. edn (1926), 355–6 · F. C. Danvers and W. Foster, eds., *Letters received by the East India Company from its servants in the east*, 6 vols. (1896–1902), vol. 5, pp. 126–7, 143, 321–2 · PRO, SP 14/122, 174; SP 16/7, 65, 138 · GEC, *Peerage*, new edn, 6.441–2 · HoP, *Commons, 1509–58*, 3.16–17 · HoP, *Commons, 1558–1603*, 2.299 · S. Purchas, *Hakluytus posthumus, or, Purchas his pilgrimes*, bk 4 (1625); repr. Hakluyt Society, extra ser., 17 (1905), 363, 502–3 · BL OIOC, MS L/MAR/C2 · *DNB*, 6.624, 666 · 'Danvers, Sir John', *DNB* · exchequer, pipe office declared accounts, PRO, E351/2261, E351/2263 · J. Glanville, *The voyage to Cadiz in 1625*, ed. A. B. Grosart, CS, new ser., 32 (1883), 27, 29, 127

Herbert, Sir Thomas, first baronet (1606–1682), traveller and government official, was born in The Pavement, York, and baptized at the parish church of St Crux on 4 November 1606. He was the son and heir of Christopher Herbert (1583–1625) of York and Jane, the daughter of Henry Akroyd of Foggathorpe, East Riding, Yorkshire. His family had settled in York before 1550, making their living as merchants; several Herberts served as aldermen and mayors. Christopher Herbert, in contrast, was a failure and died prematurely leaving his family impoverished, although the young Thomas Herbert possessed a generous bequest from his grandfather. Prior to his father's death he decided to seek a career in the law. He began his studies in 1621 at Trinity College, Cambridge, where his uncle Dr Ambrose Akroyd was a fellow, then migrated to Jesus College, Oxford, to study with another relative, Jenkin Lloyd. From there he proceeded to the inns of court but without leaving an official record of his presence at any of these places.

As a young man seeking to start his career, the young Herbert sought the help of relatives in London. Eventually his father's younger brothers William and James Herbert managed to introduce him to a distant relation, William Herbert, third earl of Pembroke (1580–1630). About 1626 Pembroke secured him a place in Sir Dodmore Cotton's impending diplomatic mission to Shah Abbas of Persia. After several delays Cotton's party finally sailed from England on 23 March 1627. The mission turned out to be a diplomatic disaster. Both of its leaders, Sir Robert Shirley and Cotton, sickened and died during July 1628, while the shah's enthusiasm for Englishmen cooled. Herbert, along with the other survivors, then made the slow return to England, arriving at Gravesend on 12 January 1630. In the course of his travels he visited the notable Persian cities of Gombroon, Shiraz, Esfahan, Ashraf, Qazvin, and Qom as well as other Asian and African locales such as Surat, Mauritius, the Cape of Good Hope, and St Helena. Unfortunately for Herbert, his patron the earl of Pembroke died a few months after his return on 10 April 1630. Disappointed, Herbert made a three-month trip to France but was back at the court by the summer of 1631. There he became friends with Sir Walter Alexander, a gentleman usher to the king. It was a valuable contact and on 16 April 1632, Herbert married Sir Walter's twenty-year-old daughter, Lucy (d. 1671). He also managed to meet and to secure the help of the new earl of Pembroke, Philip Herbert (1584–1650), a well-connected courtier and privy councillor. Pembroke introduced him to Charles I and quickly Herbert was sworn as an esquire of the body, an office which he could only assume if one of the four existing esquires died or resigned. Whether he ever actually served as such is uncertain but this circumstance may help to explain why he later became one of the attendants of the captive Charles I. All of these prestigious connections also allowed Herbert to convince the College of Arms to allow him to resume using the Herbert coat of arms, a right lost by his wastrel father.

During his period of waiting for a position as esquire of the body, Herbert and his new bride lived with her parents in Petty France, Westminster. He used this leisure to good advantage. In 1634 he published the first edition of his book of travels, entitled *A description of the Persian monarchy now beinge: the orientall Indyes Iles and other parts of greater Asia and Africk*. The book appeared in an expanded second edition in 1638 under the title *Some Yeares Travels into Divers Parts of Asia and Afrique*. Beginning with the first edition Herbert inserted materials into his narrative about places he had not visited although he sometimes implied that he had, and in each succeeding edition the amount of this second-hand material increased significantly. One particularly famous digression appearing in the first edition onward was his speculation about the medieval Welsh Prince Madoc's discovering and colonizing America. This segment was apparently included to please the earl of Pembroke's own Welsh nationalist fancies. It also continued to help fuel various theories about Madoc's colonies and Welsh Indians in North America until the early years of the nineteenth century. *Some Yeares Travels* proved sufficiently popular to encourage a Dutch translation in 1658, and a French in 1663. During his years of retirement after the Restoration, Herbert produced expanded third, fourth, and fifth editions in 1665, 1675, and 1677 respectively, and the book continued to be reprinted after his death.

When the English civil war broke out in 1642, Herbert followed his patron, Pembroke, into the parliamentarian camp. He stayed unquestionably loyal to parliament, the Commonwealth, or the protectorate throughout the entire civil war and interregnum. On 26 March 1644 parliament appointed him a commissioner to the earl of Essex's army and later to the New Model Army, where Sir Thomas Fairfax valued his services highly. When Oxford surrendered in May 1646, Herbert served as a commissioner.

The beginning of 1647 saw Herbert begin his service as an attendant to the captive Charles I, an episode that only ended with the execution on 30 January 1649 and the burial of the king. Herbert was one of the few parliamentarians whom Charles I was willing to have wait on him. During those two years Herbert successfully walked the tightrope of keeping both the parliament and the army on the one hand and Charles I on the other satisfied with how he did his job. His loyalty to parliament never came under question in spite of an incident when one of his servants smuggled a forbidden letter in to the king. Nor did the captive monarch find Herbert anything but courteous and even kindly: the two had a private joke about Herbert's needing an alarm clock so that he could rise at the proper time to wake the king; a clock could be ordered for Herbert from a London craftsman, but it failed to arrive before Charles's execution. That may have been what prompted the king to make his own pocket watch a farewell gift to Herbert. Apparently Charles also wrote out a testimonial praising Herbert's conduct during this period, although the original has not survived. Modern scholarship, however, suggests that Herbert, ever the loyal parliamentarian, may have distanced himself from the king at his execution and instead let the duties of comforting him fall on Bishop William Juxon. It also appears that Herbert helped himself to other royal possessions.

In the summer of 1649 Herbert began new duties as parliamentary commissioner serving with the army in Ireland. Other offices in Ireland followed, including from December 1653 that of secretary to the governing commission for Ireland, which became in August 1654 the governing council, with Herbert serving as its clerk until 1659. During these years he met his future son-in-law the regicide Colonel Robert Phaire of Cork, who married his daughter Elizabeth on 16 August 1658. Henry Cromwell considered Herbert's services of sufficient merit to reward him with a knighthood in July 1658. He was still living in Dublin at the restoration of Charles II in 1660, but when a general pardon was announced Herbert travelled to London to accept it. On 3 July 1660 Charles II created him a baronet to reward him for his attendance on his father and to compensate him for the loss of his protectorate knighthood.

Herbert lived quietly in Restoration England. When the plague swept London in 1665 he returned to York, where he remained for the rest of his life. His first wife, Lucy, died on 19 December 1671. The couple had had four sons and six daughters but only the eldest son and heir, Henry, second baronet (*d.* 1687), and three of the daughters, Elizabeth, Lucie, and Anne, survived their father. Within a year of Lucy's death Herbert married, on 11 November 1672, his second wife, Elizabeth (*d.* 1696), daughter of Gervase Cutler of Stainbrough, Yorkshire, and niece of the earl of Bridgewater. During these years, besides working on the three expanded editions of *Some Yeares Travels*, he engaged in antiquarian scholarship mostly relating to Yorkshire and helped William Dugdale with the research for his *Monasticon Anglicanum*. Toward the end of his life former royalists persuaded him to write a narrative of his experiences during Charles I's captivity, which appeared in 1678 as *Threnodia Carolina*. After Herbert's death Anthony Wood published an extensive extract of the account in his *Athenae Oxoniensis* (1691). Herbert's complete narrative was published in 1702 with other original documents relating to Charles I's captivity as *Memoirs of the last two years of the reign of the unparalleled prince of very blessed memory, King Charles I*. It has been republished in whole or in part and in translation many times since. While Herbert's work has been used extensively by people studying the last days of Charles I, modern scholars have questioned its reliability as an accurate record. Throughout his life Herbert showed himself to be hardworking and efficient as well as having a keen eye for self-advancement and survival. He died at Petergate, York, on 1 March 1682 and was buried on 3 March at St Crux. In his will, dated 20 December 1679, he left to his grandson George Herbert 'the great silver clock my gracious Mr King Charles the first gave mee in testimony of his Royall favour' (Borth. Inst., will). Herbert's widow married on 20 October 1684 Henry Edmunds of Yorkshire, and died in 1696. RONALD H. FRITZE

Sources GEC, *Baronetage* · N. MacKenzie, 'Sir Thomas Herbert of Tintern: a parliamentary royalist', *BIHR*, 28 (1955), 32–86 · R. Davies, 'Memoir of Sir Thomas Herbert, of Tinterne, in the county of Monmouth, and of the city of York, baronet', *Yorkshire Archaeological and Topographical Journal*, 1 (1869–70), 182–214 · W. Foster, *Thomas Herbert: travels in Persia, 1627–1629* (1928) · B. Penrose, *Urbane travelers, 1591–1635* (1942) · T. Herbert, *Memoirs of the two* *last years of the reign of King Charles I*, another edn (1813) • G. A. Williams, *Madoc: the making of a myth* (1979) • M. Braaksma, *Travel and literature: an attempt at a literary appreciation of English travel-books about Persia from the middle ages to the present day* (1938) • *DNB* • will, 1679, Borth. Inst. [Sir Thomas Herbert]

Archives Bodl. Oxf., letters and papers • Cardiff Central Library, 'Herbertorum Prosapia', an autobiographical MS updating 'Origo' • priv. coll., 'Origo praeclara Herbertorum', an autobiographical and genealogical account • priv. coll., antiquarian collection • University of Kansas, Kansas City, Clendering History of Medicine Library and Museum, commonplace book

Likenesses oils, 1642, Gov. Art Coll. • Halfpenny, etching, BM, NPG • P. Lely, portrait, priv. coll.

Wealth at death see will, Borth. Inst.

Herbert, Thomas, eighth earl of Pembroke and fifth earl of Montgomery (1656/7–1733), politician and government official, was probably born at Castle Baynard, London. He was the third surviving son of Philip *Herbert, fifth earl of Pembroke (*bap.* 1621, *d.* 1669), MP for Wiltshire (1640) and Glamorgan (1640–49), councillor and president of the council of state (1651–2) [*see under* Herbert, Philip, first earl of Montgomery and fourth earl of Pembroke], and his second wife, Katherine Villiers (*d.* 1678), daughter of Sir William Villiers, bt, of Brooksby, Leicester. Thomas was the brother and heir of Philip *Herbert, seventh earl of Pembroke (1653–1683) [*see under* Herbert, Philip, first earl of Montgomery and fourth earl of Pembroke], a notorious rake 'chiefly known for deeds of drunkenness and manslaughter' (GEC, *Peerage*, 10.422), who had himself succeeded his elder brother, William Herbert, sixth earl (1640–1674), MP for Glamorgan (1661–9).

Thomas Herbert matriculated from Christ Church, Oxford, on 18 March 1673 at the age of sixteen. In 1676 he undertook a three-year tour of France and Italy, upon which he met and befriended John Locke. He is also supposed to have studied the law. He was elected on his own interest as a moderate tory MP for Wilton (1679–81). He sat on no committees, made no speeches, and was absent from the division on the Exclusion Bill. Following his accession to the peerage on 29 August 1683 he was named lord lieutenant of Wiltshire, serving almost continuously until his death in 1733. He was also JP and *custos rotulorum* of Glamorgan (1683–1728) and of Pembroke (1683–1715).

Pembroke married, first, on 26 July 1684, Margaret Sawyer, who was the daughter and heir of Sir Robert Sawyer of Highclere, Hampshire, attorney-general (1681–7), and his wife, Margaret, daughter of Ralph Suckeley of Canonbury, Islington, Middlesex. This union produced seven sons and five daughters. The countess died on 27 November 1706 and was buried on 9 December in Salisbury Cathedral. Pembroke married, second, on 21 September 1708 at St James's, Westminster, Barbara, the widow of John Arundell, Lord Arundell of Trerice, and, previously, of Sir Richard Mauleverer. She was the daughter of Sir Thomas Slingsby, bt, of Scriven, Yorkshire, and Dorothy, daughter and coheir of George Cradock of Caverswall Castle, Staffordshire. The countess gave birth to a daughter. She died on 1 August 1721 and was buried in Salisbury Cathedral on the 9th. Pembroke married, third, on 14 June 1725, Mary,

daughter of Scrope *Howe, first Viscount Howe of Ireland, and Juliana, daughter of William, third Baron Alington of Killard, Ireland. She was a maid of honour to Caroline as princess of Wales and a lady of the bedchamber to her as queen. Their marriage apparently caused 'much pleasantry' at court (GEC, *Peerage*, 10.424).

Pembroke bore the third sword at the coronation of James II and was to bear swords at those of every subsequent monarch crowned in his lifetime. In June 1685 he commanded the Wiltshire and Hampshire trained bands raised to oppose Monmouth's rebellion. In September of that year he was appointed commander of the British regiments in the Netherlands. However, in 1687, upon his refusal to put the three questions on repeal of the test and penal laws or to assist in regulating municipal corporations, he was deprived of his lieutenancy.

During the revolution of 1688–9 Pembroke played the ambiguous role of a moderate tory: though in correspondence with the prince of Orange, he offered his services to King James upon the Dutch landing. While he was one of four peers who conveyed to the prince the invitation of 11 December to summon a free parliament and suggested the expedient of a Convention on the 24th, in debate he raised the issue of the prince of Wales's claims; argued against the demise of the crown to Mary and for a regency; and finally voted against declaring William and Mary king and queen. However, when his position on the disposition of the crown was defeated he demonstrated characteristic thoughtfulness and practicality, counselling Clarendon against seceding from the Convention on the grounds that 'the government must be supported, or else we should all be ruined' (Western, 315).

Pembroke began a distinguished administrative and diplomatic career under William III by being restored to the lieutenancy of Wiltshire and by serving as ambassador to the Dutch states general from April to October 1689. In the same year he was named a privy councillor and a lord of trade and plantations. In January 1690 he became first lord of the Admiralty. He rose from the Admiralty to be lord privy seal in March 1692, then lord president of the council in May 1699. He combined the latter duty with his previous post at the Admiralty from March 1701 to January 1702, when he became lord high admiral. Pembroke was an active naval administrator and his contemporaries thought him more than competent. He was also named lord lieutenant of south Wales and Monmouth from 1694 to 1715. More substantial indications of the king's regard for him include his appointment as a lord justice during each of William's absences from England; his position as first plenipotentiary at the treaty of Ryswick in 1697; and his nomination as a knight of the Garter and grant of £1000, in addition to his official salaries, in 1700. Mary, on the other hand, thought him a 'man of honour, but not very steady' (Van der Zee and Van der Zee, 326).

At the accession of Queen Anne, Pembroke ceased to be lord high admiral in favour of Prince George, but was reappointed lord president of the council and was awarded a pension which rose by 1704 to £2500 per annum. His position as a reliable court tory who supported the War of the Spanish Succession allowed Anne to appoint him in preference to insistent Junto candidates for the lord lieutenancy of Ireland in 1707 and, at the death of Prince George, lord high admiral on 25 November 1708. Anne finally gave way to the Junto in November 1709 by asking for Pembroke's resignation, but not before raising his pension to £3000 per annum some two months previously. Apart from his appointment as a commissioner of claims for the coronation in 1714, this marked his virtual retirement from active government service.

In office, Pembroke was the very soul of moderate court toryism. According to Geoffrey Holmes, 'No Tory could object to him, and no Whig could consider his presence there in any way threatening' (Holmes, 253–4). In cabinet, he supported Marlborough and Godolphin's war strategy against his high-tory colleagues; and he was one of the few tory negotiators for the Union. He continued to defend the duumvirs during the ministerial crisis of 1708, when he followed Somerset in refusing to sit in cabinet without them. In parliament his voting record tended to be more independent. Thus, he voted for the Occasional Conformity Bill in 1703 and for Henry Sacheverell's innocence in 1710, but against the resumption bill in 1701 and in favour of the voting rights of Scottish peers of Great Britain in 1709. A Hanoverian tory, he opposed the Oxford ministry on the Hamilton peerage and No Peace Without Spain in 1711, the commercial treaty in 1713, and the Schism Bill in 1714. He was anything but doctrinaire or vindictive: in 1717 he voted against the impeachment of Oxford, an act which eventually cost him his pension, which had been reduced previously by George I to £2000. Similarly, he opposed Fenwick's attainder in 1697, though he was willing to use the bill as a threat in order to exact full disclosure from the accused.

Pembroke had a reputation as a patron of the arts and sciences, a collector, and a virtuoso. Gilbert Burnet described him as a man 'of great and profound learning, particularly in the mathematics' (Burnet, 4.361). He was elected FRS on 13 May 1685, admitted on 26 January 1687, and served as president of the society in 1689–90: initially a fairly active member, he attended not a single meeting during his presidency. He patronized Locke, who dedicated the *Essay Concerning Human Understanding* to him. He purchased most of the collection at Wilton, including the Arundell marbles. William III thought so highly of his Van Dycks that he insisted that his secretary Constantijn Huygens, who had bypassed Wilton, go back to see them during his progress to London in December 1688. Macky described Pembroke as 'a good judge in all the several sciences', but Hearne thought him 'not a man of that deep Penetration nor of that profound Learning he is taken to be' (GEC, *Peerage*, 10.424). There seems to be a similar disagreement over Pembroke's character and private life. While Macky commended him for his simplicity of life and unaffected manners, and Marlborough thought him 'a very honest man … of an extraordinary good temper' (Snyder, 1.86–7), it would appear that he possessed some of his family's hot-headedness when in drink. This may help to explain Halifax's equivocal estimation of him: 'as mad as most of his family tho' very good natured' (Western, 329).

Pembroke died at his house in St James's Square, London, on 22 January 1733. He was buried on 31 January in Salisbury Cathedral. He was survived by his third wife, who married, second, the Hon. John Mordaunt in 1735. The earl's first son and heir, Henry *Herbert, ninth earl of Pembroke and sixth earl of Montgomery (c.1689–1750), was a gentleman of the bedchamber to George II as prince of Wales (1714–27) and as king (1728–35), and groom of the stole from 1735 until his death. R. O. BUCHOLZ

Sources HoP, *Commons, 1660–90* · GEC, *Peerage* · G. S. Holmes, *British politics in the age of Anne* (1967) · R. Beddard, ed., *A kingdom without a king: the journal of the provisional government in the revolution of 1688* (1988) · *The Marlborough–Godolphin correspondence*, ed. H. L. Snyder, 3 vols. (1975) · J. R. Western, *Monarchy and revolution* (1972) · W. A. Shaw, ed., *Calendar of treasury books*, [33 vols. in 64], PRO (1904–69), esp. 10.251, 380; 14.90, 323, 347, 911; 18.117; 19.34, 97; 33.106, 352–53, 402, 492; 25.398; 27.416, 430, 453, 547; 29.431, 570; 32.258 for pensions, etc. · C. Jones and D. L. Jones, eds., *Peers, politics and power: the House of Lords, 1603–1911* (1986) · H. Van der Zee and B. Van der Zee, *William and Mary* (1973) · M. Hunter, *The Royal Society and its fellows, 1660–1700: the morphology of an early scientific institution*, 2nd edn (1994) · *Bishop Burnet's History*
Archives Wilts. & Swindon RO, personal accounts | CKS, corresp. with Alexander Stanhope · Longleat House, corresp. with Matthew Prior · NL Wales, corresp. with Mansell family · TCD, corresp. with William King
Likenesses J. Greenhill, oils, c.1676, Wilton House, Wiltshire · W. Wissing, oils, c.1685, Wilton House, Wiltshire · marble bust, TCD

Herbert, Sir Thomas (1793–1861), naval officer, second son of Richard Townsand Herbert of Cahirnane, co. Kerry (MP for County Kerry, 1783–90), and his second wife, Jane, daughter of Anthony Stoughton of Ballyhorgan, was born at Cahirnane in February 1793, 'a collateral member of the noble house of Pembroke' (*Annual Register*, 1861). In July 1803 he entered the navy on the *Excellent* with Captain Sotheron, in which he went out to the Mediterranean, and was present at the operations on the coast of Italy and in the Bay of Naples in 1806. He was afterwards moved into the frigate *Blonde* with Captain Volant Vashon Ballard. In her he was present, in December 1807, at the capture of the Danish West Indian islands, and on Ballard's recommendation was made lieutenant by Sir Alexander Cochrane on 1 August 1809 (confirmed by the Admiralty on 10 October). For the following four years he was lieutenant of the *Pompée* with Sir James Athol Wood on the West Indian, home, and Mediterranean stations; and in 1814 was appointed first lieutenant of the *Euryalus*, with Captain Charles Napier, and took part in the operations in the Potomac, after which he was promoted commander on 19 October 1814.

In September 1821 Herbert commissioned the *Icarus* for the West Indies, where in the following May he was transferred to the *Carnation* (18 guns), and on 25 November 1822 was posted to the *Tamar* (26 guns). After destroying three pirate vessels on the coasts of Cuba and Yucatán, she was brought home by him and paid off in August 1823. In 1829 he was high sheriff for co. Kerry.

Herbert had no further naval service until November 1837, when he was appointed to the frigate *Calliope* (26 guns), and was sent to the coast of Brazil. After acting as senior officer there and at the River Plate, in January 1840 he was ordered round to Valparaiso, and thence on to China which he reached in October. For a couple of months, pending the arrival of Rear-Admiral George Elliot, he was senior officer in the Canton River, and after the admiral's arrival had command of the operations against Chuenpe (Chuanbi) and the Bogue (Humen) Forts, in the steamer *Nemesis*, opening a way through creeks behind Anunghoy (Yaniangxie), and destroying a twenty-gun battery which guarded the rear of that island. Continuing in command of the advanced squadron he captured the fort in Whampoa (Huangpu) reach, and silenced the batteries commanding the approach to Canton. In June and July he was again senior officer in the Canton River, and on the arrival of Sir William Parker he was moved into the *Blenheim* (72 guns), in which he played a distinguished part in the capture of Amoy (Xiamen) and Chusan (Zhoushan), and commanded the naval brigade at the capture of Chinghae (Qinghai). He was made a CB on 29 January, and a KCB on 14 October 1841; peace having been concluded at Nanking (Nanjing) in October 1842, he returned to England in the *Blenheim* which he paid off in March 1843.

From 1847 to 1849 Herbert was commodore on the east coast of South America, with a broad pennant in the *Raleigh* (50 guns). From February to December 1852 he was a junior lord of the Admiralty under the duke of Northumberland, and on 26 October 1852 he became a rear-admiral. From July 1852 to 1857 he was MP for Dartmouth: a Conservative, he opposed 'any further concession to the Roman Catholics' (*DrodPC*, 1857). He died at his home, Cadogan Place, Chelsea, London, on 4 August 1861.

J. K. LAUGHTON, rev. ROGER MORRISS

Sources O'Byrne, *Naval biog. dict.* · Burke, *Gen. GB* · *Annual Register* (1861), 451 · *The Times* (6 Aug 1861) · G. S. Graham, *The China station: war and diplomacy, 1830–1860* (1978) · E. Holt, *The opium wars in China* (1964) · P. Mackesy, *The war in the Mediterranean, 1803–1810* (1957) · R. Muir, *Britain and the defeat of Napoleon, 1807–1815* (1996) · Boase, *Mod. Eng. biog.*
Likenesses J. H. Lynch, lithograph, BM, NPG
Wealth at death £25,000: probate, 23 Aug 1861, *CGPLA Eng. & Wales*

Herbert, William (*d.* 1333/1337?), Franciscan theologian, was probably a native of Herefordshire. In 1290, according to the Lanercost chronicle, he was studying in Paris, and he probably remained there until at least 1303, when a list of Franciscans at university in Paris mentions him as one of two Englishmen (the other was Duns Scotus). Between *c.*1315 and 1320 he was lecturing in Oxford. By 1314 he was a bachelor of theology, and by *c.*1320 had gained his doctorate. About 1317 he became the forty-third regent master of the Franciscans at Oxford. He later retired to the Franciscan convent in Hereford, as attested by a marginal inscription in a manuscript of Roger Bacon's works belonging to him. He donated this book (BL, Royal MS 7

F. viii) to the convent, and also a copy of Bede's *De temporum ratione* (Bodl. Oxf., MS Rawl. C.308).

Herbert's death has been placed in both 1333 and 1337, but neither of these can be verified. He was buried in Hereford. Leland attributed to Herbert quodlibets and commentaries on Deuteronomy and the Apocalypse. These have not survived. In addition he is known to have written sermons while in Oxford, one for the feast of the translation of St Edmund of Canterbury (9 June), another on the text 'Dixit mater Ihesu ad eum, vinum non habent'. The latter sermon was given in the church of the Blessed Virgin, and is noteworthy in that the privilege of preaching the university sermon on Sundays was usually reserved for Dominicans. Herbert also translated Latin hymns into English, including 'Vexilla regis prodeunt', 'Gloria, laus, et honor', and hymns to the Blessed Virgin. His translations (which survive in BL, Add. MS 46919) may have greater linguistic than literary value; nevertheless, the attempt of the Franciscans to use the vernacular to introduce Latin hymnography to an English audience is important evidence of the order's pastoral work. The translations were probably designed as preaching aids rather than as texts for a choir.

Herbert's interest in the history of the Franciscan English province is attested by his annotations to a copy of the *De adventu Fratrum Minorum in Angliam* of Thomas Eccleston, which include the names of Franciscan lectors at Oxford missed by Thomas, and to a copy of a chronicle *De Britannia et Britonum rebus gestis a primis ad annum 1278*. William Herbert should be distinguished from the late thirteenth-century Dominican William of Hereford.

ANDREW JOTISCHKY

Sources A. G. Little, 'The Franciscan school at Oxford', *Franciscan papers, lists, and documents* (1943), 55–71 · A. G. Little, *The Grey friars in Oxford*, OHS, 20 (1892) · J. S. Brewer, ed., *Monumenta Franciscana*, 1, Rolls Series, 4 (1858) · Emden, *Oxf.* · A. G. Little, 'The Lamport fragment of Eccleston and its connexions', *EngHR*, 49 (1934), 299–302 · T. Carleton Brown, *Religious lyrics of the fourteenth century* (1924)
Archives BL, Add. MS 46919 · BL, Royal MS 7 F.viii

Herbert, William, first earl of Pembroke (*c.*1423–1469), soldier and administrator, was from Raglan in the marcher lordship of Usk; his attachment to Richard, duke of York, and Richard Neville, earl of Warwick, the King-maker, enabled him to become Edward IV's Welsh 'master-lock' (*Gwaith Lewys Glyn Cothi*, no. 112) and to be the first full-blooded Welshman to enter the English peerage.

Background and early service to York and Warwick The son of Sir William ap Thomas (*d.* 1445) and Gwladus (*d.* 1454), daughter of the Brecon knight *Dafydd Gam (*d.* 1415), and widow of Roger Vaughan (Fychan) of Bredwardine (*d.* 1415), William was brought up at Raglan Castle in York's lordship of Usk [see also Vaughan family (*per. c.*1400–*c.*1504)]. He took the name of Herbert (pedigrees claiming descent from a companion of William I are fanciful), and secured advancement by serving York, Gloucester, the Beauchamps, and the crown in the marches. His father was in York's retinue in France (1441), and the son was there in the last years of English occupation: he witnessed the surrender of Le Mans (1448) and at the battle of Formigny (April 1450) was captured and held for ransom. At home he became steward of York's lordships of Usk and Caerleon, and when York raised the siege of Taunton and suppressed lawlessness between the earl of Devon and Sir William Bonville (in September 1451), Herbert was with him. By 1453 he was the earl of Warwick's sheriff of Glamorgan. Along with other esquires, including Henry VI's half-brothers, Edmund and Jasper Tudor, Herbert was knighted at Christmas 1452, and Edmund granted him a £10 annuity (October 1453). Thus before the Wars of the Roses, Herbert inherited his father's influence in southeast Wales; but the growing tension between York and the Lancastrians, and between Warwick and the duke of Somerset in south Wales, strained his loyalties.

Activity in the Yorkist cause, 1454–1461 York was assured in May 1454 that Herbert 'saith he is noo monis mon but only youres' (Pugh, 'The magnates', 92). Already noble rivalries were disturbing the peace in south Wales. The dispute between Warwick and Somerset over Glamorgan led to a summons for Herbert and his kinsmen to appear before the king's council in 1453. Following the battle of St Albans in May 1455 more serious trouble occurred, and there is little doubt that Herbert, Sir Walter Devereux (whose daughter Anne he married in 1449), and their affinities acted in York's interest as well as their own to dominate Herefordshire and its environs. Their most spectacular acts reasserted the duke's authority in west Wales. Herbert, Devereux, and the Vaughans led about 2000 men from Herefordshire and neighbouring lordships to seize Carmarthen Castle, of which York was officially constable; they captured and imprisoned Edmund Tudor, and then took Aberystwyth, another castle under York's constableship. Attempts to bring the culprits to book had only temporary success; though briefly consigned to the Tower of London, by October Herbert was marauding in Glamorgan, Abergavenny, Usk, and Caerleon, and a price of 500 marks was put on his head. In late March 1457 Henry VI and Queen Margaret travelled to Hereford to oversee the trial of Herbert and others. An effort may have been made to detach him from other rebels, for his punishment was comparatively light: in June he was pardoned and restored to his possessions.

Herbert was not present when York's forces were dispersed at Ludford Bridge (October 1459). Perhaps because of this he was allowed to retain the shrievalty of Glamorgan and the constableship of Usk Castle (February 1460), following Warwick's and York's attainders. But once Henry VI had been captured at Northampton in July 1460, the Yorkists employed Herbert and Walter Devereux junior to preserve order in Wales; both also represented Herefordshire in the parliament of 1460–61. Herbert's loyalties were clear when he and a force from York's estates joined Edward, earl of March, at the battle of Mortimer's Cross (2 or 3 February 1461). A month later (3 March) he was at Baynard's Castle to acclaim Edward as king.

Service to Edward IV and rewards, 1461–1469 Herbert's position after 1461 reflects his energy, loyalty, and ambition, as well as the young king's heavy reliance on a dependable tenant with a powerful affinity. He became a king's knight and Edward's intimate, and his rewards and commissions in Wales and the marches were unprecedented. In the spring and summer he and Walter Devereux were commissioned to array men in south Wales and the marches to defeat the Lancastrians and impose the new king's authority, and a fleet was put at his disposal. On 8 May he was appointed justiciar and chamberlain of the royal counties of Carmarthen and Cardigan for life. In September he and Devereux received custody of the Stafford lands in south Wales during the duke of Buckingham's minority, Herbert acting as steward of Brecon, Hay, and Huntington, and in control of Newport. Meanwhile in July Edward IV summoned him to his first parliament as one of seven new barons.

An immediate objective was the capture of Pembroke Castle. On 30 September 1461 Herbert secured its surrender, taking custody of Henry Tudor, earl of Richmond, whom he put in the care of his wife, Anne, at Raglan; he paid £1000 for the boy's wardship and marriage. Moving north he defeated a Lancastrian force near Caernarfon in October. In February 1462 he was granted the lordship of Pembroke, along with other estates of Jasper Tudor, the attainted earl. A few days later the Welsh estates of the Mowbrays—notably Gower—were placed in his hands. By the spring Herbert and his kinsmen controlled much of southern Wales and the borderland (including Goodrich and Archenfield); and after his brother Richard captured Carreg Cennen Castle, Carmarthenshire, in May, only Harlech was unsubdued.

The king's reliance on Herbert and his affinity in Wales gave him political hegemony and huge wealth: by the mid-1460s his landed income and fees amounted to £3200–£3300 per annum. His authority in Carmarthenshire and Cardiganshire was made permanent when in September 1466 his offices were extended to his male heirs. Moreover, partly in preparation for the assault on Harlech, his power was extended to north Wales: in June 1463 as justiciar of Merioneth, and in August 1467 as justiciar of the entire principality of north Wales. He already had custody (June) of the lands of Richard Grey, lord of Powys. By 1468 there were few lordships or counties in Wales and the marches (except Glamorgan) of which he was not either lord or chief official—King Edward's 'master-lock' indeed. The prize, Harlech, fell to him in August 1468. His last notable coup came in the following month, when the duke of Norfolk transferred Chepstow and Gower to him in exchange for East Anglian manors.

Marks of the king's personal favour multiplied. In 1462 Herbert was elected a knight of the Garter; in 1463 Crickhowell and Tretower were made into a separate lordship for him, and in 1465, in recognition of his valour, Edward made Raglan a lordship in its own right, the last time a Welsh marcher lordship was created; on 8 September 1468 Herbert was created earl of Pembroke. The price was Warwick's resentment. According to T. B. Pugh, the 'original cause for [Warwick's] dissatisfaction with Edward IV' (Pugh, *Glamorgan County History*, 3.198) was the placing of the Stafford lands in Herbert's hands in 1461. Herbert's gradual mastery of Wales may have made the lord of Glamorgan more uneasy, for it coincided with Warwick's disenchantment with Edward's foreign policy and his reliance on the Woodvilles. Warwick resented the grant of the Luttrell estate of Dunster, Somerset, to Herbert's eldest son, William [see below], who took the title of Lord Dunster before his marriage to the queen's sister, Mary, in September 1466. Three weeks later (26 September) the queen's father, Lord Rivers, arranged that Herbert's earlier lease (1462) of Haverford and other lands be converted into a grant to him and his male heirs. And it was Herbert who accompanied Edward IV when he deprived Archbishop Neville of the great seal in June 1467.

Death In July 1469 the king faced Robin of Redesdale's rebellion and the arrival of Warwick and the duke of Clarence from France, proclaiming Pembroke as one of the king's wicked advisers. Pembroke raised an army for the king largely in Wales; he and his brother, Sir Richard, were to join Humphrey Stafford, earl of Devon, at Banbury, Oxfordshire; a skirmish with some rebels and a quarrel with Devon over billeting weakened Pembroke's position. In the desperate fight at Edgcote on 26 July, the Welsh were overwhelmed, and Pembroke and his brother were captured; next day Warwick ordered their execution. Welsh poets lamented the deaths of such famous Welsh nobles. Contrary to his will of July 1469, the earl was buried in Tintern Abbey rather than Abergavenny Priory, where Sir Richard's body was interred. He instructed his widow to betroth Henry Tudor, earl of Richmond (afterwards Henry VII), to their daughter Maud, which would link his family to Edward III's line.

Pembroke's eldest son, **William Herbert**, second earl of Pembroke (1455–1490), magnate, inherited the earldom of Pembroke but not the ability and flair that made the first earl virtual viceroy of Wales for Edward IV. The son's youth, as well as limited abilities (or ill health), precluded his inheriting his father's position. After the battle of Barnet on 14 April 1471 Edward IV entered London with the young earl, who was welcome at court. But he received only partial exemption from the Act of Resumption of 1473, and this may have led to disturbances by the Herbert family in 1473–4. He went with the king, his brother-in-law, to France in 1475 and on their return Herbert was allowed to enter his inheritance. The establishment of the prince of Wales's council in the marches was at the earl's expense, culminating in 1479 in the enforced exchange of the earldom of Pembroke (which was transferred to the prince) for the less valuable earldom of Huntingdon. He was closer to *Richard III, whose bastard, Katherine, he agreed to marry in February 1484; he may have been chamberlain of Richard's son, Prince Edward. Yet he did not resist Henry Tudor, with whom he had been brought up. He soon made his peace with the new king, and on 22 September 1486 was formally pardoned. When he died on 16 July 1490, he left no male heir and the Herbert ascendancy in Wales had already disintegrated.

R. A. GRIFFITHS

Sources inquisition post mortem, PRO, C140/32 · inquisition post mortem, PRO, E 149/222/10 · *Chancery records* · NL Wales, Badminton collection · Cardiff Free Library, Herbertorum prosapia, 5.7 · D. H. Thomas, 'The Herberts of Raglan as supporters of the house of York in the second half of the fifteenth century', MA diss., U. Wales, 1967 · G. H. R. Kent, 'The estates of the Herbert family in the mid-fifteenth century', PhD diss., University of Keele, 1973 · G. Williams, ed., *Glamorgan county history*, 3: *The middle ages*, ed. T. B. Pugh (1971) · R. A. Griffiths, 'Wales and the marches', *Fifteenth-century England, 1399–1509*, ed. S. B. Chrimes, C. D. Ross, and R. A. Griffiths, 2nd edn (1995), 145–72 · *Gwaith Lewis Glyn Cothi*, ed. D. Johnston (1995) · 'John Benet's chronicle for the years 1400 to 1462', ed. G. L. Harriss, *Camden miscellany, XXIV*, CS, 4th ser., 9 (1972) · W. G. Lewis, 'Herbertiad Rhaglan fel noddwyr y beirdd yn y bymthegfed ganrif a dechrau'r unfed ganrif ar bymtheg', *Transactions of the Honourable Society of Cymmrodorion* (1986), 33–60, esp. 36–53 · H. T. Evans, *Wales and the Wars of the Roses*, new edn (1995) · T. B. Pugh, 'The magnates, knights and gentry', *Fifteenth-century England, 1399–1509*, ed. S. B. Chrimes, C. D. Ross, and R. A. Griffiths (1972), 86–128 · D. E. Lowe, 'The council of the prince of Wales and the decline of the Herbert family', *BBCS*, 27 (1976–8), 278–97 · M. A. Hicks, 'The changing role of the Wydevilles in Yorkist politics to 1483', *Patronage, pedigree and power in later medieval England*, ed. C. D. Ross (1979), 60–86 · *Calendar of the fine rolls*, PRO, 22 (1962) · *CPR, 1494–1509* · J. Warkworth, *A chronicle of the first thirteen years of the reign of King Edward the Fourth*, ed. J. O. Halliwell, CS, old ser., 10 (1839)
Archives Cardiff Free Library, Herbertorum prosapia, 5.7 | NL Wales, Badminton collection
Likenesses manuscript illumination, *c*.1461–1462 (with his wife), BL, J. Lydgate, 'Troy book', Royal MS 18 D 11, fol. 6
Wealth at death approx. £3200–£3300: NL Wales, Badminton collection, receivers' accounts

Herbert, William, second earl of Pembroke (1455–1490). *See under* Herbert, William, first earl of Pembroke (*c*.1423–1469).

Herbert, William, first earl of Pembroke (1506/7–1570), soldier and magnate, was the second son of Richard Herbert (*d*. 1510) of Ewyas, a gentleman usher to Henry VII, and his second wife, Margaret, daughter of Sir Matthew Cradock of Swansea. His paternal grandfather was William *Herbert, earl of Pembroke, who was executed in 1469 on the orders of the earl of Warwick for his loyalty to Edward IV.

Early career Little can be said for certain of William Herbert's early life and upbringing. His father died in 1510, and his childhood was probably spent in the household of his mother's third husband, William Bawdrip, at Splott near Cardiff. At some point he entered the service of Charles Somerset, from 1514 earl of Worcester, who was related to the Herberts through his marriage to the daughter of William's half-uncle and namesake, William Herbert, earl of Huntingdon. John Aubrey, whose account of Herbert is a better guide to the latter's reputation than to the facts of his life, records that he was known as 'Black Will Herbert', and states that he could neither read nor write. The charge of illiteracy is baseless, but there is record evidence to support Aubrey's claim that Herbert killed a man in Bristol, for he was named in a coroner's report of 1527, and there is nothing that contradicts his story that the killer then fled to France, where he joined the army and won the favour of François I, beyond the fact that in 1555 he was reported by the Venetian ambassador

William Herbert, first earl of Pembroke (1506/7–1570), by unknown artist, 1567

to have been recalled from negotiations at Calais 'as he neither speaks nor understands any other language than the English' (Nightingale, 33). But Herbert hardly needed the French king's recommendation to draw him to the attention of Henry VIII, for in January 1526 he was already numbered among the latter's spears, or gentlemen pensioners. Probably it was Worcester who had secured his entrée at court.

Herbert's activities in the years after 1526 are unclear, and he may have left court for a while. He was referred to as a member of the royal household in 1531, but as a late gentleman of the household in 1534. In 1535, however, he became an esquire of the body, and in 1539 he was named one of the fifty new gentlemen spears. A year later he appeared in a list of the gentlemen of the king's privy chamber with a salary of £50. But Herbert's career took off after his sister-in-law Katherine Parr married Henry VIII on 12 July 1543. By 3 January 1544 he had been knighted, and other grants and honours followed. Early in 1544 the lands of Wilton Abbey were granted to Herbert and his

wife, and later that year he led 100 light horse on the campaign which captured Boulogne. In 1545 he was returned to parliament as one of the knights of the shire for Wiltshire, and on 21 February 1546 he was made steward for life of the duchy of Lancaster estates in that county. In October that year he was promoted to share with Sir Anthony Denny the position of chief gentleman of the privy chamber, and was consequently in a position to gain substantially, in terms of both influence and wealth, from his closeness to the centre of power in Henry VIII's last days. He was in attendance on 30 December 1546 when the king had his last will and testament stamped, witnessed, and sealed, and was named both an executor and one of the council of regency for Edward VI. He was also a beneficiary under the will, with a legacy of lands worth £200, later raised to 400 marks; in fact the estates he received were worth far more, including, for instance, the house in Hackney once owned by the sixth earl of Northumberland, which Herbert was able to sell for £1000.

Herbert's first marriage was clearly crucial to his promotion at court. **Anne Herbert** (b. before 1514, d. 1552) was the younger daughter of Sir Thomas *Parr (d. 1517) of Kendal [see under Parr family] and his wife, Maud Green (d. c.1531). The date of her marriage to Herbert is not recorded, but it may well have been to her that John Husee referred when he told Lady Lisle on 3 August 1537 that 'it is thought Mrs Parre will shortly marry' (LP Henry VIII, 12/2, no. 424). Like her sister she was well educated, though her Latin seems to have become rusty later—when Roger Ascham entered Princess Elizabeth's household in 1548, he urged Anne to improve it, and lent her a copy of Cicero's De officiis for the purpose. When *Katherine became queen, she made Anne her maid-in-waiting and the keeper of her jewels, and the two sisters remained close. According to Foxe, when the religious conservatives struck at the queen in 1546, 'they thought it best, at first, to begin with some of those ladies, whom they knew to be great with her, and of her blood; the chiefest whereof, as most of estimation and privy to all her doings, were these: the lady Herbert, afterward countess of Pembroke, and sister to the queen, and chief of her privy chamber' (Acts and Monuments, 5.557). Then, when Katherine saved herself by a timely submission to the king, she went to him 'waited upon only by the lady Herbert her sister, and the lady Lane, who carried the candle before her' (ibid., 559). Like the queen, Anne Herbert patronized the Flemish miniaturist Levina Teerlinc, who became another member of Katherine's privy chamber.

Relations with Protector Somerset Herbert continued to prosper during the protectorate of Edward Seymour, successively earl of Hertford and (from 16 February 1547) duke of Somerset. The two men became rivals for preeminence in Wiltshire, but at the beginning of Edward's reign Herbert was a strong supporter of Seymour. In spiritual matters he does not appear to have shared the protector's evangelicalism, but throughout his life took an essentially Erastian position, whereby the English crown assumed responsibility for the direction of the nation's religious observance. Thus he reaped material benefits from the dissolution of the monasteries (he was granted the lease of Abergavenny Priory on 16 May 1537), and even carried out the work of dissolution himself in Wales. In 1538 he was employed by Thomas Cromwell to destroy the famous shrine of the Virgin at Pen-rhys, in the Rhondda valley. Such a stance made it easier for him to adapt to changed circumstances than for some of his contemporaries.

Herbert was returned to parliament for Wiltshire in 1547, and in May 1548 crossed to Boulogne to muster its garrison. He was clearly a skilful and energetic soldier and commander, as he showed in the following year. When rebellions broke out in several parts of England, Herbert first took vigorous action against insurgents in Wiltshire, where Edward VI recorded in his journal how 'Sir William Herbert did put them down, overrun, and slay them' (Jordan, 12). By this time the men of Devon and Cornwall were also up, and around 10 July the council ordered Herbert to be ready to proceed thither. On the 24th he was instructed to march west with all his power, on the 28th to take two or three thousand men from Wales and two thousand from Gloucestershire and Wiltshire. He had not yet arrived when the royal army defeated the insurgents at Honiton and relieved Exeter, but on 18 August he was given command of the vanguard for the battle of Sampford Courtenay in which the western men were defeated again, and shortly afterwards destroyed a rebel force near Tiverton. The commander of the king's army, John, Baron Russell, described Herbert as having 'served notably' (Sil, 116).

The widespread disturbances of summer 1549 did much to undermine Somerset's authority, and led to a political campaign to remove him from office. In this context it was of crucial importance that Herbert and Russell commanded the largest field army in the country, one, moreover, that they were leading back towards London. Somerset himself, feeling the ground insecure under his feet, appreciated the potential significance of this force and tried to ensure its support, appealing three or four times to its leaders from 25 September onwards. But Herbert and Russell, having by 8 October marched as far as Andover, finally turned against the protector and withdrew to Wilton. In a letter sent to Somerset on that day they told him of their fears that if civil war broke out, 'the querell once begonne will never ende tyll the realme by dyssendyd to that wofull Calamytie that all our posterytie shall lament the chaunce', and of their perception that 'this great extremytie procedeth only upon pryvate causes' (Sil, 118). Their defection ruined the protector, who resigned his office and was sent to the Tower.

Rise to greatness Herbert was swift to ally himself with John Dudley, earl of Warwick and later duke of Northumberland, who on 2 February 1550 became lord president of the council and effective head of the government. His rewards were substantial. As compensation for his expenditure in 1549 he was licensed on 28 October to have 2000 pounds of fine silver turned into coin of the realm, an operation which brought him a profit of just over £6700. On 2 December 1549 he was made master of the king's horse, and on 8 April 1550 he was appointed lord president of the council in the marches of Wales. To support himself in this new dignity he was granted lands worth 500 marks in Glamorgan and Monmouthshire. He was indeed indefatigable in building up his estates, and bought properties (notably those of dissolved chantries) in many counties, and particularly in south Wales and Wiltshire. In his largest purchase, in co-operation with William Clerk of Punsborn, an outlay of £10,000 in 1553 brought him estates in Wales and the English counties of Somerset, Dorset, and Wiltshire worth £782 11s. 6d. per annum. Eventually the revenues from his lands, together with those from a number of valuable wardships and from the fees of his various offices, brought him an estimated annual income of between £4000 and £5000.

Office and lands made Herbert a man of power in Wales, the grants of 1550–51 causing him to be described (by way of an arcane reference to a late eleventh-century ruler) as 'the greatest lord that ever owned lands in Glamorgan either before or after Iestyn ap Gwagan's time' (Williams, *Glamorgan*, 31). In 1551 he was made lord lieutenant for all the Welsh counties, and it was far from inappropriate that having been ennobled as Baron Herbert of Cardiff on 10 October that year, he should have been further promoted to become earl of Pembroke on the following day. But probably even more important to him were his estates, and his position, in Wiltshire. There he faced competition for pre-eminence both from successive barons Stourton, heads of a long-established county family, and from the Seymours. But the Stourtons increasingly lacked the means to compete, and the fall of Somerset left Herbert without an effective rival; his superiority was confirmed after the duke's execution in 1552, when Herbert received a large grant of Seymour lands in north Wiltshire. Men formerly in Somerset's affinity now acknowledged Herbert's superiority, and he acted as an arbitrator in local disputes, including one involving the bishop of Salisbury. Herbert's power-base in the county lay at Wilton, in the south of the county, where he gave visible expression to his power in a splendid house. According to tradition he consulted Holbein before starting to build, but the fact that Holbein died in 1543, whereas Herbert only acquired the freehold of Wilton in 1544, rules against the story. Herbert clearly took a close personal interest in the process of construction, for John Knox rebuked him for spending his time with masons and architects, instead of listening to sermons. The detail of the original house at Wilton is almost entirely lost (except perhaps for the arms of Henry VIII reset in the north front), but the overall shape of Herbert's house, quadrangled with two forecourts, has survived.

The earl of Pembroke was not a man to hide his light under a bushel, indeed his obvious liking for display seems to have been both an accompaniment to and a manifestation of a personal charisma which made men willing to follow him. From the early 1550s there are frequent references to the scale and splendour of his retinues and way of life. When the Scottish queen-dowager Mary of Guise visited London in November 1551, among her escort rode the earl of Pembroke with 100 horsemen, their 'cotes gardy[d] with velvet, and chynes, hats and whyt fethers, and every [man] havyng a new gayffelins [javelin] in ther hands, and a bage [badge]' (*Diary of Henry Machyn*, 11–12). Nearly a year later the young king was entertained by Pembroke at Wilton. The imperial ambassador was greatly impressed by the magnificence of the reception, the king being served off pure gold, the council and privy chamber off silver gilt, and the rest of the royal household off silver. When Edward left, his host presented him with 'a very rich camp-bed, decorated with pearls and precious stones' (*CSP Spain, 1550–52*, 565–6). The ceremonies marking the death of his wife, who died at Baynard's Castle on 20 February 1552 and was buried in St Paul's on the 28th, probably also reflect her husband's penchant for magnificence. Machyn records the funeral of 'the good lade contes of Penbroke', attended by 100 poor men and women, by 'mornars boyth lordes and knyghts', and by the heralds responsible for all the panoply of aristocratic exequies. She was interred beside John of Gaunt's tomb, 'and after her banars wher sett up over her [and her] arnes sett on dyvers pelers' (*Diary of Henry Machyn*, 15–16). In 1554 Pembroke was reported to have 1000 men wearing his livery, and when he greeted Philip of Spain at Southampton that year, he was attended by a body of archers wearing the livery of the house of Aragon, and by 200 mounted gentlemen dressed in black velvet and wearing heavy gold chains.

Pembroke and Northumberland Following Somerset's fall Herbert was closely involved in the earl of Warwick's government. In autumn 1549 he inventoried the royal chattels, and in April 1550 he was among the privy councillors trusted by Warwick to keep order in the provinces. He was later one of a group of noblemen paid £2000 per annum each to maintain 100 horsemen to that same end. In September 1551 he was also a member of an informal committee dealing with the currency and the king's debts, and presumably in that capacity helped to uncover the shortcomings of Sir Martin Bowes, the under-treasurer of the Tower mint, in January 1551. Herbert and Warwick became earl and duke respectively on the same day, and it is a measure of the closeness of the two men that when Northumberland struck at the duke of Somerset in autumn 1551, Somerset's ally the twelfth earl of Arundel confessed that there had indeed been a plot to arrest both Pembroke and Northumberland, as well as the marquess of Northampton. Pembroke sat on the jury which condemned Somerset, despite the latter's objections. The rumours of a rift between Pembroke and Northumberland which in autumn 1552 circulated as far as Ireland seem to have been groundless, and in the following year Pembroke concurred in the plans made by Edward VI and Northumberland to divert the succession to the throne from Princess Mary to Lady Jane Grey; on 21 May 1553 Jane married the duke's son Guildford, and on the same day her sister Katherine married Henry *Herbert (*b.* in or after 1538, *d.* 1601), Pembroke's son and heir. Pembroke subsequently signed both Edward's 'device' for the limitation of

the succession and the subsequent 'engagement' undertaking to uphold it.

Northumberland is later said to have accused Pembroke of having thought up the scheme to make Jane queen. That is highly unlikely, but it seems clear that he went along with the plan as long as he reckoned it had any chance of success. He was a signatory of the letter to Mary of 9 July ordering her to cease resistance, and had Jane proclaimed queen at Beaumaris and Denbigh. He even stood godfather, with Jane and her father, the duke of Suffolk, to the daughter of the ardent protestant Edward Underhill. But as support for Mary grew, Pembroke began to have second thoughts. After Northumberland had left London to confront Mary on 13 July, Arundel and Pembroke headed the party of defection. Their headquarters was Pembroke's house at Baynard's Castle, and there, after Arundel had made a lengthy oration on Mary's behalf, Pembroke made a much briefer one, concluding: 'If my Lord of Arundell's perswasions cannot prevaile with you, eyther this sword shall make Mary Qwene, or Ile lose my life' (Nichols, 120). He and his supporters then proclaimed Mary in Cheapside.

The reign of Mary At first Mary took more account of Pembroke's slowness to support her than of his eventual rallying to her cause. He was briefly placed under house arrest and lost his Welsh presidency, but was admitted to the privy council on 13 August 1553. He had his son's marriage annulled, but lost ground with the new queen for favouring her marriage to Edward Courtenay, rather than to Philip of Spain. His opportunity to win Mary's favour came on 1 February 1554, when he was appointed her 'cheyfe capten and generall agauynst ser Thomas Wyatt and ys felous' (Sil, 140–41). Notwithstanding the cowardice and treachery of others, Pembroke kept his nerve and blocked the approaches to London, confident that Wyatt's men would lose heart and melt away—as they did. The earl was duly earmarked for rewards, but gave offence in the spring when he supported Baron Paget (another favourer of Courtenay over Philip) in opposing the heresy bill, out of fear of the consequences for lay holders of former ecclesiastical lands. Pembroke had already clashed with Stephen Gardiner, bishop of Winchester, on this issue. But he showed himself sufficiently confident of his position to come to parliament in November with all his old flamboyance, followed by 200 horsemen 'in velvet cottes and cheynes, the cotes with iij lasses of gold, and lx reseduw in bluw cotes gardyd with velvet, and badge a gren dragon' (*Diary of Henry Machyn*, 74).

Pembroke's wealth, power, and experience probably made him indispensable to Mary's government. Early in 1555 he was once more made president of the council in Wales, and although he was pursued for debt in the exchequer chamber, he was ultimately pardoned his obligations. He also managed to gain the confidence of King Philip, albeit not without some difficulty, and was one of the noblemen who received a Spanish pension. He advocated the king's involvement in government, and may have favoured his coronation. In September 1555 he accompanied Philip to Brussels for a meeting with the latter's father, Charles V, and shortly afterwards was made governor of Calais. In religious matters he acted in accordance with his habitual Erastianism, defending Sir Edward Hastings when the latter spoke up for the government's bill against religious exiles, and alienating many of his own retainers in the process. Presumably they had expected him to act otherwise, but in fact the earl was following his long-held principles. Aubrey's story of Pembroke's restoring the nuns to Wilton is without foundation, but he did make at least a gesture towards Catholic restoration, when in January 1557 one Thomas Bowes made over to him the site of the former house of Observant Franciscans in Southampton, so that Pembroke could restore it to its former use; the friars returned briefly in 1558, but there is no evidence for Pembroke's involvement in this.

Pembroke's principal services to Mary's regime were military. In 1557 he was appointed to lead an English army of just over 7000 men to assist Philip's forces in northern France. His forces arrived too late to take part in the battle of St Quentin on 10 August, but distinguished themselves in the capture of that town on the 27th. In the military emergency of 1558 that followed the loss of Calais, Pembroke was lieutenant for Wiltshire and Somerset. It was probably these commitments that made it impossible for him to attend to his responsibilities in Wales, for in August he wrote to the queen offering to resign as president of the council there, in response to her letters 'stating that the Marches of Wales are in disorder for want of a president residing there' (*CSP dom.*, *1547–80*, 106). He was nevertheless sufficiently trusted by Mary to be named one of the executors of her will.

Last years under Elizabeth When Mary died on 17 November 1558 Pembroke proceeded to Hatfield, and there took part in what was in effect the first privy council meeting of Elizabeth's reign. Then when the new queen entered London on the 28th he bore the sword before her. He clearly had Elizabeth's trust and respect. He entertained her at Baynard's Castle in 1559 and 1562, and substituted for her at the St George's day feast of 1560. A few days later he was one of the judges at a court joust, and risked injury when pieces of a shattered stave flew up and hit him. Politically he supported Sir William Cecil, the queen's secretary, at this time, both in favouring English intervention in Scotland in 1560, and in opposing suggestions that Elizabeth should marry Lord Robert Dudley in the following year. When the queen nearly died of smallpox in 1562, the Spanish ambassador reported that Pembroke supported the claims of the protestant earl of Huntingdon to the succession, which if true would suggest that the earl had adapted loyally to the new religious settlement. He also strengthened his links with the Talbot family. About May 1552 he married Anne (1524–1588), widow of Peter Compton and daughter of George Talbot, fourth earl of Shrewsbury. In 1563 his eldest son married Katherine, daughter of the sixth earl of Shrewsbury, while his daughter Anne married Lord Francis Talbot.

Pembroke's health deteriorated in the 1560s, and he was reported to be seriously ill in June 1560 and September 1564. But this did not stop his continuing pursuit of wealth, or his engagement in court politics. He was prepared to take risks for money. In 1552 he bought shares in the expedition led by Sir Hugh Willoughby which set off in pursuit of the north-east passage to China, and three years later was among the merchant adventurers of England for the discovery of lands unknown. In 1563 he invested in the *Jesus* of Lübeck, sailing to Africa and America, and shortly afterwards did the same for a slaving expedition led by John Hawkins. Closer to home, in 1568 he was a shareholder in the mines royal and mineral and battery companies, and may have been responsible for the establishment of carpet-weaving at Wilton, perhaps by fugitives from the Netherlands.

At court Pembroke moved increasingly into the camp of Robert Dudley, created earl of Leicester in 1564, and with him risked burning his fingers by involving himself in Anglo-Scottish politics. Made lord high steward of the royal household in 1568, in the same year Pembroke gave his support to proposals that the fugitive Mary, queen of Scots, should marry Thomas Howard, fourth duke of Norfolk, and then be restored to her throne with a husband acceptable to English interests. But when Elizabeth learned of the scheme in 1569 she would have nothing to do with it or its backers. Pembroke was briefly detained at court, but successfully pleaded his innocence and good intentions, and was soon allowed to retire to Wilton. But he was further embarrassed when the earls of Northumberland and Westmorland rose in revolt. They had their own reasons for favouring Mary's marriage to Norfolk, and now they claimed Pembroke as one of their backers. The earl protested his loyalty—'For God forbid I shoulde lieve the Howre, nowe in myne olde Age, to staine my former Lief with one Spott of Disloyaltie' (Sil, 175)—and Elizabeth was convinced, for he was named general of a large force levied to defend her at Windsor. But he was not required to take the field, and died at Hampton Court, aged 63, on 17 March 1570. The queen wrote a letter of condolence to his widow.

Pembroke had drawn up his will on 28 December 1567. He left £200 for distribution to the poor in London, Salisbury, Wilton, and Hendon. His daughter Anne was to have money and jewels worth 500 marks, his second son Edward 500 marks in plate and household stuff and £500 in cash. His eldest son Henry was sole executor and residuary legatee. The four overseers of the will, who were to receive £50 each, included Leicester and Sir Walter Mildmay. On the night before he died Pembroke added Sir James Croft and Sir William Cecil to the overseers, and made some further bequests: his wife was to have clothes, jewels, and £500; the queen 'his best jewell which he names his greate ballace and his newe faireste and richeste bedd'. The earl's best and second-best gold swords were to go to Leicester and the marquess of Northampton respectively. Later still Pembroke made further provision for his wife, and remembered some of his servants, also advising his son to 'entertaigne his householde and kepe them together' (Sil, 223). In 1567 he had required 'such funerall solemnitie about my said burial as to myne estate and callinge apperteynethe and I will some honorable tome and monumente shalbe upon my bodie' (ibid., 220). If he died in London he asked for burial beside his first wife in St Paul's, and there he was interred on 18 April. His exequies were of a piece with his life. The dean, Alexander Nowell, preached, his eldest son was chief mourner, and among those present were Cecil, Leicester, Mildmay, Sir Nicholas Bacon, and Bishop Edmund Grindal. His household turned out in force, including two chaplains, two secretaries, and his steward, treasurer, and comptroller. His monument, destroyed in 1666, commemorated both Pembroke and his first wife. Her virtues were said to have included religious devotion as well as conjugal fidelity, but her husband's epitaph listed only his secular honours and achievements, his services to four monarchs and above all his martial valour, at home and abroad.

NARASINGHA P. SIL

Sources DWB · HoP, Commons, 1509–58, 2.341–4 · S. J. Gunn and W. R. B. Robinson, 'The early life of William Herbert, earl of Pembroke (d. 1570)', Welsh History Review / Cylchgrawn Hanes Cymru, 18 (1996–7), 509–19 · W. R. B. Robinson, 'Sir William Herbert's acquisition of offices in Wales on the death of Henry, earl of Worcester', Historical Research, 70 (1977), 266–83 · S. E. James, Kateryn Parr: the making of a queen (1999) · Sidney, sixteenth earl of Pembroke, A catalogue of the paintings and drawings in Wilton House (1968) · N. P. Sil, William Lord Herbert of Pembroke (c.1507–1570): politique and patriot, 2nd edn (1992) · Straton, Survey of the lands of William, first earl of Pembroke, 2 vols. in 1 (Roxburghe Club, 1909) · M. M. Reese, The royal office of master of the horse (1976), chap. 11 · N. P. Sil, Tudor placemen and statesmen: select case histories (2001) · GEC, Peerage · J. E. Nightingale, Some notice of William Herbert, first earl of Pembroke of the present creation (1878) · CSP dom., 1547–80 · The acts and monuments of John Foxe, ed. J. Pratt, [new edn], 5 (1877) · W. Dugdale, The baronage of England, 2 vols. (1675–6) · VCH Wiltshire, vols. 5–6 · Wiltshire, Pevsner (1971) · J. G. Nichols, 'Life of the last Fitz-Alan, earl of Arundel', GM, 1st ser., 103/2 (1833), 10–18, 118–24, 209–15 · The diary of Henry Machyn, citizen and merchant-taylor of London, from AD 1550 to AD 1563, ed. J. G. Nichols, CS, 42 (1848) · The chronicle and political papers of King Edward VI, ed. W. K. Jordan (1966) · CSP Spain, 1550–52 · D. Starkey, ed., The inventory of King Henry VIII (1998) · F. Roth, The English Austin friars, 1249–1538 (1966), 1 · E. Auerbach, Tudor artists (1954) · L. V. Ryan, Roger Ascham (1963) · F. Rose-Troup, The western rebellion of 1549 (1913) · D. Loades, The reign of Mary Tudor: politics, government and religion in England, 1553–58, 2nd edn (1991) · D. Loades, John Dudley, duke of Northumberland, 1504–1533 (1996) · D. E. Hoak, The king's council in the reign of Edward VI (1976) · W. T. MacCaffrey, The shaping of the Elizabethan regime: Elizabethan politics, 1558–1572 (1968) · L. Stone, The crisis of the aristocracy, 1558–1641 (1965) · G. Williams, ed., Glamorgan county history, 4: Early modern Glamorgan (1974) · G. Williams, Wales and the Reformation (1997) · H. Miller, 'Henry VIII's unwritten will: grants of lands and honours in 1547', Wealth and power in Tudor England: essays presented to S. T. Bindoff, ed. E. W. Ives, R. J. Knecht, and J. J. Scarisbrick (1978), 87–105

Archives V&A NAL, household inventory · Wilts. & Swindon RO, survey of his lands in Wiltshire, Somerset, Devon, and Dorset

Likenesses oils, 1557; on loan to Holyrood House, Edinburgh · oils, 1567, Wilton House, Wiltshire [see illus.] · group portrait, oils, 17th cent. (Edward VI granting Bridewell charter), Bridewell Royal Hospital, Witley, Surrey · Passe, line engraving, BM; repro. in H. Holland, Herōologia (1620) · Stephen of Holland, silver medal, BM

Wealth at death approx. £3250 income from land; approx. £2000 income from sinecures; approx. £522 profits from wardships: also Straton, Survey

Herbert, Sir William (c.1553–1593), colonist in Ireland and author, was born about 1553 at St Julians, Monmouthshire, the only child of William Herbert (d. 1567), landowner, of St Julians, and his first wife, Jane (d. c.1554), daughter and heir of Edward Griffith of Penrhyn, Caernarvonshire. He was the great-grandson of Sir George Herbert, third son of William Herbert, first earl of Pembroke (c.1423–1469), a pedigree upon which he placed considerable emphasis. Herbert was, in fact, the earl's only surviving legitimate male heir. Between about 1568 and 1573 he attended Oxford, where he received private instruction from Laurence Humphrey, president of Magdalen College and an ardent protestant, quickly earning himself a reputation as a poet and intellectual. The poet Thomas Churchyard dedicated 'Churchyard's Dream', the ninth labour of 'the first part of Churchyard's Chippes', to Herbert in 1575 while the astrologer and mathematician John Dee gladly accepted the young man's notes on his astrological and alchemical work Monos hieroglyphica in May 1577. About this time Herbert married Florence (d. in or after 1596), daughter of William Morgan of Llantornan, Monmouthshire, and his wife, Elizabeth. They had two sons who died young—reputedly from consuming poison left in Herbert's library to protect his precious books from rats. In 1578 Florence gave birth to their only surviving child, Mary Herbert (1578–1634).

Herbert first entered political life as sheriff of Glamorgan from 1577 to 1578 and, in an effort to consolidate his position further, leased Newport Castle and then Liswerry and Lebenith manors. He was knighted by Elizabeth I at Richmond Palace on 21 December 1578 and was appointed deputy constable of Conwy Castle, Caernarvonshire, in 1579. In 1579 or 1580 he was named JP for Monmouthshire; he served as sheriff of the county from 1579 to 1580 and was, in 1583, appointed chief steward of Rhymni manor in south Wales. He was appointed custos rotulorum of Monmouthshire by 1583. Yet political advancement did not diminish Herbert's intellectual pursuits. He regularly visited Dee, who was his neighbour at Mortlake, Surrey, and undoubtedly availed himself of the large library Dee kept there. Herbert maintained an interest in astrology and alchemy and in early 1582 Dee's alchemical assistant requested to live with him. This seamless combination of the disparate roles of intellectual, country gentleman, and political servant distinguished him from many other Welsh MPs when he sat for Monmouthshire in the parliaments of 1584 and 1586. In the former, Herbert was on nine committees dealing with a wide range of political matters; in the latter he introduced a bill concerning orphans in Monmouthshire and delivered what was the first recorded speech by a Welsh MP. It concerned Mary, queen of Scots, and he was consequently chosen, with forty-five others, to present Elizabeth with a petition calling for her cousin's execution. Shortly afterwards, however, in a dramatic departure from his hitherto Welsh-based endeavours, Herbert embarked on a colonization venture in Ireland.

In May 1586 Herbert undertook, with a consortium, to plant areas of Munster which had come into the crown's hands following the attainder of Gerald Fitzjames Fitzgerald, fourteenth earl of Desmond. The catalyst for the undertaking may have been Sir James *Croft, Herbert's distant relation and former lord deputy of Ireland, but he was certainly alive to the opportunities available across the Irish Sea. In addition to the possibility of financial gain, Ireland presented an intellectual and a religious challenge to which he could devote himself. In June 1586 Herbert applied for three 'seignories' in co. Kerry, amounting to roughly 24,000 acres, but their allotment was delayed for nearly a year while the lands were surveyed. During this time he displayed his protestant convictions by composing *A letter written by a true Christian catholike to a Romaine pretended catholike, upon occasion of a controversie touching the catholike churche* (1586). This was followed in 1587 by a work, no longer extant, in praise of Sir Philip Sidney entitled *Sidney, or, Baripenthes: briefly shadowing out the rare and never ending landes of that most honourable and praiseworthy gent. Sir Philip Sidney.* Herbert finally arrived in Cork in April 1587, but received just 13,276 acres at Castleisland, co. Kerry.

On paper, the colonization scheme was promising: the plantations were to represent English islands of stability and civility inhabited and inexpensively defended by settlers drawn from those English counties where the colonists wielded influence. However, they inherited a myriad of rents and exactions previously due to Desmond, which were now due, in part, to the crown. These rents had been levied without any regularity and the land on which they were due was depopulated and wasted. Herbert identified the problem, noting a:

> continual vexation and disquietness between the undertakers and the natural inhabitants of the country, upon whom these things must be levied, but cannot be had, because they have not wherewith to pay it; the other an incumbrance to the gentleman whose lands both in England and Ireland shall stand charged in the Exchequer for these sums, which they shall never be able to levy.   (PRO, SP 63/135/58)

Dissension quickly arose among the colonists as they quarrelled over the boundaries of their lands and the retention of tenants. Herbert became embroiled in a particularly bitter dispute with Sir Edward Denny, who alleged that he had lured away some of his tenants.

The settlers had a proclivity to drift towards better land in co. Limerick and Herbert became increasingly reliant on enticing neighbouring settlers onto his lands and utilizing the existing Irish population. This latter development, coupled with his knowledge of the success of Tudor reform in Wales, had a profound influence on his treatment of the Irish and contrasted sharply with that of his colleagues. He found the Irish to be tractable enough, lacking only the 'sweet taste of civility'. He insisted that prayers be said in Gaelic and that the Lord's prayer and the ten commandments be translated for their benefit. Herbert's principal goal was doubtless their conversion to

protestantism, but his unexpected and unpopular effort to procure the release from Dublin Castle in March 1588 of the noted rebel Patrick Fitzmaurice—a member of the Old English contingent long settled in Munster—reflected his willingness to put native concerns ahead of New English interests to achieve 'stability and civility'. In doing so, however, he alienated many of his colleagues and was accused of being contaminated by the Irish, to which he responded:

> though I have ever more esteemed of the nobility of virtue, yet have I little cause to think myself blemished by my blood being the heir male of that Earl [Pembroke] that hath this day living nine earls and barons descended out of his body. (PRO, SP 63/135/81(i))

The dispute with Denny and his fellow undertakers worsened and by December 1588 quarter sessions were being disrupted. Herbert positioned himself to return home, but this was delayed while he acted as vice-president in Munster during Sir Thomas Norris's absence. Though his departure was imminent, he still held out the hope of making 'Kerry and Desmond a little England beyond Ireland' just as 'some worthy gentlemen in times past [had] made Pembrokeshire a little England beyond Wales' (PRO, SP 63/140/11). He wrote copiously on the state of Munster with prescriptions for its reform. Having served successively as JP and sheriff in co. Kerry and also as a member of the provincial council, Herbert returned to Wales in early summer 1589 with commendatory letters from leading Irish officials.

In the months following his return Herbert spoke at length with Croft about his experiences in Ireland. Croft died on 4 September 1590, but their conversations formed the basis for Herbert's lengthy treatise *Croftus, sive, De Hibernia liber.* Completed in early 1591, the work represents a collection of views formed by Croft during his deputyship, but modified and updated by Herbert's recent first-hand colonial experience in Ireland. The main thrust of *Croftus* is its belief that the colonization of Munster would succeed in introducing 'English civility' to the natives. Support was found for this argument among classical texts—Cicero in particular—or the scriptures; passages were highlighted which advocated colonization schemes to 'civilize' 'primitive' peoples. 'Civilizing' the natives, however, could not be achieved without the abolition of native customs, which *Croftus* held to be the greatest threat to the colonists:

> colonies degenerate assuredly when the colonists imitate and embrace the habits, customs and practices of the natives. There is no better way to remedy this evil than to do away with and destroy completely the habits and practices of the natives.   (*Croftus*, 81)

The introduction of protestantism and of education—the latter facilitated by the establishment of universities at Dublin and Limerick—would combine to draw the natives from their customs and ensure their Anglicization. Yet *Croftus*, while offering a window into the intellectual arguments concerning Tudor plantation schemes in Ireland, also served as a detailed piece of propaganda justifying the settlement of Ireland by New English officials. It set the tone for writings on the subject and was followed by works from two other colonists, Richard Beacon and Sir Edmund Spenser respectively, advocating similar colonization, although it reflected the more reasonable colonial mindset more fully than Spenser's work did.

In the years following his return to Wales, Herbert's energies and writings were not confined to the subject of Ireland. He attempted unsuccessfully to secure a seat on the queen's council of Wales and the marches, but was returned for parliament, again for Monmouthshire, in January 1593. Perhaps his experiences in Ireland explain his appointment as deputy lieutenant of Monmouthshire by 1593, but he was more than qualified for office by his local consequence. He wrote a love poem first published in the *Phoenix Nest* in 1593 (Park, vol. 2) and replied to Edmund Campion's *Decem rationes* (1587) in a work entitled *Sir William Herbert's confutation of Campion the Jesuit's ten reasons dedicated to Queen Elizabeth*. He also penned an aggressive letter to one Morgan who foolishly issued him a challenge. Herbert died on 4 March 1593, at St Julians, Monmouthshire, and was buried in Monmouth; he was survived by his wife and daughter. In his will (dated 12 April 1587) he bequeathed all his estates, including lands in Ireland, to his daughter, Mary. In an effort to ensure that his descendants would share both his blood and surname he inserted a clause requiring her to marry someone surnamed Herbert. If, however, the clause was ignored she would inherit a meagre living from a small portion of his lands in Anglesey and Caernarvonshire. In February 1599 she fulfilled this condition, marrying Edward *Herbert, later first Baron Herbert of Cherbury (1582?–1648). At the instigation of Sir William Herbert's widow and daughter a new survey of his Irish lands was conducted, and the rent was reduced in 1596. Throughout his career he was convinced of the benefits of Tudor government and worked tirelessly towards its implementation in Wales. His efforts to put Tudor theories of government into practice in Ireland, however, were less successful and his house and possessions were ultimately swept away by rebellion in 1598. *Croftus*, his greatest legacy, which continued to influence English colonial thought about Ireland for a decade, was in many ways an intellectual attempt to achieve Tudor reform in Ireland where his plantation had failed. CHRISTOPHER MAGINN

Sources BL, Lansdowne MS 27, no. 7 · [W. Herbert], *A letter written by a true Christian catholike to a Romaine pretended catholike* (1586) · W. Herbert, *Croftus, sive, De Hibernia liber*, ed. A. Keaveney and J. A. Madden (Dublin, 1992) · PRO, SP 63 · 'A letter of Sir William Herbert … to a gentleman of the name of Morgan', *GM*, 1st ser., 55 (1785), 32 · HoP, *Commons, 1558–1603* · *The Irish fiants of the Tudor sovereigns*, 4 vols. (1994) · J. S. Brewer and W. Bullen, eds., *Calendar of the Carew manuscripts*, 6 vols., PRO (1867–73) · *CPR, 1572–5* · *The diaries of John Dee*, ed. E. Fenton (1988) · G. Bradney, *A history of Monmouthshire*, 4/2 (1932) · W. R. Williams, ed., *The history of the parliamentary representation of Wales* (1895) · B. P. Park, ed., *Heliconia comprising a selection of English poetry of the Elizabethan age: written or published between 1575 and 1604*, 3 vols. (1815) · DNB · M. MacCarthy-Morrogh, *The Munster plantation: English migration to southern Ireland, 1583–1641* (1986) · S. G. Ellis, *Ireland in the age of the Tudors* (1998) · N. Canny, *Making Ireland British, 1580–1650* (2001)

Archives BL, Herbert's confutation of Campion, MS Lansdowne xcvii, 7, fols. 120–126a · BL, English translation of *Croftus*, Harley MS 35, item 2, fols. 154–178a · Powis Castle, 'Croftus' MS
Likenesses oils, Powis Castle; repro. in Herbert, *Croftus*
Wealth at death estates in Monmouthshire, Anglesey, Caernarvonshire, and Kerry, Ireland; shortly before death, fortune est. £5000: 'A letter', *GM*

Herbert, William, third earl of Pembroke (1580–1630), courtier and patron of the arts, was the son of Henry *Herbert, second earl of Pembroke (b. in or after 1538, d. 1601), and his third wife, Mary Sidney (1561–1621) [see Herbert, Mary, countess of Pembroke], sister of Sir Philip *Sidney and of Robert *Sidney, earl of Leicester. A tablet erected by his grateful father in St Mary's Church, Wilton, Wiltshire, noted William's birth before noon on 8 April 1580. The baby was baptized there on 28 April. Queen Elizabeth and his mother's influential uncles Robert Dudley, earl of Leicester, and Ambrose Dudley, earl of Warwick, stood as his godparents, testifying to the importance of the infant heir to the Pembroke title.

Education and early life Following the tradition of his mother's family, Lord Herbert received a careful education. Herself an accomplished writer and poet, the countess educated her son at home, employing Hugh Sanford, and later Samuel Daniel, a poet of some renown, as his tutors. Their influence, as well as the example of his mother and Sidney uncles, bred a lifelong appreciation for literature and the arts in the young man. Herbert composed poetry—which remained unpublished until after his death—but more importantly he was the best-known patron of his generation. Ultimately his education would make him the 'greatest Maecenas to learned men of any peer of his time, or since' (Brennan, 150). He received his first dedication, a theological work by William Thorne, when he was twelve, in 1592. In the same year he and his father travelled to Oxford, where in the queen's presence they banqueted at Magdalen College—the beginning of an association with the university which would continue for the rest of his life. On 9 March 1593 he matriculated at New College, where he was tutored by John Lloyd and garnered more dedications. One, Thomas Moffet's *Nobilis, or, A view of the life and death of a Sidney* (c.1594), began what would become a consistent theme in Herbert's life: comparisons with his uncle Sir Philip Sidney. In 1595 he left Oxford without a degree (though he was in 1605 awarded an MA), but retained an affection for the institution which would endure.

With his heir approaching manhood, Pembroke embarked upon the first of several abortive negotiations for his son's marriage—to Elizabeth, daughter of Sir George Carey. This alliance, along with proposals for women of the Cecil, Vere, and Howard families, all failed thanks to the earl's steep terms and Herbert's reluctance. More important for Herbert at this stage of his life was the acquisition of military glory. Some scholars have placed him in Essex's Cadiz expedition (1596), though there is no hard evidence to prove this. In 1597 he planned a trip to the continent, and two years later asked his uncle Robert Sidney for the loan of horses and weapons so that he could

William Herbert, third earl of Pembroke (1580–1630), by Sir Anthony Van Dyck

'follow the camp' (Sydney and others, 2.113). In 1598 his military interests prompted yet another dedication, this time to Robert Barret's *Theory and Practice of Modern Wars*. On the whole, however, it is unlikely that Herbert did much, if any, soldiering. His proposed campaign in 1599 was unhinged by his father's fragile health.

Elizabethan courtier In any event, Herbert's real interests lay neither in the university nor on the battlefield, but at court. Polite education however deep—as it undoubtedly was in his case—and a martial veneer were means to an end: a successful career as a courtier. His first brief visit to court was in 1595, and the experience whetted his appetite for more. He was again at court in the summer of 1597, and a sustained campaign eventually won his father's permission for longer-term residence in London, but not until the spring of 1598. Increasingly feeble, and unable to travel to court, the earl hoped that his son might represent his extensive political interests there.

Once in London, Herbert lost no time establishing himself. He courted Robert Devereux, earl of Essex, and Sir Robert Cecil, rivals for the queen's favours, and ingratiated himself with both. By the autumn of 1599 he had

made remarkable progress: 'My lord Herbert is exceedingly beloved at court of all men', wrote his uncle's man Richard Whyte in November (Sydney and others, 2.143). On 29 November the queen granted him an hour-long private audience before he returned to Wilton for the holidays. Back at court by the spring of 1600, he again turned heads: 'he will prove a great man', wrote Whyte. His father's illness soon forced a reluctant Herbert back to Wilton. He told Cecil that he hated the rustic life, but that Pembroke's weakness demanded constant attendance. Moreover, to his son's horror, the earl's approaching end spurred unwelcome generosity in him: the old man gave away £1000 on a single day during Herbert's absence. But though the earl's illness lasted far too long to suit his ambitious son, death finally released Pembroke early in the morning of 19 January 1601.

William Herbert was now third earl of Pembroke, lord of vast estates, especially in Wales and the marches. The second earl had been a knight of the Garter and lord president of the council of Wales, and his son had every hope that his successful début at court would ensure an easy succession to those honours. Unfortunately the young earl's plans fell foul of his own passions and the queen's defence of female virtue. On 14 June 1600, during his last stay at court before inheriting his title, he attended the wedding of his cousin Henry, Lord Herbert (the earl of Worcester's heir). Prominent among the performers in a masque celebrating the occasion was Mary *Fitton (*bap.* 1578, *d.* 1641). Daughter of Sir Edward Fitton, a prominent Cheshire gentleman, Mary had been at court since about 1597. Some have speculated that she was Shakespeare's 'dark lady'; whatever the truth of this, it is clear that she was a captivating young woman. Courtiers took much surreptitious amusement in the infatuation with her of the fifty-year-old treasurer of the household, Sir William Knollys—attentions which she rejected. Apparently, however, she welcomed Herbert's approach, and they began an affair, probably shortly after the wedding. Rumour alleged that Mary, disguised in men's clothing, visited his lodgings. In August, Whyte noticed William's lack of attention to family business—he seemed depressed and distracted. For this he had good reason; by this time Mary was pregnant. Under the circumstances, his trip to his father's deathbed might have come as a relief from his troubles at court. On the day the old earl died he wrote to Cecil complaining of the scandalous stories circulating about him. By the end of January 1601 Fitton's predicament was common knowledge. The queen ordered Pembroke to the Fleet prison by 25 March, where he remained until 26 April, after which he was banished to Wilton. His son was born in late March and died almost immediately. Throughout his ordeal Pembroke showed no concern for his lover and adamantly refused to marry her. This behaviour incensed the queen, who thereafter declined to name him to his father's offices. Pembroke's career at Elizabeth's court was finished.

But though the Fitton affair was a personal disaster, Pembroke was fortunate in its timing. Caught in the toils of his own scandal, he escaped any taint in the catastrophe that overwhelmed Essex at the same time. Essex counted Pembroke as a friend and expected his support in his rising, but Pembroke's political sense, even in the midst of his troubles, kept him out of danger. Though he lost the queen's favour, he at least kept his head. In October 1601, still denied access to court, Pembroke discovered a role for himself as one of the most assiduous members of the House of Lords. This period in the wilderness taught Pembroke the value of a parliamentary power base, and he began the process of building a following there important enough to oblige even kings to respect him.

Royal favourite and cultural patron For the remainder of Elizabeth's life Pembroke laboured in obscurity; 1602 passed by with virtually no mention of the earl or his whereabouts. But he was by no means prepared to abandon his hopes and to retire. The queen's death on 24 March 1603 gave Pembroke a second chance, and he wasted no time in seizing it. He and his brother, Philip *Herbert joined the rush of courtiers northward to escort the new king to London. James showed both brothers particular favour from the start. After his exclusion under Elizabeth, the Stuart accession marked a dramatic turn in Pembroke's fortunes. James, open-handed by nature, did not stint the avid courtier. The king visited Wilton twice in 1603, and clearly enjoyed Pembroke's company. In May Pembroke became a gentleman of the privy chamber and keeper of Clarendon Forest—the latter a source of income and patronage. On 9 July he succeeded in his father's place as knight of the Garter.

For all his cultural interests, Pembroke was well suited for the boisterousness of the Jacobean court. He participated enthusiastically in every accession day tilt until 1615, and performed in many masques celebrating courtly milestones. His personal relationship with James drew comment from the Venetian ambassador, who recounted a scene from the coronation: 'The earl of Pembroke, a handsome youth, who is always with the king and always joking with him, actually kissed His Majesty's face, whereupon the king laughed and gave him a little cuff' (Brennan, 105). On one of his many stays at Wilton, James, aware that Pembroke detested frogs, put one down his favourite's neck to general hilarity. Nothing abashed, Pembroke later took his revenge by sneaking a live pig into the king's close stool.

Pembroke's relationship with James continued to flourish, and he was equally popular with Queen Anne. His new year's gift to the king in 1604 was a jewel allegedly worth £40,000. Finding the wherewithal for such extravagances became easier in the same year. On 18 January James made him high steward of the duchy of Cornwall and lord warden of the stannaries; a few months later he became lord lieutenant of Cornwall—a major expansion of Herbert influence as well as sources of considerable income. On 4 November he further advanced his fortunes with his marriage to Lady Mary Talbot (d. 1650), daughter of Gilbert *Talbot, seventh earl of Shrewsbury. The match was a natural one between two important families—Pembroke's father and grandfather had both married Talbot women,

and he received an impressive dowry with his new wife. Not everyone approved of the bargain, however. Years later Clarendon—who began his parliamentary career as a Pembroke client—said that the earl 'paid much too dear for his wife's fortune by taking her person into the bargain' (Brennan, 106). Their union produced only one child, a boy who died at less than a month old.

Pembroke's success at court attracted increasing attention from those searching for a patron. During the early years of James's reign an extraordinary range of books were dedicated to Pembroke: works of theology, military affairs, history, diplomacy, law, and poetry were all offered to him; no one outside the royal family gathered as many dedications in the early seventeenth century. Pembroke obviously enjoyed his reputation as a patron of arts and letters, which appealed to his love of scholarship as well as enhancing his lustre at court. John Burton wrote that 'his vigorous and restless mind ranged over the whole life of his age' (Brennan, 148–9) and the list of his clients reads like a biographical dictionary of the Jacobean arts. In 1603 Ben Jonson dedicated his *Sejanus* to the earl, beginning a long association between the two men. Pembroke gave Jonson £20 a year to buy books, and in 1605 came to the playwright's rescue when his *Eastward Ho!* landed him in gaol for its tactless assault on the Scots. George Chapman, the famous translator of Homer, benefited from the earl's attentions. Shakespeare's sonnets, published by Thomas Thorpe in 1609, bore a dedication to W. *H., and some scholars have suggested that this was Pembroke. In any case it is certain that he and his brother Philip were the dedicatees of the first folio in 1623. Pembroke's personal relationship with Shakespeare is a murky subject, but he certainly knew and patronized some of the bard's associates, such as Richard Burbage and Edward Alleyn. The earl may also have protected Thomas Middleton when in 1624 his anti-Spanish play *A Game at Chess* appeared. George Herbert, the poet and a kinsman, received a living in the church and a seat in the House of Commons thanks to the earl. Nor did Pembroke confine his patronage to literature alone; he befriended Inigo Jones—thereby walking a tightrope between the architect and his enemy Jonson. Some time before 1605 Jones apparently toured Italy at Pembroke's expense. The earl also commissioned portraits by Nicholas Hilliard, Marcus Gheeraerts the younger, and Daniel Mytens. Among his many other clients were Thomas Tompkins and John Dowland, two of the best-known composers of the day.

While his broad popularity among writers and artists reflected Pembroke's cultural interests, it was built upon the foundation of his success at court. He steadily accumulated favours from the king, increasing his attractions as a patron. In January 1608 he became constable of St Briavel's Castle and warden of the Forest of Dean; in October 1609, captain of the Tower and Isle of Portsmouth and constable of Portchester Castle. On 29 September 1611 he joined the privy council. But Pembroke could never count on James's unalloyed favour; there were always potential rivals at court. Henry Howard, earl of Northampton, for instance, detested Pembroke as a 'Welsh juggler' who threatened the Howard family's position (O'Farrell, 73–4). But a more significant bar to Pembroke's progress was Robert Carr. James's infatuation with Carr left Pembroke angry and frustrated, as he saw more and more of the rewards of favour diverted from himself and his brother. Carr's dominance at court further inflamed Pembroke's dislike of Scottish courtiers: '… the Scots and he were ever separate' (Lloyd, 917) and in 1610 he quarrelled over a matter of precedence with the earl of Argyll. Pembroke's difficulties mounted between 1611 and 1614 as the deaths of Prince Henry, and the earls of Salisbury and Northampton promised an extensive reordering of power and patronage at court. Were it not for Carr, Pembroke believed himself well placed to fill the vacuum created by these deaths. On his deathbed, vindictive to the last, Northampton warned Carr, now earl of Somerset, to prevent Pembroke's succession to any of his offices. Pembroke's attempts to secure the offices of master of the horse, lord chamberlain, and, less importantly, the keepership of Waltham Forest, all failed during this period.

The public antagonism with Somerset led to Pembroke's identification as the leader of a faction determined to reduce the favourite's influence. In 1611 Jonson dedicated his *Catiline* to Pembroke. A story of the decline of the Roman republic, the unstated—but unmistakable—contrast was between Pembroke, the noble Roman, and Somerset, the corrupt politician. Nevertheless, Pembroke's aims were more practical: the extension of his power and patronage. By the autumn of 1612 Sir Robert Naunton was writing that Pembroke sought a truce with Somerset, whose influence seemed to grow daily. In the spring of 1613 he played a small role in the downfall of Somerset's erstwhile friend Sir Thomas Overbury when, along with the lord chancellor, Thomas Egerton, Lord Ellesmere, he told the hapless knight of his commission as ambassador to Russia. In November 1613 he assisted in the creation ceremony for Somerset's earldom, and performed at his wedding masque a month later. Amicable relations with the favourite, wary though they were, continued until July 1614, when Somerset became lord chamberlain, an office Pembroke had long coveted.

The rise of Buckingham, 1615–1621 Smarting over this setback, Pembroke was a willing participant in a plan to undermine Somerset. In April 1615 he hosted a meeting at his London home, Baynard's Castle, where he and several of the favourite's enemies, including Archbishop George Abbot, agreed to promote the career of George Villiers, a handsome—but poverty-stricken—young man who had recently caught James's eye. Pembroke lent Villiers clothing for his appearances at court, and worked with Abbot to gain the queen's favour for the young man. They succeeded, on 23 April, in arranging Villiers's knighthood, a ceremony carried out in the queen's chamber. Anne's prophetic remark to Abbot at the time was:

> My lord, you and the rest of your friends know not what you do: I know your master better than you all; for if this young man be once brought in, the first persons that he will plague must be you that labour to him. (Rushworth, 1.456)

Pembroke would soon come to realize the truth of the queen's prediction. Nevertheless, in the short term his scheme was remarkably successful. Somerset's influence waned and ended with his dramatic fall from grace in the Overbury murder scandal.

Somerset's eclipse resulted in Pembroke's achieving one of his long-standing ambitions: on 23 December 1615 he received his wand of office as lord chamberlain. This office, one of the three most important at court, greatly expanded Pembroke's authority. The lord chamberlain had an important role to play in the life of the court. He presided over the household above stairs, and supervised some 600 officers. He arranged entertainment—masques, plays, and musical performances. He supervised the office of works and licensed theatres. Additionally he gained more patronage in the church. As important as the patronage attached to the office were its very considerable profits: over £4800 annually. Pembroke must have organized the Christmas revels of 1615 well pleased by the events of the year, but the threat to his position represented by his erstwhile client Villiers grew far more quickly than the new lord chamberlain could have expected. James gave the young man a handsome new year's gift on 4 January 1616, making Villiers master of the horse. When, that summer, James visited Wilton, it was with Villiers in tow. Pembroke's appointment as a commissioner to execute the office of earl marshal in September was hardly adequate compensation for the prominence of the newly ennobled Viscount Villiers.

These political troubles might explain why at about this time Pembroke embarked upon an affair with his widowed cousin, Lady Mary *Wroth (1587?–1651/1653), who over the next several years gave birth to two children, William and Katherine. Although their existence was not widely known, Pembroke, and later his brother, helped establish his offspring as adults. At the same time Pembroke became a particularly active freemason—in 1617 as grand warden and in the next year grand master. His masonic associations might have been due to his connection with Inigo Jones, but they could also represent an attempt to broaden his power base as conflict with the new favourite loomed. A particularly galling moment for Pembroke must have been in 1618, when a new edition of Sir John Harrington's epigrams appeared on London's bookstalls. Its 1615 dedication to Pembroke had been replaced by a fulsome tribute to Villiers, now marquess of Buckingham.

But Buckingham's rise did not completely overshadow Pembroke. On 29 January 1617 Pembroke's long-standing relationship with Oxford University reached its apogee when he was elected chancellor. He took his office there seriously, intervening on the university's behalf in disputes with the town, settling squabbles among the faculty, and siding against the more strident Arminians there. Not surprisingly his role as chancellor prompted a flood of dedications and pleas for patronage. He secured fellowships for clients, and was a generous benefactor to the Bodleian Library, donating £100 towards its construction. More importantly, in 1629 he donated a collection of 250 Greek manuscripts he had purchased for £700. The rest of his Greek manuscripts made their way into the Bodleian in 1654. In 1624 Broadgates Hall honoured him by changing its name to Pembroke College. As he had no legitimate heir, the shrewd academics of the college expected, in the fullness of time, a handsome bequest. In the end they were forced to make do with (depending upon the story) a single piece of plate or a napkin for their pains. Pembroke's relationship with Oxford is commemorated in the bronze statue of him by Hubert Le Sueur which now stands in the quadrangle of the Bodleian; originally placed at Wilton, it was presented to the university by Thomas Herbert, eighth earl of Pembroke, in 1723.

Buckingham's enemies at court expected Pembroke to lead them, and their hopes increased following Queen Anne's death on 13 May 1619. Pembroke had always been close to the queen and without her influence at court Buckingham's influence burgeoned. In September he and Buckingham clashed openly over the appointment of the groom porter and a gentleman usher, both positions within the earl's purview as chamberlain. Buckingham's attempted seizure of some of Pembroke's patronage touched the earl in a particularly sensitive place. Yet the hopes of Buckingham's enemies for outright warfare with Pembroke took some time to be realized. As early as December 1617 Archbishop Abbot, bitter at the disastrous consequences of pushing Buckingham forward, turned on his ally. Writing to Dudley Carleton, he said that 'Pembroke looketh only to his own ends, and whatsoever leagues, promises, and confederations are made within one hour they come to nothing' (Cogswell, 131). After his experience with Somerset, however, it seems likely that Pembroke preferred compromise with Buckingham to an open breach.

Friendship with Buckingham brought its rewards; James paid another summer visit to Wilton in 1620, and in 1621 appointed Pembroke lord lieutenant of Somerset and Wiltshire, further consolidating his already significant power in the west. Additionally, from May to July 1621 he acted as a commissioner for the great seal. Yet Buckingham and Pembroke could not stay allies for long. This was in part due to the increasing monopoly Buckingham exercised over the king's favour, but also over matters of policy. Pembroke had long been associated with the anti-Spanish 'protestant' faction at court; it was a matter of pride to him that his famous uncle Sir Philip had died fighting the Spaniard. Northampton's pro-Spanish attitude had reinforced Pembroke's natural predilections. He consistently sought ways to challenge Spanish interests, at home and abroad. An early investor in colonial enterprises—Pembroke was the Virginia Company's second-largest investor—he put money into many other schemes that would curb Spanish power. These included investments in the Guiana Company, the Somers Islands Company, the discovery of the north-west passage, and the East India Company. In 1618 he had argued on Sir Walter Ralegh's behalf after his abortive incursion into Spanish America. Buckingham's support for a Spanish marriage for Prince Charles increased tension between the two men. Pembroke's opposition to the match was no secret.

Thomas Scott, an anti-Spanish polemicist, was one of his chaplains.

Pembroke's anti-Spanish views coincided with those of many members of parliament, and although he always supported the crown's parliamentary agenda, he was, unlike Buckingham, a popular figure there. In fact the earl welcomed sessions of parliament, for he commanded a formidable interest in both houses. In December 1621 he argued against a dissolution in council, opposing both Prince Charles and Buckingham. Ever since his exclusion from Queen Elizabeth's presence, he had recognized the value of parliamentary patronage, and could plausibly claim by 1621 to be the kingdom's foremost patron after the crown itself. The number of members identified with him varied from parliament to parliament but in the Commons it was never less than a dozen, rising to over thirty at times. Pembroke's extensive properties gave him control over several seats in the Commons, as in Cardiff and Wilton, and his many offices—his lieutenancies, the wardenry of the stannaries, the chancellorship of Oxford—further extended his reach. He sponsored the selection of old friends, such as Sir Benjamin Rudyerd, relatives like George Herbert, and dependants, such as his secretaries, for seats in the Commons. Moreover, he systematically collected proxies in the House of Lords; rarely did he have fewer than five, and at key moments he could deploy as many as ten. This parliamentary faction gave Pembroke an important advantage in his struggle with Buckingham, for though the latter (who had been elevated to duke in 1623) might have the king's heart, Pembroke could, when necessary, defend his position at court through his influence at Westminster. By 1624 the tension between the two peers was especially high, sparking yet another clash over patronage when Buckingham attempted to intervene in the appointment of court musicians.

That Pembroke could use his extensive parliamentary influence to threaten Buckingham was clear to at least one shrewd observer. Francis Bacon advised Buckingham to come to some arrangement with Pembroke, despite the low opinion he had of the earl: 'For his person, not effectual; but some dependences he hath which are drawn with him' (Ruigh, 263). The duke seems to have taken this advice to heart, if only briefly. Pembroke and his following refrained from challenging the favourite in the parliament of 1624, aided no doubt by Buckingham's conversion to the anti-Spanish cause. Friendship with the duke encouraged James to name Pembroke warden of the New Forest, a place he had wanted for some time, on 30 December 1624. A superficial amity characterized the earl's relationship with Buckingham until James's death on 25 March 1625. Pembroke was present at the royal deathbed, and James asked him to testify that he died a good protestant. Given Pembroke's popular reputation as the most prominent protestant at court, the king's last request was politically wise.

The reign of Charles I Charles I's accession presented new challenges. Buckingham was as firmly entrenched as ever, and Pembroke did not enjoy the same easy friendship

with the king as with his father—there would be no practical jokes between master and servant in this reign. But
Charles understood the importance of the man whom
Lucy Russell, countess of Bedford, described as 'the only
honest harted man imployed that I know now left to God
and his countrie' (Cogswell, 317). John Chamberlain
reported rumours that Pembroke would be a member of
Charles's cabinet council, and on his part the earl obliged
Charles by denouncing the doctrine of predestination at
the York House conference. The king named him to his
council of war but the constant tension with Buckingham
resulted in yet more quarrelling in August 1625. In October Charles visited Wilton in an effort to heal the breach.
The king's stay resulted in rumours of significant changes
at court, the outlines of which were not, in the end, fanciful.

The royally inspired truce lasted up to Charles's coronation on 2 February 1626, at which Pembroke bore the
crown. But the earl launched his most effective assault on
his rival in the new session of parliament. There Dr Samuel Turner, a Pembroke client in the Commons, raised
questions about Buckingham that would lead to formal
charges against him. Pembroke's parliamentary influence
was at its peak—with as many as thirty-eight friends, relatives, and clients in the Commons and no fewer than ten
proxies, including that of the disgraced John Digby, earl of
Bristol, from his peers. He took care to support Charles's
war, speaking on 10 March to a joint session of the need
for supply. But he did nothing to rein in the pursuit of the
duke. In June Pembroke joined three other privy councillors in a petition to the king, urging against parliament's
dissolution.

By early summer 1626 it was clear that Pembroke had to
be mollified, and once again Charles brokered a treaty—
this time a lasting one. The arrangement contained two
key provisions: a marriage alliance and an exchange of
offices at court. Buckingham betrothed his daughter Mary
to Pembroke's nephew Charles, son and heir of his
brother Philip, earl of Montgomery. Charles would, in the
course of time, inherit the Pembroke earldom as well as
his father's title. Pembroke promised the couple land
worth £4000 a year, rising to £10,000 after their marriage,
which would not take place for some time owing to the
children's ages—Mary was four and Charles seven. Buckingham promised a £20,000 dowry. The wedding finally
took place in January 1635, by which time both principals
were long dead. More important than the marriage from
Pembroke's perspective was the king's contribution to
the peace. Charles appointed Pembroke lord steward of
the household, and allowed the earl to pass his chamberlain's wand to his brother Montgomery. In early August
there were reports that Pembroke was having second
thoughts about the arrangement, but nevertheless the
exchange of offices was complete by 18 August. Now the
Herbert family, as lord steward and lord chamberlain,
controlled the royal household both above and below
stairs. Only Buckingham, as master of the horse, could
rival Pembroke. Pembroke's income was estimated at

£22,000 a year, his patronage network was the most extensive in the kingdom, and his popularity higher than ever.
The earl's long career as a courtier at last brought him—
and his family—the position he had sought since his first
introduction at Queen Elizabeth's court over thirty years
before.

Charles made another visit to Wilton in October 1626,
reflecting the newly established understanding between
the king and his servants. Pembroke withdrew his favour
from some of Buckingham's most strident opponents,
such as William Coryton and Sir Robert Phelips. He even
allowed Buckingham to poach in his Cornish patronage
preserve, appointing a ducal client vice-warden of the
stannaries. He dutifully—if unenthusiastically—supported the forced loan. But events showed that Pembroke
still found it difficult to work harmoniously with Buckingham. On 23 November, in Charles's presence, he fiercely
attacked Buckingham's leadership of the disastrous Île de
Ré expedition. Buckingham's failure encouraged Pembroke to press his advantage, and he argued for a new parliament and peace with France. Charles's reluctant agreement to call a parliament seems at least in part to have
been based upon an understanding that Pembroke's following would not support an attack on Buckingham. He
kept his side of the bargain, allowing Buckingham's
friends to dominate elections in Cornwall and Somerset,
to the dismay of many of his clients such as Coryton. Yet
Pembroke remained, at best, only a grudging friend of the
duke—only Buckingham's assassination in August 1628
would put an end to their rivalry.

Death and assessment Many observers saw Pembroke as
the most important figure at court after the duke's passing, and he continued to receive marks of royal favour: in
September 1628 he was appointed to the admiralty commission, and on 8 September 1629 Charles named him
chief justice in eyre south of Trent and vice-admiral of
Wales. But Pembroke's long enmity with Buckingham, his
advocacy of moderation and compromise as a privy councillor, and, not least, his willingness to pressure the king
with his parliamentary influence, could hardly ingratiate
him with Charles. The king was now determined to pursue a more vigorous line with his opponents, and Pembroke would not be sympathetic. He would no longer be at
the centre of Charles's counsel. Additionally Pembroke's
health was, by 1629, failing. He had been subject to occasional sharp attacks of the stone since 1623, and of gout
since 1625. Throughout most of 1627 and 1628 his health
was poor. On 9 April 1630 he dined cheerfully with his old
friend Catherine, countess of Bedford, in London. Pembroke turned fifty the day before, and an amusing subject
of their conversation was a fortune teller's prophecy that
he would not live to see his fifty-first birthday. At eight
o'clock the following morning he collapsed and died of
apoplexy at Baynard's Castle. He was buried in Salisbury
Cathedral on 7 May. He was succeeded by his brother, who
became fourth earl of Pembroke.

Pembroke was 'the very picture of nobility: his person
rather majestick than elegant, his presence whether quiet
or in motion, full of stately gravity, his mood generous,

and purely heroick' (Lloyd, 918). His generosity was well known, as countless writers and artists from Ben Jonson and Inigo Jones down could testify, and his love of scholarship was unquestionable. But while he supported the protestant cause in Europe and moderate courses at home, he never lost sight of his own, and his family's, interests. Pembroke's career was remarkable. The son and grandson of nobles adept at accumulating power through royal favour, he surpassed them both, holding his own against the two great favourites of the Stuart court—the earl of Somerset and the duke of Buckingham. If his Herbert inheritance was an appreciation of power and its use, the legacy of his Sidney mother was a lifelong passion for literature and the arts. The combination made William Herbert the greatest patron of his generation and one of the most durable, and successful, courtiers of his age.

VICTOR STATER

Sources M. Brennan, *Literary patronage in the English Renaissance: the Pembroke family* (1988) • B. O'Farrell, 'Politician, patron, poet: William Herbert, 3rd earl of Pembroke', PhD diss., U. Cal., Los Angeles, 1966 • GEC, *Peerage* • D. Taylor jun., 'The third earl of Pembroke as a patron of poetry', *Tulane Studies in English*, 5 (1955), 41–67 • D. Taylor jun., 'The earl of Pembroke and the youth of Shakespeare's sonnets: an essay in rehabilitation', *Studies in Philology*, 56 (1959), 26–54 • H. Sydney and others, *Letters and memorials of state*, ed. A. Collins, 2 vols. (1746) • V. A. Rowe, 'The influence of the earls of Pembroke on parliamentary elections, 1625–41', *EngHR*, 50 (1935), 242–56 • [T. Birch and R. F. Williams], eds., *The court and times of Charles the First*, 2 vols. (1848) • T. Cogswell, *The blessed revolution: English politics and the coming of war, 1621–1624* (1989) • C. Russell, *Parliaments and English politics, 1621–1629* (1979) • R. P. Cust, *The forced loan and English politics, 1626–1628* (1987) • R. E. Ruigh, *The parliament of 1624: politics and foreign policy* (1971) • R. Zaller, *The parliament of 1621: a study in constitutional conflict* (1971) • D. Lloyd, *State worthies* (1769), 917–19 • *Hist. U. Oxf.* 4: 17th-cent. Oxf. • J. D. Wilson, *An introduction to the sonnets of Shakespeare for the use of historians and others* (1964) • M. Wroth, *The poems of Lady Mary Wroth*, ed. J. Roberts (1983) • J. Rushworth, *Historical collections*, new edn, 1 (1721), 456 • M. Wroth, *The first part of the countess of Montgomery's Urania*, ed. J. Roberts (1995) • T. Lever, *The Herberts of Wilton* (1967)
Archives Berkeley Castle, Gloucestershire, letter to lord Berkley • PRO, lord chamberlain's papers • PRO, state papers, domestic
Likenesses I. Oliver, miniature, 1611, Folger • A. Blijenberch, oils, 1617, Powis Castle, Powys • P. van Somer, oils, 1617, Royal Collection • H. Le Sueur, bronze statue, Bodl. Oxf. • D. Mytens, oils, Wilton House, Wiltshire; versions, NPG, Audley End House, Essex • A. Van Dyck, oils, Wilton House, Wiltshire [*see illus.*]
Wealth at death common talk asserted that he had £80,000 in debts: Birch, *Court and times of Charles the First*, 73

Herbert [Harbert], **William** (1583?–1628), poet and adventurer, was born in Glamorgan, the son of Nicholas Herbert (1543–1601), writer, pirate, merchant, and public official, and either his first wife, Mary Morgan, or his second wife, Catherine or Jennett Herbert (*née* Edward). He attended Eton College as a servitor during 1598–1600 and he matriculated '*arm. fil.*' (that is, esquire's son) at Christ Church, Oxford, on 17 October 1600, though he was in residence from March onward, and remained for most of 1601. Following a prenuptial settlement in 1601 Herbert married Blanche Morgan, the daughter of Catherine Morgan of Llanrumney, a widow, in April 1602. In 1603 he was placed in attendance upon Prince Henry as groom of the privy chamber extraordinary, apparently for a period of twelve months. In that same year, upon reaching legal age, he inherited the administration of his estates. Throughout his adulthood he was an apparent conformist in religion, as attested by extant signed oaths.

The first of Herbert's two major publications, both of them extended mytho-historical poems, was *A Prophesie of Cadwallader, Last King of the Britaines* (1604), which has won critical favour over the years. Written in part to celebrate James I's accession, *Cadwallader* traces his lineage to ancient times, relying heavily (though without acknowledgement) on George Owen Harry's *Genealogy of the High and Mighty Monarch, James* (1604). In 1605 either he or his uncle William Herbert (d. 1609) wrote the commendatory poem 'In Laudem Authoris' as a preface to *The French Garden* by Peter Erondell (Pierre Erondelle), a friend of the young poet's father and uncle. In 1606 appeared Herbert's second major work, *Englands Sorrowe, or, A Farewell to Essex*, which had been entered in the Stationers' register on 30 April 1605 as *Honors epitaphes, or, The lamentation of Brittaine, for the untimely loss of many worthy late personages*, and the abbreviated headline, *Honors Epitaphs*, appears at the top of each page.

Verse that is plausibly attributable to Herbert includes two poems in *England's Helicon* (1600, 1614), 'Wodenfrides Song in Praise of Amargana' and 'Another of the Same'; the bawdy 'To the Uncapable Reader' that prefaces Robert Anton's *Moriomachia* (1613); and two commendatory poems written for William Browne's *Brittania Pastorals* (1625). Herbert is clearly a Spenserian, yet he also demonstrates (and acknowledges) indebtedness to Drayton, Daniel, and Chapman. In 1613 his friend William Gamage published a laudatory epigram on Herbert and *Cadwallader* in *Linsi-Woolsie*; this also contains an epigram on Herbert's father that provides the otherwise vanished information that Nicholas Herbert was the author of *Lle y Kymero*, now presumably lost. During his period as a poet Herbert lived with his wife at Llanrumney; they moved from there to his seat at St Fagans where they lived until 1616. (Herbert's other principal seat was Cogan Pill; both these properties came down to him from his father.) In 1607 he was under sheriff for Monmouthshire. A son, William, was born in 1609 (d. 1638).

In 1616 Herbert sold St Fagans to raise investment cash for Ralegh's doomed expedition to Guiana in search of goldmines. (He knew Ralegh through the Gamages of Coety, including the epigrammatist William.) Herbert financed a quarter of this venture, in the amount of £1200, much of the rest being an investment by Lady Ralegh herself, and Herbert apparently contributed several hundred pounds more upon Ralegh's subsequent request. In 1617, after also investing in a voyage to America by the *Flying Harte*, he left with Ralegh for Guiana, where, among other misadventures, he nearly lost his life in a gunfight during the final, failed assault on the supposed mine site. Ralegh wrote of 'my cosen Herbert' that he was 'a very valiant and honest gentleman' and 'of singular courage' (*Letters of Sir Walter Ralegh*, ed. A. Latham and J. Youings, 1999, 349, 352). Herbert and Ralegh sailed back separately in 1618, with

Herbert commanding a shipload of dissident Guiana veterans, whom Ralegh termed 'scumme' (ibid., 352), at his despairing commander's behest.

Upon his return Ralegh was placed under a sort of house arrest in the custody of Sir Lewis Stucley. Knowing he was headed for the block, he made a feebly conceived attempt to escape on 19 August. Herbert betrayed Ralegh in this attempt, and in fact he and two others had apparently conspired with Stucley to lead Ralegh into the escape, in order to give James yet another pretext for executing the popular old hero. On 17 September Herbert betrayed Ralegh yet again by turning king's evidence in his testimony, contradicting and discrediting Ralegh on key points (BL, Harleian MS 6846, fol. 16). On 4 October Ralegh insisted as a matter of honour that Lady Ralegh pay Herbert what was properly owed him on his investment in the Guiana voyage from her own returns (*Letters of Sir Walter Ralegh* ed. A. Latham and J. Youings, 1999, 371–2), but following the execution she baulked at doing so—most likely because she knew of Herbert's betrayals. She got most of her own money back from the government (which had confiscated the ship *Destiny*), but Herbert was given a minimal £700 award that was detained in the exchequer owing to a claim against it, and it is unclear whether he was ever repaid. In 1619–20 he invested in an elaborate scheme to export Welsh butter by sea, and in 1620 he purchased a house in Gosfield, Essex, where his family later moved from Cogan Pill to join him. A 1624 document reports him as involved in 'outlawry' (NL Wales, Bute L2/57) and he was in Newgate prison in 1625. Three years later he was lodged in king's bench, Southwark, apparently for debt, and he died either there or in Cardiff on 20 November 1628.

Care must be taken in order to distinguish this William Herbert from his several contemporaries who bore the same name, most of them his kinsmen, some of them also writers, and with all of whom he has been understandably confused in one way or another by researchers. Among these are his uncle Sir William Herbert of Swansea (*d.* 1609); his first cousin William Herbert of White Friars (*d.* 1645); William Herbert, first Baron Powis, sometimes styled 'of the Red Castle', his second cousin once removed; William Herbert, third earl of Pembroke (1580–1630), another second cousin once removed; Sir William Herbert of St Julian's (*d.* 1593), his third cousin once removed; William Herbert of Coldbrook, his distant cousin but near-contemporary; his own son William Herbert (1609–1638); the William Herbert (*fl.* 1634–1662) who wrote various religious and 'self-help' manuals; and the W. Har. who published the funeral poem *Epicedium* (1594).

LEO DAUGHERTY

Sources NL Wales, Bute A10/237; C21; D1/3; D1/5; D1/13; D77/1, 35; D260/5–6, 8; L2/35, 57; L3/5–6, 9–16, 34–5, 56, 77, 81, 85, 86 · inquisition post mortem, PRO, C42/447/57 · *CSP dom., 1619–23*, 428; 1628, 589 · *APC, 1619–21*, 177 · Christ Church Oxf., SM: D.P. ia.1, fol. 110 · Christ Church Oxf., SM: X(2) C.36.37 · matriculation register, 1564–1614, Oxf. UA, SP/Reg P · subscription register, 1581–1615, Oxf. UA, SP/38/Reg.A6 · 'The examination of William Herbert, esq., taken before the lords at Whitehall', BL, Harley MS 6846, fol. 16 · T. Birch, ed., *The life of Henry, prince of Wales* (1760) · G. T. Clark, *Limbus patrum Morganiae et Glamorganiae* (1886) · HoP, *Commons, 1558–1603* ·

J. Haslewood, *British bibliography* (1810), vol. 1 · *An inventory of the ancient monuments in Glamorgan*, 4/1: *Domestic architecture from the Reformation to the industrial revolution, the greater houses*, Royal Commission on Ancient and Historical Monuments in Wales and Monmouthshire (1981), 4, pt 1 · J. H. Matthews, ed., *Cardiff records: being materials for a history of the county borough from the earliest times*, 6 vols. (1898–1911), vol. 6 · T. Nicholas, *Annals and antiquities of the counties and county families of Wales*, 2 (1872) · W. Sterry, ed., *The Eton College register, 1441–1698* (1943) · G. Williams, ed., *Glamorgan county history*, 4: *Early modern Glamorgan* (1974) · *The Carl H. Pforzheimer library: English literature, 1475–1700* (1940), vol. 1 · W. R. Williams, *The parliamentary history of the principality of Wales* (privately printed, Brecknock, 1895) · W. Rees, *Cardiff: a history of the city* [1962] · M. Brennan, *Literary patronage in the English Renaissance: the Pembroke family* (1988) · DNB · A. B. Grosart, *The poems of William Harbert of Glamorgan* (1870), vol. 1 of *Miscellanies of the Fuller Worthies Library in four volumes* · wards, 7/38/138 · admin. book, 1603, PRO, PROB 6/6, fol. 146 · Chancery records

Archives BL, Harley MS 6846, fol. 16 | NL Wales, Bute MSS, letters and papers
Wealth at death seemingly bankrupt: probate, 1630, NL Wales, Bute D260/5–6 · some effects: NL Wales, Bute D/13 · PRO, C 142/447/57

Herbert, William (*fl. c.*1606–1662), translator and author of religious tracts, was born at 'Margis in Flanders', the son of Andrew Herbert the younger (HLRO, naturalization of William Herbert, 1620/21). His great-grandfather James Herbert had settled in Calais where his son Andrew the elder became an alderman and justice of the peace. With the fall of Calais in 1558, the family fled to Flanders, where his father was later executed for his protestant beliefs when William was still young. Herbert returned to England and about 1606 joined the Dutch congregation in London, being listed with the merchant members in 1617. However, in 1640 he was employed as tutor to the two sons of Montague Bertie, second earl of Lindsey.

On 27 April 1635, Herbert married Frances Sedgwicke, at Poyntington, Somerset, where they lived; they had three children, John (buried 1637), Elizabeth (*bap.* 1639), and Benjamin (*b.* 1645). His religious writings were initially intended for his family and underlined his Reformed beliefs: *Herberts Beleefe and Confession of Faith made … for the Instruction of his Wife and Children* (1646); *Herberts Careful Father and Pious Child* (1648) to instruct his daughter in the catechism; and for his wife a devotional work for women in childbirth, *Herberts Child-Bearing Woman*, which was published after her death. He seems to have returned to London a couple of years after his wife's death in March 1645. He maintained his links with the exile churches, dedicating *Herberts Quadripartit Devotion* (1648) to the pastors, elders, and deacons of the French and Dutch churches, presenting a copy to the Dutch church for which he received 20*s.* He attacked the rival French church at Westminster in his *Response aux Questions de Mr. Despagne* (1657) and defended the exile communities in his *Considerations in the Behalf of Foreiners* (1662).

Herbert translated religious manuals; *La malette de David* by Daniel Featley was published in Geneva in 1650. He also published French language works such as the fourth edition, 'exactly corrected, much amplifi'd and better ordered', of Paul Cogneau's *A Sure Guide to the French Tongue* in 1658 and in 1660 *Herberts French and English Dialogues*. His publishing was delayed by illness in 1660; the last reference to him is the dedication in *Considerations in the Behalf of Foreiners* dated 18 June 1662 at the Charterhouse, London.   ANDREW SPICER

Sources W. Herbert, *Herberts beleefe and confession of faith*, 2nd edn, 1648 (1646) • W. Herbert, *Herberts quadripartit devotion* (1648) • W. Herbert, *Herberts careful father and pious child* (1648) • W. Herbert, *Herberts child-bearing woman* (1648) • W. Herbert, *Considerations in the behalf of foreiners* (1662) • W. Herbert, *Herberts French and English dialogues* (1660) • W. Herbert, *Response aux Questions de Mr. Despagne* (1657) • naturalization of William Herbert, 1620/21, HLRO • parish register, Poyntington, Somerset, 1618–1713, Dorset RO, PE/POY: RE1/1 • R. E. G. Kirk and E. F. Kirk, eds., *Returns of aliens dwelling in the city and suburbs of London, from the reign of Henry VIII to that of James I*, Huguenot Society of London, 10/3 (1907), 150 • *Third report*, HMC, 2 (1872), appx, pp. 3–36, esp. 19 [House of Lords]

Herbert, William, styled first marquess of Powis and Jacobite first duke of Powis (*c*.1626–1696), Jacobite courtier, was the only son and heir of Percy *Herbert, second Baron Powis (1598–1667), and his wife, Elizabeth (*bap*. 1600, *d*. 1662), daughter of Sir William *Craven (*c*.1545–1618), sometime lord mayor of London. He was educated privately in his youth, possibly at home at Powis Castle. The Herbert family were Roman Catholics who espoused the royalist cause during the civil war; some of their estates were subsequently confiscated and others were sold to pay parliamentary fines levied against them. Lord Powis received scant reward for his services following the Restoration, but his son eventually gained the favour of Charles II. He succeeded to his father's title on 19 January 1667 and on 4 April 1674 received an earldom. His religion, however, debarred him from a very active place in politics. Although he owned large estates in Wales and the marches, for example, he held no office—even that of justice of the peace—during Charles II's reign. As one of a handful of Roman Catholic peers, and among the highest-ranking, Powis was from the beginning a target of the manufacturers of the Popish Plot. According to Titus Oates, the pope intended Powis to be lord treasurer of the government that would seize power after the king's assassination. He was also accused of planning to restore the monasteries and to subject England to papal domination. Parliament impeached him and four other Catholic lords, and on 25 October 1678 all five went to the Tower, where Powis would remain until February 1684, although his confinement did not prevent him from attacking his opponents. In May 1679 an armed mob invaded his London home at midnight, searching for Roman Catholic traitors.

Powis seems to have been the author of *Some Reflections upon the Earl of Danby, in Relation to the Murther of Sir Edmundbury Godfrey*. Danby, he argued, wanted Godfrey dead because he feared that his own role in the Popish Plot might be revealed. The theory was far fetched, but no more so than the one peddled by Oates. Printed by a London Catholic bookseller in 1679 and distributed clandestinely, the pamphlet accused Danby of orchestrating the murder. Powis's wife, Elizabeth (*c*.1633–1691), daughter of Edward *Somerset, second marquess of Worcester (*d*. 1667), whom he had married in July 1654, joined in her husband's defence. She too was Catholic, and she published a ballad denouncing the plot:

> The Presbyter has bin so active of late
> To twist himself into the Mysteries of State,
> Giving birth to a Plot to amuse the dark world.
> (E. Herbert, 1)

More significantly, she inflamed popular opinion against her husband and his co-religionists even further with an ill-advised attempt to invent a rival 'Presbyterian Plot'. The so-called Meal-Tub Plot, hatched in conjunction with a Catholic midwife named Elizabeth Cellier, backfired. The two women approached Thomas Dangerfield, hoping he would accuse Shaftesbury and his allies of an assassination conspiracy against Charles II and the duke of York. But while the kingdom was perfectly prepared to believe in a popish plot, a presbyterian one was a different matter. When Dangerfield realized that his 'evidence' against Shaftesbury was going nowhere, he turned upon his erstwhile employers. He accused them of plotting Shaftesbury's murder, as well as of concocting their fictional 'plot'. The countess joined her husband in the Tower on 4 November 1679. Charged with treason, she remained in prison until granted bail on 12 February 1680. In May, sceptical of the evidence presented against her, the Middlesex grand jury refused to indict and she was released. Although parliamentary proceedings against her husband petered out in the same year, not until February 1684 was Powis granted bail, with the dukes of Norfolk and Beaufort, and the earls of Pembroke and Peterborough as sureties. A few months later in October, his troubles increased when his Lincoln's Inn Fields house burnt down. He and his family barely escaped the conflagration, although two page boys were said to have died.

James II's accession reversed Powis's fortunes. In May 1685 parliament formally withdrew his impeachment, and in June 1685 the king assented to a private bill allowing him to rebuild Powis House. More concrete rewards followed. In March 1686 the king granted him a dispensation from the provisions of the Test Act, and in July named him to the privy council. In March 1687 he advanced a step in the peerage, becoming marquess of Powis. James also gave him command of a regiment of foot. Though inexperienced in government, the king gave Powis a great deal of responsibility. He became lord lieutenant of Cheshire and the city of Chester, and deputy lieutenant of Sussex in February 1687. He played an important part in the campaign to regulate the corporations, both as steward and recorder of Denbigh and steward of Shrewsbury, and as a member of the commission which oversaw the wider purge of local government. In June 1688 James made the marchioness his son's governess.

Powis exercised a moderating influence in James's counsels. He had already gained a reputation for tolerance, acting as a patron to Quakers in trouble with the law. He hoped to limit the enthusiasm of the more headstrong Catholics around the king such as Father Petre and the earl of Tyrconnell, but had little success. When regulating the corporations, he spoke out against the bullying tactics of some of his fellow commissioners. The earl of Ailesbury said that he urged James to name Powis lord lieutenant of Ireland instead of Tyrconnell, a suggestion the king rejected, alleging that Powis had 'a very weak head' (*Memoirs of … Ailesbury*, 1.148). Weak-headed or not, Powis remained conspicuously loyal to James. His prominence insured that in the revolution he would again be the target of the mob, and in December 1688 Powis House narrowly escaped demolition thanks to the intervention of the militia.

Powis accompanied his master to St Germain in late 1688, and on 12 January 1689 os James granted him a dukedom, which was never recognized in England. He headed the list of Jacobites whom parliament planned to attaint for treason in the summer of 1689. Although this bill never passed, in February 1690 he was outlawed and his lands seized. Some of these went to William III's Dutch favourite, the earl of Rochford, including the family seat Powis Castle. Powis House went to Lord Somers. The marquess's son William *Herbert, Viscount Montgomery (later second marquess of Powis and Jacobite second duke of Powis) (1657x61–1745), was jailed in the Tower as a Jacobite and fought a long battle in the courts to retain some of his property, resulting in the restoration of his family's estates and the marquessate in 1722.

In 1690 Powis landed in Ireland with James, where he acted as one of his principal advisers. James appointed him to his Irish privy council and made him lord chamberlain. He remained in Ireland until the king's flight back to France after the battle of the Boyne, and settled again at St Germain. Powis was a prominent figure in the Jacobite court, serving as lord steward and lord chamberlain of the household, but he seems to have been rather marginal in the king's counsels. The marchioness continued as royal governess until her death on 11 March 1691 os, and James made Powis knight of the Garter in April 1692. Nevertheless others exercised more influence at court as Powis struggled to maintain the dignity of a royal household on an insufficient income. Having lost estates valued at £10,000 a year, he had given up more than most for the Jacobite cause. He died, aged about seventy, on 12 July 1696 NS, after a riding accident in St Germain, and was buried there the next day. His son William succeeded to his titles. His daughter, Lady Lucy *Herbert followed her parents' religious bent and became the prioress of St Augustine, Bruges.   VICTOR STATER

Sources GEC, *Peerage* · N. Luttrell, *A brief historical relation of state affairs from September 1678 to April 1714*, 6 vols. (1857) · *The manuscripts of the House of Lords*, 4 vols., HMC, 17 (1887–94), vols. 1–2 · *Calendar of the manuscripts of the marquess of Ormonde*, new ser., 8 vols., HMC, 36 (1902–20), vol. 4 · *The manuscripts of Sir William Fitzherbert … and others*, HMC, 32 (1893) · *CSP dom.*, 1676–7; 1683; 1686–9; 1691–3 · *The manuscripts of the duke of Leeds*, HMC, 22 (1888) · W. Herbert, earl of Powis, *Some reflections upon the earl of Danby* (1679) · E. Herbert, countess of Powis, *A ballad upon the Popish Plot* (1679) · *Memoirs of Thomas, earl of Ailesbury*, ed. W. E. Buckley, 2 vols., Roxburghe Club, 122 (1890)
Archives BL, household accounts, Add. MS 38864 · NL Wales, papers

Likenesses oils, 1675, Powis Castle, Powys

Herbert, William, second marquess of Powis and Jacobite second duke of Powis (1657x61–1745), Jacobite sympathizer, was the only son of William *Herbert, styled first marquess of Powis and Jacobite first duke of Powis (c.1626–1696), and Lady Elizabeth (d. 1691), younger daughter of Edward *Somerset, second marquess of Worcester. He was known as Lord Herbert from 1674 to 1687, and as Viscount Montgomery from 1687 to 1690, and afterwards, informally. He was a trainbearer to James II at his coronation. In May 1685 he married Mary (d. 1724), elder daughter and coheir of Sir Thomas Preston, bt, of Furness, Lancashire; six of the couple's children, two sons and four daughters, reached adulthood. Having gained experience at the siege of Buda, Montgomery was appointed on 8 May 1687 colonel of an infantry regiment taken from his protestant cousin Charles, marquess of Worcester. He was a deputy lieutenant of the twelve Welsh counties and Monmouthshire from 26 February until December 1688. At the revolution of 1688 his regiment garrisoned Hull; but on the night of 3 December the protestant officers seized the fortress and him. Soon released, Montgomery crossed with William's pass of 25 December to France, but returned before war was declared, largely to defend the family estates at law against government confiscation—unsuccessfully.

Montgomery's Jacobite activity was concentrated in London rather than Wales. He was imprisoned in the Tower from 6 May to 7 November 1689. Named in a proclamation of 14 July 1690, he escaped capture. That autumn James appointed a committee to manage his affairs, the Select Number (BL, Add. MS 47608, fols. 120, 165v), comprising four Anglican tories and two moderate Catholic peers' sons, Montgomery and Lord Brudenell. Montgomery's main correspondent was Mary of Modena; his code names included Mr Thompson, Mr Mun, and William Sibson. In March 1692 James appointed him colonel of a cavalry regiment for the rising to accompany the invasion from La Hogue, which he secretly recruited. From 1693, in Jacobite disputes over policy, the Select Number were the leaders of the 'non-compounders', who opposed major constitutional concessions by James and called for a French invasion. Montgomery's draft survives for their memorial of 21 February 1694 declaring that 20,000 troops would suffice, and he lukewarmly supported Robert Charnock's 1695 mission to France. For the latter treason, a proclamation of 23 March 1696 offered £500 rewards for him and Sir John Fenwick, both then in hiding, and on 27 May he was indicted. Succeeding his attainted father in July, he remained legally a commoner until 1722. He ignored advice to escape overseas, conscious that if he were outlawed the 1695 grant of the family estates to the earl of Rochford would become virtually irreversible. On 15 December 1696 Montgomery surrendered and was committed to Newgate. Some Williamites, who claimed that he already was outlawed, found that the sheriffs of London had omitted necessary formalities. According to Thomas, earl of Ailesbury, William pressed the sheriffs to falsify the record. Montgomery was bailed on 17 June 1697, only because gaol fever made Newgate unsafe.

Refused a licence to remain in England under the act 9 Wm III c. 1, Montgomery crossed in February 1698 to Flanders. The holy Roman emperor interceded for him as head of the English lay Catholics, but Rochford's influence prevailed. He settled at Ghent and avoided visiting France (except Paris in 1701, while the Jacobite court was at Bourbon), though educating his sons there under aliases. Rochford, still unable to obtain full possession, finally sold back the estates. Powis (as he was generally known) returned to England in May 1703. He immediately resumed his father's alterations at Powis Castle and constructed its terrace gardens. Having sold old Powis House to the duke of Newcastle in 1705 for £7000, he built a new Powis House in Great Ormond Street, London. Leased in 1712 to the French ambassador, the duc d'Aumont, it mysteriously burned down on 26 January 1713, but Louis XIV paid for an even more palatial rebuilding. From 1705 onwards Powis petitioned the government to reverse his father's outlawry. He therefore avoided Jacobite activity, though his female relatives later became slightly involved. Nevertheless, during the rising of 1715 he was imprisoned in the Tower from September 1715 to May 1716. A Francophile, he spent the next decade largely in France.

Powis's eldest child, Lady Mary *Herbert (1686–1775), a pioneer female international speculator and entrepreneur, dominated him, and brought their semi-princely family to ruin in Europe's uncharted new financial markets. In 1718 Lord Panmure (and, obliquely, she herself) suggested her as a possible bride for the Pretender. During 1719 her speculations in French Mississippi Company shares made her a *millionaire* on paper. She rejected the future duc de Bouillon's proposal, though the regent and, it seems, Powis supported it—apparently determined to wed either a reigning prince, as Pope's 'Epistle to Bathurst' implies, or her fellow *millionaire* Joseph Gage. In 1720 she undertook, and drew her father and brothers into, even vaster speculations on borrowed money. The collapse of John Law's system left them liable for most of her French and English debts of over £170,000. Powis was briefly imprisoned for debt in Paris, and his elder son, William, then Lord Montgomery (1688–1748), in London. They were never again free, despite a 1726 estates settlement, from bailiffs, lawsuits, and the need for financial trickery. Only the rich lead mines which Powis had since 1705 developed at Llangynog, Montgomeryshire, and now exploited oppressively to exhaustion, averted total ruin. The family split apart: his sons denounced Powis's continuing trust in Lady Mary's incorrigible overoptimism. He largely financed her and Gage in their unscrupulous and varied counter-suits against their main creditor, Richard Cantillon, and in their mining operations in Spain.

In 1722 Powis finally had his father's outlawry reversed, recovering the marquessate and, formally, his estates. Jacobites styled him duke of Powis, and he prepared but did not press a legal statement claiming that title. He was summoned to parliament on 8 October 1722 but, as a Catholic, never sat. Although he briefly considered a protestant match for Lord Montgomery he did not convert to Anglicanism, as several Catholic general histories assumed. Yet he took little part in Catholic national affairs or Welsh tory politics. He died between 20 and 22 October 1745 at his house in Frith Street, Soho, and was buried on 28 October at Hendon, the family's Middlesex estate. His will and trusts bequeathed £4000 to Catholic charities and missions, partly to honour belatedly his father's will.

Powis's estranged elder son, William, third marquess, died unmarried. He unexpectedly left his estates to his cousin Henry Arthur, Lord Herbert of Cherbury, a protestant and aggressive whig, immediately created earl of Powis: one motive was to preserve Powis Castle. The bequest virtually extinguished Montgomeryshire Catholicism. The younger son, Lord Edward Herbert (d. 1734), had married Henrietta, daughter of his formerly Catholic schoolfellow James, first Earl Waldegrave, and left a posthumous daughter, Barbara. To forestall her possible rival claim, the earl of Powis gained custody with Lady Mary's bribed assistance, and married her in 1751.

Paul Hopkins

Sources NL Wales, Powis Castle papers · PRO, Powis MSS, PRO 30/53 · wills and trusts, PRO, C 54/5739, C54/5786, PROB 31/267/936 · 'Herbertiana', *Montgomeryshire Collections*, 5 (1871–2), 153–98, 353–92; 9 (1875–6), 381–402; 11 (1877–8), 341–72; 18 (1884–5), 119–30, 353–92; 19 (1885–6), 81–96 · 'Herbert manuscripts at Powis Castle', *Montgomeryshire Collections*, 20 (1886–7), 81–282 · W. J. Smith, ed., *Herbert correspondence* (1963) [almost entirely extracts from NL Wales and PRO collections] · C. Rowell, *Powis Castle, Powys*, rev. edn, rev. J. Gallagher (1996) [National Trust guidebook] · A. E. Murphy, *Richard Cantillon, entrepreneur and economist* (1986) · M. Murphy, 'Maria's dreams: Lady Mary Herbert, 1685–1775', *Montgomeryshire Collections*, 85 (1997), 87–100 · M. Murphy, 'Maria's dreams: the reckoning', *Montgomeryshire Collections*, 86 (1998), 65–80 · Sir John Fenwick's confessions, 1696, *JHC*, 11 (1693–7), 557–9 · *Memoirs of Thomas, earl of Ailesbury*, ed. W. E. Buckley, 2 vols., Roxburghe Club, 122 (1890) [Jacobite colleagues] · J. Macpherson, ed., *Original papers, containing the secret history of Great Britain*, 2 vols. (1775) · P. A. Hopkins, 'Aspects of Jacobite conspiracy in England in the reign of William III', PhD diss., U. Cam., 1981 · *CSP dom.* · PRO, SP 35/75 · N. Luttrell, *A brief historical relation of state affairs from September 1678 to April 1714*, 6 vols. (1857) · A. Pope, 'Epistle III: to Allen Lord Bathurst', *Epistles to several persons*, ed. F. W. Bateson (1951) · *Calendar of the Stuart papers belonging to his majesty the king, preserved at Windsor Castle*, 7 vols., HMC, 56 (1902–23), vols. 1, 3, 7 · *Report on the manuscripts of Allan George Finch*, 5 vols., HMC, 71 (1913–2003), vol. 2 · *Calendar of the manuscripts of the marquis of Bath preserved at Longleat, Wiltshire*, 5 vols., HMC, 58 (1904–80), vol. 3 · *The manuscripts of the earl of Buckinghamshire, the earl of Lindsey … and James Round*, HMC, 38 (1895) · *Miscellanea, VI*, Catholic RS, 7 (1909) · R. Hill, letters to J. Vernon, 1698–9, BL, Add MS 4199 · papal transcripts, CUL, Add MS 4879, fol. 508 · C. Cole, *Historical and political memoirs* (1735), 387 · Powis to [earl of Dysart], 29 Jan 1723, BL, Add MS 23251, fol. 62 · GEC, *Peerage* · PRO, DEL 2/65/1/543 · D. Lysons, *The environs of London*, 4 vols. (1792–6), vol. 3, p. 15

Archives NL Wales, Powis Castle archive (PC) · PRO, Powis MSS, 30/53 | BL, Caryll MSS

Likenesses group portrait, engraving (James II's coronation), repro. in F. Sandford, *The history of the coronation of … James II …* (1687), pl. 18 · oils, Coughton Court, Warwickshire

Herbert, William (1718–1795), bibliographer and printseller, was born on 29 November 1718, the second of

William Herbert (1718–1795), by William Say, pubd 1809

five children of Thomas Herbert (c.1691–1721), a dyer and hosier of Gravel Lane, Southwark, and his wife, Sarah (d. 1748). His parents were Londoners and Presbyterians. What is known of his first thirty years derives from Richard Gough's obituary of him in the *Gentleman's Magazine*, namely that he was educated at Hitchin, went to India in 1738 with a cargo of pepper, as purser's clerk to three of the East India Company's ships; was stranded at Tellicherry, and, after a series of misadventures, returned to London about 1745; that, on his return, the East India Company paid him £300 for his drawings of 'plans of the several settlements' (*GM*, 65/1, 262) which he had seen on his Indian travels, which were later published. While in India he adopted Indian costume and grew his beard. He was 'in person, rather below the middle stature; stout, and inclined to corpulency. His complexion was fair … his physiognomy remarkable for an expression of sweetness and benevolence' (Dibdin, 1.87). Among his small eccentricities was that of always using lower case 'i' when writing in the first person.

Herbert was freed by patrimony at Drapers' Hall as a dyer on 16 November 1748. Gough states that he abandoned his trade of hosiery and dyeing, and learned the art of painting on glass. There was a tradition of print engraving and selling in the Drapers' Company, and, combining his alleged experience as traveller, draughtsman, and glass painter, and with contacts in the trade and among nautical men, Herbert set up in one of ten newly built houses on London Bridge in 1749 as a seller and publisher of prints, maps, and charts. He bound and later freed two apprentices at Drapers' Hall—John Pace (bound 3 August

1751) and Thomas Wright (bound 20 July 1756). Having witnessed a number of fires on the banks of the Thames, Herbert suggested to Captain Hill of the Royal Exchange Assurance that there should be a floating fire-engine, and published a proposal in *The Gazetteer*; his plan was later adopted. When London Bridge caught fire in 1758 Herbert had the initiative to publish *A chronological and historical account from the first building a bridge across the River Thames, from London to Southwark, till the late conflagration of the temporary bridge* (1758).

Herbert moved from the bridge in 1759 (the bridge houses were pulled down between 1758 and 1762), first to Leadenhall Street. In 1765 he took a house at 27 Goulston Square, Whitechapel, where he continued to publish and issue lists of books, maps, and charts for sale. In 1773 he bought a country residence in Albury Lane, Cheshunt, Hertfordshire, and added a library wing, where he used to sit, wearing a white hat, 'under a circular skylight, in the intervening period between each meal' (Dibdin, 1.75). Being then fifty-eight years old, having succeeded in business and made three lucrative marriages, he retired from trade, still keeping the Goulston Square address until 1776 when he sold off his stock and his chart and printselling business to Henry Gregory for 1000 guineas. He continued to reissue his publications and at the end of his life he sold part of his library through his nephew Isaac.

While he was still living on the bridge Herbert published the first edition of William Nichelson's *Sundry Remarks and Observations Made in a Voyage to the East Indies* (1758) and Nichelson's *A New Directory of the East-Indies with General and Particular Charts for the Navigation of those Seas* (1758). He reissued the latter in 1759, 'with additions, corrections, and explanatory notes … printed for the editor' which started him on a method of publishing which combined business acumen with his love of research and book collecting. He would acquire the stock, copyright, and blocks of a work, then, incorporating new material, publish a greatly improved edition. Thus he annotated an interleaved copy of the 1765 edition of the *New Directory* (which was sold in 1798 after his death) and his writing and editorial career began to take off. The *New Directory* and *Sundry Remarks* published as one work went into a further four editions between 1759 and 1780. In 1765 he bought up the remaining stock and plates of Sir Robert Atkyns's history of Gloucestershire (1712), most of which had been destroyed in a fire at William Bowyer's printing office.

Herbert married three times; nothing is known of his first marriage, said to have taken place while he lived on London Bridge, nor of the second, allegedly to a niece of Thomas Newman, a dissenting minister in the City, 'a woman of weak intellect' (*DNB*) who brought him a good jointure. His last wife was Philippa Croshold (d. 1808) who came from a prosperous Norfolk family with connections among the antiquarian circle who included several of Herbert's friends. She, too, brought him a useful fortune.

Herbert began to be active in the Drapers' Company after he was admitted to the livery in 1763; he was elected to the court of assistants and made junior warden on 26

September 1781 and progressed up the court until he became master warden on 7 October 1792. He was punctual in his court attendances until six weeks before he died, shortly before being due to be elected master. His thriving trade and City connections took him to Stationers' Hall, where he bound his nephew Isaac, son of his deceased brother Thomas, apprentice to the bookseller Samuel Hayes on 4 September 1787 with the very large premium of 100 guineas.

A heraldic book-plate, dated 1745 and engraved by John June, marks the start of Herbert's book collecting, and probably his return from India. He rarely used it, however, preferring to write his name or initials in his books. In 1760 he bought Joseph Ames's interleaved and annotated copy of the *Typographical Antiquities, being an Historical Account of the Origin and Progress of Printing in Great Britain* (1749) from Sir Peter Thompson who had acquired it at Ames's posthumous sale for £9, together with the copyright, plates, and blocks. Herbert seems to have intended the kind of revision that had been so successful and satisfying with the *New Directory*; he thought to present 'the lovers of science' with a republication of Ames 'with the author's own improvements' in the interleaved copy 'and what further could be collected from my own observations, and those of my learned friends' (Herbert, 'Preface', 1.vi). In the event, the purchase revolutionized his life.

With Ames's work as a guide Herbert set systematically to work to fill the gaps in his collection of bibles and blackletter books. His livery company and East India Company connections, and the print and chart dealing, brought him into the centre of a bibliophilic and bibliographical coterie. Surviving correspondence shows that after 1760 he increasingly mixed business with pleasure, book hunting for friends who were also customers or fellow dealers, borrowing books, and, after 1774, offering hospitality at Cheshunt to other learned gentlemen with whom he corresponded. He was given free access to libraries which included that of the king, George III, and the great public collections at Oxford, Cambridge, and Lambeth. Whereas Joseph Ames had failed to gain entrance to the Stationers' Company, Herbert dined in their hall and through the good offices of his friend, the bookseller Lockyer Davis, was permitted not only to see, but to borrow, the three earliest volumes of their jealously guarded entry books and apprentice registers which he meticulously copied out. His transcriptions, which are now in the muniment room at Stationers' Hall, provided key material for his revision of Ames's *Typographical Antiquities*, which transformed it into the first history of the sixteenth-century English book trade and a major, even seminal work on English book provenance.

Herbert was an enthusiastic scholar: 'it was his custom to come to town' from Cheshunt 'for a week or ten days during moonlight nights' to take 'extracts from Caxtonian volumes in His Majesty's library' (Dibdin, 1.88), then to attend Drapers' Company courts, and the posthumous sales of those volumes whose 'owners had given me free access during their lives' (Herbert, 'Preface', 1.vi). In

1780 Herbert printed proposals for a two-volume edition of Ames but five years passed before the first volume of this edition appeared in 1785; volume two came in 1786 and three in 1790. Herbert was still at work at the time of his death and his own interleaved and annotated copy in six volumes eventually came into T. F. Dibdin's hand and is now in the British Library. Dibdin's typographically imposing reissue of Ames's work, with a memoir of Herbert and a few biographical notes, has robbed Herbert of the acclaim that should be his. Having expanded Ames's original single volume into three published volumes, Herbert continued to make manuscript additions which expanded his three volumes to six, making his arguably the most valuable of the three editions for study of the sixteenth- and seventeenth-century book trade.

Herbert's collection of some thousands of books ranging from manuscripts and incunabula to contemporary works, which he admitted had 'employed no inconsiderable part of my life and, i may add, my fortune in forming it' (Herbert, 'Preface', 1.vi), rivalled many of the libraries he had used. It was sold by his nephew in three sales during 1796 to 1798, and volumes with his signature or, occasionally, book-plate are to be found in many libraries on both sides of the Atlantic.

Herbert died at his house in Cheshunt on 18 March 1795 and was buried in Cheshunt churchyard. His widow survived him and was bequeathed his house and all contents, except for his books, together with his South Sea stock and annuities.   ROBIN MYERS

Sources *GM*, 1st ser., 65 (1795), 261–2 · Nichols, *Lit. anecdotes*, 5.264–6 · R. Myers, 'Stationers' Company bibliographers: the first 150 years: Ames to Arber', *Pioneers in bibliography*, ed. R. Myers and M. Harris (1988), 40–57, esp. 42–5 · R. Myers, 'William Herbert: his library and his friends', *Property of a gentleman: the formation, organisation and dispersal of the private library, 1620–1920*, ed. R. Myers and M. Harris, St Paul's Bibliographies (1991), 133–59 · *DNB* · J. Ames, T. F. Dibdin, and W. Herbert, eds., *Typographical antiquities, or, The history of printing in England, Scotland and Ireland*, 4 vols. (1810–19), vol. 1, pp. 73–95 · Nichols, *Illustrations*, vols. 4–7 · BL, Herbert MSS · Bodl. Oxf., MSS Herbert · CUL, Herbert MSS · Norfolk RO, Herbert papers · W. Herbert, preface, in J. Ames, *Typographical antiquities, or, An historical account of the origin and progress of printing in Great Britain and Ireland*, ed. W. Herbert, 1 (1785) [annotated copy in BL, C.133.ee.2] · J. Ames, *Typographical antiquities, being an historical account of printing in England* (1749) · W. Herbert, 'Typographical antiquities', notes, transcripts, letters, and book lists, CUL, Add. MSS 3313–3318 · records of the Drapers' Company, Drapers' Hall, London · *Catalogue of the library of William Herbert* (1796) [sale catalogue, Leigh and Sotheby, London, 10 March 1796; Maddon's annotated copy, BL, SCS 28 (7)] · *A catalogue of the entire and curious library of a late well-known collector … removed from his country residence* (1798) [sale catalogue, Mr Postan, London, 2–8 April 1798] · *A catalogue of a choice and valuable library, the property of a gentleman … to which is added the … manuscripts of … the late Mr William Herbert* (1798) [Arrowsmith and Bowley, London, 21 Nov 1798] · rentals and accounts, 1741–65, CLRO, Bridge House accounts, vols. 43–4 · freedom certificate, CLRO · *IGI*

Archives BL, copy of Joseph Ames's annotated *Typographical antiquities* with his MS notes and additions, C.60.0.5 · BL, notebooks relating to history of printing, Add. MS 18202 · BL, notices of early English printers, Egerton MSS 1835–1839 · Bodl. Oxf., account of 'a collection of tracts in black letter printed by Robert

Wyer' · Bodl. Oxf., notes in a copy of the New Testament by John Wycliffe · CUL, papers relating to *Typographical antiquities* · Drapers' Hall, London, index to bindings, redemption register, court minutes · Stationers' Company, Stationers' Hall, London, manuscript notebook transcriptions of 'Book of entries' and of apprentices | Bodl. Oxf., letters to John Price

Likenesses W. Say, mezzotint, pubd 1809, BM, NPG [*see illus.*] · T. Smyth, line engraving, NPG · engraving (William Herbert?), repro. in Dibdin, ed., *Typographical antiquities*, vol. 1 (1810), following introduction

Wealth at death value not given; house at Cheshunt, money at bank, South Sea stock, chattels, large library of books: will, PRO, PROB 11/1259

Herbert, William [*formerly* William Herbert Wilderspin] (1772–1851), antiquary and librarian, was born William Herbert Wilderspin on 18 May 1772 at Worship Street, Curtain Road, Shoreditch, London, the only son of John Wilderspin (c.1717–1781), clockmaker and smith, and his third wife, Elizabeth (Kirby?), who died c.1800. They had six children: William's two elder sisters died in childhood. Samuel *Wilderspin (1791–1866), the promoter of the infant school system, was the son of his stepbrother. The name Herbert came from a godfather; and by the time of his marriage William had ceased to use his father's surname. His memoirs give a vivid description of his early life and work in the theatre. His father died in an accident in 1781, leaving the family in poverty. William earned money by working in the households of such men as the Revd John Newton, a leading evangelical minister and friend of Cowper, and especially by reading to them. He attended briefly a school run by a Baptist clergyman, Thomas Mabbott, and was taught languages, literature, and religious studies by his patrons and associates. He studied palaeography, law Latin, and Norman French while apprenticed to a law stationer, worked for several London solicitors, and developed an interest in London history.

Herbert married Sarah Youens, a professional singer, on 14 July 1795 and they were both engaged to perform at the Bermondsey Spa Gardens in that year. Between 1795 and 1801 they were employed at the Royal Circus, St George's Fields, London, William as an actor of melodrama and singer of popular ballads. From 1796 they lived at numerous addresses in Lambeth, the longest stay being probably at Globe Place, Westminster Bridge Road, near the Marsh Gate (c.1805–1810). They are known to have had two daughters and three sons between 1796 and 1812. In 1801 William became a reader at the Lyceum for the unsuccessful spectacle *Egyptiana*, and then gave up the theatre except for part-time work as a prompter at the New Royal Circus between 1806 and 1812. His wife carried on as a singer with greater success.

After 1801 Herbert concentrated on researching and writing London history and, until about 1815, selling books and prints. His earliest published work was a contribution to Longman's *Annual Review* (1802). Between 1803 and 1805 he worked for the publishers Vernor and Hood compiling a miscellany with Edward Wedlake Brayley, *Syr Reginalde, or, The Black Tower* (1803), editing Thomas Thornton's *Sporting Tour through the North Part of England* (1804),

and writing his first substantial book—*Antiquities of the Inns of Court and Chancery* (1804)—and the descriptions to accompany Storer and Grieg's *Select Views of London and its Environs* (1804–5). He collaborated again with Brayley to publish *A Concise Account … of Lambeth Palace* (1806), which John Britton said was written mostly by Brayley. Aiming at the vogue for prints to extra-illustrate popular topographical works, in 1808 Herbert launched the first number of his own publication, a series of engraved copies of old illustrations of London under the title *Londina illustrata*. The next five numbers were published with Robert Wilkinson, who continued the series alone, adding contemporary views. In 1817–18 Herbert returned to his original scheme with a grandiose and unsuccessful series of prints, *London before the Great Fire*, which failed after the second number.

Herbert gave up his bookselling business to concentrate on historical research and writing, sometimes for others who failed to acknowledge his work. He claimed that he wrote most of John Parton's *Some Account of the Hospital and Parish of St. Giles in the Fields, Middlesex* (1822), and Charles Dawson said that he wrote the text of *History … of Hastings* (1824), credited to the book's illustrator, William George Moss. Through the bookseller Thomas Thorpe, Herbert was employed to study Lord Chichester's archives relating to his land at Hastings (1821–3); he conducted excavations of Hastings Castle in 1824 and compiled an illustrated account which was extensively used by Dawson for his *History of Hastings Castle* (1909).

In 1828, at the age of fifty-six, Herbert acquired a salaried post to which he was admirably suited, on the recommendation of the antiquary William Upcott. He was appointed first librarian of the City of London's Guildhall Library. Primarily concerned with building up the collections on London, he increased the library's stock from about 1700 books to over 10,000, adding numerous prints and drawings, some miscellaneous antiquities, and manuscripts including one of the most notable purchases, the deed signed by William Shakespeare. While librarian, Herbert compiled the catalogue of 1840 and its 1842 supplement, wrote *The Illustrations of the Site and Neighbourhood of the New Post Office* (1830), *The History … of St. Michael Crooked Lane* (1832), and his best-known work, *History of the Twelve Great Livery Companies of London* (1836–7). His memories of the Paternoster Row booksellers were published in W. Pinnock's *Guide to Knowledge* (1834). He resigned through ill health in 1845.

Herbert died of a strangulated hernia on 18 November 1851 at 40 Brunswick Street, Haggerston, Middlesex. His death was reported by his granddaughter Eliza, and he was buried at Nunhead cemetery on 23 November. His *School Education, or, The Young Academical Orator* was published posthumously in 1853.   BERNARD NURSE

Sources D. Dawe and E. W. Padwick, *William Herbert, 1772–1851* (1997) · B. Adams, *London illustrated, 1604–1851* (1983) · C. Dawson, *History of Hastings Castle* (1909) · J. Britton, 'A brief memoir of Edward Wedlake Brayley', *GM*, 2nd ser., 42 (1854), 582–6 · GL, Noble collection · d. cert.

Archives E. Sussex RO, antiquarian notebooks relating to Hastings Castle and Hastings rape · GL, autobiographical papers · Hastings Museum, Hastings Castle excavations | LPL, letters to C. Bedford relating to his book on Lambeth Palace

Herbert, William (1778–1847), classical scholar and Church of England clergyman, was born at Highclere Castle, Hampshire, on 12 January 1778, the third son and fifth child of Henry Herbert, first earl of Carnarvon (1741–1811), and Lady Elizabeth Alicia Maria (1752–1826), eldest daughter of Charles *Wyndham, earl of Egremont. He was educated at Eton College (1790–95), where he edited a volume of poems entitled *Musae Etonenses* in 1795. On leaving Eton he obtained a prize for a Latin poem entitled *Rhenus* which was published; a translation appeared in *Translations of Oxford Prize Poems* (1831). In 1795 Herbert matriculated at Christ Church, Oxford, but soon migrated to Exeter College, where he graduated BA in 1798. Subsequently moving to Merton, he proceeded MA in 1802, BCL in 1808, DCL in 1808, and BD in 1840. Inclining to a political career, he served as MP for Hampshire in 1806–7, after a very expensive campaign, and for Cricklade in 1811–12; he also practised at the bar as a member of Doctors' Commons. On 17 May 1806 he married the Hon. Letitia Emily Dorothea, second daughter of Joshua, fifth Viscount Allen; they had a son, Henry William *Herbert, and three other children.

Soon after retiring from parliament in 1812 Herbert changed course. In 1814 he was ordained, and was nominated to the valuable rectory of Spofforth in the West Riding of Yorkshire. He left Spofforth in 1840 on his promotion to the deanery of Manchester. He died suddenly at his house in Hereford Street, Park Lane, London, on 28 May 1847.

As a classical scholar, a linguist, and a naturalist, Herbert acquired a high reputation. In 1801 he brought out *Ossiani darthula*, a small volume of Greek and Latin poetry. In 1804 he published part 1 of his *Select Icelandic Poetry, Translated from the Originals with Notes*. Part 2 followed in 1806. Both are noteworthy for containing the first adequate illustration of ancient Scandinavian literature to appear in England. Herbert's efforts secured sufficient attention to induce Byron to mention him in his *English Bards and Scotch Reviewers* (1809):

> Herbert shall wield Thor's hammer, and sometimes
> In gratitude thou'lt praise his rugged rhymes.

Other translations from German, Danish, and Portuguese poems, with some miscellaneous English poems (1804), attest Herbert's exceptional command of foreign languages. He continued his literary career with articles of a non-political character in the *Edinburgh Review*. He also wrote a number of narrative poems, including *Helga* (1815); *Hedin, or, The Spectre of the Tomb*, a tale in verse from Danish history (1820); *Pia della pietra* (1820); *Iris*, a Latin ode (1820); and the *Wizard Wanderer of Jutland* (1820–22). *Attila, or, The Triumph of Christianity*, an epic poem in twelve books with a historical preface, came out in 1838, the fruit of many years' labour, and was followed by a final volume of poems, *The Christian*, in 1846.

Early attached to the study of natural history, and a good

shot, Herbert helped J. Rennie to edit White's *Selborne* in 1833, and E. T. Bennett's edition of the work in 1837 was also indebted to him for many notes, particularly on ornithology. For many years he contributed articles to the *Botanical Register* and the *Botanical Magazine*, particularly on the subject of bulbous plants. He cultivated a large number of these plants at Spofforth, Yorkshire, and at Mitcham, Surrey; many have since been lost to cultivation. His standard volume on this group of plants, *Amaryllidaceae*, was issued in 1837, and reprinted in 1966. This important work also provides examples of Herbert's skill as an artist. His 'Crocorum synopsis' appeared in the miscellaneous portion of the *Botanical Register* for 1843-4-5. Extremely valuable contributions on hybridization made by him to the *Journal of the Horticultural Society* in 1846 and 1847 were the outcome of close observation and experiment. He considered hybridization a factor in evolution and his acquaintance with Charles Darwin led to numerous references to his findings in Darwin's *Natural Selection*. His *History of the Species of Crocus*, edited by J. Lindley in 1847, was reprinted separately from the journal just after his death. The genus *Herbertia* of Sweet appropriately commemorates his name. His chief works, including his sermons, reviews, and scientific memoirs, besides his early poetical volumes, appeared in two volumes in 1842.

B. D. JACKSON, *rev.* RICHARD SMAIL

Sources HoP, *Commons* · GM, 2nd ser., 28 (1847), 425–6 · Desmond, *Botanists*, rev. edn · GM, 2nd ser., 19 (1843), 115–33 · R. A. Austen-Leigh, ed., *The Eton College register, 1753–1790* (1921) · Allibone, *Dict.* · DSB · *Gardeners' Chronicle* (10 April 1847), 234 · *Journal of Botany, British and Foreign*, 27 (1889), 83
Archives Royal Horticultural Society, London, letters and drawings | Bodl. Oxf., letters to Richard Heber · RBG Kew, letters to Sir William Jackson Hooker
Likenesses W. Beechey, oils, Eton College, provost's lodgings; repro. in Austen-Leigh, ed., *Eton College register*

Herbertson, Andrew John (1865–1915), geographer, was born on 11 October 1865 at Church Bank, Galashiels, Selkirkshire, the eldest of four children of Andrew Hunter Herbertson, a prosperous building contractor, and Janet Matthewson. He attended Galashiels Academy (1872–9) and the Edinburgh Institution, later Melville College (1879). On leaving school he worked briefly for a firm of surveyors in Edinburgh before matriculating at the University of Edinburgh in 1886. He studied sciences at Edinburgh in 1886–9 and 1891–2 with considerable success, but took no degree. The single greatest influence on him was exerted by Patrick Geddes, whom he met at Edinburgh. In the 1890s he worked enthusiastically with Geddes in Edinburgh and followed him to Dundee as his demonstrator in botany in 1892. He undertook meteorological research in 1892–3 at the Ben Nevis and Fort William observatories which, with further work at Paris and Montpelier, bore fruit in the publication with Alexander Buchan of the important *Atlas of Meteorology* (1899). At the same time he worked on the *Challenger* enterprise which had its offices in Edinburgh. He visited the University of Freiburg-im-Breisgau in 1895 and 1898 and graduated PhD of that university with a dissertation on world rainfall patterns in

1898: the work was published by the Royal Geographical Society (RGS) in 1901.

On 5 October 1893 at 3 North Fort Street, North Leith, according to the rites of the Evangelical Union church, Herbertson married Fanny Louisa Dorothy (1864–1915), classics mistress, daughter of the late John Collingwood Richardson, journalist, and Louisa Moore. Dorothy was a scholar who wrote a biography of Le Play as well as collaborating with her husband in his geographical work. They had one son, Andrew Hunter (1894–1917), and one daughter, Margaret Alice Louise.

Herbertson was lecturer in political and commercial geography at the University of Manchester (1894–6), and from 1896 to 1899 lecturer in industrial and commercial geography at Heriot-Watt College, Edinburgh, during which time he was an active member of the Royal Scottish Geographical Society.

In June 1899 Herbertson went to the newly founded school of geography in Oxford as assistant to the reader (Halford Mackinder, who had personally sought him out after hearing that he had been offered a post in America) and lecturer in regional geography. He stayed at Oxford until his death, succeeding Mackinder as reader in 1905 and being appointed to a personal chair in geography in 1910. On arrival in Oxford he was highly unusual in having a higher degree in geography and an active research interest: yet in Oxford he effectively abandoned research to throw himself into promoting geography in the university, in schools, and among those in professional life. In the university he worked tirelessly, not least because Mackinder was so often preoccupied with other interests. He lectured badly but doggedly, gave countless tutorials, and led numerous field excursions which his pupils remembered warmly. In 1910 he secured money from Abe Bailey, a South African entrepreneur, which allowed the school of geography to rent larger premises at Acland House, Broad Street, in addition to its rooms on the upper floor of the Ashmolean Museum, and to establish a library of colonial geography and history. Though he had abandoned research he did see awarded the first Oxford research degrees in geography (the BSc and BLitt), and was an active member of the RGS's research department from its foundation in 1903 (he had been elected fellow in 1892). Though no explorer himself he encouraged explorers such as Nansen, Shackleton, and Hedin to visit the school.

University geographers, like practitioners of other new disciplines, had to establish their subject in secondary schools to secure it a future at university. Through unremitting work, considerable powers of organization, and genuine enthusiasm Herbertson made a distinguished contribution to school geography. Following Mackinder he organized biennial summer schools at Oxford at which distinguished university teachers from Britain and abroad taught schoolmasters and schoolmistresses in the class and in the field. The schools were inspired by those of Geddes where the Herbertsons had first met, and R. N. Rudmose Brown described the couple during the summer courses:

> Herbertson … the small active man, the eager encouraging teacher, restless, continually at work, never learning to play or rest; or Mrs Herbertson, busy, energetic—even more so than Herbertson, a driving force at the summer schools, always everywhere, keeping everyone up 'to scratch'. (Brown, 107)

More than 850 teachers attended the five schools organized by Herbertson between 1909 and 1914 and the influence he thus exerted on British school geography was immense. The Herbertsons were prolific authors of school textbooks: more than 1.4 million copies of their textbooks were used in the specialist secondary school teaching required under the 1902 Education Act. He produced a new series of wall maps (published 1914–15). He was secretary of the Geographical Association (the professional society for geography teachers) from 1900 to 1915 and founding editor of its journal, *Geographical Teacher*, from 1901 to 1915; he used both roles to argue for more and better geographical education in schools, particularly through field classes and practical work. He successfully argued for the extension of the association's membership, hitherto confined to teachers from public schools, to those from council schools and persuaded the Ordnance Survey to supply sheet maps to schools at reduced cost so that less well funded schools could undertake map work. His patient negotiations won the support of the RGS for the association which might otherwise have seemed a rival.

Herbertson also promoted geography among professional men on imperial service. He organized lectures for Indian Civil Service probationers and taught surveying to probationers for the Egyptian and Sudan civil service. The school of geography provided facilities for colonial civil servants on furlough. Herbertson was concerned about the geographical ignorance of those in positions of influence in the empire. In his presidential address to the geographical section of the British Association for the Advancement of Science in 1910 he suggested that each colonial government have a geographical-statistical department supplying information to a central imperial intelligence department, staffed by university trained geographers.

The imperial theme underlay all his activity. For university geographers he edited with his colleague O. J. R. Howarth the six-volume *Oxford Survey of the British Empire* (1914), described by Symonds as 'a fascinating picture of Oxford's perception of the empire at its highest tide' (Symonds, 147): and he dreamed (in vain) of setting up an institute of imperial geography and history in Oxford. Works presented to the school of geography during Herbertson's readership by the India Office, the War Office, and various colonial governments gave Oxford geography a clear imperial focus. The imperial theme was also evident in his school textbooks and from his work for those on imperial service, but it was more complex than has sometimes been suggested. He argued that geography should foster first a local patriotism, and then successively affection for and loyalty to country, empire, and the world (in 'Geography' in *The Practice of Instruction*, ed. J. W.

Adamson, 1907, 191–248). Later commentators interpret this as a vision of geography as a tool of empire (Symonds, 143), but earlier observers saw instead a vision of geography as a medium for understanding between peoples at a time when imperialism and militarism were at their height (Cossar, 486–90; W. L. G. Joerg, 'Recent geographical work in Europe', *Geographical Review*, 12, 1922, 432). Similar differences of opinion surround his regional geography. Inspired by Geddes, Herbertson's classic statement of regional geography in 'The major natural regions of the world' (*GJ*, 25, 1905, 300–12) long governed geographical practice. He argued for the delimitation of natural regions which 'should have a certain unity of configuration, climate and vegetation' (p. 309). In his lifetime and afterwards regional geography degenerated into an oversimplified and often racist matching of human type on to physical, usually climatic, region. Even Gilbert in a very kind memoir admitted that he had been 'surprised … by the crudity of some of [Herbertson's] deterministic statements' (Gilbert, *Geography*, 326). Yet Herbertson had intended his regions to be natural as opposed to artificial and hoped that their use would help students, particularly school pupils, make sense of the world, not just learn facts about it, and draw together the physical and human sides of geography. Indeed towards the end of his life his concern for regions had a rather visionary quality, rejecting the 'superficial geographical inventory' in favour of a 'regional psychology' based on a 'loving familiarity' with the region (A. J. Herbertson, 'Regional environment, heredity and consciousness', *Geographical Teacher*, 8, 1915–16, 153).

Herbertson was short, fair, and stocky and wore a pince-nez above a drooping moustache. His long-standing heart problems worsened greatly towards the end of his life, but did not stop his drilling with the reservists during the war, or lead him to cut back his teaching. He died suddenly at his country house at Spriggs Holly, Radnage, Buckinghamshire, on 31 July 1915 and was buried in St Cross churchyard, Oxford, on 2 August. His widow died at Spriggs Holly just over a fortnight later, on 15 August 1915. His sudden death, combined with the effects of war, left geography at Oxford without an honour school, let alone the grand institute of which he had dreamed. His death also left him with no award or medal from any learned society and without having taken up his seat on the RGS council. It was marked by only brief obituaries from colleagues obviously greatly saddened, but none the less caught up in the war.

He is remembered by the Herbertson memorial lecture, founded in 1917 by the Geographical Association (the last was given in 1994); the Herbertson Society founded in 1924 as the undergraduate geography society at Oxford, and in its early days with a life members' section to organize the excursions which Herbertson enjoyed (it survived for some fifty years and is still periodically revived); and the Herbertson prize offered in the geography final honour school at Oxford.   ELIZABETH BAIGENT

Sources L. J. Jay, 'Andrew John Herbertson, 1865–1915', *Geographers: biobibliographical studies*, 3, ed. T. W. Freeman and P. Pinchemel (1979), 85–92 • E. W. Gilbert, 'Andrew John Herbertson, 1865–1915: appreciation of his life and work', *Geography*, 50 (1965), 313–31 • L. J. Jay, 'A. J. Herbertson: his services to school geography', *Geography*, 50 (1965), 350–61 • b. cert. • d. cert. [Fanny Louisa Dorothy Richardson, wife] • m. cert. • d. cert. • d. cert. [Fanny Louisa Dorothy Herbertson, wife] • *CGPLA Eng. & Wales* (1916) • R. Symonds, *Oxford and empire: the last lost cause?* (1986) • D. N. Livingstone, *The geographical tradition* (1992) • J. Cossar, *Scottish Geographical Magazine*, 31 (1915), 486–90 • R. N. R. Brown, 'Scotland and some trends in geography: John Murray, Patrick Geddes, and Andrew Herbertson', *Geography*, 33 (1948), 107–20 [Herbertson memorial lecture] • H. J. Mackinder, N. E. MacMunn, and E. F. Elton, *Geographical Teacher*, 8 (1916), 143–6 • E. W. Gilbert, 'Andrew John Herbertson, 1865–1915', *GJ*, 131 (1965), 516–19 • H. J. Fleure, 'The later developments in Herbertson's thought: a study in the application of Darwin's ideas', *Geography*, 37 (1952), 97–103 [Herbertson memorial lecture] • H. O. Beckit, 'Andrew John Herbertson, 1865–1915', *GJ*, 46 (1915), 319–20 • L. J. Jay, 'The published works of A. J. Herbertson: a classified list', *Geography*, 50 (1965), 364–70 • H. J. Fleure, 'Recollections of A. J. Herbertson', *Geography*, 50 (1965), 348–9 • C. H. Firth, *The Oxford school of geography* (1918) • J. F. Unstead, 'A. J. Herbertson and his work', *Geography*, 50 (1965), 343–7 • D. I. Scargill, *The Oxford school of geography*, School of Geography Research Papers, 55 (1999) • L. D. Stamp, 'Major natural regions: Herbertson after fifty years', *Geography*, 42 (1957), 201–16 [Herbertson memorial lecture]

Archives U. Oxf., school of geography and environment, papers | NL Scot., corresp., incl. to Sir Patrick Geddes • RGS, letters to Royal Geographical Society

Likenesses J. R. Freeman & Co., photograph, School of Geography and the Environment, Oxford

Wealth at death £2224 14*s.* 5*d.*: administration with will, 11 Aug 1916, *CGPLA Eng. & Wales*

Herbison, David [*called* the Bard of Dunclug] (1800–1880), poet, was born on 14 October 1800 at Mill Street, Ballymena, co. Antrim, the fourth child of William Herbison (*d.* 1825), an innkeeper, and his wife, Elizabeth Wilson. At the age of three, following an attack of smallpox, he lost his sight. For four years he remained totally blind, but regained the sight in one eye after medical treatment. His education was adversely affected by his weak eyesight and poor health. He attended school for barely two years, and considered himself to be self-educated. In 1810 his father gave up his inn and moved to a small farm at Laymore, Ballymena. At the age of fourteen David Herbison was apprenticed to the loom, and began a lifelong association with linen weaving.

Herbison's father died in 1825. Seeking to improve their prospects, he and an elder brother decided to emigrate to Canada, and sailed from Belfast on 5 April 1827. However, the vessel foundered and sank in the St Lawrence. Although they were rescued, his brother's wife was among the many who drowned. The shock of this experience, together with an unfamiliar climate, made it difficult for him to settle in Quebec. After a few weeks he decided to return to Ballymena, and resumed his occupation as a weaver. In 1830 he married Margaret Archbold (1805–1881), the daughter of a neighbouring farmer, and he and his family lived in their weaver's cottage at Dunclug, near Ballymena, until his death.

From an early age Herbison had a love of books and an affinity for poetry. With his first wages he walked to Belfast to buy a copy of Ramsay's poems, and the next year repeated the journey to acquire the works of Burns. Like many Ulster Presbyterians he looked to Scotland for cultural and literary models, since the two regions shared a similar religious and linguistic heritage. His first published poem appeared in the *Northern Whig* in 1830, and he became a regular contributor to local newspapers and periodicals. His first collection, *The Fate of M'Quillan and O'Neill's Daughter*, appeared in 1841 and was favourably reviewed. He published four more volumes during his lifetime: *Midnight Musings* (1848), *Woodland Wanderings* (1858), *The Snow-Wreath* (1869), and *The Children of the Year* (1876). A posthumous collected edition of his works was published in 1883.

Herbison wrote in his vernacular Ulster Scots as well as in standard English. Prejudice against dialect increasingly constrained him to abandon Ulster Scots, and this deprived him of his most distinctive voice. He was one of the last of a group of rural bards known as the Rhyming Weavers, and exchanged poetical epistles with Thomas Beggs of Ballyclare, James McKowen of Lambeg, and Robert Huddleston of Moneyreagh. Herbison was acclaimed by his fellow poets as the Bard of Dunclug. His work provides a valuable commentary on the decline of hand-loom weaving and its transformation from rural craft to factory-based industry, with the consequent emigration and urbanization. Poems such as 'The Auld Wife's Lament for her Teapot' (Herbison, *Select Works*, 45) and 'My Ain Native Toun' (ibid., 305–8) record this social and cultural change. Of all the rural bards, Herbison came closest to establishing a wider literary reputation. As the Bard of Dunclug, he became a minor literary celebrity. He corresponded with Sir Samuel Ferguson, contributed to periodicals in Dublin, Edinburgh, and London, as well as Belfast, and had a considerable readership in Canada and South Carolina. His literary success enabled him to survive the effects of the Irish potato famine and industrialization. He became an agent for a firm of Belfast linen merchants. Yet he retained an attachment to radical causes, supporting electoral reform and tenant rights.

Herbison died on 26 May 1880 at Dunclug, and was buried on 28 May in the new cemetery, Cushendall Road, Ballymena, where in 1881 a monument was erected to his memory by public subscription.   IVAN HERBISON

Sources D. Herbison, *The select works of David Herbison, with life of the author by Rev. David McMeekin* (1883?) [incl. his five pubd vols. and uncollected verse] · D. Herbison, *Webs of fancy: poems of David Herbison, the Bard of Dunclug*, ed. I. Herbison (1980) · I. Herbison, *David Herbison, the Bard of Dunclug: a poet and his community, 1800–1880* (1988) · J. Fullarton, 'Sketches of Ulster poets: David Herbison, the Bard of Dunclug', *Ulster Magazine*, 2/23 (1861), 457–64 · J. Hewitt, *Rhyming Weavers and other country poets of Antrim and Down* (1974) · I. Herbison, 'The rest is silence': some remarks on the disappearance of Ulster-Scots poetry* (1996) · N. Vance, *Irish literature, a social history: tradition, identity and difference* (1990) · B. Walker, 'Country letters: some correspondence of Ulster poets of the nineteenth century', *An uncommon bookman: essays in memory of J. R. R. Adams*, ed. J. Gray and W. McCann (1996), 119–39 · gravestone inscription, new cemetery, Cushendall Road, Ballymena, co. Antrim · *Ballymena Observer* (29 May 1880)

Likenesses bust on monument, 1881, new cemetery, Cushendall Road, Ballymena; repro. in Herbison, *Webs of fancy*, frontispiece

Wealth at death under £500: probate, 1880, *CGPLA Eng. & Wales*

Herbison, Margaret McCrorie [Peggy] (1907–1996), politician, was born on 11 March 1907 at 46 Shotts Kirk Road, Shotts, Lanarkshire, the fourth of the six children of John Herbison, coalminer, and his wife, Maria Jane, *née* McCrorie. Her mother was 'from Northern Ireland—in fact from [Ian] Paisley's Bannside. My father, a gentle and tolerant man, was shocked when after visiting cousins there I brought home some Orange songs. But I'd also learnt some Irish rebel songs' (*The Independent*). Thought by Harold Wilson to be indecisive, Herbison, in a creditably caring way, recognized that there were at least two sides to every question.

Herbison enjoyed a happy childhood. After attending Dykehead public primary school the strict traditional dominies of her secondary school, Bellshill Academy, saw to it that this intelligent, assiduous miner's daughter entered Glasgow University. The university inculcated in her generation the expectation that they should repay the country for privileged education by service to society, and it was for service to society that in 1970 the university bestowed on her an honorary doctorate of laws. She gained her first degree in English, and in 1930 became a schoolteacher. From then until 1945 she taught English and history, first at Maryhill primary school in Glasgow and then at Allan Glen's secondary school. Her pupils recalled her with that mixture of affection and awe which is the mark of the really successful professional teacher. 'A right proper bantamweight' was the verdict of a pupil who himself later became an international boxer (*The Independent*).

As an undergraduate at Glasgow, Herbison chaired the university's Labour branch, and she remained active in local Labour politics; she also lectured in economics for the National Council of Labour Colleges. After her father had been killed in the pit his miners' lodge, unprompted, nominated her as a candidate for the Labour selection conference in the North Lanarkshire constituency. She won the nomination, and in the general election of July 1945 took the seat from the incumbent Conservative, Sir William Anstruther Grey. She made her maiden speech on 17 October 1945, in which she said:

> In my constituency of North Lanark, where I am faced with a gigantic housing problem, we have suffered little or nothing from war damage … My people for a long time have been suffering deplorable conditions. That cannot be put on this Labour government; it is the result of governments not tackling this problem as it ought to have been tackled a long time ago … In many parts of my constituency there are people living in houses in which the Minister of Health or the Minister of Agriculture would not allow cattle to live. They would say, 'You must now house your cattle in them; if you do, we won't be willing to accept the milk for the children.' Yet, our children and their parents have to live in them. (*The Independent*)

The fight for better conditions encapsulated the essence of Herbison's political career.

Herbison soon caught the eye of the government whips. In 1947 she was chosen to second the Commons address in reply to the king's speech, an honour which had fallen to a woman only once before. Two years later she was chosen

Margaret McCrorie [Peggy] **Herbison** (1907–1996), by Elliott & Fry, 1956

to be the only woman member of the first British delegation to the consultative assembly of the Council of Europe. When the Attlee government was returned again, with a small majority, in February 1950 she became joint parliamentary under-secretary of state for Scotland, under Hector McNeil. In eighteen months she made her mark—espousing in particular the crusade to build new primary schools to replace many early Victorian ones. Following Labour's defeat in the October 1951 general election she flourished effectively on the opposition front bench, shadowing successively Scottish and pension affairs. Elected a member of the national executive committee of the Labour Party in 1948, she was a prominent Gaitskellite loyalist. She presided with skill over the 1957 Labour Party conference.

In October 1964, when the Labour Party was returned to power, Harold Wilson appointed Herbison minister of pensions and national insurance (from August 1966 minister of social security). She wished to raise pensions at once, as the Labour Party in opposition had repeatedly and explicitly promised. She was furious when told by civil servants that for administrative reasons the increase could not be made payable in less than six months. However, she was able to abolish the national assistance scheme, so loathed by socialists, and replace it with the new device of supplementary benefits. In July 1967 she resigned office in protest at the government's refusal to increase children's allowances. Characteristically she

refused to comment further, saying that she had no intention of 'giving the Tory press a story which would do harm to the Labour Party' (*The Scotsman*). Wilson, praising her warm humanity, expressed regret that she felt unable to accept decisions which commended themselves to her colleagues. She became chairman of the select committee on overseas aid in 1969 but retired from parliament at the general election of 1970. In the same year she was voted Scotswoman of the year.

A devout member of the Church of Scotland throughout her life, Herbison was thrilled to serve as the queen's representative, the lord high commissioner to the general assembly of the Church of Scotland, in 1970–71, the first woman ever to be thus appointed. It was deemed highly appropriate when in 1974 she was appointed to the royal commission on standards of conduct in public life. She also served from 1976 as the first lay observer appointed to investigate allegations against the handling of complaints by the Law Society of Scotland. She died at St Mary's Hospital, Lanark, of cancer, on 29 December 1996. She was unmarried.   TAM DALYELL

Sources *The Independent* (31 Dec 1996) · *The Guardian* (31 Dec 1996) · *The Times* (31 Dec 1996) · *The Scotsman* (31 Dec 1996) · *Daily Telegraph* (31 Dec 1996) · personal knowledge (2004) · private information (2004) · *WWW* · b. cert. · d. cert. · NA Scot., SC/CO 1007/40 **Likenesses** photograph, 1950, repro. in *The Independent* · Elliott & Fry, photograph, 1956, NPG [*see illus.*] · group photograph, 1957, repro. in *The Times* · photograph, repro. in *The Guardian* · photograph, repro. in *The Scotsman* **Wealth at death** £75,742.19: confirmation, 22 May 1997, NA Scot., SC/CO 1007/40

Herd, David (*bap.* 1732, *d.* 1810), song collector and editor, was born at Balmakelly in the parish of Marykirk in Kincardineshire, and baptized there on 23 October 1732, the son of John Herd, a farmer, and his wife, Margaret Low (1691–1751). Little is known of his education. He spent much of his career as a law clerk with David Russell, an Edinburgh accountant, and was described in later life as a 'writer' (or solicitor). He was unmarried, but was reputed to have had a natural son, a Captain John Dickson of the King's Own Scottish Borderers who was the principal legatee of Herd's estate.

Herd's classic collection *Ancient and Modern Scots Songs, Heroic Ballads &c* was published in Edinburgh in 1769 and later reissued in expanded two-volume form (1776). Containing nearly 60 'heroic ballads' and more than 300 miscellaneous songs, it appeared at a time of spectacular literary discovery and realignment. James Macpherson's publication of the poems of Ossian (1761–5), claiming to represent a line of heroic Gaelic poetry dating from the third century AD, not only appeared to demonstrate the superior antiquity of Scottish poetry, but also that contemporary 'British liberties' were descended from Celtic rather than Anglo-Saxon roots. Urged on by Samuel Johnson, Thomas Percy responded with *Reliques of Ancient English Poetry* (1765). With lavish editorial apparatus and carefully 'antiqued' orthography, Percy asserted that English constituted the dominant strand in British literature and that its roots were firmly Teutonic. Percy was happy to include Scottish material within a context of Anglo-Saxon hegemony and had received much material from correspondents in Scotland. But relations quickly cooled, and in 1769 David Herd and his coadjutor and printer John Wotherspoon published *Ancient and Modern Scots Songs*, with the implication that Scottish tradition ran truer than the English, featuring songs and ballads that were older, better, and more 'authentic' than anything Percy could show.

Herd and Wotherspoon insisted on the antiquity of some at least of their material—the collection was the first of its kind published in Scotland to include the word 'ancient' in its title (Crawford, *Society*, 217–18)—and they presented the heroic ballads as the 'epic tales' of the lowlands, although the inclusion of songs from the recent Jacobite risings suggested that the heroic mode was very much an ongoing concern. Hitherto collections of popular songs had typically contained a heterogeneous mixture of Scots, English, and Irish material, but Herd and Wotherspoon's concentration on songs deriving from the Scottish popular tradition—with lyrics in the vernacular or, where English verses were unavoidable, at least written by Scottish writers—anticipated the rising tide of cultural nationalism that was to mark the early Romantic revival in Europe. Song, they thought, was not merely a uniquely accurate indicator of 'the character, genius, taste and pursuits of a people' but enjoyed a dynamically formative role in collective self-definition; it was the very substance of national distinctiveness. Every ancient and 'unmixed' nation (an allusion to the traditional view of the English as a mongrel race):

> hath its peculiar style of musical expression, its peculiar mode of melody; modulated by the joint influence of climate and government, character and situation ... Thus each of the states of ancient Greece had its characteristic style of music ... and thus the moderns have their distinct national styles, the Italian, the Spanish, the Irish, and the Scottish.
> (D. Herd, 'Preface' to *Ancient and Modern Scots Songs*, 1769)

Herd and Wotherspoon stressed the high quality of the music, and their insistence on songs as things to be sung, rather than merely as verses intended to be read, contrasted strongly with Percy. They did not publish the airs, probably on grounds of expense and their already wide diffusion, and when this was done by James Johnson and Robert Burns in *The Scots Musical Museum* (1787–1803), the latter superseded *Ancient and Modern Scots Songs* as the standard edition. Hailed as a classic by Sir Walter Scott and by Joseph Ritson, who praised its scrupulousness and fidelity to tradition, *Ancient and Modern Scots Songs* was reissued in revised form in 1791 and again in 1869, 1870, and 1973. A selection of songs from Herd's manuscripts was published by Hans Hecht in 1904 with extensive scholarly apparatus and this remains the best single source on Herd's life and work.

Herd arrived at a unitary text for each song by collating multiple variants from a range of published and manuscript sources, correspondents and oral tradition. The social organization of contemporary Edinburgh helped him to build a network of informants. He was a leading light in the Cape Club, one of many quaintly named convivial societies where much of the cultural production of Edinburgh in its golden age was conceived. He was the third sovereign (president) of the Cape and many of its records are in his hand. Members included the poet Robert Fergusson; painters Alexander Nasmyth, Henry Raeburn, and Alexander Runciman (who was Herd's closest friend); John Wotherspoon, his printer; musicians such as F. G. C. Schetky and Stephen Clarke (Burns's friend and the arranger of the music for *The Scots Musical Museum*); leading representatives of the Edinburgh stage; and people from many different trades and professions, including the notorious Deacon William Brodie. The club met nightly in James Mann's howff (tavern) in Craig's Close for good ale and conversation, stories, and songs. Herd also frequented John Dowie's tavern in Liberton's Wynd, near to his office in Gosford's Close, where he will have met Robert Burns, whose own club, the Crochallan Fencibles, gathered there. Burns certainly seems to have enjoyed access to Herd's manuscripts, which provided the sources of several of his songs. Herd was also friendly with Walter Scott, the publisher Archibald Constable, and the antiquary and book collector George Paton.

David Herd was austere in appearance with hawk-like features and, in later life, a profusion of grey hair. In character he was affable and unpretentious, generous with time and scholarly advice, and held in affectionate esteem by those who knew him. He died in his lodgings in Potterrow, Edinburgh, on 10 June 1810 and was buried in the nearby Buccleuch parish kirkyard.

WILLIAM DONALDSON

Sources H. Hecht, ed., *Songs from David Herd's manuscripts* (1904) · *Scots Magazine and Edinburgh Literary Miscellany*, 72 (1810), 638 · R. Chambers, *Traditions of Edinburgh*, new edn (1868) · A. Jervise, *Epitaphs and inscriptions from burial grounds and old buildings in the north-east of Scotland*, 2 vols. (1875–9) · *The correspondence of Thomas Percy and George Paton*, ed. A. F. Falconer (1961), vol. 6 of *The Percy letters*, ed. C. Brooks, D. N. Smith, and A. F. Falconer (1944–88) · T. Crawford, *Society and the lyric* (1979) · T. Crawford, 'Lowland song and popular tradition in the eighteenth century', *The history of Scottish literature*, ed. C. Craig, 2: *1660–1880*, ed. A. Hook (1988), 123–39 · W. Donaldson, *The Jacobite song* (1988) · W. Donaldson, 'Their songs are of other worlds: Ossian and the Macpherson paradigm', *The highland pipe and Scottish society, 1750–1950* (2000), 5–9
Archives BL, MSS, Add. MS 22311 (MS I) · BL, MSS, Add. MS 22312 (MS II) · Hornel Library, Broughton House, Kirkcudbright, letters · NL Scot., corresp. and papers · U. Edin., corresp. and papers | NL Scot., letters to G. Paton
Wealth at death £475 12s. 8½d.: inventory of personal estate

Herd, John (1511–1584), doctor and Church of England clergyman, was born in February 1511 in Southwark, Surrey. He was educated at Eton College and at King's College, Cambridge, where he was admitted a scholar in 1529 and elected a fellow in 1532; he graduated BA in 1534. He left Cambridge in 1536, and in 1540 moved to Rochester. But he retained links with Cambridge, proceeding MA probably in 1546, and contributing verses to the volume marking the death of Martin Bucer in 1551. By that time he had trained as a doctor and become physician to Archbishop Thomas Cranmer—in July 1551 he nearly died of sweating sickness at Croydon Palace. He attended the archbishop in Oxford until August 1555, and also took possession of some of Cranmer's books. This did not prevent his conforming in religion under Mary, for though not in orders he was installed as prebendary of Lafford in Lincoln Cathedral on 19 October 1557, and in 1558 was presented to two Welsh benefices. He proceeded MD at Cambridge in the latter year.

Herd conformed under Elizabeth as well, and in April 1559 was installed in the prebend of South Newbald in York Minster. He then demonstrated both his versatility and his ambitions by writing a verse history of England between 1461 and 1509, with a fulsome dedication to Sir William Cecil dated 1 October 1562. Heavily dependent on the histories of Edward Hall and Polydore Virgil, and probably also using at least one London chronicle, Herd's work survives in two full texts (one of them published by the Roxburghe Club in 1868) and a heavily revised account of the reign of Henry VII. Historically its value is slight, and Herd himself suggested that its principal value lay in its being written in verse, and therefore more pleasing to the ear than a work in prose. A passing allusion to storm damage to St Paul's Cathedral late in Henry VII's reign prompted a reference to the disastrous fire of 1561, leading to a eulogy of Queen Elizabeth as the defender of true religion and liberty against Roman tyranny. But the trumpet Herd was most anxious to hear blown was probably his own, for his text is prefaced by a number of verses in praise of himself by former Cambridge colleagues.

No preferment resulted from his approach to Cecil, though it may have served to remind the queen's secretary of Herd's existence, for on 14 April 1563 he wrote requiring him to deliver up 'certain collections and common place notes made by the late Archbishop Cranmer' (*CSP dom.*, 1547–80, 222); five or six volumes were accordingly surrendered. Thereafter Herd pursued an ecclesiastical career. Ordained priest by the bishop of Lincoln on 1 June 1564, on 13 September 1565 he was instituted rector of Waddington, where he was recorded in 1576 as a conscientious resident clergyman. He also continued to act as a medical practitioner. No doubt it was for his parishioners that he prepared treatments to draw out thorns, heal people bitten by mad dogs, and cure murrain in 'beastes'. He also moved in more exalted circles, presumably in Lincoln Cathedral close, where he retained his prebend. He attended a number of cathedral dignitaries—in May 1582 the precentor and the chancellor both received purges—together with lay eminences such as Lord Sheffield, Sir Edmund Peckham, and Lady Wingfield. He also borrowed recipes for medicines, including an eyewater provided by Mrs Aylmer, wife of the future bishop of London.

Herd died in December 1584, probably at Waddington and most likely on the 21st. He was buried at Waddington and was commemorated in his church by a brass inscribed with verses showing every sign of having been written by their dedicatee. They acclaimed him as doctor, minister, historian, and author of a verse catechism to teach Christian doctrine to the young, and declared that Herd's achievements would bring him an enduring fame. The catechism has not survived, while both church and brass were destroyed in the Second World War.

HENRY SUMMERSON

Sources Venn, *Alum. Cant.*, 1/2.344 • Cooper, *Ath. Cantab.*, 2.40–41 • *Historia quatuor regum Angliae … authore Johanne Herdo*, ed. T. Purnell, Roxburghe Club (1868) • BL, Cotton MSS Julius C.ii; Sloane 1818 • Bodl. Oxf., MSS Lincoln College Lat. 122, 127, 138 • *CPR*, 1557–8 • *CSP dom.*, 1547–80 • R. E. G. Cole, ed., *Lincolnshire church notes made by Gervase Holles, A.D. 1634 to A.D. 1642*, Lincoln RS, 1 (1911) • C. W. Foster, ed., *Lincoln episcopal records*, Lincoln RS, 2 (1912) • *Fasti Angl., 1541–1857*, [York; Lincoln] • D. MacCulloch, *Thomas Cranmer: a life* (1996)

Herdman, James (1809–1901), flax-spinning mill proprietor, was born at 15 Mill Street, Smithfield, Belfast, in 1809, the eldest child of the three sons and one daughter, Eliza, of James Herdman (1781–1817), tannery owner, and his wife, Sarah, *née* Griffith (d. 1848), of Wales; his brothers were **John Herdman** (1811–1862) and George. Sarah Herdman carried on her husband's business after his early death. James married Elizabeth Suffern (1816–1891) in 1840, and they are recorded as living at 13 Mill Street, next door to his mother. In 1841 the first of their family of nine, four sons and five daughters, was born.

In the early 1830s James and his brother John sold their father's tannery business and founded J. and J. Herdman & Co., flax and tow spinners, with premises at Winetavern Street and Francis Street, Smithfield, Belfast. It is probable that these premises used the technique of dry spinning, which could process only coarse yarn. They had some financial backing from members of the Mulholland family, who also owned steam-powered flax-spinning mills in Smithfield, and the encouragement of their success may have prompted the search for an alternative site with water power where finer yarns could be spun. The Francis Street mill was sold, possibly to finance this development.

In March 1835 they commenced negotiations with the agent of the duke of Abercorn to acquire a lease of 'the old mill at Seein' as the duke intended to build a new water-powered flour mill, higher up the River Mourne in co. Tyrone. (Seein or Sion is an Anglicization of the Irish word 'Sián', meaning fairy mound.) The lease was for 'three lives and thirty one years', a common form of land lease of the period, on condition that the company would not build another flour mill and that the Abercorns would not permit another flax-spinning mill on their property. Subsequently the lease was converted to one of 500 years. Two other partners were admitted, the youngest Herdman brother, George, and Robert Lyons. Later in the same year the firm of A. and K. Mulholland, flax spinners of Belfast, who already had a financial interest in the Winetavern Street mill, took two shares in the Sion venture. The significance of the development of water power for both landlord and tenant can be seen in the fact that they shared equally the cost of a new weir and watercourse. On 14 November 1835 the first bundles of yarn were produced at Sion Mills.

The Herdmans bought out Robert Lyons in 1840 and the

Sion Mills premises began trading as Herdmans & Co. while the premises in Winetavern Street, Belfast, became known as the Smithfield Mill and traded under the name of J. and J. Herdman. In 1849 the Herdman brothers bought out the Mulhollands' shares and became sole proprietors of both premises. The village of Sion Mills came into being as the company built houses to attract and accommodate mill workers. James Herdman lived at Liggartstown near the village until his marriage in 1840 when he moved back to Mill Street in the heart of Belfast. His family, including his mother, moved between various suburban addresses in Belfast and co. Down between then and 1846. In 1846 he commissioned the architect Charles Lanyon to design Sion House, a square stucco building with a big pillared porch, as a family home in the village, and he and his family lived there for three years. However, after the Herdman brothers became sole proprietors of their business in 1849 it was arranged between them that James and John would look after the Smithfield Mill in Belfast and George would manage the Sion Mills premises and live in Sion House. The village of Sion Mills continued to expand as the Herdman family built more dwellings for the workers, whose numbers increased from at least 500 in the 1840s to 940 by 1866. The housing was part of a planned mill-village layout, which included a school and shop developed and maintained by the company and in 1843 was acclaimed by the Halls in their published *Ireland, its Scenery and Character*.

James Herdman and his family moved back to Belfast in 1849, and were recorded as living at 8 Royal Terrace, Lisburn Road, Belfast, the next year. There was an arrangement that James and John would visit Sion Mills once a week. James recorded in the mill diary that the 80-mile journey involved travel overnight by ship from Belfast to Londonderry and carriage from Londonderry to Sion Mills. He applauded the opening in 1855 of the railway connection via Londonderry, with a station beside the mill, which reduced the journey time to 5½ hours.

The family's apparently sensible organization of the business changed substantially within one decade. With the sudden death of George Herdman in January 1856 through illness, James and his family returned from Belfast to manage the Sion Mills premises, and to live at Sion House. The Smithfield Mill premises in Belfast were left in the charge of his brother John. However, on 15 May 1862 John Herdman was accidentally shot dead by his cousin. After this tragedy the business was formally divided in two. The Belfast firm was run by Alexander, the eldest son of John's thirteen surviving children. Sion Mills continued to be run by James Herdman and two of his sons, John and Emerson Tennant Herdman, who were minors.

This period of immense change in the family's circumstances coincided with a boom period for the Irish linen industry because of the increased demand for linen cloth and flax yarns as a substitute for the shortage of cotton during the American Civil War, 1861–5. Perhaps because of the combination of prosperity and the extreme family difficulties over the preceding years, in 1865 James Herdman decided to retire from the business when he was fifty-

six. On 31 March 1866 he handed over complete control to his sons, John and Emerson, and company records note that, among other provisions, he was to receive an annual retiring salary of £500 for the remainder of his life. Emerson Tennant Herdman moved into Sion House and in the 1880s it was remodelled in a Tudor Gothic style in sympathy with the arts and crafts movement.

In 1867 James and Elizabeth Herdman retired to 18 Camden Crescent, Bath, Somerset. They appear to have lived there quietly until Elizabeth's death in 1891 when she was seventy-five. James lived on at the same address for a further ten years, dying at home of old age and heart failure at the age of ninety-two on 23 October 1901. His death was registered by his second daughter, Agnes, who also lived in Bath. He was buried on 26 October 1901 at Lansdowne cemetery, Bath.   BRENDA COLLINS

Sources R. Herdman, *They all made me* (1970) · Herdmans mill diaries (photocopy), 1842–6, PRO NIre., T 1650 [original in company hands] · Herdmans mill diaries, 1847–1977, Herdmans Ltd, Sion Mills, co. Tyrone · 'Review of the previous century', *Tyrone Constitution* [supplement] (10 Nov 1950) · Mr and Mrs S. C. Hall, *Ireland, its scenery and character* (1843) · *North-west Ulster: the counties of Londonderry, Donegal, Fermanagh and Tyrone*, Pevsner (1979) · *Belfast Street Directory* (1819); (1842–57); (1862) · *Martin's Belfast Directory* (1841–2) · *Belfast News-Letter* (16 May–1 Aug 1862) [John Herdman] · *Belfast News-Letter* (26 Oct 1901) · *CGPLA Ire.* (1862)
Archives PRO NIre., mill diary, T1650 [photocopy of original in company hands]
Wealth at death £29,188 7s.: probate, 29 Nov 1901, *CGPLA Ire.* · £18,000—John Herdman: probate, 1862, *CGPLA Ire.*

Herdman, John (1762?–1842), physician, born in Scotland, became a member of the Medical Society of Edinburgh on 14 December 1793 and a member of the Royal College of Surgeons of the City of Edinburgh on 26 December 1797, of which he was subsequently elected a fellow. Herdman practised for twelve years at Leith and was a supporter of the Brunonian system (albeit in a modified form) of John Brown (1735–1788). On 12 July 1800 he took the degree of MD at Aberdeen, and on 31 March 1806 he was admitted a licentiate of the Royal College of Physicians. After moving to London he was made physician to the City Dispensary and physician to the duke of Sussex.

Herdman withdrew from practice upon entering Magdalene College, Cambridge, in 1809; he migrated to Trinity College in 1811, where he graduated BA in 1814 and MA in 1817. He was ordained deacon in the Church of England in 1816, and he preached occasionally at Alnwick, Howick, and other towns in Northumberland. His marriage to the daughter of C. Hay of Lesbury brought him considerable wealth, a large portion of which he spent on charitable causes.

In 1795 Herdman published *An Essay on the Causes and Phenomena of Animal Life*, in which he examined the physical properties of animal life: the senses, the nervous system and the structure of the body, and the external means required to sustain life. A second edition was published in 1806. He also wrote *Dissertations on White swelling of the Joints and the Doctrine of Inflammation* (1802); *Discourse on the Epidemic Disease Termed Influenza* (1803); *Discourses on the Management of Infants and the Treatment of their Diseases* (1804);

and *A Letter proposing a Plan for the Improvement of Dispensaries and the Medical Treatment of the Diseased Poor* (1809). Herdman died at Lesbury House, near Alnwick, Northumberland, on 26 February 1842, aged eighty.

GORDON GOODWIN, *rev.* KAYE BAGSHAW

Sources Munk, *Roll* · Venn, *Alum. Cant.* · *GM*, 2nd ser., 17 (1842), 447 · *A new biographical dictionary of 3000 cotemporary [sic] public characters, British and foreign, of all ranks and professions*, 2nd edn, 3 vols. in 6 pts (1825)

Herdman, John (1811–1862). *See under* Herdman, James (1809–1901).

Herdman, Robert (1828–1888), painter, was born at Rattray, Perthshire, on 17 September 1828, the fourth and youngest son of the Revd William Herdman, minister of that parish, and his wife, Sophia Walker. Herdman attended Rattray parish school until his father died in 1838. The family then moved to St Andrews where he studied for five sessions at Madras College. In 1843 he entered the University of St Andrews, taking the full arts curriculum, and he was a promising Greek scholar. At this time he spent the summer vacations back in Rattray where he enjoyed sketching and painting. This became Herdman's true vocation although he retained a deep belief in the importance of scholarship for the rest of his life. In June 1847 Herdman moved to Edinburgh and entered the Trustees' Academy. He studied first under Robert Ballantyne and later under the inspirational teaching of Robert Scott Lauder. He was one of a group of particularly gifted students which included William McTaggart, George Paul Chalmers, and John Pettie, and he was successful himself, winning prizes in 1848, 1850, 1851, and 1852. He attended the Royal Scottish Academy life school between 1852 and 1855 under the tuition of James Drummond. In 1854 Herdman won the academy's newly established Keith prize for the best historical picture in the Royal Scottish Academy's annual exhibition by a student and in 1855 he won the academy's bronze medal.

In the mid-1850s the Royal Scottish Academy was expanding its collection of copies of old masters for use as teaching aids. At Herdman's request Robert Scott Lauder recommended him to the academy's council to undertake the task of making old master copies. Herdman was duly commissioned to travel to Florence to copy one of Masaccio's frescoes in the Brancacci Chapel, Santa Maria del Carmine. On his return to Edinburgh further watercolours after Masaccio, Perugino, Raphael, and others were shown to the council who duly purchased a total of nine paintings including *The Agony in the Garden, after Perugino* (*c.*1855–1856; Royal Scottish Academy, Edinburgh). The impact of Herdman's months in Italy was profound. Not only did his study of early and high Renaissance art have a deep impact on his own work but the light, colours, and exoticism of everyday Italian life inspired a lengthy series of paintings over the next few years. As well as painting the street life of itinerant musicians or *pifferari*, he painted more general subjects such as *The Mandolin Player* (1856;

Perth Museum and Art Gallery) in which a woman instrumentalist is seated in a window before a distant landscape reminiscent of Italy.

Robert Herdman first exhibited at the Royal Scottish Academy annual exhibitions in 1850 and remained a regular contributor for the rest of his life. On 17 September 1857 he married Emma Catherine Abbott (*b.* 1836/7) in Edinburgh. He rapidly became an established figure in the Edinburgh art world and was elected an associate of the Royal Scottish Academy in 1858 and an academician in 1863 when he was only thirty-four. His diploma work, *La culla* (1864; Royal Scottish Academy), shows the continuing influence of Italy in its title and treatment of a Madonna-like mother and child set amid the suggestion of Roman ruins. Painted in a broad, direct manner it is characteristic of his style. During this period Robert Herdman also built up a successful portrait painting practice in Edinburgh. Among his sitters were Lady Shand (1867; NG Scot.) and Thomas Carlyle (1875; Scottish National Portrait Gallery, Edinburgh) as well as many artists and their families.

Robert Herdman was profoundly interested in Scottish history and he painted many works on such subjects as the life of Mary, queen of Scots, and the covenanters. *The Conference between Queen Mary and John Knox at Holyrood Palace, 1561* (1875; Perth Museum and Art Gallery) presents a dramatic rendering of a moment in Scottish history that also underlines the issue of historical religious divisions within the country; his covenanting subjects such as *After the Battle: a Scene in Covenanting Times* (1870; NG Scot.) deal with the hardships and human loss suffered in the name of religion. These Scottish subject paintings were very popular, indeed *After the Battle* was commissioned by the Royal Association for the Promotion of the Fine Arts in Scotland (RAPFAS) to be engraved and disseminated to a wide audience. Between 1863 and 1878 Herdman contributed to twelve RAPFAS volumes of engravings, mostly subjects based on the novels of Sir Walter Scott. Another area of interest was Celtic legend and religion, particularly the life of St Columba, for example *St Columba Rescuing a Captive* (1883; Perth Museum and Art Gallery).

Unlike many of his contemporaries, Herdman did not settle in London although he did exhibit at the Royal Academy between 1863 and 1878. He remained in Edinburgh but also spent time on Arran, painting landscapes, and also visited Mull. He spent the winter of 1868–9 in Italy and made many watercolour studies of Venice. His continuing interest in watercolours led him to become a founder member of the Royal Scottish Society of Painters in Watercolour in 1878.

Robert Herdman died suddenly on 10 January 1888 at his home at St Bernard's, 12 Bruntsfield Crescent, Edinburgh, and was buried in Grange cemetery, Edinburgh, on 14 January. He was survived by his wife and children among whom were the painter Robert Duddingstone Herdman and the marine zoologist Sir William Abbott *Herdman. In the last few days of his life he had been preparing an address to the art students of the board of manufactures' school in Edinburgh (the Trustees' Academy). Published posthumously, for distribution to the students, it summarizes Herdman's belief in the importance not only of mastering the technical and aesthetic aspects of fine art but also of developing a wider cultural awareness and understanding.   JOANNA SODEN

Sources L. Errington, *Robert Herdman* (1988) · *DNB* · *Annual Report of the Council of the Royal Scottish Academy of Painting, Sculpture, and Architecture*, 61 (1888), 10–12 · J. L. Caw, *Scottish painting past and present, 1620–1908* (1908), 174–6 · W. D. McKay, *The Scottish school of painting* (1906), 352–5 · D. Irwin and F. Irwin, *Scottish painters at home and abroad, 1700–1900* (1975), 349–50 · C. B. de Laperriere, ed., *The Royal Scottish Academy exhibitors, 1826–1990*, 4 vols. (1991), vol. 2, pp. 271–5 · Graves, *RA exhibitors*, 4 (1906), 80 · J. Halsby, *Scottish watercolours, 1740–1940* (1986), 104–6 · R. Herdman, *Address to art students* (1888) · P. J. M. McEwan, *Dictionary of Scottish art and architecture* (1994), 275 · R. Brydall, *Art in Scotland, its origin and progress* (1889), 414–18 · b. cert. · d. cert. · m. cert.

Archives NL Scot., sitters' book [copy] · Royal Scot. Acad., letter collection | NL Scot., Blackie MSS · NL Scot., Joseph Noel Paton diaries

Likenesses R. Herdman, self-portrait, oils, 1883, Aberdeen Art Gallery · R. D. Herdman, oils, 1886, Scot. NPG · Nesbitt & Lothian, photograph, NPG

Herdman, Sir William Abbott (1858–1924), marine zoologist, was born at 32 Danube Street, Edinburgh, on 8 September 1858, the eldest of the four sons of the artist Robert *Herdman (1828–1888), and his wife, Emma, *née* Abbott, of Maryborough, Queen's county, Ireland. He was educated at Edinburgh Academy and from 1875 at the University of Edinburgh, where he obtained the gold medal for comparative anatomy in 1878. After graduating in 1879 he was awarded the Baxter natural science scholarship, and assisted his professor, Charles Wyville Thomson, in work on the deep-sea zoological collections made during the voyage of HMS *Challenger*. Herdman took as his special study the Tunicates, a group of marine organisms that includes salps and sea squirts, on which he became the leading authority. He acted as secretary of the *Challenger* expedition committee.

From 1880 to 1881 Herdman was demonstrator in zoology in the University of Edinburgh, before being appointed late in 1881 as first Derby professor of natural history in the University (then University College) of Liverpool. In Edinburgh he had been active in local field work, carrying out dredgings in the Firth of Forth and publishing several papers on its fauna. In Liverpool he undertook similar studies, but sought to implement more ambitious and wide-ranging objectives, the long-term aim being to bring scientific studies of the Irish Sea to bear on the practical problems of the fishing industry. This became his life's work. In 1885, with support from the local scientific community, he founded the Liverpool Marine Biology Committee, which two years later opened a research laboratory at Puffin Island, off Anglesey. Herdman's enthusiasm inspired many amateur naturalists besides his own students, and led to a series of publications on the fauna of Liverpool Bay and the Irish Sea. In 1892 the station was moved from Puffin Island to a more advantageous position at Port Erin, Isle of Man, where it was later rebuilt to meet the growing demands of research workers. The move also reflected Herdman's growing attachment to

the Isle of Man, where he had a summer home for forty years. He made a considerable contribution to the life of the island, and involved the Manx government in the work of the Port Erin laboratory. As a result, a grant of £2000 was given in 1901 to rebuild the laboratory (which included a government-run sea-fish hatchery). Herdman had few interests that were not in some way related to his work, but he developed an active interest in the prehistory of the island. With his friend P. M. C. Kermode he carried out several archaeological investigations, and their book *Manx Antiquities* was published in 1904. Herdman was largely instrumental in the foundation of the Manx Museum at Douglas and became one of the trustees.

Herdman was first married on 6 July 1882 to Sarah Wyse Douglas (1861–1886), daughter of David Douglas, an Edinburgh publisher and bookseller. They had two daughters. Following her death, he married on 28 December 1893 Jane Brandreth Holt (*d.* 1922), daughter of Alfred *Holt, a Liverpool shipping magnate. They had a son and a daughter.

In 1891 the recently founded Lancashire Sea Fisheries Committee invited Herdman to lecture to fishermen. This led to the organization of a marine research laboratory in the University of Liverpool, and, in 1897, to the establishment of a biological station and fish hatchery at Piel Island near Barrow in Lancashire. The latter soon became a centre of instruction for fishermen in biology, navigation, and seamanship, and much faunistic and statistical work was carried out. Specially noteworthy were the researches into plankton, which were carried out in collaboration with the Irish fishery authorities.

In 1901 Herdman went to Ceylon, at the request of the Colonial Office, to investigate and report on the pearl oyster fisheries of the Gulf of Mannar. His work resulted in various recommendations being made to the government of Ceylon regarding the future of the fisheries, and led to the establishment of a marine research station at Trincomalee.

Returning to his investigations in the Irish Sea, Herdman concentrated on a study of the plankton; using his steam yachts, he extended the survey northwards to the west coast of Scotland. When the First World War restricted work at sea, he became chairman of the grain-pests committee of the Royal Society. In 1916, with his wife, he founded the George Herdman chair of geology in the University of Liverpool, in memory of their son, who was killed at the battle of the Somme; and in 1919 they endowed a chair of oceanography at Liverpool, of which Herdman became the holder for one year, after resigning in 1919 the chair of natural history. In retirement he briefly served as vice-chancellor of Liverpool University. When his second wife died in 1922 he donated money to build a geological laboratory for the university in her memory.

Herdman was a mainstay of the British Association for the Advancement of Science, serving as general secretary from 1903 to 1919, and as president at the Cardiff meeting of 1920, when the theme of his address was a plea for a new *Challenger* expedition. He received honorary degrees from several universities, and was elected a fellow of the Royal Society in 1892, served on its council from 1898 to 1910, and was foreign secretary from 1916 to 1920. He was president of the Linnean Society from 1904 to 1908. He was made a CBE in 1920 and was knighted in 1922.

As well as numerous scientific papers and the section on Ascidia in the *Cambridge Natural History*, Herdman published a work of more general interest, *The Founders of Oceanography* (1923). He died suddenly from heart failure at 161 Drummond Street, London, on 21 July 1924, and was buried in Highgate cemetery, Middlesex, later that month.

Herdman was described as 'a very pleasant companion, never ruffled, cheerful and bright' (Shipley). 'In physique he was rather small, but he had an arresting eye and somewhat of a presence' (ibid.). Shipley also described him as 'a man of simple habits, a doer rather than a philosopher'. Cole speaks of him as a man of 'volcanic energy' who by force of character brought and held together 'a heterogeneous and industrious company of marine biologists'. He was at his best in the Isle of Man, working at sea or in the laboratory with his associates. But he also made firm friendships with various scientists, such as William E. Rutter and Charles A. Kofoid from the University of California, and enjoyed being part of the wider British scientific scene, especially at the meetings of the British Association. Ill health in his final years was exacerbated by the loss of his son and his wife.

R. N. RUDMOSE BROWN, rev. MARGARET DEACON

Sources S. J. H. [S. J. Hickson], *PRS*, 98B (1925), x–xiv · J. J. [J. Johnstone], 'Sir William A. Herdman', *Nature*, 114 (1924), 165–6 · A. E. Shipley, 'Sir William Abbott Herdman', *Proceedings of the Linnean Society of London*, 137th session (1924–5), 78–80 · E. C. Herdman, biographical notes on W. A. Herdman, c.1925, U. St Andr. L., special collections department, D'Arcy Wentworth Thompson MS 40640 · W. A. Herdman, letter to James Cossar Ewart, 25 June 1915, U. Edin. L., special collections division, Cossar Ewart MSS, Gen. 139 · *The Times* (23 July 1924) · J. Johnstone, introduction and general account of the scientific work, *Report for 1924 on the Lancashire Sea-Fisheries Laboratory at University College, Liverpool* (1924), 1–23 · F. J. Cole, '"J. J." — a biographical note', in *James Johnstone memorial volume*, Lancashire Sea-Fisheries Laboratory (1934), 1–11 · T. A. Norton, 'Fisheries research at Port Erin and Liverpool University', *British marine science and meteorology: the history of their development and application to marine fishing problems* (1996), 47–60 · *Proceedings of the Isle of Man Natural History and Antiquarian Society*, 2 (1924), 364–6 · *Isle of Man Examiner* (25 July 1924) · *Isle of Man Weekly Times* (26 July 1924)

Archives U. St Andr., corresp. | Marine Biological Association of the United Kingdom, Plymouth, letters to E. T. Browne · Oxf. U. Mus. NH, letters to Sir E. B. Poulton

Likenesses photograph, c.1892, RS · W. Stoneman, photograph, 1917, NPG · R. D. Herdman, oils, U. Lpool · photograph, repro. in, 'Sir William A. Herdman', facing p. 10

Wealth at death £38,282 2s. 11d.: probate, 5 Nov 1924, *CGPLA Eng. & Wales*

Herdman, William Gawin (1805–1882), landscape painter and writer, was born on 13 March 1805 at Liverpool (probably in Stanley Street), where his father was a corn merchant. He was active in the Liverpool Academy, being admitted as a student in 1824 and serving as secretary from 1845 to 1848, but in December 1857 he was expelled,

nominally for protesting against the academy's award of its annual prize to J. E. Millais for his painting *The Blind Girl*. He continued to oppose Pre-Raphaelitism through letters to the press in Liverpool and London, and helped to start a rival establishment to the Liverpool Academy, the short-lived Liverpool Society of Fine Arts. In 1859 he was involved in setting up the country's first shilling art union in Liverpool, as an alternative to the more exclusive art unions with guinea subscriptions. He was an art teacher for many years in his native town.

Herdman exhibited several landscapes in London at the Royal Academy and the Suffolk Street Gallery between 1834 and 1861, and numerous works at the Liverpool Academy from 1822, chiefly landscapes and views of architectural subjects in various parts of the British Isles and northern Europe. Most of his known works are watercolours; his oils are relatively rare. His outstanding achievement was as a topographical artist, recording the changing streets of his native town and copying earlier pictures of its vanished buildings. He began producing such works at the age of about thirteen and published them in the form of lithographs as *Pictorial Relics of Ancient Liverpool* in 1843 and 1856; two further volumes appeared in 1878. Many of these watercolours are now in the Central Library, Liverpool, some having been transferred there from the Walker Art Gallery in the same city. He also published a selection of continental views under the title *Studies from the Folio of William Herdman* (1838), and *Views of Fleetwood-on-Wyre* (1838), and wrote on such diverse subjects as perspective, cosmology, and skating, as well as composing hymns and poetry.

Herdman was married to Elizabeth Darley Innes, and they had eleven sons and five daughters. Four sons—William, W. Patrick, J. Innes, and Stanley—worked as topographical artists and assisted their father with some of his publications. The younger William published a volume *Views of Modern Liverpool* in 1864. Herdman died at 41 St Domingo Vale, Everton, Liverpool, on 29 March 1882 and was buried on 3 April in Anfield cemetery, Liverpool.

JOSEPH SHARPLES

Sources R. Stewart-Brown, 'The Herdman drawings of old Liverpool', *Transactions of the Historic Society of Lancashire and Cheshire*, 63 (1911), 5–18 · H. C. Marillier, *The Liverpool school of painters: an account of the Liverpool Academy from 1810 to 1867, with memoirs of the principal artists* (1904), 136–42 · M. Bennett, *Merseyside painters, people and places*, 2 vols. (1978) · E. Morris and E. Roberts, *The Liverpool Academy and other exhibitions of contemporary art in Liverpool, 1774–1867* (1998) · *Liverpool Mercury* (1 April 1882) · *Liverpool Mercury* (24 May 1882) · Walker Art Gallery, Liverpool, Liverpool Academy records · burial register, Anfield cemetery, Lpool RO · grave, Anfield cemetery, Liverpool

Archives Liverpool Central Library, Liverpool Society of Fine Arts records · Walker Art Gallery, Liverpool, Liverpool Academy records

Likenesses T. Hargreaves, miniature, watercolour on ivory, 1826–7, Walker Art Gallery, Liverpool · H. E. Kidson, oils, 1895 (after photograph?), Walker Art Gallery, Liverpool

Wealth at death £83: probate, 2 Feb 1883, *CGPLA Eng. & Wales*

Herdson, Henry (b. c.1611), writer on mnemonics and memory, matriculated as a sizar from St John's College,

Cambridge, in 1626 and graduated BA in 1629–30. According to Venn he may have been rector of Harkstead, Suffolk, in 1632. As self-styled professor of the art of memory (at least 'by Publick Authority', if not according to any more conventional body), he taught in London, at or near to the Green Dragon by St Antholin Church (just east of St Paul's). Shortly before his books appeared (though possibly as early as 1647) he made an appearance at the church of St Dunstan-in-the-East, where he accosted Dr Thomas Fuller as the latter was leaving the pulpit. Fuller, describing the event some ten years later, wrote: 'when I came out of the pulpit of St Dunstan's East, one (who since wrote a book thereof) told me in the vestry, before credible people, that he in Sydney College had taught me the art of memory'. Fuller denied this, saying that he did not remember ever having seen Herdson before—'which, I conceive, was a real refutation!' In his *Life of Thomas Fuller* (1874) Bailey describes Herdson (perhaps uncharitably but hardly inaccurately) as 'the Memory-mountebank'.

Herdson's books both appeared in 1651; the two are generally found bound together. The first, whose dedication is dated 21 October 1651, is the Latin *Ars mnemonica, sive, Herdsonus Bruxiatus, vel, Bruxus Herdsoniatus*; this is in fact no more than a republication of part of Adam Brux's *Simonides redivivus* (1610). The second (this one in English), is *Ars Memoriae; the Art of Memory Made Plaine*, a summary of the principles of the art of mnemonics. According to Herdson, his is an art based on simple precepts; but he is insistent that it should not be less esteemed on these grounds—he considers that 'he must needs be malicious and unworthy, that will contemne this Art of Memory for the meanness of the Fundaments thereof'. This second book was reprinted in full in the second edition (1813) of Gregor von Feinaigle's *Art of Memory*. Though considered (by Herdson himself at least) his greatest work, it has not been much thought of by posterity; even Feinaigle described it as 'in small compass'.   DANIEL HAHN

Sources H. Herdson, *Ars mnemonica, sive, Herdsonus Bruxiatus, vel, Bruxus Herdsoniatus* (1651) · H. Herdson, *Ars memoriae; the art of memory made plaine* (1651) · G. von Feinaigle, *Art of memory*, 2nd edn (1813) · J. E. Bailey, *The life of Thomas Fuller* (1874) · T. Cooper, 'Dr Thomas Fuller, Henry Herdson, and "The art of memory"', *N&Q*, 3rd ser., 3 (1863), 383–4 · *DNB* · BL, Add. MS 5871, fol. 195 · Venn, *Alum. Cant.*

Hereberht [St Hereberht, Herebert, Herbert] (*d.* **687**), hermit, resided on the island in Derwent Water which still bears his name. He was a disciple and close friend of St Cuthbert, to whom he paid an annual visit for spiritual advice. The two friends both died on 20 March 687. In 1374 Thomas Appleby, bishop of Carlisle, directed the vicar of Crossthwaite to hold a yearly mass on St Herbert's Isle on his feast day (20 March), and granted forty days' indulgence to those who visited it then. The ruins of a circular stone building on the island may be associated with Hereberht.

C. L. KINGSFORD, *rev.* MARIOS COSTAMBEYS

Sources Bede, *Hist. eccl.*, 4.29 · P. Grosjean, 'The supposed Irish origin of St Cuthbert', *The relics of St Cuthbert*, ed. C. F. Battiscombe (1956), 144–54 · B. Colgrave, ed. and trans., *Two lives of Saint Cuthbert* (1940) · D. H. Farmer, *The Oxford dictionary of saints* (1978)

Hereford. For this title name *see* Ralph, earl of Hereford (*d.* 1057); Breteuil, Roger de, earl of Hereford (*fl.* 1071–1087); Gloucester, Miles of, earl of Hereford (*d.* 1143); Roger, earl of Hereford (*d.* 1155); Bohun, Henry de, first earl of Hereford (1176–1220); Bohun, Humphrey (IV) de, second earl of Hereford and seventh earl of Essex (*d.* 1275); Bohun, Humphrey (VI) de, third earl of Hereford and eighth earl of Essex (*c.*1249–1298); Bohun, Humphrey (VII) de, fourth earl of Hereford and ninth earl of Essex (*c.*1276–1322); Devereux, Walter, first Viscount Hereford (*c.*1489–1558).

Hereford, Nicholas (*b. c.*1345, *d.* after 1417), ecclesiastic and Wycliffite, may have been a native of Hereford. He is first recorded in September 1369, by when he was a fellow of Queen's College, Oxford, where he was treasurer in 1374/5. In the meantime he had been ordained priest on 8 June 1370, which suggests that he was born no later than 1345. He incepted as DTh in 1382. He must have either formed or maintained some connection with Hereford, where he became chancellor of the diocese by papal provision in 1375, an appointment confirmed by the king on 20 February 1377; however, this was later nullified through Pope Gregory XI's reservation of all cathedral dignities.

Although in the following century Hereford would be accused of having been a source of inspiration to John Ball at the time of the peasants' revolt, and also of having given retrospective support to the murder of Archbishop Sudbury, his public career as a follower of John Wyclif is reliably recorded only from 1382. By early in that year the mendicants in Oxford, and especially the Carmelites, considered him their principal enemy. Two of his sermons preached that spring suggest they were right to do so. In the first, a Lenten university sermon delivered in Latin in St Mary's, Oxford, he argued that no one from a religious order ought to receive a degree from the university. In the second, a public sermon delivered in English to town and gown in St Frideswide's churchyard on 15 May, Ascension day (it survives in Bodl. Oxf., MS Bodley 240, fols. 848–50, a notarial *reportatio* commissioned by his Carmelite opponents, and now edited), Hereford freely acknowledged his opposition to the friars, and argued that monks and canons, too, should be disendowed, and all religious set to manual work. This, he claimed, would produce social peace and lower taxation. And he called on the faithful Christians in his audience to put their hands to the wheel to bring this change about.

On 12 June 1382 Hereford, who had lately been one of a group preaching and teaching Wycliffite theses in and around Odiham, in Hampshire, was suspended from preaching and study by Archbishop Courtenay, whose decree was published by Chancellor Robert Rygge in Oxford three days later. Meanwhile Hereford and his associate Philip Repyndon, who had been summoned to the Blackfriars Council held in London on 14 June, had there refused to sign a condemnation of twenty-four heresies and errors attributed to Wyclif. On 16 June they applied for help to John of Gaunt, duke of Lancaster, who, under pressure from the church authorities, rebuffed them.

They were then summoned to the third session of the council, held on 18 June, and given until 20 June to reply concerning the twenty-four heresies and errors. Hereford and Repyndon responded with an evasive written statement in which they condemned equivocally five of the ten heresies and five of the fourteen errors. But for the remainder they agreed only to the condemnations in so far as the doctrines at issue were contrary to named decrees from canon law (in four cases), or in so far as those decrees circumscribed the legal or theological basis of the theses they had been propounding (in the remaining cases). With regard to thesis 17, for instance, which states that 'temporal lords may, by their judgment, take away temporal goods from clerics who habitually offend', Hereford and Repyndon conceded that this was an erroneous thesis, but only 'beyond those cases [already] defined in the laws of the church and of kingdoms' (*Fasciculi zizaniorum*, 323). The council examined them on their statement, and in the proceedings that followed Hereford, who was nothing if not excitable, declared that he was prepared to be burnt in defence of one particular thesis. Both he and Repyndon were found guilty of heresy, but sentence was deferred for a week. On 27 June once more no decision was reached, and so they were summoned to Canterbury chapter house for 1 July. Neither appeared, and both men were condemned and excommunicated.

Unlike Repyndon, Hereford chose to pursue matters by an appeal to the pope in person. He evaded possible arrest and went to Rome. But once Hereford had presented his case, Urban VI and the cardinals in consistory condemned him to life imprisonment. However, in June 1385 he escaped from gaol during the popular uprising that accompanied the siege of Pope Urban in Nocera by Charles II, king of Naples, and returned to England, where he may have been sheltered at Shenley by Sir John Montagu, a strong Lollard sympathizer. Archbishop Courtenay renewed his excommunication, and on 15 January 1386 requested a writ for Hereford's capture. Hereford was arrested and imprisoned in Nottingham town gaol in January 1387, probably transferred to the castle gaol in February, and presumably thence to the archbishop's custody. But he appears to have been free again by the summer of 1387, since on 10 August Bishop Wakefield of Worcester forbade him to preach in his diocese, on the grounds that he and others were spreading heresy in Bristol and elsewhere.

Bale's statement that Hereford was further imprisoned by the archbishop at Saltwood, Kent, in 1396 is unlikely to be correct, for he appears to have made his peace with Courtenay in 1391. Indeed, on 12 December 1391 he was granted royal protection for 'his zeal in preaching privately and openly in opposition to false teachers who subverted the Catholic faith' (*CPR, 1391–6*, 8). Since 22 January 1391 he had been rector of St Mary in the Marsh (in the Romney Marshes, Kent), and held this living until he was appointed chancellor of St Paul's Cathedral, London, on 1 July 1395, subsequently resigning in December 1396. He was briefly rector of Somerton, Oxfordshire, from August

to December 1397, and held prebends in St David's Cathedral from December 1396 to August 1397, and in Abergwili College (also in south-west Wales), also from December 1396. But his primary residence appears to have been Hereford, where in 1393 he was one of the local assessors appointed by Bishop Trefnant for the trial of Walter Bryt, and where on 16 February 1394 a royal grant restored him to the chancellorship of the diocese; shortly afterwards he received the prebend of Pratum Majus. A royal grant of trees for fuel in 1395 was conditional on his residing at Hereford. In November 1401 Henry IV added a yearly tun of wine. On 30 March 1397 Hereford was collated to the treasurership of the cathedral. Ceasing to be chancellor, he held his latest office until 2 November 1417, when he resigned it. Perhaps in the previous year he had exchanged Pratum Majus for Pratum Minor; now he resigned this as well. Instead he entered the Charterhouse in Coventry, and there he died as a monk, at an unrecorded date.

In the period 1382–91 Hereford had been an important protagonist of Wycliffite ideas in writing as well as by preaching. In July 1382 an investigation was ordered into books he was editing or compiling, and a commission of April 1388 was instructed to examine and confiscate all kinds of writings by him and by Wyclif. An injunction of 23 May 1388 referred more specifically to compilations and writings in English and Latin. Hereford and Repyndon are also said to have nailed a list of theses to the door of St Paul's Cathedral in 1382, and to have distributed broadsheets to solicit support in London. More significantly, Hereford was almost certainly one of the group of scholars who worked on the translation of the Bible into English. However, his contribution should not be exaggerated. Although a phrase in one manuscript has been construed as claiming that he translated the Old Testament up to Baruch 3: 20, such an interpretation misrepresents what was essentially a collaborative project, involving a number of scholars, of whom Hereford was reportedly one.

In the last resort, Hereford's contribution to the early development of Lollardy lay primarily in his role in the dissemination of Wyclif's ideas to a wider public outside Oxford. He played a key role in winning support from lay lords. John of Gaunt ultimately proved unreliable, but after 1382 Hereford may have been directly involved with two of the so-called 'Lollard knights', Sir William Neville (who had custody of Hereford when he was a prisoner at Nottingham) and Sir John Montagu. His beliefs and preaching in 1382, and especially his Ascension day sermon, with its call for the disendowment of the church and its return to apostolic poverty, were attractive to such lords, and to the laity in general, and in their public and practical articulation of Wyclif's idealism may justly be described as revolutionary. SIMON FORDE

Sources Emden, *Oxf.*, 2.913–15 • [T. Netter], *Fasciculi zizaniorum magistri Johannis Wyclif cum tritico*, ed. W. W. Shirley, Rolls Series, 5 (1858) • A. Hudson, *The premature reformation: Wycliffite texts and Lollard history* (1988) • S. Forde, 'Nicholas Hereford's Ascension day sermon, 1382', *Mediaeval Studies*, 51 (1989), 205–41 · A. Hudson, *Lollards and their books* (1985) · *Fasti Angl., 1300–1541*, [Hereford] · *CPR, 1391–6*

Archives Bodl. Oxf., MS Bodley 240, pp. 848–50

Hereford, Roger of [*called* Roger Infans, Roger Puer] (*fl.* 1176–1198), astronomer, is of unknown origins, but his association with Hereford is confirmed by the fact that he arranged a set of astronomical tables for the meridian of Hereford in 1178, and he is probably to be identified with the Roger Infans who witnessed several Hereford charters between 1186 and 1198. For the former bishop of Hereford, Gilbert Foliot (*d.* 1187), he wrote an ecclesiastical computus (for calculating the church calendar) in 1176. This criticizes the standard work of Gerland, a product of the late eleventh century, and refers to the Hebrews and 'Chaldeans' (by which is usually meant 'Arabs'). Roger's astronomical tables were adapted from the tables for Marseilles composed by Raimond de Marseille in 1141, which were, in turn, an arrangement of the Toledan tables, a Latin translation of an Arabic set of tables drawn up by ar-Zarqala in Toledo in 1080. Roger also wrote a comprehensive text on astrology which he may never have completed—the *Liber de quatuor partibus judiciorum astronomie*, which draws not only on a corresponding work by Raimond de Marseille, but also on the translations of Arabic astrological texts made by Juan de Sevilla and Hermann of Carinthia. Other works of astrology and alchemy are attributed to him in manuscripts. To him (as Roger Puer) is dedicated the translation (from Arabic) and commentary on the pseudo-Aristotelian *De plantis* made by Alfred of Shareshill, a leading figure in the introduction of Aristotle's natural philosophy into England in the years around 1200. To Roger of Hereford may be attributed the invention of a new way of calculating horoscopes mathematically. He did much to further the study of the mathematical sciences in England, and provides a link between the early twelfth-century pioneers in this study, Adelard of Bath and Petrus Alfonsi, and Robert Grosseteste (*d.* 1253), who joined the bishop's household in Hereford while Roger was still active there.

CHARLES BURNETT

Sources C. H. Haskins, *Studies in the history of mediaeval science*, 2nd edn (1927), 123–6 · J. C. Russell, 'Hereford and Arabic science in England, *c.*1175–1200', *Isis*, 18 (1932–3), 14–25 · J. D. North, *Horoscopes and history* (1986), 39–41 · R. W. Southern, *Robert Grosseteste: the growth of an English mind in medieval Europe*, 2nd edn (1992), lii–liii · R. French, 'Foretelling the future: Arabic astrology and English medicine in the late twelfth century', *Isis*, 87 (1996), 453–80

Heren, Louis Philip (1919–1995), journalist, was born on 6 February 1919 in Shadwell, in the docklands of Wapping, London, the second son and third and youngest child of William Heren (*d.* 1923/4), a machine minder on *The Times*, and his wife, Beatrice, *née* Keller. His life was a true *Times* romance of the messenger boy who almost became editor. His paternal grandfather was a French Basque; his maternal grandfather a German Jew; and he also had Irish blood. He grew up in the East End during the depression. His father died when Heren was four, and his mother supported the family by running a greasy-spoon café near the

gates of London Docks. She was offended when Heren called his autobiography *Growing up Poor in London*. She said that 'Growing up among the poor in London' would have been accurate.

Heren was educated at St George's, the local grammar school, where his English teacher introduced him to Dickens, G. A. Henty, and Conrad, and kindled his lifelong interest in gripping narrative and rattling good yarns. He became an autodidact and avid borrower of books from the public library. In those days *The Times* was a paternalist club that looked after '*Times* men'. So in 1933 it hired Heren, when he left school aged fourteen, as a messenger in the publicity department. *The Times* proved a substitute for secondary and university education. An assistant editor spotted the messenger boy reading Conrad's *Nostromo* in a corner, and mentioned the prodigy to his colleagues. Stanley Morison, the *éminence grise* of *The Times*, took an interest in the boy and helped him to become a reporter. Heren's first assignment for *The Times* in 1937 was to report the East End parties celebrating the coronation of George VI. As a junior reporter he would volunteer for weekend duty in Printing House Square, which he described as 'a very cushy job'. He loved having the old house to himself, sleeping in a bed with crisp linen sheets after a dinner served by 'a manservant from the chief proprietor's house', being called on Sunday morning with a cup of tea, and then having a breakfast of bacon and eggs in the editorial sitting room while reading the Sunday papers and marking stories worth following up (Heren, *Growing up Poor in London*, 136).

In 1939 Heren volunteered for the Royal Artillery, and served as a gunner non-commissioned officer in France, Iceland, and Greenland. He was then commissioned into the Royal Tank regiment, serving in India, Burma, the Yunnan province of China, and south-east Asia. War service gave him a taste for travel. So *The Times* transferred him to the foreign department, and in 1947 he was appointed the *Times* correspondent to India, where he described the massacres of partition with the sensitivity and courage of a front-line reporter. On 16 June 1948 he married Patricia Cecilia Regan (1924/5–1975), daughter of Thomas Francis Regan, a civil servant in the Air Ministry. They had one son and three daughters.

Heren was next posted to Palestine, which had become a shambles of terrorism and bloodshed, culminating in the birth of Israel in 1948, when Britain withdrew from its mandate. When Ian Morrison, the staff correspondent covering the Korean War, was killed by a landmine, Heren was sent to replace him. For the next quarter of a century Heren flew towards the sound of the guns and the political drums as brilliantly as his predecessor on *The Times*, William Howard Russell, the first professional war correspondent, a century before. While he was in Korea, Heren compared the relief of having filed a story under gunfire and deadline to 'having a good shit'. He was subsequently based in Singapore (1951–3), Delhi (1953–5), and Bonn (1955–60). While he was covering the communist uprising in Malaya he had serious brushes with the Templar administration. The reputation of *The Times* being what it then was, the good and the great regarded its staff as just another arm of the establishment. Neither Heren's working-class background nor his bolshie temperament responded to this old boy network. He said: 'Always ask yourself why these lying bastards are lying to you' (Heren, *Growing up on 'The Times'*, 26). From every country where he reported his office was bombarded with complaints from those in authority, whose feathers he had ruffled.

In 1960 Heren was appointed head of the Washington bureau. He arrived there in time for the inauguration of President Kennedy, but the succeeding Johnson era was more suited to Heren's skills than the glitter of Camelot. He reported the upsurge and climax of racial tension and civil rights disturbances, and the rise in opposition to American involvement in Vietnam, recording the anguish and divisions that split the American nation as it became bogged down in a war that could not be won. His decade in Washington was the pinnacle of Heren's career. By 1970 he was ready to come home out of the cold, mainly because his wife was ill (in fact dying). He returned as deputy editor (foreign). But he found life in London anticlimactic and frustrating. Like many foreign correspondents he was something of a lone wolf and a prima donna. He would not write leaders because they were unsigned. He was not a team player in the court of office politics, for he was still at heart a reporter from the front lines. He caused outrage in some quarters when he invited Menachem Begin to lunch at *The Times*. At the time Begin was leader of the Israeli opposition, and still *persona non grata* with the British government because of his terrorist activities during the British mandate in Palestine. In 1979 he provoked similar outrage when he invited Anthony Blunt to a *Times* lunch immediately after Blunt's traitorous activities had been exposed. Both lunches brought the paper front-page scoops.

Heren was reckoned a favourite to succeed William Rees-Mogg as editor when Kenneth Thomson sold *The Times* to Rupert Murdoch in 1981. He applied for the post, and wrote a long memorandum to the new proprietor about changes that he believed were necessary to make the paper profitable and to restore its former glories. That appointment would have made Heren a legend in his own *Times*, worthy of a Samuel Smiles or Horatio Alger penny novel about the virtuous apprentice. But Heren's bid was unsuccessful, and he suffered a second disappointment when he was deprived of the deputy editorship. His final year at *The Times* became embittered, and in 1981 he left the paper to which he had devoted his life to concentrate on writing more books about himself, the press, and America.

Heren was a stocky, pugnacious, chippy man, with a dangerous look in his eye. He enjoyed good company and good food in fine surroundings, especially his beloved Garrick Club. He would recommend his favourite restaurant in any city in the world. He was the best war correspondent of his generation, and a proper '*Times* man'. He died of a heart attack at his home, Fleet House, Vale of Health, Hampstead, London, on 26 January 1995. After a funeral at

St Mary's Roman Catholic Church, Hampstead, he was cremated at Golders Green crematorium on 2 February. He was survived by his son and three daughters. A memorial service was held at St Bride's, Fleet Street, London, on 28 March 1995.   PHILIP HOWARD

Sources WWW, 1991–5 · J. Grigg, *The history of The Times*, 6 (1993) · News Int. RO, *The Times* archive · *The Times* (27 Jan 1995) · *The Guardian* (28 Jan 1995) · *The Independent* (28 Jan 1995) · L. Heren, *Growing up poor in London* (1973) · L. Heren, *Growing up on 'The Times'* (1978) · L. Heren, *Memories of Times past* (1988) · O. Woods and J. Bishop, *The story of 'The Times'* (1983) · m. cert. · *The Times* (3 Feb 1995) · *The Times* (29 March 1995)
Archives News Int. RO, MSS |FILM BFI NFTVA, 'The light of experience', BBC2, 20 March 1977
Likenesses photograph, repro. in *The Times* (27 Jan 1995) · photograph, repro. in *The Independent* · photograph, repro. in *The Times* (3 Feb 1995)
Wealth at death £541,223: probate, 10 May 1995, *CGPLA Eng. & Wales*

Herewald (*d*. 1104/1107), bishop in south-east Wales and the border, had jurisdiction over an area that by the early twelfth century had been assimilated to Llandaff. No certain details are known about his consecration. In the twelfth-century Book of Llandaff, he is treated as the successor to Bishop Joseph (*d*. 1045) and called bishop of Llandaff, but the title is anachronistic and the statements as to the personnel present at his consecration, and its date and place, are contradictory and formulaic. There survives, moreover, a claim originating from St David's that he was consecrated neither by Archbishop Cynesige of York, nor by Archbishop Lanfranc of Canterbury (as the Book of Llandaff variously states), but by Joseph of St David's. All three versions may belong to the context of the dispute between St David's and Llandaff over episcopal jurisdiction in the twelfth century. It is possible that Herewald did not, in fact, succeed Joseph. The Anglo-Saxon Chronicle records the death of a Welsh bishop Tremerig in 1052, who also seems to have been active in south-east Wales. He may have been Herewald's predecessor. Circumstances on the Herefordshire–Wales border at this time, particularly the death in battle of Bishop Leofgar of Hereford in 1056, make the involvement of Cynesige in Herewald's consecration more plausible, as the bishop of Worcester, who administered Hereford for four years after Leofgar's death, was traditionally subordinate to York rather than Canterbury.

Very little is known of Herewald's career, outside his temporary suspension by Archbishop Anselm between 1093 and 1100, for reasons now obscure. His name suggests that he may not have been Welsh by birth, or at least that he had partly English ancestry. Accounts of his actions described in the narrations of charters in the Book of Llandaff cannot be taken as completely reliable. It may be that the attempt in these charters to associate him with all the overlords of Morgannwg in the later eleventh century, from Gruffudd ap Llywelyn (*d*. 1063/4) to Roger de Breteuil, is particularly suspicious, as it has the effect of associating him not only with the whole range of territory claimed by Llandaff in the twelfth century, but also with almost all the secular sources of power. A list of churches consecrated by him, found in the same volume, appears, interestingly, to locate him mainly in the border area of Ergyng. Again, however, the reliability of this material cannot be assumed: it might represent an attempt to promote Llandaff's claims against the see of Hereford. The Book of Llandaff credits Herewald with two sons, Mai and Lifris. The latter is associated with the church of Llancarfan, and is probably the author of the life of Cadog. The former may perhaps be identifiable with the Maius who testified to Pope Honorius II regarding the extent of the diocese of Llandaff c.1129. It may be, therefore, that one or both of Herewald's sons were involved in promoting Llandaff's claims (and contributed, therefore, to the problems surrounding the evidence for their father's career).

Herewald died on 6 March 1104, according to the Book of Llandaff; an interpolated entry in *Brenhinedd y Saesson* places his death in 1107. The former is more likely.

K. L. MAUND

Sources J. G. Evans and J. Rhys, eds., *The text of the Book of Llan Dâv reproduced from the Gwysaney manuscript* (1893) · *Gir. Camb. opera*, 3.57 · *S. Anselmi Cantuariensis archiepiscopi opera omnia*, ed. F. S. Schmitt, 6 vols. (1938–61), vol. 4 · T. Jones, ed. and trans., *Brenhinedd y Saesson, or, The kings of the Saxons* (1971), 104–8 [another version of *Brut y tywysogyon*] · C. N. L. Brooke, *The church and the Welsh border in the central middle ages* (1986), 92–4 · W. Davies, 'The consecration of the bishops of Llandaff in the tenth and eleventh centuries', *BBCS*, 26 (1974–6), 53–73

Hereward [*called* Hereward the Wake] (*fl.* **1070–1071**), rebel, is a figure on whom there is little reliable, and much suspect, information. It has been suggested that his epithet, the Wake, signifies 'the wakeful one'. It is, in fact, late, first appearing in the mid-thirteenth-century chronicle of John of Peterborough without gloss, and is more likely to be derived from Hereward's supposed relationship with the manor of Bourne in Lincolnshire, which from the mid-twelfth century was held by the Wake family.

Contemporary or near-contemporary sources for Hereward's life with some claim to unimpeachable authority are confined to the D version of the Anglo-Saxon Chronicle and to Domesday Book. They are sufficient to demonstrate his existence and a celebrated role in the English resistance to Norman rule in and around the Isle of Ely in 1070–71, but little more. The more detailed accounts of his life are all later and of equivocal value. An early twelfth-century interpolation into the E version of the Anglo-Saxon Chronicle, a closely related passage in Hugh Candidus's history of Peterborough Abbey dating from the mid-twelfth century, and the twelfth-century *Liber Eliensis*, expand on Hereward's resistance and clearly encapsulate the traditions of the two foundations of Peterborough and Ely at the time. But neither is uninfluenced by a contemporary chanson cycle inspired by Hereward's renown. Elements of this cycle survive in Gaimar's *Lestoire des Engles* dating from the 1140s, and in the late medieval *Historia Croylandensis* from Crowland. It is, however, most fully represented in the early twelfth-century *Gesta Herewardi*. An elaboration of the *Liber Eliensis*, this deals with Hereward's birth and early career as well as his resistance to the Normans. It manifestly draws on literary devices and heroic topoi, and, seemingly contradicting the few details afforded by the contemporary sources, it has been almost universally execrated. Nevertheless, it may embody some authentic detail.

It is impossible to determine Hereward's family background with any certainty. The chanson tradition identifies him as the son of a Leofric of Bourne (variously said to be a kinsman of Ralph the Staller, Ralph, earl of Hereford, and Brand, abbot of Peterborough) and of an Eadgyth, the great-great-great-niece of Oslac, earl of Northumberland. None of these assertions can be substantiated. Nevertheless, it seems likely that Hereward was of high social status. Domesday Book seemingly reveals that he held only a small estate in Laughton in his own right (there is no reason to believe that the Hereward who held lands in Warwickshire and Worcestershire in 1066 and 1086 was the same man), but he was otherwise a tenant of Peterborough Abbey in Witham on the Hill and Barholme and Stowe, and of Crowland Abbey in Rippingale, all in a small area of Kesteven in southern Lincolnshire. Nevertheless, the annual rent which he paid for Rippingale was a kind of tenure more typical of a political ally than of a subordinate. There are, moreover, indications that Hereward conferred title on Oger the Breton for much of his lands in 1086, and he can therefore probably be identified as a king's thegn. Whether he ever held Bourne is unclear; Domesday Book ascribes the manor to Earl Morcar in 1066, but much of Morcar's estates in south Lincolnshire was apparently forfeitures held by him as earl or by his representative.

Leofric (*fl.* 1070–1071), priest, who should not be confused with Hereward's father, is named by the author of the *Gesta Herewardi* as Hereward's priest at Bourne and the writer of an Old English life of the rebel which provided much of the information in the first part of the *Gesta*; authentic detail there may indicate the existence of such a source or a similar one.

According to the *Gesta Herewardi*, Hereward was a quarrelsome child and youth; and at the age of eighteen he was exiled for his unruliness at the petition of his exasperated father. He is then said to have wandered in Northumberland, Cornwall, Ireland, and Flanders. On his return to England, Hereward found that his brother had been murdered and his patrimony seized by Normans. Revenge quickly ensued, and he gathered around him a small band of discontented Englishmen. He was knighted 'in the English manner' by Abbot Brand of Peterborough; and he then encountered and slew a certain Frederick, before returning to Flanders. After a further adventure there he returned to England for good. Much of this must be romance, although an account of an expedition into 'Scaldimariland' (that is, Zeeland) by Manasses (I), count of Guînes, can be placed in a contemporary historical context; and Hereward's murder of Frederick, who can be identified as the brother of Gundrada, wife of William (I) de Warenne, is, in a seemingly independent source, substantiated by the Hyde chronicle.

Hereward comes into focus as a historical figure with the siege of the Isle of Ely as recorded in the Anglo-Saxon Chronicle. In the spring of 1070, a Danish fleet arrived in the Humber and roused the country to revolt against the Normans. At the same time the abbey of Peterborough was plundered 'by the men that Bishop Æthelric had excommunicated because there they had taken all that he had' (*ASC*, s.a. 1071, text D). In the following year earls Eadwine and Morcar rebelled against Norman rule and retreated into the fenland with various discontented Englishmen. In reply King William dispatched a fleet and land force and besieged the Isle of Ely. The rebels were forced to submit 'except Hereward alone and those who could escape with him and he led them out valiantly' (*ASC*, s.a. 1072, text D).

The later sources are more fulsome, but there is no reason to doubt the essential veracity of the account they give. All are in agreement that Hereward led the assault on Peterborough Abbey as the leader of the abbey's tenants who resented the appointment of the Norman Turold to the house. Hereward at this time seems to have been in alliance with the Danes, and Peterborough tradition saw the action as one motivated by pure greed. There is, however, perhaps some truth in Hereward's concern, reported by Hugh Candidus, for the well-being of the foundation; as a prominent tenant of the abbey he may well have considered that he was acting in its best interests. Nevertheless, much of the treasure of the abbey was taken by the Danes after Hereward retreated to Ely.

There is no information on Hereward's activities in the next few months, but after Eadwine and Morcar's resort to the Isle, he is portrayed as a principal actor in the opposition to the besiegers by the author of the *Liber Eliensis* in an account that apparently draws on local knowledge. The monks of Ely are said to have feared that their abbot, Thurstan, was to be replaced by a foreign cleric and called upon Hereward to defend them. However, given the high status of the rebels, it seems unlikely that Hereward was the actual leader. His valiant escape, though, must suggest that he was a daring soldier who impressed the rebels with his courage and ingenuity.

There is no contemporary evidence for Hereward's fate after his escape from the Isle of Ely. The later sources all agree that he was reconciled with William the Conqueror and regained his patrimony. Gaimar asserts that he was subsequently killed by a band of Englishmen, but the *Gesta Herewardi* and the *Historia Croylandensis* imply that he died in his bed. He is said to have been buried at Crowland. According to the *Historia*, he was succeeded in his estates by a daughter. Hereward had married an aristocratic Flemish woman called Turfrida before his return to England (Gaimar alone reports a second marriage—to Alftruda). Their daughter is not named, but she is said to have married Hugh d'Evermue, and they in their turn were succeeded by a daughter who married Richard de Rullos. This descent is not wholly consistent with the known history

of the barony of Bourne which incorporated Hereward's lands. However, title thereto continued to inform a dispute between the lords of Bourne and Peterborough Abbey into the mid-twelfth century, and it might therefore be suspected that the story contains a germ of truth.

The legend of Hereward developed at an early period. The laconic reference to him in the D version of the Anglo-Saxon Chronicle suggests that within a few years of the event his daring escape was so famous that it required no further explanation. More clearly, the E version of the Anglo-Saxon Chronicle and Hugh Candidus's history drew on an English source written before 1121, and one of the three sources employed in the *Liber Eliensis* appears to have been written in English. The audience was probably always local in the middle ages, but by the early twelfth century it was not exclusively English; Gaimar's history was written for an Anglo-Norman audience that could celebrate its English antecedents. The legend remained alive and probably vital into the later middle ages, as attested by the *Historia Croylandensis*, and as late as 1407 a genealogy was drawn up tracing the supposed descent of Edmund Holland, earl of Kent, from Hereward. Hereward owes his current popularity as an archetypal English hero in the mould of Robin Hood to the publication of the *Gesta Herewardi* in the nineteenth century and to Charles Kingsley's novel *Hereward the Wake* (1866) which is largely based upon it.

DAVID ROFFE

Sources *ASC*, s.a. 1071–2 [text D]; s.a. 1070, 1071 [text E] • A. Farley, ed., *Domesday Book*, 2 vols. (1783) • *The chronicle of Hugh Candidus, a monk of Peterborough*, ed. W. T. Mellows (1949) • E. O. Blake, ed., *Liber Eliensis*, CS, 3rd ser., 92 (1962) • *L'estoire des Engleis by Geffrei Gaimar*, ed. A. Bell, Anglo-Norman Texts, 14–16 (1960) • Ingulf, 'Historia Ingulphi', *Rerum Anglicarum scriptorum veterum*, ed. [W. Fulman], 1 (1684), 1–107 • Ingulf and Petrus Blesensis, 'Petri Blesensis continuatio ad Historiam Ingulphi', *Rerum Anglicarum scriptorum veterum*, ed. [W. Fulham], 1 (1684), 108–32 [see also pp. 449–593] • 'Gesta Herwardi incliti exulis et militis', *Lestorie des Engles solum la translacion Maistre Geffrei Gaimar*, ed. T. D. Hardy and C. T. Martin, 1 (1888), 339–404 • E. Edwards, ed., *Liber monasterii de Hyda*, Rolls Series, 45 (1866) • D. R. Roffe, 'Hereward "the Wake" and the barony of Bourne: a reassessment of a fenland legend', *Lincolnshire History and Archaeology*, 29 (1994), 7–10 • C. Hart, *The Danelaw* (1992) • J. H. Round, *Feudal England: historical studies on the eleventh and twelfth centuries* (1895) • E. M. C. Van Houts, 'The memory of 1066 in written and oral traditions', *Anglo-Norman Studies*, 19 (1996), 167–79 • E. M. C. Van Houts, 'Hereward and Flanders', *Anglo-Saxon England*, 28 (2000), 201–23 • E. King, 'The origins of the Wake family: the early history of the barony of Bourne in Lincolnshire', *Northamptonshire Past and Present*, 5 (1973–7), 166–76

Herfast (*d.* 1084), administrator and bishop of East Anglia, was a Norman. He appears first as chaplain to William, duke of Normandy. The only anecdote from his early career is William of Malmesbury's, probably apocryphal, story of a humiliating clash with Lanfranc, prior of Bec (before 1063). After the Norman conquest of England, Herfast subscribed royal charters as chancellor in 1068–9; and after papal legates had deposed the English bishops unacceptable to the Conqueror, at Easter 1070, he was at Whitsun rewarded with the diocese of East Anglia, replacing the married Æthelmaer, Archbishop Stigand's brother. He was consecrated by an unknown prelate before Lanfranc's consecration (at which he assisted) to Canterbury on 29 August.

Herfast's large and binary diocese, comprising the counties of Norfolk and Suffolk, had had a chequered history and no settled ecclesiastical centre; and in 1070 it was disturbed by a Danish invasion and Hereward's rebellion. Herfast seems to have called himself indifferently bishop of Elmham, Thetford, or Norwich. None had a church grand enough for one of the new bishops, and Herfast from the start had two major ambitions: to establish his see in a more suitable church and to enforce his spiritual authority over the abbeys. His attempt to enter Bury St Edmunds, ruled by the distinguished Baldwin, was, however, implacably resisted. Baldwin visited Rome and obtained in 1071 a protective bull from Alexander II; he commissioned the fabrication of useful royal charters, promoted the cult of St Edmund, and even exploited his medical skill. When the bishop badly damaged his eyes on a branch while riding through a wood, the abbot offered treatment in return for Herfast's renunciation of his scheme. And at Easter 1081, in a court summoned to London, after Herfast had produced his predecessor's kennelman as witness and Baldwin an abbot and some doctored charters, the king decided in Baldwin's favour and imposed a heavy financial pledge for Herfast's compliance. Still grieving at this defeat, Herfast died in 1084 and was remembered at Norwich on 27 January.

Monks inevitably regarded Herfast unfavourably. Lanfranc charged him with disrespectful behaviour and days spent in dicing, 'to name nothing worse' (*Letters of Lanfranc*, no. 47). He recommended study of the scriptures and canon law. William of Malmesbury thought him both unintelligent and uneducated and reported the prognosticon at his consecration as: 'Not this man, but [the robber] Barabbas' (John 18: 40), doubtless *bene trovato*. Although Herfast was unversed in that literary culture which these two monks so prized, as a ducal and royal chaplain he is unlikely to have been illiterate, and his having sons—in 1086 two or more were in possession of St Mary's, Thetford, while possibly another, Richard fitz Erfast, possessed churches near York—was no disqualification for episcopal orders. His servant Hermann, who wrote kindly of him in his miracles of St Edmund, thought him, by the standards of his time, a man intent on doing good, but led astray, as regards St Edmunds, by bad counsel. Indeed, he would seem to have attempted the reform of an ill-organized and distracted diocese, only to collide with an immoveable obstruction.

FRANK BARLOW

Sources Hermann the Archdeacon, 'De miraculis Sancti Eadmundi', *Memorials of St Edmund's Abbey*, ed. T. Arnold, 1, Rolls Series, 96 (1890), 26–92 · *Willelmi Malmesbiriensis monachi de gestis pontificum Anglorum libri quinque*, ed. N. E. S. A. Hamilton, Rolls Series, 52 (1870) · *The letters of Lanfranc, archbishop of Canterbury*, ed. and trans. H. Clover and M. Gibson, OMT (1979) · A. Gransden, 'Baldwin, abbot of Bury St Edmunds, 1065–1097', *Anglo-Norman Studies*, 4 (1981), 65–76 · M. Gibson, *Lanfranc of Bec* (1978) · A. Farley, ed., *Domesday Book*, 2 vols. (1783)

Herford, Anne Laura (1831–1870), painter, was born on 16 October 1831, probably in Altrincham, Cheshire, the ninth and youngest child of John Herford (1789–1855), wine merchant and philanthropist, and his wife, Sarah (1791–1831), artist and teacher, daughter of Edward Smith and his wife, Sarah, of Birmingham. Edward *Herford (1815–1896), Charles James Herford (1817–1891), William Henry *Herford (1820–1908), and Brooke *Herford (1830–1903)—who have been described as 'strenuous fighters in various fields of social service' (Herford, 4)—were her brothers. Both Anne Laura Herford's parents were from Unitarian families.

After the death in 1831 of Sarah Herford, who had run a prosperous girls' school in Altrincham, John Herford moved with his family into Manchester. In the 1850s Anne Laura Herford settled in London. She studied from the antique in the sculpture galleries of the British Museum and was a pupil both at Heatherley's academy in the late 1850s and at Eliza Bridell Fox's life drawing class. Arthur Paterson, Anne Laura Herford's nephew, wrote: 'Never was a Herford known who did not enjoy speaking his mind to those in authority above him' (Sharpe, 120). In 1859, when Lord Lyndhurst remarked in a speech on the benefits made available to all the queen's subjects by the Royal Academy Schools, Herford—referred to by E. C. Clayton as 'a most earnest and energetic student' (Clayton, 2.2)—wrote to him pointing out that women were excluded. Following communication with the president of the Royal Academy, Sir Charles Eastlake, she organized a petition signed by thirty-eight professional women artists and submitted a qualifying drawing signed simply A. L. Herford. Having accepted this, the Royal Academy was finally persuaded to admit women students. Herford became a probationer and entered the antique school in December 1860; in January 1862 she progressed to the school of the living draped model. A contemporary woman artist later commented: 'All the women students there owe much to Miss Herford's courage and talent' (Clayton, 2.3).

Herford exhibited a total of thirty-seven genre paintings and portraits, in oil and watercolour, at the Royal Academy (1861–7), Royal Manchester Institution (RMI) (1861–9), Royal Glasgow Institute (1861), Liverpool Academy and Liverpool Institute of Fine Arts (LIFA) (1862–5), British Institution (1863), Society of British Artists (SBA) (1864–8), Dudley Gallery, London (oil) (1867–9), and the Royal Scottish Academy (1869–70). Her genre scenes were chiefly domestic, such as *Girl Drawing* (exh. LIFA 1863) and *The New Book* (exh. SBA and RMI 1866); *A Garibaldian* (exh. LIFA 1864 and RMI 1865) and *Viva Garibaldi* (exh. SBA 1867) suggest political interests; another group, including *Rosalind* (exh. British Institution 1863), *Imogen* (exh. RMI 1866), and *Falstaff* (ex Parke-Bernet, Los Angeles, 22–3 May 1972), depicted characters from Shakespeare's plays. Herford's portraits included *The Reverend Dr. Sadler*, minister at Rosslyn Hill Unitarian Chapel in Hampstead (exh. RA, 1864), *Miss Macleod*, probably the genre painter Jessie Macleod (exh. Dudley Gallery 1868), and *Mrs. Scott Siddons*, the actress (exh. Royal Scottish Academy 1870). Between 1861 and 1865 Herford lived at various addresses in Hampstead and from 1866 to 1870 occupied 40 Fitzroy Square, where in January 1867 her niece Helen Paterson (later Mrs William Allingham), herself an art student, went to live with her. She died there, unmarried, on 28 October 1870 at the age of only thirty-nine. A post-mortem found that she had died of a 'fatty disease of the heart'.

CHARLOTTE YELDHAM

Sources d. cert. • E. C. Clayton, *English female artists*, 2 vols. (1876) • C. H. Herford, 'Memoir of W. H. Herford', in W. H. Herford, *The student's Froebel*, ed. D. B. and C. H., rev. edn, 2 vols. (1911–15) • *Art Journal*, 33 (1871), 80 • *The Athenaeum* (19 Nov 1870), 662 • M. Huish, *Happy England* (1903) • C. Yeldham, *Women artists in nineteenth-century France and England*, 1 (1984), 29 • Graves, *RA exhibitors* • Graves, *Brit. Inst.* • C. B. de Laperriere, ed., *The Royal Scottish Academy exhibitors, 1826–1990*, 4 vols. (1991) • R. Billcliffe, ed., *The Royal Glasgow Institute of the Fine Arts, 1861–1989: a dictionary of exhibitors at the annual exhibitions*, 4 vols. (1990–92) • E. Morris and E. Roberts, *The Liverpool Academy and other exhibitions of contemporary art in Liverpool, 1774–1867* (1998) • J. Johnson, ed., *Works exhibited at the Royal Society of British Artists, 1824–1893, and the New English Art Club, 1888–1917*, 2 vols. (1975) • exhibition catalogues (1867–9) [Dudley Gallery, London] • exhibition catalogues (1861–2); (1865–6); (1869) [Royal Manchester Institution] • cuttings on the Herford family, Man. CL, Manchester Archives and Local Studies • H. Sharpe, *The meeting house on Red Lion Hill and Rosslyn Hill Chapel* (1914) • council minutes, RA, vol. 11, 3 Aug 1860, 371

Wealth at death under £1500: probate, 3 Jan 1871, CGPLA Eng. & Wales

Herford, Brooke (1830–1903), Unitarian minister, was born in Altrincham, Cheshire, on 21 February 1830, the fourth son and eighth child of the surviving children of John Herford, a wholesale wine and spirit merchant in Manchester, and his wife, Sarah, daughter of Edward Smith of Birmingham. Edward *Herford and William Henry *Herford were her brothers. Sarah Herford died on 30 October 1831 at the age of forty, following the birth of a daughter, Anne Laura *Herford. John Herford subsequently married Helen Ryland (1803–1875), to whom Brooke Herford was deeply devoted.

Herford was educated in the school of the Unitarian minister John Relly Beard, and at the end of 1843 entered the counting-house of his father, who had also taken on an insurance agency. There he learned all aspects of both businesses, and in 1846 he was sent for six months to Paris, where he lived with the family of an agent of the venerable Bordeaux house of Barton et Guestier. He became fluent in French, and a month in Bordeaux acquainted him with the production side of the trade. His father, virtually retired by 1846, expected him to take over the businesses. He had, however, followed his elder brothers in Sunday school teaching in the schools connected with the Unitarian chapel in Mosley Street, and he formed a strong tie with Philip Pearsall Carpenter, minister at Warrington, who converted the younger man to teetotalism. In 1847 he told his father that he could not undertake any long-term commitment to the business and that he wanted to enter the ministry, an ambition that provoked considerable scepticism in the elder Herford, though he was later reconciled to his son's choice of career. He continued to work while studying for the entrance examinations for Manchester New College, then in Manchester. His determination on the ministry was strengthened by a close friendship with the charismatic and tragic figure of Travers Madge (1823–1866), youngest son of the well-known minister at Essex Street, London, Thomas Madge; after the younger Madge's untimely death Herford wrote a valuable memoir (1867).

In September 1848 Herford entered Manchester New College and acquitted himself impressively, but preaching was even more to him than scholastic attainment: he did missionary work in vacations, and as the college authorities refused to sanction combining his studies with a regular engagement as preacher at Todmorden, he withdrew in February 1851 to become the settled minister there. On 22 June 1852 he married Hannah (d. 1901), daughter of William Hankinson, of Hale, Cheshire; they had three sons and six daughters. In 1855 he resigned from Todmorden, finding the post too much like a private chaplaincy to the Fielden family, who had founded the church and still dominated congregational affairs. In January 1856 Herford became minister at Upper Chapel, Sheffield. The success of his ministry there was in part based upon his intelligent sympathy with the working classes; his lecture in 1861 to a chapel crowded with working men, entitled 'Trade outrages', was a striking example of plain and bold speaking. He did much missionary work here too, in Sheffield (leading to the formation of the Upperthorpe congregation) and Rotherham, and in Yorkshire and Derbyshire villages. This effort led in 1859 to his appointment as missionary tutor to the newly founded Unitarian Home Missionary Board (later College, and then Unitarian College), Manchester, adding this engagement to his Sheffield work. In 1861 he was one of the founders and editors of the *Unitarian Herald* and in 1865, with William Gaskell, bought out the other two editors, John Relly Beard and John Wright (1824–1900), minister at Bury. In 1862 he began the publication of *Home Pages*, a popular series of religious tracts.

In November 1864 Herford succeeded Beard in the ministry of New Bridge Street Chapel, Strangeways, Manchester. He had insisted, as a condition of his coming, that the congregation move to a system of free sittings—a question then much canvassed among Unitarians—and that his income be dependent only on the offertory. Sheffield had recently raised his salary to £400, and, as subscriptions at Strangeways had never amounted to £200, a considerable risk was being run. But the congregation agreed, and Herford accepted, although the reality appears to have been rather different from the expectation: he received a stipend augmented by offertories, and additional special offertories were called on two occasions when an upward adjustment was necessary, one in 1873, when they were eager to persuade him to stay. By that time he was seriously overworked. On the death of John Harland in 1868 Herford took over the preparation of the second volume of a new edition of the well-known guide to Lancashire by Edward Baines (1774–1848); the volume was published in 1870, but his travels throughout the county had damaged his health. A proposal that his ministry be shared, by alternating services with Philip Henry Wicksteed of Dukinfield and another minister, came to naught, and it was clearly a matter of time until he departed.

Herford visited the United States in 1875, and moved there later in the same year, having been called to the church of the Messiah, Chicago, where he began his ministry in January 1876. In 1881 he declined an invitation to the First Church in Cambridge, Massachusetts, but in 1882 agreed to become the minister of Arlington Street Church, Boston, where stern custom was unyielding to his views on seat holding; he remained there until January 1892. In America his forceful but genial personality found scope for abundant activities. He was chairman of the council of the American Unitarian conference (1889–91), and in 1891 became preacher to Harvard University, which conferred on him the degree of DD in June 1891.

Herford returned to England in February 1892 to succeed Thomas Sadler at Rosslyn Hill Chapel, Hampstead, at a salary of £600, more than halving the $10,000 he had received in Boston. His ministry was full of vigour. He also put new life into the British and Foreign Unitarian Association, doubling its income and acting as its president in 1898–9. In June 1901, his health failing, he retired from active duty and was presented with a testimonial raised on both sides of the Atlantic of over £3000. He died at his home at 1A Christchurch Road, Hampstead, on 20 December 1903. His body was cremated and the ashes were buried with his wife's in the burial-ground of the chapel at Hale on 24 December.

Herford's position in his denomination was that of an open-minded and warm-hearted conservative, especially in biblical matters; his relations with members of other churches and of no church were extremely cordial. His biographer, the American minister (of English origin) John Cuckson (1846–1907), recalled that his sermons were not rhetorical, but clear and devout and 'packed with good sense'. He had an extraordinary capacity to make the complexities of a rapidly shifting theological scene understandable to ordinary readers and hearers, in contrast to the impressive and moving but often very difficult language of the great representatives of the previous generation of Unitarian ministers, J. H. Thom and James Martineau; this accessibility is wonderfully captured in the titles of two of his many published tracts and lectures: *The Small End of Great Problems* (1902) and *What is Left after the Questionings of our Time?* (n.d.). But he also had a gift for delicate teasing: in 1861–2, in the *Unitarian Herald*, he published a charming series of essays, republished in 1905 as *Eutychus and his Relations*, on the venial lapses in pulpit and pew, from sleeping in church (Eutychus, in Acts 20: 9–12, had fallen into a deep sleep during an overlong sermon by the apostle Paul) to lateness in arriving to unsocial worship.
R. K. WEBB

Sources P. H. Wicksteed, in B. Herford, *Anchors of the soul* (1905) [biographical sketch] • J. Cuckson, *Brooke Herford* (1904) • The *Inquirer* (2 Jan 1904) • *The Inquirer* (9 Jan 1904) • letter to the committee and congregation of Strangeways Unitarian Chapel, Manchester, 12 May 1864, Man. CL, Manchester Archives and Local Studies, Strangeways MSS • Strangeways Unitarian Chapel, committee minutes, Man. CL, Manchester Archives and Local Studies, Strangeways MSS • W. Meadows, 'History of the chapel from 1817', *Rosslyn Hill Chapel: a short history, 1692–1973* (1974) • *Unitarian Herald* minute book, DWL • d. cert. • *Monthly Repository*, new ser., 5 (1831), 859–60 [obit. of Sarah Herford]
Archives Harris Man. Oxf., personal and family corresp. and papers • JRL, sermons
Likenesses photograph, repro. in Herford, *Anchors of the soul*, frontispiece • photograph, DWL, trustees' album
Wealth at death £186 8s. 7d.: probate, 19 Feb 1904, *CGPLA Eng. & Wales*

Herford, Caroline (1860–1945). *See under* Herford, William Henry (1820–1908).

Herford, Charles Harold (1853–1931), literary scholar and university teacher, was born at Manchester on 18 February 1853, the eldest son of Charles James Herford (1817–1891), wine merchant, and his wife, Mary Jane. The Herford family were prominent Unitarians when that persuasion included many of Manchester's business and intellectual élite: Herford's mother was the daughter of John Gooch *Robberds (1789–1854), minister of Cross Street Chapel, Manchester, and among his uncles were Brooke Herford (1830–1903), the prominent Unitarian clergyman and preacher, and William Henry Herford (1820–1908), the pioneering educationist. Herford was educated first at Castle Howell School, Lancaster, and then from 1867 to 1869 at Owens College, Manchester, before working with the architect Thomas Worthington. In 1875 he went to Trinity College, Cambridge, where he won academic distinction and obtained a first-class degree in classics in 1879.

Herford's early life is an interesting example of the intellectual opportunities available to a young man of his period and background. His extended family would have provided him with examples of the practical application of intellectual enquiry, reinforced as it was by the ethical inheritance of unitarianism. Herford was to achieve academic distinction as a Renaissance scholar, but as a young man his enthusiasm for Carlyle, and then for Browning, places him in the tradition of nineteenth-century progressive thinking, and this was to be reinforced by a knowledge of a wide range of European literature, notably the German Romantic philosophers and poets, and Dante. Herford's Germanic and Italian enthusiasms were to lie at the core of his intellectual being. He was a founder of both the English Goethe and the Manchester Dante societies.

Herford was appointed to a chair of English language and literature at University College, Aberystwyth, in 1887. In 1888 he married Marie Betge (d. 1930), who was German: it was a tragic irony that their son, Siegfried, was killed in the First World War; their other child, Mary, was to survive both her parents. In 1901 Herford moved to the University of Manchester, where he was professor of English literature from 1901 until his retirement in 1921, and then honorary professor. In 1900 he was Percy Turnbull lecturer at Johns Hopkins University, Baltimore, an early example of an English scholar being so honoured in the United States. Herford's British Academy lecture, 'Is there a poetic view of the world?' (1916), epitomizes the extent to which for him English literature was only part of a larger European cultural experience: it takes in Homer and Lucretius, Virgil, Dante, and Goethe before concluding with a discussion of Wordsworth, Shelley, and Blake. As well as the classical languages, and German and Italian, Herford knew French and Russian, together with Norwegian well enough to have translated Ibsen. Herford received honorary degrees from the universities of Manchester (1899), Wales (1921), and Innsbruck; he was elected fellow of the British Academy in 1926.

Herford's academic career united man and moment. While a young man in Manchester he came under the influence of Adolphus Ward, who was to precede him in a Manchester chair, and of Richard Holt Hutton, the prominent literary critic. He later met Henry Morley, another pioneer of English studies, and was introduced to Frederic Harrison, the leading positivist thinker. Herford's years as a professor, both at Aberystwyth and at Manchester, covered the period when his subject became a university discipline in its own right. Professors of the subject at that time were able to establish the parameters of their own activities; at the same time they felt heavily the responsibility of establishing the scholarly credentials of the new discipline. Herford was an enthusiastic teacher; his books often reflect this dimension of his work. Much of his prolific output expressed his larger interests in Romantic literature: he published book-length studies of Wordsworth both early and late in his life (*The Age of Wordsworth*, 1895; *Wordsworth*, 1930), of Goethe (1913), and of Browning (1905). His first major work, however, was *The Literary Relations of England and Germany in the Sixteenth Century* (1886). The product of extensive research, some of it undertaken during periods of study at Vienna and Berlin, its title reflects both his comparativist interests and his expertise in a period in which he was to become identified as a specialist scholar. He undertook or supervised editions *inter alia* of Spenser's *Shepherd's Calendar* (1895), of Shakespeare (both the Eversley Shakespeare, 1899, and the Warwick Shakespeare, known to generations of school students) and of works by Sir Thomas Browne, Lord Herbert of Cherbury, and Ben Jonson, culminating in his collaboration with Percy Simpson in the major edition of Ben Jonson (11 vols., 1925–52), of which only the first three volumes, initiated by his biographical introduction, were published before his death.

Herford's academic work did not inhibit his involvement in larger cultural activities. He reviewed frequently for the *Manchester Guardian* and after his retirement he wrote extensively on contemporary European subjects. A number of these essays were collected in *The Post-War Mind of Modern Germany and other European Studies* (1927); the title essay of this volume was particularly forthright. As his colleague Samuel Alexander said at a ceremony to mark his departure from Manchester: 'He had strong opinions about various subjects which not all shared, and he expressed himself strongly, and never shrank from expressing himself upon subjects which excited public interest' (*Bulletin of the John Rylands University Library*, 12, 1928, 5). In the light of later events Herford's political judgements can be seen to have been sadly optimistic: he remained above all an internationalist, repudiating the view that the defeated Germany would revert to 'Militarism, race-arrogance, imperialism'. 'The culture of Bolshevist Russia', published in the same volume, is a remarkable account of its subject: while acknowledging the negative aspects of Leninist communism it nevertheless argues for a sympathetic understanding of the problems and the potential of the post-revolutionary decade. Herford's death, on 25 April 1931 in Oxford (where he lived at 24 Old Road, Headington), came just as his more sanguine hopes for international understanding were to be horribly confounded. ALAN SHELSTON

Sources *Manchester Guardian* (29 Oct 1927) · *Manchester Guardian* (27 April 1931) · J. G. Robertson, 'Charles Harold Herford', *PBA*, 17 (1931), 401–13 · 'Library notes and news', *Bulletin of the John Rylands University Library*, 12 (1928), 1–21 · L. Abercrombie, 'Herford and international literature', *Bulletin of the John Rylands University Library*, 19 (1935), 216–29 · *The Times* (27 April 1931) · K. Speight, 'A short account of the first fifty years', *Manchester Dante Society* (1957) · *Ben Jonson*, ed. C. H. Herford, P. Simpson, and E. M. Simpson, 11 vols. (1925–52), vol. 4 · *CGPLA Eng. & Wales* (1931)

Archives Harris Man. Oxf., corresp. and papers relating to his biography of P. H. Wicksteed | BL, corresp. with W. Archer, Add. MS 45292 · BL, corresp. with Macmillans, Add. MS 55030 · NL Scot., letters to D. N. Smith

Likenesses T. Dugdale, oils, University of Manchester · W. Weatherby, drawing, Man. City Gall.

Wealth at death £23,876 5s. 4d.: probate, 11 July 1931, *CGPLA Eng. & Wales*

Herford, Edward (1815–1896), lawyer and public servant, was born in Birmingham, the eldest surviving son of the nine children of John Herford, a wine merchant, and Sarah, only daughter of Edward Smith of Birmingham, notary public and Presbyterian dissenter. His younger brothers and sisters included William Henry *Herford, Brooke *Herford, and Anne Laura *Herford.

While an articled clerk in the firm of Kay and Darbishire, Marsden Street, Manchester, Herford became one of the founding members of the Law Students Society in 1833. An active and enthusiastic supporter of the incorporation movement, Herford was one of the first members of the town council (after incorporation in 1838) at the age of twenty-three. As assistant town clerk he was required, among his other duties, to act as public prosecutor. One of the first prosecutions he undertook was brought against Chartists, including Bronterre O'Brien. From March 1849 until he was forced to retire some thirteen years before his death, Herford held the post of borough coroner. His decision to continue in his role as assistant town clerk as well as acting as borough coroner caused disagreement between himself and the Manchester Law Association and led to his resignation from that body in 1850. Herford resigned as assistant town clerk in August 1851.

Edward Herford was an active supporter of the movement to establish lyceums and played a part in the establishment of the Statistical Society to which he contributed many papers. He was a founder member of the English Church Union formed in 1859 to defend and promote high-church principles in the Church of England; in 1861 he became chairman of the National Association for Promoting the Freedom of Worship. An often controversial figure, he was a prolific author of pamphlets on economic and financial questions, most of which were published in the *Transactions of the Manchester Statistical Society*. A founder of the Lancashire and Cheshire Association of Mechanics Institutes, he was also an organizer of the Young Men's Anti-Monopoly Association (an offshoot of the Anti-Corn Law League). His private life is obscure: although he was married, it is not known if he and his wife, Harriet, had any children. Herford died at his residence, West Bank, Upton, near Macclesfield on 8 May 1896.

V. R. PARROTT

Sources E. Herford, journals, Man. CL · V. R. Parrott, 'Pettyfogging to respectability: a history of the development of the profession of solicitor in the Manchester area, 1800–1914', PhD diss., University of Salford, 1992 · *Manchester Guardian* (11 May 1896) · d. cert.
Archives Man. CL, diaries | UCL, letters to Society for the Diffusion of Useful Knowledge
Wealth at death £1070 4s. 6d.: probate, 16 July 1896, *CGPLA Eng. & Wales*

Herford, William Henry (1820–1908), educationist, was born at Coventry on 20 October 1820, the third surviving son in a family of six sons and three daughters of John Herford and his first wife, Sarah (d. 1831), daughter of Edward Smith of Birmingham, uncle of Joshua Toulmin *Smith. Edward *Herford, coroner for Manchester, was his elder brother; Brooke *Herford was a younger brother. Two other brothers, Charles and William, were active in local public life promoting liberal causes. His youngest sister was Anne Laura *Herford. His father, who was throughout life a strong Liberal and convinced Unitarian, became a wine merchant in Manchester in 1822, and sat on the Manchester town council from 1838 to 1846. He lived at Altrincham, where his wife, a woman of cultivation and an accomplished artist, conducted a successful girls' school.

After attending a school kept by Charles Wallace, Unitarian minister at Hale Barns, Cheshire, Herford was from 1831 to 1834 a day-boy at Shrewsbury School under Samuel Butler. From 1834 to 1836 he was at Manchester grammar school. Then, being destined for the Unitarian ministry, he was prepared for entry at the ministerial college at York by John Relly Beard, from whom he 'first learned by experience that lessons might be made interesting to scholars' (Herford, 6). From 1837 to 1840 he studied at Manchester College in York, during the principalship of John Kenrick, and there came into contact with German philosophy and theology. He removed with the college from York to Manchester in the summer of 1840, and thus came under the influence of three new professors, Francis Newman, James Martineau, and John James Tayler, the last of

whom he regarded as his spiritual father. Graduating BA of London University in the autumn of 1840, he began to preach in Unitarian pulpits, but declined a permanent engagement as minister at Lancaster in order to accept a scholarship for three years' study in Germany. In 1842 he went to Bonn, where he attended the courses of E. M. Arndt, A. W. Schlegel, and F. C. Dahlmann, and formed a close friendship with his contemporary, Wilhelm Ihne. After two years at Bonn he spent eight months in Berlin, where he was admitted to the family circles of the church historian Neander and the microscopist Ehrenberg. After a brief period as preacher to the Unitarian congregation at Edinburgh, he accepted in the summer of 1845 an invitation from a Unitarian congregation at Lancaster, where he remained for a year. In 1846 Lady Noel Byron, widow of the poet, invited him, on James Martineau's recommendation, to undertake the tuition of Ralph King, younger son of her daughter, Ada, countess of Lovelace. Early in 1847 he accompanied the boy to Wilhelm von Fellenberg's Pestalozzian school at Hofwyl, near Bern. Herford developed a close association with Wilhelm von Fellenberg, becoming a temporary teacher on the staff, and accepting with enthusiasm Pestalozzi's and Froebel's educational ideas.

In February 1848 Herford resumed his pastorate at Lancaster, marrying in September 1848 Elizabeth Anne (d. 1880), daughter of Timothy Davis, minister of the Presbyterian chapel at Evesham. Meanwhile he resolved to work out in a systematic way the ideas which he had developed at Hofwyl. In January 1850 Herford, while retaining his ministerial duties, opened at Lancaster a school for boys on Pestalozzian principles. There were no prizes or merit marks, and much stress was laid on self-government by the pupils. Fresh air and physical exercise were essential elements of the regime. Prosperous on the whole, but never large, the school continued with some distinction for eleven years, when a decline in its numbers caused him to transfer it to his brother-in-law, David Davis (1821–1897), a Unitarian minister, under whom the school was later renamed Castle Howell School.

Resigning his pastorate at the same time, Herford with his wife and five children went for eighteen months to Zürich in charge of a pupil. On his return in September 1863 he filled the pulpit of the free church in Manchester until 1869, acquiring increasing reputation as a teacher and lecturer, especially to women and girls, teaching at the Ladies' College, Victoria Park. Some of his teaching was given at Brook House School, Knutsford, whose headmistress, Louisa *Carbutt (later to become Herford's second wife), was educating girls on principles very similar to his own. Herford and his wife formed a plan of a co-educational school for younger children. In April 1873 they opened their co-educational school for pupils aged between seven and thirteen at Fallowfield, Manchester, and afterwards moved it to Lady Barn House, Withington. For twelve years it was run with an individuality of method which had an important local influence. The regime at the school was in opposition to the contemporary emphasis on learning by rote; handwork and physical exercise were part of the curriculum. A supporter of training for kindergarten teachers, Herford was a founder in 1872 of the Manchester Kindergarten Association. At the 1885 conference on education under healthy conditions, he criticized overpressure on elementary school pupils. He was also a prominent supporter of the opening of universities to women, making a courageous speech during the debates in 1878 on allowing women to take London degrees, replying to opposition from the medical faculty with an attack on the double standard in relations between the sexes.

In 1886, following the death of his first wife and his marriage in 1884 to Louisa Carbutt, Herford resigned the school to his second daughter, Caroline Herford [see below]. In retirement Herford devoted his time to authorship and to travel, publishing in 1889 his chief work, *The School: an Essay towards Humane Education*, a masterpiece of English educational writing, which he described as 'the fruits of more than forty years of teaching; various in the sex, age, class and nation of its objects'. In 1893 he published *The Student's Froebel*, adapted from *Die Menschenerziehung* of F. Froebel (1893; revised edn, posthumous, with memoir by C. H. Herford, 1911). This was the best English account of the educational doctrine which it summarized and expounded. In 1890 he settled at Paignton in south Devon. In 1902 he published *Passages from the Life of an Educational Free Lance*, a translation of the *Aus dem Leben eines freien Pädagogen* of Dr Ewald Haufe. He died at Torbay Lodge, Paignton, on 27 April 1908, and was buried at Paignton.

Herford spoke of himself as having been for the first quarter of a century of his teaching an unconscious follower of F. Froebel, and for the following fifteen years his professed disciple. With Pestalozzi he urged the teacher never to deprive the child of 'the sacred right of discovery', and to seek to bring things, both abstract and concrete, into actual contact with the pupil's senses and mind, putting words and names, 'those importunate pretenders', into a subordinate place. Moral training, 'practised not by preaching and as little as possible by punishment, but mainly by example and by atmosphere', he held to be of supreme importance, and its primary purpose to be 'an intellectual clearing and purifying of the moral sense'. To physical training (including play, gymnastics, singing, and handwork) he attached importance only less than that which was assigned to moral culture. Himself a teacher of genius, he disdained any compromise with educational principles or conventions of which he disapproved.

Caroline Herford (1860–1945), subsequently Caroline Herford Blake, was born on 1 November 1860 at 19 Queen Square, Lancaster, and educated at various schools in Manchester, including Lady Barn House, before attending the women's college at Brunswick Street, Manchester, which provided higher education for women before Owens College was opened to them. Resident in 1885 at Newnham College, Cambridge, she later graduated MA at Manchester University. As headmistress of Lady Barn from 1886, she was notable as a pioneer of lacrosse as a school sport. She resigned in 1907 to look after her father following the

death of his second wife. After his death, she was briefly a lecturer at University College, Reading, and then lecturer in education at Manchester University from 1910 to 1918. She was a founding member of the Manchester University branch of the British Federation of University Women. Following the family tradition of public service, she was a member of Manchester city council, where she exercised a progressive influence on the education committee until her defeat by a Conservative candidate in 1923. During the war she was a Red Cross commandant in Lancashire, and was appointed MBE in 1919. Leaving Manchester in 1924 on her marriage to Robert Blake (*d.* 1931), JP, of Yeabridge House, South Petherton, Somerset, husband of her deceased sister, she became a member of Somerset education committee. After her husband's death Caroline Herford Blake lived with a Manchester friend and colleague, Julia Sharpe, at St Martins, Grimms Hill, Great Missenden, Buckinghamshire, where she died on 16 March 1945.

M. E. SADLER, *rev.* M. C. CURTHOYS

Sources C. H. Herford, 'Memoir of W. H. Herford', in W. H. Herford, *The student's Froebel*, ed. D. B. and C. H., rev. edn, 2 vols. (1911–15) · W. C. R. Hicks, *Lady Barn House and the work of W. H. Herford* (1936) · *The Castle Howell School record* (1888) · *Manchester Guardian* (19 March 1945), 6 [Caroline Herford] · [A. B. White], ed., *Newnham College register*, 1: *1871–1923* (1964) [Caroline Herford] · Kelly, *Handbk* (1942) [Caroline Herford] · d. cert. [Caroline Herford] · M. Boyd, *Lacrosse: playing and coaching* (1959)
Likenesses photograph, *c.*1885, repro. in Hicks, *Lady Barn House*, frontispiece · double portrait, photograph, 1886 (with L. Carbutt), repro. in W. H. Herford, *In memoriam: Louisa Carbutt and Brook House* (1907), frontispiece · H. Reed, medallion, 1887, Lady Barn House School, Manchester
Wealth at death £5194 16s. 9d.: administration with will, 17 June 1908, *CGPLA Eng. & Wales* · £15,557 17s. 5d.—Caroline Herford: probate, 1945, *CGPLA Eng. & Wales*

Hericke, Sir William. *See* Herrick, Sir William (*bap.* 1562, *d.* 1653).

Hering, George Edwards (1805–1879), landscape painter, was born in London, the younger son of Charles Ernest Christian Hering, a German bookbinder who belonged to the baronial family of von Heringen in Brunswick and who died when George was young. He was probably the child of that name baptized on 19 May 1805 at St Martin-in-the-Fields, London, the son of Charles and Eliza Hering. He first worked in a bank but was soon permitted by his family to adopt art as his profession, and in 1829 he studied at the Akademie der Bildenden Künste in Munich. His patron, Lord Erskine, travelled with him in the Tyrol, and sent him to Venice. After staying there for about two years, he travelled in Italy, and round the Adriatic Sea to Constantinople and Smyrna.

On his return to Rome, Hering became acquainted with John Paget and a Mr Sanford; together they toured the Carpathian mountains. While living in Rome, Hering met Bertel Thorvaldsen and Horace Vernet, and was able to bring together the antagonistic colonies of German and English artists in that city. Hering returned to England in 1836 and published *Sketches on the Danube, in Hungary and Transilvania* in 1838. He also illustrated Paget's *Hungary and Transylvania*, published in 1839. He settled in London, where for the rest of his life he practised as a landscape painter, though he continued to pay occasional visits to Italy. On 6 July 1839 he married Catherine, daughter of William Bromley, a solicitor. She was also an artist, and exhibited, as Mrs G. E. Hering, at the Royal Academy between 1840 and 1853. About 1850 the couple adopted a young girl, Marion Hamilton [see Acton, Marion Jean Catherine Adams-], whose mother gave her up for adoption to the Herings to improve her material and social position.

Hering habitually painted Italian landscapes with bright, cloudless skies, often highly finished. In 1836 he first exhibited at the Royal Academy, sending *The Ruins of the Palace of the Cæsars, Rome*, and was a regular contributor thereafter to the academy and the British Institution, exhibiting landscapes of Rome, Naples, Genoa, Venice, La Spezia, Como, Piedmont, and Monte Rosa. In 1841 he exhibited a painting of Amalfi, which, through the agency of Samuel Rogers, was purchased by Prince Albert; it was engraved by Edward Goodall for the *Art Journal* in 1856. He occasionally showed scenes of England, the Austrian Tyrol, and Greece, and Scotland became a frequent subject in the 1870s. In 1847 he published a set of twenty coloured lithographs, *The Mountains and Lakes of Switzerland, the Tyrol and Italy*.

George Edwards Hering died at his home, 45 Grove End Road, St John's Wood, London, on 18 December 1879; he was survived by his wife. Two sales of his works were held at Christies, London, on 7 May 1880 and 25 April 1881.

L. H. CUST, rev. KENNETH BENDINER

Sources Graves, *RA exhibitors*, 4 (1906), 81–2 · *Art Journal*, 23 (1861), 73–5 · *Art Journal*, 42 (1880), 83 · G. E. Hering, *Sketches on the Danube, in Hungary and Transilvania* (1838) · G. E. Hering, *The mountains and lakes of Switzerland, the Tyrol and Italy* (1847) · *Apollo*, 88 (1968), back cover [painting by J. F. Hering sen.] · J. Paget, *Hungary and Transylvania* (1839) · *IGI* · m. cert. · *CGPLA Eng. & Wales* (1880)
Wealth at death under £2000 effects in England: probate, 13 Jan 1880, *CGPLA Eng. & Wales*

Hering, Jeanie. *See* Acton, Marion Jean Catherine Adams- (1846–1928).

Heriot, George (1563–1624), jeweller and philanthropist, was born in Edinburgh on 15 June 1563, the eldest son of George Heriot (1539/40–1610), goldsmith and MP, of Edinburgh and his first wife, Elizabeth Balderstone. Heriot was apprenticed to his father's trade, and on 14 January 1586 he was contracted to marry Christian, daughter of Simon Marjoribanks (d. 1603?), an Edinburgh merchant. They had two sons who were drowned at sea (possibly on their way to England in 1603). Heriot's father gave him 1500 merks (about £80) to set up business as a goldsmith and moneylender, allowing him to open a small booth or shop attached to St Giles's Cathedral. On 19 January 1588 he was admitted a burgess of Edinburgh, and on 28 May 1588 he was admitted a member of the guild of Edinburgh goldsmiths. In 1590 Heriot was living in Fishmarket Close in Edinburgh. By January 1594 he was 'deacon convener' (*Reg. PCS*, 6.314) of the incorporated trades of Edinburgh, and on 17 July 1597 James VI appointed Heriot goldsmith to Queen Anne. In this role he lent money to the queen, often using her jewels as security, having supplied the

George Heriot (1563–1624), by David Scougall (after Paul van Somer)

jewels in the first place. Between 1593 and 1603 Heriot's business dealings with the queen may have amounted to £50,000. On 4 April 1601 Heriot was appointed jeweller to James VI. In December that year he was a member of a syndicate commissioned by the government to issue a replacement Scottish coinage. In January 1603 he was a farmer of the customs.

Heriot's entrenched position in the Scottish crown's financial affairs was threatened by James VI's accession to the English crown as James I in March 1603. Heriot duly followed the king to London, dwelling at the New Exchange. On 9 November 1603 he received a patent as one of three jewellers to the king, with a salary of £150 per annum. On 24 August 1609 Heriot married in Edinburgh Alison (1591/2–1612), eldest daughter of James Primrose of Carrington, clerk to the Scottish privy council, with a portion of 5000 merks. According to the marriage contract of 26 September 1608, 20,000 merks were to be laid out on land. They had no children before his wife died on 16 April 1612. By 1609 Heriot was receiving 10 per cent interest on his loans to the queen, which totalled £18,000, although he seems to have had some difficulty recovering the capital. However, his position at court saw him sell jewels to other members of the royal circle such as the first duke of Buckingham and the earl of Somerset. In November 1620 he was granted the imposition on sugar for three years. Heriot was now living in the parish of St Martin-in-the-Fields, and had an estate at Roehampton, Surrey.

Heriot had no legitimate children, and on 3 September

1623 he executed a 'disposition and assignation' (*Inventory*, 2) to Edinburgh council announcing his intentions to found a hospital in the city. Heriot died in London on 12 February 1624, and was buried on the 20th in St Martin-in-the-Fields, the funeral oration being delivered by Walter Balcanquhall. Heriot provided for two illegitimate daughters, aged about ten and four, by his will of December 1623. He also left bequests to his step-mother, Christian Blawe, and his half-brothers and -sisters, as well as his nieces and nephews, especially the daughter of his deceased brother, Patrick, whom he feared would challenge his will and its main beneficiary. Heriot left the residue of his estate to the 'provost, bailiffs, ministers and council' of Edinburgh, 'for and towards the founding and erecting of an hospital', and for purchasing lands for the 'maintenance, relief bringing up and education of so many poor fatherless boys freemen's sons' as the funds allowed (will). In all £23,625 was bequeathed to the hospital and school which bears his name, as does Heriot-Watt University, formed from part of the George Heriot Hospital and trust.   STUART HANDLEY

Sources W. Steven, *History of George Heriot's Hospital, with a memoir of the founder*, 3rd edn, ed. F. W. Bedford (1872) • will, PRO, PROB 11/143, fols. 56v–61r • *Inventory of original documents in the archives of George Heriot's Hospital* (1857) • C. B. B. Watson, ed., *Roll of Edinburgh burgesses and guild-brethren, 1406–1700*, Scottish RS, 59 (1929), 249–50 • H. Paton, ed., *The register of marriages for the parish of Edinburgh, 1595–1700*, Scottish RS, old ser., 27 (1905), 325 • *CSP dom., 1603–23* • A. Constable, *Memoirs of George Heriot jeweller to King James VI* (1822) • E. C. Williams, *Anne of Denmark wife of James VI of Scotland: James I of England* (1970) • *Seventh report*, HMC, 6 (1879), 256 • *Reg. PCS*, 1st ser., 5.542–3
Archives George Heriot's Hospital, Edinburgh, papers • NA Scot., personal and family corresp. and papers
Likenesses J. & C. Esplens, mezzotint, pubd 1743 (after D. Scougall; after P. van Somer), BM, NPG • D. Scougall, oils (after P. van Somer), George Heriot's Hospital, Edinburgh [*see illus.*] • portrait (aged twenty-six), George Heriot's Hospital, Edinburgh

Heriot, John (1760–1833), newspaper editor and writer, was born on 22 April 1760 in Haddington, East Lothian. His father was sheriff-clerk of East Lothian and he had an older brother, George (1759–1839), later postmaster-general in Canada and travel writer. The family moved to Edinburgh in 1772, and Heriot attended Edinburgh high school. He began studying at Edinburgh University but had to leave in 1777 when his father's business failed. The family dispersed, and Heriot travelled to London, seeking a military commission. The army lists show that he was appointed second lieutenant in the marines on 13 November 1778 and was promoted to first lieutenant of the Plymouth division on 15 August 1781. He served on board the *Vengeance*, the *Preston*, and the *Elizabeth* off the coast of Africa and the West Indies. In the *Elizabeth* he was wounded in a battle on 17 April 1780 between the English fleet under Sir George B. Rodney and the French fleet under Admiral De Guichen. He transferred to the *Brune* frigate in July 1780 and was exposed to the hurricane that devastated Barbados on 10 October 1780. During the peace of Versailles in 1783 Heriot was put on half pay, which he mortgaged to help his parents, leaving him destitute.

Heriot turned to authorship, and wrote *The Sorrows of the Heart* in 1787 and a semi-autobiographical novel, *The Half-Pay Officer*, in 1789. He lived on the proceeds of these works for two years. At twenty-eight, on 29 May 1788 at St Martin-in-the-Fields, Westminster, he married Alison Shiriff. The *Annual Biography* describes this as 'apparently a very imprudent step; but … a step of which he never had occasion to repent' (*Annual Biography*, 44). They had two daughters, and Heriot is described in this article as 'a kind and affectionate husband and father' (ibid., 50).

In 1788 Heriot was employed by Thomas Steele, secretary of the treasury, to write pamphlets and articles for *The Times* in support of the government. By 1791 he was one of the principal treasury writers and was awarded an annual salary of £200. He was for a while on the staff of other treasury newspapers: *The Oracle* newspaper and then *The World*. In 1792, at the suggestion of Edmund Burke, and with the support of Pitt's ministry, Heriot established a newspaper designed to counteract 'the mischievous principles of revolutionary France' (Rose, 8.291). *The Sun*, a daily evening journal, appeared on 1 October 1792. It was covertly funded by the government ministers James Bland Burges and Charles Long. Within months it had a circulation of over four thousand copies daily, making it second only to *The Times*. This success has been attributed to the hundreds of copies bought and freely distributed by government. Heriot was then invited by George Rose, clerk of parliaments, to start the *True Briton*, a daily morning newspaper, on 1 January 1793. This paper took over the presses of the radical newspaper *Argus* after its closure by the government in December 1792. In this capacity Heriot's salary reached a height of £2000. The *True Briton* continued for eleven years, and then suffered a 'financial crash' (Dean, 270). Heriot continued his literary career in these years. In 1792 he wrote *An Historical Sketch of Gibraltar*, a narrative to accompany the artist Poggi's drawing of the rock. Heriot's manuscript journal entry describing his presentation of this book to George III and Queen Charlotte is quoted in the *Annual Biography*. In 1798 he edited an *Account of the Battle of the Nile* from the notes of an officer present at the battle, which went through several editions.

In 1806 Heriot left the newspapers to accept the role of commissioner of the lottery. One biographer records this as an apt position for a 'born gambler' (Dean, 270). This contrasts with the character description in the *Gentleman's Magazine* of 'a straight-forward, honourable character, warm and zealous in his political principles and attachments' (*GM*, 1st ser., 103/2, 1833, 184). In 1810 Heriot was made deputy paymaster-general of the troops in the Windward and Leeward Islands, and was stationed at Barbados. In 1816 the duke of York appointed him comptroller of Chelsea Hospital. Heriot died there from sudden paralysis on 29 July 1833, three days after his wife's death and a month after his daughter, who died in Trinidad on 30 June 1833. He was buried next to his wife in the burial-grounds of Chelsea Hospital, London, on 2 August 1833.

                    CAROLINE DAVIS

Sources *Annual Biography and Obituary*, 18 (1834), 41–51 • L. Werkmeister, *The London daily press, 1772–1792* (1963) • Chambers, *Scots.*, rev. T. Thomson (1875) • *GM*, 1st ser., 103/2 (1833), 184 • H. J.

Rose, *A new general biographical dictionary*, ed. H. J. Rose and T. Wright, 12 vols. (1848), vol. 8, pp. 291–2 · C. G. T. Dean, *History of the Royal Hospital Chelsea* [n.d.] · J. Black, *The English press in the eighteenth century* (1987), 185 · J. Grant, *The newspaper press: its origins, progress, and present position* (1871–2), 330–45 · *The Sun* (20 Feb 1793–March 1800) · *True Briton* (1 Jan 1793–5 June 1797) · J. Heriot, *An historical sketch of Gibraltar* (1792) · Army Files, correspondence of John Heriot, letter of 12 July 1780, PRO, PRO 3 U/2 · Army Files, correspondence of John Heriot, letter of 31 Dec 1793, PRO, FO95/4/6 · Army Files, correspondence of John Heriot, letter of 26 Sept 1792, PRO, ADM1/5120/20 · *IGI*

Archives BL, *Sorrows of the heart* [copy]

Herkomer, Sir Hubert von (1849–1914), painter and illustrator, was born on 26 May 1849 in Waal, Bavaria, the only child of Lorenz Herkomer (1825–1888), a builder and woodcarver, and his wife, Josephine Niggl (1826–1879), born in the nearby village of Denklingen, Bavaria, who was a gifted pianist and music teacher. The Herkomers were of peasant stock, the family having for generations practised the craft skills of woodcarving and weaving. Lorenz Herkomer, accompanied by his wife and the infant Hubert, emigrated to America in 1851, joining other relatives in Cleveland, Ohio. In 1857 they returned to Europe, and settled in Southampton, England.

The young Herkomer had only six months of formal schooling because of childhood illnesses. He received his early art instruction from his father and in 1863 was enrolled at the Southampton School of Art, where he studied for two years. The experience embittered him: he often criticized the art teaching methods of the day later in life. After briefly attending the Munich Academy in 1865, he studied at the Department of Science and Art, South Kensington, in London for two summer terms, in 1866 and 1867. With the encouragement of his friend and fellow South Kensington student Luke Fildes, Herkomer took up black and white illustration. In 1868 his illustrations to poems and short stories began to appear in a number of popular periodicals such as *Good Words for the Young*, *Fun*, the *Sunday Magazine*, *The Quiver*, and the *Cornhill Magazine*, and from 1870 in *The Graphic*, a weekly founded the year before by William Luson Thomas. Herkomer's *Graphic* engravings, which often depicted scenes of poverty and hardship, were collected by Vincent Van Gogh. Van Gogh admired Herkomer's work and mentioned him often in his letters; the subject matter and expressive style of his engravings influenced the Dutch painter's own work.

Herkomer's paintings were exhibited annually at the Royal Academy, London, from 1869. In 1873 he exhibited his first major oil painting, a Bavarian peasant subject entitled *After the Toil of the Day* (exh. RA, 1873; priv. coll., Wales). It was painted in Germany, where, from 1871, he usually resided during the summer months. In 1885 in Landsberg-am-Lech (4 miles from his birthplace, Waal), he completed the Mutterturm, a tower house built in memory of his mother, which became his summer home. Other Bavarian peasant paintings, which were made primarily for the English market, include *At Death's Door* (exh. RA, 1876; priv. coll., Wales), *Der Bittgang: Peasants Praying for a Successful Harvest* (exh. RA, 1877; Parc Howard Museum,

Sir Hubert von Herkomer (1849–1914), self-portrait, *c*.1888

Llanelli), and *Light, Life, and Melody* (exh. Grosvenor Gallery, 1879; priv. coll., Wales). Some of these works reveal the influence of contemporary German realism, particularly that of Wilhelm Leibl on the one hand, and on the other, the more delicate idealism of the English painter Frederick Walker, whom Herkomer ardently admired: he fluctuated between these two stylistic extremes for most of his career.

In 1875 Herkomer exhibited *The Last Muster: Sunday in the Royal Hospital, Chelsea* (exh. RA, 1875; Lady Lever Art Gallery, Port Sunlight), based on his *Graphic* engraving (18 February 1871, 152) *Sunday at Chelsea Hospital*. Its depiction of a group of Chelsea pensioners seated during a service in the Chelsea Hospital chapel was greatly admired for its bold realism and poignant central motif—an old soldier reaching for the pulse of his comrade, who has died beside him. In 1878 the painting was shown at the Universal Exhibition in Paris, where Herkomer was awarded a medal of honour. The phenomenal success of *The Last Muster*, which was frequently shown at national and international exhibitions over the next forty years, assured the artist lasting fame during his lifetime.

Herkomer painted several important works that revealed his sympathy for the impoverished or disadvantaged, a trait fostered in part by his own humble origins. These included *Eventide: a Scene in Westminster Union* (exh. RA, 1878; Walker Art Gallery, Liverpool), which showed elderly women in a workhouse; *Pressing to the West: a Scene in Castle Garden, New York* (exh. RA, 1884; Museum of Fine Arts, Leipzig), a depiction of poverty-stricken immigrants, inspired by a visit to America in 1883; *Hard Times, 1885* (exh. RA, 1885; Manchester City Galleries), which showed an unemployed labourer and his family resting by a road; and *On Strike* (exh. RA, 1891; RA), Herkomer's diploma picture on election to full membership of the Royal Academy.

In 1873 Herkomer settled with his parents in the village of Bushey, Hertfordshire, partly because his first patron,

Clarence Fry—who owned many of the artist's early watercolours and was the original owner of *The Last Muster*—resided in nearby Watford. On 30 December that year Herkomer married Anna Weise, the German-born daughter of a Berlin lawyer; they had two children, Siegfried and Elsa. The couple lived intermittently apart from 1877, and after his wife's death in 1883 Herkomer married, on 14 August 1884, a Welsh nurse, Lulu Griffiths (*b.* 1849), who had been a member of his household since 1874. He was devastated by her sudden death a year later. On 3 August 1888 the artist married a third time in Landsberg-am-Lech; because his bride, Margaret Griffiths (1857–1934), was his sister-in-law, Herkomer had to renounce his British citizenship, its being illegal in England at that time to marry a deceased wife's sister (he was renaturalized as a British citizen in 1897). The couple had two children, Lawrence and Gwendydd.

During the 1880s Herkomer painted several large landscapes in north Wales in the company of his lifelong friend and patron, the Welsh landowner and painter Charles William Mansel Lewis. These works included *Homeward* (exh. RA, 1882; Altes Rathaus, Landsberg-am-Lech, Germany) and *Found* (exh. RA, 1885; Tate collection), which was purchased by the Chantrey Bequest. Although he continued to exhibit subject pictures the focus of his art after 1881 was portraiture. Herkomer regarded his portraits as historical records and painted many of the most important and accomplished citizens of his day, fulfilling commissions in Britain, America, and Germany. Among his noteworthy portraits are *John Ruskin* (1879; exh. Grosvenor Gallery, 1881; NPG); *Archibald Forbes* (exh. RA, 1882; Kunsthalle, Hamburg); *Miss Katherine Grant* ('The Lady in White'; exh. RA, 1885; priv. coll.); *Henry Hobson Richardson* (1886; priv. coll., Boston, Massachusetts); and *Prince Regent Luitpold of Bavaria* (1896; exh. RA, 1899; Neue Pinakotek, Munich). Herkomer also produced several very large group portraits including his last work, *The Managers and Directors of the Firm Friedrich Krupp, Essen, Germany* (exh. RA, 1914; Villa Hügel, Essen).

Like some other portrait painters of his generation, Herkomer made a great deal of money, earning over £250,000 from portraiture alone. He was able to work with remarkable speed and enjoyed talking to his sitters to animate their expressions. He made preliminary sketches to set the pose and used photographs on occasion. The portraits he painted early in his career favoured a murky palette, tonal subtlety, and non-descriptive backgrounds, similar to the realist trends he admired in the Munich and Paris schools. For his later portraits he employed a freer brushstroke and lighter colours.

Herkomer's earnings from portraiture enabled him to build Lululaund, his huge castle-like residence at 43 Melbourne Road in Bushey, which was named in memory of his deceased second wife. This arts and crafts house, begun in 1856, was built as a homage to the traditional skills of his Bavarian forebears, and featured an exterior design by the celebrated American architect Henry Hobson Richardson; the artist and his family took up residence in 1894. The house, the only Richardson design in the United Kingdom, was demolished in 1939 in a wave of anti-German sentiment. The village of Bushey inspired several of the artist's later subject pictures such as *The First Born* (exh. RA, 1887; Forbes Magazine Collection, London) and *Our Village* (1889; exh. RA, 1890; Aberdeen Art Gallery).

Despite his childhood illnesses, Herkomer grew into a sturdy adult of medium height and slim athletic build, who enjoyed bicycling and mountain hiking. He ate little meat and neither drank alcohol nor smoked, abstemious habits he had learned from his father. Until 1890 (after which he remained clean shaven) his face was covered in a thick black beard. His piercing eyes and humourless demeanour produced a rather sinister appearance. Herkomer's wide-ranging interests, energy, and capacity for work were prodigious. He lectured tirelessly on numerous social issues and art-related topics, and he succeeded John Ruskin (at Ruskin's suggestion) as the Slade professor of art at Oxford University, a position he held from 1885 to 1894. The Herkomer Art School, founded by him in Bushey in 1883 (closed 1904), taught students from countries as far flung as Sweden, South Africa, America, and Australia. He was knighted in 1907.

Herkomer was also the author of several books, and wrote his two-volume memoir, *The Herkomers* (1910–11), with the encouragement of his friend Thomas Hardy. Herkomer also wrote and composed the music for the 'pictorial-music-plays' he performed at his private theatre in Bushey. His innovative theatre sets and lighting methods influenced the theatrical concepts of Edward Gordon Craig, who acknowledged his debt to Herkomer's ideas.

Herkomer was also an early film-maker, who pioneered the technology of this new art form in Great Britain: he acted in, and directed, several films which were released commercially in 1913 and 1914. Additionally, he experimented with printmaking techniques and enamelling, though he gave up the latter in 1901, after he destroyed his enamel portrait of Wilhelm II because the German emperor expressed dissatisfaction with it.

Herkomer was active in the affairs of the Royal Academy and the Royal Society of Painters in Water Colours; his reputation was also secure in Germany, where he energetically exhibited and executed portrait commissions. His sponsoring of an automobile race in Bavaria, the Herkmerkonkurrenz (from 1905 to 1907), brought him further recognition and endorsed his fascination with the possibilities of modern technical inventions.

In the last years of his life, Herkomer was plagued by stomach ulcers and other serious illnesses, and in 1912 he survived critical stomach surgery. He died suddenly on 31 March 1914 at Matford, Budleigh Salterton, Devon, where his family had taken him for a seaside cure. He was buried in Bushey parish churchyard on 4 April.

Herkomer's enthusiasm for all he undertook and his desire to impart the knowledge he acquired in the process rendered him a more sympathetic personality than his contemporaries could (or wanted to) appreciate. Unlike his fellow portraitists and former colleagues at *The Graphic* magazine, Luke Fildes and Frank Holl, whose commitment to social realism ended in the 1870s, Herkomer never completely abandoned the social recording that had shaped his early career: there is no question that *On Strike* is his most important work of the 1890s, despite the huge demand for his portraits. While, for example, his contemporary John Everett Millais painted portraits selectively, Herkomer took on a prodigious workload. As a result, the quality varied greatly and often depended on the artist's rapport (or lack of it) with his sitters. After the turn of the century, John Singer Sargent's bravura portraits began to dominate the academy, and Herkomer's more conservative style came to be seen as increasingly out of date.   LEE MACCORMICK EDWARDS

Sources L. M. Edwards, *Herkomer: a Victorian artist* (1999) · L. M. Edwards, 'Hubert von Herkomer and the modern life subject', PhD diss., Columbia University, 1984 · H. von Herkomer, *My school and my gospel* (1908) · H. von Herkomer, *The Herkomers*, 2 vols. (1910–11) · A. L. Baldry, *Hubert von Herkomer, R. A.* (1901) · L. Pietsch, *Herkomer* (1901) · J. S. Mills, *The life and letters of Sir Hubert Herkomer, C.V.O., RA: a study in struggle and success* (1923) · W. Meynell, 'Our living artists: Hubert Herkomer', *Magazine of Art*, 3 (1879–80), 259–63 · R. Pickvance, *English influences on Vincent Van Gogh* (1974) · H. von Herkomer, *Etching and mezzotint engraving: lectures delivered at Oxford* (1892) · H. von Herkomer, *A certain phase of lithography* (1910) · H. von Herkomer, 'Drawing and engraving on wood', *Art Journal*, new ser., 2 (1882), 133–6, 165–8 · H. von Herkomer, 'How we teach at Bushey', *Universal Review* (Sept–Dec 1889), 50–55 · H. von Herkomer, 'Scenic art', *Magazine of Art*, 15 (1891–2), 259–64, 316–21 · H. von Herkomer, 'J. W. North, painter and poet', *Magazine of Art*, 16 (1892–3), 297–300, 342–8
Archives Bayerische Staatsbibliothek, Munich, corresp. · Bodl. Oxf., corresp. · Bushey Museum Trust, Hertfordshire, diary, archival photographs, newspaper clippings · Christopher Wood Gallery, London, corresp. · CUL, corresp. · Dorset County Museum, Dorchester, corresp. · Friedrich Krupp GmbH, Essen, Historisches Archiv, corresp. · Herkomerstiftung, Mutterturm, Landsberg-am-Lech, corresp., newspaper clippings, recital programmes, photographic inventory of works · Herts. ALS, letters · Jeremy Maas Gallery, London, corresp. · RA, letters to Royal Academy · Tate collection, corresp. [copies] · Yale U., corresp., newspaper clippings, photographs, drawings | BL, letters to G. L. Craik, Add. MS 61894 · BL, corresp. with Macmillans, Add. MSS 55230, 61894 · Hertford College, Oxford, letters to principal and bursar of Hertford College, Oxford · JRL, letters to M. H. Spielmann · NPG, Heinz Library and Archive, letters to George Frederic Watts · U. Leeds, Brotherton L., letters to Sir Edmund Gosse · V&A NAL, letters to A. L. Baldry and lecture notes · Llanelli, Mansel Lewis MSS
Likenesses H. von Herkomer, self-portrait, etching, 1879, NPG · H. von Herkomer, self-portrait, watercolour, c.1888, Bushey Museum and Art Gallery, Hertfordshire [*see illus.*] · G. Grenville Marton, group portrait, watercolour, 1891 (*Conversazione at the Royal Academy, 1891*), NPG · R. Lehmann, drawing, 1891, BM · E. B. Johnson, chalk drawing, 1892 (study for posthumous portrait), BM · E. B. Johnson, oils, 1892, NPG · H. von Herkomer, self-portrait, oils, 1895, Uffizi Gallery, Florence · E. Onslow Ford, bronze bust, c.1897, NPG · H. von Herkomer, self-portrait, oils, 1907, Altes Rathaus, Landsberg-am-Lech · H. von Herkomer, group portrait, oils, 1908 (*The council of the Royal Academy*), Tate collection · G. Harcourt, oils, c.1915, Southampton City Museum and Art Gallery · F. G. [F. Goedecker], caricature, watercolour, NPG; repro. in *VF* (26 Jan 1884) · E. B. Johnson, oils (posthumous), Nottingham Castle Museum · H. von Herkomer, self-portrait, oils, Mutterturm, Landsberg-am-Lech · E. Walker, photogravure (after G. Andrews), NPG · cabinet photograph, NPG · photographs, Bushey Museum Trust, Bushey, Hertfordshire
Wealth at death £41,319 7s. 0d.: probate, 2 June 1914, *CGPLA Eng. & Wales*

Herland, Hugh (d. 1406?), master carpenter, was the presumed son of **William Herland** (d. 1375), master carpenter to Edward III. William first appears c.1332 as a sawyer of moulds at St Stephen's Chapel, Westminster, where William Hurley was master carpenter. He was also employed at the Tower, where his duties involved the maintenance of siege engines, and in 1338 he conveyed a 'great engine' to Scotland. By 1347 Herland's status had risen to that of Hurley's warden (*apparillator*) at St Stephen's; later he held the same post at Windsor c.1350, receiving the normal warden's salary (6d. to 8d. a day) for his work on the choir stalls of St George's Chapel and the ceiling of the chapter house between October 1351 and July 1352. Herland was simultaneously employed on the stalls at St Stephen's Chapel, Westminster. Upon Hurley's death in 1354, Herland received the full master's salary of 1s. a day, succeeding Hurley as head carpenter both at Westminster and at Windsor, where he worked in the 1360s on Edward III's new apartments in the upper bailey. William Herland's designation as 'chief carpenter' suggests he was in charge of the major Windsor carpentry, which included a new hall, kitchen, kitchen gate, alterations to the chapel, and the conversion of Henry III's hall into a chamber. He certainly made the roof of the cloister in the lower bailey (1355–7) and, although it is not documented, it is probable that he designed (c.1361) the elaborate open-timber roof of St George's Hall (now destroyed, but its appearance is recorded in an engraving by W. Hollar, 1663), executed by his warden following the completion of the undercroft in 1362/3. It is not known whether Hugh Herland was among the carpenters involved with this important decorative roof.

As Edward III's chief carpenter and administrator, William Herland contracted carpenters for the king's works, for instance at Hadleigh Castle, Essex (June 1358); the king's house at Rotherhithe, Surrey (1361–75), where he was comptroller; Eltham Palace, Kent; and the new castle of Queenborough on the Isle of Sheppey (1367–72), where William Wykeham was the initial overseer and where Hugh Herland was paid 8d. a day for making 'springalds', catapults for hurling stones which had become semi-portable weapons by the late fourteenth century. Since both Herlands worked as military 'engineers', clearly this aspect of the craft remained an important component of a carpenter's skills at that time.

As a reward for his long service, in 1371 William Herland was given a tenement in London and it was probably here that he died, in 1375. His office of 'disposer of the king's works' was then transferred to Hugh Herland. William's will, enrolled in the court of hustings (16 July 1375) indicates that he was survived by his wife, Agnes, but mentions no children.

Hugh Herland's career began c.1360 as the king's under-carpenter at Westminster, the Tower, and Windsor Castle, at the last of which he probably met his future patron, William Wykeham. In 1360 both Herlands were issued with robes from the great wardrobe and in 1369 each received a mourning robe for the funeral of Philippa of Hainault, at which time William Herland ranked among the 'esquires of great estate', while Hugh was an esquire of craftsman's rank (*de mistere*). Given this close association with the royal household, they may have collaborated on the wooden tester above Philippa's fine alabaster effigy in Westminster Abbey, prepared before her death by the sculptor, Jean de Liège; similarly, Hugh may have executed the tester above the tomb of Edward III, also in Westminster Abbey, following the king's death in 1377.

In 1375 Hugh succeeded his father as chief carpenter, and after a brief hiatus (1377/8) received a new patent 'for life' from Richard II in 1379 as one of two chief carpenters. He remained 'disposer of the king's works of carpentry' until his retirement in 1404/5. During his long career Hugh Herland executed numerous works for the crown and supervised the royal castles south of the rivers Trent and Humber, including Carisbrooke, Isle of Wight (1384/5), Winchester (1390), and Portchester, Hampshire (c.1385 and 1396–9), where Herland and Henry Yevele presumably administered the works for Richard II's new domestic range, employing Thomas Clevere, who received the warden's wage of 6*d.* a day.

Herland's most important work in the 1390s was unquestionably the new roof for the Norman aisled hall at Westminster Palace, the largest medieval hall in England. For this vast *renovatio* Herland was not only the master carpenter but also served as comptroller to John Godmaston, clerk of the works (Herland's account survives as BL, Add. Roll 27018). Herland made the oak framing during 1394–6 at a site near Farnham, Surrey, after which the timbers were transported piecemeal to London for assembly in 1397. The complex roof structure (ingeniously preserved by Sir Frank Baines in the early twentieth century) spans nearly 68 feet internally and combines a massive arch structure with angels and hammer beam brackets, each bearing the royal arms of Richard II. In 1399 Hugh was reappointed by Henry IV to act as comptroller to Godmaston for repairs made to the great hall and to the outer gate of the palace at Westminster, for which he was instructed to report directly to the exchequer.

In addition to works for the crown, Herland was employed in 1387 by William Wykeham, bishop of Winchester, at the latter's manor of Highclere, Hampshire, and also worked at Wykeham's collegiate foundations at Winchester and New College, Oxford (founded 1379). Accompanied by his servants, Herland dined at New College nine times in 1390/91. While little original work remains, the chapel vault at St Mary's College, Winchester (1393/4) survives; moreover, Herland's likeness (with inscription) appears in the east window of the chapel, along with representations of the master mason, William Wynford, and of Simon Membury, clerk of the works. At Oxford, contextual evidence suggests that the New College chapel roof (rebuilt by Gilbert Scott), possibly designed by Herland, was of a low-pitched angel hammer beam type. The William Herland of Kingston, Surrey,

listed as one of Wykeham's original scholars of Winchester College and admitted as a scholar to New College in July 1397, was very likely Hugh's son.

In recognition of his long and expert service, Herland received various annuities and grants. As early as 1383 he received a patent of 1*s.* a day for life, and in 1391, in return for his good service, he was granted an additional 10 marks a year for life from the fee farm of Winchester. In 1397 Richard II granted Herland an annual pension of £18 5*s.* from the exchequer. These patents were reconfirmed by Henry IV (1399 and 1403). Herland not only increased his income but was also given a house 'in the little outward ward' of Westminster Palace about 1386, to keep his tools and moulds. A property transaction of July 1391 records the quitclaim to a certain Hugh Herlande, his wife, Joan of 'Upchirche of Kent', and their heirs, of a substantial property at Kingston upon Thames, Surrey. Given Master Hugh's income and status, and the proximity of Kingston to Herland's framing site, it is very likely that this refers to Hugh Herland, the king's carpenter. The last recorded payment of Herland's pension was made on 13 May 1406, suggesting that he died within the year. He appears to have had three sons, Thomas, William, and John.

LYNN T. COURTENAY

Sources Chancery records · F. Devon, ed. and trans., *Issues of the exchequer: being payments made out of his majesty's revenue, from King Henry III to King Henry VI inclusive*, RC (1837) · R. Brown, H. M. Colvin, and A. J. Taylor, eds., *The history of the king's works*, 1–2 (1963) · L. T. Courtenay, 'Westminster Hall and its fourteenth-century sources', *Journal of the Society of Architectural Historians*, 43 (1984), 295–309 · R. Custance, ed., *Winchester College: sixth-centenary essays* (1982) · E. A. Gee, 'Oxford carpenters, 1370–1530', *Oxoniensia*, 17–18 (1952–3), 112–84, esp. 112–13 · J. Harvey and A. Oswald, *English mediaeval architects: a biographical dictionary down to 1550*, 2nd edn (1984) · J. H. Harvey, 'The king's chief carpenters', *Journal of the British Archaeological Association*, 3rd ser., 11 (1948), 13–34 · J. H. Harvey, 'The mediaeval carpenter and his work as an architect', *RIBA Journal*, 45 (1937–8), 733–43 · W. Hayter, *William of Wykeham, patron of the arts* (1970) · W. H. St J. Hope, *Windsor Castle, an architectural history*, 2 vols. (1913) · T. F. Kirby, *Annals of Winchester College, from its foundation in the year 1382 to the present time* (1892) · W. R. Lethaby, *Westminster Abbey and the king's craftsmen* (1906) · L. F. Salzman, *Building in England down to 1540* (1952) · A. H. Smith, *New College, Oxford, and its buildings* (1952) · Emden, *Oxf.* · CCIR, 1402–5
Archives BL, Add. Roll 27018
Likenesses portrait, c.1393, Winchester College chapel

Herland, William (d. 1375). *See under* Herland, Hugh (d. 1406?).

Herle, Charles (1597/8–1659), Church of England clergyman and political theorist, was born at Prideaux Herle, near Lostwithiel, Cornwall, the third of six sons of Edward Herle of Prideaux and his wife, Anne, daughter of John Treffry. On 23 October 1612, aged fourteen, he matriculated from Exeter College, Oxford. He graduated BA on 7 July 1615 and proceeded MA on 10 June 1618. Perhaps owing to ancestral connections with Lancashire, he subsequently became a tutor to James Stanley, Lord Strange. In 1625 he was instituted rector of Creed, Cornwall, but on 27 June 1626, following presentation by Sir Thomas Stanley, he was instituted rector of Winwick, Lancashire. It is not clear how soon he took up residence in this potentially rich benefice: the parsonage was still in the occupation of the widow of his predecessor, who had been locked in long-running litigation over some of its income, and Herle too became embroiled in this until the dispute was resolved two or three years later. In the meantime, while serving as chaplain in the household of Elizabeth Stanley, countess of Derby, he wrote her will, dated 19 February 1627; she died at Richmond, Surrey, on 10 March, and was subsequently buried at Westminster Abbey, so it seems likely that Herle spent some time in and around London at this period.

A 'long and hopelesse sickness', and 'the weary houres' of recuperation, gave rise to Herle's first publication, *Contemplations and devotions on the severall passages of our blessed Saviours death and passion* (1631). In dedicating the work to Strange, to whom he attributed his recovery, Herle explained that his aims were to vindicate protestantism from the Catholic charge that 'she spends all her devotion on the Pulpit, and keepes none for the Closet' (sig. A5*v*). The meditations, arranged in twenty-seven sections, ran from Jesus's 'bloudy sweat in the Garden' to the involvement of Joseph and Nicodemus with the burial of his body, in a manner resembling the stations of the cross. By this time Herle had married and was living in Winwick; his wife was possibly called Margaret. He had ten children, including Edward (*b*. 1632) and Henry (*b*. 1633).

In 1642 Herle and his three curates took the protestation oath, and on the outbreak of war found themselves in opposition to Derby's and Strange's powerful local interest. When Warrington was garrisoned for the king, Herle took refuge in London; in his absence his parsonage was fortified by Sir John Fortescue, a Catholic, though it subsequently changed hands according to the fortunes of war in the area. Apparently on the initiative of John Moore, MP for Liverpool, who that spring had helped organize resistance to Strange in Lancashire, on 26 October the Commons voted to invite Herle to preach before them at St Margaret's, Westminster. The resulting fast sermon, delivered on 30 November, and published as *A Payre of Compasses for Church and State* (1642), revealed high approval for the institution he addressed: 'good Parliaments have always beene observ'd to be like sharpe searching Frosts, which sound bodies like, as the healthiest weather; but such as are rotten, feare as too subtle and searching for their conscious prognosticke bones' (p. 10). His theme was truth and peace. Since 'that iron chayne of meere necessity is too short' and 'men's lives are God's, and may not be adventured upon any other warrant or end then God's' (p. 41), war was not to be undertaken lightly, but without truth, 'true peace cannot be had' (p. 14). Rejecting the Machiavellian counsel of balancing threats and divisions, he advocated concerted action against three categories of errors of ascending seriousness: the diversive errors of the 'Inconformists' or separatists, the perversive errors of the Arminians, and the subversive errors of the papists. The first were to be dealt with by argument, the second by burning their books, and the third by securing their persons.

Herle was soon engaged in pamphlet controversy. Taking up the themes in Charles I's *Answer to the Nineteen Propositions* of June 1642, royal chaplain Henry Ferne published in November as *The Resolving of Conscience* a defence of the king's position. By 29 December, when George Thomason obtained a copy and named its author, Herle had issued anonymously *A Fuller Answer to a Treatise Written by Dr Fearne*. In it he advanced three propositions: that a 'Parliament of England may with good conscience, in defence of King, Laws, and Government establisht, when imminently endangered … take up Armes without, and against the Kings personal commands, if he refuse'; that the final arbiters of whether such a situation had arisen were the two houses of parliament; and that the people were 'to rest' with parliament's judgement 'and in obedience thereto may with good conscience, in defence of the King, Lawes, and Government, beare and use Armes' (p. 2). Explaining that 'Englands is not a simply subordinative, and absolute, but a Coordinative, and mixt Monarchy' (p. 3), Herle went further than contemporary theorist Philip Hunton, whose position was in many respects similar, in exploring what would happen if co-operation between king and parliament, ideally equals in law making, broke down. Drawing on the idea of the king's two bodies, he propounded 'the ingenious formula of the king's virtual presence at Westminster' (Weston and Greenberg, 56) to cover his assent to parliamentary legislation. Herle complemented this in the second week of January 1643 with *An Answer to Mis-Led Dr Ferne According to his Own Method*, an extremely allusive point-by-point refutation drawing on wide historical precedent. Ferne's rejoinder, *Conscience Satisfied*, appeared in mid-April, and Herle's *An Answer to Dr Fernes Reply* by 17 May. Developing his theory of co-ordination to a position nearer to William Prynne's than Hunton's, Herle awarded parliament 'close to a monopoly' (ibid., 55) in the making and execution of laws.

On 17 February the Commons approved Herle as a Thursday afternoon lecturer in a new church at Tothill Fields, Westminster; he also gave a regular morning lecture at the abbey church and some time between 1642 and 1644 was a minister at St Olave, Southwark. Gaining in eminence, by the summer he was being spoken of in the same breath as Edmund Calamy and Stephen Marshall, and like them appeared to have gained the trust of the men around John Pym in parliament. On 15 June he encouraged the house with a fast sermon published as *Davids Song of Three Parts* (1643); five days later he was named with Calamy and Obadiah Sedgwick to license books of divinity. Nominated with William Heyrick to represent Lancashire in the Westminster assembly, he was placed on its grand committee on 29 September. Active, influential, and apparently clear-thinking, he soon emerged as one of the leading presbyterians but, although he consistently adopted a Reformed position in both doctrine and ecclesiology, his approach in debate was generally conciliatory. Earlier that year in *The Independency on Scriptures of the Independency of Churches* he had argued 'temperately' not against the Independents' contention that church government should be biblically based, which he entirely shared, but against their interpretation of what that government should be. In the assembly he supported a full exploration of their arguments, and sometimes ranged himself on their side in discussion, while in due course he authorized the publication of the Independent *An Apologeticall Narration*.

His political commitment was uncompromising, however. In *The Convinced Petitioner*, issued on 13 January 1644, he rejected a return to pre-war policy:

> when absolute prerogative gets upon the Throne, and the Pope upon the Church, what subjects then but slaves? what Christians but Papists? … no peace is to be had, but either we must fight for it in hope of victory, or purchase it by perpetuall slavery. (p. 15)

The undoubted sacrifice demanded in prosecuting the war further, and the reward from God, was outlined in *Abrahams Offer Gods Offering* (1644), preached before the lord mayor on Easter Tuesday. In the preface to *Ahab's Fall by his Prophets Flatteries* (1644), a collection of three sermons on the same text, including one at the abbey church, 'where it was much acquarrelled by some', Herle rather unsuccessfully disclaimed his critics' construction that 'what is spoken of King Ahab and Jezebel' was 'any way to be meant of our dread Soveraigne and his Consort' (sig. A2v), although he placed much emphasis on legality. Implicit in an appendix, *A Short Answer, by Way of a Postscript, to Dr Ferne's Last Reply*, was again the power invested in parliament to act without the king. *Davids Reserve and Rescue* (1645), preached to the Commons on 5 November 1644, celebrated freedom from tyranny.

On 22 July 1646 Herle was elected prolocutor of the assembly in succession to William Twisse, but by this time, his parish being securely in parliamentarian hands, he seems to have been periodically in Lancashire. His ties had never been entirely broken: in autumn 1644 he had administered collections made in London for the relief of distress caused by war in the county, while in December that year a parliamentary ordinance enabled him and other ministers to conduct ordinations there. When on 2 October 1646 Lancashire was divided into nine classical presbyteries, Herle's name headed the list of those in the fourth classis. On 25 December Robert Baillie, who as one of the Scottish commissioners at the assembly had not always approved Herle's contribution, perhaps surprisingly placed him first in a list sent to the earl of Loudoun of the ablest English clergy suitable to serve as royal chaplains. In 1647 Herle, with Marshall, accompanied the parliamentary commissioners on their mission to Scotland. In January that year one Margaret Herle was buried in Westminster Abbey; if this was his wife, Herle married again within a few months, for his daughter Mary was baptized at Winwick on 3 September 1648.

The king's execution in January 1649 seems to have been a watershed, however, and the event which persuaded Herle to leave London permanently and perhaps to alter his political stance. Retiring to Winwick, he faced two years of litigation with Fortescue. He cannot initially have enjoyed easy relations with the earl of Derby, who claimed to be the patron when tithes were calculated in

1650, but it seems that the breach was later healed. As the royalist army passed through Lancashire in August 1651 he took some of its wounded soldiers into his house and seems to have been among the local presbyterian ministers who made overtures to Derby while he was occupying Wigan for the king. Rumours were circulating in the Warrington area that Herle and his son had armed themselves and followed the royal forces, and even that Herle was a royalist spy. Probably shortly after the royalist defeat at Worcester on 3 September, Herle was among a group of distinguished Lancashire ministers arrested on suspicion of correspondence with the king and taken to Liverpool. Plague later led to their removal to Ormskirk, but their imprisonment seems to have been relatively short and their rehabilitation fairly rapid. In the summer of 1652 Herle played the leading role in the ordination at Winwick of John Howe, later domestic chaplain to Oliver Cromwell, and in 1654 he was appointed an assistant to the Lancashire commission of triers and ejectors.

Herle's final publications indicate a detachment from political matters. *Wordly policy and moral prudence, the vanity and folly of the one, the solidity and usefulnesse of the other* (1654) was a self-proclaimed 'moral discourse' advancing different aspects of personal integrity. *Wisdomes Tripos* (1655) added a third discussion, on Christian wisdom; conventionally pious, its only engagement with topical issues was to lament the 'Academy of Atheisme' which 'goes up apace … in these times' (p. 52). Herle died in late September 1659, and was buried on 29 September in the chancel of his church at Winwick. VIVIENNE LARMINIE

Sources Foster, *Alum. Oxon.* • J. L. Vivian and H. H. Drake, eds., *The visitation of the county of Cornwall in the year 1620*, Harleian Society, 9 (1874), 95 • J. E. Bailey, *The life of a Lancashire rector during the civil war* (1877) • Wood, *Ath. Oxon.*, new edn, 3.477–9 • R. S. Paul, *The assembly of the Lord: politics and religion in the Westminster assembly and the 'Grand debate'* (1985) • G. Ormerod, ed., *Tracts relating to military proceedings in Lancashire during the great civil war*, Chetham Society, 2 (1844), 207–8 • W. A. Shaw, ed., *Minutes of the Manchester presbyterian classis*, 1–2, Chetham Society, new ser., 20, 22 (1890–91), • *CSP dom.*, 1651, 397 • James, seventh earl of Derby, *The Stanley papers, pt 3*, ed. F. R. Raines, 3 vols., Chetham Society, 66–7, 70 (1867), vol. 1, p. v • *Walker rev.*, 60 • J. L. Chester, ed., *The marriage, baptismal, and burial registers of the collegiate church or abbey of St Peter, Westminster*, Harleian Society, 10 (1876), 141 • C. C. Weston and J. R. Greenberg, *Subjects and sovereigns: the great controversy over legal sovereignty in Stuart England* (1981) • *The letters and journals of Robert Baillie*, ed. D. Laing, 2 (1841), 201, 415 • J. P. Rylands, ed., *Lancashire and Cheshire wills and inventories, 1563 to 1807, now preserved at Chester*, Chetham Society, new ser., 37 (1897), 70 [will of Edward Herle, d. 1709] • W. Beaumont, *A history of Winwick*, ed. P. Riley (1995) • J. P. Pearce, *The church of St Oswald, Winwick, in legend and history* (1935)

Herle, Sir William (b. in or before 1270, d. 1347), justice, was probably born some time before 1270, since his first appointment as an attorney for litigation in the common bench was in 1291, and he must already then have been of age. His surname is apparently derived from Kirkharle in Northumberland. He may be the William Herle who acquired property there in 1304; he is certainly the William Herle who was granted free warren in his demesne lands there in 1332 and who also acquired lands elsewhere in Northumberland. He may be the William, son of William Herle, who is mentioned as the tenant of one-fifth of a knight's fee at Kirkharle in an inquisition *post mortem* of 1310, and whose father, another William (grandfather of William the justice), is known to have died in 1307. William and his brother Robert are both known to have acquired extensive properties in Leicestershire from the last decade of the thirteenth century onwards, and Robert was described in a conspiracy case of 1299 as a 'conspirator' active in Leicestershire, Warwickshire, and Staffordshire. It seems possible that the brothers had inherited some connection with Leicestershire, perhaps through their mother.

William Herle began practising as one of the serjeants of the common bench in Michaelmas term 1299, and seems to have been one of several serjeants called to the common-bench bar at that time. Final concord authorizations and law reports show him in regular attendance in the court until 1320. His success at the bar is also shown by the fact that early in the reign of Edward II he was retained by the city of London as one of its counsel, and that in 1315 he became a king's serjeant. Early in Michaelmas term 1320 he replaced John Benstead as a junior justice of the common bench and around this time he was knighted. For three terms in 1321 he was absent from the court while sitting as a justice of the London eyre, hearing civil pleas and *quo warranto* cases with the chief justice, Hervey Staunton. Otherwise he served continuously as a junior justice of the common bench, until he replaced Staunton as chief justice of the same court early in Hilary term 1327. He left court after Trinity term 1329 to serve as chief justice of the Nottinghamshire and Derbyshire eyres of 1330–31, but returned to the common bench, as its chief justice, in Easter term 1331; he relinquished this post at the end of Trinity term 1335, though he lived for another twelve years.

Herle's wife, Margaret, is first mentioned in a final concord relating to their joint acquisition of the reversion to lands at Bourton-on-Dunsmore in Warwickshire in 1311. She was dead by 1339, when William sought a licence to grant property to Garendon Abbey in Leicestershire in return for the provision of a monk to celebrate mass for William, his son Robert, the deceased Margaret, and William's deceased brother Robert. There seems to be no contemporary evidence to support Nichols's suggestion that Margaret was the daughter of Philip Courtney, or other later suggestions which make her the daughter and heir of one William Polglas. Herle died on 26 March 1347. His heir was his son Robert, who died without issue in 1364, when the Herle lands passed to Ralph Hastings, the son of Robert's sister Margaret.   PAUL BRAND

Sources *Chancery records* · court of common pleas, feet of fines, PRO, CP 25/1 · Common Bench plea rolls, PRO, CP 40 · *Report on the manuscripts of the late Reginald Rawdon Hastings*, 4 vols., HMC, 78 (1928–47), vol. 1 · F. M. Maitland and others, eds., *Year books of Edward II*, 26 vols. in 28, SeldS (1903–69) · law reports of the reign of Edward I, BL · A. J. Horwood, ed. and trans., *Year books of the reign of King Edward the First*, 5 vols., Rolls Series, 31 (1863–79) · J. Nichols, *The history and antiquities of the county of Leicester*, 4 vols. (1795–1815) · *CIPM*, 9, no. 39

Archives Hunt. L., Hastings MSS, property deeds
Wealth at death see *CIPM*

Herle, William (*d.* 1588/9), political agent, was the son of Thomas Herle of Montgomery and his wife. His father was a half-brother to Sir Richard Herbert (1468–1539). He had at least one brother and a sister. His early life is obscure but he was well educated with a good knowledge of languages, including Latin, Flemish, and Italian, and probably also French and Spanish.

Herle was in Antwerp in February 1559 when he sent Sir William Cecil, principal secretary, a letter containing news from the Low Countries. Disguised as a merchant, he travelled in 1560–62 to northern Germany where he established contacts with the nobility. He was back in London in July 1564, begging Cecil for his assistance in the case of Augier de l'Estrille who had been illegally captured by Herle and his fellow petitioners following an act of piracy. Herle continued to dabble with piracy and the privy council sent him to the Marshalsea prison on 13 November 1570. He entreated, both in English and Latin, for Cecil's help. From April 1571 he acted as a prison spy for Cecil. He played an important role in supplying information against Charles Bailly, a participant in the Ridolfi Plot of 1572. At the beginning of the year he uncovered a plot by Kenelm Berney and Edmund Mather to assassinate Cecil—having probably encouraged them in their plotting in order to impress his patron all the more by the revelation of it.

Herle was sent by Cecil, now Lord Burghley, to the Low Countries and returned in June 1573 with a long dispatch recording his conversations with William, prince of Orange. Cecil used this dispatch as an argument for aiding the Dutch, but Elizabeth I was not prepared, at this time, to quarrel with the Spanish. Herle spent the next few years in London, at Redcross Street, where he busied himself on behalf both of Paul Buys, the Dutch envoy, and of the English merchants trading with the Low Countries. He probably did not marry but he had a relationship with Rosa Jones and they had at least one illegitimate daughter, Jana, who was baptized at Guilsfield, Montgomeryshire, on 23 October 1576. In February 1582, when Robert Dudley, earl of Leicester, escorted François, duke of Alençon, as far as Antwerp on his return to France, Herle accompanied them. He later claimed that he had been left in Antwerp as Leicester's agent. He was assiduous, during the spring and summer of 1584, in supplying information to Burghley and to Sir Francis Walsingham, principal secretary, on affairs in the Low Countries. Fear of imprisonment for debt rather than a desire for public service kept him in Antwerp and his letters frequently plead for assistance with his debts. In April 1583 the Spanish ambassador noted that the queen had sent Herle to Cologne. He was appointed ambassador to Emden on 8 June 1584 and instructed to reconcile Count John and Count Edzard of Emden, the joint rulers of East Friesland, and he remained there until the spring of 1585.

On his return to England, Herle was again involved in English policy towards the Low Countries. Disagreements between Burghley and Leicester are probably behind a series of letters in which Herle explained that Burghley's role in Anglo–Dutch relations was unpopular and the queen's vacillating attitude unhelpful. Burghley took this candour in good part and justified his stance. He wished to explain his position and Herle was well placed to make the contents of these letters generally known. However, Burghley was not pleased when he discovered that Herle had shown the letters at court. Herle may have been acting on Leicester and Walsingham's behalf in trying to induce Burghley into more actively supporting the protestant cause in the Low Countries. Despite this his relationship with Burghley was reinforced by joint economic ventures.

Leicester led an English army to the Low Countries in December 1585 and Herle followed him in February 1586. The privy council ordered Leicester to send him again to Emden in order to mediate in the quarrel between Emden and the states of Holland and West Friesland, which was preventing English trade. The embassy met with little success and Leicester himself had to overcome the difficulties over trading. Despite his failure, Herle was sent in July 1586 as an envoy to Utrecht. He returned to London on 22 August 1586. He was elected MP for Callington, Cornwall, on his return, probably through Burghley's influence, enabling him to avoid his creditors. While Herle supplied both Walsingham and Burghley with information during 1587 and 1588, he failed to receive any further commissions. An appeal to Burghley on 3 May 1588 for employment and for help with his debts was answered with an annuity from the exchequer. Herle died in the parish of St Clement without the bars of the New Temple towards the end of 1588 or at the beginning of 1589; the administration of his estate was granted on 8 February 1589.

Herle's mastery of foreign languages enabled him to play a small part in England's relations with the Low Countries. Except for his embassies to Emden and to Utrecht, neither of which was notably successful, his role while abroad was to provide information, which he did in many prolix letters. A great part of his life was spent battling against ill health and in coping with his debts. In 1571 he obtained the office of rhaglaw of Cardiganshire and he believed that the profits of this office would provide him with financial security; after years of struggle, the Cardiganshire gentry defeated him. Still in debt, Herle was content to go to the Low Countries where he could avoid his creditors. His many requests for a permanent position were ignored by his powerful friends and this suggests that they considered him useful but not entirely trustworthy.   DAVID LEWIS JONES

Sources BL, Harley MS 6102, fol. 24*r* · W. V. Lloyd, 'The sheriffs of Montgomeryshire', *Montgomeryshire Collections*, 4 (1871), 402 · *CSP for.*, 1560–86 · *CSP Spain*, 1568–86 · *CSP dom.*, 1547–90 · F. Edwards, *The marvellous chance* (1968) · C. Read, *Lord Burghley and Queen Elizabeth* (1960) · D. L. Jones, 'William Herle and the office of rhaglaw in Elizabethan Cardiganshire', *National Library of Wales Journal*, 17 (1971–2), 161–82 · *HoP, Commons, 1558–1603* · *Index to administrations in the prerogative court of Canterbury*, 3: 1581–1595 (1954), 79
Archives Bodl. Oxf., papers relating to East Friesland, MS Rawl. c. 424 | BL, Cotton MSS, letters

Herman, Henry (1832–1894), playwright and novelist, was educated at a military college in Alsace. He later emigrated to the United States, fought in the Confederate ranks during the American Civil War, and lost an eye at the battle of Bull Run in Virginia. He had returned to England by 1875, as on 15 May of that year he produced *Jeanne Dubarry*, a drama in three acts, at the Charing Cross Theatre in London. On 25 July 1877 he married Eugenie Adelaide, the only daughter of Frederick Henry Edwards. She was an actress, and later played in two of Herman's pieces. His first conspicuous dramatic success, after producing several more plays, was *The Silver King*, a drama in five acts, written in conjunction with Henry Arthur Jones, which opened on 16 November 1882. Disputes regarding which collaborator had done more work on *The Silver King* ensued. Jones argued at first that Herman 'did not write a line of it' (Jones, 68), though he later acknowledged that Herman had at least written 'the end of the second act' (ibid., 73). Herman also collaborated with Jones on *Breaking a Butterfly*, an adaptation of Ibsen's *A Doll's House*, which opened at the Prince of Wales Theatre on 3 March 1884, and *Chatterton* (Princess's, 22 May 1884). In collaboration with William Gorman Wills he wrote *Claudian*, a three-act play performed at the Princess's on 6 December 1884. *The Golden Band*, in four acts (Olympic, 14 January 1887), was by Herman and Freeman Wills. Herman is responsible for two untraceable dramas, *For Old Virginia* (1891) and *Eagle Joe* (1892), and for *The Fay o' Fire*, a romantic opera, with music by Edward Jones (Opera Comique, 14 November 1885).

Herman collaborated with David Christie Murray in writing six novels between 1887 and 1891, including the melodramatic *Bishop's Bible* (1890), and *He Fell among Thieves* (1891). His name alone appears as the author of more than ten novels, including *His Angel* (1891), a story which begins vividly with a lynching in New Mexico, and *Eagle Joe* (1892), 'a Wild West Romance'. His novels were hastily written but exciting, and he wrote stories up to his death.

Freeman Wills noted that although Herman 'had not a trace of humour himself … he was fertile in invention and teemed with melodrama, and had … an excellent and refined judgment' (Wills, 220), especially regarding the work of others. He observed that Herman was 'an exacting collaborator' and that 'his manner was that of the irritable foreigner, but he was thoroughly kind-hearted and chivalrous in his domestic life, and well maintained the dignity of a literary man' (ibid., 227).

Herman's choice theatrical library was sold at Sothebys on 23 January 1885, when 234 lots fetched over £16,000. The high prices were due in great measure to the large number of grangerized books, illustrated with prints or engravings taken from other books. He died at Gunnersbury, Middlesex, on 24 September 1894 and was buried at Kensal Green cemetery, in a plot purchased by his erstwhile collaborator Henry Arthur Jones.

JOSEPH KNIGHT, rev. MEGAN A. STEPHAN

Sources *English Catalogue of Books* (1887–91) · F. C. Wills, *W. G. Wills: dramatist and painter* (1898) · D. A. Jones, *The life and letters of Henry Arthur Jones* (1930) · Boase, *Mod. Eng. biog.* · J. Coleman, *Fifty years of*

an actor's life, 2 (1904), 656–60 · personal knowledge (1901) · *The Era* (29 Sept 1894)

Herman, Josef (1911–2000), artist, was born on 3 January 1911 in Warsaw, Poland, the eldest of the three children of David Herman (*d.* 1942), a partner in a shoe factory, and his wife, Sarah Krukman (1893?–1942). He was brought up in great poverty, mostly on the streets of the Jewish quarter, for his illiterate father was persuaded to make his mark on a document which gave his absconding partner the right to sell their shared shoe factory and flee to America. David Herman sank into deep depression, incapable even of feeding himself, and his young wife, Sarah, was forced to take control of the household, fetching in other people's washing and cleaning their houses. Eventually, David managed to pull himself together sufficiently to take up cobbling, but he remained a broken man. As a consequence of this early experience, however successful he was in later years, Josef Herman would always worry about money.

Herman attended a school in Warsaw until he was thirteen. He had already engaged in a long series of temporary jobs, the first of which was as a seller of soda water in a local cinema. As a child he adopted the habit of rising early, at 4 a.m. every day, in order to have some time to himself in the single crowded room where the family slept, before the bustle of the day began. It was a habit he maintained all his life, whatever time he went to bed, and helps to account for his prodigious output of drawings and paintings. At this time he also made the acquaintance of a wandering artist, Master Xavery Rex, and a Dr Saltzman, both of whom settled in their street. From one he learned the magic of art, from the other the lesson of true humanity.

Not until he was sixteen did Herman settle in a job, as apprentice typesetter to the one-time anarchist and printer Felix Yacubowitch. For the next three years he studied his trade until he fell ill with lead poisoning. Disbarred from printing on medical grounds, he became a freelance graphic designer, and enrolled for an eighteen-month stint at the Warsaw School of Art and Decoration (1930–32). In 1932 Herman held his first exhibition of pictures, in a frame-maker's shop, and began to enjoy a slight reputation as an artist. He joined the Phrygian Bonnet, a group of socially aware artists who painted the peasants of the Carpathian mountains in an expressionist manner. Although a lifelong and committed man of the left, Herman belonged to no political party, but the authorities considered all artists Bolsheviks. Warsaw was unwelcoming and antisemitic. In 1938 Herman left Poland for Belgium. He was never to see his family or his homeland again.

In Brussels, Herman enrolled at the Brussels Academy of Fine Arts and fell under the formative influence of Constant Permeke (1886–1952), a painter of peasants in a weighty, earthy style. The Nazi invasion of Europe cut short his stay. Herman fled through France to La Rochelle, where he was mistaken for a Polish airman because of his black leather coat and beret. He was put on a ship to England, arriving in Liverpool in June 1940. From there he was sent, speaking no English, to the Polish consulate in Glasgow.

Wartime Glasgow was surprisingly lively; Herman was befriended by the sculptor Benno Schotz, and renewed his acquaintance with the painter Jankel Adler. He met J. D. Fergusson, got to know Joan Eardley, then a student at Glasgow School of Art, and designed sets and costumes for Margaret Morris's Celtic Ballet company. In 1942 he learned through the Red Cross that his family had been destroyed in the Nazi Holocaust; he began to transmute this tragedy into a melancholy but powerful celebration of Jewish themes and memories, a kind of visual autobiography. In that same year he met and married Catriona MacLeod (*d. c.*1990), a whisky heiress and also an artist, and helped to found the *Jewish Quarterly*. In 1943 the newlyweds moved to London, and Herman held his first exhibition there, at the Lefevre Gallery, shared with another unknown, L. S. Lowry.

As yet, Herman had not discovered his mature voice as an artist. He achieved this when first visiting the Welsh mining village of Ystradgynlais in the summer of 1944. There he experienced a key moment of recognition when he saw a group of miners returning from work briefly outlined on a bridge against a copper-coloured sky. That image stayed with him and provided a subject. For the next eleven years Herman lived in Ystradgynlais and painted and drew the miners. He was swiftly accepted into the community and nicknamed Joe Bach, and the work he subsequently produced made his name as a distinct artistic force in Britain.

Herman did not paint the miners at work in the pit—as Henry Moore had done—but captured them in the canteen or walking home, exhausted after their labours. More often than not, they are anonymous, and represent the universal rather than the particular: they stand for the dignity of labour, of the working man. There are portraits of individual miners, such as Mike, but these are portraits first, miners second. Herman was a subtle and perceptive portraitist—see, for instance, his portrait of Arnold Wesker in the National Portrait Gallery—but he rarely accepted commissions. For a decade the miner was his principal subject, but by no means his only one. His range was always far wider than commonly thought. Apart from fishermen and peasants at work, he also drew and painted ballet dancers and sportsmen (playing football, tennis, or snooker), while a chief preoccupation for many years was with the female nude. In later life Herman was just as likely to paint a single tree or bird, or a refulgent vase of flowers.

Although his reputation grew rapidly in the 1950s, not everything was well with Herman. His wife suffered a mental breakdown at the birth of a stillborn child, and Herman's own health suffered from the damp Welsh climate. Foreign travel was advised: over the next decade Herman visited Israel, France, Italy, and Spain. Early in 1955 and back in London, Herman met Dr Eleanor Marie (Nini) Ettlinger (*b.* 1925), who became his model and soon his mistress. That year he was accorded his first retrospective at the Wakefield City Art Gallery (further retrospectives followed in 1956 at the Whitechapel Gallery in London, then in Glasgow in 1975, and at Camden Arts Centre in London in 1980).

In 1960 Herman divorced Catriona MacLeod, and the following year, on 11 March, married Nini Ettlinger. A son had been born to the couple in 1957, and they soon decided to forsake London for Suffolk. But disaster pursued them. In the mid-1960s Herman found he could not work and suffered from severe depression. In 1966 the Hermans' infant daughter died. Herman became suicidal and was given electroconvulsive therapy and drug treatment, recovering only gradually. He moved back to London on his own, and it was not until 1974 that the family was reunited.

Herman was really happy only when he was working. Admittedly his habit of early rising allowed him a head start on most people ('six masterpieces before breakfast, my dear!' he would boast), but his industry rarely flagged. He drew in pencil and ink, worked rapidly in watercolour and mixed media, and painted more slowly in oils. He read widely, particularly relishing the autobiographies of artists, and wrote voluminously himself. Mostly his writing took the journal form. His first book, entitled *Related Twilights* (1975), was subtitled 'Notes from an artist's diary', and is a vivid evocation of people, places, and art. Herman was also famous for his internationally acclaimed collection of African miniature sculptures, an enthusiasm that grew from his friendship with Jacob Epstein.

Herman received various honours, including an OBE in 1980, and was elected a Royal Academician in 1990. A generous and charming man, he was much loved by a wide circle of friends. Habitually dressed in brown cords, topped with a white lab coat when in the studio, he was a man of few worldly needs. In later years he mostly occupied a cosy bed-sitting room situated handily at the top of steep steps leading down to the picturesque studio full of his own work and his African sculpture. His profoundly humanistic vision has an inspiring boldness and monumental grandeur that will survive. He died at his home, 120 Edith Road, London, on 19 February 2000, and was cremated on 23 February at Golders Green. His works are held in numerous British collections, including the Art Gallery and Museum, Glasgow; the Glyn Vivian Art Gallery, Swansea; the National Museum and Gallery of Wales, Cardiff; The Scottish National Gallery of Modern Art, Edinburgh; the Tate collection and the British Museum, London; Birmingham City Art Gallery; Leeds City Art Gallery; the City Art Gallery, Bristol; and Aberdeen Art Gallery.

ANDREW LAMBIRTH

Sources N. Herman, *Josef Herman: a working life* (1996) • *The Independent* (22 Feb 2000) • *The Guardian* (22 Feb 2000) • *Daily Telegraph* (21 Feb 2000) • personal knowledge (2004) • A. Lambirth and others, *Josef Herman* (1998) • J. Herman, *Related twilights* (1975) • J. Herman, *Notes from a Welsh diary* (1988) • B. Taylor, *Josef Herman: drawings* (1956) • E. Mullins, *Josef Herman: paintings and drawings* (1967) • M. Merchant, *Josef Herman: the early years* (1984) • *Josef Herman: memory of memories* (1985) • R. Heller, *Josef Herman: the work is* the life (1998) • P. Davies, *Josef Herman's drawings and studies* (1990) • CGPLA Eng. & Wales (2000)

Archives priv. coll., archive | FILM BBC Wales, various documentary programmes [video copies in Nini Herman's collection] | SOUND BL NSA

Likenesses J. Herman, self-portrait, oils, 1946, repro. in Herman, *Josef Herman*, cover • photograph, repro. in *The Independent* • photograph, repro. in *Daily Telegraph* • photograph, repro. in *The Guardian*

Wealth at death £1,637,450—gross; £1,636,600—net: probate, 14 June 2000, CGPLA Eng. & Wales

Hermand. For this title name *see* Fergusson, George, Lord Hermand (1743–1827).

Hermann (d. 1078), bishop of Ramsbury and of Sherborne, came from the continent to England early in the reign of Edward the Confessor. His parentage, date of birth, and precise place of origin are all unknown. According to the chronicle of John of Worcester, he came from Lotharingia, although William of Malmesbury in his *Gesta pontificum* says that he was Flemish by birth. However, Philip Grierson has argued that the name Hermann, common in Lotharingia, is rare in Flanders, and that William may have been misled by the fact that Hermann spent part of his career at the abbey of St Bertin. He became one of Edward the Confessor's chaplains by 1044, and in 1045 Edward appointed him to succeed the deceased Brihtwold as bishop of Ramsbury or Wilton, a diocese corresponding in extent to Wiltshire and Berkshire and with its see based at Ramsbury (a small settlement of no economic or political significance and with a cathedral community which can only have been tiny). In 1050 Hermann, together with Bishop Ealdred of Worcester, was sent to Rome by Edward the Confessor to negotiate with the pope. Edward made the decision to send the two bishops at the mid-Lent council of London in 1050 and the pair arrived in Rome on 14 April. The subject of the negotiations is unclear; claims in twelfth-century Westminster forgeries that Edward was trying to release himself from a vow to go on pilgrimage are unlikely to be valid. None the less it is obvious that Hermann was highly thought of by Edward.

Hermann himself, however, was frustrated by the limited resources of his diocese, and in 1055 requested that Edward should allow him to take over Malmesbury Abbey as his see church. In this he may have been influenced by Bishop Leofric of Crediton's decision to move his see to Exeter, a move permitted by Edward, whose charter allowing this had been witnessed by Hermann, among others. However, the monks of Malmesbury put up a much tougher fight than the clerks of Exeter had done; Edward refused Hermann's request and the latter decided to leave England for Flanders and to become a monk at the abbey of St Bertin. Meanwhile, Bishop Ealdred of Worcester took over responsibility for Ramsbury. In 1058 Ealdred wished to leave England to go on pilgrimage to Jerusalem, and Hermann was persuaded to return to his diocese. On the death of Bishop Ælfwold of Sherborne, who last occurs in a charter of 1059, Hermann was appointed to succeed him and the two sees of Sherborne and Ramsbury were united. He encouraged a young monk of

St Bertin, Goscelin, to travel to England and join his episcopal household. Although Goscelin eventually found a more permanent home at St Augustine's, Canterbury, he maintained ties with the diocese of Sherborne until shortly after Hermann's death, when he completed a life of St Wulfsige (Bishop Wulfsige of Sherborne) which Hermann had commissioned, and, shortly afterwards, a life of St Edith of Wilton. Hermann himself had close contacts with Wilton, whose new abbey church he dedicated in 1065 at the request of Queen Edith, who had paid for the rebuilding.

After the Norman conquest Hermann continued to be held in esteem. He probably attended the Council of Windsor in April 1070, since its decrees were soon afterwards copied into a Romano-Germanic pontifical of French origin used at Sherborne in his day, and on 29 August 1070 he assisted at Lanfranc's consecration. In the following year, however, Lanfranc expressed unease about Hermann's health in a letter to Pope Alexander II in which he stated that Hermann might wish to be released from his diocesan duties to become a monk once more. Lanfranc tried, not quite successfully, to dismiss a rumour that Hermann was weighed down by injuries done to him and by services owed to the king. Lanfranc did not specify Hermann's problems, though they may possibly be the demands placed on him by the king's judges which Goscelin refers to in a miracle story at the end of his life of St Wulfsige: apparently Hermann defended his rights with the aid of Wulfsige's relics. At all events, Hermann decided to persevere as bishop. He attended the Council of Windsor at Whitsun 1072 and in 1075 at the Council of London he won permission to move his see to a more important site: the borough of Old Sarum, now being refortified by William I with a castle. However, little progress could be made in building a cathedral there in the few years that remained to Hermann, who died on 20 February 1078. His place of burial is unknown; a tradition that he was buried at Old Sarum and then moved to Salisbury is almost certainly false, and it is possible that his resting place was Sherborne.   JULIA BARROW

Sources John of Worcester, *Chron.*, 2.542–3, 554–5, 578–9, 584–5 · *Willelmi Malmesbiriensis monachi de gestis pontificum Anglorum libri quinque*, ed. N. E. S. A. Hamilton, Rolls Series, 52 (1870), 39, 67–8, 182–3, 420 · *ASC*, s.a. 1045, 1046, 1049, 1051, 1077 [(texts C, D)] · 'The life of Saint Wulsin of Sherborne by Goscelin', ed. C. H. Talbot, *Revue Bénédictine*, 69 (1959), 68–85, esp. 83–4 · D. Whitelock, M. Brett, and C. N. L. Brooke, eds., *Councils and synods with other documents relating to the English church, 871–1204*, 2 vols. (1981), pt 1, 525–33, 535–6, 542; pt 2, 567, 588, 603, 609, 612 · F. Barlow, ed. and trans., *The life of King Edward who rests at Westminster*, 2nd edn, OMT (1992) · *The letters of Lanfranc, archbishop of Canterbury*, ed. and trans. H. Clover and M. Gibson, OMT (1979), 2, 34–7, 40–41, 49, 74–7, 79n. · P. Grierson, 'The relations between England and Flanders before the Norman conquest', *TRHS*, 4th ser., 23 (1941), 71–112, esp. 101 n. 4 · *Fasti Angl., 1066–1300*, [Salisbury], 1 · M. A. O'Donovan, ed., *Charters of Sherborne*, Anglo-Saxon Charters, 3 (1988), xxxi · N. R. Ker, 'Three Old English texts in a Salisbury pontifical, Cotton Tiberius C.i', *The Anglo-Saxons: studies in some aspects of their history and culture presented to Bruce Dickins*, ed. P. Clemoes (1959), 262–79, esp. 267 · F. E. Harmer, ed., *Anglo-Saxon writs* (1952), 121, 123, 131, 133, 191 (n. 4), 288–9, 559, 563–4 · A. J. Robertson, ed. and trans., *Anglo-Saxon charters*, 2nd edn (1956), 214–15, 218–19, 466 · *Reg. RAN*, 1.9, 22–3, 26, 28, 34, 64, 108–9, 113, 148 · A. Farley, ed., *Domesday Book*, 2 vols. (1783), 1.58b, 66a

Hermann (*fl.* 1070–1100), Benedictine monk and hagiographer, who may have been rightly named Bertrann, probably came from the Paris region of France. He was secretary to Herfast, bishop of East Anglia (1070–84), and after Herfast's death secretary to Baldwin, abbot of Bury St Edmunds (1065–97/8). He then became a monk of Bury St Edmunds. He wrote the *De miraculis sancti Eadmundi* (*c.*1100), which includes a few autobiographical details. During Herfast's dispute with Baldwin over his attempts to move his see to Bury he wrote the bishop's letters and read those received. He was with Herfast when he injured an eye on a branch while riding through a wood and, having heard of Baldwin's reputation as a physician, persuaded the bishop to go to him for treatment.

The identification of Hermann is problematical. No archdeacon named Hermann has been found in the records of Norwich Cathedral, nor can the hagiographer be convincingly identified with any known monk of Bury St Edmunds. The earliest known attribution of the *De miraculis* to Hermann the archdeacon is in an inscription of *c.*1370 by Henry Kirkestede, on the first page of the copy (of *c.*1100) of the *De miraculis* in the British Library (Cotton MS Tiberius B.ii, fol. 20). Possibly Kirkestede derived this name by misreading a (perhaps damaged) inscription in some now lost copy which attributed the work to Bertrann, the contemporary hagiographer whom Goscelin praises and describes as 'in sua patria ut ferebatur archidiaconus' ('archdeacon, as he was called in his homeland').

The *De miraculis* recounts the miracles ascribed to St Edmund in the eleventh century, set in the framework of the history of St Edmund's church and community. Although Hermann wrote to promote the cult of St Edmund and as a partisan of Baldwin in his struggle with Herfast, the *De miraculis* is a valuable historical source for the history of Bury St Edmunds Abbey. It also has sidelights on Cnut, who sanctioned the introduction of the Benedictine rule at Bury in 1020, and on the abbey's patrons, Edward the Confessor, William I, and William II, in their contacts with abbot and monks. The author drew on oral information and on written, including documentary, sources, most of which are now lost. He was a conscientious historian, highly educated, and a gifted Latinist.

The *De miraculis* survives in two versions, one long, the other short. The long version culminates in 1095, with the translation of St Edmund to Baldwin's new church. The only extant copy known is in the British Library (Cotton MS Tiberius B.ii, fols. 20–85v). The short version abbreviates the long version and ends *c.*1050. It survives in two copies both of *c.*1100 (Paris, Bibliothèque Nationale, MS Lat. 2621, fols. 84–92v; and Bodl. Oxf., MS Digby 39, fols. 24–39v, from Abingdon Abbey). Judging from the dearth of medieval copies, *De miraculis* itself contributed little to the spread of St Edmund's cult. But the long version was an important source for later hagiographers of St Edmund at Bury. Particularly noteworthy is the amplified, updated version produced in the late twelfth century and associated with Samson, abbot of Bury St Edmunds from 1182 to 1211 (BL, Cotton MS Titus A.viii).

ANTONIA GRANSDEN

Sources T. Arnold, ed., *Memorials of St Edmund's Abbey*, 1, Rolls Series, 96 (1890), 26–92 · F. Liebermann, ed., *Ungedruckte anglonormannische Geschichtsquellen* (1879), 231–81 [prints extracts from the long version] · E. Martène and U. Durand, eds., *Veterum scriptorum et monumentorum historicorum, dogmaticorum, moralium, amplissima collectio*, 6 (1729), cols. 821–34 [prints the short version] · A. Gransden, 'The composition and authorship of the *De miraculis sancti Eadmundi* attributed to "Hermann the Archdeacon"', *Journal of Medieval Latin*, 5 (1995), 1–52 · R. M. Thomson, 'Two versions of a saint's life from St. Edmund's Abbey', *Revue Bénédictine*, 84 (1974), 383–408 · BL, Cotton MS Tiberius B.ii, fols. 20–85*v* · Bibliothèque Nationale, Paris, MS Lat. 2621, fols. 84–92*v* · Bodl. Oxf., MS Digby 39, fols. 24–39*v*

Archives Bibliothèque Nationale, Paris, MS Lat. 2621, fols. 34–92*v* · BL, Cotton MS Tiberius B.ii, fols. 20–85*v* · Bodl. Oxf., MS Digby 39, fols. 24–39*v*

Hermes, Gertrude Anna Bertha (1901–1983), printmaker, sculptor, and designer, was born on 18 August 1901 at Altena, Bickley, Kent, the second of five children of German-born parents, Louis August Hermes (1866–1949) and his wife, Helene, *née* Gerdes (1872–1949), of Altena, near Dortmund. Her father, who had lived in England since the age of four, was artistic director of Sambrook Whitting, manufacturers of patterned silkwear.

Gertrude Hermes was educated at Belmont School, Bickley, where she shone at art, botany, and sports, although her schooldays were coloured by anti-German abuse directed at her family by neighbours in the early years of the First World War. Later in her school career she played hockey for Kent. On leaving school she considered farming as a career, and in 1920 spent nearly a year working on a farm in Essex. Her interest in art remained dominant, however, and about 1921 she enrolled at Beckenham School of Art. She made intermittent visits to relations in Germany at this time, which broadened her experience, and introduced her to the sculpture of Wilhelm Lehmbruck (1881–1919) and to German expressionism.

Although Hermes had ambitions to study at the Slade School of Fine Art, London, its intake was full when she applied in 1922, and she joined instead the unorthodox school of painting and sculpture run by Leon Underwood in Hammersmith. Here her fellow students included Eileen Agar, Raymond Coxon, Blair Hughes-Stanton, and Henry Moore. Throughout her life Hermes acknowledged her debt to Underwood, who taught life drawing and direct carving, and introduced her to African sculpture and the work of Constantin Brancusi and Henri Gaudier-Brzeska. At Easter 1925 she visited Paris, and was particularly struck by the Far Eastern sculpture in the Musée Guimet. Later that year Underwood took his pupils to Dalmatia, and although the trip was curtailed through illness in the party, it introduced Hermes to the manner of direct carving then practised in Split, and already known to English audiences through the work of the Serbian sculptor Ivan Mestrovic.

Hermes felt no instinct for painting, but her grasp of

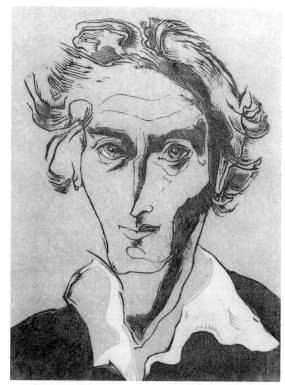

Gertrude Anna Bertha Hermes (1901–1983), self-portrait, 1949

two-dimensional form became manifest when she and fellow students at Underwood's school taught themselves wood-engraving, a subject not then on the syllabus. Her experiments in this medium led rapidly to technical mastery, and the development of an inventive and exuberant cutting style which owed much to her craftsmanship, vision, and steadiness of eye and hand. In 1925 and 1926 she qualified for the finals of the prix de Rome in engraving, but withdrew before the 1926 examinations to marry her fellow student Blair Rowlands Hughes-Stanton (1902–1981).

The couple lived together in a basement flat at 10 Hammersmith Terrace, Chiswick, London, and soon became part of the local literary and artistic milieu that included Raymond Coxon, Robert Graves, A. P. Herbert, Eric Kennington, and Dick and Naomi Mitchison. They had very little money, and depended for their living on what they earned from their art, and from Hughes-Stanton's teaching. Their first child, Judith, was born in April 1927, and although the baby's upbringing consumed the greater part of Hermes's time and energy, she made small sculpture and wood engravings, some on commission, including four wood engravings for *Pilgrim's Progress* (Cresset Press, 1928). Their flat was devastated by the Thames flood of January 1928, causing a disastrous loss of work, but none the less they exhibited the following month at St George's Gallery, where Hermes launched herself, significantly, as a sculptor rather than a wood engraver. After the birth of their second child, Simon, in September 1928 the couple left London for Hacheston, Suffolk, where they rented Chetwynd House and had more space to work. At Hacheston, Hermes completed twenty wood-engravings for *A Florilege* (Swan Press, 1930).

Hermes's marriage had by now become increasingly unhappy, her husband having continuing affairs in London. Despite this, however, they went together in 1930 to Montgomeryshire, where Hughes-Stanton had been appointed wood-engraver to the Gregynog Press. The press also contracted Hermes to engrave for them, but their production was frustrated by her inability, through deep unhappiness, to complete wood-engravings for *A Natural History of Selborne* by Gilbert White, and the edition never appeared. The marriage ended in 1931, and Hermes went back to Chiswick with their children, to live at 27A St Peter's Square. The couple were divorced in 1933.

An important new aspect of Hermes's career opened up on her return to London. She was commissioned by the architects Scott, Chesterton, and Shepherd to carve a stone fountain and design a mosaic pool bottom and door furniture for the new Shakespeare Memorial Theatre at Stratford upon Avon. This led to further commissions for decorative and functional devices for architecture, such as letter boxes, door knockers, pub signs, and, in 1936, the Britannia window for the Paris Exhibition. She was admitted to the Register of Industrial Designers in 1937. Another new avenue opened for her when she made a portrait bust of A. P. Herbert (1932). This led to commissions over the subsequent decades for a series of penetrating bronze portraits of sitters (many of whom were by now among her friends), including David Wright (1954–5), David Gascoigne (1956), and Naomi Mitchison (1958).

Hermes also found a new vivacity in other areas of her art in the 1930s. She took wood-engraving to new depths of expression, and although some of her prints revealed an underlying dark mood, reflecting the turbulence of her private life, others celebrated her joy in creativity and her understanding of the complexity of human relationships. She exhibited widely in the 1930s, notably at the Royal Academy, with the London Group, and with the Society of Wood Engravers, but her work came to popular audiences through commissions from Penguin Books, including *The Compleat Angler* (1939) by Isaak Walton. She was chosen with seven other wood-engravers to represent Great Britain at the Venice Biennale planned for 1940, but cancelled on the outbreak of the Second World War.

Hermes's relationships were complex and extensive. She had lovers, central among them the writer Francis Watson, but her expression of sexual pressures and gender identity in her art was cautious, even allegorical. She was greatly moved by poetry, indeed poets were among her closest friends, and some of her wood-engravings were directly inspired by the writings of John Donne, D. H. Lawrence, Kenneth Muir, John Pudney, and others. Hermes's sculpture of this period, in which she characteristically chose subjects which she also treated in wood-engraving, celebrated human and animal physicality. Like her wood-engraving, the sculpture is highly personal and has no stylistic allegiance.

In 1940 Hermes moved with her children to Montreal, and she then travelled on to New York to seek art commissions. After returning to Montreal, she found work as a draughtsman in aircraft production and shipbuilding. This, as she later recalled, made her 'heartily sick of black and white'. After her return to London in 1945 she moved to 31 Danvers Street, Chelsea, where she eschewed wood-engraving and began to make colour linocuts. She achieved complete mastery of this medium and pioneered a large-scale format, notably in *Rooks and Rain* (1950), *The Ram* (1958), and *Stonehenge* (1959), which won the Giles bequest prize from the Victoria and Albert Museum (1960). Her later sculpture also developed in scale, and explored growth and change in animal and plant forms.

Hermes was a natural maker and keeper of friends. She made regular visits to Carradale, the Scottish home of her lifelong friend Naomi Mitchison, and remained close to her former husband until he died. She became an able teacher of drawing and printmaking at Camberwell, St Martin's, the Central School, and the Royal Academy Schools of Art. She suffered a stroke in 1969, and produced little thereafter. Retrospective exhibitions were held at the Whitechapel Art Gallery (1967) and at the Royal Academy in London and the Mappin Art Gallery, Sheffield (1981). She was elected an associate of the Royal Society of Painter-Etchers and Engravers in 1949, and a fellow in 1951; an associate of the Royal Academy (1963), and a Royal Academician (1971); and appointed OBE (1981). A complete collection of her wood-engravings and her surviving sketchbooks is held at the Ashmolean Museum, Oxford, and her work is represented in many other public collections in Great Britain and throughout the world. Her friend the poet and wood-engraver Marion Mitchell wrote that Hermes was 'one of the few *totally* honest human beings I have known in my long life. Not even a microscopic trace of phoniness in her spirit' (letter to James Hamilton, 1987). She died of cancer at her daughter's house, 5 Sion Hill, Bristol, on 9 May 1983, and was cremated at Canford, Bristol, on 13 May 1983. A memorial service was held in London at St James's Church, Piccadilly.

JAMES HAMILTON

Sources J. Russell, ed., *The wood-engravings of Gertrude Hermes* (1993) · J. Hamilton, unpublished biography of Gertrude Hermes, priv. coll. · J. Hamilton, *Wood engraving and the woodcut in Britain, c.1890–1990* (1994) · B. Robertson, ed., *Gertrude Hermes* (1967) [exhibition catalogue, Whitechapel Art Gallery, London] · D. Brown, *Gertrude Hermes* (1981) [exhibition leaflet, RA] · J. Hamilton, postscript, *Gertrude Hermes: Selborne* (1988) · K. Eustace, *The wood engravings of Gertrude Hermes and Blair Hughes-Stanton* (1995) · P. Hughes-Stanton, *The wood-engravings of Blair Hughes-Stanton* (1991) · private information (2004) [Judith Russell, daughter] · *DNB* · *Blair Hughes-Stanton, William McCance, Gertrude Hermes, Agnes Miller-Parker* (1928) [exhibition catalogue, St George's Gallery, London] · *CGPLA Eng. & Wales* (1983)

Archives Henry Moore Institute, Leeds, Centre for the Study of Sculpture, corresp., photographs, papers · priv. coll., family papers · priv. coll., letters, notes, and research papers | Bodl. Oxf., corresp. with Sir J. L. Myres · NL Wales, Thomas Jones papers

Likenesses R. Coxon, oils, 1930–39, priv. coll. · G. Hermes, self-portrait, linocut, 1949 · G. Hermes, self-portrait, wood-engraving, 1949, NPG [*see illus.*] · photographs, repro. in Russell, ed., *Wood-engravings of Gertrude Hermes*

Wealth at death £52,449: probate, 25 July 1983, *CGPLA Eng. & Wales*

Herne [Heron], **John** (*c.*1593–1649), barrister, was the younger son of Richard Herne (*d.* 1625), alderman, and later sheriff, of London and his wife, Alice, daughter of John Paske. He was subsequently adopted by William Robson, salter of London. He was probably the John Heron who matriculated from Clare College, Cambridge, during Lent 1608. From Cambridge he entered Lincoln's Inn on 27 January 1611, receiving his call to the bar in 1618. On 4 August of that year he married, at St Bartholomew by the Exchange, Susanna (*fl. c.*1600–1660), daughter of John Woodward, grocer of London. On 5 March 1628 he was elected to parliament for Newport, Cornwall, but was unseated on petition.

During the ensuing two decades Herne assumed a prominent role in a series of important state trials, the most dramatic of which were the proceedings in the Long Parliament in the years 1641–5 against William Laud, archbishop of Canterbury (1633–45), on charges of high treason and misdemeanour. In 1632 he defended the barrister Henry Sherfield, recorder of Salisbury, on a charge in Star Chamber for defacing an offending stained-glass window in St Edmund's Church, Salisbury. In February 1634 he served as counsel for William Prynne, the outspoken barrister of Lincoln's Inn, during his Star Chamber trial for the publication of his controversial work against female players, *Histriomastix*. During the following year Herne is known to have held the manor of Hendon, Middlesex, paying rent on 32 acres with outbuildings and adjacent land. He became a bencher of his inn in 1637 and in 1640 he was residing in Aldersgate ward, London. In 1641 he acted as one of the counsel for the ship money judges, Sir John Bramston the elder and Sir Robert Berkeley, during proceedings against them in the Long Parliament.

Herne was one of Archbishop William Laud's original choices for counsel at his impeachment, being named in the prelate's petition of 1 March 1641. Ultimately he shared the archbishop's defence with the Long Parliament's appointee as co-counsel, Sir Matthew Hale. He may also have been the Mr Herne who appeared in defence of the impeached lord mayor Sir Richard Gurney in July 1642. On 11 October 1644 Herne delivered to the House of Lords an argument in law, probably a joint composition with Hale, in which he denied the existence of 'constructive treasons' under the English law as set out in Edward III's statute of treasons (1352). Moreover, Herne's argument recognized that Laud's aggrandizement of the forensic and legislative jurisdictions of the clerical estate during his tenure as archbishop of Canterbury constituted at best a mere *praemunire*. The charges that Laud had 'subverted the fundamental laws of the land' in maintaining his jurisdiction over and above that of the king closely resembled in substance and language those against Wolsey and Lingham during Henry VIII's reign and rested on the conflation of high treason with the lesser, non-capital cause of *praemunire*. On 6 November 1644 Herne visited

Laud in the Tower and returned his prayer book that William Prynne had possessed since the Long Parliament's seizure of the prelate's papers in May 1643.

His precise religious convictions are not known but a provision of his will asking that Archbishop Ussher preach his funeral sermon suggests certain episcopal sympathies. Herne died in London in 1649 leaving properties worth £300 per annum but complained that a suretyship for an improvident brother had left him with little to distribute among his heirs.

Another **John Herne** (*fl.* 1636–1660), probably the elder Herne's son, entered Lincoln's Inn on 11 February 1636. He appears to have been the translator from law French of *The learned reading of John Herne esq., late of the honourable society of Lincoln's Inn, upon the statute of 23 H. 8, cap. 3, concerning commissions of sewers* (1659). He also published a collection of precedents called *The Pleader* (1657); *The Law of Conveyances* (8 vols., 1658); *The Modern Assurancer* (1658); and *The Law of Charitable Uses* (8 vols., 1660).   D. A. ORR

Sources DNB · Venn, *Alum. Cant.*, 1/2.345 · W. R. Prest, *The rise of the barristers: a social history of the English bar, 1590–1640* (1986), 368–9 · *The manuscripts of the House of Lords*, new ser., 12 vols. (1900–77), vol. 11, pp. 364–467 · W. Prynne, *Canterburies doome, or, The first part of a compleat history of the commitment, charge, tryall, condemnation, execution of William Laud, late arch-bishop of Canterbury* (1646) · *The works of the most reverend father in God, William Laud*, ed. J. Bliss and W. Scott, 7 vols. (1847–60), vols. 3–4 · JHL, 4 (1628–42), 174, 176; 6 (1643–4), 271, 282, 381 · V. Pearl, *London and the outbreak of the puritan revolution: city government and national politics, 1625–1643* (1961), 156 · *Premunire*, 12 Coke Report 37, 77 ER 1319 · *State trials*, 4.576–86 · D. A. Orr, 'Sovereignty, state, and the law of treason in England, 1641–1649', PhD diss., U. Cam., 1997, 106–55 · W. P. Baildon, ed., *The records of the Honorable Society of Lincoln's Inn: admissions*, 1 (1896), 154 · parish register (marriage), St Bartholomew by the Exchange, 4 Aug 1618
Archives Worcester College, Oxford, entry for 11 Oct 1644, Clarke MS LXXI

Herne, John (*fl.* 1636–1660). *See under* Herne, John (*c.*1593–1649).

Herne, Sir Joseph (*bap.* 1639, *d.* 1699), merchant and financier, was born in London and baptized on 17 April 1639, the eighth son of Nicholas Herne, a merchant tailor, and the fourth son of Susan, his second wife. His early career is obscure, but in 1671 he became a freeman of the East India Company, and on 23 July 1672 he married Elizabeth, the daughter of Sir John Frederick of Old Jewry, London. Frederick was himself a major figure in trade with the Peninsula, and Herne succeeded him as head of their joint firm in 1685. The Hernes had seven sons and three daughters.

In 1678 Herne was elected to the committee of the East India Company, on which he served continuously down to 1686, and then from 1687 to 1694 and from 1698 until his death. In 1686 he became a London alderman, sitting for Broad Street; but he discharged himself the following year, probably in anticipation of the purging of Anglicans from the bench. Membership of the Mercers' Company followed in 1687.

It was after the revolution of 1688, however, that Herne

emerged to some prominence. He was elected MP for Dartmouth on 28 November 1689 (and represented the constituency until his death), and was knighted on 15 September 1690. He invested widely in a number of the new industrial and trading concerns of the early 1690s and, in partnership with the goldsmith–banker Sir Stephen Evance and others, used his international trading connections to handle the government's military remittances, first to Ireland (1690–91) and then, between May 1691 and October 1694, to the continent. This latter business was undertaken in the most difficult financial circumstances and, even after the newly founded Bank of England had taken over from Herne, it was his credit that kept the artillery train in Flanders from starving late in 1694.

After being elected governor of the East India Company for 1690–92, Herne defended the company's monopoly and the record of its previous governor, Sir Josiah Child, in the Commons. With Sir Thomas Cooke, his successor as governor, he appears to have been party to some extremely shady deals to break up the opposition group in 1693–4, and to have engaged in bribery to help secure a new charter for the company in 1694; all this brought a parliamentary storm on his head in the spring of 1696. But when in 1698 a new company finally won the trade in return for a loan of £2 million, Herne broke with Child and brought the 'old' company into the subscription so that it could continue in the trade.

East India affairs apart, Herne's parliamentary career was limited to sitting on a number of committees (the committee set up early in 1695 to prevent the clipping of the coin being probably the most notable). During 1696 he was appointed one of the commissioners to receive subscriptions for a land bank, but the subscription failed; and in 1697 he was made one of the trustees for circulating exchequer bills. It fell to Herne, as chairman of the trustees, to face the parliamentary attack of early 1698 on the fraudulent endorsements of these bills by Charles Duncombe. About the same time, and rather surprisingly for a tory committed to the old East India Company and one who had lost the remittance contract to the newly founded Bank of England, Herne also joined the so-called tobacco contractors. These contractors had won from Peter the Great the right to export tobacco from England to Russia, but many were 'whiggish' and closely connected with both the Bank of England and the soon to be established 'new' East India Company. (Possibly this connection has some bearing on Herne's break with Child.)

Herne died suddenly of a brain haemorrhage on 26 February 1699, worth 'near £200,000', and received a sumptuous funeral.

Herne's brother **Sir Nathaniel Herne** (c.1629–1679), the eldest son of Nicholas Herne and his second wife, Susan, was apprenticed to Sir John Frederick and took his freedom in the Barber–Surgeons' Company in 1655. On 1 September 1656 he married Frederick's daughter Judith and entered into partnership with his father-in-law. The firm was principally engaged in the Spanish trade and suffered under Cromwell's policy; Herne was probably the 'stout

and active young citizen' concerned in cavalier plots in the City in 1657.

Herne led an extremely busy life spanning business and politics. His firm's west country connections led him to engage in parliamentary politics in support of Joseph Williamson in 1667. His attendance at East India Company committee meetings from 1667 onwards was exemplary: he held the deputy governorship from 1672 and the governorship from 1674 until his death, and engaged in covert intelligence gathering for the company and the government. In the City he was elected sheriff in 1674–5, common councilman in 1675–6, and alderman from 1676 until his death. Maintaining his links with Dartmouth, where it is believed that he expended no less than £1000 per annum on improving the town's water supply, he was elected its MP in 1679. In parliament he sat on seventeen committees, the most important being that for securing the king and kingdom against popery. Herne died after a short illness on 10 August 1679, leaving a substantial holding of East India Company stock, valued at the revolution of 1688 at £10,838.

D. W. Jones, *rev.* Anita McConnell

Sources J. R. Woodhead, *The rulers of London, 1660–1689* (1965) · J. P. Ferris, 'Herne, Joseph', HoP, *Commons, 1660–90*, 2.537–8 · D. W. Jones, *War and economy in the age of William III and Marlborough* (1988) · J. M. Price, *The tobacco adventure to Russia: enterprise, politics, and diplomacy in the quest for a northern market for English colonial tobacco, 1676–1722* (1961) · will of Sir Nathaniel Herne, PRO, PROB 11/360, sig. 107 · will of Sir Joseph Herne, PRO, PROB 11/464, sig. 77
Archives GL, family accounts and papers | BL, letters to Robert Southwell, Add. MS 38015
Wealth at death approx. £200,000: *DNB*

Herne, Sir Nathaniel (c.1629–1679). *See under* Herne, Sir Joseph (*bap.* 1639, *d.* 1699).

Herne, Thomas (*d.* 1722), tutor and religious controversialist, was the eldest son of Francis Herne of Suffolk. He was admitted as a pensioner at Corpus Christi College, Cambridge, on 29 October 1711 and elected to a scholarship in 1712. After graduating BA in 1715, Herne was incorporated at Oxford on 21 February 1715. Soon afterwards the duchess of Bedford appointed him tutor to her sons Wriothesley and John, successively third and fourth dukes of Bedford. In 1716 Herne was elected to a vacant fellowship at Merton College, Oxford, and on 11 October 1718 proceeded MA.

Herne took part in the Bangorian controversy, publishing *The False Notion of a Christian Priesthood* (1717) under the pseudonym Phileleutherus Cantabrigiensis in response to William Law's high-church rebuttal of Benjamin Hoadly's sermon on the nature of the church. He published further pamphlets that questioned the principle of subscribing to articles of religion imposed by a state church. More particularly he upheld the right of private judgement in the controversy concerning the Trinity, and wrote two pamphlets in reply to an anti-Socinian sermon preached by Dr Thomas Mangey in 1719. In 1719 and 1720 he printed accounts of the principal works on both sides of the Bangorian and Trinitarian controversies.

Herne did not marry, or take holy orders, and died at Woburn Abbey, Bedfordshire, in 1722.

W. C. SYDNEY, *rev.* S. J. SKEDD

Sources Venn, *Alum. Cant.* · R. Masters, *The history of the College of Corpus Christi and the B. Virgin Mary … in the University of Cambridge* (1753) · Foster, *Alum. Oxon.* · A. Chalmers, ed., *The general biographical dictionary*, new edn, 17 (1814), 399

Heron, Denis Caulfield (1824–1881), lawyer and politician, was born at Newry, co. Down, the eldest son of William Heron, merchant, and his wife, Mary, daughter of Thomas Maguire, merchant, of Enniskillen, co. Fermanagh. He was educated at St Gregory's, Downside, near Bath, from April 1834 probably until 1835, and went on to Trinity College, Dublin, where he was admitted on 16 October 1840, and awarded BA in 1845, and LLB and LLD in 1857. A distinguished student, he achieved particular notice when, having been refused a scholarship in June 1843 owing to his Roman Catholicism, he appealed to the visitors, who heard the case on 11–12 December 1845 but upheld the original decision. Though his *Constitutional History of the University of Dublin* (1847) called for the abolition of tests, he later favoured the establishment of a separate denominational university.

In 1849 Heron was appointed professor of jurisprudence and political economy at Queen's College, Galway. His lectures there formed the basis for *An Introduction to the History of Jurisprudence* (1860), partly republished as *The Principles of Jurisprudence* (1873). Heron resigned his chair in 1859 to concentrate on his legal practice. Admitted to King's Inns in Dublin in 1843, and to Lincoln's Inn in 1845, he was called to the Irish bar in 1848 and joined the Munster circuit. An able *nisi prius* advocate, he was appointed QC in 1860, law adviser at Dublin Castle (April–July 1866) during the Fenian troubles, bencher of King's Inns, JP for co. Armagh and co. Down in 1872, and third serjeant-at-law in 1880.

In 1847 Heron was a founder member of the Dublin Statistical Society, from 1862 the Statistical and Social Inquiry Society of Ireland. He was appointed Barrington lecturer in 1849, and he read and published a number of papers, notably on the landlord–tenant relationship (1862, 1864). He was elected vice-president of the society in 1871, and attended the eighth International Statistical Congress at St Petersburg in August 1872.

Heron contested the by-election for co. Tipperary on 27 November 1869, as a Liberal candidate, supporting tenant rights, denominational education, and full amnesty for Fenian prisoners. He was defeated by the Fenian Jeremiah O'Donovan Rossa, who was subsequently declared ineligible as a convicted felon. At the second election on 23 February 1870, Heron overcame the Fenian Charles J. Kickham by a majority of four. In parliament, Heron's interventions were mainly limited to Irish issues, though he made spirited speeches supporting women's franchise (1 May 1872, 30 April 1873). He stood down at the general election of 1874. He was one of the counsel for the crown in the state trial of Parnell and the other Irish Land League

leaders in December 1880, and his brother-in-law was a judge in the case.

In 1854 Heron married Emily Fitzgerald (1826/7–1863), sister of John David Fitzgerald (1816–1889), later Baron Fitzgerald of Kilmarnock. The couple established a permanent residence at 7 Upper Fitzwilliam Street, Dublin. Emily Heron died on 2 August 1863, aged thirty-six. Heron survived his wife by almost twenty years. He collapsed on 15 April 1881 while salmon-fishing on the River Corrib, at Galway, and died a few hours later. He was buried at Glasnevin cemetery, Dublin, on 19 April 1881.

PHILIP SCHOFIELD

Sources *The Times* (16 April 1881) · *Irish Law Times and Solicitors' Journal* (23 April 1881) · *Law Times* (30 April 1881) · Hansard · J. F. Waller, *Report of the case of Denis Caulfield Heron, appellant, against the provost and senior fellows of Trinity College, Dublin, respondents* (1846) · R. D. C. Black, *The Statistical and Social Inquiry Society of Ireland centenary volume, 1847–1947* (1947) · J. W. Stubbs, 'During the nineteenth century', in J. P. Mahaffy and others, *The book of Trinity College, Dublin, 1591–1891* (1892), 91–129 · R. V. Comerford, 'Tipperary representation at Westminster, 1801–1918', *Tipperary: history and society: interdisciplinary essays on the history of an Irish county*, ed. W. Nolan (1985), 325–8 · *Calendar of Queen's College, Galway* (1851) · E. Keane, P. Beryl Phair, and T. U. Sadleir, eds., *King's Inns admission papers, 1607–1867*, IMC (1982) · *The Times* (20 April 1881)

Likenesses A. Gibbs, oils (presumed to be Denis Heron), King's Inns, Dublin · portrait, repro. in *ILN* (15 Jan 1881)

Wealth at death £5366 5s. 6d.: probate, 9 May 1881, CGPLA Ire.

Heron, Haly (*c*.1550–1591), author and soldier, matriculated in November 1565 as a sizar at Queens' College, Cambridge, whence he graduated BA in 1570. At some point in the 1570s he became tutor to John Kaye the younger, whom he perhaps met at Cambridge and for whom he wrote his sole literary effort, *A Newe Discourse of Morall Philosophie, Entituled, the Kayes of Counsaile* (1579). By 1581 he had entered the service of Sir Nicholas Malby, newly appointed president of Connaught, and he probably began his soldiering career as a member of the armed forces suppressing rebellion in Ireland. Married by 1583 to the widow of George Fitz Garret, he returned from Ireland late in 1585. In December of that year Thomas Randolph, under pressure from his wife, a relative of Heron, grudgingly brought him to the attention of Sir Francis Walsingham, under whose auspices he travelled to the Low Countries. In a letter of 16 February 1587, which he bore to Walsingham, Heron was praised by Sir William Russell, commander of the cavalry under the earl of Leicester and governor of Flushing, as 'a man of very good desert, for his service in these parts' (*CSP for.*, 1586–7, 364). In August 1590 Heron, now a captain, was put in charge of a company, which proceeded to Bergen-op-Zoom. Leading an assault in Brittany on 19 or 20 May 1591 he 'was thrust through the throte at the pushe of the pike whereof he died presently' (*Rutland MSS*, 1.291–2).

A Newe Discourse, described on the title-page as 'not so pleasant as profitable for younge courtiours', is one of the earliest courtly conduct books written by an English author. Heron is, however, critical of life at court; and the advice he provides consists largely of conventional moral guidance on subjects such as 'humilitie', 'company and fellowship', 'talke & communication', and 'self love'. With regard to 'wine and women', he accepts 'the use of them both' as 'very necessarie, pleasant and profitable', condemning only their abuse as 'filthy, tedious, and inconveniente' (Heron, sig. E6v). His alliterative, schematic, and ornamented prose style, liberally scattered with classical allusions, elaborate similes, and proverbs, is an early representative of 'euphuism' and was strongly influenced by George Pettie's *The Petite Pallace of Pettie his Pleasure* (1576).

JILL KRAYE

Sources V. B. Heltzel, 'Haly Heron: Elizabethan essayist and euphuist', *Huntington Library Quarterly*, 16 (1952–3), 1–21 • H. Heron, *The kayes of counsaile: a newe discourse of morall philosophie* (1579), ed. V. B. Heltzel (1954), Introduction, ix–xviii • C. Uhlig, *Hofkritik im England des Mittelalters und der Renaissance* (1973), 327–9, 382–3, 389 • J. Carré, *The crisis of courtesy: studies in the conduct-book in Britain, 1600–1900* (1994), 12 • *DNB* • *CSP dom.*, 1581–90 • *CSP for.*, 1586–7 • *The manuscripts of his grace the duke of Rutland*, 4 vols., HMC, 24 (1888–1905), vol. 1

Heron, Sir John (*b.* before **1470**, *d.* **1522**), administrator, was born, probably in London, son of the haberdasher William Heron and his wife, Joan, widow of the mercer Thomas Packer. Younger sons of a prominent Northumberland family, William and his brother Richard had settled in London, where the latter also served as surveyor of the customs. John and his wife, Margaret (*d. c.*1532), whom he had married no later than 1504, had at least six sons and three daughters: their eldest son, Giles, married a daughter of his guardian Sir Thomas More, and was executed for treason in 1540. John should be distinguished from his cousin and namesake John Heron (*d.* 1501), a servant of Lady Margaret Beaufort whom Henry VII appointed keeper of writs and rolls in common bench.

Heron commenced his career in royal service as deputy to Sir Thomas Lovell, appointed treasurer of the chamber in 1485. From July 1487 he was keeping Lovell's accounts, and by August 1492 had succeeded his master as treasurer. Under Heron's stewardship the chamber grew steadily in fiscal importance until it was handling the bulk of royal revenues, including those from loans and subsidies, as well as income from most crown lands; by 1506 its annual revenues exceeded £200,000. Exempted from exchequer audit, Heron's accounts were scrutinized by the king himself.

Despite Henry VII's close involvement with the chamber system, the accession of his son did not diminish Heron's responsibilities; indeed his status as the king's 'trusty servant John Heron his general receiver' (*Statutes of the Realm*, 3.2) was confirmed by statute in 1509. Under Henry VIII Heron continued to oversee most areas of crown expenditure, while exercising wider responsibilities: in 1514 he was one of the councillors appointed to compound with the king's debtors, and two years later he joined Wolsey in loan negotiations with Italian bankers on the king's behalf. Appointments as clerk of the hanaper (1513) and as an exchequer chamberlain (1516) enhanced his position as the crown's chief financial official. By November 1515 the treasurer had been rewarded with a knighthood; and in 1520 he attended the king at the Field of Cloth of Gold at Calais.

From his father Heron inherited lands in Lincolnshire,

and he himself accumulated considerable estates around London, purchasing Aldersbrook (Essex) in 1517 and leasing the royal manor of Higham Hill at Walthamstow (Essex) three years later. His principal residence was at Hackney (Middlesex), where he owned the manors of Shacklewell and Homerton (from 1511). He also had a house within the sanctuary at Westminster, and lands in London and Richmond (Surrey). Heron contributed to the rebuilding of Hackney parish church, and in 1516 he and his wife endowed a guild of priests at the London church of St Michael, Crooked Lane.

Heron took time from final preparations for the Field of Cloth of Gold at Calais to draw up his will on 2 June 1520. Within a year his health was probably failing, for he began surrendering his many responsibilities: in June 1521 a new clerk of the hanaper was appointed, and by early December he was no longer active as treasurer of the chamber. Heron died on 15 January 1522 and was buried at the Whitefriars, London.

P. R. N. CARTER

Sources S. B. Chrimes, *Henry VII* (1972) • G. R. Elton, *The Tudor revolution in government* (1953) • W. C. Richardson, *Tudor chamber administration, 1485–1547* (1952) • *CPR, 1485–1509* • *LP Henry VIII* • F. C. Dietz, *English public finance, 1485–1641*, 2nd edn, 2 vols. (1964) • PRO, PROB 11/21, fols. 262–3 • *VCH Essex*, vol. 6 • *VCH Middlesex*, vol. 10 • M. K. Jones and M. G. Underwood, *The king's mother: Lady Margaret Beaufort, countess of Richmond and Derby* (1992) • HoP, *Commons, 1509–58* • A. Luders and others, eds., *Statutes of the realm*, 11 vols. in 12, RC (1810–28), vol. 3 • A. P. Newton, 'The king's chamber under the early Tudors', *EngHR*, 32 (1917), 348–72 • S. J. Gunn, *Early Tudor government, 1485–1558* (1995) • D. Grummitt, 'Henry VII, chamber finance and the "new monarchy": some new evidence', *Historical Research*, 72 (1999), 229–43 • chancery, inquisitions postmortem, PRO, ser. 2, C 142/40, no. 72

Archives BL, Add. MSS 21480–21481 • PRO, account books, treasurer of chamber, E 101/414/6, E 101/414/16, E 101/415/3 • PRO, state papers, SP 1

Heron, Sir Joseph (1809–1889), lawyer and town clerk, was born in Deansgate House, Manchester, the fourth of the ten children of James Holt Heron (1777–1847), a cotton merchant, on 3 January 1809 (or, according to one source, in January 1807). Heron was educated at the Moravian school, Fairfield, and Mr Hulme's school, Burnley. He was articled to John Hampson, a Manchester attorney, and afterwards became a pupil in London of Nassau Senior, the political economist. Heron was admitted as an attorney in 1830 at the age of twenty-one, and set up practice with his brother William at 21 Princess Street in Manchester. In 1838, after the battle for the incorporation of the city had been fought and won, Richard Cobden proposed Joseph Heron for the new post of town clerk. This was a position which Heron held for forty years, earning the epithet 'father of the town clerks in England'.

An acknowledged authority on English municipal law, Heron was reputed never to have lost a case for the corporation and was recognized as one of the leading parliamentary lawyers of his day. As an attorney he was precluded from pleading his cause directly before a parliamentary committee—that task fell to a barrister. Heron, however, always instructed the counsel (whom he had employed) to call him as a witness, and in this way he was able to plead and invariably win the case in hand. In 1858, in recognition of the prominent part he played in procuring the Mersey Conservancy and Docks Act, which effectively stopped Liverpool benefiting from the taxation of shipping houses in Lancashire, Heron was awarded a silver casket and the sum of £5000. His salary as town clerk was raised from £1500 to £2500 per annum, and after his retirement in 1877 he continued to receive £1500 per annum until his death. Knighted by the queen in 1869, Heron was acknowledged by Manchester borough council in a formal resolution which testified to the high character, ability, and long services rendered that had earned him the honour.

Joseph Heron, sometimes known as Joe Heron, was a flamboyant figure. In his youth he was described as 'a swell', who wore kid gloves, tight boots, glossy curls, and all the adornments of a ladies' man. Listening to Joseph Heron on public occasions was said to have been like hearing the opinions of a consummate man of the world. He had the ability to express the most complex issues in a clear and colloquial manner. It was claimed that many a man entered the council chamber with the purpose of teaching Joe Heron his place but was converted to full acquiescence by Heron's undoubted eloquence. In answer to an exasperated councillor who exclaimed 'What right have you to speak—what ward do you represent?', Heron retorted 'A larger ward than yours, sir—I represent the entire city!' (*Manchester Faces and Places*, 1889–90).

Joseph Heron eventually married in 1881, at the age of seventy-two. His bride was Susan Preston Willert (*b.* 1809/10), *née* Beale, of Headington Hill, Oxford, the widow of an old friend and colleague. During the winter months they resided in the Hotel Californie at Cannes, where Heron died on 23 December 1889. According to his wishes he was buried in the cemetery at Cannes.

V. R. PARROTT

Sources *Manchester Faces and Places*, 1 (1889–90), 49–52 · J. T. Slugg, *Reminiscences of Manchester 50 years ago* (1881) · A. Redford, *The history of local government in Manchester*, 3 vols. (1939–40) · V. R. Parrott, 'Pettyfogging to respectability: a history of the development of the profession of solicitor in the Manchester area, 1880–1914', PhD diss., University of Salford, 1992 · m. cert.
Archives Man. CL
Likenesses J. R. Knight, portrait, *c.*1870, Manchester town hall · W. Woods, bust, Manchester town hall
Wealth at death £41,673 12s. 6d.: resworn probate, June 1891, *CGPLA Eng. & Wales* (1889)

Heron, Mary (*fl.* 1786–1792), poet and writer, seems to have lived in the north of England but whether this was her place of birth and upbringing is not known. All her books were published at Newcastle: she was described as 'Mary Heron of Durham' on the title-page of her *Sketches of Poetry* (1786) and her preface to *Odes, etc, on Various Occasions* (1792) is dated from there. She also published *Miscellaneous Poems* (1786) and *The Conflict: a Sentimental Tale in a Series of Letters* (1790).

Heron took the French Revolution among her subjects in *Odes*, and even her ode on the apparently conventional subject of the new year plunges into the topic of social inequality and injustice. Her preface shows her awareness

that this would be controversial and defends it with a mixture of apology and defiance: 'When rebellion spreads its ravages, and war renders the land one horrid scene of devastation, are not women often the first victims? Why then should they be excluded from giving their humble opinion?' (Heron, vii). This extensive preface shows that she had thought carefully about gender politics and that her opinions were advanced for their time. Her political views (under a deeply reactionary government) were liberal: deploring slavery and regarding France's 'arbitrary sway' as 'ample cause' for a revolution, she lamented that by 1792 things had gone too far into 'anarchy, confusion and disgrace' (ibid., 31, 48–9). England's constitution is praised for enshrining more liberty than that of France's *ancien régime*, but the remedies for inequality and injustice, which still exist in England, are 'Patience and Faith' (ibid., 13). Her *Ode to Music* is romantic and Radcliffe-esque.

JULIA GASPER

Sources M. Heron, *Odes, etc, on various occasions* (1792) · ESTC

Heron, Patrick (1920–1999), painter and art critic, was born at 12 Hollin Lane, Headingley, Leeds, on 30 January 1920, the eldest child in the family of three sons and a daughter of Thomas Milner Heron (1890–1983), textile and garment manufacturer, and his wife, Eulalie Mabel (1891–1986), daughter of Michael Davies, an uncompromisingly pacifist Unitarian minister from Bradford. The history of Heron's family on both sides was of a combative nonconformism and a high-minded culture of the mind and spirit. His father was a Christian socialist, and had been a pacifist conscientious objector in the First World War. A deeply cultured man, he loved art and poetry, and his business life was devoted to the integration of the ethical and the aesthetic into the commercial production of the useful. If Heron inherited his political idealism and his fearless activism from his father, he owed to his mother his intensity of visual response, his preternaturally passionate eye for the natural world. His parents remained deeply important to him throughout his life, the original source of his confidence in his own creative powers, and the continuing inspiration of his ethical and political engagement in the affairs of the world. Intensely political in temperament, Heron was a lifelong socialist and pacifist, and a founding member, in 1959, of the Campaign for Nuclear Disarmament.

Early life In 1925 the Heron family moved from Leeds to Newlyn in Cornwall, where Tom Heron was to run Crysede Silks, a modest textile business. He arranged its move to expanded premises on the island at St Ives, and rapidly built up the firm with extraordinary flair. Patrick's early years in West Penwith were idyllic: he never forgot the impressions of light, colour, and landscape that streamed in upon him in what he called the 'sacred land' of his childhood. The winter of 1927–8 was spent at Eagles Nest, the house on the promontory above the Zennor cliffs, to which he was to return to live in 1956. The house was borrowed by his parents from Hugh Arnold-Forster, the Labour luminary, in the hope that the altitude and atmosphere would be good for Patrick's asthma. Arnold-

Forster's planting of the extraordinary garden was already well advanced, but the many southern-hemisphere flowering trees and shrubs that were to be the glory of the mature garden were as yet no taller than small bushes, and its huge granite outcrops and boulders were still starkly visible.

Following a breakup with his business partner, Tom Heron left St Ives in late 1929 to set up his own firm, Cresta Silks, at Welwyn Garden City. From 1932 to 1937 Patrick attended St George's School, Harpenden, a co-educational boarding-school. There he was encouraged by a remarkable art master, Ludvig van der Straeten, who on one memorable afternoon drove his thirteen-year-old pupil to the National Gallery and stood him, enthralled, in front of Cézanne's *Mont St Victoire*, then on loan from the Courtauld collection. At St George's Heron was allowed to paint through the afternoons while his contemporaries played compulsory games. From 1934 onwards his father commissioned from him designs for silk scarves and dress textiles (and for several years after the war he was Cresta's principal designer). He left school without formal qualifications to go directly to the Slade School of Fine Art in London. In spite of the precocious accomplishment that had secured his place there, his time at the Slade was unhappy and unproductive, and he left after only two years.

At the outbreak of the Second World War Heron registered as a conscientious objector and from 1940 spent three years as a labourer for the Cambridgeshire War Agricultural Executive Committee. Frequently appalling conditions exacerbated the asthma for which he had refused to claim exemption. Late in 1943, ill and exhausted, he was ordered by doctors to cease agricultural work, and in early 1944, at the invitation of Bernard Leach, a family friend from the years in St Ives, he took up an approved work placement at the St Ives Pottery, where he worked happily as a journeyman potter for the next fourteen months. The example of Leach's creative integrity, and his subtlety as an artist with the 'power to materialize a concept' (*Painter as Critic: Patrick Heron, Selected Writings*, ed. M. Gooding, 1998, 69) were formative of Heron's own artistic philosophy.

The artist In April 1945 Heron married Delia Reiss (1920–1979), whom he had met at his first school in Welwyn Garden City in 1929. They had two daughters, Katharine (*b.* 1947), and Susanna (*b.* 1951). Delia's father, Richard Reiss (1883–1959), an active and practical proponent of the garden city ideal, had been a founding director of the successive companies that created Welwyn Garden City in 1919 and 1920. In Delia, Patrick found a companion whose feeling for art and nature perfectly matched his own. Beautiful, intelligent, and artistic, she was utterly committed to his work as a painter and writer, but retained a fierce independence of spirit. In his own words, she was his 'best and most essential critic' (Gooding, 46). Until 1956 they lived at 53 Addison Avenue, Holland Park, west London, but between 1947 and 1954 they spent some months every year in St Ives, at 3 St Andrews Street, a cottage on the harbour wall, whose interior with its view of the bay, with the figures of Delia and their two daughters, was to feature in many of Heron's paintings over that period. These were usually completed in the London studio. As a figurative artist Heron rarely drew or painted from the motif, feeling that memory was a crucial element in the invention of images that should not merely register appearances, but

Patrick Heron (1920–1999), by Jorge Lewinski, 1964

record their impact upon the receiving imagination. The exceptions to this rule were a handful of portraits of T. S. Eliot (1949), Herbert Read (1950), Jo Grimond (1986), and Antonia Byatt (1997), which began with drawings or oil sketches from the life; these, too, were always finished in studio solitude. 'Seeing', he wrote in 1956, 'is not a passive but an active operation … all art is a convention, an invention. Painting may literally claim to alter the look of the world for us. We only see nature through a system of images, a configuration which painting supplies' (Gooding, 8).

In 1955, by a surprising turn of events, Heron was able to buy Eagles Nest, to which he moved with his young family in April 1956, to be enchanted by the springtime azaleas and camellias, and find his work immediately take on a new spirit and new forms. From that moment he moved decisively, once and for all, from a Braque-influenced figuration to a fully liberated abstraction, capable of infinite development. For the rest of his life the house and its garden were to be the centre of his imaginative existence; it was, he wrote much later, 'very nearly the greatest passion of my life' (Knight, 19). Animated by Delia's personality, Eagles Nest became a magical centre of hospitality for the brilliant and sometimes turbulent company of artists and writers that made St Ives and its environs a place of extraordinary artistic vitality during the 1950s, 1960s, and 1970s. Among frequent visitors were Ben Nicholson, Barbara Hepworth, Roger Hilton, Bryan Wynter, Terry Frost, and Peter Lanyon. When Delia died, suddenly, in 1979, Heron was devastated, and for many months he was unable to work.

Heron knew from a very early age that he wanted to be an artist, a vocation encouraged with great seriousness by his parents. He spoke without affectation or irony of his infant efforts, signed and dated from the age of five, and carefully preserved in large buff envelopes, as 'early drawings'. His artistic journey was constantly eventful and unpredictable, marked by sudden intuitive breakthroughs to new expressive possibilities, new ways of response to the light and colour of the world. As for others of his generation, the immediate post-war London exhibitions of modern French masters were revelatory, and Heron's painting in the later 1940s was much influenced by the wartime still-life and interior paintings of Picasso. It was from late Braque, however, that he learned the abstracting separation of descriptive line and decorative colour that gave the best figurative paintings of his early maturity (such as *Harbour Window with Two Figures, St Ives: July 1950* and *Christmas Eve: 1951*) their exhilarating graphic rhythms and chromatic brilliance, and their complex cubistic spatial ambiguities. In the early 1950s, as both painter and writer, Heron was much preoccupied by the potentialities of abstraction, but it was not until 1956 that the logic of his development led him to a completely non-figurative painting. 'The pictures I have painted since last January', he wrote in January 1957,

> have much in common with my figurative paintings: but they lack the linear grid of figurative drawing. This has freed me to deal more directly and inventively … with every single

aspect of the painting that is purely pictorial, i.e. the architecture of the canvas, the spatial interrelation of each and every touch (or stroke, or bar) of colour, the colour-character, the paint-character of a painting—all these I now explore with a sense of freedom quite denied me while I had to keep half an eye on a 'subject'. (*Painter as Critic: Patrick Heron, Selected Writings*, ed. M. Gooding, 1998, 121)

From that time on Heron was adamantly abstract, though in later life he was prepared to admit that the experience of the phenomenal world had always somehow entered and affected even the purest of his abstract paintings.

Sometimes Heron systematically explored a pictorial idea over several years, producing numerous variations on a theme, as with the atmospheric colour abstractions of the early 1960s, with their floating soft-edged 'square-round' shapes, and the optically dazzling 'wobbly hard-edge' paintings of the following decade, with their distinctive jigsaw-like interlock of opaque high-colour zones. 'Painting', he wrote in 1962, 'has still a continent left to explore, in the direction of colour (and in no other direction)' (*Painter as Critic Patrick Heron: Selected Writings*, ed. M. Gooding, 1998, 154). At other times, under the pressure of a particular experience, he produced a spate of new work at great speed, as with the *tachiste* 'garden' paintings of 1956, the 'horizon' and 'stripe' paintings of 1957-8, and the astonishing series of small gouaches and large oils made when he was artist in residence at the Art Gallery of New South Wales in Sydney in 1989-90. The late series of so-called big paintings were made in bursts of intensive activity in the first eight months of 1994. Shown that year at Camden Arts Centre, their ecstatic energy and insouciant mastery thrilled and astonished a generation of artists fifty years younger than Heron. His career was crowned by a timely and highly acclaimed retrospective, in 1998, at the Tate Gallery.

Underlying every phase of Heron's painting were constant preoccupations: with colour as space; with line as an indicator of dynamic relations as well as a means to describe form; with the primacy of decorative order in the composition of images that begin and end at the four edges of the paper or the canvas. Behind these critical-creative ideas lay the deeper thought: that pictorial dynamics are signs and epiphanies of a greater natural ordering, that painting is a revelation of a beautiful cosmic harmony. 'The ancient valid response of the painter to the world around him', he wrote, 'is one of delight and amazement, and we must recapture it' (Gooding, 9). Like those of his acknowledged masters, Braque, Matisse, and Bonnard, his paintings were at once evocations and celebrations of the visible, discoveries of what he called 'the reality of the eye' (Knight, 24).

The writer and controversialist Many of Heron's artist friends, William Scott, Alan Davie, Roger Hilton, Bryan Wynter, Terry Frost, and Peter Lanyon among them, owed much to Heron's intelligent critical championship of their work, writing intermittently as the *New Statesman and Nation* art critic from 1947 to 1954, and then as London correspondent for *Arts* (New York) between 1955 and 1958. He was an exciting writer, capable of subtle analysis and great clarity of utterance. By nature a celebratory critic, he had a gift for precise description of the plastic qualities of painting, and of the specific aspects of technique and manner that distinguish one artist from another: his talents as an art critic were those of one whose knowledge was derived from creative practice. His critical career began with a series of remarkably authoritative reviews for the *New English Weekly* in 1945 and 1946, on Nicholson, Braque, Klee, and Picasso, among others; later he wrote brief monographs: *Vlaminck* (1947), *Ivon Hitchens* (1955), and *Braque* (1958). Edited writings and lectures were published in 1955 as *The Changing Forms of Art*, and a further selection, *Painter as Critic*, appeared in 1998. In 1958 Heron gave up criticism, taking 'a vow of silence' (Gooding, 160); notwithstanding this, in later years, among much else, he wrote illuminating essays on the drawings of Bonnard (1972) and Constable (1994), and on late Picasso (1988) and late Matisse (1993).

Heron was an inveterate controversialist, a courageous conservationist, and a master of trenchant polemical prose. Beginning with three famous articles for *Studio International*, in 1966, 1968, and 1970, he conducted a bravely sustained campaign against the programmatic critical promotion in Europe of American art, culminating in October 1974 with the publication over three days of a closely argued, 14,000 word article in *The Guardian*. As a distinguished artist outside the education system, his disinterested writings in the press against the merger of the English art schools with the polytechnics in the early 1970s, and on subsequent developments in the administration of art education, earned him enduring respect and affection among artist teachers. In the 1960s and 1970s he conducted several successful campaigns in defence of the historically unique landscape of West Penwith, including a celebrated fight in 1961 against the proposal by the Admiralty to requisition the Zennor headlands and moors as a military exercise area. From his eyrie at its highest point above the sea he maintained until his dying day an eagle eye on the twisting road that leads from St Ives to St Just, watching for any sign of straightening to its ancient track-line or of 'improvement' to its green walls and banks.

The energizing convictions behind these time-consuming political and public actions were those of a profoundly decent man, inalienably patriotic without any disfiguring prejudice, who justly saw himself as upholding a native radical tradition that went back to Ruskin, Morris, and Shaw, exemplified in his own time by Herbert Read and Bertrand Russell. At its heart was a vital sense of the centrality of art and imagination to the fully experienced life. Heron was a handsome, elegant man, disarmingly charming and attentive to others, not without an almost childlike vanity. He was an emphatic and witty conversationalist, a marvellous story-teller and mimic. The range of his friendship was exceptionally broad and inclusive, for he was capable of inspiring great love and affection on the slightest acquaintance. He died, of a heart attack, at Eagles Nest on 20 March 1999, and was buried on 27 March at Zennor parish church. He was survived by his two daughters. MEL GOODING

Sources V. Knight, ed., *Patrick Heron* (1988) · M. Gooding, *Patrick Heron* (1994) · D. Sylvester, ed., *Patrick Heron* (1998) [incl. essay by A. S. Byatt and interview by M. Gayford; exhibition catalogue, Tate Gallery, London] · *The Times* (22 March 1999) · *Daily Telegraph* (22 March 1999) · *The Guardian* (22 March 1999) · *The Independent* (23 March 1999) · WWW · personal knowledge (2004) · private information (2004) [family]
Archives NL Wales, corresp. with Emyr Humphreys · Tate collection, letters to Reg Butler · Tate collection, transcripts of interviews for TV South West | FILM BFI NFTVA, *Omnibus*, BBC, 13 March 1983 · BFI NFTVA, *South Bank Show*, London Weekend Television, 9 Feb 1986 · BFI NFTVA, documentary footage | SOUND BL NSA, 'Artists' lives', C 466/49/01–05 · BL NSA, *Front row*, BBC Radio 4, 16 June 1995, H10052/7
Likenesses photographs, 1959, repro. in *Daily Telegraph* · J. Lewinski, photograph, 1964, NPG [*see illus.*] · S. Herron, prints, 1998, NPG · photograph, repro. in *The Guardian* · photograph, repro. in *The Times* · photograph, repro. in *The Independent* · photographs, repro. in Knight, ed., *Patrick Heron* · photographs, repro. in Gooding, *Patrick Heron* · photographs, repro. in Sylvester, ed., *Patrick Heron*
Wealth at death £6,585,999: probate, 1999, CGPLA Eng. & Wales

Heron, Sir Richard, first baronet (1726–1805), Treasury official, was the fourth son and youngest child of the six children of Robert Heron (1686/7–1753) of Newark, Nottinghamshire, and Elizabeth (*d.* 1764), daughter of Thomas Brecknock of Thorney Abbey, Cambridgeshire.

Heron was described by a writer in the *Hibernian Magazine* as 'rather above the middle size, well made, and of good constitution' (*Hibernian Magazine*, 742). He was educated for the legal profession and, through the patronage of the duke of Newcastle, he gained his first government post in 1751 when he was appointed a commissioner of bankruptcy. He ascended through the ranks, first becoming a sworn clerk in the remembrance office and subsequently the lord treasurer's remembrancer in the court of exchequer. In December 1776 he was appointed principal secretary to the lord lieutenant of Ireland, John Hobart, second earl of Buckinghamshire.

Heron arrived in Dublin on 24 January 1777 and the following day was sworn of the privy council there. His career was a happy one. Despite labouring under the difficulties caused by the English government's attitude towards commercial concessions for Ireland, Heron's affability, integrity, and devotion to duty won him a position of esteem. On 25 July 1778 he was created a baronet and shortly afterwards rewarded with a pension of £700 p.a. as the searcher, packer, and gauger in Cork.

A severe illness in the spring of 1779 led to Heron's retirement from active politics in 1780, and so complete was his removal from power that he spent 1798, the year of the Irish rising, compiling and publishing a genealogical table of the Herons of Newark. Heron married Jane, *née* Hall, the widow of S. Thompson. He died on 18 January 1805 at his house in Grosvenor Square, London. He was survived by his wife and, as they had no children, was succeeded in the baronetcy by his nephew Robert Heron of Stubton, Lincolnshire.

ROBERT DUNLOP, *rev.* ROSEMARY RICHEY

Sources GM, 1st ser., 75 (1805), 93–4 · *Public Register, or, Freeman's Journal* (1777) · *Hibernian Magazine* (1779) · H. Grattan, *Memoirs of the life and times of the Rt Hon. Henry Grattan*, 5 vols. (1839–46), vol 2, pp.

175, 183 · R. Heron, *A genealogical table of the family of the Herons of Newark* (1798)

Archives BL, corresp. as an executor, Add. MSS 3524–3525 · Lincs. Arch., family corresp. · NL Ire., corresp. and papers | Bodl. Oxf., letters to Lady Sandys

Likenesses attrib. J. Reynolds, oils, 1770, Princeton University Art Museum, Princeton, New Jersey · F. Wheatley, group portrait, oils (*The Irish House of Commons, 1780*), Leeds City Art Gallery, Lotherton Hall, West Riding of Yorkshire

Heron, Robert. *See* Pinkerton, John (1758–1826).

Heron, Robert (1764–1807), journalist and author, son of John Heron, a weaver, was born in New Galloway, Kirkcudbrightshire, on 6 November 1764. He was taught privately by his mother until his ninth year, when he was sent to the parish school. He was precocious, and at the age of eleven became a pupil-teacher; at fourteen he was appointed master of the parochial school of Kelton. By the end of 1780 he had saved sufficient money to enable him, with the help of his parents, to enter the University of Edinburgh, with the view of studying for the church. While pursuing his studies he supported himself partly by teaching, but chiefly by working for booksellers. While a divinity student Heron, in the autumn of 1789, paid a visit at Ellisland to Robert Burns, who entrusted him with a letter to Dr Thomas Blacklock, which he failed to deliver. In a rhyming epistle to Blacklock, Burns attributes Heron's faithlessness either to preoccupation with 'some dainty fair one', or to partiality for drink (*The Poems and Songs of Robert Burns*, ed. J. Kinsley, 1968, no. 273b). Heron's *Memoir of Burns* (1797), reprinted from articles in the *Monthly Magazine* and published the year after Burns's death, was the first such written and was consequently highly influential throughout the nineteenth century. Modern scholarship has, on the whole, found it inaccurate and regrettable, unfairly portraying the poet as degenerating into as drunken, wayward, and profligate a character as Heron himself.

Heron was for a time assistant to Dr Hugh Blair, the rhetorician, but his habits were already irregular and his interests chiefly literary. Heron's first independent literary venture was a small edition in 1789 of Thomson's *Seasons*, with critical comments on his poetry. A larger edition appeared in 1793. In 1790–91 he announced a course of lectures entitled the 'Law of nature, the law of nations, the Jewish, the Grecian, the Roman and the canon law, and then on the feudal law', intended as an introduction to the study of law, but the scheme was unsuccessful. Borne down by drink and debt, he was thrown into prison by his creditors. On their suggestion he undertook a *History of Scotland* for Morrisons of Perth. After making some progress he was freed from prison on condition of using two-thirds of his remuneration to paying 15s. in the pound. The first volume, which appeared in 1794, was nearly all written in gaol. The *History* was completed in six volumes, 1794–9. In 1798 Heron produced at the Theatre Royal, Edinburgh, a comedy, which was shouted down before the second act. Attributing its failure to a conspiracy against him, he published it as *St Kilda in Edinburgh, or, News from Camperdown, a comic drama in two acts, with a critical preface, to which is added an account of a famous ass race* (1798). Being returned as a ruling elder for New Galloway, Heron was for several years a member of the general assembly of the Church of Scotland, and frequently spoke—and from time to time preached—with fluency and ability. In 1799 he moved to London, seeking a new start in literature. There he wrote frequently for the periodicals, was for some time editor of *The Globe*, the *British Press*, and other newspapers, and also acted as a parliamentary reporter.

Despite personal set-backs, Heron, both in Edinburgh and London, maintained a steady flow of publications on a wide variety of subjects. In 1792, his best year, he translated C. Niebuhr's *Travels through Arabia* and, from the French, Jacques Cazotte's *Arabian Tales* and *Continuations of Arabian Tales* (an important source for R. Southey's *Thalaba* of 1801), also writing *Elegant Extracts of Natural History* and *Observations Made in a Journey through the Western Counties of Scotland in 1792* (still an account of interest). In 1794 he published two works on the war against France and *General View of the Natural Circumstances of the Hebrides*. He showed an interest in chemistry, translating A. F. Fourcroy's *Chemistry* (1796) and writing *Elements of Chemistry* in 1800. He published a four-volume *New and complete system of universal geography, to which is added a philosophical view of universal history* in 1798, and an edition of the letters of Junius, 1802, in Robert Watt's *Bibliotheca Britannica*. It is there erroneously credited to John Pinkerton (*N&Q*, 6, 1852, 445); however, Pinkerton himself was the author of *Letters of Literature* by 'Robert Heron' (1784). Heron also published on the slave trade and other topics, and made other translations. He was employed by Sir John Sinclair during his compilation of the (first) *Statistical Account of Scotland* and contributed to the *Encyclopaedia Britannica* and to periodicals.

In 1806 Heron began a newspaper entitled *The Fame*, which was unsuccessful. Its failure and his improvident habits led to his confinement by his creditors in Newgate prison, where, according to his own statement, he was reduced 'to the very extremity of bodily and pecuniary distress'. From Newgate he, on 2 February 1807, wrote a letter to the Literary Fund, recounting his services to literature, and appealing for aid (printed in Isaac Disraeli, *Calamities of Authors*, 1812), but the appeal met with no response. Attacked by fever, Heron was moved to the hospital of St Pancras, where he died on 13 April 1807. He left a manuscript, 'Journal of my conduct', which was later deposited in the library of the University of Edinburgh.

T. F. HENDERSON, *rev.* H. C. G. MATTHEW

Sources *GM*, 1st ser., 77 (1807), 595 · R. Heron, journal, U. Edin. L. · Chambers, *Scots.* (1835) · *N&Q*, 6 (1852), 389–90, 445 · *N&Q*, 7 (1853), 167 · C. Carswell, 'Heron: a study in failure', *Scots Magazine*, 18 (1932–3), 37–48 · I. McIntyre, *Dirt and deity: a life of Robert Burns* (1995)
Archives U. Edin. L., journal

Heron, Sir Robert, second baronet (1765–1854), politician, born at Newark on 27 November 1765, was the only son of Thomas Heron of Chilham Castle, Kent, recorder of Newark (who died on 28 April 1794), and his first wife, Anne, the elder daughter of Sir Edward Wilmot, bt, MD. In childhood he was very feeble. His mother died on 30 April 1767, and he was brought up by strangers. He was educated from the age of eight by the Revd John Skynner, who lived near Stamford, and proceeded afterwards to St John's College, Cambridge, but did not stay long enough to take a degree. For two summers he travelled on the continent with an eccentric tutor, Robert Pedley (afterwards known as Robert Deverell). On 9 January 1792 he married Amelia (d. 1847), second daughter of Sir Horatio Mann of Broughton Malherbe. They had no children. He succeeded to the baronetcy on the death of his uncle Sir Richard *Heron, in 1805. On the death of another uncle, the Revd Robert Heron of Grantham, on 19 January 1813, he succeeded to considerable property, which was augmented by the widow's death shortly afterwards.

In politics Heron was a whig, though he voted for income tax in 1815 and had little faith in the whig leaders. He abandoned an intention to contest Lincolnshire in 1812 in order to canvass the borough of Grimsby, and was duly returned for that constituency. At the next general election in 1818 he stood for Lincolnshire, but he was in a hopeless minority and withdrew on the third day of the poll. Through Lord Fitzwilliam's interest he was returned in December 1819 for Peterborough, and was re-elected until 1832 without opposition. After that date he was frequently opposed, but continued to sit for Peterborough until his retirement in 1847. Heron was a constant speaker in the House of Commons, supporting slave-trade abolition, Catholic emancipation, and retrenchment in the 1820s; among his later proposals was a motion 'respecting the vacating of seats in parliament on the acceptance of office', on which the marquess of Northampton published a pamphlet of *Observations* in 1835. A quirky, quixotic politician, Heron embodied the spirit of the independent country gentleman.

Heron's wife died on 12 December 1847 and he died suddenly at his home, Stubton Hall, near Grantham, Lincolnshire, on 29 May 1854, the baronetcy becoming extinct. A monument to their memory was erected in Stubton churchyard by George Neville, the successor to the property; Heron had built the nave and tower of Stubton church about 1800. A volume of his *Notes* was printed anonymously for private circulation at Grantham in 1850, and published in 1851. They dealt mainly with politics and social economy, but included observations on natural history, drawn from the curious animals collected together in what was locally known as his 'menagerie'. In one passage he spoke of J. W. Croker as 'one of the most determined jobbers', and in another referred to a 'most malicious article' of that critic in the *Quarterly Review*. Croker revenged himself by a savage onslaught on the volume in the *Quarterly* (1852, 90.206–25).

W. P. COURTNEY, rev. H. C. G. MATTHEW

Sources R. Heron, *Notes by Sir Robert Heron*, 2nd edn (1851) · HoP, *Commons* · 'Biographical account of the late Mr Flood', *GM*, 1st ser., 62 (1792), 44–8 · *GM*, 2nd ser., 42 (1854), 74–5
Archives Lincs. Arch., corresp.; notes | Notts. Arch., papers relating to election petition

Likenesses S. Freeman, mixed media print, NPG · G. Hayter, group portrait, oils (*The House of Commons, 1833*), NPG · W. Walker, mezzotint (after W. Boxall), BM, NPG

Herrick, Nicholas (1542–1592), goldsmith, was born in Leicester, the fifth of twelve children of John Herrick or Heyricke (1513–1589) of Leicester, ironmonger and alderman, and his wife, Mary, daughter of John Bond of Wardene, Warwick. Nicholas was apprenticed in 1564 to Edward Gylberd, a goldsmith on Cheapside in the city of London. His elder brother Robert (1540–1618) stayed in Leicester to run his father's successful ironmongery business.

A year after completing his apprenticeship in 1572 Nicholas took over his master's apprentice John Prynne and subsequently also took on his younger brother William *Herrick (*bap.* 1562, *d.* 1653), indicating that he had assumed control of his own business or of Gylberd's at the sign of the Grasshopper in Cheapside. From entries in the Goldsmiths' Company registers it is clear that Herrick was running a busy jewellery shop that also involved pawning. In 1578 he was accused of gilding a latten chain and then using it as a pawn, and bestowing new trimming on a jewel which was used in the same way. This did not stop him becoming assistant to the Goldsmiths' Court in 1592.

Letters which survive from Nicholas and William's parents in Leicester to their sons in London reveal how closely family and business affairs were linked. Although technically free to work independently as a journeyman William was still working for his brother three years after his freedom. Their sister Mary was sent to London to 'keep house' for them. By 1582 Nicholas Herrick must have felt himself sufficiently secure to marry Julian (1561–1629), second daughter of William Stone of Segenhoe, Bedford. Three years later their first child, named William, was born. Their fourth son and sixth child was Robert *Herrick the poet. There is some indication from the family correspondence that Nicholas not only caught the plague in 1575, but also fell ill with an 'ague' in 1583. The symptoms may have recurred, resigning him to make his will on 7 November 1592, in which he described himself as 'of perfect memorie in soule, but sicke in body'. He requested that he be buried in St Vedast's, Foster Lane, and that his estate of £3000 be divided between his wife and their children.

On 9 November 1592 Herrick fell to his death from an upper window of his house in Cheapside. In a deed poll of 29 November 1592 it was assumed that he 'did kill and destroye himself', but 'from reasons of charity and other causes' his property was not confiscated. His wife must have been pregnant, for in 1593 she gave birth to their seventh child, christened William after their first child who had died in infancy. Three of Herrick's sons, Thomas, Robert, and William, became members of the Goldsmiths' Company.

It is clear from the inventory of his stock-in-trade and jewellery shop made after his death that Herrick had established a large and successful business. The contents of the shop included elaborate pieces of gem set jewellery, gold and enamel buttons, and a few pieces of wrought silver including spoons and salts amounting to £1700. The comfort of his home can be judged by glancing at the furnishings which included embroidered stools, velvet cushions, and taffeta curtains. The total of his shop and house contents and good debts amounted to £3053, suggesting that he had a clear idea of his estate before his death. Doubtful debts owing to the testator amounted to £1210, and desperate debts to just over £500 from over 185 individuals including Lord Compton, the countess of Rutland, Sir Thomas Manners, Sir Henry Harrington, Lord Henry Howard, and Lady Mordant. Herrick's brother William assumed control of his brother's family affairs and business, which laid the foundations for his future success as a goldsmith and jeweller in London.   HELEN CLIFFORD

Sources J. Nichols, *The history and antiquities of the county of Leicester*, 2/2 (1798) · W. G. D. Fletcher, *Some early notices of the Herrick family* (1885) · H. Ellis, *In the olden time: being some notices of the Herrick family* · E. H. Milhouret, *The Herrick family in England and America* (1984) · Leics. RO, Herrick papers · inventory, 1593, Leics. RO, DG 9/2409 · will, 7 Nov 1592, Leics. RO, DG 9/2407 [probate copy] · will, 26 Nov 1601, Leics. RO, DG 9/2406 [probate copy] · deed poll, 29 Nov 1592, Leics. RO, DG 9/2410 · Goldsmiths' Company registers, London
Archives Bodl. Oxf. · Leics. RO | Goldsmiths' Company, London, registers
Wealth at death £3053 18s. 6d.: Herrick MSS, Leics. RO, DG 9/2409

Herrick, Robert (*bap.* 1591, *d.* 1674), poet, was born in 'the Golden-cheap-side' (*Poetical Works*, 316). This was Goldsmith's Row on the south of Cheapside, between Bread Street and the Eleanor Cross, 'the most beautiful frame of fayre houses and shoppes that bee within the Walles of London, or elsewhere in England' (Stow, 1.345). The fifth surviving child of Nicholas *Herrick (or Heryck) (1542–1592) and Julian Stone (1561–1629), he was baptized in St Vedast's, Foster Lane, on 24 August 1591.

Family and early years The Herricks were wealthy Leicester ironmongers, but Nicholas had been apprenticed in London as a goldsmith to Edward Gylberd. Julian's father was a London mercer, William Stone. At Robert's birth, Nicholas was a successful jeweller and moneylender, but before he was two Robert was effectively deprived of both parents. On 9 November 1592, two days after making his will 'of perfecte memorie in soule but sicke in Bodie' (Herrick family papers, Leics. RO, DG 9/2406), his father allegedly 'did throwe himself forthe of a garret windowe … whereby he did kill and destroye himself' (deed poll, ibid., DG 9/2410). Harsh laws concerning suicide, including burial outside hallowed ground, were then strictly enforced, and it was probably through the influence in the city of Julian's family in particular (her brother-in-law Stephen Soame was sheriff in 1593, lord mayor in 1598) that Nicholas was hurriedly buried in St Vedast's next day, apparently in an unmarked grave.

Nicholas's presumed suicide clearly haunted Robert, whose poetry shows an obsession with the proper rites of burial that goes beyond the uncharacteristically sombre poem addressed to Nicholas's 'reverend shade' thirty-five years ('seven lustres') later, in which he apologizes for not

Robert Herrick (*bap.* 1591, *d.* 1674), by William Marshall, pubd 1648

doing 'the *Rites* to thy Religious Tombe' since he did not know 'Whether thy bones had here their Rest, or no' (*Poetical Works*, 27). Nicholas's family pressed for a verdict of accidental death. On 13 November the privy council, alerted that 'the matter is by som endevored to be found casuall' (*APC*, 1592, 290–91), warned the lord mayor that no verdict should be reached until the royal almoner, to whom a suicide's estate was forfeit, had collected evidence. The almoner, Richard Fletcher, bishop of Bristol (father of John, whose 'Incomparable Playes' Herrick was to praise over fifty years later), settled for the relatively small sum of £220 'whither the death … be found by the Coroners enquest to have been casuall & accidentall or ells a wilfull murdering & making away of himself' (23 Nov 1592; Herrick family papers, Leics. RO, DG 9/2410). The coroner's verdict is lost, but Fletcher's decision freed an estate worth £3053 (excluding doubtful and desperate debts), of which Nicholas left one-third to his wife, and two-thirds to be divided among his six children, with his brothers Robert and William as overseers.

The will was challenged by Julian: the elder Robert noted in 1602 'a suite … concerning the validitie of the testator's will and revokinge an administration of the testators goodes formerly Comitted to Julian Hericke … upon supposition that he died intestate' (Herrick family papers, Leics. RO, DG 9/2415). In March 1593 an agreement was reached between Robert and William, on behalf of the children, and Julian, who accepted £1300, rather more than a third of the residual estate, in full settlement. Nicholas's brothers agreed to 'have fowre childeren of the said Nicholas and Julian with their portions' while 'the sayd Julian shall have tow other of the childeren with theire portions as shee shall best like' (ibid., DG 9/2413). Julian kept the newly born William and her only surviving daughter, Mercy. She lived initially with her sister Christian Campion at Hampton, and subsequently with another sister, Anne Soame, at Little Thurlow, Suffolk.

Robert, still only about nineteen months old, and his elder brothers Nicholas and Thomas were thus henceforth brought up by their uncles, in practice by the London-based William *Herrick. The effective loss of both parents may have been less traumatic than might be assumed, since Robert had probably been boarded out with a wet-nurse, a normal course in wealthy London families, and one indicated in his case by an undated note from Julian asking William to 'send for the courall from Robardes nource and send it me for Will' (Bodl. Oxf., MS Eng. hist. c.474, fol. 110). William Herrick, having been apprenticed to Nicholas, had by 1593 begun his own immensely successful business as goldsmith, jeweller, and moneylender. In 1596 he married Joan May, a lady of strong presbyterian leanings. Through her, Robert acquired the future privy councillor Humphrey May as an adoptive uncle, and the poet Tom May as adoptive cousin.

Robert's childhood in this household must have had a pious presbyterian slant. He later wrote of the law's intent:

To free the Orphan from that Wolfe-like-man,
Who is his *Butcher* more then *Guardian*
(*Poetical Works*, 201)

but, though the birth of William's and Joan's own twelve children between 1598 and 1615 would have diverted attention from their nephews, these lines are not necessarily autobiographical. William did, however, put all three nephews to apprenticeships, while designing more gentlemanly careers for most of his own sons. This suggests some inequality of treatment, as does the fact that the nephews are rarely mentioned in surviving family documents. It is significant in a poet so conscious of family relationships that Herrick never addresses poems to William, the elder Robert, or any member of their families, while addressing several to his mother's relatives.

Herrick did nevertheless receive a sophisticated education before being apprenticed to William in September 1607. A poem written about 1611–12 to his brother Thomas (*Poetical Works*, 34), some time before he went to Cambridge, bears witness to this. It invokes a wide range of classical authors, and imitates Ben Jonson's then-unpublished 'To Sir Robert Wroth', suggesting that he knew Jonson before his presumed contact with the latter's circle in the mid-1620s. The tradition that Herrick received this education at Westminster is groundless, as is one that he lived at Hampton. It is more likely that, like William's own sons, he went to the nearby Merchant Taylors' School, but no registers survive for the years 1598–1603 when Herrick is most likely to have been there. All that is certain is that his reading was wide, and his characteristically easy use of literary allusion well established, by the time he was twenty.

Apprenticeship and Cambridge If Herrick did leave school in 1602–3 he may, like his father and William, have worked in his uncle's shop before his apprenticeship began. Since William records payments to Herrick's cousin, William Pearson, for his 'apparill' and diet in 1611–12 (Bodl. Oxf., MS Eng. hist. c.474, fol. 117), it seems that by the time he was nineteen, and perhaps earlier, Herrick was lodging with Pearson, who worked for William. Bound for ten years, he had served only five when, in the early summer of 1613, he entered St John's College, Cambridge, as a fellow-commoner. At least two of his Soame uncles had been students there, at one, Robert, twice becoming vice-chancellor. The change of career followed Herrick's coming of age. In March 1613 the City's orphan court (chaired by Sir Stephen Soame) recognized his majority, he being twenty-one 'and upwards' and Robert acknowledged his inheritance of £424 8s., which William immediately borrowed back, paying Robert a quarterly allowance of £10 as interest during his time at Cambridge.

In return for higher fees and a gift of silver plate, fellow-commoners shared dining privileges and other marks of status with the fellows. Robert was establishing his gentlemanly rank at one of the most expensive colleges in Cambridge. His cousin Richard Stone (*Poetical Works*, 185) followed him to St John's as a fellow-commoner in 1614, as over the next two years did the future earl of Northumberland, Algernon Percy, and Sir Clipseby Crewe, son of the lord chief justice, who became a patron and friend. A still more important patron, Mildmay Fane, later the second earl of Westmorland, was at Emmanuel in 1618. Other Cambridge friends or patrons included Thomas Southwell (ibid., 53), George Parry (ibid., 322), William Alabaster (ibid., 256), and perhaps Edward Sackville, earl of Dorset (ibid., 187). Oliver Cromwell, Hugh Peters, Oliver St John, James Shirley, John Cosin, and Gilbert Sheldon were also contemporaries. Herrick's tutor was probably William Beeston, but more significant was another fellow near his own age, the Devonian John Weekes, who had graduated in 1612. They were to remain close friends at least until the publication of *Hesperides* in 1648 (ibid., 132, 321). Still connected with St John's was another fellow, John Williams, whom Herrick later accused of being 'unkind' in some unspecified way (ibid., 52, 413), and who was in 1613 just beginning his upward climb at court.

Herrick's only surviving prose dates from these years: fifteen letters to Sir William Herrick (*Poetical Works*, 445–53) request money in a tone reflecting the deferential attitude of nephews to guardians in early modern England. Their obsequiousness obscures the fact that they are mainly reminders of the interest due on his inheritance. Although an income of £40 a year made Herrick a relatively wealthy student, it was not enough to keep him in style at St John's. Simonds D'Ewes, a fellow-commoner there in 1618, found that £50 a year caused him 'much want and discontent' (*Autobiography*, 1.118–19). In 1616 Herrick asked Sir William 'whether it were better for me to direct my study towards the lawe or not' (*Poetical Works*, 452) and migrated to the smaller and cheaper Trinity Hall, apparently not as a fellow-commoner. Here again his career intersected with that of an upwardly mobile courtier politician, Sir Robert Naunton, who resigned his fellowship that year. Herrick may have intended to move on to an inn of court, but instead, after graduating BA on 10 April 1617, he stayed on to take his MA in July 1620, although residence for the MA was no longer necessary. He may have stayed still longer: he was described as a fellow of Trinity Hall at his ordination in 1623. He was not a fellow, but possibly kept a room there after graduation, like his friend Sir Simeon Steward (ibid., 126). He is still listed in the college steward's accounts as owing over £10 in 1630.

Few poems can be dated to these years (only a tiny proportion of the 1400 poems in *Hesperides* can be dated), but the beginnings of a reputation are detectable. In 1619 Herrick contributed a poem on behalf of Trinity Hall (his only surviving holograph poem, BL, Harley MS 367, fol. 154) to a memorial collection for John Browne, a fellow of Gonville and Caius. Manuscript miscellanies belonging to the Spelman, Alston, St John, and Daniell families, all of which have Cambridge connections, contain a substantial number of his poems (Beal, 532–3). Another manuscript miscellany from this period, the 'Herrick Commonplace Book' (Texas MS), contains, along with two Herrick poems, entries in a hand which may be his. There are, however, further entries in many other hands, suggesting it was widely circulated. The case for Herrick's association with the miscellany, if not ownership of it, however, is strengthened by the fact that it contains common material with the Alston manuscript (Yale University, Osborn collection, b 197). The Alstons were a Suffolk family, connected to St John's and Trinity Hall. The Soames also owned a number of estates in Suffolk, the main one at Little Thurlow, from where Herrick's sister Mercy (*Poetical Works*, 269) married John Wingfield (ibid., 131) in 1611. The Wingfields, and Herrick's mother, subsequently lived at Brantham, a few miles away, and Robert must have visited both places in the 1620s, being in touch also with the Crofts at Saxham (ibid., 267) and the Alstons at Sudbury.

Ordination and the Île de Ré expedition It was in Peterborough, the cathedral city near Cambridge, that the next documented step took place: Herrick and Weekes were ordained deacon and priest by Bishop Thomas Dove on 24 and 25 April 1623. Ordinations on successive days were common during this period, but the ordination of the two friends at the same time implies that some opportunity had opened for them. Both were in their early thirties,

suggesting a career in the church was not their first choice, though Herrick's 'Farwell unto Poetrie' (*Poetical Works*, 410) suggests he took his vows seriously. Since neither man was presented to a living, they probably became domestic chaplains. Weekes later described himself and his wife as combining to form an 'epicene chaplain' to Endymion Porter (*CSP dom.*, 1633, 230). Herrick dedicated a number of poems to Porter, but in April 1623 the latter was in Spain. Though both could nevertheless have been appointed to his household, the influence of Herrick's family, or of such Cambridge contemporaries as Crewe, Fane, Sackville, Naunton, or Williams, may have helped him to a chaplaincy elsewhere. All that is clear is that he was in London in January 1624, when he sent 'A New-Yeares Gift' (*Poetical Works*, 126) to Sir Simeon Steward, and in July 1625, when he wrote the 'Nuptiall Song' (ibid., 112) for Crewe's marriage to Jane Pulteney in Westminster. In 1625 Richard James, in *The Muses Dirge*, gave the unpublished Herrick his first recorded praise: perhaps having read the splendid 'Nuptiall Song', he lamented that James I had not been celebrated by 'Some *Jonson*, *Drayton*, or some *Herick*'. In 1626 Mildmay Fane addressed two friendly poems to Herrick, one of which places him in London (*Poetry*, 58–9, 61).

In July 1627 Herrick and Weekes were chaplains to the duke of Buckingham on the ill-fated expedition to relieve the Huguenots at La Rochelle (cf. Herrick's petition of 1630, PRO, SP 16/173/93). It is possible that they had been in Buckingham's service before this: several influential patrons could have promoted the connection, but since Buckingham came from Leicestershire, contact could have come through the Herrick family there. Porter, John Mennes, James Smith, and a future patron, Viscount Scudamore, were also associated with the expedition, all returning safely in November, unlike the 4000 Englishmen sacrificed to international protestantism on the islands of Ré and Oléron. Weekes almost immediately became rector of Shirwell in north Devon, but Herrick probably continued in Buckingham's service until the latter's assassination in August 1628 left him looking for a new place, which he was to find, like Weekes, in Devon.

Dean Prior Herrick was presented to the vicarage of Dean Prior, on the southern edge of Dartmoor, in September 1629. A previous vicar, Scipio Stukeley, had been Weekes's uncle, while the patron of the living, Sir Edward Giles, was also related to Weekes (Herrick was himself very distantly related to Giles, through the marriage of his cousin Tobias to Elizabeth Yarde). In 1629, however, Dean Prior was in the king's gift, its incumbent, Barnaby Potter, having become bishop of Carlisle. Charles approved Herrick's appointment on 1 October, and he was instituted by Joseph Hall, bishop of Exeter, on 26 October 1629, in the London house of Hall's patron, the earl of Norwich.

Valued at £21 a year, Dean Prior was not a rich living: nearby Buckfastleigh was valued at £29, while Weekes's parish at Shirwell was worth over £30. Compared with this, let alone the £700 a year that Robert's presbyterian cousin Richard Heyrick later received as warden of Manchester College, Dean Prior did not represent worldly success for the 38-year-old poet. It did, however, represent security, and Herrick, typically Romanizing his experience, was to celebrate the 'beloved privacie' of his 'poore Tenement' (*Poetical Works*, 200), as well as cursing 'the dull confines of the drooping West' (ibid., 242). The Île de Ré expedition, Buckingham's assassination, Weekes's move to Shirwell, and his mother's impending death may all have contributed to the move, which in any case he may have seen as merely a stepping-stone.

Since Potter held the vicarage *in commendam* until Michaelmas 1630, Herrick did not move there until late that year. The 'Mr Robbert Hyrick' who was meanwhile recommended to Lady Vere by the puritan John Davenport in January 1629 (*Letters of John Davenport*, ed. I. Calder, 1937, 29, 31) was probably his cousin, the same who married Jane Gibbons at St Clement Danes in June 1632. Between 24 August 1629, when she made her will, and 5 November 1629, when it was proved, Julian Herrick died at Brantham, leaving most of her estate to the two children she had brought up, William and Mercy. Robert and Nicholas (Thomas presumably having died) received only a token ring each (PRO, PROB 11/156/97). Herrick was probably at Whitehall in May 1630, when his pastoral on the birth of Prince Charles was 'Presented to the King, and Set by Mr. Nic: Laniere' (*Poetical Works*, 85). About June 1630 he wrote an epitaph on the death of his niece Elizabeth (ibid., 145), which, placed in St Margaret's, Westminster, appeared as his first published poem in the 1633 continuation of Stow's *Survey* (Stow, 812). A poem on the approaching death of his younger brother William (*Poetical Works*, 73), dating from early November 1630 (William was buried on 8 November), implies that Herrick was then still in London, and probably living with William in Westminster. William's death prompted a poem to Porter (ibid., 72) describing William as 'The staffe, The Elme, the prop, the shelt'ring wall' of Herrick's vine, a role he hoped Porter would now take on.

If Herrick did stay in London until November 1630, William's widow, Elizabeth, may have travelled with him to Dean Prior, where she was to keep house for him until her death in 1643 (*Poetical Works*, 13, 23). Herrick's other female company in Dean Prior was his maid, Prudence Baldwin (ibid., 151), who outlived him, dying in 1678, but for whom he nevertheless wrote a graceful epitaph at least thirty years premature (ibid., 262). 'His Grange, or Private Wealth' (ibid., 246) adds details of a number of pets and fowls, but fails to mention his curate, William Greene, who may also have accompanied him to Devon in November, since his hand, confusingly similar to Herrick's, first appears in the parish register for that year, continuing until 1636. Greene also signed the bishop's transcripts for 1630, 1632, and 1634, and appeared with Herrick before the bishop's visitation of 22 March 1631, the earliest date at which Herrick can definitely be placed in Dean Prior. At the 1638 visitation, however, Herrick was alone.

In Devon, Herrick supplemented his aristocratic patrons by more modest local ones: apart from Giles and his relatives at nearby Dean Court, such gentry as John Weare (*Poetical Works*, 201), John Warr (ibid., 48), John Merrifield (ibid., 90), and Thomas Shapcot (ibid., 119) were:

Writ in the Poets Endlesse-Kalendar:
Whose velome, and whose volumne is the Skie.
(ibid., 168)

Less fortunate parishioners were recorded by name in epigrams which imitate Martial and Jonson. Greene and his successors as curates made regular visits to London possible for Herrick, and it was probably from there, for example, that Herrick wrote on the imprisonment of John Williams (ibid., 52) in or about 1637. If so, he was back in Dean Prior for the visitation of 1638, and in September 1639, when he married Lettice Yarde, the great-niece of Sir Edward Giles, to Henry Northleigh, a ceremony followed, perhaps uniquely, by a second, more classical one, composed and conducted by Herrick in the porch of the house, presumably Dean Court, where the marriage was consummated (ibid., 124).

An undated note in the domestic state papers (PRO, SP 16/474/77) from 'Mr Delles man' (Laud's secretary, William Dell) endorsed 'abt mr Henrique: a minister' suggests that a long and eventful visit to London followed this wedding. The informer's report that 'Thomsen Parsons hath had a Bastard lately shee was brought to bedd at Greenwch.' is followed by a statement whose contiguity implies Herrick played some part in this event:

Mr Herrique a Minister possest of a very good Living in Devonshire hath not resided thereon having noe Lycence for his non-residence & not being Chapline to any Noble man or man qualified by Law as I heare, his Lodging is at Westminster in the little Amrie at Nicholas Weilkes his house where the said Thomsen Parsons lives.   (ibid.)

A further implication is that Herrick had been living in the Little Almonry for some time. Born in 1618, Thomasin was the daughter of John Parsons (*d.* 1623), organist at Westminster Abbey. Herrick had written on Thomasin's beauty as a child (*Poetical Works*, 304), and, more amorously, to her elder sister Dorothy (ibid., 186).

It was probably on this visit that Herrick began moves to publish his poems. Though they had achieved considerable manuscript currency, apart from the adventitious publication of the epitaph on Elizabeth, only four had appeared in print, all probably unauthorized: in 1635 'Oberon's Feast' (*Poetical Works*, 119) was in *A Description of the King and Queen of Fayries*, and in 1640 Benson added three poems, along with those of other 'excellent gentlemen', to his edition of Shakespeare's poems. Then, in April 1640, Andrew Crooke entered for publication '*The severall Poems* written by Master ROBERT HERRICK' (Arber, *Regs. Stationers*, 4.483). It may have been Crooke's publication of Jonson, Shirley, Fletcher, and Killigrew that same year that led Herrick to him, or him to Herrick, and the installation of Prince Charles (to whom the volume was to have been dedicated) as prince of Wales would have made the moment timely. The edition never appeared, perhaps because of the information given to Dell. Herrick must have returned to Dean Prior, probably before the opening of the Long Parliament in November, and witnessed from there the movement towards civil war.

Civil war and publication of *Hesperides* Devon was a centre of conflict during the war. Herrick's loyalties were royalist, as were those of most of his local patrons, but poems such as 'Liberty' (*Poetical Works*, 153) show that he understood what was at stake. A number of poems witness that:

Sick is the Land to'th' heart; and doth endure
More dangerous faintings by her desp'rate cure
(ibid., 214)

while others offer comfort to and confidence in the king and queen. Family sickness counterpoised that of the land: in April 1643, a few days before he congratulated 'brave Hopton' on the first royalist victory in the southwest (ibid., 310), he buried his sister-in-law Elizabeth (ibid., 23). Conflict came closest to Dean Prior when in January 1646 Cromwell surprised the royalist cavalry at Bovey Tracey, and then moved on to Totnes, while Fairfax took Dartmouth. The tide of parliamentary success swept Herrick away with it: by 25 March 1646, before Exeter surrendered, the county commissioners had replaced him with a presbyterian minister, John Syms, who was to remain in place until 1660.

Homeless and without income, Herrick's first move was to Weekes at Shirwell:

To whose glad threshold, and free door
I may a Poet come, though poor.
(*Poetical Works*, 321)

By 1647 he was in London, which he greeted enthusiastically as his true home, from which he had been:

by hard fate sent
Into a long and irksome banishment.
(ibid., 242)

By the time his welcome to the king was sung at Hampton Court in August 1647 (ibid., 300), the printing of his poems, as *Hesperides, or, The Works both Humane & Divine of Robert Herrick Esq.*, was already under way. It was published in 1648, probably early in that year, and sold by John Williams at the Crown and by Francis Eglesfield at the Marigold, both in St Paul's Churchyard. Copies were also printed for Thomas Hunt at Exeter, implying the existence of a local market. Although Herrick spent some time at the last minute composing epigrams to fatten the religious part of his collection, 'His Noble Numbers', he presented himself on the main title-page as a lay gentleman, 'Robert Herrick *Esq.*', and presumably lived thus in London. The striking bust engraved by Marshall as frontispiece, also denies any clerical connections: placed in profile on a classical altar, it shows a heavy, thickset man wearing a toga, with a strong neck, a thin moustache, a prominent hooked nose, and a mass of curly hair which is suspiciously full for a man of about fifty-six. It is possible that hair and nose are exaggerated as suitably Roman characteristics, but in other respects the portrait is sufficiently idiosyncratic to suggest that it is an authentic likeness.

Walker implies that Herrick remained in London from 1647 to 1660, and writes that 'having no Fifths paid him

[he] was subsisted by Charity' (Walker, 263). Some of this charity came from Fane, to whom Herrick addressed a 'Christmas Carroll' in 1647. Fane sent £5 that November, and apparently paid £2 quarterly until 1660. To this was added an 'Annual Charity' from Viscount Scudamore, and probably something from Henry Pierrepoint, the 'gallant *Newark*' bracketed with 'Noble *Westmorland*' (Fane) as having a 'large heart and long hand' (*Poetical Works*, 301). Herrick's only surviving brother, Nicholas, a Levant merchant in London whose travels he celebrates (ibid., 330), would have been an obvious supporter and host, more so than Sir William Herrick, long retired to Leicestershire, whose sympathies were no longer royalist. Those of the Soame and Stone families were, however, and Sir William Soame (ibid., 131) at Little Thurlow and Sir Richard Stone at Stukeley were also probably supporters of their cousin. Two earlier patrons could not have helped him much: Crewe, with whom Herrick seems in any case to have quarrelled (ibid., 161), died in 1648, and Porter in 1649.

Even though he saw *Hesperides* as a definitive life's work, it is unlikely that Herrick stopped writing after its publication. Very little has survived, however: apart from the 'Christmas Carroll', he contributed to the Beaumont and Fletcher folio of 1647 (*Poetical Works*, 415), and to the elegies on Hastings in *Lachrymae musarum* of 1649 (ibid., 416). When this elegy, his last known poem, was written he still had twenty-five years to live, years which from 1660 are partially documented by the Exeter diocesan records. Despite having sworn never to return to Dean Prior until 'Rockes turn to Rivers, Rivers turn to Men' (ibid., 29), he was one of the 570 clergy who petitioned the House of Lords in 1660 to secure the revenues of their livings while awaiting restitution. That came in September with the Act for Settling Ministers. Aged sixty-nine, Herrick returned to Dean Prior, where he was again supported by a curate, David Mole, who described himself as a 'lecturer' (chanter 151, 41, Devon RO) and who had been curate at nearby South Brent since 1633. Herrick signed a certificate of orthodoxy for an Edward Goswell on 12 October 1661 (basket D/67/99, Devon RO), and subscribed to the Act of Conformity in August 1662, but did not appear before the bishop's visitation of November that year, or ever again: in August 1665 and 1668 he was represented by David Mole, the bishop excusing him; while in 1671, apparently without a curate, he was excused as extremely aged ('valde senex'). In August 1674 a new curate, 'Mr Colwell', represented him. It was presumably Colwell who buried him at the church of St George the Martyr, Dean Prior two months later, when the parish register records 'Robert Herrick Vicker was buried the 15th day of October'.

Reputation It has been argued that in 1648, aged about fifty-six, and with publication probably coinciding with the second civil war, Herrick launched *Hesperides* at an inauspicious time, his poetry too old-fashioned and too harmonious for 'the untuneable Times' (*Poetical Works*, 84). The evidence does not wholly support this. Wood remembered that *Hesperides* made some impact, and that Herrick's poems 'made him much admired in the time when they were published, especially by the generous and boon loyalists' (Wood, 2.122–3). The dedication to Prince Charles and the explicitly royalist poems suggest why *Hesperides* was timely for such readers, as less obviously does Herrick's emphasis on the continuity and shaping powers of ceremony, ritual, and tradition, and on the importance of friendship and family loyalty. Even the harmonies of the well-tuned lyric must have had a powerful nostalgic impact on readers whose world had been turned disharmoniously upside down. Seventy-five poems from *Hesperides* were included in the 1650 edition of the anthology *Witt's Recreations*, with ten more in 1663, and Herrick continued to appear in anthologies and songbooks throughout the century. He was praised as 'Yong Herric' in *Musarum deliciae* (1655, 2), and in *Naps upon Parnassus* (1658) as the only English lyric poet comparable to Horace (sig. A3*v*). But *Hesperides* did not establish him as the distinctive master of lyric that he undoubtedly was, and he was largely unknown throughout the eighteenth century. Herrick was willing to wait, however, making clear that *Hesperides* was aimed more at a future than a present audience:

That each Lyrick here shall be
Of my love a Legacie,
Left to all posterity.
(*Poetical Works*, 88)

Posterity has not always known how to take the legacy: critics have found Herrick's characteristic virtues of playfulness, generosity, gracefulness, self-mockery, the very ease of his verse, difficult to deal with. A similar anxiety about such 'trivial' qualities informs both Edward Phillips's description, 'now and then a pretty Floury and Pastoral gale of Fancy' interrupted by 'trivial passages' (*Theatrum poetarum*, 1675, 62), and F. R. Leavis's judgment that Herrick is merely 'trivially charming' (*Revaluation*, 1936, 36). His high reputation in Victorian times was, conversely, all too often based on a view of him as a simple poet of an innocent world of daffodils, quaint customs, and blossoming village beauties which itself trivialized his achievement.

Containing almost 1400 poems, probably almost all that he could find to print in 1647, *Hesperides* was and remains the only effort by an important English poet to publish his entire *œuvre* in one organized collection. For despite the appearance of being a 'heterogeneous mass' (Nichols, 2/2.634) *Hesperides* is organized: with its versified 'Argument' (*Poetical Works*, 5), and even its versified errata, and bounded by addresses 'To his Booke', it consciously imitates that enclosed garden, outside time, after which it was named. In this and other respects the struggle with 'Times trans-shifting' ('The Argument of his Book', ibid.) is Herrick's most characteristic and most profound preoccupation. Not only does he explore all the ways in which 'Poetry Perpetuates the Poet' (ibid., 265), but his lyrics typically pin down a transient moment, as in 'The Comming of Good Luck' (ibid., 100), or, most unusually at this date, transplant the material of biography—family, friends, his maid, his parishioners, his dog—into his timeless garden. Consequent upon this latter process is a fictionalizing of Herrick as a character whose Anacreontic, genial, and self-

mocking persona dominates *Hesperides*. Other poets, notably his greatest mentors, Horace and Jonson, had projected versions of themselves in their work, but Herrick was the first English poet to do so in such a thoroughgoing way. He was deeply original too in the ways he deployed his strategies against 'Times trans-shifting'. His awareness of the importance and continuity of ceremony, and of the ways in which rituals and calendar customs order inchoate experience, informs poems like 'Corinna's going a Maying' (ibid., 67), 'The Hock-Cart' (ibid., 101), and 'Ceremonies for Candlemasse Eve' (ibid., 285). These three poems also display his almost pantheistic insight into the interpenetration of human and natural worlds, and of the time-defeating forces of regeneration at work in both of them. The last lines of each also display, in their very different ways, his acceptance that in the end age and death cannot be defeated, that both human and natural worlds must 'glide / Into the Grave' ('To Blossoms', ibid., 176).

TOM CAIN

Sources *The poetical works of Robert Herrick*, ed. L. C. Martin (1956) · Leics. RO, Herrick family papers, DG 9/2405–2439 · bishop's visitations, Devon RO, Chanter 218 · Sir William Herrick's papers, Bodl. Oxf., MSS Eng. hist. b. 216, c. 474–484 · F. Delattre, *Robert Herrick: contribution à l'étude de la poésie lyrique en Angleterre au dix-septième siècle* (1912) · J. Nichols, *The history and antiquities of the county of Leicester*, 4 vols. (1795–1815) · U. Texas, Texas MS, MS file (Herrick, R) works B · Venn, *Alum. Cant.* · P. Beal and others, *Index of English literary manuscripts*, ed. P. J. Croft and others, [4 vols. in 11 pts] (1980–), vol. 2, pt 1, pp. 527–66 · *Walker rev.* · *The visitation of London, anno Domini 1633, 1634, and 1635, made by Sir Henry St George*, ed. J. J. Howard and J. L. Chester, 2 vols., Harleian Society, 15, 17 (1880–83) · W. A. Littledale, ed., *The registers of St Vedast, Foster Lane, and of St Michael le Quern, London*, 1, Harleian Society, register section, 29 (1902) · J. Tuckett, *Devonshire pedigrees recorded in the herald's visitation of 1620* (1859–61) · W. Camden, *The visitation of the county of Leicester in the year 1619*, ed. J. Fetherston, Harleian Society, 2 (1870) · *IGI* · J. Walker, *An attempt towards recovering an account of the numbers and sufferings of the clergy of the Church of England*, 2 pts in 1 (1714) · *The poetry of Mildmay Fane*, ed. T. Cain (2001) · J. Stow, *A survey of London* (1603); with introduction and notes by C. L. Kingsford (1908) · *Warren's book (collectanea ad collegium, sive, Aulam sanctae Trinitatis)*, ed. A. Dale (1911) · Bishop Joseph Hall's register, 1627–37, Devon RO, Chanter 22 · parish register, Church of St George the Martyr, Dean Prior · subscriptions book, Exeter diocese, Devon RO, Chanter 131 · bishops' transcripts, Dean Prior, Devon RO, reel 12 [microfilm] · subscriptions book, 1, 1613–38, CUL, department of manuscripts and university archives · HLRO, Main papers collection, HL, 23 June 1660 · ordination register, diocese of Peterborough, Northants. RO · Wood, *Ath. Oxon.*, 2nd edn · T. Cain, 'Herrick's "Christmas carol": a new poem and its implications for patronage', *English Literary Renaissance*, 29 (1999), 131–53 · M. Eccles, 'Herrick's inheritance', *N&Q*, 230 (1985), 74–8 · H. Clifford, 'The inventory of Nicholas Herrick, goldsmith', *Apollo*, 147 (Jan 1998), 19–24 · Arber, *Regs. Stationers* · W. Pole, *Collections towards a description of the county of Devon*, ed. J. W. De La Pole (1791) · M. Gibson, *A view of the ancient and present state of the churches of Door, Home-Lacy, and Hempsted* (1727) · *The autobiography and correspondence of Sir Simonds D'Ewes*, ed. J. O. Halliwell, 2 vols. (1845) · R. Rollin, 'Robert Herrick', *Seventeenth-century British nondramatic poets: second series*, ed. M. Thomas Hester, DLitB, 126 (1993), 168–81 · W. A. Copinger, *The manors of Suffolk*, 7 vols. (1905–11), vol. 5 · E. Hageman, *Robert Herrick: a reference guide* (1983) [bibliography] · M. Moroney, 'Recent studies in Herrick', *English Literary Renaissance*, 29 (1999), 154–76 [bibliography]

Archives BL, 'Chorus', Harley MS 367, fol. 154 · Bodl. Oxf., corresp. and related material, MSS Eng. hist. b. 216, c. 474–484 ·

Leics. RO, family papers, DG 9/2405–2439 | Bodl. Oxf., letters to Sir William Herrick, MS Eng. c. 2278 • Devon RO, Exeter diocesan records, chanter 22, 131, 218 • U. Texas, Texas MS, works B
Likenesses W. Marshall, line engraving, pubd 1648, NPG [*see illus.*] • N. Schiavonetti, line engraving (after unknown artist), NPG

Herrick [Heyricke], **Sir William** (*bap.* 1562, *d.* 1653), moneylender and royal official, was baptized on 9 December 1562 at St Martin's, Leicester, the fifth and youngest son of John Herrick or Heyricke (1513–1589) of Leicester and Mary, daughter of John Bond. He was born into a successful business family in Tudor Leicester, and was apprenticed to an elder brother, Nicholas *Herrick, who was a London goldsmith. Having become free of the Goldsmiths' Company in 1587, and taking over the business in 1592, he soon became active as a moneylender on both a large and a small scale. On one occasion the explorer and naval commander Martin Frobisher requested an overnight loan of £5, or even £3 (presumably to pay a gambling debt), but was lent only £2. By 1595 Herrick was able to buy the country house and estate of Beaumanor, near Leicester, from the financially embarrassed royal favourite, Robert Devereux, second earl of Essex. On 6 May 1596 he married Joan, daughter of Richard May of Mayfield Place, Sussex; they had twelve children, of whom eight survived infancy, including Richard *Heyrick (1600–1667), the Presbyterian minister.

Elected MP for the borough of Leicester in the last Elizabethan parliament, Herrick was also to sit in the first and third parliaments of James I (on a vacancy from 1605 to 1610, and in 1621). Soon after the new monarch's accession he was knighted, became one of the king's jewellers, gained exemption from civic office, and secured a reversion to a tellership in the exchequer of receipt. The latter grant was confirmed in 1611 and he succeeded to the office in 1616. By then he had, perhaps unavoidably, become a large-scale lender to the crown. His papers, which have survived in considerable bulk, are a potential source for the workings of the Jacobean exchequer. They include a series of begging letters from his nephew, Robert *Herrick, the poet, then a student at Cambridge, as well as the portage book of Herrick's exchequer fees during his tellership, from which can be derived approximate totals of his earnings, over and above any stipendiary fees from the crown; in a good year the sum was as large as £400, but often less than that. His so-called 'account book' (Leics. RO, MS DG 9/2049) spans the 1590s to 1630s, but is only a ledger of in and out payments in his capacity as a goldsmith and moneylender during the years 1610–19. It shows that very considerable sums were being deposited with him by other wealthy individuals, as well as recording a wide variety of loans and payments large and small. In the way in which he borrowed as well as lent, Herrick could be said to have anticipated the scrivener and goldsmith bankers of the mid- and later seventeenth century who kept 'running cashes'.

It has been suggested that Herrick's criticism of royal patents granting monopolies, such as that for gold and silver thread, during the 1621 parliament was unacceptable

to the court, and that this led to his loss of office. He was, however, allowed to sell the tellership and (though on worse terms) his post as jeweller, and vacated both in the course of 1623–4. There is evidence earlier than this of his having been in financial difficulties, probably because his loans to the crown had not been repaid. He had begun to sell property, rather than buying more, even before the 1620s, parting with a Northamptonshire rectory and its associated rights for £1700. His role as executor to the master of the great wardrobe, Sir Roger Aston (*d.* 1612), proved vexatious; Herrick was still being harassed over this more than twenty years later, causing him to minute on a letter 'that I have not a peny of Sir Roger Aston's estait in my handes' (Bodl. Oxf., MS Eng. hist. c. 480, fol. 288).

By the early 1630s Herrick had fallen into real impoverishment. This may have been worsened by his wife's extreme outspokenness and involvement in potentially slanderous disputes over religion. Lady Herrick was the sister of Sir Humphrey May (1573–1630), chancellor of the duchy of Lancaster, and a privy councillor, a connection which had been an asset earlier in the century. As against Lady Herrick's iconoclastic removal of a painted church window, and Sir William's later refusal to pay ship money on a holiday home in East Anglia, he had, however, subscribed to the forced loan of 1627 and did pay ship money on his main midland property. Yet in 1638 two of the more constitutionalist and anti-Laudian of the judges ordered a stay of any proceedings against Herrick and his eldest son for unpaid taxes—an echo perhaps of the famous Hampden ship money case decided earlier in that year. Meanwhile Sir William had surrendered his rights to the woodlands on and around the Beaumanor estate, and seems in effect to have made the management of his affairs over to trustees. The alleged plundering of his property by royalist soldiers in 1644 and 1645, because he and his wife were regarded as 'rebels' (parliamentarians), may have been, as it were, the last straw but is unlikely to have been of decisive importance. The family kept Beaumanor and a town house in Leicester, though they were still in difficulties during the later seventeenth century.

Uncertainty surrounds some aspects of Herrick's life. He died on 2 March 1653 and is sometimes said to have lived to the age of ninety-six; this would place his date of birth in 1556 or 1557 and make him nearly six when he was baptized, which, though not impossible, is extremely unlikely. The statement of his age at death is probably the result of a misreading of the inscription on his tombstone (in St Martin's, Leicester), which properly interpreted indicates that he died at the age of ninety. Obscurity also surrounds the cause of the belief, held by his family and some local historians in the eighteenth and nineteenth centuries, that he had been sent on a mission from Queen Elizabeth I to the sultan of Turkey. The state papers foreign and the records of the Levant Company reveal no trace of him; unfortunately, the portrait, said to have been of Herrick with a lady companion, both in oriental dress, which might have confirmed this story, has not survived.

More important questions concern his wealth and the reasons for his straitened circumstances and decline. He was probably never rich on the scale of his wife's brother-in-law, Baptist Hicks (1551–1621), later Lord Campden, or the greatest London tycoons of the time, such as Sir Paul Pindar (1565–1650), or some of the other farmers of the customs duties. Over-involvement in crown finance seems a likelier reason for his decline than loss of office, due to political and religious opposition to royal policy. With little evidence save the handwriting and certain entries in his papers, a decay in his mental faculties cannot be ruled out. The final picture is of an old man cajoled, possibly even swindled, out of his property rights by his own and his wife's families, and then the victim of looting by the cavalier army. At very much the same time, Herrick's poetical nephew lost his Devon church living at the hands of the victorious puritans.   G. E. AYLMER

Sources Herrick MSS, Bodl. Oxf., MSS Eng. hist. b., fols. 244–9; c., fols. 474–84, 1292–318; MS Eng. c., fol. 2278 · parish register, Leicester, St Martin's, 9 Dec 1562, Leics. RO [baptism] · Leics. RO, MS DG 9/2409 · *CSP dom.*, 1595–1638 · *Second report*, HMC, 1/2 (1871); repr. (1874), appx [Trinity Hall, Cambridge] · *Fourth report*, HMC, 3 (1874), House of Lords, 2–114; De La Warr MSS · *The manuscripts of the Earl Cowper*, 3 vols., HMC, 23 (1888–9), vol. 1, p. 296 · *Calendar of the manuscripts of the most hon. the marquis of Salisbury*, 5, HMC, 9 (1894), 296 · *Diary of the marches of the royal army during the great civil war, kept by Richard Symonds*, ed. C. E. Long, CS, old ser., 74 (1859), 183 · exchequer decrees, 1650, PRO, E 215/126/5, 128/121 · J. Nichols, *The history and antiquities of the county of Leicester*, 3/1 (1800), 99, 150–55 · J. Nichols, *The history and antiquities of the county of Leicester*, 1/2 (1815), 601 · J. Nichols, *The history and antiquities of the county of Leicester*, 2/2 (1798), 61 · J. Nichols, *The history and antiquities of the county of Leicester*, 3 (1800–04), 158 · J. G. Nichols, *Transactions of the Leicestershire Architectural and Archaeological Society*, 2 (1870) · 'The letters of Alderman Robert Heyricke of Leicester, 1590–1617', ed. T. North, *Transactions of the Leicestershire Architectural and Archaeological Society*, 5 (1882), 108–62 · S. H. Skillington, 'Beaumanoir and its lords and their connexions', *Transactions of the Leicestershire Archaeological Society*, 22 (1944–5) · C. E. Welch, *Leicestershire Archaeological and Historical Society Transactions*, 35 (1959) · DNB · HoP, *Commons* · P. Watson [for forthcoming House of Commons, 1604–1629, ed. A. Thrush] · *Poetical works of Robert Herrick*, ed. L. C. Martin (1956), appx, 445–53 · R. Ashton, *The crown and the money market, 1603–1640* (1960), 160, 169 · E. Kerridge, *Trade and banking in early-modern England* (1988) · private information (2004)
Archives BL, accounts as teller of the exchequer, Add. MS 41578 · Bodl. Oxf., accounts and corresp., estate and family papers; exchequer, compotus rolls, orders, receipts, etc. · Leics. RO, formal papers; receipt for jewels made for the prince's highness | Leics. RO, autograph account book and payment to Robert Herrick
Likenesses line drawing, 1628 (after portrait, 1628), repro. in Nichols, *History and antiquities*, vol. 3, pl. 28; formerly at Beaumanor

Herries. For this title name *see* individual entries under Herries; *see also* Maxwell, John, fourth Lord Herries of Terregles (c.1512–1583); Maxwell, William, of Terregles, fifth Lord Herries of Terregles (c.1555–1603).

Herries, Sir Charles John (1815–1883), financier, was born in Chelsea, London, on 14 June 1815, the eldest son of John Charles *Herries (1778–1855), the politician, and his wife, Sarah Dorington (d. 1821). He was educated at Eton College and at Trinity College, Cambridge, where he graduated BA in 1837 and proceeded MA in 1840. He was admitted at the

Inner Temple in 1836 and called to bar in 1840. In November 1842 Sir Robert Peel made him a commissioner of excise. In 1856 he was appointed by Sir George Cornewall Lewis as deputy chair of the Board of Inland Revenue, and in August 1877 Disraeli promoted him to the chairmanship. In 1871 he was made CB, and in October 1880 (on Gladstone's recommendation) KCB. He retired in November 1881. His public services were acknowledged in a Treasury minute of 2 December 1881, which was subsequently presented to parliament. Herries died unmarried, on 14 March 1883, at his country house, St Julian's, near Sevenoaks, and was buried in the family vault at Sevenoaks. He wrote an introduction to the *Memoir of the Right Hon. J. C. Herries, by Edward Herries, C.B.* (2 vols., 1880).

FRANCIS WATT, *rev.* M. C. CURTHOYS

Sources *The Times* (16 March 1870), 8 · Burke, *Peerage* (1883) · Venn, *Alum. Cant.* · Boase, *Mod. Eng. biog.* · *CGPLA Eng. & Wales* (1883)
Archives BL, corresp. and papers, Add. MSS 57466–57468 | BL, corresp. with W. E. Gladstone, Add. MSS 44394–44764, *passim*
Wealth at death £26,557 0s. 5d.: probate, 28 April 1883, *CGPLA Eng. & Wales*

Herries, Herbert, first Lord Herries of Terregles (b. c.1460, d. in or after 1503), landowner, was the eldest son and heir of Sir David Herries of Terregles (d. 1495) and Margaret, daughter of Sir Robert Crichton of Sanquhar. Some unspecified illness seems to have been hereditary in this important Dumfriesshire family. In 1478 Herries, along with his first wife, Mariot (daughter of John, first Lord Carlyle), and his great-uncle, George Herries of Terraughtie, replaced his father as curators of his grandfather, John Herries of Terregles (d. 1483), who was 'incompos mentis'. By 1483 the same trio were curators for Herbert's father. On 1 June 1486 James III confirmed Herbert's resignation of Terregles, Hoddom in Annandale, and other Dumfriesshire lands to his son and heir, Andrew; this was done without stated reason, though if it was due to Herbert's illness, this did not prevent him from remarrying by 4 June 1493; his second wife was Mariot Cunningham.

In the parliament of February 1490 Herbert, who had been knighted in May 1483, was styled Lord Herries of Terregles. His elevation was perhaps in recognition of his family's importance to the maintenance of royal authority, and of order, in south-west Scotland; or it may have been a means for the government, dominated by Hepburns and Humes, to be seen to be distributing patronage more evenly after the rebellion of 1489–90 in the Lennox, while at the same time undermining the interests of Archibald Douglas, fifth earl of Angus (d. 1514). However, by December 1494 Herries was under the curatorship of Sir Robert Crichton (after January 1488 Lord Crichton of Sanquhar), Lord Carlyle, and George Herries of Terraughtie. The second two disputed the gift of marriage of Herbert's heir, Andrew, and on 25 November 1495 Andrew resigned Terregles, Hoddom, with its castle, and various other lands in the south-west to the then chancellor, the earl of Angus, expecting a full regrant and marriage to

Angus's daughter, Janet. But Andrew revoked this resignation on 3 December 1498 as Angus had regranted these lands to Janet alone. On 14 January 1502 Andrew became his father's sole curator. Herbert Herries was last recorded as alive in February–March 1503. He and Mariot Carlyle had four sons and one daughter.

MICHAEL A. PENMAN

Sources J. M. Thomson and others, eds., *Registrum magni sigilli regum Scotorum / The register of the great seal of Scotland*, 11 vols. (1882–1914), vol. 2 · G. Burnett and others, eds., *The exchequer rolls of Scotland*, 9–12 (1886–9) · *APS*, 1424–1567 · T. Dickson and J. B. Paul, eds., *Compota thesaurariorum regum Scotorum / Accounts of the lord high treasurer of Scotland*, 1–4 (1877–1902) · [T. Thomson] and others, eds., *The acts of the lords of council in civil causes, 1478–1503*, 3 vols. (1839–1993) · [T. Thomson], ed., *The acts of the lords auditors of causes and complaints, AD 1466–AD 1494*, RC, 40 (1839) · W. Fraser, ed., *The book of Carlaverock: memoirs of the Maxwells, earls of Nithsdale*, 2 vols. (1873) · *Scots peerage* · N. Macdougall, *James III: a political study* (1982) · N. Macdougall, *James IV* (1989) · *Eighth report ... county of East Lothian*, Royal Commission of Ancient and Historical Monuments of Scotland (1924) · W. Fraser, ed., *The Douglas book*, 4 vols. (1885)

Herries, John Charles (1778–1855), politician, was born in November 1778 in London, the eldest son of Charles Herries, merchant, and Mary Ann Johnson. His father was descended from a long line of Dumfriesshire lairds and in the course of his career in London had become colonel of the light horse volunteers, a select and prestigious London defence force that was to have an important bearing on his son's career.

Early life: a government 'man of business' Herries was educated at Cheam and at Leipzig University, becoming proficient in French and German, and returned to London in the first half of 1798 to find that his father was bankrupt. On 5 July 1798 he was appointed a junior clerk in the Treasury at £100 p.a., and in the unusually short space of six months was promoted to a post in the revenue department at three times that salary. How far this swift progress was due to his father's connections in the volunteers is unclear, but there was no doubt about Herries's talents for business and for economics. In 1801 he was employed to draw up for Pitt his counter-resolutions against Tierney's financial proposals, and in 1803 published a pamphlet, *A Reply to some Financial Mistatements in and out of Parliament*, which was a riposte to attacks on Addington's government by Lord Grenville and Cobbett. Earlier (in 1802) he had demonstrated other talents by publishing the first of six editions of his translation from Gentz's treatise, *On the state of Europe before and after the French Revolution, being an answer to 'L'état de la France à la fin de l'an VIII'*.

By this time Herries had become, in February 1801, the private secretary of Nicholas Vansittart, who, besides being the secretary of the Treasury in Addington's government, was also associated with the volunteers. This was a position he held while Vansittart was in office until March 1807, and it might have led to a customs appointment in Buenos Aires, worth £1000 p.a., had not Lord Grenville's government fallen before it could be implemented. When Vansittart declined to join Portland's government, Herries found himself unemployed. His father therefore wrote on his son's behalf to Perceval, the new chancellor

of the exchequer and the honorable treasurer of the volunteers, with the result that Herries became his private secretary at £300 p.a.

It was under Perceval's patronage that Herries began to attract wider notice for his administrative and financial skills. During 1807–9 he produced two short-lived government newspapers with John Wilson Croker, and in October 1809 was entrusted with the unsuccessful negotiations with Vansittart for the latter's accession to the government. In 1810 he did the spadework for the budget presented by Spencer Perceval, who as prime minister appointed him secretary to the chancellor of the Irish exchequer, William Wellesley Pole, in June 1811. His time in Ireland, however, was brief: having refused Wellesley Pole's offer to become a lord of the Irish treasury, he returned to London to be appointed commissary-in-chief with a salary of £2700 (1 October 1811). Perceval had earlier demonstrated his faith in Herries's services by having him appointed to the lucrative and influential sinecure of secretary and registrar to the Order of the Bath (January 1809), and in July 1811 recommended him to the regent for an appointment that he never took up—the comptroller of army accounts—on the grounds that he was 'one of the best men of business' that he knew (Perceval to the prince regent, 16 July 1811, *Correspondence of George, Prince of Wales*, 8.46–7).

Herries's career in the high-profile role of commissary consolidated his reputation. The main problems he faced were the corruption and inefficiency attendant on supplying the troops in the Peninsula. Building on the work of his predecessor, Herries tackled them with enthusiasm and skill, referring on one occasion to his having found his 'natural place', which was 'in the working class of politicians' (Gray, 326). Tests in English and mathematics were established to select new clerks, and the staff at headquarters in Great George Street grew to 53, with 20 commissaries-general and 1000 clerks serving at home and abroad. How far he was successful in a post that he held until October 1816 has been a matter of debate. In the case of three aspects of his work—the running of his department, the rooting out of corruption, and the settlement of subsidy payments to the allies—there has been no dispute. Herries was exceptionally able in all three fields, particularly in the settlement of subsidies amounting to the enormous sum of £42.5 million, half of which was handled by Nathan Meyer Rothschild and most of which was paid, for the first time, in advantageous foreign currencies. There has been some debate, however, about the supplies of cash to Wellington's armies. Napier, following Wellington himself, alleged that the armies' operations had been restricted by lack of specie, but more recent writers have judged that Wellington never appreciated Herries's difficulties in this department and that the latter's efforts did improve, most notably when he formed a plan with Rothschild at the end of 1813 to provide the army with French specie. Thus although the judgement that Herries was 'the unsung Carnot of Whitehall' (Gray, 330) may be an exaggeration, the sensible conclusion is that Herries's work was an important and largely neglected aspect of the war effort. It was certainly seen as such by the government when the office was abolished after the war (24 October 1816), Herries being complimented in word and deed, the latter taking the form of a pension of £1350 and the new post of auditor of the civil list. In 1817 Vansittart, the chancellor of the exchequer, went so far as to claim in the Commons that the great allied push of 1812–13 had depended on his friend's efforts.

Although his marriage on 8 February 1814 to Sarah, a daughter of John Dorington, clerk of the fees of the House of Commons, had been within his own social class, Herries was now moving in powerful circles and forging connections which caused some controversy. The friendship with Vansittart, and earlier Perceval, associated him with the evangelical and intemperate wing of the tory party and, more particularly, with Vansittart's economic thinking, which in its opposition to the resumption of cash payments and a bi-metallic currency was the reverse of Huskisson's, the most influential political economist of the post-war era. Moreover the collaboration with Rothschild and the fact that his brother owned a bank suggested that he had strong interests in the City, while being secretary to the Order of the Bath and auditor of the civil list meant that he was in frequent contact with the regent and his influential secretary, Sir William Knighton.

For the moment these associations did not interrupt his career as 'a man of business'. On 27 February 1821 he suffered the personal tragedy of the death of his wife (who had borne three sons, including the financier Sir Charles John *Herries, and three daughters), but in July of that year he was appointed a member of the commission of inquiry into the Irish revenue and wrote the report (28 June 1822) which was the basis for the eventual amalgamation of the British and Irish revenue services. This provided the impetus for his elevation to high office. Thus, when the financial secretaryship of the Treasury became vacant in that year Charles Arbuthnot, the patronage secretary, having consulted Canning and checked with Huskisson, recommended Herries as the replacement, and Lord Liverpool agreed to the appointment in February 1823. In the same month he was returned as a colleague of Canning's for the Treasury borough of Harwich and some time that year took a lease on Montreal, Lord Amherst's seat near Sevenoaks, while the latter was in India (1823–8). By that time he had resigned his secretaryship of the Order of the Bath.

Into parliament: Canning's ministry and the fall of Goderich, 1823–1828 Although he made no mark as a speaker, Herries played an important background role in the development of free-trade policies in Liverpool's government. One of his achievements was the consolidation of the customs laws and another was an engineered revival in the Lancashire silk industry. In general, the leading authority on the subject argues that he did as much to advance free trade in these years as Robinson, the president of the Board of Trade, although always with pragmatic as opposed to ideological motives (Hilton, 183–4). On the other hand, he was unable to shake off the faint whiff of scandal generated by his friendship with Rothschild and Knighton. Suspicious minds therefore worked overtime when Herries proposed that the banking crisis of 1825–6 was best dealt with by an inflationary policy that included the Bank of England and City financiers buying exchequer bills in the market place to keep them at a premium. The back-bench tory squires, who distrusted the City, were also alarmed, remembering, perhaps, that Herries had argued since 1819 for the re-establishment of a property tax.

In the first few months of 1827 Herries was beginning to feel the strain of what he called his 'laborious vocation' (Herries to Knighton, 27 Feb 1827, *Letters of George IV*, 3.200). He continued in the same office in the government that Canning formed in April, but in July asked to resign his post for one with fewer duties as a result of ill health. Canning agreed, asking him to delay until a successor could be found, but must have been disappointed, as Herries had earlier outlined an imaginative economic recovery plan which included revisions to the hallowed Sinking Fund, drastic reductions in expenditure, and the setting up of a Commons' finance committee to recommend such reductions. Indeed there are some grounds for thinking that Canning wanted to promote Herries to the chancellorship. He nevertheless had Herries appointed in the interim as one of the commissioners for supervising the restoration of Windsor Castle.

It was at this point that Canning died. By this time the king had become, of necessity, the guardian of the fragile coalition government that Canning had formed out of his own followers, the pro-Catholic tories and the Lansdowne whigs. He therefore asked Goderich to stay in office and become prime minister and, having failed to persuade Sturges Bourne to become chancellor of the exchequer, accepted Goderich's suggestion that Herries take the post, arguing later that he understood Canning to have regarded him as the best man to deal with the economic situation. The offer, which was accompanied by Herries's appointment to the privy council (17 August), created a storm of public controversy, the terms of which would have destroyed lesser men. No one questioned that Herries, to quote Lansdowne's acolyte, James Abercromby, was 'an excellent man of business' (Abercromby to Huskisson, 26 Aug 1827, BL, Add. MS 38750, fols. 95–6), but there was a widespread feeling, especially among the coalition whigs, that his connections in the City and at Windsor would make him a Trojan horse for Rothschild and the king, and that this was sufficient to disqualify him. Tories also greeted the prospective appointment with alarm; Arbuthnot referred to the narrowness of his 'mind' (Arbuthnot to Peel, 15 Aug 1827, BL, Add. MS 40340, fol. 174), and others asked what would happen if Huskisson, the leader of the Commons, was unwell, and Herries, who was regarded as a poor speaker, had to fill his shoes.

Herries, for his part, initially pleaded ill health and noted that the chancellorship was 'far above my pretensions and so much beyond my wishes' (Herries, *Memoir*, 2.51). He therefore urged Goderich to appoint Huskisson to the post—the man with whom he had been most at loggerheads over economic policy. This, together with the whigs' objections, led the prime minister to search for an alternative, but as his efforts became increasingly confused the king's determination in favour of Herries hardened, with the result that he was appointed on 3 September 1827. The controversy, however, did not end there. While Herries prepared his first budget, in which he apparently decided to include a property tax, a quarrel broke out over the appointment of a chairman of the projected finance committee. In November, without any prior consultation with Herries, and at Tierney's instigation, Goderich and Huskisson agreed to the nomination of Lord Althorp, one of the leading non-coalition whigs, as chairman. Herries resented this slight and insisted upon resigning if Althorp was placed in the chair, while Huskisson said he would do likewise if Althorp was not appointed. The real point of controversy was what happened next—an issue complicated by Goderich's confused negotiations and by the prime minister's decision to provide a place in the cabinet for Lord Holland, a non-coalition whig detested by the king. On two points all sides are agreed: first, that Herries stated on 28 December that he would resign if the policy or the composition of the government abandoned or compromised the principles of Lord Liverpool's administration—a statement that was taken to mean opposition to Althorp as finance committee chairman and to Holland as a cabinet member; and, second, that it was over this issue that Goderich resigned. Herries's view, which was articulated at length in the Commons the following year, was that the circumstances justified his action. Huskisson, however, detected a plot by the king to use 'his' chancellor to bring the government down, and argued that Herries changed his mind on the Althorp affair, having agreed to his appointment prior to the overtures to Lord Holland. Moreover, a leading authority has recently alleged that Rothschild and other financiers were becoming nervous about what a finance committee might recommend, and in December put pressure on Herries to put his foot down over the chairmanship (Hilton, 243–5).

In the current state of the evidence, it is not possible to add to this account. Given Herries's modesty and his practical abilities as a man of business, it seems unlikely that he was ever party to a plot by either the king or Rothschild. On the other hand, it is quite conceivable that, being new to the feverish state of high politics, he allowed the king's views and the fears of Rothschild to play a part in his thinking without fully realizing the capital that could be made out of it. Goderich's ineptitude and Huskisson's paranoia could also not have helped matters.

Cabinet minister and opposition front-bencher, 1830–1853

The immediate effect of Herries's action was the formation of Wellington's government and his own appointment to the cabinet as master of the Royal Mint, Huskisson insisting that the price of his own inclusion was that Herries should not be chancellor. From this undemanding position he advised the government generally on economic policy and supervised the proceedings of the finance committee on its behalf. Although there is no conclusive evidence, the likelihood is that his advice played a part in the government's decisions to cut military expenditure and to abandon the Sinking Fund; and he certainly wrote the financial statement which accompanied the committee's fourth report, on which Sir James Graham commented that it made the public accounts 'intelligible' for the first time. In February 1830 he added the presidency of the Board of Trade to his portfolio and was disappointed when the cabinet decided not to introduce a property tax as part of its budget that year—the third plank of the recovery programme that he had put to Canning. Moreover his stock fell as his weaknesses as a speaker became more apparent, with Arbuthnot remarking in July that he would be better employed below cabinet level.

Following the government's resignation in November 1830, Herries spent the next two years using his considerable managerial skills to re-establish the tories as an effective force. Initially he managed relations with the press and later established the party meeting-place in Charles Street, which was the precursor of the Carlton Club. In addition he was said to have taken the initiative in framing the motion on the timber duties in March 1831 that foreshadowed the defeat of Grey's government and the calling of the 1831 general election; and in January and July 1832 he moved a series of resolutions condemning the Russian-Dutch loan which, coming from such a knowledgeable source, inflicted considerable damage on the government.

The important role that Herries played in refashioning the tories as the Conservative Party was one of the reasons why Peel appointed him secretary at war in his short-lived 1834–5 ministry, although the fact that the army estimates which he framed for 1835 were lower than any voted since 1793 was an indication of his fitness for the post from a political angle. Thereafter, he cut an increasingly influential figure in the Commons—the theatre in which he had not previously shone. He was a prominent member of the select committee on metropolitan improvements and wrote the greater part of the second report for 1838. He also played an important part in debate during 1840–41 as a trenchant critic of the whigs' financial and commercial policies. His efforts, however, were not rewarded. At the 1841 general election he was unable to continue as candidate for Harwich, as a result of the Treasury influence wielded by the whigs, and was defeated in his candidature for Ipswich. Moreover, although Peel would have put him in the cabinet at one point, Herries declined an opportunity to be returned for Ripon, preferring by that stage to be consulted unofficially, as he was over the introduction of the income tax.

Herries was returned for Stamford as a protectionist in the 1847 election and, although he was now nearly seventy, his reputation as an economist was such that he quickly became one of the troika that shared the leadership of the party in the Commons, the other two being Disraeli and Lord Granby. It was in that capacity that he made a major speech in 1849 against the repeal of the navigation laws, Lord Stanley reporting that he spoke 'very slowly, sometimes hesitating, his voice feeble, but he made every argument tell upon the House' (Vincent, 5). In February 1851 Derby offered him the chancellorship of the exchequer in a government he failed to construct, and twelve months later said that his presence in another cabinet he was attempting to form was 'indispensably necessary' (memorandum, 23 Feb 1852, appended to Herries's letter to Lord Derby of the same date, Herries MSS). On this occasion, however, Derby wanted Disraeli as chancellor, and offered Herries the Colonial Office or the Board of Trade. Herries responded by saying that if he could not have the office for which he and the public felt he was qualified—the chancellorship—he would prefer one 'with small labour and responsibility' (Herries to Derby, 23 Feb 1852, Herries MSS). He therefore agreed to be president of the Board of Control—the position he held until the government fell in December 1852. He was returned again for Stamford at the general election of 1852 but retired from parliament at the end of the session the following year, his last speech (11 July 1853) being made on the Government of India Bill. He died suddenly at St Julians, near Sevenoaks, Kent, on 24 April 1855, and was buried in the family vault there.

Assessment Until comparatively recently assessments of Herries have focused on the controversy surrounding his holding of the chancellorship in Goderich's administration and, to a lesser extent, on the criticisms levelled by Wellington over supplying his Peninsular army with cash. A broader and more favourable view is taken now. It is therefore clear that he played a significant role in politics for more than fifty years, his most notable contributions being the reform of the commissariat in 1809–12, the settlement on favourable terms of the huge subsidy payments to the allies in the fourth coalition, the advancing of free trade in the 1820s, the reorganization of toryism during the reform period, and almost continuously (and well into his seventies) the giving of expert and pragmatic advice on the economy. This was no mean achievement for someone born a member of the professional classes. The last words can be left to his political opponent, Lord Brougham, who on Herries's retirement from parliament wrote that Alexander Baring, Lord Ashburton (1774–1848), the banker, had told him that 'you were, of all the men he had ever seen in the finance department, and I think he added, transacted business with, by far the most competent' (Herries, *Memoir*, 2.277).   P. J. JUPP

Sources E. Herries, *Memoir of the public life of the Right Hon. J. C. Herries*, 2 vols. (1880) · B. Hilton, *Corn, cash, commerce: the economic policies of the tory governments, 1815–1830* (1977) · G. K. Clark, *Peel and the conservative party* (1964) · D. Gray, *Spencer Perceval: the evangelical prime minister, 1762–1812* (1963) · J. Sherwig, *Guineas and gunpowder* (1969) · B. Jenkins, *Henry Goulburn, 1784–1856* (1996) · *The letters of King George IV, 1812–1830*, ed. A. Aspinall, 3 vols. (1938) · *The correspondence of George, prince of Wales, 1770–1812*, ed. A. Aspinall, 8 vols. (1963–71) · J. E. Cookson, *Lord Liverpool's administration: the crucial years, 1815–1822* (1975) · *Disraeli, Derby and the conservative party: journals and memoirs of Edward Henry, Lord Stanley, 1849–1869*, ed. J. R. Vincent (1978) · *DNB* · priv. coll., Herries MSS (transcripts) · priv. coll.,

Arbuthnot MSS (transcripts) · BL, Add. MS 38750 · BL, Add. MS 40340
Archives Chatsworth House, Derbyshire, papers | BL, corresp. with William Huskisson, Add. MSS 38745–38753 · BL, corresp. with second earl of Liverpool, Add. MSS 38297–38302, 38411, *passim* · BL, corresp. with Sir Robert Peel, Add. MSS 40357–40607, *passim* · BL, corresp. and papers, Add. MSS 57366–57465 · Bodl. Oxf., letters to Benjamin Disraeli · Castle Howard, Yorkshire, Carlisle MSS · Lpool RO, letters to fourteenth earl of Derby · U. Southampton L., letters to first duke of Wellington
Likenesses S. Freeman, print, NPG · G. Hayter, oils (*The House of Commons, 1833*), NPG · W. Walker, mezzotint (after W. Boxall), BM, NPG

Herries, Sir Robert (*c*.1731–1815), merchant and banker, was the eldest son of William Herries of Halldykes in Dryfesdale, Dumfriesshire, a distant descendant of the lords Herries of Terregles, and his first wife, Catherine, *née* Henderson. He had two brothers, two half-brothers, and one half-sister.

In 1750 Herries was sent out as an apprentice to his uncles Robert and Charles, who were merchants in Rotterdam. His ability was noted by the Amsterdam bankers and traders Hope & Co., whose connections were to serve him well. In 1754 he set himself up in Barcelona as a brandy merchant and took out his two younger brothers, Charles and William. He also acquired business interests in Montpellier and Valencia. While visiting Edinburgh in 1761 he was persuaded by John Coutts to become a partner in the Coutts' London commission house in Jeffrey's Square. This firm became Herries, Cochrane & Co. in 1762 with a sudden loss of Coutts family interests, caused partly by their attention to the new Coutts Bank in the Strand.

Herries soon quarrelled with the Coutts brothers over control at Jeffrey's Square. The brothers had retained a right of recruiting to the partnership, but Herries felt they were no more entitled to appoint him a colleague than to choose him a wife. In January 1766, with Cochrane removed, the firm was restyled Herries & Co., in which the Coutts' Edinburgh house was represented by William Forbes and James Hunter. With Forbes as a confidant, Herries evolved his idea for a new monetary service for the grand tour, a market which he estimated as worth £1.5 million per annum. Bills of exchange and the more usual letters of credit were both disadvantaged, the former by inflexibility, the latter by fees paid at each withdrawal. A network of agencies was to be set up across Europe where travellers could encash sterling 'circular notes' (forerunners of travellers' cheques) without deduction. The agents were paid commission by Herries, whose own profit was in the use of money taken for the notes before a journey began. Other types of instrument, especially a 'transferable note', were also introduced.

In 1769 Herries tried to implement his plan through Messrs Coutts. Rebuffed, he set up the London Exchange Banking Company at 16 St James's Street, and advertised his new service; partners included his uncle Robert Herries, and Forbes and Hunter. With the help of Hope & Co., some eighty agencies were established across Europe by 1770, rising to 141 some twenty years later, with two in Asia. Herries was at first resented by other bankers, who feared, quite rightly, that he was also poaching a client base for a conventional private bank. When he was knighted in 1774, the Exchange Bank became known as Sir Robert Herries & Co. The circular note scheme, soon widely copied, was temporarily checked by the French wars, but restarted in 1815.

Within Britain and the West Indies, Herries tried other monetary innovations, all abortive. He also pursued mercantile interests, especially in Barcelona, while his English commission house acquired a contract from the Farmers-General of France to buy for them tobacco, which was imported via Glasgow from North America. This was a volatile arrangement, with allegations of intrigue and price manipulation on all sides. In 1775 the French made a sly contract with a different intermediary, and Herries failed to negotiate an equally sly private deal with their leader. His reputation was already suffering: Joshua Johnson, a London merchant, referred to Herries & Co. in 1774 as 'damned rascals' (Price, 141). Sharp practice was too much for Forbes and Hunter, who resigned from Herries's commission house, as well as from the bank. In most affairs Herries can be accused of acting without scruple and too independently of his colleagues.

By 1793 Herries was married to Catherine Foote (1762–1808) of Charlton Place, Bishopsbourne, Kent; she was some thirty years his junior but predeceased him. They had no children. In 1793 Captain Edward James Foote, Catherine's brother, married Nina, whom Herries described in his will as 'my natural daughter by Martha Scott'. Foote divorced Nina in 1803 and remarried immediately; Herries took virtual custody of Caroline Foote, one of his three grandchildren. In 1798 Herries retired from his bank (which then became known as Herries, Farquhar & Co.) but not from wider business. He bought a small estate at Cheltenham, where he died in February 1815, some £340 in debt to his old firm. He also owed £400 to Forbes, whose friendship he had never forfeited. An untypically sensitive request was that his executor (Foote, by then a rear-admiral) should send Forbes two hampers, each of four dozen bottles of cider and perry, as there was no money in the estate to repay him. The bank, still at 16 St James's Street, was absorbed by Lloyds Bank in 1893.

JOHN BOOKER

Sources W. Forbes, *Memoirs of a banking-house*, ed. [R. Chambers], [2nd edn] (1860) • J. Booker, *Travellers' money* (1994) • R. S. Sayers, *Lloyds Bank in the history of English banking* (1957) • F. G. Hilton Price, *A handbook of London bankers*, enl. edn (1890–91) • *Joshua Johnson's letterbook, 1771–1774: letters from a merchant in London to his partners in Maryland*, ed. J. M. Price, London RS, 15 (1979) • E. Healey, *Coutts & Co., 1692–1992: the portrait of a private bank* (1992) • H. B. McCall, *Some old families: a contribution to the genealogical history of Scotland* (1890) • Lloyds/TSB Group, London, archives, Herries, Farquhar & Co. records • will, PRO, PROB 11/1567, fol. 188 • will, PRO, PROB 11/1274, fol. 223 [Charles Sackville]

Archives Lloyds/TSB Group, London, TSB archives, Herries, Farquhar & Co. records

Wealth at death virtually nothing: Lloyds TSB, London, archives, A26b/9; will, PRO, PROB 11/1567, fol. 188

Herring, Francis (*d.* 1628), physician, a native of Nottinghamshire, matriculated from Christ's College, Cambridge in 1582, graduating BA in 1585, and MA in 1589. On 3 July 1599, two years after obtaining his MD, he was admitted a fellow of the College of Physicians. He was censor in 1609, 1618, 1620, 1623, 1624, 1626, and 1627. He was named an elect on 5 June 1623.

Herring's first published work was *Anatomyes of the True Physition and Counterfeit Mounte-Banke* (1602), a translation from the work in Latin by Johann Oberndoerffer. He took the opportunity to add, by way of appendix, 'A short discourse, or discovery of certaine stratagems, whereby our London-empericks have bene observed strongly to oppugne, and oft times to expugne their poore patients purses'.

Herring's later writings concentrate on the plague and on anti-Catholic propaganda. In *Certaine rules, directions or advertisements for this time of pestilentiall contagion: with a caveat to those that weare impoisoned amulets* (1603, rev. edns 1625 and 1665), he asserted that although the plague was a punishment from God, there were practical precautions that could be taken. These included cleaning the streets, burying the dead outside the city, fumigation, and keeping people away from public places. He also noted that arsenic amulets were of no use. In 1604 he published *A Modest Defence of the Caveat Given to the Wearers of Impoisoned Amulets*.

Herring's other interest was verse of an anti-Catholic bent. His *Pietas pontificia* (1605), dealing with the Gunpowder Plot, appeared in several editions and was translated into English twice, as *Popish Pietie* (1610) and *Mischeefes Mysterie* (1617). Herring died in the early part of 1628.

GORDON GOODWIN, rev. SARAH BAKEWELL

Sources Venn, *Alum. Cant.* • Munk, *Roll* • C. F. Mullet, *The bubonic plague and England* (1956), 123–4

Herring, George (1832–1906), businessman and philanthropist, of unknown parentage, is said to have begun his career as a carver in a boiled-beef shop on Ludgate Hill, though this has been disputed. By saving money and judicious betting on horse races he soon built up his income. He then established himself as a turf commission agent, gradually increasing his business. In 1855 he was an important witness against William Palmer (1824–1856), the Rugeley Poisoner, an owner and breeder of racehorses who was convicted of poisoning a fellow gambler, John Parsons Cook. At Tattersall's and at the Victoria Club Herring built up a reputation as a man of strict integrity, and was entrusted with the business of many leading speculators, who included the twelfth earl of Westmorland, Sir Joseph Hawley, and the duke of Beaufort. Briefly Herring also owned racehorses, and in 1874 Shallow, his best horse, was a winner of the Surrey stakes, Goodwood Corinthian plate, Brighton Club stakes, and Lewes autumn handicap, four out of the ten races in which he ran. Although remaining an *aficionado* of the turf and interesting himself in athletics, Herring left the racing world for that of high finance in the City, where, in association with Henry Louis Bischoffsheim (1829–1908), he made a fortune. He was chairman of the City of London Electric Lighting Company, and was connected with many similar ventures. His powers of calculation were exceptionally rapid and accurate.

A 'rough diamond' with an unassuming lifestyle, Herring spent his remaining years and large fortune on a range of charities. From 1899 until his death he guaranteed to contribute to the London Sunday Hospital Fund either £10,000 in each year or 25 per cent of the amount collected in the churches. In 1899, 1900, and 1901 the fund, exercising its option, took £10,000 annually; in 1902, £11,575; in 1903, £12,302; in 1904, £11,926; in 1905, £12,400; in 1906, £11,275. The form of the benefaction spurred subscribers' generosity. Herring also supported a Haven of Rest: almshouses for the aged in Maidenhead, where he had a house. With Howard Morley he started the Twentieth Century Club at Notting Hill for working gentlewomen, and was a generous benefactor to the North-West London Hospital at Camden Town, of which he was treasurer. In 1887 he first discussed with 'General' William Booth the Back to the Land Scheme, the Salvation Army's plan for relieving the unemployed. In 1905 he proposed to advance £100,000 to the Salvation Army for the purpose of settling poor people on marginal land in the United Kingdom. Once established as petty cultivators, able to support their families, the settlers were expected to pay back the advance, which was then to be given by the Salvation Army to King Edward's Hospital Fund in twenty-five annual instalments. Herring eagerly defended the scheme when it was criticized as impracticable, and it was put into operation. The sum actually received from Herring was £40,000 under a codicil to his will. With this an estate was purchased at Boxted, Essex, comprising about fifty holdings, which Herring had visited and approved shortly before his death. In accordance with a decision of the court of chancery, the entire control of the scheme was vested in the Salvation Army, with Booth as sole trustee.

Herring, who lived a retired life and eschewed public recognition, died on 2 November 1906 at his Bedfordshire residence, Putteridge Park, Luton, after an operation for appendicitis. He also had residences at 1 Hamilton Place, Piccadilly, London, and Bridge House, Maidenhead. The urn containing his remains, which were cremated at Woking, was buried under the sundial at the Haven of Rest Almshouses at Maidenhead. After legacies to his brother William, to other relatives, friends, and charities, the residue of his estate was left to the Hospital Sunday Fund, which benefited to the extent of about £750,000. The bequests to charities under the will reached a total of about £900,000. On 15 June 1908 a marble bust of Herring, by George Wade, presented by the Metropolitan Sunday Hospital Fund as residuary legatees under his will, was placed in the Mansion House. On a brass plate beneath the bust is inscribed a letter received in 1905 by Herring from Edward VII, who warmly commended Herring's quiet and modest philanthropy.

CHARLES WELCH, rev. CARL CHINN

Sources *The Times* (3 Nov 1906) · *The Times* (10 May 1907) · *The Times* (19–20 Dec 1907) · *The Times* (13 Feb 1908) · *The Times* (16 June 1908) · *The Times* (3 Nov 1908) · *Sporting Life* (3 Nov 1906) · *WW*

Likenesses G. Wade, marble bust, 1906–8, Mansion House, London

Wealth at death £1,371,152 18s. 8d.: double probate, 23 July 1907, *CGPLA Eng. & Wales*

Herring, John Frederick, senior (1795–1865), sporting painter, was born on 12 September 1795 in Blackfriars, London, the eldest of nine children of Benjamin Herring (d. 1871) and Sarah Jemima (d. 1831), née Howard. His father was a fringe maker and upholsterer working from Newgate Street in the City of London. The Herring family were of Dutch origin and both his father and grandfather, Jan Frederick, pursued unsuccessful claims to family property in Curaçao.

Herring was never apprenticed to his father and was, therefore, ineligible to work in the trade. At the age of eighteen he was producing both inn signs and paintings (his parents had one of the Hampton Court coach); he had also learned to drive a team of horses. In September 1814 he took the Royal Leeds Union stage and arrived at Doncaster in time to attend the Great St Leger horse race. Lodging in the town, he came upon a coach builder's finishing shop and helped an employee complete the painting of a horse on one of the coaches. The coach builder was impressed and asked him to paint the insignia on the Royal Forrester. On the trial run of the latter he met the proprietor, Mr Hill, and begged of him the vacant post of coachman to the Nelson. He was given the job and followed the arduous profession for six years, ending up on the box of the prestigious High Flyer plying between York and London.

Within a year of arriving in Doncaster Herring had set up house with Ann Harris (1796–1838)—no record of their marriage has been found—and had seen the birth of the first of their children, John Frederick junior [*see below*]. In his leisure time Herring played the clarinet, composed music, and continued to paint. As the public became aware of his talent in the latter direction, he was increasingly pressed to turn full-time to art. Among his early patrons were his contemporary Mr (afterwards the Revd) Charles Stanhope, a severe critic whose opinion he dreaded; Mr Clarke of Barnby Moor, owner of the High Flyer; and Mr Hawkesworth of Hickleton Hall, whose repeated appeals eventually persuaded him to give more time to painting and who found commissions for him in the first year of his new vocation from the Hon. E. Petre, Sir Bellingham Graham, and others.

Herring's first exhibit at the Royal Academy was *A Dog* in 1818; in the following year he had his drawing of the fractured leg of a racehorse reproduced in the *Sporting Magazine*. The year 1825 saw the start of the scheme that made the name Herring a household word. The *Doncaster Gazette* arranged for him to paint the winners of the St Leger from 1815 onwards. The pictures were then engraved and published first by Messrs Sheardown & Son, owners of the *Gazette*, and subsequently by S. and J. Fuller, and then by Baily Bros. In all, Herring painted thirty-four winners, thirty-one of which were made into prints. A series of twenty Derby winners followed two years later in 1827. 'As a

John Frederick Herring senior (1795–1865), by unknown photographer, *c*.1860 [in his studio at Meopham Park]

pourtrayer of the thoroughbred horse in high condition, he is, and long has been unrivalled' (*Memoir*). In the same year Muir records that he took lessons from Abraham Cooper RA:

> For a man of thirty-two with an established reputation to take such a step is indication of an unusual strength of character, for successful artists rarely realise their limitations. Herring's studies under Cooper taught him all that his work had hitherto lacked in technicality. (Muir)

This is doubted by Oliver Beckett, but certainly his subject matter changed and increasingly he produced rural studies with more than a touch of the Romantic and sentimental.

By 1830, his fame as a painter of the turf established, Herring moved to Six Mile Bottom, near Newmarket, the headquarters of racing. He stayed there for three years before departing for Camberwell on the outskirts of London. He now had seven surviving children, three of whom became artists: John Frederick junior, Charles (1828–1856), and Benjamin (1830–1871). Another Benjamin (1806–1830), Herring's brother, was also an artist.

Although apparently successful, Herring was in fact in financial difficulties and was rescued by William Taylor Copeland, the owner of the Spode China Company. Copeland paid off his debts of £500, commissioned a number of paintings, and used Herring's images of fox-hunting to decorate the company's wares. Ann, aged forty-two, died in 1838 and Herring moved from Park Street to Cottage Green in the same village. He did not totally abandon

racing subjects and in 1840 visited France to paint the racehorses of the duc d'Orléans. Further renown came when he was appointed animal painter to the duchess of Kent (Queen Victoria's mother) and received commissions from Queen Victoria.

After twenty years in Camberwell, now married to Sarah Gale (1794–1882/3), he revolted against the smell from both the nearby manure factory and the house drains, and the hungry and thirsty uninvited guests, and made an instant decision to move to the country. He rented Meopham Park near Tonbridge, Kent. In this idyllic refuge, with outbuildings and 30 acres, he soon installed his favourite model, the white Arab Imaum, once given to Queen Victoria, together with other horses, a miniature pony that wandered around the house eating ginger nuts, ten cows, two pigs, geese, peacocks, fowl, duck, rabbits, and two dogs. This Noah's ark of animals soon featured in his immensely popular genre paintings of the farmyard which were no sooner completed than sold to the London dealers. Satisfaction at his success was marred by the death in 1856, after a long illness, of his favourite son, Charles, who had lived with him and worked as his assistant, for which he had been paid £500 a year.

Herring himself had suffered since his youth from asthma and bronchitis—as a result, he thought, of his early exposure, when a night coachman, to the bitter winter weather of the north of England. His health now began to deteriorate and for the last few years of his life he was confined to a wheelchair. He continued to send paintings to the British Institution and the Royal Academy until his death.

Although his work was disparaged by some—'Velocipede is cleverly painted but it wants effect; the background has not been sufficiently attended to' (*Sporting Magazine*, 1830, p. 175)—nevertheless it was eagerly sought by the increasingly prosperous middle classes. Engravings of over 350 of his paintings were made in his lifetime. Although suspicious that other artists might steal his ideas and apprehensive of forgers, he did collaborate with a number of his contemporaries—James Pollard, A. F. Rolfe, Henry Bright, Sir Edwin Landseer, C. E. Boutibonne, G. B. Campion, John Faed, W. P. Frith—to produce paintings in which he portrayed the animals and the others the background. He exhibited twenty-two pictures at the Royal Academy, eighty-three at the Society of British Artists, and forty-four at the British Institution.

Herring died at his home on 23 September 1865 and was buried at Hildenborough, Kent. Examples of his work are in the Tate collection, Doncaster Museum and Art Gallery, and a private collection in Kent. **John Frederick Herring junior** (1815/1821–1907), sporting painter, is generally thought to have been born in the parish of St George's, Doncaster, on 21 June 1815, the eldest son of John Frederick Herring senior and Ann Harris, and to have been baptized on 22 October 1815. However, another baptism is recorded: of John Frederick Herring junior and his sister Sarah Herring on 22 May 1821; the date of birth of the former is undecipherable. It seems probable that the first child baptized John Frederick Herring junior died and that the second was born between 1816 and 1821. Herring junior was still with his parents when they left Doncaster for Newmarket; he lived in Cambridgeshire for the rest of his life. He married Catherine Augusta (Kate) Rolfe (1828–1928), herself an artist and sister of A. F. Rolfe, who collaborated with Herring senior. She exhibited one picture at the Royal Academy and a second at the British Institution. He was not on good terms with his father; of all his surviving children, J. F. Herring junior was the only one not to be mentioned in his father's will.

Herring painted the same subjects and very much in the style of his father, in both oil and watercolour. His pictures were, however, inferior; they lacked the firmness and confidence of his father's composition and contained too much finicky detail.

Of all sporting artists the problem of attribution is probably greater with the Herrings than any others. Herring senior often made a number of copies of a popular painting, some unsigned; there were many forgeries of his work, both in his lifetime and in the twentieth century, and signatures of father and son are often confused. Herring junior sometimes signed his work J. Fred. Herring, sometimes J. F. Herring, and less often J. F. Herring junior. He exhibited fifteen paintings at the Royal Academy and thirty-five of his works were reproduced in the *Sporting Magazine*. Herring junior died on 6 March 1907. Examples of his work are in the British Sporting Art Trust Gallery, Newmarket.   ROBERT FOUNTAIN

Sources O. Beckett, *J. F. Herring and sons* (1981) · *A memoir of J. F. Herring esq.* (1848) · H. H. Dixon, *Scott and Sebright* (1862), 85–91 · A. M. W. Stirling, *A painter of dreams and other biographical studies* (1916), 256–86 · J. B. Muir, *The engraved work of J. F. Herring senior* (1893) · *Famous hunting scenes in Spode china: a unique and permanent record of the art of John Frederick Herring*, W. T. Copeland & Sons [1955] · *CGPLA Eng. & Wales* (1865) · *Sporting Magazine*, 2nd ser., 1/3 (July 1830), 175 · S. Mitchell, *The dictionary of British equestrian artists* (1985) · C. W. Graham-Stewart, 'Out of the shadows: Henry Leonidas Rolfe, master painter of fish', *Water-log*, 10 (June–July 1998), 29–31 · W. S. Sparrow, *British sporting artists: from Barlow to Herring* (1922)
Likenesses G. Jackson, watercolour, 1822, NPG · J. B. Hunt, stipple, pubd 1848 (after W. Betham), BM, NPG · photograph, c.1860, priv. coll. [*see illus.*] · J. B. Hunt, engraving (after W. Betham), repro. in *Memoir of J. F. Herring* (1848) · carte-de-visite, NPG · wood-engraving, NPG; repro. in *ILN* (1865)
Wealth at death under £4000: probate, 13 Nov 1865, *CGPLA Eng. & Wales*

Herring, John Frederick, junior (1815/1821–1907). *See under* Herring, John Frederick, senior (1795–1865).

Herring, Julines (1582–1644), Church of England clergyman and Reformed minister in the Netherlands, was born at Llanbrynmair, Montgomeryshire, and received his first education from his mother's kinsman, a Mr Perkin, minister at More chapel in Shropshire. Herring later joined his parents in Coventry, where his father served as sheriff and mayor, and he attended the school there. As a schoolboy he was unusually pious; he not only read the scriptures diligently but also engaged with two or three friends in religious exercises before going to play. In 1600 he was admitted as a scholar to Sidney Sussex College, Cambridge, from where he graduated BA in 1604. He subsequently returned to Coventry and was encouraged to study divinity by the renowned nonconformist minister Humphrey Fenn. Herring, along with his friend John Ball of Whitmore in Staffordshire, deliberately chose to be ordained by an Irish bishop in order to avoid subscription to the Thirty-Nine Articles.

With the influence of Arthur Hildersham, the prominent nonconformist vicar of Ashby-de-la-Zouche, Leicestershire, Herring was employed from about 1610 at the parish of Calke, Derbyshire, which was a peculiar jurisdiction exempt from the bishop's authority. Herring was a popular preacher, attracting auditors from twenty towns and villages in the area, and on Sundays so many people attended his sermons that they had to listen at the windows outside the chapel. Fortunately they could hear what he said, because Herring's voice was 'clear and strong'. At Calke Herring also influenced the young Simeon Ashe, who later became a prominent pro-parliamentarian minister during the civil war. Herring remained at Calke for eight years, but was eventually forced out, according to Clarke, by 'prelatical power' and by 'ill-affected men' (Clarke, 463). While he was at Calke Herring married Christian Gellibrand, daughter of a former preacher to the English company at Flushing; they had thirteen children. Through his wife's relatives Herring was connected with a network of godly preachers: one of her sisters was married to Robert Nicolls, minister at Wrenbury, Cheshire, another sister married Oliver Bowles of Sutton, Bedfordshire, and a third married a Mr Barry of Cottesmore, Rutland.

In 1618 Herring was invited by the corporation of Shrewsbury to be the lecturer at St Alkmund's, where he preached every Tuesday and every Sunday. Under his influence Shrewsbury gained a reputation as the centre of a puritan network which stretched from Cheshire through Shropshire and into Herefordshire. Herring repeated his Sunday sermon in the evening in rotation at the houses of the leading godly members of the corporation, Edward Jones, George Wright, and William Rowley. He also attracted puritan preachers from further afield to preach in the town, including Thomas Pierson of Brampton Bryan, Herefordshire, and his brother-in-law Nicolls. Herring was also welcomed to the house at Sheriffhales, Shropshire, of Lady Margaret Bromley, who entertained at religious exercises eminent puritan ministers from neighbouring counties, including Pierson, Ball, and Nicolls.

Herring spent seventeen years at Shrewsbury, but during that time the conformists in the town, led by Peter Studley, vicar of St Chad's, mounted a campaign to remove him and complained on numerous occasions about his nonconformity. In 1620, for example, he was presented to the church authorities for failing to read the prayer book and not administering or receiving the sacrament. As a result Herring was suspended from preaching several times and when in the 1630s his actions were drawn to the attention of Archbishop William Laud, the archbishop declared 'I will pickle up that Herring of Shrewsbury' (Clarke, 466). During his suspensions Herring took refuge in conducting private fasts and regularly expounded the scriptures three times a day to his family and neighbours. He also made a practice of attending church services on Sundays, in order to demonstrate his opposition to separation, and he was an early opponent of the Shropshire separatists Daniel and Katherine Chidley. In 1637 Herring was one of thirteen clerical signatories (who also included John Dod, Simeon Ashe, and John Ball) to a letter addressed to ministers in New England, which expressed the fear that they were adopting separatist practices. Eventually Herring gave up hope of being reinstated in Shrewsbury and he moved to Wrenbury in Cheshire where he lived with his widowed sister-in-law Mistress Nicolls. At Wrenbury he lived privately and comforted individuals with afflicted consciences.

In 1636 Herring was invited to succeed the ageing John Paget as minister of the English Reformed church in Amsterdam. After much 'seeking of God' and consultation with 'godly brethren', Herring accepted this post, although it meant leaving many friends and relatives in England, whom he feared he would never see again (Clarke, 468). He was also forced to take ship from Great Yarmouth to Rotterdam in secret in order to avoid a ban on travel without a licence. On 24 August 1637, before his departure, he drew up a will leaving bequests to his wife, his sons John, Jonathan, Samuel, and James, and his daughters Christian, Dorcas, Mary, and Joanna. He burnt many of his manuscripts and correspondence with other puritan ministers to avoid their seizure *en route* by the authorities. He arrived in Rotterdam on 20 September and his first sermon was so satisfactory that the English congregation accepted him immediately. At Amsterdam Herring was able to officiate within a functioning presbyterian system and he used his position to comment on the religious and political situation in England. He declared that he was not an enemy to the bishops personally, but only to their 'Pride and Prelatical rule'. He favoured a presbyterian church government, which he described as 'the Government of Jesus Christ' and drew attention to the errors of the English Independents. He prayed that the Scots might be an instrument of good in England and on hearing of the battle of Edgehill in 1642 he prayed to God to 'preserve thine own People, and maintain thine own cause' (ibid., 471). After a lingering illness Herring died on 28 March 1644 in Amsterdam. His will was proved by his widow on 26 March 1646. His lifelong refusal to yield to the authority of the English bishops made Herring a significant figure to the presbyterians in England during the civil war period.   JACQUELINE EALES

Sources S. Clarke, 'The life of Master Julines Herring, who died anno Christi, 1644', *A generall martyrologie … whereunto are added, The lives of sundry modern divines* (1651), 462–72 · will, PRO, PROB 11/195, sig. 29 · P. Lake, 'Puritanism, Arminianism, and a Shropshire axe-murder', *Midland History*, 15 (1990), 37–64 · Venn, *Alum. Cant.* · Julines Herring to Thomas Pierson, [n.d.], BL, Add. MS 70109/71 · N. Tyacke, *The fortunes of English puritanism, 1603–1640* (1990), 18–19

Wealth at death see will, PRO, PROB 11/195, sig. 29

Herring, Thomas (1693–1757), archbishop of Canterbury, was the son of John Herring, rector of Walsoken in Norfolk, who had previously been vicar of Foxton, near Cambridge, and his wife, Martha Potts. Herring attended Walsoken School before moving to Wisbech grammar school. From there he went in 1710 to Jesus College, Cambridge, where he was a contemporary of Matthew Hutton, who was to succeed him in all three of his episcopal offices. He proceeded MA in 1717. He moved to Corpus Christi College as a fellow (1716–23) where he taught classics, and where he was ordained priest in 1719.

Herring was a fervent whig supporter in university politics (as in national affairs). Having been appointed a preacher at Ely House by Bishop Fleetwood of Ely (to whom he was chaplain), Herring became known to Philip Yorke, then solicitor-general, who, later as Lord Chancellor Hardwicke, was to be his close friend and adviser. At this stage he also held a number of livings: Holy Trinity, Cambridge; Rettendon in Essex; Great Shelford; Stow cum Quy; and, very briefly, All Hallows-the-Great. But he resided at one living only, Barley, near Royston. In 1728 a DD was conferred on Herring, and he was appointed chaplain to George II. Preaching at Ely House earned him a considerable reputation, and he achieved notoriety particularly for attacking as immoral John Gay's *Beggar's Opera* (1728). This episode marked the beginning of a friendship and correspondence with William Duncombe, the published letters to whom form an important source for a judgement on Herring's public role and private sentiment. In 1731 he was appointed rector of Bletchingley through the patronage of Sir William Clayton, and advanced to the deanery of Rochester, the patronage of Hardwicke being instrumental in his promotion. He resigned Bletchingley, but retained the deanery, when he was appointed in 1737 to the bishopric of Bangor. There he performed his duties faithfully each summer, leaving charming accounts of his journeys, with a deep appreciation of natural beauty. In 1743 he was appointed archbishop of York—bishops Edmund Gibson and Thomas Sherlock having refused that preferment.

Herring's time at York was notable first for his visitation of the diocese in 1743, a detailed report on the contemporary church in an extensive area of the north providing important evidence on the condition of the Georgian church. The second notable feature was his leadership of the county when volunteers were raised and a county fund—supported by 'men of all parties'—established to resist the Jacobite uprising of 1745. (It was feared that the Jacobites would pass through Yorkshire as they advanced south.) Although a convinced whig, Herring's attitude to tories softened after the unity he had helped to create when danger was apparent. His leadership had been dependent on a close relationship with the three lords lieutenant of the Ridings of Yorkshire.

In 1747 Herring reluctantly accepted the archbishopric of Canterbury, bishops Gibson and Sherlock having refused the offer. He soon found himself in disagreement with the duke of Newcastle, the 'ecclesiastical minister', Herring favouring a more narrow range of (politically)

Thomas Herring (1693–1757), by William Hogarth, 1744

orthodox whigs. For the second half of his tenure of the primacy he was afflicted by increasing ill health. There was an early difference with Newcastle over the summoning of convocation (though both were agreed that that body should confine its activities to expressions of loyalty to the regime). On ecclesiastical appointments Herring often found himself at odds with the duke (whose nominations tended to be less narrow in range than those of the archbishop). Although attractive as a person and a warm friend, Herring was a weak primate, disliking the responsibilities of office, and following Hardwicke on matters of policy—the Marriage Act of 1754, the establishment of the British Museum, the reformed calendar—but also in the enactment and repeal of the Jewish Naturalization Bill of 1753, and the abandonment of a scheme for bishops in America. Talk on unity with dissenters came to nothing, as did correspondence with Swiss protestants.

Herring was a kindly man, promoted to his last office beyond his desires (or his capacities), and dominated, however benignly, by Hardwicke, and, impatiently, by Newcastle. He failed to see the emerging pastoral needs of his northern diocese where large industrial areas were growing. His tendency to appoint his relations to offices prompted the pun that York was a good sea for herrings. The archbishop never married. He died at his house in Croydon on 23 March 1757, and was buried in Croydon parish church.

Herring was uninterested in theological debate, his own convictions being concerned with conduct rather than doctrine. His sermons reflected this practical emphasis. With the exception of the sermon preached in York Minster during the Jacobite uprising, his discourses were plain and unadorned. His theology was latitudinarian in spirit, if weak in substance, reflecting an aversion to metaphysical speculation. His evident sincerity and charm make him one of the most attractive, as he was among the most reluctant, archbishops of Canterbury. But the relationship with Newcastle cast a shadow over his tenure of office, and his dependence on Hardwicke effectively deprived him of initiative, had he been disposed to exercise it.

William Herring (1718–1774), dean of St Asaph, born in Norwich, was the son of William Herring (*d.* 1762), a Church of England clergyman who was probably the brother of Archbishop Thomas Herring. Educated at Clare College, Cambridge, he graduated BA in 1740 and proceeded MA in 1743; he held a fellowship of the college from 1741 to 1743. In 1750 he married Elizabeth Cotton in Lambeth Palace chapel. In 1751 he was made a Lambeth DD.

In the early part of his career Herring was rector of the Norfolk villages of Alburgh (1742–3) and Edgefield (1743–7). In 1747 he became rector of Bolton Percy, Yorkshire, and in 1751 he was elected dean of St Asaph. Herring held both posts until his death in Yorkshire on 23 May 1774.

ROBERT T. HOLTBY

Sources Nichols, *Illustrations*, vol. 3 · BL, correspondence with Lord Hardwicke and the duke of Newcastle, Add. MSS · S. L. Ollard and P. C. Walker, eds., *Archbishop Herring's visitation returns, 1743*, 5 vols., Yorkshire Archaeological Society, 71–2, 75, 77, 79 (1928–31) · R. T. Holtby, 'Thomas Herring as archbishop of York', *Northern History*, 30 (1994), 105–21 · P. C. Yorke, *The life and correspondence of Philip Yorke, earl of Hardwicke*, 3 vols. (1913) · R. Browning, 'Thomas Herring, the court whig as pastor', *Political and constitutional ideas of the court whigs* (1982) · Venn, *Alum. Cant.* · *GM*, 1st ser., 44 (1774), 239 · *DNB*

Archives Borth. Inst., corresp. and papers · LPL, corresp. and papers | BL, letters to Nathaniel Forster, Add. MS 11275 · BL, corresp. with earl of Hardwicke, Add. MSS 35598–35599 · BL, corresp. with duke of Newcastle, etc., Add. MSS 32695–32870, 33058, *passim* · CCC Cam., Canterbury and York chapter and diocesan records · CCC Cam., corresp. with Sir George Lee · Hunt. L., letters to Edmund Gibson · U. Nott. L., letters to William Herring [copies] · W. Yorks. AS, Leeds, corresp. with Lord Irwin

Likenesses W. Hogarth, oils, 1744, Tate collection [*see illus.*] · attrib. J. Willis, oils, before 1745, LPL; version, Bishopthorpe Palace, York · attrib. T. Hudson, oils, *c.*1748, NPG; version, CCC Cam. · attrib. J. S. Webster, oils, *c.*1757, LPL · J. Macardell, mezzotint, BM

Herring, William (1718–1774). *See under* Herring, Thomas (1693–1757).

Herringham [*née* Powell], **Christiana Jane**, Lady Herringham (1852–1929), artist and copyist, was born on 8 December 1852 at Blackheath Park, Kent, the daughter of Thomas Wilde Powell (1818–1897) and his wife, Mary Elizabeth, *née* Marten. She was doubly fortunate as her father, stockbroker, art collector, and philanthropist, believed in women's financial independence. Well before the Married Women's Property Act of 1882 he assigned generous sums to each of his five daughters for their exclusive use. Upon his death in 1897 Christiana's inheritance attained a total sum of £45,000. Her husband, the physician Sir

Christiana Jane Herringham, Lady Herringham (1852–1929), by unknown photographer, *c*.1880

Wilmot Parker *Herringham (1855–1936), whom she married at St Nicholas's Church, Guildford, Surrey, on 21 September 1880, encouraged her interests in art. These included a study of early Italian tempera techniques, when oils were generally regarded as the serious painter's medium. In 1899 she published her translation of Cennino Cennini's treatise *Il libro dell'arte*, compiled probably in the 1390s. Following its publication in 1821 and translation into English by Mrs Mary Merrifield in 1844, this became the standard text on tempera and fresco painting techniques. By the 1890s many tempera paintings in the National Gallery, London, had become so obscured by dirt and discoloured varnishes that assessment of their true quality was difficult. Inspired by the writings of Morris and Ruskin, and using Cennini's treatise as a guide, she tried to recover what she called the lovely 'bloomy' quality of early Italian painting and to convince the public of its beauty. In 1901 she became a co-founder of the Society of Painters in Tempera, set up with the declared object of 'Improvement in the art of Tempera painting by the interchange of the knowledge and experience of the members'. Royal academicians ignored the society, but the technique proved popular among followers of the arts and crafts movement and in particular with the Birmingham group of painters and craftsmen, notably Joseph Southall.

In 1903, however, an urgent art crisis arose with the belated realization that because of new income-tax laws, masterworks in the great private collections were steadily leaving England for galleries and private collectors in Germany, France, and the United States. A new organization emerged slowly from D. S. MacColl's rather tentative suggestion after the Paris Exhibition of 1900 for a 'Friends of the National Gallery', to make acquisitions more systematically than the ad hoc committees and private subscriptions relied on hitherto. It was not only the National Gallery that needed assistance: the crisis expanded with public controversy over the administration of the Tate Gallery's Chantrey Bequest. June 1903 began a new era, when Christiana Herringham offered £200 to launch a National Art Collections Fund (NACF) to assist acquisitions for all of Great Britain's national collections. 'It is easy to make suggestions', MacColl wrote in retrospect. 'Lady Herringham, by this act, became the real Founder of the Fund.' The distinguished provisional committee first met on 7 July 1903, at the Herringhams' home, 40 Wimpole Street, with Lord Balcarres as chairman and Isidore Spielmann as volunteer secretary offering office space and staff. Christiana Herringham assumed (or was assigned) other secretarial duties. The inaugural meeting of the NACF took place on 14 July at 74 Brook Street, Balcarres's London residence. It began immediately to raise funds to supplement the government's inadequate appropriations. The crucial event was the acquisition in 1905 of Velázquez's *Toilet of Venus*, from the Rokeby Hall collection, on sale at Agnews for £45,000, in 1905 a staggering sum. By the most intense public and private efforts and Agnews' extended deadline, the NACF raised that sum from donors in all sectors of the society—not without some public suspicions about whether committee members profited privately. On 24 January 1906 the Rokeby *Venus* assumed its proud place in the National Gallery. This drama settled a major issue: the *national* collections were the *nation's* responsibility. The NACF receives no government funds for acquisitions; by 1999 its assets exceeded £32,000,000.

Christiana Herringham, who was uncomfortable about her position as the only woman on the committee, now moved on to another art-rescue effort. In 1906 the Herringhams toured India, and in Hyderabad state visited the Ajanta caves. They were appalled at the condition of the wall paintings of the life and times of the Buddha, the work of Buddhist monks who had lived and worked there from the first to the sixth centuries AD. The neglected paintings had deteriorated as a result of the effects of damp, droppings of countless bats and other creatures, and smoke from wandering hunters' campfires. In 1829 an inquisitive Englishman actually tried to remove parts of the paintings from the walls. Ill fortune dogged two attempts to copy what remained: in 1844 the East India Company and in 1872 the government of India authorized copies; both sets were destroyed by fire.

In January 1910 Ernest Havell protested at the Royal Society of Arts that the government's schools of art, while teaching that India had no fine arts, had Indian students copying mediocre European art instead of pursuing indigenous designs and subjects. Havell's protest inspired William Rothenstein together with Havell to found the

India Society in London. That winter Christiana Herringham went to India in a new effort to secure copies of the remaining Ajanta paintings. The nizam of Hyderabad provided a camp, servants, and guards, and Havell arranged for four art students to assist. Rothenstein, who shared her enthusiasm for Indian art, accompanied her, to see Ajanta and to look for Indian painters who used indigenous motifs. She returned in 1911 to continue copying, but something unexplained occurred and she became convinced that, as with the earlier copies, hers too were threatened by fire. That conviction, real or imagined, disabled her and prevented further work. After 1914 she lived at private nursing homes. Christiana Herringham died on 25 February 1929 at St George's Retreat, Ditchling, Sussex. Her Ajanta copies, bequeathed to the India Society for keeping in England, were loaned to the Victoria and Albert Museum and subsequently given by the India Society to the nizam of Hyderabad's collection.

MARY LAGO

Sources *The book of the art of Cennino Cennini*, trans. C. J. Herringham (1899) · M. Lago, *Christiana Herringham and the Edwardian art scene* (1996) · W. Rothenstein, *Men and memories: recollections, 1872–1938, of William Rothenstein*, ed. M. Lago, abridged edn (1978) · D. S. MacColl, 'Art at the Paris Exhibition', *Saturday Review*, 90 (1900), 326–7, 358–9 · b. cert. · m. cert. · d. cert. · J. Dunkerton, 'Tempera painting in England, 1880–1950', report for the diploma in conservation of paintings, Courtauld Inst., 1979 · *CGPLA Eng. & Wales* (1929)
Archives V&A | Harvard U., Rothenstein papers · NL Scot., Crawford papers
Likenesses photograph, *c.*1880, repro. in Lago, *Christiana Herringham* [*see illus.*] · photographs, priv. coll.
Wealth at death £66,042 5*s.* 11*d.*: probate, 23 July 1929, *CGPLA Eng. & Wales*

Herringham, Sir Wilmot Parker (1855–1936), physician, was born at Guildford, Surrey, on 17 April 1855, the elder son of William Walton Herringham (1824–1905), of Old Cleve, Somerset, then curate of St Nicholas's Church, Guildford, and later prebendary of Wells Cathedral, and his wife, Matilda Anne, youngest daughter of Colonel John Boteler Parker, commandant, Woolwich. He was educated at Winchester College and at Keble College, Oxford, where he was an exhibitioner and obtained a second class in classical moderations (1875) and in *literae humaniores* (1877). In 1931 he was elected an honorary fellow of his college.

After leaving Oxford, Herringham settled in London, where he was for a few months in 1876 a student of Lincoln's Inn, but gave up law for medicine and entered St Bartholomew's Hospital medical school in October 1877. He qualified MRCS in 1881, BM (Oxon.) and MRCP in 1882, and graduated DM (Oxon.) in 1888. He was elected FRCP in 1889. At St Bartholomew's he was Kirkes gold medallist and house surgeon to Thomas Smith; he became medical registrar, casualty physician, and in 1883 demonstrator of anatomy. Herringham was not appointed to the staff as assistant physician until 1895. He was physician from 1904 to 1919. He was also physician to the West London Hospital from 1883 to 1893 and to the Paddington Green Children's

Hospital from 1888 to 1900, and then consulting physician. After qualification he was also in private practice until the First World War.

In 1886 Herringham contributed to the *Proceedings of the Royal Society* (vol. 41) a paper entitled 'The minute anatomy of the brachial plexus', which was referred to with appreciation when in 1930 he received the second quinquennial award of the Osler bronze medal. In 1883 he succeeded F. H. H. A. Mahomed of Guy's Hospital, London, as honorary secretary of the British Medical Association's organization for the collective investigation of disease, and in 1884 he brought out the second volume of the reports containing the analysis of the collected cases of acute pneumonia. In 1894 he published with Archibald Garrod and W. J. Gow *A handbook of medical pathology, for the use of students in the museum of St Bartholomew's Hospital.*

Herringham's special interest was in diseases of the kidney, and he published many papers on this subject in the *Saint Bartholomew's Hospital Reports* and other medical journals. In 1912 he wrote a monograph, *Kidney Diseases*, which included chapters on renal disease in pregnancy by his colleague Herbert Williamson. The work was 'solid, substantial, and instructive' (*BMJ*, 915). At an informal meeting in May 1906, at Herringham's house, William Osler suggested a new professional association: the Association of Physicians of Great Britain and Ireland was formed a year later and Herringham agreed to act as its honorary general secretary. The other and related project which was discussed at this meeting, attended by Garrod and J. Rose Bradford as well as by Osler, was the founding of the *Quarterly Journal of Medicine*, which became the official journal of the association.

Herringham was also active in the chief medical societies in London which became amalgamated into the Royal Society of Medicine in 1907. In 1929 he delivered the Harveian oration before the Royal College of Physicians without notes, a *tour de force*. This was published in *The Lancet* (vol. 2, 1929), under the title of 'Circumstances in the life and times of William Harvey'; an extended version was later printed in the *Annals of Medical History* (vol. 4, 1932), in which Herringham described his discovery of a hitherto unknown portrait of Harvey. In addition Herringham was vice-chancellor of the University of London from 1912 to 1915, and he was knighted in 1914 for his services as honorary general secretary to the International Medical Congress held in 1913.

At the outbreak of the First World War Herringham was lieutenant-colonel in command of the medical unit of the London University Officers' Training Corps. As temporary colonel, Army Medical Service, he went to France as consulting physician to the forces overseas and attended Lord Roberts in his last illness. Until spring 1916 he was the only consulting physician at the front. He became attached to general headquarters, was made surgeon-general in 1917, and promoted major-general in 1918. He was appointed CB (mil.) in 1915, and KCMG in 1919. His book *A Physician in France* (1919) made a wide public aware of the part played by the medical services in an army at war. He was one of the four sectional editors of the *History of the Great War Based on Official Documents: Medical Services* (1922–4).

In 1918 Herringham unsuccessfully contested the London University seat as an independent. When he resigned his post as physician to St Bartholomew's Hospital in 1919 he became chairman of the reconstruction committee of the hospital, which was responsible for the creation of the posts of directors (subsequently professors) of medicine and surgery in the hospital. In 1920, the year after Osler's death, Herringham was offered the regius chair of medicine at Oxford in succession to Osler, but he declined as he felt that he was unsuited for the position. He was chairman of the General Nursing Council for England and Wales (1922–6), masterfully guiding it from the crisis which led to his appointment to its existence as an elected body. He was also chairman of the governors of the Old Vic (1921–9) and of the council of Bedford College, London. In 1909 he was made an honorary MD of Trinity College, Dublin.

Herringham married in 1880 Christiana Jane [see Herringham, Christiana Jane (1852–1929)], eldest daughter of Thomas Wilde Powell, stockbroker, of Piccard's Rough, Guildford; she was an accomplished artist in tempera and watercolour, and the translator of the *Book of the Art of Cennino Cennini* (1899). They had two sons; the elder died in childhood and the younger was killed at Messines in 1914. Herringham died at Heathcote House, Lymington, Hampshire, on 23 April 1936.

Herringham was a classical scholar, spoke French and Italian well, and learned Spanish late in life. With his pointed beard and deep voice he was a formidable personality: 'His temper, when he was a younger man, was not well under control, and was partly responsible for the fear and dislike which he inspired among those who did not know him well' (*BMJ*, 916). Herringham made his mark on medicine principally as an organizer, administrator, and teacher.   HUGH CLEGG, rev. PATRICK WALLIS

Sources Foster, *Alum. Oxon.* · Munk, *Roll* · *BMJ* (2 May 1936), 915 · *BMJ* (9 May 1936), 965 · *The Lancet* (2 May 1936), 1030–32 · *St Bartholomew's Hospital Reports*, 69 (1936), 27–39 [incl. bibliography] · *CGPLA Eng. & Wales* (1936)

Likenesses W. Rothenstein, oils, 1935, Keble College, Oxford · photograph, repro. in *BMJ* (2 May 1936)

Wealth at death £21,093 7s. od.: probate, 12 June 1936, *CGPLA Eng. & Wales*

Herringman, Henry (*bap.* 1628, *d.* 1704), bookseller, was born in Carshalton, Surrey, the son of John Herringman, yeoman, and was baptized on 14 March 1628 at the Carshalton parish church. His mother's name may have been Margaret. He served an apprenticeship with the London bookseller Abel Roper from 1 August 1644 until 28 June 1652, when he became free of the Stationers' Company.

Herringman is probably best-known as the publisher of John Dryden, but his first enterprising move was to purchase the stock of John Holden, who had died in May 1652, and to set up business at Holden's former shop at the Blue Anchor in the Lower Walk, New Exchange, London, during 1653. Samuel Pepys writes of several occasions when

he met friends and had news of Herringman's authors there. He married Alice Abel on 29 September 1653 at the church of St Dunstan-in-the-West, London, and with her had five daughters and four sons. At about the same time he began buying copyrights: the first book to bear his imprint was an edition of Horace's *Lyrics*, published in 1653; the first copyright he registered with the Stationers' Company was a translation by Sir Kenelm Digby of Albert the Great's *Treatise Adhering to God*, entered on 19 September 1653. By the late 1660s it is almost certain that, as Thomas Shadwell suggests in *The Medal of John Bayes* (1682), Herringman began employing the young Dryden to write prefaces, commencing a relationship that developed through the 1660s and 1670s when Herringman bought up the copyrights to most of Dryden's work. Dryden briefly mentions his publisher in *MacFlecknoe* (1682), describing Herringman as captain of a guard of 'Bilk't *Stationers*' (Dryden, 57).

Herringman's early association with the established literary publisher Humphrey Moseley was another important element of his career. The two published a number of works together, and after Moseley's death in 1661 Herringman purchased from Moseley's estate copyrights to the poems of Abraham Cowley, Richard Crashaw, Sir John Denham, John Donne, Sir John Suckling, and Edmund Waller, as well as some of the plays of Ben Jonson and Sir William Davenant. Although numerous entries in the Stationers' Company register attest to the variety of Herringman's early trade list, he concentrated on the publication of *belles-lettres* from the 1660s.

Herringman's middle career was assisted in some ways by the great fire of London, which saw the disruption of his competitors' businesses and the destruction of whole editions of many books, including much of Shakespeare's third folio. Herringman was instrumental in the publication of the fourth. Herringman bought few copyrights after 1678, concentrating instead on republishing popular literary works and bringing out collected editions—Francis Beaumont and John Fletcher in 1679, Shakespeare in 1685, Jonson in 1692. In 1684 he turned over the retail side of his business to Francis Saunders and his partner Joseph Knight. A year later he became master of the Stationers' Company.

It is evident from his will, written the day before his death, that Herringman's hope was to keep his publishing business in the family. He stipulated that his kinsman John Herringman should have 'my Coppyes and partes of Coppys of Books as they stand entered in the Register Booke of the Company of Staconers … provided that he serves out his seaven years of Apprentishipp justly and truly' (PRO, PROB 11/474, fol. 322v). Instead the younger Herringman abandoned a book trade career for the wardenship of the Carshalton parish church. Many of these copies were acquired by Jacob Tonson, who developed even more strongly the line of fine literary publishing begun by Moseley and Herringman.

Herringman probably retired to Carshalton in the mid-1690s, when his name no longer appears in the poor rate ledgers for the parish of St Martin-in-the-Fields. He died in Carshalton on 15 January 1704 and was buried at the parish church, where a memorial was erected.

C. Y. FERDINAND, *rev.*

Sources C. W. Miller, 'Henry Herringman, Restoration bookseller-publisher', *Papers of the Bibliographical Society of America*, 42 (1948), 292–306 · H. R. Plomer and others, *A dictionary of the book-sellers and printers who were at work in England, Scotland, and Ireland from 1641 to 1667* (1907) · parish register, Carshalton, Central Library, Sutton, Surrey, Sutton heritage [baptism, burial] · parish register, London, St Dunstan-in-the-West, 29 Sept 1653, GL [marriage] · poor rate ledgers, parish register, London, St Martin-in-the-Fields, GL · will, PRO, PROB 11/474, sig. 40 · IGI · *The works of John Dryden*, 2: *Poems, 1681–1684*, ed. H. T. Swedenberg (1972)

Herriot, James. *See* Wight, James Alfred (1916–1995).

Herron, Ronald James (1930–1994), architect and university teacher, was born at 330 Southwark Park Road, Bermondsey, London, on 12 August 1930, the son of James Herron and his wife, Louisa (*née* Leakey). Ron Herron's family circumstances were modest—his father was a leatherworker and amateur artist. He was educated at a local elementary school and, from 1944, at Brixton School of Building, where his exceptional skills as a draughtsman (which had been encouraged by his father) flourished. Originally set to become a carpenter and joiner, he was enrolled in the school's general course. A period of employment with the architectural practice of Leighton and Higgs—where Herron discovered the work of Lutyens—was terminated by two years of national service (spent mostly in Germany).

On his return to civilian life Herron resolved to train as an architect and returned first to the Brixton school, where he attended evening classes between 1950 and 1954. His training was completed at the Regent Street Polytechnic (1954–6). In 1954 he secured a post with the London county council (LCC), working in the schools division of the council's architects' department. He continued to work for the LCC until 1961 and these years were crucial to his professional development; at this period the public sector, particularly in London, employed some of the country's most talented young architects. On 20 December 1952 Herron married Patricia Marguerite Ellen (*b.* 1928/9), daughter of William Ginn, a leatherworker.

Herron worked on a number of school projects for the LCC—the school at Sidmouth Street, off Gray's Inn Road, designed with P. J. Nicoll, was internationally noted—before moving to the council's general division, then headed by one of his former tutors at Brixton, Geoffrey Horsfall. He was immediately set to work on plans for a new arts centre at the South Bank, adjacent to the Festival Hall (1951). The first scheme for what became the Queen Elizabeth Hall/Hayward Gallery complex drew some inspiration from the Mappin Terraces at London Zoo, and was conceived as a series of inhabited mounds. The scheme was subsequently redesigned under the influence of Corbusier and the new brutalism; Herron envisaged the Queen Elizabeth Hall as 'a highly tunable concrete box with a perfect view and an Eames chair'. It was further amended and developed before being constructed by the Greater London council in 1965–8, though the basic concept of 'an informal and accidental environment' persisted.

Herron's friends and collaborators at the LCC included Warren Chalk and Dennis Crompton, with whom he entered a number of major competitions. Some of these competition schemes were published in architectural periodicals and attracted the attention of Peter Cook, Mike Webb, and David Greene, who collectively formed the nucleus of Archigram. (The name was initially that of a magazine, founded by Cook in 1960, but was adopted by the group following the 'Living City' exhibition at the Institute of Contemporary Art in 1963.) Herron, Chalk, and Crompton were recruited as members of the most influential movement in post-war British architecture. Archigram's optimistic vision was of a built environment freed from the traditional constraints of time and place by the application of new technology: its futuristic images of portable or 'plug-in' cities fed into the high-tech movement of the 1970s. Herron's own 'Walking city' project (1964) remains one of the most memorable images of the Archigram years.

Herron's departure from the LCC was prompted by the offer of a position in the design team set up by Taylor Woodrow to redevelop Euston Station; the other members of Archigram were subsequently recruited. Between 1965 and 1968 Herron worked for Halpern & Partners and then for Colin St John Wilson before setting up his own office. Two years in California followed, initially teaching at the University of California at Los Angeles and subsequently working as director of design for the practice of William Pereira. This was to be the first of a series of visits to the USA. Victory in the competition of 1970 for a leisure centre in Monte Carlo led to the formal establishment of Archigram Architects (with Cook and Crompton as partners with Herron) in 1970, but to the trio's dismay the scheme was cancelled and the practice was eventually dissolved.

Teaching—at the Architectural Association and the North-East London Polytechnic—came to occupy much of Herron's time during the 1970s. He became a partner in the design practice Pentagram in 1977 (until 1980) and in Derek Walker Associates (1981–2) before re-establishing his own office in 1982 at North Gower Street. His architect sons Andrew and Simon joined the practice in 1985 and 1988 respectively.

Herron's most significant built work, the Imagination building in Store Street, Bloomsbury, was constructed in 1988–9, a radical conversion of an Edwardian school. The former playground at the centre of the building was roofed over in PVC-coated fabric, producing a lofty and luminous internal space, with slender bridges providing vertiginous connections across the void. The building, a practical embodiment of some of Archigram's preoccupations, won a number of awards and its success led to a merger of Herron's practice with Imagination, of which Herron became a director. In 1989 an exhibition at the Royal Institute of British Architects' Heinz Gallery, 'Sets and Things', explored the Herrons' pioneering use of computers in the design process. Following the termination of the Imagination partnership in 1993 Herron became professor of architecture at the University of East London.

Ron Herron built relatively little and seemed ill at ease in the constrained world of architectural partnerships, though his facility as a draughtsman and his extraordinary energy made him an asset to any office. A hands-on designer, he scorned conventions of dress, working hours, and position. Architecture, he believed, was 'the fusing of building and art to make something special'. His sudden death, as a result of heart disease, at his home at 20A King's Avenue, Woodford Green, Essex, on 2 October 1994 was unexpected: many felt that his best built work was yet to come. His wife survived him. In 2002 the Archigram group was awarded the RIBA's royal gold medal. Herron's son received the medal on behalf of his father.   KENNETH POWELL

Sources *The Independent* (5 Oct 1994) · *The Times* (13 Oct 1994) · *Architect's Journal* (6 Oct 1994) · S. Lyall, *Imagination headquarters* (1992) · *Sets and things* (1989) [exhibition catalogue, Heinz Gallery, London, 1989] · private information (2004) [Peter Cook, Simon Herron] · b. cert. · m. cert. · d. cert.

Herschel, Alexander Stewart (1836–1907), astronomer, was the fifth of twelve children (and second son) of Sir John Frederick William *Herschel, first baronet (1792–1871), and Margaret Brodie, second daughter of the Revd Dr Alexander Stewart of Dingwall, Ross-shire, and grandson of Sir William *Herschel. He was born on 5 February 1836 at Feldhausen, near Cape Town, Cape Colony, where his father was engaged in his influential astronomical observations of the southern hemisphere. The family returned to England in 1838, and after some private education the young Herschel was sent to Clapham grammar school in 1851, where Charles Pritchard, afterwards Savilian professor of astronomy, was headmaster. In 1855 Herschel proceeded to Trinity College, Cambridge, where he graduated BA as twentieth wrangler in 1859, proceeding MA in 1877. While an undergraduate he helped Professor James Clerk Maxwell with his illustrations of the mechanics of rotation by means of the apparatus known as 'the devil on two sticks'. From Cambridge Herschel passed in 1861 to the Royal School of Mines, London, and began the observation of meteors which he continued to the end of his life and which represents his main claim to fame. However, his early writing included much on meteorology.

From 1866 to 1871 Herschel was lecturer on natural philosophy and professor of mechanical and experimental physics in the University of Glasgow. From 1871 to 1886 he was the first professor of physics and experimental philosophy in the University of Durham College of Science, Newcastle upon Tyne. At the Durham College Herschel provided, chiefly by his personal exertions, apparatus for the newly installed laboratory, some being made by his own hands. When the college migrated as Armstrong College to new buildings, the new Herschel Physical Laboratory was named after him.

Throughout his life Herschel kept extensive records of his own observations of meteors. He also accomplished important work in the compilation, reduction, and discussion of the results of other observers with whom he corresponded in all parts of the world. With R. P. Greg he constructed extensive catalogues of the radiant points of meteor streams. These were published as reports of the British Association. From 1862 to 1881 he was reporter to the committee of the British Association on 'observations of luminous meteors'. He provided annual reports of bright meteors observed, and of the progress of meteoric science. From 1874 to 1881 he also submitted reports of a committee, consisting of himself, his colleague at Newcastle, Professor A. G. Lebour, and J. T. Dunn, which was formed to determine the thermal conductivities of certain rocks. In the same way he prepared annual reports on meteoric astronomy for the Royal Astronomical Society from 1872 to 1880. At this time, there was great interest in the link between meteor showers and comets. In 1872, Herschel predicted there would be a major shower from Biela's comet—a prediction that was fulfilled in November that year. His great precision in noting the paths of meteors among the stars was of use to others. From his determination of the radiant point of the November Leonids, G. V. Schiaparelli (1835–1910) deduced the identity of their orbit with that of Tempel's comet of 1866.

Herschel was interested in many branches of physical science. One example is spectroscopy, which he also applied to his meteor observations. Like his father, he had a keen interest in photography and photographic processes. He was elected FRS in 1884, an honour already conferred on his grandfather, his father, and his younger brother John. In 1886 he gave up his professorship, and was made DCL of Durham University. In 1888, with other members of his family, he went to live at Observatory House, Slough, the house where his grandfather, Sir William Herschel, had lived. There he became increasingly reclusive (though he visited Spain to observe the solar eclipse of 1905), and also increasingly neglected his health. Yet he continued observing meteors: his final observations were made only months before his death.

Herschel died, unmarried, at Observatory House on 18 June 1907, and was buried in St Lawrence's Church, Upton, near Slough, where his grandfather was also buried.   H. P. HOLLIS, *rev.* A. J. MEADOWS

Sources H. H. T. [H. H. Turner], *Monthly Notices of the Royal Astronomical Society*, 68 (1907–8), 231–3 · G. Buttmann, *The shadow of the telescope: a biography of John Herschel*, ed. D. S. Evans, trans. B. E. J. Pagel, [another edn] (1974)
Archives Yorkshire Museum, York, corresp. | Air Force Research Laboratories, Cambridge, Massachusetts, letters to Lord Rayleigh · U. Newcastle, letters to Sir Walter Trevelyan
Likenesses photograph, 1893, Sci. Mus.
Wealth at death £3964 8s. 1d.: probate, 5 Sept 1907, CGPLA Eng. & Wales

Herschel, Caroline Lucretia (1750–1848), astronomer, was born at Hanover on 16 March 1750, the eighth child and fourth daughter of Isaac Herschel (1707–1767) and his wife, Anna Ilse Moritzen, of Neustadt. Isaac, a former gardener, was an oboist in the Hanoverian foot guards, and though his formal education was limited he possessed an

Caroline Lucretia Herschel (1750–1848), by George Müller, 1847

intellectual curiosity that he successfully communicated to Caroline's brothers. Her illiterate mother, however, had no doubt that a daughter's place was in the home, helping with the housework; she opposed all attempts by Caroline to acquire anything more than the most rudimentary education, and resented even the occasional violin lesson given by her father. Caroline tried to acquire some ability in needlework from a kindly neighbour, but for this they had to meet at dawn, for at 7 a.m. her household chores would begin.

Hanover childhood Caroline's childhood was overshadowed by the defeat in 1757 of the Hanoverian army by the French in the Seven Years' War and the resulting occupation of Hanover. Her elder brother William [see Herschel, Sir William], though in the same band as their father, was too young to be under oath, and so was free to flee to England. In 1767 Isaac, whose health had been poor for many years, died, leaving Caroline's fate in the hands of her mother and brothers. Eventually she was given grudging permission to attend a dressmaking school, but this lasted only a few weeks, after which she resumed her role of household drudge.

Meanwhile William, who by now was established as organist of a chapel in Bath, devised a scheme to liberate his sister from her Hanoverian servitude. He proposed that she be allowed to join him in Bath, at least for a period, to see whether she could be trained as a singer to assist him in his concerts. At first opinion within the family was favourable, but then her eldest brother, Jacob, began to ridicule the idea. Eventually, in August 1772, William travelled to Hanover and prevailed on their mother to release his sister, smoothing the way by the promise of an annuity to pay for a substitute servant.

Music in Bath The couple left Hanover later in the month, and after an eventful and sometimes perilous journey reached London. There William took the opportunity to visit the shops of opticians: his thoughts were turning away from music and towards astronomy.

In Bath, Caroline took over the running of the household, no easy task as she was virtually uneducated and had limited English. She found it still more difficult to integrate herself into the fashionable society whose members came to take the waters at Bath. But at least her natural abilities were now given free rein: her brother gave her two singing lessons daily, sometimes three, as well as teaching her English and arithmetic, and she had coaching from a dancing-mistress to give her the stage presence required for oratorios. Before long she was appearing at Bath or Bristol as many as five nights a week, singing leading soprano parts in works such as *Messiah*, *Samson*, and *Judas Maccabaeus*. The transformation wrought by William was dramatic: only a short while before, Caroline had been qualified to work only as a housemaid.

But the brother who had rescued Caroline was now to prove so self-centred as to destroy her new career without so much as noticing. William was becoming obsessed with the ambition to explore what he later termed 'the construction of the heavens', and in order to study distant and faint celestial objects he would need telescopes as big as possible. These, he found, he would have to make for himself. Caroline, he assumed, would do whatever was necessary to help. Thus she found the summer of 1775 'taken up with copying Music and practising, besides attendance on my Brother when polishing [telescopic mirrors], that by way of keeping him alife, I was even obliged to feed him by putting the vitals by bits into his mouth' (Lubbock, 68).

Their lives were transformed by William's discovery in March 1781 of the planet Uranus, which he chanced upon as he was systematically familiarizing himself with all the brighter stars. His scientific friends seized the opportunity to persuade the king to grant him a pension that would enable him to give up music for astronomy, his only duties being to show the heavens to the royal family when requested. William eagerly accepted, taking it for granted that Caroline would give up her career in music and partner him in his new vocation.

The apprentice astronomer William and Caroline arrived at their new home at Datchet, near Windsor Castle, in August 1782. Caroline was dismayed at the dilapidated condition of the house William had taken and at the high price of the local food. But these were the least of her problems. 'I found', she wrote later,

> I was to be trained for an assistant Astronomer; and by way of encouragement a Telescope adapted for sweeping … was given to me. I was to sweep for comets. … But it was not till the last two months of the same year before I felt the least encouragement for spending the starlight nights on a grass-plot convered by dew or hoar frost without a human being near enough to be within call.   (Lubbock, 150)

By the following summer William had built her a telescope expressly designed for the discovery of comets. 'Its movements', he wrote, 'are so convenient, that the eye remains at rest while the instrument makes a sweep from the horizon to the zenith' (W. Herschel, *PTRS*, 90, 1800, 71). In 1791 this sweeper was superseded by a more powerful instrument, of 9 inches aperture and 5 foot focal length. Two years later the astronomer royal, Nevil Maskelyne, visited the Herschels and left the following description of Caroline at work:

> [The sweeper] is a very powerful instrument, & shews objects very well ... The height of the eye-glass is altered but little in sweeping from the horizon to the zenith. This she does and down again in 6 or 8 minutes, & then moves the telescope a little forward in azimuth, & sweeps another portion of the heavens in like manner. She will thus sweep a quarter of the heavens in one night.   (RAS, Pigott MSS, letter 60)

Caroline was to become famous as the discoverer, or co-discoverer, of no fewer than eight comets, four with the sweeper made in 1783, three with its successor, and the last, found in 1797, with the naked eye. However, her earliest sweeps, in the winter of 1782–3, yielded not comets but comet-like nebulae, to add to the hundred or so already known. Later in 1783 she was to discover the companion to the Andromeda nebula.

Excited by these discoveries, Caroline quickly became reconciled to her new career. William, duly impressed, himself began to sweep for nebulae with a small refractor. But whereas the detection of newly arriving comets was an urgent task calling for small instruments with wide fields of view, the study of the permanent nebulae was best done, slowly and methodically, with the most powerful telescope available. In October 1783 William completed the ideal instrument for the purpose, a reflector of 20 foot focal length and 18 inches aperture, and with a stable mounting; and a few days later he and Caroline began to sweep the visible sky, strip by strip, in the search for nebulae. The instrument was directed to the south, at a particular elevation, and at the eyepiece William watched the sky drift past, waiting for a nebula to come into view. He then shouted out a description to Caroline, who was seated at a desk in a room nearby, next to an open window, 'with Flamsteed's Atlas open before her. As he gives her the word, she writes down the declination and right ascension and the other circumstances of the observation' (Lubbock, 138). Afterwards, Caroline would write up a fair copy and carry out the necessary calculations. Her many other duties included preparing lists of stars for use in the sweeps as position indicators and making fair copies of the resulting papers for publication in *Philosophical Transactions*.

Caroline was an indispensable member of a most remarkable team that, in one of the greatest campaigns known to observational astronomy, swept the whole of the visible sky. In twenty years of unremitting toil, brother and sister increased the number of known nebulae from about a hundred to 2500. In 1787 Caroline too received a royal pension, of £50 a year; revealingly, this was the first money that she felt she could consider her own. Meanwhile she continued to manage their domestic affairs as the mistress of William's household. In 1788 this

well-established routine received what was to Caroline a most unwelcome disruption, when at the age of forty-nine William decided to marry the widow of a neighbour. Caroline, who until then had been his inseparable companion in every aspect of his life, now had to move into lodgings; and although she eventually became reconciled to the change and doted on her nephew John, born in 1792, she later destroyed her diary for the period.

Respected astronomer   The standard catalogue of stars was the *British Catalogue* of John Flamsteed, published in 1725. William had found his work increasingly hampered by errors in the catalogue, and in 1796 he persuaded Caroline to assemble a list of these errors, a task that took her twenty months. Her list, with an index to Flamsteed's observations, was published by the Royal Society in 1798.

This, and her cometary discoveries, earned Caroline the profound respect of the professional astronomers of the day; thus she spent a week in August 1799 at Greenwich as guest of the astronomer royal. She was also friendly with various members of the royal family, one of the queen's ladies-in-waiting having been a fellow student of Caroline's in a dressmaking class in Hanover. In 1787 Fanny Burney described 'the celebrated comet-searcher' as 'very little, very gentle, very modest, and very ingenuous; and her manners are those of a person unhackneyed and unawed by the world, yet desirous to meet and return its smiles' (*Memoir and Correspondence*, 125).

Return to Hanover   William was older than Caroline and lacked her physical toughness, and in the second decade of the new century his health began to decline. He died in August 1822, and in her grief Caroline made the impulsive decision to quit England and return to Hanover. It was a mistake, for in the half-century since her departure the town had changed beyond recognition. She thought she had returned home to die, but in fact she had many more years of good health left to her, yet the astronomical research that had motivated her life in England was no longer possible: 'at the heavens there is no getting, for the high roofs of the opposite houses' (*Memoir and Correspondence*, 131).

There was, however, one last contribution to astronomy that Caroline could make. In his declining years William had persuaded his son John to abandon his intended academic career and take over his father's work as a student of the heavens. But revision of the great catalogues of nebulae was made difficult by their organization by class rather than position. To facilitate her nephew's re-examination of the nebulae, Caroline therefore undertook the massive task of rearranging the catalogues into a more suitable form. It was work that called for her immense industry and capacity for taking pains, a chore gladly undertaken because it would enable her nephew to bring still greater glory to her departed brother. For this achievement she was awarded a gold medal of the Astronomical Society. Sir David Brewster termed her catalogue 'an extraordinary monument of the unextinguished ardour of a lady of seventy-five in the cause of abstract science' (*Memoir and Correspondence*, 132).

The sturdy health Caroline had enjoyed throughout life, except for a childhood attack of typhus fever, continued. When John visited her in 1832, before leaving for the Cape of Good Hope to survey the southern skies, he recorded that his 82-year-old aunt

> runs about the town with me and skips up her two flights of stairs … In the morning till eleven or twelve she is dull and weary, but as the day advances she gains life, and is quite 'fresh and funny' at ten or eleven p.m. and sings old rhymes, nay, even dances to the great delight of all who see her. (Lubbock, 372)

On his return from Africa he visited his aunt again; but, unable to face the emotion of a final farewell, he slipped away before dawn, leaving her devastated. She lived long enough to hold in her hands John's magnificent volume of Cape *Observations*, which completed the pioneering work that she and William had carried out for the skies visible from England.

Declining years Caroline was a local celebrity, visited by passing scientists of the calibre of Humboldt and Gauss. For her ninety-sixth birthday Humboldt presented her with the gold medal for science, in the name of the king of Prussia; a year later she entertained the crown prince and princess for two hours, and sang them a song by William.

Caroline Herschel had devoted her life unstintingly to the brother who had rescued her from poverty and servitude in Hanover, and her gratitude had known no bounds. During the sweeps for nebulae, as she spent her nights acting as scribe and running errands for her brother on the platform of the telescope, 'I had … the comfort to see that my brother was satisfied with my endeavours to assist him' (*Memoir and Correspondence*, 52). In later life she would allow nothing to detract from William's reputation, constantly downplaying her own part in their achievement: 'I did nothing for my brother, but what a well-trained puppy-dog would have done' (Clerke, 140). After her death, a cousin wrote to John: 'She looked upon progress in science as so much detraction from her brother's fame' (*Memoir and Correspondence*, 346). Nevertheless, she was too intelligent to be unaware that she could have carved out her own career if her mother had not blocked her every attempt at education, and if her brother had not sacrificed her musical vocation to his own ambitions in astronomy: 'I have been throughout annoyed and hindered in my endeavours at perfecting myself in any branch of knowledge by which I could hope to gain a creditable livelihood' (ibid., 31). Yet it would be hard to identify a single original thought that passed through her mind. Her greatest assets lay in her inexhaustible industry, loyalty, and dedication; although William was one of the greatest astronomers in history, his achievement would have been wholly impossible without the partnership of his devoted sister.

Caroline Herschel died peacefully in Hanover on 9 January 1848, aged ninety-seven, and was buried in the churchyard of the Gartengemeinde, Hanover, alongside her parents and with a lock of her brother's hair in her coffin.

MICHAEL HOSKIN

Sources Mrs J. Herschel, *Memoir and correspondence of Caroline Herschel* (1876) • C. A. Lubbock, ed., *The Herschel chronicle: the life-story of William Herschel and his sister Caroline Herschel* (1933) • A. M. Clerke, *The Herschels and modern astronomy* (1895) • J. F. W. Herschel, *Memoirs of the Royal Astronomical Society*, 17 (1847–8), 120–22 • M. Hoskin and B. Warner, 'Caroline Herschel's comet sweepers', *Journal for the History of Astronomy*, 12 (1981), 27–34 • *The scientific papers of Sir William Herschel*, ed. J. L. E. Dreyer, 2 vols. (1912) • A. J. Turner and others, *Science and music in eighteenth-century Bath* (1977) [exhibition catalogue, the Holburne of Menstrie Museum, Bath, 22 Sept – 29 Dec 1977] • RAS, Pigott MSS

Archives priv. coll. • Ransom HRC, corresp. and papers • RAS, corresp. and papers | BL, letters to Sir John Herschel, Egerton MSS 3761–3762 • Harvard U., Houghton L., scientific papers

Likenesses silhouette, before 1772, MHS Oxf. • M. F. Tielemann, oils, 1829, priv. coll. • G. Müller, engraving, 1847, AM Oxf. [*see illus.*] • J. Brown, stipple (aged ninety-two), NPG • engraving (after portrait, aged ninety-seven), repro. in Lubbock, ed., *Herschel chronicle*

Wealth at death books and minor personal effects: inventory, Herschel, *Memoir*, appx

Herschel, Sir John Frederick William, first baronet (1792–1871), mathematician and astronomer, was born on 7 March 1792 in Slough, the only child of the marriage in 1788 of Sir William *Herschel (1738–1822), astronomer, and the widow Mary Pitt, *née* Baldwin (1762/3–1832?). His father was of German ancestry, his mother English.

Early life and education, 1792–1813 At the time of John Herschel's birth, his father, William Herschel, had set aside his musical career and had established himself as an internationally prominent astronomer by his discovery in 1781 of the planet Uranus, his construction of the most powerful telescopes of the period, and his pioneering studies of stellar astronomy. To these efforts his sister Caroline Lucretia *Herschel (1750–1848) made important contributions, as she also did to his son's upbringing. After attending Mr Bull's school at Newbury, and a short period of study at Eton College in 1800, John Herschel enrolled at Dr Gretton's private school at Hitcham, Buckinghamshire. More important, he received private instruction, especially in mathematics, from Alexander Rogers.

On 19 October 1809 John Herschel entered St John's College, Cambridge. Widely recognized as very gifted, he graduated in 1813 as senior wrangler and first Smith's prizeman and was soon elected to a fellowship at St John's. In May 1813 the Royal Society elected Herschel, already a published mathematician, to membership.

John Herschel's gift for mathematics, which brought such success in the Cambridge mathematical competitions, was also evident in his efforts, along with his fellow undergraduates and long-time friends Charles *Babbage and George Peacock, to induce Cambridge University to set aside the Newtonian, fluxional methods of mathematical analysis in favour of instruction based on continental, Leibnizian techniques. The Analytical Society, which these undergraduates formed under Herschel's leadership, emerged as a significant force for the reform of British mathematics. In 1813 Herschel and Babbage pressed this programme by publishing their *Memoirs of the Analytical Society* to exemplify the methods they favoured. Herschel, Babbage, and Peacock further supported this

Sir John Frederick William Herschel, first baronet (1792–1871), by John Jabez Edwin Mayall, *c*.1848

cause by translating from the French and publishing a calculus text written by Silvestre Lacroix as *An Elementary Treatise on the Differential and Integral Calculus* (1816).

Between Cambridge and the Cape, 1813–1833 Influenced in part no doubt by the difficulties in securing a position as a mathematician, Herschel was admitted to Lincoln's Inn in 1814 to prepare for the bar. None the less, his interests in empirical science increased during this period, stimulated by contacts with the chemist William Hyde Wollaston and the physician–astronomer James South. Herschel's study of chemistry progressed to the point that in 1815 he came within one vote of being elected to the vacant professorship in chemistry at Cambridge. He returned to Cambridge as a sub-lector but, finding himself dissatisfied with 'pupillizing', he left Cambridge, writing to Babbage on 10 October 1816 that 'I am going, under my Father's directions, to take up the series of his observations where he has left them (for he has now pretty well given over regularly observing) and continuing his scrutiny of the heavens with powerful telescopes' (Buttmann, 20). Mathematics was not, however, entirely set aside, some significant publications by him appearing before 1820. The Royal Society recognized the importance of Herschel's mathematical work by awarding him in 1821 its Copley medal. Nor was chemistry completely abandoned; in fact, in 1819 he published the first and most important of a number of contributions he made to photochemistry. This was his detection that hyposulphite of soda (sodium thiosulphate or 'hypo') dissolves silver salts, a major discovery in the prehistory of photography.

In 1820 Herschel played a key role in the creation of the Astronomical Society (from 1831 the Royal Astronomical Society). From its founding until 1827 he served as its foreign secretary, a role for which he was especially suited because of his numerous visits to the continent during the 1820s; increasing fame, and his gift for correspondence, made him very well known in international scientific circles. Herschel's continuing importance for that society is reflected in the fact that its members thrice (1827, 1839, and 1847) elected him to its presidency, the term of office extending for two years, and twice (1826 and 1836) awarded him the society's gold medal.

Herschel's decision to take up astronomy under his father's tutelage attained expression in their collaboration in 1820 in the construction of a 20 foot focal length, 18.25 inch aperture reflecting telescope, very similar to the instrument that his father had used so productively. Herschel employed this as his main telescope for his observational astronomy, which centred on the period from 1820 to 1838. The son took over not only the elder Herschel's telescopic technology, but adopted much of his father's research programme, especially in regard to stellar astronomy. William Herschel had pioneered the observational study of nebulous patches and star clusters, having sighted and catalogued between 1780 and his death in 1822 approximately 2500 of these objects, whereas scarcely more than a hundred had been recognized by 1780. Moreover, William Herschel had catalogued 848 double stars, hoping thereby to detect stellar parallax and to show that some double stars were gravitationally linked. The first quest failed, but the second was successful. No less important, the elder Herschel had raised questions fundamental for stellar astronomy. What is the size and structure of the Milky Way? Are nebulae 'island universes', immensely distant systems of stars comparable in size and structure to our Milky Way? Can one trace the history of the stellar region? Are gravitational forces the key to deciphering this history? Gradually, from 1820 on, John Herschel took up this legacy, while simultaneously making an array of contributions to other areas of science.

From polymath to physical scientist During the 1820s John Herschel emerged as Britain's first modern physical scientist. Possessing not only exceptional mathematical expertise but also extensive knowledge of and experimental dexterity in such areas as chemistry, mechanics, optical science, acoustics, and electricity, not to mention his unrivalled command of matters astronomical, he was in many ways the model for future British physical scientists. His most important contribution to physics during the 1820s consisted of his book length article 'Light', written for the *Encyclopaedia metropolitana* and completed in 1827. In it Herschel provided a mathematical treatment of most of physical optics in terms of the wave theory of light as recently worked out by Thomas Young and (more mathematically) by Augustin Fresnel. Continental scientists expressed their enthusiasm for Herschel's synthesis by having his treatise translated into French and German. His articles (also book length) titled 'Physical astronomy' and 'Sound' for the *Encyclopaedia metropolitana* were, especially the former, major contributions to science.

The broadest and most synthetic of all Herschel's writings appeared in 1830 as his *Preliminary Discourse on the Study of Natural Philosophy*. Now recognized as a classic in the empiricist tradition of the philosophy of science, it was also a major statement of the important place of natural science in culture and society. A number of major scientists and philosophers were strongly influenced by it, including Charles Darwin, Michael Faraday, John Stuart Mill, and William Whewell. Written with the credibility accorded an accomplished scientist and with a quality of style rare among natural philosophers, Herschel's *Preliminary Discourse*, soon translated into Danish, French, German, and Italian, emerged as a powerful force in gaining recognition for the importance of scientific inquiry.

Twentieth-century scholarship on the methodology of science tended to downplay the importance of Herschel's *Preliminary Discourse*, noting that William Whewell's *Philosophy of the Inductive Science* (1840) broke more successfully from the Baconian tendencies of the period and that John Stuart Mill's *System of Logic* (1843) was far more influential than either Herschel's or Whewell's volumes. Among the responses made to these claims are that Herschel's *Preliminary Discourse* actually did depart in major ways from the Baconian tradition, that Herschel very significantly influenced both Whewell and Mill, and that Herschel's intended audience was different from and broader than the philosophical audience addressed by Whewell and Mill.

Although known for his judiciousness, tactfulness, and modesty, Herschel in the period around 1830 found himself at the centre of a controversy about science in England. His close friends Charles Babbage and James South had been outspoken in claiming not only that science had declined in England, but also that Britain's foremost scientific society, the Royal Society, needed major reform, not least rejection of the practice of electing to membership (and frequently to high office) aristocrats who typically possessed only limited interests in and even less knowledge of science. These criticisms reached the peak of intensity in 1830 when Herschel's friends persuaded him to allow his name to be put forward for the presidency of the Royal Society. His opponent in the election was the duke of Sussex, the brother of George IV. Although Herschel lost the election 119 to 111, the programme of the reformers was eventually largely adopted.

On 3 March 1829 John Herschel married Margaret Brodie Stewart (1810–1884), daughter of Alexander Stewart DD, a Scottish Presbyterian minister and Gaelic scholar. Their marriage, uniformly reported to have been fulfilling for both, was undoubtedly fruitful. Three sons— the eldest, Sir William James *Herschel, became a judge and developer of fingerprinting—and nine daughters came from the union, the youngest child, Constance, having been born when her father was sixty-three years of age. Herschel, who until his late fifties had been essentially without paid employment, managed the costs involved in raising and educating such a large family through inherited wealth, which seems to have come mainly through his mother. The high esteem in which nearly all his contemporaries held Herschel is reflected in the fact that in 1831 William IV raised him to knighthood in the Royal Guelphic Order.

Stellar astronomy In the period between 1820 when Herschel erected his new 18.25 inch aperture reflecting telescope and 1833 when he disassembled it to take it to south Africa, Herschel's observational interests centred on double stars and nebulae, the latter gradually drawing the greater share of his interests. In March 1821, working in collaboration with James South and at first using refracting telescopes supplied by South, Herschel began searching for double stars. The first of their catalogues appeared in 1824, listing and describing 380 doubles and winning both the Lalande prize from the French Academy of Sciences and a gold medal from the Astronomical Society. This could be frustrating work, as he lamented in a letter of 23 July 1830 to his wife, Margaret: 'Two stars last night and sat up till two waiting for them. Ditto the night before. Sick of star-gazing—mean to break the telescopes and melt the mirrors' (Clerke, 154). By the time in 1833 when Herschel set aside this work six catalogues had been published, recording observations of 3346 double and multiple stars. The mathematically astute astronomer also published in 1832 a graphical method of calculating the orbits of gravitationally linked doubles. This contribution, which won him a gold medal from the Royal Astronomical Society, was hailed as one of his greatest achievements, a proof of his father's 1803 determination, based on his observations of double stars, that Newton's laws of gravitational attraction rule remote stellar systems as they do our solar system.

On 18 April 1825 Herschel announced to his Aunt Caroline his intention to take up the study of nebulae: 'These curious objects … I shall now take into my especial charge—nobody else can see them' (*Memoir and Correspondence of Caroline Herschel*, 188). The first fruits of this resolve took the form of a careful study published in 1826 of the prominent nebulous patches in the constellations Orion and Andromeda. Another object studied by him with special care was Messier Object 51, which in his observation book for 1830 he described as a 'Brother System', indicating that he viewed it as a stellar system comparable to the Milky Way. By 1833 he had completed and published a catalogue of 2306 nebulae and star clusters, 525 of which he had himself discovered. Included in this publication were drawings of nearly a hundred of these objects. Recognizing the importance of this catalogue, the Royal Astronomical Society awarded Herschel its gold medal and the Royal Society bestowed its royal medal, both in 1836.

The year 1833 saw the publication of Herschel's *Treatise on Astronomy*, which for nearly two decades was deemed the authoritative presentation in English of astronomical science. It was soon translated into Danish, French, and German. Herschel devoted only 10 per cent of that volume to stellar astronomy, which even at that date had as yet attracted few advocates. This section was, however, sufficient to indicate his convictions that most nebulous objects consist of stars, but that some may be formed of what his father had described as a shining fluid. During the period leading up to 1833 Herschel must have come to realize that the most important and timely extension that he could give to his father's nebular research programme, which had been confined to objects visible from England, would be to complement it by observing the comparable objects of the southern heavens. This vast project he took up in 1833.

Years at the Cape, 1833–1838 On 13 November 1833 Herschel, along with his wife, their three small children, and his giant reflecting telescope, sailed from Portsmouth on the *Mountstuart Elphinstone*, bound for the Cape of Good Hope at the southern tip of Africa. One can easily imagine the anticipation experienced by Herschel on this voyage as gradually the spectacular celestial objects of the southern heavens, especially the Magellanic Clouds, revealed themselves to him. On 15 January 1834 the Herschel party arrived at Cape Colony where, a few days earlier, Thomas Maclear, the new director of Britain's Royal Observatory at the Cape, had disembarked. The challenges that Herschel and Maclear faced in this outpost of the British empire are suggested by the facts that the founding director of the Cape observatory had died in a scarlet fever epidemic a few years after taking his post and his successor (and Maclear's predecessor) had resigned after thirteen months in protest at the poor living conditions.

Soon after arriving at the Cape, Herschel leased (and later purchased) a house, Feldhausen, 5 miles from Cape Town, where he set up his telescopes, most notably his 20 foot reflector. It was on 22 February 1834 that he began observing with this telescope, with systematic sweeps, as the Herschels called them, commencing on 5 March. Herschel was not far advanced in his search for southern nebulae when he experienced a major disappointment. He had carried with him a catalogue of nebulae published in 1828 by the astronomer James Dunlop, who had observed from Parramatta in New South Wales. Herschel's distress resulted from his recognition of the unreliability of Dunlop's catalogue; in fact, Herschel found that he could confirm only 206 nebulae reported by Dunlop, whereas another 629 seemed to be spurious. The locations to which Dunlop had assigned southern stars also proved unreliable, a problem that was resolved when Maclear agreed to remeasure the location of key stars.

In Herschel's slightly more than four years at the Cape he observed and catalogued 1708 nebulae, all but 439 of which had not previously been reported. Moreover, these observations, when combined with his earlier observations of nebulae in the northern heavens, allowed him to prepare a chart forcefully demonstrating the theoretically important fact that nebulae appear to lie toward the poles of the Milky Way. Herschel's evidence for this distribution eventually created a very serious problem for those who identified nebulae as island universes comparable to the

Milky Way; if this were the case nebulae should be randomly scattered over the heavens rather than oriented in terms of our Milky Way. Regarding the Milky Way itself, Herschel's Cape observations led him to back away from the traditional disc structure assigned to it in favour of a ring, or annulus.

Herschel scrutinized various spectacular nebular objects of the southern skies with particular attention. Chief among these were the nebulae around Eta Carinae (or, as it was then known, Eta Argus), as well as the Large and Small Magellanic Clouds. For the first of these objects Herschel catalogued 1216 stars and provided a drawing of it, which like many of his drawings shows exceptional ability. He not only attempted a sketch of the Large Magellanic Cloud, but also catalogued 919 stars, nebulae, and clusters in it, whereas in the Small Magellanic Cloud (itself far larger than any northern hemisphere nebula) he catalogued 244. The most theoretically significant aspect of his observation of these objects was his detection within the Large Magellanic Cloud of nebulous structures alongside stars of nearly comparable brightness, which observation led later astronomers to doubt the claim that nebulae are island universes. How, it was asked, could these nebulous structures consist of millions of stars if adjacent individual stars rival in brightness the entire nebula?

Although nebulae were the objects he most assiduously and systematically sought, Herschel also discovered and catalogued 2103 double star systems. Aware of the possibility that some of these could be gravitational doubles and would correspondingly have orbital motions, he made micrometrical measures of 417, thereby leaving an invaluable historical record of their relative positions. Three features of Herschel's work on nebulae and multiple stars are especially noteworthy. First, historians of astronomy, who typically write from the northern hemisphere, have perhaps not adequately recognized the importance of Herschel's opening up the southern heavens. Second, with Herschel's survey of the southern skies, he became and would long remain the only astronomer who had personally scrutinized with a major telescope the entire heavens. Third, Herschel's goal in observing and cataloguing so many thousands of nebulae and double stars systems was, like that of his father, not simply to locate nebulae and double star systems, but also to establish and record their appearance at the time of observation so that future observers could determine the degree to which these massive celestial objects change or evolve. Thus, a major legacy of the Herschels was not only to reveal the richness of the region beyond the solar system, but also to show that its objects should be seen as historical, possibly evolving entities.

Although Herschel devoted most of his observational energies at the Cape to nebulae and double stars, other objects received attention. Both he and Maclear anxiously awaited a predicted apparition of Halley's comet, an event made special both by the brilliance of the comet and the rareness of its appearances, the last having occurred in 1758. Herschel observed the comet with care and proceeded to provide a valuable dynamical analysis of the changes it was seen to undergo. He also devoted a portion of ninety-five nights of observing to the Saturnian system, especially two of Saturn's satellites, Enceladus and Mimas. These very faint moons, although discovered by William Herschel in 1795, had never subsequently been sighted by another astronomer. These observations not only confirmed the existence of these satellites, but also allowed Herschel to establish their periods of revolution.

The intensity of Herschel's dedication during his Cape period and the quality of the weather in the area are both suggested by the fact that in his four years there he completed a total of 382 stellar and nebular sweeps. This total can be compared with the 410 stellar sweeps Herschel had completed in the nine-year period between 1825 and 1833. Moreover, he actively contributed to the intellectual life of the colony, serving, for example, as president of the South African Literary and Scientific Institution. An ardent naturalist in regard to not only the heavens but also the earth, Herschel explored the flora, fauna, and geology of the region, making in the process a number of significant contributions in those areas. Not the least of his activities in regard to biological science took the form of two letters Herschel wrote from the Cape to Charles Lyell on the question of the evolution of organic forms. These letters, scholars have concluded, significantly influenced Charles Darwin in working out his ideas on biological evolution.

The Herschel family, which in about four years at the Cape had expanded by three additional children, began their return voyage on 11 March 1838 aboard the *Windsor Castle*, arriving in London on 15 May 1838. Herschel's return to England was immediately hailed by a dinner in his honour on 15 June, attended by 400 scientists and other notables. This dinner and, thirteen days later, Herschel's elevation to the baronetcy at the coronation of Queen Victoria support the contemporary view of John Herschel as the foremost scientist of the period. He returned with masses of observations that required painstaking analysis and reduction. This process, from which other responsibilities and interests repeatedly distracted him, took nearly a decade. It was in 1847 that Herschel's *magnum opus* appeared as a splendidly printed volume funded by the duke of Northumberland: *Results of astronomical observations made during the years 1834, 5, 6, 7, 8 at the Cape of Good Hope; being the completion of a telescopic survey of the whole surface of the visible heavens, commenced in 1825 by Sir J. F. W. Herschel*. Honours and praise were showered on the volume, the Royal Society, for example, awarding Herschel his second Copley medal.

The most eminent scientist in Britain, 1838–1850 The honours and offices offered Herschel in the period after his return from the Cape indicate the esteem in which his contemporaries held him. By the end of 1839 he had been urged to stand for Oxford's Savilian professorship of astronomy, which he declined, and offered its degree of DCL, which he accepted. He also declined the presidencies of the Royal Society and the Geological Society, but accepted the presidency of the mathematics section of the British Association for the Advancement of Science

and the presidency of the Royal Astronomical Society. Responsibilities, many of which accompanied these titles, began to take up a large portion of his life. Over the period from 1838 to about 1845 he served on the royal commission on standards, prepared two major reports on constellation reform, actively advised on James Ross's south polar expedition and on efforts to establish a worldwide network of magnetic and meteorological observatories, and in 1843 agreed to serve on the board of visitors for the Royal Observatory and as a trustee of the British Museum. All this was possible because with his return from the Cape, Herschel had terminated his large scale observational programme in astronomy.

Despite such extensive service to British science, Herschel remained during this period creatively involved with science, especially the new science of photochemistry. In the years immediately after the announcement in early 1839 by L. J. M. Daguerre of his new photographic process and shortly thereafter by W. H. Fox Talbot of a different process, Herschel sought ways to improve and advance photographic science. His efforts, which involved hundreds of experiments, yielded three major papers (1839, 1840, and 1842) published by the Royal Society, for the first of which he was awarded the society's royal medal. It was in this period that Herschel's sodium thiosulphate came to be recognized as the most useful of all the chemicals proposed as the fixer for silver based photographic images. His other important contributions include his extensive experimentation on the light sensitivity of various metals and vegetable dyes, his working out of techniques of making photographs in colour or on glass plates, and his advancing of various terms now standard in photographic science, namely, 'positive', 'negative', 'snap-shot', and 'photographer'.

Herschel's experiments in photography, which had interrupted his efforts to write up his Cape observations, were themselves interrupted when, in April 1840, the Herschel family moved from Observatory House in Slough to a large home in Hawkhurst in Kent, which they named Collingwood House and which served as the chief family residence for the remainder of Herschel's life. Another distraction came in 1845 when Herschel served as president of the British Association meeting held that year in Cambridge. In the controversy that occurred in 1846–7 concerning the discovery of the planet Neptune, Herschel became involved in many ways, not least as a peacemaker but also as a person who before the discovery had urged astronomers to look for the planet and after the discovery had suggested that William Lassell should search (as he successfully did) for a satellite.

Herschel published two major books in 1849. One of these was the *Admiralty Manual of Scientific Enquiry*, for which he served as editor and to which he contributed an important essay on meteorology. Far more significant was his *Outlines of Astronomy*, which was based partly on his earlier and shorter *Treatise on Astronomy*. Hailed as the definitive presentation of astronomy available in English, Herschel's *Outlines* had by 1871 gone through eleven editions and also translations into Chinese and Arabic.

Changes in these later editions record the evolution of Herschel's thought. For example, in the first edition Herschel, aware of the resolutions of nebulae into stars achieved by Lord Rosse and others, inclined to the view that all nebulae are composed of stars, but in the 1869 edition of *Outlines*, by then aware that William Huggins had spectroscopically shown the gaseous nature of at least some nebulae, Herschel returned to his father's notion that true nebulosity can and does exist.

Master of the mint, 1850–1855 Possibly it was the prestige associated with a position once held by Isaac Newton that led Herschel in late 1850 to agree to accept the mastership of the Royal Mint. More probably, this decision was motivated either by his readiness to assume responsibility for overseeing a planned reform of the mint or by the financial needs of a man who in the first fifty-eight years of his life had never held a paid position, but who had responsibility for the support and education of his (by 1846) eleven children, a twelfth being born in 1855. Whatever the reason and with whatever reluctance may have been generated by his already frail health and by the necessity of taking up residence in London away from his beloved family, Herschel in December 1850 took up the appointment. The planned reform was both major and disruptive. Moreover, the need to expand production of coinage, to explore its decimalization, and to establish an Australian branch of the mint at Sydney, compounded his difficulties in serving as master. Tensions grew ever more severe, bringing Herschel by late 1854 to the verge of a nervous breakdown, and leading him to submit his resignation in early 1855. In April that year he returned to his family in Collingwood and sought to restore his health. The consensus among scholars is that Herschel was successful in bringing off the much needed reform in the mint, but that the toll that it took on his energies was excessive.

Final years, 1855–1871 During the final seventeen years of Herschel's life problems of health—gout, rheumatism that periodically confined him to a wheelchair, and severe bronchitis—prevented extended travel and lessened the degree to which he could be present in person in the scientific community. But such difficulties did not stop him from writing or from corresponding. Eight books and monographs as well as over a hundred shorter writings published during this period attest to the continued vitality of his intellect. A number of the books and monographs from these years drew together earlier work. This was the case for his *Essays from the Edinburgh and Quarterly Reviews, with Addresses and other Pieces*, published in 1857 but incorporating the most important of the essays that he produced before that time. One example of the important writings appearing in this volume is Herschel's review, written in 1849, of Adolphe Quetelet's *Theory of Probabilities*. Recent scholarship has shown that this essay not only significantly influenced the development of social science in Britain, but also was a key factor in leading James Clerk Maxwell to the creation of the statistical approach to heat phenomena. Another significant compilation was Herschel's *Familiar Lectures on Scientific Subjects*, which

appeared in 1866. This volume consisted mainly of essays that Herschel had written in the period after 1855 for such journals as *Good Words* and the *Cornhill Magazine*. Two of the fourteen essays in this volume were written as part of Herschel's extended campaign against Britain's adoption of the metric system. In this cause, Herschel was not alone, nor did he lack reasonable arguments.

In 1861 Herschel published synthetic books on three separate topics, all of which had been written initially as major articles for the *Encyclopaedia Britannica*. These were *Meteorology*, *Physical Geography*, and *The Telescope*. Rather than presenting new research these studies drew on Herschel's decades of activity in these areas. Another production, which appeared in 1866, indicates his lifelong love of poetry and of foreign, including classical, languages: this was his translation of Homer's *Iliad* into hexameter verse.

John Herschel's dedication to his father's legacy as well as to observing nebulae and double stars led him to devote much effort during the last decade of his life to compiling observations of these objects into two large catalogues. The first of two large compilations was published in 1865 in the Royal Society's *Transactions* as 'A catalogue of nebulae and clusters of stars', and listed 5079 known nebulae, all but 450 of which had been discovered by William and John Herschel. At the time of his death in 1871 John Herschel had nearly finished his other project, a catalogue of 10,320 double and multiple stars; completed by Charles Pritchard and Robert Main, it was published in 1874 in the Royal Astronomical Society's *Memoirs*.

For approximately twenty-seven of the last thirty-one years of his life, Herschel lived at Collingwood House in Hawkhurst, over 40 miles from London. He may have been somewhat introverted by nature and isolated by location, but during those decades he was certainly no recluse, corresponding widely, even in the last decade of his life. In general he was extremely active as a correspondent, as is shown by the fact that over ten thousand letters to him, many from leading British and foreign scientists, have been preserved. His responses show remarkable breadth of learning, generosity, and judiciousness.

Herschel died at Collingwood on 11 May 1871. Bronchial problems, which had beset him for many years, were probably the main cause of his death. His funeral, which took place in London on 19 May, was attended by most of the leading British scientists of the mid-Victorian period. Such was the esteem in which Herschel's contemporaries held him that he was buried in Westminster Abbey next to Newton, with whom he had at times been compared. In fact, in T. Romney Robinson's obituary notice on Herschel, he remarked that with the death of Herschel, 'British science has sustained a loss greater than any which it has suffered since the death of Newton' (Robinson, xvii).

Herschel's exceptional human qualities, which made him almost universally liked and respected among his contemporaries, may have led Robinson and others to speak of Herschel in terms that overstate his significance. The judgement of history has been that Charles Darwin,

James Clerk Maxwell, and possibly other British scientists of the nineteenth century surpassed John Herschel in the number of fundamental insights attained and discoveries made. None the less, few, if any, of his contemporaries surpassed Herschel in range of contributions, from astronomy to chemistry, from mathematics to meteorology, from physics to philosophy of science. Nor did any nineteenth-century astronomer of any nation surpass Herschel in range of knowledge of the heavens or in the magnitude of their contribution to extending the foundations for stellar and extra-galactic astronomy that William Herschel had laid. In this, the Herschels were prophetic because stellar astronomy was the astronomy of the future. Moreover, historians of science have come to recognize that many, perhaps most, of Herschel's British contemporaries saw his writings and his exemplary scientific life as providing a model for the future.

MICHAEL J. CROWE

Sources A calendar of the correspondence of Sir John Herschel, ed. M. J. Crowe, D. R. Dyck, and J. J. Kevin (1998) · G. Buttmann, The shadow of the telescope: a biography of John Herschel, ed. D. S. Evans, trans. B. E. J. Pagel (1970) · B. Warner, ed., John Herschel 1792–1992: bicentennial symposium (1994) [incl. bibliography] · D. S. Evans, T. J. Deeming, B. H. Evans, and S. Goldfarb, eds., Herschel at the Cape: diaries and correspondence of Sir John Herschel, 1834–1838 (1969) · B. Warner and N. Warner, eds., Maclear and Herschel: letters and diaries at the Cape of Good Hope, 1834–1838 (1984) · RS, Herschel papers · A. M. Clerke, The Herschels and modern astronomy (1895); repr. (1901) · D. G. King-Hele, ed., John Herschel 1792–1871: a bicentennial commemoration (1992) · M. Hoskin, 'John Herschel's cosmology', Journal for the History of Astronomy, 18 (1987), 1–34 · L. J. Schaaf, Out of the shadows: Herschel, Talbot and the invention of photography (1992) · W. F. Cannon, 'John Herschel and the idea of science', Journal of the History of Ideas, 22 (1961), 215–39 · A. Chapman, 'An occupation for an independent gentleman: astronomy in the life of John Herschel', Vistas in Astronomy, 36 (1993), 71–116 · G. Good, 'John Herschel's optical researches and the development of his ideas on method and causality', Studies in History and Philosophy of Science, 18 (1987), 1–41 · C. J. Ducasse, 'John Herschel's methods of experimental inquiry', Theories of scientific method: the renaissance through the nineteenth century, ed. E. H. Madden (1960), 153–82 · D. S. Evans, 'Herschel, John Frederick William', DSB, 6.323–8 · C. A. Lubbock, ed., The Herschel chronicle: the life-story of William Herschel and his sister Caroline Herschel (1933) · J. R. Panter, 'Sir John F. W. Herschel and scientific thought in early nineteenth-century Britain', PhD diss., University of New South Wales, 1976 · S. S. Schweber, 'John F. W. Herschel: a prefatory essay', Aspects of the life and thought of Sir John Frederick Herschel, ed. S. S. Schweber (1981), 1.1–158 · DNB · M. J. Crowe, ed., The letters and papers of Sir John Herschel: a guide to the manuscripts and microfilm (1991) [at the Royal Society] · L. J. Schaaf, Tracings of light: Sir John Herschel and the camera lucida (1989) · Mrs J. Herschel, Memoir and correspondence of Caroline Herschel (1876) · [T. R. Robinson], PRS, 20 (1871–2), xvii–xxiii · Astronomical Register, 9 (1872), 140–41

Archives Belgian Royal Academy · BGS, geological notebook relating to Isle of Wight · BL, notes on chemistry and acoustics, M/552–553 [microfilm] · Bucks. RLSS, papers relating to a pew in Upton parish church, Buckinghamshire · CUL, papers and poems · Harvard U., Houghton L., corresp., notebooks, and papers · Kodak Museum, Harrow, England · MHS Oxf., corresp. and papers relating to photography · National Archives of South Africa · NMM, accounts, corresp., papers; vistors's book · Ransom HRC, corresp. and papers · RAS, corresp. and papers · Royal Mint Library, London · RS, corresp. and papers · Sci. Mus., notebook · Smithsonian Institution, Washington, DC · University of Cape Town Library, corresp. and papers relating to education in Cape Colony · Wellcome L. | American Philosophical Society, Philadelphia, letters to Sir Charles Lyell · American Philosophical Society, Philadelphia, letters to W. H. Smyth · Birr Castle, co. Offaly, archives, letters to earl of Rosse · BL, corresp. with Charles Babbage, Add. MSS 37182–37199, passim · Bodl. Oxf., corresp. with Mary Somerville · CUL, Royal Observatory Archive, corresp. with Sir George Airy · CUL, letters to Sir George Stokes, etc. · GS Lond., letters to Sir R. I. Murchison · PRO, letters to Sir Edward Sabine, BJ3 · RBG Kew, letters to Sir William Hooker · Royal Institution of Great Britain, London, letters to John Tyndall · Sci. Mus., letters to Fox Talbot · TCD, letters to Sir William Rowan Hamilton · Trinity Cam., letters to William Whewell · U. Edin. L., letters to Sir Roderick Murchison · U. St Andr. L., letters to James Forbes

Likenesses silhouette, c.1813, St John Cam. · A. E. Chalon, miniature, 1829, priv. coll. · H. W. Pickersgill, drawing, c.1835, NPG · H. W. Pickersgill, oils, c.1835, St John Cam. · J. J. E. Mayall, daguerreotype, c.1848, NPG [see illus.] · E. H. Baily, marble bust, 1850, St John Cam.; copy, NPG · J. M. Cameron, photograph, 1867, NPG · J. M. Cameron, photograph, 1867 (The astronomer), National Museum of Photography, Film and Television, Bradford, Royal Photographic Society collection · J. M. Cameron, photograph, 1867, Deutsches Museum, Munich · F. Croll, stipple (after daguerreotype by J. Mayall), NPG; repro. in Hogg's instructor · G. Gabrielli, engraving, repro. in P. Moore, Sir John Herschel: explorer of the southern sky (1992) · C. Herschel Gordon, oils (after photograph by J. M. Cameron) · C. A. Jensen, oils, RS · T. Webster, portrait (after photograph, 1871) · drawing, repro. in ILN (28 June 1845), 404 · plaster medallion (after W. Tassie), NG Scot.

Wealth at death under £30,000: probate, 20 June 1871, CGPLA Eng. & Wales

Herschel, Sir William (1738–1822), musician and astronomer, was born at Hanover on 15 November 1738, and baptized Friedrich Wilhelm. He was the fourth of the ten children (and the third of six to survive infancy) of Isaac Herschel (1707–1767), a former gardener who was then an oboist in the Hanoverian foot guards, and his wife, Anna Ilse Moritzen. All the children, except the eldest, inherited their father's musical talent; and, although the family lived in humble circumstances, the boys were encouraged to take a lively interest in scientific and philosophical questions. Herschel attended the garrison school, where he proved an apt pupil.

The musician At the age of fourteen Herschel followed his father into the band of the guards, after passing a test on the violin and oboe. His salary helped to pay for lessons in French. In 1756 the guards were stationed for some months in England, where Herschel took the opportunity to learn the language and purchased a copy of Locke's Essay on Human Understanding. The guards were then recalled to Hanover, and in July 1757 were heavily defeated in the battle of Hastenbeck. On his father's advice the young Herschel quit the scene and fled to Hanover, where he found himself in danger of being pressed into service as a soldier. He therefore returned to his regiment, to find no one interested in a boy bandsman. His father proposed that he leave for England; he was not under oath, and his father undertook to secure his formal discharge, a promise he fulfilled in 1762.

William Herschel, as he called himself when he settled in England, arrived in London in company with his elder brother Jacob, with

> not half a Guinea in the world. He went to a music shop in town and asked to write music. An opera was put into his

Sir William Herschel (1738–1822), by Lemuel Francis Abbott, 1785

hands to copy, and he returned it with such dispatch as amazed his employer, who from that time kept him in full employ till he found a more profitable line of labour. (*Scientific Papers*, 1.xvi)

After a couple of years Herschel came to the conclusion that London was overstocked with musicians, and so he accepted an invitation to take charge of the little band of the Durham militia. His talents were quickly recognized, and he was soon in demand as a performer and teacher across the north of England. He now began to compose music, and by the end of 1760 had completed six symphonies. In due course his *Eccho Catch* and *Six Sonatas for the Harpsichord with Violin and Cello Obbligato* were published. A considerable number of his works survive in manuscript: the instrumental ones include several symphonies, and concertos for oboe, violin, and viola, along with two concertos and other pieces for organ. They are judged to display 'strong concern for formal structure but limited inspiration' (*New Grove*).

In August 1766 Herschel successfully competed for the post of organist of Halifax parish church, when he produced a pleasing volume of sound by placing lead weights on the lowest key and on the key an octave above, and improvised a suitable harmony with his two hands. His musical career was now proving embarrassingly successful, for only a few days earlier he had been offered the post of organist at the new Octagon Chapel in Bath. After some hesitation, in October Herschel gave notice of resignation from his Halifax post. He was immediately offered an increased salary to stay, but was not to be persuaded, and he arrived in Bath before the year's end.

By now he had learned some Italian, as the knowledge would be of use in music. With Herschel one thing led to another: from Italian he passed to Latin, and even to Greek. By the same token, he had studied the mathematical theory of harmony in the *Harmonics* of Robert Smith, lately professor of astronomy at Cambridge, and from this he passed to other works in mathematics, and to Smith's *Opticks*. Herschel's father had long ago introduced his children to the stars, and in *Opticks* Herschel learned not only about the theory of the subject, but also how to construct telescopes, and something of what might be seen in the heavens with the finished instruments. Early in 1766 his memoranda include entries that read: 'Observation of Venus', and 'Eclipse of the moon'.

At Bath Herschel's musical career blossomed. He accepted an invitation to join the musicians who played in the Pump Room and elsewhere, he took innumerable pupils, and he was much involved in the staging of *Messiah* and other oratorios. Before long his annual income was in excess of £300.

Bath now proved a magnet for Herschel's siblings. In 1767 his brother Jacob arrived and stayed for two years; in 1768 Dietrich came for a year; and in 1770 Alexander arrived and put down his roots. But his sister Caroline [*see* Herschel, Caroline Lucretia] was languishing in Hanover, a drudge in the family household. Herschel proposed that she join him in Bath, train as a singer, and collaborate in his concert work. There was family opposition, but Herschel visited Hanover in August 1772 and brought Caroline back with him to Bath.

The amateur astronomer Herschel's musical duties were now competing with what was fast becoming an obsession for astronomy. That spring he bought a copy of James Ferguson's celebrated *Astronomy*, along with a quadrant and components for telescopes. His sister had hoped to see more of him with the ending of the season:

> But I was greatly disappointed; for, in consequence of the harassing and fatiguing life he had led during the winter months, he used to retire to bed with a bason of milk or glass of water, and Smith's *Harmonics* and *Optics*, Ferguson's *Astronomy*, etc., and so went to sleep buried under his favourite authors; and his first thoughts on rising were how to obtain instruments for viewing those objects himself of which he had been reading. (*Memoir and Correspondence of Caroline Herschel*, 34–5)

He experimented with refractors, but these had to be of excessive length in order to minimize the effect of chromatic aberration, while the lenses themselves were severely limited in size by the available glass technology. He therefore hired a small reflector. This was encouragingly convenient to handle, but its 'light-gathering power' was wholly inadequate for Herschel's ambitions. Conventionally trained astronomers saw it their business to examine the individual members of the solar system and to monitor their movements against the largely unchanging background of the stars. Herschel, knowing no better, set out to investigate the large-scale structure of the universe, what he termed 'the construction of the heavens'; and for the study of distant and faint objects he would need reflectors with massive mirrors to collect as much light as possible.

In September 1773 Herschel had his first disc cast, and, guided by Smith's *Opticks*, set about shaping and polishing it with some second-hand tools he had bought. For the rest of the decade, much of the time not occupied by his round of musical engagements was devoted to the grinding and polishing of telescopic mirrors. As the eager experimentation proceeded, Herschel gradually became a craftsman without peer in the construction of sizeable reflecting telescopes. To her sorrow, Caroline saw almost every room turned into a workshop.

A large reflector had three features of fundamental importance: a mirror of speculum metal, ideally of parabolic shape, that would reflect the incident light back to a focus; an eyepiece, in effect a microscope with which to inspect the image; and a wooden mounting, to permit the observer to direct the telescope in the desired direction and then to look through the eyepiece. Herschel's fundamental advance in the mounting was to come later; for the present he contrived a simple stand for the smaller instruments, and slung from a pole in rudimentary fashion the reflector of 20 foot focal length that he completed in 1776. In making his eyepieces he found no difficulty in obtaining magnifications of hundreds, and even thousands, exceeding in this the ambitions of most contemporary opticians. But it was in the grinding and polishing of mirrors that Herschel proved the supreme craftsman. His limitless energy encouraged an unsophisticated approach: the production of great numbers of mirrors, and the selection of the most successful for use in his telescopes.

For several years word of this extraordinary organist-astronomer had been spreading among friends of his neighbours and pupils, and in 1777 Herschel had been visited by Nevil Maskelyne, the astronomer royal, and by Thomas Hornsby, professor of astronomy at Oxford. His scientific isolation ended in December 1779, when a passer-by, Dr William Watson FRS, saw Herschel observing in the street and asked to be allowed to look through his telescope. The two became close friends, and Watson proved a faithful ally. A society, the Bath Literary and Philosophical Society, was being formed 'for the purpose of discussing scientific and phylosophical subjects and making experiments to illustrate them' (Porter, 30), and Watson drafted Herschel—'optical instrument maker and mathematician'—to be a founder member. During the next fifteen months he furnished the Bath society with some thirty-one papers on a variety of subjects. Four of them were communicated by Watson to the Royal Society in London and published in *Philosophical Transactions*.

By 1781 Herschel's ambitions for large mirrors to see further into space had outrun even the capacities of the local foundries to cast the blanks. He therefore converted the basement of his home into a foundry, at first with the intention of casting a mirror that would have been a staggering 4 feet in diameter. He later reduced this to 3 feet, but even so the mirror would have been the largest in the world. Not only the family but eminent visitors were pressed into service to pound the horse dung required for the mould. Unfortunately, the first mirror cracked on cooling, and in the second casting the mould fractured and the molten metal spilled out over the flagstones, with near-fatal consequences for Herschel and his brother.

Meanwhile Herschel found time for an occasional look at the heavens. In March 1774 he began his first observing book, and on the opening page he drew a sketch of the Orion nebula, remarking that the shape of this 'lucid spot' was not as delineated by Smith in his *Opticks*. He was quick to see the momentous implications that would result if the change was confirmed by careful observation. A list of six of the milky patches in the sky known as 'nebulae' had been published by Edmond Halley in 1715. Halley believed them to be clouds of a lucid medium that Herschel would later term 'true nebulosity'. Others thought them star clusters so distant that the individual stars could not be distinguished with the available instrumentation. But a distant star cluster that nevertheless appeared to be spread across the sky would be vast indeed, too vast to alter shape noticeably in only a few decades. A change in the shape of the Orion nebula, therefore, would show it to be formed, not of stars, but of true nebulosity.

The discovery of Uranus In the 1770s Herschel several times observed the Orion nebula, and became convinced that it was indeed changing shape. But as a novice observer he faced the more urgent task of familiarizing himself with the brightest stars of the night sky. After examining in turn each of the brighter stars, in August 1779 he embarked on a second and more thorough 'review'. This led him on 13 March 1781 to examine stars in the constellation Gemini, where he came across one whose appearance instantly struck him as 'curious'. Returning to it a few days later, he found that it had altered position: it was not a distant star, but a nearby member of the solar system, presumably—since it was not one of the known planets—a comet.

Herschel at once informed Maskelyne and Hornsby, but neither could see anything unusual in that part of the sky. When eventually Maskelyne identified the object by its movement, he suspected it might in fact be a planet, and after its orbit had been calculated this indeed proved to be the case. Herschel thus became the first person in history to discover a planet of the solar system.

Pensioner of the crown Worldwide fame quickly followed. In November 1781 Herschel was presented with the Copley medal of the Royal Society; the following month he was elected a fellow and, in a pleasing gesture, was exempted from the normal annual payment on the grounds that the money saved would be spent on science. More significantly, the discovery gave Herschel's allies at the English court the opportunity to lobby George III—himself a Hanoverian—on Herschel's behalf. In 1769 the king had established an observatory at Kew, and the incumbent observer, S. C. T. Demainbray, was now advanced in years. Herschel seemed to Sir Joseph Banks, president of the Royal Society and confidant of the king, to be a suitable successor, though it transpired that the king had promised the post to Demainbray's son. Nevertheless, in April 1782 Herschel was told that the king wished to see him, and on 20 May he packed up the 7 foot reflector with which he had discovered the planet and set off for London. The king then ordered the telescope to be set up at the Royal Observatory, Greenwich, where it remained throughout June, giving Maskelyne and other astronomers ample opportunity to compare it with the professionally made observatory instruments. Of Herschel's supreme skill as a maker of reflecting mirrors and eyepieces there could no longer be any question. 'Double stars which they could not see with their instruments I had the pleasure to show them very plainly' (Lubbock, 115).

At the beginning of July, Herschel was at Windsor, showing planets to the royal family. Shortly thereafter it seems he made an application for financial support from the crown, and was immediately offered a pension that would make him independent of music. It was not a large amount: £200 yearly, much less than he was earning from music, but attractive enough compared to the £300 paid to the holder of the onerous post of astronomer royal. His only duties were to reside near Windsor Castle and be available to show the heavens to the royal family when asked to do so. This transformation in Herschel's life would also mean the end of Caroline's career in music; but it never occurred to her brother to consult her before accepting.

Long before, Galileo had cemented his relationship with his Medici patrons by giving their name to his newly discovered satellites of Jupiter. Herschel, under advice, named his planet after the king; but continental astronomers resisted this departure from tradition, and the name Uranus was adopted, although Herschel himself always referred to it as the Georgian Planet.

At the end of July, Herschel returned to Bath and with precipitate speed organized the move to Datchet, near Windsor, where he had taken a house that was in ruinous condition but had the space he needed for all his apparatus. By 5 August he was making observations there, and by 22 August Caroline found herself under orders to sweep for comets. For a time the royal family not infrequently exercised their right to require Herschel's presence at Windsor of an evening. This involved him in transporting a telescope there in the daytime, and back home again in the darkness. He then had to set up the telescope for the night's serious work, for he was now engaged in a third review of the heavens.

The third review, like the second, had a subsidiary aim of great significance: the search for double stars. Herschel knew from Galileo of a method whereby observations of a double star—two stars that lie in almost the same direction from earth and so appear at first glance to be a single star—might be used to circumvent some of the daunting obstacles confronting any astronomer who wished to measure the distances of stars. As a contribution to this method he published in 1782 a list of 269 double stars, no fewer than 227 of which he had found himself, and in 1785 a further list of 434. The consequences were very different from those he intended. In 1784 John Michell pointed out in print (for the second time) that double stars were far too

numerous to be explained as resulting from chance alignments, that is, virtual coincidences of the directions of the two members of a double as seen from earth. Instead, most doubles must be binary stars, companions in space lying at the same distance from earth, and therefore useless for Galileo's method. And when, after an interval of two decades, Herschel re-examined a number of his doubles, he did indeed find several in which the two stars had moved in orbit around each other, so confirming that they were companions bound together by attractive forces.

In collecting double stars, Herschel imported into astronomy the methodology of the natural historian: he had become a gatherer and classifier of astronomical specimens. Contemporaries found this hard to accept. Herschel had from the start been a controversial figure, a rank amateur unfamiliar with the niceties of scientific discourse, and an observer incapable of giving a coherent definition of the position of a new planet when he had been lucky enough to find one. The draft of his paper on mountains on the moon had included highly inappropriate speculations about lunar inhabitants, while his claims to have eyepieces that magnified thousands of times had seemed nothing short of lunatic. Now he was turning a physical science into a biological one.

Friends such as Watson did their best to coach their protégé in the scientific conventions and to defend him against detractors. Meanwhile, at Datchet, Caroline was having no luck in detecting new comets, but she was encountering a significant number of nebulae. Herschel began himself to sweep for nebulae with a small refractor, before it occurred to him that they were permanent features of the night sky, and so should be tackled without haste, and with the most powerful instrumentation that Herschelian ingenuity could contrive. And he was now completing a 20 foot reflector with 18 inch mirrors and, more significantly, a stable and convenient mounting.

The construction of the heavens The 'large' 20 foot came into service in October 1783, and Herschel embarked on a systematic search of the skies visible from Windsor that was to take him and Caroline two decades to complete. By the end of the year a suitable technique of 'sweeping' had been devised. With the telescope facing south, Herschel stood on the platform laying an ambush for any nebula that might drift into the field of view as the skies turned overhead, while his sister was indoors at a desk near an open window ready to write down its position and description. The telescope, whose field of view was typically ¼° in diameter, was constantly being raised and lowered a little by a workman, so that each 'sweep' covered a strip of sky some 2° wide. In an observational campaign that is second to none in the history of astronomy, brother and sister increased the number of known nebulae from about a hundred to 2500.

Herschel's earliest observations of the Orion nebula had suggested that the object altered shape and so was a small nearby cloud of 'true nebulosity'. But how to distinguish true nebulosity from the appearance of nebulosity generated by a vast, distant star cluster? Herschel decided that the apparent nebulosity of a star cluster was irregular or 'mottled', while true nebulosity was uniform or 'milky'. He discussed his current programme in 'Account of some observations tending to investigate the construction of the heavens', read before the Royal Society in June 1784. In this remarkable paper he also initiated the method of stellar statistics that is fundamental in modern astronomy. Like several mid-century speculators, Herschel believed that the Milky Way seen in the sky is the optical effect of the earth's immersion in a layer of stars (the galaxy). But Herschel wished to know the actual shape of the galaxy, and for this the earth's interior location is most unhelpful. He saw that he could make progress on the question if he made two assumptions: first, that his telescope could reach to the borders in every direction (for unless this was so the task was hopeless), and, second, that within the galaxy the volume of space was uniformly stocked with stars. The second assumption implied that, the more stars that could be counted in a given field of view, the greater the distance to the border of the galaxy in that direction. It was, of course, an assumption that was not strictly true; Herschel hoped it would be true enough for his purposes.

In a second paper, published in 1785, Herschel gave the results of his star counts to date. So much of his time was taken up with sweeping that he could offer no more than a sample of star counts; but he listed the results for a great circle of the sky, and sketched the resulting cross-section of the galaxy. In later years he abandoned both the assumptions on which the sketch was based: with more powerful telescopes he found he was able to see stars invisible in the 20 foot, while increasing familiarity with star clusters convinced him that the assumption of uniform distribution was seriously misleading. But for much of the nineteenth century, for want of anything to put in its place, writers were to reproduce the sketch that had been disowned by its author.

No sooner had the 1784 paper been read than Herschel came across two nebulae in which he could see both milky and mottled nebulosity; indeed, in the second nebula he believed he could see stars as well. While stubborn in the face of criticism from others, Herschel was very ready to reform his own ideas, and he now concluded that he had been over hasty in accepting the existence of true nebulosity and that all nebulae were indeed distant star clusters: mottled nebulosity indicated the presence of a star cluster only just too far away for his telescope to 'resolve' the cluster into its component stars, while milky nebulosity revealed the presence of innumerable stars at a very much greater distance. The supposed changes he had observed in the Orion nebula he now chose to ignore.

But clustering implied the action of attractive forces: the more dense the cluster, the longer attractive forces had been at work on it. And so Herschel arrived at the revolutionary concept of the age of a star cluster. In the 1785 paper he described how a widely scattered collection of stars would eventually condense into clusters, and these would become more and more concentrated as time went on. His contemporaries were once more at a loss: not

only was the methodology revolutionary, but only Herschel, with his 20 foot reflector, had access to the evidence.

A further paper on the construction of the heavens followed in 1789, but the following year Herschel's identification of nebulae with star clusters received a fatal blow. On 13 November he was sweeping as usual when he came across 'A most singular phaenomenon', a star surrounded by 'a faint luminous atmosphere' (*Scientific Papers*, 1.421–2). It was in fact an unusually near example of a type of object that Herschel had discovered and termed 'planetary nebula', with a disc like a planet but pale light like a nebula. In the 1790 example Herschel could see a central star, and he at once concluded that the star was condensing out of the surrounding cloud of nebulosity.

The impact on Herschel's theorizing was dramatic. He had previously viewed the earth's galaxy as one among many; for if (say) the Orion nebula was so distant that the component stars could not be seen, and yet it occupied so much of the sky, it must be vast indeed, and 'may well outvie our milky-way in grandeur' (*Scientific Papers*, 1.255). Now it reverted to being a cloud of nearby and changeable nebulosity, a minor component within the galaxy.

More importantly, the evolutionary process among star clusters had to be extended backwards in time. In a series of papers published towards the end of his life, Herschel pictured the process as beginning with widely diffused nebulosity that gradually condensed, here and there, into clouds, out of which in time stars began to be born, to form star clusters. As time went on these condensed more and more—perhaps ending in a cataclysmic gravitational collapse that would contribute to the cycle beginning all over again. Each stage in this theoretical picture Herschel illustrated with examples from his catalogues of nebulae and star clusters, remarking that the difference between one stage and the next was perhaps less than there would be 'in an annual description of the human figure, were it given from the birth of a child till he comes to be a man in his prime' (*Scientific Papers*, 2.460).

Until 1786 there is no hint to be found in Herschel's life of romantic attachments. But that year his friend and neighbour John Pitt died, leaving a widow, Mary (1762/3–1832?), and two years later, on 8 May 1788, William and Mary (*née* Baldwin) were married. Their only child, Sir John Frederick William *Herschel, was born in 1792. Mary was of serene and pleasant nature, and brought with her money enough to relieve the pressure on her husband to supplement his income by the manufacture of telescopes for sale. The pace of life slackened, and in the years to come holidays away from Slough became a regular event.

In 1785 Herschel had requested royal funding for the monster reflector he had long coveted. In the event he received two grants of £2000 each, with £200 per annum for running costs, and Caroline was also given a small pension. Herschel had invited the king to choose between an instrument of 30 foot focal length and one of 40 foot. The king, not surprisingly, opted for the larger size, but this proved to be an unfortunate choice. Towards the end of the century Herschel was to build for the king of Spain a

25 foot, with 2 foot mirrors, and in trials at Slough this reflector proved an outstanding success: Herschel's technology was equal to a challenge on this scale. But the monster he built for himself proved of limited use. He found the tube cumbersome to manage, and the 4 foot mirrors, weighing many hundredweight, had to be made of an unusual alloy to prevent their deforming under their own weight when tilted in use. As a result they tarnished easily.

In any event, a prime purpose of the telescope had doubtless been to endorse Herschel's identification of nebulae with star clusters, by 'resolving' additional nebulae into their component stars, and the Orion nebula was the first object he examined with the unfinished instrument. But within months of the completion in 1789 Herschel changed his mind and decided that true nebulosity existed after all. Supervising the mammoth construction task had absorbed a disproportionate amount of his energies; and, although the instrument was visited by kings and archbishops as well as continental astronomers, a wonder of the age worthy of indication on the Ordnance Survey map, it proved a disappointment.

The solar system and nearby stars Except for a token paper that Herschel published in extreme old age as first president of the Astronomical Society, all his researches appeared in *Philosophical Transactions*, to whose pages he acquired almost automatic right of access. Many of his papers concerned the solar system. He argued that, when looking at the sun, observers see, not the surface of the star, but its luminous outer atmosphere, through gaps in which are seen (as 'sunspots') portions of the cool inner atmosphere that shields the inhabitants of the planet-like body of the sun from the heat of the outer atmosphere. He discovered two satellites of Uranus in 1787, after he had contrived to dispense with the secondary mirror of the 20 foot in its normal, Newtonian configuration and so avoid the loss of light that this entailed; instead, he tilted the primary mirror slightly and positioned the eyepiece inside the end of the tube, so that he stood with his back to the sky, looking directly at the image formed at the focus. In 1798 he made the astonishing announcement that the motion of the two satellites was retrograde. He subjected Saturn to frequent examination, and in 1789 discovered the satellites Mimas and Enceladus. When the supposed planets Ceres and Pallas were discovered on the continent after the turn of the century, he showed that they were far too small to be considered planets, and proposed instead the name 'asteroid'.

In 1783, in an exercise of analysis carried out at his desk, Herschel claimed to have identified the direction in which the entire solar system is travelling. It was a masterly analysis, though the striking similarity of his direction to that of modern astronomy is partly a matter of luck. In the late 1790s he put the study of variable stars onto a sound observational basis by publishing catalogues in which the brightness of a given star of a constellation was compared to that of stars of very similar brightness in the same constellation, so that a future change in the brightness of the given star would reveal itself by disturbing the published

comparisons. In 1800 he discovered infra-red rays from the sun; and he more than once passed the light of stars through a prism, though he could of course offer no explanation of the spectra thus obtained. Between 1807 and 1810, deaf to all advice, he published three long and misguided papers entitled 'Newton's rings'.

Final years, death, and reputation As he moved into his later seventies, the consequences of the long nights spent in the 1780s and 1790s observing in the cold and damp began to take increasing toll on Herschel's health, and in 1816 he persuaded his son John to abandon his career as a Cambridge don and return home, so that he could pass his astronomical skills and experience on to him before it was too late. John accepted the completion and revision of his father's work as a sacred duty, and was himself to acquire lasting fame as he discharged this duty. Over the next six years his father became increasingly frail, and on 25 August 1822, after some days in bed, Herschel died at Observatory House, his Slough home. He was buried on 7 September at St Lawrence's, Upton, near Slough. His epitaph included the words 'Coelorum perrupit claustra' ('he broke through the barriers of the heavens'). To the poet Thomas Campbell, in 1813, Herschel had remarked: 'I have looked further into space than ever human being did before me. I have observed stars of which the light, it can be proved, must take two million years to reach the earth.' 'I really and unfeignedly felt at the moment', wrote Campbell to a friend, 'as if I had been conversing with a supernatural intelligence' (Lubbock, 336).

Herschel had risen from the obscurity of his Hanoverian origins to become, first, a musician and composer of more than average competence and then a pioneer in astronomy who changed the very nature of the science. He was in the first rank as telescope builder, as observer, and as theorist, a combination of talents unique in the history of astronomy. His achievements were widely recognized: he received doctorates from the universities of Edinburgh (1786) and Glasgow (1792), was a member of the American Philosophical Society and of innumerable societies across Europe, and in 1816 was appointed a knight of the Royal Guelphic Order. Yet several contemporary astronomers, unable even to see many of the objects he discussed, were uncertain what to make of his revolutionary methodology and novel theories. Being self-taught, he had not known that astronomers were expected to focus on the solar system. Instead, he explored the construction of the universe, and it was on later generations that the questions he asked and the methods he devised to answer them were to have profound influence.

MICHAEL HOSKIN

Sources C. A. Lubbock, ed., *The Herschel chronicle: the life-story of William Herschel and his sister Caroline Herschel* (1933) • *The scientific papers of Sir William Herschel*, ed. J. L. E. Dreyer, 2 vols. (1912) • Mrs J. Herschel, *Memoir and correspondence of Caroline Herschel* (1876) • A. M. Clerke, *The Herschels and modern astronomy* (1895) • F. Arago, 'Analyse historique et critique de la vie et des travaux de Sir William Herschel', *Annuaire pour l'an 1842 publié par le Bureau des Longitudes*, 2nd edn (Paris, 1842), 249–608 • E. S. Holden, *Sir William Herschel* (1881) • M. Hoskin, 'Herschel, William', *DSB* • J. A. Bennett,

'"On the power of penetrating into space": the telescopes of William Herschel', *Journal for the History of Astronomy*, 7 (1976), 75–108 · M. Hoskin, *William Herschel and the construction of the heavens* (1963) · C. Cudworth and S. Jeans, 'Herschel, William', *New Grove* · A. J. Turner and others, *Science and music in eighteenth-century Bath* (1977) [exhibition catalogue, the Holburne of Menstrie Museum, Bath, 22 Sept – 29 Dec 1977] · R. Porter, 'William Herschel, Bath, and the Philosophical Society', *Uranus and the outer planets*, ed. G. Hunt (1982), 23–34 · J. A. Bennett, 'Herschel's scientific apprenticeship and the discovery of Uranus', *Uranus and the outer planets*, ed. G. Hunt (1982), 35–53 · S. Schaffer, 'Uranus and the establishment of Herschel's astronomy', *Journal for the History of Astronomy*, 12 (1981), 11–26 · S. Schaffer, 'Herschel in Bedlam: natural history and stellar astronomy', *British Journal for the History of Science*, 13 (1980), 211–39 · M. Hoskin, 'Herschel and the construction of the heavens', *Uranus and the outer planets*, ed. G. Hunt (1982), 55–66 · M. Hoskin, 'William Herschel's early investigations of nebulae: a reassessment', *Journal for the History of Astronomy*, 10 (1979), 165–76

Archives Harvard U., Houghton L., papers · MHS Oxf., journal and papers · NMM, household accounts; visitors book · Ransom HRC, corresp. and papers · RAS, corresp. and papers · RS, papers | NRA, priv. coll., letters to Sir Joseph Banks

Likenesses attrib. J. Flaxman, Wedgwood medallion, *c*.1781, Wedgwood Museum, Barlaston, Staffordshire · L. F. Abbott, oils, 1785, NPG [*see illus.*] · J. C. Lochée, Wedgwood medallion, *c*.1785, Wedgwood Museum, Barlaston, Staffordshire · J. Russell, oils, 1795, NMM · J. Godby, stipple, pubd 1814 (after F. Rehberg), BM, NPG · W. Artaud, oils, RAS · C. Ford, watercolour (after L. F. Abbott), Holburne of Menstrie Museum, Bath · J. C. Lochée, plaster bust, NPG · J. Sharples, pastel, Bristol City Art Gallery

Wealth at death under £60,000: PRO, death duty registers, IR 26/913 Reg. 4, No. 1136

Herschel, Sir William James, second baronet (1833–1917), developer of fingerprinting and judge, was born on 9 January 1833, probably in Slough, the eldest child of the three sons and nine daughters of Sir John *Herschel, first baronet (1792–1871), astronomer and chemist, and his wife, Margaret Brodie, daughter of Alexander Stewart, Presbyterian minister of Blair Atholl.

Herschel was educated at Clapham grammar school and the East India Company's college at Haileybury. He arrived in Bengal in 1853 and was posted to Malda as an assistant magistrate. In later years he served as magistrate of Midnapore (1866–71), district judge of Dinajpur (1871–2) and Nadia (1872–4), commissioner of Cooch Behar (1874–5), and magistrate of Shahabad (1875–7) and Hooghly (1872–8). On 19 May 1864 he married (Anne) Emma Haldane, youngest daughter of Alfred Hardcastle of Hatcham House, Surrey. She died at the birth of their second son on 5 October 1873, leaving two older girls, a boy, and the baby in Herschel's care.

In 1858 at Jangipur, while still a relatively junior civilian, Herschel realized that taking and recording fingerprints could prevent impersonation. Over the next fifteen years he noted that not only were the ridge and furrow patterns of each individual's prints unique, but they never changed. In 1877, as magistrate of Hooghly, he instituted the first known system of fingerprinting as a means of combating fraudulent contracts, false pension claims, and prisoner substitution. Although the scheme enhanced his reputation among local Bengalis as an incorruptible administrator, he received no official encouragement for his work and in 1878 he resigned the service and

Sir William James Herschel, second baronet (1833–1917), by unknown photographer

returned to England. Fingerprinting was not to be formally adopted in India until 1897.

Despite claims to prior discoveries made by Henry Faulds, who was the first to publish on the subject, Herschel is generally recognized as the pioneer of fingerprinting. His work was built upon by Sir Francis Galton and Sir Edward Henry, whose systematic methods had practical applications for the detection of criminals, and to whom with characteristic modesty he paid tribute in his book *The Origin of Finger-Printing* (1916).

Back in England, Herschel settled at Oxford. There he became an unattached member of the university and in 1881, at the age of forty-eight, was awarded a first-class degree in theology. Typical of him, wrote a friend, was his readiness to 'clothe himself in the humility of the commoner's gown' (*Oxford Magazine*, 2 Nov 1917). For a few years he lectured in divinity at Hertford College and in 1911 published *A Gospel Monogram*. Living at Lawn Upton, Littlemore, he undertook many philanthropic and religious activities, including work for the Temperance Society, and set about recording the local dialect, a task subsequently taken up by his younger daughter, Emma Dorothea. He was a member of the Oxfordshire county council from 1895 to 1904. Inspired perhaps by his father's early photographic inventions, he took a special interest in colour photography and presided at the national photographic convention in Oxford in 1901.

In 1908 Herschel moved to Warfield, Berkshire. He died at home in Rectory House, Warfield, on 24 October 1917 and was buried in the family vault in Hawkhurst, Kent, on the 27th. His elder son, John Charles William (*b*. 1869), succeeded him as third baronet. On his death in 1950 the baronetcy became extinct.

A. SPOKES SYMONDS, *rev.* KATHERINE PRIOR

Sources F. R. Cherrill, *The fingerprint system at Scotland Yard* (1954) · G. Lambourne, *The fingerprint story* (1984) · BL OIOC, Haileybury MSS · Burke, *Peerage* (1949) · *East-India Register and Army List* (1855–60); *Indian Army and Civil Service List* (1861–76); *India List, Civil and Military* (1877–8) · *The Times* (25 Oct 1917) · *The Times* (26 Oct 1917) · A. Spokes Symonds, 'Herschel's "retirement" years', *Fingerprint Whorld*, 16/62 (Oct 1990), 41–3 · private information (1993) ·

C. Sengoopta, *Imprint of the raj: how fingerprinting was born in colonial India*
Archives BL OIOC, corresp. and papers, incl. accounts and memoranda relating to India, MS Eur. D 860 · Bodl. Oxf. · U. Cal., Berkeley, Bancroft Library, corresp. and papers relating to fingerprinting
Likenesses S. Acland, photograph, Bodl. Oxf. · photograph, London Metropolitan Police; repro. in Lambourne, *Fingerprint story* · photograph, repro. in Cherrill, *The fingerprint system* [*see illus.*]
Wealth at death £1132 15*s.* 10*d.*: probate, 24 Dec 1917, *CGPLA Eng. & Wales*

Herschell, Farrer, first Baron Herschell (1837–1899), lord chancellor, was born at Brampton, Huntingdonshire, on 2 November 1837, the eldest son of the Revd Ridley Haim *Herschell (1807–1864) and his first wife, Helen Skirving (*d.* 1853), daughter of William Mowbray, an Edinburgh merchant. Raised in a non-denominational form of dissent, he later adhered to the Church of England, with broad-church leanings.

On leaving his grammar school in south London Herschell was taken by his mother to Bonn in 1853 to complete his education at the university, but with her death a few months later this idea was abandoned. Following travels with his father he matriculated at London University in July 1855. In October he entered University College and graduated BA with honours in classics in 1857. A keen advocate of the extension of university provision, he afterwards served the university as examiner in common law (1872–6), on the senate (from 1883), and from 1894 as chancellor. From early youth Herschell had proclaimed his vocation for the law. On 12 January 1858 he entered Lincoln's Inn and was called on 17 November 1860; he later became a bencher (8 May 1872) and was treasurer in 1886. He was a pupil of Thomas Chitty, the famous special pleader, and found a place in the chambers of James Hannen.

Herschell started out on the northern circuit with no connections and at first had to supplement his income by contributing to the *New Reports* (1863–5). He soon gained a reputation, especially in commercial cases, and was able to confine his excursions to Liverpool and Manchester, eventually becoming Charles Russell's leading rival there. Blessed with a remarkable memory which usually enabled him to dispense with notes, he was not a great jury advocate but had few equals as a lucid presenter of facts and law. He took silk on 8 February 1872 and served as recorder of Carlisle from 10 October 1873 to June 1880. On 20 December 1876 he married Agnes Adela, third daughter of Edward Leigh Kindersley of Clyffe, Dorset, and granddaughter of the judge Richard Torin Kindersley.

Courted by both political parties, Herschell embraced Liberalism and at a by-election on 13 June 1874 became a member for Durham City. He recommended ambitious barristers to enter parliament, but few adapted their courtroom style to the very different requirements of the Commons as successfully as he. Herschell made his mark with an impressively grave and dignified speech on a controversial Admiralty circular concerning the surrender of fugitive slaves (24 February 1876) and thereafter commanded general respect, though he could not persuade

Farrer Herschell, first Baron Herschell (1837–1899), by unknown photographer

the house to support his bill to discourage actions for breach of promise of marriage. His steadfast adherence to Gladstone's views on the Eastern question and Ireland bore fruit when the latter returned to power in 1880 and made him solicitor-general (3 May); he was knighted ten days later.

Herschell and the attorney-general, Sir Henry James, proved an unusually effective team of law officers. They met unprecedentedly heavy demands, particularly from the Foreign Office. The presentation of their opinions was admirably adapted to lay readers, and unlike many of their predecessors, they regularly attended the house. Herschell in particular was much admired for his stamina in combining onerous public duties, including leading roles in the Irish Land Bill (1881) and the Bankruptcy Bill (1883), with an enormous load of private work—he appeared in almost every major case in the Lords and privy council at this time. The effect on his health became apparent only later.

Herschell had turned down a puisne judgeship in 1879 and subsequently declined offers to be a lord of appeal, to succeed Sir George Jessel as master of the rolls, and to be speaker. His judgement was called into question when, having had to vacate his seat through the changes wrought by the third Reform Act, he was defeated for Lonsdale North (Lancashire) at the election of November 1885. However, the ensuing political upheavals worked greatly to his advantage. When Gladstone formed his third administration Selborne and James declined to serve in a ministry planning Irish home rule and thus Herschell became lord chancellor, created Baron Herschell of the City of Durham on 8 February 1886. The defeat of the Government of Ireland Bill ended his brief tenure of office (3 August) and even his noted talents for conciliation, deployed at the 'round-table conference' of January 1887, failed to bring Chamberlain and the Liberal Unionists back into the fold.

In opposition, Herschell was enabled to indulge his love of travelling—spending, for example, part of the winter of 1891-2 with the Gladstones at Biarritz—but he was not idle in public affairs. After his masterly speech against the appointment of the Parnell commission in 1888 he dropped out of political life to some extent, but besides his judicial work he presided over royal commissions into the Metropolitan Board of Works, Indian currency, and vaccination, demonstrating his 'prodigious powers of acquisition and assimilation' (Atlay, 2.459) and impressive drafting skills. When Gladstone formed his last government in 1892, Herschell was the obvious choice for lord chancellor, and resumed the great seal on 15 August, staying on under Lord Rosebery until his ministry resigned on 22 June 1895.

Herschell had quickly learned how to manage the Lords from the woolsack, though 'an unfortunate tendency to distil a spirit of acrimony' (A. Fitzroy, *Memoirs*, 1926, 1.11) was noticed, and he grew irked by the crushing weight of the Conservative majority, which led him to espouse reform of the upper house. Always an enthusiast for codification and consolidation, he had encouraged his former pupil McKenzie Chalmers in his Bills of Exchange Act (1882), and was now able to pass his Sale of Goods Act (1893), also assisting the parliamentary counsel with the Merchant Shipping Act of 1894. He also secured the passage of two measures to restrict betting and continued to press, in modified form, Halsbury's plans to extend title registration and assimilate real and personal property, though they were not enacted until 1897.

Although advocating reforms to coroners' courts, Herschell showed little inclination to tackle the defects of the superior courts, ignoring proposals for a court of criminal appeal and making only minor adjustments to the assizes. His dispensation of judicial patronage, however, was praised as scrupulously unpartisan. Having categorically refused to pack Liberals into the magistracy to reduce the tory majority, he was driven to distraction and uncharacteristic petulance by the persistent importunities of his parliamentary party.

It was said that Herschell aspired to a more overtly political office and many considered him admirably qualified, but the only offer he received was viceroy of India. He was however made GCB in 1893 and was held in high regard by the queen and by the Liberal Party.

Though he clashed with Halsbury over the latter's handling of the great Labour case of *Allen* v. *Flood* (1898), Herschell's services were again in demand by the Conservatives. In 1898 he agreed to sit on two commissions arising from disputes with the USA over the boundaries of Venezuela and Alaska respectively. After presiding over an inquiry into the National Society for the Prevention of Cruelty to Children, of which he was a vice-president, he went to Washington for the Canadian arbitration in August 1898 and there, the following February, he was injured in a fall and died unexpectedly in the Shoreham Hotel on 2 March 1899. His body was brought home and buried at Tincleton church, Dorset. He was survived by his wife, who died at Pau on 23 February 1902, two married daughters, and an only son, Richard Farrer (*d.* 1929).

Herschell was of middle height and slightly built, with regular features and dark eyes. He derived his taste for music, his principal recreation, from his mother. Sociable, ready with anecdotes, and generous to unsuccessful barristers, he was generally well liked. On the bench he became somewhat overbearing and was notorious in later years for interrupting counsel, but contemporaries rated his judgments very highly. However, he conceived the judicial function narrowly: 'we have to interpret the law, not make it' (*Salomon* v. *Salomon*, 1897). This espousal of strict formalism, and the unornamented and utilitarian style of his judgments, has diminished his reputation in some quarters. Nevertheless his judgments, ranging across most important areas of the common law, remain admirable specimens of accurate legal reasoning and include several of great importance in the development of company and commercial law, such as *Derry* v. *Peek* (1889) and *Salomon* v. *Salomon*.

Herschell had an unusually wide range of interests outside the law. He was on the council of the National Association for the Promotion of Social Science; was president of the Society of Comparative Legislation (1894); an original member and later president of the Selden Society; president of the Imperial Institute; a freemason and company director. He was honoured by the universities of Durham (DCL, 1882), Oxford (DCL, 1886), and Cambridge (LLD, 1893); and he was captain of Deal Castle from 1890 and deputy lieutenant for Kent and Durham.

PATRICK POLDEN

Sources R. F. V. Heuston, *Lives of the lord chancellors, 1885-1940* (1964) · J. B. Atlay, *The Victorian chancellors*, 2 (1908) · memoirs by various authors, *Journal of the Society of Comparative Legislation*, new ser., 1 (1899), 201-14 · E. Manson, *Builders of our law during the reign of Queen Victoria*, 2nd edn (1904) · W. C. Gully, 'Lord Herschell: a reminiscence', *Law Quarterly Review*, 15 (1899), 123-7 · R. B. O'Brien, *The life of Lord Russell of Killowen* (1901) · R. Stevens, *Law and politics: the House of Lords as a judicial body, 1800-1976* (1979) · J. L. J. Edwards, *The law officers of the crown* (1964) · *Law Times* (11 March 1899), 444-5 · GEC, *Peerage* · Boase, *Mod. Eng. biog.* · G. B. Sanderson, *Memoir of Ridley Haim Herschell* (privately printed, London, 1869) · H. S. Herschell, *Far among rubies*, ed. R. H. Herschell (1854) · V. V. Veeder, 'A century of English judicature', *Select essays in Anglo-American legal history*, 1 (1907), 730-836 · F. Herschell, *The political situation* (1898) · R. B. S. [R. B. Stevens], 'Herschell, Farrer', *Biographical dictionary of the common law*, ed. A. W. B. Simpson (1984) · M. Pope, ed., *Public servant* (1960) · R. F. V. Heuston, 'Judicial prosopography', *Law Quarterly Review*, 102 (1986), 90-113 · Gladstone, *Diaries* · *London street directories* (1881-1927)

Archives BL, corresp. with W. E. Gladstone, Add. MSS 44179-44648, *passim* · Bodl. Oxf., corresp. with Sir William Harcourt · Bodl. Oxf., corresp. with Lord Kimberley · LPL, corresp. with

Edward Benson • NL Scot., corresp. with Lord Rosebery • NL Scot., letters to Lord Kimberley • U. Birm. L., corresp. with Joseph Chamberlain

Likenesses R. Lehman, crayon drawing, 1893, BM • W. & D. Downey, woodburytype photograph, repro. in W. Downey and D. Downey, *The cabinet portrait gallery*, 1 (1890) • S. P. Hall, pencil sketches, NPG • Spy [L. Ward], watercolour caricature, NPG; repro. in *VF* (19 March 1881) • G. J. Stodart, stipple (after H. T. Wells), BM • oils, Harvard Law Library, Cambridge, Massachusetts • photograph, NPG [*see illus.*] • photographs?, repro. in Atlay, *Victorian chancellors*, facing p. 454 • photographs?, repro. in Heuston, *Lives of the lord chancellors*, facing p. 86

Wealth at death £153,136 10s. 5d.: probate, 12 May 1899, *CGPLA Eng. & Wales*

Herschell, Ridley Haim (1807–1864), missionary and Independent minister, was the third son and fourth child of Judah Herschell, a brewer, and his wife, Ghetal, of Strzelno (about 30 miles north of Torun, Poland), where he was born on 7 April 1807. Before his birth his mother was in danger because of the French occupation of the town and this suggested the name Haim ('life') for her son. His grandfather, Rabbi Hillel, lived with the boy's parents, who were pious Jews, and his simple but tolerant faith was a significant influence on the boy. From the age of eleven he attended two rabbinical schools, but owing to ill health he returned a few years later to work in his father's business. From about 1822 he attended Berlin University, supporting himself by teaching. He began to learn English as a visitor to England in 1825 and, having finished his university studies, he again went to London and then to Paris. As a student he had begun to question some of his earlier beliefs, and exposure to some English writings and the temptations of Paris now furthered the process of alienation. However, with the news of his mother's death, his religious feelings revived, and he began to study the New Testament, though his instincts were hostile to the rituals of French Catholicism.

About 1829 Herschell again came to England and on 14 April 1830 he was baptized in St James's, Westminster, by the bishop of London, one of his sponsors being the Revd Henry Colborne Ridley, whose name he adopted. Working as a lay evangelist to Jews in the London area Herschell felt restricted by the conservatism of the Anglican authorities in the London Society for Promoting Christianity amongst the Jews; he established an independent group, which gathered informally in Kensington for study and prayer, with encouragement from Edward Irving. At one of these house meetings Herschell met Helen Skirving Mowbray. Her father, William, a merchant from Leith, strongly opposed the ensuing friendship, with support from influential church leaders such as Thomas Chalmers, who claimed that Herschell had a 'shady past, including several romantic liaisons' (Brown, 217). Nevertheless, on 29 September 1831 they were married, and Herschell continued to work among Jews in Woolwich and later in Camden Town. In 1835 Lady Olivia Sparrow, who, like Herschell, had become disillusioned with the charismatic developments in Irving's church, persuaded him to take responsibility for the schools and mission work which she

Ridley Haim Herschell (1807–1864), by Thomas Fairland, pubd 1850

had established in Leigh-on-Sea, and later, near her home in Brampton, Huntingdonshire. His preference for a non-liturgical form of evangelical Christianity is reflected in his request in 1835 and 1836, for birth-notes for his daughters from the Witham Quaker monthly meeting, in preference to having them baptized.

Returning to London in 1838 Herschell began to preach in Founders' Hall Chapel, Lothbury. The following year he gathered a non-sectarian congregation at Chadwell Street Chapel, Islington, and in 1844 he took charge of Trinity Chapel, which had been built for him in John Street, Edgware Road, with help from such friends as Sir Culling Eardley Eardley. His hearers included both Anglicans and nonconformists who appreciated his respect for Judaism and his refusal to interpret the Old Testament as merely a prelude to the New Testament. His eschatology was more fully expounded in several publications, including his popular *Brief Account of the Present State and Future Expectations of the Jews* (1833; 5th edn, 1841), and in *The Voice of Israel* which he edited from 1844 to 1847. He travelled widely, visiting synagogues and preaching in eastern Europe, France, Italy, America, and Palestine. Typical of his non-denominational evangelicalism was his involvement in the establishment of both the British Society for the Propagation of the Gospel among the Jews (1844) and the Evangelical Alliance (1845). After the death of his first wife in 1853 he married Esther Fuller Maitland (d. 1882) on 3 July 1855. He died at 105 King's Road, Brighton, on 14 April 1864. His three surviving children were Farrer *Herschell, first Lord Herschell; Mary, who married John Cunliffe, the uncle of Walter Cunliffe; and Ghetal, who married John Scott Burdon Sanderson. His son Ridley had died unmarried in 1862. TIMOTHY C. F. STUNT

Sources G. B. Sanderson, *Memoir of Ridley Haim Herschell* (privately printed, London, 1869) · C. Binfield, 'Jews in evangelical dissent: the British society, the Herschell connexion and the premillenarian thread', *Prophecy and eschatology*, ed. M. Wilks, SCH, Subsidia, 10 (1994) · R. H. Herschell, ed., *Far above rubies* (1854) [memoir of Helen S. Herschell by her daughter] · S. J. Brown, *Thomas Chalmers and the godly commonwealth in Scotland* (1982), 217 · C. F. M. [C. F. Maitland], *How we went to Rome in 1857* (1892) · Burke, *Peerage* · m. cert. [R. M. Herschell and E. F. Maitland]

Likenesses T. Fairland, lithograph, pubd 1850, BM, NPG [*see illus.*] · Meisenbach, portrait, repro. in J. Dunlop, *Memories of gospel triumphs among the Jews* (1894), frontispiece

Wealth at death under £5000: probate, 28 May 1864, CGPLA Eng. & Wales

Hershon, Paul Isaac (1817–1888), Hebrew scholar, was born of Jewish parents in Galicia but converted to Christianity at an early age. As a protestant missionary he became an active member of the London Society for Promoting Christianity among the Jews in England and the East. He worked successively as director of the House of Industry for Jews at Jerusalem and of the model farm at Jaffa.

In 1859 Hershon retired from the mission field in order to devote himself to work on the Talmud and Midrashim. He published a number of texts on the Talmud, including *Extracts from the Talmud* (1860); *The Pentateuch According to the Talmud … Genesis* (1878); and *A Talmudic miscellany … or, A thousand and one extracts [translated] from the Talmud, the Midrashim, and the Kabbalah* (1880), which was published as volume 19 in Trübner's Oriental series. He translated from the Judaeo-Polish (the language most widely spoken by Jews in Europe) Jacob ben Isaac of Janowa's rabbinical commentary on Genesis (1885). He also translated the New Testament into Judaeo-Polish, and compiled an unpublished digest of marginal references in Hebrew for the whole Bible, which became the property of the London Jews' Society. He died, comparatively suddenly, on 25 September 1888, at his home, 9 Park Avenue, Wood Green, Middlesex. GORDON GOODWIN, rev. GERALD LAW

Sources *The Times* (15 Oct 1888) · CGPLA Eng. & Wales (1888) · d. cert.

Wealth at death £195: probate, 15 Oct 1888, CGPLA Eng. & Wales

Hertelpoll, Hugh of. *See* Hartlepool, Hugh of (*c.*1245–1302).

Hertford. For this title name *see* Clare, Roger de, second earl of Hertford (d. 1173); Clare, Gilbert de, fifth earl of Gloucester and fourth earl of Hertford (*c.*1180–1230); Clare, Richard de, sixth earl of Gloucester and fifth earl of Hertford (1222–1262); Clare, Gilbert de, seventh earl of Gloucester and sixth earl of Hertford (1243–1295); Joan, countess of Hertford and Gloucester (1272–1307); Clare, Gilbert de, eighth earl of Gloucester and seventh earl of Hertford (1291–1314); Seymour, Edward, first earl of Hertford (1539?–1621); Seymour, Katherine, countess of Hertford (1540?–1568); Stuart, Frances, duchess of Lennox and Richmond [Frances Seymour, countess of Hertford] (1578–1639); Seymour, William, first marquess of Hertford and

second duke of Somerset (1587–1660); Conway, Francis Seymour-, first marquess of Hertford (1718–1794); Conway, Francis Ingram-Seymour-, second marquess of Hertford (1743–1822); Conway, Maria Emily Seymour-, marchioness of Hertford (1770/71–1856) [*see under* Conway, Francis Ingram-Seymour-, second marquess of Hertford (1743–1822)]; Conway, Francis Charles Seymour-, third marquess of Hertford (1777–1842) [*see under* Conway, Francis Ingram-Seymour-, second marquess of Hertford (1743–1822)].

Hertslet, Sir Edward (1824–1902), librarian and archivist, was born on 3 February 1824 at 16 Great College Street, Westminster, the youngest son of Lewis *Hertslet (1787–1870) and his wife, Hannah Harriet, known as Jemima (d. 1828), the daughter of George Cooke. Educated at private schools in Hounslow, Middlesex, in 1840 Hertslet began work in the Foreign Office, where his father was librarian, at the early age of sixteen, as an unpaid assistant. After being appointed to the permanent establishment of the library in 1842, he rose rapidly through its ranks. When his father retired in November 1857 he became librarian, a position he held for the rest of his working life, before eventually retiring in 1896 after his tenure of office was extended seven years beyond normal retiring age. The Hertslet name thus became synonymous with that of the library for the nineteenth century. This remarkable long-lived connection began in 1801, when Hertslet's grandfather, who was a king's messenger, secured a position for his son in the library as sublibrarian. Lewis Hertslet became librarian in succession to Richard Ancell in 1810 because of a misapprehension on the part of Lord Wellesley, who thought that Hertslet was on the establishment and that by promoting him he would create a vacancy. It was noted that this 'choice youth had put on the great man' and become 'quite the jack in office' (FO 95/8/14, f. 900, 14 March 1810).

Hertslet's family originally came from Switzerland and had Anglicized their name from Hiertzelet. By 1849, when (on 10 April) Edward Hertslet married Eden Bull (b. 1826), the daughter of the archetypically named John Bull, the clerk of the journals of the House of Commons, the family had become part of the administrative and professional bureaucracy of Victorian England. They had nine sons and three daughters; the third son, Godfrey, inevitably made his career in the library and succeeded his father as editor of the *Foreign Office List*. Eden died in 1899.

The Hertslets fought a long battle to improve the status of their department within the office and only after a complaint before a parliamentary committee was the librarian given equivalent rank and salary to the senior clerks in the office in 1872. By this time the library had ceased to be the final repository of the dispatches and had become the pivot upon which the office machinery turned. The traditional function of the librarian was to provide the office with historical background memoranda, his work being separated from the political departments by a fifteen year rule. However, this distinction became blurred in practice and Hertslet's memoranda became as much current as

Sir Edward
Hertslet (1824–
1902), by Elliott &
Fry, pubd 1902

town's provisional mayor. A man of great probity, he possessed an Old World grace and dignity of bearing. His portrait at the Foreign Office library reflects the longevity of his service there and shows a strong aquiline face dominated by a high forehead scored by two deep furrows. It came as something of a surprise that he died so soon after retirement, when he succumbed to shock at his home, Bellevue, Richmond, on 4 August 1902, following an operation. R. A. JONES

Sources *The records of the foreign office, 1782–1939* (1969) · C. R. Middleton, *The administration of British foreign policy, 1782–1846* (1977) · R. Jones, *The nineteenth-century foreign office: an administrative history* (1971) · E. Hertslet, *Recollections of the old foreign office* (1901) · *The Times* (5 Aug 1902) · E. G. Petty-Fitzmaurice, *The life of Granville George Leveson Gower, second Earl Granville*, 2nd edn, 2 vols. (1905) · S. Hall, 'Sir Edward Hertslet and his work as librarian and keeper of the papers of the foreign office, 1857–1896', MA diss., U. Lond., 1958 · S. H. Hodges, 'The Hertslet family in service to the crown', uncorrected proofs, 1991, Foreign Office Library · DNB
Archives BL, memoranda and letters to W. E. Gladstone, Add. MSS 44290–44629, *passim* · PRO, letters to Odo Russell, FO 918 · RGS, corresp. relating to C. D. Cameron
Likenesses Elliott & Fry, photograph, NPG; repro. in *ILN* (1902) [*see illus.*] · photograph, Foreign Office, London
Wealth at death £10,877 4s. 9d.: probate, 10 Sept 1902, CGPLA Eng. & Wales

historical as more and more work devolved to the library from the political departments. In the office hierarchy the next person in importance to the under-secretaries in advising the secretary of state was J. B. Bergne, of the treaty department. When Bergne died in 1873, Hertslet came to occupy this position. By the time he retired, Hertslet calculated that he had provided the office with close to 3000 memoranda.

In 1878 Disraeli entertained his cabinet with an account of the subtle differences between a truce and an armistice, taken from a Hertslet memorandum, and in consequence Hertslet was attached to the British delegation on the Eastern question at Berlin. In 1889 he served on the British–Netherlands boundary commission on Borneo. For his services at the Berlin congress he was created a knight bachelor in 1878 and in 1892 he was created KCB, having previously been appointed CB in 1874. The anonymous writer of the *Times* obituary on Hertslet (5 August 1902), obviously one of his colleagues at the Foreign Office, paid the following tribute:

> He not only possessed a more intimate knowledge than perhaps any other man living of the literature of diplomacy but his long experience and judgment lent more than a technical value to the advice he was constantly called upon to give.

In addition to the famous dictionary of diplomatic biography, the *Foreign Office List*, published semi-annually and then annually from 1852 to 1966, and of which he became the editor in 1864 after the untimely accident that ended Francis Cavendish's career, Hertslet published volumes 12–19 of Hertslet's Commercial Treaties, the series begun by his father in 1820, and volumes 27–82 of the British and Foreign State Papers series begun in 1824. He put much of this treaty material in his *Map of Europe by Treaty* (1875) and a companion volume, *Map of Africa by Treaty* (1895). Altogether in a different style is the engaging *Recollections of the Old Foreign Office* (1901).

Hertslet lived all his life in Richmond and played a prominent part in local politics. When Richmond was incorporated as a royal borough in 1890 he became the

Hertslet, Lewis (1787–1870), librarian and editor of state papers, was born in November 1787, the eldest son of Jean Louis Pierre Hertslett (formerly Hiertzelet). His father was a Swiss settled in England, who became a king's messenger in May 1797. Lewis Hertslet was appointed sublibrarian in the Foreign Office on 8 February 1801; almost nine years later, on 6 January 1810, he succeeded Richard Ancell as librarian and keeper of the papers. He remained in this post until his retirement on 20 November 1857.

Hertslet was responsible for administering not only the Foreign Office's printed book collection, but also its records; in time he became a considerable authority on all matters of historical and geographical interest pertaining to British policy overseas. According to one foreign secretary, he was 'a Walking State Paper', while the historian Harold Temperley later observed that on occasion he exercised a powerful influence on policy. Research into records was facilitated by his introduction of a library system of registering and indexing manuscript correspondence, and his department provided secretaries of state with a steady stream of memoranda, offering guidance on precedents and information on international issues of the day. During the Crimean War these included papers on such topics as the status of the Aland Islands, the Russian occupation of Moldavia and Wallachia, and the Ottoman firman on the independence of Circassia.

In 1813 Hertslet began compiling a newspaper scrapbook, containing cuttings from reputable journals recording important political developments, which he called his 'Public documents book'. But of more lasting significance was his work on diplomatic documents. In 1820 he published, as a private undertaking but with a guaranteed order from the Foreign Office, two volumes of *A Complete Collection of the Treaties and Conventions*, relating to commerce, navigation, and the slave trade. Six years later appeared his classic work of reference under the title *British and Foreign State Papers*. Originally intended only for distribution to members of the government and British missions abroad, this collection of treaties and other commercial and political documents went on general sale in 1831 and continued as a series until 1968.

Hertslet married Hannah Harriet, daughter of George Cooke of Westminster; their youngest son, Sir Edward *Hertslet (1824–1902), later succeeded him as librarian at the Foreign Office. Hertslet died at his house, 16 Great College Street, Westminster, on 15 March 1870. A second wife, Mary Spencer Hertslet, survived him.

FRANCIS WATT, *rev.* RICHARD BONE

Sources *The Times* (17 March 1870) • E. Hertslet, *Recollections of the old foreign office* (1901) • S. Hall, 'Sir Edward Hertslet and his work as librarian and keeper of the papers of the foreign office, 1857–1896', MA diss., U. Lond., 1958 • *FCO records: policy, practice, and posterity, 1782–1992* (1992) • *FCO library: print, papers, and publications, 1782–1995* (1995) • *CGPLA Eng. & Wales* (1870) • Boase, *Mod. Eng. biog.*

Archives PRO, accounts and MSS relating to foreign office messengers, FO 351

Wealth at death under £12,000: probate, 17 June 1870, *CGPLA Eng. & Wales*

Hertz, Fanny (1830–1908), educationist, was born in Hanover, Germany, the daughter of Bram Hertz, a diamond merchant, who settled in London in 1837. On 6 September 1851, still a minor, she married at St James's parish church, Westminster, her cousin William David Hertz (1825–1890). Her husband, a native of Hamburg in Germany and a naturalized British subject, was a yarn merchant in Bradford, Yorkshire. They had three children: Ann (Amy) Rose (1853–1868), Helen Augusta (*b.* 1854), and Victor Francis William (1855–1863).

Fanny and William's homes at Ashfield Place then Vicar Lane, Bradford, became well-known meeting-places for writers, artists, and thinkers, and those with an interest in radical causes. She met and was much influenced by the positivist J. H. Bridges, who was then in medical practice in Bradford. Another visitor, Frederic Harrison, became a lifelong friend. Though Jewish by birth, she embraced the positivist philosophy of Auguste Comte (1798–1857) and published her own translation of a chapter of his *System of Positive Polity* in 1876.

Fanny Hertz became involved in women's educational causes, particularly the development of education for working-class factory women through the mechanics' institute movement. The vocational rationale of the movement operated to deny women's claims to an institute education, particularly when allied to what she referred to as 'the deeply rooted prejudice that woman has neither the same powers nor the same aspirations as man' (*Transactions of the National Association for the Promotion of Social Science*, 1859, 347). She helped to establish the Bradford Female Educational Institute in 1857, both she and her husband serving on the institute's committee. She was also associated with the female institute founded at Huddersfield in 1847. She was responsible for establishing the Bradford Ladies' Educational Association in 1868, from which developed the movement for the establishment of the Bradford Girls' Grammar School.

From this grew Fanny Hertz's involvement in the national movement to further the education of women. She gave a paper entitled 'Mechanics' Institutes for working women, with special reference to the manufacturing districts of Yorkshire' at the annual meeting of the National Association for the Promotion of Social Science held at Bradford in October 1859. She represented Bradford on the North of England Council for Promoting the Higher Education of Women and also became a member of the central committee of the National Union for Improving the Education of Women of All Classes, founded by Maria Grey in 1871.

Fanny Hertz's view that reading, writing, arithmetic, and needlework represented 'the necessaries' of female education was a conventional one, but, unusually for her time, she condemned the narrow and utilitarian perspective which saw the purpose of women's education as preparation 'for the duties of wives and mothers, of mistresses and servants' (*Transactions of the National Association for the Promotion of Social Science*, 1859, 348). A suitable education for working-class women in her view was one which included a wide range of subjects such as physical science, physiology (taught on George Combe's system), history, geography, poetry, choral singing, and drawing. Much influenced by Pestalozzi's educational theories, she also condemned the common attitude that teaching was a matter of filling the mind with facts. What was required was lively and interesting teaching that could engage the attention of the exhausted women and girls who attended the classes after an extended and strenuous day's work and would strengthen their reasoning powers through 'a chain of nicely calculated questions, adapted to their understandings, and elucidated by examples that come home to them' (ibid., 353).

The roles assigned to women in the positivist 'religion of humanity' gave emphasis to their moral responsibilities within the home and family and, despite her liberal educational views, Fanny Hertz cannot be said to have challenged conventional gender ideologies of the period. She also shared the class assumptions of her time, in her perception that the contact with 'superior and more developed minds' would exercise a beneficial influence on working-class women, in leading to a 'taste for self-improvement' (*Transactions of the National Association …*, 1859, 352). Yet she strongly rejected the common notion that only women in the higher social ranks should be educated, and her writing also shows a practical sympathy with the hardships of women's lives in an industrial town like Bradford. Her claim that membership of the Bradford Institute made working women 'part proprietors and managers' (ibid., 351) of the establishment may have been exaggerated, but, unusually, women members did have voting rights in the Bradford Institute and the importance she gave to 'common pride' and 'mutual goodwill' seems to signal a sincere attempt to build a genuine cross-class alliance between all the women involved with the institute.

Fanny Hertz was a member of that small band of nineteenth-century feminists who worked indefatigably to improve the conditions of women's lives, employment, and education. As she recognized herself, progress was slow and difficult, and, indeed, even at the Bradford Institute the conventional view that needlework was a subject of great importance to working-class women was not challenged, and curriculum provision did not achieve the range and quality that she advocated. Through her involvement with local and national committees for women's education and through her writing, however, Fanny Hertz did much to advance a broader, more liberal philosophy on the education of working-class women and some recognition of women's claims for equality of educational opportunities.

In the early 1870s the Hertzs settled in Harley Street, London, where Fanny Hertz held regular literary receptions. Robert Browning, Walter Pater, Henry James, and James Scully were among the men of letters entertained at her salon. Fanny survived her husband, William, by eighteen years, dying at her home, 40 Lansdowne Crescent, Notting Hill, London, on 31 March 1908, leaving a widowed daughter, Helen Augusta (Mrs G. P. Macdonnell), and a granddaughter. She was cremated at Golders Green crematorium on 3 April.   MEG GOMERSALL

Sources E. S. Beesly and S. H. Swinny, 'Recollections of Mrs Hertz', *Positivist Review*, 16 (1908), 115–17 · census return for Ashfield Place, Little Horton, Bradford, 1861 · *Bradford Observer* (19 Feb 1863) · *Bradford Observer* (13 Aug 1865) · M. S. Vogeler, *Frederic Harrison: the vocations of a positivist* (1984) · S. R. Wills, 'Social and economic aspects of the higher education of women, 1844–1870', MA diss., U. Lond., 1952, 129 [letter from Sir Gerald Hurst to S. R. Wills, 25 May 1951]

Wealth at death £33,527 7s. 8d.: resworn probate, 24 April 1908, *CGPLA Eng. & Wales*

Hertz, Joseph Herman (1872–1946), chief rabbi, was born on 25 September 1872 in the village of Rebrin, near Michalovce in Slovakia, then part of Hungary, the second son of Simon Hertz (1847–1913) and his wife, Esther Fanny Moskowitz (1848–1936). The elder Hertz was a Jewish teacher and was Joseph's first tutor. In 1883, in the wake of anti-Jewish disturbances, the family moved to New York, USA, settling in the Lower East Side, where Simon Hertz resumed teaching. He gained some fame as a writer of Hebrew poetry and a Hebrew grammar.

Hertz graduated at New York City College and gained his doctorate at Columbia with a thesis on James Martineau's ethical system. In 1894 he became the first rabbinic graduate of the Jewish Theological Seminary in New York. Hertz retained a sense of indebtedness to its principal founder and his teacher, Sabato Morais, whom he later called 'the leader of Orthodox Judaism in America'. His respect for his alma mater survived its steady 'leftward' movement into conservative Judaism.

In 1898, after four years as rabbi in Syracuse, New York, Hertz accepted a call to the rabbinate of the Witwatersrand Old Hebrew Congregation in Johannesburg, Transvaal republic. His support for the 'Uitlanders' and his attacks on civil disabilities of religious minorities in the Transvaal led to his expulsion in 1899. On his return to the

Joseph Herman Hertz (1872–1946), by Walter Stoneman, 1943

country in 1901 he resumed his self-appointed role as principal Jewish spokesman and activist, enjoying the confidence of the high commissioner, Sir Alfred Milner. In 1904 he married Rose Freed (1880–1930) of New York, a former student at Columbia. Highly cultivated and popular, his wife engaged widely in social work. They had six children. In 1911 Hertz returned to New York to be rabbi of the Orach Chayim Synagogue.

On 16 February 1913, in a contested election, Hertz was chosen as chief rabbi of the United Hebrew Congregations of the British Empire in succession to Hermann Adler. His age, experience, and reputed powers of leadership told in his favour. It was hoped that he would prove able to bridge 'West End' and 'East End', which had eluded the self-consciously Anglicized Adler. His candidacy was undoubtedly helped by Milner's private recommendation to Lord Rothschild, president of the United Synagogue, which dominated the election. Hertz became a naturalized British subject in 1915.

In his powerful installation sermon on 14 April 1913 Hertz spoke forthrightly of serious inadequacies in the Anglo-Jewish educational system, all the graver in an age of 'doubt and disillusionment'. The outbreak of war in 1914 delayed major remedial action. In October 1920 he embarked on an eleven-month tour of Jewish communities in the empire. He returned eager to advance educational standards, improve the levels of Jewish teacher training, and promote the enlargement of facilities for the recruitment and training of rabbis and ministers. However, his schemes for many-sided educational reorganization did not elicit the required financial support, and with unprecedented invective Hertz railed against the neglect of these causes by lay leaders. Nor had the expected aid from the imperial tour materialized.

The major lay figure with whom Hertz dealt was Sir Robert Waley Cohen (1877–1952), president of the United Synagogue. Each suffered from the other's imperious temperament. They neither welcomed nor proved able to overcome their pattern of public and private discord over communal management. Hertz's onslaughts on the radical Liberal synagogue in 1925–6, described by one critic as 'a hymn of hate', shocked many, including the lay heads of the United Synagogue, by their ferocity. Hertz had a robust notion of the chief rabbi's place in communal government. Where others looked to precedent, he relied on his own perception of needs.

While Hertz raised to new heights the prestige of his office, his early ambitions were not fulfilled. Among the reasons were the impact of two world wars, communal disharmony in high places, and the fact that the Victorian emancipationist habits of mind died hard. Nor did Hertz always take adequate account of the limited value of abrasiveness as an instrument of communal debate. Rabbinic and ministerial recruitment and training remained under-resourced.

In March 1930, on the sixtieth anniversary of the United Synagogue, Hertz famously pronounced that 'by its example and influence' the United Synagogue had made 'Progressive Conservatism' the Anglo-Jewish position in theology. He defined this at the time as 'religious advance without loss of traditional Jewish values and without estrangement from the collective consciousness of the House of Israel'.

Hertz frequently declared his belief in the Mosaic authorship of the Pentateuch under divine inspiration. Its legislation was 'divine will'. Judaism, he wrote, 'stands or falls' with belief in the 'historic accuracy' of the biblically portrayed revelation at Sinai. He accepted that at times the Bible speaks allegorically. Nor was there anything in Genesis that was 'necessarily in conflict' with evolutionary concepts. Within the pre-eminence of his affirmations of faith he cited, sometimes approvingly, the certainties and hypotheses of archaeologist, scientist, and historian, and expressed admiration for the scholarship of the great exponents of Jewish new learning.

While asserting the binding authority of the oral law, he acknowledged its inner capacity to develop through rabbinic search for the meaning of the biblical text. Nevertheless, he feared 'anarchy' in religion and opposed 'revolt'. He saw his office as a bulwark of tradition. That did not deter him from personal friendship with prominent heterodox protagonists or from co-operation on practical matters of common Jewish concern.

Hertz's attendance in 1934 at the opening of the hall of the parent Reform synagogue, accompanied by his expression of preference for 'difference' to 'indifference',

caused dismay among the Orthodox outside the United Synagogue and some surprise within. These reactions were not wholly eroded by the possibility that he was moved by a desire to show some measure of a united front in the face of public manifestations of antisemitism.

The significant effect of Hertz's support for the Balfour declaration of 1917 is universally acknowledged. His eloquent condemnations of the persecution of Jews in tsarist Russia and by the Soviet Union, and his outspoken attacks on the racial policies of Nazi Germany, attracted world attention. He was deeply shaken by the fate of European Jewry during the Second World War. Hertz was a religious Zionist (Mizrachist), whose stringent criticisms of the British government's restrictions on Jewish immigration into Palestine were in October 1945 joined by his public call to synagogues to unite in a day of 'solidarity' with Jewish refugees seeking entry thereto. The appeal was publicly countermanded by the lay heads of the United Synagogue as an attempt to introduce politics into the synagogue. For Hertz Jewish needs could not properly be excluded from synagogal life. The impasse remained unbroken at the date of his death.

Between 1914 and 1931 Hertz was the leading figure in the successful worldwide movement against proposals at the League of Nations for calendar reform entailing a moveable Sabbath, harmful to the religious observance of Jews and others. Among numerous posts held by him, Hertz was chairman of the Religious Emergency Council, of which his son-in-law, Solomon Schonfeld, was director. Hertz had founded this organization in 1937, and its operations included the rescue and welfare of Jewish scholars and others from Europe, in which he was personally much involved. In October 1942 he became a founder president of the Council of Christians and Jews on receiving assurances that conversionism was to be excluded.

Cecil Roth referred to Hertz's 'prodigiously wide reading and retentive memory', and aptly described 'his genius' as a writer as 'eclectic rather than original' (*DNB*). Hertz's literary legacy, in addition to innumerable articles, included his annotated edition of the Pentateuch, described by the *Jewish Chronicle* as 'a communal institution'; an annotated edition of the Jewish prayer book (1941–6); five volumes of sermons and addresses; and *A Book of Jewish Thoughts*, published in 1917 for Jewish servicemen, which went into a number of editions and several translations, and was justly described as a 'Jewish *Golden Treasury*'.

Hertz was a short, broadly built man, with purposeful gait. His full beard did not hide his firm features or his genial smile among his many personal friends or when with young people. It was said of him that he had a brusque manner and kindly nature. His strong voice had a remote American twang, a combination which some found rasping. He laboured long in preparing his sermons but, according to a memoir by E. Levine, they often lacked a human touch or homely atmosphere. Hertz was made a Companion of Honour in 1943. He was also a commander of the order of Leopold II. He was made an honorary LLD of London University (1938).

Hertz increasingly felt the burdens of office. He died in his sleep on 14 January 1946 at his home, 103 Hamilton Terrace, St John's Wood, London. He was buried on 16 January at the cemetery of the United Synagogue in Pound Lane, Willesden, London. ISRAEL FINESTEIN

Sources H. W. Meirovich, *A vindication of Judaism: polemics of the Hertz Pentateuch* (New York, 1998) • M. F. Kandel, 'The theological background of Dr. J. H. Hertz', *Le'Ela*, 48 (Dec 1999), 25–33 [London School of Jewish Studies] • R. D. Q. Henriques, *Sir Robert Waley Cohen* (1966) • J. E. Sacks, *Community of faith* (1995) • J. H. Hertz, *Affirmations of Judaism* (1927) • J. H. Hertz, *Sermons, addresses, and studies*, 3 vols. (1938) • J. H. Hertz, *Early and late* (1943) • J. H. Hertz, *Notes, commentary, and essays on Pentateuch* (1929–37) • J. H. Hertz, *In memoriam* (1947) [with 'Memoir' by E. Levine pp. 1–32 and bibliography pp. 79–87] • I. Jakobovits, 'The attitudes to Zionism of Britain's chief rabbis as reflected in their writings', *If only my people: Zionism in my life* (1984), 209–42 • G. Saron and L. Hotz, eds., *The Jews in South Africa: a history* (1955) • A. N. Newman, *Joseph H. Hertz C.H.* (1972) • *Jewish Chronicle* (18 Jan 1946) • personal knowledge (2004) • private information (2004) [family] • *CGPLA Eng. & Wales* (1946)
Archives LMA, corresp. and papers • U. Southampton, corresp. and papers
Likenesses J. Oppenheimer, oils, 1938, London College of Jewish Studies' library • Vandyk, photograph, 1938, repro. in Levine, 'Memoir' • W. Stoneman, photograph, 1943, NPG [*see illus.*]
Wealth at death £16,138 7s. 9d.: probate, 7 Aug 1946, *CGPLA Eng. & Wales*

Hertz, Mathilde Carmen (1891–1975), animal psychologist and sensory physiologist, was born on 14 January 1891 at Quantiusstrasse 13, Bonn, Germany, the second of two daughters of physicist Heinrich Rudolf Hertz (1857–1894), famous for discovering electromagnetic waves, and his wife, Elisabeth (1864–1942?), daughter of geodesy professor Max Doll of Karlsruhe. Following her father's death her mother, to supplement meagre resources, kept boarders, among whom was Maria Gräfin von Linden. One of the first women to hold a senior scientific research post in a German university von Linden strongly influenced the Hertz daughters.

Mathilde Hertz attended the state Realgymnasium (high school) in Bonn until Easter 1910, then studied art in Weimar, Karlsruhe, and Berlin. She became a sculptor, but from 1918 until 1923 also worked in the Deutsches Museum in Munich. When assisting palaeontologist Ludwig Döderlein in modelling fossil teeth she became interested in zoology, and in 1921 enrolled at Munich University. She was awarded a doctorate *summa cum laude* in 1925, following research on primitive mammalian teeth.

Mathilde Hertz remained in Munich working on zoological classification until 1927, when, having become increasingly interested in animal psychology, she moved to the Kaiser-Wilhelm Institute for Biology in Berlin-Dahlem as visiting scientist. She became a permanent assistant in 1929 following publication of several notable papers on shape perception and memory in crows and jays. Work on perception capabilities in a variety of animals followed, including outstanding studies on contour and colour recognition in bees. At the German Zoological Society's 1929 Marburg Congress she set out her approach, in which she used the gestalt psychology concept of the learned organized whole in understanding sensory development; her theories de-emphasized the role of instinct. Now prominent nationally she was appointed lecturer at Berlin University in 1930, one of few women to hold such a post. Her programme of lectures and seminars in animal psychology and sensory physiology ended in 1933 when her teaching licence was withdrawn because of National Socialist government regulations restricting the employment of women and Jews. One quarter Jewish by ancestry (although protestant by baptism and upbringing), she nevertheless succeeded in keeping her research position at the Kaiser-Wilhelm Institute until 1935 when she emigrated to Britain.

With help from her father's friend, physicist J. J. Thomson, and from biologist A. D. Imms, Mathilde Hertz settled in Cambridge, supported by an Academic Assistance Council grant. Further financial aid came from the radio industry in recognition of her father's pioneering work. In 1936 her mother and sister joined her. Although she never held a formal position at Cambridge University, for a time she collaborated with Imms at the zoological laboratory in investigations on migratory locusts, while also continuing her own studies on bees. In 1939, however, after ten years of productive work and more than thirty notable publications, she gave up research. Poor health and shortage of money were hindrances, but also her field was changing; the work of Konrad Lorenz and other continental ethologists, which emphasized the role of instinct, was largely displacing the gestalt theoretical approach she had followed. Fifty years were to lapse before neurophysiologists rediscovered her studies on optical perception in bees.

Throughout the Second World War Mathilde Hertz remained committed to Germany and kept her German citizenship, although her stubbornly held views in these matters caused a serious family quarrel. Some financial assistance continued, and she had at least occasional meetings with Cambridge biologists. In 1956 she was contacted by physicist Max von Laue, then organizing the Heinrich Hertz centenary celebrations. He found her partly blind and too proud to ask for help, barely subsisting on an income more suited to the 1930s. He arranged a German government pension for her plus additional support channelled through the Max Planck Society.

During her last twenty years Mathilde Hertz rarely left Cambridge except for occasional visits to Hamburg relatives, who knew her as 'Crow-auntie'. At the time of her death from heart failure, at her home, 3 St Margaret's Road, Girton, Cambridge, on 20 November 1975, she was co-editing a second edition of memoirs of her father. She was buried in the Hertz family plot in Olsdorfer cemetery, Hamburg. MARY R. S. CREESE

Sources S. Jaeger, 'Vom erklärbaren, doch ungeklärten Abbruch einer Karrier: die Tierpsychologin und Sinnespsychologin Mathilde Hertz (1891–1975)', *Passauer Schriften zur Psychologiegeschichte*, 11 (1996), 229–62 • *Heinrich Hertz: memoirs, letters, diaries*, ed. J. Hertz and others, trans. M. Hertz and C. Susskind, 2nd edn (1977) • *The Times* (26 Nov 1975), 30 • d. cert. • W. H. Thorpe, *Learning and instinct in animals* (1956) • Otto, Graf zu Stolberg-Wernigerode, ed., *Neue deutsche Biographie* (Berlin, 1953–) • L. S. Hearnshaw, *A short history of*

British psychology, 1840–1940 (1964) · A. Timm, 'Zwischen Emanzipation und Emigration—Jüdische Hochschullehrerinnen an der Berliner Universität bis 1933', *Zur Geschichte des Frauenstudiums und weiblicher Berufskarrieren an der Berliner Universität* [Berlin, 1995], ed. G. Jähnert (Berlin, 1996), 87–8
Archives Bodl. Oxf. · U. Cam., department of zoology
Likenesses photograph, repro. in Jaeger, 'Vom erklärbaren, doch ungeklärten Abbruch einer Karrier'
Wealth at death £84,574: probate, 12 Jan 1976, *CGPLA Eng. & Wales*

Hertzog, James Barry Munnik (1866–1942), prime minister of South Africa, was born at his father's farm, Zoetendal, near Wellington, Cape Colony, on 3 April 1866, the fifth son and eighth surviving child of Johannes Albertus Munnik Hertzog (1826–1895) and his wife, Susanna Maria Jacoba Hamman (1831–1921). The family moved to the diamond fields at Kimberley in 1872 and then to Jagersfontein in the Orange Free State in 1879. Hertzog attended Victoria College, Stellenbosch, from 1881, and there met Wilhelmina Jacoba (1863–1942), daughter of Charles Marais Neethling, a Stellenbosch farmer, whom he was to marry on 9 October 1894. In 1889 he left for the Netherlands to study law at the University of Amsterdam, where he obtained his doctorate in 1892. Unable to practise at the Cape with Dutch qualifications, he became a lawyer in Pretoria, and in 1895 he was appointed a judge on the bench of the Orange Free State. In Bloemfontein he became a close friend of President M. T. Steyn.

When the Second South African War broke out in 1899 Hertzog was appointed legal adviser to the Free State forces and did administrative work in the field, before Steyn appointed him a combat general in June 1900. Hertzog was one of those who argued that the war against the British should be continued by guerrilla tactics, and he successfully persuaded many burghers who had laid down their arms to take them up again. Having assembled a commando of 1200 men, he attacked various British positions in the Free State before, in December 1900, leading his men on a daring raid into Cape Colony. He advanced to the Atlantic Ocean before being forced to retreat. In the latter stages of the war he was active both as a fighter in the south-western Free State and as legal adviser to, and representative of, the Free State government. He was one of those who negotiated with British officials at Klerksdorp and Pretoria, and was at the meeting of Boer representatives at Vereeniging in May 1902. Hertzog was one of the signatories of the treaty signed in Pretoria on 31 May which ended the war.

Rejecting the offer of a chair in the law of South Africa at Leiden in the Netherlands, General Hertzog, as he was known after the war, went into politics in what had become the Orange River Colony. He challenged the policy of Anglicization which Lord Milner sought to impose on the former republics and demanded that Dutch should be put on an equal footing with English. He was a strong advocate of mother-tongue education in the schools. Arguing that the Orange River Colony should be given full self-government, he was a co-founder of the Orangia Unie party in 1906, and worked hard to achieve the sweeping victory it won in the election of June 1907. Elected for the

James Barry Munnik Hertzog (1866–1942), by Howard Coster, 1937

Smithfield constituency, which he was to represent for thirty-one years, he became attorney-general, then minister of education in the government of the colony from 1907 to the advent of union in 1910. While many British people came to regard him as an anti-British racialist, many Afrikaners saw him as their foremost champion. His Education Act of 1908 required English and Dutch to be used equally as languages of instruction in the colony; as a delegate to the national convention which met in 1908–9 he argued strongly that Dutch and English should have equal status as the two official languages of the new united country. He was, therefore, an architect of the clause which entrenched equal language rights in the South Africa Act. He was too prominent a figure for Louis Botha to pass over when he put together a virtual coalition cabinet in May 1910. After Hertzog had refused a seat on the appeal court he was made minister of justice.

In Hertzog's view, Botha and Jan Smuts had sold out the interests of the Afrikaners by giving in to imperial wishes and accepting a second-class status for Afrikaans; but he accepted office under Botha in order to be able to do what he could to promote what he saw to be Afrikaner interests. In a series of widely reported speeches, he called for a new South African nationalism, not British or Afrikaner but based on the principle of South Africa first, and he called on the white population to put the interests of the new country before those of the empire. Hertzog spoke of two equal streams, English and Afrikaner, flowing in the same direction; but he also called some English-speaking South

Africans foreign adventurers, and said that his aim was to make Afrikaners masters in the union. In December 1912 he called 'conciliation', the term which Botha used for his policy of bringing English and Afrikaner together, an idle word. When Hertzog refused either to moderate his language or to resign from the cabinet, Botha himself resigned in December 1912 and formed a new ministry without him.

For a time Hertzog remained in Botha's party, but when he was censured at the annual party congress in November 1913 he walked out with his supporters, and in January 1914 formed his own party, which he called the National Party, at a meeting in Bloemfontein. Initially, support for the new party came almost exclusively from Afrikaners, most of them from the Orange Free State, but over time a majority of Afrikaners would come to identify the National Party with the defence of their language and culture. And some English speakers would accept that Hertzog did not intend his nationalism to be exclusively Afrikaner.

When the First World War broke out Hertzog opposed the invasion of South-West Africa and refused to condemn those Afrikaners who took up arms against the government, but he was careful not to lend them active support. He capitalized on the bitterness caused by the failure of the uprising, and in the general election of 1915 support for the National Party grew not only in the Free State but now also in Transvaal and the Cape. After the 1920 election, at a time of economic downturn, the party became the largest party in the house of assembly. But an attempt at a 'reunion' between Smuts and Hertzog failed, and Smuts turned to the Unionists. Hertzog then accused him of siding with British imperialism. The Rand revolt of 1922 strengthened co-operation between Hertzog and Colonel F. H. P. Creswell's Labour Party. Hertzog went so far as to say that Smuts, whom he saw as being in league with the mine magnates, had incited men so that he could shoot them, and that his footsteps 'dripped with blood'. After making an election pact with Labour in 1923 Hertzog led his party to victory in the 1924 election and became prime minister. He then set out to protect white labour, to put in place further segregationist measures, and to obtain a more independent position for the union in the empire/commonwealth.

When Hertzog led an abortive National Party mission to the peace conference at Versailles in 1919, he hoped that President Woodrow Wilson might consider a plea for the re-establishment of Transvaal and Orange Free State independence, or for South Africa's secession from the British empire. By the time he became prime minister he had accepted that South Africa would remain in a reformed empire/commonwealth, and at the Imperial Conference of 1926 he was largely instrumental in wording the Balfour declaration, which spoke of 'sovereign independence' for the dominions. On his return to South Africa he took steps to give the country the symbols that went with such an independence: its own flag, nationality, and diplomatic relations with other countries. After the Imperial

Conference of 1930 he told his followers that the imperial relationship had been revised sufficiently to allow Dutch- and English-speaking South Africans to work together in a new South African nation. Among the other achievements of his first ministry, Afrikaans took the place of Dutch as one of the two official languages, an iron and steel corporation (Iscor) was established, and a 'Colour Bar Act' was passed to protect white workers against competition from cheap black labour.

After falsely accusing Smuts of aiming to create a 'black Kaffir state', in which 'white civilisation' would be 'swamped', Hertzog won an absolute majority in the house of assembly in the 1929 general election. But then came the depression and economic crisis, which led him in December 1932 to do what he said he would not do and abandon the gold standard. By early 1933 support for his government was draining away and Hertzog feared that he would be forced out of office. He therefore agreed to enter into a coalition with the South African Party of his old political enemy Smuts. Smuts allowed Hertzog to remain prime minister when, in 1934, coalition became fusion and the United Party was born. The Status Act of that year seemed to place the independence of the union beyond doubt, but Hertzog's decision to join Smuts led many former members of the National Party to view him as a traitor, and they rallied behind his former deputy, D. F. Malan, who formed a Purified National Party.

The so-called Hertzog bills which, as minister of native affairs, Hertzog had proposed in 1926, provided for political segregation and, as compensation, a new land deal for Africans. But until early 1936 he was not able to achieve the two-thirds majority in parliament which the constitution required in order for the Cape African franchise to be abolished. He rejected African appeals for the retention of that franchise, and, amid much controversy, the legislation was passed in 1936–7. As a quid pro quo for losing their vote on the common voters roll, Africans were given indirect communal representation by white citizens in parliament and an advisory Natives Representative Council was established. The promised additional land was not provided, and when in 1938 Hertzog insisted on appointing to the senate as a 'Native Representative' a man clearly unsuited for that position, the liberal Jan Hofmeyr resigned from the cabinet, unable to stomach any longer the prime minister's obvious lack of interest in the fate of the majority of the country's population.

Believing that South Africa should assert its independence, Hertzog opposed South Africa's entry into the Second World War in September 1939, and argued that the country should remain neutral, for its interests were not directly threatened and going to war would irretrievably embitter relations between English speakers and Afrikaners. Smuts won a majority for entry in the house of assembly, however, and Sir Patrick Duncan, the governor-general, refused to dissolve parliament, as Hertzog requested him to do, and instead asked Smuts to try to form a government. Hertzog then offered his resignation, which was accepted when Smuts reported that he had been able to form a government. Had there been an election, it is possible Hertzog would have been returned to power.

Hertzog's last years were tragic. He joined the Purified National Party led by Malan, but Malan did not welcome him, and when his plea that English speakers should enjoy equal rights was rejected, he left the National Party and resigned from parliament in December 1940. He was given the figurehead role of honorary leader of the new Afrikaner Party, but retreated to his farm near Witbank in Transvaal. In October 1941, under the influence of Oswald Pirow, who had been his minister of defence and was to be one of his biographers, he spoke of national socialism as the answer for South Africa. The following year, seven months after the death of his wife, he died at Waterkloof, Pretoria, on 21 November 1942, and was buried on 24 November at Pretoria. Of their three sons, the eldest, Albert, became a cabinet minister in a future National Party government, but in 1969 led a right-wing breakaway; as his father had done in 1912, he formed a new party, but one which never won seats in parliament.

Hertzog was a skilful political tactician and fluent speaker—in English as well as in Afrikaans—though he was often tortuous and his meaning far from clear, and he was given to emotional outbursts. An essentially modest man, he did much to promote Afrikaner culture while at the same time helping to create a new patriotism open to English-speaking white inhabitants as well as Afrikaners. He established the most important Afrikaans literary prize, and in 1952 a periodical, *Hertzog-Annale*, was founded as a tribute to him. A man of deeply conservative views, he could behave as a political opportunist and be openly antisemitic, as he was especially in the late 1930s. He had no real concern for the well-being of the majority of the country's population and encouraged white South Africans in the fallacy that South Africa could be a 'white man's country'. He did much to further elaborate and entrench racial segregation, preparing the way for full-scale apartheid.   CHRISTOPHER SAUNDERS

Sources D. W. Krüger, 'Hertzog, James Barry Munnik', *DSAB* · L. E. Neame, *General Hertzog, prime minister of the union* (1930) · F. Spies, D. Kruger, and J. Oberholster, eds., *Die Hertzog toesprake*, 6 vols. (1977) · C. M. van den Heever, *Generaal J. B. M. Hertzog* (1954) · C. M. van den Heever, *General J. B. M. Hertzog* (1946) · M. J. Burger, *Generaal J. B. M. Hertzog: 'n bibliografie* (1953) · O. Pirow, *James Barry Munnik Hertzog* (1957) · W. K. Hancock, *Smuts*, 2 vols. (1962–8) · T. D. Moodie, *The rise of Afrikanerdom* (1975) · A. van Wyk, *Vyf Dae: oorlogskrisis van 1939* (1991) · G. D. Scholtz, *Generaals Hertzog en Smuts en die Britse ryk* (Cape Town, 1975) · P. J. Nienaber and others, eds., *Gedenkboek Generaal J. B. M. Hertzog* (1965) · *Hertzog-Annale* (1952–66) · *DNB* · M. C. E. van Schoor, ed., 'Gen. J. B. M. Hertzog's war experiences', *Christiaan de Wet-Annale*, 10 (Oct 2000)
Archives National Archives of South Africa, Bloemfontein | BL, corresp. with Lord Gladstone, Add. MSS 46070–46074 · NA Scot., corresp. with Lord Lothian | FILM BFI NFTVA, documentary footage · BFI NFTVA, news footage
Likenesses H. Coster, photograph, 1937, NPG [*see illus.*] · G. Canitz, oils, National Museum, Bloemfontein · M. Kottler, bronze bust, Houses of Parliament, Cape Town · E. Roworth, oils, Houses of Parliament, Cape Town · C. Steynberg, bronze bust, repro. in Pirow, *James Barry Munnik Hertzog*, frontispiece · caricature, repro. in L. E. Neame, *Some South African politicians* (1929), facing p. 1 · photographs

Hervey (*d.* 1131), bishop of Ely, was a Breton by birth. He became a clerk in the service of William Rufus, and, at a time of rapid Norman advances into Wales, was promoted to the bishopric of Bangor in 1092, being consecrated by Archbishop Thomas of York (*d.* 1100). However, as Welsh resistance stiffened, Hervey was unable to maintain his position, despite his employment of secular force and excommunication, and he soon fled back to the English court, probably in 1095. Retaining his episcopal title, he attended Archbishop Anselm's general council at Westminster in 1102, and became confessor to Henry I, who in 1106 tried unsuccessfully to transfer him to the see of Lisieux. Hervey then became involved in plans to create a new bishopric at Ely.

The very large diocese of Dorchester–Lincoln, to which Ely had belonged since at least 1000, consisted of the seven archdeaconries of Lincoln, Stow, Bedford, Buckingham, Leicester, Oxford, and Huntingdon. From 1072, when Bishop Remigius (*d.* 1092) removed his see from Dorchester in Oxfordshire, the diocese was governed instead from Lincoln, where a new cathedral was dedicated in 1092. The large and wealthy Benedictine monastery at St Albans had by the end of the eleventh century virtually succeeded in establishing its independence of the diocesan at Lincoln, owing instead direct obedience to the pope, and it is possible that Abbot Richard was inspired to similar tactics on behalf of Ely. He could expect to have at his disposal very considerable monastic property, which must have seemed an ample endowment for a bishopric. But there were also problems to be solved before his scheme could be put into effect. He had to reckon with the substantial degree of autonomy enjoyed by his own religious house, where the sacrist's administrative powers had created in the Isle of Ely what was virtually an independent enclave. And there was also the fact that not far from Ely there were two large and fairly wealthy monasteries, at Thorney and Chatteris, which could have presented a threat to a new diocesan organization, and might even have been centres of hostility to it.

In any case, although Abbot Richard declared that the house of Ely owed no allegiance to Lincoln, and refused after his election to seek benediction from Bishop Robert Bloet (*d.* 1123), his campaign was not at first successful. Henry I drove him from Ely, probably in 1102, and caused him to seek the aid of Pope Paschal II (*r.* 1099–1118), who persuaded the king to restore Richard to his abbacy, apparently in the following year. But by the time of his death, in July 1107, Richard had completed both the rebuilding of the monastic church, begun under his predecessor, Abbot Simeon, and the translation of the relics of St Etheldreda and other Ely saints—two important steps towards the establishment of a new see. Following Richard's death Hervey was directed by the king to administer Ely's endowments until a decision was reached about their disposal. His actions seem to have won the approval of the monks, although they were not, it seems, aware of his instructions from the king, who late in 1108 sent him to seek papal approval for the creation of a bishopric in Ely. A papal mandate to the king to create the new see and install Hervey as the first bishop was issued on 21 November. The creation of the new see was finally approved in council at Nottingham on the feast of St Etheldreda's translation, 17 October 1109. The consent of the monks was, it seems, partly won by Henry I's grant to them of freedom from toll throughout England, which was to be confirmed in a charter guaranteeing to them the liberties granted by Edward the Confessor. Meanwhile, and more importantly, the consent of Bishop Bloet was assured—apparently through Hervey's management—by the grant to the church of Lincoln of the important Ely manor of Spaldwick in Huntingdonshire.

The administration of the new diocese was necessarily left in the hands of the archdeacon, Nicholas of Huntingdon, who plainly resented the new diocesan administration, and in 1110 departed to Rome to appeal against it, but he died before he had gone far. This enabled Hervey to appoint his own nephew, William the Breton, as archdeacon, and to endow him with the manors of Pampisford and Little Thetford. There is nothing to show whether Hervey made any attempt to interfere with the monks' claims to archidiaconal administration in the isle, although the persistence of the sacrist's claim to it as late as the fourteenth century suggests that he made no progress in asserting either his own powers or those of William. But there is some evidence that he tried to assert his control over the other two monastic houses in his diocese. Two royal writs show the king intervening to protect Thorney from Hervey's demands, though in 1128 the bishop was prepared to define Thorney's rights in its manor of Whittlesey, apparently on the occasion of his dedicating the abbey's church. And a writ of 1127, in which Henry I remitted to Chatteris 6s. 7d. due for wardpenny, also records that the king had given the nunnery to Ely, which would therefore have received the money in question.

The royal mandate for the creation of the new diocese enjoined upon Hervey an equal division between himself and the monastery of the Ely properties, and this division was embodied in a charter c.1116–17, of whose authenticity, however, there is some doubt. The Ely chronicle makes clear that the monastic income was subsequently inadequate: there was enough for only sixty monks instead of the old figure of seventy-two, and the bishop himself retained £1800 in revenues. Some concession was at least provided by the royal charter freeing the monks from toll on any sources of stone and lead for the church building. Hervey meanwhile (probably in 1130) prudently arranged with the king, in his own interest, to be free of castleguard at Norwich, which had been a serious burden on his finances. The pipe roll of 1130, listing debts owed to the crown by the bishop which amounted to some £1500, shows that he promised £1000 for the remission of castleguard. A reduction of the scutage owed from Ely's fees, from £100 to £60, cost him £240. No doubt the other royal grants of privileges and exemptions which he

obtained, including a yearly fair at Ely itself, cost similar sums. A few traces also survive of the arrangements made by Hervey to administer his new revenues and household, such as the creation of an official baker's fee, and the assembly of the episcopal reeve's fee in Fen Ditton. It seems likely, too, that the parish church of St Mary in Ely was created to serve the bishop's men living in the vicinity of his barton, or farming centre, at the top of Back Hill, which led down to the river. In the same way the episcopal vineyard, and a series of large holdings like Lisle Place, were established at an early date on the north side of Fore Hill.

There are few traces of Hervey's activity as a diocesan after his appointment of William as archdeacon. He was present in 1127 at a legatine council at Worcester, and at a royal council in 1129 when clerical marriage was condemned; he witnessed an act by which Walter *grammaticus* granted to the priory the church of Stretham; he gave to the church a silk alb, a flowered chasuble, two great cloths, and a gold pastoral staff; finally in 1131, when his death was imminent, he prepared to enter monastic life. It is not clear where he died, and the dates of his palace buildings have not been established. The many miracles wrought by St Etheldreda continued and increased in his time, not unassisted by the creation, at his insistence, of a causeway from Exning to Ely which facilitated the journeys of pilgrims. The chronicle of Orderic Vitalis contains a lengthy account of a miracle worked by the saint in 1116—the release from prison of Bricstan of Chatteris, unjustly accused before the king's justices of concealing treasure trove—which was apparently circulated in writing on the bishop's instructions. The same chronicle, under the year 1118, relates a strange story of Hervey's having a pregnant cow slaughtered and opened, to find three piglets within, a prodigy interpreted as foretelling the deaths of three great men and other dreadful events. Hervey died on 30 August 1131, and was buried in his cathedral on the following day.   DOROTHY M. OWEN

Sources E. Miller, *The abbey and bishopric of Ely*, Cambridge Studies in Medieval Life and Thought, new ser., 1 (1951), 75–112, 199–246, 280–85, 288 · E. O. Blake, ed., *Liber Eliensis*, CS, 3rd ser., 92 (1962), 204–36, 238–40 · J. Bentham, *The history and antiquities of the conventual and cathedral church of Ely*, ed. J. Bentham, 2nd edn (1812), 119–36 · N. Coldstream and P. Draper, eds., *Medieval art and architecture at Ely Cathedral*, British Archaeological Association Conference Transactions [1976], 2 (1979) · D. M. Owen, ed., *A history of Lincoln Minster* (1994), 1–46, 112–19 · *Reg. RAN*, vol. 2 · Ordericus Vitalis, *Eccl. hist.*, 3.6 · A. W. Haddan and W. Stubbs, eds., *Councils and ecclesiastical documents relating to Great Britain and Ireland*, 1 (1869), 299, 303–6 · M. Brett, *The English church under Henry I* (1975) · F. Barlow, *The English church, 1066–1154: a history of the Anglo-Norman church* (1979) · J. A. Green, *The government of England under Henry I* (1986) · D. M. Owen, *The medieval development of the town of Ely* (1993) · R. R. Davies, *Conquest, coexistence and change: Wales, 1063–1415*, History of Wales, 2 (1987); repr. as *The age of conquest: Wales, 1063–1415* (1991) · *Radulfi de Diceto … opera historica*, ed. W. Stubbs, 2: 1180–1202, Rolls Series, 68 (1876)

Archives CUL, Ely dean and chapter charters and cartularies, EDC

Hervey of Boreham. *See* Boreham, Hervey of (*b.* before 1228?, *d.* 1277).

Hervey, Lord Arthur Charles (1808–1894), bishop of Bath and Wells, fourth son of Frederick William Hervey, first marquess and fifth earl of Bristol (1769–1859), and his wife, Elizabeth Albana Upton (1775–1844), daughter of Clotworthy Upton, Lord Templetown, was born at his father's London house, 6 St James's Square, on 20 August 1808. From 1817 to 1822 he lived abroad with his parents, chiefly in Paris, and was taught by a private tutor, Samuel Forster, former head of Norwich grammar school. He entered Eton College in 1822, where his friends included Gladstone, and he remained there until 1826. In 1827 he entered Trinity College, Cambridge, as a fellow-commoner and obtained a first class in the classical tripos, graduating BA in 1830. In 1828 he was awarded a college prize, and in 1830 a Latin declamation prize. Hervey was an active sportsman, and was a champion tennis player.

Having been ordained both deacon and priest in October 1832, Hervey was instituted in November to the small family living of Ickworth-cum-Chedburgh, Suffolk; as Chedburgh was in 1844 separated from Ickworth and joined to Horningsheath or Horringer, he also became curate of Horringer, until in 1856 he was instituted to the rectory which he held with Ickworth. On 30 July 1839 he married Patience, daughter of John Singleton of Hazeley, Hampshire, and Mell, co. Louth. They had twelve children. He took a leading part in the organization of educational institutions in the neighbouring town of Bury St Edmunds as president of the Bury Athenaeum, and was an early proposer of a system of university extension (extramural teaching) in a pamphlet entitled *A suggestion for supplying the literary … institutes … with lecturers from the universities* (1855). In 1862 he was appointed by Bishop Turton of Ely to the archdeaconry of Sudbury.

On the resignation of Robert John Eden, Lord Auckland, bishop of Bath and Wells, in 1869, Hervey was offered the bishopric on the recommendation of W. E. Gladstone, and was consecrated on 21 December. In consequence of his refusal to institute a clergyman of intemperate habits, who had presented himself to a benefice, he was in 1877–9 involved in a lawsuit, which was carried before the privy council. Judgment was given in his favour with costs, but being unable to recover them he had to pay £1558, of which £978 was raised by subscription in the diocese. As a bishop he was of moderate views on church matters, though inclined to evangelicalism. He set about making Wells the centre of the diocese, and founded church-building and choral societies.

Hervey researched the chronologies of Jewish history, publishing *The Genealogies of Our Lord* in 1853. As well as publishing sermons, he contributed to William Smith's *Dictionary of the Bible* and to the Speaker's Commentary. He was a member of the committee for the revision of the Old Testament, receiving an honorary DD from Oxford University in 1885 in recognition of his work, complementing the DD received from Cambridge in 1870. Though not intellectually brilliant he was accurate and painstaking. Archaeology and family history attracted him. He wrote several papers and addresses on these subjects and served as president of the Royal Archaeological

Lord Arthur Charles Hervey (1808–1894), by Lock & Whitfield, pubd 1880

Institute. He died on 9 June 1894 at Hackwood House, near Basingstoke, the house of his son-in-law, C. Hoare. He was buried at Wells. His wife, five sons, and three daughters survived him.   WILLIAM HUNT, *rev.* ELLIE CLEWLOW

Sources J. F. A. Hervey, *A memoir of Lord Arthur Hervey DD* (1896) · Venn, *Alum. Cant.* · Burke, *Peerage* (1857) · Boase, *Mod. Eng. biog.* · Gladstone, *Diaries*

Archives Bodl. Oxf., corresp. · Suffolk RO, Bury St Edmunds, corresp. and papers | BL, corresp. with W. E. Gladstone, Add. MS 44207 · LPL, corresp. with Edward Benson · LPL, corresp. with A. C. Tait

Likenesses W. C. Ross, miniature, 1851, repro. in Hervey, *Memoir of Lord Arthur*, frontispiece · H. Graves, oils, 1871, Athenaeum, Bury St Edmunds, Suffolk · W. B. Richmond, oils, 1889, town hall, Wells; copy, bishop's palace, Wells · Elliott & Fry, photograph, repro. in Hervey, *Memoir of Lord Arthur* · Lock & Whitfield, woodburytype photograph, NPG; repro. in T. Cooper, *Men of mark* (1880) [see illus.] · engraving, repro. in Hervey, *Memoir of Lord Arthur* · engraving, repro. in *Wedmore Chronicle*, 2 (1898), 6 · wood-engraving (after photograph by J. Watkins), NPG; repro. in *ILN* (8 Jan 1870)

Wealth at death £27,731 1*s.* 6*d.*: resworn probate, Aug 1894, *CGPLA Eng. & Wales*

Hervey, Augustus John, third earl of Bristol (1724–1779), naval officer and politician, was born on 19 May 1724, the second son of John *Hervey, Baron Hervey of Ickworth (1696–1743), courtier and politician, and his wife, Mary *Hervey, *née* Lepell (1699/1700–1768), and grandson of John *Hervey, first earl of Bristol. He entered Westminster School in January 1733, and he probably remained there until May 1735 when he entered the navy as a captain's servant in the *Pembroke* (60 guns), commanded by his uncle, the Hon. William Hervey. He subsequently served in other ships as a midshipman. Early in the war of Jenkins's Ear

Augustus John Hervey, third earl of Bristol (1724–1779), by Sir Joshua Reynolds, 1762–3

(1739–43) he was again with his uncle, this time in the *Superb* (60 guns). On 31 October 1740, after three quarrelsome officers had been dismissed from the ship, Hervey, aged sixteen, passed for lieutenant and was commissioned to fill a vacancy. Later that year a refit in the Tagus gave him the opportunity to initiate a Casanova-like campaign of amorous adventure, often involving young married women.

In 1741 Hervey took part in Vernon's attack on Cartagena. The capture in November of a Spanish vessel yielded him £1500 in prize money which sufficed to settle his debts. In 1742 his intemperate uncle William was dismissed from the navy, but Hervey had already acquired a new patron, Captain the Hon. John Byng. A firm friendship began between these two contrasting characters, Hervey being of an impetuous, cocksure, convivial disposition and Byng of opposite tendency. In 1742–3 Hervey was with Byng in the *Sutherland* (50 guns) and *Captain* (70 guns), and Byng much admired his professional flair.

While waiting in 1744 to go to Jamaica in Thomas Davers's flagship, Hervey contracted a reckless secret marriage which eventually became notorious. Having just turned twenty, he met in Hampshire Elizabeth *Chudleigh (c.1720–1788). Stemming from the Devon gentry, she was lively, beautiful, and a maid of honour to the princess of Wales but, as it transpired, was inclined to marital intrigue and promiscuity. Hervey married her before a few witnesses late at night on 4 August 1744 in the church at Lainston, near Salisbury. Hervey's finances were totally inadequate to support the marriage. A son was baptized Augustus Henry Hervey at Chelsea on 2 November 1747

but he soon died. By 1749 Hervey, alienated by reports of his wife's misconduct, had finally separated from her, but the marriage, though not widely suspected for many years, ultimately prevented him from acquiring a legitimate heir.

Meanwhile, on 16 September 1746, Hervey was promoted to command the sloop *Porcupine*, and on 15 January 1747 he was posted, prospectively as Byng's flag captain, to the *Princessa* (74 guns), which he justly deemed 'a glorious ship' (*Hervey's Journal*, 47). He sailed for the Mediterranean where Byng finally decided to hoist his flag in the *Boyne* (80 guns). Byng sent the *Princessa* on three highly profitable cruises and, by the coming of peace in 1748, Hervey had accumulated prize and freight money to the tune of £9000. He was naturally grateful to Byng and remained steadfastly loyal to him. Visits to various Italian ports allowed Hervey to engage in amorous affairs faithfully recounted in his richly informative, if tendentious, *Journal*. Meanwhile, however, at Leghorn in March 1748, he bravely went in his barge and boarded a burning merchantman, heavily laden with gunpowder, which no one else would approach. He cut her free and towed her clear of the mole and the many endangered ships and storehouses. Thereupon she blew up. Hervey's coat was burned but everyone escaped injury. The governor and the merchants thanked him for averting a calamity.

With the war ending Hervey, hoping to remain employed, shifted in May 1748 into the *Phoenix* (20 guns). However, he was ordered to pay off in England. While on half pay in 1749 he was unduly prominent among the officers who protested against the new Navy Bill. However, in 1752, thanks to Lord Anson's tolerance, he was reappointed to the *Phoenix*. In time of peace bullion and coinage still awaited safe transportation, and Hervey did well out of freight money. On the proceeds he much enjoyed himself among the ladies of Genoa, Naples, Leghorn, and Lisbon.

In July 1755 Hervey, while stationed at Genoa, began sending intelligence to the Admiralty of warlike French preparations at Toulon. In September he sailed to Minorca. Already many warnings had been received there of the impending French invasion. In February 1756, as the senior naval officer in Minorca, he tried to energize the governor's council. Then Commodore Edgcumbe arrived and sent him to Villefranche for intelligence. On 12 April he heard that the French had sailed from Toulon. By 16 May Hervey had joined Byng's fleet on its way up to Mahon. From the *Phoenix* (primed as a fireship) Hervey witnessed the battle of Minorca on 20 May. At Byng's subsequent council of 24 May Hervey alone among the captains argued that, though damaged, the fleet should remain off Minorca and land a reinforcement for the besieged garrison, but he did not persist with his dissent. Notoriously the fleet fell back on Gibraltar with dire consequences for Admiral Byng.

On 2 July Sir Edward Hawke superseded Byng at Gibraltar. Hervey, now in the *Hampton Court* (64 guns), favourably impressed Hawke during the fleet's unrewarding Minorcan cruise. In the autumn, having returned to England with officers required for Byng's court martial, Hervey wrote several pamphlets on the admiral's behalf and, at his trial, testified warmly in support of his isolated friend. Hervey campaigned in vain against the iniquitous death sentence. His *Journal* is enlivened by recurrent shafts of invective aimed at 'that prejudiced weak head' Anson, 'that wasp of power and snake of ministerial dirt' Lord Barrington, and 'that infernal black demon, Mr Fox' (*Hervey's Journal*, 239, 253).

In the summer of 1757 Hervey again commanded the *Hampton Court* in the Mediterranean, where Vice-Admiral Osborn accepted much of his advice on strategic matters. In July Hervey destroyed the French frigate *Nymphe* (32 guns) on the rocks of Majorca. In February 1758 his ship's slowness prevented Hervey from reaching the *Monmouth* (64 guns) before she silenced the mighty *Foudroyant* (80 guns). Captain Gardiner having died in the fight, Hervey soon afterwards shifted into the faster sailing *Monmouth*. In July he destroyed the French frigate *Rose* (36 guns) outside the grand harbour of Malta. By October he was back at Portsmouth.

In December 1758 Hervey went to Ickworth and, at great expense, entertained the corporation of Bury St Edmunds, which had made him a member. In May 1757 he had been elected a member of parliament for that family borough by 11 votes to 10; he took his seat in January 1759.

From May 1759 Hervey, again in the *Monmouth*, played a notable part in Hawke's all-important blockade of Brest. In July Hawke wished to tighten his blockade of the port and chose Hervey to command the inshore squadron. Hervey displayed great zest, resolution, audacity, and resource. On 22 July he earned Hawke's warm commendation when, by a characteristic bluff, he foiled a French attempt to loosen the British stranglehold. In October Hawke's fleet was blown off station, but Hervey's little squadron clung on. Hervey was now suffering from gout in both feet and, on 3 November, only a fortnight before the crowning triumph at Quiberon Bay, Hawke had to order the *Monmouth* to return home. 'I heartily regret your being obliged to go in', wrote the admiral (Mackay, *Admiral Hawke*, 235).

In 1761 Hervey, in the *Dragon* (74 guns), served at the capture of Belle Île, and from December he was with Rear-Admiral Rodney in the Leeward Islands. There he was active at the capture of Martinique and in February 1762 he was detached, as commodore, to take St Lucia. This he did with typical boldness, imagination, and skill. In the same year Hervey took a prominent and distinguished part in the capture of Havana. His attack from seaward on the commanding Morro Castle was a gallant, if unsuccessful, episode. Finally Hervey's share of the enormous prize money was £1600.

His health somewhat impaired, Hervey began to turn away from the sea and seek advancement in politics. His seat at Bury was in the gift of his elder brother George *Hervey who had succeeded as the second earl of Bristol in 1751, but Hervey disliked Bristol's political associates, notably Newcastle, Fox, and, until his death in 1762, Lord

Anson. Hervey was at first attached to the friends of George III and was, on 6 November 1762, appointed colonel of the Plymouth division of marines, a near-sinecure worth £800 a year. In February 1763 he vacated his seat at Bury but was elected for Saltash, an Admiralty borough, in December. Having been a loyal supporter of George Grenville's (1763–5) ministry, Hervey avoided open opposition to Rockingham, though he did criticize the new administration's proposals for repeal of the Stamp Act in 1766. Hervey was meanwhile designated commodore to command in the Mediterranean but for political reasons became instead a groom of the bedchamber, a post worth £500 a year. In October 1766 Hervey was appointed secretary to his brother Lord Bristol, the lord lieutenant, and was sworn of the Irish privy council, but he never went to Ireland. In July 1767 he resigned, having quarrelled with his brother over his own continuing attachment to George Grenville. However, in 1767 Hervey moved in the Commons a badly needed increase in the half pay of naval lieutenants, and this was approved. In 1768 he was again elected a member for Bury; he held that seat until, on 18 March 1775, he succeeded his brother as earl of Bristol.

Meanwhile by 1767 Hervey was aiming for a seat on the Board of Admiralty, perhaps as first lord. He had for a long time been a member of Lord Sandwich's convivial set and shared the latter's strong interest in naval policy. At the end of 1770 Hervey encouraged Sandwich in his efforts to replace the ailing Hawke as first lord. In the wake of criticism of the unreadiness of the guardships during the Falklands crisis Hawke resigned in January 1771 and Sandwich was appointed in his stead. On 2 February Hervey became a lord commissioner at the Admiralty. He had a wide and trenchant knowledge of naval personnel and Sandwich openly acknowledged the value of his advice on the key matter of the guardships. Otherwise, however, he appears to have made no great contribution to the first lord's reforms. As the solitary naval lord, Hervey's record of attendance at the board, affected by ill health, was unimpressive. On succeeding to the peerage in 1775, Hervey resigned from the Admiralty. At the time of his ennoblement, Bristol was pilloried in a 'Tête-à-tête' pen portrait for his ongoing relationship with the courtesan Mary *Nesbitt (1742/3–1825) which had begun four years earlier, the couple living together at his properties in St James's Square, Westminster, and at Ickworth. The earl's divorce petition having been dismissed in 1779, he was prevented from marrying Nesbitt, whom in his will (for which she was an executor and legatee) he described as his 'dear valuable and best friend' (PRO, PROB 11/1059, fols. 98–100).

As earl of Bristol, Hervey now had an income of over £10,000 a year. In politics he veered away from his association with Sandwich and, in a long speech of April 1779 in the House of Lords, he recommended Sandwich's removal from his post. He even had the effrontery to extol the list of guardships bequeathed to Sandwich by Hawke. Meanwhile in 1775 he had been promoted to rear-admiral of the blue and he automatically progressed finally in 1778 to vice-admiral of the blue.

Largely on the strength of his *Journal* (covering the years 1746–59 but not composed from his original records until 1767–70) Hervey has emerged as a naval Casanova. Among contemporaries his reputation suffered through his having seemed to collude with his wife when she was declared a spinster, in February 1769, before an ecclesiastical court. In 1776 the House of Lords found her guilty of bigamy in her marriage of 1769 to the duke of Kingston. But it is for his remarkable seagoing record, especially in the Seven Years' War, that Hervey should be remembered.

Though quite small, he was lithe and athletic in appearance. Until gout supervened he loved singing, dancing, and pulling at an oar. His bearing was that of a haughty aristocrat and in most things he lacked moderation.

Hervey died of 'gout of the stomach' (*Hervey's Journal*, xi) at St James's Square, London, on 23 December 1779 and was buried at Ickworth five days later. The title and estates passed to his brother Frederick Augustus *Hervey (1730–1803), but Hervey alienated from him as much wealth as he could. He thus provided for his ultimate mistress, Mary Nesbitt, and for 'little' Augustus Henry Hervey (1764?–1782), his natural son by Kitty Hunter (later the wife of Sir Alured Clarke).   RUDDOCK MACKAY

Sources [earl of Bristol], *Augustus Hervey's journal*, ed. D. Erskine (1953) · M. Holmes, *Augustus Hervey* (1996) · N. A. M. Rodger, *The wooden world: an anatomy of the Georgian navy* (1986) · N. A. M. Rodger, *The insatiable earl: a life of John Montagu, fourth earl of Sandwich* (1993) · R. F. Mackay, *Admiral Hawke* (1965) · *The Hawke papers: a selection, 1743–1771*, ed. R. F. Mackay, Navy RS, 129 (1990) · D. Syrett, ed., *The siege and capture of Havana, 1762*, Navy RS, 114 (1970) · *The private papers of John, earl of Sandwich*, ed. G. R. Barnes and J. H. Owen, 4 vols., Navy RS, 69, 71, 75, 78 (1932–8) · H. W. Richmond, ed., *Papers relating to the loss of Minorca in 1756*, Navy RS, 42 (1913) · *DNB* · D. Spinney, *Rodney* (1969) · *HoP, Commons*
Archives BL, journal, Add. MS 28157 · BL, logs, account of his part in attack on Cartagena, 1741, Add. MS 12129 · Bodl. Oxf. · PRO, admiralty records · Suffolk RO, Bury St Edmunds, corresp., diaries, and papers | NMM, Sandwich MSS · priv. coll., letters to Lord Shelburne
Likenesses group portrait, oils, c.1750 (*The earl of Bristol taking leave*), Ickworth House, Suffolk · J. Reynolds, oils, 1762–3, Manor House Museum, Bury St Edmunds [*see illus.*] · T. Gainsborough, oils, c.1768, Ickworth House, Suffolk · R. Cosway, miniature, Ickworth House, Suffolk · J. Reynolds, oils (after J. Reynolds, c.1762), Wilton House; copy, NPG
Wealth at death over £10,000 income on becoming earl of Bristol, 1775: Holmes, *Augustus Hervey*, 262

Hervey, Carr, Lord Hervey (1691–1723). *See under* Hervey, John, first earl of Bristol (1665–1751).

Hervey, Frederick Augustus, **fourth earl of Bristol** (1730–1803), Church of Ireland bishop of Derry, was born at Ickworth House, Bury St Edmunds, Suffolk, on 1 August 1730, the third son of John *Hervey, Baron Hervey of Ickworth (1696–1743), courtier and writer, and his wife, Mary *Hervey, Lady Hervey (1699/1700–1768), courtier and wit, the daughter of Brigadier-General Nicholas Lepell and Mary Brooke. The manor of Ickworth had been in Hervey's family since the fifteenth century, but the earldom of Bristol came to him in 1779, from his grandfather John Hervey (1665–1751), a noted politician who received the title in 1714. Hervey's father had briefly been lord privy

Frederick Augustus Hervey, fourth earl of Bristol (1730–1803), by Angelica Kauffman, 1790

seal but his political career was cut short by his death. Despite the continuing presence of his distinguished grandfather it is believed that Hervey's mother was the principal influence that shaped his character and those of his seven siblings. He received a conventional education, first at Dr Newcome's private school in Hackney, and later at Westminster School. There he was taught by the Latinist Vincent Bourne, in the company of William Cowper, Charles Churchill, and William Hamilton. After seven years at Corpus Christi College, Cambridge, he graduated MA, as a nobleman, in 1754. During this period, and in the face of joint family opposition, he formed a love match with Elizabeth Davers (1732/3–1800), whom he married on 10 August 1752; she was one of the legitimate children of the tory Sir Jermyn Davers, of Rushbrook Hall, Suffolk, and his wife, his former long-term mistress Margaretta Green. Hervey, as a third son, had a small fortune; even so his wife's unpopularity with his family was not offset by her dowry of £3000. They had three daughters and four sons; their middle daughter was Elizabeth Christiana *Cavendish, duchess of Devonshire.

Following a failed attempt to secure a parliamentary seat for his elder brother Augustus John *Hervey, later third earl, with whom he was to remain on bad terms, Hervey abandoned an intended career in law and took holy orders. He was ordained deacon on 24 August 1754 and priest on 26 January 1755. His family background enabled him to proceed smoothly to a clerkship of the privy seal in 1756 and to a royal chaplaincy in 1763. He had sufficient leisure to undertake the first of several tours of the continent in 1765–6, during which he travelled to

Brussels, Geneva, Naples, Rome, and Florence. A visit to Vesuvius with William Hamilton when a minor eruption was in progress led to a lifelong interest in geology, even though he was hit by a hot volcanic rock and had to recuperate for a few weeks. He travelled on to Corsica, where he met General Pasquale Paoli, and returned to England via the Veneto and Switzerland. He was deeply affected by the death of his eldest son, George, who died in Spa, aged nine.

Despite its element of prestige Hervey's chaplaincy to George III was a post of poor emolument, and as his family grew so did his financial difficulties. A point of peculiar irritation was the continual failure of his brother-in-law Sir Robert Davers, a man dogged by family tragedies and suicides, to meet the terms of Hervey's marriage settlement. The situation improved dramatically, if briefly, when Hervey's eldest brother, George William *Hervey, second earl of Bristol, accepted the lord lieutenancy of Ireland in August 1766 and appointed Hervey his first chaplain. It was Hervey's first contact with Ireland.

Lord Bristol held the Irish viceroyalty for less than a year, and never visited the country. But short as his tenure was it was sufficient to put his brother's foot on the lucrative ladder of Irish preferment. Hervey was given the bishopric of Cloyne, which he held for nine months while he and his brother waited for the death of Dr William Barnard, bishop of Derry, whose position was worth at least £7000 a year. Barnard in fact outlived Bristol's term of office but the subsequent Irish viceroy approved the appointment, and Hervey succeeded to the see of Derry in February 1768. Two days earlier the degree of doctor of divinity had been conferred on him by Trinity College, Dublin. In 1770 a second such doctorate was conferred on him by Oxford University.

While Hervey's passion for politics clearly was inherited from his father's side of the family it is believed that his lifelong interest in religion was kindled by his mother. His early contacts with Irish Roman Catholic leaders indicate that his views on the issue of relief from the penal laws were well developed, as he explained to an unnamed Catholic in October 1767: 'My object is to leave you your faith entire but to secure your allegiance to the present government and to make you independent of all foreign jurisdiction whatever' (Walsh, 12). At this time the Catholic Committee, a patrician-led body that represented Irish Roman Catholic interests, was struggling to formulate an oath of allegiance that, it was hoped, would be acceptable both to the government and to the Catholic clergy and laity. Hervey's sympathetic attitude toward Catholics, and his powerful family connections, made him an attractive intermediary, and he was soon in close consultation with the Catholic Committee.

On his second European tour (April 1770–October 1772), Hervey had at least one audience with Pope Clement XIV, visited Irish Catholic seminaries in France, and took soundings on the suitability of a Catholic oath of allegiance. He formulated an oath that not merely contained a statement of allegiance to the government but also attempted to address the most common protestant fears.

It required from Catholics detailed denials of the pope's infallibility, his avowed temporal supremacy, and his supposed power to absolve subjects from their allegiance to 'heretic' kings; the Stuart pretender and his heirs were likewise to be repudiated. Hervey communicated his proposal to protestant as well as Catholic parties, but his over-strenuous efforts to persuade protestants to sanction the oath have damaged his historical reputation. He sought to win protestant support by suggesting that his oath was deliberately calculated to divide Catholics and so strengthen the protestant interest. Despite support from the Catholic gentry for his endeavours Hervey's protestant correspondents, both lay and ecclesiastical, were either opposed to his proposals or pessimistic of his chances of success. The papal internuncio wrote from Brussels to the Irish Catholic bishops, condemning the oath with its denials of papal powers. The hierarchy, fearful of the effects of their own internal disagreements on these issues and even more fearful of the effect of the internuncio's views on the government, suppressed the letter while they made vain attempts to work out with the internuncio some alternative course of action. To the consternation of his colleagues one of the bishops who was opposed to Hervey's oath eventually (in 1772) published the internuncio's letter. Despite these developments the supporters of the oath continued to press the issue until the substance of Hervey's oath was embodied in a piece of legislation in 1774. The divisions among both bishops and laity on the issue now became stark and obvious, and the Catholic Committee became split between jurors, who were prepared to take the oath, and nonjurors, who were not; as a result the committee collapsed.

Notwithstanding the disastrous effects of his involvement on the Catholic community Hervey continued to play off one side of the Irish sectarian divide against the other for the rest of the decade. To a prominent protestant politician he suggested that recognition should be extended to all jurors, that Catholic bishops and clergymen should be state-appointed, and that the (still illegal) religious orders should be allowed monasteries and that these should be run as seminaries with state funding. Hervey was aware that these ideas, if put into practice, would lead to further divisions among Catholics but he felt that such divisions could only be of value to the establishment in view of the approaching war with France.

Hervey chose to detach himself from Irish politics in the late 1770s. In 1777 he set out on his third trip to Italy, this time accompanied by his wife and youngest daughter, Louisa (1767–1821), the future wife of Robert Banks *Jenkinson, second earl of Liverpool. By November 1777 he had settled in Rome, where he indulged his passion for art and architecture. On this and on his three subsequent visits to Italy he cultivated a taste for Roman antiquities and early Italian Renaissance paintings but he also commissioned works from many contemporary artists, including portraits of himself and his family by Pompeo Batoni, Wilhelm Tischbein, Anton Maron, Elizabeth Vigee Le Brun, and Angelica Kauffmann. As he wrote to his eldest daughter, Mary: 'I cannot resist the temptation of being extravagant here especially when it is with a view of beautifying dear Ireland' (Fothergill, 53). His purchases were destined for the house at Downhill, in co. Londonderry, that was built in 1776–9 by Michael Shanahan. Hervey, however, often proved a troublesome patron; John Soane, for instance, had a wasted journey to Downhill when the promised commission for a new dining-room failed to materialize.

Hervey's fickleness contributed to his reputation for eccentricity. His extravagant dress invited both comment and ridicule; he attended the Sistine Chapel on Maundy Thursday 1779 in full canonical dress, and had a penchant for puce and golden robes. The painter Thomas Jones described how Hervey adorned himself at his levee: 'I found him combing and adjusting a single curl which was fixed to his own short hair' (Fothergill, 65). His singular appearance was matched by his unconventional religious beliefs. Though Emma Hamilton's statement that he was 'an avowed sceptic in religion' (ibid., 37) is probably an exaggeration, he seems to have been a freethinker, and he courted the friendship of Voltaire, whom he visited at Ferney. He shocked polite company by swearing freely in public and on one occasion made fools of the candidates for a wealthy living in his diocese by making them race each other after they had feasted at his table.

In December 1779 Hervey's elder brother, Augustus John Hervey, died, and he succeeded as fourth earl of Bristol, acquiring estates with an annual rental value of £20,000 and thereby doubling his income. Without obvious cause he and his wife separated in 1782, never to be reconciled. Perhaps to divert himself the Earl-Bishop, as he was known, left his inherited estate of Ickworth, in Suffolk, and returned to Londonderry, where he became a committed volunteer commander. His volunteers were among the many Irish who realized the necessity to copperfasten the legislative independence secured in 1782 with a measure of parliamentary reform. In the northern Irish counties, where volunteering was at its most articulate, informed, and enthusiastic, the issue of parliamentary reform became inextricably linked with the liberation of Catholics from the political as well as the social and economic strictures of the penal laws. As colonel of the Londonderry corps Bristol joined together with 500 Ulster corps delegates who met in Dungannon in 1783 to plan a grand general convention of volunteers for Dublin in November. At this convention it was intended to press the government to reform the allegedly corrupt Irish legislature.

But despite their frequent parliamentary stance in opposition to government the aristocratic colonels of the other volunteer corps were closely wedded to the protestant establishment, and were concerned to exercise control over their armed followers and to redirect or contain their more radical aspirations. Notwithstanding Bristol's high-profile triumphal procession from Londonderry to Dublin in November 1783, a journey interrupted by several civic receptions, care was taken once he reached Dublin that he was not elected president of the convention. In the event parliamentary reform, a multi-faceted issue,

was subordinated to the sectarian concerns of the Irish establishment and to the morbid fears of individual protestant delegates. The powerful parliamentary orator Henry Flood, on whose support Bristol had counted heavily, baulked at the proposal to enfranchise Catholics. An address from the revived Catholic Committee, embodying their wishes for further relief concessions, blunted itself against the government's determination to divide and confuse the delegates. A letter, allegedly from one of the leading Catholic gentry, was produced by a government supporter and asserted the satisfaction of Catholics with their current lot. Bristol's uncertain temper let him down more than once during the convention, and the majority of the delegates, like Flood, were unable to swallow the proposal to extend the vote to Catholics; such Catholics, it was feared, might then fill the Irish parliament to the exclusion of protestants. The delegates eventually produced a reform bill that was vague in regard to detail and pro-protestant in character. The Irish House of Commons rejected it by a large majority, and the convention dissolved itself.

The end of the American War of Independence and the renewed confidence that the return of a reasonably-sized army lent to the government had played a part in the contemptuous rejection of the Reform Bill. The government now also felt able to discourage volunteering. In the event, however, having lost much of its political *raison d'être*, volunteering went into a steady voluntary decline. Bristol, bitter beyond words at the failure of all his political ambitions, retreated further into eccentricity and nihilism. His intemperate replies to the many addresses presented to him by volunteer corps in the aftermath of the convention attracted the attention of the government, but he escaped impeachment. A close official eye was kept on him for as long as he remained in Ireland, but the government refused to be provoked by his extravagant utterances. It is said that Bristol preferred his retreat at Downhill to his English home at Ickworth. Built on a windswept clifftop it had two main entrances, north and south, so that guests might avoid the worst of the gales. For Ickworth he had many grandiose plans, which, due to his travels and divided attentions, were never completed. He commissioned Francis Sandys, an Irish architect, to build a large oval rotunda with quadrant wings, and work began in 1796; it succeeded, then as now, more as a storehouse of art treasures than as a comfortable residence. Throughout his life Bristol was moved to design and build houses in which he was destined never or seldom to live. He spent only a matter of weeks in his newly built house at Ballyscullian, co. Londonderry, in 1790–91, after which it was left empty; visitors rated it as more splendid and more pleasingly designed even than Downhill. These projects did, however, provide much-needed local employment. His determination to leave his mark on the landscape in the form of bricks and mortar was visible also during his early enthusiastic years as bishop of Derry, when as part of an assiduous visitation exercise he insisted on the building of glebe houses.

Bristol's health began to fail, and he left for Europe

again in 1785. His visits to Ireland thereafter were increasingly short, and throughout the 1790s he travelled without purpose. His increasingly outrageous behaviour and his long absence from his diocese began to cause concern. The early days of his incumbency—when his personal charity had been a byword, when he had encouraged improved farming techniques, when he had received the approbation of John Wesley, and when he had supported financially not only his own church but those of his Catholic and Presbyterian neighbours—had become a distant memory. He spent the last nine years of his life abroad, and became an intimate of Emma Hamilton and a dabbler in the affairs of the Prussian court. His reaction to the death of his estranged wife, on 19 December 1800, was characterized by its coldness and indifference; he was heard to comment scathingly on her will. While on the road from Albano to Rome on 8 July 1803 Bristol was seized with a stomach complaint and died. His body was sent to England for burial at Ickworth Park.

GERARD O'BRIEN

Sources J. R. Walsh, *Frederick Augustus Hervey, 1730–1803* (Maynooth, 1972) · B. Fothergill, *The mitred earl: an eighteenth-century eccentric* (1974) · W. Childe-Pemberton, *The Earl Bishop*, 2 vols. (1924) · C. L. Falkiner, *Studies in Irish history & biography* (1902) · *The manuscripts and correspondence of James, first earl of Charlemont*, 2 vols., HMC, 28 (1891–4) · *Eighth report*, 1, HMC, 7 (1907–9) · Burke, *Peerage* (1938) · G. Sampson, *Statistical survey of the county of Londonderry* (1802) · P. Fagan, *Divided loyalties: the question of the oath for Irish Catholics in the eighteenth century* (Dublin, 1997) · Colvin, *Archs.* · J. Ingamells, ed., *A dictionary of British and Irish travellers in Italy, 1701–1800* (1997) · *DNB*
Archives NL Ire., Bristol/Hamilton MSS, MS 2262 · PRO NIre., corresp. and papers; family corresp. · PRO NIre., papers, D 1514/9 · Suffolk RO, Bury St Edmunds, corresp. and papers | BL, corresp. with first earl of Liverpool, Add. MSS 38233–38235, 38311, 38473 · BL, letters to John Strange, Egerton MSS 1970, 2001–2002 · JRL, letters to James Caldwell · NL Ire., letters to Sir William Hamilton · NRA, priv. coll., letters to Lord Shelburne · Representative Church Body Library, Dublin, letters to Lord Townshend · Royal Irish Acad., Foster papers, MS 23.G, 39 · Wilts. & Swindon RO, corresp. with eleventh earl of Pembroke
Likenesses P. Batoni, oils, 1768, repro. in Fothergill, *Mitred earl*; priv. coll. · C. Hewetson, marble bust, *c*.1778, NPG · J. Sayers, caricature, etching, pubd 1785 (*A whisper cross the Channel*), NPG · A. Kauffman, oils, 1790, Ickworth House, Suffolk [*see illus.*] · Mme Vigée Le Brun, oils, 1790, Ickworth House, Suffolk; repro. in Fothergill, *Mitred earl* · T. Burke?, mezzotint (after A. Kauffman), NG Ire. · H. D. Hamilton, oils, repro. in Fothergill, *Mitred earl*; priv. coll. · H. D. Hamilton, pastel drawing, Ickworth House, Suffolk · W. Hoare, group portrait, oils, Ickworth House, Suffolk; repro. in Fothergill, *Mitred earl* · S. Shelley, miniature, Ickworth House, Suffolk · G. Spencer, miniature, Ickworth House, Suffolk · J. Zoffany, oils, Ickworth House, Suffolk

Hervey, Frederick William John Augustus, seventh marquess of Bristol (1954–1999), wastrel, was born on 15 September 1954 at 35 Weymouth Street, St Marylebone, London, the eldest son of Victor Frederick Cochrane Hervey, Earl Jermyn and sixth marquess of Bristol (1915–1985), and his first wife, Pauline Mary Ames (1923–1996), the daughter of the businessman Herbert Coxon Bolton. Although his parents separated in 1959, he shuttled happily enough between them and his supportive step-parents, Lady Juliet Fitzwilliam and Teddy Lambton. He

was less happy with his father's third wife, a former secretary whom he dubbed Miss Crimplene. He was educated at Harrow School and the University of Neuchâtel, Switzerland. His downfall came at the age of eighteen with the premature inheritance of a trust fund of over £1 million, and further millions, oil wells in Louisiana, and a 57,000 acre Australian sheep farm when he was twenty-one. From 1978 he lived in tax exile in Paris, Deauville, Monte Carlo, Florida, and New York, and when in England in a leased wing of the family's eccentric stately home, Ickworth in Suffolk, owned by the National Trust. His chief occupations were building up his millions in oil, shipping, and property deals and dissipating them in cocaine, heroin, fast cars, rent boys, and a large retinue of camp followers. He attempted to arrest this dizzy downward course on 14 September 1984 by marrying Marie Louise Francesca Fisher, the twenty-year-old daughter of a Marbella property developer, but his erratic behaviour and their failure to produce an heir soon put paid to the marriage, which was dissolved in 1987.

In 1985 his inheritance of the marquessate and the main family estates only fuelled the fire. Bristol was notorious for mean-spirited practical jokes, most famously sending out a young Texan woman on to the lake at Ickworth in a rubber dinghy and then sinking her with an air rifle. Up until now his brushes with the law had been minor and almost cost-free; the closest call had come in 1983 when felony charges of conspiracy to distribute heroin during a trip to New York were dropped. But in 1988 he had to serve nine months in a Jersey prison for bringing in cocaine by helicopter. In 1993 he was sentenced to five months for possession of cocaine and heroin. The sentence was postponed while he sought treatment, but he fled instead to the south of France. Rearrested, he served six months; released in May 1994, he was arrested again within forty-eight hours for possession of heroin. Given two years' probation to seek treatment, he retreated to Ickworth. Even there he proved incompatible with the National Trust, whose visitors were disturbed by his dogs and racing cars. By April 1998 he had relinquished his lease and sold all his remaining acreage and household contents. At this stage his health as well as his fortune was in ruins. Living out his final months in a small manor house, Little Horringer Hall, near Ickworth, Bristol died there in his sleep on 10 January 1999. Rumours of AIDS had circulated, but the coroner recorded 'multiple organ failure brought about by chronic drug abuse'. After the funeral, on 23 February 1999 at Bury St Edmunds Cathedral, he was buried at Ickworth church. His schizophrenic brother Nicholas having died in the previous year, the title passed to a third brother, then living a blameless life as an undergraduate at the University of Edinburgh. Bristol's chief legacy, besides the ruin of his family's fortunes, was a gift to obituarists, who made an imaginary genetic link with the eccentricities of assorted eighteenth-century Herveys. But the true fatality lay not in the genes, rather in too much money too early, too many drugs, and, possibly, too little love.

PETER MANDLER

Sources *The Times* (11 Jan 1999) · *Daily Telegraph* (11 Jan 1999) · *The Independent* (12 Jan 1999) · *The Guardian* (18 Jan 1999) · N. Ashley, 'My friend the marquess of depravity', *Daily Mail* (14 Jan 1999) · I. Katz, 'The smack of failure', *The Guardian* (2 April 1994) · *The Times* (1972–99) · *Daily Mail* (1972–99) · *Daily Telegraph* (1972–99) · *Mail on Sunday* (1972–99) · private information (2004) · b. cert. · m. cert. · d. cert.

Hervey, George William, second earl of Bristol (1721–1775), diplomatist, born on 3 August 1721, was the eldest son of John *Hervey, Baron Hervey of Ickworth (1696–1743), politician, and Mary Lepell (1699/1700–1768), political hostess [see Hervey, Mary]. He became ensign in the 38th, or duke of Marlborough's, regiment of foot on 2 June 1739 and ensign in the 1st regiment of foot guards on 11 May 1740. He was travelling in Italy when he was recalled on his promotion to captain in the 48th, or Cholmondeley's, regiment of foot, and he returned home in May 1741 but resigned this commission in August 1742. On 5 August 1743 Hervey succeeded his father as third Baron Hervey of Ickworth, and on the following 1 December he took his seat in the House of Lords. He became second earl of Bristol on the death of his grandfather John *Hervey (1665–1751) on 20 January 1751, and hereditary high steward of Bury St Edmunds.

Bristol was gazetted envoy-extraordinary to Turin on 5 April 1755; he resigned his post in August 1758 on being appointed ambassador-extraordinary and plenipotentiary to Madrid. On the ratification of the family compact between the houses of Bourbon he left Madrid without taking leave on 17 December 1761. A court whig, he was nominated lord lieutenant of Ireland and a privy councillor on 26 September 1766, but he threw up the post of lord lieutenant the next year without visiting Ireland, although he received the usual allowance of £3000 for the voyage, as well as the annual salary of £16,000. On 2 November 1768 he was chosen lord keeper of the privy seal, an office he retained until 29 January 1770 when he became groom of the stole and first lord of the bedchamber to the king. He died, unmarried, in Bath on 18 March 1775 of palsy, and was buried on 26 March at Ickworth. He was succeeded by his brother Augustus John *Hervey as third earl. GORDON GOODWIN, rev. R. D. E. EAGLES

Sources John, Lord Hervey, *Some materials towards memoirs of the reign of King George II*, ed. R. Sedgwick, new edn, 3 vols. (1952), 13–23 · Burke, *Peerage* (1980) · Walpole, *Corr.* · H. Walpole, *Memoirs of the reign of King George the Third*, ed. G. F. R. Barker, 3 (1894), 98 · D. B. Horn, ed., *British diplomatic representatives, 1689–1789*, CS, 3rd ser., 46 (1932) · A. Collins, *The peerage of England: containing a genealogical and historical account of all the peers of England* · J. Ingamells, ed., *A dictionary of British and Irish travellers in Italy, 1701–1800* (1997), 490 · IGI
Archives Suffolk RO, Bury St Edmunds, corresp. and papers | BL, corresp. with duke of Newcastle, Add. MSS 32458, 32726–32992, *passim* · PRO, corresp. with first earl of Chatham, PRO 30/8
Likenesses J. Zoffany, oils, 1769, Ickworth House, Park, and Garden, Suffolk · by or after R. Mengs, oils, Ickworth House, Park, and Garden, Suffolk · G. Townshend, caricature, NPG · J. Zoffany, portrait (after engraving)

Hervey, James (1714–1758), Church of England clergyman and writer, was born on 26 February 1714 at Hardingstone, near Northampton, son of William Hervey (1679/80–1752), rector of Collingtree and Weston Favell. He was taught by his mother until aged seven, and was then sent to the free grammar school in Northampton, where he learnt Latin and Greek under a Mr Clarke. In 1731 he went up to Lincoln College, Oxford, where his tutor was Richard Hutchins, later to become rector; the then rector, Dr Euseby Isham, appointed him shortly after he entered the college to a Creweian exhibition of £20 p.a., which he held until September 1736. He was for four years a student of civil law, but he changed faculties after the college told him that to qualify for holy orders he must hold the degree of BA. For the first two years he was idle, receiving little guidance from his tutor. In 1733 he joined the Oxford Methodists and came under the powerful influence of John Wesley, who unofficially taught him Hebrew. Having been admitted in April 1736 to the degree of BA, he was ordained deacon on 19 September by John Potter, bishop of Oxford.

Accounts differ as to whether Hervey now returned home to serve for a short time as his father's curate. By the end of 1736 he was curate to Charles Kinchin, one of the Oxford Methodists, at Dummer, near Basingstoke, Hampshire; the curacy was briefly held before him by another Oxford Methodist, George Whitefield. In June 1737 he refused the invitation of the inhabitants of Collingtree to settle among them. In 1738 he moved for two years to Stoke Abbey, Devon, the estate of Paul Orchard, another Oxford friend; they signed a pact on 28 November 1738 stating that they had been brought together by providence and agreeing to watch over each other's conduct. After Orchard's death Hervey provided a sketch of his friend's character in the dedication of the second volume of *Meditations and Contemplations* (1747) to his godson, Orchard's son Paul. In December 1739 he was ordained priest at Exeter, and from 1740 he was curate of Bideford, Devon, for two and a half years. During this period he firmly committed himself to the doctrines of free grace and justification by faith that he was to teach for the rest of his life, and embarked on what was to be an extraordinarily successful literary career. His friends collected money to raise his small stipend to £60 p.a. In 1743 the new rector of Bideford, who disliked his views, dismissed him, and although the parishioners offered to maintain him he returned to Weston Favell to act as curate to his father. His health, always precarious, became much worse, and in June 1750 his friends tricked him into staying in London in order to convalesce, partly with Whitefield and partly with his brother, William, in Miles's Lane. He did not return until May 1752, when on his father's death he succeeded to the family livings of Weston Favell and Collingtree. In order to hold both livings, jointly worth £160 or £180 p.a. (out of which he paid his curate, Abraham Maddock), he had by a tortuous and expensive process to obtain an MA at Cambridge and dispensation from the archbishop of Canterbury before being instituted by the bishop of Peterborough. He was thus able to support his mother and sister, with whom he lived at Weston for the rest of his life.

As an evangelical or gospel clergyman Hervey thought differences between denominations over forms of prayer and manner of worship unimportant; what mattered was correct doctrine. He told Isaac Watts in an admiring letter of 10 December 1747 that he had introduced Watts's hymns into his church services. In a letter of 18 August 1748 to an unidentified recipient he wrote, 'Though I am steady in my Attachment to the established church, I would have a Right-hand of Fellowship, and a Heart of Love, ever ready, ever open, for all the upright evangelical Dissenters' (Hervey, *Collection of Letters*, 1.264). There seem to have been particularly open relationships between churchmen and dissenters in Northampton and the surrounding area. His friends and correspondents in the established church were mostly Methodists or of an evangelical persuasion: Wesley, Whitefield, James Stonhouse, Thomas Hartley, Moses Browne, the countess of Huntingdon, and Lady Frances Shirley. His chief friends among the dissenters were Philip Doddridge (who dedicated *Christ's Invitation to Thirsty Souls* to him in 1748), Risdon Darracott, John Collett Ryland, Richard Pearsall, and William Cudworth. He sent many of these friends manuscript copies of his works in progress, asking for comments and corrections both theological and literary.

As a writer Hervey had two main aims: to propagate the Reformation theology that he believed, like other members of the evangelical movement, had been abandoned by the Church of England, and to draw on the intellectual and aesthetic interests of the wealthy and polite in order to draw them to Christ—'to bait the Gospel-Hook, agreeably to the prevailing Taste' (Hervey, *Collection of Letters*, 2.101). With this end in view he combined his extensive interest in physico-theology (derived mainly from Keill's *Anatomy*, Derham's *Physico-Theology* and *Astro-Theology*, and Pluche's *Spectacle de la nature*) and classical and modern poetry (especially Homer, Virgil, Milton, Thomson, and Edward Young) with a commitment to the Bible as the central text of literature as well as religion. His most popular work, *Meditations and Contemplations* (1746–7; rev. edn., 1748), consisted in its final form of six parts in two volumes. The first volume contained 'Meditations among the tombs', 'Reflections on a flower-garden', and 'A descant upon creation', and the second 'Contemplations on the night', 'Contemplations on the starry heavens', and 'A winter-piece'. The first two parts, dedicated to the daughter of George Thomson, vicar of St Gennys, Cornwall, were first printed as pamphlets by Samuel Richardson. Hervey's peculiar ecstatic style, which delighted huge numbers of readers and disgusted some critics, was the result of his attempt to combine the language of puritan meditation with that of *The Spectator* and Shaftesbury's *Moralists* (though he never mentioned the latter). His ideal was what he called Christ's style: 'Majestic, yet familiar; happily uniting Dignity with Condescension; it consists, in Teaching his Followers the *sublimest Truths*, by spiritualizing on the most *common Occurrences*' (Hervey, *Meditations*, 2.xiv). He reinterpreted for the eighteenth century the ancient notion of God's two books of nature and scripture, teaching his readers 'the Christian's *Natural Philosophy*' by encouraging them to view the world with an evangelical telescope and with an evangelical microscope (ibid., 1.185–6).

Hervey's second substantial work, *Theron and Aspasio* (3 vols., 1755; two rev. edns in the same year), which was intellectually far more demanding than the *Meditations*, was devoted to what he regarded as the key gospel doctrine, the imputation of Christ's righteousness to sinners (the importance of this doctrine was flagged in a note to the *Meditations*, 1.274–5n.). The narrative, in the form of seventeen dialogues and twelve letters, portrays the slow conversion to Reformation Christianity of the polite and cultivated Theron by his friend Aspasio (who resembles Hervey in his earlier literary tastes and his preference for the Bible). Theron thinks this is not a religion for gentlemen. The process whereby he is brought to believe otherwise is a skilful combination of the puritan conversion narrative with Shaftesburian dialogue. The argument is supported both by analysis of the precise meaning of biblical texts and by much quotation from Milton and Young. The polite reader is enticed by descriptions of landscape and works of art and by physico-theological illustrations, a process Hervey called setting apples of gold in pictures of silver. He intended to write a further volume on gospel holiness, for which he sketched a plan, but instead he felt obliged to defend his theological principles from Wesley's attack.

Though Hervey described himself as a moderate Calvinist, when Wesley read *Theron and Aspasio* in print (he had commented on the first three dialogues in manuscript) he decided that Hervey was 'a deeply-rooted Antinomian' (*Letters of the Rev. John Wesley*, 3.230) whose views would dangerously undermine holiness. Hervey ignored Wesley's lengthy critical letter of 15 October 1756, so Wesley included it in *A Preservative Against Unsettled Notions in Religion* (1758). With encouragement from Cudworth, whom Wesley intemperately described to Hervey as 'an evil man' (29 November 1758, ibid., 4.47), Hervey spent his dying months preparing a clear and carefully argued defence of his theological principles, supported by much discussion of biblical texts in Hebrew and Greek. Shortly before his death he told his brother William not to publish it, as its transcription for the press was not complete, but after a surreptitious edition appeared William brought it out as *Eleven Letters from the Late Rev. Mr Hervey, to the Rev. Mr John Wesley* (1765) (in later editions it was entitled *Aspasio Vindicated*). The deeply wounded Wesley said that Hervey died 'cursing his spiritual father' (ibid., 4.295).

Hervey had mixed feelings about writing mainly for the polite. His aim was to be a polished shaft in God's quiver (Isaiah 49: 2), an image he often referred to in correspondence. He was reluctant to cut *Theron and Aspasio*, 'lest it should be like wiping the Bloom from the Plumb, or taking the Gold from the Gingerbread' (Hervey, *Collection of Letters*, 2.125), but at the same time he was anxious to reach a wide audience who would be discouraged by the size and cost of a three-volume edition. These fears proved groundless. Both *Meditations* and *Theron and Aspasio* were printed in two sizes at different prices, octavo and duodecimo, and achieved enormous sales, usually in editions of 5000 or 6000. He gave away all the proceeds of his publications in charity to the poor; the *Meditations* brought c.£700. An extempore preacher who rarely used notes, he published only a few sermons in his lifetime, *The Cross of Christ the Christian's Glory*, preached at the visitation of the archdeacon of Northampton (1753), and three fast sermons (1757). These were evangelical in content and deliberately plain in style. He wrote critical *Remarks on Lord Bolingbroke's Letters on the Study and Use of History* (1752) at Lady Frances Shirley's request, originally as private letters. He was passionately interested in seventeenth-century puritan and Calvinist writing, his favourites being Walter Marshall, Benjamin Jenks, and the Dutch theologian Witsius. As a result of his recommendation in the third edition of *Theron and Aspasio* of Marshall's *Gospel-Mystery of Sanctification* as his desert-island choice besides the Bible, it was republished with a statement dated 5 November 1756 that until he resumed his own account of holiness it was to be regarded as the fourth volume of his own work. He also provided recommendations for Richard Burnham's *Pious Memorials* and Jenks's *Meditations*.

Hervey died on Christmas day 1758 in Weston Favell and was buried three days later in the parish church. William Romaine, in a funeral sermon preached at St Dunstan-in-the-West, London, on 4 January 1759, gave a full account of his activities as a clergyman but left his writings to speak for themselves. Their popularity held until the middle of the nineteenth century—*Meditations* had reached twenty-six editions by 1800—and then evaporated. Critical reaction was mixed. Evangelical dissenters such as John Collett Ryland and Thomas Gibbons saw Hervey as an exponent of the true sublime. The *Gentleman's Magazine* (30, 1760, 379) described his manner and writings, particularly his published letters, as conceited and effeminate. William Cowper thought him 'one of the most Spiritual & truly Scriptural Writers in the World', but later laughed at an acquaintance who formed his style on *Theron and Aspasio* (*Letters and Prose Writings of William Cowper*, ed. J. King and C. Ryskamp, 5 vols., 1979–86, 1.141, 2.360). John Newton warned ministerial students not to imitate him: 'though his luxuriant manner of writing has many of the excellencies both of good poetry and good prose, it is in reality neither the one nor the other' (J. Newton, *Plan of Academical Preparation for the Ministry*, 1782, 48). Modern distaste should not deprive him of his role as one of the most widely read writers of the evangelical revival.

ISABEL RIVERS

Sources L. Tyerman, 'Rev. James Hervey, M.A., the literary parish-priest', *The Oxford Methodists* (1873), 201–333 · J. Hervey, *A collection of the letters … to which is prefixed, an account of his life and death*, 2 vols. (1760) [by T. Birch] · J. Hervey, *The works of the late Reverend James Hervey, A.M.* (1789) · *The letters of the Rev. John Wesley*, ed. J. Telford, 8 vols. (1931), vols. 1, 3, 4 · J. Ryland, *The character of the Rev. John Hervey … with sixty-five of his original letters* (1791) · W. E. M. Brown, 'Hervey: a study of an eighteenth-century ideal', *The polished shaft: studies in the purpose and influence of the Christian writer in the eighteenth century* (1950) · A. D. McKillop, 'Nature and science in the works of James Hervey', *University of Texas Studies in English*, 28 (1949), 124–38 · [A. C. H. Seymour], *The life and times of Selina, countess of Huntingdon*, 2 vols. (1844) · G. M. Ella, *James Hervey: preacher of righteousness* (1997) · I. Rivers, 'Shaftesburian enthusiasm and the evangelical revival', *Revival and religion since 1700: essays for John Walsh*, ed. J. Garnett and C. Matthew (1993), 21–39 · 'Some account of the life of the late Rev.

Mr James Hervey', *GM*, 1st ser., 30 (1760), 377–81, 468–9, 553–6 [letter correcting some of the errors in the 'Account' plus other comments on Hervey] · *The works of John Wesley*, 25, ed. F. Baker (1980), 614 · Foster, *Alum. Oxon.*

Archives JRL, diary · Yale U., Osborn collection, MSS

Likenesses J. M. Williams, portrait, 1750 · J. Dixon, mezzotint (after J. M. Williams), BM, NPG · four mezzotints (after J. M. Williams), NPG · three portraits, NPG

Wealth at death very little remained; left future profits of works to charity: Hervey, *Collection*, vol. 1, p. xlv

Hervey, James (1750/51–1824), physician, was born in London, the son of William Hervey. After being taught at a school in Northampton, and later at home by a private tutor, he matriculated at Oxford, from Queen's College, on 19 November 1767 aged sixteen; he proceeded BA (1771), MA (1774), MB (1777), and DM (1781). He was elected physician to Guy's Hospital in 1779 and was admitted a candidate of the College of Physicians on 1 October 1781 and a fellow on 30 September 1782. He was Goulstonian lecturer in 1783, censor in 1783, 1787, 1789, 1795, 1802, and 1809, registrar from 1784 to 1814, Harveian orator in 1785, Lumleian lecturer from 1789 to 1811, and elect on 4 May 1809. He resigned from his post at Guy's in 1802. Hervey was the first appointed registrar of the National Vaccine Establishment set up in 1808. Financial independence freed Hervey from the necessity of building an extensive practice and enabled him to visit Tunbridge Wells each summer for recreational rather than professional purposes. He died in 1824.

GORDON GOODWIN, *rev.* MICHAEL BEVAN

Sources Munk, *Roll* · S. C. Lawrence, *Charitable knowledge: hospital pupils and practitioners in eighteenth-century London* (1996) · Foster, *Alum. Oxon.*

Hervey, John (1616–1680), politician and courtier, was born on 18 August 1616 and baptized at Ickworth church on the 27th. He was the eldest son and heir of Sir William Hervey (d. 1660) of Ickworth, Suffolk, MP for Bury St Edmunds in 1628–9, and Susan, daughter of Sir Robert Jermyn, kt, of Rushbrook, Suffolk. Hervey was attached to the household of Robert Sidney, second earl of Leicester, as ambassador to France in 1636, with whom he contracted a warm friendship. He was educated and travelled abroad, including a period at Leiden in 1637. He served as a gentleman of the privy chamber and a captain of horse in the royalist forces, raising a troop for the king, from *c*.1642 to 1646. He compounded in 1646 for goods and chattels worth £240. In 1658 he married Elizabeth (d. 1700), daughter and heir of Sir William Hervey, later Baron Hervey of Ross, co. Wexford, and Kidbrooke, Kent. She brought an estate worth £30,000.

At the Restoration, Hervey was named a JP for Suffolk and a commissioner for assessment for that county and Westminster. Subsequently, he served in the same capacity for Middlesex and Norfolk, being named in 1673 and 1677 respectively. In 1662 Hervey was named a commissioner for loyal and indigent officers for Suffolk. But he preferred life at court to his local responsibilities, leaving the management of his estate to his brother, Sir Thomas Hervey, kt (1625–1694), later MP for Bury St Edmunds. A client of his cousin, the earl of St Albans, John Hervey was named in 1662 treasurer of the household and receiver general to the queen. On 7 December 1664 he was elected a fellow of the Royal Society, but never presented himself for admission. In 1675 he became a commissioner for recusants for Suffolk and, in 1677, a charter member of the Royal Fishery Company.

Hervey was elected MP for Hythe in 1661 on the recommendation of the lord warden and the earl of Sandwich. He was not an active member. Burnet relates an anecdote about Hervey, who was much in favour with Charles II, which illustrates the parliamentary dilemma faced by court members. Having voted against the court in an important division, Hervey was rebuked by the king. The next day, upon entering the government lobby after a more compliant vote, the king remarked 'You were not against me to day.' Hervey replied, 'No sir, I was against my conscience to day' (Burnet, 2.73). Hervey was a patron of Abraham Cowley and a shareholder in the Duke of York's Theatre. He died on 18 January 1680 and was buried in Ickworth church on the 23rd. His Latin epitaph has been translated as 'distinguished in character, powerful in intellect, bountiful in favour, impeccable in judgment, abundant in blessings' (Hervey, 2.147; Henning, 3.540). He was survived by his wife, Elizabeth, who died in 1700. They had no children.   R. O. BUCHOLZ

Sources B. D. Henning, 'Hervey, John', HoP, *Commons, 1660–90* · W. Hervey, *The visitation of Suffolke*, ed. J. J. Howard, 2 (1871), 141–9 · *The manuscripts of the House of Lords*, 4 vols., HMC, 17 (1887–94), vol. 2, p. 264 · *The manuscripts of Rye and Hereford corporations*, HMC, 31 (1892), 457–8 [Wodehouse MSS] · *Bishop Burnet's History*, 2.73

Likenesses P. Lely, oils, Ickworth House, Park, and Garden, Suffolk · R. Tompson, mezzotint (after P. Lely), BM, NPG · oils, Ickworth House, Park, and Garden, Suffolk

Wealth at death legacies totalling £12,000; remainder of estate to brother on condition that he brought the value of the land to £20,000: Henning, 'Hervey, John', 540

Hervey, John, first earl of Bristol (1665–1751), politician and landowner, was born at Bury St Edmunds, Suffolk, on 27 August 1665, and baptized there on 29 September of that year. He was the second son of Sir Thomas Hervey, MP for Bury St Edmunds, and his wife, Isabella (d. 1665), the daughter of Sir Humphrey May, vice-chamberlain of the household to Charles I. He was educated at the grammar school at Bury St Edmunds and then at Clare College, Cambridge, where he matriculated on 5 July 1684. He did not take his degree but was awarded an LLD by the university on 16 April 1705.

On 1 November 1688 Hervey married Isabella (1670–1693), the daughter of Sir Charles Carr, bt, MP and landowner. According to Robert Halsband, the marriage was 'extraordinarily happy' and produced three children, two daughters and one son, Carr Hervey [see below]. Isabella died giving birth to their second daughter on 7 March 1693. On 27 May the following year his father—his 'best and dearest friend'—also died, and Hervey inherited his estates and the office of high steward of Bury St Edmunds. He held this position as well as being deputy lieutenant of Suffolk, to which he had been appointed two years earlier (10 May 1692), and, from March 1694, one of the MPs for Bury St Edmunds.

On 25 July 1695 Hervey married his second wife, Elizabeth Felton (1676–1741), the daughter of Sir Thomas Felton (later Lord Felton), MP for Playford Hall, Suffolk, and Elizabeth Howard, the daughter and coheir of the third earl of Suffolk. His marriage to Elizabeth, whom he described as his 'ever-new Delight', produced seventeen children. Their first child, John *Hervey (later Lord Hervey), became a courtier in George II's household, and their second son, Thomas *Hervey, became an MP and pamphleteer. A younger son, Henry Hervey *Aston, became a poet and Church of England clergyman.

Hervey continued to serve as MP for Bury St Edmunds until 23 March 1703, when he was created Baron Hervey of Ickworth in the county of Suffolk. An earlier Hervey barony had become extinct on the death of William, Baron Hervey of Kidbrooke, in June 1642. He took his seat in the House of Lords on 22 June 1703, a position that owed much to the political intrigue of the duke and duchess of Marlborough. He was a staunch whig, and an eager supporter of the revolution of 1688 and the Act of Settlement. Hervey displayed his support for the Hanoverians and his dislike of the tories in a number of ways: the ordering of medals of the elector and his family, his hosting of a dinner in honour of the recently disgraced duke of Marlborough, and his opposition to the treaty of Utrecht drafted by the tory government. At the accession of the elector he was created earl of Bristol (19 October 1714).

Lord Bristol's links with the king were broken by the royal split in November 1717, when he supported the prince of Wales. Early in the following year his wife, who was a friend and correspondent of Lady Mary Wortley Montagu, was appointed one of the ladies of the bedchamber to Princess Caroline. In the 1720s Bristol was an opponent of the Walpole government, and in March 1733 spoke in favour of a reduced standing army. His anti-Walpole stance led him to oppose the political position of his son John, while still defending him against the personal attacks made by William Pulteney and Alexander Pope.

His closeness to John was in contrast to the often strained relations between Bristol and his son from his first marriage, **Carr Hervey**, Lord Hervey (1691–1723), who was born on 17 September 1691, and educated at Clare College, Cambridge, where he graduated MA in 1710. In the following year he embarked on a grand tour, which included a meeting with Marlborough in Flanders and an introduction to the elector of Hanover. He was elected MP for the borough of Bury St Edmunds. Following the accession of George I he was granted the courtesy title of Lord Hervey, and was appointed one of the gentlemen of the bedchamber to the prince of Wales, whom he followed into opposition in 1717. To Horace Walpole he was the 'elder brother of the more known John, Lord Hervey, and reckoned to have superior parts'. However, his life was clouded by scandal. Writing in the 1830s Lady Louisa Stuart maintained that Carr was the true father of Walpole, a claim countenanced by the *DNB* but for which there is no contemporary evidence and which most probably derived from Stuart's hostility to Walpole. Carr continued to sit as an MP until March 1722, when, on account of his neglecting his parliamentary duties, he was defeated. He died at Bath, unmarried, in debt, and, in his father's words, 'drowned in drink', on 14 November 1723, aged thirty-two, and was buried on 24 November at the church at Ickworth, Suffolk.

Away from politics, the first earl of Bristol was a keen trainer and breeder of racehorses at his Newmarket stud. John Macky described him as 'a great sportsman, lover of Horse-matches and play ... a handsome Man in his Person, fair complexion, middle stature, Forty years old' (*Memoirs of the Secret Services of J. Macky*, 1733). His character was also sketched by Queen Caroline and John, Lord Hervey, in the third volume of his *Memoirs*. Bristol was in addition an accomplished author and scholar, and his diary (1688–1742) and family correspondence (1651–1750), including occasional verse and his father's letters, were published in 1894. Bristol's wife died on 1 May 1741, aged sixty-four. He himself died on 20 January 1751 and was buried at Ickworth church on 27 January.   PHILIP CARTER

Sources GEC, *Peerage*, new edn · R. Halsband, *Lord Hervey: eighteenth-century courtier* (1973) · Venn, *Alum. Cant.* · *GM*, 1st ser., 11 (1741), 275 · *GM*, 1st ser., 21 (1751), 42 · *The diary of John Hervey, first earl of Bristol*, ed. S. H. A. Hervey, 4 vols. (1894) · *Letter-books of John Hervey, first earl of Bristol*, ed. S. H. A. Hervey, 3 vols. (1894) · F. Harris, *A passion for government: the life of Sarah, duchess of Marlborough* (1991) · R. R. Sedgwick, 'Hervey, Carr', HoP, *Commons*
Archives Suffolk RO, Bury St Edmunds, corresp., diaries, and notebooks | CAC Cam., corresp. with Thomas Erle
Likenesses G. Kneller, portrait, 1699, Guildhall, Bury St Edmunds · J. B. van Loo, oils, 1742, Ickworth House, Suffolk · E. Seeman, portrait, Ickworth House, Suffolk · portrait (Hervey, Carr), Ickworth House, Suffolk · two oils, Ickworth House, Suffolk

Hervey, John, second Baron Hervey of Ickworth (1696–1743), courtier and writer, the eldest child of John *Hervey, first earl of Bristol (1665–1751), and his second wife, Elizabeth Felton (1676–1741), was born on 15 October 1696 at Jermyn Street, London, and baptized on 25 October. Known as Jack in his youth, he had two half-siblings, including a brother, Carr *Hervey [see under Hervey, John, first earl of Bristol], and sixteen full siblings, ten of whom survived to adulthood, among them the politician and pamphleteer Thomas *Hervey.

Early life and entry into politics, 1710–1750 In childhood Hervey honed his skills as a jockey and a card player. But since his health was poor, he acquired much of his formal education at the hands of private tutors at Ickworth in Suffolk, entering Westminster School only in 1712 at the age of fifteen. A year later he matriculated at Clare College, Cambridge, and in 1715 graduated MA. Queen Anne died while he was at university, and a Latin poem he penned to commemorate the accession of George I, besides being the first surviving piece of his writing, is evidence that he had already accepted the family's allegiance to whiggery. On the accession of the house of Hanover his father was made earl of Bristol.

Following university, Hervey visited continental Europe, staying in Paris and then Hanover. The latter was an unusual spot on the grand tour, but Lord Bristol hoped

John Hervey, second Baron Hervey of Ickworth (1696–1743), by Jean Baptiste van Loo, *c.*1740–41

that attendance on the new king, who was spending a vacation at Herrenhausen, might be politically useful for his son. In addition to George I, Hervey met two other persons at Hanover who would play important roles in his later life: the king's grandson, Prince Frederick, and Lady Mary Wortley Montagu, the wife of Edward Wortley Montagu, Britain's minister to Constantinople. For a while there was talk of a career in the army, but these designs came to nothing. On 21 April 1720 Hervey married the attractive but unwealthy Mary Lepell [see Hervey, Mary (1699/1700–1768)], the daughter of an army officer and one of the maids of honour to the princess of Wales. Because the marriage was financially imprudent, Hervey kept it a secret from all but his closest relatives for six months. The first of the couple's eight children was born on 3 August 1721 and given the redoubtably whiggish name of George William *Hervey. Their second son, Augustus John *Hervey, became a naval officer and politician. Meanwhile, by selling South Sea stock in a timely way, Hervey realized a £20,000 profit from the stock's meteoric appreciation. When his half-brother Carr died unmarried on 14 November 1723, Hervey acquired the courtesy title of Baron Hervey of Ickworth and became heir to the Bristol earldom. On 2 April 1725 he was elected MP for Bury St Edmunds, virtually a family seat previously held by his father and by Carr Hervey.

Soon thereafter Hervey purchased a house in Great Burlington Street, London, and entered the Commons as a supporter of Sir Robert Walpole. He represented the chamber in a conference with the Lords and wrote a public tract on the government's behalf. He sealed his close political friendship with Walpole in 1727 by supporting the first minister even when most observers thought the accession of George II meant the end of Sir Robert's career. But then in July 1728, just when it appeared that political opportunities were opening up for him, Hervey left England for the continent, visiting Paris, Rome, and Florence. Publicly he pleaded ill health to explain the trip; in fact it was designed to allow him to be with Stephen Fox, brother of Henry Fox, later Baron Holland, the young man for whom he had developed a passion. On his return to England in October 1729 Hervey was a reinvigorated man and resumed his activities in support of Walpole, especially during the fierce debates over French construction at Dunkirk. On 7 May 1730, in recognition of several years of assistance, Lord Hervey became vice-chamberlain to the king's household and, consequently, a member of the privy council.

Vice-chamberlain and lord privy seal, 1730–1743 Hervey's duties as vice-chamberlain obliged him to spend much time with Queen Caroline, a person whom he liked and respected. She reciprocated, appreciative of the pleasures that his intelligent conversation introduced into a court of dullards. Soon they were almost inseparable. Hervey hoped the vice-chamberlaincy would be a stepping stone to higher office, but, precisely because his influence with the queen was considerable and his value as a conduit between court and ministry was deemed irreplaceable, Walpole kept him in his office as long as the queen was alive. The most important professional assignment to come his way during his tenure was to oversee the arrangements for the marriage of Princess Anne, the princess royal, to the prince of Orange in 1737. But Hervey also had important political assignments, serving Sir Robert during these years as a reliable member of parliament. His loyal defence of the prime minister in the heated debates over the Excise Bill in 1733 earned him elevation, in his father's barony, to the House of Lords on 12 June of that year. In subsequent years he regularly endorsed the ministry's military and financial measures, even when he privately doubted the wisdom of Sir Robert's policies. Meanwhile, in 1733 he began writing the work now known as his *Memoirs*.

The most celebrated aspects of Hervey's life in the early 1730s, however, turned upon three notorious quarrels. The earliest involved William Pulteney and concerned politics. In casting his political lot with Walpole, Hervey had broken with Pulteney, a rising whig politician who, before 1727, had been so close a friend to Hervey that he had stood as godfather to one of Hervey's daughters. The break became violent on 25 January 1731, when the two men, having already been associated with an exchange of personal insults in a pamphlet debate, duelled at swordpoint in Green Park, London. Each wounded the other; indeed, had Pulteney not slipped before the seconds intervened, he would probably have killed Hervey. The second quarrel involved Frederick, prince of Wales, and turned in part on Anne *Vane (d. 1736), a woman with whom Hervey

and the prince conducted concurrent affairs in 1731. Like Pulteney, the prince began his relationship with Hervey on friendly terms, but the covert character of the simultaneous liaisons further complicated a friendship already burdened by Hervey's close ties with Frederick's distant mother, the queen, and the two men became cordial enemies. By the mid-1730s a common contempt for Frederick, bordering on hatred, bound Hervey and Queen Caroline. The third and most famous quarrel involved Alexander Pope and turned both on politics, Pope being a tory and Hervey a whig, and on sex, Pope having been a disappointed admirer of both Mary Lepell and Lady Mary Wortley Montagu. It suffices for the present to say that by incurring the enmity of Pope, Hervey became one of literature's most celebrated satiric targets.

Late in 1737 Queen Caroline died. Hervey attended her during much of her brief but difficult ordeal. Shaken by the loss of his close friend, he ended the memoirs he had been drafting for a decade. He also reminded Walpole that the passing of the queen removed the chief obstacle that had stood between him and higher office. Walpole was not unappreciative of Hervey's claim upon his good offices, but he had to contend with a second obstacle—the hostility of the duke of Newcastle to any promotion for Hervey—and so elevation was again deferred. Hervey was thus obliged to pay the price for too openly mocking the public awkwardnesses of the aristocratic minister. Despite the disappointment, he remained faithful to the ministry, effectively defending its Spanish policies both when the convention of Pardo was drafted and then when war could no longer be resisted; he also loyally denounced opposition efforts to require MPs to declare publicly whether they received government pensions. Walpole finally determined to face down Newcastle, and on 1 May 1740, on the resignation of Lord Godolphin, Hervey became lord privy seal.

In his new office Hervey was entitled to attend the meetings of the cabinet council and, when the king was in Hanover, of the lords justices, but his presence was irregular. As Walpole's policy towards Spain became increasingly controversial, however, Hervey resumed his role as an unembarrassed and indomitable advocate of the ministry in the House of Lords. In return for this loyalty Walpole authorized the elevation of Stephen Fox to the rank of Lord Ilchester. But, as parliamentary opposition to the government's foreign policy mounted, Walpole's hold on power began to slip, and early in 1742 Sir Robert resigned his office. Hervey tried to retain the privy seal, but the new ministry had little trust in the sedulous defender of the fallen Walpole, and on 12 July 1742 Hervey yielded the privy seal, simultaneously declining, as a mark of his indifference to favour, the royal offer of a substantial pension. With this dismissal from the office he had so long sought, Hervey was out of the government for the first time in thirteen years.

Political commentator Politics was an abiding interest of Lord Hervey's; his comments upon it recur throughout his letters, his political tracts, and the *Memoirs of the Reign of King George II*. Although he claimed that Tacitus and

Machiavelli were his instructors about political matters, he was suspicious of the utility of political theory, and his views, while often entertainingly expressed, rarely rose above the commonplace. He defined the task of government to be the sustaining of a suitable balance between civil order and personal liberty, and he approved of Walpole's court whig administration precisely because it realized that goal. He saw potential enemies of liberty lurking in all quarters—in an unbounded crown, in an unrestrained church, in an unregulated army, in an unchecked mob. The responsibility of governors was to find the means to confine the tendency of king, prelate, soldier, and zealot to sacrifice liberty to their own cause or need. Walpole was successful because he read human nature aright, and by recognizing that people 'feel sensibly for nothing but what is conducive some way or other to their pleasure, or their interest, or their pride' (Fox-Strangways, 132), he usually contrived to create the combination of sweeteners and threats necessary to effect the confinement.

As a public polemicist Hervey was bold and direct, and his three greatest tracts, while striking different tones, are alike in moving quickly to an aggressive assertion of their claims. In *Ancient and Modern Liberty Stated and Compared* (1734) he popularized the standard court whig argument that England had not been free until liberated by the revolution of 1688 and that the court whigs, as the true heirs of the revolutionary whigs, were the only qualified defenders of its legacy. In *The Conduct of the Opposition and the Tendency of Modern Patriotism* (1734) he mocked Walpole's opponents for their blindness to the dangers of allowing an army to be insubordinate to the monarch. In *Miscellaneous Thoughts* (1742) he defended the recently dissolved Walpole administration against charges of corruption, incompetence, and selfishness. These are not subtle works, but they were widely deemed effective. Indeed, Horace Walpole called some of Hervey's polemical efforts 'equal to any that ever were written' (Hervey, *Some Materials*, 1.xxxiv).

Hervey's *Memoirs*, which describe various happenings at the court of George II from 1727 to 1737 (with a gap for 1730–32), are an entirely different kind of work. Though they were probably intended for a general audience, Hervey did not publish them in his lifetime, and they then languished unseen (though not unknown) for a century until the first marquess of Bristol, after suppressing some sections that spoke slightingly of the royal family, authorized their appearance in 1848. A fuller version, based on documents in the Windsor archives and including some of the earlier excisions, appeared in 1931. Even in this later edition, however, a hole remains, leading to the hypothesis that at some point someone who controlled the manuscript—the same Lord Bristol looms large as a candidate—destroyed some of its pages. The motive for the destruction is uncertain, though suspicion attaches itself to a concern that excessive candour about the character of Hervey's close relationship with Prince Frederick would damage the author's or the prince's posthumous reputation.

For historians of the eighteenth century the *Memoirs* are an indispensable work. 'I am determined to report everything just as it is', Hervey declared, 'or at least just as it appears to me' (Hervey, *Some Materials*, 2.347). Despite his resort to the third person in discussing himself as a player in the drama of court life, Hervey's *Memoirs* are in fact very personal, direct, and even earthy. They provide ironic and amusing character sketches of the men and women who exercised power in the 1730s and memorable accounts of such events as the marriage of Princess Anne to the prince of Orange, Frederick's virtual abduction of his wife as she went into labour, and—their great set piece—the hideous death of Queen Caroline. They also allow the historian to understand some of the methods Walpole employed to exercise power and especially how, in collusion with Queen Caroline, he managed George II. They tell the tale of friendships shattered, policies undone, and ambitions thwarted. Because Hervey is a good story-teller, with an eye for the useful detail and an ear for good conversation, the stories are human and gripping. Hervey's is a personal view of politics, and, if his limning of Walpole pulls forward the manipulative aspect of the prime minister's character, he still wants his readers to understand that by and large Sir Robert used his immense talent at political management for essentially useful ends.

Hervey and Pope In 1735 Alexander Pope published his *Epistle to Arbuthnot*, which contained, in its section on Lord Hervey, one of literature's most celebrated examples of venomous invective. Hervey was cast as Sporus, the castrated boy whom Nero had transformed into his wife. Pope excoriated Hervey's politics, his sexual ambivalence, and his morality. Each of his words drew blood. Hervey was a 'mere white curd of ass's milk', a 'bug with gilded wings', a 'painted child of dirt that stinks and stings', 'one vile antithesis', an 'amphibious thing', a:

Fop at the toilet, flatterer at the board,
[who] now trips a lady, and now struts a lord

He bore 'a cherub's face—a reptile all the rest', an almost fitting body for a 'familiar toad'. He spoke only 'in florid impotence', for his 'buzz the witty and the fair annoys'. Two couplets in particular captured Pope's vision of his subject. The first was his grand gesture of dismissal:

Satire or sense, alas! Can Sporus feel?
Who breaks a butterfly upon a wheel?

The second was a summary of his contempt:

Beauty that shocks you, parts that none can trust,
Wit that can creep, and pride that licks the dust!

It was Hervey's fault that the assault occurred. Although Pope and he had long since abandoned whatever friendship they may once have had when both sought the favour of Mary Lepell, the poet had in general over the years ignored the courtier in his lacerating works. The torrent of invective that cascaded into public attention in 1735 had been invited two years earlier when Hervey, in support of Lady Mary Wortley Montagu, an earlier target of Pope's verbal sword, had associated himself with the cruel allusions to Pope's physical deformity in *Verses addressed to the Imitator of Horace*. Among its lines are these, representative both of the work's tone and of the authors' capacity:

> Like the first bold assassin be thy lot,
> Ne'er be thy guilt forgiven nor forgot
> But as thou Hat'st, be hated by mankind,
> And, with the emblem of thy crooked mind
> Mark'd on thy back, like Cain by God's own hand,
> Wander, like him, accursed through the land.

After the *Epistle to Arbuthnot* appeared, Hervey acknowledged his poetic and satiric inadequacy and withdrew from all efforts to match Pope in the art of verbal warfare. Pope, however, continued to take pleasure in savaging Hervey, even after Hervey's death, and Henry Fielding resumed many of the same themes of political, sexual, and moral depravity in his Hervey-based depiction of Beau Didapper in *Joseph Andrews* (1742). In many ways it is fair to say that through his withering barrages Pope created the persona of Lord Hervey that has endured ever since.

Hervey's personal life In appearance Hervey was slender, a bit below average height for his era, and youthfully handsome even into his forties. The poor health that had dogged him in his childhood returned intermittently throughout his life. Though an exact diagnosis of his malady is impossible at a distance of 250 years, he appears to have been subject to epileptic seizures and to the acute pain of gallstones. The diet that he adopted in an effort to mend his body—milk, tea, many vegetables, no meat—was so famously bland that it became one of the peculiar habits his critics mocked. Perhaps it was some ailment and a disfiguring appearance that may have followed from it that account for another of the eccentricities for which he was famous, a fondness for applying powder to his face. (It is known by way of additional explanation for this habit that one of the facial blemishes he so disliked was a legacy of surgery he had endured while in Italy.) By the age of forty he had lost all his teeth.

Although not a scholar, Hervey was learned in the manner of an educated eighteenth-century gentleman, proud of his command of Latin and at ease in French. His acquaintance with, in his youth, Dr Robert Freind, headmaster of Westminster School, and, in his later years, with the noted classicist Conyers Middleton, assured that he remained in contact with scholarly circles throughout his life. He even assisted Middleton in the preparation of the scholar's *Life of Cicero*, for which help Middleton lavished praise on Hervey in the dedication.

The friendship that has left the fullest evidentiary basis—in the form of a published correspondence—is Hervey's tie with Lady Mary Wortley Montagu. From the days of Hervey's visit to Hanover in 1716 (and perhaps earlier) to the last months of his life in 1743 he found in Lady Mary a person in whom he could comfortably confide. They liked and disliked the same people, they took pride and pleasure in versifying, they enjoyed gossip, and they shared a somewhat ironic view of life. Above all, they accepted each other for the flawed but interesting human beings that they respectively were, Lady Mary as a woman who at times wanted to be a man and Lord Hervey as the opposite. In his last letter to her (and almost the last surviving letter he wrote), dated 18 June 1743, a declining Hervey betrayed his fondness when he wrote that 'the last stages of an infirm life are filthy roads … May all your ways (as Solomon says of wisdom) be ways of pleasantness and all your paths peace … Adieu' (Halsband, 304).

Hervey and his father remained close throughout the son's life, even though, as a country whig, Lord Bristol disapproved of Hervey's court whig politics. With his mother, however, Hervey enjoyed a less happy and ultimately poisonous relationship, in part because Lady Bristol did not like Mary Lepell, in part because she supported Frederick, prince of Wales. At one point he called her 'the vehicle of all the ills I ever complained of' (Hervey, *Some Materials*, 3.962). Hervey's relations with his wife are more difficult to assess. She was loyal, and they often appeared to enjoy each other's company; they had eight children, whom he doted upon; but she was also very visibly his intellectual inferior, and he was frequently away from her—perhaps because she did not care for London, but perhaps too because he had other romantic interests. His callous treatment of her in his will shows that at the end they were severely estranged.

Lord Hervey was bisexual. It is necessary to state this point directly because changing senses of propriety over the years, combined with the bite of Pope's caricature, have obscured a proper understanding of the nature of his sexual orientation. There can be no doubt that he found women attractive. In addition to his marriage to Mary Lepell, he wooed and bedded Anne Vane and claimed (along with others) to be the father of the child she bore in 1733. He may have had an affair with Lady Mary Wortley Montagu and perhaps one with Princess Caroline. But there can also be no doubt that he found men attractive. He followed Stephen Fox to Italy in 1728 and frequently lived with him over the next decade. He wrote passionate love letters to Francesco Algarotti, the multi-talented Italian intellectual whom he first met in 1736 and for whose affections his chief English rival was, of all people, Lady Mary. He may have had a sexual affair with Prince Frederick before their friendship dissolved.

While the laws of the eighteenth century prescribed harsh penalties for men who engaged in homosexual activities, high society generally preferred being amused to being outraged when the miscreant was one of their own. Hervey, moreover, was happy to play the role of amuser, sometimes striking feminine attitudes and happily conjoining them with feminine behaviours. He was undisguisedly, even proudly, androgynous. He thus was the frequent target of salacious humour. William Pulteney called him 'Mr *Fainlove* … such a nice Composition of the two Sexes, that it is difficult to distinguish which is more praedominant' (Norton, 149), while an anonymous tract styled him the 'Lady of the Lords' (ibid., 152). And, leaving Pope's contributions aside, Lady Mary Wortley

Montagu delivered the most celebrated of the contemporary judgements when she wrote that humankind was divided into three sexes: men, women, and Herveys (Hervey, *Some Materials*, 1.xiv).

Hervey's death Hervey's dismissal from government in 1742 preceded his death by only a year. He spent some of that time defending the work of the administration he had served and some of it trying to mobilize his friends and family to resist the actions of the new ministry. This latter activity cost him his friendship with Stephen Fox, who preferred place to loyalty. Hervey took ill in the spring of 1743, withdrew to Ickworth in hopes of recuperating, and died there on 5 August. He was buried at Ickworth on 12 August; Conyers Middleton later contributed the Latin epitaph for his monument. The precise nature of the disease that took his life is not known, but because he had suffered bouts of poor health since childhood, his demise was not entirely a surprise, even though he was only forty-six years of age.

Hervey drew up a will in the last month of his life. Although conventional with respect to his children, with his eldest son being designated sole heir and the other children receiving annuities, it was astonishingly savage in its treatment of Lady Hervey. She received only the minimum required by their marriage contract—a jointure of £300 per year—and was further humiliated by stipulations suggesting that she might, if given freedom to dispose of property, seek to deprive their children of an inheritance. The grounds for such pettiness provoked much speculation in the succeeding months, and no generally accepted explanation for Hervey's vindictive treatment of his wife has appeared. Perhaps—there is evidence of a measure of disorientation in his final year—he succumbed to loss of wit before loss of life. The size of his estate is unknown, but since it was not divided upon his death and since his heirs prospered, observers concluded that it had been unencumbered.   REED BROWNING

Sources R. Halsband, *Lord Hervey: eighteenth-century courtier* (1973) · R. Browning, *Political and constitutional ideas of the court whigs* (1982) · John, Lord Hervey, *Some materials towards memoirs of the reign of King George II*, ed. R. Sedgwick, 3 vols. (1931) · J. Hervey, *Memoirs of the reign of George the Second*, ed. J. W. Croker, 2 vols. (1848) · *Lord Hervey and his friends, 1726–38*, ed. earl of Ilchester [G. S. Holland Fox-Strangways] (1950) · *The complete letters of Lady Mary Wortley Montagu*, ed. R. Halsband, 3 vols. (1965–7) · J. R. Dubro, 'The third sex: Lord Hervey and his coterie', *Eighteenth-Century Life*, 2 (1975–6), 89–95 · R. Norton, *Mother Clap's molly house: the gay subculture in England, 1700–1830* (1992) · C. Paglia, 'Lord Hervey and Pope', *Eighteenth-Century Studies*, 6 (1972–3), 348–71 · *Pope: poetical works*, ed. H. Davis (1966)
Archives BL, Holland House MSS · BL, corresp. with Lord Holland, Add. MS 51396 · BL, corresp. with Conyers Middleton, Add. MS 32458 · priv. coll., Murray MSS · Suffolk RO, Bury St Edmunds, corresp. and papers
Likenesses C. Jervas, double portrait, oils, 1723 (with Lady Hervey), Mulgrave Castle · miniature, *c*.1723, Ickworth House, Suffolk · J. Fayram, oils, *c*.1728–1730, Ickworth House, Suffolk · E. Bouchardon, marble bust, 1729; formerly at Melbury · W. Hogarth, group portrait, oils, *c*.1738–1739 (*The Holland House group*), Ickworth House, Suffolk · J. B. van Loo, oils, *c*.1740–1741; Sothebys, 11–12 June 1996, lot 447 [*see illus.*] · studio of J. B. van Loo, oils, *c*.1740–1741, NPG · J. L. Natter, agate medallion on gold and enamel box, Ickworth House, Suffolk · attrib. J. B. van Loo, oils, Ickworth House, Suffolk · oils (as a child), Ickworth House, Suffolk · portraits, repro. in Halsband, *Lord Hervey*
Wealth at death estate unencumbered; heirs prospered

Hervey [*née* Lepell]**, Mary, Lady Hervey of Ickworth** (**1699/1700–1768**), courtier, was born on 26 September 1700, according to an inscription in Ickworth church, the daughter of Nicholas Wedig Lepell (*b.* 1665/6, *d.* in or before 1731), courtier and army officer, and his wife, Mary (*d.* 1742), the daughter and coheir of John Brooke of Rendlesham, Suffolk. However, the baptism of a Mary Lepell, daughter of Nicholas and Mary Lepell, is recorded at St Martin-in-the-Fields, Westminster, on 16 September 1699. Her father was born in Santau, Germany, and had arrived in England from Denmark as groom of the bedchamber to Prince George of Denmark, husband of Queen Anne, in 1683. He was commissioned lieutenant-colonel in Lord Paston's regiment of foot on 1 March 1704, was colonel of his own regiment of foot from 25 March 1705, and was promoted brigadier-general on 1 March 1710. Later that year he became commander of all British forces in Spain, but in 1712 was placed on half pay.

According to a letter written by Sarah Churchill, duchess of Marlborough, in December 1737, Mary Lepell was made a cornet by her father 'in his regiment as soon as she was born … and she was paid many years after she was a maid of honour' (*Letters of Horace Walpole*, 1.clii), but no Lepell other than Nicholas appears in the army lists and commission registers for the period. On about 9 February 1715, through family connections with the Hanoverian ministers of George I and her father's friendship with the duchess of Marlborough, she was appointed maid of honour to Caroline, princess of Wales. She rapidly became part of the literary and intellectual circle surrounding the princess. John Gay hailed her as 'youth's youngest daughter, sweet Lepell', and on 17 July 1717 she was mentioned in a poem sent by Gay and William and Ann Pulteney to her fellow maid of honour Mary Bellenden. Alexander Pope described how he was taken 'into protection' by the two maids of honour on a visit to Hampton Court that September; Miss Lepell allegedly 'walk'd all alone with me three or 4 hours, by moonlight' (*Correspondence of Alexander Pope*, 1.427). In March 1720 she stayed with Pope at his house in Twickenham, Middlesex, for the benefit of her health. Other friends made at the princess's court were Henrietta Howard, later countess of Suffolk, John Arbuthnot, and Philip Stanhope, fourth earl of Chesterfield.

Mary Lepell had already refused at least one proposal of marriage, from Colonel Adolphus Oughton, a former aide-de-camp to the duke of Marlborough, in 1716. At the time she stayed with the Popes she may have already accepted John *Hervey (1696–1743) as her husband. Hervey was the eldest son of John *Hervey, first earl of Bristol, and his second wife, Elizabeth Felton. The two were married secretly on 21 April 1720, in order for Mary to continue to collect her quarterly payments as a maid of honour; they announced their marriage on 25 October that year and moved to a house on Bond Street in the fashionable West End of London. They had four daughters and four sons,

Mary Hervey, Lady Hervey of Ickworth (1699/1700–1768), by Allan Ramsay, 1762

among whom were George William *Hervey, later second earl of Bristol; Augustus John *Hervey, later third earl of Bristol; and Frederick Augustus *Hervey, eventually fourth earl of Bristol and bishop of Derry.

Mary became known as Lady Hervey when her husband's elder half-brother Carr died in 1723. She and her husband were perhaps the most celebrated couple in the court of the prince and princess of Wales. In the words of the second verse of a ballad by Pulteney and Chesterfield:

Bright Venus yet never saw bedded
So perfect a beau and a belle
As when Hervey the handsome was wedded
To the beautiful Molly Lepell.
(Stuart, 64)

When Lady Hervey bought a new house for her growing family on Great Burlington Street in 1725, the duchess of Marlborough alleged that she had found the money by aggressively flirting with George I, leading the ministry and the duchess of Kendal to buy her off with £4000; Robert Halsband thought it more likely that she had instead called in her debts and asked for money from her husband's father. She was in a position to act as an intermediary for patronage requests, and in summer 1726 successfully won for an aunt's servant the reversion of a place in St Katherine's Hospital, reflecting 'I confess that my request runs somewhat high to desire that an old woman may not be forgot; it is more than most people can promise for a young one!' (ibid., 63).

Following the accession of George II, Lady Hervey was unhappy with the continuation of Sir Robert Walpole in power, and in September 1729 tried to bring Lord Hervey into opposition alongside their old friend Pulteney, but was unsuccessful. Lord Hervey rarely mentions her in his memoirs, and she appears mainly as an obstruction to his political ambitions. Her status at court was enhanced when her husband became vice-chamberlain in 1730; her dairy allowance at Hampton Court in 1731 was the sumptuous three pats of Richmond butter and a quarter-pint of cream per day. She became estranged from Pope, but remained friendly with Pulteney even as he moved further into opposition to Walpole, and with Lady Suffolk before and after her removal from court. In 1732 she recommended to Lady Suffolk Matthew Tindal's *Christianity as Old as the Creation*, expressing her whiggish interest in rationalism; she would later name Benjamin Hoadly as a friend.

Lady Hervey seems to have tolerated her husband's bisexuality, and became a close friend of his lover Stephen Fox, to whom she sold her house in 1730, although in 1740 she allegedly lent a later passion of her husband's, Francesco Algarotti, the money he needed to leave London and move to Berlin, thereby removing him from her husband's orbit. The 1730s saw some differences emerge between the couple. Lady Hervey damaged the friendship between her husband and Lady Mary Wortley Montagu when she testified to the sanity of the countess of Mar in April 1731; the countess's sister, Lady Mary Wortley Montagu, would thus have lost custody of the countess. Despite her pregnancy with her last child, Caroline (b. 1736), Lady Hervey spent most of summer 1735 in France, allowing Hervey to revive his affair with Anne Vane. A few years later her mother-in-law, Elizabeth, countess of Bristol, who was close to Lord Hervey, described her as a 'fals, bold Wife' (Halsband, 239). None the less Lady Hervey continued to have responsibilities at court commensurate with her position as wife of the vice-chamberlain, and in 1738 chose servants for the household of Amalie Sophie Marianne von Wallmoden, mistress of George II.

Lady Hervey's relationship with her husband was to observers good, but he refused to see her for several weeks before his death, on 5 August 1743, and the fashionable world was shocked by the terms of his will, which left Lady Hervey no more than her jointure of £300 a year. The will did not reflect a breach in the family. Lady Hervey lived at Ickworth with her father-in-law, Lord Bristol, almost until his death in 1751, and remained closely involved in supervising the careers of her children. Her letters to the Revd Edmund Morris, tutor to her sons Frederick and William, were written between 1742 and 1768. As edited by John Wilson Croker and published in 1821, they reveal her as widely informed of the world of letters as well as politics, frequently quoting in Latin and Italian, and concerned for the intellectual welfare of her daughters as well as her sons. In a letter of 17 December 1743 she expressed her disillusion with whig politicians, including the Pelhams and her friend Pulteney, whom she felt had been tainted by the proximity of power. Her Francophilia became more pronounced in return, and during the War of the Austrian Succession she referred to France as 'my country' (*Letters of Mary Lepel*, 64). Over two years of letters, from April 1745 to October 1747, were missing from the manuscript, possibly because Lady Hervey expressed Jacobite sympathies in them. Her interest in early Christianity had led her to conclude that Catholicism was only in error as far as the authority of the papacy was concerned, and all other Catholic doctrines were not superstitious but expressions of the beliefs and practices of the early church. These freely expressed opinions, together with her increasingly obsessive enthusiasm for all things French, may have embarrassed her sons. Her eldest son, George, thought his youngest sisters, Emily and Caroline, were educated as 'rank Jacobites' (Halsband, 307), and he arranged for them to be separated from her. In 1748 she built a new town house in the French style, designed by Henry Flitcroft, in St James's Place, where she entertained a circle of cultural friends and clients which at various times included David Mallet, Edward Gibbon, Chesterfield, Charles and Sarah Lennox, duke and duchess of Richmond, and William Douglas, later fourth duke of Queensberry, among others. She was well known for holding select dinners for six people with common interests.

The maturity of her children, and the death of Lord Bristol, allowed Lady Hervey to spend extended periods in France, where among her circle were the *philosophe* Claude-Adrien Helvetius and Louise-Anne de Bourbon-Condé de Charolais, a granddaughter of Louis XIV. She was at Paris in October 1750 when Chesterfield commended her to his son Philip Stanhope:

> She has been bred all her life at Courts; of which she has acquired all the easy good-breeding, and politeness, without the frivolousness. She has all the reading that a woman should have; and more than any woman need have; for she understands Latin perfectly well, though she wisely conceals it. (*Letters of … Chesterfield*, 4.1594)

Her friendships in France were admired and were to some extent adopted by Horace Walpole. Walpole's 'devotion to her was that of a much younger brother rather than a son, and she did not hesitate to take him down a peg when she thought it advisable' (Walpole, *Corr.*, 31.ix). Walpole later dedicated the first three volumes of his *Anecdotes of Painting in England* to her (1762–3). She also became a friend of David Hume, making introductions for him in London and Paris, and an admirer of Jean-Jacques Rousseau. By the 1750s she had become reconciled to Pulteney and his wife, now earl and countess of Bath, and during the Seven Years' War her admiration for France was tempered by her regard for Frederick the Great. She became a friend, correspondent, and political confidante of Henry Fox, and acted as an intermediary between Fox and other politicians when Fox was attempting to strengthen his position in the administration following Henry Pelham's death in 1754. She was no friend of the old corps whigs, and expressed great hopes of George III on his accession.

Lady Hervey suffered from gout, and in the 1750s and 1760s spent long periods immobile at her home or at Ickworth. She last visited France in 1755–6. Her sometimes unconventional behaviour had compromised her role as family matriarch, and although from 1754 she was on good terms with her eldest and second sons, she became permanently estranged from her third son, Frederick, and her daughters, particularly her eldest, Lepell Phipps, Lady Mulgrave. The reasons for the estrangement are unclear. The second earl of Bristol was appointed lord lieutenant of Ireland in 1766 under the Chatham administration, but she was unable to obtain an Irish bishopric for Edmund Morris from her son. After a long decline, she died at her home in St James's Place, London, on 2 September 1768. She was buried on 9 September at the parish church in Ickworth, where Walpole wrote a verse epitaph for her tombstone. Her will excluded her third son, Frederick, and all her daughters except her second, Lady Mary Fitzgerald, and left an annuity of £60 to her maid Amy Allen, among other bequests to servants and friends, including Henry Fox and Horace Walpole.   MATTHEW KILBURN

Sources D. M. Stuart, *Molly Lepell* (1936) · *Letters of Mary Lepel, Lady Hervey, with a memoir*, ed. J. W. Crooker (1821) · John, Lord Hervey, *Some materials towards memoirs of the reign of King George II*, ed. R. Sedgwick, 3 vols. (1931) · R. Halsband, *Lord Hervey, eighteenth-century courtier* (1973) · Walpole, *Corr.* · *The letters of Philip Dormer Stanhope, fourth earl of Chesterfield*, ed. B. Dobrée, 6 vols. (1932) · *Letters to and from Henrietta, countess of Suffolk, and her second husband, the Hon. George Berkeley, from 1712 to 1767*, ed. J. W. Croker (1821) · J. C. Sainty, 'Office-holders in modern Britain: household of Princess Caroline, 1714–27', www.ihrinfo.ac.uk/office/caroline.html, 21 June 2002 · GEC, *Peerage* · I. Grundy, *Lady Mary Wortley Montagu* (1999) · *The correspondence of Alexander Pope*, ed. G. Sherburn, 5 vols. (1956) · *The correspondence of Jonathan Swift*, ed. H. Williams, 5 vols. (1963–5) · C. Dalton, ed., *English army lists and commission registers, 1661–1714*, 5 (1902) · C. Dalton, ed., *English army lists and commission registers, 1661–1714*, 6 (1904) · *Report on the manuscripts of Mrs Frankland-Russell-Astley of Chequers Court, Bucks.*, HMC, 52 (1900) · *Report on the manuscripts of the late Reginald Rawdon Hastings*, 4 vols., HMC, 78 (1928–47), vol. 3 · *Report on the manuscripts of the earl of Denbigh, part V*, HMC, 68 (1911) · *DNB* · *The letters of Horace Walpole, earl of Orford*, ed. P. Cunningham, 9 vols. (1857–9)

Archives BL, corresp., Add. MS 51345 · Suffolk RO, Bury St Edmunds, family MSS | BL, corresp. with Lord Holland, Add. MS 51397 · BL, corresp. with Lady Suffolk, Add. MS 22628, fols. 13–39

Likenesses group portrait, oils, *c*.1750 (*The earl of Bristol taking leave on his appointment to the command of a ship*), Ickworth House, Park, and Garden, Suffolk · A. Ramsay, portrait, 1762, priv. coll. [*see illus.*] · J. Heath, line engraving (after unknown artist), BM, NPG; repro. in Lord Oxford, *Works* (1798) · attrib. A. Ramsay, oils, Ickworth House, Park, and Garden, Suffolk · H. Watelet, etching (after C. N. Cochin junior, 1752), BM · oils, Ickworth House, Park, and Garden, Suffolk · pastel drawing, Ickworth House, Park, and Garden, Suffolk · two miniatures, Ickworth House, Park, and Garden, Suffolk

Hervey, Thomas (1699–1775), politician and pamphleteer, was born on 20 January 1699 at Ickworth, Suffolk, the second son of John *Hervey, first earl of Bristol (1665–1751), and his second wife, Elizabeth Felton (1676–1741). His elder brother was the courtier John *Hervey, Baron Hervey of Ickworth. Hervey matriculated on 8 June 1717 at Christ Church, Oxford, where he was a companion in dissipation and gambling to his brother Henry, both sons causing great tribulation and expense to their father. After leaving Oxford without taking a degree he was sent to Lincoln's Inn to study law, but gave himself up to a life of heavy drinking, partly to alleviate the chronic and painful ill health which dogged him all his life. In 1722 he developed an ambition to enter politics, hoping to stand for the borough of Bury St Edmunds, a seat to which he was eventually elected on 29 June 1733, replacing his brother Jack who had taken his seat in the House of Lords. He was elected unanimously and without bribery, to the great pleasure of his father, though his complete absence during the election campaign did attract adverse notice. He held the seat until 1747 when his brother Felton was elected. His mother's intense dislike for his fellow member for Bury, Colonel Norton, caused Thomas considerable family difficulties, though the story of this antipathy leading to disinheritance is untrue. He held a series of appointments at court, first in 1727 as equerry to Queen Caroline, and the following year as vice-chamberlain to the queen's household. This post ended with the death of the queen and in 1738 he was appointed as superintendent of the royal gardens.

Thomas was increasingly prey to eccentric behaviour, which in later life developed into mental instability. According to Horace Walpole, when asked why in 1741 he had voted against his party, Hervey replied that he had no idea: 'Jesus knows my thoughts; one day I blaspheme, and pray the next' (Walpole, *Corr.*, 17.244).

A prominent and scandalous aspect to Hervey's life was his relationship with Elizabeth, second wife of his godfather Sir Thomas Hanmer. Considerably younger than Hanmer, she eloped with Hervey shortly after a rift with her husband in 1737. She compounded the scandal by writing to Hanmer requesting him to leave to Hervey the estate at Great Barton, Suffolk, she had brought to the marriage, an audacious demand which understandably Hanmer refused.

Elizabeth Hanmer died in 1741 leaving Thomas £1400 after settlement of his debts. He then published a notorious 'Letter from the Honourable Thomas Hervey to Sir Thomas Hanmer' which is extraordinary for its scurrilous and indiscreet accusations. Ripostes were published, and the affair caused a great public stir. The experience of publication proved infectious: 'Tom now acquired a taste for pamphleteering' (Ponsonby, 104). For the rest of his life he regularly published letters and pamphlets, with the common theme of injustices he believed he had suffered, often at the hands of his family or the courts, and which titillated the public taste for scandal.

In 1744 Hervey married Ann, the daughter of Francis Coghlan, an Irish barrister. She was known to be a spirited woman; one day before the marriage when the couple were in Bath the novelist Fielding, seeing them across a public room, called out 'Why don't you take that bold girl into some bye-place and give her what she wants?' (Ponsonby, 105).

The marriage is said to have taken place in the Fleet prison, not because either party was imprisoned, but because it reduced cost and official process. Thomas's father had cut off communications with him, owing partly to his marrying without the earl's consent or even knowledge. The spirited Ann lost no time in writing to

him seeking financial assistance, for she was as improvident as her new husband. The request was rebuffed, but a partial reconciliation was achieved in 1750, shortly before the earl died.

Hervey had a legitimate son, William, whom he later disinherited. His natural sons, however, he treated well: Thomas (by Lady Hanmer) and George, by an unknown mother, whose death in 1758 at Ticonderoga caused his father much grief. The marriage to Ann palled, and Thomas began publishing scandalous letters on the misery of married life. He applied to have the marriage set aside, but this device failed. Samuel Johnson, who had first met Hervey and his brother Henry in Lichfield in 1730, had retained a liking for him, and wrote expressing his concern. Hervey published his reply: 'Mr Hervey's answer to a letter he received from Dr Samuel Johnson to dissuade him from parting with his supposed wife' (1772). It is characteristically vituperative: 'Sir ... you are a very good man, but you have thought fit to be an advocate for the most worthless woman that ever was on Earth' (Boswell, *Life*, 2.480).

Much of the intemperate and contradictory behaviour of Thomas Hervey might be attributable to his lifelong ill health. In the letter to Hanmer he comments on his physical and mental frailty: 'In over two and twenty years I have never been in a natural state of mind or body ... I have not been in all that time out of pain, or in the calm possession of my understanding.' His writing is eccentric and intemperate, but not without quality. In Horace Walpole's opinion Hervey's pamphleteering style 'beats everything for madness, horrid indecency, and folly, and yet has some charming and striking passages' (Walpole, *Corr.*, 38.202).

Thomas Hervey died towards the end of January 1775 in Bond Street, London. On his deathbed he acknowledged Ann as his legal wife. Johnson commented on his death: 'Tom Hervey ... though a vicious man, was one of the genteelest men that ever lived' (Boswell, *Life*, 2.341).

WILLIAM R. JONES

Sources D. A. Ponsonby, *Call a dog Hervey* (1949) · Boswell, *Life*, vol. 2 · *DNB* · Walpole, *Corr.* · L. Moore, *Amphibious thing: the life of Lord Hervey* (2000) · *The correspondence and other papers of James Boswell relating to the making of the Life of Johnson*, ed. M. Waingrow (1969), vol. 2 of *The Yale editions of the private papers of James Boswell*, research edn (1966–) · *IGI*

Archives PRO, letters to first earl of Chatham, PRO 30/8

Likenesses J. Fayram, oils, Ickworth House, Suffolk; repro. in Ponsonby, *Call a dog Hervey* · miniature, Ickworth House, Suffolk

Hervey [*formerly* Hervie], **Thomas Kibble** (1799–1859), poet and journalist, was born at Paisley, Renfrewshire, on 11 February 1799, one of the sons of James Hervie, a drysalter who settled in Manchester in 1803, and his wife, Isobella Kibble. He was baptized in the parish of Abbey on 26 February 1799. After attending Manchester grammar school he was articled to Sharp, Eccles & Co., a firm of solicitors in Manchester, and subsequently to another firm in London. He then read law in the chambers of a well-known barrister, Mr (later Sergeant) Scriven and, from 1818 to 1820, at Trinity College, Cambridge, which he left without taking a degree. His best-known literary production, a long poem in two parts entitled *Australia*, was published during his second year at Trinity. Much admired both there and in London, where it appeared in new editions, along with some of his shorter poems, in 1824, 1825, and 1829, *Australia* reads as if written for an undergraduate prize, as it in fact was; Hervey's ideas about Australia and its neighbouring islands, largely drawn from newspapers and from a few books which are cited in pseudo-scholarly notes, are fanciful in the extreme. His reputation was enhanced by lyrics such as 'The Convict Ship', 'Floranthe', and the four *Illustrations of Modern Sculpture* (1832); some of these continued to find their way into anthologies until the mid-Victorian period. A longer poem, *The Devil's Progress*, was published in 1830. He edited and contributed to two fashionable literary annuals, *Friendship's Offering* in 1826 and 1827, and *The Amaranth* in 1839. On 17 October 1843 he married Eleanora Louisa Montagu (*b.* 1811?), the daughter of George Conway Montagu of Lackham, Wiltshire. The couple had a son, Frederick Robert James.

From 1831 to 1853 nearly all of Hervey's literary energy appears to have been devoted to reviews and other articles in *The Athenaeum*, ranking in the number of his contributions with the prolific H. F. Chorley and Hepworth Dixon. The subjects of his reviews included Browning, Tennyson, Dickens, and French literature. His obituarist in the *Gentleman's Magazine* (April 1859, 433) conceded that as a reviewer he was 'characterized by a causticity of censure and a costiveness of praise, scarcely worthy of a journal of high standing'. He nevertheless became editor of *The Athenaeum*, in succession to C. W. Dilke, on 23 May 1846. Under his editorship the paper departed from its previous policy by championing humanitarian causes, among them prison reform, one of Hervey's own interests. Its sales apparently increased, at least during his last three years as editor, but the quality of its reviews deteriorated (Marchand, 76–81). The *Gentleman's Magazine* considered that his 'acknowledged qualifications' for the editorship were counterbalanced by his 'desultory and procrastinating habits'; these it attributed to the chronic asthma from which he had suffered for many years and which led to his resignation in the autumn of 1853 (p. 432).

In the remaining five years of his life Hervey contributed frequently to the *Art Journal*. Together with a single article in the *Dublin Review* (December 1836), a few brief tales in the annuals, and his contributions to *The Athenaeum*, these appear to comprise virtually the whole corpus of his published writings in prose. He died at 8 Ponsford Terrace, Haverstock Hill, London, on 17 February 1859, from asthma and bronchitis. He was survived by his wife, and was buried at Highgate cemetery, Middlesex.

At the time of his death Hervey was preparing a collected edition of his poems. This was completed by his widow and published in 1866 as *The Poems of T. K. Hervey*, with an introductory memoir. Before her marriage to Hervey she had been an established poet in her own right, having produced a long poem, *Edith of Graystock* (1833), a five-act play in verse, *The Landgrave* (1839), and a number of

short poems, some of which had appeared in the annuals edited by her future husband; after Hervey's death she produced a three-volume novel, *Snooded Jessaline* (1865).

P. D. EDWARDS

Sources 'Memoir', *The poems of T. K. Hervey* (1866) · GM, 3rd ser., 6 (1859), 431–3 · L. A. Marchand, *The Athenaeum: a mirror of Victorian culture*, new edn (1971) · Boase, *Mod. Eng. biog.*, 1.1451 · d. cert. · DNB · bap. reg. Scot.

Hervey, William, Baron Hervey of Kidbrooke and Baron Hervey of Ross (*d.* 1642), naval officer, was the only son of Henry Hervey, of Kidbrooke, Kent, and his wife, Jane, daughter of James Thomas of Llanfihangel, Monmouthshire. As a young man Hervey served aboard the lord admiral's flagship during the Armada campaign of 1588, earning renown in the action off Calais. In 1596 he commanded his own vessel, the *Darling* of Portsmouth, on the expedition to Cadiz, and was knighted by the earl of Essex. The following year he sailed on the voyage to the Azores as commander of the *Bonaventure*. In September 1598 he was one of several candidates for the comptrollership of the navy, though he failed to secure appointment. During 1599 he served as captain of the *Garland*, in the fleet based in the Downs under the command of Lord Thomas Howard. It is possible that he played some part in the war in Ireland in 1600. He served as MP for Horsham in 1601, when he was a member of a committee which was considering the Irish situation, and for Petersfield in 1604.

As a veteran of the Elizabethan sea war Hervey retained links with the navy during the early Stuart period. In 1618 he was a member of a committee investigating the ordnance office. On the outbreak of war with Spain in 1625 he was appointed to the council of war; he played an active role in advising the lord admiral on the Cadiz expedition. In December 1626 he became one of the special commissioners who were investigating the state of the navy. He was involved in a survey of naval vessels in January 1627, and in February he was consulted about the number of ships to be employed in the guard of the channel. Later in the year he served as rear admiral aboard the *Repulse* on the expedition to the Île de Ré, to relieve La Rochelle.

Hervey acquired various offices and honours during his career. He became a gentleman pensioner at the court of Elizabeth I some time before 1587. In 1598 he was made keeper of St Andrew's Castle in Hampshire, with a fee of £19 3s. 4d., although he surrendered the post in 1604. He was granted the office of remembrancer of first fruits and tenths in 1603. He was created a baronet on 31 May 1619 and became Baron Hervey of Ross, in co. Wexford, on 5 August 1620. He was made an English baron on 27 February 1628, reportedly to strengthen the royal cause in the upper house (*Buccleuch MSS*, 3.324). As Baron Hervey of Kidbrooke he was rarely absent from the House of Lords during the session of 1628, and he sat on a wide range of committees.

In 1598 Hervey married Mary (*d.* 1607), daughter of Anthony *Browne, first Viscount Montagu, and widow of Henry Wriothesley, second earl of Southampton (1545–1581), and of Thomas Heneage (*d.* 1595). The negotiations concerning the match were shrouded in mystery, probably because of hostility from the third earl of Southampton, whose 'discomfort and discontentment' with the marriage were conveyed to his mother by the earl of Essex in November 1598 (*Salisbury MSS*, 14.80). Following the death of his first wife in 1607 Hervey married in 1608 Cordelia, daughter and coheir of Brian Annesley of Leigh in Kent. They had three sons and four daughters before her death in 1636. Hervey was survived by only one of his daughters, Elizabeth, who married a cousin, John Hervey of Ickworth. At his death in London in 1642 he owned land in Wexford, a house at St Martin-in-the-Fields, Westminster, as well as the manor of Kidbrooke. The latter was valued at £1000 before 1614. A respected and well connected naval officer, Hervey has sometimes been identified as a possible candidate for William Shakespeare's 'Mr. W. H.'. He was buried in Westminster Abbey on 8 July 1642.

JOHN C. APPLEBY

Sources CSP dom., 1595–1601; 1603–10; 1625–49 • CSP Ire., 1615–25; 1633–60 • *Calendar of the manuscripts of the most hon. the marquis of Salisbury*, 6, HMC, 9 (1895); 8–9 (1899–1902); 14 (1923); 22–3 (1971–3) • R. C. Johnson and others, eds., *Proceedings in parliament, 1628*, 5 (1983) • J. S. Brewer and W. Bullen, eds., *Calendar of the Carew manuscripts*, 5: 1603–1623, PRO (1871) • APC, 1618–19, 1627–8 • J. K. Laughton, ed., *State papers relating to the defeat of the Spanish Armada, anno 1588*, 2 vols., Navy RS, 1–2 (1894) • J. K. Laughton, ed., *The naval miscellany*, 1, Navy RS, 20 (1902) • *The naval tracts of Sir William Monson*, ed. M. Oppenheim, 5 vols., Navy RS, 22–3, 43, 45, 47 (1902–14) • *Report on the manuscripts of his grace the duke of Buccleuch and Queensberry … preserved at Montagu House*, 3 vols. in 4, HMC, 45 (1899–1926), vol. 3 • HoP, Commons, 1558–1603 • *Twelfth report*, HMC (1890), pt 1

Archives PRO, state papers, James I and Charles I

Wealth at death land in Wexford; house at St Martin-in-the-Fields, Westminster; manor of Kidbrooke

Herzen, Alexander [*formerly* Aleksandr Ivanovich Gertsen] (**1812–1870**), radical publicist, was born at what is now 25 Tverskoy bulvar, Moscow, on 25 March 1812 OS (6 April 1812 NS), the illegitimate son of the rich nobleman Ivan Alekseyevich Yakovlev (1767–1846) and his young German consort, Henriette Louise Haag (1795–1851); the surname Herzen is commonly explained as meaning heart-child. After a conventional education with tutors and at Moscow University Herzen entered government service, but was twice exiled from the capitals for his democratic, Westernizing views. He became a writer, publishing essays and fiction under the pen-name Iskander, notably the novel *Kto vinovat?* (*Whose Fault?*) of 1845–6.

After inheriting a considerable fortune on his father's death in 1846 Herzen left Russia in 1847, never to return, together with his wife, Natalya Aleksandrovna, *née* Zakharina (1817–1852), whom he had married in 1838, and their children Aleksandr (Sasha; 1839–1906) and Natalya (Tata; 1844–1936), to whom was later added Olga (1850–1953). Herzen's excitement over the 1848 revolution in France and contemporary turmoil in Switzerland and Italy gave way to political disappointments and personal tragedies, culminating in his wife's affair with the poet Georg Herwegh and her death in 1852. Encouraged by friends to visit London, he first set foot on English soil at dawn on 24 August 1852, thinking to stay a few days; he remained in fact for over twelve years, residing at numerous addresses, including Laurel House, Putney High Street (1856–8), and Orsett House, Westbourne Terrace, Paddington (1860–63).

Herzen's watchword was *semper in motu*: he transformed the frustrations of exile into moral force by his constant activity. At first sad and lonely as he wandered about London, he came to respect that teeming anthill of a city. Although he despised the hypocrisy and duplicity of the British, and hated the pious tedium of their Sunday, he valued their tradition of minding one's own business. As a strongly built, broad-featured Slav, with dark hair and beard and a brilliant gaze, he was conspicuous enough, but even during the Crimean War he encountered surprisingly little hostility. He was free to associate with fellow émigrés such as Mazzini, Ledru-Rollin, Worcell, and Kossuth, and gave a magnificent luncheon for Garibaldi on 17 April 1864. His ever shifting home became a Mecca also for Russian visitors such as Chernyshevsky, Bakunin, Tolstoy, Dostoyevsky, and Turgenev. Although he took little part in British affairs, Herzen did attend the houses of parliament and the law courts, participated in some meetings, and wrote letters to the press. He met the Carlyles and Robert Owen, and was acquainted with assorted liberals and radicals including the Milner Gibsons, James Stansfeld, George Jacob Holyoake, William Linton, Charles Bradlaugh, and the younger Joseph Cowen. He read *The Times*, drank pale ale, and sang 'Rule Britannia' when the fancy took him.

While in England, Herzen wrote prolifically. Early on, in an effort to come to terms with his personal disillusionment and the failure of revolution, he embarked on the amorphous body of memoirs by which he is perhaps best known, *Byloye i dumy* (*Reflections on Times Past*), the first two volumes of which came out in London in 1861. But he also applied his satirical and polymathic pen to the cause of political reform and agrarian socialism in Russia. In 1853 he published articles on Russian serfdom in *The Leader*; his letter to Michelet appeared as a separate pamphlet, *The Russian People and their Socialism*, in 1855, and that same year an English translation entitled *My Exile in Siberia* provoked a critical stir. Meanwhile, in June 1853, he had set up the Russian Free Press as a platform of opposition to tsarist rule. At first it chiefly printed his own pamphlets, but then, following the unexpected death of Nicholas I, launched the irregular serial *Polyarnaya Zvezda* (*Pole Star*), which opened in August 1855 with a challenge to Alexander II to liberate the peasants and allow freedom of speech.

In April 1856 Herzen's lifelong friend the poet and publicist Nikolay Ogaryov (1813–1877) arrived in London with his second wife, Natalya Alekseyevna, *née* Tuchkova (1829–1913). Natalya promptly fell in love with Herzen and a painful triangle developed; but, despite the fact that she bore Herzen three children, the two men remained close allies. It was Ogaryov who suggested they create the journal *Kolokol* (*The Bell*). First issued in June 1857, this soon became a powerful voice for change. Disseminated in thousands of copies, it kept readers closely informed about events of concern to Russians and attacked oppressors and abuses. Copies smuggled into Russia were read avidly if furtively, even in official circles. *Kolokol* undoubtedly hastened the emancipation of the serfs, an event fêted by the Herzen ménage on 10 April 1861 with red flags, 7000 multicoloured gaslights, and speeches in Russian, English, German, French, Italian, Polish, and Welsh.

When the cruel limitations of the reform were properly perceived, the tone of *Kolokol* became more indignant, but Herzen's views on the future of Russia were rapidly overtaken by those of younger and more violent contemporaries, less concerned than he with individual freedom and responsibility. *Kolokol's* influence and circulation declined dramatically, especially after its unpopular support for the Polish rebellion of 1862–3. Herzen decided to shift it to Geneva, where a large colony of Russian exiles seemed a promising base; in the event this failed. He himself finally left England on 15 March 1865 and lived thereafter in Switzerland, Italy, and France. He died suddenly in Paris on 21 January 1870 and, after temporary burial in Père Lachaise cemetery, his remains were laid to rest in Nice beside (the first) Natalya. PATRICK WADDINGTON

Sources A. I. Gertsen [A. I. Herzen], *Sobraniye sochineniy v tridtsati tomakh*, 30 vols. (1954–65) · *My past and thoughts: the memoirs of Alexander Herzen*, trans. C. Garnett, rev. edn, 4 vols. (1968) · *Literaturnoye Nasledstvo*, 96 (1985) [*Gertsen i zapad* [Herzen and the west]] · *Literaturnoye Nasledstvo*, 109 (1997) [*Gertzen i Ogarev v krugu rodnykh i druzey*, 2 vols.] · M. Partridge, *Alexander Herzen* (1984) · M. Partridge, *Alexander Herzen: collected studies*, 2nd edn (1993) · E. H. Carr, *The Romantic exiles: a nineteenth-century portrait gallery* (1933) · G. Terry, *Alexander Herzen in English: a bibliography* (1992) · E. Acton, *Alexander Herzen and the role of the intellectual revolutionary* (1979) · M. Partridge, 'Aleksandr Gertsen i yego angliyskiye svyazi', *Problemy izucheniya Gertsena*, ed. V. P. Volgin and others (1963), 348–69 · M. Partridge, 'Herzen, Ogaryov and the Free Russian Press in London', *Anglo-Soviet Journal*, 27/1 (1966), 8–13 · N. A. Ogaréva-Tuchkova, *Vospominaniya, 1848–1870* (1903) · M. Malia, *Alexander Herzen and the birth of Russian socialism, 1812–1855* (1961) · I. Berlin, *Russian thinkers* (1978) · M. von Meysenbug, *Rebel in a crinoline: memoirs* (1937) · B. F. Egorov and others, *Letopis' zhizni i tvorchestva A. I. Gertsena*, 4 vols. (1974–87)

Archives Bibliothèque Nationale, Paris, family MSS · Central State Archive, Moscow · Central State Historical Archive, Moscow · Institute of Russian Literature (Pushkin House), St Petersburg · Internationaal Instituut voor Sociale Geschiedenis, Amsterdam, corresp. and papers · Russian State Library (Lenin Library), Moscow · State Literary Archive, Moscow

Likenesses portraits, repro. in Gertsen, *Sobraniye sochineniy*, frontispieces · portraits, repro. in *Literaturnoye nasledstvo 96*

Heseltine, James. *See* Heseltine, James (*c.*1692–1763).

Heseltine, Philip Arnold [*pseud.* Peter Warlock] (1894–1930), music scholar and composer, was born on 30 October 1894 in the Savoy Hotel, London, the only child of Arnold Heseltine (1852–1897), solicitor, of London, and his second wife, Bessie Mary Edith Covernton (1861–1943). In 1903 Bessie was married again, this time to Walter Buckley Jones (1864–1938), and five years later the family moved from London to his family home, Cefn Bryn-talch, near Aber-miwl, Montgomeryshire. At the age of nine Heseltine was sent to Stone House, a preparatory school in Broadstairs, Kent, and he proceeded to Eton College (1908–11). An early infatuation with the music of Frederick

Philip Arnold Heseltine [Peter Warlock] (1894–1930), by unknown photographer, 1915

Delius led to a meeting with the composer at a concert of his music in London in 1910. This resulted in a lifelong friendship and a formative musical influence.

Although it was intended that Heseltine should eventually enter the civil service, after finishing at Eton he was allowed to spend a few months in Cologne studying music and German. It was during this time that he first began composing short songs. In October 1913 he proceeded to Christ Church, Oxford, but, after an unhappy and unproductive year, he transferred to London University in October 1914. A tempting offer of work as a music critic on the *Daily Mail* in February 1915 resulted in an abrupt end to his formal studies. Mounting frustrations, however, caused him to resign this post after barely four months. Letters from this period display a deeply disturbed and melancholy figure, unsure of both his musical abilities and direction in life. A meeting with D. H. Lawrence in November 1915 temporarily fired new enthusiasms and ambitions, and he followed Lawrence to Cornwall early the next year. The spell of Lawrence's philosophies and personality was, however, soon broken, and a disillusioned Heseltine returned to London at the end of February.

Another important influence soon manifested itself in the person of the Anglo-Dutch composer Bernard Van Dieren. As a result of a brief period of study with him, Heseltine's music now became clearer, less complex, and more contrapuntal in character. On 22 December 1916 Heseltine married an artist's model, Minnie Lucy (Puma) Channing (1894–1943), daughter of Robert Stuart Channing, variously described as a mechanical engineer and a hotel waiter. A son, Nigel, had been born in July 1916. He also had a relationship from the early 1920s with Barbara Peache. Although not a declared conscientious objector, to avoid conscription Heseltine lived in Dublin from August 1917 to August 1918, during which time he became involved in occult studies, at the same time composing a number of fine songs, including 'Take, O take these lips away' and 'Sweet content'. On his return to London some of these were successfully published under the name Peter Warlock, a pseudonym he used for his musical compositions throughout his life. The choice of the name Warlock is significant, given his involvement with the occult during this period. He reserved his real name only for critical and scholarly writings. His next venture was the editing of *The Sackbut* (May 1920–June 1921), a lively music journal often containing material of a controversial nature by Heseltine himself and other members of his circle. As a result of one of these controversies Heseltine was replaced as editor, and, finding himself out of work, he returned to the family home in Wales, where he remained until 1924.

These years in Wales proved some of Heseltine's most productive: besides composing much original work, he transcribed and edited a vast amount of early English music as well as writing a book on Delius. Some time during this period he officially separated from his wife, though they had not lived together for many years, the marriage having been doomed almost from the start. He moved to London briefly in June 1924, and eventually went to live opposite the village pub in Eynsford, Kent, in early 1925 together with the composer E. J. Moeran. From this period arose much of the Warlock legend about his often wild, Bohemian lifestyle. It is not surprising that he was used as the basis for characters in novels by several authors, including Lawrence and Huxley. There was, however, also a sensitive, introvert side to his personality (as exemplified in his passion for cats). This led to a widespread myth that his was a Jekyll and Hyde split personality. He moved back to London in late 1928 (after a brief spell in Wales); his last days were haunted by ever darkening fits of black depression and declining creative confidence. He died at his home, 12A Tite Street, Chelsea, on 17 December 1930 as a result of coal-gas poisoning. The jury at the inquest gave an open verdict, though it is generally believed that his death was suicide. He was buried on 20 December at the old cemetery in Godalming.

Heseltine's compositions include more than 100 songs, mostly with piano accompaniment, though some have instrumental accompaniment, notably his acknowledged masterpiece *The Curlew* (1915–22), a song-cycle of poems by Yeats for tenor, flute, cor anglais, and string quartet. It is a work which shows the influence of Bartók, whose music he was championing at the time. Other instrumental works include *An Old Song* (1917–23), a serenade for string orchestra (1921–2), and the popular *Capriol* (1927). He also composed a number of short choral works. His scholarly output includes a large collection of Elizabethan and Jacobean vocal solo, choral, and instrumental transcriptions as well as an edition of Henry Purcell's string fantasias. He was also the author of a number of books, including *Frederick Delius* (1923), *The English Ayre* (1926), and, together with Cecil Gray, *Carlo Gesualdo: Musician and Murderer* (1926).

Heseltine's gifts as a composer were most successfully expressed through the medium of miniature song-settings in an idiosyncratic harmonic language that comprised an unusual mixture of Edwardiana, Delius, Van Dieren, Elizabethan, and folk music, features that give his music a strongly personal voice. Many commentators have seized on the contrast between the extrovert and gentler features of his music as confirmation of a split within the Heseltine–Warlock persona, an element that Cecil Gray exploited in his memoir (1934). Such a simplistic interpretation is, however, contradicted by acquaintance with Heseltine's complex life story, with its constant family pressures and lack of regular work and income, want of musical self-confidence, and frequent evidence of manic depression. At any rate his closest friends always rebutted the split personality theory, humorously summing up his change of character as 'Philip drunk and Philip sober'.   BARRY SMITH

Sources B. Smith, *Peter Warlock: the life of Philip Heseltine* (1994) · C. Gray, *Peter Warlock: a memoir of Philip Heseltine* (1934) · N. Heseltine, *Capriol for mother: a memoir of Philip Heseltine (Peter Warlock)* (1992) · I. A. Copley, *The music of Peter Warlock: a critical survey* (1979) · B. Collins, *Peter Warlock: the composer* (1996) · B. Smith, *Frederick Delius and Peter Warlock: a friendship revealed* (2000) · CGPLA Eng. & Wales (1931) · b. cert. · m. cert.

Archives BL, music collections, corresp. and papers, Add. MSS 52547–52549, 52904–52912, 54197, 57958–57970, 58127 | BL, music collections, corresp. with E. A. Dowbiggin, Add. MS 60748 · BL, music collections, corresp. with R. M. B. Nichols, Add. MS 57795 · BL, music collections, corresp. with Bernard Van Dieren, Add. MS 65187 | SOUND BL NSA, 'A conversation … about Peter Warlock', 17 Nov 1994, C4941/301–302 T1–2 · BL NSA, documentary recording · BL NSA, 'More sunlight in a simple song', 1994, H5603/1 · BL NSA, oral history interview · BL NSA, 'Peter Warlock', BBC, 12 Dec 1964, NP890R C1

Likenesses photograph, 1915, priv. coll. [*see illus.*] · E. Procter, pencil drawing, 1929, NPG

Wealth at death £10,252 13s. 5d.: resworn probate, 21 Feb 1931, *CGPLA Eng. & Wales*

Hesilrige [Haselrig], **Sir Arthur, second baronet** (1601–1661), army officer and politician, was born at Noseley, Leicestershire, the second son of Sir Thomas Hesilrige, baronet (*d.* 1630), of Noseley, and his wife, Frances, daughter of William Gorges of Alderton, Northamptonshire. He matriculated as a fellow-commoner from Magdalene College, Cambridge, in 1617 and was admitted at Gray's Inn in 1623. In 1624 Hesilrige married his first wife, Frances, daughter of Thomas Elmes of Lilford, Northamptonshire. On his father's death in 1630 he succeeded to both the family baronetcy and its extensive midlands estates. In 1632 his first wife died and two years later he married Dorothy, daughter of Fulke Greville of Thorpe Latimer in Lincolnshire, and sister of Robert *Greville, second Baron Brooke (1607–1643). His republican associate Edmund Ludlow commented of his character that he was 'a man of disobliging carriage, sower [sour] and morose of temper, liable to be transported with passion, and to whom liberality seemed to be a vice' (*Memoirs of Edmund Ludlow*, 2.133–4). Ludlow also, however, pointed to 'the rectitude and sincerity of his intentions' and to his constant concern 'to prevent arbitrary power wheresoever he knew it to be affected and to keep the sword subservient to the civil magistrate' (ibid.).

Opposition to personal rule and parliamentary career to 1642 From the early 1630s Hesilrige's radical political and religious views brought him into conflict with Charles I's personal-rule government. In 1632 he was summoned

Sir Arthur Hesilrige, second baronet (1601–1661), by unknown artist, 1640

before the privy council for failing to pay his muster fees. While waiting to make his appearance he reportedly remarked to one of the deputy lieutenants who had presented him: 'If such a gentleman as you shall be suffered to shark the country of their money, it will be a very pretty thing' (*CSP dom.*, 1631–3, 445–6). He was afterwards forced to kneel before the privy council to ask pardon for this comment and was imprisoned for a short time in the Tower of London. Through his marriage into the Greville family in 1634 he became closely associated with the puritan group led by Lord Saye and Sele and John Pym which was working in secret to oppose Charles I's government. He was heavily involved in this group's colonial ventures and was one of the original patentees of the town of Saybrook in New England. He also seriously considered emigrating to America himself at this stage. In 1635 he quarrelled with William Laud over the payment of some ecclesiastical fees and was forced to appear before the court of high commission on several occasions. In the later 1630s he publicly opposed the collection of ship money in Leicestershire. His objection to government policy during the 1630s seems to have been primarily religious in nature; at the Restoration a hostile commentator argued that religion was the 'pretence' of his 'discontent' (Gent).

In 1640 Hesilrige was returned to both the Short and Long parliaments as one of the knights of the shire for Leicestershire, and during the next eighteen months he remained a close associate of Pym and the other leaders of the opposition to Charles I's government. He strongly supported the moves to bring Thomas Wentworth, earl of Strafford, to trial, and when the impeachment proceedings against Strafford appeared to be faltering in the spring of 1641 he advocated the drawing up of a bill of attainder as an alternative way of finding him guilty of treason by statute. This was a very radical tactic about which initially even Pym was hesitant. Hesilrige was also one of the fiercest parliamentary critics of the Laudian church. In May 1641, following the defeat of a bill to exclude the bishops from the House of Lords, he joined with Oliver Cromwell and Sir Henry Vane in introducing into the House of Commons a bill to abolish bishops altogether. The bill was given a second reading, but was abandoned later that year. In December 1641 Hesilrige introduced the Militia Bill into the House of Commons and the following month he was one of the five members whom Charles I accused of treason and attempted to arrest in the Commons' chamber.

Civil war, regicide and republic On the outbreak of the first civil war in 1642 Hesilrige raised a troop of horse for parliament and in October 1642 he fought at the battle of Edgehill as part of the regiment of Sir William Balfour. By 1643 he was serving as the second in command to Sir William Waller and his regiment of cuirassiers, known as the lobsters because of their three-quarter armour, and fought at both Lansdowne and Roundway Down. In both these battles he and his men were in the thick of the action; Hesilrige himself was wounded on both occasions and nearly died of the injuries he sustained during the second engagement. In 1644 he fought at Cheriton and the second battle of Newbury.

Away from the battlefield Hesilrige played an active part in political developments at Westminster. Following Pym's death at the end of 1643, he for a time assumed the leadership of the war party in parliament. In the winter of 1644–5 he backed Oliver Cromwell in his quarrel with the earl of Manchester and in early 1645 he supported the self-denying ordinance, thereafter laying down his military commission. During the abortive peace negotiations at Uxbridge in 1645 one of parliament's terms for a settlement was that Hesilrige should be made a lord and given lands worth £2000 a year. Following the parliamentarian victory in the first civil war, Hesilrige took the side of the New Model Army in its quarrel with parliament. He was believed to have persuaded William Lenthall, the speaker of the Commons, to join the army in 1647, and after the New Model had arrived in the capital in the late summer he helped to organize the ejection from the Commons of its most prominent presbyterian critics.

In December 1647 Hesilrige was appointed governor of Newcastle and given overall responsibility for the military forces in that region. His duties in the north kept him away from London during the crucial revolutionary months of December 1648 and January 1649. He was opposed to the army's purge of parliament and, despite his republican sympathies, did not support its subsequent decision to put Charles I on trial. He turned down an invitation to sit as one of the king's judges and subsequently refused to sign the engagement, the oath of loyalty to the new regime. He none the less took up his seat in the Rump in late February 1649, and subsequently became a prominent member of the government of the republic, serving as a member of the council of state until 1653. While he was critical of the Rump Parliament's reluctance to embrace constitutional reform, he strongly supported its constitutional role and backed it in its power struggle with the army during 1652. He vehemently opposed the army's forcible dissolution of the Rump in April 1653 and thereafter remained a bitter opponent of Cromwell and the protectorate.

Control of the north-east Throughout the period from 1647 to the mid-1650s Hesilrige was governor of Newcastle and as such was one of the most powerful men in the counties of Durham and Northumberland. Following his appointment he quickly established his authority over this area and helped to keep it secure for parliament during the second civil war and the invasion of the Scots in 1648. At the beginning of July 1648 he defeated a force of Northumbrian royalists under the command of Colonel Edward Grey, and the following month he recaptured the castle at Tynemouth, after its garrison commander, Henry Lilburne, had defected to the king. In October 1648 he accompanied Cromwell to Edinburgh. He was again with him in Scotland during the 1650 campaign and was given charge of the Scottish prisoners following the English victory at Dunbar.

Hesilrige remained powerful in the north-east of England throughout the early 1650s and amassed a large personal fortune by purchasing lands which had been sequestered from local royalists and the bishop of Durham; his acquisitions included the manors of Bishop's Auckland, Easington, and Wolsingham, which between them cost him in the region of £19,000. During his period of pre-eminence in the north-east he was frequently accused of corruption and of dishonestly using his power to enrich himself. In 1650 John Musgrave published a tract entitled *A true and exact relation of the great and heavy pressures and grievances the well affected of the northern bordering counties lye under, by Sir Arthur Haslerigs misgovernment*, in which he labelled him the 'Nimrod of the North' (Musgrave, 1) and accused him of appointing delinquents to positions of power and of acquiring a vast personal fortune by extortion and the purchase of sequestered lands at a fraction of their true worth. Hesilrige was similarly accused by John Hedworth in *The Oppressed Man's Outcry* of acting unjustly and oppressively to gain control of some collieries at Harraton in Durham which had been confiscated from the Hedworth family. He also became involved in a protracted lawsuit with the Collingwood family about the rightful ownership of the manor of Esslington in Northumberland, with the courts eventually deciding against him.

In 1649 the Leveller leader John Lilburne claimed in the tract *A Preparative to an Hue and Cry after Sir Arthur Haslerig* that Hesilrige had attempted to murder him and had cheated him out of about £2400 'by the meer power of his own will' (Lilburne, 1). Lilburne asserted that Hesilrige had 'overstept' even Charles I's hated minister, Thomas Wentworth, earl of Strafford, by 'traitorously subverting the fundamentall liberties of England and (in time of peace)

exercising an arbitrary and tyrannical government over and above law' (ibid.). Two years later Lilburne again accused him of conducting a vendetta against his father and uncle, Richard and George Lilburne, and of unjustly sequestering some of the family's lands in Durham. In early 1652 a committee of the Rump declared that Lilburne's charges were false and sentenced the Leveller to a heavy fine and banishment. Hesilrige could also be extremely uncompromising in his dealings with the royalist clergy; on one occasion he ejected Alexander Davison and his family from the rectory of Norham in the middle of the night, throwing their belongings in the churchyard.

Following the establishment of the protectorate in December 1653 and Hesilrige's decision to break with Cromwell, he lost influence in the north. His dominance passed to Robert Lilburne and Charles Howard, who acted as governors of York and Carlisle respectively, and as John Lambert's deputies as major-generals for the north in 1655 and 1656.

Protectorate and Restoration Throughout the period from 1653 to 1658 Hesilrige remained an implacable opponent of Oliver Cromwell and his protectoral state. He refused to pay taxes not sanctioned by parliament and on several occasions had his property distrained as a result. In September 1654 he was elected to the first protectorate parliament as one of the members for Leicestershire, and in the early days of the session was one of the government's most outspoken critics. Edmund Ludlow remarked that during this period he was 'very instrumental in opening the eyes of many young members who had never before heard their interest so clearly stated; so that the commonwealth-party increased daily and that of the sword lost ground' (*Memoirs of Edmund Ludlow*, 1.391). When these activities prompted Cromwell to intervene and to demand that the MPs subscribe to a recognition of the government, Hesilrige refused to do so and subsequently withdrew from Westminster. Two years later he was again elected as MP for Leicestershire, for the second protectorate parliament. On this occasion he was excluded even before the assembly had met, and subsequently signed a protest about this action. In late 1657 Cromwell appointed him to the newly established other house, but he refused to accept this position and when the parliament reassembled for its brief second session in January 1658 he provocatively took up his seat in the Commons. Once again he proved a fierce critic of the government, attacking in particular the new second chamber as unconstitutional and unrepresentative.

Following Oliver Cromwell's death in September 1658, Hesilrige was elected to Richard Cromwell's parliament, once again as member for Leicestershire. He continued to attack the protectorate, and spoke against recognizing Richard as the new head of state. By the early spring of 1659 he appears to have been conspiring with the leaders of the army to bring down the regime and he was one of those behind the army's declaration calling for the recall of the Rump. Following Richard Cromwell's resignation and the subsequent return of the Rump, Hesilrige once more began to play a very prominent role in public affairs. He was a member of both the committee of safety and the council of state. He effectively controlled parliamentary proceedings and took part in the appointment of army officers. He was also put in command of a regiment which had been taken away from Charles Howard.

Hesilrige soon, however, fell out with his new army colleagues, both by exaggerating the constitutional authority of parliament and by taking insufficient notice of the concerns of the military with regard to appointments and indemnity. He was also very suspicious of John Lambert, whom he suspected of wanting to re-establish a military regime and to assume power himself. He was behind the move in parliament to cashier Lambert and seven other officers, an action which in turn persuaded Lambert forcibly to close the Rump for a second time. Following Lambert's putsch, Hesilrige based himself at Portsmouth and attempted to gather together a force to resist him. After the Rump had met again in late December 1659, he returned to London and resumed his position on the council of state.

A close ally of George Monck, whose march from Scotland to London had precipitated the return of parliamentary government, Hesilrige was slow to realize that Monck did not share his republican outlook and was considering recalling Charles Stuart from exile. When he did come to see the way events were leading, he attempted to dissuade Monck from this course of action. According to some reports he tried to persuade him to take the crown himself, before dropping his opposition in return for a promise that his own life would be spared following a restoration of the monarchy. After Charles II's return in May 1660, Hesilrige was none the less exempted from the Act of Indemnity and imprisoned in the Tower of London. He died six months later, on 7 January 1661, before he could be brought to trial for treason. A short character sketch published at the Restoration labelled him as a 'church-thief' and denounced him for his enthusiastic iconoclasm and plundering of church wealth.

Reputation and influence Hesilrige was one of the most committed and prominent republicans within mid-seventeenth-century England. He remained throughout his career a staunch supporter of the rights of the English parliament, and he opposed with equal vigour what he regarded as the unrepresentative rule of both Charles I in the 1630s and Oliver Cromwell in the 1650s. While he was undoubtedly a man of great courage and strong political and religious principles, he gained an unfortunate, but probably justified, contemporary reputation as someone who took advantage of the positions of power he enjoyed in the 1640s and 1650s both to oppress his enemies and to enrich himself. This inclination towards bullying and greed confirmed the worst prejudices of his conservative enemies about the character and origins of republicanism and did much to discredit it as a political philosophy.

CHRISTOPHER DURSTON

Sources Memoirs of Edmund Ludlow, ed. C. H. Firth, 2 vols. (1888) · The writings and speeches of Oliver Cromwell, ed. W. C. Abbott and C. D. Crane, 4 vols. (1937–47) · Diary of Thomas Burton, ed. J. T. Rutt, 4 vols. (1828) · F. B. Gent, The character of Sr. Arthur Haslerig, the church-thief [1660] · J. Bruce and D. Masson, eds., The quarrel between the earl of Manchester and Oliver Cromwell, CS, new ser., 12 (1875) · J. Lilburne, A preparative to an hue and cry after Sir Arthur Haslerig [1649] [Thomason tract E 573(16)] · J. Musgrave, A true and exact relation of the great and heavy pressures and grievances the well affected of the northern bordering counties lye under, by Sir Arthur Haslerigs misgovernment (1650) · J. Musgrave, Musgrave muz'ld (1651) · J. Hedworth, The oppressed man's outcry (1650) · A. Fletcher, The outbreak of the English civil war (1981) · C. H. Firth and G. Davies, The regimental history of Cromwell's army, 2 vols. (1940) · CSP dom., 1631–3; 1635; 1641–3 · JHC, 4 (1644–6) · JHC, 5 (1646–8) · DNB

Archives Leics. RO, corresp.

Likenesses oils, 1640, NPG [see illus.] · E. Dyer, oils (after R. Walker), Palace of Westminster, London · R. Grave, line engraving, BM, NPG

Hesketh [née Cowper], **Harriet**, **Lady Hesketh** (bap. 1733, d. 1807), cousin and intimate friend of the poet William Cowper, was baptized in St Mary's, Hertingfordbury, Hertfordshire, on 12 July 1733, the eldest of three daughters of Ashley Cowper (1701–1788), clerk of the parliaments, and Dorothy, daughter of the Revd John Oakes of Bluntisham, Huntingdonshire. Her paternal uncle, the Revd John Cowper, had married Anne Donne, a descendant of the poet John Donne.

As a child Harriet lived at Southampton Row, between Bloomsbury and Holborn, where the young William *Cowper, her cousin and two years her senior, was a frequent visitor. Her sister, Theodora Jane, entered into an unhappy love affair with Cowper. Explicit evidence in letters passing between Harriet and Cowper refutes any possibility that a romantic attachment existed between them also. Accounted a beauty in her youth, she became engaged to Thomas Hesketh (1726/7–1778) of Rufford Hall, near Ormskirk, Lancashire, about 1754; they were later married in Oxford Chapel, Cavendish Square, London. Early in their relationship the couple accompanied Cowper on a visit to Southampton, where the poet spent several months recuperating from an early bout of the chronic mental illness which dogged his adult life. On 5 May 1761 Thomas Hesketh was created baronet.

An estrangement between Harriet Hesketh and her cousin, lasting nineteen years, commenced in March 1766. Cowper's letters indicate that the breach was initiated by Hesketh. During this interval the poet sought retirement in Olney, Buckinghamshire, and Hesketh accompanied her husband for periods abroad from 1769. Sir Thomas died on 4 March 1778, aged fifty-one, after an illness lasting three years, leaving his wife in comfortable circumstances with £800 a year. Hesketh resumed contact with Cowper early in October 1785, when she wrote to congratulate him on publication of the second volume of Poems, and in June 1786 she visited the poet at his home in Olney. Her cheerful, generous nature helped alleviate Cowper's depression and she provided the financial means to enable him to quit his gloomy dwelling for Weston Park, a vacant house on the edge of the village, in October. She took up residence at Weston Park herself during Cowper's final mental collapse in 1793, but was unable to prevail upon Mrs Mary Unwin, who cohabited with Cowper, that he should be placed at Gretford, near

Stamford, in the care of the celebrated Dr Francis Willis, the physician credited with curing the madness of George III. After Hesketh's offer to pay for Cowper's treatment was refused she nursed Cowper, to the detriment of her own health, for a period of two years. Following the poet's death in 1800 she supplied his friend William Hayley (1745–1820) with most of the materials for his biography, *The Life, and Posthumous Writings of William Cowper, Esq.*, published in 1803.

Between April 1780 and July 1796 Hesketh was living in New Norfolk Street, Grosvenor Square. She suffered ill health in her last years and divided her time between Bath, Clifton, and Weymouth. A period of convalescence at Weymouth between August and October 1804 coincided with a visit by the royal family, amid widespread fears of a French invasion. These events form the subject of several candid letters to a female friend, Mrs Ricketts, composed at the end of August, which reveal Hesketh's redoubtable personality in advancing years, and her strongly held opinions. She was an ardent tory whose idolatrous loyalty to her sovereign, whom she called 'the king of kings', was matched only by her unbridled revulsion for the prince of Wales, whom she censured as 'a Drunken brat' (BL, Add. MS 30007, fols. 55v–60v).

Fanny Burney, an acquaintance of Hesketh, described her as 'well-informed, well-bred, sensible … somewhat too precise and stiff, but otherwise agreeable' (*Diary and Letters of Madame D'Arblay*, 1.445). In a letter to Hayley dated 28 January 1802, Hesketh admitted that she knew herself to be troublesome and impertinent but having 'acquir'd a *decided* Character' she felt she had no alternative but to live up to it. Her conduct throughout her life and her surviving correspondence would seem to bear out her own estimate of her qualities as a friend. In a letter to Mrs Ricketts she confided: 'I have often thought that I posses[s]'d one sentiment in common with Deane Swift—who says somewhere that "he hates the world in general, but loves Tom-Dick-&Harry". This is very much my case' (BL, Add. MS 30007, fol. 57r). She died, childless in Clifton, on 15 January 1807, and was buried in Bristol Cathedral.

JAMES WILLIAM KELLY

Sources parish register, Hertingfordbury, St Mary's, Herts. ALS, D/P 50 1/1 · abstract of will, London Records Office, DDF 413.2 [Sir Thomas Hesketh] · Hesketh pedigree, BL, Add. MS 44026 · *GM*, 1st ser., 77 (1807), 94 · *Rufford Old Hall*, National Trust (1955) · W. A. Abram, *A history of Blackburn: town and parish* (1877), 532–58 · E. Baines and W. R. Whatton, *The history of the county palatine and duchy of Lancaster*, 4 vols. (1836), vol. 4, pp. 426–32 · D. Cecil, *The stricken deer, or, The life of Cowper* (1929) · *Diary and letters of Madame D'Arblay (1778–1840)*, ed. C. Barrett and A. Dobson, 1 (1904), 445 · W. Hayley, *The life and letters of William Cowper, Esq.*, 3 vols. (1803–6) · *Letters of Lady Hesketh to the Rev. John Johnson, LL.D. concerning their kinsman William Cowper the poet*, ed. C. B. Johnson (1901) · J. King, *William Cowper: a biography* (Durham, NC, 1986) · *VCH Huntingdonshire*, vol. 2 · J. Rogan, *Cathedral portraits* (1990) · R. Clutterbuck, ed., *The history and antiquities of the county of Hertford*, 3 vols. (1815–27) · tombstone and memorial, Bristol Cathedral

Archives BL, corresp. with William Cowper, Add. MS 39673, fols. 8–17 · BL, corresp. with W. Hayley, Add. MS 30803, A and B · BL, corresp. between the families of Ricketts and Jervis, Add. MS 30007, fols. 55–62 · Cowper Memorial Library, Olney, Buckinghamshire, corresp., incl. with William Cowper · Herts. ALS, corresp. with William Cowper

Likenesses F. Cotes, oils? (as a young woman), repro. in *Letters of Lady Hesketh*, ed. Johnson, frontispiece · H. Raeburn, stipple (after F. Cotes, *c.*1755), NPG · H. Robinson, engraving (as a young woman; after drawing by W. Harvey), Cowper and Newton Museum, Olney, Buckinghamshire

Wealth at death over £7000 in investments, over £600 in cash; plus sundry items and unaccounted property: will, PRO, PROB 11/1456, fols. 135v–142v

Hesketh, Henry (1636/7–1710?), Church of England clergyman, was born in Cheshire. He was admitted as a plebeian to Brasenose College, Oxford, where he matriculated on 26 May 1653, aged sixteen, and graduated BA on 13 October 1656. He was incorporated MA at Cambridge in 1664. He held the living of Ashton upon Mersey, Cheshire, between 1662 and 1663, and Long Ditton, Surrey, from 1662. From 1663 until his death he was rector of Charlwood, Surrey, having married Sarah Mulcaster, the daughter of his predecessor, the year before. In 1677 he bought the complete presentation rights to the church of Sts Peter and Paul in Nutfield, Surrey, which he later sold to William Hollingworth. On 11 November 1678 he was chosen vicar of St Helen, Bishopsgate. He also became chaplain to Charles II. Following the death of his first wife, Hesketh married again on 11 February 1687, at St Helen, Bishopsgate; his second wife was Mary Pillet of that parish.

Hesketh was a popular preacher and several of his sermons were printed, including one given before the lord mayor and aldermen of London on 9 September 1683 after the failure of the Rye House plot, and another given in the Chapel Royal on 26 July 1685, the day of thanksgiving for the defeat of the Monmouth rebellion. In the latter sermon he attacked the distinction both between the private and public person of the king as offering a justification for resistance, and, more controversially, between giving active and passive obedience. It was not loyalty, he argued, simply to disobey the laws but submit to their penalties. He also produced a number of other works, including a case of conscience, *The Charge of Scandal and Giving Offence by Conformity* (1683), which aimed at convincing nonconformists to return to the Church of England. He argued in this case that dissenters were already committing a greater sin, that of schism, by separating from the Anglican church than they could possibly incur by conforming and perhaps offering a scandalous example to others.

In spite of his earlier preaching efforts in support of James II, Hesketh took the oaths to William and Mary and enjoyed ecclesiastical promotion under the new regime. He never offered any explanation for this dramatic volte-face. He was appointed chaplain to King William and in 1690 he was nominated, but not consecrated, bishop of Killala. In January 1694 he resigned the vicarage of St Helen, Bishopsgate. He appears to have died in December 1710.

EDWARD VALLANCE

Sources Foster, *Alum. Oxon.* · *DNB* · Wood, *Ath. Oxon.*, new edn, 4.604 · A. R. Bax, 'The plundered ministers of Surrey', *Surrey Archaeological Collections*, 9 (1888), 233–316, 256 · *VCH Surrey*, 3.229 ·

J. Spurr, *The Restoration Church of England, 1646–1689* (1991), 246 · Venn, *Alum. Cant.* · [C. B. Heberden], ed., *Brasenose College register, 1509–1909*, 2 vols., OHS, 55 (1909) · J. L. Chester and J. Foster, eds., *London marriage licences, 1521–1869* (1887)

Hesketh, Richard (*c.*1475–1520), lawyer, was the second son of Robert Hesketh of Rufford, Lancashire, a family long settled in those parts. His younger brother Hugh Hesketh became bishop of Sodor and Man in 1513. Richard was admitted to Gray's Inn in the late fifteenth century and is mentioned as an attorney in a common pleas case of 1500. A private dictum attributed to 'Hasket' occurs in the year books for the same year but is probably attributable to 1502. Hesketh gave his first reading about 1508 on the *carta de foresta*, and a written version of this exposition of the forest law made the name of Hesketh familiar to all lawyers in the sixteenth and early seventeenth centuries. Although never printed, the reading had a wide circulation and still survives in at least twelve manuscript texts, some of them translated from French into English. The texts are anonymous, but the author is identifiable from an internal allusion when he puts a case concerning an indictment of someone called Hesketh, omitting the name Richard. John Manwood cited 'M. Hesket' several times in his *Forest Law* (1598), though on folio 21 he wrongly confused him with Bartholomew Hesketh, who was clerk of the peace at Lancaster.

By the time of his first reading, Richard Hesketh was king's attorney and serjeant in the county palatine of Lancaster, and deputy chief steward in the north parts for the duchy of Lancaster. In 1515 he gave his second reading in Gray's Inn, on the Statute of Merton, and the following year was appointed a baron of the exchequer at Lancaster. His wife was named Elizabeth; no other details are known of her. He died in 1520, when he was probably still in his forties. By his will, dated 11 August and proved on 13 November 1520, he desired to be buried in the family chapel at Rufford, where he had founded a free school.

J. H. BAKER

Sources R. Somerville, *History of the duchy of Lancaster, 1265–1603* (1953), 426, 483, 485 · J. H. Baker, *Readers and readings in the inns of court and chancery*, SeldS, suppl. ser., 13 (2000) · will, PRO, PROB 11/20, sig. 3 · *Les reports des cases* (1679), Michaelmas 15, Henry VII, fol. 14, plea 3 [year books] · Gray's Inn, MS 25, fol. 61 · J. Manwood, *Forest law* (1598) · LP Henry VIII, 1, no. 438(4/m.19) · *The reports of Sir John Spelman*, ed. J. H. Baker, 1, SeldS, 93 (1977), 171, 213 · PRO, CP 40/951

Hesketh, Richard (1553–1593), merchant and conspirator, was born on 24 or 25 July 1553, according to a horoscope drawn up by John Dee. He was the fourth son of Gabriel Hesketh (*d.* 1573), a landowner of Aughton New Hall, Lancashire, and his first wife, Jane, daughter of Sir Henry Halsall of Halsall. His eldest brother, Bartholomew, inherited his father's substantial estates. A Roman Catholic, Bartholomew was questioned by the privy council in 1581 for sheltering the Jesuit Edmund Campion. The second brother, Thomas Hesketh, was a duchy of Lancaster attorney and escheator at Lancaster, and rose rapidly within the duchy and at Westminster for the vigour with which he enforced the Elizabethan religious settlement in Lancashire. Both brothers were frequently listed among the guests of Henry Stanley, fourth earl of Derby, at nearby Lathom House, where the earl and his council played a prominent role in the government of the north-west of England.

Richard Hesketh was apprenticed to Hugh Fayreclough, and in 1578 became a freeman of the Clothworkers' Company in the city of London. He seems to have been a merchant involved in the export of cloth, and in 1581 he was mentioned by John Dee in his diary as his friend and Antwerp agent who diligently searched for books and carried Dee's correspondence to his many contacts in Antwerp. Richard Hesketh probably shared the views of Dee and this Antwerp circle, including an interest in alchemy, hermetism, and religious toleration as practised by the Family of Love.

About 1586 Richard Hesketh married Isabel Shaw and became involved in litigation on behalf of Isabel and her children from her two previous marriages to Thomas Richardson and Roger Ambrose over her considerable inherited wealth and Ambrose Hall, contested in the duchy chamber, Star Chamber, and before the privy council. In October 1589 Richard Hesketh was involved in the affray at Lea Hall, near Preston, in which Thomas Hoghton and Richard Baldwin were killed; for his part in this riot Hesketh was forced into exile for three years. He travelled through Germany to Prague, then centre of the Holy Roman empire, where a group of English exiles led by Edward Kelly then enjoyed the patronage of the emperor Rudolf II, who shared Kelly's delight in alchemy and made him an *eques auratus*. In May 1591, however, Kelly fell out of favour; he was imprisoned and his circle threatened. Hesketh and others were offered the protection of the English Jesuit Thomas Stephenson, then resident in the College of the Clementinum in Prague.

In 1592 Hesketh was on the payroll of the regiment of Sir William Stanley in Flanders, then fighting in the service of Spain. Listed among the *entretenidos* or staff officers of the regiment, he was involved in the intelligence side of the regiment's work and must be the agent described in the letter of Emanuel D'Andrada to Lord Burghley. Both Colonel Stanley and Cardinal Allen were then promoting the claims of Henry Stanley, fourth earl of Derby, to the English crown. Richard Hesketh was briefed by Colonel Stanley that they had the support of the pope and the king of Spain for this claim, and by Thomas Worthington, chaplain to his company, who had experience of working in a hostile England. In the summer of 1593 Hesketh returned to England via Prague and Hamburg to merge with returning merchants. In Canterbury he was joined by Richard Baylye, also an experienced *entretenido* in Stanley's regiment, who posed as Hesketh's servant in London and on his return to Lancashire.

About 25 September 1593 Hesketh arrived at Lathom House, supposedly to show his passports to the earl of Derby in his capacity of lord lieutenant; unfortunately this was the day of the earl's death. Hesketh found the opportunity to propose that Ferdinando Stanley, the new fifth earl, should lead a revolt to claim the English crown before the death of the queen, and begin negotiations by sending a representative to Flanders. Ferdinando arranged to meet ten days later at Brereton Hall in Cheshire, and Hesketh was to join his entourage *en route* for the court at Windsor. It soon became apparent, however, that Hesketh was not accompanying his lord as his courtier but as his prisoner. Hesketh was held at Ditton House near Windsor Castle and interrogated there by William Wade, clerk to the privy council. By 15 October a confession was extracted, seemingly without torture, Hesketh claiming that his sole motivation was to further the interests of his lord. As there was plague in London his trial for treason was speedily carried out by the attorney-general, Sir Thomas Egerton, on 24 November at St Albans. From the scaffold on 29 November 1593 Hesketh is said to have bitterly renounced those who had sent him on the mission, and to have denied that he was ever a Catholic.

Four months after the execution of Richard Hesketh the apparently healthy earl of Derby died at Lathom. Ferdinando himself believed he had been bewitched, while others believed he had been poisoned as a revenge for his part in Hesketh's execution. Ferdinando had claimed that Thomas Hesketh, with the powers of the duchy of Lancaster, had strenuously opposed his rule. Ferdinando's sudden death now brought about a disputed inheritance which did enormous damage to the earldom that Richard Hesketh had sought to promote. Although later earls of Derby regained many of the lost estates and titles, they never regained the dominance they once held in the region, which now came more directly under the control of central government.   DAVID BRINSON

Sources Bodl. Oxf., MS Ashmole 451, fol. 294 • *Calendar of the manuscripts of the most hon. the marquis of Salisbury*, 4, HMC, 9 (1892); 13 (1915) • C. Devlin, 'The earl and the alchemist', *The Month*, new ser., 9 (1953) • R. St George, *Visitation of the county palatine of Lancaster, made in the year 1613*, ed. F. R. Raines, Chetham Society, 82 (1871) • *APC*, 1581–4, 184, 257, 270 • N. M. Sutherland, 'Hesketh, Thomas', HoP, *Commons, 1558–1603*, 2.305–6 • W. Ffarington, *The Derby household books*, ed. F. R. Raines, Chetham Society, 31 (1853) • J. J. Bagley, *The earls of Derby 1485–1985* (1985) • B. Coward, *The Stanleys, lords Stanley and earls of Derby, 1385–1672: the origins, wealth and power of a landowning family*, Chetham Society, 3rd ser., 30 (1983) • *The Clothworkers' Company freedom list, 1550–1600*, Clothworkers' Hall • *The private diary of Dr John Dee*, ed. J. O. Halliwell, CS, 19 (1842), 12 [12 Aug 1581] • R. S. France, ed., *The parish registers of Kirkham, 1539–1600*, 1, Lancashire Parish Register Society, 83 (1944) • H. Brierley, ed., *The parish registers of Garstang church*, 1, Lancashire Parish Register Society, 63 (1925) • PRO, DL 1/155(R3); STAC 5/47/11 • *VCH Lancashire*, 7.131 • R. J. W. Evans, *Rudolf II and his world: a study in intellectual history, 1576–1612* (1973) • E. Fucikova, ed., *Rudolf II and Prague* (1997) • A. J. Loomie, *The Spanish Elizabethans* (1963), appx 3, p. 251 • Archivo Histórico de Simancas, Valladolid, MS E 606–213 • *The letters and despatches of Richard Verstegan, c. 1550–1640*, ed. A. G. Petti, Catholic RS, 52 (1959), 203–4

Hesketh, Roger (1643–1715), Roman Catholic priest, was born on 11 June 1643, a younger son of Gabriel Hesketh, gentleman, of Whitehill, Goosnargh, Lancashire, and Anne, daughter of Robert Simpson of Barker in Goosnargh. He received his education at the English College at Lisbon, where he arrived on 9 November 1660, and was ordained priest in 1665 after a dispensation because under age. He became procurator of the college on 18 July 1667

and confessor on 7 March 1672. He began to teach philosophy on 12 January 1676 and divinity on 14 September 1677. On 6 December 1678 he was appointed vice-president, and he held that office until 1686, when he was recalled to England by Bishop John Leyburn. He left Lisbon on 29 April in that year, being then a doctor of divinity. When Dr Watkinson desired to resign the presidency of the college at Lisbon, Hesketh was nominated his successor, but Watkinson was induced to retain the presidency. In 1694 Hesketh was elected a member of the old chapter and in 1710 he assisted at its general meeting. He served on the mission in Lincolnshire, probably at Hainton, the seat of the Heneage family, and died on 4 March 1715. According to Charles Dodd he wrote a treatise on transubstantiation, one of the numerous anonymous tracts published in the reign of James II. Dodd reports that it was written in answer to the prominent controversialist John Patrick, preacher at the Charterhouse, and that a reply to Hesketh's treatise was published by Edward Bernard. More recent authorities are hesitant in attributing the tract to Hesketh.

THOMPSON COOPER, *rev.* MICHAEL E. WILLIAMS

Sources M. Sharratt, ed., *Lisbon College register, 1628–1813*, Catholic RS, 72 (1991), 86 • Gillow, *Lit. biog. hist.*, 3.287–9 • G. Anstruther, *The seminary priests*, 3 (1976), 97 • *Catholic Magazine and Review* (1835), vi, 105 • C. Dodd [H. Tootell], *The church history of England, from the year 1500, to the year 1688*, 3 vols. (1737–42)

Hesketh, Thomas (*bap.* 1560, *d.* 1613), botanist and physician, was baptized on 15 May 1560 at Great Harwood, Lancashire, near to Martholme Hall. He was the second son of Sir Thomas Hesketh of Rufford (1526–1588) and Alice, daughter of Sir John Holcroft of Holcroft. Sir Thomas was high sheriff in 1562, and the family was prominent in the affairs of the county palatine, owning several large estates. After his father's death, Thomas inherited a part of these estates, including the honour of the castle of Clitheroe and 18 acres of land in the town where he practised as a physician and surgeon. Like many of the gentry of this part of Lancashire, he seems to have been a Roman Catholic, and he appears with his neighbours on the recusant rolls for 1594–5 and 1595–6. His religion would have debarred him from many of the public offices that his family had previously held. It appears that he never married. From 1593 he spent much time at Martholme Hall, on the family's Great Harwood estate, where his actively recusant mother also lived and kept a seminary priest, and where Thomas cultivated what must have been a remarkable garden on the banks of the River Calder.

About this date Thomas Hesketh began to correspond with John Gerard, and he became the source of a great deal of the botanical information used in Gerard's famous *Herball*. Hesketh also corresponded with Lord Burghley, for whom the Cheshire-born Gerard acted as gardener at his houses in the Strand and at Theobalds. Hesketh seems to have supplied many of the famous late Elizabethan London gardens and nurseries with seeds and plants from the herb gardens, moorlands, and mosses of the north of England. Many of these plants were the 'simples' or the herbs and medicines used in his Clitheroe medical practice.

One of the ways to identify the mass of botanical information supplied by Hesketh for Gerard's *Herball* lies in the locations of the plants listed, with the Hesketh estates and their surroundings given as the habitat for many of these specimens. One berry (*Herba Paris*), along with purple goat's beard (*Tragopogon purpureum*), red bird eyne, *Primula veris flore rubro*, and the bird cherry tree or wild black berry tree (*Prunus padus*), were all to be found at Martholme, and the double white rose could be found at Rufford, the Hesketh family's main seat. According to Gerard, Hesketh introduced the double wild crowfoot from the fields around the village of Hesketh into London gardens. Hesketh also made many plant-gathering expeditions to the remoter moorlands of Pendle, Craven, and Lunedale, where he famously recorded the cloudberry, known also as the whinberry or bilberry. On the Lancashire seashore Hesketh recorded such plants as the wild rose campion and English sea campion, but most commonly he recorded many plants in his own garden, such as pepperwort or Dittander.

As one of the earliest north-country botanists, Thomas Hesketh recorded a landscape with a great profusion of wild plants, especially flowers. Much of this landscape was obliterated by the agricultural and industrial revolutions. With the draining of the huge moss lands that were once the predominant feature, plants such as the Lancashire bugloss, the butterwort, Lancashire bog asphodel, and many others recorded by Hesketh as growing in profusion, have now become rarities. In Clapdale, near Settle in Yorkshire, Hesketh recorded the primula which became known as *Primula veris Hesketi*, or 'Mr Hesketh's Primrose', when it was included by Johnson in the 1636 edition of Gerard's *Herball*. It was also illustrated in Parkinson's *Theatrum botanicum* of 1640. Some confusion surrounds 'Mr Hesketh's Primrose', which later could not be found in Clapdale, but flourished in Gerard's and Johnson's and other fashionable London gardens. Perhaps a hybrid of the primrose and cowslip, it now seems to have disappeared.

Gerard often acknowledged Thomas Hesketh in his *Herball*. The cloudberry, for instance, had been discovered in a mountain habitat by 'a curious gentleman in the knowledge of plants, called Mr. Hesketh, often remembered' (Gerard, 1396). The same volume noted that:

> there is a strange primrose found in a wood in Yorkshire growing wild, by the travels and industry of a learned gentleman of Lancashire called Mr Thomas Hesketh, a dilligent searcher of simples who hath not only brought to light this amiable and pleasant Primrose but many others also never before remembered or found out. (Gerard, 780)

Hesketh died at Clitheroe Castle on 7 December 1613, according to the inquisition post mortem taken there on 10 January 1614. His heir was his brother Robert.

DAVID BRINSON

Sources A. Sparke, ed., *The parish register of Great Harwood, 1547–1812*, Lancashire Parish Register Society, 75 (1937) • W. A. Abram, 'Thomas Hesketh of Martholme and Clitheroe', *Palatine Note-Book*, 5 (1885), 7–14 • J. Gerard, *The herball, or, Generall historie of plantes*, rev. T. Johnson, another edn (1636), 241, 780, 1396 • H. Bowler, ed., *Recusant roll no. 3 (1594–1595) and recusant roll no. 4 (1595–1596)*, Catholic RS, 61 (1970), 38, 40, 161 • R. Dean, *Rufford Old Hall* (1991), 51 • R. Pulteney, *Historical and biographical sketches of the progress of botany in England*, 1 (1790), 124 • J. Parkinson, *Theatrum botanicum* (1640), 766, 1015

Wealth at death inquisition post mortem, quoted in Abram, 'Thomas Hesketh'

Heskyns, Thomas (*fl.* 1540–1565), Roman Catholic priest, was born at Heskin, in the parish of Eccleston, Lancashire. He is said to have studied for twelve years at Oxford before removing to Cambridge, where he commenced MA in 1540, being then a priest and a fellow of Clare College. He graduated BTh at Cambridge in 1548. When it was proposed in 1549 to suppress Clare College in order to unite it with Trinity Hall, Heskyns signed a paper consenting to the dissolution, even though this was contrary to his oath to the college. He was rector of Hildersham, Cambridgeshire, from 1551 to 1556, and was admitted canon of Salisbury and prebendary of Torleton in 1554. He proceeded DTh in 1557. On 18 October 1558 he was appointed chancellor of Sarum by Cardinal Pole, and on 16 November the same year he became vicar of Brixworth, Northamptonshire—a benefice in his own gift as chancellor.

After the accession of Queen Elizabeth, Heskyns was deprived of all his offices in August 1559 for refusing to swear to the royal supremacy, and took up residence in Flanders. The often repeated assertion that he became a Dominican is based on dubious evidence. He secretly returned briefly to England in 1565, when Philip Baker, provost of King's College, Cambridge, was charged with having entertained him under cover of darkness. His most important work, published at Antwerp in 1566, was *The Parliament of Chryste*, a response to the sermon delivered at Paul's Cross in November 1559, in which John Jewel challenged his Catholic opponents to produce evidence of the antiquity of the doctrine of transubstantiation and the real presence. The book, written in 'plain' style for the general reader, prompted a riposte by William Fulke, *Heskins 'Parleament' Repealed*, printed in Fulke's *D. Heskins … Overthrowne* (1579). The date of Heskyns's death is not known.

G. MARTIN MURPHY

Sources Venn, *Alum. Cant.*, 1/2.360 • A. C. Southern, *Elizabethan recusant prose, 1559–1582* (1950), 109–12 • P. Milward, *Religious controversies of the Elizabethan age* (1977), 16–17 • G. Anstruther, *A hundred homeless years: English Dominicans, 1558–1658* (1958), 12 • A. F. Allison and D. M. Rogers, eds., *The contemporary printed literature of the English Counter-Reformation between 1558 and 1640*, 2 (1994), 429 • Cooper, *Ath. Cantab.*, 3.292–4 • C. H. Cooper and J. W. Cooper, *Annals of Cambridge*, 2 (1843), 225; 5 (1908), 282–63 • Emden, *Oxf.*, vol. 4

Archives BL, Add. MS 5808, fol. 112; Add. MS 5871, fols. 107, 154 | BL, Lansdowne MS 980, fol. 261

Hesletine [Heseltine], **James** (*c*.1692–1763), organist and composer, was trained by Dr John Blow of the Chapel Royal. He left the choir there when his voice broke in 1707. In January 1711 he was appointed organist of Durham Cathedral, which post he held until his death. He is reported to have been additionally organist of St Katharine by the Tower, London, meeting his obligations there by use of a deputy. Much of his music has been destroyed:

in a fit of pique over some misunderstanding at Durham, he apparently tore all his own compositions from the cathedral choirbooks, but not before six of them had been published in Durham in *A Collection of Anthems* (1749). An anthem, 'Unto thee will I cry', dated 17 September 1707, is in the British Library (Add. MS 30860), and other manuscript pieces are in Lambeth Palace Library. On 24 February 1730 he married Frances Wheler, daughter of Sir George *Wheler, canon of Durham. He died in Durham a childless widower on 20 June 1763, and was buried in the galilee of Durham Cathedral. His property was claimed by a nephew and niece in America.

L. M. MIDDLETON, rev. K. D. REYNOLDS

Sources W. Shaw, 'Heseltine, James', *New Grove* · 'Heseltine, James', Grove, *Dict. mus.* (1927) · J. Hawkins, *A general history of the science and practice of music*, 5 vols. (1776) · *IGI* · private information (2004) [B. Crosby]
Likenesses Taylor, portrait, Examination Schools, Oxford · oils, faculty of music, Oxford

Heslop, Harold (1898–1983), coalminer and author, was born on 1 October 1898 in the village of Rough Lea, Hunwick, co. Durham, the second of the eight children of William Heslop, coalminer, and his wife, Isobel (or Isabella), *née* Whitfield. The Heslops had been miners for several generations; Heslop's father was deputy at Rough Lea colliery (managed by his grandfather) and later an overman at neighbouring Bitchburn colliery. Heslop won a scholarship to King James I Grammar School in Bishop Auckland. When he was fourteen, however, his father was appointed manager of an ironstone mine at Boulby on the north Yorkshire coast; the nearest grammar school, at Guisborough, was too far to walk, so he began working underground at Boulby.

Within a few months his mother died in labour. William Heslop remarried almost immediately and accepted a job as manager of a reopened seam at Wylam in Northumberland. The family moved again and Heslop started work there, but his stepmother had children of her own and encouraged her stepchildren to leave home. Heslop moved to South Shields and started work at Harton colliery, where he remained for the next eleven years, apart from a few months' training with the 110th Royal Hussars at the end of the First World War. He was secretary of his Independent Labour Party branch and active in his union lodge, which he represented on the council of the Durham Miners' Association.

In 1923 Heslop applied for a Durham Miners' Association scholarship to study at the Central Labour College in London, earning the highest marks out of a hundred candidates that year, and he studied at the college from 1924 to 1926. It seems likely that he joined the Communist Party while he was in London. He met Phyllis Hannah Varndell, a young ledger clerk at Selfridges from a family active in the Social Democratic Federation; her father, Samuel Varndell, was a sculptor. They married at Lambeth register office on 27 March 1926.

While at the college Heslop wrote a novel about the activities of the communist-led minority movement in the Durham coalfield. He could not find a publisher for it,

but Ivan Maysky, secretary to the Soviet legation in London, arranged for it to be published in 1926 as *Pod vlastu uglya* ('Under the sway of coal') in the Soviet Union, where it sold over half a million copies.

The Heslops returned to South Shields in October 1926, in time to see the Durham miners go back to work, defeated again after a stoppage lasting nearly seven months. Because he refused a clerical job at Harton colliery it was another five months before he was working. He taught classes in Marxism and economics for the National Council of Labour Colleges in South Shields and Newcastle, and contested the Shields ward (unsuccessfully) for the Labour Party in local elections of 1927. He was also active in the minority movement inside the Durham Miners' Association, and wrote two penny-pamphlets attacking the anti-trade union sentiments of the local Northern Press newspapers, *Who are your Masters?* (1927) and *Who are your Masters Now?* (1927).

At the end of 1927 Harton colliery made 900 men redundant, including Heslop. He and Phyllis moved to live with her mother in London, where he found occasional work as a labourer between long periods of unemployment. He published two novels, *The Gate of a Strange Field* (1929) about the general strike and *Journey Beyond* (1930) about unemployment in London. He returned north during the general election campaign in 1929 to support the Communist Party general secretary, Harry Pollitt, who stood against Ramsay MacDonald for the Seaham division of Durham. He also helped Bob Ellis to write and edit the minority movement paper *The Worker*.

In November 1930 Heslop and Ellis attended the second conference of the International Union of Proletarian and Revolutionary Writers in Kharkov in Ukraine; there he met senior Comintern literary intellectuals including Mikhail Sholokhov, Louis Aragon, and Alexander Fadayev. He returned a convinced admirer of Soviet communism. At the same time he was important to the Soviet literary apparatus. Four of his novels were published in the Soviet Union, including *Red Earth* (1931), a utopian novel about a successful revolution in Britain which was never published in the UK. The Soviets even considered filming *Pod vlastu uglya* with a script by the novelist Yevgeny Zamyatin, whom Heslop met in Leningrad in 1930.

Back in London, Ivan Maysky found Heslop work at Arcos, the Soviet trading mission in London; in 1935 he moved to the London office of Intourist. Four more books followed, to very considerable critical acclaim: *Goaf* (1934), an English version of *Plod vlastu uglya*; a detective novel, *The Crime of Peter Ropner* (1934); *Last Cage Down* (1935); and (as Lincoln J. White) *Abdication* (1937), a study written with Bob Ellis about the abdication crisis, which sold over 40,000 copies.

During the Second World War the Heslops and their two children, Maril and Michael, moved to Taunton in Somerset. There he finished his last and most successful novel, *The Earth Beneath* (1946). It was a rich and scholarly history of work and family life in the Durham coalfield in the nineteenth century, Methodism and socialism, poaching and preaching, and the bitter struggles to establish trade unionism. The novel sold 9000 copies and was translated into Italian. It was published in the USA, where it was entered for the MGM movie contest; the novelist Pearl Buck declared it 'one of the best novels I have read' (letter to Heslop, 1947, Heslop MSS).

In 1948 Heslop began working for the Ordnance Survey in Taunton. He was still active in the Labour Party: secretary of the Taunton constituency Labour Party, he twice stood for Taunton council and contested North Devon as Labour candidate in the general election of 1955. Although he continued to write for the rest of his life (including an autobiography) he never had anything published again. He died in Tone Valley Hospital, Taunton, on 10 November 1983.

Almost single-handed Heslop created the mining novel in Britain. Other miner-novelists were later able to build on his achievements. But it was Heslop who first proved that it was possible to write about life in a pit village without D. H. Lawrence's scorn or George Orwell's sentimentality.   ANDY CROFT

Sources Heslop MSS, priv. coll. · A. West, 'Harold Heslop and the gate of a strange field', *Crisis and criticism* (1937) · E. Elistratova, 'The work of Harold Heslop', *International Literature*, 1 (1932) · G. Klaus, 'Harold Heslop: miner novelist', *The literature of labour: two hundred years of working-class writing* (1985) · A. Croft, introduction, *Out of the old earth*, ed. A. Croft and G. Rigby (1994) · A. Croft, *Red letter days: British fiction in the 1930s* (1990) · b. cert. · m. cert.
Archives priv. coll. | Durham City Library, Local Studies Collection · Durham National Union of Mineworkers archive, Durham · Marx Memorial Library, London · People's History Museum, Manchester, Communist Party archive
Likenesses caricature, repro. in Croft and Rigby, eds., *Out of the old earth*

Heslop, Luke (1738–1825), Church of England clergyman, was born and baptized on St Luke's day (18 October) 1738, in Yorkshire. He was admitted as a sizar at Corpus Christi College, Cambridge, on 3 May 1760 and was appointed chapel clerk on 31 October following; he also acted as temporary librarian for an interval, a responsible position for an, admittedly older, undergraduate. Heslop was subsequently elected to the Archbishop Sterne scholarship on 19 October 1764 and also held a Spencer scholarship. He became a fellow of Corpus on 26 January 1769. He was senior wrangler in 1764, and graduated BA in 1764, MA in 1767, and BD in 1775. Heslop was an unsuccessful candidate for the professorship of chemistry in 1771, but served as moderator of the university for the tripos examinations of 1772 and 1773. He was ordained deacon (Norwich diocese) on 13 May 1764 and subsequently priest, serving as curate of Gislingham, Suffolk, in 1764.

On 31 December 1772 Heslop married Dorothy, daughter of the Revd Dr Thomas Reeve FRCP (1700–1780), and thereafter his career took shape outside Cambridge. On 28 September 1776 he was collated prebendary in St Paul's Cathedral, having been previously collated to the vicarage of St Peter-le-Poer (within the jurisdiction of the peculiar of the dean and chapter of St Paul's) on 21 June 1775. Heslop owed much to the patronage of John Green,

bishop of Lincoln (1761–79) and formerly master of Corpus (1750–63), who appointed Heslop his examining chaplain and, on 2 September 1778, collated him to the archdeaconry of Buckingham, to which a prebendal stall at Lincoln (Heydour-cum-Walton) was attached. Heslop was inducted, on 9 January 1777, to the benefice of Adstock, Buckinghamshire (also in the gift of the bishop of Lincoln), which he held until 1803 with the rectory of the adjacent village of Addington, to which he was presented by Dame Anne Tynte and inducted on 31 March 1792, thereupon resigning the benefice of St Peter-le-Poer. He also acted as a magistrate in Buckinghamshire.

In 1804 Heslop resigned his living of Addington on becoming rector of Fulmer, Buckinghamshire, on the presentation of the dean and chapter of Windsor. The same year he additionally accepted the valuable rectory of Bothal, Northumberland, which he was awarded through the influence of the third duke of Portland, his neighbour in Buckinghamshire and lord president of the council in Henry Addington's administration. Heslop resigned Bothal in 1809 on being appointed rector of the extra-episcopal parish of St Marylebone, Middlesex, also in Portland's gift. He at once removed to London to devote himself to his overgrown parish (the rectory and its patronage were sold by the fourth duke to the crown in 1817). Heslop saw the necessity of parochial reorganization. In 1820 he proposed to the commissioners for building new churches that his parish should be split into four parts with district chapels in each one, the whole under the jurisdiction of the bishop of London. In 1810 he was awarded his last piece of patronage when he was named rector of both St Stephen's and St Augustine's, Bristol. His constitution was vigorous and he hardly suffered from ill health until aged over eighty, though he held no visitation of the Buckingham archdeaconry after 1809. He died, at 27 Nottingham Place, Marylebone, Middlesex, on 23 June 1825, aged eighty-six, and was buried in the new church of St Marylebone, opened in 1817 and designed to fit into the grand Regent's Park scheme of Thomas Nash. Despite his numerous preferments he died a comparatively poor man. Dorothy Heslop died at Bury St Edmunds on 28 December 1827, aged seventy-nine, and was survived by one son and one daughter.

Heslop was the author of two sermons and a charge (1807). He took a lifelong interest in political economy and published *Observations on the Statute of 31 Geo. II, c. 29, Concerning the Assize of Bread* (1799); *A Comparative Statement of the Food Produced from Arable and Grass Land and the Returns from each, with Observations on Inclosures and the Effect of an Act for Enclosing Commons* (1801); and *Observations on the Duty of Property, Professions, & c. to Render its Assessment Simple, and to Improve it* (1805). He was awarded a Lambeth DD by Archbishop Manners-Sutton in 1810.   NIGEL ASTON

Sources *GM*, 1st ser., 96/1 (1826), 89–90, 386 · *Fasti Angl., 1541–1857*, [St Paul's, London], 38 · Venn, *Alum. Cant.*, 1/3.439; 2/3.345–6 · *Masters' History of the college of Corpus Christi and the Blessed Virgin Mary in the University of Cambridge*, ed. J. Lamb (1831), 409–10 · G. Lipscomb, *The history and antiquities of the county of Buckingham*, 4 vols. (1831–47), vol. 2, p. 516 · G. Mackenzie, *Marylebone: great city north of Oxford*

Street (1972) • A. Burns, *The diocesan revival in the Church of England, c.1800–1870* (1999), 42, 68
Archives BL, Add. MS 37069, fol. 294; Add. MS 38277, fol. 322; Add. MS 38283, fol. 382; Add. MS 38284, fol. 50; Add. MS 38299, fol. 115 • Bristol RO, presentation and nomination, St Augustine the Less • CCC Cam., admissions register, chapter book • GL, dean and chapter of St Paul's muniment book • St George's Chapel, Windsor

Heslop, Richard Henry [*alias* Xavier] **(1907–1973)**, army officer and resistance organizer, was born on 22 January 1907 at Cierp, Haute Garonne, France, the only son and younger child of William Heslop, horse trainer, and his wife, Vera Molesworth Muspratt. He was educated at Shrewsbury School, where he distinguished himself as a sportsman, being good at golf, tennis, boxing, and swimming, and keen on all team games. He played football for his school and later with the Corinthian Casuals. Between leaving school and 1939 he had two years in Siam, followed by two years first in Spain, then Portugal, before returning to England during the depression and finding a job as secretary to a golf club in Devon.

At the outbreak of war Heslop joined a unit of the Devonshire regiment but as he spoke several languages he was transferred to the field security police, later known as the field security corps. While stationed at Freetown, west Africa, he was selected for officer training and sent to Dunbar. There he was seen by an officer who instructed him to report to Room 055A, the War Office, which was in fact the interviewing room for the Special Operations Executive (SOE).

It was obvious to the recruiting officer that Heslop was the right type of man. Richard Heslop became Raymond Hamilton and started a six-month training. He passed out with the assessment: 'Has the great qualities of fearlessness, discipline, diplomacy, and leadership. Le chef idéal.' In July 1942 he was landed by felucca near Cannes and received by Peter Churchill. He made his way to Limoges, where he was arrested and interrogated, and, after passing through various prisons, he finished up in a camp near Lyons. In November 1942, as the Germans entered the unoccupied zone, the French commandant enabled British prisoners to escape. Heslop contacted Peter Churchill who informed London. He was told to join a group at Angers and await a Lysander pick-up. There he took charge of five dropping operations before being flown out on 23 June 1943.

This abortive mission proved that Heslop could withstand severe interrogation, solitary confinement, and physical hardship. He had also gained experience of working in France. He was chosen as the man to co-ordinate the scattered Resistance groups in the Ain, Isère, Savoie, and Haute Savoie as the representative of the allied high command and, in preparation for this mission, was sent on specialist courses in sabotage and air operations. He was flown out by Hudson on 21 September 1943 accompanied by 'Cantinier', a member of the Free French section under General de Gaulle, to survey the area and make a report. They flew back on 16 October and returned to the field on 18 October with Heslop placed in charge of a British/ French/American mission.

Now began a period of intense activity. The Maquis were in the high mountains, scattered over approximately 700 square miles, and very inaccessible. Morale was at a low ebb and the various groups lacked cohesion and leadership. Heslop formed separate Maquis supported by groups of 'armée secrète'—men living in the villages who supplied food and blankets, acted as couriers, and searched out dropping zones. In November the first supply drops took place and morale improved at the sight of arms and explosives. By January 1944 Heslop had 3500 armed and trained men under his orders. He toured the camps ceaselessly to inspect, question, praise, and organize actions against targets.

The chief operation brought the ball-bearing factory at Annecy to a standstill for two-and-a-half months, after which it operated at only about 10 per cent capacity. The railways were constantly under attack. Over 160 locomotives, three turntables, two signal boxes, and numerous railway lines, bridges, and tunnels were sabotaged. Raids took place on German stores for food and clothing and German convoys were harassed. In April 1944 continuous attacks on German troop movements began. Four troop trains, one oil-tanker train, and three trains conveying war *matériel* were derailed. German convoys and patrols were ambushed. The Germans counter-attacked and their losses while fighting in the mountains were estimated at 500 killed and 700 wounded. Guerrilla activities pinned down a large number of enemy troops. A British surgeon, flown out to deal with Maquis casualties, set up a hospital which was kept very busy in the summer of 1944, by which time the number of men under arms had grown to over 5000.

By the spring of 1944 small pockets of the countryside were under Maquis control. Supplies had come in forty-eight dropping operations, and at dawn on 25 June Flying Fortresses, in a 'daylight' operation, delivered 420 containers. There was a similar operation on 1 August when 468 containers came floating down. 'Xavier's Express' ran Dakotas and Hudsons in and out of an airstrip with impudent ease. A plane carrying heavy machine-guns and mortars, too weighty to be dropped by parachute, landed on a plateau and was hidden for twenty-four hours before taking off again under cover of darkness the following night.

After D-day the Germans were determined to secure a safe escape route for their units stationed in the south of France. The battle against the Maquis, which lasted seventeen days, dislodged some of the camps, but did not achieve its objective. The Americans then landed in the south and were assisted by the Maquis. By mid-September the whole of the area had been liberated by the allies. Heslop returned to England on 24 September 1944, his mission accomplished.

Heslop had the mesmeric quality of a quietly strong man who could be trusted and whose leadership none would wish to question. He was outposted from SOE in May 1945 in the rank of lieutenant-colonel. He was appointed to the DSO for 'a record of success beyond all praise'. He was also awarded the Croix de Guerre with bronze palm in July 1944 and was later made a chevalier of the Légion d'honneur. He received the American medal of freedom with bronze palm. In 1947 Heslop married Joan Violet Clack, daughter of a London Transport official; they had two daughters and two sons.

Heslop then joined the colonial service, spending two years as a district officer in Tanganyika, followed by two years in Malaya where his experience of underground warfare was most valuable in conducting jungle battles against Chinese infiltrators. Later he had a period in the British Cameroons and then went to settle in Kent. He wrote an account of his wartime missions—*Xavier* (1970). He died in Canterbury on 17 January 1973. His ashes were interred in a monument on the Plateau d'Echallon, in the foothills of the Alps in the Ain, erected in the memory of the allied airmen who had flown so many dangerous missions with supplies for the French Resistance.

V. M. ATKINS, rev.

Sources R. Heslop, *Xavier* (1970) · G. E. Parker, *The black scalpel* (1968) · G. R. Millar, *Horned pigeon* (1946) · personal knowledge (1986) · private information (1986) · *The Times* (18 Jan 1973) **Archives** SOUND IWM SA, oral history interview

Heslop, Thomas Pretious (1823–1885), physician, was born in Bermuda, the son of Thomas Heslop, a Scottish officer of the Royal Artillery, and his wife, formerly Miss Owen, a native of Dublin. He was apprenticed to his uncle, Dr Thomas Underhill, of Tipton, Staffordshire, and then continued his medical studies at Trinity College, Dublin, in 1844; he also attended courses at some of the minor Irish medical schools. In 1847 he went to the University of Edinburgh, where he took, among other courses, midwifery with J. Y. Simpson. Heslop left Edinburgh in 1848 having graduated MD, his thesis being 'On morbid conditions of the heart occurring during fever'.

Heslop then went to Birmingham, where he spent the rest of his life. He was appointed house physician to Birmingham General Hospital in 1848, and he held this office until 1852, when he left to enter private practice in Temple Row. A shortage of patients, however, induced him to lecture on physiology at Queen's College, Birmingham, from 1853 to 1858, and to act as physician to the Queen's Hospital from 1853 to 1860. He resigned from the former after objecting to William Sands Cox's administration of the college, and from the latter in consequence of conflicts in the management of the hospital. During his time at the hospital Heslop had nevertheless had the opportunity of experimenting with certain iron salts, the results of which were the subject of his first publication, a pamphlet entitled *Suggestions Relative to the Employment of the Tincture of Sesquichloride in Puerperal Peritonitis, Iritis, and Allied Disorders* (1858). The following year Heslop became a member of the Royal College of Physicians, of which he was made a fellow in 1872. In 1870 he was persuaded to serve a second term of office at Queen's Hospital, where he occupied the position of senior physician until 1882.

Throughout his life Heslop also undertook several significant acts of charity. His first was the establishment in 1861 of the Free Hospital for Children, of which he remained a medical officer. He had founded the hospital with C. E. Mathews after recognizing Birmingham's excessive infant mortality levels and becoming convinced that the diseases of children could not be adequately treated in general hospitals. A decade later, in 1871, the Women's Hospital also came into existence through his initiative. A third foundation, the Skin and Lock Hospital, was established in 1880 at Heslop's expense. He was a member of the William Dudley Trust and an active participant in the Birmingham health lectures, opening the series with a paper entitled *Ways and Means of Health* (1883). His other publications include, *On the Present Rate of Remuneration of the Medical Officers to Sick Assurance Societies* (1867), and *The Realities of Medical Attendance on the Sick Children of the Poor in Large Towns* (1869), both of which he read before branches of the British Medical Association.

Heslop's interest in education was made clear in the address *A Glance at the History and Prospects of Education* while president of the Harborne and Edgbaston Institute in 1882. Soon after arriving in Birmingham, Heslop had established the Midland Medical Society, and along with George Yates he was one of its honorary secretaries. At a later date he founded and managed the Birmingham Philosophical Society. His most important educational work, however, was done as a governor of King Edward's School, and as chairman of Mason College (of which he had been appointed a trustee in 1873). From the opening of the college until 1884 Heslop occupied the position of chairman of the educational committee; he became bailiff in 1884 and also president of the council, an office he retained until his death. In his final years he helped to establish the institution's library, providing it with 11,000 books, including several complete sets of scientific and literary periodicals.

Heslop died as a result of heart disease, on 17 June 1885, while travelling 'on the High Road coming to Braemar from Glenshee' (death cert.). His body was transported to Dublin, where it was buried alongside that of his mother, on 20 June. Heslop bequeathed £100 to both the Queen's Hospital and the Free Hospital for Children, Birmingham, and a more substantial sum to Mason College.

JONATHAN REINARZ

Sources *Birmingham Daily Post* (18–20 June 1885) · E. W. Vincent, *The University of Birmingham: its history and significance* (1947) · R. K. Dent, *Old and new Birmingham: a history of the town and its people*, 3 vols. (1879–80) · J. A. Langford, ed., *Modern Birmingham and its institutions: a chronicle of local events, from 1841–1871*, 2 vols. (1873–7) · *The Lancet* (27 June 1885) · Munk, *Roll* · J. T. J. Morrison, *William Sands Cox and the Birmingham medical school* (1926) · d. cert. · U. Edin. L., special collections division · *DNB* **Archives** U. Birm. · U. Edin. L., special collections division **Likenesses** bust, c.1886, U. Birm. L., Heslop Room **Wealth at death** £10,492 4s. 9d.: resworn probate, May 1886, CGPLA Eng. & Wales (1885)

Hess, Dame (Julia) Myra (1890–1965), pianist, was born in London on 25 February 1890, the daughter of Frederick Solomon Hess, a textile merchant, and his wife, Lizzie, daughter of John Jacobs, shopkeeper and moneylender of London. She was the youngest of four children of whom the eldest was her only sister. She grew up in a typical Jewish home in north London.

Dame (Julia) Myra Hess (1890–1965), by Alice Boughton, 1925

Myra Hess's general education, to her lasting regret, was of the superficial kind then deemed adequate for a young girl. But thanks to her obvious musical talent she was given piano and cello lessons from the age of five. The cello was abandoned when she began more serious study at the Guildhall School of Music, where her teachers were Orlando Morgan (piano) and Julian Pascal (theory). By far the most formative musical influence in her life, however, was that of Professor Tobias Matthay, with whom she studied piano for five years after winning the Ada Lewis scholarship at the Royal Academy of Music in 1903. She always maintained that he was her 'only teacher', and he regarded her as his 'prophetess'.

Hess's official début took place on 14 November 1907, when she gave an orchestral concert at the Queen's Hall in London, conducted by the young Thomas Beecham. She played concertos by Saint-Saëns and Beethoven (the G major, with which she was later so often associated), together with an obligatory group of solos. Newspaper reports of the concert, and of her first solo recital given at the Aeolian Hall two months later, were mainly enthusiastic. Yet engagements came in slowly and were rarely well paid, so for some years her livelihood depended to a large extent on teaching.

Hess's first great success came in the Netherlands in 1912, when she took the place of an indisposed colleague to play the Schumann concerto in A minor with the Concertgebouw Orchestra under Willem Mengelberg. This advanced her career in England, where engagements with music clubs and orchestras steadily increased. Visits

abroad became impracticable during the First World War, but on 17 January 1922 she made a highly successful American début with a recital at the Aeolian Hall, New York. Thereafter, up to 1939, she divided each year between a North American tour in the winter, concerts in England and the Netherlands in the spring and autumn, and a working holiday, often in the country, during two summer months.

In the early part of her career Hess played a considerable amount of contemporary music, although even then she tended to favour the classical and Romantic repertory. This, and her abiding lack of interest in virtuosity, might suggest a rather forbidding character. But her strength of character was tempered by graciousness and by an enchanting sense of humour, which bubbled out irresistibly not only in everyday life but also whenever she played a light-hearted Scarlatti sonata or Mozart finale. Moreover, in spite of agonies of nerves before every concert, as soon as she stepped on a platform (a shortish but comfortable-looking woman, invariably dressed in black) her deceptive air of serenity made audiences feel that they were her friends, and that the only thing which mattered was the music they were about to enjoy together.

Myra Hess delighted in taking part in chamber music. In the 1920s she regularly joined the London String Quartet for a week's music-making at the Bradford chamber music festival; in the 1930s she had a sonata partnership with the Hungarian violinist Jelly d'Aranyi; and she appeared at the Casals summer festivals in Perpignan and Prades in 1951 and 1952. More important, and wholly characteristic, was her decision on the outbreak of war in 1939 to cancel an American tour in order to remain in England and organize, and take part in, the remarkable series of daily chamber music concerts which she instituted at the National Gallery in London, with the assistance of Sir Kenneth Clark, the director. They ran uninterruptedly for six and a half years (apart from a short break at the end of the war), were attended by over three-quarters of a million people, and ceased (to her bitter disappointment) only when repairs to the war-damaged gallery became inevitable.

The end of the concerts allowed Myra Hess to resume her regular tours in the Netherlands and the United States where she was greeted as a beloved, long-absent friend, and as one who had served music and her country so selflessly. Audiences sensed, too, that her powers of interpretation had acquired a new simplicity, directness, and depth. Whereas formerly her quest for sheer beauty of sound had sometimes interfered with her sense of musical line, she had now achieved such complete technical control that she could concentrate entirely on the shape and meaning of a work, knowing that her fingers would reproduce exactly what her inner ear dictated. Furthermore, her instinctive understanding of whatever music awakened her love and interest had become unerring.

From the late 1950s Myra Hess became increasingly troubled by arthritis of the hands and severe circulatory problems. Her last concert appearance was on 31 October 1961 at the Royal Festival Hall, London, when she played the Mozart concerto in A major K488 under Sir Adrian Boult. Although she still managed to give occasional lessons to a few gifted pupils, she lacked the physical and mental strength to reorientate her life in a way which might have made retirement tolerable. It was a sad end to a great career. She died at her home, 23 Cavendish Close, St John's Wood, London, on 25 November 1965. She never married.

The gramophone recordings made between 1928 and 1959 give little idea of the quality of Hess's playing. She hated recording and, as Professor Arthur Mendel wrote, 'performance for her was *essentially* communication to an audience' (Lassimonne and Ferguson, 39). The recording which comes closest to capturing her beauty of tone, human warmth, and deep musical understanding is probably the Beethoven sonata in E major, op. 109, issued in 1954. Of her few publications, immense popularity was achieved by her piano transcription (1926) of the chorale-setting from Bach's cantata no. 147, familiarly known as 'Jesu, joy of man's desiring' (the score of her arrangement is now in the British Library, Add. MS 57486). Few artists have been so closely associated with one piece of music.

For her services to music Myra Hess was appointed CBE (1936), DBE (1941), and commander of the order of Orange-Nassau (1943). She received the gold medal of the Royal Philharmonic Society (1942) and honorary degrees from the universities of Manchester (1945), Durham, London, St Andrews (all 1946), Reading (1947), Cambridge (1949), and Leeds (1951). HOWARD FERGUSON, rev.

Sources D. Lassimonne and H. Ferguson, eds., *Myra Hess by her friends* (1966) · M. C. McKenna, *Myra Hess, a portrait* (1976) · personal knowledge (1981) · W. S. Mann, 'Hess, Dame Myra', *New Grove* · notebooks of concert engagements, 1907–62, BL, Add. MSS 57730–57731 · *The Times* (27 Nov 1965) · *CGPLA Eng. & Wales* (1966)
Archives BL, notebooks of concert engagements, Add. MSS 57730–57731 | State Historical Society of Wisconsin, Madison, letters to Edith Frank · Tate collection, corresp. with Lord Clark |FILM BFI NFTVA, documentary footage · BFI NFTVA, performance footage |SOUND BL NSA, 'Dame Myra Hess talking to James Fassett', NP4028R BD1 · BL NSA, documentary recordings · BL NSA, 'Interview', 7 June 1962, NP8122WR TR1 C2 · BL NSA, performance recordings · BL NSA, recorded talk · BL NSA, 'Servant of the music', 1977, P12294 TR1
Likenesses J. S. Sargent, charcoal drawing, 1920; on loan to Museum of Fine Arts, Boston · A. Boughton, photograph, 1925, NPG [*see illus.*] · H. Coster, photographs, 1930–39, NPG · E. Kapp, drawing, 1931, U. Birm. · W. Stoneman, photograph, 1957, NPG · J. Epstein, bronze bust, Royal Academy of Music, London · J. Epstein, plaster bust, North Carolina Museum of Art, Raleigh
Wealth at death £64,768: probate, 18 Feb 1966, *CGPLA Eng. & Wales*

Hessel [*née* Smith], **Phoebe** (1713–1821), female soldier and centenarian, was probably born in Stepney, London. Her father was a 'drummer in the king's service' (*Circulator*, 147), but further details of her parents and upbringing are unknown. A tombstone in St Nicholas's churchyard, Brighton, relates that Phoebe Hessel was born in Stepney in 1713 and

> served for many years as a private Soldier in the 5th Regiment of foot in different parts of Europe, and in the year 1745 fought under the command of the Duke of Cumberland

at the battle of Fontenoy, where she received a bayonet wound in her arm. (Incompletely cited in *N&Q*, 1852, 170)

According to one account of 1825, the young Phoebe Smith accompanied her father to Flanders when her mother died, learned to play the fife, and enlisted in the regiment (cited in Wheelwright, 42–3). Other accounts describe her enlisting in 1728 to accompany a private, Samuel Golding, with whom she had 'formed a strong attachment', serving with him in the West Indies and Gibraltar (Hone, 210). One biographical sketch has the couple marrying when Golding leaves the army; she later married William Hessel, although no further details are known. Various nineteenth-century accounts portray Hessel as a well-known 'character' living in Woburn Place, Brighton, and relate stories of her soldiering reportedly recorded from her own telling. One notice of 1817 describes an encounter between the old and impoverished Hessel and the visiting prince regent (*GM*, 550). Another report, on Brighton's celebration of the prince's coronation as George IV in July 1821, refers to the participation of the 107-year-old Hessel and gives a summary of her military career (Musgrave, 164–5). According to her tombstone she died on 12 December 1821. She was buried four days later at St Nicholas's Church, Brighthelmstone (Brighton).

Hessel probably did serve in the military, like many other women, and attained a great age. However, stories of her soldiering are contradictory and legendary, conforming more to conventions of the eighteenth-century preoccupation with cross-dressing women in popular songs and prose accounts than to the official records of military history. At the same time, legends about the masquerading Hessel supply an important, if partially fanciful, glimpse of a noteworthy individual from the lowest social ranks for whom by definition more substantial documentation was not created or preserved.

DIANNE DUGAW

Sources *Circulator of Useful Knowledge* (5 March 1825), 147 · D. Dugaw, *Warrior women and popular balladry* (1989) · J. Erredge, *The ancient and modern history of Brighton* (1867) · *GM*, 1st ser., 87/2 (1817), 550 · W. Hone, *The yearbook of daily recreation and information* (1841) · H. Martin, *The history of Brighton and environs* (1871) · C. Musgrave, *Life in Brighton* (1970) · *N&Q*, 6 (1852), 170 · *N&Q*, 4th ser., 12 (1873), 221–2 · *N&Q*, 5th ser., 1 (1874), 221–3 · J. Wheelwright, *Amazons and military maids* (1989) · tombstone, St Nicolas's churchyard, Brighton
Likenesses etching, after 1821, BM; repro. in Wheelwright, *Amazons and military maids* · E. Chatfield, engraving, repro. in Hone, *Yearbook*, 210 · soft-ground etching, BM

Hessey, James Augustus (1814–1892), headmaster and Church of England clergyman, was born in St Bride's, London, on 17 July 1814, the eldest son of James Augustus Hessey and his wife, Catherine. His father, a bookseller and printer in partnership with John Taylor at 93 Fleet Street, had published early work by Keats and owned the *London Magazine* (1821–5). Hessey was educated at Merchant Taylors' School from 1823 until 1832, when he matriculated at St John's College, Oxford. He graduated BA in 1836, taking a first class in the classical school, MA in 1840, BD in 1845, and DCL in 1846. A fellow of his college from 1832 to 1846, he was an examiner at Oxford (1842–4), and published an analysis of Aristotle's *Rhetoric* for undergraduate use (1845). In 1839 he held the vicarage of Hellidon, Northamptonshire, relinquishing the living on his appointment to a college lectureship.

On 23 July 1845 Hessey was appointed headmaster of Merchant Taylors' School. His period of office was one of 'unspectacular modernisation' (Draper, 163). His natural charm helped to persuade both the boys and the autocratic governing body, the Merchant Taylors' Company, to accept changes in existing customs and practices, bringing the school more into line with other public schools. He gave evidence to the Clarendon commission (28 June 1862). On 27 July 1847 he married Emma, second daughter of the stockbroker Philip *Cazenove of Clapham Common. He was preacher of Gray's Inn from 1850 to 1879, and was appointed by A. C. Tait, bishop of London, to the prebendal stall of Oxgate, in St Paul's Cathedral, which he held until 1875.

Hessey resigned the headmastership in December 1870, shortly after his appointment by the bishop of London, John Jackson (1811–1885), as one of his examining chaplains. An orthodox churchman, he was particularly active in opposing changes to the laws of marriage, publishing in 1850 *A Scripture Argument Against Permitting Marriage with a Wife's Sister* (3rd edn, 1855). He preached the Bampton lectures at Oxford, published as *Sunday, its Origin, History, and Present Obligation* (1860; 5th edn, 1889). In 1865 and again in 1867 he was elected Grinfield lecturer on the Septuagint at Oxford. His Boyle lectures for 1871–3 were entitled *Moral Difficulties Connected with the Bible* (1871–3). In June 1875 he was appointed archdeacon of Middlesex. A scholarly and urbane clergyman he was elected in 1879 a member of the club Nobody's Friends. In 1878 and 1879 he was select preacher in the University of Cambridge. He was also one of the three permanent chairmen of the Society for Promoting Christian Knowledge, and an active member of nearly all the church societies. In 1884 the University of the South, Tennessee, conferred upon him the degree of DD. Hessey died at his home, 41 Leinster Gardens, Hyde Park, London, on 24 December 1892.

THOMPSON COOPER, *rev.* M. C. CURTHOYS

Sources Boase, *Mod. Eng. biog.* • Foster, *Alum. Oxon.* • F. W. M. Draper, *Four centuries of Merchant Taylors' School, 1561–1961* (1962) • 'The club of Nobody's Friends': biographical list of the members since the foundation, 21 June 1800, to 30 September 1885*, new edn (privately printed, 1920) • *GM*, 2nd ser., 28 (1847), 423–4 • *CGPLA Eng. & Wales* (1893) • parish register (baptism), London, St Bride, 1 Sept 1814
Archives BL, corresp. with W. E. Gladstone, Add. MSS 44378–44472 • BL, letters to W. C. Hazlitt, Add. MSS 38899–38906 • LPL, corresp. with Frederick Temple
Likenesses Ape [C. Pellegrini], chromolithograph caricature, NPG; repro. in *VF* (17 Oct 1874)
Wealth at death £19,296 12s. 2d.: resworn probate, May 1893, *CGPLA Eng. & Wales*

Hester, John (d. 1592), distiller and translator, lived for several years in London but nothing is known of his parentage or place of birth. One Hester family, location unknown, bore arms (argent on a bend sable three swans of the field); another shield of arms (a chevron between three horses' heads erased, a crescent for difference) is appended to Hester's *Short Discours* (1580), but the significance of this is not apparent. A follower of Paracelsus, John Hester is noticed first through his book *The True and Perfect Order to Distill Oyles* (1575). George Baker, a London surgeon, commended four distillers, including Hester, who 'is a painful [painstaking] travailer in those matters' (Baker, preface). Hester carried on business under the sign of the Furnaces (1581) or the Stillatory (1591), at his house on Paul's Wharf, on the Thames waterfront, south of St Paul's Cathedral, in the parish of St Benet Paul's Wharf.

Hester advertised his preparations by distributing printed broadsheets of folio size: one example (it bears Gabriel Harvey's signature and the date 1588 in ink) lists his stock-in-trade, mostly under the items' Latin names. The heading states that 'These oils, waters, extractions, or essence[s,] salts and other compositions are … ready made to be sold by John Hester', who was willing to give instruction in his art, 'for a reasonable stipend'. 'Oils' included cinnamon, aniseed, gum ammoniac, and *Fraxini* (probably manna ash, *Fraxinus ornus*). 'Waters' included frankincense, honey, and (spirits of) hartshorn. 'Salts' included ginger, sage, and mugwort (*Artemisia vulgaris*). 'Extracts or essences' were such as rhubarb, Alexandrian senna (*Cassia acutifolia*), and agaric (from the fungus *Fomes officinalis*). 'The compositions of divers authors' included flowers of sulphur and oil of camphor. Many items could have appeared in an English *materia medica* of the 1880s but 'Certain compositions of Leonardi Phirovanti' belong to this earlier period: *La petra philosophale nostra* ('The philosophers' stone medicine'), and *Elixer vitae* ('Elixir of life'). Although virtually all these wares were medicinal or culinary, there were rare exceptions, such as 'Divers compositions of most strange [and] terrible fireworks, made by the Sp[age]rical art' (alchemy), and 'a certain kind of pitch for trimmin[g] ships'.

In the period 1575 to 1591 Hester was producing medical books. He edited *A Joyfull Jewell* ([1579]) by L. Fiorovantie, and translated from the Italian by Thomas Hill, but mostly he translated books from Latin or Italian into English, including one on the 'French pox' (syphilis), and another on gunshot and other wounds. He translated two of Paracelsus's works as *The Key of Philosophie* (1580) and *114 Experiments* (1583?). His *Short Discours … uppon Chirurgerie*, translated from the work by L. Fiorovantie, was dedicated to the earl of Oxford, and *Sclopotarie* (1590) to Essex.

Hester is unlikely to have been wealthy. His name is absent from lay subsidy assessments; in 1586 he was assessed for two-fifteenths at the modest sum of 8d., when the highest rate in St Benet Paul's Wharf was 3s. 4d. The dates of his death and burial have not been ascertained but administration of his estate, as late of St Benet Paul's Wharf parish, was granted to his widow, Elizabeth, on 29 August 1592. However, Hester's high reputation survived him. Gabriel Harvey, in his *Pierces Supererogation* (1593), named six men who had been foremost in their professions: 'a mathematical mechanician' (Humphrey Cole), a shipwright (Matthew Baker), an architect (John Shute), a 'navigator' (Robert Norman), a gunner (William Bourne), and John Hester, a chemist (Grosart, 2.289). In *The Pearle of Practise* (1595), James Fourestier acknowledged that his material had been 'Found out by I[ohn]. H[ester].', though 'Since his death it is garnished and brought into some method by a wellwisher of his' (title-page): it had even been 'wanting a name (which I have given unto it)' (ibid., dedication). As to the numerous compounds contained therein:

> The greater part of them were prepared by John Hester … a man that spent much, and endangered his body, about such works, whereof many excellent men have enjoyed the benefit. … All which as not long since I bought of the survivor. (ibid., epistle to the reader)

JOHN BENNELL

Sources J. Hester, *These oiles, waters*, broadsheet, 1585?, BL, C.60.o.6 • *STC, 1475–1640*, 3.82 • J. Du Chesne, *The sclopotarie*, trans. J. Hester (1590), dedication • administration, John Hester, 1592, GL, MS 9168/14, fol. 242v • L. Phioravanti [L. Fioravantie], *A short discours … uppon chirurgerie*, trans. J. Hester (1580), prefatory matter, colophon • St Benet Paul's Wharf, London, receipts, 1572–96, GL, MS 877/1, fol. 363 • J. Fourestier, *The pearle of practise* (1595), title-page, dedication, epistle to the reader • G. Baker, *The newe Iewell of Health* (1577), preface • G. Harvey, 'Pierces supererogation', *The works of Gabriel Harvey*, ed. A. B. Grosart, 2 (1884), esp. 289
Wealth at death £31 5s. 6d.: administration, 29 Aug 1592, GL, MS 9168/14, fol. 242v

Heston, Walter (*d.* in or before **1359**), Carmelite theologian and philosopher, joined the order in Stamford. He studied at Cambridge University and had achieved his doctorate there by 10 September 1337, when he was licensed to hear confessions for two years in Ely diocese. He continued to lecture at Cambridge, receiving further licences to hear confessions on 21 January 1340, 27 December 1341, and 29 November 1345. Later he returned to Stamford where he was given permission to hear confessions in the Northampton deanery on 26 March 1347 and 28 October 1347. He died in Stamford some time between 1347 and 1359. John Bale describes him as

> studious and learned in religious doctrine and by no means ignorant in the secular sciences: he was gifted with a keen intelligence and clear speech, and gave himself wholeheartedly to the study of philosophy. In this field, he made valuable discoveries and was responsible for some well-prepared texts, with original interpretations and many interesting, intricate observations. (BL, MS Harley 3838, fol. 70v)

Bale appears to have seen only one work by Heston, *quaestiones* on Aristotle's *De anima*, in three books which he records with incipit.

Heston has at various times been mistakenly identified with Walter Kellaw, Carmelite provincial in the 1350s, and with Walter Kesso, prior at Bruges in the late thirteenth century. Francis Peck, the historian of Stamford, claimed that Heston was prior in Stamford, and possibly lectured in the breakaway university there in 1344. But Heston was then in Cambridge, and there is no evidence that he was ever prior.

RICHARD COPSEY

Sources J. Bale, Bodl. Oxf., MS Bodley 73 (SC 27635), fols. iv, 208v • J. Bale, BL, MS Harley 3838, fols. 70v, 177 • J. Bale, *Illustrium Maioris Britannie scriptorum … summarium* (1548), 250 • Bale, *Cat.*, 2.47 • Emden, *Oxf.* [Walter Eston] • Emden, *Cam.* • Norbert a St Julian, *De scriptoribus Belgicis et viris illustribus ex ordine Carmelitarum*, Royal Library, Brussels, MS 16492, xxii–xxv • J. Pits, *Relationum historicarum de rebus Anglicis*, ed. [W. Bishop] (Paris, 1619), 468–9 • C. de S. E. de Villiers, *Bibliotheca Carmelitana*, 2 vols. (Orléans, 1752); facs. edn, ed. P. G. Wessels (Rome, 1927), vol. 1, p. 579 • F. Peck, *Academia tertia Anglicana, or, The antiquarian annals of Stanford* (1727)

Heth, Thomas (*fl.* **1563–1583**), writer on astrology and mathematician, was admitted to Merchant Taylors' School in 1563, where he became head scholar, under Richard Mulcaster. He entered Oxford in 1567 as a probationer fellow of All Souls and graduated BA in 1569 and MA in 1573. Heth was a friend of the mathematicians John Dee and Thomas Allen, and a follower of Sir George Carey (later Lord Hunsdon), knight marshal to the queen. He is best known for *A manifest and apparent confutation of an astrological discourse, lately published to the discomfort (without cause) of the weake and simple sort* (1583), which he dedicated to Carey. It was a vigorous response to Richard Harvey's recent *Astrological Discourse* on the impending conjunction of Saturn and Jupiter, which had predicted apocalyptic upheavals. Heth dismissed such fears. He brushed Harvey aside as ignorant in the science of astrology, and claimed that continental writers had similarly miscalculated the event (which he fixed at 3 a.m. on 29 April) and its likely effects. Insisting that such conjunctions occurred every twenty years, Heth anticipated no extraordinary consequences. His aim was not simply to calm public anxiety but to protect astrology from the derision he saw would surely follow when the apocalypse failed to arrive; by repudiating Harvey before the event, he hoped to ensure 'that no indifferent person will thinke the worse of so excellent a science' (sig. A3v). The tract is also striking for its protestant optimism. Observing that eclipses might have good effects, Heth noted that the solar eclipse of 1536 had heralded the birth of Edward VI—'a great joye to the whole Lande' (sig. D5v)—and the public provision of English bibles. Heth's work was erudite and powerfully argued, and all the more impressive, as Thomas Nashe observed, for having been written 'pell mell' (*Works of Thomas Nashe*, 3.83). Nothing further is known of him, and he probably died young.

BERNARD CAPP

Sources T. Heth, *A manifest and apparent confutation* (1583) • Wood, *Ath. Oxon.* • *DNB* • *The works of Thomas Nashe*, ed. R. B. McKerrow, 5 vols. (1904–10); repr. with corrections and notes by F. P. Wilson (1958), vol. 3 • C. Hill, *Intellectual origins of the English revolution* (1965) • H. B. Wilson, *The history of Merchant-Taylors' School*, 2 vols. (1812–14) • C. J. Robinson, ed., *A register of the scholars admitted into Merchant Taylors' School, from AD 1562 to 1874*, 2 vols. (1882–3)

Hetherington, (Hector) Alastair (**1919–1999**), journalist, was born on 31 October 1919 at The Spinney, Llanishen, Glamorgan, the younger son of Sir Hector James Wright *Hetherington (1888–1965), philosopher and university administrator, and his wife, (Mary Ethel) Alison (1886–1966), daughter of William Reid, headmaster of Shettleston Academy, Glasgow. At the time of his birth his father was professor of logic and philosophy at University College, Cardiff; he was later, from 1936 to 1961, principal of the University of Glasgow. Hetherington's elder brother, Thomas Francis Scott Hetherington (*b.* 1916), was a civil servant, mainly in the Scottish home department.

Education, war service, and early career Although both his parents were Scottish, Hetherington rarely lived in Scotland for any prolonged period of time until the last part of his working life. He was educated in England, at Gresham's School, Holt, and Corpus Christi College, Oxford. Nevertheless the young Hetherington instinctively felt himself a Scot, and always retained his Scottish accent and love of the country he thought of as home.

Hetherington's first experience of journalism, for three months in 1940 between a truncated philosophy, politics, and economics course at Oxford and military service, was as a trainee sub-editor on the *Glasgow Herald*; but the war, inevitably, came first. He had initially volunteered for the army in 1939 but, because of family-inherited short-sightedness, found himself assigned to the pay corps. Then a change of army policy enabled him to join the Royal Armoured Corps and eventually, after a series of transfers, the 2nd Northamptonshire yeomanry, which was the armoured reconnaissance regiment of the 11th armoured division. He was a captain and tank commander during the operation Goodwood advance on Vire, soon after the Normandy landings, when his tank was destroyed and one crew member killed. Hetherington himself was lightly wounded, but the carnage in the regiment was so intense that it had to be disbanded. He was swiftly promoted major and appointed as an intelligence officer to corps headquarters, where he continued until VE-day.

Following demobilization Hetherington could have returned to university, but instead accepted a posting to Hamburg with the task—based on those three months in Glasgow—of establishing a new, politically free newspaper, *Die Welt*, as its first managing editor. It was fine experience for him and settled any doubts about what he should do next. He had always wondered about a career in academic life. Now he would become a journalist. He rejoined the *Glasgow Herald* in 1946, sub-editing again, then carving out a reputation as a defence specialist and leader writer. In 1950 those two skills helped him move to the *Manchester Guardian*. He was quickly at home under the tutelage of A. P. Wadsworth, an editor who saw great potential in him. Wadsworth helped his rising star win a year in America on a Commonwealth Fund fellowship and then, not yet thirty-five, made him foreign editor of the paper and an assistant editor.

Editor of the (*Manchester*) *Guardian* When Wadsworth became terminally ill in 1956, there were at least three other more senior journalists ahead of Hetherington for the editor's chair and he did not expect the ultimate promotion. The choice, however, belonged to Laurence *Scott, the chairman of the *Manchester Guardian*—and Scott had already privately embraced the dream and necessity of saving the paper by uprooting it from Manchester and turning it into a fully national *Guardian*, with national advertising revenues. Scott needed a dynamic editor to help him bring that about. Hetherington, just thirty-six, was his man.

First, though, there was a crisis: Suez. Hetherington—heading the leader-writing team in Wadsworth's absence—was already convinced of the futility of Eden's policy. Now he was his own master and the line became starker still. 'This act of folly, without justification in any terms but brief expediency' was roundly denounced in October 1956—and, for a few days, the roof seemed to cave in on the fledgeling editorship as thousands of readers called to signal their disapproval and government supporters attacked its disloyalty. Hetherington, however, had Scott's backing. The Suez adventure foundered and a circulation figure which had seemed in free-fall recovered. This editor had been tested at the outset and not found wanting. He was, within weeks of taking over, an established national figure and a hero to his staff. Within a year of change, too, he had married, on 27 June 1957, (Helen) Miranda (*b.* 1934/5), librarian and later probation officer, the only daughter of Richard Alexander Cavaye Oliver, professor of education at the University of Manchester from 1938 to 1970. They had met when she was working in the cuttings library of *The Guardian*. They set up home in Didsbury and had two sons and two daughters.

Hetherington used the strength Suez had brought him well, starting campaigns against the poverty gap between north and south, campaigning for social and industrial reform, and (as CND's influence grew) arguing for the creation of a 'non-nuclear club' which Britain, abandoning the bomb, might join and thus curb proliferation. In *Guardian* terms, though, the next great test was internal: the dropping of 'Manchester' from the masthead in 1959 and then, two years later, the creation of a London headquarters with full printing capacity, which would enable the south of England to receive later, more up-to-date editions without the typographical literals which had littered the old *Manchester Guardian*. Laurence Scott, whose family had long since given away their ownership of the *Guardian* and its sister *Manchester Evening News* to a specially created Scott Trust in order to save the papers from a slow enfeeblement by death duties, knew that Manchester alone could never provide the resources his precious *Guardian* would need to develop the foreign and political reporting qualities it must have. London printing was inevitable: it was also a huge gamble, much akin to the founding of a new paper.

That, at least, is what Hetherington discovered in the fraught years after 1961. Any assumption that the existing reputation of *The Guardian* would suffice in a metropolitan climate was soon destroyed. He was terribly stretched, and had to commute by night train between London and Manchester two or three times a week. *The Guardian* grew in sales, but nowhere near enough in advertising take. It was still seen as an unfashionable 'provincial' interloper in London's agency world. Worse, the profits of the *Manchester Evening News* were no longer enough to rescue it through bad economic times. Scott despaired and began to look for a rescue merger: first, in 1965, with Lord Astor's *Times*; then, two years later, with *The Times* after its purchase by the Canadian newspaper magnate Roy Thomson, who cheerily advised *Guardian* managers that 'you boys should get back to Manchester quick' (private information). Hetherington was out of the office on a short trip to

Israel and out of the action because he had not yet been made a member of the governing trust. The years of struggle had eroded his rapport with Scott; and Scott saw no need to involve him. The trust was secretly convened and gave Scott *carte blanche* to drive through a merger which would certainly have meant the end of *The Guardian* and its liberal tradition. Hetherington came home and, with eloquence and fury, dispatched an eleven-page memorandum demanding that the trust reconvene. Richard Scott, its chairman, joined with the editor, and his cousin Laurence Scott was defeated. There was a price to pay in staff redundancies and in the hiring of a new management team which effectively sidelined Laurence Scott himself. But *The Guardian* was saved. Hetherington personally had saved it.

The task henceforth was to build a paper and a group around it which could compete and endure at national level. Though few, perhaps, realized it at the time, it also involved the invention of the British broadsheet daily in its late twentieth-century form. Peter Gibbings, the new managing director hired from *The Observer*, wanted *The Guardian* to be a 'complete' newspaper, which meant adding coverage—such as horse race cards—which had never found space in the old *Guardian*. Hetherington himself plumped for greatly expanded features: the first recognizable 'op-ed' page of news analysis in a British daily and a full page on women's interests each morning. There was the beginning, too, of specialist supplements on subjects such as education, where the paper had strong readership and might hope to attract advertising to match. The paper was also redesigned by its London advertising agency—rather to Hetherington's chagrin—but it soon found expanded readership in this new form. He was named journalist of the year in 1971.

The policy side of the paper was sometimes less happy. Hetherington had come to the editorship well briefed on foreign and defence affairs, but relatively unversed in politics or the devious world of Westminster. He was informally tutored by R. H. S. Crossman, with whom he lodged during the commuting years in the early 1960s, and made a close, natural friend in Jo Grimond, the Liberal leader, who became a member of the Scott Trust after his retirement from politics. *The Guardian*, at successive elections, tended to advocate a vote for Labour, with a good Liberal showing in relevant seats, or some variant on that theme, and there were no difficulties there. It was very much *The Guardian* 'as heretofore' (the only instructions traditionally given to a new editor when he takes over). But Hetherington was also courted zealously by Harold Wilson during his four terms in Downing Street, and that relationship produced strains.

One was membership of the EC, first opposed by *The Guardian* and then gingerly embraced as Wilson came to recognize the inevitable. Another, later in Hetherington's editorship, was Northern Ireland (where some staff naturally took a republican stance and others, including Hetherington's deputy, John Cole, a more unionist perspective, with Wilson counselling in between). But the most incendiary issue was Vietnam. At the beginning of the war the paper, perhaps echoing its Suez stance, argued against American intervention and found common cause with much of the British left. Downing Street, though, valued its links with President Lyndon Johnson, and Hetherington was persuaded to take a short fact-finding trip to Saigon himself. His military experience put him instinctively on the same wavelength as America's commanders in the field and when he returned to London the anti-war policy changed. Many torrid debates in the leader-writing room ensued and the writer responsible for the *Guardian*'s original policy, Frank Edmead, resigned. It was an unhappy period, but Hetherington backed his judgement with customary courage. He could not be right all the time, but he was always straightforward and honest, his occasionally stubborn integrity never in question.

The early 1970s brought more glory and more problems. On the one hand, buoyed by the keen interest in politics the Heath government brought in train and the months of confrontation with trade-union power (which led Hetherington to raise with senior staff the hitherto unimaginable prospect of the paper backing the Conservatives in the general election of February 1974), the sales of a revitalized *Guardian* moved to over 340,000, a national force in the truest sense. On the other hand, a deteriorating economic climate once again produced alarming loss figures which the group was not yet robust enough to bear with equanimity. Hetherington, moreover, had been at the helm for a decade and a half. He was openly tired after 'a rugged winter' and, in his middle fifties, faced the prospect only of retirement at sixty if he stayed. It did not seem appealing. He needed a fresh beginning, perhaps into academic life (the rumours of vice-chancellorships sought were rife in the newsroom). In the end, though, a friendship with the BBC chairman, Michael Swann, brought him to the attention of a corporation casting around for new Scottish leadership as devolution appeared to draw nearer, and he was made controller for BBC Scotland, announcing that transition almost simultaneously with news of the closure of *The Guardian*'s Manchester office as a centre of live typesetting. His *Guardian* career, in a sense, had come full circle. The London operation he had started in 1961 was now the heart of the paper; Manchester after 1975 was little more than a peripheral branch office.

Later career Hetherington's BBC years did not go well. His wife and family decided to remain in Blackheath, sadly confirming that, after many years of late nights and absences, the marriage had disintegrated. He found the bureaucracy of the corporation deeply frustrating after a lifetime of being able to issue his own orders, and was soon seen as an enemy by successive directors-general in Broadcasting House. Devolution did not, after all, happen. By 1979 he faced the choice of quitting or hanging on to some much smaller responsibility as head of Highland Radio in Inverness. He dug in for a while, fighting yet another battle to get the tiny station its own piano before quitting the BBC in 1980.

In 1982 Hetherington became research professor in media studies at the University of Stirling. Some happier years followed. In Inverness, preparing for the general election campaign, he had met Sheila Janet Cameron (*b.* 1926), a political consultant working in the Conservative cause. He and Sheila, the widow of Hamish Cameron and daughter of Douglas Heyde, head postmaster, married on 26 October 1979, Hetherington's first marriage having ended in divorce the previous year. They moved together to Bridge of Allan, near Stirling, when the university appointment became active, and remained there until his death. Hetherington had been a member of the Scott Trust since 1970 and, after the retirement of Richard Scott in 1984, was the latter's obvious successor as trust chairman, a task he performed zealously until his own retirement in 1989. He wrote industriously during this time: two memoirs about his *Guardian* and BBC years respectively, three academic studies of media issues, and two books about aspects of his beloved Scotland, including *A Walker's Guide to Arran* (1994), where he and his second wife had a cottage at the foot of Goat Fell. He also formed a small television production company and practised, with delight, some of the new techniques he had learned at the BBC. His four children and three stepchildren were regular visitors. The two families remained on good terms.

Hetherington had always been physically vigorous and mentally rigorous, punctiliously chronicling the day-to-day doings of his working life, but in the middle 1990s his memory began to fail. It was Alzheimer's, a particularly cruel disease for a man who had prided himself on his powers of memory. He was nursed devotedly through these final years by Sheila Hetherington. He died on 3 October 1999 at Bannockburn Hospital, Bannockburn, Stirling; the funeral service was held at Logie kirk, Bridge of Allan, on 8 October. He was survived by his wife, Sheila, his three stepchildren, and the four children of his first marriage. A few days before he died Stirling University initiated an annual Hetherington lecture as a tribute to a fine journalist and great Scot.

Assessment For all the industry of his last twenty-five years, it was Hetherington's *Guardian* years which defined his career; and his contribution to the whole of British journalism in the second half of the twentieth century cannot be underestimated. Before Hetherington, editors of broadsheet (or 'quality') newspapers tended to be remote figures to their day-to-day staff, usually more interested in political issues and the rhythms of London clubland than they were in the physical production of newspapers. C. P. Scott, the greatest *Manchester Guardian* editor, had for a time combined that job with being a Liberal MP. It was expected, on papers such as *The Times* and *Daily Telegraph*, that the editor, a gentleman, would attend to matters of high policy but go home or to the club soon after six, leaving the players to bring out the paper. Hetherington, sleeves perennially rolled up for office action, changed all that. The *Guardian* he created was perhaps too small and too embattled for such divisions of responsibility, but he nevertheless made himself a master of both policy and production. It was he, night after night, who would be there on the composing room 'stone', cutting the leader column of lead slugs to fit. He was responsible not for part of the paper; he was responsible for all of it. He took the early evening conferences which decided news priorities and was always on hand to see them interpreted as the pages were produced. In this, as in much else, he was an essentially modern editor, adapting the old routines he had inherited from the *Manchester Guardian* to address the harsher imperatives of producing what was effectively a new national newspaper in the teeth of bitter competition. He did not in any strict sense invent the modern *Guardian*, and through it the broadsheet of the early twenty-first century; but his interest in features as well as news, in the development of arts and women's coverage, together with a specialist focus on the needs of particular segments of a paper's readership—for instance, in education—became standard elements throughout British nationals.

Hetherington possessed other attributes any editor needs. He had the skill to hire great writing talent, from Michael Frayn and Arthur Hopcraft to Peter Jenkins and Clare Hollingworth. He was cool under fire, but also capable of the passionate commitment which helped saved *The Guardian* from merger with *The Times*. There was a simple, almost schoolboyish integrity to him which won the trust of staff and readers alike. He was a good advertisement for his profession, partly because he was always natural, unaffected, and serious, lacking any trace of cynicism. He lived simply, with an instinctive austerity, eating plain food, rarely touching alcohol, and watching every penny of expenses with dour Scottish attention. He never took the honours which Wilson offered him.

Such qualities, of course, always had potential downsides. Hetherington's seriousness could also occasionally equal a lack of humour which, for instance, made his frequent brushes with the National Union of Journalists seem more serious than they were. His austerity sometimes verged on parsimony. ('I see you're wearing your demob suit again, Alastair', said Brian Redhead, surveying a basic green tweed suit at a society wedding ceremony in 1975: and it was, indeed, the suit the army had given him thirty years before.) There was a certain naïvety to some of his personal dealings—particularly with politicians—which made him vulnerable to manipulation. Innocent of baseness himself, he did not see it in others. One reason for the finality of the move to London was his realization that Manchester, or any other regional centre, was too far from the salons of gossip and rumour which were an indispensable aid to forming a newspaper's judgement on topical issues. In Manchester, writing his editorials, Hetherington had taken John Profumo's denials of any liaison with Christine Keeler at face value. These, though, were minor flaws. On the big issues, from war and peace to devolution and industrial regeneration, Hetherington was often right and always trenchant. And on the biggest issue of all, the transformation of the *Manchester Guardian* into a *Guardian* which became the dominant, tolerant voice of the left in British society, he was not merely right, but the essential, triumphant visionary.

PETER PRESTON

Sources *The Guardian* (4 Oct 1999) · *The Guardian* (8 Oct 1999) · *The Guardian* (15 Oct 1999) · *The Times* (4 Oct 1999) · *Daily Telegraph* (4 Oct 1999) · *The Scotsman* (4 Oct 1999) · *The Independent* (5 Oct 1999) · D. Ayerst, *Guardian: biography of a newspaper* (1971) · G. Taylor, *Changing faces: a history of 'The Guardian', 1956–88* (1993) · A. Hetherington, *Guardian years* (1991) · A. Hetherington, *Inside BBC Scotland: a personal view* (1992) · *WWW* · personal knowledge (2004) · private information (2004) · b. cert. · m. certs. · d. cert.
Archives BLPES, interview notes · University of Stirling, corresp. and papers | JRL, Manchester Guardian archives, letters to the *Manchester Guardian* · U. Edin., letters to Michael Meredith Swann, Baron Swann · University of Bristol, corresp. and statements relating to the trial of *Lady Chatterley's Lover*
Likenesses photograph, repro. in *The Guardian* (4 Oct 1999) · photograph, repro. in *The Times* · photograph, repro. in *Daily Telegraph* · photograph, repro. in *The Scotsman* · photograph, repro. in *The Independent*

Sir Hector James Wright Hetherington (1888–1965), by Lafayette, 1928

Hetherington, Sir Hector James Wright (1888–1965), university administrator, was born at Cowdenbeath, Dunfermline, on 21 July 1888, the elder son of Thomas Hetherington who in 1889 moved to Tillicoultry where he ran a business as a pharmaceutical chemist and became a JP, and his wife, Helen Mundell, a farmer's daughter. Hetherington was educated at Dollar Academy and at the University of Glasgow (1905–10), where, having a career in the church in mind, he took honours degrees, first in classics and then in philosophy and in economics (1910). In 1911 he won a Ferguson scholarship in philosophy, open to graduates of all Scottish universities. His social conscience was sharply aroused by the poverty and squalor he saw in Glasgow, and this concern for his fellow men was strongly reinforced by the influence of his professor of moral philosophy, Sir Henry Jones, of whom he wrote a biography. In 1910 Jones appointed him as lecturer in his department, a post he occupied until 1914, apart from a short time in 1912 when he resided at Merton College, Oxford, to study with H. H. Joachim. During these years he also acted as secretary and then as warden of the Glasgow University Settlement. In 1914 he became a lecturer in philosophy at the University of Sheffield and on 28 March that year he married (Mary Ethel) Alison (1886–1966), of Alva, near Tillicoultry, daughter of William Reid, the rector of Alva Academy and later headmaster of Shettleston Academy, Glasgow. She herself was a Glasgow graduate and a friend of his student days; they had two sons. From 1915 to 1920 he was professor of logic and philosophy at University College, Cardiff.

The turning point in Hetherington's career was his appointment in 1920, at the early age of thirty-two, as principal and professor of philosophy at the small and struggling University College in Exeter, where his noteworthy achievement was to secure from the University Grants Committee academic recognition and financial support for the college. The delicate and persistent negotiations involved in this episode he later recalled in his racy and illuminating brochure, *The University College at Exeter*

(1963). His evident flair and liking for academic administration did not prevent him, however, from accepting the chair of moral philosophy in Glasgow in 1924, and he found great satisfaction in being (after A. D. Lindsay) a successor to his former chief. But in 1927 his interest in administration prevailed and he took up the post of vice-chancellor of the University of Liverpool where, by his conciliatory skill and his social adroitness, he smoothed away long-standing but petty antagonisms between the senate and the lay council of the university, and strengthened the links between the university and the city. In co-operation with Frederick Marquis, the treasurer of the university, he placed the finances on a much firmer footing and secured benefactions for an extension to the students' union and a handsome new building for the university library. He also played a prominent part in the amalgamation of the four voluntary hospitals in the city and brought them into closer relationship with the faculty of medicine.

Hetherington's success at Liverpool made him a clear choice in 1936 for the post of principal of the University of Glasgow, which is a regius appointment. He had now come home to his own university, over which he presided with conspicuous wisdom, tact, and firmness until his retirement in 1961. During his long tenure, which spanned the years of the Second World War and an era of unprecedented university expansion, he transformed the university by his vision of what its function should be in a modern setting. By 1961 it was a vastly different place from that to which he had come as principal twenty-five years earlier: it was three times the size in staff and student members, enriched with many new buildings, much wider in the range of its activities, and of greater standing in every respect. With a realistic sense of priorities he actively encouraged the modernization of many existing departments, and initiated or fostered the establishment of a goodly number of new ones in every faculty. In furtherance of his policies he devoted unremitting personal attention to the making of sound academic appointments at all levels, and during his reign he was involved in the selection of more than 100 new incumbents of professorial chairs. He concerned himself also with the siting and planning of the new buildings, an interest which led to his election as an honorary associate of the Royal Institute of British Architects. He was skilful too, as he had been in Liverpool, in attracting generous financial support from private and corporate benefactors. Yet the task he envisaged for himself was not a wholly easy one. Hetherington, astute academic politician though he was, had need of a resolute determination on many occasions when quasi-autonomous heads of departments were in his view obtuse or unreasonably obstructive. But it says much for his qualities that his senate soon came to take pride in his leadership and increasingly admired and respected him. He won its affection too by his human sympathies and his pastoral interest in his staff and their families. With the student body he had especially friendly relations; and the interest of graduates in their university was kept alive by his annual Christmas letter written to them in an engagingly chatty manner and having a worldwide circulation. The one problem he was not able to solve completely was the relationship between the university and the partially affiliated Royal Technical College, which later became the University of Strathclyde. On the other hand he was brilliantly successful in effecting a renaissance in the medical school which he had 'found in a perilous state' and bedevilled by rivalries between the university, two other independent medical schools, and two teaching hospitals.

In wider arenas of academic affairs outside Glasgow, Hetherington came to play a progressively influential role, not least when questions of academic freedom and the independence of universities were concerned. He was chairman of the Committee of Vice-Chancellors and Principals from 1943 to 1947 and again from 1949 to 1952, and his close personal friendship with four successive chairmen of the University Grants Committee was invaluable in ensuring a mutual understanding between the two bodies. He also had easy high-level contacts with a number of government departments which frequently proved useful to universities. University interests also benefited from his association with various trusts and foundations, including the managing trustees of the Nuffield foundation (vice-chairman, 1947–65), the research awards committee of the Leverhulme trust (chairman 1933–58), and the Carnegie UK trust (life trustee). At the same time these trusts themselves gained much from the fertility of his ideas for expanding the fields of their beneficence. He visited the universities of Canada and the USA on many occasions and formed particularly enduring links with those in the USA. Very appropriately he was chairman from 1951 to 1956 of the committee on awards to Commonwealth (Harkness) fellowships, tenable in the USA. In 1955 he visited India to advise the Indian government about universities, and in 1957 was chairman of a commission on the constitution of the University of Malta. He took a prominent part in organizing the quinquennial congresses of Commonwealth universities, every one of which he attended from 1921 to the first overseas gathering in 1958 in Montreal, where he gave the keynote address, 'Expanding education'; indeed it was very largely due to him that the congresses were revived after the war, in 1948. He interested himself also in the founding of new universities in developing countries and was chairman of the colonial universities grants committee from 1942 to 1948. As the years went by his exceptionally wide experience, his balanced judgement on all aspects of universities' aims and problems, and his personal popularity gave him a unique position so that he came to be recognized as the unchallenged doyen of vice-chancellors throughout the Commonwealth.

In the domain of more general public service Hetherington practised the good citizenship that he preached, and was frequently called upon for help. He was a member of the royal commission on unemployment insurance from 1930 to 1932; member and chairman of various trade boards from 1930 to 1940; chairman of an inquiry into wages in the cotton industry in 1935 and 1937; chairman of a royal commission on workmen's compensation, 1939; member of the National Arbitration Tribunal from 1940 to 1948; vice-chairman of the Council on Adult Education in HM Forces from 1942 to 1948; and member of the Industrial Disputes Tribunal from 1948 to 1959. He was also chairman of the committee on hospital policy in Scotland in 1942; president of the National Institute of Social and Economic Research from 1942 to 1945; president of the Scottish Council of Social Service from 1945 to 1949; and president of section L (education) of the British Association at its Edinburgh meeting in 1951. He was chairman too of the Royal Fine Art Commission for Scotland (1957–64) and of the Schools' Broadcasting Council for Scotland. In all he held office as chairman, president, or deputy of more than fifty educational and charitable bodies, and was a member of the committees of many more.

Hetherington's career was such that the philosophical studies in which it was expected he would become eminent came to claim less and less of his attention, and in any case his major interest had always been in the practical applications of moral philosophy and its relation to the general welfare, and relatively less in logic and metaphysics. In 1918 he published *Social Purpose* (with J. H. Muirhead); in 1920 *International Labour Legislation*, based on his participation in the League of Nations Labour Conference (1919) in Washington; and in 1924 *The Life and Letters of Sir Henry Jones*. Apart from these three books many of his more important addresses on education and on economic and social topics were published in the transactions of the societies concerned or as pamphlets. In writing, as in public speaking, he had a distinctive and felicitous style which combined precision with elegance and a marked warmth of feeling. His many memoranda, reports, and addresses on a wide variety of occasions were models of their kind.

Tall and well-built and always physically in good trim, Hetherington had a commanding presence, a frank and open countenance, a generally relaxed demeanour, a ready smile, a genial sense of humour, and an easy friendliness which made him welcome everywhere. Much that he did seemed to be effortless or almost casual but it was invariably based on mastery of the facts and careful preparation. When advocating any policy or cause which he supported he relied on quiet reason and eschewed emotional appeals. Although often enough he did battle with hard-hitting opponents, he had few, if any, personal enemies. It was his knowledge, shrewdness, fair-mindedness, and wide sympathies, which gave him the standing he was accorded. He was from early years frugal in his personal life, and his chief relaxation and only addiction was golf, a game in which he was more than usually proficient. His wife was as popular everywhere as he was, and afforded him great support and happiness throughout his life. Their younger son, (Hector) Alastair *Hetherington (1919–1999), was editor of *The Guardian* from 1956 to 1975.

Created a knight in 1936, Hetherington became KBE in 1948 and GBE in 1962. He was an honorary graduate of eighteen universities in Britain, Canada, and the USA, and an honorary fellow of a number of professional bodies. In 1958 he received the Howland memorial prize from Yale 'in recognition of marked distinction in the art of government'; and in 1961 he was made an honorary freeman of Glasgow. The portrait by William Hutchison (1938) is strikingly lifelike; that commissioned by his Glasgow colleagues in 1961 and painted by David Donaldson controversially depicts him as a man of stern and masterful character. Hetherington died suddenly in the Westminster Hospital on 15 January 1965, while on a visit to London.

JAMES MOUNTFORD, rev.

Sources C. Illingworth, *University statesman: Sir Hector Hetherington* (1971) · *The Times* (16 Jan 1965) · private information (1981) · personal knowledge (1981)

Archives JRL, letters to *Manchester Guardian* · U. Glas., corresp. and university papers · U. Lpool, corresp. and papers relating to University of Liverpool | BLPES, corresp. with Violet Markham · ICL, corresp. with Lord Jackson · NL Wales, corresp. with Thomas Jones

Likenesses Lafayette, photograph, 1928, NPG [*see illus.*] · W. Stoneman, photograph, 1931, NPG · W. O. Hutchison, oils, 1938, U. Lpool · W. Stoneman, photograph, 1948, NPG · S. Cursiter, oils, 1950–59, Royal College of Physicians and Surgeons, Glasgow · W. Stoneman, photograph, 1958, NPG · D. Donaldson, oils, 1961, U. Glas.

Wealth at death £44,200 5s. 9d.: confirmation, 23 March 1965, *CCI*

Hetherington, Henry (1792–1849), publisher and journalist, was born in Compton Street, Soho, London, the eldest of the three children of John Hetherington, a tailor. He may have been the Henry John William Hetherington baptized at St Anne's, Soho, on 1 September 1792, in which case his mother was probably Elizabeth Rundle, who had married a John Hetherington at the same church on 18 June 1789. Little is known about his early life. At the age of thirteen Hetherington was apprenticed to Luke Hansard, the parliamentary printer. In 1811 he married, and subsequently he and his wife had nine children. For a time he worked as a printer in Belgium. About 1815 he returned to London and established a printing business on Kingsgate Street, near Holborn. He remained there until the beginning of 1834, when he moved his business to the Strand.

Henry Hetherington (1792–1849), by unknown engraver

During the final fifteen years of his life he worked and resided at two other locations in central London.

Hetherington's career as a journalist took form in the 1820s. He became active in the London Mechanics' Institution and in organizations which supported the ideas of Robert Owen, including the Co-operative and Economical Society, formed in 1821, and the British Association for Promoting Co-operative Knowledge, which was founded in 1829. Hetherington also took up the cause of universal suffrage, seeking to infuse it with a vision of economic and social justice. As his views became increasingly radical, he immersed himself in the political culture of working-class London. He became active in three organizations, all of which were engaged in the struggle for political democracy: the Radical Reform Association, led by Henry Hunt; the Metropolitan Political Union, whose council Hetherington served on; and the National Union of the Working Classes, which opposed the whig Reform Bill of 1832 because it did not provide for universal suffrage.

During the 1820s Hetherington was little known. He published several radical tracts and pamphlets, but none won him particular attention. Then, in October 1830, he took up the cause with which his name will always be identified: that of a penny press. The issue involved the repeal of the taxes on newspapers and other printed materials, which had first been imposed in 1712. These duties had become more onerous since 1819, when the 4d. newspaper duty was applied to all journals issued on a regular basis. For Hetherington the 'taxes on knowledge' became the defining issue of his career because he thought they unfairly punished the poor and obstructed the advancement of political and economic knowledge. He began to publish weekly unstamped journals, which were illegal. The most famous and important of these was the *Poor Man's Guardian*, first issued in July 1831, in 'defiance of the "law" to try the power of "right" against "might"'. It remained in circulation until December 1835.

Beginning in 1831 Hetherington engaged in full-scale political warfare against the whig government. He hired shop-owners and street vendors to sell the *Poor Man's Guardian* and his other illegal papers, which included the

Republican (1831–2), the *'Destructive' and Poor Man's Conservative* (1833–4), and *Hetherington's Twopenny Dispatch, and People's Police Register* (1834–6). He employed various ruses in the distribution of these papers, including physical disguises and the making up of dummy runs. He also gave numerous speeches to groups of radicals in London, the English provinces, and Scotland, taunting the authorities for maintaining a system of inequality between rich and poor. Repeatedly he attacked 'old corruption' and appealed to a vaguely defined working-class consciousness based on an alleged dichotomy between industrious producers and idle consumers.

Hetherington was prosecuted several times for seditious libel and selling unstamped newspapers. He was fined, had his presses seized, and on three occasions between 1831 and 1836 was imprisoned. He spent a total of about sixteen months in the king's bench prison and in New prison, Clerkenwell. At his trials Hetherington defended himself vigorously, and printed cheap verbatim accounts of his legal battles. Other radical journalists followed his lead, and between 1830 and 1836, when the 4*d.* stamp duty was reduced to a penny, more than 500 unstamped periodical titles were published. Hundreds of street vendors were also incarcerated for distributing illegal papers. Hetherington formed close friendships with other working-class radical reformers during this 'war of the unstamped', notably James Watson and William Lovett. While he did little writing himself, Hetherington hired talented editors for his journals, including Bronterre O'Brien (*Poor Man's Guardian*) and William J. Linton (*The Odd Fellow*).

After 1836 Hetherington remained a powerful advocate of universal suffrage and economic co-operation. He also began to champion more mainstream reform issues, such as the repeal of the corn laws and temperance legislation. Along with Watson, Lovett, and other working-class reformers, he became a leader of the moderate 'knowledge' wing of the Chartist movement which emerged in 1837. He was a founder of the London Working Men's Association, which promoted self-reformation and the 'march of intellect' as an alternative to political revolution. Hetherington toured cities and towns throughout the country as a 'missionary' on behalf of the association, helping to build up local Chartist organizations. In 1839 he was elected to represent London and Stockport at the first Chartist convention. There he attacked Feargus O'Connor's National Charter Association and advocated the fusion of the 'moral' and 'physical' wings of Chartism. He was active at the Complete Suffrage conferences of 1842 in support of this objective. Hetherington also worked closely with Lovett, W. J. Linton, Thomas Cooper, and other reformers to promote working-class literary and temperance activities at the John Street Institute in London and elsewhere. In the 1840s he took up international causes, for instance supporting the French revolutionaries of 1848 and the efforts of Giuseppe Mazzini, the Italian nationalist, to bring about the unification of Italy. He was active in the People's International League,

an organization which opposed the radical ideas of Karl Marx.

Hetherington's final years were dominated by yet another cause. This was religious freethinking, which he had advocated since the 1820s. At that time he had been involved with an organization of freethinking Christians who espoused a radical unitarianism. After being expelled by the group in 1828 he took up a modified rationalist creed based upon the ideas of primitive Christianity. In 1840 Hetherington was prosecuted for blasphemy, after publishing a cheap edition of C. J. Haslam's *Letters to the Clergy of All Denominations*. This was a gratuitous act by the whig government; Hetherington did not specifically endorse the ideas in the book, which was largely an attack on the Old Testament. At his well-publicized trial, Hetherington energetically championed the cause of religious freedom. He was convicted and sent to prison for four months. Two years later, in 1843, he reprinted a pamphlet, *Cheap Salvation, or, An Antidote to Priestcraft*, which he had first written in 1832. In it he made the case for a 'Church of Christ', devoid of superstition and priestcraft. In his *Last Will and Testament*, published just before his death in 1849 by George Jacob Holyoake and a group of secularists, he reaffirmed his belief in rational religion and requested that he be buried in unconsecrated ground.

Hetherington possessed some of the defects common to the self-educated artisan: a lack of humour, a touch of self-righteousness, and a tendency to equate personal morality with political conviction. Francis Place, a quondam ally, criticized him for being 'one of those men whose peculiarities fit them for martyrs' (BL, Place MSS). Other reformers with whom he quarrelled, such as Richard Carlile, were even harsher in their criticism. Yet, in retrospect, it is perhaps best to see Hetherington as a man of genuine conviction and courage who sacrificed a measure of personal comfort for his beliefs. He was not an original thinker, but as a symbol of conscience in the face of numerous political obstacles he loomed large in the history of working-class radicalism.

During his final years Hetherington fell heavily into debt. Eight of his nine children predeceased him and only his wife and one son, David, survived him. In 1849 Hetherington became a victim of cholera. Acting out of personal conviction he eschewed all medical treatment, which almost certainly hastened the spread of the disease. He died at 57 Judd Street, Hanover Square, London, on 24 August 1849, and was buried in Kensal Green cemetery two days later. About two thousand friends and admirers attended the service, which consisted of speeches by radicals and freethinkers. No clergyman was present at the burial. Fittingly, the hearse which carried Hetherington's body to the cemetery was emblazoned with his own words: 'We ought to endeavour to leave the world better than we found it.'   JOEL H. WIENER

Sources J. H. Wiener, *The war of the unstamped* (1969) · P. Hollis, *The Pauper Press* (1970) · E. P. Thompson, *The making of the English working class* (1963) · G. J. Holyoake, *The life and character of Henry Hetherington* (1849) · A. G. Barker, *Henry Hetherington, 1792–1849* [1938] · W. J.

Linton, *James Watson* (1880) • R. G. Gammage, *History of the Chartist movement, 1837–1854*, new edn (1894) • *IGI*
Archives PRO, Home Office MSS, 64/11 and 64/12 | BL, Francis Place collection
Likenesses engraved miniature, repro. in Gammage, *History of the chartist movement* [*see illus.*]
Wealth at death personal estate £1200; was exceeded by his debts: *BDMBR*

Hetherington, William Maxwell (1803–1865), poet and minister of the Free Church of Scotland, was born on 4 June 1803 in the parish of Troqueer, near Dumfries, the son of Robert Hetherington, gardener, and his wife, Anne Maxwell. Having received a parish-school education, he was trained as a gardener, but entered the University of Edinburgh in 1822, and became a distinguished student. Before completing his studies for the church he published *Twelve Dramatic Sketches Founded on the Pastoral Poetry of Scotland* (1829). These eulogies of Scottish peasantry were all inspired by or imitated traditional popular lyrics.

Hetherington became minister of Torphichen, Linlithgow, in 1836; and on 29 May 1836 he married Jessie, daughter of the Revd Dr Meek, of Hamilton. His *History of the Church of Scotland from the Introduction of Christianity to the Period of the Disruption, May 18, 1843*, was published in 1843. It was preceded by an essay 'On the principles and constitution of the Church of Scotland', and was reprinted several times. Its avowed purpose was to defend the newly created Free Church, of which he was one of the founder members. In 1844 he was appointed to a charge in St Andrews; there he established the *Free Church Magazine* which he edited for four years. He also contributed to religious periodicals, especially the *British and Foreign Evangelical Review*, and published sermons, poems, and some small religious and historical works. He became minister of Free St Paul's, Edinburgh, in 1848; and was appointed professor of theology at New College, Glasgow, in 1857. He was made LLD by the College of New Brunswick, Canada, and DD by Jefferson College, Pennsylvania. He died at 13 Oakfield Terrace, Hillhead, Glasgow, on 23 May 1865, survived by his wife, and was buried in the Grange cemetery, Edinburgh.

T. W. BAYNE, *rev.* S. R. J. BAUDRY

Sources A. Trotter, *East Galloway sketches, or, Biographical, historical and descriptive notices of Kirkcudbrightshire, chiefly in the nineteenth century* (1901) • C. Rogers, *The modern Scottish minstrel, or, The songs of Scotland of the past half-century*, 6 vols. (1855–7) • *IGI* • J. G. Wilson, ed., *The poets and poetry of Scotland*, 2 vols. (1876–7) • *Fasti Scot.* • m. reg. Scot. • d. cert.
Likenesses photograph, repro. in Trotter, *East Galloway sketches*
Wealth at death £1709 1*s.* 6*d.*: confirmation, 18 Sept 1865, NA Scot., SC 36/48/54, 252–4

Hetley [Hedley], **Sir Thomas** (*c.*1570–1637), serjeant-at-law, was the eldest son of William Hetley of Brampton, Huntingdonshire, a tanner, and his wife, Janet, daughter of Percival Worme of Peterborough. After spending some time at Staple Inn, Hetley was admitted to Gray's Inn in 1587 and called to the bar in 1595. Though he was made an ancient of the inn in 1603, his early practice seems to have been centred on his locality; he was appointed to several commissions of sewers and remained on the commission

of the peace for Huntingdonshire from 1601 until the end of his life. In 1604 he was returned to parliament for the town of Huntingdon, where he held the position of recorder.

An active MP, Hetley served on a number of committees dealing with technical, but important, legal matters, including that investigating complaints against the Marshalsea court, that for regulating attorneys, and that concerned with the restitution of property in the wake of forcible entries. In debate, he strongly opposed the 'perfect' union of England and Scotland that was being promoted by James VI and I, claiming that it would lead to an alteration of the common laws, customs, and privileges of England. He also rejected the idea that Scots born after 1603 should be naturalized and allowed to hold land under English law. One danger was that the Scots might eventually overrun England. Another in his view was the fact that Scots freeholders would have the English franchise and hence become in effect 'lawmakers in Parliament' (*JHC*, 1.1017), who might grant subsidies and pass laws while still retaining the capacity to return to Scotland, and thereby escape the jurisdiction of those same laws.

In the session of 1610 Hetley spoke out against John Cowell's recently published law dictionary, *The Interpreter*, and he attacked the ecclesiastical canons of 1604 because they had never been approved by the House of Commons. He also made one of the most notable contributions to the lengthy and learned debates in this session on the (unparliamentary) impositions that had recently been levied by the crown and declared legal by the judges in their decision in *Bate's case* (1607). Citing Tacitus, he concluded that Rome had been strongest when there was a mixture between the sovereignty of the king and the freedom of the subjects, and he warned that if liberty were taken away from the commons, and they found that their goods were not really their own, then the military might of the nation would be reduced to a 'drooping dismayedness' (Foster, 2.196). In addition he made an eloquent case for the role of the immemorial common law, tested by time, in shaping the constitution and defending the rights of the subject. While custom was a part of the common law, the common law of England was not the same as custom. Unlike customs, laws were to be tested against their convenience or inconvenience to the commonwealth. Reason was the essence of the common law, and the most effective way to test reason was to use the test of time, which was wiser than judges, wiser than parliament, and wiser than the wit of man.

Perhaps attracted by this philosophical turn of mind, in 1617 Sir Francis Bacon, now lord keeper, appointed Hetley to the newly created position of official law reporter of decisions made by the judges in the royal courts. The post carried a relatively meagre stipend of £100 p.a., and, though Hetley may have held it at least until 1623, there is no evidence that he was very active in its exercise. No manuscript reports of any stature can be attributed to him. The one set published under his name seems likely to have been composed by Humphrey Mackworth.

Hetley appeared at the bar of the Commons in 1621 to

defend Bacon, who was about to be impeached, from charges of misusing his authority as lord keeper, but he did not again sit in the house. In 1623 he was knighted and made a serjeant-at-law, an appointment that created some controversy within the profession because it was decided that he should not have any precedence in court since he had not, as was customary, given a law reading at Gray's Inn prior to his elevation. In 1626 he was appointed counsel for the earl of Bristol in connection with the impeachment that was being brought against him in the House of Lords, but at this point in his career he appears to have concentrated most of his attention on developing a lucrative practice. First appointed in 1617, he acted as recorder of Godmanchester until his death, and he was made surveyor of the estates of Trinity College, Cambridge, in 1631. Having purchased the manor of Brampton in 1613, he bought the rectory of Chatteris in the Isle of Ely in 1624. He and his wife, Elizabeth, daughter of Richard Gore, a merchant tailor of Bow Lane, London, had two sons and three daughters. After a painful illness, he died at Serjeants' Inn in Fleet Street, London, on 13 February 1637 and was buried at St Dunstan-in-the-West. CHRISTOPHER W. BROOKS

Sources 'Hetley, Sir Thomas', HoP, *Commons, 1604–29* [draft] · W. R. Prest, *The rise of the barristers: a social history of the English bar, 1590–1640* (1986) · E. R. Foster, ed., *Proceedings in parliament, 1610*, 2 vols. (1966) · *JHC*, 1 (1547–1628) · J. H. Baker and J. S. Ringrose, *A catalogue of English legal manuscripts in Cambridge University Library* (1996) · J. H. Baker, *The legal profession and the common law: historical essays* (1986) · Baker, *Serjeants* · *The diary of Sir Richard Hutton, 1614–1639*, ed. W. R. Prest, SeldS, suppl. ser., 9 (1991) · W. B. Bidwell and M. Jansson, eds., *Proceedings in parliament, 1626*, 4 vols. (1991–6) · will, PRO, PROB 11/173, sig. 30
Wealth at death affluent, but unspecified; owned several properties: will, PRO, PROB 11/173, sig. 30

Heton, George (*b. c.*1515, *d.* in or after **1598**), merchant and religious activist, was described in the memorial inscription of his son Martin *Heton, bishop of Ely, as *armiger* (esquire), and as descended from the family of Heton of Lancashire. If so he was evidently a younger son. Apprenticed to and made free of the Merchant Taylors' Company by the end of 1538, he settled in the London parish of St Dionis Backchurch, where on 20 January 1539 he married Elizabeth Paget. Only one child of the marriage is recorded in the register—Ann, baptized on 24 April 1540—and Elizabeth was buried on 12 September 1546.

Heton appears to have prospered early. In the London subsidy assessment of 1541 he was rated on the basis of an income of £60, and was thus reckoned one of the half-dozen wealthiest parishioners of St Dionis. His suitability as a son-in-law was not lost on London's merchant élite and on 24 January 1547 he married Joan Roocke, widowed daughter of Sir Martin *Bowes, lord mayor of London in 1545. Five children quickly followed—William (1547), Elizabeth (1548), Grace (1550), Thomas (1551), and finally Martin (1554), the future bishop. Joan Heton was buried ten days after Martin's baptism.

In 1551 Heton bought a substantial estate in Bromley St Leonard and Stratford Bow, Middlesex, from another former lord mayor, Sir Henry Hoblethorne. Like his father-in-law, he was by this time deeply committed to protestantism. He and his brother Thomas *Heton were among the principal 'sustainers' of London protestants under Mary. Two letters from the martyr John Bradford to George, his 'dear friend and brother in the lord', were afterwards published (Bickersteth, 342–6).

Heton contrived to combine this clandestine activity with the mastership of the Merchant Taylors in 1556–7. Henry Machyn describes the company feast which ended Heton's mastership on 30 June 1557. Continuing to prosper under Elizabeth, Heton was rated in the higher assessment of London of 1559 on the basis of a taxable sum of £80 and was thus reckoned among its 700 wealthiest citizens. Yet he had evidently overstrained his resources in the protestant cause. He sold his Middlesex estate to Nicholas Culverwell in 1561 and disaster struck soon afterwards. On 17 May 1563 he made 'humble request' to his company for an annuity for his relief and that of his 'poor children, being in great need and necessity … by reason of the great losses that he hath of late … had and sustained as well by sea as by land' (Clode, 1.192). He was granted an annual pension of 20 marks.

This reversal, coupled with his godly reputation, perhaps prompted the corporation to offer Heton the post of chamberlain of London, the city's principal financial officer, which he took up on 1 August 1563. In August 1565 he witnessed his father-in-law's will, which released him from a debt of £300, and in 1569 he was granted the gaugership of wine and oils for thirty years at £40 per annum.

In 1572 Heton relinquished his pension from the Merchant Taylors on the grounds that 'God hath otherwise well provided for him' (Clode, 1.192). It was, however, restored between April 1576 and June 1577, for disaster had struck again. On 13 December 1577 Heton was dismissed from the chamberlainship for undisclosed reasons. It may be significant that Elizabeth had recently complained that loan money dispatched for repayment to certain city officials had failed to reach them. Heton was, moreover, once again heavily in debt to private creditors and to the city itself, owing the latter no less than £1463. Attempts to settle the debt and audit his accounts dragged on through numerous committees until, on 26 April 1598, a final one was appointed to examine and close them.

Since no more is heard of the matter, nor of Heton himself, this may be evidence that he had recently died. Unless the description of him on Bishop Heton's tomb was merely an attempt to obliterate the memory of his financial disasters, it perhaps suggests that he had in the interim retired to a small estate in decent obscurity among his Lancashire relatives. Heton's second son, Thomas (*d.* 1606), MP for Southampton in 1593, was in 1600 appointed bailiff of the Isle of Ely by his brother Martin. BRETT USHER

Sources parish record, St Dionis Backchurch, GL, MS 17602 [unfoliated] · *VCH Lancashire* · B. R. Masters, *The chamberlain of the city of London, 1237–1987* (1988) · B. R. Masters, ed., *Chamber accounts of the sixteenth century*, London RS, 20 (1984) · E. Bickersteth, ed., *The letters of the martyrs, collected and published in 1564* (1837) · R. G. Lang,

ed., *Two Tudor subsidy assessment rolls for the city of London, 1541 and 1581*, London RS, 29 (1993) • CPR, 1550–53; 1560–63 • *The diary of Henry Machyn, citizen and merchant-taylor of London, from AD 1550 to AD 1563*, ed. J. G. Nichols, CS, 42 (1848) • higher assessment of London, GL, MS 2859, fol. 21r • will, PRO, PROB 11/49, sig. 3 [Sir Martin Bowes] • B. Willis, *A survey of the cathedrals*, 3 vols. (1742), vol. 2, pp. 361–2 [memorial inscription of Martin Heton, bishop of Ely] • C. M. Clode, *The early history of the guild of Merchant Taylors*, 2 vols. (1888) • P. Hyde, 'Heton, Thomas', HoP, *Commons, 1558–1603*
Archives CLRO, financial records as chamberlain of London
Wealth at death possibly bankrupt or at least insolvent: Masters, ed., *Chamber accounts*

Heton, Martin (1554–1609), bishop of Ely, was born in the London parish of St Dionis Backchurch and baptized there on 10 March 1554, the youngest child of George *Heton (*b. c.*1515, *d.* in or after 1598), merchant, and his second wife, Joan (*née* Bowes, formerly Roocke). That his mother was buried there ten days later lends credence to the statement on his memorial inscription in Ely Cathedral, composed by his chancellor William Gager, that, dying in childbirth, she had dedicated him to the service of God and the protestant cause ('Deo & ecclesiae reformatae'). In other respects, however, Gager's inscription has proved misleading, above all in twice misstating the bishop's age, giving it as thirty-six in 1589 and fifty-seven at his death. All former accounts have therefore assumed that he was born in 1552.

Educated at Westminster School, Heton matriculated at Christ Church, Oxford, in 1571. He graduated BA on 17 December 1574 and proceeded MA on 2 May 1578, meanwhile winning a reputation as an able and subtle disputant in philosophy and afterwards in theology. Granted letters patent in 1580 for the next vacant stall in Christ Church, he was instituted canon of the seventh prebend on 2 December 1582. He proceeded BD on 6 July 1584, was nominated vice-chancellor of Oxford on 16 July 1588, and in February 1589, not yet thirty-five years old, succeeded Laurence Humphrey as dean of Winchester. Instituted by Bishop Thomas Cooper on the crown's presentation, Heton owed his promotion to Robert Devereux, second earl of Essex, who at his majority in 1588 began an assiduous courtship of the London godly community and their families.

Heton commenced DD on 6 July 1589, and when Elizabeth visited Oxford in 1592 he was one of those who preached before her at Christ Church. Present at convocation on 16 March 1593, he was one of the deans of the formerly monastic cathedral chapters who petitioned for confirmation of their grants. In August 1596 Essex perhaps considered urging Heton's claims as dean of Westminster if Gabriel Goodman were to be elevated to the bench of bishops.

After the death on 20 September following of William Day, bishop of Winchester, fifteen Hampshire gentlemen petitioned Essex to support Heton's candidacy as his successor. Respectfully thanking Essex for securing him the deanery, they praised his preaching, his hospitality and the 'wise direction' of his life. No predecessor's 'severity' had been as effective in promoting religion (*Salisbury MSS*, 14.11). In the event Essex supported Thomas Bilson, the

Martin Heton (1554–1609), by unknown artist

successful candidate, and it must be doubted whether Elizabeth would have considered conferring so senior a bishopric on a man of only forty-two.

On 3 February 1600, however, Heton was consecrated bishop of Ely, vacant since the death of Richard Cox in 1581. The promotion had been recently refused by Lancelot Andrewes, who declined to alienate episcopal estates as the price of his elevation. Sir John Harington, a courtier who was in a position to know, believed that Heton was 'compelled in a sort to take the bishoprick on these terms' (Harington, 2.111), but Thomas Fuller later observed that 'his memory groaneth under the suspicion of simoniacal compliance' (Fuller, *Worthies*, 2.199).

The truth is more complex. Whilst the lord treasurer, Lord Buckhurst, fully admitted to Robert Cecil that he drove a hard bargain, the negotiations were carried through under the terms of the Act of Exchange (1559), by which the crown was obliged, during the vacancy of any see, to compensate it with 'spiritualities' (impropriate rectories) of equivalent value if it elected to withhold any temporal possessions from the next incumbent. Although Cecil finally achieved his objective by the simpler method of granting Heton all Ely's ancient estates on the understanding that once in office he would convey to the crown those which it wanted—hence Fuller's reference to 'simoniacal compliance'—the agreed exchanges did in fact take place and the official valuation of the see remained at £2124 18s. 5d., the figure at which it had been assessed in the *valor ecclesiasticus* of 1535.

Thus the treasury evidently did not believe that the arrangement would lead to the impoverishment of the diocese, and Buckhurst further agreed to Heton's stipulation that he would enter into bonds to pay first-fruits only on condition that Buckhurst secured him a royal warrant of exoneration. This Heton duly received on 16 May 1600. Elizabeth's stated reasons for waiving her right to more than £1900 in taxes was her usual one: that the new bishop would be 'better able to keep good hospitality and serve God and the queen' (PRO, E337/12, no. 117). Since Lancelot Andrewes finally accepted the see after Heton's death it would also seem to follow that by 1609 he recognized that Ely's financial resources had not been seriously impaired by the exchanges of ten years earlier.

A successful and popular bishop, Heton was esteemed 'inferior to few of his rank for learning and other good parts belonging to a prelate' (Harington, 2.111). His hospitality, as at Winchester, earned him the reputation of being 'the best housekeeper within man's remembrance' (Fuller, *Worthies*, 2.199)—further evidence, perhaps, that the government's original demands on the see had been realistic rather than outrageous. He engaged conscientiously in every aspect of episcopal government and also appeared annually as a judge at assize. He formally visited his diocese in 1601, 1604, and 1607, conducting proceedings himself and preaching regularly. His own generous hospitality was willingly returned. On progress in 1607 he and his retinue dined in the houses of local clergy, his hosts being excused their visitation procuration fees in lieu.

As a disciplinarian Heton evidently showed great tact. He heard sensitive cases in private rather than in consistory, and was sparing in his use of the penalties available to him under canon law. After 1604, when James I reintroduced subscription to Archbishop Whitgift's articles as his badge of inclusion within the established church, Heton seems to have handled the situation with skill: he was obliged to deprive none of his clergy for nonconformity.

James admired Heton, now grown stout, for his eloquence in the pulpit. Whilst 'fat men were wont to make lean sermons, his were not lean, but larded with much good learning' (Harington, 2.111). Although he published none, the sermon preached at Whitehall on 10 April 1603 on the text 'Come unto me all ye that labour' is preserved in summary in John Manningham's diary. Heton never lost touch with his roots within the London godly community. One of the (in the event, unneeded) sureties for his episcopal first-fruits was the future Sir Thomas Smith (d. 1625), who became governor of the East India Company, and he contributed £40 towards the purchase of books for Sir Thomas Bodley's newly established library in Oxford. The fathers of both Smith and Bodley had been close associates of his own father and of his uncle Thomas *Heton.

Heton died at Mildenhall, Suffolk, where he had retired for health reasons, on 14 July 1609. His brief and curious will, made four days earlier, contains no formal or religious preamble and no bequests. His funeral was to be conducted 'without any pomp or show'. He requested a 'convenient tomb', either in Ely Cathedral or in Downham

parish church. That expense discharged, his goods were to be sold and the profits divided into five equal parts, two going to his wife, Alice, and the other three to be equally divided between his daughters Anne and Elizabeth. Alice was named sole executrix, no overseers being appointed (PRO, PROB 11/115, fol. 225v). Since she was not granted probate until 26 April 1610 it is possible that the document was not accepted until it had been established that no more formal last will and testament existed.

Heton was buried in the south aisle of the presbytery of Ely Cathedral. His life-size alabaster effigy wears a rich cope embroidered with figures of the apostles. As well as William Gager's Latin epitaph there are verses by his nephew George, BD of Cambridge, the son of his brother Thomas (d. 1606), whom in 1600 he had appointed bailiff of the Isle of Ely. Heton's daughter Anne married Sir Robert Filmer (d. 1653) and Elizabeth Sir Edward Fish of Bedfordshire.   BRETT USHER

Sources parish registers, St Dionis Backchurch, GL, MS 17602 [unfoliated] · *Fasti Angl., 1541–1857,* [Canterbury] · *Fasti Angl., 1541–1857,* [Bristol], 103 · Wood, *Ath. Oxon.,* new edn, 2.847 · B. Willis, *A survey of the cathedrals,* 3 vols. (1742), vol. 2, pp. 361–2 · exchequer, first-fruits and tenths office, composition books, PRO, E334/12, fol. 142v · state papers domestic, Elizabeth I, PRO, SP 12/274/104 · *Calendar of the manuscripts of the most hon. the marquis of Salisbury,* 24 vols., HMC, 9 (1883–1976), vol. 6, p. 346; vol. 10, p. 120; vol. 14, p. 11 · K. Fincham, *Prelate as pastor: the episcopate of James I* (1990) · *The diary of John Manningham of the Middle Temple, 1602–1603,* ed. R. P. Sorlien (1976), 233 · J. Harington, *Nugae antiquae,* ed. T. Park and H. Harington, 2 vols. (1804) · Fuller, *Worthies* (1840) · F. Heal, *Of prelates and princes: a study of the economic and social position of the Tudor episcopate* (1980) · F. Heal, 'The bishops of Ely and their diocese, c.1515–1600', PhD diss., U. Cam., 1972 · F. A. Blaydes, ed., *The visitations of Bedfordshire, annis Domini 1566, 1582, and 1634,* Harleian Society, 19 (1884), 170 · exchequer, first-fruits and tenths office, plea rolls, PRO, E 337/12, no. 117 · will, PRO, PROB 11/115, sig. 32

Archives CUL, Ely diocesan records, 1600–1609

Likenesses alabaster effigy, Ely Cathedral · oils, Christ Church Oxf. [*see illus.*]

Heton, Thomas (b. *c.*1520, d. in or after **1587**), merchant and religious activist, was probably the Thomas Etton made free of the Mercers' Company in 1539 as late apprentice of William Locke. Such a date suggests he was born about 1520. Like his brother George *Heton, he became a 'sustainer' of protestants after the accession of Mary. Unlike George, he quickly chose exile and on 4 April 1554 petitioned the council of Strasbourg for burgher rights. Thereafter he kept open house for fugitive fellow countrymen, such as James Pilkington and Thomas Sampson. In September 1557 he signed Strasbourg's letter of reconciliation with the Frankfurt exile community and on 5 December 1558 thanked the Strasbourg magistrates for their hospitality since 1554.

On his return to the England of Elizabeth, Heton settled in the London parish of St Lawrence Jewry. In April 1560 he stood surety for Edwin Sandys's firstfruits as bishop of Worcester and in June was present at the election of elders for the re-established French protestant church in London. It was probably he rather than George whom John Jewel described later that year as his 'friend Mr Heton' (BL, Egerton MS 2533, fol. 5r). Heton had advanced him £307, the entire sum needed to discharge Jewel's initial instalment of his first fruits as bishop of Salisbury.

As 'governor of the merchants' Heton was involved after 1562 in negotiations for adopting the port of Emden as an alternative to Catholic Antwerp for the export of English cloth. In these Edmund Grindal, bishop of London, acted as intermediary between William Cecil and Jan Utenhove, lay leader of the foreign protestant community in London and agent for Anna, countess of East Friesland.

Heton remained on close terms with Thomas Sampson. Both men were appointed overseers of the will of Nicholas Culverwell in 1569, and in 1573 Sampson interceded with Cecil on Heton's behalf, asking that he be allowed to transport English cloth without paying customs duties. Strype's assumption that this indicated a terminal decline in his fortunes is wide of the mark, although it may point to a temporary set-back after the final failure of the Emden scheme.

At the time of the sack of Antwerp by Spanish troops in November 1576, Heton was governor of the English merchant adventurers there. The poet George Gascoigne, who wrote an eye-witness account of the sack and subsequent massacre, described him as 'a comely aged man ... whose hoary hairs might move pity ... especially the uprightness of his dealing considered' (Pollard, 447). The English were nevertheless held to ransom and left at the mercy of Spanish troops. Two letters from Heton to the English government, describing the plight and tribulations of the Antwerp merchants and begging for assistance, are printed along with Gascoigne's *The Spoil of Antwerp* in *Tudor Tracts* (1903).

In 1582, still of St Lawrence Jewry, Heton was rated at the high figure of £70 in the London subsidy assessment and in 1586 became master of the Mercers. In such circumstances Grindal's bequest to him in 1583—the 'fifty pounds which he oweth me'—is not good evidence that his 'loving friend' was once more in financial difficulties (Strype, *Grindal*, 604).

Having completed his year as master of the Mercers in July 1587, Heton makes only one further appearance in their court records, on 15 November following. Although he probably died shortly afterwards, the exact date is unknown and like his brother he seems to have left no will. The identity of his wife, who was with him in Antwerp, has not been established. The will of a contemporary namesake (Eton), citizen and grocer of London, was proved on 16 February 1571. To judge from its bequests, which included money for sermons at Kinver, Staffordshire, his birthplace, the two men were unrelated.

BRETT USHER

Sources C. H. Garrett, *The Marian exiles: a study in the origins of Elizabethan puritanism* (1938) · A. F. Pollard, ed., *Tudor tracts, 1532–1588* (1903) · P. Collinson, *Archbishop Grindal, 1519–1583: the struggle for a reformed church* (1979) · A. Pettegree, *Foreign protestant communities in sixteenth-century London* (1986) · exchequer, first-fruits and tenths office, composition books, PRO, E334/7, fol. 58v · G. D. Ramsay, *The City of London in international politics at the accession of Elizabeth Tudor* (1975), 229–44 · J. Strype, *Annals of the Reformation and establishment of religion ... during Queen Elizabeth's happy reign*, new edn, 4 vols. (1824) · J. Strype, *The history of the life and acts of the most reverend father in God Edmund Grindal*, new edn (1821) · Mercers' Company acts of court, 1560–95, Mercers' Hall, London · Mercers' Company acts of court, 1595–1629, Mercers' Hall, London · freedom register, Mercers' Hall, London · R. G. Lang, ed., *Two Tudor subsidy assessment rolls for the city of London, 1541 and 1581*, London RS, 29 (1993) · PRO, PROB 11/53

Heugh, Hugh (1782–1846), United Secession church minister, was born in Stirling on 12 August 1782, the ninth of ten children of John Heugh (1731–1810) and his wife, Anne Ross (d. 1807), and grandson of John Heugh (1688–1731), parish minister of Kingoldrum, Forfarshire. His father was minister of the Viewfield church in Stirling, an Anti-Burgher congregation. Heugh attended Stirling grammar school and Edinburgh University, before entering the Divinity Hall of the General Associate Synod at Whitburn in 1799. He spent the session of 1800–01 at Anderson's Institution, Glasgow. He was licensed by the General Associate Presbytery of Stirling on 22 February 1804. Calls were received from congregations at Greenloaning, Perthshire, and Hawick, Roxburghshire, but the synod were disposed to accept that which took him to Stirling, where he was ordained as colleague to his aged father on 14 August 1806. He married, on 21 June 1809, Isabella Clarkson (d. 1877), the daughter of an Anti-Burgher minister, with whom he had five daughters and two sons.

Heugh became an influential figure in his church and was moderator of the General Associate Synod in 1819, the last before the two main bodies of seceders merged to form the United Secession church. In 1821 he was called, for the third time, to a congregation at Regent Place, Glasgow. He was loath to leave his native Stirling, and it was only by the narrowest majority that the synod preferred the call to Regent Place, to which he was inducted on 9 October 1821. In addition to an active pastoral ministry, Heugh engaged in many of the public questions and controversies of the day. He swiftly became involved in arguing the case against church establishments in the voluntary controversy, and when his own denomination became agitated over the question of the atonement he issued a pamphlet, *Irenicum* (1845), which sought to conciliate the warring factions. While his sympathies naturally lay with the church's professor, John Brown, who was his personal friend, his action was characteristic of a man who, while he did not shrink from controversy, deplored the personal rancour which accompanied it. Among his other publications were *The Importance of Early Piety* (1826), *Considerations on Civil Establishments of Religion* (1833), and *Notices on the State of Religion in Geneva and Belgium* (1844). Heugh was also a keen advocate of home and foreign missions, and he was awarded the degree of DD by the college of Pittsburgh, Pennsylvania, in 1831.

From 1837 Heugh's health gave cause for concern, and a trip to Geneva in 1843 was one of a number of recuperative journeys he undertook. His health finally gave way, and he died at his home, 126 Montrose Street, Glasgow, on 10 June 1846, and was buried in Glasgow necropolis on 16 June.

LIONEL ALEXANDER RITCHIE

Sources H. M. Macgill, *The life of Hugh Heugh DD* (1850) · Chambers, *Scots.* (1835) · Anderson, *Scot. nat.* · W. Mackelvie, *Annals and statistics* *of the United Presbyterian church*, ed. W. Blair and D. Young (1873), 304, 632 • R. Small, *History of the congregations of the United Presbyterian church from 1733 to 1900*, 2 (1904), 55–7, 672 • G. Blair, *Biographic and descriptive sketches of Glasgow necropolis* (1857), 270–82 • private information (1891) • *DNB*

Likenesses E. Burton, mezzotint (after D. Macnee), BM • Fenner, Sears & Co., stipple (after J. R. Wildman), BM, NPG; repro. in *Evangelical Magazine* (1830)

Wealth at death £2376 3s. 9d.: inventory, NA Scot., SC 36/48/32, fol. 473

Heurtley, Charles Abel (1806–1895), theologian, born on 4 January 1806 at Bishopwearmouth, in co. Durham, was the son of Charles Abel Heurtley (1740–1806), a banker at Sunderland, and his wife, Isabella Hunter (d. 1816), of Newcastle upon Tyne. After his father's death Heurtley's mother married Mr Metcalfe, shipbuilder of South Shields. On his father's side he was directly descended from one Charles Abel Herteleu, a Huguenot, who in the early days of the eighteenth century migrated from his home at Rennes in Brittany in order to secure liberty to profess the protestant faith. Heurtley, who was himself a staunch protestant, always rejoiced in his descent from one who had thus suffered for his faith.

In 1813 Heurtley was sent to a school at West Boldon, near Gateshead, and in 1817 he passed on to another at Witton-le-Wear, near Bishop Auckland, a private school which at that time had a considerable reputation. Here he stayed for four years, and, as his guardians were extremely desirous that he should become a man of business, he was sent in 1822 to Liverpool as a clerk in the office of Messrs Brereton and Newsham, timber merchants. After nine months' trial, he was confirmed in his original purpose of going to university with a view to entering the church. Accordingly he returned to education at Louth grammar school in Lincolnshire, Sedbergh being too full to take him, and after ten months' work there was elected in 1823 to a scholarship at Corpus Christi College, Oxford, open to boys born in the diocese of Durham.

Heurtley graduated BA with first-class honours in mathematics in June 1827, winning the Ellerton theological essay prize in the following year. He was an unsuccessful candidate for a fellowship at Oriel in 1828, but, after spending four years as second master at the newly founded Brompton grammar school (1828–31), he succeeded to a fellowship at Corpus in 1832, which he held until 1841. In 1831 he graduated MA, was ordained, and served the curacy of Wardington, near Cropredy, Oxfordshire, until 1840, when he was appointed to the college living of Fenny Compton, Warwickshire. During this period he was also reader in Latin at Corpus (1832–5), select preacher before the university (1834 and 1838), and junior dean of his college (1838). He graduated BD in 1838 and DD in 1853. On 10 April 1844 he married Jane (d. 1893), daughter of Revd William Bagshaw Harrison, vicar of Goudhurst, Kent. He was Bampton lecturer in 1845, and on 2 July 1853 was elected Margaret professor of divinity at Oxford, which was tenable with a canonry at Christ Church, Oxford. He held the chair and canonry for forty-two years, combining them with the rectory of Fenny Compton until 1872.

Learned, courteous, retiring, reading and thinking much, but writing little, Heurtley represented the older type of Oxford scholar, whose influence depended rather upon his personal relations with members of the university than upon the effect of his written works on the world at large. He set great store by his university sermons, preaching over sixty during his lifetime. He sat as one of the theological assessors in the court that tried Archdeacon Denison for unsound eucharistic doctrine (1856). He contributed to *Aids to Faith* (1861), the orthodox response to the controversial *Essays and Reviews*. In 1873 he entered a strong protest, on theological grounds, against the granting of an honorary degree upon Professor John Tyndall, and in the same year he protested against the precedence accorded to Cardinal Manning at the jubilee dinner of the Oxford Union. His action in these matters was typical of his theological position. He had a profound devotion to the Church of England, and conceived its position mainly on the lines of the evangelical party. But he was not a party man, as was shown in a very striking way when in advanced years (1890) he preached a sermon in the cathedral deploring hasty and unmeasured condemnation of the 'higher criticism'. His practical gifts were displayed in his parish at Fenny Compton, where he successfully organized a small company to provide a proper water supply for the village.

Heurtley's written work consisted largely of sermons. Of these the most considerable volume is his Bampton lectures, *Justification* (1845), in which he adopted 'a moderate and learned Evangelical Protestant position' (Toon, 60). But he also published a series of works on creeds and formularies of faith, the main subject of his study and of his lectures, of which *De fide et symbolo* (1864) was widely used in theological colleges. His latest work, revealing his patristic scholarship, was *A History of the Earlier Formularies of the Western and Eastern Churches* (1892). Many of his parochial sermons were published, and he was the writer of a number of tracts circulated by the Society for Promoting Christian Knowledge.

Heurtley died at Christ Church, Oxford, on 1 May 1895 and was buried beside his wife at Osney cemetery on 3 May. He left one son, Charles Abel Heurtley, who became rector of Ashington, Sussex, and three daughters, of whom the eldest, Isabella, married Sydney Linton (1841–1894), the first bishop of Riverina, Australia. To his memoirist Heurtley's life exemplified a combination of deep personal religion and critical theological study within the secularized academy.

T. B. STRONG, rev. M. C. CURTHOYS

Sources W. Ince, Memoir, in C. A. Heurtley, *Wholesome words*, ed. W. Ince (1896) • Boase, *Mod. Eng. biog.* • J. Foster, *Oxford men and their colleges* (1893) • P. Toon, *Evangelical theology, 1833–1856: a response to Tractarianism* (1979) • J. S. Reynolds, *The evangelicals at Oxford, 1735–1871: a record of an unchronicled movement*, [2nd edn] (1975)

Archives Pusey Oxf., diary, notes, and corresp.; further corresp. and autographs | LPL, corresp. with Charles Golightly

Wealth at death £35,128 15s. 6d.: probate, 8 June 1895, *CGPLA Eng. & Wales*

Heuston, Robert Francis Vere (1923–1995), jurist and biographer, was born on 17 November 1923 in Dublin, the elder son of Vere Douglas Heuston, managing clerk at Guinness's brewery in that city, and his wife, Dorothy Helen, *née* Coulter. He was baptized into the Church of Ireland, of which he was throughout his life a communicant member. He was a collateral descendant (and proud to be so) of Robert Emmett, the Irish protestant patriot, executed in 1803 for leading an unsuccessful rebellion against the British, and famed among his countrymen for his defiant speech from the dock. After schooling at St Columba's College, Rathfarnham, Heuston read law at Trinity College, Dublin (1941–6), gaining first-class honours, and being auditor (president) of the Historical Society (the student debating society) in 1945. Called to the bar by King's Inns, Dublin (1947), but deciding on an academic career he, like many similarly minded Trinity graduates, went as a research student to St John's College, Cambridge.

Heuston left Cambridge within a year on his election in 1947, at the age of twenty-three, as Pembroke College, Oxford's first law fellow. Then one of the university's smallest, poorest, and least distinguished colleges, little had changed at Pembroke since the nineteenth century—as John Betjeman observed in 'The Death of Dr. Ramsden' (1947). Old men dominated, while a tiny group of middle-aged and young fellows, led by R. B. McCallum, did the work. This atmosphere (not unlike that of the Trinity he had left) was quite congenial to Heuston who—shy, reserved, and fastidious, but far from unsocial—valued formality. He remained at Pembroke for eighteen years, living in college for fifteen of them as a bachelor don responsible for student discipline as well as for teaching law. He was an austere but caring tutor. His pupils included a future lord chief justice of Northern Ireland (Robert Carswell) and a future attorney-general of the Republic of Ireland (J. M. Kelly, whose pioneering study *The Irish Constitution* (1963) was begun under Heuston's supervision). During these years the college prospered, and he did most of the writing on which his reputation within both the practising and the academic legal communities was based.

An elegant lecturer, Heuston brought an Irish perspective to constitutional law (his lectures published as *Essays in Constitutional Law*, 1961, remained in print until 1997). He then turned to torts, the law governing entitlement to compensation for injuries to person, property, business interests, or reputation wrongfully caused, or, in some circumstances, not prevented—an area of law based almost entirely on judicial decisions rather than legislation. This shift of interest resulted from his undertaking (on the recommendation of the influential A. L. Goodhart) the editing (that is, the keeping up to date) of the classic textbook *Salmond on Torts* (first published in 1907 by Sir John Salmond, a New Zealand judge) when its previous editor (and Oxford's vice-chancellor), W. T. S. Stallybrass, had died in an accident. This book, giving an accurate and clear account of the rules the courts were applying, was much relied on throughout the Commonwealth by practitioners and judges as well as by students. Heuston's eminently judicious editing, grounded in his deep respect for the collective wisdom (or common sense) of the judiciary, extended over eleven editions from 1953 to 1996 (from 1987 with R. A. Buckley). During this period the book was reshaped and largely rewritten, and maintained its authoritative status. Footnotes frequently indicated that a passage had been endorsed by a named court or judge. This was traditional legal scholarship, concerned with what judges said rather than with the consequences and desirability of what they did; while still valued by the practising profession, it came even in Heuston's lifetime to seem somewhat old-fashioned. Although a member both of the English Law Reform Committee (1968–70) and the Irish Law Reform Commission (1975–81), his instincts were not those of the law reformer.

In *The Lives of the Lord Chancellors, 1885–1940* (1964), Heuston's interests in political and constitutional history and his fascination with the English judiciary were combined. Designed as a continuation of J. B. Atlay's account of the Victorian holders of this hybrid (part political, part judicial) office, which had in its turn continued Lord Campbell's notorious volumes, it included important reassessments of, among others, lords Halsbury, Sankey, and (in a second, less satisfactory, volume, published in 1987 and covering the years 1940–70) Jowitt. Its publication made him a natural choice as the memoirist of twentieth-century judges, both in the *Dictionary of National Biography* and elsewhere.

Widely regarded as the obvious candidate when the All Souls readership in English law became vacant in 1959, Heuston was, perhaps for this very reason, passed over. Three influences help to explain his move to a professorship at Southampton in 1965: this disappointment; a feeling that he should play his part in the great expansion of English universities and their law faculties then taking place; and his marriage. On 2 July 1962 he married Bridget Nancy Ward-Perkins, daughter of Bernard Godfrey Clarke Bolland, Egyptian government official, and widow of his close friend and colleague at Pembroke, the economist Neville Ward-Perkins, thereby assuming a stepfather's responsibilities for four children.

Heuston returned to Trinity College, Dublin, as regius professor of laws in 1970. This Irish university, by now burgeoning, was very different from the Anglo-Irish protestant college he had left a quarter of a century earlier. Administrative responsibilities, controversies about the reorganization of legal education in Dublin, internal wranglings, and a certain lack of sympathy for his values and standards among younger colleagues (who included two future presidents of Ireland, Mary Robinson and Mary McAleese, and South Africa's first post-apartheid minister of education, Kader Asmal) made his tenure of the chair less happy and fruitful than had been hoped. On reaching sixty he opted for early retirement.

Heuston was a visiting professor at the University of Melbourne (1956), the University of British Columbia (1960 and 1985), and the Australian National University

(1977), Gresham professor in law (1964–70), and Arthur Goodhart professor of legal science at Cambridge (1986–7). He was made an honorary fellow of Pembroke College, Oxford (1982), an honorary bencher of King's Inns, Dublin (1983), and Gray's Inn, London (1988), a corresponding fellow of the British Academy (1993), and a QC *honoris causa* (1995). He enjoyed the English and the Irish countryside, visits to places with historical and legal associations, race meetings, and dining clubs. He kept his many English friendships in good repair, and his conversation, like his lectures and his writings, was enriched with anecdotes harvested from a wide reading of political memoirs and diaries. He died of cancer at Our Lady's Hospice, Harold's Cross, Dublin, on 21 December 1995, and was buried on 31 December at St Patrick's, Tara, Meath. He was survived by his wife and four stepchildren.   P. R. GLAZEBROOK

Sources *The Times* (27 Dec 1995) · *The Guardian* (1 Jan 1996) · *The Independent* (3 Jan 1996) · *Pembroke College, Record, 1995–1996* (1996), 68–72 [Oxford] · *WWW, 1991–5* · personal knowledge (2004) · private information (2004) · m. cert.
Likenesses photograph, 1970, Pembroke College, Oxford

Heveningham. For this title name *see* Shelton, Mary [Mary Heveningham, Lady Heveningham] (1510x15–1570/71).

Heveningham, Sir Arthur (*c.*1546–1630), local politician, was probably born at Ketteringham, Norfolk, the first of five children of Sir Anthony Heveningham (1507–1557) and his second wife, Mary *Shelton (1510x15–1570/71), daughter of John Shelton of Shelton, Norfolk, and his wife, Anne. About 1575 he married Mary (d. 1635), daughter of Thomas Hanchet, and settled at Ketteringham. The Heveninghams of Heveningham, Suffolk, had been established among that county's élite since the fourteenth century. Although they had inherited the Ketteringham estate in the late fifteenth century they had played no part in Norfolk affairs until Arthur Heveningham succeeded his stepbrother in 1574 and determined to fill the political vacuum created in East Anglia by Thomas Howard's execution in 1572. Since the duke's influence had been greater in Norfolk than in Suffolk, and since the power structure in Elizabethan Suffolk militated against that county's domination by a single magnate, perceptively Arthur Heveningham transferred the family's political centre of gravity from Suffolk to Norfolk. Appointed JP in Suffolk (1578) and Norfolk (1579), he served assiduously on both benches down to 1603 and remained in both commissions until incapacitated by ill health about 1625, but only in Norfolk was he appointed sheriff (1581–2 and 1602–3) and deputy lieutenant (1587–96 and 1605–30). Perhaps symbolically, the queen knighted him in Norwich during her progress of 1578.

Unfortunately Heveningham's face did not fit in his adopted county. A proud man, for him prestige depended upon lineage. Despite his having an acceptable one, he commissioned a pedigree which traced his descent from 'Arphaxad who was one of the knights that watched Christes Sepulchre' (Smith, 158) and which has been described as 'the most absurd of all concocted pedigrees of the Elizabethan period'. Conservative, albeit conformist in religion, he consorted with some of the leading recusants in East Anglia, notably with Nicholas Hare and Thomas Cornwallis. Intemperate by nature, he readily resorted to direct action. In a private quarrel with his neighbour, Sergeant Edward Flowerdew, he ambushed him as he rode to quarter sessions and, in his own words, gave the 'knave sergeant a knock on the cockscombe' (Smith, 198). Subsequently, in open sessions he boasted that he would 'hunt and drive him out of the county' (ibid., 158). In similar vein, in county government he preferred to act on the authority of the crown rather than through what he perceived as tortuous legal processes embodied in parliamentary statute. Thus he asserted his powers as a deputy lieutenant not only to reorganize the county militia, as justifiably he might, but also, less justifiably, to overawe recalcitrant rate-payers who flouted his attempts to levy money under a patent of 1588 which empowered him to repair the highway between Wymondham and Attleborough. Such warrants, effectively licensing private persons as opposed to statutorily appointed officials to undertake specific administrative tasks, were in his eyes direct and efficient. He held at least one other patent and lent the weight of his authority to the holders of several more.

There were, not surprisingly, gentry in the county with a different mind-set—notably Edward Flowerdew, Nathaniel and Nichols Bacon, Edward Coke, Francis Wyndham, Bassingbourne Gawdy, and Thomas Knyvett. By no means homogeneous in background, they had enough in common to make them antithetic to this newcomer. Most had received a humanistic education with its emphasis on analysis and reasoned argument in pursuit of neighbourly accord; most had gained respect for common law through study at the inns of court; most inclined to moderate puritanism; and most were 'new men' whose pedigrees rarely reached back even to 1500.

Predictably in these circumstances, between 1580 and 1600 the Norfolk bench was convulsed with a series of bitter controversies concerning militia organization, the detested activities of patentees, the arrangements to compound for purveyance, and the collection of ship money. Underlying all these disputes lurked the issue of who paid; this in turn underlined the inequities of the county rating system. Of the latter Heveningham approved, to the disquiet once more of his opponents.

In the conduct of these controversies Heveningham received support notably from Edward Clere and the Heydons of Baconsthorpe. Principally, however, he relied upon backing at court from Henry Carey, Lord Hunsdon, whom the queen appointed lord lieutenant of Norfolk and Suffolk in 1585. 'Whatsoever Sir Arthur informeth, my Lord [Hunsdon] will nedes have that true' (*Papers of Nathaniel Bacon*, 3.120), Francis Wyndham ruefully remarked when reporting on court affairs. Such was his standing at court that in the late 1590s he headed the Norfolk section in a list of 'principal gentlemen that dwell usually in their countrie'. His opponents for their part harried him and his associates in every court from quarter sessions to the high court of parliament. This they did with some success; at the county court they four times thwarted his return as knight of the shire for Norfolk; by one act of parliament in 1593 they defeated the patentees who came near to divesting Norwich Cathedral of most of its lands; and by the repeal of another they deprived the patentees for Sheringham piers of the source of their cash.

Neither side won; rather, Heveningham gave up. His aspirations had always outrun his means; never well endowed with land, by the late 1590s he had run into debt and was forced to sell his wife's jewels. Through his lack of an extensive patronage network his influence at court collapsed after Hunsdon's death in 1596, and, although he continued his involvement in local administration, it was in a much lower key. Age and the influence of his family may also have mellowed him: in 1622 he visited his old opponent Nathaniel Bacon on his deathbed; in 1626 he joined with his son John in opposition to the forced loan; and in 1649 his grandson William *Heveningham sat among the regicides. He was buried at Ketteringham on 8 October 1630. A. HASSELL SMITH

Sources D. MacCulloch, *Suffolk and the Tudors: politics and religion in an English county, 1500–1600* (1986) · A. Hassell Smith, *County and court: government and politics in Norfolk, 1558–1603* (1974) · J. Hunter, 'The history and topography of Ketteringham', *Norfolk Archaeology*, 3 (1852), 245–314 · G. L. Owens, 'Norfolk, 1620–1641: local government and central authority in an East Anglian county', PhD diss., University of Wisconsin, 1970 · *The papers of Nathaniel Bacon of Stiffkey*, ed. A. H. Smith and G. M. Baker, 3: *1586–1595*, Norfolk RS, 53 (1990) · W. A. Shaw, *The knights of England*, 2 vols. (1906) · parish register, Ketteringham, 8 Oct 1630 [burial]

Archives PRO, star chamber cases *sub* Heveningham, Arthur | Norfolk RO, Aylsham collection

Likenesses portrait, repro. in Smith, *County and court*; priv. coll.

Wealth at death assessed for subsidy at £20 in 1609; incl. Norfolk and Suffolk estates

Heveningham, Mary. See Shelton, Mary (1510x15–1570/71).

Heveningham, William (1604–1678), regicide, was the eldest son of Sir John Heveningham (1578–1633) of Ketteringham, Norfolk, and his second wife, Bridget (d. 1624), daughter of Christopher Paston of Paston, Norfolk. He matriculated at Pembroke College, Cambridge, in 1621. During the 1620s his father was a justice of the peace for Norfolk; Heveningham was a captain in the Norfolk militia and in the 1630s served as a deputy lieutenant, justice of the peace, and sheriff (1633–4). He inherited at least fifteen manors on his father's death. On 23 November 1629 he married Catherine (d. 1648), daughter of Sir Henry Wallop, an extremely wealthy resident of Hampshire and Wiltshire, and MP in numerous parliaments. Following Catherine's death Heveningham married in 1650 Mary (d. 1696), daughter of John Carey, fifth Baron Hunsdon and second earl of Dover; they had one son, Sir William Heveningham (d. 1674), who married Barbara, daughter of George Villiers, third Viscount Graham, and a daughter, Abigail, who married John Newton.

Heveningham, along with his father, refused to pay the forced loan of 1627 but, unlike his father, avoided imprisonment. Later he showed more discretion when in 1637 he

admitted royal agents on his lands to obtain saltpetre, and when he paid the ship money assessment for 1640. In the elections for the Long Parliament he backed a moderate candidate, John Potts, for one of the county seats against Sir John Holland. Thanks to his father-in-law's influence, Heveningham himself was elected MP for Stockbridge, Hampshire, in the Short Parliament (1640) and again in the Long Parliament (1640), but rarely attended sessions. After the civil war began he served on the county committees for Norfolk and Cambridgeshire. With Sir Edmund Moundeford, MP for Norfolk, Heveningham supervised seven Norfolk hundreds on behalf of parliament in 1642. He advanced £250 for the support of the parliamentarian garrison at Newport Pagnell, Buckinghamshire.

In the 1640s Heveningham may have leant towards a presbyterian religious position and was an elder in a church of the Dunwich classis. Politically, however, he was an 'independent', favouring the claims and programme of the New Model Army in 1648. As an army sympathizer, he survived Pride's Purge (December 1648) and, with his brother-in-law, Robert Wallop, was named a judge for Charles I's treason trial. He attended thirteen sessions and, like Wallop, refused to sign the royal death warrant, though he later swore approval of the king's trial and execution [*see also* Regicides]. An anxiety to curb military rule appears to have prompted his greater involvement in politics at Westminster in 1649. He was elected to the first two councils of state under the Commonwealth in 1649 and 1650, though he expressed doubts about the engagement, a 1650 loyalty oath required of officeholders and clergy. He was named vice-admiral of Suffolk in 1651.

A heavy speculator in buying army debentures, Heveningham also bought several confiscated episcopal properties (the manors of Dalston, Rose Castle, and Linstock in the diocese of Carlisle), and purchased or leased various confiscated royalist properties, including Stainton Manor, Norfolk (1653), and the duke of Hamilton's Chelsea mansion. However, some of these purchases of royalist lands did not benefit him personally since they were bought on behalf of Norfolk's county committee to cover debts. He maintained a London residence at St Martin-in-the-Fields during the 1650s and became quite wealthy, probably realizing an annual income of at least £1000.

Heveningham was perhaps the first regicide to surrender to the crown at the restoration of Charles II in June 1660, was tried in October as a regicide at the Old Bailey, and sentenced to death. His four petitions for mercy during 1660–62, supported by his wife's family connections, claimed that despite serving as a judge he had opposed the execution of Charles I. Admitting that he deserved death, Heveningham's petitions also noted his appeals before the committee for compounding on behalf of his royalist brother, Sir Arthur Heveningham, in 1656 during the interregnum. Heveningham also claimed to have contributed £500 to support Sir George Booth's royalist rising in 1659. Though Heveningham was spared execution, his wife's appeals that he be removed to her house in Suffolk failed and he remained a prisoner at Windsor Castle until his death there on 21 February 1678. His property, however, though initially confiscated, was eventually held in trust for his wife. He was buried at Ketteringham church on 25 February 1678.   DANIEL WEBSTER HOLLIS, III

Sources R. W. Ketton-Cremer, *Norfolk in the civil war: a portrait of a society in conflict* (1969) · W. Rye, *Norfolk families*, 2 vols. in 5 pts (1911–13) · Keeler, *Long Parliament* · Venn, *Alum. Cant.* · *Eighth report*, 1, HMC, 7 (1907–9) · *Ninth report*, 2, HMC, 8 (1884) · *CSP dom.*, 1648–52; 1660–62 · *State trials*, vol. 5 · *The writings and speeches of Oliver Cromwell*, ed. W. C. Abbott and C. D. Crane, 4 vols. (1937–47) · D. Underdown, *Pride's Purge: politics in the puritan revolution* (1971) · M. A. E. Green, ed., *Calendar of the proceedings of the committee for compounding … 1643–1660*, 5 vols., PRO (1889–92) · B. Worden, *The Rump Parliament, 1648–1653* (1974) · D. W. Hollis III, 'Heveningham, William', *Greaves & Zaller, BDBR · DNB*
Archives Norfolk RO, personal and estate corresp. and papers · Suffolk RO, Ipswich, corresp. with bailiffs of Ipswich | Bodl. Oxf., Holkham MSS, includes 'Precepts of William Heveningham of Heveningham, Suffolk', 1633

Heward, Leslie Hays (1897–1943), composer and conductor, was born in Littletown, Liversedge, Yorkshire, on 8 December 1897, the son of Henry Heward, railway porter, and Amy, *née* Hays. He was playing the piano by the age of two, the organ at four, and at eight he played the organ accompaniment for a performance of Handel's *Messiah*, conducted by his father at the Moravian church, Lower Wyke, in 1906. In 1911, while competing in the Morecambe Festival, his talents were discovered by Sydney Nicholson, organist of Manchester Cathedral. He subsequently joined the choir at Manchester and was given personal music tuition by Nicholson. His talent for composition started to manifest itself during these years, his works including the hymn-tune 'Wyke' (*Hymns Ancient and Modern*), and a Te Deum and evening canticles in B♭ (1916). In 1917 Heward won a scholarship to the Royal College of Music to study with Sir Charles Villiers Stanford, supplementing his income as assistant music master at Eton College from 1917 to 1919. He graduated in 1920, gaining the Manns memorial prize. Heward's involvement in Adrian Boult's conducting classes at the Royal College of Music were to inspire his own career as a conductor: he was first at the British National Opera Company (BNOC) (1922–4), then with the Cape Town Orchestra (1924–7), before returning to the BNOC (1927–30); he was also director of stage music at Covent Garden (1928), and was finally music director of the City of Birmingham Orchestra from 1930 until 26 December 1942. He had accepted the post of music director to the Hallé Orchestra, but his death deprived him of this important step forward in his career. He was a recording artist for Decca as a piano accompanist from 1928 to 1930, and for EMI as a conductor from 1938 to 1943. In 1925 he married (Hilda Viola) Lenore Buchanon Shephard (1903–1970), a dancer in the corps de ballet at the BNOC, with whom he had a daughter. Throughout his life Heward suffered from poor health, in particular from eczema and asthma, which in later life was worsened by smoking. The seeds of tuberculosis were apparent after his return from South Africa in 1927 and an operation at the Queen Elizabeth Hospital, Birmingham, in 1942, under the supervision of Lord Horder, failed to extend his

life for much longer. He died at his home, 43 Harborne Road, Five Ways, Birmingham, on 3 May 1943 at the age of forty-five; he was cremated on 6 May at Lodge Hill crematorium, Birmingham.

Heward's compositions reveal an exceptional degree of innate musicality, sensitivity and skill in melodic and harmonic development, reflecting European trends of the 1920s and 1930s, but always within a tonal framework. His best work reveals an original voice still awaiting recognition. Among his orchestral works were *The Mermaid* (1915), *Dance Suite* (1920), *South African Patrol* (1925), *Nocturne* (1927), and *Quodlibet* (1931): the last three works received broadcasts under the composer's baton. He also wrote various songs for voice and orchestra; music for the film *The Loves of Robert Burns* (1929); some church music; *Variations on an Original Theme for Two Pianos* (1916); and an unfinished opera, *Hamlet* (1916). Heward's exceptional musical ability, manifest at so early an age, should have destined him for a brilliant career; but constant ill health and lack of opportunities were frequent obstacles to recognition. After his death his abilities were commemorated in forty testimonials from prominent musicians of the time in a memorial volume, first published in 1944.   MICHAEL JONES

Sources E. Blom, *Leslie Heward, 1897–1943: a memorial volume* (1944) · M. Jones, 'Leslie Heward " … a true disciple of Orpheus"', *British Music*, 19 (1997), 45–60 · B. King-Smith, *Crescendo! 75 years of the City of Birmingham Symphony Orchestra* (1995) · *Music Review*, 4 (1943) · *New Grove* · private information (2004) [S. Heward; K. Heward; F. Young; M. Mitchell]
Archives Royal College of Music, London, MSS | SOUND BL NSA, *Vintage years*, BBC Radio 3, 3 May 1997, H8787/1 · BL NSA, performance recordings
Likenesses portrait, CBSO Archive
Wealth at death £2025 17s. 8d.: probate, 11 June 1943, *CGPLA Eng. & Wales*

Hewart, Gordon, first Viscount Hewart (1870–1943), judge, was born at Bury, Lancashire, on 7 January 1870, the eldest son of Giles Hewart, draper, and his wife, Annie Elizabeth Jones. Hewart was educated at Manchester grammar school and University College, Oxford, where he won an open classical scholarship. He obtained a second class in classical moderations (1889) and in *literae humaniores* (1891). He was married on 5 October 1892 to Sara Wood (*d.* 1933), daughter of Joseph Hacking Riley, engineer and machinist, of Bury. They had one daughter and two sons, the elder of whom was killed in the First World War.

Hewart early fixed on the law as his career, but in order to supplement a meagre income he joined the parliamentary reporting staff of the *Manchester Guardian* and subsequently became principal leader writer on the *Morning Leader*. Pressure of journalistic work delayed his call to the bar (Inner Temple) until 1902. Then, however, he joined the northern circuit, where his name was known, and his rise was rapid. Only ten years later, in 1912, he took silk, and in 1913 was elected Liberal member of parliament for Leicester (sitting for the East division of Leicester from 1918 to 1922).

Hewart was an effective advocate in court and a skilled debater in the House of Commons. He was thought of as an 'advanced' Liberal in politics, and was in favour of votes for women and home rule for Ireland. By the time he achieved office in 1916, the Liberal government of Asquith was giving way to the Lloyd George coalition and he moved steadily to the right, in line with changing government policy. In 1916 he became solicitor-general (and was knighted); he was made a member of the privy council in 1918; and he became attorney-general in 1919, with a seat in the cabinet from 1921. During these years he was offered both the Irish secretaryship and the home secretaryship. He stayed on as attorney-general since, at the time, it was presumed to give a right of reverter to the lord chief justiceship, and that latter office had always been his goal.

Hewart had wanted to become chief in 1921 when Lord Reading resigned. Lloyd George, however, was reluctant to lose his services. An unattractive device was resorted to under which A. T. Lawrence was created lord chief justice (Lord Trevethin) and required to furnish an undated letter of resignation. Even Lord Birkenhead—not a stranger to dubious intrigue—regarded the plan as 'illegal' and the judges were so offended they refused to attend Lord Reading's farewell ceremony. In 1922, as the government fell, Lord Trevethin read of his resignation in *The Times*.

Hewart was created Baron Hewart of Bury on 24 March 1922. His period as lord chief justice was not distinguished. It is true that, in the area of criminal law, he took a keen interest in the jury and in the nature of criminal prosecutions. Unfortunately, his behaviour as a judge lacked many basic judicial qualities. He made up his mind early and was frequently boorish and rude to counsel. Out of court, he extended his discourtesy to fellow members of the bench and to the lord chancellor and the members of his office. Hewart may well have been disappointed to discover how little power the lord chief justice actually had, but his feuds during the 1920s and 1930s became famous, as did his frequent changes in politics.

During the First World War, Hewart had been responsible for passing many functions to the executive which had previously belonged to the judiciary. As chief justice he sought to recover those powers. That was not all bad, as the judges of the 1980s and 1990s have shown. The problem was that Hewart lacked political judgement. Thus Sir Claud Schuster, permanent secretary to the Lord Chancellor's Office, wrote a memorandum to the Conservative lord chancellor Lord Hailsham in 1929 warning that:

> it is not too much to say that, in recent years, the weight of prejudice against the State in the minds of many members of the Court of Appeal and Judges of the High Court has been such as seriously to affect the Administration of Justice.

The more public political debates had begun a year earlier when Hewart had described as 'petty larceny' the government's refusal to create two more king's bench judges (Stevens, 30). In 1929 Hewart published a book, *The New Despotism*, vigorously attacking the growth of delegated legislation and quasi-judicial decision-making by the civil service. The government attempted to blunt the force of the book by establishing the Scott–Donoughmore committee which produced a politically powerful, albeit intellectually indefensible, report. While later in the century the book's arguments might have had the better of the day, its tone and the impact on the England of the day were almost wholly negative.

The atmosphere was not helped by Hewart's public utterances. Hewart took personally the establishment of the commission on the dispatch of business at the common law in 1934, claiming he had not been consulted. In fact, it appears, he had failed to read the appropriate correspondence. He took even greater umbrage with the

Gordon Hewart, first Viscount Hewart (1870–1943), by Sir Oswald Birley, 1935

Supreme Court of Judicature Bill of the same year. While it created new High Court judgeships, he felt parliament had been left with too much power in deciding when they might be filled. He also was upset, with more reason, by the arrangement for a presiding judge in the new panel of the Court of Appeal, but the reaction was again inappropriate. After a hastily called meeting of the judges, Hewart delivered an unprecedented speech in the House of Lords attacking the lord chancellor's permanent secretary and making a more veiled attack on Lord Chancellor Sankey. In addition to the litany of complaints, Hewart added the ministry of justice (which had not been seriously talked about since Haldane's day) as further evidence of the executive's plan to take over the judiciary. In a delayed debate Hailsham elegantly and Sankey (less so) defended the traditional view that, while ministers may be attacked, civil servants may not. The substantive arguments were also rejected. The whole episode was, however, sadly, typical of Hewart's infelicitous lack of judgement (Stevens, 35–9).

In the latter half of the 1930s Hewart was less publicly involved in controversy, partly because his health was poor, and partly because he was considering a return to politics. It was typical of his lack of good sense that he was surprised by the outcry when he was appointed as a member of a Liberal Party committee. After the death of his first wife the previous year, on 29 December 1934 he married Jean, daughter of James Reid Stewart of Wanganui, New Zealand; they had no children. In 1936 Hewart was busy plotting with Lloyd George about the Liberal return to power. By this time, he had decided that *The New Despotism* had been a mistake and, for the welfare state to succeed, civil servants needed wider discretion. Ironically, his undistinguished term, somewhat like that of his predecessor, came to an end in 1940 when he received a telephone call from 10 Downing Street asking for his resignation. The end says much about the England of the interwar years.

Despite the judgement of history, Hewart was showered with honours in his day. Honorary degrees were conferred on him by the universities of Manchester (1922), Oxford (1926), Toronto, Sheffield (1927), Birmingham (1928), and Witwatersrand (1936). He was elected an honorary fellow of his college in 1922. He became a bencher of the Inner Temple in 1917 and was treasurer in 1938. He died at his home, Garden Hill, Totteridge, Hertfordshire, on 5 May 1943. He had been advanced to a viscountcy on 1 November 1940, in which title he was succeeded by his surviving son, Hugh Vaughan Hewart (b. 1896).

ROBERT STEVENS

Sources R. Jackson, *The chief: the biography of Gordon Hewart, lord chief justice of England, 1922–40* (1959) · R. F. V. Heuston, *Lives of the lord chancellors, 1885–1940* (1964) · R. Stevens, *The independence of the judiciary: the view from the lord chancellor's office* (1993) · Burke, *Peerage* (1959) · *DNB* · *CGPLA Eng. & Wales* (1943)
Archives JRL, letters to *Manchester Guardian* · PRO, lord chancellor's office papers | Bodl. Oxf., letters to Lord Hanworth · Bodl. Oxf., corresp. with Lord Sankey · HLRO, corresp. with David Lloyd George

Likenesses J. St H. Lander, oils, *c*.1925, University College, Oxford · O. Birley, oils, 1935, NPG [*see illus.*] · G. C. Jennis, drawing, sketch, V&A · D. Low, cartoons, pencil drawings, NPG
Wealth at death £150,947 4s. 2d.: probate, 11 June 1943, *CGPLA Eng. & Wales*

Hewat, Alexander (1738/9?–1824?), Church of Scotland minister and historian, was probably born in or near Kelso. It is not known who his parents were. He was educated at Kelso grammar school and Edinburgh University. He emigrated to America in 1763 to serve as minister of the First Presbyterian or Scots church in Charles Town, South Carolina. He developed a close friendship with Governor William Bull II, and was admitted to the St Andrew's Society in November 1763. He probably meant to settle permanently, since he bought 1000 acres of land in 1772.

In 1775 all citizens of South Carolina were required to sign an association for the defence of the colony, but this did not demand explicit support for the revolutionary cause. The following summer, however, Hewat's congregation began to disperse after some members had been imprisoned for their loyalism, and on 3 August 1776 ministers were forbidden to continue praying for the king. Hewat merely changed the formula to pray for 'those in Lawful authority over us'. Finally it was demanded that he should clearly renounce his loyalty to the king. He refused to do so, and was given sixty days to depart or be imprisoned. He sailed for London in summer 1777, where he was awarded a temporary pension of £100 p.a.

In 1779 Hewat published in London *An Historical Account of the Rise and Progress of the Colonies of South Carolina and Georgia*, concentrating largely on South Carolinan society in 1700–40. Although considerably flawed because of Hewat's lack of access to vital sources, all subsequent works depended on it until the twentieth century. Through his often passionate criticisms of slavery and defence of loyalism Hewat intended his *Account* to provide moral and political guidance for those who wished to preserve South Carolina's close ties with the British monarchy. Edinburgh University awarded him a DD on 12 July 1780. By this time Charles Town had been recaptured by British forces, and Hewat prepared to return in summer 1781; but he changed his mind when he learned that his congregation was still scattered. Instead he served in the gospel mission in London. He claimed £3500 in compensation for his property in America in 1785, but this was eventually disallowed, and he had to be content with an allowance of £120 p.a. from 1788. He was invited to help William Robertson select a new minister for the Charles Town (now Charleston) congregation in 1792, but he declined on account of his practical and emotional distance from Edinburgh. He published three fast day sermons between 1795 and 1797, and two volumes of sermons in 1803–5.

At some time after he settled in London, Hewat married Mrs Eliza Barksdale, or Barkside, a widow from Charles Town who had come to England for her children's health. She died on 18 April 1814. Hewat himself probably died on 3 March 1824, leaving a legacy of £50 to the Scots church in Charles Town.

EMMA VINCENT MACLEOD

Sources G. M. Meroney, 'Alexander Hewat's "Historical account"', *The colonial legacy*, ed. L. H. Leder, 1: *Loyalist historians* (New York, 1971), 135–63 · E. D. Johnson, 'Alexander Hewat: South Carolina's first historian', *Journal of Southern History*, 20 (1954), 50–62 · S. Herstad, 'Hewat, Alexander', *ANB* · G. Palmer, *Biographical sketches of loyalists of the American revolution* (1984) · W. B. Sprague, *Annals of the American pulpit*, 3 (1859) · *Fasti Scot.*, new edn, 7.663 · E. McCrady, *The history of South Carolina under the proprietary government, 1670–1719* (1897) · E. McCrady, *The history of South Carolina under the royal government, 1719–1776* (1899) · H. E. Egerton, ed., *The royal commission on the losses and services of American loyalists, 1783 to 1785. Being the notes of Mr Daniel Parker Coke, M.P.* (1915) · *GM*, 1st ser., 84/1 (1814), 517 · J. H. Easterby, *History of St. Andrew's Society of Charleston, South Carolina, 1729–1929* (1929)
Likenesses portrait, repro. in *The centennial celebration of the dedication of the First Presbyterian Church, Charleston, South Carolina* (1915), 118
Wealth at death £50 legacy to First Presbyterian church, Charleston: Sprague, *Annals*, 252

Hewer, Dorothy Gertrude (1888–1948). *See under* Grieve, Sophia Emma Magdalene (*b.* 1858, *d.* after 1933).

Hewer [Ewers], **William** (1642–1715), naval administrator, was born in the parish of St Sepulchre, Holborn, on 17 November 1642, the eldest son of Thomas Hewer (*d.* 1665), stationer, and Anne Blackborne (*d.* after 1679), sister of Robert Blackborne, navy and admiralty secretary during the Commonwealth and subsequently secretary of the East India Company. It was at Blackborne's prompting that on 18 July 1660 the new clerk of the acts, Samuel Pepys, took on Hewer as his clerk in the Navy Office and as a domestic employee. The relationship with Pepys would mature into professional collaboration and lifelong friendship. In the early days Hewer was occasionally rebuked for small failings in dress and drink, but was soon the trusted aide and favoured companion of Pepys and his wife, Elizabeth. His private resources—derived at first from his uncle but greatly augmented by his own efforts—ensured his independence and from 1663 he set up in his own lodgings. He later gave Elizabeth an ornament worth £40 when his official salary was only £30 p.a. Pepys defended him against accusations of leaking office secrets and incivility to a bishop. In 1668 there was an awkward but inconclusive charge of corrupt dealing in naval supplies. In the same year Hewer competently mediated between Pepys and Elizabeth when their marriage was troubled. Hewer himself claimed preference for bachelorhood when Pepys offered him the hand of his sister Paulina; he remained true to his profession.

When Pepys moved to the Admiralty at midsummer 1673 he took Hewer with him as clerk; he became chief clerk in the following year. Hewer's private trading with the East India Company is recorded from 1669. By 1674 he was advancing finance for naval shipbuilding and by 1675 his fortune was reckoned at £16,500. In August that year he accompanied Sir Anthony Deane to deliver yachts to the French court; during the Popish Plot it was alleged that on this visit he had passed naval secrets to his hosts. Hewer made a counter-accusation against the informant John Scott for betraying military information. Since 1677 Hewer had been deputy judge-advocate of the fleet and a member of the Royal Fishery Company. In 1680 he succeeded Pepys as treasurer of Tangier and in 1683–4 took part in the mission to disband the colony. He and Pepys also paid a private visit to Spain. In 1684 Hewer became an assistant of the Clothworkers' Company, serving as master in 1686–7. In 1685 he was elected MP for Yarmouth, Isle of Wight; his parliamentary activities (including membership of a dozen committees) earned him the recommendation of James II for return in 1688 for the parliament that never met. On 31 January 1686 he was named an inaugural member of the Shipwrights' Company of Rotherhithe. On 17 April he was appointed a special commissioner of the navy with responsibility for accounts. From 12 October 1688 he and Deane were retained to wind up the affairs of the 1686 Admiralty commission. He declined the king's suggestion, underwritten by Pepys, that he and Deane should continue the same work indefinitely as 'inspectors' on the French model. The administrative framework was, he believed, already adequately in place. All that was needed was 'industry and knowledge' in its operation (Magd. Cam., Pepys Library, MS 1490, p. 384); Hewer had demonstrated his qualifications in both these respects. In 1687–9 he sat on the commission of the peace for several counties. The revolution of 1688 ended his public career. He declined the oath to William and Mary, and was penally taxed. On 4 May 1689 he was arrested, together with Pepys and Deane, on suspicion of treason; he was released uncharged six weeks later. In November 1692 the public accounts committee exonerated him of mismanagement in the previous reign, and he continued to defend the work of the 1686 commission. He remained a successful businessman. In April 1689 his East India Company stock was £3500; by 1702 he was worth £24,000. He was deputy governor of the old company in 1704–6 and 1708–9, and a director of the successor body in 1709–13. In 1701 he received a public pension for past service. On 15 August 1702 he was named a deputy lieutenant of Surrey.

In 1677 Hewer had moved to York Buildings, Westminster. Pepys came to live there in 1680 and from 1685 was householder, with Hewer his occasional guest. Hewer, meanwhile, had acquired an interest in a handsome house on the north side of Clapham Common, built in 1660 by Sir Denis Gauden, the navy victualler. Hewer secured the property in 1688 and filled it with 'Indys & Chineze curiositys' (Evelyn, 5.427). Here Pepys came to live in his old age and to die in 1703. From then until 1724 Pepys's library was housed there. Hewer was Pepys's executor, and Pepys's heir later married the sister of Hewer's heir, Hewer Edgley Hewer. William Hewer, who had lived 'very handsomly and friendly to every body' (ibid., 5.111) and who had in particular assisted Pepys's wayward in-laws, was a benefactor to the school, church, and parish of Clapham. He died at his house there on 3 December 1715 and was buried in the church, where a memorial was erected. C. S. KNIGHTON

Sources Pepys, *Diary* · Evelyn, *Diary*, 4.176, n. 1; 5.111 · P. Watson, 'Hewer, William', HoP, *Commons, 1660–90*, 2.542 · J. M. Collinge, *Navy Board officials, 1660–1832* (1978), 4, 110 · J. C. Sainty, ed., *Admiralty officials, 1660–1870* (1975), 131 · B. Pool, *Navy board contracts, 1660–*

1832 (1966), 14–19 • P. Norman, 'Pepys and Hewer', *Occasional papers … of … the Samuel Pepys Club*, 2 (1925), 53–77 • E. B. Sainsbury, ed., *A calendar of the court minutes … of the East India Company*, 11 vols. (1907–38), vol. 8, p. 164; vol. 9, pp. 113, 298; vol. 11, p.154 • *CSP dom.*, 1667, 1; 1675–6, 252; 1682, 211; 1686–7, 21; 1687–9, 276; 1689–90, 90; 1702–3, 393 • BL, Add. MS 22185, fol. 14 • BL, Add. MS 38871, fols. 13v, 14v, 15v–16, 17r–v • will, 9 Sept 1715, PRO, PROB 11/549, fols. 229–32 • Magd. Cam., Pepys Library, MS 1490, pp. 378–9, 383–6, 415–18, 431–5 • H. T. Heath, ed., *The letters of Samuel Pepys and his family circle* (1955) • H. B. Wheatley, *Pepysiana* (1899)

Archives Harvard U., Houghton L., diary fragments, MS Eng. 991.1 • Magd. Cam. • PRO, SP Dom. and Adm. classes

Likenesses G. Kneller, oils, NMM

Wealth at death see will, 9 Sept 1715, PRO, PROB 11/549, fols. 229–32

Hewes, George Robert Twelves (1742–1840), cordwainer and revolutionary activist in America, was born on 25 August 1742 at the sign of the Bull's Head and Horns, Water Street, Boston, Massachusetts, the sixth of nine children of George Hewes (1701–1749), tallow chandler and erstwhile tanner, and his wife, Abigail Seaver (1711–c.1755). His father was descended from a migrant to Massachusetts from Wales. His uncommon third forename, Twelves, most likely honoured the maiden name of his mother's grandmother. He was from a family of artisans and farmers; his brothers also entered the lower trades. His 'whole education', he told a biographer, 'consisted only of a moderate knowledge of reading and writing' (Hawkes, 17–18) which he received at the local common school. Orphaned at an early age and uncommonly short (he was 5 feet 1 inch when fully grown), he was apprenticed to a shoemaker and eventually opened a small shop near Griffin's Wharf where he made and mended shoes. In January 1768 he married Sarah Sumner (c.1751–1828), a washerwoman, with whom he had fifteen children, eleven of whom survived childhood. Never prosperous, in 1770 he was imprisoned briefly for a small debt. Hewes is known to history because in the 1830s, when he was in his nineties and the traditions of the American revolution were being recovered, he was thought to be one of the last survivors of the Boston Tea Party and became the subject of two memoirs. One biographer found his memory 'so extraordinary' that at times it 'absolutely astonished' him (Thatcher, 250).

Hewes was aroused to activism in 1768 by the presence of British soldiers in Boston and was present at the Boston massacre (5 March 1770), at which crowd agitation provoked British troops into firing into a crowd, and a victim of the soldiers' fire fell into his arms. He was one of a large number of self-invited participants in the Boston Tea Party (16 December 1773) who had time only to blacken their faces with soot and was active, he insisted, side by side with the wealthy patriot merchant John Hancock. In January 1774, in the course of protecting a boy from a beating by John Malcolm, a customs official, Hewes was wounded; this precipitated the tarring and feathering of Malcolm, a riveting event dramatized in London caricatures. In these and other street events Hewes was not a member of any organization but responded to grievances felt by the mechanic classes. An article signed 'Crispin' which began 'I am a shoemaker, a citizen, a free man and a

freeholder' (*Massachusetts Spy*, 16 Jan 1772) expressed Hewes's spirit. He attended town meetings only after patriot leaders opened them to 'the whole body of the people', bringing in lower tradesmen and journeymen.

When war broke out Hewes took his family to rural Wrentham, south of Boston. Between 1776 and 1781 he served four stints in the militia and two as a seaman on a privateering vessel in a fruitless quest for wealth. His shoemaker's shop in Boston destroyed, he continued his trade in Wrentham and raised a large family, some of whom migrated in search of opportunity. At the start of the Anglo-American War in 1812 Hewes, at the age of seventy, allegedly made several unsuccessful attempts to enlist. After the war he and his wife moved to Richfield Springs in Otsego county, New York, joining several children. In 1832 the federal government rewarded him with a pension for nine of his twenty months of revolutionary military service. In 1834 James Hawkes, a former democratic congressman, discovered him, taking down his life story, partly in his own words. In 1835 he was invited back to Boston where he was the guest of honour at the city's Fourth of July festivity, the subject of a three-quarter-length oil portrait by Joseph G. Cole entitled *The Centenarian*, and the subject of a second memoir by Benjamin Bussey Thatcher, a whig lawyer who treated him condescendingly as one of 'the humble classes', and masked his militancy. Hewes, who believed he was ninety-nine (although he was only ninety-three), was celebrated for his longevity and his remarkable memory, and as one of the last survivors of the Tea Party, an event conservative élites were then appropriating to counter claims of mechanic participation made by radical journeymen trade unionists. He returned to Richfield Springs, where he died on 5 November 1840, aged ninety-eight, after an accident while on the way to an Independence day celebration. He was buried in Richfield Springs Presbyterian cemetery; in 1896 his remains were reinterred in the Grand Army of the Republic plot in the town's Lakeview cemetery.

Hewes's memories reveal a man transformed by his experiences in the American revolution to active citizenship and a sense of his personal worth. He remembered the war as a moment when he could claim to being the equal of his betters. In the recent historical recovery of ordinary people of the era, Hewes has received recognition from scholars. In Boston his portrait has been hung prominently in the Old State House and a mannequin created for an exhibit in the Old South Meeting-House, scene of the mass meetings in which he took part.

ALFRED F. YOUNG

Sources A citizen of New York [J. Hawkes], *A retrospect of the Boston Tea Party, with a memoir of George R. T. Hewes* (1834) • A Bostonian [B. B. Thatcher], *Traits of the Tea Party: being a memoir of George R. T. Hewes* (1835) • E. Putnam, ed., *Lieutenant Joshua Hewes: a New England pioneer and some of his descendants* (1913) • National Archives, Washington, DC, military service records, pension application no. 14748 • A. F. Young, *The shoemaker and the Tea Party: memory and the American Revolution* (1999) • D. Hoerder, *Crowd action in revolutionary Massachusetts, 1765–1780* (1977)

Likenesses J. G. Cole, oils, 1835, Bostonian Society, Boston, Massachusetts

Hewetson, Christopher (1737/8–1798), sculptor, was born at Thomastown, co. Kilkenny, Ireland, the son of Christopher Hewetson JP (d. 1744) and his second wife, Elizabeth, daughter of Thomas Hewetson of Cloughsutton, co. Carlow. The Hewetson family can be traced back to Christopher Hewetson, an Elizabethan gentleman who settled in Ireland. His son, also Christopher, was MP for Swords, 1642–61, and served Charles I during the civil war, for which he was awarded a grant of the watermills, fairs, and markets at Thomastown, co. Kilkenny, and 500 acres in 1666. The Hewetsons continued in public service: Christopher Hewetson's father served as a lieutenant in the troop of horse before becoming justice of the peace for co. Kilkenny. The death of Hewetson's father in June 1744 seems to have precipitated a decline in the family's fortunes, and the family estate was inherited by Amyas Hewetson, Christopher's half-brother from his father's first marriage to Eleanor Bushe. In September 1745 Christopher Hewetson enrolled at Kilkenny College, giving his age as eight years. His uncle, the Revd Thomas Hewetson, was master at the college, which may explain the privileged education despite the financial problems within the family. He is said to have then studied under John van Nost the younger (c.1712–1780), the leading monumental sculptor in Dublin at the time. Nothing more is known of his early training.

Hewetson is recorded as arriving at Rome in 1765 with the American painter Henry Benbridge (1743–1812). He was to remain in the city until his death, leaving only for brief visits to Naples in 1766 and 1797. With the assistance of Thomas Jenkins, by then established as the most influential art dealer and agent active within the British community at Rome, Hewetson attracted the patronage of the most fashionable and famous British and Irish grand tourists. His earliest busts included Charles Townley (1769; BM), Frederick Hervey, bishop of Derry and earl of Bristol (c.1770; NPG), and Sir Watkin Williams Wynn (1769; NG Ire.). His terracotta portrait of the duke of Gloucester was reported in the London press (*London Chronicle*). The bust is now in the Royal Collection at Windsor. These early pieces exhibit the highly refined technique, and the naturalistic treatment of the sitters' features within a classical format, that were hallmarks of his work.

In 1771 Hewetson received the commission for his best-known work, the monument to Provost Baldwin for the examination hall of Trinity College, Dublin. This occupied him for twelve years, and the monument was finally erected in Dublin in 1784, having been exhibited in Rome the previous year. This was the sculptor's only large-scale monument. During these years, Hewetson's reputation as a maker of portrait busts rose among a truly international clientele, which included the papal authorities. His most notable commissions included the monument to Cardinal Giambattista Rezzonico (1783–6; San Nicolo in Carcere, Rome) and portrait busts of Pope Clement XIV (the earliest version, dated 1771, at Beningbrough Hall, Yorkshire), the Spanish ambassador Don José Nicolas de Azara y Perera (1779; Bibliothèque Mazarine, Paris), and the Scottish painter Gavin Hamilton (1784; Glasgow University). In 1786 he exhibited the bust of Hamilton at the Royal Academy in London, and in 1790 he exhibited a bust of 'A Nobleman' at the same institution. The bust of Hamilton appears in the portrait of Hewetson by Sefano Tofanelli (Wallraf Richartz Museum, Cologne).

Although at first considered a serious rival to Antonio Canova (1757–1822), who started working in Rome in 1779 and quickly became the most acclaimed sculptor of the period, Hewetson's practice seems to have declined in later years. In 1789–90 he produced a colossal marble bust of Leibniz (Leibniz Haus, Hanover) and he received commissions from Prince Augustus and Frederick Hervey, now fourth earl of Bristol, in the 1790s. He continued to play an active part in Rome's artistic community, signing the letter of thanks addressed to Prince Augustus by British artists in Rome in 1794, following his part in arranging tax relief for artists' imports into Britain. His name appears in the lists of artists circulated in Rome at the time. In 1796 he was commissioned by Lord Bristol to produce a statue of William Pitt, Lord Chatham. This was never completed. With the threatened invasion of Rome by the French, Hewetson fled to Naples in June 1797 where he enjoyed the protection of Sir William and Emma Hamilton. He returned to Rome at the end of that year and died there in 1798. He was recorded as a bachelor at death and was buried near the tomb of Caius Cestius at Rome.

MARTIN MYRONE

Sources T. W. I. Hodgkinson, 'Christopher Hewetson, an Irish sculptor in Rome', *Walpole Society*, 34 (1952–4), 42–54 · B. de Breffny, 'Christopher Hewetson', *Irish Arts Review*, 3/3 (1986), 52–75 · J. Ingamells, ed., *A dictionary of British and Irish travellers in Italy, 1701–1800* (1997) · R. Gunnis, *Dictionary of British sculptors, 1660–1851* (1953); new edn (1968) · W. G. Strickland, *A dictionary of Irish artists*, 2 vols. (1913) · *London Chronicle* (30 April–2 May 1772)
Likenesses S. Tofanelli, oils, c.1790, Wallraf-Richartz-Museum, Cologne · attrib. H. Benbridge, pencil drawing, priv. coll.

Hewett, Sir George, first baronet (1750–1840), army officer, was born on 11 June 1750, the only son of Major Shuckburgh Hewett (1719–1759), a descendant of an old Leicestershire family, and his wife, Ann Ward; both his parents died when he was young. He was sent to the grammar school at Wimborne, Dorset, and in 1761 was entered as a cadet at the Royal Military Academy, Woolwich. On 27 April 1762 he was given an ensigncy in the 70th foot, whose colonel, Cyrus Trapaud, had served with his father. On 20 April 1764 he was promoted lieutenant and joined his regiment in Grenada where he commanded a detachment and two howitzers. In 1771 he was sent to New York with invalids and to recruit, and was brigade-major of the troops sent to St Vincent during the Carib uprising of 1772. Returning to England with his regiment in 1774, he obtained his company (the grenadiers) on 2 June 1775, and went with the corps to Halifax, Nova Scotia, whence he was detached with his company to Long Island. In 1780 he served as part of the 2nd battalion of grenadiers at the siege of Charles Town. His company afterwards embarked as marines on board Admiral Digby's flagship, in which Prince William, afterwards William IV, was serving as a midshipman. He obtained a majority by purchase in the

43rd foot on 1 December 1781 and, as deputy quartermaster-general, accompanied a brigade of reinforcements under General O'Hara to the West Indies. He returned to New York after Rodney's defeat of the French fleet at the battle of the Saints (12 April 1782) and commanded the 2nd battalion of grenadiers until invalided home. While convalescing in Bath he met and married, on 26 July 1785, Julia (1761–1848), daughter of John Johnson of Blackheath; they had five sons and six daughters.

In 1786, when the 43rd were stationed at Windsor, George III inspected them and Hewett received praise for their appearance. Through the king's intervention he became lieutenant-colonel of the 43rd in October 1787 and, in 1791, when commanding his regiment there, adjutant-general in Ireland, a post which he held until 1799. In 1794 he raised an Irish regiment, numbered the 92nd, which was drafted soon after. He became a major-general on 3 May 1796. He established a permanent commissariat staff in Ireland, and is credited with originating the idea of a brigade of instruction in light duties, the command of which was given to John Moore. In August 1799 he became both head of the recruiting department, with a district command at Chatham and Maidstone, and colonel-commandant of the 2nd battalion of the 5th foot. In 1801 the headquarters of the recruiting department were moved from Chatham to Parkhurst, Isle of Wight, and Hewett was appointed to command the island as part of the south-western district. He was transferred to the colonelcy of the 61st foot, on 4 April 1800. In 1803 he was made inspector-general of the royal army of reserve, and in November 1804 barrackmaster-general. In 1806 he was appointed commander-in-chief in the East Indies, sailing on 17 April 1807 and landing in India on 17 October. In May 1809 he had to take over the government of India in Calcutta while the governor-general dealt with the mutiny among the company's officers in Madras. He set up commissariat departments in each presidency, encouraged the building of cantonments, and reorganized the staff of the Madras army. In 1810–11 he organized the dispatch from India of the expeditions against Bourbon (Réunion), the Isle of France (Mauritius), and Java. He left India on 18 December 1811 and reached Lymington, Hampshire, on 12 May 1812.

Hewett was promoted full general in June 1813, created a baronet on 6 November 1813, and the following month became commander of the forces in Ireland, being sworn of the Irish privy council on arrival. He left Ireland in 1816, and was created a GCB on 16 May 1820. In 1823 he purchased Freemantle Park, near Southampton, and settled there. He had expressed a particular desire to see the 61st, of which he had been colonel for forty years, on its return from Ceylon, but he died suddenly at his home on the day the regiment landed at Southampton, 21 March 1840. He was buried in Shirley church, near Southampton, and a monument was erected to him in the adjacent parish church of Millbrook. He was described as a tall, soldierly old man, much beloved in private life.

H. M. CHICHESTER, rev. PETER B. BOYDEN

Sources Private record of the life of the Right Honourable General Sir George Hewett (1840) · R. G. A. Levinge, Historical records of the forty-third regiment, Monmouthshire light infantry (1868) · H. W. Pearse, History of the 31st foot, Huntingdonshire regiment—70th foot—Surrey regiment, 1 (1916) · Burke, Peerage (1978) · GM, 2nd ser., 14 (1840), 539 · GM, 2nd ser., 29 (1848), 328 · Lord Minto in India: life and letters of Gilbert Elliot, first earl of Minto, from 1807 to 1814, ed. E. E. E. Elliot-Murray-Kynynmound (1880), 226
Archives NAM, corresp. and papers relating to Ireland | BL, letters to Sir Robert Peel, Add. MSS 40233–40244 · NA Scot., letters to Sir Alexander Hope · NA Scot., corresp. with first earl of Minto
Likenesses portrait, c.1811, Calcutta town hall · S. W. Reynolds senior and S. Cousins, mezzotint, 1820 (after S. W. Reynolds junior), BM, NAM · portrait

Hewett, Sir John Prescott (1854–1941), administrator in India, was born at Barham, Kent, on 25 August 1854, the eldest son of John Hewett (1830/31–1911), vicar of Babbacombe, Torquay, and his wife, Anna Louisa Lyster, daughter of Captain William Hammon of the East India Company's navy. He was educated at Winchester College and at Balliol College, Oxford, where he passed the Indian Civil Service examination in 1875. In 1877 he was posted to the North-Western Provinces and for four years served as an assistant magistrate and collector in Agra, Bulandshahr, and Mathura. On 18 December 1879 he married Ethel Charlotte (d. 1945), second daughter of Henry Binny Webster of the Bengal civil service; they had three children.

By 1881 Hewett was worn down by fever and was relieved to be posted to the foothills as assistant commissioner of the Tarai; there, in the Himalayan jungles, he recovered his health and engaged in a passionate pursuit of tigers, often fitting in big-game shoots by rising at 4 a.m. to clear his official work. Hewett was an ambitious man, keen to rise above the ruck of the civil service. In 1883–4 he was placed in charge of the Provincial Gazetteer of the North Western Provinces and Oudh, to which he contributed chapters on Jaunpur and Fatehpur, and in 1886, following a stint as junior secretary to the provincial board of revenue, he was appointed under-secretary to the government of India's home department. He was promoted deputy secretary in 1890 and secretary in mid-1894, serving between these posts as secretary to the royal commission on opium (1893–4). For a year from October 1898 he was on deputation in India and England as a member of the Indian plague commission.

Lord Curzon, viceroy from 1899 to 1905, had some reservations about Hewett's character: 'an able, plausible, self-seeking, not too loyal, individual, who plays for his own hand' (Curzon to Lord George Hamilton, 7 Feb 1901, BL OIOC, MS Eur. F111/160, fol. 38). Nevertheless, in 1902 he decided to try Hewett out as the officiating chief commissioner of the Central Provinces and was pleasantly surprised by his administrative ability and efficiency. Hewett was very happy in the Central Provinces. He toured widely, especially in the famine-stricken eastern districts, and took a particular interest in education, industry, and agricultural innovation. There is no doubting, however, that his love of hunting helped to keep him on tour.

In 1904 Curzon persuaded a reluctant secretary of state

Sir John Prescott Hewett (1854–1941), by Walter Stoneman, 1918

to sanction the creation of a new department of commerce and industry with a chief who would sit on the executive council. Hewett was delighted to be given the job and, as Curzon had intended, travelled all over India assessing what incentives were needed to foster new industries, including the Tata steel processing experiments at Jamshedpur in Orissa. He consistently argued for protective tariffs for indigenous industry and in later years complained that the government's miserliness had severely hampered India's economic growth.

In 1907 Hewett was knighted and appointed lieutenant-governor of his old province, by then renamed the United Provinces of Agra and Oudh. His first task was to assess the province's commercial capacity and, through the medium of the annual industrial conference which in 1907 was held at Naini Tal, he proposed radical increases in government spending on industry, but Lord Minto, Curzon's successor, would not provide the necessary funds. Hewett did get money for an agricultural college at Cawnpore, and in 1910 he organized a trade and agriculture exhibition at Allahabad modelled on Europe's big empire exhibitions.

Hewett's interest in vocational education stemmed in part from his political conservatism. Believing that Britain had a duty to protect India's peasant millions from the Western-educated professional men who dominated the new mouthpiece of Indian political aspirations, the Indian National Congress, he much preferred vocational training to liberal education modelled on Western lines.

He doubted that Indians could ever make sound civil servants and on a visit to London in 1906 did his best to persuade John Morley, the secretary of state, that he was moving too fast on political reform. When Morley refused to sanction money for a technological college in Allahabad, Hewett was convinced that, in putting political reform before industrial progress, Morley had completely misunderstood India's needs. As terrorism flared in the wake of Curzon's inflammatory partition of Bengal (1905), Hewett wrote doom-laden letters to friends complaining of weak leadership and the demoralization of the civil service. In his administration of the United Provinces this gloom bore fruit in an ominous surveillance of the press, public meetings, and political associations, and in a clumsy attempt to separate the young Muslim League from Aligarh College, the premier institution of higher education for Indian Muslims. Hewett was worried that the largely loyalist constituency of Aligarh might be infected by the untested politics of the Muslim League, and in 1910 he pressured the League into shifting its headquarters to Lucknow. It was a short-sighted move. At Aligarh an older, more conservative form of Muslim politics prevailed, but at Lucknow young Muslim lawyers, more inclined to radicalism and to co-operate with the Indian National Congress, soon captured the League's leadership.

In early 1911 Hewett was relieved from his gubernatorial duties to arrange the coronation durbar of George V and Queen Mary at Delhi at the end of the year. His creation of a tent city housing 200,000 people, spread over 25 square miles, was an organizational marvel and won him promotion to GCSI, but it was not all smooth sailing and he briefly tendered his resignation when Lord Hardinge insisted on some last-minute changes.

In 1912 Hewett retired and returned to Britain. He became chairman of several tea and rubber companies in Assam, and of the North Borneo, Hyderabad Deccan, and Russo-Caucasian companies. From 1914 he chaired the Indian Soldiers' Fund committee (for which he was made KBE in 1917), and presided over Lady Lansdowne's Officers' Families Fund. He was active in hospital work through the order of St John of Jerusalem, and was the founder chairman of the governing body of the School of Oriental and African Studies.

Throughout the First World War, Hewett kept a wary eye on the proposals for political reform in India. Lord Montagu, the secretary of state, and Lord Chelmsford, the viceroy, both knew him to be flirting with Lord Sydenham's ultra-conservative Indo-British Association which opposed their scheme of dyarchy (responsible government at the provincial level with strong British control at the centre), but they trusted that he would avoid embarrassing the government. They were to be disappointed. In September 1918 the War Office dispatched Hewett to Mesopotamia to report on the financial implications of transfer from military to civilian rule; once out of Montagu's reach, Hewett took the chance to speak out against the reforms to a publicly advertised meeting of army officers in Baghdad. Montagu was incensed and refused to have any further informal meetings with him—a reaction which may have toned down Hewett's opposition, for he accepted the result gracefully when the reforms were passed by parliament. He had a brief parliamentary career himself, being elected as the Unionist candidate for Luton in 1922, but he lost the seat a year later. With age, his political stance mellowed. He returned frequently to India on business and hunting trips, and in March 1930 he wrote to *The Times* declaring himself astonished at the pace of change in India and appealing for trust in the judgement of Lord Irwin, the viceroy. He was critical of the India Act of 1935 but refused to join the India Defence League, the 1930s equivalent of Lord Sydenham's old organization. By then he had largely accepted the inevitability of Indian self-rule.

A solid, heavy-jowled man, known to friends as Jack, Hewett looked the very essence of a colonial administrator. In private he was a strong, often despairing, critic of political opponents, but he enjoyed a reputation for generous and cordial hospitality. In 1938 he relived the deaths of many unfortunate tigers in a memoir entitled *Jungle Trails in Northern India*, a chatty volume which is curious for its exceedingly peripheral references to his wife. Lord Curzon had once complained that Hewett's domestic history was not edifying, and it is possible that it was Hewett's younger daughter, Lorna, who acted as his chief companion. Lorna, who was widowed in the First World War, features in *Jungle Trails* as an intrepid hunter in her own right and also for an unchaperoned trek she undertook to Ladakh in 1921. Hewett died on 27 September 1941 at his home, The Court House, at Chipping Warden, near Banbury, and was buried at Chipping Warden on 1 October. Lady Hewett died in 1945. Of their two other children, Mabel Ada married Brigadier-General Anthony Courage and their son, Bunty, joined the firm of Messrs Andrew Yule & Co. in Calcutta.   KATHERINE PRIOR

Sources M. N. Das, *India under Morley and Minto* (1964) · *List of the private secretaries to the governors-general and viceroys from 1774 to 1908* (1908) · *The Times* (30 Sept 1941), 1, 9 · *The Times* (8 March 1930), 13 · BL OIOC, Curzon MSS · BL OIOC, Chelmsford MSS, MS Eur. E. 264 · BL OIOC, Erle Richards MSS · B. C. Busch, *Hardinge of Penshurst* (1980) · C. A. Bayly, *The local roots of Indian politics: Allahabad, 1880–1920* (1975) · F. Robinson, *Separatism among Indian Muslims: the politics of the United Provinces' Muslims, 1860–1923* (1974) · Foster, *Alum. Oxon.* · ecclesiastical records, BL OIOC · J. B. Wainewright, ed., *Winchester College, 1836–1906: a register* (1907) · *DNB* · Venn, *Alum. Cant.*
Archives Bodl. Oxf., 'Some impressions about Mesopotamia' | BL OIOC, Chelmsford MSS · BL OIOC, Curzon MSS · BL OIOC, corresp. with Sir Henry Richards, MSS Eur F122 · Bodl. Oxf., letters to Lord Kimberley · CUL, corresp. with Lord Hardinge, etc.
Likenesses W. Stoneman, photograph, 1918, NPG [*see illus.*] · photograph, repro. in *The Times* (30 Sept 1941)
Wealth at death £19,950 4s. 7d.: probate, 1 May 1942, *CGPLA Eng. & Wales*

Hewett, Sir Prescott Gardner, first baronet (1812–1891), surgeon, son of William N. W. Hewett of Bilham Hall, near Doncaster, was born on 3 July 1812. Hewett was educated in Paris, where he studied painting, though subsequently he abandoned the idea of following art as a profession, turning his attention to medicine instead. While in Paris,

Hewett also studied anatomy at the École de Médecine and became thoroughly grounded in the principles and practice of French surgery. After his return to England he was admitted a member of the Royal College of Surgeons, on 15 July 1836, and he worked for a while as demonstrator of anatomy at the school of anatomy in Little Windmill Street, London. His excellent dissections attracted the attention of Sir Benjamin Brodie, who soon offered Hewett the post of demonstrator of anatomy at St George's Hospital, when Hewett was on the point of accepting a commission in the service of the East India Company. Hewett accepted the post at St George's, where his half-brother Cornwallis Hewett, Downing professor of physic at Cambridge, had served as physician from 1825 to 1833. Hewett became curator of the museum at St George's Hospital towards the end of 1840. He was appointed lecturer on anatomy in 1845, and on 4 February 1848 he was elected assistant surgeon to the hospital; he became full surgeon on 21 June 1861 and consulting surgeon on 12 February 1875. On 13 September 1849 Hewett married Sarah Cowell (d. 1874), eldest daughter of the Revd Joseph Cowell of Todmorden, Lancashire; they had one son, Harry Hammerton Hewett (1853–1891), who survived him only a few weeks, and two daughters.

At the Royal College of Surgeons of England, Hewett was elected a fellow on 11 December 1843. He was Arris and Gale professor of human anatomy and physiology (1854–9), a member of the council (1867–83), chairman of the board of examiners in midwifery (1875), vice-president (1874 and 1875), and president (1876). In 1863 Hewett was elected president of the Pathological Society of London, and in 1873 he was elected president of the Clinical Society. On 4 June 1874 he was chosen a fellow of the Royal Society.

Hewett was appointed surgeon-extraordinary to the queen in 1867, serjeant-surgeon-extraordinary in 1877, and serjeant-surgeon in 1884. He also held the appointment from 1875 of surgeon to the prince of Wales. He was made a baronet on 6 August 1883. He then retired to Horsham, Sussex, where he devoted much of his time to watercolour painting and to country pursuits, though he still paid occasional visits to London for professional purposes. His collection of watercolour drawings was presented to the nation, and was exhibited at the South Kensington Museum in 1891. Hewett exhibited sixteen landscape watercolours at the Old Watercolour Society and four landscapes at the Grosvenor Gallery, London. His watercolour of Newquay Bay, Cornwall, was acquired by the Tate Gallery. Hewett died on 19 June 1891 at his home, Chestnut Lodge, Horsham.

Contemporaries admired Hewett for both his teaching and surgical abilities. He first became known in professional circles, as one of the most able anatomists, skilful organizers, and best lecturers in London; the general public came to consider him an accomplished surgeon. He also published numerous papers on hernia, aneurysm, injuries of the head, and pyaemia, in the journals of the various societies to which he belonged. The results of his most valuable work on the injuries and surgical diseases of the head are embodied in his article, 'Injuries of the head', in T. Holmes's *System of Surgery* (4 vols., 1860–64).

D'A. POWER, *rev.* JEFFREY S. REZNICK

Sources *BMJ* (27 June 1891), 1410–11 · *The Lancet* (27 June 1891) · Burke, *Peerage* · *CGPLA Eng. & Wales* (1891) · private information (1901) · *Medico-Chirurgical Transactions*, 75 (1892) · *St George' Hospital Gazette*, 3 (1895) · Wood, *Vic. painters*, 2nd edn · V. G. Plarr, *Plarr's Lives of the fellows of the Royal College of Surgeons of England*, rev. D'A. Power, 2 vols. (1930)
Likenesses W. Ouless, oils, St George's Hospital, London
Wealth at death £45,133 14*s.* 6*d.*: probate, 29 July 1891, *CGPLA Eng. & Wales*

Hewett, Sir Thomas (1656–1726), architect and landowner, was born on 9 September 1656, eldest son of William Hewett, landowner, and Anne, daughter of Sir Richard Prince. After schooling at Shrewsbury School and Christ Church, Oxford, he travelled extensively on the continent, visiting France, the Netherlands, Switzerland, Italy, and Germany. He returned accompanied by 'a wife, atheism, and many eccentricities' (Holland, 175–7). His wife, whom he married in Geneva on 7 September 1689, was Frances (*c.*1668–1756), daughter of Richard Bettenson of Scadbury, Kent. Hewett's letters reveal a secretive and cantankerous streak: he was said to have disinherited his only daughter when she ran off with a local fortune-teller. The family estate at Shireoaks, where he laid out extensive ornamental grounds, was on the borders of Nottinghamshire and Yorkshire. At the death of Hewett's wife it passed to his godson John Thornhagh, who took the name Hewett.

A staunch whig, Hewett was a vehement opponent of Roman Catholicism, commenting that 'there is but one way' to drain the Roman Campagna, 'that is, Restore the Roman Liberty; no great public work can succeed under the worst of tyrannies, I mean Church Tyranny for Life' (*Various Collections*, 8.368). A series of minor government offices—receiver-general of crown rents in Lincolnshire, Warwickshire, and Leicestershire in 1695, surveyor-general of woods north of the Trent in 1696, and surveyor-general of woods north and south of the Trent in 1715—were his reward.

Hewett's close links with the whig establishment, perhaps aided by his Nottinghamshire neighbour the first duke of Kingston, are revealed by the list of his architectural clients. As well as Kingston, lord president of the council, these included the first earl of Portland; the third earl of Sunderland, first lord of the Treasury, for whom he built a celebrated library in Piccadilly; and the first Viscount Macclesfield, the lord chancellor, whom he advised on the antiquarian reconstruction of Shirburn Castle, Oxfordshire. It was Sunderland who appointed him surveyor-general of the office of works in 1719 (he was also knighted that year), after he had been dismissed from his other posts by Sir Robert Walpole in 1716.

These were years of intense architectural debate, as British architects reacted against continental baroque and sought a more austere and classical national architecture. Together with two Yorkshire neighbours, the first

Viscount Molesworth and his son John, and with Sir George Markham, Hewett had formed the new junta for architecture aimed at its reformation. Both Lord Molesworth and (from 1721) Hewett were fellows of the Royal Society and their ideals were strongly influenced by Lord Molesworth's close friend, the whig philosopher the earl of Shaftesbury. Little came of their endeavours: the Florentine architect Alessandro Galilei, encouraged to Britain in 1714 with hopes of building a new Whitehall Palace, returned disillusioned to Italy in 1719. As surveyor-general under George I, Hewett had few opportunities to build, and his vision of a purer classicism 'according to the Rules of Arts & Sciences, proportions & good sense' (Hewett to Hugh Howard, 12 Jan 1725, National Library of Ireland, Howard of Shelton Abbey MSS, PC 227) was eclipsed by the greater success of the neo-Palladian movement, causing him to complain in 1723 that 'we have no prospect of fine buildings and, if there were monys and inclination to build a palace … there are so many weak pretenders, wrong-headed mules that it is impossible to have anything good and of a fine taste' (*Various Collections*, 8.368).

As so little is known of Hewett's work, it is hard to be sure what his architectural vision encompassed. His one important surviving design is the Cube Room at Kensington Palace, London, in a 'fine Grecian taste' (*Various Collections*, 8.368). Its close parallels with the illustration of the interior of the baths of the ancients in Claude Perrault's 1684 translation of Vitruvius' *Ten Books of Architecture*—coupled with his denunciation of the work of Andrea Palladio and Inigo Jones—suggests that his architectural approach may have been influenced by the theoretical writings of seventeenth-century French architects on ancient Roman architecture. This may help explain his failure in popularizing his ideas at a time of growing national confidence and anti-French feeling. Hewett had little time for contemporary architects, including in his criticism not only Inigo Jones but also Sir John Vanbrugh—'Sr. J-V- nether doth or knows anything, arbitrary, without regarding right or wrong, negligent to the last degree and cares not what he doth to carry on his Interest & support his Creatures' (Hewett to Hugh Howard, 2 Oct 1725, National Library of Ireland, Howard of Shelton Abbey MSS, PC 227)—and Nicholas Hawksmoor—'the most illeterate magotty & dishonest Fellow living' (ibid., 12 Jan 1725). It was with despair that he wrote to Galilei in 1726, saying that if he wanted to prosper in Britain he must copy Palladio. He died on 9 April 1726 at his home, Shireoaks Hall, Nottinghamshire, and was buried in Wales church, Yorkshire.

GILES WORSLEY

Sources H. M. Colvin and others, eds., *The history of the king's works*, 5 (1976), 71–3, 198 · J. Holland, *History of Worksop* (1826), 175–8 · E. McParland, 'Sir Thomas Hewett and the new junta for architecture', *The role of the amateur architect*, ed. G. Worsley (1994), 21–6 · Colvin, *Archs.* · *The parish of St James, Westminster*, 2/2, Survey of London, 32 (1963), 368 · W. Musgrave, *Obituary prior to 1800*, ed. G. J. Armytage, 3, Harleian Society, 46 (1900), 416 · HoP, *Commons* · V. W. Walker, biographical index, *Poll-books of Nottingham and Nottinghamshire, 1710*, Thoroton Society Record Series, 18 (1958), 92–185, esp. 134 · I. Toesca, 'Alessandro Galilei in Inghilterra', *English miscellany: a symposium of history, literature and the arts*, ed. M. Praz (1952),

187–220 • Vertue, *Note books*, 2.36; 3.17, 56 • *Report on manuscripts in various collections*, 8 vols., HMC, 55 (1901–14), vol. 8 • inscription, Wales church, Yorkshire • NL Ire., Howard of Shelton Abbey MSS **Archives** Arundel Castle, West Sussex, Arundel Castle MSS, ln.4 • NL Ire., Howard of Shelton Abbey MSS • Notts. Arch.

Hewett, Sir William (*c.*1508–1567), mayor of London, was born in the hamlet of Laughton-en-le-Morthen in the West Riding of Yorkshire to Edmund Hewett, whose family hailed from Derbyshire. Hewett served an apprenticeship to a clothworker from *c.*1522 and was admitted to the freedom of the Clothworkers' Company of London at some time before 1529, when he began taking apprentices himself. Like other textilers, he was also a merchant adventurer. Several relatives, including his brother Thomas and nephew Henry, migrated from Yorkshire to work in his successful business on Candlewick Street. Stow estimated Hewett's worth at £6000 per year at the time of his death.

Hewett became master of the Clothworkers' Company in 1543, but when he was elected alderman of Vintry ward on 16 September 1550, he refused to serve in office. The court of aldermen remanded him to Newgate, which seems to have changed his perspective about civic responsibility. Hewett represented Vintry until July 1554 and then transferred to Candlewick ward. He was elected sheriff in 1553 and, with other city leaders, countersigned the letters patent of Edward VI leaving the crown to Lady Jane Grey. Just a few months later Hewett carried out the sentences of execution on Lady Jane and her husband after Thomas Wyatt's rebellion. Given the dangers of political prominence, Hewett resisted mayoral duties until prevailed upon by a committee appointed in June 1557 to persuade him. In September 1559 he became lord mayor, the first member of the Clothworkers' Company to attain the office and the first mayor elected after the accession of Elizabeth I. As was the custom, accompanied by scarlet-clad aldermen, he was knighted by the queen after travelling by water to the court in Greenwich on 21 January 1560.

Hewett's new post imposed many responsibilities. The privy council directed him to reform the city's morality by enforcing sumptuary laws, ending gaming, and persuading retailers to moderate their prices; he was to make weekly reports. Hewett also presided at the treason trial of Captain Chamberlain, commander of the castle in Calais, on 8 June 1560. The queen instructed Hewett later that year to affix the marks of a greyhound and portcullis to the silver testons in circulation in order to detect counterfeit money. In August 1562, along with other prominent Londoners, Hewett sat in judgment on several counterfeiters at the Guildhall; four were condemned to death.

At some time after 1536 Hewett married Alice, the third daughter of Nicholas Leveson of Halling, Kent, a rich London mercer who was chosen sheriff in 1534. She was known for her pious and charitable works. The Hewetts had several children, but only Anne, born in 1543, survived her parents. Stow recounts that young Anne, playing near a window in her family house on London Bridge, fell into the river and was rescued by Edward Osborne, her father's apprentice, whom she later wed. Later historians

called the story apocryphal, since the date attributed to the incident, 1536, is before the Hewetts' wedding, and as there is no evidence that the family ever lived on London Bridge. None the less, Osborne, later lord mayor himself, did marry Anne Hewett and inherited through her most of her father's estates. Lady Alice Hewett died on 8 April 1561 and was buried at St Martin Orgar.

Hewett lived in Philpot Lane, but also had a country house at Highgate; in 1565 he served as one of the governors of Sir Roger Cholmeley's newly established grammar school there. His name appears on the register of admissions to Gray's Inn and his arms, inscribed with his name, are in Gray's Inn Hall. Hewett's enterprises embroiled him in litigation on occasion. John Isham, London mercer and fellow merchant adventurer, sued him for debts; Hewett sought to collect £2000 from William, Lord Dacre, in 1558 and received judgment in the exchequer following arbitration by the privy council. He represented George Talbot, sixth earl of Shrewsbury, at the baptism of Robert Dethyke, son of Sir Gilbert Dethick or Dethyke, at St Giles Cripplegate in July 1561. He also acted as a business agent for the earl: raising money, sending in accounts, and in 1563 reminding Shrewsbury that the earl's house in London needed repair. Hewett owned Parsloes Manor in Dagenham, Essex, and various estates in Yorkshire, Derbyshire, and Nottinghamshire. He died on 25 January 1567 in London and was buried next to his wife in St Martin Orgar. His will, dated 3 January 1567, was proved on 11 March 1567. He bequeathed his business, at the sign of the Three Cranes in Candlewick Street, to Thomas and Henry Hewett, and to Anne Osborne his tenements in London and Canterbury.   ELIZABETH LANE FURDELL

Sources DNB • *The diary of Henry Machyn, citizen and merchant-taylor of London, from AD 1550 to AD 1563*, ed. J. G. Nichols, CS, 42 (1848); repr. (1968) • will, PRO, PROB 11/49, sig. 9 • J. Stow, *The survey of London* (1912) [with introduction by H. B. Wheatley] • A. B. Beaven, ed., *The aldermen of the City of London, temp. Henry III–[1912]*, 2 vols. (1908–13) • S. J. Madge, ed., *Abstracts of inquisitiones post mortem relating to the City of London*, 2: 1561–1577, British RS, 26 (1901); repr. (1968) • C. Jamison, G. R. Batho, and E. G. W. Bill, eds., *A calendar of the Shrewsbury and Talbot papers in the Lambeth Palace Library and the College of Arms*, 1, HMC, JP 6 (1966) • G. D. Ramsay, *The City of London in international politics at the accession of Elizabeth Tudor* (1975) • G. D. Ramsay, *John Isham* (1962) • APC, 1556–8, 322–3, 394–5
Likenesses attrib. A. Moro, oils, 1554–1555?, Museum of London
Wealth at death approx. £6000 p.a.: Stow, *The survey of London*

Hewett, Sir William Nathan Wrighte (1834–1888), naval officer, son of Dr William Wrighte Hewett, physician to William IV, was born at Brighton on 12 August 1834. He entered the navy in March 1847, and served as a midshipman in the Second Anglo-Burmese War of 1852–3. In 1854, while acting mate of the gun-vessel *Beagle*, he was attached to the naval brigade in the Crimea, and on 26 October was in command of a Lancaster gun in the battery before Sevastopol. A column of Russians threatened its flank, and hurried orders were sent to spike the gun and withdraw the men. Hewett boldly answered that he took no orders that did not come from Captain Lushington, the commander of the brigade; and, breaking down the side parapet of the battery, he slewed the gun round, and

Sir William Nathan Wrighte Hewett (1834–1888), by Lock & Whitfield, pubd 1882

opened a terrible fire of grapeshot on the Russian column, then barely 300 yards distant. The effect in that part of the field was decisive. A few days later his gallant conduct at the battle of Inkerman (5 November) was reported by Captain Lushington, and he was immediately promoted lieutenant, with seniority of 26 October. He was also appointed to command the *Beagle*, in which he served during the war, especially in the operations against Kerch and in the Sea of Azov, and which he held after the peace until the summer of 1857. Hewett was one of the first recipients of the Victoria Cross, his conduct on 26 October and 5 November 1854 being equally named in the *Gazette* (24 February 1857). Hewett married, in 1857, Jane Emily, daughter of Mr T. Wood, consul for the Morea; they had two daughters and three sons, two of whom, William Warrington Hewett and Edward Matson Hewett, became lieutenants in the navy.

Hewett's rank had for all this time been only provisional; he then passed his examination at Portsmouth, and was appointed to the royal yacht, from which he was promoted commander on 13 September 1858. He then successively commanded the *Viper* on the west coast of Africa, and the *Rinaldo* on the North America and West Indies station. On 24 November 1862 he was made captain. He afterwards commanded the *Basilisk* on the China station, from 1865 to 1869; was flag captain to Sir Henry Kellett in the *Ocean* on the China station from 1870 to 1872; was captain of the *Devastation* from 1872 to 1873; and from October 1873 to October 1876 was commodore and commander-in-chief on the west coast of Africa, in charge of naval operations during the Second Anglo-Asante War (1873–4),

being present at Amoaful and the capture of Kumasi. He was made KCB on 31 March 1874. In time he was also KCSI, chevalier of the Légion d'honneur, and a member of the order of the Mejidiye, and of the Abyssinian order of Solomon.

In May 1877 Hewett was appointed to the *Achilles*, and commanded her in the Mediterranean and the Sea of Marmora under Sir Geoffrey Hornby. He attained his flag on 21 March 1878, and in April 1882 was appointed commander-in-chief in the East Indies. During the Egyptian campaign of 1882 he conducted naval operations in the Red Sea, notably the occupation of Suez and the seizure of the canal in August. The war in eastern Sudan again called him to the Red Sea. After the rout of Valentine Baker Pasha's Egyptian force at al-Teb (4 February 1884) Hewett landed with a force of seamen and marines for the defence of Suakin, on 6 February 1884, and on 10 February was formally appointed governor by Valentine Baker, as representative of the khedive. On 29 February he was present, unofficially, it would seem, at the second battle of al-Teb. In April, accompanied by John Wylde, he went on a mission to King John of Abyssinia, whom, by judicious concessions on trade, he induced to sign a treaty of friendship, at Adowa (3 June 1884), and to agree to assist the evacuation of Egyptian garrisons in his neighbourhood, and more especially Kassala.

On 8 July 1884 Hewett became vice-admiral, and from March 1886 to April 1888 was in command of the Channel Fleet. He had been for some months in very delicate health, which became seriously worse after his retirement from his command; he was sent as a patient to Haslar Hospital, Gosport, where he died on 13 May 1888.

J. K. Laughton, *rev.* Roger Morriss

Sources private information (1891) · *Navy List* · A. W. Kinglake, *The invasion of the Crimea*, [new edn], 5 (1877) · H. Brackenbury, *The Ashantee War*, 2 vols. (1874) · T. Archer, *The war in Egypt and the Soudan*, 2 (1887) · C. Royle, *The Egyptian campaigns, 1882 to 1885*, rev. edn (1900) · A. D. Lambert, *The Crimean War: British grand strategy, 1853–56* (1990) · B. Robson, *Fuzzy-wuzzy: the campaigns in the eastern Sudan, 1884–85* (1993) · Gladstone, *Diaries* · CGPLA Eng. & Wales (1888)

Archives NMM, papers

Likenesses Barraud, photograph, NPG; repro. in *Men and Women of the Day*, 1 (1888) · Lock & Whitfield, woodburytype, NPG; repro. in T. Cooper, *Men of mark: a gallery of contemporary portraits*, 6 (1882) [see illus.] · photograph, NPG

Wealth at death £2765 15s. 1d.: probate, 18 June 1888, CGPLA Eng. & Wales

Hewins [*married name* Bowtell], **Mary Elizabeth** (1914–1986), autobiographer, was born at 1 Pimms Court, Stratford upon Avon, Warwickshire, on 14 December 1914, the youngest among the eight children of George Henry Hewins (1879–1977), bricklayer, and Emily (Emma) Hewins, *née* Bayliss (1882–1951), domestic servant. George Hewins, a reluctant conscript in the Royal Warwickshire regiment when Mary was born, returned from the First World War severely disabled, unable to resume bricklaying, and fond of drink. He was a stranger to his daughter, and their relationship never recovered from this long early separation.

The family had been rehoused as a result of slum clearance in 1915, Emma's forcefulness—'you didn't argue with our Mother' (M. E. Hewins, 74)—having secured one of Stratford's 'council cottages' in Park Road. Overcrowding still caused difficulties, and family rows were frequent. George Hewins had relinquished his disablement pension for a tiny lump sum, and despite his disabilities did not shrink from work—taking a series of casual, ill-paid jobs. When presenting himself for confirmation at Holy Trinity Church, he attracted the attention of the officiating bishop and was offered the steady job of caretaker at the Church of England school, Alcester Road, on the understanding that his wife and children would help him. With the job came a small schoolhouse.

Mary Hewins's meagre education at the Alcester Road school suffered from at least two handicaps: her poor eyesight was undiagnosed until her late teens, when spectacles revealed to her a world that 'was a different place, so bright, shining' (M. E. Hewins, 48); and she was exhausted through having to help clean the school. On her fourteenth birthday she left school to work at the aluminium factory, Birmingham Road, polishing pans. It was filthy work, but she moved up after six months to bottle-washing in what seemed a better workplace—Flowers brewery—though working conditions remained harsh. When an auburn-haired, grammar-school educated young man came to work there, she fell in love, likening her feelings to a river current 'pulling you away from the bathing place, pulling you where you don't want to go, where you know it's dangerous' (ibid., 44). The workforce did not know that the young man's father published the *Birmingham Gazette* and allied newspapers. The son was attracted not only to Mary, with her dark looks and cheeky attitude towards authority, but also to her family, who were dismissed by his horrified mother as 'scruffs'.

When she became pregnant, one of Mary's brothers gave him a public beating, and he fled to his mother's family. After a failed attempt at abortion she was dismissed from her job on a trumped-up charge of fetching beer for the older women (an established practice), and took a series of rough casual jobs so as to qualify for unemployment benefit. It was while cleaning the school on 22 May 1938 that she gave birth to her son, Brian; the vicar threatened the expulsion of mother and child from the family home until a sympathetic doctor intervened. None the less, Mary had to incur the public humiliation of seeking maintenance through the police court. Brian's father admitted paternity, but paid maintenance only spasmodically and then got caught up in the Second World War. Thereafter Mary thought he had been killed, and he had been mistakenly informed that she had married.

Rejecting Brian at first, Mary Hewins was pushed by her mother into breastfeeding him, and eventually began to feel a warm possessiveness, 'the most wonderful feeling I'd ever had' (M. E. Hewins, 70). In 1939 she volunteered for war work, hoping thereby to avoid conscription or being sent further afield. She was sent to the aluminium factory where her working life had begun, but ailing visibly she was soon transferred to Stratford upon Avon Canners Ltd

next door. There she at last found work she liked and did well. Punctual, keen, and adept with machinery, she was soon promoted to mechanic's mate. Meanwhile her parents looked after Brian, who came to view Emma, not Mary, as his mother.

Mary left the canning factory at the end of the war, and while working at collating for Edward Fox, printers in Stratford, she got to know Fred Bowtell (1898–1983), a bookbinder, and married him on 20 March 1948. They lived in Stratford, but had no children. Thereafter Mary did cleaning jobs and casual work, keeping a spotless home and getting much pleasure from her wide network of friends in Stratford. Brian remained the centre of her life, left school at fifteen, and after an apprenticeship qualified as an electrician, moving on to become a lecturer at the Mid-Warwickshire College, where he spent thirty-two years. There, and through voluntary probation work, he tried to give teenagers the sort of help and encouragement he had never himself received at that age.

Mary's life took another unexpected turn after Fred Bowtell died. For Brian's wife, Angela, after getting a degree in history at the Open University, had come under the influence of the movement for 'oral history'. She recorded, edited, and published the story of Mary's father George Hewins in *The Dillen* (1981), thereby penetrating to lower levels within the working class than usually enter the historical record. Encouraged by the social historian Raphael Samuel, she went on to compile Mary's autobiography, published by Oxford University Press as *Mary, after the Queen: Memories of a Working Girl* (1985), and based entirely on oral evidence. The book gained much from its direct reporting of working-class dialogue, with vivid visual metaphors, earthy language, and salty wisdom. It captures, sometimes movingly, the ups and downs of an inter-war working girl's day-to-day life at a social level which rarely moved from speech into print. Indeed the autobiography's honest and understated presentation of life's tragicomedy lends it the timeless quality that is latent in the life of everyone, but becomes known only if they are lucky enough to find the right interviewer.

Nor did Mary Hewins's remarkable story end there. Brian traced his father to Los Angeles, and went to see him. It turned out that after the war he had become a highly skilled, well-paid, and hard-drinking toolmaker, and that he had been married briefly in the 1970s. As a result of Brian's visit, his father talked to Mary over the telephone and eventually came to Stratford, meeting Mary again after nearly half a century apart. 'It was quite a dignified meeting', Brian recalled, 'and quite touching'. Her vivacity and instinctive kindness broke the ice, and she and Brian's father were soon chatting as if they had parted only a few days before. Mary had by then become used to living on her own, but Brian's father lived with his son and daughter-in-law for several years before getting a council flat nearby. Mary saw the Royal Shakespeare Company's production of *Mary, after the Queen* (1985) many times and loved it, and Brian's father saw it once. He visited Mary when she was in the Myton Hamlet Hospice,

Warwick, suffering from the cancer which killed her there on 24 January 1986. He lived on, sociable to the end, dying in 1992 of cirrhosis of the liver.

BRIAN HARRISON

Sources M. E. Hewins, *Mary, after the queen: memories of a working girl*, ed. A. Hewins (1985) · G. H. Hewins, *The Dillen: memories of a man of Stratford-upon-Avon*, ed. A. Hewins (1981) · private information (2004) · b. cert. · d. cert.
Likenesses photographs, repro. in M. E. Hewins, *Mary, after the queen* (1985)

Hewins, (Margaret) Nancy (1902–1978), theatre director and actress, was born on 14 February 1902 at The Rowans, Putney Common, London, the daughter of Professor William Albert Samuel *Hewins (1865–1931), economist, and his wife, Margaret Slater. She had a sister and a brother. Nancy founded and led what seems to have been Britain's first all-women professional theatre company. She introduced Shakespeare to many audiences, often of schoolchildren, in industrial towns and remote villages.

Nancy Hewins was educated in London at Queen's Gate School, and then at St Hugh's College, Oxford (1921–4). Here she became fascinated by the theatre, and by lighting and sets in particular. On graduating in 1924, she started an amateur company called the Isis Players which played Shakespeare in tough east London schools, using floodlights made from old biscuit tins. A switch to professionalism brought a change of name. The Osiris Players' first production was *The Merchant of Venice* in December 1927. Until it ceased touring in 1963, the company performed against all the odds throughout Great Britain and Ireland.

Nancy Hewins devoted her life to Osiris. It was always all-women, and never had more than seven players at a time. Everybody did everything: acting, props, cooking; Nancy also played the flute. Shakespeare was the heart of the repertory. Scenes were cut and minor speeches transposed to make the doubling work. Lady Macbeth was one of Nancy's parts and, applying a fresh makeup at speed, she could change from this to the Porter within a few lines. Osiris travelled in black and white Rolls-Royces, usually two at a time. Nancy Hewins said they were the only cars that could take the strain when they were piled high with bedding and scenery, on which players lay flat, learning their parts. They also accommodated her Belgian griffons, which she always took with her, one playing Moon's dog in *A Midsummer Night's Dream*.

Nancy Hewins's family came from the Black Country. She was proud of her midlands origins and liked to think she was a relative of the John Hewins who married Shakespeare's aunt Agnes. She built on her family connections, starting her out-of-London tours in Wolverhampton, where her father had attended the grammar school; from the late 1930s she based herself and the company in the Cotswolds near Broadway. Her father was the first director of the London School of Economics and briefly a Conservative MP. He knew Lord Rothermere who gave Nancy £40 which helped her to launch Osiris. Her godmother was the pioneer socialist Beatrice Webb, whose christening present of a silver teapot she kept all her life. Through her Nancy gained helpful introductions to local co-operative society education departments.

Nancy Hewins's finest hour, perhaps, came during the Second World War. She put on 1534 performances of thirty-three plays (sixteen of them by Shakespeare) in wartime, with the company travelling for a time by horse and dray because of petrol restrictions. She celebrated Osiris's twenty-first birthday at a women's institute in Kent with *Twelfth Night* in the morning, *Everyman* at lunchtime, *Macbeth* in the afternoon, Shaw's *Captain Brassbound's Conversion* after tea, and *Badger's Green*, R. C. Sherriff's comedy about village cricket, in the evening.

Nancy Hewins reckoned she had eventually played 128 Osiris parts herself. She was not a subtle actress; sets and lighting remained her first love. But her productions left an indelible impression on her young audiences, many of whom had never seen any professional theatre outside the music hall or the Christmas pantomime. Her principle was that no one could understand Shakespeare unless they enjoyed it. 'The play had to come alive to the children', she wrote in her unpublished autobiography. Osiris also played to other local audiences, including unemployed miners in the Rhondda and munitions workers. If there was no proper stage, the company would play in the round. Few players, outside the steady core of three or four, survived more than a few years. On tour they slept in barns, on school floors, even a park café. 'Digs' were too expensive. If emotional complications arose, Nancy Hewins's remedies were sal volatile or a teaspoon of brandy.

Theatre was a mission to Nancy Hewins. Everything was subordinated to the task of keeping Osiris on the road. To begin with, she augmented the funds by working as lighting director on other productions, especially pageants. The company was never publicly subsidized. Nancy Hewins was ahead of her time in acting in improvised venues to regional audiences, though she was also in the great tradition of strolling players. 'I dare say if the company had had a Russian name', she wrote, 'it would have been regarded as a remarkable experiment.' The costumes had a bright, Renaissance glamour: hessian or canvas, painted in vivid reds or golds. They were uncomfortable to wear, but they folded flat. Everything had to be tough and durable. When she played Claudius in *Hamlet*, she wore the Ghost's armour underneath, for quick changing. In her later years, she made a modest living by renting the costumes out.

Nancy Hewins was stubborn, even dogmatic, and said what she thought, but she evoked great loyalty among her actresses. She never married and had no personal vanity. She loved practical things. Interviewing one would-be actress, she made it clear that the important thing was to be able to change a car wheel. To many young people, for more than thirty years, the arrival of her Osiris company brought the first experience of theatrical magic into their lives.

Nancy Hewins died of heart failure at the Radcliffe Infirmary, Oxford, on 17 January 1978. She was buried at St Peter's Church, Willersey, Gloucestershire.

PAUL BARKER

Sources N. Hewins, 'Well, why not? The story of the Osiris players', unpublished autobiography, Theatre Museum, London • personal knowledge (2004) • *The Times* (15 June 1978) • b. cert. • d. cert. • P. Barker, 'A woman of some importance', *Independent on Sunday* (4 June 1995) • Oxford, St Hugh's College register • *The Fritillary* [St Hugh's College magazine] [obituary] • *The Times* (1 Feb 1978) • *Daily Telegraph* (19 Jan 1978)
Archives Theatre Museum, London, 'Well, why not? The story of the Osiris players', unpublished autobiography in 2 typescript vols.
Likenesses R. Saidman, five colour photographs (Osiris Players), Popperfoto Agency; repro. in *Illustrated* (29 May 1943) • drawing (in old age), repro. in *Birmingham Post* (31 Dec 1977) • photograph, priv. coll.
Wealth at death £18,187: probate, 2 June 1978, *CGPLA Eng. & Wales*

Hewins, William Albert Samuel (1865–1931), economist and politician, was born on 11 May 1865 near Wolverhampton, the second son and fourth of the ten children of Samuel Hewins (1833–1899), iron merchant, and his wife, Caroline (d. 1901), daughter of John Green of Bampton, Oxfordshire, and his wife, Sarah. He fondly traced his ancestry back to generations of midland yeomen, whence came (he believed) the imperial spirit which he in turn sought to re-evoke in Edwardian England. He was educated at Wolverhampton grammar school (1875–84) and, having won the Hatherton scholarship, at Pembroke College, Oxford, where he gained a second in mathematics in 1887.

Historical economist at the London School of Economics His father's business difficulties had given Hewins a strong interest in economics, and at Oxford the influence of Ruskin, Kingsley, and Carlyle infused him with a vision of a new social order. Originally destined for the church, he joined the Guild of St Matthew, but in 1886 he helped set up the Oxford Social Science Club; this promised the solution to social questions through practical investigation rather than ecclesiastical action. He also became an active member of the Oxford Economics Society, whose *Economic Review* was turning from the study of economics as an abstract discipline to its study as a branch of history. In this vein, in 1887 he took up the study of history, with economics as a special subject and Sir Charles Firth as his mentor. This proved a long-lived friendship, and its fruits included a notable collection of ballads, now in Sheffield University Library. From 1888 Hewins became heavily involved in the university extension movement, frequently lecturing in the north of England and organizing summer conferences in Oxford, while his historical research led in 1892 to the publication of his monograph *English Trade and Finance, Chiefly in the Seventeenth Century*. At the same time his work for the *Dictionary of National Biography* and Palgrave's *Dictionary of Political Economy*, particularly on English economists before Smith, gave him a growing appreciation of mercantilism and of an imperial

William Albert Samuel Hewins (1865–1931), by F. A. Swaine

and state-directed alternative to Victorian individualism and *laissez-faire*.

On 25 August 1892 Hewins married his long-standing fiancée, Margaret Slater (d. 1940), the daughter of James Slater, of Bescot Hall, Walsall. Their three children included the theatre director Nancy *Hewins (1902–1978). Still he sought a secure academic future. Too young to gain a chair at King's College, London, in 1891, he also found his attempts to teach economic history at Oxford thwarted by a conservative faculty. But by a happy chance he was consulted in 1894 by Sidney Webb about the organization of the embryonic London School of Economics (LSE), and in 1895 he became its first director. This proved a highly successful appointment, for Hewins's intellectual and academic ambitions dovetailed neatly with the Webbs' desire for an institutional basis for the promotion of the five 'e's': economics, efficiency, equality, education, and empire. Hewins proved an extremely able and energetic, if sometimes moody, administrator, whose enthusiasm and self-belief did much rapidly to establish the LSE as an international centre for research in the social sciences and as a central part of the University of London.

Tariff reform Increasingly disillusioned with Gladstonian Liberalism, Hewins continued to develop a 'neo-mercantilistic' approach to the state and economy, sharing many concerns of the German historical economists. Ultimately the Second South African War convinced him that Britain's future as a great power could be secured only through a new imperial policy, in which the interests of consumers so central to free-trade Liberalism would be subordinated to the needs of the new imperial community. This credo, articulated in the privately circulated *Imperialism and its Probable Effect on the Commercial Policy of the United Kingdom* (1899) and published by Schmoller's Verein für Sozialpolitik, has been considered 'the most cogent statement of the historical economists' position on the importance of the empire' (E. H. H. Green, *The Crisis of Conservatism*, 1993, 376). For the realization of such a policy Hewins was increasingly drawn to Joseph Chamberlain, while in January 1902 he had already put forward to the Coefficients the case for imperial preference. When Chamberlain himself championed the tariff case, Hewins soon became its major publicist, launching the 'crusade' with an influential series of articles in *The Times* as well as leaders in the *Morning Post* and other papers. But his role as confidential adviser to Chamberlain increasingly conflicted with the Webbs' desire to keep the LSE politically neutral, and in November 1903 Hewins resigned as its director in order to become secretary of the tariff commission; he was, Beatrice Webb noted, 'an ideal henchman for Joe, fanatical, well-informed, unveracious and loyal' (*Diary*, vol. 2, 18 Nov 1903).

The tariff commission was very much Hewins's creation, and later his creature. While formally distinct from the propagandist Tariff Reform League, it had been set up—largely, it seems, on Hewins's own suggestion—in order to provide the expert knowledge through which a 'scientific' British tariff could be devised. It was to do so through the detailed investigation of particular trades and industries. Hewins proved, as at the LSE, highly adept at setting up an efficient bureaucracy and at public relations. The reports of the commission soon did much to sustain the case for tariff reform, though rather less towards constructing a 'scientific' tariff. On behalf of Chamberlain, Hewins visited Canada in late 1905, preparing the groundwork for the pursuit of imperial preference to which much of his subsequent career would be devoted. By the election of 1906 the commission's work was far from complete, and the decimation of the Unionists left Hewins temporarily demoralized; Beatrice Webb perceptively noted:

> he thought, I am convinced, that in a few years, if not immediately, he would be arranging tariffs, and tariff wars, and tariff treaties, at the Board of Trade—hurrying from continent to continent, in close and confidential intercourse with Ministers and great financial personages—one long delightful intrigue with the World Empire as the result. (*Diary*, vol. 3, 28 Jan 1906)

Yet Hewins, ever 'the fanatic and the manipulator' (*Diary*, 2.196) and obsessively devoted to the cause of an empire united by a preferential tariff, was soon eagerly preparing for the Colonial Conference of 1907. The tariff commission continued its investigative activities (especially with regard to agriculture), though Hewins increasingly laid aside the mask of expert for the part of Unionist

politician. In particular he was much consulted by Balfour, who was impressed by 'a fiscal reformer who really knows something about his case' (Balfour to Sandars, 24 Jan 1907, quoted in F. Coetzee, *For Party or Country*, 1990, 88). Aspiring to enter parliament, he now spoke more widely on tariff reform in the country but failed in 1908 to secure the nomination for West Wolverhampton. In January 1910 he fought the unpromising seat of Shipley, and in December he contested Middleton (Lancashire), a seat he again failed to win at a by-election in 1911. Unionist failure led him to attach growing importance to social as well as tariff reform, and he helped found the Unionist Social Reform Committee in 1911.

Unionist politician Eventually in 1912 Hewins was elected for Hereford. This enabled him to play a growing role in parliamentary debate, especially in opposing home rule for Ireland, while pushing the 'Whole Hogger' tariff reform case for agriculture and imperial preference. He was also deeply involved in his own spiritual odyssey, wrestling with the legacy of his father's lapsed Catholicism, combined with his own deepening sense that the greatness of England and her empire had been as a Catholic nation. After lengthy discussions, especially with Father Pollen, he was received into the Roman Catholic church in September 1914.

The First World War, and the need for the state to intervene widely in the economy and to mobilize imperial resources, vindicated in Hewins's eyes the policies he had outlined since 1901. Exploiting his own wide contacts in the business world, he became a leading member of the influential back-bench Unionist Business Committee (UBC)—active on munitions, dyestuffs, conscription, and economic warfare—and was elected its chairman in December 1915. He put the tariff commission at the disposal of the UBC (the government having failed to take up his offer of its resources) and kept up a sustained campaign for the more efficient deployment of Britain's economy for war. Above all, Hewins became the leading proponent of 'trade war' after war, intending to destroy the 'German economic octopus' (*Apologia*, 2.59) through the greater co-ordination of the empire. His parliamentary motion promoting this policy was accepted by the Liberal government in January 1916, while Hewins also prepared for Asquith an important scheme for an 'Imperial Economic Council'. His secretive but influential personal diplomacy with France also helped prepare the groundwork for the endorsement of post-war economic 'warfare' in the Paris economic resolutions of 1916.

With the UBC at his back Hewins supported the formation of the Lloyd George coalition in 1916, and was now at the pinnacle of his political influence, believing himself 'a kind of Warwick, a maker and destroyer of governments' (W. H. Hancock, *Survey of British Commonwealth Affairs*, 1940, 2.138). 'Habitually "castle-building"' (*Diary of Beatrice Webb*, 2.266) and caricatured as the Mad Hatter, he schemed for the tariff commission—and, of course, himself as the only man who really understood it—to become part of the machinery of government, an illusion he cherished well into the 1920s. More practically, as a member of the Balfour of Burleigh committee he successfully pressed the case for imperial preference as the basis of Britain's post-war economic policy. He also now worked tirelessly to ensure that the Imperial Conference of 1917 would back this cause, pressing both Bonar Law and Lloyd George in this direction. Ultimately, though he believed Law had earlier kept him out of office, in September 1917 he became under-secretary of state at the Colonial Office; this was probably more an attempt to spike Hewins's guns than to reload them. In tandem with his friend Walter Long, a like-minded imperial enthusiast, he undertook much work on trade relations with the empire, and helped organize the 1918 Imperial Conference and develop post-war emigration policy. As a member of the 'indemnity committee' in December 1918 he urged, against the advice of Keynes, maximum reparations from Germany, but Balcarres probably exaggerated his role in recalling 'Hewins says Germany can pay our debts, and being a professor in status and pompousness, was taken at his word with lamentable results' (*Crawford Papers*, ed. J. Vincent, 1984, 9 April 1919, 401). Hewins's period in office was, however, brought to an abrupt end, for in 1918 he was not invited to contest Hereford (he believed on religious grounds, others believed because he had neglected to nurse the seat), and he became the only Unionist minister not reappointed by the Lloyd George coalition.

Political isolation Hewins's career now waned rapidly, though he remained indefatigable in his search to promote empire and tariffs, while also playing an important role in lay Catholicism, particularly as adviser to Cardinal Bourne. But, crucially, he failed to re-enter parliament—kept out, he believed, by anti-Catholic prejudice at Westminster, obliged to withdraw at Barnstaple, and unsuccessful three times at Swansea West against Sir Alfred Mond, erstwhile free-trader, now archetypal proponent of imperial economic unity. Hewins retained a strong belief in his own indispensability: for example, he aspired to the role of intermediary in the Irish troubles of 1919. In 1920 he attempted to reinvigorate the crumbling Tariff Reform League, before in 1922 launching with Long the short-lived Empire Development Union. He was occasionally consulted by Baldwin on tariff policy and was appointed to Milner's tariff advisory committee in 1923. He restated the tariff reform case in *Trade in the Balance* (1924), and helped formulate the policy of the Empire Industries Association before falling out with its key supporters, a more hard-nosed breed of business protectionist, increasingly dismissive of Hewins's quaint imperial enthusiasm. Thereafter he was largely confined to rehearsing his *idées fixes*, especially through lectures for Conservative hopefuls at the Philip Stott (later Bonar Law) College. He represented the Vatican in 1929 at the Universal Postal Union Congress. A lucrative directorship of the Victoria Wine Company gave him the leisure to write his *Apologia of an Imperialist* (2 vols., 1929), which reflected his imperial ideals but also his egoism and self-delusion: 'a monumental exhibition—an inside record of all his intrigues', as Sidney Webb accurately put it (*Letters*, vol. 3, 14 Oct 1924).

Hewins had achieved most in close association with greater men (Webb, Chamberlain, and Long), but in the 1920s was an isolated and marginal figure. He died at his home, 75 Chester Square, London, on 17 November 1931, ironically the day on which the National Government introduced its Abnormal Importations Bill, a stage towards the 'scientific tariff' for which Hewins had so long and so fanatically striven. He was buried at Kensal Green Roman Catholic cemetery on 20 November.

A. C. HOWE

Sources W. A. S. Hewins, *The apologia of an imperialist: forty years of empire policy*, 2 vols. (1929) • Sheffield University, Hewins MSS • A. Marrison, *British business and protection, 1903–1932* (1996) • BLPES, tariff commission MSS • *The diary of Beatrice Webb*, ed. N. MacKenzie and J. MacKenzie, 4 vols. (1982–5) • A. Kadish, *The Oxford economists in the late nineteenth century* (1982) • R. Dahrendorf, *LSE: a history of the London School of Economics and Political Science, 1895–1995* (1995) • G. M. Koot, *English historical economics, 1870–1926* (1987) • J. C. Wood, *British economists and the empire* (1983) • A. Sykes, *Tariff reform in British politics, 1903–1913* (1979) • *Hansard 5C* (1912–18) • R. Bunselmeyer, *The cost of war: British economic war aims and the origins of reparations* (1975) • *DNB*
Archives BLPES, corresp. with London School of Economics • BLPES, letters relating to London School of Economics • BLPES, corresp. relating to Royal Economic Society • BLPES, letters to tariff commission • University of Sheffield Library, diaries, corresp., papers, working notes | BL, corresp. with Arthur James Balfour, Add. MS 49779 • Wilts. & Swindon RO, Walter Long MSS
Likenesses H. A. Budd, oils, London School of Economics • F. A. Swaine, photograph, repro. in Hewins, *Apologia*, frontispiece [*see illus.*]
Wealth at death £1366 14*s*.: administration, 19 March 1932, *CGPLA Eng. & Wales*

Hewit, John. *See* Hewitt, John (*bap.* 1614, *d.* 1658).

Hewitson, William Chapman (1806–1878), naturalist, was born in Percy Street, Newcastle upon Tyne, on 9 January 1806, the second son of Middleton Hewitson (*d.* 1845). His early education began at Kirkby Stephen, and was completed at York, where he was articled to John Tuke, a land surveyor. About 1828 or 1829, he returned to Newcastle to pursue his career.

Hewitson was devoted to the study of natural history, a subject for which he had developed a taste during childhood. His friends included a number of like-minded natural history enthusiasts such as the marine zoologist Albany Hancock (and his brother, John), the zoologist Joshua Alder, and the geologist William Hutton. With his fellow students, Hewitson founded a society for the study of natural history (the Natural History Society of Northumberland, Durham and Newcastle upon Tyne), which first met on 19 August 1829. He was a member of the society's committee and honorary curator of its entomological department.

In early life, Hewitson had formed collections of British coleoptera and lepidoptera; he then devoted attention for some years to the study of birds' eggs. In 1831 he began his work *British Oology* (1833–42), and in 1832 he undertook a journey to the Shetland Islands, and in 1833 went on an expedition to Norway to discover the breeding places of some migratory species. He was accompanied on this trip by his friends John Hancock and Benjamin Johnson, with the aim of gathering plants, birds, and insects. During their visit to the Arctic circle, they were forced by the harshness of their circumstances, to live on the birds they shot. Hewitson's diary of this expedition was used for pieces on ornithology which appeared in Sir William Jardine's *Magazine of Zoology*.

Hewitson moved from Newcastle to Bristol in 1840, where he was employed under George Stephenson on the railway between Bristol and Exeter, as a surveyor. However, by the end of April 1845, two uncles and his father had died, leaving him as their heir, and considerably wealthy. He took up residence at Hampstead, and devoted his life to scientific research, his poor health also playing a role in his decision to give up business.

From about this time, Hewitson's attention became focused again on lepidoptera. He travelled with his friend John Hancock to Switzerland and the Alps, where he gathered a fine series of diurnal lepidoptera. He bought specimens from travellers and naturalists all over the globe, whose expenses he often paid, forming in the process what was probably the most complete collection of diurnal lepidoptera of his time. He published *The Genera of Diurnal Lepidoptera* in conjunction with the entomologist Edward Doubleday (1846–52), followed by *Illustrations of Diurnal Lepidoptera* (1863–78). He also wrote on the same subject in a number of journals. His other best-known works include the *Illustrations of New Species of Exotic Butterflies* (1851–76) and his *Descriptions of some New Species of Lycaenidae* (1868). Hewitson was also accomplished as an artist and draughtsman, and as a pictorial describer of butterflies and birds' eggs, he was considered unrivalled.

About 1848 Hewitson married, but his wife died soon after. They had no children. In the same year he purchased part of Oatlands Park, Surrey, where he lived for thirty years, in a house designed for him by the architect John Dobson. Having joined the Entomological Society in 1846, he also became a member of the Zoological Society (1859) and the Linnean Society (1862).

When Hewitson died on 28 May 1878 at Oatlands, there was no heir to his fortune. He made a bequest of £10,000 to the Newcastle Infirmary, and left his library of works on natural history, with a legacy of £3000, to the Natural History Society of Northumberland, Durham and Newcastle. He also left a large sum to the Müller Institute, Bristol. The rest of his fortune he bequeathed to various charities, and £20,000 in legacies was divided among fifty-eight of his friends. His estate at Oatlands was bequeathed to his closest friend, John Hancock, while to the British Museum was left his butterfly collection, some pictures, and watercolours, in addition to his stuffed birds. He was buried at Walton-on-Thames.   YOLANDA FOOTE

Sources *The Entomologist*, 11 (1878), 166 · private information (1891) · Boase, *Mod. Eng. biog.* · R. Welford, *Men of mark 'twixt Tyne and Tweed*, 3 vols. (1895) · W. H. Mullens and H. K. Swann, *A bibliography of British ornithology from the earliest times to the end of 1912* (1917) · *Entomologist's Monthly Magazine*, 15 (1878–9), 44–5

Archives Oxf. U. Mus. NH, drawings of butterflies · U. Newcastle, Hancock Museum, catalogues and drawings | U. Newcastle, Robinson L., letters to Sir Walter Trevelyan

Likenesses portrait, repro. in *Transactions of the Natural History Society of Northumberland, Durham and Newcastle*, 7 (1880), 223–35

Wealth at death under £70,000: probate, 14 June 1878, *CGPLA Eng. & Wales*

Hewitt, Cecil Rolph [*pseud.* C. H. Rolph] (1901–1994), police officer and writer, was born on 23 August 1901 at 28 Ilfracombe Buildings, Southwark, London, the middle child of the three sons of Frederick Thompson Hewitt (*b.* 1869), a City of London police officer, and his wife, Edith Mary Speed (*d.* 1910), a seamstress. Before he was a year old the family moved to Finsbury Park, Middlesex, and it was there that he went to two successive London county council (LCC) elementary schools before going on to the LCC central school in Fulham, where his father had taken his sons (together with his widowed sister-in-law, whom he subsequently married), following the death of his first wife in 1910.

Having failed to win an LCC scholarship, Hewitt completed his formal education at the age of fourteen. He first went to work as a counting-house clerk at a ladies' dress and coat manufacturers in the City. But he lost this job within two years after being accused of devoting far too much of his time to scribbling away on pieces of paper (he had made the mistake of consigning too many of them to the office waste-paper basket). Encouraged by a payment of £1 for a diary item from the *Daily Chronicle* in 1915, he developed a desire to become a journalist, even on one occasion submitting an article to *Punch*, whose editor, Sir Owen Seaman, rejected it but in warmly encouraging terms.

Out of work and already something of an autodidact at sixteen, Hewitt initially tried to become a junior reporter—he had learned shorthand at school—but failed to find any openings. Through the good offices of his father, who had meanwhile become a chief inspector, he secured a post instead with a firm of chartered accountants in Victoria Street, only to bring about a family crisis conclave when it was established that to be accepted as an articled clerk would require a premium of £500. Even on a chief inspector's pay this was not a realistic option, and, although his father toyed with the idea of surrendering his life endowment policy in order to make it possible, the young Hewitt was anxious to prevent the putting into effect of any such self-sacrificing gesture, and announced his intention of following his father into the police. Turned down on medical grounds by the Metropolitan Police—he later came to believe mainly because at nineteen he was a year under the age at which that force normally liked to recruit—he then blundered into applying to join the quite separate force of the City of London police, which accepted him. It was a decision that immediately prompted his father to resign on the rather overfastidious ground that father and son could not possibly serve together in the same relatively small law enforcement body overseeing the Square Mile.

Hewitt's youthful impetuosity had another consequence. It delayed his entry into what was plainly his vocation of journalism for more than twenty-five years. His time with the City of London police—in which, like his father, he ultimately rose to the rank of chief inspector—was not, however, wasted. It gave him his grounding and background in those areas of writing that he was eventually to make his speciality: cases of injustice, the rights of the individual against authority, the treatment of offenders, the workings of the legal system, and the whole mid-twentieth-century campaign for penal reform.

Even as a serving policeman, Hewitt could not entirely overcome the temptation to air his views (despite the provision in the police disciplinary code forbidding any such practice). Hence the invention of his pseudonym—the transposition of his initials and the substitution of his second name for his surname—to make the byline C. H. Rolph, which first appeared in print (in the *Children's Newspaper*) in 1924. He was years afterwards to discover that his choice of *nom de plume* had fairly soon been seen through by his superiors, but fortunately he had by then made himself sufficiently indispensable (not least by acting as speech writer to the commissioner of his force) for them not to wish to make an example of him.

On 21 August 1926 Hewitt had married Audrey Mary Buttery (1900/01–1982), a civil servant; they had one daughter. The marriage was dissolved in 1946. On 10 January 1948 he married (Ann) Jenifer Wayne (1917/18–1982), a BBC producer and scriptwriter whom he had met while working as a consultant on her radio show *This is the Law*. Their marriage was a happy one, producing a daughter and a son.

Hewitt retired from the police at the age of forty-five, in 1946, and a year later joined the left-wing political weekly the *New Statesman*, to which he had been surreptitiously contributing for almost a decade. He was recruited to its staff by the paper's most illustrious editor, Kingsley Martin, who, disliking the name Cecil, insisted on calling him Bill (in a rather painful play on his police past). Hewitt was later to write the official biography of this somewhat quixotic figure, whom he greatly admired: *Kingsley: the Life, Letters and Diaries of Kingsley Martin* (1973). In addition to producing regular pieces for the *New Statesman* until 1978, and writing for nearly 60 years weekly columns for the *Police Review* and latterly for the *New Law Journal*, Hewitt became a prolific author, publishing no fewer than twenty-eight books. Inevitably, these tended to be of variable quality, but at least three were classics: his own autobiography, *Living Twice* (1974), and his two evocations of Edwardian London, *London Particulars* (1980) and *Further Particulars* (1987).

In 1969, at the request of the home secretary, James Callaghan, Hewitt also wrote the Home Office white paper *People in Prison*, what he himself described as 'one of the most important pieces of writing I have had the chance to do'; from 1966 to 1970 he served as a member of the original Parole Board. He took an active and energetic part in such voluntary organizations as the Howard League for Penal Reform, the National Committee for the Abolition of Capital Punishment, and the Albany Trust (of which he was chairman). For many years, with his resonant bass speaking voice, he was an accomplished radio broadcaster, and during the long period of his retirement he recorded many 'talking books' for blind people. The Callaghan government of 1976–9 offered to make him a CBE, but he declined the honour. Hewitt died of cancer at the Royal Surrey County Hospital in Guildford, on 10 March 1994.   ANTHONY HOWARD

Sources C. H. Rolph [C. R. Hewitt], *Living twice: an autobiography* (1974) · C. H. Rolph [C. R. Hewitt], *Kingsley: the life, letters, and diaries of Kingsley Martin* (1973) · *The Times* (12 March 1994) · 'Still with us', *The Oldie* (28 May 1993) · personal knowledge (2004) · private information (2004) · b. cert. · m. certs. · d. cert. · *CGPLA Eng. & Wales* (1994)

Archives BLPES, papers; corresp. and papers relating to AEGIS · U. Sussex, corresp. and papers relating to *New Statesman* and biography of Martin Kingsley | BL, letters to Baron Gardiner relating to abolition of capital punishment, Add. MSS 56455–56460 *passim* · Bodl. Oxf., letters to Frank Hardie · U. Reading, letters to Longman Group · U. Sussex, corresp. with B. W. Levy · University of Warwick, Coventry, letters to Victor Gollancz | SOUND BL NSA, 1969 BBC Radio 4 'World of Books' ser. · U. Sussex Library, interviews about Kingsley Martin, recorded on cassette (1971)

Wealth at death £231,387: probate, 17 June 1994, *CGPLA Eng. & Wales*

Hewitt, Sir Edgar Rainey Ludlow- (1886–1973), air force officer, was born at Eckington, Worcestershire, on 9 June 1886, the second son and second of the five children of Thomas Arthur Ludlow-Hewitt (1850–1936), of Clancoole, co. Cork, and later vicar of Minety, Wiltshire, and his wife, Edith Annie (d. 1944), the daughter of Alfred Ricketts Hudson, of Wick House, Worcestershire. Educated at Radley College and the Royal Military College, Sandhurst, he was commissioned into the Royal Irish Rifles in 1905. He learned to fly at the Central Flying School, Upavon, a few weeks before the outbreak of the First World War, and in August 1914 he became a probationary member of the infant Royal Flying Corps. Early in 1915 he was posted to 1 squadron in France, where he gained a reputation as an exceptionally able and courageous pilot. He won an MC (1916), was six times mentioned in dispatches, and was rapidly promoted to command 3 squadron. In February 1916 he was promoted wing commander and took over 3 corps wing at Bertangles. He became a chevalier of the Légion d'honneur in 1917, and was appointed to the DSO the following year. By the end of the war, a brigadier at the age of thirty-one, he was marked by Sir Hugh Trenchard as one of the outstanding brains of the newly created Royal Air Force.

Between the wars, Ludlow—as he was always known—served as commandant of the RAF Staff College at Andover (1926–30), air officer commanding in Iraq (1930–32), director of operations and intelligence in the Air Ministry (1933–5), and air officer commanding in India (1935–7). He was an austere, sombre figure whose intelligence and devotion to duty were widely recognized, but his lack of humour and teetotal dedication to Christian Science did not encourage good fellowship. The tall, lanky figure of Ludlow-Hewitt striding across the tarmac of an airfield was respected, but loved only by those who knew him well. 'Most knowledgeable; very sound on paper; probably more detailed knowledge of service matters than anyone in the RAF', Air Chief Marshal Sir Hugh Pughe Lloyd wrote of him in his diary. 'As a commander a hopeless bungler and fuddler; unable to make up his mind and will change it five times in as many minutes; easily flustered'.

This may be a little ungenerous. But as a commander on the eve of war, Ludlow-Hewitt became the victim of his own intelligence. In 1937 he was recalled from India to become air officer commanding Bomber Command and was promoted air chief marshal. Since 1918, like almost every senior RAF officer of the period, he had shared that mystical faith held by Viscount Trenchard in the power of a bomber offensive to win wars. Yet in his new post he was quickly forced to terms with the fact that no hard thinking had ever been done about how the bombers were to find their targets; how they were to aim their bombs; how the bombs were to destroy large structures; above all, perhaps, how a credible offensive was to be mounted with the very small force at Bomber Command's disposal. From 1936 onwards, Fighter Command profited greatly from the attention of politicians and scientists—above all Sir Henry Tizard—who addressed themselves determinedly to the problems of creating a workable air defence system for Britain. Perhaps principally because so many politicians and civilians found the concept of a bomber offensive repugnant, no parallel outside stimulus was applied to Bomber Command. Ludlow-Hewitt pressed the Air Ministry in vain for the creation of a bombing development unit. He met Tizard for the first time only in July 1939.

It was Ludlow-Hewitt's thankless task to identify frankly and accurately, on the very edge of the war, the grave shortcomings of his command. His relentless minutes to the Air Ministry exposed him to the charge of pessimism, even defeatism, yet they were perfectly confirmed by battle experience. He wrote reporting that air-gunners possessed no confidence in their ability to use their equipment. After a generation in which the theory of the 'self-defending bomber formation' had been at the heart of RAF policy, he declared his conviction that fighter escorts would be essential in war. He stated a few weeks before the opening of hostilities that, if his force were ordered to undertake an all-out offensive against Germany, the medium bombers—the Blenheims—would be destroyed in three and a half weeks and the heavies—Hampdens, Whitleys, and Wellingtons—would be eliminated in seven and a half weeks. The air staff reluctantly accepted the view that the government had anyway reached for political reasons, that the RAF should not embark on an immediate strategic offensive. In September 1939 Bomber Command began the war with a programme of leaflet-dropping which confirmed Ludlow-Hewitt's worst fears about his command's aircraft navigation, and also carried out operations against the German fleet at sea and in support of the British expeditionary force in France. When the first disastrous operations of 3 group's Wellingtons against the German fleet caused heavy casualties, Ludlow-Hewitt flew personally to visit the squadrons, and astonished his men by his own sensitivity to the losses. He was too passionately humanitarian to maintain the confidence of others and too realistic about the shortcomings of his own force. An officer was needed of less sensitivity and more positive faith in his command's powers, however ill-founded. In April 1940, before the war began in earnest, Ludlow-Hewitt was removed to become inspector-general of the RAF, a post in which he served with great insight and dedication until 1945. Sir C. F. A. Portal replaced him at Bomber Command.

Ludlow-Hewitt was appointed CMG (1919), CB (1928), KCB (1933), GBE (1943), and GCB (1946). From 1943 to 1945 he was principal air aide-de-camp to the king. In 1945 he became chairman of the board of the new College of Aeronautics, a position he held until 1953. One of the founding fathers of the RAF, an exceptionally thoughtful service officer, he lacked the steel for high command in war.

Ludlow-Hewitt married on 5 February 1923 Albinia Mary (d. 1972), the daughter of Major Edward Henry Evans-Lombe, of Marlington Hall, Norwich, and the widow of Francis William Talbot Clerke and of Captain Anthony Henry Evelyn Ashley, both of the Coldstream Guards. There were no children of the marriage. Ludlow-Hewitt died at Queen Alexandra's RAF Hospital, Wiltshire, on 15 August 1973. MAX HASTINGS, rev.

Sources RAF Museum archives, Hendon · C. Webster and N. Frankland, *The strategic air offensive against Germany, 1939–1945*, 4 vols. (1961) · M. Hastings, *Bomber command* (1979) · private information (1986) · Burke, *Gen. GB* (1958)

Archives FILM IWM FVA, actuality footage | SOUND IWM SA, oral history interview

Likenesses K. Green, oils, 1929, Royal Air Force Staff College, Bracknell · W. Stoneman, photograph, 1946, NPG · T. C. Dugdale, oils, IWM

Wealth at death £155,237: probate, 4 Jan 1974, *CGPLA Eng. & Wales*

Hewitt, Sir Frederic William (1857–1916), anaesthetist, was born on 2 July 1857 at 52 Westbourne Park Villas, London, the eldest of six children (there were three brothers and two sisters), of George Frederick Hewitt (1832–1869), agricultural chemist, and his wife, Elizabeth (b. 1833), daughter of Thomas and Elizabeth Day of Stratton St Margaret, Wiltshire. Hewitt was educated at Merchant Taylors' School, London, from 1869 to 1874. He then attended the Royal School of Mines for two years and shortly afterwards won a scholarship to Christ's College, Cambridge. After graduating BA with a third class in the natural science tripos he became a medical student at St George's Hospital, London, in 1880. While there he won prizes in medicine and surgery, and he qualified MRCS in 1882, MB (Cantab) in 1883, and MD in 1886. He intended to practise in London as a physician and joined a colleague, Marmaduke Sheilds, in rooms in Somerset House, Portman Square. However, a defect in Hewitt's eyesight, which had begun to trouble him at Cambridge, became worse, and he decided to take up anaesthetics. He was appointed anaesthetist to Charing Cross Hospital, London, in 1884, to the National (later the Royal Dental) Hospital in 1885, and to the London Hospital in 1886.

Hewitt's first paper was published in *The Lancet* in 1885; it was the first of many describing apparatus for the safe administration of nitrous oxide anaesthesia and demonstrated by detailed experiments the value of combining it with oxygen—work which received the acclaim of the physiologist J. S. Haldane. Hewitt rapidly became known as an outstanding anaesthetist and teacher, writing many

Sir Frederic
William Hewitt
(1857–1916), by
Elliott & Fry, pubd
1907–9

papers and delivering many lectures on improving apparatus and techniques in anaesthesia. Always concerned that students and doctors should receive proper instruction in the subject, he was foremost in persuading the General Medical Council that the study of anaesthetics should form part of the medical curriculum. Hewitt wrote three textbooks, of which the most important, *Anaesthetics and their Administration*, was published in 1893. It reached its fifth edition in 1922, six years after his death.

In 1902, when Edward VII became ill with an appendicular abscess two days before his projected coronation, Hewitt administered the anaesthetic for the necessary operation. Afterwards, the king appointed him MVO. From that time, his practice became so busy that he gave up his appointments at the Charing Cross and Royal Dental hospitals. In 1902 he was given the honorary position of consulting anaesthetist at the London Hospital and returned to his alma mater, St George's Hospital, as physician anaesthetist.

Hewitt was appointed anaesthetist to Edward VII and later to George V. In 1907 he was honoured with a knighthood for his services to medicine. Much of the later part of his life was devoted to efforts to ensure that only medically qualified persons should be permitted to administer anaesthetics, and he was largely responsible for organizing a bill to be presented to parliament which would legalize the position. Unfortunately, pressure of business and the outbreak of the First World War in 1914 caused the bill to be dropped and it was never reconsidered.

A photograph of Hewitt, which remained in the Royal College of Physicians, shows a balding man with a rather triangular face and a moustache, and bearing a solemn appearance. Even family photographs never show him smiling, yet he had a lively sense of humour. He was a popular student at Cambridge and at St George's, where he wrote many humorous poems and sketches which appeared in the hospital's *Gazette* even after he had achieved fame.

On 24 December 1891 Hewitt married Emmie (Eve) Elizabeth (1868/9–1950), daughter of George Clare. They had three children, two daughters and one son, who died in

infancy. The Hewitts lived in London first at 10 George Street (later St George Street), Hanover Square; in 1901 they moved to 14 Queen Anne Street, where they lived for the next fourteen years. In 1902 Hewitt bought a house in Peppard, near Henley-on-Thames, which the family visited as often as possible. In 1915 the Hewitts' London residence became 24 Harcourt House, Cavendish Square.

Hewitt died of stomach cancer on 6 January 1916, at 146 King's Road, Brighton, a town to which the family frequently went on holiday; he was buried in the Brighton and Preston cemetery four days later. A memorial service was held at St George's Hospital Chapel on 12 January 1917. Lady Hewitt died on 2 April 1950 and was buried in the same grave as her husband.

Frederic Hewitt's work was a major factor in establishing anaesthesia as a subject requiring the full attention of specially trained medical men and women. He is commemorated by a lectureship at the Royal College of Surgeons, since 1991 held at the Royal College of Anaesthetists.   D. D. C. HOWAT

Sources *The Lancet* (15 Jan 1916), 157–61 · *BMJ* (15 Jan 1916), 113–14 · Merchant Taylors' School archives, London · ICL, archives · Christ's College archives, Cambridge · St George's Hospital archives, London · b. cert. · m. cert. · d. cert. · G. Edwards, 'Frederic William Hewitt, 1857–1916', *Annals of the Royal College of Surgeons of England*, 8 (1951), 233–45 · B. A. Sellick, Frederick Hewitt Lecture, Royal College of Surgeons, 21/3/1973 · D. D. C. Howat, 'Anaesthesia as a career', *Anaesthesia*, 52 (1997), 979–95 · *Kelly's Post Office directory* (1885–1915) · Brighton and Preston cemetery records · private information (2004)
Archives ICL
Likenesses Elliott & Fry, photograph, pubd 1907–9, NPG [*see illus.*] · photograph, RCP Lond. · photographs, priv. coll.
Wealth at death £35,378 9s. 6d.: probate, 13 April 1916, *CGPLA Eng. & Wales*

Hewitt, James, first Viscount Lifford (1709x16–1789), lord chancellor of Ireland, was born probably in Coventry, the son of William Hewitt, a mercer and draper, who was mayor of Coventry in 1744, and his wife, Hannah Lewis. He was apprenticed to James Birch, an attorney and receiver-general for Warwickshire, but soon afterwards decided to become a barrister and entered the Middle Temple in 1737. He was called to the bar in November 1742 and soon developed a substantial practice. He stood for Coventry, unsuccessfully, in 1754 but won the parliamentary seat at the general election in 1761. In 1755 he became a serjeant-at-law, and four years later he was appointed king's serjeant.

On 6 November 1766 Hewitt was appointed a judge of the king's bench, with the promise of further promotion, and on 9 January 1768 he received letters patent as lord chancellor of Ireland. On the same day he was created Baron Lifford in the Irish peerage, and he was made a viscount in January 1781. Lifford was lord chancellor of Ireland during the struggle between the two parliaments that resulted in the short-lived independence of the Irish legislature. He held the office for twenty-two years, longer than any of his predecessors since the time of Edward I. His income as lord chancellor was estimated at £12,000 per annum.

Hewitt married, first, Mary (d. 1765), the only daughter of the Revd Rice Williams DD, rector of Stapleford Abbots, Essex, prebendary of Worcester, and archdeacon of Carmarthen. Of their children James (1750–1830), who succeeded to the viscountcy, was dean of Armagh for more than thirty years; Joseph (1754–1794) was a judge of the king's bench in Ireland; and John (d. 1804) was dean of Cloyne. On 15 December 1766 Hewitt married, as his second wife, Ambrosia (d. 1807), daughter of the Revd Charles Bayley of Navestock, Essex, with whom he had further children. Lifford had intended to resign on a pension but died in Dublin on 28 April 1789, of a 'malignant sore throat' caught at the House of Lords (GEC, *Peerage*). He was buried in Christ Church, Dublin, where there is a memorial to him.

Lifford was known for the accuracy of his technical knowledge and for his general professional skill. He was said to be formal in manner and with old-fashioned ideas but he was also patient and urbane, and those qualities gained him general respect. He was the first lord chancellor of Ireland whose judgments have been preserved. A volume entitled *Reports of select cases argued and determined in the high court of chancery in Ireland, principally in the time of Lord Lifford* was published in 1839; it was edited by James Lyne from a manuscript prepared by John Wallis KC. The decisions reported are from the years 1767 to 1786. Many of Lifford's judgments remained in manuscript and probably perished in the Four Courts fire of 1922 but some may survive in the library of King's Inns (Osborough, 100).

ANDREW LYALL

Sources F. E. Ball, *The judges in Ireland, 1221–1921*, 2 vols. (1926); repr. (1993) · GEC, *Peerage*, new edn, vol. 6 · J. Wallis, *Reports of select cases argued and determined in the high court of chancery in Ireland, principally in the time of Lord Lifford; together with some cases determined in the other superior courts, during the same period*, ed. J. Lyne (1839) · O. J. Burke, *The history of the lord chancellors of Ireland from AD 1186 to AD 1874* (1879) · W. N. Osborough, 'Puzzles from Irish law reporting history', *The life of the law* [Oxford 1991], ed. P. Birks (1993), 89–112 · Foss, *Judges* · J. R. O'Flanagan, *The lives of the lord chancellors and keepers of the great seal of Ireland*, 2 vols. (1870) · A. Davies and E. Kilmurray, *Dictionary of British portraiture*, 4 vols. (1979–81)
Archives Coventry City RO, personal and public papers and corresp. · King's Inns Library, Dublin, MS notes of cases · LUL, papers and corresp. with William Hewitt relating to his work in the West Indies | NRA, priv. coll., letters to Lord Shelburne · PRO NIre., corresp. with George Macartney · Yale U., Farmington, Lewis Walpole Library, Townshend MSS
Likenesses R. Dunkarton, mezzotint, pubd 1790 (after Reynolds), BM · J. Reynolds, oils, Smithsonian Institution, Washington, DC · R. L. West, oils (after Reynolds), NG Ire.

Hewitt [Hewytt, Hewett], **John** (*bap.* 1614, *d.* 1658), Church of England clergyman and royalist conspirator, was baptized at Eccles, Lancashire, on 4 September 1614, the fourth son of Thomas Hewett, clothworker, of Eccles. Educated at Bolton-le-Moors School and Pembroke College, Cambridge (where he matriculated sizar on 13 May 1633), Hewitt took no degree, and his whereabouts are largely unclear during the following years. He may have been living in London, where he married, on 18 December 1636, Elizabeth Skinner (*d.* in or before 1649), daughter of Robert Skinner, a merchant taylor of St Botolph, Aldgate.

Hewitt is next recorded during the civil wars, at Oxford, where he was created DD on 17 October 1643 and by 1649 was serving as chaplain to his brother-in-law, Montague *Bertie, second earl of Lindsey; Hewitt had recently married Lady Mary Bertie (1618–1669), daughter of Robert, first earl of Lindsey (*d.* 1642), and his wife, Elizabeth Montague (*d.* 1655). It was perhaps at this time that Hewitt became minister of St Gregory by Paul, London, and rector of St Mary Magdalen, Old Fish Street. A popular and influential preacher, his sermons were attended by many leading royalists, and Oliver Cromwell allegedly told him that he 'was like a flaming Torch in the midst of a sheaf of Corn: he meaning, I being a publick Preacher, was able to set the Citie on fire by sedition and cumbustions, and promoting designs' (*Speech and Prayer*, 4).

Hewitt's prayer-book Anglicanism was tolerated by the Cromwellian regime, but during the mid-1650s his congregation became the centre for less acceptable royalist endeavours. Hewitt was reputedly responsible for collecting hundreds of pounds for the king, and his house became a meeting place for royalists and the focal point for conspiracy. In late 1657 he became involved in a plot in which were implicated or rumoured to be implicated old royalists and presbyterians, including John Stapley of Sussex, Sir William Waller, and Sir Thomas Fairfax, who were to raise a force in support of a Spanish invasion. This plot was arguably based on wishful thinking rather than genuine potential, and senior royalists such as Ormond concluded that it was 'managed by honest but unskillful men' (Carte, 2.118). Another contemporary claimed that Hewitt was 'rather a Tully than a Cataline, and hath been more prevalent with his tongue than his brain' (Underdown, 1.718). Furthermore, the Cromwellian regime knew of the plot from an early stage, thanks to a double agent, and kept Hewitt under close surveillance until ready to make their move. When Stapley was questioned in the spring of 1658 he made a full confession, and Hewitt was arrested on 8 April and sent to the Tower. The government's powerful intelligence system ensured that, while some expected Hewitt to be acquitted, the secretary of state John Thurloe felt confident that the evidence was damning. It soon became clear that the high court of justice would make an example of the plotters, and the ground was laid by an officially inspired tract, *The Horrible and Bloody Conspiracy*.

Hewitt was tried on 1 June 1658, charged with 'minding and intending to embroil this commonwealth in new and intestine wars'. The prosecution said that he 'did traiterously, advisedly and maliciously plot, contrive and endeavour to stir up, force and levy war' (*State trials*, 5.884). Although without counsel Hewitt was tutored by the leading presbyterian royalist, William Prynne, who later published an account of the trial as *Beheaded Dr John Hewytts Ghost*. Under his tuition Hewitt refused to recognize the authority of the court, and he refused to enter a plea on twelve occasions, in spite of pleas by his wife. The court had little option but to sentence him to death, realizing that he was intent on becoming a martyr. Royalists such as Joseph Jane certainly considered him to have been 'very glorious in his defence', and that he was 'most heroic and

Christian, no man yet exceeding him, scarce equalling' (Warner, 4.41, 55). On 4 June Hewitt petitioned for twenty days' reprieve in order to be able to make a confession, but he was granted only two days, and even the intercession of Cromwell's daughter failed to secure clemency. He was beheaded at Tower Hill on 8 June, after making a long speech in which he denied having been a plotter, and said:

> I here give up myself willingly and freely to be a state martyr for the public good, and I had rather die many deaths myself than betray my fellow freemen to so many inconveniences that they might be like to suffer by being subject to the wills of them that willed me to this death. (*Speech and Prayer*, 2)

Hewitt's funeral sermon was preached by his friend Dr George Wilde.

In death Hewitt achieved a degree of celebrity which he had not achieved in life. His scaffold speech was quickly published, as was an account of the trial, and before the end of the year there also appeared an elegy, together with editions of his works, entitled *Repentance and conversion, nine select sermons, certain considerations against the vanities of this world*, and *Prayers of Intercession*, the first of which was apparently edited by Wilde and another friend, John Barwick. However, Nathaniel Hardy, who ventured into print in order to complain about the appearance of what purported to be the text of the sermon he had planned for Hewitt's funeral, claimed that some of these works were published by interlopers, against Hewitt's wishes.

During the parliament of Richard Cromwell, a petition was presented on behalf of Hewitt's widow (on 17 March 1659), praying for justice upon the 'murderers' of her husband. The house agreed to hold a hearing with Lady Mary Hewitt's counsel, Prynne, who chose this moment to publish the account of Hewitt's defence. However, the committee for grievances laid aside the petition, on the grounds that some of Hewitt's judges were members of parliament, and thus privileged. Following the restoration of Charles II, Lady Mary Hewitt issued another petition seeking the exception of the judges from the Act of Oblivion, though she added that members of the court had been asked to attend by the families of the plotters in order to assist their cause. In February 1661 Hewitt's son, who issued a petition seeking money to set up in trade, was granted a royal pension of £100. Hewitt's widow later married Sir Abraham Shipman (d. 1665), and later, in 1667, Thomas Lee of Islington.   J. T. Peacey

Sources State trials, vol. 5 · D. Underdown, *Royalist conspiracy in England, 1649–1660* (1960) · Thurloe, *State papers*, vols. 1, 7 · *A collection of original letters and papers, concerning the affairs of England from the year 1641 to 1660. Found among the duke of Ormonde's papers*, ed. T. Carte, 2 vols. (1739) · *The Nicholas papers*, ed. G. F. Warner, 4, CS, 3rd ser., 31 (1920) · *The Clarke papers*, ed. C. H. Firth, 3, CS, new ser., 61 (1899) · *Calendar of the Clarendon state papers preserved in the Bodleian Library*, ed. O. Ogle and others, 5 vols. (1869–1970) · *CSP dom.*, 1650–62 · *Fifth report*, HMC, 4 (1876) · J. P. Earwaker, ed., *Local gleanings relating to Lancashire and Cheshire*, 2 vols. (1875–8) · C. Hopper, 'Dr John Hewitt', *N&Q*, 2nd ser., 12 (1861), 409–16 · *The true and exact speech and prayer of Doctor John Hewytt* (1658) · *DNB*
Likenesses line engraving, in or before 1655, BM, NPG; repro. in W. Winstanley, *The Loyall martyrology* (1655) · attrib. R. Gaywood, etching, BM, NPG; repro. in J. Hewitt, *Nine select sermons* (1658) · M. Vandergucht, line engraving, BM, NPG; repro. in E. Ward, *History of the Rebellion* (1713) · engraving, repro. in J. Hewitt, *Nine select sermons* (1658)

Hewitt, John (1719–1802), magistrate, was born in Coventry, Warwickshire, the son of John Hewitt, a city linen draper, a trade he was later to follow himself. He lived all his life in Coventry, from 1746 onwards in a newly built house in Cross Cheaping. He served as mayor in 1755, 1758, and 1760 and, as one of the city's ten aldermen, was a magistrate for some thirty years. He was probably the uncle of James *Hewitt, first Viscount Lifford (1709x16–1789), whom he assisted by providing a lavish banquet in 1754 when the latter contested a Coventry parliamentary seat. On 7 February 1768, at Hinckley, Leicestershire, he married Catherine Dyer, the daughter of the Revd Dyer, a descendant of a former lord chief justice, Sir James Dyer.

Hewitt was an exceedingly zealous magistrate, prosecuting felons and transporting criminals. He carried on lengthy exchanges of letters with leading government figures of the day, soliciting their support for his actions to keep the peace. The 1750s and 1760s undeniably were decades of widespread civil disorder in the midlands, especially on account of the price of bread, and Hewitt made a stand against the rioters. His experiences of the disorders seem to have encouraged him to publish in 1779 a journal of his proceedings as magistrate, which was a strange mixture of cases he had brought successfully to justice, explanations of criminal law, and descriptions of some notorious local murders and thefts. His chief ambition, however, was to catch the Coventry gang, a group of highly skilled and well-known coiners led by Thomas Lightoler, who ultimately turned king's evidence and fled to Austria, leaving his fellow criminals to be executed at Lancaster in 1768. Lightoler, originally a carpenter, and his brother, Timothy, a skilled carver, in 1752 had created a chimney-piece for Hewitt's Coventry house, after working at Warwick Castle. Hewitt also tried to stop prostitution in Coventry and to enforce appropriate behaviour on Sundays, and he published a handbook for the use of constables (1779). His writings have a distinct tone of his efforts being unappreciated by those in power, and he always seemed very anxious to contact influential contemporaries, such as Sir John Fielding. He was a trustee of several city charities and became chamberlain in 1747 and sheriff in 1750; he also served as master of the Weavers' Company (1759–61).

Hewitt died at his home in Cross Cheaping, Coventry, on 20 April 1802, leaving no will. He was buried in the north aisle of Holy Trinity, Coventry, and was commemorated there by a flat stone that is no longer visible.

Joan Lane

Sources *A journal of the proceedings of J. Hewitt, Coventry … in his duty as a magistrate during a period of twenty years*, 2nd edn (1790) · F. L. Colvile, *The worthies of Warwickshire who lived between 1500 and 1800* [1870] · Coventry City Archives, Lifford family MSS, PA 1484 · Coventry poll book, 1774 · Coventry poll book, 1790 · *Jopson's Coventry Mercury Extraordinary* (26 April 1802) · parish registers, Coventry, Holy Trinity · IGI · DNB

Hewitt, John (1807–1878), antiquary, was born in Beacon Street, Lichfield, the son of John Hewitt (1772–1848), preceptor, organist, and music teacher, and his wife, Betsy Warren. Educated at Lichfield grammar school, he studied music in his youth, and was for some time organist of St Mary's Church in that city. On 27 June 1840 he was appointed to the post of a clerk to the Board of Ordnance storekeeper, whose department, in the Tower of London, was responsible for the storage and issue of all arms and equipment for the army, including the national collection of historical arms and armour, then classified as 'obsolete stores'. This did not then have an official curator, and Hewitt, having a bent towards the study of antiquities, was apparently encouraged to take a special interest in it. In 1841 he published *The Tower: its History, Armouries, and Antiquities; before and since the Fire*, which set a new standard of scholarship for works of this kind and also appears to have been the first government-sponsored guide to any historical site in Britain. This was followed in 1855 by the first volume, and in 1860 by the second and third volumes, of his *Ancient armour and weapons in Europe from the iron period of the northern nations to the end of the seventeenth century* (reprinted 1967), which, although it owed much to Sir Samuel Meyrick's pioneering *Critical Inquiry into Antient Armour* (1824), can be regarded as the first modern work of scholarship on this subject. Based mainly on documentary sources, it still remains a valuable work of reference for the post-conquest period. His other major contribution to the study of arms and armour was the first *Official Catalogue of the Tower Armouries* (1859), which established the system of classification of the exhibits still in use, although he also published numerous articles on this and other antiquarian subjects, mostly in the *Archaeological Journal* and *The Reliquary*.

Hewitt had already engaged in literary pursuits while in Lichfield, and these he continued, under the pen-name Sylvanus Swanquill, during his time in London, where he enjoyed the friendship of a number of well-known literary figures. His verse was described as 'racy and descriptive, suggesting the style of the elder Hood' (*The Reliquary*, 18, 1877–8, 229). He was a considerable scholar in several languages, both ancient and modern, a skilled artist, and had a wide knowledge of many subjects besides arms and armour. His publications in other fields include *Old Woolwich* (1860), handbooks to the city of Lichfield (1874) and its cathedral (1875), and a new edition of C. A. Stothard's *Monumental Effigies of Great Britain* (1876), with greatly expanded commentaries. Hewitt retired to Lichfield, where in 1873–4 he served on the committee of the Lichfield Industrial Fine Art and Loan Exhibition, for which he also arranged a display of microscopes. He died in Lichfield on 10 January 1878, and was buried five days later in the cathedral close.

THOMPSON COOPER, *rev.* CLAUDE BLAIR

Sources *The Reliquary*, 18 (1877), 228–30 · *Lichfield Mercury* (25 Jan 1878) · J. P. Anderson, *The book of British topography: a classified catalogue of the topographical works in the library of the British Museum relating to Great Britain and Ireland* (1881), 259 · A. D. Parker, *A sentimental journey in and about the ancient and loyal city of Lichfield* (1925), 158–9 · 1866, PRO, WO 47/, 8198–9 · 1867, PRO, WO 47/, 8890 · census returns for Lichfield, 1841, PRO, HO 107/1008, fol. 32, p. 23 · C. Blair, Introduction with bibliography to J. Hewitt, *Ancient armour and weapons in Europe* (1967)

Wealth at death under £3000: probate, 13 March 1878, CGPLA Eng. & Wales

Hewitt, John Harold (1907–1987), poet, was born in Belfast on 28 October 1907, the younger child and only son of Robert Telford Hewitt, principal of Agnes Street national school, and his wife, Elinor Robinson. He was educated at his father's school (*c.*1912–1919), the Royal Belfast Academical Institution (1919–20), and the Methodist college, Belfast (1920–24). In 1924 he entered the Queen's University, Belfast, to read English and graduated in 1930 with a BA degree, having also (in 1927–9) taken a teacher training course at Stranmillis College, Belfast. Hewitt's lifelong engagement with literature, art, and politics was fostered from the start by his parents, particularly by his father, a dedicated socialist. It was on his father's bookshelves that he discovered the English dissenting tradition which decisively influenced his political and literary development, as well as the magazines which stimulated his love of art. He wrote his first poems in 1924 and his earliest to appear in print were contributed (in 1928–9) to a wide variety of left-wing newspapers.

In November 1930 Hewitt was appointed art assistant at the Belfast Museum and Art Gallery. During an exhibition there (probably in the autumn of 1932) he met Roberta Black (born in Larne, co. Antrim, on 30 October 1904, the daughter of Robert Black, watchmaker); they were married in Belfast on 7 May 1934. Hewitt's energies found expression throughout the 1930s in a range of cultural activities. In 1934, for example, he helped to form the Ulster Unit, a progressive art group, and in 1937 he was involved in the founding of the *Irish Democrat* newspaper, acting as literary editor and occasional contributor. In 1936 he finished 'The Bloody brae: a Dramatic Poem', his first extended treatment of the troubled relationship between English and Scottish planters and native Irish in the north of Ireland, thereafter a major theme in his writings.

During the Second World War, Hewitt's work in the Belfast Museum and Art Gallery significantly broadened what he later described as his 'local imaginative mythology', in particular inspiring a lasting enthusiasm for the radical strain in Ulster Presbyterianism of the later eighteenth century. Hewitt's discovery of his own region, especially the Glens of co. Antrim, made him acutely receptive to the 'regionalist' idea he encountered at this time in the works of Lewis Mumford and others. Throughout the 1930s and 1940s Hewitt wrote numerous poems, publishing many in periodicals, and transcribing many more in his notebooks. He issued his first pamphlet of poems, *Conacre*, in 1943 and his second, *Compass: Two Poems*, in 1944, both privately published; and his first book-length collection, *No Rebel Word*, was published in 1948. Another key work of the period was the long autobiographical, 'regionalist' poem 'Freehold', which appeared in the literary magazine *Lagan* in 1946. In this and other poems he emerges as the liberal Ulsterman of planter stock searching for equilibrium and an abiding place in a province where his forebears were originally interlopers, and as the city-dweller whose spiritual home is the country, however marginalized he may sometimes feel there.

Having been promoted, in 1950, to deputy director and keeper of art at the Belfast Museum and Art Gallery, Hewitt had high hopes of being appointed director when the incumbent retired, but in 1953 he failed to gain this appointment, almost certainly because his radical and socialist ideals were unacceptable to the Belfast Unionist establishment. He remained as deputy director for four more years, then applied successfully for the directorship of the Herbert Art Gallery and Museum in Coventry, a post he held from 1957 to 1972. Coventry, recovering from the devastating air raids of 1940 and 1941, offered an exciting challenge to a man of his energies and ideals, though he maintained close contact with the north of Ireland. He travelled extensively during this period, and shortly before his retirement his *Collected Poems, 1932–1967* (1968) and *The Day of the Corncrake: Poems of the Nine Glens* (1969) were published.

Hewitt and his wife returned to Belfast in 1972 at a time of violent unrest but also unprecedented creativity in Ulster, especially in the field of poetry. He produced new work as poet and art historian, salvaged and revised several decades of verse from his notebooks, published books more frequently than at any other time in his life, and enjoyed a degree of recognition and homage previously denied him. The bearded, silver-haired poet, who wore glasses, smoked a pipe, and carried a walking-stick, became a familiar figure at cultural gatherings in Belfast. Roberta Hewitt died on 19 October 1975. In the following year Hewitt became the first writer-in-residence at the Queen's University, Belfast, serving until 1979, and in 1983 he was made a freeman of Belfast. He died on 27 June 1987 in the Royal Victoria Hospital, Belfast, and in 1988 the John Hewitt international summer school was established in his memory. FRANK ORMSBY, *rev.*

Sources T. Clyde, ed., *Ancestral voices: the selected prose of John Hewitt* (1987) • F. Ormsby, ed., *The collected poems of John Hewitt* (1991) • G. Dawe and J. W. Foster, eds., *The poet's place: essays in honour of John Hewitt* (1991) • *The Times* (1 July 1987) • *The Independent* (8 July 1987) • *CGPLA NIre.* (1987)

Archives PRO NIre., papers • University of Ulster Library, literary MSS and notebooks

Wealth at death £112,465: probate, 19 Nov 1987, *CGPLA NIre.*

Hewitt, Margaret (1928–1991), sociologist and churchwoman, was born on 25 October 1928 at 63 Seedley Road, Pendleton, Salford, Lancashire, the daughter of Robert Henry Hewitt, who worked in the local education office, and his wife, Jessie, *née* Jones. She was educated at Pendleton girls' high school and Bedford College, University of London, where she read sociology and graduated in 1950 with a first-class degree. She moved to the London School of Economics, where she took a PhD in 1953.

In 1952 Margaret Hewitt was appointed an assistant lecturer in sociology at the University College of the South West, which became Exeter University in 1955, and she spent the rest of her career there, as lecturer in sociology from 1954 to 1965, senior lecturer from 1965 to 1970, and reader in social institutions from 1970. She became head of the department of sociology in 1990. As a member of the council and senate she also played an important part in the development of the university. Her main interest was in women and the family, in the days before women's studies became a respectable academic discipline. She published two important works: *Wives and Mothers in Victorian Industry* (1958), in which she concentrated on the Lancashire cotton industry, and—with Ivy Pinchbeck, her former tutor at Bedford College—*Children in English Society* (2 vols., 1969 and 1973), a study of the changing social attitudes towards children, and the development of legislation affecting them, from Elizabethan times to the passing of the Children Act of 1948.

A member of the house of laity of the church assembly of the Church of England from 1961, Margaret Hewitt was elected to the house of laity of its successor, the general synod, in 1970, and was appointed to the standing committee in 1976. In 1977 she was elected to the Crown Appointments Commission for the appointment of bishops, where she served for ten years. She served on many subcommittees, and was on the panel of chairmen, chairing working parties and committees. She chaired the working group on the roles of women and men in the Church of England (1983–4), which left aside the question of admitting women to the priesthood, and wrote the report *Servants of the Lord* (1986). She also chaired the working group considering the compatibility or otherwise of freemasonry and Christianity (1986–7) and the general synod infrastructure review group (1987–8).

An Anglo-Catholic, Margaret Hewitt was a leading member of the Catholic group in the synod, and was strongly committed to traditional Anglican doctrine and practice. She was a member of the Prayer Book Society, adhering to the prayer book of 1662, but she did not like the high-church ritual practised by some of the clergy. The Church of England's move towards the ordination of women to the priesthood began in 1966 with *Women in Holy Orders* (1966), the report of a church assembly committee. It advanced through debates in the synod in 1975 and 1978 until the synod in 1984 instructed the standing committee to bring forward legislation to authorize the ordination of women. Margaret Hewitt, a passionate opponent, began to marshal the opposition. She and the other opponents of ordaining women believed that the general synod did not have the authority to make such a change alone; it required the authority of an ecumenical council, as the Anglican church was part of the universal church. She accused those in favour of change of risking church unity by pandering to the women's movement. She argued that to remain faithful to centuries of Christian tradition the Church of England must continue to perpetuate a male priesthood, as a woman priest could not represent the male Christ at the altar. She was a founder of Women Against the Ordination of Women, formed in 1986 with the support of Graham Leonard, bishop of London, a leading opponent of the ordination of women. As national co-ordinator, she travelled round the country addressing meetings, and spoke frequently on the radio and television, concentrating on winning the support of the laity. By 1991 the movement had 5500 women members, more than the Movement for the Ordination of Women, which admitted men. She did not live to take part in the debate of the general synod in November 1992, which passed legislation to admit women to the priesthood.

Despite her opposition to a female priesthood, Margaret Hewitt believed in expanding the opportunities for women in other fields, and she was president of the Exeter branch of the National Council of Women from 1978, and chairman of the Reid Trust for the Education of Women from 1980. She was also on the governing bodies of Trinity Theological College, Bristol, from 1980 to 1985, and Salisbury and Wells Theological College from 1985. Famous for the extravagant hats she sported at meetings of the general synod, she was small, but formidable. Margaret Hewitt died, unmarried, on 7 June 1991 in the Exeter Nuffield Hospital, Wonford Road, Exeter.

ANNE PIMLOTT BAKER

Sources K. Armstrong, *The end of silence: women and the priesthood* (1993) · *The ordination of women to the priesthood: a second report by the house of bishops of the general synod of the Church of England* (1988) · *The Times* (18 April 1986) · *The Times* (12 June 1991) · *The Independent* (18 June 1991) · WW · b. cert. · d. cert.
Likenesses photograph, repro. in *The Times* (12 June 1991) · photograph, repro. in *The Independent*
Wealth at death under £125,000: administration, 19 July 1991, *CGPLA Eng. & Wales*

Hewitt, Thomas Peter (1848–1933), watchmaker and businessman, was born in Fall Lane, Prescot, Lancashire, on 1 December 1848, son of Joseph Hewitt (1823–1880) and his wife, Elizabeth, *née* Moses. His great-grandfather, Joshua Hewitt (c.1740–1802), with his sons Joseph (1771–1835) and George (c.1772–c.1840), Thomas's grandfather, and numerous relatives, established themselves as makers of watch and chronometer movements in or near Prescot. Hewitt was apprenticed to his father from 1863 to 1866 and then to Thomas Lowe, of Messrs Roskell & Sons, Church Street, Liverpool (1866–9). He returned to Prescot to take over the family business in 1869–70. Details of his marriage to Rachel (b. 1847/8) are unknown. They had four daughters and two sons.

Hewitt's significance in the history of horology derives from his energetic but ultimately unsuccessful efforts between 1870 and 1910 to reverse the commercial decline of British watch making. By 1870 Britain had lost extensive domestic and imperial markets to Swiss firms and American watch factories, which applied the 'American system of manufacturing' to make watches with standardized—and therefore interchangeable—parts. British watchmakers persisted with inefficient methods of production using outworkers.

Hewitt experimented first by making 'keyless' watches. Then, in 1882, he bought the rival firm of John Wycherley of Prescot. The new company won a gold medal at the inventions exhibition in London in 1885, which helped him secure local financial support (notably from the earl

of Derby). In 1888 he studied production methods at the great American watch factories in Waterbury, Waltham, and Elgin, and bought specialized machine tools for the Lancashire Watch Company, Prescot, of which he was managing director and moving spirit. Despite his best efforts the company, founded in 1888, collapsed in 1910. It was unable to adopt fully the new technology or absorb new production and business methods. He employed several relatives to design movements and machine tools, notably his brothers George (b. 1845), director of studies at Prescot's School of Technical Instruction, and Charles (b. 1860). His uncle James (b. 1827) superintended movement manufacturing.

Hewitt was prominent in Prescot affairs (admitted to the Lodge of Loyalty, 1883), and helped establish the School of Technical Instruction. He was chairman of the Prescot Watchmakers' Trade Association. His international horological reputation arose from his relentless writings about the need to adopt new manufacturing technologies. He strongly supported the reform of the Merchandise Marks Act (1887) and later Joseph Chamberlain's protectionist campaign. His polemic *English Watchmaking under Free Trade* (1903) blamed free trade for the collapse of British watch making and, by implication, his own business difficulties. He died at 10 Billy Lows' Lane, Potters Bar, Hertfordshire, on 24 January 1933. ALUN C. DAVIES

Sources D. Moore, ed., 'Watchmakers in s. w. Lancashire, 1520–1870', Prescot Horological Museum Archives [ongoing since 1984; entries for various members of the Hewitt family] · *The Lancashire Watch Company: its rise and progress* (1893) · A. Smith, 'Introductory essay', *The Lancashire Watch Company, Prescot, Lancashire, 1889–1910* (1973), 11–43 · *Horological Journal*, 19–54 (1887–1911) · T. P. Hewitt, *English watchmaking under free trade* (1903) · A. C. Davies, 'British watchmaking and the American system', *Business History*, 35/1 (1993), 40–54 · A. C. Davies, 'Time for a change? Technological persistence in the British watchmaking industry', *Material History Review*, 36 (1992), 57–64 · *Catalogue of the whole of the valuable watch and clockmaker's machine tools … to be sold at auction by Mr Geo. K. Dixon* (1911) [sale catalogue, 22 March 1911] · 'The Lancashire Watch Company: chat with Mr T. P. Hewitt', *St Helen's Lantern*, 2/42 (17 Jan 1889) · R. Shenton [Ansdell William], 'The Lancashire Watch Company: a dream destroyed', *Clocks*, 6 (June 1984), 13–17 · b. cert. · d. cert.
Archives Prescot Museum, Demi Hunter pocket watch, 18 carat gold, L/22/1 [movement is signed 'Thomas P. Hewitt, Prescot'; serial no. of movement 33903; case maker's initial F.K.]
Likenesses Meisenbach, photograph, c.1892, repro. in *Lancashire Watch Company*, 38

Hewlett, Ebenezer (*fl.* **1737–1747**), religious writer, lived at the New Pales in Sun Street, without Bishopsgate, London, and was for a time employed by the East India Company. Between 1737 and 1747 he wrote and published approximately twenty theological tracts, the doctrines of which, he says, brought him 'only poverty, disgrace, and loss of friends'. Hewlett's pamphlets, which often attacked trinitarian orthodoxy, include *A Harmony in Christianity*, a response to the deist Thomas Chubb's *True Gospel of Jesus Christ* (1738); *The Deist Turned Christian* (1740); and *Miracles Real Evidence* (1741), which was written against Chubb's *Discourse on Miracles* (1741). He published answers to the works of many theologians, most notably Edward

Elwall, the nonconformist James Foster, Samuel Clarke, and Caleb Fleming, and did not refrain from joining in debates over Baptist and Methodist doctrines.

GORDON GOODWIN, *rev.* ADAM JACOB LEVIN

Sources F. J. G. Robinson and others, *Eighteenth-century British books: an author union catalogue*, 5 vols. (1981), vol. 3, p. 106

Hewlett, Esther. *See* Copley, Esther (1786–1851).

Hewlett, James (1768–1836), flower painter, was born on 15 September 1768, and was baptized on 5 November at Chippenham, Wiltshire, the son of Stephen Hewlett or Hewlitt, a gardener, and his wife, Mary. His father was an associate in boyhood of John Britton, the Wiltshire antiquary. Hewlett practised chiefly at Bath, painting flowers in watercolours in an ornate Dutch style; his paintings are noted for good drawing, colour, and botanical accuracy. One of his botanical studies was exhibited at Martin Gregory, St James's, London, in November 1999. On 14 February 1808 Farington noted in his diary that the collector

> Thomas Hope has bought a picture of Flowers by Hewlet of Bath, for 500 guineas. It was sent to the British Institution. This was mentioned a few days ago at a dinner … where Hoppner was, & it was added that Hewlet had painted another picture for which he asked 900 guineas. Hoppner out of patience sd. 'Hewlet ought to be smothered'. (Farington, *Diary*, 9.3223)

In 1814, together with the Bath painter Benjamin *Barker, Hewlett purchased a plot of land on Bathwick Hill where Barker built Smallcombe Villa, which was much visited by John Britton, and Hewlett also built a property for himself. They were both visited by Queen Charlotte in 1817. He occasionally painted other subjects, such as gypsies, and contributed to the Royal Academy and other exhibitions. He painted a watercolour portrait of William Millard, the Bath peeler (Victoria Art Gallery, Bath). He moved to Isleworth, Middlesex, c.1826 and died at Park House, Isleworth, on 18 August 1836; he was buried in Isleworth church, where a monument was erected by his widow, Elizabeth. There are four drawings of flowers by Hewlett in the Victoria and Albert Museum, London. Another painter of the same name, whose relationship to Hewlett is undetermined, practised at Bath at an earlier date. It is difficult to distinguish their works. The elder Hewlett died at Notting Hill, Middlesex, in 1829.　　ANNETTE PEACH

Sources IGI · will, PRO, PROB 11/1869, fols. 73*v*–74*r* · private information (2004) [S. L. Sloman] · Farington, *Diary* · Desmond, *Botanists* · Mallalieu, *Watercolour artists*
Likenesses J. Hewlett, self-portrait, oils (middle-aged), Victoria Art Gallery, Bath · J. Varley, profile pencil drawing, Victoria Art Gallery, Bath
Wealth at death personal and real estate: will, PRO, PROB 11/1869, fols. 73*v*–74*r*

Hewlett, John (1762–1844), biblical scholar, was the son of Timothy Hewlett, of Chetnole, Dorset. After taking priest's orders he was admitted a sizar at Magdalene College, Cambridge, on 18 January 1786, at the age of twenty-four. He proceeded BD in 1796. He kept a school at Shackleford, Surrey, which he ultimately sold, became morning preacher at the Foundling Hospital, London, about 1802, and in 1819 he was appointed rector of Hilgay, Downham,

Norfolk. He was at one time professor of belles-lettres at the Royal Institution of Great Britain. He died at 55 Hunter Street, Brunswick Square, London, on 13 April 1844, and was buried in the catacombs of the Foundling Chapel, London.

Hewlett was well known for his *Vindication of the Parian Chronicle*, published in 1789, in which he displayed great knowledge of the Arundel marbles. He also took over from George Gregory (1754–1808) the editing of the Bible, published in monthly parts. He published various volumes of sermons and other theological works and an *Introduction to Reading and Spelling* (1816). His chief monuments were his edition of the Bible in three volumes (1812) and his commentaries on it in five volumes (1816).

G. C. BOASE, *rev.* H. C. G. MATTHEW

Sources Venn, *Alum. Cant.* · *GM*, 2nd ser., 21 (1844), 217 · *The Pulpit* (1809), 1.57–65 · *Norwich Mercury* (20 April 1844) · J. Brownlow, *The history and objects of the Foundling Hospital* (1865)
Archives LMA, notes, accounts, incl. account book of continental tour, corresp., and bills
Likenesses mezzotint, pubd 1795 (after H. Ashby), BM, NPG · J. P. Quilley, mezzotint, pubd 1829 (after W. Brough), BM, NPG

Hewlett, Joseph Thomas James (*bap.* 1800, *d.* 1847), novelist and Church of England clergyman, son of Joseph Hewlett and Frances Batchelor of the parish of St Pancras, London, where he was born, was baptized on 31 May 1800 at St Pancras Old Church, Pancras Road, London. He was educated at the Charterhouse, London, where he was placed by the earl of Eldon, the lord chancellor. He matriculated from Worcester College, Oxford, on 13 May 1818, and graduated BA on 5 February 1822 and MA on 25 May 1826. After taking holy orders, he married. His wife was not wealthy and, unfortunately, subsequently became an invalid. Soon after, he was appointed headmaster of Abingdon grammar school. His career there was a failure, made worse by his wife's constant illness. He did not hold the post long, and his subsequent life was a prolonged struggle with poverty.

Hewlett retired to Letcombe Regis, Berkshire, to take the curacy at Wantage, which was close by, and while there endeavoured to gain an income by writing novels. Some of his efforts include *The Life and Times of Peter Priggins, the College Scout and Bedmaker* (1841, with illustrations by Phiz (Hablot K. Browne)), *The Parish Clerk* (1841), *College Life, or, The Proctor's Notebook* (1843), and *Great Tom of Oxford* (1846). It is clear from the titles of these novels that he based much of his fiction on his own experience, but nowhere is this more evident than in *Parsons and Widows* (1844; 2nd edn, 1857), in which he presents a semi-autobiographical portrait under the name of the Curate of Mosbury. He also contributed many articles to the *New Monthly Magazine*.

In 1840, through the intercession of Fox Maule (afterwards Lord Panmure), an old schoolfellow, Lord Chancellor Cottenham presented Hewlett to the rectory of Little Stambridge, near Rochford, Essex, of the annual value of £175. The climate in Essex adversely affected his health, and he died at the rectory in Little Stambridge on 24 January 1847. His body was interred at the expense of his masonic brethren of the True Friendship lodge at Rochford. As he died in relative poverty, a public subscription was taken up for the four sons and five daughters who survived him.   THOMPSON COOPER, *rev.* REBECCA MILLS

Sources *IGI* · *GM*, 2nd ser., 27 (1847), 441–2 · Foster, *Alum. Oxon.* · Ward, *Men of the reign*, 424 · D. Bank and others, eds., *British biographical archive* (1984–98), 274, 547 [microfiche; with index, 2nd edn, 1998]

Hewlett, Maurice Henry (1861–1923), novelist and poet, was born at Oatlands Park, Weybridge, Surrey, on 22 January 1861. His father, Henry Gay Hewlett (*d.* 1897), of Huguenot extraction, had the civil service appointment of keeper of land revenue records, but was also an amateur poet and critic. Henry Gay Hewlett married Emmeline Mary, daughter of James Thomas Knowles, an architect, and sister of James Thomas Knowles (1831–1908), founder and editor of the *Nineteenth Century*. They had eight children, of whom Maurice was the eldest.

In 1872 Maurice Hewlett's parents moved to Farningham, Kent, and he became a day boy at Sevenoaks School. In 1874 he went as a boarder to Palace School, Enfield, Middlesex, and in 1875 to the International College, Spring Grove, Isleworth. In 1878 he joined his cousin, W. O. Hewlett, in the family law business at 2 Raymond Buildings, Lincoln's Inn, London. On 3 January 1888 he married Hilda Beatrice (*b.* 1864/5), daughter of the Revd George William Herbert, vicar of St Peter's, Vauxhall. With her he had a son, Cecco, in 1890, and a daughter, Pia, in 1895. Hilda Beatrice Hewlett later became a pioneer aviator, the first British woman to obtain a pilot's licence. Hewlett was called to the bar by the Inner Temple in 1890, and in 1897 succeeded his father as keeper of land revenue records, a post which he held until 1901.

In 1898 Hewlett's career changed dramatically when his first novel, *The Forest Lovers*, was published to immediate popular and critical acclaim. Fame exacted its price, however, as Hewlett was labelled a writer of historical romance, a label against which he rebelled throughout his career, as he wished to be taken seriously as a poet. He asserted that 'The truth is, I write everything and approach everything as a poet—history, psychology, romance, novels, everything'. Nevertheless, Hewlett's success enabled him from 1901 on to devote himself fully to his writing, which may be divided into three periods. During the first, from 1895 to 1905, he produced mainly Italian and historical short stories and romance novels. The most important of the latter are *The Life of Richard Yea-and-Nay* (1900), about Richard I, and *The Queen's Quair* (1904), on Mary, Queen of Scots. In the second period, to the outbreak of war in 1914, Hewlett wrote Regency novels, and contemporary thesis novels which reflected his growing interest in socialism and issues such as universal suffrage; notable among these is a trilogy beginning with *Halfway House* (1908) and concerning itself with marriage and the freedom of the sexes. During the third period, from 1914 to his death, he developed his poetry,

and penned wide-ranging, unaffected essays, including *Extemporary Essays* (1922).

Hewlett was a warm-hearted man of sardonic speech, who abhorred publicity about his private life. Nevertheless, he did publish a curious volume of autobiographical reminiscences, *Lore of Proserpine* (1913), which reveals his dividedness and his typically Edwardian fascination with the spirit world. Hewlett died at Broad Chalke, Salisbury, Wiltshire, on 15 June 1923. He was cremated, and a memorial service was held at the Broad Chalke parish church.

To his death Hewlett believed that his reputation would rest on his poetry, and in particular on *The Song of the Plow* (1916), an epic poem that praises the English peasantry as the only hope for England. It has been almost completely forgotten, although as recently as 1972 the critic Samuel Hynes hailed it as 'one of the best *terza rima* poems in English' (Hynes, 187). Hewlett now appears to have come at the end of the traditions in which he wrote. If he is remembered at all, it will be for bringing to the historical romance a certain depth of knowledge and insight about the historical periods he portrayed, while maintaining an entertaining tone. If his plots now seem derivative and predictable, and his style unfashionably affected, his characterization retains a delightful and broadly humane quality. This strength undoubtedly stems from his vivid personality, paid tribute to by a number of contemporaries, including J. C. Squire:

> He was an extraordinarily full man....He never said a thing twice in different words, and never pretended to knowledge that he did not possess. The knowledge that he did possess sufficed him. It was almost impossible to mention to him in conversation a thing which he did not know about; and everything was alive to him. His knowledge and imagination working together made the whole past, and the whole of literature, live for him.   (Squire, 363)

GEORGE MALCOLM JOHNSON

Sources *The letters of Maurice Hewlett*, ed. L. Binyon (1926) · S. Hynes, 'Maurice Hewlett: an Edwardian career', *Edwardian occasions: essays on English writing in the early twentieth century* (1972), 173–90 · J. C. Squire, 'Maurice Hewlett, man of many talents', *Language Arts* (25 Aug 1923), 363–4 · G. M. Johnson, 'Maurice Hewlett', *British short-fiction writers, 1880–1914: the romantic tradition*, ed. W. F. Naufftus, DLitB, 156 (1996) · M. Bronner, *Maurice Hewlett: being a critical review of his prose and poetry* (1910) · P. H. Muir, 'A bibliography of the first editions of books by Maurice H. Hewlett (1861–1923)', *Bookman's Journal*, 15 (1927) [supplement] · D. P. Moutz, 'Hewlett, Maurice', *The 1890s: an encyclopedia of British literature, art, and culture*, ed. G. A. Cevasco (1993)
Archives BL, extracts from diaries, Add. MS 41075 · BL, corresp. with Society of Authors, Add. MS 56722 · Harvard U., Houghton L., corresp. and papers · Ransom HRC, papers · U. Cal., Berkeley, letters | BL, corresp. with Macmillans, Add. MSS 54946–54948 · BL, corresp. with Mary Stopes, Add. MS 58496 · BLPES, letters to Frederic Harrison · Bodl. Oxf., corresp. with Robert Bridges · Harvard U., Houghton L., letters to Curtis Brown · Harvard U., Houghton L., letters to Harold Munro · U. Leeds, Brotherton L., letters to Sir Edmund Gosse
Likenesses W. Rothenstein, chalk drawing, 1898, NPG · G. C. Beresford, photograph, 1903, NPG · J. K. Lawson, oils, 1904, NPG · J. K. Lawson, pencil study, *c.*1904 (after J. K. Lawson, 1904), NPG ·

M. Beerbohm, caricature, 1908, AM Oxf.; repro. in *British novelists, 1890–1929: traditionalists*, DLitB, 34, 193 · A. L. Coburn, photogravure, 1914, NPG · V. Tittle, portrait, 1922, repro. in A. B. Sutherland, *Maurice Hewlett* (1938) · W. Tittle, lithograph, 1922, NPG · W. Hester, mechanically reproduced caricature, NPG; repro. in *VF* (5 March 1913) · photograph, repro. in *Letters of Maurice Hewlett*, frontispiece · photograph, repro. in Bronner, *Maurice Hewlett*, frontispiece

Wealth at death £4449 15s. 0d.: probate, 21 Aug 1923, *CGPLA Eng. & Wales*

Hewley [*née* Wolrych], **Sarah**, **Lady Hewley** (1627–1710), benefactor, was the only daughter and heir of Robert Wolrych (*d.* 1661), attorney of Ipswich, Suffolk, and Gray's Inn, Middlesex. Her mother's maiden name was Mott. Her husband, Sir John Hewley (*d.* 1697), whom she married some time during the 1650s, was admitted into Gray's Inn on 4 February 1638; however he suspended his legal career during the 1640s to play an active role in parliament's struggles against the king. He was the only son of a minor Yorkshire West Riding gentleman, and the couple resided in Yorkshire after their marriage, alternating between their town house in York and Bell Hall, their country residence in nearby Naburn purchased in 1663. Their two children, Wolrych and John, both died in infancy, and the bulk of the Hewleys' considerable estate was subsequently given over to charity or divided among their extended kin—including Hewley Baines, Thomas Wolrych, and Mercy Mott—by Sarah.

The Hewley marriage was characterized by religious and professional compatibility and a strong sense of public duty. Both Sarah and John held strong puritan convictions before and after the Restoration; John was a legal associate—and probably a protégé—of Sarah's father. The union facilitated their prominent role in public affairs from the 1650s onwards. John came to public prominence in York when he was employed by the corporation to administrate their purchase of the dean and chapter jurisdiction in 1656. However, he had been actively involved in county government since 1646, held the recorderships of Pontefract and Doncaster in the later 1650s, and represented Pontefract in the 1659 parliament. At the Restoration he was excluded from public office, though he maintained his nonconformist networks. However in the 1670s he once again contested Yorkshire parliamentary seats, culminating in his representation of York at the three Exclusion Parliaments on an exclusionary and reformatory ticket. True to form, he supported bills for the prevention of swearing, drunkenness, and sabbath-breaking, and security against popery.

Of course, as a woman Sarah Hewley was unable to hold public office; however, along with other prominent York women, she was no less influential than her politically active husband. She was the first and most powerful patron of nonconformist meetings in York after the Restoration, protecting and befriending preachers and providing a meeting-place for nonconformists from across the county. She was the hub of a network of friends and associates—or her 'sosiety', as she described it—who were drawn from the religious and legal circles within which she and her husband moved (Raine, 11). These meetings and networks had direct political significance, as evidenced during the exclusion crisis (1679–81) when Yorkshire nonconformists assembled to pray in the houses of dissenting York matriarchs before voting for the 'whig' platform at the shire elections in York Castle.

However, Sarah Hewley is best remembered for her charitable activities, which provided the main outlet for her reformatory and godly inclinations after the death of her husband. Although these inclinations were firmly grounded in the presbyterianism typified by Edward Bowles and Richard Baxter, the Hewleys also maintained connections with the circle of Samuel Hartlib and literary networks which included John Rushworth, Matthew Poole, Sir William Dugdale, and Andrew Marvell. The Hewley Trust, which was specifically designed as a northern charity of national significance, was founded by the deeds of 13 January 1705 and 26 April 1707: it institutionalized the support of 'poor and godly Preachers' and their 'poor and godly widows'; the education of 'young men designed for the ministry'; and the propagation of the gospel in 'poor places'; and provided a York hospital for 'widows or unmarried women' fifty-five years old or over. It was financed in large part by properties purchased from royalists by Sarah's father during the 1650s, marking it as a final legacy of the family's puritan activism of the mid-seventeenth century (North Yorkshire County RO, ZTP 1, 16–18).

Although a board of male presbyterian trustees was appointed in 1705, it is clear Sarah maintained a powerful discretionary influence over the charity's activities until at least a year before her death. However, she was also willing to entrust other institutions with the administration of reformation and 'improvement'. She was the largest anonymous contributor to the meeting-house in St Saviourgate, York, and in her will she provided a fund of £500 to the York corporation for the annual 'laying in coals' for 'poor housekeepers [and] necessitous persons' and £200 for the maintenance and construction of schools for boys and 'poore girles' respectively. She died at her house at St Saviour's, York, on 23 September 1710, after a long illness, 'leaving my vile Body to be disposed by my Executors with as little cost and ceremony as may be' (will of Sarah Hewley, Sept 1710). She was buried in St Saviourgate Chapel, York. The charity was the subject of considerable dispute and parliamentary concern in the 1840s (see G. I. T. Machin, *Politics and the Churches in Great Britain, 1832 to 1868*, 1977).

P. J. WITHINGTON

Sources wills, administrations, settlements, and deeds, 1662–98, N. Yorks. CRO, ZTP 1, 16–18 · wills of Sir John and Sarah Hewley, both prerogative, Oct 1697 and Sept 1710, Borth. Inst. · J. Raine, ed., 'A brief memoir of Mr Justice Rokeby', *Miscellanea*, SurtS, 37 (1861), 10–11, 6, 10–11 · *The Rev. Oliver Heywood … his autobiography, diaries, anecdote and event books*, ed. J. H. Turner, 4 vols. (1881–5) · *The diary of Ralph Thoresby*, ed. J. Hunter, 2 vols. (1830) · *The poems and letters of Andrew Marvell*, ed. H. M. Margoliouth, 2nd edn, 2 (1952), 314, 355 · Dugdale, *Monasticon*, vol. 1 · M. Poole, *Synopsis criticorum aliorumque s. scripturae interpretum*, 1 (1669) · T. Coulton, *The funeral sermon for*

Dame Sarah Hewley (1836) · J. Hunter, *An historical defence of the trustees of Lady Hewley's foundation* (1834) · D. Scott, 'Sir John Hewley', HoP, *Commons* [draft] · D. Scott, 'Politics, dissent and Quakerism in York, 1640–1700', DPhil diss., University of York, 1990 · HoP, *Commons, 1660–90* · housebook, vol. 36, York City Archives · *Memoirs of Sir John Reresby*, ed. A. Browning, 2nd edn, ed. M. K. Geiter and W. A. Speck (1991) · W. Dugdale, *The visitation of the county of Yorke*, ed. R. Davies and G. J. Armytage, SurtS, 36 (1859)
Wealth at death see investments in trusts; will, Sept 1710, Borth. Inst.

Hewson, John, appointed Lord Hewson under the protectorate (*fl.* 1630–1660), army officer and regicide, rose to prominence from low social origins. During the 1630s he was employed as a shoemaker or cobbler in Westminster and Edward Hyde later claimed that he was also for a time a brewer's clerk. In 1642 he enlisted in the parliamentarian forces and subsequently served under the earls of Essex and Manchester. On the formation of the New Model Army in 1645 he was appointed lieutenant-colonel of Colonel Pickering's regiment and in July of that year he took part in the storming of Bridgwater in Somerset. On Pickering's death in December 1645 Hewson succeeded him as colonel. In 1646 while stationed in the Oxford area, he illegally preached several times in a local parish church, denouncing the incumbent minister as an agent of Antichrist.

During 1647 Hewson was heavily involved in the political struggle between the army and parliament. In April he was chosen as one of the commissioners to represent the army's grievances to parliament and he subsequently presented the army's charges against the eleven presbyterian members. In November he took part in the debates of the army council at Putney, and at their close was one of those charged with drawing up instructions to be communicated to the army at the proposed general rendezvous. In December 1647 he joined his fellow officers in a prayer meeting at Windsor.

In the summer of 1648 Hewson helped to put down the royalist uprising in Kent. His regiment fought at Maidstone, assisted in the relief of Dover, and captured castles at Deal, Walmer, and Sandwich. In December 1648 he assisted Colonel Pride in his purge of parliament and at the subsequent debates of the army council at Whitehall he argued that the magistrate had a right to enforce the moral law. He was subsequently named as one of Charles I's judges and attended the court regularly during January 1649 and signed the king's death warrant [*see also* Regicides].

For all his religious radicalism Hewson was a staunch opponent of the Levellers, and in May 1649 helped Cromwell crush them at Burford. The following autumn he was part of Cromwell's expeditionary force sent to reconquer Ireland. He took part in the sack of Drogheda—subsequently commenting that if the Irish did not submit 'the lord by his power shall break them in pieces like a potter's vessel' (*Perfect Occurences*). He was involved in the relief of Arklow, helped to take Ballyronan and Leighlinbridge, and was wounded during the unsuccessful storming of

Kilkenny. It may have been here that he lost an eye. In 1650 he was appointed to the strategically vital position of governor of Dublin, a post he held until 1656.

A godly Independent and supporter of religious toleration, Hewson joined the radical John Rogers's gathered church in Dublin. Rogers later included in his tract *Ohel or Bethshemesh* an account of Hewson's testimony before the congregation, in which he had spoken of how he had lived originally as a 'child of wrath' in a 'wicked and profane family in London' before being converted through the influence of a godly preacher (Rogers, 395–6). In 1652 Hewson was recalled to London to discuss the best way to provide godly preachers for Ireland. He strongly supported the policies of Charles Fleetwood as lord deputy, and following the latter's replacement in 1655 by the protector's son Henry he unsuccessfully petitioned for Fleetwood's return. His relationship with Henry Cromwell thereafter remained tense and uneasy and in 1656 he was ordered to return to England.

In the summer of 1653 Hewson was chosen to represent Ireland in Barebone's Parliament. He took an active part in the assembly's work and in December was involved in the moderate members' plan to bring the assembly to an end. On the establishment of the protectorate he reluctantly supported the new constitutional order, but the republican Edmund Ludlow claimed that he was induced to do so only by the payment of his arrears of pay. In lieu of some of these arrears, he was granted land at Luttrellstown near Dublin.

Hewson represented Dublin in the first protectorate parliament in 1654, and Guildford in the second in 1656. In spring 1657 he bitterly opposed the moves in parliament to offer Cromwell the crown. In December 1657 he was knighted by Cromwell and chosen as a member of the new second chamber, where he took his seat in January as Lord Hewson; according to Ludlow the earl of Warwick refused to take his seat in this house because it contained figures of such mean extraction as Hewson. After the resignation of Richard Cromwell, Hewson was chosen by the Rump in July 1659 as commander-in-chief of the foot in Ireland. By the autumn he was back in England and, following John Lambert's closure of parliament, was named to the army committee of safety. In December he was ordered to suppress a demonstration in London in favour of a free parliament, and in the course of the action several demonstrators were killed and about twenty injured. As a result Hewson became a target of a great deal of criticism and was satirized in several ballads and lampoons, including Thomas Flatman's *Don Juan Lamberto*, where he appeared as the one-eyed giant, Hussonius, and Edmund Gayton's *Walk Knaves Walk*, a mock sermon by his chaplain on how to wax boots. According to Samuel Pepys, in January 1660 a gibbet was erected in Cheapside with Hewson's image nailed to it.

After the Rump's return on 26 December 1659 Hewson was deprived of his command but escaped more serious punishment. In May, as the return of Charles II became increasingly more likely, he fled to the continent. He was exempted from the Act of Indemnity but remained at liberty until his death. The Oxford antiquarian Anthony Wood claimed that he died at Amsterdam in 1662, but a pedlar who was arrested and questioned in 1665 on suspicion of being Hewson stated that he had died at Rouen in 1662 or 1663.   CHRISTOPHER DURSTON

Sources I. Gentles, *The New Model Army in England, Ireland, and Scotland, 1645–1653* (1992) · C. H. Firth and G. Davies, *The regimental history of Cromwell's army*, 2 vols. (1940) · *The Clarke Papers*, ed. C. H. Firth, 2, CS, new ser., 54 (1894) · Clarendon, *Hist. rebellion* · *CSP dom., 1654* · T. C. Barnard, *Cromwellian Ireland: English government and reform in Ireland, 1649–1660* (1975) · J. Rogers, *Ohel or Bethshemesh, or, The tabernacle of the sun* (1653) · A. Woolrych, *Commonwealth to protectorate* (1982) · *Memoirs of Edmund Ludlow*, ed. C. H. Firth, 2 vols. (1888) · C. H. Firth, *Cromwell's army* (1902) · Thurloe state papers, Bodl. Oxf., MS Rawl. A · *The writings and speeches of Oliver Cromwell*, ed. W. C. Abbott and C. D. Crane, 4 vols. (1937–47) · T. Flatman, *Don Juan Lamberto* (1659) · E. Gayton, *Walk knaves walk* (1660) · *Perfect occurences* (28 Sept–4 Oct 1649) · GEC, *Peerage*

Archives Bodl. Oxf., Thurloe state papers, MS Rawl. A

Likenesses M. Vandergucht, line engraving, BM, NPG · woodcut caricature, repro. in Flatman, *Don Juan*

Hewson, William (1739–1774), surgeon and anatomist, one of the eleven children of William Hewson (*d.* 1767), surgeon, and his wife, whose maiden name was Heron, was born at Hexham, Northumberland, on 14 November 1739. After attending Hexham Royal Free Grammar School, he was apprenticed to his father, and was also pupil to Richard Lambert, who had formed a medical charity in a house in Gallowgate, Newcastle, which later became Newcastle Infirmary. In 1759 Hewson travelled to London, lodged with John Hunter while attending the anatomical lectures of William Hunter, and studied at St Thomas's and Guy's hospitals. He also took classes in midwifery with Colin Mackenzie and in physic with Hugh Smith. When John Hunter went abroad with the army in 1760 he left Hewson to instruct the other pupils in the dissecting room. William Hunter afterwards proposed to Hewson to take him into partnership as a lecturer if he would undertake a year's study in Edinburgh. Hewson did so, and in the autumn of 1762 he returned to London and began to share in the lectures and the profits of William Hunter's anatomical school, which was then in Litchfield Street, Soho. In 1765 Hewson went to France, Flanders, and the Netherlands to visit the hospitals, but returned to give the winter lectures on anatomy.

In 1768 Hewson visited the coast of Sussex to study the lymphatic system in fishes, and made his researches the subject of a paper communicated in the following year to the Royal Society; his efforts were rewarded with the Copley medal. On 8 March 1770 he was elected FRS.

Hewson's researches on the lymphatic system gave rise to an acrimonious controversy with Alexander Monro secundus of Edinburgh, who, in a letter addressed to the Royal Society, read on 19 January 1769, and in a pamphlet (*A state of facts concerning paracentesis of the thorax, &c., and concerning the discovery of the lymphatic system in oviparous animals, in answer to Mr. Hewson*, 1770) claimed the priority in these discoveries. Hewson's reply was given in an appendix to his *Experimental Inquiries*, part 1. The minor point of

William Hewson (1739–1774), by Robert Stewart, pubd 1780

the operation of paracentesis had no reference to the other question; and in regard to this Hewson frankly admitted that he had been anticipated by Monro. But in the more important matters he successfully vindicated his own priority.

In 1769 William Hunter opened the celebrated anatomical school in Windmill Street, where a room was provided for Hewson, who continued in partnership as lecturer, receiving a larger share of profits than before. He also acquired a substantial practice in surgery and midwifery. On 10 July 1770 he married Mary (Polly) Stevenson (1739–1795), who described herself as having 'no pretensions to beauty, nor any splendid fortune' (Richardson, 151). She was, however, a friend of Benjamin Franklin, the American statesman and natural philosopher, who had lodged in her mother's house since he went to London in 1757. She described Hewson as being of slender build, above average height

> with a good air and pleasing countenance, expressive of the gentleness and sagacity of his mind. … His manners were gentle and engaging; his ambition was free from ostentation, his prudence was without meaness, and he was more covetous of fame than fortune. (Richardson, 175)

On his marriage Hewson moved to a house of his own in Craven Street, and this was made by William Hunter a ground for giving notice of breaking off their partnership. This was a blow to Hewson, especially as the building and anatomical museum necessary for carrying on the lectures were exclusively Hunter's property. A disagreement arose about the right of Hewson to make preparations for his own use, but this was smoothed over by the mediation of Franklin. Hewson used his leisure during the year of notice provided for by the terms of partnership in making preparations for future use in his own lectures, and the museum thus formed was so valuable that it subsequently sold for £700. In September 1772 Hewson began to lecture on his own account at a theatre which he built adjoining his home. His reputation was now so high, especially since the publication of various researches by him in the *Philosophical Transactions* and of his *An Experimental Inquiry into the Properties of the Blood* (1771), that he had no difficulty in attracting a large class, and he lectured for two winter sessions with great success. Early in 1774 he brought out the second part of his *Experimental Inquiries*, and his increase of reputation as a lecturer and anatomist was accompanied by a considerable increase in the size of his practice.

Hewson was an excellent anatomist and a physiologist of great originality. His researches on the blood were valuable in establishing the essential character of the process of coagulation, and the forms of the red corpuscles in different animals. They were a good example of the experimental method characteristic of the school of the Hunters. The third part of his *Experimental Inquiries*, relating to the blood, was published after his death by Magnus Falconar, who compiled four chapters of Hewson's observations which the latter had never committed to writing.

On 18 April 1774 Hewson wounded himself in making a dissection. Serious symptoms followed, and he died on the morning of Sunday, 1 May 1774, in his thirty-fifth year. According to Mary Hewson 'His last moments of recollection were embittered by the idea of leaving me with three children scantily provided for' (Richardson, 151). He was buried at St Martin-in-the-Fields, London, but his grave was later lost. His widow, who was left with two sons, gave birth to a daughter, Elizabeth, in the August following her husband's death; she went, on the advice of Benjamin Franklin, to America. The second son, Thomas Tickell Hewson (*d.* 1848), after studying at Edinburgh, became an eminent physician and president of the College of Physicians in Philadelphia. Hewson's works were collected and admirably edited by George Gulliver for the Sydenham Society in 1846. A collective Latin edition, *Opera omnia*, was published in Leiden in 1795. In 1998 the remains of a number of bodies were discovered during building work at 36 Craven Street; these may have been the remnants of some of Hewson's anatomical researches.

J. F. PAYNE, rev. MICHAEL BEVAN

Sources B. W. Richardson, 'William Hewson FRS', *The Asclepiad*, 8 (1891), 148–77 · H. Wilford, 'The life and work of William Hewson, haematologist and immunologist', *Medicine in Northumbria: essays on the history of medicine in the north-east of England*, ed. D. Gardner-Medwin, A. Hargreaves, and E. Lazenby (1993) · *Evening Standard* (10 Feb 1998) · P. J. Wallis and R. V. Wallis, *Eighteenth century medics*, 2nd edn (1988)
Archives RCP Lond., lecture notes · RCS Eng., lecture notes · RS, papers
Likenesses R. Stewart, mezzotint, pubd 1780, BM [*see illus.*] · R. Stewart, stipple, 1780, Wellcome L.; repro. in Richardson, 'William Hewson' · T. Rowlandson, group portrait (*The dissecting room*), RCS Eng.

Hewson, William (1806–1870), theological writer, was born on 12 April 1806 and baptized at St Margaret's, Westminster, on 28 December in the same year, the son of William Hewson of 7 Tottenham Court New Road, London, clerk in a bank. He entered St Paul's School, London, on 9 October 1815. He won an exhibition and proceeded to St John's College, Cambridge, in 1826, where he was elected to a scholarship in 1826 and graduated BA in 1830 and MA in 1833. He was ordained deacon (London) on 6 June 1830 and priest (York) in 1831, holding the curacy of Bishop Burton in the East Riding of Yorkshire from June 1830 to 1833. He married on 2 November 1830 Mary Ann (*d.* 1861), only child of Samuel and Mary Reckster, and widow of Lieutenant Alfred A. Yeakell. They had two children, Frances Ann (*b.* 1833) and John Singleton (1835–1850).

From January 1834 Hewson was curate of Spofforth, Yorkshire, for one year, and then became headmaster of Sherburn grammar school, Yorkshire, in 1835, with Sunday duty as a curate in Sherburn parish. From January 1838 until June 1844 he was headmaster of the cathedral school of St Peter's, York. He had little teaching ability and presided over a decline in pupil numbers, loss of discipline, and staff unrest. The dean and chapter set up a committee to inquire into the state of the school in 1842. After the dean withdrew his support for Hewson in 1844 he was dismissed, although he was later granted a pension.

In 1848 the archbishop of York presented Hewson to the perpetual curacy of Goathland, worth only £53 a year, with permission to reside at Whitby, as there was no house for the incumbent in the parish. Hewson succeeded in obtaining an increased stipend of £275 a year. He began to build a house, which was nearly completed at the time of his death.

Hewson was a laborious writer, and produced twenty-six publications, mainly on comparative religion and on prophecy and its fulfilment. His method of exposition was not lucid, and his works were little read. His favourite belief was that the book of Revelation was an inspired interpretation of the spirit of Jewish prophecy. He died from disease of the heart at 1 St Hilda Terrace, Whitby, on 23 April 1870, and was buried, as had been his wife and son, in York cemetery. His daughter completed the publication of her father's Hebrew and Greek scriptures in 1870.

G. C. BOASE, rev. ELLIE CLEWLOW

Sources *The Guardian* (4 May 1870), 513 · *Whitby Times* (29 April 1870), 4 · G. Smales, *Whitby authors and their publications* (1867) · private information (1891) · Boase, *Mod. Eng. biog.* · Venn, *Alum. Cant.* · F. J. Wiseman, *The recent history of St Peter's School, York* (1967) · A. Raine, *History of St Peter's School, York* (1926)
Wealth at death under £5000: administration, 3 June 1870, *CGPLA Eng. & Wales*

Hexham, Henry (*fl.* 1601–1650), soldier and author, born in Holland, Lincolnshire, was possibly the son of the Edward Hexham who served ten years in the Netherlands as an ensign and accompanied the English expedition to Cadiz in 1596 with the rank of lieutenant. Either his mother, or a sister of his father, was a sister of Jerome Heydon, merchant, of London, who was probably related to Sir Christopher *Heydon. The cousin, John Heydon, to whom Hexham dedicates his *Appendix of Lawes*, seems to be Sir John *Heydon (*d.* 1653), Sir Christopher's son. Further support for the connection exists in the fact that Sir Christopher's daughter, Frances, married Philip *Vincent, who wrote the commendatory verses prefixed to Hexham's translation of Gerardus Mercator's *Atlas*.

As a young man Hexham was attached as a page to the service of Sir Francis Vere, commander of the English troops in the United Provinces; he was with Vere throughout the siege of Ostend in 1601, and his narrative of that event, which is printed at the end of Sir Francis Vere's *Commentaries* (1657), supplies some unique details about the siege. Hexham seems to have served with Sir Francis until Vere's return to England in 1606, whereupon he remained in the Netherlands, possibly in one of the towns garrisoned by the English. Hexham's continued residency in the Netherlands accounts for his personal acquaintance with Prince Maurice of Nassau and his brother, Frederick Henry. Hexham transferred his services to Sir Horace Vere, who had succeeded his brother Sir Francis and was governor of the town of Brill in 1610 when Hexham translated into English and published his first book, a protestant religious work entitled *The Refutation of an Epistle, Written by a Certain Doctor of the Augustins Order*—the epistle by Dutch theologian Johannes Polyander. Hexham dedicated it to Vere and it contained an 'epistle to the Christian reader' by John Burges, minister to the English at the Hague.

The following year Hexham published three more translations in the cause of international protestantism, including a Dutch translation of Thomas Tuke's *The Highway to Heaven*, under the title *De konincklicke wech tot den hemel* and an English translation of Johannes Polyander's *Dispute contre l'Adoration des Reliques des Saincts*, as *A Disputation Against the Adoration of the Reliques of Saints*, dedicating the latter to the puritan-inclined Mary, Lady Vere, and signing it as from 'our garrison of Dordrecht, 18 Oct. 1611' (Hexham, *A Disputation*, sig. A2). Hexham undertook the translation 'so that the grave men of our nation may see that the ministers of other reformed churches marches with them unto the Lords combate' (ibid., sig. A3), and he hoped that even those infected with the 'deadly contagion' (ibid., sig. A3–4) of Catholicism would read it. Hexham was still in the Netherlands some twelve years later when his religious motivation in fighting for the Dutch was further confirmed by his *A tongue combat lately happening between two English souldiers ... the one going to serve the king of Spain, the other to serve the states generall* (1623), which he was prompted to write after reading a pamphlet disparaging the policies of Elizabeth I and James I and 'the truth of the reformed religion wherein I was educated' (Hexham, *A Tongue Combat*, sig. A2).

Hexham acted as quartermaster to Vere's regiment at the relief of Breda in 1625. By October the same year he had obtained the rank of captain. He also acted as quartermaster under Vere during the siege of Bois-le-Duc ('s-Hertogenbosch) in 1629, at the capture of Venloo, Roermond, and Strale, and at the siege of Maastricht in 1631–2.

After Vere's death he became quartermaster to the regiment of George (afterwards Baron) Goring, with whom he served at the siege of Breda in 1637.

In the 1630s Hexham stopped his overtly religious publications in favour of military and other writing. His most solid literary work was his edition of Mercator's *Atlas*. This was a translation into English of the edition by Jodocus Hondius, but Hexham made additions of his own, and was further assisted by Hondius's son, Henry. The preface is dated Amsterdam, 1 January 1636 *stilo veteri* [os], and the work is dedicated by Hexham to Charles I; it was published in Amsterdam in 1636–7 (2 vols), contains many maps and coloured plates, and remains the standard edition of Mercator. He also wrote and translated a number of battle narratives and technical military treatises.

In 1637 Hexham contributed significantly to the theory of the art of war, by publishing *The Principles of the Art Militarie Practised in the Warres of the United Netherlands* (1637), a work similar to Jacob de Gheyn's *Wapenhandelinge* ('Exercise of arms') (1607); both books consisted of engraved plates representing the drill movements for pikemen, musketeers, and arquebusiers, and were specifically designed for the use of captains in the drilling of their men. Hexham's work heavily influenced *Directions for Musters* (1638), a pamphlet printed for the use of town militias, on the eve of the first bishops' war, as part of Charles I's 'perfect militia program' (begun in 1628). Hexham's translation, *The Art of Fortification* (1638), from the original by Samuel Marolais, is said to be the first work on fortification printed in English in which the subject is treated scientifically.

In 1640 Hexham was in England, and on 27 July 1641 Edward, Viscount Conway, wrote to Secretary Nicholas that he had known Hexham as long as he could remember, and was sure he was a good protestant and would take the oath of allegiance and supremacy, which he did four days later, being then described as 'of St. Clement Danes' (*CSP dom.*, 1641–3, 59, 60). Four days after taking the oath he was granted permission to retire to the Netherlands. Hexham therefore took no active part in the civil wars in England. After returning to the Netherlands Hexham remained in Dutch service and busied himself with his literary work. In his book on army discipline, *An Appendix of Lawes, Articles, and Ordinances* (1643), he referred to the English civil war, writing that he wished to prevent the pillage committed on both sides by showing the means taken by the Dutch to check it; he also remarked that he had served forty-two years in the army and had never been wounded. Another important work was his *A copious English and Netherduytch dictionarie ... as also a compendious grammar of the instruction of the learner* published at Rotterdam in 1647–8, which he claimed was the first of its kind. It has a preface dated 21 September 1647. Hexham is last heard of in 1650 when he was recorded acting in the position of quartermaster to one of the regiments of the Anglo-Dutch brigade on monthly pay of 25 guilders.

A. F. POLLARD, rev. M. R. GLOZIER

Sources *CSP dom.*, 1627–8, 118; 1640, 516; 1641–3, 59, 60 • M. G. D. Cockle, *Bibliography of military books up to 1642* (1900), 108–9, 111 • I. J.

Maclean, ed., *Het Huwelijksintekeningen van Schotse militairen in Nederland, 1574–1665* (Zutphen, 1976), 321 • H. Hexham, *A journall of the taking of Venlo, Roermont, Strale, the memorable siege of Mastricht, the towne and castle of Limbruch … anno 1632* (1633) • G. Markham, *The fighting Veres, lives of Sir Francis Vere, general of the queen's forces in the Low Countries … and of Sir Horace Vere … Baron Vere of Tilbury* (1888), x, 508 • J. Ferguson, ed., *Papers illustrating the history of the Scots brigade in the service of the United Netherlands, 1572–1782*, 1, Scottish History Society, 32 (1899), 491 • A. J. van der Aa, *Biographisch Woordenboek* (1857–78), 8.764–5 • *DNB*

Hexham, John of (*d.* before 1209), historian and prior of Hexham, was born at Hexham and became a canon of the Augustinian priory there. The records of the house suggest that he became prior *c.*1160, that he was still prior in 1189, and that he died (presumably at Hexham) before 1209. Apart from these dates little is known about him. His chronicle, which is found as a continuation of the work of Symeon of Durham, extends from 1130 to 1154, and was probably compiled *c.*1170, and certainly at some date after May 1162. It survives in a twelfth-century manuscript (Cambridge, Corpus Christi College, MS 139), in a text that contains a number of interpolations and which was once in the possession of Sawley Abbey. Although the work borrows from other writings, including the chronicles of John of Worcester, Henry of Huntingdon, and Richard of Hexham, who was John's predecessor as prior, it contains a substantial amount of original material, and constitutes an important source for early and mid-twelfth-century history, particularly as regards the ecclesiastical history of northern England. Despite being written more than twenty years after the event, it contains the most reliable account of the dispute at York in 1140–41, when the election of William fitz Herbert as archbishop was opposed by a section of the York chapter as well as by the Cistercians of the diocese and by Bernard of Clairvaux. John's description of the struggle at Durham in the early 1140s when the newly elected bishop, William de Ste Barbe, formerly the dean of York, attempted to force his way into the see which was occupied by William Cumin, is also valuable. If in his work John of Hexham reveals little of his own personality, his chronicle illustrates none the less the contacts that existed between the Hexham canons and other ecclesiastical bodies, which explain the well-informed nature of his narrative. Thus, although on certain matters the canons came within the jurisdiction of the bishops of Durham, they were also a part of York's Durham franchise. The priors of Hexham had a seat in the York chapter, and were well acquainted with events at York. Cistercian contacts also provided a source of information. The most famous English Cistercian of his day, Ailred (*d.* 1167), was a native of Hexham, and would have been known personally to Prior John. In a border region where the canons owed what independence they enjoyed largely to the king of Scots, their relationship with David I (*r.* 1124–53) again ensured that information about the Scottish ruler featured prominently in their chronicle. Although John of Hexham's work is primarily of value for its account of northern history, it deals with matters of more than local

interest, and includes notices of events elsewhere in England and in Europe. Together with the chronicle of Richard of Hexham it marks the beginning of an important tradition of historical writing by Augustinian canons in the north of England. JOHN TAYLOR

Sources J. Raine, ed., *The priory of Hexham*, 2 vols., SurtS, 44, 46 (1864–5), 107–72 • Symeon of Durham, *Opera*, 2.284–332 • P. H. Blair, 'Some observations on the *Historia regum* attributed to Symeon of Durham', *Celt and Saxon: studies in the early British border*, ed. N. K. Chadwick (1963), 63–118 • J. M. Todd and H. S. Offler, 'A medieval chronicle from Scotland', *SHR*, 47 (1968), 151–9 • A. Gransden, *Historical writing in England*, 1 (1974), 261
Archives CCC Cam., MS 139

Hexham, Richard of (*d.* 1155×67), prior of Hexham and chronicler, was a canon of the Augustinian priory of Hexham, who succeeded Robert Biset as prior in 1141, when the latter left to become a monk at Clairvaux. His own short account of the early history of Hexham from its foundation by Wilfrid to *c.*1138, labelled subsequently as the 'short chronicle' (*brevis annotatio*), mentions one Richard as being a canon by 1138, and it is reasonable to infer that this is the author himself. If so, he was present that year when Eilaf, the father of Ailred of Rievaulx (*d.* 1167) and last of the hereditary priest–guardians of the relics of the Hexham saints, surrendered a silver reliquary cross containing their bones to the canons of Hexham as he lay dying at Durham.

Richard seems to have enjoyed cordial relations with Ailred himself, who was also present on this occasion and had close connections with Hexham. When on 3 March 1155 Richard supervised the solemn translation of the relics of Acca, Ahlmund, and others, Ailred preached the sermon that formed the basis of his own *De sanctis ecclesiae Hagustaldensis* ('On the saints of Hexham'). Ailred's tract, completed after Richard's death, may incorporate an earlier but unfinished work by Richard himself on the miracles of saints of Hexham. Throughout his writings Richard was anxious to stress the continuity between the Augustinian priory, founded in 1113, and the glories of Hexham's Anglo-Saxon past.

Richard's best-known work, *De gestis regis Stephani et de bello Standardii* ('The deeds of Stephen and concerning the battle of the Standard') is a largely firsthand account of contemporary events from 1135 to 1139, focusing on the repeated incursions by David I, king of Scots (*r.* 1124–53), into northern England, which he was particularly well placed to observe. For a time in early 1138 the Scottish army was camped at Corbridge, only 4 miles from Hexham, and Richard may well have had contact with King David and his son Earl Henry when they granted a charter of immunity from hostilities to the priory. Stressing the protective power of its tutelary saints, Richard noted that refugees flocked to Hexham, fleeing the slaughter and enslaving committed by the Galwegian and Scottish troops which he describes in impassioned if exaggerated detail.

Containing many biblical quotations, Richard's chronicle is strongly edificatory in tone, regarding the Scots' ravagings as resulting from the sins of the people. Nevertheless, the climax of his narrative is the rout of David I's forces by an Anglo-Norman army at the battle of the Standard, fought close to Northallerton in Yorkshire on 22 August 1138, in which the English erected a ship's mast as their rallying point and hung from it a silver pyx and the banners of the Northumbrian saints. To Richard, God and the saints had requited the Scots for their atrocities and sacrilege. His succinct account formed the basis of Ailred of Rievaulx's later *Relatio de Standardo* ('Account of the Standard'), composed about 1155–7, which adds little save inflated rhetoric and lengthy pre-battle orations.

Richard concludes his narrative with the Anglo-Scottish peace negotiations of 1138–9. He had met the papal legate Alberic, a key intermediary in these discussions, when in September 1138 the legate, together with bishops Robert of Hereford and Athelwold of Carlisle, visited Hexham, and Richard includes a biographical sketch of him. It is unknown whether Richard accompanied Prior Robert Biset, who formed part of Alberic's legation to David I, though he was well informed about the negotiations, which included David's indemnification of Hexham Priory for the losses it had suffered in the war.

Richard stimulated, if he did not create, Hexham as a centre for historical writing. His successor as prior, John of Hexham (*d.* before 1209), incorporated much of Richard's chronicle in his continuation of Symeon of Durham's *Gesta regum* ('Deeds of the kings'), which he took up to 1154. Both had access to a considerable number of contemporary histories, and Richard cited in full several important documents such as Henry I's coronation charter, Stephen's charter of liberties of 1136, and the canons of the Council of Westminster in 1138.

Richard was posthumously praised by Ailred for a purity and sobriety that was almost monastic—high praise from the Cistercian abbot of Rievaulx—noting that from youth his life had been honourable and worthy of veneration. The prior's personal reputation did not, however, prevent Henry Murdac (*d.* 1153), archbishop of York, from imposing a stricter discipline on the canons during an extended visitation in 1152. The date and circumstances of Richard's death (1155x67) are unknown, though it is probable he was buried in Hexham Priory.   MATTHEW STRICKLAND

Sources J. Raine, ed., *The priory of Hexham*, 2 vols., SurtS, 44, 46 (1864–5) · *The life of Ailred of Rievaulx by Walter Daniel*, ed. and trans. M. Powicke (1950) · A. Gransden, *Historical writing in England*, 1 (1974)
Archives CCC Cam., MS 139

Hey, Donald Holroyde (1904–1987), organic chemist, was born in Swansea on 2 September 1904, the second of three sons (there were no daughters) of Arthur Hey, professional musician, who had gone to Swansea from Yorkshire in 1888 to become organist at St James's Church, and his wife, Frances Jane Baynham, from an established Swansea family. Donald Hey was brought up in a cultured home, where he gained his lifelong love of music. He played the piano and organ and was a chorister, winning a choral scholarship to Magdalen College School, Oxford. Since the school was a traditional classical establishment, with little opportunity to study science beyond school certificate, he thereafter taught himself. Such was his determination that he enrolled for the intermediate London science course while still at school. Because family finances did not allow him to go to Oxford University, he opted for the new college at Swansea. In 1924 he obtained a BSc pass as an external student of London University. A first-class degree in chemistry followed in 1926 when, remarkably, he published his first scientific paper and sold his invention of a new type of chemical indicator to Imperial Chemical Industries. This was before he had even begun research for his PhD, which he gained in 1928. In 1931 he married a botanist, Jessie (*d.* 1982), daughter of Thomas Jones, chemist. They had a son and a daughter.

Hey began his academic career in 1928 in the University of Manchester, as a temporary assistant lecturer. He was promoted to lecturer in 1930, with a three-year contract. In 1930 W. S. M. Grieve became his first research student. Out of their collaboration came one of two papers on the reactions of what Hey called phenyl radicals with benzene derivatives to give biphenyls. Up until then all chemical reactions in solution were assumed to involve positively charged (2-electron deficient) or negatively charged (2-electron rich) species. Grieve and Hey put forward the bold suggestion that in their reactions a third species, hitherto unsuspected, was involved—an electrically neutral phenyl radical carrying one unpaired electron. This was received with disbelief and ridicule, which persisted until 1948 in some quarters. The foremost British organic chemist, Robert Robinson, examined Grieve for his PhD and remained unconvinced. Hey as sole author published his famous paper on the reactions of dibenzoyl peroxide in the *Journal of the Chemical Society* (1934, pt 2).

It was typical of Hey that he was prepared to take the offensive rather than retreat. In this he had an ally in W. A. Waters at Durham and, later, Oxford. Waters was attracted by Hey's paper and looked at his own work in its light. In 1937 they co-authored one of the great reviews in chemistry—'Some organic reactions involving the occurrence of free radicals in solution'—in which they postulated for the first time that a very large number of known chemical reactions proceeded via free radicals. They ended their review with an extraordinarily perceptive understatement: 'there may exist also several other reactions in organic chemistry in which transient free neutral radicals intervene' (*Chemical Review*, 21, 1937).

The study of free radicals henceforth dominated Hey's research career. He was a lecturer in chemistry at Manchester University from 1930 to 1938, and at Imperial College, London, from 1939 to 1941. In 1941 he became director of the British Research Institute, where he directed drug research. He was university professor of chemistry at King's College, London, from 1945 to 1950, when he became Daniell professor of chemistry, University of London, until his retirement in 1971.

By 1955 the importance of free radicals was universally accepted, critics disappeared or were silenced, and Hey was elected a fellow of the Royal Society. Then followed a period of remarkable administrative success, characterized by his inspired choice of supporting colleagues. His department at King's was small, with some fourteen staff, but in the 1960s six of his younger colleagues gained chairs in other departments and more were to follow in the period to his retirement. He did not shirk his responsibilities in the day-to-day operation of the college and the University of London. He served in every academic position, including that of assistant principal of the college and, as a devout Anglican, was particularly concerned with theological activities. He became a fellow of Imperial College in 1968 and an honorary fellow of the Intra-Science Research Foundation (1971), Chelsea College (1973), and University College, Swansea (1986). The University of Wales made him an honorary DSc in 1970. As the first to publish experimental evidence for the existence of reactive free radicals (molecular species carrying an unpaired electron—the source of high unselective reactivity), Hey made a truly seminal contribution to science. His demonstration, and recognition, in 1934 that dibenzoyl peroxide decomposes in solution via phenyl radicals was the very genesis of the vast compass and knowledge of free radical chemistry, biochemistry, and biological processes.

Hey used to muse ruefully in his later years that if only he had realized the commercial implications of his discovery he could have become a rich man, but the success of his pupils and colleagues was the only reward he sought. His face had an unassuming expression; he was an accomplished pianist and organist. He kept his academic and home lives quite separate, and liked a simple way of life. He was a keen gardener, who loved Wales, family life, and family holidays. He was an unselfish, gentle, and modest scholar, with a great desire to help others. Hey died on 21 January 1987 at Wray Common Nursing Home, Reigate, Surrey.   JOHN CADOGAN, *rev.*

Sources J. I. G. Cadogan and D. I. Davies, *Memoirs FRS*, 34 (1988), 293–320 • personal knowledge (1996) • *CGPLA Eng. & Wales* (1987) **Archives** King's Lond., corresp. and papers | Bodl. Oxf., corresp. with C. A. Coulson

Wealth at death £104,468: probate, 7 Sept 1987, *CGPLA Eng. & Wales*

Hey, John (1734–1815), divine, was born on 12 July 1734 at Pudsey, near Leeds, the second (eldest surviving) son and third child of Richard Hey (1702–1766), drysalter, of Pudsey and his wife, Mary (1702–1768), daughter of Jacob Simpson of Leeds, a surgeon. He maintained a lifelong correspondence with his older sister Rebecca (1731–1811), and affectionate relations with his younger brothers Samuel, William *Hey (1736–1819), surgeon, Richard *Hey (1745–1835), essayist, and his younger sisters, Dorothy and Sarah. His early education was at Heath, near Wakefield, after which he became a pupil of the Revd Wynne Bateman at Sedbergh School before going up to St Catharine's College, Cambridge, as a pensioner in 1751.

Hey graduated BA as eighth wrangler of 1755, and was ordained deacon by the bishop of Bangor in 1757 and priest by the bishop of Ely in 1760. He resided at St Catharine's College until 1758, when he graduated MA and was

elected foundation fellow of Sidney Sussex College. In 1763 he won the Seatonian prize for his poetical essay 'The Redemption'; in 1765 he proceeded to the BD; and in 1775 performed a 'public act', a scholastic disputation in Latin, which was unusual by that date, for the DD to which he was admitted in 1780. He was tutor of Sidney Sussex from 1760 to 1779 and at various times filled most other college offices, including dean, praelector, and seneschal. He lectured on Greek, Hebrew, and algebra, and in the 1770s gave a series of lectures for his Sidney Sussex pupils on moral and political philosophy which attracted the voluntary attendance of undergraduates from other colleges, including William Pitt. Hey was one of the preachers at the Royal Chapel, Whitehall, from the early 1770s and curate of Madingley from 1773 to 1780, being permitted by the bishop of Ely to hold this stipendiary appointment (£30 p.a.) in conjunction with his fellowship.

Like his college friend the Revd Thomas Twining, Hey was a devoted and knowledgeable musician, and made many friends of both sexes through singing and playing at private musical parties in Cambridge and elsewhere. In the 1750s he travelled to Bedford to hear an early performance of *Messiah*. Despite much anxious deliberation, confided to his sister Rebecca in the 1770s, Hey never married.

In 1780 Hey was presented to the rectory of Passenham, near Stony Stratford, by his friend Viscount Maynard, and afterwards to the adjacent rectory of Calverton through the patronage of Thomas Villiers, earl of Clarendon; he resigned his college fellowship on Lady day 1780. In 1780 he was also elected as first Norrisian professor of divinity, and was re-elected in 1785 and in 1790 for further five-year terms. Hey resided at Passenham, then a very rural parish, from 1782, when his parsonage house became vacant, until he resigned the benefice at Michaelmas 1814, ministering faithfully to his two small congregations and absenting himself only for his divinity lectures in Cambridge.

After his Seatonian prize poem Hey published several sermons, *Heads of Lectures in Divinity* (1794), his Norrisian *Lectures in Divinity* (4 vols., 1796–8), *Discourses on the Malevolent Passions* (1801), and a pamphlet criticizing a bill respecting parish registers (1811). He is reported in the *Dictionary of National Biography* to have printed but not published *General Observations on the Writings of St Paul* (1811), and his manuscript lectures on moral and political philosophy, in nine bound volumes, were deposited in Sidney Sussex College archives after his death by his surviving brothers.

Hey's historical importance lies chiefly in his Norrisian lectures, reprinted in second (1822) and third (1841) editions, and widely influential in the first half of the nineteenth century. But in the latter part of that century, Hey's reputation, like that of his Cambridge contemporaries of the 'intellectual party', Richard Watson and William Paley, suffered drastic depreciation. According to Sir Leslie Stephen, Hey maintained that 'talk about the Trinity is little better than unmeaning gibberish' (Stephen, 1.426).

Overton and Relton—who seem to have had no knowledge of Hey's work—said of him that 'he was even more inclined to liberalism in theology than either Watson or Paley' (Overton and Relton, 262).

These readings—or non-readings—of Hey and his Cambridge colleagues have lately become subject to reappraisal. The purpose of Hey's Norrisian lectures was to defend subscription to the Thirty-Nine Articles. The key to understanding his method lies in the lecture 'Of assenting to propositions, which are unintelligible'. Its underlying assumption is that we do indeed 'have things communicated from above by Language' (*Lectures in Divinity*, 2.94). Therefore if God 'sends a message, whether it be understood or not, it is to be carefully preserved' (ibid., 2.97). The church must inevitably embody 'the expression' (2.99) of Scripture 'into … doctrine or devotion'—including creeds, which few if any can fully comprehend. 'All ranks must join in creeds, catechisms, and Liturgies' (ibid., 2.99). In assenting to that which is unintelligible—including the doctrine of the Trinity—they acknowledge the *mysterious* in religion: 'a design of God not yet executed or made manifest' (ibid., 2.100). Hey's lectures were recommended to their pupils by the Tractarians. Both his scrupulous reasoning and his frank acknowledgement of mystery left their mark upon the Oxford Movement.

Hey retired to Marylebone for the last few months of his life, died in St John's Wood on 17 March 1815, and was buried in St John's Chapel, St John's Wood. His patrons and parishioners erected a memorial tablet which corroborates other testimony to the love and esteem in which he was held by all.   A. M. C. WATERMAN

Sources [R. Hey], 'Memoir of the Rev. John Hey', *GM*, 1st ser., 85/1 (1815), 371 · letters of John Hey to his sister Rebecca, 1757–1815, Sidney Sussex College, Cambridge, Hey MSS · college records, Sidney Sussex College, Cambridge, MR.41, MR.2, ME.31 · MS genealogy of Hey family, *c*.1990, Sidney Sussex College, Cambridge, Hey MSS · *Recreations of a country clergyman of the eighteenth century: being recollections from the correspondence of the Rev. Thomas Twining MA* (1882) · *DNB* · A. M. C. Waterman, 'A Cambridge "via media" in late Georgian Anglicanism', *Journal of Ecclesiastical History*, 42 (1991), 419–36 · L. Stephen, *History of English thought in the eighteenth century*, 2nd edn, 2 vols. (1881) · J. H. Overton and F. Relton, *The English church, from the accession of George I to the end of the eighteenth century* (1906)
Archives Sidney Sussex College, Cambridge
Likenesses oils, *c*.1795, Sidney Sussex College, Cambridge; repro. in '400 years of Sidney Sussex College, 9 April–7 July, 1996' [exhibition guide, FM Cam.]

Hey, Richard (1745–1835), essayist and mathematician, was born on 11 August 1745 at Pudsey, near Leeds, the son of Richard Hey (1702–1766), drysalter, and his wife, Mary, *née* Simpson (1702–1768). He was the younger brother of the Revd John *Hey DD (1734–1815) and of William *Hey FRS (1736–1819). He matriculated at Magdalene College, Cambridge, in 1764, became a scholar in 1765, and graduated BA in 1768 as third wrangler, obtaining the chancellor's medal. In 1771 he took the degree of MA as fellow of Sidney Sussex College, and in 1779 was created LLD by royal mandate. On 8 November 1771 he was called to the bar at the Middle Temple. There is a fiat, dated 7 December

1778, for his admission to the court of arches, but no warrant was issued. He was admitted into Doctors' Commons, but obtaining no practice retired from the bar.

Hey had started his literary career with *Observations on the Nature of Civil Liberty and the Principles of Government*, (1776), but his chief work was the *Dissertation on the Pernicious Effects of Gaming* (1783; 3rd edn 1812) by which he gained a prize of 50 guineas offered through the University of Cambridge. In 1784 Hey gained a second prize, offered by the same anonymous donor, for his *Dissertation on Duelling*, which also reached a third edition in 1812, and his *Dissertation on Suicide* gained him a third prize of 50 guineas (1785). The three dissertations were published together in 1812. In 1792 Hey published *Happiness and Rights*, in reply to Paine's *Rights of Man*. He also wrote a tragedy in five acts called *The Captive Monarch* (1794) and a novel entitled *Edington* (1796). Hey had been fellow and tutor of Magdalene College from 1782 until his marriage in May 1796 to Martha, the daughter of T. Browne. Hey's last work was *Some principles of civilisation, with detached thoughts on the promotion of Christianity in British India* (1815). He had at various times contributed papers to the *Philosophical Transactions* and other magazines, and he also assisted in editing a pamphlet which gives a scientific account of an Egyptian mummy, with anatomical and other details. Hey died on 7 December 1835 at Hertingfordbury, near Hertford.

R. E. ANDERSON, *rev.* REBECCA MILLS

Sources *IGI* · Venn, *Alum. Cant.*, 2/3.351 · H. R. Luard, ed., *Graduati Cantabrigienses*, 6th edn (1873), 232 · [D. Rivers], *Literary memoirs of living authors of Great Britain*, 1 (1798), 255–6 · [J. Watkins and F. Shoberl], *A biographical dictionary of the living authors of Great Britain and Ireland* (1816) · H. A. C. Sturgess, ed., *Register of admissions to the Honourable Society of the Middle Temple, from the fifteenth century to the year 1944*, 1 (1949), 368 · G. D. Squibb, *Doctors' Commons: a history of the College of Advocates and Doctors of Law* (1977), 209 · Watt, *Bibl. Brit.*, 1.493 · Allibone, *Dict.* · will, PRO, PROB 11/1856, sig. 29
Archives CUL, corresp. with James Plumptre

Hey, Samuel (1815–1888). *See under* Hey, William (1772–1844).

Hey, Spurley (1872–1930), educational administrator, was born on 31 March 1872 in Stocksbridge, Yorkshire, one of the eight children of Benjamin Smith Hey and Ann Birkenshaw. Family life was humble but secure, dominated by an intelligent but austere steelworker father and a strong-minded, caring mother. Hey was destined for the steelworks but went for four years (*c*.1877–1882) to a small school at Midhopestones, where the eccentric master made a strong impression on him. At ten he became a part-time worker in Fox's steelworks but disliked the job; a master at Stocksbridge elementary school persuaded his parents to allow him to become a pupil teacher there (*c*.1885–91).

Hey gained a queen's scholarship to St John's Diocesan Training College, York, where he was educated from 1891 to 1893, and in later years reminisced that the life of the college had a major effect on his character. While there he developed a love of football, which led later to paid employment with Barnsley Football Club at weekends;

this helped to support his part-time BA of London University, which was awarded in 1898. From college he was appointed to Kimberworth board school, Rotherham, where he achieved a remarkable series of promotions to become director of education in 1907. With the creation of the Rotherham local education authority in 1902, he became a co-opted member representing teachers. Single-mindedness, self-confidence, and a certain aloofness were already present and made him an unusually formidable young man. Interest in the Froebel Society for the Promotion of the Kindergarten System symbolized that keenness for children's welfare in which his passion for social justice had its origins. The idea of central schools (higher elementary schools), then a rudimentary concept, caught his imagination while at Rotherham and a start was made to extend elementary schooling for children above standard five.

From 1911 to 1914 Hey was director of education for Newcastle upon Tyne, and comments on his service testify to a strong personality and dynamic, independent leadership. It was the early years of a new and potentially influential public office and Hey, with his contemporaries James Graham of Leeds and Percival Sharp of Sheffield, together nicknamed the 'three musketeers' for their attacks on the 'Richelieu' of the Board of Education, was determined that education would not be the poor relation of social policy.

For sixteen years from 1914 Hey was director of education for Manchester, where his leadership of the progressive education committee greatly enhanced Manchester's prestige as an education authority. His magisterial style was well caught by the future Lady Shena Simon, a member of the Manchester education committee, who commented admiringly that 'Spurley Hey was an autocrat who made no attempt to disguise the fact' (S. Simon, *A Century of City Government*, 1938, 263). The high regard in which he was held by the radical Labour chairman of the education committee, Alderman Wright Robinson, in part accounted for his freedom of action, even extending to such overtly political statements as criticism of the Geddes financial 'axe', which was, he believed, 'a serious menace to the present generation of pupils' (Hey MSS, 'Notes on education finance and the attempt to reduce expenditure', 1922, 15). During this period a stream of documents bore the distinctive stamp of his reasoned and comprehensive attitude to education policy. The intensity with which he made the environment of children his starting point was remarkable so early in the century (see his *Parental Neglect and Juvenile Crime*, 1919). He made use of existing health and welfare provision, as well as the 1918 permissive legislation on continuation schools, which provided opportunities for working-class young people who had no opportunity to remain at school full-time. Concern for the mentally and physically handicapped, slow learners, and those who were disadvantaged by poverty and, 'during the short five years' journey from the cradle to the school, fought an almost continuous battle for mere existence', were automatically part of his inclusive approach (Hey MSS, 'Notes on the aim of education in elementary

schools', 1923, 5). In order to establish positive habits of work and behaviour and to change parental attitudes he developed infant classes in elementary schools, not waiting until resources would enable primary schools to be provided. As the school was a stage in life, he tackled youth unemployment energetically and extended the jurisdiction of his department to include the juvenile employment bureaux. His determination that these be associated with education rather than the Ministry of Labour was argued in *Juvenile Unemployment and Aftercare* (1920). He was unapologetic that this would enlarge local education authority powers and maintained that 'all questions of decision relative to the social, as well as the educational, side of the development of young people should be vested in the LEA' even if this necessitated 'compulsory measures' ('Development of the education of wage earners', 1917, Manchester Central Library, Hey MSS, 16).

Hey's decision to maximize school building and diversify access during a time of recession was driven by a profound consciousness that existing transfer schemes to secondary schools were inadequate. He wrote of 'the deprivation from many children of a better opportunity of training for citizenship, and the condemnation of many to circumstances from which better education alone could lift them' ('The central school', 1924, Manchester Central Library, 11). A solution was to introduce selective central schools, first envisaged in Hey's 1918 blueprint for the local education authority, *Manchester's Education Problem*, and with which his reputation has been rightly but too narrowly associated. Resisted by some on the ground of cost or competition with secondary schools, central schools enabled more elementary school children to experience an education which, at its best, narrowed the gulf between elementary and secondary schools by providing a course of schooling beyond the age of eleven. Through policies for a primary stage, central and secondary schools, and post-compulsory provision Hey steered Manchester towards the recommendations of the 1926 Hadow committee on the education of the adolescent, which foreshadowed the 1944 Education Act. As reform depended on the quality of teachers, high priority was given to the reform of training procedures, maximum freedom for heads, and close co-operation with classroom teachers, from which evolved the possibly unique advisory committee of teachers and elected members of the education committee. Membership of the Burnham committee and two departmental inquiries, evidence to the royal commission on local government, senior positions in such professional organizations as the Association of Education Committees, and contributions to the journal *Education* made him an increasingly influential national figure. In 1919 he received an honorary MA degree from Manchester University.

Hey's limited leisure was spent walking and collecting antiques. His sudden death from pneumonia on 7 May 1930 at his home in Elm Road, Didsbury, Manchester, occasioned many tributes both affectionate and admiring, of which the most fitting was that he had 'never been surpassed by any of the great public servants' who had served

Manchester (*Manchester Guardian*). He was buried on 10 May at Harlow Moor cemetery, Harrogate, Yorkshire, and honoured with a memorial service in Manchester Cathedral. Two schools were named after him. His wife, Ada Annie Hey, survived him.   A. B. ROBERTSON

Sources Man. CL, Manchester Archives and Local Studies, Hey MSS · T. H. Williams, 'Spurley Hey's contribution to the origin and development of central schools', MA diss., University of Sheffield, 1938 · W. N. Anderton, 'Wright Robinson of Manchester', MEd diss., University of Manchester, 1966 · W. A. J. Stanton, 'Spurley Hey and priorities in English education, 1914–1930', MEd diss., University of Manchester, 1985 · minutes, City of Manchester council and education committee, Manchester town hall · *Education* (1914–30) · *Manchester Guardian* (8 May 1930) · *Manchester City News* (10 May 1930) · *The Times* (9 May 1930) · *Rotherham Advertiser* (10 May 1930) · *CGPLA Eng. & Wales* (1930)
Archives Man. CL, Manchester Archives and Local Studies
Likenesses Lafayette, photograph, repro. in *Education* (16 May 1930)
Wealth at death £10,397 7s. 3d.: resworn probate, 14 Oct 1930, *CGPLA Eng. & Wales*

Hey, William (1736–1819), surgeon, was born on 23 August 1736, in the village of Pudsey, near Leeds, Yorkshire, the fourth of the eight children of Richard Hey, drysalter (*d.* 1766), and his wife, Mary (1702–1768), daughter of Jacob Simpson, a surgeon apothecary. Richard *Hey (1745–1835) and John *Hey (1734–1815) were his brothers. His father's family had been prosperous drysalters (suppliers of oils and chemicals to clothiers) in Pudsey for several generations. His father, known as 'honest Mr Hey', was a man of unbending probity and great piety. At every important point in his early career William followed his father's advice and benefited from his financial help. When Hey was three years old his clothing caught fire and he nearly burnt to death; the next year he wounded his eye with a penknife and lost his sight in that eye. In 1743 Hey and his brother John were sent to the short-lived Heath Academy near Wakefield, where he received an excellent education in natural philosophy, mathematics, French, and music. Hey had a lifelong love of music. In 1750 he was apprenticed to William Dawson, a surgeon apothecary in Leeds, and joined the Methodists about 1754. At this time Methodists considered themselves to be members of the Church of England and Hey was always an Anglican; he parted from the Methodists in 1781. In 1757 Hey went to London, where he became a student of William Bromfield at St George's Hospital. He was an unusually determined and able student who devoted many hours to dissection. He returned to Leeds in 1759, declined an offer of partnership from Dawson, and set up his own practice. After one year as apothecary to the Leeds workhouse Hey began to campaign for an infirmary at Leeds, serving as a surgeon in a temporary building that opened on Michaelmas day 1767 and becoming a staff surgeon when the infirmary building opened in 1771. In 1773 he became the senior surgeon, serving until his retirement in 1812.

Hey's London training made him far better qualified than locally trained surgeons to undertake difficult operations. However, the demand for such surgery was limited, and his career was also impeded by his devout Methodism and the competition of rivals. It was ten years

before he earned enough to support his growing family. Hey's marriage on 30 July 1761 to Alice (*c.*1737–1820), daughter of Margaret and Robert Banks of Giggleswick, had brought him a modest fortune and was a lifelong comfort; they had thirteen children, of whom eleven died either in infancy or early adulthood. Their daughter Margaret (*d.* 1816) married Robert Jarratt, vicar of Wellington, Somerset, in 1797; John (*d.* 1801) became a fellow of Magdalene College, Cambridge; Robert died in 1802; and William *Hey (1772–1844) became a surgeon and succeeded his father in his medical practice. About 1769 Hey formed a close friendship with the natural philosopher Joseph Priestley, who described Hey as 'the only person in Leeds who gave any attention to my experiments' (Bell, 1066). Hey published two criticisms of Priestley's theological tracts; however, this did not impair their friendship, and it was Priestley who successfully proposed Hey for a fellowship of the Royal Society in 1775. Hey injured his knee in 1773 and an injury to the same leg in 1778 left him permanently lame, forcing him to make all his professional visits in a carriage. He was never again able to stand for more than a few minutes or to walk any further than the length of a room without a crutch.

Hey became a councilman in Leeds in 1781 and an alderman in 1786. He twice served as mayor, in 1787–8 and in 1802–3. His vigorous efforts to enforce the proclamation against vice, profaneness, and immorality (1787) created resentment in the town. Not only was Hey burnt in effigy, but a mob stopped his carriage while his wife was inside, cut the traces, and stabbed one of his horses. The episode 'much disordered' his wife's health (Pearson, 2.31), but did not deter his activities. Hey was also forced to defend the actions of his constables at the York assizes, but his legal expenses were defrayed by his friend William Wilberforce, who supported his efforts. Hey founded the Leeds Medical Society in 1768 and in the same year he became a member of the London Medical Society. He also served as president of the Leeds Philosophical and Literary Society in 1783, and was a member of the Manchester Literary and Philosophical Society. He supported the abolition of slavery, criminal law reform, the Lancastrian school movement, and various missionary activities, but deprecated some of the views expressed by the Society for the Propagation of Christian Knowledge. Unlike Wilberforce, he opposed Catholic emancipation. He founded the *Christian Observer* as a response to the dissenters' *Leeds Mercury*. After his death, a volume entitled *Tracts and essays, moral and theological, including a defence of the divinity of Christ, and of the atonement* (1822) collected several religious tracts that he had published during his life.

Hey was a skilled, observant, and innovative surgeon. His published papers in *Medical Observations and Inquiries* included accounts of extra-uterine pregnancy (1766), rupture of the bladder (1768), and the use of electricity to treat blindness. His electrical experiments, which took place between 1766 and 1771, may have been inspired by John Wesley's advocacy of electrotherapy as well as by his friendship with Priestley. Hey's book *Observations on the*

Blood (1779) disputed the views of William Hewson concerning the effect of inflammation on the coagulation of blood. His most important book was *Practical Observations in Surgery* (1803). He developed small saws for trephination instead of drills; these were later named after him, as were Hey's operation, a partial amputation of the foot in front of the tarso-metatarsal joint; Hey's hernia, encysted hernia; Hey's internal derangement of the knee, a partial dislocation of the knee; and Hey's ligament, a band of fibrous tissue which forms the edge of a hole in the covering of the muscle just below the groin, through which the saphenous vein passes to join the femoral vein. He was the first fully to describe and name the soft malignant bleeding tumour known as fungus haematodes. In his last publication (1816) he argued that syphilis could be transmitted from a mother to her unborn children.

In amputations Hey followed the work of Edward Alanson and Benjamin Bell, and strongly emphasized the importance of healing the wound by first intention (without suppuration). He also valued conservative surgery. In one dramatic case, a nine-year-old boy broke his elbow joint and humerus. Hey dissected out the broken part of the humerus and placed the arm on a pillow, bent at the elbow. The child recovered well, and could use the injured arm. Hey was an extremely gifted anatomist who gave well attended public lectures using the bodies of executed criminals. These lectures took place at the Leeds Infirmary, to which he donated the profits. Even very late in life he was so dedicated to anatomical research that he twice travelled to London to consult with Astley Cooper on the anatomy of hernias. Hey's achievement is remarkable in light of the fact that he could see with only one eye, and was barely able to stand erect for the final forty years of his life. In his prime he was reserved, inattentive, and forbidding, but as he grew older and more comfortable with his success, he became friendly, open, and cheerful. He remained alert and active until shortly before his death in Leeds on 23 March 1819. His body was placed in the crypt of St Paul's Church, Park Square, Leeds. His devoted student Richard Pearson attributed his longevity to his temperate life, even temper, and deep religious convictions.

MARGARET DELACY

Sources J. Pearson, *The life of William Hey, Esq. F.R.S.*, 2nd edn, 2 vols. (1823) · W. G. Rimmer, 'William Hey of Leeds, surgeon (1736–1819): a reappraisal', *Proceedings of the Leeds Philosophical and Literary Society*, 9 (1959–62), 187–218 · B. Bell, 'The life, character, and writings of William Hey of Leeds', *Edinburgh Medical Journal*, 12 (1866–7), 1061–80 · *IGI* · *DNB* · private information (2004) [J. Lloyd] · M. Rowbottom and C. Susskind, *Electricity and medicine, the history of their interaction* (1984), 18–23 · S. T. Anning, 'William Hey, F.R.S.: the father of Leeds surgery', *Proceedings of the Leeds Philosophical and Literary Society*, 17 (1979–80), 101–11

Archives Leeds City Archives · U. Leeds, Brotherton L., philosophical papers · U. Leeds, Brotherton L., scientific papers and notes on medical cases; case histories | Bodl. Oxf., corresp. with William Wilberforce

Likenesses W. Holl, stipple, pubd 1816, BM, NPG, Wellcome L. · F. Chantrey, statue, *c*.1820, Leeds General Infirmary, W. Yorks. · E. Scriven, stipple, 1823 (after Allen), Wellcome L. · W. Allen, group portrait, oils (with Lady Harewood and a child), Leeds General Infirmary · Bullock, bust (executed for Mr Gott of Armley, near Leeds) · engraving (after Allen), repro. in Pearson, *Life of William*

Hey · stipple (after Allen), Wellcome L. · two portraits, Leeds General Infirmary

Hey, William (1772–1844), surgeon, the eldest surviving son of William *Hey (1736–1819), surgeon, and Alice, *née* Banks (*c*.1737–1820), was born in the family home, an apothecary's shop and premises in the Slip-in Yard, off the Briggate in Leeds, on 19 February 1772, and was baptized at St Peter's Church, Leeds, on 19 March. He became apprenticed to his father in 1787 and was groomed to take over the medical, surgical, and midwifery practice after the death of his elder brother Richard in 1789. From 1792 to 1794 Hey trained as a surgeon at St Bartholomew's Hospital in London, becoming a member of the Company of Surgeons in 1794. He returned to Leeds and began as a partner to his father from new premises in Albion Street. On 12 January 1796 he married Isabella Hudson (his maternal first cousin) of Huddersfield. They had five children, William [*see below*], Mary (b. 1798), John (b. 1802), Richard (b. 1803), and Samuel (b. 1805). Isabella died of consumption in August 1805; William did not remarry. In 1796 Hey sustained an injury to his ankle which caused him to be lame for four years. He was elected an officer of the Leeds House of Recovery in 1804, and five years later his father made him an equal partner. Hey succeeded his father in 1812 as the principal surgeon at the Leeds Infirmary, retaining the post until his resignation in 1830. Hey's book *A Treatise on the Puerperal Fever* was written in 1813, but not published until 1815.

Hey carried on the extensive midwifery practice begun by his father. The account books show midwifery receipts until 1843, six months prior to his death. He was elected as one of the original 300 fellows of the Royal College of Surgeons in 1843. Hey took his two sons John and William into his practice, his son Richard became a surgeon in York, and his son Samuel (a bachelor) became rector of Sawley in Derbyshire. His only daughter, Mary, married John Atkinson, a solicitor in Leeds. John married, in 1824, Jane, sister of Joseph Croser, one of Hey's apothecaries. He was affectionately known by his vast family as the Governor.

Hey was an active member of the Leeds Philosophical and Literary Society. A lifelong devout Christian he was an active member of the new St Paul's Church in Park Square, Leeds. He was a tory mayor of Leeds on two occasions and as mayor was chairman at a public meeting held on 9 January 1832 in the Mixed Cloth Hall in Leeds which had been called to discuss the reduction of the working hours of children. From March 1833 William had further periods of serious illness until his death at his home, 36 Albion Street, Leeds, in March 1844. He was buried in the family vault in St Paul's Church, Leeds, on 13 March 1844.

William Hey (1796–1875), surgeon, the eldest son of William and Isabella, was born at 36 Albion Street, Leeds. He was apprenticed to his father and became an equal partner after the death of his brother John in 1836. Hey married Rebecca Roberts on 13 November 1821; they had no children. On the retirement of his father in December 1830 Hey was elected surgeon at the Leeds Infirmary. He was a founder member of the Leeds school of medicine in

1831 and lectured on the principles and practice of surgery. He was president of the medical school from 1836 to 1837 and was president of the British Medical Association in 1843-4 when their annual meeting was held in Leeds. He remained on the staff of the infirmary until March 1851. Hey became a member of the Royal College of Surgeons in 1818 and was one of the original 300 fellows in 1843. He was an active member of the Leeds Philosophical and Literary Society and did much to promote the cultivation of music in Leeds. He died on 10 May 1875 at his estate, Gledhow House, Gledhow Wood, Leeds, a substantial property to the north of Leeds town. He was buried in the vault of St Paul's Church, Park Square, Leeds. His wife predeceased him.

Samuel Hey (1815-1888), surgeon, was born on 22 August 1815 and was baptized on 22 September at Ockbrook, Derbyshire. He was the second son of the Revd Samuel Hey, vicar of Ockbrook, and Margaret Hey (née Gray) of York. The Revd Samuel Hey was the youngest and second surviving son of William *Hey (1736-1819). Samuel junior attended Cox's School in Gainsborough. When he was sixteen he became an apprentice dresser at the Leeds Infirmary to his paternal uncle William Hey (1772-1844), and was one of the first group of students to join the Leeds medical school in 1831, attending the very first lecture, given by Mr Teale. On 3 September 1836 Samuel became a pupil at both the North London Hospital (later University College Hospital) and St George's Hospital in London. He then had three years' medical training in Paris and Germany before returning to Leeds in 1841, when he entered into partnership with his uncle William Hey and his cousin William Hey (1796-1875) in the family medical surgical and midwifery practice in Albion Street, Leeds. Hey became a lecturer in anatomy and surgery at the Leeds medical school in 1841, a post he retained until his resignation in August 1870. He was also president of the Leeds school of medicine in 1848-9 and was treasurer for twelve years up to 1865. He married, in 1842, Martha Jane Jowett, who died childless. He married, in 1868, Sarah Jane Pratt (1836-1874); the couple had four children. Samuel Hey was a talented musician and frequently played the organ of St Paul's Church, Park Square, Leeds. He became a member of the Royal College of Surgeons in 1838 and a fellow in 1855. In 1850 he was elected surgeon to the Leeds Infirmary, holding the post until his resignation in 1872. Hey died at his home in North Hill Road, Headingley, Leeds, on 22 January 1888.   JOSEPHINE M. LLOYD

Sources J. Pearson, *The life of William Hey*, 1 and 2 (1821) • U. Leeds, Brotherton L., MS 505, MS 567, MS 1975/1-218, MS 1990/5 no. 22 • U. Leeds, school of medicine, Leeds Infirmary MSS, 3/8 ff to 3/300 • council books 1 and 2, U. Leeds, school of medicine • W. Hey, *Treatise on the puerperal fever* (1815) • S. T. Anning, *The General Infirmary at Leeds*, 1 and 2 (1966) • S. T. Anning, *The history of medicine in Leeds* (1980) • S. T. Anning and W. K. J. Walls, *A history of the Leeds School of Medicine* (1982) • S. Burt and K. Grady, *The illustrated history of Leeds* (1994) • *IGI* • W. Yorks. AS, Leeds, Hey family papers, 75/1-75/28 • parish records, St Peter's Church, Leeds

Archives U. Leeds, Brotherton L., mayoralty papers • U. Leeds, Brotherton L., medical notes • W. Yorks. AS, family MSS, 75/1-75/28 | U. Leeds, papers relating to memoir of his father, William Hey, and draft memorandum

Likenesses J. Russell, pastel drawing, Leeds City Art Gallery • portrait (in late life)

Wealth at death owned 36 Albion Street, Leeds, and various other properties in Leeds; stocks, bonds, bank deposits, goods chattels, paintings, church pews, and vaults • £40,000

Hey, William (1796-1875). *See under* Hey, William (1772-1844).

Heydinger, Carl (*fl.* 1766-1784), printer and bookseller, may have come from Silesia, possibly Breslau; however, nothing else is known about his early life. He is first heard of as a London bookseller at the sign of the Moor's Head in Moor Street (at the end of Compton Street in Soho) in 1766. Three titles with Heydinger's name in the imprint were issued during that year, two in German and one in French. One of the German imprints associates him with 'Mr. W. Faden, printer of the Public-Ledger', suggesting perhaps an early business partnership. This title, *Eines Christen Reise* (1766), a German translation of *Pilgrim's Progress*, also contains a dedication signed by Heydinger himself and dated: 'London, den 25. Julii 1766', providing the earliest firm date for his presence in the city.

On 26 October 1767 Charles Heydinger married Jane (or Jeanne) Favre (*b.* 1749/50), the seventeen-year-old daughter of Huguenots, at St Anne's, Soho. The marriage clearly suggests a commitment to remain in London—a commitment strengthened no doubt by the birth of four children, two daughters and two sons, between 1768 and 1775. A growing family and an expanding business probably led to the acquisition in 1767 or 1768 of new premises in Grafton Street, at no great distance from Moor Street, where Heydinger in effect established himself as the successor of the German printer Johann Christoph Haberkorn and the booksellers Andreas Linde and Christlob Gottreich Seyffert. There were further moves to 274 Strand, opposite Essex Street, about 1771, and to 6 Bridges Street, Strand, opposite the Theatre Royal, Drury Lane, about 1776. Both Soho and the Strand were traditionally occupied by the German-speaking community and associated printers and booksellers.

By 1768 Heydinger was referring to himself in imprints as 'imprimeur et libraire' or 'Buchdrucker und Buchhändler' ('printer and bookseller'); from that year date his first surviving advertisements on leaves forming part of the final gatherings of books printed and sold by him. One of these lists works in German, French, and Latin, mostly imported; another includes a number of German and English items, some originally printed or sold by Heydinger's German predecessors in the London trade, offered at prices between 4*d.* and 10*s.* 6*d.* He supplemented his work as a printer and bookseller with translations of German texts into English. From 1770 to 1773 Heydinger was present at the Leipzig book fairs, the first London-based bookseller to be so. He used his Leipzig visits to establish contacts with authors and publishers in German-speaking Europe, for example with the Swiss botanist Albrecht von Haller at Bern.

Heydinger issued *A catalogue of books in all arts and sciences in the German, Latin, French and English language* in 1769, although no copy appears to have survived. According to

Nichols, Heydinger issued further catalogues of the books he printed and sold, though copies survive only of the 1773 catalogue. He appears to have reduced his publishing activities after 1777, and no imprints bearing his name have so far been recorded for the years between 1778 and 1782. A letter from Georg Forster to his friend Johann Karl Philipp Spener dated 17 February 1778 hints at financial difficulties in this period: apparently 'der arme Heydinger' ('poor Heydinger') was among the London creditors of the notorious Rudolf Erich Raspe (Forster, 118). Of Heydinger's known titles, the largest single category consists of theology or devotional literature, mostly in German and associated with the Lutheran congregations in London. The second largest category, medical and scientific literature, includes Albrecht von Haller's *Bibliotheca botanica* (1771–2). After the mid-1770s Heydinger normally appears in imprints as sole printer and bookseller.

A final move to 7 Queen's Court, Great Queen Street, Lincoln's Inn Fields, London, must have taken place in summer 1780 as Heydinger took out an insurance policy with the Sun Fire Office on 7 June that year. However, none of its details suggests the 'distressed circumstances' reported by Nichols (Nichols, *Lit. anecdotes*). Premiums on this property continued to be paid at least until 1783; Heydinger's last recorded imprints are from the following year. It may have been shortly after this that he died. The occasional revival of the imprint 'bey Carl Heydinger' into the 1790s can probably be attributed to one or both of his sons. Whatever the date or circumstances of Heydinger's death, there was certainly a contemporary perception that he had been unsuccessful in business.

As a specialist German printer Heydinger enjoyed an effective monopoly after Haberkorn's departure in the late 1760s. As an importer of German titles (and Latin titles printed in Germany) he must have enjoyed a near monopoly; certainly no other London bookseller enjoyed his links with the German trade. The demand for German-language books, however, remained small in this period, and for Heydinger, as for his precursors, diversification meant printing and selling books in foreign languages other than German (principally, of course, French) and establishing a niche for himself in the publication of books in English. Heydinger's career reveals much about the opportunities and risks facing foreign booksellers in London and sheds light on an important but neglected aspect of the reception of German culture in eighteenth-century England. GRAHAM JEFCOATE

Sources City Westm. AC, marriages 1767, St Anne's Soho, vol. 15, fol. 199 · Sun Fire Office policy, 7 June 1780, GL, MS 11936/284, fol. 51 · *A catalogue of all the English books* (1764) · *Catalogus librorum latinorum, graecorum, hebraicorum, &c. … qui venales prostant Londini apud C. Heydinger, bibliopol. in platea vulgo dicta the Strand* (1773) · *Allgemeines Verzeichniss derer Bücher, welche in Frankfurter und Leipziger Ostermesse [Michaelismesse] des [17.] Jahres entweder ganz neu gedruckt, oder sonst verbessert, wieder aufgelegt worden sind, auch inskünftige noch herauskommen sollen* (Leipzig, 1771–3) · Nichols, *Lit. anecdotes*, 3.644 · C. H. Timperley, *Encyclopaedia of literary and typographical anecdote*, 2nd edn (1842), 744 · G. Forster, *Sämtliche Schriften, Tagebücher, Briefe*, ed. S. Scheibe, 13 (Berlin, 1978)

Heydon, Sir Christopher (1561–1623), soldier and writer on astrology, was born in Surrey on 14 August 1561, the eldest son of Sir William Heydon (1540–1594) of Baconsthorpe, Norfolk, and his wife, Anne (*fl. c.*1540–1603), daughter of Sir William Woodhouse of Hickling, Norfolk. The family had risen in the fifteenth century through the law, and enjoyed a powerful position in Norfolk affairs, with extensive lands and a palatial mansion at Baconsthorpe. Heydon was educated at Peterhouse, Cambridge, where he associated with the young earl of Essex, and after proceeding BA in 1579 travelled widely on the continent. In 1586, while still a young man, he stood for the Norfolk county seat, probably at his father's behest, against a family rival, Thomas Farmer. Though he was defeated his father appealed to the privy council, which ordered a fresh poll, and this time Heydon was declared elected. The Commons however challenged the council's constitutional right to interfere in electoral disputes, and the election was quashed. Heydon stood again for parliament in 1588, this time successfully.

Heydon married twice. His first wife, Mirabel, daughter of the London alderman Sir Thomas Rivet, died on 15 July 1593 aged only twenty-two and was buried at Saxlingham, another of the family estates. Heydon erected a massive and ornate tomb which virtually filled the chancel, covered with symbolic hieroglyphs and carvings explained in a treatise now lost. Like most of his family, Heydon was both extravagant and hot-tempered, and he was already embroiled in a bitter feud with his father. Deep in debt, Sir William had been forced to mortgage Baconsthorpe and only a series of royal protections kept his creditors at bay. In 1590 he decided to sell part of his property, a plan his son challenged on the grounds that the estates were entailed to him. When Sir William then threatened to demolish Baconsthorpe itself, out of spite, the younger man secured a prohibition from the privy council which condemned the plan as unnatural and likely to set a bad example. The dispute, which drew in many of the leading Norfolk families, dragged on for several years and led to a lawsuit between father and son in 1593. Sir William died the following year, bequeathing his estate to his widow instead of his son, and Heydon then went to law against her. She appealed to the queen, on whose order the lord keeper settled the dispute. Heydon was left liable for inherited debts of £11,000, adding to his own of over £3000. A second marriage, to Anne (*d.* 1642), daughter of John Dodge and widow of John Potts of Mannington, Norfolk, in or before 1599, brought him personal happiness but a large and growing family exacerbated his financial problems.

For many years Heydon was active in local government, serving as a justice from 1586 and again from 1598, and he was also a commissioner for musters in the late 1590s. However, his martial spirit and pressing debts eventually persuaded him to play for higher stakes. Throwing in his lot with the court favourite, the earl of Essex, he served in the Cadiz expedition of 1596, where he was knighted, and he would have joined Essex in Ireland in 1599 but for domestic entanglements. His younger brother John, who had earlier fought with Leicester in the Netherlands, did accompany Essex to Ireland, and was knighted there. By this time the Heydons were mired in both court and county rivalries, inflamed by their own combative spirit. In October 1600 Heydon challenged Sir John Townshend to a duel, averted only by the privy council's intervention. The council was too late to prevent a bloody duel near Norwich in the same month between Sir John Heydon and Sir Robert Mansell, when one of Heydon's hands was completely severed.

The declining fortunes of Essex were reflected in the shrinking local influence of the Heydons. Sir Christopher was forced to mortgage Baconsthorpe, and his attempt to block Mansell's election to the parliament called for 1601 backfired, Mansell jeering that his rival was shunned by the leading Norfolk families. The Heydons' prominent part in the Essex revolt in February 1601, when they both led rebel troops through Ludgate, spelt the end of their public careers: John fled to the Netherlands, while Heydon went into hiding, and opened a correspondence with Sir Robert Cecil in which he offered to surrender if Cecil would promise his favour. He swore he had joined Essex on the spur of the moment, ignorant of the real design, and that while devoted to his patron he had never intended any disloyalty to the queen. He offered to pay a fine, though pleading that massive debts and fourteen children left him with few resources. Perhaps surprisingly, Cecil accepted his protestations and worked to secure a pardon. Heydon was held in the Fleet prison for a time, but was eventually pardoned on paying a fine of £2000. His brother returned to England in April 1602 to avoid outlawry. Heydon's financial plight remained desperate. In 1603–5 Sir Edward Coke wrote several times to Cecil on behalf of the brothers, asking for Heydon to be given the farm of the customs for Norfolk, and Heydon himself petitioned his neighbour Sir Bassingbourne Gawdy, Cecil, and James I to similar effect. His problems remained unresolved, and in 1614 he was forced to mortgage the rest of his estates. In 1620 Heydon came to the council's attention once more, after reporting that a group of Norfolk recusants was collecting money to aid the Habsburgs against the protestants in Bohemia and Germany. He remained a champion of militant protestantism to the end.

Heydon enjoyed more lasting fame as a champion of astrology, an interest kindled by his friends Richard Forster, formerly physician to the earl of Leicester, and Richard Fletcher of Gonville and Caius College, Cambridge, mathematician, physician, and astrologer. His major publication was *A Defence of Judiciall Astrologie* (1603), a massive work drawing on his own extensive library, in which he rebutted John Chamber's *A Treatise Against Judiciall Astrologie* (1601); Heydon's domestic chaplain, William Bredon, himself a prominent astrologer, helped with the composition. In reply to Chamber, who had called for legislation to outlaw astrology, Heydon insisted it was a valid science, vindicated by experience and fully compatible with Christianity. His work demonstrated familiarity with Tycho Brahe and other modern authors, and he described some of his own astronomical observations with instruments made by his friend the mathematician Edward Wright.

Heydon's work was the most substantial English defence of astrology in its time, given additional weight by his social eminence and the absence of challenges. A critical response by Chamber remained unpublished, while a rejoinder by George Carleton, later bishop of Chichester, was published only twenty years later in 1624 as *The Madnesse of Astrologers*. In it Carleton pointed out, with some justice, that Heydon's work was more impressive for its learning than its logic. Heydon also composed an important treatise on the effects of the great conjunction of Saturn and Jupiter in 1603, and later phenomena up to the comet of 1618. His commentary on European political developments was strongly protestant and in apocalyptic vein. He predicted that the Dutch would crush their Arminian and Spanish enemies, and that Spain would also lose the Indies. From the upheavals in Bohemia he concluded that the Austrian Habsburgs would fall in 1623 and Rome in 1646, leading to the ruin of the Ottomans and the rise of Christ's kingdom, 'the fifth Monarchie of the World', about 1682 (Bodl. Oxf., MS Ashmole, 242, fol. 65). In a letter to Forster in 1603 he had mused whether the conjunction, the new star, and the great eclipse of the sun in 1605 might also foreshadow 'a new Democracy or Aristocraty of the Church and Commonwealth' (Bodl. Oxf., MS Ashmole 242, fol. 16), a radical idea he incorporated in his treatise which also looked for a return to apostolic simplicity. Not surprisingly, his work remained unpublished. He also composed 'An astrological discourse with mathematical demonstrations', written around 1608, a defence of astrology drawing heavily on Kepler, with a briefer account of the 1603 conjunction. The manuscript remained in the possession of Forster until his death, when it passed to the astrologer Nicholas Fiske. Fiske's attempts to publish it were blocked, but it appeared in revised form in 1650, in the more favourable climate of the Commonwealth. Elias Ashmole subsidized the venture, with William Lilly supplying an admiring preface. Heydon also compiled elaborate prognostications for 1608 and 1609, which remained unpublished. He had astronomical as well as astrological interests, and for many years maintained a warm friendship with the eminent mathematician Henry Briggs and the astronomer John Bainbridge, sending them astronomical papers, lending instruments, and inviting them to Baconsthorpe.

Heydon died intestate in 1623 and was buried at Baconsthorpe. His widow, who died in 1642 aged seventy-five, chose to be buried beside him rather than by her first husband, in tribute to his 'conjugal affection' (Blomefield, 509). Heydon had several children by his first wife, and four daughters and a son by his second. His eldest son, Sir William, was killed on the Île de Ré expedition of 1627; his second, Sir John *Heydon, also a soldier, became lieutenant-general of the ordnance to Charles I during the civil war. Sir Christopher Heydon, though blessed with many talents, was far too impulsive to succeed in public life. In the world of learning, however, he played a significant part in fostering the renaissance of English astrology, while in fusing astrology with apocalyptic protestantism he foreshadowed some of the developments of the revolutionary era.

BERNARD CAPP

Sources HoP, *Commons* · C. Heydon, *A defence of judiciall astrologie* (1603) · C. Heydon, 'A recitall of the caelestiall apparitions of this present trigon', Bodl. Oxf., MS Ashmole 242 · C. Heydon, correspondence, Bodl. Oxf., MSS Ashmole 242, 1729 · C. Heydon, *An astrological discourse*, ed. N. Fiske (1650) · F. Blomefield and C. Parkin, *An essay towards a topographical history of the county of Norfolk*, [2nd edn], 11 vols. (1805–10), vol. 6 · A. Hassell Smith, *County and court: government and politics in Norfolk, 1558–1603* (1974) · *The private diary of Dr John Dee*, ed. J. O. Halliwell, CS, 19 (1842) · *Report on the manuscripts of the family of Gawdy, formerly of Norfolk*, HMC, 11 (1885) · *Calendar of the manuscripts of the most hon. the marquis of Salisbury*, 24 vols., HMC, 9 (1883–1976) · CSP dom., 1598–1618 · APC, 1592–1621 · *The papers of Nathaniel Bacon of Stiffkey*, ed. A. H. Smith and G. M. Baker, 3: 1586–1595, Norfolk RS, 53 (1990)

Archives Bodl. Oxf., MSS Ashmole 242, 1729

Heydon, Sir Henry (d. 1504), lawyer, was the son of John *Heydon (d. 1479) of Baconsthorpe, Norfolk, the well-known opponent of the Paston family, and of Eleanor, daughter of Edmund Winter (d. 1448) of Barningham in the same county. A Norfolk JP from 1473, he frequently acted as a feoffee, arbitrator, and adviser for other land-owners. During his career he also served on various *ad hoc* commissions, mainly in Norfolk but sometimes elsewhere. He married, probably after 1463, Anne (d. 1509/10), the second daughter of Sir Geoffrey Boleyn, a wealthy London mercer of Norfolk origin and the great-grandfather of Henry VIII's queen Anne Boleyn. Heydon inherited at least sixteen manors from his father, but began buying land in Norfolk (sometimes in competition with the Pastons) and Kent during John's lifetime. As Kent landowners the Boleyns perhaps encouraged Heydon to buy manors at West Wickham and elsewhere in the county in 1469, and he served as a JP there in the late 1480s and 1490s. A trustee for the Kent purchase was Henry Stafford, duke of Buckingham, for whose widow Heydon was an estate steward in Norfolk by the 1490s. By this date Heydon had also become steward of the household and chief bailiff of the honour of Eye on behalf of Cecily, duchess of York, whose will of 1495 he supervised.

Although he was knighted at Henry VII's coronation, Heydon remained in Norfolk rather than obey the king's summons for help against Lambert Simnel in 1487. Later, however, he attended several court occasions, including the reception of Katherine of Aragon into England in 1501, but he was primarily a local servant of the crown, rather than a courtier. Heydon died at Baconsthorpe between 20 February and 22 May 1504 leaving eight children. He was buried beside his father in a family chapel, long since vanished, at Norwich Cathedral. John, the eldest of his three sons, became a leading Norfolk gentleman of Henry VIII's reign.

A wealthy sheep farmer, Sir Henry could afford considerable building projects. In Norfolk he completed the castle his father had begun at Baconsthorpe, restored the church at Kelling, and constructed a causeway between Thursford and Walsingham and a new church at Salthouse. In Kent he built a fortified manor house and rebuilt the parish church at West Wickham. The church has a window, said to be a memorial to him, depicting a kneeling human skeleton and the Heydon arms.

C. E. MORETON

Sources M. Gregory, 'Wickham Court and the Heydons', *Archaeologia Cantiana*, 78 (1963), 1–21 · will, PRO, PROB 11/14, sig. 23 · Chancery records · *The Paston letters*, AD 1422–1509, ed. J. Gairdner, new edn, 6 vols. (1904), vol. 5, nos. 803–4; vol. 6, no. 1014; repr. in 1 vol. (1987) · F. Blomefield and C. Parkin, *An essay towards a topographical history of the county of Norfolk*, [2nd edn], 11 vols. (1805–10), vol. 6, pp. 505–6 · D. Gurney, ed., *The record of the house of Gournay*, 4 vols. (1848–58), 822, 823–31 · PRO, C 140/72/72 [inquisition post mortem of John Heydon] · C. Rawcliffe, *The Staffords, earls of Stafford and dukes of Buckingham, 1394–1521*, Cambridge Studies in Medieval Life and Thought, 3rd ser., 11 (1978), 204 · will, 1448, Norfolk RO, NCC 147 Wylbey [Edmund Winter] · PRO, E 179/150/251

Wealth at death see PRO, E 179/150/251

Heydon [*formerly* Baxter], **John** (d. 1479), lawyer, was the son of William Baxter, a free peasant or yeoman at Heydon in north-east Norfolk in the early fifteenth century. Heydon's humble origins were known to contemporaries and although throughout his career he used the surname Heydon, possibly in order to disguise his origins, legal records as late as 1450 refer to him as John Heydon of Baconsthorpe alias John Baxter of Heydon. Means were found to secure him an education at an inn of court. His first patron was the neighbouring gentleman Edmund Winter of Town Barningham, with whom he is found acting in 1428 and whose daughter Eleanor he married; he probably assisted Winter in his dispute with the Pastons over the manor of East Beckham, Norfolk, in the 1430s.

Heydon's first appointment was to the recordership of Norwich in 1431, from which he was dismissed before May 1437. Unpopular with the townsmen, he was accused in 1450 of having as recorder passed to Norwich Cathedral priory details of the city's case in its legal dispute with the priory. He was the priory's counsel by the mid-1430s and its chief steward by 1445. Heydon found employment with Sir John Clifton (as counsellor, chief steward, and executor, c.1435–47) and with William Phelip, Lord Bardolf (as counsellor and executor, c.1431–8). His rise to prominence, however, was principally owing to service with the duchy of Lancaster and with William de la Pole, first duke of Suffolk (d. 1450), whose officials and clients dominated East Anglian affairs from c.1437 until 1450. Heydon, in association with Sir Thomas Tuddenham (with whom in 1443 he received a grant of the stewardship of the duchy of Lancaster in Norfolk, Suffolk, and Cambridgeshire), was Suffolk's chief agent in East Anglia. From 1438 he was on numerous local commissions and between 1441 and 1450 a justice of the peace in Norfolk; he represented the county in parliament in 1445–6. He was chief steward of Bishop Brouns and Bishop Lyhert of Norwich and was steward of the duke of Buckingham's East Anglian estates by 1447. He enjoyed a flourishing practice as an attorney.

When Suffolk fell from power in January 1450 Heydon's local enemies—principally John (I) Paston and his patron

Sir John Fastolf—seized the opportunity to attack him. Heydon had been a supporter of Robert, Lord Moleyns, in the latter's aggressive pursuit of his claim to the Paston manor of Gresham, and had also backed some of Fastolf's opponents in lawsuits arising from disputes over estates purchased by Fastolf. Furthermore, he had attracted popular hostility, particularly among the tenants of the duchy of Lancaster, and seems to have feared for his safety. Heydon's sudden vulnerability in 1450 enabled Paston and Fastolf to launch prosecutions against him. In October of that year it was reported in the Paston correspondence that Heydon had offered £1000 for the appointment of a favourably disposed sheriff, and £2000 for the duke of York's goodwill. However, by the beginning of 1451 it was clear that Heydon and the rest of Suffolk's affinity were regaining their local influence under the leadership of Thomas, Lord Scales, a courtier and north-east Norfolk landowner, and of the widowed duchess of Suffolk, whom Heydon served as steward of Costessey manor in 1450–51.

Thereafter Heydon remained important in Norfolk affairs but was not as powerful as he had been under Suffolk's patronage. Although not reappointed to the peace commission until 1455, he was on other Norfolk commissions between 1452 and 1460 and seems to have represented Great Yarmouth in the parliament of 1459. His association with Lancastrian courtiers like Lord Scales jeopardized his position on the accession of Edward IV in 1461 but he obtained a general pardon at the cost of 500 marks in April 1462. He served on two Norfolk commissions during Henry VI's readeption in 1470–1. His main activities after 1461, however, were his legal practice and the management of his landed estate.

Heydon purchased property at and near the north-east Norfolk village of Baconsthorpe and was first described as 'of Baconsthorpe' in 1443; but in the absence of family papers little is known of the chronology and value of these acquisitions. At his death in 1479 he owned thirteen manors in Baconsthorpe, Heydon, Hempstead, Northrepps, Oulton, Salthouse, and elsewhere, which passed to his son and heir, Henry *Heydon (d. 1504). John Heydon's marriage was troubled. He seems to have believed that the second child born to his wife, Eleanor, was not his; in July 1444 Margaret Paston reported that Heydon 'wille nowt of here, nerre of here chyld', and that he had threatened to cut off her nose 'to makyn here to be know wat sche is' and kill the infant if they came near him (*Paston Letters and Papers*, 1.220). Heydon appears to have remained on good terms with his father-in-law, but his marital problems clearly continued, for in October 1450 he is said to have paled visibly when Chief Justice Markham remarked that he 'levid ungoodly in puttyng awey of his wyff and kept another' (ibid., 2.51). His will, made in March 1478 and proved in 1480, makes no reference to his wife or to any child besides Henry, though it is otherwise a pious and conscientious document. The sum of £20 was dedicated to his burial in the Heydon Chapel which he endowed at Norwich Cathedral. Benefactions were made to clergy and religious, the poor and sick, to the guild of St Peter at

Heydon, to his poor tenants, and to sixteen parish churches on his estates, while £200 was set aside for the marriages of his granddaughters.

Henry Heydon, also a common lawyer, was knighted at Henry VII's coronation in 1485 and married Anne (d. 1510), daughter of Sir Geoffrey Boleyn of Blickling, Norfolk. He was survived by three sons, the eldest of whom, John Heydon (1468–1550), inherited the Norfolk and Kent estates, and five daughters, for whom he arranged good marriages.

Many prominent sixteenth-century East Anglian families (such as the Townshends, Pastons, and Jenneys) owed their rise to a successful fifteenth-century lawyer of humble origins, but even by these standards the rapid ascent of the Heydons is remarkable and owed much to the opportunities and tenacity of the first John Heydon. In the pedigree devised by Clarenceux king of arms for Sir Christopher Heydon in 1563, the family tree before the first John Heydon is fictitious: and the arms of Sir Christopher himself were derived from those of the Hertfordshire Heydons, who were unrelated to the Norfolk family.

ANTHONY SMITH

Sources private information (2004) · *Chancery records* · will, PRO, esp. C140/72/72; PROB 11/14, sig. 23 [Henry Heydon] · N. Davis, ed., *Paston letters and papers of the fifteenth century*, 2 vols. (1971–6) · *The Paston letters, AD 1422–1509*, ed. J. Gairdner, new edn, 6 vols. (1904) · C. Richmond, *The Paston family in the fifteenth century: the first phase* (1990) · C. Richmond, *The Paston family in the fifteenth century: Fastolf's will* (1996) · A. R. Smith, 'Aspects of the career of Sir John Fastolf (1380–1459)', DPhil diss., U. Oxf., 1982 · F. Blomefield and C. Parkin, *An essay towards a topographical history of the county of Norfolk*, [2nd edn], 11 vols. (1805–10) · E. Hasted, *The history and topographical survey of the county of Kent*, 2nd edn, 12 vols. (1797–1801); facs. edn (1972) · will, Norfolk RO, NCC wills 1479–88, Caston 49–50
Wealth at death see will, Norfolk RO, Norwich, NCC wills 1479–88; PRO, C 140/72/72

Heydon, Sir John (*bap.* 1588, *d.* 1653), royalist army officer and mathematician, was baptized at Saxlingham, Norfolk, on 13 June 1588. He was the second son of Sir Christopher *Heydon (1561–1623) of Baconsthorpe, writer on astrology, and his first wife, Mirabel (*bap.* 1561, *d.* 1593), daughter of Sir Thomas Rivet or Ryvett of Chippenham, Cambridgeshire. By 1613 Heydon was keeper of the stores at Sandown Castle, Kent, perhaps owing his appointment to the patronage of Henry Howard, earl of Northampton, lord warden of the Cinque Ports. Heydon held the rank of captain and may have served abroad, perhaps as a gunner, for he acquired a reputation for his military ability and as a mathematician. He also attracted attention for his wit at court, especially for his exchanges with Lady Carey. About 1627 he married Mary Philips (d. 1658), daughter of William Philips; five of their children were alive in 1653.

John's elder brother Sir William Heydon was drowned in the expedition to the Île de Ré in 1627. John inherited the family estates and also succeeded Sir William as lieutenant of the ordnance, the senior executive officer and treasurer of the ordnance office, with a remuneration of 2.5 per cent of the business transacted. He took practical charge of the office, where the clerk, Francis Morrice, had virtually held control until disgraced in 1628. Problems arose from the office's structure and internal feuds among the principal officers. As lieutenant, Heydon was responsible for supplying the ship money fleets of 1635–9 and the armies in the bishops' wars. He also followed his brother in being appointed a paymaster of the posts and in 1629 was made one of the commissioners for forfeited bills of exchange. He was knighted in 1629.

Heydon joined the king at York in July or early August 1642 and had charge of the royalist artillery during the Edgehill campaign. He served as lieutenant-general of the ordnance at Oxford throughout the first civil war, acting as the effective head of the ordnance office, responsible for supplying the Oxford army and garrisons with military *matériel*. Heydon drew praise from leading royalists, including Clarendon and Sir Kenelm Digby, for his dedication and military ability, and in 1645 was mentioned as a possible governor of Oxford. His house in the Minories, London, was searched in 1642, when his books were seized. Heydon's lands were confiscated in 1642–3 and, following his unsuccessful application in 1646 to compound for his delinquency, he was in 1648 fined £294 10s. His landed income was assessed at £147 5s. per annum.

Heydon was created a DCL of Oxford University in December 1642. He seems to have shared his father's interest in astrology and was a friend of Elias Ashmole. Heydon died at Heston, Middlesex, on 16 October 1653 and was buried there on 19 October. In his will he mentioned outstanding suits in chancery and debts, directing that two remaining properties in Norfolk be sold. He did not name an executor and so that task was carried out by his wife, from whom he was estranged. She was buried at St Bride's, Fleet Street, on 28 November 1658.

STEPHEN PORTER

Sources M. Toynbee, ed., *The papers of Captain Henry Stevens, waggon-master-general to King Charles I*, Oxfordshire RS, 42 (1962), 57–9 · G. E. Aylmer, *The king's servants: the civil service of Charles I, 1625–1642* (1961), 289–90 · G. E. Aylmer, 'Attempts at administrative reform, 1625–40', *EngHR*, 72 (1957), 229–59, esp. 240–46 · I. Roy, ed., *The royalist ordnance papers, 1642–1646*, 2 vols., Oxfordshire RS, 43, 49 (1964–75), 16–17, 20–21 · M. C. Fissel, *The bishops' wars: Charles I's campaigns against Scotland, 1638–1640* (1994), 90–91, 97 · *Elias Ashmole (1617–1692): his autobiographical and historical notes*, ed. C. H. Josten, 5 vols. (1966 [i.e. 1967]), vol. 1, p. 28; vol. 2, pp. 363, 646–8, 656 · will, PRO, PROB 11/239/344 · *APC*, 1628–9, 96–7, 166–7, 340 · I. Roy, 'The libraries of Edward, second Viscount Conway, and others: an inventory and valuation of 1643', *BIHR*, 41 (1968), 35–46 · M. A. E. Green, ed., *Calendar of the proceedings of the committee for compounding … 1643–1660*, 2, PRO (1890), 1500–01 · *CSP dom.*, 1645–7, 59 · W. J. Thoms, ed., *Anecdotes and traditions, illustrative of early English history and literature*, CS, 5 (1839), 23–4, 69 · IGI

Heydon, John (*b.* 1629, *d.* in or after 1670), writer on astrology and alchemy, and occultist, was born on 10 September 1629 in Green Arbour, London, the son of Francis Heydon of Sidmouth, Devon, and Mary Chandler of Worcestershire. He was the grandson of Sir Christopher *Heydon of the Norfolk branch of the family, author of the learned and influential *A Defence of Judiciall Astrologie* (1603). He was privately educated at either Tardebigg, Worcestershire, or Golton, Warwickshire, or both. The civil war, in which his father became lieutenant-general of the ordnance to Charles I, ended his intention to attend university. His

John Heydon (*b.* 1629, *d.* in or after 1670), by unknown engraver, pubd 1664

claim to have commanded a troop of royalist cavalry, though, must be accepted (as with many of his own accounts) with reservations; he would have been aged thirteen.

In 1651 Heydon travelled abroad, perhaps as far as Spain, Italy, Egypt, and Turkey, and the following year returned and, after studying the law, was articled as an attorney at Clifford's Inn. By 1655 he was practising law at the court of king's bench, and began writing his first books (though these were not published until later). He must also have been practising astrology, however, because in 1657 or 1658 he was imprisoned in Lambeth House for foretelling Cromwell's death from his nativity. According to a letter written to the duke of Ormond on 2 March 1667, Richard Cromwell and John Thurloe went to him disguised as cavaliers and asked him for his prediction, and it was as a result of this that he was imprisoned.

On 4 August 1656 Heydon married Alice Culpeper, widow of the famous astrologer–physician and radical, Nicholas *Culpeper. He moved into her house in Spitalfields, near Bishopsgate, next door to the Red Lion. In July 1663 he was again imprisoned for several weeks—this time, despite his staunch royalism, by Charles II for 'seditious practices' (*CSP dom.*, 1663). He was released at the instigation of the duke of Buckingham, but repeated the experience on 23 January 1667. This time he and the duke were both arrested for suspicion of plotting, the charge against Heydon being that he had obliged Buckingham by astrologically inferring the date of the king's death.

Tantalizingly, the *Calendar of State Papers* for February 1667 also records 'Astrological predictions on the questions to Peter Heydon, astrologer of London, as to whether the fanatics shall have toleration in England, and whether the English may be compelled to a neutral place for a treaty of peace'. His predictions were apparently in the affirmative. The record continues with the statement that 'though these answers are according to the rules of his art, he is committed to the Tower for them' (*CSP dom.*, 1666–7, 541).

Heydon stoutly maintained his innocence, and when the evidence became increasingly threadbare the case was dropped. It seems to have been an attempt by Lord Arlington to get his rival, Buckingham—and, as the latter's ally, Heydon—out of the way. At Heydon's arrest, an inventory of his goods noted five hundred books, a sword and an expensive watch; the latter two articles ended up in the possession of the paid witness against him.

The last thing written by Heydon is dated 1670. There are no reports of him afterwards, and nothing is known of when or how he died. His chief books are: *A New Method of Rosicrucian Physick* (1658); *The Rosie Crucian* (1660), which supplies a Rosicrucian–Pythagorean cosmogony; *The English Physitians Guide, or, A Holy Guide* (1662), his principal work of alchemical and mystical medicine; *The Harmony of the World* (1662), his main metaphysical work which outlines his Neoplatonic cosmos; *Theomagia, or, The Temple of Wisdome* (1664), which contains much astrological material; and *The Wise Man's Crown, or, The Glory of the Rosie Cross* (1664) and *El havareuna, or, The English Physician's Tutor* (1665), both of which concentrate on alchemy. He occasionally used a Rosicrucian pen-name, Eugenius Theodidacticus.

All these works are essentially variations on a single theme: Rosicrucianism as a universal wisdom and, as such, the way to an ultimate spiritual, physical, and social harmony. Heydon never claimed to be a member of the Rosicrucian brotherhood, a mysterious group whose actual existence has been questioned, and whose supposed 'manifestos' of 1614–15 were first translated into English in 1652 by Thomas Vaughan. Rather he was an apologist and publicist for Rosicrucian ideas—which is to say, an amalgam of Neoplatonism, hermeticism, the Kabbalah, Pythagoras, Paracelsian medicine, alchemy, and astrology. To that end, he borrowed heavily, and usually without acknowledgements, from Thomas Vaughan, Francis Bacon, Sir Thomas Browne, Cornelius Agrippa (on occult philosophy), Paracelsus (on medicine), Elias Ashmole (on alchemy), and William Lilly (on astrology). For Heydon, the resulting philosophy, with its spiritual sympathies and antipathies, mystical number symbolism, and hierarchies of spirits linking any number of earthly phenomena (and ultimately ruled by God, as the One), supplied medicines equally for society, the individual

soul, and the physical body, all of which were ultimately reflections of the divine order.

The context for Heydon's arguments was the extraordinarily fertile and chaotic intellectual milieu of England in the mid-seventeenth century, in which the new mechanical and experimental philosophies, the old Aristotelianism, and the magico-religious world-view and practices of the radical sectaries, were all contending for supremacy. For many of his contemporaries, he apparently embodied much of the latter, with its 'Familistical-Levelling-Magical temper' (Hall, 199) stigmatized, especially after 1660, as 'enthusiasm'. With William Lilly, Heydon was a model for the astrologer Mopus in John Wilson's popular play of 1663, *The Cheats*. On a more learned level, he was attacked by name in the bishop of Oxford, Samuel Parker's, *A Free and Impartial Censure of the Platonick Philosophy* (1667), and by implication in Robert Boyle's *Free Inquiry into the Vulgarly Received Notion of Nature* (1665), despite (or perhaps on account of) Heydon's syncretic gesture towards Boyle's belief in the production of terrestrial phenomena by the motions of corpuscles.

Ironically, Heydon himself was far from being a radical sectary but was a lifelong, even fanatical, monarchist, who believed (to put it crudely) that a king was necessary to reflect the power of God. His monarchism and relatively well-born social status were insufficient, however, to overcome the political suspicions engendered by his 'enthusiastic' religious and metaphysical cosmology. At the same time, his politics set him at odds with the radical groupings who were similarly inclined to magic, alchemy, and astrology.

Heydon's earlier books were apparently commended by the astrologers John Gadbury and John Booker, although there is an element of doubt, since according to John Aubrey, Heydon was not above pirating praise composed for other authors' books; within a few years, however, he was attacking and being criticized by both Lilly and Booker. He even denounced Paracelsus and Jakob Boehme, despite his borrowings from them, probably for having drawn unacceptably 'levelling' conclusions from their Neoplatonic premises. 'The recent years of the [Cromwellian] tyranny', he complained, 'admitted stocking-weavers, shoe-makers, millers, masons, carpenters, bricklayers, gunsmiths, porters, butlers, etc. to write and teach astrology and physick' (*Theomagia*, 1664, C3v).

To add to the complexity of his position and seal his almost complete isolation, Heydon was himself, despite his adherence to hierarchy and his contempt for the sectaries, something of a populist in his approach. *The Rosie Crucian* contained 'Infallible Axiomata, or, Generall Rules to know all things past, present, and to come' (title-page) and *The Harmony of the World* described itself as 'a Discourse wherein the Phaenomenoa of Nature are Consonantly Salved and Adapted to Inferior Intellects' (title-page). Perhaps this was simply an attempt to spread the word and promote his programme, or perhaps it was partly compelled by the general hostility he met at a more learned level; in any case, together with his inveterate plagiarism and flamboyant self-promotion, the result was to alienate his last potential allies, namely conservative and royalist occultists such as Gadbury and Ashmole. The latter dismissed him as 'an ignoramus and a cheate' (*DNB*), a verdict that was probably widely accepted at the time, but has too readily obscured Heydon's complexity and historical interest.   PATRICK CURRY

Sources J. H. [J. Heydon], *The English physitians guide, or, A holy guide, leading the way to know all things* (1662) [incl. autobiographical account] · L. Johnson, 'Platonism, physick and politics: John Heydon and universal wisdom, 1650–70', PhD diss., U. Cam., 1987 · H. G. Dick, 'Students of physic and astrology: a survey of astrological medicine in the age of science', *Journal of the History of Medicine and Allied Sciences*, 1 (1946), 300–15 · *DNB* · F. Talbot, 'The life of John Heydon', in J. Heydon, *El Havareuna* (1665) [unpaginated] · *CSP dom.*, 21 July, 4 Aug 1663; Feb 1666–7, 541 · T. Hall, *Histrio-mastix* (1654), 199

Archives PRO, state papers | BL, Egerton MSS · BL, Sloane MSS, MS 2285, fols. 122v–123v · Bodl. Oxf., Carte MSS · Bodl. Oxf., Clarendon MSS · Althorp MSS, Halifax corresp.

Likenesses T. Cross, line engraving, BM, NPG; repro. in J. Heydon, *Holy guide* · W. Sherwin, line engraving, NPG · line engraving, BM, NPG; repro. in Heydon, *Theomagia, or, The temple of wisdome* (1664), frontispiece [*see illus.*]

Heyer [*married name* Rougier], **Georgette** (1902–1974), novelist, was born in Wimbledon, Surrey, on 16 August 1902, the daughter of George Heyer (*d.* 1925), writer, and his wife, Sylvia, *née* Watkins (*d.* 1962). George Heyer was formerly a member of the Wimbledon Literary and Scientific Society and the author of a well-received translation of the poems of François Villon published in 1924. Georgette Heyer's future literary career was influenced by her close friendship during her teenage years with two older girls, Joanna Cannan and Carola Oman; all three young women published novels in the early 1920s. Heyer, the youngest of the three, began her own literary career with the publication of *The Black Moth* (1921) which originally had been composed as a story to entertain her younger brother Boris, a haemophiliac. It was published with the encouragement of her father when Heyer was only nineteen.

The author of nearly sixty volumes, Georgette Heyer is primarily known today as the most substantial progenitor of the 'regency' or historical novel, although her career features notable forays into a variety of genres, including novels of romance and of mystery and suspense. Heyer's novels are defined particularly by her careful attention to the sociological nuances which impinge upon her characters—an element of her fiction which clearly reveals her affinity with the novels of Jane Austen. Austen's sizeable influence upon Heyer's canon is likewise affirmed by Heyer's extraordinary attention to matters of historical detail, including the style of her characters' dress and their use of language, an attention demonstrated by the voluminous notebooks left after her death in 1974—notebooks which often included detailed drawings and notes for her projected novels. Although her novels rarely received critical acclaim, particularly because regency novels have been assailed critically for the rigidity of their narrative formula, they always sold extremely well; as her biographer, Jane Aiken Hodge, notes, Heyer was 'that rare thing, a steady best-seller' (p. 9). In fact, upon her death, Heyer's fiction had been translated into more than ten

Georgette Heyer (1902–1974), by Howard Coster, 1939

languages, and perhaps even more remarkably, more than fifty of her novels were still in print at that time. Perhaps even more significantly, Heyer's novels allow us, in the words of A. S. Byatt, to retreat into a 'Paradise of ideal solutions, knowing it for what it is, comforted by its temporary actuality, nostalgically refreshed for coping with the quite different tangle of preconceptions, conventions and social emphases we have to live with. Which is what good escape literature is about' (Byatt, 265).

Following the commercial success of *The Black Moth*, Heyer quickly became a prolific young writer—publishing eleven volumes by 1930—although this period in her career can be more adequately defined by the four experimental novels that she later suppressed, *Instead of the Thorn* (1923), *Helen* (1928), *Pastel* (1929), and *Barren Corn* (1930). A string of intense personal events also marked this period in Heyer's life, particularly her father's sudden death in the spring of 1925 of a heart attack after playing tennis with Heyer's fiancé, Ronald Rougier. Because her father's career promised little in the way of a pension, Heyer's fiction suddenly became the family's only visible means of financial support. Her father's death was followed quickly by her marriage to Rougier on 18 August 1925, and her new identity as Mrs Ronald Rougier afforded her the sort of anonymity that she coveted as Georgette Heyer, for her novels were already receiving widespread attention among her budding coterie of readers. Her marriage to Rougier—an association which would last the balance of her lifetime—proved useful to Heyer as an artist, for it allowed her to visit a variety of cultures and locales.

Rougier, as a mining engineer and later a successful barrister, had to live in east Africa until 1928, later in Yugoslavia, before settling in The Albany, in London, where their neighbours included such luminaries as the actress Dame Edith Evans and the novelist and literary critic J. B. Priestley.

The publication of *Barren Corn* preceded an era of intense artistic and personal flux for Heyer—a period which included her first major attempt at traversing the historical novel, *The Conqueror* (1931), the birth of her son, Richard, in 1932, and her commercially successful experimentation with mystery novels. During the following decade Heyer produced nearly a dozen such novels, including *Footsteps in the Dark* (1932), *Why Shoot a Butler?* (1936), *The Unfinished Clue* (1934), *Death in the Stocks* (1935), *Behold, Here's Poison!* (1936), *They Found him Dead* (1937), and *A Blunt Instrument* (1938). Although she appeared to abandon the genre in the early 1940s, Heyer published the popular mystery novel *Detection Unlimited* in 1953. Critics often consider her mysteries to be uneven in quality—although Heyer's mystery novels, like her historical novels, remain in print because of her substantial popular audience.

The 1940s brought substantial changes in Heyer's life: in addition to the advent of the Second World War, her son was slowly requiring less of her attention, her husband was beginning to find success as a barrister in London, and Heyer and her family settled in Brighton. In this period Heyer produced four of her most substantial and fully realized novels, including *The Spanish Bride* (1940), *The Corinthian* (1940), *Faro's Daughter* (1941), and *Friday's Child* (1944). *Friday's Child*, a regency novel, was Heyer's personal favourite, and upon its publication in 1944 she defended it to her critics in a blaze of self-deprecation:

> I think myself I ought to be shot for writing such nonsense, but it's unquestionably good escapist literature, and I think I should rather like it if I were sitting in an air-raid shelter, or recovering from the flu. Its period detail is good; my husband says it's witty—and without going to these lengths, I will say that it is very good fun. (Hodge, 8)

Following a string of successes with *Arabella* (1949), *The Grand Sophy* (1950), and *The Quiet Gentleman* (1951), Heyer published *Cotillion* in 1953, a novel which resembles *Friday's Child* in both plot and characterization. Heyer's 1970 novel *Charity Girl* followed a string of successful novels, including *April Lady* (1957), *Venetia* (1958), *The Nonesuch* (1962), and *Cousin Kate* (1968). Diagnosed with lung cancer in May 1974, Heyer died on 5 July 1974 at Guy's Hospital, London. In its obituary *The Guardian* called her 'one of the great queens of historical fiction', while the *Sunday Telegraph* noted that she was 'sometimes known as the twentieth-century Jane Austen'. In 1975 *My Lord John*, a medieval novel about the house of Lancaster that she had researched and planned for many years, was published posthumously with the aid of her family. Heyer's novels have been the subject, moreover, of a few notable film and stage adaptations. In addition to Bernard Knowles's film version of her 1946 novel *The Reluctant Widow* (Fine Arts Films, 1951), Chicago's Lifeline Theatre has produced three stage productions of Heyer's works, including *The*

Talisman Ring (1997), *Cotillion* (1998), and *Pistols for Two* (2000). Heyer's literary achievement is difficult to assess; her novels are repetitious and did not win critical approval. Yet they remain notable (particularly her regency romances) because of her phenomenal sales records and her consistent concern for matters of style, characterization, and description.

KENNETH WOMACK

Sources E. F. Bargainnier, *Clues* (1982), 30–39 · J. A. Hodge, *The private world of Georgette Heyer* (1984) · E. Pall, *New York Times Book Review* (30 April 1989), 1, 37 · *The Guardian* (July 1974) · *Sunday Telegraph* (July 1974) · A. S. Byatt, 'An honourable escape: Georgette Heyer', *Passions of the mind: selected writings* (1991) · b. cert. · d. cert.
Archives Duke U. | BL, corresp. with Society of Authors, Add. MS 63262
Likenesses H. Coster, photograph, 1939, NPG [*see illus.*]
Wealth at death £68,989: probate, 6 Dec 1974, *CGPLA Eng. & Wales*

Heygate, William Edward (1816–1902), Church of England clergyman and writer, was born on 11 August 1816 at Hackney, Middlesex, the second son of James Heygate (1784–1873) and his wife, Anna (d. 1867), second daughter of Edward Longdon Mackmurdo of Old Ford, Middlesex. He had two brothers and three sisters. Sir William Heygate (1782–1844), MP for Sudbury 1818–26 and lord mayor of London 1822–3, created baronet in 1831, was Heygate's only uncle on his father's side. He entered Merchant Taylors' School, London, in 1831, and matriculated as Andrew's exhibitioner at St John's College, Oxford, in 1835. Taking a third class in *literae humaniores*, he graduated BA in 1839 and MA in 1842.

Ordained deacon and then priest in 1840, Heygate went first as curate to Great Wakering, Essex, before being invalided for two years with chest problems. He then served curacies at South Gerrans in Cornwall, and at Hadleigh and Leigh, both in Essex, supplementing mostly meagre stipends by teaching and writing. On 15 July 1846 he married Mary Elizabeth Penny, daughter of the Revd Edmund Henry Penny, rector of Great Stambridge, Rochford, Essex. They had seven sons and four daughters. In 1869, reputedly after John Keble had commended him to Gladstone as a parish priest deserving of promotion, Heygate was presented to the living of Brighstone (or Brixton) on the Isle of Wight by Samuel Wilberforce, bishop of Winchester.

A voluminous writer, Heygate was perhaps best known for his fiction, which contributed to the canon of high-church religious and social tales popularized by the Tractarian writers William Gresley and Francis Edward Paget. Typical of these was *William Blake, or, The English Farmer* (1848), which set out the paternal responsibilities of that class, while *Godfrey Davenant: a Tale of School Life* (1847) and *Godfrey Davenant at College* (1849), which chronicled the early moral trials of their protagonist and set out Heygate's educational ideals, also enjoyed some notice. *Sir Henry Appleton, or, Essex during the Great Rebellion* (1857) drew upon Heygate's local historical knowledge and evinced hostility to puritanism, while a better received sequel, *The Scholar and the Trooper, or, Oxford during the Great Rebellion*, appeared the following year. The first of these led to a correspondence with the prominent American manufacturer, banker, and politician Nathan Appleton (1779–1861), a distant descendant of the book's subject who claimed puritan ancestry. Their dialogue was published anonymously in the USA in 1859 as *The Doctrines of Original Sin and the Trinity Discussed in a Correspondence.* Two anti-revolutionary novellas were *Pierre Poussin, or, The Thought of Christ's Presence* (1851) and the anonymous *Alice of Fobbing, or, The Times of Jack Straw and Wat Tyler* (1860). As well as various individual tales Heygate published eight collections of children's stories, of which *Allegories and Tales* (1873) and *An Old Parson's Anecdotes and Tales* (1892) are typical. A collection of his poetry, *The Fugitive and other Poems,* appeared in 1870.

Heygate also published numerous devotional works. Well-known general guides included *Ember Hours* (1857), *The Good Shepherd* (1860) (which W. E. Gladstone used to read while dressing for dinner), and *The Eucharist* (1874), though others were intended for specific audiences, such as *The Manual: a Book of Devotion Chiefly Intended for the Poor* (1853) and *The Evening of Life, or, Meditations and Devotions for the Aged* (1856). He issued several statements of theology, such as *Catholic Antidotes* (1858), as well as a collection of sermons and various pamphlets on subjects of the day.

Made an honorary canon of Winchester in 1887, Heygate remained at Brighstone until his death there on 12 December 1902; he was buried in Brighstone churchyard. An ardent high-churchman and Tractarian sympathizer, he volunteered to assist the Revd Bryan King, rector of St George-in-the-East, London, during the ritualist riots of 1859–60, and was a lifelong friend and correspondent both of Keble and, after his settlement at Brighstone, of E. B. Pusey, who had a house at nearby Chale. Of his immediate family, his younger brother Thomas Edmund (*b.* 1826) and three of his seven sons—the eldest, William Augustine (*b.* 1847), the third, Ambrose (*b.* 1852), and the fifth, Reginald Thomas (*b.* 1858)—all followed him into Anglican orders.   S. A. SKINNER

Sources J. Foster, *The peerage, baronetage, and knightage of the British empire for 1883,* 2 [1883], 312 • *Church Times* (19 Dec 1902) • *Church Times* (24 Dec 1902) • *The Guardian* (17 Dec 1902) • C. J. Robinson, ed., *A register of the scholars admitted into Merchant Taylors' School, from AD 1562 to 1874,* 2 (1883), 245 • Mrs E. P. Hart, ed., *Merchant Taylors' School register, 1561–1934,* 2 vols. (1936) • Crockford (1902) • Foster, *Alum. Oxon.* • IGI
Archives rectory, Brighstone, Isle of Wight, parish record book | Keble College, Oxford, letters to J. Keble
Likenesses photograph, Brighstone church, Isle of Wight
Wealth at death £34,877 3s. 0d.: probate, 19 Jan 1903, CGPLA Eng. & Wales

Heylyn, John (1684/5–1759), theologian, was baptized on 2 August 1685 at St Martin-in-the-Fields, Westminster, the eldest son of John Heylyn (*d.* 1736), saddler, and Susanna Sherman, sister of Thomas Sherman of St Andrew's, Holborn. His father is said to have acquired a large fortune by army contracts. He was educated at Westminster School, where he became a king's scholar in 1700. He was admitted to Trinity College, Cambridge, as a pensioner on 7 June

1705 and was elected a scholar on 12 April 1706. He graduated BA and MA in 1709, and DD in 1728. Ordained priest, in London on 18 December 1709, he was vicar of Haslingfield, Cambridgeshire, between 1714 and 1719; Edward Rud records that Heylyn 'preach'd a very fine sermon' at the archidiaconal visitation of Dr Bentley in December 1716 (*Diary ... of Edward Rud,* 19). He became the first rector of the modern St Mary-le-Strand on 1 January 1724 and held that living until his death. On 2 July 1729 he was chosen lecturer of All Hallows, Lombard Street. Heylyn was a chaplain in ordinary to George II (1733–48) and was also rector of Sunbury, Middlesex (1742–7). He was collated to prebendal stalls at St Paul's on 11 October 1736, and at Westminster on 21 March 1743.

From his indulgence in mysticism Heylyn was known as the Mystic Doctor. His principal work was *Theological lectures at Westminster Abbey, with an interpretation of the four gospels, to which are added some select discourses upon the principal points of revealed religion* (1749). A second part of this work, entitled 'An interpretation of the New Testament', was prepared by Heylyn for the press but was not published until 1761, after his death. He also published six single sermons, one of which was delivered by him at the consecration in 1738 of his friend Joseph Butler, bishop of Bristol.

Heylyn married twice; his second wife, Elizabeth Ebbutt of St Margaret's, Westminster, died on 9 June 1747, aged forty-nine. He himself died on 11 August 1759, aged seventy-four, and was buried six days later in the south transept of Westminster Abbey, where there is a monument to his memory. He bequeathed £1000 to the lying-in hospital in Brownlow Street. He was survived by a son, John, who was a merchant in Bristol.

G. F. R. BARKER, *rev.* ADAM JACOB LEVIN

Sources *Old Westminsters,* 1.455 • will, PRO, PROB 11/848, fols. 253–4 • Venn, *Alum. Cant.* • *Fasti Angl.* (Hardy), 2.416, 3.366 • *Fasti Angl., 1541–1857,* [St Paul's, London] • *Fasti Angl., 1541–1857,* [Ely] • J. L. Chester and J. Foster, eds., *London marriage licences, 1521–1869* (1887), 676 • *The diary (1709–1720) of Edward Rud,* ed. H. R. Luard (1860), 19 • IGI
Wealth at death approx. £2000: will, PRO, PROB 11/848, fols. 253–4

Heylyn, Peter (1599–1662), Church of England clergyman and historian, was born in Burford, Oxfordshire, on 29 November 1599, the second son of Henry Heylyn (*d.* 1622), a minor country gentleman, and his wife, Elizabeth Clampard (*d.* 1616). He was educated at Burford grammar school and was admitted initially to Hart Hall, Oxford, in 1614, but was then elected a demy of Magdalen College in 1615; he matriculated on 19 January 1616.

Oxford and early influences Heylyn soon clashed with other members of the college: such was his diligence in the office of 'impositor of the Hall' that, as he later reported, he was dubbed 'the perpetual dictator', and the 'heart burning' of both the other demies and the senior fellows towards him 'break out into whipping and other base usuage' (Heylyn, xiv). He gained early renown for his geographical works. After graduating BA in October 1617 he

PETRUS HEYLYN S.T.P.
Ecclesiæ Collegiatæ Sancti Petri Westmonasteriensis
Canonicus, Martyri & superstiti CAROLIS Patri ac Filio.
Magnæ Britanniæ etc. Monarchis dum viveret à Sacris.

Peter Heylyn (1599–1662), by Robert White, pubd 1681

began to lecture on historical geography in the college, and was elected a fellow of Magdalen in the following year. After proceeding MA in 1620 he published his lectures as *Microcosmos: a Little Description of the Great World* (1621) and secured its presentation to its dedicatee, Prince Charles, at Theobalds. This proved his most popular work, going through no fewer than eight editions by 1639. From his early years Heylyn was also active as a poet. At a later age he recollected his early poems with pleasure, and continued writing them into the early 1630s, when he dedicated poems to Charles I and William Laud. He had a particular taste for satire, enthusiastically translating epigrams by Martial as well as composing a Latin comedy, *Theomachia*, and a derisory poem against Barten Holyday entitled 'Whoop Holiday', and in 1625 he composed a lengthy satirical account of his trip to France, which went through several editions in the 1650s.

Heylyn's background was not that of a straightforward divine. Moreover, despite his later association with the Laudian movement, there is no obvious indication of early associations with such ideas. On the contrary his earlier connections would seem to have been with figures more linked to puritanism. One of his kinsmen was the famous puritan sheriff of London and member of the feoffees for impropriations, Rowland *Heylyn; his early schoolteacher, Edward Davys, retained his living during the protectorate; he studied at the godly inclined Magdalen College; one of his tutors was the 'verie zealous and

pragmaticall Puritan' (Heylyn, *Memorial*, xii) Walter Newberry; and he received early patronage from the puritanically inclined earl of Danby, and support from the Calvinist dean of Winchester, John Young. The religious views apparent in the early editions of the *Microcosmos* are those of a conventional anti-Catholic Calvinist, and include many opinions that he would later condemn, including the claim that the pope was Antichrist, that continental iconoclasm was praiseworthy, and that the Albigensians were worthy predecessors of English protestants.

Pursuit of patronage and activities as an apologist Heylyn's progress seems to have been disrupted by a disputation at the divinity schools in Oxford in 1627, where he incurred the wrath of the regius professor of divinity, John Prideaux. While Heylyn later sought to present this conflict as an ideological clash, this seems to be a profitable gloss on what seems more to have been a combination of misunderstanding and personal animosity. The most important consequence of this event is that it may have first brought Heylyn to the attention of his later patron William Laud, whose patronage he was actively soliciting by 1629, the year he proceeded BD. Heylyn had in the meantime been ordained in 1624 and married, on 28 October 1628, Letitia, daughter of Thomas Highgate of Hayes, Middlesex, whose elder sister had already married Heylyn's elder brother. He continued to hold his fellowship for a year after the marriage, leading to later charges that he had married clandestinely. Heylyn's anxious search for preferment in the wake of his marriage led to a trip to the Channel Islands in 1629 as chaplain to the earl of Danby, but he used the opportunity to send an exposé of the disorders of Guernsey presbyterianism to Laud (undoubtedly against Danby's wishes). His search for public employment under Laud continued in 1630, when he prompted the government's attack upon the feoffees for impropriations in a very public and highly provocative sermon in Oxford, a copy of which he sent, bound in vellum, to Laud. Again, Heylyn demonstrated his ability to discern puritan subversion where others had not thought to find it, and condemned his kinsman Rowland Heylyn in the process.

Heylyn also sought to appeal to the king, to whom he became a chaplain-in-ordinary in 1630. As well as publishing anonymously a curious work—*Augustus*—which described how Augustus Caesar used devious methods to establish an absolute monarchy, Heylyn adopted a more direct and less controversial route in the form of his *History of St George* (1631) with an eye to Charles's particular and well-known enthusiasm for the Order of the Garter (the work was presented to the king by Laud in February 1631). Heylyn was soon put to work as a hitman against the regime's opponents. In 1632 he was charged in the king's name with reviewing William Prynne's *Histriomastix*, and came up in record time with a vitriolic review which secured Prynne's prosecution for sedition. In the previous year Heylyn had been presented to a prebendal stall in Westminster Abbey (as well as a living in Hemingford Abbots) clearly with the intention that he should dig up information on Laud's opponent, the dean, John Williams. Within seven months he was already offering to secretary of state Sir John Coke information against Williams which he had wheedled out of the civil lawyer Dr William Spicer. Two years later he again played a prominent role in the drawing up of thirty-six articles of complaint against the dean by the prebendaries. At the hearing of the commission into the grievances in February 1636 Williams commented prophetically 'If your Lordships will hear that young fellow prate, he will presently persuade you that I am no Dean of Westminster'. Just a matter of months after this hearing Heylyn embarked on a pamphlet battle with Williams over the government's altar policy, in the course of which he composed what were the principal defences of this Laudian policy, *A Coale from the Altar* (1636) and *Antidotum Lincolniense* (1637).

Heylyn also levelled his guns at Laud's opponent and his own nemesis, the Oxford regius professor of divinity John Prideaux. Having himself proceeded DD on 13 April 1633 and been licensed to preach, he accused Prideaux of heterodoxy after the act that summer, and the following year he mischievously published in translation an earlier lecture that Prideaux had given on sabbatarianism. Heylyn supplied his own preface to the work and presented the lecture as if it defended the newly reissued Book of Sports. His own substantial defence of the Book of Sports—*History of the Sabbath*—was submitted to the press the following year, to be followed by a general defence of the policies of the personal rule in 1637, the *Briefe and Moderate Answer*: each was an officially sponsored apologetic work, the former designed to complement the work of Bishop Francis White, the latter the published speech of Archbishop Laud. He also made a substantial contribution to Laud's judgment in the case of Henry Burton, John Bastwick, and William Prynne.

In career terms these various pieces of hatchet work and polemical writing paid major dividends. Further crown appointments followed: Heylyn was presented to the rich benefice of Houghton in Durham in 1633, which he substituted for that of Alresford, Hampshire, allegedly on the specific instructions of the king, so that he would be nearer to court to do his bidding. Here he substantially expanded the parsonage house and built a new chapel.

After the imprisonment of Williams, Heylyn was appointed treasurer of the Westminster chapter in December 1637, and was soon afterwards appointed to the parsonage of Islip, which he exchanged for the rectory of South Warnborough, Hampshire (a living in the gift of St John's College, Oxford, and the exchange therefore conceivably aided by Laud's intervention). Soon afterwards, however, he and his family at Alresford fell seriously ill. On Heylyn's recovery he immersed himself in researching the history of the Church of England. It was presumably about this time that he made substantial notes on proceedings of convocation, copies of which survive at Lambeth Palace Library. He also contributed materials to Laud's revised and expanded version of his *Conference with Fisher*. Like other Laudians he did not write official defences of royal policy during the Scots crisis, as the

defence of episcopacy fell to Joseph Hall, although he contributed his own *The History of Episcopacie* (1642) under the pseudonym of Theophilus Churchman.

Crisis of 1640–1642 and the civil war Heylyn attended the notorious convocation of 1640, where he seems to have played an important role in proposing and drawing up a standard set of visitation articles to be adopted for the whole country and in proposing the canon calling for greater observance of the king's accession day, as well as providing the necessary precedent of 1586 to justify the continued sitting of convocation after the dissolution of parliament.

The assembling of the Long Parliament in November 1640 made it likely that Heylyn, like other supporters of the Laudian regime, would be called to account for his actions. He was confronted first by John Williams, the released dean of Westminster, who dramatically interrupted a sermon that Heylyn was giving in the abbey by knocking on the pulpit with his staff and exclaiming 'No more of that point'. Heylyn's account of their subsequent exchanges claims that they reached a cautious cease-fire. At the same time Heylyn found himself cross-examined before a committee investigating Prynne's prosecution, which found him guilty as a delinquent, although the failure to prosecute Heylyn any further may have been partly due to his pointed reminder to Charles of 'how much it doth concerne the king in honour to justifie the intimacion of his owne commands' (PRO, SP 16/476/97). After composing a paper justifying the right of the bishops to take part in the trial of the earl of Strafford, Heylyn retired to Alresford.

It was there, late in 1642, that Heylyn found his house attacked by the troops of Sir William Waller, who had orders to bring him a prisoner to Portsmouth. Heylyn escaped and joined the king at Oxford, where he was instructed to remain and to write on the king's behalf. He was the first editor of the royalist newsbook *Mercurius Aulicus*, which began with Heylyn's characteristic claim to be seeking to deliver the dispassionate and objective truth. He was reportedly happy to pass the work on to Sir John Berkenhead when this was recommended by Sir Kenelm Digby in September 1643, although he returned to work on it for a few weeks in June 1644 during Berkenhead's absence. Later in 1643 Heylyn wrote *The Rebells Catechism*, as well as *The Stumbling Block of Schisme*, although the latter work was not published until the 1650s. He responded to news of Laud's execution with a heartfelt *Briefe Relation of the Death and Sufferings of … L. Archbishop of Canterbury* (1645) which celebrated him in verse as a martyr. In the meantime Heylyn was declared a delinquent by the Commons in 1644, was sequestrated from Alresford in 1644 and from South Warnborough in 1645, and had his estates and goods seized, and his books carried away to Portsmouth. In early May 1645 Heylyn gained the king's leave to retire to Winchester, although he soon had to flee to stay with friends in Wiltshire, before settling at Minster Lovell, Oxfordshire, in 1648 the seat of his deceased elder brother, which he farmed of his nephew for several years.

Writings of the 1650s There Heylyn resumed his writing. He published the strongly clericalist *The Undeceiving of the People in the Point of Tithes*, his substantial commentary on the creed (*Theologia veterum*), and perhaps his most famous work, the *Cosmographie*. Published in 1652 this was an enormous and highly popular expansion of his earlier *Microcosmos* into a folio volume of nearly a thousand pages, and was sufficiently well regarded that the council of state saw fit to obtain a copy for their better instruction. In the meantime Heylyn had compounded for his sequestrated estate in December 1646, and contrived to live sufficiently well (in comparison with other deprived clergy, and despite the complaints of his successor at Alresford) to purchase, in 1653, Lacy's Court, near Abingdon, Berkshire, within convenient distance of Oxford. Here he built a small private chapel in which prayer book services were conducted and he also became occupied in local affairs, successfully intervening with the courts to prevent the demolition of the church of St Nicholas, Abingdon. He was less fortunate in his attempts to avoid the decimation tax, however.

Heylyn's taste for combat also began to emerge once more in his published work as he became involved in a number of controversial exchanges with several authors, picking over the bones of the religious and political history of the pre-war period, and sometimes defending his own actions. His anonymous *Observations on Mr Hamon L'Estrange's Life of Charles I* (1656) were attacked in their turn, and further defended in Heylyn's *Extraneus valupans* (1656). Another opponent was Nicholas Bernard, who had published an exposition of the late Archbishop James Ussher's views on the sabbath, which opposed the work of Heylyn (among others). Heylyn replied with his *Respondet Petrus*, which the council ruled should be burnt for its attack on the morality of the fourth commandment, although Heylyn claimed that this sentence was not in fact carried out by the London authorities to whom it was entrusted. The *Respondet Petrus* also contained attacks on another historian, William Sanderson, whose *History of Charles I* Heylyn also attacked in a further work, *Examen historicum*. It was in this latter work that Heylyn also famously took up the cudgels against Thomas Fuller's *Church History*, accusing him of pro-puritan bias. Other opponents whom Heylyn confronted in these works included Henry Hickman, Richard Baxter, and John Harrington. In every case Heylyn showed himself to be an unapologetic defender of the ecclesiastical policies of the personal rule and an implacable critic of its puritan opponents, whom he considered to be directly responsible for the calamities that had overtaken the country.

It would be misleading, however, to imply that Heylyn had retreated into a scholarly shell, wedded to discredited ideas and apathetic to the prevailing political situation. His *Ecclesia vindicata* of 1657 suggests a more intriguing agenda. A collection of a number of works published in the 1640s, along with almost all his previously unpublished works, it is a compendium of defences of the Church of England as Heylyn saw it. Despite its uncompromising tone, however, it is not presented as a simple

rant in the wilderness. It is dedicated, curiously, to his old (and hitherto neglected) Burford schoolmaster, perhaps singled out because he was the only acquaintance of Heylyn's who had retained a living in the interregnum church. A copy of the work in the Bodleian Library (Bodl. Oxf., 4° Rawlinson 152) contains a further remarkable manuscript dedication by Heylyn to no less a figure than Oliver Cromwell. Doubtless buoyed up by hopes that Cromwell would accept the crown Heylyn argued that a re-establishment of the Church of England would provide the most effective support and accompaniment to a civil settlement. A presentation copy of his *Examen historicum* also survives bearing an unsigned manuscript dedication to Richard Cromwell, although, like the *Ecclesia vindicata*, the text provides an unapologetic endorsement of Laudian policies. *The Stumbling-Block of Disobedience* (1657) had initially been intended for the royalist cause, but Heylyn published it as a warning to the leaders of the Commonwealth not to trust popular spirits. In other works, such as the *Observations*, Heylyn also demonstrated a less than wholehearted dedication to the Stuart monarchs (and Charles in particular), in contrast to his consistent devotion to Laud's memory. Charles might have died for the Church of England, but Heylyn was not convinced that the Church of England should die for the Stuart dynasty (although he was shrewd enough to present another copy of the *Ecclesia vindicata* to Charles II with a completely different manuscript dedication, as well as contributing historical introductions to two collections of Charles I's works in the period immediately prior to the Restoration).

Restoration With the restoration of Charles II in 1660 Heylyn was restored to his livings, but did not receive any further promotion, despite his undoubted expectations. As subdean of Westminster he presented the royal sceptre to the king at the coronation, but this constituted the limit of his role in the Restoration. Many reasons may lie behind his lack of promotion: his blindness (the *Cosmographie* of 1652 was the last book which he completed with his own hand, and by 1660, while he could discern shapes, he was unable to read or write); his lack of obvious patrons at court; his 'very mean port and presence' and lack of courtly graces (according to Anthony Wood); or perhaps his inflexible nature at a time when compromises needed to be sought with presbyterians. Despite his acid remark 'Much good may it do the new Bishops: I do not envy them' (Barnard, clxxxii), Heylyn did what he could to ensure that the political power of the church was re-established: in correspondence with the earl of Clarendon he urged the calling of convocation so that the church would be re-established on a proper footing rather than re-emerging from the Savoy conference; he advised on the organization of the convocation itself (although he did not participate as a member); and in a sermon commemorating the Restoration in 1661 he warned of the urgent need to ensure that churchmen were present on the privy council.

Heylyn's most important contribution to the Restoration church, however, came in the form of the trilogy of historical works that he completed during these final years. Principal among these was *Ecclesia restaurata*, his history of the English Reformation, which he had first begun to research in the late 1630s. It provides an emphatically Laudian view of the Reformation, withering in its attacks on the excesses of the Edwardian reformation, and presenting a settlement that was essentially complete by 1560, although threatened by the emerging puritan movement, whose advent looms over the final pages of the work. His *Aerius redivivus* (published posthumously) took this account of the misdeeds of the presbyterian movement forward in a European context, and presented the upheavals of the civil war and interregnum as the culmination of a puritan plot that could be traced back to the earliest days of the vestiarian controversy; Calvinism was presented as the natural ally of civil unrest. The final and most famous part of the trilogy was Heylyn's biography of Laud, *Cyprianus Anglicus*. Not only a sustained apology for the life and policies of the archbishop this work also provides a historical defence of the Laudian church itself. It is prefaced by an account of the English Reformation which emphasizes its moderate Melancthonian nature, so that both the Arminian doctrine and the ceremonial policies of Laud and his followers can be represented as a heroic and rearguard defence of the historical orthodoxies of the English Reformation in the face of puritan sabotage. Heylyn did not live to see the publication of these final two works, however: he died in Westminster on 8 May 1662 and was buried under the subdean's seat in Westminster Abbey. His wife survived him, dying about March 1667.

Reputation The polarized view of the Church of England that Heylyn propounded has meant that he has been alternately praised and vilified by succeeding generations of scholars and churchmen. His works found their most enthusiastic audiences in the midst of the polarized religious politics of the 1670s and 1680s. His major works were regularly reprinted in the 1670s, and in 1681 a substantial collected volume of his previous works was published, followed by two biographies. He was attacked by John Locke and Algernon Sidney, and his monument in the abbey was defaced, but he was eulogized by many tories. His *Ecclesia restaurata*, with its condemnation of the excesses of the Reformation, was alleged by Gilbert Burnet to have played a role in converting the future James II to Catholicism. In the eighteenth century his *Historia quinquarticularis* was translated into Dutch and praised by the Arminian party, and acted as a focus for contemptuous attacks on his reputation by Augustus Toplady and others during the controversies over the Calvinism of the Church of England. In the nineteenth century he was listed as an authority in John Keble's *Tract 78*, and his *Ecclesia restaurata* was published by the Ecclesiastical History Society in 1849, but the Anglo-Catholic movement seems to have had mixed feelings about him. He was listed as a divine whose works were intended to be included in the Library of Anglo-Catholic Theology, but these volumes never appeared.

While there has been no shortage of writers ready to accept Heylyn's view of the lineage of high-church Anglicanism, it has also been common to treat him as merely an unscrupulous polemicist. It would be unfair, however, simply to disregard Heylyn's scholarly pretensions. He was certainly no theologian, but he did regard himself as a historian, and in this guise he devoted himself to the service of the church and state. His works display an increasing obsession with the view that all disputes could ultimately be reduced to matters of historical fact, and, for all his distortions, he usually deployed a more assured command of much greater bodies of materials than did his rivals. His conviction that scholarship should serve direct political purposes was in step with the convictions of the time. The fact that he is so often presented by historians as a uniquely cynical and untrustworthy scholar, rather than one among many in a tumultuous age, may perhaps be explained by the fact that his rendering of events has become so influential. Heylyn's partisan view of the Church of England and her Reformation has proved so persistently attractive and influential among high-church Anglican groups that the need to focus on his shortcomings and distortions has always seemed an urgent task.

ANTHONY MILTON

Sources J. Barnard, *Theologo-Historicus, or, The true life of … Peter Heylyn D.D.* (1683), ed. J. C. Robertson, in P. Heylyn, *Ecclesia restaurata*, 2 vols. (1849), 1.xxix–ccxii • G. Vernon, *The life of the learned and reverend Dr Peter Heylyn* (1682) • Bodl. Oxf., MS Wood E. 4 • P. Heylyn, *Memorial of Bishop Waynflete*, ed. J. R. Bloxam (1851), x–xxiv [incl. partial transcription of Bodl. Oxf., Wood MS E.4] • J. H. Walker, 'A descriptive bibliography of the early printed works of Peter Heylyn', PhD diss., U. Birm., 1978 • A. Milton, *Catholic and Reformed: the Roman and protestant churches in English protestant thought, 1600–1640* (1995) • A. Milton, 'Canon fire: Peter Heylyn at Westminster', *Westminster Abbey reformed, 1540–1640*, ed. R. Mortimer and C. S. Knighton (2003) • *Athenae Oxonienses … containing the life of Wood*, ed. P. Bliss, another edn, [1] (1848) • PRO, SP 16/476/97 • *Walker rev.* • *Foster, Alum. Oxon.*

Archives Bodl. Oxf., MS Rawl. D.353 | BL, Wood MSS • Magd. Oxf., MS 312

Likenesses R. White, engraving, NPG; repro. in *The historical and miscellaneous tracts of … Peter Heylyn*, ed. G. Vernon (1681), frontispiece [*see illus.*]

Heylyn, Rowland (1562–1632), ironmonger and church benefactor, was born in Shrewsbury, the son of David Heylyn, who was of Welsh ancestry, and his wife, Alice. After attending the free school there from 1571 he went to London, where in 1576 he became an apprentice ironmonger. He was admitted to the company in 1584 and subsequently served twice as its master, in 1614 and 1625. Elected an alderman from Cripplegate in April 1624, later that year he was also elected sheriff of London. At an unknown date he married Alice (*d.* 1641), daughter of Richard Aldworth of Reading; they had no surviving children.

A man of deep religious convictions, Heylyn was a particularly good example of a puritan layman whose sense of vocation moved him to take an active role in the church and in society. According to John Stow he was responsible for printing the Bible in Welsh 'in a more portable bulk' (Beaven, 2.178). In 1626 he became one of the feoffees for impropriations, a group of puritan lawyers, ministers, and merchants whose goal was to buy up church livings and staff them with godly divines. Heylyn, who can be considered as one of the two most important lay members, served as treasurer and then in 1629 as president; in 1628 the feoffees met at his house. He raised funds, and in an early list of donors is listed as giving £500, the largest single donation. In 1628 he obtained for the feoffees the advowson of the vicarage of St Alkmund in his native Shrewsbury, a lease of the tithes of St Mary's, and a barn at Cotton near the same town. Ironically, it was his kinsman Peter *Heylyn who, as chaplain to Archbishop William Laud, waged a determined and vocal attack against the group, describing them as plotters and conspirators.

From 1631 Heylyn served as president of the Bethlem and Bridewell hospitals. His will, dated 5 September 1629, contains many charitable benefactions. He left significant sums for the poor to the corporation of Shrewsbury and for imprisoned debtors in London, and sums for the ill and indigent, as well as a large donation for poor ministers. His books were donated to Shrewsbury Library. His generosity to the Ironmongers' Company included a gift for young men and a stipend for a yearly sermon on the date of the Gunpowder Plot.

Heylyn died in London in February 1632. His will was proved on 15 February by his widow, who inherited much of the residue of his estate; the remainder went to his sisters, nephews, nieces, and cousins. The feoffees did not long survive him, being suppressed by Laud in 1633.

MARC L. SCHWARZ

Sources I. M. Calder, *Activities of the puritan faction of the Church of England, 1625–33* (1957) · E. W. Kirby, 'The lay feoffees: a study in militant puritanism', *Journal of Modern History*, 14 (1942), 1–25 · C. Hill, *Economic problems of the church from Archbishop Whitgift to the Long Parliament* (1956) · P. Heylyn, *Examen historicum* (1659) · J. Nicholl, *Some account of the Worshipful Company of Ironmongers*, 2nd edn (1866) · A. B. Beaven, ed., *The aldermen of the City of London, temp. Henry III–[1912]*, 1 (1908), 132; 2 (1913), 57, 178 · will, PRO, PROB 11/161, sig. 23
Likenesses H. Cocke, oils, 1640, Ironmonger's Hall, London · portrait; in possession of W. Congreve, Charlton, Kent, 1804
Wealth at death assets: will, PRO, PROB 11/161, sig. 23

Heyman, Sir Peter (1580–1641), politician, was born on 13 May 1580, the eldest son of Henry Heyman (d. 1613) of Sellinge, Kent, and his wife, Rebecca, the daughter and coheir of Robert *Horne, bishop of Winchester. Admitted to Emmanuel College, Cambridge, in 1597, he studied under the puritan William Bedell. Shortly afterwards he served as a volunteer in Ireland, and was rewarded by the queen with some land there. By 1606 he had married Sarah (d. in or before 1613), the daughter and coheir of Peter Collett, a Merchant Taylor of London, with whom he had four children. Heyman was probably the William Hamond knighted on 20 December 1607. He married again in November 1613, when he took as his wife Mary, the daughter and coheir of another Merchant Taylor, Randolph Wolley, with whom he had six children. He succeeded to his patrimony in 1614.

Heyman was returned to the 1621 parliament as member for Hythe, the borough closest to Sellinge, after being recommended for the seat by the lord warden of the Cinque Ports, Lord Zouche. During the winter sitting he expressed dissatisfaction at the absence from the Commons of one of its leading figures, Sir Edwin Sandys, suspecting that it stemmed from the king's displeasure. Although the house received an assurance on 23 November from secretary of state Sir George Calvert that Sandys had not been committed for anything he had said or done in parliament, Heyman, on 27 November, repeated his demand that Sir Edwin be sent for. Consequently, he and William Mallory were dispatched to fetch Sandys or to obtain from him a written statement signifying whether his commitment was connected with parliament. The paper with which they returned was never reported because the king reiterated the assurance already given by Calvert, and on 19 December Heyman was ordered by the house to burn the document.

Heyman courted further royal displeasure in early 1622, when he was summoned before the council for refusing to contribute to the benevolence raised for the defence of the Palatinate. As a punishment—and since he also declined to serve as a soldier at his own expense—he was made to accompany Sir Arthur Chichester's eleventh-hour diplomatic mission to Heidelberg. He represented Hythe again in the Commons in 1624, when he seconded Mallory's proposal of 1 March to forbid the clerk of the Commons from entering the names of members responsible for motions. He also helped to draw up the charges of impeachment against the lord treasurer, Lionel Cranfield, earl of Middlesex, and was among the deputation sent to Archbishop Abbot to express the house's concern at the publication of Richard Montagu's anti-Calvinist tract, *A New Gag for an Old Goose*. Following the prorogation he captained a company of foot in Ireland, and though he returned to Kent to help muster the soldiers raised for Mansfeld's expedition his continued absence in Ireland meant that he was not elected to parliament in 1625. On relinquishing his commission in 1626 he resumed his parliamentary career. As member for Hythe he deplored the handling of the war with Spain, denied that shortage of money was to blame for recent failures, and supported the attempt to impeach the duke of Buckingham. Following the dissolution he was summoned before the council for refusing to contribute to the forced loan, but escaped imprisonment.

Heyman was re-elected for Hythe in 1628, when he participated in the debates on the liberties of the subject, expressing concern on 6 June at the king's first, unsatisfactory answer to the petition of right. He earned notoriety on 2 March 1629, when he rounded on the speaker, Sir John Finch, a fellow Kentishman, after Finch attempted to adjourn the house in obedience to the king's commands despite the wishes of many members. Heyman considered the speaker first and foremost the servant of the Commons, and 'bitterly inveighed against him, and told him he was sorry he was a Kentishman, and that he was a disgrace to his country and a blot to a noble family' (Notestein and Relf, 105). He was so incensed that he proposed that Finch should be brought to the bar and a new speaker chosen in his stead. The following day he and eight others were summoned to appear before the council to answer for their effrontery. Through the favour of Dudley Carleton, Viscount Dorchester, secretary of state, he was freed soon afterwards, but he was then swiftly recommitted to the Gatehouse prison on the instructions of the king. When asked what he would have done had he been ordered as speaker to announce the adjournment, he declared that he would have thrown himself at his majesty's feet and have given him to understand that, 'in respect he was the Speaker, he was the most improper and unfit person to deliver any such message, and therefore have supplicated his Majesty to command some other to perform that part' (BL, Lansdowne MS 93, fol. 138). Charges were subsequently laid against him in Star Chamber, and on 22 May he put in his plea and demurrer. However, soon afterwards he was released after making a full submission, though he continued to be attended by one of his gaoler's men.

In 1640 Heyman was elected for Dover to both the Short and the Long parliaments. He died intestate early in 1641 and was buried at Sellinge on 11 February. He was succeeded by his son Henry, who had taken his former seat at Hythe and recently purchased a baronetcy.

ANDREW THRUSH

Sources 'Heyman, Sir Peter', HoP, Commons, 1604–29 [draft] • C. Thompson, 'The reaction of the House of Commons in November and December 1621 to the confinement of Sir Edwin Sandys', HJ, 40 (1997), 779–86, esp. 783–5 • W. A. Shaw, Knights of England, 3 vols. (1906), 2.144 • W. Notestein and F. H. Relf, eds., Commons debates for 1629 (1921) • answers by Heyman and others showing the meaning of their speeches in parliament, 1628, BL, Lansdowne MS 93, fol. 138 • Venn, Alum. Cant.

Heymann, Lewis (1802–1869), lace merchant and manufacturer, was born on 3 March 1802 at Teterow in the grand duchy of Mecklenburg-Schwerin (later part of Germany), one of the three children of Gabriel Heymann and his wife, Nascha. For some years he travelled from Germany to England in connection with the textile trade which had been established by German merchants in Manchester and Bradford. Two of the firms, Alexander Brothers and A. J. Saalfeld, extended their activities to Nottingham in the early 1830s, when the lace industry there was growing rapidly. Heymann moved to Nottingham as manager for A. J. Saalfeld in 1834. On 23 July that year he married Henrietta Hirsch (1814–1874), the daughter of A. Hirsch, almost certainly in Germany, and on 12 February 1836 he became a naturalized British subject by private act of parliament. After his marriage he formed a partnership, Heymann and Alexander, lace merchants; his partner was a Mr Alexander who remained in Hamburg.

Heymann and his wife lived for a time on High Pavement, Nottingham, where their two eldest children were born in 1835 and 1837. Like other German Jews, he became a member of the Unitarian chapel on High Pavement, and served as warden in 1839 and 1840. His business partnership must have prospered quite early, as by 1840 he had moved to Bridgford Hall, an eighteenth-century mansion a mile out of town; in 1841 he and his wife, with their five children, were attended by seven resident servants there.

Heymann's economic success was a result of his combining his lace merchant activities with the design and manufacture of lace curtains, which he marketed on the continent as well as in Britain. He employed the designs of a local artist, Samuel Oscroft (1834–1924), and was the real creator of the Nottingham lace curtain industry. His success at the great exhibitions of 1851 and 1862 gave great impetus to his international sales. *The Art Journal Illustrated Catalogue of the International Exhibition of 1862* declared, in reference to Heymann's productions, that in 'this important manufacture the productions of Nottingham now surpass those of France' (p. 239).

Little is known of Heymann's private life. He was respected by the residents of West Bridgford, who knew him as an affable, courteous, and kindly man; these qualities were extended to his employees, and his firm became one of the pre-eminent lace merchants in Nottingham. Heymann was said to be industrious, walking to and from his business six days a week. On Sundays he attended chapel, where he was regarded as a liberal and generous man. In 1862 he helped to endow a daughter church. From 1850 some of his time was devoted to Nottingham town council, as he had been elected alderman in that year. This was an unusual honour, as he had not previously been a councillor and was one of very few men who were elected aldermen in this way. He was obviously highly regarded by members of the council, since he was made mayor in 1857, the first former German Jew to achieve this distinction in Britain. This was at a time when there was considerable unemployment in Nottingham, and within days of his being elected mayor he had to negotiate with the leaders of a large crowd which had assembled outside the council's headquarters. His well-known generosity was shown when he personally paid for bread and soup for more than 2000 poor persons in honour of the marriage of the princess royal.

Although he was re-elected as alderman in November 1868, Heymann resigned his office a month later because of failing health. He died on 15 February 1869 and was buried on 19 February in Nottingham general cemetery. He made bequests to relatives in Germany, to servants, and to several charitable institutions in Nottingham.

His eldest son, Albert Heymann (1837–1924), had a distinguished public career as a magistrate, county councillor, chairman of West Bridgford council, and deputy lieutenant of the county. It is supposed that he or his brother Henry was the anonymous donor of £10,000 to launch University College, Nottingham.

GEOFFREY OLDFIELD

Sources G. Oldfield, The Heymann family of West Bridgford (1983) • R. Mellors, Old Nottingham suburbs, then and now (1914), 351 • R. Mellors, Men of Nottingham and Nottinghamshire (1920), 221 • J. C. Warren, Biographical catalogue of portraits and a list of books, documents and relics relating to our congregational history (1934) • S. D. Chapman, 'The international houses: the continental contribution to British commerce, 1800–1860', Journal of European Economic History, 6 (1977), 5–48 • CGPLA Eng. & Wales (1869) • The Art Journal illustrated catalogue of the International Exhibition, 1862 [1862], 239 • d. cert.
Likenesses portrait, U. Nott., manuscripts department, High Pavement Chapel deposit

Wealth at death under £250,000: probate, 16 July 1869, *CGPLA Eng. & Wales*

Heynes, Simon. *See* Haynes, Simon (*d.* 1552).

Heyrick [*née* Coltman], **Elizabeth** (1769–1831), slavery abolitionist and philanthropist, was born in St Nicholas Street, Leicester, on 4 December 1769, the elder daughter and second child in a family of two girls and three boys (one of whom died young). Her parents were dissenters. Her father, John Coltman (*d.* 1808), a pupil of John Aikin (1713–1780), was a scholarly worsted manufacturer; her mother, Elizabeth Cartwright (1737–1811), was a skilled craftswoman, a published poet and book reviewer, and a friend of Robert Dodsley (1703–1764) and William Shenstone (1714–1763). John Wesley visited their house, which in the riots of 1785 was plundered by a machine-breaking mob. Elizabeth, known as Bess when young, 'was singular in her childhood' (Hutton, 61): anecdotes depict her giving scarce pennies to a beggar and choosing for rescue a plain kitten in preference to a pretty one. Her talent for landscape painting gave her father 'half a mind' to 'make an Angelica Kauffman of her' (Hutton, 61). Instead, on 10 March 1789, aged nineteen, she married John Heyrick, eldest son of John Heyrick, Leicester town clerk, and descendant of the poet Robert Herrick. He soon exchanged a legal career for a cornetcy in the 15th light dragoons, and he and his wife lived thereafter in English and Irish barracks. He died of angina on 18 June 1797 (while Elizabeth was out at church), in the act of proof-reading a sheet of his own poems. The marriage was said to have been stormy, but she mourned fervently, with lifelong observance of the anniversary of his death. They had no children.

Elizabeth rejoined her family, left the Methodists to become a member of the Society of Friends, and 'stepped boldly forward the champion of black men and tortured beasts' (Hutton, 63). Her twenty or more books and pamphlets also address war, prisons, corporal punishment, the level of wages and the plight of the industrial poor, election issues, and vagrancy legislation. In 1809 she stopped a bull-baiting at Bonsall in Derbyshire by purchasing the bull; with her friend Susannah Watts (1768–1842) she canvassed large areas of Leicester, promoting the boycott of West Indian sugar. She visited prisons and liberated long-incarcerated poachers by paying their gaol fees. Late in life she campaigned against capital punishment, in alliance with William Allen of Guy's Hospital.

Elizabeth Heyrick published anonymously at Leicester and London. Her first work, *The Warning* (1805), opposed war: '*multitudes*, equally unacquainted with the origins and the object, are always eager to rush to the standard of blood' (p. 18). She imitated Hannah More in *Bull-Baiting: a Village Dialogue between John Brown and John Simms* (1809), and treated public as well as private morality in *Familiar Letters Addressed to Children and Young Persons of the Middle Ranks* (1811), written for a sister-in-law's children. Her anti-slavery works included appeals directed to British women

and '*not* to the Government, but to the People of England'. The best known is *Immediate, not gradual abolition, or, An inquiry into the shortest, safest, and most effectual means of getting rid of West Indian slavery* (1824), a pamphlet which broached the idea of speedy abolition while William Wilberforce and other male leaders were still gradualist. It sold hundreds of thousands of copies in Britain and the USA.

Elizabeth Heyrick's philanthropy has been better recognized than her executive acumen, her grasp of power systems and of pressure-group politics, and her forceful analysis of the interdependence of social evils. She left 'a mass of unpublished manuscripts, chiefly consisting of essays, sermons, prayers, etc.' (Beale, 215). Of a manuscript list of eighteen titles she published, thirteen are untraced (though three other known works are omitted from the list). She died in Leicester on 18 October 1831, and was buried there.   ISOBEL GRUNDY

Sources C. H. Beale, ed., *Catherine Hutton and her friends* (1895) · C. Hutton, 'A sketch of a family of originals, by an original', *Ainsworth's Magazine*, 5 (1844), 56–63 · *A brief sketch of the life and labours of Mrs Elizabeth Heyrick* (1862) · family papers, Leics. RO · K. Corfield, 'Elizabeth Heyrick: radical Quaker', *Religion in the lives of English women, 1760–1930*, ed. G. Malmgreen (1986), 41–67 · C. Midgley, *Women against slavery: the British campaigns, 1780–1870* (1992)
Archives Leics. RO

Heyrick, Richard (1600–1667), Church of England clergyman, was born in London on 25 May 1600, the third son of Sir William *Herrick (Heyrick) (*bap.* 1562, *d.* 1653), a London goldsmith and alderman, and his wife, Joan Mary (or May). In 1614 he entered Merchant Taylors', London, the school attended by his lifelong friend and career associate, Thomas Case, and in 1617 entered as a fellow-commoner St John's College, Oxford, from where he graduated BA in 1619 and proceeded MA in 1622 and BD at some undisclosed date. On 14 January 1625, he was chosen a fellow of All Souls: a crucial factor in obtaining this prize was the king's recommendation, which, in turn, should be traced to his father's loans to the crown. About this time Heyrick was ordained and on 9 June 1626 he took up the benefice of North Repps, near Cromer, in Norfolk, where Case served as his curate. Heyrick married in Norfolk, probably soon afterwards, Helen (*d.* 1642), daughter of Thomas Corbet of the county, with whom he had four sons and three daughters.

Like Case, Heyrick developed a career interest in the Manchester area. Indeed, his life exemplifies a certain tension between high principle and ambitious careerism. Perhaps on 14 November 1626, Charles I awarded him the reversion of the wardenship of Manchester's collegiate church, a position whose value was estimated variously at between £700 and £70. For Heyrick to secure this position when it became vacant in 1635 required not only a powerfully composed petition from him but also intervention by Archbishop William Laud—high-church patronage which seems ironic in the light of his subsequent career. Heyrick combined the wardenship with other church appointments in Cheshire and near Manchester.

Despite his secure position within the church establishment, from the time of his appointment as warden Heyrick 'quickly assumed a leading role in Lancashire puritanism' (Richardson, 45n.). He attacked puritanism's adversary Catholicism from at least 1638 and in 1641 was preaching vehemently against Lancashire's 'infectious' 'Popery … multiplied abundantly' as a result of Catholic gentry patronage. His strident anti-episcopal tone aligned him with the Long Parliament, which in 1642 made him one of the two Lancashire ministers to be consulted on ecclesiastical affairs, and by 1643 he had emerged as a proponent of the presbyterian form of church government. This in Lancashire crystallized out of earlier puritanism which was centred on Manchester, 'a town famous for religion ever since the Reformation' as Heyrick himself put it (Richardson, 9–10), where prototypes of presbyterian church organization were created both in the 1580s and 1630s. With a ministerial colleague Heyrick was also appointed by parliament to look into the doctrines and financing of the Lancashire clergy.

By the mid-1640s Heyrick's activities were divided between Lancashire and London, where he was principally occupied as a member of the presbyterian-dominated Westminster assembly of divines. However, when in the north-west, while prominent in the establishment of the presbyterian system in 1646, Heyrick at that time declared himself 'so perfect a Lattitidinarian that the Episcopall, Presbyterians and Independents might all preache, yet each by Divine right' (Shaw, 2.13): although his attitude offended clergy of the region who sought a more exclusively presbyterian form of church government, Heyrick's remarks were aimed at devising a comprehensive ecclesiastical system to embrace mainstream protestants, probably with the aim of countering Lancashire's deeply embedded Catholicism. Yet in a fast sermon, of the same year, *Queen Esthers Resolves* (1646), he pleased his audience of MPs with his thunder against 'the Tyranny of Prelacy', meaning episcopal Anglicanism (*Fast Sermons*, 23.342). The authorship of the harmonious consent of 1648, an accord between London and Lancashire presbyterian ministers on upholding the presbyterian solemn league and covenant and suppressing dissidence, is attributed either to him or to his ministerial colleague, Richard Hollinworth (*bap.* 1607, *d.* 1656).

Heyrick's presbyterian–parliamentarian views stopped well short of a republican position and in April 1647 he lodged a strong protest when, at a meeting of clergy of the area, a proposal in favour of government without a king was mooted. Until the beginning of the 1650s these political convictions did him no harm and when the Manchester collegiate church was dissolved in 1650 he was compensated with the award of a pension of £100 a year out of sold college lands. In the following year, though, along with Case, he was imprisoned for his involvement in Christopher Love's presbyterian–royalist plot: he may have been spared disaster as a result of association between Cromwell and the north-western presbyterian lay leader George Booth. By 1654 he was back in favour and on the Lancashire commission for ejecting unworthy ministers and teachers, and in 1658 he was involved in a controversy over presbyterian excommunication.

Although Heyrick did not actively support Booth's 1659 royalist rising, he was, predictably, an ardent advocate of the Restoration, at which point powerful patronage, this time in the person of the presbyterian-inclined second earl of Manchester, came to his aid to reinvest him with the wardenship. He seems to have refused the anti-presbyterian oaths in the Act of Uniformity of 1662 but he did not scruple to use the Book of Common Prayer, while his bold claim that the warden's post had been granted to him inalienably in discharge of royal debts succeeded in keeping him in place.

Heyrick died in Manchester on 6 August 1667, a wealthy man in money (£1095) and acreage. His second wife, Anna Maria, daughter of Erasmus Breton of Hamburg, with whom he had had four daughters and two sons, commissioned a 'comely monument' (Wood, *Ath. Oxon.*, 3.780) in the collegiate church where he was buried on 9 August, with a florid Latin tribute by Thomas Case. This memorial gave Heyrick a reputation for indifference to preferment. Cast as an 'amiable man' (Raines, 127), he was in fact a combative careerist capable of pressing home his own case with great force and possessed a knack of finding influential patrons at key moments of his career. At the same time, though, Heyrick was a vigorous and eloquent preacher, whose sermons could be both earnest and learned.

MICHAEL MULLETT

Sources Wood, *Ath. Oxon.*, new edn, 3.780 • W. A. Shaw, *A history of the English church during the civil wars and under the Commonwealth, 1640–1660*, 2 vols. (1900) • R. Jeffs, ed., *Fast sermons to Parliament*, 23, 316–50 • F. R. Raines, *The rectors of Manchester, and the wardens of the collegiate church of that town*, ed. [J. E. Bailey], 2 vols., Chetham Society, new ser., 5–6 (1885) • J. Wheeler, *Manchester: its social … history* (1836) • *BL cat.*, vol. 103 • R. C. Richardson, *Puritanism in north-west England: a regional study of the diocese of Chester to 1642* (1972)
Archives Bodl. Oxf., Herrick MSS, family and estate MSS, accounts and corresp. of subject's father Sir William Heyrick or Herrick, MSS Eng. hist. b 244–48 (R); b 249, c 1292–1318
Wealth at death £1095 in personalty; £160 in books; 51½ acres: Raines, *Rectors of Manchester*, 138

Heyrick, Thomas (*bap.* 1649, *d.* 1694), poet and clergyman, was baptized at Market Harborough, Leicestershire, on 4 March 1649, the son of Thomas Herrick or Heyrick, tradesman, of Market Harborough, and great-nephew of the poet Robert Herrick. He was educated at the local grammar school and matriculated in 1667 as sizar of Peterhouse, Cambridge, his BA dating from 1671 and MA from 1675. After ordination as deacon in September 1672 and as priest in December 1681 he became curate and lecturer of St Dionysius, Market Harborough. When in addition he obtained the mastership of his old school, where he instructed some sixty boys in Greek, Latin, and Hebrew, the three posts assured him a comfortable income.

After publishing two sermons (1681, 1685), Heyrick brought out anonymously, in response to Dryden's *The Hind and the Panther*, a verse satire called *The New Atlantis* (1687) which in three books derided the state of English Catholicism and lampooned its new apologist. A second edition issued in 1690 under a new title and his own name also failed to provoke any reply from the victim. In the following year the Cambridge press published his *Miscellany Poems*, a collection mainly distinguished by its celebration of fishing and hunting, and its pictures of the more exotic forms of wildlife, from crocodiles and whales to peacocks and the 'Indian Tomineios'. The final item in the volume, introduced by a separate title-page, is a sixty-seven-page Pindaric ode entitled *The Submarine Voyage* that describes Neptune's court and the marine life of the seven seas.

Heyrick was buried at Market Harborough on 9 August 1694. A post-mortem inventory was drawn up on 21 August (Leics. RO, PR1/99/89), administration being granted three days later to his widow, Rebecca (Leicestershire district probate registrary, 1694, no. 56).

W. H. KELLIHER

Sources Venn, *Alum. Cant.* · J. Nichols, *The history and antiquities of the county of Leicester*, 4 vols. (1795–1815) · *VCH Leicestershire*, vol. 5 · H. Macdonald, *John Dryden: a bibliography of early editions and of Drydeniana* (1939)
Wealth at death see post-mortem inventory, 21 Aug 1694, Leics. RO, PR1/99/89

Heysham, John (1753–1834), physician and demographer, was born on 22 November 1753 in Lancaster, the son of Gyles Heysham, shipowner, and Anne Cumming, daughter of a substantial yeoman 'statesman farmer' of Holme, Westmorland. The Heyshams were a junior branch of the Cornet (later Gernet) family, ancient lords of the manor of Heysham parish, Morecambe Bay. Heysham was educated in the Quaker school at Yealand, near Burton, Westmorland, followed by apprenticeship to Mr Parkinson, surgeon, at Burton, Westmorland, from 1769 to 1774, while being tutored in classics and mathematics by D. R. Hutton, the vicar of Burton. He then spent three years under Alexander Monro *Secundus*, Joseph Black, and the great nosologist William Cullen, at Edinburgh's celebrated medical school, taking his MD in 1777 through a thesis on rabies. After a year visiting London and Holland, including the Leiden medical school, Heysham settled in Carlisle, Cumberland. On 4 May 1789, in London, he married Elizabeth Mary Coulthard (1765–1803), the only child of Alderman Thomas Coulthard, a wealthy tanner and twice mayor of Carlisle; they had four sons and three daughters.

Though Heysham's private practice was never worth more than £400 a year, his professional income was augmented through his many business interests, which included land ownership, a cotton works (Cowan, Heysham & Co.), an iron foundry, and chairmanship of both the Carlisle Canal Company and Carlisle Gas and Coke Company. He also held numerous public offices; he was county commissioner for assessed taxes, commissioner for lighting and improvements, and chairman of the police commissioners. Until the election of 1832, when he backed reform, his political allegiance had always been to the all-powerful Lowther tories, from which followed a lucrative commission as magistrate in 1808 and then appointment as a deputy lieutenant of the county.

Heysham was a strong, energetic man who traversed the fells of the Lake District regularly, becoming the area's premier naturalist and ornithologist. He was elected an associate of the Linnean Society at its second meeting in 1788 and provided a major contribution on the subject to W. Hutchinson's *History of Cumberland* (2 vols., 1794). Heysham was on close terms with the area's principal landed families and Carlisle's eminent churchmen—Archdeacon Paley and the cathedral's successive deans: Percy, Law, and Milner. These connections were of great assistance in his promotion of the town's public health. With Percy's help, a dispensary for the poor was founded in 1782 and the wealthy Robert Mounsey of Castletown provided a fever hospital.

Heysham is principally remembered, however, for his *Observations on the Bills of Mortality in Carlisle* (1780–88), accessibly reproduced in Glass, *The Development of Population Statistics* (1973). This was a meticulous public health and demographic record of Carlisle in the 1780s which significantly improved upon John Haygarth's pioneering medical survey and census of Chester in 1774. Heysham took a census of the age and sex of every household member in 1780 and in 1787, while carefully recording the date, age, sex, and cause of every fatality from 1779 to 1787. Apart from aiding his own medical practice, this subsequently enabled the actuary of the Sun Life Assurance Society, Joshua Milne (with Heysham's vital assistance, recorded in Lonsdale's appendix detailing their correspondence) to publish in 1815 the only accurate life table for an English population for the entire period before the 1840s. The Carlisle table was rapidly adopted commercially and officially as a money saving replacement for Richard Price's faulty Northampton table. Heysham's path breaking survey directly inspired James Cleland's important innovation in 1821, whereby Glasgow became the first rapidly industrializing city in the world to have its health record rigorously monitored.

Heysham was, in fact, generally innovative in his approach to medicine. He was a leading advocate of both inoculation and Jennerian vaccination against smallpox. He anticipated by half a century the practice of feeding, rather than starving fevers, advocated in his *Account of the Jail Fever or Typhus carcerum; as it Appeared at Carlisle in the Year 1781* (1782). His focus from the start on a sophisticated health survey and the leading role he took in promoting collective public health measures amounted to his informal adoption of the role of town medical officer of health, over half a century before such a position had been statutorily defined. Heysham died at his home in St Cuthbert's Lane, Carlisle, on 23 March 1834 and was buried in St Mary's Church. A memorial window was placed at the east end of the south aisle of the cathedral.

S. R. S. SZRETER

Sources *The life of John Heysham ... and his correspondence with Mr Joshua Milne relative to the Carlisle bills of mortality*, ed. H. Lonsdale (1870) · D. V. Glass, *Numbering the people: the eighteenth-century population controversy* (1973) · D. V. Glass, *The development of population statistics* (1973) · P. Honeyman, 'John Heysham MD, 1753–1834', *Medicine in Northumbria: essays on the history of medicine in the north-east of England*, ed. D. Gardner-Medwin, A. Hargreaves, and E. Lazenby (1993), 151–63 · 'The late Dr Heysham', *Carlisle Journal* (29 March 1834) ·

H. Barnes, 'President's address: the medical history of Carlisle', *BMJ* (1 Aug 1896), 245–51 · *DNB* · M. W. Flinn, introduction, in E. Chadwick, *Report on the sanitary condition of the labouring population of Great Britain*, ed. M. W. Flinn (1965), 1–73
Archives Carlisle Library
Likenesses M. L. Watson, bust, priv. coll.; in possession of the Revd John Heysham, vicar of Lazenby, Cumberland, 1870 · lithograph (aged sixty-six; after miniature), repro. in Lonsdale, *Life of John Heysham, MD*, frontispiece · watercolour drawing (in early manhood)

Heytesbury. For this title name *see* A'Court, William, first Baron Heytesbury (1779–1860).

Heytesbury, William (*d.* 1372/3), logician and natural philosopher, was probably born in Wiltshire. He was educated at Oxford, and was a fellow of Merton College in 1330. He was active in college life: in 1337 or 1338, for instance, he travelled with a colleague from Oxford to his college's church at Ponteland in Northumberland, and the record of their journey shows that they covered 246 miles in seven or eight days, at an average speed of over 30 miles a day, and also provides details of their food and drink, the fodder bought for their horses, and the cost of crossing the rivers of Trent and Ouse. In 1338/9 Heytesbury was college bursar. In 1341 he was named a Queen's College foundation fellow, but he was still a fellow of Merton in 1348. Records from the same year show that he was a doctor of theology. He was chancellor of the university probably from Whitsun 1370 to Whitsun 1372, and possibly also earlier, from 1352 to 1354. Outside Oxford he held a variety of ecclesiastical benefices, mainly in Kent, though he was also canon of Salisbury and of Chichester. His longest association seems to have been with Ickham, Kent. He first became rector there in 1354, and it was in Ickham church that he requested burial, in a will drawn up in December 1372 and proved on 5 February 1373. He travelled outside England at least once, for in 1349–50 he was imprisoned in France 'by the king's adversaries' (*CClR, 1349–1354*, 152), probably while on his way to the papal court in Avignon.

No theological writings by Heytesbury are known, but he was an extremely successful writer of textbooks in logic and natural philosophy. Readers particularly admired his extensive use of sophisms—puzzle cases (often quite bizarre) designed to test the validity of logical principles—and his main contribution was his application of this procedure to natural philosophy. Along with the other 'Oxford calculators' (Richard Swineshead, Thomas Bradwardine, and John Dumbleton), Heytesbury was instrumental in developing the logic of continua and infinite divisibility, and in applying quantitative analysis to such qualities as heat and colour. Although Heytesbury mainly used the techniques of supposition theory and propositional analysis to solve his sophisms, he none the less helped prepare the way for the wider application of mathematics to the physical world.

Heytesbury's three main works are the *Regulae solvendi sophismata*, the *Sophismata*, and *De sensu composito et diviso*. The *Regulae*, written in 1335 for the use of first-year logic students, contains separate chapters on insolubles (semantic paradoxes); the epistemic terms *scire* and *dubitare*; the supposition or reference of relative pronouns; the terms *incipit* and *desinit*; maxima and minima; and the three categories of place, quantity, and quality (these being the categories in which motion occurs). Thirty-three manuscripts which contain all or part of the *Regulae* are known, and there are three early printed editions (1481, 1491, 1494). Apparently only partial adaptations of the work were used in England in the later fourteenth and fifteenth centuries. The work *Termini qui faciunt* is an adaptation of chapter 2, and *De terminis relativis* of chapter 3. One version of the latter is by Richard Lavenham, and another was printed as part of the *Libellus sophistarum ad usum Cantabrigiensium* (1497, 1501–2, 1510, 1524). An adaptation of chapters 2–5, *De probationibus conclusionum*, possibly by Heytesbury himself, survives mainly in Italy and was twice printed there, once separately (Pavia, 1483), and once as part of the large Venice edition of 1494. The *Regulae* was particularly popular in Italy. The Paduan logician Gaetano da Thiene wrote a full commentary which was printed in 1483, and which formed part of the edition of 1494. Mesino de' Codroncho and Angelo da Fossombrone, who both wrote in Bologna at the end of the fourteenth century, commented on parts of chapter 6, as did Bernardus Tornius. These commentaries all appeared in the edition of 1494, and Angelo's commentary, of which a separate edition had appeared in 1482–3, was printed with Gaetano's in the volume of 1483.

Heytesbury's other main works were also more popular in Italy than in England, though an epitome of the *Sophismata* was prepared at Merton College in 1388. The *Sophismata* was included with the three Italian editions of the *Regulae*, and Gaetano da Thiene's commentary on the *Sophismata* was printed along with his commentary on the *Regulae* in 1483 and 1494. Partial commentaries were written by Gaetano's contemporaries, Simon de Lendenaria (printed 1494) and Paolo da Pergola. *De sensu composito et diviso* (printed with the *Regulae* in 1491 and 1494) was the subject of three Italian commentaries printed together in 1500, and of a fourth by Benedetto Vettori (Bologna, 1504).

Heytesbury's other works include a treatise on consequences, printed in 1517 along with treatises by Richard Feribrigge and Ralph Strode, and known in England mainly through an adaptation by Robert Alyngton called *Iuxta hunc textum*. This adaptation was printed in both the Oxford and Cambridge versions of the *Libelli sophistarum*. The *Sophismata asinina*, known in four versions, is an early collection of sophisms each of which proves the claim 'Tu es asinus' ('You are an ass'). The *Termini naturales*, a beginner's text on definitions and divisions in natural philosophy, is known in several adaptations, including one by John Garisdale. Finally there are the brief *Casus obligatorii* and the *De propositionibus multiplicibus*. Two separate works on insolubles have been attributed to Heytesbury, but one is an anonymous reworking of his text and the other is by John Venator. *De veritate et falsitate propositionum*, also attributed to Heytesbury, is in fact by Henry Hopton.

In the fifteenth century Heytesbury's work was found

on the official curriculum in many European universities, including Erfurt, Leipzig, Padua (1496), and Vienna. However, his most enthusiastic readers were in Italy, as the history of commentary and printing shows.

E. J. ASHWORTH

Sources Emden, *Oxf.* · E. J. Ashworth and P. V. Spade, 'Logic in late medieval Oxford', *Hist. U. Oxf.* 2: *Late med. Oxf.*, 35–64 · P. V. Spade, 'The manuscripts of William Heytesbury's *Regulae solvendi sophismata*: conclusions, notes and descriptions', *Medioevo*, 15 (1989), 271–313 [includes list of 33 manuscripts containing the *Regulae*, list of 3 incunabula edns, list of spurious manuscripts, bibliography] · J. A. Weisheipl, 'Repertorium Mertonense', *Mediaeval Studies*, 31 (1969), 174–224 [incl. list of Heytesbury MSS] · C. Wilson, *William Heytesbury: medieval logic and the rise of mathematical physics* (1956); repr. (1960) · J. North, 'Natural philosophy in late medieval Oxford', *Hist. U. Oxf.* 2: *Late med. Oxf.*, 65–102 · *Guillaume Heytesbury 'Sophismata asinina': une introduction aux disputes médiévales*, ed. F. Pironet (Paris, 1994) · T. H. Aston, 'The external administration and resources of Merton College to circa 1348', *Hist. U. Oxf.* 1: *Early Oxf. schools*, 311–68 · L. M. de Rijk, '*Logica Oxoniensis*: an attempt to reconstruct a fifteenth century Oxford manual of logic', *Medioevo*, 3 (1977), 121–64 · J. A. Weisheipl, 'Ockham and some Mertonians', *Mediaeval Studies*, 30 (1968), 163–213 · J. D. North, 'Astronomy and mathematics', *Hist. U. Oxf.* 2: *Late med. Oxf.*, 103–74 · W. Heytesbury, *On maxima and minima: chapter 5 of rules for solving sophismata, with an anonymous fourteenth century discussion*, ed. and trans. J. Longeway (1984) · W. Heytesbury, *On 'insoluble' sentences: chapter one of his rules for solving sophisms*, trans. P. V. Spade (1979) · N. Kretzmann and E. Stump, trans., *Logic and the philosophy of language* (1988), vol. 1 of *The Cambridge translations of medieval philosophical texts* [incl. trans. of works by Heytesbury] · E. J. Ashworth, 'Traditional logic', *The Cambridge history of Renaissance philosophy*, ed. C. B. Schmitt and others (1988), 150 · A. Maierù, *Terminologia logica della tarda scolastica* (1972), 35–8, 601–6 · D. Buzzetti, 'Linguaggio e ontologia nei commenti di autore Bolognese al *De tribus praedicamentis* di William Heytesbury', *L'insegnamento della logica a Bologna nel XIV secolo*, ed. D. Buzzetti, M. Ferriani, and A. Tabarroni (1992), 579–604 · E. J. Ashworth, 'The *Libelli sophistarum* and the use of medieval logic texts at Oxford and Cambridge in the early sixteenth century', *Vivarium*, 17 (1979), 134–58 · Paul of Pergula, '*Logica' and 'Tractatus de sensu composito et diviso*', ed. M. A. Brown (1961), xii · *Tractatus Gulielmi Hetisberi de sensu composito et diviso*, ed. J. M. Mapellus (Venice, 1494)

Heywood, Abel (1810–1893), newsagent and publisher, was born on 25 February 1810 in Prestwich, Lancashire, the youngest son of the four children born to Betty and John Heywood, whose second marriage it was. John Heywood, a 'putter out' for weavers, died in 1812. In 1819 his widow moved to Manchester and the nine-year-old Abel began working for a local manufacturer, Thomas Worthington, at the weekly wage of 18*d*. The energy and application which were to distinguish his long life were already evident and by fourteen he was in charge of sixty other boys and attending the Lion Hill Sunday school in Bennet Street. He left the Sunday school over a perceived injustice but continued his self-education by becoming one of the first members of the mechanics' institution.

In 1831, having been summarily dismissed, Heywood took the bold step of opening a penny reading-room for the working class in Oldham Street. This was rapidly followed by his setting up as a wholesale newsagent and acquiring the agency for the *Poor Man's Guardian*. Because this paper refused to pay the government stamp duty designed to make newspapers too expensive for the working class, its sale was deemed illegal and Heywood was duly charged and sentenced. He was fined £54, which he refused to pay because he believed the charge unjust. He was, therefore, sent to the Salford New Bailey for four months. His mother and family kept the business going and, when released, he returned to selling the illegal paper, incurring two further fines in 1834 and 1836, both of £18—which this time he paid. His commitment to cheap newspapers for the working class and resistance to the 'taxes on knowledge' continued unabated. In 1834 he printed almanacs on cotton handkerchiefs to avoid the tax and in 1838 he was selling 18,000 copies weekly of the *Northern Star*, the Leeds-based radical paper.

Despite selling what one contemporary described as 'insurgent literature … for sans culottes' (Manchester City Library, cuttings file), Heywood's business prospered and the rental of his shop was enough to make him eligible for the post of a commissioner of police to which he was elected in 1836. He claimed that this—and all his subsequent public work—was undertaken in the interests of the working class who 'knew of my sympathy with them' (ibid.). He took a leading role in the bitter struggle for incorporation of the city and was elected to the new city council when it was finally created in 1843.

For the rest of his life, Heywood was active on that council, as alderman in 1853 and twice as mayor, in 1862–3 during the cotton famine when he was on the Lancashire Relief Committee, and in 1876–7. In 1859 and 1865 he stood unsuccessfully for parliament as a Liberal. His major public work was, therefore, as a member of Manchester city council, particularly on the paving, sewering, and highways committee which he chaired for forty-seven years. His concern for the conditions of the poor was a motive force in overseeing Manchester's ambitious waterworks and sewage building programme and the later development of its tramway system.

Heywood's other major achievement was in initiating and seeing to completion the building he hoped would symbolize Manchester's greatness, the new town hall, opened in his second period as mayor. The queen's refusal to attend the opening and to give Heywood an honour led to a storm of rumours about his publishing past which were indignantly refuted by his friends. Instead of a royal visit, there was a procession of trades in his honour and, at his invitation, citizens paraded through their new town hall. On 28 November 1891 he was given the freedom of the city, the third man to be so honoured.

Despite his other activities, Heywood kept a close hold on the running of the Oldham Street business, which by 1851 was the largest wholesale newsagency in the country, as well as a general bookshop and publishing house, with a subsidiary interest in paper-making. When the 1851 parliamentary select committee on newspaper stamps met, Heywood provided detailed accounts of the sales of cheap periodicals in the Manchester region which his firm supplied. He handled probably 10 per cent of the national sales of the cheapest papers. Defending the quality of this press to the committee, he argued not only that the remaining tax on news should go but that the working class wanted good papers and would choose them in preference to immoral or seditious publications, if they could. Here the radical politician and the print entrepreneur were at one.

With his publisher brother, John, Heywood also played a crucial role in regional culture, publishing local writers, both in standard English and dialect, and producing local periodicals including *Ben Brierley's Journal*. Heywood took his son, also named Abel (*b.* 1840), into partnership in 1864 (and later his grandson), thus ensuring the family control of the business he had built up from his penny reading-room.

Throughout his life, Heywood was a supporter of a range of social and political causes, a ready speaker at public events where he would be found on his legs, and notable for his fluency or long-windedness, depending on the nature of the debate. In private conversation, however, he was more taciturn, a trait which offended those who believed their status merited more regard. A rationalist, with an interest in the ideas of Robert Owen, Heywood promoted the Hall of Science at Campfield and was treasurer of the Rational Sick and Burial Club.

Heywood was married twice, first to Ann Shelmerdine, and then to Elizabeth, widow of Thomas Goadsby, his fellow alderman. He had four children. A tall, somewhat gaunt though handsome man, Heywood was careless of his appearance and often looked dishevelled at public events. One contemporary described him as like some horses who are 'bad at grooming' but have plenty of 'go' in them (*City Jackdaw*). In the 1870s Heywood moved out from Manchester to the suburb of Bowdon in Cheshire. He died of heart disease at Summerfield, Rosehill, his home there, on 19 August 1893, leaving a reputation in the city as a true 'Manchester Man'. MARGARET BEETHAM

Sources [J. Johnson], *Clever boys of our time, and how they became famous men* [1861] · [W. E. A. Axon], *The mayor of Manchester and his slanderers* (1877) · parish register (baptisms), Prestwich, Lancashire (St Mary's), 22 April 1810 · *The City Jackdaw* (14 Sept 1877) · d. cert. · Manchester City Library, cuttings file **Likenesses** photograph, repro. in Abel Heywood & Son Ltd, *Abel Heywood: notes from a history of the firm* **Wealth at death** £27,306 19s. 1d.: resworn probate, March 1894, CGPLA Eng. & Wales (1893)

Heywood, Sir Benjamin, first baronet (1793–1865), banker, was born at St Ann's Square, Manchester, on 12 December 1793, the eldest son of Nathaniel Heywood (1759–1815), a banker, and his wife, Ann, the daughter of Thomas *Percival MD FRS. Thomas *Heywood (1797–1866) and James *Heywood (1810–1897) were his younger brothers. After attending Glasgow University (1809–11) he entered his father's bank. He was admitted a partner in 1814 and eventually became head of the firm and, from 1828, its sole proprietor. In 1816 he married Sophia Ann (*d.* 1852), the daughter of Thomas Robinson of The Woodlands, Manchester; they had numerous children, of whom several died young. A man of considerable piety, Heywood took a keen interest in the welfare and education of the

working classes. He was one of the founders of the Manchester mechanics' institution and served as president from its inception in 1825 until 1840; on his retirement from this office, the various addresses which he had delivered were published (1843).

Heywood was elected MP for Lancashire in 1831 as a whig, to support the government measure for reform, but he felt that his health was suffering, and when parliament dissolved after passing the Reform Act in 1832 he retired from this aspect of public life. He was, however, active in the Manchester Statistical Society, and conducted an inquiry into the condition of the working classes in Manchester which was made public in 1834. He was created a baronet on the occasion of Queen Victoria's coronation in 1838, and in 1843 he was elected FRS. In 1860 Heywood left the bank and passed the business to four of his sons. After several years in declining health he died at his home, Claremont, near Manchester, on 11 August 1865, and was buried, alongside his wife and deceased children, at St John's Church, Pendlebury, Manchester. His eldest son, Thomas Percival Heywood, succeeded as second baronet. ANITA MCCONNELL

Sources T. Heywood, *A memoir of Sir Benjamin Heywood* (1888) · C. Knight, ed., *The English cyclopaedia: biography*, 6 vols. (1856–8) · *CGPLA Eng. & Wales* (1865) **Likenesses** W. Bradley, oils, exh. 1844, Man. City Gall. · portrait, repro. in Heywood, *Memoir* **Wealth at death** under £400,000 in England: probate, 22 Sept 1865, CGPLA Eng. & Wales

Heywood, Ellis (1529–1578), author and Jesuit, was born in London, third of five children of John *Heywood (*b.* 1496/7, *d.* in or after 1578) and his wife, Joan (*d.* before 1574), daughter of John *Rastell and Elizabeth More, Sir Thomas More's sister. Educated early at court, where his father (a protégé of More) was a playwright and music tutor, Heywood later attended Oxford. In 1548 he was elected fellow of All Souls College and graduated BCL on 18 July 1552. Thereafter he departed England to become secretary to Reginald, Cardinal Pole, in Italian exile. In 1556 at Florence, Heywood published *Il Moro*, a dialogue dedicated to Pole. In the humanist tradition of treatises on the *summum bonum*, the book represents Thomas More after he resigned as lord chancellor, jesting and conversing philosophically at his house in Chelsea, his imprisonment impending.

Before publishing *Il Moro*, Heywood had returned to England on the succession of Queen Mary; from 1554 he was prebendary of Eccleshall in Lichfield Cathedral. After the advent of Elizabethan protestantism, with his father and mother he departed England again, joining other members of his family in 1564 at Louvain. His uncle William *Rastell, dying on 27 August 1565, bequeathed to Heywood the bulk of the family's estate. Near the end of 1566 he visited his brother Jasper *Heywood, a Jesuit stationed at Dillingen in Bavaria, proposing himself to join the Jesuits and in turn to will them his inheritance. Despite concerns about his health Heywood was received into the Society of Jesus at Dillingen in December 1566. After several Bavarian postings he was transferred to Antwerp, where he served until his final days.

Before this last phase of Heywood's life he is said to have visited England, possibly to protect property against government confiscation. He returned without success to Antwerp in 1573; by 1574 his estate was forfeit to the crown. Heywood's ageing father was admitted into the Antwerp Jesuit community, but with other Jesuits both father and son were deported from Antwerp in May 1578, narrowly escaping death at the hands of Dutch troops and fleeing again to Louvain, where Ellis died on 2 October 1578.   DENNIS FLYNN

Sources T. M. McCoog, ed., *Monumenta Angliae*, 2: *English and Welsh Jesuits, catalogues, 1630–1640* (1992) • A. W. Reed, *Early Tudor drama* (1926) • E. Heywood, *Il Moro*, ed. R. L. Deakins (1972) • W. Bang, 'Acta Anglo-Lovaniensia', *Englische Studien*, 38 (1907), 234–50 • O. Braunsberger, *Beati Petri Canisii, Societatis Jesu, epistulae et acta*, 8 vols. (1896–1923), vol. 5 • T. Harwood, *The history and antiquities of the church and city of Lichfield* (1806) • Foster, *Alum. Oxon.* • J. Wegg, *The decline of Antwerp under Philip of Spain* (1924)

Archives Archivum Romanum Societatis Iesu, Rome, corresp., etc., Anglia 30.1, Germ. 106, Germ. 107, Germ. 148, Germ. 150, Germ. 151

Heywood, James (*bap.* 1687, *d.* 1776), writer and poet, son of John Heywood, was born at Cheetham Hill, Manchester, and baptized at Manchester on 21 February 1687. He was educated at the Manchester grammar school. For many years he carried on the business of a wholesale linen-draper in Fish Street Hill, London. He was a governor of St Bartholomew's, Christ's, Bridewell, and Bethlem hospitals, and was elected alderman of Aldgate ward, but paid the customary fine of £500 rather than serve the office. In his earlier years he contributed to *The Freethinker*, *The Plain-Dealer*, and other publications, and a letter of his is printed in no. 268 of *The Spectator*. These pieces, with some verses, he collected in a small volume, *Letters and Poems on Several Subjects* (1722; 2nd edn, with additions, 1726). The poems had previously been published with the title *Original Poems on Several Occasions* (1721). Many of his poems are addressed to 'Lucinda', and other titles include 'Advice to a Bashful Lover' and 'To a Very Old Batchelor'. His letters, which are mostly humorous, deal with contemporary conduct, especially that between the sexes. Heywood made no secret of his own keen interest in the female sex. He wrote: 'For my Part, when I see a beautiful young Lady, the sight of her diffuses a secret Satisfaction, and strikes my Mind with an inward Joy, and causes a sudden cheerfulness, and a Secret Delight' (Heywood, 51).

Heywood is alluded to by Steele in *The Guardian* as a politician and brisk little man, who had the habit of twisting off the buttons of persons he conversed with. He died at his house in Austin Friars on 23 July 1776, aged eighty-nine. His wife, Catherine, referred to in his will, predeceased him.   C. W. SUTTON, *rev.* MICHAEL BEVAN

Sources J. Heywood, *Letters and poems on several subjects* (1726) • H. Drake, *Essays, biographical, critical, and historical, illustrative of the 'Tatler', 'Spectator', and 'Guardian'* (1805), 3.331 • will

Archives Man. CL, Manchester Archives and Local Studies, corresp. with Edward Chetham

Heywood, James (1810–1897), university reformer and philanthropist, was born in Everton, Liverpool, on 28 May 1810, the fifth son of Nathaniel Heywood, a partner in the Manchester bank of Benjamin Heywood & Sons, and his wife, Ann, daughter of Thomas *Percival, MD FRS. Sir Benjamin *Heywood and Thomas *Heywood were his elder brothers. His early education was at Manchester, followed by a period at Lant Carpenter's school at Bristol, and attendance at the universities of Edinburgh and Geneva. He entered Heywood's bank at Manchester, but on inheriting a fortune from his uncle (B. A. Heywood) he gave up banking and returned to study, entering Trinity College, Cambridge, in 1829. Although ranked twelfth senior optime in the mathematical tripos (1833), Heywood, being a Unitarian, was debarred from taking his degree by the religious tests then in force. He was called to the bar of the Inner Temple in 1838, but did not practise.

After settling in Manchester, where he was one of the trustees of the Cross Street Chapel, Heywood became a member of the Unitarian network which played a prominent role in the cultural institutions of the city. He devoted his time to learned societies, of which his house in Mosley Street was often the centre. He was elected in 1833 to membership of the Manchester Literary and Philosophical Society, of which his maternal grandfather had been a founder, and was himself one of the founders, with Richard Cobden and William Langton, of the Manchester Athenaeum, which opened in 1839 to provide reading rooms and lectures. Heywood envisaged the Athenaeum as bringing the culture of science, literature, and philosophy to young men working in commercial occupations in Manchester. A founder also, in 1838, of the Manchester Geological Society, he was elected a fellow of the Royal Society in 1839, and was a local secretary when the British Association met in Manchester in 1842. He was a fellow of the Statistical Society, a member of the first council of the Chetham Society, and president (1853–8) of the Unitarian Manchester New College. From 1845 to 1860 he was a trustee of the non-denominational Owens College, Manchester.

A radical in politics, Heywood was a member of the Anti-Corn Law League. Reform of the ancient universities, whose religious and social exclusiveness hindered the diffusion of culture, became his principal interest. He edited a collection of Cambridge university and college statutes (1840) and gave financial support to the publication of translations of early statutes of Oxford colleges to expose the extent of their neglect. In 1850 he paid his Trinity College contemporary, Thomas Wright, to produce translations of the statutes of Eton College and King's College, Cambridge, and later (1855) to produce an edition of Cambridge University documents from the period of the puritan controversies of the sixteenth and seventeenth centuries. Heywood himself compiled and published statistics on the state of the English universities in the 1840s. As MP for North Lancashire from 1847 to 1857, he became the leading parliamentary promoter of state intervention to reform the universities; his motion in April 1850 was the occasion for Lord John Russell to announce the appointment of royal commissions into both Oxford and Cambridge. The climax of his parliamentary career was in June 1854 when he carried an amendment removing religious tests for those matriculating or taking BA degrees at Oxford; a similar amendment to the Cambridge University Bill in June 1856 enabled him to graduate BA (1857) from his old university.

Heywood married in June 1853 Annie (d. 1872), widow of Gustav Albert Escher of Zürich and daughter of John Kennedy of Ardwick Hall, Lancashire. They had one daughter, Anne Sophia. They were resident from 1859 in Kensington, where Heywood was active in the Notting Hill Unitarian congregation. He was an early promoter of the free public library movement, speaking in favour of the Public Libraries Act in 1850 and maintaining at his own expense a public library in Notting Hill High Street from 1874 until 1887 when he donated it to the parish of Kensington and Chelsea. He was a founder member in 1875 of the Sunday Society to promote the opening of museums, art galleries, and public libraries on Sundays.

Having secured the admission of dissenters to the universities, Heywood, who was a supporter of women's suffrage, worked to make university education available to women. Nominated by the crown a member of the senate of London University, he advocated opening London degrees to women. In 1869 he was one of the original members of Emily Davies's committee for the foundation of a college for women, which led to the establishment of Girton College, Cambridge. He was a member of the council of the college from 1872 until his death.

Heywood was an early member of the Royal Historical Society, contributing to its transactions articles on Swiss freedom and the progress of free thought; his presidency of the society's council from 1878 to 1880 immediately preceded the displacement of the older generation of antiquaries and amateurs, to which he belonged, by university teachers of history. Though not conspicuous as a scholar in his own right, Heywood held a Unitarian faith in the power of reason, and throughout his life used his substantial wealth to support the spread of knowledge. He died at his London home, 26 Kensington Palace Gardens, on 17 October 1897, and was buried in Barnes cemetery. M. C. CURTHOYS

Sources *Memoirs of the Literary and Philosophical Society of Manchester*, 42 (1897–8), lx–lxi · W. R. Ward, *Victorian Oxford* (1965) · Venn, *Alum. Cant.* · Boase, *Mod. Eng. biog.* · Burke, *Peerage* · T. Baker, *Memorials of a dissenting chapel* (1884) · B. Stephen, *Girton College, 1869–1932* (1933) · B. Curle, *Libraries for all* (1987) · P. Joyce, *Democratic subjects: the self and the social in nineteenth-century England* (1994) · *Hist. U. Oxf.* 6: *19th-cent. Oxf.*
Archives U. Edin. L., letters to James Halliwell-Phillipps
Likenesses J. Adams-Acton, marble medallion, 1897, Manchester Athenaeum · drawing, repro. in Curle, *Libraries for all*, 3 · portrait, repro. in *ILN* (27 Nov 1847), 356 · portrait, repro. in *Biographical Magazine*, 10 (1889), 125
Wealth at death £61,745 5s. 7d.: administration, 23 Dec 1897, *CGPLA Eng. & Wales*

Heywood, Jasper (1535–1598), poet and Jesuit, was born in London, fourth of five children of John *Heywood (b. 1496/7, d. in or after 1578) and his wife, Joan (d. 1574), daughter of John *Rastell and Elizabeth More, Sir Thomas More's sister. Heywood was a schoolmate to Princess Elizabeth at court, where his father (a protégé of More) was a playwright and music tutor. He went to Oxford in 1547, graduated BA on 15 July 1553, and was elected a fellow of Merton College, gaining repute as a 'quaint poet' (Wood, *Ath. Oxon.*, 1.663). On 4 April 1558 his promising career at Merton ended when, in conflict with authority as usual, he had to resign his fellowship after repeated admonitions by the college's warden. Nevertheless Heywood proceeded MA on 10 June 1558 and was in November elected to a fellowship at All Souls College following in his brother Ellis *Heywood's footsteps.

At All Souls Heywood justified the esteem accorded him by publishing the first English translations of three tragedies by Seneca—*Troas* (1559), *Thyestes* (1560), and *Hercules furens* (1561)—thus making an important contribution to the development of Elizabethan and Jacobean drama. Some of Heywood's poems of this period were later published in Elizabethan miscellanies. Heywood's tenure at All Souls ended when, refusing to comply with Elizabethan religious reforms, he left Oxford to live briefly at Gray's Inn with his uncle William Rastell. He then went into exile at Rome, where he became a Jesuit on 21 May 1562. In Rome Heywood taught and studied for the priesthood until he was sent to the university at Dillingen, Bavaria, in March 1564. On 1 September 1564 he graduated BTh and was ordained a priest on 16 October. Heywood was later chosen to preach on 15 June 1567 at a synod of the diocese of Augsburg held for the purpose of promulgating reforms of the Council of Trent. Having defended a dissertation on the seven sacraments he graduated DTh from Dillingen on 12 August 1567. He professed the fourth vow of the Jesuits on 25 July 1570.

During the 1570s Heywood grew discontented with his situation in Bavaria, deprived of the stimulating intellectual culture he had enjoyed at Oxford and Rome. He suffered from gout and experienced terror at night, an affliction he called a 'demon' (Duhr, 229), which was not cured by exorcism. A further vexation was friction with his Jesuit superior, Paul Hoffaeus, in a controversy over the contracting of loans at 5 per cent interest by Bavarian merchants. Heywood, with many Jesuit colleagues, thought the loans usurious.

In the spring of 1580, while Heywood was in Munich attached to the court of Wilhelm V, duke of Bavaria, he met Edmund Campion, passing from Prague toward Rome to undertake the secret Jesuit mission to England. Campion later wrote to the pope that Heywood could be valuable to the mission. Heywood himself travelled to Rome at the end of 1580, lobbying his case against the 5 per cent loans over the head of Hoffaeus. But Heywood's energetic opposition did not prevent the success of Hoffaeus's policy. With a letter from the pope to Duke Wilhelm, Heywood was reassigned to the English mission.

Having left Rome on 6 May 1581 Heywood arrived at Newcastle in June, then travelled toward London to meet Campion and Robert Persons, both in England since the previous spring. Returning after twenty years in exile, Heywood brought to the English mission an outlook and style of missionary work quite different from those of Persons, his superior. Born and bred at the court of Henry VIII, Heywood had personal acquaintance not only with Queen Elizabeth but with other aristocrats in England and abroad—experience that led him, unlike Persons, to think of the mission as largely a matter of influencing great noble houses. This contrast is partly reflected in Heywood's re-entering England through Newcastle, the port controlled by Henry Percy, eighth earl of Northumberland, a leading pro-Catholic peer.

By the time Heywood came south to meet with Persons, Campion had been arrested, a severe loss to the mission. After the uneasy meeting Heywood returned to the north, where pro-Catholic feeling ran strong. In three months he was able to convert hundreds to Roman Catholicism. In October 1581 he returned to London bearing alms for imprisoned Catholics from the northern nobility and gentry. By this time Persons had retired to France for consultations about the crisis of the mission, leaving Heywood in charge.

In December 1581 Campion was executed. Alone, as deputy superior of the mission, Heywood followed his success in the north with a campaign at Oxford and Cambridge designed to make the universities 'perpetual aqueducts' (Jesuit Archives, Rome, Anglia 30.1, 119) through which would pass young English scholars bound to finish their studies at continental seminaries. Heywood also took up Persons's earlier contact with the Spanish ambassador, Mendoza, himself in touch with Northumberland and the pro-Catholic lords. One of Mendoza's concerns was to divert the stream of Heywood's 'aqueducts' toward filling the need for officers to lead a contingent of English exiles and deserters attached to the duke of Parma's army in the Spanish Netherlands. These troops were to take part in an invasion of England and restore Catholicism. In this plan, Northumberland's participation was thought essential.

For his part Heywood worked to develop contacts with what he called 'big fish'. By early 1583 he had made efforts toward reconciling to Catholicism the three most ancient earldoms of the realm, in the persons of the earls of Arundel, Derby, and Northumberland. Politically the most important of these was Northumberland, who at this time dispatched his trusted aide, Captain William Pullen, to be ordained a priest at Rheims and then to serve as chaplain to the company of English fugitives in Parma's army. Arundel and Northumberland themselves, after contact with Heywood, were formally converted to Catholicism. Despite these successes, Heywood encountered increasingly severe difficulties dealing with a split among the Catholic priests in England. Those ordained abroad sought to conduct affairs by regulations of the Council of Trent; but Marian and earlier priests insisted that, until Tridentine reforms were promulgated in England, the ancient rules of English Catholicism should pertain.

These tensions, aggravated under government persecution, culminated in a synod called to settle differences, at which Heywood's attempted rulings were challenged and protested so sharply that he was recalled for consultation with Persons in France.

Heywood had embarked at Rye and was approaching Dieppe when a squall drove his ship back to Queenborough. On 9 December 1583 he was arrested and sent to London for imprisonment in the Clink. On 5 February 1584 he was indicted for treason and on 8 February was transferred into the Tower and subjected to torture. On 6 May his trial was begun but suspended *sine die*. At Christmas 1584 Heywood was visited in the Tower by his replacement on the Jesuit mission, William Weston, disguised as a family member in the company of Heywood's sister Elizabeth Donne. Heywood's nephew John Donne was present on this occasion and witnessed a discussion between Weston and Heywood about petitioning the queen for toleration of Catholicism.

On 21 January 1585 Heywood, with other priests, was deported to France. Travelling from Rouen to Paris to Rheims, he was debriefed by Persons but was judged 'out of step' and prevented from returning to England. Instead he was summoned to Rome, where he arrived in June 1585. In April 1586 he was sent to Naples, where, determinedly protesting against the policies of Persons, he remained until his death on 19 February 1598.

DENNIS FLYNN

Sources T. M. McCoog, ed., *Monumenta Angliae*, 2: *English and Welsh Jesuits, catalogues, 1630–1640* (1992) · A. W. Reed, *Early Tudor drama* (1926) · O. Braunsberger, *Beati Petri Canisii, Societatis Jesu, epistulae et acta*, 8 vols. (1896–1923), vols. 5–8 · B. Duhr, 'Die deutschen Jesuiten im 5%-Streit des 16. Jahrhunderts', *Zeitschrift für Katholische Theologie*, 24 (1900), 209–48 · H. Vocht, *Jasper Heywood and his translations of Seneca's 'Troas', 'Thyestes', and 'Hercules furens'* (1913) · H. E. Rollins, ed., *The paradise of dainty devices, 1576–1606* (1927) · Foster, *Alum. Oxon.* · Wood, *Ath. Oxon.*, new edn, 1.663 · T. M. McCoog, *The Society of Jesus in Ireland, Scotland, and England, 1541–1588* (1996) · J. Donne, *Pseudo-martyr* (1610) · D. Flynn, 'The English mission of Jasper Heywood, S. J.', *Archivum Historicum Societatis Iesu*, 54 (1985), 45–76 · Jesuit Archives, Rome, Anglia, 8, 9, 14, 30.1 · Bodl. Oxf., MS Tanner 79/187 · D. Flynn, '"Out of step": six supplementary notes on Jasper Heywood', *The reckoned expense: Edmund Campion and the early English Jesuits*, ed. T. M. McCoog (1996), 179–92 · *Miscellanea, I*, Catholic RS, 1 (1905) · *Miscellanea, II*, Catholic RS, 2 (1906) · *Miscellanea, IV*, Catholic RS, 4 (1907) · *Miscellanea VII*, Catholic RS, 9 (1911) · L. Hicks, ed., *Letters and memorials of Father Robert Persons*, Catholic RS, 39 (1942) · *Letters of William Allen and Richard Barret, 1572–1598*, ed. P. Renold, Catholic RS, 58 (1967)

Archives Roman Archives of the Jesuits, Anglia 8, 9, 14, 30.1; Germ. 1; Hist. Soc. 42, 43, 61; Rom. 169, 170

Likenesses C. Weld, pencil drawing (after portrait), Stonyhurst College, Lancashire; repro. in McCoog, *Society of Jesuits*

Heywood, John (*b.* 1496/7, *d.* in or after 1578), playwright and epigrammatist, is thought to be the son of William Heywood, a lawyer of Coventry who acted as a temporary coroner there in 1505–6. His mother's name and family are not known, but his father's association with the Rastell family at Coventry was important later in John's life. It is known that John had three brothers: William (*d.* 1568), a yeoman of Stock in Essex, was his elder; Richard (1509–1570) entered Lincoln's Inn in 1534 and died prosperous,

John Heywood (b. 1496/7, d. in or after 1578), by unknown engraver, pubd 1556

bearing arms; and Thomas, an Augustinian friar pensioned at the dissolution from St Osyth's Monastery in Essex, was executed on 14 June 1574 for illegally saying mass.

Most of Heywood's early years remain obscure, though Anthony Wood claims that he found his studies at Broadgates Hall, Oxford, rather uncongenial. He must in youth have acquired musical skills: one unsupported tradition holds that he was a chorister. The first positive references to him at the court of Henry VIII call him a singer: as such he was granted six quarterly payments of £5 between Michaelmas 1519 and Christmas 1520, making an annual salary of £20. By 1525, when the quarterly payment rose to £6 13s. 4d., he was designated a 'player of the virginals', and this remained his denomination for many years afterwards in court documents. An annual pension of £10 was set up in November 1528, and though the records are not continuous he received this at least until 1551. As the 1528 warrant indicates that he was 'discharged from the King's court', this pension probably marked a change of status, perhaps a release from regular employment. From then on it is apparent that his activities diversified considerably from the profession of musical performer; it is not clear that he had ever composed music, though some of his lyrics have survived.

By the time this pension was set up Heywood was approximately thirty, his family connections had developed considerably, and there are signs of prosperity and a social status which could hardly have resulted solely from his musical duties, whatever they may have comprised. When Sir Thomas More became a privy councillor in 1518 he already had a connection with Heywood, and the latter's initial steps at court may have stemmed from his

patronage and growing influence in the early 1520s. In any case there was already a closer family tie, as John Rastell had married More's sister Elizabeth (probably before 1504), and Heywood himself married the Rastells' daughter Joan (d. before 1574) at some point before 1523. It was in that year that Heywood became a freeman of the city of London in the Stationers' Company, the common council having received a letter from the king in support. Meanwhile John Rastell had been gaining royal favour on his own behalf: a man of many parts, he had worked at the Field of Cloth of Gold in 1520, and created a pageant in Cheapside for the visit of the emperor Charles V in 1522. This dramatic interest, together with his status as a stationer—his activity in the printing business went back at least as far as 1512—were doubtless of value to his son-in-law. Rastell built a house with a stage in Finsbury Fields in 1524, and at some point after 1526 he printed Gentleness and Nobility, a play of his own composition, which may have contained a contribution by Heywood. Most of what survives of Heywood's work as a dramatist apparently dates from the next few years.

The marriage of Joan Rastell and John Heywood produced at least four children. Both Ellis *Heywood (1529–1578) and Jasper *Heywood (1535–1598) had successful academic careers at Oxford before becoming Jesuit priests in exile. Jasper was especially distinguished in the field of drama, publishing translations of two plays by Seneca; Ellis was gifted in languages. Joan Heywood married Christopher Stubbe; John and his wife conveyed property in Tottenham to them in 1542, possibly as a marriage settlement. Elizabeth Heywood married John Donne, a successful London ironmonger, and gave birth to the poet John Donne (1572–1631). Like their children John and Joan remained lifelong Catholics, and this loyalty played a large part in Heywood's subsequent fortunes, and in his literary output. He managed to survive political and religious turmoil in Tudor court circles, occasionally being paid for specific musical and dramatic entertainments, until he and his wife went into exile to Brabant in 1564. There are very few personal writings to indicate what Heywood felt about these changes, but it seems clear from subsequent events that the crisis of Henry VIII's heretical break with Rome over his divorce caused Heywood much concern, and that his personal loyalty to Princess Mary was publicly rewarded when she became queen. Through these years he must have been anxious over the fates of his immediate family: the imprisonment and execution of More, his wife's uncle (1535); the death of John Rastell, her father, imprisoned as a protestant heretic (1536); and the exile of her Catholic brother William Rastell (1508–1565) in the reign of Edward VI. During this time Heywood acquired land and property in Middlesex, Essex, and Kent, and achieved a higher social status. In 1530 he became a common measurer of the Mercers' Company in the city of London. At new year 1533 he received a royal gift of a gilt cup.

Heywood's political and religious interests during the remainder of the reign of Henry VIII may be judged by two elements: his activities as a playwright up to 1534 and his indictment for treason in 1544. The canon and dating of the plays have been objects of much conjecture. Besides the possible contribution to *Gentleness and Nobility* six complete plays are attributed to him. Of these 'Witty and Witless' remained in a manuscript, not in Heywood's hand, with his name at the end. *The Play of the Wether* (1533) and *A Play of Love* (1534) were both printed by William Rastell (son of John Rastell) and named Heywood on the title-page. *Four PP* was similarly named, but the first extant edition is by Thomas Middleton (c.1544). William Rastell also printed *Johan Johan* (a translation and adaptation of *La farce du pasté*) and *The Pardoner and the Friar* in 1533, both anonymous. Dates of composition remain conjectural, and there is no positive evidence about if and when performances took place, though a stage direction in 'Witty' mentions the expected presence of the king. There is little doubt that Heywood was actively engaged in performance later on, and the probability remains high that he was similarly involved in these years of tension surrounding the controversy over protestantism and the king's divorce.

The comic style of the plays, with their persistent interest in the clash of different points of view, has led to their being characterized as debates rather than as true drama, but recent criticism and performances have shown that there is much that is visual in them and that they frequently contain structures and situations which gain enormously by being physically enacted on a stage. The cunning blend of characters of different types, together with the versatile and resourceful dialogue are important features in performance. There is also a tendency to include extensive passages of dramatic narrative at key points in the plays, such as Vice's tale of the mocker mocked in *Love*, and these provide an opportunity for performance skills including movement and the imitation of dialogue by the narrators. Although the subject matter is often centred on apparently trivial comic topics like the appropriateness of the weather, or whether a witty or a witless man has more pleasure in life, there are underlying issues which come close to the heart of major contemporary controversy. Heywood avoids the morality play structure popular in many interludes, but consistently engages with his subject matter in such a way that Catholic doctrine is upheld. Though he is often satirical about some practices like the exploitation by pardoners (following Chaucer verbatim in some passages) his main objectives seem to be to see the world so as to vindicate his Catholic beliefs, albeit sustained and tempered by a humanism which probably goes back to Erasmus, via the early work and opinions of Sir Thomas More. In real life he was well known for his jesting and his witty inventiveness, as witnessed by his biographer Pitseus, even in the form of a deathbed quip; his treatment of doctrinally serious matters in the plays is always coloured by the same predisposition. Sometimes the jokes seem dangerously near the mark, as when the devil, attired for tennis in his shirt, seems to suggest the king himself in *Four PP*, but this boldness in invention may have been found allowable and indeed valuable in life at court and on stage.

While a purely allegorical interpretation of Heywood's work has not been found to be consistent, there are internal grounds for believing that the characterization of Jupiter in *Wether* is based upon Henry VIII, and when one considers the probable date of composition early in 1533, it seems that the argument about the weather may really be directed at the religious controversy surrounding Henry's marriage to Anne Boleyn in January. As Jupiter is enjoined to judge the weather from his own authority, so Henry is covertly urged to rise above the factions surrounding him and leave religion where it was. From Heywood's viewpoint at this time the shift to protestantism was not necessarily inevitable. Perhaps the comic tone of this statement of Heywood's concern is also to be associated with an attempt to mollify the growing storm, for More had resigned the chancellorship and his opposition to change was now revealed in a series of trenchant polemics.

For the rest of the 1530s Cromwell was in power, and Heywood's objections were apparently muted, except for his loyalty to Princess Mary, to whom he wrote 'A Song in Praise of a Lady' (1534, printed in *Tottel's Songes and Sonnettes*, 1557). After Cromwell's fall in 1540, however, Heywood took a public step which might well have been disastrous. With John More he became involved in a conspiracy to discredit Cranmer. As a result he was attainted, lost a good deal of his property, and must for some time have been in mortal danger. He was pardoned, and had to make a public recantation at Paul's Cross on 6 July 1544 of what were now regarded as heretical views regarding the royal supremacy.

Perhaps as some kind of peace offering a few months later Heywood wrote a play for Cranmer, 'The Parts of Man', some lines of which are preserved in the autobiography of his pupil, Thomas Whythorne. Heywood was concerned with entertainments at court on a number of other occasions. Cromwell paid him for a 'Masque of King Arthur's Knights', which was performed twice in February 1539. For Princess Elizabeth he and Sebastian Westcott presented a play using the children of St Paul's in February 1552. In the following year his 'play of children' had to be postponed from Shrovetide to Easter on account of the failing health of King Edward. In August 1559, after Elizabeth's accession, there was another performance of a play using children at Nonsuch, but by then, as will be seen, the political climate was beginning to turn against him.

Probably Heywood's best years were spent under Queen Mary. At her coronation in 1553 Stow records that Heywood was in St Paul's Churchyard where he 'sat in a pageant under a vine and made to her an oration in Latin and in English'. In this same year he received a gift of £50 from the queen. Some witty exchanges with Mary personally are recorded by William Camden and Ben Jonson. On her marriage to King Philip of Spain the following year he wrote a ballad beginning 'The eagle's bird hath spread his wings' in celebration. In 1555 his pension was increased to £50 per annum. Just before Mary's death this was cancelled and replaced by a grant of the manor of Bulmer, near Malton in Yorkshire.

A number of literary activities were now coming to fruition. Heywood's allegorical poem *The Spider and the Flie* was printed by Thomas Powell in 1556. Apparently it had been started some years before, and as Mary was a central figure in this political and religious fiction, Heywood must have judged that this was a good moment to finish it. He has an authorial presence in this poem, reflected in a number of pictures in the original text showing him observing events. The frontispiece provides us with a full-length portrait of him in academic address, showing that he was a tall man.

Apart from a handful of lyrics, Heywood was also hard at work on his proverbs and epigrams. Beginning with *A Dialogue Containing the Number in Effect of All the Proverbs in the English Tongue* in 1546, he built up a series of epigrams on proverbs in hundreds over editions in 1549, 1555, 1556, 1560, and 1561, culminating in his *Works* of 1562 (the plays were not included). Though perhaps not containing all the known English proverbs, the collection, estimated at over 1260, was indeed the largest to have appeared. It derived from many sources, including Erasmus's *Adages* (1508), but there is a sense that Heywood's sensitive ear for demotic speech played a significant part. The *Works* were well enough liked to be reprinted in 1566, 1576, 1587, and 1598.

At the beginning of Elizabeth's reign Heywood was prosperous and for a time he seems to have maintained some status in court entertainment, but the commission set up to enforce the Act of Uniformity against Catholics in 1564 precipitated a crisis for Heywood and his circle. He fled to Brabant on 20 July, leaving his interests in the care of his son-in-law, John Donne. Early in the 1570s commissions were set up enquiring into the possessions of exiles, and the transference of money must have been interrupted. Heywood, a widower, 'being now 78 years of age … a poor, honest, quiet old man', wrote to Burleigh from Malines on 18 April 1575 asking for help with the arrears (Reed, 237–8). Ellis Heywood had taken up a position at the English College in Antwerp, and John joined him there in 1576. The final crisis came two years later when the college was sacked. John and Ellis fled to Catholic Louvain, where Ellis died on 2 October 1578. John followed shortly afterwards, jesting to the last. His wit, which the protestant John Bale had acknowledged in his *Summarium* long before in 1548, was subsequently celebrated by Gabriel Harvey, William Webbe, George Puttenham, John Harington, Camden, and Jonson. His contribution to English comedy has proved to be inimitable. PETER HAPPÉ

Sources A. W. Reed, *Early Tudor drama* (1926) · A. Feuillerat, *A document relating to the revels at court in the time of King Edward VI and Queen Mary* (1908) · *The plays of John Heywood*, ed. R. Axton and P. Happé (1991), xi–xvii, 1–10, 309–30 · *LP Henry VIII*, vols. 3, 6, 14, 16–20 · *John Heywood's 'Works' and miscellaneous short poems*, ed. B. A. Milligan (1956), vii–ix, 1–15 · R. C. Johnson, *John Heywood* (1970), 11–35 · *The autobiography of Thomas Whythorne*, ed. J. M. Osborn (1961), 73–4 · Wood, *Ath. Oxon.*, new edn · R. Axton, ed., *Three Rastell plays* (1979), 20–26 · J. Stow and E. Howes, *Annales, or, A generall chronicle of England … unto the end of this present yeere, 1631* (1631), 617 · J. Bale, *Illustrium Maioris Britannie scriptorum … summarium* (1548), 235 · J. Pits, *Relationum historicarum de rebus Anglicis*, ed. [W. Bishop] (Paris, 1619), 234

Likenesses woodcut, AM Oxf., BM, NPG; repro. in J. Heywood, *The spider and the flie* (1556) [*see illus.*]

Wealth at death presumably retained property at Hinxhill, Kent; complained of poverty: letter to Burleigh, 18 April 1575

Heywood, Nathaniel (*bap.* 1633, *d.* 1677), clergyman and ejected minister, fourth son of Richard Heywood (1595/6–1677) of Little Lever, near Bolton, Lancashire, and his first wife, Alice Critchlaw (*c.*1593–1657), was born at Little Lever and baptized at Bolton parish church on 16 September 1633. Heywood's father was a fustian weaver who subsequently became a landowner in Bolton with mining and milling interests. Nathaniel's parents were strongly puritan, and another presbyterian minister, the diarist Oliver *Heywood, was one of his elder brothers.

From school at Horwich he was admitted to Trinity College, Cambridge, entering in May 1648 and graduating BA in 1652. He was brought to a spiritual commitment under the preaching of Samuel Hammond. He spent some time in London before he went to study for two years under Edward Gee, rector of Eccleston, Lancashire. There he met and married Elizabeth Parr, a relative of Richard Parr, bishop of Sodor and Man, and Gee's predecessor. They had nine children, and she outlived him.

Heywood was called to Illingworth Chapel, Halifax parish, where he suffered many hardships and setbacks, having 'not sought the peace of the place, but the good of it' (Ashurst, 7–8). He received a call from Ormskirk, Lancashire, and in January 1656 the classis met in Wigan to hear the petitions of parishioners from Ormskirk and Illingworth, finding in favour of Ormskirk. Heywood was presented to the vicarage on 7 August 1656 by the countess of Derby, installed by the fifth classis of Lancashire, and approved by the parliamentary commissioners. His ministry was active and successful. A royalist in politics, he welcomed the Restoration with a sermon on thanksgiving day (10 May 1660), taking an odd text (2 Samuel 19: 30). He was urged by the local gentry to print it but refused. Heywood was ejected from the living by the Act of Uniformity but continued to preach in the church until a Mr Ashworth, a local teacher, was installed. Heywood's biographer commented that the new vicar was non-resident and that 'Mr. Heywood still seemed to have the sole charge of that Town and parish', as well as preaching in Wigan, Warrington, Liverpool, Preston, and Eccleston (Ashurst, 14).

On the declaration of indulgence of 1672 Heywood was licensed as a presbyterian to minister at the chapel at Bickerstaff 'adjoining Lady Stanley's house' and one at Scarisbrick. To protect him from the effects of the annulment of the indulgence in 1673, Lady Stanley had the service of common prayer read before his sermon. His fiercely anti-Catholic sermons enraged local Catholics and may have had something to do with the ferocity of the persecution he experienced: in the first four months of 1674 he had thirty-four warrants presented against him. Later in the year he recorded that meetings could still be held in both chapels, though the congregation 'met in fear'. In late December 1674 he was taken by soldiers at Bickerstaff, despite Lady Stanley's personal attempt to intervene. He was tendered the Oxford oath by the JPs and given until the next quarter sessions at Wigan to consider his response, when the oath would be put to him again. Although he was supported by Lady Stanley and Henry Houghton in Wigan, what saved him was the affection of the people of Ormskirk. The Five Mile Act could not be applied because no one could be found to swear that he lived in Ormskirk.

Heywood died at Ormskirk on Sunday 16 December 1677. It was a measure of the respect and affection in which he was held that his funeral sermon was preached by the ejected nonconformist John Starkie in Ormskirk parish church, 'no man forbidding him; nay all that were any way concerned consenting'. He was buried on Wednesday 19 December in the vault of the Stanleys of Bickerstaff in the chancel of Ormskirk church. His elder brother Oliver Heywood described him as 'the flower of our family for learning, parts, piety, singularly beloved of God and man, sorely afflicted, seasonably delivered' (*Rev. Oliver Heywood*, 1.38). Heywood's biographer, usually taken to be Sir Henry Ashurst, but perhaps Oliver, emphasized Nathaniel's allegiance to the presbyterian party: 'he was (according to his Education) a strict Presbyterian', avoiding the extremes of prelacy and congregationalist democracy (Ashurst, 71). 'He loved and used sound speech that cannot be condemned, as well as sound and orthodox Truth: standing at an equal distance from Arminians on the one hand, and Antinomians on the other' (ibid., 90–91). Heywood published nothing but after his death two of his sermons were printed, with the title *Christ Displayed* (1679).

The younger **Nathaniel Heywood** (1659–1704), Heywood's eldest son, Presbyterian minister, was born on 6 June 1659 and baptized at Ormskirk eight days later. He entered Richard Frankland's academy on 25 April 1677 and graduated MA from Edinburgh University in 1680. He then studied with his uncle Oliver, becoming a chaplain to a Mr Dickins in Staffordshire in 1683–4. He was ordained at Attercliff, Yorkshire, on 1 June 1687, by Oliver Heywood and Richard Frankland, and probably succeeded in his father's ministry about this time. He suffered from melancholia and experienced lengthy illnesses, which prevented him from preaching. At the Lancashire quarter sessions held at Ormskirk on 22 July 1689 he registered 'Bury's House nr Ormeske ... for a pl. of meeting for him the sd Nathanial Heywood & his Congregation' (Register of dissenting meeting-houses, 1689, Lancs. RO, QDV 4). He is probably the Mr Heywood mentioned in the United Brethren minutes for the meeting held at Manchester on 4 September 1694.

Heywood was married three times. His first wife, Isabel Lynford of Brinscall, near Blackburn, died in childbirth in January 1688. From the son whom she died giving birth to, Benjamin Heywood of Drogheda, descended Sir Benjamin Heywood and the Heywood banking family of Liverpool, Manchester, and Wakefield. Nathaniel then married Rebecca Angier of Warrington, a marriage pointing to ties of kinship within the nonconformist ministry. Nathaniel's uncle Oliver had married the daughter of the puritan clergyman John Angier, whose nephew and grandson, both named Samuel, were ministers at Dukinfield near Manchester and Toxteth Park Chapel near Liverpool respectively. Rebecca's place within the family is unclear, but 'S. A.' (almost certainly the latter Samuel) baptized the son born to her and Nathaniel in April 1695. Nathaniel, his uncle recorded, 'greatly rejoyced in having a living wife and son Nathl. Lord's Day after left her well, preacht; in afternoon sent for out of chapel after he had been half an hour, ran fast, found her dead, April, 1695' (Turner, 64). Heywood's third marriage, the licence for which was dated 24 May 1699, was to Mary Trueman of Liverpool. He died on 26 October 1704 and was buried at Ormskirk two days later. Administration of the will was granted to his widow on 12 May 1711. JONATHAN H. WESTAWAY

Sources H. Ashurst, *Some remarks upon the life of that painful servant of God Mr. Nathaniel Heywood, minister of the gospel of Christ at Ormskirk in Lancashire. Who died in the 44th year of his age* (London, for Thomas Cockerill, 1695) • *The Rev. Oliver Heywood ... his autobiography, diaries, anecdote and event books*, ed. J. H. Turner, 1 (1881), 9, 38; 2 (1883), 48 • *Calamy rev.*, 259 • E. Calamy, ed., *An abridgement of Mr. Baxter's history of his life and times, with an account of the ministers, &c., who were ejected after the Restauration of King Charles II*, 2nd edn, 2 vols. (1713), vol. 2, p. 304 • E. Calamy, *A continuation of the account of the ministers ... who were ejected and silenced after the Restoration in 1660*, 2 vols. (1727), vol. 1, p. 560 • *DNB* • F. Nicholson and E. Axon, *The older nonconformity in Kendal* (1915), 546 • B. Nightingale, *Lancashire nonconformity*, 6 vols. [1890–93], vol. 3, pp. 180–99 • J. Arrowsmith, ed., *The registers of the parish church of Eccleston in the county of Lancaster: christenings, burials, and weddings, 1603–1694*, Lancashire Parish Register Society, 15 (1903) • J. Dixon, 'The burial list of the Ormskirk clergy and ministers', *Transactions of the Historic Society of Lancashire and Cheshire*, 3rd ser., 5 (1876–7), 125–38 • J. Dixon, 'Nathaniel Heywood, the nonconformist vicar of Ormskirk', *Transactions of the Historic Society of Lancashire and Cheshire*, 3rd ser., 6 (1877), 159–63 • M. Duggan, *Ormskirk: the making of a modern town* (1998) • M. Duggan, 'Urban change in a Lancashire market town: Ormskirk, 1660–1800', PhD diss., University of Lancaster, 1992, 146–67 • R. Halley, *Lancashire: its puritanism and nonconformity*, 2 vols. (1869), vol. 2, p. 126 • N. Heywood, *Christ displayed, as the choicest gift, and best master ... Being some of the last sermons preached by ... Mr. Nathaniel Heywood* (1697) • J. Hunter, *Familiae minorum gentium*, ed. J. W. Clay, 1, Harleian Society, 37 (1894), 61–6 • J. Hunter, *The rise of the old dissent, exemplified by the life of Oliver Heywood* (1842), 40 • W. F. Irvine, ed., *Marriage licences granted within the archdeaconry of Chester in the diocese of Chester*, 8, Lancashire and Cheshire RS, 77 (1924), 251 • W. A. Shaw, ed., 'Minutes of the United Brethren, 1693–1700', *Minutes of the Manchester presbyterian classis*, 3, Chetham Society, new ser., 24 (1891), 349–65 • *The nonconformist's memorial ... originally written by ... Edmund Calamy*, ed. S. Palmer, [3rd edn], 2 (1802), 371 • A. Sparke, ed., *The registers of the parish church of Bolton* (1913), 134 • J. H. Turner, T. Dickenson, and O. Heywood, eds., *The nonconformist register of baptisms, marriages, and deaths* (1881), 64, 235 • *Venn, Alum. Cant.* • T. Williams, ed., *The registers of the parish church of Ormskirk, part 2, 1626–1678*, Lancashire Parish Register Society, 98 (1960), 56, 60, 68, 73, 113, 210, 216

Archives DWL, Walter Wilson MSS • Lancs. RO, register of dissenting meeting-houses

Heywood, Nathaniel (1659–1704). *See under* Heywood, Nathaniel (*bap.* 1633, *d.* 1677).

Heywood, Oliver (*bap.* 1630, *d.* 1702), clergyman and ejected minister, was the third son of Richard Heywood

(1595/6–1677), yeoman, of Little Lever in the parish of Bolton, Lancashire, and his first wife, Alice Critchlaw (1593–1657) of Longworth; he was baptized in the parish church at Bolton on 15 March 1630. The neighbourhood had a long tradition of evangelical protestantism stretching back to the Edwardian preacher and Marian martyr John Bradford, and Oliver's parents were leading members of the puritan godly, ensuring that the sign of the cross was not used at their son's baptism. Oliver's mother participated in iconoclasm at Bolton in 1641 and introduced her son to the round of sermon attendance characteristic of puritan piety. His father, who prospered in the cloth trade, also built up a library of godly authors and reformation classics and Oliver was sent to Bolton grammar school and to study with William Rathband, the suspended curate at Little Lever. By his own account, however, his most important teacher before going up to Cambridge was a Mr Rudal, probably George Rudhall, schoolmaster of Horwich in the adjacent parish of Deane, from whom he went to Trinity College, Cambridge, where he was admitted in July 1647. His tutor there was Alexander Akehurst, who later became a Quaker, and Heywood joined fellow students in a religious society which met in the rooms of Thomas Jollie, who became a lifelong friend and associate. As a student he was greatly influenced by the preaching of Samuel Hammond at St Giles's Church.

Coley Chapel, 1650–1662 Heywood graduated BA in 1650 and returned home intending to enter the household of John *Angier of Denton, Lancashire, as part of his further training for the ministry. He soon began to preach in the neighbourhood and at Skipton in Yorkshire, near where other members of the family lived. As a result of this, and on the recommendation of his uncle, Francis Critchlaw, Heywood came to the attention of the congregation at Coley, one of twelve chapelries in the extensive parish of Halifax and, after preaching there at Michaelmas, he accepted the invitation to become its preacher on 26 November 1650 at a stipend of £30 a year, £20 of which came from contributions by the congregation. The parish of Halifax, and its chapelries, had been a noted puritan centre before the civil wars and at his arrival there Heywood would find several like-minded clergy in the area. Even so he was very young to assume ministerial responsibilities but, although under age, was ordained by the Bury classis on 4 August 1652. He soon enjoyed the support and company of his brother Nathaniel *Heywood, who had been appointed to the chapelry of Illingworth in the same parish and with whom he shared a house, and of another old Cambridge friend, Eli Bentley, who became assistant minister at Halifax in 1653. On 24 April 1655 Heywood married Elizabeth (d. 1661), the daughter of John Angier, in her father's church at Denton, and they moved to live at Northowram. In the same year Heywood introduced a monthly celebration of the communion to Coley for the first time since the outbreak of the civil wars and in 1657 he linked this to the setting up of an eldership and presbyterian church discipline. This split the congregation, with many of the more prosperous members opposing him, though the majority remained on his communicants' list.

Despite these divisions Heywood persisted in establishing the discipline and was determined to remain at Coley, rejecting offers to undertake ministries at York and Preston which his reputation as a pastor and his wide connections among the northern godly had put his way.

By the late 1650s Heywood had become a royalist presbyterian and was arrested and threatened with deprivation for refusing to give public thanksgiving for the suppression of the insurrection led by George Booth in 1659. When he heard of Monck's declaration for the king he recorded the news in his diary with a psalm of praise, but the Restoration soon brought his official ministry to an end. He quickly ran into conflict with Richard Hooke, the new vicar of Halifax, over rights of baptism in the outlying chapelries, and at the beginning of 1661 a private fast he was conducting was stopped by authority. Within his own congregation there was a group, headed by Stephen Ellis of Hipperholme, the most substantial resident, who wanted to restore the Book of Common Prayer and a copy was placed before Heywood in the church on 25 August 1661. Heywood ignored it and was cited before the church courts on 13 September for nonconformity; proceedings dragged on until 29 June 1662 when he was suspended from ministering within the diocese. He continued to preach for a few weeks but was excommunicated following the Act of Uniformity of 1662, the decree being read at Halifax and Bolton. His first wife died on 26 May 1661, leaving him with two young sons, John and Eliezar, another having died in infancy; on 27 June 1667 he married Abigail Crompton, daughter of James Crompton of Breightmet in Lancashire, who died in 1707.

Roving ministry, 1662–1685 Heywood was formally excluded from preaching but, in the years immediately following, his extensive family connections and his reputation led to his being invited to several pulpits on both sides of the Pennines. In addition he continued to hold conventicles and private fasts in the homes of presbyterian gentry and farmers throughout the region and at York, where Sarah, Lady Hewley, was a supporter. Following the Five Mile Act he left his home at Coley and became an itinerant preacher throughout the north, returning in January 1668 to his old chapel, where he preached to a large congregation. He was arrested on 13 March 1670 after preaching at Little Woodhouse near Leeds, but released two days later; however, in July his goods were distrained to meet the fine required under the Conventicle Act, which had just come into force. Following the declaration of indulgence in 1672 he took out two licences as a presbyterian teacher, one for his own house at Northowram and the other for the house of John Butterworth of Warley in Halifax parish. On 12 June over 100 of his former congregation entered into a church covenant with him, which though presbyterian in inspiration was sufficiently broad to enable the members of the congregational chapel at Sowerby, leaderless since the death of Henry Root, to join with them on 19 June. On 29 October that year Heywood took part in a presbyterian ordination in the house of Robert Eaton, another ejected minister, at Deansgate, Manchester.

The licences were revoked in February 1675 and Heywood set off on his travels once again, covering several hundred miles a year on his preaching tours. His labours were critical in keeping the dissenting congregations in touch with each other, and on 8 July 1678 he assisted at the first presbyterian ordination in Yorkshire. During these years he was also active in furthering his message through print, and published a number of books of practical divinity in the puritan mode which he distributed widely, and for free, among his friends and congregations: among the more important of these were *Heart-Treasure* (1667), based on sermons preached at Coley and dedicated to the congregation there, *Closet Prayer, a Christian Duty* (1671), and *Life in God's Favour* (1679), and the distribution lists for these provide a valuable insight into dissenting networks and patrons throughout the north. He continued this pattern of roving ministry from the base at his house in Northowram, occasionally harassed by the authorities but escaping serious persecution until 1685. On 16 January that year he was arrested for riotous assembly at his house and he spent the rest of the year, until 19 December, as a prisoner in York Castle for his refusal to pay the £50 fine.

Northowram Chapel, 1688–1702 The declaration of indulgence granted by James II in 1687 provided Heywood with the opportunity to regularize his position once again, and he set about building a meeting-house in Northowram on land he had provided, which was opened on 8 July 1688; a school was added in 1693. The meeting-house was licensed under the Toleration Act on 18 July 1689. Throughout his life Heywood was interested in cases of witchcraft and possession, noting many in his diaries and attending fasts and prayers associated with some cases. In September 1689 he joined with several other nonconformist divines in attending fasts associated with the case of Richard Dugdale, the Surey Demoniack, but took no part in the defence of those ministers subsequently implicated in what was later revealed as a fraud.

In September 1691 Heywood played a leading role in introducing into Yorkshire the 'happy union' between Presbyterians and Independents agreed in London earlier that year, preaching to a meeting of ministers and licensed preachers of both denominations at Wakefield on 2 September when heads of agreement were adopted. Further meetings were arranged throughout the West Riding at which ordinations were arranged and preaching licences granted. Having weathered his difficulties with the established church Heywood spent much of the 1690s concerned about the extent to which he perceived some of his fellow dissenters had departed from the strict Calvinist tradition in which he had been formed, and though his views on individuals remained for the most part characteristically generous he regretted the falling away in doctrinal orthodoxy which the Toleration Act had permitted. He continued his pastoral activities and preached throughout the Pennine region throughout the decade, being viewed as something of a patriarchal figure by younger colleagues, many of whom sought his advice and whose pulpits he often shared. The extent of his labours in this work were recorded by him in a list covering the years

from 1665 until his death: in 1690, in addition to his Sunday preaching, he preached 135 sermons, conducted forty fasts and seventeen days of thanksgiving, and travelled a total of 1100 miles, a lesser distance than he recorded in the three previous years. In 1700 his asthmatic condition deteriorated but he continued to preach forty-five weekday sermons, conduct twenty-two fasts and three days of thanksgiving, and attend eight conferences of ministers, travelling in all 145 miles.

By this date, though more closely restricted to his Northowram congregation, Heywood's wider ministry was maintained through the writing of seven treatises and an extensive correspondence of 147 letters written in that, his seventieth year. This public preaching ministry was complemented by a pastoral one in which Heywood's status as a healer and the reputation he had for powerful prayer meant that he was often asked to attend those who were ill or in distress, one on occasion being so moved by the tears of a mother for her son who had been hanged that he went off to pray with her and her family. More commonly he regularly attended the elderly and women in childbed, and was frequently asked to give advice on personal matters by nonconformists throughout the region, many of them calling at his home in Northowram. Despite his failing health Heywood continued to preach in his meeting-house there, though from 5 December 1701 he had to be carried to it in a chair—as had Calvin, he noted in his diary. He died at Northowram on 4 May 1702 and was buried three days later in Halifax parish church, being laid in his mother's tomb in Holdsworth's chapel in the south aisle. It says much for his reputation throughout the region that the funeral was attended by a large gathering of clergy, from both the established church and the dissenting congregations.

Heywood's life formed a bridge between the puritan tradition of early and mid-century England, the years following the Restoration when dissent was outlawed and many ministers, Heywood included, suffered imprisonment as a result of their preaching, and the years after the revolution of 1688 when toleration was granted and dissenting ministers could operate from settled congregations with their own chapels. Though never party to discussions at national level in a significant way Heywood was the pre-eminent figure in northern nonconformity throughout these years and, as such, his life itself represents a key point of access to the religious history of the period, but even more important than the events of his life is the way in which Heywood recorded them.

Writings and spirituality This he did in a variety of volumes which owed much to the well-established puritan tradition of recording and interpreting God's providences to both the individual and the wider community, and Heywood's wide kinship networks and public position within dissent make his volumes uniquely important for their mix of both public and private. That mix is revealed in the writings themselves which consist of a diary, begun with his removal from Coley in 1666 following the Five Mile Act and continuing until his death, an autobiographical account of the years preceding that, reflections of providences and 'returns of prayer' covering the years from 1682 until his death, commonplace notes from the sayings of other preachers, biographical notes of his family, notes of church covenants and ministerial meetings in the West Riding, and a 'register' of his congregation giving biographical sketches of his neighbours, his fellow dissenters, and other notable individuals. Taken together they reveal more than the internal preoccupations of a dedicated Calvinist minister—an abiding awareness of the force of evil in the world, manifested through witchcraft, drunkenness, or other licentious behaviour, and a conviction that prayer and fasting were the only sure means of overcoming this, and a recording of divine judgement on the ungodly, and the providential reconciling of the misfortunes of the godly; they also record his public activities—relations with his congregation, with his wide cousinage within dissent, and with the authorities in both church and state. In these writings Heywood reveals the depth of his providential Calvinism and the extent to which the events of mid-century had formed his views. Delighted as he was by the declarations of indulgence by Charles II and James II, he noted with concern the implications of these royal edicts for parliamentary government, and the encouragement they gave to papists, one group which always remained outside his inclusive humanity.

Heywood's ministry was founded on prayer, recorded almost daily in his diary and often conducted in company with others. This lay at the heart of his healing ministry, and his conviction in its power led to much deliberation on the workings of God's providence, both in his personal life and in the public life of the church, as well as in the lives of the common stock of humanity. This was revealed in his close recording and meditations on the sudden deaths of those whom he knew personally or of which he learned from others, and especially on those of the ungodly persecutors of nonconformists. Such stress on divine intervention in the world brought Heywood into conflict with the Anglican clergy of the area, and in particular with Dr Hooke, who increasingly looked to natural causes in the explanation of misfortune. Heywood himself eventually became more cautious about invoking divine intervention, especially in cases which related to members of the established church, but it remained true that his life was marked by a constant awareness of his own and his associates' relationship with their maker. This clearly drew on the puritan tradition of the earlier seventeenth century, but it also reflected his contemporary position for much of his life as a minister barred from following his true vocation and regularly harassed by the authorities for attempting to practise it. He recorded his views in *Israel's Lamentation after the Lord* (1683) when he wrote, 'It is dreadful indeed to see debauchery in the land abounding, and the basest of men vent personal malice against God's dearest children for no other fault than worshipping God, and praying for their persecutors' (p. 390). It is no surprise that he began his diary after the introduction of the Five Mile Act.

Heywood was a prominent figure among his fellow ministers, often presiding at their meetings. He recorded the lives of his contemporaries, providing Edmund Calamy with much material for his study of those ejected in 1662. He published a life of his father-in-law, John Angier, and also wrote a biography of Richard Frankland, who ran the dissenting academy attended by his sons. His pastoral writings continued to the end of his life, with a flurry of publications, most of which he financed himself, from the later 1690s when his health made travel less easy. They continued in the vein of practical divinity established in his earlier works, though with an increasing concern with preparation for death, comfort for mourners and the after-life, and they make frequent reference to the writings of contemporaries such as Richard Baxter and Henry Newcome, as well as reminding his readers of their heritage going back to the Marian martyrs. It was this which formed the argument of his final volume, entitled *The Two Worlds; Present and Future, Visible and Invisible* (1701) and dedicated to his relations living in Lancashire, in which he urged them to hold fast to the observance of their ancestors.

Heywood's legacies Heywood's sons both proceeded to the ministry, John at Rotherham and Pontefract, and Eliezar in the Sheffield area. Heywood's income from his congregation was always modest but he acquired an extensive library, numbering 265 titles when listed in 1664 and valued at £20 at his death. This he left to be divided between his two sons, his widow first having choice of ten volumes. He also acquired lands in Ovenden and Sowerby in the parish of Halifax to add to his property at Northowram and to the estate at Little Lever which he had inherited. His widow was given a life interest in certain of the properties and the estate then passed to his two sons, with the house in Ovenden going to a grandson, Timothy. Heywood's goods were valued at £132 at the time of his death, and reveal a modest if well-appointed house, with a portrait of himself hanging in the parlour. No monument was erected to him, though the chapel in Northowram, rebuilt in the nineteenth century, bears his name. In the absence of an epitaph his own review of his life, written on 15 March 1695, can stand as an assessment of his motives and achievement:

that I should be a publick preacher above 44 yeares, have such measure of health, liberty, opportunitys, more then most of my brethren, some good successe and fruit of my poor labours, marry famous Mr Angier's daughter, print so many bookes, injoy so many comforts of life, bring up two sons to be ministers, build a chappel, help so many ministers and Christians in their necessitys by my self and others, and yet have a competency my self and wife to live upon, nothing more improbable then these things and many more experiments I might produce, which I record not for ostentation but to set off the riches of grace. (*Oliver Heywood*, ed. Turner, 3.297)

WILLIAM JOSEPH SHEILS

Sources *The Rev. Oliver Heywood … his autobiography, diaries, anecdote and event books*, ed. J. H. Turner, 4 vols. (1881–5) · *The whole works of the Rev. Oliver Heywood … with memoirs of his life*, ed. R. Slate and

W. Vint, 5 vols. (1825–7) · J. Hunter, *The rise of the old dissent, exemplified by the life of Oliver Heywood* (1842) · *Calamy rev.* · writings of Oliver Heywood, BL, Add. MSS 45963–45981 [mostly printed in Heywood, *Autobiography …*, ed. J. H. Turner] · original wills, June 1702, Borth. Inst. [will and inventory] · J. H. Turner, T. Dickenson, and O. Heywood, eds., *The nonconformist register of baptisms, marriages, and deaths* (1881) · W. Notestein, *Four worthies* (1956) · *The diary of Ralph Thoresby*, ed. J. Hunter, 2 vols. (1830) · [J. Hunter], ed., *Letters of eminent men, addressed to Ralph Thoresby*, 2 vols. (1832) · W. J. Sheils, 'Oliver Heywood and his congregation', *Voluntary religion*, ed. W. J. Sheils and D. Wood, SCH, 23 (1986), 261–77 · D. Harley, 'Mental illness, magical medicine and the devil in northern England, 1650–1700', *The medical revolution of the seventeenth century*, ed. R. French and A. Wear (1989), 114–45 · J. Smail, 'Local politics in Restoration England: religion, culture, and politics in Oliver Heywood's Halifax', *Protestant identities: religion, society and self-fashioning in post-Reformation England*, ed. M. McClendon, J. R. Ward, and M. MacDonald (1999), 234–48

Archives BL, notebooks, diaries, and papers, Add. MSS 45963–45981; 46172; Add. Ch. 71437–71490 · Halifax Central Library, notebook · NRA, diaries · W. Yorks. AS, Calderdale, notebook | BL, Add. MSS 45963–45981 · W. Yorks. AS, Leeds, Yorkshire Archaeological Society, letters to Ralph Thoresby

Likenesses stained-glass window, 20th cent. (after engraving), Northowram chapel, West Yorkshire · engraving, repro. in Notestein, *Four worthies*

Wealth at death £132 in goods, excl. lands: will and inventory, 1702, Borth. Inst., original wills

Peter Heywood (1772–1831), by John Simpson, 1822

Heywood, Peter (1772–1831), naval officer, was born at the Nunnery, near Douglas, Isle of Man, on 6 June 1772, the youngest of the seven children of Peter John Heywood (1739–1790), deemster of the Isle of Man and son of a former chief justice there, and Elizabeth, daughter of James Spedding of Whitehaven, Cumberland. His uncle was Captain Thomas Pasley RN, and probably for this reason Heywood entered the navy, on 11 October 1786, after schooling in Cheshire and Westmorland. Friendship between the Heywoods and Richard Betham, William Bligh's father-in-law, persuaded Bligh to take Heywood as a volunteer aboard the *Bounty* on 27 August 1787 and on 28 October to promote him to midshipman.

When the mutiny broke out on 28 April 1789, Heywood's attitude was ambiguous. At his court martial he claimed to have been asleep, without knowledge of the mutiny until that moment, and then kept below by force until the launch was ready to receive Bligh and his party. But later statements, by John Adams in 1825 and in the journal of James Morrison, boatswain's mate, indicate that Heywood knew of Christian's plans to desert or take the ship by force. Heywood was unable, convincingly, to refute statements that he had laughed at Bligh while held captive, had held a cutlass and helped hoist out the launch. In the confusion of the moment he may well, as a boy of sixteen, have done so. He admitted at his trial that he was afraid of going to almost certain death in the launch with Bligh and since it could not hold all those who wished to go, remained in the *Bounty*.

The mutineers landed at Tahiti and then split into two parties, some, including Heywood, remaining on land, and the others taking to sea again in the *Bounty*. When, on 23 March 1791, the *Pandora*, under Captain Edward Edwards, arrived in search of the mutineers, Heywood at once surrendered. The remainder were arrested by the next day and all fourteen were immediately put in irons, and into a specially built roundhouse, nicknamed 'Pandora's box', 11 by 18 feet, built on the after part of the quarter-deck, ventilated through two small iron gratings. Here they were kept under a 24-hour guard, though on full rations. Captain Edwards was afraid the prisoners would infect his own crew with mutiny and his harsh treatment was meant to prevent this. Nothing was discovered of the mutineers who had quitted Tahiti in the *Bounty*, despite a prolonged, though increasingly perfunctory, search. On 28 August the *Pandora*, while negotiating the Endeavour Strait, struck on the reef since known by her name. Three prisoners were released to man the pumps and all the remaining prisoners, bar one, were released in the last minutes, but four were drowned as the ship sank rapidly. For nineteen days the survivors remained on a small nearby key, preparing to sail on to the nearest European settlement, the Dutch colony of Timor. All were in great distress but the prisoners were left naked, without shelter or sufficient food. Both at Batavia, and on the passage to the Cape of Good Hope in a Dutch merchant ship, this severe treatment continued. Yet at Batavia, Heywood was permitted to send his family the first news of his survival they had received.

At the Cape, Heywood was transferred to the *Gorgon*, where he was allowed daily exercise on deck, and was less rigorously confined. On arrival at Spithead on 19 June 1792 Heywood was sent on board the *Hector* (74 guns) whose captain, afterwards Sir George Montagu, a close friend of Captain Pasley, treated him with humanity. Pasley arranged legal advice for his nephew and a counsel, Aaron Graham, former deputy judge-advocate at courts martial on the Newfoundland station. But in letters to Heywood's sister, he regretted that Heywood had made no public protestation of loyalty during the mutiny and at best had appeared neutral, which alone was sufficient to condemn him. Heywood's request for a separate trial was rejected and on 12 September he, with the other prisoners, was court-martialled on the *Duke*. Heywood was fortunate in his connections for, among the members of the court, were Captain George Montagu and Captain Albermarle Bertie, a relation by marriage, both of whom had already shown him much kindness, while his family used all the interest at their command to support and protect him. The trial lasted for six days, and on 18 September they were all sentenced to death; but Heywood was strongly recommended to mercy and received a royal pardon on 27 October.

Lord Hood, who had been president of the court, advised Heywood to continue in the service, and offered to take him with him in the *Victory*. But on 17 May 1793 he joined his uncle Pasley's ship, the *Bellerophon*, later moving to the frigate *Niger* with Captain Legge. On 23 September 1793 he was moved into the *Queen Charlotte*, bearing the flag of Lord Howe, with Sir Roger Curtis, captain of the fleet, Captain Sir Andrew Snape Douglas, and Captain Sir Hugh C. Christian, all of whom had been members of the court martial, and who remained his friends and patrons. In the actions of 28 and 29 May and 1 June 1794 Heywood acted as captain's aide-de-camp, and on the return of the fleet to Spithead was one of the two midshipmen appointed to attend the side when the king came on board the *Queen Charlotte*.

Once doubts as to Heywood's fitness to hold naval rank after his court martial were resolved, Lord Howe gave him an acting commission as lieutenant in the *Robust* in August 1794, which was confirmed on 9 March 1795, when he was appointed to the fire-ship *Incendiary*. On 23 June he was lieutenant of the *Nymphe* in the action off Lorient. He joined the East India station in the *Fox*, early in 1796, remaining in her until 18 June 1798 when he was moved with his captain and cousin, Pulteney Malcolm, into the *Suffolk* bearing the flag of Vice-Admiral Rainier. Heywood had been recommended to Rainier by Earl Spencer, then first lord of the Admiralty, who believed Heywood's conviction should not debar him from further promotion, especially in consideration of his subsequent good behaviour. In August 1800 Heywood was accordingly promoted commander of the bomb-vessel *Vulcan* and thereafter by acting orders from Rainier commanded various post ships until 5 April 1803, when he was confirmed in post rank. In January 1805 as a result of ill health and the death of his eldest brother, Admiral Rainier gave him leave to return home, warmly commending his services and character.

On 20 October 1806 Heywood was appointed flag captain to Rear-Admiral George Murray in the *Polyphemus* first at the Cape of Good Hope and later in the River Plate. In May 1808 he commanded the *Donegal* off Brest and in the Bay of Biscay. While in company with the *Caesar* and *Defiance*, on 25 February 1809 he attacked and destroyed three French frigates, part of a squadron which had escaped earlier from Brest and taken shelter in Sables d'Olonne. For this he received the Admiralty's thanks, on 18 March, and in the following May took command of the *Nereus*, a newly built frigate, in which he went out to the Mediterranean, and in April 1810 brought Lord Collingwood's body back to England. In retirement Heywood considered Collingwood had been a brave, able, refined, and cultivated man, equal in merit to Nelson, whom he thought a 'rough kind of fire-eater'.

Heywood remained in the *Nereus*, employed on the east coast of South America, receiving the thanks of British merchants at Buenos Aires twice in 1811 and again in 1813, for his protection of their interests. He returned to England, in October 1813, in the *Montagu* to take command in the North Sea until April 1814. Having accompanied Louis XVIII to France and evacuated part of the British army from Bordeaux, at the subsequent naval review the *Montagu*, wearing the flag of Sir Thomas Byam Martin, led the fleet in manoeuvres before the allied sovereigns.

On Napoleon's escape from Elba, Heywood, still in the *Montagu*, joined Lord Exmouth in the Mediterranean on 20 May 1815, and transported British and imperial troops from Naples to Genoa and Marseilles. Heywood then served as senior officer at Gibraltar until February 1816 when he rejoined Exmouth in his first mission to the Barbary States. The *Montagu* was paid off at Chatham on 16 July, and Heywood did not serve again, though in 1818 he was offered the command of the Canadian lakes and later the post of Admiralty hydrographer, for which he successfully recommended Rear-Admiral Francis Beaufort. This offer indicates the respect in which his abilities as a hydrographer were held. While in the East Indies he had surveyed much of the east coast of Ceylon and the adjoining mainland. Admiralty charts published later were based on this work Heywood presented to the Admiralty in 1805. In South America he carried out a number of surveys, the best known being of the River Plate. His work here and in the East Indies was used by James Horsburgh, hydrographer to the East India Company. After his court martial Heywood had prepared a Tahitian vocabulary, based on over two years' contact with the language. This useful work was presented to the first British missionaries sent there in 1796. Though it survives only in fragments, chiefly in the correspondence of the London Missionary Society, it is historically important for the period when the European impact on Tahitian culture was first felt.

On 31 July 1816 Heywood married Frances Joliffe (1782–1863), the daughter of Colonel Graham of Stirlingshire and widow of an East India Company servant. Mrs Joliffe may have heard of Heywood from her uncle Aaron Graham, but she first met him in the scientific and literary circle she entertained at Dulwich, where she lived with her only child, Diana, and which included Sir Joseph Banks and other fellows of the Royal Society. After their marriage the Heywoods lived first at Clapham, then at Highgate, where their house was a centre for political, religious, and literary discussions. Among their friends were Sir Thomas Phillips, collector of manuscripts, and

San Martín, the South American patriot, and they were early patrons of the painter Clarkson Stanfield. Heywood was attached to his stepdaughter and in 1830 promoted her marriage to Captain Edward Belcher RN.

Heywood was at his best in conversation with small groups of friends, when 'his serious sort of countenance … brightened in argument' (*United Service Journal*, 1831, 481). A contemporary description of him as 'rather above middle size, of a spare habit' (ibid.) but with good features, is confirmed by his portrait. In politics he was a whig who favoured Roman Catholic emancipation. He became ill in 1827, possibly with a heart complaint, since he reputedly found Highgate Hill too taxing. For this reason, in 1829, the family moved to the recently built Cumberland Terrace, where Heywood caught a chill in 1831. He died there, at number 26, after a short illness, on 10 February and was buried on 18 February at St Michael's Church, Highgate.

Heywood once declared he would be glad to live his life over again, exactly as it had been. For most men, the mutiny on the *Bounty* and its aftermath would have proved an irreparable block to future advancement, but strong naval interest and connections, in the customary eighteenth-century manner, ensured Heywood not only a pardon but an honourable and modestly distinguished career, with few of the gaps in employment and thus promotion most naval officers experienced. Heywood did not forgive Bligh for jeopardizing his life, and his lengthy contribution to Marshall's *Royal Naval Biography* in 1825 is, in part, an attack on Bligh's fitness to command, in justification of Heywood's part in the mutiny. This provided the basis for the subsequent, traditional picture of Bligh as an incompetent tyrant, reinforced by, among others, Lady Belcher in her book of 1870 on the mutineers. Yet Heywood's advancement was also the result of his professional abilities, and he formed one of a group of more scientific naval officers devoted to improvements in charting and surveying an expanding empire and to wider intellectual and liberal concerns.

J. K. LAUGHTON, rev. P. K. CRIMMIN

Sources J. Marshall, *Royal naval biography*, 2/2 (1825), 747–97 · A. G. K. L'Estrange, *Lady Belcher and her friends* (1891) · *A memoir of the late Captain Peter Heywood … with extracts from his diaries and correspondence*, ed. E. Tagart (1832) · J. Barrow, *The eventful history of the mutiny and piratical seizure of H.M.S. Bounty* (1831) · BL, Heywood MSS, vol. 12, Add. MS 45974, fols. 44–56b · *United Service Journal*, 1 (1831), 468–81 · *United Service Journal*, 1 (1833), 92 · D. Syrett and R. L. DiNardo, *The commissioned sea officers of the Royal Navy, 1660–1815*, rev. edn, Occasional Publications of the Navy RS, 1 (1994), 217 · D. Lyon, *The sailing navy list: all the ships of the Royal Navy, built, purchased and captured, 1688–1860* (1993) · will, PRO, PROB 1/1785 · parish register (burials), St Michael, Highgate, London, 1831 · G. S. Graham and R. A. Humphreys, eds., *The navy and South America, 1807–1823*, Navy RS, 104 (1962) · A. C. F. David, notes, *Mariner's Mirror*, 73 (1987), 213 · A. C. F. David, *Mariner's Mirror*, 74 (1988), 107 [review of R. E. Du Rietz, *Banksia 3: Peter Heywood's Tahitian vocabulary and the narratives by James Morrison* (1986)] · Burke, *Gen. GB* · G. Kennedy, *Bligh* (1978) · C. Cairne, *A history of the churches of the rural deanery of Whitehaven* (1916) · parish register (births), St James, Whitehaven, 1772 · A. C. F. David, 'From mutineer to hydrographer: the surveying career of Peter Heywood', *International Hydrographic Review*, new ser., 3/2 (2002), 6–11

Archives Admiralty Library, extracts from Heywood's journal · Manx National Heritage Library, Douglas, Isle of Man, corresp. and papers relating to his court martial as a *Bounty* mutineer · Newberry Library, Chicago, MSE SH5078
Likenesses J. Simpson, oils, 1822, NMM [see illus.]

Heywood, Robert (1573/4–1646/7), poet, was probably born in Heywood, in the parish of Bury, Lancashire, the eldest son of Peter Heywood of Heywood, gentleman (d. 1600) and his wife, Margery (d. 1602), daughter of Roger Gartside, gentleman. He was educated locally, and on 11 July 1589, aged fifteen, he entered Brasenose College, Oxford, although he does not appear to have gained a degree. He subsequently returned to Lancashire and upon his father's death in 1600 he inherited the estate of Heywood Hall and property throughout south-east Lancashire.

At some point before 1607 Heywood married Margaret Ashton (d. 1665), daughter and coheir of John Ashton of Penketh, Lancashire, gentleman. The couple settled at Heywood Hall, which was reportedly rebuilt in 1611, and had six surviving children. From this point onwards Heywood gradually acquired wealth and an improved social standing. In 1618 he was appointed high constable for Salford hundred in Lancashire, and by 1622 he was listed as the second wealthiest landowner in his parish. In 1631 he paid £10 for his distraint of knighthood fine.

Heywood also secured a local reputation as a prominent patron of godliness and learning. Between 1618 and 1624 he procured joint ownership of the advowsons of the nearby parishes of Radcliffe and Middleton, Lancashire. The later appointment of two puritan ministers in these parishes suggests that he moved easily within nonconforming circles. About 1640 he rebuilt Heywood Chapel, which lay upon his estates, at an estimated personal cost of £150. At that time he was also composing poetry, although only one work has survived. His *Observations and Instructions, Divine and Moral* was a lengthy visionary piece, divided into five 'centuries' that reflected his own godly perspective on the nature of faith and works. It may have been this work that attracted the scholar and poet Richard James to Heywood Hall during his tour of Lancashire about 1636. In his *Iter Lancastrense*, James recalled fondly to Heywood 'the fairnesse of thy seat and courtesie', and his welcome there:

> Such things I sawe and thought, in Lancashire,
> At Heywood hall to trading Rachdale neere.
> My safe bould harbour Heywood, much I owe,
> Of praise and thanks to yᵉ where ere I goe.
> (James, 2, 12)

After the outbreak of the civil wars in Lancashire, Heywood supported the parliamentarian cause, although he played no active part in the conflict. He became vexed by the behaviour of his sons Peter and John, both of whom were prominent local royalists, and in his final will of 8 October 1646 he stated that their legacies were to be paid only after their submission to parliament. He was buried in Bury parish on 19 January 1647. His godly reputation was affirmed by a distant relative, the nonconformist divine Oliver Heywood, who remembered him as 'a pious reverend old gentleman and an excellent poet' (*Oliver Heywood*, 1.17).

S. J. GUSCOTT

Sources VCH Lancashire, 5.66, 136, 138–40, 204 • R. Heywood, *Observations and instructions, divine and moral, in verse*, ed. J. Crossley, old ser., Chetham Society, 76 (1869) • W. J. Lowenberg, H. Brierley, and A. Sparke, eds., *The registers of the parish church of Bury in the county of Lancaster: christenings, burials and weddings*, 3 vols., Lancashire Parish Register Society, 1, 10, 24 (1898–1905) • R. James, *Iter Lancastrense: a poem, written AD 1636, by the Rev. Richard James*, ed. T. Corser, Chetham Society, 7 (1845) • Foster, *Alum. Oxon.* • J. H. Stanning and J. Brownbill, eds., *The royalist composition papers*, 3, ed. J. H. Stanning, Lancashire and Cheshire RS, 29 (1896) • W. Dugdale, *The visitation of the county palatine of Lancaster, made in the year 1664–5*, ed. F. R. Raines, 2, Chetham Society, 85 (1872), 113 • *The Rev. Oliver Heywood … his autobiography, diaries, anecdote and event books*, ed. J. H. Turner, 1 (1881), 17 • *Miscellanies, relating to Lancashire and Cheshire*, 1, Lancashire and Cheshire RS, 12 (1885), 161, 216

Wealth at death see *VCH Lancashire*; Raines, ed., *The visitation*

Heywood, Robert (1786–1868), cotton manufacturer, was born on 30 June 1786 at Little Bolton in Lancashire, the only son of John Heywood (1756–1832), quilting manufacturer, and his first wife, Betty (d. 1789). Robert Heywood had two half-sisters from his father's second marriage, Hannah and Mary. The Heywood family had been dissenters for several generations, and were probably related to the descendants of Oliver Heywood, the celebrated seventeenth-century Presbyterian clergyman. At the age of seven, Robert Heywood went to Bolton grammar school under the tuition of the Revd Joseph Lemprière. However, Lemprière appears to have kept a strict regime at the grammar school, and Heywood was withdrawn by his father. Following a short spell at a clergyman's school, he attended a new Unitarian school in Bolton. His Unitarian education instilled in him principles that he was to maintain for the rest of his life—they dictated much of his later work, and provided him with the friends, business partners, and political allies who were to prove vital during his adult life.

Although he was a Liberal in politics, Heywood's business ventures were remarkably conservative. John Heywood had been in partnership with a Thomas Naylor, manufacturing fustians and quiltings, but when Naylor died in 1803, Robert Heywood became a partner in the new firm of John Heywood & Son, quilting manufacturers. The firm prospered, though Robert was clearly the junior partner. John Heywood had effective control of the business, but when his health began to fail in the early 1820s, Charles Darbishire (1798–1874) was brought in as manager, keeping this position until he retired in 1842. There was little capital re-investment in the business enterprise, and even when Robert Heywood stopped manufacturing cloth in 1854 he was still relying on handlooms. However, the Heywoods did lend heavily, and it was by this means that Heywood acquired the Crescent Bleach works in Salford; forced to foreclose on a bad debt and unable to find a willing tenant, he appointed a manager and added bleaching to his business portfolio.

Robert Heywood had an almost morbid attachment to his father, in spite of, or possibly because of, being very much under his control. Even when he was in his thirties, he had to plead for permission to visit Paris. He lived with his father until the latter died in 1832, leaving Robert £21,000. On this occasion Robert noted in his diary 'I lost the greatest friend on earth this forenoon.' For months afterwards he recorded dreams of his father and it was fifteen months after his father's death that he could first record a day when he had not wept. By 1834, however, he had recovered sufficiently to take a further trip abroad. In 1848 Heywood married Elizabeth Shawcross (b. c.1816), the daughter of a Manchester cotton merchant. They had three children, John, Mary, and Robert.

Heywood was ultimately a very widely travelled man. As well as several trips to Scotland, Ireland, and France, he undertook rigorous journeys to more distant destinations. His first major overseas journey was to Italy in 1826. This was followed by America in 1834, the Levant in 1845, a three-month honeymoon tour round revolutionary Europe in 1848, and Russia in 1858. It was his habit to keep travel diaries of all his trips; four were published in 1919. It would appear that these journeys were taken purely for leisure, as there are very few mentions of trade in the diaries and correspondence relating to his trips abroad. Heywood never saw travel as an opportunity to expand his business empire.

Heywood's public life began with his Unitarianism. He was a chapel trustee from the age of twenty-five, and a Sunday school teacher for over fifty years. He championed numerous public causes; although he was a rather reluctant political figure, not a notable orator, and not interested in self-glory, the efficiency and businesslike attitude with which he approached his public life made him rather more effective than many of his contemporaries. His main political concerns were dictated by his belief in the necessity of democratizing local and national government and creating a better environment for the people of Bolton. To this end he was involved in almost every act of public philanthropy in the town, and almost every institution promoting social welfare in Bolton benefited from his time and money. He was secretary of the Bolton Dispensary from 1813 until his death; co-founder of the exchange news room in 1829; long-standing benefactor of the mechanics' institution, being president in 1852 and vice-president until his death; and trustee of Great Bolton from 1826, acting as treasurer from 1831 to 1843. He was also instrumental in obtaining for Bolton its charter of incorporation in 1838, being one of the deputation which presented the petition to parliament, and in 1840 he became the town's second mayor (Charles Darbishire, his friend and business manager had been the first). He was an earnest supporter and advocate of teetotalism, and gave evidence to parliament in favour of the Ten Hours Bill. He provided land for one of Bolton's first public parks and also gave large sums of money to the building of the Bath assembly rooms, among other public buildings and institutions.

Heywood died at his home, The Pike, Bolton Moor, on 22

October 1868 and was buried four days later at Bolton cemetery. He was survived by his wife. One of his contemporaries noted that he was 'the tried friend of popular liberty, popular enfranchisement, popular enlightenment, and popular progress'. Indeed, his contribution to Bolton life was such that an obituarist declared 'To give a detailed biography of such a life would be to write the local history of our town' (*Bolton Journal*). A. J. GRITT

Sources W. E. Brown, *Robert Heywood of Bolton, 1786–1868* (1970) · *Bolton Journal* (26 Oct 1868) · biographical cuttings, Bolton Library · W. Brimelow, *Political and parliamentary history of Bolton* (1882) · R. Poole, *Leisure in Bolton, 1750–1900* (1982) · P. Taylor, 'A divided middle class: Bolton, 1790–1850', *Manchester Region History Review*, 6 (1992), 3–15 · J. C. Scholes, *History of Bolton* (1892) · G. M. Ramsden, *A responsible society: the life and times of the congregation of Bank Street Chapel, Bolton, Lancashire* (privately printed, 1985) · *CGPLA Eng. & Wales* (1869)
Archives Bolton Central Library, personal, political, and business papers
Likenesses photograph, *c.*1850–1860, Bolton Library · photograph, *c.*1850–1860, Bank Street Chapel, Bolton
Wealth at death under £140,000: probate, 18 June 1869, *CGPLA Eng. & Wales*

Heywood, Samuel (1753–1828), judge and author, was born on 8 October 1753 at Liverpool, the eldest of four children of Benjamin Heywood (1731–1795), merchant, and his wife, Phoebe (*b.* 1729), daughter of Samuel Ogden of Liverpool. He was educated at the dissenting academy at Warrington, where the prevailing religious ethos tended towards Unitarianism, and subsequently at Trinity Hall, Cambridge. At Trinity Hall he incurred the displeasure of the college authorities, and in particular the future bishop Samuel Hallifax, by absenting himself from Anglican worship in the college chapel. In order to avoid the subscription to the Thirty-Nine Articles required on graduation at Cambridge, he did not take a degree. Making the law his career, he studied at the Inner Temple, was called to the bar in 1778, and became a serjeant-at-law in 1794. He practised extensively on the northern circuit, where he became friendly with John Scott, the future Lord Eldon, and John Lee. His vehement dissenting and whig principles were amusingly recounted by Eldon, who quoted Lee as saying: 'Well, Sam … thou art, in Truth a Dissenter! dissenting more than anybody I ever knew!—for thou agreest with nobody about any thing!' (Lincoln and McEwen, 112).

Heywood married Susanna (*bap.* 1758, *d.* 1822), the daughter of John Cornwall, merchant, of London, at St Bride's, Fleet Street, on 1 January 1781. They had one son and four daughters; only their daughter Ann, who married Colonel Granville Eliot, survived Heywood. The debates over the attempts to secure repeal of the Test and Corporation Acts in the late 1780s spurred Heywood into a powerful attack on the system of religious tests which were designed to exclude dissenters from public office. This took the form of *The Right of Protestant Dissenters to a Compleat Toleration Asserted* (1787; 2nd edn, 1789), a scholarly history of the Test and Corporation Acts infused with a radical polemic against the Anglican hegemony. Writing under the pseudonym A Layman, he concluded:

> We may congratulate a country on the wonderful uniformity which takes place as to the employments within this Act, when not even a bug can be destroyed within the purlieus of the royal household but by the hallowed fingers of a communicant; nor a post letter conveyed to any part of the kingdom by horses belonging to a Protestant Dissenter. (p. 76)

In 1790 he took his arguments further in *High Church Politics*, in which he blamed a 'high church party', and Bishop Samuel Horsley in particular, for bringing a new climate of intolerance into public life.

His opinions and his prowess in expressing them brought Heywood to the centre of radicalism in religion and whiggism in politics. He supported, and was a trustee of, the Unitarian chapel opened by Theophilus Lindsey in Essex Street, London. He became a friend of Charles James Fox, and contributed material to the latter's *History of the Early Part of the Reign of James II* (1808) and, in his *Vindication of Mr Fox's History* (1811), defended his late friend's book against the strictures of the Pittite George Rose. He was consulted by Charles Grey, Lord Howick, in 1807 over the Catholic relief (and its possible extension to dissenters) proposed by the 'ministry of all the talents'. It was through Grey's influence that Heywood was made a judge of the Carmarthen circuit in 1807 and hence became one of the very few professed dissenters to hold national office under the Test Act (Ditchfield). He already enjoyed the reputation of an expert on electoral law, publishing *Digest of the Law Concerning County Elections* in 1790 and *Digest of the Law Respecting Borough Elections* in 1797.

Heywood was taken ill with 'paralysis'—probably a stroke—while on circuit at Haverfordwest in August 1828. He died at Tenby on 11 September and was buried at Bristol on 19 September. He lived just long enough to see the repeal of the sacramental provisions of the Test and Corporation Acts which he had so sharply denounced. His career, like that of his friend John Lee, symbolizes the political alliance between whigs and dissenters, and the rising social status of the legal profession.

G. M. DITCHFIELD

Sources G. M. Ditchfield, 'A Unitarian view of English dissent in 1807', *Transactions of the Unitarian Historical Society*, 18/2 (1807), 1–16 · J. Hunter, *Familiae minorum gentium*, ed. J. W. Clay, 1, Harleian Society, 37 (1894) · H. W. Woolrych, *Lives of eminent serjeants-at-law of the English bar*, 2 vols. (1869) · *Lord Eldon's anecdote book*, ed. A. L. J. Lincoln and R. L. McEwen (1960) · Allibone, *Dict.* · W. Field, *Memoirs of the life, writings and opinions of the Rev. Samuel Parr*, 2 vols. (1828), vol. 1, p. 235 · W. Prest, 'Law, lawyers and rational dissent', *Enlightenment and religion: rational dissent in eighteenth-century Britain*, ed. K. Haakonssen (1998), 169–92 · A. Lawyer, 'The deeds of Essex Chapel', *Transactions of the Unitarian Historical Society*, 1 (1916–18), 260–65 · J. R. Dinwiddy, 'Charles James Fox as historian', *HJ*, 12 (1969), 23–34 · *Monthly Repository*, 9 (1814), 387 · C. J. Fox, *A history of the early part of the reign of James the Second, with an introductory chapter, to which is added an appendix* (1808) · *IGI* · will, PRO, PROB 11/1747, fols. 338r–391r
Archives BL, Add. MS 35095 · Shrops. RRC, diaries and papers | JRL, Theophilus Lindsey corresp. · U. Durham, Grey MSS
Wealth at death property in Bedford Place, Russell Square, London and in co. Armagh; also long dated annuities: will, PRO, PROB 11/1747, fols. 338r–391r

Heywood, Thomas (*c*.1573–1641), playwright and poet, was probably born late in 1573 in Lincolnshire. On 3 October 1623 he gave his age as '49 or thereabouts' and as '50 yeares, or neare upon' (Sisson, 58), and on five separate occasions in his writings he refers to himself as a native of Lincolnshire. A. M. Clark presents convincing evidence, much of it unknown to earlier biographers, that the dramatist was the son of Robert Heywood (*c*.1543–1593), rector of Rothwell and Ashby-cum-Fenby, Lincolnshire, and his wife, Elizabeth. The family came originally from Mottram, Cheshire, but Robert Heywood moved to Lincolnshire after being ordained by the bishop of Chester in 1562; he had been educated at Magdalene College, Cambridge. Heywood's paternal uncle Edmund Heywood (*d*. 1624) worked for many years in the office of the exchequer and was granted a coat of arms before 1616.

Thomas Heywood matriculated as a pensioner from Emmanuel College, Cambridge, in 1591; in 1658 William Cartwright claimed that he had been a fellow of Peterhouse. Heywood later wrote in *An Apology for Actors* (1612) that during his time at Cambridge he saw 'tragedyes, comedyes, historyes, pastorals and shewes, publickly acted, in which the graduates of good place and standing have bene specially parted' (*An Apology*, 28). However, his education was probably cut short by the death of his father in February 1593, after which he moved to London and plunged into the literary scene there. Thus began a literary career astonishing not only for its length (nearly fifty years), but for the sheer range of Heywood's output, covering nearly all the genres available to him.

Early career Heywood's first published effort was a narrative poem, *Oenone and Paris* (1594), drawn from Ovid's *Heroides* and to a lesser extent from Lucian. Both classical authors would exert a strong influence on Heywood throughout his career. The poem is also a close imitation of Shakespeare's *Venus and Adonis* (1593), marking the beginning of Shakespeare's pervasive influence on Heywood's writing. It has been argued that Heywood wrote early versions of several later plays in 1594–5 (particularly *The Rape of Lucrece*, based partly on Shakespeare's poem, and *The Four Prentices of London*), and it may have been about this time that he contributed to *Sir Thomas More* (BL, Harley MS 7368), a play whose Hand D is widely accepted as Shakespeare's.

The first concrete evidence of Heywood's playwriting is a payment in Philip Henslowe's *Diary* in October 1596 for 'hawodes bocke' (*Henslowe's Diary*, 50), by which time he was probably also working as an actor. On 25 March 1598 Heywood signed an agreement to act exclusively for Henslowe over the next two years, and between December 1598 and February 1599 he wrote at least two plays for Henslowe's Admiral's Men: 'War without Blows and Love without Suit' and 'Joan is as Good as my Lady' (both now lost). In the autumn of 1598 Francis Meres's *Palladis tamia* listed Heywood among 'the best for Comedy' along with other writers for Admiral's Men.

Heywood's one surviving play from this period—the two-part *King Edward IV* (first printed 1599, with five later editions)—was performed not by Henslowe's company, but by the rival Derby's Men. Both parts are distinguished by features which would become characteristic of Heywood's drama: episodic plots, sympathetic treatment of tradesmen and apprentices, strong female characters, and a focus on Christian mercy and forgiveness rather than revenge. Part one depicts King Edward mingling among his loyal subjects in disguise (in the manner of Shakespeare's *Henry V*), then wooing and winning goldsmith's wife Jane Shore as his mistress. Part two opens with Edward's conquest of France, but is mainly concerned with Jane Shore's fall from grace under Edward's successor Richard III, and the mercy shown by her loyal husband, Matthew, and by Edward's widow, Elizabeth.

By the autumn of 1601 Heywood had become a leading member of the earl of Worcester's company of players, which became Queen Anne's Men in 1603. This company moved among the Boar's Head, Rose, and Curtain theatres before finally finding a permanent home at the Red Bull in 1607. Meanwhile Heywood had married and settled in St Saviour's parish, Southwark. His wife's name is unknown, but *contra* Clark, he was not the Thomas Heywood who married Anne Buttler, servant, in St Antholin's in 1603. As Thomas 'Hayward', player, he had at least four children baptized at St Saviour's: Mary (5 October 1600), Joseph (5 June 1603), Alice (16 September 1604), and Richard (5 September 1605). He was probably also the father of Frances (4 March 1598) and Edie (23 December 1610). With a stable family life and a steady income as a sharer in the Queen's Men, Heywood entered into the most productive period of his dramatic career. Several of the plays he wrote at Henslowe's Rose in 1602–3 are preserved only as titles '1 Lady Jane', 'Cutting Dick', 'Christmas comes but once a year', 'The Blind Eat many a Fly', but many more of his plays from this era survive, showing him exploring favourite themes and blossoming as a playwright.

Success on the stage: Heywood's prime as a playwright Heywood achieved his greatest popular success (and ensured his modern reputation) with his domestic dramas. These recall medieval morality plays in their structure, generally contrasting a prodigal spouse with a patient, virtuous one, but they add layers of complexity. The earliest of Heywood's domestic plays, the dark comedy *How a Man may Choose a Good Wife from a Bad* (*c*.1601, printed 1602) tells the story of Arthur, who tries to poison his loyal wife in order to marry a prostitute but unwittingly gives her a sleeping potion instead. While fleeing from the authorities, he meets his wife but does not recognize her, and only when Arthur is about to be executed for his crime does the wife reveal herself and save him. In *The Wise Woman of Hogsdon* (written *c*.1604, published 1638), by contrast, Heywood turns the prodigal husband story into a farce. Reluctant groom Chartley flees on the eve of his wedding to gamble with his dissolute friends, but the wise woman of the title (actually a witch) orchestrates a series of comic plots whereby Chartley contracts marriage with two other women but ends up married to his original bride. Heywood may have had a hand in *The Fair Maid of the Exchange* (written c.1602, published 1607), another domestic comedy with a strong heroine, but is probably not its primary author.

The masterpiece among Heywood's domestic plays is the tragedy *A Woman Killed with Kindness* (written 1603). The play begins with the marriage of Anne Acton to John Frankford, but here (as in *Edward IV*) it is the wife who is prodigal, having an affair with Frankford's best friend, Wendoll. Upon discovering the affair Frankford curbs his impulse for revenge and instead banishes his wife to his country estate with full provisions. Remorseful, Anne starves herself to death, but not before receiving Frankford's forgiveness on her deathbed. In a parallel subplot, Anne's brother Sir Francis Acton pays the debts of his disgraced enemy Sir Charles Mountford, whereupon Mountford offers Acton his virtuous sister Susan in marriage. The play was printed in 1607 with Heywood's name on the title-page for the first time, and with a self-deprecating prologue reflecting the modesty which was to be a hallmark of Heywood's writing.

Among Heywood's most interesting plays from this period are a series of adventure-romances, all written in the first decade of the seventeenth century but not published until many years later. The earliest of these, *The Four Prentices of London* (written 1599–1600, published 1615) opens with Godfrey of Bulloigne and his three noble brothers living in London as apprentices after their father's dispossession. They set off on a crusade to Jerusalem carrying the arms of their respective trades (a feature later satirized in Francis Beaumont's *Knight of the Burning Pestle*), trailed by their disguised sister Bella Franca, and encounter many improbable adventures before their reunion and ultimate victory in Jerusalem.

Fortune by Land and Sea and *The Fair Maid of the West, Part 1* (both written either in 1601–2 or in 1609) are more ambitious, being aptly described by Clark as 'half adventure play, half domestic tragicomedy' (Clark, 213). In both plays a middle-class hero (young Forrest and Spencer respectively) kills a powerful adversary in a tavern duel and is forced to flee overseas, and each hero loves an impossibly virtuous heroine (Anne Harding and Bess Bridges) with whom he is reunited after a series of wild adventures. *Fortune* centres its twin plots around the feuding Forrest and Harding families, while *The Fair Maid* focuses squarely on Bess Bridges, who rises from barmaid to become captain of a warship, exemplifying the kind of heroic woman who fascinated Heywood throughout his career. *Fortune* was not printed until 1655 (attributed to Heywood and William Rowley), *The Fair Maid* not until 1631, when it appeared along with its much later sequel (written c.1630).

Heywood also continued to integrate domestic situations into plays about royalty, as he had done in *Edward IV*. In *The Royal King and the Loyal Subject* (written c.1600, printed 1637), he adapts a novella from *Painter's Palace of Pleasure* about a king cruelly testing the loyalty of his steward, but changes the setting to England and adds a subplot with close parallels to *How a Man may Choose* and *Fortune by Land and Sea*. Heywood is probably also the author

of the manuscript play 'Tom a Lincoln' (BL, Add. MS 61745), a romance about the eponymous bastard son of King Arthur and his own two sons. It is based on Richard Johnson's 1607 pamphlet of the same name, but is also influenced by Shakespeare's *The Winter's Tale* and *The Tempest*.

Heywood's favourite monarch, however, was Queen Elizabeth. His two-part drama about Elizabeth, *If you Know not me, you Know Nobody* (c.1604–5, first printed 1605–6), is a veritable smorgasbord of his favourite themes. Part one (based closely on John Foxe's *Acts and Monuments*) deals with the trials of Elizabeth during the reign of her half-sister, Mary, ending with her triumphant accession to the throne. In part two the focus shifts to Sir Thomas Gresham, who builds the Royal Exchange while his prodigal nephew John cavorts with French prostitutes. Hobson the honest haberdasher teaches everyone the true meaning of charity before, abruptly, Queen Elizabeth is saved from assassination and defeats the Spanish Armada. The results, while less than satisfying dramatically, were extremely popular: part one went through eight printed editions, and part two went through four. All these editions were published anonymously, but Heywood was to recycle the material of part one many times in the coming decades, in works such as the prose *Gunaikeion* (1624) and *England's Elizabeth* (1631), and the rhymed *Life and Death of Queen Elizabeth* (1639).

Heywood's next play, *The Rape of Lucrece* (printed 1608), was also very popular, despite being a distinct oddity to modern eyes. It is a Roman revenge tragedy about the bloody rise of Tarquin Superbus and his wife, Tullia, and their fall at the hand of Brutus after Tarquin's son Sextus rapes Collatine's chaste wife, Lucrece. The rape itself closely follows Shakespeare's poem, leading Holaday to date the earliest version of the play to 1594, though 1606–7 is a more generally accepted date. The play contains many lighthearted songs, most sung by the nobleman Valerius, which many critics have found jarring and out of place. Five editions were printed by 1638, the last of these containing five additional songs.

Branching out: translations, non-dramatic poetry, and prose
Perhaps inspired by the success of *Lucrece*, Heywood next made a bid for literary respectability by immersing himself in the classics. In 1608 he published a prose translation (from the French of Lois Meigret Lyonnais) of Sallust's *Conspiracy of Catiline* and *War of Jugurtha*, with a prefatory epistle translated from Jean Bodin's *Methodus ad facilem historiarum cognitionem* and a dedication to Sir Thomas Somerset, the son of the earl of Worcester. Perhaps about this same time, an anonymous edition of Heywood's youthful translation of Ovid's *Ars amatoria* appeared, entitled *Love's School*. Though Heywood later complained angrily that it had been published without his consent, this translation became extremely popular, going through at least twelve printings in the seventeenth century.

More ambitious than either of these was *Troia Britannica* (1609), an original narrative poem of seventeen cantos, dedicated to Heywood's former patron the earl of Worcester. It begins with the Creation and goes through classical mythology and the fall of Troy, ending with a whirlwind history of Britain, from Brute's founding of London (or 'New Troy') to the accession of James I. Heywood drew on various classical and modern sources for this poem, including Chapman's translation of Homer, and also inserted several Ovidian poems and digressions praising music and poetry.

Soon afterwards Heywood set out to dramatize classical mythology in a series of spectacular, pageant-like plays known as *The Ages*. *The Golden Age* (printed 1611) tells the story of Saturn, Titan, and Jupiter; *The Silver Age* (printed 1612) concerns the further adventures of Jupiter and the early labours of Hercules; *The Brazen Age* (printed 1613) concerns the later labours of Hercules, and Jason and the golden fleece; and the two-part *The Iron Age* (printed 1632) tells the story of the Trojan War, strongly influenced by Shakespeare's *Troilus and Cressida*. Large portions of these plays (especially *The Golden Age*) are dramatizations of *Troia Britannica*, though there is also much new material, which Holaday ('Ages') suggests may be recycled from lost plays for Henslowe. *The Ages* became quite popular; according to Heywood's preface to *The Iron Age*, they were performed by two companies combined (probably the King's and Queen Anne's) and 'thronged three severall Theaters' (*Iron Age*, ed. Weiner, 2).

Heywood's first and best-known original prose work, *An Apology for Actors* (written *c*.1608, printed 1612) is a spirited and learned defence of the theatre against its enemies, filled with classical allusions and anecdotes, but also quite valuable for discussing recent stage history. It was published with a dedication to the earl of Worcester and commendatory verses from fellow playwright John Webster, fellow actors Richard Perkins, Christopher Beeston, and Robert Pallant, and John Taylor the Water-Poet. In a famous epistle to the printer, his friend Nicholas Okes, Heywood complains about William Jaggard's sloppy printing of *Troia Britannica* and Jaggard's inclusion of two poems from that work in the third edition of Shakespeare's *The Passionate Pilgrim* (1612), causing Shakespeare to be 'much offended' with Jaggard.

In 1612 Heywood wrote a commendatory poem for his Cambridge contemporary Henry Peacham's *Minerva Britanna*, followed by a funeral elegy for Prince Henry (1613), dedicated to Worcester and printed together with elegies by Webster and Cyril Tourneur. A few months later he published *Marriage Triumph* (1613), a poem honouring the marriage of Princess Elizabeth and the elector palatine. In 1614 he edited the play *Greenes Tu quoque* by John Cooke, praising both the deceased author and the recently deceased star of the play, fellow Queen's Man Thomas Greene. Heywood himself was praised in print by Webster, Thomas Freeman, and Richard Brathwaite between 1612 and 1614, and in 1614 he probably also travelled to Venice and Germany in the entourage of another former Cambridge contemporary, the earl of Southampton, as suggested by Holaday ('Low Countries'). About this time he also began compiling 'The lives of all the poets modern and foreign', which he worked on intermittently for two decades but unfortunately never published.

After this burst of activity and recognition, however, Heywood drops virtually out of sight for nearly a decade, publishing nothing between 1615 and 1624. This withdrawal from literary life may have resulted from the troubles of his acting company, Queen Anne's Men, which went into a long decline after the death of its leading actor and manager, Thomas Greene, in 1612. Heywood was one of several sharers who received black cloth for Queen Anne's funeral in May 1619, but the company was moribund by then; for the rest of his life Heywood belonged to no single company, though he often wrote for his former fellow actor Christopher Beeston's companies at the Cockpit. By October 1623 Heywood was living in St James's, Clerkenwell, London, where he remained for the rest of his life. His wife was still alive in 1624, when his uncle Edmund's will left a bequest to 'Thomas Heywoode and his wife', but on 18 January 1633, a 'Thomas Hayward & Jane Span' were married in St James's, Clerkenwell (Clark, 102).

Return to literature: *History of Women* and new plays In 1624 Heywood ended his long literary silence with *Gunaikeion, or, Nine Books of Various History Concerning Women*. This 466-page folio volume celebrates strong women throughout history, from mythological goddesses to earthly leaders such as Queen Elizabeth and Queen Anne, both of whom Heywood praises highly. In the dedication to his former patron the earl of Worcester, Heywood implies that he has had financial difficulties, and in the Latin colophon he claims that the book was conceived, written, and published within seventeen weeks. Some of the book is recycled from Heywood's earlier writing, but it also draws on a wide variety of other sources, documented by Martin and Clark. In the following year, Heywood published a *Funeral Elegy* for King James, also dedicated to Worcester, and in 1628 he wrote a commendatory poem for Matthew Mainwaring's *Vienna*.

Heywood was also writing plays again by this time, but not yet publishing them. On 2 September 1624 Sir Henry Herbert licensed 'a new Play, called The Captive, or, The Lost recovered: Written by Hayward' (Merchant, 19) for performance by Lady Elizabeth's Men at the Cockpit. This play, normally known as 'The Captives', survives only in Heywood's autograph manuscript (BL, Egerton MS 1994, fols. 52–73). The main plot, based on Plautus's *Rudens*, involves two Englishwomen imprisoned in a Marseilles brothel who escape from their evil pimp after a shipwreck and eventually marry their rescuers; the darkly farcical sub-plot, paralleled in *Gunaikeion*, depicts the corpse of a murdered abbot being used as a prop in a twisted series of revenge plots. 'The Escapes of Jupiter', an adaptation of scenes from *The Golden Age* and *The Silver Age*, immediately follows 'The Captives' in BL, Egerton MS 1994 (fols. 74–95), and is also in Heywood's handwriting. Heywood has often been credited with yet another play preserved in the same manuscript, but in a different hand: 'Dick of Devonshire', an adventure play with a romantic sub-plot, based on the

Spanish adventures of Richard Pike of Tavistock in 1625–6.

The English Traveller exhibits close similarities to 'The Captives', and must have been written about the same time, though it was not published for nearly a decade. Like 'The Captives' it has one plot drawn from Plautus (here *Mostelleria*), and another retold in *Gunaikeion*. The main plot is superficially parallel to that of *A Woman Killed with Kindness*, except that the prodigal woman is married to one man (Wincott) while being courted by another (Geraldine); she thus betrays both men, and is generally a much less sympathetic figure. In the complementary sub-plot a prodigal son destroys his absent father's house through debauchery, but is ultimately forgiven when the father returns from his travels.

After virtually abandoning print for fifteen years, in 1631 Heywood began preparing several of his unpublished early plays for the press, adding a fascinating and sometimes conflicting running commentary on the publication process itself. In part one of the two-part *The Fair Maid of the West* (printed 1631), Heywood notes that his plays have been published not in 'a large volume; but singly (as thou seest) with great modesty, and small noise' (Turner, 4). Yet in the following year, in the two-part *The Iron Age* (printed 1632), Heywood announced his intention to publish all five *Ages* plays in an elaborate annotated volume, an intention which he never realized. In 1633 he published *The English Traveller* with a famous preface in which he claims to have had 'either an entire hand or at the least a main finger' in 220 plays, saying that this one had only come 'accidentally to the press' and that 'it never was any great ambition in me to be in this way voluminously read' (Merchant, 108). Heywood also edited a reissue of Sir Richard Barckley's 33-year-old *Discourse of the Felicity of Man* (1631), and the first edition of Marlowe's *Jew of Malta* (1633), adding prologues and epilogues for the play's recent revivals at court and at the Cockpit.

Also in 1631 Heywood wrote and published the first of his lord mayors' pageants, *Londons jus honorarium*, for the Haberdashers' Company. By the end of the decade he had written and published six more lord mayors' pageants, all steeped in classical lore as well as religious imagery: *Londini artium & scientiarum scaturigo* (1632, for the Haberdashers'); *Londini emporia* (1633, Clothworkers'); *Londini sinus salutis* (1635, Ironmongers'); *Londini speculum* (1637, Haberdashers'); *Porta pietatis* (1638, Drapers'); and *Londini status pacatus* (1639, Drapers'). Heywood had been a booster of apprentices and tradesmen since his earliest plays, and his commentary in the printed editions shows him to have been on good terms with the guilds which sponsored the pageants.

Final years and Heywood's legacy Religious imagery and themes had always informed Heywood's work, but they became especially prominent in the 1630s—not only in his pageants, but in his second long narrative poem, *The Hierarchy of the Blessed Angels*, published in 1635 in a 630-page folio dedicated to Queen Henrietta Maria. This learned poem's nine books are each named after an angel or archangel; it begins by arguing for the existence of God,

describes the elaborate Christian hierarchy of angels and spirits, and recounts the temptations offered by evil spirits. Among the many digressions is a famous one in which Heywood warmly recalls famous English poets, including Shakespeare, Jonson, and Marlowe. At roughly the same time that he was writing about evil spirits for *The Hierarchy*, Heywood collaborated with Richard Brome on the journalistic play *The Late Lancashire Witches* (1634), written for the King's Men and published quickly to capitalize on a recent witchcraft scare in Lancashire. The same authors also apparently collaborated on the lost plays 'Sir Thomas Skink' and 'The Apprentice's Prize'.

The religious convictions displayed in *The Hierarchy* were both sincere and orthodox; Clark's argument that Heywood became a puritan late in life has been decisively refuted by Holaday ('Puritans'). Heywood waged a public battle in the 1630s against William Prynne, the puritan author of the anti-theatrical diatribe *Histriomastix* (1633), who had attacked Heywood and his *Apology for Actors* by name. Heywood had promised a reply to Prynne in the *English Traveller* preface (1633); in the preface to *A Maidenhead Well Lost* (printed 1634), he further denounces 'that most horrible Histriomastix', and in *A Challenge for Beauty* (printed 1636) he alludes to Prynne's 1634 imprisonment and punishment. Heywood never did reply at length to *Histriomastix*, though Clark argues that he satirized Prynne in his play *Love's Mistress, or, The Queen's Masque* (performed 1634, printed 1636).

The three plays just mentioned exhibit many similarities to Heywood's earlier work, but they abandon his usual middle-class protagonists in favour of royalty and courtly spectacle. *A Maidenhead Well Lost* is a dark comedy featuring Heywood's typical sexual misunderstandings and concern with honour, but its Italian court setting and loose morality mark it as distinctly Caroline. *A Challenge for Beauty* involves a hero (Lord Bonavida) who is banished overseas and falls in love with a strong woman (Hellena), much as in Heywood's early adventure plays. But the characters are all Spanish courtiers, and Baines considers the play a parody of the Fletcherian tragicomedies so popular in the Caroline era. The openly allegorical *Love's Mistress*, based on Apuleius's *The Golden Ass*, recalls Heywood's *Ages* plays but adopts the conventions of the Caroline court masque. It was quite successful, being presented before the king and queen three times in eight days with scenery designed by Inigo Jones, and was revived after the Restoration.

Following the publication of these new plays Heywood undertook to preserve more of his earlier works for posterity. In 1637 he issued *Pleasant Dialogues and Dramas*, a miscellaneous collection of mostly occasional verse dedicated to Henry Carey, earl of Dover. This volume includes translations of fifteen of Lucian's dialogues, fragments of two plays and a masque performed for Carey, prologues written for court performances of Heywood's plays, and various elegies, epitaphs, and acrostics. Heywood next published his early plays *The Royal King and the Loyal Subject* (1637) and *The Wise Woman of Hogsdon* (1638), and revised versions of *The Rape of Lucrece* (1638) and *If you Know not me, you Know Nobody* (1639) with prefaces complaining about the low quality of the earlier editions. He also wrote prefaces for several old plays published by his friend John Okes, including Henry Shirley's *The Martyred Soldier* (1639).

In addition to all this, Heywood published an astonishing quantity of new material in these last years, albeit nothing of any literary merit. He wrote commendatory verses for Mary Fage's *Fames Roule* (1637); Thomas Jordan's *Poetical Varieties* (1637); Shakerley Marmion's *Cupid and Psyche* (1637); Randulph Mayeres's *Mayeres his Travels* (1638); Humphrey Mill's *A Night's Search* (1640); and James Yorke's *The Union of Honour* (1640). He also wrote more than a dozen prose works, many largely recycled from his earlier writings. These include, among others, fantastic broadsides (*The Three Wonders of the Age*, 1636); defences of women (*Curtain Lecture*, 1637); religious pamphlets (*The Black Box of Rome Opened*, 1641); and the royally commissioned *True Description of his Majesty's Royal Ship* (1637). His last substantial work was *Nine the most Worthy Women of the World* (1640), published in a handsome quarto with admiring verses from friends. Heywood was buried on 16 August 1641 at St James's, Clerkenwell, bringing to a close one of the most prolific and varied careers in the history of English letters.

Heywood's reputation gradually faded in the decades after his death. Because his works were not published in folio like those of Shakespeare, Jonson, and Fletcher, and because several of his most popular works were published anonymously, his canon remained dispersed and uncertain; even at the end of the twentieth century Pearson's outdated 1874 edition remained the closest thing to a collection of his works. Despite Lamb's famous characterization of Heywood as 'a sort of prose Shakespeare' (C. Lamb, 'Heywood', 99), critics in the nineteenth and early twentieth century tended to be lukewarm in their praise, if they gave it at all. However, the flowering of feminist and new historicist criticism in the late twentieth century brought a new appreciation of Heywood for his vigorous defence of women and his interest in the lives of ordinary people. Revivals of his plays, including Stratford productions of *The Fair Maid of the West* (1986) and *A Woman Killed with Kindness* (1991), demonstrated the skill of his theatrical instincts. Though Heywood is unlikely to ever match the popularity of Shakespeare or Jonson, his works provide an invaluable glimpse into the literary world in which he worked, and his insights into human nature can still be affecting after 400 years. DAVID KATHMAN

Sources A. M. Clark, *Thomas Heywood: playwright and miscellanist* (1931) • B. Baines, *Thomas Heywood* (1984) • M. Grivelet, *Thomas Heywood* (1958) • F. S. Boas, *Thomas Heywood* (1950) • P. Merchant, ed., *Thomas Heywood: three marriage plays* (1996) • K. E. McLuskie, *Dekker and Heywood: professional dramatists* (1994) • Venn, *Alum. Cant.*, 1/2.343 • *Henslowe's diary*, ed. R. A. Foakes and R. T. Rickert (1961) • C. J. Sisson, 'The Red Bull company and the importunate widow', *Shakespeare Survey*, 7 (1954), 57–68 • G. E. Bentley, 'Shakespeare's fellows', *TLS* (15 Nov 1928), 856 • '*Oenone and Paris', by T. H.*, ed. J. Q. Adams (1943) • *Thomas Heywood's 'The four prentices of London': a critical, old-spelling edition*, ed. M. A. W. Gasior (1980) • *Thomas Heywood's '*The rape of Lucrece*', ed. A. Holaday (1950) • A. Holaday, 'Thomas Heywood's *Troia Britannica* and *The ages*', *Journal of English and Germanic Philology*, 45 (1946), 430–39 • A. Holaday, 'Thomas Heywood and the puritans', *Journal of English and Germanic Philology*, 49 (1950), 192–203 • A. Holaday, 'Thomas Heywood and the Low Countries', *Modern Language Notes*, 66 (1951), 16–19 • *Thomas Heywood's 'Art of love': the first complete English translation of Ovid's Ars amatoria*, ed. M. L. Stapleton (2000) • *Thomas Heywood's The iron age*, ed. A. W. Weiner (1979) • R. G. Martin, 'A critical study of Thomas Heywood's *Gunaikeion*', *Studies in Philology*, 20 (1923), 160–83 • R. Proudfoot, ed., *Tom a Lincoln* (1992) • *Thomas Heywood's pageants: a critical edition*, ed. D. M. Bergeron (1986) • R. C. Shady, ed., *Love's mistress, or, The queen's masque* (1977) • C. Lamb, 'Thomas Heywood', *Specimens of English dramatic poets, who lived about the time of Shakespeare, with notes* (1808), 99–123 • D. A. Brooks, *From playhouse to printing house: drama and authorship in early modern England* (2000), 189–220 • T. Heywood, *The fair maid of the west, parts I and II*, ed. R. K. Turner (1968)

Heywood, Thomas (1797–1866), antiquary, third son of Nathaniel Heywood (*d.* 1815), banker, and his wife, Ann Percival (*d.* 1847), younger brother of Sir Benjamin *Heywood, and elder brother of James *Heywood, was born at Manchester on 3 September 1797. He was educated at Manchester grammar school, which he entered on 2 August 1811. In 1818 he became a partner in his father's bank, but retired in 1828 as a result of the changed circumstances following his elder brother's assumption of control. He purchased Hope End, Ledbury, Herefordshire, where he lived until his death. Heywood married, on 2 October 1823, Mary Elizabeth (*d.* 1870), daughter of John Barton of Swinton, Lancashire; they had one son and two daughters, the youngest of whom was Mary Elizabeth *Sumner, founder of the Mothers' Union.

Before leaving Manchester Heywood had collected a remarkable library of local books, which was dispersed in 1835: his collection of tracts and pamphlets is now in Chetham's Library, Manchester. He served the office of boroughreeve of Salford in 1826, and that of high sheriff of Herefordshire in 1840. He was an early member of the council of the Chetham Society, to which his financial knowledge was a valuable asset, and edited several of its publications. Three of these—*The Norris Papers* (1846), *The Moore Rental* (1847), and *The Diary of the Rev. Henry Newcome* (1849)—still have some value. He was also the author of a small number of antiquarian articles in journals.

Heywood died at Hope End on 20 November 1866 and was buried at Wellington Heath, Herefordshire. His general library was sold in Manchester in 1868.

C. W. SUTTON, rev. ALAN G. CROSBY

Sources Annual Report [Chetham Society] (1867) • L. H. Grindon, *Manchester banks and bankers: historical, biographical, and anecdotal* (1877) • Burke, *Gen. GB* • J. F. Smith, ed., *The admission register of the Manchester School, with some notes of the more distinguished scholars*, 3/1, Chetham Society, 93 (1874), 74–6
Wealth at death under £4000: probate, 15 Dec 1866, *CGPLA Eng. & Wales*

Heyworth, Geoffrey, Baron Heyworth (1894–1974), industrialist, was born on 18 October 1894 at Oxton, near Birkenhead, the third of four sons (the second son had a twin sister) of Thomas Blackwell Heyworth, a Liverpool businessman, and his wife, Florence, daughter of Thomas

Francis Myers, of Bolton, Lancashire. Geoffrey Heyworth's father died in 1904 when he was quite young. In order to provide for her family his mother took charge of a boarding-house at the Dollar Academy, Clackmannanshire, and the Heyworth boys were educated at that school.

In September 1912 Geoffrey Heyworth joined Lever Brothers Ltd at Port Sunlight, starting as a clerk at a wage of 15s. a week. After a short while in the accounts department he was sent abroad to work for the company's Canadian subsidiary. Canada had a great influence on Heyworth's life; not only did he get his business grounding in that vast territory, but he also served with the 48th highlanders in the Canadian army from 1915 to 1918, receiving a leg wound which troubled him for the rest of his life. In 1924 he married Lois (d. 1983), daughter of Stevenson Dunlop, of Woodstock, Ontario.

In Canada Heyworth was at first concerned with sales and distribution. He experienced the business methods of the efficient and highly competitive American industry over the border. For the rest of his career he kept closely in touch with American business developments, firmly believing that a healthy operation in the United States was essential to Unilever's strength in the rest of the world.

In 1924 Heyworth returned to London, first to look after Lever Brothers' export trade and later to head the UK soap company based at Port Sunlight. In 1931 he became a director of Lever Brothers and Unilever Ltd, and was at once entrusted with the task of reorganizing the Lever soap interests in the British market. The first Viscount Leverhulme had acquired many of his competitors' businesses in building up the home soap trade. This left a disparate collection of companies still competing among themselves and jealous of their individual identities. The job of rationalizing this group of independent companies was a delicate one. Regional strengths had to be maintained, order instilled, and managers appraised and appointed in accordance with business needs. Heyworth's programme of reorganization was a pioneering move for those times and a model for the future.

Heyworth clearly made his mark on the board and when D'Arcy Cooper, who had succeeded Lord Leverhulme as chairman of Lever Brothers in 1925, died in 1941, Heyworth—though only forty-seven—was the natural successor. He was chairman from 1942 to 1960. During the war years his job was essentially to keep supplies flowing but as soon as the war was over he faced the massive task of rebuilding the business at home and abroad.

By then the 1930 amalgamation of Lever Brothers with the English and Dutch Margarine unions had become fully effective. In the reconstruction of Unilever, the group was fortunate in having had at its head a talented team—Geoffrey Heyworth with his extensive business experience and capacity for logical analysis, and, from the Dutch side, Paul Rykens, an internationalist of wide vision. Together they assembled and trained the senior staff (many recently returned from the forces) to restore the strength of the Unilever companies. In the post-war

period the family dominance in great industrial companies was giving way to the age of the employee–manager. Heyworth established an international reputation as an expert in the field of professional management. This included not only technical and production skills but also accounting, distribution, marketing, and personnel management. His speeches dealing with these topics at the Unilever annual general meetings became management models.

Heyworth realized that industry would have to work closely with the universities to ensure a better flow of graduates to its ranks. This interest in management education involved him in the establishment of the Administrative Staff College at Henley, and he became the first chairman of its court of governors. His advice on industrial matters was widely sought. His public duties were numerous. He sat on the royal commission on the taxation of profits and income (1951–5), and the company law amendment committee of the Board of Trade in 1943. He was a part-time member of the National Coal Board from 1950 to 1953 and of the board of London Passenger Transport from 1942 to 1947.

In the years after the war, as Unilever grew rapidly to become one of the largest companies in the world, Heyworth's clarity of thought informed all the major decisions. He kept personal contact with the subsidiary companies at home and abroad. He had boundless energy, despite the pain he suffered from arthritis, which made him increasingly dependent on his walking-sticks. He did not spare himself on his visits to overseas units, ascending the steepest steps in the factory and bearing the heat of the day in the local bazaar.

Despite a shy manner Heyworth was always approachable. There was no pomposity or self-importance in him and he could talk easily with men and women of all ranks. He had a real interest in people which was reflected in the attention he gave to management development. He created challenging opportunities for young managers but had little patience with any who shirked the demands of the job. He was not naturally a gifted speaker. He spoke haltingly and frequently left his sentences incomplete, but because of his lively imagination and his profound knowledge he always communicated clearly.

Heyworth realized earlier than most other industrialists that business could not stand aside from the far-reaching changes taking place in society around it. New relationships had to be formed with government, and new links with the educators. A better understanding of the consumer was also required. He helped to enhance the standing of the National Council of Social Service and was its president from 1961 to 1970. As chairman of the Leverhulme Trust, which had been founded under the will of the first Viscount Leverhulme for purposes of education and research, he encouraged support for the social sciences.

Heyworth was a member of the University Grants Committee from 1954 to 1958. A special interest was Nuffield College and in 1947 he became a visiting fellow. He remained on the governing body of Nuffield well after his retirement from Unilever and in 1961 was elected to an honorary fellowship. He received the honorary degree of LLD from St Andrews (1950), Manchester (1950), London (1962), Bristol (1966), Sussex (1966), and Southampton (1970), an honorary DCL from Oxford (1957), and an honorary DLitt from Warwick (1967). He received a knighthood in 1948 and was created Baron Heyworth of Oxton in 1955. He was appointed grand officer in the order of Orange Nassau by the queen of the Netherlands in 1947.

Heyworth died at his home at 29 Sussex Square, London, on 15 June 1974. There were no children and the barony became extinct. DAVID ORR, rev.

Sources *The Times* (17 June 1974) • C. Wilson, *The history of Unilever: a study in economic growth and social change*, 2 vols. (1954) • A. M. Knox, *Coming clean* (1976) • private information (1986) • personal knowledge (1986) • d. cert.
Likenesses W. Stoneman, photograph, 1955, NPG • M. Codner, portrait, Unilever House, London
Wealth at death £195,574: probate, 15 July 1974, *CGPLA Eng. & Wales*

Heyworth, Peter Lawrence Frederick (1921–1991), music critic, was born on 3 June 1921 in New York city, the son of Lawrence Ormerod Heyworth (1890–1954), a rubber dealer, and his wife, Ellie, *née* Sterne (1891–1927). He was educated at Charterhouse School (1935–9) and, after six years' army service that included a period in Vienna, at Balliol College, Oxford (1947–9), from where he graduated with a second-class degree in politics, philosophy, and economics. He next spent six months at the University of Göttingen, where his leanings towards German culture and music received the firm grounding that gave his subsequent work much of its character. In 1952 he joined the *Times Educational Supplement*. His ambitions then lay with a career in political journalism or as a foreign correspondent, and his writing remained marked by strongly pro-European attitudes but also a political stance well to the right of centre: he later treasured a signed photograph of Margaret Thatcher. However, tuberculosis, followed by the diagnosis of Addison's disease, set too great a constraint on his energies, which throughout his life were harboured with self-discipline and courage. Music was an enthusiasm, an art for which he never had any formal training, but he now discovered an ability for applying his sharp intelligence to concert criticism.

After moving to *The Observer* Heyworth at first wrote concert reviews, inheriting the paper's championship of new music from a predecessor, William Glock, but coming into conflict with his more traditionalist senior, Eric Blom. He succeeded Blom as chief critic in 1955. Now with greater liberty to develop his own critical stance, he made the paper a pioneer in the cause of new music, especially when it was of sufficient intellectual and imaginative energy and was detached from what he saw as insular establishment values. This brought great allegiance to Tippett, little or none to Britten. An article attacking Walton led the composer to strike him with a walking stick at a concert, and it was typical of both men's qualities that this sealed a burgeoning personal friendship in which no quarter was given on either side. Heyworth was one of the first critics to champion Harrison Birtwistle, to whose music he remained loyal throughout his life (he commissioned a David Hockney drawing of Birtwistle, who dedicated the opera *Gawain* to him). He also welcomed Glock's appointment of Pierre Boulez as conductor of the BBC Symphony Orchestra, writing eloquently of the invigoration of English musical life which this brought about. His lack of musical training denied him technical appreciation of the scores of these composers, and this he always admitted, claiming that instead he could hope to lead the equally untutored reader towards experiences that had excited and moved him. His scrupulous background work, which included assiduous attendance at rehearsals, prepared him well for such a role.

Heyworth's devotion to the German tradition found another strong focus in the Beethoven concerts given in London by Otto Klemperer from the mid-1950s. His admiration led to personal friendship and, mutual trust established, to radio interviews later published in book form as *Conversations with Klemperer* (1973). These in turn led to Heyworth's most enduring achievement, the full-scale critical and biographical study of Klemperer which overtook tentative previous plans for a study of music under the Weimar republic. Immensely thorough, alert to political considerations and to the predicament of a Jewish conductor making his career in a Germany turning towards Nazism, the book also recorded a tempestuous, depressive character whose interpretations of new music, especially at the Kroll Opera in Berlin, and of the Austro-German classics were among the greatest of their time. Volume 1 of *Otto Klemperer: his Life and Times* was published in 1983; the second and concluding volume was completed after Heyworth's death by John Lucas (1996).

Heyworth was by nature a demanding man, quick to compare aspects of British public life unfavourably with German orderliness, capable of severity to those who fell short of his high standards, from performers and composers to secretaries and waiters. Welcome as his enlivening company always was, these qualities could make him an exacting guest; he was the best of hosts and travelling companions. His highest standards were reserved for himself, and no trouble was too great in the preparation of his weekly article or in the selection of the correct wine at his table. He was a man of deep and perceptive generosity, loyal, thoughtful about his friends' tastes, sympathetic to the problems of others and reticent about his own. In turn he inspired great loyalty and affection. Among his warmest friends was W. H. Auden, whom he met in Berlin in 1964 and who dedicated *City without Walls* to him:

> At Twenty we find our friends for ourselves, but it takes Heaven
> To find us one when we are Fifty-Seven.

He died in Athens, of a stroke, on 2 October 1991, and was buried in Hinton St Mary, Dorset, on 12 October.
JOHN WARRACK

Sources WWW [forthcoming] • *The Times* (4 Oct 1991) • private information (2004) • personal knowledge (2004)
Archives SOUND BL NSA, performance recordings
Likenesses photograph, repro. in *The Times*

Wealth at death £836,523: probate, 20 Dec 1991, *CGPLA Eng. & Wales*

Hezlet [*married name* Ross], **Mary Elizabeth Linzee** [May] (1882–1978), golfer, was born in Gibraltar on 29 April 1882, one of eight children of Richard Jackson Hezlet (*b.* 1840), a major in the Royal Artillery, and his English-born wife, Emily Mary Linzee Owen. Richard Hezlet inherited Bovagh House in co. Londonderry on the death of his brother in 1887 and retired later as a lieutenant-colonel. Most of May Hezlet's formative years were spent in Ulster, her time divided between Bovagh and the resort town of Portrush about 15 miles away, where both her parents played golf. It was here also that May and her five surviving siblings learned the sport. She is said to have started at the age of nine and she had no professional tuition. In 1895 both the Irish ladies' close and British ladies' open championships were held at Portrush. Competing along with her mother and her older sister Emmy, thirteen-year-old May made her début in both events but lost her first match in each. It was three years before she made another attempt at championship golf. On this occasion she reached the final of the 1898 Irish close and lost to Jessie Magill by just one hole.

In the following year the Irish close and the British championships were held in Newcastle, co. Down, in successive weeks. On 6 May 1899 May Hezlet won her first Irish title by defeating Rhona Adair in the final. Two days later the British championship began with the preliminary stroke competition, which she won, and on 12 May she emerged as champion. At the age of seventeen years and thirteen days she set a record that lasted throughout the twentieth century as the youngest winner of the event. She defended the two titles unsuccessfully in 1900, when her friend and arch-rival Rhona Adair claimed both. In 1901, in a team which included her mother, May represented Ireland for the first time, in a friendly match against England. In later years her younger sisters Violet and Florence were to become regular members of the national team; in 1904 May, Violet, Florence, and their mother all played in the Irish team. Much later her brother Charles became a leading amateur golfer who reached the final of the British championship in 1914 and played on the Walker cup side three times in the 1920s.

May Hezlet took a second British title in 1902, when she beat Elinor Nevile on the twentieth hole in the final at Deal in Kent. In 1904 she won the Irish championship a second time and reached the final of the British again, but on this occasion lost to Lottie Dod by one hole. Parallel to her success as a golfer, May Hezlet developed a reputation as a commentator on the game by writing articles in periodicals such as the *Irish Golfer*. Her one book, *Ladies' Golf*, first published in 1904 and updated in 1907, included instruction for lady golfers and touched on etiquette as well as commenting on the skills of leading players and recording the results of important events throughout the world. Her style was lucid and her book provided one of the few first-hand insights into the early years of ladies' golf.

In 1905 May Hezlet defeated her sister Florence in the final of the Irish close, and on 25 May both played in the historic first international between the British Isles and America at Cromer in Norfolk, the match which led eventually to the biennial Curtis cup series. The home side won, with May Hezlet defeating Margaret Curtis. In 1907 the British championship returned to Newcastle, co. Down. Preceding the event, Ireland won the ladies internationals, but May Hezlet lost her matches against England and Wales. However, in the championship she advanced to the final, where again she overcame her sister Florence to claim her third and final British title. She won the last of her five Irish close championships in 1908 with another final victory over Florence. She did not compete in either championship in 1909 because of her marriage on 27 April that year to Arthur Edwin Ross (1869–1923), then Church of Ireland rector of Portrush parish, the son of David Ross of Glenageary, co. Dublin. Though they had no children, her subsequent participation in important golf events was noticeably reduced. There is a suggestion that this was because her husband thought competitive golf unbecoming for a clergyman's wife.

May Hezlet's last appearance for the Irish team was in 1912; she also contributed to Horace Hutchinson's *The New Book of Golf*, published in that year. Also in 1912 her husband was appointed rector of Ballymena. After serving as an army chaplain in the First World War he became rector of Holywood, co. Down, in 1919 and in January 1920 he was elected bishop of Tuam, Killala, and Achonry. He died on 24 May 1923. As a 41-year-old widow, Mrs Ross returned to Portrush for a time before moving to London, where she worked for the Society for the Propagation of the Gospel. In later years she shared the house of her sister Violet in Wiltshire, but in the late 1970s she moved to a nursing home, St Bart's, Dover Road, Sandwich, Kent, where she died on 27 December 1978.

May Hezlet was one of the most accomplished and successful players of the early days of ladies' golf. As a writer she contributed to the popularity of the sport and to the development of the ladies' game. Her commentary on her contemporaries provides a valuable record for golf historians.   PAUL GORRY

Sources P. Gorry, 'May Hezlet: golf heroine', *Ireland of the Welcomes*, 48/4 (1999), 14–20 · private information (2004) [Sir Arthur Hezlet, nephew; Mrs R. Hoare, niece] · *The Times* (1895–1912) · *Irish Times* (1895–1912) · *Belfast News-Letter* (1895–1912) · b. cert. · m. cert. · d. cert. · Walford, *County families* (1894) · *Church of Ireland Directory* (1921) · WWW [Arthur Edwin Ross] · R. Cossey, *Golfing ladies* (1984) · L. Mair, *One hundred years of women's golf* (1992)
Likenesses H. R. Douglas, oils, *c.*1899, Royal Portrush Ladies' Golf Club, co. Antrim · photograph, *c.*1900, Women Golfers' Museum; repro. in Cossey, *Golfing ladies*, 44

Hibbart [Hibbert], **William** (*bap.* 1725, *d.* 1808), printmaker, the son of James Hibbart, was born in Bath and baptized there on 29 November 1725. He practised in the city for over fifty years, etching and engraving book illustrations, maps, plans, and bookplates. He was apprenticed to the Bath engraver Jacob Skinner in 1738, but was greatly influenced by the presence of Thomas Worlidge in the city between 1744 and 1766; his small etched portraits imitate

Worlidge's drypoint technique. The majority of these portraits appear as frontispieces, typical examples being his two portraits of Richard Nash ('Beau Nash') for the 1762 and 1763 editions of the *New Bath Guide*. An etching, *The Knights of the Baythe, or, The One Headed Corporation*, satirizing Ralph Allen's role within the Bath council, dated 1763 and fancifully signed William O'Gaarth, is attributed to Hibbart. A handsome brass commemorative plaque signed by him and dated 1764 is still affixed to the wall of the Pump Room in Bath, next to the Tompion clock. His maps are generally confidently executed, especially his etching of Thomas Thorpe's *A Map of 5 Miles Round the City of Bath* of 1773. Not all of Hibbart's work was so successful: the amateur artist Coplestone Warre Bampfylde greatly disliked Hibbart's etchings after his illustrations for the poet Christopher Anstey's *An Election Ball* and was not placated by Anstey's assurance that 'Mr Hoare [the Bath portrait painter William Hoare] has taken a great deal of pains and has corrected many parts of them …' (Som., ARS, DD/GC 103).

Hibbart married Elizabeth Hibbart (1724–1797), who was probably a cousin, in 1748. A trade card designed by Bartolozzi for 'Hibbert, Engraver' of 8 Bridge Street, Bath, and engraved by J. Hibbert must have been for his son John (1768–1848), who invariably spelled his name Hibbert rather than Hibbart and took over his father's business; a copy of the card is now in the Banks collection in the British Museum. Another son, Charles (1765–1819), also a printmaker, travelled to Rome with the painter Thomas Barker in 1790; he was later convicted of forging banknotes and was hanged at Ilchester in 1819. Hibbart died on 13 July 1808 in Bath.　　　　SUSAN SLOMAN

Sources R. W. M. Wright, 'Index of Bath artists', Victoria Art Gallery, Bath · parish registers, Bath Abbey and St Michael's Church, Bath, Bath RO · T. Dodd, 'Memorial of engravers in Great Britain, 1550–1800', BL, Add. MS 33401 · J. Strutt, *A biographical dictionary, containing an historical account of all the engravers, from the earliest period of the art of engraving to the present time*, 2 (1786), 17 · Engraved Brit. ports., 2.30, 42, 206, 225, 270, 456; 3.548, 602 · *The Barkers of Bath* (1986), 14 [exhibition catalogue, Victoria Art Gallery, Bath, 17 May–18 June 1986] · C. Anstey, *Ad C. W. Bampfylde, epistola poetica familiaris*, 2nd edn (1777) · C. Anstey, letter to C. W. Bampfylde, 5 Jan 1777, Som. ARS, DD/GC 103 · collection of Bath trade cards, Bath Central Library, nos. 124, 125, 126, 127 · *Bath Chronicle* (10 Feb 1774) · *Bath Chronicle* (2 May 1776) · *Bath Chronicle* (14 July 1808) · apprenticeship books, Inland Revenue, PRO, IR 1, IR 17

Hibberd, (James) Shirley (1825–1890), journalist and writer on horticulture, was the son of a retired sea captain who had served under Nelson. He was born in the parish of St Dunstan and All Saints, Stepney, and following the early death of his father gave up his wish for a medical career in order to be apprenticed to a Stepney bookseller. After several years of bookselling he married, moved to Pentonville, and turned to horticultural journalism, in which he soon became a leader of middle-class fashionable taste. His earliest essays were on brambles, quickly followed by a practical gardening book, *The Town Garden: a Manual for the Management of City and Suburban Gardens* (1855). Sensing a market among the advice books and gardening manuals of the era, Hibberd followed up with the

(James) Shirley Hibberd (1825–1890), by unknown photographer

very successful *Rustic Adornments* (1856) and *Garden Favourites* (1858). In 1858 he became the first editor of the newly established magazine *Floral World*, which he managed until 1875 with considerable success. From then onwards he turned his energies towards writing popular gardening manuals, making horticultural experiments, and creating a succession of specialist gardens in various parts of north London. In Stoke Newington he created one garden for fruit, another for vegetables, another for roses, and so on. Eventually lack of space encouraged him to move to 74 The Hermitage, a private road in Muswell Hill. By the time of his death this too was filled with his gardens.

Hibberd reported the results of his experiments in a series of fluent and engagingly personal books which contributed greatly to the new, highly decorative, ornamental fashion in gardens. He wrote with the experience of trial and error. His *Profitable Gardening* (1863), *Rose Book* (1864), and *Fern Garden* (1869) were particularly successful. Among other things, Hibberd grew shrubs and trees in pots, built up a collection of specimen hollies and ivies, gave a number of popular lectures, and wrote on greenhouse design, interior flower arrangements, water gardens, seats, arbours, Wardian cases, and ferneries. As a social historian of internal and exterior furnishings his work is almost unchallenged. From 1861 he was also connected with the *Gardener's Magazine*, becoming editor towards the end of his life. He was an active member of the Royal Horticultural Society, often exhibiting specimen plants from his own collection and judging others, and also wrote on seaweeds and aquarium plants. In the 1880s, his fame as a practical plantsman was sufficient for him to be consulted by the government about potatoes and the potato blight.

Hibberd was a pronounced temperance advocate and a vegetarian; he wrote *An Epitome of the War* (1856), an account of the Crimean War, before concentrating on botanical writing. He died at 1 Priory Road, Kew, on 16 November 1890 and was buried six days later in Abney

Park cemetery at Stoke Newington. The *Gardeners' Chronicle* printed an obituary with a portrait, regretting that he was 'a victim to his own zeal' (*Gardeners' Chronicle*, 22 Nov 1890, 596). Hibberd was married twice, and had one daughter from his second marriage.   JANET BROWNE

Sources *Gardeners' Chronicle*, new ser., 20 (1883), 298–9, 305 · *Gardeners' Chronicle*, 3rd ser., 8 (1890), 596–7 · *Journal of Botany, British and Foreign*, 28 (1890), 382 · B. Massingham, *A century of gardeners* (1982), 54–66 · d. cert.
Archives Linn. Soc., papers
Likenesses engraving, repro. in 'Shirley Hibberd', 305 · photograph, Royal Horticultural Society, London [*see illus.*] · portrait, repro. in *Country Life* (13 March 1980), 750–51 · portrait, repro. in *Gardeners' Chronicle*, 596–7
Wealth at death £2006 17s. 11d.: resworn probate, Sept 1891, *CGPLA Eng. & Wales*

Hibberd, (Andrew) Stuart (1893–1983), radio broadcaster, was born at Village Canford, Dorset, on 5 September 1893, the youngest child of William Henry Hibberd, farmer and corn dealer of Village Canford, and his second wife, Mary Catherine Edney. He had one brother and seven half-brothers. From Weymouth College he won a science exhibition to St John's College, Cambridge. He had a fine tenor voice and became one of four choral scholars. He enlisted in 1914, after only a year and a half at Cambridge, and was awarded a wartime degree. He served in the Dorset regiment at Gallipoli, and later in Mesopotamia, then with the Punjabi regiment of the Indian army until it was disbanded in 1922. He married on 31 July 1923 Alice Mary (1892/3–1977), daughter of Lieutenant-Colonel Gerard Chichester, of the North Staffordshire regiment. They had no children.

In November 1924 Hibberd joined the two-year-old British Broadcasting Company Ltd at Savoy Hill as an announcer. His cultivated voice and clear enunciation typified what came to be known between the wars as the BBC accent. The words he spoke were usually written by others, and announcers then were anonymous. Nevertheless he soon acquired a special position in the affection of listeners, and was generally known as the BBC's chief announcer, in recognition of his seniority and the respect he enjoyed, although during his twenty-six years of the same work he was never officially appointed to such a post.

Hibberd's diary recorded the eminent speakers and musicians invited to broadcast in the early days, and the national events in which he was involved. It formed the basis of his book *'This—is London …'* (1950) which gives a vivid picture of the BBC's first quarter-century. He noted that on 4 January 1926 the evening announcer first wore a dinner jacket as a courtesy to the people broadcasting, many of whom were similarly clad. Hibberd himself found evening dress unsatisfactory for reading the news; he wanted nothing tight round his neck, and the microphone sometimes transmitted the creak of his starched shirt-front.

After he had closed down the Savoy Hill studio at 10.30 p.m. Hibberd would walk up to the Savoy Hotel to announce, from back stage, the dance-band tunes played

(Andrew) Stuart Hibberd (1893–1983), by Felix H. Man, 1943 [in the BBC canteen]

at the end of the broadcasting day. Microphones suspended from the ceiling, well above the band of Debroy Somers or Carroll Gibbons, would pick up the music and the swish of dancing feet, giving listeners at home a vicarious evening out. Deliberately there was no visible stand microphone which might tempt dancing couples to send greetings to friends, or—heaven forfend—to put over an advertisement. Meanwhile at nearby Charing Cross Station friendly railway staff would sometimes delay the departure of a train for Hibberd's Kent home when the much-loved familiar figure was seen racing to the platform, his white scarf trailing.

In May 1926 the general strike began, and with it the first broadcast of news before 6 p.m. Before this time an irksome restriction, imposed by the news agencies in the interest of the newspaper proprietors, had permitted the BBC access to agency news only on condition that it neither gathered news itself nor transmitted it before the evening papers were on sale. During the strike, when no newspapers appeared save the *British Worker* and the *British Gazette*, edited by Winston Churchill, this restriction was temporarily lifted; it took the Second World War to remove it altogether. On each day of the strike the BBC broadcast five news bulletins, mostly read by Hibberd. Their calm tone, markedly different from that of the *British Gazette*, helped to steady a divided nation. Broadcasting became responsibly established, and the way was paved for the private company to be transformed, at the end of that year, into a public corporation operating under royal charter, still with the initials BBC.

Apart from newsreading, Hibberd's main work in the 1920s was to present musical programmes. He was a kindly, courteous man whose best-remembered announcement was his rendering of the bulletin issued by the doctors of George V on the evening of 20 January 1936: 'The King's life is moving peacefully towards its close'. With all other programmes cancelled, Hibberd poignantly repeated the words each quarter-hour, following the chimes of Big Ben, until Sir John Reith announced the death of the monarch at midnight.

During the Second World War it was clear that Hibberd had passed his peak. A critic in *The Listener* noted in 1943, 'He frequently misses his footing as he delivers a bulletin'. However he continued to retain the affection of many listeners, especially when he began to present, in 1949, a Thursday afternoon programme, *The Silver Lining*, which brought comfort to people handicapped or housebound, and reflected his own strong Christian faith. Hibberd retired from the BBC to Budleigh Salterton in 1951, suffering from fatigue, but he continued to introduce *The Silver Lining* each week from a small self-operated studio in Exeter until the programme ended in 1964. He also gave much time to recording talking books for blind people.

Hibberd was appointed MBE in 1935. He died in St Cecilia Nursing Home, Budleigh Salterton, on 1 November 1983. LEONARD MIALL, *rev.*

Sources *The Times* (2 Nov 1983) · *The Times* (7 Nov 1983) · *Daily Telegraph* (2 Nov 1983) · *The Listener* (29 July 1943) · S. Hibberd, 'This—is London …' (1950) · private information (1990) · personal knowledge (1990) · *CGPLA Eng. & Wales* (1984) · *DNB* · m. cert.
Archives FILM BFI NFTVA, documentary footage · BFI NFTVA, performance footage | SOUND IWM SA, performance recordings
Likenesses F. H. Man, photograph, 1943, Hult. Arch. [*see illus.*]
Wealth at death £433,027: probate, 4 Jan 1984, *CGPLA Eng. & Wales*

Hibbert [*née* Burford], **Eleanor Alice** [*pseuds.* Jean Plaidy, Victoria Holt] (**1906–1993**), novelist, was born on 1 September 1906 at 20 Burke Street, Canning Town, West Ham, the daughter of Joseph Burford, a dock labourer, and Alice Louise Burford, *née* Tate. She left school at the age of sixteen and went to work as a typist for a jeweller in Hatton Garden, London. In the 1930s she married George P. Hibbert, a wholesale leather merchant some twenty years older than herself. Her long and happy marriage gave her the confidence and financial support to embark on a writing career, which had always been her ambition.

When her first attempts at novel writing were rejected by publishers, Hibbert turned to short stories, a number of which were published in the *Daily Mail* and *Evening News*. A literary agent who had formerly been literary editor of the *Daily Mail* encouraged her to try writing romantic fiction. She had never read anything in this genre, but now read twenty romantic novels in quick succession, and then wrote one—*Daughter of Anna*—which was immediately accepted and published in 1941 under her maiden name Eleanor Burford. She used that name for thirty romantic novels published over the next two decades.

It was the beginning of a literary career notable for its length (over fifty years) and for its sheer productivity. Hibbert was accustomed to write seven days a week for five hours a day, starting at 7.30 a.m. and producing an average of 5000 words per day. Towards the end of her life she estimated that she had written about 200 books, but was unsure of the exact number. Also notable is the fact that she used as many as seven pseudonyms (including her maiden name), often publishing under two or three different names within a single year. She had a keen awareness of the commercial aspects of writing and publishing and knew that writers tended to be identified with the genres in which they wrote. Since Eleanor Burford had become established as a writer of romantic fiction, Hibbert chose a new pseudonym, Jean Plaidy, for her first historical novel, *Beyond the Blue Mountains* (1947). She was by now living in Cornwall and Plaidy was the name of a beach near her home.

As she hoped, Jean Plaidy became well known as the author of popular but carefully researched historical novels centred on real women in history. Historical events in these novels are rendered through the perceptions of the central character, who is either a monarch, like Mary, queen of Scots, or Queen Victoria, or the consort, mistress, daughter, or sister of a powerful man. The novels are often grouped in series, not necessarily published in historical order, such as the Plantagenet series (fifteen volumes, 1976–82) or the queens of England series (nine volumes, 1983–90). Some eighty titles were published in all.

Hibbert realized that her historical novels, though in steady demand by readers, were never going to be bestsellers. She therefore tried writing other genres of fiction, using different pseudonyms, during the 1950s and early 1960s. As Elbur Ford (1950–53) she wrote four novelized reconstructions of famous Victorian crimes. As Kathleen Kellow (eight novels, 1952–60) and Ellalice Tate (five novels, 1956–61) she produced lighter historical romances. By 1991 she was unable to remember exactly what these *alter egos* had written, or why, except that she had been experimenting in search of best-seller status.

Hibbert's quest finally succeeded with the publication in 1960 of a Gothic romance, *Mistress of Mellyn*, under a further new pseudonym, Victoria Holt. The identity of Holt was kept a closely guarded secret until six novels had appeared, and the authorship of *Mistress of Mellyn* was attributed by some readers to Daphne du Maurier, possibly because of its Cornish setting and a certain thematic similarity to du Maurier's *Rebecca*. (Wilkie Collins and *Jane Eyre* have also been cited as influences.) Thirty-one Victoria Holt novels were published and Hibbert's work under this pseudonym attained immense popularity in both Britain and America, sparking off a new interest in a type of novel combining romance, suspense, and Gothic or dark elements, sometimes known as 'women's Gothic'.

Hibbert continued to write also under the name of Jean Plaidy, generally producing two Plaidy historical novels and one Holt Gothic per year. She adopted her final pseudonym, Philippa Carr, for *The Miracle at St Bruno's* (1972) and its sequels in the daughters of England series which eventually ran to nineteen titles. These 'historical Gothics' form an extended family saga, focusing on women in different generations of the same family from the Reformation to the Second World War.

Hibbert has never been considered a literary novelist, and did not claim to be one. She considered that her novels were 'what people want to read … a good story, first and foremost'. She wrote 'to help people switch off … and there's no reason why they shouldn't' (Bennett, 23–4). Her Holt novels have been widely translated and it was estimated in 1991 that their sales in twenty languages exceeded 75 million.

Hibbert, or more likely her publisher, adapted her image to suit the genre of each series. Photographs show an attractive dark-haired woman, well-groomed and lady-like in the publicity for Jean Plaidy novels, in a more relaxed pose for the romantic Victoria Holt books. Hibbert lived simply and protected her privacy, considering that her personal life was less important than her books. Her one extravagance was the purchase during the 1970s of King's Lodging, a historic house in Sandwich, Kent, which had been visited by several English monarchs. She restored it and furnished it lavishly, like a house from one of her own novels, but found it too big and 'a bit weird', and spent her last years in a small flat in Kensington, London.

George Hibbert had died during the 1960s and in later life Eleanor Hibbert was accustomed to spend the winter months of each year on a world cruise. She died at sea on 19 January 1993 on board the cruise liner *Sea Princess* in the Mediterranean, between Athens and Port Said. A memorial service was held in London on 6 March 1993, at St Peter's Church, Kensington Park Road.

MOIRA BURGESS

Sources C. Bennett, 'The prime of Miss Jean Plaidy', *The Guardian* (4 July 1991), 23–4 · *The Times* (21 Jan 1993) · *St James guide to contemporary popular writers* (1997) · b. cert. · d. cert.
Likenesses photograph, 1991?, repro. in Bennett, 'The prime of Miss Jean Plaidy' · photograph, repro. in *The Times*
Wealth at death £8,790,807: probate, 22 June 1993, *CGPLA Eng. & Wales*

Hibbert, George (1757–1837), merchant, was born on 13 January 1757 in Manchester, the fifth son of Robert Hibbert, merchant, of Manchester, and his wife, Abigail, daughter of William Scholey of Leeds. His grandfather and father were prominent merchants in Manchester, and his uncle Thomas Hibbert was one of the leading planters and merchants in Jamaica. He was educated in Liverpool and at the Revd Booth's school in Woolton, Lancashire. With £1500 from his father on coming of age, he moved to London in 1780 and became a junior partner in the West Indies house of Hibbert, Purrier, and Horton, at 9 Mincing Lane, which was headed by his elder brothers Thomas and Robert. On inheriting £1000 at the death of his father, he married Elizabeth Margaret Fonnereau, daughter of Philip Fonnereau, on 30 August 1784. Together they raised five sons and nine daughters. During the 1780s and 1790s Hibbert pursued the work of his firm, by 1800 known as Hibberts, Fuhr, and Purrier and highly regarded in the

Jamaica trade. In the 1790s he assumed direction of the firm. At the same time he and two brothers formed a separate partnership, which operated from the same address, but appears to have been more involved in finance. The former firm was concluded in 1815, but the latter survived his death.

At the age of forty Hibbert entered public service. He was elected an alderman of London in 1798 and served until 1803; most notably, he sided with the government by successfully backing a resolution in favour of a tax on property in 1798. The following year, he began his lifelong tenure as a director of the West India Dock Company. Several times chairman, he became the leading proponent, alongside Robert Milligan, of completing the new dock scheme. He manoeuvred for a seat in parliament in 1802, but to no avail; he was luckier in 1806, when he was selected without opposition for Seaford, Sussex. In the Commons, he took strong stands as a member of the opposition. He was most noted for his opposition to the abolition of the slave trade, which was memorialized in *The Substance of Three Speeches on the Abolition of the Slave Trade* (1807). By 1810 he had accepted the demise of the trade, and was calling for measures to end it in a more effective manner. In 1806, and again from 1807 to his retirement in 1812, he was parliament's principal West Indies supporter: he backed the continuation of the tax exemption on dividends for foreigners in 1808; he backed a ban on grain distillation in 1809; and he supported the provision of free labour from the East Indies to the West Indies in 1811. After his retirement from parliament in 1812, Hibbert acted as the agent for Jamaica until 1830, and headed the West India Committee as its chairman. In both capacities, he ardently argued the case of Caribbean planters and merchants.

Hibbert was also a renowned collector of paintings, sculpture, and books, and at his house in Clapham he brought together a unique collection of botanical exotica. In 1805 he helped to found the London Institution. In 1811 he was elected a fellow of the Royal Society and, the following year, a fellow of the Society of Arts. In 1819, as a member of the Roxburgh Club, he edited Caxton's translation of Ovid, *Six Books of Metamorphoses*. Later he edited the anonymous *Narrative of a Journey from Santiago de Chile to Buenos Ayres* (1824), and supported the publication of *Correspondence between George Hibbert, esq., and the Rev. T. Cooper, relative to the condition of the negro slaves in Jamaica* (1824). When his wife's uncle Rogers Parker died in 1828, he succeeded to Parker's Munden estate near Watford, to which he removed after auctioning off most of his art and library. He died there on 8 October 1837 and was buried at Aldenham.

DAVID HANCOCK

Sources J. H. Markland, *Sketch of life and character of George Hibbert* (1837) · A. E. Furness, 'George Hibbert and the defence of slavery in the West Indies', *Jamaican Historical Review* (1965), 56–70 · V. L. Oliver, ed., *Caribbeana*, 4 (1915–16), 193–202, 258–265, 324–330, 342–349 · T. Cooper, *Correspondence between George Hibbert, Esq., and the Rev. T. Cooper* (1824) · [G. Hibbert], *A catalogue of the library of George Hibbert* (1829) · *Catalogue of a superb assemblage of prints and books of prints* [sale catalogue, T. Philipe, London, 1809] · J. Hunter, *Familiae minorum gentium*, ed. J. W. Clay, 1, Harleian Society, 37 (1894), 270–

72 • A. B. Beaven, ed., *The aldermen of the City of London, temp. Henry III–[1912]*, 2 vols. (1908–13) • *GM*, 1st ser., 99/2 (1829) • *GM*, 2nd ser., 9 (1838) • J. E. Cussans, *History of Hertfordshire*, 3 (1881), 268 • S. Lambert, ed., *House of Commons sessional papers of the eighteenth century* (1975), vol. 72, pp. 93–111 • will, PRO, PROB 11/1889, sig. 27
Archives Cambs. AS, financial records and corresp. relating to Tharp family's estates in Jamaica | BL, letters to second Earl Spencer • Derbys. RO, letters to Sir R. J. Wilmot-Horton • Institute of Jamaica, Kingston, agent's letters, vols. 2–3, letters to Jamaican Assembly • NL Wales, letters to Nathaniel Phillips
Likenesses T. Lawrence, oils, 1811–12, Port of London Authority, London • J. Hoppner, oils • J. Ward, mezzotint (after J. Hoppner), BM

Hibbert, Henry (*d.* 1678), clergyman, was born at Marple in Cheshire, the son of William Hibbert, gentleman, and his second wife, Alice, daughter of Geoffrey Mottershead of Mottram, Cheshire. He matriculated from Brasenose College, Oxford, on 21 January 1620 and graduated BA in 1622. He was instituted in 1625 to the vicarage of Preston in Holderness, Yorkshire, where he remained undisturbed until the outbreak of civil war when he fled from the parliamentarian forces, who removed him from his living. He served briefly as a chaplain in the royalist army and in 1643 he petitioned the crown for the living of Hotham, which had been abandoned by the incumbent. By 1647 he had made his peace with parliament and was back in Cheshire as vicar of Mottram, where his mother's family resided, but by 1651 he had returned to Yorkshire as minister at Settrington in the East Riding. He was appointed vicar at Holy Trinity, Kingston upon Hull, in 1652, when he seems to have held presbyterian views, although his fellow minister John Shaw did not make him welcome. For the next few years the ministers and congregations at Hull were divided between the presbyterians and the Independent followers of John Canne, chaplain to the garrison there, so that the chancel and nave of Holy Trinity were partitioned by a brick wall to provide separate spaces for worship for each group. While at Hull Hibbert published *Waters of Marah* (1654), based on two funeral sermons for the children of William Lyne, who had died the previous year.

At the Restoration Hibbert was removed from Hull, possibly as a result of his unwillingness to conform, but his views soon adapted to the new regime. On Restoration day 1661 he preached a loyal sermon at St Paul's Cathedral before the lord mayor, which was published as *Regina dierum, or, The Joyful Day*. He was made a chaplain to James, duke of York, to whom his theological treatise, *Syntagma theologicum* (1662), was dedicated, and honours soon followed. He was made a BD at Cambridge in 1664, as a member of St John's College, and a DD of Oxford the following year. In 1662 he had been instituted to the rectory of All Hallows-the-Less in London, and on 22 September that year was added the vicarage of St Olave Jewry. He was collated to the prebendal stall of Chamberlainwood in St Paul's on 12 January 1669, which he held along with his parochial livings until his death in September 1678. He was buried in St Olave's Church on 24 September. Hibbert had married Mary, daughter of William Kirkman of Toadhole in Derbyshire, with whom he had two sons who died

young and seven daughters, four of whom survived him, as did his wife, who died on 1 November 1705. Hibbert's career provides an example of one who negotiated the religious troubles of mid-century effortlessly, and he died a prosperous cleric. WILLIAM JOSEPH SHEILS

Sources Venn, *Alum. Cant.* • J. P. Earwaker, *East Cheshire: past and present, or, A history of the hundred of Macclesfield*, 2 (1880) • *Miscellanea*, 1, Yorkshire Archaeological Society, 61 (1920) • *VCH Yorkshire East Riding*, vol. 1 • *Fasti Angl., 1541–1857*, [St Paul's, London] • Wood, *Ath. Oxon.*, new edn, vol. 3
Likenesses D. Loggan, line engraving, BM, NPG • Loggin, engraving, repro. in H. Hibbert, *Syntagma theologicum* (1662)

Hibbert, Sir John Tomlinson (1824–1908), politician, born on 5 January 1824 at Lyon House, Oldham, was the eldest son of Elijah Hibbert, one of the founders of the firm of Hibbert, Platt & Sons, machinists, and his wife, Elizabeth (Betty), daughter of Abraham Hilton of Cross Bank, near Oldham. At thirteen he was sent to a private school, Green Brow, Silloth, Cumberland. Entered at Shrewsbury School in June 1837, under Benjamin Hall Kennedy, he there distinguished himself as an athlete. In later life he was chairman of the governors of the school. He was admitted at St John's College, Cambridge, on 15 May 1843 and graduated BA as next above the 'wooden spoon' in the mathematical tripos in 1847, proceeding MA in 1851.

Called to the bar at the Inner Temple in the Easter term 1849, Hibbert at once developed a keen interest in politics. In 1857 he unsuccessfully contested his native town as a Liberal, but was returned unopposed at a by-election on 6 May 1862. Being re-elected after contests on 13 July 1865 and 18 November 1868, he lost the seat in February 1874, but regained it at a by-election on 1 March 1877, having in the interval unsuccessfully contested Blackburn. He was re-elected for Oldham on 31 March 1880 and on 25 November 1885, was defeated in 1886, regained the seat on 6 July 1892, and lost it finally on 15 July 1895. In all he was candidate for Oldham eleven times.

An enthusiastic supporter of W. E. Gladstone, he held minor office in Gladstone's four administrations, being parliamentary secretary of the Local Government Board from 1871 to 1874, and again from 1880 to 1883; under-secretary of the Home department (1883–4); financial secretary to the Treasury (1884–5 and 1892–5); and secretary to the Admiralty (1886). He was a businesslike administrator, a competent Liberal of the third rank. He also served on three royal commissions: the sanitary commission (1868); the boundary commission (1877); and the Welsh Sunday closing commission (1890). He served as well on the parliamentary committee on secondary education (1893). He materially helped the passing of the Execution within Gaols Act (1868), the Married Women's Property Act (1870), the Clergy Disabilities Act (1870), and the Municipal Elections Act (1884). Always keenly interested in poor-law reform, he was long president of the north-western poor-law conference.

To his native county, where he became JP in 1855 and deputy lieutenant in 1870, Hibbert's services were extensive, and he was more effective in local than in national government. On the passing of the Local Government Act, 1888, he was elected a county councillor for Cartmel, was chosen an alderman on 24 January 1889, was first chairman of the Lancashire county council on 14 February following, and was first chairman of the County Councils Association. Other local offices included that of governor of Owens College, Manchester, and of the courts of the Victoria University (where he was made DCL in 1902) and of Liverpool University. Hibbert was sworn of the privy council in 1886, and made KCB in 1893. He was appointed constable of Lancaster Castle in May 1907. Hibbert married first, in 1847, Eliza Anne (d. 1877), eldest daughter of Andrew Scholfield of Woodfield, Oldham; and second, in January 1878, Charlotte Henrietta, fourth daughter of Admiral Charles Warde, of Squerryes Court, Westerham, Kent. He died at his home, Hampsfield Hall, Grange-over-Sands, on 7 November 1908, and was buried at Lindall in Cartmel. His second wife, one son, and one daughter survived him.   T. C. HUGHES, rev. H. C. G. MATTHEW

Sources The Times (9 Nov 1908) · Dod's Peerage · 'The Right Hon. Sir John T. Hibbert', Manchester Faces and Places, 10 (1899), 221–4 · C. Hibbert, Memories of … Sir J. T. Hibbert, by his wife (1911) · private information (1912)
Archives BL, W. E. Gladstone MSS, Add. MSS 44429–44494 · Bodl. Oxf., corresp. with Sir William Harcourt · Bodl. Oxf., letters to J. E. Thorold Rogers
Likenesses R. E. Morrison, oils, Royal Albert Hospital, Lancaster · R. E. Morrison, oils, Lancashire county council offices, Preston · J. J. Shannon, oils, Oldham Art Gallery · wood-engraving, NPG; repro. in ILN (27 Aug 1892)
Wealth at death £58,204 1s. 10d.: probate, 30 March 1909, CGPLA Eng. & Wales

Hibbert, Robert (1769–1849), philanthropist, was born on 25 October 1769 in Jamaica, the third and posthumous son of John Hibbert (1732–1769), a Jamaica merchant, and his wife, Janet (d. 1778), daughter of Samuel Gordon. Following his mother's death he returned to England and was enrolled at Eton College in 1779. For a period in the 1780s he was a pupil, at Nottingham, of Gilbert Wakefield, who greatly influenced him. When Wakefield was imprisoned in 1801 for political pamphleteering, Hibbert sent him £1000.

Hibbert entered Emmanuel College, Cambridge, in 1787, where he formed a lifelong friendship with William Frend and graduated in 1791. He went to Kingston, Jamaica, the same year as partner in a family business. There he married, on 12 September 1792, Elizabeth Jane (1776–1853), daughter of John Nembhard MD. There were no children of the marriage. Hibbert and his wife returned to England in 1803, and in 1806 he bought the estate of East Hyde, near Luton, Bedfordshire. In 1819 he founded a charity at Luton to provide almshouses for twenty-four widows.

In Jamaica Hibbert owned slaves and was unconvinced by the arguments of Frend that this was immoral. In 1817 he sent out a Unitarian minister, Thomas Cooper, as a missionary to his slaves; he stayed in Jamaica until 1821 in the attempt to improve their moral and religious condition. Controversy attended the publication of Cooper's report

describing his failure. Hibbert sold his Jamaica holdings at a loss in 1836, having previously disposed of his Bedfordshire estate in 1833 and moved to London. He died at his home, 13 Welbeck Street, London, on 23 September 1849, and was buried in Kensal Green cemetery.

Hibbert's importance centres on the deed he executed in 1847, to come into effect after his death and that of his wife. A trust was to be set up to apply the income from capital 'in such manner as the trustees deem most conducive to the spread of Christianity in its most simple and intelligible form, and to the unfettered exercise of the right of private judgment in matters of religion'. He saw this formula as synonymous with Unitarianism, and the trust was originally called the Antitrinitarian Fund, the object of which was to provide divinity scholarships to encourage learning and culture among heterodox ministers.

However, his legal adviser, Edwin Wilkins Field, widened the founder's purpose, and in the early decades of the trust's history, after its formation in 1853, was mainly instrumental in expanding its scope. Throughout its history the trust has consistently supported pioneering ventures. An annual Hibbert lecture was commenced in 1878, given by a leading thinker of the day and subsequently published. These became an established institution, and, while they were discontinued for periods in the twentieth century, were reintroduced on BBC radio in the 1980s.

The Hibbert Journal was first published in 1902 under the editorship of Revd L. P. Jacks, who remained in the post until 1947. Unique at its inception, it was for half a century one of the main theological and philosophical journals published in the United Kingdom; the 1909 issue, entitled Jesus or Christ?, is considered a key document in twentieth-century theological scholarship. The journal ceased publication in 1968.

The trust has consistently given grants towards learned publications, and supported scholars and fellows at universities both in the UK and abroad. Since the 1850s the trust has given regular support to Manchester College, located first in London and then at Oxford, and its students. During the Second World War it set up Hibbert Houses at several places in the Middle East to provide for the welfare and support of military personnel, an activity which continued into the 1960s within Great Britain.

ALAN RUSTON

Sources J. Murch, Memoir of Robert Hibbert (1933) · A. Ruston, The Hibbert Trust, a history (1984) · GM, 2nd ser., 32 (1849), 552 · E. W. Field, 'Hibbert's Trust, or Antitrinitarian Fund', Christian Reformer, or, Unitarian Magazine and Review, new ser., 9 (1853), 246–9 · V. L. Oliver, ed., 'Family tree of the Hibberts', Caribbeana, 4 (1915–16) · S. G. Lee, 'Robert Hibbert and his religious background', Hibbert Journal (1953), 319–28 · Venn, Alum. Cant. · VCH Bedfordshire, vol. 2 · H. G. Tibbutt, 'Some Bedfordshire links with Unitarians and liberal Christians', Transactions of the Unitarian Historical Society, 14/3 (1967–70), 123–5 · J. E. Cussans, History of Hertfordshire, 3/2 (1881); facs. repr. (1972), 179–80
Wealth at death Hibbert Trust to be set up after wife's death; wealthy: will, proved 15 October 1849, PRO, PROB 11/2101, sig. 763; Murch, Memoir, 111–22

Hibbins, Ann (d. 1656), convicted witch, whose early years are obscure, may have been the sister of Richard Bellingham, a governor of Massachusetts. Claims to this effect are perhaps based on John Winthrop's statement that Bellingham was the brother-in-law of her husband, William Hibbins (d. 1654). A church register in Boston, Lincolnshire, lists William Hibbins's marriage to a Hester Bellingham, who may have been Richard's sister, on 4 March 1633. However, the date of that marriage is so close to William and Ann Hibbins's departure for Massachusetts in 1634 that it suggests the possibility that Hester and Ann were the same person. Ann Hibbins's will lists three sons with the surname Moore, indicating that she had a prior marriage and was probably widowed before marrying William Hibbins.

William and Ann Hibbins were two of many who followed the minister John Cotton to the new colony, arriving in the *Mary and John* in 1634. Both were admitted to Boston's First Church in September 1639. William rose quickly to eminence in the colony, serving as deputy to the general court in 1640–41, emissary to parliament in 1641, and as an assistant (or magistrate) from 1643 to 1654. The colony's esteem for William was not transferred to Ann, who was regarded as obstinate and proud. A protracted dispute between Ann and some carpenters over the fair price for work on the Hibbins's home remained unresolved after numerous attempts at arbitration by their fellow church member John Davis. When Hibbins charged Davis with collusion and dishonesty, the case came before the church. At issue also was Hibbins's treatment of her husband, whom she had 'against nature usurped authority over' (J. Demos, ed., *Remarkable Providences*, 1991, 238). Her failure to show sincere repentance for her behaviour resulted in excommunication in February 1641.

William Hibbins's death in 1654 removed his protection from his wife; within the year she was accused of practising witchcraft. It has been noted that Hibbins shared characteristics of other women accused as witches: she was outspoken, contentious, and a widow in a position to interrupt 'the orderly transition of property from one generation of males to another' (C. Karlsen, *The Devil in the Shape of a Woman*, 1987, 116). Hibbins was found guilty by the jury at her trial but the court of assistants sought to overturn the verdict. The case was referred to the general court, where the deputies outvoted the assistants, confirming her condemnation. She was executed as a witch on 19 June 1656, one of the first to suffer that fate in Massachusetts Bay Colony. Many opposed the proceedings. The Boston minister John Norton complained that Hibbins 'was hanged for a witch only for having more wit than her neighbours' ('Abstracts of the earliest wills', 283). The minister William Hubbard believed Hibbins was not 'well settled in her mind' and lamented, 'persons of hard favour and turbulent passions are apt to be condemned by the common people for witches, upon very slight grounds' (Hubbard, 574). Between her conviction and hanging Hibbins made out her will, in which she left her estate of £344 14s. to her three sons, John, Joseph, and Jonathan Moore,

all living in Ireland. Days before her execution her son Jonathan arrived in Massachusetts. Her will notes his 'more yn ordinary affection & paines … in the times of my distresse'. On behalf of his brothers Jonathan received the proceeds of the estate on 30 July 1656 in Boston.

JENNY HALE PULSIPHER

Sources 'Abstracts of the earliest wills on record in the county of Suffolk', *New England Historical and Genealogical Register*, 6 (1852), 283 • R. D. Pierce, ed., *The records of the First Church in Boston, 1630–1868*, 3 vols. (1961) • J. Savage, *A genealogical dictionary of the first settlers of New England*, 4 vols. (1860–62) • C. E. Banks, *Planters of the commonwealth* (1930) • G. B. Roberts, *English origins of New England families*, 2 (1985) • W. Hubbard, *A general history of New England from the discovery to MDCLXXX* (Cambridge, MA, 1815), 574 • *John Winthrop's journal: 'History of New England', 1630–1649*, ed. J. K. Hosmer, 2 vols. (1908) • N. B. Shurtleff, ed., *Records of the governor and company of the Massachusetts Bay in New England*, 5 vols. in 6 (1853–4) • R. Keayne, 'Notes on John Cotton's sermons', Mass. Hist. Soc. • J. Kamensky, *Governing the tongue: the politics of speech in early New England* (1996) • M. Peterson, 'Hibbins, Ann', *ANB*
Archives Mass. Hist. Soc., Robert Keayne, 'Notes on John Cotton's sermons'
Wealth at death £344 14s.: 'Abstracts of the earliest wills'

Hibbs, Richard (1812?–1886), writer on poverty, came from Hampshire, and studied at St John's College, Cambridge (of which he was scholar), matriculating in 1837 and proceeding BA in 1841 and MA in 1844. He took orders in 1842 and was curate of Bishop Hatfield, Hertfordshire (1841–3), and of Corton, near Lowestoft (1843–8); teacher and preacher at Lowestoft (1848–52); curate of St Paul's, Covent Garden (1852); and assistant minister of St John's Chapel, Edinburgh (1852–4). His connection with this last terminated somewhat suddenly. A bitter controversy with the incumbent led him to establish the New Church of England Chapel, St Vincent Street, where he ministered for some years and of which he published an account (1858). He was subsequently British chaplain at Lisbon, Rotterdam, and Utrecht. Hibbs's chief work, founded on personal investigation, is *Prussia and the poor, or, Observations upon the systematised relief of the poor at Elberfeld in contrast with that of England* (1876; 4th edn, 1883). Besides separate sermons, he also published works on Scottish church controversies and baptism, and *God's Plea for the Poor* (1851). He died at his home, 13 St Lawrence Road, North Kensington, London, on 26 March 1886, his wife, Fanny, surviving him.

FRANCIS WATT, rev. H. C. G. MATTHEW

Sources *The Academy* (10 April 1886), 255–6 • Venn, *Alum. Cant.* • Boase, *Mod. Eng. biog.* • *CGPLA Eng. & Wales* (1886)
Wealth at death £3640 7s.: resworn probate, June 1886, *CGPLA Eng. & Wales*

Hibernia, Peter de [Peter Hibernicus] (fl. 1239–1266), natural philosopher, was probably of Anglo-Irish origins, a member of a family that had settled in the Norman kingdom of Sicily. Little is recorded of the events of his life, and that little has in the past been obfuscated by scribal and exegetical errors confusing him with his contemporary and near namesake, the jurist Peter de Isernia. There can be no doubt that it was the latter whom Frederick II, probably in 1224, invited to become professor of civil law at the University of Naples. It has been plausibly argued that Peter de Hibernia trained in the natural sciences at

Oxford, and in logic at Paris, but nothing certain is known of his career until the period 1239–45, when, as a master at the University of Naples, he taught logic and natural philosophy to the young Thomas Aquinas. Aquinas later referred to an opinion of his former master, when commenting on the *Sentences* at Paris. Peter came to enjoy a high reputation at Naples. The proem to a *determinatio* which he delivered before King Manfred, some time between 1258 and 1266, describes him as 'the jewel of masters', while to Rabbi Moses ben Solomon of Salerno, who a few years earlier discussed with him proposals for a Latin translation of the *Guide for the Perplexed* of Maimonides, Peter was 'a wise Christian'.

Three of Peter de Hibernia's philosophical works are known to survive, his *determinatio* before Manfred, and commentaries on the *Perihermeneias* and *De longitudine* of Aristotle. Three other attributions have been rejected. Heavily influenced by Averroes, though not to the extent of accepting the latter's heterodox opinions, Peter's commentaries show him to have been a man of wide reading, especially in Arabic and Jewish sources, and some independence of mind. A striking characteristic of his philosophical work is its lack of reference to Christian doctrine—just a single allusion to Jesus' bloody sweat, as proof of his humanity. A few eccentricities like a belief that barnacle geese are hatched from trees notwithstanding, Peter was a natural philosopher of impressive learning and depth, and a master of the form of commentary that combined exposition (*lectio*) with discussion of disputed or difficult points (*quaestiones*). His analysis of the *Perihermeneias* probably influenced that of his famous pupil. Thomas Tanner records that Peter de Hibernia, whom he describes as the author of theological quodlibets (not known to survive), apparently died at Naples. This seems likely enough, but neither the place nor the date of Peter's death is now capable of demonstration.

HENRY SUMMERSON

Sources *Magistri Petri de Ybernia expositio et quaestiones in Aristotelis librum de longitudine et brevitate vitae*, ed. M. Dunne (Louvain-la-Neuve, 1993) · M. Dunne, 'Petrus de Hibernia: a thirteenth century Irish philosopher', *Philosophical Studies*, 33 (1991–2), 201–29 · J. McEvoy, 'Maître Pierre d'Irlande, professeur *in naturalibus* à l'université de Naples', *Actualité de la pensée médiévale*, ed. J. Follon and J. McEvoy (Louvain-la-Neuve, 1994), 146–58 · J.-L.-A. Huillard-Bréholles, ed., *Historia diplomatica Friderici secundi*, 2/1 (Paris, 1852), 448–53 · Tanner, *Bibl. Brit.-Hib.*, 595 · R. Sharpe, *A handlist of the Latin writers of Great Britain and Ireland before 1540* (1997), 428

Hibernicus, Thomas [Thomas of Ireland] (*c.*1270–*c.*1340), theologian, was born in Ireland. He was already a master of arts in 1295, which suggests that he could have been born as early as 1265, but certainly no later than 1275. He may have studied in England for a short time, and it was certainly in England that he learned to copy books, because those examples of his handwriting that survive display many features that are distinctively English. However, he left England early in his scholarly career and studied arts in Paris, at the Sorbonne. He had graduated as master of arts by 9 June 1295, when as such he witnessed a document concerning college business. He went on to study theology and probably took the bachelor degree. His formal theological studies went no further, however, and he probably left the Sorbonne by 1306, because the earliest manuscript of his work, which dates from that period, describes him as 'one-time fellow' of the college. He may have been appointed to a benefice, and he certainly remained in Paris, closely associated with the Sorbonne, for the rest of his life. He wrote almost exclusively on matters of pastoral theology, concerns that suggest he had experienced the work of pastoral care at first hand. He may have received a benefice from Nicolas de Bar-le-Duc, bishop of Mâcon, for whom he made a copy of his *Manipulus florum*. He died in Paris probably in the 1330s or 1340s, and left the Sorbonne at least seven books from his considerable library, including copies of his own works. He also bequeathed a substantial cash gift of 16 livres.

Thomas Hibernicus's best-known and most influential work was the *Manipulus florum*, a handbook of pastoral theology and preaching material intended for the parish priest. He probably completed the text about the time he left the Sorbonne, and it was certainly in circulation by 1310. As Hibernicus explains in the prologue, the *Manipulus* was the product of many hours of research spent in the library of his old college. It gathered together some 6000 extracts from classical and patristic sources, along with a bibliography listing over 350 different works. The work was in every sense a compilation—Hibernicus borrowed his subject list and extracts from many existing works, including the popular *Liber exceptionum* and the well-known collections of literary *exempla*, the *Florilegium Anglicanum* and *Florilegium Gallicanum*. But his organization of the extracts did represent a significant step forward. Arranged alphabetically under a comprehensive list of subject headings, and with a vast index, it was by far the most sophisticated and yet easy to use of contemporary reference works.

Hibernicus also wrote three shorter works probably intended to complement each other, *De tribus punctis*, on the work of the secular clergy, *De tribus hierarchiis*, which expands the discussion of hierarchies included at the end of *De tribus punctis*, and *De tribus sensibus sacre scripture*, which explains the four senses of scripture. Hibernicus was notable for the extent to which he copied, reworked and edited his own works; at least two of the earliest copies of the *Manipulus* are in his own hand.

The *Manipulus* exercised a vast influence on preachers, theologians, and bibliographers in late medieval Europe; almost 200 manuscripts are known to survive in English, French, and eastern European sources. It became the model for many later preaching handbooks and florilegia, and was a favourite source for late medieval sermons. It seems also to have played a practical role in the continuing work of pastoral care. In 1349 the text was incorporated into the first provincial statutes of the new archdiocese of Prague, and it continued to be a popular sourcebook for pastoral duties throughout the fifteenth century. Canon lawyers, such as the Englishman William Pagula (*d.* 1332), also made extensive use of it in their compilations. The *Manipulus* remained popular during the Renaissance, and a large number of editions were printed in the late fifteenth and sixteenth centuries.

Thomas de Hibernia (*d. c*.1270), a Franciscan friar also from Ireland, has often been confused with Hibernicus. He spent the greater part of his career in Italy where he studied under Peter de Hibernia. He was the author of the *Promptuarium morale*, a text on pastoral theology, but he was apparently reluctant to enter the priesthood himself—so much so that he is said to have cut off his own left thumb to make himself ineligible. He died *c*.1270 and was buried in the convent at Acquila. Thomas Hibernicus has also been wrongly identified with another Franciscan, Thomas Palmer, or Palmerstown, from Palmerstown, Kildare, who was active in England in the later fourteenth century. He was a member of the Winchester convent in 1371, prior provincial of the order in England from 1393 to 1396, and prior of the London convent from 1397 to 1407. He probably died in 1415.   JAMES G. CLARK

Sources R. H. Rouse and M. A. Rouse, *Preachers, florilegia and sermons: studies on the 'Manipulus florum' of Thomas of Ireland* (1979), esp. 93–112 • F. Stegmüller, ed., *Repertorium biblicum medii aevi*, 5 (Madrid, 1955), 365–6 • P. Glorieux, *La faculté des arts et ses maîtres au XIII siècle* (1971), 371–2 • Bale, *Index*, 440 • L. Wadding, *Annales minorum*, ed. J. M. Fonseca and others, 2nd edn, 4 (1732), 321
Archives Bibliothèque Nationale, Paris, MSS lat. 15985, 15986
Wealth at death 16 livres, left to the Sorbonne, Paris

Hichens, (William) Lionel [Nel] (1874–1940), public servant and industrialist, was born on 1 May 1874, at St Leonards, posthumous second son of John Ley Hichens, army surgeon, and his wife, Catherine Bacchus (1843–1924). He was educated at Winchester College, New College, Oxford, and in Paris and Germany. He taught at Sherborne School between 1898 and 1899, before enlisting with the City Imperial Volunteers during the 'black week' of British defeats in the Second South African War and serving for six months as a dispatch rider.

Lord Cromer appointed Hichens to the Egyptian ministry of finance in 1900. After nine months he was recruited by Lord Milner as a member of his 'kindergarten' formed for reconstruction work in the conquered South African colonies. As town treasurer of Johannesburg (1901–2) and colonial treasurer of the Transvaal (1902–7) Nel Hichens proved a shrewd, deft, and tactful administrator. He visited India in 1907–8 as a member of the royal commission on decentralization, and chaired a board of inquiry into the public service of Southern Rhodesia in 1909. During his visit to that country he ensured the preservation of the Zimbabwe ruins. He was a founder of the round table group of Milnerite imperialists, and after 1910 was much involved in the contents of its quarterly journal, the *Round Table*. At this stage he had ambitions for a parliamentary career, and in 1914, together with Lionel Curtis and Edward Grigg, he evolved a proposal for a federated British Isles, which was accepted by several Conservative leaders as a solution of the Irish constitutional crisis.

Lord Selborne and his wife were mentors to Hichens, and it was doubtless through Selborne's intervention that in 1910 Hichens became chairman of Cammell Laird, shipbuilders, steelmakers, and armaments manufacturers. As

he had no industrial experience, it seemed a quixotic appointment, but Hichens steered the company from desperate straits to solid ground and remained chairman until his death. He was a director of Cammell Laird's associated companies, and served as chairman of the English Electric Company (1927–30).

Together with his friend Robert Brand, Hichens went on an official mission to Canada in 1915 and assisted in forming the imperial munitions board. As chairman from 1916 of the Central Council of Associations of Controlled Firms, he represented some 2700 controlled establishments in their dealings with the Ministry of Munitions. Unlike other big armaments companies, Cammell Laird subordinated questions of profit to the public interest and avoided any suspicion of war profiteering. Hichens despised money-grubbing or idolatry of wealth. He regarded industry as a form of national service and industrial problems as essentially moral.

Hichens served on many public bodies, including the committee on the national debt (1924), Lord Colwyn's committee on economies in the fighting services (1925), the royal commission on licensing (1929), and the royal commission on lotteries and betting (1932). Among many educational interests he was from 1927 an active chairman of the governors of Birkbeck College, London University. In 1929 he bought North Aston Hall, North Aston, near Oxford, and henceforth kept a close connection with university men. He was a fellow of Winchester College from 1933.

Lionel Hichens married in 1919 (Mary) Hermione (1894–1985), third daughter of General Sir Neville Lyttelton. It was a devoted marriage. She was a woman of great character who shared his qualities and ideals; they had three sons and three daughters. Hichens was killed by a German bomb which fell on Church House, Westminster, on 14 October 1940, and was buried at North Aston church on 19 October.

Tall, handsome, and vigorous, with a commanding presence and decisive manner, Hichens was a powerful public speaker and persuasive colleague. His counsel was widely sought, and his opinions were worth hearing. He was excessively modest, and could seem austere, but had no trace of priggishness. He was self-confident, candid, affectionate, cheerful, and steadfast. He lived according to Christian ideals. He deplored pusillanimity, double-dealing, or disloyalty: his honesty was inexpugnable.

RICHARD DAVENPORT-HINES

Sources private information (2004) [Mrs Hermione Hichens] • *Round Table*, 31 (Dec 1940), 5–16 • *The Times* (17 Oct 1940) • W. Nimocks, *Milner's young men: the 'kindergarten' in Edwardian imperial affairs* (1970) • J. E. Kendle, *The Round Table movement and imperial union* (1975) • D. Lavin, *From empire to commonwealth* (1995) • *The Observer* (27 Oct 1940) • *The crisis of British power: the imperial and naval papers of the second earl of Selborne, 1895–1910*, ed. D. G. Boyce (1990) • *The Leo Amery diaries*, ed. J. Barnes and D. Nicholson, 2 vols. (1980–88) • C. Addison, *Politics from within*, 2 vols. (1924)
Archives Bodl. Oxf., corresp., diaries, and papers • Derbys. RO, papers relating to British South Africa Company • priv. coll. | Bodl. Oxf., corresp. with Lionel Curtis • Bodl. Oxf., Lord Milner MSS • Bodl. Oxf., earl and countess of Selborne MSS • Bodl. Oxf., letters to Lady Selborne • Hopton Hall, Wirksworth, Derbyshire,

Philip Lyttelton MSS · NA Scot., corresp. with Lord Lothian · University of Cape Town Library, corresp. with Patrick Duncan
Likenesses photograph, c.1925, repro. in R. P. T. Davenport-Hines, 'Hichens, William Lionel', *DBB*
Wealth at death £5463 5s. 0d.: resworn probate, Dec 1942, *CGPLA Eng. & Wales*

Hichens, Robert Smythe (1864–1950), writer, was born on 14 November 1864 at the rectory, Speldhurst, Kent, the eldest of the five children of the Revd Frederick Harrison Hichens and Abigail Elizabeth, *née* Smythe. His father's family was from Northamptonshire and his grandfather founded the firm of Hichens and Harrison. His mother was from co. Westmeath, Ireland, but grew up in Pau, France, where she met her husband. Hichens was at Hurstleigh School in Tunbridge Wells before attending Clifton College after the family moved to Bristol. While at Clifton College, Hichens found that he had talent for both music and writing. His family moving to Kent in 1884, Hichens took the opportunity to move to London and attend the Royal College of Music. He had some minor success as a lyricist but soon realized that he 'was not highly gifted in a musical sense' (Hichens, 30). In 1886 he published *The Coastguard's Secret*, written when he was seventeen years old. In 1888 he asked his father to secure him a place at the London School of Journalism, where he found favour with its director, David Anderson. After a year he left and began to contribute to various periodicals including *Mistress and Maid* and the *Pall Mall Magazine*.

In 1893 Hichens became seriously ill and nearly died of peritonitis. Upon recovering, he travelled to Egypt to complete his convalescence. Meeting Lord Alfred Douglas and Oscar Wilde while there, he became intrigued with the notion of the aesthete. His time in Egypt was spent writing *The Green Carnation*, which was published anonymously by Heinemann in 1894 and was an immediate success, indeed 'un succès de scandale' (Hichens, 71). Labelled 'the finest Satire of the Nineties' (Weintraub, 1), *The Green Carnation* satirizes the aesthete and contains a fictionalized portrait of Oscar Wilde. Although Hichens found that 'a certain amount of unpleasantness was caused to [him] by the many criticisms of well-known living people' (Hichens, 74) the novel assured him a place in the highest literary circles and he was friendly with the likes of Max Beerbohm, Marie Corelli, and Henry James.

Returning to London, Hichens continued his journalistic endeavours and succeeded George Bernard Shaw as music critic of the London *World*. He also wrote several plays, including *Becky Sharp* written, in collaboration with Cosmo Gordon-Lennox, for Marie Tempest. Several novels and short stories published before the First World War stand out as excellent, including *An Imaginative Man* (1895), *The Londoners: an Absurdity* (1898), and 'How Love Came to Professor Guildea' (*Tongues of Conscience*, 1900). The *Londoners* consolidated his position as a satirist as Edwardian society was alternately shocked, thrilled, and intrigued.

Eventually giving up journalism in order to travel abroad and write, Hichens returned again and again to Egypt and north Africa. These locales provided him with the seemingly exotic settings for his romances. *The Slave: a Romance* (1900), *The Woman with the Fan* (1904), and *The Barbary Sheep* (1909) all bear testament to his interest in the Near East. However, it was *The Garden of Allah* (1905) which provided him with his greatest success. The romance between a socialite seeking solace in the desert and a Trappist monk who has left his monastery was an instant success. Hichens also wrote several travel narratives about Egypt and the Near East, including *The Spell of Egypt* (1910) and *The Holy Land* (1913).

During the First World War, Hichens was a member of the special constabulary in Tankerton and London. It was at this time that he became friendly with the Swiss novelist John Knittel. For the next twenty-five years Hichens lived in numerous locales with Knittel, his wife Frances, and their children. Rather than returning to England permanently, Hichens and the Knittels divided their time between Africa, the French riviera, and Switzerland.

Several novels by Hichens were dramatized for stage and screen. *The Garden of Allah* was filmed three times, the best-known being the 1936 film starring Marlene Dietrich and Basil Rathbone (directed by Richard Boleslawski). As well, in 1947, Alfred Hitchcock directed Gregory Peck and Charles Laughton in the adaptation of Hichens's courtroom thriller *The Paradine Case*.

During the Second World War Hichens lived in Zürich and wrote his autobiography, entitled *Yesterday* (1947). It is an entertaining and self-critical narrative. He had an excellent ear for conversation and much of the book is spent describing encounters with diverse high-ranking members of both social and literary circles. Although the aristocratic name-dropping becomes repetitive, the self-deprecating descriptions are amusing. His acquaintance, whether it was in passing or a long friendship, with such notables as Sarah Bernhardt, Howard Carter, W. Somerset Maugham, and Elizabeth von Arnim is wittily depicted. He was a great admirer of André Gide and thought him 'one of the most remarkable of living writers' (Hichens, 155).

Hichens never married. He was a professional writer, writing quickly and with little fuss when a piece was required. He died in hospital at Zürich on 20 July 1950.

M. R. BELLASIS, *rev.* STACY GILLIS

Sources R. Hichens, *Yesterday* (1947) · *The Times* (22 July 1950) · www.indiana.edu/~victoria [Victorianist discussion e-list] · S. Weintraub, introduction, in R. Hichens, *The green carnation* (1970)
Archives Royal Society of Literature, London, letters to the Royal Society of Literature · U. Leeds, Brotherton L., letters to Bram Stoker | FILM BFI NFTVA · Metro-Goldwyn-Mayer Archives, California
Likenesses M. Beerbohm, caricature, 1898, V&A · J. Russell & Sons, photograph, c.1915, NPG · photograph, repro. in Hichens, *Yesterday*

PICTURE CREDITS

Haydon, Benjamin Robert (1786–1846)—© National Portrait Gallery, London

Hayek, Friedrich August (1899–1992)—© National Portrait Gallery, London

Hayes, Catherine (1825–1861)—© National Portrait Gallery, London

Hayes, Edward Brian (1935–1973)—Redferns

Hayes, Patricia Lawlor (1909–1998)—© reserved; British Film Institute

Hayes, Philip (*bap.* 1738, *d.* 1797)—Faculty of Music, University of Oxford

Hayes, William (*bap.* 1708, *d.* 1777)—© National Portrait Gallery, London

Hayman, Francis (1707/8–1776)—Exeter City Museums & Art Gallery

Hayter, Sir George (1792–1871)—© National Portrait Gallery, London

Hayter, Stanley William (1901–1988)—© Burlington / Lewinski Archive; collection National Portrait Gallery, London

Hayter, Thomas (*bap.* 1702, *d.* 1762)—by kind permission of the Lord Bishop of London and the Church Commissioners of England. Photograph: Photographic Survey, Courtauld Institute of Art, London

Hayter, Sir William Goodenough, first baronet (1792–1878)—© National Portrait Gallery, London

Hayter, Sir William Goodenough (1906–1995)—© National Portrait Gallery, London

Hayward, Abraham (1801–1884)—© National Portrait Gallery, London

Hayward, Sir Isaac James (1884–1976)—© National Portrait Gallery, London

Hayward, Sir John (1564?–1627)—© National Portrait Gallery, London

Hayward, John Davy (1905–1965)—© National Portrait Gallery, London

Haywood, Eliza (1693?–1756)—© National Portrait Gallery, London

Hazlitt, William (1778–1830)—Maidstone Museums and Art Galleries / Bridgeman Art Library

Head, Antony Henry, first Viscount Head (1906–1983)—© National Portrait Gallery, London

Head, Sir Francis Bond, first baronet (1793–1875)—© National Portrait Gallery, London

Headlam, Stewart Duckworth (1847–1924)—© National Portrait Gallery, London

Headlam, Walter George (1866–1908)—King's College Archives, Cambridge

Heal, Sir Ambrose (1872–1959)—© Charlotte & Stephen Halliday; by kind permission of Heal and Son Ltd

Healy, Cahir (1877–1970)—© National Portrait Gallery, London

Healy, Timothy Michael (1855–1931)—private collection; photograph © National Portrait Gallery, London

Hearn, Mary Anne [Marianne Farningham] (1834–1909)—© National Portrait Gallery, London

Hearne, Thomas (*bap.* 1678, *d.* 1735)—© National Portrait Gallery, London

Heath, Ambrose (1891–1969)—© National Portrait Gallery, London

Heath, George Edward [Ted] (1902–1969)—© David Wedgbury; collection National Portrait Gallery, London

Heath, (Seifield) Gordon (1918–1991)—Collection Stephen Bourne

Heath, Henry [Paul of St Magdalen] (*bap.* 1599, *d.* 1643)—© National Portrait Gallery, London

Heath, Neville George Clevely (1917–1946)—© reserved; photograph National Portrait Gallery, London

Heath, Nicholas (1501?–1578)—© National Portrait Gallery, London

Heath, Sir Robert (1575–1649)—private collection; photograph Christie's Images Ltd

Heathcoat, John (1783–1861)—© National Portrait Gallery, London

Heathcote, Sir Gilbert, first baronet (1652–1733)—unknown collection; photograph Sotheby's Picture Library, London / National Portrait Gallery, London

Heathcote, Sir William, fifth baronet (1801–1881)—© National Portrait Gallery, London

Heaton, Sir John Henniker, first baronet (1848–1914)—Ashmolean Museum, Oxford

Heaviside, Oliver (1850–1925)—Institution of Electrical Engineers Archives Department

Heber, Reginald (1783–1826)—All Souls College, Oxford

Heber, Richard (1774–1833)—© National Portrait Gallery, London

Heberden, William (1710–1801)—by permission of the Royal College of Physicians, London

Hector, Sir James (1834–1907)—Glenbow Archives, Calgary, Alberta (NA 588-1)

Heenan, John Carmel (1905–1975)—© National Portrait Gallery, London

Heffer, Eric Samuel (1922–1991)—© News International Newspapers Ltd

Heidegger, Johann Jakob (1666–1749)—© National Portrait Gallery, London

Heilbron, Sir Ian Morris (1886–1959)—© National Portrait Gallery, London

Heinemann, Margot Claire (1913–1992)—© The Guardian; photograph National Portrait Gallery, London

Heinemann, William (1863–1920)—© reserved; collection Heinemann Ltd

Heins, John Theodore (1697–1756)—© Norwich Castle Museum & Art Gallery

Heke Pokai, Hone Wiremu (*c.*1807/8–1850)—Alexander Turnbull Library, National Library of New Zealand, Te Puna Matauranga o Aotearoa (PUBL-0014-44)

Helpmann, Sir Robert Murray (1909–1986)—© Estate of Pamela Chandler / National Portrait Gallery, London

Helps, Sir Arthur (1813–1875)—© National Portrait Gallery, London

Hemans, Felicia Dorothea (1793–1835)—© National Portrait Gallery, London

Hempson, Denis (1694/5?–1807)—© National Portrait Gallery, London

Henchman, Humphrey (*bap.* 1592, *d.* 1675)—private collection, on loan to Plymouth Art Gallery; © reserved in the photograph

Henderson, Alexander (*c.*1583–1646)—Scottish National Portrait Gallery

Henderson, Arthur (1863–1935)—© National Portrait Gallery, London

Henderson, Sir David (1862–1921)—© National Portrait Gallery, London

Henderson, David Willis Wilson (1903–1968)—Godfrey Argent Studios / Royal Society

Henderson, Eugénie Jane Andrina (1914–1989)—photograph reproduced by courtesy of The British Academy

Henderson, Sir Hubert Douglas (1890–1952)—© National Portrait Gallery, London

Henderson, John (*bap.* 1747, *d.* 1785)—© National Portrait Gallery, London

Henderson, Sir Nevile Meyrick (1882–1942)—© National Portrait Gallery, London

Henderson, Nigel Graeme (1917–1985)—© reserved; Henderson Estate; photograph National Portrait Gallery, London

Henderson, Sir William MacGregor (1913–2000)—© reserved; Universal Pictorial Press & Agency; photograph National Portrait Gallery, London

Hendriks, Rose Ellen (*fl.* 1845–1856)—© National Portrait Gallery, London

Hendrix, James Marshall [Jimi] (1942–1970)—Getty Images – Hulton Archive

Hendy, Sir Philip Anstiss (1900–1980)—© National Portrait Gallery, London

Hengler, (Frederick) Charles (1820–1887)—V&A Images, The Victoria and Albert Museum

Hengler, Jenny Louise (*b.* 1849)—V&A Images, The Victoria and Albert Museum

Henley, Anthony (1666/7–1711)—© National Portrait Gallery, London

Henley, Robert, first earl of Northington (*c.*1708–1772)—All Souls College, Oxford

Henley, William Ernest (1849–1903)—© National Portrait Gallery, London

Henley, William Thomas (1813?–1882)—Institution of Electrical Engineers Archives Department

Hennell, Sara Sophia (1812–1899)—Herbert Art Gallery and Museum

Hennessy, (Richard) James Arthur Pope- (1916–1974)—© Lucian Freud; private collection; photograph National Portrait Gallery, London

Hennessy, Sir John Wyndham Pope- (1913–1994)—© National Portrait Gallery, London

Henrici, Olaus Magnus Friedrich Erdmann (1840–1918)—DH57, College Collection Photographs, UCL Library Services

Henrietta Maria (1609–1669)—The Royal Collection © 2004 HM Queen Elizabeth II

Henriette Anne, Princess, duchess of Orléans (1644–1670)—© National Portrait Gallery, London

Henrion, (Frederick) Henri Kay (1914–1990)—© Wolfgang Suschitzky / National Portrait Gallery, London

Henry I (1068/9–1135)—Corpus Christi College, Oxford / Bridgeman Art Library

Henry II (1133–1189)—photograph: AKG London

Henry III (1207–1272)—© Dean and Chapter of Westminster

Henry IV (1366–1413)—by kind permission of the Dean and Chapter of Canterbury Cathedral; photographer Dr Christopher Wilson

Henry V (1386/7–1422)—The Royal Collection © 2004 HM Queen Elizabeth II

Henry VI (1421–1471)—© National Portrait Gallery, London

Henry VII (1457–1509)—© National Portrait Gallery, London

Henry VIII (1491–1547)—© National Portrait Gallery, London

Henry VIII, privy chamber of (*act.* 1509–1547) [Sir Henry Neville (*c.*1520–1593)]—© reserved

Henry Benedict [Henry Benedict Stuart] (1725–1807)—private collection

Henry Frederick, prince of Wales (1594–1612)—The Royal Collection © 2004 HM Queen Elizabeth II

Henry Frederick, Prince, duke of Cumberland and Strathearn (1745–1790)—The Royal Collection © 2004 HM Queen Elizabeth II

Henry of Lancaster, first duke of Lancaster (*c.*1310–1361)—The British Library

Henry, Matthew (1662–1714)—© National Portrait Gallery, London

Henry, Philip (1631–1696)—© National Portrait Gallery, London

Henry, William (1774–1836)—© National Portrait Gallery, London

Henschel, Sir George (1850–1934)—Christie's Images Ltd. (2004)

Henslow, John Stevens (1796–1861)—Ipswich Borough Council Museums and Galleries

Henson, Herbert Hensley (1863–1947)—© National Portrait Gallery, London

Henson, Leslie Lincoln (1891–1957)—© National Portrait Gallery, London

Henty, Edward (1810–1878)—La Trobe Picture Collection, State Library of Victoria

Henty, George Alfred (1832–1902)—© National Portrait Gallery, London

Hepburn, Audrey (1929–1993)—© National Portrait Gallery, London

Hepburn, James, fourth earl of Bothwell and duke of Orkney (1534/5–1578)—Scottish National Portrait Gallery

Hepburn, Patrick George Thomas Buchan-, Baron Hailes (1901–1974)—© National Portrait Gallery, London

Hepworth, Dame (Jocelyn) Barbara (1903–1975)—© Alan Bowness, Hepworth Estate; collection National Portrait Gallery, London

Hepworth, Cecil Milton (1874–1953)—Elmbridge Museum / © private collection

Herbert, Arthur, earl of Torrington (1648–1716)—Normanby Hall Country Park, North Lincolnshire Museums Service

Herbert, Auberon Edward William Molyneux (1838–1906)—© National Portrait Gallery, London

Herbert, Aubrey Nigel Henry Molyneux (1880–1923)—private collection

Herbert, Edward, first Baron Herbert of Cherbury and first Baron Herbert of Castle Island (1582?–1648)—National Trust Photographic Library / Powis Estate Trustees

Herbert, Edward, second earl of Powis (1785–1848)—National Trust Photographic Library / John Hammond

Herbert, Elizabeth, countess of Pembroke and Montgomery (1737–1831)—Collection of the Earl of Pembroke and Trustees of Wilton House Trust, Wilton House, Salisbury, UK

Herbert, (Mary) Elizabeth, Lady Herbert of Lea (1822–1911)—© National Portrait Gallery, London

Herbert, George (1593–1633)—by permission of the Houghton Library, Harvard University (from MS Eng. 1405)

Herbert, George Edward Stanhope Molyneux, fifth earl of Carnarvon (1866–1923)—Griffith Institute, Oxford

Herbert, Henry, second earl of Pembroke (b. in or after 1538, d. 1601)—© National Museums and Galleries of Wales

Herbert, Sir Henry (bap. 1594, d. 1673)—Powis Castle, The Powis Collection (The National Trust). Photograph: Photographic Survey, Courtauld Institute of Art, London

Herbert, Henry Howard Molyneux, fourth earl of Carnarvon (1831–1890)—© National Portrait Gallery, London

Herbert, John Rogers (1810–1890)—© National Portrait Gallery, London

Herbert [Sidney], Mary, countess of Pembroke (1561–1621)—© National Portrait Gallery, London

Herbert, Philip, first earl of Montgomery and fourth earl of Pembroke (1584–1650)—Collection of the Earl of Pembroke and Trustees of Wilton House Trust, Wilton House, Salisbury, UK

Herbert, Sir Robert George Wyndham (1831–1905)—© National Portrait Gallery, London

Herbert, Sidney, first Baron Herbert of Lea (1810–1861)—© National Portrait Gallery, London

Herbert, William, first earl of Pembroke (1506/7–1570)—Collection of the Earl of Pembroke and Trustees of Wilton House Trust, Wilton House, Salisbury, UK

Herbert, William, third earl of Pembroke (1580–1630)—Collection of the Earl of Pembroke and Trustees of Wilton House Trust, Wilton House, Salisbury, UK

Herbert, William (1718–1795)—© National Portrait Gallery, London

Herbison, Margaret McCrorie [Peggy] (1907–1996)—© National Portrait Gallery, London

Heriot, George (1563–1624)—courtesy of George Heriot Trust, Edinburgh

Herkomer, Sir Hubert von (1849–1914)—courtesy of Bushey Museum and Art Gallery

Hermes, Gertrude Anna Bertha (1901–1983)—© Simon Hughes-Stanton & Judith Russell; collection National Portrait Gallery, London

Heron, Patrick (1920–1999)—© Burlington / Lewinski Archive; collection National Portrait Gallery, London

Herrick, Robert (bap. 1591, d. 1674)—© National Portrait Gallery, London

Herring, John Frederick, senior (1795–1865)—private collection; photograph © National Portrait Gallery, London

Herring, Thomas (1693–1757)—© Tate, London, 2004

Herringham, Christiana Jane, Lady Herringham (1852–1929)—photograph National Portrait Gallery, London

Herschel, Caroline Lucretia (1750–1848)—Ashmolean Museum, Oxford

Herschel, Sir John Frederick William, first baronet (1792–1871)—© National Portrait Gallery, London

Herschel, Sir William (1738–1822)—© National Portrait Gallery, London

Herschel, Sir William James, second baronet (1833–1917)—private collection; photograph © National Portrait Gallery, London

Herschell, Farrer, first Baron Herschell (1837–1899)—© National Portrait Gallery, London

Herschell, Ridley Haim (1807–1864)—© National Portrait Gallery, London

Hertslet, Sir Edward (1824–1902)—© National Portrait Gallery, London

Hertz, Joseph Herman (1872–1946)—© National Portrait Gallery, London

Hertzog, James Barry Munnik (1866–1942)—© National Portrait Gallery, London

Hervey, Lord Arthur Charles (1808–1894)—© National Portrait Gallery, London

Hervey, Augustus John, third earl of Bristol (1724–1779)—Manor House Museum, Bury St Edmunds

Hervey, Frederick Augustus, fourth earl of Bristol (1730–1803)—unknown collection / Christie's; photograph National Portrait Gallery, London

Hervey, John, second Baron Hervey of Ickworth (1696–1743)—© National Portrait Gallery, London

Hervey, Mary, Lady Hervey of Ickworth (1699/1700–1768)—private collection; photograph National Portrait Gallery, London

Heseltine, Philip Arnold [Peter Warlock] (1894–1930)—© reserved; private collection; photograph National Portrait Gallery, London / Oxford University Press

Hesilrige, Sir Arthur, second baronet (1601–1661)—© National Portrait Gallery, London

Hess, Dame (Julia) Myra (1890–1965)—© National Portrait Gallery, London

Hetherington, Sir Hector James Wright (1888–1965)—© National Portrait Gallery, London

Hetherington, Henry (1792–1849)—© National Portrait Gallery, London

Heton, Martin (1554–1609)—Christ Church, Oxford

Hewart, Gordon, first Viscount Hewart (1870–1943)—© National Portrait Gallery, London

Hewett, Sir John Prescott (1854–1941)—© National Portrait Gallery, London

Hewett, Sir William Nathan Wrighte (1834–1888)—© National Portrait Gallery, London

Hewins, William Albert Samuel (1865–1931)—© National Portrait Gallery, London

Hewitt, Sir Frederic William (1857–1916)—© National Portrait Gallery, London

Hewson, William (1739–1774)—© Copyright The British Museum

Heydon, John (b. 1629, d. in or after 1670)—© National Portrait Gallery, London

Heyer, Georgette (1902–1974)—© National Portrait Gallery, London

Heylyn, Peter (1599–1662)—© National Portrait Gallery, London

Heywood, John (b. 1496/7, d. in or after 1578)—Ashmolean Museum, Oxford

Heywood, Peter (1772–1831)—© National Maritime Museum, London

Hibberd, (James) Shirley (1825–1890)—Royal Horticultural Society, Lindley Library

Hibberd, (Andrew) Stuart (1893–1983)—Getty Images – Felix H. Man